MW00605202

A COMPENDIOUS
SYRIAC DICTIONARY

FOUNDED UPON THE

THESAURUS SYRIACUS

OF

R. PAYNE SMITH, D.D.

EDITED BY

J. PAYNE SMITH

(MRS. MARGOLIOUTH)

Wipf and Stock Publishers
EUGENE, OREGON

Wipf and Stock Publishers
199 West 8th Avenue, Suite 3
Eugene, Oregon 97401

A Compendious Syriac Dictionary
By Smith, J. Payne
ISBN: 1-57910-227-1
Publication date: February, 1999
Previously published by Oxford University Press, 1902.

PREFACE

It was hoped that this abridgement of Dean Payne Smith's *Thesaurus Syriacus* would have appeared together with or earlier than the last part of that work. I deeply regret the long delay, due chiefly to my father's death in 1895, and to the consequent necessity of laying aside my own papers, in order to labour, in conjunction with D. S. Margoliouth, at the completion of the greater work.

It is a pleasure to offer grateful acknowledgement to various kind helpers; to my valued old friend, Dr. Neubauer, for encouragement from the beginning; to M. Rubens Duval and to Dean Maclean for their extreme patience and kindness in reading all the proofs. Those of the first part were also revised by my father, and most of the latter portions by my husband.

I wish to thank the Delegates of the Press also, and Mr. Doble in particular, for unfailing consideration, and Mr. Pembrey for unstinted pains and many suggestions.

ARRANGEMENT

As this abridgement is meant chiefly for beginners I thought alphabetical rather than scientific order to be preferred, all the more because ideas of scientific arrangement vary.

Participial adjectives are placed with passive participles under the Peal conjugation because of the difficulty of distinguishing one from the other, also because the verbal, adjectival, and substantival uses of these forms slide into each other.

When the same English translation is given to more than one conjugation of a verb, it will be understood that the Pael meaning is intensive, that the Ethpeel is used of a single action and the Ethpaal of frequent or repeated action.

I do not give Greek words unless in use, and only a few proper nouns; exceptions are when a true Syriac word has the same form as a Greek word or as a proper noun, in such cases I have put the Greek or the name to avoid any possible confusion. Also proper nouns when an adjective is derived from them.

I include true Syriac words from the native Lexica even when examples have not yet been found in use. These are usually marked 'Lexx., BA., or BB.'

I have only in a few instances given East-Syrian forms, for the differences consist chiefly in pronunciation. Note, however, the E-Syr. use of ـَ, Zkâpâ, for W-Syr. ـܳ, *a*) before ܘ, e.g. in Paels of ܥܘ verbs, E-Syr. ܥܳܘܰܪ, W-Syr. ܥܰܘܰܪ; *b*) with the final Alep of foreign words, ܵܐ, W-Syr. ܰܐ, and often elsewhere in foreign words. But in Greek words E-Syr. writes ܘ݂, W-Syr. ܘܳ.

Pe, ܦ, in E-Syr. is hard except in a diphthong, as ܰܦ, *au*, and then has the form ܦ̮.

The *linea occultans* which in W-Syr. is usually below the consonant, in E-Syr. is placed above, while a short line below signifies a half-vowel.

JESSIE PAYNE MARGOLIOUTH.

OXFORD,
September 2, 1902.

ABBREVIATIONS AND EXPLANATIONS

abbrev.	abbreviated form.
abs., absol.	the absolute state, absolutely.
acc.	accusative case.
act.	active.
adj.	adjective.
adv.	adverb, adverbial.
alchem.	according to alchemists.
anom.	anomalously.
APH.	Aphel conjugation.
apoc.	apocopated form.
Ar., Arab.	Arabic.
arith.	in arithmetic.
astrol.	in astrology.
astron.	in astronomy.
BA., BB.	see Lexx.
botan.	botanically.
B.V.M.	the Blessed Virgin Mary.
c., com. gen.	common gender.
cf.	confer, compare.
Chald.	Chaldee.
chem.	in chemistry.
col.	column.
coll., collect.	collectively, collective noun.
comp.; compos.	compound; in composition.
conj.	conjugation.
constr. st.	construct state.
contr.	contracted, contraction.
dat.	dative case.
denom.	denominative.
deriv.	derived, derivative, derivation.
dial.	dialect.
dim., dimin.	diminutive.
eccl., eccles.	ecclesiastically.
ellipt.	elliptically.
emph.	in the emphatic state.
ESHTAPH.	Eshtaphal conjugation.
esp.	especially.
E-Syr.	East-Syrian.
ETHPA.	Ethpaal conjugation.
ETHPE.	Ethpeel conjugation.
ETTAPH.	Ettaphal conjugation.
f., fem.	feminine gender.
fut.	future.
gen.	gender.
geom., geomet.	geometrical.
Germ.	in German.
Gr.	Greek.
gram.	in grammar.
Heb.	Hebrew.
Hex.	in the Hexapla version of the O. T.
imp., imper.	imperative.
impers.	impersonal.
indef.	indefinitely.
inf.	infinitive.
interj.	interjection.
interrog.	interrogative.
intr., intrans.	intransitive.
irreg.	irregular.
Jac.	Jacobite, following the teaching of the Monophysite Jacobus Baradaeus.
Lat.	Latin.
Lexx.	various Syriac Lexica; the two chief compilers of these are Jesus Bar-Ali, end of ninth century, and Bar-Bahlul, a native of Tirhan, middle of the tenth century, the latter's lexicon is the fullest, it has been edited by R. Duval, Paris.
lit.	literally.

ABBREVIATIONS AND EXPLANATIONS

lit., liturg.	liturgically.
log., logic.	in logic.
m., masc.	masculine gender.
med.	in medicine.
met., metaph.	metaphorically.
milit.	in military use.
Nasar.	Nasaraean (Mandaic, Sabaean).
Nest.	Nestorian.
opp.	opposite, opposed to.
PA.	Pael conjugation.
p., part.	participle, participial.
pass.	passive.
PE.	Peal conjugation.
perh.	perhaps.
Pers.	Persian.
pers.	person, personal.
Pesh.	in the Peshitta version.
pl.	plural.
pr. n.	proper noun.
prep.	preposition.
pres.	present.
pret.	preterite.
prob.	probably.
pron.	pronoun, pronominal.
prop.	properly.
refl.	reflexive.
rel., relat.	relative.
rit.	ritual, ritually.
rt.	root.
s., sing.	singular number.
SHAPH.	Shaphel conjugation.
st.	state.
subst.	substantive.
suff.	suffix.
Syr.	Syriac.
Tacrit, Tekrit or Tagrit	a city on the Tigris.
theol.	theologically.
Tirhan	a district East of the Tigris.
tr., trans.	transitive.
Turk.	Turkish.
vernac.	vernacular.
W-Syr.	West-Syrian.

* denotes that a root is not found in the Peal conjugation.

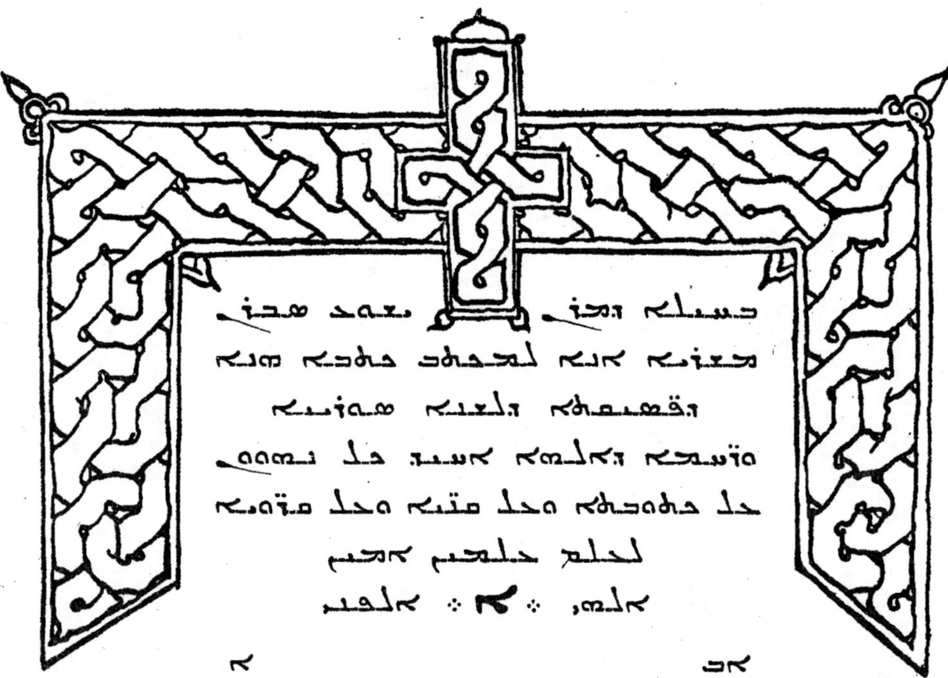

ܐ *Alep* or *Olaph* ܐܳܠܰܦ or ܐܰܠܰܦ, the first letter in the Syriac alphabet, used as the cardinal numeral 1; with ܕ prefixed the ordinal, *the first;* with a point beneath ܐ݂ it stands for 1,000; with a line beneath ܐ̱ 10,000; with two points beneath ܐ̤ 10,000,000.

ܐ has in Syriac very little power as a consonant, and when initial without a vowel is not pronounced. It is then in forming a compound thrown away, as in ܐ̱ܢܳܫ, ܟܽܠܢܳܫ; it is lost also in common words such as ܢܶܫ̈ܶܐ fem. of ܐ̱ܢܳܫܳܐ, and frequently in the imperative of ܦܐ verbs, as ܙܶܠ, ܬܳܐ, from ܐܶܙܰܠ, ܐܶܬܳܐ. Medial Olaph also frequently disappears when preceded by a consonant which can support the vowel, e. g. ܒܺܝܬ for ܒܺܐܝܬ, ܐܶܩܦܶܡ for ܐܶܦܶܐ. In many words it is indifferent whether ܐ be retained or not, Aphel participles and Pael pts. of ܦܐ verbs are commonly found written either way. ܐ is often used as an initial in nominal formations beginning with a weak letter or a sibilant, as ܐܶܝܡܰܢ from ܝܡܢ, ܐܶܫܬܰܠܳܐ from ܫܬܰܠ; in old MSS. and in the Jerusalem dialect it is very frequent even before stronger consonants. It is generally found in Greek words beginning with a double consonant, as ܐܶܟܣܢܳܝܳܐ ξένος, ܐܶܣܛܽܘܠܳܐ στολή.

ܐ often represents the Hebrew ה as in the causative conj. Aphel, which is equivalent to the Heb. Hiphil, and the Ethpaal, which answers to Heb. Hithpael. In Syriac it often interchanges with ܗ or ܝ. See instances in verbs having either of these letters for initials.

ܐܳܐܰܪ pl. ܐܳܐܪ̈ܶܣ com. gen. ἀήρ, *air, breeze.*

ܐܳܐܪܳܝܳܐ f. ܐܳܐܪܳܝܬܳܐ pl. m. ܝ̈ܶܐ, f. ܝ̈ܳܬܳܐ adj. *airy, aerial, of the air, volatile.*

ܐܳܐܪܢܳܐ same as ܐܳܐܪܳܝܳܐ.

ܐܳܒ sometimes ܐܳܒ݂ m. *August,* ܐܳܒ ܝܰܪܚܳܐ *the month Ab, the month of August.*

ܐܰܒ, ܐܰܒܳܐ pl. ܐܰܒ̈ܳܗܶܐ and ܐܰܒ̈ܳܗܳܬܳܐ irreg.; with pron. suff. 1 pers. ܐܳܒܝ, before other suffixes in the sing. it takes the form ܐܰܒܘ, in the pl. ܐܰܒ̈ܳܗܰܝ m. *father, parent, progenitor, forefather,* ܐܰܒ̈ܳܗܳܬܳܐ ܪܺܫ *a patriarch;* eccl. *a monk, abbot,* or *bishop,* ܐܰܒ̈ܳܗܳܬܳܐ ܪܘܚܳܢܳܝܶܐ *spiritual fathers,* ܪܺܫ ܐܰܒ̈ܳܗܳܬܳܐ *bishops,* ܐܰܒܳܐ ܕܐܰܒ̈ܳܗܳܬܳܐ *the patriarch.* ܐܰܒܽܘܢ *Our Father,* i.e. *the Lord's Prayer, the Paternoster,* in full ܨܠܘܬܳܐ ܕܐܰܒܽܘܢ ܕܒܰܫܡܰܝܳܐ;

also a title of reverence, e.g. applied to a patron saint. Metaph. *a founder* or *inventor* of arts, customs, heresies; *an originating principle.* Derivatives, ܐܒܗܘܬܐ, ܐܒܗܝܐ, ܐܒܗܝܢ.

ܐܒܐ and ܐܒܒܐ pl. ܐܒ̈ܐ, ܐܒ̈ܝܐ and ܐܒܒ̈ܝܐ E-Syr. ܐܒܐ or ܐܒܒܐ (rt. Chald. *to grow up*) m. *the produce of the earth*, esp. *fruit;* ܐܝܠܢ̈ܐ ܕܐܒܐ *fruit trees.* Cognate words, ܐܒܘܒܐ and ܒܘܒܐ.

ܐܒܕ fut. ܢܐܒܕ, act. part. ܐܒܕ, emph. and fem. ܐܒܕܐ, pass. part. ܐܒܝܕ, ܐܒܝܕܐ, ܐܒܝܕܬܐ, pl. m. ܝܢ, f. ܝ̈ܬܐ. *to perish, come to nought, fall to decay; to be lost;* ܡܐܒܕ ܐܒܕܝܢ ܐܢܬܘܢ *ye shall utterly perish:* with ܡܢ *to be deprived of, miss, lose.* Pass. part. *lost, strayed, gone astray; perished, perishing;* ܐܒܝܕ ܡܕܥܐ *distracted, out of his mind:* with ܡܢ *deprived of, lacking;* f. pl. *lost things* or *property.* Aph. ܐܘܒܕ *to bring to nought, do away with, cause to cease; to lose, waste, destroy, slay:* with ܡܢ *to cast out* or *away.* Derivatives, ܐܒܕܢܐ, ܐܒܕܐ, ܐܒܝܕܘܬܐ, ܡܘܒܕܢܘܬܐ, ܡܘܒܕܢܐ.

ܐܒܕܝܢܐ, ܐܒܕܝܢ with ܒ prefixed. *a) alike, like,* ܟܐܒܕܝܢ ܛܠܝ̈ܐ *like children. b) continually,* ܐܒܪܝܘ ܟܐܒܕܝܢ *stir it without intermission.*

ܐܒܕܐ, ܐܒܕܢܐ, ܐܒܕܢ rt. ܐܒܕ. m. *loss, perdition, destruction, ruin;* ܒܪ ܐܒܕܢܐ *a son of perdition* = *one who is ruined, hopeless, abandoned.*

ܐܒܕܬܐ pl. ܐܒ̈ܕܬܐ rt. ܐܒܕ. f. *a loss, a lost thing.*

ܐܒܗܘܠ Ar. and Pers. = Syr. ܕܒܘܬܐ *juniperus sabina, dwarf savin.*

ܐܒܗܘܬܐ from ܐܒܐ. f. *fatherhood*, often used with suff. 2 pers. as a title of reverence of priests, bishops, and patriarchs, ܐܒܗܘܬܟ = *Thee, O Father.*

ܐܒܗܝܐ f. ܐܒܗܝܬܐ pl. m. ܝ̈ܐ, f. ܝ̈ܬܐ adj. from ܐܒܐ. *fatherly, paternal, from a father, of his forefathers, patriarchal;* ܪܒܘܬܐ ܐܒܗܝܬܐ *inherited eminence.*

ܐܒܘܒܐ, ܐܒܘܒ pl. ܐܒܘ̈ܒܐ m. ܐܒܘܒܝܬܐ pl. ܝ̈ܬܐ f. see ܐܒܐ. *a reed, flute, pipe, a channel, canal.*

ܐܒܘܬܐ pl. ܐܒ̈ܘܬܐ m. *a) a bricklayer's rule, a mason's trowel. b) a pole* armed with an iron goad at one end and at the other an iron blade to scrape off anything adhering to the ploughshare. *c) a waterpipe, canal, duct.*

ܐܒܚ Aphel of ܢܒܚ; *to make bark.*

ܐܒܝܕܘܬܐ rt. ܐܒܕ. f. *loss, abandonment, depravity:* with suff. 1 pers. sing. often used by Syriac writers as an expression of humility, ܒܥܝ ܠܐܒܝܕܘܬܝ *seek for me who am lost,* ܚܘܣ ܥܠ ܐܒܝܕܘܬܝ *have pity on my lost condition.*

ܐܒܝܠܘܬܐ rt. ܐܒܠ. f. *mourning, sorrow,* esp. for sin, hence *penitence, the ascetic life,* ܐܬܟܬܫ̈ܐ ܕܐܒܝܠܘܬܟ *the conflicts of thy life of penitence,* ܫܠܡ ܠܗ ܙܒܢܐ ܕܐܒܝܠܘܬܗ *his solitary life of penance was ended.*

ܐܒܒܐ pl. ܐ̈ m. *a cock;* the usual word is ܬܪܢܓܠܐ.

ܐܒܠ Pe. only pass. part. ܐܒܝܠ, ܐܒܝܠܐ, ܐܒܝܠܬܐ pl. m. ܝܢ, ܝ̈ܐ, f. ܝ̈ܬܐ. *mourning, bewailing, lamenting; a mourner,* hence *an anchorite, monk, nun,* as leaving the world to bewail their sins. Ethpe. ܐܬܐܒܠ *to mourn,* esp. for the dead, *bewail, make lamentation.* Derivatives, ܐܒܠܐ, ܐܒܝܠܘܬܐ, ܐܒܠܢܐ.

ܐܒܠ, ܐܒܠܐ pl. ܐܒ̈ܠܐ rt. ܐܒܠ. m. *mourning, lamentation for the dead; a sorrow, cause of sorrow, calamity,* ܣܓܝ̈ܐܐ ܫܚܠܦ̈ܢ ܐܒ̈ܠܐ ܢܦܠܘ *many different misfortunes befel them.*

ܐܒܠܢܐ f. ܐܒܠܢܝܬܐ pl. m. ܝ̈ܐ, f. ܝ̈ܬܐ adj. rt. ܐܒܠ. *mournful, of mourning.*

ܐܒܠܬܐ pl. ܐܒ̈ܠܬܐ Ar. f. *a herd, drove,* properly of camels.

ܐܒܢܐ com. gen. *a stone;* the common word in Heb. for stone, but rare in Syr.; ܐܒ̈ܢܝ ܒܪܕܐ *hail stones;* ܐܒܢܐ ܕܫܥ̈ܐ *a sun-dial.*

ܐܒܘܣ, ܐܒܐܣ or ܐܒܒܘܣ a Graecised form of ܐܒܐ *Abba, Father; an abbot;* see ܐܒܐ.

ܐܒܥ Aphel of ܢܒܥ; *to bring forth, cause to spring forth, abound.*

ܐܒܩܐ m. *fine dust* or *sand,* such as the wind whirls along.

ܐܒܪܐ m. *lead.*

ܐܒܪܐ m. *a feather;* usually pl. ܐܒܪ̈ܐ *feathers, wings, pinions,* ܐܒ̈ܪܐ ܦܫܝ̈ܛܬܐ *expanded wings;* ܐܒ̈ܪܐ ܕܪܘܚܐ *the wings of the wind.*

ܐܒܪܬܐ *a rush, reed-grass.*

ܐܒܫ or ܐܒܐܫ Aphel of ܒܐܫ; *to do evil:* with ܡܢ *to be* or *do worse than.*

ܐܓܕܝܣ ἴγδη, *a mortar.*

ܐܓܐ and ܐܓܐ *laserpitium, ferula, asa foetida.*

ܐܓܗ Aphel of ܢܓܗ; *to shine; to wait for the morning light.*

ܐܓܘܓ, ܐܓܘܓܐ or ܐܓܘܓܐ ܕܡܝܐ pl. ܐ̈ m. ἀγωγός, *a watercourse, canal, an aqueduct;* metaph. *a stream,* ܐܓܘܓܝ ܕܡܐ *streams of blood.*

ܐܓܘܢ, ܐܓܘܢܐ pl. ܐ̈ m. ἀγών, *a trial of skill* or *strength, a contest, struggle,* ܥܒܕܘ ܐܓܘܢܐ ܚܕ ܥܡ ܚܕ *they wrestled together,* ܓܢܒܪܐ ܕܐܓܘܢܐ *a champion;* see ܐܬܠܝܛܐ. Metaph. *a mental struggle, perplexity; ascetic training, the ascetic life,* ܐܓܘܢܐ ܕܡܕܒܪ ܐܢܐ *the discipline which I practise.*

ܐܓܘܢܝܣܛܣ pl. ܐ̈ m. ἀγωνιστής, *one who strives, a wrestler.*

ܐܓܘܪ the form of 1 pers. sing. fut. of three verbs, *a)* ܐܓܘܪ from ܐܓܪ *to hire; b)* ܐܓܘܪ from ܓܪ *to commit adultery; c)* ܐܓܘܪ from ܓܪܪ *to drag.*

ܐܓܘܪܐ pl. ܐ̈ rt. ܐܓܪ. m. *one who hires.*

ܐܓܘܪܣܐ pl. ܐ̈ m. ἀγρός, *a field, land, a hospital; an estate, a farm; a village.* An ܐܓܘܪܣܐ is larger than a ܩܘܪܝܬܐ, smaller than a ܡܕܝܢܬܐ.

ܐܓܘܦܛܝܐ also spelt ܐܓܘܦܬܝܐ, ܐܓܝܦܛܝܐ etc. *Egyptian.*

ܐܓܝܪܘܬܐ rt. ܐܓܪ. f. *hiring, hired service.*

ܐܓܠܝܕܐ oftener ܓܠܝܕܐ m. *ice, frost.*

ܐܓܡܐ pl. ܐ̈ m. *a pool, standing water; a reed,* esp. *the Egyptian papyrus.*

ܐܓܡܘܢܐ or ܐܝܓܡܘܢܐ, see ܗܓܡܘܢܐ, ἡγεμών, *a prefect.*

ܐܓܢ Aphel of ܓܢܢ; *to abide* or *rest upon,* &c.

ܐܓܢܐ pl. ܐ̈ f. *a large bowl* or *wine vessel; a waterpot; the crater* of a volcano; *the capital* of a pillar; *the base* of a vessel; ܐܓܢܐ ܕܝܕܥܬܐ *the cup of knowledge.*

ܐܓܣ Aphel, see ܓܣܣ; *to recline* or *seat* at table.

ܐܓܪ with Qushoi, Aphel of ܢܓܪ; *to lengthen; to wait:* with ܪܘܚܐ *to be patient.* ܐܓܪ with Rukokh, Pael of ܐܓܪ.

ܐܓܪ fut. ܢܐܓܘܪ, imper. ܐܓܘܪ, act. part. ܐܓܪ, ܐܓܪܐ, pass. part. ܐܓܝܪ, ܐܓܝܪܐ, ܐܓܝܪܬܐ, pl. m. ܐܓܝܪܝܢ, ܐܓܝܪܐ, f. ܐܓܝܪܬܐ. *to hire:* with ܒ of the wage: with ܥܠ *against* an enemy: with ܠ and a pers. pron. expresses personal advantage, ܘܐܓܪܘ ܠܗܘܢ ܚܝܠܐ *to hire forces on his side; to bribe,* ܐܓܪ ܠܗ ܠܕܝܢܐ *he suborned the judge.* Pass. part. m. *an hireling, a hired servant;* f. emph. *money received on engaging in service, earnest money, Handgeld.* Ethpe. ܐܬܬܓܪ *to be hired, to hire oneself* with ܒ of the wage. Pa. and Ethpa. same as Pe. and Ethpe. Aph. ܐܘܓܪ *to hire out, receive hire,* ܗܘ ܕܐܘܓܪ ܘܗܢܘܢ ܕܐܘܓܪܘ *he* (Judas) *who took, and they who gave the hire.* Derivatives, ܐܓܪܐ, ܐܓܝܪܘܬܐ.

ܐܓܪ, ܐܓܪܐ pl. ܐ̈, rt. ܐܓܪ. m. *a wage, fee, fare; hire, reward;* ܡܪܐ ܐܓܪܐ *a contractor, paymaster.*

ܐܓܪܐ pl. ܐ̈, rt. perh. ܢܓܪ *to stretch out,* m. *a roof, house-top, the top of an altar;* ܒܪ ܐܓܪܐ pl. ܒܢܝ ܐܓܪܐ *a demon of lunacy,* hence with ܕ preceding *a lunatic;* ܕܝܘܢܐ ܘܒܢܝ ܐܓܪܐ *demoniacs and lunatics.* The name is derived from a custom of worshipping these demons on the flat roofs of houses; they were supposed to have more influence at the beginning and end of a month.

ܐܕܪܓܙܪܐ and ܐܕܪܓܙܪܝܐ rt. Assyrio-Babylonian; corrupted from the Chald., Dan. iii. 2, 3; *chief judges.*

ܐܓܪܬܐ pl. ܐܓܪܬܐ f. *a letter, an epistle:* with ܠܘܬ *to.*

ܐܕܫ Aphel of ܕܫ; *to grow deaf.*

ܐܕܘܢܐ m. *a portable stove.*

ܐܕܘܠܐ or ܐܕܘܠܐ *palm fibre, the fibrous involucre of the palm-tree.*

ܐܕܠܐ *lepidium latifolium, pepperwort.*

ܐܕܠܟܬܐ f. *minium.*

ܐܕܪܟܬܐ or ܐܕܪܟܬܐ f. pl. *double doors, a door with two leaves or flaps.*

ܐܕܡ Heb. m. *Adam, man;* ܒܢܝܢܫܐ ܕܐܕܡ *the human race;* ܐܕܡ ܩܕܡܝܐ *the first man.*

ܐܕܡ denom. verb Aphel conj. from ܕܡ; *to fetch blood,* &c.

ܐܕܡܣ, ܐܕܡܘܣ, ܐܕܡܣ m. ἀδάμας, *adamant.*

ܐܕܡܬܐ E-Syr. ܐܕܡܬܐ f. *earth, soil.*

ܐܕܡܬܢܐ *earthly.*

ܐܕܡܬܢܝܐ *earthy, made of earth.*

ܐܕܢܐ pl. ܐܕܢ̈ܐ, ܐܕܢ̈ܝܢ, rarely ܐܕܢܬܐ and ܐܕܢܝܬܐ f. *the ear;* a fish's *gills; anything which stands out*, as *a handle, a promontory*, a *bay* of the sea.

ܐܕܩ part. ܡܕܩ, ܡܕܩܐ, Aphel of ܕܩ; *to break to pieces.*

ܐܕܪ, ܐܕܪܐ pl. ܐ̈ m. *a threshing-floor, granary,* hence *that which is on the floor;* ܐܕܪ̈ܐ ܫܩܠܘ *they carried away the threshing-floors,* i.e. *the corn from the threshing-floor,* ܐܕܪ̈ܐ ܐܘܩܕܘ *they set fire to the threshing-floors,* i.e. *to the corn and straw;* ܐܕܪ̈ܐ ܕܡܕܝܢܬܐ *farms near a town.*

ܐܕܪ, ܐܕܪܐ *ilex, the prickly evergreen oak.*

ܐܕܪ m. *Adar, the seventh month of the Syrian year,* answering nearly to March with us. Deriv. Pers. from *Adhar, the god of fire,* to whom this month was dedicated.

ܐܕܪܘܢܐ Pers. m. *an inner room, a bedroom;* ܐܕܪܘܢܐ ܥܠܝܐ *an upper storey.*

ܐܕܪܘܫܐ pl. ܐ̈ *fire altar,* probably Pers.; see ܐܕܪ.

ܐܕܪܙܓܐ pl. ܐ̈ deriv. Pers. m. *a tailor, maker* or *mender of clothes.*

ܐܕܪܝܢܛܐ m. ἀνδριάντα, *a statue, likeness.*

ܐܕܪܩܣ ἀδάρκη, *the salt crust* on reeds in marshy places.

ܐܕܫ* Pa. ܐܕܫ act. part. ܡܐܕܫܐ and ܡܐܕܫ. *to be careless, disregardful, to neglect; to stop* the ears; *to be silent;* hence is derived

ܐܕܫܐ m. *negligence, indifference.*

ܐܕܫ, ܐܕܫܐ pl. ܝܢ, ܐ̈ m. perhaps from εἶδος, *a sort, kind, species;* pl. *of many kinds, various,* ܕܟܠ ܐܕܫܝܢ *of all sorts; race, kindred, character,* ܐܕܫܐ ܐܢܫܝܐ *the human race;* ܐܕܫܐ ܕܡܡܠܠܐ *style* of expression in speech or writing; ܫܘܦܪܐ ܕܐܕܫܗ ܫܘܝܐ ܥܒܕܗ ܠܗܕܐ ܪܒܘܬܐ *the dignity of his character rendered him worthy of so dignified an office;* ܠܐ ܫܘܐ ܐܕܫܗ ܠ *he was not the kind of man, he was unfit for. A mode, way, form; the form of administration* of baptism, chrism, &c., *the form of words used* opp. ܗܘܠܐ or ܗܘܠܝܘܬܐ *the material, the elements,* the water, oil, &c., e.g. bread and wine are the ܗܘܠܝܘܬܐ of the Holy Eucharist, the words of Christ are the ܐܕܫܐ. *Fruit* ellipt. for ܐܕܫ̈ܐ ܕܦܐܪ̈ܐ *the different kinds* of fruit *according to the seasons of the year,* ܐܕܫ̈ܐ ܕܚܩܠܐ *wild fruits;* ܢܚܠܐ ܚܣܝܢܐ ܐܕܫܐ *fruitful pastures.* Hence are derived the two following:

ܐܕܫܢܝܐ pl. ܐ̈ adj. *after its sort* or *species, special, essential.*

ܐܕܫܢܝܘܬܐ f. *a specific property, fashion.*

ܐܗܐ ܐܗܐ interj. of derision, *he-he! ha-ha!*

ܐܗܢܓ or ܐܗܢܓ perh. Pers. *a crocodile.*

ܐܗܠ Aphel of ܗܠܠ; *to deride,* with ܒ.

ܐܗܪ Aphel of ܗܪ; *to harm, irritate.*

ܐܘ, ܐܘ the point distinguishes it from the interj. ܐܘ, ܐܘ. *a*) disjunct. particle, *or, either;* ܐܘ ܐܘ *either—or, if or no. b*) sometimes used for emphasis, *also, yea, or rather, the rather. c*) interrog. particle, not always expressed in English, and usually having negative force, *whether,* ܐܘ ܕܠܡܐ *lest:* in comparison *than, rather than.*

ܐܘ interj., expressing the vocative, and wonder, grief, reproof; - *O! Oh!* often with ܠ of the person or thing.

ܐܘ interj. *Oh! woe! alas!*

ܐܘܐ root-meaning in Heb. and Ar., *a*) *to turn towards a place, to stay anywhere,* hence are derived ܐܘܝܐ, ܐܘܝܘܬܐ, ܬܘܝܐ; *b*) *to turn towards any one with affection,* hence *to be on friendly terms, in harmony with any one.* Pe. only act. part. ܐܘܐ, emph. and fem. ܐܘܝܐ, fem. emph. irreg. ܐܘܝܬܐ; pl. m. ܐܘܝܢ, ܐܘ̈ܝܐ or ܐܘ̈ܝܐ, f. ܐܘܝ̈ܬܐ *agreeing, in concord, of one mind* or *will, united, friends;* ܐܬܘ̈ܬܐ ܐܘܝ̈ܬܐ letters *agreeing* in sound=*rhyming;* ܡܦܩܬܐ ܦܫܝܛܬܐ ܠܥܒܪܝܐ ܐܘܝܐ *the Pschitta agrees with the Hebrew text;* ܩܠܐ ܐܘܝܐ *a harmonious voice;* ܪܥܝܢܐ ܐܘܝܐ *a like opinion.* Ethpe. ܐܬܐܘܝ *to agree, make alliance* ܥܡ ܦܠܢ *with any one.* Pa. ܐܘܝ inf. ܡܐܘܝܘ, part. ܡܐܘܐ for ܡܐܘܐ *to unite, reconcile, ally.* Ethpa. ܐܬܐܘܝ *to make alliance, join, agree, consent, conspire; to be reconciled; to be a follower of, belong to the party of;* construed with ܥܡ of the person, or with ܠ of a party or side: with ܥܡ or ܥܡ ܚܕ̈ܕܐ *together, to each other.* Derivatives, ܐܘܝܐ, ܐܘܝܐܝܬ, ܐܘܝܘܬܐ, ܐܘܝܐ, ܬܘܝܐ, ܬܐܘܝܐ, ܬܘܝܐ, ܬܘܝ.

ܐܘܒ, not used in Pe., is the same as several mimetic roots in Heb. meaning first, *to breathe* or *pant after,* and hence *to be eager, to desire;* see ܝܐܒ. Ethpa. ܐܬܐܘܒ the same as ܐܬܝܐܒ and ܐܬܝܐܒ *to desire greatly, love fervently.*

ܐܰܘܟܶܡ APHEL of ܐܟܡ.

ܐܘܟܘܡܪܘܢ and ܐܟܘܪܝ a) *cichorium silvestre, cichorium intybus, wild chicory; b) leontodon taraxacum, dandelion.*

ܐܘܟܒܝܐ ὤ βια (Duval). *Alas, woe to thee!* with ܠܗ and pers. pron.

ܐܰܘܒܶܠ APHEL of ܝܒܠ; *to lead, bring, bring forth.*

ܐܰܘܒܶܫ APHEL of ܝܒܫ; *to dry up, wither* tr.

ܐܘܓܐ or ܐܘܓܝܐ a) *rhus coriaria, the sumac tree; b) ocymum basiliscum, basil.*

ܐܰܘܓܶܐ APHEL of ܓܘܐ imper. ܐܘܓܐ; *to drive away, send off.*

ܐܰܘܓܶܪ APHEL of ܐܓܪ; see above.

ܐܘܕܐ pl. ܐ̈ m. *a brand, firebrand,* hence *a stick for stirring the fire, an oven rake;* ܐܘܕܐ ܡܫܚܪܐ *a charred stick;* ܐܘܕܐ ܕܬܢܢܐ *a smoking brand.*

ܐܰܘܕܺܝ denom. verb APHEL conj. from ܝܕ. *to confess, believe, praise,* &c.; see under ܝܕ.

ܐܰܘܕܰܥ APHEL of ܝܕܥ; *to make known,* &c.

ܐܘܗ interj. usually of sorrow, sometimes of wonder or joy, *Ah! Oh! Alas!* used alone or with ܠ, ܥܠ or ܠܟ.

ܐܘܙܢܐ, ܐܘܙܢܐ or ܐܙܢܐ m. *a laver* generally of stone, *a font,* ܐܘܙܢܐ ܕܡܥܡܘܕܝܬܐ *the baptismal laver.*

ܐܘܘܢܐ or ܐܘܢܐ constr. st. ܐܘܢ pl. ܐ̈, m. rt. ܐܘܢ*. *a lodging, an inn,* hence *an abode, habitation, dwelling-place, mansion;* ܐܘ̈ܢܐ ܕܓܙܘܬܐ *storehouses, store-rooms.* Often metaph. of heaven, probably in allusion to John xiv. 2, 23; ܐܘ̈ܢܐ ܕܠܥܠ—ܕܠܐ ܥܒܪܝܢ *the heavenly habitations—that pass not away;* the Holy Spirit ܐܘܢܐ ܠܗ ܥܒܕܟ *made thee to be His habitation;* ܦܓܪܐ ܐܘܢܗ *the body the mansion* of the soul.

ܐܰܘܙܶܦ APHEL of ܝܙܦ; *to lend,* esp. *at interest.*

ܐܰܘܚܶܕ APHEL of ܐܚܕ; see below.

ܐܘܚܕܢ, ܐܘܚܕܢܐ pl. ܝ̈ܢ, ܐ̈ rt. ܐܚܕ. m. *a grasp, hold, laying hold,* ܗܘܐ ܕܠܐ ܐܘܚܕܢ ܠܐܝܕܐ *it could not be laid hold of, held in the hand; power, force* of the wind, sea, &c.; political *power, jurisdiction,* ܬܪܬܥܣܪܐ ܐܦܪ̈ܟܝܣ ܗܘܝ ܒܐܘܚܕܢܐ ܕܡܦܪܝܢܐ twelve dioceses were *under the jurisdiction of the Maphrian of Tagrit; a possession,* esp. of land, *district, territory, kingdom, realm, empire.*

ܐܘܚܕܢܝܬܐ or ܐܘܚܕܢܝܬܐ pl. ܐܘܚܕ̈ܢܝܢ oftener ܐܘܚܕ̈ܢܝܬܐ rt. ܐܚܕ. f. *that which is kept close,* esp. *a dark saying, a riddle, enigma, proverb.*

ܐܰܘܚܶܠ APHEL of ܚܝܠ*; *to become enfeebled, to be unable,* &c.

ܐܰܘܚܰܪ APHEL of ܐܚܪ; see below.

ܐܘܚܠܐ *lilium agreste.*

ܐܘܚܪܢܐ or ܐܘܚܪܢܐ pl. ܐ̈ m. *veteranus, the chief men* of a city, *nobles.*

ܐܘܝ Ar. *a jackal.*

ܐܘܝ interj. to call attention or to express grief or threatening, *Ho! Oh!*

ܐܘܝܐ see ܐܘܐ. ܐܘܝܐܝܬ adv. *unanimously, with one accord, altogether, harmoniously.*

ܐܘܝܘܬ, ܐܘܝܘܬܐ rt. ܐܘܐ. f. *concord, accord, unity, unanimity, harmony, agreement;* ܒܐܘܝܘܬܐ *in agreement, in concord;* ܐܘܝܘܬܐ ܚܕܐ *with one consent;* ܠܐ ܐܘܝܘܬܐ *discord.*

ܐܘܟܝܬ = ܐܘ ܟܝܬ *that is to say, or, i.e. as, as also.* It is constantly used in lexicons when a word is explained by a synonym in the same language.

ܐܰܘܟܶܠ APHEL of ܐܟܠ; see below.

ܐܘܟܠܐ rt. ܐܟܠ. m. *food, gorging; that which has been devoured* or *gorged.*

ܐܘܟܠܬܐ rt. ܐܟܠ. f. *gangrene, an eating sore.*

ܐܰܘܟܶܡ APHEL of ܐܟܡ; see below.

ܐܘܟܡܐ f. ܐܘܟܡܬܐ pl. m. ܐ̈, f. ܬ̈ܐ rt. ܐܟܡ. adj. *black, sunburnt;* metaph. *obscure;* ܐܘܟ̈ܡܐ ܡܬܠ̈ܐ *dark sayings;* ܪܘܚܐ ܐܘܟܡܬܐ *a stormy wind;* subst. *a negro, Moor, Nubian;* the races of mankind are, ܐܘܟ̈ܡܐ *black* = *Hamites,* ܚܘ̈ܪܐ *white* = *Japhetites,* or ܣܡܘ̈ܩܐ *olive-coloured* = *Semites.* Pl. m. *black garments* worn by Abassides and judges, and by others for mourning, ܢܠܒܫܘܢ ܐܘܟ̈ܡܐ *they shall wear black.*

ܐܘܟܡܘܬܐ rt. ܐܟܡ. f. *blackness, dark colour of the skin.*

ܐܘܟܦܐ *a pack-saddle.*

ܐܘܟܦ, ܐܘܟܦܐ rt. ܐܟܦ. m. *care, anxiety.*

ܐܘܟܪܣܛܝܐ, ܐܘܟܪܣܛܝܐ εὐχαριστία, *thanksgiving,* esp. *the thanksgiving at that part of the* baptismal office when the chrism is consecrated, hence *the baptismal anointing; the eucharist, the sacrament of the Lord's supper*, hence *the host, the consecrated bread*, ܣܳܐܶܡ ܟܳܣܳܐ ܘܫܳܩܶܠ ܐܽܘܟܰܪܶܣܛܺܝܰܐ *he sets down the chalice and takes the eucharistic bread*, ܡܪܰܚܶܦ ܥܰܠ ܐܽܘܟܰܪܶܣܛܺܝܰܐ the Holy Spirit *broods over the eucharistic elements.*

ܐܰܘܠܶܕ Aphel of ܝܠܰܕ; *to beget, procreate; to help* or *cause to bring forth.*

ܐܽܘܠܓ̈ܶܐ m. pl. *barns, shelters.*

ܐܰܘܠܽܘܢ, ܐܰܘܠܺܝܘܢ or ܐܽܘܠܺܝܘܢ *lignum aloes, lign-aloes.*

ܐܰܘܠܳܘܢܳܐ or ܐܰܘܠܳܢܳܐ and ܐܰܠܳܘܢܳܐ m. and f. αὐλών, *a valley, open land* or *a broad valley between mountain ranges;* ܐܰܘܠܳܘܢܶܝܗ̇ ܕܒܰܣܺܝܡܽܘܬܳܐ *her pleasant valleys, happy fields.*

ܐܰܘܠܳܘܢܳܝܳܐ *a lowlander, an inhabitant of valley* or *plain.*

ܐܽܘܠܺܝܬܳܐ pl. ܐܽܘܠܝܳܬ̈ܳܐ rt. ܐܠܝ. f. *lament, lamentation, wailing, mourning,* esp. for the dead. ܣܶܦܪ ܐܽܘܠܝܳܬܳܐ *the Lamentations* of Jeremiah; ܩܳܠܶܐ ܕܐܽܘܠܝܳܬܳܐ *cries of sorrow.*

ܐܰܘܠܝܣܺܝܣ *the aloe.*

ܐܽܘܠܨܳܢ, ܐܽܘܠܨܳܢܳܐ pl. ܐܽܘܠܨܳܢ̈ܶܐ rt. ܐܠܨ. m. *narrowness,* ܒܺܐܪܳܐ ܕܐܽܘܠܨܳܢܳܐ *a narrow well;* hence, *a*) *a strait, necessity, distress, calamity, suffering, illness;* ܐܰܠܺܝܨܺܝܢ ܣܰܓܺܝ ܐܽܘܠܨܳܢ *deeply afflicted,* ܥܶܕܳܢܳܐ ܕܐܽܘܠܨܳܢܳܐ *a time of calamity,* ܠܰܚܡܳܐ ܕܐܽܘܠܨܳܢܳܐ *bread of affliction;* ܐܽܘܠܨܳܢ̈ܶܐ ܡܓܰܪ̈ܓܺܝܢ *the prolonged sufferings* of the martyrs; ܐܶܫܟܰܚܘ ܗܘܰܘ ܦܽܘܢܳܝܳܐ ܡܶܢ ܐܽܘܠܨܳܢܰܝܗܽܘܢ *they found relief from their afflictions.* *b*) *a being shut up closely, a siege, restraint.* ܘܠܳܐ ܡܶܢ ܐܽܘܠܨܳܢܳܐ *without compulsion=willingly, freely.*

ܐܰܘܡܥܳܐ or ܐܽܘܡܥܳܐ *sour buttermilk.*

ܐܰܘܡܝ Aphel of ܝܡܳܐ; *to bind by oath, adjure,* &c.

ܐܽܘܡܳܢ, ܐܽܘܡܳܢܳܐ rt. ܐܡܢ. m. *a workman, maker, craftsman, artificer; a carpenter; a surgeon;* ܐܽܘܡܳܢܶܗ *his* or *its maker;* ܐܽܘܡܳܢ ܥܳܠܡ̈ܶܐ *the Artificer of the worlds;* ܐܽܘܡܳܢ̈ܶܐ ܕܐܺܝܕ̈ܰܝܳܐ *manual workers;* ܐܽܘܡܳܢ̈ܶܐ ܥܳܒ̈ܕܰܝ ܕܰܗܒܳܐ *workers in gold, goldsmiths;* used also as an adj. *skilful.*

ܐܽܘܡܳܢܳܐܺܝܬ adv. *skilfully, with art, elaborately;* metaph. *craftily;* ܠܳܐ ܐܽܘܡܳܢܳܐܺܝܬ *ignorantly.*

ܐܽܘܡܳܢܽܘܬ, ܐܽܘܡܳܢܽܘܬܳܐ pl. ܐܽܘܡܳܢܘ̈ܳܬܳܐ, ܐܽܘܡܳܢ̈ܘܳܬܳܐ rt. ܐܡܢ. f. *art, craft; workmanship, skill; artifice, craftiness, guile;* pl. *engines of war.* ܐܽܘܡܳܢܽܘܬܳܐ ܕܩܪܳܒܳܐ *the art of war;* ܐܽܘܡܳܢܽܘܬܳܐ ܕܐܳܣܝܽܘܬܳܐ *the healing art, medicine.* ܐܽܘܡܳܢܽܘܬܳܐ ܕܟܺܝܡܺܝܰܐ, ܐܽܘܡܳܢܽܘܬܳܐ or abs. *alchemy, chemistry,* ܡܰܠܦܳܢ ܐܽܘܡܳܢܽܘܬܳܐ *an alchemist, chemist;* ܒܰܪ ܐܽܘܡܳܢܽܘܬܶܗ *a fellow-craftsman;* ܒܐܽܘܡܳܢܽܘܬܳܐ *by art;* ܒܐܽܘܡܳܢܽܘܬܳܐ ܕܕܰܓܳܠܽܘܬܳܐ *by false arts, by a deceitful artifice;* ܐܽܘܡܳܢܘ̈ܳܬܳܐ ܕܫܺܐܕ̈ܶܐ *the wiles of devils.*

ܐܽܘܡܳܢܳܝܳܐ f. ܐܽܘܡܳܢܳܝܬܳܐ pl. ܐܽܘܡܳܢܳܝ̈ܶܐ, ܐܽܘܡܳܢܳܝ̈ܳܬܳܐ, rt. ܐܡܢ. adj. *of* or *belonging to any art* or *handiwork, formed by art, cunningly wrought, workmanlike, skilful:* used with ܠ or ܒ, ܐܽܘܡܳܢܳܝܶܢ ܦܰܠܳܚ̈ܶܐ *skilled husbandmen.*

ܐܽܘܡܬܳܐ pl. ܐܽܘܡ̈ܶܐ, ܐܽܘܡܘܳܬܳܐ, ܐܽܡܘ̈ܳܬܳܐ, ܐܽܘܡ̈ܳܬܳܐ rt. ܐܡ com. gen. *a*) *race, nation, people,* ܪܺܝܫ ܐܽܘܡܬܳܐ *a prince* or *chief;* *b*) *a class, genus.*

ܐܳܘ, ܐܽܘ interj. of calling, imploring, sorrow, remonstrance, exclamation or admiration.

ܐܰܘܝ, ܐܰܘܝܳܐ; see ܐܽܘܘܳܐ above.

ܐܽܘܩ abbreviation for ܐܽܘܢܩܝܳܐ s. and pl. *oz.*

ܐܶܘܰܢܓܶܠܝܳܝܳܐ f. ܐܶܘܰܢܓܶܠܝܳܝܬܳܐ pl. ܐܶܘܰܢܓܶܠܝܳܝ̈ܶܐ, ܐܶܘܰܢܓܶܠܝܳܝ̈ܳܬܳܐ. Gr. adj. *of the gospels, evangelical,* ܢܳܡܽܘܣܳܐ ܐܶܘܰܢܓܶܠܝܳܝܳܐ *the law of the gospels,* ܦܽܘܩܕ̈ܳܢܶܐ ܐܶܘܰܢܓܶܠܝܳܝ̈ܶܐ *gospel precepts,* ܟܰܟܪ̈ܶܐ ܐܶܘܰܢܓܶܠܝܳܝ̈ܶܐ *the talents spoken of in the gospels.*

ܐܶܘܰܢܓܶܠܝܽܘܢ pl. ܐܶܘܰܢܓܶܠܝ̈ܶܐ and ܐܶܘܰܢܓܶܠܝܽܘ̈ܢܶܐ m. εὐαγγέλιον (the Syriac word for *gospel* is ܣܒܰܪܬܳܐ), *the gospel, a copy of the gospel,* ܐܶܘܰܢܓܶܠܝܽܘܢ ܫܠܶܡ ܠܢܳܡܽܘܣܳܐ *the gospel is in harmony with the law,* ܐܶܘܰܢܓܶܠܝܽܘܢ ܕܰܐܝܟ ܥܶܒܪ̈ܳܝܶܐ *the gospel according to the Hebrews.*

ܐܶܘܰܢܓܶܠܺܝܣܛܳܐ pl. ܐܶܘܰܢܓܶܠܺܝܣܛ̈ܶܐ (often spelt without the ܢ) εὐαγγελιστής=Syr. ܡܣܰܒܪܳܢܳܐ. m. *evangelist.*

ܐܶܘܢܽܘܟܳܐ pl. ܐܶܘܢܽܘܟ̈ܶܐ m. εὐνοῦχος, *a eunuch;* the Syriac words are ܡܗܰܝܡܢܳܐ and ܡܣܰܪܣܳܐ.

ܐܽܘܢܩܝܳܐ pl. ܐܽܘܢܩܝܳܣ, ܐܽܘܢܩܝܽܘܣ, ܐܽܘܢܩܺܝܣ or ܐܽܘܢܩܝܳܐ *uncia, an ounce, a weight equal to eight drachms;* abbreviated form ܐܽܘܩ.

ܐܘܢܝܬܐ f. (rt. ܐܢܝ, not otherwise found in Syr.; in Chald. and Heb. *to lament, mourn*) *grief, sadness.*

ܐܘܣܝܐ pl. ܐܘܣܝܐܣ, ܐܘܣܝܣ or ܐܘܣܝܣ f. οὐσία, *a*) *essence, substance,* ܒܪ ܐܘܣܝܐ and ܚܕ ܒܐܘܣܝܐ *consubstantial, of one* or *the same substance;* ܐܘܣܝܣ ܫܡܝܢܝܬܐ *heavenly substances,* ܐܘܣܝܣ ܡܬܟܝܬܐ *metallic substances. b*) *wealth, substance, estate, income,* ܐܒܕܢܐ ܕܐܘܣܝܣ ܕܝܠܗܘܢ *the loss of their property.*

ܐܘܣܝܐܝܬ adv. *of* or *belonging to the essence* or *substance, essentially, substantially.*

ܐܘܣܝܢܝܐ f. ܐܘܣܝܢܝܬܐ pl. m. ܐܘܣܝܢܝܐ, f. ܐܘܣܝܢܝܬܐ adj. *of the essence* or *substance, essential;* gram. *radical;* ܕܝܠܝܬܐ ܐܘܣܝܢܝܬܐ *essential properties.* ܡܢܘܬܐ ܐܘܣܝܢܝܬܐ *the essential* parts of holy baptism are water, oil, the priest, prayers said by a priest; the words of Christ are ܡ̈ܠܐ ܐܘܣܝܢܝܬܐ *essential to* or *of the substance* of the Holy Eucharist.

ܐܘܣܦ APHEL of rt. ܝܣܦ*; *to add, to be more* or *greater:* with another verb it has adverbial force, *more, again.*

ܐܘܥܒ APHEL of ܥܒܐ; *to make grow* or *sprout.*

ܐܘܦܛܘܣ pl. ܐܘܦܛܘܣ usually ܗܘܦܛܘܣ ὕπατος, *a consul.* See under ܗܘ also for other Greek words spelt occasionally with initial ܐ instead of ܗ.

ܐܘܦܩ APHEL of ܦܩ*; *to be able, sufficient; to vanish away; to do away with, bring to an end.*

ܐܘܦܝܩܝܢ or ܐܘܦܝܩܝܢ ὀφφίκιον, *officium*, sc. *officiales*, f. used collectively for *officials, attendants, train, suite,* ܩܡ ܕܝܢܐ ܘܟܠܗ ܐܘܦܝܩܝܢ *the judge and all the court rose up,* ܐܘܦܝܩܝܢ ܕܝܠܟ *the officials,* ܐܘܦܝܩܝܢ ܕܝܠܟܘܢ *your attendants, your retinue.*

ܐܘܦܠ Pers. *lilium aquaticum, the water-lily.*

ܐܘܦܢܐ pl. ܐܘܦܢܐ m. Heb. *wheels,* Ez. x. 15.

ܐܘܦܪܟܐ pl. ܐܘܦܪܟܐ ὕπαρχος, *procurator, prefect, governor,* ܐܘܦܪܟܐ ܕܣܘܪܝܐ *the Governor of Syria.*

ܐܘܨܪ, ܐܘܨܪܐ pl. ܐ̈ rt. ܐܨܪ. m. *a place where anything is laid up, a storehouse;* ܐܘܨܪܐ ܕܡܝܐ *a reservoir.* Pl. generally *a barn, granary,* hence *corn;* also *stores* in general. ܐܘܨܪ̈ܐ ܕܬܠܓܐ *the treasures of the snow,* ܐܘܨܪ̈ܐ ܢܗܝܪ̈ܐ ܕܒܣܝܡܘܬܗ *the shining treasuries of His bliss,* i.e. in the heavenly kingdom.

ܐܘܩܕ APHEL of ܝܩܕ; *to set on fire; to excite,* &c.

ܐܘܩܝܢܐ or ܐܘܩܝܢܘܣ pl. ܐܘܩܝܢܐ and ܐܘܩܝܢܐܣ ὄγκινος, *uncinus, an anchor, a sounding-lead;* in both senses it is used with the verb ܫܪܐ *to let down.*

ܐܘܩܝܢܘܣ, ܐܘܩܝܢܘܣ or ܐܘܩܝܐܢܘܣ ὠκεανός, *the ocean;* ܐܘܩܝܢܘܣ ܪܒܐ. ܗܘ ܕܚܕܪ ܠܟܠܗ ܐܪܥܐ *the great ocean which surrounds the whole earth.*

ܐܘܩܘܢܘܡܐ or ܐܘܩܘܢܘܡܘܣ pl. ܐ̈ οἰκονόμος, *a steward.*

ܐܘܩܪ APHEL of ܝܩܪ; *to make heavy* or *dull; to make precious,* &c.

ܐܘܪ pr. n. *Ur,* usually ܐܘܪ ܕܟܠܕܝܐ *Ur of the Chaldees.*

ܐܘܪܒ APHEL of ܪܒܐ; *to magnify, raise to honour,* &c.

ܐܘܪܓܐ pl. ܐܘܪܓܐ m. *spotted, piebald* of horses.

ܐܘܪܓܢܘܢ, ܐܘܪܓܢܘܢ pl. ܐܘܪܓܢܐ and ܐܘܪܓܢܐ m. ὄργανον, *an instrument, a vessel, an organ,* e.g. of the body; ܐܘܪܓܢܐ ܕܢܦܫܐ *the organs of respiration;* ܐܘܪܓܢܐ ܕܩܪܒܐ *engines of war;* ܐܘܪܓܢܐ ܕܐܣܛܪܘܢܘܡܝܐ or ܐܘܪܓܢܘܢ ܕܐܣܛܪܘܠܒܐ or ܐܘܪܓܢܐ ܕܡܬܒܩܝܢܘܬܐ astronomical *instruments for taking observations.*

ܐܘܪܙܝܐ and ܐܘܪܙܢܐ *a packing needle, a coarse needle* ܡܚܛܐ ܕܣܩ̈ܐ used for making sacks.

ܐܘܪܙܕܐ pl. ܐܘܪܙܕܐ f. *a frog, the frog of a horse's foot.*

ܐܘܪܗܝ *Edessa,* a city of Mesopotamia held in honour by the Syrians on account of king Abgar, and called ܡܕܝܢܬܐ ܡܗܝܡܢܬܐ or ܡܕܝܢܬܐ ܡܒܪܟܬܐ *the believing city, the blessed city.*

ܐܘܪܗܝܐ, ܐܘܪܗܝܬܐ pl. m. ܐ̈, f. ܐ̈, *Edessene, of Edessa;* ܡܡܠܠܐ ܐܘܪܗܝܐ *the Edessene dialect,* which was considered the purest Syriac. S. James of Edessa is sometimes named simply

ܐܘܪܗܝܐ *the Edessene*, and his style of writing is held to be perfect.

ܐܘܪܘܙܐ or ܐܘܪܙܐ ܕܐ *a weasel.*

ܐܘܪܚ, ܐܘܪܚܐ pl. ܐܘܪܚܬܐ rt. ܐܪܚ. f. *a*) *a way, road, journey*, ܐܘܪܚܐ ܥܒܪ *a wayfarer;* ܐܘܪܚ ܡܠܟܐ *the king's highway, the high road;* ܐܘܪܚܐ ܕܕܝܫܬܐ *a trodden path* or *way;* ܦܘܪܫܢ ܐܘܪܚܬܐ *a place where two roads meet;* ܡܢ ܐܘܪܚܐ ܐܬܐ ܗܘܐ *he had just returned from a journey.* *b*) *a custom, way, manner* of life, ܒܐܘܪܚܐ ܕܡܨܪܝܐ *after the manner of the Egyptians;* ܒܐܘܪܚܐ ܕܐܠܗܐ *in the way of God*, i.e. *in a life well-pleasing to God*, ܐܘܪܚܐ ܕܥܠܡܐ *the worldly life;* ܐܘܪܚܐ ܡܨܥܝܬܐ *a middle course, via media;* ܐܘܪܚܐ ܕܝܚܝܕܝܘܬܐ—ܕܪܝܫܢܘܬܐ *the monastic life, the life of a solitary.* *c*) *religion, the service of God;* cf. in the Acts of the Apostles, *the Way.* ܐܘܪܚܐ ܫܪܝܪܬܐ—ܕܟܪܣܛܝܢܘܬܐ *the true religion, the Christian faith*, ܐܘܪܚܐ ܕܛܝܝܘܬܐ *the religion of the Arabs.* *d*) *legal right*, ܡܛܠ ܕܐܘܪܚܗ ܗܝ ܐܘܪܚܐ *because it is his right;* ܒܐܘܪܚܐ ܟܢܘܢܝܬܐ *canonical, according to church order.*

ܐܘܪܝܐ pl. ܐܘܪܘܝܢ, ܐܘܪܘܝܬܐ (rt. ܐܪܝ*, Ar. *to stall an animal*), m. *a stall, crib, manger*, esp. the manger where our Lord was laid, hence metaph. *a cradle.*

ܐܘܪܝܙܘܢ m. ὁρίζων, *the horizon.*

ܐܘܪܝܬܐ (from the same Heb. root as that from which *the Torah* = *the Law*, is derived) *the law, the Law* of Moses, *the Pentateuch*, ܐܘܪܝܬܐ ܡܫܒܥܢܝܬܐ ܕܫܒܥܝܢ *the Pentateuch according to the Septuagint version;* often used inclusively of the whole of the Old Testament.

ܐܘܪܝ Aphel of ܐܪܝ; see below.

ܐܘܪܟܐ rt. ܐܪܟ. m. *length, longitude;* ܒܘܪܟܬܐ ܒܐܘܪܟܐ ܣܓܝܐ—marriage *blessings, written at great length;* ܐܘܪܟܐ ܕܡܕܝܢܬ ܒܒܠ *the longitude of the city of Babylon.*

ܐܘܪܟܢܝܐ adj. *longitudinal.*

ܐܘܪܥ, ܐܘܪܥܐ rt. ܐܪܥ. m. *a meeting, encounter, attack;* usually with a verb of motion, ܢܦܩ—ܣܠܩ—ܩܡ ܠܐܘܪܥܗ *he went out—rose up—to meet him.*

ܐܘܪܩ Aphel of ܝܪܩ; *to grow pale* or *green.*

ܐܘܪܩܥܬܐ = ܪܘܩܥܬܐ *a strip of cloth, a patch; rags, tatters.*

ܐܘܪܪܐ pl. ܐܘܪܪܐ *orarium.* *a*) *a cloth, a handkerchief*, ܡܫܘܗܝ ܗܘܐ ܠܕܡܥܘܗܝ ܒܐܘܪܪܐ *he wiped away* his tears *with his handkerchief.* *b*) *a stole;* deacons of the Greek church wore it over the left shoulder, floating on either side like wings; the Latin deacons tied the ends under the right arm. Among the Syrians it was worn, *a*) by subdeacons both Nestorian and Maronite, folded round the neck, *b*) by deacons of the Nestorian, Maronite, and Malabar Syrians, hanging from the left shoulder, *c*) by priests round the neck pendent in front, *d*) Maronite readers wore it hanging from the right shoulder. ܐܢܫ ܠܒܝܫ ܐܘܪܪܐ ܕܡܫܡܫܢܘܬܐ *habited in the deacon's stole*, ܡܫܡܫܢܐ ܛܥܝܢܝ ܐܘܪܪܐ *the deacons wearing their stoles.*

ܐܘܪܫܠܡ (Heb. foundation or possession of peace) *Jerusalem.*

ܐܘܪܬ Aphel of ܝܪܬ; *to leave by will, to give an inheritance* or *possession.*

ܐܘܫܛ rt. ܫܛ* only used in the Aphel conj. *to move, stretch out;* usually with ܐܝܕܐ and with ܒ of the thing or ܠܘܬ of the person, *to lay hands on, seize, steal, do harm;* cf. the following.

ܐܘܫܛ Aphel of ܫܛ*; *to hold out, stretch out;* usually with ܐܝܕܐ and with ܒ or ܠܘܬ of the thing or person, in a good or bad sense; see under ܫܛ for examples.

ܐܘܫܟܦܐ m. *a cobbler;* see ܐܫܟܦܐ.

ܐܘܫܢܐ pl. ܐܘܫܢܐ m. *an animal kept for breeding, a stallion;* metaph. *lustful, wanton.*

ܐܘܫܥܢܐ pl. ܢܐ (from Heb. *Save now!* through a Greek form) *Hosanna;* pl. *palm-branches*, ܚܕ ܒܫܒܐ ܕܐܘܫܥܢܐ—ܕܣܘܟܐ—ܕܐܘܫܥܢܐ or absol. *Palm Sunday.*

ܐܘܬܒ Aphel of ܝܬܒ; *to make inhabit* or *to be inhabited; to constitute* to an office, &c.

ܐܘܬܢܛܝܐ αὐθεντία, *authority, jurisdiction, rule*, hence *a diocese, province*, ܐܘܬܢܛܝܐ ܕܐܢܛܝܘܟܝܐ *the province of Antioch.*

ܐܘܬܢܛܝܩܐ, ܐܘܬܢܛܝܩܘܢ αὐθεντική, αὐθεντικόν, *authentic, original, an original* document.

ܐܘܬܪ Aphel of ܝܬܪ; *to be left over; to increase; to be of profit.*

ܐܘܙܓܐ or ܐܙܓܐ m. *the hair that sprouts out at puberty*, ܛܠܝܐ ܕܠܐ ܐܙܓܐ *beardless boys.*

ܐܙܓܢܐ adj. *hairy, shaggy.*

ܐܙܓܘܪܐ or ܐܙܓܘܪܐ m. *bos taurus, the buffalo.*

ܐܙܓܐ pl. ܐܙܓ̈ܐ Ar. m. *the arch of a door* or *roof, an arched building; a porch, portico,* ܐܙܓܝ̈ܗ ܘܐܣܛܘܢ̈ܘܗܝ *the porticoes and columns* of a church.

ܐܙܓܕܘܬܐ usually ܐܝܙܓܕܘܬܐ *an embassy, a message.*

ܐܙܓܘܡܐ, ܐܘܙܓܘܡܐ and ܙܘܓܘܡܐ ζύγωμα, *a crossbar to fasten a door.*

ܐܙܓܘܢܐ pl. ܐܙܓܘܢ̈ܐ m. dim. of ܐܙܓܐ. *a little* or *low arch* or *vault.*

ܐܙܘܠܐ pl. ܐ̈ rt. ܐܙܠ. m. *a traveller*, esp. *a pilgrim;* ܐܙܘܠ̈ܐ ܘܐܬܘ̈ܝܐ *comers and goers.*

ܐܘܙܠ Aphel of ܙܠ; *to despise, debase, seduce.*

ܐܙܠ fut. ܢܐܙܠ, ܬܐܙܠ, ܐܐܙܠ, inf. ܡܐܙܠ and less properly ܡܐܙܠ, pres. part. ܐܙܠ, ܐܙܠܐ, past part. ܐܙܝܠ, ܐܙܝܠܐ. *to go, walk, journey; to go away, be gone,* hence *to die.* Opp. ܐܬܐ; ܐܙܠ ܘܐܬܐ *to come and go,* i.e. *habitually.* With ܠ or ܠܘܬ of the place or action, e.g. ܠܥܕܬܐ—ܠܒܠܢܐ *to church, to the bath;* ܠܩܪܒܐ *to go to war;* ܐܙܠ ܠܬܫܡܫܬܐ *he went to attend upon* or *do allegiance to.* Used also of inanimate things; *ships, letters, boundaries, rumours,* &c.; ܐܙܠ ܝܘܡܐ *the day was over;* ܘܐܫܬܠܡܘ ܐܦܣܩܘ̈ܦܐ: ܬܐܙܠ ܠܡܕܝܢܬܐ ܡܠܟܘܬܐ ܡܢ ܐܦܣܘܣ ܟܘܪܣܝܐ ܕܦܛܪܝܪܟܘܬܐ the Synod decreed *that the Patriarchal See should be transferred from Ephesus to the capital, Byzantium;* ܦܘܫܩܐ ܐܙܠ ܠܒܠܛܫܐܨܪ *the interpretation was carried to Belteshazzar.* With ܒ, ܐܙܠ ܒܐܘܪܚܐ *to journey, travel, go in the direction of;* ܒܫܒܝܐ *to go into captivity, be carried away;* ܒܒܙܬܐ *to be for a prey;* with ܒܬܪ *to follow,* metaph. *to serve* false gods, vanity, &c.; ܣܓܝܐܐ ܐܙܠܝܢ ܒܬܪ ܛܘܥܝܝܗܘܢ *many shall follow their errors, shall err like them;* with ܠܘܬ or ܓܒ of the person, *to go with, draw near;* with ܥܠ *to march against, assault, invade;* with ܥܡ *to go with, accompany* any one; with ܩܕܡ *to go before, precede.*

When directly preceding another verb ܐܙܠ signifies intention or command; ܐܙܠ ܐܢܐ ܐܨܘܕ ܢܘܢܐ *I go a fishing;* ܐܙܠܘ ܢܚܬܘ *they went down;* with the copula ܘ it expresses continuous action, ܐܙܠ ܘܪܒܐ *he went on growing, increased more and more;* ܘܐܙܠܘ ܪܟܒܘ *they rode away;* with ܠ or ܕ preceding the second verb, *to be about to,* ܐܢܐ ܐܙܠ ܐܢܐ ܠܡܡܬ *I am going to die,* i.e. *I shall die soon;* like other verbs of motion such as ܢܦܩ, ܩܡ, ܐܬܐ, it is often used with ܠ and the pron. affix to form a pleonastic or ethical dative, ܐܙܠ ܠܟ—ܠܟܝ—ܠܟܘܢ *go away, take yourself off.* Part. pres. with ܠ, *fit, good for, convenient,* ܡܢܐ ܐܙܠ ܠܝ ܚܝܐ *what good is my life to me, of what use or advantage is this life?* ܠܡܢܐ ܐܙܠ ܠܝ *what good is it to me, what do I want with it?* ܠܡܕܡ ܠܐ ܐܙܠܐ *it is good for nothing.* The part. pres. fem. ܐܙܠܐ is often used as a subst. *going, departure.*

Wherever a vowel belongs to the ܠ the ܠ is otiose and ܙ takes the vowel, ܐܙܠܬ, ܐܙܠܝܢ *ezath, ozin* for ܐܙܠܬ, ܐܙܠܝܢ *ezlath, ozlin;* but when the vowel belongs to the ܙ, ܠ is retained, ܐܙܠ, ܐܙܠܢܢ *ezal, ezalnan.* But in the sense of *helping, being of use* the ܠ is not deprived of its vowel, ܐܙܠܝܢ *ozlin, helping.* Derivatives, ܐܙܘܠܐ, ܡܐܙܠ, ܡܐܙܠܢܐ, ܡܐܙܠܬܐ, ܡܘܙܠܢܐ, ܡܘܙܠܢܘܬܐ.

ܐܙܡܪܓܕܐ; see ܙܡܪܓܕܐ *emerald.*

ܐܚܐ 1 pers. fut. Peal, ܐܚܐ 1 pers. fut. Aphel, ܐܚܐ imper. Aphel of ܚܝܐ *to live.*

ܐܚܐ pl. ܐܚܐ, ܐܚܝܢ. fem. ܚܬܐ having dropped the Alep which is found in the cognate languages and in the pl. ܐܚܘܬܐ. See ܚܬܐ *a sister.* Takes affixes like ܐܒܐ; 1 pers. sing. ܐܚܝ 2 p.s. ܐܚܘܟ, ܐܚܘܟܝ 3 p.s. ܐܚܘܗܝ, ܐܚܘܗ pl. 1 p. ܐܚܘܢ 2 p. ܐܚܘܟܘܢ 3 p. ܐܚܘܗܘܢ, ܐܚܝܟܘܢ, &c. *a) a brother,* ܐܚܐ ܩܫܝܫܐ *an elder brother;* ܐܚܐ ܙܥܘܪܐ *a younger brother;* ܐܚܘܗ ܒܪ ܐܡܗ, ܐܚܘܗ ܒܪ ܐܒܘܗ *her step* or *half-brother on the mother's, on the father's* side. *b)* sometimes used in a wide sense for any kinsman or for one of the same tribe or nation. *c) a friend, neighbour, companion, colleague, associate,* and in a still more general sense, *another;* repeated or with ܚܕ or ܚܒܪܗ, *one and another;* ܝܡܘ ܚܕ ܥܡ ܐܚܘܗܝ *they swore to each other;* ܐܚܝܢ ܠܘܬ ܐܚܝܗܘܢ *amongst themselves.* *d)* later, *a monk, friar,* ܐܚܐ ܡܫܡܫܢܐ *a lay brother;* ܐܚ̈ܐ ܕܗܝܟܠܐ ܘܕܐܟܣܢܕܘܟܝܐ *monks Templars and Hospitallers.* Derivatives, ܐܚܝܐ, ܐܚܘܬܐ, ܐܚܝܢ, ܐܚܝܢܘܬܐ, ܚܬܐ, ܚܝܢ.

ܐܚܶܒ݂ Aphel of ܚܒ; *to love; to kindle.*

ܐܶܚܰܕ fut. ܢܺܐܚܽܘܕ, imper. ܐܶܚܽܘܕ, pres. part. ܐܳܚܶܕ, ܐܳܚܕܳܐ (this participle is seldom used except with ܗ̄ܘܳܐ or a pronoun to express the present and imperfect tenses, ܐܰܚܺܝܕ takes its place elsewhere, having an active besides passive sense); pass. part. ܐܰܚܺܝܕ, ܐܰܚܺܝܕܳܐ, m. ܐܰܚܺܝܕܳܐ, ܐܰܚܺܝܕܬܳܐ f., pl. m. ܐܰܚܺܝܕܺܝܢ, ܐܰܚܺܝܕܶܐ f. ܐܰܚܺܝܕܳܢ, ܐܰܚܺܝܕܳܬܳܐ. *a) to take, seize on, lay hold of,* usually with ܠ but also with ܒ, see ܒܐܝܕܐ and other examples below; with ܥܰܡ *to strive with;* often metaph. of various passions, of pain, fire, &c.; ܐܶܚܕܰܬ ܐܶܢܽܘܢ ܕܶܚܠܬܳܐ ܠܟ݂ܽܠܗܽܘܢ *fear seized upon them all;* ܐܶܚܕܰܬ ܐܶܫܳܬܳܐ ܚܰܪܺܝܦܬܳܐ ܠܚܰܕ *a sharp fever laid hold of some one,* i.e. *he had a sharp attack of fever. b)* of inanimate things, e.g. of custom, heresy, peace, war, *to obtain, prevail. c) to hold, contain, keep, possess, retain, comprehend;* ܒܰܝܬܳܐ ܐܳܚܶܕ ܡܳܐܐ ܒܢܰܝܢܳܫܳܐ a house *capable of receiving a hundred persons;* ܡܶܢܝܳܢܳܐ ܕܙܰܒ̈ܢܶܐ ܕܰܐܚܺܝܕܺܝܢܰܢ *the chronology which we follow;* ܡܶܠܶܐ ܐܳܚܕ̈ܳܢ ܗܳܕܶܐ ܦܽܘܫܳܩܳܐ *the words admit of this explanation, may be taken in this sense. d) to shut, shut up, close, fasten, keep closed,* often with ܬܰܪܥܳܐ *the door* or *gate* and ellipt.; ܐܶܚܰܕ ܒܐܰܦ̈ܰܘܗܝ *to shut the door in the face of any one;* ܐܶܚܰܕ ܐܽܘܪ̈ܚܳܬܳܐ *to close the ways, hold the roads,* i.e. *in time of war,* but ܐܶܚܰܕ ܐܽܘܪܚܳܐ *to hold on his way, continue a journey;* ܐܶܚܰܕ ܒܟܬܳܒܳܐ *he closed the book;* metaph. with ܪ̈ܰܚܡܶܐ *to restrain his compassion,* but ܐܶܚܰܕ ܡܳܪܝܳܐ ܪܰܚܡܳܗ̇ the Lord *had shut up her womb.*

With ܐܰܝܟ *to behave like* or *as,* e.g. ܐܰܝܟ ܒܥܶܠܕܒܳܒܳܐ *as an enemy;* with ܐܽܘܚܕܬܳܐ *to propose an enigma* opp. ܦܫܰܩ, ܫܪܳܐ or ܦܰܪܶܫ *to disclose, solve, declare it;* ܚܶܡܬܳܐ ܐܶܚܰܕ ܠܘܳܬ *to be enraged with;* ܐܶܚܕܳܗ̇ ܒܐܺܝܕܳܗ̇ *he took her by the hand,* metaph. *to help* and ܐܶܚܰܕ ܐܺܝܕܶܗ ܡܶܢ *he closed his hand,* i.e. *refused to help;* ܒܐܝܩܳܪܳܐ *to receive with honour;* ܒܡܨܝܕܬܳܐ *to net, catch in a net;* ܓܰܘܣܳܐ *to take refuge;* ܩܪܳܒܳܐ ܥܰܡ *to make war;* ܕܽܘܟܬܳܐ *to succeed to an office;* ܡܰܠܟܽܘܬܳܐ *to obtain, succeed to* or *govern a kingdom;* ܢܽܘܡܶܐ or ܢܽܘܡܬܳܐ *an ulcer eats into* or *spreads;* ܥܶܠܬܳܐ *to adduce a reason* or *pretext;* ܫܶܬܩܳܐ *to be silent;* ܨܰܘܡܳܐ *to observe a fast;* ܗܰܝܡܳܢܽܘܬܳܐ *to embrace the faith.*

The second participle is used with an active besides its passive sense. Passive, *held, grasped, fastened, barred, shut,* esp. with ܬܰܪܥܳܐ; ܪ̈ܽܘܚܶܐ ܕܰܐܚܺܝܕܳܢ ܗ̄ܘܰܝ ܒܫܝܽܘܠ the spirits *who were kept shut up in the lower regions,* 1 Pet. iii. 19; *besieged, closed, barren, sterile, retained,* metaph. *tangled, captured,* e.g. ܒܛܽܘܥܝܰܝܢ *in error;* ܐܰܚܺܝܕ ܐܶܫܳܬܳܐ *taken with a fever;* ܒܫܶܢܬܳܐ *overcome by sleep, fast asleep.* Active, *a) taking, laying hold of, seizing, holding, bearing,* hence ܐܰܚܺܝܕܰܝ ܣܰܝܦܳܐ or ܣܰܦܣܪܳܐ *sword bearers, armed with swords;* ܐܰܚܺܝܕܰܝ ܪܽܘܡܚܳܐ *spearmen;* ܐܰܚܺܝܕܺܝܢ ܗ̄ܘܰܘ ܚܰܕ ܒܐܺܝܕ ܚܰܒܪܶܗ *holding each others' hands;* ܐܰܚܺܝܕ ܟܽܠ *is constantly used of God* =*omnipotent, holding* or *upholding all. b) possessing, having, holding,* i.e. *having power over, governing,* sometimes with ܫܽܘܠܛܳܢܳܐ; hence in the emph. state, subst. *one in power, a ruler, noble, prince;* and adj. *powerful, honourable;* with ܥܺܕܬܳܐ *presiding over the church* = *being bishop,* or *patriarch;* metaph. e.g. of peace, *to rule, obtain,* with ܒ of the place, with ܥܝܳܕܳܐ *the custom holds* or *obtains, prevails;* n. b. construction ܫܶܬܩܳܐ ܐܰܚܺܝܕ ܗ̄ܘܳܐ ܠܟ݂ܽܠ *silence ruled over all* = *all kept silence;* with ܒܢܰܦܫܶܗ *being master of* or *containing himself* = *being in his right senses. c) holding* or *adhering to the truth, a doctrine, opinion, mode of worship;* ܗܰܘ ܕܰܐܚܺܝܕ ܟܰܠܩܺܝܕܽܘܢܳܝܽܘܬܳܐ *an adherent of the Council of* Chalcedon; ܐܰܚܺܝܕܰܝ ܬܰܘܕܺܝܬܝ *my co-religionists, those who hold as I do; keeping* or *observing* a feast, the law. *d)* ܐܰܚܺܝܕ ܓܰܘܣܳܐ *a refugee;* ܙܳܟܽܘܬܳܐ *a conqueror;* ܛܽܘܦܣܳܐ *being a type, typifying;* ܬܶܫܡܫܬܳܐ *serving, being a minister.*

Ethpe. ܐܶܬ݁ܚܶܕ for ܐܶܬ݂ܐܚܶܕ, *a) to be seized, caught, taken,* e.g. by lot, *to be taken captive, taken possession of;* with ܓܢܳܒ݂ܬܳܐ or ܓܢܽܘܒܝܳܐ *to be caught* or *found stealing;* ܒܟܽܘܪܗܳܢܳܐ *to fall ill;* ܡܶܢ ܠܐܽܘܬܳܐ *to be weary;* ܒܡܨܝܕܬܳܐ *to be ensnared by* false *teaching;* ܒܦܰܚܳܐ *to be ensnared;* ܒܪܰܓܬܳܐ *to be seized with desire, be captivated;* ܒܪܚܡܬܳܐ *to fall in love. b) to be held, held captive,* ܡܶܢ ܡܰܘܬܳܐ *by death,* ܒܫܝܽܘܠ *in Sheol.* ܒܩܽܘܠܳܪ̈ܶܐ *to be thrown into chains, imprisoned; to be shut up, shut, closed, fastened,* esp. with ܬܰܪܥܳܐ *a door* or *gate;* and of other places, e.g. ܐܶܬ݁ܚܶܕ ܩܰܒܪܳܐ *the sepulchre was closed;* ܫܡܰܝܳܐ *the churches were closed* during the Decian persecution; with ܦܘܡܗܘܢ *to be silent;* with ܥܝܕܐ *it is a custom, a custom prevails.*

PA. ܐܰܚܶܕ part. ܡܐܚܕ and ܡܚܰܕ, *to put in possession, to shut closely;* ܡܐܚܕ ܥܝ̈ܢܐ *one who closes* or *holds the eyes,* i.e. *from seeing what is really there = one who deceives by magic arts.* APH. ܐܘܚܶܕ *a) to make lay hold,* esp. of fire *= to kindle, set fire to* with ܒ of the object. *b) to give to hold, give into the hand, to hand to any one,* ܐܘܚܶܕ ܩܪ̈ܢܬܐ ܒܐܝ̈ܕܝܗܘܢ *he gave them trumpets to hold. c) to close up, fasten together.* DERIVATIVES, ܐܘܚܕܢܐ, ܐܘܚܕܬܐ, ܐܚܕܐ, ܐܚܕܘܬܐ, ܐܚܕܐ see part., ܐܚܝܕܘܬܐ, ܡܐܚܕ, ܡܚܕܢܘܬܐ, ܡܐܚܕܢܘܬܐ, ܡܐܚܕܢܝܬܐ.

ܐܰܚܕܳܐ rt. ܐܚܕ. m. *the hollow of a door into which the bolt is fastened, a bar* or *bolt.*

ܐܰܚܘܳܕܳܐ f. ܐܰܚܘܳܕܬܳܐ pl. m. ܐܰܚܘ̈ܳܕܶܐ rt. ܐܚܕ. subst. *he* or *that which holds* or *keeps, a governor, ruler,* ܐܰܚܘܳܕܳܐ ܕܩܠܺܝ̈ܕܶܐ *keeper of the keys,* a title of the patriarch; *a lictor.* adj. *strong, restraining, binding, comprehending, collective.*

ܐܚܘܢܐ dim. of ܐܚܐ. m. *a little brother.*

ܐܰܚܘܽܬܳܐ f. *a) brotherhood, fellowship;* ܪܚܡܬܐ ܕܐܚܘܬܐ *brotherly love. b) a fraternity, a monastic community,* ܟܗܢܐ ܕܐܚܘܬܐ *the priest of a friary;* collect. *the brethren;* ܟܠܗ ܐܚܘܬܐ *all the brethren;* ܟܢܫܐ ܕܟܠܗ ܐܚܘܬܐ *the assembly of all the brethren, the whole fraternity. c) a title,* either sing. or pl. *by which a patriarch addresses a bishop and a bishop the clergy or monks,* ܠܚܟܝܡܬܐ ܐܚܘܬܟ *to thee, O wise Brother.*

ܐܰܚܺܝ APHEL of ܚܝܐ; *to give life, restore to life.*

ܐܚܝܕܘܬܐ f. rt. ܐܚܕ. *holding, taking possession;* ܐܚܝܕܘܬ ܝܪܬܘܬܐ *entering on an inheritance;* ܐܚܝܕܘܬ ܩܢܝܢܐ *being in possession, occupancy.*

ܐܚܝܢ, ܐܚܝܢܐ m. pl. ܐܚܝ̈ܢܐ, ܐܚܝ̈ܢܝܢ f.s. ܐܚܝܢܬܐ pl. ܐܚܝ̈ܢܬܐ, ܐܚܝ̈ܢܢ. rt. ܐܚ in ܐܚܐ. *one near of kin, a relation* or *connection, the next of kin;* metaph. *allied, related, like, similar;* ܣܒܪܐ ܘܚܘܒܐ ܐܚܝܢܗ *hope, and love which is akin to her;* ܘܐܚܪ̈ܢܝܬܐ ܐܚܝܢ̈ܬܐ ܠܗܝܢ *other like things.*

ܐܚܝܢܘܬܐ pl. ܐܬܐ f. *kinship, consanguinity, affinity, relationship, similarity;* ܐܚܝܢܘܬܗ ܕܚܟܡܬܐ *an alliance with wisdom.*

ܐܚܝ̈ܢܐ f. ܐܚܝ̈ܢܬܐ *similar;* ܗܠܝܢ ܘܐܚܝ̈ܢܬܗܝܢ *these and the like;* gram. *cognate* nouns; also *nouns in relation with others,* i.e. *in the construct state.*

ܐܰܚܶܠ APHEL of ܚܠ; *to profane* the Sabbath.

ܐܚܠܐ or ܐܘܚܠܐ m. *dorycnium, an alkaline plant.*

ܐܰܚܶܡ APHEL of ܚܡ; *to heat.*

ܐܰܚ, ܐܰܚܰܚ see ܚܐ, APHEL; interj. of exultation, *Hurrah! Aha!*

ܐܚܪ Heb. root-meaning *to tarry,* not used in PE. or PA. APHEL ܐܘܚܪ part. ܡܘܚܪ *a) to tarry, delay, to be tardy, late, slow* with ܠ and an infin.; ܡܘܚܪ ܠܡܐܬܐ *he delays his coming, tarries;* ܡܘܚܪ ܠܡܡܠܠܘ *slow to speak;* ܡܘܚܪܝܢ ܠܡܬܢܝܚܘ *they are late to take rest;* but with ܒ *to be a long while over anything,* ܟܕ ܐܘܚܪ ܒܡܡܠܠܘ ܣܓܝܐܐ *when he had spoken at great length. b) to sojourn, stay,* with ܠܘܬ of a person or ܒ of a place; ܟܡܐ ܙܒܢܐ ܐܢܘ ܐܦܝܣܩܦܐ ܢܘܚܪ ܠܒܪ ܡܢ ܡܕܝܢܬܗ *how long may a bishop absent himself from his see?* SHAPH. ܫܘܚܪ *to be slack, linger, delay, defer, hinder,* generally with ܠ and infin., ܠܐ ܫܘܚܪ ܨܒܝܢܐ ܠܓܘܡܪܗ *his desire had immediate effect.* ESHTAPH. (1st form) ܐܫܬܘܚܪ *to delay, linger;* intr. *to spend time, stay, remain* in a place; *to be tardy, slow, late* or *long;* ܠܐ ܬܫܬܘܚܪܘܢ ܗܪܟܐ *do not tarry here;* ܘܬܐܬܐ ܘܠܐ ܬܫܬܘܚܪ *to come without delay. To remain, be left over.* (2nd form) ܐܫܬܚܪ and ܐܫܬܐܚܪ usually abbreviated ܐܫܬܚܪ *to remain, be left, be left over,* with ܕ *the remainder, the rest,* pl. *the others, the survivors;* ܫܪܟܐ ܕܡܫܬܚܪܢܐ *the remaining company;* ܫܪܟܐ ܕܐܫܬܚܪܘ ܥܪܩܘ *the rest fled;* ܐܝܠܝܢ ܕܐܫܬܚܪܘ ܡܢ ܟܦܢܐ *those whom the famine had spared.* DERIVATIVES, ܐܚܪܝܐ, ܐܚܪܝܘܬܐ, for ܐܚܪܢ see under ܐܚܪܢ, ܐܚܪܝܢ, ܐܚܪܢܝܐ, ܡܘܚܪܢܐ, ܡܘܚܪܢܘܬܐ, ܫܘܚܪܐ, ܫܘܚܪܢܐ, ܡܫܬܚܪܢܘܬܐ, ܐܫܬܚܪܘܬܐ.

ܐܚܪܝ, ܐܚܪܝܐ, ܐܚܪܝܬܐ pl. m. ܐܚܪ̈ܝܐ f. ܐܚܪ̈ܝܬܐ rt. ܐܚܪ. *the latter, the last;* opp. ܩܕܡܝܐ in several senses, *later, after, hinder;* ܝܡܐ ܐܚܪܝܐ *the Mediterranean sea;* after a proper name, *the younger,* ܒܢܝ̈ܟܘܢ ܐܚܪ̈ܝܐ *your younger children;* ܟܢܘܢ ܐܚܪܝ *later Conun* i.e. *January;*

ܬܫܪܝܢ ܐܚܪܝ *the later Teshrin* i.e. *November;* ܝܘܡ̈ܬܐ ܐܚܪ̈ܝܐ *the last days;* ܝܘܡܐ ܐܚܪܝܐ *the Last Day.*

Fem. used as subst. as in Heb. *the latter* or *last* part, state, &c.; ܐܚܪܝܬܗ ܕܐܝܘܒ *the latter part of Job's life* opp. ܩܕܡܝܬܗ *his former state.* Adverbially, ܐܚܪܝܬ *afterwards, at last, at length;* ܐܚܪܝܬ ܟܠ *last of all;* ܠܐܚܪܝܬܐ *after, afterwards, hereafter, at the end, finally;* ܒܝܫ ܐܚܪܝܬܐ *utterly bad.*

ܐܚܪܝܘܬܐ f. rt. ܐܚܪ. *coming after,* hence *the latter part, the end;* ܠܐܚܪܝܘܬܗ ܕܣܬܘܐ *towards the end of winter.*

ܐܚܪܝܢ, ܐܚܪܢܐ f. ܐܚܪܬܐ pl. m. ܐܚܪ̈ܢܐ, ܐܚܪܢܝܢ f. ܐܚܪ̈ܢܝܬܐ, ܐܚܪ̈ܢܝܢ rt. ܐܚܪ. *other, another, the other, the next;* with ܡܢ *different;* ܐܚܪ̈ܢܐ ܘܐܚܪ̈ܢܐ *various;* ܩܠܝܠ ܐܚܪܝܢ *yet a little while, soon after;* ܝܘܡܐ ܐܚܪܢܐ *the next day, the day after;* ܫܢܬܐ ܐܚܪܬܐ *the next* or *following year.*

ܐܚܪܢܐܝܬ adv. *otherwise.*

ܐܚܪܝܢ, ܐܚܪܝܢܐ, ܐܚܪܝܢܝܬܐ pl. m. ܐܚܪ̈ܝܢܐ, ܐܚܪܝܢܝܢ rt. ܐܚܪ. *other, another, different, strange;* ܐܚܪܝܢ ܥܡܡܐ *of another nation, foreign;* ܐܚܪܝܢܝܬܐ ܡܠܬܐ a word *of various meanings.*

ܐܚܪܝܢܐܝܬ adv. rt. ܐܚܪ. *otherwise, on the other hand, contrariwise.*

ܐܚܫ Aphel of ܚܫ; *to pain, cause grief.*

ܐܚܫܡܝܬܐ rt. ܚܫܡ. f. *supper, a banquet, meal, repast.*

ܐܚܬ Aphel of ܢܚܬ; *to let fall, send down, cast out.*

ܐܛܒ *a*) Aphel of ܛܐܒ; *to do good. b*) Aphel of ܛܒ; *to announce, make known abroad.* Both these Aphels have the fuller form ܐܘܛܒ.

ܐܛܘ̈ܢܐ m. pl. *reins, thongs.*

ܐܛܘܡܘܣ and ܐܛܘܡܘܢ pl. ܐܛܘ̈ܡܐ m. ἄτομος, ἄτομον, *indivisible, an atom, body, individual,* hence

ܐܛܘܡܝܐ, ܐܛܘܡܝܬܐ adj. *individual.*

ܐܛܝܡܘܬܐ rt. ܐܛܡ. f. *solidity;* ܐܛܝܡܘܬܐ ܕܫܘ̈ܥܐ *the hardness of the rocks;* ܐܛܝܡܘܬܐ ܕܥܝ̈ܢܐ *opacity of the eyes* in blindness.

ܐܛܠܠ Aphel of ܛܠܠ; *to give shade, overshadow.*

ܐܛܠܣ m. *satin.*

ܐܛܡ root-meaning *to close,* only past part. ܐܛܝܡ, ܐܛܝܡܐ, ܐܛܝܡܬܐ pl. m. ܐܛ̈ܝܡܐ f. ܐܛ̈ܝܡܬܐ *closed, narrow, dense, compact;* ܟܘ̈ܐ ܐܛ̈ܝܡܬܐ *narrow windows;* ܒܘܣܡܐ ܐܛܝܡܐ metaph. *firm, hard, harsh;* ܚܡܬܐ ܐܛܝܡܬܐ *obstinate anger;* ܟܝܢܐ ܩܫܝܐ ܘܐܛܝܡܐ *a hard and inexorable nature;* ܗܠܟܬܐ ܐܛܝܡܬܐ *a firm step* or *tread.* ܐܛܝܡܐܝܬ *closely, briefly.*

ܐܛܢ Aphel of ܛܢ; *to arouse zeal* or *jealousy.*

ܐܛܦ Aphel of ܢܛܦ; *to distil, let fall drops, drop down, to instil.*

ܐܛܪ Aphel of ܢܛܪ; *to lay by.*

ܐܛܪܘܓ, ܐܛܪܘܓܐ pl. ܐ̈ m. *citron, orange,* tree and fruit.

ܐܛܪܘܓܝܐ m. *citrago, a sweet-smelling plant.*

ܐܛܪܝܐ ἴτρια, *vermicelli.*

ܐܝ Words of which the first radical is a Yud, often have an alternative spelling with ܐ prefixed. See ܐܝܠܝܕܐ, ܐܝܕܐ, ܐܝܫܢܐ.

ܐܝܓܪܬܐ an older spelling of ܐܓܪܬܐ *a letter.*

ܐܝܕܐ fem. of ܐܝܢܐ *what?*

ܐܝܕܐ emph. state of ܝܕ, constr. st. ܐܝܕ pl. ܐܝ̈ܕܝܢ, ܐܝ̈ܕܐ, ܐܝ̈ܕܝܬܐ, ܐܝ̈ܕܘܬܐ, ܐܝ̈ܕܘܬܐ, constr. pl. ܐܝ̈ܕܝ. See ܝܕ *the hand.*

ܐܝܕܝܥ, ܐܝܕܝܥܐ, ܐܝܕܝܥܬܐ another spelling of ܝܕܝܥ pass. part. of ܝܕܥ *to know.*

ܐܝܘ εὖ, adv. of praise or admiration: *Good! well, well done, rightly.*

ܐܝܘܢܐ, ܐܝܘܢ Ar. *a palace, court, portico.*

ܐܝܡܒܘܒܐ or ܐܝܡܒܘܒܐ usually ܐܒܘܒܐ m. *a buffalo bull.*

ܐܝܙܓܕܐ sometimes ܐܙܓܕܐ pl. ܐܝܙ̈ܓܕܐ deriv. Pers. m. *an ambassador, envoy, messenger;* ܐܝܙܓܕܐ ܩܠܝܠܐ *a swift messenger.*

ܐܝܙܓܕܘܬܐ pl. ܘ̈ܬܐ from the above. f. *an embassy, a message, intercession;* ܟܕ ܫܡܥ ܗܕܐ ܐܝܙܓܕܘܬܐ *on hearing such a message;* ܐܝܙܓܕܘܬܗ ܕܪܒ ܟܘܡܪܐ ܕܝܠܢ *the intercession of* our *High Priest* Christ.

ܐܝܙܕܐ pl. ܐ̈ *hedysarum alhagi, a thorny plant.*

ܐܝܙܪܐ m. *a linen girdle.*

ܐܝܙܪܘܬ or ܐܝܙܪܘܬܐ *a Persian gum used in dressing wounds.*

ܐܝܚܝܕܝܐ generally without the Alep. See ܝܚܝܕܝܐ under ܝܚܕ, *only*, i.e. *son*.
ܐܝܚܝܕܐܝܬ adv. *after the manner of hermits*.
ܐܝܚܝܕܝܐ = ܝܚܝܕܝܐ *solitary, only*.
ܐܝܚܝܕܝܘܬܐ = ܝܚܝܕܝܘܬܐ *the solitary* or *monastic life*.

ܐܝܛܐ εἶτα, *afterward, then, thereupon, therefore*; used with ܐܝܟܢܐ to introduce an objection, *granting this, how is it? so how is it? now if this be so—how* or *wherein?*

ܐܝܟ *as, as if, as it were, almost, about*, ܐܝܟ ܫܥܬܐ ܩܕܡܝܬܐ *about the first hour, about* 1 *o'clock. According to*, ܐܝܟ ܐܢܫܝܢ *as some think*; ܐܝܟ ܕܘܐܝ *in due form*. With ܕ and a verb expresses the subjunctive with *that* or *to*, *that I may, that thou mayest*, &c.; ܐܝܟ ܕܐܡܪ *as I may say, so to say, as is said*; ܐܝܟ ܕܢܫܬܒܩܘܢ ܢܒܢܘܢ *they may be permitted to build, they may build*. ܐܝܟܢܐ ܐܝܟ pl. ܐܝܟ ܗܠܝܢ usually with ܕ prefixed, *such, such as, what, how*; ܒܐܝܟ ܗܢܐ ܕܘܒܪܐ *by this means, in this way*; ܐܝܟ ܗܠܝܢ ܡܚܫܒܬܐ *such thoughts, what manner of thoughts*; ܐܝܟ ܕܣܒܪ ܐܢܐ *as I think*; ܐܝܟ ܗܘ ܕ *as it were, as if, in a manner*; ܐܝܟ ܕܟܬܝܒ *as it is written*; ܐܝܟ ܡܐ ܕ *as far as, inasmuch as*; ܐܝܟ ܕܣܘܓܐܐ *generally, for the most part*; ܐܝܟ ܕܡܢܢ *as from us, in our name*; ܐܝܟ ܡܢ ܕ *as he who, as one who*. Derivatives, ܐܝܟܢܐ, ܐܝܟܢܐܝܬ, ܐܝܟܢܝܐ, ܐܝܟܢܝܘܬܐ, ܐܝܟܐ, ܐܝܟܢ.

ܐܝܟܐ adv. of place: *a*) interrog. *where?* ܐܝܟܐ ܐܢܬ *where art thou?* ܐܝܟܐ ܗܘ and contr. ܐܝܟܘ *where is? where is he? whence, how* or *why is it? wherefore?* ܐܝܟܐ ܐܢܘܢ *where are they? where are?* *b*) esp. with ܕ, relative; ܟܠ ܐܝܟܐ *wherever*; ܠܐܝܟܐ *whither, how far? how long?* ܡܢ ܐܝܟܐ *whence?* ܐܝܟܐ ܕ *some, sometimes*.

ܐܝܟܘܣ m. ἦχος, *a tone* in music = Syr. ܩܠܐ and ܩܝܢܬܐ. Hymns were sung to 8 tones, hence a hymn-book is called an ܐܘܟܛܘܐܝܟܘܣ *octoechus*; ܒܐܝܟܘܣ ܬܠܝܬܝܐ *to the third tone*.

ܐܝܟܢ, ܐܝܟܢܐ from ܐܝܟ and ܗܢܐ. Cf. ܗܟܢ. adv. *how? in what manner?* ܐܝܟܢܐ ܢܥܒܕ *after what manner shall we act? what shall we do?* ܐܝܟܢ ܐܝܬܝܟ *how art thou?* ܐܝܟܢ ܗܘ ܡܬܟܣܐ *how is he dressed?* ܐܝܟ, ܐܝܟܢܐ, ܐܝܟ ܐܝܟܢ *how? in what manner? after what fashion? such, for example.* ܐܝܟܢܐ ܕ usually with ܕ following, *what sort? what manner? as, even as, so that, lest.* ܐܝܟܢ ܕܗܘ *anyhow, some way or other*; ܟܠ ܐܝܟܢ ܕܗܘ *howsoever*.

ܐܝܟܢܝܘܬܐ from the above. f. *quality, condition, manner*; ܡܛܠ ܐܝܟܢܝܘܬܐ ܕܩܘܕܫܐ ܕܡܫܚܐ *of the manner of the consecrating of the oil*.

ܐܝܠ (Ar., Heb. and Chald. *El*) m. *God*; ܐܠܫܕܝ or ܐܝܠ ܫܕܝ transliterated from the Hebrew or ܐܝܠ ܚܝܠܬܢܐ translated, *El Shaddai, God Almighty*. Frequently used in the composition of proper names.

ܐܝܠ, ܐܝܠܐ m. *a*) *help, succour, aid, assistance*; ܐܬܐ ܠܐܝܠܗ *he came to his aid*; ܩܪܐ ܐܝܠܐ *to implore aid*; ܐܝܠܗ ܕܐܠܗܐ *the help of God*; ܒܐܝܠܐ ܕܐܠܗܐ ܫܠܡ *by the help of God this is finished*. *b*) *a helper, defender*, generally used of God; ܕܚܠܬܐ ܕܐܠܗܐ ܒܠܒܗ *the fear of God is in his heart*.

ܐܝܠܐ pl. ܐܝܠܐ m. *a stag, a hart*; ܐܝܠܬܐ pl. ܐܝܠܬܐ f. *a hind*.

ܐܝܠܕܘܬܐ = ܡܘܠܕܐ rt. ܝܠܕ. f. *being born, birth*.

ܐܝܠܘܠ m. *Elul, the twelfth Syrian month*, answering to most of September and part of October with us.

ܐܝܠܝܢ pl. com. of ܐܝܢܐ *who, what*.

ܐܝܠܠ Aphel of ܝܠܠ; *to howl, cry out*.

ܐܝܠܢ, ܐܝܠܢܐ pl. ܝܢ, ܐ m. *a tree, the trunk of a tree*; ܐܝܠܢܐ ܕܦܠܚܘܬܐ *cultivated trees*; ܐܝܠܢܐ ܕܦܐܪܐ or ܥܒܕܝ ܦܐܪܐ *fruit-trees*; ܐܝܠܢ ܛܠܠܐ *a shady tree*; ܐܝܠܢܐ ܕܛܪܦܐ *a leafy tree*.

ܐܝܠܢܝܐ f. ܐܝܠܢܝܬܐ adj. from the above. *wooded; shrubby, arborescent*; ܚܘܒܙܐ ܐܝܠܢܝܐ *the tree-mallow*.

ܐܝܠܘܙܐ pl. *nuces castaneae, avellanae* or *Ponticae, the chestnut* or *filbert*.

ܐܝܠܢܘܢ, ܐܝܠܢܘܢܐ pl. ܐܝܠܢܘܢܐ f. *a*) dim. of ܐܝܠܢܐ. *a bush, shrub*, perh. *a branch*. *b*) see ܐܝܠܐ.

ܐܝܡܟܐ adv. of place. *whence? where?*

ܐܝܡܡ, ܐܝܡܡܐ pl. ܝܢ (see ܝܘܡ) m. *the day, the day-time*, opp. ܠܠܝܐ *the night*; ܦܠܓܗ ܕܐܝܡܡܐ *mid-day, noon-tide*; ܠܢܘܗܪܐ ܩܪܐ ܐܝܡܡܐ *the light was called day*.

ܐܝܡܡܝܐ, ܐܝܡܡܝܬܐ pl. m. ܝܶܐ f. ܝܳܬܐ. adj. *belonging to the day, of to-day;* ܨܘܡܐ ܐܝܡܡܝܐ *a fast lasting through the whole day*, opp. ܫܗܪܐ ܠܠܝܐ *an all-night vigil.*

ܐܝܢ *a*) an affirmative particle, *yes, yea,* opp. ܠܐ, *no, not;* ܐܝܢ ܐܝܢ ܠܐ ܠܐ *yea, yea, nay, nay;* ܐܝܢ ܐܘ ܠܐ ܦܢܐ ܠܝ *answer me yes or no. Certainly, truly, it is, it is so;* at the beginning of a sentence, *yea, rather, well, be it so;* at the end of a prayer, ܐܝܢ ܘܐܡܝܢ *so be it, Amen. b*) adversative particle, *but, however;* ܐܢ ܐܝܢ *but if. c*) interrogative, *whether? if?*

ܐܝܢܐ m. ܐܝܕܐ f. ܐܝܠܝܢ pl. c. pron. *a*) interrog. *who? which? what? of what sort?* ܐܝܢܐ ܗܘ contr. ܐܝܢܘ, *who is? who is he?* ܒܐܝܢܐ ܫܘܠܛܢܐ *by what authority?* ܒܐܝܕܐ ܫܥܬܐ *at what hour? b*) relative, often with ܕ following, *he who, &c.;* ܟܠ ܐܝܢܐ ܕ *whosoever;* ܐܝܢܐ ܕܗܘ, ܐܝܕܐ ܕܗܝ *whoever, a certain, some—or other;* ܐܚܪ̈ܢܐ ܐܝܠܝܢ ܕܗܘܝ *certain others.* With ܐܝܟ; ܐܝܟ ܐܝܢܐ pl. ܐܝܟ ܐܝܠܝܢ *what sort, what manner.* ܒܐܝܢܐ ܙܒܢܐ *at which time;* ܒܐܝܢܐ ܥܡܠܐ *with what labour;* ܡܢ ܐܝܢܐ ܕܗܘ ܥܠܬܐ *from what cause soever.* Derivatives, ܐܝܢܝܐ, ܐܝܢܝܘܬܐ.

ܐܝܢܕܝܩܛܝܘܢ f. Lat. *an Indict*, i.e. *a space of* 15 *years.* See ܐܢܕܝܩܛܐ.

ܐܝܢܝܐ pl. ܐܝܢܝ̈ܐ adj. *qualifying, special;* ܫܡܐ ܐܝܢܝܐ *an adjective.* Metaph. with ܠܐ, *undivided, pure;* ܚܘܒܐ ܠܐ ܐܝܢܝܐ *absolute love, love in itself;* ܙܠܝܩ̈ܐ ܕܢܘܗܪܐ ܠܐ ܐܝܢܝ̈ܐ *pure rays of light.*

ܐܝܢܝܘܬܐ pl. ܐܝܢܝܘ̈ܬܐ f. *quality, sort.*

ܐܝܢܩ irreg. Aphel of ܝܢܩ; *to give suck.*

ܐܝܣܘܢ pl. ܐܝܣܘ̈ܢܐ ἴσον, *a copy* of a book or writing.

ܐܝܣܦܝܣ from Heb. through Greek, m. *jasper.* See ܝܫܦܗ.

ܐܝܣܪ for ܝܣܪ *covetous.*

ܐܝܦܘܟܝ, ܐܦܘܟܝ or ܐܦܘܟܐ pl. ܐܝܦܘܟ̈ܝܣ f. ἐποχή, astron. *the position of a star or other heavenly body.*

ܐܝܥܐ for ܝܥܐ *to grow, shoot up*, &c.

ܐܝܩܐ or ܐܝܩܝ εἰκῆ, *in vain, rashly, at random.*

ܐܝܩܪ, ܐܝܩܪܐ rt. ܝܩܪ. m. *a*) *honour, glory, magnificence;* ܠܒܘܫ̈ܐ ܕܐܝܩܪܐ *magnificent raiment;* ܡܪܟܒܬܐ ܕܐܝܩܪܐ ܕܐܠܗܐ *the chariot of God's glory*=*God's glorious chariot.* With ܝܗܒ or ܥܒܕ *to do, show* or *pay honour;* ܐܬܩܒܠ ܒܐܝܩܪܐ *he was received with honour. b*) *observance, reverence,* funeral *pomp; worth. c*) *a mark of honour, an honorarium, fee, donation, gift, wedding present, household stuff, the margin* of a book.

ܐܝܩܪܘܬܐ=ܝܩܪܘܬܐ rt. ܝܩܪ. f. *baggage, belongings*, &c.

ܐܝܪ sometimes mis-spelt ܐܝܪ m. *Iyor*, a month answering to the greater part of May with us, but beginning earlier.

ܐܝܪܐ m. ܐܝܪܬܐ f. pl. ܐܝܪ̈ܐ *a pot* or *cauldron* with rings for handles, generally made of brass.

ܐܝܪܛܝܘܢ m. ἱερατεῖον, *the sanctuary* of a church.

ܐܝܪܚ for ܝܪܚ *a month.*

ܐܝܪܘܣܐ or ܐܝܪܝܣܐ pl. ܐ̈ f. *a*) ἶρις, *a lily, lily-bulb. b*) αἶρα, *lolium, darnel.*

ܐܝܪܘܢܐ see ܠܓܝܘܢܐ, *a body of soldiers.*

ܐܝܫܝ, ܐܝܫܝ or ܐܫܝ *Jesse*, the father of David, hence the adj. ܐܝܫܝܐ; ܢܘܪܒܐ ܐܝܫܝܐ *the branch of Jesse*, the Messiah.

ܐܝܬ indeclinable, when standing alone is of either gender and number, *is, are*, Germ. *es war, es gab;* coalesces with the negative ܠܐ=ܠܝܬ *there is not, there is no;* takes the affixes of a plural noun and then has gender and number according, ܐܝܬܝ c. *I am;* ܐܝܬܝܟ m. and ܐܝܬܝܟܝ f. *thou art;* ܐܝܬܘܗܝ *he is;* ܐܝܬܝܗ *she is;* ܐܝܬܝܢ c. *we are;* ܐܝܬܝܟܘܢ m. and ܐܝܬܝܟܝܢ f. *you are;* ܐܝܬܝܗܘܢ m. and ܐܝܬܝܗܝܢ f. *they are.* With ܗܘܐ following, a past tense is formed, *was, were*, this ܗܘܐ does not always agree with its nominative, ܐܝܬܝܗܘܢ ܗܘܘ or ܐܝܬܝܗܘܢ ܗܘܐ *they were, there were;* ܚܝ̈ܠܘܬܐ ܕܐܝܬ ܗܘܐ ܒܐܘܪܫܠܡ *the forces that were at Jerusalem.*

ܐܝܬ is much used in indefinite expressions of place, time or people, ܐܝܬ ܕܐܡܪ *one says, some one says;* ܐܝܬ ܕܐܡܪܝܢ *some say;* ܐܝܬ ܐܝܟܐ *somewhere, at some time;* ܐܝܬ ܐܡܬܝ ܕ *sometimes.* With ܠ and the pron. suffix: *a*) *to have,* ܐܝܬ ܠܝ, ܐܝܬ ܠܗ *I have, he has, c'est à moi, c'est à lui,* &c.; *it is my part, office, duty;* esp. with an infin., ܐܝܬ ܠܢ ܠܡܐܠܦ *we have to learn, it is our part to learn.* *b*) *to be* in existence, in life, ܠܐ ܐܝܬܘܗܝ ܠܗ *he is not,* i.e. *he is not in life, he is dead;* contr. ܠܝܬ, ܠܝܬܝܗܘܢ *they are not, they are dead;* with ܠܘܬ and pron. suff. *to be with, to have, be found, be found guilty;* with ܥܠ *to be incumbent on, obligatory, expected from.* Derivatives, ܐܝܬܘܬܐ, ܐܝܬܝܐ, ܐܝܬܐ, ܐܝܬܝܐܝܬ.

ܐܝܬܝ Aphel of ܐܬܐ; *to bring,* &c.

ܐܝܬܘܬܐ pl. ܐܝܬܘܬܐ from ܐܝܬ. f. *a*) *being, essence, substance* = οὐσία; ܒܪܐ ܐܝܬܘܬܐ ܚܕܐ ܥܡ ܐܒܘܗܝ the Son *is consubstantial—of one substance—with the Father;* often *the Divine Substance* or *Being,* hence *the Godhead,* ܐܝܬܘܬܐ ܡܠܘܐܠܗܘܬܐ *the Eternal Being, the Godhead.* *b*) *substance* =ὑπόστασις, ܨܠܡܐ ܕܐܝܬܘܬܗ Hebr. i. 3. *c*) *existence, being, actuality,* ܒܝܫܬܐ ܠܝܬ ܠܗ ܐܝܬܘܬܐ *evil has no actual existence, does not truly exist;* ܥܘܬܪܐ ܕܐܝܬܘܬܐ *true riches, actual riches.*

ܐܝܬܘܬܢܝܐ f. ܐܝܬܘܬܢܝܬܐ pl. m. ܐܝܬܘܬܢܝܐ f. ܐܝܬܘܬܢܝܬܐ adj. *essential, actual, pertaining to being* or *existence, natural.*

ܐܝܬܝܐ f. ܐܝܬܝܬܐ pl. ܐܝܬܝܐ: *a*) *being, existing,* esp. *self-existent,* hence *eternally existing, sempiternal,* often used as an epithet of God; ܡܠܬܐ ܐܝܬܝܬܐ *the Eternal Word* and abs. *the Eternal One;* ܐܝܬܝܐ ܟܣܝܐ *the unseen Being.* *b*) *a being, entity, a cause, principle, a substance, an aeon.* *c*) *necessaries of existence.*

ܐܝܬܝܐܝܬ adv. *essentially, eternally, in eternity.*

ܐܝܟܐܕܝܐ, ܐܝܟܕܝܐ or ܐܝܟܐܕܝܐ ἠχάδια, same as ܐܝܟܘܣ *a tone.*

ܐܟܐ for ܐܟܝ Aphel of ܟܐܐ; *to pain, afflict.*

ܐܟܒܪ or ܐܟܒܪ = ܟܒܪ *perhaps, perchance.*

ܐܟܕܢܝܐ m. ܐܟܕܢܝܬܐ f. *a cock, a hen.*

ܐܟܕܢܐ pl. ܐܟܕܢܐ ἔχιδνα, f. *a viper.*

ܐܟܘܠܐ pl. ܐܟܘܠܐ m. rt. ܐܟܠ. *devouring, voracious; an eater, glutton.*

ܐܟܘܠܬܢܘܬܐ rt. ܐܟܠ. f. *gluttony, voracity.*

ܐܟܘܠܬܐ rt. ܐܟܠ. f. *gangrene;* ܐܟܘܠܬܐ ܕܒܣܪܐ *cancer.*

ܐܟܦܬܢܐ rt. ܟܦ. *solicitous, caring for* or *about.*

ܐܝܟ constr. st. of an abstract noun ܐܝܟܘܬܐ from ܐܝܟ, only used with suffixes as a prep. *as, such as, like;* ܐܝܟܘܬܝ *like me, my equal, such as I am;* ܐܝܟܘܬܟ *such as thou art, like thee,* &c.; ܐܝܟܘܬܗ *in like manner, according to;* ܐܝܟܘܬܗܝܢ ܐܝܟܘܬܗܝܢ *such and such things.*

ܐܟܙܪܝܐ or ܐܟܙܪܐ *hard, pitiless.*

ܐܟܙܢܐ, ܐܟܙܢ from ܙܢܐ and ܐܝܟ. *in like manner, as, for example;* generally followed by ܕ and with ܗܟܢܐ in the corresponding part of the proposition *as—so.*

ܐܟܦ Aphel of ܟܦ; *to blow, puff.*

ܐܟܚܕܐ, ܐܟܚܕ from ܚܕܐ and ܐܝܟ and sometimes thus written in two words. *at the same time* or *place, at once, together, with; likewise, with one consent, unanimously;* often represents σύν in composition.

ܐܟܚܕܐܝܬ adv. *at once, at the same time.*

ܐܟܚܕܢܝܘܬܐ f. *simultaneousness, a happening at the same time;* ܐܟܚܕܢܝܘܬܐ ܕܒܪܝܬܐ ܕ *the simultaneous creation of;* with ܒ preceding *collectively.*

ܐܟܝ fut. ܢܟܐ or ܢܐܟܐ, imper. ܐܟܐ, ܐܟܝ, ܐܟܘ. Aphel of ܟܐܐ; *to hurt, harm, pain.*

ܐܟܦܬܐܝܬ adv. rt. ܟܦ. *carefully, earnestly, sincerely.*

ܐܟܦܬܘܬܐ f. rt. ܟܦ. *care, pains, taking pains, diligence.*

ܐܟܠ fut. ܢܐܟܘܠ, imper. ܐܟܘܠ, act. part. ܐܟܠ, ܐܟܠܐ, ܐܟܠܬܐ, pass. part. ܐܟܝܠ, ܐܟܝܠܐ, ܐܟܝܠܬܐ. *to eat, devour, corrode,* metaph. *to consume, squander, embezzle;* ܗܒ ܠܗ ܢܐܟܘܠ *give him food, feed him;* ܢܘܪܐ ܐܟܘܠܬܐ *consuming fire.* Act. part. = subst. *an eater,* hence *a moth, bookworm, weevil, maggot, cheese-mite.*

With ܒܣܪܐ *to eat flesh,* metaph. *to be ferocious, to slay, butcher;* ܛܝܒܘܬܐ *to be ungrateful;* ܠܚܡܐ *to dine, sup,* metaph. *to be intimate,* ܐܟܠܝ ܦܬܘܪܟ *thy table companions, they who eat at thy table;* ܩܪܨܘܗܝ metaph. *to be vexed, sorry;* ܩܪܨܐ ܕ *to accuse, slander.* With ܒ of the cause, ܐܟܠ ܩܪܨܘܗܝ ܠܘܬ ܟܠܝܦܐ *he accused him to the caliph;* ܐܟܠ ܩܪܨܘܗܝ ܕܟܪܡܐ *he reproached the vineyard* (alluding to Isaiah v).

ETHPE. ܐܬܐܟܠ to be eaten, devoured, consumed, e.g. by moth, fire, the sword. With ܩܪ̈ܨܐ and ܠ of the pers. to be accused. APHEL ܐܘܟܠ to give to eat, feed, induce to take food; ܝܘ̈ܢܝܐ ܡܚܠܛܝܢ ܗܘܘ ܟܠܫܐ ܒܩܡܚܐ ܘܐܘܟܠܘ ܠܦܪ̈ܢܓܝܐ the Greeks mixed lime with flour and made the Franks eat it. DERIVATIVES, ܐܟܘܠܐ, ܐܟܘܠܬܐ, ܐܘܟܠܐ, ܐܘܟܠܘܬܐ, ܐܘܟܠܬܐ, ܐܟܠܬܐ, ܐܟܠܩܪܨܐ, ܡܐܟܘܠܬܐ, ܡܐܟܠܐ, ܡܐܟܘܠܬܐ, ܡܐܟܠܩܪܨܐ, ܡܐܟܘܠܬܐ.

ܐܟܠܐ or ܐܟܘܠܐ a hammer; ܐܟܠܘܢܐ dim. a small hammer.

ܐܟܠܘܣ or ܐܘܟܠܘܣ ὄχλος, a multitude, crowd, mob, the people.

ܐܟܠܐ m. rt. ܐܟܠ. a devouring. ܐܟܠܐ ܕܫܢ̈ܐ a hollow or cavity in the teeth.

ܐܟܠܩܪܨܐ pl. m. ܐܟ̈ܠܝ ܩܪ̈ܨܐ pl. f. ܐܟ̈ܠܬ ܩܪ̈ܨܐ an accuser, a slanderer, adversary, esp. the devil.

ܐܟܡ (the root is probably another form of ܚܡ to be hot, hence to be sunburnt) fut. ܢܐܟܡ, part. ܐܟܡ, ܐܟܡܐ. to be or become black; ܐܟܡ ܒܡܫܟܬܐ every speckled one among the sheep, Gen. xxx. 32, 33. APHEL ܐܘܟܡ to blacken, darken, make sunburnt, to become dark or black, put on black garments, be darkened, to blot a book; ܥܝܢܐ ܕܐܟܡܐ ܘܢܩܦܐ ܝܬܝܪ ܒܫܝܦܐ ܕܟܘܚܠܐ the eye which is made darker and more pleasing by the use of kohl; ܡܘܟܡܝܢ ܐܦ̈ܝܗܘܢ blackening their faces as a sign of grief. DERIVATIVES, ܐܘܟܡܐ, ܐܘܟܡܘܬܐ.

ܐܟܡܐ from ܡܐ and ܐܝܟ, generally followed by ܕ, as, as long as; ܐܟܡܐ ܙܒ̈ܢܝܢ sometimes.

ܐܟܡܢ ܕ from ܡܢ and ܐܝܟ as one who, as he who, as, as if, that, in order to.

ܐܟܣ fut. ܢܐܟܣ and ܢܟܣ APHEL of ܟܣ; to reprove, confute.

ܐܟܣܕܪܐ pl. ܐܟܣܕܪ̈ܐ f. ἐξέδρα, a gallery, corridor, balcony, a cloister, a cell or chamber.

ܐܟܣܘܢܓܝܢ f. ἀξούγγιον, fat, grease; ܐܟܣܘܢܓܝܢ ܕܚܙܝܪܐ lard, hog's grease.

ܐܟܣܢܘܕܘܟܝܢ pl. ܐܟܣܢܘܕܘܟܐ̈ܣ, ܐܟܣܢܕܘܟܣ and other spellings f. ξενοδοχεῖον, a hospital= Syr. ܒܝܬ ܡܩܒܠ.

ܐܟܣܢܘܕܘܟܐ or ܐܟܣܢܕܘܟܐ &c. m. the curator of a hospital.

ܐܟܣܘܪܝܐ pl. ܐܟܣܘܪܝܐ̈ܣ f. ἐξορία, exile, hence is derived the verb ܐܟܣܪ and the following noun.

ܐܟܣܘܪܝܣܛܐ pl. ܐܟܣܘܪܝܣܛ̈ܐ m. cf. ἐξορισθῆναι, an exile; ܡܢ ܦܪܕܝܣܐ ܕܥܕܢ ܐܟܣܘܪܝܣܛ̈ܐ ܗܘܝܢ we are exiles from the Garden of Eden.

ܐܟܣܝܢ, ܐܟܣܝܢܐ pl. ܐ̈ a great axe or hatchet for hewing stone.

ܐܟܣܝܘܡܐ ἀξίωμα, an axiom, dignity.

ܐܟܣܝܘܣ pl. ܐܟܣܝܘܬ̈ܐ f. ἄξιος, worthy, honourable.

ܐܟܣܝܣ f. ἕξις, habit, custom.

ܐܟܣܝܣܝܐ f. ܐܟܣܝܣܝܬܐ pl. m. ܐ̈ f. ܬ̈ܐ. from the above, habitual. With ܗܘܢܐ it is variously explained as the mental power inherent in man apart from instruction or the faculty of acquiring habits of virtue.

ܐܟܣܢܝܐ, ܐܟܣܢܝܐ f. ξενία, a strange or foreign country, a living abroad or travelling; exile, banishment; a guest-house or place for entertaining strangers; metaph. the life of an anchorite as being estranged from the things of this life.

ܐܟܣܢܝ, ܐܟܣܢܝܐ f. ܐܟܣܢܝܬܐ pl. m. ܐܟܣܢܝ̈ܐ f. ܐܟܣܢܝ̈ܬܐ. ξένος, subst. a foreigner, stranger, pilgrim, guest, ܪܚܡ ܐܟܣܢ̈ܝܐ given to hospitality; adj. strange, unusual, ܐܟܣܢܝ ܐܣܟܡܐ of anomalous form.

ܐܟܣܢܝܘܬܐ f. from the above, the condition of a stranger or traveller; travelling, travels; the entertaining of strangers, hospitality.

ܐܬܐܟܣܢܝ denom. verb from ܐܟܣܢܝܐ. to travel or reside abroad; to accept hospitality.

ܐܟܣܩܦܛܘܪܝܣ exceptores, notaries.

ܐܟܣܪ denom. verb from ܐܟܣܘܪܝܐ. to exile, banish. ETTAPH. ܐܬܬܐܟܣܪ to be exiled, banished.

ܐܟܣܪܟܐ m. ἔξαρχος, an exarch; the overseer of a monastery.

ܐܟܦ fut. ܢܐܟܦ rarely ܢܐܟܘܦ, part. ܐܟܦ, ܐܟܦܐ and ܐܟܝܦ, ܐܟܝܦܐ, ܐܟܝܦܬܐ often used impersonally with ܠ, to have regard to, be solicitous, careful, to take care; to urge, be urgent on. 2nd participle, anxious, busied, solicitous, urgent; ܠܗ ܐܟܝܦ ܗܘܐ ܐܟܣܢܝܐ he busied himself about the entertainment of strangers; ܐܟܝܦܝܢ ܠܡܫܡܥ anxious to hear. PA. ܐܟܦ to urge, incite. DERIVATIVES, ܐܘܟܦܐ, ܐܟܝܦܐܝܬ, ܐܟܝܦܘܬܐ, ܐܟܦܐ.

ܐܟܦܐ m. rt. ܐܟܦ. *care, necessity;* ܠܐ ܐܟܦܐ ܕ *it is not needful* or *necessary.*

ܐܟܪ part. ܡܐܟܪ denom. verb Aphel conj. from ܐܟܪܐ. *to plough, cultivate, plant.*

ܐܟܪܐ pl. ܐ (root-meaning *to dig*) m. *a ploughman, husbandman;* often metaph. of the apostles, of the ministers of evil, &c. Hence are derived verb ܐܟܪ and ܐܟܪܘܬܐ.

ܐܟܪܘܬܐ f. from ܐܟܪܐ. *agriculture, husbandry, rusticity.*

ܐܟܫ Aphel of ܟܫ; *to scare, drive away* birds, bees, &c.

ܐܟܬܐ pl. ܐܟܬܬܐ m. *wrath, lasting anger; a grudge;* with ܢܛܪ *to keep* or *nurse one's anger.*

ܐܟܬܢ, ܐܟܬܢܐ pl. ܝܢ, ܬܐ; from the above, *angry, wrathful.*

ܐܟܬܢܘܬܐ f. from ܐܟܬܐ. *ill-will, animosity, malice;* with ܠܐ, *forgetfulness of injuries.*

ܐܠܐ (contr. from ܠܐ *not* and ܐܢ *if*) conj. often with ܐܢ following; *if not, unless, only, except, however, but, although;* ܐܠܐ ܐܢ *only that, but that;* ܐܠܐ ܕ *but that;* ܐܠܐ ܠ *except.*

ܐܠܐ E-Syr. ܐܠܐ (mimetic; cf. ܝܠܠ and Eng. *to howl*) fut. ܢܐܠܐ, imper. ܐܠܝ, E-Syr. ܐܠܝ, act. part. ܐܠܐ, ܐܠܝܐ pl. ܐܠܝܢ, ܐܠܝܢ *to mourn, lament* with ܥܠ or ܠ of the pers. or thing lamented, with ܠ also of the pers. before whom; ܐܠܝܢ ܩܕܡܝܟܘܢ *we have mourned before you;* ܐܠܝ ܐܠܝܬܐ *make lamentation;* ܟܕ ܐܠܝܢ ܠܐܢܫܝܗܘܢ *making moan for their kindred.* Ethpe. ܐܬܐܠܝ pass. Derivatives, ܐܠܝܐ, ܐܠܝܬܐ, ܡܐܠܝܢܘܬܐ.

ܐܠܐ fut. ܢܐܠܐ; see ܐܠܝ and ܠܐܐ.

ܐܠܗ emph. ܐܠܗܐ pl. abs. ܐܠܗܝܢ emph. ܐܠܗܐ (Heb. *El*, Chald. *Elah*, Ar. *Allah*) m. *a) God, the Supreme Deity;* ܐܠܗ ܐܠܗܝܢ *God of gods;* ܐܠܗ ܫܡܝܐ *the God of heaven;* ܐܠܗܐ ܕܥܠܡܐ *the God of ages, the eternal Godhead;* ܐܠܗ ܒܪܢܫ *the God-man;* ܐܠܗܢ ܥܡܢ *Emmanuel;* ܠܐ ܐܠܗ *that which is not God;* ܕܠܐ ܐܠܗܝܢ *which are no gods;* ܕܠܐ ܐܠܗ *atheistic, godless.* ܕܐܠܗܐ and ܩܕܡ ܐܠܗܐ used as epithets, *most high, very great, exalted, distinguished; very greatly, mightily;* ܪܒܐ ܕܐܠܗܐ *a mighty prince,* Gen. xxiii. 6; ܐܬܚܒܠܬ ܐܪܥܐ ܩܕܡ ܐܠܗܐ *the earth was exceedingly corrupt,* Gen. vi. 11, 12. *b) a false god, heathen deity;* ܐܠܗܐ ܢܘܟܪܝܐ *strange gods;* ܐܠܗܐ ܕܢܣܟܐ *molten gods, idols;* ܝܘܡܬܐ ܕܐܠܗܐ *the days of the week* as bearing the names of various deities. Derivatives, the five following words, ܡܐܠܗܢܐ and ܡܐܠܗܢܘܬܐ.

ܐܠܗ denom. verb Pael conj. from ܐܠܗܐ. *to deify, attribute divine power;* ܠܗܘܢܐ ܡܐܠܗܝܢ *they count the mind divine;* ܡܐܠܗܝܢ ܠܡܠܐ *they attribute divine efficacy to these words.* Ethpa. ܐܬܐܠܗ *to be made God, become divine, be made a partaker of the Divine Nature;* ܐܬܐܠܗ ܒܪܢܫܐ *man became God.*

ܐܠܗܐܝܬ adv. *divinely, as God, theologically.*

ܐܠܗܘܬܐ f. *Godhead, deity, divinity;* collect. *heathen deities;* ܠܐ ܐܠܗܘܬܐ *atheism, paganism;* ܡܡܠܠܘܬ ܐܠܗܘܬܐ *theology.*

ܐܠܗܝ, ܐܠܗܝܐ, ܐܠܗܝܬܐ pl. m. ܐ f. ܬܐ. adj. from ܐܠܗܐ. *divine, godlike, godly, sacred, holy;* ܦܘܠܘܣ ܐܠܗܝܐ *Saint Paul;* ܦܘܠܚܢܗܘܢ ܐܠܗܝܐ *their holy service,* i. e. the pious life of monks; ܦܢܩܝܬܐ ܐܠܗܝܬܐ *a divine volume,* i.e. revered and precious; ܟܬܒܐ ܐܠܗܝܐ or ܟܬܒܘܬܐ ܐܠܗܝܬܐ *the Holy Scriptures;* ܡܡܠܠܐ ܐܠܗܝܐ *theology;* philosoph. *metaphysical,* opp. ܟܝܢܝܐ *physical.* Aristotle wrote ܟܬܒܐ ܕܟܝܢܝܬܐ ܘܕܐܠܗܝܬܐ *on Physics and Metaphysics.*

ܐܠܗܬܐ f. of ܐܠܗܐ. *a goddess, an idol;* ܥܐܕܐ ܕܐܠܗܬܐ *feasts of idols.*

ܐܠܘ *if; Oh that!* often followed by ܕ. ܠܐ ܐܠܘ or ܐܠܘܠܐ *unless, if not.*

ܐܠܘܠ generally ܐܝܠܘܠ, *Elul, September.*

ܐܠܘܨܐ pl. ܐ m. rt. ܐܠܨ. *an oppressor, besieger, torturer.*

ܐܠܛ Aphel of ܠܛ; *to importune, trouble.*

ܐܠܝ Aphel of ܠܐܐ; part. ܡܠܐܐ or ܡܠܐ, *to weary.*

ܐܠܝ (rarely ܐܠܐ = ܠܐܐ) fut. ܢܐܠܐ *to labour, take pains;* ܐܠܝܘ ܛܒ ܒܟܪܡܐ *they had laboured well in the vineyard;* ܣܓܝܐܐ ܕܐܠܝܘ ܒܩܪܝܢܐ *many who had read indefatigably.*

ܐܠܝ, ܐܠܝܐ rt. ܐܠܐ m. *mourning, lamentation;* ܒܩܠܐ ܕܐܠܝܐ *with sounds of sorrow.*

ܐܠܝܐ adj. *lamenting.*

ܐܠܝܬܐ pl. ܐܠܝ̈ܬܐ rt. ܐܠܐ. f. *a mourner*, esp. *a woman hired to make lamentation over the dead.*

ܐܠܝܠܘܬܐ rt. ܐܠܠ. f. *feebleness, low estate; ܐܠܝܠܘܬܝ my humble* or *my unworthy self.*

ܐܠܝܨܐܝܬ adv. rt. ܐܠܨ. *necessarily, necessitously, in straits, in misery.*

ܐܠܝܨܘܬܐ f. rt. ܐܠܨ. *narrowness;* metaph. *straits, necessity, poverty.*

ܐܠܝܬܐ f. *a*) (perh. rt. ܐܠܐ or a mis-spelling of ܐܠܠܝܬܐ) *a demon which is said to appear under the form of a wailing woman. b*) *the fat tail* of a sheep.

ܐܠܠ only participial adj. ܐܠܝܠ, ܐܠܝܠܐ, ܐܠܝܠܬܐ pl. m. ܐܠܝ̈ܠܐ f. ܐܠܝ̈ܠܬܐ. *a*) = ܡܚܝܠܐ in meaning and use, *weak, feeble, low, vile,* ܨܒܝܢܐ ܐܠܝܠܐ *a weak will;* ܐܠܝܠ ܡܗܠܟܝܢ *walking feebly;* ܐܠܝܠܐ ܕܣܘܪ̈ܝܝܐ *an obscure Syrian; b*) *a spy, searcher, inquisitor,* ܐܠܝ̈ܠܘܗܝ ܕܟܐܢܘܬܐ *the inquisitors of justice. c*) *an enticer, instigator, abettor,* ܕܚܫ̈ܐ *of the passions;* ܐܠܝ̈ܠܘܗܝ ܕܡܫܒܩ̈ܐ *into the paths of error;* ܐܠܝܠܬܐ ܕܟܠܗܝܢ ܛܢܦ̈ܬܐ *a temptress to all foul wickedness.* DERIVATIVE, ܐܠܝܠܘܬܐ.

ܐܠܡ part. ܐܠܝܡ *to keep anger.*

ܐܠܡܐ pl. ܐܠܡ̈ܐ m. *lasting anger, ill-will.*

ܐܠܥܐ pl. ܐܠܥܝܢ, ܐܠܥ̈ܐ f. *a rib;* metaph. *a wife;* mathemat. *a side;* ܣܓܝܐܬ ܐܠܥ̈ܐ *polylateral.*

ܐܠܦ PA. of ܝܠܦ; *to teach, inform, show.*

ܐܠܦ or ܐܠܦ *Alep* or *Olaph, the first letter of the Syriac alphabet;* ܐܠܦ ܒܝܬ or ܐܠܦ ܒܝܬܐ *the alphabet;* with ܠ, *alphabetically, in alphabetical order.*

ܐܠܦܐ *Alpha, the first letter of the Greek alphabet;* ܐܠܦܐ ܒܝܬܐ *the Greek alphabet.*

ܐܠܦ, ܐܠܦܐ pl. ܐܠܦ̈ܐ and ܐܠܦܝܢ m. *a thousand;* ܐܠܦ ܐܠܦܝܢ *a thousand thousand;* ܐܠܦ̈ܐ ܕܥܕ̈ܬܐ *thousands of churches.*

ܐܠܦ, ܐܠܦܐ pl. ܐܠܦ̈ܐ f. *a ship, a galley;* ܐܠܦܐ ܩܪܒܬܢܝܬܐ *a ship of war;* ܐܠܦܐ ܕܬܐܓܪ̈ܐ *a merchantman;* metaph. ܐܠܦܐ ܕܦܓܪܐ *the body* the vehicle of the soul. The B. V. Mary is called ܐܠܦܐ ܡܨܒܬܬܐ *the adorned vessel;* ܐܠܦܐ ܕܢܗܘܪܐ = *the moon;* astron. *the constellation Argo;* ܡܥܪܒܐ ܕܐܠܦܐ *the setting of the Pleiades.*

ܐܠܦܘܢܝܬܐ pl. ܐܬ̈ܐ f. dimin. of ܐܠܦܐ; *a boat, a light bark.*

ܐܠܦܪܐ pl. ܐܠܦܪ̈ܐ m. *the owner* or *captain of a ship, the ship-master, pilot; a sailor.*

ܐܠܨ fut. ܢܐܠܘܨ, act. part. ܐܠܨ, ܐܠܨܐ, pass. part. ܐܠܝܨ, ܐܠܝܨܐ, ܐܠܝܨܬܐ root-meaning *to press close. a*) *to be pressing, press earnestly, urge strongly, compel, force. b*) *to straiten, hem in,* e.g. ܒܟܦܢܐ *by famine;* ܒܡܨܪܐ *to closely besiege; to oppress, afflict, torment by crushing. c*) *to be pressing, urgent, necessary* in this sense usually impers. 3 f. sing. or act. part. m. or f. The act. part. is used also in a passive sense, *straitened, closely pressed, crowded together, afflicted;* f. pl. ܐܠܨܢ, ܐܠܨܬܐ *necessaries;* ܐܠܨܬܐ ܕܡܣܢܩܘܬܐ *privation;* ܠܝܬ ܐܠܨܐ ܥܠ *there is no need of;* ܡܢ ܐܠܨܐ *necessary, necessarily, of necessity.* Pass. part. *strait, narrow;* ܐܬܪܐ ܐܠܝܨܐ *a narrow place* but metaph. *a poverty-stricken country; afflicted, tormented, oppressed, anxious; compelled, necessary;* gram. *short in pronunciation, abbreviated.* ETHPE. ܐܬܐܠܨ *to be strait, narrow, to be reduced to straits, straitened, afflicted, tormented, weighed down* with illness, hunger, thirst; *to be compelled, constrained.* PA. ܐܠܨ same as PE. ETHPA. ܐܬܐܠܨ *to be compelled, constrained, troubled,* e.g. ܡܢ ܪ̈ܘܚܐ ܛܢܦ̈ܬܐ *with unclean spirits; to suffer afflictions.* DERIVATIVES, ܐܠܘܨܐ, ܐܠܨܐ, ܐܠܝܨܐܝܬ, ܐܠܝܨܘܬܐ, ܐܠܨܐܝܬ, ܐܠܨܝܐ.

ܐܠܨܐܝܬ adv. rt. ܐܠܨ. *necessarily.*

ܐܠܨܝ, ܐܠܨܝܐ, ܐܠܨܝܬܐ no pl. m., pl. f. ܐܠܨܝ̈ܬܐ rt. ܐܠܨ. adj. *pressing, urgent, necessary, obligatory;* ܣܘܢܩܢܐ ܐܠܨܝܐ *urgent need;* ܐܠܨܝ ܐܝܬܘܬܐ *of necessary existence,* an epithet of God, hence it stands alone for *God;* ܒܛܝܠܘܬܐ ܕܐܠܨܝ ܐܝܬܘܬܐ *Divine Providence;* pl. *necessaries, requisites.*

ܐܡ, ܐܡܐ pl. ܐܡܗ̈ܬܐ rarely ܐܡ̈ܗܐ f. *a mother, grandmother, parent;* metaph. *an abbess; a mother-city, metropolis, a city which is the see of a patriarch;* ܐܡܐ ܕܪܫܐ *the crown of the head.* DERIVATIVES, ܐܡܗܘܬܐ, ܐܡܐ, ܐܡܬܐ, ܐܡܘܡܘܬܐ, ܐܡܘܡܐ, ܐܡܡܐ.

ܐܰܡܳܐ, ܐܰܡܬܳܐ pl. ܐܰܡܺܝܢ, ܐܰܡܶܐ f. *the fore-arm, the arm from the elbow to the tip of the middle finger, a cubit* = ܬܪܶܝܢ ܙܰܪ̈ܬܺܝܢ *two spans;* ܐܰܡܳܐ ܕܡܰܝ̈ܳܐ or without ܡܰܝ̈ܳܐ *a conduit, a pool.* DERIVATIVE, ܐܰܡܙܪܳܐ.

ܐܰܡܒܳܐ Pers. *anbah, an Indian fruit.*

ܐܡܒܘܒܐ, ܐܡܒܘܒܘܣ; see ܐܒܘܒܐ.

ܐܰܡܒܰܪ Ar. *amber, ambergris.*

ܐܡܰܕ fut. ܢܶܐܡܰܕ or ܢܺܐܡܰܕ (root-meaning *to reach, arrive at, be able,* cf. ܡܛܳܐ); with ܡܶܢ *to flee, escape,* ܡܶܢ ܣܰܝܦܳܐ *from the sword,* ܡܶܢ ܗܶܪܶܣܺܝܣ *from heresy.* APH. ܐܰܘܡܶܕ fut. ܢܰܘܡܶܕ. *a) to be able, sufficient,* ܠܳܐ ܡܰܘܡܕܺܝܢ ܗܘܰܘ ܠܡܶܩܒܰܪ ܠܚܰܕ̈ܕܶܐ *there were not enough to bury each other;* ܪܗܶܛܘ ܟܽܠ ܡܳܐ ܕܰܐܘܡܶܕܘ *they ran as long as they could. b) to free, set free. c) to escape, flee away,* ܡܶܢ ܦܰܚܳܐ *from the snare,* ܡܶܢ ܬܒܰܥܬܳܐ ܕܕܡܳܐ *from blood vengeance.*

ܐܰܡܺܕ or ܐܰܡܺܝܕ *Amida, a city on the Tigris,* now *Diarbekr* or *Kara Amid.*

ܐܡܒܪܐ = ܐܰܡܒܳܪ̈ܐ *cellars, store-rooms.*

ܐܰܡܗܽܘܬܳܐ from ܐܰܡܬܳܐ. f. *service, attendance of a maidservant.*

ܐܰܡܗܳܝܳܐ, ܐܰܡܗܳܝܬܳܐ from ܐܶܡܳܐ. adj. *of a mother, motherly, maternal.*

ܐܰܡܗܳܬܳܐ pl. of ܐܶܡܳܐ *mother,* and of ܐܰܡܬܳܐ *handmaid.*

ܐܳܡܽܘܠܽܘܓܺܝܰܐ pl. ܐܡܘܠܘܓܝܣ ὁμολογία, *a confession of faith, defence.*

ܐܽܘܡܳܢܳܐ pl. ܐ̈ܶ m. rt. ܐܶܡ (cf. matrix from mater) *a shape, mould* in which things are cast or into which they fit.

ܐܰܡܽܘܪܳܐ pl. ܐ̈ m. rt. ܐܡܪ. *a speaker, orator; a preacher; one who chants* or *intones; one who says* or *affirms.*

ܐܰܡܽܘܪܽܘܬܳܐ pl. ܐ̈ܘܳܬܳܐ f. rt. ܐܡܪ. *speech, manner of speech; a homily, a category.*

ܐܰܡܽܘܬܽܘܣܬܽܘܣ ἀμέθυστος, *amethyst.*

ܐܰܡܙܪܳܐ pl. ܐܰܡܙܪ̈ܳܐ m. *a pigmy,* said to be derived from ܐܰܡܬܳܐ *cubit* and ܙܪܬܳܐ *a span.*

ܐܰܡܺܝܢ (Heb. rt. ܐܡܢ) adv. *Amen, verily, a)* used at the beginning of a sentence for emphasis or solemnity, ܐܰܡܺܝܢ ܐܰܡܺܝܢ ܐܳܡܰܪ ܐ̱ܢܳܐ ܠܟܽܘܢ *Verily, verily, I say unto you. b)* at the end of a sentence to signify assent, *so be it, amen;* hence *c)* subst. *general consent, unanimity, agreement, assent, concord, desire, wish;* ܒܰܐܡܺܝܢ ܕܰܨܒܽܘܬܳܗ ܕܥܺܕܬܳܐ *by the unanimous desire of the Church.*

ܐܰܡܺܝܢܳܐܺܝܬ rt. ܐܡܢ. adv. *continually, ever, always, unceasingly, constantly.*

ܐܰܡܺܝܢܽܘܬܳܐ rt. ܐܡܢ. f. *perpetuity, continuance;* used adverbially with ܒ, *in perpetuity, continually, continuously, permanently, habitually, constantly;* ܒܰܐܡܺܝܢܽܘܬܳܐ ܫܢܺܝ̈ܢ ܚܰܡܫܺܝܢ *for fifty continuous years;* with ܕ, adj. *continual, customary.*

ܐܰܡܺܝܪ pl. ܐܰܡܺܝܪ̈ܶܐ rt. ܐܡܪ. *an emir, commander, prince, prefect;* ܐܰܡܺܝܪ ܕܒܰܓܕܰܕ *the prefect of Baghdad.*

ܐܰܡܒܳܐ pl. ܐ̈ *a pool, a swamp* such as remains here and there in the bed of a torrent during the dry season.

ܐܰܡܺܝܬܳܐ pl. ܐܰܡܺܝܬ̈ܳܐ f. *a hoe, shovel.*

ܐܰܡܶܠ denom. verb from ܐܰܡܠܳܐ. *to enwrap, cover.*

ܐܰܡܠܳܐ pl. ܐܰܡܠ̈ܶܐ f. *tapestry, a rug, a mantle* usually figured with needlework; ܕܡܺܝܟ ܥܰܠ ܐܰܡܠ̈ܶܐ *asleep on rugs;* ܐܰܡܠ̈ܶܐ ܒܳܒܠܳܝ̈ܶܐ *Babylonian hangings* or *carpets.*

ܐܡܰܡ by enallage of the radicals, for ܡܰܐܶܠ, fut. ܢܶܐܡܰܡ and ܢܺܐܡܰܡ *to be weary of.*

ܐܡܶܢ and ܗܰܝܡܶܢ root-meaning *to make firm,* PE. only used in the part. as adj. ܐܳܡܺܝܢ, ܐܰܡܺܝܢܳܐ, ܐܰܡܺܝܢܬܳܐ pl. m. ܝܢ, ܐ̈ f. ܐ̈ܬܳܐ. *a) true, lasting, never-ceasing, never-ending, eternal, perpetual, continual, ever;* ܐܰܡܺܝܢܬܳܐ ܒܬܽܘܠܽܘܬܳܐ *perpetual virginity;* ܚܰܕ ܐܰܡܺܝܢܺܝܢ ܗܘܰܝܢ *we were ever one. b) constant, persevering, assiduous,* with ܒ of an occupation, habit, or place; ܒܨܰܘܡܳܐ *in fasting;* ܒܨܠܽܘܬܳܐ *in prayer;* ܐܰܡܺܝܢ ܒܡܶܫܬܝܳܐ ܕܚܰܡܪܳܐ *an habitual wine-drinker;* ܐܰܡܺܝܢ ܗܘܳܐ ܒܒܺܝ̈ܫܳܬܳܐ *he was persistent in evil-doing, given to evil habits. c) remaining, stopping, being constantly with,* with ܠܘܳܬ of a pers. or ܒ of a place. See ܐܡܢ. ETHPE. ܐܶܬܐܡܶܢ imper. ܐܶܬܐܰܡܰܢ, part. ܡܶܬܐܡܰܢ, ܡܶܬܐܰܡܢܳܐ. I. *a) to persevere, persist in, continue in, to be constant, stedfast,* with ܒ; ܒܬܰܫܡܫܬܳܗ ܕܰܐܠܳܗܳܐ *in the service of God;* ܒܕܘܒܪ̈ܐ *in virtuous conduct;* ܒܡܫܚܩܐ ܕܦܣ̈ܐ *in playing dibs. b) to frequent, go frequently to,* with ܠ; ܠܥܕܬܐ or ܠܥܕ̈ܬܐ *to go to church regularly, be constant in attendance at church. c) to remain, continue,* with ܒ of the place, with ܠܘܬ or ܥܡ of a person; ܨܒܐ ܐܢܐ ܕܐܬܡܢ ܠܘܬ ܐܠܗܐ *I desire to be continually with God.* II. denom. from ܐܘܡܢܐ, *to do anything with art, carry out skilfully.* PAIEL ܗܝܡܢ act. part. ܡܗܝܡܢ, ܡܗܝܡܢܐ, ܡܗܝܡܢܬܐ; pass. p. ܡܗܝܡܢ other forms same as act.; *to believe,* with ܒ *to believe in,* ܒܐܠܗܐ *in God,* ܒܫܡܗ *in the Name; to put faith in, have confidence in, trust, entrust,* with pers. suff., ܒ or ܠ. Act. p. *a believer, Christian;* ܡܗܝܡܢܐ ܫܪܝܪܐ *a true* or *orthodox believer;* pl. *the faithful;* pass. p. with ܠ or ܥܠ of the obj. *to be trusted with, have charge of.* Adj. *faithful, trustworthy; sure, firm, enduring; entrusted,* hence subst. *a minister, steward, eunuch.* ETHPAIAL ܐܬܗܝܡܢ *a) to be believed;* with ܠ of the pers. *to believe;* ܕܐܬܗܝܡܢ ܠܟ *that I may believe;* ܠܐ ܡܟܝܠ ܡܬܗܝܡܢܐ ܠܐܝܠܝܢ ܕܒܕܪܐ ܐܚܪܢܐ *perhaps this will not be credible to those who live in another age;* ܫܘܐ ܠܡܬܗܝܡܢܘ *worthy of credence, trustworthy. b) to be verified, found true; to be faithful, true, trustworthy; to be entrusted* with any office or ministry, *to receive the charge* or *care of anything,* with ܥܠ; *to be made an eunuch;* ܕܒܪܬܐ ܕܐܬܗܝܡܢܬܘܢ ܥܠܝܗ *the stewardship which is entrusted to you.* DERIVATIVES, ܐܡܝܢ, ܐܡܝܢܐ, ܐܡܝܢܘܬܐ, ܐܡܝܢܐܝܬ, ܐܘܡܢܐ, ܐܡܢ, ܐܡܢܐ, ܐܡܢܘܬܐ, ܐܡܢܝܬ, ܗܝܡܢܘܬܐ, ܡܗܝܡܢܐܝܬ, ܡܗܝܡܢܘܬܐ, ܡܬܗܝܡܢܘܬܐ.

ܐܡܢܐ pl. ܐܡܢ̈ܐ rt. ܐܡܢ. m. *that which is done constantly* or *habitually, a pursuit, habit, practice;* ܐܡܢ̈ܐ ܛܒ̈ܐ—ܡܫܒܚ̈ܐ *good habits, honourable pursuits. A craft, trade, profession, employment, office;* ܒܪ ܐܡܢܐ *a fellow-craftsman.*

ܐܡܦܘܡܐ or ܐܡܦܘܡܐ ἔμφωμα, *a window; white lead, ceruse;* ܡܝ̈ܐ ܕܐܡܦܘܡܐ *lime-water.*

ܐܡܩܬܐ f. *a lizard.*

ܐܡܪ APHEL of ܡܪ; *to make bitter, to anger, sadden, grieve.*

ܐܡܪ (in Ar. *to command;* cf. pass. part. used substantively) fut. ܢܐܡܪ 1 pers. ܐܡܪ, infin. ܠܡܐܡܪ, imper. ܐܡܪ, act. part. ܐܡܪ, ܐܡܪܐ, pass. part. ܐܡܝܪ, ܐܡܝܪܐ, ܐܡܝܪܬܐ *a) to say, speak,* with ܠ of the pers. A quotation or oblique narration is introduced by ܕ, ܐܡܪܬ ܠܟܘܢ ܕܠܐ ܐܢܫ *I told you that no one* &c.; ܗܘ ܕܐܡܪܬ *he of whom I spoke.* With ܒܝܢܬ, ܐܡܪܘ ܒܝܢܬܗܘܢ *they said among themselves* or *to each other;* ܠܘܬ *to any one;* ܡܢ *to renounce,* Germ. *absagen;* ܥܠ or ܥܠ *to speak about;* ܥܡ *to* or *with* any one. *b) to tell, affirm, assert, intend; to intone, chant.* ܐܡܪ ܒܠܒܗ—ܒܢܦܫܗ *to think, muse, imagine, devise, purpose;* with ܕܝܢܐ *to go to law;* ܐܡܪ ܟܪܘܙܘܬܐ *to preach;* ܦܘܫܩܐ or ܬܘܪܓܡܐ *to expound;* ܡܢ ܩܕܡ ܐܡܪ *to foretell, predict. c)* ܐܡܪ often stands after verbs of sending, answering, writing, &c.; ܫܕܪ or ܫܠܚ ܐܡܪ *he sent word.* Pass. part. *said, mentioned, the above-named* ellipt. for ܕܐܡܝܪ ܡܢ ܠܥܠ; *composed, written,* ܐܡܝܪ ܠܝܘܚܢܢ the gospel *of St. John;* ܐܡܝܪ ܪܘܚܢܐ *inspired.* See ܐܡܝܪ. The infin. with ܠ is used for, *that is to say, seeing that, to wit, namely, granted, doubtless;* ܟܕ ܠܡܐܡܪ *in a word.* ETHPE. ܐܬܐܡܪ or ܐܬܡܪ the radical ܐ being omitted, *to be said, told, related, mentioned; to be foretold* with or without ܩܕܡ; *to be spoken, preached, recited; to be called, named* = ܐܬܩܪܝ or ܐܫܬܡܗ; ܡܬܐܡܪܐ ܥܒܪܐܝܬ ܓܓܘܠܬܐ *called in Hebrew Golgotha,* John xix. 17; 3 ms. and part. f. impers. *it is said.* DERIVATIVES, ܐܡܘܪܐ, ܡܐܡܪܐ, ܡܐܡܪܢܐ, ܐܡܝܪ, ܐܡܝܪܐ, ܐܡܘܪܘܬܐ.

ܐܡܪܐ, ܐܡܪܐ pl. ܐܡܪ̈ܐ, ܐܡܪܝܢ m. *a lamb;* ܐܡܪܗ ܕܐܠܗܐ *the Lamb of God;* astron. *Aries,* a sign of the Zodiac.

ܐܡܬܐ, ܐܡܬܐ pl. ܐܡܗ̈ܬܐ rt. ܐܡ. f. *a) a maidservant, handmaid. b)* ܐܡܬܐ emph. st. of ܐܡܐ *a cubit.*

ܐܡܬܝ *a)* interrog. adverb, *when?* ܥܕܡܐ ܠܐܡܬܝ *how long? b)* relat. and indef. with ܕ preceding ܕܐܡܬܝ *at that time, at which time;* with ܕ following *when, at what time;* ܐܝܟ ܐܡܬܝ ܕ *sometimes;* ܟܠ ܐܡܬܝ ܕ *whensoever, so often as. c)* ܐܡܬܝ ܗܘ interj. of great desire and impatience, *when will it be? would it were!*

ܐܢ *a)* conj. *if, if it be, whether it be, however, howsoever, whensoever;* ܐܢ—ܐܢ or ܐܢ—ܐܘ *whether—or;* ܐܦܢ *even if;* ܐܢ, ܐܢ ܗܘ ܕ

now if, but if, even if; ܐܠܐ ܐܢ contr. ܐܠܐ and sometimes with ܐܢ repeated ܐܢ ܐܠܐ, *if not, or else, unless, except, surely;* in indirect questions *whether, if,* &c. In making an asseveration ܐܢ stands for *not;* ܐܢ ܐܬܠ ܫܢܬܐ ܠܥܝܢܝ *I will give no sleep unto mine eyes.* b) interj. *O!* ܐܢ ܐܪܡܝܐ ܢܒܝܐ ܡܢܐ ܒܟܝܬ *O Jeremiah the prophet, wherefore hast thou wept!* c) = ܐܝܢ *yea, truly.*

ܐܢܐ, ܐܢܐ (in MSS. ܐܢܐ, ܐܢܐ) pl. ܐܢܚܢ, ܚܢܢ pron. 1 pers. com. *I, we;* for the gen. ܕܝܠܝ *my,* ܕܝܠܢ *our* is used, acc. and dat. ܠܝ, ܠܢ *me, us; to me, to us;* abl. ܡܢܝ, ܡܢܢ *by* or *from me, us.* The second form is used as a copula, ܐܢܐ ܐܢܐ *I am;* ܐܢܐ ܗܘ *I am that* or *I am he;* with participles forms a present tense and is often contracted, ܐܡܪ ܐܢܐ and ܐܡܪܢܐ *I say;* ܐܡܪܝܢ ܚܢܢ or ܐܡܪܝܢܢ *we say;* ܒܥܐ ܐܢܐ or ܒܥܢܐ *I beg, I beseech;* ܝܕܥܝܢܢ *we know;* ܡܩܒܠܝܢܢ *we receive.*

ܐܢܒܒܙܘܢ ἀναβιβάζων, astrol. *the ascendant.*

ܐܢܒܝܩ Ar. *alembic, still.*

ܐܢ ܗܘ = ܐܢܗܘ *even if.*

ܐܢܕ Aphel of ܢܕ; *to put to flight; to arouse from sleep.*

ܐܢ ܕܝܢ = ܐܢܕܝܢ *but if, even if.*

ܐܢܕܝܩܛܝܘܢܐ, ܐܢܕܝܩܛܘܢܐ, ܐܢܕܝܩܛܝܘܢܐ, &c., f. ἰνδικτιῶνα, *an Indict, a space of fifteen years.* This reckoning is thought to have been introduced by Constantine the Great. Greek numerals are generally used with it.

ܐܢܕܪܝܐܢܛܐ, ܐܢܕܪܝܢܛܐ or ܐܕܪܝܢܛܐ pl. ܐ̈ ἀνδριάντα, *a bronze statue.*

ܐܢܗܘ; see ܐܢ.

ܐܢܘܢ pron. 3 p. m. pl. *they, them, there;* see ܗܢܘܢ.

ܐܢܘܢܐ pl. ܐܢܘܢܣ, ܐܢܘܢܣ, ܐܢܘܢܘܣ f. *annona; a yearly pension; soldiers' pay, an allowance of food; a yearly tribute of corn.*

ܐܢܘܢܩܐ or ܐܢܝܢܩܐ f. rt. ܐܢܩ. *distress, anguish* of heart.

ܐܢܚ mimetic, not used in Pe. Ethpa. ܐܬܐܢܚ *to groan.* Ettaph. ܐܬܬܐܢܚ for ܐܬܬܐܢܚ *to groan, sigh, lament.* Derivative, ܬܐܢܚܬܐ.

ܐܢܚܢ an early form of ܚܢܢ, only found in ancient MSS.; see ܐܢܐ.

ܐܢܛܘܠܝܩܘܢ, ܐܢܛܘܠܝܩܘܢ ἐντολικόν, *an injunction, assignation, power of attorney.*

ܐܢܛܝܓܪܦܘܢ or without the ܘ, ἀντίγραφον, *a copy, transcript; a reply in writing.*

ܐܢܛܝܕܘܛܘܣ ἀντίδοτος, *an antidote.*

ܐܢܬܘܦܛܘܣ *the vice-praefect of a province.*

ܐܢܝܢ 3 pl. f. pers. pron.; see ܗܢܝܢ.

ܐܢܟ imper. ܐܢܟ, act. p. ܐܢܟ, pass. p. ܐܢܝܟ denom. verb from ܐܢܟܐ *to tin over.* Ethp. ܐܬܐܢܟ pass.

ܐܢܟܐ m. *tin.*

ܐܢܠܘܡܐ pl. ܐܢܠܘܡܐ ἀνάλωμα, *expense, an allowance for expenses.*

ܐܢܦܘܪܐ, ܐܢܦܘܪܐ, ܐܢܦܘܪܐ and other spellings; pl. ܐ̈, ܐܣ and ܐܣ ἀναφορά, *anything addressed to superior authority,* as *a report, petition. The Liturgy, mass, anaphora; the veil wherewith the chalice and paten are covered;* astron. *the rising of a constellation.*

ܐܢܢܩܐ or ܐܢܢܩܝ pl. ܐܢܢܩܣ, ܐܢܢܩܣ, ܐܢܢܩܣ, ܐܢܢܩܣ, &c. f. ἀνάγκη, *necessity, exigency, need, distress;* ܡܢ ܐܢܢܩܝ *of necessity, necessarily;* ܐܢܢܩܝ ܗܘ *it must needs be, it is necessary, unavoidable.* Derivatives, the three following:

ܐܢܢܩܐܝܬ adv. *of necessity, necessarily.*

ܐܢܢܩܝܐ, ܐܢܢܩܝܐ pl. m. ܐ̈, f. ܬܐ̈ *necessary;* ܐܢܢܩܝܐ ܚܫܒܬ *I thought it necessary;* ܐܢܢܩܝܬܐ *axioms.* pl. f. *necessary expenses.*

ܐܢܢܩܝܘܬܐ f. *necessity.*

ܐܢܢܩ *to press, compel.* Ethpe. ܐܬܐܢܢܩ *to be compelled, urged, distressed.* Pa. ܐܢܢܩ *to force.* Derivative, ܐܘܢܩܐ or ܐܢܘܢܩܐ.

ܐܢܦ, ܐܢܦܐ pl. ܐܦܐ, ܐܦܝܢ f. *the nose, the nostrils;* only used in the pl.; see ܐܦܐ.

ܐܢܦܐ Heb. *a hoopoe.*

ܐܢܩ (mimetic, cf. the cognate rt. ܐܢܚ) Ethpa. ܐܬܐܢܩ *to groan, sigh.* Hence is derived

ܐܢܩܬܐ pl. ܐܢܩܬܐ f. *a groan, deep groan, sorrowful sighing,* ܕܐܣܝܪ̈ܐ *of prisoners,* Ps. lxxix. 11, &c.; ܕܝܬܡ̈ܐ *of orphans.*

ܐܢܩܢܝܐ or ܐܢܩܢܝܐ *encaenia; a festival of dedication* or *of consecration.*

ܐܢܩܘܩܠܝܘܢ or ܐܢܩܘܩܠܝܘܢ ἐγκύκλια, *an encyclical letter; a complete codex of the Holy Scriptures; a Book of Offices for the whole year; a cycle of hymns* = ܩܘܩܠܝܘܢ.

ܐܢܫ, ܐܢܫܐ, ܐܢܫܐ pl. ܐ̈ܢܫܝܢ, ܐ̈ܢܫܐ com. gen. takes affixes in the pl., not in the sing. *a*) *a man, human being, mortal* = *homo* as ܓܒܪܐ = *vir*. In this primary sense of the word ܒܪ generally stands with ܐܢܫ, ܐܢܫܐ; ܒܪ ܐܢܫܐ contr. ܒܪܢܫܐ pl. ܒ̈ܢܝ ܐ̈ܢܫܐ or ܒ̈ܢܝܢܫܐ. *b*) with affixes, *kinsfolk, relations*, esp. *parents; people, inhabitants;* ܐ̈ܢܫܘܗܝ ܕܡܕܝܢܬܐ *the people of the city, citizens;* ܐ̈ܢܫ ܐܬܪܐ *the dwellers in that place*. *c*) when followed by another noun with the possessive affix = *each;* ܐܢܫ ܒܕܘܟܬܗ *each in his place; any one, one, whoever, whosoever, a certain;* ܐܢܫ ܡܢ ܫ̈ܠܝܚܐ *one of the apostles;* ܠܝܬ ܐܢܫ *there is no one;* ܐܢܬܬܐ ܐܢܫ ܡܢ ܐܘܪܗܝ *a certain woman in Edessa;* ܡܠܟܬܐ ܐܢܫ *a certain queen;* ܐ̈ܢܫܝܢ ܛ̈ܠܝܐ *some boys;* ܐܢܫ ܐܢܫ *each, one by one;* ܐܢܫ — ܚܒܪܗ *one — the other;* ܟܠ ܐܢܫ *every one, whosoever;* ܠܐ ܐܢܫ *no one*. *d*) often used pleonastically; ܐ̈ܢܫܐ ܪ̈ܘܪܒܢܐ, ܐ̈ܢܫܐ ܪ̈ܫܢܐ *princes, nobles;* ܐܢܫ ܟܪܘܙܐ *a herald*. Derivatives, ܐܢܫܐܝܬ, ܐܢܫܘܬܐ, ܐܢܫܝܐ, ܒܪܢܫܐ, ܒܪܢܫ.

ܐܢܫܐܝܬ adv. *as a man; in human* or *mortal form; humanely, benignly, courteously*.

ܐܢܫܘܬܐ from ܐܢܫ f. *a*) *human nature, manhood* e.g. of our Lord, opp. ܐܠܗܘܬܗ. *b*) *the human race, mankind;* ܒܥܝܪܐ ܘܪܚܫܐ ܘܐܢܫܘܬܐ *cattle and creeping things and man*. *c*) collect. *men, people, inhabitants, citizens, the populace; relations, servants, family;* ܣܘܓܐܐ ܕܐܢܫܘܬܐ *a multitude of people*.

ܐܢܫܝܐ, ܐܢܫܝܬܐ pl. m. ܝ̈ܐ, f. ܝ̈ܬܐ from ܐܢܫ. adj. *human*.

ܐܢܬ f. ܐܢܬܝ pl. m. ܐܢܬܘܢ f. ܐܢܬܝܢ pron. 2 pers. *thou, you;* used as a copula, ܐܢܬܘܢ ܒܝ ܐܢܬܘܢ *ye are in me;* ܡܢ ܐܝܟܐ ܐܢܬ *whence art thou?* but for *thou art* ܐܢܬ ܐܢܬ is not used, but ܐܢܬܘ *atu* and pl. ܐܢܬܘܢ, ܐܢܬܘܢ *ye are*. With a participle or adjective ܐܢܬ forms a present tense, and as it is pronounced together with the preceding part. it is often also written in one word, ܕܚܠܐ ܐܢܬ = ܕܚܠܬ, ܡܫܟܚ ܐܢܬ = ܡܫܟܚܬ, ܡܫܒܚ ܐܢܬ = ܡܫܒܚܬ, ܡܥܒܕ ܐܢܬ = ܡܥܒܕܬ. The oblique cases are formed with ܕܝܠܟ and ܠ; ܕܝܠܟ f. ܕܝܠܟܝ pl. ܕܝܠܟܘܢ f. ܕܝܠܟܝܢ *thy, thine, your, yours;* ܠܟ f. ܠܟܝ pl. m. ܠܟܘܢ f. ܠܟܝܢ *thee, you, to thee, to you*.

ܐܢܬܘܦܛܘܣ, ܐܢܬܘܦܛܘܣ or ܐܢܬܘܦܛܐ ἀνθύπατος, *a proconsul*.

ܐܢܬܬܐ, ܐܢܬܬܐ pl. ܢܫ̈ܐ f. *a woman*, esp. *married, a wife;* ܐܢܬܬ ܐܒܐ *a stepmother;* ܐܢܬܬ ܐܚܘܗܝ *a sister-in-law*.

ܐܣܐ Pe. only act. part. used as subst.; see ܐܣܝܐ and ܐܣܝܘܬܐ. Pa. ܐܣܝ fut. ܢܐܣܐ 1 pers. fut. ܐܐܣܐ, imper. ܐܣܐ *to heal;* rarely metaph. *to restore*. Ethpe. ܐܬܐܣܝ or ܐܬܐܣܝ *to be healed, restored*. Derivatives, ܐܣܝܐ, ܐܣܝܘܬܐ, ܐܣܝܬܐ, ܐܣܝܐܝܬ, ܡܐܣܝܢܘܬܐ, ܡܐܣܝܢܐ, ܐܣܘܬܐ.

ܐܣܝܐ, ܐܣܝܐ pl. ܐ̈ܣܘܢ, ܐ̈ܣܘܬܐ Peal part. of ܐܣܐ = subst. m. *a healer, physician, leech;* ܐ̈ܣܘܬܐ ܕܡܠܟܘܬܐ *court physicians*.

ܐܣܐ, ܐܣܬܐ pl. ܐ̈ܣܐ f. *a wall, a partition* or *inner wall*. Derivative, ܐܣܬܐܝܬ.

ܐܣܐ pl. ܐ̈ܣܐ Ar. m. *the myrtle;* ܦܐܪ̈ܐ ܐܣܐ *myrtle-berries*.

ܐܣܒܠ = ܐܣܒ.

ܐܣܒ 1 pers. s. fut. of ܢܣܒ *to take*.

ܐܣ̈ܕܐ m. only pl., for the sing. ܒܣܕܪܐ is used, *pillows*, ܡܘܬܐ ܩܡ ܠܐܣ̈ܕܘܗܝ *death stood by his bedside*.

ܐܣܘܛܐ, ܐܣܘܛܐ and ܐܣܘܛܘܣ ἄσωτος, *a glutton, a prodigal*.

ܐܣܘܛܐܝܬ *immoderately, intemperately*.

ܐܣܘܛܘܬܐ pl. ܐܣܘܛ̈ܘܬܐ f. *intemperance, gluttony, debauchery, licentiousness*.

ܐܣܘܪܐ pl. ܪ̈ܐ rt. ܐܣܪ. m. *a band, bond, chain; fetters, handcuffs, imprisonment, bondage; an obligation, binding promise, oath*.

ܐܣܘܪܝܐ pl. ܐܣܘܪ̈ܝܐ rt. ܐܣܪ. m. *bondage, captivity, a prohibition, interdict*.

ܐܣܛܐܣܝܣ; see ܣܛܣܝܣ.

ܐܣܦܗܒܕ corruption of Pers. *spahpat, the master of the soldiery*.

ܐܣܛܒܠܐ, ܐܣܛܒܠܝܢ or ܐܣܛܒܠܐ *stabulum, a stable*.

ܐܣܛܒܪܩܐ or ܐܣܛܒܪܩܐ *rich silk*.

ܐܣܛܕܐ pl. ܐܣܛܕ̈ܘܢ, ܐܣܛܕ̈ܘܬܐ m. στάδιον,

a) a stadium, cxxv paces, ⅛th of a Roman mile. b) a parasang or *farsang=three or four miles.*

ܐܣܛܕܝܘܢ pl. ܐܣܛܕܝܘܬܐ, ܐܣܛܕܝܘܢ m. rarely f. *a stadium* (see above); *a gymnasium; a race-course; a field of battle; a course, orbit.*

ܐܣܛܘܐ pl. ܐܣܛܘܝܢ, ܐܣܛܘܐ m. στοά, *a porch, portico.*

ܐܣܛܘܟܣܐ pl. ܐܣܛܘܟܣܐ, ܐܣܛܘܟܣܐ m. στοιχεῖον, *an element, a first principle; a verse* or *part of a hymn.*

ܐܣܛܘܟܣܝܐ f. ܐܣܛܘܟܣܝܬܐ pl. m. ܐܣܛܘܟܣܝܐ f. ܐܣܛܘܟܣܝܬܐ adj. from the preceding; *elemental, elementary, primary, primitive.*

ܐܣܛܘܡܟܐ pl. ܐܣܛܘܡܟܐ στόμαχος, m. *the stomach.*

ܐܣܛܘܠܣ, ܐܣܛܘܢܐ pl. ܐ̈ m. στῦλος, *a column, pillar, support, prop.* Hence is derived

ܐܣܛܘܢܝܐ and ܐܣܛܘܢܝܐ pl. ܐ̈ m. *a stylite, a pillar-saint.*

ܐܣܛܘܦܪܐ *a time, season.*

ܐܣܛܘܪܟܐ m. *storax, a sweet-smelling gum.*

ܐܣܛܘܟܣܝܬܐ pl. ܐܣܛܘܟܣܝܬܐ *a Station,* i.e. *a doctrinal hymn.* The Syr. word for the same is ܡܘܬܒܐ.

ܐܣܛܝܪܐ *ostiarius, doorkeeper, usher.*

ܐܣܛܠܐ, ܐܣܛܠܐ pl. ܐܣܛܠܐ f. στολή, *a stole, vestment, garment, robe, habit.*

ܐܣܛܣܝܣ, ܐܣܛܣܝܐ or ܐܣܛܣܝܢ στάσις, *sedition.*

ܐܣܛܣܝܢܐ *seditious men, roughs.*

ܐܣܛܦܠܝܢ f. σταφυλῖνος, *a parsnip.*

ܐܣܛܦܛܐ pl. ܐܣܛܦܛܐ m. *stacte, the gum storax.*

ܐܣܛܪܘܠܒܘܢ, ܐܣܛܪܘܠܒܝܘܢ or ܐܣܛܪܘܠܒܝܘܢ ἀστρολάβιον, *an astrolabe.*

ܐܣܛܪܘܠܘܓܘܣ pl. ܐܣܛܪܘܠܘܓܐ ἀστρολόγος, *an astrologer.*

ܐܣܛܪܘܠܘܓܝܐ f. ἀστρολογία, *astrology.*

ܐܣܛܪܘܢܘܡܘܣ and ܐܣܛܪܘܢܘܡܐ pl. ܐܣܛܪܘܢܘܡܐ ἀστρονόμος, *an astronomer.*

ܐܣܛܪܘܢܘܡܝܐ ἀστρονομία, *astronomy,* one of the four primary sciences, the others being geometry, arithmetic, and music.

ܐܣܛܪܐ pl. ܐܣܛܪܛܐ *stratum, a street, road.*

ܐܣܛܪܛܝܐ στρατεία, *military service, warfare.*

ܐܣܛܪܛܓܐ and ܐܣܛܪܛܓܐ, pl. ܐ̈ m. στρατηγός, *a leader, commander* of an army; *a governor, magistrate.*

ܐܣܛܪܛܝܘܛܐ pl. ܐܣܛܪܛܝܘܛܐ and ܐܣܛܪܛܝܘܛܐ m. στρατιώτης, *a soldier.*

ܐܣܛܪܛܠܛܐ, ܐܣܛܪܛܠܛܐ, or ܐܣܛܪܛܠܛܝܣ pl. ܐܣܛܪܛܠܛܐ m. στρατηλάτης, *a commander, general.*

ܐܣܛܪܢܓܠܐ, ܐܣܛܪܢܓܠܐ and ܐܣܛܪܢܓܠܐ deriv. uncertain. *Estrangelo,* the most ancient of the three Syriac alphabets. The others are ܡܕܢܚܝܐ or ܢܣܛܘܪܝܐ *Eastern* or *Nestorian,* and ܦܫܝܛܐ or ܡܥܪܒܝܐ *Western* or *simple* writing, used by the Jacobites or Maronites.

ܐܣܛܪܢܝܐ corrupted from στρῆνος, *luxury, debauchery.*

ܐܣܝܐ, ܐܣܝܬܐ pl. m. ܐܣܝܐ f. ܐܣܝܬܐ rt. ܐܣܐ. adj. *of medicine, medicinal, medical.*

ܐܣܝܘܬܐ, ܐܣܝܘܬܐ pl. ܐܣܝܘܬܐ rarely ܐܣܘܬܐ rt. ܐܣܐ. f. *the healing art, medical science; medicine, a remedy, cure; Heilung;* ܕܠܐ ܐܣܝܘܬܐ or ܕܠܝܬ ܠܗ ܐܣܝܘܬܐ *incurable.*

ܐܣܝܪܘܬܐ rt. ܐܣܪ. f. *a being linked, joined, fettered; a bond, bondage, captivity.*

ܐܣܝܬܐ part. Pe. of ܐܣܐ f. emph. st. *healing; a nurse, midwife;* subst. *medicine, salve.*

ܐܣܟܘܠܐ and ܐܣܟܘܠܝ pl. ܐܣܟܘܠܐ and ܐܣܟܘܠܐ, ܐܣܟܘܠܝܢ, ܐܣܟܘܠܣ σχολή, *a school; teaching, knowledge.*

ܐܣܟܘܠܝܐ pl. ܐ̈ m. *a scholar, student, disciple, learner.*

ܐܣܟܘܠܣܛܝܩܐ or ܐܣܟܘܠܣܛܝܩܐ pl. ܐ̈ and ܐܣܟܘܠܣܛܝܩܘܣ m. *a scholar, disputer, pleader, an advocate.*

ܐܣܟܘܦܬܐ pl. ܐܣܟܘܦܬܐ f. *the threshold, a doorpost; a porch, vestibule; a guard-room.*

ܐܣܟܝܡ, ܐܣܟܡܐ or ܐܣܟܝܡ, ܐܣܟܡܐ pl. ܐ̈, ܐ̈ m. σχῆμα, *the form, shape. a) attire, raiment, dress, habit;* ܐܣܟܝܡ ܟܗܢܘܬܐ *priestly apparel;* ܐܣܟܡܐ ܕܟܘܡܪܘܬܐ—ܕܕܝܪܝܘܬܐ *the pontifical—the monastic habit;* ܒܐܣܟܝܡ ܝܘܢܝܐ *in Greek dress. b) manners, ways,* as the outward habit of mind; ܐܶܣܟܺܝܡܳܐ ܢܳܡܽܘܣܳܝܳܐ, ܐܶܣܟܺܝܡܳܐ ܫܰܦܺܝܪܳܐ or ܐܶܣܟܺܝܡܳܐ absolutely, *good manners, decorous, right* or *graceful behaviour, propriety.* c) *appearance, outward show,* esp. *false;* ܥܳܒܶܕ ܐܶܣܟܺܝܡܳܐ *a dissembler, hypocrite;* ܐܶܣܟܺܝܡܳܐ ܕܰܟܝܳܢܽܘܬܳܐ or ܐܶܣܟܺܝܡܳܐ ܕܰܓܳܠܳܐ *dissimulation, pretence, hypocrisy.* d) *a way, manner;* ܒܰܐܣܟܺܝܡܳܐ *like;* ܒܚܰܕ ܡܶܢ ܐܶܣܟܺܝܡܺܝܢ *in any way, some way;* with a negative, *in no way, in no wise;* ܒܟܽܠ ܐܶܣܟܺܝܡ *of all sorts* or *kinds, in manifold ways;* ܒܰܐܣܟܺܝܡ ܐܶܣܟܺܝܡ, ܐܶܣܟܺܝܡ ܐܶܣܟܺܝܡ *in many ways, variously;* hence are derived the two following words:

ܐܶܣܟܺܝܡܳܢܳܐ and ܐܶܣܟܺܝܡܳܬܳܢܳܐ f. ܬܳܐ pl. m. ܢܶܐ, f. ܬܳܐ. a) *a dissembler, hypocrite; hypocritical.* b) *of good behaviour, honest, honourable.*

ܐܶܣܟܺܝܡܳܬܳܢܽܘܬܳܐ pl. ܬܳܐ f. *hypocrisy.*

ܐܶܣܟܳܦܬܳܐ and ܐܶܣܟܳܦܳܬܳܐ pl. ܐܶܣܟܳܦܳܬܳܐ or ܬܳܐ f. *a mattock, spade* or *fork.*

ܐܶܣܰܡ and ܐܶܣܰܠ fut. ܢܶܐܣܽܠ, pass. part. ܐܰܣܺܝܡ, ܐܰܣܺܝܡܳܐ *to lay by, pile up, store up,* esp. *of corn.* Ethpe. ܐܶܬ݁ܐܶܣܶܡ *to gather up* or *together,* refl. *to be gathered up, piled up.* Derivative, ܐܣܡܳܐ.

ܐܶܣܡܳܐ pl. ܐܶܣܡܶܐ rt. ܐܣܡ. m. *a heaping up, a store, victuals; provision* for a garrison.

ܐܶܣܡܽܘܬܳܐ rt. ܐܣܡ. f. *harvesting.*

ܐܶܣܦܳܐ *a wine-can.*

ܐܶܣܦܳܘܓܳܐ or ܐܶܣܦܳܘܓܳܘܣ pl. ܓܶܐ f. σπόγγος, *a sponge.*

ܐܶܣܦܳܘܓܳܝܳܐ *spongy.*

ܐܶܣܦܳܘܪܳܐ pl. ܐܶܣܦܳܘܪܶܐ m. *a messenger who rides post.*

ܐܶܣܦܶܘܩܠܳܛܳܪ, ܐܶܣܦܶܘܩܠܳܛܳܪܳܐ pl. ܝܶܢ, ܪܶܐ m. *spiculator.* a) *a body-guard, an attendant, a guard.* b) *an executioner, hangman.*

ܐܶܣܦܺܝܢ ܚܶܘܳܪܳܐ *white mustard.*

ܐܶܣܦܺܝܢܳܐ and ܐܶܣܦܺܢܳܐ m. σφήν, *a wedge.*

ܐܶܣܦܰܢܳܬܳܐ and ܐܶܣܦܺܢܺܝܬܳܐ pl. ܬܶܐ adj. *dyed red.*

ܐܶܣܦܺܝܪ, ܐܶܣܦܺܝܪܳܐ and ܐܶܣܦܺܪ, ܐܶܣܦܺܪܳܐ, E-Syr. ܐܶܣܦܺܝܪܳܐ pl. ܪܶܐ f. a) σπεῖρα, *a company of soldiers, a cohort, band, company.* b) σφαῖρα, *anything of a round shape,* e.g. *a round cake; a sphere, globe, circle, ball;* hence

ܐܶܣܦܺܝܪܳܝܳܐ f. ܐܶܣܦܺܝܪܳܘܢܳܝܬܳܐ and ܐܶܣܦܺܝܪܳܢܳܐ f. ܢܺܝܬܳܐ *spherical, round.*

ܐܶܣܦܺܝܪܳܢܽܘܬܳܐ f. *sphericity.*

ܐܶܣܦܠܺܢܺܝܢ or ܐܶܣܦܠܺܢܺܝܢ pl. ܢܶܐ f. σπλήνιον, *a compress, bandage; a plaster, salve;* chem. *a paste.*

ܐܶܣܦܢܳܐ *a timber, a balk;* cognate ܣܦܢܳܐ.

ܐܶܣܦܶܣ f. ἀσπίς, *an adder, asp, the Egyptian cobra.*

ܐܶܣܦܰܪ &c.; see ܐܶܣܦܺܝܪ.

ܐܶܣܦܰܪܓܠܳܐ m. *the quince, the quince-tree.*

ܐܶܣܦܺܪܺܝܣ pl. ܝܶܢ, ܣܶܐ m. σπυρίς, *a round plaited basket.*

ܐܶܣܦܳܪܰܝܳܐ E-Syr. = ܐܶܣܦܺܝܪ *a ball.*

ܐܶܣܦܺܪܚܳܛܳܐ from ܐܶܣܦܺܝܪ, *a caestus.*

ܐܶܣܦܰܛܳܪܳܐ pl. ܐܶܣܦܰܛܳܪܶܐ m. σπαθάριος, *a sword-bearer, one of the imperial guard.*

ܐܰܣܶܩ irreg. Aphel of ܣܠܶܩ; *to raise, place above; to offer sacrifice* or *praise.*

ܐܶܣܩܽܘܛܳܐ pl. ܐܶܣܩܽܘܛܶܐ m. σκῦτος, *a leathern whip, scourge.*

ܐܶܣܩܽܘܦܳܐ pl. ܐܶܣܩܽܘܦܺܝܢ m. σκύφος, *a cup; the bowl of a candlestick* or *lamp.*

ܐܶܣܩܪܺܝܒܳܘܢ or ܐܶܣܩܪܺܝܒܳܘܢܳܘܣ same in pl.; σκρίβων, *an imperial messenger* or *commissioner.*

ܐܶܣܰܪ fut. ܢܶܐܣܽܘܪ and ܢܶܐܣܽܘܪ, inf. ܠܡܶܐܣܰܪ, imper. ܐܶܣܽܘܪ, act. part. ܐܳܣܰܪ, ܐܳܣܪܳܐ, pass. part. ܐܰܣܺܝܪ, ܐܰܣܺܝܪܳܐ, ܐܰܣܺܝܪܬܳܐ. a) *to bind, make fast, fasten, tie, append, annex;* with ܒ of the bond or of that to which anything is fastened, ܒܚܰܒܠܶܐ *with ropes,* ܒܫܰܫܠܳܬܳܐ *in chains,* ܒܨܰܘܪܳܐ *to the neck; to yoke* oxen; with ܓܶܫܪܳܐ *to form a bridge by lashing boats together.* b) *to bind prisoner, take into bondage, keep.* c) *to bind on* or *up;* with ܣܰܥܪܳܐ *to bind up the hair, bind with a fillet; to gird, gird on,* ܣܰܝܦܳܐ *a sword,* ܚܰܨܳܐ *the loins,* ܐܶܣܳܪܳܐ *a girdle;* ܐܶܣܰܪ ܚܰܨܰܝܗܽܘܢ ܒܐܶܣܳܪܳܐ *to bind their loins with a girdle;* ܐܶܣܰܪ ܚܰܨܳܐ metaph. *to submit, be ready to obey; to bandage* a wound. d) with ܡܶܐܡܪܳܐ or ܡܰܘܡܳܬܳܐ *to bind with a bond* or *oath; to compel, conspire; to bind* by magic arts; ܐܶܣܰܪ ܡܶܐܣܰܪ *to bind closely, restrict within limits;* opp. ܫܪܳܐ *to bind and loose* both in the simple sense and metaph., general metaph. sense *to possess authority.*

Pass. part. *girt*, ܐܣܝܪܐ or ܐܣܝܪܝ ܚܨܐ *armed men; bound, fettered, captive, ensnared, entangled, hindered*, hence subst. *a captive, prisoner*; ܒܝܬ ܐܣܝܪܐ *a prison*; metaph. ܠܫܢܐ ܐܣܝܪ *impeded speech*; ܐܣܝܪ ܒܨܒܘܬܐ *entangled in the affairs of the flesh*; ܒܩܢܝܢܐ ܐܣܝܪ ܗܘܐ *in bondage to his possessions, hampered by his wealth; under an oath, obligation, bond, engagement*, or *penance, excommunicate*; ܒܪܘܚܐ *constrained by the Spirit*. Ethpe. ܐܬܐܣܪ or ܐܬܬܣܪ imper. ܐܬܐܣܪ, with ܒ or ܥܡ *to be bound, a*) pass. *to be fastened up, closed, attached*; ܛܝܒܘܬܐ ܕܥܠ ܐܬܐ ܗܢܐ ܐܬܐܣܪܬ *the grace attached to this symbol* or *sign; to be ensnared, taken captive, imprisoned*, ܒܪܓܬܐ *by lust*, ܒܚܘܒܐ *by love; to be under penance; to be joined* in marriage or copulation; *to be kept apart* from a wife by magic arts. *b*) refl. *to gird oneself; to conspire*. Derivatives, ܐܣܘܪܐ, ܐܣܪܐ, ܐܣܝܪܘܬܐ, ܐܣܘܪܐ, ܡܐܣܪܐ, ܡܐܣܪܬܐ.

ܐܣܪ, ܐܣܪܐ pl. ܐܣܪܝܢ m. ἀσσάριον, *a small* or *half as*, a Roman copper coin.

ܐܣܪ, ܐܣܪܐ pl. ܐܣܪܐ rt. ܐܣܪ. m. *a bond, tie, fastening*; with ܚܨܐ or ellipt. *a belt, band, girdle*; ܐܣܪ ܟܬܦܬܐ *a hood, superhumeral. A joining together, union, alliance, conspiracy; a vow; an interdict, penance*.

ܐܣܘܪ, ܐܣܘܪܐ pl. ܐܣܘܪܐ rt. ܐܣܪ. m. gram. *a conjunction* or *copula*, but in a wider sense than in English grammar, the ancient Syrian grammarians only counting three parts of speech, ܫܡܗܐ *nouns, pronouns, adjectives*, and most *prepositions*, ܡܠܐ *verbs*, and ܐܣܘܪܐ *particles* i.e. *adverbs, conjunctions, the prefix preps., interjections*. ܐܣܘܪܐ *have no gender nor state but admit of the Bdul* i.e. ܒ, ܕ, ܘ, ܠ *prefixes*.

ܐܣܬܐ emph. st. of ܐܣܬܐ *a wall, a party-wall*.

ܐܣܬܝܪ, ܐܣܬܝܪܐ and ܐܣܬܐܪܐ, ܐܣܬܐܪܐ pl. ܝܢ f. *a stater* = *a shekel*, a coin or weight worth four ܙܘܙܐ or three silver denarii.

ܐܣܬܡܐ m. *the handle* of a sickle, *the hilt* of a sword.

ܐܥܒܝܕ, ܐܥܒܝܕܐ, ܐܥܒܝܕܬܐ usually for pass. part. of ܥܒܕ, *double, one* place *within another, a square*; ܡܥܪܬܐ ܐܥܒܝܕܬܐ *a double cave*, such as the cave of Machpelah.

ܐܥܒܝܕܐܝܬ rt. ܥܒܕ. adv. *doubly*.

ܐܥܦܝܦܘܬܐ rt. ܥܦ. *repetition*; ܒܐܥܦܝܦܘܬܐ *repeatedly*.

ܐܥܠ Aphel of ܥܠ; *to bring, bring in* in many senses; see under ܥܠ.

ܐܥܡܘܪܐ rt. ܥܡܪ m. *cultivated land*.

ܐܥܦܐ = ܥܘܦܐ and ܥܦܐ rt. ܥܦ. *double, twice as much*; ܐܥܦܐ ܟܣܦܐ or ܟܣܦܐ ܐܥܦܐ *double money*; ܩܒܠ ܐܥܦܐ ܕܪܘܚܐ *he received a double portion of the Spirit*; ܬܪܝܢ ܐܥܦܝܢ *twice as much*; ܐܪܒܥܐ ܐܥܦܝܢ *four times as much, quadruply, fourfold*; ܫܒܥܐ ܐܥܦܝܢ *seven times as much*; ܐܥܦܐ ܣܓܝܐܐ *many times as much*.

ܐܦ copulative conjunction, often coalesces with another particle; *also, and, truly, even, nevertheless*; ܐܦ—ܐܦ *both—and, and—also*; ܐܦ—ܘܠܐ after ܠܐ *neither—nor*; ܐܦ ܐܢ *even if, although*; ܐܦܠܐ *nor, not even*; ܐܦܠܐ ܐܢ *not even if*; ܐܦܠܐ ܚܕ *not even one, not a single one*; ܐܦܠܐ—ܘܐܦܠܐ and ܠܐ—ܐܦܠܐ *neither—nor*; ܐܦܢ contr. of ܐܢ and ܐܦ *although, albeit, even if*.

ܐܦܐ, ܐܦܝܢ, ܐܦܝ, pl. of ܐܦ, ܐܦܐ (not used in the sing.) f. *the nostrils, the face, countenance*, hence *the presence*; ܠܐܦܝܢ *to our face, in our presence, before us*; ܠܚܡܐ ܕܐܦܐ *shew-bread* as being placed before the Mercy-Seat; *a person*, ܐܦܐ ܢܘܟܪܝܬܐ *strange faces* i.e. *strange persons*; of inanimate things, *the surface, front, fore-part, outer part, covering* e.g. a book-cover; *the side* or *face of a question under discussion*; ܐܦܝ ܬܪܥܐ *a curtain, hanging, veil*; with preps. ܒܐܦܐ *in public, before, against; outwardly, in show* or *pretence*; ܐܦܝܢ ܠܘܩܒܠ ܐܦܝܢ *face to face, openly*. With ܕ, *before, in the presence*, ܠܐܦܘܗܝ ܕܡܕܒܚܐ *before the altar*; with ܠ; ܠܐܦܝ *towards, about*, esp. in expressions of time and place; ܠܐܦܝ ܪܡܫܐ *towards evening*; ܠܐܦܝ ܬܫܥ ܫܥܝܢ *about the ninth hour*; ܠܐܦܝ ܬܝܡܢܐ *southwards*; ܠܐܦܝ ܒܐܡܐ *before* or *facing the bema*; ܠܐܦܝ ܪܝܫ ܐܒܐ *at the beginning of spring*; with ܠܘܩܒܠ *before, in front, opposite to, openly, in sight of*; with ܥܠ *on the surface, upon, at; in front of, before; for, for the sake of, on account of*; ܥܠ ܐܦܝ ܬܗܘܡܐ *upon the face of the deep*; ܥܠ ܐܦܝ ܬܠܬ ܫܥܝܢ *at the third hour*; ܥܠ ܐܦܝ ܚܛܗܝܢ—ܦܘܪܩܢܢ *for our sins, for our salvation*; ܥܠ ܐܦܝ ܗܝܡܢܘܬܐ *for the faith*;

ܡܶܛܽܠ ܐܳܦ ܟܽܠܗܽܘܢ *for the sake of all, because of all;* ܡܶܛܽܠ ܐܳܦ ܗܳܢܳܐ *for which cause, wherefore.*

ܐܦܳܐ fut. ܢܐܦܶܐ, imper. ܐܦܺܝ, act. part. ܐܳܦܶܐ, f. ܐܳܦܝܳܐ m. pl. ܐܳܦܶܝܢ f. ܐܳܦܝܳܢ, pass. part. ܐܦܶܐ f. ܐܦܝܳܐ m. pl. ܐܦܶܝܢ *to bake* bread. Ethpe. ܐܶܬܐܦܺܝ *to be baked.* Derivative, ܐܦܳܝܳܐ.

ܐܰܦܺܝܩ Aphel of ܦܩ; *to take away, deprive of,* with ܡܶܢ.

ܐܦܰܕܢܳܐ pl. ܢ̈ܶܐ Heb. m. *a palace, a citadel,* often met.; ܠܶܒܳܐ ܐܦܰܕܢܳܐ ܕܢܰܦܫܳܐ *the heart is the citadel of the soul;* ܒܪܺܝܟ ܕܫܰܒܶܩ ܐܦܰܕܢܰܝ ܡܰܠܟܳܐ *blessed be He who forsook the king's palaces.*

ܐܳܦܗܳܫܳܐ = ܐܳܦ ܗܳܫܳܐ *even now.*

ܐܦܽܘܕܳܐ Heb. f. *an ephod;* ܦܰܕܬܳܐ is the usual word in Syriac.

ܐܦܽܘܕܶܝܟܣܺܝܣ, ܕܺܝܩܣܺܝܣ or ܕܺܝܩܣܳܐ f. ἀπόδειξις, *a demonstration.*

ܐܦܽܘܕܺܝܰܩܢܳܐ pl. ܢ̈ܶܐ or ܐܦܽܘܕܺܝܰܩܢܽܘܣ m. ὑποδιάκονος, *a subdeacon,* oftener ܗܽܘܦܕ̈ܝܩܢܐ.

ܐܦܽܘܠܳܘܓܺܝܰܐ f. ἀπολογία, *a defence, a speech in defence.*

ܐܦܽܘܣܺܝܰܐ m. and f. ἀπουσία, *excretions, excrement.*

ܐܦܽܘܦܰܛܺܝܩܳܐ f. ܛܺܝܩܬܳܐ ἀποφατικός, *negative, critical, decisive.*

ܐܦܽܘܦܰܣܺܝܣ, ܐܦܽܘܦܳܣܺܝܣ and ܐܦܳܦܰܣܺܝܣ f. ἀπόφασις, *a decision, sentence,* e.g. ܕܡܰܘܬܳܐ *of death; a negative, negation.*

ܐܦܽܘܩܪܺܝܣܺܝܣ f. ἀπόκρισις, *a decision, an answer.*

ܐܦܽܘܪܣܡܳܐ m. *balsam;* ܐܺܝܠܳܢܶܐ ܕܦܽܘ *balsam-trees.*

ܐܦܠܺܝܠܳܐ or ܐܦܺܝܠܳܐ m. *an uneven number, odd,* opp. ܙܰܘܓܳܐ.

ܐܦܚܢܰܢ = ܐܳܦ ܚܢܰܢ *we also.*

ܐܦܺܝܒܽܘܠܺܝ f. ἐπιβολή, *an impost, a mulct* in penalty for murder or bodily harm.

ܐܦܺܝܛܪܽܘܦܳܐ, ܐܦܺܝܛܪܽܘܦܽܘܣ or ܐܦܺܝܛܪܳܦܳܐ pl. ܦ̈ܶܐ m. ἐπίτροπος, *a procurator,* e.g. ܥܰܠ ܝܺܗܽܘܕ *over Judaea; a steward* of a church or monastery; *a guardian* of orphans.

ܐܦܺܝܛܪܽܘܦܽܘܬܳܐ and ܐܦܺܝܛܪܽܘܦܺܝ f. *office of a procurator, governorship, stewardship, guardianship.*

ܐܦܣܺܝܩܺܝܢ and ܐܦܣܺܝܩܺܝܘܢ, from Lat. *obsequium* through Greek ὀψίκιον, *the imperial officials, retinue.*

ܐܦܺܝܣܩܽܘܦܳܐ, ܐܦܺܝܣܩܳܦܳܐ or ܐܦܺܝܣܩܽܘܦܽܘܣ, E-Syr. ܐܦܶܣܩܽܘܦܳܐ pl. ܦ̈ܶܐ m. ἐπίσκοπος, *an overseer, prefect, a bishop.*

ܐܦܺܝܣܩܽܘܦܽܘܬܳܐ f. *a bishopric, the office of a bishop.*

ܐܦܺܝܩܽܘܣ f. ἱππικός, *horse-races, a race-course, hippodrome.*

ܐܦܺܝܪܳܐ *pulse, porridge.*

ܐܦܺܝܠܬܳܐ f. *a nun's cloak,* so-called by the Nestorians; the Jacobite names are ܡܰܦܪܳܐ and ܐܠܠܳܐ.

ܐܰܦܶܠ Aphel of ܢܦܰܠ; *to make fall, cast down.*

ܐܦܠܳܐ contr. of ܠܳܐ and ܐܳܦ, *nor, not even;* see ܐܳܦ.

ܐܦܠܰܢ contr. of ܐܳܦ, ܠ and pron. suff. 1 pl. *us also.*

ܐܰܦܶܣ Aphel of ܦܣ; *to give permission, to cast lots.*

ܐܦܣܽܘܢܝܳܐ and ܐܦܣܽܘܢܺܝܬܳܐ pl. ܢܝ̈ܳܬܳܐ f. ὀψώνια, *stipend, salary, wages, hire; keep, maintenance.*

ܐܦܣܺܢܬܺܝܢ or ܐܦܣܺܢܬܺܝܢܽܘܢ *absinthium, wormwood, a bitter medicine.*

ܐܦܣܩܽܘܦܳܐ *a bishop,* &c.; see ܐܦܺܝܣ.

ܐܦܣܳܪܳܐ m. *a halter, a cord* to lead a packhorse.

ܐܦܽܘܦܰܣܺܝܣ and ܐܦܽܘܦܳܐܣܺܝܣ ἀπόφασις, *a judicial decision, a sentence.*

ܐܦܥܳܐ pl. ܥ̈ܶܐ f. *an hyena.*

ܐܦܨܳܐ pl. ܨ̈ܶܐ *oak galls.*

ܐܰܦܶܩ Aphel of ܢܦܰܩ; *to bring forth.*

ܐܦܩܪܳܣܳܐ pl. ܣ̈ܶܐ m. *a felt overcoat.*

ܐܦܩܪܺܝܣܺܝܣ f. ἀπόκρισις, *an answer.*

ܐܦܪܶܝܡܳܝܳܐ m. ܝܬܳܐ f. adj. from ܐܦܪܶܝܡ; *of Ephrem;* ܡܫܘܚܬܳܐ ܐܦܪܶܝܡܳܝܬܳܐ *the metre of Ephrem,* i.e. *the heptasyllabic metre employed by S. Ephrem Syrus.*

ܐܦܪ̈ܨܳܬܳܐ f. pl., has no sing. form; *raisins,* probably corrupted from ܐܒܶܫܬܳܐ rt. ܝܒܫ *to dry.*

ܐܦܬܳܐ rt. ܦܬܳܐ. *space, place, delay, cause, occasion, opportunity;* with ܝܗܒ *to give, allow,* ܗܰܒ ܠܺܝ ܐܦܬܳܐ *allow me;* ܐܦܬܳܐ ܪܰܒܬܳܐ ܗܘܳܬ ܠܗܽܘܢ *it was a great opportunity for them;* ܠܳܐ ܐܺܝܬ ܐܦܬܳܐ *the opportunity had passed, it could no longer be done;* ܕܠܳܐ ܬܶܗܘܶܐ ܐܦܬܳܐ ܠܡܰܦܳܠܽܘܬܰܢ (*lest*) *it cause us to fall;* ܝܰܗܒ ܠܗܽܘܢ ܐܦܬܳܐ ܫܒܥܳܐ ܝܰܘܡܺܝܢ *granted them seven days' grace, delay.*

ܐܦܬܺܝܩܺܐ ἀποθήκη, *a store.*

ܐܩܘܛܐ, ܐܩܛܐܐ pl. ܐ̈ f. *a qualm, nausea, wearisomeness;* ܐܩܘܛܐ ܗܘܐ with ܠ and pron. suff. *to be sick of anything.*

ܐܙܝܪ Aphel of ܙܪ; *to fix the eyes.*

ܐܠܘܙܬܐ pl. ܐܠܘܙܬܐ f. *a kneading-trough, dough, a lump* of dough, *a mass.*

ܐܣܛܪ Aphel of ܣܛܪ; *to express in writing, publish abroad, write out,* hence is derived

ܐܣܛܪܐ pl. ܐ̈ = ܐܣܛܪܐ, *a copy* of a book or MS., *a codex.*

ܐܙܕܒܢ Ethp. of the verb ܙܒܢ. The Ethpeal and Ethpael of all verbs beginning with ܙ are thus formed.

ܐܙܗܦ rare for ܙܗܦ *to be careful, anxious.*

ܐܙܪ root-meaning *to shut in* or *up, heap up;* in Syr. the verb is found only in the Jerusalem dialect. Derivative, ܐܘܙܪܐ.

ܐܨܬ part. ܡܨܬ Aphel of ܨܘܬ; *to hearken, listen.*

ܐܩܓܐ Turk. *white;* ܐܩܓܐ ܕܣܐܡܐ *a coin of small value.*

ܐܩܠ Aphel of ܩܠ; *to lighten* a burden or load, *make less heavy, take away,* with ܡܢ *from; to hasten; to think lightly of, despise.*

ܐܩܘܠܘܬܝܐ and ܐܩܘܠܘܬܝܐ f. ἀκολουθία, *prescribed form, order, arrangement;* rit. *the office* or *liturgy proper to the day.*

ܐܩܠܝܕ, ܐܩܠܝܕܐ pl. ܬܐ, ܐ̈ m. rare for ܩܠܝܕܐ *a key;* metaph. ܐܩܠܝܕܐ ܕܡܠܟܘܬܐ ܕܫܡܝܐ *the keys of the kingdom of heaven.*

ܐܩܠܝܣܝܣܛܝܩܝ, ܐܩܠܣܝܣܛܝܩܐ, ܐܩܠܝܣܝܣܛܝܩܐ &c. ἐκκλησιαστική, *Church history;* ܐܩܠܣܝܣܛܝܩܐ ܕܐܘܣܒܝܘܣ *the Ecclesiastical History of Eusebius.*

ܐܩܠܝܦܣܝܣ, ܐܩܠܝܦܣܝܣ &c. f. ἔκλειψις, *an eclipse* of the sun or moon.

ܐܩܠܪܐ *cellars, store-rooms.*

ܐܩܠܐ and ܐܩܠܐ pl. ܐ̈ m. *an ankle-chain, a bangle.*

ܐܩܡܐ ἀκμή, *the acme, highest point, culmination;* ܐܩܡܐ ܕܛܠܝܘܬܗ *the bloom of his youth.*

ܐܩܪܒ Aphel of ܩܪܒ; *to be near, draw near, begin, add, proceed,* &c.

ܐܩܪ act. part. ܡܩܪ or ܡܩܪ Aphel of ܩܪ; *to cool.*

ܐܩܝܡ act. part. ܡܩܝܡ or ܡܩܝܡ Aphel of ܩܡ; *to fix,* &c.; with ܫܘܪܐ, ܣܝܓܐ or ܟܠܝܠܐ or with ܦܘܠܐ.

ܐܪܐ ἆρα, ἄρα, vocative and interrog. particle *O! O that! now, then, whether;* often follows other interrog. particles such as ܟܡܐ, ܡܢܐ, ܠܡܢܐ.

ܐܪܒܥܝܢܝܐ f. ܐܪܒܥܝܢܝܬܐ adj. from ܐܪܒܥܝܢ, *quadragesimal,* ܨܘܡܐ ܐܪܒܥܝܢܝܐ *the Lenten fast, the forty days' fast.*

ܐܪܒܝܬܐ *a sea-shrimp.*

ܐܪܒܐ, ܐܪܒܐ pl. ܐ̈ *the papyrus reed; the spathe* of a palm.

ܐܪܒܥ f. ܐܪܒܥܐ and ܐܪܒܥܬܐ m. *four;* with ܕ *the fourth,* ܢܗܪܐ ܕܐܪܒܥܐ *the fourth river.* ܐܪܒܥܐ ܒܫܒܐ or ܚܕ ܒܫܒܐ ܕܐܪܒܥܐ *the fourth day of the week, Wednesday,* ܨܘܡܐ ܕܐܪܒܥܐ *the Wednesday fast;* ܐܬܐ ܥܡ ܐܪܒܥܐ ܐܘ ܚܡܫܐ ܓܒܪܝܢ he came *with four or five men;* ܚܝܘܬܐ ܕܐܪܒܥ ܪܓܠܝܢ *four-footed beasts, quadrupeds;* ܐܪܒܥܬܝܗܘܢ *the four of them;* coalesces with other numbers or with nouns, ܐܪܒܥܣܪ rarely ܐܪܒܥܣܪܐ f. and ܐܪܒܥܬܥܣܪ or contr. ܐܪܒܬܥܣܪ m. *fourteen;* ܐܪܒܥܡܐܐ *four hundred;* ܐܪܒܥ ܦܢܝܢ *the four quarters of the world.*

ܐܪܒܥܝܢ *forty;* ܨܘܡܐ ܕܐܪܒܥܝܢ *the fast of forty days.*

ܐܪܕܟܠܐ pl. ܐ̈ m. *a stone-mason.*

ܐܪܓܘܢ, ܐܪܓܘܢܐ pl. ܐ̈ m. *the violet* or *hyacinthine hue obtained from the Tyrian murex, purple, a purple garment;* ܐܪܓܘܢܐ ܕܡܠܟܘܬܐ *royal purple;* ܒܪ ܐܪܓܘܢܐ ܕܡܠܟܐ *born in the purple.*

ܐܪܓܘܢܝܐ pl. ܐܪܓܘܢܝܢ, ܐܪܓܘܢܝܬܐ adj. *purple.*

ܐܪܓܘܪܘܦܪܛܝܣ and ܐܪܓܘܪܘܦܪܛܣ pl. ܐ̈ ἀργυροπράτης, *a silversmith.*

ܐܪܓܝܓ, ܐܪܓܝܓܐ, ܐܪܓܝܓܬܐ = ܪܓܝܓ, ܪܓܝܓܐ Pe. pass. part. of ܪܓ *desirable, choice, appetising;* ܦܐܪܐ ܐܪܓܝܓܐ *choice fruits;* ܟܪܡܐ ܐܪܓܝܓܐ *pleasant vineyards;* f. emph. pl. *desirable things, pleasures, lusts, desires.*

ܐܪܕܒܐ *a kind of drum.*

ܐܪܕܝܢܐ pl. ܐ̈ m. = ܪܕܝܢܐ *a bridal veil;* ܐܢܬܬܐ ܬܬܟܣܐ ܒܐܪܕܝܢܐ *the woman shall be veiled.*

ܐܪܕܝܟܠܐ and ܐܪܕܟܠܐ pl. ܐ̈ Ar. m. *a stone-mason, builder, master-builder;* metaph. ܐܪܕܝܟܠܐ ܕܒܢܝܢܐ

the Architect of the Universe; ܦܘܠܘܣ ܐܪܕܝܟܠܐ ܕܥܕܬܐ *Paul the master-builder of the Church.*

ܐܪܕܝܟܠܘܬܐ f. *stone-cutting.*

ܐܪܘܙܐ = ܪܘܙܐ rt. ܪܘܙ m. *exultation, joy.*

ܐܪܘܚܬܐ = ܪܘܚܬܐ rt. ܪܘܚ *room, open* or *free space;* opp. ܐܘܠܨܢܐ metaph. *relief* from illness or anxiety, *alleviation;* ܒܐܪܘܚܬܐ ܘܒܐܘܠܨܢܐ *in good and evil fortune.*

ܐܪܘܝܚܐ f. ܐܪܘܝܚܬܐ = ܪܘܝܚܐ rt. ܪܘܚ. *wide, spacious;* ܐܪܥܐ ܐܪܘܝܚܬܐ *open country;* ܡܕܒܪܐ ܐܪܘܝܚܐ *a vast desert.*

ܐܪܘܢ, ܐܪܘܢܐ pl. ܐ̈ m. *a calf, a young bullock;* ܐܪܘܢܝܬܐ pl. ܐܪ̈ܘܢܝܬܐ f. *a cow-calf, heifer.*

ܐܪܘܢ, ܐܪܘܢܐ rarely ܐܪܘܢܐ Heb. m. *a*) *the ark* of the covenant; ܐܪܘܢ ܕܐܠܗܐ *the Ark of God.* *b*) *a chest, strong-box* to hold money or books.

ܐܪܘܥܘܬܐ f. rt. ܐܪܥ. *a meeting, encounter; a disputation, controversy;* ܐܪܘܥܘܬܐ ܕܡ̈ܠܐ *a discussion;* ܐܪܘܥܘܬܐ ܕܟܠܩܐܕܘܢܝܐ *a refutation of the Council of Chalcedon; a controversial treatise;* ܟܬܒܐ ܕܐܪܘܥܘܬܐ ܠܘܩܒܠ ܢܣܛܘܪ̈ܝܢܐ *the Polemics* of Bar Salibi *against the Nestorians.*

ܐܪܙ Aphel of ܪܙܙ from ܪܙ; *to signify mystically.*

ܐܪܙ, ܐܪܙܐ pl. ܐܪ̈ܙܐ, W-Syr. ܪܐܙܐ rt. ܪܙ. m. *a secret, a*) *an agreement, a council;* ܐܪܙܐ ܐܚܕ ܥܡܗ *he conspired with her.* *b*) *anything having a secret* or *mystical meaning, a type, figure, sign, symbol, likeness;* ܥܕܬܐ ܒܐܪܙܟ *the Church is in Thy likeness, is like Thee;* ܐܪܙ ܡܥܡܘܕܝܬܐ *baptism, which is a figure of;* ܪܫܡܝܢ ܒܐܪܙܐ ܕܨܠܝܒܐ *they sign with the symbol of the Cross.* *c*) *a mystery, sacrament, the Holy Eucharist;* ܫܡܫ ܠܗܘܢ ܒܐܪ̈ܙܐ *he administered the Holy Communion to them;* ܥܘܢܝܬܐ ܕܐܪ̈ܙܐ *an anthem sung during the Liturgy.* *d*) *magic rites;* ܒܐܪ̈ܙܐ ܕܚܢܦܐ ܡܫܬܘܬܦܝܢ ܗܘܘ *they took part in pagan rites.* With preps. ܒܐܪܙ or ܒܐܪܙܐ *in secret, secretly, mystically.*

ܐܪܙܐ pl. ܐ̈ m. *the cedar* or *pine;* ܐܝܟ ܐܪܙܐ ܕܠܒܢܢ *as a cedar of Lebanon.*

ܐܪܙܘܢ or ܐܪܙܢ E-Syr. *low price of corn.*

ܐܪܙܦܬܐ pl. ܐ̈ rt. ܪܙܦ. *a hammer, mallet, the mallet with which a bell is struck; a stroke with a hammer;* ܐܪܙܦܬܐ ܩܕܡܝܬܐ ܕܢܦܚܐ ܗܘܐ *the first blow which the smith struck;* ܠܡܡܚܐ ܒܐܪܙܦܬܐ *to forge.*

ܐܪܚ root-meaning *to go, travel.* Pa. ܐܪܚ *a*) *to go away, depart, withdraw;* ܐܪܚ ܡܢܗ ܘܐܙܠ ܠܐܘܪܚܗ *he departed from him and went on his way;* ܐܪܚ ܕܚܠܬܐ *fear left* them. *b*) denom. from ܐܘܪܚܐ, *to stay on the way, stop on a journey.* Derivatives, ܐܘܪܚܐ, ܐܪܚܐ, ܡܐܪܚܐ.

ܐܪܚܐ rt. ܐܪܚ. m. *a*) *a wayfarer, traveller, passer-by, guest;* ܐܪܚܐ ܠܐܝܐ *a weary traveller;* metaph. *transient.* *b*) = ܐܘܪܚܐ *a way.*

ܐܪܛܒܐ or ܐܪܛܒܘܣ pl. ܐܪܛܒܣ f. *a Persian measure,* equal to six bushels and a quart.

ܐܪܛܚܫܫܬ, ܐܪܛܚܫܫܬܐ or ܐܪܛܚܫܫܬ a Hebrew corruption of the Persian name *Ardishir, Artaxerxes.*

ܐܪܛܝܩܘܣ and ܐܪܛܝܩܐ f. ܐܪܛܝܩܝܬܐ pl. m. ܐܪܛܝܩܝ̈ܐ αἱρετικός, *heretical, an heretic.*

ܐܪܝ root-meaning found in Arabic, conj. II. *to tie up an animal in its stall.* Syr. only the derivative ܐܘܪܝܐ.

ܐܪܝܐ pl. ܐܪ̈ܝܘܬܐ, ܐܪ̈ܘܬܐ f. ܐܪܝܘܬܐ pl. ܐܪ̈ܝܘܬܐ. Heb. *a lion, lioness;* metaph. *a*) *Leo, the sign of the Zodiac for August.* *b*) ܟܐܒܐ ܕܐܪܝܐ *a sort of leprosy, lepra leonina* or *elephantiasis,* ܐܬܟܪܗ ܟܐܒܐ ܕܐܪܝܐ *he was consumed with elephantiasis.* Derivatives, ܐܪܝܢܐ, ܐܪܝܢܘܬܐ.

ܐܪܝܘܣ pr. name *Arius;* ܐܪܝܘܣ ܠܝܛܐ or ܐܪܝܘܣ ܡܠܥܢܐ *the cursed Arius.*

ܐܪܝܟܘܬܐ rt. ܐܪܟ. f. *lengthiness;* ܐܪܝܟܘܬ ܡ̈ܠܐ *prolixity, the use of many words;* ܦܠܛ̈ܐ ܡܛܠ ܐܪܝܟܘܬܐ ܫܒܩܢ ܐܢܝܢ particulars *which we leave out because of their length.*

ܐܪܝܢܐ f. ܐܪܝܢܝܬܐ pl. m. ܐܪ̈ܝܢܐ, ܐܪܝܢܘܣ, ܐܪܝܐܢܘܣ *an Arian, a follower of the heresy of Arius.*

ܐܪܝܢܐ f. ܐܪܝܢܝܬܐ pl. m. ܐܪ̈ܝܢܐ from ܐܪܝܐ. *leprous, a leper;* metaph. ܣܐܡܐ ܐܪܝܢܐ *scaly silver* = lead.

ܐܪܝܢܘܬܐ = ܟܐܒ ܐܪܝܐ f. *leontiasis* or *elephantiasis,* a kind of leprosy, said to be that from which Job suffered.

ܐܪܝܣܢܐ f. ܐܪܝܣܢܝܬܐ adj. *Arian.*

ܐܪܝܣ *Ares, Mars; the planet Mars.*

ܐܪܝܣܛܘܛܠܝܣ, ܐܪܝܣܛܘܛܠܣ and other spellings, pr. n. *Aristotle.*

ܐܪܝܣܛܘܛܠܝܐ f. ܐܪܝܣܛܘܛܠܝܬܐ *Aristotelian;* ܟܬ

ܐܪܣܛܘܛܠܝܐ ܐܪܝܣܛܘܛܠܝܐ a *follower of the teaching of Aristotle.*

ܐܪܣܡܣܐ; see ܐܪܣܡܣܐ.

ܐܪܟ Aphel of ܪܟ; *to soften, mollify.*

ܐܪܟ = ܐܪܟ. fut. ܢܐܪܘܟ, act. part. ܐܪܟ, ܐܪܟܐ, pass. part. ܐܪܝܟ, ܐܪܝܟܐ, ܐܪܝܟܬܐ *to be long, prolonged; to lengthen;* pass. part. *long, wide,* said of the hair, beard, stature, of life, and time; ܐܪܝܟ ܐܝܕܗ ܠܡܣܒ *he stretches out his hand to take;* ܐܢܬܬܐ ܕܐܪܝܟ ܠܫܢܗ *a woman with a long tongue;* ܐܪܛܚܫܫܬ ܐܪܝܟ ܐܝܕܐ Artaxerxes *Longimanus;* ܐܪܝܟ ܓܦܐ an eagle *with wide-spread wings;* ܡܕܝܢܬܐ ܐܪܝܟܬܐ *a spacious city;* rit. often with ܩܠܐ understood, *prolonged, slow;* gram. ܐܪܝܟܐ ܚܒܨܐ—ܚܒܨܐ *long i* and *u* as in ܚܒܨܐ. ܒܐܪܝܟܘܬܐ *at length, freely;* opp. ܒܟܪܝܘܬܐ; see ܟܪܐ. Pa. ܐܪܟ the same. Aphel ܐܘܪܟ *to lengthen, stretch out, thrust out,* e.g. the tongue; ܐܘܪܟܬ ܓܦܝܗ *she spread her wings;* metaph. *to be lengthy in talking* or *writing;* ܕܠܐ ܢܘܪܟ ܡܠܬܐ *not to make too long a story;* ܡܘܪܟܝܢܢ ܒܡܠܬܐ *we speak at too great length, at the risk of being tedious;* ܡܘܪܟܝܢ ܨܠܘܬܗܘܢ *they make long prayers;* ܡܘܪܟܝܢ ܚܛܗܝܗܘܢ *they add to their sins, make* the list of *their sins long, as a cord is made longer,* Is. v. 18; ܐܘܪܟ ܪܘܓܙܝ *I will delay my anger* to allow a long time for repentance, Is. xlviii. 9. Derivatives, ܐܘܪܟܐ, ܐܘܪܟܢܐ, ܐܪܝܟܘܬܐ.

ܐܪܟܐ pl. ܐܪܟܐ, ܐܪܟܣ, ܐܪܟܘܣ f. ἀρχή, *a beginning; a magistrate; authority, rule, principality.* The last form of the pl., ܐܪܟܘܣ or ܐܪܟܐܣ, is used for *principalities,* the name of the seventh Order of Angels.

ܐܪܟܐ with ܒܝܬ. τὰ ἀρχεῖα, *the archives, the public library;* ܒܝܬ ܐܪܟܐ ܕܥܕܬܐ *the library of the church—of the monastery.*

ܐܪܟܘܢ, ܐܪܟܘܢܐ pl. ܐܪܟܘܢܐ and ܐܪܟܘܢܐܣ m. ἄρχων, *a prince, ruler, governor;* ܐܪܟܘܢܐ ܕܚܕܝܒ *the governor of Adiabene;* ܐܪܟܘܢܗ ܕܥܠܡܐ ܗܢܐ *the prince of this world,* John xii. 31, xiv. 30.

ܐܪܟܘܢܛܐ pl. ܐܪܟܘܢܛܐ, ܐܪܟܘܢܛܣ and ܐܪܟܘܢܛܣ ἄρχοντα, *a prince, leader, ruler;* ܐܪܟܘܢܛܐ ܕܪܘܚܐ *the prince of evil spirits.*

ܐܪܟܘܢܛܪܢܐ pl. ܐܪܟܘܢܛܪܢܐ dim. of ܐܪܟܘܢ. with ܕܒܝܫܐ or ܕܒܝܫܬܐ *princes of evil,* i.e. *the devil and his followers.*

ܐܪܟܕܝܩܘܢ, ܐܪܟܝܕܝܩܘܢܐ or ܐܪܟܕܝܩܘܢܐ pl. ܐܪܟܕܝܩܘܢܐ m. Lat. *an archdeacon.*

ܐܪܟܕܝܩܘܢܘܬܐ or ܐܪܟܝܕܝܩܘܢܘܬܐ f. *archidiaconate, office of an archdeacon.*

ܐܪܟܝܣܛܘܬܐ f. ὀρχηστύς, *dancing with music and singing.*

ܐܪܡ Heb. pr. n. *Aram,* hence *Aramea* = *Syria;* ܐܪܡ ܢܗܪܝܢ *Mesopotamia.*

ܐܪܡܐܝܬ adv. *in the Aramaic* or *Syriac language.*

ܐܪܡܝܐ pl. ܐܪܡܝܐ from ܐܪܡ as is also ܐܪܡܝܐ, both were the same Gentilic name, *Aramean,* but some time after the epoch of the Seleucidae the name *Syria,* a shortened form of *Assyria,* came into use instead of *Aramea,* and *Syrian* for *Aramean.* The ancient name was now restricted to the *Arameans of the East,* and when they did not receive Christianity the name became a synonym for *pagan* or *Sabian,* the following is a later form.

ܐܪܡܝܐ f. ܐܪܡܝܬܐ pl. ܐܪܡܝܐ; see the preceding, *an Aramean, a Syrian;* adj. *Aramaic, Syriac,* ܠܫܢܐ ܣܘܪܝܝܐ ܐܘ ܐܪܡܝܐ *the Syriac or Aramaic tongue.*

ܐܪܡܠ fut. ܢܐܪܡܠ, part. ܡܐܪܡܠܐ pl. f. ܡܐܪܡܠܢ perh. denom. from ܐܪܡܠܐ; *to widow, cause to be a widow; to be widowed, left a widow;* ܐܢܬܬܐ ܕܡܐܪܡܠܐ *a widow-woman;* metaph. ܥܕܬܐ ܡܐܪܡܠܐ *a widowed church,* i.e. left without a Bishop. Ethpa. ܐܬܐܪܡܠ *to be left* or *made a widow.*

ܐܪܡܠ, ܐܪܡܠܐ E-Syr. ܐܪܡܠܐ pl. ܐܪܡܠܐ m. *a widower;* ܐܪܡܠܬ, ܐܪܡܠܬܐ pl. ܐܪܡܠܬܐ f. *a widow;* ܐܢܬܬܐ ܚܕܐ ܐܪܡܠܬܐ *a certain widow;* ܢܫܐ ܐܪܡܠܬܐ *widow-women;* used also of animals, birds, of sterile ground or trees without fruit, and metaph. of churches left without a pastor.

ܐܪܡܠܘܬܐ f. *widowhood.*

ܐܪܡܢܘܢ or ܐܪܡܢܘܢ pl. ܐܪܡܢܐ ἄρμενον, *tackle, tackling, a sail, the topsail.*

ܐܪܢܐ sometimes misprinted ܐܪܙܐ (Heb.) m. and f. *a mountain-goat.*

ܐܪܢܒܐ a) f. *a hare.* b) *a tumour.*

ܐܪܣܝܣ (usually ܗܪܣܝܣ) pl. ܐܪܣܝܣ f. *heresy.*

ܐܪܣܣܐ pl. ܐ̈ = ܪܣܣܐ rt. ܪܣ. m. *a sprinkling; dew, fine rain, moisture;* ܐܪܣܣܐ ܕܛܠܐ *drops of dew.*

ܐܪܣܐ *barley-water.*

ܐܪܥ fut. ܢܐܪܘܥ, part. ܐܪܥ, ܐܪܥܐ *to meet, encounter;* a) ܒܣܝܦܐ or ܒܣܟܪ̈ܐ *with the sword* or *with shields = to attack,* also *to sustain* or *meet an attack, resist;* ܠܝܬ ܗܘܐ ܡܢ ܕܐܪܥ ܠܗ *no one could resist him; to resist* disease or cold; met. *to meet in argument, refute, confute.* b) *to happen, befall, come upon,* usually of misfortune; ܐܪܥܐ ܠܟܘܢ ܒܝܫܬܐ *evil will happen unto you,* Deut. xxxi. 29. Derivatives, ܐܪܥܐ, ܐܘܪܥܐ.

ܐܪܥ, ܐܪܥܐ pl. ܐܪ̈ܥܬܐ f. *the earth,* opp. ܫܡܝܐ *the heavens* and ܝܡܡ̈ܐ *the seas,* Gen. i. 1–10; *a country, land, a piece of land, field, ground, soil, the floor* of a house; ܐܪܥܐ ܕܡܨܪܝܢ *the land of Egypt;* ܐܪܥܐ ܛܒܬܐ *good ground;* ܐܪ̈ܥܬܐ ܕܒܝܬܐ *the floors of the house;* ܒܪ ܐܪܥܐ *an earthworm.* Derivatives, ܐܪܥܢܐ, ܐܪܥܝܐ.

ܐܪܥܢܐ pl. ܐܪ̈ܥܢܐ from ܐܪܥܐ adj. and subst. *earthly, terrestrial; an earthly being, a dweller on the earth;* ܪܘܚ̈ܐ ܐܪ̈ܥܢܝܐ *land winds.*

ܐܪܥܢܝܐ f. ܐܪܥܢܝܬܐ pl. m. ܐ̈ f. ܝ̈ܬܐ from ܐܪܥܐ adj. *earthly, terrestrial;* ܚܟܡܬܐ ܐܪܥܢܝܬܐ *earthly wisdom.*

ܐܪܦܐ for ܪܦܐ Ar. *a nest, a flock* of birds, *shoal.*

ܐܪܩܥ Aphel of ܪܩܥ; *to beat out thin.*

ܐܪܩܝܥܐ rt. ܪܩܥ. m. *the expanse of heaven, the firmament.*

ܐܪܩܫ fut. ܢܐܪܩܘܫ, inf. ܡܐܪܩܫ *to strike, beat, hammer* as a blacksmith.

ܐܪܫܩܝܐ, ܐܪܫܩܝ or ܐܪܫܩ̈ܝ f. ܐܝܬܐ adj. from *Arsaces,* the name or title of the founder of the Parthian empire. *Seleucia* and *Ctesiphon,* the chief cities of the Arsacian kings are called ܡܕܝܢ̈ܬܐ ܐܪܫܩܝܬܐ hence *royal, chief, principal;* ܕܝܪܐ ܐܪܫܩܝܐ *the chief monastery.*

ܐܪܬܕܘܟܣܐ f. ܐܪܬܕܘܟܣܝܬܐ pl. ܐܪܬܕܘܟܣܐ, ܐܪܬܕܘܟܣܐ, &c. Gr. = Syr. ܬܪܝܨ ܫܘܒܚܐ adj. *orthodox, holding the right faith.*

ܐܪܬܕܘܟܣܐܝܬ adv. *orthodoxly.*

ܐܪܬܕܘܟܣܘܣ pl. ܐܪܬܕܘܟܣܘ, ܐܪܬܕܘܟܣܘܢ or ܐܪܬܕܘܟܣܘܢ m. ὀρθόδοξος, *orthodox;* see ܐܪܬܕܘܟܣܐ above.

ܐܪܬܕܘܟܣܝܐ Gr. = Syr. ܬܪܝܨܘܬ ܫܘܒܚܐ. *orthodoxy, holding the right faith;* ܗܝܡܢܘܬܐ ܕܐܪܬܕܘܟܣܝܐ *the orthodox faith.*

ܐܪܬܝܬܐ = ܪܬܝܬܐ rt. ܪܬ. f. *trembling, fear.*

ܐܪܬܡܐ, ܐܪܬܡܐ or ܐܪܬܡܘܣ ἄριθμος, *a troop of soldiers.*

ܐܪܬܒܠܐ or ܐܪܬܒܠܐ pl. ܐ̈ m. *a large spoon.*

ܐܫܒ part. ܡܫܒ and ܡܫܒ Aphel of ܢܫܒ; *to blow, cause the wind to blow.*

ܐܫܕ fut. ܢܐܫܘܕ, inf. ܡܐܫܕ, imper. ܐܫܘܕ, act. part. ܐܫܕ, ܐܫܕܐ, pass. part. ܐܫܝܕ, ܐܫܝܕܐ, ܐܫܝܕܬܐ (cognate roots in Heb. and cf. ܫܕܐ) *to shed, pour out* or *down* water, rain, blood, tears; ܡܐܫܕ ܕܡܐ *bloodshed, manslaughter;* ܐܫܕ ܕܡܐ *a manslayer, homicide; bloodthirsty;* ܐܫܕ ܚܡܬܐ *breathing out poison;* metaph. *to throw up* a mound; ܐܫܕ ܥܠ ܦܐܘܗܝ *to upset; to pour out* the heart or soul in prayer; wrath or evil; gifts, the grace of God, the Holy Spirit; ܐܫܕ ܢܦܫܗ ܠܡܘܬܐ *he gave himself up of his own will unto death;* ܠܡܐܫܕ ܪ̈ܚܡܐ *to shed forth mercy;* pass. part. metaph. *shed* or *scattered abroad, dissipated, diffuse, fluid;* ܢܘܗܪܐ ܐܫܝܕܐ *diffused, scattered light;* ܪܥܝܢܐ ܐܫܝܕܐ *a distracted mind;* ܓܘܫܡܐ ܐܫܝܕܐ *a fluid body.* Ethpe. ܐܬܐܫܕ imper. ܐܬܐܫܕ *to be shed, poured out,* esp. of blood, but also of dry things, corn, ashes, stones; metaph. *to give oneself up to; to be spread abroad, diffused;* ܐܝܟ ܢܚܠܐ ܕܡܬܐܫܕ ܒܚܝܠܬܢܘܬܐ *as a torrent rushing impetuously;* ܣܒܪܐ ܕܪ̈ܫܝܥܐ ܡܬܐܫܕ *the hope of the wicked is poured out,* i.e. *flows away like water;* ܡܬܐܫܕܐ ܡܠܬܐ ܐܠܗܝܬܐ *the divine word is spread abroad.* Derivatives, ܐܫܕ, ܐܫܝܕܘܬܐ, ܡܬܐܫܕܢܐ.

ܐܫܕ, ܐܫܕܐ m. *the shedding* of blood.

ܐܫܘܦ, ܐܫܘܦܐ pl. ܝ̈, ܐ̈ rt. ܐܫܦ. *a user of charms and incantations,* esp. *a snake-charmer.*

ܐܫܘܦܘܬܐ rt. ܐܫܦ. f. *snake-charming, enchantment.*

ܐܫܛܪܐ = ܫܛܪܐ *a writing, document, bond;* ܐܫܛܪ ܚܘܒܐ *a bill, bond.*

ܐܫܝܕܘܬܐ rt. ܐܫܕ a) *a being shed, spread far and wide, diffused* as liquids, sand, light; ܐܫܝܕܘܬ ܕܡܐ *bloodshed;* metaph. ܐܫܝܕܘܬܐ ܕܝܕܥܬܐ *the diffusion of knowledge.* b) *fluidity, liquidness.*

ܐܫܬܐܝܠܐ f. ܐܫܬܐܠܬܐ = ܫܐܝܠܐ rt. ܫܐܠ. *borrowed, assumed, presumed;* ܐܒܐ ܐܫܬܐܝܠܐ *the supposed father.*

ܐܫܬܐܠܐܝܬ = ܫܐܝܠܐܝܬ rt. ܫܐܠ. *apparently, in appearance, by supposition, falsely, in pretence.*

ܐܫܝܡܘܢ, ܐܫܝܡܘܢ Heb. *a desert* or *waste.*

ܐܫܬܢܝܘܬܐ rt. ܫܢܐ. f. *assuaging, ease.*

ܐܫܟܐ pl. ܐܫܟܐ m. ܐܫܟܬܐ pl. ܐܫܟܬܐ f. *a testicle.*

ܐܫܟܦܐ or ܐܫܟܘܦܐ pl. ܐ̈ m. Ar. *a cobbler, shoemaker.*

ܐܫܟܦܘܬܐ from the above; f. *cobbling, shoemaking.*

ܐܫܟܪ, ܐܫܟܪܐ f. ܐܫܟܪܬܐ pl. ܐ̈ f. ܐ̈ *a yoke of land = about two-thirds of an acre; a field, a piece of land, a farm;* ܐܫܟܪ̈ܐ ܕܟܪܡܐ *acres of vineyard;* ܐܫܟܪ̈ܐ ܕܥܕܬܐ *Church lands* or *endowments;* metaph. ܐܫܟܪܐ ܕܥܕܬܐ *the Church's field of labour;* ܐܫܟܪܐ ܕܗܝܡܢܘܬܐ *the plot of faith;* ܫܠܝܚ̈ܐ ܐܫܟܪܐ ܗܢܐ ܦܠܚܘ *the Apostles laboured in this track.*

ܐܫܟܪܥܐ m. perh. *the wood of the acacia,* but the word is variously used to translate *box, beech, teak,* and *almug = sandal-wood;* ܕܐܫܟܪܥܐ ܕܦ̈ܐ *beechen planks.*

ܐܫܦ APHEL of ܫܘܦ and of ܫܦܐ.

ܐܫܦ (cognate roots ܢܫܦ and ܫܦܐ) fut. ܢܐܫܘܦ, part. ܐܫܦ, ܐܫܦܐ *to stroke, soothe, charm serpents,* ܐܫܦܐ ܕܚܘ̈ܝܐ *a snake-charmer, user of charms.* DERIVATIVES, ܐܫܘܦܐ, ܐܫܘܦܘܬܐ, ܐܫܦܐ.

ܐܫܦܐ rt. ܐܫܦ. m. *a charm, incantation.*

ܐܫܦܝܙܐ or ܐܫܦܝܙܐ m. *a lodging, inn, house of entertainment for travellers.*

ܐܫܫ rt. found in Heb., Chald., Ar., verb only used in Heb. Hithpoal and in Chald. Ithpael; root-meaning *to make firm, support, found,* hence is derived

ܐܫܬ, ܐܫܬܐ pl. ܐܫܬܬܐ f. rt. ܫܬ. *the bottom, the deepest part;* ܐܫܬܗ ܕܒܐܪܐ *the bottom of the well;* ܐܫܬܗ ܕܓܘܒܐ *the bottom of the pit;* ܐܫܬܗ ܕܝܡܐ *the depth of the sea;* ܐܫܬܬܐ ܕܫܘܪܐ *foundations of the walls,* Is. xvi. 7.

ܐܫܬ, ܐܫܬܐ pl. ܐܫܬܘܬܐ from a Heb. and Chald. word for fire, f. *fever;* ܐܫܬ ܝܘܡܐ *quotidian fever;* ܐܫܬܐ ܕܐܪܒܥܐ ܝܘܡܝܢ *quartan fever;* metaph. ܐܫܬܐ ܕܦܠܓܘܬܐ *the fever of schism.*

ܐܫܬܐ = ܫܬ, ܫܬܐ *six;* with ܕ *the sixth;* ܝܘܡܐ ܕܐܫܬܐ *the sixth day;* ܐܫܬܐ ܝܘܡܝܢ *the six days* of the Creation; ܐܫܬܥܣܪ = ܫܬܥܣܪ *sixteen;* ܐܫܬܝܢ = ܫܬܝܢ *sixty.*

ܐܫܬܘ generally followed by ܕܝܢ. interj. expressing desire and longing, *O that! would that!*

ܐܫܬܩܕܡ and ܐܫܬܩܕܡܝܢ from ܩܕܡ and ܫܢܬܐ. adv. of time; *last year;* ܡܢ ܐܫܬܩܕܡܝܢ *a year ago, for a year past.*

ܐܬ, ܐܬܐ pl. ܐܬܘܬܐ f. *a*) *a sign, mark, pledge, token;* ܐܬܐ ܕܩܝܡܐ *the sign* or *token of the covenant,* Gen. ix. 12; *circumcision,* Gen. xvii. 11. Used in John ii. 11–18 and throughout this Gospel of the signs whereby our Lord manifested Himself; ܐܬܘܬܐ ܘܬܕܡܪ̈ܬܐ *signs and wonders;* ܟܠ ܕܠܐ ܐܝܬ ܥܠܘܗܝ ܐܬܐ ܕܝܠܝ ܠܐ ܢܥܘܠ *whosoever has not my token let him not enter;* ܐܬܐ ܕܡܘܬܐ *a sign of approaching death;* ܐܬܐ ܕܨܠܝܒܐ *the sign of the cross;* cf. ܪܘܫܡܐ *signing, making* the sign of the cross. *b*) *a standard;* ܫܩ̈ܠܝ ܐܬܘܬܐ *standard-bearers.* *c*) pl. *a figure, description* of a pers. or thing; ܝܠܦ ܡܢܗ ܐܬܘܬܐ *he learnt the design* i.e. of a garden *from her.* *d*) *a constellation;* ܐܬܘܬܐ ܕܪܩܝܥܐ *the signs of the heavens, the figures* or *constellations of the heavens; an astronomical figure* or *symbol.* COGNATE, ܬܘܐ, ܬܘ.

ܐܬܐ fut. ܢܐܬܐ 1 pers. ܐܬܐ, inf. ܡܐܬܐ, imper. ܬܐ, ܬܝ pl. ܬܘ, ܬܝܝܢ, act. part. ܐܬܐ, ܐܬܝܐ pl. m. ܐܬܝܢ f. ܐܬܝܢ, pass. part. ܐܬܐ f. ܐܬܝܐ or ܐܬܝܬܐ *to come, arrive,* opp. ܐܙܠ *to go;* ܐܬܬ ܫܥܬܝ *my hour is come;* ܐܬܬ ܐܓܪܬܗ ܠܘܬܢ *his letter has reached us.* With preps. ܒ of the manner, ܐܬܘ ܒܐܠܦܐ *they came by ship;* ܒܚܝܠܐ ܪܒܐ *with a great army;* ܠܩܘܪܒܘܬܐ ܕ *to the neighbourhood of = near to;* with ܒܬܪ *to follow,* ܬܘ ܒܬܪܝ *follow me;* ܐܬܝܬ ܒܬܪ ܡܠܦܢܘܬܝ *thou hast followed my teaching;* with ܚܕܪ *to surround.* With ܠ *a*) *of place* or *result;* ܠܓܠܝܠܐ *to Galilee;* ܠܐܬܪܗ *to his place;* metaph. ܐܬܐ ܠܓܠܝܐ *it was apparent;* ܠܡܗܘܐ, ܠܥܒܕܐ, ܠܡܫܘܕܥܘ *to come to be, come to pass, come to something, result in;* ܠܡܦܩܢܘܗܝ *to turn out to advantage;* ܠܡܦܓܥ ܕ *to meet.* *b*) with pers. pron. suff. has ethical force, ܐܶܬܳܐ ܠܶܗ *he went his way.* With ܠܘܳܬ or ܒܶܝܬ of the pers.; metaph. ܐܶܬܳܐ ܠܘܳܬ ܢܰܦܫܶܗ *to come to himself, to a right mind;* with ܡܶܢ, from a place or pers. ܡܶܢ ܐܰܝܟܰܐ ܐܳܬܶܐ ܐܰܢ̱ܬ *whence comest thou?* ܐܶܬܰܘ ܗܳܠܶܝܢ ܐܶܓܰܪ̈ܳܬܳܐ ܡܶܢ ܡܰܠܟܳܐ *letters came from the king;* with ܥܰܠ, *to attack, invade; to befall, come upon,* said of good or of evil; ܥܰܠ ܥܰܠ ܠܶܒܳܐ *to take to heart, grieve;* with ܩܕܳܡ, *to go in front, precede,* hence *to make progress, prosper, succeed.* Act. part. ܥܰܐܕܳܐ ܕܐܳܬܶܐ *the approaching feast;* ܗܰܘ ܕܐܳܬܶܐ *He who is to come* i.e. *the Messiah;* gram. W-Syr. ܕܐܳܬܶܐ *the future,* opp. ܕܩܳܐܶܡ *the present* and ܕܥܒܰܪ *the past;* fem. used impers. with ethical ܠ, *to serve, be of use, advantage;* ܠܳܐ ܐܳܬܝܳܐ ܠܶܗ *it is of no use to him, it will do him no good;* with ܠܩܽܘܒܠܶܗ *to prosper, succeed;* ܐܰܝܟ ܕܐܳܬܝܳܐ *as it may happen, by chance, heedlessly.* Infin. = subst. *advantage, profit;* ܠܳܐ ܡܶܐܬܳܐ ܐܝܬ ܠܗܘܢ ܡܶܕܶܡ *they are worthless.* Pa. ܐܰܬܺܝ *to come* (rare). Aph. ܐܰܝܬܺܝ fut. ܢܰܝܬܶܐ, inf. ܠܡܰܝܬܳܝܘܼ, imper. ܐܰܝܬܳܐ, part. ܡܰܝܬܶܐ f. ܡܰܝܬܝܳܐ; *to make come,* with ܠ or acc. of the thing or person brought, with ܠ or ܠܘܳܬ of the pers. to whom it is brought; *to summon, bring, have some one brought,* ܫܰܕܰܪ ܐܰܝܬܺܝ *to send for; to bring forward* an argument, complaint, *to allege, cite, quote.* With ܒ, *to bring into* e.g. difficulties; with ܥܕܪܐ and ܕ of the person, *to accuse;* with ܥܰܠ ܥܰܠ *to bring upon, inflict;* with ܥܰܠ ܥܰܠ ܠܶܒܳܐ *to bring to mind, take to heart* = *to notice, care;* with ܫܘܳܠܳܐ, ܣܒܰܪܬܳܐ or ܡܶܠܬܳܐ *to bring news, tell, relate, recount;* ܠܥܽܘܗܕܳܢܳܐ *to remind, mention;* ܦܺܐܪ̈ܶܐ *to bear, yield, bring forth fruit.* Imper. used adverbially, *thus, so:* ܐܰܝܟ ܐܰܝܬܳܐ ܠܡܶܐܡܰܪ *so to speak, as we may say, thus for instance.* Ettaph. ܐܶܬܐܰܝܬܺܝ *to be brought, led, carried;* ܠܗܳܪܟܳܐ ܘܠܗܳܪܟܳܐ ܡܶܬܐܰܝܬܝܳܐ ܗܘܳܬ *it was carried hither and thither;* ܐܶܬܐܰܝܬܺܝ ܦܰܓܪܶܗ ܠܐܽܘܪܗܳܝ *his body was brought to Edessa* for burial; *to be brought to pass, succeed, turn out;* ܠܳܐ ܡܶܬܐܰܝܬܝܳܐ ܗܘܳܬ ܐܰܝܟ ܨܶܒܝܳܢܶܗ *the event did not meet his desires; to happen to,* with ܥܰܠ, ܟܽܠܗܶܝܢ ܕܡܶܬܐܰܝܬܝܳܢ ܥܰܠ ܒܢܰܝ̈ܢܳܫܳܐ *everything brought upon men, everything that can befall human beings.* Derivatives, ܐܳܬܽܘܝܳܐ, ܐܰܬܺܝܬܳܐ, ܡܰܐܬܝܳܐ, ܡܰܝܬܝܳܢܳܐ, ܡܰܝܬܝܳܢܽܘܬܳܐ, ܡܰܝܬܝܳܐ, ܡܶܬܐܰܝܬܝܳܢܳܐ, ܡܶܬܐܰܝܬܝܳܢܽܘܬܳܐ.

ܐܳܬ, ܐܳܬܽܘܬܳܐ pl. ܐܳܬ̈ܘܳܢ, ܐܳܬ̈ܘܳܬܳܐ f. = ܐܳܬܳܐ. *a sign, a character, a letter* of the alphabet; ܒܰܐܳܬܽܘܬܳܐ *in alphabetical order;* ܐܳܬܽܘܬܳܐ ܕܪܺܝܫܳܐ *an initial letter;* ܡܶܬܩܰܠܢܺܝܬܳܐ a letter *pronounced with a vowel,* opp. ܫܠܺܝܬܳܐ *a silent* or *otiose letter;* ܐܳܬܽܘܬܳܐ ܦܬܺܝܚܬܳܐ *having the vowel Pethacha* ◌ܰ, ܙܩܺܝܦܬܳܐ *having Zekapa* ◌ܳ, ܪܒܺܝܨܬܳܐ *having Revaza* ◌ܶ; ܐܳܬ̈ܘܳܬܳܐ ܡܰܩܠܳܢܝܳܬܳܐ *vowel letters* as ܝ, ܘ, ܐ; ܐܳܬ̈ܘܳܬܳܐ ܥܶܩܳܪܳܝܳܬܳܐ *radicals* also called ܐܺܝܬܝܳܝܳܬܳܐ *essential* or ܟܝܳܢܳܝܳܬܳܐ *natural,* opp. ܬܽܘܠܳܐ or ܡܫܰܡܠܝܳܢܝܳܬܳܐ *formative;* ܡܶܬܬܰܘܣܦܳܢܝܳܬܳܐ *affixed* or *prefixed,* ܕܡܶܬܕܰܒܩܳܢ *suffixed* to denote gender or number, as ܐ, ܘ, ܝ, ܬ; or possession, as ܝ, ܟ, ܗ.

ܐܳܬܽܘܝܳܐ pl. ܐܳܬܽܘܝ̈ܶܐ rt. ܐܬܐ. m. *a comer, an arrival;* opp. ܐܳܙܽܘܠܳܐ *a goer.*

ܐܰܬܽܘܢܳܐ rt. ܐܬܢ. m. *an oven, furnace.*

ܐܳܬܽܘܪ f. *a*) *Assyria.* *b*) *the province and diocese of which Mosul was the capital;* hence

ܐܳܬܽܘܪܳܝܳܐ pl. ܐܳܬܽܘܪ̈ܳܝܶܐ *a*) *an Assyrian.* *b*) in later times ܡܰܘܨܶܠ ܐܳܬܽܘܪܳܝܳܐ *the see of the city of Mosul.*

ܐܰܬܺܝܪ, ܐܶܬܺܝܪܳܐ *a*) ἀθήρη, *pottage.* *b*) αἰθήρ, m. *the air, the atmosphere;* hence

ܐܶܬܶܝܪܳܝܳܐ pl. ܝ̈ܶܐ *ethereal, celestial.*

ܐܰܬܠܺܝܛܳܐ pl. ܐܰܬܠܺܝܛ̈ܶܐ m. ἀθλητής, *an athlete, warrior, champion,* esp. used of those who strive for God and the truth. ܐܰܬܠܺܝܛ̈ܶܐ ܢܳܨܽܘܚ̈ܶܐ *victorious athletes* = *martyrs;* ܣܰܒܪܳܐ ܕܐܰܬܠܺܝܛ̈ܰܘܗܝ (*Christ*) *the Hope of those who strive for Him.*

ܐܰܬܠܺܝܛܳܐܺܝܬ adv. *as an athlete, athletically, boldly, bravely.*

ܐܰܬܠܺܝܛܽܘܬܳܐ f. ἄθλησις, *athletic contests, wrestling,* hence *a contest, struggle, an heroic deed; courage, constancy, martyrdom;* ܐܰܬܠܺܝܛܽܘܬܳܐ ܪܰܘܪ̈ܒܳܬܳܐ ܥܒܰܕ *he did great exploits.*

ܐܰܬܠܰܐ or ܐܰܬܠܺܝ αἰθάλη, *a*) *ashes,* *b*) *an alembic.*

ܐܰܬܠܺܝܛܽܘܣ = *a*) ܐܰܬܠܺܝܛܳܐ. *b*) ܐܰܬܠܽܘܣ.

ܐܰܬܠܺܝܣܽܘܬܳܐ pl. ܐܰܬܠܺܝܣ̈ܘܳܬܳܐ f. ἄθλησις, *a contest, trial; constancy, fortitude; brave* or *heroic deeds,* esp. of the martyrs.

ܐܰܬܠܽܘܣ pl. ܐܰܬܠܽܘ̈ܣܶܐ m. *a*) ἄθλος, *contest, trouble, toil;* ܐܰܬܠܽܘ̈ܣܰܘܗܝ ܕܗܶܪܰܩܠܺܝܣ *the labours of Hercules.* *b*) ἆθλον, *a prize of victory.*

ܐܬܠܡܣܬܐ = ܐܬܠܡܣܬܐ; see above.

ܐܬܐܡ denom. verb Aphel conj. from ܬܐܘܡܐ. *to bear twins, to be double.*

ܐܬܡܠ, ܐܬܡܠܝ; see ܬܡܠ. adv. of time, *yesterday.*

ܐܬܢ Aphel of ܬܢ; *to smoke.*

ܐܬܢܐ pl. ܐܬܢܬܐ f. *an ass;* ܐܣܪ ܥܠ ܐܬܢܗ *he saddled his ass.* Cf. ܚܡܪܐ.

ܐܬܪ Aphel of ܬܪ; *to shed its leaves.*

ܐܬܪ, ܐܬܪܐ pl. ܐܬܪܘܢ, ܐܬܪܘܬܐ m. *a) the place = a special place;* ܐܬܪܐ ܩܕܝܫܐ *the holy place;* ܒܪܝܟ ܐܝܩܪܗ ܕܡܪܝܐ ܡܢ ܐܬܪܗ *blessed be the glory of the Lord from His place,* Ez. iii. 12; metaph. *place, position, office. b) a region, district, country;* ܐܬܪܐ ܡܕܒܪܐ *a desert place;* ܐܬܪܘܬܐ ܪܚܝܩܬܐ *distant places* or *countries;* ܐܬܪܐ ܕܗܘܢܝܐ *the country of the Huns;* ܐܬܪܐ ܕܦܪܣܝܐ *Persia;* ܐܬܪܐ ܕܒܘܣܡܐ *the realms of bliss. c)* indef. *a* or *any place,* ܐܬܪ ܕ or ܒܐܬܪܐ ܕ *in the place where, wherever, where;* ܐܬܪ ܕܗܘ *where he is;* ܒܐܬܪ ܐܬܪ *in various places;* ܒܟܠ ܐܬܪ *everywhere;* ܡܢ ܐܬܪ *whence, wherewith;* ܠܐܬܪܐ ܘܠܐܬܪܐ *hither and thither. d)* metaph. *space, room, time, delay, opportunity;* ܒܥܐ ܗܘܐ ܠܗ ܐܬܪܐ ܕ *he sought opportunity to;* ܥܕ ܐܝܬ ܐܬܪܐ ܠܬܝܒܘܬܐ *while there is room for repentance;* ܥܕ ܐܝܬ ܠܢ ܐܬܪܐ *while we have opportunity, while we are able;* ܐܝܬ ܐܬܪܐ ܠܡܣܩ *there is a way to climb up, it is possible to ascend;* with ܝܗܒ *to give way, place, time* or *opportunity, to yield, permit;* ܗܒ ܠܝ ܐܬܪܐ ܩܠܝܠ *grant me a little space, let me wait a little;* ܠܐ ܬܬܠ ܠܗ ܐܬܪܐ ܥܠܝ *do not let him get an advantage over me.* Derivatives, ܐܬܪܢܐ, ܐܬܪܝܐ, ܡܐܬܪ.

ܐܬܪܝܐ, ܐܬܪܝܬܐ pl. ܝܐ, f. ܝܬܐ. *local, provincial;* ܡܡܠܠܐ ܐܬܪܝܐ *dialect;* gram. ܫܡܗܐ ܐܬܪܝܐ *adverbs of place.*

ܐܬܪܢܝܐ, ܐܬܪܢܝܬܐ pl. ܝܐ, f. ܝܬܐ. from ܐܬܪ. adj. *local, of the place, belonging to a special place;* gram. *of place,* i.e. adverbs.

܀ ܫܠܡܬ ܐܠܦ ܐܠܗܐ ܡܥܕܪܢܐ ܀

܀ ܒܫܡ ܡܪܝܐ ܕܒܥܘܕܪܢܗ ܫܪܝܢ ܒܐܬܘܬܐ ܒܝܬ ܀

܀ ܒ ܀

ܒ

ܒ the letter *Beth* ܒܝܬ, ܒܝܬܐ. One of the BeGaDCePaTh or aspirated letters; having a hard sound *b* at the beginning of a word or syllable, soft sound *v* or *w* after a vowel sound, as ܒܒܪܐ *bavro.*

Beth interchanges with *Mim* (ܡ) and *Pe* (ܦ) in cognate roots, Heb. Chald. or Ar. In Greek names it often stands for υ or π. Thus names beginning with *Eu* are transliterated by ܐܘ. *Beth* also expresses the number 2; with ܕ *the second;* with a line beneath ܒ̱ 2,000, E-Syr. ܒ 2,000, ܒ̱ 20,000.

ܒ prep. inseparable prefix, *in, among, with, at, to, into, on, upon; by, according to, for, because, about.* ܒ is sometimes omitted before another ܒ, ܐܪܡܝܘ ܐܢܘܢ ܒܒܝܬ ܐܣܝܪܐ for ܒܒܝܬ ܐܣܝܪܐ *they threw them into prison.* ܒ with a substantive sometimes implies *with that only,* as ܒܫܡܐ ܕ *nominally, in name only.* ܥܪܩܘ ܒܢܦܫܗܘܢ *they fled for their lives, they escaped with their bare lives.* ܒ following an adj. forms a superlative, ܒܪܝܟܬܐ ܒܢܫܐ *blessed art thou amongst women, most blessed of all women.* ܒ frequently helps to form adverbs, as ܒܛܘܫܝܐ *secretly*, ܒܢܡܘܣܐ *legally*, ܒܬܪܝܬ or ܕ ܒܥܓܠܐ *quickly, immediately*; ܒܫܠܝܐ *quietly, tranquilly*; ܒܡܫܘܚܬܐ *abundantly*.

ܒܐܬܪܝܗ, ܒܐܬܪܝܢ; see ܐܬܪܐ.

ܒܐܪܐ m. *a*) *the beam of an oil-* or *wine-press*. *b*) Heb. *bath*, a liquid measure, about 8½ gallons. *c*) *spina alba*.

ܒܐܛܘܣ βάτος, *rubus vulgaris* or *fruticosus*, *the common bramble*.

ܒܐܝܕܐ see ܝܕ. *through, by means of*; ܒܐܝܕܐ ܒܐܝܕܐ *one after another, in order, by degrees, little by little*.

ܒܐܡܐ ܒܐܡܐ f. pl. ܒܐܡܐ̈; see ܒܡܐ. *judgement-seat*, &c.

ܒܐܪ, ܒܐܝܪܐ or ܒܐܝܪܐ, f. ܒܐܝܪܬܐ pl. m. ܒܐܝܪ̈ܐ, f. ܒܐܝܪ̈ܬܐ = ܒܝܪ̈ܐ. rt. ܒܘܪ. *neglected, barren, unfruitful*, of land; metaph. *confused, stupid*.

ܒܐܠܢܝ, ܒܠܢܝܘܣ &c.; see ܒܠܢܐ.

ܒܐܠܢܝܐ m. see ܒܠܢܐ. *the keeper of the bath*.

ܒܐܠܝ or ܒܠܝ ܕ ܡܝܪܒܠܢܐ *myrobalanum*.

ܒܐܪ, ܒܐܪܐ pl. ܒܐܪ̈ܐ, spelt also ܒܪ, ܒܪܐ. f. *a well, a pit*.

ܒܐܪܘܕ Pers. *saltpetre*.

ܒܐܪܬܐ pl. ܒܐܪ̈ܬܐ same as ܒܝܪܬܐ f. *a fortress, palace*, &c.

ܒܐܫ fut. ܢܒܐܫ, pres. part. ܒܐܫ f. ܒܐܫܐ impersonal verb, *to be* or *seem evil, to displease, to harm*; ܢܒܐܫ ܠܟܘܢ ܡܢ ܕܠܗܘܢ *it shall be worse for you than for them*; ܒܐܫܝܢ ܡܢ ܚܝܘܬܐ *we do more harm than wild beasts*. Ethpe. ܐܬܒܐܫ also spelt ܐܬܒܫ and ܐܬܒܐܫ *to be* or *seem evil, to displease*, with ܠ, ܒܥܝܢܐ or ܩܕܡ; *to suffer evil*, with ܡܢ. Aph. ܐܒܐܫ and ܐܒܫ *to do evil, to hurt, harm, afflict*, with ܠ or ܠܘܬ; *to be* or *do worse than*, with ܡܢ; ܠܐ ܡܒܐܫܝܢ ܐܦܠܐ ܡܛܐܒܝܢ *idols do neither harm nor good*; ܐܒܫ ܡܒܐܫܘ ܠܥܡܗ *he hath brought much evil on his people*. Derivatives, ܒܐܫܬܐ, ܒܝܫܐ, ܒܝܫܐ, ܒܝܫܘܬܐ, ܒܝܫܬܐ, ܡܒܐܫܢܐ, ܡܒܐܫܢܘܬܐ.

ܒܐܫܬܐ rt. ܒܐܫ. f. *a misfortune*.

ܒܒ, ܒܒܐ oftener ܒܒܐ, ܒܒܬܐ pl. ܒܒ̈ܬܐ f. *the pupil* of the eye; ܛܘܦܐ ܕܒܒܝ *the drops of my eyes*.

ܒܒܓܐ *a parrot*.

ܒܒܘܢܐ dim. of ܒܒܐ.

ܒܒܘܫܐ pl. ܒܒܘ̈ܫܐ m. *a*) *a little boy, baby*. *b*) *a valet, lad*; f. ܒܒܘܫܬܐ pl. ܒܒܘ̈ܫܬܐ *a little girl*; ܐܝܟ ܒܒܘ̈ܫܐ *like children*.

ܒܒܒ interj. *O strange! wonderful!*

ܒܒܝܠ or ܒܒܝܠ Babylonian, *Bab-Il*, the Gate of God; *Babylon*.

ܒܒܠ, ܒܒܠܝܐ f. ܒܒܠܝܬܐ pl. m. ܝ̈ܐ f. ܝ̈ܬܐ adj. from the above. *Babylonian; a Babylonian, an astrologer*; ܐܪܥܐ ܕܒܒܠܝ̈ܐ *the country of the Babylonians*.

ܒܒܘ interj. of entreaty, *I pray thee*; see ܒܒܘ.

ܒܒܪ, ܒܒܪܐ m. Pers. *the panther, tiger*.

ܒܓ Turkish *Bey, prince*.

ܒܓܒܘܓܐ pl. ܒܓܒܘ̈ܓܐ m. mimet. from the sound made in pouring out, *a narrow-necked jug*.

ܒܓܒܘܓܝܬܐ pl. ܒܓܒܘܓ̈ܝܬܐ f. dim. of the above, also *a bubble*.

ܒܓܕܐܕ, ܒܓܕܐܕ or ܒܓܕܕ f. Ar. *Baghdad*, built by Almanzor, the second Abasside Khalif, A.D. 763, on the ruins of Seleucia and Ctesiphon.

ܒܓܕܟܦܬ *BeGaDCePaTh*, a memoria technica of those letters which take the points Rukokh or Qushoi; see ܒ, ܓ, &c.

ܒܓܘ prep. *within, inside*; see ܓܘ.

ܒܓܠܢܐ f. ܒܓܠܢܝܬܐ pl. m. ܒܓܠ̈ܢܐ, f. ܒܓܠܢܝ̈ܬܐ rt. ܒܓܠ. *an idle talker, babbler*; f. pl. *nonsense, silliness*.

ܒܓܘܢܐ m. rt. ܒܓܢ. *lamentation, complaint*.

ܒܓܠ ܒܓܠ act. part. ܒܓܠ, ܒܓܠܐ, pass. part. ܒܓܝܠ, ܒܓܝܠܐ, ܒܓܝܠܬܐ pl. m. ܝ̈ܢ, f. ܝ̈ܢ. *to cry out, prate, rail, rail at*, with ܒ or ܠܘܬ; pass. part. *foolish, absurd*. Derivatives, ܒܓܠܘܬܐ, ܒܓܠܐ.

ܒܓܠܐ m. ܒܓܠܬܐ f. Ar. *a mule*.

ܒܓܠܐ m. rt. ܒܓܠ. *babble, idle talk*.

ܒܓܢ ܒܓܢ 3 m. pl. ܒܓܢܘ, fut. ܢܒܓܢ, part. ܒܓܢ. *to cry, complain, appeal*. Pa. ܒܓܢ *to cry, call for help, complain, appeal against*, with ܡܢ or ܠܘܬ; ܣܓܝܐܐ ܡܒܓܢܝܢ ܠܘܬܗ ܡܢ ܡܕܡ *many made complaint* or *appealed* against him to the emperor. DERIVATIVES, ܒܓܐ, ܒܓܝܐ, ܒܓܝܘܬܐ.

ܒܓܐ or ܒܓܝ, ܒܓܝܐ pl. ܒܓܝ̈ܐ m. an appeal, used with ܩܪܐ to call for help, appeal unto; ܒܓܝ ܩܪܝܬ ܠܩܣܪ thou hast appealed to Caesar; ܒܓܝ̈ܝܟ ܡܪܢ ܝܫܘܥ of Thy mercy, Lord Jesus; rt. ܒܓܐ or ܒܓܝ; see ܒܓܐ.

ܒܓܪ fut. ܢܒܓܪ, imp. ܒܓܘܪ, pass. part. ܒܓܝܪܐ. to make fast a door with bolt or stone, to bar in; ܡܬܒܓܪܝܢ ܘܡܬܒܓܪܝܢ the waters are reined in and curbed. ETHPE. ܐܬܒܓܪ to grow thin, to dry up of water. PA. ܒܓܪ a) to make fast a door, to close or hem in, hold back; ܒܓܪܘܗܝ ܒܛܘܪܐ they hemmed him in in the mountain; ܣܡ ܢܝܪܗ ܥܠ ܣܦܝܪܐ—ܘܒܓܪܗ He laid His yoke on the sphere and held it in. b) to be weak or emaciated. ETHPA. ܐܬܒܓܪ to be held fast, restrained, stopped or closed. DERIVATIVES, ܒܓܪܐ, ܡܒܓܪܐ.

ܒܓܪ, ܒܓܪܐ rt. ܒܓܪ. m. a bar, bolt, or stone to hold a door.

ܒܕ causal particle, compound of ܒ and ܕ. in that, i.e. on that account, because; usually joined to the following word, ܒܕܣܒܪ because he thought; ܒܕܛܒ because—very.

ܒܕ to mix. PALPEL ܒܕܒܕ to confuse, toss about, trouble; ܡܒܕܒܕ ܗܘ ܒܪܥܝܢܗ he is confused, perplexed in his mind. ETHPALPAL, passive of Palpel, ܐܠܦܐ ܡܬܒܕܒܕܐ ܡܢ ܥܘܫܢܐ ܕܓܠ̈ܠܐ a ship tossed about by the violence of the billows.

ܒܕܐ fut. ܢܒܕܐ, imp. ܒܕܝ, inf. ܡܒܕܐ, act. part. ܒܕܐ, ܒܕܝܐ, pass. part. ܒܕܝܐ, to feign, devise, pretend, speak falsely; ܗܪ̈ܛܝܩܐ ܒܕܝܢ ܡܢ ܠܒܗܘܢ ܦܘܚ̈ܡܐ heretics devise evil inventions in their hearts; pass. part. fictitious, spurious; ܐܘܢܓܠܝ̈ܘܢ ܒܕܝ̈ܐ spurious gospels. DERIVATIVES, ܒܕܘܝܐ, ܒܕܝܐ.

ܒܕܐ same as ܒܕܪܐ the beam of an oil- or wine-press.

ܒܕܗܘ therefore, for that cause, on that account; see ܗܘ.

ܒܕܘܝܐ pl. ܒܕܘ̈ܝܐ Ar. Bedawee, nomad.

ܒܕܘܝܐ pl. ܒܕܘ̈ܝܐ rt. ܒܕܐ. m. a foolish talker, trifler.

ܒܕܘܟܬ prep. for, instead of; see ܕܘܟ.

ܒܕܘܠ Bdul, a memoria technica of the prefix particles. These are prefixed without a vowel when the first letter of the word has a vowel, except with initial Olaph which quiesces, its vowel being taken by the prefix, e.g. ܠܐܠܗܐ; also when a word or adjective has only one vowel, and that being on the initial, the ܒܕܘܠ letter takes Pethacha, e.g. ܕܡܐ, ܒܫܡܐ. But particles follow the general rule, ܘܟܠ, ܒܟܠ. When the first letter has no vowel, the prefix particle takes Pethacha, thus ܠܡܫܝܚܐ, ܒܡܫܝܚܐ. Or if two of the ܒܕܘܠ particles are prefixed, the first takes Pethacha; if three, the second takes the vowel.

ܒܕܘܠܐ pl. ܒܕܘ̈ܠܐ m. ܒܕܘܠܬܐ, pl. ܒܕܘ̈ܠܬܐ f. rt. ܒܕܠ. babbling, foolish, garrulous; ܣܒܬܐ ܒܕܘܠܬܐ a garrulous old woman.

ܒܕܘܠܝܐ m. pl. f. ܒܕܘܠܝ̈ܬܐ adj. from ܒܕܘܠ; ܦܠܚ̈ܬܐ ܒܕܘܠܝ̈ܬܐ cases formed by the addition of these particles and governed by them.

ܒܕܘܠܘܬܐ m. rt. ܒܕܠ. empty chatter.

ܒܕܘܩܐ pl. ܒܕܘ̈ܩܐ m. searcher, trier; teacher; restorer.

ܒܕܝܐ pl. ܒܕܝ̈ܐ rt. ܒܕܐ. babbling, folly; fabrication, humbug, foolish inventions; ܡ̈ܠܐ ܕܒܕܝܐ feigned words, fictions; ܚ̈ܙܘܢܐ ܕܒܕܝܐ pretended visions; often used of heretical teaching.

ܒܕܝܪܐܝܬ rt. ܒܕܪ. adv. here and there.

ܒܕܝܪܘܬܐ rt. ܒܕܪ. f. a scattering, that which is scattered.

ܒܕܠ to speak foolishly, invent folly, senseless tales. DERIVATIVES, ܒܕܘܠܐ, ܒܕܘܠܘܬܐ, verb ܒܕܠ, ܡܒܕܠܢܘܬܐ.

ܒܕܠܐ compound of ܒ, ܕ, and ܠܐ. because—not.

ܒܕܡܢ compound of ܒ, ܕ, and ܡܢ. because—from.

ܒܕܩ fut. ܢܒܕܘܩ, imp. ܒܕܘܩ, inf. ܡܒܕܩ, act. part. ܒܕܩ, ܒܕܩܐ a) to search, spy out, explore; ܒܕܩܝܢ ܕܝܢܐ or ܟܐܢܘܬܐ searching out judgement or justice, i.e. inquiring so as to judge justly. b) to repair, restore; ܒܕܩ ܠܬܪ̈ܥܐ he repaired the gates; metaph. ܠܡܒܕܩ ܟܝܢܐ ܦܨܝܚܐ to restore ruined nature. c) to show, point out, declare; ܒܕܩ ܗܘܐ ܕܥܬܝܕ ܗܘܐ he showed what would happen; ܩܕܡ ܒܕܩ to predict.

Pa. ܒܰܨܺܝ a) *to search out, examine.* b) and c) same as Peal; ܡܳܢܳܐ ܡܒܰܨܶܐ *what does it mean, signify?* ܗܰܘ ܕܡܰܣܓܶܐ ܡܶܠܰܝܗܘܽܢ ܡܒܰܨܶܐ ܠܗ ܒܨܺܝܪܽܘܬ ܪܶܥܝܳܢܶܗ *he who uses many words shows his little wit.* Ethpa. ܐܶܬܒܰܨܺܝ; passive of Pa. a) and b); also *to become known, be shown, come forth, appear;* ܕܠܳܐ ܢܶܬܒܰܨܘܽܢ ܢܶܣܝܳܢܶܐ ܪ̈ܘܪܒܶܐ *lest great temptations arise.* Derivatives, ܒܨܳܝܳܐ, ܒܽܘܨܳܝܳܐ, ܒܨܳܝܽܘܬܳܐ, ܡܒܰܨܝܳܢܳܐ, ܡܒܰܨܝܳܢܽܘܬܳܐ.

ܒܳܨܽܘܝܳܐ pl. ܒܳܨܽܘܝܶܐ rt. ܒܨܐ. m. a) *a searcher, trier;* b) *a restorer.*

ܒܽܘܨܳܝܳܐ pl. ܒܽܘܨܳܝܶܐ rt. ܒܨܐ. m. a) *searching out;* b) *repairing;* c) *showing forth, publishing.*

ܒܕܰܪ fut. ܢܶܒܕܽܘܪ, imp. ܒܕܽܘܪ, inf. ܡܶܒܕܰܪ, part. ܒܳܕܰܪ, ܒܳܕܪܳܐ, ܒܕܺܝܪ, ܒܕܺܝܪܳܐ. *to scatter, put in disorder, sprinkle, shed, spread* salve on wounds; metaph. ܐܶܒܕܽܘܪ ܥܰܠ ܦܰܪ̈ܨܽܘܦܰܝܗܘܽܢ ܒܰܣܡܳܐ ܕܬܰܝܳܒܽܘܬܳܐ *I will overspread their faces with the medicine of repentance;* ܡܶܫܚܳܐ ܒܳܕܰܪ ܪܺܝܚܳܐ *ointment that sheds a strong odour abroad.* Pa. ܒܰܕܰܪ *to scatter abroad, disperse, distribute, dissipate;* ܒܰܕܰܪܬ ܐܽܘܪ̈ܚܳܬܳܟ *thou hast scattered thy ways,* i.e. *wandered in many directions;* ܒܰܕܪܺܝܗܝ ܠܘܳܬ ܣܢܺܝܩܶܐ *distribute it amongst the needy.* Ethpa. ܐܶܬܒܰܕܰܪ *to be scattered abroad, dispersed, routed; to be overspread.* Derivatives, ܒܳܕܽܘܪܳܐܺܝܬ, ܡܒܰܕܪܳܢܳܐ, ܡܒܰܕܪܳܢܽܘܬܳܐ, ܡܒܰܕܪܳܢܳܐܺܝܬ, ܒܽܘܕܳܪܳܐ, ܒܕܳܪܽܘܬܳܐ.

ܒܕܒܕ mimetic. Ethpa. ܐܶܬܒܰܕܒܰܕ *to be confused, perplexed.* Derivative, ܒܽܘܕܒܳܕܳܐ.

ܒܰܗܘܽܪ, ܒܰܗܘܽܪܳܐ pl. ܒܰܗܘܽܪܶܐ m. ܒܰܗܘܽܪܬܳܐ pl. ܒܰܗܘܽܪ̈ܳܬܳܐ, f. rt. ܒܗܪ. adj. *dusky, dim, obscure;* ܓܰܘܢܶܗ ܒܰܗܘܽܪ ܗ̱ܘ *its colour is pale* or *dim;* ܥܢܳܢܳܐ ܒܰܗܘܽܪܬܳܐ *a shadowy cloud;* ܪ̈ܡܙܶܐ ܒܰܗܘܽܪܶܐ *obscure indications, dim hints.*

ܒܰܗܘܽܪܳܐܺܝܬ rt. ܒܗܪ. adv. *dimly, indistinctly, obscurely.*

ܒܰܗܘܽܪܽܘܬܳܐ rt. ܒܗܪ. f. *dimness, faint* or *pale light.*

ܒܰܗܬܳܢܳܝܳܐ f. ܒܰܗܬܳܢܳܝܬܳܐ pl. f. ܒܰܗܬܳܢܳܝ̈ܳܬܳܐ rt. ܒܗܬ. *shamefaced, modest.*

ܒܰܗܬܳܢܽܘܬܳܐ f. rt. ܒܗܬ. *modesty, bashfulness.*

ܒܰܗܝ ܕ causal particle, *because, in that.*

ܒܰܫܝܳܐܺܝܬ rt. ܒܫܠ. adv. *quietly, simply;* ܢܶܩܒܪܽܘܢܳܗ̇ ܒܰܫܝܳܐܺܝܬ *let them bury her quietly,* i.e. *with no pomp.*

ܒܽܘܫܳܠܽܘܬܳܐ rt. ܒܫܠ. f. *quiet, quietness, calm, rest, tranquillity, silence;* ܒܽܘܫܳܠܽܘܬܳܐ ܕܡܶܢ ܡܰܚܫ̈ܒܳܬܳܐ ܒܝ̈ܫܳܬܳܐ *rest from evil thoughts.*

ܒܗܶܬܬܳܢܳܐܺܝܬ adv. rt. ܒܗܬ. *with shame.*

ܒܰܫ fut. ܢܶܒܫܽܘܠ and ܢܶܒܫܰܠ, act. part. ܒܳܫܶܠ, ܒܳܫܠܳܐ, pass. part. used as an adj. ܒܰܫܺܝܠ, ܒܰܫܝܠܳܐ, ܒܰܫܺܝܠܬܳܐ, pl. m. ܒܰܫܝܠܺܝܢ, f. ܒܰܫܝܠܳܢ. *to cease* from action, *leave off, become quiet, be stayed, rest,* with ܡܶܢ; hence *to stay* or *remain quiet, dwell quietly;* ܫܠܺܝ ܫܰܠܗܶܒܺܝܬܳܐ ܕܪܕܽܘܦܝܳܐ *the flame of persecution was stayed, quieted down;* ܒܩܶܠܳܝܬܳܟ ܬܶܬܒ ܘܬܶܫܠܶܐ *thou shalt settle down and abide quietly in thy cell;* p. p. *free from disturbance, tranquil, secure; abstinent, calm, serene, gentle;* ܫܳܠܶܝܢ ܒܫܰܝܢܳܐ *settling down to a quiet life;* ܬܺܐܢܶܐ ܒܫܰܝܢܳܝܬܳܐ *figs growing in a sheltered garden;* a Byzantine title of Caesar, ܩܶܣܰܪ ܒܰܫܺܝܠܳܐ *Serene Caesar.* Ethpe. ܐܶܬܒܫܶܠ *to be at peace, have peace,* esp. from active warfare, with ܡܶܢ; *to be* or *remain quiet, tranquil;* e.g. ܡܶܢ ܛܰܝܳܝܶܐ *to have peace from the Arabs, be no longer harassed by the Arabs;* in the opposite sense ܟܰܕ ܐܶܬܒܫܶܠ ܨܠܳܚܶܐܕܺܝܢ ܡܶܢ ܐܽܘܪܶܫܠܶܡ *when Saladin had peace at Jerusalem,* i.e. *held it firmly.* Pa. ܒܰܫܶܠ *to make to leave off, to set at ease, pacify.* Derivatives, ܒܫܺܝܠܳܐܺܝܬ, ܒܫܺܝܠܽܘܬܳܐ, ܒܽܘܫܳܠܳܐ.

ܒܽܘܫܳܠܳܐ or ܒܽܘܫܠܳܐ rt. ܒܫܠ. m. *leaving off, abstinence; a pause, quiet;* ܒܒܽܘܫܳܠܳܐ *quietly;* ܕܠܳܐ ܒܽܘܫܳܠܳܐ *unceasingly.*

ܒܗܩ Aphel ܐܰܒܗܶܩ; *to shine white, glitter;* ܠܒܽܘܫܳܐ ܡܰܒܗܩܳܐ ܐܰܝܟ ܬܰܠܓܳܐ *raiment shining like snow;* ܦܰܓܪܶܗ ܡܰܒܗܶܩ ܗ̱ܘܳܐ ܘܚܰܘܳܪ ܒܓܰܪܒܳܐ *his body was glittering and white with leprosy;* hence is derived

ܒܽܘܗܩܳܐ m. *a ray of light,* and

ܒܰܗܰܩܬܳܐ f. *a skin disease, shiny spots* not leprous but like leprosy.

ܒܗܪ root-meaning *to shine.* Pe. only p. part. ܒܗܺܝܪ, ܒܗܺܝܪܳܐ, ܒܗܺܝܪܬܳܐ *dim, uncertain;* ܝܺܕܰܥܬܳܐ ܒܗܺܝܪܬܳܐ *dim knowledge.* Shaph. ܫܰܒܗܰܪ *to glorify.* Eshtaphal ܐܶܫܬܰܒܗܰܪ *to glory, glorify oneself, boast,* with ܒ; ܠܳܐ ܬܶܫܬܰܒܗܰܪ ܕܥܒܰܕܬ ܡܶܕܶܡ *boast not that thou hast achieved aught;* ܒܫܡܳܟ ܝܶܫܽܘܥ ܐܶܫܬܰܒܗܰܪ *in Thy name, O Jesus, will I glory.*

DERIVATIVES, ܒܗܝܪܐ, ܒܗܝܪܘܬܐ, ܒܗܝܪܘܬܐ, ܒܗܪܐ, ܡܒܗܪܢܐ, ܡܒܗܪܢܘܬܐ, ܡܒܗܪܐ, ܡܒܗܪܢܘܬܐ.

ܒܘܗܪܐ pl. ܒܘܗܪܐ rt. ܒܗܪ. m. *dawn, twilight.*

ܒܗܬ fut. ܢܒܗܬ, imp. ܒܗܬ, inf. ܡܒܗܬ, act. p. ܒܗܬ, ܒܗܬܐ, pass. p. ܒܗܝܬ, ܒܗܝܬܐ, the other form ܒܗܬ is less common. *to be ashamed, confused,* with ܒ; *to stand in awe of, revere,* with ܡܢ; ܓܝܪܬܐ ܕܒܗܝܬܐ ܟܕ ܩܝܡܐ *an adulteress standing in confusion at her trial;* ܠܐ ܒܗܬ ܒܫܫܠܬܝ *he was not ashamed of* my *chains;* ܠܐ ܬܒܗܬ ܡܢܝ *do not be in awe of me,* i.e. *afraid to speak;* ܒܗܬܝܢ ܗܘܘ ܐܦܝܗܘܢ *they were ashamed.* APH. ܐܒܗܬ *to put to shame, dishonour, confound;* ܐܒܗܬ ܣܒܪܗܘܢ *he frustrated their hope;* the Nicene Fathers ܐܒܗܬܘ ܠܐܪܝܘܣ *confounded Arius.* DERIVATIVES, ܒܗܬܬܐ, ܒܗܬܬܘܬܐ, ܒܗܬܬܐ, ܡܒܗܬܢܐ.

ܒܗܬܬܐ, ܒܗܬܬܐ rt. ܒܗܬ. f. *shame, disgrace;* often with ܐܦܐ *confusion of face;* ܠܐ ܒܗܬܬܐ *shamelessness;* ܕܠܐ ܒܗܬܬܐ *shameless, impudent;* with ܥܒܕ or ܗܠܟ *to behave himself unseemly;* metaph. *an idol.*

ܒܘܓܐ *a*) Pers. m. *pottage;* *b*) *a shirt, garment.*

ܒܘܒ and ܒܒ abbrev. for ܒܒܐ.

ܒܘܒܢܐ pl. ܒܘܒܢܐ *a*) m. *a canal;* ܡܢ ܒܘܒܢܐ ܡܫܬܝܗܘܢ *their drink is from the canal.* *b*) *a cooking-pot, pan, dish.* *c*) f. with soft ܒ, ܒܘܒܢܐ *a she-buffalo.*

ܒܘܒܠܐ pl. ܐ̈ m. ܒܘܒܠܬܐ pl. ܬ̈ܐ f. *a wild bull, a buffalo.*

ܒܘܥܝܐ pl. ܐ̈ rt. ܒܥܐ. m. *calling out, calling for help, complaint.*

ܒܘܥܝܐ pl. ܐ̈ m. *a foundation, a great stone;* ܫܪܐ ܒܘܥܝܗ ܕܐܪܥܐ *He cast the foundation of the earth.*

ܒܘܣܡܐ rt. ܒܣܡ found in Chaldee. m. *cheerfulness.*

ܒܘܨܝܐ pl. ܐ̈ rt. ܒܨܐ. m. *searching, research; a crucible; declaration, showing forth;* ܒܘܨܝܐ ܕܟܣܝܬܐ *the making known of hidden things;* ܒܘܨܝܐ ܡܩܕܡܝܐ ܕܢܒܝܐ *the predictions of the prophets.*

ܒܘܕܪܐ rt. ܒܕܪ. m. *a*) *dispersion, scattering.* *b*) *dispersed parts, scattered particles;* ܒܘܕܪܘ ܕܚܠܒܐ *spilt milk.* *c*) *distribution;* ܒܘܕܪ ܩܢܝܢܗ the distribution of *his wealth.*

ܒܘܗܘ f. Heb. Gen. i. 2. *chaos, emptiness.*

ܒܘܗܝܐ or ܒܘܗܝܐ rt. ܒܗܝ. m. *perturbation, embarrassment, terror.*

ܒܘܗܪܐ rt. ܒܗܪ. m. *twilight, daybreak;* ܒܒܘܗܪܐ ܕܨܦܪܐ *in the twilight of dawn.*

ܒܘܙܚܐ rt. ܒܙܚ. m. *scorn, a laughing-stock; derision, delusion.*

ܒܘܙܐ or ܒܙܐ pl. ܒܘܙܐ m. *a hawk, falcon.*

ܒܘܨܠܐ or ܒܘܨܠܐ pl. ܒܘܨܠܐ m. *an onion,* probably a provincial form of ܒܨܠܐ.

ܒܘܙܢܛܝܐ rarely ܒܘܙܢܛܝܘܢ *Byzantium.*

ܒܘܙܥܐ pl. ܐ̈ m. rt. ܒܙܥ. *a*) *a hole pierced through, a perforation;* ܒܘܙܥܐ ܕܓܢܐ *the holes pierced* in the hands and feet of the Lord *by nails.* *b*) gram. *a slight pause or opening between two consonants, neither having a vowel.*

ܒܘܚ fut. ܢܒܘܚ, inf ܡܒܚ, part. act. ܒܐܚ. *a*) *to be weak* or *broken down with age,* of human beings, of trees, &c. *b*) *to be over-ripe, overdone,* of food, fruit, &c.

ܒܘܚܢܐ pl. ܐ̈ m. rt. ܒܚܢ. *examination, inquiry into, a query, a disputation;* ܒܘܚܢܐ ܕܠܘܩܒܠ ܚܠܩܝܕܘܢܝܐ *a disputation against the adherents of the Council of Chalcedon.*

ܒܘܚܪܢܐ pl. ܐ̈ rt. ܒܚܪ. m. *a*) *trial, visitation, proving;* ܒܘܚܪܢܐ ܕܗܝܡܢܘܬܐ *the proving* or *trial of faith.* *b*) *crisis* of an illness. *c*) *a crucible;* ܐܪܡܝܗ ܒܒܘܚܪܢܐ *cast it into the crucible.*

ܒܘܚܫܐ rt. ܒܚܫ. m. *stirring.*

ܒܘܚܫܢܐ *tender grass* or *young blades of corn, the first growth of crops* or *of weeds* which withers before harvest.

ܒܘܛܠܐ pl. ܐ̈ rt. ܒܛܠ. m. *a*) *abolition, annulling,* of debts, wills, &c. *b*) *infirmity, loss* of physical vigour. *c*) *deposition* of bishops.

ܒܘܝܐܐ pl. ܒܘܝܐܐ m. rt. ܒܝܐ with affixes keeps one Olaph. *comfort, consolation;* pl. often *hortatory* or *consolatory discourses.*

ܒܘܝܐܢܐ f. ܒܘܝܐܢܝܬܐ rt. ܒܝܐ. adj. *consolatory.*

ܒܘܝܢܐ pl. ܐ̈ ـ m. rt. ܒܝܢ. *understanding, discernment;* ܠܐ ܒܘܝܢܐ *want of judgement, senselessness;* ܕܠܐ ܒܘܝܢ often as adv. or adj. *without consideration, devoid of understanding, senseless;* ܥܡܠܐ ܣܪܝܩܐ ܕܠܐ ܒܘܝܢܐ *with vain labour.*

ܒܘܝܬܐ m. rt. ܒܝܬ. *delay, deferring; a hindrance;* ܕܠܐ ܒܘܝܬ *incessantly.*

ܒܘܟܐ *white* or *black spots on the nails.*

ܒܘܟܪܐ pl. ܒܘܟܪ̈ܐ m. *native,* whether aborigines or earliest settlers, then *settlers, inhabitants;* ܥܡܡ̈ܐ ܒܘܟܪ̈ܐ *the native races.*

ܒܘܟܪܐ pl. ܐ̈ ـ m. rt. ܒܟܪ. *the first-born* of man or beast; hence Isa. lx. 6 *a young camel.* Metaph. Moses ܒܘܟܪܐ ܕܢܒܝ̈ܐ *first-born of the prophets;* Stephen ܒܘܟܪܐ ܕܣܗ̈ܕܐ *first-born of the martyrs;* Sunday ܒܘܟܪܐ ܕܝܘܡ̈ܬܐ *first of the days,* &c. Very often used of Christ, hence in Nestorian Liturgies, the holy bread is called ܒܘܟܪܐ, in allusion to Christ the First-born of all creatures; ܟܗܢܐ ܩܨܐ ܠܒܘܟܪܐ ܠܬܪܬܝܢ ܡܢ̈ܘܢ *the priest shall break the Bukhra into two portions.*

ܒܘܟܪܐܝܬ adv. rt. ܒܟܪ. *first.*

ܒܘܟܪܘܬܐ f. rt. ܒܟܪ. *right of the first-born, right of primogeniture.*

ܒܘܟܡܐ *a weaned camel-foal.*

ܒܘܟܡܐ m. *a great stone.* Cf. ܒܟܡܐ.

ܒܘܠܐ, ܒܘܠܐ, ܒܘܠܝ a) βουλή, *Council, Senate;* with ܒܝܬ *the court-house, council-chamber;* ܣܘܥܪ̈ܢܐ ܕܒܘܠܐ *affairs of state.* b) *the spout* of a jug.

ܒܘܠܒܘܣܐ, ܒܘܠܒܘܣ, ܒܘܠܒܘܣ or ܒܘܠܒܘܣܐ pl. ܒܘܠܒ̈ܘܣܐ m. βολβός, *bulb, onion;* ܒܘܠܒ̈ܘܣܐ ܕܫܘܫ̈ܢܐ *lily bulbs;* ܒܘܠܒ̈ܘܣܐ ܡܓܥܝܢ̈ܐ *emetic bulbs.*

ܒܘܠܒܠܐ pl. ܒܘܠܒ̈ܠܐ m. rt. ܒܠܒܠ. *confusion, disorder; disturbance; corruption;* ܒܘܠܒܠܐ ܕܡܓܕܠܐ *the confusion at the tower* of Babel.

ܒܘܠܗܝܐ pl. ܒܘܠܗ̈ܝܐ from ܒܠܗ. m. *terror, dismay, stupefaction.*

ܒܘܠܘܛܐ and ܒܘܠܘܛܝܣ pl. ܒܘܠܘ̈ܛܐ m. βουλευτής, *a counsellor, senator; honourable.*

ܒܘܠܝ̈ܬܐ f. pl. no sing. *signet-rings, gems of rings, pebbles.*

ܒܘܠܝܩܐܝܬ adv. rt. ܠܩ. *suitably, rightly.*

ܒܘܡܐ f. or com. Ar. *an owl.*

ܒܘܡܣܐ βωμός, m. pl. *high places, hill-shrines;* ܒܘܣܡܐ 2 Chr. i. 13 by metathesis.

ܒܝܢ root-meaning *to separate.* COGNATE ܒܝܢ, ܒܝܢܐ. PA. ܒܝܢ *to show, point out, to give instruction, understanding; to discern;* ܐܠܗܐ ܗܘ ܒܝܢ ܐܘܪܚܬܗ *God has shown us His ways,* Job xxviii. 23. ETHPA. ܐܬܒܝܢ *to notice, take notice of, regard, consider, understand, have discretion,* with ܒ or ܥܠ; pass. *to be tried, inquired into;* ܐܬܒܝܢܬ ܒܚܪܬܗܘܢ *I understood their end,* Ps. lxxiii. 16; ܐܬܒܝܢ ܕܝܢܗ *his cause was tried;* part. m. *understanding, discreet, considerate.* DERIVATIVES, ܒܘܝܢܐ, ܡܒܝܢ, ܡܒܝܢܐ, ܡܬܒܝܢܐ, ܡܬܒܝܢܘܬܐ.

ܒܘܢܐ *a ball, globule;* ܒܘ̈ܢܐ ܕܩܝܪܐ *balls of wax;* ܒܘܢܝܐ dim. *a little ball, pellet.*

ܒܘܒܘܢܘܣ or ܒܘܒܘܢܘܣ βουβῶνες, *a swelling* or *sore in the groin.*

ܒܘܝܐ *congratulation, rejoicing, the leading home of a bride.*

ܒܘܣܐ a) *base, foot, candlestick.* b)=ܒܘܣܐ.

ܒܘܣܩܣ, ܒܘܣܩܐ pl. ܒܘܣ̈ܩܐ m. *being torn* or *rent in pieces, laceration.*

ܒܘܣܛܪܢ basterna, *a closed litter.*

ܒܘܣܡܐ pl. ܒܘܣ̈ܡܐ m. *gladness, delight, felicity; a banquet;* pl. *delights, pleasures;* ܡ̈ܠܐ ܕܒܘܣܡܐ *sweet* or *kind words.*

ܒܘܣܪܐ pl. ܒܘܣ̈ܪܐ m. *contempt, confuting.*

ܒܘܣܬܢܐ m. Pers. *a garden;* ܒܘܣܬܢܝܬܐ f. dim. *a little garden.*

ܒܘܬ only found in Pa. or Aph. part. ܡܒܘܬ *to delay, hinder, put off.* DERIVATIVE, ܒܘܬܐ.

ܒܘܥܒܥܐ *saliva from the mouth of one possessed with a devil.*

ܒܘܥܛܐ m. rt. ܒܥܛ. *kicking, knocking, stroke.*

ܒܘܥܛܬܐ pl. ܒܘܥ̈ܛܬܐ f. *kick, knock, blow.*

ܒܘܥܝܐ pl. ܒܘܥ̈ܝܐ m. rt. ܒܥܐ. *wallowing* or *tumbling on the ground.*

ܒܘܥܪܐ m. rt. ܒܥܪ. *gleaning grapes* or *corn.*

ܒܘܥܬܐ rt. ܒܥܬ. m. *fear, terror, punishment.*

ܒܘܨܐ m. byssus, *fine white linen;* hence is derived

ܒܘܨܝܐ f. ܒܘܨܝܬܐ adj. *of fine white linen.*

ܒܘܨܝܢܐ ܒܘܨܝܢ pl. ܐ̈ m. dim. of ܒܘܨܐ. *a) a wick,* hence *a lamp, a light. b) verbascum thapsus,* a plant from which wicks were prepared. *c) cucumis anguinus.*

ܒܘܨܪ, ܒܘܨܪܐ pl. ܒܘܨܪ̈ܐ rt. ܒܨܪ. m. *failing, lessening, waning* of the moon; *mistake, defect, omission* in a manuscript; *fault;* ܒܘܨܪ ܕܡܐ *letting of blood;* ܕܠܐ ܒܘܨܪ *without omission, fully;* ܕܠܐ ܬܘܣܦܬܐ ܘܒܘܨܪ *neither more nor less.*

ܒܘܨܪ, ܒܘܨܪܐ f. *a) Bosra* or *Bostra,* the capital of Arabia Petraea. *b)* = ܒܨܪܐ *Bassora* on the Tigris, below Baghdad.

ܒܘܩܝܐ m. rt. ܒܩܐ. *trial, proof, experience;* with ܢܣܒ *to try, prove, make trial of.*

ܒܘܩܝܢܐ m. rt. ܒܩܐ. *trial, inquiry, examination by torture.*

ܒܘܩܠܐ pl. ܐ̈ m. *a)* baculum, *a staff, cudgel. b)* bucolicus, *a pastoral poet. c) the germ before the seed has sprouted.*

ܒܘܩܠܠܪܝܘ buccellarii, *body-guards.*

ܒܘܩܠܛܘܢ buccellatum, *soldiers' bread.*

ܒܘܪ fut. ܢܒܘܪ, part. act. ܒܐܪ, ܒܝܪܐ. *to lie uncultivated, waste, neglected;* metaph. ܐܬܪܗ ܕܚܟܡܬܐ ܒܝܪܐ ܗܘܐ *the domain of wisdom was unreclaimed; to be devoid, dismayed, confused;* ܒܐܪ ܐܢܐ ܡܢ ܒܘܝܐܐ *I am left without comfort, in dismay.* Aph. ܐܒܝܪ *to leave uncultivated, lay waste.* Ethpauel ܐܬܒܘܪ *to be amazed, confused.* Derivatives, ܒܝܪܐ, ܒܘܪܐ, ܒܘܪܐ, ܒܘܪܝܘܬܐ, ܒܝܪܐ.

ܒܘܪܐ pl. ܒܘܪ̈ܐ m. ܒܘܪܬܐ, pl. ܒܘܪ̈ܬܐ f. rt. ܒܘܪ. *a waste;* ܒܘܪܐ ܕܟܘܒܐ *a thorny waste; simple, unlearned, foolish, rude;* ܒܘܪܐ ܒܡܠܬܐ *rude in speech.*

ܒܘܪܐܝܠܐ or ܒܘܪܐܝܠܝ *calumus aromaticus.*

ܒܘܪܐܝܬ adv. *ignorantly, without civilization.*

ܒܘܪܓܐ pl. ܒܘܪ̈ܓܐ m. πύργος, *a tower, turret; a pigeon-cote, pigeon-turret;* astron. *a sign of the zodiac;* ܬܪܥܣܪ ܒܘܪ̈ܓܐ *the twelve signs.*

ܒܘܪܕܥܢܐ from the following. *Baradaeus,* a nickname of James, Bishop of Edessa A.D. 551, the leader of the Jacobites. He is said to have been so named from wearing a horse-cloth for his cloak.

ܒܘܪܕܥܬܐ f. oftener ܒܪܕܥܬܐ pl. irreg. ܒܘܪ̈ܕܥܐ. *a pack-saddle, saddle-cloth, horse-cloth, rags.*

ܒܘܪܘ, ܒܘܪܘܬܐ rt. ܒܘܪ. f. *a waste place; rudeness, ignorance;* ܨܠܘ ܥܠ ܒܘܪܘܬܝ *pray for me a rough ignorant man.*

ܒܘܪܝܐ pl. ܐ̈, ܬܐ or ܬܐ f. *mats made of split reeds* or *rushes.*

ܒܘܪܝܐ *a)* Chald. *holiness, purity. b) distance, remoteness. c)* for ܒܘܪܩ *borax.*

ܒܘܪܟ, ܒܘܪܟܐ rt. ܒܪܟ. m. *a blessing, benediction;* esp. rit. ܒܘܪܟ ܡܝܐ *the Blessing of the Waters* at the Feast of the Epiphany; ܒܘܪܟ ܣܘܟܐ *the Blessing of the Branches* on Palm Sunday; ܕܚܒܠܐ and ܕܟܠܝܠܐ *the Blessing of the Ring* and *of the Crowns,* i.e. the chief parts of ܛܟܣܐ ܕܒܘܪܟܐ *the Order of Marriage.*

ܒܘܪܩܐ and ܒܘܪܩ m. Ar. *nitre, borax.*

ܒܘܪܟ, ܒܘܪܟܐ pl. ܐ̈ rt. ܒܪܟ. f. *the knee, kneeling, a genuflexion;* ܥܠ ܒܘܪ̈ܟܘܗܝ ܐܬܪܒܝܬ *I was brought up at his knees;* ܣܝܡ ܒܘܪ̈ܟܐ *kneeling, genuflexion;* ܒܪܟܘ ܒܘܪܟܐ ܚܕܐ *they made one genuflexion.*

ܒܘܪܟܬܐ pl. ܟܢ, ܟܬܐ rt. ܒܪܟ. f. *a blessing;* often with ܕ as adj., ܡܛܪܐ ܕܒܘܪܟܬܐ *blessed rain.* Metaph. *bounty, a gift, present;* ܗܒ ܠܝ ܡܕܡ ܒܘܪܟܬܐ *give me somewhat for a present;* ܦܠܓܘ ܒܘܪܟܬܗ ܠܟܠܗ ܥܡܐ *they distributed his bounty to all the people;* ܡܫܘܬܦܐ ܕܒܘܪܟܬܐ ܗܘ ܐܪ̈ܙܢܝܬܐ *he is a partaker of the sacramental gift.*

ܒܘܪܢܝܐ pl. ܐ̈ m. *a stone jar;* ܕܦܚܪܐ *a crock, earthen jar.*

ܒܘܪܢܫܐ from ܒܪܢܫܐ. *the incarnation, the taking of human nature.*

ܒܘܪܣܝܐ pl. ܐ̈ m. ܒܘܪܣܝܬܐ, pl. ܝܬܐ f. βυρσεύς, *a tanner.*

ܒܘܪܣܝܘܬܐ f. *tanning.*

ܒܘܪܣܡܐ or ܒܘܪܣܡܐ m. pl. Pers. baresma, *a bundle of date, pomegranate,* or *tamarisk twigs,* held by Magian priests or worshippers during service.

ܒܘܪܣ, ܒܘܪܣܐ and ܒܘܪܣܘܢ; see ܒܘܪܩܐ *borax.*

ܒܘܫܠܐ pl. ܐ̈ rt. ܒܫܠ. m. *pottage, boiled* or *cooked food; digestion; the ripening* of fruit.

ܒܬ, ܒܐܬ fut. ܢܒܘܬ, imper. ܒܘܬ, inf. ܡܒܬ, part. ܒܐܬ, pl. ܒܝܬܝܢ probably denom. from ܒܝܬܐ. *to lodge, pass the night, remain all night;* with ܠܘܬ of the pers. and ܒ of the place; ܒܬܢ ܠܘܬܗ ܟܠܢ ܒܠܠܝܐ *we all stayed with him that night;* metaph. *to dwell quietly, lodge, stay;* ܢܦܫܗ ܒܛܒܬܐ ܬܒܘܬ *his soul shall dwell at ease,* Ps. xxv. 13. Aph. ܐܒܝܬ *to leave* or *to keep through the night,* hence *to withhold;* ܐܠܗܐ ܠܐ ܡܒܝܬ ܐܓܪܟܘܢ *God will not keep back your wages;* cf. Lev. xix. 13. Derivative the following—

ܒܝܬܘܬܐ pl. ܬ̈ܐ, ܐ̈ m. *passing the night, a vigil;* ܒܬ ܒܝܬܘܬܐ ܒܠܠܝܐ ܗܘ *he kept vigil that night.*

ܒܙ fut. ܢܒܘܙ, imper. ܒܘܙ, inf. ܡܒܙ, act. p. ܒܐܙ, pl. ܒܐܙܝܢ or ܒܙܝܢ, pass. p. ܒܙܝܙ. *to spoil, take spoil, plunder;* ܒܙܘܗ ܟܠ ܕܐܝܬ ܠܗ *they despoiled him of everything.* Ethpe. ܐܬܒܙܝܙ *to be despoiled, pillaged;* ܐܬܒܙܝܙܬ ܡܕܝܢܬܐ *the city was pillaged;* metaph. ܘܐܬܒܙܙ ܠܠܝܐ ܒܫܗܪܐ *to rob the night by vigils.* Pa. ܒܙܙ *to plunder with violence.* Aph. ܐܒܙ *to spoil, despise.* Palpel ܒܙܒܙ *to waste, seize again and again.* Ethpalpel ܐܬܒܙܒܙ pass. Derivatives, ܒܙܘܙܐ, ܒܙܘܙܘܬܐ, ܒܙܘܙܝܐ, ܒܙܐ, ܒܙܝܙܘܬܐ, ܒܙܬܐ, ܡܒܙܙܢܐ, ܡܒܙܙܢܘܬܐ.

ܒܙܐ pl. ܐ̈ m. Ar. *a teat, pap, nipple;* ܒܙ̈ܐ ܓܘܝܝܐ *the inner teguments of the paps;* ܒܙ̈ܐ ܕܟܠܒܐ *dogs' paps, the sebestena* or *myxae,* a medicinal plant.

ܒܙܘܙ, ܒܙܘܙܐ pl. ܐ̈ m. ܒܙܘܙܬܐ pl. ܬ̈ܐ f. rt. ܒܙ. *a spoiler, destroyer;* Thou, O Lord, ܠܒܙܘܙܢ ܒܙܬ *hast spoiled our spoiler.*

ܒܙܘܙܘ, ܒܙܘܙܘܬܐ rt. ܒܙ. f. *robbery, rapacity.*

ܒܙܘܙܝܐ pl. ܐ̈ rt. ܒܙ. m. *plundering, pillage;* ܡܫܡܗܐ ܒܩܛܠܐ ܘܒܒܙܘܙܝܐ *famous for murder and pillage.*

ܒܙܘܥܐ rt. ܒܙܥ. m. *a piercer, one who bores holes,* e. g. in pearls.

ܒܙܙܐ pl. ܐ̈ m. Ar. *a mercer, linen-draper;* ܫܘܩܐ ܕܒܙܙ̈ܐ *the silk-market.*

ܒܙܐ m. ܒܙܬܐ f. rt. ܒܙ. *spoiling, plundering.*

ܒܙܚ Pa. ܒܙܚ, part. act. and pass. ܡܒܙܚ, ܡܒܙܚܐ, pl. m. ܡܒܙܚܝܢ. *to mock, scoff at, insult; to ravish;* generally with ܒ, sometimes ܠ; ܒܙܚܘ ܢܫ̈ܐ *they ravished the women.* Ethpa. ܐܬܒܙܚ *to be scoffed at, put to shame;* Herod ܐܬܒܙܚ ܡܢ ܡܓܘܫ̈ܐ *was mocked by the Magi.* Derivatives, ܒܙܚܐ, ܒܘܙܚܐ, ܡܒܙܚܢܐ.

ܒܙܚܐ pl. ܒܙܚ̈ܐ m. rt. ܒܙܚ. *mocking, disgrace, reproach, shameful language;* ܥܒܕ ܐܢܘܢ ܒܙܚܐ *he made them a laughing-stock;* ܒܒܙܚܐ *delusively.*

ܒܙܝܙܘ, ܒܙܝܙܘܬܐ f. rt. ܒܙ. *being plundered, pillaged.*

ܒܙܩܐ and ܒܘܙܩܐ pl. ܐ̈ m. *hawk, falcon.*

ܒܙܩܝܪܐ m. *a falconer.*

ܒܙܥ fut. ܢܒܙܘܥ, inf. ܡܒܙܥ, act. part. ܒܐܙܥ, ܒܐܙܥܐ, pass. part. ܒܙܝܥ ܒܙܝܥܐ *to cleave, break, pierce* or *bore through; to penetrate;* ܒܙܥ ܠܗ *it pierces his hand;* ܒܙܥ ܠܫܪܝܢܗ *broke through* his *cuirass;* ܐܐܪ ܒܐܙܥܐ an arrow or a bird *cleaves the air;* with ܒ of the instrument. Ethpe. ܐܬܒܙܥ *to be pierced through.* Pa. ܒܙܥ *to cut* or *scratch deeply, rend* or *pierce through and through; to burst through;* ܐܙܩܐ ܡܒܙܥܝܢ *rent* or *burst wine-skins.* Ethpa. ܐܬܒܙܥ *to burst open, be driven asunder, be broken up;* ܥܢܢܐ ܡܬܒܙܥܐ *a cloud is rifted, dispersed.* Derivatives, ܒܘܙܥܐ, ܒܙܥܐ, ܡܒܙܥܢܐ.

ܒܙܥ, ܒܙܥܐ rt. ܒܙܥ. m. *a rent, cleft, opening;* ܒܙܥܐ ܕܛܘܪܐ *a cleft in the mountain.*

ܒܙܪ *to scatter, sow.* Pa. ܒܙܪ the same.

ܒܙܪܩܐ pl. ܐ̈ rt. ܒܙܪ. m. *a small pebble,* smaller than ܟܐܦܐ or ܟܠܟܐ; *a wart;* pl. *chips.*

ܒܙܪܩܘܢܐ pl. ܐ̈ m. dim. of ܒܙܪܩܐ. *tiny pebble.*

ܒܙܪܐ = ܐܦܘܕܐ *a receipt.*

ܒܙܬ, ܒܙܬܐ pl. ܒܙ̈ܬܐ f. rt. ܒܙ. *prey, spoil; robbery, spoiling;* ܒܙܬܐ ܕܡܣܟܢ̈ܐ *robbery of the poor.*

ܒܙܬܐ fem. of ܒܙܐ *pap, breast.*

ܒܚܘܪܐ pl. ܐ̈ m. *assayer* of metals, *trier* of the heart, the thoughts; *one who weighs, examines;* adj. *that which tries, tests.*

ܒܚܘܪܘܬܐ f. rt. ܒܚܪ. *trial, searching out.*

ܒܚܝܪܐܝܬ rt. ܒܚܪ. adv. *carefully, accurately, skilfully;* ܒܚܝܪܐܝܬ ܫܕܝܢ ܒܩܫܬܐ *they are skilful archers;* ܛܒ ܒܚܝܪܐܝܬ ܐܬܬܪܓܡ *it was most accurately translated.*

ܒܚܝܪܘܬܐ rt. ܒܚܪ. f. *test, trial.*

ܒܚܝܫܘܬܐ rt. ܒܚܫ. f. *wantonness, lustfulness.*

ܒܚܢ fut. ܢܒܚܢ, inf. ܠܡܒܚܢ *to test* metal; *to try, test.* Pa. ܒܚܢ *to try, test* metal; *to examine, dispute;* ܡܒܚܢܝܢ ܠܦܪܚܬܐ *observing a bird* for augury; ܠܡܒܚܢܘ ܣܘܥܪܢܐ *to test actions.* Ethpa. ܐܬܒܚܢ *to be tried, proved, examined; to investigate* judicially. Derivatives, ܒܘܚܢܐ, ܡܒܚܢܢܐܝܬ, ܡܒܚܢܢܐ, ܡܒܚܢܢܘܬܐ.

ܒܚܪ fut. ܢܒܚܘܪ and ܢܒܚܪ, imp. ܒܚܘܪ, inf. ܡܒܚܪ, act. part. ܒܚܪ, ܒܚܪܐ, pass. part. ܒܚܝܪ, ܒܚܝܪܐ. *to try, prove* as silver by fire; metaph. *to examine, observe,* as ܠܒܐ, ܟܘܠܝܬܐ, ܡܚܫܒܬܐ *the heart, the reins, the thoughts;* ܐܕܢܐ ܒܚܪܐ ܡܠܐ *the ear tries words;* pass. part. *tried, approved, accurate; expert, renowned;* with ܠܐ *base, rejected, inaccurate;* ܨܚܚܐ ܒܚܝܪܐ *a tested* or *accurate copy* of a MS.; ܡܠܦܢܐ ܒܚܝܪܐ *an approved* or *renowned teacher;* impers. ܒܚܝܪܐ ܠܗ *it was proved, ascertained.* Ethpe. ܐܬܒܚܪ *to be tried;* with ܒ *in, by* or *concerning;* ܐܬܒܚܪܬ ܒܡܣܟܢܘܬܐ *thou art tried by poverty;* impers. *to be proved, ascertained;* with ܠ and pers. pron. *to prove himself to be;* ܬܬܒܚܪ ܠܟ *thou shalt be proved capable.* Ethpa. ܐܬܒܚܪ *to be tried, proved.* Derivatives, ܒܚܘܪܐ, ܒܚܘܪܘܬܐ, ܒܚܝܪܐܝܬ, ܒܚܝܪܘܬܐ, ܒܘܚܪܢܐ.

ܒܚܫ and ܒܚܫ fut. ܢܒܚܘܫ and ܢܒܚܫ, imp. ܒܚܘܫ and ܒܚܫ, act. part. ܒܚܫ, ܒܚܫܐ, pass. part. ܒܚܝܫܐ, ܒܚܝܫܬܐ *to stir, shake, agitate;* ܒܚܫ ܦܟܐ *to stir the jaws* = to eat; *to move quickly, hasten;* ܒܚܫܢ ܕܢܩܘܡ ܠܬܫܡܫܬܐ *we hastened to arise for service;* metaph. *to excite with desire.* Pa. ܒܚܫ *to stir up, incite;* ܒܚܫܬܗ ܚܘܐ ܠܐܕܡ *Eve incited Adam.* Aph. ܐܒܚܫ *to stir* or *shake thoroughly.* Derivatives, ܒܚܫܐ, ܒܚܝܫܘܬܐ, ܒܘܚܫܐ.

ܒܚܫܐ *the front of a shirt.*

ܒܚܫܐ m. rt. ܒܚܫ. *stirring, shaking.*

ܒܛܐ pl. ܒܛܐ. m. *a duck* or *drake.*

ܒܛܐ pl. ܒܛܐ m. *sparks* from red-hot coals or from iron.

ܒܛܘܒܛܐ no sing. *military roads* or *journeys.*

ܒܛܘܣ or ܒܐܛܘܣ βάτος, rubus fruticosus, *the bramble.*

ܒܛܘܝܬܐ pl. f. perhaps of ܒܐܛܝܐ *a bowl* or *wine-vessel,* or of ܒܛܝܬܐ.

ܒܛܝܚܐ perhaps Ar. *a small round melon.*

ܒܛܝܠܐܝܬ rt. ܒܛܠ. adv. *carefully, accurately, diligently, instantly.*

ܒܛܝܠܐܝܬ rt. ܒܛܠ. adv. *in vain, idly.*

ܒܛܝܠܘܬܐ rt. ܒܛܠ. f. *care, forethought, diligence;* with ܒ, *diligently, carefully.* ܣܡ ܒܛܝܠܘܬܐ ܠܘܬ *to endeavour, give oneself up to.* ܒܛܝܠܘܬܐ ܐܠܗܝܬܐ *Divine Providence,* sometimes ellipt., ܡܠܐܟܐ ܕܒܛܝܠܘܬܐ *a guardian angel.*

ܒܛܝܢܘܬܐ rt. ܒܛܢ. f. *conception;* ܒܛܢܘܬܐ is more commonly used.

ܒܛܝܬܐ f. *a wine-jar.*

ܒܛܠ fut. ܢܒܛܘܠ, inf. ܡܒܛܠ, act. part. ܒܛܠ, ܒܛܠܐ, pass. part. ܒܛܝܠ and ܒܛܝܠ, ܠܐ, ܠܬܐ. *a) to cease work, be idle, at leisure; to come to an end, come to nought, fail; to be void, of no effect; to cease,* especially with ܡܢ *from,* ܝܗܘܕܝܐ ܒܛܠܝܢ ܚܕܐ ܒܫܬܐ ܝܘܡܝܢ *the Jews ceased work once in six days.* If two bishops are consecrated to one see, ܗܘ ܩܕܡܝܐ ܢܫܡܫ ܘܐܚܪܢܐ ܢܒܛܘܠ *he who is prior shall serve, and* the consecration of *the other be void.* *b) to take care of, attend to;* pass. part. 1) impers. with ܠ and pers. pron. *it concerned,* hence *to care, be concerned,* ܥܠ *about, for; to be addicted to,* with ܒ, ܠ, or ܠܘܬ. 2) adj. usually in the old form ܒܛܝܠ *void, obsolete, of no effect, unavailing, vain, unprofitable, idle, unoccupied, out of employment;* ܡܐܢܐ ܒܛܝܠܐ *an empty vessel;* ܣܒܪܐ ܒܛܝܠܐ *a vain hope;* ܝܪܚܐ ܒܛܝܠܐ *months without lawsuits;* rit. *common.* Ethpe. ܐܬܒܛܠ impers. with ܠ and pers. pron., with ܕ or ܥܠ of the object, *to care, take care of, attend to; to be concerned, careful, diligent;* ܬܠܡܝܕܐ ܗܘܘ ܡܬܒܛܠܝܢ ܥܠ ܟܢܫܐ *the disciples were concerned about the multitude; to idle, trifle away time.* Pa. ܒܛܠ *to cause to cease, bring to nought* or *to an end, withdraw from, remove;* ܬܒܰܛܠܽܘܢ ܚܡܺܝܪܳܐ ܡܶܢ ܒܳܬܰܝܟܽܘܢ *ye shall put away leaven from your houses; to make void, useless, of no effect, to abolish, abrogate; to desist, leave off.* Ethpa. ܐܶܬ݁ܒܰܛܰܠ *to cease, fail, have nothing to do with, leave off; to be vain, be brought to nought.* Derivatives, ܒܛܠܐ, ܒܛܺܝܠܳܐܝܬ݂, ܒܛܳܠܳܐ, ܒܛܳܠܬ݂ܳܐ, ܒܘܼܛܳܠܳܐ, ܒܛܶܠܬ݂ܳܐ, ܡܒܰܛܠܳܢܳܐ, ܡܒܰܛܠܳܢܽܘܬ݂ܳܐ.

ܒܰܛܺܝܠ, ܒܰܛܺܝܠܳܐ m. ܒܰܛܺܝܠܳܐ, ܒܰܛܺܝܠܬ݂ܳܐ f.; pl. m. ܒܰܛܺܝܠܺܝܢ, ܒܰܛܺܝܠܶܐ, f. ܒܰܛܺܝܠܳܢ, ܒܰܛܺܝܠܳܬ݂ܳܐ rt. ܒܛܠ. adj. *idle, vain, empty.*

ܒܘܼܛܠܳܐ pl. ܒܘܼܛܠܶܐ. m. *a carved ornament* in Solomon's temple.

ܒܰܛܺܝܠܳܐܝܬ݂ rt. ܒܛܠ. adv. *without any object, needlessly.*

ܒܛܳܠܳܐ, ܒܛܳܠܳܢ rt. ܒܛܠ. m. *suspension of labour,* especially on holy days, *loss of time through illness; leisure, idleness.*

ܒܶܛܡܬ݂ܳܐ, ܒܶܛܡܳܐ f. *the oak, terebinth;* pl. ܒܶܛܡܶܐ *terebinth-berries.*

ܒܛܶܢ fut. ܢܶܒܛܰܢ, act. part. ܒܳܛܶܢ, ܒܳܛܢܳܐ, pass. part. ܒܛܺܝܢ, ܒܛܺܝܢܳܐ, ܒܛܺܝܢܬ݂ܳܐ. *to conceive, be with child, bear;* metaph. ܓܰܪܒܝܳܐ ܒܳܛܢܳܐ ܡܶܛܪܳܐ *the north wind is heavy with rain.* Ethpe. ܐܶܬ݂ܒܛܶܢ imper. ܐܶܬ݂ܒܛܰܢ and Ethpa. ܐܶܬ݂ܒܰܛܰܢ *to be conceived;* metaph. ܐܶܬ݂ܒܛܶܢܰܬ݂ ܡܶܠܬ݂ܳܐ ܒܗ̇ ܒܠܶܒܳܗ̇ *the Word was conceived in her heart.* Pa. *to engender, breed.* Derivatives, ܒܶܛܢܳܐ, ܒܛܺܝܢܽܘܬ݂ܳܐ, ܒܛܺܝܢܬ݂ܳܐ.

ܒܶܛܢܳܐ m. rt. ܒܛܢ. *conception;* metaph. ܒܶܛܢܰܝ ܚܶܡܬ݂ܳܐ *the conceptions of anger.*

ܒܛܺܝܢܳܐ, ܒܛܺܝܢܬ݂ܳܐ pl. ܒܛܺܝܢܳܢ ܒܛܺܝܢܳܬ݂ܳܐ rt. ܒܛܢ. adj. f. *pregnant, with child.*

ܒܛܺܝܢܽܘܬ݂ܳܐ rt. ܒܛܢ. f. *conception.*

ܒܰܝ contracted form of ܒܰܝܬ݂ܳܐ *house;* ܡܶܢ ܒܰܝ ܠܒܰܝ *from house to house.*

ܒܰܝܳܐ E-Syr. ܒܰܝܺܝ Pa. *to console, comfort;* fut. ܢܒܰܝܶܐ or ܢܒܰܝܳܐ, imp. ܒܰܝܳܐ, inf. ܠܡܒܰܝܳܝܽܘ or ܠܡܒܰܝܳܝܽܘܬ݂ܶܗ, ܠܡܒܰܝܳܝܽܘܬ݂ܳܐ, pres. part. ܡܒܰܝܶܐ or ܡܒܰܝܳܐ, f. ܡܒܰܝܳܐ pl. m. ܡܒܰܝܶܐܝܢ. One Olaph is kept in all the inflections and with affixes. Ethpa. ܐܶܬ݂ܒܰܝܳܐ fut. ܢܶܬ݂ܒܰܝܶܐ and ܢܶܬ݂ܒܰܝܳܐ, inf. ܠܡܶܬ݂ܒܰܝܳܝܽܘ or ܠܡܶܬ݂ܒܰܝܳܝܽܘܬ݂ܶܗ, imper. s. m. ܐܶܬ݂ܒܰܝܳܐ f. ܐܶܬ݂ܒܰܝܳܝ pl. m. ܐܶܬ݂ܒܰܝܳܘ f. ܐܶܬ݂ܒܰܝܳܝܶܝܢ and ܐܶܬ݂ܒܰܝܳܝܢ, part. ܡܶܬ݂ܒܰܝܳܐ pl. ܡܶܬ݂ܒܰܝܶܐܝܢ *to be comforted, receive comfort.* Derivatives, ܒܘܝܳܐ, ܒܘܝܳܝܳܐ, ܡܒܰܝܳܝܳܐ.

ܒܰܝܒܳܬ݂ܳܐ f. pl. *small watercourses;* cf. ܐܒܘܒܳܐ.

ܒܺܝܒܠܺܝܘܬ݂ܺܝܩܺܝ pl. ܒܺܝܒܠܺܝܘܬ݂ܺܝܩܶܐ, ܒܺܝܒܠܺܝܘܢ, ܒܺܝܒܠܺܝܘܢܶܐ *bibliotheca, library.*

ܒܝܰܕ *through, by means of;* see ܝܰܕ.

ܒܰܝܙܶܩ Paiel conj. of ܒܙܩ. Ethpaial ܐܶܬ݂ܒܰܝܙܰܩ *to play the fool, totter, stagger;* ܡܒܰܝܙܰܩ ܗ̄ܘܳܐ ܥܰܠ ܬܰܪܥܶܐ *he scrabbled.*

ܒܺܝܛܳܢܳܐ *a woollen tunic.*

ܒܺܝܟܺܝܘܢ βήχιον, *coltsfoot.*

ܒܺܝܠ or ܒܶܝܠ *a) Bel,* the supreme deity of the Babylonians. *b)* the planet *Jupiter; tin.*

ܒܺܝܠܠܳܘܣ βίλλος, *a bill, notice.*

ܒܺܝܠܕܳܪܳܐ or ܒܺܝܠܰܕܳܪܳܐ deriv. Pers. m. *a letter-carrier, courier.*

ܒܶܝܠܳܢܺܝܕܳܘܣ *the inner bark of the acorn.*

ܒܺܝܠܬ݂ܺܝ or ܒܶܝܠܬ݂ܺܝ f. the planet *Venus; copper.*

ܒܺܝܡܳܐ f. ܒܶܝܡܳܐ, ܒܺܝܡ pl. ܒܶܝܡܶܐ, ܒܶܝܡܳܬ݂ܳܐ, ܒܺܝܡܘܣ βῆμα. *a) the judgement-seat. b) a bishop's throne;* ܒܺܝܡ ܡܫܺܝܚܳܐ ܐܰܢܛܺܝܘܟܳܝܳܐ *the glorious throne = see, of Antioch. c) a part of a church, the space between the sanctuary and the nave.*

ܒܰܝܶܢ Pa. of ܒܝܢ; *to discern, make discern.*

ܒܰܝܢܳܬ݂, ܒܶܝܢܳܬ݂ rt. ܒܝܢ. prep. (the form ܒܶܝܢܳܬ݂ takes the pron. affixes of a noun in the sing., ܒܰܝܢܰܝ those of a noun in the pl. In construction with another noun the form ܒܶܝܢܳܬ݂ is most often used; see ܒܶܝܢ the commonest form of all). *between, among, within, in the midst.* Often used with ܠ and ܡܶܢ of direction to and from, where in English it is not needed, ܡܶܢ ܒܶܝܢܳܬ݂ ܥܶܣܒܳܐ *among the grass,* Isa. xliv. 4; so with ܠ acc., e.g. ܒܰܝܢܰܝ ܠܟܰܪܡܺܝ *between me and my vineyard.* Idioms, ܒܰܝܢܰܝ, ܒܰܝܢܳܝ &c. used with ܠ and a pron. suff. *particularly, privately,* German *unter vier Augen;* ܒܰܝܢܰܝ ܘܰܠܟ݂ *between me and thee;* with ܠܢܰܦܫܶܗ, ܠܢܰܦܫܳܟ݂ &c. *within thyself, himself, in thy, in his heart,* &c.; ܒܰܝܢܰܝܢ ܠܢܰܦܫܰܢ ܡܶܬ݂ܚܰܫܒܺܝܢܰܢ *we think in* or *to ourselves.*

ܒܝܳܢܩܬ݂ܳܐ pl. ܒܝܳܢܩܳܬ݂ܳܐ f. *a phial, vessel, jug, pot.*

ܒܺܝܢܬ݂ܳܐ or ܒܺܝܬ݂ܳܐ pl. ܒܺܝܢܳܬ݂ܳܐ, ܒܺܝܢܝܳܢ or ܒܺܝܢܝܳܐ,

ܒܶܥܬ݂ܳܐ f. *egg;* ܒܶ̈ܥܐ ܬܰܪ̈ܬܶܝ ܚܶܠܡܳܘ̈ܳܬܳܐ *eggs with double yolks.* Metaph. *the top of an arch; the crown of the head; testicle;* the form of pl. ܒܶ̈ܥܐ is used of eggs, ܒܶ̈ܥܬܳܐ in the other meanings.

ܒܶܥܬܳܢܳܝܳܐ or ܒܶܥܬܳܝܳܐ f. ܒܶܥܬܳܢܳܝܬܳܐ or ܒܶܥܬܳܝܬܳܐ adj. *eggshaped, arched.*

ܒܽܘܪܳܐ m. ܒܽܘܪܬܳܐ f. rt. ܒܘܪ. adj. *barren, uncultivated, unsown.*

ܒܽܘܪܽܘ, ܒܽܘܪܽܘܬ݂ܳܐ f. rt. ܒܘܪ. *barrenness.*

ܒܺܝܪܽܘܣ, ܒܺܝܪܽܘܣܳܐ m. βηρίον = birrus, *a mitre* or *cloak*, esp. of a bishop; ܒܺܝܪܽܘܣܳܐ ܕܣܰܥܪܳܐ *a shaggy cloak.*

ܒܺܝܪܬܳܐ, ܒܺܝܪܬܳܐ or ܒܺܝܪܬܳܐ constr. ܒܺܝܪܰܬ pl. ܒܺܝܪ̈ܳܬܳܐ f. *a palace, castle, court, camp.*

ܒܺܝܫ, ܒܺܝܫܳܐ f. ܒܺܝܫܳܐ, ܒܺܝܫܬܳܐ pl. m. ܒܺܝܫܺܝܢ, ܒܺܝܫ̈ܶܐ f. ܒܺܝܫܳܢ, ܒܺܝܫ̈ܳܬܳܐ rt. ܒܐܫ. *bad, evil;* ܡܰܘܬܳܐ ܒܺܝܫܳܐ *a cruel death;* ܫܽܘܚܢܳܐ ܒܺܝܫܳܐ *a malignant ulcer; sad, unfortunate* or *unlucky;* ܒܺܝܫ ܓܰܕܳܐ *unlucky; the Evil One;* ܒܺܝܫܳܐ ܘܡܰܫܪܝܳܬܶܗ *the Evil One and his hosts.* Fem. used as subst. *evil, wickedness, misfortune;* ܥܳܒ̈ܕܰܝ ܒܺܝܫ̈ܳܬܳܐ *evil-doers;* ܒܺܝܫ ܒܺܝܫ *very badly;* ܒܺܝܫ ܒܺܝܫ ܚܠܺܝܫ *diseased.*

ܒܺܝܫܳܐ pl. ܒܺܝ̈ܫܶܐ rt. ܒܐܫ. m. *poor; a poor man.*

ܒܺܝܫܳܐܺܝܬ adv. *wickedly.*

ܒܺܝܫܽܘܬ݂ܳܐ f. *evil, harm; wickedness, envy;* ܒܺܝܫܽܘܬ ܐܰܦ̈ܶܐ, ܒܺܝܫܽܘܬ ܠܶܒܳܐ &c. *sadness;* ܒܺܝܫܽܘܬ ܓܰܕܳܐ *ill-luck;* ܒܺܝܫܽܘܬ ܡܰܘܕܥܳܢܽܘܬܳܐ *wrong opinion, heterodoxy.*

ܒܶܝܬ pl. ܒܶܝܬܺܝܢ *Beth*, the second letter of the alphabet; *two* or *second;* see ܒ.

ܒܰܝܬܳܐ, ܒܶܝܬ pl. ܒܳܬܶܐ, ܒܳܬܺܝܢ constr. ܒܳܬܰܝ f. rt. ܒܘܬ. *a house; room; temple* or *church,* generally with the name ܒܶܝܬ ܡܳܪܬܝ ܡܰܪܝܰܡ *St. Mary's Church;* metaph. *family,* hence *a nation, race, people;* astron. *mansion;* rit. *a verse of a hymn, versicle, short hymn, introit,* ܒܳܬܶܐ ܕܥܪܘܒܬܐ *versicles used in the services of Good Friday.* ܒܶܝܬ is often used to form compound nouns: *a*) names of places, as ܒܶܝܬ ܐܝܠ *Bethel,* ܒܶܝܬ ܠܰܚܡ *Bethlehem,* &c.; of countries, as ܒܶܝܬ ܐܳܬܽܘܪ̈ܳܝܶܐ *Assyria;* ܒܶܝܬ ܡܶܨܪ̈ܳܝܶܐ *Egypt. b*) to mean those belonging to or associated with in any way, *companions, followers,* especially with ܕ, as ܕܒܶܝܬ ܐܰܠܳܗܳܐ *the faithful, the servants of God;* ܕܒܶܝܬ ܝܰܘ̈ܢܳܝܶܐ *the Greeks;* ܕܒܶܝܬ ܡܺܝܟܳܐܝܶܠ *the archangels;* ܕܒܶܝܬ ܢܽܘܚ *the men of Noah's age;* ܕܒܶܝܬ ܥܶܠܺܝ *Eli and his sons;* ܕܒܶܝܬ ܦܬܠܡܐܘܣ *the army, the dynasty of the Ptolemies.* Sometimes without ܕ, especially the names of sects, as ܒܶܝܬ ܐܰܪܺܝܳܘܣ *the Arians;* ܒܶܝܬ ܦܰܘܠܳܐ *the followers of Paul of Samosata. c*) the place where anything is to be found, kept or done. The gender of these compound nouns often agrees with the second part. Instances where ܒܶܝܬ is best translated *place* or *house* are not given in the following list. The prep. ܒ is rarely found before ܒܶܝܬ in construction with another noun, never before any word for prison; ܝܳܬܶܒ ܒܶܝܬ ܡܰܟܣܳܐ *sitting at the custom-house.* ܒܶܝܬ is sometimes redundant, as ܡܰܘܬܶܗ ܕܒܶܝܬ ܦܰܘܠܳܐ *the death of Paul.*

ܒܶܝܬ ܐܰܒܳܗܽܘܬܳܐ *the patriarchal house* or *see.*

ܒܶܝܬ ܐܝܠ *the house of God, Bethel.*

ܒܶܝܬ ܐܽܘܠܨܳܢܳܐ *house of correction.*

ܒܶܝܬ ܐܰܬܪܳܐ *the people of a town* or *country.*

ܒܶܝܬ ܐܰܣܺܝܪ̈ܶܐ *a prison.*

ܒܶܝܬ ܐܰܦܕܶܕܪܳܐ *a latrine, privy.*

ܒܶܝܬ ܐܰܪܟܶܐ or ܒܶܝܬ ܐܰܪܟܶܐ *archives, library.*

ܒܶܝܬ ܒܰܘܬܳܐ *a caravansary, lodging for the night.*

ܒܶܝܬ ܒܶܟܝܳܐ *wailing* for the dead, *lamentation.*

ܒܶܝܬ ܒܶܣܡ̈ܶܐ *a censer.*

ܒܶܝܬ ܓܰܘܣܳܐ *a refuge.*

ܒܶܝܬ ܓܰܙܳܐ *a treasury; the sanctuary* of a church; E-Syr. *a recess in the north wall of the sanctuary.*

ܒܶܝܬ ܓܰܢܽܘܢܳܐ *the bride-chamber.*

ܒܶܝܬ ܕܽܘܪܳܫܳܐ *a gymnasium, school.*

ܒܶܝܬ ܕܺܝܢܳܐ or ܒܶܝܬ ܕܺܝܢܳܐ *a tribunal, law-court.*

ܒܶܝܬ ܕܶܢܚܳܐ *Epiphany.*

ܒܶܝܬ ܕܳܪܫܳܐ; see ܒܶܝܬ ܕܽܘܪܳܫܳܐ.

ܒܶܝܬ ܗܰܠܟܳܐ or ܒܶܝܬ ܗܶܠܟܳܬܳܐ *a gallery, corridor.*

ܒܶܝܬ ܘܰܥܕܳܐ *a trysting-place; assembly.*

ܒܶܝܬ ܙܰܪܥܳܐ *a portion of land sown* or *fit for sowing.*

ܒܶܝܬ ܚܒܽܘܫܝܳܐ *a prison.*

ܒܶܝܬ ܚܙܳܘܳܐ *a tower, look-out.*

ܒܶܝܬ ܚܙܳܝܳܐ *a theatre.*

ܒܶܝܬ ܚܰܠܽܘܠܳܐ *a marriage-feast.*

ܒܝܬ ܡܫܬܝܐ *a banqueting-hall.*

ܒܝܬ ܛܒܚܐ *a kitchen.*

ܒܝܬ ܝܘܠܦܢܐ *a school.*

ܒܝܬ ܝܠܕܐ *birthday,* especially *the Nativity of Christ; a horoscope; the rising* of the sun or moon.

ܒܝܬ ܟܪܝܗܐ *hospital.*

ܒܝܬ ܠܚܡ *house of bread, Bethlehem.*

ܒܝܬ ܡܐܢܐ *a store-room.*

ܒܝܬ ܡܒܫܠܬܐ *a kitchen.*

ܒܝܬ ܡܩܒܪܬܐ *a cemetery.*

ܒܝܬ ܡܛܪܬܐ *a cellar.*

ܒܝܬ ܡܕܘܣܐ *a footprint.*

ܒܝܬ ܡܐܚܕ (ܐܝܕܐ *a hilt, handle.*

ܒܝܬ ܡܘܬܒܐ *a) a dwelling; b) session;* see under ܒܝܬ prep.

ܒܝܬ ܡܝ̈ܬܐ *the grave, Sheol.*

ܒܝܬ ܡܟܣܐ *a custom-house.*

ܒܝܬ ܡܠܟܐ *a palace.*

ܒܝܬ ܡܠܟܘܬܐ *kingdom, royal palace.*

ܒܝܬ ܡܣܡܟ *a prop, support.*

ܒܝܬ ܡܥܡܘܕܝܬܐ *baptistery.*

ܒܝܬ ܡܥܡܪܐ *habitation, house.*

ܒܝܬ ܡܩܕܫܐ *temple, sanctuary.*

ܒܝܬ ܡܚܙܐ *a fortress, castle.*

ܒܝܬ ܡܫܟܒܐ *a bedchamber.*

ܒܝܬ ܡܫܟܢܐ *tabernacle.*

ܒܝܬ ܡܫܪܝܐ *habitation, resting-place, lodging.*

ܒܝܬ ܡܫܩܝܐ *a place for watering cattle; a banquet.*

ܒܝܬ ܢܘܪܐ or ܢܘܪܬܐ *temple of fire; stove.*

ܒܝܬ ܢܛܘܪܬܐ *prison.*

ܒܝܬ ܢܫ̈ܐ *the harem, the women's apartments.*

ܒܝܬ ܣܗܕ̈ܐ *a church dedicated to* or *containing relics of martyrs.*

ܒܝܬ ܣܡܠܐ *those on the left hand, rejected at the Last Day.*

ܒܝܬ ܥܒܘܪܐ *barn, granary.*

ܒܝܬ ܟܬ̈ܒܐ *record-office.*

ܒܝܬ ܥܝ̈ܢܐ *the forehead.* ܒܝܬ here is a prep.; see below.

ܒܝܬ ܟܠܚܘܬܐ pl. ܒ̈ܬܐ ܕܟܠܚܘܬܐ *temple on a high place, temple of idols.*

ܒܝܬ ܩܒܘܪܐ *sepulchre.*

ܒܝܬ ܥܡܕܐ *baptistery.*

ܒܝܬ ܥܢܝܐ *Bethany, house of echo* or *answering.*

ܒܝܬ ܦ̈ܓܐ *Bethphage, house of figs.*

ܒܝܬ ܦܬܟܪ̈ܐ *temple of idols.*

ܒܝܬ ܦܘܪܣܐ *rendezvous, goal.*

ܒܝܬ ܨܝܕܐ *Bethsaida, place of the fisher.*

ܒܝܬ ܩܒܘܪܐ *sepulchre.*

ܒܝܬ ܩܘܕܫܐ *sanctuary.*

ܒܝܬ ܩܘܪܒܢܐ *treasury.*

ܒܝܬ ܪܥܝܐ *pasture, grazing-country.*

ܒܝܬ ܓܙܐ *store-room, barn.*

ܒܝܬ ܪܓܠܐ *stirrup.*

ܒܝܬ ܙܝܢܐ *armoury.*

ܒܝܬ ܪܚܝܐ *a mill.*

ܒܝܬ ܪܡܫܐ *evening, sunset.*

ܒܝܬ ܫܘܒܬܐ *the morrow after the sabbath.*

ܒܝܬ ܫܒܬܐ *synagogue; refectory.*

ܒܝܬ ܫܘܠܛܢ̈ܐ *dominions.*

ܒܝܬ ܫܩܝܐ *well-watered land.*

ܒܝܬ ܫܘܩܐ *fair, market.*

ܒܝܬ ܬܚܘܡ̈ܐ *the borders, marches.*

ܒܝܬ ܬܢܘܪܐ *bakehouse.*

ܒܝܬ ܬܪܥܐ *porch, vestibule;* cf. below.

Derivatives, ܒܝܬܐ, ܒܝܬܝܐ, ܒܝܬܝܐܝܬ, ܒܝܬܝܘܬܐ, ܒܝܬܝܬܐ, ܒܝܬ verb, ܒܝܬܘܬܐ, ܒܝܬܘܬܐ, ܡܒܝܬܢܐ, ܡܒܝܬܢܘܬܐ.

ܒܝܬ contracted from ܒܝܢܬ; see ܒܝܢ rt. ܒܝܬ. prep. *between, among, at, while, whilst;* ܒܝܬ—ܒܝܬ, ܒܝܬ—ܠܒܝܬ, ܒܝܢܬ—ܠܒܝܢܬ &c. *between—and;* ܒܝܬ ܐܠܗܐ ܠܒܝܬ ܟܠ ܢܦܫܐ ܚܝܬܐ *the covenant between God and every living creature,* Gen. ix. 16, cf. ver. 17; ܡܢ ܒܝܬ *from, from among, out of;* often with ܠ, ܒܝܬ ܡܝ̈ܬܐ *half-dead;* ܒܝܬ ܫܢܬܐ ܠܡܫܬܗܪ *half-asleep;* ܒܝܬ ܪܓܠܐ ܠܦܪ̈ܫܐ *between infantry and cavalry;* with ܠ twice, ܒܝܬ ܠܝ ܘܠܟ *between me and thee;* ܐܢܫ ܒܝܬ ܠܢܦܫܗ *each to himself;* ܒܝܬ ܠܗ ܠܢܦܫܗ *by* or *to himself;* ܒܝܬ ܐܝܕܝ *by, by the help of* (see ܐܝܕ); ܒܝܬ ܒܝܬܐ *from house to house;* ܒܝܬ ܡܘܬܒܐ *collects said during the singing of the* ܡܘܬܒܐ, at Nocturns; ܒܝܬ ܢܗܪ̈ܝܢ *Mesopotamia;* ܒܝܬ ܓܒܝ̈ܢܐ *the forehead;* ܒܝܬ ܬܪ̈ܥܐ *a gateway, porch.*

ܒܝܬܝܐܝܬ from ܒܝܬܐ. adv. *civil, privately;* ܒܝܬܝܐܝܬ ܘܐܘܣܝܐܝܬ *properly and essentially.*

ܒܝܬܘܢܐ m. dim. of ܒܝܬܐ *a small house* or *building; a cell.*

ܒܝܬܘܬܐ from ܒܝܬܐ. f. only in ܪܒ ܒܝܬܘܬܐ *stewardship.*

ܒܝܬ denom. verb from ܒܝܬܐ, fut. ܢܒܝܬ, inf. ܡܒܝܬܘ, part. act. ܡܒܝܬܢܐ, f. ܡܒܝܬܢܝܬܐ *to bring home, admit into a family,* ܒܝܬ ܠܡܒܕܪ̈ܐ ܕܥܢܟ *bring home those of Thy flock who are dispersed abroad; to tame, domesticate; to take for one's own, appropriate;* with ܠܗ or ܠܢܦܫܗ *to win, take* or *gain for oneself;* ܒܝܬ ܠܡܪ̈ܘܕܐ *to win over rebels.* Ethpa. ܐܬܒܝܬ *to make a friend of, become intimate* or *familiar with, accustomed to; to be like, related,* ܡܡܠܠܗܘܢ ܠܟܠܕܝܐ ܐܬܒܝܬ *their language is related to Chaldee;* gram. *to be cognate, derived from,* as ܐܬܥܒܕܢܐ from ܐܬܥܒܕ.

ܒܝܬܝ, ܒܝܬܝܐ m. ܒܝܬܝܬܐ, f. pl. m. ܒܝܬܝ̈ܐ, ܒܝܬܝ̈ܬܐ, pl. f. ܒܝܬܝ̈ܢ, ܒܝܬܝ̈ܬܐ from ܒܝܬܐ. adj. *belonging to the family* or *household, domestic, familiar, an associate, intimate friend; private, peculiar, proper, inbred, suitable, convenient, like, related to, near, akin;* ܡܛܠ ܨܒܘ̈ܬܐ ܒܝܬܝ̈ܬܐ *for family reasons, private business;* ܐܝ̈ܕܝ ܒܝܬܝ̈ܬܐ *my own hands;* ܠܡܠܠܘ ܒܝܬܝܐܝܬ ܝܬܝܪ ܐܘ ܚܬܝܬܐܝܬ *to speak more properly* or *exactly;* ܗܕܐ ܬܪܥܝܬܐ ܒܝܬܝܐ ܠܫܪܪܐ *this opinion is nearer to the truth.*

ܒܝܬܝܘܬܐ f. *being of the same household;* collect. *household;* hence *a*) *relationship, friendship, intimacy, familiarity;* ܒܝܬܝܘܬܐ ܕܗܝܡܢܘܬܐ *the household of faith;* ܒܝܬܝܘܬܐ ܕܠܘܬ ܐܠܗܐ *friendship with God.* *b*) *ownership; likeness, affinity;* gram. *relation of one word to another, by derivation;* ܐܬܘܬܐ ܒܝܬܝܘܬܐ or ܐܬܘ̈ܬܐ ܕ *letters by which one word is formed from another,* especially Yud and Nun ܝ and ܢ, e.g. ܥܦܪܢܝܐ and ܥܦܪܢܝܬܐ from ܥܦܪܐ *dust;* and with foreign words ܐܘ ܣ ܘ and ܣ.

ܒܟܐ fut. ܢܒܟܐ, imp. ܒܟܝ, inf. ܡܒܟܐ, pres. part. ܒܟܐ, f. ܒܟܝܐ, pl. m. ܒܟܝܢ, f. ܒܟܝ̈ܢ, ܒܟܝ̈ܬܐ *to weep* with suff. and ܠ acc., or with ܥܠ of the cause; ܒܝܬ ܒܟܝܐ lit. place of those that weep, *lamentation, mourning.* Ethpe. ܐܬܒܟܝ *to be bewailed, lamented for.* Pa. ܒܟܝ *to greatly bewail, weep copiously; to cause to weep* or *lament;* with suff. and ܠ acc., or with ܥܠ of the cause. Ethpa. ܐܬܒܟܝ *to be deeply lamented.* Aphel ܐܒܟܝ *to make weep.* Derivatives, ܒܟܝܐ, ܒܟܬܐ, ܒܟܘܬܐ, ܡܒܟܝܢܐ.

ܒܟܐ m. ܒܟܬܐ f. *a cock, a hen;* cf. ܐܒܟܐ.

ܒܟܘܪܐ pl. ܐ̈ rt. ܒܟܪ. m. *a weaned camel foal.*

ܒܟܝܐ rt. ܒܟܐ. m. *weeping, mourning, lamentation.*

ܒܟܝܐ pl. ܒܟܝ̈ܐ, m. ܒܟܝܬܐ pl. ܒܟܝ̈ܬܐ f. rt. ܒܟܐ. *a mourner,* especially *women hired to make lamentation.*

ܒܟܝܪܐܝܬ adv. rt. ܒܟܪ. *precociously, for the first time.*

ܒܟܝܪܐ f. ܒܟܝܪܬܐ pl. m. ܐ̈, f. ܬܐ̈ rt. ܒܟܪ. adj. *the earliest, primitive, primary;* pl. *early lambs* or *kids;* ܡܛܪܐ ܒܟܝܪܐ *early rain,* opp. ܠܩܫܐ; ܡܚܫܒܬܐ ܒܟܝܪܬܐ *primary thought.*

ܒܟܝܪܘܬܐ rt. ܒܟܪ. f. *priority.*

ܒܟܠܘ̈ܬܐ f. no sing. *unripe grapes, sour grapes; galls.*

ܒܟܡܐ comp. of ܒ and ܟܡܐ. interrog. adv. *for how much?*

ܕܘܝܬܐ or ܕܘܝܬܐ vulg. Arab. m. *an ink-pot.*

ܒܟܪ act. p. ܒܟܪ. *to bring forth early* flowers or fruit. Ethpe. ܐܬܒܟܪ *to be first-born.* Pa. ܒܟܪ *to be the first, go first* or *before;* with ܒ, *to do* or *attempt first;* the almond-tree ܡܒܟܪ ܒܦܪܚܗ *is the earliest to blossom;* ܗܘ ܩܕܡܝܐ ܒܟܪ ܠܘܬܗ *he was the first to come to him,* i.e. was his first disciple. Derivatives, ܒܘܟܪܐ, ܒܘܟܪܘܬܐ, ܒܟܝܪܐ, ܒܟܝܪܘܬܐ, ܒܟܝܪܐܝܬ, ܒܟܪܐ.

ܒܟܪܐ f. ܒܟܪܬܐ pl. m. ܐ̈, f. ܬܐ̈ rt. ܒܟܪ. *early, first-ripe;* pl. m. *first-fruits;* metaph. ܥܐܕܐ ܒܟܪܐ *the first feast-day,* i.e. the Nativity of our Lord.

ܒܟܫܐ m. *a great stone to close a door, a boundary-stone;* cf. ܟܫܐ, ܟܘܫܐ and ܟܘܫܐ.

ܒܟܐ part. f. ܒܟܝܬܐ *to weave for hire;* hence ܒܟܝܬܐ f. pl. ܬܐ̈ *a hired weaveress,* and Neo-Syriac ܒܟܬܐ pl. ܒܟ̈ܬܐ *a woman, spinster.*

ܒܟܝܬܐ fem. of ܒܟܝܐ rt. ܒܟܐ. *weeping, mourning, lamentation.*

ܒܠܒܠ act. part. ܒܐܠ, pl. ܒܠܝܢ or ܒܐܠܝܢ, pass. part. ܒܠܝܠ, ܒܠܝܠܐ, ܒܠܝܠܬܐ. *to confuse, confound;* ܒܐܠܝ ܐܘܣܝܐ—ܟܝ̈ܢܐ *those who confound the substances, the natures* of Christ; pass. part. as adj. *mixed, confused.* Metaph. *disorderly, irregular, irrational;* ܠܐ ܒܠܝܠ, *in right order;* ܣܘܪ̈ܛܐ ܒܠܝ̈ܠܐ *lines confusedly written;* ܟܝܢܐ ܒܠܝܠܐ *irrational nature;* ܒܠܝܠ ܒܚܘܒܐ Germ. *verwirrt, out of his mind with love;* subst. m. *mixed fodder; cleansed wheat.* Palpel ܒܠܒܠ *to confound, confuse, mar, spoil;* ܒܠܒܠ ܡܪܝܐ ܠܫܢܐ ܕܟܠܗ ܐܪܥܐ *the Lord confounded the languages of all the earth,* Gen. xi. 9; ܚܘܝܕܐ ܕܠܐ ܡܒܠܒܠܘܬܐ *union without confusion* (in the Person of Christ). Ethpalpal ܐܬܒܠܒܠ *to be confused, disordered, disturbed, troubled.* Derivatives, ܒܘܠܒܠܐ, ܒܠܝܠ, ܒܠܝܠܐ, ܒܠܝܠܘܬܐ, ܒܠܝܠܐܝܬ, ܡܒܠܒܠܢܐ, ܡܒܠܒܠܢܘܬܐ.

ܒܠܐ or ܒܠܝ fut. ܢܒܠܐ, inf. ܡܒܠܐ, pres. part. ܒܠܐ, ܒܠܝܐ *to grow old, wear out,* especially of clothes; ܙܩܐ ܒܠܝ̈ܬܐ *torn wine-skins;* chronicles ܕܒܠܝ ܗܘܘ ܘܐܬܚܒܠܘ *which had grown old and worn out.* Metaph. *to wear* or *waste away, to be consumed;* ܒܠܝܬ ܒܟܘܪܗܢܝ *I wear away in my grief.* Ethpe. ܐܬܒܠܝ *to be consumed, to waste away.* Pa. ܒܠܝ *to fail with age, waste away;* ܡܒܠܐ ܠܗ ܥܠܡܐ *the world waxes old, wears away.* Ethpa. ܐܬܒܠܝ *to fail.* Aph. ܐܒܠܝ *to cause to waste away* or *fail.* Derivatives, ܒܠܝ, ܒܠܝܐ, ܒܠܝܐ, ܒܠܝܘܬܐ.

ܒܠܐ m. *the heart;* ܣܡ ܥܠ ܒܠܐ *to take to heart, consider, care;* ܣܠܩ ܥܠ ܒܠܐ *it entered his heart;* ܣܡ ܒܒܠܐ *to notice, apply his mind, set his mind on, resolve;* ܡܢ ܒܠܐ *by heart, by rote.*

ܒܠܐܢܐ, ܒܠܐܢܐ, ܒܠܐܢܝ, ܒܠܐܢܘܣ, ܒܠܐܢܘܣ, ܒܠܐܢܝܣ; see ܒܠܢܐ m. *a bath, bath-house.*

ܒܠܣܡ, ܒܠܣܡܘܢ *balsam.*

ܒܠܒܘܠܝܬܐ pl. ܒܠܒܘ̈ܠܝܬܐ f. *a wick.*

ܒܠܒܠܬܐ f. *the uvula;* see ܠܒܠܒܬܐ.

ܒܠܗ act. part. ܡܒܠܗ, pass. part. ܡܒܠܗ. *a) to terrify, stun, astonish. b) to hasten, advance, bring up* troops; *encourage.* Ethpa. ܐܬܒܠܗ *to be astonished, dismayed, terrified.* Derivatives, ܒܘܠܗܐ, ܡܒܠܗܢܐ.

ܒܠܘܛ, ܒܠܘܛܐ pl. ܒܠܘ̈ܛܐ m. *the oak,* quercus ballota; *the ilex;* ܒܠܘܛ ܦܪܣܐ *the date-palm;* ܒܠܘܛ ܡܠܟܐ *the chestnut.*

ܒܠܘܛܐ pl. ܒܘܠܘܛ̈ܐ = *a counsellor.*

ܒܠܘܡܒܛܐ *plumbata, scourges loaded with lead.*

ܒܠܘܥܐ pl. ܒܠܘ̈ܥܐ m. *a) a hook, fish-hook. b) a small hoop* to fasten torn wine-skins.

ܒܠܘܥܐ pl. ܒܠܘ̈ܥܐ rt. ܒܠܥ. m. *one who swallows up, a devourer;* adj. *voracious.*

ܒܠܘܥܬܐ pl. ܒܠܘ̈ܥܬܐ or ܒܠܘ̈ܥܝܬܐ rt. ܒܠܥ. f. *a sink, sewer.*

ܒܠܘܪ̈ܐ pl. *a) chains, bracelets* of gold; *plaits* of hair. *b)* = ܒܘܪܘܠܐ *beryl.*

ܐܬܒܠܚܘܕ denom. verb from ܒܠܚܘܕ, *to be the only one;* gram. *to be in the singular number.*

ܒܠܚܘܕ adv. formed from ܒ, ܠ, and rt. ܚܕ; see ܚܘܕ. *only, alone;* ܒܠܚܘܕܝ or ܐܢܐ ܒܠܚܘܕܝ *I only.*

ܒܠܚܘܕܝܘܬܐ prob. mistake for ܚܘܕܝܘܬܐ. *loneliness, being in the singular number.*

ܒܠܛ Peal and ܒܠܛ Pael. *a) to shut* the eyes, *bolt* gates. *b) to be worm-eaten, moth-eaten. c) to have prominent eyes* or *ulcerated eyes.* Ethpa. ܐܬܒܠܛ *to be bolted.* Aph. ܐܒܠܛ *a) to breed worms, become carious, rot* as wood; ܩܝܣܐ ܕܠܐ ܡܒܠܛ *sound timber, wood that will not rot. b)* ܥܝ̈ܢܐ ܡܒܠܛ̈ܬܐ *prominent eyes.* Derivatives, ܒܠܛܝܬܐ, ܒܠܛܘܬܐ, ܡܒܠܛܘܬܐ.

ܒܠܛܐ = ܒܠܐ m. *the knop* or *cup* of a flower; *the bowl* of a candlestick, *a sconce.*

ܒܠܛܝܐ *the wood* or *shaft* of a spear.

ܒܠܛܝܬܐ rt. ܒܠܛ. f. teredo xylophagus, *a boring-worm; caries.*

ܒܠܝ root ܒܠܐ. negative particle, generally used with ܡܢ, *without, for want of, for lack of, lacking;* ܡܢ ܒܠܝ ܠܒܘܫܐ, ܝܕܥܬܐ *for lack of clothing, of knowledge,* &c.; ܩܡ ܒܠܝ ܙܘܥܐ *he stood motionless.*

ܒܠܝ, ܒܠܝܐ pl. ܒܠ̈ܝܐ rt. ܒܠܐ. m. *a) the wearing-out* of clothes; *worn-out clothes, rags. b)*

=ܒܠܝ failing, lack, scarcity, want; ܡܢ ܒܠܝ ܣܦܪ̈ܐ for lack of scribes.

ܒܠܝܐ pl. ܝ̈ܐ m. and ܒܠܝܐ pl. ܒ̈ܠܝܐ, ܒ̈ܠܝܢ m. rt. ܒܠܐ. old, worn-out.

ܒܠܝܘܬܐ rt. ܒܠܐ. f. wearing away, waxing old, being worn-out.

ܒܠܝܠ m. mixed fodder; see ܒܠ.

ܒܠܝܠܐܝܬ rt. ܒܠ. adv. confusedly, without any order, incorrectly.

ܒܠܝܠܘܬܐ rt. ܒܠ. f. mixture, confusion, mistake. Metaph. ܚܛܝܬܘܬܝ ܘܒܠܝܠܘܬܝ my sinful and distracted self.

ܒܠܝܥܘܬܐ rt. ܒܠܥ. f. greediness; avidity, absorption, e.g. ܒܪܚܡܬܐ ܕܝܘܠܦܢܐ in the love of learning.

ܒܠܡ fut. ܢܒܠܘܡ, act. part. ܒܠܡ, ܒܠܡܐ, pass. part. ܒܠܝܡ, ܒܠܝܡܐ. to muzzle, check. Metaph. ܒܠܡ ܦܘܡܗ ܕܗܪܛܝܩܐ he muzzled—stopped—the heretic's mouth. Ethpe. ܐܬܒܠܡ imp. ܐܬܒܠܡ to have the mouth stopped, to be struck dumb, checked, bridled; to be obstructed of the womb. Derivative the following—

ܒܠܡܐ pl. ܡ̈ܐ m. a halter, headstall, bridle.

ܒܠܢܐ or ܒܠܢܝ pl. ܒܠܢܘܬܐ, also ܒܐܠܐܢܝ, ܒܐܠܐܢܝܣ, ܒܠܢܝܣ, and ܒܐܠܐܢܝܣ, ܒܢܐ &c. βαλανεῖον, a bath. Derivative, ܒܠܢܝܐ.

ܒܠܣܐ βλαισός, splay-footed.

ܒܠܣܓܐ m. a white ass of Egyptian or Georgian breed, small and swift.

ܒܠܣܛܪܘܣ, ܒܠܣܛܝܣ or ܒܠܣܛܐ balistae, an engine of war to throw darts or stones.

ܒܠܣܡܘܢ, ܒܠܣܡܘܢ, or ܒܠܣܡ balsam, balm.

ܒܠܥ fut. ܢܒܠܥ, act. part. ܒܠܥ, ܒܠܥܐ, ܒܠܥܬܐ, pass. part. ܒܠܝܥ, ܒܠܝܥܐ, ܒܠܝܥܬܐ. a) to swallow up, devour, usually metaph. ܒܠܥܬ ܐܢܘܢ ܐܪܥܐ the earth swallowed them up; ܫܘܚܬܐ ܒܠܘܥܬܐ the devouring pit; pass. part. devoured, engulphed, immersed; ܒܠܝܥ ܒܚܘܒܐ immersed in debt; ܒܠܝܥܐ ܗܘܬ ܒܪܚܡܬܗ she was devoured by love of him; gram. mute. b) to be struck, smitten, beaten, wounded, with ܒ, ܡܢ, or ܥܠ; ܒܪܓܠܗ in the foot; ܒܣܝܦܐ with a sword; ܒܠܥܝ ܚܒܪܝܗܘܢ those who bully, wrong, injure their neighbours. Metaph. with various passions, ܒܠܥ ܒܬܗܪܐ he was struck with admiration; ܒܚܣܡܐ smitten with envy; ܒܟܪܝܘܬܐ stricken with grief. Ethpe. ܐܬܒܠܥ imp. ܐܬܒܠܥ a) to be absorbed, swallowed up, carried away; gram. Jac. to be omitted in pronunciation, mute. b) to be struck, wounded. Pa. ܒܠܥ a) to lap water from one's hand; b) to be beaten, slain. Aph. ܐܒܠܥ to strike, wound. Derivatives, ܒܠܘܥܐ, ܒܠܥܐ, ܒܠܝܥܐ, ܒܠܘܥܬܐ.

ܒܠܥܐ pl. ܥ̈ܐ rt. ܒܠܥ. m. swallowing; gram. ܟܕ ܒܠܥ ܗܘ when ܗ is not pronounced, as ܗܘܐ, opp. ܟܕ ܡܒܠܐ when it has a point under it and is pronounced ܗܘܐ.

ܒܠܥܕ prep. takes suffixes like a plural noun. without; often with ܡܢ preceding or following; ܒܠܥܕ ܡܢ without.

ܒܠܘܥܬܐ rt. ܒܠܥ. f. one who devours, swallows down; a sinking away, subsidence. Metaph. of the setting sun, receding tide.

ܒܠܨ to bud, blossom; pass. part. ܒܠܝܨ, ܒܠܝܨܐ uttered, opp. ܒܠܝܥܐ mute. Ethpe. ܐܬܒܠܨ to be explained, expounded. Ethpe. and Ethpa. gram. to be uttered, pronounced. Aph. ܐܒܠܨ to make bud or sprout; to disclose, discover, to teach or expound; gram. to make a letter capable of pronunciation by adding a vowel. Ettaph. ܐܬܬܒܠܨ to explain, declare; gram. to utter, pronounce.

ܒܠܨܐ, ܒܠܨ m. rt. ܒܠܨ. enunciation of a letter; cf. ܒܠܝܥܐ.

ܒܠܨܐ pl. ̈ a grain; ܒܠܨܐ ܕܪܘܡܢܐ a pomegranate seed.

ܒܠܨܘܨܝܬܐ pl. ܝ̈ܬܐ f. a spark.

ܒܠܩ fut. ܢܒܠܘܩ and ܢܒܠܩ, act. part. ܒܠܩ, ܒܠܩܐ with ܥܠ. to come unawares or unlooked for, fall suddenly upon; to come quickly, arrive; to happen, occur unexpectedly; used of illness, war, &c.; to rise as a star, light; to desire eagerly. Ethpa. ܐܬܒܠܩ to be eager about anything, eagerly desire. Aph. part. ܡܒܠܩ coming unexpectedly, falling on by night, E-Syr. Derivative the following—

ܒܠܩܐ m. an unexpected occurrence.

ܒܠܩܐ m. pl. thieves, marauders.

ܒܠܩܬܐ m. a perfume or ointment-box.

ܒܢܠܝܢ; see ܒܢܠܝܢ.

ܒܢܐ fut. ܢܒܢܐ, imp. ܒܢܝ, act. part. ܒܢܐ, ܒܢܝܐ pl. m. ܒܢܝܢ, f. ܒܢܝܢ, pass. part. ܒܢܐ, ܒܢܝܐ pl. m. ܒܢܝܢ, f. ܒܢܝܢ. *to build.* Metaph. *to build up, edify, to construct; to compose* or *adapt* canticles, expressions, &c.; act. part. *a builder.* Ethpe. ܐܬܒܢܝ *to be built, erected, founded;* ܥܠ ܫܡ *to the name* or *in memory of.* Pa. ܒܢܝ *to restore;* seldom except metaph. *to exhort, encourage, edify;* ܒܢܐ ܠܒܟܘܢ *comfort your heart.* Ethpa. ܐܬܒܢܝ pass. Derivatives, ܒܢܝܐ, ܒܢܝܢܐ, ܒܢܝܘܬܐ, ܒܢܝܐ, ܒܢܝܢܐ, ܒܢܘܝܐ, ܡܒܢܝܢܐ, ܡܒܢܝܢܘܬܐ, ܒܢܝܬܐ.

ܒܢܐ m. pl. ܒܢܝܐ, ܒܢܘܬܐ *a bath;* ܫܚܢ ܒܢܐ *he who heats the bath;* cf. ܒܠܢܐ. Derivative, ܒܢܝܐ.

ܒܢܕܐ and ܒܢܕܐ pl. ܒܢܕܐ f. Pers. *a banner, standard.*

ܒܢܕܪ part. ܡܒܢܕܪܐ denom. verb from ܒܢܕܪܐ. *to roll up, make into a ball.*

ܒܢܕܪܐ *a ball;* cf. ܒܘܢܕܪܐ.

ܒܢܘܝܐ pl. ܐ̈ rt. ܒܢܐ. m. *a builder.*

ܒܢܝ, ܒܢܝܐ, ܒܢܝܢ; see ܒܪ *son,* probably from ܒܢܐ.

ܒܢܝܐ pl. ܐ̈ rt. ܒܢܐ. m. *a builder, founder.* Metaph. ܫܠܝܚܐ ܒܢܝܐ ܕܐܦܣܩܘܦܘܬܐ *the Apostles were founders of sees.*

ܒܢܝܐ rt. ܒܢܐ. m. *building.*

ܒܢܝܘܬܐ rt. ܒܢܐ. f. *the art of building.*

ܒܢܝܢ, ܒܢܝܢܐ pl. ܐ̈ rt. ܒܢܐ. m. *building; a building, edifice.* Metaph. *superstructure, edification, instruction.*

ܒܢܝܢܬܐ pl. of ܒܢܝܬܐ.

ܒܢܝܬܐ rt. ܒܢܐ. f. *a building, structure, edifice.*

ܒܢܝܬܐ, ܒܢܬ pl. of ܒܪܬܐ *daughter;* see ܒܪ, ܒܪܐ.

ܒܢܢܐ m. ܒܢܢܝܬܐ f. pl. m. ܒܢܢܐ, f. ܒܢܢܝܬܐ *keeper of a bath.*

ܒܣܐ fut. ܢܒܣܐ, imp. ܒܣܝ, act. part. ܒܣܐ, ܒܣܝܐ pl. m. ܒܣܝܢ, f. ܒܣܝܢ. *to disdain, despise, scorn,* with ܒ or ܥܠ; pass. part. ܒܣܐ, ܒܣܝܐ pl. m. ܒܣܝܢ, ܒܣܝܐ, f. ܒܣܝܢ, ܒܣܝܬܐ. *despised, despicable, of no value.* Ethpe. ܐܬܒܣܝ *to be despised, neglected.* Pa. ܒܣܝ *to despise, neglect.* Ethpa. ܐܬܒܣܝ *to be despised, scorned.* Aph. ܐܒܣܝ *to despise, neglect, slight, disregard;* ܐܒܣܝܘ ܥܒܕܘܗܝ ܠܡܙܒܢ *his servants had neglected to buy* bread; ܗܘ ܕܠܐ ܡܒܣܐ ܒܥܘܬܟ *He who does not despise thy petition.* Derivatives, ܒܣܝܐ, ܒܣܝܐܝܬ, ܒܣܝܘܬܐ, ܒܣܝܢܐ, ܡܒܣܝܢܐ, ܡܒܣܝܢܐܝܬ, ܡܒܣܝܢܘܬܐ, ܡܬܒܣܝܢܐ.

ܒܣܒܣ Palpel of ܒܣ unused; fut. ܢܒܣܒܣ, imp. ܒܣܒܣ, act. part. ܡܒܣܒܣ, pass. ܡܒܣܒܣ. *to tear in pieces* as wild beasts. Metaph. *to outrage.* Ethpalpal ܐܬܒܣܒܣ *to be torn* or *rent in pieces.* Metaph. *to run wildly into sin.* Derivatives, ܒܘܣܒܣܐ, ܡܒܣܒܣܐ.

ܒܣܛܪܐ pl. ܐ̈ m. *a gold* or *silver coin worth* 700 *drachmas.*

ܒܣܛܪܐ pl. ܐ̈ and ܒܣܛܪܘܬܐ *a pillow, cushion;* cf. ܐܣܛܐ.

ܒܣܘܡܐ pl. ܐ̈ rt. ܒܣܡ. m. *given to pleasure, effeminate.*

ܒܣܘܪܐ rt. ܒܣܪ. m. *a despiser, contemner.*

ܒܣܝܐ rt. ܒܣܐ. m. *vile, vileness.*

ܒܣܝܐܝܬ rt. ܒܣܐ. adv. *disdainfully, carelessly, neglectfully.*

ܒܣܝܘ, ܒܣܝܘܬܐ rt. ܒܣܐ. *neglect, poverty, meanness,* especially of clothes.

ܒܣܝܠܝܩܐ and ܒܣܝܠܝܩܐ pl. ܒܣܝܠܝܩܐ, ܒܣܝܠܝܩܘܣ and ܒܣܝܠܝܩܘܣ f. βασιλική, *a palace, court of justice, church;* ܒܥܘܬܐ ܕܒܣܝܠܝܩܐ *an anthem* sung when Christian kings or emperors were at service.

ܒܣܝܡܐܝܬ rt. ܒܣܡ. adv. *pleasantly, kindly, moderately.*

ܒܣܝܡܘܬܐ rt. ܒܣܡ. f. *sweetness, pleasantness, kindness, gladness;* ܒܣܝܡܘܬܐ ܕܪܝܚܐ *fragrance.*

ܒܣܝܢܐ rt. ܒܣܐ. m. *despising, negligence,* ܐܦܣܝܢ ܡܢܗ ܒܣܝܢܐ *they shall fine him for negligence; anything despicable;* ܒܣܝܢܐ ܕܥܡܐ *the dregs of the people.*

ܒܣܝܣ pl. the same. f. βάσις, *the base, foot* of a candlestick.

ܒܣܝܪܐܝܬ rt. ܒܣܪ. adv. *with contempt, scornfully.*

ܒܣܝܪܘܬܐ rt. ܒܣܪ. f. *contempt, baseness, vileness.*

ܒܣܡ fut. ܢܒܣܡ, act. part. ܒܳܣܶܡ, ܒܳܣܡܳܐ, pass. part. ܒܣܺܝܡ, ܒܣܺܝܡܳܐ, ܒܣܺܝܡܬܳܐ a) *to be fragrant, sweet.* Metaph. with ܠ *to please;* ܒܣܺܝܡ ܠܶܗ ܕ *it pleases him to;* ܡܳܐ ܕܒܳܣܡܺܝܢ *when they please; to enjoy, delight in* with ܒ; *to make merry, be glad;* ܒܣܶܡ ܠܶܒܶܗ *his heart is merry.* b) denom. from ܒܶܣܡܳܐ. *to burn incense, perfume.* Verbal adj. *sweet, fragrant;* especially with ܘܰܪܕܳܐ ܒܰܣܺܝܡܳܐ, ܒܰܣܺܝܡ *the sweet rose;* ܩܝܣܳܐ ܕܒܰܣܺܝܡ or ܕܒܶܣܡܶܐ *sweet-smelling wood.* Metaph. *merry, pleasant, kind, mild, gentle;* ܪܘܚܳܐ ܒܰܣܺܝܡܬܳܐ *a gentle breeze;* ܒܰܣܺܝܡ ܐܳܪܚܳܐ *of pleasing manners;* ܡܡܰܠܠܳܐ ܒܰܣܺܝܡܳܐ *a pleasant* or *smooth style.* Pa. ܒܰܣܶܡ a) *to make cheerful;* with ܠܶܒܳܐ *to soften, soothe; to delight, cause to rejoice* with ܒ; b) *to sweeten, perfume, prepare perfume* or *incense;* ܒܡܶܠܚܳܐ *to season with salt;* ܡܒܰܣܶܡ ܠܣܰܥܪܳܐ *perfuming the hair;* ܡܶܫܚܳܐ ܡܒܰܣܡܳܐ *aromatic oil;* ܡܒܰܣܶܡ ܙܡܺܝܪ̈ܳܬܳܐ *composing sweet psalms.* Ethpa. ܐܶܬܒܰܣܰܡ *to refresh oneself, take delight in, enjoy* with ܒ or ܥܰܡ; ܕܢܶܬܒܰܣܰܡ ܒܡܶܡܠܠܶܗ *to enjoy his conversation* or *company.* Aph. ܐܰܒܣܶܡ *to yield fragrance.* Derivatives, ܒܣܳܡܳܐ, ܒܶܣܡܳܐ, ܒܣܺܝܡܘܬܳܐ, ܒܣܺܝܡܳܐܺܝܬ, ܒܣܳܡܳܐ, ܒܣܺܝܡܳܐ, ܒܣܺܝܡܘܬܳܐ, ܒܣܺܝܡܳܐܝܬ, ܒܰܣܳܡܳܐ, ܒܶܣܡܳܐ, ܡܒܰܣܡܳܢܳܐ, ܡܶܬܒܰܣܡܳܢܳܐ.

ܒܶܣܡܳܐ, ܒܣܶܡ pl. ܒܶܣܡܶܐ, ܒܶܣܡܘܢܶܐ, and ܒܶܣܡܳܢܶܐ rt. ܒܣܡ. m. *sweet spices, ointment, perfume, sweet odour, incense;* with ܣܳܡ or ܐܰܣܶܩ *to burn incense;* ܬܶܢܳܢܳܐ ܕܒܶܣܡܶܐ *smoke, fumes,* or *vapour of incense;* ܒܶܝܬ ܒܶܣܡܶܐ or ܕ ܒ̈ *a censer;* ܩܰܢܝܳܐ ܕܒܶܣܡܳܐ *sweet calamus.*

ܒܰܣܳܡܳܐ pl. ܶܐ rt. ܒܣܡ. m. *a maker* or *seller of ointments and perfumes.*

ܒܘܣܳܡܳܐ pl. ܒܘܣܳܡܶܐ rt. ܒܣܡ. m. *pleasure, luxury; enjoyment, feasting,* ܥܒܰܕ ܒܘܣܳܡܳܐ *he made a banquet.*

ܒܶܣܡܘܢܳܐ and ܒܶܣܡܳܢܳܐ; see ܒܶܣܡܳܐ, ܒܣܡ.

ܒܣܳܣܳܐ; see ܒܣܳܣܳܐ. f. *base, shaft,* or *stem.*

ܒܣܰܪ fut. ܢܶܒܣܽܘܪ, imp. ܒܣܽܘܪ, inf. ܡܶܒܣܰܪ, act. part. ܒܳܣܰܪ, ܒܳܣܪܳܐ, pass. part. ܒܣܺܝܪ, ܒܣܺܝܪܳܐ, ܒܣܺܝܪܬܳܐ *to despise, scorn* with ܠ or ܥܰܠ, *to blame, reprove, condemn;* ܕܢܶܒܣܽܘܪ ܡܰܟܺܝܟܘܬܳܐ ܠܗܳܝ ܪܳܡܘܬܳܐ *that humility may reprove this arrogance;* ܪܶܢܝܳܐ ܕܺܝܠܳܟ ܒܳܣܰܪ ܠܳܟ *your own opinion condemns you;* pass. part. *despised, rejected, despicable;* ܡܦܰܩ ܒܪܽܘܚܳܐ ܒܣܺܝܪ *a rejected excuse.* Ethpe. ܐܶܬܒܣܰܪ and Ethpa. ܐܶܬܒܰܣܰܪ *to be despised.* Pa. ܒܰܣܰܪ *to despise* with ܠ or ܥܰܠ; ܥܰܠ ܡܰܘܬܳܐ, ܥܰܠ ܩܘܽܪܒܳܢܶܐ *to scorn death, despise dangers; to dare.* Derivatives, ܒܣܳܪܳܐ, ܒܣܺܝܪܳܐܺܝܬ, ܒܘܣܳܪܳܐ, ܒܣܺܝܪܘܬܳܐ, ܡܒܰܣܪܳܢܳܐ, ܡܒܰܣܪܳܢܘܬܳܐ.

ܒܰܣܰܪ Pael denom. from ܒܶܣܪܳܐ. *to clothe with flesh, to incarnate;* ܠܳܐ ܡܒܰܣܪܳܐ *incorporeal;* ܡܶܠܬܳܐ ܡܒܰܣܪܬܳܐ *the incarnate Word.* Ethpa. ܐܶܬܒܰܣܰܪ *to have taken flesh, to become incarnate.*

ܒܣܰܪ, ܒܶܣܪܳܐ pl. ܶܐ m. a) *flesh,* hence *the body;* ܒܒܶܣܰܪ *in the flesh, according to the flesh, carnally;* ܡܰܘܬܳܐ ܕܒܶܣܪܳܐ *natural death;* ܒܶܣܪܳܐ ܝܰܬܺܝܪܳܐ *a fleshy growth, excrescence;* pl. f. ܒܶܣܪ̈ܳܬܳܐ *carcasses, the fleshy parts* of the body. b) *pulp, fleshy part* of fruit; pl. m. *unripe fruit,* especially *sour grapes;* ܡܰܝ̈ܳܐ ܒܶܣܪ̈ܶܐ *the juice of unripe grapes.* Derivatives, verb ܒܰܣܰܪ, ܒܶܣܪܳܢܳܐܺܝܬ, ܒܶܣܪܳܢܘܬܳܐ, ܒܶܣܪܳܢܳܐ, ܡܒܰܣܪܳܢܘܬܳܐ, ܡܶܬܒܰܣܪܳܢܘܬܳܐ, ܡܶܬܒܰܣܪܳܢܳܐܺܝܬ.

ܒܶܣܪܳܢܳܝܳܐ f. ܒܶܣܪܳܢܳܝܬܳܐ pl. m. ܝܶܐ, ܝܺܢ f. ܝܳܬܳܐ rt. ܒܶܣܪܳܐ. *of flesh, fleshy; corporeal, carnal;* ܗܰܕ̈ܳܡܶܐ ܒܶܣܪ̈ܳܢܳܝܶܐ *the fleshy parts of the body.*

ܒܶܣܪܳܢܳܐܺܝܬ from ܒܶܣܪܳܐ adv. *carnally, according to the flesh.*

ܒܶܣܪܳܢܘܬܳܐ from ܒܶܣܪܳܐ. f. *incarnation;* med. *the granulation of flesh.*

ܒܶܣܪܳܢܳܐ, ܢܳܝܳܐ pl. m. ܶܐ f. ܝܳܬܳܐ from ܒܶܣܪܳܐ. a) adj. *of flesh, animal* food; *according to the flesh, fleshly, carnal; earthly, terrestrial;* ܙܰܘܥܶܐ ܒܶܣܪ̈ܳܢܳܝܶܐ *the impulses of the flesh;* ܠܳܐ ܡܶܐܟܘܠܬܳܐ ܒܶܣܪܳܢܳܝܬܳܐ ܗܘ *it is supernatural,* or *celestial food.* b) med. *a species of dropsy.*

ܒܣܬܳܐ = ܒܘܣܬܳܐ, cf. the following:

ܒܶܣܬܽܘܩܳܐ and ܒܣܬܩܳܐ. Pers. *a bottle;* ܒ̈ ܕܦܰܚܳܪܳܐ *an earthen bottle.*

ܒܶܣܬܪܳܐ, ܒܶܣܬܰܪ Pers. m. subst. *the back, hinderpart;* ܒܶܣܬܰܪ ܪܺܫܳܐ *the occiput, back of the head;* ܠܒܶܣܬܪܳܗ ܐܰܙܶܠ *hindside-foremost.* Prep. *behind, following, after;* with ܠ *at the back, backward;* with ܡܶܢ *behind, at the back, on the outside;* ܠܩܘܕܡܰܝܗܘܢ ܘܰܠܒܶܣܬܪܳܐ *forwards* and backwards; with ܗܦܟ to return, retire; ܦܩܝܢ ܠܒܣܬܪܗ, ܠܒܣܬܪܗܘܢ with thy, his, hands tied behind. Derivatives the following—

ܐܬܒܣܬܪ denom. to turn backwards or round.

ܒܣܬܪܐܝܬ usually ܠܒܣܬܪܐܝܬ adv. backwards; ܡܗܦܟܢܘܬܗ ܠܒ̈ his return journey.

ܒܣܬܪܝܐ, ܒܣܬܪܝܬܐ pl. m. ܒܣܬܪ̈ܝܐ adj. at the back, latter, placed after; ܒܣܬܪܝܬܐ ܥܩܘܨܐ having a sting in its tail; ܠܒܣܬܪܝܐ backward, moving backward, retrograde.

ܒܣܬܪܢܝܐ, ܒܣܬܪܢܝܬܐ same as ܒܣܬܪܝܐ.

ܒܣܬܪܘܡܐ Turk. a coarse horse-cloth, a rug.

ܒܥܐ keeps Olaph in perf. 3 m. pl. and in imp. 2 m. pl. ܒܥܐܘ, fut. ܢܒܥܐ, imp. ܒܥܝ, inf. ܡܒܥܐ, pres. part. ܒܥܐ, ܒܥܝܐ. Contractions with pers. prons., ܒܥܝܢܐ usual form ܒܥܐܢܐ = ܒܥܐ ܐܢܐ, ܒܥܝܐܢܬ = ܒܥܝܐ ܐܢܬ, ܒܥܝܢܢ = ܒܥܝܢ ܚܢܢ. to seek with acc. or ܠ; to pray, beseech with ܡܢ; to seek, desire, endeavour with ܕ, ܠ, or a verb; with ܢܦܫܐ to seek to slay; with ܥܡ to dispute, argue. The pres. part. is used impers. of the near future, ܒܥܐ ܕܢܗܘܐ ܪܡܫܐ it was about to be evening, towards evening. Ethpe. ܐܬܒܥܝ to be sought, needed, required, summoned; to be inquired into or discussed; ܐܬܒܥܝ ܘܠܐ ܐܫܬܟܚ it was sought but could not be found; ܐܬܒܥܝܘ ܐܦܝܣܩܘܦܐ ܟܠܗܘܢ all the bishops were summoned; impers. ܐܬܒܥܝܬ it was required, necessary; part. necessary, needed, wanting, lacking; impers. with ܗܘܐ, ܗܘ, or ܗܘܐ, with ܠ and pers. pron. suff. or absol. ܡܬܒܥܝܐ ܠܝ, ܠܟ, &c., it is required of me, I ought; with ܠܐ it is not necessary, I need not; ܟܠ ܡܐ ܕܡܬܒܥܐ ܠܗ or ܕܡܬܒܥܝܐ whatever is wanted. Derivatives, ܒܥܘܬܐ, ܒܥܘܬܢܐ, ܒܥܘܬܐ, ܒܥܘܝܐ, ܒܥܝܐ, ܡܬܒܥܝܢܘܬܐ, ܒܥܝܐ, ܒܥܐ; Cognate, ܐܬܒܥܝ.

ܒ̈ܥܝܐ pl. of ܒܥܝܬܐ.

ܒܥܒܘܥܝܬܐ pl. ܒܥܒܘ̈ܥܝܬܐ f. a bubble, especially of rain or mist; cf. ܦܩܦܘܩܬܐ.

ܐܬܒܥܒܥ denom. verb from the above; of rain to rush down so as to raise bubbles.

ܒܥܓܠ adv. directly, quickly; see ܥܓܠ.

ܒܥܕ Aph. ܐܒܥܕ to drive or send far away; to be, go, or depart afar, with ܡܢ; pass. part. far, distant, remote; ܐܘܪ̈ܚܬܐ ܡܒܥܕ̈ܬܐ far journeys; ܣܒܪܐ ܕܡܒܥܕܐ a distant hope. Derivatives, ܡܒܥܕܢܘܬܐ, ܡܒܥܕܘܬܐ.

ܒܥܘ, ܒܥܘܬܐ pl. ܒܥ̈ܘܢ, ܒܥ̈ܘܬܐ rt. ܒܥܐ. f. a request, petition, intercession, rogation; ܒܥܘܬܐ ܕܢܝܢܘܝ̈ܐ Rogation of the Ninevites, a fast of three days occurring three weeks before Lent; ܫܒܘܥܐ ܕܒܥܘܬܐ Rogation week. ܒܒܥܘ usually followed by ܡܢ, interj. I pray thee.

ܒܥܘܐ m. camels' hair.

ܒܥܘܛܬܐ rt. ܒܥܛ. f. kicking, a kick.

ܒܥܘܝܐ pl. ܒܥܘ̈ܝܐ rt. ܒܥܐ. m. a seeker, disputant.

ܒܥܘܪܐ pl. ̈ܐ m. more commonly ܒܥܘܠܬܐ pl. ̈ܬܐ f. unripe fruit, especially grapes; a species of vine.

ܒܥܘܪܐ pl. ̈ܐ. globular dung; ܒܥܘܪ̈ܐ ܕܓܡ̈ܠܐ camels' droppings.

ܒܥܘܬܢܐ rt. ܒܥܐ. humbly desiring.

ܒܥܛ fut. ܢܒܥܘܛ or ܢܒܥܛ to kick, urge on with the heel; to kick over or against, resist, thrust, knock; ܕܠܐ ܢܒܥܘܛ ܠܟܝܢܐ not to kick against nature. Pa. ܒܥܛ to kick often or violently; ܠܥܘܩܣܐ ܒܥܛ to kick against the pricks. Derivatives, ܒܥܘܛܬܐ, ܒܥܛܐ, ܡܒܥܛܢܐ.

ܒܥܝܐ f. ܒܥܝܬܐ pl. m. ̈ܐ, f. ̈ܬܐ rt. ܒܥܐ. he who desires, entreats, or sues; a seeker, suppliant, advocate; a lewd person; ܗܘܢܐ ܒܥܝܐ an inquiring mind; ܗܘܐ ܒܥܝܐ ܠܐܒܝ̈ܕܐ He became a seeker of the lost; ܗܘܘ ܒܥܘ̈ܝܐ ܚܠܦܝ be suppliants for me.

ܒܥܘܝܐ f. ܒܥܘܝܬܐ pl. m. ̈ܐ, f. ̈ܬܐ rt. ܒܥܐ. an intercessor, advocate.

ܒܥܠܘܬܐ rt. ܒܥܠ. f. marriage, married state.

ܒܥܝܪܐ rt. ܒܥܪ. m. collect. noun, with or without Siami. sheep, cattle, beasts of burden, animals; domestic animals opp. ܚܝܘܬܐ; ܒܥܝܪܐ ܕܟܝܐ—ܛܡܐܐ clean and unclean beasts.

ܒܥܝܪܐܝܬ rt. ܒܥܪ. adv. irrationally, like a beast.

ܒܥܝܪܝܐ, ܒܥܝܪܝܬܐ rt. ܒܥܪ. adj. animal, of or like animals.

ܒܥܺܝܪܳܝܳܐ, ܒܥܺܝܪܳܝܬܳܐ rt. ܒܥܪ. adj. *animal, of* or *belonging to animal life, brutal.*

ܒܥܨ participial adj. ܒܥܺܝܨܳܐ. *trampled on, stunted, wretched, spoilt.* Ethp. ܐܶܬܒܥܶܨ uncertain, perhaps a mistake for ܐܶܬܒܥܶܬ. *to be bruised, vexed by a devil.*

ܒܥܶܠ fut. ܢܶܒܥܽܠ, act. part. ܒܳܥܶܠ, pass. part. ܒܥܺܝܠ, ܒܥܺܝܠܬܳܐ, denom. from ܒܥܶܠ. *to own, take for one's own,* i.e. *to marry.* Ethpe. ܐܶܬܒܥܶܠ *to take a husband, be married.*

ܒܥܶܠ, ܒܰܥܠܳܐ pl. ܒܰܥܠܺܝܢ m. *lord, owner, head of a family,* hence *husband;* ܒܥܶܠ ܐܶܡܳܐ or ܒܰܥܠܳܐ ܕܐܶܡܳܐ *step-father;* ܒܥܶܠ ܐܰܢ̈ܬܳܐ *husband;* ܒܥܶܠ ܒܪܰܬ *son-in-law;* ܒܥܶܠ ܚܳܬܳܐ *brother-in-law.* ܒܥܶܠ is often used in construction with other nouns: ܒܥܶܠܕܪܳܐ, ܒܥܶܠܕܪܳܐ, or ܒܥܶܠ ܕܪܳܐ pl. ܒܰܥܠܰܝ ܕܪ̈ܳܐ *enemy, adversary;* ܒܥܶܠܕܒܳܒܳܐ m. ܒܥܶܠܕܒܳܒܬܳܐ f. *enemy, adversary,* especially *the devil;* ܒܥܶܠܕܒܳܒܳܐܺܝܬ adv. *in a hostile manner;* ܒܥܶܠܕܒܳܒܽܘܬܳܐ f. *enmity;* ܒܥܶܠܕܒܳܒܳܝܳܐ, ܒܥܶܠܕܒܳܒܳܝܬܳܐ adj. *hostile, adverse;* ܒܥܶܠܕܺܝܢܳܐ f. ܒܥܶܠܕܺܝܢܬܳܐ pl. m. ܒܰܥܠܰܝ ܕܺܝܢܳܐ *adversary at law;* ܒܥܶܠ ܡܶܠܟܳܐ *counsellor;* ܒܥܶܠ ܩܝܳܡܳܐ *confederate;* ܒܥܶܠ ܪ̈ܳܙܶܐ *counsellor, sharer of counsels* or *secrets;* ܒܥܶܠ ܫܡܳܐ *having the same name;* ܒܥܶܠ ܬܚܽܘܡܳܐ *neighbour, borderer.*

ܒܥܠܳܐ m. *unripe grapes;* cf. ܒܣܪܳܐ.

ܒܥܶܠܰܬ; see ܥܶܠܬܳܐ. *because, on account of.*

ܒܥܰܩ act. part. ܒܳܥܶܩ *to rend, tear up* or *asunder, tear with the teeth;* ܪܽܘܚܳܐ ܒܺܝܫܬܳܐ ܒܥܰܩܬ ܠܛܰܠܝܬܳܐ *an evil spirit rent the girl.* Ethpe. ܐܶܬܒܥܶܩ *to be torn, convulsed.* Pa. ܒܰܥܶܩ *to convulse, tear, agitate violently, confound;* ܒܰܥܶܩ ܠܰܐܠܳܗܰܝܗܽܘܢ Moses *confounded their gods.* Ethpa. only part. ܡܶܬܒܰܥܩܳܐ *torn, convulsed.* Derivative the following—

ܒܽܘܥܩܳܐ m. *convulsions, a convulsive fit.*

ܒܥܰܪ part. ܒܳܥܪܳܐ. *to pluck one by one, pick out, graze; to be fierce* or *cruel;* ܣܰܝܦܳܐ ܒܳܥܪܳܐ *the cruel sword.* Pa. ܒܰܥܰܪ *to pluck, root up, gather out, glean, search diligently;* ܒܰܥܰܪ ܘܰܫܕܳܐ ܒܺܝܫ̈ܳܬܳܐ *he picked out and cast away the bad.* Ethpa. ܐܶܬܒܰܥܰܪ *to search out, inquire diligently, gather, glean.* Palal ܒܰܥܪܰܪ *to make fierce* or *cruel,* or *as brute beasts.* Ethpalal ܐܶܬܒܰܥܪܰܪ *to grow wild, fierce, cruel, to rage,* with ܒ or ܥܰܠ; ܐܺܝܙܰܒܶܠ ܐܰܝܟ ܡܫܰܢܝܬܳܐ ܐܶܬܒܰܥܪܪܰܬ Jezebel *raged like a maniac.* Derivatives, ܒܥܺܝܪܳܐ, ܒܥܺܝܪܳܐܺܝܬ, ܒܥܺܝܪܳܝܳܐ, ܒܥܺܝܪܳܝܳܐܺܝܬ, ܒܥܺܝܪܽܘܬܳܐ, ܒܰܥܪܳܪܳܐܺܝܬ, ܒܰܥܪܳܪܳܝܳܐ, ܒܰܥܪܳܪܽܘܬܳܐ.

ܒܰܥܪܳܪܳܐܺܝܬ adv. *fiercely, savagely.*

ܒܰܥܪܳܪܽܘܬܳܐ f. *brutality, rage, fury.*

ܒܰܥܪܳܪܳܝܳܐ, ܒܰܥܪܳܪܳܝܬܳܐ f. pl. m. ܒܰܥܪܳܪܳܝ̈ܶܐ, f. ܒܰܥܪܳܪܳܝ̈ܳܬܳܐ rt. ܒܥܪ. adj. *wild, fierce, cruel, raging,* as ܓܰܠ̈ܠܶܐ *billows,* ܚܶܒ̈ܠܶܐ *pains,* ܡܰܚܫ̈ܒܳܬܳܐ *thoughts.*

ܒܰܥܪܳܪܳܝܽܘܬܳܐ f. *raging, fury, boisterousness.*

ܒܰܥܪܰܪ Palal of ܒܥܰܪ.

ܒܥܰܬ *to be formidable, assault suddenly, terrify.* Aph. ܐܰܒܥܶܬ *to terrify.* Derivatives, ܒܽܘܥܳܬܳܐ, ܒܥܳܬܽܘܬܳܐ.

ܒܥܳܬܳܐ f. no pl. rt. ܒܥܳܐ. *search, desire, request; disputation; debate;* ܢܦܰܩܘ ܠܒܥܳܬܶܗ *they went in search of him.*

ܒܰܥܬܳܐ or ܒܶܥܬܳܐ (rare) *an egg;* see ܒܺܝܥܬܳܐ.

ܒܰܥܬܳܢܳܝܳܐ, ܒܰܥܬܳܢܳܝܬܳܐ from ܒܰܥܬܳܐ. adj. *egg-shaped.*

ܒܥܳܬܽܘܬܳܐ rt. ܒܥܬ. f. *terror.*

ܒܨܳ *to pine away;* part. ܒܰܨܺܝ, ܒܰܨܝܳܐ *meagre, sickly.* Ethpa. *to grow thin, emaciated.* Derivative, ܒܨܝܽܘܬܳܐ.

ܒܨܳܐ fut. ܢܶܒܨܶܐ, imp. ܒܨܺܝ, inf. ܡܶܒܨܳܐ, act. part. ܒܳܨܶܐ, ܒܳܨܝܳܐ, pass. part. ܒܨܶܐ. *to search into* or *out, trace out, inquire into, investigate;* ܡܳܪܝܳܐ ܒܨܰܝܬܳܢܝ *Lord, Thou hast searched me out.* Ethpe. *a*) *to be inquired into, investigated,* mentally; *b*) *to inquire* or *examine into;* ܐܶܬܒܨܺܝܘ ܕܰܝܪ̈ܳܬܳܐ ܘܥܺܕ̈ܳܬܳܐ *they inquired into the monasteries and churches;* ܟܝܳܢܳܐ ܕܠܳܐ ܡܶܬܒܨܶܐ *an inscrutable nature.* Pa. ܒܰܨܺܝ same as Peal. Aph. ܐܰܒܨܺܝ *to inquire, desire, demand.* Derivatives, ܒܨܽܘܝܳܐ, ܒܨܳܝܳܐ, ܒܨܳܝܬܳܐ, ܡܒܰܨܝܳܢܽܘܬܳܐ, ܡܶܬܒܨܝܳܢܳܐ.

ܒܨܽܘܝܳܐ pl. ܒܨܽܘ̈ܝܶܐ, m. ܒܨܽܘܝܬܳܐ f. rt. ܒܨܳܐ. *an inquirer, explorer,* often in a bad sense of those who are too curious as to hidden or divine matters, such as heretics; *a guardian* of orphans.

ܒܨܽܘܪܳܐ rt. ܒܨܪ. m. *a fault, failing.*

ܒܨܽܘܪܬܳܐ *a counterpane.*

ܒܨܳܝܳܐ, ܒܨܳܝ rt. ܒܨܳܐ. m. *inquiry.*

ܒܰܨܝܽܘܬܳܐ rt. ܒܨܳ. f. *leanness, emaciation.*

ܒܨܝܪܐܝܬ rt. ܒܨܪ. adv. *less, very little, too little;* ܒܨܝܪܐܝܬ ܐܬܚܫܒܘ ܗܘܘ *they held low opinions.*

ܒܨܝܪܘܬܐ rt. ܒܨܪ. f. *fewness, meanness, paucity, deficiency;* ܒܨܝܪܘܬ ܡܛܪܐ *want* or *scarcity of rain;* ܒ̈ ܡܠܘܬܐ *fewness of words,* i.e. moderation in speech; ܒ̈ ܕܓܢܣܢ *our poor* or *vile race;* ܒܨܝܪܘܬܝ *my humble self.*

ܒܨܝܪܢܝܬܐ rt. ܒܨܪ. adj. *very thin, very slight.*

ܒܨܠܐ pl. ̈ m. *an onion;* ܒ̈ ܕܡܥܐ *scilla maritima.*

ܒܨܠܘܠܬܐ or ܒܨܠܘܠܝܬܐ *glowing charcoal.*

ܒܨܪ fut. ܢܒܨܘܪ, imp. ܒܨܘܪ, inf. ܡܒܨܪ, act. part. ܒܨܪ, ܒܨܪܐ, pass. part. ܒܨܝܪ, ܒܨܝܪܐ, ܒܨܝܪܬܐ *to take away, subtract, lessen;* ܐܢܒܨܘܪ ܐܝܠܝܢ ܕܐܘܣܦ *to take back those things which he had added;* with ܡܢ, e.g. ܡܢ ܕܛܝܡܐ *to set a lower price; to fail, be diminished, decrease, wane, withdraw,* of the moon, opp. ܪܒܐ *to wax and wane;* ܒܨܪ ܡܢ ܫܘܥܒܕܐ ܕܣܘܠܛܢ *he withdrew his allegiance from the Sultan.* Participial adj. *wanting, imperfect;* ܦܘܚܡܐ ܒܨܝܪܐ *an imperfect copy;* gram. *defective;* metaph. *low, humble, unworthy; poor, mean, thin;* ܐܢܫܝܢ ܒܨܝܪ̈ܐ *men of low estate;* ܬܘܪܣܝܬܐ ܒܨܝܪܬܐ *poor* or *scanty food.* Adverbial use, with ܡܢ *less* in size, age, number, or value; with ܒ or ܕ *least;* ܠܐ ܡܕܡ ܒܨܝܪ *none the less;* with numbers, *less, minus;* ܐܪܒܥܝܢ ܒܨܝܪ ܚܕܐ *forty* stripes *save one;* ܟܡܐ ܒܨܝܪ and ܒܨܝܪ ܩܠܝܠ *almost, about.* Fem. *too little, not enough, much less;* ܒܨܝܪܐ ܗܝ ܗܕܐ *this is but a little, this is not enough.* Ethpe. ܐܬܒܨܪ *to become less, be subtracted.* Pa. ܒܨܪ *to make less, diminish, take away, subtract;* ܒܨܪܬ ܝܘܡܘܗܝ *thou hast shortened* his *days;* see Apoc. xxii. 19 bis; *to omit, leave out, neglect,* with ܡܢ *from,* ܥܠ *regarding;* ܠܐ ܢܒܨܪ ܡܢܗ ܚܕܐ ܝܘܕ *let him not omit one jot.* Ethpa. ܐܬܒܨܪ *to be diminished, deprived of, omitted; to come short, fail, be inferior;* e.g. ܡܢ ܥܘܬܪܐ *to be deprived of wealth;* ܡܢ ܕܠܡܥܒܕ ܦܐܪ̈ܐ *to fail to yield fruit.* Derivatives, ܒܨܝܪܐܝܬ, ܒܨܝܪܘܬܐ, ܒܨܝܪܢܝܬܐ, ܒܨܘܪܐ, ܒܨܪܐ, ܡܒܨܪܢܐ, ܒܨܪܐ.

ܒܨܪܐ rt. ܒܨܪ. m. *a little, a small portion, particle;* ܒܨܪܐ ܡܢ ܟܠܐ *a part of the whole; the little finger.*

ܒܨܬܐ rt. ܒܨܐ m. no pl. *search, inquiry, question, examination;* ܒܨܬܐ ܕܝܕ *question the 14th;* ܒܨܬܐ ܕܫܪܪܐ *the search for truth.*

ܒܩ rit. abbrev. of ܒܩܝܢܬܐ or ܒܩܠܐ *to the chant.*

ܒܩ fut. ܢܒܘܩ, act. part. ܒܐܩ, pass. part. ܒܩܝܩ and ܒܩܒܩ, ܒܩܝܩܐ, &c. *to be worm-eaten, rotten; to decay;* ܩܝܣܐ ܒܩܝܩܐ *rotted wood;* ܒܩܒܩܝܢ ܡܢ ܐܪܟܐ ܕܫܢܝܐ *decayed with age.* Aph. ܐܒܩ *to fret, consume.* Derivatives, ܒܩܒܩܘܬܐ, ܒܩܐ.

ܒܩܐ fut. ܢܒܩܐ, imp. ܒܩܝ, inf. ܡܒܩܐ, act. part. ܒܩܐ, ܒܩܝܐ, pass. part. ܒܩܐ, ܒܩܝܐ *to try, search, prove, examine, inquire into,* with ܒ or ܠ; ܟܕ ܒܩܐ ܠܨܒܘܬܐ *after he had tried the matter, inquired into it;* ܒܩܝܢܢ ܠܐܠܗܐ *we were proved,* or *approved, by God.* Ethpe. ܐܬܒܩܝ *to be tried, proved;* ܒܬܪ ܫܢܬܐ ܕܡܬܒܩܐ *after a year's trial, novitiate.* Pa. ܒܩܝ *to prove,* seldom used, the Ethpa. ܐܬܒܩܝ having an active sense, *to prove, consider, observe* with ܒ; ܐܬܒܩܘ ܒܫܘܫܢ̈ܐ *consider the lilies.* Derivatives, ܒܩܘܝܐ, ܒܘܩܝܐ, ܒܩܝܐ, ܒܩܝܢܐ, ܡܬܒܩܝܢܘܬܐ.

ܒܩܐ pl. ̈ rt. ܒܩ. m. *a gnat.*

ܒܩܒܩ *to boil, bubble;* mimetic, cf. ܒܥܒܥ.

ܒܩܘܝܐ (rt. ܒܩܐ Arabic *to last, endure*) m. adj. *lasting, permanent.*

ܒܩܘܪܙܐ some article of apparel, perh. = *pectorale.*

ܒܩܝܐ rt. ܒܩܐ. m. *trial, investigation.*

ܒܩܝܢܐ rt. ܒܩܐ. m. *trial.*

ܒܩܒܩܘܬܐ rt. ܒܩ. f. *rottenness* of wood.

ܒܩܠܬܐ pl. ̈ f. *a cutaneous eruption, white spots on the skin.*

ܒܩܪ fut. ܢܒܩܘܪ, imp. ܒܩܘܪ, inf. ܡܒܩܪ, act. part. ܒܩܪ, pass. part. ܒܩܝܪ *to ask, question, seek; attend to;* ܐܣܝܐ ܒܥܝܢܢ *we seek a physician;* ܒܥܘܬܗܘܢ ܠܐ ܒܩܝܪ̈ܢ *their complaints were neglected.* Ethpe. and Ethpa. ܐܬܒܩܪ and ܐܬܒܩܪ *to be searched, examined.* Pa. ܒܩܪ *to examine.* Derivatives, ܒܘܩܪܐ and probably the four following words, the primary meaning of the root being *to cleave open,* hence, *a*) *to plough; b*) *to find out.*

ܒܩܪܐ pl. ̈ f. collect. noun, *a herd, drove,* esp. of kine, but also of swine; *an ox.*

ܒܩܪܐ pl. ܐ̈ m. *a herdsman, cowherd.*

ܒܩܪܐܝܬ adv. *by herds* or *shoals.*

ܒܩܪܢܝܐ f. ܒܩܪܢܝܬܐ pl. m. ܝ̈ܐ, f. ܝ̈ܬܐ adj. *gregarious.*

ܒܪ, ܒܪܐ m. *the open country;* with ܕ or a noun in the constr. st. *of* or *belonging to the open country, wild;* ܚܝܘܬܐ ܕܒܪܐ *the beasts of the field.* Metaph. *that which is outside, the outside;* ܠܒܪ adv. *without, outside,* opp. ܠܓܘ *within, inside; outer, out of doors.* Metaph. *strange, foreign;* ܠܒܪ ܡܢ *except, without, besides, beyond;* ܡܢ ܒܪ oftener ܡܢ ܠܒܪ *on the outside,* opp. ܡܢ ܠܓܘ or ܡܢ ܓܘ *on the inside.* Derivatives, ܒܪܝܐܝܬ, verb ܒܪܝ see ܒܪܐ, ܒܪܝܢܐܝܬ, ܒܪܝ, ܒܪܝܐ see ܒܪܝܢܐ, ܒܪܝܬܐ, ܒܪܝܬܐ, ܒܪܝܢܘܬܐ.

ܒܪ, ܒܪܐ f. ܒܪܬܐ, ܒܪ̈ܬܐ, pl. m. ܒܢܝܢ, ܒܢ̈ܝܐ, constr. st. ܒܢܝ, f. ܒܢܬ, ܒܢ̈ܬܐ, constr. st. ܒܢ̈ܬ. *son, daughter; the young of animals;* ܒܪܐ ܒܘܟܪܐ *firstborn son;* ܒܪܐ ܪܒܐ—ܙܥܘܪܐ *elder, younger, son;* ܒܪ ܒܪܐ or ܒܪܬ ܒܪܐ *grandson* or *daughter;* ܒܪ ܕܕܐ or ܒܪܬ ܕܕܐ *cousin;* ܒܪ ܐܚܐ or ܒܪܬ ܐܚܐ *nephew, niece.* Fem. metaph. *suburbs, dependent villages* or *towns;* collect. *the people of one race* or *inhabiting one town* or *country;* poet. ܒܪܬ ܥܒܪܝܐ or ܒܪܬ ܐܒܪܗܡ *the Hebrews.*

ܒܪ is used in construction with various nouns: *a*) to express age; ܒܪ ܫܢܬܐ ܚܕܐ *one year old;* ܒܪ ܬܠܬ ܫܢܝܢ, &c. *b*) to form patronymics and surnames, with the name of the father or head of the race, and often metaph. *c*) to express any close relation, subjection, or similarity.

ܒܪ ܐ̈ܓܪܐ; see ܐ̈ܓܪܐ, *a demon;* ܕܒܪ ܐ̈ܓܪܐ *lunatic.*

ܒܪ ܐܕܘܡ pl. ܒܢܝ ܐܕܘܡ *Edomite.*

ܒܪ ܐܢܫ *any one;* pl. *men.*

ܒܪ ܐܕܫܐ *of the same sort, like.*

ܒܪ ܐܘܡܢܘܬܐ *agreeing, allied.*

ܒܪ ܐܘܡܢܘܬܐ *of the same trade.*

ܒܢܝ ܐܘܡܬܐ *those of one nation.*

ܒܪ ܐܙܡܠܐ *a chisel, tool; a dagger; a handbook, manual.*

ܒܪ ܐܝܬܘܬܐ *consubstantial.*

ܒܪ ܐܟܪܐ *a fellow-workman.*

ܒܪ ܐܢܫܐ; see ܐܢܫ and ܒܪܢܫ. *a man, a son of man.* As a title of our Lord it is generally written ܒܪܗ ܕܐܢܫܐ *the Son of man.*

ܒܪ ܐܣܟܘܠܐ *scholar, schoolfellow.*

ܒܪ ܐܪܙܐ see ܒܪ ܐܪܙܐ.

ܒܪ ܐܬܢܐ *foal of an ass.*

ܒܪ ܐܬܪܐ *native, inhabitant.*

ܒܪ ܒܝܬܐ *bondslave, one born in the house; a steward, dispenser;* ܒܢܝ ܒܝܬܐ *the household.*

ܒܪ ܒܣܪܐ *man, human being;* pl. *kindred.*

ܒܪ ܒܩܪܐ *calf, bullock that has not yet been yoked.*

ܒܢܝ ܒܪܐ *sons of the desert; Bedouin.*

ܒܪ ܓܒܐ *adherents of a sect* or *party, companions.*

ܒܪ ܓܘܪܐ *bastard.*

ܒܢܝ ܓܢܘܢܐ *sons of the bride-chamber,* i.e. *friends admitted to the marriage.*

ܒܪ ܓܢܣܐ *of the same race, kindred,* or *sort;* pl. *kindred.*

ܒܢܝ ܕܘܒܪܐ *of one way of life.*

ܒܪ ܕܡܘܬܐ *like.*

ܒܢܝ ܕܪܐ *contemporaries, of the same generation.*

ܒܪ ܕܪܝܫ; see ܕܪܝܫ. *again.*

ܒܪ ܗܦܪܟܝܐ *provincial, diocesan.*

ܒܪ ܗܝܡܢܘܬܐ *holding the same faith;* pl. *the faithful.*

ܒܪ ܙܒܢܐ *contemporary.*

ܒܪ ܙܘܓܐ *yokefellow, companion; like, likeminded; husband, wife.*

ܒܪ ܙܢܩܐ pl. ܒܪܙܢܩܐ *greaves;* see ܙܢܩ.

ܒܪ ܙܪܥܐ *a seed, grain of seed.*

ܒܪ ܚܐܪܐ *free, free-born, noble;* used also of *a freed slave.*

ܒܪ ܚܕܝܐ *breast-plate.*

ܒܪ ܚܘܒܐ *friend.*

ܒܪ ܚܛܝܐ or ܚܛܗܐ *sinner,* pl. *wicked men.*

ܒܪ ܚܝܠܐ *man of worth; soldier.*

ܒܪ ܚܢܢܐ *Son of the Merciful One,* i.e. Christ.

ܒܢܝ ܚܣܢܐ *garrison.*

ܒܪ ܚܫܘܟܐ *lover of darkness.*

ܒܪ ܛܒܐ *Son of the Good,* i.e. Christ.

ܒܪ ܛܘܗܡܐ *cognate, of the same race; noble.*

ܒܢܝ ܛܘܥܝܝܢ *lovers of error;* opp. ܒܢܝ ܫܪܝܪܘܬܐ *lovers of the truth.*

ܒܪ ܬܠܡܝܕܐ *disciple.*

ܒܰܪ ܝܰܘܡܶܗ *on the same day, immediately;* compare ܒܰܪ ܝܰܘܡܳܢܳܐ *lasting only a day;* pl. *born on the same day.*

ܒܰܪ ܝܰܘܢܳܐ *young dove.*

ܒܰܪ ܝܰܡܺܝܢ or ܒܰܪ ܝܳܡܺܝܢ probably a confusion of the Heb. name ܕܶܒܪܰܝ ܝܰܘܡܺܝܢ *Chronicles* with ܒܰܪ ܝܰܘܡܶܗ (see above).

ܒܰܪ ܝܰܡܺܝܢܳܐ *he who stands* or *sits at the right hand;* pl. especially *those set at our Lord's right hand at the last judgement.*

ܒܢܰܝ ܝܳܪ̈ܬܽܘܬܳܐ *co-heirs.*

ܒܰܪ ܟܝܳܢܳܐ *of one nature, consubstantial.*

ܒܰܪ ܠܘܳܝܳܐ *companion, fellow-traveller.*

ܒܰܪ ܠܶܠܝܳܐ *lasting only one night, that same night; an evil-doer.*

ܒܢܰܝ ܡܘܰܠܟܳܢܳܐ *sharers of the promise, having the same promise.*

ܒܰܪ ܡܰܘܬܳܐ *guilty* or *condemned to death.*

ܒܰܪ ܡܰܘܬܒܳܐ *consort; assessor.*

ܒܰܪ ܡܶܠܟܳܐ *counsellor.*

ܒܰܪ ܡܰܠܟܽܘܬܳܐ *heir of the kingdom.*

ܒܰܪ ܡܢܳܬܳܐ *partaker, sharer;* ܒܰܪ ܬܪ̈ܶܝܢ ܡ̈ܢܰܘܳܢ *receiving a double portion* of the inheritance.

ܒܪܳܐ ܕܡܰܥܡܽܘܕܺܝܬܳܐ *godson.*

ܒܰܪ ܡܪܰܒܝܳܢܳܐ *foster-brother.*

ܒܢܰܝ ܡܰܪܥܺܝܬܳܐ *subjects,* especially of a spiritual ruler.

ܒܢܰܝ ܢܒ̈ܺܝܶܐ *disciples of the prophets, those educated to be teachers.*

ܒܰܪ ܢܽܘܗܪܳܐ *a child of light, spiritually enlightened; the blessed, the angels.*

ܒܰܪ ܢܽܘܟܪܳܝܳܐ *stranger, foreigner.*

ܒܰܪ ܢܺܝܪܳܐ *bearing the same yoke, fellow-pupils;* pl. f. *women married to the same man.*

ܒܢܳܬ ܝܰܥܢܳܐ *ostriches.*

ܒܰܪܢܳܫܳܐ pl. ܒܢܰܝܢܳܫܳܐ; see under ܒܪܢܫ.

ܒܰܪ ܣܺܝܥܬܳܐ *colleague.*

ܒܢܰܝ ܥܶܕ̈ܬܳܐ *the clergy.*

ܒܰܪ ܥܽܘܡܪܳܐ *one brought up* or *living in a monastery, monk.*

ܒܰܪ ܥܽܘܒܳܐ *intimate friend* or *companion.*

ܒܰܪ ܥܰܠܡܳܐ *layman, secular.*

ܒܰܪ ܥܰܡܳܐ *of the same race;* ܒܪܰܬ ܥܰܡܳܐ collect. *the people;* pl. *laity, the common people.*

ܒܰܪ ܥܰܡܡܳܝܳܐ *gentile, heathen.*

ܒܰܪ ܥܶܢܝܳܢܳܐ *gossip, intimate acquaintance.*

ܒܢܰܝ ܥܶܪ̈ܘܒܳܐ *mixed race.*

ܒܰܪ ܦܽܘܠܚܳܢܳܐ *partner in labour, mate.*

ܒܰܪ ܦܶܚܡܳܐ *like, equal.*

ܒܢܰܝ ܦܰܠܳܛܝܢ *courtiers.*

ܒܢܰܝ ܦܽܠܚܽܘܬܳܐ *soldiers,* especially *mercenaries; servants.*

ܒܢܰܝ ܦܬܳܟܪ̈ܳܐ *idolators;* ܕܒܢܰܝ ܦܬܳܟܪ̈ܳܐ *things offered to idols.*

ܒܰܪ ܨܰܘܪܳܐ *a collar.*

ܒܢܰܝ ܩܽܘܡܬܳܐ *those of the same age.*

ܒܢܰܝ ܩܽܘܫܬܳܐ *lovers of truth.*

ܒܰܪ ܩܝܳܡܳܐ *a monk;* ܒܪܰܬ ܩܝܳܡܳܐ *a nun.*

ܒܪܰܬ ܩܳܠܳܐ or ܩܳܠܳܐ pl. ܒܢܳܬ ܩ̈ܳܠܳܐ *sound, echo; voice, word, saying, language;* gram. *a term, expression, word;* ܒܪܰܬ ܩܳܠܳܢܳܐ adj. gram. *belonging to a word, verbal.*

ܒܢܰܝ ܩܠܺܝܪܽܘܣ or ܩܠܺܝܪܽܘܣ *the clergy.*

ܒܢܰܝ ܩܪܺܝܬܳܐ *inhabitants of a village* or *town; fellow-townsmen.*

ܒܰܪ ܪܳܙܳܐ or ܪ̈ܳܙܶܐ *sharer of a secret,* hence *admitted to counsels* or *purposes, counsellor; partaker of Holy Communion.*

ܒܰܪ ܪܶܥܝܳܢܳܐ *holding the same tenets, of one faith* or *sect.*

ܒܰܪ ܫܽܘܪܳܐ *outwork.*

ܒܰܪ ܫܰܠܡܽܘܬܳܐ *one in accord* or *agreement.*

ܒܰܪ ܫܡܳܐ *of the same name.*

ܒܰܪ ܫܢܳܐ *of the same age;* ܒܰܪ ܫܢܺܝܢ with a number, so many *years old;* ܒܰܪ ܫܰܢ̱ܬܳܐ *of one year's age* or *growth.*

ܒܰܪ ܫܳܥܬܳܐ *one hour old;* ܒܰܪ ܫܳܥܬܳܗ and ܒܰܪ ܫܳܥܬܶܗ *immediately.*

ܒܰܪ ܫܰܪܒܬܳܐ *of the same tribe* or *stock;* pl. *kindred, fellow-countrymen.*

ܒܰܪ ܬܰܘܕܺܝܬܳܐ *of the same faith.*

ܒܰܪ ܬܽܘܪܳܐ *bullock.*

ܒܰܪ ܬܚܽܘܡܳܐ *living on the borders, neighbour.*

ܒܰܪ ܬܘܪܣܺܝܬܳܐ *pupil, one adopted* or *educated;* pl. *fellow-pupils, companions.*

ܒܰܪ ܬܪܥܺܝܬܳܐ *holding the same tenets* or *opinions.*

ܒܰܪ ܬܶܫܡܶܫܬܳܐ *fellow-servant* or *minister, colleague.*

DERIVATIVES, ܒܪܘܢܐ, ܒܪܘܬܐ, ܒܪܘܬܢܘܬܐ, ܒܪܢܝܐ, &c.

ܒܳܪ, ܒܳܪܳܐ same as ܒܺܐܪ. f. *a well, a pit.*

ܒܪܐ Pa. ܒܰܪܺܝ denom. from ܒܰܪ, ܒܳܪܳܐ. *to leave out, omit, remove;* ܡܶܢ ܝܰܨܦܳܬ݂ܳܐ ܕܥܰܠܡܳܐ ܡܒܰܪܝܳܐ ܢܰܟ݂ܦܽܘܬ݂ܳܐ temperance *exempts* or *sets free from daily cares;* pass. part. ܡܒܰܪܳܝ, ܡܒܰܪܝܳܐ *beyond, remote, exempt, excluded, foreign, alien;* ܗܰܘܢܳܐ ܡܒܰܪܝܳܐ *the mind freed* or *apart from* the body; ܡܒܰܪܳܝ ܡܶܢ ܫܽܘܚܠܳܦܳܐ *not subject to change.*

ܒܪܐ fut. ܢܶܒܪܶܐ, imper. ܒܪܺܝ, inf. ܡܶܒܪܳܐ *to create;* act. part. ܒܳܪܶܐ, ܒܳܪܝܳܐ subst. *the Creator;* pass. part. ܒܪܶܐ, ܒܪܺܝܳܐ, fem. ܒܪܺܝܬ݂ܳܐ, pl. m. and f. ܒܪܺܝܶܐ, emph. f. ܒܰܪܺܝܬ݂ܳܐ oftener ܒܪܺܝܬ݂ܳܐ. *a creature, the Creation,* hence *the world, the earth;* ܣܶܦܪܳܐ ܕܒܪܺܝܬ݂ܳܐ *the Book of Genesis.* Ethpa. ܐܶܬ݂ܒܪܺܝ *to be created.* Derivatives, ܒܪܽܘܝܳܐ, ܒܪܽܘܝܽܘܬ݂ܳܐ, ܒܪܺܝܬ݂ܳܐ, ܒܪܺܝܬ݂ܳܐ, ܒܪܺܝܬ݂ܳܢܳܐ, ܒܪܺܝܬ݂ܳܢܳܐ, ܡܶܬ݂ܒܪܝܳܢܽܘܬ݂ܳܐ.

ܒܪܐ emph. st. of ܒܰܪ *a son.*

ܒܰܪܳܐܺܝܬ݂ and ܒܰܪܳܝܳܐܺܝܬ݂ rt. ܒܰܪ, ܒܳܪܳܐ. adv. *outwardly, in appearance.*

ܒܰܪܐ̱ܢܳܫܳܐ; see ܒܰܪ or ܒܪܢܫ. adj. *human.*

ܒܰܪܒܰܪܳܐܺܝܬ݂ adv. *barbarously.*

ܒܰܪܒܰܪܳܝܳܐ f. ܝܬ݂ܳܐ pl. m. ܝܶܐ, f. ܝܳܬ݂ܳܐ. *barbarian.*

ܒܰܪܒܰܪܳܝܽܘܬ݂ܳܐ f. *barbarism.*

ܒܰܪܕܳܐ m. *hail;* ܟܺܐܦܶܐ ܕܒܰܪܕܳܐ *hail-stones.*

ܒܰܪܕܳܐ pl. ܒܰܪܕܶܐ m. *speckled, spotted, a disease of the eyelids, small hard tubercles* forming on them; *variegated.*

ܒܰܪܕܽܘܬܳܐ pl. ܒܰܪܕܽܘܬܶܐ m. *mule.*

ܒܰܪܕܥܬ݂ܳܐ f. *pack-saddle, saddle-cloth;* see ܒܽܘܪܕܥܬ݂ܳܐ.

ܒܰܪܗܳܝܽܘܬ݂ܳܐ rt. ܒܪܗ. *clearness, brightness.*

ܒܳܪܽܘܝܳܐ m. ܒܳܪܽܘܝܬ݂ܳܐ f. rt. ܒܪܐ. *the Creator;* ܡܶܠܬ݂ܳܐ ܒܳܪܽܘܝܬ݂ܳܐ *the Creating Word.*

ܒܳܪܽܘܝܽܘܬ݂ܳܐ f. rt. ܒܪܐ. *creative power, creation, creatorship.*

ܒܪܽܘܟ݂ *a*) imper. of verb ܒܪܟ. *b*) abs. st. of ܒܽܘܪܟܳܐ *knee.*

ܒܶܪܽܘܠܳܐ pl. ܒܶܪܽܘܠܶܐ generally m. in the sing. and f. in the pl. *beryl.*

ܒܰܪܽܘܠܚܳܐ m. *pearl;* ܓܶܐܦܳܐ ܕܒܰܪܽܘܠܚܳܐ *beryl.*

ܒܪܽܘܢܳܐ *a*) dim. of ܒܰܪ, *little son.* *b*) for ܒܪܽܘܝܳܐ.

ܒܪܽܘܬ݂ܳܐ f. *a*) *the cypress, juniper.* *b*) or ܒܪܽܘܬ݂ܽܘܬ݂ܳܐ rt. ܒܪ. *sonship, sons;* ܡܰܘܟ݂ܠܳܦܳܐ ܕܒܪܽܘܬ݂ܗ *the becoming extinct of all his sons.*

ܒܰܪܺܝ Pa. parts. act. and pass. ܡܒܰܪܺܝ pl. ܡܒܰܪܝܳܢܶܐ, f. ܡܒܰܪܝܳܢܺܝܬ݂ܳܐ *clear* or *transparent.* Ettaph. ܐܶܬ݂ܒܰܪܝ *to be made clear, shown clearly.*

ܒܰܪܝܳܐ pl. ܝܶܐ m. *a he-goat, a buck.*

ܒܰܪܳܝܳܐ f. ܒܰܪܳܝܬ݂ܳܐ pl. m. ܝܶܐ, f. ܒܰܪܳܝܳܬ݂ܳܐ rt. ܒܰܪ, ܒܳܪܳܐ. *a*) *outer, distant, further; foreign;* opp. ܓܰܘܳܝܶܐ ܠܒܰܪܳܝܶܐ *those within and those without, besieged and besiegers, citizens and foreigners.* *b*) *outward, literal;* ܗܽܘܦܳܟ݂ܳܐ ܒܰܪܳܝܳܐ *the literal meaning.* *c*) *specious, in outward appearance.* *d*) *foreign to the Church,* hence *secular, profane, pagan;* ܚܶܟ݂ܡܬ݂ܳܐ ܒܰܪܳܝܬ݂ܳܐ *heathen wisdom.* *e*) f. emph. *extraneous, superfluous matter* in writing. *f*) *wild* animals or plants.

ܒܳܪܝܳܐ; see ܒܪܐ part. act. *creator.*

ܒܰܪܳܝܳܐܺܝܬ݂ rt. ܒܰܪ, ܒܳܪܳܐ. adv. *outwardly, in appearance.*

ܒܰܪܳܝܽܘܬ݂ܳܐ f. rt. ܒܰܪ, ܒܳܪܳܐ. *the outer part, appearance* or *form;* ܒܰܪܳܝܽܘܬ݂ܗ ܕܡܰܫܟܳܐ *the outer cuticle, epidermis.*

ܒܪܺܝܽܘܬ݂ܳܐ f. rt. ܒܪܐ. *creation, formation.*

ܒܳܪܳܝܳܐ m. ܒܳܪܳܝܬ݂ܳܐ f. rt. ܒܪܐ. adj. *of the creator.*

ܒܰܪܝܳܐܺܝܬ݂ from ܒܰܪ, ܒܳܪܳܐ. adv. *simply.*

ܒܰܪܝܽܘܬ݂ܳܐ from ܒܳܪܳܐ. f. *simplicity, ignorance.*

ܒܪܺܫܺܝܬ݂ E-Syr. ܒܪܺܫܺܝܬ݂ Gen. i. 1. *In the beginning;* see ܪܺܫ.

ܒܰܪܺܝܬ݂ܳܐ fem. of ܒܰܪ, ܒܳܪܳܐ, pl. ܝܳܬ݂ܳܐ *fields, wilds, desert places.*

ܒܪܺܝܬ݂ܳܐ pl. ܝܳܬ݂ܳܐ f. *a street, broad place.*

ܒܪܺܝܬ݂ܳܐ; see ܒܪܐ fem. pass. part. *a creature, the Creation.*

ܒܪܺܝܬ݂ܳܢܳܝܳܐ pl. ܝܶܐ from the above. adj. *of* or *referring to the Creation, created.*

ܒܪܟ and ܒܪܶܟ ܒܪܟ fut. ܢܶܒܪܽܘܟ݂ and ܢܶܒܪܽܘܟ݂, parts. ܒܳܪܶܟ݂, ܒܳܪܟܳܐ; ܒܪܺܝܟ݂ and ܒܪܺܝܟ݂, ܟܳܐ, ܟܬ݂ܳܐ *to bend the knee, kneel, bow down;* often with ܥܰܠ ܒܽܘܪܟܰܝܗܽܘܢ; ܒܳܪܟܳܢ ܘܝܳܠܕܳܢ the hinds *bow themselves to bring forth young,* Job xxxix. 4. The old form of pass. part. is used for a present part. ܒܪܺܝܟ݂ ܥܰܠ ܐܰܪܥܳܐ *kneeling on the earth,* but the form ܒܪܺܝܟ݂ is used as a participial adj. *blessed,* also in the form ܒܪܺܝܟ݂ ܗܽܘ = ܒܪܺܝܟ݂ܽܘ as a benediction; ܡܕܺܝܢܬ݂ܳܐ ܒܪܺܝܟ݂ܬ݂ܳܐ *the blessed city;* cf. Pa. part. rit. ܒܪܺܝܟ݂ܽܘ ܡܫܺܝܚܳܐ *Blessed be Christ.* Pa. ܒܰܪܶܟ݂ *to bless;* rit. *to give* or *pronounce the blessing;* ܒܰܪܶܟ݂ ܡܳܪܝ *Bless O my Lord,* a formula of frequent use before and during prayer; pass. part. ܡܒܰܪܰܟ, ܡܒܰܪܟܳܐ f. ܡܒܰܪܟܬܳܐ pl. m. ܝܢ̈ـ, f. ܝܳܬ̈ـ. *blessed, the Blessed One;* ܒܪܶܗ ܕܡܒܰܪܟܳܐ *the Son of God;* f. frequently used of the Blessed Virgin and of Christian cities, especially of Edessa. Ethpa. ܐܶܬ݂ܒܰܪܰܟ *to be blessed, receive* or *seek a blessing, to visit holy places* and *tombs, to say farewell;* ܨܰܠܺܝ ܘܶܐܬ݂ܒܰܪܰܟ ܡܶܢ ܩܰܒ݂ܪܳܐ ܩܰܕܺܝܫܳܐ *he prayed and received blessing at the Holy Sepulchre.* Aph. ܐܰܒܪܶܟ *to make to kneel down, cause to bow.* Metaph. ܐܰܒܪܶܟ ܥܰܡ̈ܡܶܐ ܬܚܶܝܬ ܣܰܝܦܳܐ *I will make the heathen bow beneath* thy *sword.* Derivatives, ܒܘܪܟܳܐ, ܒܘܪܟܬܳܐ, ܒܘܪܟܬܳܢܳܐ, ܒܪܟܐ, ܡܒܰܪܟܳܢܳܐ, ܡܒܪܟܢܘܬܐ.

ܒܪܳܟ, ܒܪܳܟ݂ܳܐ rt. ܒܪܟ. m. rit. *a genuflexion, a blessing, benediction.*

ܒܪܰܚܡܰܢ̈ܶܐ m. pl. *Brahmins.*

ܒܪܰܡ *but, but yet, however, nevertheless,* with ܐܶܠܳܐ, ܠܳܐ, or ܟܠ.

ܒܪܰܡ fut. ܢܶܒܪܽܘܡ, act. part. ܒܳܪܶܡ, ܒܳܪܡܳܐ, pass. part. ܒܪܺܝܡ *to gnaw, eat into* of worms, moths, locusts, &c. Metaph. of hunger, pain, &c. Ethpe. ܐܶܬ݂ܒܪܶܡ *to be gnawed, eaten into.* Pa. part. ܡܒܰܪܡܳܐ *carious, worm-eaten, moth-eaten.*

ܒܪܽܘܡܳܐ m. perh. βρῶμα, *erosion;* ܒܪܽܘܡܳܐ ܕܡܰܪܢܺܝܬܳܐ *fretting cares,* hence the verb ܒܪܡ.

ܒܳܪܳܢܳܐܝܬ rt. ܒܪ. *outwardly, openly;* cf. ܒܪܳܝܬ.

ܒܰܪܢܳܫܳܐ pl. ܒܢܰܝܢܳܫܳܐ m. comp. of ܒܰܪ ܐ݈ܢܳܫܳܐ, f. ܒܪܰܬ݂ ܐ݈ܢܳܫܳܐ pl. ܒܢ̈ܳܬ݂ ܐ݈ܢܳܫܳܐ. *son of man, man;* ܒܰܪܢܳܫܳܐ ܕܠܓܰܘ *the inner being.* Derivatives, ܒܰܪܢܳܫܽܘܬ݂ܳܐ, ܡܬܒܪܢܫܢܐ, ܒܪܢܫܝܐ, ܒܪܢܫܝܐܝܬ, ܒܘܪܢܫܐ, and the denom. verb—

ܐܶܬ݂ܒܰܪܢܰܫ *to become man;* ܡܶܠܬ݂ܳܐ ܐܶܬ݂ܒܰܣܰܪ ܘܰܐܠܳܗܳܐ ܐܶܬ݂ܒܰܪܢܰܫ *the Word took flesh and God became man.*

ܒܪܰܙ fut. ܢܶܒܪܽܘܙ and ܢܶܒܪܰܙ, imper. ܒܪܽܘܙ, part. ܒܳܪܶܙ *a) to bore* the ears, *pierce, transfix;* ܠܳܐ ܒܪܰܙ ܠܶܟܝ ܥܰܩܬ݂ܳܐ *no sorrow pierced thee, entered thy heart. b) to lay open, explain clearly.* Pa. and Aph. *to make apparent, clear;* part. *lucid, luminous.* Ettaph. ܐܶܬ݁ܒܪܰܙ *to be clearly proved, demonstrated.* Derivatives, ܒܪܙܳܐ, ܡܒܪܙܢܘܬܐ, ܡܒܪܙܢܐܝܬ.

ܒܪܳܙܳܐ m. *a perforation; clear evidence.*

ܒܪܰܩ fut. ܢܶܒܪܽܘܩ, parts. ܒܳܪܶܩ, ܒܪܺܝܩ. *a) to shine, flash, lighten. b) to be set on edge* as the teeth, *be benumbed, blighted, stupefied.* Aph. ܐܰܒܪܶܩ *to cause to shine, flash, lighten;* ܢܰܝܙܟ݂ܳܐ ܕܡܰܒܪܶܩ *a glittering spear.* Ettaph. ܐܶܬ݁ܒܪܶܩ *to shine, lighten, coruscate.* Derivatives, ܒܪܩܐ, ܒܪܘܩܐ, ܒܪܩܢܐ.

ܒܰܪܩܳܐ pl. ܝܢ̈ـ rt. ܒܪܩ. m. *lightning, a flash of lightning.*

ܒܳܪܩܳܐ m. *emerald.*

ܒܪܳܩܳܐ rt. ܒܪܩ. m. *grating* of the teeth.

ܒܪܩܐ *pebbles.*

ܒܰܪܩܽܘܩܳܐ *the apricot.*

ܒܰܪܩܳܢܳܐ, ܢܳܝܬܳܐ ـ rt. ܒܪܩ. adj. *pertaining to lightning;* ܥܢܳܢܳܐ ܒܰܪܩܳܢܳܝܬܳܐ *a thunder-cloud.*

ܒܰܪܩܳܩܳܐ m. *a canal, a cut to draw off water from a river.*

ܒܪܪ from ܒܰܪ, ܒܳܪܳܐ, only pass. part. ܒܪܺܝܪ, ܒܪܺܝܪܳܐ, ܒܪܺܝܪܬܳܐ *in a natural state, simple, innocent, foolish, rude;* ܝܰܘܢܳܐ ܒܪܺܝܪܬܳܐ *the innocent dove.*

ܒܪܰܬ݂, ܒܪܰܬ݂ܳܐ pl. ܒܢܳܬ݂, ܒܢܳܬ݂ܳܐ, fem. of ܒܰܪ, ܒܪܳܐ. *daughter; egg, young;* ܒܢܳܬ݂ܳܐ ܕܚܶܘܝܳܬ݂ܳܐ *the serpent's brood.*

ܒܺܝܪܬܳܐ f. *castle, palace;* see ܒܺܝܪܬܳܐ.

ܒܣܒܣ or ܒܰܣܒܳܣܳܐ m. *ruta sylvestris, wild rue.*

ܒܫܝܠܘܬܐ f. *ripeness, perfection.*

ܒܫܶܠ fut. ܢܶܒܫܰܠ, imp. ܒܫܰܠ, inf. ܡܶܒܫܰܠ, act. part. ܒܳܫܶܠ, ܒܳܫܠܳܐ, pass. part. ܒܫܺܝܠ, ܒܫܺܝܠܳܐ, ܒܫܺܝܠܬܳܐ *to ripen, grow ripe, to boil, melt;* part. pass. *ripe, boiled, sodden.* Ethpe. ܐܶܬ݂ܒܫܶܠ *to be boiled.* Pa. ܒܰܫܶܠ *to ripen, make ripe, boil.* Ethpa. ܐܶܬ݂ܒܰܫܰܠ *to be ripened, brought to ripeness; boiled, digested.* Derivatives, ܒܘܫܠܐ, ܒܫܠܐ, ܒܫܝܠܘܬܐ, ܡܒܫܠܢܐ, ܡܒܫܠܢܘܬܐ.

ܒܫܳܠܳܐ m. rt. ܒܫܠ. *ripeness, perfection of growth.*

ܒܳܬ; see ܒܘܬ. *to spend the night.*

ܒܰܬܺܝܠܶܐ Ar. *a bottle, wine-vessel;* cf. ܒܛܝܠܐ.

ܒܬܘܠܳܐ, ܒܬܽܘܠܳܐ pl. ܝܢ̈ـ. m. *an unmarried man, celibate;* adj. *chaste, virgin;* pl. *tokens of virginity, the virgin state;* ܛܰܒ݂ܥ̈ܶܐ ܕܒܬ݂ܽܘܠܽܘܬ݂ܳܗ ܕܡܰܪܝܰܡ *the seals of virginity of Mary;* ܕܦܩܝܥܝܢ ܒܬܘ̈ܠܘܗܿ *a deflowered virgin.* Derivatives the following words—

ܒܬܘܠܬܐ, ܒܬܘ̈ܠܬܐ pl. ܒܬܘܠܢ, ܒܬܘܠܬܐ f. subst. and adj. *virgin, maiden;* ܐܪܥܐ ܒܬܘܠܬܐ *virgin soil. Virgo,* a sign of the Zodiac.

ܒܬܘܠܐܝܬ adv. *modestly, like a virgin.*

ܒܬܘܠܘܬܐ f. *chastity, virginity, celibacy;* ܡܪܝܡ ܦܫܬ ܒܒܬܘܠܘܬܐ *Mary remained a virgin;* with ܐܬܢܕܪ *to be vowed to virginity* or *celibacy.*

ܒܬܘܠܝܐ f. ܒܬܘܠܝܬܐ pl. m. ܝ̈ܐ, f. ܝ̈ܬܐ. adj. *virginal, of* or *belonging to a virgin, chaste.*

ܒܛܝܠܬܐ f. *a bottle;* cf. ܒܛܐܠ.

ܒܬܠ Pa. denom. from ܒܬܘܠܐ; *to deflour, violate* a virgin. Ethpa. ܐܬܒܬܠ *to be deflowered, violated.*

ܒܬܪ prep. from ܒ and ܐܬܪ, takes suffixes like a noun in the sing., rarely those of the pl., *after, following;* ܐܝܠܝܢ ܕܒܬܪܢ *our successors;* ܕܒܬܪ *next;* ܒܬܪ ܚܕ̈ܕܐ *in turn, one after another;* ܒܬܪ ܩܠܝܠ *soon after;* ܒܬܪ ܒܬܪ *in order, one after another;* ܠܒܣܬܪܐ *backwards;* often with ܡܢ, ܡܢ ܒܬܪ *after, following;* ܡܢ ܒܬܪ ܕ *after that;* ܒܬܪ ܝܘܡܐ or ܠܒܨܦܪܗ ܕܝܘܡܐ *the next day;* ܒܬܪ ܙܒܢܐ *some time after;* so with ܫܢܬܐ *year.* ܕܒܬܪ ܡܝܢܝܩܐ *metaphysics;* ܒܬܪ ܪܫܐ *head downwards.* With verbs, following ܐܙܠ or ܐܬܐ *to follow;* ܐܟܠ *to accuse;* ܒܥܐ *to find an opportunity of complaint against;* ܩܪܐ or ܢܗܡ *to summon;* ܩܡ *to succeed,* &c.

ܒܬܪܝܐ adj. from ܒܬܪ. *coming after, happening later, subsequent.*

ܒܬܪܝܘܬܐ from ܒܬܪܝܐ f. *backwardness, posteriority,* opp. ܩܕܡܝܘܬܐ *priority.*

ܒܬܪܟܢ comp. of ܒܬܪ and ܟܢ. *afterwards, following.*

: ܫܘܠܡܗ ܕܐܬܘܬ ܒܝܬ :

: ܒܪܝܟ ܐܝܕܐ ܕܐܫܠܡܢ ܐܬܘܬܐ ܕܒܝܬ: ܘܫܪܝܢ ܐܬܘܬܐ ܕܓܡܠ :

: ܓ :

ܓ — ܓܐܐ

ܓ letter *g,* ܓܡܠ *Gamal* or *Gomal.* The cardinal number 3; with ܕ the ordinal, *the third.*

ܓܐܝ Pael conj. of ܓܐܐ, fut. ܢܓܐܐ, part. m. ܡܓܐܐ, pl. ܡܓܐܝܢ *to rejoice, take pleasure, live luxuriously,* with ܒ. Ethpa. ܐܬܓܐܝ fut. ܢܬܓܐܐ or ܢܬܓܐܐ, imp. ܐܬܓܐܝ or ܐܬܓܐܝ, part. m. ܡܬܓܐܐ, or emph. ܡܬܓܐܝܐ, f. ܡܬܓܐܝܐ *to bear oneself grandly, magnificently, with pride, pomp,* or *luxury;* with ܥܠ *to exult over; to luxuriate, enjoy pleasures* or *delights;* ܡܒܘܥܐ ܡܬܓܐܝܢ ܒܪܘܝܚܘܬܐ *springs gush forth luxuriantly;* ܒܪܩܐ ܕܡܬܓܐܐ ܘܥܒܪ *the lightning which shines forth magnificently and disappears;* ܕܢܐܪܬ ܒܡܕܝܢܬ ܩܕܝܫܐ ܦܘܢܩ̈ܐ ܡܓܐ̈ܝܐ *that he may possess full pleasures in the City of the Saints.* Aph. ܐܓܐܝ *to treat luxuriously;* ܡܓܐܐ ܦܓܪܗ ܒܡܦܢܩܘ̈ܬܐ ܘܒܦܘܢܩ̈ܐ *he pampers his body with luxuries and delicacies.* Derivatives, ܓܐܐ, ܓܐܘܢ, ܓܐܘܬܐ, ܓܐܝܘܬܐ, ܓܐܝܬ, ܓܐܝܘܬܐ.

ܓܐܐ, ܓܐܝܐ, ܓܐܝܬܐ pl. m. ܓܐ̈ܝܐ, f. ܓܐ̈ܝܬܐ rt. ܓܐܐ. adj. *delightful, pleasant, gay, glorious, stately, proud;* ܒܪܘܝܗ ܕܢܘܗܪܐ ܓܐܝܐ *Creator of joyous light;* ܓܐܝܐ ܒܡܪ̈ܘܡܐ *glorious in the heights;* used in the emph. state of God.

ܓܐܪ̈ܐ pl. m.; see ܓܐܪܐ.

ܓܐܘܓܪܐܦܝܐ *geography.*

ܓܐܘܡܛܪܝܐ *geometry.*

ܓܐܘܡܛܪܝܩܝܐ m. ܓܐܘܡܛܪܝܩܝܬܐ f. adj. *geometric.*

ܓܐܘܡܛܪܐ *a geometrician.*

ܓܐܘܬܢܐ rt. ܓܐܐ. adj. m. *luxurious.*

ܓܐܘܬܢܐ, ܓܐܘܬܬܢܐ pl. m. ܓܐܘܬܢ̈ܐ, f. ܓܐܘܬܢܝܬܐ rt. ܓܐܐ. adj. *proud;* ܥܩܪܗ ܕܓܐܘܬܢ̈ܐ ܥܩܪ ܡܪܝܐ *the Lord hath plucked up the roots of the proud.*

ܓܐܘܬܢܘܬܐ rt. ܓܐܐ. f. *pleasures, delights, grandeur.*

ܓܐܙ, ܓܐܙܐ or ܓܐܙܐ pl. ܓܐܙܝܢ, ܓܐܙܢ pres. part. of ܓܙ *to shear;* ܓܐܙ, ܓܐܙܐ, ܓܐܙܐ pl. ܓܐܙܝܢ, ܓܐܙܢ pres. part. of ܓܙܐ *to fail.*

ܓܐܐ not used in Pe.; see ܓܐܐ.

ܓܐܐ, ܓܐܐܝ another form of ܓܐܐ adj.

ܓܐܝܐܝܬ; see ܓܐܐ. adv. *luxuriously, in state* or *pomp.*

ܓܐܝܘܬܐ pl. ܓܐܝܘ̈ܬܐ, ܓܐܝܘܬܐ rt. ܓܐܐ. f. *state, stateliness, magnificence, luxury, pomp, pride* of person, bearing, clothing, life; *joys, delights;* ܦܬܘܪܗ ܡܠܐ ܗܘܐ ܟܠ ܓܐܝܘܢ *his table was supplied with all kinds of luxuries;* ܓܐܝܘܬܐ ܕܙܒܢܐ *temporal delights.*

ܓܐܠܐ; see ܓܠܐ *a cloak;* ܓܠܐ *a heap of stones, a tortoise;* ܓܠܐ *straw, chaff.*

ܓܐܠܩܘܢ, ܓܐܠܩܘܢܐ, ܓܐܠܩܘܢ or ܓܐܠܩܘܢܐ m. γαλλικόν, *soap used to wash* and *darken the hair.*

ܓܐܡܣ, ܓܐܡܣܘܣ, ܓܐܡܘܣ; see ܓܡܘܣܐ.

ܓܐܪ, ܓܐܪܐ, ܓܐܪܐ pres. part. of ܓܪ *to net,* and of ܓܘܪ *to hunt.*

ܓܐܦܐ; see ܓܦ, ܓܦܐ *a*) *the arm, armpit.* *b*) *a wing.*

ܓܐܪ, ܓܐܪܐ, ܓܐܪܐ act. part. of ܓܪ; ܓܐܪ, ܓܐܪܐ, ܓܐܪܐ act. part. of ܓܘܪ.

ܓܐܪܐ or ܓܐܪܐ pl. ܓܐܪ̈ܝܢ, ܓܐܪ̈ܐ m. *an arrow, dart, shaft, bolt; a thunderbolt; a dart* or *gore* of a garment.

ܓܐܪܘܢܐ pl. ܓܐܪ̈ܘܢܐ m. dim. of ܓܐܪܐ. *a dagger; a critical mark.*

ܓܐܫܝܫ Ar. *a saddle-cloth, housing.*

ܓܒ sometimes ܓܝܒ, emph. ܓܒܐ pl. ܓܒ̈ܐ, ܓܒ̈ܝܢ m. *the side.* *a*) *the hump* of a camel; *the bank* of a river, shore, coast; *the spoke* of a wheel; *the wing* of an army; ܓܒܐ ܩܕܡܝܐ *the prow;* ܓܒܐ ܐܚܪܝܐ *the stern.* *b*) *a place, country;* ܓܒܐ ܕܡܕܢܚܐ *the East.* *c*) ܐܩܝܡ ܓܒܐ or ܩܡ *to take sides, rebel, take up arms, set up a faction;* ܕܡܢ ܓܒܐ *those adhering to one side* or *party;* ܡܢ ܓܒܐ ܕܦܪ̈ܝܫܐ *on the Pharisees' side;* ܕܡܢ ܣܡܠܐ *those* whom our Lord will set *on* His *left hand* at the last judgement. *d*) ܠܚܘܕ ܓܒ *on one side, privately;* ܡܢ ܟܠ ܓܒ or ܡܢ ܟܠ ܓܒ̈ܝܢ *on* or *from every side;* ܡܢ ܓܒ ܠܓܒ *from one end to another;* ܡܢ ܓܒ ܐܚܪܢܐ *on the other side;* ܠܘܬ ܓܒ *beside, near* (the Pschitta generally has ܠܘܬ ܓܒ; see ܓܝܒ).

ܓܒܐ fut. ܢܓܒܐ, inf. ܡܓܒܐ, imper. ܓܒܝ, pres. part. ܓܒܐ, ܓܒܝܐ, pass. part. ܓܒܐ, ܓܒܝܐ spelt ܓܒܝܐ Deut. xii. 1; with pron. suff. 1 p. E-Syr. ܓܒܝܢ pl. ܓܒ̈ܝܢ, W-Syr. ܓܒܝܢ, ܓܒܝܢ, *my chosen one, mine elect; to choose, approve, appoint,* with ܠ *to* an office, or with dat., ܓܒܘ ܠܟܘܢ *choose for yourselves; to prove, purge; to collect, exact* tribute; pass. part. *chosen, elect, approved; choice, pure, eminent;* ܓܒܐ ܗܘ ܡܢ *it is preferred to, acceptable rather than;* ܡܐܟܘܠܬܐ ܓܒܝܬܐ *choice food;* ܦܛܪܝܪܟܐ ܓܒܝܐ *the Patriarch elect;* ܦܝܠܘܣܘܦ̈ܐ ܓܒ̈ܝܐ *eminent philosophers.* Ethpe. ܐܬܓܒܝ *to be chosen, purified; to be taxed, exacted* of usury. Pa. ܓܒܝ *to choose, select, collect; to clean corn;* ܓܒܘ ܙܝܙܢ̈ܐ *gather out the tares;* part. ܡܐܡܪ̈ܐ ܡܓܒܝ̈ܐ *select homilies.* Ethpa. ܐܬܓܒܝ *to be chosen out, gathered together;* ܘܐܬܚܫܒܘ ܐܝܟܢܐ ܡܬܓܒܝܐ ܗܢܐ ܟܣܦܐ *to consider how this sum might be collected.* Aph. ܐܓܒܝ *to choose;* with ܢܦܫܐ *to vow oneself,* ܐܝܠܝܢ ܕܐܓܒܝܘ ܢܦܫܗܘܢ ܠܐܠܗܐ *those who have devoted themselves to God;* ܡܓܒܝܢܐ ܗܘܐ ܕܐܣܛܘܪܟܐ *he was a gatherer of storax.* Derivatives, ܓܒܝܐ, ܓܒܝܢ, ܓܒܝܢܐ, ܡܓܒܝܢܐ, ܓܘܒܝܐ, ܓܒܝܬܐ, ܓܒܝܘܬܐ, ܓܒܝܢܘܬܐ.

ܓܒܘܠܐ pl. ܓܒܘܠ̈ܐ m. see below for fem. rt. ܓܒܠ. *a maker, framer, potter, founder;* ܐܠܗܐ ܓܒܘܠܐ ܕܦܓܪܐ *God the fashioner of the body.*

ܓܒܘܠܘܬܐ rt. ܓܒܠ. f. *the potter's art, modelling, fashioning.*

ܓܒܘܠܬܐ pl. ܓܒܘܠ̈ܬܐ rt. ܓܒܠ. m. *fiction, fable.* There are five sorts of poetic fiction—*a*) ܡܬܠܐ *fable;* *b*) ܡܬܠܐ ܦܠܐܬܐ *parable;* *c*) ܚܒܪܘܬܐ ܡܕܪܫܝܬܐ

impersonation; d) ܓܒܠܬܐ ܕܠܐ ܙ̈ *simple composition,* i. e. without fable or parable; *e)* ܕܚܕܡܘܬܐ ܐܝܟ ܕܒܦܘܚܡܐ ܦܘܚܡܐ *similitude* or *types.*

ܓܒܘܠܬܐ rt. ܓܒܠ. f. adj. *plastic;* subst. *a lump.*

ܓܒܘܬܐ m. *a vessel, water-pot.*

ܓܒܚܐ m. *bald in front.*

ܓܒܚܘܬܐ f. *baldness on the forepart of the head.*

ܓܒܝܐ pl. ܐ̈ m. rt. ܓܒܐ. *a tax-gatherer, collector.*

ܓܒܝܐܝܬ rt. ܓܒܐ. adv. *freely, spontaneously, voluntarily.*

ܓܒܝܘܬܐ rt. ܓܒܐ. f. *election,* often used as a title with pron. suff. ܓܒܝܘܬܗ *he who is elected, designate.*

ܓܒܝܠܘܬܐ rt. ܓܒܠ. f. *a) framing, fashioning;* ܙ̈ ܕܐܕܡ *the forming of Adam. b) plausibility.*

ܓܒܝܠܬܐ pl. ܬ̈ܐ rt. ܓܒܠ. f. *a) that which is formed* or *moulded, formation, creation;* ܙ̈ ܕܐܠܗܐ *the human body fashioned by God;* ܡܢ ܫܘܪܝ ܓܒܝܠܬܗ ܕܒܓܘ ܟܪܣܐ *from the beginning of his being formed in the womb. b) the substance to be moulded, a lump, a mass* of dough or clay; ܪܫܐ ܕܓܒܝܠܬܢ *the Head of our substance, of those formed like us.*

ܓܒܝܢܐ pl. ܐ̈ rt. ܓܒܢ. m. *the eyebrow.* With ܐܪܝܡ *to be supercilious, haughty;* metaph. *superciliousness.* ܒܝܬ ܙ̈ *the space between the eyebrows, the brow; a ridge, brow of a hill.*

ܓܒܝܬܐ rt. ܓܒܐ. f. 1) *choice, election;* coll. *the chosen, the elect;* ܒܓܒܝܬܐ ܕܡܫܝܚܐ *among the elect of Christ.* 2) usually pl. ܓܒܝ̈ܬܐ *the collection* of tribute, alms, &c.; *tribute, exacted offerings;* ܓܒܝ̈ܬܐ ܕܟܣܦܐ *tribute of silver.*

ܓܒܠ fut. ܢܓܒܘܠ, inf. ܡܓܒܠ, act. part. ܓܳܒܶܠ, ܓܳܒܠܳܐ, pass. part. ܓܒܝܠ, ܓܒܝܠܐ, ܓܒܝܠܬܐ. *to form, fashion, mould; to mix* or *make up* medicine; ܒܪܢܫܐ ܕܓܒܠ *the man whom he had formed;* with ܬܘܒ *to fashion anew, reform;* ܓܒܠ ܡ̈ܠܐ *speaking feigned words, of artful speech;* pass. part. metaph. *fictitious, feigned;* ܕܚܠܬ ܐܠܗܐ ܓܒܝܠܬܐ *feigned godliness;* gram. *a noun of action having a definitely active or passive meaning,* as ܩܛܠܐ ܓܒܝܠܐ *slaughtering, the act of slaying;* opp. ܚܬܝܡܐ *accurately defined,* i. e. a noun including both active and passive meaning, as ܬܘܪܣܝܐ *nourishing* or *being nourished.* ETHPE. ܐܬܓܒܠ pass. of Peal. PA. ܓܒܠ intensive of Peal; pass. part. ܡܓܒܠ *strong, sturdy; feigned* words; ܡ̈ܠܐ ܡܓܒܠܬܐ *fables.* DERIVATIVES, ܓܒܘܠܐ, ܓܒܘܠܬܐ, ܓܒܘܠܘܬܐ, ܓܒܝܠܘܬܐ, ܓܒܝܠܬܐ, ܓܒܠܐ, ܡܓܒܠܢܘܬܐ, ܡܬܓܒܠܢܐ.

ܓܒܠܐ m. ܓܒܠܬܐ f. rt. ܓܒܠ. *a noun of action;* cf. ܓܒܠ pass. part.

ܓܒܢ pass. part. ܓܒܝܢܐ *curdled, coagulated.* ETHPE. ܐܬܓܒܢ *to be thick* or *curdled.* PA. ܓܒܢ *to curdle;* part. ܡܓܒܢܐ *bulging, ridged.* ETHPA. ܐܬܓܒܢ same as Ethpe. DERIVATIVES, ܓܒܝܢܐ, ܓܒܢܐ, ܓܒܘܢܐ, ܓܒܝܢܐ, ܡܓܒܢܢܐ.

ܓܒܢܐ rt. ܓܒܢ. m. *a cheese-press; rind, skin.*

ܓܒܣܘܣ; see ܓܒܣܘܣ.

ܓܒܪ, ܓܒܪܐ pl. ܓܒܪ̈ܝܢ, ܐ̈ m. *man* (especially *a strong* or *mighty man* = Lat. *vir,* while ܒܪܢܫܐ = *homo*), *husband* ܗܘܐ ܠܓܒܪܐ *to be married;* ܓܒܪܐ ܢܫܐ or ܓܒܪ ܢܫܐ pl. ܓܒܪ̈ܝ ܢܫܐ *an hermaphrodite, a eunuch, effeminate;* ܓܒܪ ܣܥܪ *a man* wearing a garment *of haircloth,* i. e. *a prophet;* ܓܒܪܐ ܡܫܡܠܝܐ *an adult;* ܙ̈ ܕܡܫܟܚܬܟ *thy acquaintances; a man, one, a certain . . . ;* ܓܒܪ ܓܒܪ *each, every one, one by one;* ܓܒܪ— ܚܒܪܗ *one and another, a man and his neighbour;* ܓܒܪܐ ܡܫܡܫܢܐ *a certain deacon;* often redundant, ܓܒܪܐ ܣܘܪܝܝܐ *a Syrian;* ܙ̈ ܬܓܪ̈ܐ *merchants.* DERIVATIVES, verb ܓܒܪ, ܓܒܪܐܝܬ, ܓܒܪܘܢܐ, ܓܒܪܘܢܘܬܐ, ܓܒܪܢܐ, ܓܒܪܢܝ, ܓܒܪܘܬܐ, ܓܒܪܬܐ, ܓܒܪܐ, ܓܒܪܬܐ, verb ܐܬܓܒܪ, ܓܒܪܬܐ, ܓܒܪܐ, ܡܬܓܒܪܢܘܬܐ.

ܓܒܪ denom. verb from ܓܒܪܐ, *to use force.* PA. ܓܒܪ *to come to man's estate; to strengthen, embolden.* ETHPA. ܐܬܓܒܪ imper. ܐܬܓܒܪ *to be grown up; to be valiant;* with ܥܠ *to prevail over, excel, exceed in power.*

ܓܒܪܐܝܬ from ܓܒܪܐ, adv. *manfully, firmly.*

ܓܒܪܘܢܐ, ܓܒܪܘܢܘܢܐ or ܓܒܪܘܢܘܢܐ m. dim. of ܓܒܪܐ. *a shabby little scrub.*

ܓܒܪܘܬܐ pl. ܓܒܪ̈ܘܬܐ, from ܓܒܪܐ. f. *vigour, force, manhood; the virile member;* pl. *exploits, deeds of renown, mighty acts, miracles;* ~ ܕܪ̈ܫܝܥܐ *the violence of wicked men.*

ܓܢܒܪܢܐ, ܓܢܒܪܢܝܬܐ pl. m. ܢܐ̈, f. ܢܝܬܐ̈, from ܓܢܒܪܐ. adj. *masculine, valiant, heroic;* subst. *a valiant man* or *woman, hero, heroine;* ܐܝܟ ܓܢܒܪܢܝܬܐ ܐܬܕܒܪܬ *the maiden bore herself heroically.*

ܓܢܒܪܢܝܐܝܬ, ܓܢܒܪܢܝܐ, f. ܢܝܬܐ adj. *male, manly,* and the same as ܓܢܒܪܢܐ; ܠܒܘܫܐ ܓܢܒܪܢܝܐ *male attire;* ~ ܕܘܒܪܐ *manly conduct;* ܢܦܫܐ ܓܢܒܪܢܝܬܐ *a valiant soul.*

ܓܢܒܪܢܘܬܐ; see ܓܢܒ. adj. *effeminate, enervating.*

ܓܢܒܪܬܐ fem. of ܓܢܒܪܐ. *a strong, virile* or *valiant woman, one of masculine mind* or *courage.*

ܓܒܬܐ contr. for ܓܒܝܢܬܐ rt. ܓܒܢ. f. *cheese, curd.*

ܓܘܓܠܐ m. ܓܘܓܠܬܐ f. *a fornicator, harlot.*

ܓܓܘܠܬܐ pr. n. *Golgotha.*

ܓܓܠܐ pl. ܠܐ̈ m. *a) pitch. b) a heavy burden, a weight. c) melissophyllum.*

ܓܓܪܘܬܐ rt. ܓܓܪ. f. *gluttony.*

ܓܓܪܢܐ pl. f. ܓܓܪ̈ܢܝܬܐ (ܐܬܘ̈ܬܐ) *guttural* consonants.

ܓܓܪܢ, ܓܓܪܢܐ, f. ܓܓܪܢܝܬܐ and ܓܓܪܘܢܐ, pl. m. ܢܐ̈, f. ܢܝܬܐ̈ rt. ܓܓܪ. *a glutton; gluttonous.*

ܓܓܪܬܐ pl. ܓܓܪ̈ܬܐ contracted for ܓܓܪܬܐ rt. ܓܓܪ. f. *the throat;* ~ ܕ ܚܢܘܩܝܬܐ *a quinsey;* ܓܓܪܬܐ ܡ *a gargle.*

ܓܕ fut. ܢܓܕ or ܢܓܘܕ, act. part. m. ܓܐܕ, pl. ܓܕܝܢ, pass. part. pl. ܓܕܝܕܝܢ, is conjugated like ܓܙ. *to weave, to cut off, put an end to* especially with ܢܘܠܐ *a web;* ܐܝܟܢܐ ܢܓܘܕ ܢܫܐ ܟܘܪܬܐ *how to cut out honeycomb* without being stung. Ethpe. ܐܬܓܕܕ, with ܢܘܠܐ ܕܚܝ̈ܐ *the web of life was sundered.* Derivatives, ܓܕܐ, ܓܕܝܕܐ, ܓܕܘܕܐ, ܓܕܝܕܘܬܐ, ܓܕܘܕܝܬܐ.

ܓܕ, ܓܕܐ pl. ܓܕ̈ܐ or ܓܕ̈ܝܐ m. rt. ܓܕ. *a) fortune, luck, success;* ~ ܛܒ *happy, fortunate;* ~ ܒܝܫ *unlucky, unfortunate;* ܓܕܐ ܒܝܫܬܐ *misfortune, evil fortune, ill-luck;* ܡܛܠ ܓܕܝ ܒܝܫܐ *because of my ill-luck;* ܡܫܠܡܢܐ ܕܓܕܗܘܢ *betrayers of their fortune, unworthy of their good-luck. b) a genius* or *god of fortune;* ܒܣܡܐ ܠܓܕܐ ܣܡ ܗܘܐ *he offered incense to Fortune;* ܐܩܝܡܘ ܠܓܕܐ ܥܠ ܐܣܛܘܢ̈ܐ *they erected images of Fortune on pillars.*

ܓܕܘܕ imper. of ܓܕ *to draw.*

ܓܕܐ fut. ܢܓܕܐ, part. ܓܕܐ, ܓܕܝܐ. *a) to ascend, to rise* or *mount up* as smoke, fire, birds. *b) to cast up, belch forth;* ܓܒܠ̈ܐ ܕܢܘܪܐ ܓܕܝܢ ܟܐܦ̈ܐ volcanoes *belching forth red-hot stones.* Derivatives, ܓܕܝܐ, ܓܕܝܬܐ, ܡܓܕܝܐ.

ܓܕܕ, ܓܕܕܐ pl. ܓܕ̈ܕܐ and ܓܕ̈ܝܕܐ m. rt. ܓܕ. *thrums, the ends of a weaver's threads; the cutting off of a web;* ܓܕܕ ܡܩܕܡ *a web;* ܡܛܐ ܢܘܠܐ ܠܡܓܕܕ *the web was nearly woven = death was near.*

ܓܕ̈ܕܐ only pl., generally m. *wormwood, bitter medicine.* Metaph. *bitter sorrow* or *trouble.*

ܓܕܘܕ, ܓܕܘܕܐ pl. ܝܢ, ܢܐ̈ m. *an unmarried youth, a boy from ten to eighteen years of age;* cf. ܥܠܝܡܐ *a young man over eighteen years.*

ܐܬܓܕܘܕ denom. verb from ܓܕܘܕ. *to become a youth, to live as a youth.*

ܓܕܘܠܐ pl. ܠܐ̈ m. rt. ܓܕܠ. generally pl. except as the name of certain constellations, *the plaiting of the hair, plaits* or *tresses of hair; a necklace* or *chain;* ܓܕܘܠܐ ܕܕܗܒܐ *golden chains.*

ܓܕܘܠܘܬܐ rt. ܓܕܠ. f. *weaving.*

ܓܕܝܐ pl. ܓܕܝܢ, ܓܕܝ̈ܐ m. *a kid;* a sign of the Zodiac, *Capricornus.*

ܓܕܝܐ pl. ܓܕܝ̈ܐ rt. ܓܕܐ. *mounting up, leaping up;* pl. *earthquakes* when the earth mounts and sinks perpendicularly without lateral motion.

ܓܕܝܕܐ adj. from ܓܕ̈ܕܐ. *bitter.*

ܓܕܝܘܢܐ dim. of ܓܕܝܐ m. *a little kid. The third star* in the tail of the Little Bear, which we call the pole-star.

ܓܕܝܠܬܐ pl. ܠܢ, ܠܬܐ̈ f. rt. ܓܕܠ. *a plait* or *braid of hair, curled* or *frizzed tresses;* ܐܚܕܗ ܒܓܕܝܠܬܗ *he seized him by his tresses; wreathen, twisted* or *plaited work;* ܓܕܝܠܬܐ ܕܩܢ̈ܝܐ *a reed-mat;* pl. *fringes.*

ܓܕܝܫܐ pl. ܫܐ̈ rt. ܓܕܫ. m. *a) a heap, pile* of wood, *shock* of corn, *a hay-loft. b) a chance, casualty.*

ܓܕܰܠ fut. ܢܶܓܕܽܘܠ, inf. ܡܶܓܕܰܠ, act. part ܓܳܕܶܠ, ܓܳܕܠܳܐ, pass. part. ܓܕܺܝܠ, ܓܕܺܝܠܳܐ, ܓܕܺܝܠܬܳܐ. *to twist, plait, interweave* the hair, a crown, a nest, rope, &c.; ܥܒܳܕܳܐ ܓܕܺܝܠܳܐ *twined* or *wreathen work.* Metaph. *a*) *to compose* or *arrange* words with art; with ܡܰܚܫܰܒ̈ܬܳܐ *to make intricate plans;* ܢܶܓܕܽܘܠ ܩܳܠܶܐ ܕܬܶܫܒܽܘܚܬܳܐ *let us weave sounds of praise.* *b*) *to circle in the air, gyrate, soar;* ܐܘܿ ܢܶܫܪ̈ܶܐ ܕܓܕܰܠܘ ܘܣܠܶܩܘ ܠܰܡܪܰܘܡܳܐ *O eagles, which have circled and ascended on high;* ܓܳܕܶܠ ܠܡܶܥܡܪ̈ܶܐ ܕܠܳܐ ܡܶܬܡܫܚܳܢܶܐ my mind *ascends towards the immeasurable habitations.* Ethpe. ܐܶܬܓܕܶܠ passive; ܡܨܺܝܕܬܳܐ ܕܐܶܬܓܕܠܰܬ ܡܶܢ *a net woven of . . . .* Pa. ܓܰܕܶܠ *to plait* a crown or the hair. Aph. ܐܰܓܕܶܠ same as Pael. Part. ܡܰܓܕܠܳܐ f. ܡܰܓܕܠܬܳܐ, ܡܰܓܕܠܳܢ ܥܰܪ̈ܣܳܬܳܐ bowers *of interwoven flowers.* Bar-Bahlul says that Mary Magdalene was so-named ܡܰܓܕܠܳܐ ܕܡܓܰܕܠܳܐ ܗܘܳܬ ܣܰܥܪܳܗ̇ *because of her braided hair.* Ethpaual ܐܶܬܓܰܘܕܰܠ *to be piled up.* Derivatives, ܓܕܺܝܠܳܐ, ܓܕܺܝܠܬܳܐ, ܓܕܽܘܠܬܳܐ, ܓܳܕܽܘܠܳܐ, ܡܓܰܕܠܳܢܳܐ, ܡܓܰܕܠܳܐ.

ܓܕܺܝܠܳܐ pl. ܶ̈ܐ rt. ܓܕܠ. m. *plaiting, twining; anything twisted* or *plaited, wickerwork, a garland;* ܓ̈ܕܺܝܠܶܐ ܕܫܽܘܒܚܳܐ *a wreath* or *crown of glory.*

ܓܕܰܡ fut. ܢܶܓܕܽܘܡ, inf. ܡܶܓܕܰܡ, act. part. ܓܳܕܶܡ, pass. part. ܓܕܺܝܡ, ܓܕܺܝܡܳܐ, ܓܕܺܝܡܬܳܐ. *to mow, cut* or *hew down;* ܐܰܝܟ ܚܳܨܽܘܕ̈ܶܐ ܠܫܶܒ̈ܠܶܐ ܓܳܕܡܺܝܢ *as reapers cut down the ears of corn;* ܓܶܫܪܳܐ ܓܕܰܡܘ *they broke down the bridge;* pass. part. *cut down* in battle; *circumcised;* gram. *apocopated; a noun in the absol. st.*, as having its last letter hewn off. Ethpe. ܐܶܬܓܕܶܡ *to be hewn* or *smitten off, to be broken down* or *open;* ܡܶܬܓܰܕܡܺܝܢ ܡܽܘܬ̈ܠܶܐ ܕܡܰܘܬܳܐ *the bars of death are broken down;* gram. *to be contracted,* as ܟܰܠ for ܟܰܠܬܳܐ. Pa. ܓܰܕܶܡ *to batter, dash in pieces.* Ethpa. ܐܶܬܓܰܕܰܡ *to be broken in pieces, battered down;* gram. *to be contracted.* Derivatives, ܓܕܳܡܳܐ, ܓܕܺܝܡܽܘܬܳܐ, ܡܓܰܕܡܽܘܬܳܐ, ܡܓܰܕܡܳܢܽܘܬܳܐ.

ܓܕܳܡ, ܓܕܳܡܳܐ pl. ܶ̈ܐ rt. ܓܕܡ. m. *a hewing off, a cut palm-branch;* gram. *aphaeresis, contraction* as in the abs. or constr. st. of a noun; ܫܡܳܐ ܓܕܳܡܳܐ a noun *in the abs.* or *constr. st.*

ܓܕܳܢܳܝܳܐ f. ܓܕܳܢܳܝܬܳܐ from ܓܰܕܳܐ. *fortunate, lucky.*

ܓܕܳܢܳܝܽܘܬܳܐ from ܓܰܕܳܐ. *good fortune, good luck.*

ܓܕܳܢܳܝܳܐ rt. ܓܕܠ. *textile.*

ܓܕܳܢܳܝܳܐ pl. ܶ̈ܐ m. *a narrowed* or *a jutting-out part of a building; a rebatement, entablature, corbel, coping, bracket; a ledge, crag;* ܓܰܘܣܳܐ ܒܓܰܘ ܓܕܳܢ̈ܶܐ *a refuge among the crags.* Metaph. ܗܦܰܟ ܘܰܣܚܦܳܗ̇ ܠܓܕܳܢܳܗ̇ ܕܥܳܠܡܳܐ *he ruined and cast down the heights of this world, worldly haughtiness.*

ܓܕܰܦ Pa. ܓܰܕܶܦ *to revile, blaspheme* with ܒ, ܠ, or ܥܰܠ. Ethpa. ܐܶܬܓܰܕܰܦ *to be reviled, blasphemed.* Derivatives, ܓܽܘܕܳܦܳܐ, ܡܓܰܕܦܳܢܳܐ, ܡܓܰܕܦܳܢܽܘܬܳܐ.

ܓܕܺܝܪܳܐ Ar. m. *a pond, pool.*

ܓܕܰܫ fut. ܢܶܓܕܽܘܫ, inf. ܡܶܓܕܰܫ, pres. part. ܓܳܕܶܫ, ܓܳܕܫܳܐ, pass. part. ܓܕܺܝܫ. I) *to heap up.* II) *to chance, happen, occur* with ܒ, ܠ, and with pron. suffix. Pret. 3 s. and pres. part. m. and f. and fut. impers. ܓܕܰܫ ܠܶܗ *it happened to him;* ܓܕܰܫ ܥܰܠ ܪܶܥܝܳܢܶܗ *it occurred to him, came into his mind;* ܟܽܐܒ̈ܶܐ ܕܓܳܕܫܺܝܢ ܡܶܢ ܩܽܘܪ̈ܳܫܳܐ *illnesses arising from colds;* ܗܳܠܶܝܢ ܕܓܳܕܫܳܢ *events;* ܕܰܠܡܳܐ ܓܳܕܶܫ, ܕܰܠܡܳܐ ܓܕܰܫ *by chance, perhaps.* Derivatives, ܓܶܕܫܳܐ, ܓܶܕܫܳܝܳܐ, ܓܶܕܫܳܐܺܝܬ, ܓܕܺܝܫܳܐ.

ܓܶܕܫܳܐ pl. ܶ̈ܐ rt. ܓܕܫ. m. *a*) *a chance, an accident;* ܓܶܕ̈ܫܶܐ ܐܶܢܽܘܢ ܟܽܠܗܽܘܢ ܨܒ̈ܘܳܬܳܐ *all things are fortuitous;* ܓܶܕܫܳܐ ܒܺܝܫܳܐ *a mischance, misfortune; an event, an achievement;* in logic, *accident;* ܒܓܶܕܫܳܐ *by chance, accidentally.* *b*) *a heap,* Job xxi. 32. Cf. ܓܕܺܝܫܳܐ.

ܓܶܕܫܳܐܺܝܬ adv. rt. ܓܕܫ. *by chance, accidentally.*

ܓܶܕܫܳܝܳܐ pl. ܓܶܕܫܳܝ̈ܶܐ m. rt. ܓܕܫ. *fortuitous, accidental, occasional.*

ܓܗܳܐ fut. ܢܶܓܗܶܐ, inf. ܡܶܓܗܳܐ. *to flee, escape* with ܡܶܢ, especially from bodily or mental pains or evils; ܙܳܕܶܩ ܕܢܶܓܗܶܐ ܩܕܡ ܡܶܢ ܟܽܠ ܡܰܘܟܣܳܢܳܐ *he must first eschew all things blameworthy;* ܕܢܶܓܗܶܐ ܡܶܢ ܒܶܗܬܬܳܐ ܗ̱ܘܳܐ *he might flee from shame.* Ethpe. ܐܶܬܓܗܺܝ *to be delivered, set free.* Pa. ܓܰܗܺܝ *to go out, be quenched* of fire. Aph. ܐܰܓܗܺܝ *a*) *to set free, deliver, to eschew.* *b*) *to be delivered, free* or *at rest* from labour, suffering, evil; ܡܶܢ ܓܰܪܒܳܐ *from leprosy;* ܐܰܓܗܺܝ ܡܶܢ ܕܶܚܠܬܳܐ ܕܡܰܘܬܳܐ *from the fear of death;* ܐܰܓܗܺܝ ܡܶܢ ܛܰܢܦܽܘܬܳܐ ܕܒܶܣܪܳܐ *he shunned fleshly defilements.* *c*) *to be released, dispensed from;*

excused, *quit of* an obligation, suretyship, &c.; ܐܬܓܗܝ ܡܢ ܚܝܐ *to be free from life, at rest.* Derivatives, ܓܗܝܬܐ, ܡܓܗܝܢܐ, ܡܓܗܝܢܘܬܐ.

ܓܗܢܐ Pers. *a*) *time.* *b*) *a room adorned with rich hangings, a bridal-chamber.*

ܓܗܝܠܘܬܐ rt. ܓܗܠ. f. *wantonness.*

ܓܗܝܪܘܬܐ rt. ܓܗܪ. f. *dullness, obscurity.*

ܓܗܝܬܐ rt. ܓܗܐ. f. *deliverance, flight, escape,* especially from pain, weariness, life on earth.

ܓܗܠ particip. adj. ܓܗܝܠܐ or ܓܗܠܐ f. ܓܗܝܠܬܐ *amorous, wanton.* Derivative, ܓܗܝܠܘܬܐ.

ܓܗܢ or ܓܗܢ fut. ܢܓܗܘܢ, parts. ܓܗܐܢ, ܓܗܝܢ, *to bend* or *bow, to stoop, incline;* ܓܗܢ ܒܨܠܘܬܐ ܒܨܠܘܬܐ *bending in prayer.* Ethpe. ܐܬܓܗܢ *to bend, incline, prostrate oneself,* with ܥܠ; ܐܬܓܗܢ ܥܠ ܐܪܥܐ *he bowed himself down upon the earth.* Pa. ܓܗܢ *to bend* or *sink down.* Ethpa. ܐܬܓܗܢ same as Ethpe. Aph. ܐܓܗܢ *to make to bend* or *stoop.*

ܓܗܢܐ f. *Gehenna;* see ܓܗܝܢܐ.

ܓܘܗܢܐ m. and ܓܘܗܢܬܐ pl. ܓܘܗܢܝܬܐ f. rt. ܓܗܢ. *an inclination, bowing, bending,* especially rit. *a prayer of inclining,* said by the priest with bent head and low voice=Lat. *oratio secreta.*

ܓܗܪ fut. ܢܓܗܘܪ, act. part. ܓܗܐܪ, ܓܗܪܐ, pass. part. m. ܓܗܝܪܐ, f. ܓܗܝܪܬܐ. *to be dazzled, dimmed,* usually with ܪܥܝܢܐ or some word for mind. Metaph. *to be amazed;* ܓܗܪܐ ܥܝܢܗ ܡܢ ܩܪܝܢܐ *his eye is dim from study;* ܫܘܒܚܐ ܠܡܢ ܕܒܪܒܘܬܗ ܓܗܝܪ ܗܘܢܐ *glory by whose greatness the understanding is dazzled.* Aph. *to obscure, dim,* or *eclipse with light;* ܕܡܓܗܪ ܠܫܡܫܐ ܙܠܝܩܘܗܝ *whose brightness makes the sunlight dim.* Derivatives, ܓܗܝܪܘܬܐ, ܓܗܪ, ܓܗܪܐ, ܓܘܗܪܬܐ.

ܓܗܪ *dim-sighted, lacking sight, wanting insight;* ܓܗܪ ܡܢ ܝܕܥܬܐ *devoid of knowledge.*

ܓܘܗܪܐ pl. ܓܘܗܪܐ rt. ܓܗܪ. m. *dimness of vision; dim, faint.*

ܓܘܗܪܬܐ rt. ܓܗܪ. f. *weak sight, a suffusion of the eyes.*

ܓܘ, ܓܘܐ m. *the inside, inward parts,* hence *the inside, midst, inner part;* with ܒ, ܠ, ܡܢ, ܥܠ forms preps. and adverbs of place and time; ܒܓܘ and ܠܓܘ *within, inside;* ܒܓܘܝ *within me;* ܒܓܘܗ *within her;* ܒܓܘ ܬܪܬܝܢ ܫܢܝܢ *within two years;* ܡܢ ܠܓܘ or ܡܠܓܘ *within, on the inner part* or *side, inwardly, from within;* ܡܢ ܓܘ *inside, within,* opp. ܡܢ ܒܪ *outside, without.*

Emph. st. ܓܘܐ *the belly, inner part;* ܟܐܒ ܓ̈ *dysentery;* ܡܐܢܝ ܓܘܐ *the viscera, inwards;* ܓܘܗ ܣܪܝܩ ܗܘܐ *it was hollow within;* ܒܓܘ ܠܒܟܘܢ *within your heart.* Metaph. *a body of people, congregation, community;* ܟܠܗ ܓܘܐ *the whole body; all;* ܓ̈ ܕܩܠܝܪܝܩܐ *the clergy;* ܓ̈ ܕܟܪܝܣܛܝܢܐ *the Christian community;* ܓ̈ ܕܡܗܝܡܢܐ *the company of the faithful; the laity; a monastery* or *religious community;* ܕܓܘܐ *common;* ܓܘܝܐ *held* or *used in common, general, inner;* logic. *the general.* Derivatives, ܓܘܝ, ܓܘܝܐ, ܓܘܝܐ, ܓܘܝܘܬܐ, ܓܘܝܬܐ, ܓܘܝܬܐ, ܓܘܢܐ, ܓܘܝܢܐ, ܡܓܘܝܢܘܬܐ, ܡܓܘܝܢܐ.

ܓܘܒ Aph. ܐܓܝܒ, inf. ܡܓܒܘ, act. part. ܡܓܝܒ *to answer;* ܠܡܓܝܒܘܬܗ *to answer him;* ܡܓܝܒ ܗܘܐ ܠܗܘܢ *he answered them.* Ettaph. *to be answered, receive answer.* Derivatives, ܓܘܒܐ, ܡܓܘܒܢܘܬܐ.

ܓܘܒ, ܓܘܒܐ pl. ܝܢ, ܐ̈ *a*) m. *a well, cistern, pit, den.* *b*) f. *a beam, joist, plank.*

ܓܘܒܝܐ rt. ܓܒܐ. m. *a selection; the cleaning, winnowing* of corn.

ܓܘܒܢܐ pl. ܝܢ, ܐ̈ rt. ܓܒܢ. m. *a cheese; a cake* of raisins, figs, dates, &c.; ܚܕ ܒܫܒܐ ܕܓܘܒܢܐ=*Quinquagesima Sunday,* until which day cheese and eggs may be eaten; *a cheese-press* or *mould.*

ܓܘܒܣܝܢ *white lime;* see ܓܒܣܝܢ.

ܓܘܒܬܐ pl. ܓܘܒܝܬܐ f. cf. ܓܘܒܐ *a*) *a pit, hole, den, cavern.*

ܓܘܓܐ, ܓܘܓܝܐ or ܓܘܓܝܐ rt. ܓܓܐ. m. *whispering, speaking softly;* like a child or as in prayer.

ܓܘܓܝܬ pl. ܓܘܓܝܬ f. *a spider;* ܢܘܠܐ ܕܓ̈ *a cobweb, spider's web.*

ܓܘܓܢܝܐ *silly, fatuous.*

ܓܘܕ, ܓܘܕܐ pl. ܝܢ, ܐ̈ com. but oftener f. *a band, company, rank, choir; the wing* of an army; ܓ̈ ܕܓܝܣܐ *a band of robbers;* ܓ̈ ܕܫܠܝܚܐ, ܓ̈ ܕܣܗܕܐ *the company of the Apostles, of the Martyrs;* ܓܘܕܐ ܡܠܐܟܝܐ

angelic choirs; ܬܫܡܫܬܐ ܕܥܕܬܐ ܒܬܪܝܢ ܓܘܕܝܢ ܬܬܩܪܐ *the church services shall be intoned by two choirs;* ܓܘܕܝܢ ܓܘܕܝܢ *by companies.*

ܓܘܕܐ f. *a leathern bottle;* ܐܝܟ ܓܘܕܐ ܡܢ ܝܡܐ proverb *as a bottle-full from the sea,* Angl. *a drop in the ocean.*

ܓܘܕܪܐ m. *a hedge, a mound;* ܝܬܒ ܒܛܠܠܐ ܬܚܝܬ ܓܘܕܪܐ *sitting in the shade under a hedge.*

ܓܘܕܦܐ pl. ܓܘܕܦܐ, ܓܘܕܦܝܢ, ܓܕܘܦܐ rt. ܓܕܦ. m. *blasphemy, reviling.*

ܓܘܗܪܐ m. *the dawn, morning light.* Cognate, ܢܓܗ.

ܓܘܙܠܐ or ܓܘܙܠܐ pl. ܐ̈ from ܓܙܠ. m. *flame, heat; the kindling of a fire;* ܡܕܠܩܝܢ ܓܘܙܠܐ *they make the fire blaze up;* ܓܘܙܠܐ ܕܢܘܪܐ *fiery meteors.*

ܓܙܪ, ܓܙܪ fut. ܢܓܙܪ, inf. ܡܓܙܪ, part. ܓܙܪ, ܓܙܪܐ *to hasten away, to be lacking, fail,* especially of water, often joined with ܝܒܫ *to dry up;* ܕܠܐ ܓܙܪ *never-failing;* ܓܙܪܝ ܥܝܢܝ *mine eyes fail.* Pa. ܓܙܪ *a) to be barren. b) to bereave, deprive of;* ܡܓܙܪ ܠܗ ܠܨܗܝܐ ܡܢ ܫܬܝܐ *he will deprive the thirsty of drink;* ܡܓܙܪܐ ܡܢ ܡܝܐ *waterless, arid, sterile.* Ethpa. ܐܬܓܙܪ *to be diminished; to be missing, felt as a want.* Aph. ܐܓܙܪ *to lay* or *leave waste; to bereave;* ܡܢ ܐܓܙܪ ܡܒܘܥܝܟ *who hath stopped thy flowing waters, made thine abundance to fail.* Derivatives, ܓܙܪܐ, ܡܓܙܪܐ.

ܓܘܙ, ܓܘܙܐ pl. ܓܘ̈ܙܐ m. *the nut* tree and fruit, especially *the walnut;* ܫܒܘܛܐ ܕܓܘ̈ܙܐ *nut branches;* ܓ ܕܒܣܡܐ or ܕܡܘܫܟܐ *the nutmeg;* ܓ ܗܢܕܘܝܐ *the cocoa-nut;* ܓ ܕܩܝܐ *nux vomica;* ܓ ܦܘܢܛܝܩܐ *the filbert, chestnut.*

ܓܘܙ, ܓܘܙܝ, ܓܘܙܘ, ܓܘܙܝܢ imper. of ܓܙ *to shear.*

ܓܘܙܓܘܢ f. *a garment.*

ܓܘܙܪܐ m. rt. ܓܙܪ. *barrenness, the being without children, the loss of children.*

ܓܘܙܠ a Pauel conjugation, *to kindle, set on fire, inflame, excite, irritate;* metaph. ܐܢ ܡܓܘܙܠܝܢ ܐܢܬܘܢ ܚܡܬܐ ܥܠܝ *if ye excite anger against me.* Ethpaual ܐܬܓܘܙܠ *to be on fire, break out in flames; to be inflamed, incensed,* ܒܚܡܬܐ, ܒܚܘܒܐ, *with rage, with love;* ܐܬܓܘܙܠ ܪܘܓܙܗ ܥܠܝܢ *his anger is hot against us.*

Derivatives, ܓܘܙܠܐ or ܓܘܙܠܐ, ܓܘܙܠܬܐ, ܡܓܘܙܠܢܘܬܐ, ܡܓܘܙܠܢܐ, ܡܓܘܙܠܢܝܬ.

ܓܘܙܠܐ m. *lefthanded, ambidexter;* cf. ܓܕܠܐ.

ܓܘܙܠܐ = ܓܘܙܠܐ.

ܓܘܙܠܬܐ pl. ܐ̈ from ܓܙܠ. f. *a flame, a fiery coal; fire, heat;* pl. *fiery meteors.* Metaph. ܓ ܕܪܕܘܦܝܐ *the flame of persecution.*

ܓܘܙܥܐ pl. ܐ̈ rt. ܓܙܥ. m. *the trunk* or *stump* of a felled tree; *a shoot* or *rod* thicker than a ܫܒܛܐ; gram. *a root, primitive form.*

ܓܘܙܥܢܝܐ rt. ܓܙܥ. adj. *radical.*

ܓܘܙܝܬܐ pl. ܐ̈ f. of ܓܘܙܐ *a nut-tree, walnut-tree.*

ܓܚ, ܓܚ fut. ܢܓܘܚ, inf. ܡܓܚ, act. part. ܓܐܚ, ܓܝܚܐ *to gush out, pour forth* as water; *to rush out eagerly;* ܓܚ ܥܡܐ *the populace poured forth.* Aph. ܐܓܝܚ *to make flow, gush* or *pour forth;* ܐܓܝܚ ܡܪܝܐ ܡܝܐ *the Lord made waters to gush forth;* ܡܓܝܚ ܒܘܪܟܬܐ *pouring forth blessings;* ܐܓܝܚܘ ܬܪ̈ܥܐ ܕܪܥܝܢܟܘܢ *open the doors of your mind.* Ethtaph. ܐܬܬܓܝܚ *to be poured forth, sent abroad.* Derivatives, ܓܘܚܐ, ܓܝܚܐ, ܡܓܝܚܢܐ, ܡܓܝܚܢܘܬܐ.

ܓܘܚܐ prob. a vulgar form of ܓܘܚܐ *terror, horror, ruin; a clap of thunder, earthquake.*

ܓܘܚܟܐ rt. ܓܚܟ. m. *laughter, laughing, sport, ridicule;* ܕܓܘܚܟܐ *absurd, ridiculous.*

ܓܘܚܟܢܐ rt. ܓܚܟ. m. *risible, laughable.*

ܓܘܐ Pa. denom. verb from ܓܘܐ. *to take* or *bring in, admit;* pass. part. ܡܓܘܐ, ܡܓܘܝܐ *admitted to counsel, instructed; beyond, remote, innermost; secret, esoteric;* ܐܝܬ ܡܓܘܝܢ ܒܗ ܠܬܝܡܢܐ ܠܓܘ *there lie to the far South.* Ethpa. ܐܬܓܘܝ *to go far in, enter, penetrate.* Metaph. *to be deeply versed, have attained a high degree; to be castrated;* ܐܬܓܘܝܘ ܠܓܘ ܡܕܒܪܐ *they retired to the interior of the desert;* ܡܬܓܘܐ ܠܓܘ ܟܣܝܬܐ *he penetrates far into hidden things.*

ܓܘܝܐ f. ܓܘܝܬܐ, pl. m. ܓܘܝܐ, ܓܘܝܝܢ, f. ܓܘܝܬܐ rt. ܓܘ. *inner, internal, farther, remote;* ܕܪܬܐ ܓܘܝܬܐ *the inner court;* ܗܢܕܘ ܓܘܝܬܐ *farther India;* opp. ܒܪܝܐ *outer;* ܓܘܝܐ—ܒܪܝܐ *citizens—foreigners; the besieged—the besiegers; sacred—profane.*

ܓܘܐܐ pl. ܓܘ̈ܐܐ rt. ܓܘܐ. m. *the inwards, intestines; an eunuch.*

ܓܘܕܐ m. *a ball.*

ܓܘܒܠܐ rt. ܓܘܒ. m. *an answer.*

ܓܘܝܘܬܐ rt. ܓܘܐ. f. *the inner* or *farther part; possession;* ܕܚܫܘܟܐ ~ *innermost recess of darkness.*

ܓܘܠܬܐ pl. ܓܘ̈ܠܬܐ rt. ܓܘܠ. f. *a*) *a ball.* *b*) pl. *piles, hemorrhoids.*

ܓܘܠ or ܓܐܠ, fut. ܢܓܘܠ, act. part. ܓܐܠ, ܓܐܠܐ root-meaning same as ܓܠܠ *to wind* or *twine round,* hence *to stir, be moved* only with ܪ̈ܚܡܐ and ܥܠ of the object; *to be moved with compassion;* ܓܝܠܝܢ ܪ̈ܚܡܐ ܕܟܐܢܘܬܐ ܥܠ ܬܝܒܐ *the bowels of justice are moved towards the penitent.* Aph. ܐܓܝܠ *to cast out* or *forth, eject, reject* often coupled with ܐܥܒܪ; ܛܝܒܘܬܐ ܡܓܝܠܐ ܘܡܥܒܪܐ ܦܠܓܘܬܐ *grace will repel and expel dissensions;* part. ܡܓܝܠ used in both senses, *a*) act. the sea after a storm ܠܬܪܡܘܬܗ ܡܓܝܠ *casts forth its dregs;* fishes' gills ܡܓܝܠܝܢ ܠܡ̈ܝܐ *move aside the waters;* *b*) pass. ܥܘܬܪܐ ܡܓܝܠ ܘܥܒܝܪ *riches poured forth and heaped up.* Ethtaph. ܐܬܬܓܝܠ *to be rejected.* Derivatives, ܓܘܠܐ, ܓܘܠܬܐ, ܡܓܝܠܘܬܐ.

ܓܘܠܐ pl. ܓܘ̈ܠܐ m. *a*) *a wild beast,* perh. *the hyaena.* *b*) *terror.* *c*) pl. of ܓܘܠܬܐ *garments.*

ܓܘܠܐܒ Pers. *julep.*

ܓܘܠܓܠܐ rt. ܓܠܓܠ. m. *a veil.*

ܓܘܠܓܘܣ *an ape;* see ܓܠܓܠܐ.

ܓܘܠܕܢܐ pl. ܐ̈ rt. ܓܠܕ. m. *deprivation, want, lack;* ~ ܕܡܐܟܘܠܬܐ *abstinence, fasting.*

ܓܘܠܝܐ rt. ܓܠܐ *a*). m. *captivity, forced emigration;* ~ ܕܐܬܪ̈ܘܬܐ *the carrying away of regions,* i.e. *of all the population.*

ܓܘܠܟܐ m. *a lathe.*

ܓܘܠܢܐܪ Pers. *a pomegranate blossom.*

ܓܘܠܩܐ pl. ܐ̈ m. *a sack.*

ܓܘܠܬܐ pl. ܓܘ̈ܠܐ f. rt. ܓܘܠ. *a cowl, a woollen cloak* worn by monks or shepherds; ܐܠܒܫܗ ܓܘܠܬܐ ܕܐܪܟܝܡܢܕܪܝܘܬܐ *he clad him in the Archimandrite's cowl;* E-Syr. *an altar-cloth.*

ܓܘܡ, ܓܐܡ same as ܓܡܡ *to cut off.*

ܓܘܡܣܐ pl. ܝ̈ܢ, ܐ̈ m. *a bean;* used for *a measure of weight,* a Greek bean equalled two oboli, an Alexandrian bean three, an Egyptian bean four.

ܓܘܡܚܐ rt. ܓܡܚ. m. *impudence, presumption, rashness.*

ܓܘܡܚܢ, ܓܘܡܚܢܐ f. ܓܘܡܚܢܝܬܐ pl. m. ܐ̈, f. ܬ̈ܐ rt. ܓܡܚ. *bold, daring, impudent, shameless.*

ܓܘܡܚܢܐܝܬ rt. ܓܡܚ. adv. *presumptuously, frowardly.*

ܓܘܡܚܢܘܬܐ rt. ܓܡܚ. f. *impudence, perversity, frowardness.*

ܓܘܡܚܢܝܐ f. ܓܘܡܚܢܝܬܐ adj. same as ܓܘܡܚܢ.

ܓܘܡܛܪܝܐ, ܓܘܡܛܪܘܣ; see ܓܐܘܡܛܪܐ.

ܓܘܡܛܪܝܐ, ܐ̈, ܓܘܡ̈ܛ, ܓܘܡܛܪܘܬܐ *geometry,* &c.; see under ܓܐܘܡܛܪܝܐ.

ܓܘܡܝܙܐ *a wild fig, sycamore.*

ܓܘܡܢܣܝܘܢ and various other spellings, γυμνάσιον, *a*) *a place for athletic exercises.* *b*) *exercise, practice.*

ܓܘܡܨܐ m. ܓܘܡܨܬܐ f. pl. m. ܝ̈ܢ rt. ܓܡܨ. m. *a hollow, a pit;* ܕܡ̈ܝܐ ~ perh. *a whirlpool.*

ܓܘܡܨܐ pl. ܐ̈ m. *a*) *a pit, pitfall,* with ܚܦܪ *to dig a pit.* Metaph. ܡܢ ܓܘܡܨܐ ܠܓܘܡܨܐ *from depth to depth* of sin; ܓܘܡܨ̈ܐ ܬܚܬܝ̈ܐ *the lower regions.* *b*) *a trench* to plant trees in. *c*) ܕܠܚܡܐ ~ *a chunk, a big lump* of food.

ܓܘܡܪܐ rt. ܓܡܪ. m. *perishing, slaughter.*

ܓܘܡܪ̈ܝܢ, ܓܘܡܪ̈ܐ irreg. pl. of ܓܘܡܪܬܐ *burning coals.*

ܓܘܡܪܢܝܐ, ܢܝܬܐ adj. *of* or *from fiery coals.*

ܓܘܡܪܙܐ pl. ܐ̈ m. *a weasel.*

ܓܘܡܬܐ pl. ܬ̈ܐ f. *a den, slough; a hollow, ditch, trench;* ~ ܕܐܪܥܐ *a ditch in the ground;* ܒܓܘܡܬܐ ܕܨܘܐܗ ܐܝܟ ܚܙܝܪܐ ܡܬܦܪܦܪ *he revels in the slough of his filth like a pig.*

ܓܘܢ denom. verb Pa. conj. from ܓܘܢܐ. *to colour, dye.* Ethpa. ܐܬܓܘܢ *to be coloured;* ܡܐܢ̈ܐ ܡܓܘܢ̈ܝܢ *dyed raiment.*

ܓܘܢ, ܓܘܢܐ W-Syr. ܓܘܢ, ܓܘܢܐ, E-Syr. pl. ܝ̈ܢ, ܐ̈ and ܓܘܢ̈ܘܢܐ m. Pers. *gûn.* *a*) *colour,* hue, ܣܡܘܩܐ ܓܘܢ ܫܡܝܐ sky blue, azure; ܣܘܡܩܐ vermilion; ܓܘ̈ܢܝܢ ܓܘ̈ܢܝܢ various colours; ܓܒܪܐ ܛܒܐ ܣܘܡܩ ܓܘܢܗ ܗܘܐ the good man was of a florid complexion. Metaph. ܚܘܒܐ ܕܨܒܝܥ ܒܓܘܢ ܚܡܬܐ love tinged with anger. b) appearance, sort, kind, ܓܘܢܐ ܚܘܪܐ the white sort; ܬܠܬܐ ܓܘ̈ܢܐ ܕܒܫܠܐ three kinds of stewed food (or ܓܢܣ throughout). Derivatives, verb ܓܘܢ and ܓܘܢܝ, ܓܘܢܝܐ, ܡܓܘܢܢܘܬܐ.

ܓܘܢ, ܓܘܢܐ pl. ܓܘܢܘ̈ܬܐ m. a great brazen vessel for washing.

ܓܘܢ perh. γοῦν, always with ܒ and ܕ, ܒܓܘܢ therefore, then, forasmuch as, for that cause, on that account.

ܓܘܢܐܝܬ adv. rt. ܓܘܢ. in common, in general, together.

ܓܘܢܒܐ pl. ܐ̈ rt. ܓܢܒ. m. theft, stealth, a clandestine action.

ܓܘܢܛܣܛܒܠ and other spellings. French, connétable, comes stabuli.

ܓܘܢܚܐ pl. ܝ̈ܢ, ܐ̈ rt. ܓܢܚ. m. a terrible event, stupendous deed; the terror caused by earthquake; pl. horrors, atrocities, such as slaughter and carnage; terror, grief, confusion of mind; ܬܕܡܘܪܬܐ ܘܓܘܢܚܐ a wonderful and terrible thing.

ܓܘܢܝܐ, ܓܘܢܝܐ or ܓܘܢܝܬܐ pl. ܓܘܢܝܣ, ܓܘܢܝܘܬܐ, ܓܘܢܝܐܣ emph. ܓܘܢܝܬܐ, ܓܘܢܝܘܬܐ or ܓܘܢ throughout. f. γωνία, a corner; the angle or side of a triangle or other geometric figure; ܫܘܝ ܓܘܢܝܘܬܐ equal-sided; ܓ̈ ܚܪܝܦܬܐ an acute, ܦܬܝܬܐ an obtuse, ܬܪܝܨܬܐ a right angle; ܓܘܢܝܐ ܕܥܝܢܐ or ܩܪܢܐ the inner corner of the eye.

ܓܘܢܚ, ܓܘܢܚܐ pl. ܐ̈ rt. ܓܢܚ. m. blame, reproach, contumely, calumny, complaint; ܥܠ ܓܘܢܚܢ our complaint.

ܓܘܢܝ, ܓܘܢܝܐ, ܓܘܢܝܬܐ pl. m. ܝ̈ܢ, ܐ̈ f. ܬ̈ܐ rt. ܓܘܢ. adj. common, general, universal; ܐܒܐ ܓ̈ or ܐܒܘܢ a patriarch or metropolitan bishop; ܐܓܪܬܐ ܓ̈ a general or catholic epistle; ܡܡܠܠܐ ܓ̈ the vulgar tongue; ܨܠܘܬܐ ܓ̈ Jac. a ferial prayer, daily office, opp. ܕܝܠܢܝܐ special, for special occasions; ܐܝܟ ܡܠܬܐ ܓ̈ according to the literal sense. ܓܘܢܝܐ prob. inner sc. under-garments.

ܓܘܝܢ Pauel same as ܓܘܢ Pael to colour. Ethpau. ܐܬܓܘܝܢ = Ethpa. ܐܬܓܘܢ.

ܓܘܢܐ pl. of ܓܘܢܐ m. colours.

ܓܘܢܕܘܣ Pers. m. orchis.

ܓܘܢܕܪܐ m. a) a blow with the fist. b) the throat. Cognate, ܓܢܕܪܐ.

ܓܘܣ Ethpa. ܐܬܓܘܣ to take refuge, flee for succour, help, or relief, with ܒ or ܠܘܬ of place or person; ܒܝܘܢܝܐ with the Greeks; ܒܦܬܟܪܐ to idols; ܠܘܬ ܥܕܬܐ in the church. Pa. ܓܝܣ denom. verb from ܓܝܣܐ, see below. Derivatives, ܓܘܣܐ, ܓܘܣܝܐ, ܡܬܓܘܣܢܘܬܐ.

ܓܘܣܐ rt. ܓܘܣ. m. seeking refuge; a place of refuge, asylum, ܒܝܬ ܓܘܣܐ the same; ܐܚܕ ܓܘܣܐ to take refuge.

ܓܘܣܩܬܐ pl. ܬ̈ܐ rt. ܓܣܩ. f. a vessel to pour out of.

ܓܘܣܝܐ or ܓܘܣ pl. ܐ̈ rt. ܓܘܣ. m. he who flees for succour, a refugee, fugitive; ܓܘ̈ܣܘܗܝ those who took refuge with him.

ܓܘܦ interj. of contempt, Pooh!

ܓܘܥܠܢ, ܓܘܥܠܢܐ pl. ܐ̈ rt. ܓܥܠ. m. a deposit, trust, charge; ܡܪܐ ܓ̈ or ܡܪܐ the owner of that which is committed in trust; ܠܐ ܡܟܦܪܝܢ ܒܓܘܥܠܢܐ they do not deny a deposit; ܢܦܫܟ ܓ̈ ܡܓܥܠܐ ܠܟ ܡܢ ܐܠܗܐ thy soul is entrusted to thee by God; ܓ̈ ܕܦܝܠܣܘܦܐ the charges or precepts of philosophers.

ܓܘܥܬܐ rt. ܓܥܬ. m. vomit.

ܓܘܦܠܬܐ pl. ܓܘ̈ܦܠܬܐ f. gleaning.

ܓܘܦ, ܓܦ fut. ܢܓܘܦ, act. part. ܓܐܦ, ܓܝܦܐ to hunt, take in a net. Metaph. rhet. to captivate. Pa. ܓܘܦ the same. Ethpa. ܐܬܓܘܦ to shut or fasten. Derivatives, ܓܘܦܐ, ܓܘܦܬܐ.

ܓܘܦܐ, ܓܘܦ or ܓܘܦ pl. ܓܘ̈ܦܐ m. a net, drag-net.

ܓܘܦܢܐ pl. ܐ̈ rt. ܓܦܢ. f. a vine, ܓ̈ ܐܘܟܡܬܐ ܘܚܘܪܬܐ black bryony, white bryony; see ܓܦܬܐ.

ܓܘܦܢܐ rt. ܓܦܢ. m. digging.

ܓܘܣܩܣ gypsum; see ܓܦܣܘܣ.

ܓܘܦܢܐ m. *a*) Ar. *the spathe* of a palm, *involucre* of a blossom. *b*) *a bulb*. *c*) ܓ̅ ܕܝܡܐ *a marine aromatic drug*.

ܓܘܦܬܐ = ܓܘܦܬܐ f. *a fowling-net*.

ܓܘܪ, ܓܪ fut. ܢܓܘܪ, inf. ܡܓܪ, act. part. ܓܐܪ, ܓܐܪܐ with pron. aff. or ܒ of the person; *to commit adultery*. Pa. ܓܝܪ and Aph. ܐܓܝܪ *to commit adultery*. Ethpa. ܐܬܓܝܪ *to go a whoring*. Derivatives, ܓܘܪܐ, ܓܝܘܪܐ, ܓܝܘܪܐ, ܓܝܪܐ, ܓܝܪܘܬܐ.

ܓܘܪܐ pl. ܐ̈ rt. ܓܘܪ. m. *a*) *adultery*; ܒܪ ܓܘܪܐ *a bastard*. *b*) *the column* of a book or account, ܬܬܟܬܒ ܒܓܘܪܐ ܕܚܝܒܐ *thou shalt be inscribed among the debtors*. *c*) Ar. *a jar*.

ܓܘܪܒܐ pl. ܒ̈ܐ m. Pers. *a stocking, sock*.

ܓܘܪܓܐ, ܓܘܪܓܠܐ or ܓܘܪܓܠܐ m. *a capsule, seed-vessel, pod*.

ܓܘܪܕܐ m. *a knave, cheat*.

ܓܘܪܓܝܐ pl. ܝ̈ܐ rt. ܓܪܓ. m. *an incentive, inducement; encouragement, provocation;* one of the six parts of rhetoric.

ܓܘܪܓܫܐ pl. ܫ̈ܐ m. *a bowing down, falling down* to pray; *the rolling* of thunderclouds; *a vibrating sound*.

ܓܘܪܕܝܕܐ *ambidexter*.

ܓܘܪܕܡܐ *the gnawing of a bone, getting the marrow out*.

ܓܘܪܙܐ pl. ܐ̈ m. *a faggot, bundle of wood; the load of pollen* which a bee brings from flowers.

ܓܘܪܝܐ pl. ܓܘܪ̈ܝܐ m. *a whelp*, ܓ̅ ܕܐܪܝܐ *a lion's whelp*, used metaph. of Christ in allusion to Gen. xlix. 9.

ܓܘܪܡܕܐ *the fore-arm, a cubit*.

ܓܘܪܡܘܫܬܐ or ܓܘܪܡܘܫܐ *a double* or *lined garment*.

ܓܘܪܢܐ pl. ܢ̈ܐ generally fem. γοῦρνα, *a large vessel, a stone bath, an urn;* ܓܘܪܢܐ ܕܩܒܘܪܐ *funereal urns*.

ܓܘܪܢܝܐ dialect of Tacrit, *a plane*.

ܓܘܪܢܝܐ m. *a little pig*.

ܓܘܪܣܐ rt. ܓܪܣ. m. *breaking up, destruction*.

ܓܘܪܦܐ pl. ܦ̈ܐ m. γορφίον, *a cutting* or *slip of the olive-tree; a hollow* in a tree.

ܓܘܙ ܩܝ *nux vomica, strychnine*.

ܓܘܪܓܪܐ rt. ܓܪܓܪ. m. *a*) *clamour, shouting, vociferation*. *b*) *rumination, chewing the cud*.

ܐܬܓܘܪܓܪ denom. verb from the above *a*) *to make guttural sounds*. *b*) *to chew the cud*, ܚܝܘܬܐ ܕܡܬܓܘܪܓܪܢ *ruminants*. Metaph. *to ruminate, meditate*.

ܓܘܪܫܢܐ *digestive medicines*.

ܓܘܫ imper. of ܓܫ *to touch*.

ܓܘܫܬܐ m. *the bottom* of a well, *hollow* in a river, *a ford*. Metaph. *profundity*, ܒܢܝ ܓܘܫܬܐ *men of deep learning*.

ܓܘܫܡ emph. ܓܘܫܡܐ pl. ܓܘܫ̈ܡܝܢ, ܡ̈ܐ m. *a body, solid; a metal;* ܓ̅ ܐܣܦܝܪܐܢܐ *a spherical form;* ܓܘܫܡܐ ܕܠܐ ܡܬܦܠܓܝܢ *atoms;* ܕܠܐ ܓܘܫܡ *incorporeal*. Metaph. *a corporate body, community; the whole*, ܓ̅ ܕܐܬܘܬܐ ܟܠܗ *the whole alphabet; the text* of the Scriptures; *a system* of doctrine; ܓ̅ ܕܦܪܟܣܝܣ *the text of the Acts* of the Apostles; ܓ̅ ܕܡܠܦܢܘܬܐ ܕܐܘܢܓܠܝܘܢ *the text of the teaching of the Gospel;* logic. *substance*. Derivatives the four following words, verb ܓܫܡ, ܓܫܝܡܐ, ܓܫܝܡܘܬܐ, ܡܓܫܡܢܘܬܐ, ܡܓܫܡܢܘܬܐ.

ܓܘܫܡܢܝ, ܓܘܫܡܢܐ, ܢܝܬܐ adj. from ܓܘܫܡܐ. *bodily, corporeal;* with ܠܐ *incorporeal*.

ܓܘܫܡܢܐܝܬ from ܓܘܫܡܐ. adv. *bodily*. Metaph. *literally* opp. ܪܘܚܢܐܝܬ *spiritually* with reference to exposition of the Scriptures.

ܓܘܫܡܬܢ, ܢܐ, ܢܝܬܐ pl. m. ܢ̈ܐ, ܢܝ̈ܢ, f. ܢ̈ܝܢ, ܢ̈ܝܬܐ adj. *fleshy, corpulent, material, corporeal, literal;* ܣܘܟܠܐ ܓܘܫܡܬܢܝܐ *the literal sense*.

ܓܘܫܡܬܢܘܬܐ from ܓܘܫܡܐ. f. *bulkiness, corporeality*.

ܓܘܫܡܬܐ f. *a net, a covering of network* for the head.

ܓܘܫܦܐ, ܓܘܫܦܬܐ, ܓܘܫܦܫܬܐ, ܓܘܫܦܫܦܬܐ, ܓܘܫܦܫܦܘܬܐ f. *a counterpane*.

ܓܘܬܐ f. *the inner bark* of the oak, used in dyeing.

ܓܘܬܝܐ f. ܓܘܬܝܬܐ pl. m. ܓܘܬ̈ܝܐ *a Goth*.

ܓܙ fut. ܢܓܘܙ and ܢܓܙ, inf. ܡܓܙ, imper. ܓܘܙ, act. part. ܓܐܙ, ܓܐܙܐ or ܓܙܐ, pl. m. ܓܙܝܢ, f. ܓܙܝܢ,

pass. part. ܓܙܝܙ, ܙܐ, ܙܬܐ. *to clip* or *cut* the hair; *to shear* sheep, part. pl. f. emph. ܓܙܝܙܬܐ *shorn sheep.* Ethpe. ܐܬܓܙܝܙ *to be mown, shorn; to be cut off, concluded.* Aph. ܐܓܙ same as Pe. Derivatives, ܓܙܐ, ܓܙܬܐ, ܓܙܘܙܐ, ܓܙܙܐ, ܓܙܙܬܐ, ܡܓܙܘܙܐ, ܡܓܙܙܐ.

ܓܙ 3 m. s. of ܓܘܙ *to fail.*

ܓܙܐ or ܓܙܙܐ pl. ܓܙܐ contr. from ܓܢܙܐ *to hide.* m. *treasure, a treasury.* Metaph. *the eucharist* or *the consecrated bread,* ܕܠܐ ܢܫܒܘܩ ܓܙܐ ܥܠ ܡܕܒܚܐ *he may not leave the host on the altar* till the second day; ܒܝܬ ܓܙܐ E-Syr. *a recess in the north wall of the sanctuary* where the holy bread is placed.

ܓܙܬܐ m. ܓܙܬܐ f. pl. c. ܓܙܐ rt. ܓܙ. m. *a mowing, shearing.* f. *a fleece, wool.*

ܓܙܙܐ rt. ܓܙ. m. *a shearer.*

ܓܙܐ seldom used in Pe. *to deprive,* Pa. ܓܙܝ or ܓܙܝ act. *to bereave, deprive of;* pass. *to be bereaved;* Elijah ܐܚܕ ܠܫܡܝܐ ܘܓܙܝ ܠܐܪܥܐ *bound heaven and made the earth barren;* pass. part. ܡܓܙܝ, ܡܓܙܝܐ, ܡܓܙܝܬܐ *destitute, sterile, lonely, bereaved;* ܡܕܝܢܬܐ ܡܓܙܝܬܐ *a deserted city;* ܡܓܙܝܬܐ ܡܢ ܡܝܐ *waterless, arid;* legal ܡܓܙܝܐ ܝܠܕܐ ܕܡܬܓܙܝܐ *a feigned issue;* f. emph. *a childless woman;* m. pl. emph. *anchorets, ascetics.* Ethpa. ܐܬܓܙܝ *to be bereaved* esp. of husband or children; *to be left destitute,* ܐܬܓܙܝܬ ܐܪܥܐ ܡܢ ܡܛܪܐ *the land was barren for lack of rain.* Derivatives, ܓܙܝܐ, ܡܓܙܝܘܬܐ, ܡܓܙܝܢܐ.

ܓܙܒܪܐ or ܓܝܙܒܪܐ pl. ܐ, perh. for ܓܢܙܒܪܐ with ܝ lengthened to ܘ to compensate the loss of ܢ; m. *a treasurer, a steward;* cf. ܓܙܐ.

ܓܙܒܪܘܬܐ or ܓܝܙ f. from the above, *treasurership.*

ܓܙܘܙܐ pl. ܐ rt. ܓܙ. m. *a shearer.*

ܓܙܘܡܬܢܐ, ܓܙܘܡܬܢܝܬܐ rt. ܓܙܡ. adj. *comminatory, threatening.*

ܓܙܘܡܬܢܘܬܐ rt. ܓܙܡ. f. *boldness.*

ܓܙܘܪܐ pl. ܐ rt. ܓܙܪ. m. *cutting, piercing;* ܦܪܙܠܐ ܓܙܘܪܐ *lancets; one who performs the rite of circumcision.*

ܓܙܘܪܬܐ pl. ܓܙܘܪܢ, ܓܙܘܪܬܐ rt. ܓܙܪ. f. *circumcision, the foreskin;* ܥܡܐ ܕܡܢ ܓܙܘܪܬܐ *the Jews.*

ܓܙܙܐ rt. ܓܙ. m. *shearing.*

ܓܙܝܬܐ rt. perh. ܓܙܐ; cf. ܓܙܐ. m. *an inner chamber.*

ܓܙܝܡܬܐܝܬ rt. ܓܙܡ. adv. *sharply.*

ܓܙܝܪܐܝܬ rt. ܓܙܪ. adv. *decisively; severely.*

ܓܙܝܪܬܐ rt. ܓܙܪ. f. *a decree, sentence, ordinance; a space parted off* or *separated; a partition wall; split wood, a pile of wood;* ܓ̈ ܕܬܪܥܐ *the door-knocker.*

ܓܙܝܬܐ f. *a poll-tax, capitation tax;* ܓܙܝܬ ܪܫܐ the same.

ܓܙܠܐ, ܓܙܠܢܝܬܐ adj. *left-handed;* cf. ܓܘܙܠܐ.

ܓܙܡ fut. ܢܓܙܘܡ, inf. ܡܓܙܡ, act. part. ܓܐܙܡ, ܓܐܙܡܐ, pass. part. ܓܙܝܡ root-meaning like that of ܓܙ, ܓܙܝ, ܓܙܪ &c.; *to cut off,* hence *a*) *to determine, decree;* impers. ܓܙܝܡܐ ܠܗ *it was determined;* *b*) with ܥܠ *to rush upon, assault;* *c*) *to threaten;* ܓܙܡ ܕܢܣܚܘܦ ܥܡܪܗ the flood *which threatened to tear away his dwelling;* ܓܗܢܐ ܓܙܝܡܬܐ ܠ *Gehenna which is decreed* or *threatened to* or *for.* Ethpe. ܐܬܓܙܡ *to be threatened.* Pa. ܓܙܡ *to threaten.* Derivs. ܓܙܡܐ, ܓܙܘܡܬܢܐ, ܓܙܘܡܬܢܘܬܐ, ܓܙܝܡܬܐܝܬ, ܓܙܡܬܐ, ܓܘܙܡܐ.

ܓܙܡܐ pl. ܐ rt. ܓܙܡ. m. *an assault, threat.*

ܓܙܡܐ rt. ܓܙܡ. m. *a branch cut off.*

ܓܙܡܝܙܐ Pers. *the fruit of the tamarisk.*

ܓܙܦܐ Pers. *vain, futile.*

ܓܙܪ fut. ܢܓܙܘܪ, inf. ܡܓܙܪ, imper. ܓܙܘܪ, act. part. ܓܐܙܪ, pass. part. ܓܙܝܪ, ܪܐ, ܪܬܐ. *to cut* or *hew stone; to tear; to probe* a wound; *to circumcise, be circumcised; to determine, decree;* ܓܙܪܘ ܐܢܘܢ ܦܪ̈ܚܬܐ *birds of prey tore them;* ܓܙܪܬ ܥܠ ܡܘܬܗܘܢ *she determined upon their death;* with ܨܘܡܐ *to proclaim a fast;* pass. part. ܓܙܝܪ̈ܝ ܠܒܐ *circumcised in heart;* ܡܢܝܢܐ ܕܝܪ̈ܚܘܗܝ ܓܙܝܪܝܢ *the number of his months is determined;* pl. f. *hewn stones.* Ethpe. ܐܬܓܙܪ *to be cut* or *hewn out; to undergo a surgical operation; to be circumcised; to decree, appoint.* Aph. ܐܓܙܪ *to bestow, confer upon.* Derivatives, ܓܙܘܪܐ, ܓܙܘܪܬܐ, ܓܙܝܪܐܝܬ, ܓܙܝܪܬܐ, ܓܙܪܐ, ܓܙܪܐ, ܓܙܪܐ, ܓܙܪܐ, ܓܙܪܬܐ, ܡܓܙܪܐ.

ܓܙܪܐ rt. ܓܙܪ. m. *one who performs the rite of circumcision.*

ܓܙܪܐ pl. ܐ rt. ܓܙܪ. m. *a cut, notch; a slit,*

e.g. in the bark of a vine; *an incision, excision; a surgical operation; a prey,* ܐܝܟ ܐܪܝܐ ܥܠ ܓܙܪܬܐ *as a lion over the prey.*

ܓܙܪ, ܓܙܪܐ m. with ܕܒܪܐ *the wild parsnip;* ܓܙܪ ܓܢܬܐ *the garden parsnip.*

ܓܙܪܐ m. *nimble, agile.*

ܓܙܪܐ pl. ܝܢ, ܐ rt. ܓܙܪ. m. *a) surgery. b) a judgement, sentence,* generally ܓܙܪ ܕܝܢܐ pl. ܓܙܪܝ ܕܝܢܐ with the verbs ܐܬܦܣܩ or ܢܦܩ, with ܥܠ of the pers. ܓܙܪܐ ܡܪܝܪܐ ܐܬܓܙܪܘ ܥܠܝܗܘܢ *bitter sentences were decreed upon them;* ܓܙܪ ܨܘܡܐ *the appointment of a fast. c) a flock, sheepfold.* Metaph. *a mandra, monastery;* ܕܝܪܝܐ ܕܒܓܙܪܐ *the monks in the mandra;* ܓܙܪܝܢ ܓܙܪܝܢ *by flocks,* i.e. *in good order.*

ܓܙܪܬܐ pl. ܓܙܪܢ, ܓܙܪܬܐ often misprinted ܓܙܝܪܬܐ rt. ܓܙܪ. f. *an island.*

ܓܙܪܬܘܢܝܬܐ f. dim. of ܓܙܪܬܐ *a little island.*

ܓܙܬܐ pl. ܓܙܐ rt. ܓܙ. f. *a fleece, wool;* see ܓܙܐ.

ܓܚ 3 m. s. of ܓܘܚ *to rush out.*

ܓܚܘܟܘܬܐ rt. ܓܚܟ. f. *laughter, the faculty of laughter;* ܓ ܕܒܪܢܫܐ ܕܝܠܝܬܐ *laughter is peculiar to man.*

ܓܚܟ and ܓܚܟ, fut. ܢܓܚܘܟ, inf. ܡܓܚܟ, imper. ܓܚܘܟ, part. ܓܚܟ, ܓܚܟܐ *to laugh,* with ܒ or ܥܠ; *to be merry, dance.* Metaph. of an amalgam, *to be bright.* Ethpe. ܐܬܓܚܟ act. *to laugh at, deride;* pass. *to be laughed at, derided.* Pa. ܓܚܟ *to mock, ridicule,* with ܒ or ܥܠ *to sport, jest.* Ethpa. ܐܬܓܚܟ *to be ridiculed, mocked.* Aph. ܐܓܚܟ *to cease to laugh.* Derivatives, ܓܘܚܟܐ, ܓܚܘܟܐ, ܓܚܘܟܘܬܐ, ܡܓܚܟܢܐ, ܡܓܚܟܢܐܝܬ, ܡܓܚܟܢܘܬܐ, ܡܬܓܚܟܢܐ.

ܓܚܢ *to discharge pus.*

ܓܚܣܐ, ܓܚܣܐ or ܐܓܚܣܐ *a) deprived of one testicle. b) heritage, succession.*

ܓܚܦܐ pl. ܐ m. *a vault;* ܒܝܬ ܓ or ܓܚܦܐ ܕܓܚܦܐ *a vaulted room; a brothel.*

ܓܝܓܠ, ܓܝܓܠܐ pl. ܝܢ, ܐ, contr. from ܓܠܓܠܐ rt. ܓܠ. f. *a) the wheel* of a carriage, well, mill; *a potter's wheel;* ܡܗܦܟ ܓܝܓܠܐ ܥܠܝܗܘܢ *he turns the threshing-wheel over them;* proverb. ܬܗܦܘܟ ܥܠܝܗܘܢ ܓ *their turn will come. b) a round stone rolling in a groove* to close the opening of a sepulchre. *c) an instrument of torture. d) a circle, ring,* ܓ ܕܣܐܡܐ *a silver ring; a row* ܕܓܘܪܓܐ *of embroidery; a ball* of cotton or thread. *e)* rit. *cycle, course. f)* astron. *disc, sphere, cycle.* Metaph. *angels* in allusion to their swiftness, ܓ ܟܪܘܒܝܐ *the cherubic wheels;* ܓ ܙܒܢܐ *the wheel of time;* ܓ ܫܢܬܐ *the circle of the year;* ܓܝܓܠܬܐ ܪܒܬܐ the constellation *Ursa Major.*

ܓܝܓܪܬܐ pl. ܓܝܓܪܬܐ m. γίγαρτον, *grape-stones* and *skins, refuse from the wine-press; date-stones.*

ܓܝܕ denom. verb Pael conj. from ܓܝܕܐ *to hough, ham-string.* Metaph. *to unnerve.* Ethpa. ܐܬܓܝܕ pass.

ܓܝܕܐ pl. ܐ m. *a) a nerve, tendon, sinew;* ܓ ܕܚܙܘܐ *the optic nerve;* ܓ ܡܫܡܥܢܐ *the auditory nerve, nerve of hearing;* ܓ ܢܫܝܐ *the sciatic nerve;* metaph. ܓܝܕܐ ܕܦܪܙܠܐ *iron thews. b) the fibres* of a tree; *a string* of a musical instrument; *a tie, ligament.*

ܓܝܕܢܝܐ adj. from ܓܝܕܐ. m. *sinewy.*

ܓܝܗܢܐ, ܓܗܢܐ or ܓܗܢܐ Heb. f. *Gehenna, the place of torment.*

ܓܝܘܚܘܬܐ rt. ܓܘܚ. f. *a gushing forth, overflowing* of water.

ܓܝܘܠܐ m. *a bird,* perh. *a magpie.*

ܓܝܘܠܐܝܬ adv. from the above; ܠܐ ܬܬܨܒܬ ܓܝܘܠܐܝܬ ܒܨܒܬܐ ܕܠܐ ܘܠܝܢ *be not adorned like a magpie with unsuitable adornments.*

ܓܝܘܣܘܬܐ with ܕܪܚܡܐ rt. ܓܘܣ. f. *an impulse* of compassion, *tender feeling.*

ܐܬܓܝܪ denom. verb from the following. *to be a pilgrim, a stranger.*

ܓܝܘܪܐ m. ܓܝܘܪܬܐ f. pl. m. ܐ, f. ܬܐ rt. ܓܘܪ. *a)* subst. *an alien, foreigner, stranger; proselyte;* liturg. *a farcing* or *inserted verse. b)* adj. *alien, foreign, strange.*

ܓܝܘܪܐ m. ܓܝܘܪܬܐ f. pl. m. ܐ, f. ܬܐ rt. ܓܘܪ. *an adulterer, adulteress;* gram. *false, foreign,* e.g. ܪ is counted with the gutturals but as a ܓܝܘܪܬܐ, ܥ, ܚ, ܗ being true gutturals.

ܓܝܙܒܪܐ pl. ܐ m. rt. perh. ܓܙ. *a treasurer;* cf. ܓܙܒܪܐ.

ܓܝܪܬܐ from pres. part. of ܓܘܪ. f. *failing,* ܣܗܪܐ ܓܝܪܬܐ *the waning moon.*

ܓܺܝܳܚܳܐ rt. ܓܘܚ. m. *a breaking forth, running over* of water, tears, &c.

ܓܺܝܚܳܘܢ perh. rt. ܓܘܚ. *Gihon*, the second river of Eden.

ܓܺܝܠܳܘܣ or ܓܺܝܠܳܘܣܳܐ pl. ܐ̈ m. *a monkey, an ape.*

ܓܺܝܢܳܐ; see ܓܶܢܳܝܳܐ.

ܓܰܝܶܣ Pael denom. from ܓܰܝܣܳܐ. *to seize suddenly, take as prey, plunder, rob.*

ܓܰܝܣܳܐ pl. ܐ̈ m. *a*) *a band of robbers; a troop* esp. *of light horse.* *b*) *a marauding expedition, a foray.* Derivatives, ܓܝܣ verb, ܓܝܣܝܐ, ܓܝܣܝܐܝܬ, ܓܝܘܣܐ.

ܓܰܝܣܳܝܳܐ pl. ܓܝܣܝܶܐ, ܐ̈ m. *a robber, pirate.*

ܓܰܝܣܳܝܳܐܝܺܬ adv. *like robbers, in the manner of robbers.*

ܓܰܝܳܣܳܐ pl. ܐ̈ m. *a wife's sister's husband.*

ܓܝܘܣܐ adj. *rapacious, ravening.*

ܓܶܝܪ γάρ, causal conj. *for, but, indeed, however;* ܐܳܦ ܓܶܝܪ *even if;* ܘܳܐܦ ܓܶܝܪ *and even;* ܠܳܐ ܓܶܝܪ *not so;* ܟܰܕ ܓܶܝܪ *while, whereas.*

ܓܳܝܽܘܪܳܐ m. ܓܳܝܽܘܪܬܳܐ f. pl. m. ܐ̈ f. ܬ̈ܐ rt. ܓܘܪ. *one who commits adultery*, esp. *openly.*

ܓܺܝܪܳܐ pl. ܐ̈ m. *bird-lime.*

ܓܳܝܽܘܪܽܘܬܳܐ rt. ܓܘܪ. f. *adultery;* ܡܰܚܫܒܳܬܳܐ ܕܓܳܝܽܘܪܽܘܬܳܐ *impure thoughts.*

ܓܺܝܫܽܘܬܳܐ f. *difficulty in swallowing.*

ܓܶܫܪܳܐ or ܓܶܝܫܪܳܐ E-Syr. ܓܶܫܪܳܐ pl. ܐ̈ m. *a bridge, plank.*

ܓܰܠ *to be in a state of motion, to be put in motion;* cf. ܓܘܠ. pass. part. ܓܠܝܠ, ܐ, ܬܐ *round.* Pa. ܓܰܠܓܶܠ or perh. denom. from ܓܰܠܠܳܐ. *to rise in waves, to surge, swell.* Ethpa. ܐܶܬܓܰܠܓܰܠ *to be moved, tossed, rolled about;* ܕܰܡܬܓܰܠܓܠܳܐ ܒܥܰܠܥܳܠܶܐ *tempest-tossed.* Aph. ܐܰܓܶܠ *to roll, unfold.* Ethpalpal ܐܶܬܓܰܠܓܰܠ *to be made round, to be wreathed* or *twirled about* as vapour. Derivatives, ܓܠܝܠܐ, ܓܠܓܠܬܐ, ܓܠܓܠܐܝܬ, ܓܠܓܘܠܬܐ, ܓܠܠܐ, ܓܠܠܐ, ܡܓܠܐ, ܡܓܠܐ, ܡܓܠܬܐ.

ܓܳܠ 3 m. s. of ܓܘܠ with ܪܶܥܝܳܐ *to be moved.*

ܓܶܠܳܐ pl. ܓܶܠܶܐ m. same as ܓܰܠܠܳܐ, ܓܠܠܐ and

ܓܽܘܠܒܳܝܬܳܐ rt. ܓܠܒ. *a cloak, a coarse outer garment*, esp. *a monk's cloak.*

ܓܶܠܳܐ pl. ܓܶܠܶܐ, ܓܶܠܠܶܐ or ܓܶܠܠܶܐ m. *a straw, chip; straw, hay, dry stalks* or *twigs;* ܡܳܐܢܳܐ ܕܓܶܠܶܐ ܓܶܠܶܐ ܓܕܝܠܐ *a coat of hay-bands* or *stalks woven together.*

ܓܰܠܳܐ pl. ܓܰܠܶܐ often spelt ܓܰܠܠܳܐ, ܓܰܠܠܶܐ rt. ܓܠܠ. m. *a*) *a mound* of stones or earth, *a dam;* ܓܰܠܳܐ ܕܪܶܥܳܐ *gravel.* *b*) m. and f. *a tortoise, turtle.*

ܓܠܳܐ fut. ܢܶܓܠܶܐ, inf. ܡܶܓܠܳܐ, imper. ܓܠܺܝ, ܓܠܳܝ, ܓܠܰܘ, ܓܠܰܝܶܝܢ, act. part. ܓܳܠܶܐ, ܓܳܠܝܳܐ, pass. part. ܓܠܶܐ, ܓܠܝܳܐ. *a*) *to uncover, reveal, lay open, declare, show, make known* with ܠ or ܥܰܠ; ܓܠܳܐ ܪܺܫܶܗ *he bared his head;* ܓܠܳܐ ܕܰܗܒܳܐ *he came upon gold;* ܓܠܳܐ ܐܪܳܙܳܐ *he made known the secret, told his counsel, revealed the mystery;* ܓܠܳܐ ܣܰܟܠܽܘܬܶܗ *he openly confessed his sin;* gram. *to pronounce.* Pass. part. *uncovered, open, manifest, evident, public;* opp. ܟܣܶܐ and ܛܡܺܝܪܳܐ *hidden, concealed;* with ܠܳܐ *obscure;* ܐܳܬܳܐ ܓܰܠܝܳܬܳܐ *a manifest miracle;* ܬܰܘܕܺܝܬܳܐ ܕܗܰܝܡܳܢܽܘܬܳܐ ܓܰܠܝܬܳܐ *a public profession of faith;* ܗܳܝ ܕܠܰܣܓܺܝܐܶܐ ܓܰܠܝܳܐ *which was known to many;* ܓܰܠܝܳܐ or ܓܠܶܐ ܕ *it is evident.* Idioms, ܓܠܶܐ ܒܓܠܶܐ or ܓܠܶܐ ܥܰܝܢ *face to face, openly, clearly, boldly;* ܒܰܓܠܝܳܐ ܓܰܠܝܳܐܝܺܬ *manifestly, evidently;* ܓܰܠܝܽܘܬ ܦܰܪܨܽܘܦܳܐ *with open* or *unveiled face* i. e. *boldly, confidently;* ܒܰܓܠܶܐ ܥܰܝܢ ܠܳܐ ܐܶܬܒܰܗܬܽܘ *they had no need to be ashamed;* ܒܓܠܶܐ ܪܰܘܡܳܐ *publicly, openly;* gram. ܡܓܰܠܝܳܢܺܝܬܳܐ *a letter added to the verb to show* the gender or person, as ܬ in ܬܶܟܬܽܘܒ. *b*) *to go into exile.* In this sense the form ܓܠܳܐ is more usual. Ethpe. ܐܶܬܓܠܺܝ passive and reflexive of Peal; ܐܶܬܓܠܺܝܘ ܫܶܬܶܐܣܶܐ ܕܬܶܒܶܝܠ *the foundations of the world were uncovered;* ܐܶܬܓܰܠܝܰܬ ܗܶܪܶܣܺܝܣ *the heresy was revealed;* ܛܽܘܥܝܳܐ ܐܶܬܓܠܺܝ *the error was confessed;* refl. ܐܶܬܓܠܺܝ ܝܰܘܣܶܦ ܠܰܐܚܰܘܗܝ *Joseph made himself known to his brethren.* Pa. ܓܰܠܺܝ i) *to uncover, reveal.* ii) *to lead* or *go into captivity* or *exile.* Ethpa. ܐܶܬܓܰܠܺܝ pass. Aph. ܐܰܓܠܺܝ *to uncover, bring forth.* Derivatives, ܓܠܝܘܢܐ, ܓܠܝܘܢ, ܐܬܓܠܝ verb, ܓܠܝܢܐ, ܓܠܝܘܬܐ, ܓܠܝܬܐ, ܓܠܝܐ, ܓܠܝܐܝܬ, ܓܠܝܢܐ, ܓܠܝܘܬܐ, ܓܠܝܢܐ, ܡܓܠܝܢܝܬ, ܓܠܐ ܐܦܐ, ܓܠܝܢܐ, ܡܓܠܝܢܝܬ, ܡܓܠܝܢܘܬܐ, ܡܓܠܝܢܐ, ܡܓܠܝܢܝܬ, ܡܓܠܝܢܘܬܐ.

ܓܠܐܪܝܢ γαλάριον, *curds.*

ܓܠܒܐ *a dagger* or its *sheath.*

ܓܠܓܘܪܐ m. *a bier.*

ܓܠܐ fut. ܢܓܠܐ, inf. ܡܓܠܐ, imper. ܓܠܝ, act. part. ܓܠܐ, ܓܠܝܐ, pass. part. ܓܠܐ, ـܝܐ, ـܝܬܐ. *to draw aside* a veil; *to uncover* the eye; *to disperse* mist; ܓܠܝܢ ܐܦ̈ܝ ܦܪܣܐ *the curtains of the sanctuary are drawn back.* Pa. ܓܠܝ *to unveil, lay bare;* ܓܠܝ ܫܩܠ ܬܟܣܝ̈ܬܐ *he drew aside and took away the coverings;* med. *to dry up the orbit of the eye, make the pupil project;* ܡܓܠܝܐ *prominent, protruding.* Ethpa. ܐܬܓܠܝ pass. of Peal. Derivatives, ܓܠܝܘܢܐ, ܓܠܘܝܐ, ܓܠܝܐ.

ܓܠܝܘܢܐ pl. ـܐ rt. ܓܠܐ. m. *a curtain cord* or *rod.*

ܓܠܘܝܐ rt. ܓܠܐ. m. *the drawing up* or *aside* of a curtain; *opening* of the eyes, *elevation* of the eyebrows.

ܐܬܓܠܓܠ Ethpalpal conj. of ܓܠܓܠ; see above.

ܓܠܕ perh. denom. verb from ܓܠܝܕܐ. *to freeze;* ܡ̈ܝܐ ܓܠܝܕܝܢ *freezing waters.* Pa. ܓܠܕ *to freeze.* Aph. ܐܓܠܕ *to be frozen, to freeze, congeal;* ܡܓܠܕܝܢ ܢܛܦ̈ܐ *rain-drops are congealed.*

ܓܠܕܐ pl. ـܐ m. *skin, hide, fur;* ܬܛܠܝܠ ܓܠܕ̈ܐ *a roof of hides.*

ܓܠܕܘܢܐ dim. of the above, m. *a little skin, thin membrane.*

ܓܠܕܢܝܐ from ܓܠܕܐ. adj. *leathery, membranaceous.*

ܓܠܘܙܐ m. ܓܠܘܙܬܐ f. pl. m. ـܐ, f. ـܬܐ rt. ܓܠܙ. *a spoiler, an unjust person.*

ܓܠܘܝ quadrilit. verb from Pael of ܓܠܐ ii with the same meaning, *to carry away, lead into captivity; to go into exile.* Ethp. ܐܬܓܠܘܝ *to be carried into captivity, exiled; to remove from one place to another.*

ܓܠܘܝܐ pl. ܓܠܘ̈ܝܐ rt. ܓܠܐ ii. m. *an exile.*

ܓܠܘܓܠܐ Pers. *a pair of compasses.*

ܓܠܘܣ; see ܓܠܘܣܘܣ and ܓܠܣܐ *an ape.*

ܓܠܘܣܩܐ a) Chald. *fine white flour, dough.* b) *chestnuts.*

ܓܠܘܣܩܘܡܐ pl. ـܐ m. γλωσσόκομον, *a case, money-box, coffin,* esp. a case wherein the remains of saints were preserved, *a shrine, a reliquary.*

ܓܠܘܦܐ pl. ـܐ rt. ܓܠܦ. m. *a carver, sculptor.*

ܓܠܘܦܘܬܐ rt. ܓܠܦ. f. *the art of carving.*

ܓܠܘܬܐ rt. ܓܠܐ ii. *captivity;* collect. *captives, exiles.*

ܓܠܙ fut. ܢܓܠܘܙ, inf. ܡܓܠܙ, parts. ܓܐܠܙ, ܓܠܙܐ; ܓܠܝܙ, ـܐ, ـܬܐ. *to cheat, purloin, seize, take away; to disinherit, deprive* with ܡܢ; ܢܗܦܘܟ ܡܕܡ ܕܓܠܙ *let him return what he has wrongfully taken;* ܠܐ ܬܓܠܘܙ ܪ̈ܚܡܝܟ ܡܢܢ *take not away Thy mercies from us;* ܡܢ ܐ̈ܠܝܢ ܕܓܠܝܙܢ *what things are canonically prohibited.* Ethpe. ܐܬܓܠܙ with ܡܢ of the object or sometimes of the pers. passive; a) *to be deprived of, be destitute, disinherited,* ܘܠܐ ܐܬܓܠܙ ܡܢ ܗܘ ܝܪܬܘܬܐ ܕܥܕܬܐ ܕܒܫܡܝܐ *lest I lose my inheritance of the Church in Heaven;* ܡܬܓܠܙܝܢ ܡܢ ܝܘܬܪܢܝܗܘܢ *they are deprived of their profits.* b) *to separate oneself, depart,* ܡܢ ܢܫܝܗܘܢ ܡܬܓܠܙܝܢ *separating themselves from their wives.* Derivatives, ܓܠܘܙܐ, ܓܠܙܐ, ܓܠܝܙܘܬܐ, ܓܠܝܙܐܝܬ, ܡܬܓܠܙܢܘܬܐ, ܡܓܠܙܢܐ.

ܓܠܫ fut. ܢܓܠܘܫ, act. part. ܓܐܠܫ, pass. part. ܓܠܝܫܐ, ܓܠܝܫܬܐ. *to spread out, show, explain,* ܓܠܘܫ ܠܒܘܫ̈ܐ ܒܫܡܫܐ *spread out the clothes in the sun.* Pa. ܓܠܫ and Aph. ܐܓܠܫ *to declare, show forth.* Derivatives, ܓܠܝܫܐܝܬ, ܓܠܝܫܘܬܐ, ܡܓܠܫܢܘܬܐ.

ܓܠܛܐ Ar. m. *a mistake* in writing.

ܓܠܝ another form of ܓܠܐ; see above.

ܓܠܝܐ rt. ܓܠܐ i. m. *a manifestation, a declaring* or *showing openly;* ܒܓܠܝܐ ܐܬܐ *to appear openly, publicly, to be evident;* ܒܓܠܝܐ *openly, publicly.*

ܓܠܝܐ f. ܓܠܝܬܐ pl. m. ܓܠ̈ܝܐ, f. ܓܠ̈ܝܬܐ rt. ܓܠܐ ii. *a captive, exile.*

ܓܠܝܐܝܬ rt. ܓܠܐ i. adv. *clearly, openly, publicly, outwardly;* opp. ܟܣܝܐܝܬ *secretly.*

ܓܠܝܕܐ m. *ice, crystal;* ܐܓܠܝܕܐ is an older form. Derivative, verb ܓܠܕ, ܓܠܝܕܝܐ, ܡܓܠܕܢܐ, ܓܠܕܢܐ.

ܓܠܝܕܐ or ܓܠܝܕܢܐ f. ܓܠܝܕܢܝܬܐ, pl. m. ܝܐ, f. ܝܬܐ. adj. *frozen, glacial, icy, stiff;* ܪ̈ܘܚܐ ܓܠܝܕܢܝ̈ܬܐ *icy winds.*

ܓܠܝܘܢܐ pl. ܐ̈ m. = ܓܠܝܢܐ. rt. ܓܠܐ i. *a vision, revelation.*

ܓܠܝܘܢܐ pl. ܐ̈ m. rt. ܓܠܐ i. *a writing-tablet.*

ܓܠܝܘܦܐ pl. ܐ̈ m. rt. ܓܠܦ. *a writing-tablet.*

ܓܠܝܘܬܐ rt. ܓܠܐ i. f. *an uncovering, revealing, showing openly;* ܓܠܝܘܬ ܪܝܫܐ *the uncovering* or *baring of the head;* ~ ܐܦ̈ܐ *the uncovering of the face=confidence;* ~ ܕܡ̈ܠܐ *plain words;* ~ ܕܐܣܟܡܐ *the external appearance.*

ܓܠܝܙܘܬܐ rt. ܓܠܙ. f. *non-existence, negation; absence, lack, deprivation, abstinence;* ܓܠܝܙܘܬ ܪܚܡܐ *cruelty;* gram. *omission.*

ܓܠܝܙܘܬܢܐ rt. ܓܠܙ. adj. *negative.*

ܓܠܝܫܐܝܬ rt. ܓܠܫ. adv. *clearly.*

ܓܠܝܫܘܬܐ rt. ܓܠܫ. f. *spreading out* clothes; *explanation.*

ܓܠܝܠܐܝܬ rt. ܓܠ. adv. *in a round form.*

ܓܠܝܠܘܬܐ rt. ܓܠ. f. *rotundity, sphericity.*

ܓܠܝܠܢܐܝܬ rt. ܓܠ. adv. *spherically, rounding into a full circle* as the moon.

ܓܠܝܡܐ or ܓܠܘܡܐ Pers. m. *a woollen outer garment, a cloak.*

ܓܠܝܢܐ pl. ܐ̈ m. rt. ܓܠܐ a). *a revelation, appearance, manifestation; the Apocalypse;* ܥܐܕܐ ܕܓܠܝܢܐ *the Feast of the Transfiguration.*

ܓܠܝܢܐܝܬ rt. ܓܠܐ. adv. *by revelation.*

ܓܠܝܢܝܐ, ܝܬܐ pl. m. ܝ̈ܐ, f. ܝ̈ܬܐ rt. ܓܠܐ i. adj. *revealed, open, plain, sensible;* with ܕܡܘܬܐ *a shape really visible,* opp. ܚܙܘܢܝܬܐ *seen in a dream.*

ܓܠܝܪܐ pl. ܐ̈ m. *galearius, a soldier-servant, camp-follower.*

ܓܠܝܪܘܬܐ f. *a crowd of galearii, a rabble.*

ܓܠܝܬܐ fem. of ܓܠܝܐ *a captive.*

ܓܠܠ Pael of ܓܠ. *to swell, surge.*

ܓܠܠܐ pl. ܓܠܠܝܢ, ܓܠ̈ܠܐ rt. ܓܠ. m. *a wave, a billow.*

ܓܠܠܐ = ܓܠܐ m. *hay, stubble.*

ܓܠܠܐ pl. ܐ̈ m. subst. *ground liable to be flooded, a valley;* adj. *round.*

ܓܠܡܐ m. *a rocky place* or *ridge; a shapeless mass.*

ܓܠܡ part. ܓܠܝܡܐ *to cut, circumcise.*

ܓܠܡܬܐ pl. ܬ̈ܐ f. *the foreskin.*

ܓܠܦ fut. ܢܓܠܘܦ, imper. ܓܠܘܦ, act. part. ܓܠܦ, ܓܠܦܐ, pass. part. ܓܠܝܦ, ܐ, ܬܐ. a) *to carve* wood or stone, *to engrave, fashion, adorn;* ܓܠܦܝܢ ܢܣܟ̈ܐ *fashioning molten images;* ܟܐܦ̈ܐ ܓܠܝ̈ܦܬܐ *engraved gems;* ܓܠܝܦܘܬܗܘܢ *their graven images.* Metaph. ܡܠܬܐ ܓܠܝܦܬܐ *polished speech.* b) m.= ܡܓܠܦܐ, ܫܘܫܡ̈ܐ ܓܠܝ̈ܦܐ *husked sesame seeds.* Ethpe. ܐܬܓܠܦ *to be carved.* Derivatives, ܓܠܘܦܐ, ܓܠܦܐ, ܓܠܘܦܐ, ܓܠܘܦܘܬܐ.

ܓܠܦܐ pl. ܐ̈ rt. ܓܠܦ. m. *engraving, carving* or *embossing; the engraving* on gems, gold, &c.; ~ ܕܥܙܩܬܐ *the engraving on a signet;* pl. *scales, spangles.*

ܓܠܦ̈ܢܐ m. pl. *feathers, fins.*

ܓܠܨ fut. ܢܓܠܨ a) *to wrinkle, frown.* b) *to show the teeth.* Pa. ܓܠܨ *to have the lips wide apart; to gape* as the edges of a wound; part. ܡܓܠܨܐ *splay-mouthed.* Derivative, ܡܓܠܨܘܬܐ.

ܓܠܩܐ pl. ܐ̈ m. *a tub, jar.*

ܓܠܫ *to scratch, tear with nails.* Ethpe. ܐܬܓܠܫ pass.

ܓܡ fut. ܢܓܘܡ, act. part. ܓܐܡ, ܓܡܡܐ, pass. part. ܓܡܝܡ, ܐ, ܬܐ. a) *to cut off, to lop* branches. Metaph. ܐܬܐ ܡܘܬܐ ܓܡܡ *death comes to cut thee down;* ܢܓܘܡ ܡܘܬܪ̈ܘܬܐ *let him prune away superfluities.* b) *to be full* as a measure; pass. part. *filled, full.* Ethpe. ܐܬܓܡܡ *to be cut down, cut off;* ܐܬܓܡܡ ܚܝܘܗܝ ܐܝܟ ܢܨܒܬܐ *his life was cut down like a plant.* Pa. ܓܡܡ a) *to cut down.* b) *to fill.* Derivative, ܓܡܡܐ.

ܓܡܐ pl. ܓܡ̈ܐ m. Ar. *a vessel, an earthen pot.*

ܓܡܕ act. part. ܓܡܕ *to mangle* clothes, *press heavily.* Pa. ܓܡܕ rare, same as Aphel ܐܓܡܕ *to dare, be shameless, persist obstinately.* With another verb has adverbial force; *boldly, rashly;* ܐܓܡܕ ܘܥܢܐ *he answered boldly.* Derivatives, ܓܡܕܐ, ܓܡܕܐܝܬ, ܓܡܕܢܐܝܬ,

ܓܡܘܪܘܬܐ, ܓܡܝܪܐ, ܓܡܝܪܘܬܐ, ܓܡܝܪܐܝܬ, ܡܓܡܪܢܘܬܐ.

ܓܡܘܫܐ m. ܓܡܘܫܬܐ f. rt. ܓܡܫ. *shameless.*

ܓܡܘܫܘܬܐ rt. ܓܡܫ. f. *mangling* or *smoothing* linen.

ܓܡܘܪ m. *an omer.*

ܓܡܘܪܐ, ܓܡܘܪܬܐ pl. m. ܐ̈ f. ܬܐ̈ rt. ܓܡܪ. *he* or *that which finishes, accomplishes, effects; efficient.* Used of a bishop because by him the ordination of priests is *performed, effected* or *made valid;* of the priesthood whereby the sacraments are *accomplished;* ܟܗܢܘܬܐ ܓܡܘܪܬܐ ܕܟܠ ܐܪ̈ܙܐ *the priesthood whereby all the sacraments are effected;* ܬܓܐ ܕܓܡܘܪ̈ܐ *the crown of bishops. The corporal* on which the portions of the host are placed after the fraction; see ܓܡܘܪܬܐ.

ܓܡܘܪܝܐ rt. ܓܡܪ. m. *end, destruction;* ܕܦܬܐܡܐ ~ *a speedy end;* ~ ܕܠܐ *unfinished, imperfect;* ܫܪܓܐ ܕܥܐܟ ܒܓܡܘܪܝܐ ܕܡܫܚܐ *the lamp goes out when the oil is used up.*

ܓܘܡܪܬܐ pl. ܓܘܡܪ̈ܝܢ, ܓܘܡܪ̈ܐ f. *a) a coal, live coals,* ܓܘܡܪ̈ܐ ܕܢܘܪܐ *fiery coals;* metaph. with pl. ܓܘܡܪ̈ܬܐ or ܓܘܡܪ̈ܬܐ the *particles of consecrated bread* are so-called in Syriac liturgies in allusion to Isa. vi. 6, the live coals on the altar being interpreted as a type of Christ. *b) red-hot stones* thrown up by a volcano. *c) ulcers, carbuncles.*

ܓܡܘܫܐ pl. ܐ̈ m. *a buffalo bull.*

ܓܡܝܫܘܬܐ rt. ܓܡܫ. f. *impudence.*

ܓܡܝܪܐܝܬ rt. ܓܡܪ. adv. *perfectly, completely, thoroughly;* arith. *even, equal.*

ܓܡܝܪܘܬܐ rt. ܓܡܪ. f. *perfection, completeness, full growth.*

ܓܡܠ *Gamal,* the letter *g.*

ܓܡܠܐ, ܓܡܠܐ pl. ܝܢ̈, ܐ̈ com. gen. *the camel, dromedary;* ܓܡܠ ܢܡܪܐ m. *the camelopard, the giraffe;* ܓܡܠܐ ܕܒܝܬܐ *a great beam* which supports the rafters.

ܓܡܠܐ pl. ܐ̈ m. *a) a camel-driver* or *keeper. b) flat-nosed.*

ܓܡܠܝܘܬܐ from ܓܡܠ f. *camel-herding;* ܠܓܡܠܝܘܬܐ ܕ *attending to the camels.*

ܓܡܡܐ rt. ܓܡ. m. *a) pruning, felling. b) fullness, running over* of a measure.

ܓܡܣ act. part. ܓܡܣ, ܓܡܣܐ *to plunge under water, immerse, dive,* ܠܟܠܗ ܐܚܝ̈ܢ ܓܡܣܝܢ ܬܠܬ ܓܡܣ̈ܝܢ ܒܡܥܡܘܕܝܬܐ *we immerse thrice at baptism.* Aph. ܐܓܡܣ *to dip, immerse.* Derivatives, ܓܡܘܣܐ, ܓܡܘܣܬܐ, and the following—

ܓܡܣܐ m. and ܓܡܣܬܐ f. rt. ܓܡܣ. *a) immersion, a dip, dive;* ܒܓܡܣܬܐ ܚܕܐ ܡܥܡܕܝܢܢ *we baptize with one immersion. b) a handful.*

ܓܡܣܬܐ f. *mire, dirt.*

ܓܡܨ perh. denom. from ܓܘܡܨܐ. *to throw into a pit.* Ethpe. ܐܬܓܡܨ *to fall into a pit; to be overwhelmed among ruins.*

ܓܡܪ fut. ܢܓܡܘܪ in the active sense; ܢܓܡܪ passive, inf. ܡܓܡܪ, imper. ܓܡܘܪ, act. part. ܓܡܪ, ܓܡܪܐ, pass. part. ܓܡܝܪ, ܐ, ܬܐ. Trans. *a) to perfect, finish, accomplish, effect, perform; to cause to become;* ܓܡܪ ܟܠܗ ܟܝܠܐ ܕܫܢ̈ܘܗܝ *he accomplished the measure of his life;* ܓܡܪܗ ܠܡܘܠܟܢܗ *he fulfilled his promise;* ܝܫܘܥ ܓܡܪ ܟܠ ܒܫܘܠܡܐ ܒܪܘܫܡܐ ܕܨܠܝܒܗ *Jesus who perfects, brings all to perfection, by the sign of His Cross;* ܪܘܚܐ ܕܩܘܕܫܐ ܚܡܪܐ ܕܒܟܣܐ ܢܓܡܘܪ ܕܡܐ *may* the Holy Spirit *cause the wine in the chalice to become blood. b) to consume, put an end to,* in this sense the Pael is more common. Intrans. *a) to be perfected, finished, accomplished. b) to be consumed, spent, done away with; to fail, cease;* arith. *to be divisible without any remainder;* ܓܡܪ ܗܘܐ ܚܝܠܗ ܡܢ ܨܗܝܐ *his strength failed from thirst;* ܥܘܬܪܐ ܕܠܐ ܓܡܪ *infinite riches;* pass. part. *perfect, mature, complete, whole, quite, final;* ܟܝܠܐ ܓܡܝܪܐ *a full measure;* ܢܚܬܐ ܓܡܝܪܐ ܕܬܟܠܬܐ *a garment all of blue;* ܥܠܬܐ ܓܡܝܪܬܐ *a whole burnt-offering;* ܦܣܩܐ ܓܡܝܪܐ *the final sentence.* Ethpe. ܐܬܓܡܪ *to be perfect, perfected, finished, accomplished;* ܚܠܡ̈ܘܗܝ ܠܐ ܐܬܓܡܪܘ *his dreams did not come to pass;* ܐܬܓܡܪܘ ܒܡܝܬܪܘܬܐ *they were of perfect virtue.* In the consecration of a bishop, the Syrians say ܐܬܓܡܪ (ܒܣܝܡܐܝܕܐ) *he is perfected* (*by the imposition of hands*), where we should say *the consecration is effected* or *completed.* Pa. ܓܡܪ *to make perfect, bring to an end, finish; to spend, waste; to put an end to, destroy, lay waste, root out, extirpate;*

ܐܓܡܪܟܘܢ ܡܢ ܐܪܥܐ *I will destroy you from off the earth;* ܟܕ ܓܡܪ *when it had made an end.* Denom. from ܓܘܡܪܬܐ; *to heat over red-hot coals.* Ethpa. ܐܬܓܡܪ *a) to be accomplished, to come to pass* as prayers, dreams. *b) to fail, be destroyed.* Aph. ܐܓܡܪ *a) to accomplish. b) to do away with, destroy.* Derivatives, ܓܡܘܪܐ, ܓܘܡܪܐ, ܓܡܝܪܐ, ܓܡܘܪܬܐ, ܓܡܝܪܐܝܬ, ܓܡܝܪܘܬܐ, ܓܡܪܐ, ܡܓܡܪܢܐ.

ܓܡܪ, ܓܡܪܐ rt. ܓܡܪ. m. *a perfecting, making perfect, perfection.* With ܠ prefixed an adverb is formed, ܠܓܡܪ *utterly, entirely, altogether.*

ܓܢ not used in Pe.; root-sense *to lie down* or *upon.* Aph. ܐܓܢ part. ܡܓܢ or ܡܓܝܢ *to make descend* or *rest upon.* With ܒ or ܛܠܠܐ and ܥܠ *to cover with the hand,* hence *to protect;* ܐܝܕܟ ܗܘܬ ܡܓܢܐ ܥܠܝܗܘܢ *Thy hand protected them;* ܨܠܘܬܟ ܬܓܢ ܥܠ ܡܪܥܝܬܟ *may thy prayer protect thy flock.* The causative sense is often lost. With ܒ or ܥܠ *to lie down, rest in* or *on, to dwell within;* often said of the Holy Spirit, *to descend* or *enter gently* with ܒ; *to abide, rest upon, overshadow* with ܥܠ; ܐܓܢ ܪܘܚܐ ܥܠ ܒܬܘܠܬܐ *the Spirit descended upon the Blessed Virgin;* ܒܣܪܝ ܢܓܢ ܥܠ ܣܒܪܐ *my flesh shall rest in hope;* ܚܫܘܟܐ ܡܓܢ ܥܠܝ *darkness overshadows me.* Derivatives, ܓܢ, ܓܢܐ, ܓܢܘܢܐ, ܓܢܬܐ, ܓܢܝܐ, ܓܢܝܢܐ, ܡܓܢܢܐ, ܡܓܢܢܘܬܐ and ܡܓܢܢܘܬܐ.

ܓܢܢ, ܓܢܢܐ rt. ܓܢ. *a refuge, protection,* always with ܒ; ܒܓܢܢܟ ܡܪܚܡܢܐ *to Thy protection, O merciful One.* Cf. ܓܢܝ.

ܓܢܐ pl. of ܓܢܬܐ *gardens.*

ܓܢܐ fut. ܢܓܢܐ, inf. ܡܓܢܐ, imper. ܓܢܝ, pass. part. ܓܢܐ, f. ܓܢܝܐ, ܓܢܝܬܐ, pl.m. ܓܢܝܢ, f. ܓܢܝܢ. *a) to lie down, recline* or *sit down* ܥܠ ܦܬܘܪܐ *at table; to lie* or *lean upon;* ܓܢܝܬ ܒܐܘܪܝܐ *Thou didst lie in the manger;* ܝܘܚܢܢ ܕܓܢܐ ܥܠ ܚܕܝܗ ܕܡܪܢ *John who lay on our Lord's breast. b) to withdraw* or *depart secretly, to lie concealed.* Pass. part. ܟܕ ܓܢܐ ܗܘܐ *when he was lying down, in bed;* ܡܫܘܚܬܗ ܕܓܢܝܐ ܕܣܗܪܐ *the extent, surface* of the moon *which is obscure to us.* Ethpe. ܐܬܓܢܝ reflexive of *b.* Pa. ܓܢܝ *to blame, find fault with, rebuke;* ܐܝܠܝܢ ܕܡܓܢܝܢ ܠܢ ܒܚܡܝܠܘܬܐ *those who accuse us of sloth;* the pass. part. also means *hidden, retired.* Ethpa. ܐܬܓܢܝ *a) to be blamed, rebuked* with ܡܢ of the agent and ܒ of the reason. *b) to withdraw himself, conceal himself* with ܡܢ *from.* Aph. ܐܓܢܝ *a) to make recline* or *sit down, place* at table, ܢܓܢܐ ܠܡܣܟܢܐ ܒܒܬܝܢ *let us receive the poor into our houses; to lie, be laid upon; to overshadow. b) to conceal oneself, withdraw oneself;* ܡܓܢܐ ܗܘܐ ܢܦܫܗ *he hid himself.* Derivatives, ܓܘܢܝܐ, ܓܢܝܐ, ܡܓܢܝܐ, ܡܓܢܝܘܬܐ.

ܓܢܕܪܐ *dross* of silver, *slag* of iron.

ܓܢܬܘܣ and ܓܢܘܣ Greek pl. forms of ܓܢܬܐ *a garden.*

ܓܢܒ fut. ܢܓܢܘܒ, inf. ܡܓܢܒ, act. part. ܓܢܒ, ܓܢܒܐ, pass. part. ܓܢܝܒ, ܓܢܝܒܐ, ܓܢܝܒܬܐ. *a) to steal, to go* or *do* anything *secretly, furtively, by stealth;* ܓܢܒ ܕܡܥܘܗܝ *concealing his tears;* ܓܢܒܐ ܐܟܠܐ *she eats furtively;* ܠܡܓܢܒ ܨܒܘܬܐ ܡܢܟ *to conceal* the affair *from thee;* ܓܢܒܝܢ ܗܘܘ ܥܐܠܝܢ ܘܥܠܝܢ *they entered furtively* or *they seized an opportunity of going in secretly. b) to conceal; to abstract, avert* the mind, ܓܢܒ ܝܥܩܘܒ ܠܒܗ ܕܠܒܢ *Jacob stole the heart of Laban,* the Orientals considered the heart to be the seat of the intellect, and so *to steal a man's understanding = to elude his observation. c) to deceive, to present a false appearance,* ܫܒܠܐ ܓܢܒܢ ܡܠܝܘܬܐ ܐܝܟ ܗܘ ܕܡܠܝܢ *ears* of corn *which had a false appearance of fullness. d) to take away, go away by stealth, steal away,* especially with ܢܦܫܐ; ܦܪܣܝܐ ܓܢܒܘ ܢܦܫܗܘܢ *the Persians withdrew secretly.* Gram. *to elide* a letter, as the first ܒ of ܐܒܝܕܐ. Pass. part. ܡܝܐ ܓܢܝܒܐ ܚܠܝܢ *stolen waters are sweet;* ܐܬܘܬܐ ܓܢܝܒܬܐ *elided letters.* Ethpe. ܐܬܓܢܒ *to be stolen, kidnapped, seduced; to steal away;* ܡܬܓܢܒܐ ܒܢܡܘܣܗ ܕܚܛܝܬܐ *seduced, captivated, by the law of sin.* Gram. ܡܬܓܢܒܢܐ *elided,* i.e. letters written but not pronounced, as ܗ in ܡܢܗ. Pa. ܓܢܒ *to steal, to do secretly* or *furtively, to deceive;* ܡܓܢܒ ܚܙܐ *to glance furtively.* Ethpa. ܐܬܓܢܒ gram. *to be omitted in pronunciation.* Derivatives,

ܓܢܘܒܐ, ܓܢܘܒܘܬܐ, ܓܢܝܒܐ, ܓܢܒܐܝܬ, ܓܢܒܐ, ܓܢܒܘܬܐ, ܓܢܝܒܘܬܐ, ܓܢܘܒܐܝܬ, ܡܓܢܒܢܐ.

ܓܢܒ, ܓܢܒܐ = ܓܒ, ܓܒܐ (the root is probably ܓܒ and the nasal ܢ a later strengthening) m. *the side, bank, shore;* ܠܘܬ ܓܢܒ *by the side* or *shore;* ܠܘܬ ܓܢܒܐ ܕܦܪܬ *on the bank of the Euphrates;* ܠܘܬ ܓܢܒ ܩܣܪܝܐ *near Caesarea;* ܡܢ ܓܢܒ ܦܬܘܪܐ *at the side of the table.*

ܓܢܒܐ m. ܓܢܒܬܐ f. rt. ܓܢܒ. *a thief, spoiler, depredator.*

ܓܢܒܐܝܬ rt. ܓܢܒ. adv. *by stealth, furtively, like a thief.*

ܓܢܒܘܬܐ rt. ܓܢܒ. f. *a theft.*

ܓܢܒܪ, ܓܢܒܪܐ pl. ܝܢ, ܐ m. intensive form of ܓܒܪܐ. adj. *mighty, strong, great, excelling,* with ܒ *distinguished;* ܓܢܒܪ ܠܥܠܡܝܢ *God mighty for evermore;* subst. *a mighty man, giant, hero, champion;* ܓܢܒܪܐ ܚܝܠܐ *warriors, mighty men;* astron. *the constellation Orion.*

ܓܢܒܪ denom. verb from the above. Pa. part. ܚܝܠܐ ܡܓܢܒܪܢܐ *power working mighty wonders.* Ethp. ܐܬܓܢܒܪ *to act manfully, mightily, earnestly; to vaunt* or *brag;* ܐܬܓܢܒܪܘ *quit you like men.*

ܓܢܒܪܐܝܬ adv. from the above. *manfully, valiantly.*

ܓܢܒܪܘܬܐ pl. ܘܬܐ from the same. f. *manliness, manly strength, fortitude, heroism;* pl. *mighty deeds, wonders;* ܪܫ ܓ̈ *strong point, peculiar faculty;* ܥܒܕܐ ܕܓܢܒܪܘܬܐ *mighty* or *magnificent erections.*

ܓܢܒܪܬܐ pl. ܬܐ, fem. of ܓܢܒܪ. *a lady, a heroine; brave, valiant, strong, fortified;* ܡܕ̈ܝܢܬܐ ܓܢܒܪ̈ܬܐ *fortified cities.*

ܓܢܒܘܪܐ in the Tagrit dialect. *round.*

ܓܢܒܘܪܬܐ or ܓܢܒܘܪܘܬܐ f. *a ball, sphere, globe.*

ܐܬܓܢܒܪ denom. verb from the above. *to roll.*

ܓܢܒܘܪܐ *a small flask.*

ܓܢܘܒܐ pl. ܐ rt. ܓܢܒ. m. *a thief.*

ܓܢܘܒܝܐ rt. ܓܢܒ. m. gram. *the omission* of a letter in pronunciation as ܢ and ܕ in ܡܕܝܢܬܐ, ܫܢܬܐ, or in writing as ܘ in ܟܠ and ܡܠܟܘܬ.

ܓܢܘܒܘܬܐ rt. ܓܢܒ. f. *a theft.*

ܓܢܘܡܐ pl. ܓܢܘܡܣ m. γνῶμα, *a decree, judgement, sentence, maxim.*

ܓܢܘܢ, ܓܢܘܢܐ pl. ܐ rt. ܓܢ. m. *a bed* or *couch,* esp. *a bridal bed* or *chamber.* Metaph. *the heavenly resting-place,* or *bridal feast;* ܓ̈ ܕܚܕܘܬܐ *the feast of gladness;* ܓ̈ ܚܝܐ *the abode of life,* &c.

ܓܢܘܣܝܣ or ܓܢܘܣܣ γνῶσις, *a schedule, notice, inventory.*

ܓܢܘܢܝܬܐ rt. ܓܢ. f. dim. *a little garden.*

ܓܢܙ Pe. only pass. part. ܓܢܝܙ, ܓܢܝܙܐ, ܓܢܝܙܬܐ *hidden, kept close, unknown; occult, secret, mystic,* constantly used of God, e.g. with ܐܝܬܝܐ *the Being,* ܫܡܐ *the Name,* ܐܒܐ *the Father,* ܝܠܝܕܐ *the Begotten;* ܓܢܝܙܐ *an invisible being, a demon, genius, jinn;* ܝܘܠܦܢܐ ܓܢܝܙܐ *occult sciences;* ܩܠܐ ܓܢܝܙܐ rit. Jacob. probably *mystic hymns;* gram. a letter *not uttered.* Ethpe. ܐܬܓܢܙ *to be hidden, go out of sight, disappear* with ܡܢ. Derivatives, ܓܢܝܙܐܝܬ, ܓܢܙܘܬܐ.

ܓܢܚ fut. ܢܓܢܚ, pass. part. ܓܢܝܚ, ܐ, ܬܐ. *to sigh, wail, sob; to be moved, touched;* part. with ܠܒܐ *pricked to the heart, feeling compunction; terror-stricken; grievous, violent, terrible;* ܝܡ̈ܡܐ ܓܢܝܚ̈ܐ *terrible seas;* ܡܘܬܐ ܓܢܝܚܐ *a violent death.* Ethpe. ܐܬܓܢܚ *to be pricked, touched, moved* in mind or heart. Pa. ܓܢܚ *to strike to the heart, to disquiet sorely.* Ethpa. ܐܬܓܢܚ *to be wounded* or *smitten* with sorrow, often with ܠܒܐ. Aph. ܐܓܢܚ *to move* the heart, *to incite.* Derivatives, ܓܘܢܚܐ, ܓܢܚܐ, ܓܢܚܐܝܬ.

ܓܢܚ, ܓܢܚܐ or ܓܢܚ ܠܒܐ rt. ܓܢܚ. m. *a pricking of heart, compunction.*

ܓܢܝ Pa. conj. of ܓܢܐ. *to blame.*

ܓܢܝܐ m. but has pl. fem. ܓܢܝ̈ܬܐ rt. ܓܢܐ. *a hiding, concealing; a secret place, a*) for the worship of idols, hence Ashtaroth is translated by ܓܢܝ̈ܬܐ in 1 Sam. vii. 3, 4 and elsewhere; *b*) *a hiding* or *lurking-place* in the mountains, *a defile; a shelter, shadow;* ܓ̈ ܕܪܘܚܐ *a shelter from the wind;* ܟܕ ܣܗܪܐ ܒܓܢܝܗ ܕܐܪܥܐ *when* the moon *is covered by the shadow of the earth.*

ܓܢܝܐܝܬ rt. ܓܢܐ. adv. *secretly, mystically.*

ܓܢܝܘܬܐ rt. ܓܢܐ. f. *a being concealed, remote from observation, invisibility, secrecy,* generally used of God; gram. *the omission* of a letter written but not pronounced, as the ܝ in ܠܐܝܒܪܐ.

ܓܢܝܚܐܝܬ rt. ܓܢܚ. adv. *terribly.*

ܓܢܢܐ pl. ܐ̈ rt. ܓܢ. m. *a gardener.*

ܓܢܢܐ rt. ܓܢ. m. *rest.*

ܓܢܣ Pa. denom. verb from ܓܢܣܐ. *a) to make cognate, connect. b) to make known the genus;* part. ܡܓܢܣ, ܡܓܢܣܐ *cognate, similar.* Ethpa. ܐܬܓܢܣ *to be cognate, similar.*

ܓܢܣ, ܓܢܣܐ pl. ܓܢܣܐ̈, ܓܢ̈ܣܐ m. γένος, *a) family, race, nation;* ܓ̄ ܐܢܫܐ *the human race, mankind;* ܕܡܢ ܓܢܣܐ ܕܢܡܪܘܕ *a descendant of Nimrod;* ܐܢܫ ܢܘܟܪܝ ܓܢܣܐ *a foreigner. b) order, sort, kind;* ܓܢܣ ܓܢܣ *various, manifold;* ܓ̄ ܕܡܪܟܒܬܐ *a sort of chariot. c) sex;* ܡܫܡܫܢܝܬܐ ܬܠܦ ܘܬܥܒܕ ܠܒܢ̈ܬ ܓܢܣܗ̇ — a deaconess *shall instruct and teach those of her sex.* gram. *gender,* ܕܟܪܢܝܐ *masc.,* ܢܩܒܬܢܝܐ *fem.,* or ܓܘܢܝܐ *common.* Derivatives, verb ܓܢܣ, ܓܢܣܝܐ, ܓܢܣܐܝܬ, ܓܢܣܝܘܬܐ, ܓܢܣܢܐ.

ܓܢܣܢܐ pl. ܝ̈ m. *family, nation, sort;* ܡܢ ܓܢܣܢܗ ܬܠܝܐ *by origin from Tela;* ܟܠ ܓܢܣ̈ܢܝ ܕܣܡ̈ܡܢܐ *all sorts of medicines.*

ܓܢܣܢܐܝܬ adv. *generically.*

ܓܢܣܢܘܬܐ from ܓܢܣܐ. f. *kindred, likeness.*

ܓܢܣܢܝ, ܓܢܣܢܝܐ, ܓܢܣܢܝܬܐ pl. m. ܝ̈ܢ, ܝ̈ܐ f. ܝ̈ܢ, ܝ̈ܬܐ adj. from ܓܢܣܐ. *of the same race; of every sort, general, generic;* ܢܣܝܘܢ̈ܐ ܓܢܣܢܝ̈ܐ *general* or *usual temptations;* ܫܡܐ ܓ̄ *a generic name,* e.g. ܚܝܘܬܐ *living creature;* gram. ܐܬܘ̈ܬܐ ܓܢܣܢܝ̈ܬܐ *radicals;* opp. ܐ̄ ܡܘܣܦܢܝ̈ܬܐ *additional,* i.e. formative *letters;* ܦܘܠܚܢܐ ܓ̄ *the genitive case;* ܢܘܩ̈ܙܐ ܓ̄ *radical points,* i.e. those which form part of the letter as the points in ܪ and ܕ.

ܓܢܣܣ γένεσις, *horoscope.*

ܓܢܪܐ m. *the dewlap* of an ox; *a goître.*

ܓܢܫܝܐ *the sinew of the hip,* Gen. xxxii. 32; *the thigh;* ܟܐܒܐ ܕܓܢܫܝܐ *sciatica.*

ܓܢܬܐ pl. ܓܢ̈ܐ, ܓܢܝܢ and ܓܢܘܢ rt. ܓܢ. f. *a sheltered place, garden;* ܓܢܬ ܥܕܢ, ܓ̄ ܢܝܚܬܐ or absolutely *the garden of Eden, Paradise.*

ܓܢܬܘܢܝܬܐ, ܓܢܬܘܢܬܐ or ܓܢܬܘܢܘܬܐ f. dim. of ܓܢܬܐ. *a little garden.*

ܓܣܐ Aph. ܐܓܣܝ part. ܡܓܣܐ or ܡܓܣܐ denom. verb from ܓܣܐ. *to make recline, to seat; to lean on the elbow, lie down on one's side, sit down* at table; *to fling oneself down;* ܐܓܣܝ ܠܡܣܡܟ *he sat down to dine;* ܕܘܟܬܐ ܕܡܓܣܝܐ *a place to lie down in;* ܩܒܪܐ ܕܡܓܣܝܐ ܒܗ̇ ܗܘܬ *the sepulchre wherein she lay.*

ܓܣܐ pl. ܐ̈ m. *a) the side, flank, haunch; lateral surface;* ܓ̈ܣܝ ܠܫܢܐ *the sides of the tongue. b)* ܓܣܐ ܕܕܗܒܐ *a girdle* ornamented with silver or gold, worn round the loins by boys or women. *c)* pl. *riches.* Derivatives, verb ܐܓܣܝ, ܡܓܣܝܐ, ܡܓܣܝܢܐ.

ܓܣܐ fut. ܢܓܣܐ, inf. ܡܓܣܐ, imper. ܓܣܝ, act. part. ܓܣܐ, ܓܣܝܐ, pass. part. ܓܣܐ. *to vomit, throw up, reject; to find vent, shed forth; to belch forth* curses, *to prate;* ܝܡܐ ܓܣܐ ܫܠܕܗ ܕܣܗܕܐ *the sea threw up* a martyr's body; ܝܪ̈ܚܐ ܓܣܘ ܦܩܥܐ *the months shed forth blossoms;* ܡܒܘܥܐ ܕܓܣܐ ܡܝ̈ܐ ܚܝ̈ܐ *a fountain bringing forth living water.* Ethpe. ܐܬܓܣܝ *to be vomited up.* Pa. ܓܣܝ *to throw up, spit out, disgorge.* Derivatives, ܓܣܝܐ, ܓܣܝܢܐ, ܓܣܝܘܬܐ.

ܓܥܝܪܐ m. ܓܥܝܪܬܐ f. rt. ܓܥܪ. *bellowing, howling.*

ܓܥܪܬܐ f. *a whip.*

ܓܣܛܪܢ κιστέρνα, *a cistern.*

ܓܣܝܐ and ܓܣܝܢܐ rt. ܓܣܐ. *eructation.*

ܓܣܝܬܐ pl. ܝ̈ܬܐ rt. ܓܣܐ. f. *belching, vomiting.*

ܓܥܦܐ m. pl. *fins.*

ܓܥܪ fut. ܢܓܥܪ, inf. ܡܓܥܪ. *to roar, howl, bellow,* said esp. of a lion, also of a wolf, camel, ox. Derivative, ܓܥܝܪܐ.

ܓܥܐ fut. ܢܓܥܐ, inf. ܡܓܥܐ, imper. ܓܥܝ onomatop. *to low, bellow* as a bull, hence *to call out, call upon, implore* with ܠܘܬ, ܥܠ or ܠ; ܩܠܐ ܕܕܡܐ ܕܐܚܘܟ ܓܥܐ ܠܘܬܝ ܡܢ ܐܪܥܐ *the voice of thy brother's blood calls to me from the ground.* Derivatives, ܓܥܝܐ, ܓܥܝܐ, ܓܥܬܐ.

ܓܥܝܢܐ pl. ܐ̈ rt. ܓܥܐ. adj. *lowing, bellowing.* Metaph. ܙܘ̈ܥܐ ܓܥܝ̈ܢܐ *rumbling earthquakes.*

ܓܥܠ pass. part. ܓܥܝܠܐ, ܓܥܝܠܬܐ. *a) to be oppressed with grief. b) to abominate, shun.* Ethpa. ܐܬܓܥܠ *to be an abomination;* part. ܡܬܓܥܠܢܐ *nauseous, abominable.* Aphel ܐܓܥܠ *to spit out, eject.*

ܓܥܝܐ rt. ܓܥܐ. subst. m. *lowing, bellowing.*

ܓܥܝܪܘܬܐ rt. ܓܥܪ. f. *disgust, loathing.*

ܓܥܝܪܘܬܐ rt. ܓܥܪ. f. *disgrace, opprobrium.*

ܓܥܠ not used in Pe. or Pa. Ethpe. ܐܬܓܥܠ with ܠ *to be committed, entrusted* to the care of any one; ܡܢܝܐ ܕܐܬܓܥܠ ܠܝ *the talent entrusted to me;* ܡܪܥܝܬܐ ܕܐܬܓܥܠܘ ܡܢ ܡܪܢ *the flocks committed into his hands by our Lord.* Aph. ܐܓܥܠ with ܠ or ܒܐܝܕܗ *into his hand; a) to commit* to any one, *to entrust;* ܐܓܥܠ ܢܦܫܟ ܠܚܟܡܬܐ *devote yourself to wisdom;* ܐܓܥܠ ܪܘܚܗ ܠܐܠܗܐ *he committed his spirit to God; b) to commend,* rit. *to commend to God;* ܦܛܪܝܪܟܐ ܡܓܥܠ *the Patriarch gives the benediction.* Ettaph. ܐܬܬܓܥܠ *to be deposited;* ܠܘܬ ܐܚܪܢܐ *with another, to the care of another.* Derivatives, ܓܘܥܠܐ, ܡܓܥܠܢܘܬܐ, ܡܓܥܠܢܘܬܐ.

ܓܥܣ fut. ܢܓܥܘܣ *to vomit.* Pa. ܓܥܣ *to cause to vomit.* Derivatives, ܓܘܥܣܐ, ܡܓܥܣܐ.

ܓܥܪ fut. generally ܢܓܥܪ, but ܢܓܥܘܪ is also found; act. part. ܓܥܪ, ܓܥܪܐ, pass. part. ܓܥܝܪ, ܐ, ܬܐ. *to loathe, abhor* with ܒ or ܡܢ; ܓܥܪܘ ܒܫܠܡܗ *they rejected his greeting with loathing;* ܓܥܝܪܝܢ ܗܘܘ ܡܢ ܡܪܕܘܬܐ *they loathed instruction;* pass. part. *abominable, hateful, loathsome, detested.* Aph. ܐܓܥܪ *to fill with loathing, cause to abhor.* Derivative, ܓܥܝܪܘܬܐ.

ܓܥܪ fut. ܢܓܥܘܪ, act. part. ܓܥܪ, pass. part. ܓܥܝܪܐ, ܓܥܝܪܬܐ with ܒ *to chide, reprove, rebuke;* ܢܓܥܘܪ ܒܟ ܡܪܝܐ *the Lord rebuke thee;* pass. part. *vile, abominable, odious.* Derivatives, ܓܥܝܪܘܬܐ, ܓܥܪܬܐ.

ܓܥܪܬܐ rt. ܓܥܪ. f. *groaning, complaint.*

ܓܥܬܐ pl. ܓܥܝܬܐ rt. ܓܥܐ. f. *a bellow, bellowing, shout, call, calling;* ܓܥܬܐ ܐܝܟ ܬܘܪܐ *a bellow like a bull's;* ܓܥܝܬܐ ܕܐܪܥܐ *rumblings of the earth.*

ܓܦ (cf. ܓܦܦ) part. m. ܓܐܦ pl. ܓܐܦܝܢ *to hunt.* Metaph. *to catch, couple, fasten.*

ܓܦ, ܓܦܐ and ܓܐܦܐ pl. ܓܦܝܢ, ܓܐܦܐ m. *an arm, an armful.*

ܓܦ, ܓܦܐ and ܓܐܦܐ pl. ܓܦܝܢ, ܓܦܐ m. *a wing;* ܒܥܠܝ ܓܦܐ *winged creatures; a bird; pen;* fish's *fin.*

ܓܦܘܬܐ rt. ܓܦܦ m. *a hut made of branches.*

ܓܦܘܦܐ m. ܓܦܘܦܬܐ f. pl. m. ܐ f. ܬܐ adj. *bent, crooked;* subst. m. *a winding hollow* excavated by water; ܓܦܘܦܐ ܕܢܚܠܐ Job xxi. 33 *deep hollows in* the beds of *torrents; a cave.*

ܓܦܘܦܬܐ f. *an enclosed space* or *a pavement.*

ܓܦܦ Pa. i) ܓܦܦ *to dig.* ii) denom. from ܓܘܦܢܐ. *to take layers from a vine, propagate by layers.* Ethpa. ܐܬܓܦܦ *to be dug.* Derivatives, ܓܘܦܢܐ, ܓܘܦܐ, ܓܦܘܦܐ, ܓܦܘܬܐ.

ܓܦܢܢܐ m. ܓܦܢܢܬܐ f. pl. m. ܢܐ, f. ܬܐ adj. from ܓܦܐ. *winged, swift.*

ܓܦܣܝܣ, ܓܘܦܣܝܣ or ܓܘܦܣܝܣ m. γύψος, *gypsum, white lime, plaster;* ܩܠܝܘ ܓܦܣܝܣ *lime-burners, plasterers;* ܛܘܫ ܓܘܦܣܝܣ *whitewash it.*

ܓܦܦܐ pl. ܐ m. *the back.*

ܓܦܬܐ pl. ܓܘܦܢܝܢ, ܓܘܦܢܐ contr. from ܓܦܢܬܐ rt. ܓܦܦ, the other form ܓܘܦܢܐ is seldom used in the sing., f. *a vine;* ܦܐܪܐ ܕܓܦܬܐ *the fruit of the vine;* ܓܦܬܐ ܕܚܩܠܐ *wild vine* or *gourd;* ܟܬܢܐ ܕܓܘܦܢܐ *linen* or *cotton.* Metaph. ܓܦܬܐ ܐܕܡܝܬܐ *the vine sprung from Adam.*

ܓܪ m. *lime, mortar, plaster.*

ܓܪ fut. ܢܓܘܪ, inf. ܡܓܪ, act. part. ܓܐܪ, ܓܪܐ with or without ܐ in the pl., pass. part. ܓܪܝܪ. *a) to drag. b)* of water, *to leak, trickle;* ܓܪܝܢ ܕܡܥܐ ܕܬܪܘܝܗܘܢ *the tears of both trickle down. c)* ܓܪ ܥܠܬܐ ܥܠܘܗܝ *to lay a charge against, to accuse;* the pass. part. has also act. signif. ܠܡܢܐ ܓܪܝܪܝܬܘܢ ܠܝ *why do you tear me away?* Ethpe. ܐܬܓܪ *to be dragged* or *torn away.* Aph. ܐܓܪ *to lead, conduct* esp. with ܥܡܗ *to bring with him.* The Aphel of ܓܪ *to be lengthy* has the same form. Palpal ܓܪܓܪ *to drag, carry off by violence,* ܠܫܒܝܐ *into captivity;* ܡܓܪܓܪܐ ܓܦܝܗ ܥܠ ܐܪܥܐ *trailing her wings on the ground.* Ethpalpal

ܐܬܓܪܓܪ passive. DERIVATIVES, ܓܪܘܪܬܐ, ܓܪܓܪܐ, ܡܓܪܓܪܢܐ, ܡܓܪܓܪܢܘܬܐ, ܓܘܪܓܪܐ, verbs ܓܪܓܪ and ܓܪܓ, ܓܪܓܣ, ܓܪܘܪܐ, ܓܪܐ. COGNATES, ܓܪܐ, ܓܪܓ.

ܓܪ usually ܓܝܪ *for, but, indeed, however.*

ܓܪ 3 m. s. of ܓܘܪ *to commit adultery.*

ܓܪܐ act. part. ܓܪܐ, ܓܪܝܐ, pass. part. ܓܪܐ, ܓܪܝܐ, same meaning as ܓܪ but used chiefly metaph. *to run* or *trickle down; to be dragged, torn* or *carried away;* ܓܪܝܐ ܐܝܟ ܫܥܘܬܐ *it runs down, melts, like wax;* ܒܪܚܡܬ ܚܪܝܢܐ ܗܘ ܓܪܐ ܘܚܛܐ *he was carried away by love of strife and sinned;* ܥܠܝܡܬܐ ܕܓܪܝܐ ܒܪܚܡܬ ܨܒܬܐ *a girl carried away by love of adornment.* PA. ܓܪܝ *to provoke, incite* generally with ܒ of the pers. and acc. or ܠ of the object. ETHPA. ܐܬܓܪܝ *a) to provoke, stir up strife, pick a quarrel, contend* with ܒ or ܥܡ. *b) to withdraw* or *retire.* APH. ܐܓܪܝ *to incite* to sin. DERIVATIVES, ܓܪܝܐ, ܓܘܪܝܐ, ܡܓܪܝܢܐ, ܡܓܪܝܢܘܬܐ, ܡܬܓܪܝܢܘܬܐ.

ܓܪܝܐ pl. ܓܪ̈ܝܐ m. ܓܪܝܬܐ, pl. ܓܪ̈ܘܝܢ, ܓܪ̈ܘܬܐ f. rt. ܓܪܐ. *a lion's whelp;* the usual m. s. form is ܓܘܪܝܐ.

ܓܪܒ fut. ܢܓܪܒ, imper. ܓܪܘܒ, denom. verb from ܓܪܒܐ. *to be* or *become leprous.* ETHPE. ܐܬܓܪܒ the same. APH. ܐܓܪܒ *to be a leper, leprous.*

ܓܪܒ, ܓܪܒܐ pl. ܝܢ, ܐ (with hard b) m. *a leper.*

ܓܪܒܐ (with aspirated b) m. *leprosy,* ܡܚܘܬܐ ܕܓܪܒܐ *the plague of leprosy.* DERIVATIVES the two preceding words and ܓܪܒܢܐ.

ܓܪܒ, ܓܪܒܐ pl. ܝܢ, ܐ m. *a) a leathern bottle; any vessel, jar, pitcher;* ܓܪܒܐ ܕܚܡܪܐ *a wine-skin;* ܓܪܒܐ ܕܡܝܐ *a pitcher of water. b) a robe.*

ܓܪܒܝܐ, ܓܪܒܝ f. *the north-wind, the north;* ܡܕܢܚ ܓܪܒܝ or ܓܪܒܝ ܡܕܢܚ *north-east;* ܡܥܪܒ ܓܪܒܝ or ܓܪܒܝ ܡܥܪܒ *north-west;* ܓܪܒܝܐ ܥܫܝܢܐ *a strong N. wind;* ܡܢ ܬܝܡܢܐ ܠܓܪܒܝܐ *from south to north.*

ܓܪܒܝܝܐ m. ܓܪܒܝܝܬܐ f. from the above. adj. *northern, of the north,* often with ܦܢܝܬܐ understood, *the north side.*

ܓܪܒܢܐ pl. ܓܪ̈ܒܢܐ from ܓܪܒܐ. m. *a leper, leprous.*

ܓܪܓ (rt. related to ܓܪ and ܓܪܐ, cf. ܓܪܓܪ and ܓܪܝ), not used in Peal. PA. ܓܪܓ *to excite* desire or anger, *to provoke, stir up, stimulate; to entice, coax;* ܣܢܝܐܬܐ ܡܓܪܓܐ ܚܪܝܢܐ *hatred stirreth up strife;* ܡܓܪܓ ܠܡܘܬܐ *he will challenge death.* ETHPA. ܐܬܓܪܓ refl. DERIVATIVES, ܓܘܪܓܐ, ܓܪܓܐ, ܡܓܪܓܢܐ, ܡܓܪܓܢܘܬܐ.

ܓܪܓܐ pl. ܓܪ̈ܓܐ rt. ܓܪܓ. m. *a) the thread of a net; a snare, toil, web. b) a cupping instrument.*

ܓܪܓܘܫܬܐ pl. ܓܪ̈ܓܘܫܬܐ m. *a pomegranate seed; a husk.*

ܓܪܓܣ *to prostrate oneself.* ETHPALPAL ܐܬܓܪܓܣ *to prostrate* or *bow oneself, to fall down,* ܥܠ ܐܦܘܗܝ *upon his face;* ܥܠ ܒܘܪܟܘܗܝ *on his knees;* ܩܕܡ *before;* with ܒܨܠܘܬܐ *to bow down in prayer;* ܢܦܠ ܘܐܬܓܪܓܣ ܘܣܓܕ ܘܨܠܝ *he fell down and worshipped and prayed.* DERIVATIVE, ܓܘܪܓܣܐ.

ܓܪܓܪ PALPAL conj. of verb ܓܪ. *to drag.*

ܓܪܓܪܐ pl. ܓܪ̈ܓܪܐ rt. ܓܪ. m. *a threshing instrument* drawn by oxen, consisting of a broad plank or else of wheels furnished with stone or iron teeth.

ܓܪܕ fut. ܢܓܪܘܕ, inf. ܡܓܪܕ, act. part. ܓܪܕ, ܓܪܕܐ, pass. part. ܓܪܝܕ, ܐ, ܬܐ. *to scrape, scrape off, lay bare* leather, a bone, &c.; *to strip, lay bare,* as locusts; *to erase* or *cross out* writing. ETHPE. ܐܬܓܪܕ passive. Metaph. *to be made plain, shown plainly; to be stripped, left destitute;* ܠܐ ܢܬܓܪܕ ܪܥܝܢܢ ܡܢ ܒܘܝܐܟ *let not our mind be left bare of Thy consolation.* PA. ܓܪܕ *to scrape.* ETHPA. ܐܬܓܪܕ refl. of Pa. PALI ܓܪܕܝ fut. ܢܓܪܕܐ, act. part. ܡܓܪܕܝ, ܡܓܪܕܝܐ, pl. m. ܡܓܪܕܝܢ, f. ܡܓܪܕܝܢ, pass. part. ܡܓܪܕܝ fem. and pl. same as act. part. *to be wanting, absent, lacking, to fail, cease; to be stripped, left without, be deprived of* with ܡܢ, e.g. ܡܢ ܩܢܝܢܗܘܢ *of their possessions;* ܓܘܒܐ ܡܓܪܕܝ ܡܢ ܡܝܐ *a waterless pit;* ܚܘܛܪܐ ܕܠܐ ܡܓܪܕܝܢ ܡܢ ܟܘܒܝܗܘܢ *rods not stripped of their thorns.* Metaph. ܩܪܒܐ ܠܐ ܓܪܕܝ *war did not cease;* ܠܐ ܓܪܕܝ ܙܕܝܩܐ ܡܢ ܥܠܡܐ *the world did not lack righteous men.* ETHPALI ܐܬܓܪܕܝ *to fail, grow weak;* with ܡܢ *to be* deprived of, destitute. DERIVATIVES the three following words, ܓܪܕܐ, ܓܪܕܝܢ, ܓܪܝܕܐܝܬ, and ܓܪܝܕܘܬܐ.

ܓܪܕܐ rt. ܓܪܕ. adj. m. *bare, hairless, without wool;* cf. the following:

ܓܪܕܐ E-Syr. ܓܪܕܐ rt. ܓܪܕ. m. *the beaver.*

ܓܪܕܝܢ PALI conj. of ܓܪܕ; see above.

ܓܪܕܝܢܐ pl. ܢܐ m. γέρδιος, *a weaver.*

ܓܪܕܝܢܘܬܐ f. *the art of weaving.*

ܓܪܕܡ *to gnaw* or *scrape* bones; ܐܬܓܪܕܡ *to be broken, torn, smitten;* cf. ܓܪܕ.

ܓܪܕܬܐ *a*) rt. ܓܪܕ. f. *a chip, shaving, filing;* ܓܪܕܬܐ ܕܢܚܫܐ *copper filings.* *b*) *an eel.*

ܓܪܕܘܡܐ m. *a rolling-pin; a cotton-gin.*

ܓܪܥܘܡܐ pl. ܡܐ rt. ܓܪܡ. m. *fruit-stones,* apple or lemon-*pips,* cotton-*seeds.*

ܓܪܘܦܐ rt. ܓܪܦ. adj. m. *overwhelming.*

ܓܪܘܦܝܐ rt. ܓܪܦ. m. *an overwhelming* or *rushing flood, an inundation.* Metaph. ܓܪܘܦܝܐ ܕܫܒܝܐ *captives carried away as by a tearing flood.*

ܓܪܘܦܝܘܢ γραφεῖον, *a style.*

ܓܪܘܪܐ rt. ܓܪ. gram. *a point* placed above several members of a phrase to signify their connexion.

ܓܪܝܒ, ܓܪܝܒܐ pl. ܒܐ m. *a measure,* perh. the thirtieth part of a cor.

ܓܪܝܕܐܝܬ rt. ܓܪܕ. adv. *plainly, without circumlocution.*

ܓܪܝܡܐܝܬ rt. ܓܪܡ. adv. *decidedly, absolutely.*

ܓܪܝܣܐ rt. ܓܪܣ. m. *a morsel* of bread.

ܓܪܝܥܘܬܐ rt. ܓܪܥ. f. *tonsure, having received tonsure, monasticism.*

ܓܪܝܨܬܐ pl. ܓܪܝܨܐ, ܨܬܐ generally with ܕܠܚܡܐ. *a cake* or *loaf* of bread.

ܓܪܙܪ m. *a ballista, crossbow.*

ܓܪܡ fut. ܢܓܪܘܡ, inf. ܡܓܪܡ, pass. part. ܓܪܝܡܐ *to cut off, cut short;* usually metaph. *to decide, determine, appoint, to be decided* &c. esp. with ܒܝܫܬܐ *evil;* ܓܪܝܡܐ ܠܗ ܠܘܬ ܡܠܟܘܬܐ ܒܝܫܬܐ ܡܢ ܡܠܟܐ *evil was determined against him by the king;* ellipt. ܟܕ ܚܙܘ ܕܓܪܝܡܐ ܠܗ ܡܢ ܟܠ ܕܘܟ *when they saw that it was all up with them;* with ܦܣܩܬܐ *to make a decision, resolve;* pass. part. *appointed, decreed, ratified; crushed, carded* as cotton. ETHPE. ܐܬܓܪܡ pass.

ܓܪܡ denom. verb PAEL conj. from ܓܪܡܐ. *to break bones.*

ܓܪܡ, ܓܪܡܐ pl. ܓܪܡܝܢ, ܡܐ m. *a bone; the kernel* or *stone* of a fruit; ܓܪܡܐ ܚܨܐ *the spine;* ܓܪܡܐ ܕܦܝܠܐ or ܓܪܡܦܝܠܐ *ivory;* ܓܪܡܐ ܕܦܝܠܐ *elephants' tusks.* Metaph. *self,* ܓܪܡܗ or ܓܪܡܐ *himself,* ܓܪܡܝ *myself,* &c.; with ܒ prefixed *by myself, alone.* DERIVATIVES, verb ܓܪܡ, ܓܪܡܢܐ, ܓܪܡܢܝ, ܓܪܡܢܝܐ, ܓܪܡܢܘܬܐ.

ܓܪܡܛܝܩܐ, ܓܪܡܛܝ, ܓܪܡܛ γραμματική, *grammar.*

ܓܪܡܛܝܘܢ or ܓܪܡܛܝܘܢ *a legal document, a writ.*

ܓܪܡܛܝܩܐ pl. ܩܐ and ܓܪܡܛܝܩܘܣ m. *a grammarian.*

ܓܪܡܛܝܩܘܬܐ or ܓܪܡܛ f. *the art of grammar.*

ܓܪܡܛܝܩܐ f. cf. above; *grammar.*

ܓܪܡܛܝܩܝܐ, ܩܝܐ pl. m. ܩܝܐ, f. ܩܝܬܐ adj. *grammatical, of grammar.*

ܓܪܡܝܕܐ *an ell, cubit;* cf. ܓܘܪܡܝܕܐ.

ܓܪܡܝܕܐ Pers. m. *fine white flour.*

ܓܪܡܛܝܩܐ &c.; see under ܓܪܡܛ *grammar.*

ܓܪܡܢܐ rt. ܓܪܡ. adj. *bony, cartilaginous.*

ܓܪܡܢܝܐ, ܢܝܐ pl. m. ܓܪܡܢܝܐ, f. ܢܝܬܐ, ܢܝܬܐ rt. ܓܪܡ. adj. *bony, testaceous;* ܓܪܡܢܝܬܐ *shell-fish.*

ܓܪܢ *dearness* of corn.

ܓܪܣ fut. ܢܓܪܘܣ and ܢܓܪܘܣ, act. part. ܓܪܣ, ܓܪܣܐ, pass. part. ܓܪܝܣ, ܓܪܝܣܐ *to be broken to pieces, shattered, crumbled; innutritious;* ܡܠܚܐ ܓܪܝܣܐ *broken salt;* ܟܠܟܠܬܐ ܓܪܝܣܬܐ ܡܢ ܚܝܠܐ *innutritious produce;* pass. part. = subst. *a morsel.* ETHPE. ܐܬܓܪܣ *to be vanquished, discomfited.* PA. ܓܪܣ *to break in pieces, to diminish, do away with, devour.* APH. ܐܓܪܣ *to destroy, do away with, annihilate.* DERIVATIVES, ܓܪܝܣܐ, ܓܪܣܐ, ܡܓܪܣܢܘܬܐ.

ܓܪܣܐ rt. ܓܪܣ. m. *meal, flour;* ܓܪܣܐ ܕܣܥܪܐ *barley-meal;* ܓܪܣܐ ܕܚܛܐ *wheaten-flour.*

ܓܪܣܐ pl. ܐ̈ m. *an asp.* Metaph. ܚܣܡܐ ܓܪܣܐ *the viper envy;* ܓܪܣܐ ܪܒܐ *the devil.*

ܓܪܘܣܛܝܣ m. pl. ἄγρωστις, *grass, hay.*

ܓܪܥ fut. ܢܓܪܘܥ, inf. ܡܓܪܥ, act. part. ܓܪܥ, pass. part. ܓܪܝܥ, ܓܪܝܥܐ, ܓܪܝܥܬܐ *to shave* the hair or beard; *take the tonsure; to deprive of hair;* pass. part. *shaven, shorn* as a monk or slave, hence *a monk;* a term of contempt, perh. *slave.* Ethpe. ܐܬܓܪܥ *to be shaved, to receive tonsure.* Derivatives the four following words:—

ܓܪܥܐ rt. ܓܪܥ. m. *a barber.*

ܓܪܥܐ rt. ܓܪܥ. m. *shaving.*

ܓܪܥܘܢܐ pl. ܐ̈ rt. ܓܪܥ. m. *one shaven, a monk, a lad.*

ܓܪܥܘܬܐ rt. ܓܪܥ. f. *shaving;* ܡܐܢܐ ܕܓܪܥܘܬܐ *barbers' implements.*

ܓܪܦ fut. ܢܓܪܘܦ, inf. ܡܓܪܦ, act. part. ܓܪܦ, ܓܪܦܐ, pass. part. ܓܪܝܦܐ *to rush* as a torrent or flood, *to overflow, overwhelm, seize, carry away; to draw* water; *to wipe clean;* ܢܝܠܘܣ ܓܪܦ ܡܠܐ *the Nile overflows;* ܓܪܦ ܓܙܝܗ ܕܡܨܪܝܢ *he carried off the treasures of Egypt.* Ethpe. ܐܬܓܪܦ *to be seized, carried off* by rushing waters or billows. Metaph. *by persuasion, by folly,* &c. Aph. ܐܓܪܦ *to overflow, overwhelm.* Derivatives, ܓܪܘܦܐ, ܡܓܪܘܦܝܬܐ, ܓܪܦܐ, ܡܓܪܦܬܐ, ܓܪܘܦܝܐ.

ܓܪܦܐ rt. ܓܪܦ. m. *a flood.*

ܓܪܪ part. ܓܪܝܪ *to lay hold of.*

ܓܪܣܛܝܣ f. ἄγρωστις, *grass;* cf. ܓܪܘܣܛܝܣ.

ܓܪܪܐ rt. ܓܪ. m. *dragging,* esp. with violence.

ܓܪܫ fut. ܢܓܪܘܫ, inf. ܡܓܪܫ, act. part. ܓܪܫ *to drag, trail; to protract, prolong.* Pa. ܓܪܫ intens. and *to drive out.*

ܓܪܫܘܢ *in Carshun,* i.e. Arabic written in Syriac characters.

ܓܫ and ܓܫ fut. ܢܓܘܫ, inf. ܡܓܫ, act. part. ܓܐܫ, ܓܝܫܐ *to touch, feel, handle; to embrace; to spy, explore, try;* ܓܘܫܘܢܝ *handle me;* ܓܘܫܡܐ ܕܒܗ ܓܫܝܢ ܠܥܘܡܩܐ a plummet *to try the depth.* Metaph. ܫܪܝ ܓܐܫ ܠܗ ܠܡܠܟܐ *he began to sound the king.* Ethpe. ܐܬܓܫ *to be touched, sounded; to be tangible, palpable, apprehended;* ܪܘܚܐ ܡܬܓܫܢܝܬܐ *a perceptible wind;* ܝܡܬܐ ܕܠܐ ܡܬܓܫܢܝܬܐ *an unfathomable lake.* Metaph. ܐܦ ܠܐ ܒܬܪܥܝܬܐ ܡܬܓܫܢܐ ܐܠܗܐ God *can never be apprehended even by the mind.* Aph. ܐܓܫ *to touch, handle.* Palpel ܓܫܓܫ *to grope.* Derivatives, ܓܫܐ, ܓܫܘܫܐ, ܓܫܘܫܘܬܐ, ܓܫܬܐ, ܡܓܫܓܫܢܘܬܐ, ܡܓܫܢܐ, ܡܓܫܢܘܬܐ.

ܓܫܐ rt. ܓܫ. m. *that which is touched* or *explored,* usually *the bottom;* ܕܠܝܬ ܠܗ ܓܫܐ *bottomless;* ܡܟܣܐ ܠܒܝܫܬܐ ܕܩܒܝܥܐ ܒܠܒܗ ܡܢ ܓܫܐ ܕܓܫܐ *he hides the evil which is firmly fixed in* his *heart from being probed.*

ܓܘܫܡ constr. st. of ܓܘܫܡܐ *body;* pl. constr. ܓܘܫܡܝ; ܕܠܐ ܓܘܫܡ *incorporeal.*

ܓܫܘܫܘܬܐ rt. ܓܫ. f. *the act of touching* or *handling.*

ܓܫܘܫܐ m. ܓܫܘܫܬܐ, f. pl. m. ܝ̈, ܐ̈, f. ܢ̈, ܬܐ̈ rt. ܓܫ. subst. *a spy, scout, explorer, searcher;* adj. *searching, penetrative.*

ܓܫܘܫܘܬܐ rt. ܓܫ. f. *spying, being a spy.*

ܓܫܛ *to rub* or *graze* the skin. Pa. ܓܫܛ *to scratch, give a scratch, wound slightly.* Ethpa. ܐܬܓܫܛ *to be rubbed, barked, stripped off,* said of the skin.

ܓܫܡܢܝ, ܝܐ, ܝܬܐ pl. m. ܐ̈ f. ܬܐ̈ adj. from ܓܘܫܡܐ. *embodied, corporeal, material, solid;* ܠܐ ܓܫܡܢܝܐ *incorporeal, immaterial;* ܡܚܫܒܬܐ ܓܫܡܢܝܬܐ *thoughts expressed in writing,* opp. to those which exist in the mind only; ܩܠܐ ܓܫܡܢܝܬܐ *articulate sounds;* ܡܠܐ ܕܠܐ ܓܫܡܢܝܬܐ *metaphysics.*

ܓܫܡܢܘܬܐ f. (see the preceding) *corporeality, embodiment; the giving of outward form* or *expression, enunciation.*

ܓܫܡ denom. verb Pael conj. from ܓܘܫܡܐ. *to indue* or *clothe with a body, embody, express* as thought in writing; ܠܒܪܐ ܓܫܡ ܡܢ ܒܬܘܠܬܐ the Holy Spirit *indued the Son with a body from the Virgin;* ܠܓܫܡ ܡܠܝܟ ܒܕܝܘܬܐ ܘܒܟܪܛܝܣܐ *to embody* or *give outward expression to thy words with ink and paper;* part. *indued with a body, incarnate; figured, described;* astron. *solid;* ܬܘܕܝܬܐ ܕܚܕ ܟܝܢܐ ܡܓܫܡܐ *the confession of one incarnate nature;* ܠܐ ܡܓܫܡܐ *incorporeal.* Ethpa. ܐܬܓܫܡ a) *to be indued with a body; to take form* or *shape, be formed,* e.g. ܒܓܘ ܟܪܣܐ *in the womb;* said esp. of the

Incarnation of Christ; ܡܶܢܶܟ݂ ܐܶܬܓܰܫܰܡ ܦܳܪܽܘܩܳܐ ܕܥܳܠܡܳܐ of thee did the Saviour of the world take flesh; ܦܺܐܪ̈ܶܐ ܡܶܬܓܰܫܡܺܝܢ fruits form flesh, fill out. b) metaph. of thoughts receiving outward form by speech, paper and ink.

ܓܫܰܫ fut. ܢܶܓܫܽܘܫ, inf. ܡܶܓܫܰܫ, act. part. ܓܳܫܶܫ, ܓܳܫܫܳܐ, pass. part. ܓܫܺܝܫܳܐ (cognate rt. ܓܫܳܐ) generally with ܒ, *to touch, feel, come in contact with, lay the hand on, handle, seize upon;* ܓܫܰܫܬ ܒܗܽܘܢ ܒܺܝܫܬܳܐ *evil was close upon them;* ܕܠܳܐ ܡܶܬܓܫܫܳܐ ܠܪ̈ܓܳܫܶܐ *imperceptible to the senses;* ܟܰܕ ܓܳܫܫܺܝܢ ܠܡܰܚܺܝ̈ܠܶܐ *when* persecutions *touch the weak* brethren. Aph. ܐܰܓܫܶܫ *to bind, fasten.* Derivatives, ܓܫܽܘܫܽܘܬܳܐ, ܓܫܳܫܳܐ, ܡܓܰܫܫܳܢܳܐ.

ܓܫܳܫܳܐ rt. ܓܫܫ. m. *touch, a touch;* ܒܓܫܳܫܳܐ ܕܪܶܦܦܳܐ *in one moment.*

ܓܫܰܪ fut. ܢܶܓܫܽܘܪ, inf. ܡܶܓܫܰܪ, pass. part. ܓܫܺܝܪܳܐ *to construct a bridge, bridge over, heap up stones as for a bridge, to serve as a bridge;* ܓܫܰܪ ܓܶܫܪܳܐ *he made a bridge;* ܦܰܚܬܳܐ ܕܠܳܐ ܡܶܬܓܫܰܪ *an impassable abyss.*

ܓܶܫܪܳܐ E-Syr., ܓܶܫܪܳܐ oftener ܓܶܫܪܳܐ W-Syr. pl. ܐ̈ rt. ܓܫܪ. m. *a bridge, plank;* ܓܫܽܘܪ ܠܺܝ ܒܪܰܚܡܰܝܟ ܓܶܫܪܳܐ ܕܚܰܝ̈ܶܐ ܕܥܠܰܘܗܝ ܐܶܥܒܰܪ *make for me in thy mercy a bridge of life that thereon I may pass over.*

ܓܫܳܫܬܳܐ, const. st. ܓܫܳܫܰܬ pl. irreg. ܓܫܳܫ̈ܳܬܳܐ f. rt. ܓܫܫ. *handling, touching* or *feeling* with the hands, *contact, touch, sensation; the sense of touch; the spying out* or *exploring* of a country; ܓܫܳܫܬܳܐ ܩܰܪܺܝܪܬܳܐ ܕܦܰܓܪܳܐ *the cold touch* of a corpse; ܓܫܳܫܰܬ ܐܺܝܕܰܝ̈ܳܐ ܩܰܕܺܝ̈ܫܳܬܳܐ *the touch of holy hands;* ܐܰܠܳܗܳܐ ܠܳܐ ܐܺܝܬܰܘܗܝ ܠܓܫܳܫܬܳܐ *God is not apparent to the senses;* ܕܳܡܶܝܢ ܒܚܶܙܘܳܐ ܘܒܓܫܳܫܬܳܐ *they look and feel like.*

ܓܬ *a wine-press.*

ܫܠܡܬ ܐܬܘܬܐ ܓܡܠ
ܘܠܗ ܬܫܒܘܚܬܐ

⁘ ܫܪܝ ܥܠ ܕܘܠܬ܆ ܕܒܪܝ ܦܘܫܩ ܘܒܐܝܕܐ ܕܟܬܒܐ ܗܢܐ. ܐܡܝܢ ⁘

⁘ ܕ ⁘

ܕ

ܕ *Dolath* ܕܳܠܰܬ, the fourth letter of the alphabet; the number 4; with another ܕ *the fourth,* ܕܕ; ܕ݂ 4000; ܕ̱ 40,000.

ܕ rel. pron. of all genders and numbers *who, which, what; he, she* or *they who, that which;* ܗܽܘ ܕ *he who,* ܗܳܝ ܕ *she who, it which;* ܕ ܕܡܰܢ, ܕܗܽܘ, ܕܗܳܝ *whose;* ܕܗܽܘ, ܕܗܳܝ, ܕܗܶܢܽܘܢ *who, which;* ܕܒܶܗ, ܕܒܳܗ, ܕܒܗܽܘܢ *in whom, in which;* ܕܡܶܢܶܗ, ܕܡܶܢܗܽܘܢ, ܕܡܶܢܳܗ *from whom, from which;* with ܟܽܠ ܟܽܠ *all they who* e.g. ܟܽܠܚܰܝ *all the living.* With prepositions, *he* or *they who are;* ܕܒܳܬܰܪ *he who follows, the following;* ܕܩܕܳܡ *the preceding;* ܕܠܥܳܠܰܡ *he who is for everlasting;* ܘܕܰܠܗܰܘ ܕܩܰܕܡ *etcetera;* ܕܠܘܳܬܶܗ *his companions;* ܕܒܶܝܬ *they of the house* or *company of;* ܕܒܶܝܬ ܡܰܕܓܠܳܐ *they who are of falsehood, the false, liars.* ܕ is often redundant esp. before participles, ܕܝܳܬܶܒ *sitting;* ܛܳܒܳܬܳܐ ܕܥܬܺܝܕܳܢ *the blessings to come;* ܕ introduces a dependent sentence or a quotation, hence it is constantly prefixed to ܗܳܐ *behold.* After a verb of interrogation ܕ = *whether.* It is often preceded by the other prefix particles ܒ, ܘ, and ܠ; see ܒܕܠ.

ܕ preceding a cardinal forms an ordinal numeral, ܕܬܪܝܢ or ܕܬܪܬܝܢ *the second*, ܕܙ or ܕܫܒܥܐ *the seventh.*

ܕ relative, causal and final conj. *that, so that, in order that;* when preceding a verb in the future tense it is often rendered in English by the infinitive, ܒܗܬ ܐܢܐ ܕܐܡܪ *I am ashamed to say*, they came ܕܢܚܙܘܢ *to see.* ܕ is commonly used with other conjunctions and with adverbs ܐܝܟ ܕ, ܐܝܟܢܐ ܕ, ܐܟܙܢܐ ܕ *as, so that;* ܐܝܟ ܕܣܒܪ ܐܢܐ *in my opinion;* ܐܝܟ ܕܒܣܓܝܐܬܐ *often, generally, sometimes;* ܐܝܟܐ ܕ *where;* ܡܐ ܕ *when, at the time that;* ܡܢ ܕ *since;* ܥܕܡܐ ܕ *until;* ܗܫܐ ܕ *now that;* ܟܕ ܡܚܕܐ ܕ *as soon as;* ܙܒܢܐ ܕ *the time when.*

ܕ *of, by, about, for, against, on account of;* the sign of the genitive. Nouns with ܕ are often used as epithets, ܒܝܬܐ ܕܐܪܙܐ *a house of cedar;* ܡܪܟܒܬܐ ܕܡܠܟܘܬܐ *the royal chariot;* ܐܠܗܐ ܕܫܪܪܐ *the true God;* a substantive is often understood, ܗܘܬ ܕܬܕܡܘܪܬܐ *it was a cause of wonder, a wonderful thing;* ܕܐܪܥܐ *earthly* or *the things of earth;* ܕܫܡܝܐ *heavenly, heavenly treasures;* ܕܒܣܪ *carnal;* ܕܪܘܚ *spiritual;* ܕܙܒܢܐ *temporal;* ܕܦܣܝܩܬܐ *short;* ܕܫܪܟܐ *the others, the rest.*

ܕܐܒܐ, ܕܐܒܐ, ܕܝܒܐ or ܕܝܒܐ pl. ܐ̈ com. gen. *a wolf;* ܕܐܒܬܐ or ܕܝܒܬܐ pl. ܬ̈ܐ f. *a she-wolf.*

ܕܐܒܐ *a bear;* see ܕܒܐ.

ܕܐܘܢܐ and ܕܐܘܢܐ same as ܕܘܘܢܐ rt. ܕܘܐ. m. *misery.*

ܕܐܝܟ contr. of ܐܝܟ ܕ, *what manner, of what kind, what sort.*

ܕܐܝܢ Zend, *religion, worship;* ܕܐܝܢ ܕܡܓܘܫܘܬܐ *Magian worship.*

ܕܐܡܘܣܝܢ δημόσιον, *the public prison.*

ܕܐܡܘܣܝܢ δημόσιον, *the state treasury, the public hall.*

ܕܐܢ comp. of ܕ and ܐܢ *if.*

ܕܐܢ Spanish, *Don.*

ܕܐܦܐ *boards, tablets, leaves;* see ܕܦܐ.

ܕܐܦܢܐ, ܕܐܦܢܝ, and ܕܐܦܢܝܣ f. δάφνη, *the laurel* or *bay.*

ܕܐܩܢܐ, ܕܐܩܢܐ; see ܕܩܢܐ.

ܕܐܫ, ܕܐܫܐ; see ܕܘܫ *to observe;* ܕܐܫ, ܕܫܐ, pl. irreg. ܕܫܝܢ; see ܕܫ *to pound.*

ܕܘܩܝܕܣ δοκίδες, *meteors.*

ܕܒܪ no fem., see ܕܒܪ *to fight;* ܕܒܪ, ܕܒܪܐ, see ܕܘܪ *to dwell.*

ܕܒܪܐ pl. ܕܒܪ̈ܐ rt. ܕܒܪ. m. *a wrestling contest;* ܒܥܠ ܕܒܪܐ *an opponent;* see ܕܒܪ.

ܕܐܪܘܚܬܐ rt. ܕܪܘܚ. adj. with ܠܐ *intangible, incomprehensible.*

ܕܒܪܪܐ=ܕܒܪܪܐ rt. ܕܒܪ. m. *an athlete.*

ܕܐܬܐ, ܕܐܬܝܐ act. part. of ܐܬܐ with pron. ܕ prefixed, *he* or *that which is to come, the coming, the future.*

ܕܒ 3 m. s. of verb ܕܘܒ.

ܕܒܐ rarely ܕܐܒܐ pl. ܕܒ̈ܐ, ܕܒܝܢ com. gen. *a bear;* ܕܒܐ ܪܒܬܐ *the Great Bear;* ܕܒܐ ܙܥܘܪܬܐ *the Little Bear,* constellations.

ܕܒܐ *a wolf;* see ܕܐܒܐ.

ܕܒܒܐ or ܕܒܒܐ pl. ܐ̈ m. *a fly; a sort of locust;* ܕܒܒ ܟܠܒܐ *the dog-fly;* ܕܒܒܐ ܕܒܬܚܬܝܐ ܕܢܗܪܘܬܐ ܕܡܨܪܝܢ *the flies that are in the low parts of the rivers of Egypt.*

ܕܒܒܬܐ pl. ܬ̈ܐ f. *the gad-fly.*

ܕܒܓܐ E-Syr. ܕܝܒܓܐ see ܕܝܒܓ, *a vest of brocade.*

ܕܒܘܚܐ rt. ܕܒܚ. m. *one who offers sacrifice.*

ܕܒܘܩܐ or ܕܒܩܐ rt. ܕܒܩ. m. *viscous, viscidity, stickiness; an elm-tree.*

ܕܒܘܩܘܬܐ rt. ܕܒܩ. f. *the closing* of a wound.

ܕܒܘܪܐ pl. ܐ̈ *a*) m. *a drone; b*) com. *a wasp.*

ܕܒܘܪܐ pl. ܐ̈ rt. ܕܒܪ. m. *a guide, leader.*

ܕܒܘܪܬܐ and ܕܒܘܪܝܬܐ pl. ܬ̈ܐ f. *a bee,* pl. *bees, hornets.*

ܕܒܘܫܐ pl. ܐ̈ from ܕܒܫܐ. m. *a raisin cake, honey cake.*

ܕܒܚ fut. ܢܕܒܘܚ and ܢܕܒܚ, imper. ܕܒܘܚ or ܕܒܚ, act. part. ܕܒܚ, ܕܒܚܐ, pass. part. ܕܒܝܚ, ܚܐ, ܚܬܐ *to slay, slaughter,* esp. for sacrifice, *to sacrifice, offer sacrifice* with ܠ of the pers., pass. part. *slain, immolated, sacrificed* esp. to idols. Ethpe. ܐܬܕܒܚ *to be sacrificed, offered in sacrifice.* Pa. ܕܒܚ *to sacrifice* with ܠ of the pers., rarely with ܩܕܡ; ܕܒܚ ܩܕܡ ܦܬܟܪܗ *he offered sacrifice before his idol.* Derivatives, ܕܒܚܐ, ܕܒܘܚܐ, ܕܒܚܬܐ, ܕܒܚܘܬܐ, ܡܕܒܚܐ, ܡܕܒܚܝܐ, ܕܘܒܚܐ.

ܕܶܒܚܳܐ pl. ܶܐ rt. ܕܒܚ. m. *a sacrifice; the victim;* ܕܶܒܚܳܐ ܕܫܰܢ݈ܬܳܐ *the yearly sacrifice;* ܕܶܒܚܳܐ ܕܰܫܠܳܡܳܐ *a peace-offering,* also called ܫܠܰܡܳܝܳܐ; ܕܶܒܚܳܐ ܩܰܕܺܝܫܳܐ—ܡܶܠܺܝܠܳܐ ܘܪܽܘܚܳܢܳܝܳܐ *the holy—the reasonable and spiritual sacrifice,* i.e. the Holy Eucharist; our Lord is called ܕܶܒܚܳܐ ܚܠܳܦ ܟܽܠ *the sacrifice for all.* Metaph. ܗܘܰܘ ܕܶܒܚܶܐ ܠܚܰܝ݈ܘܳܬܳܐ *they became victims to wild beasts.*

ܕܶܒܚܬܳܐ and ܕܶܒܰܚܬܳܐ (the ܰ being adopted as a help to pronunciation) rt. ܕܒܚ. f. *a sacrifice; an offering in sacrifice* often used of the Eucharist, esp. with adjectives, ܡܠܺܝܠܬܳܐ *reasonable,* ܕܠܳܐ ܕܡܳܐ *bloodless.*

ܕܒܳܚܽܘܬܳܐ rt. ܕܒܚ. f. *sacrificing, an offering up in sacrifice.*

ܕܒܳܩܽܘܬܳܐ pl. ܳܬܳܐ rt. ܕܒܩ. f. *adhesion, closing* of a flesh wound; gram. *apposition;* pl. *affixes, suffixes.*

ܕܒܶܠܬܳܐ pl. ܕܒܶܠܶܐ, ܕܒܶܠܝܢ with ܕܬܺܐܢܶܐ or ellipt. *a cake* or *mass of dried figs.*

ܕܶܒܫ and ܕܽܘܒܫ Ar. *dibs,* grape-juice boiled down to the thickness of oil.

ܕܒܰܪ fut. ܢܶܕܒܽܘܪ and ܢܶܕܒܰܪ, imper. ܕܒܽܘܪ, act. part. ܕܳܒܰܪ, ܕܳܒܪܳܐ, pass. part. ܕܒܺܝܪ *to prick, sting* as an insect, scorpion, needle. Metaph. of the sword, sin, &c.; ܕܒܰܪ ܠܶܗ ܥܽܘܩܣܳܗ̇ ܕܚܛܺܝܬܳܐ *the sting of sin pierced* him. ETHPE. ܐܶܬ݂ܕܒܰܪ *to be pricked, stung,* ܕܽܘܟܬܳܐ ܕܡܶܬ݂ܕܰܒܪܳܐ *the part bitten* by a serpent; ܓܶܐܪܳܐ ܡܶܬ݂ܕܰܒܪܳܐ the point of an arrow *pierces the flesh.* PA. ܕܰܒܰܪ *to prick* or *sting repeatedly; to puncture* sycamore fruit; metaph. ܙܺܝܙܳܢܶܐ ܕܡܕܰܒܪܺܝܢ ܠܟܽܘܢ *the tares whose pricks trouble you.* DERIVATIVES, ܕܒܳܪܳܐ, ܕܽܘܒܪܳܐ, ܡܕܰܒܪܳܢܳܐ, ܕܽܘܒܳܪܬܳܐ.

ܕܒܳܪܳܐ pl. ܶܐ rt. ܕܒܪ. m. *stinging.*

ܕܒܶܩ and ܕܒܰܩ fut. ܢܶܕܒܰܩ, imper. ܕܒܽܘܩ, act. part. ܕܳܒܶܩ, ܕܳܒܩܳܐ, pass. part. ܕܒܺܝܩ, ܕܒܺܝܩܳܐ, ܕܒܺܝܩܬܳܐ *to cleave, adhere, touch, remain with, keep close to* with ܒ or ܠ; ܕܶܒܩܰܬ ܓܶܦܶܗ ܕܚܰܕ ܟܪܽܘܒܳܐ ܒܟܽܘܬܠܳܐ *the wing of one* cherub *touched the wall;* ܕܒܶܩ ܒܰܐܪܥܳܐ *he grovelled on the ground;* ܕܒܶܩܬ ܥܰܝܢܶܗ *his eye was fixed, dull;* metaph. ܕܠܳܐ ܕܒܶܩ *incongruous, inappropriate.* Pass. part. *close to* of place, *cleaving, adhesive, following,* ܕܒܺܝܩ ܗ̄ܘܳܐ ܠܶܗ ܟܶܢܫܳܐ ܣܰܓܺܝܐܳܐ *a great multitude followed him;* ܕܒܺܝܩܺܝܢ ܠܰܢ ܥܳܩܳܬ݂ܳܐ *troubles follow us closely;* gram. *conjunctive, relative* pronouns as ܕ, ܡܳܢ, ܡܳܐ, ܐܰܝܢܳܐ; and ܡܶܠܶܐ ܕܒܺܝܩܳܬ݂ܳܐ *intransitive verbs.* ETHPE. ܐܶܬ݂ܕܒܶܩ *to cleave unto, adhere, stick, be joined together;* ܐܶܬ݂ܕܰܒܩܰܬ ܢܰܦܫܝ ܒܳܗ̇ *my soul clave unto her.* PA. ܕܰܒܶܩ *to put, join* or *fasten together* esp. *to make a garment, arrange* or *bind* the leaves of a book; *to stick, glue;* proverb. ܡܕܰܒܶܩ ܚܰܨܦܶܐ *glueing potsherds together*=to waste labour. ETHPA. ܐܶܬ݂ܕܰܒܰܩ *a) to cleave to, remain in close connexion* with a person; ܐܶܬ݂ܕܰܒܩܽܘ ܠܶܗ ܣܰܓܺܝܐܶܐ *many accompanied him, followed him about; b) to be bound* or *fastened together* as the leaves of a codex. APH. ܐܰܕܒܶܩ *to make adhere, join, stick together; to close* a wound; *to affix.* DERIVATIVES, ܕܽܘܒܳܩܳܐ, ܕܒܳܩܳܐ, ܕܶܒܩܳܐ, ܕܒܺܝܩܽܘܬܳܐ, ܕܽܘܒܳܩܽܘܬܳܐ, ܡܕܰܒܩܽܘܬܳܐ.

ܕܶܒܩܳܐ pl. ܶܐ rt. ܕܒܩ. m. *a) edge, selvedge, seam, border, join* of curtains, clothes; *joint* of armour. *b) solder, glue, bird-lime. c) a bound volume;* ܕܽܘܒܳܩܳܐ is the commoner word.

ܕܒܳܩܳܐ pl. ܶܐ rt. ܕܒܩ. m. *a) a joining* or *fastening together; the binding up* or *closing* of a wound. *b) an elm-tree.*

ܕܒܰܪ fut. ܢܶܕܒܰܪ, imper. ܕܒܽܘܪ, parts. ܕܳܒܰܪ, ܕܳܒܪܳܐ; ܕܒܺܝܪ, ܕܒܺܝܪܳܐ *to lead* a flock *to pasture,* hence *a) to lead, take, drive, drive away; to go hither and thither, go onward. b) to guide, govern, manage,* with ܡܰܠܟܽܘܬܳܐ or ܡܰܕܒܪܳܢܽܘܬܳܐ; ܡܕܰܒܰܪ ܡܰܠܟܽܘܬܳܐ *to govern the kingdom;* ܡܰܪܟܰܒܬܳܐ *to drive;* ܣܦܺܝܢܬܳܐ *to steer a ship;* ܒܡܫܽܘܛܳܐ *to row;* ܕܒܰܪ ܐܰܟܳܪܽܘܬܳܐ *to plough,* sometimes ellipt. ܐܰܟܳܪܳܐ *a ploughman, husbandman;* metaph. Hos. x. 13 ܕܒܰܪܬܽܘܢ ܚܛܺܝܬܳܐ *ye have ploughed sin. c)* with ܐܰܢܬܬܳܐ *to take a wife. d) to act,* often with the idea of force; ܕܒܰܪ ܒܺܝܫ *to do evil, harm* any one; ܕܒܰܪ ܡܶܛܽܠ ܐܢܳܫ or ܕܒܰܪ ܒܰܩܛܺܝܪܳܐ *to act with force = to oppress;* ܕܒܰܪ ܐܰܝܟ ܚܰܝܠܳܐ ܕܰܐܠܦܳܐ *he fought with the strength of a thousand.* Part. ܕܳܒܰܪ *a)* active sense, *going about with, doing, taking, driving;* ܕܳܒܪܳܐ; ܕܳܒܰܪ ܗ̄ܘܳܐ ܠܶܗ ܣܳܛܳܢܳܐ *taking her sons with her;* ܣܳܛܳܢܳܐ *Satan governed him, impelled him. b)* passive, *led, driven, governed, moved,* &c. ETHPE. ܐܶܬ݂ܕܒܰܪ, imper. ܐܶܬ݂ܕܒܰܪ *a)* pass. *to be led, led* or *carried away* with ܒ, ܠ, ܥܰܡ; *to be taken* or *led captive;* with ܒܩܛܝܪܐ *to suffer violence, be forced, compelled; to be ploughed,* ܐܪܥܐ ܡܬܕܒܪܢܝܬܐ *ploughed land.* b) refl. *to conduct oneself, act;* ܒܥܒܕܐ ܛܒܐ ܐܬܕܒܪ *practise good works.* Pa. ܕܒܪ a) *to lead, guide, rule, manage* with ܒ, ܡܕܒܪ ܚܝܘܗܝ ܒ *one who leads a laborious life; to treat* a wound. b) *to drive, steer, plough.* c) *to govern, be in authority, have charge of; to take, receive.* d) with ܥܡ *to concert, plot.* Ethpa. ܐܬܕܒܪ a) pass. *to be led, guided, driven, led* or *carried away;* with ܡܢ ܥܠܡܐ *from this world=to die;* ܟܕ ܡܬܕܒܪ ܐܢܐ ܡܢܟ *when I am taken away from thee;* ܡܢ ܫܐܕܐ *to be driven hither* and *thither by a devil.* b) refl. *to conduct oneself, act,* hence *to live,* often with ܕܘܒܪܐ which see. Aph. ܐܕܒܪ *to do, perform, exercise power, govern;* ܡܠܟܘܬܐ ܡܕܒܪܝܢ *they govern kingdoms.* Derivatives, ܕܘܒܪܐ, ܕܒܪܐ, ܕܒܪܐ, ܕܒܪܢܐ, ܕܒܪܬܐ, ܕܒܘܪܐ, ܡܕܒܪܐ, ܡܕܒܪܐ, ܡܕܒܪܢܘܬܐ, ܡܕܒܪܢܐܝܬ, ܡܕܒܪܢܝܐ, ܡܕܒܪܢܐ, ܡܕܒܪܢܝܐ.

ܕܒܪܐ rt. ܕܒܪ. m. *the field, land, country,* opp. ܡܕܝܢܬܐ *the town;* ܕܕܒܪܐ *of the field, wild;* ܚܝܘܬܐ ܕܕܒܪܐ *a wild animal,* opp. ܒܥܝܪܐ *a domesticated* or *labouring beast;* ܥܣܒܐ ܕܕܒܪܐ *wild herbs.*

ܕܒܪܐ rt. ܕܒܪ. m. *guiding, management, driving, ploughing.*

ܕܒܪܝܐ, ܕܒܪܝܬܐ pl. m. ܐ̈, f. ܬܐ̈ adj. rt. ܕܒܪ. *belonging to the open country, rustic, wild;* ܬܐܢܬܐ ܕܒܪܝܬܐ *the wild fig.*

ܕܒܪܝ ܝܘܡܝܢ or ܣܦܪ ܕܒܪܝ ܝܘܡܝܢ and ܣܦܪ ܕܒܪܝܡܝܢ *the Book of the Chronicles;* corrupted from the Heb. name.

ܕܒܪܬܐ pl. ܬܐ̈ rt. ܕܒܪ. f. *the prey, animals driven away* from the enemy's country, opp. ܫܒܝܬܐ *the human beings taken captive.*

ܕܒܫ denom. verb Pael conj. from ܕܒܫܐ, *to become like honey;* ܟܕ ܡܕܒܫ ܐܝܟ ܗܘ *when it is as clear as honey.*

ܕܒܫ, ܕܒܫܐ pl. ܐ̈ *honey,* m. ܟܘܬܪܬܐ ܕܕܒܫܐ *honeycomb; grape-* or *date-syrup.*

ܕܒܫܢܐ pl. ܐ̈ adj. *honeyed, like honey;* ܕܒܘܪܝܬܐ ܕܒܫܢܝܬܐ *honey-bees;* ܟܐܦܐ ܕܒܫܢܝܬܐ *honey-stone.*

ܕܓ *to be deaf* or *dumb;* not used in Pe. Aph. ܐܕܓ *to grow deaf; to deafen.* Derivatives, ܕܓܐ, ܕܓܘܬܐ.

ܕܓܘܫܐ m. ܕܓܘܫܬܐ f. rt. ܕܓܫ. *he* or *that which stabs* or *pierces.*

ܕܓܠ Pa. ܕܓܠ *to lie, deceive, act deceitfully* or *treacherously; to deny, disappoint.* With ܒ *to defraud, cheat, be unfaithful;* ܒܩܝܡܐ *to a covenant;* ܒܡܘܡܬܐ *to forswear oneself, swear falsely;* with ܠ *to accuse of falsehood; to falsify;* ܒܫܘܘܕܝܐ *to break a promise;* with ܥܠ *to assert falsely.* Ethpa. ܐܬܕܓܠ *to be accused* or *convicted of falsehood, to be thought false, be suspected of deceit; to be deceived* or *disappointed,* ܡܢ ܣܒܪܗ *in* his *hope;* ܫܪܪܐ ܕܠܐ ܡܬܕܓܠ *unstained truth.* Derivatives, ܕܓܠܐ, ܕܓܠܘܬܐ, ܕܓܠܐܝܬ, ܕܓܠܢܐ, ܡܕܓܠܢܐ, ܡܕܓܠܢܘܬܐ.

ܕܓܠ, ܕܓܠܐ f. ܕܓܠܬܐ pl. m. ܝܢ, ܐ̈, f. ܢ, ܬܐ̈ rt. ܕܓܠ. adj. *false, vain, deceitful; spurious, feigned;* ܒܪܐ ܕܓܠܐ *a pretended son;* ܣܗܕܐ ܕܓܠܐ *a false witness;* ܕܓܠܐܝܬ ܡܫܬܡܗ *falsely called.*

ܕܓܠܐܝܬ rt. ܕܓܠ. adv. *falsely, deceitfully, vainly, in vain.*

ܕܓܠܘܬܐ pl. ܘܬܐ̈ rt. ܕܓܠ. f. *a falsehood, untruth, lie; treachery, unfaithfulness;* ܕܓܠܘܬܐ ܟܘܐ̈ *secret windows* or *openings;* ܡܫܝܚܐ ܕܕܓܠܘܬܐ *pseudo-Christs, false Messiahs.* Used adverbially with ܕ or ܒ prefixed, ܒܕܓܠܘ *falsely, treacherously;* ܠܕܓܠ *vainly, to no purpose.*

ܕܓܡ act. part. ܕܓܝܡ, ܕܓܝܡܐ *to inflame* or *cloud* the eyes, hence

ܕܓܡܐ m. *a swelling* or *watering* of the eyes.

ܕܓܫ fut. ܢܕܓܘܫ, act. part. ܕܓܫ, ܕܓܫܐ, pass. part. ܕܓܝܫ *to stab, pierce, transfix.* Ethpa. ܐܬܕܓܫ *to be stabbed, pierced through.* Aph. ܐܕܓܫ *to pierce through.* Derivatives, ܕܓܘܫܐ, ܕܓܫܐ.

ܕܓܫܐ rt. ܕܓܫ. m. *stabbing.*

ܕܕ, ܕܕܐ pl. ܕܕ̈ܐ m. for fem. see below. a) *a friend, a beloved.* b) *an uncle on the father's side,* opp. ܚܠܐ *the mother's brother;* ܒܪ ܕܕܐ *a first-cousin;* ܕܕܬܐ pl. ܕܕ̈ܬܐ f. *a father's sister.*

ܕܕܝܘܢ δαδίον, *a torch, torchwood.*

ܕܕܠܡܐ comp. of rel. conj. ܕ and ܕܠܡܐ; *lest, lest*

perchance, that; with ܠܐ after verbs of fearing.

ܕܕܪܐ m. *the elm.*

ܕܗܐ *behold; for behold, see now, but see;* see ܗܐ and ܕ.

ܕܗܒ, ܕܗܒܐ pl. ܐ̈ m. *a*) *gold;* ܕ ܡܨܠܝܐ *choice, fine* or *refined gold.* *b*) a tax of *one gold piece;* pl. ܕܗ̈ܒܐ ܕܕܢܪ̈ܐ *gold doubloons;* ܟܐܦܐ ܕܗܒ or ܕܗܒܐ ܟܐܦܐ *chrysolite;* ܥܪܘܒܬܐ ܕܕ *Golden Friday,* the Friday after Pentecost kept in honour of the Twelve Apostles. Derivatives the three following words and ܡܕܗܒܢܘܬܐ.

ܕܗܒ denom. verb from ܕܗܒܐ *to gild, to interweave with gold;* part. ܡܕܗܒ, ܡܕܗܒܐ *gilded, gilt, interwoven with gold; auriferous;* metaph. ܦܘܝܣ̈ܐ ܡܕܗ̈ܒܐ *gilded persuasions = bribery.* Ethpa. ܐܬܕܗܒ metaph. *to be adorned, crowned.* Aph. ܐܕܗܒ *to overlay with gold,* metaph. *to crown.* Part. ܡܕܗܒ, ܡܕܗܒܐ *golden, gilded.*

ܕܗܒܢܐ or ܕܗܒܝܐ adj. from ܕܗܒܐ. *golden, gilded.*

ܕܗܒܢܝܐ, ܕܗܒܢܝܬܐ pl. m. ܝܢ̈, ܐ̈, f. ܕܗܒܢܝ̈ܢ, ܕܗܒܢܝ̈ܬܐ adj. from ܕܗܒܐ. *golden, gold-coloured, gilded;* ܦܘܡܐ ܕܗܒܢܝܐ *golden-mouthed, eloquent.*

ܕܗܝܢܘܬܐ rt. ܕܗܢ. f. *fatness, oiliness; ductility* of metals; metaph. *brightness.*

ܕܗܢ fut. ܢܕܗܢ *to grow fat, to be anointed, oiled;* participial adj. ܕܗܝܢ, ܕܗܝܢܐ, ܕܗܝܢܬܐ *fat.* Ethpe. ܐܬܕܗܢ *to be fattened; to be fertile, fruitful, enriched;* metaph. ܐܬܕܗܢܬ ܣܝܦܐ ܡܢ ܕܡܐ *the sword is made fat with slaughter.* Aph. ܐܕܗܢ *to make fat, anoint; to consider fat,* i. e. *acceptable; to enrich.* Derivatives, ܕܗܝܢܘܬܐ, ܕܘܗܢܐ or ܕܘܗܢܐ.

ܕܘܐ and ܕܘܝ, fut. ܢܕܘܐ, imper. ܕܘܝ, with suff. 3 p. s. ܕܘܝܗܝ, parts. ܕܘܐ, ܕܘܝܐ, ܕܘܝܬܐ; ܕܘܐ, ܕܘܝܐ, ܕܘܝܬܐ, pl. m. ܕܘܝܢ, ܕܘܝ̈ܐ, f. ܕܘܝܢ, ܕܘܝ̈ܬܐ, both participles have the same pl. forms and the same meaning, *to be sad, wretched; to grieve,* refl. and trans. Parts. *sad, wretched, poor, miserable;* ܕܘܐ ܡܢ ܟܠ *most miserable.* For ܕܘܝܐ = ܕܘܝܐ see below. Ethpe. ܐܬܕܘܝ *to be laid low, shattered; to grieve, mourn.* Pa. ܕܘܝ *to lay low, make lowly.* Aph. ܐܕܘܝ *to bring low; to grieve, make wretched;* ܐܕܘܝܬܢ *thou hast made us wretched;* ܡܘܬܐ ܠܗܘܢ ܡܕܘܐ *death brings them low;* ܦܫ ܟܕ ܡܕܘܝ ܘܒܟܐ *he was left wretched and weeping.* Ettaph. ܐܬܬܕܘܝ *to be sad.* Derivatives, ܐܕܘܝܐ or ܕܘܝܐ, ܕܘܝܐ or ܕܘܝܐ, ܕܘܝܬ, ܕܘܝܐ, ܕܘܘܝܐ, ܡܕܘܝܐ, ܕܘܝܘܬܐ.

ܕܘܝܐ same as ܐܕܘܝܐ and ܕܘܘܝܐ. *misery.*

ܕܘܒ, ܕܒ fut. ܢܕܘܒ, act. part. ܕܐܒ, ܕܐܒܐ pl. m. ܕܐܒ̈ܐ. *a*) *to flow out, issue, have an issue* primarily of menstruation and of seminal discharge, esp. with ܕܘܒܐ or ܕܡܐ. *b*) *to melt, waste* or *pine away.* Part. *one that has an issue, discharge* or *flux;* metaph. *weak, failing, declining,* ܡܢ ܗܝܡܢܘܬܐ *from the faith.* Pa. ܕܘܒ *to melt, dissolve, wear* or *waste away; to consume, emaciate;* with ܦܓܪܐ or ܒܣܪܐ of the body being wasted by fasts and vigils; with ܢܦܫܐ of the soul being fretted or worn with trouble; ܡܠܚܐ ܡܕܘܒܢܐ ܠܣܪܘܚܘܬܐ *salt dispelling putrefaction;* ܡܕܘܒܐ ܠܗ ܠܫܐܘܠ ܪܘܚܐ ܒܝܫܬܐ *an evil spirit consumed Saul.* Ethpa. ܐܬܕܘܒ *to be broken up, grow thin, waste away.* Aph. ܐܕܝܒ same as Pa. ܒܣܪܐ ܡܕܘܒܐ *the flesh wastes away, decays.* Derivatives, ܕܘܒܐ, ܕܘܒܐ, ܕܝܒܐ, ܕܘܒܘܬܐ, ܡܕܘܒܐ.

ܕܘܒܐ pl. ܐ̈ rt. ܕܘܒ. m. *a*) *issue, flux, seminal discharge;* ܕ ܢܫܐ or ܢܫ̈ܐ *a woman's monthly course;* *b*) *falling in drops, distilling;* ܕ ܕܒܫܐ *liquid honey.*

ܕܘܒܚ, ܕܘܒܚܐ rt. ܕܒܚ. m. *a sacrifice.*

ܕܘܒܪܐ rt. ܕܒܪ. m. a serpent's *bite.*

ܕܘܒܪܬܐ pl. ܬܐ̈ rt. ܕܒܪ. f. *the sting* of a scorpion or of a bee.

ܕܘܒܩܐ pl. ܝܢ̈, ܐ̈ rt. ܕܒܩ. m. *a*) *glue, solder, bird-lime;* ܕܘܒܩ̈ܐ ܕܟܬܒ̈ܐ *covers* or *bindings of books,* hence ellipt. *a book, a bound volume.* Cf. Germ. *Band.* *b*) *the elm.*

ܕܘܒܪ, ܕܘܒܪܐ pl. ܐ̈ rt. ܕܒܪ. m. *the course* of the sun or moon; *order, rule, government, administration; treatment* of wounds, metals, &c.; *agreement; custom, way, manner of life, manners;* ܢܣܒ ܕܘܒܪܐ *to agree on a course of action, make an agreement;* ܕ ܣܗܪܐ—ܕܟܘܟ̈ܒܐ &c. *the due course* or *fixed order of the moon* or *stars;* metaph. ܕܘܒܪܐ ܐܠܗܝܐ *godly life;*

ܕܘܒܪܐ ܕܚܢܦܘܬܐ ‍heathen customs; ܥܛܝܢ ܕܘܒܪܐ ill-mannered; ܕܘܒܪܐ ܕܝܚܝܕܝܘܬܐ the monastic rule or way of life; pl. ellipt. discipline, the ascetic life.

ܕܘܓܐ Ar. and Pers. sour skim milk.

ܕܘܓܐ m. ܕܘܓܬܐ f. pl. ܕܘܓܐ rt. ܕܓ. a deaf person, deaf-mute. Metaph. lead.

ܕܘܓܘܬܐ rt. ܕܓ. f. deafness.

ܕܘܓܠܐ rt. ܕܓܠ. m. falsehood, lying.

ܕܘܓܡܐ pl. generally ܕܘܓܡܛܐ sometimes ܕܘܓܡܛܐ or ܕܘܓܡܐ m. δόγμα, doctrine, teaching, dogma; pl. rules, precepts.

ܕܘܓܡܛܝܩܝ dogmatics, dogmatic science; ܟܬܒܐ ܕܕ dogmatic writings.

ܕܘܕ, ܕܕ akin to seethe, Germ. sieden, not used in Pe. PAEL ܕܘܕ to trouble, disturb, perturb, ܫܘܪܝܐ ܡܕܘܕܐ ܘܡܒܠܒܠܐ a disorderly and confused beginning; ܪܘܝ ܘܡܕܘܕܝܢ ܡܢ ܚܡܪܐ drunk and disorderly. ETHPA. ܐܬܕܘܕ to be troubled, agitated, often with ܠܒܐ heart, ܪܥܝܢܐ mind. DERIVATIVES, ܕܘܕܐ, ܕܘܕܐ or ܕܘܕܐ, ܡܕܘܕܐܝܬ, ܡܕܘܕܘܬܐ, ܡܕܘܕܢܐ, ܡܕܘܕܢܐܝܬ.

ܕܘܕܐ rt. ܕܘܕ. m. a kettle, a great iron pot.

ܕܘܕܐ pl. ܕܘܕܐ; see ܕܘܕ.

ܕܘܕܩܐ and ܐܕܘܕܩܐ δώδεκα. Twelve Lections appointed for Holy Week.

ܕܘܗܢܐ and ܕܘܗܢܐ rt. ܕܗܢ. m. fat, fatness, rich food. Metaph. ܒܢܝ ܕܘܗܢܐ luxurious, effeminate.

ܕܘܘܕ, ܕܘܘܕܐ or ܕܘܕܐ pl. ܐ̈ rt. ܕܘܕ. m. trouble, confusion, contention; ܕܠܐ ܕܘܘܕ untroubled, calm, ܩܪܐ ܕܠܐ ܕܘܘܕ read distinctly, without stumbling; ܚܟܡܬܐ ܕܠܐ ܕܘܘܕ untroubled wisdom.

ܕܘܘܝ, ܕܘܘܝܐ E-Syr. ܕܘܘܝܐ pl. ܐ̈ rt. ܕܘܝ. m. wretchedness, misery.

ܕܘܙܐ m. a bracket.

ܕܘܚܠܐ pl. ܐ̈ rt. ܕܚܠ. m. making afraid, a causing or a cause of terror, a terror, horror.

ܕܘܚܢܐ m. millet or some similar grain.

ܕܘܚܩܐ rt. ܕܚܩ. m. removing.

ܕܘܛܪܐ δευτέρα, the second Indict.; see ܐܢܕܝܩܛܘܢ.

ܕܘܝ; see ܕܘܝ.

ܕܘܝܐ m. pl. Templars, the Knights Templar.

ܕܘܝܐܝܬ rt. ܕܘܝ. adv. miserably, wretchedly.

ܕܘܝܕܐ rt. ܕܘܕ. m. wasting away or pining, wasting disease, emaciation ܕܒܣܪܐ of the flesh, ܕܢܦܫܐ of the soul.

ܕܘܝܕ pr. n. David, used ellipt. for ܡܙܡܘܪܐ ܕܕܘܝܕ the Psalter; ܕܘܝܕ ܕܫܒܥܝܢ the Septuagint Version of the Psalms.

ܕܘܝܕܝܐ, ܕܘܝܕܝܬܐ E-Syr. ܕܘܝܕܝܐ pl. m. ܕܘܝܕܝܐ f. ܕܘܝܕܝܬܐ adj. from the above, Davidic, of or by David; ܫܒܛܐ ܕܘܝܕܝܐ the rod of David = Christ; ܠܡܚܐ ܠܒܪ ܡܢ ܫܢܝܐ ܕܘܝܕܝܐ to live beyond the limits set by David; cf. Ps. xc. 10.

ܕܘܝܘܢܐ dim. of participial adj. ܕܘܝܐ; see ܕܘܝ part. m. a wretched little creature, little wretch.

ܕܘܝܘܬܐ rt. ܕܘܝ. f. misery, wretchedness.

ܕܘܟܠܐ rt. ܕܘܟܠ. m. service, attendance.

ܕܘܝܪ, ܕܘܝܪܐ pl. ܐ̈ rt. ܕܘܪ. m. a sojourning, a staying, a dwelling; a place of habitation; pl. customs, way of life.

ܕܘܝܬܕܐܪ Pers. lit. Keeper of the Inkhorn, the title of the scribe whose office was to write down the edicts of the Khalif.

ܕܘܟ, ܕܘܟܐ constr. ܕܘܟܬ emph. ܕܘܟܬܐ com. gen. but generally ܕܘܟܐ m. and ܕܘܟܬܐ f. pl. ܕܘܟܝܬܐ rarely ܕܘܟܘܬܐ a) a place, spot, position, post, office; with ܡܠܐ, ܚܟܡ, or ܢܛܪ to exercise the office, fill the place or post; b) a place or passage of a book, ܐܝܟܢܐ ܕܒܕܘܟ ܐܡܪ as He says somewhere; c) ܒܕܘܟ somewhere, anywhere; ܘܠܐ ܒܕܘܟ nowhere; ܒܟܠ ܕܘܟ everywhere; ܒܕܘܟ ܕܘܟ here and there, in many places; ܠܕܘܟ ܕܘܟ to sundry places; ܡܢ ܕܘܟ ܕܘܟ from some place or other; ܡܢ ܟܠ ܕܘܟ or ܕܘܟܐ from every place, on or from every side.

ܕܘܟܬ generally with ܒ prefixed = prep. for, instead of; ܒܕܘܟܬܗ or ܡܢ, ܒ on the spot, immediately, N.B. always with the same pron. suff. 3 p. s. DERIVATIVES, ܕܘܟܬܢܐܝܬ, ܕܘܟܬܢܐ.

ܕܘܟܣ, ܕܘܩܣ pl. ܕܘܟܣܐ m. dux, commander of an army, leader, chief; a prefect.

ܕܘܟܝܐ rt. ܕܟܐ. m. cleansing, ablution, purification, purity; ܡܢ ܚܛܝܬܐ from sin; ܕܘܟܝ ܠܒܐ purity of heart.

ܕܘܟܣܐ pl. ܕܘܟܣ̈ܣ δόξα, *glory, praise;* ܕ ܠܐܠܗܐ *glory to God.*

ܕܘܟܪܢܐ, ܕܘܟܪܢܐ pl. ܢ̈ܐ rt. ܕܟܪ. m. *a) remembrance, anything kept in remembrance, a token of remembrance, keepsake, memory;* ܕܘܟܪܢܗ ܠܒܘܪܟܬܐ *whose memory is blessed, of blessed memory. b) a memorial,* that part of a sacrifice which was burnt on the altar as a sign that God was prayed to remember the offerer, Lev. ii. 2, 9, 16, &c.; ܗܕܐ ܗܘܝܬܘܢ ܥܒܕܝܢ ܠܕܘܟܪܢܝ *do this for my memorial;* Luke xxii. 19, hence the Eucharist is often called ܕܘܟܪܢܐ. *c) a memorial prayer, commemoration* esp. of the holy dead at the Lord's Supper and on special days, hence *a Saint's day, holy day;* ܕܘܟܪܢܐ ܕܣܗܕܐ, ܕܥܢܝܕܐ *Festivals of Martyrs, of the Departed.*

ܕܘܟܪܢܝܬܐ fem. emph.; see ܕܘܟܪܐ.

ܕܘܟܝܐܝܬ from ܕܘܟ. adv. *locally.*

ܕܘܟܝܐ, ܕܘܟܝܬܐ from ܕܘܟ. adj. *local, pertaining to some place.*

ܕܘܠ, ܕܠ fut. ܢܕܘܠ, inf. ܡܕܠ, act. part. ܕܐܠ, ܕܐܠܐ, pass. part. ܕܝܠ. *a) to be moved, stirred up, aroused. b) to move; to go, come, go in* or *out,* often with other verbs of motion, ܕܠ ܘܢܦܩ, ܕܠ ܘܢܚܬ *he arose and went out, he descended,* here ܕܠ expresses the beginning of the action. *c) to stir, arise* as mental impulses, ܕܠ ܡܚܫܒܬܐ ܒܪܥܝܢܗ *a thought stirred* or *arose in his mind. d) to quiver, quake,* ܡܕܠ ܬܕܘܠ ܐܪܥܐ *the earth shall quake exceedingly;* ܥܠܥܠܐ ܬܕܘܠ *a storm shall arise.* Ethpe. or Ettaph. ܐܬܕܘܠ *to be shaken, moved;* ܡܬܕܘܠ ܠܒܗ *his heart quakes, is troubled.* Pa. ܕܘܠ *to serve, attend, wait upon, minister.* Aph. ܐܕܝܠ *a) to move, stir up, arouse, excite,* ܡܕܝܠ ܗܘ ܬܘܒ ܛܢܦܘܬܐ *he stirs up filth continually;* ܐܕܝܠ ܐܠܗܐ ܒܠܒܗ *God put in his heart;* ܚܕܘܬܐ ܡܕܝܠܐ ܒܪܓܠܝܗ *joy stirs in her feet. b) to enter, to bring in.* c) gram. *to give a vowel* to a letter, e.g. when two consonants without vowels come together. Derivatives, ܕܘܠܐ, ܕܘܝܠܐ, ܕܝܠܐ, ܕܝܠܬܐ, ܡܕܝܠܐ.

ܕܘܠܐ pl. ܕܘ̈ܠܐ rt. ܕܠܐ. m. *a bucket, water-pot; Aquarius,* a sign of the zodiac.

ܕܘܠܐ m. *the woof* of a web; *a hank* of thread or silk.

ܕܘܠܒܐ pl. ܢ̈ܐ m. *the oriental plane-tree.*

ܕܘܠܠܐ rt. ܕܠ. m. *a divorce, legal separation* with ܐܓܪܬܐ or ܟܬܒܐ.

ܕܘܠܦܝܢܐ, ܕܘܠܦܝܢ m. *a dolphin.* The name of a constellation.

ܕܘܡܘܣܝܘܢ δημόσιον, ܕܘܡܣܝܢ ܒܝܬ *the public tribunal.*

ܕܘܡܝܐ rt. ܕܡܐ. m. *likeness, resemblance, similitude; the like, like action* or *behaviour; a pattern, example; appearance, likelihood;* ܕܘܡܝܗ ܠܐܒܘܗܝ *his likeness to his Father;* ܕܘܡܝܐ ܠܐ ܐܬܚܙܝ *the like has not been seen;* ܠܝܬ ܠܗ ܕܘܡܝܐ *it is unlikely;* ܕܠܝܬ ܕܘܡܝܐ *unique, incomparable.* ܒܕܘܡܝܐ adv. *apparently,* opp. ܒܫܪܝܪܘܬܐ or ܒܩܘܫܬܐ *truly, indeed;* ܒܕܘܡܝܐ ܕ *like, as.*

ܕܘܡܝܢܝܐ rt. ܕܡܐ. adj. *ideal.*

ܕܘܡܣܐ pl. ܢ̈ܐ f. domus, *a house, building; a pile* of wood or stones. Metaph. *a foundation;* ܕܘܡܣ̈ܐ ܕܡܠܟܘܬܢ *the foundations of our kingdom;* ܩܕܡܝܬܐ—ܠܐ ܥܠ ܕܘܡܣܐ ܫܪܝܪܐ ܩܝܡ *the former opinion is not based on a sure foundation.*

ܕܘܡܣܛܝܩܘܣ, ܕܘܡܣܛܝܩܘܣ or ܕܘܡܣܛܝܩܐ δομέστικος, some official of the Byzantine rule.

ܕܘܡܣܝܣܬܐ from δώμησις, f. *building.*

ܕܘܡܪܐ rt. ܕܡܪ. m. *wonder, marvel, a wondrous thing;* ܡܠܐ ܕܘܡܪܐ *wonderful, admirable.*

ܕܘܡܪܐܝܬ rt. ܕܡܪ. adv. *wonderfully, admirably.*

ܕܘܢ, ܕܢ fut. ܢܕܘܢ, inf. ܡܕܢ, imper. ܕܘܢ, act. part. ܕܐܢ, ܕܝܢܐ, pass. part. ܕܝܢ *to judge. a) to administer justice, rule. b) to pronounce* or *give judgement, condemn, acquit, vindicate; to determine, decree; to declare* a dream. *c) to plead, sue, go to law;* ܕܝܢܐ ܠܡܥܠ *to bring a suit;* with ܥܡ *to debate, strive.* Ethpe. ܐܬܕܝܢ rare, *to be judged;* with ܥܡ *to contend with.* Ethtaph. ܐܬܬܕܝܢ *a) to be administered* (of justice); *to exercise judgement* or *justice. b) to be judged, condemned, punished; determined. c) to go to law, contend with. d) to judge, decide, consider;* ܐܬܕܝܢܬ ܠܝ ܐܠܨܐ *I judged* or *thought necessary.* Derivatives, ܕܝܢܐ, ܕܝܢܐ, ܕܝܢܘܬܐ, ܕܝܢܬܐ, ܡܕܝܢܐ, ܡܕܝܢܐ, ܕܝܢܘܬܐ, ܡܕܝܢܬܐ, ܡܕܝܢܬܐ.

ܕܘܢܒܐ constr. ܕܘܢܒ and ܕܢܒ, pl. ܕܘܢܒܐ rt. ܕܢܒ. generally m. *the tail, hinder end;* ܕܘܢܒܐ ܕܢܝܙܟܐ *the hinder end of a spear;* ܕܘܢܒ ܣܘܣܝܐ *equisetum, mare's tail.*

ܕܘܢܒܬܐ and ܕܢܒܬܐ f. the same, usually metaph. *the last,* term of contempt.

ܕܘܢܐܛܝܒܐ m. *donative,* largess granted to Roman soldiers by the emperor.

ܕܘܢܩܐ rt. ܕܢܩ. m. *torment, pain.*

ܕܘܣܢܛܪܝܐ, ܕܘܣܢܛܪܝ, ܕܘܣܢܛܪܝ or ܕܘܣܢܛܪܝܐ δυσεντερία, *dysentery,* sometimes with ܕܡܥܝܐ *of the bowels.*

ܕܘܣܦܘܛܝܩܐ pl. ܐ̈ adj. δεσποτικός, *imperial, official, from* or *belonging to the Byzantine Court.*

ܕܘܥܟ, ܕܘܥܟܐ rt. ܕܥܟ. m. *quenching, assuaging,* ܕܚܡܬܐ *of anger; abolishing,* ܕܡܘܬܐ *of death.*

ܕܘܥܪ, ܕܘܥܪܐ rt. ܕܥܪ. m. *a stinging, smarting* of the eyes. Metaph. ܫܠܡܐ ܕܠܐ ܕܘܥܪ *in unvexed peace.*

ܕܘܥܬܐ pl. ܕܘܥܬܐ rt. ܕܥܬ. com. gen. *sweat, perspiration.* ܕ ܐܝܠܢܐ *gum, resin;* ܕ ܟܐܦܐ *talc;* ܕ ܦܪܓܐܓܐ *poppy juice, opium.*

ܕܘܥܬܢܝܐ, ܢܝܬܐ adj. from the above. *sudorific.*

ܕܘܦܛܘܟܘܢ *a diptych;* see ܕܝܦܛܘܟܘܢ.

ܕܘܦܢܐ m. *a mummy-case, wooden coffin.*

ܕܘܨ, ܕܨ fut. ܢܕܘܨ, inf. ܡܕܨ, imper. ܕܘܨ, act. part. ܕܐܨ, ܕܝܨܐ *to exult, leap for joy;* ܟܘܟܒܐ ܕܝܨܝܢ perh. *shooting stars.* Pa. ܕܝܨ *a) to exult, dance for joy. b) to make merry, exhilarate.* Derivatives, ܕܘܨܐ, ܕܝܨܐ, ܕܝܨܐ.

ܕܘܨܐ pl. ܕܘܨܐ rt. ܕܘܨ. m. *exultation, rejoicing;* ܕܘܨܐ ܕܡܠܐܟܐ *rejoicing of angels.*

ܕܘܩ imperative, ܢܕܘܩ fut. of ܕܩ. *to bray, pound,* and of the following:

ܕܘܩ, ܕܩ fut. ܢܕܘܩ, inf. ܡܕܩ, imper. ܕܘܩ, act. part. ܕܐܩ, ܕܝܩܐ, pass. part. ܕܝܩ *to gaze,* esp. *from afar, to take astronomical observations; to observe, regard, to look forth, upon* or *into; to pound.* But this meaning should properly belong to ܕܩ. Pa. ܕܝܩ *to regard, gaze upon.* Ethpa. ܐܬܕܝܩ *to be pounded,* a confusion with ܐܬܕܩܩ from ܕܩ. Aph. ܐܕܝܩ *to look out* or *forth;* ܡܢ ܟܘܬܐ *from the window; to look for, towards* or *up, to behold.* Metaph. *to show oneself, appear, come to light;* ܐܕܝܩܘ ܙܝܙܢܐ *tares appeared;* ܐܝܟ ܫܪܓܐ ܐܕܝܩܘ ܡܕܝܩܢ ܐܪ̈ܙܝܟ *Thy mysteries appear clearly like lamps.* Pass. part. ܡܕܝܩ *acquainted* or *familiar* with any study or subject; *instructed.* Derivatives, ܕܘܩܐ, ܕܘܩܢܐ, ܕܝܩܐ, ܡܕܝܩܘܬܐ.

ܕܘܩܐ pl. ܕܘܩܐ rt. ܕܘܩ. m. *looking forth. a) the sense of sight, vision;* ܕܘܩܐ ܚܪܝܦܐ *keen eyesight; an astronomical observation.* Metaph. *scope, prospect. b) one who observes,* esp. from a height, *a watchman;* ܕܘܩܐ often forms part of the name of a place; ܪܡܬܐ ܕܕܘܩܐ *the watchmen's hill,* 1 Sam. i. 1. Metaph. *a prophet; a bishop. c) a robber, a lier in wait. d) a watch-tower, a look-out; a wooden tower* for besieging a city.

ܕܘܩܐ rt. ܕܩ.=ܕܩܐ *a) something broken small* or *ground;* ܕܘܩܐ ܕܡܪ̈ܓܢܝܬܐ *pearls reduced to powder; dry pulse. b) a frying-pan.*

ܕܘܩܣ or ܕܘܟܣ m. dux, *a leader, governor.*

ܕܘܩܢܐ pl. ܐ̈ rt. ܕܘܩ. m. with ܐܪ̈ܓܢܐ *instruments for making astronomical observations.*

ܕܘܩܣܝܣ with ܢܣܒ. *to suffer punishment.*

ܕܘܩܪܐ pl. ܐ̈ rt. ܕܩܪ. m. *a thrust* from a cow's horn; *goring.*

ܕܘܪ imperative; ܢܕܘܪ fut. of ܢܕܪ *to vow.*

ܕܘܪ, ܕܪ root-meaning *to go round.* Pe. only used in participle ܕܐܪ, ܕܝܪܐ *dwelling;* ܪܘܚܐ ܕܝܪܐ ܒܗܘܢ *a spirit inhabits them,* i. e. idols. Pa. ܕܝܪ *a)* almost always with ܒ, *to dwell, inhabit. b) to make inhabit, to settle; to lead the life of a monk. c) to go about* or *to and fro;* metaph. ܠܡܐܢܐ ܕܠܐ ܡܕܝܪܝܢ ܒܗ ܥܠܥܠܐ a haven *where tempests stay not.* Derivatives, ܕܘܪܐ, ܕܘܪܐ, ܕܘܪܬܐ, ܕܝܪܐ, ܕܝܪܐ, ܕܝܪܘܬܐ, ܕܝܪܝܐ, ܕܝܪܝܘܬܐ, ܕܝܪܝܐ, ܕܪܐ, ܕܪܬܐ, ܡܕܝܪܐ.

ܕܘܪ, ܕܘܪܐ and ܕܘܪܐ rt. ܕܘܪ. m. *a circle;* ܕ ܕܫܢܘܗܝ *his double row of teeth;* eccles. *a procession,* ܒܕܘܪܐ ܕܩܘܪܒܐ ܕܐܪܙܐ *at the Eucharistic procession.*

ܕܘܪܬܐ, ܕܘܪܝܬܐ rt. ܕܘܪ. f. ܕ ܫܠܗܒܝܬܐ *the flame* under a pot appearing *round* the sides of it.

ܕܘܪܐ and ܕܘܪܝܐ δωρεά, *a deed of gift; the bride's jointure* or *marriage settlement* made by the bridegroom.

ܕܘܪܓܐ rt. ܕܪܓ. m. *a gradual progress, improvement,* or *attainment;* ܒܕܘܪܓܐ *step by step, by degrees.*

ܕܘܪܛܐ or ܕܘܪܐܛܐ δύρατα, *a spear, a sceptre.*

ܕܘܪܟܐ rt. ܕܪܟ. m. *the treading out* of wheat.

ܕܘܪܟܬܐ pl. ܬܐ̈ rt. ܕܪܟ. f. *a footstep, a foothold, that on which one treads,* e. g. *a floor, a pavement.*

ܕܘܪܡܐ pl. ܐ̈ m. *deceit, a fraud, cheat, trick.*

ܕܘܪܩܢܝܐ pl. ܐ̈ δωρακινόν, *the apricot* or *peach; a sort of Persian vine.*

ܕܘܪܫܐ pl. ܐ̈ rt. ܕܪܫ. m. *exercise, discipline; teaching, instruction; disputation, investigation.*

ܕܘܫ, ܕܫ fut. ܢܕܘܫ, inf. ܡܕܫ, imper. ܕܘܫ, act. part. ܕܐܫ, ܕܝܫܐ, pass. ܕܝܫ, ܕܝܫܐ *to tread, tread under foot, trample;* with ܠ or ܥܠ of the pers. or thing. With ܡܥܨܪܬܐ *to tread the wine-press;* ܥܡܐ ܕܝܫܐ *a down-trodden people.* Metaph. *to transgress,* ܠܢܡܘܣܐ *the law,* ܥܠ ܩܢܘܢܐ *a rule.* ETHPE. ܐܬܕܝܫ *to be trodden, trodden under foot, trampled upon;* metaph. ܐܬܕܝܫܘ ܩܢܘܢܐ *the canons were violated, set at nought.* PA. ܕܝܫ *to tread down, trample.* DERIVATIVES, ܕܘܫܐ, ܕܝܫܐ, ܕܝܫܐ, ܡܕܫܢܐ, ܡܕܫܢܘܬܐ.

ܕܘܫܐ rt. ܕܘܫ. m. *that which is trodden* or *trampled, trampling;* ܫܒܩܬܘܢܝ ܕܘܫܐ ܠܛܠܝܐ *ye have let* me *be trampled upon by boys.*

ܕܚܚ cognate root ܕܩܩ. PE. only particip. adj. ܕܚܝܚ, ܐ, ܬܐ *small, minute;* ܥܦܪܐ ܕܚܝܚܐ *fine dust;* subst. m. *dust;* ܓܒܝܠ ܡܢ ܕܚܝܚܐ *formed out of the dust;* ܕܚܝܚܐ ܕܗܕܡܐ ܩܕܝܫܐ *the dust of holy limbs.* PA. ܕܚܚ *to reduce to ashes.* ETHPA. ܐܬܕܚܚ *to become dust;* ܐܢܐ ܡܬܕܚܚ ܐܢܐ ܒܩܒܪܐ *I become dust in the grave.*

ܕܚܐ fut. ܢܕܚܐ, inf. ܡܕܚܐ, act. part. ܕܚܐ, ܕܚܝܐ. *a) to push, strike, thrust; to impel. b) to cast* or *thrust out, drive away* or *off; to repel, reject;* ܕܚܝܢ ܫܘܪܐ ܒܕܝܩܐ *they strike the wall with battering-rams;* ܐܐܪ ܕܚܐ ܠܐܣܛܘܟܣܐ ܕܢܘܪܐ ܠܥܠ *air causes the element of fire to rise;* ܢܕܚܘܢ ܡܢܗܘܢ ܒܝܫܬܐ *let them cast away the evil thing.* ETHPE. ܐܬܕܚܝ *a) to be hurled* or *cast;* metaph. *to be impelled. b) to be cast out, expelled;* ܩܠܥܐ ܐܬܕܚܝܬ ܠܘܬܗ *the sling was hurled against him;* ܐܬܕܚܝܬ ܢܦܫܐ ܠܫܝܘܠ *the soul was cast down to Sheol.* PA. ܕܚܝ same as Peal. ܕܚܝܘ ܠܚܟܡܬܐ *they rejected wisdom.* ETHTAPH. ܐܬܕܚܝ same as ETHPE. DERIVATIVES, ܕܚܘܝܐ, ܕܚܝܐ, ܕܚܘܝܐ, ܡܕܚܝܢܘܬܐ.

ܕܚܘܝܐ pl. ܐ̈ rt. ܕܚܐ. m. *expulsive,* having the power or effect of *causing violent motion;* pl. *earthquakes, shocks of earthquakes.*

ܕܚܘܠܐ rt. ܕܚܠ. m. *one who fears, is afraid.*

ܕܚܘܠܬܢܐ, ܬܐ rt. ܕܚܠ. *timid, fearful.*

ܕܚܘܠܬܢܐܝܬ rt. ܕܚܠ. adv. *timidly.*

ܕܚܘܠܬܢܘܬܐ rt. ܕܚܠ. f. *timidity, fearfulness.*

ܕܚܘܝܐ rt. ܕܚܐ. m. *one who drives away* or *removes, an oppressor;* ܕܚܘܝܐ ܕܒܝܫܬܐ *a dispeller of evil things.*

ܕܚܘܝܐ rt. ܕܚܐ. m. *a driving back* or *away, repulsing; banishment; repudiation, putting away* of a wife.

ܕܚܝܐ rt. ܕܚܐ. m. *repulsion, impulsion.*

ܕܚܝܚ, ܕܚܝܚܐ adj. and subst.; see ܕܚܚ.

ܕܚܝܠ and ܕܚܝܠܐ; see ܕܚܠ.

ܕܚܝܠܐܝܬ rt. ܕܚܠ. adj. *fearfully, terribly, horribly.*

ܕܚܝܠܘܬܐ rt. ܕܚܠ. f. *fearfulness, awfulness, terrible might;* a title of reverence with suff. 2 p. *thy Dread, your Mightiness.*

ܕܚܝܠܬܟ contr. of ܕܚܝܠ ܐܢܬ *awful* or *terrible art Thou;* ܥܢܝܢܐ ܕܚܝܠܬܟ anthems for special festivals, beginning with Ps. lxviii. 35.

ܕܚܠ fut. ܢܕܚܠ, inf. ܡܕܚܠ, act. part. ܕܚܠ, ܕܚܠܐ, pass. parts. ܕܚܝܠ, ܐ, ܬܐ; ܕܚܠ, ܐ, ܬܐ *to fear, dread, stand in awe of, reverence* with ܠ or ܡܢ; *to be afraid of* with ܡܢ; ܕܚܠܘ ܕܚܠܬܐ ܪܒܬܐ *they were terribly afraid;* ܕܚܠ ܐܠܗܐ *God-fearing, one who fears God;* ܕܚܠܝ ܡܪܝܐ *they who fear the Lord;* ܕܚܠܝ ܫܐܕܐ—ܦܬܟܪܐ *idolators, worshippers of demons;* pass. part. the older form keeps the passive sense, *fearing, fearful, afraid;* the form ܕܚܝܠ has active or causative signif., *fearful, formidable, terrible, dreadful, awful;* see ܕܚܝܠܐ. Pa. ܕܚܠ *to terrify, alarm, frighten, threaten.* Aph. ܐܕܚܠ same as Pa. Derivatives, ܕܚܠܐ, ܕܚܠܬܐ, ܕܚܝܠܐ, ܕܚܠܬܢܘܬܐ, ܕܚܠܬܢܐ, ܕܚܘܠܐ, ܕܚܝܠܘܬܐ, ܡܕܚܠܢܐ.

ܕܚܠܐ, ܕܚܠܬܐ pl. m. ܕܚܠܐ, f. ܕܚܠܬܐ rt. ܕܚܠ. generally f. *a) fear, dread,* pl. *panics. b)* generally constr. or emph. *awe, worship, religion* often used of false or mistaken religion, of a heresy or sect; ܕܚܠܬ ܡܪܝܐ or ܐܠܗܐ *the fear of God;* ܕܚܠܬܐ ܫܦܝܪܬܐ *piety, reverence towards God, true religion;* ܕܚܠܬ ܫܐܕܐ or ܓܠܦܐ *superstition;* ܕܚܠܬ ܦܬܟܪܐ *idolatry. c) the object of worship,* generally *a false god, an idol.*

ܕܚܠ, ܕܚܠܐ m. *a worshipper;* see ܕܚܠ.

ܕܚܠܬܐ pl. ܐ̈ rt. ܕܚܠ. m. *a fear, a terror; a scarecrow.*

ܕܚܠܢܐ = ܕܚܠ ܐܢܐ *I fear.*

ܕܚܠܬܐ fem. emph.; see ܕܚܠܐ.

ܕܚܐ, ܕܚܐ fut. ܢܕܚܐ, inf. ܡܕܚܐ, imper. ܕܚܝ, act. part. ܕܚܐ, ܕܚܝܐ, pass. part. ܕܚܐ, ܕܚܝܐ, ܕܚܝܬܐ *to thrust out, drive away; to take away, remove, reject;* pass. part. *outcast, abandoned.* Ethpe. ܐܬܕܚܝ *to be cast out, driven away, removed, expelled.* Ethpa. same as Ethpe. Derivatives, ܕܘܚܝܐ, ܕܚܘܝܐ, ܕܚܝܝܐ, ܡܕܚܝܢܐ, ܡܬܕܚܝܢܐ.

ܐܕܚܫ denom. verb Aphel conj. from ܕܚܫܐ *to harden.*

ܕܚܫܐ with ܟܐܦܐ *a millstone, hailstone; flint.*

ܕܚܫܐ only pl. m. *the guard, guardsmen; attendants, yeomen, warders, apparitors* of a tribunal.

ܕܝܐܒܝܛܐ or ܕܝܒܝܛܐ m. διαβήτης, *a pair of compasses; a carpenter's square.*

ܕܝܐܛܐܩܣܝܣ διάταξις, *a decree, edict;* ܕ ܫܠܝܚܐ *the Apostolic Constitutions.*

ܕܝܐܛܣܪܘܢ διατεσσάρων, *a diatessaron* or *harmony of the Four Gospels.*

ܕܝܐܠܠܝܐ, ܕܝܠܠܝܐ, ܕܝܠܠܝܐ, ܕܝܠܠܝܐ or ܕܝܠܠܝܣ διαλαλία, *a proclamation, sentence, judgement.*

ܕܝܐܠܘܓܘܣ pl. ܕܝܐܠܘܓܘ̈ܣ διάλογος, *a dialogue.*

ܕܝܐܠܩܛܝܩܘܣ pl. ܕܝܐܠܩܛܝܩܘ̈ܣ διαλεκτικός, *a dialectician.*

ܕܝܐܡܛܪܐܝܬ adv. *diametrically.*

ܕܝܐܩܘܢ m. *a deacon.*

ܕܝܐܩܘܢܝܐ or ܕܝܩܘܢܝܐ διακονία, *service, that which is serviceable.* Cf. ܡܫܡܫܢܐ.

ܕܝܐܬܝܣܝܣ διάθεσις, logic. *a position.*

ܕܝܐܬܝܩܐ, ܕܝܬܝܩܐ, ܕܝܬܩܐ and other spellings, pl. ܕܝܬܝܩܣ or ܕܝܐܬܝܩܐ f. διαθήκη, *a covenant, testament;* ܕ ܥܬܝܩܬܐ—ܚܕܬܐ *the Old and New Testament.*

ܕܝܒܐ, ܕܝܘܒܐ rt. ܕܘܒ. m. *a discharge, flux, issue;* with ܢܫܐ *monthly course of women;* ܕ ܕܡܐ *of blood;* ܕ ܡܝܐ *strangury.* Metaph. *weakness* of mind.

ܕܝܒܐ oftener ܕܐܒܐ *a wolf.*

ܕܝܒܓ Ar. m. *brocade.*

ܕܝܘ, ܕܝܘܐ pl. ܕܝܘܐ, ܕܝܘܝܢ m. Zend daēwa, Pers. dēw, *an evil spirit, a devil;* ܗܘܐ ܠܗ ܕܝܘܐ *he was possessed by an evil spirit.* Derivatives, verb ܐܬܕܝܘ, ܕܝܘܢܐ, ܕܝܘܢܘܬܐ, ܕܝܘܢܝܐ, ܡܬܕܝܘܢܐ.

ܕܝܘܐܢ Arab. and Pers. *diwan, a register, minute-book, bureau, session, council;* ܣܟܪܘ ܕܝܘܐܢܗܘܢ *they closed their register, finished their session.*

ܕܝܘܒܐ pl. ܐ̈ m. ܕܝܘܒܬܐ f. rt. ܕܘܒ. *liquid, moist;* ܗܘܠܐ ܕܝܘܒܬܐ *humid matter.*

ܕܝܘܒܘܬܐ rt. ܕܘܒ. m. *a flux, gonorrhea.*

ܕܝܘܠܐ, ܕܝܘܠܬܐ rt. ܕܘܠ. adj. gram. *a letter vocalized, having a vowel* opp. ܫܠܝܐ, ܫܠܝܬܐ *mute, quiescent.*

ܕܝܘܢ denom. verb from ܕܝܘܐ Ethpaial ܐܬܕܝܘܢ *to be vexed with a devil, suffer from demoniacal possession.*

ܕܝܘܢܐ, ܕܝܘܢܝܬܐ pl. m. ܐ̈ f. ܬ̈ܐ from ܕܝܘܐ *a demoniac, one vexed by a devil, a madman.*

ܕܝܘܢܘܬܐ from ܕܝܘܐ f. *demoniacal possession, madness.*

ܕܝܘܦܘܣܛܝܢ; see ܕܝܦܘܣܛܝܢ.

ܕܝܦܘܣܝܛܐ, ܕܝܦܘܣܝܛܣ or ܕܝܦܘܣܝܛܐ pl. ܐ̈ διφυσίτης, *a dyophysite*, a believer in two natures in Christ.

ܕܝܘܫܐ pl. ܐ̈ rt. ܕܘܫ. *an observer, spectator.*

ܕܝܘܪܐ rt. ܕܘܪ. m. *a dweller, settler.*

ܕܝܘܫܐ pl. ܐ̈ rt. ܕܘܫ. *a treader* of the wine-press. Metaph. *a trampler, oppressor.*

ܕܝܘܬܐ f. *ink;* ܒܝܬ ܕܝܘܬܐ *an ink-pot.*

ܕܝܘܢܝܐ adj. from ܕܝܘܐ *suggested by a demon.*

ܕܝܘܬܢܝܐ, ܕܝܘܬܢܝܬܐ adj. *in ink, of ink;* ܦܘܫܩܗ ܕ = *the expression of it in writing.*

ܕܝܐܛܓܡܐ διάταγμα, *a decree.*

ܕܝܩܘܢ *a deacon.*

ܕܝܠ a possessive particle comp. of ܕܝ an old form of the rel. pron. ܕ and the enclitic prep. ܠ; is always found with possess. suffixes. It often serves to give emphasis = *own, very,* esp. when preceded by a prep. with the same pron. suff. ܕܝܠܝ *my,* ܕܕܝܠܝ ܐܢܬ *thou art mine;* ܥܡ ܕܝܠܝ *with my own;* with sign. of the accus. ܠܕܝܠܝ *my own, that which is mine;* ܐܢܐ ܕܝܠܝ *I myself;* ܕܝܠܟ, ܕܝܠܟܝ m. and f. *thy, thine, thy own* &c., and so with the other forms; ܕܝܠܗ *his;* ܕܝܠܗ̇ *her;* ܕܝܠܢ *our;* ܕܝܠܟܘܢ, ܕܝܠܟܝܢ *your;* ܕܝܠܗܘܢ, ܕܝܠܗܝܢ *their* m. and f.; ܕܝܠܗ ܐܗܘܐ *I will be his, belong to him, be on his side;* ܕܝܠܗ or ܕܝܠܗ̇ *his* or *her own accord, expense, opinion,* &c.; ܕܝܠܗ ܡܢ ܕܝܠܗ *by the same, of the same;* ܕܝܠܗ̇ ܕܫܢܬܐ—ܕܡܕܝܢܬܐ *of that very* or *same year, of the same city.* Derivatives, ܕܝܠܢܝܐ, ܕܝܠܢܐܝܬ, ܕܝܠܝܬܐ, ܕܝܠܢܝܘܬܐ, ܕܝܠܝܐ, ܕܝܠܘܬܐ.

ܕܝܠ Pael conj. of ܕܘܠ, *to serve* or *attend.*

ܕܝܠܐ rt. ܕܘܠ. m. *a motion* of the bowels; ܕܝܠܐ ܕܡܥܐ or ܫܘܠܐ *diarrhoea, dysentery.*

ܕܝܐܠܘܣܝܣ διάλυσις, *dissolution of partnership, division of goods.*

ܕܝܠܝܐ only found in the fem. form ܕܝܠܝܬܐ adj. *one's own, peculiar;* see below.

ܕܝܠܝܘܬܐ from ܕܝܠ f. *a property, quality* or *attribute.*

ܕܝܠܝܬܐ pl. ܕܝܠܝܬܐ̈ properly adj. fem. but used as subst. It is not found in the older writers such as Ephraem Syrus; *that which is proper, natural* or *peculiar* to any thing or person; *a property, quality, characteristic.*

ܕܝܠܡܐ, ܕܝܠܡܘܣ; see ܕܝܠܠܡܐ.

ܕܝܠܢܐܝܬ adv. from ܕܝܠ *properly, peculiarly, specially, separately; for* or *by himself.*

ܕܝܠܢܝܐ, ܕܝܠܢܝܬܐ pl. m. ܕܝܠܢܝܐ̈, ܕܝܠܢܝܬܐ̈ f. ܕܝܠܢܝܐ̈, ܕܝܠܢܝܬܐ adj. from ܕܝܠ. *own, of his own, especial, peculiar to, particular;* opp. ܓܘܢܝܐ *ordinary* and *special, public* and *private* &c.; ܒܩܢܘܡܗ ܕ *in his own person;* ܐܝܟ ܕܝܠܢܝܐ ܕ *according to its special,* i.e. *allegorical, meaning.*

ܕܝܠܢܝܘܬܐ from ܕܝܠ f. *a property, peculiarity.*

ܕܝܠܬܐ rt. ܕܘܠ. f. *a descent; a swing.*

ܕܝܡܘܣܝܐ δημόσια, *public; the public prison; the public money, taxes* or *tribute.*

ܕܝܡܘܣܝܘܢ δημόσιον, f. *the public treasury, the revenue;* see ܕܝܡܘܣܝܢ.

ܕܝܐܡܛܪܘܢ διάμετρον, *diameter.*

ܕܝܡܘܣ and ܕܡܘܣ δῆμος, *the populace, plebs.*

ܕܝܡܘܣܝܘܢ, ܕܝܡܘܣܝܘܣ; see ܕܝܡܘܣܝܐ.

ܕܝܡܘܣܝܢ δημόσιον, *the public bath.*

ܕܝܡܬܐ f. *a mist;* ܕܛܠܐ ܕ *a fall of dew,* Ex. xvi. 13, 14.

ܕܝܢ pass. part. of verb ܕܘܢ.

ܕܝܢ, ܕܝܢܐ pl. ܕܝܢܐ̈ rt. ܕܘܢ. m. *a) judgement, a judgement, sentence, verdict;* ܒܝܬ ܕܝܢܐ *a tribunal;* ܬܫܘܝܪ ܕ *punishment. b) a law, rule, custom* or *manner. c) a lawsuit, a contention;* ܒܥܠ ܕܝܢܐ *an adversary;* ܓܒܪ ܕܝܢ *a man of strife.*

ܕܝܢ the Greek particle δέ, conj. *but, however, for, then;* cannot begin a sentence, very often immediately follows a demonst. pron., ܗܘ ܕܝܢ, ܗܢܘ ܕ *but he, he however, that is to say.*

ܕܝܢ, ܕܝܢܐ pl. ܕܝܢܐ̈, ܕܝܢܝܢ rt. ܕܘܢ. m. *a judge;* ܣܦܪ ܕܝܢܐ *the Book of Judges; a cadi;* ܕܝܢܐ ܕܐܬܪܐ *a praetor,* often = ܗܓܡܘܢܐ *the governor.* When written without vowels ܕܝܢܐ has a point above the Yod to distinguish it from ܕܝܢܐ = ܕܝܢܐ *judgement.*

ܕܝܢܘܬܐ rt. ܕܘܢ. f. *a judgeship, the office of a cadi; the pronouncing of a judgement, giving of a legal opinion.*

ܕܝܢܘܬܐ rt. ܕܘܢ. f. *judgement*, generally with ܕܬܐܪܬܐ *the judgement of the conscience, conscientiousness.*

ܕܝܢܝ Pehlevi, *a devotee, ascetic.*

ܕܝܢܬܐ fem. of ܕܝܢܐ *a judge.*

ܕܝܢܪ, ܕܝܢܪܐ pl. ܝܢ, ܐ̈ m. *a) a denarius, Roman penny, a silver coin* worth about 8½*d.* in English money. *b) a dinar* generally gold, sometimes silver.

ܕܝܣܢܛܪܝܐ; see ܕܘܣܢܛܪܝܐ *dysentery.*

ܕܝܣܝܣ f. δέησις, *a petition.*

ܕܝܦܛܘܟܘܢ or ܕܝܦܛܘܟܝܢ also ܕܘܦܛܘܟܘܢ and E-Syr. ܕܝܦܬܘܟܝܢ pl. ܕܝܦܛܘܟܐ δίπτυχον, *a two-leaved tablet, diptychs, tablets, a)* on which conciliar canons were inscribed. *b)* on which the names of those to be prayed for by the Church were written. This latter kind of diptych was read aloud during the Liturgy. Dionys. Bar-Salibi, Bishop of Amid, cir. A. D. 1169, says that there were six Diptychs, called by the Syrians Canons, three in commemoration of the living, sc. 1) the rulers of the Church, 2) the clergy and people, 3) kings; and three for the dead, 1) Saints, 2) Doctors and Synods, 3) the faithful departed.

ܕܝܨ Pael of ܕܘܨ; *to exult, to dance.*

ܕܝܨܐ, ܕܝܨܬܐ pl. m. ܐ̈ f. ܕܝܨܝܬܐ rt. ܕܘܨ. an animal named from its agility in leaping, probably *the rock-goat* or *ibex.*

ܕܝܨܐ rt. ܕܘܨ. m. *exultation, leaping for joy, springing.*

ܕܝܩ Pa. of ܕܘܩ; *to regard, gaze upon.*

ܕܝܩܐܘܡܛܐ or ܕܝܩܐܘܡܛܐ δικαιώματα, *legal documents.*

ܕܝܩܘܢܐ pl. ܐ̈ rt. ܕܘܩ. m. E-Syr. *a looker, observer.*

ܕܝܩܘܢܝܐ pl. ܕܝܩܘܢܣ f. διακονία, *a hospital* where the sick and paralytic were ministered to.

ܕܝܪ Pael of ܕܘܪ; *to dwell* &c.

ܕܝܪ, ܕܝܪܐ pl. ܕܝܪܐ com. rt. ܕܘܪ. *a) a cote, fold* for sheep or other animals, *a den. b) a dwelling, habitation, lodge;* ܕܝܪܝ ܡܕܒܪܐ *the camps* of shepherds *in the wilderness.* Metaph. *a mandra, monastery;* ܪܫ ܕܝܪܐ *an archimandrite, abbot.* In this sense ܕܝܪܐ is generally f. with pl. ܕܝܪܬܐ.

ܕܝܪܐ, ܕܝܪܬܐ pl. m. ܐ̈, f. ܕܝܪܝܬܐ rt. ܕܘܪ. *a dweller, inhabitant.*

ܕܝܪܘܢܝܬܐ dim. of ܕܝܪܐ. f. *a little monastery.*

ܕܝܪܝܐ, ܕܝܪܝܬܐ pl. m. ܕܝܪܝܐ f. ܕܝܪܝܬܐ rt. ܕܘܪ. *a monk, a nun;* adj. *monastic,* ܐܣܟܡܐ or ܕܝܪܝܐ ܠܒܘܫܐ *the monastic habit.*

ܕܝܪܝܘܬܐ rt. ܕܘܪ. f. *monastic life;* ܕܕ ܕܘܒܪܐ or ܕܘܒܪܐ *the monastic way* or *manner of life;* ܕܕ ܐܣܟܡܐ *the monastic* or *religious habit;* ܕܕ ܠܒܫܬܐ *the taking the habit by a monk* or *nun.*

ܕܝܪܝܩܘܣ or ܕܝܪܝܩ *a daric,* a Persian gold coin worth about £1 1s. 10*d*.

ܕܝܪܝܢܐ rt. ܕܘܪ. adj.=ܕܝܪܝܐ.

ܕܝܫ Pael of ܕܘܫ.

ܕܝܫܐ rt. ܕܘܫ. m. *a treading down* or *trampling under foot.*

ܕܝܬܐ pl. ܕܝܬܐ and ܕܝܬܐ f. *some unclean bird,* perh. *a kite* or *vulture.*

ܕܝܬܝܩܐ, ܕܝܬܝܩܐ, ܕܝܬܝܩܝ pl. ܕܝܬܝܩܘܣ and ܕܝܬܝܩܣ; see ܕܝܐܬܝܩܐ.

ܕܟܐ, ܕܟܝ fut. ܢܕܟܐ, inf. ܡܕܟܐ, imper. ܕܟܝ, act. part. ܕܟܐ *to be* or *be made pure* or *clean;* pass. part. ܕܟܐ, ܕܟܝܐ, ܕܟܝܬܐ *clean, pure; clean* from ceremonial defilement; *cleansed* from leprosy; ܕܟܐ ܠܒܐ—ܪܥܝܢܐ—*pure in heart—in mind;* ܕܟܐ ܡܢ *free from, lacking.* Pa. ܕܟܝ *to cleanse, purify, pronounce clean* according to the ceremonial law; *to offer a sacrifice for sin; to refine* metals; *prune* vines. Metaph. *to purge out, separate;* ܡܕܟܐ ܠܙܝܙܢܐ ܡܢ ܚܛܐ *he separates the tares from the wheat;* ܡܕܟܝܢܘܬ ܫܢܐ *dentifrice.* Ethpa. ܐܬܕܟܝ *a) to be cleansed, purified, made* or *declared free* from leprosy, from demoniacal possession. *b) to purify oneself* or *be purified* ceremonially. Metaph. *to be made clear, explained.* Derivatives, ܕܟܘܬܐ, ܕܟܝܐܝܬ, ܕܟܝܘܬܐ, ܕܟܝܢܐ, ܡܕܟܝܢܐ, ܡܕܟܝܢܘܬܐ, ܡܬܕܟܝܢܐ, ܬܕܟܝܬܐ.

ܕܟܝܐܝܬ rt. ܕܟܐ. adv. *purely, innocently, sincerely.*

ܕܟܝܘ, ܕܟܝܘܬܐ rt. ܕܟܐ. f. *purification; purity, clearness, transparency* e.g. of the sky; *moral purity, holiness.*

ܕܟܪ fut. ܢܕܟܪ, part. ܕܟܝܪ *to remember, call to mind, be mindful of;* part. *a*) active sense, *remembering,* ܕܟܝܪ ܐܢܐ *I remember. b*) passive, *kept in remembrance, commemorated, rehearsed, recited.* Ethpe. ܐܬܕܟܪ imper. ܐܬܕܟܪ and ܐܬܕܟܪ *to remember, call to mind, have in remembrance* or *memory, make mention of, make a memorial, commemorate.* Ethpe. ܐܬܕܟܪ *to remember, call to mind.* Aph. ܐܕܟܪ *to remind, bring to remembrance, make mention of, mention, rehearse.* Derivatives, ܡܕܟܪܢܐ, ܕܘܟܪܢܐ, ܡܬܕܟܪܢܘܬܐ, ܡܬܕܟܪܢܐ.

ܕܟܪ, ܕܟܪܐ pl. ܕܟܪܐ m. adj. and subst. *male, masculine;* chem. *arsenic; a male,* pl. *the male organs;* ܕܟܪ ܢܩܒܐ *hermaphrodite; a ram* sometimes with ܕܥܪܒܐ or ܕܥܢܐ; *Aries,* a sign of the zodiac; ܐܝܠ ܕܟܪܐ *a battering-ram.* Derivatives the seven following words—

ܕܟܪ denom. verb Pael conj. from ܕܟܪܐ; gram. *to assign the masculine gender.* Ethpa. ܐܬܕܟܪ *to be of the masculine gender.*

ܕܟܪܐܝܬ adv. gram. *masculine, in the masculine gender.*

ܕܟܪܘܬܐ f. *the masculine gender.*

ܕܟܪܢ, ܕܟܪܢܐ and ܕܟܪܝ, ܕܟܪܝܐ adj. m. *masculine, male, virile.*

ܕܟܪܢܘܬܐ f. same as ܕܟܪܘܬܐ.

ܕܟܪܢܝ, ܕܟܪܢܝܐ, ܕܟܪܢܝܬܐ same as ܕܟܪܢ.

ܕܟܪܢܝܘܬܐ f. *the male gender; virility, courage.*

ܕܠ Pe. only participial adj. *a*) ܕܠܝܠ, ܕܠܝܠܐ, ܕܠܝܠܬܐ *thin, fine, rare,* pl. *few* ܠܐ ܕܠܝܠܝܢ ܒܡܢܝܢܐ *not few in number;* ܒܕܠܝܠܬܐ with ܡܠܐ understood, *in few words, briefly. b*) ܕܠܝܠ, ܠܐ, ܠܬܐ *easy, ready* with ܠ of the thing to be done or suffered; with ܠ and an infin. *easy to do, easily* or *readily done;* ܕܠܝܠܝܢ ܠܡܫܬܥܝܘ *easily told;* ܕ ܠܡܬܘܩܕܘ *inflammable;* ܕ ܐܬܐܣܝ *he was readily cured.* Pa. ܕܠܠ or ܕܐܠܠ *a*) *to designate, mention, specify. b*) *to repudiate* e.g. ܩܝܡܐ *a covenant.* Ethpa. ܐܬܕܠܠ *a*) *to be diminished, become rare* or *few, be cut off;* ܐܬܕܠܠܬ ܡܠܬܗ ܕܡܪܝܐ the word of the Lord *became precious* i.e. *rare. b*) *to be designated, indicated, surnamed;* ܡܢ ܩܘܡܐ ܕܐܬܪܐ ܡܬܕܠܠܝܢ *they are named from their countries.* Aph. ܐܕܠ *a*) *to diminish, lessen. b*) *to show.* Derivatives, ܕܘܠܐ, ܡܕܠܠܢܐ, ܕܠܝܠܘܬܐ, ܕܠܝܠܐܝܬ, ܕܠܝܠܬܐ, ܡܕܠܠܢܘܬܐ.

ܕܠ 3 m. s. pret. of verb ܕܘܠ.

ܕܠܐ; see ܠܐ; *that not, lest; without.*

ܕܠܐ fut. ܢܕܠܐ, inf. ܡܕܠܐ imper. ܕܠܝ, act. part. ܕܠܐ, ܕܠܝܐ, pl. m. ܕܠܝܢ, f. ܕܠܝܢ *to draw* water, *to draw* or *drag out* with ܡܢ; ܕܠܐ ܠܢ ܡܝܐ *he drew* water *for us;* ܡܢ ܬܗܘܡܐ ܐܕܠܝܟ *I will draw thee out of the abyss.* Pa. ܕܠܝ *to draw up* or *out, lift up, rescue* from perils of water and metaph. from depths of sin; ܕܠܝ ܐܠܗܐ ܠܝܘܢܢ ܡܢ ܢܘܢܐ God *brought Jonah out of the fish.* Ethpa. ܐܬܕܠܝ *to be led* or *drawn out, to come* or *rise out, escape* from depths of sin or misery; ܒܟ ܐܬܕܠܐ ܕܡܛܒܥ *by Thee may I who am submerged be dragged out;* ܡܢ ܕܐܚܝܕ ܒܗ ܗܘ ܡܬܕܠܐ *whoso holds on to Him is rescued.* Derivatives, ܕܘܠܐ, ܕܠܝܐ, ܡܕܠܝܢܐ, ܡܕܠܐ, ܡܕܠܝܐ.

ܕܠܘܚܢܐ, ܕܠܘܚܢܝܬܐ pl. m. ܢܐ, f. ܢܝܬܐ rt. ܕܠܚ. adj. and subst. *he* or *that which troubles, disturbs, incites to evil; an agitator, instigator;* ܕ ܫܝܢܐ *disturber of peace.*

ܕܠܘܚܝܐ pl. ܝܐ rt. ܕܠܚ. m. *a troubling; tossing* of the sea; *disorder, tumult, commotion, confusion.*

ܕܠܚ fut. ܢܕܠܘܚ, act. part. ܕܠܚ, ܕܠܚܐ *to trouble, disturb, discomfit;* pass. part. ܕܠܝܚ, ܚܐ, ܚܬܐ *ruffled, tempest-tossed; turbid, fouled; blurred;* ܟܬܝܒܬܐ ܕܠܝܚܬܐ *blurred writing;* ܪܕܝܐ ܕܠܝܚܐ ܕܛܘܥܝܘܬܐ *turbid streams of error;* ܩܢܝܢܐ ܕܠܝܚܐ ܕܥܠܡܐ *troublesome worldly goods.* Ethpe. ܐܬܕܠܚ *to be shaken, disturbed, disquieted, ruffled, violently moved* or *agitated.* Pa. ܕܠܚ *to ruffle, agitate, disorder, disquiet, discomfit.* Ethpa. ܐܬܕܠܚ same as Ethpe. ܐܬܕܠܚ ܝܡܐ *the sea became rough;* ܐܬܕܠܚܘ ܒܡܚܫܒܬܗܘܢ *they were agitated in mind.* Derivatives, ܕܠܘܚܐ, ܕܠܘܚܝܐ, ܕܠܘܚܝܘܬܐ, ܡܕܠܚܢܐ, ܡܬܕܠܚܢܐ.

ܕܠܝ Pael of ܕܠܐ.

ܕܠܝܚܘܬܐ rt. ܕܠܚ. f. *the tossing* of waters, *troubled waters,* ܟܕ ܢܚ ܡܝܐ ܡܢ ܕܠܝܚܘܬܗܘܢ *when the waters were at rest again; opacity* of the air, opp. ܫܦܝܘܬܐ *transparency.* Metaph. *disturbance, disorder,* ܕܠܝܚܘܬܐ ܕܫܝܢܐ *discord.*

ܕܰܠܺܝܠ and ܕܰܠܺܝܠ participial adjectives; see ܕܰܠ.

ܕܰܠܺܝܠܳܐܺܝܬ rt. ܕܰܠ. adv. *rarely, scarcely.*

ܕܰܠܺܝܠܳܐܺܝܬ rt. ܕܰܠ. *easily, readily.*

ܕܰܠܺܝܠܽܘ rt. ܕܰܠ. only with ܒ prefixed, *rarely, seldom.*

ܕܰܠܺܝܠܽܘܬܳܐ rt. ܕܰܠ. f. *easiness, facility, disposition, tendency;* with ܪܽܘܓܙܳܐ or ܚܶܡܬܳܐ ܠܟܽܠ *an angry disposition, irritability.*

ܕܳܠܺܝܬܳܐ pl. ܢܳܬܳܐ rt. ܕܠܐ. f. *a shoot, young branch.*

ܕܳܠܺܝܬܳܐ pl. ܢܳܬܳܐ rt. ܕܠܐ. f. *a*) *a varicose vein. b*)=ܕܳܠܺܝܬܳܐ.

ܕܰܠܶܠ Pael of ܕܰܠ.

ܕܰܠܡܳܐ comp. of ܡܳܐ, ܠ, ܕ; *that—not, lest, not;* used after verbs of fearing, *unless, except; it may be, perhaps, perchance; why? whether? is it not? not?* in asking a question when the answer is expected to be negative.

ܕܠܰܦ fut. ܢܶܕܠܽܘܦ, mimet. cf. *drop, drip* and Germ. *tropfen, to drop, trickle down.* Derivative—

ܕܶܠܦܳܐ m. *a dropping, trickling.*

ܕܠܰܩ fut. ܢܶܕܠܽܘܩ, inf. ܡܶܕܠܰܩ, act. part. ܕܳܠܶܩ, ܕܳܠܩܳܐ *to blaze, flame, shine like fire;* ܕܠܶܩ ܫܽܘܒܚܳܐ ܐܰܝܟ ܠܰܡܦܺܐܕܶܐ *glory shone out like lamps.* Pa. ܕܰܠܶܩ *to light, set on fire.* Aph. ܐܰܕܠܶܩ *to light, set light to.* Metaph. *to inflame;* ܐܰܕܠܶܩ ܡܰܕܒܚܳܐ *he kindled the altar fire.* Derivatives the two following—

ܕܠܶܩܬܳܐ or ܕܶܠܩܳܐ pl. ܬܶܐ, ܩܶܐ rt. ܕܠܩ. m. *a flame, blaze, torch, a bright shining;* ܐܰܒܳܐ ܢܽܘܪܳܐ. ܒܪܳܐ ܕܶܠܩܳܐ. ܘܪܽܘܚܳܐ ܫܰܚܺܝܢܽܘܬܳܐ *the Father is fire, the Son the flame, and the Holy Spirit the heat of the fire,* Cod. Poc. in Bodl. Libr. cdiv. 300 r. on the Holy Trinity.

ܕܰܠܳܩܳܐ rt. ܕܠܩ. m. *a glow-worm.*

ܕܰܠܩܽܘܒ denom. verb from ܕܠܩܽܘܒܠܳܐ *to oppose, to be opposed, be in opposition, to contradict;* ܡܕܰܠܩܒܳܐ ܗܳܢܳܐ ܠܗܳܝ ܕܳܐܡܰܪ *this is contrary to what he says.* Ethpaual ܐܶܬܕܰܠܩܰܒ *to be in disagreement, opposed, repugnant; to oppose.*

ܕܠܩܽܘܒܠܳܐ comp. of ܩܽܘܒܠܳܐ, ܠ, ܕ; rt. ܩܒܠ. *that which is in front* or *opposite, opposite, opposed, repugnant; the opposite, the contrary;* ܡܶܢ *on the contrary;* ܗܰܘ ܕܠܩܽܘܒܠܳܐ *the adversary, opponent;* ܕܠܩܽܘܒܠܳܝܗܽܘܢ *his enemies.*

ܕܠܩܽܘܒܠܳܝܳܐ, ܝܬܳܐ pl. f. ܕܠܩܽܘܒܠܳܝܳܬܳܐ *a*) *an opponent, enemy. b*) *the opposite, the contrary,* ܡܶܢ *on the contrary;* logic. *the contradiction* of propositions.

ܕܠܩܽܘܒܠܳܝܽܘܬܳܐ f. *hostility, variance, contrariety;* ܡܶܢ *in the contrary manner;* logic. *contradiction.*

ܕܳܠܰܬ or ܕܳܠܰܬ *Dolath* or *Dalat,* the fourth letter of the alphabet; see ܕ.

ܕܰܡ contr. from ܕܰܠܡܳܐ *lest, that,* after verbs of fearing; *perchance, whether,* in asking a negative question.

ܕܡ, ܕܡܳܐ pl. ܕܡܶܐ m. *blood, bloodshed;* ܐܰܢ̄ܬܬܳܐ ܕܪܳܕܝܳܐ ܕܡܳܐ *the woman having an issue of blood;* ܛܺܝܡܶܐ ܕܕܡܶܗ *the price of his blood,* i. e. *the ransom for his life;* ܦܽܘܪܩܳܢܳܐ ܕܒܰܕܡܳܐ *redemption through blood;* ܒܕܡܳܐ ܕܨܰܘܪܰܝܗܽܘܢ or ܒܕܡܳܐ lit. *with the blood of their necks = at the peril of their lives;* ܩܶܛܠܳܐ ܘܕܡܳܐ *slaughter and bloodshed.* Metaph. *juice, sap* of plants. Derivatives, verbs ܐܰܕܡ and ܕܰܡܕܶܡ, ܕܡܕܡܳܢܳܐ, ܕܡܳܢܳܐ, ܡܕܡܕܡܳܢܳܐ.

ܐܰܕܡ fut. ܢܰܕܶܡ, act. part. ܡܰܕܶܡ denom. verb Aphel conj. from ܕܡ; *to fetch blood, to be imbued* or *sprinkled with blood.* Palpel ܕܰܡܕܶܡ *to bleed,* part. ܡܕܰܡܕܡܳܐ *bleeding, covered with blood.* Ethpalpal ܐܶܬܕܰܡܕܰܡ *to be bloody* or *of the colour of blood.*

ܕܡܳܐ fut. ܢܶܕܡܶܐ, inf. ܡܶܕܡܳܐ, imper. ܕܡܺܝ, part. ܕܳܡܶܐ, ܕܳܡܝܳܐ, pl. m. ܕܳܡܶܝܢ, ܕܳܡܝܳܢ, f. ܕܳܡܝܳܢ, ܕܳܡܝܳܬܳܐ *to be like, resemble.* Part. with ܠ *like, similar;* impers. ܕܳܡܶܐ ܠܗܽܘܢ ܕ *it seems to them;* ܕܳܡܝܳܐ *probably, likely;* ܠܳܐ ܕܳܡܝܳܐ *unlikely;* ܐܰܝܟ ܕܕܳܡܝܳܐ *as it seems, as is likely;* ܘܡܳܐ ܕܕܳܡܶܐ *and the like, and so on.* Ethpe. ܐܶܬܕܡܺܝ *to be* or *become like, to imitate.* Pa. ܕܰܡܺܝ *a*) *to liken, compare* with ܠ; *to estimate. b*) *to imitate, make like, become like* with ܒ; ܡܕܰܡܶܐ ܕܰܡܺܝܬܳܟ *I have supposed a likeness in thee;* ܠܥܳܠܡܳܐ ܠܚܰܩܠܳܐ ܕܰܡܺܝ *he compared the world to a field.* Ethpa. ܐܶܬܕܰܡܺܝ *to be* or *become like, be compared; to feign oneself, to imitate.* Metaph. *to represent, imagine;* ܐܳܣܝܽܘܬܳܐ ܡܶܬܕܰܡܝܳܐ *acting like a physician;* ܡܶܬܕܰܡܶܝܢ ܠܥܰܠܡܳܐ *becoming* like our Lord. Act. part. impers. ܡܬܕܡܝܐ *it seems, it is likely.* DERIVATIVES, ܕܘܡܝܐ, ܕܘܡܝܢܐ, ܕܡܘܬܐ, verb ܕܡܘܬ, ܕܡܝܐܝܬ, ܕܡܝܘܬܐ, ܕܡܝܐ, ܡܕܡܝܢܐ, ܡܕܡܝܢܐܝܬ, ܡܕܡܝܢܘܬܐ, ܠܐܕܡܝܢܐ, ܠܐܕܡܝܘܬܐ.

ܕܡܕܡܢܐ, ܕܡܕܡܢܝܬܐ rt. ܕܡ. adj. *bloody, mingled with blood.*

ܕܡܘܬܐ, ܕܡܘܬܐ constr. ܕܡܘܬ pl. ܕܡܘ̈ܬܐ, ܕܡܘ̈ܬܐ rt. ܕܡܐ. f. a) *the form, shape, figure, type, archetype* = ἰδέα; ܒܪܘܝܐ ܕܕܡܘ̈ܬܐ ܕܟܠ God is *the Maker of all archetypes.* b) *a pattern, plan, example;* ܐܥܒܕܟܘܢ ܕܡܘܬܐ ܒܝܫܬܐ ܠܟܠܢܫ *I will make an example of you for evil to every one.* c) *an image, reflection* in a mirror, *imagination;* ܦܪܘܩ ܠܝ ܡܢ ܚܠܡܐ ܒܝܫܐ ܘܡܢ ܕܡܘ̈ܬܐ ܡܣܝ̈ܒܬܐ *deliver me from evil dreams and wicked imaginations.* d) *a likeness, simile, enigma; constellation;* ܟܠ ܕܡܘ *all manner, every sort* or *way;* ܕܠܐ ܕܡܘ *shapeless;* ܕܡܘܬܐ ܕ; ܕܡܘܬ ܠ =, *like;* ܕܡܘܬܐ ܕܢܡܪܐ *like a leopard;* ܒܕܡܘܬ *like, in the likeness;* ܒܗ ܒܕܡܘܬܐ *in like manner, likewise;* ܒܕܡܘܬܐ *in appearance* opp. ܫܪܝܪܐܝܬ *really and truly;* ܕܒܕܡܘܬܐ *pretended.*

ܕܡܘܟܐ, ܕܡܘܟܬܐ rt. ܕܡܟ. *sleeping;* with ܠܐ *sleepless.*

ܕܡܘܣܝܢ δημόσιον; ܨܒܘ̈ܬܐ ܕܕܡܘܣܝܢ *public* or *state business;* ܒܕܡܘܣܝܢ *publicly;* cf. ܕܡܣ.

ܕܡܘܬ denom. verb Pauel conj. from ܕܡܘܬܐ; *to give a likeness* or *shape;* ܡܕܡܘܬ ܨܘܪܬܐ ܠܙܘܙܐ *it imprints a figure* on the coin. ETHPAUAL ܐܬܕܡܘܬ *to receive the impress of a figure* as a coin.

ܕܡܝ PAEL of ܕܡܐ.

ܕܡܝܐ act. part. fem. of ܕܡܐ.

ܕܡܝ̈ܐ, ܕܡܝ̈ܐ constr. ܕܡܝ̈ m. pl. no sing. *price, hire, ransom;* ܝܩܝܪ ܕܡܝ̈ܐ *precious;* ܪܒ ܕܡܝ̈ f. ܪܒܬ ܕܡܝ̈ *of great price, very precious;* ܕܠܐ ܕܡܝ̈ *priceless, inestimable.*

ܕܡܝܐܝܬ rt. ܕܡܐ. adv. *likewise, equally; likely, probably; apparently.*

ܕܡܝܘܬܐ rt. ܕܡܐ. f. *likeness, resemblance, similarity;* ܠܐ ܕܡܝܘܬ ܛܒܥܐ *unauthenticity of a seal.*

ܕܡܝܐ, ܕܡܝܬܐ pl. m. ܝ̈ܐ, f. ܝ̈ܬܐ, rt. ܕܡܐ. adj. *like, resembling, similar;* gram. *agreeing* in number and gender, *comparative.*

ܕܡܝܪܐܝܬ rt. ܕܡܪ. adv. *wonderfully.*

ܕܡܝܬ = ܕܡܝܐ ܐܢܬ *thou art like.*

ܕܡܟ fut. ܢܕܡܟ, imper. ܕܡܘܟ, act. part. ܕܡܟ, ܕܡܟܐ, verb. adj. ܕܡܝܟ, ܕܡܝܟܬܐ *to sleep, go to sleep, lie down;* with ܥܡ or ܠܘܬ *to come near, lie with.* Metaph. *to die;* ܠܐ ܕܡܟ ܢܘܗܪܗ ܕܚܟܡܬܐ *the light of wisdom never sets;* ܟܕ ܦܠܓ ܡܕܡܟ *half-asleep.* PA. ܕܡܟ *to send to sleep, lull to sleep.* Metaph. *to calm* e.g. ܚܫܐ *the passions.* APH. ܐܕܡܟ *to make lie down, send to sleep, cast into a deep sleep.* Metaph. *to lull, calm.* DERIVATIVES, ܕܡܟܐ, the three following words, ܡܕܡܟܐ and ܡܕܡܟܢܐ.

ܕܡܟ, ܕܡܟܐ pl. ܕܡܟܝܢ, ܕܡܟܐ often used instead of the participle of ܕܡܟ. *sleeping, asleep,* ܕܡܟܝܢܢ *we are asleep; a sleeper;* pl. emph. *the dead.*

ܕܡܟ, ܕܡܟܐ rt. ܕܡܟ. m. *a sluggard.*

ܕܡܟܘܬܐ rt. ܕܡܟ. f. *deep sleep, drowsiness, sloth.*

ܕܡܢܝܐ, ܕܡܢܝܬܐ rt. ܕܡ. adj. a) *of blood, of the same blood;* ܕܡܢܝ̈ܐ ܕܓܢܣܗ *his blood-relations.* b) *bloody, bloodshot;* ܥܝܢܐ ܕܡܢܝܬܐ *an eye suffused with blood;* ܗܝ ܡܥܡܘܕܝܬܐ ܕܡܢܝܬܐ ܕܣܗ̈ܕܐ *that baptism in blood of the martyrs.*

ܕܡܘܣ usually ܕܝܡܘܣ δῆμος, *people, populace.*

ܕܡܣ denom. verb Pael conj. from ܕܘܡܣܐ; *to build, lay foundations.*

ܕܡܣܝܐ δημόσιος, *public;* ܕܡܣܝܢ; see ܕܝܡܣܝܢ.

ܕܡܣܩܝܐ, ܕܡܣܩܝܬܐ m. and f. *Damascene, of Damascus;* see ܕܪܡܣܘܩ.

ܕܡܥ fut. ܢܕܡܥ *to weep, shed tears.* PA. ܕܡܥ *to weep vehemently, shed many tears.* DERIVATIVES the two following—

ܕܡܥܬܐ, ܕܡܥܬܐ pl. ܕܡܥ̈ܐ f. *a tear.* Metaph. *sap* or *resin* oozing out *in drops.*

ܕܡܥܬܢܝܬܐ pl. ܢ̈ܝܬܐ dim. of ܕܡܥܬܐ f. *a little tear, tear-drop.*

ܕܡܰܪ act. part. ܕܳܡܰܪ, ܕܳܡܪܳܐ, ܕܳܡܪܳܬܳܐ, pass. part. ܕܡܺܝܪܳܐ, ܬܳܐ to tremble. Pe. rare except in part. adj. wonderful, marvellous; ܠܳܐ ܕܡܺܝܪܳܐ ܐܶܢ it is no wonder if. Pael ܕܰܡܰܪ to make marvellous. Ethpa. ܐܶܬ݂ܕܰܡܰܪ to wonder, marvel, be amazed with ܒ; seldom passive, ܬܶܕܡܽܘܪܬܳܐ ܗܳܕܶܐ ܗ̄ܝ ܠܺܝ that is a marvel to me. Aph. ܐܰܕܡܰܪ to astonish, cause to wonder. Derivatives, ܕܽܘܡܳܪܳܐ, ܕܽܘܡܳܪܳܐܺܝܬ݂, ܕܡܺܝܪܳܐܺܝܬ݂, ܡܶܬ݂ܕܰܡܪܳܢܳܐ, ܡܶܬ݂ܕܰܡܪܳܢܳܐܺܝܬ݂, ܬܶܕܡܽܘܪܬܳܐ.

ܕܳܢ 3 m. s. pret. of ܕܽܘܢ.

ܕܢܳܐ part. ܕܳܢܶܐ to adhere to a doctrine. Ethpe. ܐܶܬ݂ܕܢܺܝ to assent, agree, follow, obey; to comply with, give way to, feign compliance, dissemble; to apply oneself, with ܠ; e.g. ܠܰܡܫܰܟ݂ܠܳܢܽܘܬ݂ܳܐ to take to loose living; ܠܳܐ ܗ̄ܘܳܐ ܐܶܬ݂ܕܢܺܝ ܠܗܽܘܢ he would not give way to them; ܠܰܟ݂ܬ݂ܳܒ݂ܶܐ ܩܰܕܺܝܫܶܐ ܡܶܬ݂ܕܢܶܐ ܐ̱ܢܳܐ I give assent to the Holy Scriptures. Aph. ܐܰܕܢܺܝ to yield or assent to; with ܢܰܦ݂ܫܶܗ to submit oneself, be compliant, feign compliance; to pretend.

ܕܰܢܳܐ pl. ܢܶܐ m. ܕܰܢܬܳܐ f. a) a thick branch. b) m. only; a wine-jar rounded or pointed at the bottom so as to rest in the earth.

ܕܢܒ Pa. ܕܰܢܶܒ. to make to be the tail, i.e. to put in the last place, make contemptible; to dock the tail, smite the hindmost. Derivatives, ܕܽܘܢܒܳܐ, ܕܽܘܢܒܬܳܐ.

ܕܢܕܠ Ethpalpal ܐܶܬ݂ܕܰܢܕܰܠ. to dangle. Derivative the following—

ܕܰܢܕܠܳܐ m. a centipede.

ܕܽܘܢܒܳܐ, ܕܽܘܢܒܬܳܐ; see ܕܢܒ.

ܕܢܰܚ fut. ܢܶܕܢܰܚ, imper. ܕܢܰܚ, act. part. ܕܳܢܰܚ, ܕܳܢܚܳܐ, pass. parts. ܕܢܺܝܚ, ܚܳܐ, ܚܬܳܐ and ܕܰܢܝܚ, ܚܳܐ, ܚܬܳܐ to rise as the sun, moon or stars, opp. ܥܪܰܒ to set; to break as the day; to dawn or shine upon, shine forth, spring forth, appear, to be manifest, known, illustrious; of frequent metaphorical use, esp. as applied to our Lord; ܥܳܠܡܳܐ ܚܰܕܬܳܐ ܕܢܰܚ ܥܠܰܝܢ a new world hath arisen upon us; ܕܢܰܚ ܫܽܘܥܺܝܬܶܗ ܩܕܳܡ ܝܽܘܚܰܢܳܢ His story was made manifest to John; ܕܢܰܚ ܥܠܰܝ ܡܳܪܝ ܘܶܐܕܢܰܚ ܡܶܢ ܢܽܘܗܪܳܟ ܐܰܝܟ ܐܺܝܡܳܡܳܐ shine forth on me, O Lord, and I shall shine from Thy light as the day; parts. a) old form. ܕܢܺܝܚ risen, shining, radiant, bright, brilliant. b) form. ܕܰܢܝܚ risen; clear, evident, plain. Ethpa. ܐܶܬ݂ܕܰܢܰܚ to appear, be plain, manifest. Aph. ܐܰܕܢܰܚ to make arise, make or let shine; to show forth, manifest, make clear; to give light, show clearly. With ܩܰܪܢܳܐ to make a horn sprout forth = to raise to honour; ܐܰܕܢܰܚ ܢܽܘܗܪܳܐ let light arise; ܐܰܕܢܰܚ ܨܶܒ݂ܝܳܢܶܗ he made his will clear; ܢܽܘܗܪܳܟ ܩܕܳܡܰܝܗܽܘܢ ܐܰܕܢܰܚܬ݁ Thou didst manifest Thy light before them on the Mount of Transfiguration. Derivatives, ܕܶܢܚܳܐ, ܕܰܢܝܺܚܳܐܺܝܬ݂, ܡܰܕܢܚܳܐ, ܡܰܕܢܚܳܝܳܐ, ܡܰܕܢܚܳܢܳܐ.

ܕܶܢܚܳܐ rt. ܕܢܚ. m. the rising of sun or stars, sunrise, dayspring; brightness, light. Metaph. the shining forth or manifestation of our Lord in the flesh, ܥܺܐܕܳܐ ܕܕܶܢܚܳܐ or ܥܺܐܕܳܐ ܕܕܶܢܚܳܐ the Feast of the Epiphany; ܕܶܢܚܳܐ ܕܰܐܠܳܗܳܐ the Theophany, manifestation of God. Astrolog. the ascendant or predominant star, the horoscope i.e. that part of the heavens which arises in the east at the hour of birth.

ܕܰܢܝܺܚܳܐܺܝܬ݂ rt. ܕܢܚ. adv. clearly, evidently, plainly.

ܕܰܢܝܺܚܽܘܬ݂ܳܐ rt. ܕܢܚ. f. brightness, conspicuousness; with ܠܳܐ obscurity.

ܕܢܩ root-meaning to torment. Cognate roots, ܐܢܩ, ܐܢܚ, ܥܢܩ. Ethpe. ܐܶܬ݂ܕܢܶܩ to be in pain, in torment, to be tormented. Pa. ܕܰܢܶܩ to torment. Ethpa. ܐܶܬ݂ܕܰܢܰܩ to be tormented, suffer torments. Derivative, ܕܽܘܢܩܳܐ.

ܕܰܢܩܳܐ pl. ܩܶܐ, sometimes spelt with ̈ or ̇ over the init. ܕ, m. a coin, the fourth part of a dirhem or the sixth part of a ܙܽܘܙܳܐ.

ܕܽܘܪܩܽܘܣܳܐ a partridge.

ܕܰܩܘܣܬܳܐ a kind of millet.

ܕܰܩܘܣܬܳܐ m. a handle, hilt.

ܕܰܥ imper. of ܝܺܕܰܥ to know.

ܕܥܺܝܟ݂ܳܐ, ܕܥܺܝܟ݂ܬܳܐ rt. ܕܥܟ. with ܠܳܐ unquenchable, inextinguishable.

ܕܥܶܟ݂ fut. ܢܶܕܥܰܟ݂, inf. ܡܶܕܥܰܟ݂, act. part. ܕܳܥܶܟ݂, ܕܳܥܟܳܐ, pass. ܕܥܺܝܟ݂ and ܕܰܥܝܟ݂, ܟܳܐ, ܟܬܳܐ to be put out, quenched as fire and light; to be extinguished, suppressed, obscured; to be extinct, past, at an end; ܕܥܶܟ݂ ܐܰܝܟ ܬܶܢܳܢܳܐ he vanished like smoke. Metaph. of ܟܰܦ݂ܢܳܐ famine, ܫܽܘܦ݂ܪܳܐ beauty, ܗܶܪܶܣܝܣ a heresy, ܣܰܒ݂ܪܳܐ hope, &c. Ethpe.

ܐܬܕܥܟ same as PE. PA. ܕܥܟ *to put out* or *quench; to extinguish, suppress, check,* metaph. ܒܝܫܘܬܐ *evil,* ܪܚܡܬܐ *love.* ETHPA. ܐܬܕܥܟ *to be put out, extinct, quenched, quieted.* APH. ܐܕܥܟ *to put out, quench, extinguish; to subdue, abate, allay, assuage.* DERIVATIVES, ܕܘܥܟܐ, ܕܥܟܐ, ܕܥܟܐ, ܡܕܥܟܢܐ, ܡܕܥܟܢܘܬܐ, ܡܕܥܟܢܐ.

ܕܥܟܐ rt. ܕܥܟ. m. *quenching, extinction, abolition.*

ܕܥܨ fut. ܢܕܥܘܨ, act. part. ܕܥܨ *to drive in* a nail; *to fasten, thrust in; to plant;* ܕܥܨ ܚܘܛܪܐ ܒܐܪܥܐ *he thrust* his staff *into the ground.* ETHPE. ܐܬܕܥܨ *to be planted, ingrafted.*

ܕܥܪ fut. ܢܕܥܘܪ, act. part. ܕܥܪ, ܕܥܪܐ, pass. ܕܥܝܪ *to prick, stab.* Metaph. *to irritate, wound;* ܕܠܐ ܢܕܥܘܪ ܚܫܐ ܠܪܥܝܢܟ *lest passion wound thy mind.* ETHPE. ܐܬܕܥܪ *to be irritated, disquieted.* DERIVATIVES, ܕܘܥܪܐ, ܕܥܪܐ, ܡܕܥܪܢܐ.

ܕܥܪܐ rt. ܕܥܪ. m. *a smarting* of the eyes; *an offence, vexation.*

ܕܥܬ fut. ܢܕܥܬ, act. part. ܕܥܬ, ܕܥܬܐ, pass. part. ܕܥܝܬ, ܕܥܝܬܐ *to sweat, perspire; to toil, labour.* PA. ܕܥܬ *to sweat profusely.* DERIVATIVE, ܕܘܥܬܐ.

ܕܦܐ pl. ܕܦܝܢ, ܕܦܐ or ܕܦܐ m. *a board, tablet; a table, wooden altar;* pl. *the leaves* of a diptych, of a book; ܕܦܐ ܕܐܠܦܐ *oars;* ܕܦܐ ܕܢܚܫܐ *brazen leaves.*

ܕܦܢܐ pl. ܕܦܢܬܐ f. *the side* of the body or of a building.

ܕܦܢܐ pl. ܕܦܢܘܬܐ or ܕܦܢܝܣ δαπάνας, *travelling expenses, provision for a journey.*

ܕܦܢܝܢ, ܕܦܢܝܕܝܢ δαφνίδιον, *the laurel.*

ܕܦܦܬܐ E-Syr. *the scab, itch.*

ܕܩ or ܕܩ; see ܕܘܩ.

ܕܩ fut. ܢܕܘܩ, imper. ܕܘܩ, act. part. ܕܐܩ, ܕܩܐ, pl. m. ܕܩܝܢ, pass. part. ܕܩܝܩ, ܩܐ, ܩܬܐ *to beat, to pound* or *bray* in a mortar; *to break in pieces, reduce to powder;* pass. part. *pounded, minute, fine, sifted; slight, least;* ܚܠܐ ܕܩܝܩܐ *fine sand;* ܐܫܬܐ ܕ *a slight fever.* ETHPE. ܐܬܕܩ *to be broken in pieces, pounded, ground up.* PA. ܕܩܩ *to break to pieces, grind to powder;* metaph. ܕܩܩ ܠܡܗܠܟܢܘܗܝ *he made small steps, restrained his steps.* ETHPA. ܐܬܕܩܩ *to be broken to pieces.* APH. ܐܕܩ act. part. ܡܕܩ, ܡܕܩܐ *to break in pieces, beat very small.* PALPEL ܕܩܕܩ *to pound, hammer.* ETHPALPAL ܐܬܕܩܕܩ *to be broken to pieces.* DERIVATIVES, ܕܩܐ, ܕܩܝܩܐ, ܕܩܩܐ, ܕܩܘܩܐ, ܕܩܝܩܘܬܐ, ܡܕܩܢܐ.

ܕܩ 3 m. s. pret. of ܕܘܩ.

ܕܩܐ pl. ܕܩܐ rt. ܕܩ. m. *dry pulse.*

ܕܩܝܩ, ܕܩܝܩܐ, ܕܩܝܩ pl. ܩܝܢ, ܩܐ f. ܩܐ, ܩܬܐ rt. ܕܩ. *small, minute, light;* ܫܘܢܩܐ ܕܩܝܩܐ *light punishments;* ܕܩܝܩܐ *the common people,* opp. ܪܘܪܒܢܐ *the nobles.*

ܕܩܘܩܐ rt. ܕܩ. m. *a pestle.*

ܕܩܘܪܐ, ܕܩܘܪܬܐ rt. ܕܩܪ. *butting, wont to gore.*

ܕܩܘܪܝܘܢ m. *a decurion.*

ܕܩܛܐ δεκάτη, ellipt. *the tenth* indict.

ܕܩܝܩܘܬܐ rt. ܕܩ. f. *minuteness, fineness;* ܕܩܝܩܘܬܐ ܕܟܐܦܐ *stone reduced to powder.*

ܕܩܠ part. ܕܩܠ *to sift, to clean.* ETHPA. ܐܬܕܩܠ *to be cleaned.*

ܕܩܠܐ pl. ܩܠܝܢ, ܩܠܐ m. *a palm-tree;* ܕܩܠܘܢܐ pl. ܢܐ m. dim. *a little palm-tree.*

ܕܩܠܛܝܢܬܐ f. pl. *spots, pocks.*

ܕܩܠܬ m. *the river Tigris.* Cf. Heb. *Hiddekel.*

ܕܩܢ, ܕܩܢܐ pl. ܕܩܢܐ m. *the chin, the beard.*

ܕܩܢܝܬܐ f. *a cave* or *band* of robbers.

ܕܩܢܢܐ pl. ܢܐ *bearded.*

ܕܩܢܘܣܐ pl. ܣܐ m. δεκανός, *a lictor, beadle, runner; a fixed star; a degree* = 360th *part of the zodiac.*

ܕܩܩ Pael conj. of ܕܩ.

ܕܩܩܐ pl. ܩܐ rt. ܕܩ. *a*) *anything broken small* or *beaten up,* ܕ ܒܥܘܪܐ *beaten up yolks of eggs; pulse.* *b*) *a shallow; a little island.*

ܕܩܪ fut. ܢܕܩܘܪ and ܢܕܩܪ, inf. ܡܕܩܪ, pass. part. ܕܩܝܪ. *a*) *to dig, break, pierce through.* *b*) *to stab, thrust, gore* ܒܩܪܢܬܐ *with the horns.* ETHPE. ܐܬܕܩܪ *to be thrust through.* PA. ܕܩܪ *to butt, gore, wound,* metaph. ܟܠܝ ܠܫܢܟ ܡܢ ܕܢܕܩܪ *keep thy tongue from inflicting wounds.* ETTAPH. ܐܬܬܕܩܪ *to fight, to thrust* with the horn. DERIVATIVES, ܕܘܩܪܐ, ܕܩܘܪܐ, ܕܩܪܐ, ܕܩܪܬܐ.

ܕܩܪ, ܕܩܪܐ rt. ܕܩܪ. m. *a stab, a thrust* ܕܪܘܡܚܐ *from a spear;* ܡܚܘܬܐ ܕܩܪܐ *a wound.*

ܕܘܪܫܬܐ pl. ܕܘܪ̈ܫܬܐ rt. ܕܪܫ. f. *a piercing; pleurisy.*

ܕܪܘܫܬܐ rt. ܕܪܫ. f. *fine dust, sawdust, powder.*

ܕܪ act. part. ܕܐܪ pl. ܕܐܪܝܢ *to fight.* Pa. ܕܪܪ *to fight bravely, strive hard,* ܥܡ ܚܘܦܛܐ ܕܪܓܬܐ *with the incitements of desire.* The part. is sometimes spelt ܡܕܪܪ. Ethpa. ܐܬܕܪܪ *to fight, strive.* Derivatives, ܕܪܐ, ܕܪܪܐ, ܕܪܪܐ, ܕܪܪܘܬܐ.

ܕܪ, ܕܪܐ pl. ܕܪܝܢ, ܕܪ̈ܐ rt. ܕܘܪ. m. *a)* eccles. *a procession,* cf. ܕܘܪܐ. *b) the circle* or *revolution* of the year. *c) a generation, an age, a time;* ܕܪ ܘܕܪ *in each generation;* ܡܢ ܕܪ ܠܕܪ *from one generation to another;* ܠܕܪ ܕܪܝܢ or ܠܕܪܕܪܝܢ *in seculum seculorum, for ever and ever;* ܒܕܪܢ *in our age, in our times;* ܒܟܠܗܘܢ ܕܪܝܢ *in all ages, always;* ܕܪ̈ܐ ܣܓܝܐܐ *ages after, long after;* ܠܕܪ̈ܐ ܕܐܬܝܢ *in time to come, in future ages.*

ܕܪܬܐ, ܕܪܬܐ pl. ܕܪܝܢ or ܕܪ̈ܐ or ܕܪ̈ܬܐ rt. ܕܘܪ. f. *an enclosure, a place surrounded by a fence* or *pale. a) a sheepfold, farm-yard, homestead. b) a court* of the tabernacle, temple, of a palace, house, Germ. *Hof, a chamber;* ܕܪܬܐ ܡܠܟܘܬܐ *the royal court;* ܕܪܬܐ ܠܒܪ ܐܦ *a vestibule, open court;* ܠܒܪ ܒܕܪܬܐ *without in the courtyard;* ܕܪ̈ܬܐ ܐܢܝܢ ܕܐܠܗܐ churches *are the courts of God.*

ܕܪܪܐ or ܕܐܪܐ pl. ܕܪ̈ܐ rt. ܕܪ. m. *a wrestling-match; wrestling, striving, struggling, contest;* ܠܘܬ ܚܫ̈ܐ ܐܝܬܘܗܝ ܕܪܢ *our wrestling is against the passions.*

ܕܪܐ fut. ܢܕܪܐ, act. part. ܕܪܐ, ܕܪܝܐ *to scatter, sprinkle; to winnow* corn, cf. ܐܕܪܐ *a threshing-floor;* ܕܪܘ ܥܦܪܐ ܠܥܠ ܠܘܬ ܫܡܝܐ *they sprinkled dust toward heaven.* Metaph. *to lavish;* ܬܕܪܝܘܗܝ ܠܡܣܟܢܐ *thou shalt lavish it upon the poor.* Ethpe. ܐܬܕܪܝ passive; ܥܘܪܐ ܕܡܬܕܪܐ ܡܢ ܪܘܚܐ *chaff driven by the wind.* Derivatives, ܐܕܪܐ, ܕܪܘܝܐ, ܕܪܝܐ, ܡܕܪܘܝܐ, ܡܕܪܘܢܝܬܐ, ܡܕܪܝܐ, ܡܕܪܝܢܐ, ܡܬܕܪܝܢܐ.

ܕܪܒܐ Ar. m. *a way.*

ܕܪܓ, ܕܪܓܐ pl. ܕܪ̈ܓܝܢ, ܕܪ̈ܓܐ m. *a step, stair, degree* of a dial. Metaph. *a state, condition, place, degree, rank, the order* or *degrees* of the ministry; ܗܘܘ ܡܩܒܠܝܢ ܠܡܘܬܐ ܒܕܪܓܐ *they were at the point of death;* ܡܥܠܝ ܕܪܓܐ *of exalted rank* or *position;* ܝܬܒܘ ܐܝܟ ܕܪ̈ܓܝܗܘܢ *they were seated according to their rank;* ܕܪܓ ܡܢ ܕܪܓ *by degrees.* Derivatives the following and ܕܘܪܓܐ.

ܕܪܓ denom. verb Pael conj. from ܕܪܓ; *to step forward, proceed, advance gradually, promote.* Ethpa. *a)* ܐܬܕܪܓ *to step up, march forward; to rise* or *attain gradually* e.g. to honour or knowledge. *b) to be advanced, promoted; to receive holy orders.*

ܕܪܓܠܐ pl. ܐ̈ m. *a heath-cock, partridge.*

ܕܪܓܫܬܐ pl. ܬ̈ܐ f. *a litter; a cradle.*

ܕܪܕܪܐ m. *a vulture.*

ܕܪܕܫ *to foul;* ܡܕܪܕܫܝܢ ܡܐ̈ܢܝܗܘܢ *their filthy garments.*

ܕܪܕܪܐ pl. ܕܪܕܪܝܢ, ܕܪ̈ܕܪܐ m. *a) a thistle. b) ulmus campestris.*

ܕܪܘܝܐ rt. ܕܪܐ. m. *a winnower.*

ܕܪܘܡܐ, ܕܪܘܡܬܐ pl. ܝ̈ܢ, ܬ̈ܐ f. rt. ܕܪܡ. *a) a concubine. b) sucker, layer* of vine.

ܕܪܘܫܐ pl. ܐ̈ rt. ܕܪܫ. m. *a debater, disputant, dialectician, controversialist.*

ܕܪܘܫܐܝܬ rt. ܕܪܫ. adv. *controversially.*

ܕܪܘܫܝܐ rt. ܕܪܫ. adj. *argumentative, dialectical, rhetorical.*

ܕܪܝ, ܕܪܝܐ rt. ܕܪܐ. m. *a winnowing.*

ܕܪܝܟܘܢ or ܕܪܝܟܘܢܐ pl. ܐ̈ cf. ܕܪܝܘܫ *a daric,* a Persian gold coin named from Darius Hystaspes who struck them. It is worth about a guinea.

ܕܪܡܢܐ Pers. *absinth, wormwood.*

ܕܪܟ or ܕܪܟ fut. ܢܕܪܘܟ and ܢܕܪܟ, act. part. ܕܪܟ, ܕܪܟܐ, pass. part. ܕܪܝܟ, ܕܪܝܟܐ, Germ. *treten, eintreten, to tread upon, to tread out* as corn; *to step* or *come out* or *upon; to arrive.* With ܠܘܬ *to force* a woman; with ܕܪܘܡܬܐ *to force* or *strike* scions or layers. Ethpe. ܐܬܕܪܟ *to be trodden, thrashed out;* metaph. *to comprehend, perceive;* ܠܐ ܡܬܕܪܟ *incomprehensible.* Aph. ܐܕܪܟ *to thrash* corn; *to come up to* or *arrive at* whether physically or mentally; *to follow closely, overtake, come upon, seize; to find, attain, obtain; to apprehend, understand;* ܐܕܪܟܬ ܐܢܘܢ ܒܝܫܬܐ *evil came upon them;* ܐܕܪܟܘܗܝ ܟܕ ܚܝ *they found him still alive.* With ܚܝ̈ܐ or ܩܨܐ *to reach* or *come to the end of life.* Ettaph. ܐܬܬܕܪܟ *to be apprehended* &c. Derivatives, ܕܘܪܟܐ, ܕܘܪܟܬܐ, ܕܘܪܟܬܐ, ܕܪܟܐ, ܕܪܟܬܐ, ܡܕܪܟܢܐ, ܡܕܪܟܢܘܬܐ, ܡܬܕܪܟܢܐ, ܡܬܕܪܟܢܐܝܬ, ܡܬܕܪܟܢܘܬܐ.

ܕܘܪܟܐ rt. ܕܪܟ. m. *a step, taking a step.*

ܕܘܪܟܐ, ܕܘܪܟܬܐ rt. ܕܪܟ. f. *the treading out* or *thrashing* of corn; ܬܘܪܐ ܕܕܪܟ ܕܘܪܟܬܐ *the ox that treadeth out the corn.*

ܕܪܡ only Pael pass. part. ܡܕܪܡ, ܡܕܪܡܐ, ܡܕܪܡܬܐ *cunning, crafty, tricky.* Derivatives, ܕܪܡܐ, ܡܕܪܡܘܬܐ.

ܕܪܡܐ pl. ܕܪ̈ܡܛܐ δρᾶμα, *a fable, drama.*

ܕܪܡܘܢ pl. ܕܪܡܘܢܣ f. δρόμων, *a sort of light vessel.*

ܕܪܡܘܢܪܐ or ܕܪܡܘܢܪܝܐ m. pl. dromonarii, *rowers of a dromon, boatmen.*

ܕܪܡܣܘܩ rarely ܕܪܡܫܘܩ pr. n. *Damascus.*

ܕܪܡܣܘܩܝܐ, ܝܬܐ from the above, *damascene.*

ܕܪܥ denom. verb Pael conj. from ܕܪܥܐ; *to steer, rule; to take any one by the arm.*

ܕܪܥܐ pl. ܕܪ̈ܥܝܢ, ܕܪ̈ܥܐ m. *the arm, the shoulder; a sleeve.*

ܕܪܪܐ pl. ܕܪ̈ܪܐ rt. ܕܪ. m. *a wrestler, athlete, warrior, combatant.*

ܕܪܪܘܬܐ rt. ܕܪ. f. *prowess; conflict; a contest.*

ܕܪܫ fut. ܢܕܪܘܫ, inf. ܡܕܪܫ, act. part. ܕܪܫ, ܕܪܫܐ, pass. part. ܕܪܝܫ, ܕܪܝܫܐ, ܕܪܝܫܬܐ (root-meaning *to thresh* or *tread out*) *to tread, find out* or *prepare* a path, with ܐܘܪܚܐ or ܫܒܝܠܐ. Metaph. *to practise, train, instruct,* esp. with ܢܦܫܐ; with ܥܡ *to dispute, debate.* Pass. part. *trodden, worn; common, trite;* ܠܐ ܕܪܝܫ *untrodden, pathless.* Pa. ܕܪܫ *to practise, train, instruct;* ܒܐܘܪܚܐ ܕܚܝ̈ܐ *in the way of life.* Pass. part. ܡܕܪܫ, ܡܕܪܫܐ, ܡܕܪܫܬܐ *practised, trained, learned;* ܡܕܪ̈ܫܝܢ ܒܡܠܦܢܘܬܐ—ܟܬ̈ܒܐ *learned men.* Ethpa. ܐܬܕܪܫ *to be open, trodden* of a road; *to be disputed, debated; to be exercised, trained, instructed,* with ܩܪܒܐ *to be expert in war;* ܒܕܘܒܪܐ ܕܢܙܝܪܘܬܐ *in the ascetic life.* Derivatives, ܕܪܫܐ, ܕܪܘܫܐ, ܕܪܘܫܘܬܐ, ܕܪܫܬܐ, ܕܪܫܢܐ, ܡܕܪܫܐ, ܡܕܪܫܢܐ, ܡܕܪܫܢܘܬܐ, ܡܬܕܪܫܢܘܬܐ.

ܕܪܫ, ܕܪܫܐ rt. ܕܪܫ. m. *treading* or *pounding;* metaph. with ܥܡ or ܠܘܩܒܠ *a disputation, controversy, controversial treatise;* ܒܝܬ ܕܪܫܐ pl. ܒ̈ܬܐ ܕܪܫܐ *a gymnasium, school.*

ܕܪܫܬܐ f. some herb, perh. *cyclamen* or *hellebore.*

ܕܫ 3 m. s. pret. of ܕܘܫ.

ܕܫܢ denom. verb Pael conj. from ܕܫܢܐ; *to give, grant.* Ethpa. ܐܬܕܫܢ *to be given.*

ܕܫܢܐ E-Syr. ܕܫܢܐ pl. ܢ̈ܐ Pers. m. *a gift.*

ܕܬܝܓ *a double-edged blade.*

ܕܬܐ Heb. and Chald. *an edict, judgement, law.*

⁘ ܫܠܡܬ ܐܬܘܬܐ ܕܕܠܬ ⁘

⁘ ܫܪܝܐ ܐܬܘܬܐ ܕܗܐ ⁘

⁘ ܗ ⁘

ܗ ܗܐ

ܗ the fifth letter of the alphabet. The cardinal number 5; ܕܗ ordinal *the fifth.*

ܗ̄ abbreviation for *a*) ܗܢܘ *that is, i.e.* *b*) *Hallelujah,* ܗ̄ܘ ܗ̄ or ܗ̄ܠܠ ܗ̄ *Hallelujah, Hallelujah.*

ܗܐ the letter ܗ.

ܗܐ interjection demonstrative or emphatic *Lo! Behold!* often used in expressions of time *already, now, these;* ܗܐ ܠܬܡܢܬܥܣܪ ܫܢܝܢ ܗܐ ܥܣܪܝܢ ܫܢܝܢ—*Lo these eighteen years, twenty years;* in adverbial expressions of time *here, this,* ܡܢ ܗܐ ܗܫܐ *from this very time;*

ܡܢ ܗܫܐ ܘܠܗܠ *from this time onwards, henceforth;* ܡܢ ܗܫܐ ܘܠܗܠ *henceforward.* With ܕ, ܕܗܐ *for behold, because, already;* ܠܐ ܗܐ interrog.—*not? is it not so?*

ܗܒ, ܗܒܘ, ܗܒܝ, ܗܒܝܢ imperative of verb ܝܗܒ, *give, put* &c.; interj. of encouragement or exhortation, *come.*

ܗܒܒ denom. verb Pael conj. from ܗܒܒܐ; *to bloom, blossom;* metaph. *to flourish, glitter, to be showy;* act. part. ܡܗܒܒ, pass. part. ܡܗܒܒ *florid, adorned, splendid, foaming* as new wine; ܓܘܢܗ ܕܐܦܘܗܝ ܕܡܗܒܒ ܗܘܐ *his complexion which had been florid;* ܡܗܒܒ ܗܘܐ ܒܛܪܦܐ *wreathed* or *garlanded with leaves.*

ܗܒܒܐ pl. ܝܢ, ܐ *a flower, blossom;* ܗܒܒܐ ܕܓܘܢܐ *flowers of various colours;* ܗܒܒܐ ܕܢܚܫܐ *verdigris;* ܗܒܒܐ ܕܡܠܚܐ *saltpetre.* Derivatives, ܗܒܒ verb, ܗܒܒܬܐ, ܡܗܒܒܢܐ, ܡܗܒܒܢܘܬܐ. Cognates, ܐܒܐ, ܐܒܒܐ.

ܗܒܠ, ܗܒܠܐ m. *vanity, emptiness;* ܗܒܠ ܗܒܠܝܢ *vanity of vanities;* ܚܝܝ ܕܗܒܠܟ *thy vain* or *empty life.* Derivatives, ܗܒܠܢܝܐ, ܗܒܠܢܘܬܐ.

ܗܒܠܐ pl. ܐ m. *a herd, swineherd.*

ܗܒܠܐ m. a rare form for ܗܒܠܬܐ; see below.

ܗܒܠܢܝܐ, ܗܒܠܢܝܬܐ pl. m. ܐ f. ܬܐ adj. from ܗܒܠ; *vain, empty,* pl. m. *followers of vanity.*

ܗܒܠܢܘܬܐ from ܗܒܠ. f. *vanity.*

ܗܒܠܬܐ or ܗܒܠܬܐ f. *a herd, drove, line* esp. of camels. Cognate, ܐܒܠܬܐ.

ܗܒܒܬܐ from ܗܒܒܐ. f. *a bloom, blossom.*

ܗܓܐ imper. ܗܓܝ *to meditate* with ܒ of the subject. Ethpa. ܐܬܗܓܝ *to meditate; a) to plan* or *scheme* with ܕ of the intention, with ܥܠ or ܠܘܩܒܠ *against;* ܗܢܘܢ ܐܬܗܓܝܘ *they planned this affair;* ܡܪܕܘܬܐ ܐܬܗܓܝ ܠܘܩܒܠܗ *he plotted rebellion against him. b) to read syllable by syllable, study, brood over;* gram. *to vocalize.* Derivatives, ܗܓܝܐ, ܗܓܝܢܐ, ܗܓܝܐ, ܗܘܓܝܐ, ܡܗܓܝܢܐ, ܡܗܓܝܢܘܬܐ, ܡܬܗܓܝܢܐ.

ܗܓܣ not used in Pe.; root-meaning *to dream, see visions in sleep.* Pa. ܗܓܣ *to imagine, fancy.* Ethpa. ܐܬܗܓܣ *to fancy, imagine, conceive mentally, devise;* ܫܪܝ ܠܡܬܗܓܣܘ ܦܢܛܣܝܣ ܛܢܦܬܐ *he began to conceive foul fancies.* Derivatives the seven following words, ܡܗܓܣܢܐ, ܡܬܗܓܣܢܐ, and ܡܬܗܓܣܢܘܬܐ.

ܗܓܣܐ pl. ܐ rt. ܗܓܣ. m. *an imagination, illusion, idea;* ܥܠܡܐ ܗܢܐ ܕܗܓܣܐ ܘܚܠܡܐ *this world of illusions and dreams;* ܗܓܣܐ ܕܡܢ ܟܬܒܐ *ideas from books.*

ܗܘܓܣܐ rt. ܗܓܣ. m. *a phantom, apparition, appearance, illusion;* ܠܐ ܗܘܐ ܗܘܓܣܐ the ram sacrificed instead of Isaac *was no phantom.*

ܗܓܣܐ pl. ܐ rt. ܗܓܣ. m. *imagination, the imaginative faculty,* the second of the five mental senses.

ܗܓܣܐ rt. ܗܓܣ. m. *delirium, illusion.*

ܗܓܣܐܝܬ rt. ܗܓܣ. adv. *in vain semblance, spuriously.*

ܗܓܣܬܐ pl. ܬܐ rt. ܗܓܣ. f. *a phantom, illusion, imagination; a vain fancy, show* or *pomp; the heresy of the Phantastiasts.*

ܗܓܣܢܝܐ, ܢܝܬܐ rt. ܗܓܣ. adj. *fantastic, fanciful; a Phantastiast.*

ܗܓܡܬܐ rt. ܗܓܡ. m. *ruin, destruction* in the active sense, cf. ܗܓܡܬܐ.

ܗܓܐ rt. ܗܓܐ. m. *meditation; severe suffering.*

ܗܓܝܡܘܬܐ rt. ܗܓܡ. f. *ruin, destruction* in the passive sense.

ܗܓܝܐ pl. ܐ rt. ܗܓܐ. m. *meditation, study, subject of study; reading by syllables* as a beginner, *a syllable;* ܗܓܝܐ ܠܡܩܪܐ ܫܪܝܢ *we began to learn reading;* ܚܕ ܗܓܝܐ *monosyllabic;* ܬܠܬܐ ܗܓܝܐ *trisyllabic;* ܡܫܘܚܬܐ ܕܬܡܢܐ ܗܓܝܐ *octosyllabic metre;* ܩܠܐ ܕܗܓܝܐ *an articulate sound;* ܒܗܘܢ ܒܗܓܝܐ *in these very words.*

ܗܓܡ fut. ܢܗܓܘܡ, act. part. ܗܓܡ, ܗܓܡܐ, pass. part. ܗܓܝܡ *to ruin, destroy, overthrow, break down, hew down.* Ethpe. ܐܬܗܓܡ *to be ruined.* Pa. ܗܓܡ *to break down, ruin utterly.* Derivatives, ܗܓܡܬܐ, ܗܓܝܡܘܬܐ.

ܗܓܘܡܢܐ, ܗܓܡܢ or ܗܓܡܢ pl. ܐ m. ἡγεμών, *a prefect, procurator, governor; hegoumenos* or *prior* of a monastery.

ܗܓܡܘܢܘܬܐ f. ἡγεμονία, *principality, prefecture.*

ܗܓܝܐ pl. ܐ rt. ܗܓܐ. m. *reading, the art of reading; a syllable.*

ܗܓܝܢܐ m. *a dromedary.*

ܗܓܪ pr. n. *Hagar;* ܒܢܝ ܗܓܪ or ܒܢܝ ܗܓܪ *Arabs, Saracens.* Derivatives the three following, ܡܗܓܪܝܐ and ܡܗܓܪܝܘܬܐ.

ܐܰܗܓܰܪ denom. verb Aphel conj. from the above; *to become a Mohammedan, apostatize to Islam;* ܡܰܗܓܪܳܢܳܐ *perverts to Islam.* Ethpa. ܐܶܬ݂ܗܰܓܰܪ the same.

ܗܰܓܪܳܝܳܐ pl. ܝܶܐ m. *a Mohammedan.*

ܗܰܓܪܳܝܽܘܬ݂ܳܐ f. *Islam, Mohammedanism.*

ܗܳܕ݂ (rare), ܗܳܕ݂ܶܐ fem. *this;* ܗܳܕ݂ܶܐ ܗ̱ܝ *this is;* see ܗܳܢܳܐ.

ܗܕܳܐ fut. ܢܶܗܕܶܐ, part. ܗܳܕܶܐ rare in Pe. *to lead, direct.* Pa. ܗܰܕܺܝ *to lead, direct* with ܠ; ܟܽܠܡܶܕܶܡ ܕܦܰܩܶܕ ܠܰܢ ܘܰܡܗܰܕܶܐ ܠ *everything that he hath commanded and directed us* to do. Ethpa. ܐܶܬ݂ܗܰܕܺܝ *to be led, guided;* with ܒܺܐܝܕܳܐ *by the hand; to follow,* with ܒ or ܒܳܬ݂ܰܪ; ܒܝ ܢܶܬ݂ܗܰܕܶܐ *let him follow my example.* Derivatives, ܗܕܳܝܳܐ, ܗܕܳܝܽܘܬ݂ܳܐ, ܗܰܕܳܝܳܐ, ܗܽܘܕܳܝܳܐ, ܡܗܰܕܝܳܢܳܐ, ܡܗܰܕܝܳܢܽܘܬ݂ܳܐ, ܡܶܬ݂ܗܰܕܝܳܢܳܐ, ܡܶܬ݂ܗܰܕܝܳܢܽܘܬ݂ܳܐ.

ܗܰܕܺܐܝܠ a corruption of the Heb. *harel* = mount of God; metaph. *the altar.*

ܗܰܕܽܘܣܳܐ rt. ܗܕܣ. *inquisitive, garrulous.*

ܗܰܕܳܝܳܐ, ܗܰܕܳܝܬ݂ܳܐ pl. m. ܗܰܕܳܝܶܐ f. ܗܰܕܳܝܳܬ݂ܳܐ rt. ܗܕܐ. *a leader, guide, teacher.*

ܗܶܕܝܽܘܛ, ܗܶܕܝܽܘܛܳܐ m. ܗܶܕܝܽܘܛܺܝܬ݂ܳܐ f. pl. m. ܝܶܐ, ܝܺܢ, ܝܶܐ f. ܝܳܬ݂ܳܐ ἰδιώτης, *simple, untaught, ignorant* ܒܰܩܪܳܝܳܐ *of reading;* ܒܝܽܘܠܦܳܢܳܐ *unlearned; stupid, plebeian;* pl. *common people.*

ܗܶܕܝܽܘܛܳܐܝܺܬ݂ adv. *plainly, ignorantly.*

ܗܶܕܝܽܘܛܽܘܬ݂ܳܐ f. ἰδιωτεία, *ignorance, lack of knowledge, want of experience.*

ܗܕܳܝܽܘܬ݂ܳܐ rt. ܗܕܐ. f. *leading, direction; way, manner.*

ܗܽܘܕܳܝܳܐ pl. ܗܽܘܕܳܝܶܐ rt. ܗܕܐ. m. *a leader, guide, teacher.*

ܗܰܕܺܝܪܳܐܝܺܬ݂ rt. ܗܕܪ. adv. *handsomely, splendidly.*

ܗܰܕܺܝܪܽܘܬ݂ܳܐ rt. ܗܕܪ. f. *comeliness, excellence; honour;* ܚܰܝܶܐ ܗܰܕܺܝܪܽܘܬ݂ܳܐ *an honourable life.*

ܗܕܳܡ, ܗܰܕܳܡܳܐ pl. ܝܢ, ܶܐ m. *a limb, member, part of the body;* ܗܰܕܳܡܶܐ ܓܰܠܝܳܢܶܐ *the hands and feet;* ܗܰܕܳܡܶܐ ܓܰܘܳܝܶܐ *the internal organs;* ܗܰܕܳܡܶܐ ܟܰܣܝܶܐ, ܡܰܟܣܝܳܢܶܐ, ܡܶܬ݂ܚܰܫܳܢܶܐ &c. *the genital organs;* ܦܣܳܩ ܗܰܕܳܡܶܐ *mutilation;* ܗܕܳܡ ܗܕܳܡ *limb by limb, piecemeal.* Metaph. *a part* of a discourse, *a part of speech, a word* or *syllable.* Derivative the following—

ܗܰܕܶܡ denom. verb from ܗܰܕܳܡܳܐ; *to dismember, cut in pieces,* pass. part. ܡܗܰܕܰܡ, ܡܗܰܕܡܳܐ, ܡܗܰܕܡܳܢܳܐ. Ethpa. ܐܶܬ݂ܗܰܕܰܡ *a) to be dismembered. b) to be formed* in the womb.

ܗܕܰܣ fut. ܢܶܗܕܽܘܣ, inf. ܡܶܗܕܰܣ, act. part. ܗܳܕܶܣ *to meditate,* hence *to give heed, attend, apply oneself earnestly,* generally with ܒ of the object. Derivatives, ܗܰܕܽܘܣܳܐ, ܗܶܕܣܳܐ.

ܗܶܕܣܳܐ rt. ܗܕܣ. m. *meditation, attention.*

ܗܕܰܪ Pe. only participial adj. ܗܰܕܺܝܪ, ܗܰܕܺܝܪܳܐ, ܗܰܕܺܝܪܬ݂ܳܐ *adorned, comely, acceptable, agreeable, honourable;* ܛܠܳܝܳܐ ܗܰܕܺܝܪܳܐ *a comely youth;* ܐܰܬ݂ܪܳܐ ܗܰܕܺܝܪ ܐܺܝܠܳܢܶܐ *a beautifully wooded country.* Pael ܗܰܕܰܪ parts. same form for act. and pass. ܡܗܰܕܰܪ *to adorn, glorify;* ܐܢܳܐ ܡܗܰܕܰܪ ܠܡܰܠܟܳܐ ܕܰܫܡܰܝܳܐ *I give glory to the King of heaven;* ܠܒܽܘܫܶܐ ܡܗܰܕܪܶܐ *shining garments.* Ethpa. ܐܶܬ݂ܗܰܕܰܪ *to be glorified, honoured; to receive gifts as marks of high esteem, pay* or *receive honour,* ܬܶܬ݂ܗܰܕܰܪ ܡܶܢܰܢ ܒܰܠܒܽܘܫܶܐ ܘܰܫܡܳܗܶܐ ܡܝܰܩܪܶܐ *thou shalt be honoured by us with robes and titles of honour.* Derivatives, ܗܶܕܪܳܐ, ܗܰܕܺܝܪܳܐܝܺܬ݂, ܗܰܕܺܝܪܽܘܬ݂ܳܐ, ܡܗܰܕܪܳܢܳܐ.

ܗܶܕܪܳܐ constr. st. ܗܶܕܰܪ rt. ܗܕܪ. m. *excellency, glory, honour.*

ܗܶܕܪܰܘܠܺܝܣ pl. ܶܐ m. ὕδραυλις, *some musical instrument,* perhaps *a water-organ.*

ܗܽܘ m. ܗܺܝ f. E-Syr. ܗܘ, ܗܝ pl. m. ܐܶܢܽܘܢ f. ܐܶܢܶܝܢ pron. 3 pers. *he, she, it, they; him, her, it, them; he himself, she herself* &c.; *this, that, these, those;* ܕܗܽܘ, ܕܗܺܝ *who, which; whoever, whatever, whosoever, whatsoever, some, some—or other, any one, some one, anything, something;* the pl. is found but less commonly. ܐܶܢܽܘܢ and ܐܶܢܶܝܢ are used after active verbs instead of the pronominal suffixes ܗܘܢ, ܗܶܝܢ = *them.* In poetry the first syllable is sometimes dropped for the sake of the metre, ܢܽܘܢ.

ܗܽܘ and ܗܺܝ are often pleonastic but with emphatic force, esp. with ܕܶܝܢ *but;* ܗܽܘ can stand with another pers. pron. of any number or gender, ܐܶܢܳܐ ܗܽܘ *I myself.* When ܗܽܘ follows an ܐ the ܗ takes linea occultans and the ܘ forms the diphthong *au,* the ' of the ܐ being changed to ' West-Syr.; East-Syr. keeps '; ܗܺܝ and ܝܶܐ form the diphthong *oi;* ܗܽܘ and ܶܐ *eu,* ܗܺܝ and ܶܐ *ei;* ܡܶܢ ܟܽܠܶܗ ܠܶܒܳܐ ܗܽܘ *from the heart;* ܥܰܣܩܳܐ ܗܽܘ *it is hard;* ܗܺܝ and ܗܳܕܶܐ make ܗܳܕܶܐ ܗ̱ܝ E-Syr. but ܗܳܕܶܐ ܗ̱ܝ W-Syr.; ܗܽܘ ܗܳܢܳܐ *the same;* ܗܽܘ ܕ *that which;* ܗܽܘ ܗܳܢܳܐ *this very;* ܚܰܕ ܗܽܘ *one, one only.*

ܗܽܘ often serves as a copula, the ܗ quiescing and the ܘ̇ or ܘܼ coalescing with the preceding consonant; ܐܢܳܐ ܗܽܘ, ܐ̱ܢܳܐܗܽܘ I am; ܐܢ̱ܬ ܗܽܘ or ܐܢ̱ܬܗܽܘ thou art; ܐܢ̱ܬܘܢ ܗܽܘ, ܐܢ̱ܬܘܢܗܽܘ you are; ܕܗܽܘ, ܕܗܽܘܝܘ or ܕܗܽܘ ܗ̱ܘ who is, which is; ܡܢܳܐ ܐܢܽܘܢ ܗܳܠܶܝܢ what are these? ܗ̱ܘ ܡܶܢ or ܡܢܽܘ blessed is he; ܡܳܪܝܳܐ ܠܳܟ for ܠܳܟ ܗ̱ܘ to Thee, O Lord; ܚܰܕ ܗ̱ܘ = ܚܰܕܽܘ he is one; ܡܰܢ ܗ̱ܘ = ܡܰܢܽܘ who is he? who is this? and ܡܳܢܳܐ ܗ̱ܘ = ܡܳܢܽܘ what is this? how is it? ܓܠܶܐ ܗ̱ܘ = ܓܠܶܐܘ it is evident; ܪܰܒܽܘ it is great. ܗܽܘ sometimes represents our definite article the; ܗܽܘ ܗܽܘ generally written ܗܽܘܝܽܘ and ܗ̱ܝ ܗ̱ܝ generally ܗ̱ܝܝ E-Syr. ܗܳܢܰܘ, ܗܳܝܢܽܘ that is to say, id est, the same, that very; ܕܗܽܘܝܽܘ, ܕܗ̱ܝܝ who indeed is, who or which itself.

ܗܽܘ ܗܽܘ m. ܗ̱ܝ ܗ̱ܝ f. pl. m. ܗܶܢܽܘܢ ܗܶܢܽܘܢ f. ܗܶܢܶܝܢ ܗܶܢܶܝܢ the same; ܚܰܕ ܘܗܽܘ ܗܽܘ one and the same.

ܗܰܘ E-Syr. ܗܳܘ or ܗܰܘ f. ܗܳܝ, pl. m. ܗܳܢܽܘܢ f. ܗܳܢܶܝܢ are derived from ܗܽܘ &c., with ܗܳܐ prefixed adding demonstrative force; demonst. pron. he, she, they, that, those; Germ. der, die, das; answers to the Greek def. art.; repeated one—the other, some—some; often used as antecedent, ܐܰܝܟ ܗܳܝ ܕ, ܐܰܝܟ ܗܰܘ ܕ as, as if, as though, in like manner as, so as, as one who, because, considering that, inasmuch as; ܡܶܛܽܠ ܗܳܝ ܕ therefore, on that account; ܐܶܠܳܐ ܒܠܚܽܘܕ ܗܳܝ ܕ unless; ܒܳܬܰܪ ܗܳܝ ܕ after that; ܠܰܡܶܛܳܐ ܠܗܳܝ ܕ, ܠܘܳܬ ܗܳܝ ܕ so that, so far as to; ܡܶܢ ܗܳܝ ܡܳܐ ܕ on that account; ܡܶܛܽܠ ܗܳܝ ܕ because of this. Derivatives, ܗܳܝܢܳܐܝܬ, ܗܰܘܝܘܬܳܐ, ܗܰܘܝܳܐ, ܡܗܰܘܝܳܐ, ܡܗܰܘܝܳܢܳܐܝܬ.

ܗܘܳܐ; see ܗܘܳܝܳܐ.

ܗܘܳܐ fut. ܢܶܗܘܶܐ, apoc. ܢܶܗܘܶܐ, pl. ܢܶܗܘܽܘܢ, apoc. ܢܶܗܘܽܘܢ, 2 fem. ܬܶܗܘܶܝܢ, apoc. ܬܶܗܘܶܝܢ &c., inf. ܡܶܗܘܳܐ, imper. ܗܘܺܝ (the pret. is often used as an imperative esp. in the 2nd pers.), act. part. ܗܳܘܶܐ, ܗܳܘܝܳܐ, pass. part. ܗܘܶܐ, ܗܘܶܝܳܐ, ܗܘܺܝܬܳܐ, pl. m. ܗܘܶܝܢ, ܗܳܘܝܳܐ, f. ܗܳܘܝܳܢ a) the substantive verb to be, to exist; to be, remain or live in a place esp. with adverbs of place; to be sold for with ܒ of the price; with ܒܳܬܰܪ to be with, follow; with ܚܠܳܦ to be instead of, succeed; with ܠ to have, possess; to be for, serve as, be held or considered; with ܠܓܰܒܪܳܐ to marry; ܗܘܺܝ ܢܳܛܰܪܬ beware! take care! with ܥܰܡ to be with, stay with; ܥܰܡ ܢܰܦܫܶܗ ܗܘܳܐ he was alone; with ܥܰܡ to be for one or on his side. b) to begin to be, become, be made, done or wrought, to come to pass, happen; often in exclamations with pron. suffix ܡܳܢܳܐ ܗܘܳܬ ܗܳܕܶܐ what is this? why is this? ܡܳܐ ܕܗܘܳܬ, ܡܶܕܶܡ ܕܗܘܳܬ what or that which has befallen me? ܐܳܦܶܢ ܢܶܗܘܶܐ ܕ even if it happens that. The act. part. is used impersonally, it comes to pass, takes place &c.; when used with pron. 2 pers. pl. is generally contracted ܗܳܘܶܝܬܽܘܢ you are. Pass. part. made, created; ܗܘܳܝܳܐ ܘܙܰܒܢܳܝܳܐ created and temporal; pl. beings, created things, Germ. Wesen, all things that are or that may be created; cf. ܗܘܳܝܳܐ. c) as an auxiliary verb ܗܘܳܐ, with ܗ quiescent, α) with the participle forms the imperfect tense; ܝܳܕܰܥ ܗܘܳܐ he knew; ܡܫܰܡܫܺܝܢ ܗܘܰܘ they were serving; ܗܘܳܐ ܗܘܳܐ there was, Germ. es war; β) with the pret. sometimes equals the aorist more generally the pluperfect, ܐܶܬܳܐ ܗܘܳܐ he had come. d) after ܐܺܝܬ impersonal, there was, there were, Germ. es gab, es war; ܗܘܳܐ is used with a pl. as well as with the sing.; ܗܘܳܐ is often otiose α) after another preterite, ܫܰܪܺܝ ܗܘܳܐ he began; ܠܳܐ ܗܘܳܐ ܕ not that; β) before another ܗܘܳܐ or ܗܘܰܘ; γ) before impersonal ܗܘܳܝܳܐ. Aph. ܐܰܗܘܺܝ to give existence, to create; ܚܰܝܠܳܐ ܐܰܠܳܗܳܝܳܐ ܕܐܰܗܘܺܝܬ ܟܽܠ O Divine power who hast given existence to all things. Ettaph. ܐܶܬܬܰܗܘܺܝ to receive existence or being, be made or created. Derivatives, ܗܘܳܝܳܐ, ܗܘܳܝܬܳܐ, ܡܗܰܘܝܳܐ, ܡܗܰܘܝܳܢܘܬܳܐ, ܡܬܗܰܘܝܳܢܳܐ, ܡܬܗܰܘܝܳܢܘܬܳܐ.

ܗܘܰܢܓܶܠܺܝܘܢ pl. ܗܘܰܢܓܶܠܺܝܢ εὐαγγέλιον, gospel; usual spelling ܐܶܘܰܢܓܶܠܺܝܘܢ.

ܗܘܳܓܳܓܳܐ rt. ܗܓܓ. m. a pretence, a counterfeit.

ܗܽܘܓܳܝܳܐ rt. ܗܓܐ. m. meditation, study, exercise, practice; syllabification, the addition of a letter to facilitate enunciation; a reading or spelling book; ܘܰܘ ܕܗܽܘܓܳܝܶܗ ܕܡܶܠܬܳܐ Wav in the pronunciation of ܡܶܠܬܳܐ.

ܗܽܘܓܢܳܝܳܐ or ܗܽܘܓܢܳܝܳܐ ܓܰܡܠܳܐ pl. ܓܡܰܠ̈ m. a dromedary, a strong camel. Cognate, ܗܶܓܢܳܐ.

ܗܽܘܕܳܝܳܐ pl. ܝ̈ rt. ܗܕܐ. m. a rule, direction.

ܗܘܗܘ rit. abbrev.; see ܗ̄ Hallelujah, hallelujah.

ܗܘܳܝ interj. of grief or sorrow, generally repeated, Alas! alas! woe!

ܗܘܝܐ, ܗܘܝܐ pl. ܐ̈ rt. ܗܘܐ. m. *generation, genealogy, being, birth, origin, existence;* ܗܘܝܗ ܕܒܪܢܫܐ—ܕܥܠܡܐ *the coming into existence of man, of the world;* metaph. *accession* of an emperor, of a bishop; ܡܢ ܫܘܪܝ ܗܘܝܗ *from its first beginning, from its origin;* ܐܬܐ ܠܗܘܝܐ *it came to be, it came to pass;* ܐܝܬܝ ܠܗܘܝܐ *to bring into existence, create;* pl. *substances, things* or *beings already in existence, primary elements* or *existences,* opp. ܗ̈ܘܝܐ *those things* or *beings* which derive from them.

ܗܘܝܢܘ contraction of ܗܘ ܗܘ *i.e., that is to say.*

ܗܘܝܢܘܬܐ rt. ܗܘܐ. f. *the creation.*

ܗܘܟ with ܡܢ *whence is it?* ܡܢ ܗܘܟ ܟܡܝܪ ܐܢܬ *wherefore art thou sad?*

ܗܘܠܐ or ܗܘܠܐ pl. ܗܘ̈ܠܐ, ܗܘܠܐܣ or ܗܘܠܐܣ f. ὕλη, *matter, material, the material part* e. g. of chrism, of baptism; ܥܠܡܐ ܗܘܠܝܐ *the material world;* pl. *material impulses, temptations* or *lusts.* Derivatives, ܗܘܠܢܝܐ, ܗܘܠܢܝܘܬܐ.

ܗܘܠܠܐ pl. ܐ̈ rt. ܗܠܠ. m. *praising, a shout of joy, a chant* or *hymn; a hulala* = one of the twenty sections into which the East-Syrians divide the Psalms; *a hallelujah, a chanting of hallelujah* after a psalm or portion of a psalm.

ܗܘܠܢܝ, ܢܝܐ, ܢܝܬܐ pl. m. ܐ̈ f. ܬ̈ܐ from ܗܘܠܐ. *of* or *pertaining to matter, material, carnal;* pl. *material things;* ܠܐ ܗܘܠܢܝܐ *immaterial, not subject to matter* as angels or the ministry of the Church.

ܗܘܠܢܝܘܬܐ from ܗܘܠܐ. f. *materiality;* with ܠܐ *immateriality.*

ܗܘܢ denom. verb from ܗܘܢܐ; Pael only pass. part. ܡܗܘܢ, ܡܗܘܢܐ, ܡܗܘܢܬܐ *endowed with reason, rational, intellectual, wise.* Ethpa. ܐܬܗܘܢ *to come to one's senses, regain reason, master oneself.* Palel ܗܘܢܢ *to mind, be mindful of, act wisely;* ܗܘܢܢܬ ܥܠ *she behaved wisely towards.* Ethpalal ܐܬܗܘܢܢ *to understand, be understood, be mindful of* with ܥܠ; *to regain one's reason;* ܟܡܐ ܙܒܢܐ ܘܠܐ ܠܡ ܠܐܢܬܬܐ ܕܬܬܗܘܢܢ ܥܠ ܐܪܡܠܘܬܗ *how long is a woman required to observe widowhood for her husband?*

ܗܘܢܐ pl. ܗܘܢ̈ܝܢ, ܗܘ̈ܢܐ constr. st. E-Syr. ܗܘܢ, W-Syr. ܗܘܢ m. *a) the mind, reason;* ܢܦܩ ܡܢ ܗܘܢܗ *he has gone out of his mind;* ܐܬܐ—ܗܦܟ ܠܘܬܗ ܗܘܢܗ *his reason returned unto him;* ܡܠܝ ܗܘܢܐ *intellectual, able;* ܗܘܢܐ ܟܝܢܝܐ *natural capacity;* ܠܐ ܗܘܢܐ *irrational.* *b) sense, meaning; an opinion, dogma;* ܗܘܢܐ ܕܡ̈ܠܐ *the sense* or *meaning of the words.* Derivatives, ܗܘܢ verb, ܗܘܢܢܐ, ܡܗܘܢܐܝܬ, ܡܗܘܢܘܬܐ, ܡܬܗܘܢܢܐܝܬ, ܡܬܗܘܢܢܐ, ܡܬܗܘܢܢܐܝܬ, ܡܬܗܘܢܢܘܬܐ.

ܗܘܢܒܐ = ܗܢܒܐ *an axe.*

ܗܘܢܢܝܐ, ܢܝܬܐ pl. m. ܐ̈ f. ܬ̈ܐ adj. from ܗܘܢܐ. *of, to* or *in the mind, existing in the mind, intellectual;* ܣܓܕܬܐ ܗܘܢܢܝܬܐ *the adoration of the mind;* ܓܠܝܢܐ ܗܘܢܢܝܐ *a revelation to the mind.*

ܗܘܦܐ pl. ܗ̈ܘܦܐ m. *a breath, breathing, puff of air; a vapour, odour; inbreathing, afflatus;* ܗܘܦܐ ܕܚܟܡܬܐ *the breath of wisdom;* ܥܠ ܡܘܫܐ ܫܪܐ ܗܘܦܐ *the divine afflatus rested upon Moses.*

ܗܘܦܘܕܝܩܢܐ pl. ܐ̈ spelt also ܐܦܘܕ, ܗܦܘܕ, ܗܦܘܕ, ὑποδιάκονος, *a subdeacon.*

ܗܘܦܘܕܝܩܢܘܬܐ f. *the office of a subdeacon.*

ܗܘܦܘܬܣܝܣ and ܗܘܦܘܬܣܝܣ ὑπόθεσις, *hypothesis.*

ܗܘܦܘܬܛܝܩܝ adj. *hypothetical, conditional.*

ܗܘܦܛܘܣ and ܗܦܛܘܣ pl. ܗܦܛܘ̈ܣܐ and ܗܘܦܛܘܣ ὕπατος, *a consul, prefect, man of consular rank.*

ܗܘܦܛܝܐ or ܗܦܛܝܐܣ ὑπατεία, *consulship, office* or *rank of a consul; consular largess, a scattering of money amongst the populace* as consuls or emperors were wont to do when on a progress.

ܗܘܦܟ, ܗܘܦܟܐ pl. ܟ̈ܐ, ܐ̈ rt. ܗܦܟ. m. *a going* or *turning back, round* or *about;* hence *a course* or *revolution* of the stars, *a revolving* in the mind, *deliberation, controversy; a manner* or *way of life, conversation, converse, dealing,* often pl.; ܗܘܦܟ ܡ̈ܠܐ *answering back;* legal, ܗܘܦܟ ܢܟ̈ܣܐ *disposal* or *devising* of wealth; gram. *inflection, conjugation.*

ܗܘܦܘܡܢܝܡܛܐ ὑπομνήματα, *acts, records.*

ܗܽܘܦܶܪܶܛܳܐ pl. ܶܐ ὑπηρέτης, *an attendant, inferior officer.*

ܗܽܘܦܰܪܟܳܐ or ܗܽܘܦܰܪܟܳܘܣ pl. ܶܐ or ܗܽܘܦܰܪܟܳܘܣ ὕπαρχος, *a prefect, procurator, governor of a province.*

ܗܽܘܦܰܪܟܺܝܰܐ pl. ܝܳܬܳܐ or ܗܽܘܦܰܪܟܺܝܰܣ ἐπαρχία, *a province.*

ܗܽܘܦܳܕܝܰܩܢܳܐ pl. ܶܐ E-Syr. *subdeacon;* see ܗܽܘܦܽܘܕܝܰܩܢܳܐ.

ܗܽܘܪܽܘܣ *Horus,* an Egyptian deity. εὖρος, *a south-east wind.*

ܗܽܘܬܳܐ pl. ܗܽܘܬܶܐ, ܗܽܘܬܳܬܳܐ f. *an abyss, deep; great cavern;* ܐܽܘܪܚܳܐ ܡܰܠܝܳܐ ܦܰܚܶܐ ܘܗܽܘܬܳܬܳܐ *a way full of snares and chasms;* ܗܽܘܬܳܐ ܕܡܺܝ̈ܬܶܐ *the deep wherein the dead abide.*

ܗܽܘܙܳܙܳܐ pl. ܶܐ m. *a kind of thorn, a bramble.*

ܗ̄ܝ pers. pron. 3 p. s. f. *she, her, this;* see ܗܽܘ.

ܗܳܝ demonst. pron. 3 p. s. f. *she, her, that, the;* see ܗܰܘ.

ܗܶܓܡܽܘܢܳܐ *a governor;* see ܗܶܓܡܽܘܢܳܐ.

ܗܶܓܡܽܘܢܽܘܬܳܐ *a prefecture;* see ܗܶܓܡܽܘܢܽܘܬܳܐ.

ܗܳܝܕܶܝܢ adv. of time, *at that time, then;* ܡܶܢ ܗܳܝܕܶܝܢ *henceforth, after this, afterwards;* ܗܝܕܝܢ same as ܗܳܝܕܶܝܢ.

ܗܳܝܕܶܝܢ contr. of ܗܳܝ ܐܺܝܢ, adv. of time, *then, at that time;* ܡܶܢ ܗܳܝܕܶܝܢ or ܡܶܢ ܒܳܬܰܪ ܗܳܝܕܶܝܢ *from that time, henceforward;* ܥܕܰܡܳܐ ܠܗܳܝܕܶܝܢ or ܠܗܳܝܕܶܝܢ *until now, hitherto.*

ܗ̄ܝܺܘ contr. of ܗ̄ܝ ܗ̄ܝ *that is to say, id est;* ܕܗ̄ܝܺܘ *which is* or *which itself is.*

ܗ̄ܝ̈ܬܳܐ and ܗ̄ܝ̈ܬܳܝܳܐ; see under ܗ̄ܝܽܘܢܳܝܳܐ.

ܗ̄ܝܽܘܬܳܐ from ܗ̄ܝܺܘ f. *state, condition, identity, essence, likeness, mien.*

ܗ̄ܘ ܗ̄ܘܝܽܘܬܳܐ from ܗ̄ܘ ܗ̄ܘ f. *identity, being the same;* with ܒ *in like manner, likewise, in the same way;* ܒܗ̄ܘ ܗ̄ܘܝܽܘܬܳܐ ܫܡܳܐ *by the same name.*

ܗ̄ܘ ܗ̄ܘܢܳܝܳܐ, ܗ̄ܘ ܗ̄ܘܢܳܝܬܳܐ pl. ܝܶܐ from ܗ̄ܘ ܗ̄ܘ adj. *same, of the same nature, identical, equal,* generally with ܙܰܘܥܳܐ *motion* or *movement.*

ܗ̄ܘ ܗ̄ܘܢܳܐܝܺܬ adv. *in the same* or *like manner.*

ܗܰܝܟܠܳܐ, ܗܰܝܟܠܳܐ pl. ܶܐ m. *a palace; a temple, the temple* at Jerusalem; ܗܰܝܟܠܳܐ ܕܩܽܘܕܫܳܐ *the holy temple; a church,* ܗܰܝܟܠܳܐ ܕܩܝܳܡܬܳܐ ܡܳܪܳܢܳܝܬܳܐ *the Church of the Resurrection of the Lord* = the Church of the Holy Sepulchre. E-Syr. that part of a church which is for the people = Eng. nave, see ܬܶܒܶܒܬܳܐ. Metaph. ܗܰܝܟܠܳܐ ܕܢܽܘܗܪܳܐ *the temple of light = heaven;* the B. V. M. is called ܗܰܝܟܠܶܗ ܕܐܰܠܳܗܳܐ *the temple of God.* Hence—

ܐܶܬܗܰܝܟܰܠ denom. verb; ܐܰܠܳܗܳܐ ܡܶܠܬܳܐ ܕܡܶܬܗܰܝܟܰܠ ܗ̄ܘܳܐ ܡܶܢ ܒܬܽܘܠܬܳܐ *God the Word who had,* as it were, *a temple prepared for Him in the Virgin.*

ܗܽܘܠܺܐ and ܗܽܘܠܺܐ same as ܗܽܘܠܺܐ f. *matter, material.*

ܗܰܝܡܶܢ act. part. ܡܗܰܝܡܶܢ, ܡܗܰܝܡܢܳܐ, ܡܗܰܝܡܢܳܢܺܝܬܳܐ, pass. part. ܡܗܰܝܡܰܢ Paiel conj. of ܐܶܡܰܢ see p. 19, *to believe, have faith* or *confidence in, to be faithful, trusted.*

ܗܰܝܡܳܢܽܘܬܳܐ rt. ܐܡܢ. f. In the O. T., *firmness, truth, faithfulness, an office;* ܒܗܰܝܡܳܢܽܘܬܳܐ *truly, faithfully.* N. T. and later, *faith, the Christian faith, religion, doctrine, creed;* ܗܰܝܡܳܢܽܘܬܰܢ objectively *our religion, our belief;* ܗܰܝܡܳܢܽܘܬܳܐ ܬܪܺܝܨܰܬ ܫܽܘܒܚܳܐ *the orthodox faith;* ܗܰܝܡܳܢܽܘܬܳܐ ܕܐܰܪܝܳܘܣ *Arianism;* ܠܳܐ ܗܰܝܡܶܢ *unbelief;* ܒܨܺܝܪܽܘܬ ܗܰܝܡܳܢܽܘܬܳܐ *want of faith.* After another noun it has adjectival force, ܪܳܚܡܳܐ ܗܰܝܡܳܢܽܘܬܳܐ *a true* or *faithful friend.*

ܗܳܪܟܳܐ adv. *here* (rare).

ܗܳܟܰܢܳܐ another form of ܐܰܟܰܢܳܐ *as, so, thus, likewise, as many.*

ܗܳܟܺܝܠ *now, then, thus, so, therefore, for.*

ܗܳܟܰܢ, ܗܳܟܰܢܳܐ *so, thus, in this way, after this manner, likewise, in like manner, such;* ܗܳܟܰܢܳܐ ܘܗܳܟܰܢܳܐ *such and such;* ܥܰܡܳܐ ܕܗܳܟܰܢܳܐ *a nation like this* or *such as this.* With preps. *this;* ܐܰܝܟ ܗܳܟܰܢ *this sort, of this opinion, these;* ܒܗܳܟܰܢ *at this, in this, thereby, thereat, herein;* ܒܳܬܰܪ ܗܳܟܰܢ *after this, henceforward;* ܒܳܬܰܪ ܗܳܟܰܢ ܘܗܳܟܰܢ *after such a time, after a certain time;* ܠܗܳܟܰܢ *to this;* ܡܶܛܽܠ ܗܳܟܰܢ *on this account;* ܥܰܠ ܗܳܟܰܢ *about the matter, on this business.*

ܗܽܘܠܳܐ; see ܐܶܣܽܘܪܳܐ *exile.*

ܗܰܠ; see ܠܗܰܠ *afar, beyond, aforetime, thenceforth.*

ܗܠܠ not used in Pe. Pael ܗܰܠܶܠ *to praise,*

chant praises, sing hallelujahs. Ethpa. ܐܬܗܠܠ *a) to chant, intone; b) to deride, scorn.* Aphel ܐܗܠܠ fut. ܢܗܠܠ or ܢܗܠ, part. ܡܗܠܠ or ܡܗܠ *to deride, mock* with ܒ of the person. Derivatives, ܗܘܠܠܐ, ܗܠܠܐ, ܡܗܠܠܢܐ, ܡܗܠܠܢܘܬܐ, ܬܗܠܠܐ, ܬܗܠܠܬܐ.

ܗܠܝܢ, ܗܠܝܢ unusual forms of ܗܢܘܢ 3 m. pl. *they, them, that, the;* see ܗܘ.

ܗܠܝܒܐܝܬ rt. ܗܠܒ. adv. *swiftly, speedily.*

ܗܠܟ not used in Pe. Pa. ܗܠܟ *a) to go, go on, move forward, proceed, walk, travel. b)* used of time, ܢܗܠܟܘܢ ܫܢܝܐ *let the years go on;* of business, of judgement, ܗܠܟ ܕܝܢܐ *the sentence is pronounced* or *carried out;* of leprosy *to spread. c) to act, behave. d) to make walk, lead.* Ethpa. ܐܬܗܠܟ *to be traversed;* ܛܘܪܐ ܠܐ ܡܬܗܠܟܝܢ *pathless mountains.* Derivatives, ܗܘܠܟܐ, ܗܠܟܐ, ܗܠܟܬܐ, ܡܗܠܟܐ, ܡܗܠܟܢܐ, ܡܬܗܠܟܢܐ, ܡܬܗܠܟܢܘܬܐ.

ܗܠܟܢܐ, ܗܠܟܢܝܬܐ pl. m. ܐ̈ܢ, f. ܝ̈ܬܐ rt. ܗܠܟ. *one who goes on foot, walks, a peripatetic philosopher;* ܚܝܘܬܐ ܗܠܟܢܝܬܐ *animals which walk* on the ground opp. ܡܫܚܝܢܝܬܐ and ܦܪܚܢܝܬܐ *those which swim* or *fly;* ܓܦܬܐ ܗܠܟܢܝܬܐ *a vine trained against a prop* or *tree.*

ܗܠܟܬܐ rt. ܗܠܟ. m. *a going, way, walk;* ܒܝܬ ܗܠܟܬܐ *a walk, passage, corridor.*

ܗܠܟܬܐ and ܗܠܟܬܐ pl. ܬ̈ܐ rt. ܗܠܟ. f. *a going, walking, treading, marching;* pl. *goings, steps, ways;* ܒܝܬ ܗܠܟܬܐ=ܒܝܬ ܗܠܟܬܐ.

ܗܠܠ *to praise;* see ܗܠ.

ܗܠܠܘܝܐ Heb. *hallelujah, crying of hallelujahs;* ܡܙܡܘܪܐ ܗܠܠܘܝܢܝܐ *hallelujah psalms,* i.e. those which begin, Praise ye the Lord.

ܗܠܡܐ pl. ܗܠܡܐ m. usually in the pl. *carved ornaments* on the inner walls of the Temple, perh. *gourds* or *flowers; lattice* or *fretwork;* ܗܠܡܐ ܚܒܝܟܐ *fretwork, chainwork.*

ܗܡܐ not used in Pe. Aphel ܐܗܡܝ *to turn away* or *avert* the eyes. *a) to disregard, neglect* with ܒ or ܡܢ; ܡܢ ܠܡܣܥܪܗ, ܡܢ ܨܠܘܬܐ *to neglect prayer. b) to allow; to delay;* ܐܢܐ ܟܕ ܩܠܝܠ ܐܗܡܝܬ *while I delayed a little.* Ettaph. ܐܬܬܗܡܝ *to neglect, to be neglected, disregarded.* Derivatives, ܡܗܡܝܢܐ, ܡܗܡܝܢܘܬܐ, ܡܬܗܡܝܢܘܬܐ.

ܗܡܝܢܐ, ܗܡܝܢܐ ἡμίνα, *a liquid measure, a hin; a vessel.*

ܗܡܝܢܐ, ܗܡܝܢܐ pl. ܐ̈ܢ Pers. m. *a belt, girdle.*

ܗܡܪܝܐ pl. m. ܐ̈, f. ܝ̈ܬܐ ὅμηρος, *a hostage, envoy; a pledge.*

ܗܡܟܝܠ comp. of ܗܐ, ܡܢ, and ܟܠ, *hence;* ܡܢ ܗܡܟܝܠ *on that account.*

ܗܡܝܢ f. *death* or *the place of the dead;* ܬܒܪ ܡܘܚܠܐ ܕܗܡܝܢ ܫܘܚܠܐ *he brake the bars of gloomy death.*

ܗܡܝܢܟܐ, ܗܡܝܢܟܐ or ܗܡܢܟ pl. ܐ̈ܢ m. *a necklace, neckchain.*

ܗܡܣ fut. ܢܗܡܘܣ, part. ܗܡܣ, ܗܡܝܣܐ. *a) to meditate, muse upon, think upon* with ܒ of the object; ܗܝ ܕܠܐ ܗܡܣ ܒܗ ܗܘܢܐ *that which the mind does not perceive, inscrutable. b) to seek, study, attempt* with ܠ or ܕ; ܗܡܣܝܢ ܠܡܚܘܝܘ *they seek to show;* ܘܢܗܡܣ ܒܛܘܠܗ no one *may attempt the abrogation* of these canons. *c) to attack* with ܒ; ܐܬܪܝܗܘܢ ܗܡܣܘ ܚܕ ܒܚܕ *the two* wild beasts *attacked each other.* Derivative the following—

ܗܡܣܐ or ܗܡܣܐ pl. ܐ̈ rt. ܗܡܣ. m. *meditation, thought, thoughtfulness, a thought; touch.*

ܗܢ, ܗܢܐ m. ܗܕܐ, ܗܕܐ f. ܗܠܝܢ, pl. c. demonst. pron. *this, these; him-, her-, itself;* ܒܗ ܒܗܢܐ, ܒܗ ܒܗܕܐ *in this very . . ., in the same . . .;* ܗܕܐ, ܐܝܟ ܗܠܝܢ, ܗܢܐ *such as this, such as these, of this sort;* ܟܡܐ ܗܢܐ and ܗܢܐ ܟܡܐ *so very, so great, so much, so greatly, all this, to such a degree.*

ܗܢܐ fut. ܢܗܢܐ, part. ܗܢܐ *to be agreeable, grateful, pleasant; to afford pleasure, please.* Ethpe. ܐܬܗܢܝ and Ethpa. ܐܬܗܢܝ *to gain profit* or *enjoyment* with ܒ or ܡܢ. Aph. ܐܗܢܝ *to profit, avail, benefit;* ܡܢܐ ܡܗܢܝܐ ܨܠܘܬܐ *of what good is prayer?* ܡܗܢܝܢ ܡܝܐ ܠܐܪܥܐ *water benefits the earth.* Derivatives, ܗܢܝܐ, ܗܢܝܢܐ, ܗܢܝܢܘܬܐ, and ܗܢܝܘܬܐ, ܗܢܝܐ, ܡܗܢܝܢܐ.

ܗܢܕܐ m. *an axe to hew stone.*

ܗܢܕܘ or ܗܢܕܘܝܐ *India.* The river *Indus.*

ܗܢܕܘܝܐ f. ܗܢܕܘܝܬܐ pl. m. ܐ̈, f. ܝ̈ܬܐ *an*

Ethiopian, Cushite, Nubian, a Hindoo; adj. *Indian.*

ܗܢܕܩܛܐ ἑνδεκάτη, *the eleventh* indict.

ܗܢܕܝܩܛܘܢܐ see ܐܢܕܝܩܛ *an indict*, i.e. a cycle of fifteen years.

ܗܢܘܢ contr. from ܗܘܐ ܠܗ; see ܗܘܐ.

ܗܢܘܢ another form of ܗܢܘܢ; see under ܗܘ.

ܗܢܘܢ; see ܗܘ; demonst. pron. 3 m. pl. *they, them, these; the, that.*

ܗܢܝ, ܗܢܝܐ, ܗܢܝܬܐ pl. m. ܗܢܝܐ f. ܗܢܝܢ, ܗܢܝܬܐ rt. ܗܢܐ. *sweet, fragrant, pleasant, grateful, agreeable;* ܗܢܝ ܪܝܚܐ *sweet-smelling;* ܗܢܝ ܠܟ *does it please you, do you like?* ܗܢܝܐ ܢܝܚܐ ܠܡܫܬܪܕܦܐ (contr. for ܗܢܝܐ ܗܘ) *sweet is repose to the harassed.*

ܗܢܝܘܬܐ pl. ܗܢܝܘܬܐ and ܗܢܝܢܘܬܐ pl. ܗܢܝܢܘܬܐ rt. ܗܢܐ. f. *sweetness, pleasantness, pleasure;* ܪܚܡܝ ܗܢܝܢܘܬܐ *pleasure-lovers, pleasure-seekers, luxurious;* ܪܚܡܬ ܗܢܝܢܘܬܐ *luxury;* ܕܡܟܘ ܒܗܢܝܘܬܐ *they slept sweetly.*

ܗܢܝܐܝܬ rt. ܗܢܐ. adv. *gladly, willingly;* ܗܢܝܐܝܬ ܫܡܥܬ ܗܘܬ ܠܡܠܘܗܝ *she listened gladly to his words.*

ܗܢܝܘܟܐ pl. ܐ̈ ἡνίοχος, *a charioteer, driver.* Metaph. *a cherub,* ܥܡ ܗܢܝܘܟܐ ܡܩܪܝܢܐ *with the cherubim who call upon* Thee.

ܗܢܝܘܟܘܣ ἡνίοχος, a constellation, *the Waggoner.*

ܗܢܝܢ, ܗܢܝܢܐ rt. ܗܢܐ. m. *use, profit, advantage;* ܡܢܐ ܗܢܝܢ *what good is it? what is the use?*

ܗܦܩܛܝܣ, ܗܦܩܛܝܢ or ܗܦܩ ἐπακταὶ ἡμέραι, *epacts, intercalary* days.

ܗܦܪ; see ܗܦܪ.

ܗܦܘܟܐ pl. ܐ̈ rt. ܗܦܟ. m. *changing, wavering, overturning, upsetting, ruin, perversion; return, reversal;* astron. *revolution, retrograde motion;* logic. *inversion;* ܒܗܦܘܟܐ *in inverse order, inversely.*

ܗܦܘܟܝܐ pl. ܐ̈ rt. ܗܦܟ. *perverted, contrary.*

ܗܦܘܪܐ pl. ܐ̈ rt. ܗܦܪ. m. *a babbler, prater, braggart.*

ܗܦܝܟܐܝܬ rt. ܗܦܟ. adv. *adversely, crookedly.*

ܗܦܝܟܘܬܐ rt. ܗܦܟ. f. *retrogression, reflux;* ܗܦܝܟܘܬܐ ܡܪܕܝܬܐ *retrograde motion;* ܗܦܝܟܘܬܐ ܕܝܡܐ *ebb.*

ܗܦܟܬܐ fem. emph. participle of ܗܦܟ = subst. *an overthrow, reverse, ruin; an onslaught;* ܒܚܕܐ ܗܦܟܬܐ *at one onslaught;* pl. *contradictions, contrariety, frowardness.*

ܗܦܣܩܘܦܘܣ, ܗܦܣܩܘܦܐ, ܗܦܣ &c.; see ܐܦܝܣܩܘܦܐ; *an overseer, bishop.*

ܗܦܟ fut. ܢܗܦܘܟ, inf. ܡܗܦܟ, act. part. ܗܦܟ, ܗܦܟܐ, pass. part. ܗܦܝܟ, ܐ̈, ܬܐ. *a) to turn, change, move, return;* ܐܙܠܝܢ ܘܗܦܟܝܢ *going and coming* i.e. *continually;* ܗܦܟ ܫܡܫܐ *the sun went down;* ܚܡܪܐ ܕܫܪܐ ܠܡܗܦܟ *wine that begins to turn;* ܗܦܟܬ ܚܘܒܗܘܢ ܠܣܢܐܬܐ *their love turned to hatred;* with ܒ, ܡܠܬܐ—ܒܡܘܡܬܐ—ܒܡܠܬܐ *to retract, break an oath, one's word, a promise;* with ܠ *to return, give back, restore;* metaph. *to turn, be a pervert, convert,* ܠܡܫܠܡܢܘܬܐ *to Islam;* ܡܢ ܡܓܘܫܘܬܐ *from Magianism;* with ܠܒܣܬܪܐ *to turn back* or *away;* with ܡܢ *to turn back* or *away from* often fig., ܡܢ ܫܛܝܘܬܐ *to turn from folly,* ܡܢ ܚܛܗܐ *from sin,* ܡܢ ܚܡܬܐ *to leave off from anger;* with ܠܘܬ *to change within, return to; to turn upon, attack.* *b)* with acc. or ܠ *to overthrow, ruin.* *c)* ܗܦܟ preceding another verb agreeing with it or with ܠ before the governed verb, has adverbial force, *again;* ܗܦܟ ܫܕܪ *he sent again;* ܗܦܟܘ ܐܬܘ *they came back.* Participial adj. *changed, inverted, upside-down; perverted, perverse, contrary;* ܐܦܐ ܗܦܝܟܬܐ *averted faces;* ܡܠܦܢܘܬܐ ܗܦܝܟܬܐ *perverted doctrines.* Ethpeel ܐܬܗܦܟ *a)* refl. *to turn, turn round* in bed, *spring back* like a bow, *to bow oneself, be moved, change,* often with ܡܕܥܐ *the mind,* ܠܒܐ, ܡܥܝܐ or ܪܚܡܐ *the bowels,* ܐܬܗܦܟܘ ܪܚܡܝܗ ܥܠ ܒܪܗ *her bowels yearned upon her son.* *b)* pass. *to be changed, transformed,* ܐܪܣܢܝܩܘܢ ܡܐ ܕܡܬܗܦܟ *arsenic when it is transmuted;* of wine, *to turn, grow sour.* *c) to be overturned, overthrown, cast down* or *out,* ܢܝܢܘܐ ܡܬܗܦܟܐ *Nineveh* shall be *overthrown.* Pa. ܗܦܟ *to turn, change, overthrow;* with ܐܝܕܗ *to stretch his hand out again,* i.e. *to lay hands on more, continue to seize;* with ܡܠܐ *to exchange words, converse.* Ethpa. ܐܬܗܦܟ *to turn* with ܠܘܬ or ܡܢ of place and person; *to turn about, back, round; to overturn; to go about, do, have to do, be occupied, employed, deal, live* with ܒ of the place, occupation, or mode of life; ܬܓܪܐ ܡܬܗܦܟܝܢ ܒܥܡܠܐ *merchants are busy with gain;* ܡܬܗܦܟܝܢ

ܡܗܦܟܝܢܢ *we live loosely;* also with ܒ *to receive usury;* with ܒܠܒܗ *to turn over* or *revolve in his heart;* with ܥܡ of the person, *to have to do, hold converse* or *intercourse, be intimate with.* Aph. ܐܗܦܟ *a*) *to turn, change; to lead, bring* or *move* from one place to another, e.g. ܥܢܐ *a flock. b*) with ܐܦܐ often also with ܡܢ *to turn one's face away from* = *to turn one's back,* hence *to leave* or *fail, refuse, forsake, to flee; to turn away, forbear. c*) with ܠ or ܠܘܬ *to turn oneself towards; to translate. d*) *to overthrow, upset, subvert. e*) *to bring, send* or *put back, to restore, return, cause to return. f*) esp. with ܦܬܓܡܐ *to return answer, answer, retort* with ܠܗ or ܠܘܬ, with ܫܘܐܠܐ *he brought forward an objection in the form of a question, he retorted with a question.* Derivatives, ܗܦܘܟܐ, ܗܘܦܟܐ, ܗܦܘܟܝܐ, ܗܦܝܟܐܝܬ, ܗܦܝܟܘܬܐ, ܗܦܟܢܘܬܐ, ܗܦܟܐ, ܗܦܘܟܐ, ܗܦܟܐ, ܗܦܘܟܐܝܬ, ܗܦܟܐ, ܗܦܟܢܘܬܐ, ܗܦܟܬܐ, ܡܗܦܟܢܐ, ܡܗܦܟܢܘܬܐ, ܡܬܗܦܟܢܐ, ܡܬܗܦܟܢܐܝܬ, ܡܬܗܦܟܢܘܬܐ.

ܗܦܘܟ, ܗܦܘܟܐ rt. ܗܦܟ. adj. *contrary, rebellious;* pl. f. ܗܦܘܟܝܬܐ *perversions, perversities.*

ܗܘܦܟ, ܗܘܦܟܐ rt. ܗܦܟ. m. *inversion;* with ܒ forms an adverbial expression, *vice versa, on the contrary, in an opposite way, contrary to.*

ܗܦܟ, ܗܦܟܐ rt. ܗܦܟ. m. *a*) *inversion,* ܗܦܟܐ ܕܬܘܩܢܐ *inverse order;* ܗܦܟ ܐܦܐ *averting the face. b*) *overthrow, ruin.*

ܗܦܝܟܐܝܬ or ܗܦܘܟܐܝܬ rt. ܗܦܟ. adv. *bottom-upwards, topsy-turvy, inside out, in reverse* or *retrograde order; preposterously.*

ܗܦܝܟܐ oftener ܗܦܟܐ, ܢܝܬܐ pl. m. ܢܝ̈ܢ, ܢܐ̈ pl. f. ܢܝ̈ܢ, ܢܝ̈ܬܐ rt. ܗܦܟ. *perverted, perverse, retrograde; adverse, contrary.*

ܗܦܝܟܘܬܐ rt. ܗܦܟ. f. *inversion; an objection.*

ܗܦܘܟܢܐ f. ܗܦܘܟܢܝܬܐ pl. m. ܢܝ̈ܢ, ܢܐ̈ f. ܢܝ̈ܬܐ rt. ܗܦܟ. *perverse, bending, bent.*

ܗܘܦܟܬܐ or ܗܦܟܬܐ rt. ܗܦܟ. f. *a return* or *coming again;* ܠܗܘܦܟܬܐ ܕܝܘܡܐ *the next day, the day after,* ܗܘܦܟܬܐ ܕܫܢܬܐ *the year following, the next year.*

ܗܦܟܬܐ pl. ܗܦ̈ܟܬܐ sometimes with a vowel over the first letter from carelessness; rt. ܗܦܟ. f. *a return, a coming back* or *again, a turning aside* or *away;* ܗܦܟܬܐ ܝܗܒ *to turn, flee; a retort, objection* in arguing, usually followed by ܦܘܢܝܐ *the answer* or ܫܪܝܐ *the solution; an opposite argument, an answer, an antiphon.*

ܗܦܠܘܢܐ ἁπλῆ ὠνή, *sale without warranty.*

ܗܦܠܘܣ ἁπλῶς, *simply, hastily.*

ܗܦܪ act. part. ܗܦܪ, ܗܦܪܐ, pass. part. ܗܦܝܪ, ܐ, ܬܐ *to babble, prate, brag.* Derivative, ܗܦܪܐ.

ܗܦܪܟܐ or ܗܦܪܟܐ, ܗܦܪܟܘܣ or ܗܘܦܪܟܘܣ pl. ܗܦܪ̈ܟܐ, see ܐܦܪܟܐ; ἔπαρχος, *the governor of a province.*

ܗܦܪܟܘܬܐ f. *the governorship of a province.*

ܗܦܪܟܝܐ and ܗܦܪܟܝܐ pl. ܗܦܪܟܝܣ *a prefecture, province;* cf. ܐܦܪܟܝܐ.

ܗܪ fut. ܢܗܪ, part. ܗܐܪ *to bark* or *yelp; to quarrel, fight,* with ܥܡ. Aph. ܐܗܪ fut. ܢܗܪ or ܢܗܪ, part. ܡܗܪ or ܡܗܪ *to do harm* or *hurt, molest, annoy, irritate, be at strife;* with ܠܫܢܐ *to whet the tongue.* Also pass. *to be hurt.* Derivatives, ܗܪܪܐ, ܗܪܬܐ, ܗܪܝܢܐ, ܡܗܪܢܐ, ܡܗܪܢܘܬܐ.

ܗܪܓ fut. ܢܗܪܘܓ, inf. ܡܗܪܓ, act. part. ܗܪܓ, ܗܪܓܐ *to muse upon, apply the mind, dwell upon in thought* often with ܡܚܫܒܬܐ *thought,* ܪܥܝܢܐ *mind* or the like as nominative, with ܒ of the object; *to strive after, seek for* preferment.

ܗܪܓܐ pl. ܓܐ̈ rt. ܗܪܓ. m. *study, musing.*

ܗܪܛܝܩܘ *heretics;* see ܗܪܛ.

ܗܪܘܡ, ܗܪܘܡܐ pl. ܡܝ̈ܢ, ܡܐ̈ m. ἄρωμα, *sweet spice, fragrant herb.*

ܗܪܘܡܛܝܩܝܐ adj. from the above. *sweet-smelling, fragrant, aromatic.*

ܗܪܘܡܛܝܩܘܬܐ from the above. f. *aroma, aromatic quality.*

ܗܪܛ imper. of verb ܪܗܛ *to run.*

ܗܪܛܝܩܐ or ܗܪܛܝܩܘܣ pl. ܗܪܛܝܩ̈ܐ, ܩܘܣ or ܩܘ αἱρετικός, *heretical, a heretic.*

ܗܪܛܝܩܝܐ, ܝܬܐ adj. *heretical.*

ܗܪܣܝܛܩܐ; see ܗܪܛܝܩܐ.

ܗܪܟܐ from ܗܪ particle of place and ܟܐ; adv. generally of place but also of time and cause, *here, herein, in this place, now;* ܗܪܟܐ ܗܘ, ܗܪܟܐ ܐܝܬܘܗܝ *here is, it is here;* ܠܗܪܟܐ *hither;* ܡܢ ܠܗܪܟܐ ܡܟܝܠ *hence, henceforward;* ܥܕܡܐ ܠܗܪܟܐ *so far, hitherto, hereunto;* ܗܪܟܐ like our *here below,* is often used to express *in this world, in this life* opp. ܬܡܢ.

ܗܪܩܠܝܢ same as ܗܪܩܠܐ.

ܗܪܩܘܠܝܣ or ܗܪܩܘܠܝܣ pl. ܐ̈ m. *the horse* an instrument of torture.

ܗܪܣܝܘܛܐ m. ܗܪܣܝܘܛܝܬܐ f. pl. m. ܐ̈ f. ܬ̈ܐ *heretical, a heretic.*

ܗܪܣܝܘܬܐ f. *heresy.*

ܗܪܣܝܣ pl. ܗܪ̈ܣܝܣ f. αἵρεσις, *an opinion, heresy, sect, faction.*

ܗܪܪ, ܗܪܪܐ pl. ܐ̈ rt. ܗܪ. *quarrelsome, contentious;* ܐܣܛܘܟܣܐ ܗܪ̈ܪܐ *opposing elements;* legal. *a pleader.*

ܗܪܝܪܐ pl. ܗܪ̈ܝܪܐ rt. ܗܪ. f. *a squabble, brawl, quarrel, dispute, objurgation, controversy, lawsuit;* ܗܪܝܪܐ ܥܒܕ *to strive, contend, brawl.*

ܗܪܬܡܢ *there, thither;* see ܗܪܟܐ and ܬܡܢ.

ܗܪܝܪܢܐ rt. ܗܪ. *contentious.*

ܗܫ, ܗܫܐ from ܗܕܐ ܫܥܬܐ *this hour, this same* or *very hour;* adv. of time, *at present, just now, now, lately, not long since;* ܕ ܗܫܐ *now that, as—already;* ܕܗܫܐ *of to-day, of the present, that which now is;* ܗܫܐ—ܗܫܐ *sometimes—sometimes;* ܡܢ ܗܫܐ *from this time, henceforward;* ܠܗܠ ܡܢ ܗܫܐ or ܥܕܡܐ ܠܗܫܐ *yet, until now, up to the present;* ܩܕܡ ܗܫܐ *before this time.*

ܫܠܡ ܐܬܘܬܐ ܗ

ܫܘܪܝ ܐܬܘܬܐ ܕܘ

ܘ

ܘ the sixth letter of the alphabet, ܘܐܘ or ܘܘ *Vav* or *Waw*, a vowel-consonant, as vowel *u*, as consonant *v* or *w*. The number 6; ܕܘ *the sixth.*

ܘ copulative conjunction *and, also, for, but, yet, however, since, because, that, in order that, then, or, even, again;* ܘ—ܘ *both—and, when—then;* ܘܠܐ or ܘ—ܠܐ *neither, nor, not even;* ܘܠܐ—ܘܠܐ *neither—nor;* ܘܐܠܐ *otherwise, else, if not;* ܘܐܢ ܕܝܢ *and if;* ܘܐܦ *although, nevertheless, so also;* ܘܐܦܠܐ *not even, neither, nor;* ܘܐܦܢ *even if.* ܘ is used very freely and often need not be translated, esp. when with the act. part., or it may be translated by *while, as, then,* ܘܐܡܪ *saying, then he said;* ܘܐܬܐ *coming* or *as he was coming.*

ܘܐܘ or ܘܘ *Vav* or *Waw*, the name of the letter ܘ and of the conjunction ܘ.

ܘܐܘܝܐ, ܘܐܘܝܬܐ adj. from the above, *having a Waw;* ܡ̈ܠܐ ܘܐܘܝ̈ܬܐ *words in which there is a Waw.*

ܘܐܠܐ, ܘܐܠܐ or ܘܐܠܐ *a veil;* see ܘܠܐ.

ܘܒܪܐ pl. ܐ̈, also ܘܒܪܐ and ܐܘܒܪܐ only Lexx. *spawn,* fishes' *roe.*

ܘܗܡ Ar. m. *imagination.*

ܘܗܡܢܝܐ, ܝܬܐ adj. from the above, *imaginative, imaginary.*

ܘܙܐ or ܘܙܐ seldom ܘܙܬܐ pl. ܘ̈ܙܐ f. *a goose* or *gander.*

ܘܙܝܪܐ Ar. m. *vizier, minister of state; vicegerent.*

ܘܙܝܪܘܬܐ f. *viziership, the office of prime minister* or *vizier.*

ܘܪܢܐ pl. ܐ̈ also ܐܘܪܢܐ m. *a cistern* or *bath* generally *of stone, a font;* ܒܝܬ ܘܪܢܐ *the bath-house.*

ܘܝ, ܘܝܐ *a*) interj. of anger, menace, or lamentation = ܐܘܝ. *Ah! Oh! woe! alas!* generally with ܠ, and when expressing grief with ܠ and the pers. pron. suff. ܘܝ ܠܝ *woe is me! alas for me!* so with other persons sing. or pl., often being written in one word ܫܪܒܬܐ ܕܘܝܠܗ *a generation on whom be woe, an accursed generation.* *b*) subst. with pl. ܘ̈ܝܐ, *a woe, misery, misfortune, denunciation;* ܘ̈ܝܗ

ܘܰܝ with ܒ or ܠ *to mourn, make lamentation; to denounce woe,* ܢܪܰܒܶܐ ܘܳܝܳܐ ܥܠܰܝܗܘܢ *let us heap maledictions upon.*

ܘܺܠܳܐ pl. ܘܺܠܶܐ also ܘܶܠܳܐ &c. with pl. ܘܶܠܶܐ or ܘܺܠܘܳܣ f. *velum, a veil, covering, curtain, hanging;* metaph. ܦܰܓܪܳܐ ܘܺܠܳܐ ܗ̱ܘ *the body is a veil.*

ܘܳܠܶܐ act. part. m. ܘܳܠܝܳܐ f. ܘܳܠܝܳܐ, ܘܳܠܝܽܘܬܳܐ *a*) defective verb, used impersonally with ܠ, *it is meet, fit, right, proper, convenient; it ought, it should, it must, it behoves;* with ܠ and pers. pron. suff. *I ought* or *must* &c., ܘܳܠܶܐ ܠܶܗ *he must;* ܘܳܠܶܐ ܠܰܢ *we must* or *should.* The fem. has less direct verbal force and needs the addition of a demonst. pron., ܘܳܠܝܳܐ ܗ̱ܝ ܕ, ܘܳܠܝܳܐ ܗ̱ܘܳܬ ܕ, ܘܳܠܝܽܘܬܶܗ ܗ̱ܝ ܕ *it is right* or *fitting that;* ܠܳܐ ܒܘܳܠܝܽܘܬܳܐ *unsuitably, unseemly. b*) as adv., with prefix ܒ, *fitly, rightly, of necessity, justly, fittingly;* ܒܘܳܠܝܽܘܬܶܗ, ܒܘܳܠܝܽܘܬܳܗ̇ *according to its merit, as it deserves; c*) as adj. ܐܰܝܠܶܝܢ ܕܘܳܠܝܳܢ ܠܡܶܐܟܽܘܠܬܳܐ *things fit for food; d*) as subst. *that which is right* or *due,* ܒܟܽܠܗܶܝܢ ܘܳܠܝܳܬܳܐ obedience *in all due matters, so far as is proper;* hence 1) *dues, customary offerings* or *gifts* esp. eccles., ܘܳܠܝܳܬܳܐ ܕܥܺܕܬܳܐ *the dues of the Church;* ܘܳܠܝܳܬܳܐ ܐ̱ܚܪܳܝܳܬܳܐ *the* last *duties to the departed, funeral rites.* 2) *propriety, decorum, decency;* ܗ̇ܝ ܕܥܳܒܪܳܐ ܬܚܽܘܡܶܐ ܕܘܳܠܝܽܘܬܳܐ *that which transgresses the limits of decorum,* opp. ܢܳܛܰܪ ܘܳܠܝܽܘܬܳܐ *observing decorum;* ܠܳܐ ܘܳܠܝܽܘܬܳܐ *indecorum, impropriety.* Ethpa. ܐܶܬܘܰܠܺܝ *to be fitting, to beseem,* ܢܶܬܘܰܠܶܐ ܠܰܢ *let it be fitting for us.* Derivatives the four following words—

ܘܳܠܝܳܐܺܝܬ from ܘܳܠܶܐ. adv. *fittingly, becomingly, duly.*

ܘܳܠܝܽܘܬܳܐ or ܘܳܠܺܝܢܽܘܬܳܐ rt. ܘܠܐ. f. *fitness, decorum, propriety, accordance with propriety.*

ܘܳܠܝܳܢܳܐ from ܘܳܠܶܐ. adj. *right, fitting, proper;* with ܠܳܐ *unworthy, unmeet, unseemly.*

ܘܳܠܝܽܘܬܳܐ; see under ܘܠܐ.

ܘܺܠܘܳܣ pl. of ܘܺܠܳܐ.

ܘܰܡܦܳܐ pl. ܶܐ *a stocking.*

ܘܰܣܦܳܐ m. *a captive, slave; a heavy burthen.*

ܘܰܣܦܽܘܬܳܐ f. *bondage, slavery;* ܢܺܝܪ ܘܰܣܦܽܘܬܳܐ *the yoke of bondage.*

ܘܰܥܶܕ denom. verb Pael conj. from ܘܰܥܕܳܐ; *to appoint a time* or *place for meeting, to meet, gather together,* ܠܛܽܘܪܳܐ ܕܘܰܥܶܕ ܐܶܢܽܘܢ ܝܶܫܽܘܥ the disciples met *at the mount which Jesus had appointed.* Ethpa. ܐܶܬܘܰܥܰܕ with ܠ, ܠܘܳܬ or ܥܰܡ *to meet at a fixed time* or *place, to come together, assemble, join with, be present;* ܐܶܬܘܰܥܰܕܘ ܒܢܰܝ ܐܺܝܣܪܳܝܶܠ ܠܩܪܳܒܳܐ *the Children of Israel assembled to war;* ܐܶܬܘܰܥܰܕ ܠܟܢܽܘܫܝܳܐ *he was present at the council.*

ܘܰܥܕܳܐ pl. ܶܐ m. *a*) *an appointed time, signal* or *place,* ܕܘܟܬܳܐ ܕܘܰܥܕܳܐ *a trysting-place, rendez-vous;* with ܝܰܗ݈ܒ *donner rendez-vous, to agree to meet. b*) *something agreed upon* or *promised, an agreement, a pledge,* ܘܰܥܕܳܐ ܕܡܽܘܠܟܳܢܶܐ ܫܡܰܝܳܢܶܐ *a pledge of heavenly promises. c*) *a place, space, term, boundary, approach,* ܘܰܥܕܳܐ ܕܠܶܡܺܐܢܳܐ *entrance to the port;* ܐܶܬܶܐ ܠܘܰܥܕܳܐ ܕܪ̈ܰܚܡܰܝܟ *I shall find access to Thy mercy,* with ܒ or ܠ *near, close by, towards,* ܠܘܰܥܕܳܐ ܕܒܶܝܬ ܠܚܶܡ *near Bethlehem;* ܢܦܰܩܘ ܠܘܰܥܕܗܽܘܢ *they went towards them, to meet them;* ܘܰܥܕܳܐ ܕ or ܠܘܰܥܕܳܐ ܕ *nearly, about,* ܘܰܥܕܳܐ ܕܬܪ̈ܶܝܢ ܫܢܺܝܢ *a space of two years;* ܡܛܳܐ ܛܰܠܝܳܐ ܠܘܰܥܕܳܐ ܕܬܪܰܥܣܰܪ ܫܢܺܝܢ *the boy drew near the term of twelve years;* ܠܘܰܥܕܳܐ ܕܡܳܐܐ ܫܢܺܝܢ *about* 100 *years.*

ܘܰܦܳܐ perhaps ὄψ, ὄπα, *speech.*

ܘܰܩܦ Ar. *a pious bequest, endowment* of a monastery.

ܘܰܪܕܳܐ pl. ܘܰܪ̈ܕܶܐ m. *the rose;* ܡܰܝ̈ܳܐ ܕܘܰܪܕܳܐ *rose-water,* ܘܰܪܕܳܐ ܕܒܰܪܳܐ *anemone coronaria;* chem. *films* or *skins* forming on the surface of a liquid.

ܘܰܪܕܳܢܳܝܳܐ adj. from ܘܰܪܕܳܐ. *rosy, rosaceous, of a rose.*

ܘܰܪܕܽܘܦܳܐ m. *merops, the bee-eater* bird.

ܘܰܪܙܳܐ pl. ܶܐ m. *a wild boar.*

ܘܰܪܝܳܕܳܐ Ar. pl. ܶܐ m. *a vein; a root* or *fibre* of a tree.

ܘܰܪܩܳܐ or ܘܰܪܩܬܳܐ pl. ܘܰܪ̈ܩܶܐ f. *a page, leaf* or *sheet;* ܘܰܪ̈ܩܶܐ ܕܣܺܐܡܳܐ *sheets of silver.*

✣ ܫܠܡܬ ܐܬܘܬܐ ✣

⁘ ܐܬܐ ܙܝܢ ܣܠܩܬ: ܚܠܐ ܕܒܝܫܝ ܐܠܗܐ ܗܕܪ ܘܡܟܪ ܠܫܡܝܟܘܬܐ ⁘

⁘ ܙ ⁘

ܙ the seventh letter of the Syriac alphabet, *Zain*, spelt variously ܙܝܢ, ܙܝ, ܙܐ, ܙܝܐ, and ܙܝܢ; the number 7; ܙ̈ *the seventh;* ܙ̱ 7000.

ܙܐܛܡܛܐ or ܙܐܛܡܛܐ pl. ܙܐܛܡܛܐ̈, ܙܐܛܡܛܐ or ܙܐܛܡܛܐܝܬ; see ܙܛܡܛܐ. m. *inquiry, accusation, fault.*

ܙܐܦܐ pl. ܙܐܦܝܢ rt. ܙܘܦ. m. *fraud, wile, deceit, dissimulation;* ܕܙܐܦܐ *counterfeit, fraudulent, deceitful, sham, false, simulated,* —ܚܘܒܐ ܕܙܐܦܐ ܘܗܝܡܢܘܬܐ *false love, simulated faith;* ܡܠܦܢܐ ܕܙܐܦܐ *teachers of false doctrine.*

ܙܐܦܢܐ, ܙܐܦܢܝܬܐ pl. m. ܢ̈ܐ f. ܢܝ̈ܬܐ rt. ܙܘܦ. *counterfeit, forged* as coin; metaph. *false* esp. of teaching, with ܠܐ *guileless, unfeigned,* ܣܐܡ ܙܐܦܢܐ ܚܠܦ ܫܪܝܪܐ *he puts the false for the true;* ܠܒܐ ܠܐ ܙܐܦܢܐ *a sincere heart.*

ܙܐܦܢܐܝܬ, ܙܐܦܐ or ܙܐܦ rt. ܙܘܦ. adv. *fraudulently, deceitfully.*

ܙܐܦܢܘܬܐ rt. ܙܘܦ. f. *dissimulation, deceitfulness, pretence.*

ܙܐܦܢܝ, ܙܐܦܢܝܐ, ܙܐܦܢܝܬܐ rt. ܙܘܦ. adj. *worthless, useless, dishonest, clandestine;* with ܠܐ *unfeigned, sincere.*

ܙܒܐ pl. ܙܒܣ and ܙܒܐܣ ζάβα, *a coat of mail, cuirass.*

ܙܒܕ *to endow, give a dowry.* DERIVATIVE the following—

ܙܒܕܐ pl. ܐ̈ m. *a dowry, marriage portion.*

ܙܒܘܢܐ pl. ܢ̈ܐ rt. ܙܒܢ. *a buyer, purchaser.*

ܙܒܘܪܐ or ܙܒܪܐ pl. ܙܒܪ̈ܐ, ܐ̈ m. *a pan, paten, dish, jar, vessel.*

ܙܒܝܠܐ *a basket made of rushes* or *palm-leaves;* cf. ܙܒܝܠܐ.

ܙܒܝܢܬܐ pl. ܢܬ̈ܐ rt. ܙܒܢ. f. *a purchase, possession; sale, price, ransom;* ܕܙܒܝܢܬܐ *acquired by purchase* opp. ܝܪܘܬܘܬܐ *inherited;* ܫܛܪ̈ܐ ܕܙܒܝܢܬܐ *deeds of purchase;* ܙܒܝܢ̈ܬܐ ܕܫܒܝܐ *ransoms of captives.*

ܙܒܠ, ܙܒܠܐ m. *dung, excrement; a dung-heap;* ܙܒܠܐ ܚܕܬܐ *new manure.* DERIVATIVES, verb ܙܒܠ, ܙܒܠܐ.

ܙܒܠ denom. verb Pael conj. from ܙܒܠܐ; *to dung, to manure.* ETHPA. ܐܙܕܒܠ *to be manured;* ܐܪܥܐ ܡܙܕܒܠܐ *manured ground.* APH. ܐܙܒܠ same as PE.

ܙܒܢ fut. ܢܙܒܢ, inf. ܡܙܒܢ, imper. ܙܒܢ, act. part. ܙܒܢ, ܙܒܢܐ, pass. part. ܙܒܝܢ, ܙܒܝܢܐ, ܙܒܝܢܬܐ *to buy, buy off, ransom, redeem;* ܙܒܢܘ ܢܦܫܗܘܢ ܫܬܐ ܡ̈ܢܝܢ ܕܕܗܒܐ *they paid six measures of gold for their ransom;* ܟܕ ܙܒܢ ܩܢܘܡܐ ܡܫܝܚܐ ܙܒܢܢ ܡܢ ܠܘܛܬܐ ܕܢܡܘܣܐ *Christ hath redeemed us from the curse of the law;* past part. ܥܒܕܐ ܙܒܝܢܐ *a bought slave;* ܙܒܝܢܐ ܒܕܡܐ *redeemed with blood;* cf. ܙܒܝܢܬܐ. ETHPE. ܐܙܕܒܢ *to be bought.* PA. ܙܒܢ *to sell* with ܠ of the object and ܒ of the price; *to accept a ransom.* Act. part. selling = *a merchant,* ܡܙܒܢ ܐܪܓܘܢܐ *a seller of purple;* ܡܙܒܢ ܥܡܝܪܐ *a hay-dealer.* ETHPA. ܐܙܕܒܢ *to be sold,* ܠܐ ܬܪܝܢ ܨܦܪ̈ܝܢ ܡܙܕܒܢܝܢ ܒܐܣܪ *are not two sparrows sold for a farthing?* DERIVATIVES, ܙܒܘܢܐ, ܙܒܝܢܬܐ, ܙܒܢܐ, ܙܒܘܢܐ, ܡܙܒܢܢܐ, ܡܙܒܢܢܘܬܐ.

ܙܒܢ, ܙܒܢܐ pl. ܙܒܢܝܢ, ܙܒ̈ܢܐ m. *time, a space of time; an age, epoch, era,* ܙܒ̈ܢܐ ܘܥܕܢ̈ܐ *times and seasons;* ܩܘܝ ܬܡܢ ܙܒܢܐ ܙܥܘܪܐ *he remained a while in that place;* ܒܙܒܢܐ ܕܬܠܬ ܫܢܝܢ *within three years;* ܙܒܢܐ ܕܪܡܫܐ *eventide;* ܒܙܒܢܐ ܕܐܒܝܒܐ *in the month of Abib;* ܙܒܢܐ ܢܝܣܢܝܐ *season of Nisan = spring-time;* ܙ ܬܫܪܝܢܝܐ *autumn;* ܠܐ ܗܘ ܙܒܢܐ *he is younger;* ܒܢܝ̈ ܙܒܢܐ *of the same age, contemporaries;*

ܙܒܢܐ ܕܢܘܚ *the Noachian era;* ܙܒܢܐ ܡܢ ܙܒܢܐ *in successive ages;* ܡܟܬܒܢܘܬ ܙܒܢܐ *a chronicle;* often = *the present age* opp. the life to come and so ܕܙܒܢܐ *temporal* opp. ܕܠܥܠܡ *eternal;* ܚܝܐ ܕܙܒܢܐ *this present life,* ܥܠܡܐ ܕܙܒܢܐ *the temporal world,* ܫܠܝܛܢܐ ܕܙܒܢܐ *secular rulers;* ܕܠܦܘܬ ܙܒܢܐ *temporary;* ܡܫܟܢ ܙܒܢܐ *the tabernacle;* gram. ܙܒܢܐ ܥܒܪ: ܩܐܡ ܘܥܬܝܕ *past, present, and future tense.* With preps. ܒܙܒܢܐ ܗܘ *at that time, then,* ܒܙܒܢܐ ܕ *when,* ܒܙܒܢܐ ܐܚܪܢ *at another time, again;* ܠܙܒܢܗ or ܒܙܒܢܗ *in due season;* ܒܙܒܢܐ ܘܕܠܐ ܒܙܒܢܐ *in and out of season.* Adverbial use, ܙܒܢ *formerly;* ܙܒܢ ܙܒܢ *often, frequently;* ܒܙܒܢ *sometimes;* ܙܒܢ ܒܙܒܢ *now and then, occasionally;* ܒܙܒܢܐ ܩܠܝܠ *soon;* ܒܟܠܙܒܢ *always;* ܒܬܪ ܙܒܢ or ܙܒܢܐ *afterwards, after a time;* ܒܬܪ ܙܒܢܐ *long after.* The forms ܙܒܢܐ, ܙܒܢܬܐ W-Syr. ܙܒܢܬܐ pl. ܙܒܢܝܢ, ܙܒܢܬܐ, when used to express an indefinite date or repetition of an action, are generally fem.; ܟܡܐ ܙܒܢܝܢ *often, how often;* ܚܕܐ ܙܒܢ or ܚܕܐ ܙܒܢܐ *once,* ܬܪܬܝܢ ܙܒܢܝܢ *twice,* with ܕ prefixed *for the second time, again;* so with other numerals. ܙܒܢܬܐ *first, formerly;* ܙܒܢܬܐ *many times, sometimes;* ܙܒܢܬܐ ܚܕܐ or ܟܠ ܚܕܐ ܙܒܢܬܐ *each time;* ܙܒܢܬܐ ܘܙܒܢܬܐ *once and again;* ܠܬܠܬ ܙܒܢܝܢ *for the third time;* ܬܠܬ ܙܒܢܝܢ *thrice;* so with other numbers. Cognate, ܙܡܢ. Derivatives the three following—

ܙܒܢܐܝܬ rt. ܙܒܢ. adv. *in time, temporally;* with ܠܐ *not concerned with time, eternally.*

ܙܒܢܝܐ, ܙܒܢܝܬܐ pl. m. ܝܐ— f. ܝܬܐ— rt. ܙܒܢ. *temporal, temporary, transient, transitory;* pl. m. adverbs *of time.*

ܙܒܢܢܝܐ &c. same as ܙܒܢܝܐ but less commonly used; opp. ܡܠܥܠܡܝܐ *eternal;* pl. m. *human beings.*

ܙܒܢܬܐ; see end of ܙܒܢ, ܙܒܢܐ.

ܙܒܬܐ oftener ܙܦܬܐ. f. *pitch; a hog's bristle.*

ܙܓܐ, ܙܓܓܐ m. *a bell, a mortar.*

ܙܓܘܓܐ m. *vitriol.*

ܙܓܘܓܐ pl. ܐ— m. *a glass-blower.*

ܙܓܘܓܝܬܐ pl. ܝܬܐ— f. *glass; a glass vessel.*

ܙܓܘܓܐ pl. ܙܓܘܓܐ and ܙܓܘܓܢܝܬܐ m. dim. of ܙܓܐ. *a little bell.*

ܙܓܪ fut. ܢܙܓܘܪ, inf. ܡܙܓܪ, imper. ܙܓܘܪ, act. part. ܙܓܪ, ܙܓܪܐ, pass. part. ܙܓܝܪ *to shut up, hold in, keep from, confine, curb, restrain; to hinder, forbid, find fault.* Ethpe. ܐܬܙܓܪ *to keep oneself from; to be kept back* or *under, to be confined, compressed, closed, restrained, hindered, forbidden.* Pa. ܙܓܪ *to keep back* or *under, curb, restrain.* Aph. ܐܙܓܪ same as Pa. Cognates, ܣܓܪ and ܣܟܪ.

ܙܕܘܩܝܐ pl. ܝܐ— *a Sadducee.*

ܙܕܝܩܐ, ܙܕܝܩܬܐ pl. m. ܝܢ—, ܐ— f. ܢ—, ܬܐ— rt. ܙܕܩ. *upright, righteous* opp. ܚܛܝܐ *a sinner.*

ܙܕܝܩܐܝܬ rt. ܙܕܩ. adv. *justly.*

ܙܕܝܩܘܬܐ, ܙܕܝܩܘܬ rt. ܙܕܩ. f. *righteousness; alms, beneficence.*

ܙܕܩ only act. part. ܙܕܩ, ܙܕܩܐ pl. ܙܕܩܝܢ, ܙܕܩܢ usually impersonal; *it is right, it ought, it is due;* ܙܕܩ ܘܟܐܢ *it is meet and right;* ܐܝܟ ܕܙܕܩ *as befits, as is right, worthily;* ܐܝܟ ܕܙܕܩ ܠܚܕܒܫܒܐ ܕܡܪܢ *as beseems the Lord's Day;* with ܠ and a pers. pron., *it is right for me, for thee, I ought, thou oughtest* &c.; ܡܕܡ ܕܙܕܩ ܠܟܘܢ ܠܡܥܒܕ *that which you ought to do;* ܠܐ ܙܕܩ ܠܗ ܠܡܚܐ *he is unfit to live;* ܠܝ, ܠܗ ܙܕܩܐ ܗܘܬ *it belonged to me, to him, it was mine, his, by right;* ܠܗ ܙܕܩܐ ܗܘܬ ܝܪܬܘܬܐ—ܡܠܟܘܬܐ *the inheritance, the kingdom was his by right.* Pa. ܙܕܩ *to justify, to declare righteous, give sentence in behalf of, to adjudge, attribute; to think to be right, judge right, approve; to give alms;* ܩܡ ܡܫܝܚܐ ܕܢܙܕܩܢ Christ *rose that He might justify us;* ܐܝܟ ܕܡܙܕܩܝܢ ܩܢܘܢܐ *as the canons declare;* ܐܝܠܝܢ ܕܡܙܕܩܝܢ ܐܝܟܘܬܗ *those who judge, hold opinions, like him;* ܗܢܐ ܠܥܕܬܐ ܡܙܕܩܝܢܢ ܘܡܙܕܩܝܢܢ *we adjudge this as the right of the Church.* Ethpa. ܐܙܕܕܩ *to be justified, declared righteous, acquitted; to be adjudged, assigned, attributed;* ܠܝܬܡܐ ܡܙܕܕܩ ܡܥܣܪܐ *the tithe is assigned for orphans;* metaph. ܒܥܝܪܐ ܐܙܕܕܩ ܠܗ ܕܢܬܩܪܐ *he is rightly called a brute.* Derivatives, ܙܕܝܩܐ, ܙܕܝܩܐܝܬ, ܙܕܝܩܘܬܐ, ܙܕܩܐ, ܙܕܩܬܐ, ܙܕܩܐܝܬ, ܙܕܘܩܐ, ܡܙܕܩܢܘܬܐ, ܡܙܕܩܢܐ, ܡܙܕܩܢܘܬܐ.

ܙܕܩܐ, ܙܕܩܐ rt. ܙܕܩ. m. *that which is right* or *due,* hence *a right, law, rule; a righteous act; a due, portion, allowance, appurtenance, tax, tribute, debt; a rite, service, alms* oftener ܙܕܩܬܐ; ܐܝܟ ܙܕܩܗ *duly, according to rule* or *ordinance;* ܠܒܪ ܡܢ ܙܕܩܐ *unduly;* ܒܙܕܩܐ *rightly, accord-*

ing to right, as it should; ܠܐ ܒܙܕܩܐ *unlawfully, wrongly;* ܙܕܩܐ ܕܟܗܢܐ *the priest's due* or *portion.*

ܙܕܩܐܝܬ rt. ܙܕܩ. adv. *rightly, duly, deservedly.*

ܙܕܝܩ, ܙܕܝܩܐ, ܙܕܝܩܬܐ rt. ܙܕܩ. *right, lawful, regular.*

ܙܕܩܬܐ, ܙܕܩܬܐ rt. ܙܕܩ. f. *alms* as the right or due of God or of our neighbour; see ܙܕܩܐ.

ܙܗܐ Pe. only participial adj. ܙܗܐ, ܙܗܝܐ, ܙܗܝܬܐ pl. m. ܙܗܝܢ, ܙܗܝܐ f. emph. ܙܗܝܬܐ. *shining, splendid, glorious; noble, distinguished, honourable, reverend.* Ethpe. ܐܙܕܗܝ *to be purified, made to shine, glorified.* Pa. ܙܗܝ imper. ܙܗܐ *to purify, adorn, make to shine, make to bloom.* Ethpa. ܐܙܕܗܝ *to shine, glow; to be purified, shining, resplendent.* Derivatives, ܙܗܝܐܝܬ, ܙܗܝܘܬܐ.

ܙܗܘܡ, ܙܗܘܡܐ rt. ܙܗܡ. *strong-smelling, stinking.*

ܙܗܝܐܝܬ rt. ܙܗܐ. adv. *nobly, honourably, worthily, chastely.*

ܙܗܝܘܬܐ rt. ܙܗܐ. f. *splendour, glow, resplendence; excellency, honour, virtue.*

ܙܗܝܪܐܝܬ rt. ܙܗܪ. adv. *warily, circumspectly, securely.*

ܙܗܝܪܘ, ܙܗܝܪܘܬܐ rt. ܙܗܪ. f. *watchful care, prudence, caution; an admonition; safety, guardianship;* ܠܐ ܙܗܝܪܘܬܐ *carelessness, heedlessness, imprudence;* ܒܙܗܝܪܘܬܐ *with great care, securely.*

ܙܗܡ root-meaning *to be greasy, dirty; to smell like bad fat.* Pael pass. part. ܡܙܗܡ *stinking.* Ethpa. ܐܙܕܗܡ *to be foul, evil-smelling.* Derivatives the two following and ܙܗܘܡ.

ܙܗܘܡܐ, ܙܗܘܡܬܐ pl. m. ܙܗܘܡܐ pl. f. ܙܗܘܡܢ, ܙܗܘܡܬܐ rt. ܙܗܡ. *filthy, foul, rank.*

ܙܗܘܡܘܬܐ rt. ܙܗܡ. f. *a stink, corruption, foulness.*

ܙܗܪ fut. ܢܙܗܪ 1) *to be clear, transparent, bright;* ܕܒܫܐ ܕܙܗܪ *clear honey.* 2) participial adj. ܙܗܝܪ, ܙܗܝܪܐ, ܙܗܝܪܬܐ rt. ܙܗܪ. *safe, secure, sure, circumspect, prudent, vigilant;* ܣܒܪܐ ܛܒ ܙܗܝܪܐ *a most sure hope;* with ܠܐ *imprudent, dangerous, unsafe;* ܡܬܩܦܢܘܬܐ ܠܐ ܙܗܝܪܐ *an imprudent onslaught;* ܐܘܪܚܐ—ܘܕܘܟܬܐ ܠܐ ܙܗܝܪܬܐ *an unsafe road, dangerous place;* with ܒ *careful of, intent upon, watchful over, attentive;* ܙܗܝܪܐ ܒܢܦܫܟ *watchful over thyself;* ܦܓܘܕܬܐ ܕܙܗܝܪܐ ܒܣܘܣܝܐ *the rein which restrains the horse;* ܛܝܒܘܬܐ ܕܡܫܝܚܐ ܙܗܝܪܐ ܗܘܬ ܒܗ *the grace of Christ kept him safe;* with ܠܐ or ܡܕܡ ܕ *taking heed, provident;* with ܡܢ *avoiding, keeping from;* ܙܗܝܪ ܗܘܐ ܒܡܠܬܐ ܡܢܗ *he carefully kept the matter from her;* ܐܝܢܐ ܕܙܗܝܪ ܡܢ ܛܢܦܘܬܐ *whoso keeps far from abominations.* Ethpe. ܐܙܕܗܪ imper. ܐܙܕܗܪ *to take heed, be careful, watch over, guard, keep; to beware,* with ܒ of the object cared for, esp. with ܒܢܦܫܗ *of his soul, of himself,* with ܡܢ of the object to be avoided; ܐܙܕܗܪ ܒܗ *watch over him, guard him;* ܐܙܕܗܪܘ ܕܠܐ ܬܬܛܢܦ ܗܝܡܢܘܬܐ *take heed lest the faith be defiled.* Imper. with ܠ and pers. pron. suff. *cave tibi, take care, take warning, take heed to thyself,* &c. Pa. ܙܗܪ *to warn, admonish, caution; to take precautions, provide against, make sure, keep safe.* Ethpa. ܐܙܕܗܪ *to take care, watch over, guard, guard against.* Aph. ܐܙܗܪ *a) to shine brightly, flash, lighten;* ܐܘܪܚܐ ܕܙܕܝܩܐ ܐܝܟ ܢܘܗܪܐ ܡܙܗܪܐ *the path of the just is as a shining light;* metaph. ܡܙܗܪ ܒܫܘܒܚܐ *illustrious. b) to warn, admonish.* Derivatives, ܙܗܝܪ, ܙܗܝܪܐܝܬ, ܙܗܝܪܘܬܐ, ܙܗܪܐ, ܙܗܪܝܪܐ, ܙܘܗܪܐ, ܡܙܗܪܢܐ.

ܙܗܪܐ pl. ܙܗܪܐ rt. ܙܗܪ. m. *a) brightness, brilliancy, splendour, flashing,* ܕܢܘܪܐ *of a fire;* ܙܗܪܐ ܕܟܘܟܒܐ *of the stars;* ܘܡܫܕܪ ܠܡܚܒܘܗܝ ܙܗܪܐ ܕܫܪܪܐ God *sends brilliant beams of the truth to those who love Him;* ܚܫܘܟܐ ܕܠܝܬ ܒܗ ܙܗܪܐ *unbroken gloom;* ܐܪܥܐ ܕܠܝܬ ܒܗ ܙܗܪܐ *a land with no flash of light, a gloomy land. b) a flower in full bloom. c)* Pers. *venom.*

ܙܗܪܝܪ, ܙܗܪܝܪܐ pl. ܐ̈ rt. ܙܗܪ. m. *a bright light, a flash* or *beam of light.*

ܙܘܐ act. part. ܙܐܐ *to swell.* Ethpa. ܐܙܕܘܝ *to be swollen, distended.* Pa'li ܙܘܝ *to swell.* Ethpalp. ܐܙܕܘܝ *to be puffed up* with pride, *behave haughtily, swagger.*

ܙܘܒܠܐ from ܙܒܠ. m. *spreading dung, manuring.*

ܙܘܒܢܐ pl. ܐ̈ rt. ܙܒܢ. m. *sale.*

ܙܘܓ denom. verb Pael conj. from ܙܘܓܐ; *to join together, unite* in marriage. Aphel ܐܙܘܓ *to couple, join with another.* Ethpa. ܐܙܕܘܓ *to be joined together, united* in marriage; *to marry.*

ܙܘܓܐ, pl. ܙܘܓܝܢ, ܙܘ̈ܓܐ m. ζυγόν, *a yoke,* ܙܘܓܝܢ ܙܘܓܝܢ *in couples;* esp. with ܒܪ, ܒܪܬ, ܒܢܝ *a yokefellow, companion, wife, equal,* associate; ܒܪ ܙܘܓܐ ܕܫ̈ܠܝܚܐ a fellow-worker with the Apostles; ܒ̈ܢܝ ܙܘܓܗ his equals; a pair, couple, ܙܘܓܐ ܕܐܚ̈ܐ two brothers, ܙܘܓܐ ܕܘܘ double Waw. Also a change or suit of clothes consisting of an outer and an inner garment, a chariot for two horses, a couplet, distich of two ܦܬܓܡ̈ܐ; an even number, a balance; gram. a conjugation; two even points.

ܙܘܓܠܐ pl. ̈ܠܐ m. a fledgeling, esp. a young dove.

ܙܘܓܡܐ same as ܐܙܘܓܡܐ, ζύγωμα, a bolt, bar.

ܙܘܓܢܝܐ pl. ̈ܢܝܐ from ܙܘܓܐ. even, double; ܗܕ̈ܡܐ ܙܘܓܢ̈ܝܐ the double members of the body; ܡܐܡܪ̈ܐ ܙܘܓܢ̈ܝܐ a rhymed poem, rhyming couplets.

ܙܘܕ PAEL ܙܘܕ to supply with provision for a journey, to make preparation, equip, prepare or send on a journey; metaph. to dismiss with prayer before a journey or on leaving home, to provide with, load with; ܡܙܝܢܝܢ ܘܡܙܘܕܝܢ arming and equipping; ܙܘܕ ܐܢܘܢ ܒܒܘܪ̈ܟܬܐ he dismissed them with blessings; ܨܥܪ̈ܐ ܙܘܕ ܐܢܘܢ he loaded them with contumely; ܦܪ̈ܢܐ ܕܡܙܘܕܝܢ ܠܗ̇ ܐܒܗ̈ܝܗ̇ the dowry wherewith the parents of a bride furnish her; ܡܙܘܕ ܒܝܕܥܬܐ ܕܠܫ̈ܢܐ equipped with a knowledge of languages. ETHPA. ܐܙܕܘܕ to be furnished or to furnish oneself with food for a journey, to be provided, supplied or furnished with; metaph. to receive the viaticum when dying; ܡܩܒܠܝܢ ܙܘܕܐ ܡܙܕܘܕ ܩܕܝܫܘܬܐ endued with holiness; ܢܙܕܘܕܘܢ ܒܐܓܪ̈ܬܐ ܕܫܘܘܕܥܐ let them be provided with commendatory letters. DERIVATIVE the following—

ܙܘܕܐ generally in the pl. ܙܘ̈ܕܐ m. provision for a journey, viaticum, victuals, food, support, often metaph. of the Holy Communion.

ܙܘܕܝܘܢ, ܙܘܕܝܢ pl. ܙܘܕ̈ܝܐ ζώδιον, a sign of the zodiac; see ܡܠܘܫܐ the Syriac word for the same.

ܙܘܕܩܐ rt. ܙܕܩ. m. an adjudgement, sentence; an endowment or provision for religious purposes; pl. alms.

ܙܘܗܪ, ܙܘܗܪܐ pl. ̈ rt. ܙܗܪ. m. a caution, warning, admonition, provision, prohibition; security.

ܙܘܘܓ, ܙܘܘܓܐ pl. ̈ from ܙܘܓܐ. m. marriage, coition, copulation; ܙܘܘܓܐ ܬܪܝܢܝܐ a second marriage; ܣܓܝܐܘܬ ܙܘܘܓܐ polygamy.

ܙܘܙ, ܙܘܙܐ pl. ܙܘܙܝܢ, ܙܘ̈ܙܐ m. a) a coin equal to a quarter shekel of Jewish money or to a Greek drachma or Arabic dirhem, worth nearly ten pence; ܬܪܝܢ ܙܘܙܝܢ a didrachma, half-shekel = the temple tribute. b) a measure of weight or of liquids, a dram = one-eighth of an oz.

ܙܘܙܝ PA'LI conj. of ܙܘܐ to swell.

ܙܘܙܦܐ m. the zizyphus or jujube-tree.

ܙܘܚ, ܙܚ fut. ܢܙܘܚ, act. part. ܙܐܚ, ܙܝܚܐ, pass. part. ܙܝܚ to put in motion, to move, stir or arouse oneself to action, to rise; often with ܐܬܐ to arise and come, also with ܐܙܠ or other verbs of motion; pass. part. borne; ܟܕ ܙܝܚ ܡܪܚܡܢܘܬܟ ܠܡܚܬ when Thy pitifulness moved Thee to descend; ܙܚ ܠܗ ܚܬܢܐ ܕܢܐܬܐ ܠܘܬܟܝ the bridegroom arose to come unto thee; ܒܐܝܩܪܐ ܪܒܐ ܙܝܚ ܗܘܐ he was borne with great honour to the sepulchre. PA. ܙܝܚ a) to move or lift up any one or thing, hence to carry solemnly or in procession; to bear to the grave, bear in the womb, to accompany, attend upon, escort; rit. to lift up, elevate or bear vestments or vessels, to solemnize or keep a feastday. b) to celebrate, extol, laud, glorify, adorn. ܥܠ ܟܬܦܬܟ ܙܝܚܬܗ Thou didst bear the lost sheep on Thy shoulders; ܙܝܚܘ ܥܝܪ̈ܐ ܠܥܪܣܗ̇ angels bare the bier of the B.V.M.; ܟܗܢܐ ܡܙܝܚ ܠܟܣܐ the priest carries the chalice in procession; ܡܙܝܚ ܠܦܝܪܡܐ ܥܠ ܐܪ̈ܙܐ he swings the censer over the holy elements; ܥܕܬܐ ܕܡܙܝܚܐ ܥܐܕܟ the Church which celebrates thy feastday; ܟܕ ܙܝܚܬܗ ܠܕܡܘܬܐ ܡܝܩܪܬܐ ܒܛܘܪܐ when Thou didst glorify the honourable likeness on the Mount of Transfiguration. ETHPA. ܐܙܕܝܚ to be led, borne or carried about with pomp and solemnity, to march in triumph, go in state or magnificence, to be celebrated, highly extolled; ܥܠ ܕܪ̈ܥܝܗ̇ ܕܒܬܘܠܬܐ ܐܙܕܝܚ He was borne in the Virgin's arms; ܠܥܠ ܡܢܗܘܢ ܡܙܕܝܚ ܗܘܐ ܒܝܕ ܡܠܦܢܘܬܐ ܕܢܒ̈ܝܐ He was exalted far above them by the teaching of the Prophets; ܚܢܦܘܬܐ ܕܒܥܠܡܐ ܗܢܐ ܡܙܕܝܚܐ ܗܘܬ Paganism which was highly exalted in this age. DERIVATIVES, ܙܘܚܐ, ܙܝܚܐ, ܙܘܝܚܐ, ܡܙܕܝܚܢܘܬܐ, ܡܙܝܚܐ.

ܙܘܚܐ rt. ܙܘܚ. m. a) *a solemn procession, a train* or *retinue;* ܒܙܘܚܐ ܕܥܒܕܐ ܣܓܝܐܐ *with a great train of servants.* b) *pomp, magnificence.*

ܙܘܚܬܐ pl. ܬ̈ܐ a) *a window.* b) *a battlement* or *turret.*

ܙܘܚ, ܙܘܝܚܐ pl. ܐ̈ rt. ܙܘܚ. m. a) *a procession, a solemn ceremony,* e.g. at an episcopal visitation, consecration, or enthronement, hence *the office* then used; *a funeral procession;* ܥܐܕܐ ܕܙܘܝܚܐ ܕܙܩܝܦܐ *the festival of the procession of the Cross;* ܙܘܝܚ ܐܪ̈ܙܐ *the procession of the Host.* b) *the transfiguration* or *appearance in glory* of our Lord, ܥܐܕܐ ܕܙܘܝܚܐ *the festival of the transfiguration.*

ܙܘܚܬܐ m. *winnowing* of corn.

ܙܘܝܬܐ pl. ܙܘܝܢ, ܙܘܝ̈ܬܐ f. *a corner, angle;* ܟܐܦܐ ܕܙܘܝܬܐ *a corner-stone;* used metaph. of the four *corners* of the earth, the seven *zones* or *climes,* the four *quarters* of heaven.

ܙܘܠܙܠ, ܙܘܠܙܠܐ from ܙܠܙܠ. m. *want, lack, poverty, failure of harvest, insolvency, bankruptcy.*

ܙܘܠܠܐ rt. ܙܠ. m. *meanness, ignominy; luxury.*

ܙܘܒܠܐ rt. ܙܒܠ. m. *adornment, ornament.*

ܙܘܡ, ܙܘܡܐ m. a) ζωμός, *broth;* ܡܥܒܕܝ ܙܘܡܐ *broth-makers.* b) *the humming* of gnats.

ܙܘܡܪܐ pl. ܐ̈ rt. ܙܡܪ. m. *psalmody; a psalm, chant, canticle,* esp. between the Epistle and Gospel.

ܙܢ, ܙܢ fut. ܢܙܘܢ, imper. ܙܘܢ, act. part. ܙܐܢ, ܙܐܢܐ *to feed, give food to, provide; to support, supply, sustain;* ܙܘܢ ܠܡܣܟܢܐ *feed the poor;* ܒܪܐ ܙܐܢ ܠܥܠܡܐ ܒܦܓܪܗ *the Son sustaining the ages by His Body;* ܠܐܘܢܣ ܕܙܒܢܐ ܕܪ̈ܓܐ the wheel of time *provides high degrees* for some; ܡܙܝܢ ܕܐܢܬ ܛܝܒܘܬܐ ܕܐܠܗܐ ܝܗܒܬ ܒܐܝ̈ܕܘܗܝ *that which the grace of God has given into his hands.* Pa. ܙܝܢ *to supply with arms, to arm, equip;* act. part. ܡܙܝܢ, pass. part. ܡܙܝܢ pl. m. ܡܙܝܢܝܢ, ܡܙܝܢ̈ܐ *armed men, soldiers.* Ethpe. ܐܙܕܝܢ imper. ܐܙܕܝܢ *to arm himself, be armed, equipped, accoutred, fortified, ready to attack* or *resist;* ܡܙܕܝܢ ܠܘܩܒܠ ܡܕܥܐ ܓܘܕܐ ܕܦܘܪ̈ܓܝܬܐ *a troop of allurements armed against the mind.* Derivatives, ܙܝܢܐ, ܙܘܢܐ, ܙܘܢܬܐ, ܡܙܘܢܐ.

ܙܘܢܐ, ܙܘܢܐ pl. ܙܘ̈ܢܐ, ܙܘܢܣ or ܙܘܢܣ f. ζώνη, *a zone, girdle, belt;* with ܫܪܐ *to unbelt = degrade, disgrace;* ܙܘܢܐ ܪܡܐ *the empyrean;* ܙܘܢܐ ܫܚܝܢܐ *the torrid zone.*

ܙܘܢܪܐ pl. ܐ̈ ζωνάριον, dim. of ܙܘܢܐ. f. *a girdle, belt,* worn by monks and priests and Christians generally; ܥܐܕܐ ܕܙܘܢܪܐ ܕܝܠܕܬ ܐܠܗܐ *the festival of the girdle* of the B.V.M. (West-Syr.)

ܙܥ, ܙܥ fut. ܢܙܘܥ, inf. ܡܙܥ, act. part. ܙܐܥ, ܙܝܥܐ, pass. part. ܙܝܥ, ܙܝܥܐ, ܙܝܥܬܐ, pl. m. ܙܝܥܝܢ, f. ܙܝܥ̈ܬܐ, rarely ܙܘܝܥ, ܙܘܝܥܐ, pl. f. ܙܘܝܥܢ *to be in motion, moved, shaken to and fro, agitated* physically or mentally, *to quake, quiver, totter, tremble,* ܙܥ ܠܒܗ ܐܝܟ ܕܙܝܥܝܢ ܐܝ̈ܠܢܐ *his heart quaked as trees are shaken;* ܡܙܥ ܙܥܬ ܠܟ *thou art beside thyself, over-excited;* ܙܥ ܫܘܐܠܐ *the question was moved, the subject was agitated;* ܡܥܡܪ̈ܐ ܕܠܐ ܙܝܥܝܢ *stable habitations;* pass. part. *made to quake for fear, scared, affrighted, timid; fearful, terrible, horrible;* ܙܝܥ ܐܢܐ *I tremble;* ܚܙܘܐ ܙܝܥܐ *terrific appearance;* ܩܠ̈ܐ ܙܝܥܐ ܘܕܚܝܠܐ *fearful and terrible sounds.* Ethpe. ܐܙܕܝܥ a) *to be moved, agitated* in mind or body, in a good or bad sense; *to be shaken to and fro, disturbed, troubled; to toss to and fro* in bed; with ܚܡܬܐ *to be moved with anger;* ܐܙܕܝܥܬ ܐܪܥܐ *the earth quaked;* with ܥܠ *to rise* or *be stirred up against.* b) *to be moved, impelled* ܒܚܘܒܐ *by love,* ܒܪܘܚܐ *by the Spirit; to be moved, brought forward* for discussion, *debated, determined;* gram. *to be vocalized,* pronounced with a vowel. Aph. ܐܙܝܥ *to move, set in motion, shake, affect, disturb, disquiet, terrify; to stir up, rouse, excite, instigate* as ܪܕܘܦܝܐ *persecution,* ܪ̈ܚܡܐ *mercy.* With ܓܐܪܐ *to let fly an arrow, fling a dart;* with ܢܦܫܗ *to affect himself;* with ܡ̈ܠܐ *to discourse, discuss;* with ܩܛܝܓܘܪܝܐ *to move an accusation = accuse, censure;* with ܩܠܐ *to sound, give forth sound;* with ܩܪܒܐ *to attack, charge;* gram. *to vocalize, give a vowel,* ܫܡܐ ܡܙܝܥ or ܡܙܝܥ ܐܬܐ *a noun the first letter of which has a vowel.* Palpal ܙܥܙܥ *to shake, to make to shake* or *tremble, to move* or *drive away;* ܡܠܦܢܘܬܐ ܡܙܥܙܥܬܐ *unstable, unreliable teaching.* Ethpalpal ܐܙܕܥܙܥ *to be greatly moved, stirred* or *disturbed* of animate or inanimate things; *to struggle, jostle.* Derivatives, ܙܘܥܐ, ܙܘܥܬܐ, ܙܘܥܢܐ, ܙܘܥܢܝܐ, ܙܝܘܥܐ, ܡܙܥܢܐ, ܡܙܥܢܘܬܐ, ܡܙܘܥܢܝܬܐ, ܡܙܘܥܙܥܢܐ, ܡܙܥܙܥܢܘܬܐ, ܡܙܕܥܙܥܢܐ.

ܙܘܥ, ܙܘܥܐ pl. ܙܘ̈ܥܐ rt. ܙܘܥ. m. *a moving, shaking, quaking; a*) physical, *an earthquake, the vibration* of a weapon, *tottering* of the feet, *staggering, the stirring* of ferment—ܙܘܥܐ ܝܘܡܝܐ, ܕܟܘܟܒܐ, ܫܡܫܢܝܐ—*diurnal, stellar, solar motion. b*) mental, *motion, movement, impulse,* e.g. ܕܒܣܪܐ or ܕܦܓܪܐ *a carnal impulse;* ܕܚܫ̈ܐ *of the passions;* ܕܪܥܝܢܐ or ܕܡܕܥܐ *of the mind;* pl. *the powers* or *faculties* of the mind, i. e. ܗܘܢܐ ܘܡܕܥܐ ܘܡܬܒܝܢܘܬܐ ܘܥܘܗܕܢܐ ܘܡܣܟܠܢܘܬܐ *understanding, apprehension, memory, discrimination and consideration;* ܩܕܫ ܙܘ̈ܥܝܢ *sanctify our powers;* ܐܢܗܪ ܡܪܢ ܙܘ̈ܥܐ ܕܚܘܫ̈ܒܝܢ *enlighten, O our Lord, the impulses of our thoughts. c*) *a popular movement, sedition. d*) adjectival use, ܕܙܘܥܐ or ܡܠܐ ܙܘ̈ܥܐ *terrible. e*) gram. a vowel as *moving the consonant to which it belongs,* ܡܠܐ ܙܘܥܐ *having a vowel* opp. ܫܠܝܐ *mute.*

ܙܘܥܙܥ, ܙܘܥܙܥܐ, ܙܘܥܙܥܬܐ rt. ܙܘܥ. m. *a violent disturbance, a whirlwind;* ܕܠܐ ܙܘܥܙܥܐ *unshaken; without disturbance.*

ܙܘܥܪܢܐ rt. ܙܥܪ. m. *faultfinding, blaming.*

ܙܘܥܦܐ rt. ܙܥܦ. m. *railing;* pl. *angry menaces.*

ܙܘܥܬܐ f. no pl., rt. ܙܘܥ. *quaking, trembling, terror.*

ܙܘܦ root-meaning *to clip coin, utter false coin,* not used in Pe. Pael ܙܝܦ usually metaph. except in the pass. part. *a*) *to utter false* or *counterfeit doctrine; to demonstrate* teaching *to be false* or *spurious. b*) *to charge* or *convict of falsehood* or *perjury. c*) *to suborn* witnesses, *corrupt* or *falsify;* ܠܗܕܐ ܣܒܪܬܐ ܗܘܝܢ ܙܝܦܝܢ *we demonstrated that this opinion is false;* ܡܙܝܦܝܢ ܠܫܪܪܐ *corrupting the truth.* Pass. part. *forged, counterfeit, false;* ܙܘܙܐ ܡܙܝܦܐ *false coin;* ܝܕܥܬܐ ܠܐ ܡܙܝܦܬܐ *unalloyed knowledge.* Ethpa. ܐܙܕܝܦ *to be adulterated, corrupted; to act fraudulently; to show to be a sham, worthless, a mere counterfeit;* ܚܡܪܐ ܕܡ̈ܙܕܝܦ ܒܡ̈ܝܐ *wine adulterated with water.* Ethpalan ܐܙܕܝܦܢ denom. from ܙܝܦܢܐ *to be cunning* or *wily.* Derivatives, ܙܝܦܐ, ܙܝܦܢܐ, ܙܝܦܢܝܬ, ܙܝܦܢܘܬܐ, ܡܙܝܦܢܐ, ܡܙܝܦܐ.

ܙܘܦܐ f. *hyssop;* ܕܟܝܢܝ ܒܪܣܣܐ ܕܙܘܦܟ *cleanse me with the sprinkling of Thy hyssop;* metaph. *a fuller's sprinkler.*

ܙܘܦܪܘܣ m. *a white heron* or *egret.*

ܙܘܪ, ܙܪ fut. ܢܙܘܪ, act. part. ܙܐܪ, ܙܐܪܐ *to tie tightly, hold tight in the hand, to take a handful.* Derivative the following—

ܙܘܪܐ pl. ܙܘ̈ܪܐ, ܙܘܪ̈ܝܐ rt. ܙܘܪ. m. *a handful, the hollow of the hand, palm of the hand, a blow, slap; a measure;* ܐܟܝܠܬ ܥܦܪܗ ܕܐܪܥܐ ܒܙܘܪܟ *Thou hast measured the dust of the earth in the hollow of Thy hand.*

ܙܘܪܩܐ Ar. m. *a boat.*

ܙܘܠܝܐ pl. ܐ̈ m. *a cake made of fine flour, oil, and honey,* offered to idols.

ܙܘܥܪܐ, ܙܘܥܪܢܐ *short, dwarfish.*

ܙܘܪܘܢܝܬܐ pl. ܙܘܪܘܢܝ̈ܬܐ f. *scarlet;* ܠܒܘܫܐ ܕܙܘܪܘܢܝܬܐ *a robe of scarlet;* ܙܘܪܘܢܝ̈ܬܐ ܡܢܨܚ̈ܢܝܬܐ *robes of brilliant scarlet.*

ܙܘܚܠܐ pl. ܙܘ̈ܚܠܐ m. *a crawling locust, a locust before its wings are grown.*

ܙܛܡ or ܙܛܡܐ denom. verb Pael conj. from ܙܛܡܐ; *to investigate, accuse, blame;* ܙܛ̈ܡܐ ܕܡܙܛܡܝܢ ܠܝ *the charges they bring against me.* Part. ܡܙܛܡܐ used as adj. *culpable, faulty, wrong;* ܣܒܪܬܐ ܡܙܛܡܬܐ *a wrong opinion.* Ethpa. ܐܙܕܛܡ *to be blamed, found guilty; to find fault;* ܚܣ ܕܢܙܕܛܡ *heaven forbid that he be guilty.*

ܙܛܡܐ and ܙܐܛܡܐ pl. ܙܛ̈ܡܐ, for other spellings see ܙܐܛܡܐ and ܙܝܛܡܐ. m. ζήτημα, *an inquiry, investigation, impeachment, accusation, charge; a fault, misdeed;* ܐܥܒܪ ܡܢ ܡܚܫܒܬܟ ܗܠܝܢ ܙܛ̈ܡܐ *I will efface these accusations from thy thoughts.* Derivatives, verb ܙܛܡ, ܡܙܛܡܐ.

ܙ, ܙܝ or ܙܝܢ *Zain,* the seventh letter of the alphabet.

ܙܝܓ Ar. *a calendar;* ܙܝܓ ܠܡ̈ܬܠܡܕܢܐ *a calendar for beginners.*

ܙܝܘ, ܙܝܘܐ pl. ܙܝ̈ܘܐ m. *shining, brightness* esp. with ܐܦ̈ܐ or ܦܪ̈ܨܘܦܐ *brightness of countenance = cheerfulness;* ܙܝܘܗܝ ܫܢܐ *his looks changed, his countenance fell.*

ܙܝܒܩ, ܙܝܒܩܐ also spelt ܐܝܒܩ and ܙܝܒܘܩ m. *quicksilver, mercury.*

ܙܳܘܽܢܳܐ rt. ܙܘܢ. m. *one who feeds, supports, supplies* or *sustains, a guardian, preserver, sustainer;* ܙܳܘܽܢܳܐ ܕܗܽܘܝܽܘ ܡܣܰܝܒܪܳܢܳܐ ܠܟܽܠܳܗ ܒܪܺܝܬܳܐ *He is the Preserver who supports the whole creation.*

ܙܰܘܥܬ݂ܳܢܳܝܳܐ pl. ܝܶܐ rt. ܙܘܥ. *timid.*

ܙܺܝܙܳܢܳܐ pl. ܙܺܝܙܳܢܶܐ m. ζιζάνιον, usually pl. *tares,* often metaph. of wicked men.

ܙܰܝܰܚ Pael conj. of ܙܘܚ. *to bear in state; to extol,* &c.

ܙܝܳܚܰܡܬܳܐ; see ܙܰܚܡܬܳܐ.

ܙܰܝܺܥ, ܙܰܝܺܥܳܐ another spelling of ܙܝܥ the pass. part. of ܙܘܥ. *scared, fearful.*

ܙܳܝܡܝܳܐ pl. ܙܳܝܡܝܳܘܳܬ݂ f. ζημία, *harm, injury, misfortune;* ܙܳܝܡܝܳܘܳܬ݂ ܣܰܓܺܝܐ̈ܬܳܐ ܕܰܗܘܳܝ ܥܰܠ ܟܪܺܝܣܛܝܳܢܶܐ *the many calamities which befel the Christians.*

ܙܰܝܢ *Zain;* see ܙ.

ܙܰܝܶܢ Pael conj. of ܙܘܢ. *to arm.*

ܙܰܝܢܳܐ rt. ܙܘܢ. m. *arms, armour, weapons; furniture, trappings, ornaments;* ܡܳܐܢܰܝ ܙܰܝܢܳܐ *engines of war;* ܒܶܝܬ ܙܰܝܢܳܐ *an armoury;* often metaph.

ܙܰܝܢܬ݂ܳܐ rt. ܙܘܢ. f. *a repast, victuals;* ܐܰܟ݂ܫܰܪ ܡܳܪܝܳܐ ܙܰܝܢܳܬ݂ܳܟ݂ *make lawful, O Lord, the food Thou hast provided.*

ܙܺܝܥ or ܙܰܝܺܥ, ܙܺܝܥܳܐ, ܙܺܝܥܬܳܐ pass. part. of ܙܘܥ. *fearful,* &c.

ܙܰܝܥܳܐ pl. ܝܶܐ (when written without vowels has a point above the Yod, while ܙܝܥܐ has a point beneath, ܙܝܥܐ) *trembling, fearful.*

ܙܰܝܶܦ Pael conj. of ܙܘܦ. *to falsify,* &c.

ܐܶܙܕܰܝܰܦ; see under ܙܘܦ.

ܙܰܝܦܳܐܺܝܬ rt. ܙܘܦ. same as ܙܳܐܦܳܐܺܝܬ *deceitfully.*

ܙܺܝܩܳܐ pl. ܙܺܝܩܶܐ m. *a*) *violent rain with wind, rain falling in great drops, boisterous wind. b*) *a shooting star,* metaph. *radiancy;* ܙܺܝܩܶܐ ܢܽܘܪܳܢܳܝܶܐ ܐܰܝܟ ܡܽܘܪܢܝܳܬ݂ܳܐ *fiery shooting stars like lances;* ܒܙܺܝܩܳܐ ܕܰܙܠܺܝܩܽܘܬܳܟ݂ ܐܰܢܗܰܪܰܢܝ *enlighten me with the radiancy of Thy splendour.*

ܙܺܝܩܬܳܐ f. same as ܙܺܝܩܳܐ II.

ܙܺܝܪ, ܙܺܝܪܳܐ pl. ܙܺܝܪܶܐ m. *a crescent-shaped ornament* worn by women, also by camels; *a necklace.*

ܙܰܝܬܳܐ pl. ܙܰܝܬܺܝܢ, ܙܰܝܬܶܐ m. *the olive* tree and fruit, *olive oil;* ܒܶܝܬ ܙܰܝܬܶܐ or simply ܙܰܝܬܶܐ *an olive garden;* ܡܪܰܪ ܙܰܝܬܶܐ *scum* or *lees of oil;* ܙܰܝܬܳܐ ܕܒܰܪܳܐ *the wild olive* opp. ܙܰܝܬܳܐ ܕܰܓܢܳܢܳܐ or ܛܳܒܬܳܐ *the cultivated olive.*

ܙܟ݂ܳܐ fut. ܢܶܙܟܶܐ, imper. ܙܟ݂ܝ, act. part. ܙܳܟܶܐ, ܙܳܟ݂ܝܳܐ, pass. part. ܙܟ݂ܶܐ, ܙܟ݂ܶܝܳܐ, ܙܟ݂ܶܝܬܳܐ. *a*) *to conquer, overcome;* ܢܦܰܩ ܟܰܕ ܙܳܟܶܐ ܘܰܠܡܶܙܟܳܐ *he went forth conquering and to conquer;* ܙܳܟ݂ܽܘܬܳܐ ܕܙܳܟ݂ܝܳܐ ܠܥܳܠܡܳܐ *the victory that overcometh the world. b*) *to be free from guilt, blame* or *punishment, to be declared blameless* or *innocent, to be clear* or *to clear oneself, to show oneself in the right, to justify oneself* or *others,* opp. ܐܶܬ݂ܚܰܝܰܒ *to be* or *be found guilty;* ܐܰܝܟܰܢܳܐ ܢܶܙܟܶܐ ܒܰܪܢܳܫܳܐ ܥܰܡ ܐܰܠܳܗܳܐ *how can a man be found just with God?* Ethpe. ܐܶܙܕܟ݂ܝ *to be conquered, vanquished, overcome, overpowered,* metaph. by temptation, pleasure, sleep, a bribe, &c. Pa. ܙܰܟܺܝ *a*) *to grant victory, cause to conquer, overcome* or *predominate;* ܗܰܘ ܕܰܡܙܰܟܶܐ ܠܳܟ݂ *He who giveth thee the victory. b*) *to hold* or *pronounce innocent, to acquit, justify, clear,* opp. ܚܰܝܶܒ; ܠܳܐ ܬܙܰܟܶܐ ܢܰܦܫܳܟ݂ *do not justify thyself;* ܐܶܢ ܗܽܘ ܕܡܰܠܟܳܐ ܡܙܰܟܶܐ ܠܶܗ. ܡܰܢܽܘ ܕܡܶܫܟܰܚ ܡܚܰܝܶܒ ܠܶܗ *if the king hold him innocent who can find him guilty?* Ethpa. ܐܶܙܕܰܟܺܝ *to be pronounced innocent, be justified.* Derivatives, ܙܳܟ݂ܽܘܬܳܐ, ܙܰܟܳܝܳܐ, ܙܰܟܳܝܽܘܬܳܐ, ܡܙܰܟܝܳܢܳܐ, ܡܙܰܟܝܳܢܽܘܬܳܐ, ܡܙܰܟܝܳܢܳܐ.

ܙܳܟ݂ܽܘ, ܙܳܟ݂ܽܘܬܳܐ pl. ܙܳܟ݂ܘܳܬ݂ܳܐ, ܙܳܟ݂ܘܳܬ݂ rt. ܙܟܐ. f. *a*) *victory, the reward of victory;* ܬܶܢܝܳܐ ܪܰܒܳܐ ܕܙܳܟ݂ܽܘܬܳܐ ܕܚܽܘܪܒܳܐ *the ruins of Ephesus are a great sign of victorious desolation;* ܕܶܐܣܰܒ ܙܳܟ݂ܽܘܬܳܐ ܕܩܽܘܪܳܝܳܐ ܕܰܠܥܶܠ *that I may receive the prize of the high calling. b*) *justification, acquittal, innocence;* ܣܳܗܕܶܐ ܠܙܳܟ݂ܽܘܬܳܗ *witnesses to prove her innocence.*

ܙܳܟ݂ܽܘܪܳܐ or ܙܰܟ݂ܽܘܪܳܐ pl. ܪܶܐ rt. ܙܟܪ. m. *a diviner, necromancer;* pl. *familiar spirits, demons, spirits of the dead;* ܐܰܣܶܩ ܙܳܟ݂ܽܘܪܳܐ or ܒܙܳܟ݂ܽܘܪܶܐ *to bring up a familiar spirit = to divine by one;* ܡܰܩܣܡܳܐ ܙ *one who summons a spirit to divine by.*

ܙܰܟܳܝ, ܙܰܟܳܝܳܐ pl. ܙܰܟܳܝܶܐ, ܙܰܟܳܝܺܢ rt. ܙܟܐ. *a*) *victorious,* an epithet often applied to kings; ܙܰܟܳܝܺܢܰܢ ܒܶܗ ܒܰܡܢ ܕܰܐܚܶܒܰܢ *we are conquerors through Him who loved us;* ܣܳܗܕܶܐ ܙܰܟܳܝܶܐ *victorious martyrs;*

Christ is ܡܪܐ ܕܙܟܝܐ *the Lord of those who overcome.* b) *justified, in the right; innocent, guiltless, blameless;* ܕܡܐ ܙܟܝܐ *innocent blood.*

ܙܟܝܘܬܐ rt. ܙܟܐ. f. *innocence, equity.*

ܙܡܙܡ *to use magic arts.*

ܙܠ fut. ܢܙܘܠ and ܢܙܠ, act. part. ܙܐܠ, ܙܐܠܐ, pl. m. ܙܐܠܝܢ, f. ܙܐܠܢ or ܙܠܝܢ, participial adj. ܙܠܝܠ, ܠܐ, ܠܬܐ *to weigh light* in the balance, thence *to be of little weight* or *value, less than it should be; to be despised; to slacken, become less* often with ܒܡܣܐܬܐ *in the scales;* ܒܥܝܢܝܐ *in the eyes* of any one; ܟܟܪܐ ܕܥܬܝܪܐ ܙܠ *the talent of Dives was found wanting;* ܙܠܬ ܬܝܒܘܬܢ *our penitence was too slight;* ܙܠ ܟܐܒܝ ܡܢ ܕܝܠܗ *my pain is lighter than his;* ܠܐ ܚܐܪ ܘܠܐ ܙܐܠ *he looks not back nor slackens;* part. adj. *of light weight, value* or *behaviour; cheap, base, despised; luxuriant, luxurious, loose, debauched, licentious;* ܡܐܢܐ ܙܠܝܠܐ *luxurious furniture;* ܓܘܦܦܐ ܙܠܝܠܐ ܕܪܘܩܕܐ *the licentious embraces of the dance;* f. emph. pl. *loose women.* Pa. ܙܠܠ *to lessen, to make light* or *frivolous, to corrupt;* ܪܘܩܕܐ ܠܡܫܡܠܝܢܘܗܝ ܡܙܠܠ *dancing makes those who pursue it frivolous.* Ethpa. ܐܙܕܠܠ a) *to think little of; to become* or *be considered of little value, contemptible;* ܐܝܟ ܕܐܝܬ ܥܠܡܘܬܟ ܡܙܕܠܠ ܐܢܬ *thou art thought little of because of thy youth;* ܛܒ ܐܙܕܠܠ ܒܥܝܢܝ *he was very contemptible in my eyes.* b) *to be luxurious, extravagant, debauched, unrestrained;* ܕܠܐ ܢܙܕܠܠܘܢ ܒܡܦܩܬܐ ܕܢܦܩܬܐ *lest they become extravagant and spendthrift;* ܡܐ ܕܡܙܕܠܠ ܛܘܘܣܐ *when the peacock wantons in pride.* Aph. ܐܙܝܠ a) *to hold in no esteem, to despise, debase,* ܡܢ ܕܡܙܝܠ ܢܦܫܗ *he who thinks lightly of his own soul;* ܐܙܝܠ ܠܡܝܩܪܬܝ *he has despised my honourable things.* b) *to seduce.* Derivatives, ܙܠܝܠܐܝܬ, ܙܠܝܠܘܬܐ.

ܙܠܐ m. *a rush, reed.*

ܙܠܓ not used in Peal. Aph. ܐܙܠܓ *to shine forth, be radiant, effulgent;* ܢܘܗܪܗ ܕܫܪܪܐ ܐܙܠܓ ܒܝ *the light of the truth broke in brightness upon me;* ܡܚܙܝܬܐ ܡܙܠܓܢܝܬܐ *shining glass.* Ettaph. ܐܬܬܙܠܓ *to be enlightened, illuminated;* ܢܦܫܬܐ ܚܛܝܬܐ ܠܐ ܡܬܩܒܠܢ ܒܟܝܢܗܝܢ ܠܡܬܬܙܠܓܘ *sinful souls are by nature incapable of enlightenment.* Cognate, ܙܠܩ. Derivatives, ܙܠܓܐ, ܡܙܠܓܢܝܬܐ.

ܙܠܓܐ pl. ܐ̈ = ܙܠܝܩܐ. m. *the brightness* or *shining* of light, *the sparkling* of fire, *sparkling rays;* pl. *meteors;* often metaph. *splendour; a comment* or *gloss;* ܙܠܓ̈ܐ ܕܕܗܒܐ *the rays of light* reflected *from gold;* ܙܠܓ̈ܐ ܕܙܝܘܐ ܡܠܟܘܬܐ *dazzling splendours of royalty.*

ܙܠܗܡ *to cut short,* said of time. Ethpaial ܐܙܕܠܗܡ *to be shortened,* esp. of time; *to come short, be reduced, fail* in quantity, strength or wealth, *to be bankrupt;* ܟܕ ܡܙܕܠܗܡ ܙܒܘܢܐ *when the purchaser fails, goes bankrupt;* ܐܙܕܠܗܡ ܚܨܕܐ ܘܩܡ ܟܦܢܐ *the harvest failed and caused dearth;* ܐܙܕܠܗܡ ܡܬܘܩܢܗ *his constitution was broken.* Derivatives, ܙܠܗܡܐ, ܡܙܕܠܗܡܢܘܬܐ.

ܙܠܚ fut. ܢܙܠܘܚ, imper. ܙܠܘܚ, act. part. ܙܐܠܚ, ܙܐܠܚܐ, pass. part. ܙܠܝܚ, ܚܐ, ܚܬܐ *to pour out, shed* or *cast abroad; to sprinkle, bedew, moisten* with ܠ of the accusative and with ܒ, e.g. ܒܕܡܐ *with blood,* ܒܕܡܥܐ *with tears,* ܒܫܠܗܒܝܬܐ *to envelop in flame.* With ܚܫܐ *to grieve, to pain,* with ܣܡܡܢܐ *to apply medicine* or *salve,* with ܥܕܠܬܐ *to blame,* with ܒܗܬܬܐ *to cast shame, insult,* with ܪܘܩܐ *to spit.* Particip. adj. *sprinkled, scattered, covered with;* ܐܣܛܠܐ ܙܠܝܚ ܒܕܡܐ *a vesture spotted with blood;* ܡܫܪܝܐ ܙܠܝܚܝ ܒܣܡܡܢܐ *perfumed* dwellings. Ethpe. ܐܙܕܠܚ *to be poured out, sprinkled, shed, cast abroad.*

ܙܠܚܐ pl. ܙܠܚ̈ܐ m. *a thin plate* of metal.

ܙܠܝܠ, ܠܐ, ܠܬܐ participial adj.; see ܙܠ.

ܙܠܝܠܐܝܬ rt. ܙܠ. adv. *lustfully, lasciviously.*

ܙܠܝܠܘܬܐ rt. ܙܠ. f. *luxury, license, licentiousness; baseness.*

ܙܠܝܡܐܝܬ rt. ܙܠܡ. adv. *obliquely.*

ܙܠܝܡܘܬܐ, ܙܠܝܡܘܬܗ rt. ܙܠܡ. f. *obliqueness, obliquity, oblique position, slant;* ܬܪܬܝܢ ܢܘܩܙܢ ܒܙܠܝܡܘܬܐ *two points placed slanting;* metaph. ܙܠܝܡܘܬܐ ܕܬܪܥܝܬܐ *mental obliquity.*

ܙܠܝܩܐ pl. ܐ̈ rt. ܙܠܩ. m. *a ray* or *flash* of light, *dazzling, flashing* or *twinkling light;* ܙܠܝܩ̈ܝ ܨܦܪܐ *the rays of dawn;* metaph. ܙܠܝܩ̈ܐ ܕܚܙܘܐ ܐܠܗܝܐ *the dazzling glory of the vision of God.*

ܙܰܠܶܠ Pael conj. of ܙܰܠ.

ܙܠܰܡ fut. ܢܶܙܠܽܘܡ, pass. part. ܙܠܺܝܡ, ܙܠܺܝܡܳܐ, ܙܠܺܝܡܬܳܐ to make crooked a line; to turn aside, pervert; participial adj. oblique, slanting, uneven; ܣܝܳܡܳܐ ܙܠܺܝܡܳܐ an oblique position; astron. ܡܚܽܘܕܪܳܐ ܙܠܺܝܡܬܳܐ an oblique circle; obliquity often ellipt.; gram. a letter having the vowel Revotzo or Zlama; ܫܡܳܐ ܙܠܺܝܡܳܐ a verbal noun; ܢܽܘܩܙ̈ܶܐ ܙܠܺܝܡ̈ܶܐ points placed obliquely; metaph. distorted, perverted, depraved; ܡ̈ܶܠܶܐ ܙܠܺܝܡ̈ܳܬܳܐ perversions of words. Ethpe. ܐܶܙܕܠܶܡ to be turned aside, distorted; to turn away. Derivatives, ܙܠܺܝܡܳܐܺܝܬ, ܙܠܺܝܡܽܘܬܳܐ, ܙܶܠܡܳܐ, ܙܰܠܡܳܐ.

ܙܠܳܡܳܐ pl. ܐ̈ rt. ܙܠܡ. m. a) Zlama, E-Syr. the vowel ◌ܶ = W-Syr. Revotzo; ܙܠܳܡܳܐ ܦܫܺܝܩܳܐ or = ܐܺܝܬܳܐ ܪܒܳܐ long e, ܙܠܳܡܳܐ ܩܫܺܝܩܳܐ or = ܐܺܝܬܳܐ ܙܥܽܘܪܳܐ short e. b) a fault, crooked writing.

ܙܰܠܡܳܐ rt. ܙܠܡ. m. twisting, winding; perversity.

ܙܠܰܦ fut. ܢܶܙܠܽܘܦ, inf. ܡܶܙܠܰܦ, imper. ܙܠܽܘܦ, act. part. ܙܳܠܶܦ, ܙܳܠܦܳܐ, pass. part. ܙܠܺܝܦ to draw water or wine, pour out; metaph. to empty, wash away, ܡܰܢ ܢܶܙܠܽܘܦ ܚܶܠܝܽܘܗܝ ܡܶܢ ܣܶܦܪ̈ܰܝܗܽܘܢ who can purge the filth from their books; pass. part. mingled, infected, ܡܶܢ ܡܶܪܳܪܬܳܐ ܙܠܺܝܦܳܐ ܕܚܶܘ̈ܘܳܬܳܐ mingled or infected with serpents' poison. Ethpe. ܐܶܙܕܠܶܦ to be drawn up, poured out, to flow as water; to be exhausted, wasted; ܕܠܳܐ ܡܶܬܙܰܠܦܺܝܢ ܠܚܰܕ ܡܶܢ ܓܶܒ̈ܝܢ watery particles are suspended in the air so that they do not flow away in either direction; ܝܰܡܳܐ ܕܫܰܠܝܽܘܬܳܐ ܠܳܐ ܐܶܙܕܠܶܦ the sea of tranquillity is ever full. Derivative, ܙܠܳܦܳܐ.

ܙܠܳܦܳܐ pl. ܐ̈ rt. ܙܠܦ. m. a cup, bowl; the drawing up of water.

ܙܠܰܚ = ܕܠܰܚ, fut. ܢܶܙܠܽܘܚ, inf. ܡܶܙܠܰܚ, act. part. ܙܳܠܶܚ to drop or trickle down, to rain or pour water in drops, to bale out water. Derivatives, ܙܠܳܚܳܐ, ܡܙܰܠܚܳܐ.

ܙܠܶܚܬܳܐ pl. ܙܠܶܚ̈ܝܳܬܳܐ or ܐܶܙܠܶܚܬܳܐ f. an oyster, oyster-shell; a measure of weight.

ܙܠܰܩ Aph. ܐܰܙܠܶܩ to shine brightly, dazzle; ܩܳܕܡܺܝܢ ܓܰܘܢܳܐ ܡܰܙܠܩܳܐ ܠܥܰܝ̈ܢܶܐ their colour dazzles the eyes. Ettaph. ܐܶܬܬܰܙܠܰܩ to be illuminated. Derivatives, ܙܠܳܩܳܐ, ܙܰܠܩܳܐ.

ܐܶܙܠܳܩܳܐ pl. ܐ̈ rt. ܙܠܩ. m. a flash of lightning, thunderbolt.

ܙܰܡ fut. ܢܶܙܽܘܡ, act. part. ܙܳܐܶܡ, pass. part. ܙܡܺܝܡ, ܙܡܺܝܡܳܐ. a) to sound, rescund, buzz; ܐܰܝܟ ܕܶܒܳܪ̈ܳܐ ܙܳܐܡܺܝܢ ܗܘܰܘ they buzzed like wasps; ܙܰܡ ܟܽܠܶܗ ܐܳܐܰܪ the whole air resounded. b) to tie or train a tree; pass. part. sounding, sonorous. Palp. ܐܰܙܡܙܶܡ to make resound, make a bubbling noise. Ethpalpal ܐܶܙܕܰܡܙܰܡ to be rumoured, buzzed about. Aph. ܐܰܙܺܝܡ to ring or sound as metal; to noise abroad. Derivative, ܙܡܳܡܳܐ.

ܙܡܺܝܠܳܐ or ܙܶܡܝܳܠܳܐ pl. ܙܡܺܝܠ̈ܶܐ m. σμίλη, a pruning-knife, penknife.

ܙܡܺܝܓܡܳܐ m. σμῆγμα, soap or anything else used for cleaning clothes.

ܙܡܺܝܢ, ܙܡܺܝܢܳܐ, ܙܡܺܝܢܬܳܐ; see ܐܰܙܡܶܢ. a) invited, bidden; a guest. b) ready, appointed, destined; ܙܡܺܝܢܺܝܢ ܠܗܽܘܢ ܡܰܚ̈ܘܳܬܳܐ the stripes prepared for them.

ܙܡܺܝܪܬܳܐ, pl. ܙܡܺܝܪ̈ܳܬܳܐ rt. ܙܡܪ. f. a chant, psalm, hymn, song; ܙܡܺܝܪܬܳܐ ܕܩܺܝܢܳܪܳܐ the melody of the cinyra, sound of the strings; ܙܡܺܝܪܬܳܐ ܕܙܡܺܝܪ̈ܳܬܳܐ the Song of Songs, called also ܫܺܝܪ ܫܺܝܪ̈ܺܝܢ and ܬܶܫܒ̈ܚܳܬܳܐ; ܙܡܺܝܪ̈ܳܬܳܐ ܕܕܰܘܺܝܕ the Psalms of David, oftener ܡܰܙܡܽܘܪ̈ܶܐ.

ܙܡܺܝܬܳܐ f. hoar-frost.

ܙܡܳܡܳܐ rt. ܙܡ. m. a) a buzzing or ringing sound; the sound of a trumpet, hum of voices. b) Ar. a ring or wooden bit in the nostrils. c) the tie of a vine.

ܐܰܙܡܶܢ denom. verb Pael conj. from Chald. ܙܡܳܢܳܐ = ܐܰܙܡܢܳܐ a fixed or appointed time. to summon to an appointed time or place, to prepare for the same, hence to bid, summon, call, invite, attract, induce; silversmiths used lead ܒܰܐܒܳܪܳܐ ܕܢܰܬܺܝܟܽܘܬܳܐ ܕܣܺܐܡܳܐ to induce the fusion of silver; ܠܬܰܝܒܽܘܬܳܐ ܐܰܙܡܶܢ ܐܶܢܽܘܢ he called them to repentance; ܡ̈ܶܠܶܐ ܡܰܙܡ̈ܢܳܢܝܳܬܳܐ ܠܫܰܝܢܳܐ words calling to peace; ܦܪ̈ܺܝܩܶܐ ܒܨܠܺܝܒܳܐ ܘܰܡܙܰܡ̈ܢܶܐ ܠܒܶܝܬ ܡܰܠܟܽܘܬܳܐ O saved by the cross and bidden to the king's house. Ethpa. ܐܶܙܕܰܡܰܢ to be summoned, bidden, invited; to prepare oneself, be ready, imminent. See ܙܡܺܝܢ, ܡܙܰܡܢܳܐ.

ܙܡܰܪ fut. ܢܶܙܡܽܘܪ, imper. ܙܡܽܘܪ, act. part. ܙܳܡܰܪ, ܙܳܡܪܳܐ to sing, chant, play on a stringed instrument; ܙܡܽܘܪ ܬܶܫܒܽܘܚܬܳܐ ܠܐܠܳܗܳܐ sing praise to God. Ethpe. ܐܶܙܕܡܰܪ to be chanted, sung;

ܐܝܟ ܕܐܡܪ ܡܙܡܘܪܐ ܗܘܐ ܩܕܡ ܕܡܙܡܪ *harping;* ܗܘ ܕܐܡܪ ܡܙܡܪܢܐ *as was said by the Psalmist.* Pael same as Peal; also with regard to David, *to say in the Psalms;* ܗܘ ܡܙܡܪܢܐ *the Psalmist* = David. Ethpa. ܐܙܕܡܪ *to be chanted, sung.* Derivatives, ܙܡܪܐ, ܙܡܪܬܐ, ܙܡܪܘܬܐ, ܙܡܝܪܐ, ܡܙܡܘܪܐ, ܡܙܡܪܢܐ, ܡܙܡܪܢܘܬܐ.

ܙܡܪܐ, ܙܡܪܬܐ pl. m. ܙܡܪܐ f. ܙܡܪܬܐ *a*) rt. ܙܡܪ. *a singer, flute-player;* when without vowels ܙܡܪܐ. *b*) *steel grey* generally with ܥܝܢܐ, pl. f. ellipt. *steel grey eyes.*

ܙܡܪܐ pl. ܐ̈ rt. ܙܡܪ. m. *music* vocal or stringed; *revelling.*

ܙܡܪܓܕܐ or ܙܡܪܓܕܐ pl. ܐ̈ m. σμάραγδος, *an emerald;* often with prosthetic Alep, ܐܙܡܪܓܕܐ.

ܙܡܪܘܬܐ rt. ܙܡܪ. f. *music.*

ܙܢ, ܙܢܐ pl. ܙܢܝܢ, ܙܢܝܐ m. *sort, kind, way, method, manner,* ܙܢܐ ܕܚܡܪܐ *a kind of wine;* ܙܢܝ ܪܥܘܬܐ *the ways* or *customs of shepherds;* ܙܢܝܢ ܙܢܝܢ *of various kinds* or *sorts, divers, different;* ܒܝܫ ܙܢܝܐ *evil, of evil ways;* ܙܢܘܗܝ *his wicked habits;* ܙܢܝܐ ܢܟܦܘܬܐ *chastity;* gram. *mood,* ܙܢܐ ܡܚܘܝܢܐ—ܦܘܩܕܢܐ *the indicative —imperative mood;* ܙܢܐ ܕܠܐ ܡܣܟܡܐ *the infinitive mood.* With preps. ܒܙܢܐ *by way of, in the manner of, in some way, metaphorically;* ܒܙܢܐ ܕܡܬܠܐ *by a parable;* ܒܐܝܢܐ ܙܢܐ *in whatever way;* ܒܙܢܐ ܐܚܪܢܐ *in another fashion;* ܡܢ ܚܕ ܙܢܐ *in some way or other;* ܒܟܠܗܘܢ ܙܢܝܢ *by all means;* ܐܝܟ ܙܢܐ; see ܐܝܟܙܢܐ. Derivative, ܙܢܝܐ.

ܙܢܐ fut. ܢܙܢܐ *to commit whoredom* once. Pa. ܙܢܝ *to go a whoring* habitually, *commit fornication; to accuse of prostitution.*

ܙܢܒܝܠ, ܙܢܒܝܠܐ pl. ܐ̈ Pers. m. *a basket, frail* of figs.

ܙܢܓܐ m. *the noise* of a chariot, of arms, of horses.

ܙܢܕܐ, ܙܢܕܐ m. *sleeves* or *maniples* worn by Jacobite priests and still worn by the Christians of St. Thomas in Malabar.

ܙܢܗܐ *a tumour.*

ܙܢܝ, ܙܢܝܐ f. ܙܢܝܬܐ or ܙܢܝܬܐ pl. m. ܙܢܝܐ f. ܙܢܝܬܐ rt. ܙܢܐ. *a fornicator, whoremonger, harlot.*

ܙܢܝܘܬܐ pl. ܙܢܝܘܬܐ rt. ܙܢܐ. *fornication, whoremongering;* ܙܢܝܘܬܐ ܦܓܪܢܝܬܐ *bodily fornication,* opp. ܢܦܫܢܝܬܐ ܙ *fornication of the soul* which is ܚܪܫܘܬܐ *sorcery* and ܦܘܠܚܢܐ ܕܟܘܟܒܐ *apostacy.*

ܙܢܝܢܐ m. ܙܢܝܢܬܐ f. only pl.; from ܙܢ. *various, different, of many sorts.*

ܙܢܩ fut. ܢܙܢܘܩ, inf. ܡܙܢܩ *to shoot* an arrow, *to hurl, sling,* hence *to cast off, out* or *away; to bind;* ܠܐ ܬܙܢܩܢܝ ܡܢ ܡܥܡܪܟ *cast me not out of thy dwelling;* ܙܢܩ ܘܫܕܝܗ ܠܐܬܘܢܐ ܕܢܘܪܐ *he hurled and cast him into the furnace of fire.* Derivative, ܙܢܩܐ.

ܙܢܩܐ or ܙܢܩܐ m. *a*) rt. ܙܢܩ. *a bit, bridle.* *b*) ζάγχη, *long boots.*

ܙܥ; see ܙܘܥ.

ܙܥܦܐܝܬ rt. ܙܥܦ. adv. *angrily.*

ܙܥܘܪܐ m.; ܙܥܘܪܐ, ܙܥܘܪܐ pl. ܙܥܘܪܐ, ܙܥܘܪܝܢ, ܙܥܘܪܬܐ, ܙܥܘܪܬܐ pl. ܙܥܘܪܢ f. rt. ܙܥܪ. adj. *little, less, least; small, feeble, short; younger, junior,* opp. ܪܒܐ; ܩܕܡ ܙܥܘܪ *a very small affair;* ܠܐ ܙܥܘܪ ܥܘܬܪܐ *considerable wealth;* ܙܥܘܪ ܙܒܢܐ ܩܠܝܠ *a very little while;* ܙܥܘܪ ܗܝܡܢܘܬܐ *of feeble faith;* ܙܥܘܪ ܢܦܫܐ *desponding, discouraged;* ܙܥܘܪ ܒܥܘܡܪܐ, ܫܢܝܐ *short, young;* ܒܪ ܫܢܝܐ ܙܥܘܪܬܐ *very young;* ܒܪܗ ܙܥܘܪܐ *his youngest son.* Pl. *few,* opp. ܣܓܝܐܐ; ܒܬܪ ܙܥܘܪܬܐ *soon after;* ܒܙܥܘܪܬܐ *in few words, in short, briefly, concisely.* Metaph. *inferior, low, base;* ܙܥܘܪܬܐ *things of no value.*

ܙܥܘܪܐܝܬ rt. ܙܥܪ. adv. *a little, feebly, in a small degree.*

ܙܥܘܪܘܬܐ rt. ܙܥܪ. f. *fewness* of years = *youth; feebleness;* ܙܥܘܪܘܬ ܢܦܫܐ *faintheartedness;* ܙܥܘܪܘܬ ܢܫܡܐ *failing breath;* ܙܥܘܪܘܬܝ *my feebleness* = *my feeble self.*

ܙܥܘܪܐ; see ܙܥܘܪܐ.

ܙܥܘܪܢܐܝܬ rt. ܙܥܪ. adv. *briefly, moderately, a very little.*

ܙܥܙܥ Palpel conj. of ܙܘܥ *to shake,* &c.

ܙܥܝܦܐܝܬ rt. ܙܥܦ. adv. *angrily, wrathfully.*

ܙܥܝܦܘܬܐ rt. ܙܥܦ. f. *flaring up* of fire or anger, *indignation;* ܒܙܥܝܦܘܬܐ *indignantly,* opp. ܒܢܝܚܘܬܐ *gently.*

ܙܥܡ, fut. ܢܙܥܘܡ *to find fault.* Derivatives, ܙܥܡܐ, ܙܥܡܬܐ.

ܙܥܦܬܐ rt. ܙܥܦ. f. *reproach.*

ܙܥܦ Ethpe. ܐܙܕܥܦ *to be wroth, indignant.* Derivatives, ܙܥܦܐ, ܙܥܝܦܘܬܐ, ܙܥܦܬܐ.

ܙܥܩ or ܙܥܩ fut. ܢܙܥܘܩ and ܢܙܥܩ, act. part. ܙܥܩ, ܙܥܩܐ *to call, shout* with the voice or with a trumpet. Aph. ܐܙܥܩ same as Peal. ܡܙܥܩܝܢ ܘܐܡܪܝܢ *crying out and saying; he proclaims* ܡܙܥܩ. Ettaph. ܐܬܙܥܩ *to be declared, noised abroad.* Derivatives, ܙܥܩܬܐ, ܡܙܥܩܢܘܬܐ.

ܙܥܩܬܐ rt. ܙܥܩ. f. *a shout, outcry, loud noise, clamour.*

ܙܥܪ fut. ܢܙܥܪ, inf. ܡܙܥܪ *to lessen, diminish; to become few* or *feeble, be brought low, be reduced* in strength or value; with ܢܦܫܐ *to be faint-hearted, despond.* Ethpe. ܐܙܕܥܪ *to be closed, hemmed in.* Aph. ܐܙܥܪ *to make* or *do less, to bring to nothing, to reduce, think little* or *lightly of.* Derivatives, ܙܥܘܪܐ, ܙܥܘܪܝܬ, ܙܥܘܪܝܬ, ܙܥܘܪܘܬܐ, ܡܙܥܪܢܘܬܐ.

ܙܦܐ, ܙܦܬܐ f. *a bristle;* cf. ܙܠܦܐ.

ܙܦܢܝܢ or ܙܦܢܝܢ *some, so much, so many, as many, such and such things;* ܙܦܢܝܢ ܟܘܪܝ ܚܛܐ *so many measures of wheat;* ܙܦܢܝܢ ܘܙܦܢܝܢ *and so on, these and others, and more besides.*

ܙܦܪ fut. ܢܙܦܪ *to stink* as a fox or goat. Derivatives the two following words—

ܙܦܝܪܐ or ܙܦܪܐ pl. ܐ̈ rt. ܙܦܪ. *stinking, evil-smelling;* ܚܢܝܩܬܐ ܙܦܪܐ ܕܚܢܦܐ *foul strangled food* of the heathen.

ܙܦܝܪܘܬܐ rt. ܙܦܪ. f. *stink, evil smell,* e.g. of onions; usually metaph. of sin, idols, &c.; ܙܦܝܪܘܬܐ ܕܕܒܚܐ ܛܢܦܐ *the stink of foul sacrifices.*

ܙܦܬܐ; see ܙܦܐ.

ܙܦܬܐ or ܙܦܬܐ f. *pitch; a bristle,* ܙܦܬܐ ܕܚܙܝܪܐ *a hog's bristle.*

ܙܩܐ, ܙܩܐ f. *a wineskin, leathern bottle.*

ܙܩܘܪܐ or ܙܩܘܪܬܐ pl. ܙܩܘܪܝܬܐ f. *a curry-comb.*

ܙܩܘܦܐ pl. ܐ̈ rt. ܙܩܦ. m. *a crucifier;* ܡܢܘ ܡܫܠܡܢ ܗܘܐ ܠܡܪܢ ܠܙܩܘܦܘܗܝ *who was it who delivered our Lord up to those who crucified Him?*

ܙܩܘܪܐ pl. ܐ̈ rt. ܙܩܪ. m. *texture, web, cloth, a garment;* ܙܩܘܪܐ ܕܟܬܢܐ *a linen cloth;* ܙܩܘܪܐ ܙܚܘܪܝܬܐ *a scarlet vest.* Metaph. *a composition* in prose or verse, *a treatise, volume.*

ܙܩܘܪܐ pl. ܐ̈ rt. ܙܩܪ. m. *a weaver;* metaph. *one who plots* or *contrives.*

ܙܩܘܪܘܬܐ rt. ܙܩܪ. f. *weaving, the textile craft.*

ܙܩܬܐ pl. ܙܩܬܐ̈ rt. ܙܩܬ. f. *a goad.*

ܙܩܬܐ pl. ܙܩܬܢ, ܙܩܬܐ̈ f. *a ring* to hold a bar or staff for carrying a litter, the ark, &c.; *ring-shaped handles* of a cauldron, *bolt-rings* of a door; *rings* or *links* of chain armour.

ܙܩܝܦܐ pl. ܙܩܝܦܐ̈ rt. ܙܩܦ. m. *the cross; crucifixion.*

ܙܩܝܦܘܬܐ rt. ܙܩܦ. f. *a*) *crucifixion;* metaph. *the faith of the cross, Christianity;* ܪܘܫܡܐ ܕܙܩܝܦܘܬܐ *the sign of the cross;* ܥܪܘܒܬܐ ܕܙܩܝܦܘܬܐ *Good Friday. b*) *the rising, surging* of waves.

ܙܩܦ fut. ܢܙܩܘܦ, inf. ܡܙܩܦ, imper. ܙܩܘܦ, act. part. ܙܩܦ, ܙܩܦܐ, pass. part. ܙܩܝܦ, ܙܩܝܦܐ, ܙܩܝܦܬܐ. *a*) *to lift up, set up, hang* on a tree, on a cross, *crucify. b*) *to erect, bristle, stand up* as the hair. *c*) *to rise up, swell* as the sea; metaph. *to storm, fall upon with violence;* gram. *to add the vowel Zekofo.* ܙܩܦ ܐܠܗܐ ܛܘܪܐ ܥܠ ܐܪܥܐ *God set mountains above the earth;* ܐܙܩܦ ܥܠ ܡܫܡܥܬܐ *he hung an earring in the ears;* ܙܩܦܐ ܡܢ ܣܥܪܐ ܕܒܣܪܝ *the hair of my flesh bristled;* ܙܩܦ ܥܠܥܠܐ *a tempest arose.* Pass. part. *set up, hung, poised, erect, unbending; lifted up, lofty* of waves, *swollen, puffed up;* in the N. T. *crucified* but in other books ܨܠܝܒܐ is usual; gram. *having the vowel Zekofo.* ܐܝܟ ܕܩܠܐ ܙܩܝܦܝܢ *they stand erect like palms;* ܡܢ ܕܙܩܝܦ ܩܕܡܝܗܘܢ ܠܟܠܝܘܡ ܚܫܐ *he who stands firm daily against the passions;* ܡܚܫܘܠܐ ܙܩܝܦܐ *swollen floods;* ܡܚܫܒܬܗܘܢ ܙܩܝܦܬܐ *their turgid thoughts;* ܩܠܐ ܙܩܝܦܝܢ *uplifted voices.* Ethpe. ܐܙܕܩܦ *to stand erect, be erected, to stand on end* as the hair, *to rise up, swell* as the sea; *to be hung, crucified;* metaph. *to arise, be stirred up* as war, anger, &c.; *to surge;* ܐܙܕܩܦܬ ܟܪܟܐ Joseph's *sheaf stood erect;* ܐܙܕܩܦܬ ܣܒܠܬܐ *a ladder was set up;* ܐܙܕܩܦܘ ܥܠ ܙܩܝܦܐ *they were crucified.* Pa. ܙܩܦ *to make the hair stand on end.* Derivatives, ܙܩܘܦܐ, ܙܩܝܦܐ, ܙܩܝܦܘܬܐ, ܙܩܦܐ, ܡܙܩܦܐ.

ܙܩܦ, ܙܩܘܦܐ rt. ܙܩܦ. m. *a*) *a stake.* *b*) the vowel ـܳ *o* pronounced *Zekofo* by the West-Syrians, *â* pronounced *Zkâpâ* by the East-Syrians.

ܙܩܪ fut. ܢܙܩܘܪ, inf. ܡܙܩܪ, imper. ܙܩܘܪ, act. part. ܙܳܩܰܪ, ܙܳܩܪܳܐ, pass. part. ܙܩܝܪ, ـܳܐ, ـܳܬܳܐ *to weave;* metaph. *to compose;* ܢܶܫ̈ܐ ܙܳܩܪ̈ܳܢ ܡܳܐܢ̈ܶܐ *women weaving garments;* ܡܰܬܠܳܐ ܙܳܩܰܪ *he composes a parable;* ܨܠܘܬܐ ܐܪܝܟܬܐ ܙܩܪܝܢ *they spin out a long prayer;* ܦܓܪܐ ܙܩܪ ܠܗ *He formed a body for Himself.* Pass. part. *woven, textile,* ܡܐܢ̈ܐ ܙܩܝܪ̈ܐ *textile work, fabrics;* ܡܐܢ̈ܐ ܙܩܝܪ̈ܐ ܕܕܗܒܐ *cloth interwoven with gold.* ETHPE. ܐܙܕܩܪ *to be woven, composed, formed;* ܒܩܢܘܡܐ ܕܡܠܬܐ ܐܙܕܩܪ ܠܒܘܫܐ ܕܗܕ̈ܡܐ *within the Person of the Logos was formed the robe of* human *limbs;* ܙܩܘܪܐ ܕܡܢ ܡܠ̈ܐ ܡܙܕܩܪ *music set to words.* DERIVATIVES, ܙܩܘܪܐ, ܙܩܘܪܬܐ, ܙܩܝܪܘܬܐ, ܙܩܪܐ.

ܙܩܬ fut. ܢܙܩܘܬ, inf. ܡܙܩܬ, imper. ܙܩܘܬ, act. part. ܙܳܩܶܬ, ܙܳܩܬܳܐ *to prick, goad; to stir the soil, dig;* metaph. *to vex, provoke, goad, stimulate; to be urged* or *goaded on, provoked, tormented;* ܙܩܘܬ ܠܗ ܠܒܥܝܪܟ *urge on thy beast;* ܚܣܡܐ ܙܩܬܗ ܗܘܐ *envy stimulated her;* ܟܠ ܡܕܡ ܙܩܬܢܝ ܠܗ ܘܥܒܕܬ *everything urged me to;* ܠܟܘܬܫܐ ܕܥܡ ܐܪ̈ܛܝܩܐ ܡܙܕܩܬ ܐܢܬ *thou art goaded on to a conflict with heretics.* ETHPE. ܐܙܕܩܬ metaph. *to be goaded, urged on; to be stung, tormented;* ܡܙܕܩܬ ܗܘܐ ܒܥܘܩܣ̈ܐ ܕܚܘܒܐ ܕܐܠܗܐ *he was urged on by the pricks of the love of God.* PAEL ܙܰܩܶܬ *to prick, wound;* ܚܨܘ̈ܗܝ ܡܙܩܬܝܢ ܗܘܘ ܠܗ *they wounded him in the loins.* DERIVATIVES, ܙܩܬܐ, ܙܩܘܬܐ, ܙܩܬܐ.

ܙܩܬܐ pl. ܙܩ̈ܬܐ rt. ܙܩܬ. m. *a rod, goad; the bow* of a musical instrument.

ܙܩܘܬܐ rt. ܙܩܬ. f. *tetanus; spasm* or *rigor* of fever.

ܙܪܒ fut. ܢܙܪܘܒ, act. part. ܙܳܪܶܒ, ܙܳܪܒܳܐ, pass. part. ܙܪܝܒ, ـܳܐ, ـܳܬܳܐ *to press, urge, constrain; to contract, hold in the breath* in reading; *to thrust oneself forward, thrust back, resist;* ܒܩܪܝܢܐ ܒܢܦܫܐ ܙܪܝܒܐ *they breathe shortly while reading;* ܙܪܒܝܢ ܗܘܘ ܘܕܚܩܝܢ ܠܗ *they pressed upon him, thrust themselves upon him;* ܙܪܒܬ ܐܢܘܢ ܕܚܠܬܐ *fear constrained them;* pass. part. *compressed, compact; constrained, oppressed;* ܢܚܠܐ ܙܪܝܒܐ *a torrent straightly pent in,* hence *rapid, headlong;* ܐܘܪܚܐ ܐܠܝܨܬܐ ܘܙܪܝܒܬܐ *a narrow and straight path;* ܡܨܝܕܬܐ ܕܙܪܝܒܢ ܥܘܩܕ̈ܝܗ *a net of close meshes;* ܠܚܘܫܟܐ ܙܪܝܒܐ *constrained by extreme poverty;* ܒܪܕܐ ܙܪܝܒܐ *compact hailstones.* ETHPE. ܐܙܕܪܒ *to be pressed together, to be compact, condensed, crowded together, squeezed, crushed; to be urged, pressed, constrained, compelled; to be in straits, straitened, perplexed;* ܡܙܕܪܒܝܢ ܡܢ ܩܛܝܪܐ *constrained by violence;* ܐܙܕܪܒܘ ܟܠܗ ܓܘܗ ܠܥܠ *all his inner organs were crushed upwards;* ܡܙܕܪܒ ܗܘܐ ܡܢ ܐܝܙܓܕܐ *he was urged by the ambassador.* DERIVATIVES, ܙܪܒܐ, ܙܘܪܒܐ, ܙܪܝܒܐ, ܙܪܝܒܘܬܐ.

ܙܪܒܐ rt. ܙܪܒ. m. *pressure, burden.*

ܙܪܓ fut. ܢܙܪܘܓ, act. part. ܙܳܪܶܓ, ܙܳܪܓܳܐ *to glisten, be red* with wine, said of the eyes. DERIVATIVE, ܙܪܓܐ.

ܙܪܓܐ pl. ـ̈ܐ rt. ܙܪܓ. m. *wine colour,* a colour between yellow and red, *a topaz, amethyst.*

ܙܪܕܐ pl. ـ̈ܐ m. *a coat of mail.*

ܙܘܪܒܐ pl. ـ̈ܐ rt. ܙܪܒ. m. *compression; straitness, distress;* ܒܙܘܪܒܐ *in straits;* ܙܘܪ̈ܒܝܗܘܢ ܕܡܝ̈ܐ ܒܐܘܪ̈ܚܬܐ ܐܠܝ̈ܨܬܐ waters *being pent up in narrow ways;* ܙܘܪܒܐ ܕܢܫܡܬܐ *shortness of breath.*

ܙܪܘܥܐ pl. ـ̈ܐ rt. ܙܪܥ. m. *a sower.*

ܙܪܙ root not found in Syr.; Chald. *to gird on, arm.* DERIVATIVES, ܙܪܝܙܐ, ܙܪܝܙܐܝܬ, ܙܪܝܙܘܬܐ.

ܙܪܝܒܘܬ, ܙܪܝܒܘܬܐ rt. ܙܪܒ. f. *compression, condensation, impetus;* ܙܪܝܒܘܬ ܚܝܠܐ ܕܪܥܝܢܗ *the constrained force of his mind.*

ܙܪܝܒܬܐ, ـ̈ܬܐ rt. ܙܪܒ. f. *a whirlwind, hurricane.*

ܙܪܝܙ, ـܳܐ, ـܳܬܳܐ rt. ܙܪܙ. *brave, valiant, strenuous; ready, swift, diligent;* ܙܪܝܙ ܚܠܦ ܫܪܪܐ *valiant for the truth;* ܙܪ̈ܝܙܐ ܢܨ̈ܘܚܐ *valiant conquerors;* ܙܪܝܙ ܒܚܘܪܡܐ *ready in handling the spear;* ܓܦ̈ܐ ܙܪ̈ܝܙܐ *swift pinions.*

ܙܪܝܙܐܝܬ rt. ܙܪܙ. adv. *valiantly, strenuously, readily, diligently.*

ܙܪܝܙܘܬܐ rt. ܙܪܙ. f. *valiantness, readiness, rapidity.*

ܙܪ̈ܝܢ, ܙܪ̈ܐ pl. of ܙܪܬܐ.

ܙܪܝܥ; see ܙܪܥ.

ܙܪܩܦܐ m. *a giraffe.*

ܙܪܝܦܐܝܬ rt. ܙܪܦ. adv. *violently, by force.*

ܙܪܝܦܘܬܐ rt. ܙܪܦ. f. *violence.*

ܙܪܝܦܐ, ܙܪܝܦܬܐ rt. ܙܪܦ. f. *violent rain, downpour.*

ܙܪܝܩ; see ܙܪܩ.

ܙܪܙܦ Ethpa. ܐܙܕܪܙܦ *to walk proudly, strut, swagger.*

ܙܪܢܝܟ, ܙܪܢܝܟܐ ἀρσενικόν, *yellow orpiment.*

ܙܪܥ fut. ܢܙܪܘܥ, inf. ܡܙܪܥ, imper. ܙܪܘܥ, act. part. ܙܪܥ, ܙܪܥܐ, pass. part. ܙܪܝܥ, ܙܪܝܥܐ, ܙܪܝܥܬܐ *to spread abroad, scatter,* hence *to scatter seed, to sow, beget, generate;* metaph. *to implant, disseminate, propagate;* ܙܪܘܥ ܡܠܘܗܝ ܕܐܠܗܐ *a sower of the words of God = a preacher of the Gospel;* ܙܪܝܥܝܢ ܒܥܡܡܐ *dispersed, dispersed among the Gentiles.* Ethpe. ܐܙܕܪܥ *to be scattered abroad, dispersed; to be sown, planted; disseminated.* Aph. ܐܙܪܥ *to form seed; to sow.* Derivatives, ܙܪܘܥܐ, ܙܪܥܐ, ܙܪܥܘܢܐ, ܙܪܝܥܘܬܐ, ܙܪܝܥܐ.

ܙܪܥ, ܙܪܥܐ pl. ܙܪ̈ܥܐ, ܙܪܥܬܐ (rare), rt. ܙܪܥ. m. *a) seed, grain, a cornfield;* ܒܝܬ ܙܪܥܐ *land fit for sowing,* but ܒܝܬ ܙܪ̈ܥܐ means also *among the cornfields;* ܙܪܥܐ ܕܒܪܢܫܐ—ܕܡܘܠܕܐ *seed of procreation. b) young* or *immature offspring;* birds' *eggs* or *nestlings;* ܙܪܥܐ ܕܚܝܘܬܐ *the young of animals;* ܙܪܥܐ ܕܕܒܘܪܝܬܐ *the grubs of bees;* ܙܪܥܐ ܕܩܡܨܐ *locusts' eggs. c) offspring, race,* ܙܪܥܐ ܕܡܠܟܘܬܐ *the seed royal, royal lineage.*

ܙܪܥܘܢܐ pl. ܐ̈ m. dim. of ܙܪܥܐ. *grain, pulse, dry vegetables* opp. ܝܪܩܘܢܐ *green pot-herbs; the germ* opp. ܙܪܥܐ *the entire seed.*

ܙܪܥܝܬܐ pl. ܙܪ̈ܥܝܬܐ rt. ܙܪܥ. f. generally used in the pl. *descendants, family, offspring;* ܙܪ̈ܥܝܬܐ ܕܢܘܚ *the descendants of Noah.*

ܙܪܥܢܝܐ, ܙܪܥܢܝܬܐ rt. ܙܪܥ. adj. *generative, pertaining to procreation.*

ܙܪܦ fut. ܢܙܪܘܦ *to sprinkle, shed.* Derivatives, ܙܪܝܦܐܝܬ, ܙܪܝܦܘܬܐ, ܙܪܝܦܬܐ.

ܙܪܦܐ m. *a skin disease, the scab.*

ܙܪܩ fut. ܢܙܪܘܩ, act. part. ܙܪܩ, ܙܪܩܐ, pass. part. ܙܪܝܩ, ܙܪܝܩܐ, ܙܪܝܩܬܐ *to scatter, sprinkle, disperse;* ܥܢܢܐ ܙܪܩܐ ܪܣܝܣܬܐ a cloud *sprinkles fine drops;* ܙܪܩ ܝܪܬܘܬܗ *he squandered his inheritance;* ܓܪ̈ܡܐ ܙܪ̈ܝܩܐ ܘܡܒܕܪ̈ܐ *scattered and dispersed bones.* Ethpe. ܐܙܕܪܩ *to be scattered about, dispersed.* Aph. ܐܙܪܩ *to scatter,* e.g. blood.

ܙܪܩܐ, ܙܪܩܬܐ *sky-blue, blue-eyed.*

ܙܪܬ, ܙܪܬܐ, ܙܪܬܐ pl. ܙܪܬܝܢ, ܙܪ̈ܬܐ f. *a span,* the space one can stretch from the thumb to the little finger; a ܙܪܬܐ equals ܬܪܥܣܪܐ ܨܒ̈ܥܢ *twelve fingers,* and ܬܠܬ ܙܪܬܝܢ make one ܐܡܬܐ *cubit.*

⁘ ܒܥܘܕܪܢܗ ܕܡܪܢ ܫܠܡܬ ܐܬܘܬܐ ܙܝܢ ܕܐܝܬܝܗ̇ ܫܒܥܝܬܐ: ܫܘܒܚܐ ܠܗ
ܠܐܒܐ ܘܠܒܪܐ ܘܠܪܘܚܐ ܩܕܝܫܐ ܐܡܝܢ ⁘

⁘ ܡܪܝܐ ܥܕܪܝܢܝ ܒܫܘܒܚܐ ܗܘ ܘܐܡܣܐ ܚܝܠܐ ⁘

⁘ ܚ ⁘

ܚ ܚܝܬ

ܚ i.e. ܚܝܬ *Cheth,* the eighth letter of the alphabet; the numeral 8, with ܕ prefixed *the eighth.*

ܚܐܝ pl. ܚܐܝܢ irreg. and rare form for ܚܝܐ pres. part. of ܚܝܐ *to live.*

ܚܐܘܬܐ constr. st. ܚܐܘܬ f. *thickened milk, clotted cream, butter,* ܚܐܘܬܐ ܕܓܕܝܐ *butter made from goats' milk;* ܟܬܒܐ ܕܚܐܘܬ ܚܟܡܬܐ *the book* called *the Cream of Wisdom.*

ܚܐܙܐ pl. ܚ̈ܐܙܐ; see ܚܙܐ m. *an abyss.*

ܚܐܝ act. part.; see ܚܘܐ and ܚܝܐ.

ܚܐܠܐ *unripe dates.*

ܚܐܦܐ pl. ܚܐ̈ܦܐ m. a) *the rushing* of water, hence *an onset, irruption; impetuosity, eagerness, vehemence, violence, turbulence;* ܚܐܦܐ ܕܗܘ̈ܢܝܐ *an irruption of the Huns;* ܚܐ̈ܦܐ ܕܛܠܝܘܬܐ *the passions* or *the turbulence of youth;* ܚܐܦܐ ܕܪ̈ܫܝܥܐ *turbulence of the wicked;* ܒܚܐܦܐ *impetuously, hastily, vehemently;* with ܢܦܩ or ܥܠ *to rush in* or *upon, to hasten, to do* or *go eagerly;* ܟܠܢܫ ܚܐܦܐ ܪܗܛ ܠܐܪܥܐ ܕܝܪܬܘܬܗ *each hastens eagerly to the land of his inheritance.* b) *a cock-crow,* ܒܟܠ ܚܐܦܐ ܕܩܪܝܐ ܬܪܢܓܠܐ *at each cock-crow.*

ܚܐܦ or ܚܐ̈ܦ coll. *gnats.*

ܚܐܦܢܐ, ܚܐܦܢܝܬܐ adj. from ܚܐܦܐ. *vehement, violent.*

ܚܐܪܐ (ܚܪ) pl. ̈ܐ; see ܚܐܪ.

ܚܐܪܐܝܬ rt. ܚܪ. adv. *freely, of his own accord;* with ܠܐ *basely.*

ܚܐܪܘܬܐ or ܚܐܪܘܬܐ rt. ܚܪ. f. a) *freedom, liberty* opp. ܥܒܕܘܬܐ *servitude; the being free-born, of gentle* or *noble extraction;* metaph. *nobility* of birth or mind, *good breeding, good manners, politeness, generosity.* b) *continence* esp. the period of widowhood to be observed before re-marriage, ܐܢܬܬܐ ܡܢ ܒܬܪ ܒܥܠܗ ܬܢܛܪ ܚܐܪܘܬܐ a woman after her husband's death *shall keep continent for ten months;* ܡܙܒܢܢܝܬ ܚܐܪܘܬܗ a woman *who sells her chastity.* c) ܚܐܪܘܬܐ *power over oneself;* ܚܐܪܘܬܐ ܕܢܦܫܐ usually ellipt. *freewill,* ܐܠܗܐ ܠܐ ܥܨܐ ܠܚܐܪܘܬܐ God *will not compel freewill;* ܠܐ ܡܕܡ ܡܫܥܒܕ ܚܐܪܘܬܗܘܢ ܕܣܗܕܐ *nought can subjugate the freewill of the martyrs;* ܡܘܬܐ ܕܚܐܪܘܬܐ *voluntary death;* with ܒ or ܡܢ *of his own accord, willingly;* ܒܚܐܪܘܬܗܘܢ ܘܠܐ ܡܢ ܩܛܝܪܐ *of their own accord and without coercion.*

ܚܐܪܘܬܐܝܬ adv. rt. ܚܪ. *freely.*

ܚܐܪܐ, ܚܐܪܢܐ f. ܚܐܪܬܐ or ܚܐܪܬܐ pl. m. ܚܐܪ̈ܐ, ܚܐܪܝܢ or ܚܐܪ̈ܝܢ emph. ܚܐܪ̈ܐ f. ܚܐܪ̈ܬܐ rt. ܚܪ. *free, well-born, noble; a freed slave;* ܐܣܟܝܡܐ ܕ *the garb of the free,* ܡܪܝܡ ܠܥܒ̈ܕܐ ܠܐܝܩܪܐ ܕܚܐܪ̈ܐ *He raises slaves to the dignity of the freeborn;* ܫܘܠܛܢܐ ܚܐܪܐ *self empire;* ܒܡܠܬܐ ܦܪܝܣܬܐ ܘܚܐܪܬܐ *in frank and open language;* f. *a mistress, a lady;* ܢܫ̈ܐ ܚܐܪ̈ܬܐ *noble ladies;* ܚܐܪܬܐ ܐܝܬܝܗ̇ ܗܘܬ *she was freeborn;* ܚܡܪܐ ܒܪ ܚܐܪ̈ܐ *the free wild ass;* pl. emph. *nobles, princes, men of rank;* ܒܪ ܚܐܪ̈ܐ is constantly used for ܚܐܪ.

ܚܐܪܘܟܬܐ pl. ܚܐܪ̈ܘܟܬܐ f. *a ditch, trench, canal; a fosse.*

ܚܡ fut. ܢܚܘܡ, act. part. ܚܐܡ, ܚܡܐ pass. part. and participial adj. ܚܡܝܡ and ܚܡܝܡ, ܐ, ܬܐ *to be kindled, set on fire, burn fiercely;* ܚܡܬ ܢܘܪܐ ܒ *the fire raged in* or *amongst;* ܚܡܬ ܢܘܪܐ ܡܢ ܠܬܚܬ *fire was set to it from beneath;* ܓܡܘܪ̈ܐ ܚܡܝܢ ܡܢܗ *coals are kindled at it.* Part. ܚܡܝܡ *glowing, shining, white hot;* ܚܡܝܡ *loved, beloved, dear, cherished; a friend, near relative,* ܢܦܫܐ ܚܡܝܡܬܐ ܐܝܟ ܢܦܫܗ *he was dear to him as his own soul;* ܚܡܝܡܝܢ ܠܝ *beloved by me.* Pa. ܚܡܡ *to love vehemently, embrace, caress; to keep warm, cherish* as birds their eggs; ܚܡܡܘ ܠܚ̈ܕܕܐ *they embraced each other.* Ethpa. ܐܬܚܡܡ *to be beloved, cherished, embraced.* Aph. ܐܚܡ fut. ܢܚܡ or ܢܚܡ, inf. ܡܚܡܘ or ܡܚܡܡܘ, act. part. ܡܚܡ or ܡܚܡ *to kindle; to love;* ܕܬܚܡܘܢ ܚܕ ܠܚܕ *that ye should love one another;* ܟܠ ܡܢ ܕܡܚܡ *whoso loveth.* Ethtaph. ܐܬܬܚܡ *to be loved, beloved;* ܡܬܬܚܡܢܐ ܠܐܠܗܐ *beloved of God.* Derivatives, ܚܡܝܡܐ, ܚܡܡܐ, ܚܡܝܡܘܬܐ, ܚܡܝܡܐܝܬ, ܚܡܡܐ, ܡܚܡܢܐ, ܚܡܝܡܘܬܐ, ܚܡܝܡܐܝܬ, ܚܡܡܐ, ܡܚܡܢܘܬܐ.

ܚܡ 3 m. s. of ܚܡܡ.

ܚܡܐ or ܚܡܐ pl. ܚܡ̈ܐ m. *a measure* $= \frac{1}{12}$ of a drachm.

ܚܡܘܡܐ pl. ̈ܐ rt. ܚܡ. m. *anything quickly set on fire, withered leaves* or *twigs, dry sticks, rubbish.*

ܚܡܘܨܐ m. rt. ܚܡܨ. *mixture, commingling, confusion.*

ܚܡܘܪܐ m. *smoke, steam;* metaph. ܕܡܢ ܚ ܚܡܬܟ *the fumes of thy wrath.*

ܚܡܘܣܢܐ, ܚܡܘܣܢܝܬܐ rt. ܚܡܣ. *containing, comprehensive, convincing.*

ܚܡܘܣܐ pl. ܚܡܘ̈ܣܐ m. *apple, peach.*

ܚܡܘܣܢܐܝܬ rt. ܚܡܣ. adv. *compendiously.*

ܚܡܘܣܐ, ܚܡܘܣܝܐ pl. ̈ܐ rt. ܚܡܣ. a) *a siege, blockade; imprisonment;* with ܒܝܬ written or understood, *a prison.* b) *a burrow, covert.* c) *the life of a recluse; life in the cloister; the cell of a recluse;* with ܒܝܬ *the dwelling of a recluse;* ܢܡܘܣܐ ܕܚܡܘܣܝܐ *the rule of the cloistered* life; ܦܬܚ ܬܪܥܐ ܕܚܒܘܫܝܗ he opened the door of his cell. d) metaph. distress, straitness; ܚܒܘܫܝ̈ܐ ܕܡܛܠ ܡܫܝܚܐ distresses for Christ's sake.

ܚܒܘܫܬܐ pl. ܬ̈ܐ f. an enclosure, cloister; the cell of a recluse; a prison; a stronghold; ܡܚܒܫܘ ܚܒܘܫܬܐ ܕܩܒܪܐ the cloistered grave; ܚܒܘܫܬܗ ܠܥܢܢܐ the compression, i. e. force of confined vapour, of the cloud rends it.

ܚܒܛ fut. ܢܚܒܘܛ, inf. ܡܚܒܛ, act. part. ܚܒܛ, ܚܒܛܐ, pass. part. ܚܒܝܛ, ܛܐ, ܛܬܐ to beat down like hail, to cudgel, batter, with ܒ of the instrument and ܥܠ; ܒܪܕܐ ܕܪܘܓܙܐ ܚܒܛ ܗܘܐ the hail of wrath beat down; ܟܕ ܚܒܛܐ ܥܠ ܚܕܝܗ beating her breast; ܟܪܡܐ ܕܚܒܝܛ ܒܒܪܕܐ a vineyard beaten down by hail; ܡܛܪܐ ܚܒܝܛܐ beating rain, violent rain; to thrash corn, olives, walnuts; to snatch away as a torrent. Ethpe. ܐܬܚܒܛ to be beaten out, as olives or grain. Pa. ܚܒܛ to dash or throw against the ground, to go on kicking or beating the earth; ܚܒܛܗ ܠܟܘܙܐ ܠܐܪܥܐ he dashed the jug to the ground; ܡܚܒܛ ܗܘܐ ܪ̈ܓܠܘܗܝ he kept kicking his feet. Ethpa. ܐܬܚܒܛ to be thrown down headlong. Derivative, ܚܒܛܐ.

ܚܒܛܐ rt. ܚܒܛ. m. a beating, shaking, ܕܙܝܬܐ of the olive.

ܚܒܝܒ, ܚܒܝܒ; see ܚܒ.

ܚܒܝܒܐܝܬ rt. ܚܒ. adv. kindly, affectionately, pleasantly.

ܚܒܝܒܘܬܐ rt. ܚܒ. f. loveliness, pleasantness.

ܚܒܝܟܐܝܬ rt. ܚܒܟ. adv. confusedly, without order; gram. contracted.

ܚܒܝܟܘܬܐ rt. ܚܒܟ. f. commingling.

ܚܒܝܠܬܐ fem. emph. part. of ܚܒܠ = subst. that which is twisted; metaph. ܚܒ̈ܠܐ ܕܚܒܝܠܬܗ the ropes or snares of his perversity.

ܚܒܝܨܐ rt. ܚܒܨ. m. a sort of cake made of flour and sweetened wine or honey.

ܚܒܝܨܐܝܬ rt. ܚܒܨ. adv. having the vowel ܶ.

ܚܒܝܫܐ, ܚܒܝܫܬܐ f. carded wool.

ܚܒܝܫ, ܚܒܝܫܐ m. a prisoner; a recluse; see under ܚܒܫ Peal.

ܚܒܝܫܘܬܐ rt. ܚܒܫ. f. beleaguering, siege; imprisonment; the life of a recluse; ܚܒܝܫܘܬܐ ܕܡܕܝܢܬܐ the siege of the city; ܡܕܝܢܬܐ ܕܚܒܝܫܘܬܐ a city prepared to sustain a siege.

ܚܒܝܫܝܐ m. a recluse, a monk secluded in his cell; cf. ܚܒܝܫ under ܚܒܫ.

ܚܒܝܫܬܐ f. a cloister; a recluse; see ܚܒܫ.

ܚܒܝܬܐ or ܚܒܝܬܐ f. a liquid measure = Heb. bath, about 8½ gallons; a wine-cask, butt; ܚܒܝܬܐ ܣܦܝܩܬܐ an empty butt.

ܚܒܟ fut. ܢܚܒܘܟ, act. part. ܚܒܟ, ܚܒܟܐ, pass. part. ܚܒܝܟ, ܟܐ, ܟܬܐ to mix, mingle esp. of dry things; to join, unite in intercourse; to confuse, confound esp. of confounding the substances; gram. to join letters, write two letters or words together; ܚܒܟܘ ܓܒ̈ܐ ܠܚܕ̈ܕܐ both sides got mingled; ܚܒܟܬ ܗܝ ܥܡ ܟܢܫܐ she mixed among the crowd; ܢܦܫܐ ܟܕ ܠܐ ܚܒܝܟܐ ܒܦܓܪܐ the soul when it is no longer mixed up with or united to the body. Ethpe. ܐܬܚܒܟ pass. of Peal, with ܒ or ܥܡ; ܐܬܚܒܟܘ ܩܢܘ̈ܡܐ ܬܪ̈ܝܢ the two substances were confounded. Pa. ܚܒܟ to intermix, confuse; ܡܚܒܟ ܨܒܘܬܐ ܒܨܒܘܬܐ he confuses one affair with another; ܓܘܢܐ ܕܐܪܥܐ ܡܚܒܟܐ the colour of the earth is a mingled colour. Ethpa. ܐܬܚܒܟ to be intermixed, confounded, amalgamated. Derivatives, ܚܒܟܐ, ܚܒܝܟܐܝܬ, ܚܒܝܟܘܬܐ, ܡܚܒܟܢܐ.

ܚܒܟܐ rt. ܚܒܟ. m. combination, conjunction, mingling, mixture.

ܚܒܠ fut. ܢܚܒܠ, act. part. ܚܒܠ, ܚܒܠܐ, pass. part. ܚܒܝܠ, ܠܐ, ܠܬܐ root-meaning to twist, writhe esp. in the pains of childbirth, to be in travail, to labour in birth; metaph. to be twisted, perverted; to conceive in the mind; to be pregnant, full of consequence; ܩܪܝܒܐ ܗܘܬ ܚܒܠܐ ܠܡܝܠܕ the travailing one was near delivery; ܚܕ ܡܢ ܕܚܒܝܠ ܪ̈ܥܝܢܘܗܝ one of perverted mind. Pa. ܚܒܠ a) to travail, be in pains of childbirth, labour to bring forth; metaph. ܥܢܢܐ ܚܒܠ ܡܛܪܐ a cloud brings forth rain. b) to twist or falsify a reckoning; to spoil, mar, corrupt esp. to corrupt a codex by mistakes, a place with heresy; ܒܪܕܐ ܡܚܒܠ ܦܐܪ̈ܐ hailstones spoil the fruit; ܚܡܪܐ ܡܚܒܠܐ marred wine; ܠܐ ܚܒܠ ܛܒ̈ܥܐ ܕܩܒܪܐ he did not break the seals of the sepulchre; ܚܒܠ ܪ̈ܚܡܘܗܝ he corrupted his compassion = cast forth all pity; with ܩܝܡܐ to pervert a covenant, make it useless or void by false teaching, ܚܒܠܘ ܠܐܬܪ̈ܘܬܐ i.e. ܒܝܘܠܦܢܐ *they corrupted* those *countries* with false teaching, cf. below under *d;* ܡܚܒܠ ܪ̈ܥܝܢܐ *one of corrupt opinions* = *a heretic;* ܠܐ ܡܚܒܠܐ *uncorrupt.* c) *to become corrupt, depraved,* ܚܒܠ ܥܡ ܐܢܬܬܐ *to sin with a woman.* d) *to destroy, to spoil, ravage* with ܒ, *bring destruction upon* with ܥܠ, said of war, famine or pestilence; *to ravage, devour, tear* as wild beasts; ܕܢܚܒܠ ܒܐܪܥܐ—ܒܐܬܪ̈ܘܬܐ *to ravage, make havoc in the land, in those countries;* ܟܕ ܚܒܠܬ ܒܗ̇ ܒܒܢ̈ܝ ܒܝܬܗ̇ Jerusalem *when she had destroyed those of her own household;* ܚܒܠ ܢܦܫܗ *he destroyed himself.* Ethpa. ܐܬܚܒܠ a) *to be formed in the womb, be brought forth with travail;* ܐܬܒܛܢ ܘܐܬܚܒܠ ܘܐܬܝܠܕ *he was conceived and brought to the birth and brought forth.* b) *to be corrupted, corrupt,* esp. with heresy; ܡܢ ܗܪܣܝܣ ܐܬܚܒܠܘ *they were corrupted by laxity of life;* ܐܝܠܝܢ ܕܐܬܚܒܠܘ ܒܡܕܥܗܘܢ *those who have lost their reason;* ܐܬܚܒܠ ܡܢ ܗܝܡܢܘܬܐ ܗܘܢܗ *his mind was perverted from the faith.* c) *to be destroyed,* ܒܒܪܩܐ *by lightning,* ܒܢܘܪܐ *by fire,* ܒܝܡܐ *in the sea; to be depraved.* Derivatives, ܚܒܘܠܐ, ܚܒܠܐ, ܚܒܠܐ, ܚܒܘܠܐ, ܚܒܠܐ, ܚܒܠܐ, ܡܚܒܠܢܘܬܐ, ܡܚܒܠܢܐ, ܡܚܒܠܢܐ, ܡܚܒܠܢܘܬܐ.

ܚܒܠ, ܚܒܠܐ pl. ܝܢ, ܐ̈ rt. ܚܒܠ. m. a) *a cord, rope, line, noose;* esp. *a measuring line,* hence *a portion* of land *measured* out, *a portion, allotment, tract* of land; ܐܬܬܠܝ ܒܚܒܠܐ *he was hung with a rope;* ܚܒܠܗ ܠܚܒܘܠܐ ܒܚܒܠܗ *he destroyed the destroyer with his own noose;* ܚܒܠܐ ܕܝܪܬܘܬܗ *the lot of his inheritance;* ܚܕ ܚܒܠܐ *one portion* of land; ܚܒܠ ܝܡܐ *coast-land, maritime district.* b) *a line, row, series* of persons or things; ܫܒܥܐ ܚܒ̈ܠܐ ܐܘ ܩܠܝܡ̈ܐ *seven lines or climes;* ܚܒܠܐ ܕܟܪ̈ܡܐ *a line* or *row of vines;* ܦܪܚܬܐ ܕܦܪܚܝܢ ܚܒ̈ܠܐ ܚܒ̈ܠܐ ܒܐܐܪ *birds which fly in lines* or *straight flights in the air;* ܚܒܠܐ ܕܢܒ̈ܝܐ—ܕܢܒܝܘܬܐ *the line* or *succession of prophets;* ܚܒ̈ܠܐ ܕܢܘܪܐ ܣܠܩܝܢ ܗܘܘ ܡܢ ܦܘܡܗܘܢ *lines* or *rays of fire rose from their mouths.*

ܚܒܘܠܐ, ܚܒܘܠܬܐ pl. m. ܐ̈, f. ܬ̈ܐ, rt. ܚܒܠ. *a destroyer, avenger; a corruptor* of youth; adj. *rapacious, devouring, destructive;* ܕܐܒ̈ܐ ܚܒ̈ܘܠܐ *rapacious wolves;* ܚܝܘ̈ܬܐ ܚܒ̈ܘܠܬܐ *carnivorous animals,* ܦܪ̈ܚܬܐ ܚܒ̈ܘܠܬܐ *birds of prey.*

ܚܒܠܐ pl. ܐ̈ rt. ܚܒܠ. m. usually in the pl.; *the pangs* of travail; ܟܐܒܐ ܕܚܒ̈ܠܐ *the sorrow of travail;* ܚܒ̈ܠܐ ܕܡܘܠܕܐ or ܚܒ̈ܠܐ ܕܝܠܕܬܐ *the birth-pangs;* metaph. *the pains* of death, of Sheol, or any great pain; ܚܒ̈ܠܐ ܕܕܚܠܬܐ *the pangs of fear.*

ܚܒܠ, ܚܒܠܐ pl. ܐ̈ rt. ܚܒܠ. m. *corruption, hurt, harm, destruction, desolation; adultery;* ܕܠܐ ܚܒܠܐ *incorrupted, incorruptible, immortal; incorruption;* ܚܝ̈ܐ ܕܠܐ ܚܒܠܐ *immortal life;* ܡܙܕܪܥܝܢ ܒܚܒܠܐ. ܡܬܩܝܡܝܢ ܕܠܐ ܚܒܠܐ *they are sown in corruption, they are raised in incorruption;* ܕܬܚܕܬ ܠܒܢܝܢ̈ܘܗܝ ܡܢ ܚܒܠܐ ܕܛܘܡܐܬܐ ܕܦܬܟܪ̈ܐ *that thou mayest rededicate its buildings after their defilement in idol-worship.* Interj. *woe! destruction!* ܚܒܠ ܠܝ *woe unto me!* ܚܒܠܗ̇ ܠܐܘܪܗܝ *woe to Edessa!*

ܚܒܢ not used in Pe. Ethpa. ܐܬܚܒܢ and ܐܬܚܒܢ *to be slothful, lazy; to hesitate, falter;* ܗܢܘܢ ܕܡܬܚܒܢܝܢ ܒܗܕܐ *they who are slothful in this matter.* Derivatives the three following words—

ܚܒܢ, ܚܒܢܢܐ pl. ܝܢ, ܐ̈ rt. ܚܒܢ. *slothful, lazy, negligent;* ܚܒܢܢܐ ܕܚܒܢ ܡܢ ܟܠܗܘܢ ܚܒܢ̈ܢܐ *the very laziest of all the lazy.*

ܚܒܢܢܐܝܬ adv. *slothfully, negligently.*

ܚܒܢܢܘܬܐ pl. ܬ̈ܐ f. rt. ܚܒܢ. *slothfulness, sluggishness.*

ܚܒܨ fut. ܢܚܒܘܨ, imper. ܚܒܘܨ or ܚܒܘܨ, act. part. ܚܒܨ, ܚܒܨܐ, pass. part. ܚܒܝܨ, ܐ, ܬܐ *to push, shove; to crowd together, throng, push* or *squeeze through a throng, to press onward;* ܚܒܘܨܝܗܝ ܠܒܪ *keep him outside, shut the door against him;* ܚܒܨ ܕܢܥܒܪ *he pushes his way through;* ܚܒܨܝܢ ܗܘܘ ܠܐܢܫܐ *they pushed people aside, squeezed through the crowd;* ܚܒܨܐ ܠܬܪܥܐ ܟܠܢܫ ܐܢܫ *every one crowded to the door;* metaph. *to press on, urge on, hasten, be earnest, eager, anxious;* ܚܒܝܨ ܐܢܬ ܕܬܐܙܠ *thou art in a hurry to be off;* ܚܒܝܨܐ ܕܬܐܠܦ *she was eager to learn;* ܚܒܝܨ ܐܢܐ ܕܐܫܬܥܐ ܥܠ ܥܢܝ̈ܢܝܗܘܢ *I hasten* to relate *their affairs;* ܚܒܨ ܠܒܢ̈ܘܗܝ *he urged on his sons, exhorted them;* gram. *to give the vowel Ḥvasa* ◌ܻ. Ethpe. ܐܬܚܒܨ refl. *to thrust, press, throng;* ܐܬܚܒܨܬ ܒܐܣܬܐ *she pressed against the wall;* pass. *to be pressed close together, com-*

pressed; to endeavour earnestly, to take great pains; gram. *to have the vowel* ◌ܶ. DERIVATIVES, ܚܒܝܪܐ, ܚܒܝܪܐܝܬ, ܚܒܪܐ, ܚܒܘܪܐ, ܚܒܪܐ.

ܚܒܪܐ rt. ܚܒܪ. m. *a crowd, throng;* ܚܒܪܐ ܕܓܝܣܐ *a throng of robbers.*

ܚܒܪܐ m. rt. ܚܒܪ. *a press, throng, crowd, pressure;* ܚܒܪܐ ܕܟܣܐ *thronging cups* = a carouse; ܡܛܠ ܚܒܪܐ *on account of the crowd;* gram. *the vowel Ḥvasa* ◌ܶ, ܚܒܨܐ ܐܪܝܟܐ *long Ḥvasa,* i.e. written with ܝ as in ܕܝܢ; ܚܒܨܐ ܟܪܝܐ short *i* as in ܟܪܝܐ West-Syr. = ܟܗܢܐ East-Syr.

ܚܒܪ PAEL ܚܒܪ *a) to fix* the eyes, with ܥܠ *upon. b)* with ܥܡ *to associate with, be a companion of,* ܠܐ ܢܚܒܪ ܥܡܟ ܟܘܪܣܝܐ ܕܥܘܠܐ *the throne of the wicked shall have no fellowship with thee.* ETHPA. ܐܬܚܒܪ *to be intimate, be a companion, to ally oneself* with ܠ. DERIVATIVES, ܚܒܪܐ, ܚܒܪܬܐ, ܚܒܪܘܬܐ, ܚܒܪܢܝܐ.

ܚܒܪܐ, ܚܒܪ f. ܚܒܪܬܐ, pl. m. ܐ̈, f. ܬ̈ܐ, rt. ܚܒܪ. *a companion, comrade, fellow, an intimate friend, neighbour; another, the other; equal to, like;* ܐܢ ܐܢܫ ܐܝܬ ܠܗ ܥܠ ܚܒܪܗ *if a man have anything against another;* ܒܝܬ ܟܐܦܐ ܠܚܒܪܬܗ *between one stone and another;* ܠܐ ܐܝܬ ܗܘܐ ܠܗ ܚܒܪܐ ܒܥܠܡܐ *there was not its equal in the world;* ܫܪܒܬܐ ܠܚܒܪܬܗ ܬܫܬܥܐ *one generation shall tell it to another;* rit. *an alternative* prayer or lection, *an alternate* chant, ܩܠܐ ܚܒܪܝܐ *responding tones;* ܦܠܓܘܬܐ ܩܕܡܝܬܐ ܘܚܒܪܬܗ *the first part and the following part.*

ܚܒܪܐ pl. ܐ̈ m. I. rt. ܚܒܪ. *a conjuror, a charmer.* II. *a deep pit, a pitfall, deep darkness;* ܡܥܡܩܐ ܘܚܒܪܐ *precipices and abysses;* ܚܒܪ̈ܐ ܕܡܘܒܠܝܢ ܠܒܝܫܬܐ *pitfalls leading to wickedness.*

ܚܒܪܘܬܐ rt. ܚܒܪ. f. *fellowship, boon-companionship, a partnership;* ܚܒܪܘܬܐ ܕܝܗܘܕܝܐ *the synagogue of the Jews.*

ܚܒܪܢܝܐ pl. ܐ̈ rt. ܚܒܪ. *of or belonging to partners;* ܕܝܢ̈ܐ ܚܒܪܢܝ̈ܐ *suits between partners.*

ܚܒܪܬܐ pl. ܬ̈ܐ fem. of ܚܒܪ, ܚܒܪܐ.

ܚܒܪܬܐ pl. ܬ̈ܐ f. *a bruise, sore;* ܚܒܪ̈ܬܐ ܕܪܕܝܢ *running sores;* metaph. *an error in* a manuscript; ܡܠܐ ܛܘܫ̈ܐ ܘܚܒܪ̈ܬܐ *full of blots and blurrs.*

ܚܒܫ fut. ܢܚܒܘܫ, inf. ܡܚܒܫ, imper. ܚܒܘܫ, act. part. ܚܒܫ, ܚܒܫܐ, pass. part. ܚܒܝܫ, ܐ̱, ܬܐ̱, *to shut in* or *up. a)* ܒܡܕܝܢܬܐ or ellipt. *to besiege, beleaguer, hem in; to confine, imprison* with ܥܠ of the pers., ܚܒܫ ܡܕܝܢܬܐ ܥܠܝܗܘܢ *he kept him besieged in the city;* ܚܒܫ ܐܢܘܢ ܚܫܘܟܐ ܒܕܚܠܬܐ *darkness imprisoned them in terror;* ܚܒܫܗ ܒܒܝܬ ܐܣܝܪ̈ܐ *he shut him up in prison;* ܐܚܕܗ ܠܘܙܝܪܐ ܘܚܒܫܗ *he seized the vizier and imprisoned him. b) to enclose,* with ܢܘܢܐ or ܡܨܝܕܬܐ *to net* fish; metaph. ܚܒܫܗ ܒܡܠܘܗܝ *he caught him* in the toils *of his own words. c)* with ܢܦܫܗ *to shut up close, make subject, bind;* ܚܒܫ ܢܦܫܗ ܒܫܘܘܕܝܐ *he bound himself by a promise. d) to live the life of a recluse, live the cloistered life. e)* metaph. *to contain, comprehend, include;* ܟܠ ܬܪܝܢ ... ܣܛܪ̈ܝܢ ܚܒܫܝܢ ܙܘܝܬܐ *every two* sides *contain an angle;* ܚܘܒܐ ܕܚܒܫ ܠܟܠܗ ܩܢܝܢܗ *a debt which comprises the whole of his property;* ܚܒܫܝܢ ܠܟܠܗ ܢܡܘܣܐ ܦܘܩܕ̈ܢܐ ܥܣܪܐ *the Ten Commandments comprise the* whole *Law. f) to restrain, convince, confute* by argument; pass. part. *a) besieged, imprisoned, a prisoner,* ܒܝܬ ܚܒܝܫ̈ܐ *a prison;* ܟܕ ܡܛܪܐ ܚܒܝܫ *when rain is held back, denied;* ܚܒܝܫܐ ܢܦܫܗ ܠܡܘܡܐ *subject to blame. b) a recluse* who, though living in a monastery, remained in his or her own cell and refrained from all intercourse. *c)* emph. *a cloister.* ETHPE. ܐܬܚܒܫ *a)* refl. *to shut oneself up, to remain indoors; to give oneself to the life of a recluse;* ܥܝܕܐ ܐܝܬ ܠܢ ܕܢܬܚܒܫ *it is our custom to remain indoors* during the fast. *b)* pass. *to be besieged, imprisoned;* ܟܠ ܕܐܬܚܒܫ ܐܬܐܚܕ *every one who is besieged is* as good as *taken. c)* geom. *to be contained, included;* ܐܣܟܝܡܐ ܒܓܘ ܣܛܪ̈ܘܗܝ ܡܬܚܒܫ *a figure is contained within its bounding lines.* APH. ܐܚܒܫ *to make subject, to shut up.* DERIVATIVES, ܚܒܘܫܐ, ܚܒܘܫܬܐ, ܚܒܘܫܝܐ, ܡܚܒܫܢܐ, ܚܒܝܫܐ, ܚܒܝܫܘܬܐ, ܡܬܚܒܫܢܐ.

ܚܒܘܫܐ, ܚܒܘܫܬܐ pl. m. ܐ̱, f. ܬܐ̱ *a beetle; a leech;* ܚܒܘܫܬܐ ܐܘܟܡܬܐ *black beetles.*

ܚܒܬܐ = ܚܒܘܬܐ rt. ܚܒ. f. *stubble, brushwood, husks, dry rubbish;* ܐܢ ܩܪܒܐ ܚܒܬܐ ܠܢܘܪܐ ܐܟܠܐ ܠܗ *if stubble come near the fire, it devours it;* metaph. ܚܒܬܐ ܕܝܘܠܦܢܐ *rubbishy teaching, stale trash.*

ܚܓ 3 m. s. pret. of verb ܚܘܓ.

ܚܓܐ pl. ܚܓܐ̈ m. *a feast, festal day, feasting; a festal assembly*, hence *a fair, any assembly; a company, a dance;* ܚܓܐ ܘܡܫܘܬܝܐ *feasting and mirth;* ܚܓܐ ܪܘܚܢܝܐ *a spiritual feast;* ܚܓܐ̈ ܥܡܝܛܐ̈ ܕܚܢܦܘܬܐ *the gloomy feasts of heathendom;* ܐܬܦܠܓܘ ܟܢܫܝܗܘܢ ܕܫܐܕܐ̈ ܚܓܐ̈ ܚܓܐ̈ *the crowds of devils divided themselves into bands.* Derivatives, verb ܚܓܓ, ܚܓܝܓܘܬܐ, ܚܓܝܓܐ, ܚܓܝܢܐ, ܡܚܓܓܢܐ, ܡܚܓܓܢܘܬܐ.

ܚܓܐ or ܚܓܐ m. *hedysarum alhagi, a thorny plant.*

ܚܓܐ̈ pl. of ܚܓܝܬܐ.

ܚܓܐ̈ pl. of ܚܓܬܐ.

ܚܓܓ denom. verb Pael conj. from ܚܓܐ. *to keep* a feast; ܚܓܐ ܕܡܚܓܓܝܢܢ *the feast we celebrate.*

ܚܓܝܓܘܬܐ from ܚܓܐ f. *festivity.*

ܚܓܝܪܘܬܐ f. *halting, lameness.*

ܚܓܠ fut. ܢܚܓܘܠ *to surround, go round;* ܕܢܚܓܠܘܢ ܠܗܘܢ ܠܡܕܝܢܬܐ ܫܘܪܐ *that they might erect walls round the cities;* ܚܕܪ ܩܒܪܗ ܢܦܫܗ ܚܓܠܐ ܠܗ *his soul shall wander round his grave.*

ܚܓܠ, ܚܓܠܐ also ܚܓܠܐ, pl. ܚܓܠܐ̈ com. gen. but ܚܓܠܬܐ *a hen partridge; a partridge;* ܙܘܓܐ ܕܚܓܠܐ̈ *a brace of partridges.*

ܚܓܡܐ m. Ar. *a cupper, a surgeon who applies a cupping instrument.*

ܚܓܢܝܐ adj. *a)* from ܚܓܐ, *festal;* ܒܟܢܘܫܝܐ ܚܓܢܝܐ̈ *in festal assemblies.* *b)* from ܚܓܬܐ, *thorny.*

ܚܓܪ Pe. only part. ܚܓܝܪܐ *halt, lame, maimed.* Pa. ܚܓܪ *to be lame.* Derivatives, ܚܓܝܪܘܬܐ, ܚܓܝܪܐ.

ܚܓܪܐ pl. ܐ̈ m. *a coney.*

ܚܓܪ *a)* fut. ܢܚܓܪ, part. ܚܓܪ, ܚܓܪܐ, intr. *to halt, limp, be lame;* ܚܓܪ ܝܥܩܘܒ *Jacob halted, limped.* Participial adj. ܚܓܝܪ, ܚܓܝܪܐ, *halt, lame, crippled, feeble;* often used as a nickname; ܦܪܥܘܢ ܚܓܝܪܐ *Pharaoh Claudus* = Pharaoh Necho; with ܠܫܢܐ or ܡܠܬܐ *stammering, of halting tongue;* ܛܠܝܐ ܚܓܝܪ ܠܫܢܗ *a stammering child;* metaph. *deficient, feeble;* ܚܓܝܪܐ ܠܡܥܒܕ ܨܒܝܢܗ *too weak to carry out his will.* *b)* fut. ܢܚܓܘܪ, act. part. ܚܓܪ, ܚܓܪܐ, tr. *to hinder, restrain;* ܗܘ ܕܚܓܪ ܠܗ ܘܟܠܐ ܡܢ ܡܕܢܚܘܬܗ *that which impedes and prevents its rising;* ܠܐ ܗܘܐ ܥܝܕܐ̈ ܦܓܪܢܝܐ̈ ܕܚܓܪܝܢ *it is not the habits of the body which hinder.* Ethpe. ܐܬܚܓܪ *a) to be* or *become lame;* metaph. *to be* or *become feeble, be impeded, fettered;* ܐܬܚܓܪ ܡܢ ܚܛܗܘܗܝ *he was fettered by his sins;* ܡܬܚܓܪܝܢ ܡܢ ܣܘܥܪܢܐ ܛܒܐ *they are hindered from good works.* *b) to stammer, have an impediment in his speech;* ܐܬܚܓܪ ܡܡܠܠܗ ܕܠܫܢܐ *his speech was impeded.* Pa. ܚܓܪ *to lame, cripple; to impede, fetter; to halt;* ܟܝܢܐ ܕܚܓܪܗ *nature which hath denied motion to it;* ܚܓܪܗ ܠܡܥܠܠܗ *he prevented his entrance;* ܚܓܪܗ ܠܚܐܪܘܬܐ *he fettered freewill;* ܗܢܘܢ ܕܥܕܟܝܠ ܡܚܓܪܝܢ *those who still halt* between two opinions. Ethpa. ܐܬܚܓܪ *to fall lame, be crippled; to be stopped, checked, impeded;* ܚܘܝܐ ܕܡܛܠ ܐܕܡ ܐܬܚܓܪ *the serpent which on account of Adam was deprived of feet;* ܟܕ ܡܬܚܓܪ ܡܢ ܡܪܗ *a dog when it is ordered by its master to stay still.* Aph. ܐܚܓܪ *a) to lame, to restrain. b) to be lame, feeble;* metaph. *to stumble, waver, be unsteady;* ܡܚܓܪ ܟܝܢܐ ܠܘܬ *nature is impotent, restrained from;* ܡܚܓܪ ܥܠ ܬܪܬܝܗܝܢ ܒܘܪܟܐ̈ *halting on both knees = doubly irresolute;* ܐܚܓܪܘ ܒܩܝܡܬܐ *they stumbled at the Resurrection,* were not firm in the faith.

ܚܓܬܐ pl. ܚܓܐ̈ (uncertain) f. *the shrine* or *fane* of an idol; ܟܕ ܥܒܕܝܢ ܚܓܐ ܒܚܓܐ̈ *when they make feasts in the temples of idols.*

ܚܓܬܐ pl. ܚܓܐ̈ f. *a thorn.*

ܚܕ m. ܚܕܐ f. *a) one, each, some one, any one;* used as indef. art. *a;* ܐܓܪܬܐ ܠܓܒܪܐ ܚܕ *a letter to some one, to a certain man;* ܚܕ—ܚܕ or ܚܕ—ܘܚܕ *one—the other, each;* ܚܕ ܚܕ m. or ܚܕܐ ܚܕܐ f. *each, every, every one, several;* ܟܠ ܚܕ m., ܟܠ ܚܕܐ f. *each one severally, several;* ܒܟܠ ܚܕܐ ܚܕܐ *in each and all;* ܚܕ ܚܕ ܡܢܟܘܢ *each of you;* ܚܕܐ ܚܕܐ ܡܢ ܬܪܥܐ̈ ܡܢ ܚܕܐ ܡܪܓܢܝܬܐ *each one of the several gates was of a single pearl,* Apoc. xxi. 21. *b)* with preps. ܚܕ ܒܚܕ *each one, one—the other;* ܕܚܕ *single, singular;* ܡܠܬܐ ܕܚܕ ܘܕܣܓܝܐ̈ *verb of the singular and of the plural;* ܕܚܕܐ ܥܝܢܐ *one-eyed;* ܕܚܕ ܠܚܕ *of each other, of one another;* ܚܕ ܠܚܕ *one another;* ܚܕ ܡܢ ܚܕ *one from another;* ܚܕ ܥܠ ܚܕ or

ܚܕ ܠܘܳܬ ܚܕ one towards—one with—another; ܚܕܳܐ ܚܕܳܐ ܠܚܘܕ separately, particularly. c) ܚܕ with a number and ܒ denotes *double, treble*, &c., ܚܕܳܐ ܒܬܪܶܝܢ ܡܢܳܬܳܐ a double portion; ܚܕ ܬܪܶܝܢ or ܚܕ ܒܬܪܶܝܢ double; ܚܕ ܒܐܪܒܥܳܐ fourfold; ܚܕ ܒܫܒܥܳܐ sevenfold, seven times. With ܕ or ܡܢ before the number, *a part*; ܚܕܳܐ ܡܢ ܐܪܒܥܳܐ or ܚܕ ܕܐܪܒܥܳܐ *a fourth part*; ܚܕܳܐ ellipt. for ܚܕܳܐ ܙܒܢ, is used adverbially with ܒ or ܠ *once*, e.g. ܚܕܳܐ ܒܫܢܬܳܐ *once a year*; ܚܕܳܐ—ܕܬܪܬܶܝܢ or ܚܕܳܐ—ܘܕܬܪܬܶܝܢ *firstly—secondly*; ܚܕܳܐ ܒܪܶܒܘ *once in ten thousand times*; ܒܚܕܳܐ *at once, directly*; ܒܚܕܳܐ ܡܶܠܬܳܐ *in one word*; ܡܢ ܚܕܳܐ oftener contr. ܡܚܕܳܐ *directly, immediately, suddenly*; ܡܚܕܳܐ ܕ *as soon as, at the same time as*; ܚܕ ܟܡܳܐ *how much more, how much rather*; ܚܕ ܟܡܳܐ ܕܝܢ *how much more*; ܚܕ ܟܡܳܐ ܠܐ or ܚܕ ܟܡܳܐ ܕܠܐ *how much less*; ܚܕ ܒܟܡܳܐ or ܚܕܳܐ *seldom, sometimes*; ܚܕ ܒܟܡܳܐ ܡܫܬܟܚ *it is rarely found*. Derivatives, ܚܕܳܝܳܐ, ܚܕܳܝܘܬܐ, ܚܕܳܢܳܝܳܐ, ܚܕܳܢܳܐܝܬ, ܚܕܳܐ, ܚܕܬ, ܚܕܰܝ, ܚܕܳܕܳܐ, ܚܕܳܕܶܐ, ܚܕܳܢܳܝܘܬܐ, verb ܡܚܕܳܐ, ܡܚܕܳܢܳܝܘܬܐ, ܡܚܕܳܝܳܐ, ܡܚܕܳܐܝܬ, ܚܕ.

ܚܕܳܐ or ܚܕܝ fut. ܢܶܚܕܶܐ, inf. ܡܶܚܕܳܐ, imper. ܚܕܝ, act. part. ܚܳܕܶܐ, ܚܳܕܝܳܐ, ܚܳܕܝܳܬܳܐ intr. *to be glad, rejoice*, with ܠ *over* or *at*; *to welcome, entertain* with ܒ; ܚܕܶܐ ܠܶܒܳܐ *glad of heart*. The imper. and infin. are used as salutations = χαῖρε, χαίρειν; ܚܕܝ ܪܰܒܝ *hail, master*; ܚܕܰܘ ܒܡܳܪܰܢ *rejoice in our Lord*; ܒܡܶܚܕܳܐ *greeting*; ܚܕܝ ܠܐ ܬܶܐܡܰܪ ܠܶܗ *thou shalt not salute him, shalt give him no greeting*. The act. part. is often contracted with a pron., ܚܳܕܶܝܢܳܐ *I rejoice*, ܚܳܕܶܝܢܰܢ *we rejoice*. Pa. ܚܰܕܝ *to gladden, make glad, rejoice* trs.; *to felicitate, congratulate*; ܥܶܠܠܰܝ ܡܚܰܕܝܳܢܘܬܳܐ *causes of gladness*; ܚܰܕܝ ܒܢܘܗܪܶܗ *He made glad with His light*. Ethpa. ܐܶܬܚܰܕܝ *to be gladdened, made glad*. Aph. ܐܰܚܕܝ *to gladden*, ܡܰܚܕܝܳܐ ܠܶܒܳܐ *rejoicing the heart*. Derivatives, ܚܕܘܬܳܐ, ܚܕܘܳܐ, ܚܕܘܳܝܳܐ, ܚܕܝܳܐ, ܚܕܳܝܳܐ, ܡܚܕܝܳܐ.

ܚܕܳܐ ܙܒܰܢ = ܚܕܳܙܒܰܢ f. *one only, once*.

ܚܶܕܒܳܐ or ܚܶܕܘܳܐ pl. ܐ̈ m. only lexx. *chicory, cichorium endivia*.

ܚܕܒܫܰܒܳܐ *Sunday*; for special Sundays see ܐܘܪܚܬܐ, ܚܕܬܐ, ܡܥܠܬܐ, &c.

ܚܕܳܕܶܐ from ܚܕ. *each other, one the other, one with another*; ܕܚܕܳܕܶܐ *of one another, of each other, mutual*; ܐܰܚܘܬܳܐ ܕܚܕܳܕܶܐ *brotherliness towards one another*.

ܚܕܘ or ܚܕܗܘ contr. of ܚܕ ܗܘ m. *one only, once*.

ܚܕܘܳܐ const. st. ܚܕܘܳܬ, with suff. 1 p. ܚܕܘܳܬܝ *my gladness*, with the other suffixes it is regular, ܚܕܘܳܬܳܟ *thy joy*, &c.; emph. ܚܕܘܳܬܳܐ, pl. ܚܕܘ̈ܳܬܳܐ, m. and f. rt. ܚܕܳܐ. a) *gladness, mirth, joy, rejoicing; a merrymaking, festivity, dance*; ܬܰܟܣܝܳܐ ܕܚܕܘܳܬܳܐ *brave apparel, festal raiment*; ܟܠ ܚܕܘܳܐ ܢܶܗܘܶܐ ܥܰܡܟܘܢ *all joy be with you*; ܚܕܘܳܬ ܠܶܒܳܐ *joy of heart*; ܫܠܳܡ ܠܶܟܝ ܚܳܕܝܬܳܐ ܕܝܳܠܕܰܬ ܚܕܘܳܬܳܐ ܠܟܽܠܶܗ ܥܳܠܡܳܐ *hail to thee, O joyful one, who barest the joy of the whole world*. b) *subterranean granaries, pits* for storing wheat or barley; ܚܕܘ̈ܳܬܳܐ ܘܓܘ̈ܒܶܐ ܕܚܶܛܶܐ ܘܣܥܪ̈ܶܐ *underground stores and pits of wheat and barley*.

ܚܕܘܓܳܐ pl. ܐ̈ m. *the friend of the bridegroom, best man, master of the ceremonies at a wedding, a wedding-guest*; ܚܕܘ̈ܓܶܐ ܘܡܫܰܡܫܳܢܶܐ ܕܡܶܫܬܘܳܬܳܐ *the guests and attendants of the wedding-feast*; ܚܕܘ̈ܓܰܝ ܓܰܢܢܳܐ ܪܘܚܳܢܳܝܳܐ *the guests of the spiritual bride-chamber*.

ܚܕܘܓܬܳܐ pl. ܐ̈ f. *a friend of the bridegroom*, esp. *the women who made known to His disciples that their Lord had risen*; ܠܚܕܘ̈ܓܳܬܶܗ ܚܙܳܐ ܡܰܠܰܐܟܳܐ ܕܚܰܬܢܳܐ *the angel beheld the friends of the bridegroom*.

ܚܕܘܪܳܐ f. ܚܕܘܪܬܳܐ, pl. m. ܐ̈, f. ܬܳܐ̈, rt. ܚܕܪ. *a vagrant, mendicant*; ܦܺܝܢܟܳܐ ܕܚܕܘܪܳܐ *the beggar's dish*, the name of the constellation otherwise called Corona borealis.

ܚܕܘܪܬܳܐ a) see above; b) *a door-hinge*. c) *a buttonhole*.

ܚܕܘܳܬ constr. st. of ܚܕܘܳܐ, emph. st. ܚܕܘܳܬܳܐ.

ܚܕܘܳܬܳܢܳܐ rt. ܚܕܳܐ. adj. *joyful, glad*.

ܚܰܕܚܕܳܢܶܐ m. pl. ܚܰܕܚܕܳܢܝܳܬܳܐ f. pl. from ܚܕ. *a few, a very few, some*; ܠܚܰܕܚܕܳܢܶܐ ܡܶܬܝܰܗܒܳܐ *it is granted to few*; ܒܚܰܕܚܕܳܢܝܳܬܳܐ *in a few instances, in some few cases*.

ܚܰܕܝ; see verb ܚܕܳܐ. ܚܰܕܝ Pa. of the same. *to gladden*, &c.

ܚܰܕܝܳܐ pl. ܚܰܕܝ̈ܶܐ or ܚܰܕܘ̈ܳܬܳܐ m. *the breast*; ܒܬܘܠܬܳܐ ܕܛܥܺܝܢܳܐ ܒܚܰܕܝܳܗ ܠܒܪܳܐ ܕܐܰܠܳܗܳܐ *the Virgin bearing on her bosom the Son of God*; ܒܶܝܬ ܚܰܕܝܳܐ or ܒܶܝܬ ܚܰܕܝ *a breastplate*.

ܚܕܝܐ, ܚܕܝܬܐ pl. m. ܚܕܝ̈ܐ, f. ܚܕܝ̈ܬܐ, rt. ܚܕܐ. *glad, cheerful, joyous, mirthful, merry;* often with ܠܒܐ *heart.*

ܚܕܝܐܝܬ rt. ܚܕܐ. adv. *gladly, cheerfully;* with ܩܒܠ *to welcome, to receive hospitably.*

ܚܕܝܘܬܐ f. rt. ܚܕ. *solitude; union, unity;* ܚܕܝܘܬܐ ܟܝܢܝܬܐ *natural union* as that of the elements; ܚܕܝܘܬܐ ܕܡܥܒܕܢܘܬܐ *unity in action;* ܚܕܝܘܬܐ ܠܐ ܡܬܦܫܩܢܝܬܐ *inexplicable unity.*

ܚܕܝܢܢ contr. for ܚܕܝܢ ܚܢܢ. *we rejoice;* see ܚܕܐ act. part.

ܚܕܝܪܘܬܐ rt. ܚܕܪ. f. *being surrounded;* ܚܕܝܪܘܬ ܡܕܝܢܬܐ *a siege.*

ܚܕܝܢܐ contr. of ܚܕܐ ܐܢܐ *I am glad;* see ܚܕܐ.

ܚܕܢܝܐܝܬ rt. ܚܕ. adv. *singly, singularly, with special honour; in the singular number.*

ܚܕܢܝ, ܚܕܢܝܐ, ܚܕܢܝ pl. m. ܐ̈, f. ܚܕܢܝ̈ܬܐ, rt. ܚܕ. *singular,* gram. *in the singular number;* ܚܕܢܝ ܙܘܥܐ *having only one vowel;* ܚܕܢܝ ܦܣܩܐ *monosyllabic;* ܚܕܢܝ ܦܢܝܢܐ *following the same rule.* Metaph. *unique,* ܚܕܢܝܐ ܗܘܐ ܒܐܣܝܘܬܐ ܕܙܒܢܗ *he was singularly esteemed as a physician in his time;* ܚܕܢܝ̈ ܟܝܢܐ *those who assert that there is one only nature* in Christ = *Monophysites.*

ܚܕܢܝܘܬܐ f. from ܚܕ. *oneness, unity; singularity, the singular number;* ܚܕܢܝܘܬ ܟܝܢܐ ܐܠܗܝܐ *the unity of the Divine Nature;* ܚܕܢܝܘܬ ܟܝܢܐ the doctrine of *one sole nature* in Christ, *Monophysitism.*

ܚܕܥܣܪ m. ܚܕܥܣܪܐ f. comp. of ܚܕ *one* and ܥܣܪ *ten; eleven.*

ܚܕܪ fut. ܢܚܕܘܪ and ܢܚܕܪ, imper. ܚܕܘܪ, act. part. ܚܕܪ, ܚܕܪܐ, pass. part. ܚܕܝܪ, ܐ, ܬܐ. *a) to go round* or *about, to encompass* with ܒ or ܠ; ܚܕܪ ܗܘܐ ܒܫܘܩܐ *he went about in the market-places;* ܚܕܪ ܒܓܫܘܫܐ *he groped about, spied all round;* ܡܢ ܚܕܪ *all round, round about. b) to surround, beset,* with ܡܕܝܢܬܐ *to besiege;* ܐܬܐ ܠܘܬܗ ܘܚܕܪܗ *he came against* the city *and beset it. c) to beg;* ܚܕܪ ܠܗ ܠܚܡܐ *he begs his bread. d)* with another verb, *again;* ܢܚܕܪ ܢܬܐ *let him come round again.* Pass. part. *compassed, surrounded;* ܚܕܝܪܐ ܡܝܐ *surrounded by water;* ܩܘܪܝܐ ܕܚܕܝܪܢ ܠܗ *the villages lying round about;* with ܡܕܝܢܬܐ or ܡܢ ܡܕܝܢܬܐ *beset, besieged;* ܚܕܝܪ ܠܗ ܚܝܠܐ *compassed with armies.*

Ethpe. ܐܬܚܕܪ *to be begged of.* Aph. ܐܚܕܪ *to enclose, to make go round, to set* a wall or hedge *round, to encompass* with an army, *guard round about, gird;* ܐܝܢܐ ܕܡܚܕܪ ܠܗܘܢ *he girds them with armour.* With other verbs; *again;* ܥܐܠ ܘܡܚܕܪ ܢܦܩ *he enters and again goes out;* ܐܚܕܪ ܗܘ ܠܗ *he gave him back, gave him again.* Derivatives, ܚܕܘܪܐ, ܚܕܘܪܐ, ܚܕܪܐ, ܚܕܪܬܐ, ܚܕܪܘܬܐ, ܡܚܕܪܢܘܬܐ, ܡܚܕܪܢܐܝܬ.

ܚܕܪܐ, ܚܕܪܐ pl. ܐ̈ m. rt. ܚܕܪ. *a circle; vagrancy, begging;* pl. *circumjacent places, suburbs, surroundings;* ܚܕܪ̈ܝܗ ܕܐܘܪܫܠܡ *the suburbs of Jerusalem.* The const. forms ܚܕܪ, ܚܕܪ̈ܝ are in common use as a prep. *round about, surrounding, hard by;* ܦܪܕܝܣܐ ܚܕܪ ܒܝܬܐ *a garden adjoining the house;* ܫܪܘ ܚܕܪ̈ܝ ܡܫܟܢܝ *they encamped round about my tent;* ܐܬܪܐ ܕܚܕܪ̈ܝ ܝܘܪܕܢܢ *the country round about the Jordan.*

ܚܕܪܬܐ pl. ܚܕܪ̈ܬܐ f. rt. ܚܕܪ. *a circuit; corridor; a surrounding outer wall,* hence *an out-building.*

ܚܕܬ Pa. ܚܕܬ *a) to make new, bring in unauthorized innovations, new teaching, institute new* canons, *construct new* buildings, &c., *issue new* i.e. counterfeit coin; ܠܘܩܒܠ ܡܫܝܚܐ ܚܕܬܘ heretics *brought in new teaching against Christ;* ܐܝܠܝܢ ܩܘܢ̈ܝܐ ܕܚܕܬ ܩܕܡܝܬ ܒܨܝܕ ܐܘܪ̈ܚܬܐ *the pools which he first constructed beside the roads. b) to dedicate, renew, restore, repair, revive;* ܚܕܬܘ ܠܬܪ̈ܥܐ *they renewed* or *dedicated the gates;* ܚܕܬ ܫܘܪ̈ܝܗ ܕܡܕܝܢܬܐ *he rebuilt the walls of the city.* Ethpa. ܐܬܚܕܬ *a) to arise newly, be new, recent, gain new strength;* ܐܬܚܕܬ ܥܝܕܐ *a new custom has arisen;* ܗܠܝܢ ܢܡ̈ܘܣܐ ܕܐܬܚܕܬܘ *newly-decreed laws;* ܝܘܠܦܢܗ ܟܠ ܝܘܡ ܡܬܚܕܬ ܗܘܐ *his doctrine gained fresh strength each day;* ܡܬܚܕܬ ܗܘܐ ܒܫܦܝܪ̈ܬܐ ܟܠܝܘܡ *he daily grew in beautiful virtues. b) to renew, restore, repair.* Derivatives, ܚܕܬܐ, ܚܕܬܐܝܬ, ܚܕܬܘܬܐ, ܚܘܕܬܐ, ܡܚܕܬܢܘܬܐ.

ܚܕܬܐ, ܚܕܬܐ f. ܚܕܬܬܐ pl. m. ܚܕ̈ܬܐ, f. ܚܕ̈ܬܬܐ, rt. ܚܕܬ. *new, recent, fresh;* ܚܕܬܐ ܗܝ ܡܚܘܬܐ *the scar is fresh;* ܚܝ̈ܐ ܚܕ̈ܬܐ ܕܒܬܪ ܡܘܬܐ *the new life beyond death;* ܚܕܬܐ often ellipt. for ܕܝܬܩܐ ܚܕܬܐ *the New Testament;* ܐܢܫܐ ܚܕ̈ܬܐ *novices, tiros;* pl. f. *novelties, innovations;* ܪ̈ܚܡܝ ܚܕ̈ܬܬܐ *novelty-mongers, longing for something fresh.*

ܚܘܕܬܐܝܬ rt. ܚܕܬ. adv. *lately, recently, newly, unusually.*

ܚܘܕܬܐ pl. ܚܘܕܬܬܐ f. rt. ܚܕܬ. *newness* e. g. of clothes opp. ܥܬܝܩܘܬܐ *freshness;* ܟܕ ܚܘܕܬܗ *when it was new;* ܟܕ ܚܘܕܬܢ ܠܐ ܐܬܥܬܩܬ ܒܚܛܝܬܐ *while our freshness hath not been made old by sin;* ܚܘܕܬܐ ܕܡܠܟܘܬܐ *a new reign, the beginning of a reign;* ܚܘܕܬܗ ܕܣܗܪܐ *the new moon;* pl. *novelties.*

ܚܘܐ not used in Pe. PA. ܚܰܘܺܝ, imper. ܚܰܘܳܐ, ܚܰܘܳܐ, ܚܰܘܳܐܝ, ܚܰܘܶܝܢ *to show, make manifest, manifest; to declare, demonstrate; to show oneself, appear,* generally with ܢܦܫܗ; *to make a show, exhibit; to pretend, profess; to discover, to publish;* ܚܰܘܳܐ ܠܰܢ ܡܫܒܠܐ *show us the way in;* ܚܰܘܳܐܢܝ ܕܝܢܪܐ *show me a penny;* ܐܪܥܐ ܛܒܬܐ ܚܰܘܳܐܢܝ *prove me to be good ground;* ܡܢܘ ܡܚܘܐ ܕܒܢܝ ܚܐܪܐ *who will declare that they are free = who will free them;* ܕܢܚܘܐ ܠܢ ܬܘܕܝܬܟܘܢ *that he may declare, expound, your religion to us;* ܕܓܠܐ ܡܚܘܐ ܠܗ *he declares him a liar;* ܫܡܐ ܡܚܘܐ ܟܝܢܐ *the name indicates the nature* of the thing; ܚܢܘܟ ܚܘܝ ܣܦܪܐ ܘܟܬܒܐ *Enoch discovered books and writings.* ETHPA. ܐܬܚܘܝ *to be shown, related; to show oneself, to appear; to be made manifest, spread abroad; to be discovered;* ܐܝܟ ܕܡܬܚܘܝܐ *as is reported, related.* DERIVATIVES, ܚܘܝܐ, ܡܚܘܝܢܐ, ܡܚܘܝܢܘܬܐ, ܡܬܚܘܝܢܐ, ܡܬܚܘܝܢܘܬܐ, ܬܚܘܝܬܐ.

ܚܘܒ, ܚܳܒ fut. ܢܶܚܘܒ, inf. ܡܶܚܳܒ, act. part. ܚܳܐܶܒ, ܚܳܝܒܳܐ. *a) to be unequal, unequally matched, weaker,* with ܡܢ *than,* hence *to succumb, be conquered; to be powerless, of no avail, to fail;* ܚܳܒ ܡܢ ܢܟܠܘܗܝ *his wiles effected nothing;* ܚܳܒ ܡܢ ܐܢܫܐ ܙܥܘܪܐ *he was conquered by a few men;* ܚܳܝܒܳܐ ܡܡܠܠܐ ܕܐܢܫܐ ܡܢ ܬܫܒܘܚܬܗ *human speech is unable to utter His praise;* ܠܐ ܚܳܐܶܒ ܒܩܪܒܐ *unconquered in war.* *b) to owe, to be guilty;* ܚܳܒܶܬ ܪܒܘ ܟܟܪܝܢ *I owed a myriad talents;* with ܚܛܗܐ *to commit a sin;* ܚܳܐܶܒ ܐܢܐ *I am guilty;* ܚܳܐܶܒ ܐܢܐ ܠܗ *I am guilty before him;* ܢܦܫܬܐ ܕܠܐ ܚܝܒܢ ܠܡܟܪܝܘ *souls who ought not to grieve.* ETHPE. ܐܬܚܝܒ *to be found guilty, to be owing, due.* Part. used impers.; ܡܬܚܝܒܐ *it is due, incumbent* with ܠ of the person to whom and with ܠܘܬ of that which is due to be paid or observed. PA. ܚܰܝܶܒ *to prevail;* with ܥܠ *with* or *over; to overcome, surmount; to confute; to find guilty, condemn;* with ܡܘܡܬܐ *to bind over, cause to take an oath;* ܕܢܙܟܘܢ ܘܢܚܝܒܘܢ ܚܫܐ ܕܢܦܫܐ *that they may conquer and overcome the passions of the soul.* ETHPA. ܐܬܚܰܝܰܒ *to be worsted, convinced, confuted; to be guilty, convicted, condemned.*

ܚܘܒܐ, ܚܘܒ pl. ܚܘܒܶܐ rt. ܚܘܒ. m. *a debt,* esp. ܡܪܐ ܚܘܒܐ *a creditor, usurer.*

ܚܘܒܐ, ܚܘܒ rt. ܚܒ. m. *love, charity, affection;* ܚܘܒܐ ܡܢ ܐܠܗܐ ܗܘ *love is of God;* ܚܘܒܐ ܐܚܝܐ *brotherly love;* ܕܠܐ ܚܘܒܐ *without natural affection, heartless;* ܠܐ ܒܚܘܒܐ *unwillingly;* ܚܘܒܝ ܡܪܝ *my friend;* with pron. suff. 2 p. a title of regard or courtesy, ܠܚܘܒܟ *unto thee, O Beloved;* ܚܘܒܟܘܢ *dear* or *beloved Sir.*

ܚܘܒܐܝܬ rt. ܚܒ. adv. *affectionately, amicably.*

ܚܘܒܢܐ m. *gloom, thick darkness;* ܡܢ ܚܘܒܢܐ ܢܦܩ ܗܘܐ ܠܚܝܐ *he came out of deep gloom into life.*

ܚܘܒܛܐ rt. ܚܒܛ. m. *mixture, confusion.*

ܚܘܒܠܐ pl. ܚܘܒܠܶܐ rt. ܚܒܠ. m. *a recompense, reward, remuneration, compensation, interest,* usually with ܦܪܥ, ܗܦܟ, ܝܗܒ, ܫܠܡ or ܦܪܥ; ܗܐ ܚܙܝܢ ܦܪܥܝܢ ܠܢ ܚܘܒܠܐ *behold how they reward us;* ܐܦܪܥܘ ܠܗܘܢ ܚܘܒܠܐ ܒܝܫܐ *they have rewarded evil unto them;* ܦܪܥܘ ܚܘܒܠܐ ܛܒܐ ܠܐܚܘܗܘܢ *they returned good unto their brother;* ܡܢ ܚܘܒܠܐ ܐܙܕܟܝܬ *I am overcome by that which I owe* i. e. by gratitude and affection.

ܚܘܒܠܐ rt. ܚܒܠ. m. *corruption; destruction, desolation, laying waste; torment, pestilence; passion, adultery;* ܚܘܒܠܐ ܕܒܢܝܢܫܐ ܡܢ ܗܘ ܚܘܝܐ *the slaying of men by that serpent;* ܚܘܒܠܐ ܕܗܝܟܠܐ *the desolation of the temple;* ܚܘܒܠܐ ܡܚܒܠܐ ܕܡܘܬܐ *a deadly pestilence;* ܚܘܒܠܐ ܕܢܦܫܬܐ *the destruction* or *corruption of souls;* ܚܘܒܠܐ ܕܥܕܬܐ *corruptions in the Church;* ܡܥܒܪ ܠܗܘܢ ܚܘܒܠܐ ܠܒܢܝܐ *it transmits the passions to descendants.*

ܚܘܒܢܐܝܬ rt. ܚܒ. adv. *lovingly, amicably.*

ܚܘܒܬܐ pl. ܚܘܒܬܐ rt. ܚܘܒ. f. *a debt,* pl. *dues;* ܡܪܐ ܚܘܒܬܐ *a creditor;* ܫܒܩ ܠܗ ܚܘܒܬܗ *he forgave him the debt;* metaph. *guilt, sin;* ܚܘܒܬܗ ܕܐܕܡ *the guilt of Adam.*

ܚܘܓ, ܚܳܓ act. part. ܚܳܐܶܓ, ܚܳܝܓܳܐ, pass. part. ܚܺܝܓ *to describe* or *draw* a circle, hence *to* encompass, go about; ܝܡܐ ܡܬܚܕܪ ܘܚܒܝܫ ܒܬܚܘܡܗ the sea is encompassed and bound in its limit. Metaph. with ܠܫܢܐ to stammer; with ܡܢ to avoid, stand in awe of, hold in reverence; to refuse from modesty, be modest, retiring; ܚܕܪ ܡܢ ܡܝܬܪܘܬܗ he revered his virtue. Pa. ܚܕܪ to surround. Derivatives, ܚܕܪܐ, ܚܕܝܪ, ܚܕܪܘܐ, ܚܕܪܢܐܝܬ, ܚܕܪܝܐ, ܚܘܕܪܐ.

ܚܕܪܘܬܐ m. pl. idol temples or shrines.

ܚܘܕܪܐ pl. ܐ̈ rt. ܚܕܪ. m. a circle; ܚܘܕܪ̈ܐ ܪܘܚܢܝ̈ܐ spiritual circles i. e. angelic choirs.

ܚܘܕܪܐ from ܚܕܪ. m. the celebration of a feast, festival-keeping.

ܚܘܕܪܬܐ pl. ܚܘܕܪ̈ܬܐ rt. ܚܕܪ. f. a compass, circle, orb; halo round the sun or moon; ܗܢܐ ܐܐܪ ܕܒܚܘܕܪܬܐ this encircling air; ܟܕ ܥܒܕ ܣܗܪܐ ܚܘܕܪ̈ܬܐ the moon when it forms halos; ܚܘܕܪܬ ܪܩܝܥܐ the circle of the firmament.

ܚܘܕܪܬܢܐ, ܢܝܬܐ rt. ܚܕܪ. adj. orbed, round, spherical, ܫܛܝܚܘܬܐ ܚܘܕܪܬܢܝܬܐ a curved surface, the plane of a sphere.

ܚܘܕܪܐ pl. ܐ̈ m. a tiara, head-band, head-dress; ܥܒܘܕ ܚܘܕܪ̈ܐ ܕܡܠܟܐ he was a maker of regal tiaras.

ܚܘܕܪܐ pl. ܝܢ, ܐ̈ rt. ܚܕܪ. m. a) a circle, circumference; globe; ܟܠܗ ܚܘܕܪܐ the entire circle; ܚܘܕܪܐ ܕܦܠܓܗ ܕܝܘܡܐ the meridian circle; ܚܘܕܪ̈ܐ ܢܚܫ̈ܝܐ brazen circles for taking observations of the heavenly bodies; ܚܘܕܪܐ ܕܬܒܝܠ the whole world; ܚܘܕܪܐ ܕܫܢܬܐ or ܕܫܢܝܐ the circle or course of the year. b) a circuit, course, series, esp. the Khudhra i. e. the book of proper anthems and other variable parts of the service for the festivals of the year. c) a circus, hippodrome. d) a company; ܚܘܕܪܐ ܕܩܕܝܫ̈ܐ the company of the saints. With preps.; ܒܚܘܕܪܐ round about; ܠܚܘܕܪܐ all round, round about; ܡܕܝܢ̈ܬܐ ܕܒܚܘܕܪܐ the circumjacent towns.

ܚܘܕܪܘܢܐ pl. ܐ̈ m. dim. of ܚܘܕܪܐ. a little circle, circlet.

ܚܘܕܪܢܐܝܬ rt. ܚܕܪ. adv. in circumference, all round, on every side, circular; in an orbit or course; ܐܝܟ ܐܪܒܥ ܐܡܝܢ ܚܘܕܪܢܐܝܬ about four cubits in circumference.

ܚܘܕܪܢܝܐ, ܢܝܬܐ rt. ܚܕܪ. circular, spherical; arranged by course, revolving; ܐܪܥܐ ܚܘܕܪܢܝܬܐ ܗܝ the earth is round; ܬܫܥܐ ܐܠܦܝܢ ܚܘܕܪܢܝ̈ܢ ܕܫܢܬܐ nine thousand revolutions in the course of the year.

ܚܘܕܬܐ pl. ܚܘܕܬ̈ܐ rt. ܚܕܬ. m. a) a making new, initiating, founding, institution, dedication, consecration, esp. a dedication or consecration festival, anniversary festival, Germ. Jahresfeier; ܚܘܕܬܐ ܕܡܕܒܚܐ dedication of the altar; ܥܐܕܐ ܕܚܘܕܬܐ the feast of dedication; ܚܘܕܬܐ ܕܨܠܝܒܐ ܦܪܘܩܐ the feast of the saving Cross; ܚܘܕܬܐ ܕܡܠܟܐ or ܚܘܕܬܐ ܕܚܡܝܪܐ ܩܕܝܫܐ the renewal of the holy leaven; the designation of a bishop; the founding of a kingdom; an accession; ܚܘܕܬܐ ܕܩܢܘ̈ܢܐ the institution of canons, establishing of rules; a novelty, innovation esp. of false teaching. b) rebuilding, restoration; pl. repairs; ܚܘܕܬܐ ܕܚܪ̈ܒܬܐ the rebuilding of ruins; metaph. renewal, restitution, restoration e. g. to spiritual life, ܚܘܕܬܢ our being made new at the resurrection; ܚܘܕܬܗ ܕܢܡܘܣܐ the renewal of the law, the new law i. e. the Gospel; ܚܘܕܬܐ ܕܒܪܝܬܐ the renewal of creation; ܕܟܠ ܟܠܡܕܡ or ܚܘܕܬܐ ܕܟܠ the restitution or renewal of all things.

ܚܘܘܝܐ pl. ܚܘܘ̈ܝܐ rt. ܚܘܐ. m. a demonstration, proof.

ܚܘܘܪܐ pl. ܐ̈ rt. ܚܘܪ. m. whiteness, white heat, white flame; ܚܘܘܪܐ ܕܣܟ̈ܠܘܬܐ ܕܦܪܙܠܐ ܡܫܚܢ̈ܐ the excandescence of heated iron stakes; ܠܒܫܝܢ ܚܘܘܪܐ they put on white i. e. white clothing; chem. blanching.

ܚܘܘ̈ܬܐ pl. of ܚܘܝܐ. snakes.

ܚܘܙ to be glad; particip. adj. ܚܘܝܙ, ܐ, ܬܐ cheerful, ready, apt, prompt, spirited; ܦܪܨܘܦܗ ܚܘܝܙ ܗܘܐ ܘܢܗܝܪ his countenance was radiant and cheerful; ܪ̈ܟܫܐ ܚܘܝ̈ܙܝܢ spirited horses. Ethpa. ܐܬܚܘܙ to be cheerful, ready, prompt; ܐܬܚܘܙ ܘܐܬܬܟܠ he was ready and trustful. Derivatives, ܚܘܝܙܐܝܬ, ܚܘܝܙܘܬܐ.

ܚܘܚܐ m. a thorn, thornbush.

ܚܘܛ, ܚܛ fut. ܢܚܘܛ, inf. ܡܚܛ, act. part. ܚܐܛ, ܚܝܛܐ, pass. part. ܚܝܛ, ܚܝܛܐ. a) to sew on or up, to stitch up, piece on, patch, mend; ܚܛܘܗܝ ܒܡܫܟܐ ܕܥܪܒܐ they sewed him up in a leathern coat; ܚܘܛ ܠܗ ܨܪܝܐ ܕܥܒܕܬ ܐܢܐ mend the rent I have made; ܟܘܬܝܢܐ ܕܠܐ ܚܝܛܐ a seam-

less garment. b) *to dig.* ETHPE. ܐܬܚܝܛ *to be sewn on;* metaph. *to join, come together.* PA. ܚܝܛ *to sew together;* metaph. *to join, piece together;* ܫܐܠ ܘܚܝܛ ܡ̈ܠܐ ܣ̈ܓܝܐܬܐ *he borrowed and pieced on many expressions* i.e. *he plagiarized;* ܦܚܘܪ ܘܚܝܛ Lazarus was *bound and sewn up.* ETHPA. ܐܬܚܝܛ *to be sewn on* or *together.* DERIVATIVES, ܚܘܛܐ, ܚܝܘܛܐ, ܚ̈ܝܛܐ, ܚܝܛܘܬܐ.

ܚܘܛܐ or ܚܘܛܘܬܐ m. *lasciviousness.*

ܚܘܛܐ pl. ܐ̈ rt. ܚܛ. m. *a thread, string, measuring-line; a fillet;* ܚܘܛܐ ܕܬܠܬܐ ܠܐ ܒܥܓܠ ܡܬܦܣܩ *a threefold cord is not quickly broken;* ܡܢܘ ܡܬܚ ܥܠܝܗ ܚܘܛܐ *who stretched the line upon it?*

ܚܘܛܦܐ rt. ܚܛܦ. m. *seizing* or *carrying off by violence.*

ܚܘܛܪ, ܚܘܛܪܐ pl. ܝܢ, ܐ̈ rt. ܚܛܪ. m. *a staff, rod, sceptre; a pastoral staff;* ܚܘܛܪܐ ܕܪܥܝܐ *a shepherd's staff;* ܚܘܛܪܐ ܕܡܠܟܘܬܐ *the sceptre of the kingdom;* ܛܠܝܐ ܚܘܛܪܐ ܕܣܝܒܘܬܐ *youths are the staff of old age.*

ܚܘܛܪܬܐ f. *a hump,* ܕܓܡܠܐ *a camel's hump.*

ܚܘܝ PAEL conj. of ܚܘܐ; *to show,* &c.

ܚܘܝܐ pl. ܚܘ̈ܘܬܐ, generally m. *a snake, serpent;* metaph. *the devil;* heretics are called ܒܢܝ ܚܘܝܐ.

ܚܘܝܒܐ pl. ܐ̈ rt. ܚܘܒ. m. *finding guilty, condemning; condemnation;* ܐܝܢܐ ܚܘܝܒܐ ܢܗܘܐ ܠ *what condemnation shall there be?* ܚܘܝܒܐ ܐܪܡܝ ܥܠ *he condemned, passed sentence of condemnation.*

ܚܘܝܨܐ rt. ܚܨܐ. m. *an enclosure, place of safety; a veil.*

ܚܘܝܕܐ rt. ܚܕ. m. *a uniting, joining; junction, union, unity;* ܒܚܘܝܕܟ ܕܥܡ ܒܣܪܐ *at Thy union with flesh;* ܨܠܘܬܐ ܕܚܘܝܕܐ *prayer for unity.*

ܚܘܝܠܐܝܬ rt. ܚܝܠ. adv. *gladly, cheerfully, readily, willingly;* ܚܘܝܠܐܝܬ ܐܫܬܥܒܕܘ ܠܐܢܛܝܘܟܘܣ *they willingly became subject to Antiochus;* ܚܘܝܠܐܝܬ ܡܩܒܠܝܢ *they gladly accept.*

ܚܘܝܠ, ܚܘܝܠܘܬܐ pl. ܐ̈ rt. ܚܝܠ. f. *cheerfulness, alacrity, readiness;* ܩܕܡ ܒܢܦܫܗ ܚܘܝܠܘܬܐ ܗܘܐ ܠܗ ܕܢܩܢܐ *he was glad in himself at that which he might possess;* ܕܢܣܝܡܘܢ ܒܪܥܝܢܗܘܢ ܛܝܒܘܬܐ ܕܣܦܩܐ ܠܗܕܐ *they should store up in their mind readiness sufficient for this;* ܒܚܘܝܠܘܬܐ *gladly, readily, willingly;* ܒܚܘܝܠܘܬܐ ܐܫܬܠܡܘ *they cordially assented.*

ܚܘܝܛܐ pl. ܐ̈ rt. ܚܛ. m. *a patching together, fabrication.*

ܚܘܝܠܐ from ܚܝܠ. m. *strength, strengthening, help, comforting, exhortation;* ܐܠܗܐ ܚܘܝܠܐ ܕܡܚܝܠܘܬܢ *God the strength of our weakness;* ܚܘܝܠܐ ܕܥܠ ܬܝܒܘܬܐ *exhortation to repentance.*

ܚܘܝܪܐ rt. ܚܝܪ. m. *a tight bandage, compress.*

ܚܘܝܟܐ pl. ܐ̈ m. *a weaver.*

ܚܘܟܡܐ, ܚܘܟܡܬܐ pl. ܐ̈ rt. ܚܟܡ. m. *a contrivance, subtilty, cunning device* or *composition;* pl. *guiles;* ܒܚܘܟܡܐ ܕܡ̈ܠܐ *with cunningly devised phrases;* ܚܘ̈ܟܡܐ ܐ̈ܢܫܝܐ *human wiles.*

ܚܘܠܐ m. *a common* or *unconsecrated* place or thing, opp. ܩܘܕܫܐ *a consecrated thing,* and ܚܪܡܐ *a devoted thing.*

ܚܘܠܒܐ or ܚܘܠܒܢܐ pl. ܐ̈ m. *a thorn; a goad; a chisel.*

ܚܘܠܕܐ pl. ܐ̈ rt. ܚܠܕ. m. *a mole;* ܥܘܝܪ ܐܢܬ ܐܝܟ ܚܘܠܕܐ *thou art blind as a mole.*

ܚܘܠܛܢܐ rt. ܚܠܛ. m. *a mingling, commingling, contact; meeting, intercourse, acquaintance, intimacy; confusion;* ܚܘܠܛܢܗ ܕܢܘܗܪܐ ܥܡ ܚܫܘܟܐ *the mingling of light with darkness;* ܣܢܐ ܗܘܐ ܚܘܠܛܢܐ ܕܥܡ ܗܪܛܝܩܐ *he loathed any contact with heresy, intercourse with heretics.*

ܚܘܠܒܐ rt. ܚܠܒ. m. *must, new wine.*

ܚܘܠܠ, ܚܘܠܠܐ from ܚܠܠ. m. *a washing* or *cleansing;* ܚܘܠܠ ܡܐ̈ܢܐ *the washing of vessels.*

ܚܘܠܠܐ pl. ܐ̈ rt. ܚܠ. m. *a fissure, cavity.*

ܚܘܠܡܛܐ or ܚܘܠܡܘܛܐ pl. ܐ̈ m. *a chameleon.*

ܚܘܠܡܢ, ܚܘܠܡܢܐ pl. ܐ̈ rt. ܚܠܡ. m. *convalescence, recovery, healing, health;* ܩܠܝܠ ܩܠܝܠ ܠܚܘܠܡܢܐ ܡܩܪܒܝܢ ܠܗܘܢ *little by little they lead them to convalescence;* ܡܘܗܒܬܐ ܕܟܠ ܚܘܠܡ̈ܢܐ ܐܠܗ̈ܝܐ *the gift of all divine healings.*

ܚܘܠܡܢܝܐ, ܚܘܠܡܢܝܬܐ rt. ܚܠܡ. *healing, wholesome, salutary;* ܦܐ̈ܪܐ ܚܘܠܡܢ̈ܝܐ *wholesome fruits;* ܝܘܠܦܢܐ ܕܚܘܠܡܢܝܘܬܐ *the science of healing substances.*

ܚܘܠܒܐ pl. ܹܐ m. *a cavern, a hole, hollow* or *cleft* in the ground; ܚܘܠܒܐ ܕܡܕܒܪܐ *caverns in the desert;* ܚܘܠܒܐ ܥܡܝܩܐ ܕܐܪܥܐ *deep clefts in the earth.*

ܚܘܠܦ, ܚܘܠܦܐ pl. ܹܐ rt. ܚܠܦ. m. *a*) *a change, exchange;* ܚܘܠܦܐ ܕܐܣܝܪܐ *an exchange* of prisoners; ܚܘܠܦ ܡܥܡܪܐ *a change of abode, migration.* *b*) *a changing* or *succeeding in course,* ܚܘܠܦܐ ܕܙܒܢܐ *succeeding times* or *seasons.* *c*) the name of some shrub, *the willow* or *a reed.* *d*) = ܚܠܦ prep. *for.*

ܚܘܠܨ, ܚܘܠܨܐ rt. ܚܠܨ. m. *a spoiling, robbery; a spoil, the prey.*

ܚܘܡܐ rt. ܚܡ I. m. *heat, sultriness;* ܚܘܡܐ ܨܠܝܠܐ *clear heat;* ܚܘܡܐ ܕܡܕܒܪܐ *the dazzling heat of the desert.*

ܚܘܡܬܐ rt. ܚܡ II. f. *a broom.*

ܚܘܡܡܐ rt. ܚܡ I. m. *heat;* ܕܒܘܪܐ ܡܢ ܒܬܪ ܚܘܡܡܐ ܢܦܩܝܢ *bees swarm after hot weather.*

ܚܘܡܣܢܐ rt. ܚܡܣ. m. *endurance, constancy, perseverance.*

ܚܘܡܪ, ܚܘܡܪܐ rt. ܚܡܪ. m. *shame, bashfulness, modesty;* ܕܠܐ ܚܘܡܪܐ *shameless, immodest.*

ܚܘܡܪܐ emph. ܚܘܡܪܬܐ or ܚܡܪܬܐ pl. ܚܘܡܪܝܢ, ܚܘܡܪܐ or ܚܘܡܪܬܐ f. *a bead; stone* of a necklace; *a vertebra* or *joint* of the body; *a socket* or *joint* of a column; *a berry;* ܚܘܡܪܐ ܝܩܝܪܐ or ܚܘܡܪܬܐ ܝܩܝܪܬܐ *precious gems;* ܚܘܡܪܐ ܕܚܨܐ *the vertebrae of the spine;* ܚܘܡܪܐ ܕܡܘܬܐ *the berries of the deadly nightshade.*

ܚܘܡܫܐ pl. ܹܐ from ܚܡܫ. m. *a*) *a fifth part, a fifth;* ܬܪܝܢ ܚܘܡܫܝܢ *two-fifths.* *b*) *the loins, abdomen.*

ܚܢ, ܚܘܢ fut. ܢܚܘܢ, cf. ܚܢ. *to have pity on;* ܛܝܒܘܬܐ ܕܚܢܐ ܠܚܛܝܐ grace *which takes pity on sinners;* ܚܢܗ ܣܘܠܛܢܐ *the Sultan had pity on him.*

ܚܘܢ *show us;* imper. of verb ܚܘܝ with suff. I pl.

ܚܘܢܛܬܐ rt. ܚܢܛ. f. *a mixture of spices* for embalming the dead; ܚܘܢܛܬܐ ܕܚܢܛܘܗܝ ܠܡܪܢ *the spices wherewith they embalmed our Lord.*

ܚܣ, ܚܘܣ fut. ܢܚܘܣ, inf. ܡܚܣ, imper. ܚܘܣ, act. part. ܚܐܣ, ܚܣܐ. *a*) *to pity, have pity, spare, have regard;* with ܥܠ; ܠܐ ܚܣ ܥܠ *if He spared not His Son;* ܚܘܣ ܥܠ ܢܟܣܬܟ *spare thy slaughter* i.e. *be not slaughtered;* ܚܘܣ ܥܠ ܦܓܪܟ *spare thy flesh.* *b*) *to spare,* hence *to use sparingly; to refrain from* with ܡܢ, ܚܘܣ ܡܢ ܥܣܩܘܬܐ ܕܐܟܠܩܪܨܐ *abstain from calumny;* ܚܐܣܢܐ ܕܠܡܐ *I forbear lest . . .* ܚܣ is constantly used to express deprecation of evil, generally with ܠ of the pers., *God forbid, far be it from me, let it not be;* prob. optative use of perfect ellipt. for *God save us from doing such and such a thing;* ܚܣ ܘܠܐ ܢܗܘܐ *God forbid that it should be;* ܚܣ ܠܢ *far be it from us.* DERIVATIVES, ܚܘܣܝܐ, ܚܣܘܣܐ, ܚܣܘܣܐܝܬ, ܚܣܘܣܘܬܐ.

ܚܘܣܝ, ܚܘܣܝܐ pl. ܹܐ from ܚܣܐ. m. *a*) *atonement, propitiation, pardon, remission.* *b*) *the breastplate* worn by the high-priest; *the mercy-seat,* hence ܒܝܬ ܚܘܣܝܐ *the Holy of Holies, the temple.* *c*) eccles. *absolution, the giving of absolution;* ܛܟܣܐ ܕܚܘܣܝܐ *the rite* or *office of absolution;* pl. *prayers for pardon.*

ܚܘܣܟܐ rt. ܚܣܟ. m. *restraint;* ܚܘܣܟܐ ܕܡܢ ܢܦܫܟ *that which you deny yourself.*

ܚܘܣܢ, ܚܘܣܢܐ rt. ܚܣ. m. *a*) *pity, indulgence, lenity;* ܕܠܐ ܚܘܣܢ *harsh;* ܕܠܐ ܪܚܡܝܢ ܘܠܐ ܚܘܣܢ *merciless and pitiless;* ܣܓܝ ܚܘܣܢܐ *very pitiful.* *b*) *sparing, frugality;* ܒܚܘܣܢ *sparingly;* ܕܠܐ ܚܘܣܢ *without measure.*

ܚܘܣܢܐ pl. ܹܐ rt. ܚܣܢ. m. *strength, defence,* ܐܬܕܝܫܘ ܒܚܘܣܢܐ ܕܡܪܥܝܬܐ *they were trodden down in the defence of the flock;* ܬܚܝܬ ܚܘܣܢܐ ܘܣܬܪܐ ܕܐܠܗܐ *under the defence and protection of God.*

ܚܘܣܪܢܐ pl. ܹܐ rt. ܚܣܪ. m. *want, loss, harm, damage, ruin; a fine, penalty, confiscation; expense;* ܠܝܬ ܒܕܚܠܬܗ ܕܐܠܗܐ ܚܘܣܪܢܐ *in the fear of God is no loss;* ܚܘܣܪܢܐ ܕܟܠܢ ܡܬܡܠܝܢ ܡܢ ܝܘܬܪܢܐ ܕܟܠܢ *the wants of all of us are supplied by the advantages of all of us;* ܚܘܣܪܢܐ ܕܥܘܠܐ *unjust exaction;* ܐܦܠܐ ܥܠ ܚܘܣܪܢܐ ܚܐܫ ܗܘܐ *nor did he mind expense.*

ܚܦ, ܚܘܦ fut. ܢܚܘܦ, act. part. ܚܐܦ, ܚܝܦܐ. *to sprinkle, rub, cleanse;* ܣܚܬ ܘܚܦܬ ܠܒܢܝܗ̈ *she washed and rubbed her children.*

ܚܘܦܛܐ pl. ܴ̈ܬܐ rt. ܚܦܛ. m. *exhortation, encouragement*; ܚܘܦܛܐ ܕܥܠ ܙܕܩܬܐ *exhortation to almsgiving*; ܒܚܘܦܛܐ ܕܦܪܩܠܝܛܐ *through the inworking of the Comforter.*

ܚܘܦܝ, ܚܘܦܝܐ rt. ܚܦܐ. m. *a) covering over* or *hiding*; ܚܘܦܝܐ ܕܣܗܪܐ *an eclipse of the moon*; ܚܘܦܝܗ ܕܟܘܟܒܐ *the occultation of a star. b) a stake* or *prop* for a vine; *earth heaped up* round the stem of a tree. *c)* gram. *the passing over* or *leaving unpronounced* of a letter.

ܚܘܦܢܐ pl. ܝ̈ܢ, ܴ̈ܬܐ f. properly *the hands bent for holding, the hollow of the hand, palm of the hand, a handful*, with ܡܠܐ *to fill the hand, take handfuls*; ܚܘܦܢܐ ܚܘܦܢܐ *by handfuls*; ܙܪܥܐ ܕܩܛܝܪ ܒܚܘܦܢܘܗܝ *the seed held together in his hands*; rit. ܢܣܒ ܟܗܢܐ ܦܓܪܐ ܘܕܡܐ ܡܢ ܟܣܐ ܒܚܘܦܢܘܗܝ the priest *shall take the body and blood from the cup into his hands.*

ܚܨ, ܚܳܨ fut. ܢܚܘܨ, imper. ܚܘܨ, act. part. ܚܳܐܶܨ, ܚܳܝܨܳܐ, pass. part. ܚܺܝܨ, ܚܺܝܨܳܐ, ܚܺܝܨܳܬܳܐ. *a) to bind fast, press closely, hold tight*; ܚܳܨ ܐܶܢܽܘܢ ܣܳܛܳܢܳܐ ܒܚܰܒ̈ܠܶܐ ܕܚܰܛܺܝܬܳܐ *Satan bound them fast with the cords of sin*; ܚܳܨ ܐܺܝܕܶܗ *he held his hand close* =*was close-fisted. b)* with ܩܺܝܬܳܪܳܐ *to play the cithern*; with ܡܺܢ̈ܝܳܐ *to touch the chords*; with ܪܗܛܐ *to be swift. c)* metaph. *to compel*; *to strengthen, grow strong*; ܥܕܡܐ ܕܚܳܐܶܨ ܘܡܬܚܠܡ *till he grows strong and gains health*; ܕܒܙܝܢܐ ܕܗܝܡܢܘܬܐ ܢܚܘܨ ܠܟܪܘܙܘܬܐ *that with the panoply of faith he may make strong the preaching of the Gospel.* Participial adj. *close, dense, solid, firm, robust, vigorous*; *swift, pressing*; ܐܐܪ ܚܺܝܨܳܐ *dense air*; ܬܘܪܣܝܬܐ ܕܚܝܨܐ ܘܡܝܬܪܐ ܡܢ ܚܠܒܐ *solid food and better than milk*; ܣܒܐ ܚܝܨܐ *a robust old man*; ܪܗܛܐ ܚܝܨܐ *swift running*; ܚܝܨܐ ܐܓܘܢܟ *thy combat is hard*; ܩܪܝܬܐ ܚܝܨܬܐ ܛܒ *a very pressing call*; ܡ̈ܠܐ ܚ̈ܝܨܬܐ ܘܝܩܝܪ̈ܬܐ *pressing and weighty words*; gram. *a strengthened* i.e. *a doubled* letter. Pa. ܚܰܝܶܨ *to bind together, to strengthen*; ܡܚܝܨܝܢ ܠܗ ܠܐܠܦܐ *undergirding the ship*; ܚܝܨܘ ܢܝܪܐ ܕܒܝܫܐ ܥܠ ܨܘܪܝܗܘܢ *they bound the yoke of the Evil One on their necks*; metaph. esp. of giving strength to the paralyzed; ܚܝܨ ܡܫܪ̈ܝܐ *strengthen the paralyzed*; ܡܚܝܨ ܟܪܝܗܐ *he strengthens the weak*; gram. *doubled*; ܟܠ ܐܬܘܬܐ ܕܡܚܝܨܐ ܠܒܪ ܡܢ ܐܪܒܝܐ *every letter strengthened* i.e. *having Teshdid in Arabic.* Ethpa. ܐܬܚܝܨ *to be firmly bound, closely pressed*; *to be thickened, strengthened, become firm*; gram. *to be strengthened* or *doubled*; ܐܝܟܢܐ ܕܬܬܩܫܐ ܘܬܬܚܝܨ ܚܝܠܗ ܐܝܟ ܦܪܙܠܐ *so that his strength may become hard and firm like iron*; ܕܢܬܚܝܨܘܢ ܘܢܬܠܒܒܘܢ ܩܠܝܠܐ *that the swift may be strengthened and encouraged.* Derivatives, ܚܝܨܐ, ܚܘܨܐ, ܚܝܨܐ, ܚܝܨܘܬܐ, ܡܚܝܨܢܐ, ܚܝܨܐܝܬ.

ܚܘܨܐ rt. ܚܨ. m. *the spathe* of a palm; *a palm mat.*

ܚܘܨܦܐ rt. ܚܨܦ. m. *boldness, impudence, frowardness*; *persistence*; ܚܘܨܦܐ ܘܡܪܚܘܬܐ *impudence and audacity*; ܟܒܫ ܚܘܨܦܗ ܕܐܠܘܨܐ *he checked the wantonness of the oppressor.*

ܚܩ, ܚܘܩ fut. ܢܚܘܩ, act. part. ܚܳܐܶܩ *to crack, creak*; ܢܘܪܐ ܚܳܩܰܬ *the fire crackled*; ܬܪܥܐ ܚܳܐܶܩ *the door creaks.*

ܚܘܩ, ܚܘܩܐ m. *a stair*; ܚܘܩ̈ܐ ܕܣܘܠܩܬܐ *the steps of the staircase.*

ܚܘܩ pl. ܚܘ̈ܩܐ m. *a line, verse, meaning*; ܟܠܡܕܡ ܕܐܡܝܪ ܒܚܘ̈ܩܘܗܝ ܕܟܬܒܐ *everything that is expressed in the lines of the book*; ܬܢܐ ܚܘ̈ܩܐ ܕܟܬܒܐ *it repeats the verses of Scripture.*

ܚܘܪ fut. ܢܶܚܘܰܪ, pres. part. ܚܳܘܰܪ *to be* or *become white*; *to assume white* i.e. *white* clothing as a party badge; ܢܚܬܘܗܝ ܚܘܪܘ ܐܝܟ ܢܘܗܪܐ *his garments became white like light*; ܟܠܗ ܚܘܪ ܗܘܐ *he turned white.* Pa. ܚܰܘܰܪ imper. ܚܰܘܰܪ *to whiten, bleach, clean*; metaph. *to make white* or *clear* from the stains of sin; ܢܰܟܺܝ ܘܚܰܘܰܪ ܢܚ̈ܬܐ *he cleansed and whitened garments*; ܚܰܘܰܪ ܛܘ̈ܠܫܝܢ *clean away our stains.* Ethpa. ܐܬܚܘܪ *to become* or *be made white* or *clean*; *to be blanched*; *to be whitewashed*; ܢܬܚܘܪܘܢ ܥܕ̈ܬܐ *the churches are to be whitewashed.* Aph. ܐܚܘܪ inf. ܡܚܘܪܘ, act. and pass. part. ܡܚܘܪ, f. ܡܚܘܪܐ *to make white, blanch, to cause to appear white*; ܟܒܪܝܬܐ ܕܡܚܘܪܐ *sulphur which whitens*; part. adj. *white*, with ܓܪܒܐ *white* or *pale from leprosy*; ܡܚܘܪ ܐܝܟ ܬܠܓܐ *white as snow.* Derivatives, ܚܘܪܐ, ܚܘܪܐ, ܚܘܪܘܪܐ, ܚܘܪܘܬܐ, ܡܚܘܪܢܐ, ܚܘܪܢܐ, ܡܚܘܪܢܐ, ܚܘܪܢܝܬܐ.

ܚܘܪ, ܚܳܪ fut. ܢܶܚܘܳܪ, inf. ܡܶܚܳܪ, imper. ܚܘܳܪ, act. part. ܚܳܐܰܪ, ܚܳܝܪܳܐ. *a*) *to look, behold, gaze* with ܒ, ܠܘܳܬ or ܠܥܶܠ *to look at, regard, have regard to, consider;* with ܒ *to give heed to;* with ܡܶܢ ܩܕܳܡ *to beware of;* ܢܰܥܺܝܡ ܠܡܶܚܳܪ *delightful to behold;* ܚܳܪܶܬ ܒܟܽܠ ܥܒܳܕܳܐ *I considered every work;* ܫܽܘܪܳܐ ܕܚܳܐܰܪ ܠܡܰܕܢܚܳܐ *a wall with an eastward aspect;* ܚܘܳܪ ܠܢܰܦܫܳܟ *look to thyself, be circumspect;* ܚܳܐܰܪ ܐܽܘܪܚܳܐ *a watchman.* *b*) *to look for, expect* with acc. or ܠ; *to regard, concern* with ܠ or ܠܥܶܠ; ܚܳܐܰܪ ܡܰܠܟܳܐ ܠܚܰܪܬܳܐ ܕܨܶܒܽܘܬܶܗ *the king looks for the end of his affair;* ܐܰܝܟܰܢܳܐ ܚܳܝܪܺܝܢ ܐܢ̱ܬܽܘܢ ܕܢܶܗܘܶܐ *how can you expect that...?* ܕܚܶܛܶܐ ܠܳܐ ܐ̱ܢܳܫ ܚܳܐܰܪ ܗ̄ܘܳܐ *no one regarded the wheat* i. e. crops were neglected in time of pestilence; ܠܥܶܠ ܕܒܢܰܝܢܳܫܳܐ ܚܳܐܰܪ ܗ̄ܘܳܐ ܦܽܘܪܩܳܢܳܐ *salvation concerned mankind;* ܐܰܝܢܳܐ ܕܒܳܥܶܐ ܕܠܳܐ ܚܳܝܪܺܝܢ ܒܶܗ *he who seeks what does not concern him.* Aph. ܐܰܚܺܝܪ *a*) *to cause to look at* or *regard; to show, direct;* ܡܰܚܺܝܪ ܠܗܽܘܢ ܠܰܐܪܥܳܢܳܝܳܬܳܐ ܕܠܳܐ ܢܶܚܘܪܽܘܢ ܠܫܡܰܝܳܢܳܝܳܬܳܐ *he made them look towards earthly things lest they should regard heavenly things;* ܐܰܚܺܝܪ ܠܰܢ ܒܫܒܺܝܠܰܘܗܝ *direct us in* God's *ways;* ܠܥܶܠ ܡܶܠܰܘܗܝ ܡܰܚܺܝܪ ܗ̄ܘܳܐ ܠܺܝܗܽܘܕܳܝܶܐ *he addressed his words to the Jews.* *b*) *to urge.* *c*) *to see, understand;* ܠܳܐ ܡܰܚܺܝܪ ܗ̄ܘܳܐ ܘܡܶܣܬܰܟܰܠ *he did not see and understand.* Derivatives, ܚܶܙܘܳܐ, ܚܘܳܪܳܐ, ܚܰܘܪܳܐ, ܚܺܝܪܳܐ, ܡܰܚܺܝܪܳܢܳܐ.

ܚܶܘܳܪ, ܚܶܘܳܪܳܐ pl. ܐ̈ rt. ܚܘܪ. m. *a*) *sight, a sight, aspect, look, appearance;* ܚܶܘܳܪܳܐ ܕܒܰܢܝܳܐ *a spectacle;* ܩܰܘܡܬܶܗ ܘܚܶܘܳܪܶܗ ܫܰܦܺܝܪܺܝܢ ܗ̄ܘܰܘ his *stature and appearance were pleasing;* ܚܶܘܳܪܳܐ ܡܰܪܺܝܪܳܐ *a bitter* or *sad sight;* metaph. *a likeness, model, copy, example;* ܚܶܘܳܪܳܐ ܕܬܰܠܡܺܝܕ̈ܶܐ ܩܰܕܡܳܝ̈ܶܐ *the example of the first disciples.* *b*) *a lamb of the first year, a yearling.* *c*) *a cinder.* *d*) *the white poplar.*

ܚܰܘܳܪܳܐ rt. ܚܘܪ. m. *an envious* or *gluttonous person.*

ܚܶܘܳܪ, ܚܶܘܳܪܳܐ, ܚܶܘܳܪܬܳܐ pl. m. ܝ̈ܢ, ܐ̈, f. ܢ̈, ܬ̈ܐ, rt. ܚܘܪ. *white, silvery, clear, bright;* ܥܰܡܪܳܐ ܚܶܘܳܪܳܐ *white wool;* ܡܰܚܘܳܬܳܐ ܚܶܘܳܪܬܳܐ ܐܰܘ ܕܡܶܚܘܰܪܳܐ *a white* or *whitish spot;* ܐܶܣܛܠܶܐ ܚܶܘܳܪ̈ܳܬܳܐ *white robes.* Special meanings: *a*) ܚܶܘܳܪ ܒܰܝܥܬܳܐ *the white of an egg.* *b*) m. various trees and plants, such as *the white alder, white vine.* *c*) *white metal, tin.* *d*) *silver coin;* ܪ̈ܶܒܘܳܢ ܚܶܘܳܪ̈ܶܐ *silver dinars;* ܚܰܡܫܡܳܐܐ ܐܰܠܦܺܝܢ ܚܶܘܳܪ̈ܶܐ *500,000 pieces of silver.* *e*) pl. *white garments* ellipt. for ܡܳܐܢ̈ܶܐ ܚܶܘܳܪ̈ܶܐ; ܫܰܒܬܳܐ ܕܚܶܘܳܪ̈ܶܐ *the week of white* i.e. Easter or Whitsun weeks when those who had received baptism wore white for the whole week as a symbol of baptismal purity; ܩܶܪܝܳܢܳܐ ܕܬܪܶܝܢ ܕܚܶܘܳܪ̈ܶܐ *second lesson for Easter week.* *f*) pl. f. *white hair, old age;* ܨܰܦܝܳܐ ܚܶܘܳܪ̈ܳܬܳܐ ܡܰܘܠܕܳܐ *care produces white hair;* ܚܶܘܳܪ̈ܳܬܶܗ ܡܝܰܩܪ̈ܳܬܳܐ *his honourable grey hairs.*

ܚܘܳܪ, ܚܘܳܪܳܐ rt. ܚܘܪ. m. *a look, glance; gazing, consideration, contemplation; aim, intention;* ܚܘܳܪܳܐ ܚܰܪܺܝܦܳܐ *a sharp glance;* ܚܘܳܪܳܗ ܠܥܶܠ ܐܰܪܺܝܡܰܬ *she looked up;* ܐܰܝܠܶܝܢ ܚܘܳܪ̈ܶܐ ܡܰܥܒܪܺܝܢ ܠܰܢ ܠܰܬܶܐܘܪܺܝܐ ܕܰܐܠܳܗܳܐ *what considerations lead us to the contemplation of God.*

ܚܘܳܪܳܐ pl. ܚܘܳܪ̈ܶܐ, ܚܘܳܪ̈ܺܝܢ rt. ܚܪܪ. m. *a hole, aperture;* ܚܘܳܪܳܐ ܕܰܐܣܦܺܝܣ *an asp's hole.*

ܚܘܳܪܒܳܐ pl. ܶܐ rt. ܚܪܒ. m. *a*) *a desert, plain, waste place,* hence pr. n. *the Arabah, the low desert tract* or *plain* of the Jordan from the Sea of Galilee to the Red Sea; ܐܰܬܪܳܐ ܚܘܳܪܒܳܐ *a desert place.* *b*) *emptiness, solitude, desolation, devastation; laying waste, ravaging;* ܐܳܬܳܐ ܛܰܡܐܬܳܐ ܕܚܘܳܪܒܳܐ *the abominable sign of desolation;* ܚܘܳܪܒܳܗ ܕܐܘܪܶܫܠܶܡ *the laying waste* or *the ruins of Jerusalem;* ܚܘܳܪܒܳܐ ܕܥܺܕ̈ܳܬܳܐ *the laying waste of churches.* *c*) *a stork* or *heron.*

ܚܘܳܪܒܰܩܢܳܐ m. *hellebore.*

ܚܶܘܳܪܘܳܪܳܐ, ܚܶܘܳܪܘܳܪܬܳܐ rt. ܚܘܪ. adj. *whitish;* subst. m. pl. ܚܶܘܳܪܘܳܪ̈ܶܐ *white spots* in the eye or *a web of white* obscuring the sight.

ܚܶܘܳܪܽܘܬܳܐ rt. ܚܘܪ. f. *whiteness;* metaph. *wantonness* of the eyes.

ܚܘܳܪܳܓܳܐ rt. ܚܪܓ. m. *cutting, laceration.*

ܚܘܳܪܳܓܬܳܐ, ܚܘܳܪܳܓܬܳܐ rt. ܚܪܓ. f. *a scratch, gash; laceration.*

ܚܘܳܪܳܒܳܐ pl. ܶܐ rt. ܚܪܒ. m. *parching;* ܡܩܰܪܶܪ ܐ̱ܢܳܐ ܠܟܽܠ ܚܘܳܪ̈ܳܒܶܐ *I cool all parching heats;* metaph. *ardent prayers;* astron. *occultation* of a star by reason of its passing near the sun.

ܚܘܳܪܡܳܫܳܐ from ܚܪܡܫ. m. *wagging the tail* as a dog.

ܚܘܳܪܛܳܐ pl. ܶܐ m. a kind of *vetches* or *tares* used for fodder.

ܚܘܪܙܥܐ m. *the service tree, sorbus domestica.*

ܚܘܪܢܝܐ, ܢܝܬܐ rt. ܚܘܪ. *whitish, grey;* ܐܪܥܐ ܚܘܪܢܝܬܐ *white clayey soil.*

ܚܘܪܒܬܐ f. *the white poplar,* also *the black poplar* or *alder.*

ܚܘܪܦܐ rt. ܚܪܦ. m. *a sharp edge* or *point* e.g. of a sword; ܚܘܪܦܐ ܕܢܩܝܪ̈ܐ *the points of the nails;* metaph. *the highest point, extreme, best, vigour;* ܚܘܪܦܐ ܕܛܠܝܘܬܐ *the height of youth;* ܚܘܪܦܐ ܕܚܡܘܬܐ ܕܫܡܫܐ *the extreme fierceness of the sun.*

ܚܘܪܩ, ܚܘܪܩܐ, ܚܘܪܩ rt. ܚܪܩ. m. generally with ܫܢ̈ܐ *gnashing of teeth.*

ܚܘܪܡܢܐ pl. ܐ̈ܐ rt. ܚܪܡ. m. *a limit, definition, that which is determined, an established purpose, decree;* ܐܝܟ ܚܘܪܡܢܐ ܕܟܬܒ̈ܐ ܩܕܝܫ̈ܐ ܐܝܬܝܗ̇ *our confession is according to that which is determined by Scripture;* ܒܪ̈ܝܬܐ ܒܚܘܪܡܢܗ ܕܒܪܘܝܗܘܢ ܢܛܪܢ ܛܟܣܐ ܕܝܠܗܘܢ *the creatures by the decree of their Creator hold their special order;* ܣܪܝܩܐ ܘܒܛܝܠܐ ܚܘܝܗ ܠܚܘܪܡܢܗܘܢ God *showed their purpose to be void and vain;* with ܩܕܡ *predestination;* ܙܒܢܐ ܕܚܘܪܡܢܐ *the appointed time;* ܚܘܪܡܢܐ ܕܫܢ̈ܝܐ *a fixed* or *appointed number of years.*

ܚܘܪܪ, ܚܘܪܪܐ, ܚܘܪܪ rt. ܚܪ. m. *freeing, giving freedom;* ܚܘܪܪܐ ܡܢ ܕܚܠܬܐ *freedom from fear;* ܚܘܪܪ ܥܒܕ̈ܝܟ *the manumission of thy slaves;* ܚܘܪܪ ܐܣܝܪ̈ܐ *the release of prisoners;* ܚܘܪܪ ܡܕܐܬܐ *exemption from tax* or *tribute; exemption* of monasteries from episcopal jurisdiction, *a monastery so exempt* and directly under the patriarch.

ܚܘܪܫܦܐ m. *the plum-tree.*

ܚܘܪܫܐ pl. ܐ̈ܐ rt. ܚܪܫ. m. *quinsy, sore throat, hoarseness.*

ܚܘܫܒ, ܚܘܫܒܐ, ܚܘܫܒ pl. ܐ̈ܐ rt. ܚܫܒ. m. *reckoning, thinking, thought, idea, opinion, intention, design, council;* ܟܠܗܘܢ ܚܘܫ̈ܒܝܟ ܢܨܠܚܘܢ *may all thy intentions be successful;* ܠܐ ܕܐܢ ܒܚܘܫܒ̈ܘܗܝ ܟܣܝ̈ܐ *he does not judge in his secret thoughts;* ܚܘܫܒܐ ܒܪ ܚܐܪܐ *a noble thought;* ܢܣܒܘ ܚܘܫܒܐ *they took council;* ܕܠܐ ܚܘܫܒܐ *rashly; an objection,* ܫܪܝܐ ܚܘܫ̈ܒܐ *solution* or *answer to objections;* gram. *the part understood* in an elliptical sentence.

ܚܘܫܒܢܝܐ, ܚܘܫܒܢܝܬܐ pl. m. ܐ̈ܐ, f. ܚܘܫܒܢܝ̈ܬܐ rt. ܚܫܒ. adj. *mental, in thought;* gram. *understood, not expressed.*

ܚܘܫܒܢ, ܚܘܫܒܢܐ, ܚܘܫܒܢ pl. ܐ̈ܐ, ܐ̈ܐ rt. ܚܫܒ. m. *a) a numbering, number, fixed* or *appointed number; an account, reckoning; arithmetic, calculation, computation, enumeration, census;* ܚܘܫܒܢܐ ܕܟܣܦܐ *an account of the money;* ܟܣܦܐ ܚܘܫܒܢ̈ܝܢ *money according to computation;* ܠܥܠ ܡܢ ܚܘܫܒܢܐ *beyond calculation, innumerable, immeasurable;* ܕܠܐ ܚܘܫܒܢ *innumerable, endless;* with ܥܒܕ *to take account, reckon;* with ܝܗܒ or ܥܒܕ *to give account;* ܚܘܫܒܢܐ ܚܘܪܐ *a white pebble* [Gr. ψῆφος]. *b)* Ar. *a small cushion.*

ܚܘܫܚ, ܚܘܫܚܐ, ܚܘܫܚ pl. ܐ̈ܐ rt. ܚܫܚ. m. *use;* ܚܘܫܚ̈ܘܗܝ ܕܢܡܘܣܐ ܐܬܒܛܠܘ ܒܗܘܝ ܡܐܬܝܬܗ ܕܡܚܝܢܢ *the uses of the law became void at the coming of our Saviour.*

ܚܘܛ imper. of verb ܢܚܛ *to descend.*

ܚܘܛܛܐ pl. ܐ̈ܐ from ܚܛܛ. m. *tickling, itching, longing; enticement, allurement;* ܒܚܘܛܛܐ ܕܡܫܡܥܬܗܘܢ *with itching ears;* ܡܟܐ ܕܡܫܬܓܫ ܐܢܬ ܒܚܘܛܛܗ ܕܪܓܬܐ *so much as thou art disturbed by itching desire;* ܚܘܛ̈ܛܐ ܕܠܐ ܡܠܠܐ ܕܛܠܝܘܬܐ *the speechless longings of childhood;* ܚܘܛ̈ܛܐ ܕܦܓܪܐ—ܕܚܛܝܬܐ *the enticements of the body, of sin.*

ܚܘܛܛܢܝܐ *inciting, inflammatory, enticing.*

ܚܘܬܡ, ܚܘܬܡܐ, ܚܘܬܡ pl. ܐ̈ܐ rt. ܚܬܡ. m. *the end, conclusion;* ܚܘܬܡܐ ܕܐܓܪܬܢ *the end of our letter;* ܥܕܡܐ ܠܚܘܬܡ ܡܙܡܘܪܐ *to the end of the psalm;* usually rit. *the conclusion* of an office, esp. *the final prayer* after the celebration of Holy Communion, *the conclusion, obsignation* or *final benediction;* pl. *concluding versicles, dimissory hymns* or *prayers,* sometimes ܒܪ̈ܟܬܐ; ܒܘܪܟܬܐ ܕܚܘܬܡܐ *the final* or *dimissory blessing; the recital of the whole psalter;* ܗܢܘܢ ܕܒܟܠ ܫܒܘܥܐ ܡܦܩܝܢ ܚܘܬܡܐ ܠܡܙܡܘܪ̈ܐ *those who each week recite the whole psalter to its conclusion.*

ܚܘܬܪ, ܚܘܬܪܐ rt. ܚܬܪ. m. *pride, pomp;* ܚܒܝܒ ܚܘܬܪܐ ܠܒܢ̈ܝ ܚܐܪ̈ܐ *pride is dear to the free; pride, boast, honour, glory;* ܚܘܬܪܐ ܘܫܘܒܗܪܐ ܕܟܝܢܢ *the pride and boast of our nature.*

ܚܙܐ fut. ܢܶܚܙܶܐ, inf. ܡܶܚܙܳܐ, imper. ܚܙܝ, act. part. ܚܳܙܶܐ, ܚܳܙܝܳܐ, ܚܳܙܝܳܐ, ܚܳܙܝܳܬܳܐ, pl. ܚܳܙܶܝܢ, ܚܳܙܰܝܳܐ, f. ܚܳܙܝܳܢ, ܚܳܙܝܳܬܳܐ, pass. part. ܚܙܶܐ, ܚܙܶܝܳܐ *to see. a) to perceive, consider, notice;* ܠܡܛܰܠܠܳܐ ܐܰܝܟ ܫܪܳܪܳܐ ܚܳܙܶܐ *he takes the shadow for reality. b) to provide,* ܐܰܠܳܗܳܐ ܢܶܚܙܶܐ ܐܶܡܪܳܐ ܠܥܳܠܬܳܐ *God will provide a lamb for the burnt-offering. c)* with ܐܰܦ̈ܶܐ lit. *to see the face = to appear before, visit. d) to look, take heed, watch;* ܚܙܝ ܠܳܟ *look to thyself, beware;* ܙܶܠ ܘܰܚܙܝ ܬܰܪ̈ܥܶܐ *go and watch the doors;* pass. part. ܠܳܐ ܚܙܶܐ ܠܰܢ *it did not seem to us;* as adj. *visible, respected, remarkable, well-known,* Germ. *angesehen;* ܥܺܕܬܳܐ ܚܙܺܝܬܳܐ *the visible Church;* ܡܫܰܒܚܳܐ ܘܚܙܶܝܳܐ *notable and remarkable;* ܢܶܫ̈ܶܐ ܚܙܺܝܳܬܳܐ *notable women.* ETHPE. ܐܶܬܚܙܺܝ *a) to be seen, to be visible;* ܐܰܠܳܗܳܐ ܕܠܳܐ ܡܶܬܚܙܶܐ *the invisible God;* ܡܶܬܚܰܙܝܳܢܳܐ ܕܶܐܝܬܰܝܗܽܘܢ ܗܘܰܘ ܡܶܢ ܐܰܝܠܶܝܢ ܕܠܳܐ ܡܶܬܚܰܙܝܳܢ *visible things have their being from those which are invisible. b) to let oneself be seen, show oneself, appear,* hence *to seem;* ܡܶܬܚܰܙܝܳܐ ܠܺܝ, ܠܰܢ *it seemed to me, to us,* &c.; ܐܶܬܚܙܺܝ ܠܺܝ *I think, I consider;* ܐܶܢ ܡܶܬܚܰܙܝܳܐ *if it seems good, if it is approved. c) to show* or *prove oneself,* hence *to be* strong, victorious, &c.; ܘܶܐܬܚܙܺܝܘ ܡܚܺܝܠܶܐ ܘܥܰܪܩܘ *they were weak and fled;* ܒܟܽܠܗܽܘܢ ܩܪ̈ܳܒܰܘܗ̱ܝ ܐܶܬܚܙܺܝ *he was victorious in all his wars;* ܗܽܘ ܕܡܶܬܚܰܙܝܳܢܽܘܬܳܐ ܥܰܡܶܗ ܐܺܝܬܶܝܗ̇ *he on whose side was the victory. d) to receive sight* with ܠ and pers. pron. suff. ETHPEAUAL ܐܶܬܚܰܙܘܺܝ *to obtain honour* or *glory, to distinguish oneself; to make a show* or *spectacle of oneself; to boast;* ܗܳܢܽܘܢ ܕܡܰܥܕܶܝܢ ܕܢܶܬܚܰܙܘܽܘܢ ܒܨܠܰܘ̈ܳܬܗܽܘܢ *those who are wont to make a boast of their prayers, to say prayers for appearance sake.* DERIVATIVES, ܚܶܙܘܳܐ, ܚܙܳܘܳܐ, ܚܙܘܳܝܳܐ, ܚܳܙܝܳܐ, ܚܙܳܝܳܐ, ܚܙܺܝܬܳܐ, ܚܶܙܝܳܢܳܐ, ܚܶܙܝܳܢܽܘܬܳܐ, ܚܶܙܬܳܐ, ܚܶܙܘܳܐ, ܡܶܚܙܳܐ, ܡܶܚܙܝܳܢܳܐ, ܡܶܬܚܙܳܘܝܳܢܽܘܬܳܐ, ܡܶܬܚܙܳܝܳܢܳܐ, ܡܶܬܚܰܙܝܳܢܳܐܺܝܬ, ܡܶܬܚܰܙܝܳܢܽܘܬܳܐ.

ܚܙܳܐ or ܚܙܳܝܳܐ pl. ܚܶܙ̈ܝܳܐ or ܚܶܙ̈ܳܝܶܐ m. *a depth, an abyss;* ܚܶܙ̈ܝܳܐ ܕܰܐܪܥܳܐ or ܚܙܳܝ̈ܶܗ ܕܥܽܘܡܩܳܐ *the bowels of the earth;* ܠܚܶܙ̈ܝܳܐ ܕܠܶܒܳܟ ܠܡܶܥܒܰܩ *to sound the depths of thy heart.*

ܚܙܳܒܳܐ pl. ܚܙ̈ܳܒܶܐ m. *a barrel, tub.*

ܚܶܙܘܳܐ pl. ܚܶܙ̈ܘܰܝܳܐ, ܚܶܙ̈ܘܶܐ rt. ܚܙܐ. m. *a) appearance, form, figure,* ܫܰܦܺܝܪ ܚܶܙܘܳܐ *of pleasing appearance;* ܫܰܦܺܝܪ ܚܶܙܘܳܐ *a good-looking* or *handsome man;* ܕܠܳܐ ܚܶܙܘܳܐ *shapeless, ill-favoured. b) a likeness, a vision* (ܚܶܙܘܳܢܳܐ is the usual word), ܚܶܙܘܳܐ ܕܒܽܘܠܳܐ *a phantom, apparition;* ܒܚܶܙܘܳܐ *in a vision;* also *openly, in sight.*

ܚܳܙܘܳܝܳܐ pl. ܚܳܙܘܳܝ̈ܶܐ rt. ܚܙܐ. m. *a spectator, seer, prophet* (ܚܳܙܝܳܐ is the usual word).

ܚܙܳܘܶܐ, ܚܙܳܘܳܢܳܐ pl. ܚܙܳܘ̈ܶܐ rt. ܚܙܐ. m. generally pl. *a) visions;* ܚܳܙܝ̈ܰܝ ܚܶܙܘ̈ܳܢܶܐ *seers of visions. b) remarkable* or *notable doings, sights, shows, public games* or *contests;* ܚܙܳܘ̈ܶܐ ܚܰܢ̈ܦܶܐ *pagan spectacles;* ܒܶܝܬ ܚܙܳܘ̈ܶܐ *a gymnasium, theatre.*

ܚܶܙܘܳܦ, ܚܶܙܘܳܦܳܐ rt. ܚܙܦ. *rough, shaggy* as camels' hair.

ܚܶܙܘܳܦܽܘܬܳܐ rt. ܚܙܦ. f. *hairiness, shagginess.*

ܚܳܙܽܘܩܳܐ pl. ܚܳܙ̈ܽܘܩܶܐ rt. ܚܙܩ. m. *a) a wayfarer, traveller. b) a membrane, the diaphragm, midriff.*

ܚܙܽܘܩܬܳܐ rt. ܚܙܩ. f. *setting out on a journey, a journey, departure* esp. from this life; ܐܰܝܟ ܠܚܙܽܘܩܬܳܐ ܪܰܚܺܝܩܬܳܐ *it is like a far journey;* ܙܘܳܕܳܐ ܕܰܚܙܽܘܩܬܳܐ or ܦܽܘܪܢܳܣܳܐ *viaticum.*

ܚܙܽܘܩܳܝܳܐ rt. ܚܙܩ. adj. *of* or *for travelling,* ܠܒܽܘܫܳܐ ܚܙܽܘܩܳܝܳܐ *travelling raiment.*

ܚܙܽܘܪ, ܚܙܽܘܪܳܐ pl. ܶܐ *a) the apple; other round fruits;* ܚܙܽܘܪ̈ܶܐ ܕܰܐܪܡܰܢܳܝܳܐ *apricots;* ܚܙܽܘܪܳܐ ܡܕܺܝܳܝܳܐ *the citron;* ܚܙܽܘܪܳܐ ܦܳܪܣܳܝܳܐ *the peach;* ܚܙܽܘܪ ܪܘܡܳܢܳܐ is used to translate *pomegranate* in the Song of Songs, iv. 3 and vi. 6; but it may also mean, like μῆλον, *the round part of the cheek. b) a poppy-head. c) the capital* of a column. *d) the bowl* of a candlestick.

ܚܙܺܝܙ, ܚܙܺܝܙܳܐ adj. m. *scabby, mangy.*

ܚܙܺܝܙܽܘܬܳܐ or ܚܙܺܝܙܬܳܐ f. *a) scab, ringworm. b) lichen.*

ܚܳܙܶܐ, ܚܳܙܝܳܐ pl. ܚܳܙ̈ܝܳܐ rt. ܚܙܐ. *one who sees, beholds* or *contemplates, an eye-witness, spectator* at the theatre, *looker-on; a seer* of divine visions; adj. *discerning, wise;* ܚܳܙ̈ܰܝ ܕܬܶܕܡܪ̈ܳܬܳܟ *the witnesses of Thy wonderful works.*

ܚܙܳܝܳܐ rt. ܚܙܐ. m. *sight;* ܚܰܪܺܝܦ ܚܙܳܝܳܐ *sharp-sighted;* ܠܳܐ ܚܙܳܝܳܐ *blindness.*

ܚܙܺܝܪ, ܚܙܺܝܪܳܐ, ܚܙܺܝܪܬܳܐ, ܚܙܺܝܪܶܝܢ pl. m. ܶܐ, f. ܳܬܳܐ, m. *a) a hog;* ܚܙܺܝܪ ܒܳܪܳܐ *the wild boar;* ܚܙܺܝܪܳܐ ܕܥܳܒܳܐ *a boar of the wood. b)* f. *a sow;* f. pl. *sores* or *swellings* on the neck, *scrofula.*

ܚܙܝܪܝܐ, ܚܙܝܪܝܬܐ adj. from the above, *swinish, hoggish*; ܥܕܪܐ ܚܙܝܪܝܐ *a herd of swine*; ܓܪܓܪܬܐ ܚܙܝܪܝܬܐ *swinish gluttony*; ܕܘܒܪ̈ܐ ܚܙܝܪ̈ܝܐ *hoggish manners*.

ܚܙܝܪܘܬܐ from ܚܙܝܪܐ f. *hoggishness, swinishness*.

ܚܙܝܪܢ *Khaziran*, the tenth Syrian month, answering to June with us.

ܚܙܝܬܐ pl. ܬ̈ܐ, prop. act. part. fem. emph. of ܚܙܐ; subst. *the eye*; ܕܡܥ̈ܐ ܚܙܝ̈ܬܐ *tears*; ܚܫܟ̈ܝ ܚܙܝ̈ܬܗ ܡܢ ܒܟܝܐ *her eyes were dim with weeping*.

ܚܙܡ pass. part. ܚܙܝܡ, ܚܙܝܡܐ, ܚܙܝܡܬܐ *to stop* the ears; ܢܦܫܐ ܚܙܝܡܬܐ *a dull* or *deaf soul*.

ܚܙܡܐ m. *a girth*.

ܚܙܦ root-meaning *to be rough, harsh*. Pe. not used in Syr. Ethpe. ܐܬܚܙܦ the same. Derivatives, ܚܙܘܦܐ, ܚܙܘܦܘܬܐ.

ܚܙܩ fut. ܢܚܙܘܩ, inf. ܡܚܙܩ, imper. ܚܙܘܩ, act. part. ܚܙܩ, ܚܙܩܐ, pass. part. ܚܙܝܩ, ܚܙܝܩܐ, ܚܙܝܩܬܐ. *a*) *to gird, gird up* or *on, bind on*; ܚܙܩ ܚܪܨܐ; ܚܙܩܘܢ ܙܝܢܐ ܐܢܘܢ *he girt them with armour*; ܚܙܘܩܘ ܚܪ̈ܨܝ ܪܥܝܢܝܟܘܢ *gird up the loins of your minds*. *b*) *to gird oneself* for walking, hence *to walk abroad, go, go away, go on a journey, proceed, travel, depart, depart hence* i. e. from this life; ܚܙܩ ܠܐܬܪܐ ܪܚܝܩܐ *he went to a distant country*; ܚܙܩ ܡܢ ܬܡܢ *he departed thence*; ܚܙܩܝ ܒܐܘܪܚܐ *wayfarers, travellers*; ܐܝܙܓܕܐ ܕܚܙܩ ܩܕܡ ܡܠܟܐ *an ambassador travelling to the king's presence*; ܗܘ ܕܡܫܝܚܐܝܬ ܚܙܩ *a courier, swift messenger*; ܬܚܙܘܩ ܠܘܬ ܡܪܟ *thou shalt depart hence to thy Lord*; pass. part. ܚܙܝܩ ܒܚܒܠܐ *bound with cords*; ܚܪ̈ܨܘܗܝ ܚܙܝܩܝܢ ܗܘܘ ܐܫܒܘܚܬܐ *his loins were girded gloriously*; ܚܙܝܩܐ ܒܪܓܬ ܚܘܒܟ *bound* or *enslaved by desire of thy love*. Pa. ܚܙܩ *a*) *to gird round*, Germ. *umgurten*; *to girth* a beast of burden. *b*) *to gird* for a journey, *send away*; *to arm*; ܡܚܙܩܐ ܚܦܝܛܐ *well girt, active*; ܡܫܪܝܬܐ ܡܚܙܩܬܐ ܚܝܠܬܢܐ *a fortified camp*; ܟܐܦ̈ܐ ܦܣܝ̈ܠܬܐ ܡܚܙܩܢ ܒܦܪܙܠܐ *hewn stones bound together with iron joints*; metaph. ܠܡܚܙܩܘ ܐܝ̈ܕܝܗܘܢ ܒܥܒܕܐ ܕܒܝܬܐ ܕܡܪܝܐ *to strengthen their hands in the work of the house of the Lord*. Ethpa. ܐܬܚܙܩ *to gird oneself, put on*; *to be girt round, equipped, armed*, esp. with ܬܟܣܐ *garments* or ܙܝܢܐ ܚܠܝܨܐ *armour*; *to be girt with strength, strengthened, to be ready*, often metaph. ܙܕܝܩ̈ܐ ܒܪܚܡܬܐ ܐܠܗܝܬܐ ܒܠܚܘܕ ܡܬܚܙܩܝܢ *the just are armed* fully *with divine love only*; ܠܐ ܐܬܚܙܩܘ ܠܥܒܕܐ ܗܢܘܢ *they were not ready for deeds, did not carry out their work*. Derivatives, ܚܙܘܩܐ, ܚܙܩܐ, ܚܙܩܐ, ܡܚܙܩܐ, ܚܙܩܬܐ, ܚܙܘܩܘܬܐ, ܡܚܙܩܢܘܬܐ.

ܚܙܩܐ rt. ܚܙܩ. m. *a girdle, belt*; *a band, bond*; ܚܙܩ̈ܐ ܕܚܒܠܐ *the knots of a cord*; ܬܗܘܐ ܗܝܡܢܘܬܐ ܚܙܩܐ ܕܚܨ̈ܘܗܝ *faithfulness shall be the girdle of his reins*; ܚܘܒܐ ܕܗܘܝܘ ܚܙܩܐ ܕܓܡܝܪܘܬܐ *love which is the band of perfectness*.

ܚܙܩܘܬܐ rt. ܚܙܩ. f. *setting forth, a journey*.

ܚܙܪܐ m. *flour*, esp. *flour not cleared of bran*.

ܚܙܪܐ from ܚܙܝܪ m. *a swineherd*.

ܚܙܪܐ pl. ܪ̈ܐ m. *a furrow* or *line made in sand by wind*.

ܚܙܪܝܐ or ܚܙܪܝܬܐ from ܚܙܪܐ adj. *floury, farinaceous*.

ܚܙܪܐ pl. ܚܙܪ̈ܐ or ܚܙܘܪܝܬܐ as if from a form ܚܙܘܪܝܬܐ m. *the plum* tree and fruit.

ܚܙܘܪܢܝܬܐ pl. ܝ̈ܬܐ f. *the plum* or *damson*.

ܚܙܘܪܬܐ constr. st. ܚܙܘܪܬ, pl. ܚܙܘܪ̈ܢ, ܚܙܘܪ̈ܬܐ f. *a round loaf* or *cake*; ܚܙܘܪ̈ܬܐ ܕܣܥܪ̈ܐ *barley cakes*.

ܚܙܘܬܐ pl. ܬ̈ܐ m. *a mallet for beating flax* or *hemp*.

ܚܛ fut. ܢܚܘܛ, inf. ܡܚܛ, act. part. ܚܐܛ, ܚܐܛܐ, pass. part. ܚܛܝܛܐ. *a*) *to dig, dig out*; ܒܐܪܐ ܥܒܕ ܘܚܛܗ *he hath made and dug a well*; ܚܛܝܢ ܫܬܐܣܬܐ *they dig out the foundation*. *b*) *to sew, patch*, cf. ܚܘܛ. Pa. ܚܛܛ *to plough, excavate*, with ܥܝ̈ܢܐ *to gouge* or *pluck out the eyes*; ܡܚܛܛܐ ܒܣܟܬܐ ܕܦܕܢܐ *furrowed with the ploughshare*. Ethpa. ܐܬܚܛܛ *to be dug up* or *ploughed*; ܐܪܥܐ ܡܬܚܛܛܐ *the earth is dug* or *ploughed*. Derivatives, ܚܛܘܛܐ, ܚܛܛܐ, ܚܛܝܛܘܬܐ, ܡܚܛܐ.

ܚܛܐ fut. ܢܚܛܐ, inf. ܡܚܛܐ, act. part. ܚܛܐ, ܚܛܝܐ root-meaning *to miss*, hence *to sin* with ܠ of the pers. or with ܒ of the deed; ܚܛܐ ܚܛܗܐ *he committed a sin*; ܠܐ ܐܚܛܐ ܒܠܫܢܝ *I will not sin with my tongue*. Pa. ܚܛܝ *to boast, be arrogant*; *to give oneself to sensual pleasure*. Ethpa. *to behave arrogantly*. Aph. ܐܚܛܝ *to cause to sin, lead into sin*; *to count sinful;* ܐܚܛܝ ܠܐܝܣܪܝܠ *he made Israel sin.* Derivatives, ܚܛܐ, ܚܛܗܐ, ܚܛܝܐ, ܚܛܝܬܐ, ܚܛܝܘܬܐ, ܚܛܝܢܐ, ܚܛܝܬܐ, ܚܛܝܬܢܐ, ܡܚܛܝܢܐ, ܡܚܛܝܢܘܬܐ.

ܚܛܐ rt. ܚܛܐ. m. (rare) *sin;* ܚܛܘ ܚܛܐ ܓܠܝܐ *they committed open sin.*

ܚܛܐ pl. of ܚܛܬܐ. *grains of wheat.*

ܚܛܗ, ܚܛܗܐ pl. ܐ̈ rt. ܚܛܐ. m. *sin; a sin, fault;* ܕܠܐ ܚܛܗ *sinless, innocent;* metaph. *a sin-offering,* ܡܝܐ ܕܚܛܗܐ the same; ܡܝܐ ܕܚܛܗܐ *water of expiation, lustral water.*

ܚܛܘܛܐ pl. ܐ̈ rt. ܚܛ. m. *a furrow, trench;* ܚܛܬܐ ܢܦܠܐ ܒܚܛܘܛܐ *a grain falling into the furrow;* ܒܩܒܪ̈ܐ ܐܝܟ ܕܒܚܛܘܛܐ *in graves as in furrows;* metaph. ܟܘܬܝܢܐ ܕܚܛܘܛܐ *a striped vest.*

ܚܛܘܦ, ܚܛܘܦܐ, ܚܛܘܦܬܐ pl. m. ܐ̈, f. ܬܐ̈, rt. ܚܛܦ. adj. *ravenous, rapacious;* ܚܛܘܦܝܢ ܦܪ̈ܚܬܐ *hawks are birds of prey;* subst. *an extortioner, plunderer, ravisher.*

ܚܛܘܦܘܬܐ rt. ܚܛܦ. *rapacity.*

ܚܛܘܦܝܐ rt. ܚܛܦ. m. *seizing by force, rapine, rape; the spoil;* ܥܘܬܪܐ ܕܡܢ ܚܛܘܦܝܐ ܡܟܢܫ *wealth which he gets together by violence;* ܚܛܘܦܝܐ ܕܡܣܟܢ̈ܐ *the spoil of the poor.*

ܚܛܘܦܝܐ, ܚܛܘܦܝܬܐ adj. same as ܚܛܘܦܐ.

ܚܛܘܪܐ, ܚܛܘܪܬܐ rt. ܚܛܪ. *a carder* of cotton.

ܚܛܘܪܬܐ rt. ܚܛܪ. f. *a*) *the hump* of a camel. *b*) ܚܛܘܪܬܐ ܕܐܪܥܐ *a mound, hill.* *c*) *a carder's bow.*

ܚܛܝܛܐ pl. ܐ̈ rt. ܚܛ. m. *a well.*

ܚܛܝ, ܚܛܝܐ, ܚܛܝܬܐ pl. m. ܚܛܝܐ̈, ܚܛܝܝܢ, pl. f. ܚܛܝܢ, ܚܛܝܬܐ rt. ܚܛܐ. *a sinner;* ܓܒܪܐ ܚܛܝܐ *a sinful man;* ܗܕܐ ܐܢܬܬܐ ܚܛܝܬܐ ܗܝ *this woman is a sinner.*

ܚܛܝܐܝܬ rt. ܚܛܐ. adv. *sinfully;* ܠܐ ܚܛܝܐܝܬ *apart from sin, blamelessly.*

ܚܛܝܘܬ, ܚܛܝܘܬܐ rt. ܚܛܐ. f. *sinfulness;* with pers. pron. suff. ܚܛܝܘܬܝ = *I a sinner.*

ܚܛܝܛܘܬܐ rt. ܚܛ. f. *a hole, excavation; a furrow.*

ܚܛܝܢܐ pl. ܐ̈ rt. ܚܛܐ. m. *a fault, slight sin;* ܢܛܪ ܢܦܫܗ ܘܦܓܪܗ ܡܢ ܟܠ ܚܛܝܢ *let him keep his soul and body from every sin.*

ܚܛܝܦܐܝܬ rt. ܚܛܦ. adv. *violently, hastily.*

ܚܛܝܦܘܬܐ rt. ܚܛܦ. f. *rapture, ecstasy.*

ܚܛܝܬܐ f. no pl. rt. ܚܛܐ. *sin.*

ܚܛܝܬܢܐ, ܚܛܝܬܢܝܬܐ rt. ܚܛܐ. adj. *sinful, of sin, caused by sin;* ܙܘ̈ܥܐ ܚܛܝܬܢ̈ܝܐ *sinful impulses;* ܚܫ̈ܐ ܚܛܝܬܢ̈ܝܐ *sufferings caused by sin.*

ܚܛܦ fut. ܢܚܛܘܦ, inf. ܡܚܛܦ, imper. ܚܛܘܦ, act. part. ܚܐܛܦ, ܚܐܛܦܐ, pass. part. ܚܛܝܦ, ܐ̱, ܬܐ̱ *to take by force, do violence, violate; to seize, snatch, catch at;* with ܡܠܟܘܬܐ *to usurp;* ܚܛܦ ܡܠܟܘܬܐ ܠܗ *he usurped the kingdom;* ܚܛܦ ܠܗ ܫܡ *he took* or *usurped the name of . . . ; to rob, plunder;* gram. *to draw back, attract,* e.g. the ܒܘܟܠ letters attract the vowel from the initial of a word to which they are prefixed; ܚܛܦܘ ܢܡܘܣܐ *they violated the law;* ܚܛܘܦܘ ܐܢܘܢ ܡܢ ܢܘܪܐ *snatch them out of the fire;* ܕܢܚܛܘܦ ܙܒܢܐ ܡܢ ܫܢܬܐ *to snatch a little time from sleep;* ܠܡܚܛܦ ܥܝ̈ܢܐ ܕܐܢܫ̈ܐ *to allure men's eyes;* ܚܛܦܝܢ ܠܗ ܠܗܕܐ ܡܠܬܐ ܠܥܠܬܐ *they seize on that expression as a pretext.* Pass. part. ܡܘܬܐ ܚܛܝܦܐ *sudden* or *violent death;* ܟܠܗ ܡܕܥܐ ܕܝܠܝ ܚܛܝܦ ܗܘܐ ܠܘܬ ܡܫܝܚܐ *my whole mind was forcibly attracted to Christ.* Ethpe. ܐܬܚܛܦ *to be seized, pillaged, snatched away, carried off, caught up;* ܐܬܚܛܦܘ ܟܠܗܘܢ ܩܢܝܢܝ *all my goods were forcibly seized;* ܛܠܝ̈ܐ ܕܡܬܚܛܦܝܢ ܡܢ ܩܕܡ ܙܒܢܐ *boys carried off prematurely* by death; ܙܕܝܩ̈ܐ ܡܬܚܛܦܝܢ ܒܥܢܢ̈ܐ ܠܐܘܪܥܗ *the just are caught up in the clouds to meet Him.* Pa. ܚܛܦ *to take by force.* Ethpa. ܐܬܚܛܦ *to be dragged* or *carried away by force.* Derivatives, ܚܛܘܦܐ, ܚܛܘܦܝܐ, ܚܛܘܦܘܬܐ, ܚܛܝܦܐܝܬ, ܚܛܝܦܘܬܐ.

ܚܛܪ act. part. ܚܐܛܪ, pass. part. ܚܛܝܪ. *to beat* with rods, *to card,* ܥܡܪܐ ܕܚܛܝܪ ܒܩܛܢܐ *carded cotton.* Ethpa. ܐܬܚܛܪ *to be beaten* with rods, *carded.* Derivatives, ܚܛܪܐ, ܚܛܘܪܐ, ܚܛܘܪܬܐ.

ܚܛܪܬܐ f. *the hump* of a camel or bull.

ܚܛܬܐ pl. ܚܛܐ f. *a grain of wheat, wheat;* ܬܪܒܐ ܕܚܛܐ *the fat of wheat = the best flour;* ܚܨܕܐ ܕܚܛܐ *wheat harvest.*

ܚܝ, ܚܝܐ, ܚܝܬܐ pl. m. abs. ܚܝܝܢ, ܚܝܐܝܢ or ܚܝܝܢ, emph. ܚܝ̈ܐ, pl. f. ܚܝ̈ܬܐ rt. ܚܝܐ. *a*) *living, alive,* often used verbally, ܚܝ ܐܢܐ *I live;* ܚܝ ܗܘ *he lives, is alive;* ܚܝܐ ܢܦܫܗ *whose soul liveth,* i.e. although his body be dead; the formula of an oath, ܚܝ ܐܢܐ *as I live = by my* life; ܚܰܝ ܗܽܘ ܚܰܝܳܐ ܢܰܦܫܳܟ as thy soul liveth; ܚܰܝ ܡܳܪܝܳܐ as the Lord liveth. b) living, alive, life-giving; ܚܰܝ ܠܥܳܠܡܳܐ He who lives eternally; ܟܰܕ ܚܰܝ while alive, in his lifetime; ܚܰܝܶܐ the living opp. ܡܺܝܬܶܐ the dead; ܢܰܦܫܳܐ ܚܰܝܬܳܐ a living soul = an animal; ܒܩܳܠܳܐ ܚܰܝܳܐ viva voce, with the living voice, opp. ܒܟܬܳܒܳܐ in writing; ܣܒܰܪܬܳܐ ܚܰܝܬܳܐ the life-giving Gospel; ܡܶܢ ܚܰܝܶܐ ܩܳܠܶܐ ܚܰܝܶܐ ܡܡܰܠܠܺܝܢ. ܘܡܶܢ ܩܳܠܶܐ ܚܰܝܶܐ. ܚܰܝܶܐ ܡܶܬܝܰܗܒܺܝܢ out of life do living voices speak, and by means of living voices life is given; f. emph. a midwife. c) metaph. live, living, pure; raw, unripe, immature; ܒܶܣܪܳܐ ܚܰܝܳܐ raw flesh; ܓܘܡܪܶܐ ܚܰܝܬܳܐ live coals; ܙܰܝܬܶܐ ܚܰܝܶܐ unripe olives; ܥܕܰܡܳܐ ܕܚܰܝܳܐ ܦܺܐܪܳܐ ܒܟܰܪܡܳܐ till the fruit mature in the vineyard; ܐܶܢ ܚܰܡܪܳܐ ܚܰܝ ܗܽܘ ܘܚܰܣܺܝܢ if the wine be unmixed and strong; ܡܰܝܳܐ ܚܰܝܶܐ living i.e. perennial, never-failing waters; ܚܰܝ ܠܥܳܠܰܡ the plant semper-vivum.

ܚܰܝܶܐ rarely ܚܰܝܝܢ, rt. ܚܝܐ. only pl. m.; takes a verb in either sing. or pl., ܒܶܗ ܚܰܝܶܐ ܗܘܳܐ in Him was life; ܚܰܝܶܐ ܐܺܝܬܰܝܗܽܘܢ ܢܘܗܪܳܐ the life was light; life, salvation, ܚܰܝܠܳܐ ܡܥܰܒܕܳܢ ܚܰܝܶܐ life-working power; ܚܰܝܶܐ ܙܰܒܢܳܝܶܐ or ܐܰܪܥܳܢܳܝܶܐ temporal life, this present life opp. ܚܰܝܶܐ ܚܰܕܬܶܐ or ܐ̱ܚܪ̈ܳܢܶܐ the new life, the other life; ܢܶܘܠܳܐ ܕܚܰܝܶܐ the web of life; ܡܰܕܒܚܳܐ ܚܰܝܶܐ the altar; ܫܰܠܶܡ ܚܰܝܰܘܗܝ he died. A formula of swearing with pers. pron. suff. and often with ܠܳܐ or ܒ, by the life of —.

ܚܝܳܐ fut. ܢܺܚܶܐ or ܢܺܚܝܶܐ, inf. ܡܶܚܝܳܐ or ܡܶܚܶܐ, imper. ܚܝܺܝ, part. m. ܚܳܝܶܐ, f. ܚܳܝܝܳܐ, pl. m. ܚܳܝܶܝܢ or ܚܳܝܝܺܢ and anom. ܚܰܝܶܐ to live, be alive; to revive, recover; to be saved, to live again; ܐܽܘܡܳܢܘܼܬܳܐ ܕܢܺܚܶܐ ܒܳܗ a craft by which he may live; ܚܝܳܐ ܡܶܢ ܟܽܘܪܗܳܢܶܗ he recovered from his illness; ܢܺܚܶܐ ܡܰܠܟܳܐ let the king live; ܚܝܺܝ ܠܥܳܠܰܡ live for ever; ܐܶܬܚܰܕܰܬ ܘܚܝܰܘ ܢܳܡܽܘܣܶܐ the laws were revivified and revived; ܚܝܰܘ ܡܶܢ ܫܰܪܒܬܳܐ ܗܳܕܶܐ ܡܥܰܩܰܡܬܳܐ save yourselves from this froward generation; ܒܣܰܒܪܳܐ ܗܽܘ ܓܶܝܪ ܚܝܺܝܢ we are saved by hope; ܐܳܦ ܡܫܺܝܚܳܐ ܡܺܝܬ ܘܚܝܳܐ ܘܩܳܡ Christ both died and revived and rose. Aph. ܐܰܚܺܝ, fut. ܢܰܚܶܐ and ܢܰܚܺܐ, act. part. ܡܰܚܶܐ, ܡܰܚܝܳܐ, fem. constr. ܡܰܚܝܰܬ or ܡܰܚܝܳܢܺܝܬ, pl. m. ܡܰܚܝܶܝܢ, ܡܰܚܝܳܢܶܝܢ, f. ܡܰܚܝܳܢ. to give life, save, keep alive, save alive; to quicken, restore to life; ܐܰܚܺܝ ܡܺܝܬܶܐ he gave life to the dead; ܠܳܐ ܐܰܚܺܝ ܓܰܒܪܳܐ ܐܳܘ ܐܰܢ̱ܬܬܳܐ he left neither man nor woman alive; ܕܬܰܚܽܘܢ ܝܰܬܺܝܪ ܡܶܢ ܕܬܰܘܒܕܽܘܢ that ye may save rather than destroy; ܐܶܢܳܐ ܡܰܚܶܐ ܐ̱ܢܳܐ ܘܡܡܺܝܬ ܐ̱ܢܳܐ I give life and I slay; ܟܦܰܪܘ ܒܗܰܘ ܕܡܰܚܶܐ ܠܟܽܠ they denied Him who giveth life to all. Imper. with suff. pron. 1st pers. ܐܰܚܰܝܢܝ, ܐܰܚܰܝܢ interj. Aha! Alas! Ethtaph. ܐܶܬܬܰܚܺܝ to be quickened, to be saved alive. Derivatives, ܚܰܝ, ܚܰܝܶܐ or ܚܰܝܝܢ, ܚܰܝܬܳܐ, ܚܰܝܳܐܝܬ, ܚܰܝܘܳܐ, ܡܰܚܝܳܢܳܐ, ܚܰܝܳܢܳܐ, ܚܰܝܘܬܳܐ, ܚܰܝܘܬܳܢܳܐܝܬ, ܚܳܝܘܬܳܐ, ܚܰܝܳܬܳܐ, ܡܰܚܝܳܢܘܬܳܐ.

ܚܰܝܳܐܝܬ rt. ܚܝܐ. adv. alive, raw; ܐܳܟܠܺܝܢ ܠܕܶܒܫܳܐ ܚܰܝܳܐܝܬ they eat plain honey.

ܚܰܝܶܒ Pael conj. of ܚܘܒ to condemn, &c.

ܚܰܝܳܒ, ܚܰܝܳܒܳܐ pl. ܶܐ rt. ܚܘܒ. guilty, condemned; conquered, vanquished; a debtor; ܚܰܝܳܒ ܡܰܘܬܳܐ condemned to death or deserving death; ܚܰܝܳܒ ܢܰܦܫܶܗ self-condemned; ܚܰܝܳܒܺܝܢܰܢ ܥܰܠ ܐܰܚܽܘܢ we are guilty concerning our brother; ܡܶܬܥܰܩܢܺܝܢܰܢ. ܐܶܠܳܐ ܠܳܐ ܚܰܝܳܒܺܝܢܰܢ we are harassed but unconquered; ܒܪܺܝܟ ܙܳܟܳܝܳܐ ܕܢܚܶܬ ܠܡܶܥܕܰܪ ܚܰܝܳܒܶܐ blessed be the victor who came down to help the vanquished; ܚܰܝܳܒܳܟ ܗܽܘ thy debtor; ܐܰܝܟ ܕܐܳܦ ܚܢܰܢ ܫܒܰܩܢ ܠܚܰܝܳܒܰܝܢ as we also have forgiven our debtors. Verbal use with pron. or ܗܘܳܐ and ܠ, to owe, to be due; impers. it ought, it should, it is due; ܚܰܝܳܒ ܗܽܘ it must, he ought; ܚܰܝܳܒ ܐ̱ܢܳܐ I ought; ܚܰܝܳܒܺܝܢ ܐܢ̱ܬܽܘܢ you ought; ܚܰܝܳܒܺܝܢܰܢ ܠܡܶܣܬܰܟܳܠܽܘ we must understand.

ܚܰܝܳܒܽܘܬܳܐ rt. ܚܘܒ. f. a) defeat, rout, opp. ܙܳܟܽܘܬܳܐ victory; metaph. ܒܚܰܝܳܒܽܘܬܳܐ ܕܟܽܠ ܪܶܓܬܳܐ in the defeat of any lust. b) loss, liability. c) condemnation, guilt, opp. ܙܰܟܳܝܽܘܬܳܐ innocence. With pron. suff. ܚܰܝܳܒܽܘܬܝ = I a sinner.

ܚܰܝܳܓܳܐ pl. ܶܐ rt. ܚܘܓ. m. a going round, perambulation, circuit.

ܚܰܝܶܕ act. part. ܡܚܰܝܶܕ, pass. ܡܚܰܝܰܕ, other forms ܡܚܰܝܕܳܐ, ܡܚܰܝܰܕܬܳܐ are the same for both parts; denom. verb Pael conj. from ܚܕ to make one, unite, join, adjoin; ܚܰܩܠܳܐ ܒܚܰܩܠܳܐ ܡܚܰܝܕܺܝܢ they join field to field; ܩܘܼܒܳܝܳܐ ܕܡܚܰܝܕܺܝܢ ܠܝܰܡܳܐ pools connected with the sea; ܡܚܰܝܰܕܬܳܐ ܦܰܪܣܬܳܐ an animal whose foot is not cloven; ܡܚܰܝܕܳܐ ܦܪܰܚܬܳܐ a web-footed bird. Ethpa. ܐܶܬܚܰܝܰܕ to be united, joined, with ܥܰܡ or ܠ; ܐܳܦ ܐܢ̱ܬܽܘܢ ܬܶܬܚܰܝܕܽܘܢ ܥܰܡܰܢ ye also shall join with us.

ܚܝܘܬܐ, ܚܝܘܬܐ pl. ܚܝܘܬܐ rt. ܚܝܐ. *a*) f. *life, living, vitality;* ܓܪ̈ܡܐ ܣܦܝܩܝܢ ܡܢ ܚܝܘܬܐ *the bones are devoid of life;* ܪܚܡܬ ܚܝܘܬܐ *love of life;* ܚܝܘܬܐ ܪܘܚܢܝܬܐ ܕܢܦܫܐ *the spiritual vitality of the soul.* *b*) m. and f. *a living creature, an animal,* also coll. *animals, beasts;* ܚܝܘ̈ܬܐ ܕܐܪܒܥ ܪ̈ܓܠܝܢ *quadrupeds;* ܚܝܘܬܐ ܕܒܪܐ or ܕܚܩܠܐ or ܚܝܘܬܐ ܒܪܝܬܐ *a wild animal;* opp. ܒܥܝܪܐ *a domesticated animal;* ܚܝܘ̈ܬܐ ܕܡܘܒܠܐ *beasts of burthen;* ܚܝܘܬܐ ܝܡܝܬܐ *a dolphin, whale, &c.;* ܚܝܘܬܐ ܦܪܚܬܐ *a bird,* esp. *a bird of prey;* ܚܝܘܬܐ ܡܠܝܠܬܐ *a rational creature, a human being;* ܚܝܘܬܐ ܨܡܚܝܬܐ *a zoophyte;* ܚܝܘܬܐ ܛܪܘܦܬܐ *a carnivorous animal, savage beast.*

ܚܝܘܣܐ rt. ܚܣ. *pitiful;* ܠܐ ܚܝܘܣܐ *pitiless, harsh.*

ܚܝܘܣܬܢ, ܚܝܘܣܬܢܐ, ܚܝܘܣܬܢܝܬܐ rt. ܚܣ. *pitiful, benevolent, ready to pardon;* ܐܢܬܬܐ ܚܝܘܣܬܢܝܬܐ ܝܬܝܪ ܗܝ ܡܢ ܓܒܪܐ *woman is more pitiful than man.*

ܚܝܘܣܬܢܐܝܬ adv. rt. ܚܣ. *a*) *pitifully, kindly, courteously.* *b*) *sparingly;* ܝܗܒ ܚܝܘܣܬܢܐܝܬ ܘܟܕ ܪܛܢ *he gave parsimoniously and grumblingly.*

ܚܝܘܣܬܢܘܬܐ rt. ܚܣ. f. *compassion, benevolence, kindness, indulgence, solicitude;* ܚܝܘܣܬܢܘܬܐ ܐܒܗܝܬܐ *fatherly indulgence* or *care.*

ܚܝܘܬܢ, ܚܝܘܬܢܐ, ܚܝܘܬܢܝܬܐ rt. ܚܝܐ. adj. *animal;* metaph. *brutal.*

ܚܝܘܬܢܐܝܬ adv. rt. ܚܝܐ. *after the manner of animals, brutally.*

ܚܝܘܬܢܝܐ, ܚܝܘܬܢܝܬܐ rt. ܚܝܐ. adj. *animal, vital; brutal, bestial;* ܚܝ̈ܠܐ ܚܝܘܬܢܝ̈ܐ *the animal powers;* ܥܝ̈ܕܐ ܚܝܘܬܢܝ̈ܐ *beastly customs.*

ܚܝܛ PAEL conj. of ܚܛ *to sew together.*

ܚܝܛ, ܚܝܛܐ pass. part. and ܚܝܛܐ f. act. part. of ܚܛ *to sew.*

ܚܝܛܐ rt. ܚܛ. m. *a tailor.*

ܚܝܛܐ rt. ܚܛ. m. *a seam, suture;* ܚܝܛܐ ܕܪܫܐ *the suture of the head.*

ܚܝܛܘܬܐ rt. ܚܛ. f. *tailoring.*

ܚܝܠ, ܚܝܠܐ pl. ܚܝ̈ܠܝܢ, ܚܝ̈ܠܐ m. *might, strength, power, force;* *a*) with ܥܫܢ or ܙܟܐ *to prevail with, overcome, to be able;* with ܐܬܡܨܝ *to master the power* of another, *prevail over;* ܐܬܡܨܝ ܚܝܠ ܥܡ ܡܠܐܟܐ *he had power over the angel and prevailed;* ܚܝܠ ܥܠ ܪܓܝܓܬܗ ܐܬܡܨܝ *he conquered his appetites;* ܟܠ ܚܝܠ ܡܨܐ and ܟܠ ܚܝܠ *omnipotent, almighty;* ܓܒܪܐ ܚܝܠܐ *a strong man;* ܓܒܪ̈ܐ ܕܚܝܠܐ *strong* or *able men;* ܠܐ ܚܝܠ *powerless, impotent;* ܐܝܬ ܒܗܘܢ ܚܝܠܐ *they are able, they have the power;* ܐܝܟ ܚܝܠܝ or ܐܝܟ ܡܫܟܚܢܘܬܐ ܚܝܠܟ *as I can, as thou canst—according to my—thy—power, &c.;* ܠܥܠ ܡܢ ܚܝܠܗ *beyond his power;* ܡܢ ܟܠܗ ܚܝܠܗ *with all his might.* *b*) *a host, an army;* ܪܒ ܚܝܠܐ *a captain, commander;* ܫܡܝܐ ܘܟܠܗ ܚܝܠܗܘܢ *the heavens with all their host.* *c*) pl. the fifth order of angels, *powers.* *d*) *a mighty work = a miracle,* in this sense generally f.; ܚܝ̈ܠܐ ܘܐܬ̈ܘܬܐ *mighty works and signs;* ܗܝܡܢܘܬܐ ܕܚܝ̈ܠܐ faith *which works miracles.* *e*) *potentiality, possibility.* *f*) *force, sense, import;* ܚܝܠܐ ܕܟܬܒܐ *the sense of the letter;* ܚܝܠܐ ܕܡܠܬܗ *the force of his speech* i.e. *his forcible speech, eloquence;* ܠܐ ܐܕܪܟܘ ܚܝܠܐ ܕܡܠ̈ܘܗܝ *they did not apprehend the import of his words.* *g*) *abundance, wealth.* DERIVATIVES, ܚܝܠܐ, verb ܚܝܠ, ܚܝܠܬܐ, ܚܝܠܬܢ, ܚܝܠܬܢܐܝܬ, ܚܝܠܬܢܘܬܐ, ܡܚܝܠܐ, ܡܚܝܠܐܝܬ, verb ܡܚܝܠ, ܡܚܝܠܘܬܐ, ܡܚܝܠܬܐ, ܡܬܚܝܠܢܘܬܐ.

ܚܝܠ denom. verb PAEL conj. from ܚܝܠ *to strengthen, comfort, confirm;* ܗܢܘܢ ܕܚܝܠܘ ܐܝ̈ܕܘܗܝ *those who strengthened his hands;* ܐܢܘܢ ܚܝܠ ܒܩܪܒܐ *strengthen them in the fight.* ETHPA. ܐܬܚܝܠ imp. E-Syr. same as Pret. W-Syr. ܐܬܚܝܠ *to grow strong, gather one's strength, be strengthened; to be strong, take courage;* ܡܬܚܝܠܝܢ ܒܣܒܪܐ ܛܒܐ *they are strong in a good hope.*

ܚܝܠܬܐ pl. ܚܝܠ̈ܬܐ from ܚܝܠ. f. *strength, power, force;* pl. *companies, hosts; miracles;* ܐܠܗܐ ܕܚܝ̈ܠܬܐ *the God of hosts;* ܚܝ̈ܠܬܐ ܫܡܝܢܝ̈ܬܐ *heavenly powers* or *hosts;* ܚܝ̈ܠܬܐ ܕܒܝܫܘܬܐ *powers of evil, evil spirits;* ܚܝ̈ܠܬܐ ܕܐܐܪ *the powers of the air.*

ܚܝܠܬܢ, ܚܝܠܬܢܐ, ܚܝܠܬܢܝܬܐ pl. m. ܚܝܠܬܢܝܢ, ܚܝܠܬܢ̈ܐ, f. ܚܝܠܬܢܝܢ, ܚܝܠܬܢ̈ܝܬܐ from ܚܝܠ. *strong, mighty, powerful; a mighty man;* ܚܝܠܬܢܐ ܦܠܛܘܢ *the mighty Plato;* ܚܝܠܬܢ̈ܐ ܕܐܪܥܐ *the mighty of the land;*

ܨܠܘܬܐ ܚܝܠܬܢܝܬܐ *a powerful prayer;* ܚܝܠܬܢܐ ܕܟܠ *omnipotent;* ܡܪܝܐ ܚܝܠܬܢܐ is the Peshitto equivalent for Heb. Jehovah Sabaoth, *the Lord of hosts.*

ܚܝܠܬܢܐܝܬ from ܚܝܠ. adv. *mightily, strenuously; virtually;* ܕܢܣܝܒܪ ܚܝܠܬܢܐܝܬ ܗܘ ܕܓܕܫ *that he may strenuously endure that which befalls.*

ܚܝܠܬܢܘܬܐ pl. ܬܐ from ܚܝܠ. f. *might, strength; ability, intrepidity, courage;* ܫܡܫܐ ܒܚܝܠܬܢܘܬܗ ܕܢܚܗ *the sun in his strength;* ܚܝܠܬܢܘܬܐ ܪܘܚܢܝܬܐ *spiritual strength, fortitude.*

ܚܬܢ denom. verb Pael conj. from ܚܬܢܐ. *a) to perform the duty of a kinsman* or *Goel.* *b) to connect, ally;* pass. part. ܡܚܬܢܐ ܗܘܬ ܠܕܝܢܐ *she was related to the judge;* ܥܒܕܐ ܕܡܚܬܢ ܗܘܐ ܠܕܐܚܘܗܝ *an act akin to that of his brother.* Ethpa. ܐܬܚܬܢ *to be connected, allied in marriage; to be near of kin, alike, analogous.*

ܚܙܪܐ pl. ܐ̈ rt. ܚܙܪ. m. *a swath, bandage-cloth;* ܚܙܪܐ ܕܟܬܢܐ *a linen cloth;* gram. the *doubling* of a letter.

ܚܣܝܢܐܝܬ rt. ܚܣܢ. adv. *closely, vigorously, robustly, actively, speedily;* ܡܚܝ ܚܣܝܢܐܝܬ *strike hard;* ܟܕ ܟܬܫܘ ܚܣܝܢܐܝܬ ܐܬܟܬܫܘ *when they have fought very strenuously.*

ܚܣܝܢܘܬܐ pl. ܚܣܝܢܘܬܐ rt. ܚܣܢ. f. *compactness, the curdling* of milk. Metaph. *firmness, tenacity, mental denseness;* ܚܣܝܢܘܬܐ ܕܡܚܠܫܢ ܚܝܠܘܬܐ ܕܢܦܫܐ *which weaken the forces of the soul;* ܚܣܝܢܘܬ ܩܠܐ *vehemence of a sound;* ܒܚܣܝܢܘܬܐ *strongly, firmly.*

ܚܙܘܐ, ܚܙܘܐ pl. ܚܙܘ̈ܐ rt. ܚܙܐ. m. *a sight, look, gazing, aspect, countenance.* Metaph. *appearance, presence, attention;* ܚܙܘܐ ܕܠܒܐ *the regard of the heart;* ܚܙܘ ܪܥܝܢܐ *discernment;* ܗܘܢܐ ܟܕ ܟܢܫ ܚܙܘܗ̇ *the mind when it collects itself.* With verbs, ܐܪܡܝ ܚܙܘܐ ܠ *to turn the eyes towards;* ܐܪܝܡ ܚܙܘܐ ܠ *to look up;* with ܩܡ or ܥܠ *to fix the gaze;* ܠܩܘܒܠ ܚܙܘܐ *straight forward.*

ܚܝܪܬܐ or ܚܝܪܬܐ f. *a shepherds' camp; a mandra, convent.*

ܚܝܐ, ܚܝܬܐ rt. ܚܝܐ. f. *a) life,* ܚܝܐ ܕܡܝ̈ܬܐ *resurrection* of the dead. *b) alive; a midwife.*

ܚܝܬ *Cheth,* the letter ܚ.

ܚܟ act. part. ܚܐܟ. *to rub, scratch.* Derivatives, ܚܟܘܟܐ, ܚܟܬܐ.

ܚܟܐ contr. from ܚܢܟܐ. m. *the palate;* ܡܪܝܪ ܥܠ ܚܟܐ *it is bitter to the palate;* ܩܢܝܐ ܕܚܟܐ *the larynx;* ܐܬܘܬܐ ܕܚܟܐ *the palatal letters;* metaph. ܐܦܨܝܬ ܢܦܫܝ ܡܢ ܚܟܘܗ ܕܛܥܝܘܬܐ *I have delivered myself from the jaws of error.*

ܚܟܘܡܐ rt. ܚܟܡ. m. *coition, sexual intercourse.*

ܚܟܝܡ, ܚܟܝܡܐ, ܚܟܝܡܬܐ pl. ܚܟܝܡܝܢ, ܚܟܝ̈ܡܐ, f. ܚܟܝ̈ܡܢ, ܚܟܝ̈ܡܬܐ, rt. ܚܟܡ. *wise, prudent, intelligent, sensible; learned, skilful, crafty, cunning; a wise man, sage, magician;* ܚܟܝܡ ܠܒܐ *wise-hearted;* ܐܣܝܐ ܚܟܝܡܐ *a skilled physician;* ܪܝܫ ܚܟܝ̈ܡܐ *chief of the magicians.*

ܚܟܝܡܐܝܬ adv. rt. ܚܟܡ. *wisely, with understanding, prudently, sensibly.*

ܚܟܝܡܘܬܐ rt. ܚܟܡ. f. *a) wisdom. b) coition.*

ܚܟܟܐ rt. ܚܟ. m. *itch, scab, mange.*

ܚܟܡ fut. ܢܚܟܘܡ, inf. ܡܚܟܡ, act. part. ܚܟܡ, ܚܟܡܐ, pass. part. ܚܟܝܡ only in sense *b.* See ܚܟܝܡ. *a) to know, discern.* *b) to have sexual intercourse.* Ethpe. ܐܬܚܟܡ *to be known carnally.* Pa. ܚܟܡ *to make wise, grant wisdom* or *discernment, to instruct;* ܚܟܡ ܠܗܕܝܘܛܘܬܢ *grant wisdom to our ignorance, to us who are ignorant;* ܟܬܒܐ ܡܚܟܡܝܢ ܠܢ ܕ *books instruct us that.* Ethpa. ܐܬܚܟܡ *to prove oneself wise, act wisely; to become wise, learn wisdom, be instructed; to be cunning, make artful* or *guileful attempts, conspire;* ܒܢܣܝܘܢܐ ܡܬܚܟܡ ܐܢܫ *a man learns wisdom through trials;* ܐܬܚܟܡ ܥܠ ܩܛܠܗ *he contrived his murder.* Derivatives, ܚܟܘܡܐ, ܚܟܘܡܐ, ܚܟܝܡ, ܚܟܝܡܐܝܬ, ܚܟܝܡܘܬܐ, ܚܟܡܬܐ, ܚܟܡܬܢܐ, ܡܚܟܡܢܐ, ܡܚܟܡܢܘܬܐ, ܡܬܚܟܡܢܘܬܐ.

ܚܟܡܐ const. st. ܚܟܡܬ, emph. ܚܟܡܬܐ, pl. ܚܟܡܢ, ܚܟܡ̈ܬܐ, rt. ܚܟܡ. f. the meaning differs somewhat with the forms, the abs. st. being used in a more defined and restricted sense. *a*) abs. ܚܟܡܬܐ *wisdom, counsel; a scheme, plan;* ܒܚܟܡܬܐ *cunningly, artfully. b*) emph. st. *wisdom, knowledge, science, philosophy;* ܪܫܝܬ ܚܟܡܬܐ ܕܚܠܬܗ ܕܡܪܝܐ *the fear of the Lord is the chief part of wisdom;* ܡܢܘ ܡܢܐ ܥܢܢܐ ܒܚܟܡܬܗ *who hath numbered the clouds in his wisdom?* ܚܟܡܬܐ ܕܫܠܝܡܘܢ *the Wisdom of Solomon = the Book of Wisdom. c*) *skill, art;* ܚܟܡܬܐ ܩܪܒܐ *the art of war, generalship.* Often used as a title of honour, ܚܟܡܬܟ *thou who art wise.*

ܚܟܡܬܢܝܐ, ܢܝܬܐ rt. ܚܟܡ. adj. *scientific, of science, of the wise.*

ܚܟܘܬܐ rt. ܚܟ. f. *scab, mange.*

ܚܠ root-meaning *to enter into a hollow.* Pe. only part. adj. ܚܠܝܠ, ܠܐ, ܠܬܐ *hollow, concave;* ܚܠܝܠ ܗܘܐ *it was hollow;* ܐܒܘܒܐ ܚܠܝܠܬܐ *a hollow pipe;* subst. *a hollow, hole, burrow; a dug-out, boat,* ܚܠܝܠܘܗܝ ܕܐܪܥܐ *the hollow places of the earth;* ܚܦܪܘ ܚܠܝܠܐ *they dug a hole;* ܚܠܝܠܐ ܕܚܘܘܬܐ *the serpents burrow.* Pael ܚܠܠ *to wash away, cleanse, purify;* ܢܚܠܠ ܘܢܫܘܦ ܟܠ ܨܘܐܬܐ *let him cleanse and rub away all dirt;* ܚܠܠ ܠܫܢܝ ܒܙܘܦܐ *purify my tongue with thy hyssop;* ܚܠܠܢܝ *purify me.* Ethpa. ܐܬܚܠܠ *to be washed, made clean, purified;* ܐܬܚܠܠ ܦܓܪܗ ܘܢܦܫܗ *his body was made clean and his soul made pure.* Palpel ܚܠܚܠ fut. ܢܚܠܚܠ *to move to and fro, shake violently;* ܡܚܠܚܠܝܢ ܛܘܪܐ *the mountains are shaken;* pass. part. ܡܚܠܚܠ *hollow.* Ethpalpal ܐܬܚܠܚܠ. *a*) *to be dissolved;* ܡܬܚܠܚܠ ܦܓܪܐ ܘܒܠܐ *the body wastes away and grows old. b*) *to be hollowed out.* Aph. ܐܚܠ *to infringe, break, profane* the Sabbath. Derivatives, ܚܠܐ, ܚܠܐ, ܚܠܠܐ, ܚܠܘܠܐ, ܚܠܝܠܐ, ܚܠܘܠܝܬܐ, ܚܠܚܘܠܐ, ܚܠܚܠܐ, ܚܠܐ, ܚܠܝܠܘܬܐ, ܚܠܠܐ, ܚܠܝܠܐ, ܡܚܠܚܠܢܐ.

ܚܠ, ܚܠܐ m. *vinegar;* ܚܠܐ ܕܚܡܪܐ *vinegar made from wine.*

ܚܠ, ܚܠܐ m. *sand, gravel;* ܦܪܕܬܐ ܕܚܠܐ ܕܝܡܐ ܣܦܪ ܝܡܐ *a grain of sand from the sea-shore.*

ܚܠܐ pl. ܚܠܐ m. *a mother's brother, maternal uncle,* opp. ܕܕܐ *an uncle on the father's side.*

ܚܠܐ pl. ܚܠܐ m. *a*) *dust, fine dust;* ܚܠܐ ܕܪܓܠܝ ܢܦܨ ܐܢܐ *I shake off dust from my feet;* ܚܠܐ ܕܐܓܘܢܐ *the dust of conflicts. b*) *a garment of fine linen. c*) ܚܠܐ ܕܥܝܢܐ *a white film* in the eyes, *cataract. d*) ܚܠܬܐ *a scabbard* has pl. ܚܠܐ.

ܚܠܐ, ܚܠܝܐ, ܚܠܝܬܐ *sweet;* see ܚܠܝ.

ܚܠܒ fut. ܢܚܠܘܒ, imper. ܚܠܘܒ, act. part. ܚܠܒ, pass. part. ܚܠܝܒ, ܒܐ, ܒܬܐ. *to milk, press out* or *suck milk.* Ethpe. ܐܬܚܠܒ *to be milked.* Derivatives, ܚܠܒܐ, ܚܠܒܢܐ.

ܚܠܒܐ rt. ܚܠܒ. m. *a*) *milk;* ܚܠܒܐ ܩܦܝܐ *curdled milk;* ܐܡܪܐ ܕܚܠܒܐ *a sucking lamb;* ܒܪ ܚܠܒܐ *sucking, a suckling;* metaph. *milky juice* or *sap;* ܐܝܬ ܚܠܒܐ ܒܛܪܦܝ ܬܐܢܐ *there is milky juice in fig-leaves. b*) *yielding milk, giving suck.*

ܚܠܒ, ܚܠܒܐ m. *fat; membrane, the diaphragm; peel, rind* or *shell;* ܚܠܒܐ ܕܩܠܦܐ *a fine skin* or *membrane.*

ܚܠܒܢܝܐ, ܢܝܬܐ rt. ܚܠܒ. adj. *milky, like milk;* ܟܐܦܐ ܚܠܒܢܝܬܐ *milk-stone.*

ܚܠܒܢܝܐ, ܢܝܬܐ pl. m. ܢܝܐ, ܢܝܬܐ from ܚܠܒܐ. adj. *fat, membranaceous,* ܦܪܚܬܐ ܚܠܒܢܝܬܐ ܓܦܐ *insects with transparent wings.*

ܚܠܒܢܝܬܐ f. *galbanum,* a fragrant resin.

ܚܠܕ fut. ܢܚܠܘܕ, inf. ܡܚܠܕ, act. part. ܚܠܕ, ܚܠܕܐ. *to creep, crawl, glide;* with ܒܐܪܥܐ *to burrow, to drive a mine underground;* metaph. *to insinuate* or *thrust oneself in; to lie hid, be latent;* ܚܘܘܬܐ ܕܚܠܕܢ ܒܥܦܪܐ *snakes which crawl in the dust;* ܚܠܕܝܢ ܗܘܘ ܒܒܬܐ *they crept secretly into houses;* ܚܝܠܐ ܕܒܐܣܛܘܟܣܐ ܚܠܕܝܢ *forces latent in the elements.* Pa. ܚܠܕ *to creep* or *thrust oneself in; to move in* or *through;* ܚܡܝܪܐ ܕܚܠܕ *the leaven which moves through.* Aph. ܐܚܠܕ *to drive* or *screw in.* Derivatives, ܚܠܕܐ, ܚܠܕܘܢܐ, ܚܠܕܝܢܬܐ.

ܚܠܕܝܢܬܐ rt. ܚܠܕ. f. *gangrene;* ܡܠܬܗܘܢ ܐܝܟ ܚܠܕܝܢܬܐ *their speech is like gangrene.*

ܚܠܕܘܕܐ rt. ܚܠܕ. m. *the jerboa.*

ܚܠܕܘܢܐ rarely ܚܠܕܘܢܐ rt. ܚܠܕ. m. *a mixed crowd, rabble; a swarm* of insects.

ܚܠܘܠ, ܚܠܘܠܐ pl. ܠܐ rt. ܚܠ. m. *a banquet, supper,* esp. *a marriage feast; a banqueting room;* ܐܬܐ ܚܬܢܐ ܠܒܝܬ ܚܠܘܠܐ *the bridegroom came to the marriage feast.*

ܚܠܘܦܬܐ pl. ܦܬܐ rt. ܚܠܦ. f. *a blade, knife.*

ܚܠܘܢܐ or ܚܠܝܙܘܢܐ pl. ܢܐ m. *shellfish,* esp.

the Tyrian murex; ܨܒܥܐ ܕܒܕܡܐ ܕܚܠܙܘܢܐ *dyed Tyrian purple.*

ܚܠܚܠ Palpel conj. of ܚܠ.

ܚܠܛ fut. ܢܚܠܘܛ, inf. ܡܚܠܛ, imper. ܚܠܘܛ, act. part. ܚܳܠܶܛ, ܚܳܠܛܳܐ, pass. part. ܚܠܝܛ, ܚܠܝܛܐ, ܚܠܝܛܬܐ *to mix, mingle with;* act. and refl., generally with acc. and ܒ or ܥܡ; *to add, join or unite; to take part with, to impart;* ܚܳܠܛܝܢ ܦܪܝܣܬܐ *they who mix* or *knead the Eucharistic bread;* ܚܳܠܶܛ ܡܰܝܳܐ ܒܡܶܫܚܳܐ *he adds water to the oil;* ܚܠܛ ܕܡܗܘܢ ܥܡ ܕܚܒܪܝܗܘܢ *he mingled their blood with that of their fellows;* ܕܡܐ ܒܕܡܐ ܚܠܛܘ *they have added blood to blood* i.e. *slain continually;* ܢܚܠܛܢܝ ܒܡܢܝܢܐ ܕܓܒܝܐ̈ܘܗܝ *let Him add me to the number of His chosen;* ܚܠܛ ܒܢ ܚܝܘܗܝ ܕܠܐ ܢܡܘܬ *He infused His life in us that we should die no more;* ܚܡܪܐ ܕܚܠܝܛ ܒܗ ܡܘܪܐ *wine mingled with myrrh;* ܚܠܝܛ ܥܡ ܡܝܬܪܘܬܐ ܠܐ ܚܠܝܛܬܐ *pure virtue;* ܚܠܝܛ ܥܡ *tempered with.* Ethpe. ܐܬܚܠܛ *a) to join* or *take part with. b) to be kneaded, to be alloyed.* Pa. ܚܰܠܶܛ *to mix thoroughly, to join, mingle;* ܚܰܠܶܛ ܡܪܝ ܩܠܝܢ ܕܡܠܐܟܝܟ *let our voices mingle with the voices of thy angels;* pass. part. ܡܚܠܛ *mixed, alloyed;* ܡܚܠܛܬܐ *of various sorts.* Ethpa. ܐܬܚܰܠܰܛ imper. E-Syr. same as Pret. W-Syr. ܐܬܚܰܠܛ with ܒ or ܥܡ *to be admitted, have part with, be together; to mix with, have to do with, make alliance;* ܡܬܚܰܠܛ ܕܩܠܬ ܒܦܪܬ the Tigris *mingles with the Euphrates;* ܐܬܚܰܠܰܛ ܒܥܡܡܐ Ephraim *had dealings with the nations;* ܕܢܬܚܰܠܛ ܠܓܘܕܐ ܕܩܕܝܫܐ *that he may be added to the choirs of the saints.* Derivatives, ܚܠܛܐ, ܚܠܝܛܐ, ܚܠܝܛܐܝܬ, ܚܠܝܛܘܬܐ, ܡܚܠܛܢܘܬܐ, ܚܠܛܐ.

ܚܠܛܐ pl. ܐ̈ rt. ܚܠܛ. m. *a) a mixture;* ܠܐ ܬܙܪܥ ܚܠܛܐ *thou shalt not sow mixed seed* i.e. two sorts together; ܡܐܢܐ ܕܚܠܛܐ ܕܨܒܥܝܢ *a garment of mixed material and colours* e.g. of interwoven cotton and silk; ܕܠܐ ܚܠܛܐ *unmixed. b) spelt, rye.*

ܚܠܐ fut. ܢܚܠܐ, act. part. ܚܳܠܶܐ, ܚܳܠܝܳܐ, pass. part. ܚܠܐ, ܚܠܝܐ, ܚܠܝܬܐ. *to be* or *become sweet; to speak fair;* ܚܠܘ ܡܝܐ *the waters were made sweet;* ܚܠܐ ܒܪܝܚܗ *it is sweet in odour;* part. adj. *sweet, soft, pleasant;* ܚܠܐ ܡܢ ܕܒܫܐ *sweeter than honey;* ܩܠܐ ܚܠܝܐ *sweet sounds;* ܚܠܐ ܚܙܘܐ *sweet-looking;* ܚܠܐ ܫܡܐ *of illustrious name;* pl. emph. fem. ܚܠܝܬܐ *chicory.* Pa. ܚܰܠܺܝ *to sweeten, make sweet;* ܡܚܠܐ ܡܪܝܪܘܬܗܘܢ *sweetening their bitter flavours.* Ethpa. ܐܬܚܰܠܺܝ *to become sweet.* Aph. ܐܚܠܝ same as Pa. ܐܚܠܝ ܡܘܫܐ ܡܝܐ *Moses made the waters sweet.* Derivatives, ܚܠܝܐ, ܚܠܝܘܬܐ, ܚܠܝܐ, ܡܚܠܝܢܐ.

ܚܠܝܘܬܐ rt. ܚܠܐ. f. *a) sweetness, pleasantness;* ܚܠܝܘܬܐ ܕܦܐܪܐ *the sweetness of fruits. b) sweetmeats;* ܚܠܝܘܬܐ ܠܐ ܐܟܠ ܗܘܐ *he did not eat sweets. c) must, sweet wine;* ܚܠܝܘܬܐ ܕܪܘܡܢܐ *sweet wine* or *juice of pomegranates.*

ܚܠܙܘܢܐ *shellfish;* see ܚܠܙܘܢܐ.

ܚܠܝܛܐܝܬ rt. ܚܠܛ. adv. *confusedly;* with ܠܐ *without confusion.*

ܚܠܝܛܘܬܐ rt. ܚܠܛ. f. *mingling; communion, intercourse, sociability.*

ܚܠܝܠ, ܚܠܝܠܐ m. *a hollow, hole, cavity, burrow, boat;* see part. of ܚܠ.

ܚܠܝܠܘܬܐ rt. ܚܠ. f. *a cavity, hollow; hollowness, concavity;* ܚܠܝܠܘܬܐ ܪܒܬܐ ܐܝܬ ܒܐܪܥܐ *there is a great cavity in the earth;* ܚܠܝܠܘܬܐ ܕܥܘܒܐ *the hollow of the bosom.*

ܚܠܝܡܐܝܬ rt. ܚܠܡ. adv. *well, mighty, entirely, firmly, stoutly, bravely.*

ܚܠܝܡܘܬܐ rt. ܚܠܡ. f. *health, soundness, firmness;* ܚܠܝܡܘܬܐ ܗܝܡܢܘܬܐ *a right faith;* ܚܠܝܡܘܬܐ ܕܡܕܥܐ *the right* or *true sense;* ܚܠܝܡܘܬܐ ܢܦܫܢܝܬܐ *strong resolutions of the soul, fortitude;* ܚܠܝܡܘܬܐ ܬܪܝܨܘܬܐ *uprightness.*

ܚܠܝܨܐ rt. ܚܠܨ. m. *a) a skin* to hold liquids, *a bottle made of hide;* ܚܠܝܨܐ ܕܚܠܒܐ *a skin of milk. b) strong, valiant; an athlete, combatant;* see under ܚܠܨ.

ܚܠܝܨܐܝܬ rt. ܚܠܨ. adv. *strenuously, bravely, valiantly.*

ܚܠܝܨܘܬܐ rt. ܚܠܨ. f. *hardihood, stoutness, courage, fortitude, steadfastness.*

ܚܰܠܶܠ Pael conj. of ܚܠ *to purify,* &c.

ܚܠܠܐ pl. ܐ̈ rt. ܚܠ. m. *a hole in the earth, a cave; a tunnel, trench, breach, mine;* ܚܦܪܝ ܚܠܠܐ ܬܚܝܬ ܫܘܪܐ *those who dug trenches under the wall = sappers;* ܥܒܕܘ ܚܠܠܐ *they made a breach.*

ܚܠܡ fut. ܢܶܚܠܽܘܡ, act. part. ܚܳܠܶܡ, ܚܳܠܡܳܐ, pass. part. ܚܠܺܝܡ, ܚܠܺܝܡܳܐ, ܚܠܺܝܡܬܳܐ. *to dream;* pass. part. *a*) *dreaming.* *b*) as adj. *well, healthy, whole, sound;* ܚܰܝ ܘܚܠܺܝܡ *alive and well;* ܚܠܺܝܡܺܝܢ ܒܪܶܥܝܳܢܳܐ *of sound mind;* ܗܶܘܺܝ or ܗܘܳܘ ܚܠܺܝܡ *farewell;* metaph. *sound, wholesome, firm, strong, correct;* ܚܠܺܝܡ ܒܗܰܝܡܳܢܽܘܬܳܐ *firm in the faith, orthodox;* ܪ̈ܶܥܝܳܢܶܐ ܚܠܺܝܡܶܐ *correct opinions;* ܫܶܬܶܐܣܬܳܐ ܚܠܺܝܡܬܳܐ *a sure foundation;* ܢܶܫܪܳܐ ܚܠܺܝܡ ܓܶܦ̈ܶܐ *a strong-winged eagle;* gram. *a strong* verb; ܚܠܺܝܡܰܬ ܫܽܘܠܳܡܳܐ *ending in a strong letter.* Ethpe. ܐܶܬ݂ܚܠܶܡ *a*) *to be refreshed with sleep.* *b*) *to recover health, be healed, cured, made whole;* ܨܳܒܶܐ ܐܢ̱ܬ ܕܬܶܬ݂ܚܠܶܡ *wilt thou be made whole?* Pa. ܚܰܠܶܡ *to heal.* Aph. ܐܰܚܠܶܡ *to heal, cure, restore,* &c.; ܐܰܚܠܶܡ ܠܡܰܚ̈ܘܳܬܰܢ *heal our stripes;* ܐܰܚܠܶܡ ܠܚܓܺܝܪ̈ܶܐ *he healed the lame.* Ethpalal ܐܶܬ݂ܚܠܰܡܠܰܡ *to dream; to give forth seed of generation in sleep.* Derivatives, ܚܶܠܡܳܐ, ܚܽܘܠܡܳܢܳܐ, ܚܰܠܡܳܢܳܐ, ܚܠܰܡܳܐ, ܚܠܺܝܡܽܘܬܳܐ, ܚܠܺܝܡܳܐܺܝܬ, ܡܚܰܠܡܳܢܽܘܬܳܐ, ܡܚܰܠܡܳܢܳܐ.

ܚܶܠܡܳܐ, ܚܶܠܡܳܐ pl. ܐ̈ rt. ܚܠܡ. m. *a dream;* ܒܚܶܠܡܳܐ *in a dream;* ܫܽܘܥܺܝܬ݂ܳܐ ܕܚܶܠܡܳܐ ܘܦܽܘܫܳܩܶܗ *the narration of a dream and its interpretation.*

ܚܠܰܡܚܰܠ = ܚܰܠ ܡܶܠܚܳܐ lit. *vinegar salt,* m. *pickle, brine.*

ܚܶܠܡܳܢܳܝܳܐ, ܚܶܠܡܳܢܳܝܬܳܐ rt. ܚܠܡ. adj. *dreamlike, arising from dreams.*

ܚܠܳܢܳܝܳܐ, ܚܠܳܢܳܝܬܳܐ from ܚܠܳܐ adj. *sandy, gravelly;* ܐܰܪܥܳܐ ܚܠܳܢܳܝܬܳܐ *sandy soil;* ܟܺܐܦ̈ܶܐ ܚܠܳܢܳܝ̈ܶܐ *gravel stones.*

ܚܶܠܡܳܐ, ܚܰܠܡܳܐ or ܚܶܠܡܳܐ, Ar. m. *a pad, cloth, rug.*

ܚܰܠܡܠܡܳܐ pl. ܐ̈ m. *the beard* of an ear of corn.

ܚܠܰܦ fut. ܢܶܚܠܽܘܦ, pass. part. ܚܠܺܝܦ, ܚܠܺܝܦܳܐ, ܚܠܺܝܦܬܳܐ. *a*) *to exchange, substitute.* *b*) *to pierce, shear.* Pa. ܚܰܠܶܦ *to change, exchange, renew;* ܚܰܠܶܦ ܡܳܐܢܰܘܗ̱ܝ ܥܰܡ ܥܰܒܕܶܗ *he changed clothes with his servant;* ܡܚܰܠܦܰܝ ܟܶܣܦܳܐ ܐܰܘ ܡܚܰܠܦܳܢܶܐ *money-changers;* ܠܳܐ ܡܚܰܠܦܺܝܢܰܢ ܠܗܰܝܡܳܢܽܘܬܰܢ *we will not change our faith;* ܢܚܰܠܦܽܘܢ ܚܰܝܠܗܽܘܢ *they shall renew their strength.* Ethpa. ܐܶܬ݂ܚܰܠܰܦ *to be changed, exchanged, bartered; to be renewed; to change in turn, do* anything *in turn, succeed;* ܐܶܬ݂ܚܰܠܰܦ ܕܡܽܘܬ݂ܶܗ *his likeness was changed, he was transfigured;* ܫܰܒܥܳܐ ܥܶܕܳܢܺܝܢ ܢܶܬ݂ܚܰܠܦܽܘܢ *seven seasons shall be renewed* or *shall succeed.* Aph. ܐܰܚܠܶܦ *to sprout* or *grow up again, to succeed something of a different nature; to try different ways, change one's methods;* ܐܺܝܠܳܢܳܐ ܡܰܚܠܶܦ ܘܣܳܠܶܩ *a tree sprouts again and shoots up;* ܪܶܓܬܳܐ ܡܰܚܠܦܳܐ *desire springs again.* Shaphel ܫܰܚܠܶܦ. *a*) *to change, alter; to convert, pervert.* *b*) *to translate, turn from one language into another;* ܫܰܚܠܶܦ ܡܶܠܬܶܗ ܕܡܳܪܝܳܐ *he changed the word of the Lord* i.e. *disobeyed its command;* ܫܰܚܠܶܦ ܠܶܐܓܰܪܬܳܐ *he altered, interpolated the letter;* ܫܰܚܠܶܦ ܐܶܢܽܘܢ ܡܶܢ ܗܰܝܡܳܢܽܘܬܳܐ *he perverted them from the faith;* ܡܫܰܚܠܦܺܝܢ ܡܰܟ̈ܪܙܳܢܶܐ the Evangelists *give varying genealogies;* pass. part. as adj. ܡܫܰܚܠܰܦ, ܡܫܰܚܠܦܳܐ *different, various, diverse;* ܡܰܦܩ̈ܳܢܘܳܬܳܐ ܡܫܰܚܠܦܳܬܳܐ *various versions;* ܫܘܝܽܘܬܳܐ ܠܳܐ ܡܫܰܚܠܦܬܳܐ *equality not differing.* Eshtaphal ܐܶܫܬܰܚܠܰܦ *a*) pass. *to be changed, be turned the other way.* *b*) refl. *to change, be transformed.* *c*) *to change* an opinion, *to turn* or *be perverted* from the faith; ܥܰܡ ܙܰܒ̈ܢܶܐ ܐܶܫܬܰܚܠܰܦ *he changed with the times.* Derivatives, ܚܽܘܠܳܦܳܐ, ܚܽܘܠܦܳܐ, ܡܚܰܠܦܳܢܳܐ, ܚܰܠܦܳܐ, ܚܠܳܦܳܐ, ܚܽܘܠܳܦܽܘܬܳܐ, ܚܶܠܦܳܐ, ܚܰܠܦ, ܡܫܰܚܠܦܳܢܳܐ, ܡܫܰܚܠܦܳܢܽܘܬܳܐ, ܡܫܰܚܠܦܳܢܳܐܺܝܬ, ܫܘܚܠܳܦܳܐ, ܡܫܰܚܠܦܽܘܬܳܐ, ܡܫܰܚܠܦܳܢܳܐܺܝܬ, ܐܶܫܬܰܚܠܦܽܘܬܳܐ, ܐܶܫܬܰܚܠܦܳܐ.

ܚܠܳܦ rt. ܚܠܦ. prep. takes the suffixes of a noun in the m. pl., *for, instead, because;* ܚܠܳܦ ܚܰܕܳܝܽܘܬܳܐ ܩܛܺܝܪܳܐ *instead of unity oppression;* ܚܠܳܦ ܟܢܽܘܫܬܳܐ ܗܽܘ ܢܳܨܶܐ *he contends for the Council;* ܚܠܳܦ ܕ *in the place of, on account of;* ܚܠܳܦ ܗܰܘ ܕ *because, on account of,* Germ. *dafür dass;* ܗܰܘ ܚܠܳܦ ܡܫܺܝܚܳܐ *Antichrist;* gram. ܚܠܳܦ ܫܡܳܐ pl. ܚܠܳܦ ܫܡܳܗ̈ܶܐ *a pronoun.*

ܚܰܠܦܳܐ another form for ܚܶܠܦܳܐ *b.*

ܚܶܠܦܳܐ rt. ܚܠܦ. *a*) *impious, profane.* *b*) *a reed, willow.*

ܚܽܘܠܳܦܳܐ rt. ܚܠܦ. m. *exchange, barter;* ܚܽܘܠܳܦܳܐ ܕ = ܚܠܳܦ, prep. *instead of, on account of, on behalf of;* ܚܽܘܠܳܦܳܐ ܕܫܺܐܪ̈ܳܝܶܐ *instead of silken raiments;* ܚܽܘܠܳܦܳܐ ܕܣܰܟ̈ܠܘܳܬܗܽܘܢ *on account of their sins.*

ܚܠܦܘܬܐ rt. ܚܠܦ. f. *impiety.*

ܚܠܦܬܐ rt. ܚܠܦ. f. *something given in exchange, a substitute.*

ܚܠܨ fut. ܢܚܠܘܨ, act. part. ܚܠܨ, ܚܠܨܐ, pass. part. ܚܠܝܨ, ܚܠܝܨܐ, ܚܠܝܨܬܐ. *to gird oneself, set briskly to work.* Part. adj. *a) girt;* metaph. *strong, strenuous, valiant;* ܩܪܒܐ ܚܠܝܨܐ *a hard fight;* ܠܐ ܚܠܝܨܐ *slack;* subst. *an athlete, a combatant;* ܚܠܝܨܐ ܙܪܝܙܝܢ ܒܨܠܘܬܐ *combatants armed with prayer. b) chafed* or *bare,* said of the shoulder worn by constant friction. ETHPE. ܐܬܚܠܨ *to gird oneself.* PA. ܚܠܨ *to take spoil, seize; to commit sacrilege;* ܣܦܝܢܐ ܣܓܝܐܬܐ ܚܠܨܘ ܡܢ ܛܝܝܐ *they seized many ships from the Arabs;* ܡܚܠܨܝ ܒܝܬ ܥܕܬܐ *robbers of churches;* ܡܚܠܨܝ ܩܒܪܐ *spoilers of tombs.* ETHPA. ܐܬܚܠܨ *to be spoiled, pillaged, to be taken by storm* or *by force;* with ܡܢ *to be deprived of;* ܠܐ ܡܬܚܠܨܢܐ *inviolable, secure.* DERIVATIVES, ܡܚܠܨܢܐ, ܚܠܝܨܐ, ܚܠܘܨܐ, ܡܚܠܨܢܘܬܐ, ܚܠܝܨܘܬܐ.

ܚܠܩ fut. ܢܚܠܘܩ, act. part. ܚܠܩ, ܚܠܩܐ, pass. part. ܚܠܝܩ, ܚܠܝܩܐ, ܚܠܝܩܬܐ. *to allot, to determine* by lot or fate, *to destine;* ܩܕܡ ܝܕܥ ܘܚܠܩ *he foreknew and foredestined;* ܟܘܟܒܐ ܚܠܩܘ ܘܦܠܓܘ ܠܗ ܡܘܬܐ *the stars determined and apportioned for him death;* pass. part. *fated, destined;* ܐܝܟ ܕܚܠܝܩ ܠܗ *as fate decreed for him;* ܗܠܝܢ ܚܠܝܩܢ ܕܢܗܘܝܢ *these things shall come to pass by fate.* DERIVATIVE, ܚܠܩܐ.

ܚܠܩܐ pl. ܚ̈ܠܩܐ rt. ܚܠܩ. *lot, portion; fate, destiny;* pl. *casting lots, oracles, auguries;* ܢܦܩ ܚܠܩܐ ܡܢ ܐܠܗܐ *the lot went forth from God;* ܚܙܝ ܕܚܠܩܐ ܘܡܠܚܫܝ ܚܪ̈ܫܐ *augurs and enchanters.*

ܚܠܫ denom. verb PAEL conj. from the following. *to weaken, enfeeble.* ETHPA. ܐܬܚܠܫ *to be enfeebled, discouraged.*

ܚܠܫ, ܚܠܫܐ, ܚܠܫܬܐ pl. m. ܚ̈ܠܫܐ, f. ܚ̈ܠܫܬܐ *frail, feeble, enfeebled; weak, mean, unwarlike, fainthearted, unfortunate, unlucky;* ܡܦܩ ܒܪܘܚܐ ܚܠܫܐ *a feeble apology;* ܟܝܢܢ ܚܠܫܐ *our feeble nature;* ܐܢܐ ܚܠܫܐ *I who am frail* or *unfortunate;* with ܡܢ *lacking, wanting, devoid of,* ܐܢܫ ܚܠܫܐ ܡܢ ܪܕܘܬܐ ܕܝܠܘܦܐ *one lacking the discipline of the learned = untaught.* DERIVATIVES, verb ܚܠܫ, ܚܠܫܘܬܐ.

ܚܠܫܘܬܐ from ܚܠܫ. f. *weakness, feebleness, frailty, low estate;* ܚܠܫܘܬܝ ܝܕܥ ܐܢܐ *I know my frailty;* ܐܬܪܚܡ ܥܠ ܚܠܫܘܬܝ *have mercy on my low estate, on me who am frail.*

ܚܠܬܐ pl. ܚ̈ܠܐ rt. ܚܠ. f. *a sheath, scabbard;* ܗܦܟ ܣܦܣܪܗ ܠܚܠܬܗ *he put his sword back into the scabbard.*

ܚܠܬܐ or ܚܠܬܐ rt. ܚܠ. f. *a bucket.*

ܚܠܬܐ pl. ܚ̈ܠܬܐ fem. of ܚܠܐ. *the mother's sister, an aunt on the mother's side.*

ܚܠܬܝܬܐ f. *laserpitium, silphium, assafoetida.*

ܚܡ fut. ܢܚܡ, act. part. ܚܐܡ, ܚܡܐ, pass. part. ܚܡܝܡ and ܚܡܝܡ, ܚܡܝܡܐ, ܚܡܝܡܬܐ. I. *to be hot, grow warm* or *hot,* said of the sun, of the heart, of teeming animals. Part. adj. ܚܡܝܡ *heated, hot, glowing; fervent, violent;* ܚܡܝܡ ܗܘܐ ܒܪܘܚܗ *he was stirred in spirit;* ܐܬܪܐ ܚܡܝܡܐ *a torrid region;* ܚܘܒܐ ܚܡܝܡܐ *fervent love;* ܐܫܬܐ ܚܡܝܡܬܐ *fever;* ܠܚܡܐ ܚܡܝܡܐ *hot* or *new bread;* ܡ̈ܝܐ ܚܡܝܡ̈ܐ *hot springs,* cf. ܚܡܝܡܘܬܐ. II. *to sweep,* ܚܡܐ ܒܝܬܐ *sweeping the house;* ܚܡܝܡ ܘܡܨܒܬ *swept and garnished.* PA. ܚܡܡ part. ܡܚܡܡܐ. *to warm.* ETHPA. ܐܬܚܡܡ *to be warm, to feel the heat, to become hot* with desire, zeal, &c. APH. ܐܚܡ *to warm, scorch.* PALPEL ܚܡܚܡ pass. part. ܡܚܡܚܡ *parched, arid.* ETHPALPAL ܐܬܚܡܚܡ *to dry up with heat, decay for lack of moisture.* DERIVATIVES, ܚܡܡܐ, ܚܡܝܡܐ, ܚܡܝܡܬܐ, ܚܡܝܡܘܬܐ, ܚܘܡܐ, ܡܚܡܡܢܐ, ܚܡܡܐ, verb ܚܡܬ, ܚܡܬܐ, ܚܡܬܢܐ, ܚܡܬܢܘܬܐ, ܚܡܝܡܬܐ.

ܚܡܐ, ܚܡ pl. irreg. ܚܡ̈ܘܗܐ with suff. ܚܡܘܗܝ, ܚܡܘܗ &c. m. *a father-in-law,* cf. ܚܡܬܐ f. *a mother-in-law.*

ܚܡ pr. n. *Ham.*

ܚܡܐ fut. ܢܚܡܐ, part. ܚܐܡܐ, ܚܡܝܐ. I. *to wither* with the heat, *to fade;* metaph. *to fade away, grow faint;* ܚܡܐ ܝܪܘܩܐ *the tender grass is withered away;* ܐܝܟ ܥܣܒܐ ܡܢ ܫܠܝ ܚܡܐ *it withers away suddenly like the grass;* ܐܝܟ ܠܓܘܬܐ ܚܡܐ *it passes away as vapour;* ܢܚܡܐ ܕܘܟܪܢܗ *may its remembrance fade away;*

ܫܘܦܪܐ ܕܚܡܐ *comeliness which passes away;* ܕܠܐ ܚܡܝܐ *unfading.* II. *to sweep,* ܗܘ ܡܐ ܕܚܡܝܢ ܒܒ̈ܬܝܗܘܢ، ܚܡܝܢ *that which they sweep out of their houses.* Pa. ܚܰܡܺܝ *to warm.* Aph. ܐܰܚܡܺܝ *to dry up, wither* trans., *cause to fade;* ܡܰܚܡܝܐ ܣܝܒܘܬܐ ܠܛܠܝܘܬܐ *advancing age makes youthfulness fade away.* Derivatives, ܚܡܝܐ, ܡܚܡܝܢܐ.

ܚ̈ܡܘܗܐ pl. of ܚܡ, ܚܡܐ *a father-in-law.*

ܚܡܘܥܬܐ or ܚܡܘܥܝܬܐ f. *lapathum, cress;* ܚܡܘܥܬܐ ܕܚܡܘܨܐ *sour cress.*

ܚܡܘܨ, ܚܡܘܨܐ, ܚܡܘܨܬܐ pl. m. ܚܡܘܨܝܢ, ̈ܐ, f. ܚܡܘܨܢ, ̈ܬܐ, rt. ܚܡܨ. *sour, unripe, harsh;* ܚܡܪܐ ܚܡܘܨܐ *sour wine;* ܚܠܒܐ ܚܡܘܨܐ *sour milk.*

ܚܡܘܨܘܬܐ rt. ܚܡܨ. f. *acidity, sharpness, sourness.*

ܚܡܘܨܬܢ, ܚܡܘܨܬܢܐ, ܬܢܝܬܐ rt. ܚܡܨ. *bashful, modest;* ܚܡܘܨܬܢܝܬܐ *a modest woman.*

ܚܡܘܪܬܐ pl. ܚܘܡܪ̈ܐ, ܚܘܡܪ̈ܝܬܐ f. *a globule; a round stone; a gem; a joint; a berry.* See ܚܘܡܪܐ.

ܚܡܘܬܐ pl. ̈ܐ m. *an imposthume, pustule, breaking out, the head of a sore;* ܚܡ̈ܘܬܐ ܕܢܦܩܢ ܒܦܓܪܗ *the pustules which come out on his body;* ܒܘܥܘܢܐ ܕܚܡ̈ܘܬܐ *smallpox.*

ܚܡܘܬܢܐ or ܚܘܡܬܢܐ m. *outworks, rampart.*

ܚܡܘܝܐ rt. ܚܡܐ. m. *drying up; going out* as a fire; *sweeping.*

ܚܡܝܠܘܬܐ rt. ܚܡܠ. f. *the ingathering, harvesting.*

ܚܡܝܠܬܐ rt. ܚܡܠ. f. *a rough outer garment, rug* or *wrap; a cassock.*

ܚܡܝܡ, ܡܐ, ܡܬܐ; see ܚܡ.

ܚܡܝܡܐ rt. ܚܡ. m. *hay, dry fodder.*

ܚܡܝܡܐܝܬ rt. ܚܡ. adv. *warmly, fervently, instantly.*

ܚܡܝܡܘܬܐ rt. ܚܡ. f. a) *heat, glow; fervour, zeal;* ܚܡܝܡܘܬܐ ܫܡܫܢܝܬܐ *solar heat;* ܚܡܝܡܘܬܗ ܕܠܘܬ ܐܠܗܐ *his fervent zeal towards God.* b) *sweeping, cleaning.*

ܚܡܝܡܬܐ pl. ̈ܬܐ rt. ܚܡ. f. *hot springs, warm waters; a bath.*

ܚܡܝܢܐ m. *a father-in-law;* cf. ܚܡ, ܚܡܐ; ܚܡܝܢܝ ܘܚܡܬܝ *my father and mother-in-law.*

ܚܡܝܥ, ܚܡܝܥܐ m. *leaven, leavened bread;* cf. ܚܡܝܥ pass. part.

ܚܡܝܥܘܬܐ rt. ܚܡܥ. f. *fermentation.*

ܚܡܝܪ, ܚܡܝܪܐ pl. ̈ܐ m. *leaven; leavened bread.*

ܚܡܝܫܐܝܬ adv. from ܚܡܫܐ. *fivefold;* ܕܚܠܬܐ ܚܡܝܫܐܝܬ ܗܘܝܐ *fear arises from five causes.*

ܚܡܝܫܝܐ, ܝܬܐ from ܚܡܫܐ. adj. *fifth.*

ܚܡܝܫܝܘܬܐ from ܚܡܫܐ f. *the number five; dividing into five parts.*

ܚܡܝܬ, ܚܡܝܬܬܐ *angry;* see ܚܡܬ.

ܚܡܰܠ fut. ܢܶܚܡܘܠ, inf. ܡܶܚܡܰܠ, imper. ܚܡܘܠ, act. part. ܚܳܡܶܠ ܚܳܡܠܳܐ, pass. part. ܚܡܝܠ, ̈ܐ, ܠܬܐ. a) *to gather in* esp. corn into a barn, *to amass, lay up, lay by, put away; to take up, gather in, collect, compile;* ܐܘܨܪ̈ܐ ܡܣܐܬܐ ܚܡܝܠܝܢ ܗܘܘ ܠܗ ܚܛ̈ܐ *a quantity of barns stored up wheat for him* i.e. *were heaped with corn;* ܚܡܝܠܝܢ ܗܘܘ ܒܓܙ̈ܐ ܢܟ̈ܣܐ ܕܠܐ ܡܬܡܫܚܝܢ *infinite wealth was laid up in the treasuries;* ܚܡܘܠ ܒܥܝܪܟ *gather in thy cattle;* ܦܬܚܬ ܫܝܘܠ ܦܘܡܗ ܘܚܡܠܬ *the pit opened her mouth and swallowed up;* ܡܪܝܐ ܚܡܠܢܝ *the Lord hath taken me up;* ܚܡܠܘ ܢܦܫܗܘܢ *they recollected themselves;* ܕܦܘܫ̈ܩܐ ܒܟܬܒܐ ܚܕ ܢܚܡܘܠ *that he might collect glosses into one book* i.e. *compile scholia.* b) *to withhold, restrain;* ܚܳܡܶܠ ܪ̈ܚܡܘܗܝ ܒܪܘܓܙܗ *he withholdeth mercy in his wrath;* ܐܢܬ ܫܡܫܐ ܚܡܘܠ ܙܠܝܩ̈ܝܟ *do thou, O Sun, restrain thy rays;* ܚܡܠܗ ܠܠܫܢܗ *he restrained his tongue;* ܚܡܠܬ ܢܦܫܗ *she restrained herself.* Ethpe. ܐܬܚܡܠ imper. ܐܬܚܡܠ a) *to be gathered in* as the harvest; esp. with ܠܘܬ ܐܒܗ̈ܘܗܝ *to be gathered to his fathers, to die, be buried;* ܐܬܚܡܠ ܠܫܠܝܗ ܕܩܒܪܐ *he was gathered into the quiet of the tomb.* b) *to gather together* intr., *to go* or *be put aside;* ܡܬܚܡܠܝܢ ܚܝ̈ܘܬܐ ܕܒܪܐ ܒܡܥܪ̈ܬܗܘܢ ܘܫܠܝܢ *wild beasts betake themselves to their dens and are quiet.* c) *to be withheld, restrained.* Pa. ܚܰܡܶܠ a) *to wrap up, cover closely; to enshroud;* ܟܕ ܕܡܚܡܠ ܗܘܐ ܡܐܢ̈ܐ ܩܘܕܫܐ *when he had covered the Eucharistic vessels.* b) *to hem in.* c) *to withhold, withdraw* a book from circulation. Ethpa. ܐܬܚܰܡܰܠ *to be gathered in, brought in* as the harvest, *to gather* together or *stand up in a heap; to be summed up; to be held back, restrained;* ܒܗ ܐܬܚܡܠܬ ܥܬܝܩܬܐ *the Old Testament is gathered up, is complete, in Him;* ܕܬܬܚܡܠ ܒܟܝܐ *that weeping may be restrained.* Derivatives, ܚܡܠܬܐ, ܚܡܠܐ, ܚܡܘܠܬܐ.

ܚܡܠ, ܚܡܠܐ pl. ܐ̈ rt. ܚܡܠ. m. *ingathering* of the harvest, *laying by;* ܥܐܕܐ ܕܚܡܠܐ *the feast of ingathering;* ܒܝܬ ܚܡܠܐ *a storehouse.*

ܚܡܡ Pael conj. of ܚܡ.

ܚܡܡܐ *ginger.*

ܚܡܣܢ Pamel conj. of ܚܣܢ, has the same meanings as the Pael but intensified. *a) to grasp firmly, hold fast* with ܒ; ܚܡܣܢ ܐܚܘܕ ܒܗ *take hold of him firmly;* ܠܐ ܢܚܡܣܢ ܚܝܠܗ *he shall not retain his strength. b) to be very strong, powerful* or *brave, to put force* or *restraint* on oneself, *to endure, persist, persevere; to resist, hold out against;* ܚܡܣܢ ܒܩܪܒܐ *he held out bravely, was strong in combat;* ܚܡܣܢܘ ܒܝܘܠܦܢܗ ܕܦܪܘܩܢ *they were steadfast, held fast, in the doctrine of our Saviour;* ܠܐ ܢܚܡܣܢ ܒܚܙܬܗܘܢ *let us not endure the sight of them. c)* with ܠܘܬ *to remain with* any one; with ܡܢ *to abstain from; to remain away from.*

ܚܡܥ fut. ܢܚܡܥ, act. part. ܚܡܥ, ܚܡܥܐ, pass. part. ܚܡܝܥ and ܚܡܝܥ, ܐ, ܬܐ. *to ferment, to leaven, to mix;* ܚܡܝܪܐ ܕܚܡܥܐ *dough set to leaven;* ܚܡܝܪܐ ܚܢܦܐ ܕܚܡܥ ܗܘܐ *heathen leaven which had leavened and penetrated them;* ܓܒܝܠܐ ܚܡܝܥܐ ܘܡܚܠܛܐ a mass of clay *worked up and mixed;* ܠܚܡܐ ܠܐ ܚܡܝܥܐ *unleavened bread.* Aph. ܐܚܡܥ *to cause to ferment* or *be leavened, to leaven;* ܐܚܡܥܗ ܒܚܡܝܪܐ *he leavened it with leaven.* Derivatives, ܚܡܥܐ, ܚܡܝܥܘܬܐ.

ܚܡܥܐ or ܚܡܥܐ m. *a pomegranate seed* or *grain.*

ܚܡܨ fut. ܢܚܡܨ *to turn sour,* intr.; ܕܠܐ ܢܚܡܨ ܚܡܪܐ *lest the wine turn acid.* Pa. ܚܡܨ *to make ashamed.* Ethpa. ܐܬܚܡܨ *to blush, be ashamed, be confused;* ܚܘܒܐ ܕܠܐ ܡܬܚܡܨ *unabashed love;* ܡܢ ܕܝܢ ܐܢܫ ܠܐ ܡܚܡܨ ܠܝ *no man makes me ashamed.* Aph. ܐܚܡܨ *a) to turn sour,* tr. ܐܢ ܚܡܪܐ ܡܚܡܨ ܘܗܘܐ ܚܠܐ *if the wine be turned acid and made into vinegar. b) to make ashamed, to shame,* ܡܚܡܨܝܢ *blushing and shamefaced.* Derivatives, ܚܡܝܨܐ, ܚܡܘܨܐ, ܚܡܘܨܘܬܐ, ܚܡܨܢܐ, ܚܡܨܬܐ, ܚܡܝܨܘܬܐ, ܡܬܚܡܨܢܘܬܐ, ܐܚܡܨܐ.

ܚܡܨ or ܚܡܨ pr. n. *Emesa* now *Homs,* in N. Syria.

ܚܡܨܐ pl. ܐ̈ m. *a) small pulse, vetches. b) bean meal.*

ܚܡܨܝܠܬܐ f. *the autumn crocus, meadow saffron, colchicum autumnale.*

ܚܡܪ Ethpa. ܐܬܚܡܪ *to ferment.*

ܚܡܪ, ܚܡܪܐ or ܚܡܪܐ pl. ܚܡܪ̈ܐ or ܚܡܪ̈ܐ c. gen. but more often used as masc. while ܐܬܢܐ is used for the fem. *a) an ass;* ܚܡܪܐ ܢܩܒܬܐ *a she-ass;* ܡܩܒܘܪܝܐ ܚܡܪ *the burial of an ass;* ܘܪܕܐ ܕܚܡܪܐ *the peony. b)* metaph. *the bridge* of a cithern.

ܚܡܪܐ pl. ܚܡܪ̈ܐ or ܚܡܪ̈ܘܬܐ m. *wine;* ܚܡܪܐ ܕܠܐ ܡܒܫܠ *must, unfermented juice* of the grape; ܚܡܪܐ ܚܝܐ *pure wine* i.e. unmixed with water; ܚܡܪܐ ܕܕܒܫܐ *mead;* ܚܡܪ ܕܒܫܐ *wine mingled with honey;* ܚܡܪ̈ܐ ܡܫܢܝܐ ܛܥܡܐ *wines of various flavours;* ܚܡܪܗܘܢ ܕܪܘܡܢܐ *pomegranate juice.*

ܚܡܪܐ m. ܚܡܪܬܐ f. *a wine-seller, wine-merchant.*

ܚܡܪܘܢܐ pl. ܐ̈ m. dim. of ܚܡܪܐ. *a little ass.*

ܚܡܪܢܐ or ܚܡܪܝܢܐ m. *an ass-driver, donkey-boy.*

ܚܡܫ, ܚܡܫܐ, ܚܡܫܐ, ܚܡܫܬܐ *five;* ܚܡܫ ܙܒܢܝܢ *five times;* ܕܚܡܫܐ *the fifth;* ܚܡܫܒܫܒܐ W-Syr., ܚܡܫܒܫܒܐ E-Syr. *Thursday;* ܒܢܓܗ ܕܚܡܫܐ *at dawn on Thursday;* ܚܡܫܒܫܒܐ or ܚܡܫܐ ܕܦܨܚܐ *the fifth day of Holy Week, Maundy Thursday;* ܚܡܫܡܐܐ *five hundred;* ܚܡܫܝܢ *fifty;* ܚܡܫܝܢ ܚܡܫܝܢ *by fifties.* The collective ܚܡܫܬܐ is used with suffixes, ܚܡܫܬܢ *we five;* ܚܡܫܬܝܗܘܢ *those five, the five of them,* &c. Derivatives, ܚܡܘܫܐ, ܚܡܫܝܢܝܐ, ܚܡܝܫܝܐ, ܚܡܫܘܬܐ, verb ܚܡܫ.

ܚܡܫ denom. verb Pael conj. from ܚܡܫܐ. *to take a fifth part, divide by five.*

ܚܰܡܫܰܡܫܳܐ; see ܚܡܫ, ܚܰܡܫܳܐ. 500.

ܚܰܡܶܫܬܰܥܣܰܪ and ܚܰܡܫܰܬܥܶܣܪܶܐ m. ܚܰܡܶܫܬܰܥܶܣܪܶܐ, ܚܰܡܫܰܬܥܶܣܪܶܐ f. *fifteen*.

ܚܡܬ denom. verb from ܚܶܡܬܳܐ. Pe. *to burn with anger*, part. adj. ܚܰܡܺܝܬ, ܚܰܡܺܝܬܳܐ. *enraged, angry*, usually impers. with ܥܰܠ; ܚܶܡܬܳܐ ܠܶܗ ܥܰܠ ܕܶܐܙܕܒܶܢ *he was angry because* Joseph *was sold;* ܚܡܺܝܬ ܘܢܶܦܩܶܬ *he was angry and went out;* usually impers. with ܠ, ܚܰܡܺܝܬܳܐ ܠܶܗ ܥܰܠ *he is enraged about* ... Pael ܚܰܡܶܬ *to enrage, to anger, provoke anger;* ܡܰܪܓܶܙ ܘܡܚܰܡܶܬ ܠܕܰܝܳܢܳܐ *he provokes and enrages the judge.* Ethpa. ܐܶܬܚܰܡܰܬ with ܥܰܠ of the object, *to rage, be furious; to provoke;* ܡܶܬܚܰܡܬܳܐ ܟܺܐܢܽܘܬܳܐ *justice is angered;* ܐܶܬܚܰܡܰܬ ܘܐܶܬܚܰܪܰܪ ܥܰܠ ܐܺܝܘܒ *his anger was kindled against Job;* ܫܘܓܳܫܳܐ ܥܰܠ ܟܽܠܗܘܢ ܐܶܬܚܰܡܰܬ *the tumult raged against them all.* Aph. ܐܰܚܡܶܬ *to provoke, anger, vex;* ܐܰܚܡܶܬ ܠܶܒܳܐ ܕܥܰܡܡܶܐ ܣܰܓܺܝܐܶܐ *I shall vex the hearts of many nations.*

ܚܶܡܬܳܐ pl. ܚܶܡܳܬܳܐ rt. ܚܡ. f. *heat,* ܚܶܡܬܳܐ ܕܢܽܘܪܳܐ *the heat of the fire;* metaph. *a) rage, fury, passion,* ܚܶܡܬܳܐ ܕܪܽܘܓܙܶܗ *fierce anger. b) venom, inflammation* from venom.

ܚܰܡܬܳܐ fem. of ܚܡܳܐ. *a mother-in-law;* ܚܰܡܳܘܟ ܘܚܰܡܳܬܳܟ *thy father- and mother-in-law.*

ܚܶܡܬܳܢ, ܚܶܡܬܳܢܳܐ, ܚܶܡܬܳܢܺܝܬܳܐ pl. m. ܢܶܐ f. ܢܳܝܳܬܳܐ from ܚܶܡܬܳܐ. *irascible, wrathful, passionate, furious;* ܓܰܒܪܳܐ ܚܶܡܬܳܢܳܐ ܡܓܰܪܶܐ ܚܶܪܝܳܢܳܐ *a wrathful man stirreth up strife.*

ܚܶܡܬܳܢܳܐܝܬ from ܚܶܡܬܳܐ. adv. *angrily, furiously.*

ܚܳܢ 3 m. s. of verb ܚܢܢ. *to have pity.*

ܚܳܢ fut. ܢܶܚܢܽܘܢ, inf. ܡܶܚܰܢ, imper. ܚܽܘܢ, act. part. ܚܳܐܶܢ, pass. part. ܚܢܺܝܢ, ܚܢܺܝܢܳܐ. i. *to pity, spare, to be gracious, pitiful, to have pity* or *compassion* with ܠ or ܥܰܠ of the pers. ܚܽܘܢ ܥܠܰܝ ܐܰܝܟ ܕܚܰܢܬ ܠܓܰܝܳܣܳܐ *have pity on me as Thou hadst pity on the robber;* ܚܽܘܢܳܢܳܐܝܬ ܫܡܰܥ ܠܒܳܥܽܘܬܝ *pitifully hear my request;* ܢܰܦܫܳܬܳܐ ܕܐܶܬܚܢܰܢ *souls who have obtained mercy.* ii. pass. part. ܚܢܺܝܢ see below; *to smell rank* as the body from sweat and dirt. Ethpe. ܐܶܬܚܢܶܢ *to find mercy* or *favour;* ܐܶܬܚܢܶܢ ܡܶܢܳܟ *he obtained mercy from thee.* Ethpa. ܐܶܬܚܰܢܰܢ *to seek favour* or *kindness, to make supplication;* ܡܶܬܚܰܢܰܢ ܐܢܳܐ ܡܶܢܟܽܘܢ ܐܰܚܰܝ *I beseech you, brethren.* Derivatives, ܚܢܢ, ܚܢܳܢܳܐ, ܚܢܺܝܢܳܐ, ܚܽܘܢܳܢܳܐ, ܚܢܳܢܽܘܬܳܐ, ܡܶܬܚܰܢܢܳܢܽܘܬܳܐ, ܡܶܬܚܰܢܢܳܢܳܐܝܬ, ܡܶܬܚܰܢܢܳܢܳܐ, ܬܰܚܢܳܢܳܐ.

ܚܢܳܐ fut. ܢܶܚܢܶܐ, act. part. ܚܳܢܶܐ, ܚܳܢܝܳܐ. *to bend* a bow, *to take aim, aim at, hit* the mark; *to have regard* or *look to* the end, *to notice; to incline towards* an opinion, *turn towards* a person, *come near, agree nearly; to have for an aim, bend one's mind towards, to attain, apprehend; to apply* or *accommodate* to a purpose, often used with ܢܺܝܫܳܐ; ܒܩܶܠܥܳܐ ܚܳܢܶܝܢ ܗܘܰܘ *they took aim with the sling;* ܚܳܢܶܝܢ ܘܡܦܰܠܓܺܝܢ *aiming and missing;* ܟܰܕ ܫܳܕܶܝܢ ܘܚܳܢܶܝܢ ܠܚܕܳܕܶܐ *shooting and aiming at each other;* ܚܢܳܐ ܗܘܳܐ ܠܢܺܝܫܳܐ *he bent his mind to that aim, had for his aim;* ܚܢܳܐ ܠܢܺܝܫܳܐ *he attained the aim, hit the mark;* ܚܽܘܪ ܠܢܺܝܫܳܟ ܘܠܳܐ ܬܶܣܛܶܐ ܠܛܽܘܥܝܳܐ *look at your aim lest you deflect, fall aside, to error;* ܠܳܐ ܬܶܣܒܪܽܘܢ ܕܠܰܕܗܰܒ ܒܰܠܚܽܘܕ ܚܳܢܶܐ ܐ̱ܢܳܐ *do not think that I aim only at gold;* ܕܝܰܬܺܝܪ ܚܳܢܝܳܐ ܠܫܪܳܪܳܐ *which more nearly hits the truth;* ܒܡܶܢܝܳܢܳܐ ܚܳܢܝܳܐ ܚܰܕ ܚܕܳܢܳܐܝܬ *it very nearly agrees in number;* ܠܨܶܒܝܳܢܶܗ ܕܐܠܳܗܳܐ ܚܳܢܝܳܐ *it is in accord with the will of God;* ܠܳܐ ܚܢܳܬܶܗ ܠܣܶܒܪܶܗ ܥܶܝܢܳܐ ܕܫܺܝܠܘܚܳܐ the pool of Siloam *did not answer* the expectation *of the man laid there.* Ethpe. ܐܶܬܚܢܺܝ *to be inclined* or *disposed.* Derivatives, ܚܢܳܐ, ܚܢܳܝܳܐ, ܚܢܳܝܽܘܬܳܐ, ܚܢܳܢܳܐ, ܚܢܺܝܬܳܐ.

ܚܶܢܳܐ pl. ܢܶܐ rt. ܚܢܐ. m. *a bending,* hence, *a) the hollow* of a chariot, *the lap;* ܫܳܩܶܠ ܠܗܽܘܢ ܒܚܶܢܶܗ *he takes them in his lap. b) the privy parts.*

ܚܢܓ root-meaning *to groan, pant after,* Pe. only part. adj. ܚܰܢܺܝܓ, ܓܳܐ, ܓܬܳܐ *sighing, sad, mournful, doleful, miserable, lamentable;* ܒܟܳܬܳܐ ܚܰܢܺܝܓܬܳܐ *sad weeping;* ܒܠܶܒܳܐ ܚܰܢܺܝܓܳܐ *with a sorrowful heart;* ܐܘܳܝ ܡܳܐ ܚܰܢܺܝܓܳܐ ܗܳܕܶܐ ܬܰܫܥܺܝܬܳܐ *oh! what a lamentable history this is;* ܩܺܝܢܬܳܐ or ܡܰܐܡܪܳܐ ܚܰܢܺܝܓܳܐ *a lament, dirge.* Pael ܚܰܢܶܓ only 3 p. s. f. impers. ܚܰܢܓܰܬ ܠܶܗ *it grieved him;* ܚܰܢܓܰܬ ܠܰܢ *it made us groan.* Ethpa. ܐܶܬܚܰܢܰܓ *to groan, to sigh* or *pant after, to long for;* ܗܳܕܶܐ ܡܶܬܚܰܢܰܓ ܐ̱ܢܳܐ ܘܡܶܬܚܰܢܰܓ *this I desire and long for.* Aph. ܐܰܚܢܶܓ *to cause to pant after* or *long for; to make doleful;* ܠܐܰܬܠܺܝܛܶܐ ܡܰܚܢܶܓ ܟܠܺܝܠܳܐ *the crown rouses the desire of athletes.* Derivatives, ܚܢܳܓܳܐ, ܚܰܢܺܝܓܳܐܝܬ, ܚܰܢܺܝܓܽܘܬܳܐ.

ܬܶܢܚܬܳܐ pl. ܬܶܢܚ̈ܳܬܳܐ rt. ܐܢܚ. f. *a sigh, groan;* ܒܶܟܝܳܐ ܘܬܶܢܚ̈ܳܬܳܐ *weeping and groaning.*

ܚܶܢܘܳܝܳܐ, ܚܶܢܘܳܝܬܳܐ pl. ܚܶܢܘܳܝ̈ܶܐ from ܚܳܢܽܘܬܳܐ. *a tavern-keeper; a huckster, seller of herbs, greengrocer;* ܟܰܕ ܬܳܩܶܠ ܗ̱ܘܳܐ ܚܶܢܘܳܝܳܐ ܠܥܶܢܒ̈ܶܐ *while the greengrocer weighed the grapes.*

ܚܶܢܘܽܨܳܐ m. *a young pig, sucking-pig.*

ܚܳܢܽܘܩܳܐ pl. ܐ̈ܶ rt. ܚܢܩ. *strangling, stifling, overwhelming;* ܢܰܗܪ̈ܰܘܳܬܳܐ ܚܳܢܽܘܩ̈ܶܐ *rivers which drown people;* ܐܶܬ݂ܚܰܢܩܰܬ ܒܡܰܝ̈ܳܐ ܚܳܢܽܘܩ̈ܶܐ *she was drowned in the overwhelming waters.*

ܚܢܳܩܳܐ pl. ܐ̈ܶ rt. ܚܢܩ. m. *strangling, hanging, drowning;* ܠܰܝܬ ܐܳܬ݂ܳܐ ܕܰܚܢܳܩܳܐ ܥܰܠ ܨܰܘܪܶܗ *there is no mark on his neck of his having been strangled* or *hanged;* metaph. *distress, anxiety;* ܚܢܳܩܳܐ ܢܰܦ̮ܫܳܢܳܝܳܐ *mental anxiety.*

ܚܢܽܘܬܳܐ pl. ܚܰܢ̈ܘܳܬܳܐ rt. ܚܢܐ. f. *an arched chamber, a cell, stall* or *booth; a gang* or *crew;* ܚܳܢܽܘܬܳܐ ܕܢܰܦ̮ܚܳܐ *the blacksmith's booth;* ܚܳܢܘ̈ܳܬܳܐ ܕܗܶܪ̈ܛܝܩܶܐ *gangs of heretics.*

ܚܢܰܛ fut. ܢܶܚܢܽܘܛ, inf. ܡܶܚܢܰܛ, pass. part. ܚܢܺܝܛ, ܚܢܺܝܛܳܐ, ܚܢܺܝܛܬܳܐ. *to embalm;* ܚܢܰܛܽܘܗ̱ܝ ܐܳܣܘ̈ܳܬܳܐ ܠܐܺܝܣܪܳܐܝܶܠ *the physicians embalmed Israel.* ETHPE. ܐܶܬ݂ܚܢܶܛ *to be embalmed.* PA. ܚܰܢܶܛ same as PE. DERIVATIVE, ܚܢܳܛܳܐ.

ܚܶܢܝܳܐ pl. ܚܶܢ̈ܝܶܐ rt. ܚܢܐ. m. *aim, bent, leaning, disposition, purpose;* ܚܶܢܝܳܐ ܕܢܺܝܫܳܐ *aim at a mark, direction;* ܦܰܫܶܩ ܐܶܢܽܘܢ ܐܰܝܟ ܚܶܢܝܳܐ ܕܪܶܥܝܳܢܶܗ *he explained them according to the bent of his own mind.*

ܚܶܢܝܳܐܝܬ rt. ܚܢܐ. adv. *at a venture.*

ܬܶܢܚܳܐܝܬ rt. ܐܢܚ. adv. *dolefully, sadly;* ܟܰܕ ܒܳܟܶܐ ܬܶܢܚܳܐܝܬ *weeping and groaning.*

ܬܶܢܚܳܢܽܘܬܳܐ rt. ܐܢܚ. f. *lamentation.*

ܚܰܢܺܝܢ, ܐ̱ܳ, ܬܳܐ rt. ܚܢܢ II. adj. *stale, musty, rancid;* ܡܶܫܚܳܐ ܗ̱ܘ ܕܚܰܢܺܝܢ *rancid oil;* ܩܶܢܩ̈ܢܶܐ ܨܰܐܝ̈ܳܐ ܘܚܰܢܺܝܢ̈ܶܐ ܘܒܺܝܫ̈ܰܝ ܪܺܝܚܳܐ *dirty and foul and evil-smelling bottles.*

ܚܶܢܟܳܐ pl. ܐ̈ܶ f. usually contr. to ܚܶܟܳܐ. *the palate;* ܡܰܪܺܝܪ ܚܶܢܟܳܐ *sad, embittered, morose.*

ܚܢܰܢ pers. pron. I c. pl. *we;* after a participle the initial ܚ is not pronounced; a fuller form ܐܶܢܰܚܢܰܢ or ܐܰܚܢܰܢ is found in ancient MSS.

ܚܢܳܢ, ܚܢܳܢܳܐ, ܚܢܳܢܬܳܐ rt. ܚܢ. *pitiful, tender, compassionate, clement,* with ܠܳܐ *unmerciful, pitiless;* ܒܥܶܝܬܳܟ ܒܪܶܗ ܕܚܢܳܢܳܐ *I have besought Thee, O Son of the Merciful One.*

ܚܢܳܢ, ܚܢܳܢܳܐ rt. ܚܢ. m. *pity, mercy, compassion, pitifulness, clemency, favour, grace;* ܒܚܢܳܢ ܚܽܘܒܶܗ *by His pitiful love;* ܩܰܪܶܒܬܳܢܝ ܠܘܳܬܳܟ ܒܚܢܳܢܳܟ *Thou hast in Thy pity drawn me near to Thee;* metaph. a compound of oil, dust, and water mixed with the relics of saints or with earth from holy places; this was used for anointing the sick, for anointing at betrothals, &c., by the East Syrians; cf. ܒܪܽܘܟܬܳܐ.

ܚܢܳܢܽܘܬܳܐ rt. ܚܢ. f. *pitifulness, clemency.*

ܚܰܢܶܦ denom. verb PAEL conj. from ܚܰܢܦܳܐ. *to paganize; to turn aside to idolatry.* ETHPA. ܐܶܬ݂ܚܰܢܰܦ *to be profane, irreligious.* APH. ܐܰܚܢܶܦ *to apostatize; to pervert to paganism;* ܥܳܠܡܳܐ ܕܰܐܚܢܦܶܗ ܣܳܛܳܢܳܐ *the world which Satan had reduced to paganism.*

ܚܰܢܦܳܐ, ܚܰܢܦܬܳܐ pl. m. ܐ̈ܶ f. ܬ̈ܳܐ. *godless, ungodly, profane, pagan, heathen; a Gentile, Greek;* ܚܰܢܦ̈ܶܐ ܛܳܥܝ̈ܶܐ *the erring heathen;* ܝܽܘܠܝܳܢܳܘܣ ܚܰܢܦܳܐ *Julian the apostate.* DERIVATIVES, verb ܚܢܦ, ܚܰܢܦܽܘܬܳܐ, ܚܰܢܦܳܐܝܬ, ܚܰܢܦܳܝܳܐ.

ܚܰܢܦܳܐܝܬ adv. from ܚܰܢܦܳܐ. *after the Gentile* or *heathen manner.*

ܚܰܢܦܽܘܬܳܐ from ܚܰܢܦܳܐ f. a) *impiety, godlessness, paganism, Sabaeanism,* ܚܰܢܦܽܘܬܳܐ ܕܦܳܠܚܽܘܬ ܦܰܬܟܪ̈ܶܐ *the impiety of idolatry;* ܥܒܰܪ ܡܶܢ ܚܰܢܦܽܘܬܳܐ ܕܰܐܒ݂ܽܘܗ̱ܝ ܠܗܰܝܡܳܢܽܘܬܳܐ ܕܰܐܠܳܗܳܐ *he passed over from the heathenism of his father to faith in God.* b) used as a collect. noun *heathendom, the Gentiles.*

ܚܰܢܦܳܝܳܐ, ܚܰܢܦܳܝܬܳܐ from ܚܰܢܦܳܐ. *heathen, Gentile, ethnic;* ܥܰܡ̈ܡܶܐ ܚܰܢܦܳܝ̈ܶܐ *heathen nations;* ܥܝܳܕܳܐ ܗ̱ܘܳܐ ܚܰܢܦܳܝܳܐ *it was a heathen custom.*

ܚܢܰܩ fut. ܢܶܚܢܽܘܩ, act. part. ܚܳܢܶܩ, ܚܳܢܩܳܐ, pass. part. ܚܢܺܝܩ, ܐ̱ܳ, ܬܳܐ. *to choke, stifle, suffocate, smother,* with smoke, in water, under ruins; *to strangle, hang;* metaph. *to torment, oppress;* ܚܢܰܩ ܢܰܦ̮ܫܶܗ *he hanged himself;* ܕܢܶܚܢܩܽܘܢܳܝܗ̱ܝ ܒܚܰܒ݂ܠܳܐ *that they might strangle him with a noose;* ܣܠܶܩܘ ܟܽܘܒ̈ܶܐ ܘܚܢܰܩܽܘܗ̱ܝ *thorns grew up and choked* the seed; ܚܢܺܝܩ ܒܕܶܡ̈ܥܶܐ *choked with tears;* ܚܢܺܝܩܺܝܢ ܒܡܰܝ̈ܳܐ *drowned;* ܚܢܺܝܩܺܝܢ ܒܟܰܦܢܳܐ *perished with hunger.* ETHPE. ܐܶܬ݂ܚܢܶܩ *to be choked, suffocated, drowned;* metaph. *to be overwhelmed* with cares, sorrows or difficulties; ܐܶܬ݂ܚܢܶܩ ܒܶܗ

ܐܶܬ݂ܚܢܶܩ ܒܟܪܝܘܬܐ ܬܪܥܝܬܝ my mind was overwhelmed with sorrow. Pa. ܚܰܢܶܩ to choke, suffocate, strangle, ruin. Ethpa. ܐܶܬ݂ܚܰܢܰܩ to be choked, suffocated, smothered, strangled, drowned; metaph. to be straitened. Derivatives, ܚܢܘܩܐ, ܚܢܘܩܝܐ, ܚܢܘܩܘܬܐ, ܚܢܩܐ, ܚܢܝܩܐ.

ܚܶܢܩܳܐ rt. ܚܢܩ. usually in the pl. ܚܶܢܩܶܐ bands, bonds; ܚܶܢܩܶܐ ܕܢܺܝܪܳܐ the collar of a yoke or the strings with which it is tied to the neck; the neck of a vessel; ܦܣܩܘ ܚܶܢܩܶܐ ܕܕܶܚܠܬ݂ܳܐ they cut the bands of fear.

ܚܳܣ particle of deprecation, let it not be, God forbid! see ܚܘܣ.

ܚܰܣܝܳܐ, ܚܰܣܝܳܐ, ܚܰܣܝܬܳܐ pl. m. ܚܰܣܝܶܐ f. ܚܰܣܝܳܬ݂ܳܐ adj. a) holy, just, pure, ܡܰܬ݂ܩܳܠܶܐ ܚܰܣܝܶܐ just weights; ܚܰܣܝܳܐ ܕܡܶܢ ܥܳܠܰܡ the Holy One who is from everlasting; ܦܰܓ݂ܪܶܐ ܚܰܣܝܶܐ the holy bodies of the saints; ܒܢܳܬ݂ ܩܝܳܡܳܐ ܚܰܣܝܳܬ݂ܳܐ pious nuns; ܓܘܳܕ݂ܶܐ ܚܰܣܝܶܐ ܕܡܰܠܰܐܟ݂ܶܐ ܩܰܕܺܝܫܶܐ the pure choirs of holy angels. b) venerable, reverend, right or most reverend, frequently of monks, priests, bishops, &c. c) subst. a bishop, ܚܰܣܝܳܐ ܕܗܳܝ ܡܕܺܝܢܬܳܐ the bishop of that city; ܣܘܢܗܘܕܘܣ ܕܚܰܣܝܶܐ an episcopal synod. Derivatives, ܚܣܝܘܬܐ, verb ܚܰܣܶܝ, ܚܣܝܐܝܬ, ܚܘܣܝܐ, ܡܚܣܝܢܐ, ܡܚܣܝܢܘܬܐ, ܡܚܣܝܢܘܬܐ.

ܚܰܣܳܐ, ܚܰܣܬܳܐ pl. ܚܰܣܶܐ f. a lettuce; ܛܰܪܦܶܐ ܕܚܰܣܶܐ lettuce leaves.

ܚܣܰܕ fut. ܢܶܚܣܽܘܕ, act. part. ܚܳܣܶܕ, ܚܳܣܕܳܐ. to revile, scorn with ܠ; ܠܳܐ ܢܶܚܣܽܘܕ ܐ̱ܢܳܫ ܡܶܢ ܡܓܰܕܦܳܢܶܐ let not one of the blasphemers revile. Pa. ܚܰܣܶܕ to scorn, revile, insult, taunt, reproach, defy; ܥܰܡܳܐ ܕܚܰܣܶܕ ܢܰܦܫܶܗ a people that jeoparded their lives; ܠܡܚܰܣܳܕܽܘܬ݂ܶܗ ܕܐܺܝܣܪܳܝܶܠ ܣܠܶܩ Goliath has come up to defy Israel; ܛܽܘܒܰܝܟܽܘܢ ܐܶܡܰܬ݂ ܕܢܚܰܣܕܽܘܢܳܟ݂ܽܘܢ ܒܢܰܝ ܐ̱ܢܳܫܳܐ blessed are ye when men shall revile you; pass. part. ܕܦܳܣܶܩ ܕܺܝܢܳܐ ܥܰܕ ܠܳܐ ܢܶܫܡܰܥ. ܣܰܟ݂ܠܳܐ ܗܽܘ ܘܰܡܚܰܣܕܳܐ he who pronounces judgment before he heareth is a fool and put to shame. Ethpa. ܐܶܬ݂ܚܰܣܰܕ to be mocked, reviled; to suffer blame or reproach; ܐܶܢ ܡܶܬ݂ܚܰܣܕܺܝܢ ܐܢ̱ܬܽܘܢ ܥܰܠ ܐܰܦܰܝ ܫܡܶܗ ܕܡܫܺܝܚܳܐ if ye be reproached for the name of Christ. Derivatives, ܚܶܣܕܳܐ, ܚܣܘܕܐ, ܡܚܣܕܢܐ, ܡܚܣܕܢܘܬܐ, ܡܬܚܣܕܢܐ.

ܚܶܣܕܳܐ (with hard d) rt. ܚܣܕ. a shameful thing, shame, reproach, ignominy.

ܚܶܣܕܳܐ (with aspirated dh) Heb. cf. ܚܣܝܕܐ. mercy, kindness, favour; ܒܶܝܬ݂ ܚܶܣܕܳܐ Bethesda = place of mercy.

ܚܰܣܺܝܟ݂ܳܐ pl. ܚܰܣܺܝܟ݂ܶܐ rt. ܚܣܟ. parsimonious; abstinent, frugal; ܚܰܣܺܝܟ݂ܳܐ ܕܝܰܬ݁ܺܝܪ ܠܳܐ ܡܦܰܪܢܣܳܐ ܗܽܘ the over-frugal man is not liberal.

ܚܰܣܺܝܟ݂ܽܘܬ݂ܳܐ rt. ܚܣܟ. f. parsimony, avarice; refraining, restraint; ܚܰܣܺܝܟ݂ܽܘܬ݂ܳܐ ܕܠܶܫܳܢܳܐ ܡܶܢ ܕܰܓ݁ܳܠܽܘܬ݂ܳܐ the refraining of the tongue from falsehood.

ܚܰܣܺܝܟ݂ܳܢܳܐ, ܚܰܣܺܝܟ݂ܳܢܺܝܬ݂ܳܐ rt. ܚܣܟ. parsimonious.

ܚܰܣܳܡܳܐ, ܚܰܣܳܡܬܳܐ rt. ܚܣܡ. an envious person.

ܚܰܣܚܽܘܣܳܐ m. cartilage, a tendon; ܓܰܓܰܪܬܳܐ ܡܶܢ ܬܠܳܬ݂ܳܐ ܚܰܣܚܽܘܣܶܐ ܡܬ݂ܰܩܢܳܐ the throat is formed of three tendons.

ܚܰܣܚܽܘܣܳܢܳܐ, ܚܰܣܚܽܘܣܳܢܺܝܬ݂ܳܐ gristly, cartilaginous; ܚܰܣܚܽܘܣܳܢܶܐ ܚܰܝ̈ܘܳܬ݂ܳܐ crustaceans opp. ܚܰܝ̈ܘܳܬ݂ܳܐ ܓܰܪܡܳܢܝܳܬ݂ܳܐ vertebrate animals.

ܚܰܣܺܝ denom. verb Pael conj. from ܚܰܣܝܳܐ. to make atonement or propitiation with ܥܰܠ; to absolve, give absolution, purge, pardon, condone, spare, be gracious; ܩܰܕܫܶܗ ܘܰܚܰܣܝܶܗ ܠܡܰܕܒܚܳܐ he sanctified and made atonement for the altar; ܚܰܣܺܝܘ ܥܰܠ ܚܛܳܗܶܐ ܕܒܢܰܝ ܥܰܡܗܽܘܢ they made atonement for the sins of their nation; ܕܡܳܐ ܗܽܘ ܡܚܰܣܶܐ ܥܰܠ ܢܰܦܫܳܐ it is the blood that maketh atonement for the soul; ܚܰܣܳܐ ܚܰܘܒܰܝ purge my guilt; ܚܽܘܢ ܘܰܚܰܣܳܐ pity and pardon; ܟܽܠ ܡܰܢ ܕܰܡܚܰܣܶܐ ܗܽܘ ܢܶܬ݂ܚܰܣܶܐ whosoever pardons shall himself be pardoned; ܬܶܗܘܶܐ ܡܚܰܣܰܝ ܡܶܢ ܡܰܘܡܳܬ݂ܳܐ thou shalt be free of any oath, absolved from it; ܡܚܰܣܰܝܢ ܡܶܢ ܕܡܳܐ ܕܰܒܢܰܝ̈ܢܳܫܳܐ we are innocent of human blood. Ethpa. ܐܶܬ݂ܚܰܣܺܝ to be made or declared free from guilt, pure, clear or righteous; to be loosed or set free, to go free or unpunished; to have atonement made; to be absolved, receive absolution, pardon, mercy, to seek absolution or pardon; ܗܰܘ ܕܰܡܨܰܠܶܐ ܢܶܬ݂ܚܰܣܶܐ ܡܶܢ ܡܳܪܝܳܐ whoso prays may he receive mercy from the Lord; ܬܶܬ݂ܚܰܣܶܐ ܡܶܢ ܡܰܘܡܳܬ݂ܝ thou shalt be clear from my oath; ܐܰܝܠܶܝܢ ܕܪܳܚܡܺܝܢ ܚܰܣܝܽܘܬ݂ܳܐ ܚܰܣܝܳܐܝܬ݂ ܢܶܬ݂ܚܰܣܽܘܢ they that love holiness holily shall be judged holy; ܡܶܬ݂ܚܰܣܝܳܢ ܠܳܟ݂ ܚܛܳܗܰܝܟ thy sins are absolved.

ܚܰܣܝܳܐܺܝܬ݂ from ܚܰܣܝܳܐ. adv. piously, rightly.

ܚܰܣܺܝܕܳܐ, ܚܰܣܺܝܕܬܳܐ Heb. cf. ܚܶܣܕܳܐ. gracious, winning,

full of grace; ܥܰܡܳܐ ܚܰܣܝܳܐ *the holy nation* i. e. the Hebrews.

ܚܰܣܝܽܘܬܳܐ from ܚܰܣܝܳܐ. f. *righteousness, holiness, venerableness;* ܕܽܘܒܳܪܳܐ ܕܚܰܣܝܽܘܬܳܐ *holy living;* a title of honour esp. applied to bishops, ܚܰܣܝܽܘܬܳܟ݂ *your Holiness, your Reverence,* hence *the episcopate,* ܪܺܫ ܚܰܣܝܽܘܬܳܐ *a hierarch, a prelate.*

ܚܣܺܝܟ݂, ܚܣܺܝܟ݂ܳܐ *exempt; abstinent; a glade;* see ܚܣܟ.

ܚܣܺܝܟ݂ܽܘܬܳܐ rt. ܚܣܟ. f. *abstinence, immunity;* ܚܣܺܝܟ݂ܽܘܬܳܐ ܕܡܶܢ ܟܽܠ ܡܶܢܳܝܳܢ *refraining from all intercourse;* ܚܣܺܝܟ݂ܽܘܬܳܐ ܡܶܢ ܟܽܠ ܩܳܠܶܐ ܘܫܽܘܥܝܳܐ ܘܫܽܘܓ݂ܳܫܳܐ *freedom from all rumours, noises* or *disturbances.*

ܚܣܺܝܠܽܘܬܳܐ rt. ܚܣܠ. f. *weaning, abstinence;* ܚܣܺܝܠܽܘܬܳܐ ܕܡܶܢ ܐܽܘܟ݂ܠܳܐ *abstinence from food.*

ܚܰܣܺܝܢ, ܢܳܐ, ܢܬܳܐ *mighty, serious,* in many senses; see under ܚܣܢ.

ܚܰܣܺܝܢܳܐܺܝܬ rt. ܚܣܢ. adv. *very much, violently, seriously, courageously;* ܐܶܬܒܟܺܝ ܚܰܣܺܝܢܳܐܺܝܬ *he wept violently.*

ܚܰܣܺܝܢܽܘܬܳܐ rt. ܚܣܢ. f. *fortifying; ramparts, fortifications;* ܚܰܣܺܝܢܽܘܬܳܗ ܕܡܕܺܝܢܬܳܐ *the fortifying* or *the fortifications of the city.*

ܚܰܣܺܝܪ *lacking, less, without;* see ܚܣܪ.

ܚܰܣܺܝܪܽܘ, ܚܰܣܺܝܪܽܘܬܳܐ pl. ܘܳܬܳܐ rt. ܚܣܪ. f. *want, need, necessity, deficiency, waning* of the moon; *poverty, scantiness, scarcity,* ܚܰܣܺܝܪܽܘܬ ܥܰܠܠܳܬܳܐ *failure of the crops, a bad harvest;* ܚܰܣܺܝܪܽܘܬ ܗܰܘܢܳܐ *stupidity;* ܚܰܣܺܝܪܽܘܬ ܗܰܝܡܳܢܽܘܬܳܐ *scant faith;* ܚܰܣܺܝܪܽܘܬ ܪܶܥܝܳܢܳܐ *folly, madness.*

ܚܰܣܺܝܬܳܐ emph. fem. of ܚܣܳܐ, ܚܰܣܝܳܐ *holy, a holy person.*

ܚܣܰܟ݂ fut. ܢܶܚܣܽܘܟ݂, inf. ܡܶܚܣܰܟ݂, imper. ܚܣܽܘܟ݂, act. part. ܚܳܣܶܟ݂, ܚܳܣܟ݂ܳܐ, pass. part. ܚܣܺܝܟ݂, ܟ݂ܳܐ, ܟ݂ܬܳܐ. *to keep back* or *from, to withhold, restrain, refuse; to save up;* with ܡܶܢ *to spare, preserve, set free;* ܒܰܪ ܚܳܣܶܟ݂ ܘܠܳܐ ܝܳܗܶܒ *he withheld* corn *and would not give it out;* ܐܶܚܣܽܘܟ݂ ܢܰܦ̮ܫܝ *I will preserve my life;* ܚܣܰܟ݂ ܡܶܢ ܩܶܛܠܳܐ *he spared him from slaughter;* ܚܰܣܟܶܢܝ ܡܶܢ ܨܰܥܪܳܐ *save me from dishonour;* ܡܰܘܬܳܐ ܚܳܣܶܟ݂ ܠܚܰܝܳܒܳܐ ܡܶܢ ܡܳܪܳܐ ܡܰܘܬܳܐ *death sets free the debtor from his creditor.* Part. adj. *free from, void of, apart, exempted; abstaining, abstinent;* ܚܣܺܝܟ݂ ܡܶܢ ܚܛܺܝܬܳܐ *free from sin;* ܚܣܺܝܟ݂ ܡܶܢ ܕܺܝܫܳܐ *untrodden;* ܚܣܺܝܟ݂ܳܬܳܐ ܕܐܺܝܠܳܢܶܐ *glades, coverts of trees.* Ethpe. ܐܶܬ݂ܚܣܶܟ݂ *to be withheld, preserved, free from;* ܐܶܬ݂ܚܣܶܟ݂ ܡܶܢ ܢܽܘܪܳܐ ܗܘܳܐ *it was fireproof;* ܙܰܪܥܶܐ ܡܶܬ݂ܚܰܣܟ݂ܺܝܢ ܡܶܢ ܪ̈ܰܚܫܶܐ seeds *made proof against vermin.* Pa. ܚܰܣܶܟ݂ *to reserve, store up, keep in reserve.* Ethpa. ܐܶܬ݂ܚܰܣܰܟ݂ *to be exempted, free* from obligation, from guilt; ܡܶܬ݂ܚܰܣܟ݂ܺܝܢܰܢ ܡܶܢ ܕܡܳܐ *we shall be acquitted, unstained by murder.* Derivatives, ܚܣܳܟ݂ܳܐ, ܚܣܺܝܟ݂ܽܘܬܳܐ, ܚܣܺܝܟ݂ܳܐܺܝܬ, ܡܚܰܣܟ݂ܳܢܽܘܬܳܐ, ܡܚܰܣܟ݂ܳܢܳܐܺܝܬ, ܚܰܣܟ݂ܽܘܬܳܐ, ܡܰܚܣܟ݂ܳܢܳܐ.

ܚܣܳܟ݂, ܚܣܳܟ݂ܳܐ rt. ܚܣܟ. m. *restraint;* ܚܣܳܟ݂ ܢܰܦ̮ܫܳܐ *self-restraint.*

ܚܣܰܠ fut. ܢܶܚܣܽܘܠ, imper. ܚܣܽܘܠ, act. part. ܚܳܣܶܠ, pass. part. ܚܣܺܝܠ, ܠܳܐ, ܠܬܳܐ. *to wean;* metaph. *to refrain, restrain, to teach self-control, accustom to abstinence;* ܥܽܘܠܶܠܳܐ ܚܣܺܝܠܳܐ ܡܶܢ ܚܰܠܒܳܐ *a weaned infant;* ܚܣܰܠܘ ܠܒܰܥܺܝܪܳܐ ܡܶܢ ܡܰܝܳܐ *they accustomed the beast to do without water;* ܚܣܰܠ ܦܽܘܡܶܗ ܡܶܢ ܟܽܠ ܫܽܘܐܳܠܺܝܢ *he refrained his mouth from all questions;* ܚܳܣܠܺܝܢ ܢܰܦ̮ܫܗܽܘܢ ܡܶܢ ܚܣܳܡܳܐ *they restrain themselves from envy;* ܚܣܺܝܠܺܝܢ ܡܶܢ ܪ̈ܶܓ݂ܝܳܬ݂ܳܐ *weaned from lust;* ܚܽܘܒܳܐ ܚܣܺܝܠ ܡܶܢ ܫܽܘܒܗܳܪܳܐ *love is separated from arrogance.* Ethpe. ܐܶܬ݂ܚܣܶܠ *to be weaned, trained to abstinence;* ܡܶܬ݂ܚܣܠܺܝܢ ܡܶܢ ܒ̈ܺܝܫܳܬ݂ܳܐ *weaned from evil things.* Derivatives, ܚܣܳܠܳܐ, ܚܣܺܝܠܽܘܬܳܐ.

ܚܣܳܠܳܐ rt. ܚܣܠ. m. *being weaned.*

ܚܣܰܡ fut. ܢܶܚܣܽܘܡ, act. part. ܚܳܣܶܡ, ܚܳܣܡܳܐ, pass. part. ܚܣܺܝܡ, ܡܳܐ, ܡܬܳܐ with ܒ a) in a good sense, *to emulate, rival, contend jealously* or *zealously;* ܕܚܳܣܡܺܝܢ ܥܒ̈ܳܕܶܐ ܛܳܒܶܐ *emulous of good works;* ܚܣܰܡ ܗܘܳܐ ܒܕܽܘܒܳܪܰܝܗܽܘܢ *he emulated their manner of life;* part. adj. *enviable, desirable, happy;* ܥܰܡܳܐ ܚܣܺܝܡܳܐ ܕܟ݂ܪ̈ܺܝܣܛܝܳܢܶܐ *the happy race of Christians;* ܐܽܘܪܗܳܝܶܐ ܒ̈ܢܰܝ ܡܕܺܝܢܬܳܐ ܚܣܺܝܡܬܳܐ *Edessenes, sons of the desirable city.* b) *to envy, be envious, jealous;* ܠܳܐ ܬܶܚܣܽܘܡ ܠܡܰܘܬܳܐ *be not anxious for death;* ܝܽܗܽܘܕܳܝܶܐ ܚܳܣܡܺܝܢ ܒܳܟ݂ *the Jews are envious of thee.* Ethpe. ܐܶܬ݂ܚܣܶܡ *to be envied, to incur the jealousy* or *spite of rivals;* ܐܶܬ݂ܚܣܶܡ ܕܳܢܺܝܐܝܶܠ *Daniel was envied.* Ethpa. ܐܶܬ݂ܚܰܣܰܡ *to be emulous, compete zealously.* Derivatives, ܚܣܳܡܳܐ, ܚܳܣܡܳܐ, ܚܰܣܡܳܐ, ܚܰܣܡܳܢܳܐܺܝܬ, ܚܰܣܡܳܢܽܘܬܳܐ.

ܚܳܣܽܘܡܳܐ, ܬܳܐ pl. m. ܶܐ f. ܳܬܳܐ rt. ܚܣܡ. *envious, grudging, spiteful;* ܗܰܘܢܳܐ ܚܳܣܽܘܡܳܐ *an envious mind;* ܐܺܝܕܳܐ ܚܳܣܽܘܡܬܳܐ *a grudging hand;* ܗܰܘ ܚܳܣܽܘܡܳܐ ܣܳܢܶܐ ܛܳܒ̈ܳܬܳܐ *that envious one* i. e. *hater of all good, the devil.*

ܚܶܣܡܳܐ pl. ܶܐ rt. ܚܣܡ. *emulation, zeal, competition, envy, jealousy; a grudge;* with ܕܠܳܐ *ungrudging, generous;* ܚܶܣܡܳܐ ܘܐܳܟܶܠܩܰܪܨܳܐ *envy and backbiting;* ܡܶܢ ܚܶܣܡܳܐ ܐܰܫܠܡܽܘܗܝ *out of envy* the chief priests *had delivered him up.*

ܚܳܣܽܘܡܳܐܺܝܬ rt. ܚܣܡ. adv. *enviously.*

ܚܳܣܽܘܡܽܘܬܳܐ rt. ܚܣܡ. *envy, rivalry;* with ܠܳܐ *frankness, generosity.*

ܚܶܣܰܢ and ܚܣܶܢ fut. ܢܶܚܣܰܢ, inf. ܡܶܚܣܰܢ, act. part. ܚܳܣܶܢ, ܚܳܣܢܳܐ, pass. part. ܚܣܺܝܢ and ܚܰܣܺܝܢ, ܳܐ, ܳܬܳܐ. *a)* ܚܣܶܢ intrans. *to wax strong, increase* of illness, *to be extremely ill; to have hard labour* in childbirth; *to be very difficult, be in difficulties;* ܚܣܶܢ ܟܽܘܪܗܳܢܗܽܘܢ *their sickness was very sore;* ܚܣܶܢܰܬ ܟܰܕ ܝܳܠܕܳܐ *she laboured hard to bring forth;* ܡܶܕܶܡ ܠܳܐ ܚܳܣܶܢ ܡܶܢ *nothing is more difficult than. b)* ܚܣܶܢ trans. *to be stronger than, prevail over, subdue; to force* a woman; ܚܣܶܢܬܳܢܝ ܘܶܐܬܟܰܫܰܪܬ *thou art stronger than I and hast prevailed;* ܠܡܶܚܣܰܢ ܠܚܶܡܬܳܐ *to subdue anger;* ܐܺܝܬ ܕܚܳܣܢܺܝܢ ܠܟܰܦܢܳܐ *some are stronger than hunger* i. e. when they fast. Part. adj. *a) strong, powerful, mighty* = Heb. El Shaddai, *the Almighty;* ܐܰܠܳܗܳܐ ܚܰܣܺܝܢܳܐ ܡܶܢܶܗ *are we stronger than he?* ܐܳܘ ܚܰܣܺܝܢ ܡܶܢܶܗ ܠܳܐ ܡܥܰܘܶܠ ܕܺܝܢܳܐ *doth the Almighty pervert justice?* ܐܰܡܪܰܕ ܒܚܰܣܺܝܢܳܐ *he defied the Almighty;* ܝܶܫܽܘܥ ܒܡܰܘܬܶܗ ܐܶܣܰܪ ܠܚܰܣܺܝܢܳܐ ܗܰܘ *Jesus by His death bound the strong man* i.e. Satan, referring to Luke xi. 21, 22. *b) violent, hard, difficult, severe, serious, solemn, weighty;* ܡܕܺܝܢܬܳܐ ܚܰܣܺܝܢܬܳܐ *a strong city;* ܩܳܠܳܐ ܚܰܣܺܝܢܳܐ *a violent noise;* ܓܰܪܒܝܳܐ ܚܰܣܺܝܢܬܳܐ *a violent north wind;* ܩܪܳܒܳܐ ܚܰܣܺܝܢܳܐ *a great war;* ܡܰܘܡܳܬܳܐ ܚܰܣܺܝܢܬܳܐ *a solemn oath;* ܚܰܣܺܝܢܺܝܢ ܦܽܘܩܕܳܢܶܐ *the commands are difficult;* ܚܰܣܺܝܢ ܡܶܢ ܚܒܳܠܳܐ *not subject to corruption.* Ethpe. ܐܶܬܚܣܶܢ imper. ܐܶܬܚܰܣܰܢ *to be subdued, overpowered, tyrannized over;* ܠܳܐ ܐܶܬܚܣܶܢ ܡܶܢ ܪܶܓܬܳܐ *he was not overcome by lust;* ܘܟܽܠܗܽܘܢ ܐܰܝܠܶܝܢ ܕܶܐܬܚܰܣܰܢܘ ܡܶܢ ܐܳܟܶܠܩܰܪܨܳܐ *all those who suffered the tyranny of the devil.* Pa. ܚܰܣܶܢ *to strengthen, fortify, secure, guard, to take refuge;* ܚܰܣܶܢ ܡܽܘܟܠܶܐ ܕܥܺܕܬܳܐ *he strengthened the bolts* of the church; ܠܡܚܰܣܳܢܽܘ ܟܽܠܶܗ ܩܶܢܝܳܢܶܗ *to guard all his wealth;* ܚܰܣܶܢ ܢܰܦܫܳܟ ܒܚܰܕ ܡܶܢ ܚܶܣܢܶܐ *fortify thyself in one of the fortresses.* Pass. part. ܡܚܰܣܢܳܬܳܐ ܡܕܺܝܢܳܬܳܐ *fortified cities;* metaph. ܢܰܦܫܳܐ ܠܳܐ ܡܚܰܣܢܬܳܐ *an unguarded soul* i. e. lying open to temptation. Ethpa. ܐܶܬܚܰܣܰܢ *a) to show oneself strong, to be strengthened, confirmed;* ܡܶܬܚܰܣܢܳܢ ܡܰܘܡܳܬܳܐ *oaths are confirmed. b) to fortify oneself, seek refuge;* ܐܶܬܚܰܣܰܢܘ ܒܚܽܘܪ̈ܶܐ ܘܡܥܰܪ̈ܳܬܳܐ *they sought refuge in holes and caves. c) to take by storm, to tyrannize over* with ܥܰܠ. For Pamel conj. see ܚܰܣܡܶܢ. Derivatives, ܚܶܣܢܳܐ, ܚܰܣܺܝܢܳܐ, ܚܰܣܺܝܢܳܐܺܝܬ, ܚܰܣܺܝܢܽܘܬܳܐ, ܚܣܳܢܳܐ, ܡܚܰܣܢܳܐ, ܡܚܰܣܢܳܢܽܘܬܳܐ, ܚܰܣܡܶܢ, ܚܶܣܢܳܐ, ܡܚܰܣܢܳܐ, ܡܚܰܣܢܳܐ, ܡܶܬܚܰܣܢܳܐ, ܡܶܬܚܰܣܢܳܢܽܘܬܳܐ.

ܚܶܣܢܳܐ pl. ܶܐ rt. ܚܣܢ. m. *a fortress, citadel, fortification, rampart, outwork;* ܒܶܝܬ ܚܶܣܢܳܐ *a fortified place, stronghold;* ܦܰܣܶܩܘ ܚܶܣܢܰܝ̈ܗܽܘܢ ܕܫܽܘܪܳܐ *they broke down the ramparts.*

ܚܶܣܢܳܝܳܐ pl. ܳܝܶܐ rt. ܚܣܢ. m. *the governor* of a fortress.

ܚܣܰܪ fut. ܢܶܚܣܰܪ, act. part. ܚܳܣܰܪ, ܚܳܣܪܳܐ, pass. part. ܚܰܣܺܝܪ, ܳܐ, ܳܬܳܐ. *a) to be wanting, to decrease, fail, be insufficient; to be in want, to want, lack;* ܙܰܘܕܳܐ ܠܳܐ ܚܣܰܪ ܡܶܕܶܡ *their provisions did not fail, diminish;* ܚܣܰܪ ܠܗܽܘܢ ܚܰܡܪܳܐ *the wine failed, came to an end;* ܐܶܢ ܚܳܣܰܪ ܟܳܣܳܐ *if the cup be not sufficient* i.e. if the wine fail; ܚܣܰܪܘ ܠܶܗ ܥܰܒ̈ܕܶܐ ܐ̱ܚܪ̈ܳܢܶܐ *he had no other servants;* ܚܣܰܪܘ ܗܘܰܘ ܒܡܰܬܩܳܠܳܐ *they were wanting in the balance, were less than the right weight;* ܫܰܪܺܝ ܚܣܰܪ ܠܶܗ *he began to be in want. b) to lose, suffer loss, be fined; to lay out, expend;* ܢܶܚܣܰܪ ܡܳܐܐ ܕܟܶܣܦܳܐ *he shall lose* 100 *pieces of silver;* ܚܣܰܪ ܐܰܓܪܳܐ ܕܰܛܥܽܘܢܳܐ *he had less by the hire of the porters.* Pass. part. *a)* verbal use with ܠ and pers. pron. suff. *to lack, want,* ܚܕܳܐ ܚܰܣܺܝܪܳܐ ܠܳܟ *one thing thou lackest;* ܡܶܕܶܡ ܠܳܐ ܚܰܣܺܝܪ ܠܝ *I am in want of nothing. b) in want of, lacking; incomplete,* ܚܰܣܺܝܪ ܠܰܚܡܳܐ *in want of bread;* ܫܰܢ̱ܬܳܐ ܚܰܣܺܝܪܬܳܐ *an incomplete year;* ܣܗܪܳܐ ܟܰܕ ܚܰܣܺܝܪ *the waning moon;* with a subst. it is frequently privative; ܚܰܣܺܝܪ ܗܰܘܢܳܐ *stupid;*

ܒܪܢܫܐ or ܠܡܕܥܐ ܚܣܝܪ lacking understanding, senseless, mad; ܗܝܡܢܘܬܐ ܚܣܝܪ unbelieving; ܡܪܒܝܬܐ ܚܣܝܪ low bred. c) less opp. ܝܬܝܪ more; ܚܣܝܪ ܝܬܝܪ more or less; ܟܡܐ ܚܣܝܪ how much less; ܚܕ ܚܣܝܪ ܐܪܒܥܝܢ forty less one. d) pl. f. emph. ܚܣܝܪ̈ܬܐ wants, necessaries; ܟܬܒܐ ܕܚܣܝܪ̈ܬܐ the Book of Chronicles. Pa. ܚܣܪ to suffer any one to be in want, to inflict loss, fine, damage; ܡܕܡ ܠܐ ܚܣܪܬ ܠܗܘܢ thou didst not let them lack anything; metaph. ܚܘܒܠܐ ܢܚܣܪ ܒܣܪܗ the sore will waste his flesh. Ethpa. ܐܬܚܣܪ to be fined, amerced; to be damaged. Aph. ܐܚܣܪ a) to allow to be in want; to fine, confiscate, deprive; ܡܚܣܪ ܠܗ ܠܚܐܪܘܬܗ he deprives him of his freedom. b) to do harm, to injure; ܡܕܡ ܠܐ ܡܚܣܪ ܐܢܐ ܠܟܘܢ I will do you no harm; ܡܚܣܪܐ ܠܐܕܢܐ it is hurtful to the ears; ܡܚܫܒܬܗ ܕܒܝܫܐ ܡܚܣܪܢ the thoughts of the bad man do harm. Ettaph. ܐܬܬܚܣܪ to be fined, to forfeit; to be exacted as a fine, penalty, &c., ܐܬܬܚܣܪ ܟܠ ܡܐ ܕܩܢܐ ܗܘܐ he forfeited all that he possessed; ܐܬܬܚܣܪ ܛܝܡܐ ܗܘ ܕ that price was exacted. Derivatives, ܡܚܣܪܢܐ, ܚܘܣܪܢܐ, ܚܣܝܪܘܬܐ.

ܚܦܐ and ܚܦܝ fut. ܢܚܦܐ, act. part. ܚܦܐ ܚܦܝܐ, pass. part. ܚܦܐ, ܚܦܝܬܐ to cover, hide; ܐܘܪܚܐ ܚܦܝܬܐ a secret path. Pa. ܚܦܝ to cover, veil, obscure, hide from view, bury out of sight; ܚܦܝ ܐܐܪ a swarm of locusts obscured the air; ܚܦܬ ܠܥܡܘܪ̈ܝܗ a city fell and buried its inhabitants; ܪܫܗ ܡܚܦܝ with covered head; metaph. to cover i.e. expiate a sin, to give pardon; to pass over, omit; to surpass; ܚܦܝ ܫܡܗ he concealed his name; ܒܫܬܩܐ ܚܦܐ to pass over in silence; ܚܦܝ ܒܟܠ ܝܕ̈ܥܬܐ ܠܟܠܕܝ̈ܐ Daniel reduced the Chaldaeans to silence in all the sciences. Ethpa. ܐܬܚܦܝ a) refl. to veil oneself; metaph. to be shy. b) pass. to be covered, concealed, obscured, eclipsed, ruined; ܒܫܬܩܐ ܢܬܚܦܘܢ let them be hidden in silence; ܠܡܐܢ̈ܐ ܕܐܬܚܦܝ ruined ports. c) gram. to be passed over in pronunciation, as a letter with linea occultans. Derivatives, ܚܦܝܬܐܝܬ, ܚܦܝܐ, ܚܦܝܘܬܐ, ܡܚܦܝܢܐ, ܡܚܦܝܢܘܬܐ, ܡܬܚܦܝܢܘܬܐ, ܬܚܦܝܬܐ.

ܚܦܘܦܐ m. a bitter herb; the mallow, rumex, althaea, anchusa, malva.

ܚܦܘܪܐ rt. ܚܦܪ. m. a ditcher, a labourer.

ܚܦܘܪܬܐ rt. ܚܦܪ. m. digging, excavation.

ܚܦܝܬܐܝܬ rt. ܚܦܐ. adv. secretly.

ܚܦܝܬܐܝܬ adv. barefoot.

ܚܦܛ Pe. only part. adj. ܚܦܝܛ, ܚܦܝܛܐ, ܚܦܝܛܬܐ assiduous, painstaking, diligent, worthy with ܒ or ܥܠ of the object; ܗܘܐ ܚܦܝܛܐ ܒ take pains to . . ., be diligent about . . .; ܚܦܝܛ ܠܡܠܦܢܘܬܐ ܘܠܬܠܡܝܕܘܬܐ careful in teaching; ܚܦܝܛ ܠܡܕܡ ܕܡܬܚܙܝܢ diligent about visible things, ܚܦܝܛ ܠܡܬܝܕ̈ܥܢܝܬܐ negligent of those to come; ܚܦܝܛ ܗܘܐ ܠܬܕܡܘܪܬܐ ܘܡܬܕܡܪ worthy and virtuous; ܚܦܝܛ ܗܘܐ he was worthy of admiration, admirable. Pa. ܚܦܛ to urge, exhort, incite, encourage with ܠ of the pers. and with ܥܠ or ܠܘܬ of the object; ܚܦܛܗ ܒܪܥܝܢܗ he put it into his mind; ܚܦܛܗ ܠܡܐܬܐ ܒܥܓܠ he urged him to come quickly; ܥܠ ܢܟܦܘܬܐ ܘܡܣܟܢܘܬܐ ܚܝܠܬܢܐܝܬ ܡܚܦܛ he exhorts vigorously to abstinence and poverty; ܒܥܘܬܗ ܚܦܝܛܐ ܗܘܬ his entreaty was urgent. Ethpa. ܐܬܚܦܛ imper. West-Syr. ܐܬܚܦܛ a) to take pains, to endeavour, be diligent; with another verb, to do anything with labour or great care, diligently; ܐܬܚܦܛ ܒܩܪܝܢܐ be diligent in reading; ܐܬܚܦܛ ܠܡܥܒܕ—ܠܡܣܡ—ܠܡܩܢܐ he took pains to do, in composing, to acquire. b) to work in, ܡܘܬܐ ܒܢ ܡܬܚܦܛ death worketh in us; ܨܒܝܢܗ ܕܐܠܗܐ ܕܡܬܚܦܛ ܗܘܐ ܒܗܘܢ the will of God which worked in them. Aph. ܐܚܦܛ same as Pa. Derivatives, ܚܦܝܛܐ, ܚܦܝܛܐܝܬ, ܚܦܝܛܘܬܐ, ܡܚܦܛܢܐ, ܡܚܦܛܢܐܝܬ, ܡܚܦܛܢܘܬܐ, ܡܬܚܦܛܢܐ.

ܚܦܝ verb; see ܚܦܐ.

ܚܦܝܛܐܝܬ rt. ܚܦܛ. adv. earnestly, carefully.

ܚܦܝܛܘܬܐ, ܚܦܝܛܘܬ pl. ܬ̈ܐ rt. ܚܦܛ. f. exhortation, diligence, earnest care; ܚܦܝܛܘܬܐ ܕܕܘܒܪ̈ܐ exhortation to virtuous living; ܚܦܝܛܘܬܐ ܕܒܛܠܐ ܠܡܬܕܒܪܢܘܬܐ diligence in pursuing virtue; ܒܚܦܝܛܘܬܐ with pains, diligently; ܚܦܝܛܘܬܐ ܕܥܐܕܐ preparation for or celebration of a festival.

ܚܦܝܬ ܚܦܝܬ adverbial form of the following; ܚܦܝܬ ܡܗܠܟܐ ܗܘܬ she was walking barefoot.

ܚܦܝܐ, ܚܦܝܬܐ ܚܦܝܬ barefoot, unshod; ܥܪܛܠܝ ܘܚܦܝܬ naked and barefoot.

ܚܦܝܦܘܬܐ f. *going barefoot;* ܒܚܦܝܦܘܬܐ *with bare feet.*

ܚܦܦܐ m. *soap, soaping; shampooing, rubbing* or *brushing* of the head or clothes.

ܚܦܪ I. fut. ܢܚܦܘܪ, imper. ܚܦܘܪ, act. part. ܚܳܦܰܪ, ܚܳܦܪܳܐ, pass. part. ܚܦܝܪ, ܐ, ܬܐ. *to dig, drive a mine, to burrow; to scratch* or *paw* the ground; ܚܳܦܰܪ ܒܥܝܢܐ ܒܐܪܥܐ ܨܗܝܐ *digging a fount in a thirsty land;* ܓܘܒܐ ܚܦܝܪܐ ܕܠܐ ܚܦܪܬ *wells digged which thou diggedst not.* II. fut. ܢܚܦܰܪ *to blush, be ashamed;* ܠܐ ܐܚܦܰܪ ܒܥܒܕܐ ܛܒܐ *I need not blush for good works.* Ethpe. ܐܬܚܦܰܪ *to be dug up* or *out;* ܡܶܕܶܡ ܕܡܶܬܚܦܰܪ *minerals.* Aph. ܐܚܦܰܪ I. *to dig* or *break through;* ܟܐܦܐ ܡܚܦܪܐ ܐܬܚܙܝܬ ܗܘܬ *an arch was broken through.* II. *to be put to the blush, put to shame;* ܡܚܦܪܬ ܐܢܬܝ *thou art put to shame;* ܦܪܨܘܦܝܟܘܢ ܠܐ ܢܚܦܪܘܢ *your faces shall not be ashamed;* ܐܦ ܐܝܕܝܐ ܒܪܒܪܝܬܐ ܡܚܦܪܢ *even barbarian hands are ashamed, restrained by shame.* Derivatives, ܚܦܘܪܐ, ܚܦܘܪܬܐ, ܚܦܝܪܐ, ܡܚܦܪܢܘܬܐ.

ܚܦܪ, ܚܦܪܐ rt. ܚܦܪ. m. *a ditch, trench, pit, pond, mine, grave;* ܚܦܪܐ ܒܐܪܥܐ ܕܡܝܐ *a pit* or *pond in watery land;* ܚܦܪܐ ܕܟܒܪܝܬܐ *a sulphur mine;* ܥܒܪ ܠܚܦܪܗ *he was buried.*

ܚܨܐ, ܚܨ pl. ܚܨܝܢ, ܚܨܐ m. *the loin, the back;* ܐܣܰܪ ܚܨܐ *to gird the loins;* with ܐܗܦܟ, ܝܗܒ, ܗܦܟ &c. *to turn tail, to flee;* ܢܗܦܟܘܢ ܚܨܐ ܠܘܬܗ ... ܥܠ ܚܨܐ ܕܥܝܠܐ ܥܘܬܪܗܘܢ *they shall load their riches on the backs of young asses;* ܠܐ ܝܗܒ ܚܨܐ ܠܡܘܬܐ *he did not flee death;* ܢܛܘܪܝ ܚܨܐ *the rear-guard.* Metaph. *the back, highest part, summit;* ܕܡܝܐ, ܕܝܡܐ— *the surface of the water, of the sea;* ܠܥܠ ܡܢ ܚܨܐ ܕܫܡܝܐ *above the highest ridge of heaven;* ܗܝܡܢܘܬܐ ܥܠ ܚܨ ܩܠܐ ܡܬܛܥܢܐ *faith shall be borne upon the voice,* i. e. *by the voice.*

ܚܨܐ fut. ܢܚܨܐ *to pluck out, tear out* the eyes; *to knock out* a tooth; ܐܢ ܥܝܢܝ ܚܨܝܬ *if thou pluck out mine eyes;* metaph. ܚܨܐ ܡܠܐܟܐ ܢܦܫܝ an angel *plucked out and bare my soul.* Ethpe. ܐܬܚܨܝ and Ethpa. ܐܬܚܨܝ *to be plucked* or *torn out,* said of the eyes. Pa. ܚܨܝ *to tear* or *root out* the eyes, the nails. Derivatives, ܚܨܝܐ, ܡܚܨܝܢܐ.

ܚܨܒܐ, ܚܨܒܐ pl. ܚܨܒܐ m. *an earthen vessel with two handles, a large wine-jar;* ܡܙܓܗ ܡܢ ܚܨܒܘܗܝ *he mingled it from his wine-jars.*

ܚܨܕ fut. ܢܚܨܘܕ, act. part. ܚܳܨܶܕ, ܚܳܨܕܳܐ. *to reap, cut* or *mow down;* ܥܕܡܐ ܕܚܨܕܘ ܚܨܕܐ *till they had reaped the crops.* Ethpe. ܐܬܚܨܕ *to be reaped, cut down;* ܗܘ ܕܟܒܪ ܗܘܘ ܐܬܚܨܕܘ ܚܩܠܬܗܘܢ *for already their fields had been reaped.* Derivatives, ܚܨܕܐ, ܚܨܘܕܐ.

ܚܨܕ, ܚܨܕܐ rt. ܚܨܕ. m. *reaping, the harvest, a ripe crop;* ܚܨܕܐ ܕܚܛܐ *wheat harvest;* ܚܨܕܐ ܕܣܥܪܐ *barley harvest;* ܥܐܕܐ ܕܚܨܕܐ *the feast of harvest.*

ܚܨܘܕܐ rt. ܚܨܕ. m. *a reaper; a sickle.*

ܚܨܘܨܐ rt. ܚܨ. m. *a toothpick.*

ܚܨܝܢܐ Ar. m. *a small axe.*

ܚܨܝܦܐܝܬ rt. ܚܨܦ. adv. *shamelessly, wilfully, frowardly.*

ܚܨܝܦܘܬܐ rt. ܚܨܦ. f. *being urgent* or *pressing, persistence, obstinacy, wilfulness;* ܚܨܝܦܘܬ ܐܦܐ *impudence.*

ܚܨܨܐ pl. ܐ m. *a pebble.*

ܚܨܦ fut. ܢܚܨܘܦ rare except in part. adj. ܚܨܝܦ, ܚܨܝܦܐ, ܬܐ *bold, impudent, shameless;* ܢܦܫܐ ܚܨܝܦܬܐ *a bold person;* ܐܢܬܬܐ ܚܨܝܦܬ ܥܝܢܐ *a woman with an impudent eye, shameless look.* Pa. ܚܨܶܦ *to act with impudence* or *insistency, to be impudent, persistent, to persist in, insist, be insistent* with ܥܠ *about* or *upon;* ܟܠܢܫ ܡܚܨܦ ܠܢܦܫܗ ܥܠܘܗܝ *every one urgently makes for himself;* ܐܢ ܐܢܫ ܡܚܨܦ ܠܩܘܫܬܐ *if any man impudently impugn the truth.* Ethpa. ܐܬܚܨܦ *to bear oneself impudently, behave shamelessly.* Aph. ܐܚܨܦ *to be bold, persistent, urgent* in action with ܠ of the action; often with ܐܡܰܪ *to speak boldly;* with ܐܦܐ *to set* or *harden the face;* ܡܚܨܦ ܥܠ ܥܘܕܪܢܐ one *who begs importunately for help;* ܦܘܩܕܢܐ ܡܚܨܦ *an urgent decree;* ܠܐ ܬܚܨܦ ܠܗܘܢ *do not molest them.* Derivatives, ܚܨܝܦܐ, ܚܨܝܦܐܝܬ, ܚܨܝܦܘܬܐ.

ܚܨܒܐ pl. ܐ m. *a) an earthen vessel;* ܚܨܒܐ

ܡܐܢܐ ܕܦܚܪܐ *a potter's vessel;* ܡܐܢܐ ܕܚܨܦܐ *an earthen vessel.* *b) a shell;* ܚܕ ܓܢܒܐ ܚܨܦܐ *univalves.*

ܚܨܦܢܝܐ, ܢܝܬܐ from ܚܨܦܐ *earthen; testaceous;* pl. *shell-fish.*

ܚܨܨܐ pl. ܐ̈ m. *pebble, shingle.*

ܚܨܪܐ f. *a) the little finger, the little toe;* ܥܙܩܬܐ ܕܚܨܪܐ *a ring on the little finger;* ܪܝܫ ܚܨܪܗ *the tip of his little finger;* ܡܝ̈ܐ ܡܠܐ ܚܨܪܐ *as much water as clings to the little finger* when dipped into water; ܚܨܪܐ ܕܡܝ̈ܐ *a little drop of water.* *b) a pen;* ܢܣܝܘܢܐ ܕܚܨܪܐ ܕܟܬܒܐ *trial of a quill pen.*

ܚܪܘ, ܚܪܘܐ with ܩܪܒܐ m. *the caul.*

ܚܩܐ; same as ܚܩܩ *to bound.*

ܚܩܩ fut. ܢܚܩܘܩ, act. part. ܚܩܩ. *to bound, gambol.*

ܚܩܠ, ܚܩܠܐ pl. ܚܩܠܬܐ f. *the field, the open country* opp. ܡܕܝܢܬܐ; *a field;* ܚܩܠ ܕܡܐ *Aceldama, the field of blood;* ܚܩܠܐ ܕܡܫܟܐ *parchment.*

ܚܩܪ fut. ܢܚܩܘܪ, act. part. ܚܩܪ. *to talk empty talk, boastfully, to vaunt.*

ܚܪ *to be dry* or *husky* of the throat; *to be dumb;* ܚܪܐ ܓܓܪܬܝ *my throat is rough.* Pa. ܚܪܪ *to manumit, set free* slaves or captives; *to exempt* from taxes, from episcopal jurisdiction; ܚܪܪ ܩܘܣܛܢܛܝܢܘܣ ܐܬܪ̈ܘܬܐ ܕܣܝܡܝܢ ܒܗܘܢ ܓܪ̈ܡܐ ܕܩܕܝ̈ܫܐ Constantine *exempted the places where bones of saints were laid* from taxation; ܛܝܒܘܬܐ ܕܡܚܪܪܐ ܠܢ ܡܢ ܟܠ ܚܘܒܬܐ ܘܕܝܢܐ *grace which sets us free from all guilt and judgement.* Pass. part. ܡܚܪܪ *freed, free, exempt* from tribute, jurisdiction, guilt, anxiety, &c.; ܬܪܥܝܬܐ ܡܚܪܪܐ ܡܢ ܪܚܡܬ ܫܘܒܚܐ *a mind free from love of praise;* ܢܡܘܣܐ ܕܡܚܪܪ ܡܢ ܫܘܚܠܦܐ *an invariable rule.* Ethpa. ܐܬܚܪܪ *to be freed, set free* from servitude, prison, &c., *to be relieved* from tribute; *to be disencumbered, cleared out* by the removal of rubbish or débris. Derivatives, ܚܐܪܐ (ܚܪ), ܚܐܪܐܝܬ, ܚܐܪܘܬܐ, ܚܐܪܘܬܐܝܬ, ܚܐܪܝܐ, ܚܐܪܘܬܐ, ܚܘܪܪܐ, ܚܪܘܪܐ, ܡܚܪܪܢܐ, ܡܚܪܪܐܝܬ, ܚܪܝܪܘܬܐ.

ܚܪܐ I. not used in Pe. Ethpe. ܐܬܚܪܝ *a) to gainsay, resist, contend, dispute, strive, quarrel* with ܥܡ or ܠܘܩܒܠ; ܠܐ ܢܬܚܪܐ ܘܠܐ ܢܩܥܐ *he shall not strive nor cry;* ܥܡܐ ܕܡܬܚܪܐ ܘܠܐ ܡܬܛܦܝܣ *a gainsaying and disobedient people.* *b) to contend, strive, attempt* in a good sense; ܚܠܦ ܢܡܘܣܐ ܡܬܚܪܝܢ ܗܘܘ ܝܗܘܕܝ̈ܐ *the Jews contended for the law;* ܙܒܢܐ ܡܬܚܪܐ ܠܡܚܒܠܘ ܠܥܬܝܩ̈ܬܐ *time strives to destroy ancient things.* *c) to stick against, obstruct,* ܐܬܚܪܝ ܒܓܓܪܬܗ ܓܪܡܐ ܕܢܘܢܐ *a fishbone stuck in his throat;* ܐܬܚܪܝܬ ܐܠܦܐ *the ship stuck fast, ran aground.* Aph. ܐܚܪܝ *to make ready to fight.* Derivatives, ܚܪܝܢܐ, ܚܪܝܢܐܝܬ, ܚܪܝܢܝܐ, ܚܪܝܢܘܬܐ, ܚܪܝܢܐ, ܡܬܚܪܝܢܐ.

ܚܪܐ II. imper. ܚܪܝ *to mute* as birds. Derivatives, ܚܪܘܬܐ, ܚܪܝܐ, ܒܝܬ ܡܚܪܝܐ.

ܚܪܒ fut. ܢܚܪܒ, act. part. ܚܪܒ, ܚܪܒܐ, verbal adj. ܚܪܝܒ, ܒܐ, ܒܬܐ. *to waste, dwindle; to be laid waste, be desolate, destroyed, ruined, ravaged; to lie waste;* ܐܘܪܫܠܡ ܚܪܒܬ *Jerusalem was desolate;* ܢܗܪܐ ܚܪܒ ܘܝܒܫ *the river dwindles, and dries up.* Part. adj. *ravaged, waste, desolate,* used of buildings or places whereas ܩܛܝܠܐ is said of human beings; ܡܕܝܢ̈ܬܐ ܚܪܝܒ̈ܬܐ ܕܡܠܝܢ ܦܓܪ̈ܐ ܕܩܛܝ̈ܠܐ *cities ravaged and full of corpses of the slain.*

ܚܪܒ fut. ܢܚܪܘܒ, inf. ܡܚܪܒ, act. part. ܚܪܒ, ܚܪܒܐ, pass. part. ܚܪܝܒ, ܒܐ, ܒܬܐ. *to waste, lay waste, destroy, ravage, make havoc; to slay with the sword, take by force, massacre, rout;* ܚܪܒ ܫܒܘܪ ܠܣܘܪܝܐ *Sapor laid waste Syria;* ܡܐ ܕܫܠܡ ܠܡܚܪܒܘ ܐܢܘܢ ܚܪܒܐ ܪܒܐ *when he had made an end of slaying them with a great slaughter;* ܚܪ̈ܝܒܐ *the slain.* Ethpe. ܐܬܚܪܒ *to be slain, cut down, put to flight, routed;* ܐܬܚܪܒܘ ܚܪܒܐ *they were utterly destroyed.* Ethpa. ܐܬܚܪܒ *to be brought to destruction, utterly wasted, dispersed, exterminated.* Aph. ܐܚܪܒ *to lay waste, destroy, make havoc of, make desolate; to dry up, empty* or *consume* as water, treasures, &c., ܐܚܪܒ ܫܝܢܢ *he destroyed our tranquillity;* ܐܚܪܒ ܓܙ̈ܐ *he ravaged the treasuries.* Derivatives, ܚܪܒܐ, ܚܪܒ, ܚܘܪܒܐ, ܚܪܘܒܐ, ܚܪܘܒܘܬܐ, ܚܪܒܢܐ, ܚܪܒܘܬܐ, ܚܪܝܒܐ, ܡܚܪܒܢܐ.

ܚܪܒ, ܚܪܒܐ, ܚܪܒܬܐ rt. ܚܪܒ. *desolate, waste, uninhabited; waterless, arid, dried up;* metaph.

forlorn, destitute; empty, vain, foolish; ܡܕܒܪܐ ܚܪܒܐ *an arid wilderness;* ܢܗܪܐ ܚܪܒܐ *a dried-up river;* ܫܘܩܐ ܚܪܒܝܢ *desolate streets;* ܓܪܡܘܗܝ ܚܪ̈ܝܒܝܢ *his dry bones;* ܬܗܘܐ ܥܡܪܗ ܚܪܒܐ *let his habitation be desolate;* ܚܪܒܐ ܡܢ ܝܕܥܬܐ *destitute of knowledge;* ܦܬܟܪ̈ܝܗܘܢ ܚܪ̈ܒܐ *their vain idols;* ܡܫܬܒܗܪܢܐ ܚܪܒܬܐ *a braggart.* Fem. emph. = subst. *a waste, ruin, solitary place;* ܚܪ̈ܒܬܗ ܕܐܘܪܫܠܡ *the ruins of Jerusalem;* ܐܝܟ ܩܘܦܐ ܒܚܪ̈ܒܬܐ *as an owl in the desert.*

ܚܪܒܐ rt. ܚܪܒ. com. *a*) *a sword, blade, dagger;* ܚܪܒܐ ܕܦܕܢܐ *a ploughshare;* metaph. *war, slaughter; laying waste, ravaging, devastating, destroying, ruining;* ܒܚܪܒܐ ܠܚܕ̈ܕܐ ܢܐܪܥܘܢ *to encounter each other in war;* ܚܪܒܐ ܐܪܝܡܘ *they waged war;* ܚܪܒܐ ܪܒܐ ܥܒܕܘ ܘܩܒܘ *they made great havoc, ravaged near and far;* ܚܪܒܐ ܕܕ̈ܝܪܐ *the ravaging of monasteries.* *b*) *desolation, emptiness, nought;* ܡܢ ܚܪܒܐ ܥܒ̈ܕܝܟܘܢ *your works are of nought.*

ܚܪܘܒܐ rt. ܚܪܒ. m. *demolition, destruction.*

ܚܪܒܘܩܬܐ or ܚܪܒܘܩܝܬܐ f. *a button-hole.*

ܚܪܓ fut. ܢܚܪܘܓ, inf. ܡܚܪܓ, act. part. ܚܪܓ, ܚܪܓܐ, pass. part. ܚܪܝܓ, ܓܐ, ܓܬܐ. *to rub, polish;* ܢܘ̈ܢܐ ܚܪ̈ܓܢ ܓܢ̈ܒܝܗܘܢ ܠܚܕ̈ܕܐ fishes *rub their sides against each other;* part. adj. *polished, elegant.* Pa. ܚܪܓ *to rub hard;* ܟܐ̈ܦܐ ܡܚܪ̈ܓܢ ܠܚܕ̈ܕܐ ܘܗܘ̈ܝܢ ܚܠܐ *stones rub against each other and become gravel.* Ethpa. ܐܬܚܪܓ *to be rubbed hard* or *violently.* Derivatives, ܚܪܓܐ, ܚܪܝܓܘܬܐ.

ܚܪܓܐ rt. ܚܪܓ. m. *rubbing, rubbing against* something; ܒܚܪܓܐ ܕܓܦ̈ܝܗܘܢ *in the rubbing against* each other *of their fins.*

ܚܪܓܠܐ m. *a large wingless locust;* see ܩܡܨܐ.

ܚܪܕܠܐ pl. ܠܐ̈ m. *mustard seed; black mustard.*

ܚܪܕܠܘܢܐ dimin. of ܚܪܕܠܐ m. *wild mustard, white mustard.*

ܚܪܕܘܢܐ pl. ܢܐ̈ m. *a lizard;* ܚܪܕܘܢܐ ܕܝܒܫܐ *a land crocodile;* ܚܪܕܘܢܐ ܕܝܡܐ a sort of *crab* or *crayfish;* ܚܪܕܘܢܐ ܬܢܝܢܐ *a crocodile.*

ܚܪܘܒ, ܒܐ, ܒܬܐ rt. ܚܪܒ. adj. (rare) *waste, desolate, dried up.*

ܚܪܘܒܐ pl. ܒܐ̈ m. the *locust* or *carob* tree, *ceratonia siliqua;* also its *husks* or *pods* which are used for fodder; ܚܪ̈ܘܒܐ ܗܢܘܢ ܕܐܟܠܝܢ ܗܘܘ ܚܙ̈ܝܪܐ *the husks which the swine did eat.*

ܚܪܘܒܘܬܐ rt. ܚܪܒ. f. *devastation, exhaustion;* ܚܪܘܒܘܬܐ ܕܟܦܢܐ *being wasted with hunger.*

ܚܪܘܒܝܐ rt. ܚܪܒ. m. *desolation, devastation.*

ܚܪܘܫ, ܫܐ, ܫܬܐ rt. ܚܪܫ. *harsh, coarse, rough;* ܡܪܛܘܛܐ ܚܪܘܫܐ ܕܥܡܪܐ *a coarse woollen cloak, a shaggy cloak.*

ܚܪܘܫܘܬܐ rt. ܚܪܫ. f. *coarseness, roughness, harshness;* ܚܪܘܫܘܬܐ ܕܩܠܐ *hoarseness.*

ܚܪܘܩܐ or ܚܪܘܩܐ, ܩܬܐ rt. ܚܪܩ. *yellow, pale, saffron-hued;* ܓܘܢܗ ܚܪܘܩܐ *the yellow hue* of gold; ܐܪܣܢܝܩܘܢ ܚܪܘܩܐ *arsenic;* ܦܪܚ ܚܪܘܩ *the sunflower.*

ܚܪܘܨ, ܚܪܘܨܐ or ܚܪܘܨܐ, ܨܬܐ rt. ܚܪܨ. *rough* or *harsh* to the taste, *bitter, astringent.*

ܚܪܘܨܘܬܐ rt. ܚܪܨ. f. *harshness* of taste, *astringency.*

ܚܐܪܘܬܐ pl. ܬܐ̈ rt. ܚܪ. m. *a*) generally pl. *emancipation, manumission, deeds* or *writing of manumission; freedom, deliverance;* ܡܘܗܒ ܐܢܐ ܠܟ ܚܐܪܘܬܐ *I grant thee freedom;* ܐܬܟܬܒܘ ܚܐܪ̈ܘܬܗܘܢ *their deeds of manumission were drawn up;* ܥܒܕ ܚܐܪܘܬܐ ܠܥܡܗ *he wrought deliverance for his people.* *b*) *a hole, opening, perforation; the eye* of a needle; *the cell* of a bee; *the pores* of the skin; ܚܪܘܪܐ ܕܡܫܡܥܬܐ *the orifice of the ear.*

ܚܪܘܫܐ, ܫܬܐ rt. ܚܪܫ. *hoarse.*

ܚܪܘܫܘܬܐ or ܚܪܘܫܘܬܐ rt. ܚܪܫ. f. *hoarseness, a cold.*

ܚܪܘܫܢܐ, ܢܝܬܐ rt. ܚܪܫ. *hoarse, rough, guttural.*

ܚܪܘܫܬܐ rt. ܚܪܫ. f. *the throat.*

ܚܪܘܬܐ pl. ܚܪ̈ܘܬܐ f. *a branch* esp. *a palm-branch.*

ܚܪܘܬܐ pl. ܚܪ̈ܘܬܐ f. *the upper part of the thigh, the hip-joint;* ܟܐܒܐ ܕܚܪ̈ܘܬܐ *sciatica.*

ܚܪܘܬܐ rt. ܚܪܐ I. f. *excrement, dung; the buttocks.*

ܚܪܙ fut. ܢܚܪܘܙ, imper. ܚܪܘܙ, act. part. ܚܐܪܙ, ܚܐܪܙܐ, pass. part. ܚܪܝܙ, ܙܐ, ܙܬܐ. root-meaning *to perforate for stringing together* as pearls for a necklace, hence *to hang* as a necklace or chain, *to place, arrange* or *set in order,* esp.

with ܡ̈ܠܐ *to string words together, to compose* a discourse; ܚܪܙܘ ܠܨܘܪܝ ܫܫܠܬܐ *they hung a chain round my neck;* ܢܦܫܗܘܢ ܚܪܙܘ ܠܗܘܢ ܒܫܫܠܬܐ *they associated themselves with them;* ܚܪܙ ܥܠܘܗܝ ܫܪܒܐ ܐܪܝܟܐ *he strung a long story on to it;* part. adj. *strung, composed, set;* ܣܦܝܪܬܐ ܕܚܪܝܙܐ ܒܕܪܥܗ *a basket which hung on her arm;* ܚܪܝܙ ܒܟܐܦ̈ܐ ܝܩܝܪ̈ܬܐ *set with precious stones;* ܒܬܠܬܐ ܦܢܩܝܬ̈ܐ ܚܪܝܙܝܢ *arranged in three vols.;* ܚܪܝܙ ܒܫܘܠܡܐ ܫܠܝܚܝܐ *included in apostolic succession;* gram. *inserted,* as diacritic points. ETHPE. ܐܬܚܪܙ *to be pierced through; to be set* or *arranged in right order.* DERIVATIVES, ܚܪܙܐ, ܚܪܙܐ, ܚܪܝܙܘܬܐ.

ܚܪܙܐ rt. ܚܪܙ. Ar. m. *an amulet, charm.*

ܚܪܙܐ rt. ܚܪܙ. m. *perforation* of beads, &c., *a row, series, arrangement.*

ܚܪܛ part. adj. ܚܪܝܛ, ܚܪܝܛܐ, ܚܪܝܛܬܐ *planed, filed.*

ܚܪܛܡ *to wag* the tail; *to growl, snarl, begin to bark.*

ܚܪܟ fut. ܢܚܪܘܟ, act. part. ܚܳܪܶܟ, pass. part. ܚܪܝܟ, ܚܪܝܟܐ, ܚܪܝܟܬܐ. *to scrape, scratch;* ܚܪܝܟܝܢ ܐܦܝܗܘܢ *their faces were scratched.* ETHPE. ܐܬܚܪܟ *to be scratched; to gash* or *lacerate oneself.* PA. ܚܪܶܟ *to scratch* or *tear* esp. with the nails; ܒܒܣܪܗܘܢ ܠܐ ܢܚܪܟܘܢ ܡܚܪܘܟܝܬܐ *they shall not make any cuttings in their flesh.* DERIVATIVES, ܚܪܘܟܐ, ܡܚܪܘܟܝܬܐ, ܚܪܟܐ.

ܚܪܟܐ or ܚܪܟܐ pl. ܐ̈ rt. ܚܪܟ. m. *a gash* or *scratch.*

ܚܪܛܘܡܐ m. *the snout, proboscis, the trunk* of an elephant.

ܚܪܛܘܡܦܐ, ܚܪܛܡܦܐ or ܚܪܛܡܦܐ pl. ܐ̈ m. *chick-pea.*

ܚܪܝ *a*) see ܚܪܐ I. for ETHPEAL and APHEL. *b*) construct state pl. of ܚܪܝܐ.

ܚܪܝܐ pl. ܚܪ̈ܝܐ rt. ܚܪܐ II. m. *dung, droppings;* ܚܪ̈ܝ ܝܘܢܐ *doves' dung.* Metaph. ܚܪ̈ܝ ܣܐܡܐ *dross of silver;* ܚܪ̈ܝ ܦܪܙܠܐ *iron slag.*

ܚܪܝܒ and ܚܪܝܒ; see ܚܪܒ and ܚܪܒ.

ܚܪܝܒܘܬܐ rt. ܚܪܒ. f. *devastation, desolation.*

ܚܪܝܓܘܬܐ rt. ܚܪܓ. f. *polish, refinement, eloquence.*

ܚܪܝܙܘܬܐ rt. ܚܪܙ. f. *arrangement* of words, *composition.*

ܚܪܝܢܐ, ܚܪܝܢܝܐ rt. ܚܪܐ I. *quarrelsome, contentious; a heretic;* ܣܟܘܪ ܦܘܡ̈ܐ ܕܚܪܝܢ̈ܐ ܕܡܒܨܝܢ ܠܐܠܗܘܬܐ *stop the mouths of heretics who investigate the Divinity.*

ܚܪܝܢܘܬܐ rt. ܚܪܐ I. f. *strife, contention, dispute, litigation.*

ܚܪܝܡܘܬܐ rt. ܚܪܡ. f. *red-heat,* state of *being red-hot.*

ܚܪܝܢܐ, ܚܪܝܢ pl. ܐ̈ rt. ܚܪܐ I. *controversy, dispute, contention, strife, schism;* ܚܪܝܢ ܡ̈ܠܐ *contradiction;* ܡܘܕܥܢܘܬܐ ܕܚܪܝܢܐ *a matter of dispute;* ܦܠܓܘܬܐ ܕܚܪܝܢܐ *a matter of strife;* ܕܠܐ ܚܪܝܢ *without dispute, assuredly.*

ܚܪܝܢܐܝܬ rt. ܚܪܐ I. adv. *contentiously, schismatically.*

ܚܪܝܢܝܐ rt. ܚܪܐ I. *polemic, controversial;* ܡ̈ܠܐ ܚܪܝܢܝ̈ܐ *matters of controversy.*

ܚܪܝܥܐ rt. ܚܪܥ. m. *carthamus tinctorius,* a sort of yellow thistle.

ܚܪܝܦܐ and ܚܪܝܦܐ; see ܚܪܦ part.

ܚܪܝܦܐܝܬ rt. ܚܪܦ. adv. *swiftly, suddenly, ardently;* ܒܪܩܐ ܕܚܪܝܦܐܝܬ ܥܒܪ *lightning which passes in a moment;* ܫܪܝ ܕܢܘܕܐ ܚܪܝܦܐܝܬ *he began ardently to confess* his faith.

ܚܪܝܦܘܬܐ rt. ܚܪܦ. f. *sharpness* of taste or voice; *acuteness* of bodily or mental senses; *swiftness, speed, rapidity, celerity, velocity; fervour;* ܒܚܪܝܦܘܬܐ ܕܐܪܟܢܘܗܝ *at the rapid motion of their wings;* ܚܪܝܦܘܬܐ ܕܡܚܫܒܬܐ *the swiftness of thought;* ܚܪܝܦܘܬܐ ܟܝܢܝܬܐ *natural acuteness;* ܚܪܝܦܘܬ ܚܡܬܐ *irascibility;* ܚܪܝܦܘܬ ܡ̈ܠܐ *sharpness of speech, sarcasm;* ܚܪܝܦܘܬ ܛܢܢܐ *fervent zeal.*

ܚܪܝܪܘܬܐ rt. ܚܪ. f. *huskiness* of the throat, *hoarseness.*

ܚܪܟ fut. ܢܚܪܘܟ *to burn, scorch, singe.* ETHPE. ܐܬܚܪܟ pass. ܐܦܠܐ ܚܕܐ ܡܢ ܣܥܪܐ ܕܪܫܗ ܐܬܚܪܟܬ *not one hair of his head was singed;* ܐܪܙܐ ܕܣܢܝܐ ܕܠܐ ܐܬܚܪܟ *the mystery of the bush which was not consumed.* PA. ܚܪܶܟ *to burn up, parch, dry up;* part. ܡܚܪܟ ܡܚܪܟܐ *sunburnt, parched, dried up, burnt up, charred;* ܐܦܝܗ ܕܡܚܪܟܝܢ ܒܫܡܫܐ *her face burnt with the sun;* ܐܘܕ̈ܐ ܡܚܪ̈ܟܐ *charred brands.* ETHPA. ܐܬܚܪܟ *to be singed; to be heated, warmed;* astron. *to be hidden* by rays of light; ܟܘܟܒܐ ܕܡܬܚܪܟ

heated vapour. Derivatives, ܚܪܘܟܐ, ܚܪܟܘܬܐ, ܡܚܪܟܢܐ, ܡܚܪܟܐ, ܚܪܟܐ.

ܚܪܳܟܳܐ rt. ܚܪܟ. m. *touchwood, tinder; some medicament.*

ܚܰܪܟܽܘܫܳܐ pl. ܚܶܐ from ܚܪܟܫ. m. *flattering, fawning.*

ܚܰܪܟܶܫ *to fawn upon, to wag its tail* as a dog. Derivatives, ܚܪܟܘܫܐ, ܚܪܟܫܐ.

ܚܪܰܡ Ethpe. ܐܶܬ݂ܚܪܶܡ *to be excommunicated, anathematized.* Aph. ܐܰܚܪܶܡ in O.T. *to separate from ordinary use, to devote* to God, *to destroy utterly;* ܬܰܚܪܶܡ ܩܶܢܝܳܢܗܽܘܢ ܠܡܳܪܝܳܐ *thou shalt devote their substance unto the Lord.* N. T. and later, *to excommunicate, to put under a curse* or *anathema, to curse, ban;* pass. part. ܡܚܰܪܰܡ, ܡܚܰܪܡܳܐ, ܡܚܰܪܡܬܳܐ *accursed, execrable, under anathema;* ܗܳܝܕܶܝܢ ܫܰܪܺܝ ܠܡܚܰܪܳܡܽܘ ܘܰܠܡܶܐܡܳܐ *then began he to curse and to swear;* ܗܶܪܶܣܺܝܣ ܡܚܰܪܡܬܳܐ *an execrable heresy;* ܐܰܫܒܺܝܩܳܐ ܘܡܚܰܪܡܳܐ *suspended* from office *and excommunicate.* Ettaph. ܐܶܬ݁ܬ݂ܰܚܪܰܡ *to be anathematized, excommunicated; to be threatened with excommunication;* ܟܰܕ ܡܶܬ݂ܦܰܩܰܕ ܓܰܒ݂ܪܳܐ ܒܰܚܪܳܡܳܐ ܕܢܶܗܦܽܘܟ݂ ܠܘܳܬ݂ ܐܰܢ̈ܬ݂ܶܗ *the man being commanded under pain of excommunication to return to his wife.* Derivatives, the six following words and ܡܚܰܪܡܢܘܬܐ.

ܚܪܶܡ, ܚܶܪܡܳܐ pl. ܚܶܐ rt. ܚܪܡ. m. O. T. *a devoted thing* either given to God for use in His service or to be destroyed. In other books *a votive offering; a curse, anathema; excommunication, death;* ܚܶܪܡ ܕܠܳܐ ܡܰܘܕܶܐ ܕܰܐܠܳܗܳܐ ܡܺܝܬ݂ ܥܰܠ ܨܠܺܝܒ݂ܳܐ *cursed be he who denies that God died on the Cross;* ܢܶܗܘܶܐ ܚܶܪܡ *let him be anathema;* ܚܣ ܘܚܶܪܡ ܕܢܶܗܘܶܐ *God forbid that it should be . . .*

ܚܰܪܺܝܡ, ܚܰܪܺܝܡܳܐ, ܚܰܪܺܝܡܬܳܐ rt. ܚܪܡ. *under a ban, accursed, execrable; savage, fierce, ferocious,* often applied to birds of prey; ܐܰܝܟ ܚܰܪܺܝܡܬܳܐ ܝܶܬ݂ܒܰܬ݂ ܗܘܳܬ݂ *she sat like one under a ban or curse;* ܥܰܠܥܳܠܳܐ ܚܰܪܺܝܡܳܐ *a wild storm;* ܚܰܪܺܝܡܳܬ݂ܳܐ ܘܰܐܟ݂ܳܠܰܬ݂ ܒܶܣܪܳܐ *ferocious and carnivorous* birds.

ܚܰܪܺܝܡܳܐܺܝܬ݂ rt. ܚܪܡ. adv. *savagely, cruelly;* ܚܰܪܺܝܡܳܐܺܝܬ݂ ܐܶܬ݂ܩܛܶܠ *he was cruelly slain.*

ܚܰܪܺܝܡܽܘܬ݂ܳܐ pl. ܘ̈ܳܬ݂ܳܐ rt. ܚܪܡ. f. *cruelty, ferocity, barbarity; savage* or *inhuman deeds;* ܚܰܪܺܝܡܽܘܬ݂ܳܐ ܕܥܰܠܥܳܠܳܐ *the raging of the tempest;* ܚܰܪܺܝܡܽܘܬ݂ܳܐ ܕܢܳܡܽܘܣܳܐ *harsh enactments of the Law;* ܚܰܪܺܝܡܽܘܬ݂ܳܐ ܕܣܽܘܢܗܳܕܳܘܣ ܕܟܰܠܩܺܝܕܽܘܢ *the outrageous violence of the Council of Chalcedon.*

ܚܰܪܡܳܢܳܐ pl. ܢܶܐ rt. ܚܪܡ. *a*) with ܚܶܘܝܳܐ or ellipt. *the basilisk* or *cockatrice;* ܟܠܺܝܠܳܐ ܕܚܰܪܡܳܢܳܐ *crowned with a basilisk.*

ܚܰܪܡܳܢܽܘܬ݂ܳܐ rt. ܚܪܡ. f. *harshness.*

ܚܪܺܢ pl. m. ܚܪ̈ܳܢܶܐ f. ܚܪ̈ܳܢܝܳܬ݂ܳܐ rt. ܐܚܪܢ. *another, the other;* see ܐܚܪܺܢ.

ܚܪܰܣ fut. ܢܶܚܪܽܘܣ *to roughen, to harden* by rubbing. Derivatives, ܚܪܘܣܐ, ܚܪܘܣܘܬܐ, ܚܪܣܐ, ܚܪܣܘܬܐ.

ܚܶܪܣܳܐ rt. ܚܪܣ. m. *scab, mange;* ܚܶܪܣܳܐ ܕܥܰܦ̈ܥܰܦܶܐ *a thickening of the eyelids.*

ܚܰܪܣܽܘܬ݂ܳܐ rt. ܚܪܣ. f. *roughness.*

ܚܰܪܣܳܢܳܐ pl. ܢܶܐ m. *rock-dwelling fish.*

ܚܪܰܥ fut. ܢܶܚܪܰܥ, act. part. ܚܳܪܰܥ, pass. part. ܚܪܺܝܥ, ܚܪܺܝܥܳܐ, ܚܪܺܝܥܬܳܐ. *a*) *to be cunning.* *b*) *to be yellow.* Pa. ܚܰܪܰܥ *to sophisticate;* ܦܫܺܝܛܽܘܬ݂ܳܐ ܕܠܳܐ ܡܚܰܪܥܳܐ *unsophisticated simplicity.* Ethpa. ܐܶܬ݂ܚܰܪܰܥ *to act craftily, deceitfully.* Derivatives, ܚܪܘܥܐ, ܚܪܝܥܐ, ܚܪܝܥܐܝܬ, ܚܪܝܥܘܬܐ, ܡܚܪܥܢܐ.

ܚܪܺܝܥ, ܚܪܺܝܥܳܐ, ܚܪܺܝܥܬܳܐ pl. m. ܚܪ̈ܺܝܥܶܐ f. ܚܪ̈ܺܝܥܳܬ݂ܳܐ rt. ܚܪܥ. 1) *astute, crafty, knavish.* 2) *yellow, yellowish;* ܡܰܝ̈ܳܐ ܕܚܪܺܝܥܳܐ *saffron-water.* 3) *carthamus tinctorius,* cf. ܚܰܪܥܳܐ.

ܚܪܺܝܥܳܐܺܝܬ݂ rt. ܚܪܥ. adv. *craftily, knavishly.*

ܚܪܺܝܥܽܘܬ݂ܳܐ rt. ܚܪܥ. f. 1) *cunning, craftiness, knavishness;* ܡܶܠܟܳܐ ܕܚܪܺܝܥܽܘܬ݂ܳܐ *crafty counsel.* 2) *biliousness;* ܚܪܺܝܥܽܘܬ݂ܳܐ ܕܐܶܣܛܽܘܡܟ݂ܳܐ ܘܰܟ݂ܪܺܝܗܽܘܬ݂ܳܐ *biliousness, heartburn.*

ܚܪܰܦ fut. ܢܶܚܪܽܘܦ, act. part. ܚܳܪܶܦ, ܚܳܪܦܳܐ, pass. part. ܚܪܺܝܦ and adj. ܚܰܪܺܝܦ, ܦܳܐ, ܦܬܳܐ. *to mix* drink; ܚܪܰܦ ܠܶܗ ܩܽܘ̈ܠܶܐ ܪ̈ܰܘܪܒܶܐ *he mixed great flagons for himself;* metaph. ܕܡܳܐ ܘܡܰܝ̈ܳܐ ܚܪܰܦ ܕܢܕܰܟܶܐ ܠܗܰܘ ܕܐܶܬ݂ܛܰܘܰܫ *He mingled blood and water that He might cleanse that which was defiled;* part. ܚܪܺܝܦ *a*) *mingled;* ܚܰܡܪܳܐ ܠܳܐ ܚܪܺܝܦܳܐ *undiluted wine.* *b*) *a drinking-companion, table-companion, guest,* ܠܡܶܫܬܽܘܬ݂ܶܗ ܕܰܟ݂ܝܳܐ ܐܶܥܽܘܠ ܚܪܺܝܦܳܐ ܐܢܳܐ *that I may enter His pure feast as a guest.* Part. adj. ܚܰܪܺܝܦ *sharp, sudden, swift, acute; bitter, severe;* ܐܶܫܳܬ݂ܳܐ ܚܰܪܺܝܦܬܳܐ *an acute* or *severe fever;* ܛܶܦܪ̈ܶܐ ܚܰܪ̈ܺܝܦܶܐ *sharp nails;* ܡܰܓܠܳܐ ܚܰܪܺܝܦܬܳܐ *a sharp sickle;* ܚܰܪܺܝܦ ܪܶܥܝܳܢܳܐ *agile, quickwitted, acute* in body or mind; ܚܰܪܺܝܦ ܚܶܙܘܶܗ *he is keen-sighted;* ܚܰܪܺܝܦ ܒܡܶܠܬܳܐ *ready of speech;*

ܚܰܪܺܝܦ ܠܡܶܥܢܳܐ ܦܶܢܝܳܢܳܐ *prompt to answer; a sudden change;* ܫܽܘܚܠܳܦܳܐ ܚܰܪܺܝܦܳܐ ܬܝܳܒܽܘܬ݂ܳܐ ܚܰܪܺܝܦܬܳܐ *swift repentance;* math. ܙܳܘܺܝܬ݂ܳܐ ܚܰܪܺܝܦܬܳܐ *an acute angle;* ܩܳܠܶܐ ܚܰܪܺܝܦܶܐ *shrill notes.* Pa. ܚܰܪܶܦ *a) to mix, to infuse. b) to sharpen; to stimulate;* ܡܚܰܪܶܦ ܣܰܦܣܶܪܗ *sharpening* his *sword;* ܟܰܦܢܳܐ ܕܰܡܚܰܪܶܦ ܠܐܶܣܛܽܘܡܟܳܐ hunger *which makes the stomach keen.* Ethpa. ܐܶܬ݂ܚܰܪܰܦ *to be stimulated, made eager.* Aph. ܐܰܚܪܶܦ *to sharpen; to egg* or *urge on.* Derivatives, ܚܽܘܪܦܳܐ, ܚܰܪܺܝܦܳܐܺܝܬ݂, ܡܚܰܪܦܳܢܽܘܬ݂ܳܐ, ܚܰܪܦܳܐ, ܚܰܪܺܝܦܽܘܬ݂ܳܐ.

ܚܰܪܦܳܐ or ܚܶܪܦܳܐ rt. ܚܪܦ. m. *a blade, sword.*

ܚܰܪܦܬ݂ܳܐ or ܚܶܪܦܬ݂ܳܐ f. *a patch* on a shoe; ܚܶܪܦܬ݂ܳܐ ܚܰܕܬ݂ܳܐ ܕܣܰܢܕܠܳܐ *a new patch on a sandal.*

ܚܰܪܨܠܳܐ m. *ornithogalum,* an umbelliferous plant.

ܚܰܪܨܦܬ݂ܳܐ f. *half-frozen hail, sleet.*

ܚܪܰܩ fut. ܢܶܚܪܽܘܩ, inf. ܡܶܚܪܰܩ, imper. ܚܪܽܘܩ, act. part. ܚܳܪܶܩ ܚܳܪܩܳܐ, pass. part. ܚܪܺܝܩ, ܚܪܺܝܩܳܐ, ܚܪܺܝܩܬ݂ܳܐ. root-meaning *to cut; to fix, settle, appoint, destine; to conclude,* with ܡܶܢ *to abdicate;* with ܩܕܳܡ *to predestine;* ܚܪܰܩ ܪ̈ܺܝܫܳܢܶܐ ܥܰܠ ܡܰܠܰܐܟ̈ܶܐ *He appointed princes over the angels;* ܥܕܰܡܳܐ ܠܝܰܘܡܳܐ ܗܰܘ ܕܚܪܰܩ ܐܰܠܳܗܳܐ *until that day which God determined;* ܚܳܪܩܺܝܢܰܢ ܕܣܺܗܪܳܐ ܡܶܢ ܫܶܡܫܳܐ ܡܩܰܒܶܠ ܢܽܘܗܪܳܐ ܡܶܛܽܠ ܗܳܕܶܐ *we conclude that the moon derives light from the sun from this reason . . .* Part. adj. *determined, destined, appointed, fixed, definite, express, obligatory;* ܠܽܘܛܬ݂ܳܐ ܚܪܺܝܩܬ݂ܳܐ ܥܰܠ ܗܰܘ ܕܣܳܛܶܐ ܡܶܢ ܗܰܝܡܳܢܽܘܬ݂ܳܐ *the curse determined upon whoso turns aside from the faith;* ܐܶܢ ܗܽܘ ܕܟܽܠܡܶܕܶܡ ܚܪܺܝܩ ܡܶܢ ܚܶܠܩܳܐ *if everything be destined by fate;* ܨܠܰܘ̈ܳܬ݂ܳܐ ܕܰܚܪ̈ܺܝܩܳܢ ܥܰܠ ܟܽܠ *prayers enjoined on all;* ܒܥܶܕ̈ܳܢܶܐ ܕܰܚܪ̈ܺܝܩܳܢ *at fixed times;* ܫܳܥ̈ܶܐ ܚܪ̈ܺܝܩܳܬ݂ܳܐ ܩܳܢܽܘܢܳܝܳܬ݂ܳܐ *the canonical hours.* Ethpe. ܐܶܬ݂ܚܪܶܩ *to be appointed, decreed, determined;* with ܩܕܳܡ *to be predestined;* ܡܰܥܡܽܘܕܺܝܬ݂ܳܐ ܕܡܰܝܳܐ ܠܫܽܘܒܩܳܢ ܚܛܳܗ̈ܶܐ ܐܶܬ݂ܚܪܶܩܰܬ݂ *baptism by water, appointed for the remission of sins;* ܗܳܠܶܝܢ ܕܡܶܢ ܐܰܠܳܗܳܐ ܐܶܬ݂ܚܪܶܩܝ *things which were instituted by God.* Pa. ܚܰܪܶܩ *to gnash* the teeth, *to sharpen;* ܚܰܪܶܩܘ ܟܰܟܰܝ̈ܗܽܘܢ *they sharpened their tusks;* ܡܚܰܪܩܺܝܢ ܫܶܢ̈ܰܝܗܽܘܢ ܥܠܰܝܢ *they gnash their teeth at us.* Ethpa. ܐܶܬ݂ܚܰܪܰܩ *to be cut, cut through.* Derivatives, ܚܽܘܪܩܳܐ, ܚܶܪܩܳܐ, ܡܚܰܪܩܳܢܽܘܬ݂ܳܐ, ܚܰܪܩܳܐ, ܚܶܪܩܳܐ, ܚܪܺܝܩܽܘܬ݂ܳܐ, ܚܽܘܪܳܩܳܐ, ܡܚܰܪܩܳܐܺܝܬ݂.

ܚܶܪܩܳܐ pl. ܚܶܪ̈ܩܶܐ rt. ܚܪܩ. m. *a) a division, section; b) an end, limit;* ܣܳܡ ܠܳܗ ܚܶܪܩܳܐ *he set limits to it. c) a divine decree, destiny;* ܠܰܝܬ ܚܶܪܩܳܐ ܐܳܦ ܠܳܐ ܚܶܠܩܳܐ *there is neither destiny nor fate. d)* pl. *a necklace.*

ܚܽܘܪܳܩܳܐ rt. ܚܪܩ. m. 1) *gnashing* the teeth. 2) *a judicial decision, enforcing.* 3) *an army.*

ܚܰܪܩܽܘܒܳܐ m. *the heel, the ankle; the pastern* of a horse.

ܚܰܪܩܠܺܝܣ pr. n. *Heraclea* a town of Syria.

ܚܰܪܩܠܳܝܳܐ, ܝܬܳܐ from ܚܰܪܩܠܺܝܣ. adj. *of Heraclea, Harkleian, according to the Harkleian version* i. e. that of ܬܳܐܘܡܳܐ ܚܰܪܩܠܳܝܳܐ *Thomas of Heraclea;* ܡܦܰܩܬ݂ܳܐ ܚܰܪܩܠܳܝܬ݂ܳܐ *the Harkleian version* i.e. the recension in A. D. 616 of the translation of the N. T. from Greek into Syriac by Philoxenus about 100 years earlier; ܐܶܘܰܢܓܶܠܝܽܘܢ ܚܰܪܩܠܳܝܳܐ *the Gospel according to the Harkleian Version.*

ܚܪܶܫ I. ܚܪܶܫ, fut. ܢܶܚܪܰܫ *to be silent, dumb, mute;* with ܓܰܓܪܬ݂ܳܐ *to be hoarse;* ܚܪܶܫ ܠܶܫܳܢܶܗ *his tongue was tied;* ܚܪܶܫ ܟܶܢܳܪܳܐ *the harp was mute;* ܥܶܕܳܢܳܐ ܗܰܘ ܕܶܐܚܪܰܫ ܘܠܳܐ ܐܶܡܰܠܶܠ *that time when I shall speak no more.* II. ܚܪܰܫ, fut. ܢܶܚܪܽܘܫ, pass. part. ܚܪܺܝܫܳܐ *to slay;* ܕܺܐܒܳܐ ܕܚܪܰܫ ܠܶܐܡܪܳܐ *the wolf who slew the lamb.* Ethpe. ܐܶܬ݂ܚܪܶܫ *to become deaf, to stop one's ears.* Pa. ܚܰܪܶܫ I. *a) to use enchantments, magic arts, to enchant;* ܚܰܪܫܳܗ̇ *he bewitched her;* ܒܓܶܠܝܳܐ ܡܚܰܪܶܫ ܗܘܳܐ *he practised magic arts openly. b) to silence, make dumb.* II. *to butcher.* Ethpa. ܐܶܬ݂ܚܰܪܰܫ *to enchant; to become deaf.* Aph. ܐܰܚܪܶܫ *to silence, to cause to be dumb;* ܡܰܢ ܐܰܚܪܶܫ ܟܶܢܳܪܳܟ *who has silenced thy harp.* Derivatives, ܚܽܘܪܳܫܳܐ, ܚܶܪܫܳܐ, ܚܰܪܫܽܘܬ݂ܳܐ, ܚܰܪܳܫܳܐ, ܚܰܪܳܫܽܘܬ݂ܳܐ, ܚܰܪܺܝܫ adj., ܚܰܪܳܫܳܐ, ܚܰܪܳܫܬ݂ܳܐ, ܚܰܪܫܳܐܺܝܬ݂, ܡܚܰܪܫܳܢܽܘܬ݂ܳܐ, ܡܚܰܪܫܳܢܳܐ, ܡܚܰܪܫܳܐܺܝܬ݂, ܡܚܰܪܫܳܢܳܐ.

ܚܪܺܫ, ܚܰܪܫܳܐ, ܚܰܪܫܬ݂ܳܐ rt. ܚܪܫ. *dumb, deaf; a deaf-mute;* ܚܰܝ̈ܘܳܬ݂ܳܐ ܚܰܪ̈ܫܳܬ݂ܳܐ *dumb animals;* ܦܬ݂ܟܰܪ̈ܶܐ ܚܰܪ̈ܫܶܐ *dumb idols;* ܚܶܫܽܘܟ݂ܳܐ ܚܰܪܫܳܐ *speechless darkness.*

ܚܰܪܳܫ, ܚܰܪܳܫܳܐ pl. ܚܰܪ̈ܳܫܶܐ m. rt. ܚܪܫ. *a magician, enchanter, sorcerer, wizard;* ܚܰܪ̈ܳܫܶܐ ܫܳܪܶܝܢ ܚܶܪ̈ܫܶܐ *wizards can dissolve charms;* ܫܶܡܥܽܘܢ ܚܰܪܳܫܳܐ *Simon the Sorcerer;* ܚܰܪܳܫܬ݂ܳܐ pl. ܚܰܪ̈ܳܫܳܬ݂ܳܐ f. *a sorceress, witch, enchantress.*

ܚܪܫܐ or ܚܪܫܐ pl. ܐ̈ rt. ܚܪܫ. m. *an enchantment, incantation; magic, witchcraft;* ܚܒܫܘ ܚܪ̈ܫܐ *they worked enchantments, performed incantations;* ܚܒܫ ܚܪܫܐ *an enchanter, magician.*

ܚܪܫܐܝܬ adv. rt. ܚܪܫ. *stupidly.*

ܚܪܫܘܬܐ rt. ܚܪܫ. f. *dumbness, deafness.*

ܚܪܫܘܬܐ pl. ܚܪ̈ܫܘܬܐ rt. ܚܪܫ. f. *magic, sorcery, witchcraft;* ܚܪܫܘܬܐ ܕܥܒܕܐ ܚܝܠܐ *wonder-working witchcraft;* pl. *incantations, charms.*

ܚܪܬ fut. ܢܚܪܘܬ, act. part. ܚܪܬ, ܚܪܬܐ. I. *to dig out, hollow out, furrow.* II. *to be hoarse.* ETHPA. ܐܬܚܪܬ pass. of both meanings; ܐܪܥܐ ܒܢ̈ܗܪܘܬܐ ܡܬܚܪܬܐ *the earth is furrowed by rivers.* DERIVATIVE, ܚܪܬܐ.

ܚܪܬ 2 pers. masc. sing. and ܚܪܬ 1 pers. com. sing. of verb ܚܘܪ *to behold*, &c.

ܚܪܬܐ constr. ܚܪܬ, pl. ܚܪ̈ܬܐ for ܐܚܪܬܐ rt. ܐܚܪ. f. *the latter end, extremity, furthest part; the term, event, result; remnant; the stem* of a ship; ܚܪܬܐ ܒܝܫܬܐ *an evil end, evil event;* ܚܪܬܐ ܕܛܘܒܢܘܬܐ *the term of bliss, the highest bliss;* ܒܚܪܬܐ ܕܙܒ̈ܢܐ *in the last time, at the last;* ܒܚܪܬܐ *at the end, in the lowest place, last, at last, at length, finally;* ܒܚܪܬܐ ܕܟܠܗܘܢ *last of all.*

ܚܪܬܐ pl. ܚܪ̈ܬܐ rt. ܚܪܬ. m. *a furrow, hollow* worn by the drip of water.

ܚܪܬܐ m. *vitriol;* ܚܪܬܐ ܕܐܫܟܦ̈ܐ *shoemaker's vitriol;* ܕܝܘܬܐ ܕܚܪܬܐ *ink.*

ܚܫ fut. ܢܚܫ, act. part. ܚܐܫ, f. ܚܫܐ or ܚܐܫܐ, pl. m. ܚܐܫܝܢ or ܚܫܝܢ, f. ܚܐܫܢ or ܚܫܢ, pass. part. ܚܫܝܫ and ܚܫܝܫ, ܚܫܝܫܐ, ܚܫܝܫܬܐ. *a) to suffer,* with ܡܢ at the hands of any one, *to be sad, sorrowful,* with ܥܠ *to feel sorry for, to pity;* ܠܐ ܚܐܫ ܐܢܐ *I don't care;* ܠܐ ܚܐܫ ܒܡܘܬܗ *he is not grieved at his own death;* ܚܫ ܥܠܘܗܝ *he sympathized with him. b) to be sorry, to repent;* ܠܐ ܡܕܡ ܚܫܝܢ ܗܘܘ ܥܠ ܚܛܗܝܗܘܢ *they felt no compunction at all for their sins.* c) rare uses, *to be offended;* ܚܫ ܕܠܐ ܐܣܬܟܝܘ ܠܗ *he was offended that they had not expected him; to suffer, be obliged to put up with;* ܣܘܪܗܒܐ ܕܚܫܘ *the haste to which they were compelled.* In versions from the Greek ܚܫ answers to πάσχω. Gram. ܚܐܫ *passive* opp. ܥܒܘܕ *active.*

Part. adj. *a)* ܚܫܝܫ *conscious of, cognizant of, privy to; guilty of, deserving;* ܠܐ ܡܕܡ ܚܫܝܫ ܐܢܐ ܒܢܦܫܝ *I know nothing against myself;* ܠܐ ܚܫܝܫܝܢ ܒܢܟܠܐ *they knew no guile;* ܚܫܝܫܝܢ ܗܘܝܬܘܢ ܒܩܛܠܗ *ye were privy to his murder. b)* ܚܫܝܫܐ *suffering, diseased; sad, sorrowful, full of feeling, pathetic, sympathetic;* ܗܢܘܢ ܚܫܝܫܝܢ ܒܟܘܪܗܢܐ *those suffering from sickness;* ܕܘܟܬܐ ܕܚܫܝܫܐ *the part affected, the seat of pain;* ܚܫܝܫ ܗܘܐ ܥܠܝܗܘܢ *he felt for them, compassionated them;* ܠܒܐ ܚܫܝܫܐ *a feeling heart;* ܩܝ̈ܢܬܐ ܚܫܝ̈ܫܬܐ *mournful melodies;* ܐܪܡܝܐ ܚܫܝܫܐ *sad Jeremiah.* APHEL ܐܚܫ act. part. ܡܚܐܫ or ܡܚܫ. *to pain, sadden; to cause pain* or *suffering;* ܕܢܚܫܘܢܝܗ ܠܦܓܪܐ *that he might afflict the body;* ܡܚܫܝ ܐܠܗܐ *Patripassians, Theopaschites.* ETHPALPAL ܐܬܚܫܚܫ *to be pained, afflicted.* DERIVATIVES, ܚܫܐ, ܚܫܫܐ, …

ܚܫ ܚܫܒܘܢ; see below ܚܘܫܒܢܐ.

ܚܫܐ pl. ܚܫ̈ܐ rt. ܚܫ. m. *a) pain, suffering, disease, sickness;* ܚܫܐ ܕܦܟܝܓܐ *paralysis. b) sadness, sorrow, mourning; sorrow* for sin, *contrition. c) the Passion* of our Lord; ܫܒܘܥܐ ܕܚܫܐ or *Passion week;* ܥܪܘܒܬܐ ܕܚܫܐ *Good Friday. d) passion, desire, ambition, affection;* ܚܫ̈ܐ ܢܦܫܢܝ̈ܐ *mental passions* or *affections* e.g. pallor from fear; grief, anger, fear, gladness; ܚܫܐ ܕܠܘܬ ܐܠܗܐ *a passion for God;* ܐܝܬ ܗܘܐ ܠܗ ܚܫܐ ܕܡܠܟܘܬܐ *he is ambitious to reign;* ܢܛܪ ܠܒܗ ܡܢ ܚܫ̈ܐ *he keeps his heart from passions;* ܠܡܣܒܥܘ ܚܫ̈ܝܗܘܢ *to satisfy their passions.*

ܚܫܐ or ܚܫܐ m. the herb *thyme.*

ܚܫܒ fut. ܢܚܫܘܒ, imper. ܚܫܘܒ, act. part. ܚܫܒ, ܚܫܒܐ, pass. part. ܚܫܝܒ, ܚܫܝܒܐ, ܚܫܝܒܬܐ. *a) to count, number, reckon,* ܚܫܒܘ ܕܡ̈ܝܗܘܢ *they reckoned the value of them;* ܚܫܒ ܢܦܩܬܐ *counting the cost, reckoning the expense;* ܚܫܒܝ ܙܒ̈ܢܐ *chronologers. b) to enumerate, recount. c) to take account, reckon, regard, think much of,* with ܠܐ *to make* or *think nothing of . . .;* ܚܫܒܗ ܐܝܟ ܪܘܝܐ *he thought she was drunk;* ܠܐ ܚܫܒܝܢ ܠܡܘܬܐ *they think nothing of death;* ܚܫܒܐ ܠܟܘܡܪ̈ܐ ܐܝܟ ܟܠܒ̈ܐ *she takes account of* the stars as the Chaldaeans did. d) to charge, lay to the account of any one, ascribe, lay the blame. Pass. part. highly esteemed or reputed, imputed or reckoned; ܥܕܡܐ ܠܢܡܘܣܐ . . . ܠܐ ܚܛܝܬܐ ܗܘܬ ܚܫܝܒܐ until the law . . . sin was not imputed; ܠܐ ܚܫܝܒܐ ܗܘܬ it was not reckoned, was thought nothing of; ܠܐ ܚܫܝܒܐ of no account, not thought much of; ܡܢܐ ܚܫܝܒܐ ܠܝ or ܠܘܬܝ what is it to me? = it is nothing to me. ETHPE. ܐܬܚܫܒ a) pass. to be numbered, reckoned, imputed, accounted, with ܥܡ amongst; ܠܐ ܡܬܚܫܒܐ ܠܟܘܢ ܗܕܐ ܚܛܝܬܐ ܩܕܡ ܐܠܗܐ let not this sin be imputed to you before God; ܘܠܐ ܡܬܚܫܒܝܢ innumerable, inestimable; ܠܐ ܡܬܡܢܝܢ ܐܝܟ ܕܠܐ ܡܬܚܫܒܝܢ of inestimable worth; ܡܗܝܡܢܐ ܓܝܪ ܐܬܚܫܒܘ for they were counted faithful. b) refl. to think, meditate, but in this sense the Ethpa. is usual. PAEL ܚܫܒ to count. ETHPA. ܐܬܚܫܒ to think, reckon, have in the mind; to plan, devise, design, purpose, plot with ܥܠ against any one; with ܒܠܒܗ or ܒܢܦܫܗ to purpose in his heart, think to himself; with ܡܚܫܒܬܐ to make plans, invent designs; with ܢܟܠܐ to plot, lay a plot; with ܥܠܬܐ to invent a pretext; ܐܬܚܫܒܘ ܡܚܫܒܬܐ ܒܝܫܬܐ ܥܠ they have taken evil counsel against . . .; with ܢܟܠܐ ܒܝܫܐ the same; ܐܬܚܫܒ ܕܢܩܛܠܝܘܗܝ he thought to kill him, planned his murder; ܗܠܝܢ ܕܐܬܚܫܒ those things which he purposed. APHEL only parts. a) act. ܡܚܫܒ one who computes, ܡܚܫܒܝ ܚܘܫܒܢ ܟܘܟܒܐ astrologers. b) pass. reckoned, computed. DERIVATIVES, ܚܘܫܒܐ, ܚܘܫܒܢܐ, ܚܫܝܒܐ, ܚܫܝܒܘܬܐ, ܚܫܒܬܐ, ܚܫܘܒܐ, ܚܘܫܒܢܝܐ, ܚܫܘܒܬܐ, ܚܫܒܢܝܐ, ܚܫܒܢܘܬܐ, ܡܚܫܒܢܐ, ܡܚܫܒܬܐ, ܡܚܫܒܢܘܬܐ, ܡܚܫܒܬܢܝܐ, ܡܚܫܒܢܝܐ.

ܚܫܒܬܐ pl. ܚܫܒܬܐ rt. ܚܫܒ. f. a) thought, a thought; ܕܩܠܝܠܐ ܗܝ ܡܚܫܒܬܐ ܡܢ ܡܡܠܠܐ thought is easier than speech. b) a dirge, lamentation.

ܚܫ̈ gram. abbrev. for ܚܫܘܫܐ passive.

ܚܘܫܒܢܘܬܐ rt. ܚܫܒ. f. a) the mind, powers of thought, ܐܢܗܪ ܚܘܫܒܢܘܬܢ enlighten our mind. b) computation, arithmetic.

ܚܘܫܒܢܝܐ, ܚܘܫܒܢܝܬܐ rt. ܚܫܒ. thoughtful, having the faculty of thought or reflection; ܢܦܫܐ ܡܠܝܠܬܐ ܘܚܘܫܒܢܝܬܐ the soul endowed with reason and thought.

ܚܘܫܒܢܝܘܬܐ rt. ܚܫܒ. f. the faculty of thought, logical power.

ܚܫܘܟ, ܚܫܘܟܐ, ܚܫܘܟܬܐ rt. ܚܫܟ. a) adj. dark, darkened, dim, shady; in the dark, in darkness; turbid, foul of water; ܥܢܢܐ ܚܫܘܟܐ a dark cloud; ܩܠܝܬܐ ܚܫܘܟܬܐ a dark cell; ܥܝ̈ܢܘܗܝ ܚܫܘ̈ܟܬܐ his dim eyes; ܐܢܗܪ ܠܗܘܢ ܠܚܫܘܟܝܢ I will give light to those who are in darkness. b) subst. darkness, ܥܕ ܚܫܘܟ or ܟܕ ܚܫܘܟ while it was yet dark; ܡܫܪ̈ܝܬܐ ܕܚܫܘܟܐ the hosts of darkness.

ܚܫܘܟܘܬܐ rt. ܚܫܟ. f. darkness, obscurity; ܚܫܘܟܘܬܐ ܕܚܛܝܬܐ the darkness of sin.

ܚܫܘܟܢܐ, ܚܫܘܟܢܝܬܐ rt. ܚܫܟ. dark, obscure; ignorant, blind; ܥܒ̈ܕܐ ܚܫܘܟܢ̈ܐ works of darkness; ܛܪܛܪܘܣ ܚܫܘܟܢܝܬܐ shady Tartarus.

ܚܫܘܟܬܢܝܐ rt. ܚܫܟ. shady, dark.

ܚܫܘܟܬܢܘܬܐ rt. ܚܫܟ. f. obscurity of mind, ignorance.

ܚܫܘܠܐ pl. ܝ̈ܠܐ rt. ܚܫܠ. a worker in metal, goldsmith.

ܚܫܘܠܬܐ pl. ܬ̈ܐ rt. ܚܫܠ. m. same as ܚܫܘܠܐ.

ܚܫܘܫܐ, ܚܫܘܫܬܐ pl. m. ܫ̈ܐ, f. ܫ̈ܬܐ rt. ܚܫ. a) passible, capable of or liable to feeling or suffering; ܚܫܘܫܐ ܐܟܘܬܢ of like passions with us; ܠܐ ܚܫܘܫܐ impassible, not subject to passion; ܐܠܗܘܬܐ ܠܐ ܚܫܘܫܬܐ the Godhead not subject to passion; ܝܨܝܦܘܬܐ ܚܫܘܫܬܐ anxiety pertaining to the passions = temporal care. b) sympathetic, pitiful; ܐܝܟ ܐܣܝܐ ܚܟܝܡܐ ܘܚܫܘܫܐ as a wise and pitiful physician. c) gram. passive, in the accusative case opp. ܣܥܘܪܐ active, nominative; ܫܡܗܐ ܚܫܘܫܝܐ ܒܐܣܟܡܐ nouns of passive form.

ܚܫܘܫܐܝܬ rt. ܚܫ. adv. passively; with grief; gram. in the passive voice or sense, in the acc. case.

ܚܫܘܫܘܬܐ rt. ܚܫ. f. passibility, sensitiveness; with ܠܐ impassibility, indifference; ܠܐ ܚܫܘܫܘܬܐ ܥܠܡܢܝܬܐ freedom from temporal affections; gram. the passive voice, the government of a verb or noun.

ܚܫܚ to be fit, suitable, useful usually act. part. ܚܫܚ, ܚܫܚܐ, ܚܫܚܬܐ. a) verbal use, impers. it is suitable, useful, needed, ܚܫܚܐ ܠܡܫܠܡܘܬܗ the lost sheep was wanted to complete the tale of them. b) adj. *useful, serviceable, profitable, suitable, convenient, in ordinary use, common;* ܝܬܝܪ ܡܢ ܚܫܚ *most useful;* ܠܐ ܚܫܚܐ *useless;* ܡ̈ܠܐ ܠܐ ܚܫܚܬ̈ܐ *profitable sayings;* ܠܐ ܚܫܚܐ ܗܘܬ ܠܡܬܒܐ ܐܪܥܐ the land *was not suitable for a settlement;* pl. fem. emph. ܚܫ̈ܚܬܐ *necessaries;* gram. *common* words, ܟܬܒܐ ܕܚܫ̈ܚܬܐ *a vocabulary.* Ethpa. ܐܬܚܫܚ *to be used to, familiar with; to use, employ, do, deal, treat, behave* with ܒ; *to have to do with, hold intercourse, treat* with ܥܡ of the pers.; ܒܠܫܢܐ ܣܘܪܝܝܐ ܡܬܚܫܚ ܗܘܐ *he was familiar with the Syriac language;* ܡܬܚܫܚ ܐܢܐ ܒܩܛܝܪܐ *I use violence;* ܠܐ ܐܬܚܫܚܢ ܒܡ̈ܠܐ ܕܦܘܝܣܐ *we used no enticing words;* ܐܬܚܫܚ ܥܡ ܥܡܘܪ̈ܐ *he behaved mercifully towards the inhabitants;* ܠܐ ܓܝܪ ܡܬܚܫܚܝܢ ܝܗܘ̈ܕܝܐ ܥܡ ܫܡܪ̈ܝܐ *for the Jews have no dealings with the Samaritans.* Derivatives, ܚܫܚܐ, ܚܫܚܐܝܬ, ܚܫܚܘܬܐ, ܚܫܝܚܐ, ܚܫܚܬܐ.

ܚܫܚܐܝܬ rt. ܚܫܚ. adv. *usefully, fitly.*

ܚܫܚܘܬ, ܚܫܚܘܬܐ also ܚܫܝܚܘܬ, ܚܫܝܚܘܬܐ rt. ܚܫܚ. f. *usefulness, utility, advantage;* ܕܠܐ ܚܫܚܘܬ or ܕܠܝܬ ܒܗ ܚܫܚܘܬ *useless, of no use, no good.*

ܚܫܝܚܐ, ܚܫܝܚܬܐ rt. ܚܫܚ. *useful;* gram. *used for the sake of elegance,* opp. ܐܠܨܝܐ *necessary* to the sense.

ܚܫܚܬܐ pl. ܚܫ̈ܚܬܐ rt. ܚܫܚ. f. a) *use, utility; that which is necessary for use, needed* esp. *necessaries of life;* ܠܚܫܚܬܐ ܘܠܨܒܬܐ *for use and for ornament;* ܚܫ̈ܚܬܐ ܕܡܐܟܘܠܬܐ *things necessary for food;* ܡܠܚܐ ܕܚܫܚܬܐ *ordinary salt;* ܚܫ̈ܚܬܐ ܕܡܣ̈ܟܢܐ *those things of which the poor have need;* ܚܫܚܬܗ ܕܦܓܪܐ *that of which the body has need;* ܡܠܝܘ ܚܫܚܬܗܘܢ *they supplied their necessity, their needs;* ܚܫܚܬܐ ܕܬܫܡܫܬܐ ܕܕܝܪܝܘܬܐ *the menial work of the monastic life;* ܠܝܬ ܠܢ ܡܕܡ ܕܢܡܠܐ ܒܗ ܚܫܚܬܐ ܕܚܦܪܐ *we have nothing to use for digging* (lit. *that we may fulfil with it the use of digging*). b) legal, ܚܫܚܬܐ ܕܡܘܗܒܬܐ *usufruct.* c) gram. *use, dialect, phrase,* ܚܫ̈ܚܬܐ ܣܘܪ̈ܝܝܬܐ *Syriac phrases, Syriacisms;* ܚܫܚܬܐ ܐܘܪܗܝܬܐ *the Edessene use, Edessene dialect.*

ܚܫܘܟܐ *obscure;* see ܚܫܟ.

ܚܫܝܫܐܝܬ rt. ܚܫ. adv. *sadly, mournfully; with contrition, sorrow of heart.*

ܚܫܝܫܘܬܐ rt. ܚܫ. f. *sadness, sorrow,* with ܥܠ of the cause, ܚܫܝܫܘܬܐ ܕܥܠ ܚܛܗ̈ܐ *sorrow for sin.*

ܚܫܝܫܬܐ rt. ܚܫ. *of passible nature, subject to passion.*

ܚܫܟ fut. ܢܚܫܘܟ, act. part. ܚܫܟ, ܚܫܟܐ, pass. part. ܚܫܝܟ, ܟܐ, ܟܬܐ; part. adj. ܚܫܘܟ, ܟܐ, ܟܬܐ. *to grow dark* towards evening, *to be darkened, eclipsed, obscured, dimmed;* ܫܡܫܐ ܚܫܟ ܡܢ ܣܗܪܐ *the sun is eclipsed by the moon;* ܥܝ̈ܢܝܗܘܢ ܚܫ̈ܟܢ ܡܢ ܒܟܝܐ *their eyes are dim from weeping;* ܥܝܢܐ ܚܫܘܟܬܐ *a darkened eye.* Part. adj. *obscure, under a cloud; in darkness, ignorant,* ܓܒܪܐ ܡܣܟܢܐ ܚܫܘܟܐ *a poor and obscure man.* Pael ܚܫܟ *to darken;* ܚܫܟܘ ܐܐܪ *they darkened the air; to do anything at eventide* opp. ܩܕܡ *to do anything early;* ܡܩܕܡ ܘܡܚܫܟ coming *early and late, at morn and at even.* Ethpa. ܐܬܚܫܟ *to be obscured, made dim* or *weak* of apprehension; ܐܬܚܫܟ ܠܒܗܘܢ *their heart was dull.* Aph. ܐܚܫܟ *to turn* the day *to night, darken;* metaph. with ܐܦ̈ܐ *to sadden;* with ܠܒܐ *to darken the heart = obscure the mind.* Ettaph. ܐܬܬܚܫܟ *to be obscured, darkened* as the sun in an eclipse. Derivatives, ܚܫܘܟܐܝܬ, ܚܫܘܟܘܬܐ, ܚܫܘܟܝܐ, ܚܫܘܟܐ, ܚܫܟܐ, ܚܫܟܢܐ, ܚܫܟܢܝܐ, ܡܚܫܟܢܐ, ܡܚܫܟܢܘܬܐ.

ܚܫܟܐ pl. ܐ̈ rt. ܚܫܟ. m. *darkness, an eclipse;* ܚܫ̈ܟܐ ܕܣܗܪܐ *lunar eclipses;* metaph. *darkness* or *dullness* of mind.

ܚܫܟܢܐ pl. ܐ̈ rt. ܚܫܟ. m. *a dark night, moonless night;* pl. *vertigo.*

ܚܫܟܢܝܐ, ܢܝܬܐ rt. ܚܫܟ. *dark.*

ܚܫܠ fut. ܢܚܫܘܠ, act. part. ܚܫܠ, ܚܫܠܐ, pass. part. ܚܫܝܠ, ܠܐ, ܠܬܐ. *to found, cast* or *forge;* e.g. ܕܗܒܐ *gold;* ܩܠܝܕܐ *a key;* ܙܝܢܐ *armour.* Metaph. *to frame* or *devise; to cause, contrive, plot;* with ܒܝܫܬܐ *to devise evil* with ܥܠ of the pers.; with ܢܟܠܐ *to intrigue, conspire;* ܠܒܗ ܚܫܠ ܥܘܠܐ *his heart worketh iniquity;* ܟܘܬܝܢܐ ܕܝܘܣܦ ܚܫܠܬ ܠܗ ܚܣܡܐ *Joseph's coat caused him to be envied;* with ܡܘܓܠܐ *to form pus.* Ethpe. ܐܬܚܫܠ *to be founded, cast, forged, fabricated;* metaph. *to invent, contrive;* with ܢܟܠܐ *to be resolved . . .* Pa. ܚܫܠ *to frame, make out of metal.* Derivatives, ܚܫܘܠܐ, ܚܫܘܠܬܐ, ܚܫܠܐ, ܚܫܠܬܐ, ܚܫܠܬܐ.

ܚܫܠܐ rt. ܚܫܠ. m. *a goldsmith.*

ܚܫܠܐ m. *a decoction of wheat and barley, barley-water.*

ܚܫܠܘܬܐ rt. ܚܫܠ. m. *working in gold, the goldsmith's art.*

ܚܫܠܬܐ pl. ܬܐ rt. ܚܫܠ. f. *a) any graven work, a graven image, an ornament* of metal work, generally of gold; ܚܫܠܬܐ ܕܡܢ ܐܘܦܝܪ *graven work of Ophir;* ܚܫܠܬܐ ܘܡܐܢܐ ܕܣܐܡܐ *ornaments and vessels of silver;* ܥܙܩܬܐ ܕܚܫܠܬܐ ܕܕܗܒܐ *rings of gold work. b) the casting* or *graving of metal.*

ܚܫܡ Aphel. ܐܚܫܡ *to sup, dine, take food; to eat, use as food.* Derivative, the following word—

ܚܫܡܝܬܐ or ܐܚܫܡܝܬܐ pl. ܬܐ rt. ܚܫܡ. f. *supper.*

ܚܫܘܫܐ pl. ܐ rt. ܚܫ. *liable* or *subject to passions, carried away by passion.*

ܚܫܘܫܐܝܬ rt. ܚܫ. adv. *passibly, in a passible manner; mournfully, pathetically;* ܐܢ ܚܫܘܫܐܝܬ ܐܬܝܠܕ. ܐܢ ܕܝܢ ܠܥܠ ܡܢ ܚܫܐ *if Christ was born as a passible being* or *with human passions, but if He be above passion . . .*

ܚܫܘܫܢܐ rt. ܚܫ. adj. *pertaining to the passions* or *desires,* hence *subject* or *under the dominion of natural passions* or *desires; perverted, criminal,* ܡܠܟܐ ܚܫܘܫܢܝܐ *depraved counsel;* ܡܚܫܒܬܐ ܒܝܫܬܐ ܘܚܫܘܫܢܝܬܐ *evil and perverted thoughts.*

ܚܫܒܟ from ܚܫ and ܒܟ. adv. *according to; clearly, evidently.*

ܚܫܚܫܟ some plant, perhaps *Solomon's Seal.*

ܚܬ Pe. only pass. part.=adj. ܚܬܝܬ, ܚܬܝܬܐ, ܚܬܝܬܬܐ. *a) exact, accurate, approved, found correct* as ܕܝܬܩܐ *codices;* ܡܦܩܬܐ ܚܬܝܬܬܐ *a correct version. b) true, faithful, steadfast, sure, real; that which truly is* opp. apparent; ܡܣܩܘܠܐ ܚܬܝܬܐ *the right* or *true sense;* ܡܦܫܩܢܐ ܚܬܝܬܐ *faithful translators;* ܬܘܪܬܐ ܚܬܝܬܬܐ *the true faith;* ܗܪܛܝܩܐ ܚܬܝܬܐ *thorough heretics;* ܚܢܦܘܬܐ ܚܬܝܬܬܐ *pure heathenism;* ܗܝ ܕܚܬܝܬܐ ܕܝܢ ܗܝ *the truth is that . . .;* ܢܛܘܪܬܐ ܚܬܝܬܬܐ *a sure guard;* ܫܡܐ ܚܬܝܬܐ *the real* i. e. *the proper name.* Gram. *regular, proper;* ܫܡܐ ܚܬܝܬܐ *a proper noun;* ܢܩܒܬܐ ܚܬܝܬܬܐ *a regular feminine* i.e. formed *according to rule.* Pael ܚܬܬ *to settle definitely, exactly, to ratify, prove.* Ethpa. *to be ratified, confirmed.* Derivatives, ܚܬܝܬܐܝܬ, ܚܬܝܬܘܬܐ.

ܚܬܐ for ܐܚܬܐ fem. of ܐܚܐ, pl. ܐܚܘܬܐ. *a) a sister;* ܚܬܗ ܕܠܐ ܡܢ ܐܡܗ *his step-sister on the mother's side;* ܚܬܗ ܕܐܒܐ—ܚܬܗ ܕܐܡܐ *a paternal—maternal aunt. b) a relation, companion. c) a sister, nun;* ܕܝܪܐ ܕܐܚܘܬܐ *a convent, nunnery.*

ܚܬܠܐ or ܚܬܠܬܐ pl. irreg. ܚܬܠܝܢ, ܚܬܠܐ or ܚܬܠܬܐ f. *a sack, bag;* ܚܬܠܬܐ ܕܐܝܬ ܠܗ ܬܪܝܢ ܦܘܡܝܢ *a sack with two openings. b) a plank* esp. one resting on piles or pillars, hence *a plank bridge, wooden bridge.*

ܚܬܚܬ Palpel conj. *to excite, entice, allure, solicit;* ܒܡܠܬܐ ܡܚܬܚܬܢܝܬܐ ܓܘܚܟܐ *with laughter-provoking speech;* ܐܢ ܡܚܬܚܬ ܠܢ ܚܙܘܐ ܕܐܦܐ *if a fair face attract us;* ܠܒܘܫܐ ܕܡܚܬܚܬ ܠܥܝܢܐ *a garment enticing to the eyes.* Ethpalpal ܐܬܚܬܚܬ *to be enticed, allured.* Derivatives, ܚܬܚܬܐ, ܚܬܚܬܢܐ, ܡܚܬܚܬܢܐ.

ܚܬܝܪܘܬܐ rt. ܚܬܪ. f. *pride, pomp.*

ܚܬܝܬܐܝܬ rt. ܚܬ. adv. *accurately, exactly, diligently, truly;* gram. *regularly.*

ܚܬܝܬܘܬܐ rt. ܚܬ. f. *accuracy, exactness, sincerity, genuineness, essential quality, characteristic;* gram. *regularity;* ܚܬܝܬܘܬܐ ܣܘܦܐ ܘܡܫܡܠܝܐ *the extreme of accuracy, the greatest possible exactness;* ܒܚܢ ܗܘܐ ܠܗܘܢ ܠܘܬ ܚܬܝܬܘܬܐ ܕܠܒܗܘܢ *he proved the sincerity of their heart;* ܒܚܬܝܬܘܬܐ *carefully, diligently, truly, exactly.*

ܚܬܡ fut. ܢܚܬܘܡ, imper. ܚܬܘܡ, act. part. ܚܬܡ, ܚܬܡܐ, pass. part. ܚܬܝܡ, ܐ, ܬܐ. *a) to seal, set a seal* upon; *to attest, confirm, sign, ratify, determine;* ܚܬܘܡ ܒܥܙܩܬܐ ܕܡܠܟܐ *seal with the king's seal;* ܠܐ ܬܚܬܘܡ ܠܡܠܐ ܕܢܒܝܘܬܐ ܕܟܬܒܐ ܗܢܐ *seal not the sayings of the prophecy of this book;* ܚܬܡܬ ܝܘܢܐܝܬ *I signed in Greek letters;* ܚܬܘܡ ܒܥܒܕܐ ܗܝ ܕܐܡܪܬ *confirm by action that which thou hast said. b)* with ܨܠܝܒܐ expressed or understood *to make the sign of the Cross, to sign with the Cross;* ܚܬܡ ܢܦܫܗ ܒܨܠܝܒܐ *he crossed himself;*

ܚܬܡ ܒܨܠܝܒܐ ܥܠ ܟܠܗ ܥܕܬܐ *he made the sign of the Cross over the whole congregation;* then, because the sign of the Cross was made over the congregation at the concluding prayer or benediction (cf. ܚܘܬܡܐ), *to finish, conclude,* ܚܬܡܘ ܨܠܘܬܗܘܢ *they finished* their *prayer;* ܚܬܡܬ ܫܪܒܐ ܒܬܪܝܢ ܡܐܡܪܝܢ *I have brought* my history *to a conclusion in two discourses;* ܚܬܡ ܒܢܝܡܝܢ ܠܒܢܝ ܝܥܩܘܒ Benjamin *was the last-born of the sons of Jacob. c) to close, seal, stop up; to close* a wound; ܚܬܡܗ ܒܐܒܪܐ *he sealed* the vessel *with lead;* ܚܬܡܘ ܬܪܥܐ ܒܟܐܦܐ *they stopped the gate with stones;* ܚܬܡܬ ܐܪܥܐ ܠܥܠ ܡܢܗ *the earth closed above him;* ܫܘܚܢܐ ܕܥܣܩܝܢ ܠܡܬܚܬܡ *sores which are difficult to close, slow to heal up;* ܥܦܥܦܐ ܚܬܝܡܝܢ ܒܐܒܪܐ *eyelids sealed with lead = heavy with sleep;* ܚܬܝܡܝܢ ܒܐܠܦ each phrase *ends in Alep.* Ethpe. ܐܬܚܬܡ *to be sealed, signed; closed;* ܠܐ ܐܬܚܬܡܘ ܡܥܡܕܐ the baptized *were not signed with chrism.* Pa. ܚܬܡ *a) to seal, sign, subscribe;* metaph. *to prove, certify;* ܨܒܘܬܐ ܐܚܪܢܝܬܐ ܕܡܘܕܥܢܘܬܗ ܚܬܡܘ other events besides *have proved the foreknowledge of our Saviour. b) to sign* with the Cross. *c) to bring to an end, finish, conclude* esp. divine service; *to read through to the end* e.g. the Psalter; ܨܠܝܒܐ ܡܫܪܐ ܟܠ ܘܡܚܬܡ ܟܠ *the Cross begins and finishes everything,* i.e. every rite is commenced and concluded with the sign of the Cross. Ethpa. ܐܬܚܬܡ *a) to be consummated, accomplished; to be read to the end;* ܡܙܡܘܪܐ ܚܕܐ ܙܒܢܐ ܒܫܒܬܐ ܡܬܚܬܡܝܢ the Psalms *are read through once in each week. b) to be printed.* Derivatives, ܚܘܬܡܐ, ܚܬܡܐ, ܚܬܡܐ, ܡܚܬܡܢܐ, ܡܚܬܡܢܘܬܐ.

ܚܬܡܐ pl. ܐ̈ rt. ܚܬܡ. m. *a seal, signet-ring; a seal, token* or *sign; the healing over* or *cicatrix* of a wound; ܡܣܗܕܝܢ ܒܗ ܚܬܡܐ *they witness it with their seal, they seal it;* ܚܬܡܐ ܕܡܥܡܘܕܝܬܐ *the seal of baptism;* ܩܒܠܘ ܚܬܡܐ ܕܚܝܐ *receive the sign of life.*

ܚܬܡܐ pl. ܐ̈ rt. ܚܬܡ. m. often used indifferently with the preceding ܚܬܡܐ. m. properly *sealing, signing, making the sign of the Cross, obsignation,* ܚܬܡܐ ܕܡܥܡܘܕܝܬܐ *the sealing* or *signing of baptism.*

ܚܬܢ Ethpa. ܐܬܚܬܢ denom. verb from ܚܬܢܐ. *to connect with oneself by marriage, to marry; to take in marriage, be married; to intermarry;* metaph. *to be united;* ܠܡܬܚܬܢܘ ܠܒܪܬ ܡܠܟܐ *to marry the king's daughter;* ܐܬܬ ܟܠܬܐ ܠܡܬܚܬܢܘ *the bride came to be married;* ܡܬܚܬܢܐ ܢܦܫܗ at the resurrection *to each body its soul is united.*

ܚܬܢܐ pl. ܐ̈ m. *a connection by marriage,* esp. *a son-in-law, a brother-in-law, a bridegroom;* ܚܬܢܗ ܕܡܠܟܐ *his daughter's husband;* ܚܬܢܗ ܕܚܬܢܗ *his brother-in-law;* ܚܬܢܐ ܗܘܐ ܕܒܝܬ ܐܚܐܒ *he was a connection of the house of Ahab.* Derivatives, verb ܐܬܚܬܢ, ܚܬܢܘܬܐ, ܡܚܬܢܐ.

ܚܬܢܘܬܐ from ܚܬܢܐ. f. *espousals, nuptials;* ܠܒܘܫܐ ܕܚܬܢܘܬܐ *a nuptial garment, wedding raiment.*

ܚܬܦ Pael. ܚܬܦ *to break, break down;* ܕܡܚܬܦ ܐܪ̈ܙܐ *which breaketh the cedars.*

ܚܬܪ root-meaning *to shake, vibrate; to be tremulous with pride.* Pe. only part. ܚܬܝܪܐ, ܚܬܝܪܬܐ *swollen with pride, puffed up with pride, haughty, proud;* ܚܬܝܪ ܐܢܬ = ܡܫܬܒܗܪ *thou dost glory, boast;* ܪܚܡ ܫܘܡܐ ܛܒܐ ܘܚܬܝܪ ܒܗ *loving fair fame and glorying in it;* ܐܬܚܬܪܬܘܢ ܚܬܝܪܝܢ ܐܢܬܘܢ *ye are puffed up.* Ethpe. ܐܬܚܬܪ and Ethpa. ܐܬܚܬܪ *to step proudly* or *haughtily, to swagger, be puffed up.* Aphel ܐܚܬܪ *to puff up, make proud.* Derivatives, ܚܘܬܪܐ, ܚܬܝܪܘܬܐ, ܡܚܬܪܢܐ, ܡܬܚܬܪܢܐ.

ܚܬܬܐ; see ܚܬܐ.

∴ ܫܠܡܬ ܐܝܟ ܡܚܝܠܐ ܒܚܝܠܐ ܕܫܠܡܬܐ ∴

∴ ܫܘܠܡܐ ܛܒܐ ܗܘ ܠܝ ܛܘܒܝܟ ܒܛܘܒܢܐ ܕܡܪܝܐ ܗܘܐ ܕܛ̄ ∴

∴ ܛ ∴

ܛ ܛܐ

ܛ, ܛܝܬ *Teth*, the ninth letter of the alphabet; the number 9, with ܕ *the ninth*.

ܛܐܒ fut. ܢܛܐܒ, inf. ܡܛܐܒ, act. part. ܛܐܒ. impers. and intrans. *to be good* or *well* opp. ܒܐܫ *to be* or *do evil;* usually with ܠ; ܢܛܐܒ ܠܗܘܢ *it shall be well with them;* with ܩܕܡ or ܒܥܝܢܝ *to please, seem good;* with ܠܒܐ *to be cheerful, glad, merry.* Aph. ܐܘܛܐܒ *a) to do good, deal well, treat well* generally with ܠ of the pers. *to* or *with;* ܦܩܕ ܠܒܢܘܗܝ ܕܢܘܛܐܒܘܢ ܠܟܪܣܛܝܢܐ ܘܠܐ ܢܥܠܒܘܢ *he charged his sons to deal well with the Christians and not to wrong them. b) to make* or *do better, to amend.* For Derivatives, see ܛܘܒ. For ܐܘܛܐܒ or ܐܛܝܒ, see also Aphel of ܛܒ.

ܛܐܒ, ܛܐܒܐ and ܛܒܐ pl. ܛܐܒܐ̈ and ܛܒܐ̈ rt. ܛܒ. m. *a) a message, news, tidings. b)* often pl. *rumour, fame, report;* ܛܐܒ ܡܐܬܝܬܗ *the news of his arrival;* ܠܡܘܕܥܘ ܛܐܒܗ ܠܡܠܟܐ *to announce him to the emperor;* ܡܐ ܛܐܒܟ—ܛܐܒܗ *what is the news of you—of him? how are you? how is he? what is said about him?*

ܛܐܒܠܝܘܢ or ܛܒܠܝܘܢ *cyclamen europaeum* or *leontica, leontopetalum.*

ܛܐܓܢܐ; see ܛܓܢܐ.

ܛܐܘܦܐ pl. ܐ̈; see ܛܘܦܐܘܬܐ *pollution.*

ܛܐܘܣ *τέως, at least, only, directly.*

ܛܛܪܐܦܘܠܘܢ *τετράπυλον, a building with four gates.*

ܛܐܟܣܘܣ *taxus, the yew-tree.*

ܛܐܠ, ܛܐܠܐ; see ܛܠ, ܛܠܐ. m. *dew;* metaph. ܛܠܐ ܕܪܚܡܐ *the dew of* God's *mercy;* ܛܠܐ ܕܐܣܝܘܬܐ *the dew of healing.*

ܛܐܠܝܢܘܣ, ܛܐܠܝܢܘܣ or ܛܠܠܝܢܐ *τελλίνη, a bivalve shell-fish.*

ܛܐܠܢܝܐ pl. ܐ̈ from ܛܠܐ. adj. *dewy, of dew.*

ܛܐܠܢܝܐ oftener ܛܠܢܝܐ rt. ܛܠܠ. *shady, shadowy, dim, unreal.*

ܛܐܡܐ, ܛܐܡܝܬܐ pl. f. ܛܐܡܝܬܐ̈, ܛܐܡܝܬܐ and other spellings, see ܛܡܐ. *impure, unclean.*

ܛܐܢܝܬܐ, ܛܐܢܝ m. *the body of a shirt.*

ܛܐܦܐ; see ܛܦܐ. *a thin plate* or *layer* of metal.

ܛܒ fut. ܢܛܒ, part. ܛܐܒ, ܛܒܐ, ܛܒܝܬܐ *to make inquiry, inform oneself, be informed;* part. adj. *renowned, illustrious, celebrated, famous; memorable, remarkable,* ܩܪܒܐ ܛܒܐ *the famous war;* ܛܒ̈ܐ ܕܚܢ̈ܦܐ *illustrious heathen.* Ethpe. ܐܬܛܒ *to be published, spread abroad.* Pa. ܛܒܒ *to publish* a report, *spread abroad* a rumour; pass. part. ܡܛܒܒ, ܡܛܒܒܐ *celebrated, notorious.* Ethpa. ܐܬܛܒܒ *to be published, spread abroad; to acquire fame, become* or *be renowned.* Aph. ܐܛܒ and ܐܛܝܒ *to bring news, report, tell, say; to make known, to spread a rumour* or *report.* Derivatives, ܛܐܒܐ or ܛܒܐ, ܛܒܒܘܬܐ.

ܛܒ, ܛܒܐ, ܛܒܬܐ pl. m. ܛܒܝܢ, ܛܒ̈ܐ, pl. f. ܛܒܢ, ܛܒ̈ܬܐ rt. ܛܘܒ. *a)* adj. *good* opp. ܒܝܫ *bad, evil, valuable, precious, worth* usually with a value specified; *cultivated* of a tree or plant, *excellent, honourable; kind, gracious, benevolent, beneficent, favourable;* ܛܒ ܡܢ *better than;* ܒܚܝ̈ܐ ܛܒ̈ܐ ܐܬܪܒܝܬ *I was brought up in good* or *easy circumstances;* ܟܐܦܐ ܛܒܬܐ *a precious stone;* ܡܫ̈ܚܐ ܛܒ̈ܐ *precious ointments;* ܕܛܒ ܡܐܐ *worth one hundred;* ܗܘ ܡܐ ܕܛܒ *the value, the worth;* ܙܝܬܐ ܛܒܬܐ *a good olive* opp. ܕܒܪܐ *wild;* ܪܘܚܐ ܛܒܬܐ *a fair wind;* ܛܒ̈ܐ ܕܡܕܝܢܬܐ *the chief men of the city, nobles;* used impers. ܛܒ ܠܟ or ܛܒ ܗܘ ܠܟ *it is good, useful* or *advantageous for you.* *b*) subst. *that which is good* or *desirable, excellence, virtue, goodness, kindness, benevolence, benefit, prosperity;* ܛܒܐ ܩܕܡܝܐ *the chief good;* with ܥܒܕ or ܣܥܪ *to act* or *treat kindly;* ܥܒܕ ܛܒܬܐ *a benefactor;* with ܦܪܥ *to return good, reward;* with ܐܘܕܝ *to be grateful, to thank;* with ܐܬܡܛܝܒ *to make good offers, promise advantages.* *c*) ܛܒ or ܛܒ݁ adv. *very, much, greatly, exceeding;* ܛܒ ܕܡܨܐ *as much as possible;* ܛܒ ܣܓܝܐܐ *very many;* ܛܒ ܪܒܐ *very great;* ܛܒ ܛܒ *very much, very greatly, exceedingly;* ܛܒ ܕܝܢ *though, although, however, nevertheless;* ܛܒ ܡܢ *above, over, more, more than, rather;* ܡܘܬܐ ܛܒ ܡܢ ܚܝܐ *death rather than life;* ܕܒܚܬܐ ܡܝܬܪܬܐ ܛܒ ܡܢ ܕܩܐܝܢ *a far better sacrifice than that of Cain.*

ܛܒܐ pl. ܛܒܐ oftener ܛܒܐ, ܛܒܘܬܐ rt. ܛܒ. m. *news, tidings, fame, rumour, report;* ܛܒܟ ܛܒܐ *thy fair fame.*

ܛܒܐܝܬ rt. ܛܒ. adv. *well, rightly, virtuously;* ܠܗ ܛܒܐܝܬ ܐܝܬ *it does well, it prospers;* ܠܐ ܛܒܐܝܬ ܐܝܬ ܠܗ *he is in the wrong.*

ܛܝܒ Pael conj. of ܛܒ.

ܛܝܒܘ, ܛܝܒܘܬܐ rt. ܛܒ. f. *goodness, kindness;* with ܥܒܕ and ܥܡ of the pers. *to act kindly* or *well towards* any one, *to be good, kind, gracious.*

ܛܒܘܠܪܐ m. *tabularius, the collector* or *registrar* of tribute.

ܛܒܚ fut. ܢܛܒܘܚ *to slay, strike;* ܣܦܣܪܐ ܛܒܚ ܒܝܫܬܐ *a sword which slays evil things.* Pa. ܛܒܚ *to strike down, batter, crush.* Ethpa. ܐܬܛܒܚ *to be crushed, battered.* Derivatives, the three following words and ܡܛܒܚܐ.

ܛܒܚܐ pl. ܐ̈ rt. ܛܒܚ. *a butcher, slaughterer; a cook.*

ܛܒܚܐ rt. ܛܒܚ. m. *the shambles* or *market;* ܒܝܬ ܛܒܚܐ *a kitchen.*

ܛܒܚܘܬܐ rt. ܛܒܚ. f. *slaughter, slaughtering.*

ܛܒܝܐ pl. ܛܒܝܢ, ܛܒܝܐ m. *a roe, deer;* ܛܒܝܬܐ or ܛܒܝܬܐ f. *a doe, a gazelle;* metaph. pr. n. *Dorcas, Tabitha.*

ܛܒܝܒܘܬܐ rt. ܛܒ. f. *renown, celebrity;* ܛܒܝܒܘܬ ܫܪܒܬܗ *the renown of his family, his renowned race.*

ܛܒܝܥ and ܛܒܝܥ, ܐ, ܬܐ; see ܛܒܥ.

ܛܒܝܥܘܬܐ rt. ܛܒܥ. f. *sunkenness, low state, a being sunk deep* or *immersed* in sleep, in thought, in sin, &c., ܚܘܒܐ ܕܥܠܡܐ ܪܘܚܢܝܐ ܢܥܝܪܢܝ ܡܢ ܛܒܝܥܘܬܝ ܒܨܦܬܐ ܕܥܠܡܐ *may the love of the spiritual world awaken me from my absorption* in the cares of this world; ܝܫܘܥ ܐܩܝܡ ܛܒܝܥܘܬܢ *Jesus has raised us out of our abasement.*

ܛܒܝܥܬܐ or ܛܒܝܥܬܐ fem. of ܛܒܝܥܐ.

ܛܒܠ act. part. ܛܒܠ ܛܒܠܐ denom. verb from ܛܒܠܐ. *to drum;* ܛܒܠܐ ܛܒܠܝܢ ܗܘܘ *the drums were drumming.*

ܛܒܠܐ pl. ܐ̈ m. *a drum, a tabor;* ܩܠ ܛܒܠܐ *the sound of the tabors;* metaph. *the drums* of the ear.

ܛܒܠܝܬܐ pl. ܬܐ f. *tabula.* *a*) *a tablet, plate;* ܛܒܠܝܬܐ ܕܠܓܘ ܓܠܘܣܩܡܐ *coffin-plates.* *b*) *the flat top* or *surface* of an altar, *an altar, a wooden portable altar* opp. ܡܕܒܚܐ *an altar* of stone. *c*) arith. *a table* or *column* of figures.

ܛܒܠܣܗܪܢܝ *crescent-shaped.*

ܛܒܠܪܐ, ܛܒܠܪܐ or ܛܒܠܪܐ, pl. ܛܒܠܪܐ or ܛܒܠܪܐ m. *tabellarius, a runner, letter-carrier, postman.*

ܛܒܥ fut. ܢܛܒܘܥ and ܢܛܒܥ, inf. ܡܛܒܥ, imper. ܛܒܘܥ, act. part. ܛܒܥ, ܛܒܥܐ, pass. parts. ܛܒܝܥ and ܛܒܝܥ, ܐ, ܬܐ: *a*) intr. *to sink, be sunk, immersed, swallowed up, set;* with ܒܡܝܐ *to be drowned;* ܒܫܢܬܐ *to be sunk in sleep, be in a deep slumber;* ܒܦܘܢܩܐ *to be given over to pleasures;* ܛܒܥ ܫܡܫܐ *the sun sank* or *set.* *b*) tr. *to imprint* a seal, *to mark, sign, seal;* ܒܥܙܩܬܐ *with a signet-ring;* ܛܒܥ ܕܝܬܝܩܐ ܗܕܐ *he signed this will.* *c*) *to imprint, stamp* money, *to coin;* ܛܒܥ ܗܘܐ ܙܘܙܐ ܒܫܡܗ *he issued money stamped with his name;* ܥܒܕ ܙܘܙܐ ܡܢ ܟܪܛܝܣܐ ܛܒܝܥܐ ܐܝܟ ܟܬܒܐ ܣܘܡܩܬܐ *he issued paper money printed in red;* pass. parts. both forms have the same meaning, ܛܒܝܥ is most used, ܛܒܝܥ ܒܫܢܬܐ or ܛܒܝܥ ܒܡܫܒܚܬܐ *sound asleep, in deep slumber;* ܪܓܠܘܗܝ ܛܒܝܥܢ ܗܘܝ ܒܟܒܠܐ *his feet were held fast with fetters;* ܐܢܐ ܕܒܨܦܬܐ ܛܒܝܥ ܗܘܝܬ ܥܠܡܐ *I was immersed in worldly cares;* ܛܒܝܥ ܒܛܒܥܐ ܫܒܥܐ *sealed with seven seals;* ܕܢܐ ܛܒܝܥܐ *a sealed-up jar;* ܛܒܝܥܝܢ ܒܚܕ ܡܘܡܐ *marked with the same spot;* ܣܐܡܐ ܛܒܝܥܐ *coined silver;* ܩܠܐ ܗܘ ܗܢܐ ܕܐܡܝܪ ܛܒܝܥܬܐ *it is that voice which wakens the sleepers* or *those immersed* in worldly cares. Ethpe. ܐܬܛܒܥ *a) to be plunged, immersed, drowned;* ܚܝܠܗ ܐܬܛܒܥ ܒܝܡܐ Pharaoh's *army was drowned in the sea;* ܐܬܛܒܥ ܣܦܝܢܬܐ *the ships sank;* with ܒܡܝܐ ܕܡܥܡܘܕܝܬܐ *to have been plunged in the waters of baptism;* ܢܬܛܒܥܘܢ ܒܫܠܗܒܝܬܐ *let them be plunged in the flames. b) to be sealed, signed;* metaph. *to be assured* or *confirmed* as with a seal; ܒܡܥܡܘܕܝܬܐ *to receive chrism. c) to be imprinted, engraved, coined, marked, impressed;* ܨܘܪܬܐ ܕܡܠܟܐ ܕܐܬܛܒܥܬ ܒܕܝܢܪܐ *the image of the king imprinted on the dinar;* ܐܬܛܒܥ ܒܗ ܒܛܠܝܘܬܗ ܕܢܦܠܘܚ ܠܡܠܟܐ *it was impressed on him in his youth that he was to serve the king.* Pa. ܛܒܥ *to plunge, dip, immerse, submerge, drown, sink;* metaph. *to submerge* in sin or trouble, *to swallow up, to imbue; to fix deep, to fasten;* ܒܝܡܐ ܕܚܛܗܐ ܗܐ ܡܛܒܥ ܐܢܐ *lo, I sink in a sea of sins;* ܚܘܐ ܛܒܥܬ ܠܐܕܡ *Eve plunged Adam* into trouble; ܟܐܦܐ ܕܒܢܝܢܐ ܡܛܒܥܢ ܒܐܒܪܐ *building stones strongly fixed with lead.* Ethpa. ܐܬܛܒܥ *to be sunk, submerged; to be imbued; to be sealed,* with ܒܡܥܡܘܕܝܬܐ *to receive chrism.* Derivatives, ܛܒܥܐ, ܛܒܥܘܬܐ, ܛܒܝܥܐ, ܡܛܒܥܢܐ.

ܛܒܥܐ pl. ܐ̈ rt. ܛܒܥ. m. *a) a seal, signet, the gem* of a signet, *the print* of a seal, *a sealing* or *being sealed, signature;* metaph. *the seal* or *sign* of baptism, of chrism, *bread signed* with the Cross in the Holy Eucharist or that prepared beforehand and marked with a Cross; ܛܒܥܐ ܣܝܡ ܚܕ ܥܠ ܚܕ *place the oblates above each other; seal* or *token,* ܛܒܥܐ ܕܡܛܪܬܐ ܕܒܬܘܠܘܬܗ *the tokens of her virginity being preserved intact. b) a stamp, mould, die, the impression* of a die; metaph. *character, style, authenticity;* ܕܢܬܟܬܒ ܫܡܗ ܥܠ ܛܒܥܐ ܕܙܘܙܐ ܘܕܝܢܪܐ *that his name should be inscribed on the dies of the zuzi and dinars;* ܛܒܥܐ ܡܫܦܝܐ *a polished style;* ܒܛܒܥܐ ܕܡܪܝ ܝܥܩܘܒ *in the metre or style of Saint James.*

ܛܓܢܐ, ܛܓܢܐ or ܛܓܢܐ m. *a frying-pan.*

ܛܓܢ denom. verb Pael conj. from ܛܓܢܐ. *to broil;* pass. part. ܡܛܓܢ, ܡܛܓܢܐ. Ethpa. ܐܬܛܓܢ *to be broiled;* metaph. *to be tormented;* ܒܨܦܬܐ ܡܬܛܓܢ ܐܢܐ *I am tormented with anxiety.*

ܛܓܢܐ, ܛܓܢܐ, ܛܓܢܐ or ܛܓܢܐ pl. ܢܐ̈ m. τήγανον, *a gridiron, an instrument of torture;* metaph. *pain, torture.*

ܛܓܪ Ethpe. ܐܬܛܓܪ *to do harm, deal hardly* with ܒ of the pers.; *to strive* or *brawl* with ܥܡ of the pers. Ethpa. ܐܬܛܓܪ the same; ܠܐ ܬܬܛܓܪܘܢ ܥܡ ܐܢܫ *do harm to none.* Derivative, ܛܓܪܐ.

ܛܗܡ denom. verb Pael conj. from ܛܘܗܡܐ. *to bring into relationship, make to be related;* ܡܨܥܝܐ ܗܘ ܡܫܝܚܐ ܕܢܛܗܡ ܠܬܪܝܗܘܢ Christ is a mediator *to bring* those of *both sides into relationship;* ܡܛܗܡܬܐ *a woman of good family.* Aph. ܐܛܗܡ the same; ܡܛܗܡܐ ܠܒܢܝ ܐܕܡ ܥܡ ܐܠܗܐ *she brings the sons of Adam into relationship with God.* Ethpa. ܐܬܛܗܡ *to be of kin, related, like* with ܒ; ܡܫܝܚܐ ܐܬܛܗܡ ܗܘܐ ܒܓܢܣܟ ܘܒܐܘܣܝܟ *Christ was of thy race and substance.*

ܛܗܪܐ pl. ܐ̈ m. *noon, midday;* ܛܗܪܐ ܕܩܝܛܐ *summer noonday heat;* ܐܪܣܛܘܢ ܕܛܗܪܐ *the midday meal,* Germ. *Mittagsessen.*

ܛܗܪܝܐ, ܛܗܪܝܐ pl. m. ܐ̈ f. ܝܬܐ̈ adj. *meridian, of noontide* or *noonday;* ܚܘܕܪܐ ܛܗܪܝܐ *the meridian circle;* ܚܘܡܐ ܛܗܪܝܐ *noontide heat;* f. pl. *noontide heat;* ܒܛܗܪܝܬܐ *at noon.*

ܛܗܪܐܝܬ from ܛܗܪܐ. adv. *at noontide; as at noon.*

ܛܘܐ pass. part. ܛܘܐ, ܛܘܝܐ *to be parched, broiled.* Pa. ܛܘܝ *to roast, broil, bake, scorch;* ܡܛܘܐ ܒܢܘܪܐ *roast with fire;* ܐܡܪܐ ܡܛܘܝܐ *roast lamb.* Derivatives, ܛܘܝܐ, ܡܛܘܝܢܘܬܐ.

ܛܘܒ root-meaning *to be good,* cf. cognate ܛܐܒ. Pa. ܛܝܒ pass. part. ܡܛܝܒ, ܡܛܝܒܐ *to get ready, make preparations, prepare, provide;* ܡܐ ܕܡܛܝܒ ܫܪܓܐ *when he dresses the lamps;* ܛܝܒܘ ܐܘܪܚܗ ܕܡܪܝܐ *prepare ye the way of the Lord;* ܛܝܒܘ ܦܨܚܐ *they made ready the Passover;* ܛܝܒ ܠܩܘܒܠܗ *he made preparations against him* i.e. *prepared to go to war;* pass. part. *prepared, ready, at hand, present;* ܡܛܝܒ ܗܘ ܠܡܩܛܠ ܟܠ ܚܕ ܡܛܝܒ *ready to kill;* ܟܠܝܘܡ ܡܛܝܒ *always ready;* ܗܘ ܕܡܛܝܒ ܗܘܐ ܠܟܘܢ *He who has been appointed for you;* ܐܝܠܝܢ ܕܡܛܝܒܝܢ ܗܘܘ *those who were present;*

ܡܛܝܒ̈ܐ *one of those present;* ܠܐ ܡܛܝܒ ܗܘܐ ܒܒܝܬܐ *he was not at home.* ETHPA. ܐܬܛܝܒ imper. W-Syr. ܐܬܛܝܒ *a)* pass. *to be prepared, made ready. b)* refl. *to prepare oneself, get or be ready; to be near at hand, be present, be found* with ܠܘܬ or ܥܡ of the pers., with ܒ of the place; ܟܕ ܐܬܛܝܒ ܥܡ ܣܘܩܪܛܝܣ *when he was with Socrates;* ܗܐ ܬܪܬܥܣܪܐ ܙܒܢܝܢ ܐܬܛܝܒ ܠܘܬܝ *lo, twelve times over has this been presented to me;* ܐܬܛܝܒ ܒܡܣܓܕܐ *he was in the mosque;* ܒܣܘܢܗܘܕܘܣ *he was present at the synod, attended the council;* ܟܕ ܠܐ ܡܬܛܝܒ ܗܘܐ ܒܙܒܢܐ ܗܘܐ *on some occasion when he was not present;* ܟܠ ܕܡܬܛܝܒ *whoever is within reach, every one who is there;* ܟܕ ܐܬܛܝܒ ܥܪܘܒܬܐ ܕܚܫܐ *on the eve of Good Friday;* ܡܬܛܝܒ ܩܪܒܐ *war is imminent;* but ܐܬܛܝܒ ܠܩܪܒܐ *to make ready for war.* DERIVATIVES, ܛܒ, ܛܒܐ, ܛܝܒܘܬܐ, ܛܘܒ, ܛܘܒܐ, ܛܘܒܢܐ, ܛܘܒܢܘܬܐ, ܛܝܒܘܬܐ, ܛܘܒܐ, ܛܘܒܬܢܘܬܐ, ܛܘܒܬܢܐ, ܡܛܝܒܘܬܐ, ܡܛܝܒܐܝܬ, ܡܛܝܒܐ, or ܡܬܛܝܒܢܐ.

ܛܘܒ, ܛܘܒܐ pl. ܛܘܒ̈ܝܢ, ܛܘܒ̈ܐ rt. ܛܘܒ. m. *good, good things, a) the fruits of the earth, choice produce. b) blessing, bliss, blessedness, beatitude,* with pron. suff. or with ܠ *to be blessed,* ܛܘܒܘܗܝ, ܛܘܒܝܗ, ܛܘܒܝܗܘܢ, ܛܘܒܝܗܝܢ *blessed is he, she, blessed are they, &c.,* ܛܘܒܝܟ *blessed art thou;* ܛܘܒܘܗܝ ܠܐܢܫܐ ܕ *blessed is he who;* ܛܘܒܐ ܣܓܝܐܐ *most blessed;* ܛܘܒܐ ܬܠܬ ܙܒܢܝܢ *thrice blessed;* ܫܘܐ ܠܛܘܒܐ *worthy of congratulation, felicitation, enviable;* with ܝܗܒ *to call blessed, to deem happy* or *blessed;* ܛܘܒܐ ܢܬܠܘܢ ܠܝ ܫܪܒܬܐ ܟܠܗܝܢ *all generations shall call me blessed;* ܛܘܒ̈ܐ *the Beatitudes* Matt. v. 3–12.

ܛܘܦܢܐ rt. ܛܦܢ. m. *the crusher, batterer.*

ܛܘܒܣ *a kind of red dye* or *pigment.*

ܛܘܒܣܝܐ adj. from the above, *coloured red.*

ܛܘܒܝܠܐܢܫ = ܛܘܒܘܗܝ ܠܐܢܫ *Blessed be he who,* the name of a Syrian chant.

ܛܘܒܢܐ, ܛܘܒܢܐ pl. m. ܐ̈ f. ܬܐ rt. ܛܘܒ. *blessed, the blessed* generally used as a title of honour of apostles, martyrs, prophets, patriarchs, bishops, monks, &c., ܐܝܟ ܕܐܡܪ ܛܘܒܢܐ ܦܘܠܘܣ *according to the saying of St. Paul;* ܛܘܒܢܝܬܐ ܡܪܝܡ *the Blessed* Virgin *Mary.* Cf. ܛܘܒܢܐ.

ܛܘܒܬܢܘܬܐ rt. ܛܘܒ. f. *beatitude;* ܚܪܬܐ ܕܛܘܒܬܢܘܬܐ *final bliss, the extremity of blessedness.*

ܛܘܒܥܐ pl. ܐ̈ rt. ܛܒܥ. m. *overwhelming, submersion,* ܛܘܒܥܐ *drowning;* ܫܢܬܐ ܝܩܝܪܬܐ *heavy slumber;* ܛܘܒܥܐ ܕܡܕܝܢܬܐ *the swallowing up* or *destruction of cities* by earthquakes; metaph. baptismal *immersion, absorption* in worldly affairs, *torpor;* ܕܢܬܬܥܝܪܘܢ ܡܢ ܛܘܒܥܐ ܕܡܡܚܠܢܘܬܐ *that they may be aroused from slothful negligence.*

ܛܘܒܬܢܐ, ܬܢܐ rarely ܬܢܐ pl. m. ܐ̈ f. ܬܐ rt. ܛܘܒ. adj. *blessed, blissful* used like ܛܘܒܢܐ; ܛܘܒܬܢܐ ܦܘܠܘܣ *blessed Paul;* ܛܘܒܬܢܐ ܩܕܝܫܐ ܕܝܘܕܘܪܘܣ *the most blessed saint Diodorus;* ܛܘܒܬܢܐ ܗܘ ܡܢ ܗܘ ܕܐܝܬ ܠܗ ܚܝ̈ܐ ܫܠܝ̈ܐ *happy is he who leads a quiet life* i. e. *the life of a hermit;* ܢܘܚܐ ܛܘܒܬܢܐ *blissful rest.*

ܛܘܒܬܢܘܬܐ rt. ܛܘܒ. f. *blessedness, beatitude,* used as a title of bishops and patriarchs, ܛܘܒܬܢܘܬܟܘܢ ܡܝܩܪܬܐ ܡܢ ܠܘܬܟܘܢ *your venerable Beatitude.*

ܛܘܓܐ f. *toga;* ܛܘܓܐ ܙܚܘܪܝܬܐ *a scarlet toga.*

ܛܘܓܢܐ m. *an iron chair* in which martyrs were scorched; see ܛܓܢܐ.

ܛܘܓܪܐ rt. ܛܓܪ. m. *rebuke, reproach, brawling; prejudice;* ܫܡܥܘ ܛܘܓܪ̈ܐ ܐܠܗܝ̈ܐ *hearken unto godly rebukes;* ܐܢ ܐܢܫ ܢܩܪܐ ܟܠܗ ܐܘܢܓܠܝܘܢ ܕܠܐ ܛܘܓܪܐ *if any one will read the whole Gospel without prejudice.*

ܛܘܗܡܐ pl. ܐ̈ m. *race, stock, family, lineage, descent, origin;* ܒܢܝ ܛܘܗܡܐ or ellipt. *kindred, kinsmen;* ܒܪ ܛܘܗܡܐ ܪܒܐ or ܡܥܠܝ ܛܘܗܡܐ *of noble birth;* ܪܡܘܬ ܛܘܗܡܐ *high* or *noble birth, nobility;* ܛܘܗܡ̈ܐ ܕܐܪܥܐ *the races of the earth* i.e. *all nations;* ܬܠܬܐ ܛܘܗܡ̈ܐ ܕܦܪ̈ܚܬܐ *three kinds of birds;* ܛܘܗܡܗ ܕܢܦܫܐ *the origin of the soul.* DERIVATIVES, ܛܗܡ, ܡܛܗܡܢܐ.

ܛܘܗܐ pl. ܐ̈ m. *a moment, an interval* of time, slightly longer than ܪܦܦܐ.

ܛܘܘܓܐ rt. ܛܘܓ. m. *disturbance* esp. *the surging* of the billows, *a tempest.*

ܛܘܠܒ ETHPA. ܐܬܛܘܠܒ *to make supplication.* DERIVATIVE, ܛܘܠܒܐ.

ܛܘܠܒܐ rt. ܛܘܠܒ. m. *supplication.*

ܛܘܗܠܬܐ pl. ܬ̈ܐ f. *a small bunch* or *cluster* of grapes, ܛܘܗܠܬܐ ܕܒܘܪܟܬܐ *a cluster of blessing.*

ܛܘܝܐ rt. ܛܘܐ. m. *roasting,* ܐܟܠ ܒܛܘܝܐ *to eat roast meat;* ܒܛܘܝܐ ܐܟܠܝܢܢܝ *you will eat me roast.*

ܛܘܝܒ, ܛܘܝܒܐ rt. ܛܝܒ. m. *preparation, readiness;* ܛܘܝܒ ܪܥܝܢܐ *promptitude;* with ܥܒܕ *to make preparations, prepare.*

ܛܘܟܢ, ܛܘܟܢܐ pl. ܐ̈ from ܛܟܢ. m. *a device, machination, trick, guile;* ܠܐ ܛܘܟܢܐ ܬܥܒܕ *thou shalt use no guile;* ܕܠܐ ܛܘܟܢ *straight-forwardly.*

ܛܘܟܣ, ܛܘܟܣܐ pl. ܐ̈ from ܛܟܣ. m. *a*) *ordering, arrangement, organization; regulation, instruction;* ܛܘܟܣܐ ܡܠܝܠܐ *rational arrangement;* ܛܘܟܣ ܛܠܝܐ *the training of the novices;* ܛܘܟܣ ܬܫܡܫܬܐ *the regulation* or *ordering of church services. b*) *ordinance, rule, precept;* ܛܘܟܣܐ ܥܕܬܢܝܐ *ecclesiastical rules* or *constitutions;* ܛܘܟܣܐ ܩܢܘܢܝܐ *the order* of divine service *as prescribed by the canons. c*) *a composition, tract. d*) *assisting at the Takhsa* or *liturgy, communicating.*

ܛܘܠ root-meaning *to be long.* Pa. ܛܘܠ *to walk to and fro, pace up and down* for pleasure.

ܛܘܠܝܐ m. from ܛܠܝ. *rejuvenescence.*

ܛܘܠܝܒ, ܛܘܠܝܒܐ rt. ܛܠܒ. *eminent, excellent, superior, able, distinguished* usually with ܒ; ܐܘܡܢܐ ܛܘܠܝܒܝܢ ܒܐܘܡܢܘܬܐ *able artificers;* ܣܦܪܐ ܛܘܠܝܒܐ *a distinguished writer.*

ܛܘܠܝܒܘܬܐ rt. ܛܠܒ. f. *eminence, excellence;* ܛܘܠܝܒܘܬܐ ܕܪܒܐ *great ability.*

ܛܘܠܡܐ Ar. m. *soft squashy bread, doughy bread.*

ܛܘܠܫܐ rt. ܛܠܫ. m. *heavy sleep; a soporific.*

ܛܘܠܒܐ pl. ܐ̈ m. *a troop, band, camp;* ܫܩܠܘ ܛܘܠܒܐ *they moved camp;* ܛܘܠܒܐ ܕܫܐܕܐ *a troop of demons.*

ܛܘܠܩܐ rt. ܛܠܩ. m. *end, passing away, destruction, annihilation; scattering, dissipation;* ܛܘܠܩܗ ܕܣܗܪܐ *the waning of the moon;* ܛܘܠܩܗ ܕܢܟܣܐ *the dissipation of riches;* ܛܘܠܩܐ ܕܚܝܐ *the ending of life* = *death;* ܗܘܐ ܛܘܠܩܗ ܒܫܝܘܠ Dives *ended in Sheol.*

ܛܘܠܓܢܐ m. *an iron ladle* or *frying-pan.*

ܛܘܠܫܐ pl. ܐ̈ rt. ܛܠܫ. m. *a spot, stain, defilement;* ܕܠܐ ܛܘܠܫܐ *unspotted, stainless, undefiled;* ܛܘܠܫܐ ܐܝܟ ܚܘܪܐ *some sort of white spots.*

ܛܘܠܫܐ rt. ܛܠܫ. m. *the plastering* of a house.

ܛܘܠܫܢܝܐ, ܛܘܠܫܢܝܬܐ rt. ܛܠܫ. adj. *impure, polluted.*

ܛܘܠܫܬܐ rt. ܛܠܫ. f. *pollution, defilement.*

ܛܘܡܐܐ pl. ܛܘܡܐܐ̈ or ܛܘܡܐܐ pl. ܛܘܡܐܐ̈ rt. ܛܡܐ. m. *pollution, defilement.*

ܛܘܡܣܐ pl. ܛܘܡܣܐ̈ and ܛܘܡܣܘܣ m. τόμος, *a tome, volume, document, epistle;* ܛܘܡܣܐ ܣܘܢܗܕܝܩܐ *a synodical letter;* ܛܘܡܣܐ ܕܠܐܘܢ *the tome* or *Letter of* Pope *Leo* to Flavian on Eutychianism.

ܛܘܢܒܐ pl. ܐ̈ Ar. m. *a rope, cord* esp. *a tent-cord;* metaph. ܛܘܢܒܘܗܝ ܕܥܠܡܐ ܗܢܐ *the cords which hold fast this world.*

ܛܘܢܘܣ pl. ܛܘܢܘܣ̈, ܛܘܢܘܣ or ܛܘܢܘܣ m. τόνος, *a tone* in music; *a syllable;* ܒܫܒܥܐ ܛܘܢܘܣ *in heptasyllabic metre.*

ܛܘܢܦܐ rt. ܛܢܦ. m. *pollution, defilement;* ܛܘܢܦܐ ܕܕܡܐ *by blood.*

ܛܘܣ, ܛܣ fut. ܢܛܘܣ, act. part. ܛܐܣ, ܛܝܣܐ. *a*) *to fly on high, circle in the air* as a bird of prey; ܛܣ ܐܝܟ ܢܫܪܐ *he flew mightily as an eagle;* ܘܛܝܣܐ ܒܥܦܪܘܪܐ the ostrich *rouseth herself up to flight.* Metaph. ܛܣ ܚܢܢܐ *mercy flew swiftly;* ܛܐܣ ܪܥܝܢܐ ܥܠ ܙܒܢܐ ܘܥܕܢܐ *the mind circles round times and seasons,* i. e. is anxious as to coming events. *b*) *to float;* ܐܠܦܐ ܛܝܣܐ *the ship rode* on the waves.

ܛܘܣܐ pl. ܛܘܣܐ̈ m. ταῶς, *a peacock.*

ܛܘܥܝܝܢ rt. ܛܥܐ. f. *a*) *error, mistake, false worship;* ܒܛܘܥܝܝܢ *by mistake. b*) *forgetting, forgetfulness, oblivion;* ܫܬܩܐ ܘܛܘܥܝܝܢ *silence and oblivion;* with ܐܫܠܡ or ܝܗܒ and ܫܕܐ *to give over to oblivion. c*) *deception, deceitfulness,* ܕܥܘܬܪܐ *of riches;* ܒܛܘܥܝܝܢ *by guile.*

ܛܘܦ, ܛܦ fut. ܢܛܘܦ, inf. ܡܛܦ, act. part. ܛܐܦ, ܛܝܦܐ. *a*) *to float, swim* as anything lighter than water, said of oil, eggs, the ark; hence *to sail upon, set sail for;* ܠܡܛܦ ܒܡܫܟܝܢܐ ܥܠ ܡܫܡܫܢܘܗܝ ܕܡܕܝܢܬܐ *to sail courageously* on the billows; ܛܦܘ ܦܓܪܐ ܥܠ ܡܝܐ corpses floated on the waters; to go about, go round, ܛܦ ܥܠ ܫܕܪܢܝ ܕܐܛܘܦ ܐܪܥܐ send me away to go about the land. b) to rise, overflow as water, be inundated; ܛܦܘ ܡܝܐ ܠܥܠ ܡܢ ܪܫܝ the waters rose above my head; ܐܛܛܦܬ ܛܪܣܘܣ ܡܢ ܢܗܪܐ Tarsus was flooded by the river; ܪܘܚܐ ܛܐܦܬܐ an overwhelming wind. Aph. ܐܛܝܦ a) to make float; ܐܠܝܫܥ ܐܛܝܦ ܦܪܙܠܐ Elisha made iron float on the water. b) to make overflow, to overflow, overwhelm, deluge; ܕܠܐ ܢܛܝܦܘܢ ܡܝܐ ܠܐܪܥܐ lest the waters overflow the earth; metaph. ܐܛܝܦ ܠܟܠܗ ܡܬܥܡܪܢܝܬܐ ܒܡܠܦܢܘܬܗ he deluged the whole earth with his teaching. Derivatives, ܛܘܦܐ, ܛܘܦܢܐ, ܛܘܦܬܐ, ܛܝܦܐ, ܛܘܦܢܝܐ, ܡܛܛܦܢܐ.

ܛܘܦܐ or ܛܘܦܐ (for pl. ܛܘܦܐ see ܛܘܦܬܐ) rt. ܛܘܦ. f. a) sailing, course, a voyage; ܐܠܦܐ ܒܣܘܟܢܐ ܡܬܕܒܪܐ ܠܛܘܦܐ ܬܪܝܨܐ a ship is guided by the rudder to a straight course. b) a raft.

ܛܘܦܐܙܝܘܢ, ܛܘܦܐܕܝܘܢ or ܛܘܦܐܙܝܘܢ τοπάζιον, a topaz.

ܛܘܦܘܢܝܩܘܣ adj. τυφωνικός, tempestuous.

ܛܘܦܘܣ or ܛܘܦܘܣ m. τύπος, an edict, imperial rescript.

ܛܘܦܢܐ pl. ܐ̈ rt. ܛܘܦ. m. a flood, deluge, inundation; ܡܝܐ ܕܛܘܦܢܐ the waters of the flood; ܛܘܦܢܐ ܢܘܪܢܝܐ the fiery deluge which will overwhelm the later world as ܗܘ ܛܘܦܢܐ ܡܝܢܝܐ that watery deluge covered the earlier.

ܛܘܦܣܐ pl. ܛܘܦܣܐ̈, ܛܘܦܣܐ m. τύπος, a type, figure, likeness, model, mould, example; ܪܫܡ ܛܘܦܣܐ ܕܩܫܬܐ ܘܓܐܖܐ he drew the outline of a bow and arrow; ܛܘܦܣܐ ܐܢܘܢ ܕܐܝܟܢ ܢܐܙܠ ܒܬܪܗܘܢ they are an example which we should follow; ܒܛܘܦܣܐ ܕ in the likeness, in like manner, like, as; geomet. a figure; gram. a mood. Derivatives, the two following words, verb ܛܦܣ, and ܡܛܦܣܢܐ.

ܛܘܦܣܢܐܝܬ from ܛܘܦܣܐ. adv. typically, figuratively.

ܛܘܦܣܢܝܐ, ܛܘܦܣܢܝܬܐ pl. ܐ̈, ܐ̈ from ܛܘܦܣܐ. adj. typical, symbolic.

ܛܘܦܬܐ pl. ܛܘܦܐ rt. ܛܘܦ. f. a drop; ܛܘܦܐ ܡܛܪܐ or ܡܛܪܢܝܬܐ ܛܘܦܐ raindrops; ܛܘܦܬܐ ܕܚܠܒܐ a drop of milk; gram. Ribui points.

ܛܘܪ only found in act. part. ܛܐܪ, ܛܐܪܐ, pl. f. ܛܝܪ̈ܢ to fly. Aph. ܐܛܝܪ to make fly, let take flight; ܐܛܝܪ ܪܥܝܢܢ ܠܫܡܝܐ turn our regard heavenward. Derivative, ܛܝܪܐ.

ܛܘܪܐ pl. ܐ̈ Ar. from a middle Alep root meaning to go or turn round, m. a space of time or distance, a moment, interval; measure, size, quantity; ܒܛܘܪܐ in a moment, at that moment; ܛܘܪܐ ܪܒܐ or ܣܓܝܐܐ a long time, a great distance.

ܛܘܪ, ܛܘܪܐ pl. ܛܘܪ̈ܝܢ, ܛܘܪ̈ܐ m. a mountain; ܛܘܪܐ ܕܙܝܬ̈ܐ the Mount of Olives; ܛܘܪܐ ܕܠܒܢܢ Mount Lebanon.

ܛܘܪܓܠܐ pl. ܐ̈ m. a thistle.

ܛܘܪܓܡܐ m. the noise of wind in the belly; a like sound from the depth of the earth, a rumbling noise.

ܛܘܪܓܠܐ pl. ܐ̈ rt. ܛܪܓܠ. m. seething, ebullition, raging of the sea; metaph. of persecution.

ܛܘܪܝܐ, ܛܘܪܝܬܐ pl. m. ܐ̈, f. ܐ̈ from ܛܘܪܐ. mountainous, of the mountains; a mountaineer, an ascetic living in the mountains; ܛܘܪ̈ܝܐ ܘܡܕܒܪ̈ܝܐ hermits of mountains and deserts.

ܛܘܪܝܐ rt. ܛܪܐ. m. an assault, attack, shock.

ܛܘܪܝܟ com. gen. Pahlawi turek, a jackal.

ܛܘܪܢܐ; see ܛܘܪܢܐ.

ܛܘܪܢܘܣ m. τόρνος, a turner's chisel, a lathe chisel; ܡܢܪܬܐ ܓܠܝܦܐ ܒܛܘܪܢܘܣ a candlestick chased with a chisel.

ܛܘܪܦܐ pl. ܐ̈ rt. ܛܪܦ. m. a) tossing to and fro of the billows; weariness, exhaustion, wretchedness, ill-treatment; ܛܘܪܦܐ ܕܟܦܢܐ—ܕܨܗܝܐ exhaustion from hunger, from thirst; ܛܘܪܦܐ ܕܐܘܪܚܐ weariness from the journey. b) vexation, agitation, anxiety, trouble, ܛܘܪܦܐ ܕܠܒܐ anxiety of heart; ܛܘܪܦܐ ܕܪܘܚܐ or ܕܢܦܫܐ vexation of spirit. c) the stripping or shaking off of leaves.

ܛܘܪܩܝܐ or ܛܘܪܟܝܐ pl. ܛܘܪܩܝ̈ܐ rarely ܛܘܪܩܝܢ and ܛܘܪܟܝܢ m. a Turk.

ܛܘܪܫܐ rt. ܛܪܫ. m. food which was forbidden during a fast e.g. flesh, eggs, and milk food.

ܛܳܫ, ܛܫ fut. ܢܶܛܘܽܫ, imper. ܛܘܽܫ, act. part. ܛܳܐܶܫ, ܛܳܝܫܳܐ, pass. part. ܛܝܼܫ, ܛܝܼܫܳܐ. *to besmear, rub on, daub, anoint;* ܣܰܡܳܐ ܡܰܘܬܳܐ ܥܰܠ ܓܶܐܪܰܝܗܽܘܢ ܛܳܝܫܺܝܢ *they besmear their arrows with poison;* metaph. *to fasten upon, ascribe;* ܛܳܫ ܒܗܽܘܢ ܫܡܳܐ ܗܳܢܳܐ *he nicknamed them;* ܛܳܫ ܥܒܳܕܰܘܗ̱ܝ ܥܰܠ ܡܳܪܝ ܝܰܥܩܽܘܒ *he palmed off his compositions as being those of Mar James.* Ethpe. ܐܶܬ݂ܛܝܼܫ *to be besmeared, anointed;* ܬܶܬ݂ܛܝܼܫ ܥܰܠ ܡܰܪܽܘܛܳܐ ܡܰܠܘܳܫܬܳܐ *let the salve be spread on a rag;* metaph. *to be falsely ascribed to.* Pa. ܛܰܘܶܫ *to defile, pollute, profane;* ܡܛܰܘܫܳܐ ܒܕܡܳܐ *blood-stained, guilty of slaughter;* ܐܺܝܕܰܝܳܐ ܡܛܰܘܫܳܬ݂ܳܐ *polluted hands.* Ethpa. ܐܶܬ݂ܛܰܘܰܫ *to be defiled, polluted;* ܠܳܐ ܐܶܬ݂ܛܰܘܫܰܬ݂ ܡܕܺܝܢܬܳܐ ܡܶܢ ܥܳܠܰܡ ܒܗܰܝܡܳܢܽܘܬ݂ܳܐ ܛܽܘܥܝܳܝܬܳܐ *the city has never been profaned by a false faith.* Derivatives, ܛܽܘܫܳܝܳܐ, ܛܰܘܫܳܐ, ܬܰܛܘܺܝܫܳܐ.

ܛܽܘܫܳܝܳܐ, ܛܽܘܫܳܝܬܳܐ or ܛܽܘܫܳܝܺܝܬ rt. ܛܫܐ. f. *lurking, lying in hiding;* ܐܶܢ ܢܶܛܫܶܐ ܓܰܒܪܳܐ ܒܛܽܘܫܳܝܳܬ݂ܳܐ *if any hide in secret places,* Jer. xxiii. 24; ܚܛܺܝܬ݂ܳܐ ܛܽܘܫܳܝܬܳܐ ܕܡܶܬ݂ܛܰܫܝܳܐ *secret sin, sin which lurks secretly;* ܒܛܽܘܫܳܝܳܐ or ܒܛܽܘܫܳܝܺܝܬ *secretly, in secret, in concealment.*

ܛܽܘܫܳܫܬܳܐ rt. ܛܘܫ. f. *pollution.*

ܛܰܘܳܐ *fasting,* used adverbially, ܒܳܬ݂ ܛܰܘܳܐ *he passed the night fasting.*

ܛܪܺܝܛܺܝܩܳܐ corrupted from τρίταιος. *a tertian fever* or *ague,* cf. ܛܪܺܝܛܰܝܩܳܐ.

ܛܚܺܝ pass. part. ܛܚܺܝܫ, ܛܚܺܝܫܳܐ, ܛܚܺܝܫܳܬ݂ܳܐ. *troubled, disturbed;* ܕܛܚܺܝܫ ܒܫܶܢܬܳܐ ܐܰܝܟ ܫܡܽܘܐܝܶܠ *disturbed in sleep as Samuel.* Ethpalpal ܐܶܬ݂ܛܰܚܛܰܚ *to be troubled, confused.* Derivative, ܛܽܘܚܛܳܚܳܐ.

ܛܚܳܢܳܐ=ܛܚܺܝܢܳܐ rt. ܛܚܢ. m. *grinding* e.g. of flour.

ܛܚܽܘܪܶܐ pl. ܐ̈ rt. ܛܚܪ. m. pl. *piles, hemorrhoids;* ܨܰܠܡܶܐ ܕܛܚܽܘܪܰܝܗܽܘܢ *models of their emerods,* 1 Sam. vi.

ܛܚܳܠܳܐ pl. ܐ̈ m. *the milt, spleen;* sometimes *the lungs, kidneys;* ܐܰܝܠܶܝܢ ܕܟ݂ܪܺܝܗܺܝܢ ܒܛܚܳܠܗܽܘܢ *sick of the spleen, suffering pain in the spleen.*

ܛܚܳܠܳܝܳܐ and ܛܚܳܠܳܢܳܝܳܐ pl. ܐ̈ adj. m. *splenetic, sick of the spleen.*

ܛܚܰܢ fut. ܢܶܛܚܽܘܢ, act. part. ܛܳܚܶܢ, ܛܳܚܢܳܐ, pass. part. ܛܚܺܝܢ, ܢܳܐ, ܢܳܬ݂ܳܐ. *to grind, pound, masticate;* ܣܰܒ ܪܚܝܳܐ ܘܛܚܽܘܢ ܩܶܡܚܳܐ *take the grindstone, grind meal;* ܫܶܡܫܽܘܢ ܛܳܚܶܢ ܪܚܝܳܐ *Samson grinds at the mill;* said of the ostrich grinding up nails in her stomach; metaph. ܗܳܠܶܝܢ ܕܛܳܚܢܺܝܢ ܠܟܬ݂ܳܒ݂ܶܐ ܩܰܕܺܝܫܶܐ *those who grind up,* i.e. *pervert, the word of Scripture.* Ethpe. ܐܶܬ݂ܛܚܶܢ *to be ground.* Pa. ܛܰܚܶܢ *to grind up, pound hard.* Derivatives, ܛܚܽܘܢܳܐ, ܛܚܳܢܳܐ, ܛܚܺܝܢܳܐ.

ܛܳܚܢܳܐ pl. ܐ̈ m. ܛܳܚܢܺܝܬ݂ܳܐ pl. ܬ݂ܳܐ̈ f. rt. ܛܚܢ. *a grinder, one who grinds;* ܩܳܠܳܐ ܕܛܳܚܢܳܝܳܬ݂ܳܐ *the sound of women at the mill;* ܟܟܶܐ ܛܳܚܢܳܝܳܬ݂ܳܐ *the molar teeth, the grinders.*

ܛܚܺܝܢܳܐ rt. ܛܚܢ. m. *grinding, mastication.*

ܛܚܰܪ fut. ܢܶܛܚܽܘܪ, part. ܛܳܚܶܪ, ܛܳܚܪܳܐ. *to suffer from constrained bowels.* Ethpe. ܐܶܬ݂ܛܚܶܪ and Pa. ܛܰܚܰܪ same as Pe. Derivatives, ܛܚܽܘܪܶܐ, ܛܰܚܪܳܐ.

ܛܰܚܪܳܐ rt. ܛܚܪ. m. *tenesmus, a straining at stool.*

ܛܛܰܪܰܐܘܳܢܽܘܣ; see ܛܰܛܪܰܐܘܳܢܽܘܣ *a bird.*

ܛܛܰܪܟܽܘܣ; see ܛܰܛܪܟܽܘܣ.

ܛܶܛܪܰܐ τέτταρα, *four;* ܛܶܛܪܰܐ ܐܶܘܰܢܓܶܠܝܳܘܢ, ܛܶܛܪܰܐܶܘܰܢܓܶܠܝܳܘܢ or ܛܶܛܪܰܐܘܰܢܓܶܠܝܳܘܢ τετραευαγγέλιον, *a codex containing the four Gospels.*

ܛܶܛܪܰܓܳܘܢܳܘܢ, ܛܶܛܪܰܓܽܘܢܳܘܢ or ܛܶܛܪܰܓܽܘܢܳܘܣ, m. τετράγωνον, *a quadrangle, four-sided rectangle.*

ܛܶܛܪܰܓܽܘܢܳܝܳܐ and ܛܶܛܪܰܓܳܘܢܳܝܬܳܐ the same; ܛܶܛܪܰܓܳܘܢܳܝܬܳܐ ܥܳܒܶܕ ܒܗܽܘܢ ܫܶܡܫܳܐ *the sun forms a rectangle with them.*

ܛܶܛܪܰܕܺܝܛܳܐ pl. ܐ̈ τετραδίτης, *a tetradite,* a heretic who believes in a quaternity of Persons instead of acknowledging the Holy Trinity.

ܛܶܛܪܰܛܺܐ τετάρτη, *the fourth Indict.*

ܛܶܛܪܰܦܽܘܠܺܝܣ; see ܛܶܛܪܰܦܽܘܠܺܝܣ.

ܛܶܛܪܰܪܟܳܐ or ܛܶܛܪܰܪܟܺܝܣ pl. ܛܶܛܪܰܪܟܶܐ or ܛܶܛܪܰܪܟܺܘܣ τετράρχης = Syr. ܪܺܝܫܳܐ ܕܪܽܘܒܥܳܐ m. *a tetrarch, governor of the fourth part of a country, a petty prince.*

ܛܶܛܪܰܪܟܽܘܬ݂ܳܐ f. *a tetrarchy, a principality* being the fourth part of a realm.

ܛܰܝܳܐܺܝܬ for ܛܰܝܳܝܳܐܺܝܬ adv. *in the Arabic language.*

ܛܰܝܒܽܘ, ܛܰܝܒܽܘܬ݂ܳܐ pl. ܬ݂ܳܐ̈ rt. ܛܐܒ. f. active *goodness, kindness, lovingkindness, grace; a favour, benefit;* ܒܛܰܝܒܽܘܬ݂ܶܗ ܕܐܰܠܳܗܳܐ *by the grace* of God; ܛܝܒܘܬܗ ܕܡܪܢ ܝܫܘܥ ܡܫܝܚܐ the grace of our Lord Jesus Christ; hence the doxology, prayers which begin with the doxology; with ܥܒܕ to deal kindly with ܠ or ܥܡ of the pers.; with ܣܡ to confer a favour; with ܐܘܕܝ to thank, be grateful, hence ܬܘܕܝ ܛܝܒܘܬܐ thanksgiving, see under ܝ; ܐܢܐ ܡܘܕܝܢܐ ܛܝܒܘܬܐ ܕܪ̈ܘܪܒܬܐ I have to return thanks for great favours. Special meanings, a) a gift, bounty, thankoffering. b) holy oil; ܩܪܢܐ ܕܛܝܒܘܬܐ the horn of oil of Extreme Unction; ܛܝܒܘܬܐ ܕܡܥܡܘܕܝܬܐ baptismal oil i.e. the chrism of the grace of confirmation. c) same as ܚܢܢܐ which see; ܛܝܒܘܬܐ ܕܡܪܝ ܬܐܘܡܐ the grace of St. Thomas i.e. dust from the grave of St. Thomas mixed with oil and water.

ܛܝܒܘܬܢܐ rt. ܛܝܒ. gracious.

ܛܝ̈ܝܐ; see ܛܝܝܐ.

ܛܝܘܝ and ܛܘܝ, Ar. a quail.

ܛܝܘܦܐ pl. ܐ̈ rt. ܛܘܦ. m. a) a swimmer; a sailor, seaman, mariner, seafarer; ܠܛܝܘܦ̈ܐ ܐܘܒܠ ܠܠܡܐܢܐ ܕܨܒܝܢܐ he brought seafarers unto the appointed haven. b) the adipose membrane, the caul.

ܛܝܙܐ pl. ܛܝ̈ܙܐ m. ܛܝܙܬܐ pl. ܛܝܙ̈ܬܐ and ܛܝܙܘܬ̈ܐ f. the fundament, anus.

ܛܝܚܐ only pl. ܛܝ̈ܚܐ m. white spots on the eyes, a defluxion in the eyes, blearness or soreness of the eyes.

ܛܝܚܢܐ, ܛܝܚܢܝܬܐ pl. m. ܐ̈ f. ܬ̈ܐ adj. from ܛܝܚܐ blear-eyed, suffering from the above disease.

ܛܝܛܘܣ or ܛܝܛܝܘܣ same as the following—

ܛܝܛܒܘܣ or ܛܝܛܝܒܘܣ Ar. ṭaiṭawa, all these forms are corruptions of Sans. tittibha, a sandpiper; this name has also been confused with psittacus, a parrot, and with τέττιξ, a cicada; ܛܝܛܝܒܘܣ ܗܘ ܦܪܚܬܐ ܡܠܩܛܐ ܡ̈ܠܐ the tittibha is a bird which picks up words.

ܛܝܛܠܘܣ pl. ܛܝܛܠ̈ܘܣ m. titulus, a title, superscription, inscription.

ܛܝܝܐ, ܛܝܝܬܐ pl. m. ܛܝ̈ܝܐ f. ܛܝ̈ܝܬܐ Ar. an Arab of the tribe of Tay, then any Arab, Moslem, Mohammedan; ܡܠܟܐ ܛܝܝܐ an Arab king; ܛܝ̈ܝܐ—ܐܝܟ ܕܛܝ̈ܝܐ according to Arabic chronology i.e. in the year of the Hegira; ܡܡܠܠܐ or ܠܫܢܐ ܛܝܝܐ the Arabic language, Arabic. DERIVATIVES, the two following words—

ܛܝܝܐܝܬ adv. in the Arabic language; ܦܘܫܩܗ ܕܝܠܗ ܛܝܝܐܝܬ the explanation of it in Arabic.

ܛܝܝܘܬܐ f. collect. the Arabian people, the Arabs, the Arab dominion, Islam; ܛܝܝܘܬܐ ܕܡܨܪܝܢ ܘܣܘܪܝܐ the Arabs of Egypt and Syria.

ܛܝܒ PAEL of ܛܘܒ.

ܛܝܡܐ or ܛܝܡܐ f. but masc. in the pl. ܛܝܡ̈ܐ or ܛܝܡܘܬܐ τιμή, an honour, value, fee, price; ܛܝܡܐ ܕܕܡܐ the price of blood; ܕܢܬܠ ܕܗܒܐ ܘܚܣܢ̈ܐ ܠܛܝܡܐ ܕܒܪܗ he offered to give gold and yield fortresses to ransom his son; ܝܩܝܪ ܛܝܡܐ and ܛܝܡܐ ܝܩܝܪ costly, valuable, precious; ܠܝܬ ܛܝܡܐ ܠܐ ܡܬܛܝܡ priceless, of inestimable worth.

ܛܡܝܘܢ or ܛܡܝܘܢ cf. ܛܡܝܘܢ ταμιεῖον, the exchequer; ܒܝܬܗ ܢܗܘܐ ܠܛܡܝܘܢ his house shall be confiscated.

ܛܝܢ denom. verb PAEL conj. from ܛܝܢܐ. to smear with clay; cover with clay; ܡܐܢܐ ܕܛܝܢܬ the vessel thou hast smeared with clay; ܩܕܪܐ ܡܛܝܢܬܐ a pot covered with clay.

ܛܝܢ, ܛܝܢܐ m. mud, mire, clay, dirt; ܛܝܢܐ ܕܐܪܥܐ ܕܟܪܒܬܐ mire from ploughed land.

ܛܝܢܢ, ܛܝܢܢܐ adj. of clay; muddy, miry; ܒܝܬܐ ܛܝܢܢܐ a house of clay.

ܛܝܢܢܘܬܐ and ܛܝܢܢܝܘܬܐ f. a swelling or thickness of the liver or of its artery.

ܛܝܦܐ, ܛܝܦܬܐ pl. m. ܐ̈ f. ܬ̈ܐ rt. ܛܘܦ. a superficial or shallow person.

ܛܝܦܘܬܐ rt. ܛܘܦ. f. floating, swimming on the surface.

ܛܝܪܐ pl. ܐ̈ rt. ܛܐܪ. f. a bird, esp. a bird of prey.

ܛܐܪܐ act. part. of verb ܛܐܪ. to fly.

ܛܝܪܐ pl. ܛܝܪ̈ܐ m. a place surrounded with a wall, an enclosure, encampment for flocks, pastoral village, sheepfold. Metaph. a mandra, *community of monks; the Church,* ܛܝܪܐ ܕܩܘܫܬܐ *the true fold.*

ܛܝܪܐ, ܛܝܪܘܣܐ and ܛܝܪܣܐ Pers. *the gores* of a shirt.

ܛܝܫܐ rt. ܛܘܫ. m. *smearing;* metaph. ܒܛܝܫܐ ܕܦܪܨܘܦܐ *by putting on a false veneer; covering* his real meaning *by a pretence.*

ܛܝܬ f. *Teth,* the name of the ninth letter of the alphabet.

ܛܟܐ rarely ܛܐܟܐ τάχα = Syr. ܟܒܪ. *perhaps, now, soon.*

ܛܟܛܟ *to murmur, resound, swell* as the sea.

ܛܟܢ denom. verb Pael conj. from ܛܟܢܐ. *to exercise art* or *craft, to be skilful, ingenious;* ܫܢܩܐ ܡܛܟܢܐ *subtle* or *cunningly devised torments;* ܬܚܘܝܬܐ ܡܛܟܢܢܝܬܐ *ingenious proofs.* Ethpa. ܐܬܛܟܢ usually act. *to exercise craft, act cunningly, contrive skilfully, devise, plot against, execute ingeniously.*

ܛܟܢܐ pl. ܛܟܢܝܢ, ܛܟܢܐ m. τέχνη, *craft, device* generally in a bad sense, *cunning, artifice, fraud, guile.* Derivatives, ܛܟܢܘܬܐ, verb ܛܟܢ.

ܛܟܢܢܝܐ, ܛܟܢܢܝܬܐ pl. m. ܛܟܢܢܝܐ f. ܛܟܢܢܝܬܐ adj. from ܛܟܢܐ. *crafty, cunning, cheating.*

ܛܟܣ denom. verb Pael conj. from ܛܟܣܐ. pass. part. ܡܛܟܣ, ܡܛܟܣܐ, ܡܛܟܣܬܐ. *a) to order, set* or *place in order, arrange, assign, to lay out* a corpse; ܛܟܣ ܠܗܘܢ ܟܠ ܝܘܡ ܠܚܡܐ ܬܪܬܥܣܪܐ ܠܝܛܪܝܢ ܕܠܚܡܐ *he assigned to them a daily portion of twelve pounds of bread;* metaph. *to keep in order, control, restrain* the passions; ܛܟܣ ܢܦܫܟ *compose yourself, be orderly;* ܡܛܟܣ ܚܡܬܗ *controlling his anger. b) to ordain, confer holy orders; to set over, appoint* a bishop or a secular ruler; *to institute, constitute, ordain* laws, canons, festivals; *to arrange, appoint, compose* hymns, prayers, &c.; *to take, partake of the Holy Communion.* Pass. part. *a) placed, arranged, ordered, orderly, moderate, modest, self-controlled;* with ܠܐ *disorderly, unruly,* ܪܘܓܙܐ ܠܐ ܡܛܟܣܐ *immoderate anger. b) appointed, settled;* ܐܥܕܢܐ ܡܛܟܣܐ *the appointed season, time determined; stationed* of soldiers, ܗܢܘܢ ܕܡܛܟܣܝܢ ܗܘܘ ܒܡܨܪܝܢ *those on duty in Egypt. c) composed, written;* ܦܘܫܩܐ ܡܛܟܣ ܠ *a commentary by —;* ܡܠܬܐ ܡܛܟܣܬܐ *well-ordered speech;* ܡܛܟܣܝܢ ܒܥܣܪܝܢ ܘܚܡܫܐ ܪ̈ܫܝܢ ܡܛܟܣܐ a subject *set forth* or *arranged under twenty-five heads.* Ethpa. ܐܬܛܟܣ *a) to be set* or *arranged in order, placed, ranged amongst, ranked with;* ܐܬܛܟܣ ܠܗ ܟܘܪܣܝܐ ܕܕܗܒܐ *a golden throne was set for him;* often of burial; ܐܬܛܟܣ ܦܓܪܗ ܒܥܕܬܐ *his body was laid in the church;* with ܥܡ *to be reckoned with the angels;* metaph. ܡܬܛܟܣܝܢ ܗܘܘ ܒܡܠܟܝܗܘܢ *they became temperate, well regulated. b) to be ordained, receive holy orders, be consecrated; to be instituted, constituted, ordained, appointed* to an office, of laws, festivals, &c.; ܐܬܛܟܣ ܗܘܐ ܒܪܒܘܬܐ ܗܘ ܕܐܬܩܛܠ *he was appointed* to the command *in place of him who was slain. c) to be drawn up, composed* as a lexicon. *d) to be received, consumed,* said of the eucharistic elements.

ܛܟܣܐ and ܛܐܟܣܐ pl. ܛܟܣܝܢ, ܛܟܣܐ m. τάξις, *order;* ܛܟܣܐ ܕܟܝܢܐ *the order of nature. a) series, rank;* ܛܟܣܝܢ ܛܟܣܝܢ *in ranks;* ܒܛܟܣܐ *in the place of, reckoned as* or *amongst;* ܒܛܟܣܐ ܕܒܥܠܕܒܒܐ ܚܫܒ ܠ *he reckoned as enemies those who —;* ܠܒܪ ܡܢ ܛܟܣܐ *extraordinary, unusual. b) rank, degree, station; holy orders;* ܛܟܣܐ ܥܕܬܢܝܐ *ecclesiastical orders;* ܛܟܣܐ ܕܟܗܢܘܬܐ—ܕܡܫܡܫܢܘܬܐ *the order of the priesthood, the order of the diaconate;* ܬܠܬܐ ܛܟܣܐ ܕܡܠܐܟܐ *three orders of angels. c) a rule, regulation, ordinance;* ܛܟܣܐ ܕܝܚܝܕܝܘܬܐ *monastic rule, the rules* or *ordinances of the monastic life. d)* eccles. *liturgical order, an office, rite, ritual, liturgy, takhsa;* ܐܝܟ ܛܟܣܐ ܕܒܟܠܗܘܢ ܚܕ ܒܫܒܐ *according to the rule on each Sunday, as is ordered for every Sunday;* ܛܟܣܐ ܕܫܠܝܚܐ *the Liturgy of the Apostles* Addai and Mari; ܡܫܡܫܢܐ ܕܛܟܣܐ ܐܘܟܝܬ ܕܩܐܡ ܥܠ ܛܟܣܐ *the deacon who is serving at the office. e) furniture, apparatus, equipment, ornaments* official, military, ecclesiastical; ܟܠܗ ܛܟܣܐ ܕܡܕܒܚܐ *all the array* or *furniture of an altar; official robes, vestments* esp. of priests; ܛܟܣܐ ܡܫܡܫܢܝܐ *a complete set of canonicals. f) officials, attendants;* ܒܢܝ ܛܟܣܐ ܕܝܠܗ *his attendants.* Derivatives, ܛܟܣܘܬܐ, verb ܛܟܣ.

ܛܟܣܐܘܛܐ pl. ܛܟܣܐܘܛܐ, ܛܟܣܐܘܛܐ or ܛܟܣܝܘܛܐ m. ταξεώτης, *an apparitor, serjeant, magistrate's official.*

ܛܟܣܝܣ pl. ܛܟܣܝܣܐ = ܛܟܣܐ m. τάξις. *a*) *order, rule, ordinance. b*) *degree, rank, official status. c*) *officials, public servants, attendants.*

ܛܠܠ not used in Peal. Pa. ܛܠܠ *to cover, overshadow, shade; to roof, lay rafters* or *planks;* ܒܝܬܐ ܡܛܠܠܐ *a ceiled house;* ܚܦܝܪܐ ܡܛܠܠܐ *covered* or *shady trenches.* Ethpa. ܐܬܛܠܠ *to be covered, shaded, roofed;* ܡܬܛܠܠ ܡܢ ܐܝܠܢܐ *shaded by trees.* Aph. ܐܛܠ part. ܡܛܠ or ܡܛܠܠ pl. ܡܛܠܠܝܢ *to cover over, overshadow, give shade,* with ܥܠ; ܐܝܠܢܐ ܡܛܠܠ *a shady tree;* ܚܣܢܐ ܕܡܛܠ ܥܠ ܕܩܠܬ *a fortress overhanging the Tigris;* ܟܪܘܒܐ ܕܡܛܠܠ *a cherub overshadowing* the mercy-seat. Derivatives, ܐܛܠܠܐ, ܛܠܘܠܐ, ܛܠܘܠܝܬܐ, ܛܠܠܐ, ܛܠܝܠܐ, ܛܠܝܠܘܬܐ, ܛܠܠܐ, ܡܛܠܠܐ, ܡܛܠܠܬܐ or ܡܛܠܠܬܐ, ܡܛܠܠܝܬܐ, ܡܛܠܠܐ, ܡܛܠܬܐ.

ܛܠ, ܛܠܐ and ܛܐܠ, ܛܐܠܐ m. *dew;* ܛܠܐ ܓܠܝܕܐ *half-frozen dew;* also *fine hoar-frost;* cf. ܓܠܝܕܐ. Derivative, ܛܠܠ.

ܛܠܐ, ܛܠܝܐ pl. ܛܠܝܐ, ܛܠܝܐ m. ܛܠܝܬܐ pl. ܛܠܝܬܐ, ܛܠܝܬܐ and ܛܠܝܬܐ f. *a*) *young, youthful, childish;* ܛܠܐ ܡܫܬܒܩܐ *an infant, very young child;* ܛܠܝܐ ܫܒܪܐ *young children;* ܛܠܐ ܫܒܪܐ *very young;* ܛܠܐ ܗܘܐ ܒܪܥܝܢܐ *he was childish. b*) *a child* from seven to twelve years of age, cf. ܫܒܪܐ *a child* under seven and ܥܠܝܡܐ *a youth* up to twenty-five years of age; *a child, boy, girl, maiden. c*) *a lad, handmaid, servant;* ܛܠܝܐ ܕܡܛܒܚܐ *a scullion.* Derivatives, verb ܛܠܐ, ܛܠܝܐ, ܛܠܝܘܬܐ, ܛܠܝܘܬܐ, ܛܠܝܘܬܐ, ܛܠܝܐ, ܛܠܝܘܬܐ, ܡܛܠܝܢܘܬܐ, ܛܠܝܘܬܐ.

ܛܠܐ ܕܕܒܫ *honey-dew, a sort of manna.*

ܛܠܦܣܐ pl. ܐ̈ m. *a*) *a door-hinge. b*) *a horse-shoe. c*) *sandals.*

ܛܠܝܦܪܐ *a leathern strigil* or *scraper.*

ܛܠܝܩܐ m. *a drinking-cup.*

ܛܠܘܡ, ܛܠܘܡܐ, ܛܠܘܡܬܐ pl. m. ܐ̈ f. ܬ̈ܐ rt. ܛܠܡ. *one who wrongs, injures* or *acts unjustly* by another, *an oppressor, tyrant;* Cain was the ܛܠܘܡܐ ܐܚܐ of Abel; *unjust, faithless, ungrateful;* ܕܝܬܝܩܐ ܛܠܘܡܬܐ *an unjust will;* ܛܠܘܡܐ ܕܛܝܒܘܬܐ *one who is unmindful of benefits received.*

ܛܠܘܡܐܝܬ rt. ܛܠܡ. adv. *unjustly, wrongfully.*

ܛܠܘܡܘܬܐ pl. ܬ̈ܐ rt. ܛܠܡ. f. *injustice, wrong, oppression; ingratitude, faithlessness, perfidy, calumny, stubborn unbelief,* e.g. ܕܝܗܘܕܝܐ *of the Jews.*

ܛܠܘܡܝܐ pl. ܐ̈ rt. ܛܠܡ. m. *injustice, oppression, tyranny, violence, cruelty, calumny, iniquity, injury;* ܛܠܘܡܝܐ ܒܡܘܡܬܐ *bad faith, perjury.*

ܛܠܘܢܝܬܐ a rare spelling of ܛܠܢܝܬܐ *a shadow,* &c.

ܛܠܘܫܐ pl. ܐ̈ rt. ܛܠܫ. m. *a destroyer.*

ܛܠܘܪܐ m. ܛܠܘܪܬܐ f. same as ܛܠܪܐ. *an iron spoon* or *pan.*

ܛܠܘܫܐ, ܛܠܘܫܬܐ rt. ܛܠܫ. *slimy, clogging, clammy* as ܥܡܛܐ *vapour,* ܛܝܢܐ *mud,* ܣܘܗܐ *matter* &c., ܐܪܥܐ ܛܠܘܫܬܐ *clayey earth.*

ܛܠܘܫܘܬܐ or ܛܠܫܘܬܐ rt. ܛܠܫ. f. *stickiness, clamminess.*

ܛܠܫ imper. ܛܠܘܫ *to beat out, hammer;* part. adj. ܛܠܝܫ, ܛܠܝܫܐ, ܛܠܝܫܬܐ *thin, meagre, mean; plane; flat.* Pa. ܛܠܫ same as Pe. Derivatives, ܛܠܝܫܐܝܬ, ܛܠܝܫܘܬܐ.

ܛܠܝܐ pl. ܐ̈ m. *a lazy, negligent* or *careless person.*

ܛܠܝ act. part. ܛܠܐ, pass. part. ܛܠܐ, denom. verb from ܛܠܝܐ. *to be* or *become young, new;* ܕܛܥܡ ܠܗܘܢ ܛܠܐ *he who tastes them recovers his youth;* ܛܠܐ ܐܢܬ ܒܫܢܝܐ *thou art young, of few years;* ܕܠܥܠܡ ܛܠܐ *having eternal youth;* ܓܪܡܐ ܛܠܝܐ *fresh bones.* Pael ܛܠܝ *to restore to youth.* Ethpa. ܐܬܛܠܝ *to recover youth, be restored to youth, be rejuvenated;* ܕܒܗ ܐܬܛܠܝܬ ܟܝܢܢ ܐܢܫܝܐ *whereby our human nature was restored.*

ܛܠܝܐ pl. ܛܠܝܐ m. ܛܠܝܬܐ pl. ܛܠܝܬܐ f. from ܛܠܐ. *an unmarried youth* or *maiden, a freeborn youth* or *maiden;* but the fem. is used also for *maids, handmaids;* cf. ܛܠܐ, ܛܠܝܐ.

ܛܠܝܘ, ܛܠܝܘܬܐ from ܛܠܝܐ. f. *a*) *childhood, boyhood, youth;* ܡܢ ܛܠܝܘܬܐ ܘܥܕܡܐ ܠܩܒܪܐ *from childhood to the grave;* ܐܢܬܬ ܛܠܝܘܬܟ *the wife of thy youth. b*) collect. *lads, servants; young people;* ܐܒܠܐ ܕܥܠ ܛܠܝܘܬܐ *grief for those who die in youth.*

ܛܠܝܘܢܐ dim. of ܛܠܝܐ. m. *a little boy* or *lad, a youth.*

ܛܠܝܘܣܐ pl. ܐ̈ dim. of ܛܠܝܐ. m. *a little boy;* ܛܠܝܘܣܬܐ f. *a little girl.*

ܛܠܝܘܬܐܝܬ adv. from the above. *childishly.*

ܛܠܝܘܬܢܐ adj. from ܛܠܝܘܬܐ. *childish, puerile.*

ܛܠܝܘܬܢܝܐ adj. from ܛܠܝܐ. *puerile, of* or *belonging to childish ignorance.*

ܛܠܝܚܐܝܬ rt. ܛܠܚ. adv. *thinly, narrowly;* ܛܠܝܚܐܝܬ ܡܡܠܠܝܢ *they lisp, clipping* their words.

ܛܠܝܚܘܬ, ܛܠܝܚܘܬܐ rt. ܛܠܚ. f. *thinness, tenuity, clipping* the speech, pronouncing double letters as single; *a long* and *narrow shape of the head.*

ܛܠܝܢܐ, ܛܠܝܢܝܬܐ from ܛܠܝܐ. *childish, youthful.*

ܛܠܝܡܘܬܐ rt. ܛܠܡ. f. *injustice, oppression, calumny, false accusation.*

ܛܠܝܣܡܐ, ܛܠܝܣܡܣ or ܛܠܝܣܡܛܣ pl. ܛܠܝܣܡܛܐ or ܛܠܣܡܐ τελέσματα, *incantations, magic arts, wonders worked by magic.*

ܛܠܝܬܐ *a girl;* see ܛܠܝܐ.

ܛܠܠ Pael conj. of ܛܠܠ.

ܛܠܠܐ, ܛܠܠܐ pl. ܐ̈ rt. ܛܠܠ. m. *shade, a shadow;* metaph. *protection;* ܛܠܠܐ ܕܡܘܬܐ *the shadows of death, deep darkness;* ܐܝܟ ܕܠܛܠܠܐ ܐܚܕ *he grasps the shadow;* ܐܝܟ ܕܠܛܠܠܐ ܢܣܒ ܠܦܓܪܐ *he took the shadow for the substance;* ܛܠܠܐ ܕܚܟܡܬܐ ܐܝܟ ܛܠܠܐ ܕܟܣܦܐ *wisdom is a defence as money is a defence.*

ܛܠܠܢܐ, ܛܠܠܢܝܬܐ pl. m. ܢ̈ܐ f. ܢܝ̈ܬܐ rt. ܛܠܠ. *shadowy, of* or *belonging to shade.*

ܛܠܡ fut. ܢܛܠܘܡ, act. part. ܛܠܡ, ܛܠܡܐ, pass. part. ܛܠܝܡ, ܐ, ܬܐ. *a) to oppress, wrong, cheat, defraud, deceive, deal falsely, treat wrongly, unjustly; to accuse falsely;* with ܐܓܪܐ *to cheat of his wages;* with ܛܝܒܘܬܐ *to act ungratefully;* with ܡܘܠܟܢܐ *to break a promise;* ܚܦܝܛܝܢ ܕܠܐ ܢܛܠܡܘܢ *careful to do no wrong. b) to withhold that which is due* esp. faith owed to God; *to deny, reject, refuse;* ܛܠܡܘܗܝ ܠܗܝܡܢܘܬܐ ܕܥܠ ܬܕܡܪ̈ܬܐ ܕܐܠܗܐ *they refused to believe in the wondrous works of God;* ܡܢ ܕܛܠܡ ܠܟܘܢ ܠܝ ܗܘ ܛܠܡ *he who rejecteth you rejecteth me.* With ܫܐܠܬܐ *to refuse a request;* with ܫܠܡܐ *to refuse to salute any one;* with ܢܦܫܗ *to feign oneself, pretend to be;* ܟܪܡܐ ܛܠܡ ܦܐܪ̈ܐ *a vineyard that yields no fruit;* ܐܝܠܝܢ ܕܛܠܡܝܢ ܠܡܫܠܡܘ ܓܘܥܠܢܐ *those who refuse to render a deposit entrusted to their care.* Pass. part. *defrauded, wronged, injured, oppressed, calumniated;* ܦܪܘܩܘ ܠܛܠܝܡܐ *relieve the oppressed;* ܛܠܝܡ ܚܝ̈ܐ *unjustly* or *untimely deprived of life;* ܫܘܫܢ ܛܠܝܡܬܐ *the slandered Susanna.* Ethpe. ܐܬܛܠܡ *a) to be defrauded, cheated, wronged, oppressed, falsely accused, calumniated; to be deprived of, to lack. b) to be rejected, despised;* ܫܪܪܐ ܐܬܛܠܡ ܘܐܬܕܝܫ *the truth rejected and trampled on.* Pa. ܛܠܡ same as Peal. Derivatives, ܛܘܠܡܢܐ, ܛܠܘܡܐ, ܛܠܘܡܘܬܐ, ܛܠܘܡܐܝܬ, ܛܠܝܡܘܬܐ, ܛܠܡܐ.

ܛܠܘܡܐ rt. ܛܠܡ. m. *oppression.*

ܛܠܢܐܝܬ rt. ܛܠܠ. adv. *in a shadow, figuratively.*

ܛܠܢܐ or ܛܠܠܢܐ, ܢܝܬܐ from ܛܠܐ. *dewy, of dew;* ܢܛܘܦܬܐ ܛܠܢܝܬܐ *a dew-drop.*

ܛܠܠܢܐ and ܛܠܠܢܝܐ, ܢܝܬܐ rt. ܛܠܠ. adj. *shady, shadowy;* ܢܓܗܐ ܛܠܠܢܐ *twilight;* metaph. *a) seeming, apparent, unreal;* ܛܒܬܐ ܛܠܠܢܝܬܐ *a shadowy good. b) shadowing forth* that which truly is, *figurative;* ܡܕܒ̈ܚܐ ܛܠܠܢ̈ܝܐ *altars which foreshadowed* the true sacrifice.

ܛܠܠܢܝܬܐ pl. ܢܝ̈ܬܐ rt. ܛܠܠ. f. *a) a shadow, shade* esp. metaph. *a figure, type;* ܢܡܘܣܐ ܛܠܠܢܝܬܐ ܕܛܒ̈ܬܐ ܕܥܬܝ̈ܕܢ *the law was a shadow of future blessings. b) a spectre, demon.*

ܛܠܣܡܐ τελέσματα, *magic;* see ܛܠܝܣܡܣ.

ܛܠܥ Ethpe. ܐܬܛܠܥ *to fall into a stupor, become unconscious.* Derivative, ܛܘܠܥܐ.

ܛܠܥܬܐ pl. ܥ̈ܬܐ f. *a marsh, watery mire.*

ܛܠܦܚܐ pl. ܐ̈ m. *lentils; freckles;* ܒܫܘܠܐ ܕܛܠܦܚ̈ܐ *lentil pottage.*

ܛܠܦܚܘܢܐ pl. ܐ̈ dim. of ܛܠܦܚܐ. m. *the pond* or *marsh lentil;* ܛܠܦܚܘܢܐ ܕܡܝ̈ܐ *adiantum capillus veneris;* ܛܠܦܚܘܢ̈ܐ ܕܐܦ̈ܐ *freckles.*

ܛܠܦܣ̈ܐ m. *chessmen,* the game of *chess.*

ܛܠܦܣܬܐ same as ܛܠܦܣ̈ܐ.

ܛܠܩ and ܛܠܩ, fut. ܢܛܠܘܩ, act. part. ܛܠܩ, ܛܠܩܐ. *to be spent, consumed, used up, past, ended; to fail, vanish, disappear;* ܛܠܩ ܡܢ ܚܝ̈ܐ ܗܠܝܢ *he passed away from this life;*

ܚܫܘܟܐ ܕܠܐ ܛܠܡܐ ܠܥܠܡ *endless darkness.* Ethpe. ܐܬܛܠܡ *to vanish, be dispersed* ܐܝܟ ܬܢܢܐ *like smoke; to pass away, be destroyed, perish.* Pa. ܛܠܡ *to use up, to make* or *come to an end, finish; to spend, waste* money, time, trouble, words; *to put away* a wife; *to destroy, get rid of;* ܡܐ ܕܛܠܡܬ ܠܡܠܝܟ *when thou hast made an end of speaking;* ܡܛܠܡܝܢ ܡܢܢ ܦܓܪܐ ܘܕܡܐ ܕܡܫܝܚܐ *the* Body and Blood of Christ *put death away from us.* Ethpa. ܐܬܛܠܡ *to consume away, fail, vanish, perish* as smoke, fire or by fire, *to be finished, consumed;* ܠܒܐ ܕܡܬܛܠܡ ܒܚܣܡܐ *a heart consumed with envy.* Derivatives, ܛܘܠܡܐ, ܛܘܠܡܢܐ, ܡܛܠܡܢܘܬܐ, ܡܬܛܠܡܢܐ, ܛܠܡܐ, ܛܘܠܡܢܘܬܐ.

ܛܠܡܩ *talc.*

ܛܠܪܐ pl. ܐ̈ m. *talare, talaria, sandals* = ܩܪܦܝܠܐ and ܩܪܦܝܠܝܢ.

ܛܠܫ fut. ܢܛܠܘܫ, pass. part. ܛܠܝܫ, ܫܐ, ܫܬܐ. *to be spotted, filthy, despised.* Pa. ܛܠܫ *to infect* a sheep *with mange; to make slimy, dirty.* Ethpa. ܐܬܛܠܫ *to be defiled, polluted.* Derivatives, ܛܘܠܫܐ, ܛܘܠܫܢܐ, ܛܘܠܫܢܝܬܐ, ܛܠܘܫܐ, ܛܠܘܫܘܬܐ, ܛܘܠܫܬܐ.

ܛܡܡ fut. ܢܛܘܡ root-meaning *to stop up, close.* Peal only part. adj. ܛܡܝܡܐ, ܛܡܝܡܬܐ *close, solid, opaque, dense;* ܬܘ ܛܡܝܡܬܐ *a blotted Tau* i. e. written too thickly, ܦܓܪ̈ܐ, ܓܘܫܡ̈ܐ ܛܡܝܡ̈ܐ *solid bodies, opaque substances;* ܩܪ̈ܢܐ ܕܐܝܠ̈ܐ ܒܠܚܘܕ ܛܡܝܡܢ ܘܐܚܪ̈ܢܝܬܐ ܣܪܝܩܢ *the horns of stags only are solid, others are hollow;* ܟܐܦ̈ܐ ܛܡܝܡ̈ܬܐ *stones closely packed;* ܛܡܝܡܝ ܠܒܐ *dense of heart.* Pa. ܛܡܡ *to stop up, block* a well, watercourse, cavern; metaph. *to repress, restrain* e. g. ܪܓܬܐ ܕܒܣܪܐ *the lust of the flesh.* Ethpa. ܐܬܛܡܡ *to be stopped, closed;* metaph. *to be repressed, coerced.* Derivatives, ܛܡܝܡܐܝܬ, ܛܡܝܡܘܬܐ.

ܛܡܐ or ܛܡܝ *to be unclean, defiled.* Pa. ܛܡܐ or ܛܡܝ infin. ܡܛܡܐܘ or ܡܛܡܝܘ, pass. part. ܡܛܡܐ, ܡܛܡܝܐ. *to pollute, defile, corrupt, deflour; to pronounce* or *declare unclean.* Ethpa. ܐܬܛܡܐ and ܐܬܛܡܝ *to be defiled, polluted.* Aph. ܐܛܡܝ *to pronounce unclean.* Derivatives, ܛܘܡܐܐ or ܛܘܡܝܐ, ܛܡܐ, ܛܡܐܘܬܐ, ܛܡܐܢܐ, ܛܡܐܢܝܬ, ܡܛܡܐܢܝܬ.

ܛܡܐ m. emph. and fem. abs. ܛܡܐܐ rarely ܛܡܝܐ f. emph. ܛܡܐܬܐ, pl. m. ܛܡܐܝܢ, ܛܡܐܐ f. ܛܡܐܢ, ܛܡܐܬܐ rt. ܛܡܐ. *unclean, impure, defiled, polluted;* ܡܐܟܘܠܬܐ ܛܡܐܬܐ *unclean food;* ܛܡܐܬܐ *harlots.*

ܛܡܐܘ, ܛܡܐܘܬܐ pl. ܛܡܐܘ̈ܬܐ wrongly spelt ܛܡܘܬܐ and ܛܡܝܘܬܐ rt. ܛܡܐ. f. *uncleanness* esp. *unchastity, defilement; an abomination, unclean thing* esp. forbidden food; ܛܡܐܘܬܗ ܕܥܘܠܐ ܕܚܠܬܐ ܕܐܠܗܐ *the fear of God is an abomination to the wicked.*

ܛܡܐܢܐ, ܢܝܬܐ rt. ܛܡܐ. *impure, polluted.*

ܛܡܪܘܬܐ rt. ܛܡܪ. *hiding in the earth; burial.*

ܛܡܝܘܢ m. ταμιεῖον, *the imperial treasury.*

ܛܡܝܡܐܝܬ rt. ܛܡ. adv. *solidly.*

ܛܡܝܡܘܬܐ rt. ܛܡ. f. *stopping up, closing.*

ܛܡܝܪܬܐ rt. ܛܡܪ. f. *a loaf baked in the ashes.*

ܛܡܫ pass. part. ܛܡܝܫ *to pollute.*

ܛܡܣܐ, ܛܡܣܬܐ in the dialect of Tekrit. *the first thread tied to the weaver's beam.*

ܛܡܪ fut. ܢܛܡܘܪ, act. part. ܛܡܪ, ܛܡܪܐ, pass. part. ܛܡܝܪ, ܪܐ, ܪܬܐ root-meaning *to dig deep. a) to hide* or *bury under the earth, cover with earth; to lay hidden* snares, nets, &c.; *to hide, cover, to steep* in liquid; ܛܡܪܘܗܝ ܒܓܘܫܡܐ *cover it with a ball of earth;* ܛܡܪ ܚܙܩܝܐ ܡܪܕܝܬܐ ܕܡܝ̈ܐ ܒܡܦܩܗ ܕܡܥܝܢܐ ܥܠܝܐ Hezekiah *made a conduit from the outlet of the upper spring;* ܛܡܪܬ ܚܡܝܪܐ ܒܩܡܚܐ *she hid leaven in flour;* metaph. ܛܡܪ ܚܫܘܟܐ ܠܥܠܡܐ *darkness covers the world;* ܛܡܘܪܘ ܚܘܒܐ ܒܠܒ̈ܐ ܐܝܟ ܚܡܝܪܐ *hide love in the hearts of men* like leaven. *b) to bury* under ruins, *cover* with a flood, *overwhelm, burst in, rush headlong upon;* ܢܦܠܬ ܘܛܡܪܬ ܠܥܡܘܪ̈ܝܗ *the city fell and overwhelmed its inhabitants;* ܛܡܪܗ ܢܝܠܘܣ *the Nile covered it;* ܛܡܪܬܗ ܡܚܝܠܘܬܐ *indolence overwhelmed him;* ܛܡܪ ܒܓܘ ܚܝܠܐ ܕܦܪ̈ܣܝܐ *he rushed headlong among the Persian soldiers.* Pass. part. *hidden* or *buried* under the earth; ܣܝܡ̈ܬܐ ܛܡܝܪ̈ܬܐ *hidden treasures;* ܙܪܥܐ ܕܛܡܝܪ ܗܘܐ ܒܐܪܥܐ *the seed which was hidden in the soil;* metaph. *hidden, covered, steeped* e. g. ܒܚܛ̈ܗܐ *in sins;* ܐܬܒܩܘ ܕܐܝܢܐ ܗܘ ܛܡܝܪ *consider what is the hidden meaning.* Ethpe. ܐܬܛܡܪ *a) to hide oneself* in the earth, ܒܓܘܡܨ̈ܐ *in pits. b) to be covered, overwhelmed* by falling earth or buildings. *c*) *to be watered, irrigated.* ETHPA. ܐܬܛܰܡܰܪ *to be covered with earth, buried in the earth, overwhelmed;* ܒܬܘܠܬܐ ܚܝܬܐ ܐܬܛܡܪܬ a vestal virgin *was buried alive.* DERIVATIVES, ܛܡܘܪܐ, ܛܡܪܐ, ܛܡܪܬܐ, ܛܡܝܪܐ, ܛܡܝܪܘܬܐ, ܡܛܡܪܢܘܬܐ.

ܛܡܘܪܐ pl. ܐ̈ rt. ܛܡܪ. m. *an accumulation of earth; being buried alive* under falling buildings; *a hidden thing, mystery;* ܛܡܘܪ̈ܐ ܕܚܟܡܬܐ *secrets of wisdom;* med. *an obstruction.*

ܛܡܪܐ and ܛܡܪܬܐ rt. ܛܡܪ. m. *a thigh-band; girdle round the loins.*

ܛܡܫ fut. ܢܛܡܘܫ, act. part. ܛܳܡܶܫ, ܛܳܡܫܐ, ܛܳܡܫܳܬܐ. *to dip, moisten, wet, soak,* ܒܚܠܐ *in vinegar,* ܒܟܣܐ *in a cup,* ܕܢܛܡܘܫ ܨܒܥܗ ܙܥܘܪܬܐ ܒܡܝܐ *that he may dip his little finger in water.* ETHPE. ܐܬܛܡܫ *to be soaked.* PA. ܛܰܡܶܫ same as Peal.

ܛܢ fut. ܢܛܢ, imper. ܛܢ, act. part. ܛܳܐܶܢ, pl. m. ܛܳܐܢܝܢ, pass. part. ܛܢܝܢ, ܛܢܝܢܬܐ. *to envy, be jealous, to be moved* or *burn with jealousy, zeal, zealous desire, emulation, indignation* with ܒ; ܒܡܘܗܒܬܐ ܪܘܚܢܝܬܐ *of spiritual gifts;* ܕܥܒܕ̈ܐ ܛܒ̈ܐ *of good works;* ܛܢ ܗܟܝܠ ܘܬܘܒ *be zealous therefore and repent;* ܛܢܢܐܝܬ ܝܠܦܬ *I learned zealously;* ܛܳܐܢܝܢ ܛܢܢܐ ܟܐܢܐ *moved with righteous zeal.* Pass. part. *a*) *envious;* *b*) *enviable.* PA. ܛܰܢܶܢ *to inflame with zeal, provoke to jealousy;* ܛܢܢܬ ܠܛܝܝ̈ܐ ܒܡܠܝܗ *she aroused the zeal of the Arabs by her words.* ETHPA. ܐܬܛܰܢܰܢ *to be inflamed, moved, provoked to wrath* or *zeal,* or *to burn with wrath* or *zeal* usually before a verb of action; ܐܢܫ ܡܢ ܛܝܝܐ ܐܬܛܢܢ ܘܫܕܐ ܟܐܦܐ ܥܠ *a certain Arab inflamed with zeal threw a stone at . . .* APH. ܐܛܢ *to provoke to jealousy, stir up, inflame with zeal.* DERIVATIVES, ܛܢܐ, ܛܢܢܐ, ܛܢܢܐܝܬ, ܛܢܢܘܬܐ.

ܛܢܒܘܪܐ pl. ܐ̈ Pers.-Arab. *a tambour, tambourine, drum.*

ܛܰܢܶܢ Pael of ܛܢ; see above.

ܛܢܢܐ, ܛܢܢܬܐ rt. ܛܢ. m. *jealous, zealous, a zealot;* ܐܠܗܐ ܛܢܢܐ *a jealous God;* ܛܢܢܐ ܗܘܐ ܕܐܠܗܐ *he was zealous for God;* ܛܢܢܬܐ ܕܗܝܡܢܘܬܐ *a woman zealous for the faith.*

ܛܢܢܐ rt. ܛܢ. m. *jealousy, zeal, ardent desire;* ܢܘܪܐ ܕܛܢܢܐ *the fire of jealousy;* ܛܢܢܐ ܕܗܝܡܢܘܬܐ *zeal for the faith;* with ܐܬܚܡܛ or ܩܕܚ *to be inflamed with zeal, to burn with zeal.*

ܛܢܢܐܝܬ rt. ܛܢ. adv. *zealously, ardently.*

ܛܢܢܘܬܐ rt. ܛܢ. f. *jealousy, emulation, zeal.*

ܛܢܦ PA. ܛܰܢܶܦ *to profane, pollute, defile, deflower;* ܒܕܡܐ *with blood;* ܐܝܟ ܙܢܝܬܐ ܘܡܛܢܦܬܐ *a harlot and polluted;* ܡܛܢܦܐ ܒܙܢܝܘܬܐ *defiled by fornication;* ܒܝܫܬܐ ܕܛܢܦܬ ܘܚܒܠܬ ܠܥܠܡܐ *evil which has polluted and defiled the world;* ܡ̈ܠܐ ܡܛܢܦ̈ܬܐ *polluted* i.e. *heretical words.* ETHPA. ܐܬܛܰܢܰܦ *to be defiled, polluted, corrupt; to commit abomination.* DERIVATIVES, ܛܢܦܐ, ܛܢܦܘܬܐ, ܛܢܦܘܬܐ.

ܛܢܦ, ܛܢܦܐ, ܛܢܦܬܐ rt. ܛܢܦ. *defiled, polluted, impure, filthy, foul;* ܠܚܡܐ ܘܡܝ̈ܐ ܛܢܦ̈ܐ *bread and water polluted* by heathen rites; ܪ̈ܘܚܐ ܛܢܦ̈ܬܐ *unclean spirits;* ܡ̈ܠܐ ܛܢܦ̈ܬܐ *foul language;* ܐܬܐ ܛܢܦܬܐ ܕܚܘܪܒܐ *the sign of the abomination of desolation,* Matt. xxiv. 15; cf. ܛܢܦܘܬܐ.

ܛܢܦܘܬܐ pl. ܛܢܦܘ̈ܬܐ, ܛܢܦܘ̈ܬܐ rt. ܛܢܦ. f. *defilement, uncleanness; anything polluted, abominable, an abomination,* e.g. an idol, worship offered to idols, food offered to idols; ܛܢܦܘܬܐ ܡܚܒܠܐ *the abomination that maketh desolate,* Dan. xi. 31; ܛܢܦܘ̈ܬܐ ܕܥܡ̈ܡܐ *the abominable customs of the heathen;* ܥܒܕܘܬܐ ܕܛܢܦܘܬܐ ܘܥܘܠܐ *the bondage of uncleanness and iniquity;* metaph. *heresy.*

ܛܣܐ or ܛܣܬܐ pl. ܛܣ̈ܐ m. *a*) *a thin plate* or *scale, a leaf of metal;* ܟܬܒ̈ܐ ܕܛܣ̈ܐ *writings on metal;* ܚܪ̈ܫܐ ܕܟܬܒܝܢ ܛܣ̈ܐ *wizards who write amulets.* *b*) *a basin, cup.*

ܛܣܘܓܐ *a coin* of small value, worth about four carats.

ܛܣܣ ETHPA. ܐܬܛܰܣܰܣ denom. verb from ܛܣܐ. *to be beaten into thin plates;* ܠܐ ܡܬܛܣܣ ܐܕܡܘܣ *adamant cannot be beaten thin.*

ܛܥܐ fut. ܢܛܥܐ, act. part. ܛܳܥܐ, ܛܳܥܝܐ, ܛܳܥܝܳܬܐ, pass. part. ܛܥܐ, ܛܥܝܐ, ܛܥܝܬܐ. *a*) *to wander, err, go astray, fall in error, be led into the wrong way;* ܥܪܒܐ ܛܥܝܐ *a stray sheep;* ܟܠܢ ܐܝܟ ܥܪ̈ܒܐ ܛܥܝܢ *all we like sheep have gone astray;* ܕܠܐ ܬܛܥܘܢ ܒܬܪ ܦܬܟܪ̈ܝܟܘܢ *lest ye go astray after their idols;* ܠܐ ܛܥܐ ܓܐܪܗ *he shot his arrow unerringly;* ܢܫܡܗ ܛܥܐ ܗܘܐ

she was bewildered, had lost herself, was wandering in mind. b) *to be missing, lost, to perish* as one who is lost; ܠܐ ܛܥܐ ܚܕ ܡܢܢ *not one of us is missing.* c) *to be forgotten, disregarded, escape notice; to be unmindful, forget, err, mistake;* ܐܝܟܢܐ ܛܥܬ ܠܟ *how has it escaped your notice;* ܟܕ ܛܥܐ ܗܘ ܣܟܠܐ *the stupid fellow forgetting, not noticing;* ܕܠܐ ܢܛܥܐ ܐܢܫ ܡܢܗܝܢ *thoughts which no man may disregard;* ܛܥܐ ܝܘܐܫ ܠܛܝܒܘܬܐ ܕܝܘܝܕܥ *Joash was unmindful of the kindness shown him* by Jehoiada; ܠܐ ܛܥܐ ܐܢܐ ܠܢܡܘܣܐ ܕܪܗܘܡܝܐ *I am not unmindful of Roman law;* with ܡܢ ܫܡܥܐ *to escape one's hearing, remain unknown;* with ܢܦܫܗ or ܢܦܫܗ *to forget oneself;* with ܪܚܡܐ *to forget to be merciful, be unmindful of mercy.* Act. part. with ܟܘܟܒܐ or ellipt. *a planet,* ܛܥܝܐ ܫܒܥܐ ܟܘܟܒܐ *the seven planets;* ܟܘܟܒܐ ܕܠܐ ܛܥܝܢ *fixed stars;* ܐܣܦܝܪܐ ܕܛܥܝܬܐ *the sphere of the planets;* ܕܠܐ ܡܪܟܢܝܢ ܘܛܥܝܐ ܠܒܐ *of an erring heart;* ܗܕܝܘܛܐ ܘܛܥܝܢ *the ignorant and erring;* ܪܘܚܐ ܛܥܝܬܐ *an erring* or *wayward spirit;* ܝܘܠܦܢܐ ܛܥܝܐ *erroneous doctrines;* ܡܛܥܝܢܐ ܘܛܥܝܐ *deceiving and deceived, a heretic;* ܟܢܘܫܬܐ ܕܛܥܝܐ *congregations of heretics;* ܟܠܢ ܛܥܝܢ ܡܟܪܙ *he proclaims that we are all heretics;* pass. part. *forgotten, consigned to oblivion.* Ethpe. ܐܬܛܥܝ a) *to be led astray, deceived.* b) *to be missing, out of sight, forgotten, no longer remembered, regarded,* or *mentioned,* ܫܡܘܥܐ ܕܡܬܛܥܐ ܫܡܥܬܗ *a forgetful hearer;* ܫܡܐ ܚܕ ܐܬܛܥܝ ܡܢ ܡܪܫܡܢܘܬܐ *one name* in the list *has been forgotten, is missing;* ܐܬܛܥܝܘ ܡܢ ܡܪܒܥܐ *they have been forgotten from the womb;* ܐܬܛܥܝܘ ܡܢ ܩܒܪܐ *they are out of mind in the grave.* Aph. ܐܛܥܝ a) *to cause to wander* or *err, to lead astray, deceive, seduce;* ܐܝܟ ܕܠܛܠܝܐ ܐܛܥܝܬܗ ܗܝ *she led him astray like a child;* ܠܐ ܐܫܟܚ ܕܢܛܥܝܢܝ ܠܚܛܗܐ ܕܪܘܦܣܘܬܐ *he could not lead me into the sin of apostasy;* ܢܦܫܗ ܡܛܥܐ *he deceives himself.* b) *to cause to lose* or *miss* = *deprive, rob;* ܠܐ ܐܛܥܝܢ ܡܕܡ ܡܢܗܘܢ *we missed nothing by reason of them.* c) *to cause to forget* or *be forgotten,* ܗܐ ܡܛܥܝܐ ܠܕܘܟܪܢܗܘܢ ܚܒܝܒܐ ܠܚܛܗܝ *may their dear memory cause my sins to be forgotten.* Ettaph. ܐܬܬܛܥܝ a) *to be led astray, deceived, mistaken;* ܐܬܬܛܥܝܘ ܒܣܘܟܠܗܘܢ ܕܥܠܝ *they were deceived in their opinion of me;* ܡܬܬܛܥܝܢ ܒ *they err concerning, are mistaken about.* b) *to be forgotten, consigned to oblivion;* ܐܬܬܛܥܝ ܕܘܟܪܢܗ *his memory perished.* Derivatives, ܛܥܘܝ, ܛܥܝܐ, ܛܥܝܐ, ܛܥܝܘܬܐ, ܛܥܝܐܝܬ, ܡܛܥܝܢܘܬܐ, ܡܛܥܝܢܐ, ܡܛܥܝܢܐܝܬ, ܡܬܛܥܝܢܐ.

ܛܥܘܡܐ, ܛܥܘܡܬܐ rt. ܛܥܡ. a) *that which tastes, gustatory;* ܪܓܫܐ ܛܥܘܡܐ *the sense of taste.* b) *a graft.*

ܛܥܘܡܐ pl. ܐ̈ rt. ܛܥܡ. m. a) *taste, flavour.* b) *a taste, a meal;* ܛܥܡ ܛܥܘܡܐ *he took a snack;* ܐܙܠܢ ܠܛܥܘܡܐ *we went to take food.*

ܛܥܘܬܐ pl. ܐ̈ rt. ܛܥܐ. m. *error, blunder, mistake* in composition; ܬܪܨ ܛܥܘܬܗ *he corrected his mistake;* ܛܥܘܬܐ ܕܣܦܪܐ *the error of a scribe.*

ܛܥܘܢܐ, ܛܥܘܢܬܐ pl. m. ܐ̈ f. ܬ̈ܐ a) rt. ܛܥܢ. *a bearer, carrier, porter;* ܣܪܝܘ ܡܝ̈ܬܐ ܡܢ ܣܢܝܩܘܬܐ ܕܛܥܘܢܐ *the dead rotted for want of any to bear them to the grave;* ܚܝܘ̈ܬܐ ܛܥܘ̈ܢܝܬܐ *beasts of burthen.* b) Ar. *a pestilence.*

ܛܥܘܢܬܐ pl. ܬ̈ܐ rt. ܛܥܢ. f. a) *a load, burthen, a crop* of fruit; *bearing, carrying, support;* ܒܛܥܘܢܬܐ ܕܓܡ̈ܠܐ *borne by camels, on camel-back;* ܣܘܣܝܐ ܠܛܥܘܢܬܐ ܕܪܒܘܬܟܘܢ *a horse to bear your Honour.*

ܛܥܘܝܐ, ܛܥܘܝܬܐ pl. m. ܐ̈ f. ܬ̈ܐ rt. ܛܥܐ. *erring, wandering, liable to err;* ܡܠܦ̈ܢܐ ܠܐ ܛܥܘ̈ܝܐ *infallible teachers.*

ܛܥܘܝܘܬܐ rt. ܛܥܐ. f. with ܗܘܢܐ *wandering of mind, mental derangement.*

ܛܥܘܝܐ rt. ܛܥܐ. m. *error, liability to err.*

ܛܥܝܐ rt. ܛܥܐ. m. *a deceiver.*

ܛܥܝܐ or ܛܥܝܢܐ pl. ܛܥܝܢ or ܛܥܝ̈ܢ rt. ܛܥܐ. *led astray, erring.*

ܛܥܝܐܝܬ rt. ܛܥܐ. adv. *deceitfully.*

ܛܥܝܘܬܐ or ܛܥܝܘܬܐ rt. ܛܥܐ. f. a) *erring, straying, error;* ܛܥܝܘܬܐ ܕܣܓܝܐܘܬ ܐܠܗ̈ܐ *the error of polytheism;* ܛܥܝܘܬܐ ܕܦܬܟܪ̈ܐ *the folly of idolatry;* ܗܝܡܢܘܬܐ ܕܠܝܬ ܒܗ ܛܥܝܘܬܐ *unwavering faith.* b) *misleading, deceiving, deception* e. g. of the devil; *foolish ignorance, forgetfulness.*

ܛܥܝܢܘܬܐ pl. ܬ̈ܐ rt. ܛܥܢ. f. *produce, yield;* ܛܥܝܢܘܬ ܦܐܪ̈ܐ *bearing fruit, fruitfulness.*

ܛܥܶܡ fut. ܢܶܛܥܰܡ, imper. ܛܥܰܡ, act. part. ܛܳܥܶܡ, ܛܳܥܡܳܐ, pass. part. ܛܥܺܝܡ, ܡܳܐ, ܡܬܳܐ. *to taste, take food, eat* with ܠ or ܡܶܢ; ܟܰܕ ܛܳܥܶܡ *while he was eating;* metaph. *to taste, try, touch, perceive; experience;* ܡܰܘܬܳܐ ܠܳܐ ܛܥܶܡ *he did not taste death;* ܛܥܶܡܘ ܫܘܢܳܩܶܐ *they experienced torments;* ܛܥܶܡܘ ܚܰܝܠܳܐ ܕܰܡܫܺܝܚܳܐ *they had experience of the power of Christ.* Pass. part. *a)* verbal use, ܠܳܐ ܛܥܺܝܡ ܗ̄ܘܳܐ ܡܶܕܶܡ ܠܗܽܘܢ ܝܰܘܡܳܬܳܐ ܣܰܓܺܝܐ̈ܳܬܳܐ *they had tasted nothing for several days. b)* adj. *tasting of, tasty, palatable;* metaph. *agreeable; sapient;* ܛܥܺܝܡ ܡܶܢ ܟܽܠ ܛܥܽܘܡܺܝܢ *more savoury than all savours;* ܫܶܡ ܛܥܺܝܡ *an acceptable* or *honourable name,* opp. ܫܶܡ ܦܟܺܝܗ *an insipid* or *vain name.* ETHPE. ܐܶܬ݂ܛܥܶܡ *a) to be tasted. b) to taste of, taste like. c)* metaph. *to be perceived, tried, discerned;* ܡܶܛܽܠ ܕܢܶܬ݂ܛܥܶܡ ܟܽܠܢܳܫ *every one may perceive. d) to be grafted.* ETHPA. ܐܶܬ݂ܛܰܥܰܡ *to be budded* or *grafted;* metaph. ܒܪܶܗ ܕܰܐܠܳܗܳܐ ܨܒ݂ܳܐ ܕܢܶܬ݂ܛܰܥܰܡ ܒܰܒ݂ܬ݂ܽܘܠܬܳܐ the Son of God willed *to be grafted upon the Virgin.* APH. ܐܰܛܥܶܡ *a) to make to taste, perceive* or *experience; to acquire a taste, get a taste for;* ܐܰܛܥܶܡܘ ܚܰܝܘ̈ܳܬ݂ܳܐ ܡܶܢ ܡܶܢܝܳܢܳܐ ܕܩܛܺܝܠ̈ܶܐ ܒܩܪܳܒ݂ܳܐ wild beasts from the number of those slain in battle *had acquired a taste for human flesh;* metaph. ܡܰܛܥܡܺܝܢ ܒܥܽܘܬ݂ܪܳܐ ܡܰܩܘܝܳܢܳܐ *having a taste for abiding wealth. b) to ingraft,* also *to implant firmly.* ETHTAPH. ܐܶܬ݂ܬܰܛܥܰܡ *to be ingrafted, inserted, fixed.* DERIVATIVES, ܛܥܽܘܡܳܐ, ܛܥܽܘܡܳܐ, ܛܰܥܡܳܐ, ܛܶܥܡܳܐ, ܛܥܺܝܡܳܐ, ܛܥܺܝܡܳܐܝܬ݂, ܡܰܛܥܡܳܢܽܘܬ݂ܳܐ, ܛܰܥܡܬ݂ܳܐ, ܛܥܺܝܡܳܐ, ܛܥܺܝܡܽܘܬ݂ܳܐ, ܡܰܛܥܡܳܢܳܐ, ܡܰܛܥܡܳܢܽܘܬ݂ܳܐ, ܡܶܬ݂ܛܰܥܡܳܢܳܐ.

ܛܥܳܡܳܐ, ܛܥܳܡ pl. ܡ̈ܶܐ rt. ܛܥܡ. m. *taste, taking a taste of;* ܟܰܕ ܛܳܥܶܡ ܚܰܡܪܳܐ *while he tasted wine;* metaph. *taste, perception, discernment, sapience, sense;* ܐܰܢ̄ܬ݁ܬ݂ܳܐ ܒܺܝܫܰܬ݂ ܛܥܳܡܳܐ *a woman of bad taste, without discretion;* ܚܰܝܶܐ ܕܠܳܐ ܛܥܳܡܳܐ *an insipid life;* ܛܥܳܡܳܐ ܝܳܗ̄ܒ݂ܳܐ ܠܗܶܕܝܽܘܛܶܐ *she gives discernment to the ignorant;* ܡܳܢܳܐ ܛܥܳܡܳܐ ܐܺܝܬ݂ ܒܡܶܠܬ݂ܳܐ *what sense is there in the saying?*

ܛܥܽܘܡܳܐ pl. ܡ̈ܶܐ rt. ܛܥܡ. m. *the grafting, budding* or *inoculation* of trees; ܐܳܘܢܳܐ ܕܛܥܽܘܡܳܐ *the season for making grafts; a graft, a sapling* or *shoot firmly planted.*

ܛܥܺܝܡܳܐ, ܡܬ݂ܳܐ rt. ܛܥܡ. *tasteful, of* or *in good taste, comely, agreeable, discreet, wise, witty.*

ܛܥܺܝܡܳܐܝܬ݂ rt. ܛܥܡ. adv. *wittily, discreetly.*

ܛܥܺܝܡܽܘܬ݂ܳܐ pl. ܘ̈ܳܬ݂ܳܐ rt. ܛܥܡ. f. *flavour, savour;* metaph. *sapience, discretion;* ܛܥܺܝܡܽܘܬ݂ܳܐ ܕܡܶܠܬܶܗ *the flavour* or *wit of* his *speech.*

ܛܥܺܝܡܳܢܳܐ, ܡܬ݂ܳܐ rt. ܛܥܡ. *having a strong savour, pungent;* ܡܶܠܚܳܐ ܛܥܺܝܡܳܢܳܐ *keen* or *sharp, salt;* metaph. *pleasant.*

ܛܰܥܡܬ݂ܳܐ or ܛܥܰܡܬ݂ܳܐ pl. ܛܰܥܡ̈ܳܬ݂ܳܐ or ܛܥܰܡ̈ܳܬ݂ܳܐ rt. ܛܥܡ. f. *a) taste, flavour, sweet savour. b) the sense of taste, perception, sense, appreciation, quality, property;* ܛܰܥܡܬ݂ܳܐ ܒܚܶܟܳܐ ܗ̄ܝ *the taste resides in the palate;* ܬ݁ܪܬܶܝܢ ܛܰܥܡܳܢ ܐܺܝܬ݂ ܠܶܗ *the will has two properties,* that of willing and of refusing; ܛܰܥܡ̈ܳܬ݂ܳܐ ܕܗܰܝܡܳܢܽܘܬ݂ܳܐ *the perceptions of faith. c) a taste, slight repast; a taste, specimen. d) a grafting in.*

ܛܥܰܢ fut. ܢܶܛܥܽܘܢ, act. part. ܛܳܥܶܢ, ܛܳܥܢܳܐ, pass. part. ܛܥܺܝܢ, ܢܳܐ, ܢܬ݂ܳܐ. *a) to bear,* ܒܟܰܪܣܳܐ *in the womb;* ܦܺܐܪ̈ܶܐ *fruit. b) to bear, carry* ܥܰܠ ܟ݁ܬ݂ܦ݂ܳܬ݂ܳܐ *on the shoulders;* ܒܟܰܪܟܽܘܢܳܐ *in a litter,* the dead *to burial,* ܡܰܘܒܠܳܐ *a weight,* ܣܒܰܪ̈ܬܳܐ *tidings,* ܛܳܥܢܰܝ ܙܰܝܢܳܐ *armour-bearers; to bear on high, uphold, to bring, to carry away. c) to bear with, tolerate, endure,* ܥܰܡܠܳܐ *labour;* ܒܺܝܫܶܐ *the wicked;* with ܢܰܦ̮ܫܳܐ *to be patient.* Part. ܛܳܥܶܢ *a)* active verbal sense, ܛܳܥܶܢ ܐ̱ܢܳܐ ܒܺܐܝ̈ܕܰܝ *I bear in my hands,* ܐܰܝܢܳܐ ܐܶܪܙܳܐ ܛܳܥܢܺܝܢ ܗ̄ܘܰܘ ܕܶܩܠܶܐ *what symbolical meaning did the palms bear?* ܚܡܳܪ̈ܶܐ ܛܥܺܝܢܺܝܢ *laden asses. b)* passive sense, ܛܥܺܝܢ ܥܰܠ ܟܰܬ݂ܦ݂ܳܬ݂ܳܐ *borne on men's shoulders. c)* adjectival, answering to φόρος in composition, ܐܰܪܥܳܐ ܛܳܥܢܰܬ݂ ܦܺܐܪ̈ܶܐ *fruitful land;* with ܐܳܬ݂ܳܐ *a standard-bearer;* with ܙܳܟ݂ܽܘܬ݂ܳܐ *victorious;* ܛܥܺܝܢ ܚܰܡܪܳܐ *heavy with wine,* ܚܽܘܕܪܳܐ ܛܳܥܶܢ ܚܰܝܘ̈ܳܬ݂ܳܐ *the zodiacal circle* as bearing figures of animals; ܛܥܺܝܢܺܝܢ ܚܰܝܶܐ ܗܰܕ̈ܳܡܰܘܗ̄ܝ *his limbs were full of life;* ܛܳܥܶܢ ܚܰܝܶܐ *life-bringing* opp. ܛܳܥܶܢ ܡܰܘܬ݂ܳܐ *death-bringing, deadly;* with ܣܒܰܪ̈ܬܳܐ *a messenger;* ܡܘܕܥܳܢܽܘܬ݂ܳܐ *signifying;* ܣܰܟܺܝܢܳܐ *carrying a knife, an assassin;* ܥܽܘܬ݂ܪܳܐ *enriching, wealth-bringing;* ܦܺܐܪ̈ܶܐ *fruitful;* ܢܽܘܗܪܳܐ *Lucifer;* ܥܰܩܬ݂ܳܐ *bearing annoyance, anxiety.* ETHPE. ܐܶܬ݂ܛܥܶܢ *to be carried, borne, endured; to be laden, loaded;* ܥܰܣܩܺܝܢ ܠܡܶܬ݂ܛܥܳܢܽܘ *grievous to be borne.* APH. ܐܰܛܥܶܢ *a) to load, lade, freight, make carry;* with ܛܥܳܢܳܐ *to lay a burden* on any one; with ܪ̈ܟܫܐ to load the horses; ܛܥܢܘܗܝ ܠܐܣܛܥܢܘܗܝ ܥܠ ܪܫܗ they made him carry a tray upon his head; ܥܠ ܓܡ̈ܠܐ ܐܛܥܢ ܐܢܘܢ he mounted them on camels. b) to take up, pack up, carry a load; ܐܝܟ ܕܡܨܝܢ ܠܡܛܥܢ as much as they could carry; ܡܛܥܢܝܢ ܐܝܟ ܩܠܝܠ ܩܠܝܠ ܡܐܢܐ ܕܥܨܪܬܐ making the weight of a press bear gradually. ETTAPH. ܐܬܛܥܢ to be put into the scale; to be loaded, laden; to be compelled to bear; ܐܬܛܥܢ ܦܓܪܐ ܠܥܡܠܐ his body was made to undergo labours. DERIVATIVES, ܛܥܘܢܐ, ܛܥܘܢܘܬܐ, ܛܥܢܐ, ܛܥܝܢܐ, ܛܥܝܢܘܬܐ, ܡܛܥܢܢܐ.

ܛܥܢܐ, ܛܥܢ pl. ܐ̈ rt. ܛܥܢ. m. a load, burden, package, freight, cargo; ܛܥܢܐ ܕܓܡܠܐ a camel's load; ܛܥܢܐ ܕܚܡܪܐ a load of wine; ܕܦܪܙܠܐ a freight of iron; ܐܝܟ ܛܥ̈ܢܐ ܐܬܛܥܢܘ paralytics were conveyed like luggage; with ܣܒܠ or ܫܩܠ to take care of, take charge of, take trouble about, undertake; but ܫܩܠ ܛܥܢܐ ܡܢ to relieve of a burthen; ܫܩܘܠ ܛܥܢܐ a protector; ܡܫܩܠ ܛܥܢܐ care, pain, industry.

ܛܥܢܬܐ rt. ܛܥܢ. f. a crop of fruit.

ܛܥܐ or ܛܥܝ fut. ܢܛܥܐ, act. part. ܛܥܐ. to miss, err, fall, fall into error; ܕܠܐ ܚܓܝܪܐ ܢܛܥܐ that the lame may not lose the way; ܣܒܪܐ ܕܛܥܐ ܗܘܐ a hope that has missed i.e. not reached fulfilment, failed. ETHPE. ܐܬܛܥܝ to be missed, forgotten, neglected; ܐܢܫܘܬܗ ܕܡܫܝܚܐ ܠܐ ܡܬܛܥܝܐ the human nature of Christ is not to be forgotten i.e. mistaken notions should not be entertained about it. APH. ܐܛܥܝ to lead into error. DERIVATIVES, ܛܥܝܐ, ܛܥܝܘܬܐ, ܛܥܝܝܐ, ܛܥܝܐ.

ܛܥܝܐ rt. ܛܥܐ. full of error, erring.

ܛܦ PALPEL ܛܦܛܦ to flicker as a dying lamp for want of oil. ETHPALPAL. ܐܬܛܦܛܦ to bubble, sing as boiling water; to flicker.

ܛܦܐ fut. ܢܛܦܐ, act. part. ܛܦܐ, ܛܦܝܐ, pass. part. ܛܦܐ, ܛܦܝܐ. a) to shut, close, ܥܝ̈ܢܐ the eyes; ܬܪܥܐ the door; metaph. ܢܛܦܐ ܟܠ ܐܢܫ ܪܥܝܢܗ let every one compose his mind. b) to shut oneself up, shelter oneself, huddle. c) to lay near, apply closely, ܐܝܟ ܚܒܘܫܐ like a bandage; ܛܦܝܬܗ ܠܐܓܪܬܟ ܥܠ ܥܝ̈ܢܝ I pressed your letter to my eyes. PA. ܛܦܝ to press, embrace; to lay near; to include amongst; to attach, thrust or fasten in; ܛܥܢܐ ܡܛܦܝܐ ܓܦ̈ܐ ܕܦܪ̈ܚܬܐ ܐܚܪ̈ܢܝܬܐ ܒܓܘܗ the magpie sticks the feathers of other birds among her own; ܢܛܦܐ ܠܥܝ̈ܢܘܗܝ ܡܘܬܗ let us lay before his eyes, force on his notice, the fact of his death; with ܟܪܝܘܬܐ to lay sorrow upon any one; gram. to pronounce with a close sound, to contract. ETHPA. ܐܬܛܦܝ to be included; to cleave or keep close, to shelter oneself, commit or betake oneself, be joined by a covenant; ܐܢܐ ܠܐܠܦܐ ܡܬܛܦܐ ܐܢܐ I trust myself to the ship; ܡܪ̈ܥܝܬܗ ܡܬܛܦܝܐ ܗܘܬ ܬܚܝܬ ܟܢ̈ܦܝ ܨܠܘܬܗ his flock kept close under the wings of his prayer for protection; ܚܝ̈ܐ ܚܕ̈ܬܐ ܒܗ ܡܫܬܟܚܝܢ ܠܡܬܛܦܝܘ new life is found in nearness to Him. DERIVATIVES, ܛܦܝܐ, ܛܦܝܐ.

ܛܦܚ fut. ܢܛܦܚ, act. part. ܛܦܚ. a) to stretch out, spread out; ܝܡܝܢܝ ܛܦܚܬ ܫܡܝܐ my right hand hath spread out the heavens. b) to sparkle. PA. ܛܦܚ same as Peal; ܛܘܪ̈ܐ ܘܪ̈ܡܬܐ ܛܦܚܬ Thou hast spread out mountains and heights.

ܛܦܝܬܐ and ܛܦܝܬܐ pl. ܐ̈ m. τάπης, τάπητα, a carpet.

ܛܦܪܐ rt. ܛܦܪ. m. the side ܕܥܡܘܕܐ of a pillar; ܕܛܘܪܐ of a mountain.

ܛܦܝܐ rt. ܛܦܐ. m. the shutting or closing of a gate or door.

ܛܦܠܘܬܐ rt. ܛܦܠ. f. corruption of manners, depravity.

ܛܦܠ PEAL only particip. adj. ܛܦܝܠܐ defiled, corrupt; ܚܝ̈ܐ ܛܦܝ̈ܠܐ depraved lives. PAEL part. ܡܛܦܠ the same; ܛܠܝܐ ܕܠܐ ܡܛܦܠ an innocent child. ETHPA. ܐܬܛܦܠ pass. DERIVATIVE, ܛܦܠܘܬܐ.

ܛܦܣ fut. ܢܛܦܣ and ܢܛܦܘܣ, to take or seek refuge, take shelter, shelter oneself, with ܒ, ܒܡܠܟܐ ܕܝܘ̈ܢܝܐ with the Greek emperor; ܒܬܪ̈ܝܗܘܢ behind each other; ܒܟܢܦ̈ܘܗܝ under His wings; ܒܪ̈ܚܡܘܗܝ in His mercy.

ܛܦܣ denom. verb PAEL conj. from ܛܘܦܣܐ. to typify, symbolize, signify, figure, shadow forth; ܒܥܐܕ̈ܐ ܢܝܚܗ ܕܡܫܝܚܐ ܡܛܦܣܝܢܢ by festivals we show symbolically the rest of Christ; ܡܢܐ ܡܛܦܣ what is typified thereby? ETHPA. ܐܬܛܦܣ pass. ܐܪܐܙܐ ܕܐܝܟ ܒܛܠܠܐ ܩܕܡ ܐܬܛܦܣ the mystery which was prefigured as by a shadow; gram. to be formed.

ܛܦܪܐ pl. ܐ̈ f. *a*) *a finger-* or *toe-nail;* ܛܦܪ̈ܐ ܕܥܝ̈ܢܐ *horny membranes on the corners of the eyes;* ܗܠܟ ܥܠ ܪܝܫ ܛܦܪ̈ܘܗܝ ܡܗܠܟ ܗܘܐ *walking on tiptoe;* ܐܠܦܗ ܡܢ ܛܦܪ̈ܐ ܕܛܠܝܘܬܐ *he learnt it in his tender youth.* *b*) *a hoof, claw, talon, the leg* of a locust; ܡܦܠܓܐ ܛܦܪܐ ܠܬܪܝܢ ܦܠܓܘ̈ܢ *parting its hoof into two divisions.* *c*) *a sharp instrument shaped like a finger-nail.* *d*) *onycha*, a spice. *e*) *the onyx-stone.*

ܛܪ imperative of ܢܛܪ *to keep.*

ܛܪܐ and ܛܪܝ fut. ܢܛܪܐ, act. part. ܛܪܐ, ܛܪܝܐ, pass. part. ܛܪܐ, ܛܪܝܐ usually with ܒ, I. *to strike upon, beat against* as the waves; *to strike root* as a plant; *to beat back* or *off, drive away* with ܡܢ; *to come upon, befall, assail, to settle and sting* as the bee, *to light on* as the eye; *to allow* or *leave* to settle &c.; ܫܒܘܩ ܢܛܪܐ *let it settle;* ܫܒܘܩ ܢܛܪܐ ܩܪܝܪ *let it cool;* metaph. of conscience, doubt, fear, pain, peril; ܛܪܐ ܒܟ ܩܠܝܠ *he touched thee lightly;* ܛܪܐ ܒܗ ܡܘܬܐ *death comes upon him;* ܛܪܐ ܫܢܬܐ ܥܠ ܥܝ̈ܢܝܢ *slumber falls upon our eyes;* ܚܙ̈ܘܢܐ ܕܛܪܝܢ ܒܥܝ̈ܢܝܗܘܢ *visions which come before their eyes;* ܟܠܡܕܡ ܕܛܪܐ ܒܒܢܝ̈ܢܫܐ *all that assails* or *befalls human beings.* II. *to plaster, daub* with mortar. Pass. part. *smitten, beaten, assailed* esp. *harassed* by evil spirits; ܓܦܢ̈ܐ ܛܪܝܢ ܡܢ ܒܪܩܐ *vines struck by lightning;* ܛܪܝܐ ܗܘܬ ܡܢ ܛܠܝܘܬܗ̇ *she had been harassed by evil spirits from her childhood.* Ethpe. ܐܬܛܪܝ I. with ܒ *a*) *to assail, dash* or *strike against, to stumble at* or *against, be offended, displeased: to come* or *chance upon, run against.* *b*) *to be grazed, cut* as vines by a spade, *to be hurt, agitated* ܒܪܥܝܢܗ *in his mind;* ܢܦܠܬ ܘܠܐ ܐܬܛܪܝܬ *she fell without bruising herself.* II. *to be plastered, daubed* with mortar. Pa. ܛܪܝ intensive of Peal I. *to assail severely, strike in pieces.* Ethpa. ܐܬܛܪܝ *to dash, beat* or *rush against* as floods, *to assault* in war. Derivatives, ܡܛܪܘܬܐ, ܛܪܝܐ, ܡܛܪܝܢܘܬܐ.

ܛܪܓܘܕܐ, ܛܪܓܘܕܘܣ or ܛܪܓܘܕܝܣ m. ܛܪܓܘܕܝܬܐ f. τραγῳδός, *an actor, poet, singer;* ܛܪܓܘܕܐ ܕܪܘܚܐ David *the singer of the spirit.*

ܛܪܕ fut. ܢܛܪܘܕ, act. part. ܛܪܕ, ܛܪܕܐ, pass. part. ܛܪܝܕ, ܐ, ܬܐ. *to drive away, drive out, expel, excommunicate;* with ܫܐܕ̈ܐ, ܕܝ̈ܘܐ, &c. *to drive out devils;* ܝܪ̈ܬܐ ܕܛܪܝܕܝܢ ܗܘܘ *heirs who had been driven away* from their rights; ܓܘܕ̈ܐ ܕܗܪ̈ܛܝܩܐ ܛܪܝܕܐ *troops* of heretics *put to flight;* ܛܪܝܕܐ ܒܩܛܝܪܐ *impelled forward with violence.* Ethpe. ܐܬܛܪܕ *to be driven away* or *out, expelled, rejected.* Derivatives, ܛܪܕܐ, ܛܪܘܕܐ, ܛܪܝܕܘܬܐ.

ܛܪܕܐ rt. ܛܪܕ. m. *driving;* ܡܢ ܛܪܕܐ ܣܓܝܐܐ ܕܛܪܕܘ ܐܢܘܢ ܠܐܝܘ the mules were tired *from their having driven them so far;* ܛܪܕܐ ܕܫܐܕܐ *the driving out of a devil.*

ܛܪܘܓܐ pl. ܓܐ̈ same as ܐܛܪܘܓܐ m. *a citron, orange.*

ܛܪܘܕܐ, ܛܪܘܕܐ or ܛܪܘܕܐ, ܬܐ *squinting, crook-eyed.*

ܛܪܘܕܐ rt. ܛܪܕ. m. *the driving off, chasing away* of insects or birds; ܛܪܘܕܗ ܕܩܡܨܐ *driving off the locust.*

ܛܪܘܠܐ pl. ܠܐ̈ m. τρούλλα, *a ladle; iron pan.*

ܛܪܘܢܐ pl. ܢܝܢ, ܢܐ̈ m. *a*) τύραννος, *a tyrant, lord, ruler; a rebel;* ܛܪܘܢ̈ܐ ܦܠܣܛܝܢܝ̈ܐ *the lords of the Philistines.* *b*) as if from ܛܪܢܐ hence sometimes written ܛܘܪܢܐ. adj. *hard, cruel; contumacious, refractory, rebellious;* ܐܢܫ ܛܪܘܢ ܢܦܫܐ *one of flinty-soul, a soul hard as flint;* ܠܒܘ̈ܬܐ ܩܫ̈ܝܬܐ ܘܛܪܘܢ̈ܐ *dull and rebellious hearts;* ܦܟܐ ܛܪܘܢܐ ܐܝܟ ܕܢܫܝܒܐ *a stony* i.e. *dried up jaw-bone.* Derivatives, the three following words—

ܛܪܘܢܐܝܬ from ܛܪܘܢ. adv. *tyrannically, cruelly, violently.*

ܛܪܘܢܘܬܐ from ܛܪܘܢ f. *a*) *tyranny, tyrannical rule, outrageous ways, cruelty;* ܟܠܝܗ ܠܛܪܘܢܘܬܐ ܕܚܛܝܬܐ *He put a stop to the tyranny of sin.* *b*) *rebellion, defection;* ܫܪܝ ܡܓܠܦ ܪ̈ܐܙܐ ܕܢܟܠܐ ܘܛܪܘܢܘܬܐ ܠܘܩܒܠܗ *he began to forge secret conspiracy and rebellion against him.*

ܛܪܘܢܝܐ, ܢܝܬܐ from ܛܪܘܢ. adj. *tyrannical, cruel, violent, outrageous;* ܩܛܝܪܐ ܛܪܘܢܝܬܐ ܘܡܘܗܒܬܐ ܐܚܕ *by violence and bribery he seized* the patriarchate.

ܛܪܘܦܝܩܘܣ pl. ܛܪܘܦܝܩܐ τροπικός, *the solstice,* ܛܪܘܦܝܩܘܣ ܣܬܘܝܐ—ܩܝܛܝܐ *the winter solstice, the summer solstice; the tropic;* ܛܪܘܦܝܩܘܣ ܕܣܪܛܢܐ—ܕܓܕܝܐ *the tropic of Cancer, of Capricorn.*

ܛܪܘܦܝܩܝܐ, ܝܬܐ ـ from the above. *solstitial, tropical.*

ܛܪܘܦܪܝܘܢ pl. ܛܪܘܦܪܝܐ τροπάριον, *a short hymn.*

ܛܪܛܡ *to murmur, grumble.*

ܛܪܛܦ Palpal *to seethe, swell, surge* of fire, water, clouds; of thoughts, feelings. Ethpalpal ܐܬܛܪܛܦ *to be made to boil, bubble* or *seethe up;* ܕܢܬܡܠܐ ܛܓܢܐ ܡܫܚܐ ܘܢܬܛܪܛܦ *that the frying-pan be filled with oil and heated;* metaph. as Palpal of water, of an earthquake; ܝܡܐ ܡܬܛܪܛܦ ܘܡܬܥܒܪ *the sea surges and rages savagely.* Derivative, ܛܪܛܘܦܐ.

ܛܪܛܝܩܠ, ܛܪܛܝܩܠܐ pl. ܐ̈ ـ perhaps a corrupt form of ܩܪܛܝܩܠܐ *craticula.* m. *a flat iron plate with narrow openings for baking over the coals or for holding coals, a gridiron.*

ܛܪܛܫ Palpel of ܛܪܫ *to soil, blot.*

ܛܪܝ, ܛܪܝܐ rt. ܛܪܐ. I. *beating, buffeting* of the billows; metaph. ܛܪܝܐ ܕܬܐܪܬܐ *the buffeting of conscience.* II. *daubing, plastering.*

ܛܪܝܒܘܢܐ pl. ܐ̈ ـ m. *tribunus, a tribune, officer of the emperor.*

ܛܪܝܓܘܕܐ; see ܛܪܓܘܕܐ.

ܛܪܝܓܘܢܘܢ or ܛܪܝܓܘܢܘܢ, ܛܪܝܓܘܢܐ pl. ܛܪܝܓܘܢܘܬ f. τρίγωνον, *a triangle.*

ܛܪܝܕܘܬܐ rt. ܛܪܕ. f. *expulsion.*

ܛܪܝܛܐ, ܛܪܝܛܐ, ܛܪܝܛܝ or ܛܪܝܛܝܣ pl. ܛܪܝܛ̈ܐ τρίτη, *the third* esp. *the third Indict; tertian ague.*

ܛܪܝܡܐ *a*) corrupted from θέρμη, *fever. b*) *a pear.*

ܛܪܝܡܝܣܝܘܢ τριμίσιον, *a coin* worth three dirhems or about half-a-crown.

ܛܪܝܢܐ or ܛܪܝܢܐ Pers. m. *a tray woven of palm-leaves* or *osiers.*

ܛܪܝܢܐ, ܛܪܝܢܐ or ܛܪܝܢܐ m. *whey.*

ܛܪܝܣܩܠܝܣ τρισκελής, *a tripod, a three-legged table.*

ܛܪܝܦܘܕܐ τρίπους, τρίποδα *a*) *a poem in three-foot measure. b*) pl. ܛܪܝܦ̈ܐ *mantlets* or *sheds* to protect besiegers.

ܛܪܝܩ, ܛܪܝܩܐ, ܛܪܝܩܬܐ *a contentious, mischief-making, malicious* or *sly person* esp. *the devil;* ܐܬܛܠܡܬ ܚܘܐ ܡܢ ܛܪܝܩܐ Eve *was beguiled by the mischief-maker;* ܠܫܢܐ ܛܪܝܩܐ ܥܒܕ ܫܓܘܫܝܐ *a contentious tongue causeth confusion.*

ܛܪܝܩܐܝܬ adv. from the above. *slyly, cunningly, dishonestly.*

ܛܪܝܩܘܬܐ pl. ܬ̈ܐ from ܛܪܝܩܐ f. *cunning, unfairness, knavery.*

ܛܪܝܩܘܡܫܐ or ܛܪܘܡܩܘܡܫܐ pl. ܬܐ ـ f. *soles, sandals.*

ܛܪܝܡܝܣܝܘܢ *a coin;* see ܛܪܝܡܝܣܝܘܢ.

ܛܪܫ cf. ܛܪܛܫ *to soil, spoil, blot* writing.

ܛܪܢ denom. verb Pael conj. from ܛܪܢܐ. *to harden, indurate, petrify.* Ethpa. ܐܬܛܪܢ *to become hard, indurated* or *petrified.*

ܛܪܢܐ pl. ܝܢ ـ, ܐ̈ ـ m. *flint, hard stone, rock;* ܟܐܦܐ ܕܛܪܢܐ *hard rock, flinty rock;* ܩܫܝܘܬܐ ܛܪܢܐ *the hardness of flint;* ܠܒܐ ܕܛܪܢܐ *a heart of flint;* ܐܝܢܐ ܕܛܪܢ ܠܒܗ *he whose heart is hard as flint.* Derivatives, verb ܛܪܢ, ܛܪܢܝܬܐ, ܛܪܢܝܐ.

ܛܪܢܓܒܝܢ *a sort of manna.*

ܛܪܢܘܬܐ from ܛܪܢܐ f. *stony* or *excessively hard nature* e.g. ܛܪܢܘܬܐ ܕܐܕܡܢܛܐ *the extreme hardness of adamant.*

ܛܪܢܝܐ, ܛܪܢܝܬܐ from ܛܪܢܐ *flinty, rocky, hard.*

ܛܪܦ fut. ܢܛܪܘܦ, act. part. ܛܪܦ, ܛܪܦܐ, pass. part. ܛܪܝܦ, ܐ ـ, ܬܐ ـ. *to smite, buffet, dash against; to clap, flap, wave, move* with ܥܠ, ܒ or ܠ; ܛܪܦ ܥܠ ܚܕܝܗ *smiting his breast;* ܛܪܘܦ ܥܠ ܠܒܟ *smite upon thy heart;* ܓܦܐ ܕܛܪܦܝܢ ܚܕ ܥܠ ܚܕ *wings which touch against each other;* said also of billows, wind, &c. Pael ܛܪܦ *a*) *to buffet* or *smite repeatedly, treat roughly; to shake to and fro, shake off* leaves, *strip off* leaves; *to clap* the hands; ܡܛܪܦܝܢ ܒܪ̈ܓܠܝܗܘܢ *tottering on their feet, mincing;* ܢܛܪܦ ܐܝܕܗ ܥܠܝܗܘܢ *he shall wave his hand against them;* ܠܐ ܢܛܪܦ ܟܪܡܐ *he must strip the vine* of its leaves. *b*) usually pass. part. *to shake, harass, agitate, vex* by famine, war, plague, troubles; ܡܛܪ̈ܦܐ ܢܬܢܝܚܘܢ *the weary are at rest;* ܡܛܪܦ ܒܠܒܗ *smitten in his heart;* ܦܘܢܝܐ ܕܡܛܪܦܬܐ *the return of the shattered* Church to God. Ethpa. ܐܬܛܪܦ *a*) *to be shaken to and fro, ill-treated, harassed, agitated; afflicted;* with ܢܦܫܐ or ܪܘܚܐ *his spirit was harassed, agitated. b*) *to be weary, exhausted, worn out, disabled* by hunger, thirst, fatigue, disease; metaph. ܡܬܛܪܦ ܗܘܐ ܒܥܒܕܘܗܝ *he wore himself out in prayer.* c) *to reel, stagger* in drunkenness. Aph. ܐܛܪܦ *to smite, shake violently;* metaph. *to harass, vex;* ܐܛܪܦܬ ܐ̈ܦܝ ܒܐ̈ܝܕܝ ܗܘܝܬ *I smote my face with my hands; to wag* the tail. Derivatives, ܛܪܦܐ, ܛܪܦܐ, ܛܪܦܢܐ, ܛܪܦܘܬܐ, ܡܛܪܦܢܘܬܐ, ܡܛܪܦ, ܡܛܪܦܢܘܬܐ.

ܛܪܦܐ pl. ܛܪ̈ܦܐ rarely ܛܪ̈ܦܝܢ m. *a leaf;* ܛܪܦܐ ܕܟܪܘܒܐ *a cabbage-leaf;* ܛܪܦܐ ܕܩܢܝܐ *a green reed, fresh reed;* ܛܪ̈ܦܐ ܣܩܠܐ *spinach;* metaph. a) *a leaf* of a book. b) ܛܪܦܐ ܕܐܕܢܐ *the lobe of the ear;* ܛܪܦܐ ܕܟܒܕܐ *the lobe of the liver;* ܛܪܦܐ ܕܢܚܝܪܐ *the cartilage of the nostril.* c) ܛܪܦܐ ܕܣܡܝܕܐ or ܕܚܛ̈ܐ *bran.*

ܛܪܦܐ rt. ܛܪܦ. m. *a stroke, blow; the strokes* of a bird's wings; ܛܪܦܐ ܕܙܒܢܐ *a beat of time, a moment;* ܐܝܟ ܕܒܛܪܦܐ *as at one blow, as in a moment, very suddenly.*

ܛܪܦܘܣܐ *a skiff.*

ܛܪܦܝܛܝܣ, ܛܪܦܝܛܝܛܐ pl. ܐ̈ m. τραπεζίτης, *a money-changer.*

ܛܪܦܢܝܐ rt. ܛܪܦ. *leafy, made of leaves;* ܙܪ̈ܙܐ ܛܪ̈ܦܢܝܐ *girdles of leaves.*

ܛܪܦܣܐ pl. ܐ̈ m. *a corslet, cuirass* of mail.

ܛܪܦܣܬܐ pl. ܛܪ̈ܦܣܬܐ or ܛܪ̈ܦܣܢܬܐ f. *lean flesh.*

ܛܪܦܬܐ pl. ܬ̈ܐ f. *fine flour.*

ܛܪܘܢ, ܛܪܘܢܐ, ܛܪܘܢܬܐ *chief, excellent, best of its kind* as *the bravest, most valiant, wisest, most skilled; expert, vigorous, valuable;* ܠܝܬ ܛܪܘܢܐ ܕܠܐ ܐܝܬ ܛܪܘܢ ܡܢܗ ܐܚܪܢ *there is none so good but that there may be a better;* ܛܪܘܢ ܡܢ ܟܠ *excelling, best of all;* ܐܒܪܐ ܛܪܘܢܐ *the best tin;* ܒܥܝܪܐ—ܣܘܣܝܐ ܛܪܘܢܐ—ܟܘܕܢܝܐ ܛܪܘܢܬܐ *a strong* or *valuable beast, horse, mule;* ܚܨܘ̈ܕܐ ܛܪ̈ܘܢܐ *vigorous reapers;* ܢܘܪܐ ܛܪܘܢܬܐ *a strong fire;* ܥܝܪܐ ܛܪܘܢܐ ܘܡܬܚܝܠܢܐ *watchful, valiant and brave;* ܛܪ̈ܘܢܐ ܕܟܠܕܝ̈ܐ *the wisest of the Chaldaeans;* ܛܪ̈ܘܢܐ ܕܝܘ̈ܢܝܐ *the bravest of the Greeks;* ܛܪܘܢ ܢܒܝ̈ܐ *the greatest among the prophets.*

ܛܪܘܢܐܝܬ from ܛܪܘܢ. adv. *well, wisely, excellently, skilfully.*

ܛܪܘܢܘܬܐ from ܛܪܘܢ. f. *excellence, pre-eminence,* ܛܪܘܢܘܬܐ ܕܕܘܒܪܗܘܢ *the excellence of their way of life;* ܛܪܘܢܘܬܐ ܕܛܪ̈ܘܢܐ ܒܩܪܒܐ *the valour of the valiant is* shown *in war.*

ܛܪܩܛܛܘܢ m. *tractatulus, a little treatise.*

ܛܪܩܛܘܢ, ܛܪܩܛܛܘܢ or ܛܪܩܛܘܣ pl. ܐ̈ τράκτατον, *treating, negotiation;* ܐܫܬܕܪܘ ܠܛܪܩܛܘܢ *they were sent to negotiate.*

ܛܪܝܩܠܝܢܐ or ܛܪܩܠܝܢܐ pl. ܐ̈ m. τρικλίνιον, *a dining-room, inner room;* ܪܝܫ ܛܪܝܩܠܝܢܐ *the president of a banquet, master of a feast;* ܒܚܕ ܡܢ ܛܪ̈ܝܩܠܝܢܐ ܪ̈ܘܪܒܐ ܕܦܠܛܝܢ *in one of the great banqueting-halls of the palace.*

ܛܪܫ fut. ܢܛܪܘܫ, pass. part. ܛܪܝܫ, ܐ, ܬܐ. *to scatter, sprinkle, splash;* metaph. *to spot;* ܛܝܢܐ ܕܛܪܫ ܥܠ ܦܓܪ̈ܝܗܘܢ *the mud he splashed on their bodies;* ܟܕ ܠܐ ܛܪܝܫ ܒܟ ܡܘܡ ܕܓܠܐ *there being no spot of false semblance in thee.* Pa. ܛܪܫ with ܒܐܪܥܐ *to dash against the ground.* Ethpa. ܐܬܛܪܫ passive. Palpel ܛܪܫܫ *to spot, spatter, soil, sully, stain, pollute;* ܡܛܪܫܫ ܒܕܡܐ—ܒܒܝܫܬܐ *spotted with blood, with evil;* ܢܟܠܐ ܡܛܪܫܫ ܠܒܗ *guile pollutes his heart;* used esp. by writers in expressions of humility about their work; ܐܠܗܐ ܚܘܣ ܥܠ ܥܒܕܟ ܕܛܪܫܫ ܗܠܝܢ ܣܛܪ̈ܐ *O God, pardon thy servant for sullying these lines.* Ethpalp. ܐܬܛܪܫܫ *to be spotted, stained, defiled;* ܢܫܪܘܢ ܨܘܡܐ ܘܢܫܪܘܢ ܠܡܬܛܪܫܫܘ ܒܡܐܟܘܠܬܐ [illegible] *they will break the fast and begin to pollute themselves by eating prohibited food.* Derivatives, ܛܪܘܫܐ, ܡܛܪܫܫܢܘܬܐ.

ܛܪܫܐ and ܛܪܫܢܐ m. *a barren oak; a shrub.*

ܛܫܐ or ܛܫܝ fut. ܢܛܫܐ, act. part. ܛܫܐ, pl. ܛܫܝܢ, pass. part. ܛܫܐ, ܛܫܝܐ, ܛܫܝܬܐ. *to hide, conceal; to hide oneself; lie hid;* ܥܪܩ ܘܛܫܐ *he fled and hid;* pass. part. *hidden, concealed, secret, occult;* ܛܫܝܢ ܒܡܥܪܬܐ *concealed in a cave;* pl. f. emph. ܛܫܝ̈ܬܐ *hidden* or *secret* sins, treasures, &c.; also *hiding-places;* ܡܛܫܝ̈ܬܐ ܗܘܘ ܪܡܝܢ ܒܡܛܫܝ̈ܬܐ *they lay in secret places;* gram. *understood* e.g. in an elliptical phrase as ܟܦܐ ܩܡܚܐ *a handful of flour,* where ܡܢ *of* is understood; ܐܣܘܪܐ ܛܫܝܐ *a conjunction lying hid* or *understood.* Pa. ܛܫܝ *to hide, conceal; to conceal* or *excuse* a fault; ܩܐܝܢ ܘܥܟܪ ܘܓܝܚܙܝ ܘܝܗܘܕܐ ܛܫܝܘ ܥܘܠܗܘܢ *Cain, Achar, Gehazi, Judas concealed* their wrongdoing; ܡܛܫܝܐ = ܡܛܫܝܢܐ *I conceal;* ܣܝܡܬܐ ܡܛܫܝܬܐ *hidden treasure;* also ܡܛܫܝܬܐ ellipt. the same; ܡܛܫܝ̈ܬܐ ܕܝܕܥܬܐ *hidden stores of knowledge;* ܡܠܬܐ ܡܛܫܝܬܐ *a secret saying* i.e. one in which the sense is hidden; ܡܛܫܝ̈ܬܐ ܕܡܠܟܐ *secret counsels of the king, secrets of state;* ܟܬܒ̈ܐ ܡܛܫܝ̈ܐ *the Apocryphal Books.* ETHPA. ܐܬܛܫܝ *to hide* or *conceal oneself, be hidden, lie in hiding;* ܐܬܛܫܝܘ ܐܕܡ ܘܐܢܬܬܗ ܒܝܬ ܐܝܠܢ̈ܐ *Adam and his wife hid themselves among the trees;* ܐܬܛܫܝܘ ܡ̈ܝܐ *the water disappeared* in the earth. APHEL ܐܛܫܝ *to hide, secrete; to conceal, lay up* or *store in a secret place;* ܦܘܩܕ̈ܢܝ ܐܛܫܐ ܒܠܒܟ *lay up my commandments in thine heart;* pl. f. emph. ܡܛܫܝ̈ܢܬܐ *hiding* or *lurking-places, places of concealment* opp. PA. part. ܡܛܫܝ̈ܢܬܐ *the things concealed;* ܡܥܪ̈ܐ ܕܡܛܫܝܢܘܬܗܘܢ *the caves where they lay hid;* ܚܢܩ ܚܢ̈ܝܩܐ ܒܡܛܫܝ̈ܢܬܐ *he suffocated some in* their *hiding-places.* DERIVATIVES, ܛܫܝܐ, ܛܫܝܘܬܐ, ܛܫܝܬܐ, ܡܛܫܝܢܬ, ܡܛܫܝܢܘܬܐ.

ܛܫܝܘܬܐ rt. ܛܫܐ. f. *hiding away.*

ܛܫܝܬܐ rt. ܛܫܐ. f. *an extinguisher;* ܕܫܪܓܐ *of a candle.*

ܛܫܝܬܝ mountain dialect. *indeed! really!*

✣ ܫܠܡܬ ܐܬܘܬܐ ܛܝܬ ܗܘܐ ܕܫܠܡ ܒܫܠܡܘܬܐ ✣

✣ ܬܘܒ ܡܫܪܝܢܢ ܠܡܟܬܒ ܒܝܘܕ. ܒܥܘܕܪܢܗ ܕܡܪܝܐ ܕܫܘܪܝܐ ܕܬܫܒܘܚܬܐ ✣

✣ ܝ ✣

ܝ

ܝ i.e. ܝܘܕ *Yud,* the tenth letter of the alphabet; the number 10; with a point above, ܝ̇, 100; with ܕ prefixed, ܕܝ, *the tenth.*

ܝܐ interj. *Ho! O! Oh!*

ܝܐܐ or ܝܐܝ, ܝܐܝܐ, ܝܐܝܬܐ pl. m. ܝܐܝܢ, pl. f. ܝܐܝܢ, ܝܐܝ̈ܬܐ pres. part. of a verb no longer in use; *fair, comely, becoming, seemly, suitable, meet, virtuous, noble, honourable;* ܝܐܝܬ contraction of ܝܐܝ ܐܢܬ m. and ܝܐܝܐ ܐܢܬܝ = ܝܐܝܬܝ f. *thou art fair* &c.; ܪܓܬܐ ܝܐܝܬܐ *a virtuous desire;* ܝܐܐ ܘܙܕܩ *it is meet and right;* impers. with ܠ, *it becomes, beseems, befits, is due;* ܐܝܩܪܐ ܕܝܐܐ ܗܘܐ ܠܥܡܠܗ *the honour due to his labours;* ܬܫܒܘܚܬܐ ܝܐܝܐ ܗܝ ܠܗ *praise befits him, is comely for him;* ܡܕܡ ܕܝܐܐ ܠܡܠܦܢܘܬܐ ܚܠܝܡܬܐ *things which befit, are in accordance with, sound doctrine.* DERIVATIVE, ܝܐܝܘܬܐ.

ܝܐܒ fut. ܢܐܒ, act. part. ܝܐܒ, ܝܐܒܐ, pass. part. ܝܐܝܒ, ܝܐܝܒܐ, ܝܐܝܒܬܐ PE. hardly used except in the parts. both of which have active meaning, *to pant after, desire eagerly* or *fervently; to long for;* ܟܦܢܝܢ ܘܝܐܒܝܢ ܠܗ *they hunger and pant after it;* ܝܐܒ ܗܘܐ ܠܗܕܐ *he longed for this;* ܒܥܘܬܐ ܝܐܝܒܬܐ *fervent supplication.* PA. ܝܐܒ pass. part. ܡܝܐܒ *filled with longing; full of passionate desire.* The ETHPAAL has various forms ܐܬܝܐܒ, ܐܬܝܐܒ, ܐܬܝܒ and ܐܬܝܒ *to long for, desire ardently;* ܥܢ̈ܐ ܡܬܝܐܒܢ ܠܪܥܝܟ *the sheep eagerly desire thy pasture;* ܢܦܫܝ ܐܬܝܐܒܬܟ ܒܠܠܝܐ *my soul hath desired thee in the night.* DERIVATIVES, ܝܐܒܬܐ, ܝܐܝܒܘܬܐ, ܝܐܒܐ, ܝܐܒܬܐ, ܡܝܐܒܢܘܬܐ, ܡܬܝܐܒܢܘܬܐ, ܡܬܝܐܒܢܐ, ܡܬܝܐܒܢܐܝܬ, ܡܬܝܐܒܘܬܐ.

ܝܐܝܒܐܝܬ rt. ܝܐܒ. adv. *eagerly, with desire.*

ܝܐܝܒܘܬܐ rt. ܝܐܒ. f. *eager longing, earnest desire.*

ܝܐܝܘܬܐ rt. ܝܐܐ. f. *beauty, grace, comeliness, seemliness, honourableness;* ܫܘܦܪܐ ܝܐܝܐ *fair beauty.*

ܝܐܠܐ in the dialect of Tirhan. *nightmare.*

ܝܐܣܡܝܢ jasmine.

ܝܒܒ Pael ܝܰܒܶܒ, fut. ܢܝܰܒܶܒ. *a) to make a joyful noise, sound* a trumpet, *blow* a horn. *b) to shout; to howl* as the wind. Derivative, ܝܒܒܐ.

ܝܰܒܳܝܣ *a) puberty, adolescence;* ܒܝܰܒܳܝܣ *the state of puberty. b)* ἶβις, *the ibis.*

ܝܰܒܺܝܫܽܘܬܳܐ rt. ܝܒܫ. f. *dryness, drought.*

ܝܒܠ root-meaning *to flow.* Pael ܝܰܒܶܠ *a) to do anything by course* or *in succession, to hand down, transmit from one to another;* ܠܡܰܠܟܽܘܬܳܐ ܕܥܳܠܡܳܐ ܝܰܒܶܠܬ *I have related in order of time the empire of the world;* ܡܝܰܒܠܝܢ ܐܟ̣ܠܺܝܠܳܐ *those who wore the crown in succession. b) to bring, escort; to translate; to follow in order;* ܢܒ̣ܺܝܶܐ ܕܡܝܰܒܠܺܝܢ ܗ̱ܘܰܘ ܠܗܽܘܢ ܡܶܠܬܳܐ ܐܠܳܗܳܝܬܳܐ the prophets *who had brought the divine word to them;* ܕܢܝܰܒܠܽܘܢ ܩܛܺܝܓܳܪܶܐ *that they may bring accusations;* ܡܝܰܒܠܳܢ ܫܳܥܰܝܟ *thy hours pass by.* Ethpa. ܐܶܬ݂ܝܰܒܰܠ *a) to be handed down in succession, transmitted, perpetuated;* ܗܰܝܡܳܢܽܘܬ݂ܳܐ ܕܠܘܳܬܰܢ ܐܶܬ݂ܝܰܒܠܰܬ *the faith which was handed down to us. b) to be derived, generated; to take one's origin, descend from;* ܡܰܠܟܶܐ ܕܡܶܢܳܟ ܡܶܬ݂ܝܰܒܠܺܝܢ *the kings who take their origin from thee. c) to be brought, escorted, accompanied;* ܒܡܰܪܕܺܝܬܶܗ ܡܶܬ݂ܝܰܒܰܠ ܗ̱ܘܳܐ ܡܶܢ ܐܰܬ݂ܪܳܐ ܠܰܐܬ݂ܪܳܐ *on his journey he was escorted from one place to another. d) to be translated;* ܦܶܣܽܘܩܳܐ ܐ̱ܚܪܳܝܳܐ ܐܶܬ݂ܝܰܒܰܠ *the last line has been translated* from the Greek. Aph. ܐܰܘܒܶܠ *to bring, lead, take, carry; to admit; to receive,* ܐܰܘܒܶܠܘ ܥܰܒܽܘܪܳܐ ܠܟܰܦܢܳܐ ܕܒܳܬܰܝܟܽܘܢ *carry corn for the famine of your houses;* ܢܰܘܒܶܠ ܩܽܘܪܒܳܢܶܐ ܠܡܳܪܝܳܐ a people *shall bring offerings to the Lord;* ܐܽܘܪܚܳܬ݂ܳܐ ܕܡܰܘܒܠܳܢ ܠܚܰܝܶܐ *ways leading to salvation;* ܡܰܘܒܠܺܝܢ ܗ̱ܘܰܘ ܡܶܠܰܘܗ̱ܝ *they received his words;* ܐܰܘܒܶܠ ܐܶܢܽܘܢ ܠܘܳܬ ܦܳܬܽܘܪܶܗ *he admitted them to his table.* Ettaph. ܐܶܬ݁ܬܰܘܒܰܠ *to be led, brought, carried, removed; to be translated* of a bishop; *to be driven* ܠܟܳܐ ܘܰܠܟܳܐ *hither and thither.* Derivatives, ܝܒܠܐ, ܝܒܠܐ, ܝܘܒܠܐ, ܝܘܒܠܢܐ, ܡܘܒܠܐ, ܡܘܒܠܢܐ, ܡܝܒܠܢܐ, ܡܝܒܠܢܘܬܐ, ܡܬܝܒܠܢܘܬܐ, ܡܬܘܒܠܢܘܬܐ.

ܝܰܒܠܳܐ, ܝܰܒܶܠ rt. ܝܒܠ. m. *a) a stream;* ܐܺܝܠܳܢܳܐ ܕܫܪܺܝܪ ܥܰܠ ܝܰܒܠܳܐ *a tree firmly rooted by the stream. b) couch-grass* sometimes ܝܰܒܠܳܐ ܕܝܰܡܳܐ; ܝܰܒܠܳܐ ܕܝܰܡܳܐ *seaweed, squill, rush.*

ܝܒ̣ܳܠܳܐ rt. ܝܒܠ. m. *a burden.*

ܝܰܒܠܳܐ *a measure* equal to two skins full; *a great water-pot.*

ܝܰܒܠܽܘܢ m. *a wind.*

ܝܰܒܶܡ denom. verb Pael conj. from ܝܰܒܡܳܐ *to marry a husband's widow, to fulfil the part of a brother* in raising up a son to continue the father's name.

ܝܰܒܡܳܐ, ܝܰܒܶܡ m. *a brother-in-law, the husband's brother whose duty it was to raise up heirs to his deceased brother.* Derivatives, verb ܝܒܡ, ܝܒܡܬܐ, ܝܒܡܘܬܐ.

ܝܰܒܶܡܬܳܐ const. rt. ܝܰܒܡܰܬ݂. pl. ܝܰܒܡܳܬ݂ܳܐ f. *a sister-in-law to be taken after her husband's death by his brother.*

ܝܰܒܢܳܐ pl. ܝܶܐ m. *a buzzard.*

ܝܰܒܪܽܘܚܳܐ pl. ܝܶܐ m. *mandragora, the mandrake, love-apple.*

ܝܒܶܫ rarely ܐܝܒܫ, fut. ܢܺܐܒܰܫ, infin. ܡܶܐܒܰܫ, act. part. ܝܳܒܶܫ, ܝܳܒܫܳܐ, pass. part. ܝܰܒܺܝܫܳܐ, ܝܰܒܺܝܫܬܳܐ. *a) to be dried up, arid; to dry up* intr.; *to be stanched;* ܝܒܶܫܘ ܡܰܝܳܐ ܡܶܢ ܐܰܪܥܳܐ *the waters dried up from the earth. b) to fade, wither; to be shrivelled* as trees with cold; *to droop, languish;* ܒܰܪ ܒܠܺܠܝܳܐ ܐܺܝܬ݂ܰܘܗ݈ܝ ܘܒܰܪ ܒܠܺܠܝܳܐ ܝܒܶܫ *in one night it sprang up and in one night withered;* ܝܒܶܫ ܡܶܢ ܕܶܚܠܬܳܐ *shrivelling from fear;* part. adj. ܝܰܒܺܝܫܳܐ, ܝܰܒܺܝܫܬܳܐ rt. ܝܒܫ. *dry, dried* or *burnt up, withered; having withered* or *wasted limbs;* fem. emph. ellipt. for ܐܰܪܥܳܐ ܝܰܒܺܝܫܬܳܐ *dry land.* Pael ܝܰܒܶܫ *to parch, dry up* tr., *desiccate.* Ethpa. ܐܶܬ݂ܝܰܒܰܫ *to become dried up, parched.* Aphel ܐܰܘܒܶܫ *to dry, dry up, shrivel;* ܝܰܡܡܶܐ ܐܰܘܒܶܫ *He dried up the seas,* i.e. *turned the sea into dry land;* ܩܽܘܪܳܐ ܕܡܰܘܒܶܫ ܘܚܽܘܡܳܐ ܕܡܰܘܩܶܕ *the cold which dries up and the heat which burns up.* Derivatives, ܝܒܝܫܐ, ܝܒܝܫܘܬܐ, ܝܒܫܐ, ܝܒܫܢܐ, ܝܘܒܫܐ, ܝܘܒܫܢܐ, ܡܘܒܫܢܘܬܐ, ܡܝܒܫܢܐ.

ܝܰܒܫܳܐ rt. ܝܒܫ. m. *dry land, earth,* opp. ܝܰܡܳܐ *sea,* ܐܶܙܰܠ ܒܝܰܒܫܳܐ *he went by land.*

ܝܰܒܫܳܢܳܐ, ܝܰܒܫܳܢܳܝܬܳܐ rt. ܝܒܫ. *terrestrial,* ܚܰܝܘ̈ܳܬ݂ܳܐ ܝܰܒܫܳܢܳܝܳܬ݂ܳܐ *land animals,* opp. ܚܰܝܘ̈ܳܬ݂ܳܐ ܡܰܝܳܢܳܝܳܬ݂ܳܐ *aquatic creatures.*

ܝܰܒܫܽܘܬ݂ܳܐ rt. ܝܒܫ. m. *drought.*

ܝܰܒܫܳܢܳܝܳܐ, ܝܰܒܫܳܢܳܝܬܳܐ rt. ܝܒܫ. *terrestrial, living on dry land.*

ܝܓܐ not used in Peal. Aph. ܐܰܘܓܺܝ *to send* or *drive away, to expel, reject, remove;* ܒܺܝܫܳܬܳܐ ܢܰܘܓܶܐ ܡܶܢܶܗ *he will reject evil things;* ܘܠܳܐ ܬܰܘܓܶܝܢܝ ܡܶܢ ܡܶܡܠܠܳܟ݂ *lest thou drive me away from converse with thee.* Derivatives, ܡܰܘܓܝܳܢܳܐ, ܡܰܘܓܝܳܢܽܘܬܳܐ, ܬܰܘܓܺܝܬܳܐ.

ܝܓܪ Shaphel ܫܰܓܪܺܝ. *to fling, hurl, to throw down* or *upon;* ܟܺܐܦܶܐ ܕܡܫܰܓܪܺܝܢ ܡܶܢ ܫܽܘܪܳܐ *the stones which they hurl down from the rampart.* Eshtaph. ܐܶܫܬܰܓܪܺܝ *to be hurled down; to be downcast, abject.* Derivatives, ܫܽܘܓܪܳܝܳܐ, ܡܫܰܓܪܳܢܳܐ, ܝܓܳܪܳܐ.

ܝܓܳܪ, ܝܓܳܪܳܐ pl. ܝܓܳܖ̈ܝܢ, ܝܓܳܖ̈ܐ m. *a heap of stones, a barrier.*

ܝܕ emph. ܐܺܝܕܳܐ, constr. ܐܺܝܕ, pl. ܐܺܝܕܰܝܢ, ܐܺܝܕܶܐ, ܐܺܝܕܰܘܳܬܳܐ (this last form of pl. is used for inanimate things), constr. ܐܺܝܕܰܝ. f. *a) the hand;* ܐܺܝܕܶܗ ܕܝܰܡܺܝܢܳܐ—ܕܣܶܡܳܠܳܐ *his right, his left hand;* ܐܺܝܕܳܐ ܕܡܰܘܡܳܬܳܐ *the right hand* used in taking *oaths;* ܐܺܝܕܳܐ ܛܳܒܬܳܐ ܗܘܳܐ ܟܳܬܶܒ ܒܰܟܬܺܝܒܳܬܳܐ *he wrote a good hand. b) the fist;* ܐܰܠܬܺܝܛܶܐ ܕܒܺܐܝܕܳܐ *pugilists. c) the paw, forepaw; the axle* of a wheel; *the arm* of a seat or throne; *a handle,* ܝܰܕ ܡܰܩܠܕܳܐ *the handle of a bolt; the clapper* of a bell; ܐܺܝܕܰܝܳܐ ܕܦܰܪܙܠܳܐ *iron hands* an instrument of torture. *d) the side, bank, shore;* ܝܰܕ ܐܽܘܪܚܳܐ *the roadside;* ܝܰܕ ܝܰܡܳܐ *the seashore;* ܝܰܕ ܢܰܚܠܳܐ ܕܢܰܗܖ̈ܘܳܬܳܐ— *the bank of a torrent, of rivers,* &c.

Metaph. *a) power, dominion;* ܐܺܝܕܳܐ ܐܰܚܺܝܕܬܳܐ *a mighty hand;* ܐܺܝܕܶܗ ܕܡܳܪܝܳܐ *the hand of the Lord;* ܐܺܝܕܳܐ ܕܪܽܗܘܡܳܝܶܐ *the Roman government; help, opportunity* cf. prep. below and ܥܶܕܳܢ; ܐܺܝܕܳܐ ܐܰܝܟ ܡܳܐ ܕܳܝܗܒܳܐ ܐܺܝܕܳܐ *as opportunity offers; bounty, liberality;* ܐܺܝܕܳܐ ܪܘܺܝܚܬܳܐ the same; ܐܰܝܟ ܐܺܝܕܳܐ ܕܡܰܠܟܳܐ *according to the bounty of the king. b)* ܐܺܝܕܳܐ ܪܳܡܬܳܐ *a high hand, haughtiness. c) laying on of hands, ordination;* ܐܺܝܕܳܐ ܕܟܳܗܢܽܘܬܳܐ ܕܡܫܰܡܫܳܢܽܘܬܳܐ— *ordination to the priesthood, to the diaconate;* cf. ܣܝܳܡ ܐܺܝܕܳܐ = ܫܽܘܡܠܳܝܳܐ.

Adv. ܐܺܝܕܳܐ ܒܐܺܝܕܳܐ or ܒܰܐܝܕܰܝܳܐ *on every hand, on every side, round about;* ܐܺܝܕܳܐ ܠܳܐܝܕܳܐ *one after another, in order, successively;* ܠܳܐܝܕܳܐ ܠܳܐܝܕܳܐ *little by little, gradually, in order.*

With preps. ܒܝܰܕ, ܒܐܺܝܕܳܐ and ܒܐܺܝܕܰܝ *through, by, by means of, by the help of, with, by reason of, according to, throughout, during;* ܒܝܰܕ ܐܰܠܳܗܳܐ *by the help of God;* ܒܐܺܝܕܰܝܗܽܘܢ *by their assistance, by means of them;* ܠܳܐ ܗܘܳܐ ܒܐܺܝܕܰܝ *it was not in my power, it did not depend on me;* ܒܐܺܝܕܰܝܢ *by our help, through us;* ܒܝܰܕ ܩܰܠܺܝܠ ܝܰܘܡܳܬܳܐ *for a few days;* — ܒܝܰܕ ܗܳܝ ܕ *on that account, therefore, because, that;* ܒܐܺܝܕܳܐ *in deed* opp. ܒܡܶܠܬܳܐ *in word;* ܡܶܢ ܝܰܕ ܡܶܢ ܐܺܝܕܳܐ *on account of, through, from;* ܝܰܕ ܪܽܘܚܳܐ *through the wind, by the force of the wind;* ܠܘܳܬ ܐܺܝܕܳܐ, ܠܝܰܕ *by, near, through;* ܠܝܰܕ ܬܰܪܥܳܐ *near the gate;* with ܠܒܰܪ *open, outward;* ܬܶܐܘܳܪܺܝܰܐ ܕܠܒܰܪ ܐܺܝܕܳܐ *an obvious* or *superficial theory;* with ܬܚܶܝܬ *under the power* of, *subject.*

ܝܕ root-meaning *to love,* Pael ܝܰܕܶܕ. *to love.* Ethpa. ܐܶܬܝܰܕܰܕ *to be beloved.* Derivatives, ܝܰܕܺܝܕܳܐ, ܝܰܕܺܝܕܽܘܬܳܐ.

ܝܕܐ not used in Peal. Ethpa. ܐܶܬܝܰܕܺܝ variously interpreted as *to be strengthened* or *to prophesy.* Aphel ܐܰܘܕܺܝ *to confess, acknowledge, profess, assert, affirm* with ܒ or ܠ; ܟܰܕ ܡܰܘܕܶܝܢ ܒܰܣܟܠܘܳܬܗܽܘܢ *confessing their sins;* generally of faith *to believe, believe openly;* ܡܰܘܕܶܝܢ ܒܰܡܫܺܝܚܳܐ *they believe in Christ;* ܡܶܢ ܕܠܳܐ ܚܕܳܐ ܩܢܽܘܡܳܐ ܡܰܘܕܶܐ ܒܰܡܫܺܝܚܳܐ *whoso does not confess one hypostasis in Christ;* ܠܳܐ ܡܰܘܕܶܐ ܗܽܘ ܕܗܰܝܡܳܢܽܘܬܰܢ *he is not of our faith;* ܡܰܘܕܝܳܢܶܐ *confessors.* With ܠ *to give thanks, to praise;* ܡܰܘܕܶܐ ܐ̱ܢܳܐ ܠܰܐܠܳܗܳܐ *I give thanks unto God;* ܐܰܘܕܺܝ ܠܰܚܢܳܢܳܟ ܚܰܢܳܢܳܐ *I praise Thy mercy, O merciful One.* Ethtaph. ܐܶܬܬܰܘܕܺܝ *to be confessed; to be acknowledged, declared, accepted, recognised; to be preached; to be praised;* ܬܠܺܝܬܳܝܽܘܬܳܐ ܕܰܒܬܠܺܝܬܳܝܽܘܬ ܬܶܫܒܽܘܚܬܳܐ ܡܶܬܬܰܘܕܝܳܐ *the Trinity praised with a threefold song;* ܡܶܬܬܰܘܕܝܳܐ ܫܰܪܺܝܪܳܐܝܬ *accepted as true;* ܡܶܬܬܰܘܕܶܝܢ ܗܘܰܘ ܡܶܢ ܟܽܠ ܐ̱ܢܳܫ ܕܡܰܝܬܪܺܝܢ *they were universally acknowledged excellent.* Eshtaphal ܐܶܫܬܰܘܕܺܝ *a) to confess. b) to consent;* with ܥܰܡ *to league, make alliance with. c) to promise;* ܐܶܫܬܰܘܕܺܝܘ ܠܶܗ ܕܢܶܬܠܽܘܢ ܠܶܗ ܟܶܣܦܳܐ *they promised to give him money;* ܐܰܝܟ ܡܳܐ ܕܐܶܫܬܰܘܕܺܝ *as he had promised.* Derivatives, ܡܰܘܕܝܳܢܳܐ, ܡܰܘܕܝܳܢܺܝܬ, ܡܰܘܕܝܳܢܽܘܬܳܐ, ܡܶܫܬܰܘܕܝܳܢܳܐ, ܡܶܫܬܰܘܕܝܳܢܽܘܬܳܐ, ܡܶܬܬܰܘܕܝܳܢܳܐ, ܡܶܬܬܰܘܕܝܳܢܺܝܬ, ܡܶܬܬܰܘܕܝܳܢܽܘܬܳܐ, ܬܰܘܕܺܝܬܳܐ, ܬܰܘܕܺܝܬܳܐ, ܬܰܘܕܝܳܐ.

ܝܰܕܽܘܥܳܐ or ܝܳܕܽܘܥܳܐ pl. ܶܐ rt. ܝܕܥ. m. *a wizard, soothsayer.*

ܝܳܕܽܘܥܳܐ, ܝܳܕܽܘܥܬܳܐ pl. m. ܶܐ f. ܳܬܳܐ rt. ܝܕܥ. *a) instructed, learned, experienced, skilful;* with ܠܳܐ *ignorant;* ܢܰܘܕܰܥ ܗܳܫܳܐ ܠܝܳܕܽܘܥܶܐ ܘܦܰܪܽܘܫܶܐ *inform we now such as are discerning;* ܐܰܝܟ ܡܶܢܝܳܢܳܐ ܕܝܳܕܽܘܥܶܐ *according to the computation of the learned. b) intimate; an acquaintance;* ܚܰܕ ܡܶܢ ܝܳܕܽܘܥܰܘܗ̄ܝ *one of his acquaintances. c)* ܝܳܕܽܘܥܳܐ *a soothsayer.*

ܝܳܕܽܘܥܽܘܬܳܐ rt. ܝܕܥ. f. *a) divination, soothsaying. b) knowledge* with ܠܳܐ *ignorance.*

ܝܳܕܽܘܥܬܳܢܳܐ, ܝܺܬܳܐ rt. ܝܕܥ. *a) intelligent, intellectual, wise, prudent, discerning;* ܕܰܡܫܰܡܠܝܳܐ ܕܽܘܒܳܪܳܐ ܕܝܳܕܽܘܥܬܳܢܶܐ ܚܰܣܺܝܢܶܐ *of the perfect way of life of wise ascetics. b) endowed with intelligence* or *reason, reasonable, rational, intelligible;* ܟܝܳܢܶܐ ܝܳܕܽܘܥܬܳܢܳܝܶܐ *natures endowed with reason;* ܢܰܦܫܳܐ ܝܳܕܽܘܥܬܳܢܺܝܬܳܐ *a reasonable soul.*

ܝܳܕܽܘܥܬܳܢܳܐܺܝܬ rt. ܝܕܥ. adv. *rationally, intelligently, learnedly, skilfully;* with ܠܳܐ *foolishly.*

ܝܳܕܽܘܥܬܳܢܽܘܬܳܐ rt. ܝܕܥ. f. *intelligence, reason, consciousness.*

ܝܰܕܺܝܕܳܐ rt. ܝܕ. *beloved;* ܐܰܒܳܗܰܝܢ ܕܺܝܠܰܢ ܝܰܕܺܝܕܶܐ *our beloved Fathers.*

ܝܰܕܝܳܕܳܐ m. *the hoopoe;* perh. *the centipede, multipede.*

ܝܰܕܺܝܕܽܘܬܳܐ rt. ܝܕ. f. *friendship, love.*

ܝܰܕܝܳܬܳܐ or ܝܳܕܝܳܬܳܐ some insect; see ܝܰܕܝܳܬܳܐ.

ܝܺܕܺܝܥܳܐܺܝܬ rt. ܝܕܥ. adv. *clearly, evidently; expressly;* with ܠܳܐ *secretly, without notice; ignobly.*

ܝܺܕܺܝܥܽܘܬܳܐ rt. ܝܕܥ. f. *that which may be known, knowledge, science, learning, renown, repute, the epoch when an author flourished;* with ܠܳܐ *uncertainty; obscurity.*

ܝܰܪܢܳܐ pl. ܝܰܪܢܶܐ m. and f. *a hyena;* ܝܰܪܢܬܳܐ *a she-hyena.*

ܝܺܕܰܥ also ܐܺܝܕܰܥ, fut. ܢܶܕܰܥ, inf. ܡܶܕܰܥ, imper. ܕܰܥ, act. part. ܝܳܕܰܥ, ܝܳܕܥܳܐ, pass. part. ܝܺܕܺܝܥ, ܝܺܕܺܝܥܳܐ, ܝܺܕܺܝܥܬܳܐ. *to know; to perceive, understand, be able;* ܝܺܕܰܥ ܢܰܦܫܶܗ *know thyself;* ܐܶܢ ܡܶܕܰܥ ܝܳܕܰܥ *if he know for certain;* ܐܰܝܟ ܕܝܳܕܰܥ *at his discretion;* ܟܰܕ ܝܳܕܰܥ ܘܟܰܕ ܠܳܐ ܝܳܕܰܥ ܐܢܳܐ *wittingly and unwittingly;* with ܢܰܦܫܳܐ or ܗܰܘܢܳܐ *to be of a sane mind, have possession of one's faculties;* act. part. contracted with pers. prons. ܝܳܕܰܥܢܳܐ *I know,* ܝܳܕܰܥܬ m. ܝܳܕܥܰܬܝ f. *thou knowest,* ܝܳܕܥܺܝܢܰܢ *we know,* ܝܳܕܥܺܝܬܽܘܢ *you know,* ܝܳܕܥܺܝܢ *they know;* adj. *knowing, learned, skilled, cunning; acquainted with, an acquaintance;* ܝܳܕܰܥ ܝܰܘܢܳܐܺܝܬ *knowing Greek, acquainted with the Greek language;* ܨܰܝܳܕܳܐ ܝܳܕܰܥ ܨܰܝܕܳܐ *a cunning hunter;* ܝܳܕܥܺܝܢ ܣܽܘܟܳܠܳܐ *practised in understanding.* Pass. part. adj. *a) well known, notable, noble, famous;* ܫܰܪܒܬܳܐ ܝܺܕܺܝܥܬܳܐ *a noble race* or *lineage;* ܝܺܕܺܝܥܶܐ ܕܡܕܺܝܢܬܳܐ *the notables, chief men of the city;* with ܠܳܐ *obscure, mean. b) certain, fixed, a certain* thing or person; with ܡܶܢܝܳܢܳܐ or ܡܰܕܰܐܬܳܐ *a fixed* or *certain sum of money* or *tribute;* ܫܢܺܝܢ ܝܺܕܺܝܥܳܬܳܐ *several years;* ܒܫܰܢ݈ܬܳܐ ܐܰܝ ܝܺܕܺܝܥܬܳܐ *in a certain year, in such and such a year;* ܝܺܕܺܝܥܳܬܳܐ ܡܶܢܗܶܝܢ *certain of them;* with ܝܰܘܡܳܐ or ܥܐܕܳܐ *a fixed* or *appointed day* or *feast, a special* or *solemn day. c) particular, private, special;* ܕܺܝܠܳܢܳܝܳܬܳܐ ܘܝܺܕܺܝܥܳܬܳܐ ܘܦܪܺܝܫܳܬܳܐ ܠܟܽܠܚܰܕ *things peculiar and private and special to each. d) manifest, evident, clear,* with ܠܳܐ *unknown, hidden;* ܨܽܘܪܬܳܐ ܝܺܕܺܝܥܬܳܐ *the express image;* fem. abs. impers. *it is evident, obvious.* ETHPE. ܐܶܬܺܝܕܰܥ imper. W-Syr. ܐܶܬܺܝܕܰܥ, E-Syr. same as pret. *a) to be known, recognized, ascertained; to be understood. b) to become known, be well known, famous, to flourish;* ܡܰܠܦܳܢܶܐ ܕܶܐܬܺܝܕܰܥܘ ܒܣܽܘܪܝܳܝܶܐ ܡܫܰܒܚܶܐ *famous Syriac teachers;* ܒܗܳܢܳܐ ܙܰܒܢܳܐ ܡܳܪܝ ܐܺܝܣܚܳܩ ܡܶܬܺܝܕܰܥ ܗ̄ܘܳܐ *at this time Mar Isaac flourished;* ܫܰܪܺܝ ܠܡܶܬܺܝܕܳܥܽܘ *began to be renowned. c) to be known as, be called* or *named,* ܝܰܥܩܽܘܒ ܕܡܶܬܺܝܕܰܥ ܒܘܪܕܥܳܝܳܐ *Jacob surnamed Baradaeus. d) to be made known, declared; to be meant, indicated, signified,* ܗܰܘ ܕܶܐܬܺܝܕܰܥ ܒܪܳܐ ܕܰܐܠܳܗܳܐ *who was declared the Son of God.* Fem. impers. *it is known, clear, manifest;* ܡܶܬܺܝܕܥܳܐ ܠܡܰܢ ܕܝܳܕܰܥ *it is clear to one who can understand.* PAEL ܝܰܕܰܥ *to inform, indicate.* APH. ܐܰܘܕܰܥ *to make known, to show, point out, show forth, tell, inform, instruct, announce, relate;* ܡܰܘܕܥܺܝܢܰܢ ܥܒܳܕܳܐ *we relate the affair;* ܡܰܘܕܥܺܝܢ ܬܰܡܳܢ *they say there, give out there;* ܡܰܘܕܥܳܐ ܗܳܕܶܐ ܥܰܠ *this relates to, refers to.* ETTAPH. ܐܶܬܬܰܘܕܰܥ *to be made known, announced, related, told;* ܡܶܬܺܝܕܥܺܝܢ ܘܡܶܬܬܰܘܕܥܺܝܢ *they are known and acknowledged.* SHAPHEL ܫܘܕܥ *to make clear, explain, teach; to mean, notify, indicate, signify* esp. *symbolically, to symbolize, typify, prefigure, predict;* with ܥܠ *to refer to, indicate;* ܡܢܐ ܡܫܘܕܥ ܡܘܪܐ ܕܡܫܘܚܐ *what does the expression myrrh signify?* ܡܫܘܕܥܢܐ ܕܙܒܢܐ *annals, chronicles;* gram. ܡܫܘܕܥܢܐ ܚܫܐ *expressing passion* i. e. *an interjection.* ESHTAPH. ܐܫܬܘܕܥ *to know, recognize, understand, to see, perceive;* ܐܫܬܘܕܥ ܟܘܬܝܢܐ ܐܢ ܕܒܪܟ ܗܘ *see if this coat be thy son's;* ܗܝܕܝܢ ܢܫܬܘܕܥ ܚܝܠܐ ܕܡܠܬܗ ܘܡܠܝܠܘܬܗ *he will then appreciate his power of speech and eloquence.* DERIVATIVES, ܝܕܘܥܐ, ܝܕܘܥܬܐ, ܝܕܘܥܬܢܐ, ܝܕܘܥܬܢܐܝܬ, ܝܕܥܬܐ, ܝܕܥܐ, ܝܕܥܢܐ, ܝܕܥܢܘܬܐ, ܝܕܥܢܐܝܬ, ܝܕܘܥܬܢܘܬܐ, ܝܕܥܐ, verb ܡܕܥ, ܡܕܥܐ, ܡܕܥܢܐ, ܡܕܥܢܘܬܐ, ܡܫܘܕܥܢܐ, ܡܫܘܕܥܢܐ, ܡܫܘܕܥܢܘܬܐ, ܡܫܘܕܥܢܐ, ܡܫܬܘܕܥܢܐ, ܡܫܬܘܕܥܢܘܬܐ, ܡܫܬܘܕܥܢܐܝܬ, ܡܘܕܥܐ, ܡܫܬܘܕܥܢܐܝܬ, ܡܫܬܘܕܥܢܐ, ܡܫܬܘܕܥܢܘܬܐ and ܫܘܕܥܐ.

ܝܘܕܐ, ܝܘܕܐ sometimes ܝܘܕܐ rt. ܝܕܥ. m. *a mark, sign, note;* ܢܝܫܐ ܘܩܝܡܬܐ ܘܫܘܩܠܐ ܥܠ ܓܢܒ ܐܘܪܚܐ *sign-posts and milestones by the roadside;* any *point, line* or *sign* in writing opp. ܢܘܩܙܐ *points* or *dots* only; ܢܝܫܐ ܕܩܠܐ *vowel-points.* Also *the first words of a hymn* or *canticle* given as the name of a chant or tune.

ܝܕܥܬܐ or ܝܕܥܬܐ pl. ܝܕ̈ܥܬܐ m. *a firefly.*

ܝܕܝܥܐܝܬ rt. ܝܕܥ. adv. *learnedly, skilfully; by name.*

ܝܕܥܬܐ often ܐܝܕܥܬܐ pl. ܝܕ̈ܥܬܐ rt. ܝܕܥ. f. *a*) *information, knowledge, doctrine,* ܠܐ ܝܕܥܬܐ *ignorance;* ܝܕܥܬܐ ܡܩܕܡܬܐ *foreknowledge;* ܒܠܐ ܝܕܥܬܐ *ignorantly, inconsiderately; unexpectedly;* ܒܝܕܥܬܐ ܘܒܠܐ ܝܕܥܬܐ *wittingly and unwittingly;* ܒܢܝ̈ ܝܕܥܬܐ *learned men.* *b*) = νοῦς, *mind, sense, intelligence, understanding, apprehension,* ܢܦܩ ܡܢ ܝܕܥܬܗ *he went out of his mind;* ܝܕܥܬܐ ܡܠܝܠܬܐ *logic.* *c*) *a notice, indication;* ܝܕܥܬܐ ܕܐܒܗ̈ܬܐ *a notice of the patriarchs* i. e. a table of their names.

ܝܗ the name of GOD, Heb. JAH *the Lord;* ܝܗܘܗ is sometimes found for *Jahveh.*

ܝܗ interj. *Oh! enough! woe!* ܝܗ ܠܟ *woe to thee!*

ܝܗܒ rarely ܝܗܒ or ܝܗܒ has no future form and the infin. ܡܗܒ is rare, the fut. and inf. forms of ܢܬܠ are borrowed, fut. ܢܬܠ, inf. ܡܬܠ, imper. ܗܒ, ܗܒܝ, ܗܒܘ, ܗܒܝܢ, act. part. ܝܗܒ, ܝܗܒܐ, pl. ܝܗܒܝܢ, ܝܗܒ̈ܢ, pass. part. ܝܗܝܒ, ܝܗܝܒܐ, ܝܗܝܒܬܐ. The imperative is further shortened by the omission of ܗ in pronunciation esp. after ܘ, ܘܗܒܘܗܝ *u—wu and give it to him;* in the fem. ܗ is always retained. *a*) *to give, grant, allow, permit, concede, offer; to yield, give oneself up; to apply* or *devote oneself;* ܗܒ ܠܝ ܕܐܩܪܒ ܠܟ *grant to me that I may offer to Thee;* ܐܢ ܝܗܒ ܙܒܢܐ *if time allow;* ܠܐ ܝܗܒܝܢ ܠܟ ܠܡܥܒܪ—ܝܡܡܐ *the seas do not permit thee to pass over;* ܡܢ ܕܝܗܝܒ ܠܗ *he to whom it is given.* *b*) *to put, place, set, lay upon* or *by* with ܒ or ܥܠ; ܝܗܒ ܛܝܒܘܬܐ *finding favour;* with ܩܕܡ *to set before, in sight of; to entrust, commit, bestow, assign, appoint;* ܐܒܐ ܠܣܓܝܐܘܬ ܥܡܡܐ ܝܗܒܬܟ *the father of a multitude of nations have I made thee;* ܝܗܒ ܫܠܝܡܘܢ ܣܐܡܐ ܐܝܟ ܟܐܦܐ ܘܐܪܙܐ ܐܝܟ ܫܩܡܐ *Solomon made silver to be as stones and cedars as sycamores* for abundance; ܝܗܒ ܠܝ ܙܒܢܐ *he set me a time.* Idioms, before another verb *to betake* or *take to;* ܝܗܒ ܕܢܐܬܐ *he was on the point of coming;* ܝܗܒܘ ܠܡܥܪܩ *they took to flight.*

ܝܗܒ ܐܝܕܐ *to give the hand* as a sign of good faith, *to promise; to give help,* Angl. *a helping hand; to allow, give leave* or *opportunity; to give way, submit.*

ܝܗܒ ܐܬܪܐ *to give way, make place, give opportunity.*

ܝܗܒ ܠܓܒܪܐ *to give in marriage.*

ܝܗܒ ܘܝ *to cry woe upon.*

ܝܗܒ ܚܨܐ *to turn the back, flee.*

ܝܗܒ ܛܘܒܐ ܠ *to pronounce* or *call blessed.*

ܝܗܒ ܦܬܓܡܐ *to give an answer, pledge one's word.*

ܝܗܒ ܡܫܬܡܥܢܘܬܐ *to yield obedience, submit.*

ܝܗܒ ܢܦܫܗ ܠ *to devote* or *give oneself up to; to yield oneself.*

ܝܗܒ ܦܐܪܐ *to bear* or *yield fruit.*

ܝܗܒ ܦܢܝܬܐ *to answer.*

ܝܗܒ ܩܠܐ *to cry out, proclaim, make a noise, give a sound.*

ܝܗܒ ܡܘܕܥܢܘܬܐ to show, exhibit; to promise.

ܝܗܒ ܫܠܡܐ to salute, to bid farewell.

ܝܗܒ ܬܘܪܨܐ to correct.

Ethpe. ܐܬܝܗܒ to be given, granted, permitted; to be yielded, surrendered, delivered; ܛܝܒܘܬܐ ܕܐܬܝܗܒܬ ܠܝ ܡܢ ܐܠܗܐ the grace that was given me of God; ܗܕܐ ܬܬܝܗܒ let this be granted; ܠܡܘܬܐ ܐܬܝܗܒ he was delivered to death. Derivatives, ܝܗܘܒܐ, ܝܗܘܒܘܬܐ, ܝܗܝܒܐܝܬ, ܡܘܗܒܬܐ, ܡܘܗܒܘܬܐ, ܡܬܝܗܒܢܘܬܐ.

ܝܗܘܒܐ, ܝܗܘܒܬܐ rt. ܝܗܒ. m. a giver (opp. ܢܣܘܒܐ a taker, receiver); esp. a liberal giver; ܐܠܗܐ ܝܗܘܒܐ ܠܝܗܘܒܐ ܗܘ ܡܘܗܒܬܐ God the Giver to those who give, grants gifts; ܐܪܥܐ ܝܗܘܒܬܐ ܕܦܐܪܐ the earth giver of fruits; gram. dative.

ܝܗܘܒܘܬܐ rt. ܝܗܒ. f. giving, alleging; ܝܗܘܒܘܬܐ ܕܡܘܙܦܘܬܐ advancing on loan; ܝܗܘܒܘܬܐ ܕܥܠܬܐ allegation of cause, bringing a case; ܝܗܘܒܘܬܐ ܕܨܒܬܐ ornamentation.

ܝܗܘܕܐܝܬ adv. Judaically, after the manner of the Jews.

ܝܗܘܕܝܐ and ܝܗܘܕܝܐ m. a Jew; ܝܗܘܕܝܬܐ f. a Jewess.

ܝܗܘܕܝܘܬܐ f. Judaism; collect. the Jews.

ܝܗܘ ܝܗܘ a shout of joy, hurrah! huzza!

ܝܗܝܒܐܝܬ rt. ܝܗܒ. adv. in the dative case.

ܝܗܝܒܘܬܐ or ܐܝܗܝܒܘܬܐ rt. ܝܗܒ. f. giving, assigning; a gift, donation; ܝܗܝܒܘܬܐ ܦܣܐ division by lot; ܝܗܝܒܘܬܐ ܕܢܡܘܣܐ the giving of the Law; ܝܗܝܒܘܬ ܐܝܕܐ help, assistance.

ܝܗܠ, ܝܗܠܐ pl. ܝܗܠܝܢ, ܝܗܠܐ com. a) properly a tribe of Arabs. b) a troop, band, cohort; ܝܗܠܐ ܕܩܘܪܕܝܐ bands of Kurds; ܝܗܠܐ ܫܡܝܢܝܐ heavenly cohorts.

ܝܗܠܢܝܐ m. ܝܗܠܢܝܬܐ pl. f. from ܝܗܠܐ. adj. gregarious, in troops or flocks.

ܝܘ contraction for ܝܘܢܝܐ Greek i.e. according to the Septuagint version.

ܝܘܒܐ rt. ܝܒܐ. m. eager longing, earnest desire.

ܝܘܒܐܢܐ pl. ܝܘܒܐܢܐ rt. ܝܒܐ. gram. optative.

ܝܘܒܒ, ܝܘܒܒܐ rt. ܝܒ. m. the sound of a trumpet, a shout of joy, shouting, bawling.

ܝܘܒܝܠܝܐ adj. of the Jubilee; ܫܢܬܐ ܕܝܘܒܝܠܐ the year of Jubilee.

ܝܘܒܠ, ܝܘܒܠܐ pl. ܝܘܒܠܐ rt. ܝܒܠ. m. a) a course, series, succession; ܝܘܒܠܐ ܕܡܠܟܘܬܐ succession to the empire; ܝܘܒܠܐ ܫܠܝܚܝܐ ܕܟܗܢܘܬܐ Apostolic succession of orders. b) custom, tradition, transference, translation, version; ܝܘܒܠ ܡܠܬܐ verbal tradition; ܝܘܒܠܐ ܡܢ ܝܘܢܝܐ ܠܣܘܪܝܝܐ a translation from Greek into Syriac. c) chronological order; ܝܘܒܠܐ ܕܙܒܢܐ or ܝܘܒܠ ܫܢܝܐ chronology; a division or section of a chronicle; ܝܘܒܠܐ ܩܕܡܝܐ first section. d) ܝܘܒܠܐ ܕܫܪܒܬܐ, ܝܘܒܠ ܫܪܒܬܐ or abs. genealogical succession, descent, line, posterity; generation, procreation. e) right of succession.

ܝܘܒܠܝܐ, ܝܘܒܠܝܬܐ adj. from ܝܘܒܠܐ. of tradition, traditional; genealogical; genital; etymological, an etymologist.

ܝܘܒܡܐ from ܝܒܡ m. a levirate marriage, marriage with a brother's widow.

ܝܘܓܘܢ jugum, an acre of land.

ܝܘܓܪܐ pl. ܝܘܓܪܝܢ and ܝܘܓܪܐ jugerum, a juger or acre of land.

ܝܘܕ pl. ܝܘܕܐ f. Yud, name of ܝ the smallest letter of the Syriac alphabet; a jot, the tip or point of a letter; ܝܘܕ ܚܕܐ ܐܘ ܚܕ ܣܪܛܐ one jot or one tittle; ܝܘܕܐ ܚܒܝܠܐ confused or badly-written letters.

ܝܘܕܐܝܬ adv. Judaic, after the manner of the Jews.

ܝܘܕܝܐ, ܝܘܕܝܬܐ adj. Jewish, Judaic.

ܝܘܕܝܐ, ܝܘܕܝܬܐ from ܝܘܕ. gram. written with a Yud or formed by the insertion of a servile Yud.

ܝܘܙܐ or ܝܘܙܐ m. the panther, cheetah.

ܝܘܛܐ or ܝܘܛܐ f. ἰῶτα, Greek ι.

ܝܘܠܝܢܝܣܛܐ pl. ܝܘܠܝܢܝܣܛܐ a Julianist, a follower of Julian of Halicarnassus who taught that the body of Christ was incorruptible.

ܝܘܠܦܢܐ pl. ܝܘܠܦܢܐ rt. ܝܠܦ. m. learning, study, scholarship, instruction; doctrine, a dogma, opinion; an art, science; ܒܝܬ ܝܘܠܦܢܐ a school, college; ܝܘܠܦܢܐ ܕܡܓܘܫܐ the learning of the Magians; ܝܘܠܦܢܐ ܢܘܟܪܝܐ heresies; ܝܘܠܦܢܐ ܟܝܢܝܐ ܘܒܬܪ ܟܝܢܝܐ physics and metaphysics.

ܝܘܠܦܢܝܐ, ܝܘܠܦܢܝܬܐ from ܝܘܠܦܢܐ *an adherent of a doctrine, a sectarian; scientific.*

ܝܘܡ, ܝܘܡܐ pl. ܝܘܡܝܢ, ܝܘܡܬܐ oftener ܝܘܡܬܐ m. *a day*, 24 hours from evening to evening (for *the day, daytime* opp. ܠܠܝܐ *the night* see ܐܝܡܡܐ). ܝܘܡܐ ܕܡܪܢ or ܝܘܡܐ ܡܪܝܐ or ܝܘܡܐ ܕܡܪܝܐ *the Lord's Day;* ܝܘܡܐ ܕܚܕ ܒܫܒܐ *Sunday;* ܝܘܡܐ ܐܚܪܝܐ *the last day;* ܡܠܐ ܝܘܡܝܢ *a full month, entire month;* ܝܘܡܬܐ ܩܫܝܫ or ܪܒ ܒܝܘܡܝ *advanced in years, aged;* ܕܝܘܡܬܢ *of our time, in our days;* ܒܝܘܡܝ ܦܠܢ *in the time of any one;* ܡܢ ܝܘܡܝ *in my days;* ܒܪ ܝܘܡܐ *ephemeral.* Adverbial expressions, ܝܘܡܬܐ *some time;* ܚܕ ܡܢ ܝܘܡܝܢ *one day;* ܝܘܡ ܒܝܘܡ *from day to day, continually;* ܝܘܡܐ ܒܝܘܡܐ *each day;* ܟܠܝܘܡ ܟܠܝܘܡ and ܒܟܠܝܘܡ *each day, daily;* ܒܝܘܡܐ ܕܒܬܪܗ *on the next day, on the day after;* ܠܝܘܡܐ ܐܚܪܢܐ *the next day, the day following;* ܝܘܡܐ ܕܝܘܡܐ, ܕܟܠܝܘܡ *daily;* ܠܝܘܡܬܐ *after some time;* ܝܘܡ ܡܢ ܝܘܡ or ܡܢ ܝܘܡ ܠܝܘܡ *from day to day;* ܝܘܡܬܐ or ܩܕܡ ܝܘܡܐ *yesterday, lately.*

ܝܘܡܢܝܐ, ܝܘܡܢܝܬܐ from ܝܘܡ. *daily, diurnal;* ܡܪܕܝܬܐ ܝܘܡܢܝܬܐ ܕܫܡܫܐ *the diurnal motion of the sun.*

ܝܘܡܢ, ܝܘܡܢܐ from ܝܘܡ. *to-day, this day, at this present time;* ܡܢ ܝܘܡܢܐ ܘܠܗܠ *from this day forward;* ܝܘܡܐ ܕܝܘܡܢܐ *this day, this very day, the present time.*

ܝܘܡܢܝܐ from ܝܘܡ. *diurnal, quotidian.*

ܝܘܢ f. Ἰάων, *Javan, Greece.* Derivatives, verb ܝܘܢ, ܝܘܢܝܐ, ܝܘܢܝܬ, ܝܘܢܝܘܬܐ.

ܝܘܢܐ pl. ܝܘܢܐ com. *a dove;* ܒܪ ܝܘܢܐ pl. ܒܢܝ ܝܘܢܐ *a young dove.*

ܝܘܢܐܝܬ from ܝܘܢ. adv. *in Greek.*

ܝܘܢܝܐ, ܝܘܢܝܬܐ from ܝܘܢ. *Greek, a Greek;* ܫܘܥܝܬܐ ܕܝܘܢܝܐ *fables of the Greeks;* ܡܦܩܬܐ ܕܝܘܢܝܐ *the Septuagint,* abbrev. ܡܦ; . . . ܒܫܢܬ ܕܝܘܢܝܐ or contr. ܕܝܘ *in the year . . . according to the Greek reckoning, according to the era of the Seleucidae.*

ܝܘܢܝܘܬܐ from ܝܘܢ f. *a) the Greek language, Greek learning, Hellenism;* ܝܘܠܦܢܐ ܕܝܘܢܝܘܬܐ *the teaching of Greek. b) the era* or *computation of the Seleucidae.*

ܝܘܢܢ denom. verb Palpel conj. from ܝܘܢ. *to be versed in Greek, to write in the Greek manner.*

ܝܘܩܢܐ pl. ܝܘܩܢܐ m. εἰκών, *an image, figure, likeness,* pl. *icons, images* of the saints; *a copy* of a book; ܝܘܩܢܐ ܕܡܠܟܐ ܕܛܒܝܥ ܒܕܝܢܪܐ *the king's likeness stamped on a dinar;* metaph. *a figure* of speech, *semblance;* gram. *form.* Derivatives, verb ܐܝܩܢ, ܡܝܩܢܐ, ܡܝܩܢܢܐ, ܡܝܩܢܢܘܬܐ.

ܝܘܩܢܬܐ pl. ܬܐ m. ὑάκινθος, *jacinth.*

ܝܘܩܢܬܝܢܐ or ܝܘܩܢܬܢܐ pl. ܢܐ or ܢ ὑακίνθινος, *of jacinth, hyacinthine.*

ܝܘܩܪܐ pl. ܝܢ, ܐ rt. ܝܩܪ. m. *a burden, a weight, charge;* ܝܘܩܪܐ ܕܢܦܩܬܐ *heavy expenses;* ܝܘܩܪܐ ܕܡܟܣܐ *burdensome charges, heavy exactions;* ܝܘܩܪܐ ܕܩܫܝܫܘܬܗ *the weight of his age;* ܠܐ ܗܘܐ ܝܘܩܪܐ ܥܠ ܐܢܫ ܠܐ *I will not be a burden to any one; heaviness, uneasiness.* With ܫܩܠ *a) to undertake the care, take a charge. b) to bear hardship.*

ܝܘܩܪܢܐ rt. ܝܩܪ. m. *scarcity, dearth.*

ܝܘܪܕܢܢ Heb. *the river Jordan;* metaph. *the baptismal font.*

ܝܘܪܩ, ܝܘܪܩܐ, ܝܘܪܩܬܐ rt. ܝܪܩ. *a)* adj. *tender green, greenish, yellowish, pale;* ܐܠܡܐ ܝܘܪܩܬܐ *a green lizard;* ܝܘܪܩܝܢ ܐܝܟ ܕܡܢ ܨܘܡܐ *pale as from fasting. b)* subst. *a herb, vegetable, greenstuff, greens;* ܝܘܪܩܐ ܕܓܢܬܐ *garden herbs; green pond-weed.*

ܝܘܪܩܘܬܐ rt. ܝܪܩ. f. *green grass; pallor.*

ܝܘܪܬܘܬܐ rt. ܝܪܬ. f. *inheritance, heirship.*

ܝܘܪܬܢܐ pl. ܢܐ rt. ܝܪܬ. m. *heritage, a possession, property;* ܠܝܘܪܬܢܐ ܕܠܥܠܡ *for an everlasting possession.*

ܝܘܬܪܢ, ܝܘܬܪܢܐ pl. ܢܐ rt. ܝܬܪ. m. *possession, property, use, profit, advantage, increase, gain; superabundance, superfluity;* ܕܠܐ ܝܘܬܪܢ *in vain, to no advantage;* ܣܓܝ ܝܘܬܪܢܐ or ܡܝܬܪ *very profitable.*

ܝܘܬܪܢܝܐ rt. ܝܬܪ. *advantageous, profitable.*

ܝܙܘܦܐ pl. ܦܐ rt. ܝܙܦ. m. *a borrower.*

ܝܙܝܦܐܝܬ rt. ܝܙܦ. adv. *as a borrower.*

ܝܙܝܦܘܬܐ pl. ܝܬܐ rt. ܝܙܦ. f. *borrowing;* with ܒ ܡܫܥܒܕ *in debt.*

ܝܪܠܝܓ pl. ܓܐ misspelling of ܝܪܠܝܓ Tatar, *a royal mandate.*

ܝܼܙܰܦ fut. ܢܹܐܙܰܦ, inf. ܡܹܐܙܰܦ, act. part. ܝܳܙܶܦ, ܝܳܙܦܳܐ, pass. part. ܝܙܺܝܦ, ܝܙܺܝܦܳܐ, ܝܙܺܝܦܬܳܐ. *to borrow;* pass. part. impers. ܝܙܺܝܦܳܐ ܠܝܼ ܡܶܢܶܗ *he borrowed from me;* ܡܳܢܳܐ ܝܙܺܝܦ ܗ̱ܘܳܐ ܠܶܗ *what had he borrowed?* gram. *borrowed, adopted,* opp. ܡܕܺܝܠܳܝܳܐ *proper.* Ethpe. ܐܶܬ݂ܝܙܶܦ *to be borrowed, obtained.* Aph. ܐܰܘܙܶܦ *to lend, lend on interest.* Derivatives, ܝܙܦܐ, ܝܙܘܦܐ, ܡܘܙܦܢܐ, ܡܘܙܦܢܘܬܐ, ܡܘܙܦܐ, ܡܘܙܦܢܐ.

ܝܶܙܦܳܐ, ܝܶܙܦܬܳܐ constr. st. ܝܶܙܦܰܬ pl. ܝܶܙܦܳܬܳܐ rt. ܝܙܦ. f. *a loan, investment;* ܝܶܙܦܳܐ ܕܰܫܐܶܠܘ *borrowers who have asked a loan;* ܝܶܙܦܬܳܐ ܡܒܰܕܪܬܳܐ ܕܦܰܠܳܚܳܐ *the scattered investment of the husbandman* i.e. seed sown.

ܝܰܚܡܽܘܪܳܐ pl. ܶܐ m. *dense smoke, thick dust; a funeral pyre;* ܩܕܪܐ ܡܠܝܢ ܕܟܒܪܝܬܐ ܡܦܩܢ ܝܚܡܘܪܐ *pots full of sulphur emitting dense fumes.*

ܝܚܝܕ from ܚܕ. Ethpaal ܐܶܬ݂ܝܰܚܰܕ *to be united;* sometimes by mistake for ܐܶܬ݂ܚܰܝܰܕ. Shaphel ܫܰܘܚܶܕ *to leave lonely, separate;* ܫܰܘܚܶܕ ܢܰܦܫܶܗ *he went away by himself.* Pass. part. ܡܫܰܘܚܰܕ, ܡܫܰܘܚܕܳܐ, ܡܫܰܘܚܕܳܬܳܐ *solitary, separate, deserted, desolate;* ܡܫܰܘܚܰܕ ܡܰܠܟܳܐ ܡܶܢ ܪ̈ܰܘܪܒܳܢܶܐ ܘܡܶܢ ܙ̈ܥܽܘܪܶܐ *a king is separate from both the high and low in rank;* ܗܳܝ ܕܰܡܫܰܘܚܕܳܐ ܡܫܰܘܚܕܽܘܬ݂ *the entirely desolate;* ܐܰܪܡܰܠܬܳܐ ܡܫܰܘܚܕܬܳܐ *a solitary* or *desolate widow.* Eshtaphal ܐܶܫܬܰܘܚܰܕ *to be left alone, left solitary;* with ܡܶܢ *to separate from, abstain from.* Derivatives, ܝܚܝܕܐ, ܝܚܝܕ, ܝܚܝܕܐܝܬ, ܝܚܝܕܘܬܐ, ܡܫܘܚܕܐܝܬ, ܡܫܘܚܕܘܬܐ, ܝܚܝܕܝܐ, ܫܘܚܕܐ.

ܝܚܰܛ part. f. ܝܳܚܛܳܐ, pl. ܝܳܚ̈ܛܳܢ *to cast* its young, *be abortive, have a miscarriage.* Aph. ܐܰܘܚܶܛ *to cause abortion.* Derivative, ܝܚܛܐ.

ܝܶܚܛܳܐ pl. ܝܶܚ̈ܛܶܐ often misspelt ܝܚܛܐ, rt. ܝܚܛ. m. *an abortive* or *still-born child, a premature* or *untimely birth.*

ܝܚܛܐ or ܝܚܛܐ pl. ܶܐ m. *a network veil* or *head-covering.*

ܝܺܚܺܝܕܳܐ or ܐܺܝܚܺܝܕܳܐ pl. ܶܐ from ܚܕ. m. *only-begotten; only son* with ܒܪܳܐ expressed or understood.

ܝܺܚܺܝܕܳܐܺܝܬ or ܐܺܝܚܺܝܕܳܐܺܝܬ from ܚܕ. adv. *singly, alone, apart, by oneself, solitarily, as a solitary* or *hermit.*

ܝܺܚܺܝܕܽܘܬܳܐ from ܚܕ. f. *that which is alone, only* or *sole;* ܝܺܚܺܝܕܽܘܬ݂ ܫܽܘܠܛܳܢܳܐ *monarchy, absolute power.*

ܝܺܚܺܝܕܳܝܳܐ, ܝܳܬܳܐ from ܚܕ. a) *sole, only, the only-begotten;* ܝܺܚܺܝܕܳܝܳܐ ܕܡܶܢ ܐܰܒܳܐ *the only-begotten of the Father;* ܒܪܬܳܐ ܝܺܚܺܝܕܳܝܬܳܐ *an only daughter.* b) *alone, by oneself, solitary; a solitary, hermit, anchorite* but also *a monk* or *nun* of a community. c) *singular;* gram. opp. plural. d) *of one's own, special, specific* opp. ܓܢܣܳܝܳܐ *generic.* e) f. emph. *property, quality* = ܕܺܝܠܳܝܬܳܐ the word used by later writers.

ܝܺܚܺܝܕܳܝܽܘܬܳܐ from ܚܕ. f. a) *unity; the being one* or *being alone;* ܝܺܚܺܝܕܳܝܽܘܬܳܟ݂ *thou only, thou by thyself.* b) *the solitary* or *monastic life;* ܥܰܠ ܫܽܘܪܳܝܳܐ ܕܐܽܘܪܚܳܐ ܕܝܺܚܺܝܕܳܝܽܘܬܳܐ *on the origin of the way of the solitary life.* c) *a property, special quality.*

ܝܚܠ Aphel ܐܰܘܚܶܠ with ܠ a) *to enfeeble, render weak, to relax;* ܐܰܘܚܶܠ ܠܫܰܒܬܳܐ *to give occasion to remissness in the observance of the sabbath;* ܠܦܰܓܪܳܐ ܡܰܡܚܶܠ ܘܡܰܘܚܶܠ *it enfeebles and debilitates the body.* b) *to become enfeebled, exhausted;* with ܠ or ܡܶܢ *to be unable;* with ܡܶܢ or ܥܰܠ *to despair;* ܐܰܘܚܶܠܢ ܡܶܢ ܩܪܳܒܳܐ ܐܰܡܺܝܢܳܐ *we are exhausted from constant war;* ܡܚܳܐ ܘܐܰܘܚܶܠ *he failed and grew weak;* ܐܰܘܚܶܠܶܬ ܥܰܠ ܚܰܝܰܝ *I despaired of my life.* Derivatives, ܡܘܚܠܢܘܬܐ, ܡܘܚܠܢܐ, ܬܘܚܠܬܐ.

ܝܰܚܡܽܘܪܳܐ m. *alcephalus bubalis, the bubale,* a species of antelope with short horns, long head and heavy build.

ܝܚܰܡ same as ܐܽܘܟܰܡ *to be* or *become black;* ܝܶܚܡܶܬ *I became black;* ܚܶܛܶܐ ܘܣܥܳܪܶܐ ܝܳܚܡܺܝܢ ܡܶܢ ܥܰܬܺܝܩܽܘܬܳܐ *wheat and barley turn black with age.*

ܝܺܠܶܕ fut. ܢܺܐܠܰܕ, 1 pers. sometimes ܐܺܠܰܕ, inf. ܡܺܐܠܰܕ, act. part. ܝܳܠܶܕ, ܝܳܠܕܳܐ, pass. part. ܝܠܺܝܕ, ܝܳܐ, ܝܳܬܳܐ. a) *to beget, to generate;* ܒܪܝ ܐܢܬ ܐܢܐ ܝܘܡܢܐ ܝܠܕܬܟ *thou art my son, this day have I begotten thee.* b) *to bear, to bring forth;* ܬܺܐܠܰܕ ܠܳܟ݂ ܒܪܳܐ *she shall bear thee a son; to lay eggs;* ܩܰܩܳܐ ܒܩܶܢܳܐ ܢܽܘܟ݂ܪܳܝܳܐ ܝܳܠܕܳܐ *the cuckoo lays in a strange nest.* Pass. part. ܝܠܺܝܕܰܝ ܢܶܫܶܐ *born of women;* ܝܠܺܝܕܺܝܢܰܢ *we are born;* ܝܠܺܝܕ ܒܦܽܘܪܦܽܘܪܳܐ *born in the purple;* ܝܠܺܝܕ ܒܰܝܬܳܐ *born in the house* i.e. *a slave;* ܝܠܺܝܕܰܝ ܡܶܢ ܪܽܘܚܳܐ *born of the Spirit;* ܟܝܳܢܳܐ ܝܠܺܝܕܳܐ *natural beauty, inborn grace.* Ethpe. ܐܬܝܠܶܕ *to be begotten, born, brought forth;* with ܡܶܢ ܕܪܺܝܫ *to be born again, be regenerate;* metaph. *to rise, wax* of the moon opp. ܐܶܬܒܰܨܰܪ *to wane; to be caused, derived;* ܕܢܶܬܺܝܠܶܕ ܫܶܓܝܳܐ *that a schism should arise.* Pa. ܝܰܠܶܕ *to help to bring forth.* Aph. ܐܰܘܠܶܕ *a) to beget, procreate, bear, bring forth;* ܐܰܒܪܳܗܳܡ ܐܰܘܠܶܕ ܠܐܺܝܣܚܳܩ *Abraham begat Isaac. b) to act as a midwife, give assistance at childbirth. c) to make bring forth, to cause, effect;* arith. *to give the result;* ܥܢܳܢܳܐ ܐܰܘܠܶܕ ܚܶܫܘܟܳܐ *a cloud caused darkness;* ܚܰܝܠܳܐ ܡܰܘܠܕܳܢܳܐ ܕܚܰܝܶܐ *vivifying force.* Ethtaph. ܐܶܬܬܰܘܠܰܕ *to receive the help of a midwife, to be brought to the birth.* Derivatives, ܝܳܠܽܘܕܳܐ, ܝܰܠܕܳܐ, ܝܳܠܕܳܐ, ܝܳܠܽܘܕܬܳܐ, ܝܰܠܽܘܕܽܘܬܳܐ, ܝܳܠܽܘܕܳܐ, ܝܰܠܽܘܕܳܐ, ܝܰܠܽܘܕܳܐܝܬ, ܝܰܠܽܘܕܽܘܬܳܐ, ܡܰܘܠܕܳܐ, ܡܰܘܠܳܕܳܐ, ܝܰܠܺܝܕܽܘܬܳܐ, ܝܰܠܺܝܕܳܐܝܬ, ܝܰܠܽܘܕܽܘܬܳܐ, ܬܰܘܠܳܕܳܐ, ܡܰܘܠܕܳܢܽܘܬܳܐ, ܡܰܘܠܕܳܢܳܐ, ܡܰܘܠܕܳܢܳܝܳܐ, ܡܰܘܠܕܳܢܽܘܬܳܐ.

ܝܰܠܕܳܐ, ܝܰܠܶܕ pl. ܝܰܠܕܶܐ rt. ܝܠܕ. m. *a) the act of bearing, bringing forth. b) birth, nativity;* ܝܰܠܕܳܐ ܕܡܳܪܰܢ *the birth of our Lord;* ܝܰܠܕܶܗ ܕܡܳܪܰܢ *the Nativity of Christ, Christmas; a horoscope;* ܝܰܠܕܳܐ ܚܰܕܬܳܐ *new birth, regeneration;* ܝܰܠܕܶܐ ܕܡܰܚܫܰܒܬܳܐ *results, tendencies of thought. c) that which is brought forth, offspring, a brood, produce, fruit;* ܝܰܠܕܶܐ ܕܥܺܕܬܳܐ *the children of the Church;* ܝܰܠܕܶܐ ܢܽܘܟܪܳܝܶܐ *bastards;* ܝܰܠܕܳܐ ܕܦܰܪܚܬܳܐ *an insect, a fledgeling;* ܝܰܠܕܳܐ ܕܩܰܡܨܳܐ *a brood of locusts;* pl. *inhabitants.*

ܝܰܠܕܬܳܐ pl. ܝܰܠܕܳܬܳܐ rt. ܝܠܕ. f. *a fertile mother; a midwife.*

ܝܳܠܕܬܳܐ pl. ܝܳܠܕܳܬܳܐ, emph. part. fem. of ܝܠܶܕ = subst. *a travailing woman; a mother;* ܝܳܠܕܰܬ ܫܰܒܥܳܐ *she who has borne seven, a mother of seven;* ܝܳܠܕܰܬ ܐܰܠܳܗܳܐ *Theotokos, Deipara* opp. ܝܳܠܕܰܬ ܡܫܺܝܚܳܐ *Christotokos, Christipara.*

ܝܳܠܽܘܕܽܘܬܳܐ rt. ܝܠܕ. f. *begetting; bearing; maternity.*

ܝܰܠܽܘܕܳܐ, ܝܰܠܽܘܕܬܳܐ pl. m. ܶܐ, f. ܳܬܳܐ rt. ܝܠܕ. *an infant, babe, suckling;* ܐܰܝܟ ܝܰܠܽܘܕܳܐ ܡܫܰܚܠܦܳܐ *as a crawling infant;* ܝܰܠܽܘܕܶܐ ܒܗܰܝܡܳܢܽܘܬܳܐ *babes in faith;* ܥܕܰܡܳܐ ܕܢܶܬܚܰܣܰܠ ܡܶܬܩܪܶܐ ܝܰܠܽܘܕܳܐ *until it is weaned it is called a* ܝܰܠܽܘܕܳܐ; cf. ܥܽܘܠܳܐ *a newborn babe* and ܚܰܣܺܝܠܳܐ *a weaned child.*

ܝܳܠܽܘܕܳܐ, ܝܳܠܽܘܕܬܳܐ pl. m. ܶܐ ,ܺܝܢ, f. ܳܬܳܐ rt. ܝܠܕ. *a parent, one who begets or brings forth;* ܟܽܠ ܕܪܳܚܶܡ ܠܝܳܠܽܘܕܳܐ: ܪܳܚܶܡ ܐܳܦ ܠܗܰܘ ܕܐܶܬܺܝܠܶܕ ܡܶܢܶܗ *whosoever loveth him that begat loveth him also that is begotten of him;* ܡܰܕܢܚܳܐ ܝܳܠܽܘܕܳܐ ܕܫܶܡܫܳܐ *the East bringer forth of the sun.*

ܝܳܠܽܘܕܳܐܝܬ rt. ܝܠܕ. adv. *generative.*

ܝܰܠܽܘܕܽܘܬܳܐ rt. ܝܠܕ. f. *infancy;* ܥܽܘܒܳܕܶܐ ܕܝܰܠܽܘܕܽܘܬܳܐ *infantile ways.*

ܝܳܠܽܘܕܽܘܬܳܐ rt. ܝܠܕ. f. *generating power, generating.*

ܝܳܠܽܘܦܳܐ pl. ܶܐ rt. ܝܠܦ. m. *studious; a learner, pupil;* ܡܰܠܦܳܢܶܐ ܘܝܳܠܽܘܦܶܐ *teachers and pupils, masters and disciples.*

ܝܳܠܽܘܦܳܐܝܬ rt. ܝܠܦ. adv. *as a learner, tentatively,* opp. ܪܰܒܳܐܝܬ *masterly.*

ܝܳܠܽܘܦܽܘܬܳܐ rt. ܝܠܦ. *docility;* with ܠܳܐ *indocility, unteachableness, carelessness.*

ܝܺܠܺܝܕܳܐܝܬ rt. ܝܠܕ. adv. *by birth, by right of birth.*

ܝܺܠܺܝܕܽܘܬܳܐ or ܐܺܝܠܺܝܕܽܘܬܳܐ pl. ܳܬܳܐ rt. ܝܠܕ. f. *being born* or *begotten;* ܠܳܐ ܝܺܠܺܝܕܽܘܬܳܐ is the characteristic of the Father and ܕܝܺܠܝܕܽܘܬܳܐ ܕܒܪܳܐ ܕܺܝܠܳܝܬܳܐ ܐܺܝܬܶܝܗ *the peculiar property of the Son is His being begotten; birth, race, origin;* ܐܰܪܥܳܐ ܕܝܺܠܺܝܕܽܘܬܳܐ *native country;* ܝܺܠܺܝܕܽܘܬܝ ܡܶܢ ܡܰܕܢܚܳܐ ܐܺܝܬܶܝܗ *I am of eastern origin.*

ܝܺܠܺܝܦܳܐܝܬ rt. ܝܠܦ. adv. with ܠܳܐ *ignorantly, foolishly.*

ܝܺܠܺܝܦܽܘܬܳܐ rt. ܝܠܦ. f. *knowledge, skill;* with ܠܳܐ *ignorance.*

ܝܠܠ root-meaning *to wail,* cf. ܐܠܐ, p. 17. Pa. ܝܰܠܶܠ *to howl at.* Aph. ܐܰܝܠܶܠ *to wail, lament, cry out;* ܐܰܝܠܶܠܘ ܘܰܒܟܰܘ *wail and weep;* ܡܰܝܠܶܠ ܝܶܠܠܳܐ ܪܰܒܳܐ ܘܡܰܪܺܝܪܳܐ *crying with a loud and bitter cry.* Derivatives, ܝܰܠܳܐ, ܝܰܠܠܳܐ.

ܝܰܠܳܐ rt. ܝܠܠ. m. *the hyena.*

ܝܶܠܠܬܳܐ often ܝܶܠܶܠܬܳܐ or ܝܶܠܠܳܬܳܐ, ܝܶܠܳܠܬܳܐ or ܝܶܠܠܬܳܐ, also ܐܶܠܶܠܬܳܐ, pl. ܝܶܠܠܳܬܳܐ or ܝܶܠܝܳܠܬܳܐ rt. ܝܠܠ. f. *wailing, howling, shouting; a shout, cry, outcry;* ܐܶܠܶܠܬܳܐ ܕܩܪܳܒܳܐ *a battle-cry, shout.*

ܝܠܶܦ fut. ܢܺܐܠܰܦ, 1 pers. ܐܺܐܠܰܦ, inf. ܡܺܐܠܰܦ, imper. ܐܺܠܰܦ, act. part. ܝܳܠܶܦ, ܝܳܠܦܳܐ, pass. part. ܝܠܺܝܦ or ܝܺܠܺܝܦ, takes ܠ of the pers. and ܠ of the thing *to learn,* pass. part. *learned, skilled.* Pael ܐܰܠܶܦ fut. ܢܰܐܠܶܦ but much oftener ܝܰܠܶܦ and so with the act. part. ܡܰܐܠܶܦ and ܡܝܰܠܶܦ

to teach, inform, train; ܡܝܠܦ ܩܪܒܐ *trained to war.* Ethpa. ܐܬܝܠܦ imper. E-Syr. the same, W-Syr. ܐܬܝܠܦ *to be taught, instructed; to learn, to inform oneself.* Derivatives, ܝܘܠܦܢܐ, ܡܠܦܢܐ, ܡܠܦܢܘܬܐ, ܝܘܠܦܢܐ, ܡܝܠܦܢܐ, ܝܠܘܦܐ, ܝܘܠܦܐ.

ܝܡܐ pl. ܝܡܡܐ, ܝܡܡܝܢ m. *the sea; a sea, a lake;* ܣܦܬ ܝܡܐ *the seashore, coast;* ܝܡܐ ܕܡܠܚܐ *the Salt Sea* i.e. *the Dead Sea;* ܝܡܐ ܪܒܐ *the Great Sea* i.e. *the Mediterranean;* ܝܡܐ ܕܙܓܘܓܝܬܐ ܕܕܡܐ ܠܩܪܘܣܛܠܘܣ *a sea of glass like unto crystal;* ܥܒܕ ܝܡܐ ܕܢܚܫܐ *he made the molten sea* i.e. the great laver for the temple. Metaph. ܠܐ ܡܬܡܩܐ ܝܡܐ ܕܪ̈ܚܡܘܗܝ *the sea of* God's *mercies is not exhausted;* ܝܡܐ ܕܝܕܥܬܐ *a sea of knowledge;* ܝܡܐ ܕܚܫܘܟܐ *the sea of darkness,* i. e. Gehenna.

ܝܡܐ, ܐܝܡܐ and ܝܡܐ, fut. ܢܐܡܐ, inf. ܡܐܡܐ, imper. ܝܡܝ and ܝܡܐ, m. ܝܡܝ, f. act. part. ܝܡܐ, ܝܡܝܐ. *to swear; to take an oath, swear fealty;* ܠܐ ܬܐܡܐ ܒܫܘܩܪܐ *thou shalt not swear falsely, forswear thyself, perjure thyself;* ܠܐ ܬܐܡܘܢ ܟܠ ܠܐ ܒܫܡܝܐ ܘܠܐ ܒܐܪܥܐ *swear not at all, neither by heaven nor by the earth;* ܝܡܝ ܠܝ *swear to me.* Aph. ܐܘܡܝ *a) to make swear, bind by an oath;* ܐܘܡܝ ܩܝܡܐ ܠܡܠܟܐ *to cause to swear fealty to some one. b) to call to witness, to adjure;* ܟܕ ܡܘܡܐ ܠܗ ܕܢܫܠܐ *adjuring him to stop. c) to exorcise;* ܡܘܡܝܢ ܕܡܘܡܝܢ ܥܠ ܫܐܕܐ *exorcists.* Ettaph. ܐܬܬܘܡܝ *a) to be sworn, put on oath;* ܢܬܬܘܡܘܢ ܡܗܝܡܢܐ ܒܐܘܢܓܠܝܘܢ *let the faithful be sworn on the Gospel. b) to be adjured; to be exorcised.* Derivatives, ܝܡܝܐ, ܡܘܡܬܐ, ܡܘܡܝܢܘܬܐ, ܡܘܡܝܢܐ, ܡܘܡܝܬܐ.

ܝܡܝܐ pl. ܝ̈ܡܝܐ rt. ܝܡܐ. m. *a) one who takes an oath, one who swears* esp. habitually or falsely, *a swearer, perjurer. b) of or pertaining to an oath.*

ܝܡܝܢ, ܝܡܝܢܐ pl. ܝ̈ܡܝܢܐ f. *the right,* esp. *the right hand,* rarely with ܐܝܕܐ, ܐܝܕܗ ܕܝܡܝܢܐ *his right hand* opp. ܣܡܠܐ *the left, the left hand;* ܐܕܢܗ ܕܝܡܝܢܐ *his right ear;* ܓܒܐ ܕܝܡܝܢܐ *the right side;* ܦܟܐ ܕܝܡܝܢܐ *the right cheek;* ܡܢ ܝܡܝܢܐ *on the right, on the right hand.* Metaph. *a pledge, promise, compact* as confirmed by the right hand; ܝܡܝܢܐ ܕܫܠܡܐ *a compact of peace;* ܝܡܝܢ ܚܢܢܐ *the right hand of mercy* i. e. strength or help given in mercy, cf. ܝܕ; ܝܡܝܢܐ ܕܟܗܢܘܬܐ *ordination to the priesthood* = ܣܝܡ ܐܝܕܐ ܕܟܗܢܘܬܐ. ܝܡܝܢܐ and ܣܡܠܐ are often used with reference to Matt. xxv. 33, ܒܪ ܝܡܝܢܐ *one who is set at the right hand, one who is approved, accepted, blessed.* Derivatives, ܝܡܝܢܐܝܬ, ܝܡܝܢܝܐ, verb ܝܡܢ, ܝܡܝܢܐ, ܬܝܡܢܐ, ܬܝܡܢܝܐ.

ܝܡܝܢܐܝܬ from ܝܡܝܢ. adv. *from the right hand* or *direction; rightly, well.*

ܝܡܝܢܝܐ, ܝܡܝܢܝܬܐ pl. m. ܝ̈ܡܝܢܝܐ f. ܝ̈ܡܝܢܝܬܐ from ܝܡܝܢ. *a) at the right, on the right hand* or *side;* ܡܫܡܫܢܐ ܝܡܝܢܝܐ *the deacon who stands on the right. b) judged favourably, approved, righteous, blessed,* esp. with reference to Matt. xxv. 33, cf. above; ܕܘܒܪ̈ܐ ܝܡܝܢܝ̈ܐ *conduct such as will lead to our being set at Christ's right hand* opp. ܪܚܝܩ ܡܢ ܝܡܝܢܝܬܐ ܕܘܒܪ̈ܐ ܘܪܡܐ ܠܘܬ ܣܡܠܝܬܐ *far from blessed courses and cast down towards those which lead to rejection;* ܦܘܪ̈ܥܢܐ ܝܡܝܢܝ̈ܐ *gracious recompenses.*

ܝܡܘܡܐ and ܝܡܘܡܐ m. *a kind of lake fish.*

ܝܡܡܐ, ܝܡܡܝܢ irreg. pl. of ܝܡܐ; see above.

ܝܡܝܐ, ܝܡܝܬܐ pl. m. ܝ̈ܡܝܐ from ܝܡܐ. *marine, maritime, of the sea; a seaman, mariner;* ܝܡܝܐ ܓܘܢܐ *sea-green;* ܚܝܘܬܐ ܝܡܝܬܐ *a marine animal.*

ܝܡܢ denom. verb Pael conj. from ܝܡܝܢܐ. *to take by the right hand, to handle.*

ܝܡܬܐ pl. ܝܡܘܬܐ, ܝܡܬܐ f. *a lake, pool, swamp;* ܝܡܘܬܐ ܕܡܠܚܐ *salt pools.*

ܝܢܒܝܩ corruption of ܐܢܒܝܩ *an alembic.*

ܝܢܘܩܐ; see ܝܢܘܩܐ.

ܝܢܘܩܐ pl. ܝ̈ܢܘܩܐ rt. ܝܢܩ. m. *a suckling; sucking child.*

ܝܢܘܩܘܬܐ rt. ܝܢܩ. f. *suckling, giving suck.*

ܝܢܩܐ rarely ܝܢܘܩܐ pl. ܝ̈ܢܩܐ m. νεανίσκος, *a youth.*

ܝܢܩ or ܐܝܢܩ fut. ܢܐܢܘܩ, act. part. ܝܢܩ, ܝܢܩܐ. *to suck;* ܝܢܩܝ ܬܕܝܐ *infants at the breast;* ܐܝܢܩ ܚܠܒܐ *he sucked milk.* Ethpe. ܐܬܝܢܩ *to be suckled.* Pa. ܝܢܩ *give suck* or *milk.* Aph. ܐܝܢܩ rarely ܐܘܢܩ *to suckle, to give suck* or *milk;* ܡܝܢܩܢ ܕܡܝܢܩܢ *those who give suck, nursing mothers;* ܓܡܠܐ ܡܝܢܩܢܝܬܐ *milch camels.* Derivatives, ܝܢܘܩܐ, ܝܢܘܩܘܬܐ, ܝܢܩܐ, ܝܢܩܬܐ, ܝܢܩܘܬܐ, ܡܝܢܩܢܐ, ܡܝܢܩܢܘܬܐ, ܡܝܢܩܬܐ.

ܝܢܩܐ or ܝܢܘܩܐ m. ܝܢܩܬܐ f. pl. m. ܝ̈ܢܩܐ, f. ܝ̈ܢܩܬܐ rt. ܝܢܩ. *a suckling, sucking child.*

ܝܢܩܘܬܐ or ܝܢܝܩܘܬܐ rt. ܝܢܩ. f. *suckling, lactation;* ܙܒܢܐ ܕܝܢܩܘܬܐ *the period of suckling.*

ܝܢܩܘܬܢܝܐ, ܝܢܩܬܢܝܐ rt. ܝܢܩ. *foster;* ܐܚܝܢܘܬܐ ܓܢܣܢܝܬܐ or ܝܢܩܘܬܢܝܬܐ *relationship by birth* or *fosterhood.*

ܝܣܡܝܢ ܝܣܡܐ *jasmin, jessamine,* ܡܫܚܐ ܕܝܣܡܝܢ *jasmin oil* or *salve.*

ܝܣܦ Aphel ܐܘܣܦ *to add, increase, be greater, do more* opp. ܒܨܪ *to subtract, diminish;* ܢܘܣܦܘܢ ܐܝܠܢܐ ܦܐܪܐ ܠܡܥܒܕ the fruit-trees *shall yield an abundant crop;* ܗܘ ܕܡܘܣܦ ܥܠ ܛܝܡܐ *one who puts on more to the price;* ܡܛܠ ܡܢܐ ܡܘܣܦܝܢ ܒܬܐܘܠܘܓܝܐ ܕܪܘܚܐ ܩܕܝܫܬܐ ܢܣܒܐ ܡܢ ܒܪܐ *why do they add in theology that* the Holy Spirit *receives from the Son?* Adverbial use with another verb, *again, more, abundantly;* ܐܘܣܦܘ ܠܡܣܢܝܗ *they hated him yet more;* ܐܘܣܦ ܥܢܐ *he answered again.* Ettaph. ܐܬܬܘܣܦ *to be added, to be given in addition;* with ܡܢ ܠܒܪ *to be added from without* i. e. *to be extraneous, non-essential; to wax* as the moon; *to be swollen* as a river; *to increase* in volume, in honour, in riches, &c.; ܐܬܬܘܣܦܬ ܩܠܝܠ ܩܠܝܠ *it increased by little and little;* ܪܗܛܘ ܘܐܬܬܘܣܦܘ ܒܡܢܝܢܗܘܢ ܡܢ ܟܠܗܘܢ ܦܢܝܬܗ ܕܡܕܝܢܬܐ *they ran and swelled their number from all sides of the city;* gram. ܐܬܘܬܐ ܕܡܬܬܘܣܦܢ *additional* i. e. *servile letters.* Adverbial use same as Aphel. Derivatives, ܬܘܣܦܬܐ, ܡܬܬܘܣܦܢܐ, ܡܘܣܦܢܘܬܐ, ܡܘܣܦܢܐ, ܬܘܣܦܬܐ.

ܝܣܦ ܫܒܥܐ for ܫܒܘܥܐ ܕܝܣܦܐ eccles. *the seventh Sunday after Pentecost.*

ܝܥܐ and ܝܥܝ fut. ܢܐܥܐ, inf. ܡܐܥܐ, imper. ܥܝ, act. part. ܝܥܐ, ܝܥܝܐ. *to shoot, sprout, bud; to spring* or *come up, grow* as plants, human hair, birds' feathers; ܟܕ ܕܝܢ ܝܥܐ ܥܣܒܐ *now when the grass sprang up;* ܐܝܠܢܐ ܕܝܥܘ *trees which had grown up;* metaph. ܡܢ ܪܚܡܬ ܟܣܦܐ ܝܥܝܐ ܥܠܘܒܘܬܐ *out of the love of money springs covetousness.* Aph. ܐܘܥܝ *to make grow, to bear* or *bring forth* as a tree; *to sprout* or *put forth* as feathers; ܘܐܘܥܝ ܡܪܝܐ ܐܠܗܐ ܡܢ ܐܪܥܐ ܟܠ ܐܝܠܢ *and out of the ground made the Lord God to grow every tree;* ܩܕܡ ܕܢܘܥܐ ܟܘܒܐ *before it puts forth thorns;* ܢܘܥܘܢ ܓܦܐ ܐܝܟ ܕܝܘܢܐ *they shall put forth wings like a dove;* ܢܘܥܐ ܡܪܝܐ ܙܕܝܩܘܬܐ ܘܬܫܒܘܚܬܐ *the Lord will cause righteousness and praise to spring forth.* Derivatives, ܝܥܝܐ, ܡܥܝܐ, ܡܘܥܝܐ, ܡܘܥܝܢܘܬܐ, ܡܘܥܝܬܐ.

ܝܥܐ pl. ܝܥܐ m. *a quail, a sand-grouse.*

ܝܥܝܬܐ pl. ܝܥܝܬܐ rt. ܝܥܐ. f. *a sprout, shoot, blade, herb, plant;* ܝܥܝܬܐ ܕܟܘܒܐ ܦܠܚ ܗܘܐ Adam after the fall *tended thorny plants;* metaph. *a projection, battlement, parapet;* ܝܥܝܬܐ ܕܫܘܪܐ *the battlements of the wall.*

ܝܥܠܐ pl. ܝܥܠܐ m. *the mountain goat, ibex, chamois.*

ܝܥܩܒܝܢ and ܝܥܩܘܒܝܢ *rheum ribes.*

ܝܥܢ, ܝܥܢܐ, ܝܥܢܬܐ *avaricious, covetous, greedy, grasping;* ܓܒܪܐ ܝܥܢܐ ܡܓܪܐ ܚܪܝܢܐ *an avaricious man stirreth up strife;* ܡܘܬܐ ܝܥܢܐ *insatiable death.* Derivatives, verb ܝܥܢ, ܝܥܢܘܬܐ, ܝܥܢܐܝܬ.

ܝܥܢ denom. verb Pael conj. from ܝܥܢܐ. *to make greedy, excite cupidity;* ܡܝܥܢ ܠܗܘܢ ܘܢܣܒܝܢ ܡܕܡ ܕܠܐ ܕܝܠܗܘܢ evil passion *arouses covetousness in them so that they take what is not theirs.* Ethpa. ܐܬܝܥܢ *to covet, greedily desire,* with ܠܘܬ, ܥܠ ܗܘ ܕܐܬܝܥܢ ܥܠ ܡܐ ܕܠܘܬܗܘܢ *the Sultan coveting what they had with them.*

ܝܥܢܐܝܬ from ܝܥܢܐ. adv. *greedily, gluttonously;* ܚܛܦܘ ܦܘܪܥܢܗܘܢ ܡܢ ܥܕܬܐ ܝܥܢܐܝܬ *they greedily seized their dues from the congregation.*

ܝܥܢܘܬܐ, ܝܥܢܘܬܐ from ܝܥܢܐ. f. *avarice, avidity, covetousness, cupidity, insatiableness;* ܝܥܢܘܬܐ ܕܟܪܣܘܬܗܘܢ *their insatiable bellies;* ܚܛܝܬܐ ܥܠܬ ܠܥܠܡܐ ܒܝܕ ܢܟܠܐ ܕܝܥܢܘܬܐ *sin entered the world through the enticingness of cupidity.*

ܝܥܪܐ pl. ܝܥܪܝܢ, ܝܥܪܐ m. *a thicket, a tangle of thorns* or *briars; a sucker* of a vine, *a briar;* often metaph. of sin, &c., ܝܥܪܐ ܘܟܘܒܐ *briars and thorns;* ܥܩܘܪ ܠܝܥܪܐ ܕܚܛܗܐ *root out the thorny growth of sins;* ܝܥܪܐ ܕܦܬܟܪܘܬܐ *the thorny tangle of idolatry.*

ܝܦܐ act. part. m. pl. ܝܦܝܢ, rare for ܐܦܐ. *to bake.*

ܝܦܐ Peal not in use. Aphel ܐܘܦܝ *a) to be able, enough, sufficient;* ܠܐ ܡܘܦܝܐ ܗܘܬ ܐܪܥܐ ܠܡܣܒܠܘ ܐܢܘܢ ܡܛܠ ܩܢܝܢܗܘܢ *the land was not able to bear them because of their cattle;*

ܙܥܘܪ ܠܫܢܝ ܘܒܡܢܐ ܐܣܦܩܟ *poor is my tongue and wherewith shall I be sufficient for thee?* b) *to bring to an end, complete, consume.* c) *to come to an end, pass away, cease, fail, vanish, wane;* ܐܝܟ ܬܢܢܐ ܐܣܦ *it vanished like smoke;* ܟܕ ܡܣܬܦܐ ܚܡܬܐ *when anger has ceased;* ܒܘܣܡܐ ܕܠܐ ܡܣܬܦܝܢ *unfailing joys, pleasures which vanish not away.* Derivatives, ܡܘܣܦܢܐ, ܡܘܣܦܢܘܬܐ.

ܝܦܐ from ἧπαρ (ὄνειον) *the liver of an ass.*

ܝܦܝܐ rt. ܐܦܐ. (rare) *a baker.*

ܝܨܘܦܐ *clear red.*

ܝܨܘܦܐ pl. ܐ̈ rt. ܝܨܦ. m. *a superintendent, caretaker, overseer, guardian; diligent, busy;* ܝܨܘܦܐ ܕܥܠ ܟܠ ܣܥܘܪܘܬܐ ܛܒܬܐ *diligent in every good cause.*

ܝܨܘܦܐܝܬ rt. ܝܨܦ. adv. *carefully, diligently.*

ܝܨܘܦܢܐ, ܝܨܘܦܢܝܬܐ, ܢ̈ܐ ܬ̈ܐ rt. ܝܨܦ. *careful, diligent, zealous; an overseer, warden.*

ܝܨܘܦܢܘܬܐ rt. ܝܨܦ. f. *care, solicitude.*

ܝܨܝܠܐ pl. ܐ̈ m. *a joint, the elbow.*

ܝܨܝܦ and ܝܨܝܦ; see ܝܨܦ.

ܝܨܝܦܐܝܬ rt. ܝܨܦ. adv. *carefully, exactly, with pains.*

ܝܨܝܦܘܬܐ rt. ܝܨܦ. f. *care, diligence, attention, seriousness; anxiety, guardianship;* ܝܨܝܦܘܬܐ ܥܠܡܢܝܬܐ *worldly anxieties;* ܝܨܝܦܘܬܐ ܝܬܝܪܬܐ *overmuch anxiety.*

ܝܨܨ Ethpalpal ܐܬܝܨܝܨ denom. verb from ܝܨܨܐ. *to become a nation, to be propagated.*

ܝܨܨܐ, ܝܨܨܐ and ܝܨܝܨܐ pl. ܐ̈ m. *a people, race, nation;* ܡܢ ܫܪܒܬܐ ܒܨܝܪܬܐ ܘܝܨܨܐ ܕܘܝܐ *of low family and mean nation.* Derivative, verb ܝܨܨ.

ܝܨܦ fut. ܢܐܨܦ, act. part. ܝܨܦ, ܝܨܦܐ, pass. part. ܝܨܝܦ and ܝܨܝܦ, ܝܨܝܦܐ, ܝܨܝܦܬܐ. *to be careful, be anxious about; to take care, take pains, to mind, to be diligent, earnest, solicitous;* ܠܐ ܬܐܨܦܘܢ ܠܢܦܫܟܘܢ *be not anxious about your life;* ܝܨܦܝܢ ܒܒܬܝܗܘܢ ܫܦܝܪܐܝܬ *minding their houses well;* ܝܨܦ ܘܟܬܒ *he wrote carefully.* Parts. the form ܝܨܝܦܐ has the passive sense, *cared for, studied, sought out, exquisite;* form ܝܨܝܦܐ active signif. *careful, anxious, solicitous.* Ethpe. ܐܬܝܨܦ *to be sought for, cared for, taken care of, attended to, studied, necessary;* ܒܘܣܡܐ ܕܦܓܪܐ ܡܬܝܨܦܝܢ *the pleasures of the body are cared for;* ܠܐ ܡܬܝܨܦܐ ܛܒ ܗܕܐ *it does not matter much;* ܢܬܝܨܦܢ ܣܘܢܩܢܘܗܝ *let his needs be attended to.* Pael ܝܨܦ *to take pains, attend to.* Ethpa. ܐܬܝܨܦ *to take pains, do carefully;* ܐܬܝܨܦ ܒܡܪܒܝܢܘܬܗܘܢ *he took pains in their education, instructed them carefully.* Derivatives, ܝܨܘܦܐ, ܝܨܘܦܐܝܬ, ܝܨܘܦܢܐ, ܝܨܘܦܢܘܬܐ, ܝܨܝܦܐܝܬ, ܝܨܝܦܘܬܐ, ܡܬܝܨܦܢܐ, ܝܨܦܐ.

ܝܨܪܐ pl. ܐ̈ Neo-Heb. m. *propensity* esp. towards evil, *natural disposition; bent, inclination;* ܩܫܝܘܬ ܝܨܪܐ *stubbornness;* ܝܨܪܗ ܕܟܝܢܢ *the bent of our nature;* ܒܪܢܫܐ ܕܠܐ ܟܒܫ ܝܨܪܗ *a man who does not control his inclinations;* ܠܐ ܐܫܟܚ ܝܨܪܗ *he could not do what he wished.*

ܝܩܕ or ܐܝܩܕ fut. ܢܐܩܕ, act. part. ܝܩܕ, ܝܩܕܐ, part. adj. ܝܩܝܕ, ܐ, ܬܐ. *to be burnt up, set on fire, to catch fire;* ܠܡܘܫܐ ܐܬܚܙܝ ܣܢܝܐ ܕܝܩܕ ܘܠܐ ܝܩܕ *there was shown to Moses a bush which blazed without being consumed;* ܓܐܪܐ ܝܩܕܐ *red-hot arrows;* ܗܘ ܕܢܘܗܪܐ ܝܩܕܝܢ ܡܢܗ *He from whom seraphs derive brilliance.* Metaph. *to be inflamed, enkindled; to burn* with envy, love, faith, &c. Part. adj. *burnt, burning, fiery, torrid, tawny;* ܠܐ ܗܘܐ ܗܘܐ ܠܒܢ ܝܩܕ ܒܢ *did not our heart burn within us?* ܕܨܗܝܐ ܝܩܝܕܝܢ *parched with thirst;* ܐܬܪܐ ܝܩܝܕܐ *the torrid zone.* Ethpe. ܐܬܝܩܕ *to be on fire, to burn.* Ethpa. ܐܬܝܩܕ *to be set on fire, kindled, burnt up.* Aph. ܐܘܩܕ *to set on fire, light, kindle, burn up, consume;* ܬܘ ܢܪܡܐ ܠܒܢܐ ܘܢܘܩܕ ܐܢܝܢ ܒܢܘܪܐ *come let us make bricks and burn them thoroughly;* ܐܘܩܕ ܠܡܕܝܢܬܗܘܢ *he burnt their city;* ܓܪܡܝ ܚܘܪܘ ܐܝܟ ܡܘܩܕܐ *my bones are white as if they were burnt.* Metaph. *to inflame, excite.* Ettaph. ܐܬܬܘܩܕ *to be burnt, burnt up.* Derivatives, ܝܩܕܐ, ܝܩܕܐ, ܝܩܕܢܐ, ܝܩܕܢܐܝܬ, ܝܩܕܢܘܬܐ, ܝܩܘܕܐ, ܝܩܕܢܐ, ܡܘܩܕܢܐ, ܡܘܩܕܢܘܬܐ, ܡܘܩܕܢܐܝܬ.

ܝܩܕܐ pl. ܐ̈ rt. ܝܩܕ. m. *a burning* esp. *a burnt sacrifice, burnt-offering;* ܝܩܕܐ ܡܫܡܠܝܐ *a whole burnt-offering.*

ܝܩܕܐ pl. ܐ̈ rt. ܝܩܕ. m. *fuel, kindling-wood.*

ܝܩܕܢܐ, ܝܩܕܢܐ pl. ܝ̈ rt. ܝܩܕ. m. *a) burning, a fire, conflagration;* ܢܗܘܐ ܠܝܩܕܢܐ *it shall be burnt;* ܝܩܕܢ ܗܝܟܠܐ *the burning of the temple. b) firing, fuel. c) heat, inflammation;* ܝܩܕܢܐ ܕܪܘܚܐ *a burning wind;* ܝܩܕܢܐ ܕܐܫܬܐ *fever heat.*

ܝܩܕܬܐ rt. ܝܩܕ. f. *fire, burning flame.*

ܝܩܘܕܐ, ܬܐ rt. ܝܩܕ. *flaming, fiery, fervent;* ܠܐ ܝܩܘܕܐ *incombustible;* ܬܓܡ̈ܐ ܝܩܘܕ̈ܐ *the burning ranks* of angels.

ܝܩܘܕܐܝܬ rt. ܝܩܕ. adv. *ardently.*

ܝܩܘܕܘܬܐ rt. ܝܩܕ. f. *flaming, burning;* metaph. *glow, vehemence.*

ܝܩܘܢܬܐ or ܝܩܘܢܬܐ pl. ܬ̈ܐ ὑάκινθος, *a jacinth* or *ruby;* ܝܩܘܢܬܐ ܣܘܡܩܬܐ ܘܙܚܘܪܝܬܐ *a red and scarlet ruby.*

ܝܩܘܪܐ or ܝܩܘܪܐ rt. ܝܩܪ. adj. *heavy, ponderous.*

ܝܩܠܐ or ܝܩܠܐ m. *a button-hole.*

ܝܩܢ denom. verb Pael conj. from ܐܝܩܘܢܐ. *to stamp* or *imprint a likeness* on a coin, *to coin; to form, figure, represent, describe,* esp. *by similitudes, to signify;* ܚܘܣ ܥܠ ܢܦ̈ܫܬܐ ܕܐܬܝܩܢ ܒܕܡܘܬܟ *have pity on the souls formed after Thy own likeness;* ܟܠܗܘܢ ܐ̈ܪܙܐ ܠܗ ܡܪܡܙܝܢ ܘܟܠܗܘܢ ܥܐܕ̈ܐ ܩܕܝ̈ܫܐ ܠܗ ܡܝܩܢܝܢ *all the Sacraments point to Him and all holy days are similitudes of Him.* Ethpa. ܐܬܝܩܢ *to be stamped with an image* as a coin, *to be depicted, described, expressed;* ܫܘܦܪܐ ܕܕܘܒܪ̈ܐ ܫܦܝܪ̈ܐ ܡܬܝܩܢ *the beauty of comely life is described.*

ܝܩܝܪܐܝܬ rt. ܝܩܪ. adv. *a) with difficulty, hardly, grievously;* ܝܩܝܪܐܝܬ ܫܡܥܬ *thou art hard of hearing. b) with honour, reverentially.*

ܝܩܝܪܘܬܐ rt. ܝܩܪ. f. *a) weight;* metaph. *seriousness, sobriety, dignity; honour, reverence;* ܪܘܓܙܐ ܕܝܩܝܪܘܬܐ *serious* or *severe anger;* ܝܩܝܪܘܬܐ ܕܕܘܒܪ̈ܐ *sober* or *dignified conduct. b) heaviness, sluggishness. c) furniture.*

ܝܩܪ fut. ܢܐܩܪ, act. part. ܝܩܪ, ܝܩܪܐ, pass. part. ܝܩܝܪ, ܐ, ܬܐ. *a) to be heavy* generally metaph. *to be heavy, weighed down, oppressed; to be heavy* or *dull* with age; *to be a burden, burdensome, oppressive;* ܝܩܪ ܠܫܢܗ *his tongue was slow* from palsy; ܕܠܐ ܢܐܩܪܘܢ ܠܒܘܬܟܘܢ ܒܐܟܠܘܬܐ ܘܒܪܘܝܘܬܐ ܘܒܝܨܦܬܐ ܕܥܠܡܐ *lest your hearts be weighed down with surfeiting and drunkenness and worldly care;* ܝܩܪ ܠܝ ܗܢܐ ܐܬܪܐ *this place is wearisome to me. b) to be precious, rare, costly.*

Part. adj. *a) heavy, ponderous; deep, dull, hard;* ܝܩܝܪܐ ܟܐܦܐ ܘܝܩܝܪ ܚܠܐ ܘܪܘܓܙܗ ܕܣܟܠܐ ܝܩܝܪ ܡܢ ܬܪܝܗܘܢ *a stone is heavy and the sand weighty but a fool's wrath is heavier than them both;* ܫܢܬܐ ܝܩܝܪܬܐ *heavy* or *deep sleep;* ܝܩܝܪ ܠܒܐ *dull of heart. b) weighty, honourable, honoured;* ܡܘܫܐ ܝܩܝܪ ܗܘܐ ܩܕܡ ܡܪܝܐ *Moses was honoured before the Lord. c) dear, beloved* with ܥܠ, ܠ; ܥܒܕܐ ܕܝܩܝܪ ܗܘܐ ܠܘܬܗ *a servant who was dear to him. d) precious, costly, valuable;* ܝܩܝܪܐ ܚܟܡܬܐ ܡܢ ܟܐܦ̈ܐ ܛܒ̈ܬܐ *wisdom is more precious than goodly stones;* ܝܩܝܪ̈ܬܐ ܕܥܕܬܐ *the precious things of the Church* i. e. the Sacraments; ܒܝܩܝܪ *dearly, at a high price.* Ethpe. ܐܬܝܩܪ *to be burdened.* Pa. ܝܩܪ *a) to honour, treat with reverence; to worship;* ܝܩܪ ܠܐܒܘܟ ܘܠܐܡܟ *honour thy father and thy mother;* ܡܝܩܪܝܬܘܢ ܠܢܘܪܐ *ye worship fire. b) to confer honour* or *public office; to bring gifts;* ܕܪܓܐ ܕܩܪܘܝܐ ܡܝܩܪ ܗܘܐ ܠܗ *the office of reader was conferred on him.* Part. adj. ܡܝܩܪ, ܡܝܩܪܐ, ܡܝܩܪܬܐ *a) honoured, honourable, venerable;* ܐܪܙܐ ܪܒܐ ܘܡܝܩܪ ܗܢܐ *a sacrament so great and honoured;* ܣܒ̈ܐ ܡܝܩܪ̈ܐ *venerable old men. b) precious, valuable;* ܩܢܝ̈ܢܐ ܡܝܩܪ̈ܐ *valuable possessions,* ܡܝܩܪܬܐ ܒܓܢܣܐ *of a valuable kind.* Ethpa. ܐܬܝܩܪ imper. West-Syr. ܐܬܝܩܪ *to be honoured, held in honour, accounted precious; to glory, to obtain honour; to be adorned* or *given* in honour of some one. Aph. ܐܘܩܪ *a) to make heavy* or *dull;* ܐܘܩܪܘ ܡܫܡܥܬܗܘܢ *they have made dull their hearing;* ܐܘܩܪܗ ܒܫܫܠܬܐ *he loaded him with chains. b)* with ܥܠ *to be burdensome, wearisome;* ܥܠ ܐܢܫ ܠܐ ܬܘܩܪ *do not be a bore. c) to give honour, make valuable; to appraise.* Ettaph. ܐܬܬܘܩܪ *to be burdened.* Derivatives, ܐܝܩܪܐ, ܐܝܩܪܬܐ and ܝܩܪܬܐ, ܝܩܘܪܐ, ܝܩܝܪܐܝܬ, ܝܩܝܪܘܬܐ, ܝܩܪܐ, ܡܝܩܪܐ, ܡܝܩܪܐܝܬ, ܡܝܩܪܘܬܐ, ܡܝܩܪܢܐ, ܡܝܩܪܢܐܝܬ, ܡܝܩܪܢܘܬܐ.

ܝܩܪܐ rt. ܝܩܪ. m. *weight.*

ܝܩܪܘܪܐ m. *a toad.*

ܝܩܪܬܐ and ܐܝܩܪܬܐ rt. ܝܩܪ. f. *a burthen, cumbrance, belongings, family, children, little ones, following, household stuff, baggage;* ܒܝܩܪܬܐ

ܥܓܠܬܐ ܠܢܫܝܟܘܢ ܘܠܛܠܝܟܘܢ *waggons for your wives and little ones;* ܫܒܩܘ ܡܐܢܝܗܘܢ ܘܥܪܩܘ *they left their baggage and fled.*

ܝܪܒ and ܐܪܒ cognate root to ܪܒ and ܪܒܐ, fut. ܢܐܪܒ, act. part. ܝܪܒ, ܝܪܒܐ. *to be* or *become great, to grow up, to increase* in power or dignity; *to be exalted, rise to high honour;* ܝܪܒܬ ܢܨܒܬܐ ܥܕܡܐ ܠܫܡܝܐ the plant *grew up heaven-high;* ܗܫܐ ܢܐܪܒ ܚܝܠܟ ܡܪܝܐ *now, O Lord, let Thy power be great;* ܢܐܪܒ ܫܡܟ *let Thy name be magnified;* ܐܣܝܐ ܐܫܬܡܗ ܘܝܪܒ *the physician became famous and honoured.* Aph. ܐܘܪܒ *a) to enlarge, widen;* ܐܘܪܒ ܠܐܡܝܕ *he enlarged Amid;* ܐܘܪܒ ܠܗܪܣܝܣ ܕܡܩܕܘܢܝܘܣ *he extended the heresy of Macedonius; b) to make great, raise to honour; to magnify, extol;* ܐܘܪܒܘܟ ܡܠܟܐ ܘܥܒܕܘܟ ܕܝܢܐ *emperors have raised thee to honour and made thee a judge;* ܡܘܪܒܐ ܢܦܫܝ ܠܡܪܝܐ *my soul doth magnify the Lord;* ܡܘܪܒܐ *the Magnificat;* ܡܫܝܚܐ ܢܘܪܒ ܥܘܗܕܢܟ *Christ grant thee to be long remembered.*

ܝܪܒܘܥܐ pl. ܐ̈ m. *the jerboa.*

ܝܪܘܓ, ܝܪܘܓܐ pl. ܐ̈ m. *a well* or *tank;* ܓܘܒܝܗܘܢ ܘܝܪܘܓܝܗܘܢ *their pools and tanks;* metaph. ܝܪ̈ܘܓܐ ܒܪ̈ܝܟܐ ܐܢܘܢ ܟܬܒܐ ܐܠܗܝܐ *blessed wells are the divine scriptures.*

ܝܪܘܩܐ rt. ܝܪܩ. adj. *pale, ashy, livid.*

ܝܪܘܪܐ pl. ܐ̈ usually f. *a jackal.*

ܝܪܘܛܐ or ܝܪܘܛܐ m. a tree the sap of which is used medicinally, *panaces, heracleum, ferula opopanax.*

ܝܪܬܐ, ܝܪܬܘܬܐ pl. ܝܪ̈ܬܐ rt. ܝܪܬ. m. *an heir, inheritor, master, possessor;* ܐܦ ܝܪܬܐ ܗܘ ܘܡܪܐ ܕܟܪܡܐ *he is both heir and lord of the vineyard;* ܒܝܬܐ ܕܡܝܬ ܝܪܬܗ *a house the owner of which is dead.*

ܝܪܚ, ܝܪܚܐ pl. ܐ̈ m. *a month;* ܝܪܚ ܝܘܡܬܐ *a full month;* ܪܝܫ ܝܪܚܐ *the new moon, the first of the month;* ܝܪܚܐ ܕܢܝܣܢ *Nisan, the month of flowers;* ܝܪܚܐ ܕܚܨܕܐ *the month of harvest.* The months answer nearly to our own, beginning with ܬܫܪܝ ܩܕܡ or ܐ ܬܫܪܝ *October,* ܬܫܪܝ ܐܚܪܝ or ܒ *November,* ܟܢܘܢ ܩܕܡ or ܐ *December,* ܟܢܘܢ ܒ *January,* ܫܒܛ *February,* ܐܕܪ *March,* ܢܝܣܢ *April,* ܐܝܪ *May,* ܚܙܝܪܢ *June,* ܬܡܘܙ *July,* ܐܒ *August,* ܐܝܠܘܠ *September.* Derivatives, ܝܪܚܐ, ܝܪܚܐܝܬ, ܝܪܚܘܬܐ.

ܝܪܚܘܬܐ from ܝܪܚ. f. *a monthly course.*

ܝܪܚܐܝܬ from ܝܪܚ. adv. *monthly.*

ܝܪܚܝܐ from ܝܪܚ. *monthly;* ܚܘܫܒܢܐ ܝܪܚܝܐ *a monthly reckoning.*

ܝܪܚܐ pl. ܐ̈, same as ܙܪܚܐ or ܙܪܚܐ m. *a firefly.*

ܝܪܝܥܐ, ܝܪܝܥܬܐ pl. ܝܪ̈ܝܥܢ, ܐ̈ f. *a hanging, covering, curtain, a tent, the inhabitants of a tent, a family;* ܡܬܚ ܫܡܝܐ ܐܝܟ ܝܪܝܥܬܐ *He stretched out the heaven like a curtain;* ܝܪ̈ܝܥܬܐ ܕܣܥܪܐ *haircloth tents;* ܡܐܬܝܢ ܐܠܦܝܢ ܝܪ̈ܝܥܬܐ ܕܛܘܪ̈ܟܝܐ 200,000 *tents* or *families of Turks.*

ܝܪܝܥܬܘܢܬܐ dim. of ܝܪܝܥܬܐ. *a little curtain, coverlet.*

ܝܪܝܟ *to be long;* ܒܠܘܛܐ ܕܠܐ ܝܪܝܟ *a dwarf oak;* ܝܪܝܟ ܠܗ ܡܡܠܠܐ ܥܠ ܗܢܐ ܨܒܘܬܐ *discourse on this matter is lengthy.* Cf. ܐܪܝܟ p. 29.

ܝܪܠܐ perh. *a crocodile.*

ܝܪܠܝܓ or ܝܪܠܝܓ pl. ܐ̈ Tatar. m. *a royal mandate* or *diploma.*

ܝܪܩ fut. ܢܐܪܩ *to be* or *grow pale.* Pa. ܝܪܩ *to make pale;* pass. part. ܡܝܪܩ, ܡܝܪܩܐ. *pale, pallid.* Ethpa. ܐܬܝܪܩ *to become pale.* Aph. ܐܘܪܩ *to make pale, become* or *turn pale;* ܐܘܪܩܘ ܐܦܘܗܝ *his face turned pale; to show* or *become green* i.e. to put forth leaves. Derivatives, ܝܪܩܐ, ܝܪܩܘܢܐ, ܝܪܩܘܢܝܬܐ, ܝܘܪܩܐ, ܝܪܩܢܐ, ܡܝܪܩܢܐ, ܡܘܪܩܢܘܬܐ.

ܝܪܩܐ pl. ܐ̈ rt. ܝܪܩ. m. *a herb, garden-* or *pot-herb, vegetable;* ܝܪ̈ܩܐ ܕܒܪܐ *wild herbs;* ܝܪ̈ܩܐ ܪܛܝܒܐ *fresh vegetables;* ܝܪ̈ܩܐ ܕܐܣܝܘܬܐ *medicinal herbs.*

ܝܪܩܘܢܐ pl. ܐ̈ dim. of ܝܪܩܐ. m. *a small herb.*

ܝܪܩܢ, ܝܪܩܢܐ rt. ܝܪܩ. adj. *yellowish, pale yellow.*

ܝܪܩܢܐ rt. ܝܪܩ. m. *pallor, turning yellow* from disease, *blight, mildew; jaundice; a blighting* or *withering wind.*

ܝܪܬ fut. ܢܐܪܬ, inf. ܡܐܪܬ, for act. part. see ܝܪܬܐ. *to be heir, to inherit; to take possession, possess;* ܙܪܥܗ ܢܐܪܬ ܐܪܥܐ *his seed shall inherit the land;* ܐܬܩܪܝܬܘܢ ܠܡܐܪܬ ܡܠܟܘܬܐ *ye have been called to inherit a blessing;* [illegible] *ye shall take possession of a land flowing with milk and honey;* [illegible] *that I may inherit life.* Ethpe. ܐܬܝܪܬ or ܐܬܬܪܬ *to be made heir; to be made to inherit.* Aph. ܐܘܪܬ *to give* or *leave an inheritance, leave by* will; *to divide an inheritance, cause to inherit* or *possess;* [illegible] *distribute thy riches to thy sons;* [illegible] *a good man leaveth an inheritance to his children's children;* [illegible] *he shall cause Israel to take possession of it.* Derivatives, ܝܪܘܬܘܬܐ, ܝܪܬܐ, ܝܪܬܘܬܐ, ܡܘܪܬܐ, ܡܘܪܬܢܐ.

ܝܪܬܐ pl. ܝܪ̈ܬܐ rt. ܝܪܬ. m. *an heir, inheritor, possessor;* [illegible] *inheritors of the promise;* [illegible] a bishop's *appointed successor to the see.*

ܝܪܬܘܬܐ pl. ܝܪ̈ܬܘܬܐ rt. ܝܪܬ. f. *an inheritance, portion, lot, possession, property;* [illegible] *fellow-heirs;* with ܦܪܩ *to redeem an inheritance.*

ܝܫܐ but pl. ܝ̈ܫܐ *a maggot, hopper, a worm* bred in salted meat.

ܝܫܛ only used in Aphel ܐܘܫܛ *to move, stretch out,* usually with ܐܝܕܐ and with ܒ of the object and ܠ of the pers. *to lay hands on, seize, steal, harm;* [illegible] *he laid hands on Tabriz;* [illegible] *if he have not laid his hand on his neighbour's goods;* [illegible] *they laid hands on him, handled him roughly.*

ܝܫܘܥܝܐ pl. ܝ̈ܫܘܥܝܐ from ܝܫܘܥ. *of* or *belonging to Jesus, a follower of Jesus;* [illegible] *love such as that of Jesus.*

ܝܫܛ not used in Peal. Aphel ܐܘܫܛ *to hold out, stretch out* usually with ܐܝܕܐ and with ܒ of the object or ܠ of the pers., [illegible] *lest he put forth his hand and take of the tree of life;* [illegible] *I will stretch out my hand and smite the Egyptians;* [illegible] *the destroyer laid his hand on the powerful and renowned;* [illegible] *thou stretchest forth thy hand to heal and to do wonders;* [illegible] *he brought help;* [illegible] *they address questions to their superiors;* [illegible] *he slew him with an arrow.* Ettaph. ܐܬܬܘܫܛ *to be offered, presented; to advance.* Shaphel ܫܘܫܛ *to make spring forth, cause to advance;* [illegible] *heat makes everything bring forth and shoot up;* [illegible] *the path which brings near and leads us forward towards God.* Eshtaphal ܐܫܬܘܫܛ *to reach forward, stretch forward, offer; to grow up; to advance, make progress, succeed, be advanced* esp. in dignity; [illegible] *reaching forward to the things which are before in labouring unto virtue;* [illegible] *he grew taller and stronger;* [illegible] *as time advances;* [illegible] *let him not be advanced from rank to rank.* Derivatives, ܫܘܫܛܐ, ܫܘܫܛܐ or ܫܘܫܛܐ, ܫܘܫܛܢܘܬܐ, ܡܫܬܘܫܛܢܘܬܐ.

ܫܘܫܛܐ pl. ܫܘ̈ܫܛܐ rt. ܫܛ. m. *the throat, gullet, windpipe;* [illegible] *medicines for the windpipe;* metaph. [illegible] *and that the throat of thy soul may be sweetened by the taste of our love.*

ܝܫܦܗ or ܝܫܦܐ m. *jasper.*

ܝܬ, ܝܬܐ com. *a*) *being, essence, existence; material, matter;* with ܠܐ *non-existence, nothingness;* [illegible] *He brought us into being out of nothingness.* *b*) archaism used like Heb. *eth* as sign of the accusative; [illegible] *God created the heaven and the earth.* *c*) *the self;* with pron. suff. ܝܬܟ, ܝܬܗ *thyself;* ܝܬܗ *himself;* ܝܬܗܘܢ *themselves;* [illegible] *his own body;* [illegible] *beside himself* cf. [illegible] *possessed of freewill;* [illegible] *self-empire, self-control;* [illegible] *self-disdain;* [illegible] *plants come into existence by themselves.* Derivatives, ܝܬܝܬܐ, ܝܬܝܐ, verb ܝܬ.

ܝܬܒ fut. ܢܬܒ, inf. ܡܬܒ or ܡܬܐܒ, imper. ܬܒ, parts. ܝܬܒ, ܝܬܒܐ and ܝܬܝܒ, ܝܬܝܒܐ. *a*) *to sit down, sit, be seated, repose; to incubate;* with [illegible] &c. *to ride;* with ܒܐܠܦܐ or [illegible] *to take ship, embark;* with [illegible] *on the throne* or ellipt. *to reign;* [illegible] *they who sit in the gate = judges, chief men* of the city; with [illegible] *to be in one's right mind, have possession of one's faculties.* b) *to remain, abide, settle, dwell; to encamp;* ܝܬܶܒ ܗܘܳܐ ܫܢܰܬ ܚܕܳܐ ܘܝܰܪ̈ܚܶܐ ܫܬܳܐ ܒܩܘܪܢܬܘܣ *he dwelt for a year and six months in Corinth; to lie* as snow; ܝܬܶܒ ܥܰܠ ܐܶܓܳܪ̈ܶܐ ܐܰܪܒܰܥ ܨܶܒ̈ܥܺܝܢ *it lay four fingers deep on the roofs.* c) *to be situated.* Parts. a) ܝܳܬܶܒ *sitting, situated, placed; settled, inhabited;* ܡܕܺܝܢܬܳܐ ܕܝܳܬܒܳܐ ܒܦܶܩܥܬܳܐ a city *in the plain;* ܡܕ̈ܺܝܢܳܬܳܐ ܝܳܬ̈ܒܳܢ *inhabited cities;* see also as subst. below. b) ܝܳܬܶܒ *sitting, seated;* ܝܽܘܡܳܐ ܕܝܳܬܶܒ ܗܘܳܐ ܢܽܘܪܕܺܝܢ ܐܰܝܟܳܐ ܕܝܳܬܶܒ ܐܢ̱ܬ *one day when Nur-eddin was sitting where thou art sitting.* Pa. ܝܰܬܶܒ *to cause to inhabit, people, re-people;* pass. part. ܡܝܰܬܰܒ, ܡܝܰܬܒܳܐ, ܡܝܰܬܰܒܬܳܐ *situated, settled;* with ܠܳܐ *uninhabited;* metaph. *settled, composed, occupied;* ܐܘ ܪܶܥܝܳܢܳܐ ܡܝܰܬܒܳܐ *O firmly-set mind;* ܗܰܘܢܳܐ ܡܝܰܬܒܳܐ *a composed mind.* Ethpa. ܐܶܬܝܰܬܰܒ *to be inhabited, settled; to establish* or *settle oneself; to settle, subside; to re-establish, re-people.* Aphel ܐܰܘܬܶܒ *to make dwell* or *inhabit, to cause to be inhabited, to found; to restore; to place, set, keep, station, appoint;* ܩܽܘܪ̈ܝܳܐ ܕܚܪ̈ܺܝܒܳܢ ܢܰܘܬܒܽܘܢ *they shall make desolate cities to be inhabited;* ܐܰܠܳܗܳܐ ܡܰܘܬܶܒ ܝܚܺܝ̈ܕܳܝܳܐ ܒܒܰܝܬܳܐ *God setteth the solitary in a family;* ܠܡܰܘܬܳܒܽܘ ܢܶܫ̈ܶܐ ܢܽܘܟܪ̈ܳܝܳܬܳܐ *to take strange women to dwell with, to marry strangers;* ܐܰܘܬܶܒ ܕܰܝܳܢ̈ܶܐ *to appoint judges;* ܐܰܘܬܶܒ ܥܰܠ ܟܘܪܣܝܳܐ *to set on the throne, make king;* ܐܰܘܬܶܒ ܢܛܽܘܪܬܳܐ *to station a guard;* ܡܰܠܟ̈ܶܐ ܡܰܘܬ̈ܒܰܝ ܡܕ̈ܺܝܢܳܬܳܐ *kings founders of cities.* Ethtaph. ܐܶܬܬܰܘܬܰܒ *to sojourn, settle, dwell, inhabit;* ܐܶܬܳܐ ܠܡܶܬܬܰܘܬܳܒܽܘ ܥܰܡܰܢ *he came to sojourn with us;* ܐܶܢܳܐ ܒܨܺܝܪܳܐ ܕܡܶܬܬܰܘܬܰܒ ܒܐܳܡܺܝܕ *I an insignificant person dwelling in Amid.* Derivatives, ܬܘܬܒܐ, ܝܬܒܐ, ܝܳܬܒܐ, ܝܬܘܒܐ, ܡܘܬܒܐ, ܬܘܬܒܘܬܐ, ܡܬܒܘܬܐ.

ܝܳܬܒܳܐ pl. ܝܳܬ̈ܒܶܐ, ܝܳܬ̈ܒܺܝܢ rt. ܝܬܒ. m. *an inhabited place* opp. ܡܰܕܒܪܳܐ, *a dwelling-place, habitation; seat, site;* ܒܟܽܠܶܗ ܝܳܬܒܳܐ ܕܐܰܬܪܳܐ *in all the inhabited part of the country;* ܡܬܺܝܡ ܝܳܬܒܗܽܘܢ *their habitation is situated . . .;* ܝܳܬܒܳܐ ܕܡܰܠܟܽܘܬܳܐ *the seat of empire, imperial palace.*

ܝܳܬܽܘܒܳܐ, ܝܳܬܽܘܒܬܳܐ pl. ܝܳܬ̈ܽܘܒܶܐ, ܝܳܬ̈ܽܘܒܳܬܳܐ rt. ܝܬܒ. a) adj. *inhabited.* b) subst. *an inhabitant, settler, sojourner.*

ܝܳܬܒܳܐ pl. ܝܳܬ̈ܒܶܐ rt. ܝܬܒ. part. emph. = subst. *an inhabitant, dweller;* ܒܺܝܫܽܘܬܗܽܘܢ ܕܝܳܬ̈ܒܶܝܗ̇ *the wickedness of those that dwell therein;* ܝܳܬ̈ܒܰܝ ܡܰܕܒܪܳܐ *dwellers in the desert;* ܝܳܬ̈ܒܶܐ ܣܳܡܘ ܝܳܬܒ̈ܶܐ ܕܢܶܗܘܽܘܢ ܠܢܝܳܚܳܐ ܕܝܳܬ̈ܒܶܐ *settlers established dwelling-places that dwellers therein might have rest.*

ܝܳܬܒܽܘܬܳܐ rt. ܝܬܒ. f. *a place of sojourning, resting-place.*

ܝܰܬܽܘܒܬܳܐ or ܝܬܽܘܒܬܳܐ rt. ܝܬܒ. f. *dung, excrement.*

ܝܳܬܽܘܒܬܳܐ rt. ܝܬܒ. f. *a place of habitation, the habitable earth.*

ܝܰܬܽܘܥܳܐ m. *spurge, euphorbia.*

ܝܰܬܺܝܪ, ܝܰܬܺܝܪܳܐ, ܝܰܬܺܝܪܬܳܐ, ܝܰܬܺܝܪܳܢ rt. ܝܬܪ. adj. a) *greater, overmuch, superfluous, surpassing, especial;* ܚܽܘܒܳܐ ܝܰܬܺܝܪܳܐ *superabundant love;* ܕܺܝܢܳܐ ܝܰܬܺܝܪܳܐ *greater condemnation;* ܒܚܰܬܺܝܬܽܘܬܳܐ ܝܰܬܺܝܪܬܳܐ *with especial care;* ܝܰܘܡ̈ܳܬܳܐ ܝܰܬܺܝܪ̈ܳܢ *very many days;* ܐܶܫܟܰܚ ܐܶܢܽܘܢ ܝܰܬܺܝܪܺܝܢ ܒܥܶܣܪܳܐ ܙܰܒ̈ܢܺܝܢ ܥܰܠ ܟܽܠܗܽܘܢ ܚܰܪ̈ܳܫܶܐ *he found them ten times better than all the magicians;* ܒܰܝܬܳܝܽܘܬܳܐ ܝܰܬܺܝܪܬܳܐ *undue familiarity;* ܫܡܳܐ ܝܰܬܺܝܪܳܐ *a nickname;* pl. fem. emph. *superfluous* or *needless* cares, words or deeds; *superfluities; great* or *virtuous deeds;* ܨܶܦܬܳܐ ܕܥܰܠ ܝܰܬܺܝܪ̈ܳܬܳܐ *anxiety about needless things;* adverbial use; ܝܰܬܺܝܪ ܒܨܺܝܪ and ܝܰܬܺܝܪ ܒܨܺܝܪ *more or less;* ܝܰܬܺܝܪ ܡܶܢ ܗܳܕܶܐ *still more, especially;* ܝܰܬܺܝܪ ܘܝܰܬܺܝܪ *more and more;* ܝܰܬܺܝܪ ܚܬܺܝܬܳܐܝܺܬ *most accurately.* b) *odd, uneven* opp. ܙܰܘܓܳܐ *even.* c) *far off, strange;* ܢܽܘܟܪ̈ܳܝܶܐ ܘܝܰܬܺܝܪ̈ܶܐ ܠܳܐ ܗܘܰܝܢ ܠܢܳܡܽܘܣܰܢ *we are not strangers and unacquainted with our law;* ܗܘܳܬ ܝܰܬܺܝܪܬܳܐ ܚܰܘܳܐ ܡܶܢ ܓܰܢܬܳܐ *Eve became estranged from that garden.*

ܝܰܬܺܝܪܳܐܝܺܬ rt. ܝܬܪ. adv. *more and more, increasingly, especially; the more, the rather.*

ܝܰܬܺܝܪܽܘܬܳܐ, ܝܰܬܺܝܪܽܘܬ rt. ܝܬܪ. f. a) *the best, excellence, advantage;* ܐܰܝܟ ܕܒܝܰܬܺܝܪܽܘܬ *in a better way, more excellent manner.* b) *abundance, superfluity;* ܠܳܐ ܗܘܳܐ ܒܝܰܬܺܝܪܽܘܬܳܐ ܕܩܶܢܝܳܢܳܐ ܐܺܝܬ ܚܰܝ̈ܶܐ a man's *life consisteth not in abundance of possessions;* ܡܶܢ ܝܰܬܺܝܪܽܘܬ *superfluous, needless.* c) *secretions, products;* ܝܰܬܺܝܪܽܘܬܳܐ ܕܒܥܺܝܪ̈ܳܐ *animal products* i.e. milk, butter, eggs; ܝܰܬܺܝܪܽܘܬ ܡܶܐܟܽܘܠܬܳܐ *waste products, excrement.*

ܝܬܡ, ܝܬܡܐ, ܝܬܡܬܐ *bereaved, desolate, fatherless, orphan;* ܒܢܝ̈ܐ ܝܬܡ̈ܐ ܕܐܬܝܬܡܘ ܠܝ *my orphaned children;* ܡܪܒܝܢܘܬܐ ܕܝܬܡ̈ܐ *education of orphans.* DERIVATIVES, verb ܝܬܡ, ܝܬܡܘܬܐ.

ܝܬܡ denom. verb PAEL conj. from ܝܬܡܐ. *to bereave, make an orphan.* ETHPA. ܐܬܝܬܡ *to be bereaved, orphaned.*

ܝܬܡܘܬܐ from ܝܬܡܐ. f. *orphanhood, fatherlessness, bereavement;* ܝܬܡܘܬܗ ܕܡܢ ܐܡܐ *his being motherless.*

ܝܬܐܝܬ from ܝܬܐ. adv. *of itself, by its nature.*

ܝܬܝܐ, ܝܬܝܬܐ from ܝܬܐ. *essential.*

ܝܬܩܐ pl. ܐ̈ m. *a sheet, roll, tablet, codex.*

ܝܬܪ or ܐܝܬܪ, fut. ܢܐܬܪ, imper. ܝܬܪ, act. part. ܝܬܪ. *to be left over, to have over and above, have profit, advantage; to gain, be gained, win, obtain;* ܡܕܡ ܕܝܬܪ ܡܢܗ ܠܨܦܪܐ *that which remaineth of it until the morning,* ܫܩܠܘ ܩܨ̈ܝܐ ܡܕܡ ܕܝܬܪ *they took up the fragments left over;* ܝܬܪܘ ܛܝ̈ܝܐ ܡܢ ܝܘ̈ܢܝܐ ܣܘ̈ܣܘܬܐ ܘܙܝ̈ܢܐ ܣܓܝ̈ܐܐ *the Arabs won from the Greeks a quantity of horses and arms;* ܬܓܪܐ ܐܬܪܝܢ ܘܦܠܓܘܬ ܝܬܪ *a merchant makes twice and a half profit;* ܘܝܬܪܘ ܗܘܘ ܣܓܝܐܐ ܒܚܙܬܐ ܕܚܕ̈ܕܐ *and they had great profit from seeing each other.* PA. ܝܬܪ *to make to abound; to increase;* ܡܪܝܐ ܢܝܬܪܟܘܢ ܘܢܣܓܐܟܘܢ ܒܚܘܒܐ ܚܕ ܠܘܬ ܚܕ *the Lord make you to increase and abound in love one towards another;* ܝܬܪ ܘܐܥܫܢ ܚܛܝܬܗ ܕܒܠܗ ܗܘ *he increased and intensified his sin by....* Part. a) ܡܝܬܪ, ܡܝܬܪܐ, ܡܝܬܪܬܐ *good, excellent, especial, best;* ܡܝܬܪܝܢ ܦܐܪ̈ܐ ܕܐܒܐ *the finest fruit;* ܕܒܫܐ ܕܬܫܪܝܢ ܡܝܬܪ *autumn honey is the best;* ܠܐ ܗܘܐ ܐܢܬܘܢ ܡܝܬܪܝܢ ܡܢܗܘܢ *are ye not better than they?* ܐܢܐ ܐܚܘܝܟܘܢ ܐܘܪܚܐ ܕܡܝܬܪܐ *I show you a more excellent way;* —ܡܝܬܪ ܗܘܐ ܡܢܗ ܒܥܘܬܪܐ ܒܚܝܠܐ *he surpassed him in wealth, in power;* a title of honour, ܐܘ ܡܝܬܪܐ *O excellent man.* Pl. f. ܡܝܬܪ̈ܬܐ ܡܝܬܪܘܬܐ *the most excellent things, noble deeds, virtues;* ܐܪܒܥ ܐܢܝܢ ܡܝܬܪ̈ܬܐ ܕܢܦܫܐ ܡܠܝܠܬܐ. ܚܟܝܡܘܬܐ. ܚܝܠܬܢܘܬܐ. ܢܟܦܘܬܐ. ܟܐܢܘܬܐ *there are four virtues pertaining to rational being, prudence, fortitude, temperance, justice;* ܓܒܪܐ ܕܡܠܐ ܡܝܬܪ̈ܬܐ *a man of distinguished virtues.* b) from ܝܬܪܐ. *supplied with a string, strung;* ܩܫܬܐ ܡܝܬܪܬܐ *a strung bow.* ETHPA. ܐܬܝܬܪ a) *to be made to abound, to have abundance, abound, superabound; to be increased, to grow* in power, dignity &c.; *to profit;* ܢܬܝܗܒ ܠܗ ܘܢܬܝܬܪ ܠܗ *to him shall be given and he shall have abundance;* ܐܬܝܬܪܬ ܛܝܒܘܬܐ *grace abounded;* ܐܬܝܬܪܢ *we increased* opp. ܐܬܒܨܪܘ *they decreased.* b) *to exceed, excel, surpass;* ܢܬܝܬܪ ܒܒܝܫܘܬܐ *he shall exceed in wickedness;* ܐܬܝܬܪ ܒܕܚܠܬ ܐܠܗܐ ܘܒܝܘܠܦܢܐ *he excelled in godliness and in learning.* APHEL ܐܘܬܪ a) *to have over, have enough and to spare; to leave, let remain;* ܗܘ ܕܣܓܝ ܠܐ ܐܘܬܪ *he who gathered much had nothing over;* ܡܕܡ ܕܡܘܬܪ *that which is left, the rest.* b) *to be of use, help, profit, advantage; to help, avail;* ܡܘܬܪ or ܡܢܐ ܐܘܬܪ *what use is it?* ܡܕܡ ܠܐ ܐܘܬܪ *he gained no advantage.* DERIVATIVES, ܝܘܬܪܢܐ, ܝܘܬܪܢܐ, ܝܬܝܪ, ܝܬܝܪܐܝܬ, ܝܬܝܪܘܬܐ, ܝܬܪܐ, ܡܘܬܪܢܐ, ܡܘܬܪܢܘܬܐ, ܡܘܬܪܢܐܝܬ, ܡܝܬܪܐ, ܡܝܬܪܐܝܬ, ܡܝܬܪܘܬܐ, ܡܝܬܪܢܘܬܐ, ܡܝܬܪܢܘܬܐ, ܬܘܬܪܐ.

ܝܬܪ, ܝܬܪܐ pl. ܐ̈ rt. ܝܬܪ. m. *the string* of a bow, of a musical instrument; ܐܪܡܝ ܝܬܪܐ ܒܨܘܪܗ ܘܚܢܩܗ *he put a bowstring round his neck and strangled him;* ܝܬܪܐ ܕܩܫܬܐ *the string of a bow; a sinew; the diameter* of a circle; *a beam;* ܝܬܪܐ ܕܒܝܬܐ *a beam of a house.*

ܝܬܬ denom. verb PAEL conj. from ܝܬ. *to give existence, constitute, establish.*

[Syriac colophon]

ܡܪܝ ܒܥܘܢܐ ܕܬܘܚܬܐ ܕܠܐ ܡܫܬܘܚܬܐ ܕܒܪܝܬܐ ܡܫܡܠܝܐ ܕܠܐ.
ܠܟ ܡܪܝ ܬܫܒܘܚܬܐ ܘܥܠܝܢ ܪܚܡܝܟ ܥܕܡܐ ܠܥܠܡ ܐܡܝܢ ✣

✣ ܟ ✣

ܟܐܒܬܐ

ܟܟ

ܟܟ usually thus written double when standing alone, for ܟ, the eleventh letter of the Syriac alphabet, ܟܦ or ܟܘܦ ܐܬܘܬܐ *the letter Coph* or *Cap;* the numeral 20, ܟܐ 21, ܟܒ 22, with a point ܟ݂ 200, ܟ݂ܐ 201, ܟ݂ܒ 202 &c. In words adopted from the Greek ܟ stands usually for χ and ܟܣ for ξ, e.g ܟܘܪܐ χώρα, ܟܣܢܘܣ ξένος.

ܟܐ in Heb. and Chald. adv. of place *here*, and so found in the Jerusalem dialect and in Modern Syriac, but in Ancient Syriac only in compounds with ܐܝܟ, ܠ, ܡܢ &c., as ܠܟܐ *hither*, ܡܢ ܟܐ *on this side, hence &c.* Derivatives, ܟܐ, ܐܝܟܐ, ܠܟܐ, ܗܪܟܐ, ܗܝܕܝܟܐ, ܐܝܟܢܐ, ܟܢܐ.

ܟܐܐ for ܟܐܐ, fut. ܢܟܐܐ, imper. ܟܐܝ, inf. ܡܟܐܐ, act. part. ܟܐܐ, ܟܐܝܐ. *to rebuke, reprove, chide* with ܒ of the pers. or cause; with ܕܠܐ *to forbid*, ܟܐܐ ܒܚܡܬܗ ܕܠܐ *in his anger he forbade . . .;* ܟܐܝ ܒܝܗܘܕܝܐ ܘܟܐܝ ܒܥܡܡܐ *rebuke the Jews and reprove the Gentiles;* ܟܐܝܬܗ ܒܝܢܝ ܠܒܝܢܗ ܟܐܝܐܝܬ ܛܒ *I rebuked him privately and very severely;* ܟܐܝܐ ܠܢ ܟܐܢܘܬܐ *justice reproaches us.* Ethpe. ܐܬܟܐܝ *to be rebuked, reproved, admonished;* ܠܐ ܐܬܟܐܝܘ seeing the miracle *they were not admonished.* Pa. ܟܐܝ *to reprove gravely, rebuke severely* with ܒ; ܠܐ ܡܨܝܢ ܕܢܟܐܘܢ ܒܐܫܬܐ *they have no power to rebuke the fever.* Ethpa. ܐܬܟܐܝ fut. ܢܬܟܐܐ and ܢܬܟܝܐ rare; pass. of Pael. Derivatives, ܟܐܝܐ, ܟܐܝܘܬܐ.

ܟܐܒ fut. ܢܟܐܒ, act. part. ܟܐܒ, ܟܐܒܐ, pass. part. ܟܐܝܒ, ܟܐܝܒܐ (rare). Cf. Cognate ܟܒ. *to pain, feel pain, suffer, be sorry, grieve;* with ܠ of the pers. and ܡܢ or ܥܠ of the cause; ܟܐܒ ܠܗ ܟܐܒܐ ܐܝܢܐ ܕܗܘ *suffering from whatsoever disease;* ܟܐܒܐ ܠܝ ܡܚܘܬܝ *my hurt pains me;* ܟܐܒܐ ܡܢ ܪܘܓܙܐ ܥܝܢܝ *mine eye aches from fretting;* ܟܐܒ ܠܗ *he felt sorry;* impers. ܟܐܒܐ ܠܗܘܢ *it grieved them.* Parts. *suffering; grievous, painful; sad, sorry;* ܟܐܒܐ ܡܚܘܬܗ *her wound is grievous;* ܐܝܠܝܢ ܕܟܐܒܝܢ ܠܗܘܢ ܛܚܠܝܗܘܢ *those who suffer from the spleen;* ܪܘܚܐ ܕܟܐܒܐ ܡܝܒܫܐ ܓܪܡܐ *a sorrowful spirit drieth up the bones;* ܓܒܪܐ ܟܐܝܒܝ ܢܦܫܐ *men sad of soul.* Ethpe. ܐܬܟܐܒ *to grow thin or lean.* Ethpa. ܐܬܟܐܒ *to be hurt.* Aph. ܐܟܐܒ and ܐܟܒ *to hurt, grieve, afflict, pain;* ܐܟܐܒܘ ܠܪܘܚܐ ܕܩܘܕܫܐ *they have grieved the Holy Spirit;* act. part. ܡܟܐܒ, ܡܟܐܒܢܐ, pass. part. ܡܟܐܒ, ܡܟܐܒܐ or ܡܟܒܐ, ܡܟܐܒܬܐ *sick, sorry, suffering;* ܡܟܐܒܝ ܟܐܒܐ *suffering from illness;* ܗܘ ܡܟܐܒܐ *that sick man;* ܡܟܐܒܝܢ ܪܝܫܐ *suffering from headache;* ܐܪܥܐ ܗܕܐ ܟܪܝܗܐ ܘܡܫܬܢܩܐ ܘܡܟܐܒܬܐ *this earth is sick and tormented and diseased.* Derivatives, ܟܐܒܐ, ܟܐܒܢܐ, ܟܐܒܐܝܬ, ܡܟܐܒܢܘܬܐ, ܡܟܐܒܢܐ, ܡܟܐܒܢܘܬܐ.

ܟܐܒ, ܟܐܒܐ pl. ܟܐܒܐ rt. ܟܐܒ. m. *pain, grief, sickness, disease;* ܟܐܒܐ ܕܡܫܢܩܢܐ *excruciating pain;* ܟܐܒܐ ܕܡܚܒܠܐ *the pain of travail;* ܡܐܣܐ ܟܠ ܟܐܒ ܘܟܘܪܗܢ *healing all manner of pain and sickness;* ܟܐܒ ܐܓܒܐ *pleurisy;* ܟܐܒ ܐܪܝܐ *elephantiasis;* ܟܐܒ ܡܥܝܐ *dysentery;* ܟܐܒܐ ܡܫܟܢܝܐ *fever;* ܟܐܒ ܚܨܐ *lumbago;* ܟܐܒܐ ܕܡܥܝܐ *dysentery;* ܟܐܒܐ ܕܒܘܥܐ *smallpox;* ܟܐܒ ܡܥܝܐ *colic;* ܟܐܒ ܪܝܫܐ *headache;* ܟܐܒ ܪܓܠܐ *gout.*

ܟܐܒܢܐ pl. ܟܐܒܢܐ rt. ܟܐܒ. m. *painful.*

ܟܐܒܢܝܐ pl. ܟܐܒܢܝܐ rt. ܟܐܒ. m. *painful; suffering, diseased;* ܢܘܣܝܐ ܟܐܒܢܝܐ *painful afflictions;* ܟܪܝܗܐ ܘܟܐܒܢܝܐ *the sick and suffering.*

ܟܐܘܠܐ and ܟܐܘܠܐ; see ܟܘܠܐ *the ark.*

ܟܐܘܣܝܘܬܐ rt. ܟܣܐ. f. *concealing, keeping back* property, *suppression* of facts in witness; *cheating.*

ܟܐܘܢ and ܟܝܘܢ n. pr. m. *Saturn, the planet Saturn;* chem. *lead.*

ܟܐܪܝܐ; see ܟܐܪ, participle.

ܟܐܡ for ܟܡ *soon after.*

ܟܐܝܡ a fuller writing of ܟܐܢ.

ܟܐܪܝ or ܟܪܝ rt. ܟܪܐ. *sultry, heavy;* ܐܐܪ ܟܐܪܝ ܠܟܠܝ *the air is suffocating me, weighs me down.*

ܟܐܡܘܢܐ = ܟܡܘܢܐ *a storm.*

ܟܐܡܟܠ particle of affirmation, doubt, emphasis, derision; *forsooth, indeed, that is to say, id est, scilicet, exempli gratia; forasmuch as, as it were, as if, in order, just as, just as if;* ܟܐܡܟܠ ܕ *so that;* ܐܦܢ—ܟܐܡܟܠ *although—yet;* ܟܐܡܟܠ ܕܣܘܣܝܐ ܢܐܟܘܠ ܒܣܪܐ *as if a horse could eat flesh!* ܟܐܡܟܠ ܕܠܐ ܚܙܐ ܠܕܗܘܝܐ *as if he had not seen what had happened.*

ܟܐܢ or ܟܐܢܝ Tatar. m. *khan, emperor, supreme ruler.*

ܟܐܢ, ܟܐܢܐ (or ܟܐܝܢ, ܟܐܝܢܐ), ܟܐܢܬܐ pl. m. ܟܐܢܐ, ܟܐܢܝܢ, f. ܟܐܢܢ, ܟܐܢܬܐ *upright, right, just;* ܟܐܝܢ ܗܘ ܕܝܢܝ *my judgement is just;* ܠܐ ܟܐܢ ܠܡܐܡܪ *it is not right to say;* ܠܡܕܢ ܟܐܢܬܐ ܕܝܢܗܘܢ *to judge what things are right;* ܠܐ ܟܐܢ ܠܟܘܢ ܡܠܬܐ *the saying is not approved by you, does not seem right to you;* ܥܡܪܐ ܥܡ ܟܐܢܐ *dwelling amongst the just* i. e. *the blessed dead;* ܟܐܢܐ are ranked next to ܓܡܝܪܐ *the perfect.* Derivatives, ܟܐܢܐܝܬ, ܟܐܢܘܬܐ.

ܟܐܢܐܝܬ from the above, adv. *rightly, justly, deservedly.*

ܟܐܢܘ, ܟܐܢܘܬܐ or ܟܝܢܘܬܐ from ܟܐܢ. f. *justice, rectitude, uprightness, righteousness,* ܟܐܢܘܬܐ ܕܡܕܒܪܢܘܬܐ *righteous dealing;* ܟܐܢܘܬܐ ܢܡܘܣܝܬܐ *legal righteousness;* ܕܝܢܐ ܕܟܐܢܘܬܐ *a just judge;* ܕܝܢܐ ܟܐܢܐ *just judgement;* ܒܟܐܢܘܬܐ *of right, with justice; justly, truly.*

ܟܐܢܪܐ; see ܟܢܪ *a cither.*

ܟܐܦ, ܟܐܦܐ pl. ܟܐܦܝܢ, ܟܐܦܐ f. *a stone, rock;* ellipt. for *a stone vessel, column, idol, a precious stone;* ܐܣܛܘܢܐ ܕܩܐܡ ܥܠ ܟܐܦܐ *a stylite is one who stands on a column;* ܟܐܦܐ ܚܪܫܬܐ *deaf stones* i. e. *idols;* ܗܘܐ ܟܐܦܐ *he was turned to stone;* ܐܬܪܓܡ ܒܟܐܦܐ *he was stoned;* ܡܙܝܥ ܟܠ ܟܐܦ *he leaves no stone unturned;* ܢܘܢܐ ܕܟܐܦܐ *a rock-fish;* ܟܐܦܐ ܕܒܪܕܐ *hailstones;* ܟܐܦ ܙܗܒܐ *chrysolite;* ܟܐܦ ܫܚܢܐ *grindstone, hard stone fit for grindstones;* ܟܐܦܐ ܕܫܢܝܬܐ *a whetstone;* ܟܐܦܐ ܕܪܚܝܐ *a millstone;* ܟܐܦܐ ܕܦܣܝܠܬܐ *a hewn* or *squared stone* opp. ܡܫܠܡܬܐ *a whole stone* i. e. *unhewn;* ܟܐܦܐ ܩܠܝܐ *a jeweller;* ܟܐܦܐ ܝܩܝܪܬܐ or ܡܝܩܪܬܐ *precious stones;* ܟܐܦܐ ܕܡܫܬܝܢܘܬܐ *stone in the bladder;* ܫܡܥܘܢ ܟܐܦܐ *Simon Peter.* Derivatives, ܟܐܦܢܐ, ܟܐܦܢܝܐ, ܟܐܦܢܘܬܐ, ܟܐܦܢܐ, ܟܐܦ.

ܟܐܦܘܢܐ pl. f. ܟܐܦܘܢܝܬܐ from ܟܐܦ. *stony, like stone.*

ܟܐܦܢܐ pl. f. ܟܐܦܢܝܬܐ from ܟܐܦ. adj. *stone, made of stone;* ܐܓܢܐ—ܠܘܚܐ—ܦܝܢܟܣ ܟܐܦܢܝܬܐ *stone water-pots, tablets, plaques.*

ܟܐܦܢܝܐ, ܢܝܬܐ from ܟܐܦ. *stony, rocky, hard as stone.*

ܟܐܦܢܝܘܬܐ from ܟܐܦ. f. *stony nature.*

ܟܐܦܬܢܐ, ܢܝܬܐ from ܟܐܦ. *stony.*

ܟܐܪ act. part. ܟܐܪ *to vituperate* (rare). Pael ܟܐܪ or ܟܪ rarely ܟܘܪ or ܟܪܝ, fut. ܢܟܐܪ both parts have the same irreg. form ܡܟܐܪ. *to reproach, put to the blush, put to confusion, bring reproach upon;* ܐܬܘܬܗ ܕܡܫܝܚܐ ܡܟܐܪܢ ܠܡܢ ܕܠܐ ܡܘܕܐ ܒܗ Christ's *miracles reproach him who does not confess Him;* ܟܕ ܡܟܣ ܘܡܟܐܪ ܠܒܝܫܘܬܗ *reproving and reproaching his wickedness.* Pass. part. ܡܟܐܪ for ܡܟܐܪ, ܡܟܐܪܬܐ as adj. *misshapen, ill-favoured, unsightly, marred, despised;* ܐܢܬܬܐ ܡܟܐܪܬܐ ܒܚܙܘܐ *an ill-favoured woman;* ܡܣܟܢܬܐ .... ܡܟܐܪܬܐ ܡܢ ܟܠ *poor and despised by all.* Ethpa. ܐܬܟܐܪ and ܐܬܟܐܪ *to be ashamed, put to the blush, reproached;* ܕܠܐ ܢܬܟܐܪ ܚܣ ܡܢ *lest we be put to shame;* ܗܘܘ ܡܬܟܐܪܝܢ ܡܢ ܟܠܢܫ *they were reproached by every one.* Aph. ܐܟܐܪ *to put to shame, sentence to ignominy;* ܐܟܐܪ ܠܒܨܘܝܐ God *has put vain inquirers,* i.e. *heretics, to shame.* Derivatives, ܡܟܐܪܘܬܐ, ܟܘܪܐ, ܟܘܪܐ or ܟܘܪܐ, ܟܐܪܐ.

ܟܐܪܐ m. *a vinegar-cruet.*

ܟܐܬܒ for (ܟܬܒ) ܟܬܒܐ *handwriting.*

ܟܐܪܬܐ or ܟܪܬܐ f. I. rt. ܟܐܪ. *reproof, rebuke, censure, blame;* ܟܐܪܬܐ ܢܩܝܫܬܐ *a feeble* or *ineffectual reproof;* ܥܠ ܟܐܪܬܐ ܕܬܐܪܬܐ *of the censure of conscience.* II. *an uncultivated crop, that which grows of itself;* see ܟܪܐ, ܟܪܬܐ.

ܟܐܪܬܐ f. *a clod, lump of earth;* see ܟܪܬܐ.

ܟܐܬܘܢ Turkish *a sultana, the chief wife of a ruler* = ܡܠܟܬܐ ܪܒܬܐ *a chief queen.*

ܟܒܕ denom. verb Pael conj. from ܟܒܕܐ. *to move to wrath.* Ethpa. ܐܬܟܒܕ *a) to be angry, indignant* ܥܠ *with* or *against. b) to have excited the wrath of others, be detested.*

ܟܒܕܐ or ܟܒܕܐ pl. ܟܒܕ̈ܐ f. *the liver, the seat of anger, gall, bile;* ܟܒܕܐ ܡܪܝܪܬܐ *bitter wrath;* ܡܚܝܗܝ ܡܢ ܟܒܕܐ *he smote him out of anger.* Derivatives, verb ܟܒܕ, ܟܒܕܢܐ, ܟܒܕܢܝܐ.

ܟܒܕܢܐ from ܟܒܕܐ. *irascible, irritable.*

ܟܒܕܢܝܐ, ܢܝܬܐ from ܟܒܕܐ *pertaining to the liver.*

ܟܒܘܢܐ pl. ܢ̈ܐ m. *a round cake* ܕܠܚܡܐ *of bread;* it is larger than a ܡܚܒܘܙܐ.

ܟܒܘܢܝܬܐ = ܟܒܢܝܬܐ *a cloak.*

ܟܒܘܫܐ or ܟܘܒܫܐ pl. ܫ̈ܐ rt. ܟܒܫ. m. *a) nightmare. b)* ܟܒܘܫܐ ܓܒܢ̈ܐ ܚܕ̈ܬܐ *new cheeses* i. e. *pressed together from fresh cheese.*

ܟܒܘܫܝܐ rt. ܟܒܫ. m. *the storming* of a town.

ܟܒܘܬܐ f. *dung.*

ܟܒܝܐ usually pl. ܟܒ̈ܝܐ m. *excrement, dung, filth;* ܟܒ̈ܝܐ ܕܬܘܪܐ *cow-dung.*

ܟܒܝܢܬܐ pl. ܟܒܝܢ̈ܬܐ rt. ܟܒܢ. *a) a hood. b) a girdle.*

ܟܒܝܫܘܬܐ rt. ܟܒܫ. f. *bondage, bringing into subjection; self-control* opp. ܡܫܬܪܚܘܬܐ *flurry.*

ܟܒܠ fut. ܢܟܒܘܠ, pass. part. ܟܒܝܠ. *to bind, fetter.* Pa. ܟܒܠ the same. Derivatives, the two following words—

ܟܒܠܐ pl. ܠ̈ܐ rt. ܟܒܠ. m. *a bond, fetter;* ܟܠ ܡܨܝܕ̈ܬܐ ܕܦܪܝܣܢ ܠܢ ܟܒ̈ܠܝܟ ܐܢܝܢ *all the nets laid for us are fetters for thyself.*

ܟܒܠܐ rt. ܟܒܠ. m. *binding, fettering.*

ܟܒܢ or ܟܒܢ fut. ܢܟܒܢ and ܢܟܒܘܢ, imper. ܟܒܘܢ, act. part. ܟܒܢ, pass. part. ܟܒܝܢ, ܢܐ, ܢܬܐ. *to gird on, put on* with ܣܩܐ *sackcloth;* ܐܪܓܘܢܐ ܐܟܒܢܬ ܐܢܘܢ faith *clothed them in purple;* ܟܒܢ ܣܩܐ—ܒܘܨܐ—ܦܪܙܘܡܐ *clothed in sackcloth, in fine linen, wearing a girdle;* metaph. ܟܒܢ ܡܠܐ ܥܩܬܐ ܘܡܟܣܝ ܚܫܐ *girt with* sad *words and covered with suffering;* ܚܫܐ ܟܒܢ ܡܢ ܓܘܗ *he bore suffering within, was suffering inwardly;* ܟܒܢ ܥܪܦܠܐ *thick darkness.* Ethpe. ܐܬܟܒܢ *to put on* esp. ܣܩܐ *sackcloth;* metaph. ܐܬܟܒܢܘ ܫܡܝܐ ܥܢܢܐ ܘܪܘܚܐ *the heavens became black with clouds and wind.* Aph. ܐܟܒܢ *to gird, clothe* trans. ܫܪܝܬ ܣܩܝ ܘܐܟܒܢܬܢܝ ܚܕܘܬܐ ܐܝܟ ܚܨܪܐ *thou hast loosed my sackcloth and clothed me with gladness as with a girdle.* Derivatives, ܟܒܝܢܬܐ, ܟܒܢܐ, ܟܒܢܬܐ.

ܟܒܢܐ or ܟܒܢܐ pl. ܢ̈ܐ rt. ܟܒܢ. m. *a) girding on, putting on* ܕܣܩܐ *of sackcloth. b) a girdle.*

ܟܒܢܬܐ or ܟܒܢܬܐ rt. ܟܒܢ. f. *a cloak, the habit of a monk.*

ܟܒܪ fut. ܢܟܒܪ, pass. part. ܟܒܝܪ, ܐ, ܬܐ. *to increase, abound* ܒܥܘܬܪܐ ܘܩܢܝܢܐ *in wealth and possessions;* ܒܪܝܟ ܗܘܐ ܥܠ ܒܢܝ̈ ܐܕܡ ܕܢܦܪܘܢ ܘܢܣܓܘܢ ܘܢܟܒܪܘܢ ܒܫܪܒܬܗܘܢ *a blessing was pronounced on the sons of Adam that they should increase and multiply in their generations.* Aph. ܐܟܒܪ *to increase, augment, multiply;* ܠܚܡܐ ܕܐܬܟܒܪ ܡܢ ܡܠܬܐ ܕܝܫܘܥ loaves *bred and multiplied at the word of Jesus.* Derivatives, ܟܒܪܐ, ܡܟܒܪܢܐ.

ܟܒܪ often written ܟܒܪ or ܐܟܒܪ; when with ܕ or ܘ prefixed takes ܐ or ܐ. *a)* particle of doubt or hope, *perhaps, perchance, doubtless, may be;* ܐܠܐ ܟܒܪ *unless perchance;* ܟܒܪ ܐܝܬܝܗܘܢ *they may be, they appear to be. b) formerly, of old.*

ܟܒܪܐ or ܟܒܪܐ I. rt. ܟܒܪ. m. *great increase, augmentation.* II. = ܟܘܪܐ m. *a bee-hive.*

ܟܒܪܝܬܐ or ܟܒܪܝܬܐ f. *sulphur, brimstone;* ܪܝܚܐ ܕܟܒܪܝܬܐ *the smell of sulphur;* ܚܠܐ ܕܟܒܪܝܬܐ *sulphuric acid; soap* or *lye* from the ashes of plants, ܟܒܪܝܬܐ ܕܩܨܪ̈ܐ *fuller's brimstone* or *soap.*

ܟܒܪܝܬܢܐ pl. ܢ̈ܐ adj. from the above. *sulphurous, of sulphur* or *brimstone;* ܫܪ̈ܝܢܐ ܟܒܪܝܬܢ̈ܐ *breastplates as of brimstone.*

ܟܒܪܝܬܢܝܐ, ܢܝܬܐ the same.

ܟܒܪܝܬܐ from ܟܒܪܝܬܐ pl. m. *sulphuric* or *fiery bolts.*

ܟܒܫ ܟܒܫ fut. ܢܶܟܒܽܘܫ, act. part. ܟܳܒܶܫ, ܟܳܒܫܳܐ, pass. part. ܟܒܺܝܫ, ܫܳܐ, ܫܳܬܳܐ. root-meaning *to tread down, tread under foot,* ܐܽܘܪܚܳܐ ܕܟܒܰܫܽܘܗ̇ *the path they have trodden,* hence, *a) to break up* the ground with spade or pickaxe, *to break in, subjugate, keep under;* ܐܰܝܢܳܐ ܕܠܳܐ ܟܳܒܶܫ ܟܝܳܢܶܗ *whoso does not conquer his natural disposition;* ܟܒܰܫ ܪܶܢܝܳܗ ܒܠܶܒܶܗ *he subdued his curiosity in his heart.* *b) to subdue, bring into subjection* nations, countries &c., *to seize, conquer, attack, fall upon;* ܟܒܰܫ ܐܶܢܽܘܢ ܠܡܰܕܰܐܬܳܐ *he compelled them to pay tribute, reduced them to the condition of tributaries;* ܡܛܰܝܒܺܝܢ ܕܢܶܟܒܫܽܘܢ ܐܶܢܽܘܢ *they make ready to fall upon them suddenly;* ܫܰܕܰܪ ܚܰܝܠܘܳܬܳܐ ܕܢܶܟܒܫܽܘܢ ܠܗܽܘܢ ܠܡܰܥܒܪܳܐ ܘܢܶܐܚܕܽܘܢ ܐܽܘܪܚܳܬܳܐ *he sent forces to seize* or *stop the mountain-passes and to hold the roads.* *c) to take money for one's own purposes, to filch, pilfer.* *d) to press hard upon, fall upon, crush to death, overwhelm* as a flood, ruined buildings &c., ܐܘܩܝܳܢܳܘܣ ܟܳܣܶܐ ܘܟܳܒܶܫ ܠܗ̇ ܠܰܐܪܥܳܐ *the ocean covers and presses hard upon the earth.* *e) to crush* in a wine-press, *to pickle* ܒܚܰܠܳܐ *in vinegar.* Part. adj. *a) downtrodden, oppressed, subdued, subject.* *b) broken in, tamed* as an animal, ܟܒܺܝܫ ܗܽܘ ܣܳܛܳܢܳܐ ܐܰܝܟ ܐܰܪܝܳܐ ܒܟܺܐܢܽܘܬܳܐ Satan as a lion *is held in, kept under, by righteousness.* *c) subtracted, pilfered,* ܠܡܰܢ ܕܟܒܰܫ ܗܳܢܳܐ ܟܽܠܶܗ ܟܶܣܦܳܐ *who has taken, pilfered all this money.* *d) pressed, preserved,* ܬܺܐܢܶܐ ܟܒܺܝܫܺܝܢ ܒܡܳܐܢܳܐ *figs pressed together in a pot.* *e)* astron. *set between, intercalated, an intercalary* day, month or year; ܫܢܬܳܐ ܟܒܝܫܬܳܐ *leap-year* as having an intercalated day, opp. ܫܢܬܳܐ ܦܫܝܛܬܳܐ *an usual* or *even year.* Ethpe. ܐܶܬ݂ܟ݁ܒܶܫ *a) to be broken up, ploughed.* *b) to be subdued, brought into subjection,* with ܠܡܰܕܰܐܬܳܐ *to be reduced to paying tribute, to be made tributary;* ܐܶܬ݂ܟ݁ܒܶܫܘ ܐܽܘܪܗܳܝܶܐ ܬܚܶܝܬ ܐܺܝܕܳܐ ܕܪ̈ܽܗܘܡܳܝܶܐ the Edessenes *were brought under the power of the Romans;* ܨܶܒܝܳܢܶܗ ܠܳܐ ܡܶܬ݂ܟ݁ܒܶܫ *his will is untamed.* *c) to be crushed, squeezed* in a press.

Pa. ܟܰܒܶܫ *to subdue, break in, bring into subjection, tame* animals, ܡܟܰܒܫܺܝܢ ܠܦܺܝܠܶܐ ܒܪܳܐ ܒܦܺܝܠܳܐ ܕܡܟܰܒܰܫ *they tame wild elephants by means of one already trained;* ܥܺܝܠܳܐ ܕܠܳܐ ܡܟܰܒܰܫ *an unbroken foal;* metaph. *to control, subdue* ܢܰܦܫܳܐ *the self,* ܦܰܓܪܳܐ *the body.* Ethpa. ܐܶܬ݂ܟ݁ܰܒܰܫ *to be thoroughly broken in, subjugated, brought under subjection;* ܐܶܬ݂ܟ݁ܰܒܰܫܘ ܚܽܘܫܳܒܰܘܗ̱ܝ *his thoughts were thoroughly under control.* Aph. ܐܰܟܒܶܫ *to make lie down* or *sit down.* Derivatives, ܟܒܫܐ, ܟܒܫܐ, ܟܒܝܫܘܬܐ, ܟܒܝܫܐ, ܟܒܘܫܐ, ܟܒܘܫܝܐ, ܡܟܒܫܢܐ, ܡܟܒܫܐ.

ܟܶܒܫܳܐ pl. ܫܶܐ m. *a) a wether sheep, old ram.* *b) sap of the mustard plant.* *c) the head* or *end of a bridge.* *d)* or ܟܒܫܐ *a spindle.*

ܟܒܫܐ rt. ܟܒܫ. m. *a) an assault, taking by storm.* *b)* see above *d.*

ܟܒܫܘܬܐ, ܟܒܫܘܬܐ some vegetable.

ܟܰܕ *a) when, after; although, even if; because; while;* ܟܰܕ ܗܽܘ *when indeed, although, notwithstanding that;* ܟܰܕ—ܠܳܐ *although—not;* ܡܶܢ ܟܰܕ ܡܶܢ ܟܰܕ *from the time that ...;* ܡܶܢ ܟܰܕ ܫܰܪܺܝ ܕܢܰܟܪܶܙ *from the time that he began to preach;* ܡܶܢ ܟܰܕ ܥܶܠܰܬ݂ *from the moment she came in.* ܟܰܕ before the finite verb, and esp. before a participle or adjective, denotes present action or state ܟܰܕ ܐܶܬ݂ܪܰܥܺܝ *while he was thinking;* ܟܰܕ ܡܨܰܠܶܐ *while praying, in the act of prayer;* ܟܰܕ ܐܰܣܺܝܪ *bound, he being bound;* ܟܰܕ ܟܬ݂ܺܝܒ *written, being written;* ܟܰܕ ܝܳܬ݂ܶܒ *sitting;* ܟܰܕ ܚܰܝ *alive;* ܟܰܕ ܠܳܐ ܨܳܒܶܐ *being unwilling, unwillingly;* ܟܰܕ ܝܳܕܰܥ ܘܟܰܕ ܠܳܐ ܝܳܕܰܥ *wittingly and unwittingly.* *b)* ܟܰܕ standing between two pronouns signifies identity, ܗܽܘ ܟܰܕ ܗܽܘ m. ܗܺܝ ܟܰܕ ܗܺܝ f. *the same,* ܒܗ̇ ܟܰܕ ܒܗ̇ ܫܰܢ݈ܬܳܐ *in the same year;* ܗܳܠܶܝܢ ܟܰܕ ܗܳܠܶܝܢ ܡ̈ܶܠܶܐ *the very same words;* ܕܚܰܕ ܟܰܕ ܚܰܕ ܦܰܓܪܳܐ *of the same body;* ܥܰܠ ܗܳܝ ܟܰܕ ܗܳܝ ܡܰܠܟܽܘܬܳܐ *touching this same kingdom.* Cf. ܗܽܘ and its derivative ܗܽܘܝܽܘܬܳܐ *identity.* For ܟܰܕܗܽܘ = ܟܰܕ ܗܽܘ see below.

ܟܕܒ ܟܕܒ act. part. ܟܳܕܶܒ *to be false* in word or deed. Usually Pael ܟܰܕܶܒ *a) to lie, speak falsely, be false, break faith, fail, deny* with ܒ; with ܐܰܠܳܗܳܐ or ܡܳܪܝܳܐ ܒܐܰܠܳܗܳܐ *to be unfaithful to God;* ܟܰܕܒܶܬ݂ ܒܫܪܳܪܶܗ ܕܐܰܠܳܗܳܐ *I have been false to* God's *truth;* ܟܰܕܶܒ ܒܡܳܪܝܳܐ *he was unfaithful to the Lord;* ܪ̈ܳܚܡܶܐ ܡܟܰܕܒܺܝܢ *friends fail, prove false;* ܡܶܢܗܶܝܢ ܫܰܪܺܝܪ̈ܳܢ ܘܡܶܢܗܶܝܢ ܡܟܰܕܒ̈ܳܢ *these opinions are partly true, partly false;* ܡܶܫܚܳܐ ܢܟܰܕܶܒ ܠܗܽܘܢ *oil shall fail them.* *b) to accuse of falsehood, convict of lying;* ܡܟܕܒܝܢ ܠܟܐܢܐ *they accuse true men of falsehood.* Ethpa. ܐܬܟܕܒ *a) to be deceived, violated* as a vow or promise; ܡܛܠ ܕܟܕܒܢ ܐܬܟܕܒܘ *because we were false others were false to us;* ܡܘܡܬܐ ܐܬܟܕܒܬ ܠܗ the oath *was violated by him* i.e. *he violated, was false to, his monastic profession. b) to be proved false, convicted of falsehood* or *perjury.* Aphel *to make to lie* or *be false;* ܡܠܦܢܘܬܗܘܢ ܫܢܝܐ ܗܝ. ܘܡܟܕܒܐ ܠܟܪܘܙܘܗܝ *their doctrine is mad and makes its preachers false.* Derivatives, ܟܕܒܐ, ܟܕܒܐܝܬ, ܟܕܒܘܬܐ, ܡܟܕܒܢܘܬܐ, ܡܬܟܕܒܢܐ.

ܟܕܒ, ܟܕܒܐ, ܟܕܒܬܐ rt. ܟܕܒ. *a) lying, false* as ܡܘܡܬܐ *an oath,* ܡܠܬܐ *a speech,* ܪܘܚܐ *a spirit,* ܫܡܥܐ *a report;* ܡܫܝܚܐ ܟܕܒܐ *false Christs, pseudo-Messiahs;* ܐܦܢ ܟܕܒ ܗܘ *even if it be false. b) a liar.*

ܟܕܒܐܝܬ rt. ܟܕܒ. adv. *falsely, mendaciously.*

ܟܕܒܘܬܐ rt. ܟܕܒ. f. *a falsehood, lie, breach of faith, treachery;* ܢܒܝܐ ܕܟܕܒܘܬܐ *lying prophets.*

ܟܕܘ contraction of ܟܕ ܗܘ *it suffices, is enough, sufficient, more than enough;* ܟܕܘ ܠܢ *it suffices us, is all we want;* ܐܠܐ ܐܢܫ ܕܠܐ ܡܣܬܒܥ. ܘܐܪܒܥܐ ܠܐ ܐܡܪܐ ܟܕܘ *there are three which are not satisfied, and a fourth says not, enough!* ܟܕܘ ܕܗܠܝܢ *enough of this;* ܟܕܘ ܠܟ ܫܒܘܩ *have enough, leave me;* ܠܐ ܟܕܘ ܠܟ—ܠܟܘܢ *are you not satisfied? is it not enough for you?* said in remonstrance. Sometimes added for emphasis, cf. ܗܘ; ܟܕܘ ܐܝܟ ܗܘ ܕܐܝܬ ܠܗ ܗܘܢܐ ܢܗܝܪܐ *he indeed being of enlightened understanding, possessing great perspicacity.* ܘܟܕܘ sometimes closes a paragraph or narration, *thus far, thus much and no more, enough;* ܠܐ ܢܬܩܪܐ—ܐܠܐ ܫܡܐ ܕܦܛܪܝܪܟܐ ܘܟܕܘ *the name of the patriarch only shall be recited;* ܒܠܚܘܕܘܗܝ ܘܟܕܘ *only and solely;* ܡܢ ܟܕܘ or ܡܢܟܕܘ *at that very time, even now, already, for some time;* ܐܫܟܚܘܗܝ ܕܡܢ ܟܕܘ ܡܝܬ ܠܗ *they found that he was even now dead;* ܡܢܟܕܘ ܢܦܩ ܗܘܐ ܦܣܐ ܡܢ ܐܠܗܐ *the lot had already gone forth from God.*

ܟܕܢܘܬܐ rt. ܟܕܢ. f. *yoking, coupling, joining,* ܟܕܢܘܬܐ ܕܦܕܢܐ *yoking to the plough;* ܟܕܢܘܬܐ ܕܚܝܐ ܥܡ ܒܣܪܐ ܚܫܘܫܐ *the coupling of life with passible flesh.*

ܟܕܝܪܘܬܐ rt. ܟܕܪ. f. *feebleness, weariness, fatigue.*

ܟܕܢ fut. ܢܟܕܘܢ, act. part. ܟܕܢ, ܟܕܢܐ, pass. part. ܟܕܝܢ, ܟܕܝܢܐ, ܟܕܝܢܬܐ. *to yoke, couple, join, bind* ܟܕܢ ܬܘܪܐ ܒܢܝܪܐ or ܬܘܪܐ ܠܢܝܪܐ *to the yoke,* ܟܕܢ ܬܘܪܐ *he yoked the oxen;* ܐܡܪ ܟܕܘܢ. ܘܟܕܢܘ ܬܘܪܐ ܠܡܪܟܒܬܗ *he said, harness, and they yoked* oxen *to his chariot;* metaph. *to bring into bondage, subjugate, restrain;* ܟܕܢܘ ܟܬܦܗܘܢ ܠܦܕܢܐ *they put their shoulder to the plough;* with ܠܡܕܐܬܐ *to compel to pay tribute;* ܟܕܢܬ ܠܡܠܝ *I have restrained my words;* ܟܕܢܘ ܓܘܕܐ *they formed a company walking by couples;* ܟܕܢܘ ܠܗܕܝܘܛܐ ܠܟܗܢܘܬܐ *they yoked the simple to the priesthood* i.e. *made priests of the unlearned;* with ܠܢܝܪܐ ܕܥܒܕܘܬܐ—ܕܙܩܝܦܐ *to bring under the yoke of bondage, of the cross.* Pass. part. ܟܕܝܢܐ ܚܕ ܥܡ ܚܕ *yoked in couples;* ܚܝܘܬܐ ܟܕܝܢܬܐ *draught animals;* metaph. ܟܕܝܢ ܠܥܒܕܘܬܐ *enslaved;* ܟܕܝܢ ܠܪܚܡܬ ܟܣܦܐ *enslaved by greed;* ܟܕܝܢܝܢ ܬܚܝܬ ܢܡܘܣܐ *to be subject to the law, under the law;* with ܥܡ *joined with, united* or *coupled to;* ܓܫܪܐ ܕܐܠܦܐ ܟܕܝܢܢ ܗܘܐ ܥܠ ܢܗܪܐ *a bridge* of boats *lashed together on the river;* ܟܘܪܣܝܐ ܕܟܕܝܢܢ ܒܗ ܓܝܓܠܐ ܕܢܘܪܐ a throne *to which fiery wheels are yoked.* Ethpe. ܐܬܟܕܢ *a) to be yoked, bound, harnessed, subjugated;* metaph. with or without ܢܝܪܐ; with ܠܫܘܥܒܕܐ *to be brought into subjection;* with ܠܡܫܥܒܕܘܬܐ *to be reduced to slavery. b) to be coupled, yoked, joined* ܒܙܘܘܓܐ or ܒܫܘܬܦܘܬܐ *in marriage.* Derivatives, ܟܕܢܐ, ܟܕܢܘܬܐ, ܟܕܢܐ or ܟܘܕܢܐ, ܡܬܟܕܢܢܐ.

ܟܕܢܐ rt. ܟܕܢ. m. *yoking, bringing under the yoke, subjection, subjugation.*

ܟܕܢܐ m. ܟܕܢܬܐ f. *a small narrow-necked jug.*

ܟܕܪ fut. ܢܟܕܘܪ, act. part. ܟܕܪ, verbal adj. ܟܕܝܪ, ܐ, ܬܐ. *to become weak, sickly* or *weary,* ܟܕܪ ܡܢ ܪܗܛܐ *he was wearied with running;* ܟܕܝܪܐ *the infirm.* Pa. ܟܕܪ *to enfeeble,* ܟܕܪܬ ܟܠܗܘܢ ܪܓܫܝ *thou hast enfeebled all my senses.* Derivatives, ܟܕܝܪܘܬܐ, ܟܕܪܘܬܐ.

ܟܕܪܘܬܐ rt. ܟܕܪ. f. *violence, wickedness.*

ܟܗܐ Aphel ܐܟܗܐ *to breathe out* wind or fire, *to sigh.*

ܟܗܝܢ, ܟܗܝܢܐ, ܟܗܝܢܬܐ *having abundance, opulent, rich, prosperous, flourishing;* ܐܝܠܢܐ

ܐܢܬܬܐ ܕܡܢ ܫܪܒܬܐ ܟܬܝܪܬܐ *a woman of a wealthy family;* ܫܘܪܐ ܕܟܬܝܪ ܚܝܠܐ *a wall of great strength;* ܫܠܡܐ ܟܬܝܪܐ *entire peace;* ܫܢܝܐ ܟܬܝܪܬܐ *prosperous, abundant* or *fruitful years;* with ܒ *abounding in, full of,* ܡܕܝܢܬܐ ܟܬܝܪܬܐ ܒܩܘܪܝܐ a city *rich in dependent towns;* ܟܬܝܪܐ ܗܘܬ ܡܕܝܢܬܐ ܒܒܝܫܬܐ ܘܒܪܫܝܥܘܬܐ the city *was given up to evil and impiety;* ܬܘܕܝܬܐ ܕܡܫܚܠܦܢ ܕܟܬܝܪܢ ܗܫܐ ܒܥܠܡܐ the various *confessions which at the present time abound in the world;* ܦܪܣ ܕܟܬܝܪܐ ܒܡܫܠܡܢܘܬܐ *Persia which is full of, given up to, Mohammedanism.*

ܟܘܬܪܢܘܬܐ pl. ܬܐ from the above. f. *abundance, opulence, affluence, prosperity, well-being;* ܟܘܬܪܢܘܬܐ ܥܠܡܢܝܬܐ *worldly prosperity;* ܟܘܬܪܢܐ ܕܕܝܪܐ *an abundance of monasteries.*

ܟܗܢ, ܟܗܢܐ pl. ܢܐ, ܢܝܢ m. *a priest;* ܪܒ ܟܗܢܐ or ܪܝܫ ܟܗܢܐ *a high-priest;* ܣܦܪ ܟܗܢܐ *Leviticus;* ܦܘܫܩܐ ܕܟܗܢܐ *commentary on Leviticus.* Derivatives, verb ܟܗܢ, ܟܗܢܐܝܬ, ܟܗܢܘܬܐ, ܟܗܢܝܐ, ܟܘܗܢܐ, ܟܘܗܢܝܐ, ܡܟܗܢܘܬܐ, ܡܬܟܗܢܢܘܬܐ.

ܟܗܢ denom. verb Pael conj. from ܟܗܢ *a) to be* or *serve as a priest, to fulfil the priestly office, minister, offer sacrifice as a priest,* ܐܝܟ ܢܡܘܣܐ ܡܟܗܢܝܢ ܗܘܘ *they fulfilled the priestly office according to the law;* ܗܢܘܢ ܕܡܟܗܢܝܢ ܒܒܝܬܐ ܕܡܪܝܐ *those who minister as priests in the house of the Lord;* ܗܕܝܘܛܐ ܕܟܗܢܘ ܠܐ ܟܬܪܘ *the ignorant when made priests did not abide in their ministry. b) to offer up* sacrifice, with ܕܒܚܬܐ *to celebrate Holy Communion;* ܕܒܚܐ ܪܘܚܢܝܐ *to offer up spiritual sacrifices. c) to serve, minister* said of a deacon, a preacher &c. ܗܢܘܢ ܕܡܟܗܢܝܢ ܗܘܘ ܠܟܪܘܙܘܬܐ ܕܐܘܢܓܠܝܘܢ *those who waited on the preaching of the Gospel. d) to appoint, set up, make* a priest. *e)* connected with ܟܬܝܪܐ *to abound in wealth; enrich* or *aid with wealth;* ܟܗܢ ܥܕܬܐ ܚܪܝܒܬܐ *he gave abundantly to ruined churches.* Ethpa. ܐܬܟܗܢ *a) to be offered in sacrifice, immolated, consecrated;* ܐܬܟܗܢ ܡܫܝܚܐ ܒܒܣܪ ܥܠ ܨܠܝܒܐ Christ *was offered up in the flesh upon the tree;* ܠܚܡܐ ܕܡܬܟܗܢ *consecrated* Eucharistic *bread. b) to be consecrated priest. c) to be administered, performed. d) to grow rich, abound, flourish;* ܐܬܟܗܢ ܟܠܗ ܗܘ ܐܬܪܐ ܒܣܘܪܝܝܐ *all that region abounded in Syrians;* ܐܬܟܗܢܬ ܒܕܚܠܬ ܐܠܗܐ *she was conspicuous for her piety.* Aph. ܐܟܗܢ *to offer up* ܕܒܚܬܐ *a sacrifice; to consecrate* the Eucharist.

ܟܗܢܐܝܬ rt. ܟܗܢ. *as a priest, in a priestly manner, sacerdotally.*

ܟܗܢܘܬܐ rt. ܟܗܢ. f. *a) priesthood, office* or *dignity* of a priest, ܛܟܣܐ ܕܟܗܢܘܬܐ *the priestly order;* ܪܒ ܟܗܢܘܬܐ *the high-priesthood;* ܝܗܒ—ܩܒܠ ܐܝܕܐ ܕܟܗܢܘܬܐ *he gave, he received, ordination to the priesthood;* ܡܕܝܢܬ ܟܗܢܘܬܐ = ܡܕܝܢܬܐ ܟܗܢܝܬܐ *Hierapolis. b)* collect. *the priests, the priesthood, clergy;* as a title, ܟܗܢܘܬܟ *O Priest.*

ܟܗܢܝܐ, ܢܝܬܐ rt. ܟܗܢ. *belonging to the priest's office, devoted to sacred purposes, sacred, holy, consecrated;* ܨܠܘܬܐ ܟܗܢܝܬܐ *prayers which might be recited by the priest only;* ܪܝܫ ܟܗܢܝܐ *high-priestly, pontifical;* ܡܐܢܐ ܟܗܢܝܐ *the sacred vessels;* ܟܬܒܐ ܟܗܢܝܐ *the sacred scriptures;* ܪܡܫܐ ܟܗܢܝܐ *the sacred evening* i.e. that on which our Lord instituted the Holy Communion; ܫܒܘܥܐ ܟܗܢܝܐ ܕܚܫܐ *the Holy week of the Passion.*

ܟܘ abbrev.; see ܟܘܪܣܝܐ.

ܟܘܐ, ܟܘܬܐ pl. ܟܘܝܢ, ܟܘܐ f. *an opening, aperture, hole; a) a window, lattice;* ܥܠܝܬܐ ܕܟܘܝܗ ܣܓܝܐܢ *an upper room with many windows;* ܟܘܝ ܡܫܟܢܐ *openings in the sides of tents;* ܟܘܝ ܫܡܝܐ *the windows* or *sluices of heaven;* ܟܘܝ ܗܘܢܐ *the windows of the mind. b) a pigeon-hole;* ܦܪܚܝܢ ܐܝܟ ܝܘܢܐ ܠܟܘܝܗܘܢ *they fly as doves to their windows;* i.e. *openings* in round towers. *c) a recess, hole;* ܣܡ ܟܬܒܘܗܝ ܒܟܘܬܐ *he placed* his books *in a recess;* ܟܘܬܐ ܕܡܐܢܐ *the recess* or *cupboard where the holy vessels were placed.*

ܟܘܐ pass. part. ܟܘܐ. *to sear, cauterize;* ܟܘܝܢ ܒܬܐܪܬܗܘܢ *having seared consciences.* Pa. ܟܘܝ *to cauterize, brand, scorch;* ܡܟܘܐ ܐܣܝܐ ܠܟܘܪܗܝܗܘܢ *the physician cauterizes their hurts.* Ethpa. ܐܬܟܘܝ *to be scorched, seared, cauterized.* Derivatives, ܟܘܝܐ, ܟܘܝܬܐ.

ܟܘܐܓܐ also spelt ܟܘܐܓܐ and ܟܘܓܐ. Pers. *Khowaja, master, lord, sir.*

ܟܘܒܪܐ, ܟܘܒܪܐ or ܟܘܒܪܐ rt. ܟܒܪ. m. *shame, reproach, disgrace, dishonour, ignominy.*

ܟܐܒ, ܟܒ fut. ܢܟܘܒ, act. part. ܟܐܒ, ܟܐܒܐ, same as ܟܐܒ. *to feel pain* or *sorrow;* ܢܟܘܒ ܥܡܟ ܠܒܗ *he will sorrow with thee;* ܟܐܒܝܢ ܗܘܘ ܥܝܢܘܗܝ ܡܢ ܣܘܓܐܐ ܕܒܟܝܐ *his eyes smarted, ached, from so much weeping.*

ܟܘܒܐ, ܟܘܒ pl. ܟܘܒܐ m. *a thorn;* ܟܘܒܐ ܘܐܛܕܐ *thorns and briars;* ܐܪܥܐ ܡܦܩܐ ܟܘܒܐ *land bringing forth thorns;* ܟܘܒܐ ܕܥܡܪܐ *cotton wool, cotton;* proverb ܟܘܒܐ ܒܫܘܚܢܝܢ ܡܚܝܬܘܢ *ye beat our sores with thorns, touch a raw.* Derivatives, ܟܘܒܝܐ, ܟܘܒܢܐ, ܟܘܒܢܝܘܬܐ.

ܟܘܒܐ *a cup, goblet, vessel;* ܟܘܒܐ ܕܣܐܡܐ *a silver goblet.*

ܟܘܒܝܐ pl. ܐ̈ from ܟܘܒܐ. m. *a thorn.*

ܟܘܒܢܝܐ, ܟܘܒܢܝܐ pl. m. ܐ̈ f. ܬܐ̈ from ܟܘܒܐ. *of thorns, thorny, bristly, prickly;* ܟܘܒܢܝܢ ܣܘܟܝܗܘܢ *their branches are thorny;* ܩܘܦܕܐ ܚܝܘܬܐ ܟܘܒܢܝܬܐ ܡܫܟܐ *the hedgehog is an animal with a prickly skin;* metaph. *bristling with difficulties.*

ܟܘܒܢܝܘܬܐ from ܟܘܒܐ. f. *thorniness; prickly nature of* a thorn or thistle.

ܟܘܒܫ, ܟܘܒܫܐ rt. ܟܒܫ. m. *a*) *breaking up* or *ploughing* fallow land. *b*) *subjection, subjugation;* ܕܦܓܪܐ *of the body;* ܟܘܒܫ ܢܦܫܐ *self-control.*

ܟܘܒܫܐ pl. ܐ̈ rt. ܟܒܫ. m. *a footstool;* pl. *stone sedilia.*

ܟܘܒܪܐ m. *haemorrhage* after child-birth; *the caul.*

ܟܘܕܪܐ *scur butter-milk.*

ܟܘܕܢܐ rarely ܟܘܕܢܐ m. ܟܘܕܢܬܐ f. pl. m. and f. ܟܘܕܢܘܬܐ, ܟܘܕܢܘܬܐ rt. ܟܕܢ. *a mule;* ܫܩܠܘ ܗܘܘ ܡܝܐ ܥܠ ܟܘܕܢܐ ܠܚܨܝܗܘܢ *they brought water on the backs of mules;* ܪܟܝܒ ܟܘܕܢܐ *riding a mule;* metaph. f. *a mole, mound;* ܟܘܕܢܘܬܐ ܬܪܬܝܢ ܐܩܝܡ ܩܕܡ ܡܕܝܢܬܐ *he erected two moles over against the city.*

ܟܘܕܪܐ pl. ܐ̈ m. *a vulture,* perh. *the Egyptian vulture,* in size it is between a ܢܫܪܐ and ܐܝܬܐ; ܦܪܘܓܐ ܕܟܘܕܪܐ *young vultures.*

ܟܘܕܪܬܐ, cf. ܟܘܕܪܐ. f. *a woman lately delivered; a midwife.*

ܟܘܗܢܘܬܐ or misspelt ܟܘܗܢܘܬܐ pl. ܐ̈ rt. ܟܗܢ. m. *the priesthood, the sacred ministry; the liturgy, celebration, consecration;* ܟܠܗܘܢ ܟܘܗܢܘܬܐ *all the priestly offices;* ܟܘܗܢܘܬܐ ܕܐܪ̈ܙܐ *the administration of the mysteries;* ܣܒܪܬܐ ܕܟܘܗܢܘܬܐ *the Gospel of the liturgy;* ܟܘܗܢܘܬܐ ܕܦܨܚܐ *the celebration of Holy Communion on Maundy Thursday; consecration* of a bishop, hence ܒܪ ܟܘܗܢܘܬܐ *a bishop;* ܦܛܪܝܪܟܐ ܟܠܗܘܢ ܟܘܗܢܘܬܐ *patriarchs consecrated with due form and ceremony.*

ܟܘܘܢܐ or ܟܘܘܢܐ pl. ܐ̈ rt. ܟܘܢ II. *a warning, admonition, correction.*

ܟܘܙܪܐ; see ܟܘܙܪܐ *shame* &c.

ܟܙ fut. ܢܟܘܙ, act. part. ܟܐܙ, ܟܐܙܐ *to shrink* with fear, shame or modesty; *a*) *to quail, be timid, afraid* with ܡܢ; ܡܢ ܡܘܬܐ—ܡܢ ܫܢܕܐ—ܡܢ ܪܘܫܐ—ܡܢ ܫܓܘܫܝܐ *to shrink from death, torments, from finding fault, at the uproar. b*) *to shrink* from admitting or believing; *to abhor* a heresy. *c*) *to be shamefaced, bashful, ashamed,* ܟܙ ܡܢܗܘܢ *he was ashamed of them;* ܡܢ ܕܚܠܬܗ ܩܡ ܗܘܐ ܟܙ ܡܢ ܫܡܗ *he stood in awe of his name.* Derivative, ܟܘܙܐ.

ܟܘܙܐ rt. ܟܘܙ. m. *bashfulness, shrinking modesty.*

ܟܘܙ, ܟܘܙܐ m. *a narrow-necked vessel; a liquid measure equalling the fourth part of a bath.*

ܟܘܙܙܐ Ar. m. *shivering.*

ܟܘܚܕܐ, ܟܘܚܕ rt. ܟܚܕ. m. *reverence, modesty, shame;* ܕܠܐ ܟܘܚܕ *shameless.*

ܟܘܚܕܢܐ, ܟܘܚܕܢܐ rt. ܟܚܕ. *modest, shamefaced.*

ܟܘܚܠܐ Ar. m. *kohl, stibium* a preparation of antimony used to darken the eyes.

ܟܘܚܠܐ rt. ܟܚܠ. m. *the use of kohl, application of kohl to the eyes.*

ܟܘܝܐ pl. ܐ̈ rt. ܟܘܐ. m. *branding; branding-irons;* metaph. *burning reproaches.*

ܟܘܝܘܬܐ rt. ܟܘܐ. f. *penitence.*

ܟܘܝܫܐ *having the lower eyelid weak* or *drooping.*

ܟܘܝܫܘܬܐ or ܟܘܝܫܘܬܐ f. *weakness of the lower eyelid.*

ܟܘܠܐ, ܟܘܠܐ, ܟܘܠܐ or ܟܘܠܐ pl. ܐ̈ f. *an ark* esp. *Noah's ark;* ܢܦܩܘ ܡܢ ܟܘܠܐ *they came out of the ark;* ܟܘܠܐ ܕܦܘܪܩܢܐ *the ark of safety.*

ܟܘܢܐ, ܟܘܢܐ rt. ܟܘܢ I. m. *constitution, disposition; occurrence, chance, luck;* ܟܘܢܝܐ

fortuitous, by chance; ܟܘܢܫܐ ܠܡܩܕܡܘ *a wonderful piece of luck.*

ܟܘܟܐ or ܟܘܟܐ name of the ancient city or the site later occupied by Seleucia and still in use ecclesiastically as the name of the Patriarchal See, also for the suburbs or district of Seleucia; ܟܘܪܣܝܐ ܕܟܘܟܐ *the See of Cucha;* ܥܕܬܐ ܕܟܘܟܐ ܐܡܐ ܕܣܠܝܩ ܘܩܛܝܣܦܘܢ *the Church of Cucha, mother of Seleucia and Ctesiphon.*

ܟܘܟܒܐ, ܟܘܟܒܐ, ܟܘܟܒܬܐ pl. m. ܟܘܟܒܝܢ, ܟܘܟܒܐ, ܟܘܟܒ pl. f. ܟܘܟܒܬܐ usually m., f. *the planet Venus; a star, planet;* ܟܘܟܒ ܨܦܪܐ—ܟܘܟܒܐ ܕܨܦܪܐ or ܕܢܓܗܐ *the morning star;* ܟܘܟܒܐ ܕܪܘܡܚܐ ܕܪܡܚܐ *a lance-like star* i.e. *a comet;* ܟܘܟܒܐ ܛܥܝܐ *wandering stars, planets;* ܟܘܟܒܐ ܚܫܘܟܐ *nebula;* ܟܘܟܒ ܕܘܢܒܐ *a comet;* ܡܚܫܒ ܟܘܟܒܐ *an astrologer;* metaph. ܟܘܟܒܐ ܕܕܪܗ *the star* or *shining light of his age; an asterisk* usually ܟܘܟܒܘܢܐ; ܟܘܟܒ ܐܪܟܐ *talc.*

ܟܘܟܒ denom. verb Palpel conj. from ܟܘܟܒܐ. *a) to stud* or *cover with stars;* ܡܟܘܟܒܬܐ ܚܘܕܪܐ *a starry circle. b) to mark with an asterisk.* Ethpalpal ܐܬܟܘܟܒ *to become a star;* ܐܘܪܝܘܢ ܕܐܬܟܘܟܒ *Orion who became a star.*

ܟܘܟܒܘܢܐ pl. ܢ̈ܐ dim. of ܟܘܟܒܐ m. *a little star, asterisk.*

ܟܘܟܒܢ or ܟܘܟܒܢ m. *some unclean bird,* perh. *an owl.*

ܟܘܟܒܝܠ contr. for ܟܘܟܒ ܒܝܠ *the planet Jupiter.*

ܟܘܟܒܢܝܐ pl. ܢ̈ܐ from ܟܘܟܒܐ. adj. m. *stellar, of stars.*

ܟܘܟܝܬܐ pl. ܟܘܟܝ̈ܬܐ f. *a sudden storm, tempest, whirlwind, snowstorm, sandstorm.*

ܟܘܟܠܬܐ same as ܟܘܟܠܬܐ f. *a barley cake.*

ܟܘܠ, ܟܘܠ not used in Peal. Aph. ܐܟܝܠ *to mete, measure* esp. corn. Ettaph. ܐܬܬܟܝܠ *to be measured* used of superficies, quantity, extent or time; ܙܒܢܐ ܕܡܬܬܟܝܠ ܒܪܗܛܐ ܕܫܡܫܐ ܘܣܗܪܐ time *which is measured by the course of the sun and moon;* ܚܢܢܐ ܕܠܐ ܡܬܬܟܝܠ *unmeasured mercy.* Derivatives, ܟܝܠܐ, ܟܝܠܬܐ, ܡܟܝܠܐ, ܡܟܝܠܬܐ, ܡܟܘܠܬܐ.

ܟܘܠ, ܟܘܠܐ a fuller form of ܟܠ *all, the whole.*

ܟܘܠܐ; see ܟܘܠܐ *the ark.*

ܟܘܠܒܐ or ܟܘܠܒܐ pl. ܢ̈ܐ m. *an axe, hatchet, pickaxe.*

ܟܘܠܒܘܢ m. *a worn path, a rut.*

ܟܘܠܒܬܐ pl. ܢ̈ܐ m. *a basket* for carrying grapes to the winepress.

ܟܘܠܝ χολή, *the bile, gall* = Syr. ܡܪܪܬܐ.

ܟܘܠܝܐ, ܟܘܠܝܬܐ pl. ܟܘܠܝܢ, ܟܘܠܝܬܐ, ܟܘܠܝܬܐ f. *the kidneys* or *reins;* ܚܨܐ ܕܟܘܠܝܬܐ *the flanks.*

ܟܘܠܢܝܘܬܐ from ܟܠ. f. *entirety, completeness, all;* ܟܘܠܢܝܘܬܐ ܘܡܢܘܬܐ *the whole and the parts;* ܥܡ ܟܘܠܢܝܘܬܐ ܕܒܝܬܗ *with his entire household;* ܒܟܘܠܢܝܘܬܗ *in its entirety, altogether.*

ܟܘܠܠܐ, ܟܘܠܠ rt. ܟܠ. m. *crowning, perfecting, approving, adorning. a)* the ceremony of *setting crowns* on the bride and bridegroom, *a wedding. b) the crowning* of a conqueror esp. of a martyr, *the death* or *commemoration* of a martyr or other saint; ܟܘܠܠܐ ܕܣܗܕܘܬܐ *crowning* or *martyrdom by the sword;* ܥܐܕܐ ܕܟܘܠܠܗ *the festival of his receiving the crown;* ܟܘܠܠܐ ܕܫܠܝܚܐ—ܕܡܪܝܡ *the festival of the Apostles, the translation of the B.V. Mary.*

ܟܘܠܢܐܝܬ or ܟܠܗ from ܟܠ. adv. *wholly, entirely, altogether; totally; on the whole.*

ܟܘܠܢܝܐ, ܟܘܠܢܝܐ, ܟܘܠܢܝܬܐ or ܟܠܝ from ܟܠ. adj. *entire, total; general, universal* opp. ܡܢܝܐܝܬ *particular;* ܢܣܝܘܢܐ ܟܘܠܢܝܐ *common* or *universal temptations;* ܝܡܐ ܟܘܠܢܝܐ *the ocean;* eccles. *catholic;* ܦܛܪܝܪܟܐ ܐܘ ܟܘܠܢܝܐ *the Patriarch or Catholicos.*

ܟܘܠܢܝܘܬܐ or ܟܠܢܝܘܬܐ from ܟܠ. f. *the whole, all, totality; entirety, completeness;* ܝܡܐ ܟܘܠܢܝܘܬܗܘܢ ܕܡܝܐ *the sea is the gathering together of all waters;* ܟܘܠܢܝܘܬܐ ܕܫܘܠܛܢܐ *absolute power.*

ܟܘܠܦܐ pl. of ܟܠܝܦܐ *khalif.*

ܟܘܠܫܐ from ܟܠܫܐ. *calcination;* ܟܘܠܫܗ ܕܥܦܪܐ *calcination of earths.*

ܟܡܐ, ܟܡ fut. ܢܟܡܐ, act. part. ܟܐܡ rarely ܟܐܡ, ܟܡܐ usually with ܠܒ; root-meaning *to cover up, conceal,* hence *a) to keep, lay by* or *reserve secretly; to keep oneself close; to be reserved, keep silent;* ܚܟܝܡܐ ܟܢܫ ܐܘ ܟܐܡ *the wise man collects and keeps reserves;* ܠܐ ܟܐܡ ܩܠܐ ܕܙܡܝܪܬܗ *the sound of her songs is not silent;* ܠܐ ܬܬܟܡܐ ܢܦܫܝ ܥܡ ܪܫܝܥܐ *my tongue shall not keep silence touching my faith in Thee*, but cf. *e* below. *b*) *to take away privily, appropriate*, used esp. in colophons of secretly taking possessions of books. *c*) *to lay hold secretly, fall suddenly upon;* ܟܡܣ ܡܘܬܐ ܥܠ ܟܠ ܒܣܪ *death laid hold secretly on all flesh. d*) *to make a fraudulent use of, defraud of, refuse to return* or *make good, to deny* ܦܘܩܕܢܐ *a deposit,* ܡܘܠܟܢܐ *a promise,* ܪܫܐ *the principal. e*) *to refuse to give out in due time, to keep in* or *suppress* till the thing is spoiled or corrupt, *to fail to produce* as the earth her seed, the womb a foetus, a tree its fruit; metaph. ܐܢ ܟܡܣܝܢ ܐܢܬܘܢ ܚܪܝܢܐ *if ye suppress contention;* ܗܒ ܕܐܥܒܪ. ܠܐ ܢܟܡܘܣ ܠܝ ܐܬܪܐ ܥܣܩܐ *grant that I may pass over, let not the difficult place engulf me.* This verb is sometimes confused with ܟܡܐ, ܟܡܢ, and ܟܡܫ. Derivatives, ܟܡܘܣܘܬܐ, ܟܡܣܐ, ܟܡܣܘܬܐ.

ܟܡܣܘܣ *chemistry.*

ܟܘܡܘܣ pl. ܟܘܡܘܣܐ m. χυμός, *chyme, humour, juice,* ܐܪܒܥܐ ܐܝܬ ܟܘܡܘܣܐ ܒܦܓܪܐ there are *four humours* or *fluids* in the body; ܟܘܡܘܣܐ ܡܪ̈ܝܪܐ *bilious humours;* ܟܘܡܘܣ ܕܡܐ *the blood;* ܟܘܡܘܣܐ ܕܦܐܪ̈ܐ *the juices of fruits.*

ܟܘܡܪܐ pl. ܐ̈ rt. ܟܡܪ. m. *a priest*, sometimes opp. ܟܗܢܐ *a priest* according to the Mosaic Law; ܪܫ ܟܘܡܪ̈ܐ or ܪܒ ܟܘܡܪ̈ܐ *a high-priest;* ܟܬ̈ܒܐ ܕܟܘܡܪ̈ܐ *hieroglyphics.*

ܟܘܡܪܘܬܐ rt. ܟܡܪ. f. *priesthood;* ܟܘܡܪܘܬܗ ܕܡܠܟܝܙܕܩ *the priesthood of Melchisedech;* ܪܝܫ ܟܘܡܪܘܬܐ *the episcopate;* ܟܘܪܣܝܐ ܕܟܘܡܪܘܬܐ *the patriarchal throne.*

ܟܘܡܪܝܐ, ܝܬܐ rt. ܟܡܪ. *priestly;* ܟܬ̈ܒܐ ܟܘܡܪ̈ܝܐ *hieroglyphics.*

ܟܘܡܪܬܐ pl. ܬ̈ܐ rt. ܟܡܪ. f. *a priestess, temple keeper, one having charge of a holy place* or *holy rites;* ܟܘܡܪ̈ܬܐ ܡܫܡ̈ܫܢܝܬܐ *deaconesses;* ܟܘܡܪܬܐ ܒܬܘܠܬܐ *a vestal virgin.*

ܟܘܡܬܪܐ = ܟܡܬܪܐ *a pear.*

ܟܘܢ, ܟܢ I. fut. ܢܟܘܢ, act. part. ܟܐܢ, ܟܝܢܐ. *to be, exist, begin to be;* eccles. *to come, fall* on a special day, as a festival; gram. *to be found, exist, occur;* ܠܡܕ ܚܠܦ ܕܠܬ ܟܝܢܐ *Lamadh is found instead of Daleth.* Ethpe. ܐܬܟܝܢ *to be by nature, be naturally constituted; to happen, occur;* ܐܬܟܝܢ ܐܘܢܘܟܐ *he was born a eunuch;* ܟܠ ܟܝܢܐ ܡܠܝܠܐ ܐܬܟܝܢ ܠܡܩܒܠܘ ܝܘܠܦܢܐ *every rational being is by nature capable of learning;* ܐܬܪܐ ܕܐܬܟܝܢ ܠ *a place naturally fit for ...,* ܗܠܝܢ ܕܐܬܟܝܢܝ *natural objects.* Pa. ܟܝܢ *to give existence* or *nature, to constitute; to give shape, elaborate, make fit;* ܐܠܗܐ ܡܬܩܢ ܘܡܟܝܢ ܟܠ God *forms and ordains the nature of everything;* pass. part. ܡܟܝܢ, ܡܟܝܢܐ *inborn, natural, fit;* ܟܠܗܘܢ ܗܘ̈ܝܐ ܡܟܝ̈ܢܐ *all created beings.* Ethpa. ܐܬܟܝܢ *a*) *to be by nature, be naturally constituted, ordained, formed* ܡܢ ܐܠܗܐ *by God;* ܕܒܗ ܡܬܟܝܢܝܢ ܒܪ̈ܩܐ ܘܪ̈ܥܡܐ the zone *wherein are formed lightnings and thunders. b*) *to be closely fitted, be in conjunction;* ܡܟܣܚܝܢ ܠܗܘܢ ܕܢܬܟܝܢܘܢ ܠܒܐ ܠܒܐ ܠܠܒܐ *they trim* the grafts *so that the inner heart may fit close to that* of the stem; ܟܘܟ̈ܒܐ ܡܐ ܕܡܬܟܝܢܝܢ ܥܡ ܣܗܪܐ *stars when in conjunction with the moon. c*) *to occur, fall* as a festival, a conjunction of planets, the position of a star; *to be found, stand, be extant;* ܡܫܟܚܐ ܕܬܪܝܢ ܟܘܣܦܝܢ ܢܬܟܝܢܘܢ ܠܣܗܪܐ ܒܚܡܫܐ ܝܪ̈ܚܝܢ *it is possible for two eclipses of the moon to occur within five months;* ܡܠ̈ܐ ܝܘܢܝ̈ܐ ܕܡܬܟܝܢ̈ܢ ܒܟܬ̈ܒܐ ܣܘܪ̈ܝܝܐ Greek words *occurring in Syriac books;* ܬܫ̈ܥܝܬܐ ܐܬܟܝܢ *histories are extant;* ܐܝܕܐ ܕܐܬܟܝܢܬ *whichever* woman *it happens to be.* Aph. ܐܟܝܢ *a*) *to give existence, appoint by natural law, constitute, ordain;* ܠܥܠܡܐ ܐܟܝܢ ܡܢ ܠܐ ܡܕܡ God *brought the world into existence out of nothing;* ܙܒܢܐ ܕܚܝ̈ܐ ܐܟܝܢ ܐܠܗܐ ܠܒܢܝ̈ܢܫܐ ܟܪܝܐ ܗܘ *brief is the space of life appointed unto men by God. b*) *to give shape, elaborate* a description. Pass. part. ܡܟܝܢ *natural, capable, possible* see under ܣܟ. Derivatives, ܟܝܢܐ, ܟܝܢܝܐ, ܟܝܢܐܝܬ, ܟܝܢܘܬܐ, ܟܝܢܢܐ, ܡܟܝܢܐ, ܡܟܝܢ, ܡܟܝܢܘܬܐ, ܡܬܟܝܢܢܘܬܐ.

ܟܘܢ, ܟܢ II. root-meaning *to be upright* cf. ܟܐܢܐ. Pael ܟܘܢ *to set right, correct, admonish, rebuke, convict, condemn;* ܚܙܬܗܘܢ ܕܩܕ̈ܝܫܐ ܡܟܘܢܢܐ ܠܚܙ̈ܝܐ *the sight* of holy men *is a rebuke to the beholders.* Ethpa. ܐܬܟܘܢ *a*) *to be corrected, reformed, amended; to correct, reform, amend himself* or *his ways;* ܠܐ ܐܬܟܘܢܘ ܪ̈ܫܝܥܐ *the impious would not be corrected, would not amend their ways;* ܐܢ ܬܬܟܘܢܘܢ ܒܦܘܪ̈ܫܢܐ

if they would have received reproof, been admonished, by former chastisements. Derivatives, ܡܬܟܘܢܢܐ, ܟܘܢܢܐ, ܟܘܢܝܐ or ܟܘܢܝܘܬܐ.

ܟܘܢ; see ܟܐܘܢ *Saturn.*

ܟܘܢܝ, ܟܘܢܝܐ pl. ܹܐ rt. ܟܢܐ. m. *a naming, mention; a name, title, appellation;* ܕܘܟܬܐ ܕܟܘܢܝܗ *a place called . . .;* ܒܚܕ ܟܘܢܝܐ *by the same name;* ܒܟܘܢܝܐ ܕܝܪܝܐ *a monk in name only;* ܐܝܠܝܢ ܕܟܘܢܝ ܐܒܗܘܗܝ *those whom he called his parents, his adopted parents;* gram. *a noun, the nominative;* ܦܠܘܚܘܬܐ ܕܟܘܢܝܐ *the nom. case.*

ܟܘܢܝܩܣ pl. ܹܐ or ܟܘܢܝܩܣ, ܟܘܢܝܩܝܣ χοῖνιξ, *a dry measure* = about three pints.

ܟܘܢܫ, ܟܘܢܫܐ rt. ܟܢܫ. m. *a gathering together.* a) *a collection* of alms, *amassing* of money, ܟܘܢܫܢ ܩܐܡ ܠܐܚܪܢܐ *that which we have gathered together remains for others;* ܟܘܢܫ ܟܣܦܐ ܕܡܕܐܬܐ *collecting the tribute money;* ܟܘܢܫܐ ܕܝܘܬܪܢܐ ܥܘܠܐ *amassing unfair profit;* ܟܘܢܫ ܥܠܠܬܐ *ingathering of the harvest.* b) *a summoning, assembling, convoking;* ܟܘܢܫ ܚܝܠܘܬܐ *levying the forces.* c) *a collection* of precepts, canons, laws, &c.; ܟܘܢܫܐ ܦܣܝܩܐ *an epitome;* ܟܘܢܫܐ ܕܐܒܗܬܐ ܡܠܦܢܐ *catenae of the Fathers.* d) *a logical conclusion, reasoning, summing-up, computation;* ܕܫܢܝܐ *a chronological reckoning.* e) *recollection, a recollected mind.*

ܟܘܢܬܐ usually pl. ܟܘܢܬ̈ܐ f. *spelt, rye.*

ܟܘܢܬ ܫܪܐ or ܟܘܢܬܫܪܐ and contr. ܟܘܫܪܐ *the navel, the passage of the navel.*

ܟܘܣ imper. of verb ܢܟܣ *to slay.*

ܟܘܣ χόος, χοῦς a) *earth.* b) *a liquid measure* = six sextarii, about three quarts.

ܟܘܣܒܪܬܐ f. *coriandrum sativum, the spice coriander,* ܙܪܥܐ ܕܟܘܣܒܪܬܐ *coriander seed.*

ܟܘܣܝܐ rt. ܟܣܐ. m. a) *covering, concealing* any part of the body, ܟܘܣܝ ܐܦܐ *covering the face.* b) *a covering, wrapper.*

ܟܘܣܝܬܐ pl. ܟܘܣܝ̈ܬܐ rt. ܟܣܐ. f. *a covering for the head, a conical felt cap, cowl, hood;* ܟܘܣܝܬܐ ܐܪܙ ܗܘ ܕܩܘܢܣܐ ܕܦܘܪܩܢܐ *the cowl is the symbol of the helmet of salvation.*

ܟܘܣܟܣܐ m. *cartilage; the part of a bone which contains marrow.*

ܟܘܣܛܠܐ pl. ܹܐ f. a) *a scalpel; a cupping-glass;* ܐܘܡܢܘܬܐ ܕܟܘܣܛܠܐ *the art of cupping.* b) ܟܘܣܛܠܐ ܕܒܝܬ ܟܬܦܬܐ *the space between the shoulders.*

ܟܘܦܬܐ m. *a bow, bend, curve; convexity;* ܟܘܦܬܐ ܕܚܘܕܪܐ *the bow* or *curve of a circle.* Derivatives, the two following words—

ܟܘܦܢܝ, ܟܘܦܢܝܐ, ܟܘܦܢܝܬܐ from ܟܘܦܬܐ. *convex, crooked, bowed, hunchbacked.*

ܟܘܦܢܝܐ *hunchbacked, crookbacked.*

ܟܘܦ, ܟܦ fut. ܢܟܘܦ, pass. part. ܟܝܦ same as ܟܦ. *to bend, bow* ܒܘܪܟܐ *the knee,* ܨܘܪܐ *the neck,* ܪܝܫܐ *the head.* Ethpe. ܐܬܟܝܦ *to be bent, pliable.*

ܟܘܦ imper. of verb ܟܦ *to bend.*

ܟܘܦ or ܟܦ *Coph* or *Cap,* the letter ܟ.

ܟܘܦܪ, ܟܘܦܪܐ rt. ܟܦܪ. m. a) *wiping off* or *out;* metaph. *the effacing* of sin. b) *a towel, dishcloth, clout.* c) *that which is wiped away, dirt, offscouring.*

ܟܘܦܪܐ m. I. *pitch, bitumen;* ܟܘܦܪܐ ܕܐܣܦܝܢܬܐ *pitch for calking a ship.* II. *the henna-flower, cypress-flower.*

ܟܘܦܬܐ f. *the blossom* or *calyx of the garden pomegranate, a rose-calyx.*

ܟܘܪ Peal doubtful, perh. *to be ashamed, to fear, to oppress.* Ethpa. ܐܬܟܘܪ *to feel ashamed; to grow hot, be sultry;* metaph. *to grow angry.* Derivatives, ܟܪܝܪ and ܟܪܝܪܐ, ܟܘܪܐ, ܟܘܪܐ, ܟܘܪܢܐ.

ܟܘܪ, ܟܘܪܐ or ܟܘܪܐ pl. ܹܐ m. and f. *a beehive.*

ܟܘܪ, ܟܘܪܐ or ܟܘܪܐ pl. ܟܘܪ̈ܘܣ or ܟܘܪܘܣ f. χώρα, *country, land, neighbourhood, district,* esp. *the country round a city;* ܐܘ ܒܡܕܝܢܬܐ ܐܘ ܒܟܘܪܐ *whether in the town or in the country;* ܐܢܬܬܐ ܡܢ ܟܘܪܐ *a woman from the neighbourhood;* ܡܢ ܟܘܪ ܐܚܪܢܐ *from some other quarter;* ܟܘܪܐ ܕܐܡܝܕ—ܕܚܡܨ *the district of Amida, Emesa, &c.;* ܟܘܪܐܦܝܣܩܘܦܐ *chorepiscopus,* one who ruled over village churches in the place of a bishop and appointed the lesser orders, but did not ordain priests nor deacons, and himself belonged to the priesthood.

ܟܘܪ, ܟܘܪܐ pl. ܟܘܪ̈ܝܢ rt. ܟܘܪ. m. *a fire, furnace, kiln, crucible, refining-pot;* ܟܘܪܐ ܕܦܘܪܫܢܐ *a crucible for separating;* ܟܘܪܐ ܕܒܘܚܪܢܐ—ܕܒܘܩܝܐ *the furnace of trial.*

ܟܘܪ, ܟܘܪܐ pl. ܟܘܪ̈ܝܢ, ܟܘܪ̈ܐ Heb. *a cor,* a measure both dry and liquid = 10 ephahs or 11⅑ bushels. ܟܘܪܐ ܕܚܛ̈ܐ—ܕܣܥܪ̈ܐ—ܕܕܒܫܐ—ܕܚܡܪܐ *a cor of wheat, of barley, of honey, of wine;* ܒܟܘܪܐ ܟܘܪܐ ܘܟܘܘܪܐ ܐܝܬ ܠܝ ܐܦ ܟܘܪ̈ܐ ܕܚܛ̈ܐ *in the country I have a furnace and beehive, bushels of wheat too.*

ܟܘܪܐܦܣܩܘܦܐ *chorepiscopus;* see under ܟܘܪܐ.

ܟܘܪܓܝܢ pl. ܐ̈ ,Ar. and Pers. m. *khurjin, a travelling-bag, saddle-bag, pouch; a horse-cloth, housing.*

ܟܘܪܕܝܐ, ܝܬܐ *a Kurd, Kurdish man* or *woman.*

ܟܘܪܕܝܢܐ pl. ܐ̈ m. the same.

ܟܘܪܗܢܐ, ܟܘܪܗܢ, ܟܘܪܗܢܐ pl. ܝܢ̈, ܐ̈ rt. ܟܪܗ. m. *sickness, illness, disease, infirmity, malady;* metaph. *harm, hurt, misfortune, evil, pain, mischief;* ܚܠܡ ܡܢ ܟܘܪܗܢܗ *he recovered from his illness;* ܟܘܪ̈ܗܢܐ ܡܪ̈ܟܒܐ *a complication of diseases;* ܟܘܪܗܢܐ ܡܚܒܠܢܐ *a pestilence;* ܟܘܪܗܢܐ ܕܡܥܝ̈ܐ *diarrhoea,* ܕܟܘ̈ܠܝܬܐ *disease of the kidneys,* ܟܘܪܗܢܐ ܕܡܝ̈ܐ *dropsy;* ܐܝܬ ܟܘܪܗܢܐ ܕܒܝܫܬܐ ܕܚܙܝܬ ܬܚܝܬ ܫܡܫܐ *there is a grievous evil which I have seen beneath the sun.*

ܟܘܪܗܢܢܐ, ܝܬܐ rt. ܟܪܗ. adj. *morbid, pertaining to disease.*

ܟܘܪܙܐ, ܟܘܪܙܬܐ or ܟܘܪܙܝܢܐ, Ar. f. *a satchel, provision bag, wallet, traveller's bag.* Cf. ܟܘܪܓܝܢ.

ܟܘܪܚܐ pl. ܝܢ̈, ܐ̈ m. *a hut, shed, hovel, cabin; a hermit's cell, a separate little dwelling,* opp. ܩܠܝܬܐ *a cell in a monastery;* ܕܘܒܪܐ ܟܘܪܚܝܐ *a hermit's life.*

ܟܘܪܚܝܐ m. *one who lives in a cell, a hermit.*

ܟܘܪܝܐ pl. ܐ̈ from ܟܘܪܐ m. *a chorepiscopus;* see under ܟܘܪܐ.

ܟܘܪܟܐ pl. ܐ̈ rt. ܟܪܟ. m. *a turning, circuit; a wrapping* or *binding round; enshrouding;* eccles. *a procession.*

ܟܘܪܟܝܐ pl. ܟܘܪܟ̈ܝܬܐ rt. ܟܪܟ. m. *a crane;* perh. *a swift* or *swallow* so called from its gyrations.

ܟܘܪܟܡܐ m. *crocus sativus, the saffron crocus.*

ܟܘܪܟܡܢܘܬܐ from the above, f. *saffron colour, yellowness;* metaph. *pallor.*

ܟܘܪܟܡܢܐ or ܟܘܪܟܡܝܢܐ adj. from ܟܘܪܟܡܐ. *saffron* or *crocus coloured.*

ܟܘܪܪܐ or ܟܘܪܪܐ pl. ܐ̈ rt. ܟܘܪ. m. *sultriness, dry* or *baking heat and suffocating air, a drought;* ܙܒܢܐ ܕܟܘܪ̈ܪܐ ܕܐܒ ܝܪܚܐ *the season of excessive heat in August;* ܪܘ̈ܚܐ ܫܚܝܢ̈ܬܐ ܘܟܘܪ̈ܪܐ *hot winds and sultry heats.*

ܟܘܪܪܢܐ rt. ܟܘܪ. adj. *parched.*

ܟܘܪܣܐ pl. ܝܢ̈, ܐ̈ usually m. *a*) *a quire* of paper, *section* of a book; later Syriac codices are arranged in fasciculi of 4, 6, 8, 10 or more leaves, the first page of each being numbered and thus referred to in the index, e. g. ܟܘ. ܝܕ ܦܐ. ܘ *quire* 14, *page* 6; ܡܢ ܟܘܪܣܐ ܐܚܪܝܐ *from the last quire;* cf. ܦܐܬܐ. *b*) *a pamphlet, book;* ܟܘܪܣܐ ܕܬܫܒ̈ܚܬܐ *a book of canticles;* ܟܘܪܣܐ ܕܫܡܗ̈ܐ *a vocabulary, catalogue.*

ܟܘܪܣܝܐ, ܟܘܪܣܝܐ pl. ܟܘܪ̈ܣܘܬܐ, ܟܘܪ̈ܣܘܢ m. *a*) *a seat of state, chair, throne;* ܟܘܪܣܝܐ ܡܠܟܘܬܐ *the royal throne. b*) *a bishop's throne* or *seat;* ܟܘܪܣܝܐ ܡܕܝܢܬܐ or ellipt. *a cathedral city, bishop's see, jurisdiction, authority. c*) *a sedan chair, litter* or *palanquin. d*) *the pier* of a bridge, *base* of a column.

ܟܘܪܣܬܐ pl. ܝܬܐ f. *a*) = ܟܘܪܣܐ; ܟܘܪܣܬܐ ܐܚܪܝܬܐ *the last quire* or *part* of a book. *b*) *a wallet, travelling-bag. c*) E-Syr. the part of the burial service for the day.

ܟܘܪܦܐ pl. ܐ̈ m. *an asp, a viper.*

ܟܘܪܬܐ f. *a beehive* or *a honey-comb;* cf. ܟܘܪܐ.

ܟܫ, ܟܫ fut. ܢܟܘܫ, act. part. ܟܐܫ, ܟܫܐ. *to be tranquil, stay quiet, remain quietly;* ܐܦܠܐ ܒܒܬ̈ܝܗܘܢ ܟܫܝܢ *nor will they stay quietly at home;* ܟܐܫ ܘܐܩܝܡ *at leisure, having leisure.* Pael ܟܫ *to make to stay quiet.* Derivative, ܟܘܫܐ.

ܟܘܫܐ rt. ܟܫ. m. *tranquillity, the tranquil and silent life* of a monk, *monastic retirement;* ܟܘܫܐ ܕܩܠܝܬܐ *the tranquillity of the cell;* ܕܒܪ ܒܗ ܟܘܫܐ ܒܕܝܪܐ *he led the quiet life in the monastery.*

ܟܘܫܬܐ pl. ܬ̈ܐ = ܟܘܫܬܐ. m. *a spindle.*

ܟܘܫܝܐ, ܟܘܫܝܬܐ pl. m. ܝ̈ܐ f. ܝ̈ܬܐ from Cush the son of Ham. *a Cushite, Ethiopian, Abyssinian;* ܟܘܫܝܐ ܐܘܟܡܐ ܐܘܟܡܐ *an Ethiopian i.e. a negro.*

ܟܘܫܢܐ pl. ܢ̈ܐ Pers. m. *a kind of pulse, the bitter vetch.*

ܟܘܫܦ, ܟܘܫܦܐ pl. ܦ̈ܐ rt. ܟܫܦ. m. *an earnest prayer, entreaty, supplication, intercessory prayer, intercession;* ܩܪܒ ܠܐܠܗܐ ܨܠܘܬܐ ܒܟܘܫܦ̈ܐ ܣܓܝ̈ܐܐ *he offered prayer to God with many supplications;* ܥܠ ܟܘܫܦ̈ܐ ܘܨܠܘ̈ܬܐ ܕܡܪܟܢܘܬܐ *about the intercessions and prayers of inclining in the liturgy.*

ܟܘܫܦܐ, ܟܘܫܦܬܐ or ܟܘܫܦܬܐ *a covering, blanket, rug.*

ܟܘܫܦܬܐ pl. ܬ̈ܐ f. *a coverlet, blanket, rug.*

ܟܘܫܪܐ rt. ܟܫܪ. m. *a) prosperity, success, advantage, good-fortune;* ܣܘܓܐܐ ܕܟܘܫܪ̈ܘܗܝ *his frequent successes;* ܝܬܝܪ ܟܘܫܪܐ *very fortunate. b) diligence, activity, vigour, assiduity;* ܚܘܝ ܟܘܫܪܐ ܬܡܝܗܐ *he showed admirable assiduity;* ܒܟܘܫܪܐ *actively, diligently, admirably.*

ܟܘܬ usually ܐܟܘܬ prep. *as, like,* ܣܟܠܐ ܐܟܘܬܝ *stupid like me.*

ܟܘܬܐ emph. state of ܟܘܐ f. *a window &c.*

ܟܘܬܚܐ m. *a relish prepared with vinegar, tasty food.*

ܟܘܬܝܢܐ, ܟܘܬܢܐ, ܟܘܬܝܢܬܐ pl. ܟܘܬܝܢ̈ܐ, ܟܘܬܝܢܝܢ, ܟܘܬܢܝܢܬܐ or ܟܘܬܢܝܬܐ from ܟܬܢܐ. f. *a) a linen garment, a coat or tunic;* ܟܘܬܝܢܐ ܕܐܝ̈ܕܝܢ *a long coat with sleeves;* ܟܘܬܝܢܐ ܕܒܘܨܐ *a coat of fine linen;* ܟܘܬܝܢܐ ܡܨܒܥܬܐ ܙܢ̈ܝܐ *a tunic worked in different colours;* ܟܘܬܝܢܐ ܕܡܫܟܐ *a coat of skin. b) a membrane, tegument, thin skin* covering any organ of the body; ܟܘܬܝܢ̈ܬܐ ܕܥܝܢܐ *the membranes of the eye.*

ܟܘܬܡܐ const. st. ܟܘܬܡ (rare), emph. ܟܘܬܡܬܐ, pl. ܟܘܬܡ̈ܬܐ rt. ܟܬܡ. f. *a spot or mark* on the skin, *a freckle, a pock, pock-mark; scab, mange;* ܟܘܬܡ̈ܬܐ ܟܐܡܬܐ *freckles;* metaph. *marks, spots* or *scars* of sin; with ܣܡ *to spot, defile;* ܚܘܪ ܟܘܬܡ̈ܬܢ *He made white our spots;* ܕܠܐ ܟܘܬܡܐ *spotless, unspotted, immaculate;* ܚܘܒܐ ܕܠܐ ܟܘܬܡ̈ܬܐ *pure love.*

ܟܘܬܪܐ rt. ܟܬܪ. m. *awaiting, persistence, stability, duration;* ܟܘܬܪܐ ܕܚܫܘܟܐ *the duration of an eclipse;* ܚܘܒܐ ܕܡܩܘܐ ܒܟܘܬܪܐ *love abiding in continuance, continuing* or *constant love.*

ܟܘܪܙ, ܟܘܪܙܐ Pers. m. *a bold fighter, brave warrior, champion.*

ܟܚ Aphel ܐܟܚ *to blow* the fire, *breathe, blow upon, puff, exhale.* Derivative, ܟܚܬܐ.

ܟܚܡ act. part. ܟܚܡ, pass. part. ܟܚܝܡ, ܟܚܝܡܐ, ܟܚܝܡܬܐ. *to revere, be modest;* pass. part. *a) revered, reverend, venerable. b) reverent, modest.* Pa. ܟܚܡ *to put to shame, make ashamed.* Ethpa. ܐܬܟܚܡ *to stand in awe, reverence* with ܡܢ; *to be ashamed, modest, feel shame;* ܠܐ ܡܬܟܚܡ *shameless.* Derivatives, ܟܘܚܡܐ, ܟܚܝܡܐܝܬ, ܟܚܝܡܘܬܐ, ܡܬܟܚܡܢܐ, ܡܬܟܚܡܢܘܬܐ.

ܟܚܝܡܘܬܐ rt. ܟܚܡ. f. *reverence, respect; modesty, chastity.*

ܟܚܠ fut. ܢܟܚܘܠ, act. part. ܟܚܠ, ܟܚܠܐ, pass. part. ܟܚܝܠ, ܠܐ, ܠܬܐ. *a) to paint* the lower eyelid *with kohl, to paint* or *anoint the eyes* with salve; ܟܚܝܠ̈ܢ ܥܝ̈ܢܝܗ̇ *her painted eyes. b) to gouge out* the eyes. Ethpe. ܐܬܟܚܠ *a) to be smeared* or *spread on the eyes* as salve or lotion. *b) to be gouged out, darkened* of the eyes. Derivatives, ܟܘܚܠܐ, ܟܘܚܠܬܐ, ܟܚܠܬܐ, ܟܚܠܐ, ܡܟܚܠܬܐ, ܡܟܚܠܐ.

ܟܚܠܘܬܐ, ܟܚܝܠܘܬܐ or ܟܘܚܠܘܬܐ rt. ܟܚܠ. f. *the application of kohl* or of salve to the eyes.

ܟܚܠܐ rt. ܟܚܠ. m. *kohl, antimony, collyrium.*

ܟܚܬܐ rt. ܟܚ. f. *a breath, stirring of air, a light breeze.*

ܟܝ a particle following and emphasizing expressions of doubt, desire or interrogation, *now, indeed, verily, truly;* ܐܢܫ ܟܝ ܐܢܫ *now will any one?* ܐܝܟܐ ܟܝ, ܐܝܢܐ ܟܝ *now where? now who?* ܟܡܐ ܟܝ *how much indeed?* ܐܝܢܐ ܟܝ ܐܬܐ ܗܝ *what sort of sign can it be?* ܟܡܐ ܟܝ *how much more?*

ܟܝܐ or ܟܝܐ f. χία, *a fragrant gum, mastick;* ܡܫܝܚܐ ܕܟܝܐ *mastick salve.*

ܟܝܒ, ܟܝܒܐ same as ܟܐܒ ܟܐܒܐ *pain;* ܟܝܒ ܠܒܐ *compunction.*

ܟܝܘܢܐ, ܟܝܘܢܬܐ pl. m. ܢ̈ܐ f. ܢ̈ܬܐ rt. ܟܘܢ. *fraudulent, tricky.*

ܟܘܡܣܘܬܐ rt. ܟܡܣ. f. *secret fraud, trickiness.*

ܟܡܝܪܐ pass. part. of ܟܡܪ.

ܟܡܝܢ same as ܟܡܝܪ *sultry, heavy.*

ܟܝܠܐ pl. ܟܝܠܝܢ, ܟܝܠܐ rt. ܟܘܠ. m. *a measure* of wine, oil, grain, &c., ܒܟܝܠܝܢ ܟܝܠܝܢ *by various measures;* ܟܝܠܐ ܬܪܝܨܐ or ܟܝܠܐ ܫܠܡܐ *a just* or *exact measure;* ܠܐ ܐܝܬ ܠܗ ܟܝܠܐ God *is not measurable;* metaph. *amount, quantity;* ܡܠܦܢܘܬܗ ܕܥܠ ܢܒܝܐ ܕܟܝܠܐ *his teaching on the Prophets amounted to fifty* homilies, was *fifty in amount.*

ܟܝܠܐܝܬ rt. ܟܘܠ. adv. *by measure, according to right measure.*

ܟܝܠܝܪܟܐ or ܟܝܠܝܐܪܟܐ pl. ܐ̈ χιλίαρχος, *a chiliarch, captain of a thousand.*

ܟܠܒܐ = ܟܠܒܐ *a willow.*

ܟܐܦܬܐ f. *a steep rock, abrupt bank* or *ridge.*

ܟܝܠܬܐ pl. ܟܝܠܝܢ, ܟܝܠܬܐ rt. ܟܘܠ. f. *a measure,* ܟܝܠܬܐ ܪܒܬܐ ܘܙܥܘܪܬܐ *a greater and lesser measure;* ܟܝܠܐ ܘܟܝܠܬܐ *diverse measures,* ܟܝܠܬܐ ܘܟܝܠܬܐ the same; ܒܟܝܠܬܐ *according to measure;* ܐܦܠܐ ܝܩܪܐ ܕܣܝܒܘܬܐ ܒܟܝܠܬܐ *nor is* honour of age *measured by the number of years;* ܥܕܡܐ ܕܬܬܡܠܐ ܟܝܠܬܐ ܘܡܢܝܢܐ *until the measure be full and the number completed.*

ܟܝܡܐ f. the constellation of the *Pleiades;* ܡܥܪܒܗ ܕܟܝܡܐ *the setting of the Pleiades* = September; also *Coma Berenices.*

ܟܝܡܘܢ, ܟܝܡܘܢܐ or ܟܐܡܘܢܐ pl. ܐ̈ m. χειμών, *a storm, tempest, rough weather;* metaph. ܟܝܡܘܢܐ ܕܐܘܠܨܢܐ, ܕܪܕܘܦܝܐ *a storm of distress, of persecution.*

ܟܝܡܘܢܝܐ pl. ܐ̈ from the above. adj. *stormy, tempestuous.*

ܟܝܡܝܐ, ܟܝܡܝܐ or ܟܝܡܝܐ *chemistry;* ܐܘܡܢܘܬܐ ܕܟܝܡܝܐ *alchemy.*

ܟܝܢ, ܟܝܢܐ pl. ܟܝܢܐ, ܟܝܢܐ rt. ܟܘܢ I. m. *a) nature; natural disposition, instinct* opp. ܨܒܝܢܐ *will;* ܒܟܝܢܐ *by nature, naturally;* ܟܝܢܐ ܕܚܝܠܘܬܗ *his natural* or *inborn strength;* ܟܠ ܟܝܢ, ܟܠ ܟܝܢܝܢ *every nature* or *kind of creature;* eccles. the Council of Chalcedon taught ܚܕ ܩܢܘܡܐ ܘܬܪܝܢ ܟܝܢܐ *one Person and two Natures* in our Lord; ܬܪܝܢ ܟܝܢܐ *Dyophysites. b) procreation, the procreative member, privy parts. c) essence, substance* (ܟܝܢܐ and ܐܝܬܝܐ were used by early writers before the adoption of the Greek ܐܘܣܝܐ); ܟܝܢܐ ܕܡܫܚܐ *the nature* or *substance of oil;* ܟܝܢܐ ܒܪܝܬܐ *created things* or *substances;* ܟܝܢܐ ܟܐܦܢܝܐ *stony substances;* ܟܒܪܝܬܢܝܐ *sulphurous substances;* ܚܕ ܟܝܢܐ, ܥܡ ܟܝܢܐ *consubstantial;* ܒܪ ܟܝܢܐ *of the same nature* or *essence,* ὁμοούσιος. *d)* as adj. ܕܟܝܢܐ *physical, natural, inborn;* ܠܒܪ ܡܢ ܟܝܢܐ *preternatural;* ܠܥܠ ܡܢ ܟܝܢܐ *supernatural.*

ܟܝܢܐܝܬ from ܟܝܢܐ. adj. *naturally, according to nature* or *natural order.*

ܟܝܢܝܐ, ܟܝܢܝܬܐ pl. m. ܐ̈ f. ܬܐ̈ rt. ܟܘܢ I. *a) natural, physical; of nature, according to nature;* ܟܝܢܝܬܐ ܕܢܦܫܐ ܘܕܠܒܪ ܡܢ ܟܝܢܗ ܘܠܥܠ ܡܢ ܟܝܢܗ *that which is natural to the soul and that which is preternatural and supernatural;* ܝܘܠܦܢܐ ܟܝܢܝܐ or ܬܐܘܪܝܐ ܟܝܢܝܬܐ *physical* or *natural science;* ܟܝܢܝܬܐ *physics;* ܒܬܪ ܟܝܢܝܬܐ *metaphysics;* ܦܝܠܣܘܦܐ ܟܝܢܝܐ *a natural philosopher;* ܡܡܠܠ ܥܠ ܟܝܢܝܬܐ *a physiologer;* ܟܬܘܒ ܥܠ ܟܝܢܝܬܐ *a physiographer. b) by nature, innate, inborn, native, essential;* ܐܚܐ ܟܝܢܝܐ *an own brother, brother-german;* ܗܘܢܐ ܟܝܢܝܐ *native wit;* ܕܢܦܫܐ ܟܝܢܝܬܐ *natural properties, essential attributes;* ܡܪܘܬܐ ܟܝܢܝܬܐ ܐܝܬ ܠܗ *He is Lord by nature;* ܒܪܐ ܟܝܢܝܐ ܕܐܒܐ *consubstantial with the Father. c)* gram. *substantive, radical.*

ܟܝܢܝܘܬܐ rt. ܟܘܢ I. f. *nature, natural;* ܡܡܠܠܘܬܐ ܟܝܢܝܘܬܐ *physiology;* ܚܕ ܟܝܢܝܘܬܐ *consubstantiality.*

ܟܝܣ, ܟܝܣܐ pl. ܟܝܣܐ m. *a small bag, pouch, purse;* ܟܝܣܐ ܕܡܐܢܐ *a bag* or *trunk of clothes;* ܐܠܗܝܗܘܢ ܟܝܣܝܗܘܢ ܘܟܪܣܗܘܢ *their gods are their moneybag and their belly.*

ܟܝܣܘܢܐ dim. of ܟܝܣܐ. m. *a little bag* or *purse.*

ܟܝܪܘܛܘܢܝܐ, ܟܝܪܘܛܘܢܝܬܐ or ܟܝܪܘܛܘܢܝܐ pl. ܟܝܪܘܛܘܢܝܬܐ f. χειροτονία = Syr. ܣܝܡ ܐܝܕܐ *laying on of hands, ordination* or *consecration.*

ܟܝܪܘܛܘܢܝܣܐ χειροτονῆσαι, *ordination;* with ܥܒܕ *to ordain; ordained, admitted to holy orders.*

ܟܝܪܘܛܘܢܝܬܝܣ and ܟܝܪܘܛܘܢܝܬܝܣ χειροτονηθεὶς *a) elected, appointed;* with ܩܕܡ *fore-ordained. b) ordained, consecrated.*

ܟܘܬܒܐ or ܟܬܒܐ ܐܝܕܐ pl. ܟܬܒܐ ܐܝܕܝܐ also ܟܬܒܐ and ܟܬܒܐ m. *handwriting, autograph;* with ܚܬܡ, ܣܡ or ܐܪܫܡ *to subscribe, sign* e.g. a synodical decree or anathema, ܚܬܡܬ ܒܟܬܒ ܐܝܕܝ *I have signed this with my own hand;* ܟܬܝܒܐ ܒܟܬܒܐ ܐܝܕܘܗܝ *written by the hand of.*

ܟܝܬ particle of explanation, *scilicet, that is to say, indeed;* usually compounded with ܗܘ; ܗܘܟܝܬ *i.e.*

ܟܟܐ E-Syr. ܟܟܐ pl. ܟܟܐ m. *a tooth* esp. *a molar tooth, tusk;* ܟܟܐ ܕܦܝܠܐ *an elephant's tusk;* ܟܟܐ ܢܩܝܒܐ *a hollow tooth.*

ܟܟܪܬܐ pl. ܟܟܪܬܐ and ܟܟܪܐ f. *a cake of bread;* ܟܟܪܐ ܡܪܝܪܬܐ *bitter cakes* i. e. flavoured with wormwood.

ܟܟܘܡܬܐ pl. ܟܟܘܡܝܬܐ f. *a weasel, polecat.*

ܟܟܠܢܐ or ܟܟܠܢܐ m. *spotted, speckled,* esp. *white speckled with black.*

ܟܟܠܢܝܐ *marked with spots, speckled.*

ܟܟܠܬܐ pl. ܟܟܠܬܐ f. *a) a spot;* ܢܡܪܐ ܟܟܠܬܢܝܐ *a spotted pard;* ܚܝܘܬܐ ܕܟܟܠܬܐ *a spotted beast. b) a pill, pastille.* Cf. pl. of ܟܟܘܠܬܐ.

ܟܟܪܐ pl. ܟܟܪܝܢ, ܟܟܪܐ f. *a talent* = £125 or 12,000 zuzi at 8 zuzi the oz. or 3,000 silver staters; ܥܣܪܐ ܟܟܪܝܢ ܕܟܣܦܐ *ten talents of silver;* ܟܟܪܐ ܐܘܢܓܠܝܘܢܝܐ *the talents spoken of in the Gospel.*

ܟܟܪܬܐ pl. ܟܟܪܝܬܐ f. *a) a honeycomb;* ܕܒܫܐ ܒܟܟܪܬܐ *honey in the comb. b) a disease when the skin becomes full of little holes.*

ܟܟܪܢܝܐ from ܟܟܪܐ. *weighing a talent, very ponderous.*

ܟܠ root-meaning *to complete, perfect.* Pa. ܟܠܠ *to crown, adorn with garlands;* ܡܟܠܠ ܒܘܪܕܐ *crowned with roses, rose-garlanded.* Special meanings, *a) to give the crown of martyrdom. b) to set crowns* on the heads esp. of the bride and bridegroom, *to unite in marriage. c) to surround* e.g. with a wall. *d) to crown* with praise or approval. Ethpa. ܐܬܟܠܠ *to be crowned, adorned* as a tree with foliage, a city with buildings; ܡܬܟܠܠܝܢ ܒܬܫܒܚܬܐ *crowned* or *covered with praise;* esp. *to be crowned as a bride, be wedded; to receive the crown of martyrdom, to die a holy death;* with ܒܢܘܪܐ *to be martyred by fire;* ܒܣܗܕܘܬܐ *to die as a martyr;* ܐܬܟܠܠ ܒܣܗܕܘܬܐ *he suffered as a confessor;* ܐܬܟܠܠ ܒܐܘܪܗܝ *he received the crown of martyrdom at Edessa.* Aph. ܐܟܠ *to fancy, imagine.* Shaphel ܫܟܠܠ *to complete, finish* esp. a building; *to build, restore;* ܠܫܟܠܠܘ ܕܚܘܕܪܐ ܕܫܘܪܐ *to complete the circuit of the walls;* ܡܓܕܠܐ ܕܡܚܕܪ ܒܫܘܪܐ ܘܡܫܟܠܠ ܒܟܠܝܠܐ *a tower encircled with walls and crowned with battlements;* ܫܟܠܠ ܗܘ ܕܐܣܚܦܘ *he rebuilt that which they had ruined;* ܡܫܟܠܠ ܥܠ ܚܠܐ *built upon sand* i.e. insecure, transitory. Pass. part. *a) finished, complete, perfect,* ܚܟܡܬܐ ܡܫܟܠܠܬܐ *perfect wisdom. b) adult, full-grown;* ܐܢܬܬܐ ܡܫܟܠܠܬܐ *a woman of full age.* Eshtaph. ܐܫܬܟܠܠ *to be completed, finished. a)* as the building of a house, wall, gate; *to be built, constructed, adorned. b)* as a book, *to be brought to an end, ended. c) to be brought to the end of life, to die. d) to be perfected, made perfect* e.g. ܒܪܘܚܢܝܬܐ *in spiritual things.* Derivatives, ܟܘܠܐ, ܟܠܠܐ, ܟܠܝܠܐ, ܟܠܠܐ, ܟܠܠܬܐ, ܡܫܟܠܠܢܐ, ܡܫܟܠܠܢܘܬܐ, ܫܘܟܠܠܐ.

ܟܠ emph. st. ܟܠܐ. written also ܟܘܠ, ܟܘܠܐ m. *a) the whole, the whole world, the universe, all;* ܐܚܝܕ ܟܠ *upholding all;* ܙܟܐ ܟܠ *all-victorious;* ܝܕܥ ܟܠ *omniscient;* ܒܪܘܝܐ ܕܟܠ *the Creator of the universe;* ܟܠ ܕܟܠ ܟܠ *the entirety of the whole universe,* a title of God; ܟܘܠܐ ܘܡܢܘܬܗ *the whole and its parts;* with suffixes ܟܠܗ, ܟܠܗܝܢ, ܟܠܟܘܢ, ܟܠܗ, &c.; ܟܠܗ ܕܝܠܟ ܐܢܐ *I am wholly thine;* ܟܠܟܝ ܫܦܝܪܐ ܐܢܬܝ *thou art altogether lovely;* ܟܠܗ ܛܡܐ ܐܢܐ *I am utterly unclean;* ܠܐ ܡܕܡ ܟܠ ܟܠܗ *nothing at all, absolutely nothing;* ܟܠܗ ܟܠܗ ܥܡ ܟܠܗ *entirely, utterly;* ܟܠܢ ܥܡ ܟܠܢ *the whole of us, we all without exception. b)* in construction with a pronoun or substantive *all, every, each,* ܟܠ ܐܢܫ or ܟܠܢܫ *every one, any one, each;* ܟܠܡܕܡ ܕܟܠ ܓܢܣ *of every sort, all sorts;* ܒܟܠܕܘܟ *everywhere, in every place;* ܟܠ ܚܝ *every living thing;* ܒܟܠܙܒܢ *always, ever;* ܟܠ ܚܕ, ܟܠܚܕܐ *every one, each one;* ܟܠ ܝܘܡ, ܟܠܝܘܡ *every day, daily;* ܟܠ ܝܘܡ ܕܟܠ ܝܘܡ *all, all things, everything;* ܟܠܡܕܡ ܗܢܐ ܟܠ *this universe;* ܒܟܠܙܒܢ *ever, always;* ܟܠ ܥܕܢ usually with ܡܢ preceding, *altogether, entirely, at all, in any manner, anyhow, whatever happens, at all events;* ܬܐܘ ܠܘܬܢ ܡܢ ܟܠ ܦܘܪܣ *come to us in any case;* with ܠܐ *in no wise;* ܟܠ ܫܢܬܐ or ܒܟܠܫܢܐ *every year, each year, yearly;* ܒܟܠܫܥ, ܟܠܫܥ *hourly, ever, at all times;* ܘܠܐ ܟܠܫܥ ܕܢܨܠܐ *we ought always to pray;* see ܫܢܬܐ, ܫܥܬܐ. c) in construction with relative pronouns and particles corresponds to Lat. *cumque;* ܟܠ ܡܐ ܕ, ܟܠ ܐܝܢܐ ܕ *who* or *whatsoever;* ܟܠܡܢ ܕ *whoever, whosoever;* ܟܠ ܟܡܐ ܕ *so much as; as much, how much, how long;* ܟܠܡܐ ܕ *whosoever, whatsoever; as often as, as often soever as . . .,* ܟܠ ܐܝܟܐ ܕ *wheresoever;* ܟܠ ܐܡܬܝ ܕ *whenever, whensoever.*

Before numerals ܟܠ adds distributive meaning, ܟܠ ܬܪܝܢ ܠܬܪܝܢ *each two, every couple;* ܠܟܠ ܡܐܐ *to every hundred;* ܟܠ ܫܬ ܫܢܝܢ *every sixth year, once in six years.*

ܒܟܠ after an adjective forms a superlative, ܚܟܝܡ ܒܟܠ *most wise;* ܩܕܝܫܗܘ ܒܟܠ *it is most holy.*

ܟܠ ܠܐ or ܠܐ—ܟܠ *no one, none, nothing, no, no manner of, not at all, in no wise,* ܘܠܐ ܟܠ *nor any.* Derivatives, ܟܠܢܝܐܝܬ, ܟܠܢܝܘܬܐ, ܟܠܢܝܐ, ܟܠܝܘܬܐ.

ܟܠܐ fut. ܢܟܠܐ, act. part. ܟܠܐ, ܟܠܝܐ, pass. part. ܟܠܐ, ܟܠܝܐ. a) *to withhold, forbid, hinder, restrain* usually with ܡܢ; *to detain, shut up, keep under restraint; to refuse, deny;* with ܡܢ ܝܠܕܐ *to restrain from bearing;* with ܡܢ ܡܡܠܠܘ *to forbid* or *hinder from speaking;* with ܢܦܫܐ *to hinder oneself, be in one's own way;* with ܪ̈ܚܡܐ *to refuse compassion;* with ܫܡܝܐ *to shut up the heaven* from giving rain; ܡܢ ܡܛܪܐ ܟܠܝܬ ܠܚܡܐ ܡܢ ܟܦܢܐ *thou hast withholden bread from the hungry;* ܫܐܠ ܡܢܗ ܘܠܐ ܟܠܐ ܠܟ *ask of him and he will not refuse you;* ܒܢܡܘܣܐ ܟܠܐ ܐܠܗܐ ܡܐܟܘܠܬܐ ܕܕܡܐ God *forbade in the law the eating of blood.* b) eccles. *to forbid, prohibit* e.g. ܙܘܘܓ̈ܐ *marriages* between near relations; ܠܐ ܟܠܝܐ *it is not forbidden* opp. ܠܐ ܡܫܬܠܛܐ *it is not allowed;* ܟܠܝܐ ܗܘ ܡܢ ܬܫܡܫܬܐ—ܡܢ ܡܫܡܫܢܘܬܐ ܘܬܘܪܐ *he is suspended from the ministry, excommunicated.* c) intrans. *to stay, hold back, pause;* ܠܐ ܟܠܐ ܐܠܐ ܐܙܠ *he stayed not but went quickly;* ܟܠܝܐ ܡܪܕܝܬܗ *his journey is delayed;* ܟܠܐ ܗܘܐ ܠܘܬ ܟܠ ܡܠܬܐ *he paused at each word.*

Ethpe. ܐܬܟܠܝ a) *to be withheld, kept back, restrained, hindered, forbidden, prohibited;* ܐܬܟܠܝܘ ܫܡܝܐ ܡܢ ܡܛܪܐ or ܐܬܟܠܝ ܡܛܪܐ ܡܢ ܫܡܝܐ *the heavens were stayed from rain;* ܐܬܟܠܝ ܐܘܪ̈ܚܬܐ *the roads were impassable;* ܐܢ ܡܬܟܠܝܬܘܢ *if you are hindered.* b) eccles. *to be forbidden, prohibited, suspended.* c) *to refrain, refuse, stay, pause;* ܡܢ ܡܡܠܠܐ *from speech;* ܐܬܟܠܝܬ ܕܠܐ ܠܡܫܕܪܘ *thou hast refused to send.* Pa. ܟܠܝ *to keep close, hold back.* Aph. ܐܟܠܝ same as Pael. Derivatives, ܟܠܝܐ, ܟܠܝܘܬܐ, ܡܟܠܝܢܐ, ܡܬܟܠܝܢܐ, ܡܬܟܠܝܢܐܝܬ, ܡܬܟܠܝܢܘܬܐ, ܡܟܠܝܐ.

ܟܠܒ fut. ܢܟܠܘܒ or ܢܟܠܒ, act. part. ܟܠܒ, denom. verb Peal conj. from ܟܠܒܐ. *to behave like a dog, be rabid;* ܟܠܒܐ ܕܟܠܒ *like a mad dog.*

ܟܠܒ, ܟܠܒܐ pl. ܝܢ, ̈ܐ m. *a dog;* ܟܠܒܬܐ pl. ̈ܬܐ f. *a bitch;* ܟܠܒܐ ܦܩܪܐ *a mad dog;* ܟܠܒ̈ܐ ܕܥܢܐ *sheep-dogs;* ܟܠܒ̈ܐ ܫܬܘ̈ܩܐ *dumb watch-dogs;* ܟܠܒܐ ܕܝܡܐ *a seal;* ܟܠܒܐ ܕܡܝ̈ܐ *an otter;* metaph. *a sodomite;* astron. *the dog-star, Sirius.* Derivatives, verb ܟܠܒ, ܟܠܒܐ, ܟܠܒܢܐ, ܟܠܒܘܢܐ, ܟܠܒܐܝܬ, ܟܠܒܢܝܘܬܐ, ܟܠܒܢܐ.

ܟܠܒܐ pl. ̈ܐ m. *a dog-keeper.*

ܟܠܒܐ usually ܩܘܠܒܐ m. *an axe.*

ܟܠܒܐܝܬ rt. ܟܠܒ. adv. *rabidly, like a mad dog.*

ܟܠܒܘܢܐ, ܟܠܒܘܢܝܬܐ m. and f. dim. of ܟܠܒܐ. *a puppy, whelp.*

ܟܠܒܢܐ or ܟܠܒܢܝܐ m. ܟܠܒܢܝܬܐ f. from ܟܠܒܐ adj. *canine.*

ܟܠܒܢܐ pl. ̈ܐ m. χαλβάνη, *gum galbanum.*

ܟܠܒܢܘܬܐ from ܟܠܒܐ f. *canine nature* or *behaviour, hydrophobia, rabies.*

ܟܠܒܬܐ and ܟܠܒܬܐ pl. ̈ܬܐ a) fem. of ܟܠܒܐ. b) metaph. *tongs, pincers, tweezers, nippers;* ܟܠܒܬܐ ܕܬܠܬ ܫ̈ܢܝܢ *a three-pronged fork.*

ܟܠܕܝ denom. verb Pali conj. from the following word, *to act as a Chaldaean;* ܟܡܐ ܕܡܟܠܕܝܢ ܗܘܘ ܐܬܦܪܣܝܘ *the more they played the Chaldaean the more they were exposed.* Aph. ܐܟܠܕܝ infin. ܡܟܠܕܝܘ *to consult the stars, consult an oracle.*

ܟܠܕܝܐ, ܟܠܕܝܬܐ, ܟܠܕܝ *a Chaldaean, astronomer, astrologer.*

ܟܠܕܝܘܬܐ f. *Chaldaean knowledge* i.e. *astronomy, astrology; the Chaldaean language.*

ܟܠܝܠܐ pl. ܟܠܝ̈ܠܐ m. *a tiara, mitre;* ܟܠܝܠܐ ܕܡܟܠܠ ܪܫܗ ܕܟܗܢܐ *the mitre which crowns a priest.*

ܟܠܝܬܐ m. κάλαθος, *a bowl.*

ܟܠܝܢܐ, ܟܠܝܢܝܐ rt. ܟܠܐ. *hindering, preventive, prohibitive;* ܐܚܝܢܘܬܐ ܟܠܝܢܝܬܐ *kinship within prohibited degrees.*

ܟܠܝܘ, ܟܠܝܘܬܐ rt. ܟܠܐ. f. *hindrance, impediment;* ܕܠܐ ܟܠܝܘ *unhindered, without let* or *hindrance.*

ܟܠܝܘܢܝ f. χελώνη, *a tortoise* (milit.).

ܟܠܝܘܬܢܝܬܐ pl. ܢ̈ܝܬܐ f. *anemone coronaria, colchicum autumnale, meadow saffron.*

ܟܠܝܘܣܝܬܐ pl. ܟܠܝܘܣܝ̈ܬܐ f. *wild roses.*

ܟܠܝܪܘܢ or ܟܠܝܪܘܢ m. *the chin.*

ܟܠܝܓܪܐܦܐ or ܟܠܝܓܪܦܐ a corruption of ܟܪܛܘܠܪܐ *a secretary.*

ܟܘܠܝ; see ܟܘܠܝ *bile.*

ܟܠܝܠ, ܟܠܝܠܐ pl. ̈ܠܐ rt. ܟܠܠ. m. *a) a crown, garland, chaplet; a circle* or *chaplet of gold* opp. ܬܐܓܐ *a diadem; a mitre, turban; the rim* or *border* of a table, chest, ark; *the finishing, completion* of a building; ܚܘܠ ܟܠܝܠܐ ܕܥܡܕ̈ܐ *the laying aside of the crowns of the baptized* after the octave of their baptism; ܟܠܝܠܐ ܕܡܟܝܪܘܬܐ *the crown of betrothal;* ܚܕܘܬ ܟܠܝܠܐ ܘܟܠܝ̈ܠܐ *a wedding, the nuptial rite;* ܟܠܝܠܐ ܕܣܦܪܐ *the tonsure;* ܟܠܝܠ ܙܟܘܬܐ *the crown of victory;* ܩܒܠ ܟܠܝܠ ܟܠܝܠܐ ܕܣܗܕܘܬܐ *he received the crown of martyrdom. b) a circle, company,* e.g. ܕܓܡܝܪ̈ܐ *of the perfect;* ܕܬܠܡܝ̈ܕܐ *of the disciples. c)* astron. ܟܠܝܠܐ ܓܪܒܝܝܐ—ܬܝܡܢܝܐ *the Corona Borealis, Australis;* ܡܐ ܕܥܪܒ ܟܠܝܠܐ *when the Corona has set;* ܟܠܝܠ ܡܠܘܫܐ *the circle of the Zodiac.*

ܟܠܝܠܢܝܐ rt. ܟܠܠ. adj. *coronal, of* or *belonging to a crown* or *to the crown of the head.*

ܟܠܝܡܘܢ *the ichneumon.*

ܟܠܝܢ, ܟܠܝܢܐ rt. ܟܠܐ. m. *a hindrance, stay, let, impediment, prohibition;* ܕܠܐ ܟܠܝܢ *unhindered, unstayed;* eccles. *a prohibition, suspension,* e.g. ܡܢ ܬܫܡܫܬܐ *from administering Divine service; excommunication.*

ܟܠܝܦܐ pl. ܟܠܝ̈ܦܐ Ar. m. *the Khalif,* vicegerent of the Prophet Mohammed.

ܟܠܝܦܘܬܐ f. *the Khaliphate, empire of the Khalifs.*

ܟܠܝܬܐ rt. ܟܠܐ. f. *restraint, hindrance, obstacle;* ܠܝܬ ܠܢ ܟܠܝܬܐ *nothing hinders us;* ܡܢܘ ܟܠܝܬܐ? *what prevents us? what objection is there?* ܕܠܐ ܟܠܝܬܐ *unhindered, finding no obstacle;* ܟܠܝܬܐ ܒܝܕܟ ܗܝ *it depends only on you.*

ܟܠܟܐ pl. ̈ܐ Ar. *a raft;* metaph. *a floating mass of ice.*

ܟܠܠ Pael of ܟܠ.

ܟܠܠ, ܟܠܠܐ pl. of ܟܠܬܐ; ܟܠܠ pl. of ܟܠܬܐ.

ܟܠܡܘܣ, ܟܠܡܘܣ, ܟܠܡܘܕܐ, ܟܠܡܘܕܝܢ or ܟܠܡܘܣ, ܟܠܡܘܣ, &c., χλαμύς, χλαμύδα, dim. χλαμύδιον, f. *a mantle, robe.*

ܟܠܡܢܛܝܣ; see ܩܠܡܢܛܝܣ.

ܟܠܩܝܕܘܢܝܐ, ܢܝܬܐ from ܟܠܩܝܕܘܢ *Chalcedon* in Bithynia, eccles. *an adherent of the Council of Chalcedon, a Dyophysite, Melchite;* ܦܠܓܘܬܐ ܟܠܩܝܕܘܢܝܬܐ *the schism of Chalcedon.*

ܟܠܫ denom. verb Pael conj. from ܟܠܫܐ. *to calcine, to whitewash;* ܐܣܝܬܐ ܡܟܠܫܬܐ *a whitewashed wall.* Ethpa. ܐܬܟܠܫ *to be calcined.* Aph. ܐܟܠܫ *to fill* or *cover with chalk, fill with chalk* or *lime; to plaster, whitewash;* ܩܒܪ̈ܐ ܡܟܠܫܐ or ܡܟܠܫܝܢ *whited sepulchres.*

ܟܠܫ, ܟܠܫܐ m. *lime, quicklime;* ܟܠܫ ܒܝܥ̈ܐ *powdered eggshell.*

ܟܠܬܐ pl. ܟܠܘܬܐ, ܟܠܬ̈ܐ rt. ܟܠܠ. f. *a) a bride;* ܟܠܬܐ ܡܠܟܬܐ *the royal bride;* ܟܠܬܐ ܕܢܘܗܪܐ *the bride of light. b) a daughter-in-law. c) the foreskin.*

ܟܠܬܐ pl. ܟܠ̈ܠܐ rt. ܟܠܠ. f. *a) a canopy, bed-curtain, mosquito-net. b) a piece of linen, kerchief, veil* esp. *the covering* or *pall* over the Eucharistic elements; *a linen wrap* or *covering. c) anemone coronaria,* cf. ܟܠܝܘܬܢܝܬܐ.

ܟܡܐ adv. *how much, how many;* ܟܡܐ ܕ *as much, as many, as far, as long;* ܟܡܐ ܕܡܫܟܚܝܢ *as much as they can;* ܟܡܐ ܙܒܢܝܢ *how many times?* ܟܡܐ ܕܐܝܬ *so long as;* ܟܡܐ ܕܚܝ *so long as he lives;* ܟܡܐ ܠܟܡܐ *how much more?* ܚܕܐ ܠܟܡܐ or ܡܢ ܟܡܐ *seldom, once in a while, sometimes;* ܒܟܡܐ *for how much?* ܒܟܡܐ ܐܝܟܢ *in how many ways?*

ܟܡܐܢܐ pl. ܼ̈ rt. ܟܡܢ. m. *lying-in-wait, lurking-place, lair; an ambush;* with ܣܡ or ܣܝܡ *to set ambushes;* metaph. *wiles, subtilty;* ܒܟܡܐܢܝܟ *by thy evil wiles;* ܒܟܡܐܢܐ *secretly, insidiously.*

ܟܡܐܢܐܝܬ rt. ܟܡܢ. adv. *insidiously, treacherously.*

ܟܡܫ pass. part. ܟܡܝܫ. *to fade, be flabby.*

ܟܡܗ fut. ܢܟܡܗ. *to be blinded, befogged, confused,* usually metaph. ETHPE. ܐܬܟܡܗ the same. PA. ܟܡܗ *to blind;* ܚܛܝܬܐ ܡܟܡܗܐ ܠܢܦܫܐ *sin blinds the soul.* APH. ܐܟܡܗ *to blind, darken, surround with darkness;* ܠܥܠܡܐ ܕܡܟܡܗ ܠܢ *the world which blinds us.* DERIVATIVES, ܟܡܗܐ, ܟܡܗܘܬܐ, ܡܟܡܗܢܐܝܬ.

ܟܡܗ, ܟܡܗܐ or ܟܡܝܗܐ pl. m. ܟܡܗܐ f. ܟܡܗܬܐ rt. ܟܡܗ. *blind, obscured, dark, dim.*

ܟܡܗܘܬܐ rt. ܟܡܗ. f. *blindness, darkness, obscurity, shadow;* ܟܡܗܘܬ ܠܒܐ *dullness of heart.*

ܟܡܘܢܐ or ܟܘܡܢܐ m. *cummin.*

ܟܡܝܘܬܐ from ܟܡܐ. f. *quantity, amount, sum; number; size, length;* ܟܡܝܘܬܐ ܕܚܝܐ *the average length of life;* ܐܝܟ ܡܨܥܝܘܬܐ ܕܟܡܝܘܬܐ *of small size;* ܒܟܡܝܘܬܐ ܙܥܘܪܬܐ *eighty men in all;* ܝܗܒ ܟܡܝܘܬܐ ܕܙܘܙܐ *he gave a sum of money.*

ܟܡܟܐ pl. ܼ̈ m. *a cake.*

ܟܡܝܪܐܝܬ rt. ܟܡܪ. adv. *mournfully, sorrowfully, sadly.*

ܟܡܝܪܘܬܐ, ܟܡܝܪܘܬܐ or ܟܡܝܪܘܬܐ rt. ܟܡܪ. f. *sadness, mournfulness, sorrow.*

ܟܡܝܠܐ or ܟܝܡܝܠܐ *alchemy;* ܥܒܕܝ ܟܝܡܝܠܐ *alchemists, chemists.*

ܟܡܐܠܐܘܢ or ܟܡܐܠܐܘܢ, ܟܡܐܠܝܘܢ, ܟܡܐܠܝܘܢ *the chameleon.*

ܟܡܢ fut. ܢܟܡܘܢ, act. part. ܟܡܢ, ܟܡܢܐ, pass. part. ܟܡܝܢ, ܟܡܝܢܐ and ܟܡܝܢ, ܟܡܝܢܐ. *to lay wait, lie in wait, in ambush; to be full of wiles and deceits;* ܟܡܢ ܢܟܠܐ ܒܠܒܐ *to plot secretly;* ܟܡܢ ܟܡܐܢܐ ܒܠܒܗ *in his heart lurks treachery;* ܚܛܝܬܐ ܟܡܝܢܐ ܒܗܕܡܝܢ ܕܦܓܪܐ *sin lies in wait in our bodily members;* ܐܝܟ ܕܒܐ ܟܡܝܢܐ *a bear lying-in-wait;* ܢܘܪܐ ܟܡܝܢܐ ܠܐܝܠܢܐ *fire lies in wait for the trees.* ETHPE. ܐܬܟܡܢ *to lay wait, lie in wait;* ܐܬܟܡܢܘ ܥܠ ܡܕܝܢܬܐ *they laid an ambush against the city;* metaph. *to act perfidiously.* PA. ܟܡܢ *to devise plots, lay snares;* ܟܡܢ ܥܠ ܕܠܐ ܕܝܠܗ *he lay in wait for what did not belong to him.* ETHPA. ܐܬܟܡܢ intensive of ETHPE. APH. ܐܟܡܢ usually with ܟܡܐܢܐ and with ܠ or ܥܠ *to set an ambush, lay snares, act treacherously.* DERIVATIVES, ܟܡܐܢܐ, ܟܡܐܢܐܝܬ.

ܟܡܢܝܐ adj. from ܟܡܐ. *relating to quantity.*

ܟܡܫ fut. ܢܟܡܘܫ, act. part. ܟܡܫ. *to let fade or languish, to languish, wither* said of fruit, flesh, the soul, &c.

ܟܡܪ fut. ܢܟܡܪ, pass. part. ܟܡܝܪ, ܐ, ܬܐ. *to be sad.* Part. adj. *gloomy, dark, black* as ܥܢܢܐ *a cloud,* ܢܚܠܐ *a valley,* ܠܠܝܐ *the night,* ܓܘܢܐ *the complexion;* metaph. *gloomy, sad, mournful;* ܐܣܟܡܐ ܟܡܝܪܬܐ *a mourning garment;* ܝܪܚܐ ܟܡܝܪܐ *the gloomy month* of February; ܠܒܘܝܐܐ ܕܟܡܝܪܐ *for the comfort of the sad.* ETHPE. ܐܬܟܡܪ *to be sad, to mourn.* APH. ܐܟܡܪ *to cast a gloom, sadden, make mournful;* ܫܒܛ ܟܡܝܪܐ ܕܡܟܡܪ ܟܠ *gloomy February which casts a gloom on all.* DERIVATIVES, ܟܘܡܪܐ, ܟܡܝܪܘܬܐ, ܟܡܝܪܐܝܬ, ܟܘܡܪܐ, ܟܘܡܪܘܬܐ, ܟܘܡܪܬܐ, ܡܟܡܪܢܐ.

ܟܡܫ pass. part. ܟܡܝܫܐ. *to dry up, shrivel* from drought as grapes. DERIVATIVE, ܟܡܫܘܢܐ.

ܟܡܫܘܢܐ pl. ܼ̈ rt. ܟܡܫ. m. *a grape stone;* ܟܡܫܘܢܐ ܕܩܫܡܫܐ *the stones of raisins; shrivelled grapes* which fall from the cluster.

ܟܘܡܬܪܐ pl. ܼ̈ also ܟܘܡܬܪܐ m. *a pear.*

ܟܡ sometimes ܟܝܡ and for the sake of metre ܐܟܡ *and so, and then, then, next, afterward; soon, shortly, hereupon.*

ܟܢܐ m. *a*) *the base, support, fundament; a candlestick;* ܟܢܐ ܕܬܠܬܐ ܪܓܠܝܢ *a tripod;* ܟܢܐ ܕܟܝܘܪܐ *the base of the laver;* ܡܓܕܠܐ ܡܨܒܬܐ ܟܢܢܐ *a tower with an ornamented base.* *b*) *the stem* of a tree, *stalk, root* of a plant; ܥܒܕ ܟܢܐ *to strike root;* metaph. ܠܪܓܠܝ ܟܢܐ *I set my feet firmly.* *c*) geom. *the base* of a cylinder.

ܟܢܐ PA. ܟܢܝ, fut. ܢܟܢܐ. *to give a name or title, to name, surname, nickname, call;* with ܥܠ *to name it after him;* ܐܣܪܗ—ܘܟܢܝܗ ܥܠ ܫܡܗ *he ordained him by the name of . . ., ordained* and gave him the name; ܟܰܢܺܝܗ̇ ܠܟܬܳܒܳܐ he named the book, gave a title to the book; ܐܶܢ ܐ̱ܢܳܫ ܢܟܰܢܶܝܘܗܝ ܪܰܒܳܐ if any one will call him a teacher, count him among the doctors. Ethpa. ܐܶܬܟܰܢܺܝ to be named, surnamed, called; ܝܰܘܣܶܦ ܕܶܐܬܟܰܢܺܝ ܒܰܪܢܰܒܳܐ Joseph who was called Barnabas; ܥܰܠ ܫܡܶܗ ܐܶܬܟܰܢܺܝ it was named after him. Derivatives, ܟܘܢܳܝܳܐ, ܡܟܰܢܝܳܢܳܐ.

ܟܺܐܢܳܐܺܝܬ for ܟܺܐܢܳܐܺܝܬ. adv. justly.

ܟܳܢܽܘܢ m. the name of two months, ܟܳܢܽܘܢ ܩܕܺܝܡ or ܩܰܕܡܳܝܳܐ First Conun, December; ܟܳܢܽܘܢ ܒ or ܐ̱ܚܪܳܝ Later Conun, January.

ܟܳܢܽܘܢܳܝܳܐ adj. from ܩܳܢܽܘܢܳܐ II. regular, exact.

ܟܳܢܽܘܢܺܝܬܳܐ pl. ܟܳܢܽܘܢܝܳܬܳܐ f. I. the palm of the hand, sole of the foot; ܓܰܘ ܟܳܢܽܘܢܺܝܬܶܗ within his hand, upon his palm. II. κανών, a rule for ruling lines or measuring, a plumb-line.

ܟܢܽܘܫܽܘܬܳܐ rt. ܟܢܫ. f. gathering together; ܟܢܽܘܫܽܘܬܳܐ ܕܥܰܡܡܶܐ the nations gathered together.

ܟܢܽܘܫܝܳܐ pl. ܟܢܽܘܫܝܶܐ rt. ܟܢܫ. m. a) a convocation, congregation, assembly; with ܟܢܰܫ to call together, assemble a multitude; ܟܢܽܘܫܝܶܐ ܕܬܶܫܡܶܫܬܳܐ congregations for Divine worship, ܒܶܝܬ ܟܢܽܘܫܝܶܐ places of meeting for worship. b) a council, synod; gram. a plural, plural form, ܫܰܪܒܳܬܳܐ ܟܢܽܘܫܝܳܗ̇ ܕܫܰܪܒܬܳܐ, ܫܰܪܒܳܬܳܐ is the plural of ܫܰܪܒܬܳܐ.

ܟܢܽܘܫܬܳܐ perh. contr. of ܟܽܘܢܳܫܬܳܐ m. the navel.

ܟܢܽܘܫܬܳܐ pl. ܟܢܽܘܫܳܬܳܐ, ܟܢܽܘܫܳܢ or ܟܢܽܘܫܳܢ, ܟܢܽܘܫܳܬܳܐ rt. ܟܢܫ. f. a) a coming or meeting together, a congregation, a synagogue, also ܒܶܝܬ ܟܢܽܘܫܬܳܐ; sometimes the Jews opp. ܥܺܕܬܳܐ the Christians. b) a choir, company, congregation, church.

ܟܺܐܢܽܘܬܳܐ usually ܟܺܐܢܽܘܬܳܐ justice, &c.; ܒܟܺܐܢܽܘܬܳܐ justly.

ܟܰܢܺܝ Pael conj. of ܟܢܐ.

ܟܢܺܝܪܳܐ, ܟܢܺܝܪܬܳܐ f. also ܟܢܺܝܪܳܐ, ܟܢܺܝܪܬܳܐ f. a cake.

ܟܢܺܝܟܳܐܺܝܬ rt. ܟܢܟ. adv. modestly, seriously, discreetly.

ܟܢܺܝܟܽܘܬܳܐ rt. ܟܢܟ. f. dignity, self-respect, prudence, modesty; dignified manners, grave or reverend behaviour.

ܟܢܺܝܫܳܐܺܝܬ rt. ܟܢܫ. adv. together, taken together, jointly, with one accord, in common, universally, generally; ܢܳܡܽܘܣܳܐ ܩܳܪܶܐ ܟܢܺܝܫܳܐܺܝܬ ܠܟܬܳܒܶܐ ܟܽܠܗܽܘܢ he calls the scriptures in general the law, he speaks of the law meaning the scriptures generally.

ܟܢܺܝܫܽܘܬܳܐ rt. ܟܢܫ. f. a gathering or coming together, flocking together, assembling, joining together, union, conjunction, a collection, summary; ܟܢܺܝܫܽܘܬܳܐ ܕܡܰܝܳܐ a gathering flood, a lake; ܟܢܺܝܫܽܘܬܳܐ ܠܡܰܕܥܳܐ ܡܶܢ ܦܽܘܚܳܪܳܐ a recalling of the mind from wandering thoughts, recollection; the conjunction or being present of all the essential parts of a sacrament; arith. the sum, total; ܠܰܟܢܺܝܫܽܘ together, added together.

ܟܢܰܟ Pe. only part. adj. ܟܢܺܝܟ, ܟܢܺܝܟܳܐ, ܟܢܺܝܟܬܳܐ. grave, dignified, solemn, venerable, reverend; moderate, modest, chaste, gentle; ܟܢܺܝܟ ܚܶܙܘܳܐ of venerable appearance; ܕܰܝܪܳܝܶܐ ܟܢܺܝܟܶܐ reverend monks; ܟܢܺܝܟܳܬܳܐ chaste or reverend women, recluses; ܦܰܩܰܥܬܳܐ ܟܢܺܝܟܳܐ ܥܳܒܕܳܐ the bee carries on her modest labour. Ethpe. ܐܶܬܟܢܶܟ to bear oneself with dignity, behave seriously, modestly; to give serious attention; ܐܶܬܟܢܶܟ ܦܺܝܠܳܣܳܘܦܳܐܺܝܬ he bore himself gravely as a philosopher. Pa. ܟܰܢܶܟ to render honourable; to praise; to recall to serious or dignified behaviour; ܡܟܰܢܶܟ ܪܶܓܬܳܐ he moderates desire; pass. part. dignified, honourable, venerable, adorned; ܡܟܰܢܟܳܐ ܒܣܰܝܒܽܘܬܳܐ ܡܟܰܢܟܺܝܢ venerable from great age. Ethpa. ܐܶܬܟܰܢܶܟ to bear oneself with dignity; to be honoured; to glory in, boast of. Derivatives, ܟܢܺܝܟܳܐܺܝܬ, ܟܢܺܝܟܽܘܬܳܐ, ܟܘܢܳܟܳܐ, ܡܟܰܢܟܳܢܳܐ.

ܟܢܳܟܬܳܐ f. a ball of unspun flax or cotton, clew of cotton.

ܟܰܢܶܦ Pael conj. and ܐܰܟܢܶܦ Aphel conj. denom. verb from ܟܶܢܦܳܐ. to gather under the wings.

ܟܢܰܦ, ܟܶܢܦܳܐ pl. ܟܶܢܦܶܐ and ܟܶܢܦܳܬܳܐ f. the side, edge, outer part, esp. a) a wing; ܒܰܪ ܟܶܢܦܳܐ a winged creature, a bird; ܟܶܢܦܰܝ ܡܰܕܒܪܳܝܬܳܐ the ostrich; metaph. covering, overshadowing, protection; ܛܶܠܳܠܳܐ ܕܟܶܢܦܶܐ the overshadowing of the wings. b) the arms, lap, bosom; ܫܩܰܠܬܶܗ ܒܟܶܢܦܰܝܗ̇ she took her son in her arms; ܟܶܢܦܳܬܳܐ infants-in-arms. c) the border, flap, skirt, hem of a garment; ܬܚܶܝܬ ܟܶܢܦܶܗ under his cloak; metaph. ܟܶܢܦܰܝܗ̇ ܕܐܰܪܥܳܐ the ends of the earth; ܟܶܢܦܳܐ ܕܝܰܡܳܐ a bay of the sea; ܟܶܢܦܳܬܳܐ ܕܛܽܘܪܳܐ the sides, stretches or crests of a mountain. d) a pinnacle;

the side or *horn* of an altar; *the arm* of a cross; *a branch; the wing* of an army. Derivatives, verb ܟܢܦ, ܡܟܢܦܢܘܬܐ.

ܟܢܪ, ܟܢܪܐ or ܟܢܳܪܐ pl. ܐ̈ m. *a harp, cithera, cithern, lyre;* ܟܢܪܐ ܕܫܒܥ ܢܥܡ̈ܬܗ *a seven-stringed harp;* ܕܥܣܪܐ ellipt. *ten-stringed;* ܢܥܡ̈ܐ ܣܓܝ̈ܐ *many stringed;* metaph. ܢܦܫܐ ܘܗܘܢܐ ܘܟܢܪܗܘܢ ܦܓܪܐ *the soul and mind and their harp the body;* S. Ephrem is called ܟܢܪܐ ܕܪܘܚܐ ܕܩܘܕܫܐ *the cithern of the Holy Spirit;* ܟܢ̈ܪܐ ܡܫܒܚ̈ܢܐ *harps sounding forth praise.*

ܟܢܪܐ or ܟܢܳܪܐ pl. ܐ̈ m. *the service tree, sorbus domestica.*

ܟܢܪܘܣܛܐ m. *a harpist.*

ܟܢܫ fut. ܢܟܢܘܫ, act. part. ܟܳܢܶܫ, ܟܳܢܫܐ, pass. part. ܟܢܝܫ, ܟܢܝܫܐ. *to gather together, collect;* ܐܝܟ ܬܪܢܓܘܠܬܐ ܕܟܢܫܐ ܦܪ̈ܘܓܝܗ ܬܚܝܬ ܓܦ̈ܝܗ *a hen gathering her chickens under her wings;* ܕܗܒܐ ܗܘ ܕܟܢܫܬ *the gold which you have brought together, amassed;* ܚܪܫܐ ܕܟܢܫ ܟܢܫܐ *a sorcerer, mountebank who collects a crowd;* ܟܢܫܗ ܒܡܐܡܪܐ ܚܕ *he gathered into one treatise, epitomized.* Special meanings, *a*) with ܠܘܬ ܐܒܗ̈ܘܗܝ *to gather to his fathers, to cause to die;* ܐܠܗܐ ܟܢܫܗ ܠܘܬܗ *God took him to Himself;* also *to lay out* for burial, ܟܢܫܘܗ ܘܩܒܪܘܗ *they laid her body out and buried her.* *b*) *to bring together, assemble;* ܠܥܕܬܐ ܟܢܫܝܢ ܗܘܘ *they assembled the church;* ܟܢܝܫܐ ܗܘܐ ܣܘܢܗܕܘܣ *the Council was assembled;* ܡܢܘ ܡܢܟܘܢ ܕܟܢܝܫܝܢ *which of you here assembled?* *c*) *to gather* or *collect* one's senses; *to hold oneself in;* ܟܢܘܫ ܢܦܫܟ ܙܥܘܪ *recollect yourself;* ܗܘܢܐ ܕܟܢܝܫ *a recollected mind,* ellipt. *recollected, contemplative.* *d*) *to curdle, thicken;* ܪܛܝܒܘܬܗ ܕܚܠܒܐ ܟܢܫܐ ܚܠܒܘܬܗ *the liquidness of milk thickens.* *e*) *to sweep.* *f*) with ܡ̈ܝܐ *to be dropsical, have the dropsy;* ܓܒܪܐ ܕܟܢܝܫ ܗܘܐ ܡ̈ܝܐ *a man suffering from dropsy.* *g*) metaph. of time or number *to amount, come to;* ܟܢܫܝܢ ܫܢ̈ܝܐ ܡܢ—ܠ or ܕܡܛܝܢ *the number of years from—to—are* so many. Ethpe. ܐܬܟܢܫ and Ethpa. ܐܬܟܢܰܫ *a*) *to be gathered* ܠܘܬ ܥܡܗ *to his people,* ܠܩܒܪܐ *to the grave* or ellipt. *to die;* ܐܬܟܢܫ ܡܢ ܥܠܡܐ *he was taken away from the world;* ܐܬܟܢܫܘ ܒܫܠܡܐ *they departed in peace.* *b*) *to come together, assemble* esp. as a synod; ܒܥܕ̈ܬܐ *in the churches;* ܐܬܟܢܫܬ ܟܠܗ ܡܕܝܢܬܐ *the whole city came together;* ܐܬܟܢܫܘ ܒܣܠܝܘܩ *they held a synod in Seleucia;* ܐܬܟܢܫܘ ܥܠ ܗܕܐ *they agreed on this point, met each other's wishes.* *c*) with ܠܘܬ ܢܦܫܗ *to recollect one's thoughts, enter into oneself, be recollected;* ܡܢ ܛܘܥܝܝ ܐܬܟܢܫ ܗܘܐ *he had returned from error to a right mind.* *d*) in reasoning, ܡܬܟܢܫ ܕ or ܡܬܟܢܫܐ *it follows, results, we gather that ....* *e*) arith. *to be computed, reckoned, to result, amount, come to,* ܡܢܝܢܐ ܕܡܬܟܢܫ ܡܢ ܣܘܓܐܐ *the number which results from multiplication.* *f*) astron. *to meet, be in conjunction.* *g*) *to be collected, compiled.* *h*) gram. *to form a plural, be in the plural;* ܠܐ ܡܬܟܢܫܝܢ *they have no plural form.* *i*) *to be laid waste.* Pael ܟܢܰܫ *to assemble, call together, levy* an army, *convoke* a synod; *to collect* money, tribute, alms; *to bring* or *gather together, acquire; to compile, make a digest, epitomize; to compute, reckon; to gather a conclusion* from an argument, *conclude; to recall, recollect, summon* the thoughts, *collect* the mind; ܦܫܛ ܐܝܕܗ ܘܡܟܢܫ *he stretches out his hand and draws it back;* ܐܟܣܢܝܐ ܗܘܝܬ ܘܟܢܫܬܘܢܢܝ *I was a stranger and ye took me in;* ܟܢܫ ܠܚܕܝܘܬܐ Christ *brought together into oneness* the Godhead and Manhood; ܕܡܟܢܫܝܢ ܒܡܪܢ ܡܪܢ *which are brought together in the Lord our Lord;* ܢܘܪܐ ܡܟܢܫܬܐ *a heaped-up pyre;* ܠܟܣܝܩܘܢ ܡܟܢܫܐ *a lexicon compiled from others;* ܡܟܢܫܐ ܠܟܬܘܒܐ *epitomized;* ܗܘܢܐ ܡܟܢܫܐ *a recollected* or *thoughtful mind.* Derivatives, ܟܢܘܫܐ, ܟܢܘܫܘܬܐ, ܟܢܘܫܝܐ, ܟܢܘܫܬܐ, ܟܢܫܐ, ܟܢܫܬܐ, ܟܢܝܫܐ, ܟܢܝܫܘܬܐ, ܟܢܫܬܐ, ܡܟܢܫܢܐ, ܡܬܟܢܫܢܐ, ܡܟܢܫܢܘܬܐ, ܡܬܟܢܫܢܘܬܐ.

ܟܢܫ, ܟܢܫܐ pl. ܟܢܫ̈ܐ, ܟܢܫ̈ܝܢ, rt. ܟܢܫ. m. *a gathering together* of waters; *multitude* of people; *a congregation, assembly; a company* of monks, pupils, *a school;* ܒܟܢܫܐ *together, in common;* gram. *the plural number.*

ܟܢܫ, ܟܢܫܐ with ܡ̈ܝܐ *dropsy;* in the lexx. *sweeping; assembling; death.*

ܟܢܫܬܐ rt. ܟܢܫ. f. *sweepings, rubbish;* ܟܢܫܬܐ ܕܥܦܪܐ *dust-swept together;* in the lexx. *a ball of cotton.*

ܟܢܬܐ, ܟܢܬܐ also ܟܢܘܬܐ pl. ܟܢܘܬܐ m. and f. *a companion, fellow-servant, colleague;* ܟܢܘܬܝ *my fellow-servants;* ܟܗܢܐ ܟܢܬܗ *his fellow-priest; an opponent* in an argument; metaph. *like, similar, equal;* ܪܒܢܐ ܟܢܬܗ ܕܪܗܘܡܐ *Ravenna the fellow of Rome;* wood is the ܟܢܬܗ of fire i. e. suits with its nature; ܟܢܘܬܐ ܐܝܬܝܟܘܢ ܕܒܥܝܪܐ *you are like beasts.*

ܟܢܬܐ or ܟܢܬܐ f. *a*) same as ܟܢܐ. *b*) *a basket of fruit.*

ܟܣ fut. ܢܟܘܣ and ܢܟܣ, act. part. ܟܐܣ, pass. part. ܟܣܝܣ, ܟܣܝܣܐ, ܟܣܝܣܬܐ. *a*) *to break in pieces, munch, crunch;* ܟܐܣ ܣܥܪܐ *munching dry barley;* ܐܝܠܢܐ ܥܩܝܪܐ ܘܟܣܝܣ *an uprooted and broken tree. b*) *to blame, put to shame.* Ethpe. ܐܬܟܣܣ *to be reproved, blamed, found guilty, proved to be in the wrong; convicted* ܒܗܪܛܩܘܬܐ *of heresy;* ܒܥܘܠܐ ܣܓܝܐܐ *of much wickedness;* ܐܬܟܣܣ ܗܘܐ ܕ *he was blamed for, shown to be wrong in;* ܡܢ ܗܢܐ—ܥܘܢܝܐ ܟܕܒܢܐ ܐܝܟ ܗܠܝܢ ܡܬܟܣܣܢ *by this text such wicked opinions are refuted.* Pa. ܟܣܣ *to blame, reprove.* Aph. ܐܟܣ *to show to be wrong, rebuke, reprove, convince, confute,* with ܠ or pers. affix and with ܒ, ܡܢ or ܥܠ of the cause; ܢܟܣܝܘܗܝ ܒܡܠܘܗܝ *he will rebuke his words, reprove him for what he has said;* ܠܟܐܢܐ ܢܟܣ ܠܘܩܕܡ *he will reprove the righteous first;* ܢܟܣ ܠܫܒܘܩܝ ܗܝܡܢܘܬܐ ܐܝܟ ܓܝܣܐ *let us reprove forsakers of the faith as being like robbers.* Ettaph. ܐܬܬܟܣ with ܡܢ *to be reproved, shown his faults, convinced of sin.* Derivatives, ܡܟܣܢܐ, ܡܟܣܢܐܝܬ, ܡܟܣܢܘܬܐ.

ܟܣ, ܟܣܐ pl. ܟܣܐ m. *a cup, beaker, drinking-vessel;* ܟܣܐ ܕܡܝܐ ܩܪܝܪܐ *a cup of cold water;* esp. *the Eucharistic chalice;* ܟܣܐ ܕܚܠܛ ܡܢ ܚܡܪܐ ܘܡܝܐ *the mixed cup;* ܩܕܫ ܥܠ ܟܣܐ *he consecrated the cup,* i. e. *celebrated Holy Communion.*

ܟܣܐ fut. ܢܟܣܐ, act. part. ܟܣܐ, ܟܣܝܐ, pass. part. ܟܣܐ, ܟܣܝܐ, ܟܣܝܬܐ. *to cover, veil, conceal, keep secret.* Pass. part. *concealed, hidden, secret, occult* often opp. ܓܠܝܐ *open, uncovered;* ܓܘܝܐ ܗܕܡܐ ܟܣܝܐ *the internal organs;* but ܥܝܢܐ ܟܣܝܬܐ ܕܪܥܝܢܐ *the inner sight of the mind* opp. ܥܝܢܐ ܒܪܝܬܐ *the outer bodily eyes; ineffable, mystic;* ܐܝܬ ܗܘ ܕܟܣܐ ܒܟܠܗܘܢ ܒܥܒܕܘܗܝ ܘܓܠܐ ܒܡܥܒܕܢܘܬܗܘܢ *Thou that art secret in all Thy works and manifest in their workings;* ܚܬܡܐ ܟܣܝܐ ܕܪܘܚܐ *the mystic seal of the Spirit;* ܟܣܝܬܐ ܕܐܠܗܐ *the secrets of God, the ineffable blessings of God.* Pa. ܟܣܝ *a*) *to cover, wrap up, clothe, robe;* ܥܪܛܠܝܐ ܗܘܝܬ ܘܟܣܝܬܘܢܢܝ *I was naked and ye clothed me;* ܟܣܝܬ ܐܦܝܗ̈ ܒܥܦܝܬܐ *she covered her face with a veil;* metaph. gusts arose ܕܢܟܣܘܢܗ ܠܐܠܦܐ *to overwhelm the ship. b*) *to hide, conceal; to cover, condone;* ܠܐ ܟܣܝܬ ܗܕܐ ܡܢܢ *thou hast not concealed this from us. c*) *to stop up* a fountain. *d*) *to protect;* ܟܣܝ ܡܫܪܝܬܐ ܒܪܘܡܚܐ *he protected the camps with* his *spear.* Pass. part. *a*) *covered, robed, clothed* ܣܩܐ *in sackcloth;* ܐܪܓܘܢܐ *in purple;* ܡܟܣܝ ܪܫܐ *with covered head. b*) *hidden, secret;* ܠܥܠ ܡܢ ܒܢܝ ܐܢܫܐ ܡܟܣܝܐ ܡܢܗܘܢ *beyond human beings, hidden from them;* ܐܪ̈ܙܐ ܡܟܣܝܐ *hidden mysteries. c*) *closed, shut;* ܦܘܡܐ ܡܟܣܝܐ *a closed mouth.* Ethpa. ܐܬܟܣܝ *to be covered, clothed, robed, arrayed;* ܐܬܟܣܝ ܣܩܐ *he was clothed in sackcloth; to be overwhelmed* by waves, floods, earth; ܐܬܟܣܝܬ ܐܪܥܐ ܥܠܝܗܘܢ *the earth closed upon them; to be hidden* ܡܢ ܥܝܢܐ *from sight; to be passed over, condoned* of sin; *to be sheltered, protected;* ܒܢ̈ܝܢܫܐ ܒܛܠܠܐ ܕܟܢܦܝܟ ܢܬܟܣܘܢ *men shall find shelter under the shadow of Thy wings.* Derivatives, ܟܣܝܐ, ܟܣܝܐܝܬ, ܟܣܝܐ, ܟܣܐ, ܟܣܝܐ, ܟܣܝܘܬܐ, ܡܟܣܝܢܘܬܐ, ܡܟܣܝܢܐܝܬ, ܬܟܣܝܬܐ.

ܟܣܝܐ pl. of ܟܣܝܬܐ.

ܟܣܐܐ, ܟܣܐܐ or ܟܣܐ pl. ܟܣܐܐ m. *time of full moon, the fifteenth day of the month;* ܟܣܐܐ ܣܗܪܐ ܒܟܣܐܐ ܗ. ܒܡܫܠܡܢܘܬܗ *full moons; the moon at the full i. e. in its fullness;* ܡܢ ܟܣܐܗ *from the middle of the month;* ܒܟܣܐܗ ܕܬܡܘܙ ܘܕܐܝܠܘܠ *at July* or *September full moon.*

ܟܣܘܚܐ pl. ܐ̈ rt. ܟܣܚ. m. *a pruner.*

ܟܣܛܘܣ, ܟܣܛܘܣܘ m. ξυστός, *a porch supported on pillars; a balcony, an upper room.*

ܟܣܘܪܐ m. *a huckster, costermonger.*

ܟܣܚ fut. ܢܟܣܘܚ, pass. part. ܟܣܝܚ, ܟܣܝܚܐ, ܟܣܝܚܬܐ. *to prune* esp. a vine, *to lop;* ܐܝܠܢܐ ܕܟܣܝܚܝܢ ܫܒܫܒܗܘܢ *trees with their shoots lopped off.* Ethpe. ܐܬܟܣܚ *to be pruned;* ܐܝܟ ܟܪܡܐ ܕܡܬܟܣܚ *as a pruned vineyard.*

Pa. ܦܰܣܶܩ, ܡܦܰܣܩܳܐ ܢܚܺܝܪ̈ܶܐ perh. *flatnosed* as if with lopped-off nostrils. Derivatives, ܦܣܩܢܐ, ܦܣܩܐ, ܦܣܩܬܐ, ܦܣܩܢܐ.

ܦܳܣܽܘܩܳܐ, ܦܳܣܽܘܩܺܝܬܳܐ rt. ܦܣܩ. *a pruner.*

ܦܣܳܩܳܐ rt. ܦܣܩ. m. *pruning, lopping.*

ܦܶܣܩܳܐ pl. ܦܶܣܩ̈ܶܐ rt. ܦܣܩ. *small seed-bulbs.*

ܦܶܣܝܳܐ rt. ܦܣܐ. m. *hiding, concealment* usually with prep. ܒܦܶܣܝܳܐ *in hiding, in secret, secretly;* ܡܶܢ ܦܶܣܝܳܐ ܠܓܰܠܝܳܐ ܢܺܐܬܶܐ *it shall come forth from obscurity and appear openly.*

ܦܣܳܝܳܐ pl. ܦܣܳܝ̈ܶܐ rt. ܦܣܐ. m. *an outer covering, roof* of the ark, of a tent; *the cover* of a well, *lid* of a pot; ܦܣܳܝ̈ܶܐ ܟܝܳܢܳܝ̈ܶܐ *natural coverings* such as rind, shell, bark; ܐܳܐܰܪ ܕܐܺܝܬܰܘܗܝ ܦܣܳܝܳܐ ܕܥܳܠܡܳܐ *the air which is the outer covering of the world;* ܦܣܳܝܳܐ ܩܕܳܡ ܐܰܪܡܺܝ ܦܽܘܡܶܗ *he drew some covering over his mouth.*

ܦܣܺܝܳܐܺܝܬ rt. ܦܣܐ. adv. *covertly, secretly, obscurely, mysteriously, mystically.*

ܦܣܺܝܽܘܬܳܐ rt. ܦܣܐ. f. *a covering over* or *concealing; that which is concealed* or *unseen; that which really is, within,* opp. ܒܪܳܝܽܘܬܳܐ or ܠܒܰܪܳܝܽܘܬܳܐ *external appearance;* ܦܣܺܝܽܘܬܗܽܘܢ ܕܨܶܒ̈ܘܳܬܳܐ *the true inwardness of things; secrets, mysteries, arcana.*

ܦܣܺܝܢܳܐ, ܦܣܺܝܢܳܢ or ܦܣܺܝܢܽܘܢ f. *a*) ξήριον, *powdered drugs* or *perfumes.* *b*) Ar. *elixir, the philosopher's essence* which would change lead to gold.

ܦܰܣܦܳܣܳܐ or ܦܰܣܦܰܣܳܐ m. *a*) *a basket.* *b*) ܦܰܣܦܳܣ̈ܶܐ ܕܠܶܒ̈ܢܶܐ *wooden moulds for making bricks.*

ܦܣܺܝܣܳܐ m. *plaster.*

ܦܣܢ Ettaphal ܐܶܬܰܦܣܰܢ or ܐܶܬܦܰܣܢܰܢ denom. verb from ξένος, *to travel about; to receive hospitality, be entertained as a guest.* Cf. ܐܶܦܣܢܳܝܳܐ and below.

ܦܶܣܬܳܩܳܐ pl. ܦܶܣܬܳܩ̈ܶܐ m. *fruits* usually *dried* or *preserved fruits* such as *raisins, walnuts, almonds; dessert;* but ܦܶܣܬܳܩ̈ܶܐ ܪܰܛܺܝܒ̈ܶܐ *fresh fruits.*

ܦܶܣܬܳܩܳܐ pl. ܦܶܣܬܳܩ̈ܶܐ m. *coral.*

ܦܣܢܕܘܟܝܢ or ܦܣܢܘܕܘܟܝܢ f. ξενοδοχεῖον, *a guest-house, hospital;* cf. for this and the following ܐܶܦܣܢܕܘܟܝܢ &c.

ܦܣܢܕܘܟܘܣ or ܦܣܢܕܘܟܣ m. ξενοδόχος, *the master of the guests.*

ܦܶܣܬܳܐ f. *a crust of bread.*

ܦܶܣܬܳܐ pl. ܦܶܣܬ̈ܶܐ m. *the sole* of a sandal, shoe, &c.; ܦܶܣܬ̈ܶܐ ܒܠܳܝ̈ܳܬܳܐ *worn-out soles.*

ܦܣܶܬܳܐ pl. ܦܣܶܬ̈ܶܐ and ܦܣܶܬ̈ܳܐ f. *the loin, loins, muscles of the loins.*

ܦܶܣܦ, ܦܶܣܦܳܐ pl. ܦܶܣܦ̈ܶܐ m. *silver, money, a silver coin, piece of money;* ܦܶܣܦܳܐ ܕܐܶܙܕܰܒܰܢ ܒܶܗ *the money he was bought for, his price;* ܬܠܳܬܺܝܢ ܕܦܶܣܦܳܐ *thirty pieces of silver;* ܪܳܚܶܡ ܦܶܣܦܳܐ *avaricious;* ܪܶܚܡܰܬ ܦܶܣܦܳܐ *avarice;* ܦܶܣܦ ܪܺܫܳܐ *a poll-tax, capitation tax; a census;* ܦܰܩܶܕ ܥܽܘܡܰܪ ܕܢܶܬܟܬܶܒ ܦܶܣܦ ܪܺܫܳܐ ܒܟܽܠܗܶܝܢ ܐܰܬܪ̈ܘܳܬܳܐ ܕܐܽܘܚܕܳܢܶܗ *Omar commanded a census to be taken of all the countries of his empire;* ܒܦܶܣܦ ܪܺܫܳܐ ܡܶܬܚܫܶܒ ܥܰܡܗܽܘܢ *he is enrolled amongst them, numbered with them.*

ܦܣܦ Aphel ܐܰܦܣܶܦ denom. verb from ܐܶܦܣܦܳܪܽܘܣ *to banish, exile.*

ܦܶܣܬܳܐ, ܦܶܣܬܳܐ or ܦܶܣܬܳܐ pl. ܦܶܣ̈ܬܳܐ f. (cf. ܦܶܣ, ܦܶܣܬܳܐ) *an earthen vessel* in which wine was mixed.

ܦܶܣܬܳܐ pl. ܦܶܣ̈ܬܶܐ and ܦܶܣ̈ܬܳܐ f. *provender, fodder, forage, hay;* ܡܙܰܒܶܢ ܦܶܣܬܳܐ *a dealer in hay.*

ܦܰܟ fut. ܢܶܦܟܽܘܦ, inf. ܡܶܦܟܰܦ, imper. ܦܽܘܟ, act. part. ܦܳܐܶܟ, ܦܳܟܳܐ, pl. m. ܦܳܟܺܝܢ or ܦܳܐܟܺܝܢ, pass. part. ܦܟܺܝܦ, ܦܟܺܝܦܳܐ, ܦܟܺܝܦܬܳܐ. *to bend, curve, bow* ܒܽܘܪܟܳܐ *the knee;* ܪܺܫܳܐ *the head;* ܢܰܦܫܳܐ *himself,* &c.; with ܩܰܠܥܳܐ *to stretch the sling;* metaph. *to bend, make flexible, make gentle;* ܦܰܟܦܶܟ ܦܰܟܶܦܬܳܢܝ *thou hast brought me very low;* ܦܟܺܝܦܺܝܢ ܠܘܳܬܶܗ *bowing before him.* Part. adj. *a*) *bent, bowed, crookbacked, distorted;* ܗܰܕܳܡ̈ܶܐ ܦܟܺܝܦ̈ܶܐ *bent* or *distorted limbs;* ܦܟܺܝܦ ܠܒܶܣܬܪܳܐ *bent backwards.* *b*) *arched, curved, concave;* ܩܰܪ̈ܢܳܬܳܐ ܦܫܺܝܛ̈ܳܬܳܐ ܘܦܟܺܝܦ̈ܳܬܳܐ *straight and curved trumpets;* ܡܥܰܪܬܳܐ ܦܟܺܝܦܬܳܐ ܕܟܺܐܦܳܐ *an arched stone cavern;* ܣܶܟܬܳܐ ܕܦܟܺܝܦ ܪܺܫܳܗ *a curved-headed nail;* ܦܰܪ̈ܚܳܬܳܐ ܦܟܺܝܦܳܬ ܡܰܢܩܽܘܪ—ܛܽܘܦܪ̈ܶܐ *birds with hooked beaks, talons;* ܦܟܺܝܦ ܢܚܺܝܪܳܐ *hook-nosed.* Ethpe. ܐܶܬܦܟܶܦ *to be bent* or *bowed down, to bend* or *bow oneself,* usually metaph. ܐܶܬܦܟܶܦ ܚܰܨܗܽܘܢ *their back was bent* i.e. *they were no longer inflexible.* Pa. ܦܰܟܶܦ *to bend over, bow* ܦܰܓܪܳܐ *the body;* ܢܰܦܫܳܐ *oneself.* Ethpa. ܐܶܬܦܰܟܰܦ *to bow* in adoration, *stoop* from weakness, *bend over, bulge* e.g. as buildings from the shock of an earthquake;

to be bent, crooked, hooked. No Aphel, ܐܰܟܦ݂ is Pael of ܐܶܬ݂ܟܰܦ, see p. 16, col. 2.

ܟܰܦ, ܟܰܦܳܐ pl. ܟܰܦܶ̈ܐ rt. ܟܦ. f. *the palm, hollow* of the hand; *a handful, sheaf, bundle;* ܡܠܳܐ ܟܰܦܳܐ *a handful;* ܟܰܦܳܐ ܕܡܶܠܚܳܐ *a handful of salt;* ܟܰܦܶ̈ܐ ܕܟܽܘܒܶ̈ܐ *bundles of thorns;* ܢܩܰܫ ܟܰܦܶ̈ܐ *to clap the hands;* with ܚܨܰܕ or ܟܢܰܫ *to reap, gather together a sheaf;* metaph. ܟܰܦܳܐ ܡܒܰܪܰܟܬܳܐ ܕܫܠܺܝܚܽܘܬܳܐ *the blessed sheaf,* i.e. *company, of the Apostles.*

ܟܳܦܳܐ, ܟܳܦܺܝܬܳܐ pl. ܟܳܦܶ̈ܐ rt. ܟܦ. f. *anything hollow* or *curved, a pan, bowl, saucer, snuff-dish, censer; a spoon, ladle;* ܟܳܦܳܐ ܕܬܰܪܠܳܐ or ܕܡܰܣܰܬܳܐ *the scale of a balance;* ܟܳܦܳܐ ܕܡܢܳܪܬܳܐ *the bowl of a candlestick;* ܟܳܦܳܐ ܕܩܶܠܥܳܐ *the hollow of a sling; the hollow of a vault, a vault,* ܟܳܦܰܬ ܫܡܰܝܳܐ *the vault of heaven;* ܟܳܦܺܝܬܳܐ ܕܩܶܫܬܳܐ ܕܥܢܳܢܳܐ *the arch of the rainbow;* ܬܰܪܥܳܐ ܕܟܳܦܶ̈ܐ *the door of the vaults;* ܟܳܦܶ̈ܐ ܕܬܰܚܬ ܓܶܫܪܳܐ *the hollow spaces under* the arches of *a bridge;* ܟܳܦܺܝܬܳܐ ܓܰܡܠܳܝܬܳܐ ܟܽܘܪܢܳܝܬܳܐ, *a seat carried on a camel's back, on a mule.*

ܟܽܘܦܳܐ = ܟܳܦܳܐ rt. ܟܦ. f. *a ladle, large kitchen spoon.*

ܟܦܳܐ fut. ܢܶܟܦܶܐ, act. part. ܟܳܦܶܐ, ܟܳܦܝܳܐ, pass. part. ܟܦܶܐ, ܟܦܶܝܳܐ, Cognate ܟܦ. *a) to bend, bow, incline, curve, lean over;* with ܥܰܠ ܚܰܕܝܶܗ *to bow over on one's breast;* with ܠܰܐܪܥܳܐ or ܐܰܦܶ̈ܐ ܥܰܠ ܐܰܪܥܳܐ *to bow down the face to the ground;* ܥܰܠ ܐܰܦܰܝܗܽܘܢ ܟܦܶܝܢ ܗܘܰܘ *they were lying with their faces toward the ground;* ܢܶܟܠܳܐ ܕܥܰܠ ܢܰܦܫܶܗ ܟܳܦܝܳܐ *deceit recoiling on itself;* ܟܦܳܐ ܛܰܘܦܳܐ ܪܺܫܶܗ ܘܢܰܫܶܩ ܠܫܽܘܠܰܝ ܦܰܪܕܰܝܣܳܐ *the deluge bent its head and kissed* the outskirts of Paradise; ܩܽܘܠܬܳܐ ܕܟܦܶܝܳܐ ܦܽܘܡܳܗ *a waterpot with a curved spout. b) to overturn, upset;* ܡܫܺܝܓܬܳܐ ܕܚܰܠܠܶܐ ܟܦܺܝܬ ܥܠܶܝܗ̇ *I threw the soapsuds over her, upset the washing-basin over her.* Ethpe. ܐܶܬ݂ܟܦܺܝ *a) to bend with effort, strain. b) to bow* in adoration, ܡܶܬ݂ܟܦܶܝܢ ܩܕܳܡܰܘܗܝ ܥܶܠܳܝܶ̈ܐ *before Him celestial beings bend. c) to be overturned, upset,* ܩܶܕܪܳܐ ܕܡܰܝ̈ܳܐ ܕܡܶܬ݂ܟܦܝܳܐ *a pot of water turned upside down.* Eshtaph. ܐܶܫܬ݁ܰܟܦܺܝ *to be overwhelmed.*

ܟܳܦܽܘܪܳܐ, ܟܳܦܽܘܪܬܳܐ rt. ܟܦܪ II. *a) an infidel, unbeliever, heathen, pagan;* pl. *pagans* opp. Jews but *Jews* opp. Christians; ܥܰܡܳܐ ܟܳܦܽܘܪܳܐ ܕܦܳܪܣܳܝܶ̈ܐ *the unbelieving Persian nation; an apostate;* ܛܶܟܣܳܐ ܕܚܽܘܣܳܝܳܐ ܕܟܳܦܽܘܪܶ̈ܐ *form of absolution for those who have denied the faith. b) ungrateful, unthankful;* ܟܳܦܽܘܪ ܛܰܝܒ̈ܽܘܬܳܐ *unmindful of benefits;* ܒܳܣܶܡ ܥܰܠ ܟܳܦܽܘܪܶ̈ܐ *kind to the thankless.*

ܟܳܦܽܘܪܳܐܺܝܬ rt. ܟܦܪ. adv. *as an infidel, perfidiously, denying and refuting.*

ܟܳܦܽܘܪܽܘܬܳܐ rt. ܟܦܪ. f. *denial, rejection* of Christ, of the Faith; *impiety, infidelity, paganism, apostasy;* also *renunciation* made in baptism of the devil and all his works.

ܟܽܘܦܪܳܢܳܐ rt. ܟܦܪ. m. *denial, rejection; infidelity, impiety;* ܟܽܘܦܪܳܢܳܐ ܕܰܐܠܳܗܽܘܬܳܐ *denial of the Godhead;* ܟܽܘܦܪܳܢܳܐ ܕܒܰܐܠܳܗܳܐ *apostasy* or *rejection of God.*

ܟܽܘܦܪܳܐ or ܟܽܘܦܪܡܳܐ m. *hellebore, helleborus niger* or *candidus.*

ܟܽܘܦܳܝܽܘܬܳܐ rt. ܟܦ. f. *crookedness,* ܟܽܘܦܳܝܽܘܬ ܢܚܺܝܪܳܐ *being hook-nosed.*

ܟܦܶܢ fut. ܢܶܟܦܰܢ, act. part. ܟܳܦܶܢ, ܟܳܦܢܳܐ, *to hunger;* metaph. *to hunger after, desire greedily;* the adj. ܟܦܶܢ, ܟܰܦܢܳܐ usually takes the place of the participle; see below. Ethpe. ܐܶܬ݂ܟܦܶܢ and Ethpa. ܐܶܬ݂ܟܰܦܰܢ same as Peal. ܐܶܬ݂ܟܦܶܢ ܠܥܽܘܬ݂ܪܳܐ *he hungered after wealth;* ܡܰܘܬܳܐ ܕܶܐܬ݂ܟܰܦܰܢ *death for which he had hungered.* Aph. ܐܰܟܦܶܢ *to make to hunger, afflict with hunger;* ܠܳܐ ܡܰܟܦܶܢ ܠܰܒܢܰܝ̈ܢܳܫܳܐ *Thou wilt not leave the children of men to be consumed with hunger.* Derivatives, ܟܰܦܢܳܐ, ܟܰܦܢܳܐܺܝܬ, ܟܰܦܢܽܘܬܳܐ.

ܟܦܶܢ, ܟܰܦܢܳܐ pl. ܟܰܦܢܶ̈ܐ rt. ܟܦܢ. m. *a)* subst. *hunger, scarcity, famine;* ܗܘܳܐ ܟܰܦܢܳܐ ܪܰܒܳܐ ܒܟܽܠܗܶܝܢ ܐܰܪ̈ܥܳܬܳܐ *a great famine overspread all lands;* ܟܰܦܢܳܐ ܕܬܰܘܪܳܐ lit. *the hunger of a bull,* Angl. *wolfish hunger. b)* adj. *hungry, famished;* ܟܦܶܢ ܠܰܕܡܳܐ *thirsting for blood;* ܕܶܐܒܳܐ ܟܰܦܢܳܐ *a ravenous wolf;* ܢܰܦܫܳܐ ܟܰܦܢܬܳܐ or ܕܟܰܦܢܳܐ *a hungry soul;* ܟܰܦܢܶ̈ܐ ܠܟܺܐܢܽܘܬܳܐ *thirsting for justice.*

ܟܰܦܢܳܐܺܝܬ rt. ܟܦܢ. adv. *very hungrily, in a famished state.*

ܟܰܦܢܽܘܬܳܐ rt. ܟܦܢ. f. *hunger, state of famine, being famished.*

ܟܣܬܐ m. *monthly course, menstruous discharge;* ܐܢܬܬܐ ܕܝܬܒܐ ܒܟܣܬܐ *a woman staying apart for her uncleanness.*

ܟܘܣܬܐ adj. from ܟܣܬܐ. *unclean, dirty.*

ܟܣܬܢܐ, ܟܣܬܢܝܬܐ from ܟܣܬܐ *menstruous;* ܐܘܪܚܐ ܟܣܬܢܝܐ *the monthly course; a woman during that time* or *suffering from an issue;* ܐܣܝ ܗܘܐ ܠܗܝ ܠܟܣܬܢܝܬܐ *He healed her who had a flux.*

ܟܦܦ Pael conj. of ܟܦ.

ܟܘܦܦܐ rt. ܟܦ. m. *a) being bent, bowed* with age, ܟܘܦܦܐ ܕܫܢܝܐ *being bent with years;* ܟܘܦܦ ܩܫܬܐ *the being drawn of a bow;* ܟܘܦܦܐ ܕܫܡܝܐ *the vaults of heaven, zones, spheres;* astron. *a segment* of a circle; ܟܘܦܦܐ ܕܪܒ ܡܢ ܦܠܓܗ ܕܚܘܕܪܐ *a segment larger than a half-circle;* ܡܬܚܐ ܕܟܘܦܦܐ lit. *the string of an arc* i. e. *the line dividing a circle into segments.*

ܟܦܦܬܐ pl. ܟܦܦܬܐ rt. ܟܦ. f. *anything hollow* or *curved; a coffer; the hollow part of a censer, of a bookcase;* esp. *a paten;* ܟܣܐ ܘܟܦܦܬܐ *chalices and patens;* ܟܦܦܬܐ ܕܫܢ ܦܝܠܐ *curved tusks of ivory, ivory platters.*

ܟܦܪ fut. ܢܟܦܘܪ, act. part. ܟܦܪ, ܟܦܪܐ, pass. part. ܟܦܝܪ, ܐ, ܬܐ. I. *to wipe, wipe clean, scour;* ܫܡܛܗ ܠܣܝܦܐ ܘܟܦܪܗ ܒܦܓܪܐ ܕܣܗܕܐ ܛܘܒܢܐ *he seized the sword and wiped it in the body of the blessed martyr;* ܟܦܪ ܦܘܣܩܗ *wipe its cut* i.e. *cleanse the part cut.* II. *to deny, renounce, desert the faith, apostatize* usually with ܒ e. g. ܒܨܠܝܒܐ ܕܦܘܪܩܢܢ *to deny the Cross of our salvation;* with ܒܥܠܡܐ *to renounce the world;* ܟܦܪܐ ܒܡܘܗܒܬܐ ܫܡܝܢܝܬܐ ܒܐܟܠܩܪܨܐ *the devil;* *thou didst renounce the heavenly gift;* ܠܐ ܟܦܪܝܢ ܒܫܪܪܗ ܕܗܢܐ ܬܪܥܝܬܐ *they do not deny the truth of this opinion;* with ܛܝܒܘܬܐ *to be ungrateful;* but ܠܐ ܬܟܦܘܪ ܒܢ ܛܝܒܘܬܟ *let not Thy grace reject us.* Pass. part. *a)* impers. ܟܦܝܪ ܠܟ *it is renounced as to thee* i.e. *I renounce thee;* ܟܦܝܪ ܠܗ ܐܪܛܡܝܣ *Diana is renounced;* ܟܦܝܪ ܐܢܐ ܒܐܠܗܝܟ *I deny thy gods. b) unfaithful, infidel, accursed.* Ethpe. ܐܬܟܦܪ I. *to be wiped away.* II. *to be denied; to be disannulled, declared null* as ܩܝܡܐ *a covenant.* Pa. ܟܦܪ. I. *to wipe, rub dry* as ܐܝܕܘܗܝ *his hands;* ܠܦܝܢܟܐ ܒܟܦܘܪܐ *the paten with the corporal; to wipe away* ܕܡܥܐ *tears;* ܟܘܬܡܐ ܕܚܛܝܬܐ *stains of sin;* ܟܦܘܪܬܐ ܕܡܢ ܦܬܟܪܐ ܗܘܬ *a fragment rubbed off from the idol;* metaph. *to disperse, clear off, blot out;* ܟܦܪܗ ܠܫܪܟܢܐ ܕܥܡܠܝܩܝܐ Saul *did away with the remnant of the Amalekites;* ܠܥܩܒܬܐ ܕܒܝܫܐ ܡܟܦܪ ܗܘܐ *he abolished the traces of the Evil one.* II. *to compel to apostatize, force to deny.* Ethpa. ܐܬܟܦܪ *to be wiped off, blotted out, effaced* ܒܐܣܦܘܓܐ *with a sponge;* metaph. as sin in baptism; ܬܬܟܦܪ ܕܘܟܪܢܗܘܢ *may the memory of them be blotted out; to be done away with, vanish* as ܚܡܬܐ *anger.* Aphel ܐܟܦܪ *to force to deny* ܠܐܠܗܐ *God; to compel to apostatize* ܡܢ ܟܪܣܛܝܢܘܬܐ *from Christianity; to cause* or *command to renounce,* ܡܟܦܪ ܠܗ ܟܘܡܪܐ ܠܣܛܢܐ *the priest tells* the baptismal candidate *to renounce the Evil one.* Derivatives, ܟܦܪܐ, ܟܦܘܪܐ, ܟܦܘܪܬܐ, ܟܦܘܪܘܬܐ, ܡܟܦܪܢܐ, ܟܦܘܪܐܝܬ.

ܟܦܪ, ܟܦܪܐ pl. ܟܦܪ̈ܐ m. *a village, hamlet;* usually as part of a proper name, ܟܦܪ ܢܚܘܡ *Capernaum, the village of* the prophet *Nahum.*

ܟܦܪܘܢܐ pl. ܢ̈ܐ dim. of ܟܦܪܐ. m. *a little village, hamlet, cluster of houses* esp. in the neighbourhood of a city.

ܟܦܪܝܣܐ *a) hard white candy* or *sweetmeat. b) smoke, steam.*

ܟܦܪܬܐ f. *an earthen vessel, crock.*

ܟܦܫ fut. ܢܟܦܘܫ *to boll, form into a pod* or *seed-vessel;* ܟܬܢܐ ܟܦܫ *the flax was bolled;* ܟܦܫ ܚܘܛܪܐ the rod of Aaron *put forth ripe almonds;* ܦܐܪܐ ܠܐ ܟܦܫܘ *the fruits did not form.* Ethpe. ܐܬܟܦܫ *to be formed* as fruit. Pa. ܟܦܫ *to thicken, form into a knot.* Derivative, ܟܦܫܬܐ.

ܟܦܫ ܥܪܒܝܐ *the cyclamen.*

ܟܦܬܐ rt. ܟܦ. f. *a hollowed place, arch* or *vault;* ܟܦܬܐ ܕܢܘܪܐ *the fireplace.*

ܟܦܫܬܐ rt. ܟܦܫ. m. *the calix* of a flower, *capsule, seed-vessel.*

ܟܦܬܢܐ adj. from ܟܦܬܐ. *arched, vaulted.*

ܟܪ adv. of place, *where,* usually *with the* relative, ܟܪ ܕ *where;* ܟܠ ܟܪ ܕ *wheresoever;* ܠܟܠ ܟܪ ܕ *whithersoever;* ܠܟܪ ܕ *thither where;* ܡܢ ܟܪ ܕ *whence, from that place* or *time; as soon as;* ܡܢ ܟܪ ܕܢܫܒ ܪܘܚܐ *from whatever quarter the wind blows.*

ܟܪܐ, ܟܪܝ fut. ܢܟܪܐ, act. part. ܟܪܐ, ܟܪܝܐ, pass. part. ܟܪܐ, ܟܪܝܐ. *a) to be short, narrow, brief;* ܟܪܘ ܝܘܡܝܗܘܢ *the days are few. b) to be sad, displeased, annoyed; to grieve;* usually impers. with ܠ; ܟܪܝܐ ܗܘܐ ܠܕܘܝܕ *David was sad;* ܠܐ ܢܗܘܐ ܟܪܝܐ ܠܟܘܢ ܥܠ ܐܝܠܝܢ ܕܕܡܝܟܝܢ *sorrow not for those that are asleep;* ܘܠܐ ܕܢܟܪܐ ܠܢ *we ought to feel sorry;* ܟܪܝܬ ܠܗ ܥܠܘܗܝ *he felt pity for him;* pass. part. *a) small, narrow, brief, short* opp. ܐܪܝܟ; ܡܫܚܬܐ ܟܪܝܬܐ *a brief space;* ܫܢܝܐ ܟܪܝܬܐ *few* or *brief years;* ܬܪܥܐ ܟܪܝܐ *the lesser gate;* ܟܪܝܐ ܩܘܡܬܐ *little of stature, short;* ܟܪܝܐ ܪܘܚܐ *short-tempered* opp. ܢܓܝܪ ܪܘܚܐ *long-suffering, patient;* music. ܩܠܐ ܟܪܝܬܐ *short notes;* gram. ܙܘܥܐ ܟܪܝܐ *a short vowel;* ܫܡܗܐ ܟܪܝܐ *short names* or *nouns;* adverbial, ܟܪܝܐܝܬ *briefly, shortly;* ܡܟܪܝܢܘܬܐ ܓܪܡܛܝܩܝܬܐ *a grammatical epitome. b) sad, sorrowful* f. impers. with ܠ *to grieve, be sorry,* ܟܪܝܐ ܠܢ ܥܠ ܦܘܪܫܢܟ *we are very sad at thy separation from us;* ܥܠ ܐܘܪܚܐ ܡܟܐ ܕܐܪܝܟܐ ܠܐ ܟܪܝܐ ܠܝ *I do not care how long the journey may be;* ܠܐ ܟܪܝܐ ܠܝ ܕܐܡܘܬ ܐܢܐ *I am not sorry to die.* Ethpe. ܐܬܟܪܝ *to be cut short, made brief,* ܐܬܟܪܝ ܠܗ ܫܥܬܐ *the moment was brief;* ܐܬܟܪܝܘ ܚܝܘܗܝ *his life is cut short.* Pa. ܟܪܝ *to shorten, curtail, contract,* ܟܪܝ ܡܐܢܐ ܠܡܟܣܝܘܬܗ *the garment is too short to cover him,* ܟܪܝ ܝܘܡܬܐ *it shortened the days, the time.* Ethpa. ܐܬܟܪܝ *to be shortened, cut short* as days, life; impers. *to be despondent, despairing,* ܠܐ ܐܬܟܪܝܬ ܠܟܘܢ ܒܢܣܝܘܢܝܟܘܢ *you did not lose heart in your trials;* with ܪܘܚܗ *his spirit was grieved, courage failed.* Aph. ܐܟܪܝ *a) to shorten* opp. ܐܘܪܟ; ܐܟܪܝ ܐܝܕܝܗܘܢ ܡܢ *he shortened their hands, held them back. b) to sadden, be displeased, angry;* with ܥܠ *to be sorry for, to condole with.* Derivatives, ܟܪܝܘܬܐ, ܟܪܝܘܬܐ, ܟܪܝܬܐ.

ܟܪܐ m. *the socket* or *the higher part of the arm.*

ܟܪܐ or ܟܪܝܐ m. *an iron pot for heating pitch.*

ܟܪܒ fut. ܢܟܪܘܒ, act. part. ܟܪܒ, ܟܪܒܐ, pass. part. ܟܪܝܒܐ. *to plough, till* the ground, ܟܪܘܒܘ ܠܟܘܢ ܟܪܒܐ *break up your fallow ground;* metaph. *to meditate, turn over one's thoughts.* Ethpe. ܐܬܟܪܒ *to be ploughed, tilled.* Derivatives, ܟܪܒܐ, ܟܪܒܐ, ܟܪܘܒܐ, ܟܪܘܒܐ, ܟܪܒܘܬܐ.

ܟܪܒܐ or ܟܪܒܐ m. *cabbage, cauliflower,* ܟ̇ ܕܒܪܐ *wild cabbage.*

ܟܪܒܐ pl. ܟܪܒܐ rt. ܟܪܒ. m. *ploughing, tilling* the ground; *fallow ground; a furrow,* ܠܐ ܬܙܪܘܥ ܥܠ ܟܪܒܐ ܕܥܘܠܐ *sow not in the furrow of unrighteousness.*

ܟܪܒܝܐ rt. ܟܪܒ. adj. *rustic.*

ܟܪܒܠܬܐ pl. ܟܪܒܠܬܐ f. *a bird's crest* or *tuft,* esp. ܟ̇ ܕܬܪܢܓܠܐ *a cock's comb.*

ܟܪܒܣܐ pl. ܐ̈ m. *fine cambric, muslin* or *lawn;* ܡܙܒܢ ܟܪܒܣܐ *a linendraper.*

ܟܪܗ *to suffer pain, be sad, weak, ill;* cf. cognate ܟܪܐ. Pe. only part. adj. ܟܪܝܗ, ܟܪܝܗܐ, ܟܪܝܗܬܐ *sick, sickly, ill, diseased, weak, infirm, feeble;* ܟܪܝܗ ܗܘ *he is ill;* ܒܝܬ ܟܪܝܗܐ *a hospital, infirmary;* ܟܪܝܗܬ ܚܘܒܐ *love-sick;* ܬܐܢܐ ܟܪܝܗܬܐ *rotten figs;* ܦܓܪܐ ܟܪܝܗ *the flesh is weak;* ܡܫܡܥܬܐ ܟܪܝܗܬܐ *weak hearing;* ܥܘܕܪܢܐ ܟܪܝܗܐ *ineffectual assistance;* ܐܬܪܐ ܟܪܝܗܬܐ *unhealthy country;* metaph. of wrong opinions ܟܪܝܗܝ ܫܘܒܚܐ *heterodox;* ܟܪܝܗܝܢ ܗܘܘ ܡܕܥܝܗܘܢ ܒܛܘܥܝܝ ܕܫܐܕܐ *their minds were disordered by the misleading of devils;* gram. *a feeble* syllable i.e. one containing a quiescent letter; *a defective* verb; ܫܡܐ ܟܪܝܗ ܐܬܘܬܐ a noun *having a weak letter;* ܫܡܗܐ ܟܪܝܗܝ ܩܕܡܝܬܐ—ܡܨܥܝܬܐ—ܐܚܪܝܬܐ nouns *having the initial quiescent* as ܐܟܠܐ, *the second letter quiescent* as ܫܐܠܐ, the *final* as ܟܪܐ. Ethpe. ܐܬܟܪܗ *a) to fall sick, be sick, ill, in pain. b) to grow weak, lose strength, fail, languish;* ܐܬܟܪܗ ܠܒܟ *thine heart was tender, thou didst grieve;* ܐܬܟܪܗ ܒܗܝܡܢܘܬܐ *he grew weak in faith;* ܐܝܠܝܢ ܕܡܬܟܫܠܝܢ ܘܡܬܟܪܗܝܢ *those who stumble, are perplexed, distressed at this saying.* Pa. ܟܪܗ *to make ill* or *sick;* ܡܟܪܗܝܢ ܪܥܝܢܐ *sick in mind.* Ethpa. ܐܬܟܪܗ *to fall sick, become very ill; to make oneself ill, feign sickness.* Aph. ܐܟܪܗ *to cause to be ill* or *sickly, injure, harm;* with ܢܦܫܗ *to feign sickness;* ܠܐ ܡܕܡ ܡܚܒܠ ܘܡܟܪܗ ܟܪܡܐ ܐܝܟ ܟܣܚܐ ܒܝܫܐ *nothing ruins and injures a vineyard* so much as bad pruning. Derivatives, ܟܘܪܗܢܐ, ܟܪܝܗܘܬܐ, ܟܘܪܗܢܝܘܬܐ, ܡܟܪܗܢܐ.

ܟܪܘܒܐ pl. ܝܢ̈, ܐ̈ rt. ܟܪܒ. m. *a cherub.*

ܟܪܒܐ pl. ܳܐ rt. ܟܪܒ. m. *a ploughman, husbandman; a plough.*

ܟܪܘܒܝܐ, ܳܝܬܐ from ܟܪܘܒܐ. adj. *cherubic, of* or *pertaining to cherubs;* ܦܠܚܘܬܐ ܟܪܘܒܝܬܐ *the cherubic companies.*

ܟܪܘܙܐ, ܟܪܘܙܐ, ܟܪܘܙܬܐ rt. ܟܪܙ. *a herald, public crier, proclaimer, preacher, harbinger, forerunner* esp. used of St. John the Baptist, ܠܟܪܘܙܐ ܕܡܫܝܚܐ ܬܐܠܕ Elizabeth *shall give birth miraculously to the forerunner* of Christ.

ܟܪܘܙܐ or ܟܪܘܙܐ κῆρυξ, m. *a pearly shell, mother-of-pearl.*

ܟܪܘܙܘܬܐ pl. ܳܬܐ rt. ܟܪܙ. f. *a*) *heralding, proclamation, preaching, message; the Gospel;* ܟܪܘܙܘܬܐ ܕܝܘܢܢ *the preaching of Jonah;* ܟܪܘܙܘܬܐ ܕܫܠܝܚܐ *the message* or *preaching of the Apostles.* *b*) eccles. *a proclamation, recitation, bidding-prayer, litany, a commemoration* of bishops, patriarchs, &c., *recited* during divine service; ܒܛܠܘܗ ܠܟܪܘܙܘܬܐ ܕ *they annulled the commemoration* of the name of .... *c*) *public prayers* for the khalifs = *public acknowledgement* of their sovereignty; ܡܠܟܐ ܕܛܝܝܐ ܫܡܐ ܠܚܘܕ ܗܘܐ ܠܗܘܢ ܘܟܪܘܙܘܬܐ ܕܡܠܟܐ *the khalifs of the Arabs had only the name and proclamation of kings,* not real power; ܨܒܐ ܕܢܒܛܠ ܟܪܘܙܘܬܗ ܕܡܣܥܘܕ ܘܢܟܪܙ ܠܕܘܝܕ *he wanted to annul the name of Mas'ud and proclaim Daoud* in his stead.

ܟܪܘܬܘܢܝܬܐ pl. ܟܪܘܬܘܢܝܬܐ; see ܟܪܘܬܘܢܝܬܐ *laying on of hands.*

ܟܪܘܟܐ or ܟܪܘܟܐ pl. ܳܐ rt. ܟܪܟ. m. *the piece of wood round which the weaver's thread is fastened, a weaver's beam.*

ܟܪܘܟܝܐ pl. ܟܪܘܟܝܐ rt. ܟܪܟ. m. *moving round, going* or *running about; circular* or *revolving motion; circuits, circlings* of the wind, clouds, &c., *a circle, circumference;* ܟܪܘܟܝܐ ܕܥܕܬܐ *a procession in church;* ܟܪܘܟܝܐ ܕܪܩܝܥܐ *the revolving of the firmament;* ܟܪܘܟܝܐ ܕܫܢܬܐ *the turning* or *revolving of the year;* ܟܠܡܕܡ ܕܟܪܘܟܝܐ *everything belonging to the succession* of Festivals in their order.

ܟܪܘܟܝܬܐ pl. ܳܝܬܐ rt. ܟܪܟ. f. *a whirlwind, hurricane.*

ܟܪܘܟܝܬܐ rt. ܟܪܟ. f. *a whirlpool, eddy.*

ܟܪܘܠܐ pl. ܳܐ m. *a*) *a hook,* esp. *a hook from which a lamp is suspended.* *b*) *a stick with an iron hook* for lifting lamps down; *a club hooked at the end, polo-stick.* *c*) *a curved piece of wood* attached to the end of a cord by which a load is fastened; *a saddle-bow.* *d*) ܟܪܘܠܐ ܕܠܚܡܐ *a twisted roll, twist of bread.*

ܟܪܘܠܝܐ, ܳܝܬܐ from ܟܪܘܠܐ. *deeply curved, bent;* ܣܘܪܛܐ ܟܪܘܠܝܐ *a deeply curved line;* ܣܓܕܬܐ ܟܪܘܠܝܬܐ *very deep reverences.*

ܟܪܘܡܐ, ܟܪܘܡ pl. ܳܐ m. χρῶμα, *colour;* ܐܝܟ ܟܪܘܡܐ ܕܫܡܝܐ ܒܕܟܝܘܬܐ *as the colour of heaven in its clearness;* ܟܪܘܡܐ ܡܫܚܠܦܐ *varied colours.* Metaph. *a*) *colour of the face, complexion, blushing;* ܕܠܐ ܟܪܘܡܐ *unblushing, shameless.* *b*) *countenance, aspect; boldness, impudence;* ܩܫܐ ܟܪܘܡܐ *a set face, bold look;* ܟܪܘܡܗ ܕܫܡܝܪܐ ܗܘ *his audacity is adamantine,* Angl. *he is brazen-faced.* *c*) *appearance, pretext,* ܒܟܪܘܡܐ ܘܠܐ ܒܫܪܪܐ *in appearance and not in truth;* ܒܐܝܢܐ ܟܪܘܡ ܐܟܠܝܢ ܩܪܨܘܗܝ *on what pretext do they accuse him?* *d*) *style;* ܕܡܨܒܬ ܒܟܪܘܡܐ *of ornate style.*

ܟܪܘܡܬܢܐ, ܳܢܝܬܐ adj. from the above. *bold, audacious, impudent.*

ܟܪܘܡܬܢܘܬܐ from ܟܪܘܡܐ f. *boldness, impudence; lasciviousness.*

ܟܪܘܢܝܩܘܢ, ܟܪܘܢ or ܟܪܘܢ pl. ܟܪܘܢܝܩܐ m. χρονικόν, *a chronicle.*

ܟܪܘܬܐ pl. *a*) of ܟܪܝܐ *a heap.* *b*) of ܟܪܝܬܐ *the thumb.*

ܟܪܙ Pe. only participial adj. ܟܪܝܙܐ or ܟܪܝܙܐ *proscribed, execrated, despised.* Ethpe. ܐܬܟܪܙ *a*) *to be proclaimed, announced, publicly taught, preached;* ܬܬܟܪܙ ܗܕܐ ܣܒܪܬܐ ܕܡܠܟܘܬܐ *this gospel of the kingdom shall be preached;* ܢܬܟܪܙ ܫܡܗ ܘܡܠܦܢܘܬܗ ܒܟܠܗ ܡܕܢܚܐ *his name and teaching will be celebrated in all the East.* *b*) *to be proclaimed, named* king, bishop, &c.; ܐܬܟܪܙ ܡܠܟܐ *he was proclaimed king.* *c*) *to have the name recited in public prayer* as being khalif, cf. ܟܪܘܙܘܬܐ; *to be recited, proclaimed, commemorated* as the names of bishops, &c., at divine service. Pa. ܟܪܙ *to proscribe;* with ܡܢ ܝܪܬܘܬܐ *to disinherit.* Aph. ܐܟܪܙ *a*) *to proclaim by a herald* or *messenger;* ܐܟܪܙ ܠܡܕܝܢܬܐ ܫܠܡܐ *proclaim peace to* the city. *b*) *to announce, preach;* ܐܟܪܙܘ ܠܗܘܢ ܢܒܝܐ ܩܕܡܝܐ *unto them the former prophets cried;* John the Baptist ܡܟܪܙ ܗܘܐ ܒܡܕܒܪܐ *preached in the desert. c*) *to teach, show, argue. d*) *to recite publicly* or *in a loud voice, to promulgate* a decree, with ܒ ܒܫܡܗ *to issue decrees in the name of, by the authority of . . .; to proclaim* or *make* king, caesar, khalif, sultan, *to recite the name* of a reigning khalif in public prayer; *to proclaim* a bishop, insert his name in the diptychs; *to proclaim* a feast. *e*) eccles. *to proclaim, intone* a ܟܪܘܙܘܬܐ. Pass. part. ܡܟܪܙ, ܡܟܪܙܐ *proscribed, interdicted, execrated, accursed, disinherited, exiled;* ܡܟܪܙܐ ܡܢ ܥܕܬܐ *excommunicated;* ܡܟܪܙܐ ܕܠܐ ܒܢܝܐ *cursed with childlessness.* Derivatives, ܟܪܘܙܐ, ܟܪܘܙܘܬܐ, ܡܟܪܙܢܐ.

ܟܪܙܐ m. I. *an earthen water-jar with a narrow orifice.* II. *a he-goat, a ram, head of the flock.*

ܟܪܙܘܠܐ or ܟܪܙܠܐ pl. ܐ̈ m. *a shepherd, a shepherd's crook.*

ܟܪܛܝܣܐ pl. ܐ̈ usually f. χάρτης, *writing-material, paper, a schedule, bill, deed; a record, document, treatise;* ܡܥܒܕܢܐ ܕܟܪܛܝܣܐ *a preparer of paper* or *parchment;* ܟܬܒܘܗܝ ܕܟܪܛܝܣܐ *characters formed on paper;* ܟܪܛܝܣܐ ܕܦܪܝܥܝܢ ܢܬܗܦܟܘܢ ܠܡܪܝܗܘܢ *paid bills are to be returned to their owners* i.e. *given back receipted;* ܥܒܕ ܡܟܬܒܢܘܬܐ ܠܘܩܒܠܗ ܒܟܪܛܝܣܐ *he published a treatise against him.*

ܟܪܛܘܠܪܐ pl. ܐ̈ χαρτουλάριος, *a clerk* of the revenue, *administrator* of the imperial exchequer; ܟܪܛܘܠܪܐ ܕܥܕܬܐ *keeper of the records of the Church.*

ܟܪܛܘܢܝܐ or ܟܪܛܘܢܐ *ordination;* see ܟܪܛܘܢ and ܟܪܘܢ.

ܟܪܝܐ, ܟܪܐ and ܟܪܝܐ, E-Syr. ܟܪܝܐ, pl. ܟܪ̈ܘܬܐ, ܟܪ̈ܘܬܐ f. *a pile, heap* esp. *a heap of threshed grain;* ܟܪ̈ܘܬܐ ܟܪ̈ܘܬܐ *by heaps.*

ܟܪܝܐܝܬ rt. ܟܪܐ. adv. *shortly, briefly.*

ܟܪܝܗܐܝܬ rt. ܟܪܗ. adv. *morbidly.*

ܟܪܝܗܘܬܐ rt. ܟܪܗ. f. *sickness, sickliness, infirmity, weakness, impotence;* ܟܪܝܗܘܬܗ ܕܦܓܪܐ *the flesh subject to sickness;* ܐܬܛܠܠܬܘܢ ܒܟܪܝܗܘܬܐ ܕܗܝܡܢܘܬܟܘܢ *ye were tossed about through the weakness of your faith.*

ܟܪܝܘܬܐ, ܟܪܝܘܬܐ rt. ܟܪܐ. f. *shortness, brevity;* ܟܪܝܘܬܐ ܕܙܒܢܐ—ܕܐܘܚܕܢܐ *lack of time;* metaph. *sadness, anxiety, distress; pressure, coercion;* ܐܝܟ ܕܡܢ ܟܪܝܘܬܐ *unwillingly;* ܟܪܝܘܬܐ ܕܠܒܐ *heartfelt sorrow;* ܟܪܝܘܬܐ ܗܘܬ ܠܗ ܠܪܘܚܐ ܠܘܬ ܐܢܫܘܬܐ the Holy Spirit *felt pity for mankind;* ܟܪܝܘܬܐ ܕܢܦܫܐ *impatience, sadness,* but med. ܟܪܝܘܬܐ ܕܢܫܡܐ *shortness of breath, asthma.*

ܟܪܝܟܐܝܬ rt. ܟܪܟ. adv. *round about.*

ܟܪܝܟܘܬܐ rt. ܟܪܟ. f. *girding, surrounding;* ܟܪܝܟܘܬܐ ܕܡܕܝܢܬܐ *a besieging.*

ܟܪܝܣܛܝܢܐ, ܟܪܝܣܛܝܢܐ χριστιανός, *a Christian;* ܡܢ ܩܕܡ ܐܬܩܪܝܘ ܬܠܡܝܕܐ ܒܐܢܛܝܘܟܝ ܟܪܝܣܛܝܢܐ *the disciples were called Christians first in Antioch.*

ܟܪܝܣܛܝܢܝܐ, ܟܪܝܣܛܝܢܝܐ adj. *Christian;* ܢܫܐ ܟܪܝܣܛܝܢܝܬܐ *Christian women.*

ܟܪܝܣܛܝܢܐܝܬ or ܟܪܣܛܐܝܬ from the above. adv. *as a Christian, in a Christian manner;* ܐܝܟ ܕܦܐܐ ܟܪܝܣܛܝܢܐܝܬ *as becomes a Christian, befitting a Christian.*

ܟܪܝܣܛܝܢܘܬܐ or ܟܪܣܛܘܬܐ from the above. f. *Christianity, the Christian faith;* collect. *the Christian congregation, Christian people;* ܒܫܠܡܐ ܕܟܠܗ ܟܪܝܣܛܝܢܘܬܐ *with the accord of the whole congregation.*

ܟܪܝܣܝܣ, ܟܪܝܣܝܣ, ܟܪܣܝܣ or ܟܪܣܝܣ pl. ܟܪܝܣܝܣ or ܟܪܝܣܝܣ f. χρῆσις, *a*) *use, custom, wont, experience;* ܣܗܕܐ ܟܪܝܣܝܣ *experience witnesses* to this. *b*) *testimony, evidence, proof, a passage adduced* or *cited in proof, a quotation, example;* ܟܪܝܣܝܣ ܕܡܢ ܟܬܒܐ *testimony from the Scriptures;* ܟܪܝܣܝܣ ܕܐܒܗܬܐ *citations from the Fathers.*

ܟܪܟ fut. ܢܟܪܘܟ and ܢܟܪܟ, imper. ܟܪܘܟ, pass. part. ܟܪܝܟ, ܟܪܝܟܐ, ܟܪܝܟܬܐ. *a*) *to go round, encircle, turn about* as ܬܚܘܡܐ *a boundary,* ܚܒܠܐ *a measuring-line; to turn round, move round* with ܒ, ܡܢ or ܠܘܬ; ܫܘܪܐ ܕܡܕܝܢܬܐ *the city wall all round;* ܗܘܐ ܟܪܟ ܡܢ ܟܠ ܟܪܟ

ܡܢ ܒܝܬ ܠܒܝܬ he went round from house to house; ܢܟܪܘܟ ܟܠ ܢܗܝܪ̈ܐ the subdeacon *shall go round* and see *to the lamps;* ܟܪ̈ܟܝܢ ܥܡ ܚܝ̈ܘܬܐ *going about with wild beasts* i. e. living like them. *b) to place round, gird round, encompass, surround; to stand round about, to guard, to besiege;* ܟܪܘܟ ܐܢܘܢ ܒܨܘܪܟ *hang them round thy neck;* ܫܘܪ̈ܐ ܚܣܝ̈ܢܐ ܟܪܟܘܢܝ *strong walls surrounded me. c) to roll round, roll up* or *together, to wrap round, bind, swathe;* ܟܪܟܬ ܡܟܬ̈ܒܠܬܐ ܕܣܥܪܗ̇ *she rolled up the plaits of her hair;* ܟܪܟ ܐܦ̈ܘܗܝ ܒܡܥܛܦܪܗ *he wrapped his face in his mantle;* with ܒܥܙܘܪ̈ܐ *to swaddle;* with ܟܪܟܐ *to roll a volume up, fold up a roll; to bind up* a wound; *to enshroud, prepare for burial;* ܢܟܪܟܝܗ ܟܪܟܐ ܕܡܬ̈ܟܢܫܬܐ *she put on her shroud;* ܟܪܟܝܢ ܥܡܪܐ ܕܟܠܗ̇ *they shear the fleece all over;* ܐܝܟܢ ܐܪܥܐ ܟܪܟ ܣܐܬܐ ܕܚܛ̈ܐ *how much land does a bushel of corn cover?* Part. ܟܪܝܟ *a)* active *going round, encircling; standing round* as a guard, *surrounding* or *besieging* with ܠ or ܥܠ, ܡܕܝܢܬܐ ܕܟܪܝܟ ܠܗ̇ ܫܘܪܐ a city *with a wall round it;* ܐܘܠܨܢܐ ܟܪܝܟ ܠܠܒܗ̇ *distress straitly surrounds her heart;* ܡܚ̈ܫܘܠܐ ܕܟܪܝܟܝܢ ܠܝ *the billows which surge round me;* ܐܝܩܪܐ ܟܪܝܟ ܠܟ *may honour adorn thee round about. b)* passive *fenced, surrounded* with walls; *wrapped* ܒܥܙܘܪ̈ܐ *in swaddling bands;* ܒܡܥܦܪܐ *in a veil* or *cloth;* ܥܘܠܐ ܕܟܪܝܟ ܒܫܠܝܬܐ the embryo *covered with the caul;* ܐܓܪܬܐ ܕܟܪܝܟܐ *a folded letter;* ܕܘܢܒܐ ܕܟܠܒܐ ܟܪܝܟ ܟܪܝܟ *a dog's curly tail. c)* impers. ܟܪܝܟ ܗܘܐ ܠܗܘܢ ܒ *they wandered about in* other countries. ETHPE. ܐܬܟܪܟ imper. E-Syr. same as pret., W-Syr. ܐܬܟܪܟ, with suff. 3 ps. ܐܬܟܪܟܝܗ̇ I. active = Peal *a) to go round, move about,* &c.; ܡܕܝܢܬܐ ܕܐܪܒܥܝܢ ܡ̈ܝܠܝܢ ܡܬܟܪܟܢܘܬܗ̇ a city *whose circuit is forty miles;* ܡܬܟܪܟ ܗܘܐ ܝܫܘܥ ܒܟܠܗ̇ ܓܠܝܠܐ *Jesus went about in all Galilee;* ܐܬܟܪܟܬ ܒܡܕܒܪܐ *I wandered about in the desert;* ܡܬܟܪܟܝܢ ܘܟܢܫܝܢ *they went about collecting . . .;* ܐܬܟܪܟܢ ܥܠ ܩܘܦܪܘܣ *we coasted round Cyprus.* = Peal *b) to surround, march round, stand round* as a guard; *to stand about, to delay, linger.* II. passive *a) to be turned round, driven round* as ܓܝܓܠܐ *a wheel; to be moved* or *carried round;* ܠܐ ܬܬܟܪܟ ܝܪܬܘܬܐ *the inheritance* of a Hebrew *shall not be removed* from one tribe to another; *to be stationed round. b)* pass. of Peal *c) to be rolled up, wrapped up, swathed, swaddled;* ܟܪܟܐ ܕܡܬܟܪܟ *a rolled up scroll.* III. refl. *to turn oneself round, revolve;* ܬܪܥܐ ܕܡܬܟܪܟ ܥܠ ܨܢܝܪ̈ܘܗܝ *a door which turns on its hinges; to gyrate, circle, wheel round* as a bee; *to coil, twist round* as a serpent, as a dog's tail; *to roll round, revolve, come round* of number or time; ܫܒܥܐ ܝܘܡ̈ܬܐ ܟܕ ܡܬܟܪܟܝܢ *seven revolving days.* PA. ܟܪܟ *to bind* or *twist round, tie a vine to a stake; to go* or *circle round often.* ETHPA. ܐܬܟܪܟ *a) to go hither and thither, walk up and down, go to and fro. b) to be wrapped round, bound up. c) to gird, surround, besiege.* APH. ܐܟܪܟ *a) to make revolve, make to turn round,* ܡܟܪܟ ܠܫܡܝܐ God *makes the heavens revolve;* with ܪܚܝܐ *to turn a mill-wheel;* ܠܬܪܥܐ *a door on its hinges* or *in its grooves;* ܡܟܪܟ ܚܙܝܐ *he looks all round;* ܠܐ ܬܟܪܟ ܐܪܝܐ ܒܪܚܝܐ *do not set a lion to turn a mill-wheel; to make a stone revolve from a sling, to sling. b) to roll round* in the mouth, *utter,* ܕܠܐ ܢܟܪܟܘܢ ܫܡܐ ܒܠܫܢܗܘܢ *that they should not take the name on their tongue.* DERIVATIVES, ܟܘܪܟܐ, ܟܪܘܟܐ, ܟܪܘܟܝܬܐ, ܟܪܘܟܝܐ, ܟܪܟܐ, ܟܪܟܐ, ܟܪܟܐ, ܟܪܝܟܘܬܐ, ܟܪܝܟܐ, ܟܪܝܟܐܝܬ, ܡܬܟܪܟܢܘܬܐ, ܡܬܟܪܟܢܐ, ܡܬܟܪܟܢܐܝܬ, ܡܟܪܟܢܐ.

ܟܪܟܐ pl. ܟܪܟܝܢ, ܟܪ̈ܟܐ m. *a fenced* or *walled* city, *fortified place.*

ܟܪܟܐ pl. ܟܪ̈ܟܐ rt. ܟܪܟ. m. *a) a written roll, scroll, volume, codex;* ܟܪܟܐ ܕܟܬܝܒ ܡܢ ܠܓܘ ܘܡܢ ܠܒܪ *a roll written within and without;* ܟܪ̈ܟܐ ܕܟܬܝܒܝܢ ܟܠܗܘܢ *rolls written all over;* ܟܪܟܐ ܕܩܢ̈ܘܢܐ *a volume of canons;* ܟܪ̈ܟܐ ܕܫܘܝܘܬܐ *writings of consent, written consent. b) an eddy;* ܒܡܛܪܐ ܥܒܕܬ ܟܪ̈ܟܐ *thou madest eddying pools of rain. c)* ܟܪܟܐ ܕܕܗܒܐ *a roll* or *cylinder of gold.*

ܟܪܟܐ pl. ܟܪ̈ܟܐ rt. ܟܪܟ. m. *a) revolving, revolution, circuit, course, orbit* of the sun, the heavens, the year; ܠܟܪܟܗ̇ ܕܗܕܐ ܫܢܬܐ *at the turn of this year;* ܟܪܟܐ ܕܠܐ ܫܠܝܐ *continuous revolution. b)* κρόκη, *the woof.*

ܟܪܟܕܢܐ m. *a rhinoceros, a horn.*

ܟܪܟܫ *to write badly, spoil writing.*

ܟܶܪܟܺܝܣܳܐ or ܟܰܪܟܺܝܣܳܐ m. κερκίς, ίδα. *a) a weaver's comb, shuttle. b) the point* of an arrow. *c) the fore-arm, wrist, knuckle.*

ܟܰܪܟܰܫܬܳܐ f. *the girth, buckle of the girth.*

ܟܰܪܟܶܡ denom. verb Palpel conj. from ܟܘܪܟܡܳܐ *to make yellow, tinge with saffron, turn pale* or *yellowish,* ܦܰܪܰܚܬܳܐ ܡܟܰܪܟܡܬܳܐ ܓܰܘܢܳܐ *a saffron-coloured bird.*

ܟܪܳܟܬܳܐ or ܟܰܪܳܟܬܳܐ pl. ܟܪ̈ܳܟܳܬܳܐ rt. ܟܪܟ. f. *a) a bandage, binder, swaddling-band. b) a convolution, bend, winding. c) a tendril;* ܟܪܳܟܬܳܐ ܕܰܟܪܳܡܳܐ *a tendril of a vine. d) the slough* of a snake.

ܟܪܰܡ fut. ܢܶܟܪܽܘܡ *to cut short, lop off;* pass. part. ܟܪܺܝܡܳܐ *cut off, mutilated* esp. of the nose; *stopped short.* Derivatives, ܟܰܪܡܳܐ, ܟܪܳܡܳܐ, ܟܪܺܝܡܳܐ.

ܟܪܳܡ, ܟܰܪܡܳܐ pl. ܟܰܪ̈ܡܺܝܢ, ܟܰܪ̈ܡܶܐ rt. ܟܪܡ. m. *a) a vineyard;* ܦܳܠܚ̈ܰܝ ܟܰܪܡܳܐ *vine-dressers. b) a vine;* ܟܰܪܡܳܐ ܕܚܶܘܝܳܐ *snake's vine, colocynth.*

ܟܰܪܳܡܳܐ pl. ܟܰܪ̈ܳܡܶܐ rt. ܟܪܡ. m. *a vine-dresser.*

ܟܰܪܡܳܝܳܐ rt. ܟܪܡ. adj. *of* or *from the vine, the grape;* ܚܰܡܪܳܐ ܟܰܪܡܳܝܳܐ *wine from the grape.*

ܟܰܪܡܺܝܣܳܐ pl. ܬܳܐ *a thin cake of bread.*

ܟܪܳܢܺܝܩܽܘܢ; see ܟܪܘܢ̄ *a chronicle.*

ܟܪܰܣ imper. ܟܪܽܘܣ perh. *to shut;* ܟܪܽܘܣ ܡܶܢ *leave off.*

ܟܪܶܣ, ܟܰܪܣܳܐ pl. ܟܰܪ̈ܣܶܐ, ܟܰܪ̈ܣܳܬܳܐ f. *a) the belly, the paunch;* ܓܰܘ̈ܳܝܶܐ ܕܟܰܪܣܳܐ *the intestines, entrails;* ܡܰܫܠܚܳܢܽܘܬ ܟܰܪܣܳܐ *diarrhoea;* ܡܡܰܠܠܶܝܢ ܡܶܢ ܟܰܪܣܳܐ *ventriloquists;* metaph. ܟܰܪܣܳܐ ܕܩܶܕܪܳܐ *the belly of the pot;* ܟܰܪ̈ܣܳܬܳܐ ܕܢܚܳܫܳܐ *big-bellied vessels of brass;* ܟܰܪܣܳܐ ܕܦܰܪܰܚܬܳܐ *a bird's crop;* ܟܰܪܣܳܐ ܕܐܶܓܰܪܬܳܐ *the body of a document, the middle part written on;* ܓܶܚܟܰܬ ܒܟܰܪܣܳܗ̇ *she laughed within her, secretly; appetite, hunger;* ܐܰܣܓܺܝܘܽܬ ܟܰܪܣܳܐ *gluttony;* ܟܰܪܣܳܐ ܣܪܺܝܩܳܐ *vainglory, vanity, conceit. b) the womb;* ܡܶܢ ܟܰܪܣ ܐܶܡܶܗ *from his mother's womb. c) a cavity, ventricle,* ܟܰܪܣܳܐ ܣܶܡܳܠܳܝܬܳܐ *the left ventricle* of the heart; ܟܰܪܣܳܐ ܒܶܣܬܪܳܝܬܳܐ ܕܡܰܘܚܳܐ *the posterior ventricle of the brain.*

ܟܰܪܣܦܳܢܳܐ pl. ܢ̈ܶܐ m. *a stalk, bundle of stalks;* ܟܰܪܣܦܳܢ̈ܶܐ ܕܟܶܬܳܢܳܐ *flax-stalks.*

ܟܪܶܣܛܝܳܢܳܐ, ܟܪܶܣܛܝܳܢܳܐܝܬ, ܟܪܶܣܛܝܳܢܽܘܬܳܐ or ܟܪܶܣܛ̄; see ܟܪܶܣܛ̄.

ܟܰܪܣܬܳܢܳܐ, ܟܰܪܣܬܳܢܺܝܬܳܐ from ܟܰܪܣܳܐ *big bellied,* having *a protuberant paunch.*

ܟܪܰܥ, ܟܪܳܥܳܐ pl. ܟܪ̈ܳܥܺܝܢ, ܥ̈ܶܐ m. *the leg, shank, shin* of cattle, sheep, locusts, bees, &c.; often forms part of names of plants, ܟܪܳܥܳܐ ܕܐܰܪܢܒܳܐ *hare's foot, trifolium arvense;* ܟܪܰܥ ܟܰܪܒܳܐ *wild basil, clinopodium;* metaph. ܟܪܳܥܳܐ ܕܝܰܡܳܐ *the shore* or *an inlet, arm of the sea.*

ܟܰܪܥܳܐ or ܟܪܳܥܳܐ m. *first milk after birth;* also *clotted milk.*

ܟܪܰܦܣܳܐ or ܟܪܳܦܣܳܐ m. *parsley, celery.*

ܟܪܳܨܳܐ ܐܶܟܰܠ; see ܐܶܟܰܠ ܩܪܨܳܐ.

ܟܰܪܳܐܬܳܐ or ܟܪܳܬܳܐ pl. ܟܰܪ̈ܳܘܳܬܳܐ rt. ܟܪܐ. f. *the thumb, the great toe;* ܟܪܳܬܳܐ ܕܐܺܝܕܶܗ *his thumb;* ܟܪܳܬܳܐ ܕܪܶܓܠܳܐ *the great toe;* ܪܫܰܡ ܒܟܪܳܬܶܗ *he signed with his thumb.*

ܟܰܪܳܬܳܐ pl. ܟܰܪ̈ܳܬܶܐ f. *a leek.* Derivatives, ܟܰܪܳܬܳܝܳܐ, ܟܰܪܳܬܽܘܬܳܐ.

ܟܰܪܳܬܳܝܳܐ pl. m. ܟܰܪܳܬܳܝ̈ܶܐ pl. f. ܟܰܪܳܬܳܝ̈ܳܬܳܐ adj. *leek-green, leek-coloured.*

ܟܽܘܪܬܳܐ f. *a burden for the back, a load;* ܫܪܳܐ ܟܽܘܪܬܶܗ *he laid down his load.*

ܟܰܪܳܬܽܘܬܳܐ from ܟܰܪܳܬܳܐ f. *leek-colour, greenness.*

ܟܫ not used in Pe. Aphel ܐܰܟܶܫ *to drive off, flap away* birds or bees. Derivatives, ܡܰܟܫܳܢܳܐ, ܡܰܟܫܳܢܺܝܬܳܐ.

ܟܫܳܐ fut. ܢܶܟܫܶܐ, act. part. ܟܳܫܶܐ, ܟܳܫܝܳܐ, pass. part. ܟܫܶܐ, ܟܫܺܝܳܐ. *to pile up, heap;* ܟܫܰܘ ܟܺܐܦ̈ܶܐ ܥܠܰܘܗܝ *they piled stones over him;* ܟܫܰܘ ܐܺܝܟ ܥܶܠܳܝܶܐ *vapours arose in heaps;* ܢܶܟܫܽܘܢ ܩܰܝܣ̈ܶܐ ܥܰܠ ܢܽܘܪܳܐ *let them pile wood on the fire;* ܕܟܳܫܶܐ ܩܰܝܣ̈ܶܐ *one who gathers sticks;* ܟܫܳܐ ܛܰܝܒܽܘܬܳܐ ܥܠܰܘܗܝ *he heaped kindness upon him.* Pass. part. ܥܰܦܪܳܐ ܕܟܫܶܐ ܗ̄ܘܳܐ *the earth heaped up* to form a mole; ܣܺܝܡ̈ܳܬܳܐ ܕܟܫܶܝܢ ܗ̄ܘܰܘ *the treasures they had heaped up;* ܟܫܶܐ ܗ̄ܘܳܐ ܠܗܘܢ ܠܰܚܡܳܐ *they have piles of bread, plenty of bread.* Ethpe. ܐܶܬ݂ܟܫܺܝ *to be piled* or *heaped up;* ܥܠܰܝܟ ܐܳܦ ܓܽܘܡܪ̈ܶܐ ܡܶܬ݂ܟܰܫܝܳܢ *on you too, hot coals are heaped;* ܠܳܐ ܬܶܬ݂ܟܰܫܶܐ ܚܰܘ̈ܒܰܝܟ *do not let your debts accumulate.* Pa. ܟܰܫܺܝ *to pile up a great heap.* Ethpa. ܐܶܬ݂ܟܰܫܺܝ pass. of Pael. Derivative, ܟܶܫܝܳܐ.

ܟܘܫܟܘܫܳܐ *cnicus, bastard saffron.*

ܟܫܽܘܪܳܐ, ܟܫܽܘܪܳܐ or ܟܶܫܽܘܪܳܐ pl. ܪ̈ܶܐ m. *a plank* or *beam; a one-plank bridge.*

ܟܫܰܛ fut. ܢܶܟܫܽܘܛ, act. part. ܟܳܫܶܛ, ܟܳܫܛܳܐ, pass. part. ܟܫܺܝܛܳܐ *to shoot, aim, let fly* an arrow, with ܒ; *to send* an arrow from the bow; metaph. ܠܘ ܠܩܘܒܠ ܦܪܨܘܦܐ ܡܫܬܕܐ ܡܐ ܕܟܬܒܢ *what we have written is not aimed at any special persons;* pass. part. *struck by an arrow.* Ethpe. ܐܬܩܫܬ and Ethpa. ܐܬܩܫܬ *to be pierced* or *wounded* by an arrow. Aph. ܐܩܫܬ same as Pe. Derivatives, ܩܫܬܐ, ܩܫܬܐ, ܩܫܬܐ, ܩܫܬܘܬܐ.

ܩܫܬܐ or ܩܫܬܐ = ܩܫܬܐ m. *a bow, the rainbow.*

ܩܫܬܐ pl. ܐ̈ rt. ܩܫܬ. m. *an archer, bowman;* astron. a sign of the Zodiac, *Sagittarius;* ܟܘܟܒܐ ܩܫܬܐ *a shooting star.*

ܩܫܬܐ pl. ܐ̈ rt. ܩܫܬ. m. *a)* ܓܐܪ̈ܐ *shooting with arrows, archery;* ܩܫܬܘܗܝ ܕܠܒܣܬܪܐ *his backward shots.* *b) an arrow, shaft, bolt; a shooting star.*

ܩܫܬܘܬܐ rt. ܩܫܬ. f. *archery;* the setting up of a machine for *casting darts.*

ܩܫܝܪܐܝܬ rt. ܩܫܪ. adv. *diligently, assiduously, strenuously, successfully.*

ܩܫܝܪܘܬܐ rt. ܩܫܪ. f. *success, prosperity; diligence, application, capability, business capacity;* ܘܐܠܐ ܕܢܚܘܐ ܩܫܝܪܘܬܗ *he ought to show what he is capable of.*

ܩܫܬܐ pl. ܩܫܬܐ, ܩܫܬܐ rt. ܩܫܐ. f. *a pile, heap;* ܕܩܝܣܐ *of wood;* ܕܟܐܦܐ *of stones;* ܕܩܛܝܠܐ *of the slain;* ܩܫܬܐ ܩܫܬܐ *in heaps.*

ܩܫܬܐ, ܩܘܫܬܐ or ܩܫܬܐ m. *a girth, binding-band.*

ܩܫܠ fut. ܢܩܫܘܠ root meaning *to stumble;* pass. part. usually with ܒ of the pers. or cause, *offended, angry, irate,* ܩܫܝܠܝܢ ܠܬܐܪܬܗܘܢ ܐܢܬܘܢ *you are an offence to their consciences;* ܩܫܝܠܝܢ ܗܘܘ ܒܟܢܘܫܬܐ *they took great offence at the synod.* Ethpe. ܐܬܩܫܠ with ܒ or ܥܠ *to be offended, irate, scandalized; to suspect;* ܐܬܩܫܠܬ ܒܪܥܝܢܝ *I was troubled in my mind;* ܗܘ ܛܠܝܐ ܡܝܬ ܘܐܬܩܫܠܘ ܣܓܝܐܐ ܕܐܒܘܗܝ ܘܐܡܗ ܩܛܠܘܗܝ *the boy died and many were scandalized, suspecting that his father and mother had put him to death.* Aph. ܐܩܫܠ *to give offence, cause offence, cause to offend* or *sin, scandalize, repulse;* ܐܩܫܠܬܘܢ ܠܣܓܝܐܐ ܒܢܡܘܣܐ *ye have caused many to stumble against the law;* ܐܢ ܐܝܕܟ ܐܘ ܪܓܠܟ ܡܩܫܠܐ ܠܟ *if thy hand or foot cause thee to offend;* ܡܩܫܠܢܝܬܐ ܗܘܬ ܠܣܓܝܐܐ ܒܫܘܦܪܗ *she was a cause of offence* or *temptation to many by her beauty.* Derivatives, ܡܩܫܠܢܘܬܐ, ܡܩܫܠܢܐ, ܩܫܠܐ.

ܩܫܠܐ, ܩܫܠܐ pl. ܝ̈ܢ, ܐ̈ rt. ܩܫܠ. m. *a stumbling-block, rock, reef; cause of offence, offence, scandal, scruple;* with ܢܣܒ *to take offence;* with ܣܡ *to put a stumbling-block* in the way; ܐܠܦܐ ܕܡܬܬܪܝܐ ܒܟܠ ܩܫܠܝܢ *a ship which strikes on every rock;* ܕܠܐ ܢܗܘܐ ܠܟܠ ܩܫܠܐ *lest it be a cause of offence;* ܡ̈ܠܐ ܕܡܩܪܒܢ ܩܫܠܐ *words which lead to scandal;* ܘܠܐ ܩܫܠܐ ܕܢܗܝܡܢ ܘܠܐ ܠܟܘܢ *ye ought to believe it without any scruple.*

ܩܫܩܫ root-meaning *to speak softly, whisper,* not used in Peal. Ethpa. ܐܬܩܫܩܫ *to pray in a low voice, make supplication, supplicate, deprecate; to entreat earnestly:* with ܠܘܬ; ܒܩܠܝ ܠܡܪܝܐ ܐܬܩܫܩܫܬ *with my voice I made supplication to the Lord;* ܡܬܩܫܩܫܝܢܢ ܘܡܬܟܫܦܝܢܢ *we pray and beseech.* Derivatives, ܩܫܩܫܐ, ܡܬܩܫܩܫܢܐ, ܡܬܩܫܩܫܢܘܬܐ, ܡܬܩܫܩܫܢܐܝܬ, ܐܬܩܫܩܫܐ, ܐܬܩܫܩܫܘܬܐ, ܐܬܩܫܩܫܐܝܬ.

ܩܫܪ fut. ܢܩܫܪ, act. part. ܩܫܪ, ܩܫܪܐ, pass. part. ܩܫܝܪ, ܐ, ܬܐ. *to prosper, succeed, be fortunate; to be favourable, be of use, serve well;* ܕܩܫܪ *useful, serviceable, profitable;* ܕܠܐ ܩܫܪܐ *useless, ineffectual;* ܡ̈ܠܐ ܕܠܐ ܩܫܪܢ *unprofitable talk;* ܠܡܕܡ ܠܐ ܩܫܪ *it is good for nothing, of no use;* ܚܡܪܐ ܕܩܫܪ ܢܦܩ *wine that has turned out well;* ܡܢܐ ܕܩܫܪ ܡܢ ܗܘ *what is there better than to . . .?* Part. adj. *diligent, industrious, active, assiduous, dexterous, vigorous, strenuous,* often used of ascetics; *brave, excellent; advantageous, useful, profitable, acceptable,* ܕܒܘܪܬܐ ܩܫܝܪܬܐ *the industrious bee;* ܨܒܝܢܐ ܩܫܝܪܐ *the energetic will;* ܩܫܝܪܐ ܒܡܠܦܢܘܬܐ ܕܝܘܠܦܢܐ *one who labours assiduously in imparting doctrine;* ܡܢܐ ܗܘܐ ܩܫܝܪܐ ܠܗ *of what advantage was it?* ܥܠ ܪܒܘܬ ܩܫܝܪܘܬܗ ܕܫܠܝܐ ܠܩܫܝܪ̈ܐ *on the great advantage of quiet to strenuous ascetics.* Pa. ܩܫܪ *to do with success, accomplish successfully.* Ethpa. ܐܬܩܫܪ *a) to prosper, prevail, succeed, have good success. b) to be active, vigorous; to do* or *accomplish with zeal* or *diligence;* ܐܬܩܫܪܘ ܥܠ ܥܒܕܝܟܘܢ *be diligent in your doings;* ܐܬܩܫܪܘ ܒܨܠܘܬܐ ܘܒܨܘܡܐ *they laboured zealously in prayers and fastings.* Aph. ܐܲܟܫܲܪ *to have good success, bring to success, produce good results, do well, prosper* in work, in war; *to flourish* as a tree or plant; ܗܘܰܘ ܡܰܟܫܪܺܝܢ ܡܣܰܓܺܝ *they fought with great success;* ܟܰܕ ܚܙܳܐ ܕܐܰܟܫܰܪ *when he saw he had gained the advantage;* ܒܐܰܬܪܳܐ ܚܰܢܦܳܐ ܡܰܢ ܡܰܟܫܰܪ *in a heathen land who can do well?* Derivatives, ܟܫܺܝܪܳܐ, ܟܫܺܝܪܳܐܺܝܬ, ܟܫܺܝܪܘܬܳܐ, ܟܘܫܳܪܳܐ.

ܟܰܫܳܪܳܐ pl. ܐ̈ rt. ܟܫܪ. m. *a wise* or *successful teacher.*

ܟܘܫܳܪܳܐ rt. ܟܫܪ. m. *skilful* or *successful work.*

ܟܳܬ, ܟܳܬܳܐ or ܟܳܬܳܐܬܳܐ f. I. *that which grows of itself, a crop growing from a former harvest;* ܟܳܬ ܟܳܬܳܐ *the uncultivated produce of the second year;* ܬܶܐܟܘܿܠ ܐܝܟ ܫܰܢܬܳܐ ܗܳܕܶܐ ܟܳܬܳܐ. ܘܒܫܰܢܬܳܐ ܕܬܰܪܬܶܝܢ ܟܳܬ ܟܳܬܳܐ *thou shalt eat this year that which groweth of itself, and in the second year that which springeth from the same.* II. *reproof, censure;* see ܟܳܬܳܐܬܳܐ.

ܟܬܳܐ or ܟܬܳܐܬܳܐ f. *a clod, lump* or *ball of earth; a mass of mud* for smearing walls; ܟܬܳܐ ܙܥܘܿܪܬܳܐ ܕܡܶܢܳܗ ܐܬܓܒܶܠ ܐܳܕܳܡ *the little lump of clay of* which *Adam* was formed.

ܟܬܰܒ fut. ܢܶܟܬܘܿܒ, imper. ܟܬܘܿܒ, act. part. ܟܳܬܶܒ, ܟܳܬܒܳܐ, pass. part. ܟܬܺܝܒ, ܟܬܺܝܒܳܐ, ܟܬܺܝܒܬܳܐ. *a) to write, write out, copy out; to describe, inscribe, subscribe, enroll;* ܟܳܬܶܒ ܒܐܺܝܕܶܗ *he subscribes with his own hand;* ܟܬܘܿܒܘܿ ܠܐܰܪܥܳܐ ܠܫܰܒܥܳܐ ܦܶܠܓܘܿܢ *describe the land in seven divisions;* ܟܬܰܒ ܢܰܦܫܶܗ ܬܰܠܡܺܝܕܳܐ *he enrolled himself as a disciple;* ܟܬܘܿܒܳܝܢܝ ܥܰܡ ܠܳܐ ܡܗܰܝܡ̈ܢܶܐ *write me down amongst the faithless;* ܟܬܰܒ ܒܶܐܓܰܪܬܳܐ ܩܪܳܐ ܐܶܢܘܿܢ *he summoned them by letter, wrote for them to come;* rarely with ܥܰܠ *to write of, concerning* or *about,* in this sense the Aphel is usual. *b) to decree, ordain, assign in writing, leave by will* with ܠ or ܥܰܠ; ܟܠ ܡܶܕܶܡ ܕܐܺܝܬ ܠܝ ܐܶܟܬܒܺܝܘܗܝ ܠܟ *I will leave thee in my will all which I have.* Pass. part. *written, inscribed;* ܐܰܝܟ ܕܟܬܺܝܒ *as it is written;* ܟܬܺܝܒ ܡܶܢ ܠܥܶܠ ܕܟܬܺܝܒ *above-mentioned;* ܥܶܪܒܳܐ ܟܬܺܝܒܳܐ *a marked sheep.* Fem. emph. = subst. see below. Ethpe. ܐܶܬܟܬܶܒ *a) to be written, committed to writing;* ܟܬܳܒ̈ܐ ܕܟܬܺܝܒܺܝܢ ܒܐܺܝܕܰܝܗܘܿܢ *writings in their handwriting, codices copied out by them;* ܐܶܬܟܬܶܒ ܦܢܩܺܝܬܳܐ ܗܳܕܶܐ ܐܘܿ ܐܶܬܚܰܒܪܰܬ *this volume was copied out or put together. b) to be inscribed, enrolled* e.g. as a soldier; with ܒܡܰܟܬܒܘܼܬ ܫܡܳܐ *in the census;* ܕܡܶܬܟܰܬܒܺܝܢ ܒܫܡܰܝܳܐ *enrolled in heaven. c) to be described;* ܐܶܬܟܬܶܒܘ ܥܠܰܝܗܘܿܢ ܕܐܝܬܰܝܗܘܿܢ ܡܨܠܝ̈ܢܶܐ *they were falsely described as, reported to be Messaliani.* Aph. ܐܰܟܬܶܒ *a) to write, commit to writing, write a book, compose;* with ܥܰܠ *of, concerning, about;* with ܠܘܩܒܰܠ *against;* ܐܰܟܬܶܒ ܥܰܠ ܫܢܰܝܳܐ ܘܙܰܒ̈ܢܶܐ *he wrote annals and a chronicle;* ܣܰܓܺܝܐܶܐ ܐܰܟܬܒܘ ܥܠܰܘܗܝ *many have written about him;* ܬܪܶܥܣܰܪ ܡܺܐܡܪ̈ܐ ܐܰܟܬܶܒ *he composed twelve discourses;* also *to cause to be written;* ܐܰܟܬܶܒ ܟܬܳܒܳܐ ܗܳܢܳܐ *he had this book written, caused this record to be made;* ܐܰܝܟ ܕܡܰܟܬܒܺܝܢ ܫܡܳܗܰܝܗܘܿܢ ܥܰܡܺܝܕ̈ܐ *candidates for baptism come to have their names written down. b) to issue a written decree, to inscribe, dedicate, mark;* ܠܡܰܟܬܳܒܘ ܡܰܕܰܐܬܳܐ ܥܰܠ ܟܠ ܡܕܺܝܢܳܐ ܘܐܰܬܪܳܐ *they began to impose tribute on each city and district;* ܡܶܟܺܝܠ ܡܰܟܬܶܒ ܢܰܦܫܶܗ ܠܡܳܪܝܳܐ *henceforth* (from baptism) *he dedicates himself to the Lord.* Act. part. as subst. ܡܰܟܬܶܒ ܡܰܬܠܶܐ *a writer of fables;* ܡܰܟܬܶܒ ܫܢܰܝܳܐ *a chronicler, historian* cf. part. pass. ܡܰܟܬܰܒ ܫܢܰܝܳܐ *a chronicle, history.* Derivatives, ܟܬܳܒܳܐ, ܟܬܳܒܬܳܐ, ܟܬܘܿܒܳܐ, ܟܬܳܒܘܿܢܳܐ, ܟܬܺܝܒܘܼܬܳܐ, ܟܬܳܒܳܝܳܐ, ܟܬܳܒܳܝܬ, ܟܬܳܒܬܳܐ, ܡܟܬܳܒ, ܡܟܬܰܒܬܳܐ, ܡܰܟܬܒܳܢܘܼܬܳܐ, ܡܰܟܬܒܳܢܳܐ, ܡܰܟܬܒܳܢܘܼܬܳܐ.

ܟܬܳܒ, ܟܬܳܒܳܐ pl. ܟܬܳܒܺܝܢ, ܐ̈ rt. ܟܬܒ. m. *a) writing, handwriting, script;* ܫܳܪܶܐ ܐ̱ܢܳܐ ܟܬܳܒܳܐ ܕܫܘܼܥܺܝܬܳܐ *I begin to write the book of—;* ܟܬܘܿܒ ܒܟܬܳܒܳܐ ܕܓܢܳܐ *write in common handwriting. b) superscription, inscription* on a coin, *title* of a book. *c) a writing, book, record, treatise;* ܟܬܳܒܳܐ ܕܫܢܰܝܳܐ *a book of annals;* ܟܬܳܒ̈ܐ ܕܐܰܒܳܗܳܬܳܐ *the writings of the Fathers;* esp. *the Holy Scriptures,* ܟܬܳܒܳܐ ܥܰܬܺܝܩܳܐ *the Old Testament;* ܐܰܝܟ ܣܳܗܕܘܼܬܳܐ ܕܟܬܳܒܳܐ *according to the witness of Scripture. d) a written agreement, a decree, a bill, bond;* ܟܬܳܒܳܐ ܕܫܘܼܒܳܩܳܐ—ܕܡܶܫܬܰܒܩܳܐ *a bill of divorce.*

ܟܬܳܒܬܳܐ, ܟܬܳܒܬܳܐ rt. ܟܬܒ. f. with ܐܺܝܕܳܐ *a handwriting, autograph;* ܟܬܰܒܬ ܐܶܓܰܪܬܳܐ ܒܟܬܳܒܬܳܐ ܕܐܺܝܕܳܗ *she wrote a letter with her own hand.*

ܟܬܳܒܘܿܢܳܐ pl. ܐ̈ dim. of ܟܬܳܒܳܐ. m. *a little book, booklet, pamphlet, scrap of writing.*

ܟܬܒܢܝܐ, ܟܬܒܢܝܬܐ rt. ܟܬܒ. *a*) adj. *belonging to writing, taken from a book, literary; scriptural;* ܡܡܠܠܐ ܟܬܒܢܝܐ *literary language* or *style;* ܢܡܘܣܐ ܟܝܢܝܐ ܘܟܬܒܢܝܐ *natural law and scriptural law.* *b*) subst. *a librarian.*

ܟܬܘܒܐ, ܟܬܘܒܘ rt. ܟܬܒ. m. *a writer, copyist, scribe, amanuensis, secretary, notary;* ܟܬܘܒܗ ܕܟܬܒܐ ܗܢܐ *the scribe who wrote out this book;* ܟܬܘܒܐ ܛܥܘ ܒܐܬܘܬܗ ܕܫܡܐ *the copyists mistook the letters of the name.*

ܟܬܘܒܘܢܐ dim. of ܟܬܘܒܐ m. *a little scribe;* ܐܬܕܟܪܘ ܠܝ ܝܘܚܢܢ ܟܬܘܒܘܢܐ *remember me John the paltry scribe.*

ܟܬܘܒܘܬܐ rt. ܟܬܒ. f. *writing, script; the writing out* or *copying of books; the profession of a scribe; literary pursuits.*

ܟܬܝܒܐ, ܟܬܝܒܬܐ pl. ܟܬܝ̈ܒܬܐ Peal pass. part. f. = subst. usually pl. *a*) *writing, way of writing, handwriting;* ܒܟܬܝܒܬܐ ܕܚܠܝܦܐ *in the khalif's writing;* ܫܩܠ ܒܟܬܝܒܬܐ *he transcribed;* ܢܫܕܪܘܢ ܡܫܠܡܢܘܬܗܘܢ ܒܟܬܝܒܬܐ ܕܐܝܕܝܗܘܢ *they shall send their consent in their own handwriting.* *b*) *anything written, letters, characters, the alphabet; an inscription* e.g. on stone or on coins; *a letter, epistle; a bill, bond;* ܟܬܝܒܬܐ ܕܙܒܢܐ *a bill of sale; a document, register, roll; holy scripture.*

ܟܬܝܒܘܬܐ rt. ܟܬܒ. *way of writing, script;* ܟܬܝܒܘܬܐ ܕܫܡܗܐ *the inscribing of names;* ܡܢ ܟܬܝܒܘܬܐ ܕܫܡܐ *from the way in which the name . . . is written.*

ܟܬܝܒܐ, ܟܬܝܒܬܐ rt. ܟܬܒ. adj. *written, copied; scriptural;* ܡܦܩ ܒܪܘܚܐ ܟܬܝܒܬܐ *a written apology.*

ܟܬܝܫܘܬܐ rt. ܟܬܫ. f. *excitement, excitability, perturbation, tumultuousness;* ܡܫܠܝ ܗܘܐ ܠܟܬܝܫܘܬܗ *he calmed his excitement;* ܟܬܝܫܘܬܐ ܕܫܢܝܘܬܐ ܕܚܢܦܘܬܐ *the raging madness of heathendom.*

ܟܬܟܘܬܐ f. *cartilage, gristle; bone small enough to be eaten.*

ܟܬܡ fut. ܢܟܬܘܡ, act. part. ܟܬܡ, pass. part. ܟܬܝܡ. *to mask, scar, make a mark.* Pa. ܟܬܡ *to spot, sully, befoul, defile;* ܟܬܡܬ ܐܢܐ ܠܝ ܒܚܘܒܐ *I have spotted myself with guilt.* Pass. part. ܡܟܬܡ, ܡܟܬܡܐ, ܡܟܬܡܬܐ *spotted, defiled, contaminated;* ܓܪܒܐ ܡܟܬܡܝܢ *spotted with leprosy;* ܓܒܪܐ ܕܡܟܬܡ ܒܬܪܥܝܬܐ *a man of impure thoughts;* with ܠܐ *undefiled, immaculate, &c.;* ܘܠܐ ܡܟܬܡܐ ܗܘܬ ܪܥܝܢܗ ܒܚܣܡܐ *nor was his mind sullied by envy;* ܫܠܡܘܬܐ ܠܐ ܡܟܬܡܬܐ *uninterrupted concord.* Ethpa. ܐܬܟܬܡ *to be spotted, sullied, defiled, foul;* ܒܚܛܝܬܐ *with sin;* ܐܫܬܘܝܘܬܗܘܢ ܐܬܟܬܡܬ *their harmony was interrupted;* ܠܐ ܢܬܟܬܡ ܪܥܝܢܟ ܒܚܣܡܐ ܥܠ ܡܕܡ ܕܩܢܝܢ *let not thy mind be sullied with envy of anything that we possess.* Derivatives, ܟܬܡܐ, ܡܟܬܡܢܘܬܐ, ܡܟܬܡܢܐ.

ܟܬܢܐ pl. ܟܬܢ̈ܐ m. *flax, linen, a linen cloth* or *garment;* ܙܪܥܐ ܕܟܬܢܐ *linseed.* Derivatives, ܟܬܢܝܐ, ܟܬܢܝܐ.

ܟܬܢܝܐ, ܟܬܢܝܬܐ adj. *linen, of linen;* ܠܒܝܫܝܢ ܟܬܢܝ̈ܬܐ *clothed in linen.*

ܟܬܦܐ, ܟܬܦܐ pl. ܟܬܦܐ, ܟܬܦܝܢ, ܟܬܦܬܐ f. *the shoulder, the shoulder-blade;* metaph. *the upper side, side;* ܟܬܦܬܗ ܕܦܕܬܐ *the shoulder-pieces of an ephod;* ܟܬܦܐ ܝܡܝܢܝܬܐ ܕܒܝܬܐ *the right side of the house;* ܕܢܪܕܘܢ ܚܕ ܟܬܦܐ *to invade with a united front;* or ܐܪܟܢ ܟܬܦܐ ܕܡܫܬܥܒܕܢܘܬܐ ܕܡܟܝܟܘܬܐ *to bend down the shoulder* to bear the yoke *in humility* or *obedience.* Special meanings *a*) *the alternate part of a chant* as being sung by one side of a choir. *b*) *the part of a pruned vine which will next bear fruit.*

ܟܬܪ Pael ܟܬܪ *a*) *to wait for, await, stay, continue, persist, remain* with ܠܘܬ of a person, ܒ of a place, ܥܠ of a thing; ܟܬܪ ܠܘܬܢ *stay with us;* ܟܬܪ ܥܠ ܐܦܝܣܩܘܦܘܬܗ *he continued in his bishoprick* so many years; ܡܢ ܒܬܪ ܡܘܠܕܐ ܟܬܪܬ ܒܒܬܘܠܘܬܐ the B.V.M. *after giving birth remained a virgin;* ܐܝܟܐ ܡܟܬܪܐ ܢܦܫܐ ܒܬܪ ܡܘܬܐ *where does the soul wait after death?* ܛܘܦܣܐ ܡܟܬܪ ܠܫܘܪܪܐ *the type awaits the realization.* *b*) *to wait, stay, delay, tarry;* ܕܢܟܬܪ ܩܠܝܠ *that he may wait a little while;* ܟܬܪ ܫܡܫܐ. ܣܗܪܐ ܩܡ *the sun stayed and the moon stood still;* ܛܠܐ ܘܪܣܣܐ ܠܐ ܡܟܬܪܝܢ ܠܐܢܫ *dew and drops tarry for no man.* Ethpa. ܐܬܟܬܪ *to remain, dwell;* ܐܠܗܐ ܠܐ ܡܬܟܬܪ *God does not dwell in,* is not limited to, *any place.* Derivatives, ܟܘܬܪܐ, ܡܟܬܪܢܘܬܐ, ܡܟܬܪܢܐ, ܡܟܬܪܢܘܬܐ, ܡܟܬܪܢܐܝܬ.

ܟܬܫ fut. ܢܶܟܬܽܘܫ, act. part. ܟܳܬܶܫ, ܟܳܬܫܳܐ, pass. part. ܟܬܺܝܫ, ܟܬܺܝܫܳܐ, ܟܬܺܝܫܬܳܐ. *to beat, toss, disquiet; to strive, contend, fight; to debate;* ܟܰܠܢܺܝܠܳܐ ܟܳܬܫܳܐ ܠܝܰܡܳܐ. ܒܽܘܨܳܝܳܐ ܟܳܬܶܫ ܠܪܶܥܝܳܢܳܐ *a tempest tosses the sea, inquiry disquiets the mind;* ܐܰܝܟ ܗܰܘ ܕܠܐܳܐܰܪ ܟܳܬܶܫ *as one that beateth the air;* ܟܳܬܫܺܝܢ ܒܚܶܡܬܳܐ *quarrelling hotly.* Part. adj. *beaten, tossed, agitated; unruly, turbulent, contentious;* ܓܰܠܠܶܐ ܡܟܰܬܫܳܐ *tossing billows;* ܦܪ̈ܳܐܶܐ ܡܟܰܬܫܶܐ *furious wild asses.* Especially *driven about, vexed* or *harassed by a demon,* ܡܶܢ ܪ̈ܽܘܚܶܐ ܕܫܰܢܝܳܐ ܡܟܰܬܫܺܝܢ *they were driven about by spirits of madness;* ܦܰܓܪ̈ܶܐ ܡܟܰܬܫܶܐ *bodies vexed by evil spirits;* ܟܽܘܡܪ̈ܶܐ ܘܰܡܟܰܬܫܶܐ *priests and those possessed.* Ethpe. ܐܶܬܟܬܶܫ *a) to be disquieted, be in an uproar, to roar, rage;* ܝܰܡܳܐ ܕܡܶܬܟܰܬܫ *the raging sea. b) to strive hard, make great efforts;* ܐܶܬܟܬܶܫ ܕܢܶܡܰܠܶܠ *he strove hard to speak.* Ethpa. ܐܶܬܟܰܬܰܫ *a) to strive, contend, struggle, resist, fight against* usually with ܥܡ of the pers., with ܠܘܳܬ or ܥܰܠ of the thing; ܐܶܬܟܰܬܰܫ ܥܡ ܣܳܛܳܢܳܐ *he strove with Satan;* ܓܒܽܘܠ ܒܛܺܝܢܳܐ ܕܡܶܬܟܰܬܫ ܥܡ ܢܽܘܪܳܐ *puddle it with clay that it may resist fire. b) to strive hard, endeavour painfully, take great pains;* ܡܶܬܟܰܬܰܫ ܗܘܳܐ ܕܢܰܫܠܶܐ ܠܪܶܥܝܳܢܶܗ *he strove to tranquillize his mind.* Derivatives, ܟܬܳܫܳܐ, ܟܬܽܘܫܳܐ, ܡܟܰܬܫܳܢܳܐ, ܡܟܰܬܫܳܢܽܘܬܳܐ, ܬܶܟܬܽܘܫܳܐ.

ܟܬܳܬܳܐ *ferruginous earth, iron ore.*

∴ ܫܠܡ ܣܘܪܐ ܕܟܦ ∴

∴ ܘܠܬܪܗ ܫܪܝܐ ∴

∴ ܠܡܪܢ ܕܡܫܝܚܐ ܫܘܒܚܐ. ܠܥܠܡܝܢ ܕܠܥܠܡܐ ܕܠܐ ܫܘܠܡ ܕܡܫܪܝܢ ܠܡܗܘܐ ܡܫܟܚܐ ܡܢ ܐܘܠ ܫܘܠܡܐ ∴

∴ ܠ ∴

ܠ ܠ

ܠ, ܠܳܡܰܕ *Lamad* or *Lomadh*, the twelfth letter of the Syriac alphabet. As a numeral, ܠ 30, ܠܐ 31, ܠܒ 32 &c., ܠ̱ 3000.

ܠ inseparable prefix prep. *a)* of place, *to, unto, into, towards, against;* ܠܬܰܝܡܢܳܐ ܘܰܠܡܰܕܢܚܳܐ *towards the south and east;* ܐܶܬܳܐ ܠܡܕܺܝܢܬܳܐ *he came to a city;* ܐܶܣܶܩ ܠ—ܠܘܳܬ ܠ *he went up against* i.e. *attacked. b)* of pers. *to, unto, upon; by, for, of, on account of, according to, against;* ܐܳܡܰܪ ܐܢܳܐ ܠܟ *I say unto thee;* ܣܟܠܶܬ ܠܡܳܪܝܳܐ *I have sinned against the Lord. c)* of time, *at, on, to, until, after;* ܠܥܶܣܪܳܐ ܝܰܘܡܺܝܢ *on the tenth day;* ܡܶܢ ܝܰܘܡ ܠܝܰܘܡ *from day to day;* ܠܝܰܘܡܳܢܳܐ *until to-day;* ܠܙܰܒܢܳܐ ܐ̱ܚܪܺܢܳܐ *at another time;* ܠܐܰܪܒܥܺܝܢ ܝܰܘܡܺܝܢ *after forty days;* ܚܕܳܐ ܠܐܰܪܒܰܥ ܫܢܺܝܢ *once in four years;* . . . ܒܫܢܰܬ . . . ܠܡܰܘܠܳܕܶܗ ܕܡܳܪܰܢ *in the year . . . after the birth of our Lord;* ܒܫܢܰܬ . . . ܠܝܰܘܢܳܝܶܐ *in the year . . . of the Greeks,* but ܕܝܰܘܢܳܝܶܐ is commoner.

Uses: *a)* sign of the dative; ܗܰܒ ܠܝ *give me. b)* after transitive verbs the sign of the accusative; ܩܛܰܠ ܠܓܰܒܪܳܐ *he killed the man. c)* after a verb in the passive voice the sign of the agent; ܐܶܬܟܬܶܒ ܠܕܰܘܺܝܕ—ܟܬܺܝܒ ܠܕܰܘܺܝܕ or ellipt. *ascribed to, written by David;* ܐܟܺܝܠ ܠܚܰܝܘ̈ܳܬܳܐ *torn of wild beasts. d)* after neuter verbs and with pers. prons. adds emphasis; ܦܽܘܩ ܠܟ *get out;* ܩܽܘܡ ܠܟ *abide. e)* after impers. verbs;

ܩܢܛ ܠܗ he was sorry; with ܐܝܬ or ܗܘܐ and ellipt. to have to do, to be able; ܐܝܬ ܠܝ ܣܓܝܐܬܐ ܗܘܐ ܠܝ ܠܡܟܬܒ I had many things to write; ܐܦ ܗܘ ܐܝܬ ܗܘܐ ܠܗ ܕ he was also able to . . .; ܐܝܬ ܠܟ ܠܡܐܠܦ you may learn; ܡܢܐ ܐܝܬ ܠܢ ܘܠܟ what have we to do with thee? ܡܢܐ ܠܝ ܘܠܟ what have I to do with thee? . . . ܡܢܐ ܠܟ ܠܡܥܒܕ what business have you with . . .? f) sign of the infin., ܠܡܥܒܕ to do; ܝܩܝܪ ܠܡܫܡܥ heavy of hearing. g) used with nouns or pronouns to form other preps. and adverbs, ܠܘܬ towards; ܠܒܪ, ܠܓܘ without, within; ܠܓܡܪ altogether; ܠܣܘܓܐܐ at length; ܠܝܡܝܢܐ at the right; ܠܡܢܐ, ܠܡܘܢ, ܠܡܢܐ, ܠܡܢܐ why? wherefore? ܠܡܚܣܢ hardly; ܠܣܪܝܩܘܬܐ in vain; ܠܘܩܒܠ, ܠܘܩܒܠܐ towards; ܠܩܘܪܒܐ near; ܠܓܘ within, &c. &c.

ܠܐ negative and interrog. particle no, not, is it not? ܠܐ—ܘܠܐ, ܠܐ—ܘܠܐ, ܠܐ—ܐܦܠܐ neither—nor. Formula of denying, ܠܐ ܡܫܝܚܐ by Christ, no; ܠܐ ܚܝܝܟ, ܘܠܐ ܚܝܘܗܝ by your life, by his life I deny. With ܕ prefixed, ܕܠܐ lest, that—not; without; ܕܚܠ ܕܠܐ he feared lest; ܕܠܐ ܡܢܝܢ without reckoning; ܕܠܐ ܥܕܠܐ without blame, blameless; ܕܠܐ ܐܠܗܐ godless, impious; ܕܠܐ ܚܟܝܡܐܝܬ imprudently; ܟܕ ܠܐ because—that—not, although—not.

ܠܐ in compounds=in- or un-; ܠܐ ܡܫܟܚܐ impossible; ܠܐ ܡܗܝܡܢܐ unfaithful; for ܠܐ ܐܝܬ see ܠܝܬ.

ܠܐܐ or ܠܐܝ pl. 3 m. ܠܐܝܘ f. ܠܐܝ or ܠܐܝܬܝܢ, 2 m. ܠܐܝܬܘܢ, ܠܐܝܬܘܢ, 1 c. ܠܐܝܢ, fut. ܢܠܐܐ or ܢܠܐܐ, pl. 3 m. ܢܠܐܘܢ or ܢܠܐܝܢ, inf. ܡܠܐܐ, act. part. ܠܐܐ, ܠܐܝܐ, ܠܐܝܐ, pass. part. ܠܐܐ, ܠܐܐ, ܠܐܝܐ, pl. ܠܐܝܢ, ܠܐܝܢ, ܠܐܝܬܐ. to be weary, wearied by labour, to labour; ܡܠܐܐ ܩܛܠܘ ܥܕܡܐ ܕܠܐܘ they slew till they were weary; ܬܘ ܠܘܬܝ ܟܠܟܘܢ ܠܐܝܐ come unto Me, all ye that labour; ܕܠܐ ܠܐܐ unwearied, indefatigable. Ethpe. ܐܬܠܐܝ to be wearied by labour. Aph. ܐܠܐܝ or ܐܠܐܝ part. ܡܠܐܐ, ܡܠܐܝܐ or ܡܠܐܐ f. ܡܠܐܝܐ. to weary, fatigue, trouble; ܠܡܢܐ ܡܠܐܝܢ ܐܢܬܘܢ ܠܝ why do you trouble me? Derivative, ܠܐܘܬܐ.

ܠܓܘܣ a) λαγώς, a hare. b) λόγος, word, saying, speech.

ܠܓܛܘܢ legatum, a legacy.

ܠܕܢܘܢ and ܠܕܢܐ, ܠܐܕܢܘܢ, ܠܐܕܢܘܢ, ܠܐܕܢܘܢ, λάδανον, gum ladanum.

ܠܐܘܢ m. leo, a lion.

ܠܐܘܬܐ or ܠܐܘܬܐ pl. ܠܐܘܬܐ rt. ܠܐܐ. f. labour, trouble, weariness, care, the result of labour; ܠܐܘܬܐ ܕܐܘܪܚܐ the fatigue of the journey; ܠܐܘܬܐ ܕܐܝܕܝܟ the labour of thine hands; ܠܐܘܬܐ ܕܝܬܡܐ the care of orphans; ܠܐ ܚܣܝܪ ܗܘ ܡܢ ܠܐܘܬܐ ܕܫܠܝܚܐ he does not fall short of the labours of the Apostles.

ܠܐܟ root found in Ethiopic, to send a messenger, an envoy. Derivatives, ܡܠܐܟܐ, ܡܠܐܟܘܬܐ, ܡܠܐܟܐܝܬ, ܡܠܐܟܘܬܐ, ܡܠܐܟܐܝܬ.

ܠܐܡܐܢܐ; see ܠܡܐܢܐ a port.

ܠܐܦܐ pl. ܠܐܦܐ for ܡܫܘܛܐ an oar; metaph. ܐܚܝܕ ܠܐܦܐ ܕܡܕܒܪܢܘܬܐ ܕܥܕܬܐ he holds the oars, Anglice the helm, of the Church.

ܠܒ, ܠܒܐ pl. ܠܒܐ, ܠܒܘܬܐ, ܠܒܘܬܐ m. the heart; metaph. a) the mind; the breast as the seat of intelligence and feeling; ܟܪܝܘܬ ܠܒܐ sorrow of heart; ܕܠܐ ܠܒܐ without understanding, without energy, lazy, senseless; ܒܠܒܐ rit. secretly; ܡܢ ܠܒܗ of his own accord; by heart. With verbs; ܐܣܩ ܥܠ ܠܒܗ he considered; ܒܣܡ ܠܒܐ to rejoice, cheer, make friendly; with ܗܘܐ to propose, intend; with ܟܐܒ to pity; with ܡܠܠ to be kind, speak kindly, comfort; ܣܠܩ ܥܠ ܠܒܗ to be called to mind, come to mind; ܣܡ ܒܠܒܗ to think of, consider; ܐܪܡܝ ܐܠܗܐ ܒܠܒܗ God put into his heart. b) the centre, middle, best part, pith, marrow; ܒܪ ܠܒܐ the inner part, part near the pith or centre; ܠܒܐ ܕܕܩܠܐ the pith of the palm; ܠܒܐ ܕܝܡܐ the depth of the sea; ܠܒܐ ܕܡܫܪܝܬܐ—ܕܣܕܪܐ the centre of an army, of a rank; ܠܒܐ ܕܩܛܪܢܐ rosin; ܠܒܐ ܕܚܛܐ starch; ܠܒܘܬܐ ܕܠܒܢܐ moulds for brickmaking. Derivatives, verb ܠܒܒ, ܠܒܝܒ, ܠܒܝܒܐܝܬ, ܠܒܝܒܘܬܐ, ܠܒܒܐ, ܡܠܒܒܢܘܬܐ, ܡܠܒܒܢܐ, ܠܒܘܒܐ, ܠܒܝܒܐ.

ܠܒܒ denom. verb Pael conj. from ܠܒܐ. to encourage, comfort, console, exhort, inspirit. Ethpa. ܐܬܠܒܒ to take heart, be encouraged, comforted; ܐܬܠܒܒ ܩܠܝܠ ܡܢ ܟܪܝܘܬܗ he recovered somewhat from his sorrow.

ܠܒܟ ܠܒܟ act. part. ܠܒܟ, ܠܒܟܐ, pass. part. ܠܒܝܟ, ܐ, ܬܐ. to thicken; to make dense, heavy, opaque, compact; ܪܘܚܐ ܠܒܟܢ ܠܥܢܢܐ the winds drive the clouds together; ܚܫܘܟܐ ܠܒܝܟܐ thick darkness; ܓܠܝܕܐ ܠܒܝܟܐ a heavy frost. Ethpe. ܐܬܠܒܟ to become heavy, to be condensed, solidified, congealed; ܥܢܢܐ ܡܬܠܒܕܝܢ ܘܗܕܪ ܡܬܦܪܕܝܢ clouds gather closely and disperse again; ܢܛܦܐ ܕܡܬܠܒܕܝܢ ܥܠ ܦܓܪܐ drops condensed upon bodies. Pa. to solidify, thicken; ܡܠܒܕܝܢ ܣܥܪܗܘܢ they let their hair become matted. Ethpa. ܐܬܠܒܕ to be condensed, become dense, opaque. Derivatives, ܠܒܕܐ, ܠܒܕܘܬܐ, ܡܬܠܒܕܢܘܬܐ.

ܠܒܕܐ rt. ܠܒܕ. m. condensation.

ܠܒܘܬܐ or ܠܒܘܛܐ pl. ܐ m. an equal, just or fair measure.

ܠܒܘܟܐ, ܠܒܘܟܬܐ rt. ܠܒܟ. restraining; ܪܘܚܐ ܠܒܘܟܬܐ a contrary wind.

ܠܒܘܟܝܐ rt. ܠܒܟ. m. laying or keeping hold, grasp, attainment.

ܠܒܘܢܬܐ f. a) incense, frankincense. b) Mt. Lebanon.

ܠܒܘܫܛܐ or ܠܒܘܫܬܐ an uneven measure; cf. ܠܒܘܫܐ.

ܠܒܘܫ, ܠܒܘܫܐ pl. ܝܢ, ܐ rt. ܠܒܫ. m. a garment, raiment, clothing; with ܢܣܒ to clothe oneself, dress oneself.

ܠܒܛ Pael ܠܒܛ to instigate, incite; ܡܠܒܛܝ ܚܪܝܢܐ stirrers up of strife; ܘܡܠܒܛܢ ܦܪܨܘܦܗ his countenance was excited and fuming. Ethpa. ܐܬܠܒܛ pass. of Pael. Derivatives, ܠܒܛܐ, ܠܘܒܛܐ, ܡܠܒܛܢܐ, ܡܠܒܛܢܘܬܐ.

ܠܒܛܐ or ܠܒܝܛܐ rt. ܠܒܛ. m. incitement, egging on to strife, brawling.

ܠܒܝܒ, ܠܒܝܒܐ, ܠܒܝܒܬܐ adj. from ܠܒܐ. courageous, bold, intrepid, strenuous; ܐܪܝܐ ܠܒܝܒܐ the bold lion.

ܠܒܝܒܐܝܬ adv. from ܠܒܐ. courageously, boldly.

ܠܒܝܒܘܬܐ from ܠܒܐ. f. fortitude, courageousness.

ܠܒܝܕܘܬܐ rt. ܠܒܕ. f. congelation, opacity, density.

ܠܒܝܟܘܬܐ rt. ܠܒܟ. f. apprehension; ܠܒܝܟܘܬܐ ܕܪܥܝܢܐ preoccupation of mind.

ܠܒܝܫܘܬܐ rt. ܠܒܫ. f. putting on, clothing.

ܠܒܟ fut. ܢܠܒܘܟ, act. part. ܠܒܟ, ܠܒܟܐ, pass. part. ܠܒܝܟ, ܠܒܝܟܐ, ܠܒܝܟܬܐ. to lay hold, take hold, grasp, seize, catch, capture; to take, to hold, keep, retain; to take root; to take possession; to hold a bishopric; ܡܠܐ ܠܒܟܐ ܐܝܕܐ as much as the hand can grasp; ܠܒܟܬܗ ܒܕܩܢܗ she seized him by the beard; ܩܠܝܬܐ ܙܥܘܪܬܐ ܠܒܟ ܠܗ he took possession of a little cell; [Syriac] which equals the swiftness of the deer; [Syriac] they held their former rank; with ܚܘܠܡܢܐ to regain health. Metaph. to hold to, retain, adopt thought, custom, &c.; to comprehend; to keep, last, persist; ܠܒܟܬ ܗܕܐ ܪܥܝܢܐ she held this opinion; with ܒܐܝܩܪܐ to hold in honour. Idioms; with ܐܘܪܚܐ to hold on his way, set forward; with ܕܘܟܬܗ to succeed any one; with ܢܟܦܘܬܐ to be chaste; with ܢܦܫܐ to restrain, control oneself; with ܙܒܢܐ to seize the opportunity; with ܨܘܡܐ to begin the fast; with ܪܕܝܐ to set out, start; with ܣܘܪܗܒܘܬܐ to hasten; with ܪܩܕܐ to begin to dance; with ܫܬܩܐ to be silent. Pass. part. a) active sense holding fast, keeping, upholding, ruling, being in possession; ܗܢܘܢ ܕܠܒܝܟܝܢ those in authority; ܠܒܝܟ ܕܝܪܐ ruling the monastery = being abbot; ܠܒܝܟ ܐܓܘܢܐ striving; ܗܘܐ ܠܒܝܟ ܒܥܒܕܗ he entered on his work; ܗܘܐ ܠܒܝܟ ܥܝܕܐ the custom prevailed; ܡܢܝܢܐ ܕܠܒܝܟܝܢ ܣܓܝܐܐ the chronology which many adhere to; ܠܒܝܟ ܟܬܒܐ a librarian; ܠܒܝܟ ܢܦܫܗ self-controlled. b) pass. sense (rare) taken, captured, held fast, bound. Ethpe. ܐܬܠܒܟ to be seized, caught, captured, taken, apprehended, kept; to become condensed; metaph. with ܒܐܝܩܪܐ to be held in honour; ܥܝܕܐ ܐܬܠܒܟ or ܐܬܠܒܟ ܥܝܕܐ the custom was adopted. Aph. ܐܠܒܟ to give to hold, deliver, make to take; to make to apprehend or grasp, give to learn, teach, direct; ܐܠܒܟ ܐܢܘܢ ܐܘܪܚܐ ܬܪܝܨܬܐ he made them lay hold of the right way. Derivatives, ܠܒܘܟܐ, ܠܒܘܟܝܐ, ܠܒܟܐ, ܡܠܒܟܐ, ܠܒܝܟܘܬܐ, ܡܬܠܒܟܢܐ, ܡܬܠܒܟܢܘܬܐ, ܡܬܠܒܟܢܐܝܬ.

ܠܒܟܬܐ rt. ܠܒܟ. f. a) a task, lesson. b) a handle or occasion given to an adversary.

ܠܒܠܒܬܐ f. the uvula.

ܠܒܢܐ pl. of ܠܒܢܬܐ, ܠܒܢܬܐ.

ܠܒܢܐܝܬ adv. from ܠܒܐ. in his heart, secretly.

ܠܒܢܘܬܐ f. *brick-making.*

ܠܒܢܝܐ, ܝܬܐ adj. from ܠܒܐ. *of* or *from the heart, hearty, heartfelt;* ܕܡܐ ܠܒܢܝܐ *arterial blood;* metaph. ܫܘܒܚܐ ܠܒܢܝܐ—ܨܠܘܬܐ ܠܒܢܝܬܐ *heartfelt praise, earnest prayer.*

ܠܒܢܢ pr. n. *Mount Lebanon.*

ܠܒܢܢܝܐ or ܠܒܢܢܝܐ adj. from the above. *of* or *from Lebanon;* ܢܚܫܐ ܠܒܢܢܝܐ *brass from Lebanon, fine brass.*

ܠܒܢܬܐ and contr. ܠܒܬܐ pl. ܠܒܢܐ f. *a sun-dried tile* or *brick;* ܠܒܢܐ ܕܕܗܒܐ *plates* or *ingots of gold;* ܠܒܬܐ ܕܦܪܙܠܐ *an iron plate.*

ܠܒܪ adv. of place, *out, outside, out-of-doors;* see ܒܪ.

ܠܒܫ fut. ܢܠܒܫ, act. part. ܠܒܫ, ܠܒܫܐ, pass. part. ܠܒܝܫ, ܠܒܝܫܐ, ܠܒܝܫܬܐ *to put on* armour or apparel, *to clothe oneself, endue, don;* metaph. *to take, assume, take possession of;* ܠܒܫܘܗܝ ܠܡܪܢ ܝܫܘܥ ܡܫܝܚܐ *put ye on the Lord Jesus Christ;* ܠܒܫܘ ܠܣܓܝܐܐ ܫܐܕܐ *devils entered into many;* ܠܒܫ ܡܠܟܘܬܐ *he took possession of the kingdom;* ܠܒܫ ܩܪܒܐ ܪܒܐ *he commenced a great war;* with ܦܓܪܐ *to endue a body, become corporeal;* with ܐܒܠܐ, ܟܪܝܐ, ܚܫܐ, &c. *to grieve, suffer;* with ܫܡܐ *to assume a name.* Part. adj. *clad, clothed, endued,* &c.; ܠܒܝܫ ܙܝܢܐ *armed, mailclad, corseleted;* ܠܒܝܫ ܐܘܟܡܐ—ܚܘܪܐ *clad in black, in white;* ܠܒܝܫ ܠܒܘܫܐ ܕܓܒܪܐ *in male attire;* ܠܒܝܫ ܠܐܠܗܐ *God-clad, having put on God, godly, inspired,* cf. Rom. xiii. 14; ܠܒܝܫ ܠܡܫܝܚܐ *having put on Christ;* ܠܒܝܫܝ ܪܘܚܐ *endued with the Spirit;* ܠܒܝܫ ܙܟܘܬܐ *conquering, triumphant;* ܠܒܝܫ ܚܫܐ *liable to natural passions;* ܠܒܝܫ ܡܘܬܐ *subject to death;* ܠܒܝܫܝ ܢܘܗܪܐ *clad in light;* ܦܪܙܠܐ ܠܒܝܫ ܢܘܪܐ *white-hot iron.* Ethpe. ܐܬܠܒܫ *to clothe oneself, to be clothed; to be possessed* by a demon. Aph. ܐܠܒܫ *to clothe, endue, put on; to enshroud;* metaph. ܡܠܒܫܝܢ ܛܝܒܘܬܐ *endued with grace;* ܐܠܒܫܘܗܝ ܚܫܐ ܘܟܪܝܘܬܐ *they made him sad and sorry.* Derivatives, ܠܒܫܐ, ܠܒܘܫܐ, ܠܒܘܫܐ, ܠܒܝܫܐ, ܠܒܝܫܘܬܐ, ܡܠܒܫܢܐ, ܡܠܒܫܢܘܬܐ.

ܠܒܝܫܐ pl. ܐ̈ rt. ܠܒܫ. *armed, mailed, a heavy-armed soldier.*

ܠܒܫܐ rt. ܠܒܫ. m. *a garment, clothing.*

ܠܒܬܐ; see ܠܒܢܬܐ.

ܠܓ part. ܠܓܓ. *stammering.* Palpel ܠܓܠܓ *to hesitate in speech; to lisp, stammer, prattle, chatter;* ܠܓܠܓ ܗܘܐ ܐܝܟ ܛܠܝܐ *he prattled like a child.* Derivatives, ܠܓܠܓܐ, ܠܓܠܓܢܐ.

ܠܓܐ, ܠܓܬܐ or ܠܓܝܬܐ pl. ܠܓܝܢ, ܠܓܝܬܐ f. *a dish, basin, vessel; a measure;* ܠܓܬܐ ܕܕܝܣܐ *a basin of porridge;* ܠܓܬܐ ܕܡܣܟܢܐ or ܕܚܕܪܐ a constellation *the beggar's dish* = Corona Borealis.

ܠܓܐ pl. ܐ̈ m. *a league.*

ܠܓܝܬܐ pl. of ܠܓܬܐ; ܠܓܛܘܢ see ܠܓܝܛܘܢ.

ܠܓܘ prep. takes no suffixes; *inside, within;* see ܓܘ.

ܠܓܙ Ar. *to speak in riddles.* Derivative, ܠܓܙܐ.

ܠܓܙܐ m. *an enigma, riddle, parable.*

ܠܓܛܐ, ܠܓܛܘܢ, ܠܓܛܘܢ pl. ܠܓܛܐ cf. ܠܓܝܛܘܢ, Lat. *legatum, portion of an inheritance, bequest, legacy.*

ܠܓܝܘܢ, ܠܓܝܘܢܐ pl. ܝܢ, ܐ̈ f. Lat. *a legion;* ܢܚܬܘ ܠܓܝܘܢܐ ܕܢܘܗܪܐ ܡܢ ܪܘܡܐ *the legions of light descended from on high;* ܓܒܪܐ ܕܒܗ ܠܓܝܘܢ *the man possessed with the Legion* of devils.

ܠܓܝܢܐ pl. ܐ̈ m. λάγηνος, *a flask, bottle, vessel.*

ܠܓܠܓ Palp. conj. of ܠܓ.

ܠܓܠܓܢܐ pl. ܐ̈ rt. ܠܓ. m. *a stammerer, stutterer.*

ܠܓܘܡܐ m. *a bridle, bit.*

ܠܓܡܪ adv. *utterly, entirely, altogether;* see ܓܡܪ.

ܠܓܢܐ m, *cynara scolymus, a kind of artichoke.*

ܠܓܢܐ pl. ܐ̈ m. λάγανον, *a cake made of flour and oil.*

ܠܓܬܐ *a*) emph. st. of ܠܓܐ. *b*) better ܠܓܬܐ f. *a seed-bed* or *flower-bed, parterre; a ridge* or *furrow.*

ܠܗܕܢܝ, ܠܗܕܢܐ, ܠܗܕܢ cf. ܠܕܢܝ *gum ladanum.*

ܠܗ Palpel ܠܗܠܗ *to amaze, confuse, stupefy.* Ethpalp. ܐܬܠܗܠܗ *to be amazed.* Derivatives, ܠܗܠܗܐ, ܠܗܠܗܘܬܐ.

ܠܗܐ, ܠܗܝ perhaps a harder form of ܠܐܝ. Shaph. ܫܠܗܝ part. ܡܫܠܗܝܐ *a*) perh. *wearying.* *b*) corrupt reading for ܡܫܠܝܐ in some copies of Job x. 22. Derivatives, ܫܠܗܝܐ, ܫܠܗܝܬܐ, ܠܗܝܐ.

ܠܗܒ only Shaphel ܫܠܗܒ *to inflame, glow, warm, cherish;* ܡܫܠܗܒ ܐܝܟ ܐܬܘܢܐ *glowing as in a furnace;* ܡܫܠܗܒܢܘܬܐ ܫܠܗܒܝܬܐ *glowing heat;* ܐܫܬܐ ܡܫܠܗܒܬܐ *a burning fever.* Eshtaphal ܐܫܬܠܗܒ *to be glowing, to burn with fever; to be inflamed, excited* with zeal. Derivatives, ܫܠܗܒܐ, ܫܠܗܒܝܬܐ, ܫܠܗܒܘܬܐ, ܡܫܠܗܒܢܘܬܐ, ܫܠܗܒܢܐ, ܫܠܗܒܢܝܐ, ܡܫܠܗܒܢܐ.

ܠܗܓ, ܐܬܠܗܓ denom. verb Ethpa. conj. from ܠܗܓܐ. *to be resolved* or *drawn up into vapour, to be evaporated, to exhale* ܡܝܐ ܟܕ ܡܢ ܫܠܗܒܝܘܬܐ ܡܬܠܗܓܝܢ *water when it is drawn up by heat.* Aph. ܐܠܗܓ *to evaporate, resolve into vapour.*

ܠܗܓܐ pl. ܐ̈ m. *vapour, steam, exhalation, heat;* ܠܗ̈ܓܐ ܫܚܝܢ̈ܐ—ܡܝ̈ܢܝܐ *hot fumes, watery vapours;* ܥܠܡܐ ܟܠܗ ܐܝܟ ܠܗܓܐ *the whole world is like a vapour.* Derivatives, verb ܐܬܠܗܓ, ܠܗܓܐ, ܠܗܓܢܐ.

ܠܗܓܢܝܐ and ܠܗܓܢܝܐ, ܠܗܓܢܝܬܐ adj. from ܠܗܓܐ. *vaporous, steamy;* ܡܢ̈ܘܬܐ ܠܗܓܢܝ̈ܬܐ *particles of vapour.*

ܠܗܛ Ethpe. ܐܬܠܗܛ *to be set on fire, to burn;* ܢܘܪܐ ܡܬܠܗܛܢܝܬܐ *flaming fire.* Aph. ܐܠܗܛ *to kindle, make glow.* Derivative, ܠܗܛܐ.

ܠܗܛܐ pl. ܐ̈ m. *the heat* or *flame* of fire.

ܠܗܝܦܐܝܬ rt. ܠܗܦ. adv. *eagerly, greedily.*

ܠܗܝܦܘܬܐ rt. ܠܗܦ. f. *ardent desire, eager longing; the object of desire;* ܐܝܬܝܟ ܐܢܬ ܠܗܝܦܘܬܐ ܘܡܚܠܝܘܬܐ *thou art desire and sweetness.*

ܠܗܠ comp. of ܗܠ demonstrative particle and ܠ. adv. of place and time expressing remoteness, *a*) *thither, beyond, far, far off;* ܠܗܠ ܘܠܗܠ *hither and thither;* ܦܢܘ ܠܗܠ *stand back;* ܡܢ ܠܗܠ *afar, far off, beyond;* ܡܢ ܠܗܠ *far from;* ܠܗܠ ܡܢ ܟܠ *above all, supreme, highest.* *b*) *beyond, thenceforth, from that time forth, long since;* ܡܢ ܗܫܐ ܘܠܗܠ *from this time forward;* ܕܠܗܠ *that which is beyond this life* opp. to ܕܗܪܟܐ *the things of this present life;* ܕܝܢܐ ܕܠܗܠ *the last judgement;* ܥܠܡܐ ܕܠܗܠ *the age beyond, the world to come.*

ܠܗܠܝܐ or ܠܗܠܝܐ adj. from ܠܗܠ. *of the life beyond this,* ܛܘܒܐ ܠܗܠܝܬܐ *the happiness of the far-off land* i. e. *of heaven.*

ܠܗܦ fut. ܢܠܗܘܦ, pass. part. ܠܗܝܦ, ܠܗܝܦܐ. *to pursue eagerly, seize greedily, be eager for;* part. *thirsting, longing, eagerly desiring;* ܠܗܝܦܝܢ ܠܩܛܠܐ *eager for the slaughter;* ܪܥܝܢܐ ܠܗܝܦ ܠܡܝܬܪܘܬܐ *a mind athirst for virtue.* Ethpa. ܐܬܠܗܦ *to desire ardently, seek* or *long for eagerly, thirst after;* with ܠܥܘܬܪܐ *for wealth;* with ܠܡܠܘܗܝ *to listen eagerly to his words.* Aph. ܐܠܗܦ *to devour with thirst, inflame with desire.* Derivatives, ܠܗܝܦܘܬܐ, ܠܗܝܦܐܝܬ.

ܠܗܦܝܩܝܢ; see ܠܦܝܩܝܢ *a litter.*

ܠܗܬ denom. verb Pael conj. from ܠܗܬܐ *to breathe hard, pant;* ܟܕ ܡܠܗܬܐ ܡܢ ܥܡܠܐ *breathing quickly from toil;* ܗܢܘܢ ܕܡܠܗܬܝܢ *asthmatic people.*

ܠܗܬܐ or ܠܗܬܐ m. *asthma, shortness of breath;* ܠܗܬܐ ܢܫܡܐ ܘܢܫܡܘܫܐ *panting and puffing.*

ܠܘ contr. of ܠܐ ܗܘ, negative particle *no, not; is it not? does it not?* ܠܘ—ܐܠܐ *not—but;* ܠܘ ܒܠܚܘܕ *not only;* ܠܘ ܣܓܝܐܐ *not many.* The double negative ܠܘ ܠܐ makes an affirmative; ܠܘ ܠܐ ܡܨܐ *not unable* = *able;* ܠܘ ܠܐ ܡܕܡ *somewhat.* In composition *in-, un-;* ܠܘ forms negatives but less commonly than ܠܐ; ܠܘ ܡܫܡܠܝܐܝܬ *imperfectly;* ܠܘ ܣܓܝ *very little, not much;* ܠܘ ܣܓܝ ܕܝܢ *not much less.*

ܠܘܐ, ܠܘܐ fut. ܢܠܘܐ, imper. ܠܘܝ, act. part. ܠܘܐ ܠܘܝܐ. *to go* or *come with, accompany, follow;* ܠܘܐ ܗܘܐ ܠܦܘܠܘܣ ܛܝܡܬܐܘܣ *Timothy was Paul's companion;* ܠܘܝܐ ܠܗ ܛܠܠܗ ܕܒܪܢܫܐ *a man's shadow follows him;* ܢܟܦܘܬܐ—ܩܕܝܫܘܬܐ ܠܘܝܐ ܗܘܬ ܠܗ *chastity, holiness, was his familiar companion;* ܚܝܠܗ ܕܐܠܗܐ ܠܘܐ ܗܘܐ ܠܗ *God's strength was with him.* Ethpe. ܐܬܠܘܝ *to accompany, join;* with ܩܪܒܐ *to join combat;* ܐܬܠܘܝܬ ܠܗ

ܠܐܢܛܝܒܘܬܐ grace went with him. Pa. ܠܰܘܺܝ to accompany, conduct, pursue; to follow to the grave; ܚܛܳܗܳܟ ܡܠܰܘܶܐ ܠܳܗ ܠܟ thy sin ever pursues thee; ܡܳܐ ܕܰܡܠܰܘܶܐ ܐܢܬ ܠܥܢܝܕ̈ܐ ܠܩܒܪܐ܆ ܐܶܬܕܟܰܪ ܕܳܐܦ ܐܢܬ ܡܶܫܬܰܠܘܰܝܬ ܠܬܰܡܳܢ when thou followest the departed to the grave, remember that thou also wilt be borne thither. Ethpa. ܐܶܬܠܰܘܺܝ to be accompanied, conducted; to be followed or borne to the grave; to make or be a companion of, to associate with; to be brought up together, with ܥܡ, ܠ or ܒ; ܐܶܬܠܰܘܺܝܘ ܒܰܡܰܠܦܳܢܘܬܳܐ they were fellow-learners; ܢܶܬܠܰܘܶܐ ܥܰܡܟܽܘܢ ܐܠܗܐ God be with you; ܢܶܬܠܰܘܽܘܢ ܡܰܠܰܐܟ̈ܐ let angels accompany. Aph. ܐܰܠܘܺܝ to accompany, follow esp. to the grave. Derivatives, ܠܘܝܐ, ܠܘܝܐ, ܠܘܝܐ, ܠܘܝܬܐ, ܠܘܝܐ, ܠܘܝܬܐ, ܡܠܘܝܐ, ܡܫܬܠܘܝܢܘܬܐ.

ܠܘܒܒܐ pl. ܐ̈ from ܠܒܐ m. encouragement, exhortation, consolation; ܠܠܘܒܒܐ ܕܚܕ̈ܕܐ to encourage each other.

ܠܘܒܠܐ rt. ܠܒܠ. m. an inciting, rousing.

ܠܘܓܘܬܛܐ λογοθέτης, an auditor.

ܠܘܓܝܣܡܘܣ reasoning, speech.

ܠܘܓܝܩܘܣ m. ܠܘܓܝܩܝ f. pl. ܠܘܓܝܩܘܣ adj. λογικός, rational.

ܠܘܓܝܩܝ and ܠܘܓܝܩܝܐ λογική, logic, reasoning, eloquence.

ܠܘܓܝܩܝܐ, ܠܘܓܝܩܝܬܐ from the above. adj. logical, of logic.

ܠܘܓܠܓܐ pl. ܐ̈ rt. ܠܓܠܓ. m. stammering, hesitating speech, lisping.

ܠܘܓܡܐ m. a bridle, bit, curb; the jaw; ܢܘܩܪܐ ܕܠܘܓܡܐ the hollow of the jaw.

ܠܘܕܘܢ λοῦδον, the arena, amphitheatre.

ܠܘܕܪܐ m. λουδάριος, a gladiator, player, a rough, a bad character.

ܠܘܕܪܘܬܐ from the above. f. the business of a gladiator or player.

ܠܘܕܬܐ pl. ܐ̈ f. a band, cohort, body-guard; ܛܝܒܘܬܗ ܕܐܠܗܐ ܠܘܕܬܐ ܕܡܚܝܠܘܬܢ the grace of God is the guard of our feebleness.

ܠܘܗܝܐ rt. ܠܗܐ. m. amazement, consternation.

ܠܘܘܝܐ pl. ܐ̈ rt. ܠܘܐ. m. company, accompanying, esp. attendance at a funeral, a funeral procession, obsequies; ܠܘܘܝܗ ܕܡܪܬܝ ܡܪܝܡ the burial of St. Mary; ܛܟܣܐ ܕܠܘܘܝܐ or ܡܠܘܝܐ the funeral rite, burial service.

ܠܘܙ, ܠܘܙܐ pl. ܠܘܙ̈ܐ m. the almond tree and fruit; ܠܘܙ̈ܐ ܚܠܝ̈ܐ sweet almonds opp. ܠܘܙ̈ܐ ܡܪ̈ܝܪܐ bitter almonds.

ܠܘܚ, ܠܘܚܐ pl. ܠܘܚ̈ܐ f. a tablet, writing-tablet, writing, title; ܠܘܚ̈ܐ ܕܟܐܦܐ tables of stone; ܠܘܚ̈ܐ ܕܕܝܬܩܐ—ܕܢܡܘܣܐ—ܕܣܗܕܘܬܐ the tables of the covenant, of the law; ܠܘܚ̈ܐ ܕܠܒܟ the tablets of thine heart = thy memory; ܠܘܚܐ ܕܩܪܝܢܐ a reading-book, lesson-book; ܠܘܚܐ ܕܩܪ̈ܝܢܐ a table of the lections; ܠܘܚ̈ܐ ܕܕܒܩܐ tablets or squares of glue.

ܠܘܚܡܐ rt. ܠܚܡ. m. a threat, threatening, menace, rebuke.

ܠܘܚܫܐ pl. ܐ̈ rt. ܠܚܫ. muttering, whispering, incantation.

ܠܘܚܫܬܐ pl. ܬ̈ܐ rt. ܠܚܫ. f. an incantation, a charm, an amulet; whispers of evil, detraction, disparagement.

ܠܘܛ, ܠܛ fut. ܢܠܘܛ, act. part. ܠܐܛ, ܠܝܛܐ, pass. part. ܠܝܛ, ܠܝܛܐ, ܠܝܛܬܐ. to curse; p. p. accursed. Ethpe. ܐܬܠܝܛ to be accursed, be the subject of a curse. Pa. ܠܰܘܶܛ to curse bitterly. Derivatives, ܠܘܛܬܐ, ܠܘܛܐ, ܠܝܛܐ, ܡܠܝܛܐ.

ܠܘܛܪܝܘܢ λωτάριον, zizyphus lotus, the lotus.

ܠܘܛܢܝܐ or ܠܘܛܢܝܐ; see ܠܝܛܢܝܐ a litany.

ܠܘܛܘܣ, ܠܘܛܘܣ m. λωτός, the lotus plant.

ܠܘܛܬܐ pl. ܠܘ̈ܛܬܐ rt. ܠܛ. f. a curse, malediction; imprecation; ܐܪܥܐ ܕܠܘܛܬܐ an accursed land; ܒܪ ܠܘܛܬܐ accursed, execrable.

ܠܘܝ irreg. imperative of ܠܘܐ, used as an interj. Oh that! if only.

ܠܘܝ pr. n. Levi. Derivatives, ܠܘܝܐ, ܠܘܝܘܬܐ.

ܠܘܝܐ, ܠܘܝܬܐ pl. m. ܠܘ̈ܝܐ, f. ܠܘ̈ܝܬܐ, rt. ܠܘܐ. a companion, guide, friend, follower; ܚܟܡܬܐ ܠܘܝܬܐ ܬܗܘܐ ܠܟ may wisdom accompany you.

ܠܘܝܐ pl. ܠܘ̈ܝܐ m. ܠܘܝܬܐ pl. ܬ̈ܐ from ܠܘܝ a Levite.

ܠܘܝܐ rt. ܠܘܐ. m. a company, escort, suite; ܠܘܝܘܗܝ his companions; a funeral train or procession, a funeral.

ܠܹܘܵܝܘܼܬܳܐ from ܠܹܘܵܝ. f. *the office* or *service of a Levite.*

ܠܘܳܝܬܳܐ rt. ܠܘܐ. f. *escort, attendance, company, companions, companionship, a funeral procession, funeral;* ܒܰܪ ܠܘܳܝܬܳܐ *a companion;* ܢܶܗܘܶܐ ܒܰܠܘܳܝܬܟܼܘܿܢ *may he be one of your party, may he journey together with you;* ܡܰܠܰܐܟ̈ܐ ܕܢܘܼܗܪܳܐ ܠܘܳܝܬܟܼܘܿܢ ܢܶܗܘܘܿܢ *angels of light attend you;* ܒܰܠܘܳܝܬܳܐ ܗܳܕܶܐ ܗܘܳܘ ܚܘܼܫܳܒ̈ܝ *my thoughts journeyed on this wise.*

ܠܶܘܝܳܬܳܢ or ܠܶܘܝܰܬܰܢ Heb. m. *leviathan, a sea-monster, crocodile, serpent, a whale;* metaph. *the devil.*

ܠܘܼܟܼܝܬܳܐ pl. ܠܘܼܟܼܝ̈ܳܬܳܐ f. *a spear, a broad spear.*

ܠܘܼܒܝܬܳܐ pl. ܠܘܼܒܝ̈ܳܬܳܐ f. *the point of an arrow* or *spear, a spear-head;* ܠܘܼܒܝ̈ܳܬܳܐ ܕܓܶܐܪ̈ܶܐ ܡܫܰܩܝ̈ܳܢ ܣܰܡܳܐ *points tipped with poison.*

ܠܘܼܒܝܳܬܳܢܳܝܳܐ from above. *sharp-pointed.*

ܠܘܼܒܳܕܳܐ pl. ܠܘܼܒܳܕ̈ܶܐ m. *a maker of rough cloth for tents or horsecloths.*

ܠܘܼܒܳܕܘܼܬܳܐ f. *the making of horsecloths.*

ܠܘܳܩ, ܠܘܰܩ or ܠܘܼܩ fut. ܢܠܘܼܩ, ܢܠܘܿܩ, part. ܠܳܐܶܩ, ܠܘܼܩܳܐ. *to draw nigh, come near;* ܦܳܪܰܚܬܳܐ ܐܶܢ ܐ̱ܢܳܫ ܢܠܘܼܩ ܠܦܰܪ̈ܘܼܓܶܝܗ̇ *a bird if any one approaches her young . . .;* ܫܶܢܬܳܐ ܠܳܐ ܠܘܼܩܳܐ ܠܘܳܬ ܥܰܦ̈ܥܰܦܰܝܗܘܿܢ *sleep comes not near their eyelids.* ETHPA. ܐܶܬ݂ܠܰܘܰܩ *to be brought near, agree with.*

ܠܘܼܡܳܐ pl. ܠܘܼܡܺܝܢ, ܠܘܼܡܶܐ m. *a farthing, the fourth part of an as.*

ܠܘܼܡܠܳܠܳܐ from ܠܡܠܡ. m. *enunciation, pronunciation.*

ܠܳܥ, ܠܥ or ܠܥܰ fut. ܢܠܘܼܥ, inf. ܡܶܠܥܰܥ, act. part. ܠܳܐܶܥ, pl. ܠܳܐܥܺܝܢ or ܠܥܺܝܢ. *to lick up, lap;* ܠܥܺܝܢ ܡܰܝ̈ܳܐ ܒܐܺܝܕ̈ܰܝܗܘܿܢ *lapping water from their hands;* ܠܳܐܶܥ ܕܡܳܐ *licking up blood.* DERIVATIVES, ܠܘܥܐ, ܠܘܥܬܐ, ܠܥܥܐ, ܡܠܥܠܥܢܘܬܐ, ܡܠܥܠܥܢܐ.

ܠܘܥܳܐ or ܠܘܥܳܐ rt. ܠܥܥ. *a) pondweed. b) the jaw;* ܠܘܥܳܐ ܬܰܚܬܳܝܳܐ *the lower jaw.*

ܠܘܥܬܳܐ or ܠܘܥܬܳܐ pl. ܠܘܥ̈ܳܬܳܐ *the jawbone, the jaw.*

ܠܘܥܣܳܐ rt. ܠܥܣ. m. *chewing, masticating.*

ܠܘܳܦ, ܠܘܦ fut. ܢܠܘܼܦ, act. part. ܠܳܐܶܦ, ܠܳܝܦܳܐ, pass. part. ܠܝܼܦ, ܠܝܼܦܳܐ. *to join, add.* ETHPE. ܐܶܬ݂ܠܺܝܦ *to be added, to join oneself.* APH. ܐܰܠܺܝܦ *to subjoin, connect, continue;* ܡܶܢ ܫܠܳܡܶܗ ܠܘܳܬ ܡܰܠܦܳܢܘܼܬܶܗ ܐܰܠܺܝܦ *immediately after the salutation he begins his sermon.*

ܠܘܦܳܐ m. *a) sempervivum. b) pearl barley. c) the arum;* ܠܘܦܳܐ ܩܰܦܣܳܝܳܐ *arum crispum.*

ܠܘܦܪܳܐ m. *a) a little idol, image, metal figure. b)* perh. λιπαρός, *sumptuous, wealthy.*

ܠܘܦܢܳܐ some instrument of torture.

ܠܘܩܒܰܠ = ܠܘܼܩܒܰܠ rt. ܩܒܠ. prep. *a) opposite, against;* with ܩܳܡ *to rise* or *stand against, oppose;* ܠܘܩܒܰܠ ܡܶܐܡܪܳܐ *contradiction. b) before, in front, towards;* ܠܘܩܒܰܠ ܐܰܦ̈ܶܐ *facing, fronting, in front of;* ܬܳܐܙܠܽܘܢ ܠܘܩܒܰܠܗܘܿܢ *they shall go straight forward;* ܠܘܩܒܰܠ ܪܰܡܫܳܐ *towards evening. c) in proportion, in comparison, according to;* ܠܳܐ ܡܶܕܶܡ ܐܶܢܽܘܢ ܠܘܩܒܰܠ ܗܳܕܶܐ *they are nothing in comparison with this.*

ܠܘܩܕܰܡ for ܠܘܼܩܕܳܡ rt. ܩܕܡ. *first, first of all, before;* ܡܶܢ ܠܘܩܕܰܡ *formerly.*

ܠܘܩܳܛܳܐ pl. ܠܘܩܳܛ̈ܶܐ rt. ܠܩܛ. m. *gleaning, leasing;* ܠܘܩܳܛܳܐ ܕܙܰܝ̈ܬܳܐ *olive gleaning; food* or *alms collected* by begging; metaph. *a book of extracts, selections, gleanings.*

ܠܘܼܪܳܐ pl. ܠܘܼܪ̈ܶܐ f. λύρα, *a lyre.*

ܠܘܼܪܳܐ or ܠܘܼܪ̈ܶܐ *a) a sort of pulse. b) a saddle.*

ܠܳܫ, ܠܫ fut. ܢܠܘܼܫ, act. part. ܠܳܐܶܫ, ܠܳܝܫܳܐ, pass. part. ܠܝܼܫ, ܠܝܼܫܳܐ. *to knead, to weld;* ܠܫܘ ܦܰܪܙܠܳܐ ܐܰܝܟ ܕܠܳܐܶܫ ܓܰܒܪܳܐ ܛܺܝܢܳܐ *they welded iron as a man works clay;* ܠܳܐܶܫ ܠܫܳܐ *kneading dough.* ETHPE. ܐܶܬ݂ܠܺܝܫ *to be kneaded, mixed; to be softened, moistened* as flour with water, as food with saliva. DERIVATIVES, ܠܫܳܐ, ܠܝܫܳܐ, ܠܘܫܳܐ.

ܠܘܳܬ contr. from the construct state of the unused noun ܠܘܳܝܬܳܐ *being with, association:* prep. *a) at, with, near, in comparison with;* ܠܘܳܬ ܬܰܪܥܳܐ *near the door;* ܨܶܒܥܳܐ ܕܠܘܳܬ ܒܘܼܗܳܡܳܐ *the forefinger;* ܠܘܳܬ ܡܰܠܟܳܐ *with the king;* ܠܘܳܬܳܟ݂, ܠܘܳܬܶܗ *at thy house, at his house,* Fr. *chez toi, chez lui;* ܐܺܝܬ ܠܘܳܬܝ, ܠܘܳܬܶܗ *I have, he has;* ܠܰܝܬ ܠܟܘܿܢ ܠܘܳܬܝ ܡܶܕܶܡ ܡܶܢ ܣܰܟܳܐ *you have nothing to expect from me but war;* ܠܐ ܗܘܐ ܠܘܬܢ ܫܘܠܛܢܗ *we do not acknowledge his rule;* ܡܢ ܠܘܬ *from being with, from the presence of;* ܫܒܩ ܐܢܘܢ ܘܐܙܠ ܠܘܬ ... *he left them and went to . . .;* gram. ܠܘܬ ܡܕܡ *relation;* ܕܠܘܬ ܡܕܡ *relative;* ܒܠܘܬ ܡܕܡ *in the construct state.* *b*) *to, towards, for, regarding;* ܥܕܡܐ ܠܘܬ *as far as to;* ܐܓܪܬܐ ܠܘܬ *a letter to . . .;* ܚܘܒܐ ܠܘܬ ܐܠܗܐ—ܠܘܬ ܟܠ—ܠܘܬ ܚܕ̈ܕܐ *love to God, towards all, to each other;* ܠܘܬ ܡܘܬܗ *in respect of his death;* ܐܡܪܝܢܢ ܠܘܬܗܘܢ *we say respecting them.* Derivatives, verb ܐܠܘܬ, ܡܠܘܬܐ, ܡܠܘܬܘܬܐ, ܡܬܠܘܬܢܘܬܐ, ܡܠܘܬܐܝܬ, ܡܬܠܘܬܐܝܬ.

ܠܘܬ Aphel ܐܠܘܬ denom. verb from ܠܘܬ. *to put together, join, add, unite* with ܠ or ܥܡ; ܚܘܒܐ ܡܠܘܬܐ ܠܗ ܠܟܐܢܘܬܐ *love united to justice;* gram. ܡܠܘܬܐ *in apposition;* ܫܡܗ̈ܐ ܡܠܘ̈ܬܐ *two nouns joined* i. e. one being in the construct state; ܗܘ ܕܡܠܘܬܐ *a noun in the construct state* as ܡܠܘܬܐ in ܡܠܘܬܗ. Ethtaph. ܐܬܬܠܘܬ *to join oneself; to be joined together, added, connected, referred;* ܣܘܪܛܐ ܕܡܬܬܠܘܬܐ ܒܝܢܬ ܬܪܬܝܢ ܢܘܩ̈ܙܢ *a line of connexion between two points;* ܐܠܐ ܐܢ ܠܘܬ ܡܫܝܚܐ ܡܬܬܠܘܬܐ *unless it be referred to Christ;* gram. *to be in connexion with another part of speech, to be in apposition, be placed in the construct state.*

ܠܘܬܒܬܐ pl. ܬ̈ܐ rt. ܠܬܒ. m. *guile, deceit, knavery, knavish plots; malice, ill-will;* ܠܘܬܒܬܐ ܦܪܝܫܝܬܐ *Pharisaic guile;* ܠܘܬܒ̈ܬܐ ܛܢܦ̈ܬܐ *foul designs.*

ܠܘܬܡܬܐ rt. ܠܬܡ. m. *a murmur, murmuring, muttering, incantation.*

ܠܙ ܠܙ fut. ܢܠܘܙ, part. adj. ܠܐܙ, ܠܐܙܐ. *to be importunate, tiresome, grievous;* ܛܠܝ̈ܐ ܠܐܙ̈ܐ *troublesome children;* ܫܘ̈ܬܐ ܠܐܙ̈ܐ ܕܦܬܟܪܘܬܐ *the offensive feasts of idol-worship.* Ethpe. ܐܬܠܙ *to be importuned, pestered, worried, annoyed, disquieted, harassed;* ܡܢ ܨܗܝܐ—ܟܘܪܗܢܐ—ܪܓܬܐ—ܚܫ̈ܐ *by thirst, sickness, desire, passions;* ܐܬܠܙܬ ܡܢ ܒܥܘ̈ܬܐ ܕܪ̈ܘܪܒܢܐ *she was worried by the solicitations of the nobles.* Ethpa. ܐܬܠܙ *to be disquieted.* Aphel ܐܠܙ *to importune, annoy by importunity, be pressing, tiresome, vexatious;* ܐܦܢ ܡܠܝܙܝܢ ܐܢܬܘܢ *even if ye be importunate;* ܗܪ̈ܣܝܣ ܡܠܝܙ̈ܢܝܬܐ *grievous heresies;* ܒܥܘܬܐ ܡܠܝܙܢܝܬܐ *a pressing request.* Ethtaph. ܐܬܬܠܙ *to be molested* by a devil. Derivatives, ܠܙܘܙܐ, ܠܙܐ, ܠܙܝܙܐ, ܠܙܝܙܘܬܐ, ܡܠܝܙܢܐ, ܡܠܝܙܢܘܬܐ.

ܠܙܘܙܐ rt. ܠܙ. m. *an importunate person, a bore.*

ܠܙܘܪܕ; see ܠܙܘܪܕ.

ܠܙܝܙܘܬܐ pl. ܬ̈ܐ rt. ܠܙ. *importunity, annoyance, worry.*

ܠܙܘܪܕ Pers. *lapis lazuli.*

ܠܙܬܐ pl. ܠܙ̈ܬܐ rt. ܠܙ. f. *importunity, tiresomeness, worry, annoyance, impertinence;* ܡܢ ܠܙܬܐ ܕܛܝ̈ܝܐ ܐܬܐܠܨ *he was constrained by the importunity of the Arabs;* ܡܢ ܠܙܬܐ ܕܡܚܘܬܐ ܕܥܘܒܪ̈ܐ *because of the plague of mice;* ܘܡܢ ܠܙܬܐ ܘܫܓܘܫܝܐ ܢܥܪܩܘܢ . . . *they ought to avoid worries and turmoil.*

ܠܚܐ fut. ܢܠܚܐ, inf. ܡܠܚܐ, pass. part. ܠܚܐ, ܠܚܝܐ. *to rub off, wipe away, blot out, erase, efface* e. g. ܡܘܡܐ *a blot;* ܕܡ̈ܥܐ *tears;* ܚܛܝܬܐ *sin;* ܣܘܪܚܢܐ *a mistake;* ܫܡܐ *a name.* Ethpe. ܐܬܠܚܝ *to be blotted out, wiped off, effaced, destroyed;* ܦܝܢܟܐ ܕܡܬܠܚܝܐ *a wiped dish;* ܠܡܬܠܚܝܘ ܕܘܟܬܐ ܕܩܒܪܐ *to efface the place of the sepulchre;* ܢܬܠܚܝܢ ܚܛܗ̈ܝܟܘܢ *may your sins be blotted out;* gram. *to be elided, suppressed.* Aph. ܐܠܚܝ *to blot out.* Derivatives, ܠܚܘܝܐ, ܠܚܝܐ, ܡܬܠܚܝܢܐ, ܡܬܠܚܝܢܘܬܐ.

ܠܚܘܕ from root ܚܕ and prep. ܠ takes pl. suffixes. *only, alone, sole, by oneself;* ܠܚܘܕܝ *I only;* ܐܢܬ ܠܚܘܕܝܟ *thou alone, &c.;* ܗܘ ܠܚܘܕ for ܠܚܘܕܘܗܝ *he only;* ܟܠ ܐܢܫ ܠܚܘܕܘܗܝ *each man separately;* ܐܠܦܐ ܠܚܘܕܝܗ *a ship left to itself* i.e. without a helmsman. Derivatives, ܠܚܘܕ, ܠܚܘܕܝܐ, ܠܚܘܕܝܐܝܬ, ܠܚܘܕܝܘܬܐ.

ܠܚܘܕܝܐܝܬ from ܠܚܘܕ. adv. *by oneself, separately, apart;* ܐܡܠܟ ܠܚܘܕܝܐܝܬ *he bare sole rule;* ܐܬܟܬܫ ܠܚܘܕܝܐܝܬ *he fought in single combat.*

ܠܚܘܕܝܐ, ܠܚܘܕܝܬܐ from ܠܚܘܕ. *only, alone, singular, solitary, sole;* ܠܚܘܕܝܐ ܒܡܠܟܘܬܐ *sole ruler;* ܠܚܘܕܝ ܥܝܢܐ *single-eyed;* ܕܘܒܪ̈ܐ ܠܚܘܕ̈ܝܐ *solitary* or *unsocial habits;* ܠܚܘܕܝ ܒܕܪܗ *the one man of his time;* ܠܚܘܕܝ

ܒܓܘܢܐ ܘܒܛܥܡܐ ܠܚܘܕܝܐ uniform in colour and taste; gram. singular; ܒܡܢܝܢܐ ܠܚܘܕܝܐ in the singular; separate, absolute opp. affixed.

ܠܚܘܕܝܘܬܐ pl. ܬܐ̈ from ܠܚܘܕ. f. unity opp. Trinity; a unit, oneness; solitude, solitariness opp. ܟܢܫܐ a crowd; ܩܪܒܐ ܠܚܘܕܝܐ single combat; ܫܘܠܛܢܘܬܐ ܠܚܘܕܝܬܐ sole rule; ܠܚܘܕܝܘܬܐ ܒ solely, simply; gram. the singular number.

ܠܚܘܝܐ pl. ܐ̈ rt. ܠܚܐ. m. one who erases, expunges.

ܠܚܘܡܘܬܐ rt. ܠܚܡ. f. adaptation.

ܠܚܘܫܐ pl. ܐ̈ rt. ܠܚܫ. a charmer, snake-charmer.

ܠܚܝܐ rt. ܠܚܐ. m. blotting out.

ܠܚܝܡܘܬܐ rt. ܠܚܡ. f. threatening, indignation.

ܠܚܟ fut. ܢܠܚܘܟ, act. part. ܠܚܟ, ܠܚܟܐ. to lick; ܠܚܟ ܥܦܪܐ ܒܡܘܟܟܐ he licked the dust in abjectness; ܠܚܟܬ ܫܠܗܒܝܬܐ ܕܡܐ the flame licked up blood. Pael ܠܚܟ to go on licking, lick often or continually; ܡܠܚܟ ܟܠܒܐ ܠܡܪܗ a dog licks his master. Derivatives, ܠܚܟܐ, ܡܠܚܟܢܘܬܐ.

ܠܚܟܐ or ܠܚܟܐ m. plantain, plantago major.

ܠܚܟܐ rt. ܠܚܟ. m. licking.

ܠܚܠܣ to fawn as a dog, flatter. Ethpaal ܐܬܠܚܠܣ to be flattered, wheedled. Derivatives, ܠܚܠܘܣܐ, ܠܚܠܘܣܬܢܐ, ܠܚܠܘܣܬܢܘܬܐ.

ܠܚܠܘܣܐ pl. ܐ̈ m. a fawner, flatterer, parasite.

ܠܚܠܘܣܬܢܐ rt. ܠܚܠܣ. m. a flatterer, knave.

ܠܚܠܘܣܬܢܘܬܐ rt. ܠܚܠܣ. f. fawning, flattery.

ܠܚܡ fut. ܢܠܚܘܡ, act. part. ܠܚܡ, ܠܚܡܐ, pass. part. ܠܚܝܡ, ܠܚܝܡܐ, ܠܚܝܡܬܐ. I. to eat. II. to suit with, fit, agree; ܠܚܡܝܢ ܠܚܕܕܐ agree with each other; used chiefly in the act. part. impers., it is fitting, suitable, convenient; ܒܥܕܢܐ ܕܠܚܡܐ at a convenient time. III. to menace, threaten; pass. part. active sense ܠܚܝܡܝܢ ܗܘܘ ܠܡܩܛܠܗ they threatened to kill him; ܢܘܪܐ ܠܚܝܡܬܐ ܠܚܛܝܐ fire menacing sinners. Ethpe. ܐܬܠܚܡ I. to fit, accommodate, connect, comprise, compact, form; ܐܬܪܐ ܕܡܬܠܚܡ ܠܗ ܡܢ ܥܒܘܕܗ a place made suitable to it by the maker. II. pass. to be threatened with ܥܠ or ܠ; ܐܠܦܐ ܡܬܠܚܡܐ ܗܘܬ ܠܡܬܒܪܘ the ship was in peril of being dashed to pieces. Pa. ܠܚܡ to fit, adjust, adapt, do anything suitably, join fitly together, compact, compose; ܡܠܚܡܝܢ ܕܘܟܬܐ they choose a fitting place; ܢܒܥܐ ܕܢܠܚܡ ܡܠܐ ܠܨܠܘܬܐ let us try to find suitable words for prayer; ܘܠܐ ܡܕܥ ܠܚܡܬܘܢ ܢܟܠܝܟܘܢ you have planned your guiles ignorantly; pass. part. fitly composed, congruous, well arranged; ܩܝܢܬܐ ܡܠܚܡܬܐ harmonious songs. Ethpa. ܐܬܠܚܡ I. to be adapted, adjusted; to be fitted, joined or fastened together, to unite; ܟܐܦܐ ܡܬܠܚܡܢ ܗܘܝ the stones were fitted on the mountain = squared in the quarry; ܐܬܠܚܡܘ ܠܥܡܐ ܚܕ the twelve tribes grew into one nation. II. to threaten, warn or command with threats; ܐܬܠܚܡ ܠܗ ܒܡܘܬܐ he threatened him with death. Derivatives, ܠܚܡܐ, ܠܚܡܐ, ܠܚܝܡ, ܠܚܡܐܝܬ, ܠܚܘܡܘܬܐ, ܠܚܡܘܬܐ, ܡܠܚܡܢܘܬܐ, ܡܠܚܡܢܐ, ܠܚܡܢܐ, ܡܠܚܡܢܐ, ܡܬܠܚܡܢܐ.

ܠܚܡ, ܠܚܡܐ pl. ܠܚܡܝܢ, ܠܚܡܐ rt. ܠܚܡ I. m. food, victuals, bread, a cake or loaf of bread; ܡܐܬܝܢ ܓܪܝܨܢ ܕܠܚܡܐ 200 loaves; ܠܚܡܐ ܕܣܥܪܐ barley-bread; ܥܕܢܐ ܕܠܚܡܐ supper-time; ܐܟܠ ܠܚܡܐ to sup, sit at meat; ܠܚܡܐ ܚܝܐ living bread, the bread of life; ܗܘܐ ܠܚܡܐ ܠܫܠܗܒܝܬܐ it fed the flame, added fuel to the fire.

ܠܚܡܐܝܬ rt. ܠܚܡ II. adv. fitly, aptly, justly, rightly; ܠܐ ܠܚܡܐܝܬ ܐܬܐ ܗܘܐ ܠܗ ܠܡܣܟܠܘܬܐ he had not rightly come to understanding or to his senses.

ܠܚܡܘܬܐ rt. ܠܚܡ II. f. fitness, agreement, aptitude; ܠܚܡܘܬܐ ܟܝܢܝܬܐ natural aptitude.

ܠܚܡܢܐ, ܢܝܬܐ rt. ܠܚܡ II. apt, suitable; ܡܠܬܐ ܠܚܡܢܝܬܐ a well-composed speech.

ܠܚܫ fut. ܢܠܚܘܫ and ܢܠܚܫ, act. part. ܠܚܫ, ܠܚܫܐ. to mutter incantations; to murmur, whisper, speak low ܒܐܕܢܐ in the ears of any one, to speak low in prayer, to sing softly as a lullaby; ܠܚܫ ܠܗ ܠܠܒܗ the devil whispered to her heart. Ethpe. ܐܬܠܚܫ to be told secretly, softly. Pa. ܠܚܫ to murmur softly, to whisper, *insinuate* with ܥܠ *against* any one. ETHPA. ܐܬܠܚܫ *to whisper, murmur* e.g. ܨܠܘܬܐ *prayers;* ܐܬܠܚܫܘ ܥܠܝ ܐܟܚܕܐ *they whispered together against me.* DERIVATIVES, ܠܚܘܫܐ, ܠܚܘܫܬܐ, ܠܚܫܐ, ܠܚܫܐ, ܡܠܚܫܢܐ.

ܠܚܫܐ pl. ܐ̈ rt. ܠܚܫ. m. *a charm, allurement.*

ܠܚܫܬܐ m. *a*) *the palm of the hand.* *b*) *the breath, breathing.*

ܠܛܐ fut. ܢܠܛܐ *to scrape off.* ETHPE. ܐܬܠܛܝ *to be scraped off.* DERIVATIVE, ܠܛܝܐ.

ܠܛܘܫܐ rt. ܠܛܫ. m. *one who sharpens his sword.*

ܠܛܝܐ rt. ܠܛܐ. m. *a*) *abrasion.* *b*) *a scraped* or *sharpened stake, a spike;* ܠܛܝܐ ܕܦܪܙܠܐ *an iron spike;* ܠܛܝܐ ܕܩܢܝܐ *the point of a reed.*

ܠܛܝܫܘܬܐ rt. ܠܛܫ. f. *the sharp point* or *edge* of a weapon; metaph. ܠܛܝܫܘܬ ܪܘܓܙܐ *sharp anger; acuteness, subtlety* of speech.

ܠܛܡܐ or ܠܛܡܐ m. *the pistachio nut, nux pistacia* or *avellana.*

ܠܛܦ fut. ܢܠܛܘܦ *to bark, shave, unsheath.*

ܠܛܪ *to chant, celebrate in song.*

ܠܛܫ fut. ܢܠܛܘܫ, act. part. ܠܛܫ, ܠܛܫܐ, pass. part. ܠܛܝܫ, ܠܛܝܫܐ, ܠܛܝܫܬܐ. *a*) *to hammer, rub, polish, sharpen, smear;* with ܙܝܢܐ *to hammer armour;* with ܣܦܣܪܐ *to sharpen a sword;* ܠܛܫ ܬܘܪܐ ܩܪܢܬܗ *the bull rubbed his horns on the earth.* *b*) *to provoke, incite* with ܠܚܡܐ ܠܪܘܓܙܐ—ܠܚܡܐ ܠܪܚܡܬܐ *to anger, to love.* Part. adj. *a*) *sharpened, dipped* or *smeared* with poison; ܓܐܪܐ ܠܛܝܫܐ *sharp* or *poisoned arrows.* *b*) *keen, acute, crafty.* ETHPE. ܐܬܠܛܫ imper. E-Syr. the same, W-Syr. ܐܬܠܛܫ passive of Peal in all senses. DERIVATIVES, ܠܛܘܫܐ, ܠܛܝܫܘܬܐ, ܡܠܛܫܢܐ.

ܠܝܒܐ λίψ, acc. λίβα, *a south-west wind, African wind.*

ܠܝܒܘܢܛܘܣ—ܠܝܒܐܘܢܛܘܣ—ܠܝܦܣ λιβόνοτος, *south-west wind.*

ܠܝܒܠܠܣ, ܠܝܒܠܠܘܣ pl. ܠܝܒܠܠܘܣܐ, ܠܝܒܠܠܘܢ, or ܠܒܠܠܘܣ m. *libellus; a deposition, written accusation, warrant,* ܠܝܒܠܠܘܢ ܕܗܝܡܢܘܬܐ *a confession of faith;* ܠܝܒܠܠܐ ܕܡܠܟܐ *an imperial warrant;* ܠܝܒܠܠܐ ܕܬܘܒܘܬܐ *a written recantation.*

ܠܝܛ usually repeated ܠܝܛ ܠܝܛ *quickly, directly, swiftly.* DERIVATIVES, ܠܝܛܐ, ܠܝܛܐܝܬ.

ܠܝܛܐ from ܠܝܛ adv. *swiftly, quickly, rashly.*

ܠܝܛܐܝܬ from ܠܝܛ adv. *swiftly, rapidly, directly.*

ܠܝܓܐܛܘܢ, ܠܝܓܛܘܢ, ܠܓܛܘܢ, ܠܓܐܛܘܢ pl. ܠܝܓܛܐ; see other spellings under ܠܓܛܐ m. ληγᾶτον, *a legacy, bequest.*

ܠܝܓܛܪܐ pl. ܐ̈ *legatarius, a legatee.*

ܠܝܘܛܐ rt. ܠܘܛ. m. *one who curses, declares accursed.*

ܠܝܘܛܐ pl. ܐ̈ rt. ܠܘܛ. m. *a swearer, one who curses, pronounces accursed.*

ܠܝܛܘܪܓܝܐ pl. ܠܝܛܘܪܓܝܣ λειτουργία, *liturgy.*

ܠܝܛܢܝܐ, ܠܝܛܢܝܐ and see ܠܛܢܝܐ f. λιτανεία, *a litany, solemn supplication.*

ܠܝܛܪܐ pl. ܝܢ̈, ܐ̈ usually m. but in the lexx. f. λίτρα, *libra, a pound weight;* ܠܝܛܪܐ ܒܓܕܕܝܬܐ *the Baghdad pound* weighed 400 drachmas, each drachma = 16 carats ⅔ grain, a Syrian pound equalled six Baghdad pounds.

ܠܝܟܝܢ, ܠܝܟܝܢ, ܠܝܟܢܐ, ܠܝܟܝܢܘܣ m. λειχήν, *lichen.*

ܠܠܝܐ, ܠܠܝܘܬܐ irreg. pl. of ܠܠܝܐ *night.*

ܠܠܝܐ or ܠܠܝܢܝܐ; see ܠܠܝܐ *nocturnal.*

ܠܡܛܐ pl. ܐ̈ m. *the terebinth berry; the resin of the terebinth.*

ܠܝܡܝܛܘܢ or ܠܝܡܝܛܘܢ λίμιτον, ܐܠܝ ܠܝܡܝܛܘܢ = Syr. ܬܚܘܡܐ ܐܬܪܘܬܐ *borders, confines.*

ܠܚܟܐ rt. ܠܚܟ. m. *licking.*

ܠܡܦܐ, ܠܡܦܐ, ܠܘܦܐ or ܠܡܦܐ pl. ܐ̈ *an oar;* ܓܒܪ̈ܐ ܕܠܡܦܐ *oarsmen, rowers;* metaph. *the rudder, helm,* ܠܡܦܐ ܕܡܕܒܪܢܘܬܐ *of government;* ܕܫܘܠܛܢܐ *of authority;* with ܐܚܕ *to hold the helm.*

ܠܝܫܐ or ܠܝܫܐ rt. ܠܘܫ. m. *dough, paste.*

ܠܝܫܐ rt. ܠܘܫ. m. *kneading, mixing* dough.

ܠܝܫܘܢܐ dim. of ܠܝܫܐ m. *a small bit of paste* or *dough.*

ܠܝܬ comp. of ܠܐ and ܐܝܬ (the ܬ is always hard) indeclinable verbal particle *it is not, they are not, there is not;* takes suffixes like a plural noun, ܠܝܬܘܗܝ *he is not;* ܠܝܬܝܗܘܢ *they are not;* ܡܝܐ ܠܝܬܝܗܘܢ *there is no water;* ܠܝܬ ܢܡܘܣܗܘܢ *their law does not permit;* with

ܗܘܳܐ expresses the past tense ܠܰܝܬ ܗܘܳܐ *there was not;* with ܠ *to have,* ܠܰܝܬ ܠܝ *I have not;* ܠܰܝܬ ܠܰܢ ܐܶܠܳܐ *we have only;* ܐܶܢ ܗܳܕܶܐ ܠܰܝܬܶܝܗ̇ ܐܳܦ ܠܳܐ ܗܳܝ ܠܰܝܬܰܘܗ̇ *if this be not so neither will that continue to be.* Ethpa. ܐܶܬܠܰܝܰܬ *to be reduced to nothing, annihilated; to cease, cease to be; to vanish from sight* e.g. as a star; ܡܶܬܒܰܨܪܳܐ ܥܕܰܡܳܐ ܕܡܶܬܠܰܝܬܳܐ *it diminishes till it ceases to be;* a cone ܡܶܬܠܰܝܬܳܐ ܒܪܺܫܳܗ̇ ܚܽܘܪܛܳܐ *comes to nothing at its apex.* Derivatives, ܠܰܝܬܳܐ, ܠܰܝܬܽܘܬܳܐ, ܡܠܰܝܬܳܐ, ܡܶܬܠܰܝܬܳܢܽܘܬܳܐ.

ܠܺܝܬܳܘܣ λίθος, *stone.*

ܠܰܝܬܳܝܳܐ pl. ܐ̈ from ܠܰܝܬ. *non-existent.*

ܠܰܝܬܳܝܽܘܬܳܐ from ܠܰܝܬ. f. *non-existence, nothingness, annihilation;* ܡܶܢ ܠܰܝܬܳܝܽܘܬܳܐ ܠܗܳܝܘܬܳܐ ܐܰܝܬܺܝܬܳܢ *Thou hast brought us out of nothingness into being.*

ܠܟܳܐ comp. of ܠ and ܟܳܐ. adv. of place and time *hence, hither;* ܠܟܳܐ ܘܰܠܟܳܐ *hither and thither;* ܠܟܳܐ ܘܠܗܳܠ *hither and thither, in all directions;* ܡܶܢ ܗܳܫܳܐ ܘܰܠܟܳܐ *henceforth, thenceforward, from this time forth;* ܡܶܢ ܠܟܳܐ *on this side, within* opp. ܠܗܳܠ *beyond.*

ܠܳܟܺܝ abbrev. for ܠܳܟ ܗܽܘ *to thee;* ܠܳܟܺܝ ܡܣܰܟܝܳܢ ܪ̈ܽܘܚܰܝܢ *on Thee do our spirits wait;* ܠܳܟܺܝ ܡܳܪܝܳܐ *to Thee, O Lord* (first words of a hymn of praise).

ܠܟܰܣ = ܠܚܰܟ, fut. ܢܶܠܟܽܘܣ, act. part. ܠܳܟܶܣ, ܠܳܟܣܳܐ, pass. part. ܠܟܺܝܣ. *to lick, lick up* e.g. ܥܰܦܪܳܐ *the dust;* metaph. of fire. Ethpe. ܐܶܬܠܟܶܣ pass. Pael ܠܰܟܶܣ *to lick, lick up* as a dog, *to suck* as a bee; ܡܠܰܟܣܺܝܢ ܗܘܰܘ ܠܶܗ ܐܰܪ̈ܝܳܘܳܬܳܐ *lions gobbled him up;* ܫܰܪܺܝ ܡܠܰܟܶܣ ܡܶܢ ܕܡܳܐ *he began to lick up the blood.*

ܠܟܶܡܳܐ comp. of ܠ, ܡܐ and ܟܳܐ; see ܡܳܐ and ܟܰܡ.

ܠܶܟܣܺܝܣ, ܠܶܟܣܶܣ or ܠܶܐܟܣܺܝܣ pl. ܠܶܟܣܺܝ̈ܣ f. λέξις, *a) speech, diction, style;* ܬܪܺܝܨܽܘܬܳܐ ܕܠܶܟܣܺܝܣ *correct diction. b) language, tongue; a phrase, reading;* ܠܶܟܣܺܝܣ ܐܳܪܳܡܳܝܬܳܐ—ܦܳܪܣܳܝܬܳܐ *the Aramaic, the Persian tongue;* ܦܽܘܫܳܩܳܐ ܕܠܶܟܣܺܝ̈ܣ ܥܶܒܪ̈ܳܝܳܬܳܐ ܐܰܝܠܶܝܢ ܕܒܡܰܙܡܽܘܪ̈ܶܐ *explanation of the Hebrew expressions in the Psalter.*

ܠܶܟܣܺܝܩܳܘܢ or ܠܶܐܟܣܺܝܩܳܘܢ m. λεξικόν, *a lexicon, dictionary;* ܠܶܟܣܺܝܩܳܘܢ ܐܰܘܟܺܝܬ ܦܽܘܫܳܩ ܡ̈ܶܠܶܐ *a lexicon, that is an explanation of words;* ܠܶܟܣܺܝܩܳܘܢ ܡܟܰܢܫܳܐ *a dictionary compiled from others;* ܠܶܟܣܺܝܩܳܘܢ ܦܽܘܫܳܩܳܝܳܐ *a glossary.*

ܠܰܟܣܶܩ denom. verb *to write* or *compile a lexicon.*

ܠܰܟܢܳܐ *a dish;* see ܠܰܩܢܳܐ.

ܠܰܟܠܳܟ, ܠܰܟܠܳܐ emph. m. ܠܰܟܠܳܟܳܐ, pl. m. ܠܰܟ̈ܠܳܐ, f. ܠܰܟܠܳܟܳܬܳܐ rt. ܠܟܠܟ. *a fool; foolish, fatuous, stupid, dull, brutish;* ܠܰܟ̈ܠܳܐ ܕܚܰܩܠܳܐ *the brutes of the field, brute beasts;* ܥܰܡܳܐ ܠܰܟܠܳܐ *a brutish* or *senseless people.* Derivatives, verb ܠܰܟܠܶܟ, ܠܰܟܠܽܘܬܳܐ.

ܠܰܟܠܶܟ denom. verb Pael conj. from ܠܰܟܠܳܐ. *to make* or *pronounce stupid* or *foolish.* Ethpa. ܐܶܬܠܰܟܠܶܟ, ܐܶܬܠܰܟܠܰܟ or ܐܶܬܠܰܟܠܶܟ *to be* or *become foolish, turn stupid* or *silly, make a fool of, be infatuated;* ܠܰܟܠܳܐ ܟܰܕ ܡܶܬܚܰܡܰܬ ܝܰܬܺܝܪܳܐܺܝܬ ܡܶܬܠܰܟܠܰܟ *a fool when he is irritated behaves still more foolishly;* ܐܶܢ ܡܰܘܣܶܦ ܡܶܬܠܰܟܠܰܟ *if he continues to act foolishly, if he goes on making a fool of himself.*

ܠܰܟܠܽܘܬܳܐ from ܠܰܟܠܳܐ. f. *folly, foolishness, nonsense;* ܡܶܠܬܳܐ ܕܠܰܟܠܽܘܬܳܐ *foolish talking.*

ܠܺܠܝܳܐ, ܠܺܠܝܳܐ pl. ܠܺܠ̈ܝܳܐ, ܠܺܠܰܘܳܬܳܐ, ܠܺܠܰܘܳܬܳܐ, m. *night, a night;* ܒܠܺܠܝܳܐ *by night, at night;* ܐܺܝܡܳܡ ܠܺܠܝܳܐ or ܠܺܠܝܳܐ *a day and night;* ܬܪܶܝܢ ܐܺܝܡܳܡܺܝܢ ܘܠܺܠܰܘ̈ܳܬܳܐ *two days and nights.*

ܠܺܠܝܳܝܳܐ, ܠܺܠܝܳܢܳܐ, ܠܺܠܝܳܢܳܝܳܐ, ܠܺܠܝܳܢܳܐ, ܠܺܠܝܳܝܳܐ or ܠܺܠܝܳܢܳܝܳܐ, f. ܝܬܳܐ adj. from ܠܺܠܝܳܐ. *nightly, by night, nocturnal;* ܡܰܛܰܪܬܳܐ ܠܺܠܝܳܢܳܝܬܳܐ *a night-watch;* ܫܳܥܶ̈ܐ ܠܺܠܝܳܢܳܝܳܬܳܐ ܘܺܐܝܡܳܡܳܝܳܬܳܐ *the hours of the night and day;* ܛܽܘܪ̈ܶܐ ܠܺܠܝܳܢܳܝܶ̈ܐ *dark mountains.*

ܠܺܠܺܝܬܳܐ from ܠܺܠܝܳܐ f. *lamia, a night-spectre, a phantom* or *demon in the form of a woman.*

ܠܡ particle of explanation *forsooth, to wit, namely;* serves instead of inverted commas to mark a quotation or oblique oration; ܠܚܰܛܳܝܳܐ ܓܶܝܪ ܐܶܡܰܪ ܠܶܗ ܠܡ ܐܰܠܳܗܳܐ *for to the sinner saith God;* ܐܶܡܰܪ ܗܽܘ ܕܗܽܘܝܽܘ ܠܡ ܒܪܶܗ ܩܰܫܺܝܫܳܐ ܕܟܽܘܣܪܽܘ *he gave himself out to be the elder son of Chosroes.*

ܠܡ Palpel ܠܰܡܠܶܡ *to speak, enunciate.* Ethpalpal ܐܶܬܠܰܡܠܰܡ *to stammer; to enunciate.* Derivative, ܠܽܘܡܠܳܡܳܐ.

ܠܡܳܐ comp. of ܠ and ܡܳܐ. *a)* interrogative particle, ܠܡܳܐ ܢܒܺܝܳܐ ܐܰܢ̄ܬ *art thou a prophet?*

b) negative particle = ܕܠܡܐ *that—not, lest;* ܚܙܝ ܠܡܐ ܠܐܢܫ ܬܐܡܪ *see thou tell no man.*

ܠܡܐܢ or ܠܡܝܢ, ܠܡܐܢܐ pl. ܐ̈ m. λιμήν, *a haven, port, harbour;* metaph. ܠܡܐܢ ܚܝ̈ܐ *the haven of salvation;* ܠܡܐܢ ܩܕܝ̈ܫܐ *the harbour of the saints;* ܐܬܝܬ ܠܠܡܐܢܐ ܕܫܪܒܐ *I have come to the end of the story;* ܫܒܘܥܐ ܕܡܥܠܬܗ ܕܠܡܐܢܐ *the week of entry into the haven* = the week preceding Palm Sunday.

ܠܡܕ fut. ܢܠܡܘܕ, pass. part. ܠܡܝܕ. *to put together, compile; to accord with;* ܗܘܢܗ ܠܡܕ ܠܐ ܠܡܕ *his tone of mind does not comport with solitude.* Pa. ܠܡܕ *to bring together, connect, compile;* ܠܐ ܡܠܡܕܐ *disjoined.* Ethpa. ܐܬܠܡܕ *to be connected, related, inserted, set* as a jewel, to music;—ܩܝܢܬܐ ܕܡܬܠܡܕܐ ܠܘܬ *a chant set to* certain words. Taphel ܬܠܡܕ *to make a disciple, teach the Christian faith, convert;* ܡܕܝܢܬܐ ܗܝ ܕܬܠܡܕ *the city which he brought to the Christian faith;* ܬܠܡܕ ܘܐܥܡܕ ܣܓܝ̈ܐܐ *he taught and baptized many;* ܬܠܡܝܕܐ ܗܘܐ ܠܐܒܘܠܒܪܟܬ *he was a pupil of Abulbarcat.* Ettaph. ܐܬܬܠܡܕ *a) to be instructed, taught, educated, to become a disciple, pupil, follower;* ܐܠܟܣܢܕܪܘܣ ܠܐܪܣܛܘܛܠܝܣ ܐܬܬܠܡܕ *Alexander was a pupil of Aristotle. b) to be instructed in the Christian faith, to become a catechumen, disciple, convert,* ܠܟܪܝܣܛܝܢܘܬܐ *to Christianity;* ܠܗܝܡܢܘܬܐ *to the faith;* ܡܬܬܠܡܕܢܐ *catechumens. c) to embrace* ܠܕܝܪܝܘܬܐ *the monastic life;* ܐܬܬܠܡܕ ܠܡܣܟܢܘܬܐ ܩܕܝܫܬܐ *holy poverty:* ܐܬܬܠܡܕ ܡܢ ܥܠܡܐ *he left the world = became a monk.* Derivatives, ܬܠܡܝܕܐ, ܬܠܡܝܕܘܬܐ, ܡܬܬܠܡܕܢܐ, ܡܬܠܡܕܢܐ, ܬܠܡܕܬܐ.

ܠܡܕ the letter *Lamadh;* see ܠ.

ܠܡܕܢܐ adj. from the letter ܠܡܕ gram. *preceded by Lamadh* as an accusative, an infinitive.

ܠܡܚܣܢ rt. ܚܣܢ. adv. *hardly, with difficulty, only just.*

ܠܡܛܐ m. *felt.*

ܠܡܦܐܕ, ܠܡܦܝܕ, ܠܡܦܐܕܐ emph. ܐ, rarely ܠܡܦܕܝܣ pl. ܝܢ̈, ܐ̈ m. rarely f. λαμπάς, -άδα, *a) a lamp, torch, candlestick;* ܕܝܩܕܐ *a burning torch;* ܕܢܗܝܪܐ *a lighted torch;* metaph. *splendour, brightness, shining;* ܠܡܦܐܕܐ ܕܫܡܫܐ *the shining of the sun;* ܠܡܦܐܕܐ ܕܚܘܒܐ ܐܠܗܝܐ *the brightness of Divine love. b) a flash, meteor, lightning.*

ܠܣܛܐܝܬ from ܠܣܛܐ. adv. *in the manner of robbers* or *freebooters, marauding;* ܥܠ ܠܣܛܐܝܬ ܠܐܬܪܐ ܕܝܘܢܝ̈ܐ *he made marauding incursions into the country of the Greeks.*

ܠܣܛܝ denom. verb Pali conj. from ܠܣܛܐ. *to rob, make raids, maraud, commit piracy.* Ethpali ܐܬܠܣܛܝ *to be seized by robbers, carried off by brigands;* metaph. ܦܛܪܝܪܟܘܬܐ ܐܬܠܣܛܝܬ *the Patriarchate was unlawfully occupied.*

ܠܣܛܐ or ܠܝܣܛܐ pl. ܐ̈ ληστής, *a) a robber, freebooter, brigand, pirate. b)* adj. *piratical, predatory, thievish.* Derivatives, ܠܣܛܐܝܬ, verb ܠܣܛܝ, ܠܣܛܝܘܬܐ, ܡܠܣܛܢܐ, ܡܠܣܛܢܘܬܐ.

ܠܣܛܝܘܬܐ from ܠܣܛܐ. f. *open robbery, brigandage.*

ܠܥ fut. ܢܠܥ same as ܠܚܟ, ܠܥ *to lick.*

ܠܥܒ part. ܠܥܒ *to be greedy, gluttonous, intemperate.* Ethpe. ܐܬܠܥܒ *a) to seize greedily, rush greedily on, to give oneself over to pleasure* esp. *to be gluttonous, indulge the appetite,* ܒܦܓܥܐ *with delicacies. b)* in a good sense *to be eager, delight in.* Derivatives, ܠܥܒܐ, ܠܥܒܐܝܬ, ܠܥܒܘܬܐ, ܠܥܘܒܐ.

ܠܥܒܐ, ܠܥܒܬܐ rt. ܠܥܒ. *greedy, gluttonous, voracious.*

ܠܥܒܐܝܬ rt. ܠܥܒ. adv. *greedily, immoderately.*

ܠܥܒܘܬܐ rt. ܠܥܒ. f. *avidity, greediness, gluttony.*

ܠܥܓ, ܠܥܓ, ܠܥܓܐ, ܠܥܓܬܐ perh. mimetic, cf. ܠܥܓ. *a stammerer, stutterer;*—ܠܥܓ ܡܡܠܠܐ ܠܥܓܐ *hesitating in speech.* Derivatives, verb ܠܥܓ, ܠܥܓܘܬܐ.

ܠܥܓ denom. verb Pael conj. from ܠܥܓ. *to stutter.* Ethpa. ܐܬܠܥܓ *to take to stuttering, begin to stammer.*

ܠܥܓܘܬܐ from ܠܥܓ. f. *stammering, stuttering, faltering speech, hesitation in speech.*

ܠܥܘܒܐ Ar. m. dialect. *saliva.*

ܠܥܘܒܐ m. *one whose saliva runs down.*

ܠܥܘܙܐ, ܠܥܘܙܬܐ rt. ܠܥܙ. *of indistinct* or *strange speech, of a foreign tongue.*

ܠܥܐ fut. ܢܠܥܐ, act. part. ܠܳܥܐ, ܠܳܥܝܳܐ, pass. part. ܠܥܝܐ *to make indistinct* or *soft sounds* as birds, insects, serpents; *to sing, chant, sound, give forth a sound* ܩܶܢܝ̈ܳܬܳܐ ܕ *of chants*; ܩܳܠܶܐ ܕܐܘܠܳܝ̈ܳܬܳܐ *sounds of lamentation; to lisp; to speak a foreign language; to whisper softly* said of the Holy Spirit, of grace, faith, error; ܡܶܠܶܐ ܠܳܥܝܳܢ *they utter, pronounce;* ܫܪܳܪܳܐ ܕܫܠܺܝ̈ܚܶܐ ܠܥܝܐ *the truth proclaimed by the Apostles;* ܠܥܰܘ ܥܺܝܪ̈ܶܐ ܬܶܫܒܽܘܚܬܳܐ ܚܕܰܬܳܐ angels *sounded forth a new song;* gram. *to express.* Ethpe. ܐܶܬܠܥܝ *to sound, be sounded, be heard* said of sound rather than of sense; *to be told, said, whispered;* gram. *to be pronounced, said.* Derivatives, ܠܥܘܝܐ, ܠܥܝܐ, ܠܥܝܬܐ.

ܠܶܥܝܳܐ pl. ܐ̈ rt. ܠܥܐ. m. *sound, speech, tongue, twittering* esp. inarticulate sounds as of birds and beasts; *foreign speech; dialect, way of speech, utterance, pronunciation,* ܠܶܥܝܶܐ̈ ܗܰܢܝܳܢܳܝ̈ܶܐ *pleasant sounds;* ܠܥܝܳܐ ܒܰܣܺܝܡ ܠܶܥܝܳܐ *the sweet-voiced swallow;* ܠܶܥܝܶܐ̈ ܐ̱ܚܪ̈ܳܢܶܐ *other tongues;* ܠܥܝܳܐ ܢܒܺܝܝܳܐ *prophetic utterance;* ܠܶܥܝܶܐ̈ ܕܐܪ̈ܳܙܶܐ ܕܠܳܐ ܫܶܦܘ̈ܳܬܳܐ *whispers of mysteries* i.e. of holy things, *not made known by lips.*

ܠܶܥܝܳܬܳܐ rt. ܠܥܐ. f. *speaking, sound.*

ܠܥܶܠ ܠܥܶܠ see ܠܥܶܠ; *upward, above.*

ܠܥܶܣ or ܠܥܰܣ ܠܥܣ fut. ܢܶܠܥܽܘܣ, imper. ܠܥܘܣ, act. part. ܠܳܥܶܣ, ܠܳܥܣܳܐ, pass. part. ܠܥܺܝܣ, ܠܥܺܝܣܳܐ, root-meaning *to chew, masticate* but usually *to take food, eat;* ܠܳܥܣܺܝܢܰܢ ܘܫܳܬܶܝܢܰܢ *we eat and drink;* pass. part. impers. ܠܳܐ ܠܥܺܝܣ ܠܰܢ ܝܰܘܡܳܢܳܐ *we have tasted no food to-day;* ܡܶܢ ܕܠܥܺܝܣ ܠܗܘܢ *after they had eaten.* Ethpe. ܐܶܬܠܥܶܣ *to be masticated, eaten.* Pa. ܠܰܥܶܣ *to eat hungrily, devour, gnaw.* Aph. ܐܰܠܥܶܣ *to make swallow, give to eat.* Derivatives, ܠܘܥܣܐ, ܡܠܥܣܐ, ܡܠܥܣܢܘܬܐ.

ܠܥܰܦ same as ܠܘܦ, ܠܰܦ *to join.* Ethpe. ܐܶܬܠܥܶܦ *to be joined* or *woven together.*

ܠܦܽܘܬ prep. *according to, in proportion, corresponding;* ܠܦܽܘܬ ܣܽܘܓܳܐܐ ܕܪ̈ܰܚܡܰܝܟ *according to the abundance of Thy mercies;* ܠܦܽܘܬ ܐ̱ܚܪ̈ܳܢܝܽܘܬ ܙܰܒ̈ܢܶܐ *according to the different seasons;* ܠܦܽܘܬ ܕ *because, on account of.*

ܠܶܦܛܳܐ or ܠܶܦܛܽܘܢ pl. ܠܶܦܛܶܐ̈ λεπτός, *a small thing, small coin, obolus, farthing.*

ܠܦܳܦܳܐ rt. ܠܦ. *an envelope* ܕܐܶܓܰܪܬܳܐ *of a letter.*

ܠܶܦܬܳܐ *a turnip.*

ܠܶܦܬܳܐ; see ܠܶܦܬܳܐ *an oar.*

ܠܦܽܘܡܳܠܳܐ; see ܠܦܘܡܠ.

ܠܦܽܘܪܳܐ; see ܠܦܘܪ.

ܠܰܩܳܛܳܐ rt. ܠܩܛ. m. *a gatherer, gleaner.*

ܠܩܽܘܫܬܳܢܳܐܺܝܬ = ܩܽܘܫܬܳܢܳܐܺܝܬ *true.*

ܠܩܽܘܫܬܳܢܳܐܺܝܬ from ܩܽܘܫܬܳܐ adv. *verily, indeed.*

ܠܶܩܝܳܐ m. *the confines* of a city, esp. *the land and villages under its jurisdiction, a suburb, region, surrounding country;* a monastery ܕܒܠܶܩܝܳܢܶܗ ܕܣܺܝܣ *in the region of Sis.*

ܠܩܰܛ ܠܩܛ fut. ܢܶܠܩܽܘܛ, act. part. ܠܳܩܶܛ, ܠܳܩܛܳܐ. *a) to gather, pick, pick up, collect, glean;* ܢܶܠܩܛܽܘܢ ܬܘܣܦܬܐ *they shall gather food* i.e. manna; ܠܩܛܳܐ ܗܘܳܬ ܒܚܰܩܠܳܐ *she gleaned in the field;* ܢܶܠܩܽܘܛ ܫܽܘܫܰܢ̈ܶܐ *he will gather lilies;* ܠܳܩܛܳܐ ܩܺܝܣ̈ܶܐ *picking up sticks;* ܠܳܩܶܛ ܫܩܡܶܐ̈ *a gatherer of sycamore fruit.* *b) to pick up* as a bird = *eat;* with ܡܶܠܶܐ *to pick up words* as a parrot. *c)* metaph. with ܦܽܘܫܳܩ̈ܶܐ *to collect comments, explanations.* *d)* chem. *to collect* particles, *attract, absorb.* Ethpe. ܐܶܬܠܩܶܛ *to be gleaned, gathered, collected.* Pa. ܠܰܩܶܛ *to pick up* arrows, *gather in* sheaves, *gather* honey, *collect, select;* ܠܒܽܘܫܶܗ ܡܠܰܩܛܳܐ ܗܘܳܐ ܟܽܠܶܗ ܡܶܢ ܪ̈ܽܘܩܥܶܐ *his clothing was all patches;* ܡܠܰܩܶܛ ܡܶܠܶܐ *a babbler;* ܡܶܐܡܪ̈ܶܐ ܡܠܰܩܛܶܐ *selected sermons.* Ethpa. ܐܶܬܠܰܩܰܛ *to be gathered together.* Derivatives, ܠܩܘܛܐ, ܠܩܘܛܐ, ܠܩܛܐ, ܠܩܛܐ, ܠܩܘܛܘܬܐ, ܡܠܩܛܐ.

ܠܰܩܳܛܳܐ pl. ܐ̈ m. *an embroiderer.*

ܠܶܩܛܳܐ rt. ܠܩܛ. m. *bait, crumbs, food;* ܠܶܩܛܳܐ ܕܨܰܝܳܕܶܐ *fishing-bait;* ܠܶܩܛܳܐ ܕܡܒܰܕܰܪ ܥܰܠ ܐܰܪܥܳܐ *crumbs* or *bait scattered on the ground;* metaph. ܐܳܦ ܥܰܡ̈ܡܶܐ ܒܠܶܩܛܶܗ ܕܡܰܠܦܳܢܽܘܬܳܐ ܡܶܬܨܰܝܕܺܝܢ ܠܬܝܳܒܽܘܬܳܐ *the heathen too are enticed by teaching and entrapped to repentance;* ܒܠܶܩܛܶܗ ܚܳܢܶܩ ܠܺܝ *the world strangles me with its allurements.*

ܠܶܩܛܳܐ, ܠܩܳܛܳܐ rt. ܠܩܛ. m. *ingathering, gleaning;* ܠܩܳܛ ܙܰܝܬܳܐ *olive-gathering;* ܠܩܳܛܳܐ ܕܠܶܩܛܳܗ *her gleanings.*

ܠܩܽܘܛܽܘܬܳܐ or ܠܩܛܽܘܬܳܐ pl. ܬ̈ܳܐ dimin. of ܠܩܳܛܳܐ m. *a little collection; gathering, ingathering* of fruit.

ܠܩܛܝܩܢܝܐ pl. ܢ̈ܐ adj. from ܠܩܛܝܩܝܢ *a beast trained to draw a litter.*

ܠܩܛܝܩܝܢ, ܩܝܢ and ܠܩܛܝܩܢ f. λεκτίκιον, *a litter, a bier; a pyx, portable altar.*

ܠܩܫܐܝܬ rt. ܠܩܫ. adv. *late.*

ܠܩܫܝܐ, ܝܬܐ rt. ܠܩܫ. adj. *late, latter* opp. ܒܟܝܪܐ *early;* said of rain, of animals born late in the season, of plants flowering or ripening late.

ܠܩܫܝܘܬܐ rt. ܠܩܫ. f. *lateness, tardiness.*

ܠܩܢܐ or ܠܩܢܐ pl. ܝܢ̈, ܬ̈ܐ f. λεκάνη, *a basin, bowl, laver, dish, plate, vessel;* ܠܩܢܐ ܕܐܝ̈ܕܝܐ *a washhand-basin, foot-bath;* ܠܩܢܐ ܕܢܚܫܐ *a brazen laver.*

ܠܩܫ Pael ܠܩܫ; *to bring forth late* offspring or fruit, *to gather* late fruit. Derivatives, ܠܩܫܐ, ܠܩܫܐܝܬ, ܠܩܫܝܐ, ܠܩܫܝܘܬܐ.

ܠܩܫܐ rt. ܠܩܫ. m. *late grass, aftermath.*

ܠܩܠܩܛܝܣ from χαλκῖτις, *copperas, flowers of copper.*

ܠܪܕܐ m. dialect. *a great sack, sack for litter.*

ܠܪܘܣܐ = ܠܪܣܐ.

ܠܪܣܐ pl. ܐ̈ λῆρος, m. *senseless, foolish;* ܐܝܟ ܠܪܣܐ ܕܡܡܠܠ ܘܠܐ ܫܠܐ *as a foolish person who talks unceasingly.*

ܠܪܣܘܬܐ f. *idle talk, nonsense, babbling, raving, folly.*

ܠܪܣܐ or ܠܪܝܣܐ = ܠܪܣܐ.

ܠܫܢ denom. verb Pael conj. from ܠܫܢܐ *to pronounce, sound;* ܠܐ ܡܠܫܢܝܢ ܠܗܠܝܢ ܐܬ̈ܘܬܐ ܟܠܢܐܝܬ *not pronouncing those letters at all.* Ethpa. ܐܬܠܫܢ *to be pronounced;* ܥܐ ܕܐܝܟ ܐܠܦ ܡܬܠܫܢܐ *'Ain which sounds like Alep.*

ܠܫܢܐ, ܠܫܢ pl. ܝܢ̈, ܐ̈ m. *a) the tongue;* ܐܬ̈ܘܬܐ ܕܠܫܢܐ *lingual letters* i.e. ܕܛܠܢܬ; *b) speech, language, pronunciation;* ܠܫܢܐ ܕܐܬܪܐ *dialect;* ܠܫܢܐ ܕܛܘܪܝܐ *Highland dialect* perh. the language of the Assyrian highlands opp. ܠܫܢܐ ܐܬܪܝܐ *the common speech* of Mesopotamia; ܠܫܢܐ ܝܗܘܕܝܐ *the Jew's language. c) a people, nation;* ܚܕ ܠܫܢܐ *speaking the same tongue. d)* metaph. *a stretch* of the sea, of a river, *a tongue* or *spit* of land; ܠܫܢܐ ܐܝܟ ܓܫܪܐ *a narrow isthmus;* ܠܫܢܐ ܕܫܝܘܠ *the mouth of Sheol;* ܠܫܢܐ ܕܢܘܪܐ *a tongue of flame;* ܠܫܢܐ ܡܢ ܕܗܒܐ ܐܘ ܣܐܡܐ *a wedge of gold or silver. e)* names of plants; ܠܫܢ ܐܡܪܐ *plantago, the plantain;* ܠܫܢ ܟܠܒܐ *cynoglossum, hounds-tongue;* ܠܫܢ ܟܠܒܬܐ *lolium, darnel, cockle, tares;* ܠܫܢܐ ܪܒܐ *plantago major;* ܠܫܢ ܨܦܪܐ *fraxinus ornus, a sort of ash-tree;* ܠܫܢ ܬܘܪܐ *borago officinalis, buglossum, borage, bugloss.* Derivatives, verb ܠܫܢ, ܠܫܢܢܐ, ܠܫܢܢܘܬܐ, ܠܫܢܝܘܬܐ, ܡܠܫܢܢܐ, ܡܠܫܢܢܘܬܐ.

ܠܫܢܢܐ, ܢܝܬܐ adj. from ܠܫܢܐ. *loquacious, garrulous, talkative; eloquent.*

ܠܫܢܢܘܬܐ from ܠܫܢܐ. f. *loquacity, talkativeness.*

ܠܫܢܝܘܬܐ from ܠܫܢܐ. f. *language, idiom, speech.*

ܠܫܬܐ f. *a button hole.*

ܠܬܚܬ, ܠܬܚܬ and ܠܬܚܬܝܢ adv. *below, beneath, downwards;* ܡܝ̈ܐ ܕܠܬܚܬ ܡܢ ܪܩܝܥܐ *the waters under the firmament;* ܐܝܟܐ ܕܡܢ ܠܬܚܬ ܟܬܒܐ ܡܥܗܕ *which Scripture mentions below.*

ܠܛܟ fut. ܢܠܛܘܟ, act. part. ܠܛܟ, ܠܛܟܐ, root-meaning *to stain, pollute. To agree, be convenient, fitting, suitable, becoming, worthy;* ܕܠܟܠܚܕ ܠܛܟܝܢ *becoming to each;* ܦܘܩܕ̈ܢܐ ܠܛܟܝܢ ܠܛܠܝ̈ܐ *commands suitable for children;* ܡܠܬܐ ܠܛܟܬܐ ܕܠܡܫܡܥ *a speech worthy to be listened to.* Ethpe. ܐܬܠܛܟ *to be guilty of, devise* or *act with guile, ill-will* or *malice, to conspire* with ܥܡ or ܠܘܩܒܠ *against;* ܢܦܫܐ ܡܬܠܛܟܢܝܬܐ *a malicious soul;* ܕܘܠܚܡܐ ܕܡܬܠܛܟܝܢ ܒܗ ܟܠܗܘܢ *the confusion of which all alike were guilty.* Pa. ܠܛܟ *to defile, contaminate,* ܚܫ̈ܐ ܦܓܪ̈ܢܝܐ ܗܘܐ ܡܠܛܟܐ *he was defiled with carnal passions.* Ethpa. ܐܬܠܛܟ *to act with guile* or *deceit, to be defiled.* Derivatives, ܡܠܛܟܢܐ, ܡܠܛܟܢܘܬܐ.

ܠܬܟ m. a dry measure, *a half cor, half omer.*

ܠܬܡ fut. ܢܠܬܘܡ, act. part. ܠܬܡ, ܠܬܡܐ. *a) to speak, pronounce. b) to pile up, bring together.* Pa. ܠܬܡ *a) to murmur* ܒܣܦܘܬܗ *between his lips; to disparage. c) to bring together, compile.* Ethpa. ܐܬܠܬܡ *to be coupled, fastened together.* Derivatives, ܠܘܬܡܐ, ܡܠܬܡܢܐ, ܡܠܬܡܢܘܬܐ.

⁘ ܫܠܡ ܐܬܘܬܐ ܕܠܡܕ ⁘

⁘ ܘܫܘܪܝܐ ܕܡܝܡ ⁘

܀ ܬܘܒ ܒܚܝܠ ܡܪܢ ܡܫܪܝܢܢ ܟܬܒܐ ܕܡܐܡ ܐܬܘܬܐ ܡܢ ܡܪܢ ܕܝܢ ܕܡܝܡ ܝܗܒ ܠܢ ܠܡܫܠܡܘܬܐ ܀

܀ ܡ ܀

ܡ ܡܫܪܝܢܘܬܐ

ܡ, ܡܝܡ *Mim* the thirteenth letter of the alphabet; the numeral 40, ܡ̄ ܡܐܡܪܐ *Discourse* 40; ܡ̇ 400.

ܡܐ *a*) interrog. pron. *what?* ܡܐ ܠܝ ܘܠܟ *what have I to do with thee?* *b*) rel. pron. *that, that which, what; when, then, after that, whensoever, as often as;* ܠܐ ܫܘܐ ܐܢܐ ܡܐ ܕܐܡܪܬ *I do not deserve what you say, I am not worthy of that which you say;* ܡܐ ܕܝܢ ܕ *but when;* ܐܝܟ ܡܐ *as*=ܐܝܟܢܐ; ܐܝܟ ܡܐ ܕ *as, like;* ܟܠ ܡܐ ܕ, ܟܠܡܐ=ܡܐ ܕ *whatsoever, whichever, whensoever, whenever, so often as.* *c*) particle of exclamation *how! how much!* ܡܐ ܕܚܝܠ *how terrible!* ܡܐ ܛܒ *how good!* *d*) ܡܐܢܫ; see ܡܢܫ. Derivatives, ܐܝܡܐ, ܕܡܐ, ܡܕܡ, ܟܡܐ, ܡܕܡܐ, ܡܢܘܬܐ, ܠܡܐ, ܡܝܡ, ܕܝܡܐ.

ܡܐ, many participles of ܦܐ verbs and of Aphel conjugations have alternate forms, with and without Alep after Mim. Nouns derived from such participles have the same alternative spelling.

ܡܐܐ, ܡܐܬܐ, ܡܐܐܬܐ pl. ܡܐܐ, ܡܐܘ̈ or ܡܐܘ̈, ܡܐܘ̈ܬܐ com. gen. *a hundred, a century;* ܡܐܬܝܢ or ܡܐܬܝܢ 200; ܬܠܬ ܡܐܐ or ܬܠܬ ܡܐܐ 300; ܐܪܒܥܡܐܐ 400, and so on; ܬܡܢܐ ܡܐܐ or ܬܡܢܡܐܐ 800; ܪ̈ܒܝ ܡܐܘ̈ܬܐ or ܪ̈ܒܝ ܡܐܘ̈ *centurions.*

ܡܐܒܫܠܐ; see ܡܒܫܠܐ *a cook.*

ܡܐܒܫܠܢܘܬܐ; see ܡܒܫܠܢܘܬܐ and ܡܐ above.

ܡܐܓܪܐ or ܡܐܓܪܐ; see ܡܓܪܐ.

ܡܐܘܫܐ for ܡܘܫܐ *a jackal.*

ܡܐܙܐ *μᾶζα, barley-water sweetened with refined honey; barley cakes mixed with milk.*

ܡܐܙܠܐ, ܡܐܙܠܐ rt. ܐܙܠ. m. *departure, journeying;* ܡܐܙܠܐ ܘܡܐܬܝܬܐ *going and coming;* ܡܐܙܠ ܚܕ ܝܘܡ *one day's journey.*

ܡܐܙܠܬܐ pl. ܡܐܙ̈ܠܬܐ rt. ܐܙܠ. f. *a departure, journeying, pilgrimage;* with ܚܝܠܐ *a military expedition.*

ܡܐܚܕ ܐܝܕܐ rt. ܐܚܕ. m. *grasping by the hand;* metaph. *help, assistance.*

ܡܐܟܠܢܘܬܐ and ܡܐܟܠܢܘܬܐ; see ܡܟܠܢܘܬܐ.

ܡܐܟܠܐ pl. ܡܐܟ̈ܠܐ, ܡܐܟ̈ܠܐ; see ܡܟܠܐ *a mine.*

ܡܐܘܬܐ from ܡܐܐ. f. *the number one hundred.*

ܡܐܡܝܟܐ or ܡܡܝܟܐ rt. ܡܟ. *slanting, tottering, bending over, ready to fall;* ܐܫܝܬܐ ܕܡܡܝܟܐ *a tottering wall.*

ܡܐܢܝܐ; see ܡܐܢܐ.

ܡܐܢܐ; see ܡܐܢ.

ܡܐܢܝܘܬܐ rt. ܡܐܢ. f. *sloth, laziness, lassitude, negligence, reluctance;* ܡܘܒܠܐ ܕܡܐܢܝܘܬܐ *a weary weight, distasteful burden;* ܠܐ ܡܐܢܝܘܬܐ *strenuousness;* ܕܠܐ ܡܐܢܝܘܬܐ *indefatigable, active, assiduous.*

ܡܐܢܝܐܝܬ rt. ܡܐܢ. adv. *lazily, slothfully, carelessly.*

ܡܐܝܬܐ, ܡܐܝܬܐ or ܡܝܬܐ m. ܡܐܝܬܬܐ, ܡܝܬܬܐ, ܡܐܝܬܬܐ f. rt. ܡܘܬ. *dead;* ܗܘ ܕܡܫܡܠܝܐ ܡܝܬ ܡܝܬܐ *he who is quite dead.*

ܡܐܟܘܠܬܐ pl. ܡܐܟܘ̈ܠܬܐ rt. ܐܟܠ. f. *food, victuals, provisions;* pl. *suburbs, dependent towns.*

ܡܐܣܝܢܐ, ܡܐܣ̈ܝܢܐ rt. ܢܣܐ. *noxious, injurious, harmful;* see ܡܣܝܢܐ.

ܡܐܣܝܢܘܬܐ; see ܡܣܝܢܘܬܐ.

ܡܐܟܠ ܩܪܨܐ rt. ܐܟܠ. m. *backbiting, calumny, an evil report; a backbiter, slanderer.*

ܡܐܟܘܠܬܐ and ܡܐܟܘܠܬܐ rt. ܐܟܠ. m. *food, victuals, provisions.*

ܡܐܟܘܠܬܐ pl. of ܡܐܟܘܠܬܐ.

ܡܐܟܢܐ, ܡܐܟܢܐ pl. ܡܐܟܢܘܬܐ, ܡܐܟܢܘܣ, ܡܐܟܢܣ, ܡܐܟܢܘܣ, ܡܐܟܢܐ or ܡܟܢܐ f. μηχανή, *an engine; a stratagem; a cunning* or *ingenious device;* ܟܐܦܐ ܕܡܐܟܢܐ *a stone hurled from an engine;* metaph. ܡܐܟܢܘܣ ܕܟܐܢܘܬܐ *means of justice = true arguments.*

ܡܐܟܣܢܐܝܬ rt. ܟܣ. adv. *by way of reproof, reprovingly.*

ܡܐܠܗܢܐ, ܡܐܠܗܢܝܬܐ from ܐܠܗ *deifying, making divine, making to be a partaker of the divine nature; divine.*

ܡܐܠܗܢܘܬܐ from ܐܠܗ f. *deification.*

ܡܐܠܟܝ and rarely ܡܐܠܟܝ; see ܡܠܟܝ. adv. *rather.*

ܡܐܡܘܢܐ for ܡܡܘܢܐ *mammon.*

ܡܐܡܪ, ܡܐܡܪܐ pl. ܐ̈ rt. ܐܡܪ. m. *speech, diction; a discourse, sermon, homily,* esp. *a metrical homily; a treatise, a division* of a book; *a proposition;* with ܠܘܩܒܠ *a disputation.*

ܡܐܢ fut. ܢܡܐܢ, act. part. ܡܐܢ, part. adj. ܡܐܢܐ, ܡܐܢܝܐ. *to irk, bore, be irksome, tedious; to be reluctant, unwilling, weary of;* with ܢܦܫܐ *his soul was weary of, abhorred . . .;* usually impers. with ܠ; ܡܐܢ ܠܗ ܡܢܗܘܢ *he was weary of them;* ܠܐ ܡܐܢ ܠܝ *it does not annoy me, I do not mind.* Part. adj. *slothful, inactive, lazy, negligent.* Aph. ܐܡܐܢ *to be careless, negligent, slothful, indolent, inactive; to neglect, grow weary;* ܐܝܟ ܕܐܬܪܚܡܢ ܠܐ ܡܡܐܢܝܢܢ *as we have received mercy we faint not.* Derivatives, ܡܐܢܐ, ܡܐܢܝܐܝܬ, ܡܐܢܘܬܐ.

ܡܐܢ, ܡܐܢܐ or ܡܢܐ pl. ܡܐܢܝܢ, ܡܐܢ̈ܐ m. *a vessel, utensil, implement, instrument; a garment, dress; clothing, an outfit, furniture, baggage;* ܡܐܢ̈ܐ ܕܥܡܪܐ—ܕܟܬܢܐ *cotton, woollen clothing;* ܡܐܢܐ ܝܩܝܪܐ *costly raiment;* ܡܐܢ̈ܐ ܕܐܒܠܐ *mourning;* ܡܐܢ̈ܐ ܕܕܗܒܐ *golden vessels* or *ornaments;* ܫܩܘܠ ܡܐܢܘܗܝ *his armour-bearer.* Metaph. ܡܐܢܐ ܕܐܒܕܢܐ *a vessel of perdition;* ܡܐܢ̈ܐ ܕܪܚܡܐ *vessels of mercy.*

ܡܐܢܝ ܓܘܐ *the viscera, entrails, bowels.*

ܡܐܢܝ ܡܕܒܚܐ *vessels* or *fittings of the altar.*

ܡܐܢܝ ܐܣܝܐ *weapons, arms.*

ܡܐܢܝ ܙܡܪܐ *musical instruments.*

ܡܐܢܝ ܐܘܠܕܐ *the organs of reproduction.*

ܡܐܢܝ ܚܡܪܐ *wine-vessels, wine-skins, casks.*

ܡܐܢ̈ܐ ܕܢܓܪ̈ܐ *carpenters' tools.*

ܡܐܢ̈ܐ ܕܦܚܪ̈ܐ *potters' vessels.*

ܡܐܢܝ ܡܩܕܫܐ *vessels of the sanctuary, eucharistic vessels.*

ܡܐܢܝ ܩܪܒܐ *arms, weapons.*

ܡܐܢ̈ܐ ܕܬܫܡܫܬܐ *sacred vessels, vestments.*

ܡܐܢܝ and ܡܢܝ the heresiarch *Manes* A.D. 240, founder of the Manichaean sect.

ܡܐܢܚܐ, ܡܐܢܚܐ; see ܡܢܚܐ *money.*

ܡܐܢܝܣ for ܡܢܝ *Manes.*

ܡܐܢܝܢܐ from ܡܐܢܝ *a Manichee, follower of Manes.*

ܡܐܣܐ or ܡܣܐ; see ܡܣܡܣܐ *fibre.*

ܡܐܣܬܐ and ܡܐܣܬܐ; see ܡܣܬܐ *a balance.*

ܡܐܣܛܝܟܐ; see ܡܣܛܝܟܐ *mastic.*

ܡܐܣܝܢܐ, ܡܐܣܝܢܝܬܐ rt. ܐܣܐ. *healing, therapeutic; a healer, physician.*

ܡܐܣܝܢܘܬܐ rt. ܐܣܐ. f. *healing.*

ܡܐܣܪܐ; see ܡܣܪܐ *a saw.*

ܡܐܣܪܐ rt. ܐܣܪ. m. *a band;* ܡܐܣܪ ܚܨܐ *a girdle, belt; the waist.*

ܡܐܣܪܝܛܐ; see ܡܣܪܝܛܐ and ܡܣܪܛܐ.

ܡܐܣܪܘܬܐ pl. ܡܐܣܪܝܬܐ rt. ܐܣܪ. f. *a handful, bundle, burden.*

ܡܐܣܪܬܐ *the elbow, bend of the arm, a cubit.*

ܡܐܦܬܐ; see ܡܦܬܐ, ܡܦܬܐ.

ܡܐܦܝܬܐ rt. ܐܦܐ. f. *baking; a bakeress.*

ܡܐܩܘܙܐ; see ܡܩܘܙܐ.

ܡܐܩܘܢ = ܡܩܘܢ *the poppy.*

ܡܐܩܪ or ܡܐܩܪܘܣ μάκερ, *mace.*

ܡܐܩܪܘܢ; see ܡܩܪܘܢ.

ܡܐܪܐ or ܡܪܐ m. μάρρον, *a mattock, hoe, a mallet.*

ܡܐܪܐ, ܡܐܪ act. part. of ܡܪ; ܡܐܪ, ܡܪܐ act. part. of ܡܪܪ.

ܡܐܪܘܣ; see ܡܪܘܣ.

ܡܐܪܘܪܘܬܐ rt. ܡܪ. f. *bitterness.*

ܡܐܪܘܪܐ and ܡܪܘܪܐ; see ܡܪܪܐ.

ܡܐܪܘܪܢܝܘܬܐ; see ܡܪܘܪܢܝܘܬܐ.

ܡܐܪܘܫܬܐ rt. ܪܘܫ. f. *must, the juice of the grape as it flows from the winepress.*

ܡܐܪܘܫܬܢܐ *sweet, juicy.*

ܡܐܪܝ denom. verb; see ܡܪܝ.

ܡܐܪܘܢܐ; see ܡܪܘܢܐ.

ܡܐܪܘܬܐ; see ܡܪܘܬܐ.

ܡܐܬܪܚܢܘܬܐ rt. ܬܪܚ. f. *confidence, reliance.*

ܡܐܬܐ emph. st. of ܡܐܐ *one hundred;* ܡܐܬܝܢ dual of ܡܐܐ.

ܡܐܬܐ or ܡܐܬܐ pl. ܡܐܬܐ or ܡ̈ܐܬܐ; see ܡܐܬܐ.

ܡܐܬܐܡܛܝܩܐ μαθεματικός, *mathematical.*

ܡܐܬܝܬܐ or ܡܐܬܝܐ rt. ܐܬܐ. m. *coming, arrival, advent;* ܡܐܬܝܬܗ ܕܦܪܘܩܢ *the coming of the Saviour;* ܕܡܐܬܝܬܗ ܩܫܝܐ ܠܡܩܡ ܠܘܩܒܠܗ *whose onslaught is hard to resist.*

ܡܐܬܝܬܐ and ܡܐܬܝܬܐ rt. ܐܬܐ. f. *a) coming, advent,* ܡܐܬܝܬܐ ܕܠܘܬ ܢܦܫܐ *coming to himself, recovery of consciousness;* ܡܐܬܝܬܗ ܕܡܫܝܚܐ ܬܢܝܢܬܐ *the second coming of Christ;* ܡܐܬܝܬܐ ܠܡܠܟܘܬܐ *accession to the throne. b) an attack, incursion.*

ܡܐܬܐ, ܡܐܬܝܢܐ, ܡܐܬܐܝܢ Aphel part. of ܐܬܐ.

ܡܒܝܐܢܐ, ܡܒܝܐܢܝܬܐ rt. ܒܝܐ *a comforter, consoler; comforting, consolatory.*

ܡܒܐܫܢܐ, ܡܒܐܫ rt. ܒܐܫ. *noxious; an evil-doer, malefactor.*

ܡܒܐܫܢܘܬܐ rt. ܒܐܫ. f. *harm, detriment; wickedness, evil conduct, iniquity.*

ܡܒܓܥܢܐ rt. ܒܓܥ. *clamorous.*

ܡܒܕܒܕܢܘܬܐ rt. ܒܕ. f. *uneasiness, mental disturbance.*

ܡܒܕܩܢܐ, ܡܒܕܩܢܝܬܐ rt. ܒܕܩ. *he or that which shows forth, declares; a prophet, lawgiver.*

ܡܒܕܩܢܘܬܐ rt. ܒܕܩ. f. *a) a declaration;* legal. *a deposition. b) restoration, rebuilding.*

ܡܒܕܪܐܝܬ rt. ܒܕܪ. adv. *dispersedly, here and there.*

ܡܒܕܪܘܬܐ rt. ܒܕܪ. f. *dispersion, separation;* ܡܒܕܪܘܬܢ *we who are dispersed.*

ܡܒܕܪܢܐ, ܡܒܕܪܢܝܬܐ *a scatterer, spendthrift; a medicine which dissipates swellings.*

ܡܒܗܘܩܘܬܐ rt. ܒܗܩ. f. *glittering brightness.*

ܡܒܗܘܪܢܝܬܐ rt. ܒܗܪ. f. pl. *a lattice window.*

ܡܒܗܬܢܐ, ܡܒܗܬܢܝܬܐ rt. ܒܗܬ. *causing shame, bringing to confusion,* ܣܒܪܐ ܕܠܐ ܡܒܗܬܢܝܬܐ *hope which maketh not ashamed.*

ܡܒܗܬܢܘܬܐ rt. ܒܗܬ. *confounding, confuting.*

ܡܒܘܥܐ, ܡܒܘܥܐ pl. ܡܒ̈ܘܥܐ, ܡܒܘܥܐ rt. ܢܒܥ. m. *a spring, source, fount* esp. *one gushing forth abundantly;* ܡܒܘܥܐ ܕܡܝܐ *springs of water;* ܡܒܘܥܐ ܕܚܝܐ *a source of life.*

ܡܒܙܚܢܐ pl. ܡܒܙܚ̈ܢܐ rt. ܒܙܚ. m. *a scoffer, mocker.*

ܡܒܙܚܢܘܬܐ rt. ܒܙܚ. f. *derision, mockery.*

ܡܒܙܚܢܐܝܬ rt. ܒܙܚ. adv. *mockingly, derisively.*

ܡܒܚܚܐ rt. ܢܒܚ. m. *barking.*

ܡܒܚܢܢܐܝܬ or ܡܒܚܢܢܐܝܬ rt. ܒܚܢ. adv. *subtilly, sophistically;* with ܠܐ *without discrimination* or *examination.*

ܡܒܚܢܢܐ, ܡܒܚܢܢܝܬܐ rt. ܒܚܢ. *a) one who examines, discusses, investigates, tries. b) trying, disputing.*

ܡܒܚܢܢܘܬܐ rt. ܒܚܢ. f. *investigation, examination.*

ܡܒܛܠܢܐ, ܡܒܛܠܢܝܬܐ rt. ܒܛܠ. *he* or *that which makes to cease, abolishes, confutes, destroys.*

ܡܒܝܢܢܐ rt. ܒܝܢ. m. *one who discerns, considers, examines.*

ܡܒܝܢܢܘܬܐ rt. ܒܝܢ. f. *discernment, perception, skill.*

ܡܒܝܬܐ part. of verb ܒܝܬ.

ܡܒܝܬܝܢܐ rt. ܒܝܬܐ. *domestic;* gram. *primitive* opp. derived.

ܡܒܟܝܢܐ, ܡܒܟܝܢܝܬܐ rt. ܒܟܐ. *sad, plaintive.*

ܡܒܠܒܠܐܝܬ rt. ܒܠܒܠ. adv. *in confusion, confusedly, disorderly.*

ܡܒܠܒܠܢܐ, ܡܒܠܒܠܢܝܬܐ rt. ܒܠܒܠ. *one who confuses, confounds.*

ܡܒܠܗܘܢܢܐ from ܒܠܗܘܢ. *astounding, stupefying.*

ܡܒܠܥܬܢܝܬܐ rt. ܒܠܥ. f. *the gullet.*

ܡܒܠܒܠܘܬܐ rt. ܒܠܒܠ. f. *a tubercle, small ulcer,* esp. ܕܥܝܢܐ *on the eye;* ܡܒܠܒܠܘܬܐ ܕܒܣܝܣܐ *a hemorrhoid; laxity of the anus.*

ܡܒܠܩܢܐ, ܢܝܬܐ rt. ܒܠܩ. *unexpected, sudden.*

ܡܒܢܝܢܐ, ܢܝܬܐ rt. ܒܢܐ. *a builder, founder, restorer; edifying.*

ܡܒܩܣܩܣܐ rt. ܒܩܣܩܣ. *torn, rent; dissolute.*

ܡܒܣܝܢܐ rt. ܒܣܐ. m. *a despiser, scorner.*

ܡܒܣܝܢܐܝܬ rt. ܒܣܐ. adv. *carelessly, despicably.*

ܡܒܣܝܢܘܬܐ rt. ܒܣܐ. f. *negligence, contempt.*

ܡܒܣܡܢܐ, ܢܝܬܐ rt. ܒܣܡ. a) *one who prepares perfumes.* b) *exhilarating.*

ܡܒܣܪܢܐ, ܢܝܬܐ rt. ܒܣܪ. *a scorner; scornful.*

ܡܒܣܪܢܐܝܬ rt. ܒܣܪ. adv. *with contempt, contemptuously.*

ܡܒܣܪܢܐܝܬ from ܒܣܪܐ. adv. *carnally.*

ܡܒܣܪܢܘܬܐ rt. ܒܣܪ. f. *contempt.*

ܡܒܣܪܢܘܬܐ from ܒܣܪܐ. f. *incarnation.*

ܡܒܥܐ, ܡܒܥܝܐ Aphel part. of ܢܒܥ.

ܡܒܥܕܘܬܐ and ܡܒܥܕܢܘܬܐ rt. ܒܥܕ. f. *distance, remoteness, a far journey.*

ܡܒܥܛܢܐ, ܢܝܬܐ rt. ܒܥܛ. *a kicking* horse or mule.

ܡܒܥܝܢܐ rt. ܢܒܥ. m. *one who pours forth, sheds abroad;* ܡܒܥܝܢܐ ܕܗܪܣܝܣ *a source* or *author of heresy.*

ܡܒܩܪܢܐ rt. ܒܩܪ. m. *a gleaner, gatherer.*

ܡܒܩܝܢܘܬܐ rt. ܒܩܐ. f. *inquiry, investigation.*

ܡܒܨܪܢܐ, ܢܝܬܐ rt. ܒܨܪ. *diminishing, of diminution.*

ܡܒܨܪܘܬܐ rt. ܒܨܪ. f. *deficiency.*

ܡܒܪܗܝܘܬܐ rt. ܒܪܗ. f. *clearness, transparency.*

ܡܒܪܝܢܘܬܐ rt. ܒܪ, ܒܪܐ. f. a) *abstraction, separation.* b) *settlement, quittance.*

ܡܒܪܝܢܐ, ܢܝܬܐ rt. ܒܪ, ܒܪܐ. *external.*

ܡܒܪܝܢܘܬܐ rt. ܒܪ, ܒܪܐ. f. *separation; a break, rupture between the joints.*

ܡܒܪܟܘ = ܡܒܪܟ ܗܘ Pael part. pass. of ܒܪܟ. *blessed be he.*

ܡܒܪܟܢܐ rt. ܒܪܟ. *blessing; one who blesses.*

ܡܒܪܟܢܘܬܐ rt. ܒܪܟ. f. *benediction.*

ܡܒܪܪܐܝܬ rt. ܒܪܪ. adv. *clearly, lucidly.*

ܡܒܪܪܢܘܬܐ rt. ܒܪܪ. f. *elucidation, explanation.*

ܡܒܪܩܢܐ rt. ܒܪܩ. *lightning, flashing like lightning.*

ܡܒܫܠܢܐ, ܢܝܬܐ rt. ܒܫܠ. *fit for boiling; having the power of digesting.*

ܡܒܫܠܢܘܬܐ rt. ܒܫܠ. f. *ripeness, ripening.*

ܡܓ *to grow flat, tasteless* as wine; pass. part. ܡܓܝܓ, ܓܐ, ܓܬܐ *tasteless, senseless.* DERIVATIVE, ܡܓܝܓܘܬܐ.

ܡܓܐ m. *Indian pea.*

ܡܓ̈ܠܐ = ܡܓ̈ܠܐ pl. of ܡܓܠܐ, ܡܓܠܬܐ.

ܡܓܪ Aphel part. of verb ܝܓܪ.

ܡܓܪܐ m. some sort of fruit.

ܡܓܪܐ (ܡܓܪܐ) rt. ܓܪܐ. *a spot where fire breaks forth* esp. *a vent of volcanic flames.*

ܡܓܕܠ, ܡܓܕܠܐ pl. ܠܐ rt. ܓܕܠ. m. *a tower, bulwark;* often forms part of the name of a place.

ܡܓܕܠܝܬܐ from ܡܓܕܠܐ pr. n. *Magdalen, of Magdala,* ܡܪܝܡ ܡܓܕܠܝܬܐ *Mary Magdalen.*

ܡܓܕܡܘܬܐ rt. ܓܕܡ. f. gram. *aphaeresis, contraction.*

ܡܓܕܡܢܘܬܐ rt. ܓܕܡ. f. gram. *aphaeresis, dropping of a letter* at the beginning or end of a word.

ܡܓܕܦ, ܡܓܕܦܢܐ, ܢܝܬܐ rt. ܓܕܦ. *blasphemous; a blasphemer.*

ܡܓܕܦܢܐܝܬ rt. ܓܕܦ. adv. *blasphemously.*

ܡܓܕܦܘܬܐ rt. ܓܕܦ. f. *blasphemy.*

ܡܓܗ, ܡܓܗܐ Aphel act. part. of ܓܗܐ.

ܡܓܗܐ usually pl. ܡܓܗ̈ܐ rt. ܓܗ. m. *dawn, daybreak,* ܟܘܟܒܐ ܕܡܓܗ̈ܐ ܡܕܢܚ *the star which rises at dawn;* ܠܠܝܐ ܕܡܓܗܝ ܫܒܬܐ *the night immediately preceding the Sabbath.*

ܡܓܗܝܢܐ rt. ܓܗܐ. *that which sets free, gives refuge.*

ܡܓܗܝܢܘܬܐ rt. ܓܗܐ. f. *escape, deliverance.*

ܡܓܘܓܢܘܬܐ cf. ܓܘܓܐ. f. *whispering, speaking softly.*

ܡܓܘܠܢܐܝܬ from ܓܘܠܐ. adv. *flaming, like flames.*

ܡܓܘܢܘܬܐ rt. ܓܘܢ. f. *initiation, acquaintance;* with ܒ *skill.*

ܡܓܘܫܐ pl. ܫܐ, ܫܬܐ from Zend môghu, a fire-worshipper. m. *a magian, mage, a priest of the Persian religion, one professing magianism; a magician, wizard;* ܡܓܘܫܐ ܕܡܓܘܫܐ *the Magian* i. e. *the Persian nation.* Derivatives, verb ܡܓܫ, ܡܓܘܫܐ, ܡܓܘܫܘܬܐ, ܡܓܘܫܝܐ.

ܡܓܘܫܘܬܐ pl. ܘܬܐ from ܡܓܘܫܐ f. *magianism, the doctrine of the magi, fire-worship;* pl. *magic arts, enchantments.*

ܡܓܘܫܝܐ pl. ܝܐ from ܡܓܘܫܐ. m. *a magian, fire-worshipper, Chaldaean.*

ܡܓܙܪܐ rt. ܓܙܪ. m. *a sickle, bill-hook.*

ܡܓܠܝܐ *an anchorite;* see Pa. part. of ܓܠܐ.

ܡܓܠܝܘܬܐ rt. ܓܠܐ. f. *want, lack, bereavement* esp. of children, *barrenness; penury; a penurious* or *destitute life* as that of anchorites.

ܡܓܠܝܢ, ܡܓܠܝܢܐ, ܡܓܠܝܢܝܬܐ rt. ܓܠܐ. *one who makes to be childless* or *barren.*

ܡܓܠܠܐ m. *lame;* ܡܓܠܠܬܐ f. *fat, soft.*

ܡܓܙܪܐ rt. ܓܙܪ. m. *a*) *an axe, hatchet, saw,* esp. for smoothing stone. *b*) *a dagger; a lancet, scalpel.*

ܡܓܚܟܢܐ, ܡܓܚܟܢܝܬܐ rt. ܓܚܟ. *ludicrous, ridiculous; comical, amusing, funny.*

ܡܓܚܟܢܐܝܬ rt. ܓܚܟ. adv. *comically; derisively.*

ܡܓܚܟܢܘܬܐ rt. ܓܚܟ. f. *laughter, ridicule, derision.*

ܡܓܢܒܘܬܐ pl. ܘܬܐ rt. ܓܢܒ. f. *an answer.*

ܡܓܢܒܢܐ, ܡܓܢܒܢܝܬܐ rt. ܓܢܒ. *answering, correspondent.*

ܡܓܝܓܘܬܐ rt. ܡܓ. f. *tastelessness, insipidity; brackishness.*

ܡܓܝܪܐ, ܡܓܝܪܬܐ rt. ܓܪܐ. *dried up, waterless;* ܡܒܘܥܐ ܡܓܝܪܬܐ *springs which have failed.*

ܡܓܝܣܢܐ rt. ܓܣܐ. *a liberal giver.*

ܡܓܝܣܢܘܬܐ rt. ܓܣܐ. f. *a breaking forth, overflowing.*

ܡܓܝܠܢܘܬܐ rt. ܓܠܠ. f. *ejection, rejection.*

ܡܓܝܣܛܪܘܣ, ܡܓܝܣܛܪܘܣ or ܡܓܝܣܛܪܐ m. μάγιστρος, *a master, steward, prefect; master of the horse, master of the imperial household, chief officer of the emperor's palace.*

ܡܓܝܣܛܪܝܢܐ, ܡܓܝܣܛܪܝܢܘܣ pl. ܡܓܝܣܛܪܝܢܘ or ܢܐ m. *magistrianus, provincial.*

ܡܓܝܪܘܣܐ, ܡܓܝܪܘܣܐ, ܡܓܝܪܐ, ܡܓܝܪܣܐ or ܡܓܝܪܐ pl. ܐ m. μάγειρος, *a*) *a cook, baker, butcher;* ܪܝܫ ܡܓܝܪܘܣܐ *the head-cook;* ܡܫܡܫܢܐ ܕܡܓܝܪܘܣܐ *scullions;* ܒܝܬ ܡܓܝܪܘܣܐ *the kitchen.* *b*) *a cooking-pot, kettle.*

ܡܓܠ Aphel ܐܡܓܠ denom. verb from ܡܓܠܐ. *to be purulent, discharge pus* or *matter.*

(ܐܦܐ) ܡܓܠܝܐ rt. ܓܠܐ. m. lit. *uncovering of the face, unveiling,* hence *confidence.*

ܡܓܠܐ, ܡܓܠܬܐ pl. ܡܓܠܐ rt. ܓܠܠ. f. *a sickle.*

ܡܓܠܐ m. ܡܓܠܬܐ f. pl. ܡܓܠܐ and ܡܓܠܐ rt. ܓܠܠ. *a roll, scroll, volume; a schedule, codicil; a sheet, skin, parchment;* ܡܓܠܐ ܕܟܬܒܢܘܬܐ *skins for writings.*

ܡܓܠܕܐ pl. ܐ m. *a lash, whip.*

ܡܓܠܕܢܐ, ܡܓܠܕܢܝܬܐ from ܓܠܝܕܐ. *freezing, icy.*

ܡܓܠܝܢܐ, ܡܓܠܝܢܝܬܐ rt. ܓܠܐ. *a captive, exile.*

ܡܓܠܘܠܐ pl. ܐ rt. ܓܠܠ. m. *a clod, lump of mud.*

ܡܓܠܙܢܐ rt. ܓܠܙ. *a cheat, knave.*

ܡܓܠܚܢܘܬܐ rt. ܓܠܚ. f. *an explanation; a display.*

ܡܓܠܝܐܝܬ rt. ܓܠܐ. adv. *clearly, openly.*

ܡܓܠܝܘܬܐ rt. ܓܠܐ. f. *captivity; manifestation.*

ܡܓܠܝܢܐ, ܡܓܠܝܢܝܬܐ rt. ܓܠܐ. *a*) *revealing, manifesting.* *b*) *a starling.*

ܡܓܠܝܢܐܝܬ rt. ܓܠܐ. adv. *clearly, openly.*

ܡܓܠܝܢܘܬܐ rt. ܓܠܐ. f. *uncovering, manifestation;* ܡܓܠܝܢܘܬ ܐܦܐ *unveiling of the face = confidence.*

ܡܓܠܦܘܬܐ rt. ܓܠܦ. f. *being splay-mouthed, having the upper lip drawn back exposing the teeth.*

ܡܓܠܬܐ; see ܡܓܠܐ and ܡܓܠܐ.

ܡܓܡܓܐ m. corrupt from κροκόμαγμα, *the autumn crocus.*

ܡܓܡܚܢܐ rt. ܓܡܚ. *impudent, importunate.*

ܡܓܡܚܢܘܬܐ rt. ܓܡܚ. f. *impudence.*

ܡܓܡܪܢܐ pl. ܐ rt. ܓܡܪ. m. *a destroyer, exterminator.*

ܡܓܢ adv. *gratis, freely, without expense, payment* or *recompense; empty, in vain;* legal. ܡܓܢ ܬܦܘܩ a woman divorcing her husband *shall depart empty* i. e. without her dowry.

ܡܓܢ, ܡܓܢܐ pl. ܡܓܢ̈ܝܢ, ܡܓܢ̈ܐ rt. ܓܢ. f. *a short buckler, round shield.*

ܡܓܢܢܐ rt. ܓܢ. *armed with a round shield; disk-shaped.*

ܡܓܢܒܐܝܬ rt. ܓܢܒ. adv. *secretly, by stealth.*

ܡܓܢܛܝܣ, ܡܓܢܐܛܝܣ or ܡܓܢܝܛܝܣ f. *loadstone, magnet;* ܐܬܢܓܕܐ ܕܡܓܢܛܝܣ ܠܘܬ ܦܪܙܠܐ *the attraction of the loadstone towards iron.*

ܡܓܢܝܐ rt. ܓܢܐ. m. *a retiring room, a couch* or *bed; lying* or *sitting down.*

ܡܓܢܢܐ, ܡܓܢܢܝܬܐ from ܡܓܢ. adj. *freely given, free, without payments.*

ܡܓܢܝܢܘܬܐ rt. ܓܢܐ. f. *censure, reproach.*

ܡܓܢܝܢܐ, ܡܓܢܝܢܝܬܐ rt. ܓܢܐ. adj. *reproachful, vituperative, contumelious, expressive of deserving censure* or *rebuke.*

ܡܓܢܢܘܬܐ rt. ܓܢ. f. *descent, gliding down, overshadowing, protection, abiding, indwelling.*

ܡܓܢܢ or ܡܐܓܢܢ Aphel act. part.; see ܓܢ.

ܡܓܣܐ pl. ܡܓܣ̈ܐ from ܓܣܐ. m. *a) reclining, lying down, sitting down* esp. at table. *b) a base. c) a flagon, oil-flask.*

ܡܓܘܦܐ m. *a bolt, bar.*

ܡܓܥܠܢܘܬܐ pl. ܡܓܥܠܢܘ̈ܬܐ rt. ܓܥܠ. f. *consigning, depositing, commendation;* ܐܓܪ̈ܬܐ ܕܡܓܥܠܢܘܬܐ or ܕܡܓܥܠܢܘ̈ܬܐ *commendatory letters.*

ܡܓܥܓܥܢܐ rt. ܓܥܓܥ. m. *one suffering from nausea.*

ܡܓܪܓܪܢܐ, ܡܓܪܓܪܢܝܬܐ rt. ܓܪܓ. *enticing, inciting, provocative; a seducer.*

ܡܓܪܓܪܢܐܝܬ rt. ܓܪܓ. adv. *provoking emulation.*

ܡܓܪܓܪܢܘܬܐ rt. ܓܪܓ. f. *incitement, enticement.*

ܡܓܪܕܦܘܬܐ rt. ܓܪܕܦ. *destitution.*

ܡܓܪܕܦܢܘܬܐ rt. ܓܪܕܦ. *failure.*

ܡܓܪܘܦܝܬܐ pl. ܡܓܪܘܦܝܬ̈ܐ f. rt. ܓܪܦ. *a fire shovel.*

ܡܓܪܝܢܐ, ܡܓܪܝܢܝܬܐ rt. ܓܪܐ. *stimulating, inciting; an instigator, stirrer up of strife.*

ܡܓܪܝܢܘܬܐ rt. ܓܪܐ f. *stirring up of strife, instigation; an assault.*

ܡܓܪܢܘܬܐ rt. ܓܪܢ. f. *delay; patience.*

ܡܓܪܣܐ; see ܡܓܪܣܬܐ.

ܡܓܪܣܬܐ f. *a mortar.*

ܡܓܪܣܢܐ, ܡܓܪܣܢܝܬܐ rt. ܓܪܣ. *crushing, pulverizing, destructive.*

ܡܓܪܣܢܘܬܐ rt. ܓܪܣ. f. *shattering.*

ܡܓܪܠܐ rt. ܓܪܠ. m. a stake of wood *scraped smooth.*

ܡܓܪܘܦܬܐ rt. ܓܪܦ. f. *a shovel, a ladle.*

ܡܓܪܬ ܪܘܚܐ rt. ܓܪܝ. f. *longsuffering, indulgent kindness.*

ܡܓܫ ܡܓܫ act. part. ܡܓܫ, denom. verb from ܡܓܘܫܐ. *to worship according to magian rites; to profess magianism; to mutter.* Pa. ܡܓܫ *to celebrate magian rites, practise magic arts, use enchantments.* Ethpa. ܐܬܡܓܫ *to become a fire-worshipper.*

ܡܓܫܐ from ܡܓܘܫܐ. m. *muttering.*

ܡܓܫܘܬܐ rt. ܓܫ. f. *exploration, examination.*

ܡܕ and ܡܕܐ cognate roots to ܐܡܕ. Derivatives, ܡܕܝܐ, ܡܕܝܘܬܐ, ܡܕܡܕܝܘܬܐ, ܡܬܡܕܝܢܘܬܐ.

ܡܕܝܐܝܬ from ܡܕܝ. adv. *Median, in the Medes' language.*

ܡܕܐܬܐ also spelt ܡܕܬܐ, ܡܕܐܬܐ and ܡܕܐܬܐ pl. ܡܕ̈ܐܬܐ f. *a) tribute;* ܡܕܐܬܐ ܕܡܠܟܐ *the king's tribute* or *tax;* with ܐܦܩ *to pay tribute;* with ܓܒܐ *to collect. b) a fine, penalty.*

ܡܕܒܚ, ܡܕܒܚܐ pl. ܡܕܒܚ̈ܝܢ, ܡܕܒܚ̈ܐ rt. ܕܒܚ. m. *an altar; the sanctuary, the holy place where the altar stands;* ܒܝܬ ܡܕܒܚܐ the same.

ܡܕܒܚܢܐ rt. ܕܒܚ. m. *one who offers sacrifice, the sacrificing priest.*

ܡܕܒܟܢܐ, ܡܕܒܟܢܝܬܐ rt. ܕܒܟ. *pricking, stinging.*

ܡܕܒܩܢܘܬܐ rt. ܕܒܩ. *packing up* for a journey.

ܡܕܒܩܢܐ rt. ܕܒܩ. *adhesive;* ܚܒܘܫܐ ܡܕܒܩܢ̈ܐ *bandages closing* a wound.

ܡܕܒܪ, ܡܕܒܪܐ rt. ܕܒܪ. m. *wilderness, desert;* ܡܕܒܪܐ ܕܢܛܪܝܐ *the Nitrian Desert.*

ܡܕܒܪ, ܡܕܒܪܐ Pael act. part. of ܕܒܪ. *a guide, leader;* ܡܕܒܪ̈ܝ ܐܠܦܐ *pilots.*

ܡܕܒܪܐ pl. ܡܕܒܪ̈ܐ, ܡܕܒܪ̈ܬܐ rt. ܕܒܪ. adj. *desert, deserted.*

ܡܕܒܪܝܐ, ܡܕܒܪܝܬܐ from ܡܕܒܪܐ *of* or *belonging to a desert, solitary; a hermit;* ܐܘܪܚܐ ܡܕܒܪܝܬܐ *the desert road* i.e. *road to* or *through the desert.*

ܡܕܰܒܪܳܢܳܐ rt. ܕܒܪ. m. *a leader, ruler, judge, governor, prefect;* with ܕܡܰܠܟܘܬܳܐ *a regent; a pilot; a tutor, guardian; a bishop, abbot.*

ܡܕܰܒܪܳܢܳܐܝܬ rt. ܕܒܪ. adv. *providently, prudently, discreetly; providentially, by the providence of God, according to the Divine dispensation.*

ܡܕܰܒܪܳܢܘܬܳܐ pl. ܘܳܬܳܐ rt. ܕܒܪ. f. *a) guidance, direction; steering; rule, government, administration; stewardship, leadership. b) manner of proceeding, action, course. c) prudence, foresight. d) a province, prefecture. e) the Divine dispensation, the providence, government* or *economy of God;* often used of our Lord's whole doings with mankind esp. of His incarnation and life on earth, and in the plural, of His acts in the flesh.

ܡܰܕܒܪܳܝܳܐ, ܡܰܕܒܪܳܝܬ from ܡܰܕܒܪܳܐ. adj. *of the desert, inhabiting the desert.*

ܡܕܰܒܪܳܢܳܝܳܐ, ܝܬܳܐ rt. ܕܒܪ. adj. *a) of* or *belonging to government. b) dispensatory, according to our Lord's dispensation.*

ܡܕܰܒܪܳܢܺܝܬܳܐ fem. of ܡܕܰܒܪܳܢܳܐ *an abbess, superior.*

ܡܕܰܒܛܠܳܢܳܐ rt. ܒܛܠ. m. *one who nullifies, stultifies.*

ܡܕܰܗܒܘܬܳܐ from ܕܗܒܳܐ. f. *gilding, overlaying with gold.*

ܡܕܰܗܢܳܢܳܐ rt. ܕܗܢ. m. *he* or *that which makes fat* or *oily.*

ܡܕܰܘܕܳܢܳܐܝܬ rt. ܕܘܕ. adv. *confusedly, irregularly; in confusion* or *perturbation.*

ܡܕܰܘܕܘܬܳܐ rt. ܕܘܕ. f. *trouble, disturbance;* ܡܕܰܘܕܘܬ ܬܰܪܥܺܝܬܳܐ *confusion of mind, perturbation.*

ܡܕܰܘܕܳܢܳܐ, ܢܺܝܬܳܐ rt. ܕܘܕ. *troubling, disturbing; a disturber, troubler.*

ܡܕܰܘܕܳܢܳܐܝܬ rt. ܕܘܕ. adv. *irregularly.*

ܡܕܰܘܙܳܢܳܐ E-Syr. ܡܕܰܘܙܳܢܳܐ, ܢܺܝܬܳܐ *a pander, procurer.*

ܡܕܰܘܝܳܢܳܐ, ܢܺܝܬܳܐ rt. ܕܘܐ. *afflicting, reducing to misery.*

ܡܕܰܘܪܳܐ rt. ܕܘܪ. m. ܡܕܰܘܪܳܐ ܕܪܰܟ݂ܫܶܐ *a breaker in of horses.*

ܡܕܰܘܕܳܐ, ܡܕܰܘܕܬܳܐ rt. ܡܕܘܕ. *rotten, spoiled, crusted;* ܒܺܥܶܐ ܡܕܰܘܕܳܬܳܐ *rotten eggs;* ܩܶܣܦܳܐ ܡܕܰܘܕܳܐ *dross of silver.*

ܡܕܰܘܳܬܳܐ pl. emph. of ܡܕܘܝܐ.

ܡܕܰܚܠܳܢܳܐ rt. ܕܚܠ. *terrible, inspiring terror.*

ܡܕܰܚܠܳܢܘܬܳܐ rt. ܕܚܠ. f. *horrifying, the inspiring of terror.*

ܡܕܰܚܩܳܢܳܐ rt. ܕܚܩ. m. *one who drives forth, banishes.*

ܡܕܰܚܩܳܢܳܝܳܐ rt. ܕܚܩ. adj. *of divorcement,* with ܟܬܳܒܳܐ *a writing of divorcement.*

ܡܕܰܚܩܳܢܘܬܳܐ rt. ܕܚܩ. f. *rejection, putting away;* ܟܬܳܒܳܐ ܕܡܕܰܚܩܳܢܘܬܳܐ *a writing of divorcement.*

ܡܕܰܝ or ܡܳܕܰܝ pr. n. f. *Media.* DERIVATIVES, ܡܕܝܐ, ܡܕܝܐܝܐ.

ܡܳܕܳܝܳܐ or ܡܳܕܳܝܳܐ pl. ܝܶܐ from ܡܳܕܰܝ. *a Mede, Median.*

ܡܳܕܶܐ and ܡܳܕܘܳܬܳܐ plurals of ܡܕܘܝܐ.

ܡܰܕܝܳܐ rt. ܕܝܐ. m. *flight, escape.*

ܡܕܺܝܒܳܢܳܐ, ܢܺܝܬܳܐ rt. ܕܘܒ. *consuming, causing to waste away; causing perspiration.*

ܡܕܺܝܒܳܢܘܬܳܐ rt. ܕܘܒ. f. *pining, wasting away.*

ܡܰܕܝܳܢܘܬܳܐ rt. ܕܝܐ. f. *deliverance.*

ܡܕܺܝܠܳܢܳܐ, ܢܺܝܬܳܐ rt. ܕܘܠ. *a servant, attendant, steward.*

ܡܕܝܢ or ܡܳܕܝܰܢ pr. n. *Midian.*

ܡܶܕܶܝܢ comp. of ܡܳܐ and ܕܶܝܢ *well then, so then, then, therefore.*

ܡܕܺܝܢܬܳܐ, ܡܕܺܝܢܰܬ pl. ܡܕܺܝܢܳܢ, ܡܕܺܝܢܳܬܳܐ rt. ܕܝܢ. f. *a city, town;* rarely *a province, country;* ܡܕܺܝܢܳܬܳܐ ܒܡܕܺܝܢܳܬܳܐ *in various cities;* ܡܕܺܝܢܳܬܳܐ ܬܰܪܬܶܝܢ *the two cities* = Seleucia and Ctesiphon; ܡܕܺܝܢܳܬܳܐ ܒܥܶܣܪ ܡܕܺܝܢܳܢ *Decapolis;* ܡܕܺܝܢܰܬ ܐܰܠܳܗܳܐ *the city of God* = Antioch; ܡܕܺܝܢܰܬ ܡܰܠܟܘܬܳܐ *the royal city, the capital;* ܡܕܺܝܢܰܬ ܩܘܕܫܳܐ *the holy city* = Jerusalem; ܡܕܺܝܢܰܬ ܫܠܳܡܳܐ *the city of peace* = Baghdad. The Blessed Virgin Mary is called ܡܕܺܝܢܬܶܗ ܕܒܰܪ ܐܺܝܫܰܝ *the city of the Son of Jesse.*

ܡܕܺܝܢܳܝܳܐ, ܢܳܝܬܳܐ rt. ܕܝܢ. *a) of the city, urban, civil, civic;* ܣܘܥܪܳܢܶܐ ܡܕܺܝܢܳܝܶܐ *civic affairs, municipal matters. b) a citizen.*

ܡܕܝܢܳܝܳܐ, ܢܳܝܬܳܐ from ܡܕܝܢ. *a Midianite.*

ܡܕܺܝܢܳܝܘܬܳܐ rt. ܕܝܢ. f. *civil government.*

ܡܕܺܝܢܬܘܢܺܝܬܳܐ rt. ܕܝܢ. f. *a little town.*

ܡܕܺܝܨܘܬܳܐ rt. ܕܝܨ. f. *delighting, delight.*

ܡܕܘܕܐ pl. ܐ̈ـ m. *a wallet, travelling-bag.*

ܡܕܘܩܘܬܐ rt. ܕܘܩ. f. *gazing, regarding.*

ܡܕܘܩܢܘܬܐ rt. ܕܘܩ. f. *looking, beholding.*

ܡܕܘܪܐ pl. ܝܢ̈ـ, ܐ̈ـ rt. ܕܘܪ. m. *a story* of a building, *a flat, a lofty dwelling; a habitation;* metaph. *the heavens, the zones of the heavenly spheres.*

ܡܕܘܪܢܐ rt. ܕܘܪ. *a dweller, inhabiter.*

ܡܕܟ Pael ܡܰܕܶܟ *to season, salt, compound, prepare with care;* with ܣܡܐ *to mix* or *prepare drugs;* ܐܬܡܕܟܘܗܝ ܕܡܣܡܢܐ ܡܢ ܚܠܝܘܬܐ ܘܡܪܝܪܘܬܐ *an antidote compounded of sweet and bitter* herbs; ܡܠܚܐ ܡܡܕܟܬܐ *pungent salt.* Metaph. with ܡܘܬܐ *to compass the death of* any one; with ܢܟܠܐ *to prepare wiles;* with ܦܚܐ *to lay a cunning trap;* ܡܡܕܟ ܒܡܠܚܐ ܕܫܪܪܐ *seasoned with the salt of truth;* ܡܡܕܟܐ ܗܘܬ ܡܠܬܗ ܒܚܘܒܐ ܘܝܕܥܬܐ *his speech was seasoned with love and knowledge.* Ethpa. ܐܬܡܕܟ *to be seasoned, spiced, salted;* ܡܫܚܐ ܕܒܒܣܡܐ ܐܬܡܕܟ *oil compounded with spices;* ܒܗ ܡܬܡܕܟܝܢ ܦܟܝܗܐ *the dull are seasoned by it* i.e. by instruction. Derivatives, ܡܕܘܟܐ, ܡܡܕܟܢܘܬܐ, ܡܕܘܟܐ.

ܡܕܟܝܐ ܕܫܢܐ rt. ܕܟܐ. m. *dentifrice.*

ܡܕܟܢܘܬܐ or ܡܕܟܢܘ̈ܬܐ only pl. rt. ܡܕܟ. m. *herbs, seasoning, condiments,* as pepper, cinnamon, &c.

ܡܕܟܝܢܐ rt. ܕܟܐ. m. *a razor;* ܩܡ ܥܠ ܦܘܡܐ ܕܡܕܟܝܢܐ *he stood on the edge of a razor = was in great peril.*

ܡܕܟܝܢܘܬܐ, ܡܕܟܝܘܬܐ Pael infin. of ܕܟܐ. f. *a cleansing, purging, pruning; purification; purity.*

ܡܕܟܝܢܐ, ܡܕܟܝܢܝܬܐ rt. ܕܟܐ. *purifying, purging;* ܣܡܐ ܡܕܟܝܢܐ *purgative medicine;* ܢܘܪܐ ܡܕܟܝܢܝܬܐ *purgatorial fire.*

ܡܕܟܪܢܐ rt. ܕܟܪ. m. *a recorder, chronicler.*

ܡܕܟܬܐ rt. ܕܟ (?). f. *a mortar.*

ܡܕܠܐ pl. ܡܕܠ̈ܐ rt. ܕܠܐ. *wooden door-bolts.*

ܡܕܠܐ and ܡܕܠܐ m. *a millipede, woodlouse.*

ܡܕܠܚܢܐ, ܡܕܠܚܢܝܬܐ rt. ܕܠܚ. *a*) adj. *troubling, disturbing;* ܡܚܫܒܬܐ ܡܕܠܚܢܝܬܐ *disturbing* or *agitating thoughts;* ܬܐܪܬܐ ܡܕܠܚܢܐ *a troubling conscience.* *b*) subst. *a troubler, agitator, instigator.*

ܡܕܠܝܢܐ, ܡܕܠܝܢܝܬܐ rt. ܕܠܐ. *lifting up* or *out; a pulley;* ܣܡܝܟ ܐܢܐ ܥܠ ܨܠܘܬܟ ܡܕܠܝܢܝܬܐ *I rely on thy prayers to help me out.*

ܡܕܠܠܢܐ rt. ܕܠܠ. *a*) *indicative, specifying.* *b*) *rarefying.*

ܡܕܠܛܪܢܐ from ܕܠܛܪ. *an accuser, adversary.*

ܡܕܠܛܪܢܐܝܬ from ܕܠܛܪ. adv. *in hostile opposition.*

ܡܕܡ com. gen. and both numbers, but with a pl. ܡܕ̈ܡܐ *affairs, things. Something, anything, aught, somewhat, some, some or other; any one, some one, a certain* . . .; ܐܝܢܐ ܡܕܡ *some time;* ܚܣ̈ܢܐ ܡܕܡ *some fortresses;* ܩܠܐ ܡܕܡ *a certain rumour;* ܡܕܡ ܕ *that which, anything which, something which, whatever;* ܡܕܡ ܘܡܕܡ ܡܕܡ *of some sort, different sorts, various, certain;* ܡ̈ܠܐ ܡܕܡ ܡܕܡ *certain words;* ܡܢ ܡܕܡ *some, a few;* ܒܡܕܡ *in some things, partly;* ܒܡܕܡ ܕܝܠܗ or ܡܢ ܡܕܡ ܕܝܠܗ *at his own expense;* ܟܠ ܡܕܡ *everything* cf. ܟܠ; ܡܕܡ ܠܐ or ܠܐ ܡܕܡ *nothing at all;* ܠܡܕܡ ܠܐ ܐܘܠܐ *it is good for nothing.*

ܡܕܡܝܐ, ܡܕܡܝܬܐ from ܡܕܡ. *something; a being; special.*

ܡܕܡܝܘܬܐ from ܡܕܡ. f. *the being something.*

ܡܕܡܝܢܐ, ܡܕܡܝܢܝܬܐ rt. ܕܡܐ. *an imitator; representative, typical.*

ܡܕܡܝܢܐܝܬ rt. ܕܡܐ. adv. *probably, conjecturally.*

ܡܕܡܝܢܘܬܐ pl. ܘ̈ܬܐ rt. ܕܡܐ. *imitation, resemblance.*

ܡܕܡܟܐ rt. ܕܡܟ. m. *lying down, a couch, bed;* ܡܕܡܟܐ ܕܙܘܘܓܐ *sexual intercourse;* ܡܕܡܟܐ ܕܛܗܪܐ *noontide rest, siesta;* eccles. ܡܕܡ ܡܕܡܟܐ *one of the canonical hours said before going to bed* = ܣܘܟܠܐ *compline.*

ܡܕܡܟܢܐ rt. ܕܡܟ. *soporific.*

ܡܕܡܝܢܐ from ܕܡ, ܕܡܐ. *blood red, crimson; sanguine, rubicund.*

ܡܕܡܪܢܐ, ܡܕܡܪܢܝܬܐ rt. ܕܡܪ. *wonderful.*

ܡܕܢܐ, ܡܕܢ pl. ܐ̈ـ from ܕܢܐ. m. *a wine-cellar, store-room;* metaph. ܕܒܘܪܐ ܒܡܕ̈ܢܐ ܣܐܡ ܕܒܫܐ the bee *stores up honey in cells.*

ܡܕܢܚܐ, ܡܕܢܚ pl. only constr. st. ܡܕܢܚܝ rt. ܕܢܚ. m. (rarely f. when denoting a country).

a) *the sunrise, the eastern sky, the east;* ܒܡܕܢܚܐ *in the east;* ܠܡܕܢܚܐ *towards the east;* ܡܕܢܚ ܓܪܒܝܐ *north-east;* ܠܡܕܢܚ ܬܝܡܢܐ *south-eastward;* ܡܢ ܡܕܢܚ ܠܡܕܢܚ ܬܘܒ *eastward;* ܡܕܢܚܗ ܕܡܕܒܪܐ *at the east of the desert.* *b*) in a narrower sense *the Persian empire; Syria, Assyria;* also esp. eccles. *Chaldaea* and *Assyria* opp. ܡܥܪܒܐ *Mesopotamia* and *Syria;* ܟܘܪܣܝܐ ܕܡܕܢܚܐ *the See of the East.*

ܡܕܢܚܝܐ, ܡܕܢܚܝܬܐ rt. ܕܢܚ. *a*) *east, eastern;* ܪܘܚܐ ܡܕܢܚܝܬܐ *the east wind.* *b*) pl. *Easterns, Orientals;* ܦܛܪܝܪܟܐ ܕܡܕܢܚܝܐ *Patriarch of the Eastern* Christians.

ܡܕܢܚܢܐ rt. ܕܢܚ. m. ܡܕܢܚܢܐ ܕܨܦܪܐ *He Who maketh the dawn to rise.*

ܡܕܘܫܐ or ܡܕܫܐ m. *a thread* esp. *the thread first tied to the loom.*

ܡܕܥܐ, ܡܕܥ rt. ܝܕܥ. m. *the mind, intellect, understanding;* ܡܕܥܐ ܡܠܝܠܐ *the rational mind;* ܕܠܐ ܡܕܥ and ܚܣܝܪ ܡܕܥܐ *wanting in understanding, ignorant, unwise;* ܠܒܪ ܡܢ ܡܕܥܗ *out of his mind.*

ܡܕܥ denom. verb from ܡܕܥܐ *to endow with mind.* Ethpa. ܐܬܡܕܥ *to be endowed with mind; to possess intelligence, to understand, know.*

ܡܕܥܟܢܐ, ܡܕܥܟܢܝܬܐ rt. ܕܥܟ. *quenching; an extinguisher.*

ܡܕܥܟܢܘܬܐ rt. ܕܥܟ. f. *quenching, extinction.*

ܡܕܥܢܝܐ, ܡܕܥܢܝܬܐ, ܡܕܥܢܐܝܬ from ܡܕܥܐ. *intelligent, intelligible, rational; skilful, expert.*

ܡܕܥܪܢܐ, ܡܕܥܪܢܝܬܐ rt. ܕܥܪ. *a*) *offending, contentious;* ܪܘܚܐ ܡܕܥܪܢܝܬܐ *a vexed* or *unquiet spirit.* *b*) *blinding, befogging.*

ܡܕܩ, ܡܕܩܐ, ܡܕܩܢ Aphel act. part. of ܕܩ *to pound.*

ܡܕܪܫ pl. ܡܕܪܫܝܢ Aphel pass. part. of ܕܪܫ. *instructed, expert, versed.*

ܡܕܪܫܘܬܐ rt. ܕܪܫ. f. *skill, complete aptitude.*

ܡܕܘܟܬܐ rt. ܕܘܟ. f. *a mortar.*

ܡܕܪ *to be rotten* as an egg. Pa. ܡܕܪ *to go bad, rot* as eggs or fruit. Aph. ܐܡܕܪ perh. denom. verb from ܡܕܪܐ *to crack* as parched ground. Derivative, ܡܕܘܪܐ.

ܡܕܪܐ pl. ܐ̈ com. gen. usually m. *a clod, lump of earth, mould* or *clay, soil;* ܡܕܪܐ ܕܐܕܡ *the earth whence Adam was formed;* ܡܕܪܐ ܚܘܪܐ *white clay;* ܡܕܪܐ ܕܦܚܪܐ *potter's clay.* Derivatives, verb ܐܡܕܪ, ܡܕܪܢܐ, ܡܕܪܝܐ, ܡܕܪܬܐ.

ܡܕܪܐ m. *the cord* wherewith a load is tied on a camel.

ܡܕܪܓܐܝܬ from ܕܪܓܐ ܕܪܓ. adv. *in its degree.*

ܡܕܪܘܣܐ m. rt. ܕܪܣ. *a cylinder, roller* for breaking clods.

ܡܕܪܘܣܘܢܝܬܐ pl. ܢܝ̈ܬܐ dimin. of ܡܕܪܘܣܐ f. *a small roller, hand-roller.*

ܡܕܪܝܐ pl. ܡܕܪܘܝܐ rt. ܕܪܐ. m. *a winnowing-shovel, winnowing-fan.*

ܡܕܪܢܐ from ܡܕܪܐ. *earthy.*

ܡܕܪܝܢܐ, ܡܕܪܝܢܝܬܐ rt. ܕܪܐ. *a winnower, scatterer, a spendthrift.*

ܡܕܪܟܢܐ rt. ܕܪܟ. *comprehending, intelligent.*

ܡܕܪܟܢܘܬܐ pl. ܘ̈ܬܐ rt. ܕܪܟ. f. *a*) *perception, conception, comprehension;* astron. *an observation.* *b*) *arrival, attainment* esp. *attaining puberty.*

ܡܕܪܟܬܐ rt. ܕܪܟ. f. *a*) *trodden ground; a rut.* *b*) *a footstool, step.*

ܡܕܪܡܢܐܝܬ rt. ܕܪܡ. adv. *craftily.*

ܡܕܪܡܢܘܬܐ rt. ܕܪܡ. f. *craft, slyness, cunning.*

ܡܕܪܢܐ from ܡܕܪܐ. *a creature of earth, earthly being.*

ܡܕܪܢܐ m. *a spindle.*

ܡܕܪܥܢܘܬܐ from ܕܪܥܐ. f. *stretching out the arm.*

ܡܕܪܫ, ܡܕܪܫܐ pl. ܫ̈ܐ rt. ܕܪܫ. m. *an exposition, commentary, a doctrinal hymn, hymn, ode.*

ܡܕܪܫܘܬܐ rt. ܕܪܫ. f. *skill, training.*

ܡܕܪܫܢܐ, ܡܕܪܫܢܝܬܐ rt. ܕܪܫ. *a*) subst. *schoolmaster, teacher.* *b*) adj. *disputed, debated.*

ܡܕܪܫܬܐ rt. ܕܪܫ. f. *a school.*

ܡܕܪܬܐ from ܡܕܪܐ. f. *earth.*

ܡܕܘܫܐ rt. ܐܕܫ. m. *a pestle.*

ܡܕܫܢܘܬܐ rt. ܐܕܫ. f. *silence, negligence.*

ܡܗܐ fut. ܢܡܗܐ *to cook, boil, boil up.* Derivatives, ܡܗܘܝܐ, ܡܗܝܐ.

ܡܗܒ infin. of verb ܝܗܒ.

ܡܗܘܒܐ rt. ܝܗܒ. m. *giving.*

ܡܗܒܒܐܝܬ from ܗܒܒ. adv. *gaudily, showily.*

ܡܗܒܒܘܬܐ from ܗܒܒ. f. *blossoming, bloom, prime, vigour.*

ܡܗܓܝܢܐ, ܢܝܬܐ Ar. gram. *denoting distinct utterance, forming a syllable,* ܐܬܐ ܡܗܓܝܢܬܐ *a vowel* added to facilitate pronunciation.

ܡܗܓܝܢܘܬܐ rt. ܗܓܐ. f. *syllabification, addition of a vowel.*

ܡܗܓܪܐ *a pervert to Islam;* see ܗܓܪ.

ܡܗܓܪܢܘܬܐ from ܗܓܪ. f. *Islamism; the Hegira.*

ܡܗܓܪܝܐ from ܗܓܪ. *an Arab, Mussulman.*

ܡܗܕܝܢܐ, ܢܝܬܐ rt. ܗܕܐ. *a leader, guide, director.*

ܡܗܕܝܢܘܬܐ rt. ܗܕܐ. f. *direction, guidance.*

ܡܗܕܪܢܐ rt. ܗܕܪ. m. *one who adorns, beautifies;* ܡܠܟܐ ܡܗܕܪܢܝ ܕܝܪܐ *kings who have furnished* or *embellished monasteries.*

ܡܗܕܪܢܐ, ܢܝܬܐ rt. ܗܕܪ. *becoming, honourable.*

ܡܗܘܝܢܐ rt. ܗܘܐ. m. *giving existence; a creator.*

ܡܗܘܝܢܘܬܐ rt. ܗܘܐ. f. *creation, the act of creation.*

ܡܗܘܢ, ܡܗܘܢܐ, ܡܗܘܢܝܬܐ from ܗܘܢܐ; see ܗܘܢ; *rational, endowed with reason.*

ܡܗܘܢܐܝܬ from ܗܘܢܐ. adv. *wisely, prudently, discreetly.*

ܡܗܘܢܘܬܐ from ܗܘܢܐ. f. *understanding, intelligence, discretion.*

ܡܗܘܢܢܘܬܐ from ܗܘܢܐ. f. *intelligence.*

ܡܗܘܠܡܣ, ܡܗܘܠܐܡܣ; see ܡܐܠ.

ܡܗܘܝܐ rt. ܡܗܐ. m. *boiling* esp. *boiling too long, boiling over.*

ܡܗܘܝܐ from ܡܝܐ. *watery.*

ܡܗܘܝܘܬܐ from ܡܝܐ. f. *wateriness.*

ܡܗܝܡܢ, ܡܗܝܡܢܐ, ܡܗܝܡܢܝܬܐ act. part. of ܗܝܡܢ; see ܐܡܢ; *a believer, a Christian.* ܡܗܝܡܢ pass. part. emph. and fem. forms same as those of the act. part., *faithful, trustworthy; an eunuch.*

ܡܗܝܡܢܐܝܬ from ܗܝܡܢ. adv. *faithfully, according to the Christian faith.*

ܡܗܝܡܢܝܢ ܚܢܢ = ܡܗܝܡܢܝܢܢ *we believe;* used as subst. for *the Nicene Creed.*

ܡܗܝܢܐ, ܢܝܬܐ *efficient.*

ܡܗܝܪܐܝܬ rt. ܡܗܪ. adv. *promptly, readily, skilfully, admirably.*

ܡܗܝܪܘܬܐ rt. ܡܗܪ. f. *skill, skilfulness; practice, intelligence;* ܡܗܝܪܘܬܐ ܕܒܣܘܥܪܢܐ *practical knowledge, ability.*

ܡܗܝܪ *Mechir,* the name of the sixth Egyptian month.

ܡܗܟܢܐܣ or ܡܗܟܢܝܣ pl. of ܡܟܐܢܐ *an engine.*

ܡܗܠܠ Aphel part. of ܗܠܠ.

ܡܗܠܢܟܘܠܝܩܐ μελαγχολική, *melancholy.*

ܡܗܠܢܟܘܠܝܩܝܐ pl. ܩܝ̈ adj. *melancholy.*

ܡܗܠܟܢܐ, ܢܝܬܐ rt. ܗܠܟ. *walking, able to walk.*

ܡܗܠܠܢܐ rt. ܗܠܠ. m. *a mocker, derider.*

ܡܗܠܠܢܐܝܬ rt. ܗܠܠ. adv. *derisively.*

ܡܗܠܠܢܘܬܐ rt. ܗܠܠ. f. *derisive.*

ܡܗܠܠܢܐ, ܢܝܬܐ rt. ܗܠܠ. *derisive.*

ܡܗܡܝܢܐ, ܢܝܬܐ rt. ܗܡܐ. *careless, negligent.*

ܡܗܡܝܢܐܝܬ rt. ܗܡܐ. *carelessly.*

ܡܗܡܝܢܘܬܐ rt. ܗܡܐ. f. *negligence, carelessness.*

ܡܗܢܐ, ܡܗܢܝܐ Aphel part. of ܗܢܐ. *useful, agreeable.*

ܡܗܢܐ rt. ܡܗܐ. *boiled too long, insipid, spoiled.*

ܡܗܢܝܢܐ, ܢܝܬܐ rt. ܗܢܐ. *useful, pleasant;* with ܠܐ *useless, unprofitable.*

ܡܗܦܟܐ rt. ܗܦܟ. perh. Pael pass. part. *a*) subst. *return.* *b*) adj. *perverse, froward.*

ܡܗܦܟܢܐ or ܡܗܦܟܢܐ rt. ܗܦܟ. m. *he* or *that which brings back* or *restores; subversive.*

ܡܗܦܟܢܘܬܐ rt. ܗܦܟ. f. *aversion, rejection, abolition.*

ܡܗܪ root-meaning in Heb. *to be quick, apt;* in Ar. *to give a dowry;* in Conj. II. *to buy a foal;* Conj. III. and V. *to be quick, capable, skilful.* Syr. Peal only pass. part. ܡܗܝܪ, ܡܗܝܪܐ, ܡܗܝܪܬܐ *trained, practised, skilled, skilful;* ܐܘܡܢܐ ܡܗܝܪܐ *a skilled artisan;* ܣܦܪܐ or ܣܦܪܐ ܡܗܝܪܐ *a practised scribe;* ܡܠܦܢܘܬܐ ܡܗܝܪܬܐ *wise* or *prudent instruction.* PAEL ܡܗܪ *to train.* Ethpa. ܐܬܡܗܪ *to be skilled, trained, instructed;* ܐܬܡܗܪ ܒܐܘܡܢܘܬܗ *he was a master of his art.* Derivatives, ܡܗܝܪܐܝܬ, ܡܗܝܪܘܬܐ, ܡܗܪܐ, ܡܗܘܪܐ.

ܡܘܗܪ, ܡܘܗܪܐ Aphel part. of ܗܪ *molesting, injurious.*

ܡܘܗܪܐ rt. ܡܗܪ. m. *a marriage portion* or *gift from the bridegroom to the bride, a marriage dowry.*

ܡܘܗܪܢܐ, ܡܘܗܪܢܝܬܐ rt. ܗܪ. *injurious, destructive.*

ܡܘܗܪܢܘܬܐ rt. ܗܪ. f. *molestation, disturbance.*

ܡܘܗܪܩܐ dialect. m. *a rod, whip.*

ܡܘܬܐܕܘܣ, ܡܘܬܐܕܘܣ, ܡܬܕܘܣ or ܡܬܘܕܘܣ pl. ܡܬܘܕܘ̈ܣ, f. μέθοδος, *way of acting, a stratagem.*

ܡܘ *meum athamanticum,* a medicinal herb.

ܡܘ with suff. ܡܘܗܝ irreg. form of ܡܕܡ.

ܡܘܒܕܢܐ, ܡܘܒܕܢܝܬܐ rt. ܐܒܕ. adj. *destructive, pernicious, fatal, mortal;* subst. *a destroyer.*

ܡܘܒܕܢܘܬܐ rt. ܐܒܕ. f. *ruin, destruction, being brought to naught.*

ܡܘܒܠܐ pl. ܡܘܒܠܐ̈, ܡ̈ rt. ܝܒܠ. f. *a burden, load, cargo.*

ܡܘܒܠܢܘܬܐ rt. ܝܒܠ. f. *reduction.*

ܡܘܒܫܢܘܬܐ rt. ܝܒܫ. f. *desiccation.*

ܡܘܓܚܢܐ, ܡܘܓܚܢܝܬܐ rt. ܓܚ. *that which drives away.*

ܡܘܓܚܢܘܬܐ rt. ܓܚ. f. *expulsion.*

ܡܘܓܠܐ, Neo-Gr. μοῦχλα, m. *a) pus, matter, phlegm;* ܐܕܢܐ ܕܡܪܕܝܢ ܡܘܓܠܐ *ears discharging matter. b) the juice of olive kernels.*

ܡܘܓܠܝܬ from ܡܘܓܠܝܐ. adv. *in Mogul, in the language of the Moguls.*

ܡܘܓܠܝܐ, ܡܘܓܠܝܬܐ pl. m. ܡ̈ f. ܡܘܓܠܝ̈ܬܐ *a Mongol,* explained in the native lexx. as *a Tartar* or *Hun.*

ܡܘܕܝܐ pl. ܡܘܕܝܢ, ܡܘܕܝܐ̈ and ܡܘܕܝܘ̈ܬܐ m. *modius, a peck,* a Roman measure used especially for corn, containing sixteen sextarii or nearly eight English quarts.

ܡܘܕܝܢܐ from ܐܘܕܝ. *a) one who confesses Christ, one of the faithful, a confessor;* ܣܗܕ̈ܐ ܘܡܘܕܝܢ̈ܐ *martyrs and confessors;* ܥܪܘܒܬܐ ܕܡܘܕܝܢ̈ܐ *Friday of the Confessors* under King Sapor = Friday in Easter week. *b) one who confesses his sin, a penitent. c) grateful.*

ܡܘܕܝܢܐܝܬ from ܐܘܕܝ. adv. *by way of confession* or *acknowledgement.*

ܡܘܕܝܢܘܬܐ from ܐܘܕܝ. f. *confession, acknowledgement; giving of thanks; confession* or *profession* of faith, *profession* of virginity; *confession = witnessing to the faith, confessorship;* ܟܠܝܠܐ ܕܡܘܕܝܢܘܬܐ *a confessor's crown.*

ܡܘܕܪܐ pl. ܡ̈ rt. ܡܕܪ. m. *mixing, a mixture, compound, preparation, medicament, seasoning;* ܡܘܕܪܐ ܘܛܘܝܒܐ ܕܡܫܚܐ ܡܒܣܡܐ *the mixing and preparation of fragrant oil;* ܡܘܕܪ̈ܐ ܡܛܒ̈ܩܐ *highly seasoned dishes.*

ܡܘܕܥܘܬܐ rt. ܝܕܥ. f. *knowledge, learning.*

ܡܘܕܥܢܐ, ܡܘܕܥܢܝܬܐ rt. ܝܕܥ. *a) instructive, didactic, teaching, giving information. b) a small bell, handbell.*

ܡܘܕܥ ܐܢܐ = ܡܘܕܥܢܐ Aphel part. of ܝܕܥ. with 1 pers. pron.

ܡܘܕܥܢܘܬܐ rt. ܝܕܥ. f. *a making known* or *showing, a preface, introduction, an admonition;* ܡܘܕܥܢܘܬܐ ܕܗܝܡܢܘܬܐ *an exposition of the faith.*

ܡܘܕܥܬܐ rt. ܝܕܥ. f. *a) knowledge, acquaintance. b) a learned man. c) an acquaintance,* with ܐܢܫ, ܓܒܪܐ or ellipt. *d) a crying for sale, public offering for sale.*

ܡܘܕܪܐ m. *dross;* cf. ܡܕܪܐ.

ܡܘܗܒܬܐ pl. ܡ̈ rt. ܝܗܒ. f. *a gift, present, favour;* ܡܘܗܒܬ ܚܫܚܬܐ *usufruct;* adverbial use ܡܘܗܒܬ *freely, by favour, gratis, for nothing.*

ܡܘܗܘܦܛܐ W-Syr., ܡܘܗܦܛܐ E-Syr.; see ܡܘܗܦܛܐ, *chief of the Magi.*

ܡܘܗܪܐ rt. ܡܗܪ. m. *a foal.*

ܡܘܙܓܐ rt. ܡܙܓ. m. *mixture, blending, confusion; temperature;* ܣܡ̈ܡܢܐ ܘܡܘܙܓ̈ܐ *drugs and mixtures;* ܡܘܙܓܐ ܕܦܓܪܐ *physical temperament, bodily constitution;* ܓܒܪܐ ܒܝܫ—ܛܒ ܡܘܙܓܐ *a man of bad, of good, constitution;* ܠܡܛܪ ܠܡܘܙܓܟܘܢ *to retain your health;* theol. *the combination* or *union* of the two natures in our Lord; ܕܡܘܙܓܗ ܢܚܝܐ ܠܡܝܘܬܘܬܢ *that His commingling* with our nature *might quicken our mortality;* astron. *conjunction* of stars.

ܡܘܙܓܢܐ, ܡܘܙܓܢܝܬܐ rt. ܡܙܓ. adj. *mingled, confused; constitutional.*

ܡܘܿܪܩܳܐ m. *a beak, bill;* ܦܪܰܚܬܳܐ ܚܠܳܦ ܐܺܝܕܳܐ ܐܺܝܬ ܠܗܘܿܢ ܡܘܿܪܩܳܐ *birds have a beak instead of a hand.*

ܡܘܪܒܠܬܳܐ pl. ܡܘܪܒ̈ܠܳܬܳܐ f. *a sphere, an orbit, the globe, the poles, a zone* of the heavens, *the Zodiacal circle.*

ܡܘܪܒܠܬܳܢܳܝܳܐ adj. *of the spheres* or *pertaining to the zones* of the heavens.

ܡܘܙܦܳܢܳܐ rt. ܝܙܦ. m. *a lender, one who lends on interest; a creditor.*

ܡܘܙܦܳܢܘܬܳܐ *lending, money lending.*

ܡܘܿܬܳܪܳܐ *a*) rt. ܡܬܪ. m. *stretching;* ܒܡܘܿܬܳܪܳܐ ܕܗܰܕܳܡܰܘܗܝ *while stretching his limbs. b*) *dross.*

ܡܘܚܳܐ m. *the brain, the marrow;* ܡܘܚܳܐ ܕܚܨܳܐ *the spinal marrow;* metaph. ܒܨܝܪ ܡܘܚܳܐ *of little wit.* Derivative, ܡܘܚܢܐ.

ܡܘܚܡܝܳܢܘܬܳܐ rt. ܚܡܐ. f. *setting on fire, conflagration.*

ܡܘܚܡܳܬܳܐ rt. ܚܡܐ. f. *the bezel* or *setting* of a ring.

ܡܘܚܳܢܳܐ, ܡܘܚܳܢܳܝܳܐ from ܡܘܚܳܐ. *cerebral.*

ܡܘܚܠܫܳܢܘܬܳܐ rt. ܚܠܫ. f. *exhaustion, feebleness.*

ܡܘܚܪܳܢܘܬܳܐ rt. ܐܚܪ. f. *delay.*

ܡܘܛ, ܡܳܛ fut. ܢܡܘܛ, act. part. ܡܳܐܛ, ܡܳܝܛܳܐ. *to totter, lean over, stagger;* ܐܣܝܳܐ ܕܡܳܝܛ *a tottering wall;* ܡܳܛܘ ܪ̈ܶܓܠܰܝ *my feet slipped.* Ethpe. ܐܶܬܡܘܿܛ *to be shaken, to quiver.* Derivatives, ܡܘܛܳܐ, ܡܳܝܛܳܐ.

ܡܘܛܳܐ rt. ܡܘܛ. m. *rocking, leaning over, unsteadiness.*

ܡܘܛܝܳܐ rt. ܡܛܐ. m. *arrival.*

ܡܘܝܐ or ܡܐܘܝܐ pl. ܐ̈ mimetic = ܝܳܪܘܿܪܳܐ *a jackal.*

ܡܘܝܳܩܳܐ rt. ܡܘܩ. m. *mocking, derision, laughing to scorn, sneering.*

ܡܘܟܳܟܳܐ pl. ܐ̈ rt. ܡܟܟ. m. *humiliation, affliction; abasing, abasement, submission;* ܡ̈ܠܶܐ ܡܘܟܳܟܳܐ *submissive speech, humble words;* ܡܟܺܝܟܳܐ ܐܶܢ ܢܶܓܥ ܒܶܗ ܡܘܟܳܟܳܐ ܠܳܐ ܡܶܬܡܰܟܰܟ *the humble even if affliction befall him is not cast down.*

ܡܘܿܟܠܳܐ pl. ܡܘܿܟ̈ܠܝܢ, ܐ̈ m. μοχλός, *a bar, bolt;* ܬܒܰܪ ܡܘܿܟ̈ܠܰܘܗܝ ܕܫܝܘܿܠ *he brake the bars of hell.* Derivative, ܡܟܠ.

ܡܘܟܪܳܝܳܐ pl. ܐ̈ Ar. m. *an hired servant;* ܡܘܟܪ̈ܳܝܶܐ ܕܒܰܝܬܳܐ *indoor servants.*

ܡܘܠܐ, ܡܘܠܝܳܐ and ܡܘܠܳܝܳܐ pl. m. ܐ̈ f. ܡܘܠܝܳܬܳܐ and ܡܘܠܳܝܳܬܳܐ I. *mulus, mula, a mule.* II. μύλη, *the plant mola.* III. m. *a brazen vessel* for drawing wine from a cask.

ܡܘܠܕ, ܡܘܠܳܕܳܐ rt. ܝܠܕ. m. *a*) *parturition, travail, bringing forth. b*) *birth, nativity, generation;* ܡܘܠܳܕܳܐ ܕܡܰܝܳܐ metaph. for *baptism;* ܡܘܠܳܕܳܐ ܕܡܶܢ ܪܺܝܫ *regeneration.*

ܡܘܠܕܳܢܳܐ, ܡܘܠܕܳܢܝܬܳܐ rt. ܝܠܕ. *a*) *a forefather, progenitor, parent. b*) *generative, genital. c*) *causing to bring forth* or *to be prolific. d*) *causative, efficient.*

ܡܘܠܕܳܢܘܬܳܐ rt. ܝܠܕ. f. *generation, procreation, begetting, bearing, bringing forth;* ܡܘܠܕܳܢܘܬܳܐ ܡܣܰܓܝܳܢܺܝܬܳܐ *fecundity, prolificness.*

ܡܘܠܳܕܳܝܳܐ rt. ܝܠܕ. *of* or *belonging to birth.*

ܡܘܠܘ μῶλυ, the plant *moly.*

ܡܘܠܳܚܳܐ rt. ܡܠܚ. m. *salting, pickling.*

ܡܘܠܳܝܳܐ, ܡܘܠܳܝ rt. ܡܠܐ. m. *a filling-up, fulfilling, satisfying, completion; fullness, fulfilment; the conclusion* of a treaty; ܡܘܠܳܝܳܐ ܕܙܰܒ̈ܢܶܐ *the fulfilment of times, end of time;* ܡܘܠܳܝܳܐ ܕܝܰܘ̈ܡܳܬܳܐ *completion of the days;* ܥܪܘܒܬܳܐ ܕܡܘܠܳܝ ܐܰܪ̈ܒܥܝܢ ܕܨܘܡܳܐ *Friday at the end of Lent;* ܡܘܠܳܝ ܫܰܢ̄ܬܳܐ *the end of the year;* ܡܘܠܳܝ ܚܘܕܪܳܐ *the entire circle;* ܡܘܠܳܝܳܐ ܕܣܘܢܩܳܢܳܐ *the supplying of a need;* ܡܘܠܳܝ ܣܘܥܪܳܢܳܐ *completion of an action;* ܡܘܠܳܝ ܥܺܕܬܳܐ *the entire Church, universal Church;* ܡܘܠܳܝܳܐ ܕܡܕܺܝܢܬܳܐ *the whole of the capital.*

ܡܘܠܝܣܛܐ, ܡܘܠܝܣܛܝܬܐ or ܡܘܠ̈ܣ *a pander; an hermaphrodite.*

ܡܘܠܟܝܐ or ܡܘܠܟܝ f. μολόχη, *the mallow;* ܡܘܠܟܝܐ ܐܝܠܢܝܬܐ *malva arborescens;* ܡܘܠܟܝܐ ܕܒܪܐ *malva officinalis* or *sylvestris.*

ܡܘܠܟܳܢܳܐ pl. ܐ̈ rt. ܡܠܟ. m. *a*) *a promise, declaration;* ܡܘܠܟܳܢܶܗ ܕܐܰܒܪܳܗܳܡ *the promise made to Abraham;* ܐܰܪܥܳܐ ܕܡܘܠܟܳܢܳܐ *the promised land. b*) *counsel, advice. c*) *possession in lands, property* esp. *pious foundations, bequests* to mosques or churches.

ܡܘܠܟܬܐ; see ܡܘܠܐ.

ܡܘܡ, ܡܘܡܳܐ pl. ܡܘ̈ܡܝܢ, ܐ̈ m. *a spot, mark,*

blemish, a plague-spot; a speck, flaw, infirmity; ܣܒܐ ܕܐܣܓܝ ܒܗ ܡܘ̈ܡܐ an old man whose infirmities increased; metaph. a fault, vice, defect, bad habit; ܝܕܥ ܠܗ ܡܘ̈ܡܐ ܕܢܦܫܗ he who is aware of his own offences; ܣܡ ܒܗ ܡܘܡܐ he branded him with disgrace; ܕܠܐ ܡܘܡ flawless, faultless, unblemished. Derivatives, ܡܘܡܢܐ, ܡܘܡܬܢܐ, ܡܘܡܬܢܘܬܐ.

ܡܘܡܝܐ native pitch, bitumen.

ܡܘܡܢܐ from ܡܘܡ. blameworthy, reprehensible.

ܡܘܡܝܢܐ pl. ܢ̈ܐ rt. ܝܡܐ. m. one who administers an oath; an exorcist.

ܡܘܡܝܢܘܬܐ rt. ܝܡܐ. f. exorcism, a formula of exorcising.

ܡܘܡܝܬܐ pl. ܡܘ̈ܡܝܢ, ܡܘ̈ܡܝܢܬܐ rt. ܝܡܐ. f. an adjuration, a solemn oath or charge.

ܡܘܡܬܐ in the Bible, elsewhere generally ܡܘܡܬܐ pl. ܡܘ̈ܡܬܐ rt. ܝܡܐ. f. an oath, curse, execration; a deprecation; an agreement or treaty ratified by oath.

ܡܘܡܬܢܐ, ܬܢܝܬܐ from ܡܘܡ. faulty, damaged, imperfect; ܢܩܦ ܕܡܘܡܬܢܐ ܡܙܒܢ he declares that he sells damaged goods; ܚܘܒܐ ܓܡܝܪܐ ܘܠܐ ܡܘܡܬܢܐ perfect and spotless love.

ܡܘܡܬܢܘܬܐ from ܡܘܡ. f. infirmity; ܠܐ ܡܘܡܬܢܘܬܐ ܕܦܓܪܐ soundness of body, healthiness.

ܡܘ̈ܡܝ pl. of ܡܘܡܐ.

ܡܘܢ = ܡܢ and ܡܘܢܐ interrog. and rel. pron. what, what is it? why? wherefore? ܡܘܢ ܕ that which; ܡܘܢ ܕܦܐܫ ܗܘܐ what was over; ܡܛܠ ܡܘܢ ܕܗܘܐ on account of what was done; ܟܠ ܡܘܢ, ܡܘܢ ܕܗܘ whosoever, whatsoever; ܒܡܘܢ, ܥܠ ܡܘܢ by what means? how? ܠܡܘܢ, ܒܡܘܢ why? wherefore? for what cause?

ܡܘܢܝܛܐ or ܡܘܢܝܛܐ pl. ܡܘܢܝܛܣ f. moneta, money, coin, coinage; the die, stamp; ܒܝܘܡܝ ܣܪܘܓ ܐܫܬܟܚܬ ܡܘܢܝܛܐ in the days of Serug coining or money was invented; ܡܘܢܝܛܐ ܕܩܕܡܝܐ ܕܟܣܦܐ ancient silver coin; ܡܢ ܡܘܢܝܛܐ ܕܝܠܝ ܢܬܛܒܥܘܢ the coins shall be struck from my die. Metaph. ܡܘܢܝܛܐ ܕܫܡܐ ܬܠܝܬܝܐ the impress, stamp of the triple name i.e. in baptism; ܐܝܠܝܢ ܕܛܒܝܥܝܢ ܒܡܘܢܝܛܐ ܕܐܠܗܘܬܟ those who are stamped with Thy divine impress.

ܡܘܢܣܛܝܪܝܢ, ܡܘܢܣܛܪܝܢ pl. ܡܘܢܣܛܪ̈ܝܐ μοναστήριον, a monastery.

ܡܘܢܟܐ rt. ܡܢܟ. m. setting out, coming, arrival, advent; ܒܡܘܢܟܗ at his arrival.

ܡܘܣܝܐ, ܡܘܣܝܬܐ stubborn, kicking said of a mule.

ܡܘܣܐܘܣ or ܡܘܣܐ musa, a muse; ܐܘܡܢܘ̈ܬܐ ܕܡܘܣܐܘܣ the crafts of the Muses, the liberal arts.

ܡܘܣܛܝܣ f. μύτις, μύστις, the internal sac of a mollusc.

ܡܘܣܛܪܐ m. sour wine.

ܡܘܣܛܪܘܢ, ܡܘܣܛܪܘܢ &c. μύστρον, a measure.

ܡܘܣܝܩܘܪܐ, ܡܘܣܝܩܪܐ or ܡܘܣܩܪܐ pl. m. ̈ܐ f. ̈ܬܐ μουσικός, a musician, singer, poet; ܢܩܫ̈ܐ ܡܘܣܝܩܘܪ̈ܬܐ singing women.

ܡܘܣܝܩܝ f. μουσική, music, the art of music.

ܡܘܣܝܩܝܘܬܐ and ܡܘܣܝܩܘܪܘܬܐ f. μουσικά, music.

ܡܘܣܝܩܪܝܐ, ܝܬܐ musical, singing.

ܡܘܣܦܢܐ rt. ܝܣܦ. m. one who adds on esp. to the price of any article.

ܡܘܣܩܪܐ; see ܡܘܣܝܩܘܪܐ.

ܡܘܣܩܝ a tumour esp. on the eye.

ܡܘܣܪܩܐ the Persian New Year's Day.

ܡܘܣܪܐ perh. μυσαρός, abominable, odious.

ܡܘܣ, ܡܣ fut. ܢܡܘܣ to shake esp. to shake milk to make butter.

ܡܘܥܕܐ, ܡܘܥܕ from ܥܕܐ m. an appointed time or place; arrival in port.

ܡܘܥܙܠܐ pl. ̈ܐ rt. ܥܙܠ. m. a spindle; a dish or bowl carried by a mendicant.

ܡܘܥܝܢܐ rt. ܥܝܢ. germinative.

ܡܘܥܝܢܘܬܐ rt. ܥܝܢ. f. germination, vegetation.

ܡܘܥܝܬܐ pl. ̈ܬܐ rt. ܥܝܢ. f. growth, germination, the shooting or springing up of plants; a plant; collect. growth, plants, vegetation; ܛܪ̈ܦܐ ܕܡܘܥܝܬܐ a fresh growth of leaves.

ܡܘܦܛܐ or ܡܘܦܛܐ, ܡܘܗܦܛܐ and ܡܘܗܦܛܐ pl. ̈ܐ deriv. Pers. a môbed, archmage, chief of the Magi.

ܡܘܗܦܛܘܬܐ or ܡܘܦܛܘܬܐ from the above. f. *the office of the chief Magian.*

ܡܘܦܝܢܐ, ܝܢܝܬܐ rt. ܦܝ. *evanescent, fleeting.*

ܡܘܦܝܢܘܬܐ rt. ܦܝ. f. *failure, cessation.*

ܡܘܦܣܬܐ f. *bees' dung* or *dead bees* in honey.

ܡܘܦܬܐ f. *the foreskin.*

ܡܘܨܐ rt. ܡܨ. m. *suckling, giving milk.*

ܡܘܨܪܐ rt. ܡܨܪ = ܡܘܬܪܐ m. *stretching the limbs.*

ܡܘܩ, ܡܩ act. part. ܡܐܩ *to deride.* PAEL ܡܝܩ with ܒ of the pers. *to mock, deride, make a mock of.* ETHPA. ܐܬܡܝܩ *to be mocked, derided, made a laughing-stock.* DERIVATIVES, [illegible].

ܡܘܩܐ pl. ܐ̈ m. *a shoe, slipper;* [illegible] *a woman's shoe; priest's slippers* opp. [illegible]; monks might not wear ܡܘܩܐ but only [illegible] *a sort of sandal.*

[illegible] pl. [illegible] m. μύκης, μύκητες, *a fungus.*

ܡܘܩܕܢܐ, ܢܝܬܐ rt. ܝܩܕ. *inflammable, burning, fiery hot.*

ܡܘܩܕܢܘܬܐ rt. ܝܩܕ. f. *combustion, combustibility.*

ܡܘܩܠܐ m. *bdellium, borassus flabelliformis, an odoriferous gum.*

ܡܘܩܪܐ pl. ܐ̈ m. *the yolk* of an egg.

ܡܘܪ, ܡܪ fut. [illegible], infin. [illegible], act. part. [illegible]. *to deal* in corn; *to supply, transport* or *import* provisions; [illegible] *to buy corn;* [illegible] *their ships bring all sorts of victuals.* ETHPE. [illegible] *to be carried, conveyed, imported.* APH. [illegible] *to barter* or *sell* corn. DERIVATIVE, ܡܝܪܐ.

ܡܘܪܐ or ܡܘܪܐ pl. ܡܘܪܣ or ܡܘܪܘܣ *a*) f. μοῖρα, astron. *a degree* of a circle; [illegible] when the moon is in *the sixteenth degree of Capricornus;* [illegible] *point of transit;* geograph. *a degree.* *b*) f. Μοῖρα, *a Fate.* *c*) *morus, the mulberry-tree.* *d*) m. μύρρα, *myrrh;* [illegible] *the bitterness of myrrh;* [illegible] *pure* or *refined myrrh.* DERIVATIVE, verb ܡܘܪ.

ܡܘܪܒܐ, ܡܘܪܒ Aphel act. part. of ܪܒ. *the Magnificat, a chant to which the Magnificat is sung;* [illegible] *chants to which the Magnificat is commonly sung.*

[illegible] corrupt. from μολυβδήνη, *iron* or *lead slag.*

ܡܘܪܒܢܐ rt. ܪܒ. *one who magnifies, exalts* or *extols.*

ܡܘܪܕܐ a plant, *conium maculatum.*

ܡܘܪܕܣ a plant, *harmala, ruta sylvestris.*

ܡܘܪܕܣܢܓ λιθάργυρον, *dross of silver.*

ܡܘܪܘܢ or ܡܘܪܘܢ also spelt [illegible], [illegible] and [illegible] pl. [illegible] μύρον, *an unguent, ointment, perfume, sweet oil; chrism;* [illegible] *consecration of the chrism;* [illegible] *signing with consecrated oil.*

ܡܘܪܕܢܐ, ܡܘܪܕܢܝܬܐ and ܡܘܪܕܢܝܐ *malevolent, malicious.*

ܡܘܪܕܢܘܬܐ f. *malevolence.*

ܡܘܪܝܐ rt. ܡܪܐ. m. *imitation.*

ܡܘܪܝܐ m. μυρία, *a sauce of pickled fish.*

ܡܘܪܡܪܐ rt. ܡܪ. m. *provocation, bitterness; rage;* [illegible] *burning like fury, burning furiously.*

ܡܘܪ denom. verb from ܡܘܪܐ *to perfume* or *preserve with myrrh;* [illegible] *vinegar spiced with myrrh.*

ܡܘܪܢܐ *muraena, the murena,* a fish.

ܡܘܪܢܝܬܐ or ܡܘܪܢܝܬܐ pl. [illegible] f. *a spear* esp. *used as a sceptre; a staff, a pastoral staff.*

ܡܘܪܣܐ rt. ܡܪܣ. m. *maceration.*

ܡܘܪܣܬܢܐ rt. ܡܪܣ. *ill-tempered.*

ܡܘܪܥܢܐ pl. ܐ̈ rt. ܡܪܥ. m. *sickness, ill-health, pining away, pallor;* [illegible] *his flesh took a sickly hue.*

ܡܘܪܩܐ rt. ܡܪܩ. m. *cleansing.*

ܡܘܪܩܘܬܐ rt. ܝܪܩ. f. *pallor, paleness.*

ܡܘܪܩܢܐ alch. *of a reddish gold colour.*

ܡܘܪܬܐ pr. n. *Marah.*

ܡܘܪܬܝܐ and ܡܘܪܬܝܢܐ, ܢܝܬܐ from ܡܘܪܬܐ; [illegible] *waters of Marah.*

ܡܘܪܬܢܐ rt. ܝܪܬ. *one who leaves an inheritance.*

ܡܘܫ, ܡܫ fut. ܢܡܘܫ, act. part. ܡܐܫ, ܡܐܫܐ, pass. part. ܡܝܫ. *to touch, feel, grope; to search out, explore;* [illegible] *as the blind man gropes;* [illegible] *swine routed in the mire;* with [illegible] *to search out parables;* [illegible] *He who searcheth hearts;* ܡܫܫ ܗܘܝܬ ܠܣܘܓܐܐ ܕܚܛܗܝ *I have searched out the abundance of my sins.* Ethpe. ܐܬܡܫܫ or ܐܬܡܫ *to be touched, handled, felt, searched out;* ܐܢ ܨܒܝܢ ܠܒܝܬܐ ܕܢܬܡܫܫ *if they choose that the house be searched;* ܕܝܢܘܗܝ ܕܐܠܗܐ ܠܐ ܡܬܡܫܫܝܢ *the judgements of God are inscrutable.* Pa. ܡܫܫ *to pry, search closely.* Aph. ܐܡܫ *to let feel, cause to touch.* Derivatives, ܡܘܫܫܐ, ܡܫܘܫܘܬܐ, ܡܫܘܫܐ, ܡܫܫ, ܡܬܡܫܫܢܐ.

ܡܘܫܫܐ rt. ܡܫܫ. *a) touching, groping. b)* pl. ܐ̈ some part of the date palm.

ܡܘܫܐ pr. n. *Moses.* Derivative, ܡܘܫܝܐ.

ܡܘܫܚܬܐ constr. ܡܘܫܚܬ or ܡܫܘܚܬ, emph. ܡܫܘܚܬܐ, pl. ܡܘܫܚܢ, ܡܘܫܚܬܐ, rt. ܡܫܚ. f. *a) measuring, a measure, dimension, size;* ܚܒܠܐ ܕܡܫܘܚܬܐ *a measuring-line;* ܒܬܐ ܕܡܫܘܚܬܐ *houses of* large *dimensions;* ܓܒܪܐ ܕܡܫܘܚܬܐ *tall men,* metaph. *distinguished men;* ܙܒܢܐ ܕܡܫܘܚܬܐ *a definite time;* ܒܡܫܘܚܬܐ *moderately;* ܕܠܐ ܡܫܘܚܬܐ *immoderately;* ܡܫܘܚܬܐ or ܕܠܐ ܡܘܫܚܐ *unmeasured, immense, immoderate;* ܠܥܠ ܡܢ ܡܫܘܚܬܐ *above measure;* ܗܠܝܢ ܕܠܥܠ ܡܢ ܡܘܫܚܬܟ *things that are beyond you;* ܛܥܝܬ ܡܫܘܚܬܟ *you have forgotten your size, forgotten how weak you are. b) metre,* ܡܐܡܪܐ ܕܡܘܫܚܬܐ *metrical harangues* or *sermons;* ܡܫܘܚܬܐ ܕܫܬܐ *hexameter. c) an acrostic psalm, a metrical* or *rhythmical* homily, sermon, speech; *a chant. d) stature, age;* ܬܠܬ ܡܘܫܚܢ *the three ages* of man. *e) condition, state; rank, station;* ܕܡܘܬܪܢ ܠܟܠ ܡܘܫܚܢ *useful for* men of *all conditions* or *circumstances;* ܠܡܘܪܐ ܡܫܘܚܬܐ ܐܠܗܐ ܐܘܪܒܗ *God had so highly exalted him.*

ܡܘܫܟܬܐ pl. ܐ̈ rt. ܡܫܟ. f. *an heifer.*

ܡܘܫܟ; see ܡܫܟ.

ܡܘܫܝܐ, ܝܬܐ adj. from ܡܘܫܐ. *Mosaic, Mosaical;* ܡܫܠܡܢܘܬܐ ܡܘܫܝܬܐ *the Mosaic tradition.*

ܡܘܫܟ m. *musk.*

ܡܘܫܟܠܐ or ܡܘܫܟܐ pl. ܐ̈ *a garden carrot, parsnip.*

ܡܘܬ, ܡܝܬ usually ܡܝܬ, fut. ܢܡܘܬ, poet. ܢܡܘܬ, imper. ܡܘܬ, infin. ܡܡܬ, pres. part. ܡܐܬ, ܡܝܬܐ, ܡܝܬܐ, verbal adj. ܡܝܬ, ܡܝܬܐ, ܡܝܬܬܐ, the form ܡܝܘܬ, ܡܝܘܬܐ is frequently used instead of this, *to die;* ܡܝܬ ܠܗ *he is dead, he died;* ܒܣܪܐ ܡܝܘܬܐ *mortal flesh;* ܐܘ ܡܝܘܬܝ ܡܘܬܐ ܩܫܝܐ *O ye who are to die a cruel death;* ܦܠܓ ܡܝܬ ܦܠܓ ܚܝ *half-dead;* ܡܢܬ ܥܣܪܐ ܡܝܬܐ ܒܒܝܬܐ ܗܘ *she counted ten dead in that house;* ܫܠܕܐ ܡܝܬܐ *dead bodies.* Ethpe. ܐܬܡܝܬ *to be put to death, killed, slain;* ܐܝܟ ܕܐܡܝܬܘ ܐܬܡܝܬܘ *as they had slain so were they slain;* ܐܫܟܚܗ ܕܟܒܪ ܐܬܡܝܬ *he found him dead already.* Aph. ܐܡܝܬ *to put to death, kill, slay; to mortify;* ܐܡܝܬܘ ܗܕܡܝܗܘܢ *they mortified their members;* two forms of infin. ܓܙܪ ܠܡܡܬܘܬܟ *he has decreed your death;* ܡܛܝܒܝܢ ܠܡܡܬܘܬܗ *they are ready to kill him.* Derivatives, ܡܘܬܐ, ܡܘܬܢܐ, ܡܝܬܐ, ܡܝܘܬܐ, ܡܝܘܬܘܬܐ, ܡܡܝܬܢܐ, ܡܡܝܬܢܘܬܐ, ܡܝܬܘܬܐ.

ܡܘܬ, ܡܘܬܐ (abs. form rare) pl. ܡܘܬܝܢ, ܡܘܬܐ, rt. ܡܘܬ. m. *a) death;* ܡܘܬܐ ܕܡܢ ܫܠܝ *sudden death;* ܡܘܬܐ ܡܩܕܡܐ *premature death;* ܡܘܬ ܢܦܫܗ *suicide;* ܡܘܬܐ ܟܝܢܝܐ *a natural death;* ܡܘܬܐ ܕܠܐ ܟܝܢܗ ellipt. for ܕܠܐ ܟܝܢܗ ܕܐܢܫܐ *death not according to nature, a violent death. b) way of dying, cause of death; an execution; a plague, pestilence;* ܪܒܘ ܡܘܬܝܢ *a myriad deaths;* ܒܝܫܐ ܡܘܬܐ ܗܠܝܢ ܬܡܘܬ *thou shalt die these several deaths;* ܟܦܢܐ ܘܡܘܬܐ *famine and pestilence. c)* used with ܕ as an adj. *deadly, fatal, mortal;* ܕܡܘܬܐ ܗܘܐ ܟܘܪܗܢܗ *his illness was fatal.*

ܡܘܬܒܐ pl. ܐ̈ rt. ܝܬܒ. m. *a) a site, settlement, habitation, place. b) sitting, sojourning; ascending the throne; a sitting, session, congress. c) a seat;* ܪܝܫ ܡܘܬܒܐ *a chief seat;* a bishop's *see, throne;* ܡܘܬܒܐ *thrones* = the third rank of angels. *d)* eccles. *part of a service sung sitting, a division of the Psalms;* ܒܝܬ ܡܘܬܒܐ or ܩܘܡܐ *prayers repeated between the Psalms. e) the seat, buttocks, anus.*

ܡܘܬܠܐ rt. ܡܬܠ. m. *an allegory, parable, simile.*

ܡܘܬܢܐ or ܡܘܬܢܐ pl. ܐ̈ rt. ܡܘܬ. m. *a plague, pestilence, mortality, slaughter;* ܡܘܬܢܐ ܕܪܕܝܦܐ *a raging pestilence.*

ܡܘܬܢܢܝܬܐ rt. ܡܘܬ. adj. *pestilential, deadly.*

ܡܘܬܪܢܘܬܐ rt. ܝܬܪ. f. *utility.*

ܡܘܬܪܢܐ, ܢܬܐ pl. m. ܢܐ, ܢܐ f. ܢܝܬܐ rt. ܝܬܪ. *useful, profitable, advantageous;* with ܠܐ *unprofitable, unavailing.*

ܡܘܬܪܢܐܝܬ rt. ܝܬܪ. adv. *profitably.*

ܡܘܬܪܢܘܬܐ pl. ܬܐ rt. ܝܬܪ. f. *usefulness, advantage.*

ܡܙܐ pl. of ܡܙܬܐ.

ܡܙܒܢ, ܡܙܒܢܐ, ܡܙܒܢܢܬܐ *a seller, dealer, merchant;* see Pael conj. of ܙܒܢ.

ܡܙܒܢܢܐ rt. ܙܒܢ. m. *a seller, vender.*

ܡܙܓ fut. ܢܡܙܘܓ, act. part. ܡܐܙܓ, ܡܐܙܓܐ, pass. part. ܡܙܝܓ, ܐ, ܬܐ. *to mix, mingle, blend; temper;* esp. *to mix wine with water;* ܠܐ ܡܙܝܓܐ *strong* wine, *undiluted;* ܡܙܓܗ ܠܟܣܐ ܕܡܘܬܐ *he mixed the cup of death;* ܐܠܗܐ ܡܙܓܗ ܠܦܓܪܐ *God hath tempered the body.* ETHPE. ܐܬܡܙܓ *to be mixed, mingled;* ܚܡܪܐ ܕܐܬܡܙܓ *wine mingled* ready for drinking; metaph. ܐܬܡܙܓܬܘܢ ܐܝܟ ܒܡܟܝܪܘܬܐ *ye were joined together as by betrothal;* ܟܕ ܡܝܐ ܘܢܘܪܐ ܡܬܡܙܓܝܢ *when water and fire are brought together.* PA. ܡܙܓ *a) to mingle, intermingle, compound, temper;* ܕܡܡܙܓܝܢ ܡܠܬܗ ܕܐܠܗܐ *those who adulterate the word of God;* ܠܡܠܬܗ ܡܙܓܗ ܒܡܪܬܝܢܘܬܐ *he tempered his address with admonition;* ܐܐܪ ܡܡܙܓܐ *temperate air;* ܠܐ ܡܡܙܓܐ—ܡܡܙܓܢܬܐ *intemperate, excessive, extreme.* *b)* theol. *to join* Godhead and manhood; ܡܙܓ ܟܝܢܐ *He united the Natures.* ETHPA. ܐܬܡܙܓ *a) to be mingled, commingled, tempered, temperate.* *b) to be united, to unite oneself;* ܡܬܡܙܓ ܠܦܓܪܝܢ ܒܝܕ ܒܣܪܗ ܩܕܝܫܐ ܘܕܡܗ ܝܩܝܪܐ *He communicates Himself to our bodies through His own holy flesh and precious blood.* DERIVATIVES, ܡܙܓܐ, ܡܙܓܬܐ, ܡܙܘܓܐ, ܡܙܝܓܐ, ܡܙܘܓܝܐ, ܡܙܘܓܝܘܬܐ, ܡܡܙܓܢܐ, ܡܡܙܓܢܐܝܬ, ܡܡܙܓܢܘܬܐ, ܡܬܡܙܓܢܐ.

ܡܙܓܐ pl. ܐ rt. ܡܙܓ. m. *a mixture, a drink, wine and water;* ܡܙܓܐ ܕܟܣܐ *the mixed chalice.*

ܡܙܓܬܐ pl. ܬܐ rt. ܡܙܓ. f. *a) wine mingled with water* esp. for the holy Eucharist. *b) a cup, beaker, bowl* of wine. *c) a cup, liquid measure.*

ܡܙܕܒܢܢܐ rt. ܙܒܢ. *a)* adj. *saleable.* *b)* subst. *merchandise, goods for sale.*

ܡܙܕܕܩܢܘܬܐ rt. ܙܕܩ. f. *justification, being justified* (passive sense).

ܡܙܕܗܪܢܘܬܐ rt. ܙܗܪ. f. *admonition* (passive sense).

ܡܙܕܘܓܢܐ, ܢܝܬܐ from ܙܘܓܐ. *a) generative, marriageable;* with ܠܐ *within the prohibited degrees of marriage.* *b)* of versification *arranged in double order.*

ܡܙܕܗܝܢܐ rt. ܙܗܐ. *boasting, arrogant.*

ܡܙܕܗܝܢܘܬܐ rt. ܙܗܐ. f. *boastfulness, ostentation.*

ܡܙܕܘܚܢܘܬܐ rt. ܙܘܚ. f. *a ride, going on horseback; pomp.*

ܡܙܕܟܝܢ, ܡܙܕܟܝܢܐ, ܢܝܬܐ rt. ܙܟܐ. *conquerable, easily overcome;* or with ܠܐ *invincible, unconquerable.*

ܡܙܕܟܝܢܘܬܐ rt. ܙܟܐ. f. *fleeing* or *being put to flight, defeat, overthrow;* with ܠܐ *invincibleness.*

ܡܙܕܠܠܢܘܬܐ rt. ܙܠܠ. f. *luxury.*

ܡܙܕܥܙܥ, ܡܙܕܥܙܥܐ, ܥܬܐ Ethpalpal part. of ܙܥ; *tossed to and fro, swayed, shaken;* with ܠܐ *unshaken, immovable.*

ܡܙܕܥܙܥܢܐ, ܢܝܬܐ rt. ܙܥ. *that can be moved* or *shaken, unstable;* with ܠܐ *firm, lasting, settled.*

ܡܙܕܥܙܥܢܐܝܬ rt. ܙܥ. adv. with ܠܐ *steadfastly, constantly.*

ܡܙܕܥܙܥܢܘܬܐ rt. ܙܥ. f. with ܠܐ *steadfastness, constancy.*

ܡܙܕܩܢܐ, ܢܝܬܐ rt. ܙܕܩ. m. *justifying; a justifier.*

ܡܙܕܩܢܘܬܐ rt. ܙܕܩ. f. *justification, acquittal.*

ܡܙܕܩܦܢܘܬܐ rt. ܙܩܦ. f. *standing up on end, bristling.*

ܡܙܕܪܟܢܘܬܐ rt. ܪܟܒ. f. *riding.*

ܡܙܕܪܚܒܢܘܬܐ from ܙܪܚܒ. f. *swaggering, ostentation.*

ܡܙܕܪܥܢܐ rt. ܙܪܥ. *sown, planted.*

ܡܙܗܪܢܐ rt. ܙܗܪ. *admonitory, warning; a monitor, denouncer.*

ܡܙܗܪܢܐܝܬ rt. ܙܗܪ. adv. *by way of warning.*

ܡܙܗܪܢܘܬܐ rt. ܙܗܪ. *transparency.*

ܡܙܘܓܐ m. ܡܙܘܓܬܐ f. rt. ܡܙܓ. *a bowl for mixing drink.*

ܡܙܘܓܐ, ܡܙܘܓܬܐ from ܙܘܓܐ. *married; a married man* or *woman.*

ܡܙܘܓܐܝܬ from ܙܘܓܐ. adv. *coupled, in pairs, together.*

ܡܙܘܓܘܬܐ from ܙܘܓܐ. f. *matrimony, copulation.*

ܡܙܘܓܘܬܐ rt. ܙܘܓ. f. *the combination* or *union* of two natures in our Lord.

ܡܙܘܓܢܘܬܐ from ܙܘܓܐ. f. *uniting in marriage.*

ܡܙܘܕܘܬܐ rt. ܙܘܕ. f. *making provision for a journey.*

ܡܙܘܢ, ܡܙܘܢܐ rt. ܙܘܢ. m. *food, victuals, support, maintenance, sustenance.*

ܡܙܘܪܐ rt. ܡܙܪ. m. *a mallet, a fuller's mallet.*

ܡܙܘܪܬܐ pl. ܬܐ rt. ܡܙܪ. f. *a mallet, a spiked staff; a blow from a mallet.*

ܡܙܗܡܢ, ܡܙܗܡܢܐ from ܙܗܡܐ. *an accuser, fault-finder; one who causes a fault to be committed.*

ܡܙܐ and ܡܙܐܣ pl. μάζα, *lumps.*

ܡܙܘܕܐ rt. ܙܘܕ. m. *a traveller's provision-bag.*

ܡܙܝܚܢܐ rt. ܙܘܚ. *a retainer, attendant, follower;* pl. *a retinue.*

ܡܙܝܚܢܘܬܐ rt. ܙܘܚ. f. *carrying.*

ܡܙܝܢܘܬܐ rt. ܙܘܢ. f. *armour, equipment.*

ܡܙܝܥܢܐܝܬ rt. ܙܘܥ. adv. *hastily, quaveringly.*

ܡܙܝܥܢܘܬܐ rt. ܙܘܥ. f. *confusion; absurdity.*

ܡܙܝܥܢܐ rt. ܙܘܥ. *moving, causing motion; a muscle, motor nerve.*

ܡܙܝܦܢܐ rt. ܙܘܦ. *a forger; a corrupter* of doctrine.

ܡܙܟܝܢܐ, ܡܙܟܝܢܝܬܐ rt. ܙܟܐ. *a justifier,* opp. ܡܚܝܒܢܐ *accuser.*

ܡܙܠܐ or ܡܙܠܐ pl. ܐ̈ m. *rank, station;* astron. *a station.*

ܡܙܠܓܢܘܬܐ rt. ܙܠܓ. f. *sparkling brightness, brilliance.*

ܡܙܠܓܝܬܐ f. same as ܡܙܠܐ.

ܡܙܠܚܘ, ܡܙܠܚܘܐ verbal adj. from ܙܠܚ. *short, brief; scarce, failing, little; mean, poor, bankrupt.*

ܡܙܠܚܘܬܐ rt. ܙܠܚ. f. *shortness* of time, *scarcity, rareness.*

ܡܙܠܠܘܬܐ rt. ܙܠܠ. f. *lasciviousness.*

ܡܙܠܓܐ, ܡܙܠܓܬܐ rt. ܙܠܓ. *lucid, ornamented.*

ܡܙܠܓܐܝܬ rt. ܙܠܓ. *elegantly.*

ܡܙܡܘܪܐ rt. ܙܡܪ. m. *a psalm, hymn;* ܟܬܒܐ ܕܡܙܡܘܪ̈ܐ *the Psalms, Book of Psalms;* ܡܙܡܘܪ̈ܐ ܕܡܣܩܬܐ *the psalms of degrees;* ܡܙܡܘܪ̈ܐ ܕܨܠܘܬܐ *psalms suitable for use in prayer.*

ܡܙܡܢܘܬܐ from ܙܡܢ. f. *harm, injury.*

ܡܙܡܛܐ pl. ܐ̈ m. *a) the lower saucer* or *base* of a lamp; *snuffers. b) a surgical instrument.*

ܡܙܡܢ, ܡܙܡܢܐ, ܡܙܡܢ pass. part. of ܙܡܢ. *appointed, invited, bidden; a guest.*

ܡܙܡܢܢܐ, ܡܙܡܢܢܝܬܐ from ܙܡܢ. *one who makes ready, invites, calls;* ܡܙܡܢܢ̈ܐ ܕܟܠܝ̈ܐ *servants bringing in guests;* generally metaph. *bringing, causing to attain;* ܬܝܒܘܬܐ ܡܙܡܢܢܝܬܐ ܕܫܘܒܩܢܐ *penitence bringing* us *to pardon.*

ܡܙܡܪܢܐ rt. ܙܡܪ. m. *a singer, psalmist; the Psalmist* i.e. David; *one of the lower ecclesiastical orders.*

ܡܙܡܪܢܘܬܐ rt. ܙܡܪ. f. *psalmody.*

ܡܙܡܪܢܝܐ rt. ܙܡܪ. *belonging to the Psalms;* ܦܬܓܡ̈ܐ ܡܙܡܪܢܝ̈ܐ *verses taken from the Psalms.*

ܡܙܢܐ m. *medicago sativa sicca,* a common food for cattle.

ܡܙܢܝܐ adj. from ܐܢܝܐ Nasar. *a bell,* cf. ܙܢܝܐ; *jingling, having bells on the harness.*

ܡܙܥ, ܡܙܥܐ, ܡܙܥܐ Aphel pass. part. of ܙܘܥ. *shaken, tottering.*

ܡܙܥܙܥܐ Palpal pass. part. of ܙܘܥ. *tottering, unstable.*

ܡܙܥܙܥܢܐ rt. ܙܘܥ. *a troubler, one who vexes.*

ܡܙܥܩܢܘܬܐ rt. ܙܥܩ. f. *a prayer intoned in a loud voice.*

ܡܙܥܪܢܘܬܐ rt. ܙܥܪ. f. gram. *formation of diminutives.*

ܡܙܩܦܐ, ܡܙܩܦܬܐ rt. ܙܩܦ. *rugged.*

ܡܙܪ fut. ܢܡܙܘܪ, pass. part. ܡܙܝܪ. *to stretch out; to sit* on a mule; *to bind; to stretch* in yawning. ETHPE. ܐܬܡܙܪ *to stretch oneself* as on awaking or in yawning. DERIVATIVES, ܡܙܘܪܐ, ܡܙܘܪܬܐ, ܡܙܪܐ, ܡܙܝܪܘܬܐ.

ܡܚܙܪܐ or ܡܚܙܪܐ pl. ܐ̈ rt. ܚܙܪ. m. *a) stocks for confining criminals who were to be scourged. b)* vulg. *hardy, sturdy, unflinching.*

ܡܚܙܪܘܢܐ *a rolling-pin.*

ܡܚܙܬܐ f. *hair;* pl. ܡܚ̈ܙܐ *hairs, fur.*

ܡܚܚ act. part. ܡܚܐܚ. *to smell, perceive.* Ethpe. ܐܬܡܚܚ *to blow away, go to dust.* Ethpalpal ܐܬܡܚܡܚ *to wallow in the dust, turn to dust.*

ܡܚܐ fut. ܢܡܚܐ, act. part. ܡܚܐ, ܡܚܝܐ, pass. part. ܡܚܐ, ܡܚܝܐ. *a) to strike, smite, beat, wound;* ܡܚܘ ܐܢܘܢ ܡܚܘܬܐ ܪܒܬܐ *they smote them with great slaughter;* with ܓܐܪܐ *to wound with an arrow;* ܫܡܫܐ ܡܚܐ ܥܠ ܪܫܗ *the sun beat on his head;* ܡܚܘ ܒܘܪ̈ܟܝܗܘܢ ܠܐܪܥܐ *they fell on their knees;* ܡܚܐ ܒܩܪܒܐ *he rushed into the fray;* with ܚܒ̈ܠܐ *pains smote, took hold on;* with ܒܐܪܥܐ *to seize, attack* as an illness, e.g. ܒܪ̈ܓܠܐ *in the feet;* ܡܚܐ ܒܫܘܚܢܐ *ulcerous;* with ܡܫܟܢܐ *to strike, pitch a tent;* with ܥܩܪܐ *to strike root;* with ܟܦ̈ܐ *to clap the hands;* with ܣܟܐ *to drive a nail in;* with ܩܪܒܐ *to attack, invade;* with ܩܪܢܐ *to butt,* but ܡܚܝ ܪܫܟ *recline your head, lie down. b) to strike* money. *c)* with ܪܝܚܐ *to diffuse, be apparent;* ܡܚܐ ܪܝܚܐ ܒܒܣܡܐ ܒܟܠܗ ܒܝܬܐ *the sweet smell spread through the whole house;* ܡܚܐ ܗܘܐ ܡܢܗܘܢ ܪܝܚܐ *an odour rose up from them. d) to bind* or *gird* with ܒ; ܚܨܐ *on the loins;* ܡܚܝܐ ܚܨܝܗܝܢ ܣܩܐ *she put girdles on them;* ܢܫ̈ܐ ܡܚܝ̈ܢ ܣܩܐ ܐܣܪ̈ܘܐ *women girt with sackcloth.* Ethpe. ܐܬܡܚܝ *a) to be wounded; to be attacked* by illness; ܐܬܡܚܝ ܪܟܫܐ ܒܪ̈ܓܠܝܗܘܢ *the horses were footsore. b) to be struck, coined* as money. Pa. ܡܚܝ *to wound many, wound severely;* part. ܡܡܚܝ, ܡܡܚܝܐ, ܡܡܚܝܬܐ *smitten, wounded, ill, sick, afflicted;* with ܒܫܘܚܢܐ *suffering from ulcers, full of sores.* Ethpa. ܐܬܡܚܝ *to be beaten back* or *down, struck down, smitten, sore wounded, afflicted;* with ܒܫܘܚ̈ܢܐ *with sores;* ܒܚܙܘ̈ܢܝܬܐ *with phantoms;* ܒܚܢܦܘܬܐ *with heathenism.* Aph. ܐܡܚܝ with ܪܝܚܐ *to make a smell come up.* Derivatives, ܡܚܘܬܐ, ܡܚܘܐ, ܡܚܝܐ, ܡܡܚܝܢܐ, ܡܬܡܚܝܢܐ, ܡܚܝܬܐ.

ܡܚܝܐ or ܡܚܐܝܐ irreg. infin. of verb ܚܝܐ *to live,* &c.

ܡܚܐ, ܡܚܝܐ Aph. act. part. of ܚܝܐ.

ܡܚܒܢܐ, ܡܚܒܢܝܬܐ rt. ܚܒ. *loving.*

ܡܚܒܛܐ, ܡܚܒܛܬܐ rt. ܚܒܛ. *striped, a striped tunic.*

ܡܚܒܪܘܬܐ rt. ܚܒܪ. f. *a compound, mixture.*

ܡܚܒܪܢܐ rt. ܚܒܪ. adj. *compound;* subst. *one who confounds.*

ܡܚܒܠܘܬܐ rt. ܚܒܠ. f. *sodomy, depravity.*

ܡܚܒܠܢܐ, ܢܝܬܐ rt. ܚܒܠ. *a)* adj. *destroying, corrupting; pestilential; rapacious. b)* subst. *a destroyer, spoiler, plunderer; a defiler, corrupter.*

ܡܚܒܢܐ, ܡܚܒܢ rt. ܚܒ. adj. *earnestly desiring, zealous;* subst. *a lover, a friend.*

ܡܚܒܢܘܬܐ rt. ܚܒ. f. *love.*

ܡܚܓܓܢܐ from ܚܓܐ. *festal, solemn.*

ܡܚܓܓܢܐܝܬ from ܚܓܐ. adv. *in a joyous* or *festal manner.*

ܡܚܓܪܐܝܬ rt. ܚܓܪ. adv. *lamely.*

ܡܚܕܐ *a)* contr. of ܡܢ ܚܕܐ and ܡܢ=ܡܚܕܐ; ܡܚܕܐ ܕܢܚܬ ܠܐܬܪܗ ܚܕܐ. *immediately, at once;* *as soon as he went down to his own country. b)* infin. of verb ܚܕܐ *to rejoice.*

ܡܚܕܝܢܐ, ܢܝܬܐ rt. ܚܕܐ. *he who* or *that which makes glad, gladdening, cheering, exhilarating.*

ܡܚܕܪܢܘܬܐ rt. ܚܕܪ. f. *gyration.*

ܡܚܕܬܢܐ, ܢܝܬܐ rt. ܚܕܬ. *restoring, renewing; one who restores, makes anew.*

ܡܚܘܐ, ܡܚܘܬܐ pl. ܬ̈ܐ rt. ܚܘܐ. f. *balustrade, parapet.*

ܡܚܘܐ, ܡܚܘܬܐ pl. ܡܚ̈ܘܢ, ܡܚ̈ܘܬܐ rt. ܡܚܐ. f. *a blow, wound, sore, stripe; sickness, disease; slaughter; affliction; a scourge, plague;* ܡܚܘܬܐ ܕܡܘܬܐ *a deadly wound;* ܟܐܦܐ ܕܡܚܘܬܐ *a stone of offence;* ܥܣܪ ܡܚ̈ܘܢ *the ten plagues of* Egypt; ܡܚܘܬܐ ܕܒܪܩܐ *a thunderbolt.*

ܡܚܘܙܐ, ܡܚܘܙܐ pl. ܐ̈ m. *a little fortified town* smaller than a ܡܕܝܢܬܐ; ܩܘܪ̈ܝܐ ܘܡܚܘ̈ܙܐ ܘܡܕܝ̈ܢܬܐ *villages and towns and cities.*

ܡܚܘܛܐ pl. ܐ̈ f. *phlegm, rheum, snivel, mucus.* Derivative, the following word—

ܡܚܘܛܢܐ, ܢܝܬܐ adj. from ܡܚܘܛܐ. *mucous, of phlegm.*

ܡܚܘܝܐ rt. ܚܘܐ. m. an optical instrument, *a spying-tube, the mirror of an astrolabe.*

ܡܚܘܝܢܐ, ܢܝܬܐ rt. ܚܘܐ. *he* or *that which points out* or *declares; an informer; the index* of a book; ellipt. for ܡܚܘܝܢܘܬܐ ܦܬܓܡܐ *arguments;* gram. *indicative, demonstrative* e. g. the points in ܗܘ and ܗܝ are ܡܚܘܝܢܐ.

ܡܚܘܝܢܐܝܬ rt. ܚܘܐ. adv. *logically.*

ܡܚܘܝܢܘܬܐ pl. ܘܬܐ rt. ܚܘܐ. f. *a demonstration, proof.*

ܡܚܘܠܬܐ pl. ܡܚܘ̈ܠܐ rt. ܚܘܠ. f. *a sieve.*

ܡܚܘܪܢܐ, ܢܝܬܐ rt. ܚܘܪ. *he* or *that which makes white* or *clean, a fuller.*

ܡܚܘܪܢܘܬܐ rt. ܚܘܪ. f. *bleaching, whitening.*

ܡܚܙܐ rt. ܚܙܐ. m. with ܥܝܢܐ *eye-sight, eye-service.*

ܡܚܙܝܢܐ rt. ܚܙܐ. m. *seeing, sight, considering.*

ܡܚܙܝܬܐ pl. ܡܚܙܝ̈ܢܐ rt. ܚܙܐ. f. *an example; a mirror.*

ܡܚܙܝܬܢܐ rt. ܚܙܐ. *clear, like a mirror.*

ܡܚܙܩܘܬܐ rt. ܚܙܩ. f. *being girded, readiness.*

ܡܚܙܩܬܐ pl. ܩ̈ܬܐ rt. ܚܙܩ. f. *a girdle.*

ܡܚܛܐ, ܡܚܛܐ pl. ܛ̈ܐ rt. ܚܛ. m. *a needle;* metaph. ܡܢ ܚܘܛܐ ܠܡܚܛܐ *in detail.*

ܡܚܛܒܬܐ or ܡܚܛܦܬܐ f. a many-coloured or *embroidered* garment.

ܡܚܛܝܢܐ, ܢܝܬܐ rt. ܚܛܐ. *inciting to sin.*

ܡܚܛܝܢܘܬܐ rt. ܚܛܐ. f. *incitement to sin.*

ܡܚܝܐ rt. ܡܚܐ. m. *beating; a blow.*

ܡܚܝܒܘܬܐ rt. ܚܘܒ. f. *condemnation.*

ܡܚܝܒܢܐ, ܢܝܬܐ rt. ܚܘܒ. *condemning, damnatory, pronouncing guilty.*

ܡܚܝܕܐܝܬ rt. ܚܕ. adv. *conjointly, unitedly.*

ܡܚܝܕܘܬܐ rt. ܚܕ. f. *union.*

ܡܚܝܕܢܐ rt. ܚܕ. *uniting, serving to unite.*

ܡܚܝܠ, ܡܚܝܠܐ, ܡܚܝܠܬܐ rt. ܚܝܠ. *weak, poor, lean, lank; sickly, infirm, unhealthy; dubious;* ܡܚܝ̈ܠܐ *the poor* opp. ܥܬܝ̈ܪܐ *the rich;* ܡܚܝܠ ܒܝܘܠܦܢܐ—ܒܪܘܚܐ *of scanty learning;* ܐܢܐ ܡܚܝܠܐ *I who am weak* or *ignorant;* ܡܚܝܠܐ ܠܘܬ ܥܘܕܪܢܐ *unavailing.*

ܡܚܝܠܐܝܬ rt. ܚܝܠ. adv. *weakly, impotently.*

ܡܚܝܠܘܬܐ pl. ܘܬܐ rt. ܚܝܠ. f. *weakness, infirmity, instability;* ܡܚܝܠܘܬ ܝܘܠܦܢܐ *scanty learning;* ܗܢܘܢ ܕܐܠܝܨܝܢ ܒܡܚܝܠܘܬܐ *those who are encompassed with infirmities;* often used of the 1st pers. ܡܚܝܠܘܬܝ *I who am weak, my feeble self.*

ܡܚܝܠܢܐ rt. ܚܝܠ. *one who strengthens, confirms, comforts.*

ܡܚܝܠܢܘܬܐ rt. ܚܝܠ. f. *strengthening.*

ܡܚܝܢܐ, ܢܝܬܐ or ܢܝܬܐ rt. ܚܝܐ. *life-giving, quickening, vivifying; Saviour, giver of life, quickener.*

ܡܚܝܢܐ from ܚܡܐ. *a kinsman.*

ܡܚܝܢܘܬܐ rt. ܚܝܐ. *quickening, vivifying; refreshment, nourishment.*

ܡܚܝܪܢܐ rt. ܚܘܪ. *styptic.*

ܡܚܝܪܐܝܬ rt. ܚܘܪ. adv. *providently, prudently.*

ܡܚܝܡܘܡܬܐ pl. ܐ̈ rt. ܚܡ. m. *the kinsman* whose duty it was to raise up seed for the dead.

ܡܚܟܡܢܐ rt. ܚܟܡ. m. *a*) *one who makes wise, grants wisdom. b*) *a wise man, a wizard.*

ܡܚܠ denom. verb Pael conj. from ܡܚܝܠ. *to weaken, grow weak.* Ethpa. ܐܬܡܚܠ *to be* or *become weak, feeble, unable; to lose strength; to be ruinous;* ܐܬܡܚܠ ܡܢ ܦܘܠܚܢܐ *he was unfit for work.* Aph. ܐܡܚܠ *a*) *to weaken, enfeeble. b*) *to be weakened, enfeebled, dismayed; to fall ill;* ܐܡܚܠܬ ܡܢ ܟܦܢܐ *I grew weak from hunger;* ܐܡܚܠ ܥܝ̈ܢܘܗܝ *his eyes grew feeble.*

ܡܚܠܒܐ rt. ܚܠܒ. m. *a milking-pail.*

ܡܚܠܚܠܐ see Palpal part. of ܚܠ; *loose, lax.*

ܡܚܠܚܠܢܐ rt. ܚܠ. *dissolvent, erosive.*

ܡܚܠܛܘܬܐ rt. ܚܠܛ. f. *putting together, including.*

ܡܚܠܠܐ rt. ܚܠܠ. m. *snoring;* ܡܚܠܠܐ ܕܫܢܬܐ Ruth iii. 7, perh. *deep sleep.*

ܡܚܠܠܢܐ, ܢܝܬܐ from ܚܠܠ. *detersive, cleansing.*

ܡܚܠܡܢ, ܡܚܠܡܢܐ, ܡܚܠܡܢܝܬܐ rt. ܚܠܡ. *healing, wholesome.*

ܡܚܠܡܢܘܬܐ rt. ܚܠܡ. f. *healing, recovery.*

ܡܚܠܨܢܐ rt. ܚܠܨ. m. *a spoiler, robber;* with ܕܒܝܬ ܡܩܕܫܐ or ܕܩܘܪܒܢܐ *a sacrilegious robber.*

ܡܚܡܡܐ m. ܡܚܡܡܬܐ f. rt. ܚܡ. *a pot* or *other vessel for heating water.*

ܡܚܡܝܢܢܐ rt. ܚܡܐ. m. *that which dries up, causes to wither.*

ܡܚܡܡܢܐ rt. ܚܡ. *causing heat.*

ܡܚܡܡܢܘܬܐ rt. ܚܡ. f. *incandescence.*

ܡܚܣܢܢܢܐ rt. ܚܣܢ. *constant, steadfast, self-controlled, unyielding;* with ܠܐ *incontinent, indiscreet.*

ܡܚܣܢܢܢܘܬܐ rt. ܚܣܢ. f. *constancy, fortitude, endurance, steadfastness, self-control.*

ܡܚܢܩܘܬܐ pl. ܬܐ rt. ܚܢܩ. f. *strangling, hanging; a noose, halter, rope.*

ܡܚܣܕܢܐ, ܢܝܬܐ rt. ܚܣܕ. *a reviler, taunter.*

ܡܚܣܕܢܐܝܬ rt. ܚܣܕ. adv. *reproachfully, disdainfully.*

ܡܚܣܝܢܐ, ܢܝܬܐ from ܚܣܐ. *a)* adj. *absolving, pardoning, gracious* often applied to that whereby we obtain pardon, as the Cross, the Sacraments. *b)* subst. *one who makes atonement* or *propitiation; one who gives pardon* or *absolution.*

ܡܚܣܝܢܐܝܬ from ܚܣܐ. adv. *propitiatorily, seeking pardon.*

ܡܚܣܝܢܘܬܐ from ܚܣܐ. f. *propitiation.*

ܡܚܣܝܢܢܐ from ܚܣܐ. *sanctifying, sanctificatory.*

ܡܚܣܦܢܐ rt. ܚܣܦ. *parsimonious, avaricious, close fisted.*

ܡܚܣܢܐ rt. ܚܣܢ. m. pl. *the loins, reins; the privy parts.*

ܡܚܣܢܘܬܐ rt. ܚܣܢ. f. *a stronghold, fortification.*

ܡܚܣܢܬܐ rt. ܚܣܢ. f. *the groin, the loins.*

ܡܚܣܪܢܐ, ܢܝܬܐ rt. ܚܣܪ. *hurtful, disadvantageous;* ܐܬܓܪܐ ܡܚܣܪܢܐ *a losing bargain, bad bargain.*

ܡܚܦܛܢܐ, ܢܝܬܐ rt. ܚܦܛ. *he* or *that which exhorts* or *incites.*

ܡܚܦܛܢܐܝܬ rt. ܚܦܛ. adv. *zealously, encouragingly.*

ܡܚܦܛܢܘܬܐ rt. ܚܦܛ. f. *exhortation, encouragement.*

ܡܚܦܝܐܝܬ rt. ܚܦܐ. adv. *covertly, secretly; gently, softly, in a low voice, mystically.*

ܡܚܦܝܢܘܬܐ rt. ܚܦܐ. *concealment.*

ܡܚܩܠܬܐ f. *a midwife.*

ܡܚܫܚ denom. verb Pael conj. from ܡܚܫܚܐ *to measure land.*

ܡܚܪ rarely ܠܡܚܪ *the after-time, future, to-morrow;* ܝܘܡܢܐ ܘܡܚܪ ܘܠܒܬܪܗ *to-day and to-morrow and the day after;* ܠܡܚܪ *on the morrow;* ܩܕܡ ܡܚܪ *in time to come.*

ܡܫܚ, ܡܫܚܐ pl. ܐ fully written ܡܫܚ ܐܪܥܐ m. *a land-surveyor, geometrician.* Derivative, ܡܫܚܘܬܐ, verb ܡܫܚ.

ܡܚܪܒܘܬܐ rt. ܚܪܒ. f. *desolation.*

ܡܚܪܒܢܐ pl. ܐ rt. ܚܪܒ. m. *a spoiler, ravager.*

ܡܚܪܘܩܬܐ rt. ܚܪܘ. f. *a troop of dogs; a dog-collar.*

ܡܫܚܘܬܐ from ܡܫܚܐ. f. *measurement of land, surveying, geometry.*

ܡܚܪܝܐ (ܚܪܝܐ) rt. ܚܪܐ. m. *a dung-heap, a privy.*

ܡܚܪܟܢܐ, ܢܝܬܐ rt. ܚܪܟ. *parching, scorching.*

ܡܚܪܡܢܐ rt. ܚܪܡ. m. *one who curses, anathematizes.*

ܡܚܪܦܐܝܬ rt. ܚܪܦ. adv. *separately.*

ܡܚܪܪܐܝܬ rt. ܚܪ. adv. *freely.*

ܡܚܪܪܢܐ rt. ܚܪ. *one who sets free, gives freedom, manumits.*

ܡܚܪܫܢܐ rt. ܚܪܫ. *magical.*

ܡܚܫܒܢܐ rt. ܚܫܒ. m. *one who makes calculations, an astrologer.*

ܡܚܫܒܬܐ pl. ܬܐ rt. ܚܫܒ. f. *a thought, idea, device; care, consideration; reasoning, intention, purpose;* ܕܠܐ ܡܚܫܒܬܐ *thoughtlessly, unreasonably.*

ܡܚܫܒܬܢܐ, ܢܝܬܐ rt. ܚܫܒ. *rational, pertaining to thought.*

ܡܚܫܘܠ, ܡܚܫܘܠܐ pl. ܐ rt. ܚܫܠ. m. *a storm, tempest, raging of the sea, surging of the waves;* metaph. *peril.*

ܡܚܫܘܠܢܐ rt. ܚܫܠ. *stormy, perilous.*

ܡܚܫܫܢܘܬܐ rt. ܚܫ. f. *passion, feeling.*

ܡܚܫܟܢܐ rt. ܚܫܟ. *darkening, clouding over.*

ܡܚܫܚܠ denom. verb Palpel conj. from ܡܚܫܘܠܐ *to disturb, agitate;* ܐܐܪ ܡܚܫܚܠ *it ruffles the air.* ETHPALP. ܐܬܡܚܫܚܠ *a*) *to be tempest-tossed, shipwrecked;* ܐܠܦܐ ܡܬܡܚܫܚܠܐ ܥܠ ܡܚܫܘܠܐ *it is tossed about by the floods. b*) *to be rough, boisterous* as the sea; metaph. *to waver, fluctuate.*

ܡܚܫܢܐ, ܢܝܬܐ also ܡܚܐܫܢܐ rt. ܚܫ. *painful, afflicting, causing suffering.*

ܡܚܫܢܘܬܐ rt. ܚܫ. f. *infliction of pain.*

ܡܚܫܚܬܢܐ from ܚܫܚܬ. *exciting* or *heightening desire, arousing uneasy desire.*

ܡܚܬܡܢܐ, ܢܝܬܐ rt. ܚܬܡ. *one who signs* or *seals, concludes, consummates.*

ܡܚܬܢܐ, ܡܚܬܢܢܐ from ܚܬܢ. *allying, taking in marriage.*

ܡܚܬܪܐ *young, tender.*

ܡܚܬܪܘܬܐ f. *tender growth, young herbage.*

ܡܛܐ fut. ܢܡܛܐ, act. part. ܡܛܐ, ܡܛܝܐ. *to come, arrive at, reach,* with ܠ, ܠܘܬ, ܥܠ but usually metaph. *a*) of time, season, number or amount, as rumours, &c., with ܐܥܕܢܐ *the time came;* ܡܛܐ ܩܨܗ *his end draws near;* ܡܛܐ ܠܗ ܣܘܦܐ ܕܟܠ *the end of all things is at hand;* ܡܛܐ ܛܝܡܐ ܠ *the price mounted up, came to;* ܠܐ ܡܛܝܐ ܗܘܐ ܐܝܕܗ ܕܗܒܐ *he could not come by any gold, could not lay his hand on money. b*) *to happen, befall, attain, come* with ܠ *to* or ܥܠ *upon;* with ܦܣܐ *the lot came, fell;* ܡܛܐ ܠܗ —ܡܢܬܐ—ܦܣܐ *his lot, his portion was;* ܐܝܟ ܕܡܛܐ ܠܗ ܐܢܫ *to each his portion;* ܠܐ ܡܛܐ ܠܟܠܗܘܢ *it is not enough for all;* ܕܘܟܬܐ ܕܡܛܝܐ ܠܗ ܠܡܥܡܪܐ *the place where it was his lot to dwell;* ܗܘ ܕܡܛܝܐ ܠܗ *that which befell him;* with ܚܝܠܘܬܐ *to be able;* ܐܝܟ ܕܡܛܐ ܚܝܠܘܬܗ *as far as he can.* PA. ܡܛܝ *to bring; to come, arrive* at a place, with ܠ or ܠܘܬ; *to come, arrive, reach, attain; to happen, befall,* as a day, a letter, time, number or age, good or evil fortune, temptation, end; ܩܠܝܠ ܡܡܛܐ ܠ *he had nearly arrived at;* ܡܛܝ ܠܡܥܠ *he was on the point of entering;* ܡܛܝ ܕܢܦܩ ܩܨܗ *he was nearing his end;* ܐܬܐ ܝܫܘܥ ܘܡܛܝ ܠܘܬܗܘܢ *Jesus came and met them;* ܐܬܪܘܬܐ ܡܛܝ ܠܚܨܕܐ *the fields are ready for harvest;* ܡܕܡ ܕܡܛܝܗ ܡܢ ܒܙܬܐ *that which came to him of the prey, his booty;* ܠܐ ܐܫܬܟܚ ܐܢܫ ܕܠܐ ܡܛܝܗ ܡܢ ܒܝܫܬܗܘܢ *there was not a person who did not suffer some harm from them.* ETHPA. ܐܬܡܛܝ *to be brought unto, arrive at* a place; *to attain to, fall into* or *upon,* ܠܡܝܬܪܘܬܐ *unto virtue;* ܠܣܢܝܩܘܬܐ *into penury* but ܥܩܬܐ ܣܓܝܐܬܐ ܐܬܡܛܝܬ ܥܠܝ *much sorrow has fallen upon me.* APH. ܐܡܛܝ *to bring.* DERIVATIVES, ܡܛܘܬܐ, ܡܛܝܐ, ܡܬܡܛܝܢܘܬܐ, ܡܬܡܛܝܢܐ.

ܡܛܐܪܟܐ or ܡܛܪܟܐ rt. ܛܪܟ. *a patron, leader, promoter, benefactor.*

ܡܛܐܪܟܘܬܐ rt. ܛܪܟ. f. *beneficence, kindness.*

ܡܛܐܠܐܢ pl. ܡܛܐܠܐܣ; see ܡܛܠܢ *a mine.*

ܡܛܐܠܐܝܐ; see ܡܛܠܐ.

ܡܛܐܠܐܩܣܐ; see ܡܛܠܩܣܐ *metathesis.*

ܡܛܒܥܢܐ and ܡܛܐܒܥܢܐ rt. ܛܒܥ. *a messenger, bringer of news.*

ܡܛܒܥܢܘܬܐ rt. ܛܒܥ. f. *proclaiming.*

ܡܛܒܥܢܐ, ܢܝܬܐ, ܡܛܒܥܢ rt. ܛܒܥ. *he* or *that which overwhelms, drags down, subverts, ruins; oppressive, stupefying.*

ܡܛܘܗܡܘܬܐ from ܛܘܗܡܐ. f. *high descent.*

ܡܛܘܗܡܢܐ from ܛܘܗܡܐ. *a kinsman, relation.*

ܡܛܘܫܢܝܬܐ or ܡܛܫ rt. ܡܛܫ. f. *the forefinger.*

ܡܛܘܫܢܝܬܐ rt. ܛܘܫ. f. *a drag-hook* or *net* for fishing things out of a pit or pool.

ܡܛܛܠ; see ܡܛܠ.

ܡܛܢܝܐ or ܡܛܢܘܝܬܐ pl. ܢܝܬܐ, ܢܝܣ and ܡܛܢܘܝܣ f. μετάνοια, *a genuflection* on one knee, *an obeisance;* with ܥܒܕ or ܩܒܠ *to make* or *offer obeisance;* ܢܥܒܕ ܚܕܐ ܡܛܢܘܝܬܐ ܩܕܡ ܡܕܒܚܐ *he shall make one genuflection before the altar.*

ܡܛܘܦܬܐ rt. ܢܛܦ. f. *dropping, dropping down, a splash; ointment.*

ܡܛܘܦܬܐ rt. ܢܛܦ. f. *a large drop.*

ܡܛܝܪܐ rt. ܡܛܪ. *rainy, damp.*

ܡܛܘܬܐ, ܡܛܐ or ܡܛܝܬܐ pl. ܬܐ̈ rt. ܡܛܐ. f. *a portion, part, share;* ܡܛܝܬܐ ܕܦܪܢܝܬܐ the husband's or wife's *portion according to the marriage settlements.*

ܡܛܫ fut. ܢܡܛܘܫ. *to lick* the fingers. Ethpe. ܐܬܡܛܫ *to be licked.* Pa. ܡܛܫ *to lick up greedily.* Aph. ܐܡܛܫ *to cause to lick up* or *swallow.* Derivatives, ܡܛܘܫܬܐ, ܡܛܫܬܐ, ܡܡܛܫܢܐ.

ܡܛܫܬܐ pl. ܬܐ̈ rt. ܡܛܫ. f. *a lozenge.*

ܡܛܝ, ܡܛܝܐ rt. ܡܛܐ. m. *coming, arrival.*

ܡܛܝܒܐܝܬ rt. ܛܝܒ. adv. *promptly, readily.*

ܡܛܝܒܘܬܐ rt. ܛܝܒ. f. *readiness, preparation, enterprise.*

ܡܛܝܦܘܬܐ rt. ܛܘܦ. f. *a flood, inundation.*

ܡܛܝܪܐ rt. ܡܛܪ. *rainy.*

ܡܛܟܣܐܝܬ from ܛܟܣܐ. adv. *in good order, regular;* with ܠܐ *disorderly, in an irregular manner.*

ܡܛܟܣܘܬܐ pl. ܬܐ̈ from ܛܟܣܐ. f. *a*) *order, regularity, arrangement; orderliness, moderation;* ܡܛܟܣܘܬܐ ܕܥܕܬܐ *good order, discipline;* ܠܐ ܡܛܟܣܘܬܐ *disorderliness, commotion; irregularity. b*) *an order, class;* ܡܛܟܣܘܬܐ ܫܡܝܢܝܬܐ *the heavenly orders;* ܡܛܟܣܘܬܐ ܕܥܕܬܐ *hierarchy. c*) *celebrating* or *receiving holy communion. d*) gram. *order, construction; style.*

ܡܛܟܣܢܐ, ܢܝܬܐ from ܛܟܣܐ. *one who orders, sets in order, disciplines, moderates; a prefect; a composer, author;* eccles. *celebrant;* gram. *ordinal.*

ܡܛܠ rarely written fully ܡܛܘܠ, often followed by ܕ. With pers. pron. affixes has the form ܡܛܠܬ; ܡܛܠܬܝ *because of me, on my account, for me;* ܡܛܠܬܗ ܕ *for whose sake;* ܡܛܠܬܗܘܢ *because of them,* &c. *a*) *because of, by reason of, on account of, in order that;* ܡܛܠ ܗܕܐ *for this cause, on account of;* ܡܛܠܗܕܐ, ܡܛܠ ܗܕܐ *on this account;* ܡܛܠܡܢܐ or ܡܛܠܡܢ *for what cause? on what account? wherefore?* ܡܛܠ ܕܗܐ *for behold! b*) *about, on a* subject; ܡܛܠ ܡܘܬܐ ܦܓܪܢܝܐ *On physical death;* ܬܘܒ ܡܛܠ ܫܘܠܡܗ ܕܥܠܡܐ *Another* homily *on the end of the world.*

ܡܛܠܠܐ; see ܡܛܠܠܐ.

ܡܛܠܠܘܢ, ܡܛܠܘܢ, ܡܛܠܘܢ, ܡܛܐܠܘܢ and ܡܛܐܠܘܢ, pl. ܡܛܐܠܐ, ܡܛܐܠܐ m. μέταλλον, *a mine, quarry.*

ܡܛܠܝܩܐ pl. ܩܐ̈ also ܡܛܠܝܩܘܣ, ܡܛܐܠܝܩܘܣ, ܡܛܠܝܩܘܣ μεταλλικός, *metallic, metal; a mine, quarry; a miner.*

ܡܛܠܝܬܐ f. *a booth, shed, workshop.*

ܡܛܠܠܐ rarely ܡܛܠܐ emph. st. ܡܛܠܬܐ and ܡܛܐܠܐ, pl. ܡܛܠܝܢ ܡܛܠܠܝܢ, ܡܛܠܠܐ, ܡܛܐܠܐ, ܡܛܠܬܐ or ܡܛܐܠܐ rt. ܛܠܠ. f. *a booth, hut, shed, shelter, roof, tabernacle, tent;* ܒܡܛܠܐ *in secret;* ܥܐܕܐ ܕܡܛܠܐ *the feast of booths* or *tabernacles;* ܡܛܠܬܐ ܕܒܟܪܡܐ *a hut in a vineyard;* ܡܛܠܐ ܫܡܝܢܝܬܐ *heavenly habitations.*

ܡܛܠܠܢܐ rt. ܛܠܠ. m. *a*) *a covering* for the head. *b*) *one who makes a tent* or *roof.*

ܡܛܠܡܡܘܬܐ rt. ܛܠܡ. f. *heavy slumber, unconsciousness.*

ܡܛܠܡܢ, ܢܐ, ܢܝܬܐ rt. ܛܠܡ. *consuming, destroying, dissipating.*

ܡܛܡܪܘܬܐ pl. ܬܐ̈ rt. ܛܡܪ. f. *a hiding* or *lurking-place.*

ܡܛܥܝܢܐ, ܢܝܬܐ rt. ܛܥܐ. *a*) *causing to stray* esp. from the right faith, *seducing, misleading, deceiving;* ܪܘܚܐ ܡܛܥܝܢܝܬܐ *seducing spirits. b*) *an impostor, deceiver;* pl. f. *impositions, frauds. c*) *wandering;* ܟܘܟܒܐ ܡܛܥܝܢܐ or ellipt. *the planets.*

ܡܛܥܝܢܐܝܬ rt. ܛܥܐ. adv. *deceitfully, guilefully.*

ܡܛܥܝܢܘܬܐ pl. ܬܐ̈ rt. ܛܥܐ. f. *error, misleading, fallacy, guile, deception;* ܐܘܡܢܘܬܐ ܡܛܥܝܢܘܬܗ *his misleading artifices;* ܡܛܥܝܢܘܬܐ ܣܘܦܣܛܝܩܝܬܐ *fallacious sophistries.*

ܡܛܡܛܐ *a giraffe.*

ܡܛܠܥܘܬܐ rt. ܛܠܥ. f. *lameness, halting speech.*

ܡܛܦܛܦܘܬܐ rt. ܢܛܦ. f. *oozing, issuing in drops.*

ܡܛܠܫܢܝܬܐ rt. ܛܠܫ. gram. *line of abbreviation.*

ܡܛܘܫܢܝܬܐ rt. ܛܘܫ. *befouling, polluting.*

ܡܛܘܦܣܢܝܐ, ܢܝܬܐ from ܛܘܦܣܐ. adj. *typical, figurative, symbolical.*

ܡܛܦܣܢܘܬܐ from ܛܘܦܣܐ. f. *adumbration.*

ܡܛܘܡܝܬܐ f. *mallow, malva* or *althea ficus*; cf. ܚܛܡܝܬܐ.

ܡܛܪ fut. ܢܡܛܪ, act. part. ܡܳܛܰܪ, ܡܳܛܪܳܐ. *to rain;* metaph. ܓܐܪ̈ܐ ܡܛܰܪ ܓܐܪ̈ܐ *it rained arrows.* Ethpe. ܐܬܡܛܰܪ *to be rained upon, watered with rain;* metaph. *to come down like rain.* Pa. ܡܰܛܰܪ *to give rain, moisten with rain;* ܕܠܐ ܡܛܪܐ ܢܡܰܛܰܪ *that it rain not.* Aph. ܐܰܡܛܰܪ *to cause to rain, to rain, pour* or *shower down;* ܡܛܪܐ ܐܡܛܰܪ *the rain poured down;* ܐܢܐ ܡܰܡܛܰܪ ܠܟܘܢ ܠܚܡܐ *I pour down bread for you.* Ethtaph. ܐܬܬܰܡܛܰܪ metaph. *to come down like rain; to be borne down as with rain* e.g. ܒܓܐܪ̈ܐ *with arrows;* ܡܬܬܡܛܪܢ ܥܠܝܢ ܒܘܪ̈ܟܬܐ *blessings pour down upon us.* Derivatives, ܡܛܘܪܐ, ܡܛܪܐ, ܡܛܪܢܐ, ܡܛܪܢܝܐ, ܡܛܪܢܘܬܐ, ܡܛܪܝܐ, ܡܡܛܪܢܐ, ܡܡܛܪܢܘܬܐ.

ܡܛܪܐ rt. ܡܛܪ. m. *rain;* ܢܚܬ ܡܛܪܐ *rain fell;* ܡܛܪܐ ܒܟܝܪܐ ܘܠܩܝܫܐ *early and latter rain;* ܚܣܝܪܘܬ ܡܛܪܐ *lack of rain, drought.*

ܡܛܪܢܐ; see ܡܝܛܪܢ.

ܡܝܛܪܦܘܠܝܛܝܣ, ܡܝܛܪܘܦܘܠܝܛܝܣ, ܡܝܛܪܦܘܠܝܛܘܬܐ; see under ܡܝܛܪܢ.

ܡܛܪܦܘܩܬܐ rt. ܛܪܦ. *a) a moment, the twinkling of an eye;* ܒܚܕܐ ܡܛܪܦܘܩܬܐ *in one moment;* cf. ܛܪܦܐ. *b) a shovel, ladle* (?).

ܡܛܪܛܫܘܬܐ from ܛܪܛܫ. f. *being defiled.*

ܡܛܪܛܫܢ, ܡܛܪܛܫܢܐ from Palpel of ܪܛܫ. m. *one who spots* or *spatters* in writing, *a careless scribe.*

ܡܛܪܢܝܐ, ܢܝܬܐ rt. ܡܛܪ. adj. *rainy;* ܙܒܢܐ ܡܛܪܢܝܐ *a rainy season;* ܢܛܘܦܝ̈ܬܐ ܡܛܪܢܝ̈ܬܐ *rain-drops.*

ܡܝܛܪܦܘܠܝܛܝܩܝܐ adj. *metropolitical;* with ܗܘܦܪܟܝܐ *the Metropolitan see.*

ܡܛܪܢ Ethp. ܐܬܡܛܪܢ denom. verb from ܡܝܛܪܢ; *to be made* or *become Metropolitan.*

ܡܛܪܢܘܬܐ rt. ܢܛܪ. f. *storing up, laying by.*

ܡܛܪܢܘܬܐ rt. ܡܛܪ. f. metaph. *showering down* bad words.

ܡܛܪܢܝܐ, ܢܝܬܐ rt. ܡܛܪ. same as ܡܛܪܢܝܐ.

ܡܛܪܦ rt. ܛܪܦ. m. *striking* or *clapping together;* ܡܛܪܦ ܥܝܢܐ ܕܥܝܢܐ *the twinkling of an eye;* ܐܝܟ ܡܛܪܦ *for a single moment.*

ܡܛܪܦܢܘܬܐ rt. ܛܪܦ. f. *perturbation, tribulation;* ܠܡܛܪܦܢܘܬܝ ܥܘܕܪܢܐ ܢܬܠ may God grant *help to my troubled self.*

ܡܛܪܦܢܝܐ, ܢܝܬܐ rt. ܛܪܦ. *sad, vexatious.*

ܡܛܪܩܐ Ar. m. *a strap, scourge.*

ܡܛܪܬܐ pl. ܡܛܪ̈ܢ, ܡܛܪ̈ܬܐ rt. ܢܛܪ. f. *a) a watch;* ܡܛܪܬܐ ܕܨܦܪܐ *the morning watch;* ܡܛܪܬܐ ܐܚܪܝܬܐ ܕܠܠܝܐ *the last watch of the night. b) a guard, guards, garrison. c) a post, station, camp.*

ܡܛܫܬܐ pl. ܡܛܫ̈ܐ, ܡܛܫ̈ܬܐ f. *a sandal, shoe, old shoe.*

ܡܛܫܝܐܝܬ rt. ܛܫܐ. adv. *in secret, secretly, covertly, clandestinely.*

ܡܛܫܝܘܬܐ rt. ܛܫܐ. f. *hiding, keeping close, secrecy.*

ܡܛܫܝܢܘܬܐ rt. ܛܫܐ. *hiding, concealing.*

ܡܛܬܐܣܝܣ or ܡܛܐܬܐܣܝܣ f. μετάθεσις, *metathesis, transposition* of letters.

ܡܝ̈ܐ has no sing. and is always written with ribui, constr. st. ܡܰܝ̈, abs. ܡܰܝ̈ܢ, rare ܡܰܝ̈ܶܝܢ; with affixes ܡܰܝ̈ܰܝ, ܡܰܝ̈ܰܘܗܝ, ܡܰܝ̈ܶܗ, ܡܰܝ̈ܰܢ; pl. ܡܰܝ̈ܟܘܢ, ܡܰܝ̈ܟܶܝܢ, ܡܰܝ̈ܰܝܗܘܢ, ܡܰܝ̈ܰܝܗܶܝܢ but usually the ܝ is dropped and a shortened form is used ܡܰܝ̈, ܡܰܘ̈ܗܝ, &c., 3 p. s. m. irreg. ܡܰܘ̈ܗܝ, but 3 p. s. f. ܡܰܝ̈ܶܗ; pl. ܡܰܝ̈ܗܘܢ, ܡܰܝ̈ܗܶܝܢ, &c., m. *water, waters; juice; the white* of an egg; *urine;* ܡܰܝ̈ ܣܥܪܐ *barley-water;* ܡܰܝ̈ ܓܘܒ̈ܐ *water from tanks* or *cisterns;* ܡܰܝ̈ ܙܝܬܐ *the watery part of olives, olive lees* or *scum;* ܡܝ̈ܐ ܚܪܝܦ̈ܐ *aqua fortis;* ܡܰܝ̈ ܡܛܪܐ *rain-water;* ܡܰܝ̈ ܢܝܠܘܣ *the waters of the Nile;* ܡܝ̈ܐ ܕܠܝܡܘ̈ܢܐ *juice of lemons;* ܡܰܝ̈ ܪ̈ܓܠܐ *urine;* ܡܰܝ̈ ܫܬܝܐ *water fit for drinking* or *for irrigation;* ܡܝ̈ܐ ܕܫܟܪܐ *sherbet;* ܡܰܝ̈ ܡܫܬܝܐ *drinking-water.* Derivatives, ܡܝܢܐ, ܡܝܢܘܬܐ, ܡܡܝܢܐ, ܡܡܝܢܘܬܐ.

ܡܝܒܠܢܐ rt. ܝܒܠ. m. *a) a bearer, carrier;* with ܐܓܪܬܐ *a letter-carrier, postman;* with ܫܠܝܚܐ *a messenger. b) an ancestor, founder of a line; a successor. c) a translator, interpreter.*

ܡܫܠܡܢܘܬܐ rt. ܫܠܡ. f. *succession; translation.*

ܡܫܠܦܢܐ rt. ܫܠܦ. *dessicative.*

ܒܝܬ ܡܣܝܪܘܢ *the kitchen;* cf. ܡܝܣܪܘܢܐ.

ܡܣܝܪܘܢܐ and ܡܣܪܘܢܐ; see ܡܝܣܪܘܢܐ.

ܡܫܪܝܡ *the offering of the Eucharist.*

ܡܝܘܢܝ *a Grecist, Greek scholar;* cf. ܝܘܢܝ.

ܡܡܫܫܢܘܬܐ rt. ܡܫܫ. f. *touching, stroking.*

ܡܝܘܬܐ, ܡܝܘܬܬܐ, ܡܝܘܬܝܬܐ rt. ܡܘܬ. *mortal, a mortal;* with ܠܐ *immortal.*

ܡܝܘܬܐܝܬ adv. with ܠܐ *immortally.*

ܡܝܘܬܘܬܐ f. with ܠܐ *immortality.*

ܡܬܟܐܘܣ *a goldsmith, gold-smelter.*

ܡܬܟܘܪܐ or ܡܬܟܘܪܢܐ pl. ܐ̈ Ar. m. *a girdle of hard material, an apron.*

ܡܬܪܦܢܐ rt. ܬܪܦ. *causing abortion.*

ܡܬܓܐ rt. ܡܘܓ. m. *shakiness, being ready to fall.*

ܡܬܟܣܐ m. μέταξα, *silk, raw silk.*

ܡܝܛܪܢ or ܡܝܛܪܢ also ܡܝܛܪܢ and ܡܝܛܪܢ contracted from ܡܝܛܪܘܦܘܠܝܛܐ m. *the Matran, Metropolitan.*

ܡܝܛܪܘܦܘܠܝܣ, ܡܝܛܪ̈, &c., f. *metropolis, a chief city.*

ܡܝܛܪܘܦܘܠܝܛܐ, ܡܝܛܪܘܦܘܠܝܛܝܣ and other spellings, pl. ܐ̈ or ܐ̈ m. *Metropolitan, a Metropolitan bishop.*

ܡܝܛܪܘܦܘܠܝܛܘܬܐ, ܡܝܛܪܘܬܐ, &c., f. *the office of a Metropolitan.*

ܡܬܟܒܐ; see ܡܬܟܒܐ *ohaby,* &c.

ܡܝܬ, ܡܝܬܐ = ܡܝܬ and ܡܝܬܐ; see ܡܘܬ.

ܡܝܠ, ܡܝܠܐ pl. ܝ̈ܢ, ܐ̈ m. μίλιον, *a mile, milestone.*

ܡܝܓܪܐ *a saw.*

ܡܝܓܝܢܐ some coin.

ܡܝܟܠܬܐ pl. ܬ̈ܐ f. *a carpet;* cf. ܡܛܠܐ.

ܡܝܡ *Mim* name of the letter ܡ, hence is derived—

ܡܝܡܝܐ, ܡܝܡܝܬܐ *having initial* ܡ, *beginning with the letter Mim.*

ܡܝܡܣܐ pl. ܐ̈ *a mould.*

ܡܝܡܢܢܐ *ambidexter;* see ܝܡܝܢ.

ܡܝܡܘܣ, ܡܝܡܣܐ pl. ܐ̈ m. μῖμος, *a mime, buffoon, jester; a rascal, rogue, thief.*

ܡܝܡܣܘܬܐ from ܡܝܡܘܣ. f. *pantomime, acting, buffoonery, effeminacy, obscenity.*

ܡܝܡܣܝܐ adj. from ܡܝܡܘܣ; ܓܒܪ̈ܐ ܡܝܡܣܝܐ *mimes, actors.*

ܡܝܢ, ܡܝܢܐ, ܡܝܢܝܬܐ from ܡܝܐ. adj. *of water, watery, aqueous.*

ܡܝܢ, ܡܝܢܐ m. *race, family, stock.*

ܡܝܢܘܬܐ and ܡܝܢܝܘܬܐ from ܡܝܐ. f. *wateriness, humidity.*

ܡܝܢܝܐ, ܡܝܢܝܬܐ from ܡܝܐ. *watery, aqueous, aquatic, humid;* ܡܢܘܬܐ ܡܝܢܝܬܐ *aqueous particles;* ܠܚܘ̈ܬܐ ܡܝܢܝܬܐ *moist vapours;* ܚܝ̈ܘܬܐ ܡܝܢܝܬܐ *aquatic animals.*

ܡܝܢܩܘܬܐ rt. ܝܢܩ. f. *sucking.*

ܡܝܢܩܢܐ, ܡܝܢܩܢܝܬܐ rt. ܝܢܩ. *giving milk, suckling; the teats; a nurse.*

ܡܝܢܩܬܐ rt. ܝܢܩ. f. *a wet-nurse.*

ܡܝܣܩܘܛܝܢ or ܡܝܣܩܘܛܝܢ, ܡܝܣܩܘܛܪܝܢ *a dish, dessert dish.*

ܡܝܣܘ, ܡܝܣܘܣ or ܡܝܣܘܣ μίσυ, μίσεως m. shoemaker's *vitriol.*

ܡܝܣܘܢܐ or ܡܝܣܢ m. *a water-bird.*

ܡܝܣܪܐ rt. ܐܣܪ. *a bobbin; the thread.*

ܡܝܣܩܘܪܐ pl. ܐ̈ *a musician; music.*

ܡܝܩܐ m. *the indigo plant, indigofera tinctoria.*

ܡܝܩܘܢ, ܡܝܩܘܢܐ or ܡܐܩܘܢ pl. ܡܝܩܘ̈ܢܐ m. μήκων, *the poppy.*

ܡܝܩܪܢܐ, ܡܝܩܪܢܝܬܐ from ܝܩܪ. *characteristic.*

ܡܝܩܪܢܐܝܬ rt. ܝܩܪ. adv. *with honour, showing honour.*

ܡܝܩܪܘܬܐ rt. ܝܩܪ. f. *honour, excellence;* usually as a title ܡܝܩܪܘܬܟ *your Excellency.*

ܡܝܩܪܢܐ rt. ܝܩܪ. *one who honours, shows honour, a worshipper.*

ܡܝܩܪܢܘܬܐ rt. ܝܩܪ. f. *worship, reverence.*

ܡܝܪܐ rt. ܡܘܪ. m. *corn, provisions, supplies;* ܟܣܦܐ ܕܡܝܪܢ *our corn-money.*

ܡܝܪܘܢ m. μύρον, *ointment, sweet salve.*

ܡܝܫܐ m. *a) quercus coccifera, the scarlet oak. b) celtis australis. c) a sort of raisin.*

ܡܝܫܐ rt. ܡܫܫ. m. *touching;* ܕܠܐ ܡܝܫܐ *so as not to be touched.*

ܡܝܬ, ܡܝܬܐ, ܡܝܬܬܐ; see ܡܘܬ *to die.*

ܡܡܺܝܬܽܘܬܳܐ rt. ܡܘܬ. f. *mortality, deadness, death;* ܕܢܰܚܶܐ ܡܡܺܝܬܽܘܬܰܢ *that he may quicken our mortality, raise us up from death;* ܡܶܢ ܡܡܺܝܬܽܘܬܳܐ ܠܥܺܕܬܳܐ ܐܰܥܺܝܪܳܗ̇ ܡܶܢ ܥܩܳܪܽܘܬܳܐ *he aroused the Church from deathlike barrenness.*

ܡܰܡܛܝܳܢܽܘܬܳܐ rt. ܐܬܳܐ. f. *bringing, bearing;* ܐܰܝܟ ܡܰܡܛܝܳܢܽܘܬ ܥܶܕܳܢܳܐ *as opportunity offers;* ܡܰܡܛܝܳܢܽܘܬ ܦܺܐܪ̈ܶܐ ܕܪܽܘܚܳܐ *the bringing forth of fruits of the spirit;* ܡܰܡܛܝܳܢܽܘܬܳܐ ܡܶܢ ܡܰܟܬ̈ܒܳܢܽܘܬܳܐ *compiling from books.*

ܡܰܡܛܝܳܢܳܐ, ܡܰܡܛܝܳܢܺܝܬܳܐ rt. ܐܬܳܐ. m. *he* or *that which brings* or *produces;* ܡܰܡܛܝܳܢܳܐ ܕܕܺܝܬܺܩܺܐ *the testator;* ܡܰܡܛܝܳܢ̈ܶܐ ܕܡ̈ܰܝܳܐ *aqueducts.*

ܡܰܡܛܝܳܢܽܘܬܳܐ rt. ܐܬܳܐ. f. *bringing forward, producing* e. g. ܕܣܳܗ̈ܕܶܐ *of witnesses;* ܡܰܡܛܝܳܢܽܘܬܳܐ ܕܬܰܚܘ̈ܝܳܬܳܐ *the alleging of arguments.*

ܡܡܬܩܬܐ rt. ܡܬܩ. *sweet food.*

ܡܡܰܠܝܳܐܝܺܬ rt. ܝܰܠܶܦ. *well, notably, especially, in the best way, excellently, virtuously.*

ܡܡܰܠܝܽܘܬܳܐ rt. ܝܰܠܶܦ. f. *the best, highest, extreme, peculiar excellence, virtue;* ܡܡܰܠܝܽܘܬܳܐ ܕܕܘܒܳܪܳܐ *excellent* or *virtuous conduct, the ascetic life.*

ܡܡܰܠܝܳܬܳܐ f. *virtues;* see Pael part. of ܝܰܠܶܦ.

ܡܶܟ, ܡܳܟ, or ܡܟܶܟ, fut. ܢܶܡܟܽܘܟ and ܢܶܡܟܶܟ, act. part. ܡܳܟܶܟ or ܡܳܐܟܶܟ, ܡܳܟܳܐ or ܡܳܟܳܐ, f. emph. pl. ܡܳܟܟ̈ܳܬܳܐ or ܡܳܟ̈ܳܬܳܐ, pass. parts. ܡܟܺܝܟ and ܡܟܺܝܟ, ܟܳܐ, ܟܬܳܐ. *to lie down flat, prostrate oneself, humble oneself; to be laid low, be spread* or *strewn flat;* with ܩܶܛܡܳܐ or ܣܰܩܳܐ *to put on sackcloth* or *strew ashes* on the head, *to humble oneself in sackcloth and ashes.* Part. adj. *a*) active form *low, lowly, poor;* with ܡܶܢ *lower, lesser, inferior;* ܟܰܕ ܡܳܐܟܶܟ ܦܽܘܠܽܘܣ ܡܶܢ ܐܳܦܩܳܐ *when the pole sinks below the horizon;* ܣܺܐܡܳܐ ܕܡܳܐܟܶܟ ܡܶܢ ܕܗܰܒܳܐ *silver being inferior to gold;* ܪ̈ܳܡܶܐ ܘܡܳܟ̈ܶܐ—ܡ̈ܰܠܟܶܐ ܘܡܳܟ̈ܳܐ *high and low, kings and paupers;* f. emph. pl. *poor affairs, low* or *mean circumstances, baseness;* ܡܳܟܳܟ̈ܳܬܰܢ ܢܣܰܒ *Christ took our poverty* upon Him. *b*) first passive form (rare); ܟܰܕ ܡܟܺܝܟܺܝܢ ܥܰܠ ܥܰܦܪܳܐ *lying prone in the dust.* *c*) second passive form *sunken, low, low-lying, prostrate;* ܓܽܘܦܢܳܐ ܡܟܺܝܟܳܐ ܡܟܝܟܘܬܐ *a vine of stunted growth;* ܡܶܨܪܶܝܢ ܕܡܟܺܝܟܳܐ ܗܘܳܬ ܡܶܢ *Egypt which lies lower than* the level of the Red Sea; metaph. *low, lowly, humble, meek;* ܛܽܘܒܰܝܗܽܘܢ ܠܡܰܟ̈ܺܝܟܶܐ ܕܗܶܢܽܘܢ ܢܺܐܪܬܽܘܢ ܐܰܪܥܳܐ *blessed are the meek for they shall inherit the earth.* Ethpe. ܐܶܬܡܟܶܟ *to be spread flat.* Pa. ܡܰܟܶܟ *to lay low, abase, humble, humiliate, afflict; to force* a woman; *to subdue* in war; with ܠܰܐܪܥܳܐ *to lay low to the ground;* with ܡܶܢ ܪܰܒܽܘܬܳܐ *to cast down from an office;* with ܢܰܦܫܳܐ *to humble oneself, to afflict one's own soul;* with ܪܶܢܝܳܐ ܪܳܡܳܐ *to humble a high spirit.* Part. adj. ܐܰܬܪܳܐ ܡܡܰܟܟܳܐ ; ܡܡܰܟܟܳܐ, ܡܡܰܟܟܬܳܐ, ܡܡܰܟܶܟ *low-lying ground;* ܠܰܚܡܳܐ ܡܡܰܟܟܳܐ *poor bread, bread of affliction;* ܚܰܝ̈ܶܐ ܡܡܰܟܟ̈ܶܐ *a lowly life.* Ethpa. ܐܶܬܡܰܟܰܟ. *a*) pass. *to be strewn upon; to be bowed down, brought low; to be forced, outraged* of a woman; ܟܽܠ ܕܪܳܡ ܢܰܦܫܶܗ ܢܶܬܡܰܟܰܟ *every one that exalteth himself shall be brought low.* *b*) refl. *to bow down, to behave humbly towards* with ܠܘܳܬ ; ܐܶܬܳܐ ܠܘܳܬ ܣܽܘܠܛܳܢ ܘܶܐܬܡܰܟܰܟ ܠܶܗ *he came and submitted himself to the Sultan.* Aph. ܐܰܡܶܟ *to strew; to lay low, cast down, humble, abase;* ܩܶܛܡܳܐ ܡܰܡܶܟ ܠܣܰܓܺܝܐ̈ܶܐ *ashes were strewn under many;* with ܥܰܝ̈ܢܶܐ *to lower the eyes, look down;* with ܩܳܠܳܐ *to lower the voice, speak in a low tone;* with ܢܰܦܫܳܐ *to humble himself.* Derivatives, ܡܟܘܟܐ, ܡܟܝܟܐܝܬ, ܡܟܝܟܘܬܐ, ܡܡܟܟܢܘܬܐ, ܡܟܟܐ, ܡܟܟܢܐ.

ܡܶܟܺܝܠ comp. of ܡܶܢ and ܟܺܠ adv. *a*) of time, *from this time;* ܡܶܟܺܝܠ ܠܰܐܪܒܥܺܝܢ ܝܰܘܡܺܝܢ *within forty days;* ܡܶܢ ܡܶܟܺܝܠ *from that time forth.* *b*) of place, *of* or *from this place, hence;* ܫܰܢܺܝܘ ܠܗܽܘܢ ܡܶܟܺܝܠ *they have departed hence;* ܡܶܟܺܝܠ ܘܡܶܟܺܝܠ *here and there; on this side and on that;* ܚܰܕ ܡܶܟܺܝܠ ܘܚܰܕ ܡܶܟܺܝܠ *one on this side and one on that.* *c*) logic. ܡܶܬܚܰܘܝܳܐ ܡܶܟܺܝܠ *hence, it follows.*

ܡܰܟܐܒܽܘܬܳܐ rt. ܟܐܒ. f. *infliction of pain, wounding.*

ܡܰܟܐܒܳܢܳܐ, ܡܰܟܐܒܳܢܺܝܬܳܐ rt. ܟܐܒ. *painful, grievous;* ܡܣܰܟܢܽܘܬܳܐ ܡܰܟܐܒܳܢܺܝܬܳܐ *distressing poverty.*

ܡܰܟܐܒܳܢܽܘܬܳܐ rt. ܟܐܒ. f. *pain, affliction.*

ܡܟܺܝܟܳܐܝܺܬ rt. ܡܟܟ. adv. *humbly, submissively.*

ܡܶܟܰܐܢܳܐ pl. ܡܶܟܰܐܢܶܣ, ܡܶܟܰܢܰܘܣ; see ܡܶܟܰܐܢܳܐ μηχανή, *an engine of war.*

ܡܶܟܰܐܢܳܐܝܺܬ from μηχανή. adv. *ingeniously.*

ܡܟܰܥܰܪ, ܡܟܰܥܪܳܐ, ܡܟܰܥܪܬܳܐ Pael pass. part. of ܟܥܪ. *marred, misshapen*, &c.

ܡܟܰܥܪܽܘܬܳܐ rt. ܟܥܪ. f. *disfigurement; sternness, austerity;* ܕܦܰܪܨܽܘܦܳܐ *of countenance.*

ܡܟܰܒܪܳܢܳܐ and ܡܟܰܒܪܳܢܳܐ, ܢܺܝܬܳܐ rt. ܟܒܪ. *one who makes to abound, increases* wealth or prosperity.

ܡܟܰܕܒܽܘܬܳܐ rt. ܟܕܒ. f. *mendacity.*

ܡܟܰܗܶܢ Aphel part. of ܟܗܢ.

ܡܟܰܗܢܳܢܳܐ, ܢܳܝܬܳܐ rt. ܟܗܢ. *a)* adj. *belonging to the ordination of a priest;* ܩܶܪܝܳܢܶܐ ܡܟܰܗܢܳܢܳܝܶܐ *lections read at an Ordination. b)* subst. *one who performs priestly functions, serves, ministers, offers sacrifice;* ܡܟܰܗܢܳܢܶܐ *the clergy* i. e. the three orders; ܡܟܰܗܢܳܢܳܐ ܕܕܶܒܚܬܳܐ ܚܰܝܬܳܐ *he who offers the living sacrifice, the officiating priest.*

ܡܟܰܗܢܳܢܽܘܬܳܐ rt. ܟܗܢ. f. *the priest's office, priesthood; worship, religious service.*

ܡܟܽܘܠܳܐ pl. ܶܐ m. *a measure* ܕܥܰܒܽܘܪܳܐ *of corn.*

ܡܟܺܝܟܳܐ pl. ܶܐ rt. ܡܟ. *humble, submissive.*

ܡܟܰܣܝܳܢܳܐ, ܢܺܝܬܳܐ rt. ܟܣܐ II. *one who corrects, admonishes, rebukes;* ܡܰܪܕܽܘܬܳܐ ܡܟܰܣܝܳܢܳܝܳܬܳܐ *disciplinary chastisements.*

ܡܟܽܘܢܬܳܐ pl. ܡܟܽܘܢܳܬܳܐ f. *a base.*

ܡܟܽܘܪܳܐ, ܡܟܽܘܪܬܳܐ rt. ܡܟܪ. *a suitor, bridegroom, bride, one who betroths* act. opp. ܡܟܺܝܪܳܢܳܐ *one who is betrothed;* metaph. ܡܰܟܢܺܝܟܽܘܬܳܐ ܡܟܽܘܪܬܳܐ ܕܐܺܝܩܳܪܳܐ *submission which espouses honour;* ܛܰܝܒܽܘܬܳܐ ܡܟܽܘܪܬܳܐ ܕܒܽܘܪܟܳܬܳܐ *grace which espouses to itself blessings.*

ܡܟܽܘܪ̈ܶܐ rt. ܡܟܪ. m. pl. *betrothals, espousals.*

ܡܟܽܘܪܝܳܐ pl. ܶܐ rt. ܡܟܪ. m. *betrothal, espousal;* ܥܶܙܩܬܳܐ ܪܗܒܽܘܢܳܐ ܕܡܟܽܘܪܝܳܗ̇ *the ring the pledge of her betrothal.*

ܡܟܽܘܟܽܘܬܳܐ *a)* rt. ܡܟ. f. *humility, meekness. b) stone lid* or *cover of a well. c) a floating bladder, float, raft.*

ܡܟܽܘܬܳܐ or ܡܟܽܘܬܬܳܐ rt. ܢܟܬ. f. *a bite.*

ܡܟܽܘܬܳܢܽܘܬܳܐ rt. ܢܟܬ. f. *a bite.*

ܡܟܽܘܬܳܢܳܐ rt. ܢܟܬ. m. *one who gnaws a crust of bread.*

ܡܟܽܘܬܳܢܺܝܬܳܐ rt. ܢܟܬ. f. *a bite, a mouthful.*

ܡܟܰܚܶܫ Aphel part. of ܟܚܫ.

ܡܟܚܽܘܠܳܐ rt. ܟܚܠ. m. *the stick* or *style used in applying kohl to the eyes.*

ܡܟܺܝܟ ; see ܡܟ.

ܡܟܺܝܟܳܐܺܝܬ rt. ܡܟ. adv. *humbly, in lowliness* or *humiliation, submissively, meekly, gently;* ܢܳܗܡܺܝܢ ܫܰܦܢܺܝܢܶܐ ܡܟܺܝܟܳܐܺܝܬ *turtle-doves coo softly.*

ܡܟܺܝܟܽܘܬܳܐ rt. ܡܟ. f. *lowliness, humility;* ܡܟܺܝܟܽܘܬܳܐ ܠܶܒܳܢܳܝܬܳܐ *heartfelt humility.*

ܡܟܺܝܠ comp. of ܡܢ and ܟܺܝܠ obs. Cf. ܗܳܟܺܝܠ. *a)* adv. of time, *thence, thenceforward, from that time, after this. b)* illative adv. *therefore, so then, so now, now therefore, from henceforth;* ܠܳܐ ܡܟܺܝܠ *no longer, no more, not again.*

ܡܟܺܝܠܳܢܳܐ, ܢܺܝܬܳܐ rt. ܟܝܠ. *a measurer, one who gives forth by measure.*

ܡܟܺܐܒܳܢܳܐ, ܢܺܝܬܳܐ and ܡܰܟܐܒܳܢܳܐ rt. ܟܐܒ. *noxious, hurtful, injurious, mischievous;* ܡܶܐܟܽܘܠܬܳܐ ܡܰܟܐܒܳܢܺܝܬܳܐ *unwholesome food.*

ܡܟܰܢܢܳܐܺܝܬ rt. ܟܢ. adv. *elaborately.*

ܡܟܰܢܢܽܘܬܳܐ rt. ܟܢ. f. *nature, natural constitution.*

ܡܟܐܒܽܘܬܳܐ or ܡܰܟܐܒܬܳܐ rt. ܟܐܒ. *harm, damage, injury.*

ܡܟܰܢܢܳܝܳܐ, ܢܳܝܬܳܐ rt. ܟܢ. adj. *by nature, according to nature.*

ܡܟܰܢܢܳܢܳܐ rt. ܟܢ. m. *He who calls into existence, appoints nature, the Creator, supreme disposer* ܕܥܳܠܡܶܐ *of the worlds.*

ܡܟܰܢܢܳܢܳܐܺܝܬ rt. ܟܢ. adv. *naturally, according to nature.*

ܡܟܰܢܢܳܢܽܘܬܳܐ rt. ܟܢ. f. *creation, formation.*

ܡܟܺܝܪܽܘܬܳܐ rt. ܡܟܪ. f. *betrothal, connexion by marriage.*

ܡܟܟܳܐ rt. ܡܟ. m. *a rug.*

ܡܟܰܠ denom. verb Pael conj. from ܡܟܽܘܠܳܐ. *to bar, bolt.*

ܡܟܠܳܐ = ܡܐܟܠܳܐ m. *food.*

ܡܟܰܠܠܳܢܳܐ rt. ܟܠ. m. *He who crowns, gives the crown* ܠܣܳܗ̈ܕܶܐ—ܕܩܰܕܺܝܫܶܐ—ܠܐܰܬܠܺܝܛܶܐ *to the martyrs, to the saints.*

ܡܟܰܬܢܳܐ rt. ܢܟܬ. m. *imagination, instinct.*

ܡܟܰܬܢܽܘܬܳܐ rt. ܢܟܬ. f. *opinion, supposition, imagination.*

ܡܟܡܟܡܢܐܝܬ rt. ܟܡܟܡ. adv. *in a shadow, metaphorically.*

ܡܟܡܟܡܢܐ, ܢܝܬܐ rt. ܟܡܟܡ. *gloomy, darkening.*

ܡܟܡܪܢܐ, ܪܢܝܬܐ rt. ܟܡܪ. *saddening, mournful.*

ܡܟܝܢ, ܡܟܝܢܐ Aphel pass. part. from ܟܘܢ = adj. *a*) *natural, by nature, innate;* ܕܠܐ ܡܟܝܢ *unnatural, contrary to nature;* ܠܐ ܡܟܝܢܝܢ ܒܢܘܗܝ *they are not his own sons;* ܚܫܐ ܕܡܟܝܢܝܢ ܒܒܣܪܐ *passions innate in the flesh, the natural passions of the flesh.* *b*) *existing, in existence, possible;* ܠܐ ܡܟܝܢܐ *it cannot be, is impossible.* *c*) *naturally fitted, endowed with capacity, capable, adapted* usually followed by ܕ; ܐܝܠܝܢ ܕܠܐ ܡܟܝܢܝܢ ܕܢܐܠܦܘܢ *those who have no power of learning, who are incapable of learning;* ܠܗܢܐ ܡܠܟܐ ܡܟܝܢ ܗܘܐ ܬܐܓܐ *for this king the crown was fitting.*

ܡܟܝܢܘܬܐ rt. ܟܘܢ. f. *essential nature, constitution, disposition; possibility.*

ܡܟܝܢܝܐ, ܢܝܬܐ *natural, innate, according to natural order.*

ܡܟܢܝܡܛܐ pl. μηχανήματα, *engines of war.*

ܡܟܢܝܩܐ or ܡܟܢܝܩܘܣ pl. ܡܟܢܝܩܐ or ܡܟܢܝܩܘܣ μηχανικός, *an engineer.*

ܡܟܒܪܢܐ, ܪܢܝܬܐ rt. ܟܒܪ. *he* or *that which confers honour, renders dignified.*

ܡܟܢܦܘܬܐ from ܟܢܦܐ. f. *sheltering under the wings, protection.*

ܡܟܢܫܢ, ܡܟܢܫܢܐ, ܡܟܢܫܢܝܬܐ rt. ܟܢܫ. *one who gathers together, collects;* ܥܢܐ ܕܠܝܬ ܠܗ ܡܟܢܫܢܐ *sheep that no man gathereth, sheep without a shepherd;* ܠܝܬ ܡܟܢܫܢܐ ܠܫܠܕܗ *there is no one to take up the corpse, none to bury;* ܕܝܪܐ ܕܡܟܢܫܢܘܬܢ *the monastery where we meet together; a compiler* of laws, of words; *deductive, inferential;* gram. *a collective* noun.

ܡܟܢܫܬܐ, ܡܟܢܫܬܐ or ܡܟܢܫܬܐ pl. ܡܟܢܫܬܐ or ܡܟܢܫܝܬܐ rt. ܟܢܫ. f. *a broom, besom.*

ܡܟܣܣ Aphel part. of ܟܣ.

ܡܟܣ, ܡܟܣܐ pl. ܣܐ m. *a publican, collector, tax-gatherer;* ܒܝܬ ܡܟܣܐ *toll* or *custom-house.*

ܡܟܣܐ pl. ܣܐ m. *tribute, impost, toll, tax.* Derivatives, ܡܟܣܐ, ܡܟܣܘܬܐ.

ܡܟܣܘܬܐ from ܡܟܣܐ. f. *publicanship, collectorship.*

ܡܟܣܝܢܐܝܬ rt. ܟܣܐ. adv. *secretly, mysteriously, mystically.*

ܡܟܣܢ, ܡܟܣܢܐ, ܡܟܣܢܝܬܐ rt. ܟܣ. *a reprover, rebuker, chider, confuter;* ܐܬܢܐ ܡܟܣܢܝܬܐ *the ass which reproved* Balaam.

ܡܟܣܢܐܝܬ rt. ܟܣ. adv. *reprovingly, with blame.*

ܡܟܣܢܘܬܐ or ܡܟܣܬܐ rt. ܟܣ. *reproof, admonition, refutation, confutation;* ܡܟܣܢܘܬܐ ܕܬܐܪܬܐ *the rebukes of conscience;* ܡܐܡܪܐ ܕܡܟܣܢܘܬܐ *an admonitory discourse, admonition;* ܥܒܕ ܠܘܩܒܠܗܘܢ ܡܟܣܢܘܬܐ *he issued an admonition against them.*

ܡܟܣܘܬܐ from ܡܟܣܐ. f. *the collecting* or *farming of tolls and taxes; the office of a collector* or *publican.*

ܡܟܣܪܐ m. = ܡܟܣܪܐ *a dam.*

ܡܟܣܪܝܡ *a large dish.*

ܡܟܦܪܢܐ rt. ܟܦܪ I. *a*) *one who wipes away, cleanses, effaces.* *b*) *a napkin.* *c*) *Antidoron.*

ܡܟܦܪܢܐ rt. ܟܦܪ II. *one who compels to apostatize.*

ܡܟܪ fut. ܢܡܟܘܪ, act. part. ܡܟܪ, pass. part. ܡܟܝܪ, ܐ, ܬܐ. *a*) root-meaning *to barter* hence *to betroth, espouse* often with ܐܢܬܬܐ; ܕܢܡܟܘܪ ܒܪܬܗ *to ask for his daughter in marriage;* ܡܫܝܚܐ ܒܕܡܗ ܡܟܪ ܠܗ Christ *by His blood bought* the Church *to be His bride;* pass. part. *a wooer, suitor; the betrothed, spouse, bride, bridegroom;* ܝܘܣܦ ܡܟܝܪܗ ܕܡܪܝܡ *Joseph the suitor of Mary;* ܥܕܬܐ ܡܟܝܪܬܗ ܕܡܫܝܚܐ *the Church the betrothed of Christ.* *b*) *to spring* or *split open* as the earth, *to let a spring gush forth.* Ethpe. ܐܬܡܟܪ and Ethpa. ܐܬܡܟܪ *to be betrothed;* metaph. ܢܦܫܐ ܕܙܕܝܩܐ ܡܬܡܟܪܐ ܠܐܠܗܐ the soul *of the righteous is promised to God.* Aph. ܐܡܟܪ *to betroth, promise* or *give in marriage.* Ettaph. ܐܬܬܡܟܪ pass. of Aphel. Derivatives, ܡܟܘܪܐ, ܡܟܘܪܐ, ܡܟܝܪܘܬܐ, ܡܟܝܪܬܐ, ܡܡܟܪܢܐ, ܡܬܡܟܪܢܐ.

ܡܟܪܐ, ܡܟܪܐ or ܡܟܪܐ m. *minium, red pigment;* ܡܟܪܐ ܕܢܓܪܐ *carpenter's vermilion.*

ܡܟܪܐ rt. ܟܪܐ. m. *a flagon with a small mouth.*

ܡܟܪܗܘܬܐ rt. ܟܪܗ. f. *morbidness, unhealthiness; morbid disposition.*

ܡܟܪܝܢܐ or ܡܟܪܝܢܐ rt. ܟܪܗ. *noxious, lethal.*

ܡܟܪܟܘܬܐ pl. ܡܟܪܟܘܢܝܬܐ rt. ܟܪܟ. f. *winding, turning; a crooked path.*

ܡܟܪܙܐܝܬ rt. ܟܪܙ. *publicly.*

ܡܟܪܙܢܐ pl. ܢ̈ܐ rt. ܟܪܙ. m. *a preacher, reciter of prayers* in a mosque, &c., ܡܟܪܙܢܐ ܕܐܘܢܓܠܝܘܢ *preachers of the Gospel;* ܡܟܪܙܢܐ ܕܟܐܢܘܬܐ *a herald of righteousness.*

ܡܟܪܙܢܘܬܐ rt. ܟܪܙ. f. *preaching, proclamation.*

ܡܟܪܝܘܬܐ rt. ܟܪܐ. f. *imperfection.*

ܡܟܪܬܐ f. *a burden to be carried on the back, a knapsack.* Cf. ܟܪܬܐ.

ܡܟܫܫ Aphel act. part. of ܟܫ.

ܡܟܫܘܠܐ pl. ܠ̈ܐ rt. ܟܫܠ. m. *a stumbling-block, offence, scandal, scruple, a cause of offence, occasion of stumbling;* ܠܐ ܡܫܬܠܡܝܢ ܡܟܫܘܠܐ ܡܢ ܥܠܡܐ *offences will never be wanting in the world.*

ܡܟܫܠܐ rt. ܟܫܠ. m. *a stumbling-block, offence.*

ܡܟܫܠܢܘܬܐ rt. ܟܫܠ. f. *an offence, scandal;* ܕܡܟܫܠܢܘܬܐ *scandalous.*

ܡܟܫܟܫܬܐ pl. ܫ̈ܬܐ rt. ܟܫ. f. *a fly-flap.*

ܡܟܫܫܬܐ pl. ܡܟܫܫܝܬܐ rt. ܟܫ. f. *a fly-flap, small fan.*

ܡܟܬܒ, ܡܟܬܒܐ rt. ܟܬܒ. m. *a) a writing, written narrative;* ܡܟܬܒ ܙܒܢܐ *annals, a chronicle. b) a writing-style, punch, gimlet.*

ܡܟܬܒܢܐ pl. ܢ̈ܐ rt. ܟܬܒ. m. *a writer, composer, author, compiler; a notary;* ܡܟܬܒܢܐ ܕܙܒ̈ܢܐ *a chronicler, historian.*

ܡܟܬܒܢܘܬܐ pl. ܘ̈ܬܐ rt. ܟܬܒ. f. *a writing, description, narration; a book, record, chronicle, register, account; a deed, act, contract;* ܡܟܬܒܢܘܬܐ ܐܘܢܓܠܝܬܐ *the Gospel records;* ܡܟܬܒܢܘܬܐ ܕܦܠܓܘܬ ܐܪܥܐ or ܕܐܬܪ̈ܘܬܐ *a geography-book.*

ܡܟܬܡܘܬܐ rt. ܟܬܡ. f. *defilement, uncleanness.*

ܡܟܬܡܢܐ, ܢ̈ܬܐ rt. ܟܬܡ. *defiling, polluting.*

ܡܟܬܪܘܬܐ rt. ܟܬܪ. f. *continuance;* with ܠܐ *instability.*

ܡܟܬܪܢܐ, ܢܬܐ rt. ܟܬܪ. *abiding, lasting, stable, permanent, enduring, unmoved; slow, tardy;* ܠܐ ܡܟܬܪܢܝܬܐ *unabiding, unstable things;* ܙܘܥܐ ܡܟܬܪܢܐ *tardy motion.*

ܡܟܬܪܢܐܝܬ rt. ܟܬܪ. adv. *permanently.*

ܡܟܬܪܢܘܬܐ rt. ܟܬܪ. f. *abiding, stability, permanence, duration;* with ܠܐ *transitoriness;* ܒܡܟܬܪܢܘܬܐ ܠܐ ܡܫܬܪܝܢܝܬܐ laid up with God *in steadfast continuance.*

ܡܟܬܫܐ pl. ܫ̈ܐ rt. ܟܬܫ. m. *contention, strife, trouble, turbulence, conflict;* ܡܟܬܫܐ ܕܪ̈ܫܝܥܐ *the turbulence of the impious;* ܡܟܬܫܐ ܕܠܒܗ *the trouble of his heart, his own inner strife.*

ܡܠܠ Pe. only part. adj. ܡܠܝܠ, ܡܠܝܠܐ, ܡܠܝܠܬܐ *a) endowed with speech and reason, articulate, rational, reasonable,* with ܠܐ *inarticulate, dumb, irrational;* ܢܦܫܐ ܡܠܝܠܬܐ *the rational soul;* ܒܪ̈ܝܬܐ ܡܠܝܠܬܐ *rational creatures* opp. ܠܐ ܡܠܝ̈ܠܐ *dumb animals;* ܡܕܥܐ ܡܠܝܠܐ *a mind endowed with reason;* ܡܒܘ̈ܥܐ ܡܠܝ̈ܠܐ *founts of reason* i. e. of doctrine. *b) eloquent, a rhetorician, dialectician, logician;* ܡܠܝܠܘܬܐ *logic;* ܡܟܬܒܢܘܬܐ ܕܡܠܝܠܘܬܐ *a treatise on logic.* Pael ܡܠܠ *a) to speak, say, recite;* with ܥܡ or ܠܘܬ *to talk;* ܚܝ̈ܘܬܐ ܕܠܐ ܡܡܠܠܢ *dumb animals;* ܡܠܠ ܥܠ ܟܣܐ *he said the words* of consecration *over the chalice. b) to utter a sound, sound, creak;* ܡܠܠ ܪ̈ܥܡܐ *the thunder muttered. c)* the act. part. ܡܡܠܠ answers to -λόγος in compounds; ܡܡܠܠ ܥܠ ܐܠܗܐ or ܐܠܗܘܬܐ *a theologian;* ܡܡܠܠܝ ܟܘ̈ܟܒܐ—ܟܝ̈ܢܝܬܐ *astrologers, physiologists;* ܢܫ̈ܐ ܡܡܠܠܢ ܡܢ ܟܪܣܐ *female ventriloquists.* Ethpa. ܐܬܡܠܠ *to be spoken, said, told; to be accused;* sometimes perhaps active *to speak* with ܥܡ; part. with negative ܠܐ ܡܬܡܠܠܢܐ *ineffable, unspeakable;* ܡܢܝܢܐ ܕܠܐ ܡܬܡܠܠ *an untold quantity.* Derivatives, ܡܠܐ ܡܠܬܐ, ܡܡܠܠܐ, ܡܡܠܠܢܐ, ܡܠܘܠܐ, ܡܠܘܠܘܬܐ, ܡܠܝܠܐ, ܡܠܝܠܐܝܬ, ܡܠܝܠܘܬܐ, ܡܡܠܠܐ, ܡܡܠܠܢܐ, ܡܡܠܠܢܘܬܐ, ܡܬܡܠܠܢܐ, ܡܡܠܠܢܝܐ, ܡܬܡܠܠܢܘܬܐ, ܡܬܡܠܠܢܐܝܬ, ܡܬܡܠܠܢܘܬܐ.

ܡܠܐ fut. ܢܡܠܐ, act. part. ܡܠܐ, ܡܠܝܐ, ܡܠܝܐ, pass. part. ܡܠܐ, ܡܠܝܐ, ܡܠܝܬܐ. *to fill, replenish; to complete, conclude; to be full, satisfied; to be enough, be able;* ܠܟܠ ܡܠܐ ܐܠܗܐ God *fills the universe;* ܠܐ ܡܠܝܐ ܐܕܢܐ ܠܡܫܡܥ *the ear is not satisfied with hearing.* Special meanings: with ܒ

to fill the hand with gifts, *to consecrate;* with ܙܰܒ݂ܢܳܐ *to complete a time;* ܟܰܕ ܡܠܰܘ ܠܗܽܘܢ ܬܡܳܢܝܳܐ ܝܰܘܡܺܝܢ *when eight days were completed;* ܡܠܰܘ ܝܰܘܡܰܝܢ *our days are ended;* with ܠܶܒܳܐ *to comfort, console;* with ܡܰܝܳܐ *to draw water;* with ܡܳܐܢܶܐ *to patch clothes;* with ܩܶܫܬܳܐ *to draw a bow;* ܡܠܳܐ ܠܩܶܫܬܶܗ ܓܶܐܪܳܐ *he fitted an arrow to the bow.* Pass. part. *filled, full, complete;* ܗܘܳܐ ܡܠܶܐ ܪܽܘܚܳܐ *he was filled with the Spirit;* ܫܶܒܠܶܐ ܡܠܶܐ ܦܶܐܪܳܐ *full ears of corn;* ܡܠܶܐ ܫܢܰܝܳܐ *full of years, advanced in years;* ܡܰܠܝܳܐ ܦܽܘܪܫܢܶܐ *manifold, manysided;* ܩܶܫܬܳܐ ܡܠܝܬܳܐ *a drawn bow;* in comp. *full;* ܡܠܶܐ ܒܰܝܬܳܐ *a houseful;* ܡܠܶܐ ܐܺܝܕܳܐ, ܚܽܘܦܢܳܐ or ܚܰܦܢܳܐ *a handful;* ܡܠܶܐ ܟܳܣܳܐ *a cupful;* ܡܠܶܐ ܦܽܘܡܳܐ *a mouthful;* with nouns of time and space expresses *limitation;* ܡܠܶܐ ܐܰܚܕܳܐ *a short time, little while;* ܕܡܠܶܐ ܐܰܚܕܳܐ or ܒ *for a while, temporary, temporal;* ܪܳܚܡܽܘܬܳܐ ܕܡܠܶܐ ܐܰܚܕܳܐ ܐܝܬܶܝܗ *short-lived friendship;* ܒܽܘܣܳܡܶܐ ܕܡܠܶܐ ܐܰܚܕܳܐ *temporal enjoyments;* ܡܠܶܐ ܐܰܡܬܳܐ *a cubit long;* ܡܠܶܐ ܙܰܪܬܳܐ *a span wide, narrow;* ܡܠܶܐ ܝܰܘܡܳܐ *the space of a day;* ܡܠܶܐ ܠܠܝܳܐ *one night;* ܡܠܶܐ ܪܶܦܦܳܐ *a minute's space;* ܒܡܠܶܐ ܪܶܦܦܳܐ *suddenly;* ܡܠܶܐ ܡܰܪܦܳܐ ܕܥܰܝܢܳܐ *in the twinkling of an eye;* ܡܠܶܐ ܫܳܥܬܳܐ or ܫܳܥܳܐ *a short time;* ܡܠܶܐ ܫܳܥܳܐ *for an hour, for a time.* Ethpe. ܐܶܬܡܠܺܝ *a) to be filled,* with ܚܰܕܽܘܬܳܐ *with joy;* with ܪܽܘܚܳܐ *with the Spirit;* with ܠܶܒܳܐ *to be encouraged. b) to be provided, completed, finished;* ܗܳܠܶܝܢ ܨܒ݂ܘܳܬ݂ܳܐ ܠܽܘܩܕܰܡ ܢܶܬ݂ܡܰܠܝܳܢ *these affairs must first be completed;* ܐܶܬ݂ܡܠܺܝ ܚܽܘܠܳܦܳܐ *the exchange* of prisoners *was accomplished.* Pael ܡܰܠܺܝ *a) to fill up, fulfil, complete, sate, supply, satisfy;* ܣܽܘܢܩܳܢܳܐ *a need;* ܣܽܘܢܩܳܢܶܐ *wants;* ܫܶܐܠܬܳܐ *a request;* with ܕܽܘܟܬܳܐ *to supply the place* of, but cf. *b;* with ܫܰܢܬܳܐ *to take a whole year. b) to fill* an office, ministry, position. *c) to consecrate* a bishop, cf. Peal with ܐܺܝܕܳܐ. Ethpa. ܐܶܬ݂ܡܰܠܺܝ *to be completely filled, quite full, fulfilled;* ܕܢܶܬ݂ܡܰܠܶܐ ܡܶܕܶܡ ܕܶܐܬ݂ܶܐܡܰܪ ܒܝܰܕ ܢܒ݂ܺܝܳܐ *that it might be fulfilled which was spoken by the prophet.* Aph. ܐܰܡܠܺܝ *to fill up;* act. part. ܡܰܡܠܶܐ ܠܶܒܳܐ *consolation,* cf. Peal. Shaphel ܫܰܡܠܺܝ *to do thoroughly* or *completely, to accomplish, perfect, make an end, finish, perform; to fulfil* a promise; *to offer* sacrifice; *to celebrate* a feast; *to get perfect* = *learn by heart;* with ܒܳܬ݂ܰܪ ܡܳܪܝܳܐ *to wholly follow the Lord;* with ܐܺܝܕܳܐ *to consecrate* to office; eccles. *to perform* divine service, *celebrate* the Eucharist, *to confirm* the consecration of a bishop, *to ordain.* Pass. part. ܡܫܰܡܠܰܝ, ܡܫܰܡܠܝܳܐ, ܡܫܰܡܠܰܝܬܳܐ. *full, whole, entire; perfect, complete; of full growth, adult;* ܩܽܘܡܬܳܐ ܡܫܰܡܠܰܝܬܳܐ *full growth* = the age of twenty-five years; ܫܰܢܬܳܐ ܡܫܰܡܠܰܝܬܳܐ *a full year;* gram. ܫܡܳܐ ܡܫܰܡܠܝܳܐ *a completed noun* i. e. one ending in ܐ. Eshtaph. ܐܶܫܬܰܡܠܺܝ *a) to be entirely given over, to be initiated* with ܒ *to* or *in* the rites of Baal-Peor (Num. xxv. 3–5). *b) to be fully formed* or *grown, to become perfect; to be fulfilled; to be made perfect* through martyrdom, *to be at an end* esp. of life; *to be concluded* as peace; *to be celebrated* as a feast; eccles. *to be perfected* in baptism or by receiving chrism after baptism; *to be confirmed* as a bishop by the patriarch or metropolitan after he has been consecrated; generally *to be consummated.* Derivatives, ܡܰܠܝܳܐ, ܡܶܠܬܳܐ, ܡܠܳܠܳܐ, ܡܰܠܳܐ, ܡܰܠܳܝܳܐ, ܡܰܠܳܝܬܳܐ, ܡܠܳܘܳܐ, ܡܰܠܘܳܐ, ܡܰܠܘܳܝܳܐ, ܡܰܠܘܳܝܬܳܐ and ܡܰܠܰܝܳܐ, ܡܰܠܝܳܐ, ܡܶܠܝܳܐ, ܡܰܠܝܳܢܳܐ, ܡܰܠܝܽܘܬܳܐ, ܡܰܡܠܝܳܐ, ܡܰܡܠܝܳܢܳܐ, ܡܰܠܝܳܢܽܘܬܳܐ, ܡܶܠܝܽܘܬܳܐ, ܡܫܰܡܠܝܳܢܳܐ, ܡܫܰܡܠܝܳܢܳܐܝܬ݂, ܡܫܰܡܠܝܳܢܽܘܬܳܐ, ܫܽܘܡܠܳܝܳܐ, ܡܶܫܬܰܡܠܝܳܢܳܐ, ܡܶܫܬܰܡܠܝܳܢܽܘܬܳܐ, ܡܶܫܬܰܡܠܝܳܢܳܐܝܬ݂, ܡܶܫܬܰܡܠܝܳܢܳܐ, ܡܶܫܬܰܡܠܝܳܢܽܘܬܳܐ.

ܡܠܶܐ rt. ܡܠܐ. verbal adj. *full;* used occasionally in compounds instead of the pass. part. cf. above ܡܠܶܐ ܐܰܚܕܳܐ = ܡܠܶܐ ܐܰܚܕܳܐ—ܪܶܦܦܳܐ—ܡܰܪܦܳܐ &c. *a little while;* ܡܠܶܐ ܥܽܘܒܳܐ *a lapful;* ܡܠܶܐ ܩܰܥܒܳܐ *a bowlful;* ܡܠܶܐ ܦܽܘܡ ܡܶܠܶܐ *wordy, verbose.*

ܡܶܠܬܳܐ, ܡܶܠܰܝ pl. ܡܶܠܶܐ, ܡܶܠܺܝܢ rt. ܡܠܠ. f. (cf. *b*) *a) a word, saying, sentence, precept, command;* ܩܳܠܳܐ ܚܰܝܳܐ *the living* or *spoken voice* but ܡܶܠܶܐ ܚܰܝܳܬܳܐ *the living words* of Holy Scripture; ܡܶܠܬܳܐ ܕܟܬ݂ܳܒ݂ܳܐ *the text of Scripture;* ܡܶܠܬܳܐ ܕܦܽܘܩܕܳܢܳܐ *a command.* With verbs: with ܒܥܳܐ, ܫܰܝܢܳܐ or ܫܠܳܡܳܐ *to desire an agreement* or *treaty;* ܫܰܕܰܪܘ ܡܶܠܬܳܐ ܥܰܠ ܢܰܦܫܗܽܘܢ the besieged *sent to make terms for his life;* with ܗܦܰܟ *he went back on his word, broke his promise;* with ܝܰܗ݈ܒ *to give one's word, promise, answer;* with ܫܘܳܐ, ܦܣܰܩ, ܢܣܰܒ *to consent, agree, make a compact;* with ܦܣܰܩ *to cut one's words short;* ܫܘܶܐ ܠܡܶܥܒ݂ܕܳܐ ܥܽܘܗܕܳܢܳܐ *worthy of mention;* ܥܽܘܗܕܳܢܳܐ

or ܠܥܠ ܡܢ ܡܠܬܐ *ineffable.* b) m. *the Logos;* ܡܠܬܐ ܕܡܪܝܐ *the Word of the Lord;* ܡܠܬܐ ܝܚܝܕܝܬܐ ܕܐܠܗܐ *the Only-begotten Word of God.* c) *the faculty of speech or thought, reason, energy of mind;* ܚܝܘܬܐ ܕܠܐ ܡܠܬܐ *dumb animals* but ܕܠܐ ܡܠܬܐ *a bad speaker.* d) *a thing, affair; a cause, reason,* ܒܡܠܬܗ *on his account;* ܒܟܠ ܡܠܝܢ *in all things;* ܡܠܬܐ ܙܥܘܪܬܐ *a small matter, trifling affair;* ܐܝܟ ܡܠܬܗܘܢ *according to their argument, as they reason;* ܡܠܬܐ ܕܚܟܝܡܘܬܐ *a wise reason;* with ܥܒܕ *to take into account, mention, speak about.* e) *a discourse, tract; a definition.* f) gram. *verb, voice;* ܡܠܬܐ ܥܒܘܕܬܐ—ܚܫܘܫܬܐ *the active, the passive voice;* ܡܠܬܐ ܦܘܩܕܢܝܬܐ *the imperative;* ܫܡܐ ܡܠܬܐ *a participle, adjective;* ܠܘܬ ܡܠܬܐ *an adverb.*

ܡܠܛܐ or ܡܠܛܐ, ܡܠܛܐ or ܡܠܛܝܬܐ rt. ܡܠܐ. m. *the first milk after delivery.*

ܡܠܐܐ or ܡܠܐܐ Aphel part. of ܠܐܐ *to weary.*

ܡܠܘܐ or ܡܠܘܬܐ rt. ܡܠܐ. m. *fullness;* ܬܒܝܠ ܘܡܠܘܗ *the whole inhabited earth;* ܝܡܐ ܒܡܠܘܗ *the sea with the fullness thereof;* ܡܠܘܐ ܕܥܡܘܪܝܗ *the multitude of its inhabitants;* ܥܕܬܐ ܒܡܠܘܗ *the crowded church;* ܡܬܚ ܩܫܬܗ ܒܡܠܘܗ *he drew his bow to the full.*

ܡܠܘܐ or ܡܠܘܬܐ rt. ܡܠܐ. m. *an overflow, pool, flood, inundation;* ܡܠܘܐ ܕܕܡܗ *the flow of her blood;* ܢܣܝܘܢܐ ܡܬܚܝܠܝܢ ܐܝܟ ܡܠܘܐ ܕܡܝܐ *temptations gain in strength like a water-flood.*

ܡܠܐܟܘܬܐ Ar. f. *the angelic host.*

ܡܠܐܟܐ, ܡܠܐܟ pl. ܝܢ, ܐ rt. ܠܐܟ. m. *a messenger* esp. *a messenger of God, an angel;* ܪܫ or ܪܒ ܡܠܐܟܐ *an archangel.*

ܡܠܐܟܐܝܬ rt. ܠܐܟ. adv. *angelically.*

ܡܠܐܟܘܬܐ rt. ܠܐܟ. f. *an embassy, mission, message.*

ܡܠܐܟܝܐ, ܡܠܐܟܝܬܐ, ܡܠܐܟܝܐ rt. ܠܐܟ. adj. *angelic;* ܕܡܘܬܐ ܡܠܐܟܝܬܐ *the likeness of an angel.*

ܡܠܐܦܐ, ܡܠܐܦܬܐ; see ܡܠܘܦܐ.

ܡܠܐܩܝܐ m. τὰ μαλάκια, *molluscs.*

ܡܠܒܐ m. *a kind of perfume; the crocus.*

ܡܠܒܒܢܐ, ܢܝܬܐ from ܠܒܒ *exhorting, encouraging; an encourager, instigator;* ܡܠܬܐ ܡܠܒܒܢܝܬܐ *a word of exhortation.*

ܡܠܒܒܢܘܬܐ from ܠܒܒ f. *exhortation, consolation.*

ܡܠܒܟܢܐ, ܢܝܬܐ rt. ܠܒܟ. *hortatory, stimulating;* ܦܘܩܕܢܐ ܡܠܒܟܢܐ ܘܡܟܠܝܢܐ *positive and negative commandments.*

ܡܠܒܟܢܘܬܐ rt. ܠܒܟ. f. *instigation, incitement, exhortation.*

ܡܠܒܟܐ rt. ܠܒܟ. m. *a handle, haft, hilt.*

ܡܠܒܢܐ; see ܠܒܢܐ. m. *a mould for brick-making, a brick-kiln.*

ܡܠܓ fut. ܢܡܠܘܓ and ܢܡܠܓ, act. part. ܡܠܓ, pass. part. ܡܠܝܓ, ܡܠܝܓܐ, ܡܠܝܓܐ. *to rub* ܫܒܠܐ *ears of corn* in the hands; *to pluck out* hairs or feathers; ܡܠܝܓܐ ܘܡܥܩܪܐ *plucked up and rooted out;* ܥܡܐ ܡܠܝܓܐ ܘܡܚܝܠܐ *a despoiled and weak nation.* DERIVATIVE, ܡܠܓܐ.

ܡܠܓܐ rt. ܡܠܓ. m. *plucking, plucked-out feathers;* ܥܒܝܫ ܡܠܓܗ *thickly feathered.*

ܡܠܓܡܐ pl. ܐ or ܡܠܓܡܛܐ m. μάλαγμα, *salve, soothing ointment.*

ܡܠܗܝܢܐ pl. ܐ and ܡܠܗܝܢܐ rt. ܠܗܐ. *a bore, wearisome person.*

ܡܠܗܝܘܬܐ rt. ܠܗܐ. f. *consternation.*

ܡܠܘܐ, ܡܠܘܐ, ܡܠܘܬܐ or ܡܠܘܐ pl. ܐ rt. ܡܠܐ. m. *fullness, abundance, quantity, volume, amount, sum, sum total; gain, profit; matter, material; occasion* for thought or speech; *matter, secretion;* ܝܡܐ ܡܢ ܢܗܪܘܬܐ ܡܩܒܠ ܡܠܘܐ *the sea gets its fullness from the rivers;* ܢܣܒܘ ܡܠܘܐ ܕܠܐ ܡܢܝܢ *they seized countless money;* ܡܠܘܐ ܕܐܠܦܐ *the cargo of a ship;* ܡܠܘܐ ܕܥܘܬܪܐ *riches;* ܕܢܥܒܕ ܡܠܘܐ ܒܬܐܓܘܪܬܗ *that he may make profits by his trading;* ܡܠܘܐ ܕܠܐ ܕܡܘܬ *formless matter; the material part* of the sacraments; ܒܝܕ ܡܠܘܐ ܦܓܪܢܝܐ the Eucharist is offered *through bodily material.*

ܡܠܘܚܐ or ܡܠܘܚ rt. ܡܠܚ. *sea-purslane, atriplex halimus.*

ܡܠܘܝܢܐ rt. ܠܘܐ. m. *a companion, guide, follower; one who follows a corpse to the funeral.*

ܡܠܘܟܐ, ܡܠܘܟܬܐ rt. ܡܠܟ. *a counsellor, adviser.*

ܡܠܽܘܟܽܘܬܳܐ rt. ܡܠܟ. f. *counsel.*

ܡܠܽܘܟܺܝܳܐ f. *μαλάχη, malva, althea, the mallow.*

ܡܳܠܠܽܘܢ, ܡܳܠܽܘܢ, ܡܳܠܰܠܽܘܢ rarely ܡܰܠܠܽܘܢ, *μᾶλλον, rather, the rather, more;* ܟܡܳܐ ܡܳܠܽܘܢ *how much more;* ܐܶܠܳܐ ܗ̄ܘ ܡܳܠܽܘܢ *but the rather;* ܡܳܠܠܽܘܢ ܐܶܡ *or rather.*

ܡܠܰܚܟܽܘܬܳܐ rt. ܠܚܟ. f. *licking, licking up.*

ܡܰܠܘܳܫܳܐ or ܡܰܠܘܳܫܳܐ pl. ܶܐ m. *a sign of the Zodiac;* ܡܰܠܘܳܫܳܐ ܕܐܶܡܪܳܐ—ܕܕܶܟܪܳܐ *the sign Aries, the ram; a natal star;* ܚܙܝ ܠܡܰܠܘܳܫܳܟ *regard the star under which you were born;* ܡܰܠܘܳܫܶܐ ܕܪܳܕܽܘܬܳܐ *the stars* or *zodiacal signs which have influence over mankind.*

ܡܰܠܘܳܫܳܝܳܐ, ܝܬܳܐ from ܡܰܠܘܳܫܳܐ *zodiacal, pertaining to the heavenly bodies;* ܓܰܕܳܐ ܡܰܠܘܳܫܳܝܳܐ *fortune according to the stars, horoscopic lot.*

ܡܠܰܘܳܐ, ܡܠܰܘܬܳܐ, ܡܠܰܘܝܳܬܳܐ Aphel pass. part. of ܠܘܳܐ. *joined, united.*

ܡܰܠܘܳܬܳܐ *a*) rt. ܡܠܐ. f. *a place for getting water.* *b*) pl. ܘܳܬܳܐ f. *a pear.*

ܡܠܰܘܝܳܐܺܝܬ or ܡܠܰܘܝܳܬܳܐܺܝܬ from ܠܘܳܐ. adv. *conjoinedly, together; in order.*

ܡܠܰܘܝܽܘܬܳܐ E-Syr. ܡܠܰܘܳܝܽܘܬܳܐ or ܡܰܠܘܳܐ from ܠܘܳܐ f. *conjunction, aggregation;* gram. *annexion* of two nouns, the first being in the constr. state; *the being affixed* as an enclitic.

ܡܰܠܝܳܢܳܐ, ܢܺܝܬܳܐ rt. ܠܐܐ. *importunate, tiresome, impertinent, foolish, distressing.*

ܡܰܠܝܳܢܽܘܬܳܐ rt. ܠܐܐ. *troublesomeness, annoyance.*

ܡܠܰܚ fut. ܢܶܡܠܽܘܚ, act. part. ܡܳܠܰܚ, ܡܳܠܚܳܐ, ܡܳܠܚܳܢܳܐ, pass. part. ܡܠܺܝܚ, ܡܠܺܝܚܳܐ, ܡܠܺܝܚܬܳܐ. *to be salt, to salt, season with salt, to sprinkle;* ܡܠܽܘܚ ܐܶܢܽܘܢ ܒܥܰܦܪܳܐ *sprinkle them with dust;* pass. part. *salt, nitrous.* Ethpe. ܐܶܬ݂ܡܠܶܚ *to be salted, sprinkled with salt; to sprinkle oneself; to eat salt* with ܥܰܡ. Pa. ܡܰܠܰܚ *a*) *to salt, season,* ܒܡܶܠܚܳܐ *with salt.* *b*) with ܐܶܠܦܳܐ *to steer;* metaph. *to govern, direct.* Ethpa. ܐܶܬ݂ܡܰܠܰܚ *a*) *to be seasoned with salt.* *b*) *to eat salt, be a companion, intimate* with ܥܰܡ. *c*) *to sail;* metaph. ܗܰܘܢܳܐ ܟܰܕ ܒܝܰܡܳܐ ܕܪܽܘܚܳܡܰܘܗܝ ܕܡܳܪܰܢ ܡܶܬ݂ܡܰܠܰܚ *the mind when it explores the sea of our Lord's tenderness.* Derivatives, ܡܶܠܚܳܐ, ܡܰܠܳܚܳܐ, ܡܠܳܚܳܐ, ܡܰܠܚܳܐ, ܡܰܡܠܚܳܢܳܐ, ܡܰܠܚܽܘܬܳܐ, ܡܰܠܚܬܳܐ, ܡܰܠܚܽܘܬܳܐ, ܡܶܬ݂ܡܰܠܚܳܢܳܐ, ܡܶܬ݂ܡܰܠܚܳܢܽܘܬܳܐ.

ܡܶܠܚܳܐ, ܡܶܠܚܳܐ pl. ܶܐ rt. ܡܠܚ. f. *salt;* ܩܝܳܡܳܐ ܕܡܶܠܚܳܐ *a covenant ratified with salt* i.e. not to be disannulled; ܡܶܠܚܳܐ ܕܐܰܪܥܳܐ *salt the symbol of the earth* i. e. one of the four elements.

ܡܰܠܳܚܳܐ pl. ܶܐ rt. ܡܠܚ. m. *a sailor, mariner, salt;* met. ܡܰܠܳܚܳܐ ܕܩܽܘܫܬܳܐ *the true pilot.*

ܡܰܠܚܳܐ *a winnowing-fan.*

ܡܰܠܚܽܘܬܳܐ rt. ܡܠܚ. f. *a*) *saltness, flavour of salt.* *b*) *steering, piloting, pilotage.*

ܡܠܰܚܟܽܘܬܳܐ rt. ܠܚܟ. f. *licking.*

ܡܠܰܚܡܳܐܺܝܬ rt. ܠܚܡ. adv. *aptly, fittingly, with exactitude, conveniently.*

ܡܠܰܚܡܽܘܬܳܐ rt. ܠܚܡ. f. *fitness, adaptation, proportion, harmony, symmetry;* ܡܠܰܚܡܽܘܬܳܐ ܕܗܰܕܳܡܶܐ *proportion of the limbs;* ܡܠܰܚܡܽܘܬܳܐ ܕܟܝܳܢܳܐ *the harmony of nature;* ܡܠܰܚܡܽܘܬܳܐ ܕܬܰܫܥܝܳܬܳܐ *an arrangement* or *series of stories.*

ܡܰܠܚܡܳܢܳܐ, ܢܺܝܬܳܐ rt. ܠܚܡ. *an artificer, skilful workman; a locksmith.*

ܡܰܠܚܬܳܐ pl. ܡܰܠܚܳܬܳܐ rt. ܡܠܚ. f. *salt land, a salt-marsh, salt-pit, salt-pan.*

ܡܠܰܛ fut. ܢܶܡܠܽܘܛ, act. part. ܡܳܠܶܛ, pass. part. ܡܠܺܝܛ, ܡܠܺܝܛܳܐ, ܡܠܺܝܛܬܳܐ. *a*) *to smear, rub over.* *b*) *to clothe* or *cover oneself;* ܡܠܰܛ ܢܽܘܗܪܳܐ ܐܰܝܟ ܡܰܪܛܽܘܛܳܐ *He clothed Himself with light as with a garment.* *c*) *μελετᾶν, to mix oneself up with, trouble oneself about, busy oneself with, study, practise;* with ܡܩܰܕܰܡ *to consider beforehand;* ܡܠܺܝܛ ܒܣܽܘܥܪܳܢܶܐ *accustomed to affairs, businesslike, capable;* ܡܰܢ ܕܡܳܠܶܛ ܒܠܳܐ ܨܒ݂ܘܬܶܗ *a busybody.* Pass. part. *a*) *smeared* ܒܕܡܳܐ *with blood.* *b*) *practised, studious, capable;* ܡܠܺܝܛܳܐ ܣܰܓܺܝܐܳܬ݂ܳܐ *having studied much;* ܡܠܺܝܛܳܐ ܒܝܰܘܢܳܝܽܘܬܳܐ *having studied Greek, well versed in Greek;* ܒܽܘܨܳܝܳܐ ܕܰܗܘܰܘ ܡܠܺܝܛܺܝܢ *studious research, careful investigations.* Ethpe. ܐܶܬ݂ܡܠܶܛ and Ethpa. ܐܶܬ݂ܡܰܠܰܛ *to be smeared;* metaph. *to be tinged* with heretical speculations or *to be mixed up, occupied* with them. Derivatives, ܡܶܠܛܳܐ, ܡܰܠܛܳܐܺܝܬ, ܡܰܠܛܽܘܬܳܐ.

ܡܶܠܛܳܐ, ܡܶܠܛܳܐ rt. ܡܠܛ. m. *a*) *mortar, cement; bee-glue, a gummy substance with which bees close the crevices of their hive.* *b*) *attention, study.*

ܡܰܠܛܫܬܳܐ rt. ܠܛܫ. f. *a whetstone, grindstone.*

ܡܠܝܐ, ܡܠܝܐ rt. ܡܠܐ. m. *fullness, supply;* ܡܠܝܐ ܕܣܘܢܩܢܗ *the supply of his need;* ܢܚܠܐ ܕܡܠܝܢܘܗܝ *the torrent-beds when full;* cf. ܡܠܐܐ and ܡܠܐܬܐ.

ܡܠܝܐ rt. ܡܠܐ. m. *a seamster, mender, tailor.*

ܡܠܝܐܝܬ rt. ܡܠܐ. adv. *fully, completely, wholly.*

ܡܠܝܘܬܐ pl. ܬܐ̈ rt. ܡܠܐ. f. *fullness, abundance;* ܒܡܠܝܘܬܐ ܕܣܗܪܐ *at full moon;* ܡܠܝܘܬܐ ܕܦܓܪܐ *bodily repletion;* ܡܠܝܘܬܐ ܕܒܣܪܐ *obesity, corpulence.*

ܡܠܝܚܘܬܐ rt. ܡܠܚ. f. *saltness.*

ܡܠܝܛܐܝܬ rt. ܡܠܛ. adv. *busily, studiously.*

ܡܠܝܛܘܬܐ rt. ܡܠܛ. f. *capacity, study, acumen;* ܒܪ ܡܠܝܛܘܬܐ *a man of deep study.*

ܡܠܝܛܐ pl. ܢ̈ܐ rt. ܠܛ. *one who curses, pronounces maledictions.*

ܡܠܝܠ, ܠܐ, ܠܬܐ part. adj.; see ܡܠܠ.

ܡܠܝܠܐܝܬ rt. ܡܠܠ. adv. *rationally, eloquently, expressively, well* or *skilfully put.*

ܡܠܝܠܘܢܐ dim. of ܡܠܝܠܐ. m. *a contemptible speaker* or *rhetorician.*

ܡܠܝܠܘܬܐ rt. ܡܠܠ. f. *a) the faculty of speech* or *reason, reason, prudence;* ܕܠܐ ܡܠܝܠܘܬܐ *irrational, void of understanding. b) speech, pronunciation, eloquence. c) logic, dialectic.*

ܡܠܝܠܝܐ pl. ܝ̈ܐ rt. ܡܠܠ. m. *rational, according to reason, logical, skilled in arguing* or *in oratory;* ܛܘܟܣܐ ܡܠܝܠܝܐ *logical order.*

ܡܠܝܣܛܐ, E-Syr. ܡܠܣ, *μάλιστα, especially, chiefly.*

ܡܠܝܦܘܬܐ rt. ܠܦ. f. *joining together.*

ܡܠܝܪܐ m. *μιλιάριον, a cauldron.*

ܡܠܝܬܐ Ar. f. *a woman's headdress, a long piece of silk twisted twice round the head.*

ܡܠܝܬܐ rt. ܡܠܐ. f. *a patch;* ܡܠܝܬܐ ܚܕܬܐ *a patch of new stuff.*

ܡܠܟܠܟܢܐ, ܡܠܟܠܟܢܬܐ from ܟܠܟ. *annihilating.*

ܡܠܟ fut. ܢܡܠܘܟ, act. part. ܡܠܟ, ܡܠܟܐ, pass. part. ܡܠܝܟ, ܡܠܝܟܐ. I. *to counsel, advise, exhort;* ܡܠܟܐ ܬܪܝܨܬܐ ܡܠܟܐ *she gives right counsels;* ܡܠܟܝ̈ ܡܠܟܐ *counsellors;* ܡܠܟܗ ܒܝܫܐ *the Evil One instigated him.* II. *to promise, make a promise;* ܩܝܡܝ ܕܡܠܟܬ ܠܕܘܝܕ *My covenant which I promised to David;* ܡܪܢ ܡܠܟ ܗܘܐ ܠܗܘܢ ܕܡܢ ܕܡܟܫܠ *our Lord predicted a millstone for the neck of whoso should cause offence;* ܚܝܐ ܕܡܠܝܟܝܢ *the promised life, salvation.* III. *to reign.* ETHPE. ܐܬܡܠܟ I. *to take counsel, consult;* ܐܬܡܠܟ ܥܡܝ ܡܠܟܐ *the king consulted me.* II. *to be promised.* PA. ܡܠܟ I. *to give counsel.* II. *to promise.* III. *to set up as king, as khalif.* ETHPA. ܐܬܡܠܟ imper. E-Syr. same as pret.; W-Syr. ܐܬܡܠܟ *to take counsel, consult, hold a council;* ܐܢܫܝܢ ܕܡܬܡܠܟܝܢ ܫܠܡܐ *counsellors of peace.* APH. ܐܡܠܟ I. *to give counsel, counsel.* II. *a) to reign, rule, be king, begin to reign, come to the throne;* ܒܫܢܬܐ ܕܐܡܠܟ *in the year of his accession to the throne;* metaph. *to bear rule, bear sway, dominate, take possession of;* ܢܝܪܐ ܕܚܛܝܬܐ ܡܡܠܟܐ ܒܟܘܢ *the yoke of sin bears rule over you;* ܐܡܠܟ ܒܗ ܫܐܕܐ *a demon possessed her. b) to make king, crown king, elect as ruler;* ܐܬܘ ܠܡܡܠܟܘܬܗ *they came to make him king.* ETHTAPH. ܐܬܬܡܠܟ *a) to be made king;* ܐܬܬܡܠܟ ܒܬܪܗ ܒܪܗ *his son was made king after him. b) to be reigned over, be subject to rule* or *sway;* ܐܬܬܡܠܟܘ ܡܢ ܣܛܢܐ *they became subjects of Satan.* DERIVATIVES, ܡܠܟܐ, ܡܠܟ, ܡܠܟܘܬܐ, ܡܠܟܘܬܐ, ܡܠܟܘܬܐ, ܡܠܟܘܬܐ, ܡܠܟܐܝܬ, ܡܠܟܐܝܬ, ܡܠܟܐ, ܡܠܟܬܐ, ܡܠܟܐ, ܡܠܟܢܐ, ܡܠܟܢܐ, ܡܠܟܢܘܬܐ, ܡܠܟܢܐ, ܡܠܟܘܢܐ, ܡܬܡܠܟܢܘܬܐ, ܡܬܡܠܟܢܐ, ܡܬܡܠܟܢܘܬܐ.

ܡܠܟ, ܡܠܟܐ pl. ܡܠܟܝܢ, ܡܠܟܐ rt. ܡܠܟ III. m. *a king, ruler, emperor, khalif, prince, emir, toparch, &c.;* ܐܘܪܚܐ ܕܡܠܟܐ *the king's highway;* ܣܦܪ ܡܠܟܐ *the Book of Kings;* ܡܠܟ ܡܠܟܐ *king of kings,* a title of the kings of Babylonia and Persia. Metaph. ܫܡܫܐ ܘܣܗܪܐ ܡܠܟܝ ܫܢܬܐ *the sun and moon are rulers of the year;* ܦܘܩܕܢܐ ܩܕܡܝܐ ܡܠܟܐ ܕܟܠܗܘܢ ܦܘܩܕܢܐ *the first commandment is chief of all the commandments;* eccles. the East-Syrians call the special leaven used in making new Eucharistic bread, also the priest's loaf ܡܠܟܐ; ܚܘܕܬܐ ܡܠܟܐ *renewal of the malcha.*

ܡܠܟ, ܡܠܟܐ pl. ܟ̈ܐ rt. ܡܠܟ. m. *counsel, advice;* ܒܥܠ ܡܠܟܐ or ܡܠܟܢ *a counsellor, adviser;* ܒܢܝ ܡܠܟܗ ܕܡܠܟܐ *the king's counsellors.*

ܡܠܟܐܝܬ rt. ܡܠܟ. adv. *royally.*

ܡܠܟܐܝܬ rt. ܡܠܟ. adv. *prudently.*

ܡܠܟܘ, ܡܠܟܘܬܐ pl. ܡܠܟܘܬ, ܬܐ̈ rt. ܡܠܟ. f. *reign, rule, kingdom, royal dignity, majesty;*

ܒܫܢܬܐ ... ܕܡܠܟܘܬܗ *in the year . . . of his reign;* ܡܠܟܘܬܐ ܕܫܡܝܐ *the kingdom of heaven;* ܒܢܝ ܡܠܟܘܬܐ *the children of the kingdom;* as a title, ܡܠܟܘܬܟ *your majesty;* ܡܠܟܘܬܢ *we the king;* as an epithet, ܡܕܝܢܬܐ ܕܡܠܟܘܬܐ or ܡܕܝܢܬ ܡܠܟܘܬܐ *the royal city, the capital;* ܦܘܩܕܢܐ ܕܡܠܟܘܬܐ *a royal mandate;* pl. emph. *the Books of Kings;* ܣܦܪܐ ܩܕܡܝܐ ܕܡܠܟܘܬܐ *the First Book of Kings.*

ܡܠܟܘܢܐ dim. of ܡܠܟܐ. m. *a kinglet, princeling.*

ܡܠܟܘܬܢܝܐ pl. ܐ̈ـ rt. ܡܠܟ. *royal, pertaining to the kingdom.*

ܡܠܟܝܐ, ܐܝܬܐ rt. ܡܠܟ. *royal, regal, imperial;* ܢܚܬܐ ܡܠܟܝܐ *regal raiment;* ܐܘܪܚܐ ܡܠܟܝܬܐ *the king's highway.*

ܡܠܟܝܘܬܐ rt. ܡܠܟ. f. *imperial majesty.*

ܡܠܟܢܝܐ rt. ܡܠܟ. adj. *of counsel, persuasive.*

ܡܠܟܬܐ pl. ܡܠܟܢ, ܡܠܟܬܐ rt. ܡܠܟ. f. *a queen, empress, princess;* ܡܠܟܬ ܫܒܐ *the Queen of Shebà;* used metaph. of cities, ܡܠܟܬܐ ܕܡܕܝܢ̈ܬܐ *the queen of cities* i. e. Baghdad; ܪܗܘܡܐ ܡܠܟܬܐ *imperial Rome.*

ܡܠܟܬܘܢܝܬܐ pl. ܝ̈ܬܐ dim. of ܡܠܟܬܐ. f. *a little queen.*

ܡܠܟܬܘܢܝܬܐ pl. ܝ̈ܬܐ the same.

ܡܰܠܶܠ Pael of ܡܠܠ.

ܡܠܝܠܐ; ܡܠܝܠܐ pl. ܐ̈ـ, ܐ̈ܬܐ rt. ܡܠܠ. *endowed with the power of speech, full of talk, talkative, eloquent, garrulous;* with ܠܐ *mute, speechless;* ܡܠܝܠܐ *endowed with speech,* opp. ܡܠܝܠܐ *endowed with reason;* ܡܠܝܠܘܬܐ ܡܘܗܒܬܐ *the gift of speech, faculty of speaking.*

ܡܠܝܠܐܝܬ; see ܡܠܝܠܐ.

ܡܠܝܠܘܬܐ rt. ܡܠܠ. f. *talkativeness, loquacity.*

ܡܠܝܠܝܐ, ܝܬܐ rt. ܡܠܠ. *endowed with speech, rational.*

ܡܠܝܠܘܬܐ rt. ܡܠܠ. f. *utterance.*

ܡܠܟܡܘܬܐ rt. ܠܟܡ. f. *symmetry;* with ܠܐ *ungainliness.*

ܡܠܣܛܝܐ pl. ܐ̈ـ part. of denom. verb ܠܣܛܐ, m. *a robber, freebooter, brigand.*

ܡܠܣܛܢܘܬܐ from the above. f. *robbery, brigandage;* ܡܠܣܛܢܘܬܐ ܐܘܪܚܬܐ *highway robbery.*

ܡܠܚܠܐ or ܡܠܚܠܐ pl. ܐ̈ـ m. *white spots on the eyes.*

ܡܠܥܘܣܐ pl. ܐ̈ـ rt. ܠܥܣ. m. *a) eating, nourishment, food, victuals. b) saffron dye.*

ܡܠܥܣܬܐ rt. ܠܥܣ. f. *food, eating.*

ܡܠܦ infin. of verb ܐܠܦ; ܡܠܦ, ܡܠܦ, Pael parts. of verb ܐܠܦ.

ܡܠܦܘܢܐ or ܡܠܦܦܘܢܐ pl. ܐ̈ـ μηλοπέπων, *a kind of melon shaped like an apple.*

ܡܠܦܢ, ܡܠܦܢܐ, ܡܠܦܢܝܬܐ rt. ܐܠܦ. *apt to teach, learned, a teacher, master, schoolmaster, doctor;* given as a title to many of the Fathers esp. to St. Ephrem Syrus ܡܠܦܢܐ ܪܒܐ *the Great Master,* and to St. James of Sarug ܡܠܦܢܐ ܬܒܝܠܝܐ *the Ecumenical Doctor* and ܡܠܦܢܐ ܐܠܗܝܐ *the divine Doctor.*

ܡܠܦܢܘܬܐ pl. ܘ̈ܬܐ rt. ܐܠܦ. f. *teaching, the office of a teacher; learning, scholarship; a doctrinal treatise, a homily.*

ܡܠܦܢܝܐ, ܝܬܐ rt. ܐܠܦ. *doctrinal; skilful.*

ܡܠܩܛܐ pl. ܐ̈ـ rt. ܠܩܛ. m. *tweezers, snuffers.*

ܡܠܫ = ܡܠܫ; fut. ܢܡܠܘܫ. *to peel, make smooth, pluck off* hair, feathers, &c. DERIVATIVES, the four following words—

ܡܠܝܫܐ rt. [illegible]. *peeled, bald.*

ܡܠܝܫܐ rt. ܡܠܫ. *hardworking, laborious.*

ܡܠܫܐ rt. ܡܠܫ. f. *a great brazen vessel for washing clothes.*

ܡܠܫܐ rt. ܡܠܫ. m. *baldness.*

ܡܠܬܐ emph. state of ܡܠܐ; see above.

ܡܠܬܢܝܐ rt. ܡܠܠ. gram. *verbal;* ܠܘܬ ܡܠܬܢܝܐ *adverbial.*

ܡܠܬܥܠܐܝܬ rt. ܬܥܠ. adv. *fraudulently, maliciously.*

ܡܬܥܠܘܬܐ rt. ܬܥܠ. *guile, villany, malice.*

ܡܬܛܪܢܘܬܐ rt. ܛܪܢ. f. *murmuring, detraction, disparagement.*

ܡܬܛܪܢܢܐ rt. ܛܪܢ. m. *a mutterer, disparager, traducer.*

ܡܠܬܢܝܐ rt. ܡܠܠ. *a) verbal, of words;* ܩܪܒܐ ܡܠܬܢܝܐ *a verbal war, war of words;* ܚܘܕܪ̈ܐ ܡܠܬܢ̈ܝܐ *verbal complications. b) verbose.*

ܡܡܪܩܘܬܐ rt. ܡܪܩ. f. *escape, deliverance.*

ܡܡܙܓܘܬܐ rt. ܡܙܓ. f. *a compound, mixture of equal proportions.*

ܡܡܪܩܘܬܐ rt. ܡܪܩ. f. *escape*.

ܡܡܕܥܢܐ, ܢܝܬܐ rt. ܡܕܥ. *informing* or *endowing with intelligence*.

ܡܡܕܪܘܬܐ rt. ܡܕܪ. f. *rottenness*.

ܡܡܘܠ, ܡܡܘܠܐ pl. ܐ̈ m. *a deluge, flood, cataclysm, tide*; ܡܡܘܠ ܡܛܪܐ *a flood of rain*; metaph. ܡܡܘܠܐ ܕܪܚܡܐ *a flood of pity*; ܡܡܘܠܐ ܕܪ̈ܓܝܓܬܐ *a whirlpool of lusts*; ܡܡܘܠܐ ܕܫܠܗܒܝܬܐ *a torrent of flame*.

ܡܡܘܢ, ܡܡܘܢܐ m. *μαμμωνᾶς*, *mammon, money, riches*; ܡܡܘܢ ܐܒܘܕܐ *perishing riches*.

ܡܡܙܓܐ pl. ܓ̈ܐ Pael part. pass. of ܡܙܓ = subst. m. *mingled wine and water, drink*.

ܡܡܙܓܐܝܬ rt. ܡܙܓ. adv. *temperately, proportionately*.

ܡܡܙܓܘܬܐ rt. ܡܙܓ. f. *mixing, blending, due proportion*; ܠܐ ܡܡܙܓܘܬܐ *non-confusion, non-commingling* of natures in Christ; ܡܡܙܓܘܬܐ ܐܒܝܒܝܬܐ—ܬܫܪܝܢܝܬܐ *the vernal, the autumnal equinox*.

ܡܡܚܘܬܐ rt. ܡܚܐ. f. *a blow, wound*.

ܡܡܚܝܢ, ܡܡܚܝܐ, ܡܡܚܝܬܐ; see Pael part. of ܡܚܐ.

ܡܡܛܪܘܬܐ rt. ܡܛܪ. f. *rain*.

ܡܡܛܪܢܐ rt. ܡܛܪ. *rain-giving, rain-bringing*.

ܡܡܝܩܢܐ rt. ܡܘܩ. m. *mocking, scornful; a mocker, scoffer, scorner*; ܠܫܢܐ ܡܡܝܩܢܐ *a mocking tongue*.

ܡܡܝܩܢܘܬܐ rt. ܡܘܩ. f. *scorn, mockery*; ܡܡܝܩܢܐ ܪܓܝܢ ܡܡܝܩܢܘܬܐ *scorners delight in scorning*.

ܡܡܝܪܢܝ or ܡܡܝܪܢ a plant, *chelidŏnium*.

ܡܡܝܬܐ f. a plant, *glaucium phoeniceum*.

ܡܡܝܬܢܐ, ܢܝܬܐ rt. ܡܘܬ. adj. *death-bringing, deadly*; ܣܡܐ or ܐܪܣܐ ܡܡܝܬܢܐ *deadly poison*.

ܡܡܟܟܢܐ pl. ܢ̈ܐ rt. ܡܟܟ. m. *a humiliator*.

ܡܡܟܪܢܐ rt. ܡܟܪ. m. *he who gives in betrothal, promises in marriage*.

ܡܡܠܠ; see Aphel of ܡܠܠ.

ܡܡܠܟܢܐ, ܢܝܬܐ rt. ܡܠܟ. *piloting, directing*.

ܡܡܠܝܢܐ, ܢܝܬܐ rt. ܡܠܐ. *a fulfiller, supplier; completing, fulfilling*, &c.; ܡܡܠܝܢܐ ܕܡܢܝܢܐ *that which completes a number*; ܚܘܒܐ ܡܡܠܝܢܐ ܕܢܡܘܣܐ *love which fulfils the law*; ܛܝܒܘܬܐ ܕܐܠܗܐ ܡܘܠܕܢܝܬܐ ܘܡܪܒܝܢܝܬܐ ܘܡܡܠܝܢܝܬܐ the grace of God *which gives birth and nourishes and consummates*.

ܡܡܠܠܐ rarely ܡܡܠܐ rt. ܡܠܠ. m. with pron. suff. 1 pers. W-Syr. ܡܡܠܠܝ, E-Syr. ܡܡܠܠܝ. *a*) *speech, diction, way of speaking, style, eloquence, dialect*, ܡܢܘܬܐ ܕܡܡܠܠܐ *parts of speech*; ܡܡܠܠܐ ܢܘܟܪܝܐ or ܢܘܟܪܝܬܐ *strange* or *foreign speech*; ܡܡܠܠܐ ܣܘܪܝܝܐ—ܝܘܢܝܐ *Syriac, Greek*, &c. *b*) *talk, discourse, dissertation, treatise, homily*; ܡܡܠܠܐ ܣܪܝܩܐ *idle talk*; ܡܡܠܠܐ ܕܩܕܡ ܩܪܝܢܐ *a preface, proemium*.

ܡܡܠܠܘܬܐ rt. ܡܠܠ. f. *speaking, discourse; teaching, science*; ܡܡܠܠܘܬܐ ܕܓܠܬܐ *false-speaking*; with ܐܠܗܘܬܐ *theology*; ܓܢܣܐ *genealogy*; ܟܘܟܒܐ *astrology, astronomy*; ܐܐܪ̈ܝܬܐ *meteorology*; ܫܪ̈ܒܬܐ *genealogy*; ܡܡܠܠܘܬܐ ܬܫܒܘܚܬܐ or ܫܘܒܚܐ *the doxology*.

ܡܡܠܠܢܐ, ܢܝܬܐ rt. ܡܠܠ. *speaking, declaring*.

ܡܡܣܝܢܐ, ܢܝܬܐ rt. ܡܣܐ. *putrefying, causing decay*.

ܡܡܣܡܣܘܬܐ f. *serious illness*.

ܡܡܣܡܣܢܐ *one who is seriously ill*.

ܡܡܨܥܢܐ rt. ܡܨܥ. m. *a mediator*.

ܡܡܨܪܘܬܐ rt. ܡܨܪ. f. *impregnability*.

ܡܡܪܢܐ pl. ܢ̈ܐ rt. ܡܪܐ. *one who is zealous, an imitator*; ܡܡܪ̈ܢܐ ܕܡܫܝܚܐ *imitators of Christ*.

ܡܡܪܢܐܝܬ rt. ܡܪܐ. adv. *with emulation, vying with each other*.

ܡܡܪܢܘܬܐ rt. ܡܪܐ. f. *emulation, imitation, comparison*.

ܡܡܪܡܪܢ, ܡܡܪܡܪܢܐ, ܢܝܬܐ rt. ܡܪ. *provoking, irritating, contentious, rebellious; a rebel*; ܡܡܪܡܪ̈ܢܘܗܝ ܕܪܘܚܐ *those who provoke the wrath of the Spirit*.

ܡܡܪܡܪܢܘܬܐ rt. ܡܪ. f. *contentiousness, exacerbation; a cause of bitterness, of provocation*.

ܡܡܫܚܐܝܬ rt. ܡܫܚ. adv. *temperately, moderately, commensurately, fitly, evenly*.

ܡܫܽܘܚܬܳܐ rt. ܡܫܚ. f. a) *moderation, moderate amount, state between two extremes, equipoise, balance.* b) *mensuration.* c) ܡܫܽܘܚܬܳܐ ܕܡܶܫܬܝܳܐ *a measure of drink.*

ܡܶܢܥܳܠܰܡ contr. for ܡܶܢ ܥܳܠܰܡ *from everlasting, from aforetime; ever;* with ܠܳܐ *never.*

ܡܡܰܬܠܳܢܳܐ rt. ܡܬܠ. m. *a writer of parables* or *proverbs; the author of the Book of Proverbs.*

ܡܶܢ Greek particle μέν, *indeed,* used to introduce the first member of a sentence, cf. Germ. *zwar,* usually followed by ܕܶܝܢ introducing the second; ܡܶܢ—ܕܶܝܢ μέν—δέ, *on the one hand—on the other.*

ܡܰܢ interrog. pron. com. gen. and number *who? which? what?* ܡܰܢ ܗܽܘ *who is it?* ܡܰܢ ܐܰܢ̱ܬܽܘܢ *who are ye?* ܡܰܢ ܐܶܢܽܘܢ ܗܳܠܶܝܢ *who are these?* ܡܰܢ ܡܫܟܰܚ ܠܡܶܥܒܰܕ ܗܳܕܶܐ *who is able to do this?* ܕܡܰܢ ܬܶܗܘܶܐ ܙܳܟܽܘܬܳܐ *whose shall be the victory?* ܕܡܰܢ ܢܶܗܘܝܳܢ *whose shall these things be?* ܡܰܢ ܕ *he who, any one who, whoso, whosoever;* ܕܡܰܢ ܕܰܒܝܬܶܗ *whose soever house;* ܠܰܝܬ ܡܰܢ ܕ *there is no one;* ܡܰܢ ܕܶܝܢ preceding a verb, *O that!* ܡܰܢ ܗܽܘ usually contracted ܡܰܢܽܘ *who? who is? what is? who is it? who are?* ܡܰܢ ܗܽܘ ܐܰܢܬܽܘܢ, *who are these?* ܡܰܢܽܘ ܡܶܢܟܽܘܢ *which of you?* ܕܡܰܢܽܘ *whose* used after verbs of inquiring, *who he may be, who it may be, what it is.*

ܡܶܢ prep. with affixes ܡܶܢܝ, ܡܶܢܳܟ, ܡܶܢܶܗ, &c. a) of place: *from, out of, at, on;* ܡܶܢ ܟܰܘܬܳܐ *from the window;* ܐܰܦܩܶܗ ܡܶܢ ܦܰܪܕܰܝܣܳܐ the Lord God *sent him forth from the garden;* ܠܒܰܪ ܡܶܢ ܬܰܪܥܳܐ *outside the door;* frequently with verbs of motion: ܐܶܙܰܠ ܡܶܢ—ܠ *going from—to . . .;* with ܗܦܰܟ or ܗܦܰܟ *to return from . . .;* ܢܽܘܗܪܳܐ ܕܢܳܚܶܬ ܡܶܢ ܫܡܰܝܳܐ *a light which comes down from the sky;* ܢܦܰܩ ܡܶܢ ܬܰܪܥܳܐ *he went out of the door;* ܢܦܰܩܬܽܘܢ ܡܶܢ ܐܰܪܥܳܐ ܕܡܶܨܪܶܝܢ *ye came out from the land of Egypt;* with ܐܰܦܶܩ or ܢܦܰܩ *to bring out, take from* a place or person; verbs of escaping often have ܡܶܢ ܩܕܳܡ; with expressions of position: ܡܶܢ ܝܰܡܺܝܢܳܐ—ܡܶܢ ܣܶܡܳܠܳܐ *on the right hand, on the left;* ܡܶܢ ܓܶܢܒܳܐ *at the side;* ܡܶܢ ܬܰܝܡܢܳܐ ܕܢܰܚܠܳܐ *on the south side of the valley;* ܡܶܢ ܬܰܡܳܢ *thence.* b) of origin, race, birthplace or residence: *of, from;* ܐܰܠܳܗܳܐ ܫܰܪܺܝܪܳܐ ܡܶܢ ܐܰܠܳܗܳܐ ܫܰܪܺܝܪܳܐ *very God of very God;* ܐܰܒܽܘܗ̱ܝ ܕܦܠܰܛܽܘܢ ܡܶܢ ܦܽܘܣܺܝܕܽܘܢ ܢܚܶܬ Plato's *father was descended from Poseidon;* ܡܶܢ ܫܰܪܒܬܳܐ ܕܡܰܠܟܽܘܬܳܐ *of the royal stock;* ܡܶܢ ܕܰܝܪܳܐ ܕܙܽܘܩܢܺܝܢ *from the monastery of Zuknin.* c) of material: *of, from;* ܓܒܰܠ ܡܶܢ ܐܰܪܥܳܐ. ܟܽܠܳܗ̇ ܚܰܝܘܬܳܐ the Lord God *formed out of the ground every animal;* ܥܒܺܝܕ ܡܶܢ ܐܰܒܳܪܳܐ *made of tin.* d) of agent or object, cause or reason: *by, of, from, for, on account of,* ܡܶܢ ܐܽܘܠܨܳܢܳܐ *of necessity;* ܡܶܢ ܚܰܕܽܘܬܳܐ *for joy;* ܡܶܢ ܗܳܕܶܐ ܝܺܕܺܝܥܳܐ *it is clear from this;* ܡܺܝܬܘ ܡܶܢ ܨܗܝܳܐ *they died of thirst;* ܠܐܶܝܘ ܡܶܢ ܠܡܶܩܒܰܪ *they were too weary to bury* the dead; with verbs of fear, of hindering or neglecting, of needing, asking, taking, giving: ܕܚܶܠܢ ܡܶܢ ܢܰܦܫܳܬܰܢ *we feared for our lives;* ܢܶܒܗܬܽܘܢ ܡܶܢ ܒܪܝ *they will reverence my son.* e) of time: *from, while, during, at;* ܡܶܢ ܨܰܦܪܳܐ ܠܛܰܗܪܳܐ *from morn to noon;* ܡܶܢ ܛܠܝܽܘܬܝ *from my youth;* ܡܶܢ ܪܺܫܳܐ *at the beginning, from the beginning;* ܡܶܢ ܚܰܝܰܘܗ̱ܝ *during his life;* ܐܶܓܰܪ̈ܳܬܳܐ ܡܶܢ ܐܶܦܺܝܣܩܽܘܦܽܘܬܶܗ *letters from the time when he was made bishop:* with ܕ *after;* ܡܶܢ ܕܢܦܰܩ ܫܺܐܕܳܐ *when the devil had gone out.* f) partitive: *of, out of, some of;* ܐܢܳܫܺܝܢ ܡܶܢܗܽܘܢ *some of them;* ܡܶܢܗܽܘܢ—ܘܡܶܢܗܽܘܢ *some—others;* ܡܶܢ ܛܰܝܳܝܶܐ *some of the Arabs;* ܫܰܕܰܪ ܡܶܢ ܚܰܝܠܰܘܳܬܶܗ *he sent some of his forces;* ܡܶܢܶܗ—ܘܡܶܢܶܗ—ܘܡܶܢܶܗ *one part—and another—and another;* ܡܶܢܶܗ ܡܶܢܶܗ *part of it, partly;* cf. i. g) distributive: ܡܶܢ ܚܰܡܫܳܐ ܚܰܡܫܳܐ *by fives and by tens;* ܡܶܢ ܥܶܣܪܳܐ ܥܶܣܪܳܐ ܘܡܶܢ ܠܺܝܛܪܶܐ weighing *one or two pounds each;* ܡܶܢ ܚܰܡܫܺܝܢ Hex. and Harkleian for ܚܰܡܫܺܝܢ *by fifties.* h) comparative: *than;* ܚܠܶܐ ܡܶܢ ܕܶܒܫܳܐ *sweeter than honey;* ܣܢܺܐ ܡܶܢ ܣܳܛܳܢܳܐ *more hateful than Satan;* ܕܘܳܝ ܡܶܢ ܟܽܠ *most miserable.* i) idioms: with pers. pron. or the name of a person; *on the side, of the party, in the name,* ܡܰܢܽܘ ܡܶܢ ܡܳܪܝܳܐ *who is on the Lord's side?* ܡܶܢܶܗ ܗܘܰܘ *they were on his side;* ܡܶܢ ܓܶܒܶܗ *on his side, in his own name, by his own authority;* ܡܶܢܶܗ or ܡܶܢܶܗ ܘܒܶܗ and less commonly ܡܶܢܶܗ ܠܶܗ and ܡܶܢܶܗ ܒܠܚܽܘܕܰܘܗ̱ܝ *by himself, of himself, by itself alone;* ܡܶܢܶܗ ܢܦܰܠ *it fell of itself;* ܡܶܢ ܚܰܕ ܦܽܘܡܳܐ *with one voice, with one accord.* For compounds ܡܶܢܕܶܡ, ܡܶܢܕܰܥܡ, ܡܶܢܕܰܥܡ, ܡܶܢ ܕܶܗܪܽܘܢ, see ܐܶܢܳܐ, ܟܰܕ, ܩܕܳܡ, ܗܳܪܟܳܐ, ܠܟ, ܡܶܢܥܠܰܡ, ܡܶܢܟܳܐ, &c. DERIVATIVES, ܡܢܳܐ, ܡܢܳܝܳܐ, ܡܶܢܝܳܢܳܐ, ܡܢܺܝܢܳܐ, ܡܶܢܥܠܰܡ.

ܡܢܐ, ܡܢ interrog. pron. neuter. *what? why? wherefore?* ܡܢ ܫܡܗ *what is his name?* ܡܢܐ ܠܝ ܘܠܟ *what have I to do with thee?* ܡܢܐ ܩܝܡܝܢ ܐܢܬܘܢ ܘܚܝܪܝܢ ܒܫܡܝܐ *why stand ye looking into heaven?* ܡܢ ܕ *that which;* ܒܡܢܐ *whereby? wherewith? wherefore?* ܠܡܢܐ, ܠܡܢ *to what end? why? wherefore?* ܡܛܠ ܡܢܐ *why? wherefore?* ܡܢ ܡܢܐ *whence?* ܠܘܬ ܡܢܐ *wherefore?* ܡܢܐ ܗܘ = ܡܢܘ *what is this? how is it?* ܡܢܐ ܗܝ = ܡܢܝ is a less frequent contraction. Derivative, ܡܢܝܘܬܐ.

ܡܢܬܐ usually emph. ܡܢܬܐ pl. ܡܢܝܢ, ܡܢܘܢ f. *a*) *hair, fur;* ܡܢܝܢ ܦܪ̈ܝܫܬܐ *separate hairs;* ܡܢܝܢ ܙܥܘܪ̈ܬܐ *scanty hairs.* *b*) music. *a string,* ܡܢܝܢ ܡܬܝ̈ܚܬܐ ܘܪ̈ܦܝܬܐ *tense—loose—strings;* ܥܣܪܐ ܡܢܝܢ *a decachord.*

ܡܢܐ fut. ܢܡܢܐ, act. part. ܡܢܐ, ܡܢܝܐ, pass. part. ܡܢܐ, ܡܢܝܐ, ܡܢܝܬܐ. *to number, count, reckon, enumerate, recount, repute* often with ܠ and pers. pron., ܡܢܝ ܠܝ ܠܥܡܐ *number me the people;* ܡܢܝܬ ܠܗܘܢ ܟܣܦܐ *I counted out money to them;* ܡܢܘ ܢܡܢܐ ܬܕܡܪ̈ܬܗ *who can recount* His *marvellous acts?* with ܥܡ *amongst* or *with;* ܥܡ ܪ̈ܕܘܦܐ ܡܢܘ ܢܦܫܗܘܢ *they joined the number of persecutors;* ܒܐܝܢܐ ܡܪܥܝܬܐ ܡܢܐ ܐܢܬ ܠܝ *amongst which flock do you reckon me?* ܠܐ ܝܕܘܥܐ ܡܢܝܗܝ *he reckoned him to be ignorant.* Ethpe. ܐܬܡܢܝ *to be numbered, reckoned, counted;* ܒܫܒܛܐ ܕ *in the tribe of;* ܥܡ ܥܘ̈ܠܐ ܐܬܡܢܝ *He was counted amongst the transgressors.* Derivatives, ܡܢܝܢܐ, ܡܢܝܢܘܬܐ, ܡܢܝܢܐ, ܡܢܝܢܬܐ, ܡܢܝܢܘܬܐ, ܡܢܝܢܬܐ, ܡܢܬܐ, ܡܢܘܬܐ, ܡܢܝܢܐ, ܡܬܡܢܝܢܐ, ܡܬܡܢܝܢܘܬܐ, ܡܬܡܢܝܢܐ, ܡܬܡܢܝܢܬܐ.

ܡܢܟܝܐ pl. ܐ̈ rt. ܢܟܐ. *unhealthy, numb.*

ܡܢܓܒܐ rt. ܢܓܒ. m. *having withered limbs.*

ܡܢܓܒܘܬܐ rt. ܢܓܒ. f. *paralysis.*

ܡܢܓܒܢܐ rt. ܢܓܒ. m. *parched, withered; desiccative.*

ܡܢܓܕܢܐ rt. ܢܓܕ. m. *scourging; a scourger, tormentor;* ܫܒ̈ܛܐ ܡܢܓܕ̈ܢܐ *the rods which scourge us.*

ܡܢܓܘܪ m. *a mat; a shelter of matting* esp. on a small boat.

ܡܢܓܢܘܢ, ܡܢܓܢܐ m. μάγγανον, *an engine* esp. *of war; an instrument of torture.*

ܡܢܓܢܝܩܘܣ pl. ܐ̈, ܐ̈ܣ or ܝ̈ܣ com. gen. μαγγανικός, *a ballista, torment, engine for hurling stones.*

ܡܢܕܝܐ, ܡܢܕܐ Aphel part. of ܢܕ.

ܡܢܕܝܢܘܬܐ rt. ܢܕ. f. *waving, motion.*

ܡܢܕܝܠ, ܡܢܕܝܠܐ pl. ܝ̈ܢ, ܐ̈ m. μανδήλη, μανδήλιον, *a cloth, napkin, towel.*

ܡܢܕܪܝܫ or ܡܢܕܪܫ; see under ܕܪܫ. *again, anew, afresh.*

ܡܢܗܡܢܐ, ܡܢܗܡܢܬܐ rt. ܢܗܡ. *moaning.*

ܡܢܗܪܢܐ, ܡܢܗܪܢܬܐ, ܡܢܗܪܢܝܬܐ rt. ܢܗܪ. *a*) adj. *shining, bright, enlightening, of the nature of light;* subst. *a light, a window.* *b*) *expository; a commentator, one who expounds* the Scriptures. *c*) *a torch of flax.*

ܡܢܗܪܢܘܬܐ rt. ܢܗܪ. f. *enlightening, illumination, irradiation; interpretation, elucidation;* ܐܪܙܐ ܕܡܢܗܪܢܘܬܐ ܐܘ ܕܝܢ ܥܡܕܐ ܩܕܝܫܐ *the mystery of enlightenment i. e. holy baptism.*

ܡܢܘ contr. of ܡܢ ܗܘ *who is this? who is he?*

ܡܢܘ contr. of ܡܢܐ ܗܘ *what is this? how is it?*

ܡܢܘܚܬܐ from ܢܘܚ. f. *shipwreck.*

ܡܢܘܬܐ, ܡܢܘܬ pl. of ܡܢܬܐ.

ܡܢܚܐ, ܡܢܚ Aphel part. pass. of ܢܚ. *deceased, defunct, the late.*

ܡܢܚܬ or ܡܢ ܚܬ with ܠ prefixed, *the next year,* Luke xiii. 9.

ܡܢܛܪܢܐ, ܡܢܛܪܢܝܬܐ rt. ܢܛܪ. adj. *guarding, preserving;* ܡܕܒܪܢܘܬܐ ܡܢܛܪܢܝܬܐ *watchful providence;* ܙܝܢܐ ܡܢܛܪܢܐ *arms of defence;* subst. *a guardian, preserver.*

ܡܢܛܪܢܘܬܐ rt. ܢܛܪ. f. *guardianship, care.*

ܡܢܝ *Manes,* cf. ܡܐܢܝ. Derivatives, ܡܢܝܢܐ, ܡܢܝܢܘܬܐ.

ܡܢܝܐ pl. ܡܢܝܢ, ܡܢܝ̈ܐ, ܡܢܘܬܐ m. a measure of weight and of value; *a mina, a pound.*

ܡܢܝܢܐ pl. ܐ̈ rt. ܡܢܐ. *one who counts, numbers, a reckoner, arithmetician.*

ܡܢܝܢܐ from ܡܢܬܐ. music. *stringed.*

ܡܢܝܢܘܬܐ E-Syr. ܡܢܝ rt. ܡܢܐ. f. *numbering, enumeration, arithmetic.*

ܡܢܝܘܬܐ from ܡܢܐ. f. *quiddity.*

ܡܢܝܚܢܐ, ܡܢܝܚܢܝܬܐ rt. ܢܚ. *rest-giving, ministering, useful, serviceable; a restorer; a servant,*

servant-maid, server, attendant, esp. *a worshipper, a religious;* ܡܫܡ̈ܫܢܐ ܕܡܪܢ *the saints who serve our Lord;* ܕܝܪ̈ܝܐ ܘܡܡܫܡ̈ܫܢܐ *monks or religious.*

ܡܡܫܡܫܢܘܬܐ rt. ܫܡܫ. f. *service, ministry; the rests* or *beats* of a metre.

ܡܡܫܡܫܢܝܐ rt. ܫܡܫ. *religious, ministerial.*

ܡܡܬܝܠܐ; see ܡܬܝܠܐ.

ܡܢܝܢܐ, ܡܢܝܢ pl. ܐ̈ (ܡܢܝ̈ܢܐ with Ribui is used as a collective noun) rt. ܡܢܐ. m. *a number; a few; a numbering, census; reckoning, enumeration, computation; chronology, an epoch, era;* ܒܡܢܝܢܐ ܙܥܘܪܐ *few;* ܝܘ̈ܡܬܐ ܕܡܢܝܢܐ *a few days;* ܕܠܐ ܡܢܝܢ or ܕܠܝܬ ܠܗ ܡܢܝܢ *innumerable;* ܣܟܐ ܕܡܢܝܢܐ ܕܟܣܦܐ *a sum of money;* ܟܕ ܡܛܝܬ ܠܡܢܝܢܐ ܫܒܝܥܝܐ *when I had attained my seventh year;* ܣܦܪܐ ܕܡܢܝܢܐ *the book of Numbers;* ܐܝܟ ܡܢܝܢ ܕܐܢܫܝܢ *according to the computation of some, as some have reckoned* or *computed;* ܡܢܝܢܐ ܗܢܕܘܝܐ *the Indian way of reckoning;* ܡܢܝܢܐ ܕܫܢ̈ܝܐ—ܕܙܒ̈ܢܐ *a reckoning of years* or *dates;* ܡܢܝܢܐ ܕܡܨܪ̈ܝܐ *the Egyptian era,* ܕܐܠܟܣܢܕܪܘܣ—ܕܝܘ̈ܢܝܐ *the era of Alexander, Anno Graecorum* (311 B.C.); ܡܢܝܢܐ ܕܐܦܡܝ̈ܐ *the Apamean era* (same date); ܕܝܗܘ̈ܕܝܐ—ܕܥܒܪ̈ܝܐ *the Judaic, the Hebrew chronology;* gram. *number* ܚܕܢܝܐ—ܣܓܝܐܢܝܐ *sing.* or *pl.*

ܡܢܝܢܐ, ܡܢܝܢܐ or ܡܢܝܢ m. *a worm, weevil, an insect like a locust which eats the heart out of the corn.*

ܡܢܝܟܝܢܝܐ, ܐܝܬܐ from ܡܢܝ. *Manichaean, a Manichee.*

ܡܢܝܢܝܐ pl. ܐ̈ rt. ܡܢܐ. *pertaining to number, arithmetical;* ܫܡܐ ܡܢܝܢܝܐ *a numeral.*

ܡܢܝܟܝܘܬܐ from ܡܢܝ. f. *Manichaeanism.*

ܡܢܩܝܬܐ or ܡܢܩܝܬܐ pl. ܝ̈ܬܐ rt. ܢܩܐ. f. *a bowl* for libations or in which the libation was mixed; *a ladle, table-spoon;* a measure = about half a pint.

ܡܢܣܝܣܐ m. *viola odorata, the violet.*

ܡܢܣܦܪܐ; see ܣܦܪܐ.

ܡܢܣܛܪܘܦܘܣ; see ܦܪܘܣ.

ܡܢܟܪܝܢܘܬܐ from ܢܟܪ. f. *alienation, estrangement.*

ܡܢܟܬܢܐ, ܬܢܝܬܐ rt. ܢܟܬ. adj. *biting, sharp, stinging;* subst. *one who bites, devours.*

ܡܢܠܝܘܢ; see ܠܝܘܢ.

ܡܢܢܐ or ܡܢܐ m. *manna.*

ܡܢܣܝܢܐ, ܢܝܬܐ rt. ܢܣܐ. *a tempter, the tempter* = Satan.

ܡܢܣܝܢܐܝܬ rt. ܢܣܐ. adv. *by way of experiment, tentatively.*

ܡܢܣܝܢܘܬܐ rt. ܢܣܐ. f. *experience; temptation.*

ܡܢܥ Pa. ܡܢܥ *a*) *to arrive, come* with ܒ, ܠ or ܥܕܡܐ ܠ; ܐܡܬܝ ܕܙܒܢܐ ܢܡܢܥ *when the time shall come;* ܡܢܥ ܗܘܐ ܠܗ ܙܒܢܐ ܕܨܘܡܐ *it was now Lent.* *b*) *to bring, lead;* ܐܘܪܚܐ ܕܡܡܢܥܐ ܠܐܪܥܐ ܕܒܘܣܡܐ *the way which leads to the land of bliss;* ܠܢܡܐܐ ܫܠܡܐ ܡܢܥܗ *he brought him safe to the haven.* Ethpa. ܐܬܡܢܥ *to set out, come, arrive,* with ܠ, ܥܕܡܐ ܠ; ܡܐ ܕܐܬܡܢܥ ܫܡܫܐ ܠ ... ܐܡܬܝ *when the sun has reached ...;* ܕܐܢܐ ܒܩܢܘܡܝ ܐܬܡܢܥ ܠܘܬ ܫܠܝ̈ܛܢܐ ܙܒܢ̈ܝܐ *that I should appear in person before the temporal rulers.* Derivatives, ܡܡܢܥܢܘܬܐ, ܡܢܥܐ, ܡܡܢܥܐ.

ܡܢܥܐ or ܡܢܥܐ rt. ܡܢܥ. m. *setting out, coming, arrival, attainment.*

ܡܢܦܚܘܬܐ rt. ܢܦܚ. f. *a swelling, tumour.*

ܡܢܦܚܢܐ, ܢܝܬܐ rt. ܢܦܚ. *flatulent.*

ܡܢܦܚܢܝܬܐ rt. ܢܦܚ. f. *a fan, fly-flap.*

ܡܢܦܠܘܬܐ rt. ܢܦܠ. f. *failing, feebleness.*

ܡܢܦܨܢܐ, ܢܝܬܐ rt. ܢܦܨ. *purgative, emetic, cathartic.*

ܡܢܦܨܢܘܬܐ rt. ܢܦܨ. f. *purging.*

ܡܢܦܫܐ, ܡܢܦܫܬܐ rt. ܢܦܫ. *animate, endowed with life,* with ܠܐ *inanimate, inert;* ܒܪ̈ܝܬܐ ܡܢܦܫܬܐ ܘܠܐ ܡܢܦܫܬܐ *animate and inanimate creatures.*

ܡܢܦܫܢܘܬܐ rt. ܢܦܫ. f. *breathing, respiration.*

ܡܢܨܚܢܐ rt. ܢܨܚ. *one who gives the victory, makes to triumph; a conqueror.*

ܡܢܪܓܢܐܝܬ rt. ܢܪܓ. adv. *complainingly.*

ܡܢܪܓܘܬܐ; same as ܡܢܪܓܢܘܬܐ.

ܡܢܪܓܢܐ, ܢܝܬܐ rt. ܢܪܓ. *wheedling, coaxing.*

ܡܢܪܓܢܐܝܬ rt. ܢܪܓ. *coaxingly, caressingly.*

ܡܢܪܓܢܘܬܐ rt. ܢܪܓ. *blandishment, caressing.*

ܡܢܩܒܢܘܬܐ rt. ܢܩܒ. f. gram. *the feminine gender.*

ܡܢܩܒܬܢܝܐ, ܢܝܬܐ rt. ܢܩܒ. gram. *forming the feminine, a sign of the feminine form.*

ܡܢܩܝܘܬܐ rt. ܢܩܐ. f. *the clearing* of a path.

ܡܢܩܫܬܐ; see ܡܢܩܝܫܬܐ.

ܡܢܩܫܘܬܐ rt. ܢܩܫ. f. *clattering.*

ܡܢܪܐ, ܡܢܪܬܐ pl. ܬ̈ܐ Heb. f. *a) a lamp-stand, candlestick;* ܫܒܥ ܡܢܪ̈ܬܐ ܕܕܗܒܐ *seven golden candlesticks. b) a minaret.*

ܡܢܫܝܢܐ rt. ܢܫܐ. *causing oblivion.*

ܡܢܫܝܢܘܬܐ rt. ܢܫܐ. f. *oblivion.*

ܡܢܫܠܝ, ܡܢܫܠܝܐ, ܡܢܫܠܝܐ, ܡܢܫܠܝܐ comp. of ܡܢ and ܫܠܝ. *suddenly;* see ܫܠܝܐ.

ܡܢܬܐ pl. ܡ̈ܢܘܢ, ܡ̈ܢܘܬܐ rt. ܡܢܐ. f. *a part, portion* esp. *a portion allotted, a lot;* ܕܠܐ ܡܢܬܐ *portionless;* ܒܢܝ ܡܢܬܐ *partakers;* ܒܡܢܬܐ *partly;* ܣܓܝ ܡ̈ܢܘܢ *manifold;* ܟܠܐ ܘܡ̈ܢܘܬܐ *the whole and the parts;* ܡܢܬܐ ܡܢܬܐ *severally, one by one;* ܡ̈ܢܘܬܐ ܡܦܫܦܫܬܐ *fragments;* ܡ̈ܢܘܬܐ ܕܩܕܝܫܐ or ellipt. *relics;* geogr. or mathemat. *a degree;* gram. ܡ̈ܢܘܬܐ ܕܡܠܬܐ or ܕܡܡܠܠܐ *parts of speech.*

ܡܢܬܐ; see ܡܢܝܐ.

ܡܢܬܐܝܬ rt. ܡܢܐ. adv. *partly, somewhat, a little; severally, particularly.*

ܡܢܬܝܐ, ܡܢܬܝܬܐ rt. ܡܢܐ. adj. *particular, partial, separate, private;* ܨܒܘ̈ܬܐ ܡܢܬܝ̈ܬܐ *private affairs.*

ܡܢܬܡܠ, ܡܢܬܡܠܝ, ܡܢܬܡܠ from ܡܢ and ܬܡܠ. adverb of time, *the day before yesterday, the other day.*

ܡܢܬܢܝܐܝܬ rt. ܡܢܐ. adv. *partly, partially.*

ܡܢܬܢܝܐ, ܢܝܬܐ rt. ܡܢܐ. adv. *partial, in part, particular.*

ܡܢܬܢܝܘܬܐ rt. ܡܢܐ. f. *particularization, severality* opp. ܟܠܢܝܘܬܐ *entirety.*

ܡܢܛܠܢܐ, ܢܝܬܐ rt. ܢܛܠ. *that which makes the balance turn, preponderating.*

ܡܢܛܠܢܘܬܐ rt. ܢܛܠ. f. *preponderance.*

ܡܣܐ; see ܡܣܣܐ.

ܡܣܐ fut. ܢܡܣܐ, pass. part. ܡܣܐ, ܡܣܝܐ, ܡܣܝܬܐ. *a) to putrefy, melt, waste, drip away;* ܣܪܝܐ ܘܡܣܐ *foul and fetid;* ܦܓܪܐ ܡܣܝܐ *a putrid corpse;* ܥܝܢ̈ܐ ܡܣܝ̈ܬܐ *running eyes, failing, wasting;* ܐܘܚܠܐ ܡܣܝܬܐ ܘܪܦܫܐ ܣܝܢܐ *slimy mire;* ܠܒܐ ܡܣܝܐ *a melting heart, cowardly heart. b) to be thickened, to curdle, become hard;* ܚܒܠܐ ܕܡܣܐ ܡܢ ܩܝܣܐ *a rope harder than wood.* Ethpe. ܐܬܡܣܝ *to pine, decay, rot, melt* or *consume away* as fruit, flesh; from disease, sorrow or fear; ܐܬܡܣܝ ܪ̈ܓܠܝܗܘܢ ܡܢ ܓܠܝܕܐ *their feet mortified from frostbite;* metaph. ܠܒܐ ܕܐܢܫ ܢܬܡܣܐ *every heart shall melt.* Aph. ܐܡܣܝ *to make to putrefy, cause to fall away* or *decay; to wash away, dissolve, damp off, make moist* or *wet;* ܠܐ ܡܛܪܐ ܡܡܣܐ ܠܗ *rain does not wash it away, dissolve it;* ܐܡܣܝ ܕܡ̈ܥܐ *he watered with tears.* Metaph. with ܠܒܐ *to weaken, enervate.* Derivatives, ܡܣܘܬܐ, ܡܣܘܝܐ, ܡܣܝܬܐ, ܡܡܣܝܢܐ, ܡܡܣܝܢܘܬܐ, ܐܡܣܘܬܐ.

ܡܣܐ τὸ μέσον, τὰ μέσα, *the middle* ܕܡܕܝܢܬܐ *of the city* perh. *the forum.*

ܡܣܓܠܐ rt. ܣܓܠ. m. *wooden fetters;* cf. ܡܣܓܐ.

ܡܣܐܢܐ; see ܡܣܐܢܐ *a sandal* and ܡܣܢܐ *a basket.*

ܡܣܐܪܐ; see ܡܣܪܐ *a saw.*

ܡܣܐܬܐ, ܡܐܣܬܐ, ܡܣܐܬܐ or ܡܣܐܬܐ pl. ܬ̈ܐ or ܬ̈ܐ rt. ܢܣܐ. f. *a balance, pair of scales;* a sign of the Zodiac, *Libra.*

ܡܣܐܬܢܝܐ rt. ܢܣܐ. *weighed in the balance, equal, exact, true.*

ܡܣܒ or ܡܣܒܘ, ܡܣܒܐ rt. ܢܣܒ. m. *a) taking, receiving;* ܡܣܒܐ ܘܡܬܠܐ *taking and giving = commerce, trade;* ܡܣܒܐ ܕܐܪ̈ܙܐ *receiving Holy Communion;* ܡܣܒܐ ܕܐܢܬܬܐ or ellipt. *taking a wife, marriage;* ܡܣܒܐ ܕܢܫ̈ܐ ܣܓܝ̈ܐܬܐ *polygamy. b) taking away, abstraction. c)* ܡܣܒ ܒܐܦ̈ܐ *regarding appearance, putting on an appearance; dissimulation, hypocrisy.*

ܡܣܒܗܐܝܬ rt. ܣܒܗ. adv. *in like manner, analogously.*

ܡܣܒܗܘܬܐ rt. ܣܒܗ. f. *likeness, resemblance, imitation, similarity, similitude.*

ܡܣܒܟܘܬܐ rt. ܣܒܟ. f. *adhesion.*

ܡܣܒܠܢܘܬܐ rt. ܣܒܠ. f. *the infliction of punishment.*

ܡܣܒܥܢܐ rt. ܣܒܥ. *satiating, satisfying.*

ܡܣܒܥܢܘܬܐ rt. ܣܒܥ. f. *a filling, satiating.*

ܡܣܒܪܢܐ, ܢܝܬܐ rt. ܣܒܪ. *a messenger, bearer*

of tidings; an evangelist, preacher; ܐܪܒܥܐ ܡܣܒܪܢ̈ܐ the four Evangelists.

ܡܣܒܪܢܐܝܬ rt. ܣܒܪ. adv. as we may suppose, conjecturally.

ܡܣܒܪܢܐܝܬ rt. ܣܒܪ. adv. as one who brings tidings.

ܡܣܒܪܢܘܬܐ rt. ܣܒܪ. f. opinion, surmise, supposition, suspicion, doubt.

ܡܣܒܪܢܘܬܐ rt. ܣܒܪ. f. preaching; expectation, awaiting.

ܡܣܓܐ pl. ܐ̈ m. a cord to bind a load.

ܡܣܓܕܐ rt. ܣܓܕ. m. a mosque.

ܡܣܓܝܢܐ rt. ܣܓܐ. one who multiplies.

ܡܣܓܝܢܐ rt. ܣܓܐ. one who extols, chants praises, a singer.

ܡܣܓܝܢܘܬܐ rt. ܣܓܐ. f. multiplication, abundance.

ܡܣܓܝܢܘܬܐ rt. ܣܓܐ. f. singing, chanting, magnifying.

ܡܣܓܦܢܐ, ܡܣܓܦܢܐ, ܢܝ̈ܬܐ rt. ܣܓܦ. noxious, injurious.

ܡܣܓܦܢܘܬܐ rt. ܣܓܦ. f. causing injury, injuring.

ܡܣܗܕܢܘܬܐ rt. ܣܗܕ. f. testifying, bearing witness, giving evidence.

ܡܣܗܕܢܘܬܐ rt. ܣܗܕ. f. adjuring, taking or calling to witness.

ܡܣܘܚܢܐܝܬ rt. ܣܘܚ. adv. cheerfully, with alacrity.

ܡܣܘܚܘܬܐ rt. ܣܘܚ. f. longing, desire.

ܡܣܘܚܢܐ rt. ܣܘܚ. one who excites desire.

ܡܣܘܚܢܘܬܐ rt. ܣܘܚ. f. longing, desire.

ܡܣܘܦܐ or ܡܣ̈ pl. ܐ̈ rt. ܣܘܦ. m. a flood, torrent.

ܡܣܘܦܐ, ܡܣܘܦܝܬܐ rt. ܣܘܦ. f. a syringe.

ܡܣܘܣܐ, ܡܣܘܣܢܐ act. part. of verb ܣܘܣ.

ܡܣܘܣܢܐ from ܣܘܣ. a caretaker, nurse; a groom.

ܡܣܘܣܢܘܬܐ from ܣܘܣ. f. the care of the sick; care of horses, grooming.

ܡܣܘܪܐ pl. ܐ̈ rt. ܡܣܪ. m. a delator, accuser, calumniator; a despiser, one who holds others in contempt.

ܡܣܘܪܘܬܐ rt. ܡܣܪ. f. delation, the laying of accusations.

ܡܣܘܪܝܐ pl. ܐ̈ rt. ܡܣܪ. m. delation, calumniation; a charge, accusation; ܐܓܪܬܐ ܕܡܣܘܪܝ̈ܐ a letter full of accusations.

ܡܣܪܩܐ pl. ܐ̈ rt. ܣܪܩ. m. a) a comb for the hair, weaver's comb. b) a pecten, sort of shell. c) the radiating bones of the hand or foot.

ܡܣܘܬܐ, ܡܣ̈ or ܡܣ̈ rt. ܡܣܐ. f. rennet; ܚܠܒܐ ܡܓܒܢܐ ܒܡܣܘܬܐ milk curdled by rennet.

ܡܣܘܬܐ f. the cypress.

ܡܣܚܐ m. a poker, fire-shovel, oven-rake; cf. ܡܣܚܬܐ.

ܡܣܚܘܬܐ pl. ܘ̈ܬܐ rt. ܣܚܐ. washing, ablution; conveniences for washing; ܒܝܬ ܡܣܚܘܬܐ the bath.

ܡܣܚܝܐ rt. ܣܚܐ. m. a bath-house.

ܡܣܚܦܘܬܐ rt. ܣܚܦ. f. ruin.

ܡܣܚܦܢܐ rt. ܣܚܦ. m. a destroyer.

ܡܣܛܐ m. a lancet.

ܡܣܛܒܐ = ܡܣܛܒܬܐ f. a stone bench; a square raised place in front of the altar.

ܡܣܛܝܟܝ, ܡܣܛܝܟܝܢ f. μαστίχη, mastic, gum mastic.

ܡܣܛܝܢܐ, ܢܝ̈ܬܐ rt. ܣܛܐ. averting, leading astray; a seducer; an apostate.

ܡܣܛܝܢܘܬܐ pl. ܘ̈ܬܐ rt. ܣܛܐ. error, transgression; apostasy.

ܡܣܝܒܘܬܐ pl. ܘ̈ܬܐ rt. ܣܝܒ. f. pollution; ܡܣܝܒܘܬܐ ܕܕܡܐ blood-stains.

ܡܣܝܒܪܢܐ rt. ܣܒܪ. patient, temperate, self-controlled.

ܡܣܝܒܪܢܘܬܐ rt. ܣܒܪ. f. patience, endurance, continuance, moderation, self-control, continence.

ܡܣܝܘܬܐ, ܡܣܝܘܬܐ rt. ܡܣܐ. f. decay, rottenness, foetor, an ulcer; ܡܣܝܘܬܐ ܕܪ̈ܛܝܒܘܬܐ watery dissolution, dripping away; ܡܢ ܡܣܝܘܬܐ ܕܐܐܪ ܐܬܟܪܗ he became very ill from the foulness of the air; ܕܟܪܝܗ ܡܣܝܘܬܐ suffering from running sores.

ܡܣܝܢܐ or ܡܣ̈ pl. ܢ̈ܐ, ܐ̈ m. a day's journey, a parasang or farsang; ܚܡܫܐ ܡܣܝܢ̈ܐ ܪܚܝܩ five days' journey distant.

ܡܣܝܩܘܬܐ rt. ܣܝܩ. f. setting on fire, inflaming.

ܡܣܬܝܟܐܝܬ rt. ܣܝܟ. *definitely, within limits, summarily, briefly;* ܟܠܗܘܢ ܡܣܬܝܟܐܝܬ *all together.*

ܡܣܬܝܟܘܬܐ rt. ܣܝܟ. f. *limitation, being contained within limits;* with ܠܐ *immensity;* rhet. ܡܣܬܝܟܘܬ ܡܠܬܐ *a figure of speech where the orator expresses much in few words.*

ܡܣܝܟܢܐ, ܡܣܝܟܢܝܬܐ rt. ܣܝܟ. *defining, circumscribing.*

ܡܣܝܟܢܘܬܐ rt. ܣܝܟ. f. *terminating, bringing to an end.*

ܡܣܝܡܢܐ, ܡܣܝܡܢܝܬܐ rt. ܣܝܡ. gram. *affirmative.*

ܡܣܝܥܢܐ, ܡܣܝܥܢܝܬܐ rt. ܣܝܥ. *a helper, auxiliary.*

ܡܣܝܥܢܘܬܐ rt. ܣܝܥ. f. *aid, help, support.*

ܡܣܝܦܢܐ, ܡܣܝܦܢܝܬܐ rt. ܣܘܦ. *consuming, deadly, destructive.*

ܡܣܟܐ pl. ܐ̈ rt. ܣܟܟ. m. *a)* = ܡܣܟܢܐ *a poker, rake. b) a syringe, clyster, injection.*

ܡܣܟܘܪܐ; see ܡܣܟܪܐ.

ܡܣܟܝܢ, ܡܣܟܝܢܐ, ܡܣܟܝܢܬܐ, ܡܣܟܝܢ; see ܡܣܟܢ, &c.

ܡܣܟܝܢܐ rt. ܣܟܐ. *expectant, expressing expectation.*

ܡܣܟܝܬܐ and ܡܣܟܝܬܬܐ f. *a fringe* or *mop of hair* overhanging the forehead.

ܡܣܟܬܐ pl. ܐ̈ rt. ܣܟ. m. *a plough, that part of the plough to which the share is fixed, a ploughshare.*

ܡܣܟܠܘܬܐ rt. ܣܟܠ. f. *crime, folly.*

ܡܣܟܠܢܐ rt. ܣܟܠ. *an evil-doer, wrong-doer, offender.*

ܡܣܬܟܠܢܐ rt. ܣܟܠ. *understanding; one who explains, instructs, expounds.*

ܡܣܟܠܢܘܬܐ rt. ܣܟܠ. f. *offence, perversity, iniquity, viciousness, folly, fatuity.*

ܡܣܬܟܠܢܘܬܐ rt. ܣܟܠ. f. *intelligence.*

ܡܣܬܟܡܢܐ, ܡܣܬܟܡܢܝܬܐ rt. ܣܟܡ. *a former, fashioner, modeller.*

ܡܣܟܢ Palpel conj. of ܣܟܢ. *to impoverish.*

ܡܣܟܝܢܐ, ܡܣܟܝܢܬܐ, ܡܣܟܢܐ written fully ܡܣܟܝܢ, &c. rt. ܣܟܢ. *poor, needy, meagre; poverty-stricken, wretched, miserable* opp. ܥܬܝܪܐ; ܪܚܡܬ ܡܣܟܢܐ *love of the poor.*

ܡܣܟܢܐܝܬ rt. ܣܟܢ. adv. *meagrely; like a poor person, in the guise of a pauper.*

ܡܣܟܢܘܬܐ rt. ܣܟܢ. f. *poverty, want, penury; poorness, meagreness;* ܡܣܟܢܘܬܝ *my poor self;* ܐܬܬܠܡܕ ܠܡܣܟܢܘܬܐ ܩܕܝܫܬܐ *he became a disciple of holy poverty.*

ܡܣܟܪܐ or ܡܣܟܘܪܐ pl. ܐ̈ rt. ܣܟܪ. m. *a dam, barrier, embankment.*

ܡܣܟܪܐ = ܡܣܟܪܐ m. *difficulty, great pains.*

ܡܣܠܝܘܬܐ rt. ܣܠܐ. f. *rejection, contemptibility.*

ܡܣܠܝܢܐ rt. ܣܠܐ. *one who spurns, rejects.*

ܡܣܠܝܢܐܝܬ rt. ܣܠܐ. adv. *scornfully.*

ܡܣܠܝܢܘܬܐ rt. ܣܠܐ. f. *rejection; refuse.*

ܡܣܬܠܡܘܬܐ rt. ܣܠܡ. f. *the winnowing* of grain.

ܡܣܬܠܡܢܝܬܐ rt. ܣܠܡ. f. *the bobbin* of a loom.

ܡܣܬܡܟܪܝܬܐ pl. ܝ̈ܬܐ, ܐ̈ infin. of verb ܣܡ with ܪܫܐ m. *capital punishment, punishment.*

ܡܣܡܡܘܡܐ Ar. *poisoned.*

ܡܣܡܝܘܬܐ or ܡܣܡܝܘܬܐ rt. ܣܡܐ. f. *lameness.*

ܡܣܡܝܢܐ rt. ܣܡܐ. *blinding.*

ܡܣܡܟܐ rt. ܣܡܟ. m. *retiring, repose; a couch, seat, support.*

ܡܣܬܡܟܢܐ rt. ܣܡܟ. m. *a supporter, helper, upholder.*

ܡܣܡܠܐ from ܣܡܠܐ. *ambidextrous.*

ܡܣܡܡܢܐ, ܡܣܡܡ rt. ܣܡ. m. *a poisoner.*

ܡܣܬܡܡܢܐ rt. ܣܡ. *healing, curing.*

ܡܣܬܡܟܠܢܐ, ܡܣܬܡܟܠܐ, ܡܣܬܡܟܠ from ܣܡܟܠ. *austere, ascetic, self-restrained; humbled.*

ܡܣܬܡܟܠܐܝܬ from ܣܡܟܠ. adv. *ascetically.*

ܡܣܬܡܟܠܘܬܐ from ܣܡܟܠ. f. *voluntary poverty.*

ܡܣܢܐ or ܡܣܐܢܐ, ܡܣܢܬܐ pl. ܡ̈ܣܢܐ and ܡ̈ܣܐܢܬܐ f. *a rush* or *reed basket.*

ܡܣܐܢܐ and ܡܣܢܐ pl. ܐ̈ rt. ܣܐܢ. m. *a shoe, sandal;* ܕܠܐ ܡܣܐܢܐ *unshod.*

ܡܣܬܢܩܘܬܐ rt. ܣܢܩ. f. *indigence.*

ܡܣܥܐ pl. ܐ̈ m. *a goad;* ܡܣܥܐ ܕܬܘܪܐ *an ox-goad.*

ܡܣܥܐ, ܡܣܥܐ or ܡܣܐܥܐ m. *fibre* esp. *palm fibre, a rope of fibre, cocoanut matting.*

ܡܣܦܝܠܐ *μέσπιλον, the medlar.*

ܡܣܬܦܩܢܐ rt. ܣܦܩ. *laxative.*

ܡܣܦܪܐ rt. ܣܦܪ. m. *shears, scissors, snuffers.*

ܡܣܦܪܘܬܐ rt. ܣܦܪ. f. *tonsure.*

ܡܣܦܪܢܐ rt. ܣܦܪ. m. *a) shears, scissors, a razor. b) a shearer, hair-cutter.*

ܡܣܦܪܬܐ pl. ܬܐ rt. ܣܦܪ. f. *a) shears, razors. b) an arch, vault.*

ܡܣܩ, ܡܣܩܐ rt. ܢܣܩ. m. *going* or *carrying up, ascent, sunrise;* ܡܣܩ ܫܦܪܐ *rising of the dawn; offering up* sacrifice; ܡܫܘܚܬܐ ܕܡܣܩܐ ܕܩܘܪܒܢܐ *the proper quantity of the oblate;* chem. *sublimation, distillation.*

ܡܣܩܬܐ, ܡܣܩܬܐ pl. ܬܐ rt. ܢܣܩ. f. *a) an ascent, going up, climb, pass;* ܥܣܩܘܬܐ ܕܡܣܩܬܐ *difficulty of the ascent;* ܡܣܩܬܐ ܕܡܢ ܒܝܬ ܡܝܬܐ *rising from the dead. b) taking up, translation* of the bones of saints.

ܡܣܩܘܣܬܐ pl. ܡܣܩܘܣܬܐ f. perh. *spasms.*

ܡܣܩܘܡܐܝܬ from ܣܩܡ. adv. *stiffly, symmetrically.*

ܡܣܩܘܡܘܬܐ from ܣܩܡ. f. *proportion.*

ܡܣܩܠܢܐ pl. ܢܐ rt. ܣܠܩ. *a)* subst. m. *an ascent, slope, eminence; steps, stairs;* ܡܙܡܘܪܐ ܕܡܣܩܠܢܐ *a psalm of degrees;* ܡܣܩܠܢܐ ܕܡܝܬܪܘܬܐ *the ascents of virtue. b)* adj. *impelling, making to rise;* ܙܘܥܐ ܡܣܩܠܢܐ *an upward impulse.*

ܡܣܩܠܢܘܬܐ pl. ܬܐ rt. ܣܠܩ. f. *contemplation.*

ܡܣܩܠܢܝܐ rt. ܣܠܩ. *of* or *for ascending.*

ܡܣܩܦܐ pl. ܦܐ rt. ܣܩܦ. *crouching.*

ܡܣܩܦܢܐ rt. ܣܩܦ. gram. the point ܂.

ܡܣܩܪ, ܡܣܩܪܐ rt. ܣܩܪ. *cross-eyed, squinting; azure, blue-eyed.*

ܡܣܩܪܘܬܐ rt. ܣܩܪ. f. *squinting.*

ܡܣܩܪܢܐ rt. ܣܩܪ. *one who looks askance, despises.*

ܡܣܪ fut. ܢܡܣܘܪ, act. part. ܡܣܪ, pass. part. ܡܣܝܪ. *to deliver up* to punishment or scorn, *to hold up* to contempt, *to lay an accusation against, accuse,* with ܥܠ or ܠܘܬ. ETHPE. ܐܬܡܣܪ *to be delivered up,* with ܒܐܝܕܝ ܒܥܠܕܒܒܘܗܝ or ܩܕܡ *into the hands of his enemies; to be made the scorn* or *sport of* ... with ܩܕܡ or ܡܢ *to be held in contempt;* ܐܬܡܣܪܬ ܗܝܡܢܘܬܐ *the faith was held in contempt.* PA. ܡܣܪ *to bring an accusation* with ܒ *against; to speak contemptuously.* APH. ܐܡܣܪ *a) to hold in contempt, hold lightly, set at naught, contemn,* with ܥܠ of people, but usually of ܒܗܬܬܐ *shame;* ܕܚܠܬܐ *fear;* ܚܝܐ *life;* ܡܘܬܐ *death;* ܢܡܘܣܐ *the law;* ܩܪܒܐ *war. b) to dare* with ܕ or ܠ and a verb. DERIVATIVES, ܡܣܘܪܐ, ܡܣܘܪܘܬܐ, ܡܣܘܪܢܐ.

ܡܣܪܐ also ܡܣܘܪܐ and ܡܣܪܬܐ pl. ܐ rt. ܢܣܪ. m. *a) a saw. b) a dolphin,* more probably *a sawfish. c)* see ܡܣܪܩܝܢ.

ܡܣܪܐܘܢ *the mesentery.*

ܡܣܪܓܠܐ, ܣܪܓܠܐ m. *a ruler, one who rules lines.*

ܡܣܪܕܘܬܐ rt. ܣܪܕ. f. *inspiring terror, fear.*

ܡܣܪܕܢܐ, ܣܪܕܢܐ rt. ܣܪܕ. *terrifying, terrible, frightful.*

ܡܣܪܕܢܘܬܐ rt. ܣܪܕ. f. *the causing of terror, affrighting, terrifying.*

ܡܣܪܘܚܝܬܐ, ܬܐ rt. ܣܪܚ. f. *an oil-flask.*

ܡܣܪܘܣ; see ܡܣܪܘܣ: *a good Syriac scholar.*

ܡܣܪܚܘܬܐ rt. ܣܪܚ. f. *depravity.*

ܡܣܪܚܢ, ܡܣܪܚܢܐ rt. ܣܪܚ. *a) one who gives largely. b) he who ordains, consecrates.*

ܡܣܪܚܢ, ܡܣܪܚܢܐ rt. ܣܪܚ. *a corrupter.*

ܡܣܪܚܢܘܬܐ rt. ܣܪܚ. f. *a) a request, command. b) ordination, designation, consecration. c) liberality.*

ܡܣܪܚܢܘܬܐ rt. ܣܪܚ. f. *corruption, damage.*

ܡܣܪܛܐ rt. ܣܪܛ. m. *a scalpel.*

ܡܣܪܩܝܢ and ܡܣܪܩܐ m. *a large dish, dessert dish.*

ܡܣܪܩܝܐ *ignorant, unlearned.*

ܡܣܪܝܩܐ *mesenteric.*

ܡܣܪܝܣܐ m. *an eunuch;* see verb ܣܪܣ.

ܡܣܪܩܐܝܬ rt. ܣܪܩ. adv. *in poverty, in the practice of poverty, empty-handed.*

ܡܣܪܩܘܬܐ rt. ܣܪܩ. f. *privation, poverty* esp. *voluntary renunciation of worldly goods, an austere life.*

ܡܣܪܬܐ rt. ܢܣܪ. f. *sawing.*

ܡܣܪܬܐ rt. ܐܣܪ. see ܡܐܣܪܬܐ *a bundle.*

ܡܣܬ or ܡܣܬܐ, ܡܣܬܐ only used in the const. st. m. *quantity, sufficiency, that which is sufficient, enough,* ܐܟܘܠ ܡܣܬܟ *eat so much as is sufficient for thee;* ܡܣܬ ܣܘܢܩܢܟ *enough for thy need, as much as thou needest;* ܡܣܬ ܚܘܒܐ *enough to pay a debt, the amount of the debt;* ܡܣܬ ܙܒܢܐ *for a time;* ܠܐ ܡܣܬ ܕ *it is not enough to . . .;* ܡܣܬ ܕ *as far as, in order that.*

ܡܣܬܐ *a balance;* see ܡܣܐܬܐ.

ܡܣܬܐ and less correctly ܡܣܬܐ rt. ܡܣܐ. f. *rennet, sour curdled milk; that which holds together.*

ܡܣܬܒܥܢܐ, ܢܝܬܐ rt. ܣܒܥ. with ܠܐ *insatiable; that which never palls nor causes satiety.*

ܡܣܬܓܕܢܐ rt. ܣܓܕ. *adored, adorable.*

ܡܣܬܓܦܢܐ rt. ܣܓܦ. *subject to injury.*

ܡܣܬܕܩܢܐ rt. ܣܕܩ. with ܠܐ *indivisible.*

ܡܣܬܕܩܢܐܝܬ rt. ܣܕܩ. adv. with ܠܐ *indivisibly.*

ܡܣܬܗܕܢܐ rt. ܣܗܕ. *that of which evidence is given.*

ܡܣܬܗܕܢܘܬܐ rt. ܣܗܕ. f. *the giving of testimony.*

ܡܣܬܗܪܢ, ܡܣܬܗܪܢܐ from ܣܗܪܐ. *lunatic.*

ܡܣܬܘܪܢܐ from ܣܘܪܐ. m. gram. *of narration.*

ܡܣܬܝܒܪܢܐ, ܢܝܬܐ rt. ܣܒܪ. with ܠܐ *intolerable.*

ܡܣܬܝܒܪܢܐܝܬ rt. ܣܒܪ. adv. with ܠܐ *intolerably;* ܠܐ ܡܣܬܝܒܪܢܐܝܬ ܚܕܝܐ ܡܬܓܠܓܠ *he is so excited with joy he cannot contain himself.*

ܡܣܬܝܩܢܘܬܐ rt. ܣܩ. f. *kindling, burning; being scorched, burnt.*

ܡܣܬܝܟܢܐ, ܢܝܬܐ rt. ܣܟ. *finite, limited;* with ܠܐ *infinite, unlimited.*

ܡܣܬܝܟܢܐܝܬ rt. ܣܟ. adv. with ܠܐ *infinitely.*

ܡܣܬܝܟܢܘܬܐ rt. ܣܟ. f. with ܠܐ *infinity, incomprehensibility.*

ܡܣܬܬܝܢܘܬܐ from ܣܬܘܐ. f. *wintering, passing the winter.*

ܡܣܬܟܝܢܐ rt. ܣܟ. *one in need of help.*

ܡܣܬܟܝܢܐ, ܢܝܬܐ rt. ܣܟܐ. *expected, awaited, looked for;* with ܠܐ *unexpected.*

ܡܣܬܟܝܢܐܝܬ rt. ܣܟܐ. adv. with ܠܐ *unexpectedly, unhoped for.*

ܡܣܬܟܢܢܐܝܬ rt. ܣܟܢ. adv. *firmly, immovably.*

ܡܣܬܟܠܢܐ, ܢܝܬܐ rt. ܣܟܠ. *a*) *that which can be apprehended by the intellect, intelligible, mystical.* *b*) *one against whom an offence is committed.*

ܡܣܬܟܠܢܐܝܬ rt. ܣܟܠ. adv. *mystically.*

ܡܣܬܟܠܢܘܬܐ rt. ܣܟܠ. f. *understanding, intellect.*

ܡܣܬܟܡܢܘܬܐ from ܣܟܡ. f. *formation, configuration.*

ܡܣܬܠܝܢܐ rt. ܣܠܐ. *contemptible.*

ܡܣܬܠܝܢܘܬܐ rt. ܣܠܐ. f. *rejection, reprobation.*

ܡܣܬܥܪܢܐ, ܢܝܬܐ rt. ܣܥܪ. *that which should be done, an undertaking.*

ܡܣܬܥܪܢܘܬܐ rt. ܣܥܪ. f. *visitation; action.*

ܡܣܬܦܩܪܢܐ rt. ܣܦܩܪ. *a braggart, prater, vaunter.*

ܡܣܬܪܓܢܐ rt. ܣܪܓ. *caparisoned.*

ܡܣܬܪܓܢܘܬܐ rt. ܣܪܓ. f. *the being furnished with a horse-cloth.*

ܡܣܬܪܢܘܬܐ rt. ܣܬܪ. f. *concealment.*

ܡܣܬܪܚܢܐ rt. ܣܪܚ. f. *wasted, desolate.*

ܡܣܬܪܛܢܘܬܐ rt. ܣܪܛ. f. *being scratched, scarified.*

ܡܣܬܪܢܐ, ܢܝܬܐ rt. ܣܬܪ. *a protector; protecting, concealing, sheltering.*

ܡܣܬܪܢܘܬܐ rt. ܣܬܪ. f. *protection, defence.*

ܡܣܬܪܩܢܐ rt. ܣܪܩ. with ܠܐ *that which cannot be laid aside.*

ܡܣܬܪܩܢܘܬܐ rt. ܣܪܩ. f. *laying aside, renunciation.*

ܡܣܬܬܐܝܬ rt. ܣܬ. adv. *according to natural character,* opp. ܠܐ ܡܣܬܬܐܝܬ *according to condition.*

ܡܣܬܬܘܬܐ rt. ܣܬ. f. *stability, steadfastness, constancy;* with ܠܐ *instability, inconstancy.*

ܡܣܬܬܢܐ rt. ܣܬ. *one who establishes, sets firmly.*

ܡܣܬܬܪܢܐ rt. ܣܬܪ. with ܠܐ *indestructible.*

ܡܥܐ pl. ܡܥܝܢ, ܡܥܝܐ f. *an obolus, farthing.*

ܡܥܐ emph. ܡܥܝܐ rarely ܡܥܝܐ pl. ܡܥܝܢ, ܡܥܝܐ m. pl. *a*) *the bowels, viscera, intestines;*

ܡܥܝܐ ܩܛܝܢܐ—ܥܒܝܐ *the lesser, the greater intestines;* ܡܥܝܐ ܬܪܝܨܐ *the rectum;* ܦܘܠܛ ܡܥܝܐ *dysentery;* ܒܪܝ ܕܢܦܩ ܡܢ ܡܥܝ *my son who came forth from my loins;* ܡܥܝܐ ܕܪܚܡܐ *bowels of mercy.* b) ܡܥܝܐ ܕܐܪܥܐ *earth-worms.*

ܡܥܒܕܐ rt. ܥܒܕ. m. *enchantment, sorcery; a worker of enchantments.*

ܡܥܒܕܢܐ, ܢܝܬܐ rt. ܥܒܕ. *working, causing, efficient;* ܡܥܒܕܢܝܬܐ ܕܐܒܕܢܐ ܠܐܢܫܐ *bringing destruction upon men;* with ܠܐ *ineffectual, void, of none effect;* gram. *active.*

ܡܥܒܕܢܐܝܬ rt. ܥܒܕ. adv. *causally, actually.*

ܡܥܒܕܢܘܬܐ pl. ܘܬܐ. rt. ܥܒܕ. f. *operation, working, power to efface* or *produce, energy, activity, efficacy, effect, action; instigation, motion* or *influence;* ܡܥܒܕܢܘܬܐ ܡܚܝܢܝܬܐ *life-giving power;* ܐܝܟ ܕܡܢ ܡܥܒܕܢܘܬܐ ܕܐܠܗܐ *as by the operation of God;* ܡܥܒܕܢܘܬܐ ܐܢܫܝܬܐ *human actions;* ܐܝܟ ܡܥܒܕܢܘܬܐ ܣܛܢܝܬܐ *as by Satanic influence;* ܢܦܩ ܠܡܥܒܕܢܘܬܐ *it came into operation* or *effect;* ܒܡܥܒܕܢܘܬܐ *really, actually, in effect;* pl. *the functions* of the body; gram. *action.*

ܡܥܒܕܢܢܐ rt. ܥܒܕ. adj. *efficient, effectual;* ܚܝܠܐ ܡܥܒܕܢܢܐ *efficient* or *productive force.*

ܡܥܒܪܐ, ܡܥܒܪܬܐ pl. ܡܥܒܪܬܐ rt. ܥܒܪ. f. a) *a way, pass, passage, crossing, ford, straits, a duct, canal;* ܡܥܒܪܬܐ ܕܓܒܥ *the pass of Geba;* ܒܡܥܒܪܬܐ ܕܢܗܪܐ *at the ford of the river.* b) *a public road* or *way; a ferry, ferry-boat; a passage, vestibule.* c) *a going amongst, intercourse, conversation.*

ܡܥܒܪܢܐ pl. ܢܐ rt. ܥܒܪ. m. a) *he who causes to pass over* or *by;* ܡܥܒܪܢܐ ܕܙܒܢܐ ܘܕܪܐ God *who makes times and generations to pass away.* b) *a passage, a strait* of the sea, *a ferry-boat;* ܡܥܒܪܢܐ ܕܦܓܪܐ *ducts, pores of the body.* c) *a hymn of the dead;* ܡܥܒܪܢܐ ܕܥܒܪܝܐ *a hymn of those who are passing away.*

ܡܥܐܕܢܐ pl. ܢܐ rt. ܥܐܕ. m. *keeping holiday, festive, festal;* ܡܐܡܪܐ ܡܥܐܕܢܐ *festal homilies;* ܟܬܒܐ ܡܥܐܕܢܐ *a book with hymns for festivals;* ܠܐ ܡܥܐܕܢܐ *those who do not keep Easter.*

ܡܥܕܪܢ, ܡܥܕܪܢܐ, ܢܝܬܐ rt. ܥܕܪ. a) *a helper, help, giver of assistance, fellow-worker, benefactor, protector,* ܐܝܟ ܡܥܕܪܢܐ ܕܠܘܬܗ *a help meet for him.* b) adj. *useful, helpful, advantageous, salutary;* ܣܡܡܢܐ ܡܥܕܪܢܐ *useful drugs.*

ܡܥܕܪܢܘܬܐ rt. ܥܕܪ. f. *help, assistance.*

ܡܥܕܪܢܢܐ, ܢܝܬܐ rt. ܥܕܪ. *helpful, assisting, help-giving;* ܡܥܕܪܢܢܝܬܐ *things helpful* or *salutary.*

ܡܥܗܕܢܐ E-Syr. ܡܥܗܕܢܐ pl. ܢܐ rt. ܥܗܕ. m. *a recorder, chronicler.*

ܡܥܗܕܢܘܬܐ rt. ܥܗܕ. f. *a calling to remembrance, rehearsal, recording;* ܡܥܗܕܢܘܬܐ ܕܣܘܥܪܢܐ *the recording of actions;* ܡܥܗܕܢܘܬܐ ܠܘܬ ܡܝܬܪܘܬܐ *an exhortation to virtue;* ܡܥܗܕܢܘܬܐ ܕܐܘܢܓܠܝܘܢ *a commentary on the Gospel.*

ܡܥܘܟܢ, ܡܥܘܟܢܐ, ܢܝܬܐ pl. m. ܢܐ f. ܢܝܬܐ rt. ܥܘܟ. *he* or *that which hinders, impedes, a hinderer;* ܠܐ ܬܗܘܘܢ ܡܥܘܟܢܐ ܠܥܒܕܐ *you may not hinder the work;* ܙܝܙܢܐ ܡܥܘܟܢܐ *tares which entangle* the corn or *hamper* growth; ܝܬܝܪܘܬܐ ܡܥܘܟܢܝܬܐ *embarrassing superfluity.* Pl. f. *hindrances, impediments;* ܡܥܘܟܢܝܬܐ ܕܥܠܡܐ *worldly difficulties, hindrances* to piety.

ܡܥܘܟܢܐܝܬ rt. ܥܘܟ. adv. *loiteringly.*

ܡܥܘܠܢܐ rt. ܥܘܠ. *an oppressor.*

ܡܥܝܐ, ܡܥܝܬܐ f. *an intestine, entrail.*

ܡܥܙܐ = ܡܥܙܐ *hair, fur.*

ܡܥܙܠܢܘܬܐ rt. ܚܙܠ. f. *constancy.*

ܡܥܙܠܢܐܝܬ rt. ܚܙܠ. adv. *with constancy, with fortitude.*

ܡܥܙܠܢܘܬܐ rt. ܚܙܠ. f. *fortitude, endurance.*

ܡܥܙܠܐ rt. ܥܙܠ. m. *a spindle.*

ܡܥܛܫܢܐ rt. ܥܛܫ. *sneezing, causing sneezing; a plant* used for snuff.

ܡܥܝܕܘܬܐ rt. ܥܝܕ. f. *habit, custom.*

ܡܥܝܢ, ܡܥܝܢܐ pl. ܡܥܝܢܐ ܡܥܝܢܝܬܐ from ܥܝܢܐ. f. *a spring, fount;* ܡܥܝܢܐ ܕܡܝܐ *a spring of water;* metaph. ܡܥܝܢܐ ܕܚܝܐ *the fount of life;* ܡܥܝܢܐ ܕܒܘܪܟܬܐ *a fount of blessings.*

ܡܥܝܢܝܐ from ܥܝܢܐ. adj. *of* or *from a fount* or *spring;* ܡܝܐ ܡܥܝܢܝܐ ܘܢܗܪܝܐ *spring* and *river water.*

ܡܥܟܣܘܬܐ rt. ܥܟܣ. f. some illness perh. *epilepsy.*

ܡܥܟܣܬܐ; see ܥܟܣ.

ܡܥܝܩܢܐ, ܢܝܬܐ rt. ܥܘܩ. *grievous, troublesome, distressing, vexatious;* pl. f. *annoyances, afflictions;* ܚܐܪܘܬܐ ܕܡܢ ܟܠܗܘܢ ܡܥܝܩܢܝܬܐ *freedom from all annoyances.*

ܡܥܝܪܢܐ, ܡܥܝܪܢܝ rt. ܥܘܪ. m. *a) one who awakes, arouses;* ܘܝ ܠܟ ܡܥܝܪܢܐ ܕܒܝܫܬܐ *woe to thee who stirrest up evil. b) nocturns. c) a poker.*

ܡܥܝܪܢܘܬܐ pl. ܘܬܐ rt. ܥܘܪ. f. *that which arouses the mind to attention, a monition, observation, notice.*

ܡܥܠܐ, ܡܥܠܐ pl. ܡܥܠܐ or ܡܥܠܐ rt. ܥܠ. m. opp. ܡܦܩܐ. *coming, entrance, return; beginning, commencement;* ܡܥܠܝ or ܡܥܠ ܨܘܡܐ *the entering upon* or *beginning of the fast;* ܚܕ ܒܫܒܐ ܕܡܥܠܝ ܨܘܡܐ *the Sunday before Lent;* ܒܪܡܫܐ ܕܐܝܬܘܗܝ ܡܥܠܝ ܫܒܬܐ *at vespers, that is at the commencement of the Sabbath.*

ܡܥܠܬܐ, ܡܥܠܐ rt. ܥܠ. f. opp. ܡܦܩܢܬܐ. *a) entrance, entering in* or *upon; an incursion, inroad, invasion. b) bringing in, introduction; an introduction, preface. c) entrance into office, induction, inauguration. d)* eccles. *dedication* of a church, *solemn entrance* or *procession;* ܡܥܠܬܐ ܕܩܘܪܒܢܐ—ܕܪܐܙܐ *the bringing in of the holy elements, the entrance. e) crop, produce, return.*

ܡܥܠܝܐܝܬ rt. ܥܠܐ. adv. *eminently, excellently, sublimely; on high.*

ܡܥܠܝܘܬܐ rt. ܥܠܐ. f. *loftiness, a lofty deed, high estate, excellence, elevation, exaltation, sublimity;* ܡܥܠܝܘܬܐ ܕܛܘܗܡܐ *nobility of birth;* title ܡܥܠܝܘܬܟ *your Highness, your Excellency.*

ܡܥܠܝܢܐ rt. ܥܠܐ. *a) one who raises, exalts. b) a monk's cloak.*

ܡܥܠܢܐ pl. ܢܐ, ܢܝܢ rt. ܥܠ. m. opp. ܡܦܩܢܐ. *a way in, ingress, entrance;* ܡܥܠܢܐ ܕܬܪܥܐ *the entering* or *approach to the gate.*

ܡܥܠܢܘܬܐ rt. ܥܠ. f. *an entrance; access, admittance;* with ܫܩܠ *to obtain entrance* or *admittance.*

ܡܥܠܥܠܐ, ܡܥܠܥܠܬܐ rt. ܥܠ. *tempest-tossed, troubled.*

ܡܥܠܥܠܢܘܬܐ rt. ܥܠ. f. *violent agitation.*

ܡܥܡܕܢܐ rt. ܥܡܕ. m. *one who baptizes;* esp. John *the Baptist.*

ܡܥܡܘܕܝܬܐ rt. ܥܡܕ. f. *a) a pool. b) washing. c) baptism;* ܒܪܐ ܕܡܥܡܘܕܝܬܐ *a godchild. d)* with ܒܝܬ or ellipt. *a baptistery.*

ܡܥܡܛܢܐ, ܢܝܬܐ rt. ܥܡܛ. *darkening, sullying.*

ܡܥܡܠܐ, ܡܥܡܠܬܐ or ܡܥܡܠܬܐ cf. ܐܡܠܐ. *a rug, carpet.*

ܡܥܡܥܐ *very ill, seriously ill.*

ܡܥܡܪܐ, ܡܥܡܪ rt. ܥܡܪ. m. *dwelling, sojourning* esp. in a strange land; ܒܝܬ ܡܥܡܪܐ *a dwelling-place; a dwelling, abode;* ܫܘܝܘܬܐ ܡܥܡܪܐ *fitness for habitation, habitableness;* ܡܥܡܪܐ ܕܡܫܝܚܝܐ *a monastery.*

ܡܥܡܪܢܐ rt. ܥܡܪ. *the founder* of a town.

ܡܥܢܝܢܐ, ܢܝܬܐ rt. ܥܢܐ. *a singer, precentor.*

ܡܥܢܝܢܘܬܐ rt. ܥܢܐ. f. *singing; a choral dance.*

ܡܥܢܝܬܐ pl. ܡܥܢܝܢܬܐ rt. ܥܢܐ. f. *a) familiar intercourse;* with ܒܪ *intimate, a friend. b) a chant, antiphon.*

ܡܥܟ fut. ܢܡܥܘܟ, act. part. ܡܥܟ, ܡܥܟܐ, pass. part. ܡܥܝܟ, ܟܐ, ܟܬܐ. *to dash, trample* or *knock down, to bruise;* ܡܥܟ ܐܝܟ ܐܪܝܐ ܥܘܦܝܐ ܘܥܢܒܝܐ ܐܡܐ ܥܡ ܒܢܝܐ *he tramples down branch and berries, mother and children, together;* ܫܘܚܢܐ ܕܡܥܟ ܗܘܐ ܚܝܠܗ *the ulcer which had brought his strength down.* Used of demoniacal possession esp. in the pass. part. *convulsed, distraught by a devil, raving, vile, horrid;* ܪܓܝܓܬܐ ܡܥܝܟܬܐ ܕܚܫܝܗܘܢ *the vile indulgence of their passions.* Fem. emph. *raving, distraction, aberration;* ܒܡܥܝܟܘܬܐ ܐܢܐ ܐܬܢܣܝܬ *I myself was tried by demoniacal distractions.* ETHPE. ܐܬܡܥܟ *to be knocked* or *trampled down* under the horses' feet; *to be convulsed, tormented by a demon.* PA. ܡܥܟ *to trample, crush;* ܘܡܥܟܘ ܠܥܡܘܪܝܗ *parts of the city fell and crushed the inhabitants;* metaph. *to pollute.* DERIVATIVES, ܡܥܟܐ, ܡܥܟܘܬܐ.

ܡܥܟܐ pl. ܟܐ rt. ܡܥܟ. m. *a) a twisting, griping* of the intestines, *convulsion;* ܡܥܟܐ ܕܟܪܣܐ *the colic;* ܡܥܟܐ ܕܛܠܝܐ *infantile convulsions. b) the rubbing* of ears of wheat.

ܡܥܩܣܩܣܐ rt. ܥܩܣ. *crisp, curly.*

ܡܥܣܪܐ pl. ܐ̈ from ܥܣܪ. m. *a tenth part, tithe.*

ܡܥܣܪܢܘܬܐ from ܥܣܪ. f. *tithing, the exacting* or *offering of a tithe.*

ܡܥܦܝܢܐ, ܢܝܬܐ rt. ܥܦܐ. *an undertaker, one who lays out for burial; funereal.*

ܡܥܦܦܢܘܬܐ rt. ܥܦ. f. *multiplication; plurality.*

ܡܥܦܪܐ or ܡܥܦܪܐ pl. ܐ̈ rt. ܥܦܪ. m. *a cloak* or *hood;* one of the Eucharistic vestments, *a large square linen amice* or *cope.*

ܡܥܦܪܢܐ rt. ܥܦܪ. m. *a gleaner.*

ܡܥܨܝܢܐ rt. ܥܨܐ. *stubborn.*

ܡܥܨܪܬܐ pl. ܡܥܨܪ̈ܬܐ, ܡܥܨܪ̈ܐ rt. ܥܨܪ. f. *a wine-press, wine-vat.*

ܡܥܩܐܝܬ rt. ܥܩܐ. adv. *sadly.*

ܡܥܩܒܐܝܬ rt. ܥܩܒ. adv. *curiously, inquisitively.*

ܡܥܩܒܢܐ, ܢܝܬܐ, ܡܥܩܒܢ rt. ܥܩܒ. *a tracker, one who follows the track, a searcher, investigator.*

ܡܥܩܒܢܐܝܬ rt. ܥܩܒ. adv. *inquisitively.*

ܡܥܩܒܢܘܬܐ rt. ܥܩܒ. f. *inquiry.*

ܡܥܩܒܢܝܐ rt. ܥܩܒ. *interrogative.*

ܡܥܩܝܘܬܐ rt. ܥܩܐ. f. *sadness.*

ܡܥܩܡܐܝܬ rt. ܥܩܡ. adv. *perversely.*

ܡܥܩܡܘܬܐ rt. ܥܩܡ. f. *perversity, craftiness, tortuosity.*

ܡܥܩܡܢܐ rt. ܥܩܡ. *a perverter; one who takes distorted views, a cynic.*

ܡܥܪܐ pl. ܐ̈ rt. ܥܪܐ. m. *a note, mark, sign.*

ܡܥܪܬܐ, ܡܥܪܐ pl. ܡܥܪ̈ܐ, ܡܥܪ̈ܬܐ E-Syr. ܡܥܪ̈ܬܐ rt. ܥܘܪ II. f. *a) a cave, cavern, den, hollow;* ܡܥܪܬܐ ܕܓܢܒ̈ܐ *a den of thieves;* ܡܥܪ̈ܬܐ ܕܟܦܝ̈ܠܬܐ *double caverns, caves one within the other;* ܡܥܪܬ ܓܙ̈ܐ *the Cave of Treasures* where, according to legend, the bodies of Adam and of the patriarchs were laid, where also were stored the gold, incense and myrrh offered by the Magi to Christ. *b) a cell;* ܡܥܪܬܐ ܕܒܢܗ̇ ܘܐܬܩܢܗ̇ ܡܢ ܟܐܦ̈ܐ *a cell which he built and fashioned of stones.*

ܡܥܪܒܐ also written ܡܥܪܒܐ pl. ܡܥܪ̈ܒܐ usually constr. com. gen. *the setting of the sun, the west* opp. ܡܕܢܚܐ; ܡܥܪܒ ܓܪܒܝܐ *the north-west;* ܡܥܪܒܗ ܕܫܡܫܐ *the going down of the sun, sunset;* ܒܡܥܪܒܐ ܕܐܪܒܥܫܒܐ *on Wednesday evening;* ܡܥܪܒܝܗ̇ ܕܕܩܠܬ *the western shores of the Tigris;* ܡܥܪ̈ܒܘܗܝ ܕܥܠܡܐ *the western regions of the world.*

ܡܥܪܒܐܝܬ rt. ܥܪܒ. adv. *confusedly.*

ܡܥܪܒܘܬܐ rt. ܥܪܒ. f. *a) mixing. b) sifting.*

ܡܥܪܒܝܐ, ܝܬܐ rt. ܥܪܒ. *western, occidental;* ܡܥܪ̈ܒܝܐ *Westerns, inhabitants of the west.*

ܡܥܪܒܠܘܬܐ from ܥܪܒܠ. f. *sifting, bolting.*

ܡܥܪܕܪܘܬܐ from ܥܪܕܪ. f. *corrosion* of the bones, *cariousness.*

ܡܥܪܙܘܬܐ rt. ܥܪܙ. f. *licentiousness, lasciviousness.*

ܡܥܪܙܢܐ rt. ܥܪܙ. *debauched.*

ܡܥܪܡܐܝܬ rt. ܥܪܡ. adv. *maliciously.*

ܡܥܪܡܘܬܐ rt. ܥܪܡ. f. *swelling, rising high* as water; metaph. *malice, exasperation, violence.*

ܡܥܪܦܢܐ pl. ܢ̈ܐ rt. ܥܪܦ. *a money-changer.*

ܡܥܪܦܢܝܐ adj. from the above, ܦܬܘܪ̈ܐ ܡܥܪܦܢܝ̈ܐ *money-changers' tables.*

ܡܥܪܩܐ rt. ܥܪܩ. m. *refuge;* ܒܝܬ ܡܥܪܩܐ *a place of refuge.*

ܡܥܪܩܐ rt. ܥܪܩ. *one who puts to flight, drives out.*

ܡܥܫܢܐ, ܢܝܬܐ rt. ܥܫܢ. *a champion, defender.*

ܡܥܫܢܘܬܐ rt. ܥܫܢ. f. *strengthening.*

ܡܥܫܦܐܝܬ from ܥܫܦܐ. adv. *as an axe cuts, sharply, distinctly.*

ܡܥܫܩܘܬܐ rt. ܥܫܩ. f. *insolence, madness, folly, perversity.*

ܡܥܫܩܢܐ, ܢܝܬܐ rt. ܥܫܩ, *grievous, insolent.*

ܡܥܫܩܢܘܬܐ rt. ܥܫܩ. f. *oppression, false accusation.*

ܡܥܬܕܐܝܬ rt. ܥܬܕ. adv. *ready, in readiness.*

ܡܥܬܕܘܬܐ rt. ܥܬܕ. f. *preparing, preparation.*

ܡܥܬܕܢܐ, ܢܝܬܐ rt. ܥܬܕ. *one who prepares, makes ready; introductory.*

ܡܥܬܕܢܘܬܐ rt. ܥܬܕ. f. *readiness.*

ܡܥܬܪܢܐ rt. ܥܬܪ. *enriching, making rich.*

ܡܦܓܪܢܐ rt. ܦܓܪ. gram. *points used instead of vowel points placed one above a letter, the other below but not immediately* as in ܚܒܪܐ and ܚܘܒܪܐ.

ܡܦܓܥܢܐ, ܢܝܬܐ rt. ܦܓܥ. *hindering, impeding.*

ܡܦܓܥܢܐܝܬ rt. ܦܓܥ. adv. *unwillingly.*

ܡܦܓܝܢܘܬܐ rt. ܦܓܐ. f. *an error, defect.*

ܡܦܘܚܐ rt. ܢܦܚ. m. *a pair of bellows.*

ܡܦܘܚܝܬܐ pl. ܚܝܬܐ rt. ܢܦܚ. f. *a*) *a breath, puff of air, blast, blowing, eruption* of wind or fire from the earth. *b*) *afflatus, inspiration. c*) *a fan, winnowing-shovel.*

ܡܦܘܚܢܐ rt. ܦܘܚ. *cooling, refreshing.*

ܡܦܘܚܬܐ rt. ܢܦܚ. f. *a breath, breathing, afflation, inspiration.*

ܡܦܘܠܬܐ pl. ܡܦܘܠܝܬܐ and ܡܦܠܬܐ rt. ܢܦܠ. f. *a fall, falling, ruin* e.g. of buildings; ܟܐܒܐ ܕܡܦܘܠܬܐ *epilepsy.* Metaph. *a fall, misfortune, calamity, catastrophe* esp. theol. *a fall, falling into sin;* gram. *a case.*

ܡܦܘܫܫܢܐ, ܢܝܬܐ rt. ܦܫ. *diaphoretic, dissolvent.*

ܡܦܚܐ rt. ܢܦܚ. m. *an air-ball, air-cushion.*

ܡܦܚܡܢܘܬܐ rt. ܦܚܡ. f. *comparison, analogy.*

ܡܦܚܡܢܐ, ܢܝܬܐ rt. ܦܚܡ. *comparing, analogical.*

ܡܦܛܡܢܘܬܐ rt. ܦܛܡ. f. *fattening, feeding up.*

ܡܦܛܡܢܘܬܐ rt. ܦܛܡ. f. *fattening, stall-feeding.*

ܡܦܝܓܢܐ rt. ܦܘܓ. *cooling, refreshing.*

ܡܦܝܓܢܘܬܐ rt. ܦܘܓ. f. *cooling, coolness.*

ܡܦܝܚܢܝܬܐ pl. ܢܝܬܐ rt. ܦܘܚ. f. *a pair of bellows, a fan.*

ܡܦܚܙܘܬܐ and ܡܦܚܙ rt. ܦܚܙ. f. *disdain, scorn, negligence, boldness.*

ܡܦܝܣܢܐ, ܢܝܬܐ from ܦܝܣܐ. adj. *persuasive, plausible, winning;* ܡ̈ܠܐ ܡܦܝܣܢܝܬܐ *persuasive words;* subst. *an intercessor, advocate;* gram. the accent .–.

ܡܦܝܣܢܐܝܬ from ܦܝܣܐ. adv. *persuasively, suppliantly.*

ܡܦܝܣܢܘܬܐ from ܦܝܣܐ f. *persuasion, invitation, persuasiveness, sophistry; supplication, intercession.*

ܡܦܟܗܢܐ rt. ܦܟܗ. *counteractive, acting as an antidote.*

ܡܦܠ, ܡܦܠܐ rt. ܢܦܠ. m. *falling, fall; sunset, descent;* ܟܕ ܡܦܠ ܫܢܬܐ ܥܠ ܒ̈ܢܝ ܐܢܫܐ *when sleep falleth upon men;* ܡܦܠܗ ܠܒܝܬ ܐܣܝܪ̈ܐ *his being thrown into prison.*

ܡܦܠܓܐܝܬ rt. ܦܠܓ. adv. *separately, apart.*

ܡܦܠܓܘܬܐ rt. ܦܠܓ. f. *duplicity.*

ܡܦܠܓܢܐ, ܢܝܬܐ rt. ܦܠܓ. *one who divides, separates.*

ܡܦܠܚܪܘܬܐ and ܡܦܠܚܪܢܘܬܐ from ܦܠܚܪ. f. *dispersion, scattering; mental perturbation* or *confusion.*

ܡܦܠܛܢܐ, ܢܝܬܐ rt. ܦܠܛ. *freeing, setting free.*

ܡܦܘܠܬܐ or ܡܦܠܬܐ, cf. ܡܦܘܠܬܐ rt. ܢܦܠ. f. gram. *a case; a prefix.*

ܡܦܢܛܣܝܢܐ, ܢܝܬܐ from ܦܢܛܣܝܐ. *imaginary.*

ܡܦܢܝܢܐ, ܢܝܬܐ rt. ܦܢܐ. *giving, bringing* or *leading back, restoring;* ܡܦܢܝܢܐ ܕܛܥܝ̈ܐ ܠܥܕܬܐ *one who brings back wanderers to the Church.*

ܡܦܢܝܢܐ, ܢܝܬܐ rt. ܦܢܐ. *answering, converting.*

ܡܦܢܝܢܘܬܐ rt. ܦܢܐ. f. *return, conversion.*

ܡܦܢܩܘܬܐ rt. ܦܢܩ. f. *a luxurious life, indulgence in ease and pleasure.*

ܡܦܢܩܢܐ rt. ܦܢܩ. *one who leads a luxurious* or *effeminate life.*

ܡܦܣ Aphel pass. part. of ܦܣ. *it is lawful, right.*

ܡܦܣ Aphel pass. part.; see under ܦܣܐ. *able, capable, expert,* &c.

ܡܦܣܘܬܐ from ܦܣܐ. f. *knowledge, capability;* with ܠܐ *ignorance, incapacity.*

ܡܦܣܢܘܬܐ rt. ܦܣ. f. *permission, licence, liberty;* eccles. *a permission, faculty, power;* used with ܝܗܒ, ܢܣܒ or ܗܘܐ; ܡܦܣܢܘܬܐ ܗܘܬ *it is allowed, permitted.*

ܡܦܣܩܢܐ, ܢܝܬܐ rt. ܦܣܩ *cutting, trenchant; one who lops off, amputates;* ܫ̈ܢܐ ܡܦܣܩܢܝܬܐ *the incisors.*

ܡܦܨܚܢܐ rt. ܦܨܚ. *gladdening, one who makes glad.*

ܡܦܨܚܢܐܝܬ rt. ܦܨܚ. adv. *exultingly.*

ܡܦܨܝܢܐ, ܡܦܨܝܢܝܬܐ rt. ܦܨܐ. *a deliverer, saviour.*

ܡܦܩ, ܡܦܩܐ pl. ܡܦܩܐ or ܡܦܩܢܐ rt. ܢܦܩ. m. *a*) *going out,* opp. ܡܥܠܐ. *exit, egress;* ܡܦܩܗ ܕܫܢܬܐ *the end of the year.* *b*) ܡܦܩ ܒܪܘܚܐ *apology, excuse, defence; preface.*

ܡܦܩܕܢܐ, ܡܦܩܕܢܝܬܐ rt. ܦܩܕ. *an instructor, commander; a testator.*

ܡܦܩܕܢܘܬܐ rt. ܦܩܕ. f. *a precept, injunction.*

ܡܦܩܢܐ pl. ܡܦܩܢ̈ܐ rt. ܢܦܩ. m. *a*) *going forth* or *out, departure;* ܣܦܪܐ ܕܡܦܩܢܐ *the Book of Exodus.* *b*) *outgoing, issue, flood.* *c*) *way out, passage, outlet, exit, egress.* *d*) *limit, end;* ܡܦܩܢܐ ܕܬܚܘܡܐ *the limit of the border; end* of life, *death;* ܡܦܩܢܐ ܕܢܦܫܐ *the departure of the soul;* ܫܥܬܐ ܕܡܦܩܢܐ *the hour of death.* *e*) *edition;* ܡܦܩܢܗ ܚܕܬܐ ܘܚܬܝܬܐ ܕܟܬܒܐ *new and accurate edition of a book.* *f*) *rejection.* *g*) *issue, result.* *h*) *the vent, anus.*

ܡܦܩܢܘܬܐ rt. ܢܦܩ. f. *a*) *casting out.* *b*) eccles. *procession* of the Holy Ghost. *c*) gram. *derivation.*

ܡܦܩܢܢܐ, ܡܦܩܢܢܝܬܐ rt. ܢܦܩ. *a*) *departing, said on departing;* ܡ̈ܠܐ ܡܦܩܢܝܬܐ ܕܓܥܘܐ ܠܐܠܗܐ *commendatory words; words in which one at the point of death commends himself to God.* *b*) *excretory.*

ܡܦܩܥܢܐ rt. ܦܩܥ. m. *a watchman, one who shouts to scare away thieves.*

ܡܦܩܥܬܐ rt. ܦܩܥ. m. *a sling; a watchman's rattle.*

ܡܦܩܥܬܐ rt. ܦܩܥ. f. *a blotch, pustule.*

ܡܦܩܦܩܢܐ, ܡܦܩܦܩܢܝܬܐ rt. ܦܩ. *a prater; garrulous.*

ܡܦܩܬܐ pl. ܡܦܩܢ, ܡܦܩܬ̈ܐ rt. ܢܦܩ. f. *a*) *setting out* opp. ܡܦܢܝܢܐ *return; departure, death; expulsion; a procession, an expedition.* *b*) *a version, translation;* ܡܦܩܬܐ ܦܫܝܛܬܐ *the Peshita version;* ܡܦ. ܕܫ̈ܬܐ *the Hexapla.* *c*) *a breaking out, blain, eruption* esp. on the skin of the head. *d*) gram. *utterance, pronunciation.*

ܡܦܪܐ rt. ܦܪܐ. *that which grows of itself, self-sown.*

ܡܦܪܓܢܐܝܬ rt. ܦܪܓ. adv. *solemnly.*

ܡܦܪܓܢܘܬܐ and ܡܦܪܓܢܢܘܬܐ rt. ܦܪܓ. f. *splendour, brilliancy.*

ܡܦܪܓܢܐ rt. ܦܪܓ. *entertaining.*

ܡܦܪܕܕܐ rt. ܦܪܕ. m. *a cake made of the scrapings of the kneading-trough mixed with honey or oil.*

ܡܦܪܕܢܘܬܐ rt. ܦܪܕ. f. *separation; fleeing.*

ܡܦܪܚܢܐܝܬ rt. ܦܪܚ. adv. *swiftly, speedily.*

ܡܦܪܚܢܐ rt. ܦܪܚ. *one who makes to fly;* ܡܦܪܚܢܐ ܕܩܢܝܢܗ *a spendthrift.*

ܡܦܪܝܘܬܐ rt. ܦܪܐ. f. *procreation.*

ܡܦܪܝܢ, ܡܦܪܝܢܐ, ܡܦܪܝܢܝܬܐ rt. ܦܪܐ. *a*) *fruitful, fertile, generative.* *b*) *a begetter, progenitor, parent.* *c*) eccles. among the Jacobites *the Maphrianus, Maphrian, primate.*

ܡܦܪܝܢܘܬܐ rt. ܦܪܐ. *a*) *procreation, generative power, fecundity, fertility, productiveness;* with ܠܐ *sterility.* *b*) eccles. *the Maphrianate, primacy.*

ܡܦܪܝܢܝܐ, ܡܦܪܝܢܝܬܐ rt. ܦܪܐ. *a*) *generative.* *b*) *belonging to the Maphrian.*

ܡܦܪܟܟܘܬܐ rt. ܦܪܟ. f. *rubbing, crumbling, friction.*

ܡܦܪܝܢ Ethp. ܐܬܡܦܪܝܢ denom. verb from ܡܦܪܝܢܐ *to be made Maphrian, be raised to the archiepiscopate.*

ܡܦܪܢܣܢܐ from ܦܪܢܣ. m. *a steward, caretaker, provider; a tutor, guardian, administrator.*

ܡܦܪܢܣܐܝܬ and ܡܦܪܢܣܢܐܝܬ from ܦܪܢܣ. adv. *providentially.*

ܡܦܪܢܣܢܘܬܐ from ܦܪܢܣ. f. *a*) *a stewardship, management, administration, government, direction.* *b*) *providence, forethought, dispensation.*

ܡܦܪܣ, ܡܦܪܣܐ rt. ܦܪܣ. m. *spreading out, extension.*

ܡܦܪܣܐܝܬ rt. ܦܪܣ. adv. *nakedly, barely.*

ܡܦܪܣܝܘܬܐ rt. ܦܪܣ. f. *a*) *detection.* *b*) *open prostitution.*

ܡܦܪܣܝܢܐ rt. ܦܪܣ. *one who spreads evil reports, an accuser; a betrayer of secrets.*

ܡܦܪܣܢܘܬܐ rt. ܦܪܣ. f. *stripping naked.*

ܡܦܪܣܚܘܬܐ from ܦܪܣܚ. f. *rarefaction, expansion, looseness.*

ܡܦܪܣܚܢܘܬܐ from ܦܪܣܚ. f. *expansion, dissolution.*

ܡܦܪܥܢܐ rt. ܦܪܥ. *blossoming.*

ܡܦܪܩܐܝܬ rt. ܦܪܩ. adv. *at a distance, from afar.*

ܡܦܪܩܢܘܬܐ and ܡܦܪܩܘܬܐ rt. ܦܪܩ. *separation, dispelling, removal.*

ܡܦܪܫܐܝܬ rt. ܦܪܫ. adv. *apart, separately, distinctly, differently, particularly;* with ܠܐ *indiscriminately.*

ܡܦܪܫܘܬܐ rt. ܦܪܫ. f. *separateness, distinctness, distinction.*

ܡܦܪܫܢܐ or ܡܦܪܫܢܐ, ܢܝܬܐ rt. ܦܪܫ. *a*) *one who separates, discerns* or *explains, a critic;* ܡܦܪܫܢܐ ܕܢܡܘܣܐ *an expounder of the law;* ܝܘܡܐ ܡܦܪܫܢܐ *the day which discerns* or *separates* (the day of judgement). *b*) *separating, affording ground for separation* or *divorce.*

ܡܦܪܫܢܘܬܐ rt. ܦܪܫ. f. *separation, discrimination.*

ܡܦܫܛܘܬܐ rt. ܦܫܛ. f. *extension, simplicity.*

ܡܦܫܛܢܐ rt. ܦܫܛ. *stretching out, making straight.*

ܡܦܫܩܢܐ, ܢܝܬܐ rt. ܦܫܩ. *a*) *explanatory, interpretative. b*) *an instructor, expositor, commentator. c*) *an interpreter, translator.*

ܡܦܫܩܢܐܝܬ rt. ܦܫܩ. adv. *clearly.*

ܡܦܫܩܢܘܬܐ rt. ܦܫܩ. f. *exposition, commentary.*

ܡܦܫܪܢܐ rt. ܦܫܪ. *liquefying, dissolvent.*

ܡܦܬܚ, ܡܦܬܚܐ rt. ܦܬܚ. m. *the act of opening;* ܡܦܬܚ ܦܘܡܐ *eloquence.*

ܡܦܬܚܢܐ, ܢܝܬܐ rt. ܦܬܚ. *opening, one who opens.*

ܡܦܬܝܘܬܐ rt. ܦܬܐ. f. *dilatation, expansion.*

ܡܦܬܝܢܐ, ܢܝܬܐ rt. ܦܬܐ. *amplifying, dilating.*

ܡܦܬܟܐܝܬ rt. ܦܬܟ. adv. *many-coloured, manifold, variously.*

ܡܦܬܟܘܬܐ rt. ܦܬܟ. f. *variety, diversity,* esp. of colour; *an embroidered robe* or *stuff;* ܡܦܬܟܘܬܐ ܕܢܡܪܐ *the spotted coat of a leopard.*

ܡܦܬܟܢܐ rt. ܦܬܟ. *an embroiderer.*

ܡܦܬܠܐܝܬ rt. ܦܬܠ. *obliquely, perversely.*

ܡܦܬܠܘܬܐ rt. ܦܬܠ. f. *perversity.*

ܡܦܬܠܬܘܬܐ pl. ܬܐ rt. ܦܬܠ. f, *perversity, perverse* or *froward ways.*

ܡܦܬܟܦܢܘܬܐ rt. ܦܬ. f. *commination, calumny, contumely.*

ܡܨ fut. ܢܡܘܨ, act. part. ܡܐܨ, ܡܐܨܐ. *to suck* as young animals, as an insect sucks blood, as the earth sucks up water. Derivatives, ܡܨܐ, ܡܨܘܨܐ, ܡܨܨܐ.

ܡܨܐ I. fut. ܢܡܨܐ, act. part. ܡܨܐ, ܡܨܝܐ, pass. part. ܡܨܐ. *to suck* or *draw out* esp. blood, *to lap up* water; *to dry up* as a spring. Pa. ܡܨܝ *to suck out* blood; *to drink* or *draw from* the dregs; *to dry up* with illness. Ethpa. ܐܬܡܨܝ *to be sucked* or *squeezed out, to be strained* from dregs; *to dry up, become bloodless* from disease. Aph. ܐܡܨܝ *to drain out* blood, *wring out* water; *to drain* to the dregs; *to strain* away the dregs. Derivative, ܡܨܝܬܐ.

ܡܨܐ II. (root in Heb. and Chald. *to find, arrive at*) *to be able, have the power, be allowed,* pass. part. ܡܨܐ, ܡܨܝܐ used for the third pers. m. and f. also impers. *it may, it can.* With pers. prons. and often contracted forms the present tense: ܡܨܝܢܐ or ܐܢܐ ܡܨܐ *I can,* ܡܨܐ ܐܢܬ = ܡܨܝܬ *thou canst, thou mayest,* ܡܨܝܢ ܚܢܢ = ܡܨܝܢܢ *we may* or *can;* ܡܨܝܢ ܐܢܬܘܢ = ܡܨܝܬܘܢ *you may, can,* &c.; ܡܨܐ ܗܘܐ *he could, he might;* ܡܨܝܐ ܕܢܗܘܐ *it may be, it is possible;* ܟܠܗ ܠܐ ܡܨܝܐ *it is not impossible;* ܟܡܐ ܕܡܨܝܐ or ܟܡܐ *as far as may be, as much as possible;* ܐܝܟ ܟܡܐ ܕܡܨܝܢܢ *to the best of our power;* ܡܨܐ ܟܠ *omnipotent.* Often used with ܚܝܠܐ to give emphasis, ܠܐ ܡܨܐ ܐܢܐ ܚܝܠܐ ܕܐܫܬܘܩ *I am not able to keep silent;* ܠܐ ܡܨܐ ܐܢܐ ܚܝܠܗ *I am no match for him;* ܐܢ ܡܨܐ ܐܢܐ ܚܝܠܐ ܕܐܢܐ ܠܚܕ ܡܢܗܘܢ *if I can get the better of one of them;* ܡܨܐ ܚܝܠܐ a title of the Byzantine Emperors. Ethpe. ܐܬܡܨܝ *to be able; to dare, oppose, resist* with ܠ; with ܒܚܝܠܐ or ܚܝܠܐ or with ܠܘܩܒܠ, ܒ *to prevail over, overcome;* ܐܬܡܨܝܘ ܚܝܠܟ *they were stronger than thee;* ܠܐ ܡܬܡܨܝܢ ܗܘܘ *they were unequally matched* (in war); ܠܐ ܐܬܡܨܝܘ ܠܘܩܒܠ ܡܕܝܢܬܐ *they could not take the city;* metaph. ܠܐ ܐܬܡܨܝ ܒܗ *he could not prevail upon him.* Derivatives, ܡܨܝܢܘܬܐ, ܡܬܡܨܝܢܐ, ܡܬܡܨܝܢܐܝܬ, ܡܬܡܨܝܢܘܬܐ, ܡܬܡܨܝܢܐ.

ܡܨܒܥܘܬܐ rt. ܨܒܥ. f. only in the lexx. *baptism.*

ܡܨܰܒܬܽܘܬܳܐ rt. ܨܒܬ. f. *ornament, adornment.*

ܡܨܰܒܬܳܢܳܐ, ܢܺܝܬܳܐ rt. ܨܒܬ. *one who adorns, ornaments, embellishes.*

ܡܨܛܒܥܢܐ rt. ܨܒܥ *one who deceives by false appearances, an impostor.*

ܡܨܛܒܥܢܘܬܐ rt. ܨܒܥ. f. *impersonation, imposture.*

ܡܨܕܝܘܬܐ or ܡܨܕܬܐ rt. ܨܕܐ. f. *fixing* the eyes on any object, *a fixed regard, steady gaze.*

ܡܨܛܐܐܝܬ rt. ܨܐܐ. adv. *disgustingly.*

ܡܨܛܐܝܘܬܐ rt. ܨܐܐ. f. *a*) *crapula.* *b*) *a tavern.*

ܡܨܘܨܐ or ܡܨܨܐ rt. ܡܨ. m. *a*) *a syringe for injecting oil into the nostrils.* *b*) *the plucking out of hairs.*

ܡܨܘܨܐ rt. ܨܘܨ. m. *chirping, twittering* of birds.

ܡܨܘܬܐ pl. ܡܨܘܬܐ rt. ܨܝܐ. f. *strife, contention; a brawl, quarrel, conflict, disputation.*

ܡܨܘܬܢܐܝܬ rt. ܨܝܐ. adv. *contradictorily.*

ܡܨܘܬܢܐ rt. ܨܝܐ. *contradictory.*

ܡܨܚܝ Aphel part. of ܨܚܐ.

ܡܨܚܝܢܐ, ܢܝܬܐ rt. ܨܚܐ. *foul-mouthed, abusive.*

ܡܨܚܝܢܘܬܐ rt. ܨܚܐ. f. *evil speaking, abuse.*

ܡܨܚܢܘܬܐ rt. ܨܚ. f. *transcription.*

ܡܨܛܒܝܢܐ, ܢܝܬܐ rt. ܨܒܐ. *pleasing, agreeable, delightful.*

ܡܨܛܒܝܢܘܬܐ rt. ܨܒܐ. f. *goodwill, approval, good pleasure.*

ܡܨܛܒܬܐ or ܡܨܛܒܐ f. *a raised place, platform, step, seat.*

ܡܨܛܒܬܢܘܬܐ rt. ܨܒܬ. f. *adorning, embellishment.*

ܡܨܛܒܥܢܐ, ܢܝܬܐ rt. ܨܒܥ. *of false appearances, fallacious, delusive.*

ܡܨܛܒܥܢܘܬܐ rt. ܨܒܥ. f. *imposture, delusiveness, fraudulence.*

ܡܨܛܘܒܢܐ rt. ܨܘܒ. *a wayfarer, one who frequents a road.*

ܡܨܛܘܒܢܘܬܐ rt. ܨܘܒ. f. *a being inclined towards.*

ܡܨܛܠܝܢܐ, ܢܝܬܐ rt. ܨܠܐ. *froward, prone to evil;* with ܠܐ *inflexible, firm, unperverted.*

ܡܨܛܠܝܢܐܝܬ rt. ܨܠܐ. adv. *of its natural propensity;* with ܠܐ *unbendingly, undeviatingly.*

ܡܨܛܠܝܢܘܬܐ rt. ܨܠܐ. f. *proneness, propensity, inclination, deviation, aberration;* with ܠܘܬ *towards;* ܡܨܛܠܝܢܘܬܐ ܡܢ ܗܝܡܢܘܬܐ *apostasy;* ܠܐ ܡܨܛܠܝܢܘܬܐ *unswerving rectitude;* ܕܠܐ ܡܨܛܠܝܢܘܬܐ *unswervingly.*

ܡܨܛܠܠܘܬܐ rt. ܨܠܠ. *cleansing, purification.*

ܡܨܛܢܥܘܬܐ pl. ܡܨܛܢܥܘܬܐ rt. ܨܢܥ. f. *a wile, crafty trick.*

ܡܨܛܥܝܘܬܐ or ܡܨܥ f. *rubbing, embrocation.*

ܡܨܛܪܝܢܐ rt. ܨܪܐ. *a*) *a libertine.* *b*) *fissile, cleavable.*

ܡܨܛܪܝܢܘܬܐ rt. ܨܪܐ. f. *cleavage.*

ܡܨܝܒܢܐ, ܢܝܬܐ rt. ܨܘܒ. *a leader; that which produces* or *causes.*

ܡܨܝܕܢܐ, ܢܝܬܐ rt. ܨܘܕ. *a fisher; network, lattice.*

ܡܨܝܕܬܐ pl. ܡܨܝܕܬܐ rt. ܨܘܕ. f. *a net, snare;* ܒܝܬ ܡܨܝܕܬܐ *net-work;* ܟܘܐ ܕܡܨܝܕܬܐ *lattice windows.*

ܡܨܝܕܬܢܐ rt. ܨܘܕ. *like a network* or *grating.*

ܡܨܝܢܘܬܐ rt. ܡܨܐ II. f. *power, strength.*

ܡܨܝܪܢܐ rt. ܨܘܪ. *a painter.*

ܡܨܠܠܬܐ or ܡܨܠܬܐ f. rt. ܡܨܐ I. *a wine-strainer; dregs.*

ܡܨܠܚܢܐܝܬ rt. ܨܠܚ. adv. *well, prosperously.*

ܡܨܠܚܢܘܬܐ rt. ܨܠܚ. f. *success, prosperity.*

ܡܨܠܚܢܘܬܐ rt. ܨܠܚ. *cleaving.*

ܡܨܠܚܢܐ rt. ܨܠܚ. *splitting, cleaving.*

ܡܨܠܚܢܘܬܐ pl. ܡܨܠܚܢܘܬܐ rt. ܨܠܚ. *prosperity, welfare, success, a success, victory.*

ܡܨܠܝܢܐ rt. ܨܠܐ. *a*) *protecting suppliants* a title of Jove. *b*) *one who prays* esp. *one who reads prayers in a mosque; a pilgrim to Mecca.* *c*) *a Messalian* one of a sect of heretics. *d*) astron. *relating to declension.* *e*) gram. the points ܶ or ̈.

ܡܨܠܠܐܝܬ rt. ܨܠܠ. adv. *purely.*

ܡܨܠܠܘܬܐ rt. ܨܠܠ. f. *cleansing, purification, purity.*

ܡܨܠܠܢܐ rt. ܨܠܠ. *refining, purifying.*

ܡܨܠܡܢܐ rt. ܨܠܡ. *a*) *a moulder, modeller.* *b*) *a feather with which bread is brushed over* or *ornamented.*

ܡܨܠܠܬܐ pl. ܡܨܠܠܬܐ rt. ܨܠܠ. f. *a strainer, filter; strained wine, wine-dregs.*

ܡܨܢܥܐܝܬ rt. ܨܢܥ. adv. *craftily.*

ܡܨܢܦܬܐ pl. ܡܨܢܦܬܐ rt. ܨܢܦ. f. *a mitre, turban.*

ܡܨܰܥ fut. ܢܶܡܨܰܥ *to be in the midst, place in the middle;* ܟܰܕ ܡܨܰܥ ܗܘܳܐ ܨܰܘܡܳܐ *when the fast was half through.* Pa. ܡܰܨܰܥ *a) to come between;* with ܫܳܡ *to place between* or *in the middle;* with ܩܳܡ *to stand in the middle, to halve;* with ܢܰܟܶܠ *to defraud of half; to intervene, meet, befall; to interpose, mediate;* ܡܫܺܝܚܳܐ ܨܠܺܝܒܶܗ ܡܡܰܨܰܥ Christ *places His cross in the midst, mediates by His cross;* ܡܡܰܨܰܥ ܚܰܫ̈ܶܐ *in the midst of passions, encompassed by the desires of the flesh.* Ethpa. *to be between, in the middle, to intervene, mediate, act as mediator;* ܩܡܢ ܒܝܬ ܚܝ̈ܠܘܬܐ ܡܬܡܨܥܝܢ *we stood between opposing forces;* ܐܘܪܚܐ ܕܒܗ ܡܬܡܨܥ *the road on which he is midway;* with ܩܳܡ *to stand between, be doubtful.* Aph. ܐܰܡܨܰܥ *to mediate, act as mediator.* Derivatives, ܡܨܥܐ, ܡܨܥܬܐ, ܡܨܥܝܐ, ܡܨܥܝܘܬܐ, ܡܨܥܢܐ, ܡܨܥܢܘܬܐ, ܡܡܨܥܢܐ, ܡܬܡܨܥܢܘܬܐ.

ܡܨܥܳܝܳܐܺܝܬ rt. ܡܨܥ. adv. *moderately, mildly.*

ܡܨܰܥܳܝܳܐ, ܡܨܰܥܳܝܶܐ pl. m. ܡܨܰܥܳܝܬܳܐ f. rt. ܡܨܥ. *a) middle, intermediate;* ܡܨܰܥܳܝܶܐ *the middle class; the middle line* of an *army;* ܡܨܰܥܳܝܬܳܐ *the middle finger;* ܡܨܰܥܳܝ ܩܘܡܬܐ *of middle height;* ܫܘܪܐ ܡܨܰܥܳܝܳܐ *a party-wall;* ܬܚܬܝܬܐ ܘܡܨܰܥܳܝܬܐ *the Upper and Middle* Thebaid. *b) intermediate, mediocre, subsidiary, medial. c) a go-between, intercessor, mediator;* ܡܨܰܥܳܝܳܐ ܕܫܠܡܐ *a peace-maker.*

ܡܨܰܥܳܝܽܘܬܳܐ rt. ܡܨܥ. f. *a) a middle part, state* or *position; mediocrity;* ܡܢ ܡܨܰܥܳܝܽܘܬܳܐ ܠܓܡܝܪܘܬܐ *from mediocrity to perfection. b) mediation, intervention, service, assistance, means;* ܕܠܐ ܡܨܰܥܳܝܽܘܬܳܐ ܕܐܚܪܢܐ *without further intervention;* ܝܗܒ ܒܡܨܰܥܳܝܽܘܬܶܗ ܐܣܝܘܬܐ God *gave healing through him, by his means;* ܒܥܘܕܪܢܗ ܘܒܡܨܰܥܳܝܽܘܬܶܗ *by his help and service;* ܠܐ ܐܬܚܫܒܬ ܒܡܨܰܥܳܝܽܘܬܳܐ ܕܫܠܡܐ *thou hast not cared to intervene to make* peace; ܒܡܨܰܥܳܝܽܘܬܗܘܢ ܓܘܢܝܬܐ *by their common assistance.*

ܡܨܰܥܪܳܢܳܐ, ܢܝܬܐ rt. ܨܥܪ. *an insolent, infamous* or *outrageous* person.

ܡܨܰܥܪܳܢܳܐܺܝܬ rt. ܨܥܪ. adv. *insolently, abusively.*

ܡܨܰܥܪܳܢܽܘܬܳܐ rt. ܨܥܪ. f. *abusiveness, disgrace, shamefulness.*

ܡܨܰܥܪܳܢܺܝܬܳܐ rt. ܨܥܪ. *infamous, shameful, disgraceful.*

ܡܨܰܥܬܳܐ rt. ܡܨܥ. f. *the middle, middle part, centre; an interval;* ܐܪܥܐ ܡܨܰܥܬܳܐ ܕܒܪܝܬܐ ܟܠܗ *the earth is the centre of the universe;* ܡܨܥܬ ܢܗܪ̈ܘܬܐ *Mesopotamia;* ܡܢ ܡܨܰܥܬܳܐ ܕܦܘܢܩ̈ܝܟ ܢܚܛܦܘܟ *he will snatch thee away from the midst of* thy *delights;* ܐܠܘܠܐ ܗܘܐ ܠܡܨܰܥܬܳܐ *nisi obstet, if there be no let* or *hindrance;* with ܗܘܐ *to be in, be present;* with ܐܬܐ *to bring forward publicly, to be produced before all; to meet together;* with ܐܫܬܩܠ ܡܢ *to be taken away from amongst, to be slain.* Construct state ܡܨܥܬ or ܒܡܨܥܬ prep. *in the midst, between, amongst, at;* ܡܨܥܬܗܘܢ ܠܡܝ̈ܐ *between them and the water;* ܐܛܒܥ ܒܡܨܥܬ ܓܠ̈ܠܐ *he was drowned in the waves;* ܒܡܨܥܬ ܛܗܪܐ *about noon, at noon.*

ܡܨܳܝܳܐ rt. ܡܨ. *sucking, licking out.*

ܡܨܰܪ = ܡܬܰܪ. Ethpa. ܐܶܬܡܨܰܪ *to stretch one's limbs.* Derivative, ܡܨܪܐ.

ܡܶܨܪܳܝܳܐ, ܡܶܨܪܳܝܬܳܐ *Egyptian, an Egyptian.*

ܡܶܨܪܶܝܢ f. *Misraim, Egypt;* ܡܨܪܝܢ ܓܘܝܬܐ *Inner Egypt* i.e. beyond the Thebaid; ܝܡܐ ܕܡܨܪܝܢ *the Red Sea.*

ܡܨܰܪܦܽܘܬܳܐ rt. ܨܪܦ. f. *astringency.*

ܡܨܰܪܦܳܢܳܐ and ܡܨܰܪܦ, ܢܝܬܐ rt. ܨܪܦ. *astringent, styptic, binding.*

ܡܨܰܪܦܳܢܽܘܬܳܐ rt. ܨܪܦ. f. *astringency;* metaph. *keenness, contraction, gripping.*

ܡܩܒܳܐ rt. ܢܩܒ. m. *an awl; the eye* of a needle; *a hole bored* in the lobe of the ear; ܡܩܒܐ ܕܢܚܝܪܐ *a nostril.*

ܡܩܰܒܝ or ܡܰܩܰܒܝ, ܡܩܰܒܝܳܐ *Maccabee;* ܟܬܒܐ ܕܡܩܒ̈ܝܐ *the Book of the Maccabees.*

ܡܩܰܒܠܳܢܽܘܬܳܐ rt. ܩܒܠ. f. *receptivity.*

ܡܩܰܒܠܳܢܳܐ, ܢܝܬܐ rt. ܩܒܠ. *capable of containing* or *receiving, receptive; a receiver, recipient, receptacle;* rit. *the humeral veil; a host, hostess, guest-mistress; a sponsor, God-parent;* ܡܩܒܠܢܐ ܕܡܠܟܘܬܐ *successor to the kingdom.*

ܡܩܒܠܢܘܬܐ rt. ܩܒܠ. f. *receptivity, capacity;* ܡܩܒܠܢܘܬܐ ܕܡܠܟܘܬܐ *succession to the kingdom.*

ܡܩܒܪܢܐ rt. ܩܒܪ. *one who binds sheaves.*

ܡܩܒܬܐ rt. ܢܩܒ. f. *a*) *a club, awl, drill. b*) perh. *an engine of war for boring holes through walls; a narrow defile.*

ܡܩܕܚܐ rt. ܩܕܚ. m. *an awl, borer, auger; a tinder-box.*

ܡܩܕܚܢܐ rt. ܩܕܚ. m. *pricking* or *throbbing pain.*

ܡܩܕܢܘܬܐ rt. ܩܕܢ. f. *possession.*

ܡܩܕܡܘܬܐ rt. ܩܕܡ. f. *priority, preceding;* in comp. *pre-, fore-*: ܡܩܕܡܘܬ ܚܙܬܐ *foresight;* ܡܩܕܡܘܬ ܝܕܥܬܐ *foreknowledge;* ܡܩܕܡܘܬ ܡܠܬܐ *foretelling;* gram. ܡܩܕܡܘܬ ܫܡܐ *a preposition.*

ܡܩܕܡܢܐ, ܡܩܕܡܢܝܬܐ rt. ܩܕܡ. *preceding;* ܝܕܥܬܐ ܡܩܕܡܢܝܬܐ *foreknowledge.*

ܡܩܕܡܢܐܝܬ rt. ܩܕܡ. adv. *primarily.*

ܡܩܕܫܐ rt. ܩܕܫ. m. ܒܝܬ ܡܩܕܫܐ *the sanctuary, holy place.*

ܡܩܕܫܝܐ, ܡܩܕܫܝܬܐ rt. ܩܕܫ. *an inhabitant of Jerusalem.*

ܡܩܕܫܢܐ, ܡܩܕܫܢܝܬܐ rt. ܩܕܫ. *sanctifying, hallowing, consecrating, proclaiming Holy, holy, holy; a sanctifier, one who sanctifies, makes holy;* eccles. *the consecrating priest;* ܡܠܐ ܡܩܕܫܢܝܬܐ *the words of consecration.*

ܡܩܕܫܢܘܬܐ rt. ܩܕܫ. f. *sanctification.*

ܡܩܘܪܐ or ܡܩܪ perh. corrupt for ܡܢܩܘܪܐ. m. *a bird's beak.*

ܡܩܘܝܢܐ, ܡܩܘܝܢܝܬܐ rt. ܩܘܐ. *permanent, lasting, abiding, enduring.*

ܡܩܘܝܢܘܬܐ with ܠܐ rt. ܩܘܐ. f. *mutability, instability.*

ܡܩܘܩܘܣ or ܡܩܘܩܝܣ m. *a cup.*

ܡܩܘܩܝܬܐ f. *a hen.*

ܡܩܘܪܐ and ܡܩܪ rt. ܢܩܪ. m. *a*) *a bird's beak. b*) *a canal, aqueduct, cistern.*

ܡܩܘܘܪܐ; see ܡܩܘܪܪܐ.

ܡܩܘܪܪܐ m. *a puddle, pool of rain-water.*

ܡܩܘܪܪܢܐ and ܡܩܘܪܢܐ rt. ܩܪ. *cooling, refrigerative.*

ܡܩܘܪܪܢܘܬܐ rt. ܩܪ. f. *cooling, refrigeration.*

ܡܩܚܢܘܬܐ rt. ܢܩܚ. f. *quarrelling, contention.*

ܡܩܛܝܐ pl. ܡܩܛܝܬܐ f. *a cucumber-garden.*

ܡܩܛܠܢܐ rt. ܩܛܠ. *a slayer, enemy.*

ܡܩܛܢܢܐ rt. ܩܛܢ. *lean, emaciating, subtle.*

ܡܩܛܢܢܘܬܐ rt. ܩܛܢ. f. *attenuation, rarefaction.*

ܡܩܛܥܘܬܐ rt. ܩܛܥ. f. *despondency, slackness, remissness.*

ܡܩܛܦܐ, ܡܩܛܦܬܐ rt. ܩܛܦ. f. *a covering, wrapper.*

ܡܩܛܪܓܢܐ from ܩܛܪܓ. *a*) *an accuser, plaintiff; defamer, detractor. b*) *categorical, positive, predicatory.*

ܡܩܛܪܓܢܘܬܐ rt. ܩܛܪ. f. *a*) *accusation, blame. b*) *predication, affirmation.*

ܡܩܛܪܘܬܐ (ܡܠܬܐ) rt. ܩܛܪ. *connected speech.*

ܡܩܛܪܢܐ rt. ܩܛܪ. *one who forms syllogisms.*

ܡܩܛܪܬܐ rt. ܩܛܪ. f. *stocks, fetters.*

ܡܩܝܕܘܬܐ rt. ܩܘܕ. f. *dancing.*

ܡܩܝܡܐܝܬ rt. ܩܘܡ. adv. *in reality.*

ܡܩܝܡܘܬܐ rt. ܩܘܡ. f. *fixity, stubbornness, position, state, status; the election* of a patriarch.

ܡܩܝܡܢܐ, ܡܩܝܡܢܝܬܐ rt. ܩܘܡ. *one who establishes, constitutes, an upholder, supporter; constituent, essential;* ܐܒܐ ܡܩܝܡܢܐ ܕܐܢܫܘܬܐ *the Father who upholds mankind;* ܡܩܝܡܢܐ ܕܗܝܡܢܘܬܐ *a supporter of the Faith;* ܚܝܠܐ ܡܩܝܡܢܐ *essential virtue;* ܐܣܛܘܟܣܐ ܡܩܝܡܢܝܘܗܝ ܕܟܝܢܐ *the elements which constitute nature.*

ܡܩܝܡܢܐ rt. ܩܘܡ. *a restorer, one who raises the dead; persistent, constant;* med. *astringent, tonic.*

ܡܩܝܡܢܘܬܐ rt. ܩܘܡ. f. *resuscitation; institution.*

ܡܩܫܝܘܬܐ from ܩܫܐ. f. *stiffness, tension* of the muscles, *rigidity, a rigor.*

ܡܩܠܕܢܐ *a bolt, bar, door-chain; the socket* of a bolt.

ܡܩܠܘܢ and ܡܐܩܠܘܢ m. μάκελλον, *a shambles, butchers' row, market-place.*

ܡܩܠܠܐܝܬ rt. ܩܠ. adv. *lightly.*

ܡܩܠܠܢܘܬܐ rt. ܩܠ. f. *alleviation.*

ܡܩܠܣܢܐܝܬ from ܡܩܠܣܐ. adv. *laudably.*

ܡܩܠܣܢܐ, ܢܝܬܐ from ܡܩܠܣܐ. *a*) *an applauder, one who praises.* *b*) adj. *of praise, praising, laudatory.*

ܡܩܠܥܢܐ from ܩܠܥܐ. m. *a ballista, catapult, sling; a slinger.*

ܡܩܠܩܠܢܘܬܐ rt. ܩܠ. f. *blame, reproach.*

ܡܩܡܐ rt. ܩܘܡ. m. *the act of standing, standing up.*

ܡܩܡܢܐ pl. ܝ̈ܐ rt. ܩܡܢ. *a lurker, lier-in-wait, waylayer; a marauder, plunderer; a robber band.*

ܡܩܢܘܬܐ or ܡܩܢܐܘܬܐ rt. ܩܢܐ II. f. *lividness, lead colour.*

ܡܩܢܝܢܘܬܐ rt. ܩܢܐ I. f. *acquiring, acquisition.*

ܡܩܢܝܢܐ rt. ܩܢܐ I. m. *one who grants, gives possession.*

ܡܩܢܒܢܐ rt. ܩܢܒ. *having the property of dyeing blue.*

ܡܩܢܒܬܐ rt. ܩܢܒ. f. *a long veil.*

ܡܩܦܣܘܬܐ pl. ܘ̈ܬܐ f. *spasms, convulsions;* cf. ܩܦܣܣܐ.

ܡܩܣܩܣܢܘܬܐ from ܩܣܩܣ. f. *decorum, embellishment.*

ܡܩܦܐ pl. ܝ̈ܐ m. *a wooden hook, shepherd's crook, pastoral staff.*

ܡܩܦܩ Aphel act. part. of ܢܦܩ. *proceeding,* rit. *he continues, proceeds.*

ܡܩܦܚܢܐ rt. ܩܦܚ. *buffeting; one who slaps or smites, a striker.*

ܡܩܦܚܢܘܬܐ rt. ܩܦܚ. f. *buffeting, boxing.*

ܡܩܦܢܘܬܐ or ܡܩܦܢܘ̈ rt. ܢܩܦ. f. gram. *affixing, suffixing; the connexion* of one noun with another by means of the construct state or by ܕ.

ܡܩܦܩܦܐ pl. ܝ̈ܐ rt. ܩܦܩܦ. m. *the ham, hough.*

ܡܩܨܝܢܘܬܐ rt. ܩܨ. f. *a contract, an agreement.*

ܡܩܩܪܐ rt. ܢܩܪ. m. *a*) = ܡܩܘܪܐ *a bird's beak.* *b*) *an auger, gimlet.*

ܡܩܪܐ rt. ܢܩܪ. m. *a cistern, channel.*

ܡܩܪܐ ܬܪܢܓܠܐ rt. ܩܪܐ. *cock-crow.*

ܡܩܪܒܢܘܬܐ rt. ܩܪܒ. f. *the making an offering, offering an oblation.*

ܡܩܪܒܢܐ, ܢܝܬܐ rt. ܩܪܒ. *a warrior, fighter, enemy; warlike, hostile.*

ܡܩܪܒܢܐ rt. ܩܪܒ. m. *one who offers sacrifice, an offerer; one who promotes, shows favour.*

ܡܩܪܒܢܐܝܬ rt. ܩܪܒ. adv. *in a warlike* or *hostile manner.*

ܡܩܪܒܢܘܬܐ rt. ܩܪܒ. f. *making war, the carrying on of war.*

ܡܩܪܛܢܐ *intricate, involved, subtle, sophistical.*

ܡܩܪܘܢܐ pl. ܝ̈ܐ m. *a pair of paniers.*

ܡܩܪܘܚܐ rt. ܩܪܚ. *lame, maimed.*

ܡܩܪܝܢܐ rt. ܩܪܝ. *eloquent.*

ܡܩܪܝܢܘܬܐ rt. ܩܪܝ. f. *importunity; eloquence.*

ܡܩܪܝܢܐ rt. ܩܪܐ. f. *a teacher of reading.*

ܡܩܪܡܐ or ܡܩܪܡܐ rt. ܩܪܡ. m. *a membrane, caul; the peritonaeum.*

ܡܩܪܪܢܐ rt. ܩܪ. *cooling, refrigerant; a water-cooler.*

ܡܩܪܢܐܝܬ from ܩܪܢܐ. adv. *crookedly, deviously, sideways.*

ܡܩܪܪܢܘܬܐ rt. ܩܪ. f. *cooling, refrigeration.*

ܡܩܪܥܐ m. *a*) Ar. *a lash, whip.* *b*) *fraudulent.*

ܡܩܪܛܣܢܐ from ܩܘܪܛܣܐ *a maker of earrings.*

ܡܩܪܬܐ rt. ܢܩܪ. f. *a narrow beak.*

ܡܩܫܝܢܐ, ܡܩܫܝܢܝܬܐ rt. ܩܫܐ. *hardening, indurating.*

ܡܩܫܩܫܬܐ rt. ܩܫܐ. f. *flint; pyrites.*

ܡܩܫܬܢܘܬܐ rt. ܩܫܬ. f. *a gazing intently, attentive consideration.*

ܡܩܫܬܢܐ, ܢܝܬܐ rt. ܩܫܬ. *intent, intense.*

ܡܪ fut. ܢܡܪ, act. part. ܡܐܪ, ܡܪܐ, pl. f. ܡܪ̈ܢ, verbal adj. ܡܪܝܪ, ܐ, ܬܐ. *to be bitter, sour, acid;* ܡܪܝܪ ܩܠܝܠ ܡܪܐ *slightly acid, sub-acid;* ܡܪ̈ܢ ܥܒܘܛܐ ܥܬܝܩܬܐ *old grain becomes bitter.* Verbal adj. *bitter, sour; sad, harsh, severe, cruel, ferocious;* ܪܝܚܐ ܡܪܝܪܬܐ *a sour smell;* ܩܪܐ ܡܪܝܪܐ *colocynth, wild gourd;* ܡܪܝܪ ܗܘܐ ܠܗ ܛܥܡܐ ܕܐܠܗܝ̈ܬܐ *one to whose taste divine things are bitter, who has a distaste for them;* ܒܪܕܐ ܡܪܝܪܐ *piercing hail;* ܡܪܝܪ ܚܢܟܐ *bitter of palate* = *sad, morose;* ܡܪܝܪ ܢܦܫܐ *bitter of soul, sad;* ܟܡܝܪܘܬܐ ܡܪܝܪܬܐ *bitter sorrow;* ܕܝܢܐ ܡܪܝܪܐ *a harsh judge;* ܡܪܝܪ ܗܘܐ ܥܠ *he was bitter against, acted harshly towards;* ܫܥܒܕܘܬܐ ܡܪܝܪܬܐ *bitter wrath, cruel rage;* ܐܬܘܬܐ ܡܪ̈ܬܢܝܬܐ *signs of punishment* opp. ܬܕܡܪ̈ܬܐ ܒܪ̈ܟܢܝܬܐ *miracles of blessing.* Pa. irreg. ܡܰܪܰܪ *to make bitter.* Aph. ܐܰܡܰܪ *to make bitter* or *sad; to sour, exacerbate;* ܐܰܡܪܰܪ ܡܰܪܡܰܪ ܛܰܥܡܶܗ ܠܚܶܟܳܐ *its taste is bitter to the palate.* Palpal ܡܰܪܡܰܪ *to render bitter, embitter, sour, sadden, exacerbate;* ܟܽܘܪܗܳܢܳܐ ܕܡܰܪܡܰܪ ܠܚܰܝܰܝ *the sore which embitters my life;* ܐܝܟ ܐܰܪܝܳܐ ܡܡܰܪܡܰܪ *like an enraged lion;* ܡܛܽܠ ܕܡܰܪܡܰܪܘ ܠܩܰܕܺܝܫܳܐ *because they had provoked the Holy One to wrath.* Ethpalpal ܐܶܬܡܰܪܡܰܪ *to be embittered, saddened, provoked to wrath;* with ܒܟܶܐܒܳܐ or ܒܒܶܟܝܳܐ *to weep bitterly, be in bitter sorrow;* with ܥܰܠ *to be bitter against, treat harshly.* Derivatives, ܡܪܳܪܽܘܬܳܐ, ܡܰܪܡܪܳܢܳܐ, ܡܰܪܡܪܳܢܽܘܬܳܐ, ܡܰܪܡܪܳܢܳܝܳܐ, ܡܰܪܡܰܪܬܳܐ, ܡܰܪܺܝܪܳܐ, ܡܰܪܺܝܪܽܘܬܳܐ, ܡܪܳܪܬܳܐ, ܡܪܳܪܳܐ, ܡܪܰܪܬܳܐ, ܡܰܪܬܳܐ.

ܡܪܳܐ Pael ܡܰܪܺܝ or ܡܰܐܪܺܝ *to contend, strive; to emulate, imitate* with ܠ, ܒ, ܥܰܡ; ܡܡܰܪܶܐ ܠܡܶܗܘܳܐ ܐܰܝܟܘܳܬܶܗ *he strives to become like* him; ܡܡܰܪܶܐ ܠܥܰܡܠܰܘ̈ܗܝ *he emulates his labours;* ܦܪܰܚܬܳܐ ܕܡܡܰܪܝܳܢ ܠܩܳܠܳܐ ܕܒܰܪܢܳܫܳܐ birds *which imitate the human voice.* Ethpa. ܐܶܬܡܰܪܺܝ same as Pael; ܗܳܢܽܘܢ ܕܡܶܬܡܰܪܶܝܢ ܒܐܰܣܛܕܺܝܢ *they who contend on the racecourse.* Derivatives, ܡܡܰܪܝܳܢܳܐ, ܡܶܬܡܰܪܝܳܢܳܐ, ܡܶܬܡܰܪܝܳܢܽܘܬܳܐ, ܡܶܬܡܰܪܝܳܢܳܐ.

ܡܳܪܳܐ; see ܡܳܐܪܳܐ.

ܡܳܪܳܐ abs. and constr., emph. ܡܳܪܝܳܐ and ܡܳܪܝܳܐ the latter form is used only of the Lord God, and in the Peshita Version of the O. T. represents the Tetragrammaton. Eastern Lexicons have a fanciful derivation of this form from the initial letters of ܡܳܪܽܘܬܳܐ *lordship,* ܪܰܒܽܘܬܳܐ *majesty,* and ܝܳܬܝܽܘܬܳܐ *self-existence.* Pl. ܡܳܪ̈ܰܘܳܬܳܐ, ܡܳܪ̈ܰܘܳܬܳܐ also ܡܳܪ̈ܰܘܳܢ, ܡܳܪ̈ܰܘܳܬܳܐ; with affix 1 p. ܡܳܪܝ *my Lord,* ܡܳܪܰܢ *our Lord;* m. (for fem. see ܡܳܪܬܳܐ) *a lord, owner, master, ruler, prince, satrap;* ܡܳܪܰܢ ܐܶܬܳܐ *Maranatha, our Lord hath come;* ܡܳܪܳܐ ܕܡܳܪ̈ܰܘܳܬܳܐ *lord of lords;* ܡܳܪܳܐ ܕܡܕܺܝܢܬܳܐ *the ruler of the city;* ܡܳܪ̈ܰܘܗܝ ܕܡܕܺܝܢܬܳܐ *the nobles, rulers of the city;* ܨܶܒܽܘܬܳܐ ܕܡܳܪ̈ܰܘܳܬܳܐ *an affair of the rulers, of the government;* ܡܳܪܝ *Mar, my Lord, Sir,* used not only in addressing a superior but as a title of ecclesiastics and saints; ܡܳܪܝ ܫܶܡܥܽܘܢ *Mar Simeon;* ܥܽܘܡܪܳܐ ܕܡܳܪܝ ܣܳܒܳܐ *the Convent of Mar Saba.*

ܡܳܪܳܐ in construction with another noun expresses rule, power, or ownership:—

ܡܳܪܳܐ ܐܰܓܪܳܐ *the master, hirer.*

ܡܳܪܳܐ ܐܶܠܦܳܐ *the captain, pilot.*

ܡܳܪܳܐ ܒܰܝܬܳܐ *the father of the family, head of the house.*

ܡܳܪܳܐ ܚܰܘܒܳܐ *a creditor.*

ܡܳܪܳܐ ܚܰܝܠܳܐ *endued with strength* or *fortitude.*

ܡܳܪܳܐ ܟܽܠ *Lord of all, omnipotent;* ܡܶܠܬܳܐ ܡܳܪܰܬ ܟܽܠ *the Word omnipotent.*

ܡܳܪܳܐ ܟܰܪܡܳܐ *the master* or *owner of the vineyard.*

ܡܳܪܳܐ ܟܬܳܒܳܐ *the author* or *owner of the book.*

ܡܳܪܳܐ ܢܶܟܣܶܐ *a rich man.*

ܡܳܪܳܐ ܨܰܘܡܳܐ ܘܰܨܠܽܘܬܳܐ *devoted to fasting and prayer.*

ܡܳܪܰܝ ܩܽܘܪܝܳܐ *landed proprietors, zemindars.*

Derivatives, ܡܳܪܽܘܬܳܐ, ܡܳܪܘܳܬܳܐ, ܡܳܪܬܳܐ, verb ܡܰܪܺܝ, ܡܳܪܳܝܳܐ, ܡܳܪܳܢܳܐ, ܡܳܪܳܢܳܝܳܐ, ܡܳܪܳܢܳܐܝܬ, ܡܳܪܳܢܳܝܽܘܬܳܐ.

ܡܳܪܳܐܪܳܐ also ܡܳܐܪܳܐܪܳܐ and ܡܳܪܳܐܪܳܐ from ܐܪܳܪ *one who initiates into mysteries, an instructor, teacher;* ܡܳܐܪܳܐܪ̈ܶܐ ܘܡܶܬܐܪ̈ܳܪܶܐ *teachers and taught.*

ܡܳܪܳܐܪܽܘܬܳܐ and ܡܳܐܪܳܐܪܽܘܬܳܐ from ܐܪܳܪ f. *initiation into mysteries, instruction in holy things.*

ܡܰܪܒܳܒܳܐ pl. ܐ̈ m. *folding-doors.*

ܡܰܪܒܽܘܥܬܳܐ pl. ܥ̈ܳܬܳܐ rt. ܪܒܥ. f. *a place to lie down in, a den, lair, covert; a stable, fold; a place of repose, abode, tomb; the womb;* ܒܰܪ ܡܰܪܒܽܘܥܬܶܗ *his own sister.*

ܡܪܰܒܝܳܢܳܐ, ܡܪܰܒܝܳܢܺܝܬܳܐ rt. ܪܒܐ. *a) that which makes to grow* or *increase, one who brings up, tends, rears, a nurse, foster-father* or *mother;* ܫܶܡܫܳܐ ܡܪܰܒܝܳܢܳܐ the sun *which causes germination* or *growth;* ܫܠܳܡܳܐ ܡܪܰܒܝܳܢܳܐ ܕܡܰܥܒܕܳܢܘܳܬܳܐ *peace which fosters the growth of virtues;* ܒܰܪ ܡܪܰܒܝܳܢܽܘܬܶܗ *a foster-brother. b) a money-lender.*

ܡܰܪܒܺܝܬܳܐ pl. ܝ̈ܳܬܳܐ rt. ܪܒܐ. f. *growth.*

ܡܰܪܒܥܽܘܬܳܐ and ܡܰܪܒܥܳܢܽܘܬܳܐ rt. ܪܒܥ. f. *swelling, tumidity.*

ܡܰܪܒܥܳܢܳܐ rt. ܪܒܥ. *swelling, causing to swell.*

ܡܰܪܒܥܳܐ, ܡܰܪܒܰܥ rt. ܪܒܥ. m. *the womb; the inner part, pith* of elders, rushes, &c.

ܡܰܪܒܥܳܐ rt. ܪܒܥ. m. *a cote, fold, byre;* ܡܰܪܒܥܳܐ ܕܥܳܢܳܐ *a sheep-cote.*

ܡܪܒܥܐܝܬ rt. ܪܒܥ. adv. *foursquare, quadrangular.*

ܡܪܒܥܢܐ rt. ܪܒܥ. *uterine, of the womb.*

ܡܪܓ fut. ܢܡܪܘܓ *to totter, vacillate, be weak* as the hands or feet. Aph. ܐܡܪܓ the same, also *to make to totter.*

ܡܪܓܐ pl. ܐ̈ m. *a meadow.*

ܡܪܓܐ = ܡܪܓܐ m. *red earth, red ochre.*

ܡܪܓܙܢܐ, ܢܝܬܐ rt. ܪܓܙ. *irritating, provoking, exasperating.*

ܡܪܓܙܢܘܬܐ rt. ܪܓܙ. f. *irritation, provocation, wrath.*

ܡܪܓܝܓܐ rt. ܪܓܓ. *moist, watery, rainy.*

ܡܪܓܢܐ pl. ܐ̈ f. μάραγνα, *a scourge of leathern thongs filled with sand and having sharp points.*

ܡܪܓܢܝܬܐ pl. ܝ̈ܬܐ f. μαργαρίτης, *a pearl* esp. *a single large pearl, a gem;* ܡܪܓܢܝܬܐ ܕܠܐ ܡܘܡܐ *a flawless pearl.* Metaph. *a particle of the Eucharistic bread; a relic;* used also of virginity, the faith, &c.

ܡܪܓܫܢܐ, ܢܝܬܐ rt. ܪܓܫ. *endowed with sense;* ܡܪܓܫܢܐ ܚܪܝܦ *having acute senses.*

ܡܪܓܫܢܐܝܬ rt. ܪܓܫ. adv. *sensibly;* with ܠܐ *insensibly.*

ܡܪܓܫܢܘܬܐ rt. ܪܓܫ. f. *the faculty of sense* esp. *the sense of touch, perception, sensation, sensibility, intelligence;* with ܠܐ *ignorance, stupidity.*

ܡܪܕ fut. ܢܡܪܘܕ, act. part. ܡܪܕ, ܡܪܕܐ, pass. part. ܡܪܝܕ and ܡܪܝܕ, ܐ, ܬܐ. *a) to rebel, revolt, rise against* with ܥܠ, ܡܢ; ܡܢ ܫܘܠܛܢܐ *from the power;* ܡܪܕܬ ܡܢ ܢܝܪܐ an heifer *rebelled against the yoke;* ܡܪܕܘ ܚܕ ܥܠ ܚܕ *they rose against each other. b) to defy, resist, oppose, defend against, fortify, take shelter;* ܒܡܓܕܠܐ ܕܫܘܪܐ *in the towers of the rampart;* ܡܚܘܬܐ ܕܥܠ ܟܠܗܘܢ ܐܣܘܬܐ ܡܪܕܐ *a wound which defies all physicians;* ܟܘܪܗܢܐ ܕܟܐܒܐ ܡܪܕ ܥܠܝ ܒܝܫܐ *the sore which the Evil one inflicted on me. c) to go beyond, escape, surpass;* ܡܪܕ ܡܢ ܚܝܠܐ *beyond one's strength;* ܡܪܕ ܠܡܫܘܚܬܐ *beyond measure;* ܒܪܩܐ ܕܡܪܕ ܡܢ ܚܙܬܐ *lightning which flees beyond our sight;* ܡܪܕ ܡܢ ܝܕܥܬܐ ܕܒܪܢܫܐ *it surpasses human knowledge. d)* legal. *to be emancipated, freed* ܡܢ ܫܘܥܒܕܐ *from subjection.* Pass. parts. 1st form ܡܪܝܕ *rebellious, a rebel;* ܡܪܝܕܝܢ ܗܘܘ ܒܡܠܟܗܘܢ *they rebelled against them.* 2nd form ܡܪܝܕ *a fugitive; inaccessible, secure;* ܫܘܪܐ ܡܪܝܕܐ *a stronghold;* metaph. *unattainable;* ܡܪܝܕ ܡܢ ܟܠ *beyond all.* Ethpa. ܐܬܡܪܕ *a) to rebel, revolt. b) to be oppressed, to suffer the tyranny* of sickness, passion, &c. Pa. ܡܪܕ *to rebel; to fortify;* ܡܕܝܢܬܐ ܡܡܪܕܬܐ *a fortified city.* Ethpa. ܐܬܡܪܕ *to rebel, resist, struggle against.* Aph. ܐܡܪܕ *to incite rebellion, stir up revolt; to fortify.* Derivatives, ܡܪܕܐ, ܡܪܘܕܐ, ܡܪܕܘܬܐ, ܡܪܘܕܘܬܐ, ܡܪܘܕܐ, ܡܡܪܕܢܘܬܐ, ܡܡܪܕܢܐܝܬ.

ܡܪܕܐ rt. ܪܕܐ. m. *a journey, march;* ܡܪܕܐ ܕܝܘܡܐ *a day's journey;* ܡܪܕܐ ܕܬܠܬܐ ܝܘܡܝܢ *three days' journey;* ܡܪܕܐ ܕܫܒܬܐ *a Sabbath day's journey.*

ܡܪܕܐ pl. ܝ̈ܢ, ܐ̈ rt. ܡܪܕ. m. *a) a rebellion, revolt, conspiracy. b) a fortified place, stronghold, citadel;* ܡܪܕܐ ܕܬܚܘܡܐ *frontier fortifications;* ܢܛܘܪ ܡܪܕܐ *a sentinel, soldier of the garrison.*

ܡܪܕܐ m. *a) a cord to tie up a camel. b)* rt. ܡܪܕ. *rebellion.*

ܡܪܕܘܬܐ, ܡܪܕܘ rt. ܡܪܕ. f. *rebellion, defection, revolt; insolence, impudence.*

ܡܪܕܘܬܐ, ܡܪܕܘ pl. ܘ̈, ܬܐ rt. ܪܕܐ. f. *instruction, discipline, correction, chastisement;* ܥܣܪ ܡܪܕܘܬܐ *the ten plagues* of Egypt; ܡܣܪܒܢ ܡܪܕܘܬܐ *perverse, headstrong, ignorant;* ܕܠܐ ܡܪܕܘ *ignorant, undisciplined, boorish;* ܕܠܐ ܡܪܕܘܬܐ ܬܚܣܕܘܢ ܠܢ *lest you should reproach us with incivility.*

ܡܪܕܝ, ܡܪܕܘܢܝ or ܡܪܕܝܢܝ Pers. *the root of the wild pomegranate.*

ܡܪܕܝܐ rt. ܪܕܐ. m. *disease, sickness.*

ܡܪܕܝܢܐ rt. ܪܕܐ. *running;* ܡܪܕܝܢܐ ܕܡܝܐ *fluxes, diarrhoea, dysentery.*

ܡܪܕܝܬܐ, ܡܪܕܝܬ pl. ܝ̈ܬܐ rt. ܪܕܐ. f. *a journey, voyage, course;* ܡܪܕܝܬܐ ܕܗܠܟܬܐ pleonastic *a journey;* ܡܪܕܝܬܐ ܠܒܣܬܪܐ *retrograde movement* opp. ܡܪܕܝܬܐ ܠܩܕܡܘܗܝ *direct progress;* ܡܪܕܝܬܐ ܕܝܡܐ or ܒܝܡܐ *navigation;* ܡܪܕܝܬܐ ܕܢܫܐ or ܕܘܬܐ *menstruation;* ܡܪܕܝܬܐ

ܕܫ̈ܢܝܐ *the course of years;* ܡܪܕܝܬܐ ܕܟܘ̈ܟܒܐ *the course of the stars.*

ܡܪܕܐ ܕܣܐܡܐ = ܡܪܕܘܬܐ *silver dross.*

ܡܪܕܝܢܐ rt. ܪܕܝ. m. *a spindle.*

ܡܪܗܒܢܐ, ܬܐ rt. ܪܗܒ. *terrific, affrighting.*

ܡܪܗܛܐ pl. ܐ̈ rt. ܪܗܛ. m. *a) exertion, endeavour. b) resources, property, riches.*

ܡܪܗܛܐܝܬ rt. ܪܗܛ. adv. *quickly, speedily, briefly.*

ܡܪܗܛܢܐ rt. ܪܗܛ. m. *a) the channel* of a river. *b)* gram. *marhetono, hastening* enunciation, a sign indicating absence of any vowel sound.

ܡܪܗܛܢܐܝܬ rt. ܪܗܛ. adv. *a) briefly. b) having the line marhetono.*

ܡܪܗܛܢܘܬܐ rt. ܪܗܛ. f. *speediness, molestation;* gram. *the use of the line marhetono.*

ܡܪܘܐ m. *wild marjoram.*

ܡܪܘܕܐ, ܐ, ܬܐ rt. ܡܪܕ. *a) rebellious, refractory, insolent; a deserter, rebel. b) imperious, cruel, fell; a tyrant.*

ܡܪܘܕܐܝܬ rt. ܡܪܕ. adv. *contumaciously, frowardly.*

ܡܪܘܕܘܬܐ rt. ܡܪܕ. f. *rebellion, revolt, insurrection; refractoriness, rebelliousness, disobedience, insolence, tyranny.*

ܡܪܘܚܐ pl. ܐ̈ rt. ܪܘܚ. m. *a fan;* ܡܫܡܫܢ̈ܐ ܕܛܥܝܢܝܢ ܡܪ̈ܘܚܐ *deacons bearing fans.*

ܡܪܘܚܐܝܬ rt. ܪܘܚ. adv. *widely.*

ܡܪܘܚܢܐ rt. ܪܘܚ. *refreshing, reviving.*

ܡܪܘܚܬܐ pl. ܡܪ̈ܘܚܝܬܐ f. = ܡܪܘܚܐ *a fan.*

ܡܪܘܛܘܬܐ f. and ܡܪܘܛܐ m. rt. ܡܪܛ. *plucking, tearing out.*

ܡܪܘܝܢܐ rt. ܪܘܐ. *intoxicating.*

ܡܪܘܡܐ pl. ܐ̈ Heb. *height;* or ܠܡܪܘܡܐ ܠܡܪܘܡܐ *on high;* ܕܥܡܪ ܒܡܪܘܡܐ *who dwelleth on high.*

ܡܪܘܡܢܐ rt. ܪܘܡ. *exalted, lofty, having high aims.*

ܡܪܘܡܝܡܐ rt. ܪܘܡ. *exalted, on high, heavenly.*

ܡܪܘܢܝܐ from ܡܪܘܢ *Maro; a Maronite, follower of the heresy of Maro.*

ܡܪܘܣ ; see ܡܐܪܘܣ.

ܡܪܘܣܐ m. *couch grass.*

ܡܪܘܣܣܬܐ rt. ܡܪܣ. *battered, shattered, harassed, epileptic, demoniac.*

ܡܪܘܩܐ rt. ܡܪܩ. *cleansing, detersive.*

ܡܪܘܪܐ or ܡܪܘܪܬܐ Ar. f. *wild chicory.*

ܡܪܘܬܐ pl. ܡܪ̈ܘܬܐ from ܡܪܐ. f. *a) lordship, dominion, authority, power;* ܡܪܘܬܐ ܐܢܫܝܬܐ *human authority* opp. ܡܪܘܬܐ ܐܠܗܝܬܐ *divine authority;* ܡܪܘܬܢ *our self-government, power over ourselves;* ܡܪܘܬܐ ܝܚܝܕܝܬܐ *monarchy, sole rule. b) ownership, right of possession, domain;* ܠܡܪܘܬܐ ܕܗܢܐ ܕܘܟܬܐ ܬܬܒܥܘܢ *ye shall claim the ownership of this spot. c)* a title; ܡܪܘܬܗ *his lordship. e)* pl. *dominions,* the fourth order of angels. Cf. ܐܠܦܐ.

ܡܪܙܐ or ܡܪܙܐ Pers. *the border, limit, march, frontier.*

ܡܪܙܒܢܐ pl. ܐ̈ from the above, *marzban, a marquis, margrave, warden of the marches.*

ܡܪܙܢܐ also ܡܐܪܙܢܐ and ܡܪܐܙܢܐ, ܬܐ from ܐܪܙ. *one who initiates into mysteries, an instructor, teacher;* ܡܐܪ̈ܙܢܐ ܘܡܬܐܪ̈ܙܢܐ *teachers and taught.*

ܡܪܙܦܐ, ܡܪܙܦܬܐ m. *a rolling-pin.*

ܡܪܚ ܡܪܚ fut. ܢܡܪܚ, act. part. ܡܪܚ *to be rash, headstrong.* Ethpa. ܐܬܡܪܚ same as Peal. Aph. ܐܡܪܚ *to venture, dare, be rash, hasty, headstrong, presumptuous* in a good or bad sense; ܡܡܪܚ ܐܢܐ = ܡܡܪܚܢܐ *I venture, dare,* &c.; ܥܠ ܡ̈ܠܐ ܪ̈ܘܪܒܬܐ ܐܡܪܚ *he ventured great things,* with ܠܡܐܡܪ *to venture to say, say rashly, brag.* Ettaph. ܐܬܬܡܪܚ *to be rashly* or *presumptuously done* or *committed.* Derivatives, ܡܪܚܐ, ܡܪܚܐܝܬ, ܡܪܚܘܬܐ.

ܡܪܚܐ, ܡܪܚܐ, ܡܪܚܬܐ rt. ܡܪܚ. *bold, headstrong, wilful, insolent, presumptuous; a boaster, bully.*

ܡܪܚܐܝܬ rt. ܡܪܚ. adv. *boldly, rashly, presumptuously.*

ܡܪܚܘܬܐ pl. ܬܐ̈ rt. ܡܪܚ. f. *boldness, intrepidity, audacity, effrontery, presumption;* pl. *daring acts, desperate ventures.*

ܡܪܚܡܢ, ܡܪܚܡܢܐ, ܬܐ rt. ܪܚܡ. *merciful, tender, compassionate, benevolent, conciliatory;* with ܠܐ *merciless.*

ܡܪܚܡܢܐܝܬ rt. ܪܚܡ. adv. *mercifully;* with ܠܐ *mercilessly.*

ܡܪܚܡܢܘܬܐ rt. ܪܚܡ. f. *mercy, mercifulness, lovingkindness, compassion; beneficence, alms, almsgiving, good works;* a title of the Byzantine emperors ܡܪܚܡܢܘܬܟܘܢ *your Clemency.*

ܡܪܚܦ, ܢܐ, ܢܝܬܐ rt. ܪܚܦ. *brooding, cherishing;* rit. *moving lightly to and fro;* metaph. *pitiful, compassionate,* ܐܠܗܐ ܡܪܚܦܢܐ ܘܡܪܚܡܢܐ *God is full of compassion and merciful.*

ܡܪܚܦܢܐܝܬ rt. ܪܚܦ. *hoveringly.*

ܡܪܚܦܢܘܬܐ rt. ܪܚܦ. f. *compassion, pity, commiseration.*

ܡܪܚܩܢܐ, ܢܝܬܐ rt. ܪܚܩ. *rebellious; a rebel;* ܡܪܚܩܢܐ ܡܢ ܐܠܗܐ *apostates, backsliders.*

ܡܪܚܩܢܘܬܐ rt. ܪܚܩ. *removal to a distance; defection;* ܡܪܚܩܢܘܬܐ ܕܡܢ ܥܠܡܐ *forsaking the world.*

ܡܪܚܫܢܐ rt. ܪܚܫ. *creeping.*

ܡܪܛ fut. ܢܡܪܘܛ, act. part. ܡܐܪܛ, ܡܪܛܐ, pass. part. ܡܪܝܛ. *to pluck, pull* or *tear out* hair, feathers, vegetables, &c.; ܡܪܛܬ ܣܥܪܐ ܚܘܪܐ ܕܝܠܗ *she pulled out her white hairs;* ܡܪܛܬ ܚܘܐ ܦܐܪܐ ܕܡܘܬܐ Eve *plucked the fruit of death;* ܡܪܘܛ ܩܪܢܘܗܝ ܕܐܝܠܐ *dishorn the stag;* metaph. ܡܪܘܛ ܝܘܬܪܢܐ *pluck profit;* ܝܘܢܐ ܕܡܪܝܛܢ ܓܦܝܗ̈ *a dove with torn wings.* Ethpe. ܐܬܡܪܛ *to be pulled out.* Pa. ܡܪܛ *to pluck, pull.* Ethpa. ܐܬܡܪܛ *to be torn off, pulled out* as feathers or wings. Derivatives, ܡܪܘܛܘܬܐ, ܡܪܛܐ, ܡܪܝܛܐ, ܡܪܛܘܢܐ.

ܡܪܛܐ pl. ܐ̈ and ܡܪܝܛܐ rt. ܡܪܛ. m. *the plucking out, pulling off* of the hair or feathers; *baldness; plumes, fine apparel.*

ܡܪܛܒܢܐ rt. ܪܛܒ. *making moist, bringing moisture.*

ܡܪܛܘܛܐ pl. ܐ̈ m. *a cloak, mantle, covering.*

ܡܪܛܘܢܐ rt. ܡܪܛ. m. dim. *a little feather, tiny plume.*

ܡܪܛܢܢܐ, ܢܝܬܐ rt. ܪܛܢ. *a murmurer, grumbler.*

ܡܪܛܝܣܘܡ corrupt for ܡܪܛܝܣܩܘܢ Pers. *asparagus.*

ܡܪܝ irreg. Pael of ܡܪܪ.

ܡܪܝ *my Lord;* see ܡܪܐ.

ܡܪܝܐ emph. state of ܡܪܐ.

ܡܪܝܢܢܐ rt. ܪܢܢ. *resounding.*

ܡܪܝܪ; see ܡܪܪ.

ܡܪܝܚܘܬܐ rt. ܪܘܚ. f. *tranquillity.*

ܡܪܝܚܢܐ rt. ܪܘܚ. *refreshing, soothing.*

ܡܪܝܚܢܐ rt. ܪܘܚ. *digestive.*

ܡܪܝܚܢܘܬܐ rt. ܪܘܚ. f. *the sense of smell.*

ܡܪܝܡܢܐ, ܢܝܬܐ rt. ܪܘܡ. *a) one who exalts. b) repressive, rescinding. c) an opponent. d)* gram. *negative, privative.*

ܡܪܝܡܢܘܬܐ rt. ܪܘܡ. f. *a) elevation, exaltation. b) abrogation, removal; prohibition* of animal food during a fast. *c)* gram. *negation, suppression.*

ܡܪܝܡܢܝܐ rt. ܪܘܡ. *negative.*

ܡܪܝܣܘܬܐ rt. ܪܣܣ. f. *being battered, knocked about; being vexed by a devil.*

ܡܪܝܩܐܝܬ rt. ܪܩܩ. adv. *clearly, lucidly.*

ܡܪܝܩܘܬܐ rt. ܪܩܩ. f. *cleansing, purifying, purification* of body, mind, spirit.

ܡܪܝܪ; see verb ܡܪܪ.

ܡܪܝܪܐܝܬ rt. ܡܪܪ. adv. *bitterly, harshly, cruelly, severely;* ܒܟܝܬ ܡܪܝܪܐܝܬ *I wept bitterly;* ܐܬܟܪܗ ܡܪܝܪܐܝܬ *he contracted a severe illness.*

ܡܪܝܪܘܬܐ rt. ܡܪܪ. f. *bitterness; harshness, cruelty;* ܡܪܝܪܘܬ ܪܥܝܢܐ or ܡܪܝܪܘܬ ܫܘܚܠܦܐ *moroseness, a sour* or *harsh disposition.*

ܡܪܟܒܐ; see ܡܪܟܒܬܐ.

ܡܪܟܒܐ, ܡܪܟܒܬܐ pl. ܡܪܟܒܐ, ܡܪܟܒܬܐ rt. ܪܟܒ. f. *a chariot, carriage, vehicle, conveyance; a throne; a ship.*

ܡܪܟܒܐܝܬ rt. ܪܟܒ. adv. *artificially.*

ܡܪܟܒܘܬܐ rt. ܪܟܒ. f. *structure, composition, construction, complexity.*

ܡܪܟܒܢܐ rt. ܪܟܒ. *a driver, charioteer.*

ܡܪܟܒܢܐ rt. ܪܟܒ. *a) complex. b) a compounder, composer, author, writer.*

ܡܪܟܒܢܘܬܐ rt. ܪܟܒ. f. *intermingling, coherence.*

ܡܪܟܟܢܐ rt. ܪܟ. *softening, emollient, laxative.*

ܡܪܟܟܢܐܝܬ rt. ܪܟ. adv. *pronounced softly,* i.e. with rucocho.

ܡܪܟܟܢܘܬܐ rt. ܪܟ. f. *the softening* or *aspiration* of a letter.

ܡܰܪܟܢܽܘܬܳܐ rt. ܪܟܢ. f. *inclination, bending.*

ܡܰܪܩܽܘܢܳܐ m. *black cummin, anise.*

ܡܰܪܡܽܘܬܳܐ rt. ܪܘܡ. f. *a) elevation, haughtiness. b)* gram. *suppression, elision* of a letter.

ܡܰܪܡܝܽܘܬܳܐ rt. ܪܡܐ. f. *supplanting;* ܡܰܪܡܝܽܘܬܳܐ ܕܪܶܓܠܳܐ *tripping up.*

ܡܰܪܡܝܳܢܳܐ rt. ܪܡܐ. *a whisperer, calumniator, slanderer.*

ܡܰܪܡܝܳܢܽܘܬܳܐ rt. ܪܡܐ. f. *a) setting upon, attack; a cast* or *throw* of a fisher's net or hook. *b) whispering, talebearing, slander, plotting, spite.*

ܡܰܪܡܺܝܬܳܐ pl. ܡܰܪܡܝܳܢ, ܡܰܪܡܝܳܬܳܐ rt. ܪܡܐ. f. *a subdivision of the Psalter* containing from one to four Psalms. Cf. ܗܽܘܠܳܠܳܐ.

ܡܰܪܡܳܝܳܐ pl. ܶܐ m. *candle-snuffers.*

ܡܰܪܡܰܪ Palpal conj. of ܡܰܪ.

ܡܪܰܡܪܡܳܐܝܺܬ rt. ܪܘܡ. adv. *wonderfully, exceedingly.*

ܡܪܰܡܪܡܳܢܳܐ, ܢܺܝܬܳܐ rt. ܪܘܡ. *lifter up, exalter; raising, exalting.*

ܡܰܪܰܢ denom. verb from ܡܳܪܳܐ. Ethpa. ܐܶܬܡܰܪܰܢ or ܐܶܬܡܰܪܰܐܢ *to become lord, take possession.*

ܡܳܪܳܢܳܐܝܺܬ from ܡܳܪܳܐ. adv. *authoritatively, domineeringly; rightfully, rightful, properly, accurately* opp. ܒܫܽܘܚܠܳܦܳܐܝܺܬ and ܫܳܐܝܠܳܐܝܺܬ *metaphorically, figuratively.*

ܡܳܪܽܘܬܳܐ, ܡܳܪܘܳܬܳܐ or ܡܰܪܘܳܬܳܐ pl. ܘܳܬܳܐ from ܡܳܪܳܐ. f. *domination, dominion;* pl. *angels;* see ܡܳܪܽܘܬܳܐ.

ܡܳܪܳܝܳܐ, ܡܳܪܳܢܳܝܳܐ or ܡܰܪܘܳܢܳܝܳܐ, ܢܳܝܬܳܐ from ܡܳܪܳܐ. adj. *a) of* or *pertaining to a lord* or *master, dominant, supreme, principal, pre-eminent, imperial;* God is ܐܰܒܳܐ ܡܳܪܳܢܳܝܳܐ *the Supreme Father;* ܡܶܠܰܝܟܳܬܳܐ ܡܳܪܳܢܳܝܳܬܳܐ *imperial rescripts;* ܦܽܘܩܕܳܢܳܐ ܡܳܪܳܢܳܝܳܐ *a supreme command;* ܗܰܝܟܠܳܐ ܡܳܪܳܢܳܝܳܐ *a noble temple;* ܓܰܘ̈ܢܶܐ ܡܳܪ̈ܳܢܳܝܶܐ *the primary colours. b)* spec. *of* or *belonging to the Lord;* ܦܽܘܩ̈ܕܳܢܶܐ ܡܳܪ̈ܳܢܳܝܶܐ *the commandments of our Lord;* ܚܫܳܡܺܝܬܳܐ ܡܳܪܳܢܳܝܬܳܐ *the Lord's supper;* ܫܢܰܬ ܐܓܫ ܡܳܪܳܢܳܝܬܳܐ in the year 1703 *of our Lord;* ܥܺܐܕܳܐ ܡܳܪ̈ܳܢܳܝܶܐ *the festivals of our Lord. c) one's own, proper, properly named, rightly called, actual* opp. ܫܳܐܝܠܳܐ *borrowed, assumed;* ܡܳܪܳܢܳܝܳܐ *property, possessions;* ܫܡܳܐ ܕܝܽܘܬܳܢܳܐ ܐܘ ܡܳܪܳܢܳܝܳܐ *a personal* or *proper name;* ܕܺܝܠܳܝܬܳܐ ܡܳܪܳܢܳܝܬܳܐ *the specific* or *generic property;* ܕܶܒ̈ܚܶܐ ܪܽܘܚܳܢ̈ܳܝܶܐ ܘܡܳܪ̈ܳܢܳܝܶܐ ܕܗܰܘܢܳܐ *the spiritual and actual sacrifices of the intelligence.*

ܡܳܪܳܢܽܘܬܳܐ or ܡܰܪܘܳܢܽܘܬܳܐ from ܡܳܪܳܐ. f. *a) dominion, sovereignty;* ܚܕܳܐ ܡܰܠܟܽܘܬܳܐ. ܚܕܳܐ ܡܳܪܳܢܽܘܬܳܐ. ܚܕܳܐ ܡܳܪܽܘܬܳܐ there is in the Trinity *one being from everlasting, one dominion, one lordship. b) right of property, possession. c) property, essence;* ܒܡܳܪܳܢܽܘܬܶܗ ܕܫܡܳܐ *in the name itself.*

ܡܰܪܢܳܐ, ܡܰܪܢܺܝܬܳܐ pl. ܢܝ̈ܳܬܳܐ f. *a) a lance. b)* rt. ܪܢܐ. *care, anxiety;* ܕܠܳܐ ܡܰܪܢܺܝܬܳܐ *free from care, unconcerned;* ܡܰܪ̈ܢܝܳܬܳܐ ܥܳܠܡܳܢܳܝܳܬܳܐ *worldly cares. c) thought, theory, reflection, suspicion.*

ܡܪܰܣ fut. ܢܶܡܪܽܘܣ, act. part. ܡܳܪܶܣ, pass. part. ܡܪܺܝܣ. *to crush, bruise, steep;* ܡܳܪܶܣ ܠܰܚܫܳܒ̈ܳܬܳܐ ܐܰܠܳܗܳܝܳܬܳܐ *he crushes down, represses, godly thoughts;* ܡܪܺܝܣ ܗܽܘ ܠܶܒܶܗ *his heart is harassed.* Pa. *to bruise, batter.* Ethpa. ܐܶܬܡܰܪܰܣ *to be bruised, steeped;* ܒܚܰܡܪܳܐ *in wine.* Derivatives, ܡܪܳܣܳܐ, ܡܪܽܘܣܝܳܐ, ܡܪܽܘܣܳܐ, ܡܰܪܣܳܐ, ܡܪܺܝܣܽܘܬܳܐ, ܡܰܪܣܽܘܬܳܐ.

ܡܪܳܣܳܐ rt. ܡܪܣ. m. *squeezing.*

ܡܰܪܣܽܘܦܳܐ pl. ܶܐ m. μαρσύπιον, *a pouch, purse, leathern bag.*

ܡܪܰܥ fut. ܢܶܡܪܰܥ, act. part. ܡܳܪܰܥ. *to be* or *fall ill, become sick, infirm* or *flabby;* ܡܳܪܰܥ ܒܠܶܒܶܗ *he is sick at heart;* ܦܺܐܪ̈ܶܐ ܕܥܶܕܶܢ ܠܳܐ ܡܳܪܥܺܝܢ *the fruits of Eden do not wither.* Pa. ܡܰܪܰܥ *to be ill.* Ethpa. ܐܶܬܡܰܪܰܥ *to be diseased;* ܕܠܳܐ ܢܶܬܡܰܪܥܽܘܢ ܡܶܢ ܚܽܘܡܳܐ *lest they become diseased from the heat.* Aph. ܐܰܡܪܰܥ *to cause sickness,* perh. *to nip off.* Derivatives, ܡܰܪܥܳܐ, ܡܪܺܝܥܳܐ, ܡܰܪܥܽܘܬܳܐ.

ܡܪܺܝܥܳܐ pl. ܡܪܺܝܥܶܐ, m. ܡܪܺܝܥܬܳܐ, pl. ܡܪ̈ܺܝܥܳܬܳܐ, f. rt. ܡܪܥ. adj. *sick, sickly, ill, wasting, unhealthy;* ܨܠܺܝܒܳܟ ܠܥܳܠܡܳܐ ܡܪܺܝܥܳܐ ܐܰܣܺܝ *Thy Cross has healed a sick world;* ܐܶܣܛܽܘܟܣܶܐ ܡܪ̈ܺܝܥܶܐ ܘܡܶܣܟܺܢ̈ܶܐ these *weak and beggarly elements;* ܓܽܘܦܢܳܐ ܡܪܺܝܥܬܳܐ *a drooping vine.*

ܡܰܪܥܳܐ or ܡܪܳܥܳܐ pl. ܶܐ rt. ܡܪܥ. m. *sickness, disease.*

ܡܪܟܟܐ, ܡܪܟܟܬܐ rt. ܪܟܟ. *soft, tender;* ܒܝ̈ܥܐ ܡܪܟܟ̈ܬܐ *soft-boiled eggs.*

ܡܪܟܒܘܬܐ rt. ܡܪܟܒ. f. *sickness, disease, unhealthiness;* ܐܐܪ ܡܥܒܪ ܡܪܟܒܘܬܐ ܡܢ ܦܓܪ̈ܐ *the air takes away disease from bodies.*

ܡܪܟܝܢܐ pl. ܝ̈ܢܐ rt. ܪܟܐ. *reconciling, propitiatory; a propitiator.*

ܡܪܟܝܢܘܬܐ rt. ܪܟܐ. f. *propitiation.*

ܡܪܟܝܬܐ pl. ܝܢ̈ܬܐ rt. ܪܟܐ. f. *a) pasture. b) a flock; subjects, a Christian community, a diocese.*

ܡܪܟܡܘܬܐ rt. ܪܟܡ. f. *stupefaction, being thunderstruck.*

ܡܪܟܡܢܐ rt. ܪܟܡ. *thundering.*

ܡܪܟܬܢܘܬܐ rt. ܪܟܬ. f. *froth, foam, foaming.*

ܡܪܦ Aphel act. part. of ܪܦ.

ܡܪܦܝܢܐ, ܝܢ̈ܬܐ rt. ܪܦܐ. *enervating, soft, effeminate.*

ܡܪܦܝܢܘܬܐ rt. ܪܦܐ. f. *abandonment, negligence.*

ܡܪܩܕܢܐ rt. ܪܩܕ. *a dancer.*

ܡܪܦܬܢܐ rt. ܪܦܬ. *causing to throb.*

ܡܪܩܥܐ rt. ܪܩܥ. *patched.*

ܡܪܘܝܢܐ rt. ܪܘܝ. *a trainer, breaker-in of horses.*

ܡܪܩ fut. ܢܡܪܘܩ, act. part. ܡܪܩ, ܡܪܩܐ, pass. part. ܡܪܝܩ, ܩܐ, ܩܬܐ. *to rub off rust, scour, polish, cleanse;* ܟܠܝܢܗ *his armour;* ܫܢ̈ܐ *the teeth;* metaph. *to cleanse, purify, purge away;* ܡܪܩܐ ܡܠܚܐ *salt purifies;* ܟܠܚܕ ܡܪܩ ܒܠܒܪ ܘܒܢܦܫܗ ܡܛܡܐ *every one purifies himself outwardly and in his secret* soul *is stained;* ܡܪܘܩܘ ܡܚܫܒܬܟܘܢ ܡܢ *clear your mind of . . . .* Verbal adj. ܡܚܙܝܬܐ ܡܪܝܩܬܐ *a polished mirror;* ܐܐܪ ܡܪܝܩܐ *clear air;* ܢܦܫܐ ܡܪܝܩܬܐ *a purified soul;* used especially of being *polished, prompt, cultivated* in mind, thought or expression. ETHPE. ܐܬܡܪܩ and ETHPA. ܐܬܡܪܩ *to be scoured, polished, wiped clean; to be cleansed, purified.* ETHTAPH. ܐܬܬܡܪܩ *to be cleansed, scoured.* DERIVATIVES, ܡܪܘܩܐ, ܡܪܘܩܝܐ, ܡܪܩܐ, ܡܪܩܐ, ܡܪܩܘܬܐ, ܡܪܩܐ, ܡܪܩܢܝܐ, ܡܬܡܪܩܢܐ.

ܡܪܩܐ rt. ܡܪܩ. m. *a polishing, brushing, smoothing* of clothes, pearls, &c.; ܡܪܩܐ ܕܫܘܚܢܐ *the cleansing of a sore.*

ܡܪܩܕܘܬܐ rt. ܪܩܕ. f. *mourning, lamentation.*

ܡܪܩܕܢܐ rt. ܪܩܕ. *a mourner.*

ܡܪܩܕ̈ܬܐ pl. of ܡܪܩܕܘܬܐ.

ܡܪܩܕܢܝܐ rt. ܪܩܕ. a particle *expressing lamentation* as ܘܝ *alas!*

ܡܪܩܕܬܐ pl. ܡܪܩܕ̈ܬܐ f. *sorrow, mourning, lamentation;* ܩܠ ܡܪܩܕ̈ܬܐ *the sound of lamentation.*

ܡܪܩܝܘܢܝܐ or ܡܪܩܝܘܢܝܐ pl. ܝ̈ܐ or ܡܪܩܝܘܢܝ̈ܐ from ܡܪܩܝܘܢ. m. *a Marcionite, follower of* the heretic *Marcion.*

ܡܪܩܝܘܢܝܣܛܐ same as ܡܪܩܝܘܢܝܐ.

ܡܪܩܦܐ rt. ܪܩܦ. m. *the hypochondria, upper part of the belly.*

ܡܪܩܫܝܬܐ *pyrites.*

ܡܪܪܐ usually pl. ܡܪܪ̈ܐ rt. ܡܪ. f. *bitterness, anything bitter, bitter herbs, gall, wormwood;* ܡܒܘܥܐ ܕܡܪܪ̈ܐ *a spring of bitterness;* ܒܡܪܪܘܬ ܢܦܫܐ *in bitterness of soul.*

ܡܪܪܬܐ rt. ܡܪ. f. *gall, bile, poison,* ܡܪܪܬܐ ܕܚܘܝܐ *the venom* of the serpent; ܡܪܪܬܐ ܕܒܪܐ *cucumis colocynthis, the wild gourd.*

ܡܪܫܐ, ܡܪܫܬܐ or ܡܪܫܬܐ rt. ܪܫ. *a) a pestle, a mortar. b) a strong hempen rope.*

ܡܪܫܥܬܐ, ܡܪܫܥܬܐ pl. ܡܪܫܥ̈ܬܐ rt. ܪܫܥ. f. *rebuke, complaint, accusation, charge;* ܕܠܐ ܡܪܫܥܬܐ *blameless.*

ܡܪܫܥܢܘܬܐ rt. ܪܫܥ. f. *censure, vituperation;* ܡܪܫܥܢܘܬ ܛܝܒܘܬܐ *taunting with a favour.*

ܡܪܫܠܐܝܬ rt. ܪܫܠ. adv. *negligently, slackly.*

ܡܪܫܠܘܬܐ and ܡܪܫܠܢܘܬܐ rt. ܪܫܠ. f. *paralysis.*

ܡܪܫܠܢܐ rt. ܪܫܠ. *paralyzed, feeble.*

ܡܪܫܡܢܐ rt. ܪܫܡ. *a pencil; a baker's stamp.*

ܡܪܫܡܢܘܬܐ rt. ܪܫܡ. f. *drawing, design.*

ܡܪܬܐ pl. ܡܪ̈ܘܬܐ fem. of ܡܪܐ. *a) a lady, mistress, owner, governess, princess, abbess;* ܡܪܬ ܒܝܬܐ *the mistress of a household;* ܡܪܬܐ ܝܩܝܪܬܐ *a very noble lady;* with suff. I p. ܡܪܬܝ *my lady, Mistress, Lady* a title esp. of the saints; ܡܪܬܝ ܡܪܝܡ ܝܠܕܬ ܐܠܗܐ *Saint Mary Mother of God;* ܡܪܬܢ *our Lady;* ܡܪܬܝ ܫܡܘܢܝ *Saint Samona. b)* adj. *possessing, rich;* ܐܠܗܘܬܐ ܡܬܝܪܐ ܒܣܝܡܬܐ *the Godhead rich in treasures;* ܫܢܬܐ ܡܬܝܪܐ ܒܥܠܠܬܐ *a rich* or *abundant year;* ܡܬܝܪܐ ܒܪܓܫܐ—ܗܘܢܐ *endowed with sense, rich in mental powers;* ܡܬܝܪܐ ܡܛܘܫܐ ܘܡܛܢܦܐ *exceedingly defiled and polluted.*

ܡܪܬܐ or ܡܪܪܬܐ pl. ܡܪ̈ܬܐ rt. ܡܪ. f. *bitterness, gall, bile;* ܐܪܒܥ ܡܪ̈ܬܐ *the four humours* of the body; ܡܪܬܐ ܐܘܟܡܬܐ *black bile;* ܡܪܬܐ ܫܥܘܬܢܝܬܐ *yellow bile;* ܡܪܬܐ ܣܘܡܩܬܐ *blood;* ܡܪܬܐ ܚܘܪܬܐ *phlegm.*

ܡܬܪܝܢܐ rt. ܬܪܐ. adv. *an admonisher, monitor; admonitory.*

ܡܬܪܝܢܐܝܬ rt. ܬܪܐ. adv. *warningly, admonitorily.*

ܡܬܪܝܢܘܬܐ pl. ܘܬܐ rt. ܬܪܐ. f. *an admonition, warning, exhortation, homily.*

ܡܪܬܢܐ, ܬܐ rt. ܡܪ. adj. *bilious; irritable, ill-tempered.*

ܡܪܬܢܝܐ, ܬܐ rt. ܡܪ. *bilious, bitter.*

ܡܫ 3 m. s. pret. of verb ܡܘܫ.

ܡܫ = ܡܫܫ *to touch, feel.* Derivatives, ܡܫܘܫܐ, ܡܫܡܫܐ.

ܡܫܐ fut. ܢܡܫܐ, act. part. ܡܫܐ, ܡܫܝܐ. *to lease, glean* corn, &c.; *to rub;* ܡܫܐ ܦܪ̈ܨܘܦܘܗܝ ܒܐܝܕܗ *he rubbed his face with his hand.* Pa. ܡܫܝ *to choose out, make a selection.* Derivatives, ܡܫܝܐ, ܡܫܘܝܐ.

ܡܫܐܠܢܐ, ܢܝܬܐ rt. ܫܐܠ. *asking, interrogative; an interrogator; the questioner* in a dialogue; gram. *interrogative, of interrogation;* ܦܘܚܡܐ ܡܫܐܠܢܐ *a mark of interrogation,* the points ܿ, ܼ or . .

ܡܫܐܠܢܐܝܬ rt. ܫܐܠ. adv. *interrogatively.*

ܡܫܐܠܢܘܬܐ rt. ܫܐܠ. f. *interrogation; excusing, eschewing.*

ܡܫܐܠܢܘܬܐ rt. ܫܐܠ. f. *lending, money-lending.*

ܡܫܒܐ pl. ܶܐ rt. ܢܫܒ. m. *a breath, breath of air, breeze, light wind.*

ܡܫܒܒܐ *a leathern wallet.*

ܡܫܒܚܢܐܝܬ rt. ܫܒܚ. adv. *gloriously.*

ܡܫܒܚܢܘܬܐ rt. ܫܒܚ. f. *praiseworthiness;* ܡܫܒܚܢܘܬ ܗܘܦܟܐ *laudable behaviour.*

ܡܫܒܚܢ, ܡܫܒܚܢܐ, ܢܝܬܐ rt. ܫܒܚ. *uttering praise, singing praises; a singer, chorister;* ܡܫܒܚܢܐ ܩܝܬܪ̈ܐ *resounding citherns;* ܡܫܒܚܢܐ ܬܪܝܨ ܫܘܒܚܐ *the orthodox.*

ܡܫܒܚܢܝܬܐ f. the plant *scammony.*

ܡܫܒܠܢܐ pl. ܶܐ rt. ܫܒܠ. *a guide, leader, director;* esp. *the director of the monks, hegoumenos, abbot.*

ܡܫܒܠܢܘܬܐ rt. ܫܒܠ. f. *direction.*

ܡܫܓܝܢܐ, ܢܝܬܐ rt. ܫܓܐ. *a misleader, beguiler, seducer, impostor;* ܐܓܪܬܐ ܡܫܓܝܢܝܬܐ *a beguiling epistle.*

ܡܫܓܚܢ, ܡܫܓܚܢܐ from ܫܓܚ. *changed, altered, different.*

ܡܫܓܚܢܐܝܬ from ܫܓܚ. adv. *variously.*

ܡܫܓܚܢܘܬܐ from ܫܓܚ. f. *a premiss, a proposition.*

ܡܫܓܝܢܝܬܐ dim. of ܡܫܓܬܐ. *a washhand basin.*

ܡܫܓܫܢܐ rt. ܫܓܫ. m. *a demagogue, leader of sedition.*

ܡܫܓܬܐ pl. ܡܫܓ̈ܝܬܐ rt. ܫܓܐ. f. *a washing-bowl, basin.*

ܡܫܕܝܐ Aphel part. of ܫܕܐ. m. *a cast, throw;* ܡܫܕܝܐ ܕܩܫܬܐ—ܡܫܕܝܐ ܓܐܪܐ *a bowshot;* ܡܫܕܝܐ ܟܐܦܐ *a stone's-throw.*

ܡܫܕܠܢܐ, ܢܝܬܐ rt. ܫܕܠ. *enticing, alluring; a flatterer, deceiver.*

ܡܫܕܪ, ܡܫܕܪܐ Pael pass. part. of ܫܕܪ. *a messenger, ambassador, legate.*

ܡܫܕܪܢܐ rt. ܫܕܪ. m. *a sender.*

ܡܫܕܪܢܘܬܐ rt. ܫܕܪ. f. *sending, a mission.*

ܡܫܚܢܘܬܐ rt. ܫܚܐ. f. metaph. *lukewarmness, coolness.*

ܡܫܘܚܢܐ rt. ܫܚܐ. adj. *quenching, extinguishing.*

ܡܫܘܚܢܘܬܐ rt. ܫܚܐ. f. *the act of quenching.*

ܡܫܘܫܐ m. ܡܫܘܫܬܐ, f. *a thin woollen garment worn by monks.*

ܡܫܓܪܢܐ, ܢܝܬܐ rt. ܫܓܪ. *inciting, provoking.*

ܡܫܘܕܥܢܐ, ܢܝܬܐ rt. ܝܕܥ. *signifying, indicative, expressing, denoting.*

ܡܫܘܕܥܢܘܬܐ rt. ܝܕܥ. f. *signification, denotation, indication; a token.*

ܡܫܘܙܒܢܘܬܐ rt. ܫܙܒ. f. *deliverance, preservation, salvation; a remnant saved.*

ܡܫܘܙܒܢܐ, ܢܝܬܐ rt. ܫܙܒ. adj. *saving, delivering, redeeming;* ܙܩܝܦܐ ܡܫܘܙܒܢܐ *the redeeming cross;* ܛܝܒܘܬܐ ܡܫܘܙܒܢܝܬܐ *saving grace.*

ܡܫܘܚܢܐ rt. ܡܫܚ. *an anointer; a measurer, geometrician.*

ܡܫܘܚܕܐܝܬ from Shaphel conj. of ܝܚܕ. adv. *solitarily.*

ܡܫܘܚܕܘܬܐ from Shaphel of ܝܚܕ. rt. ܝܚܕ. f. *loneliness.*

ܡܫܘܚܢܢܐ rt. ܫܘܚ. *germinating.*

ܡܫܘܚܢܢܘܬܐ or ܡܫܘܚܢܘܬܐ rt. ܫܘܚ. f. *sprouting out; an excrescence, protuberance.*

ܡܫܘܚܪܐ from Shaphel of ܐܚܪ. adj. *slow, slothful, slack.*

ܡܫܘܚܪܐܝܬ from Shaphel of ܐܚܪ. adv. *slowly, tardily, late, negligently.*

ܡܫܘܚܪܘܬܐ from Shaphel of ܐܚܪ. f. *delay, slackness.*

ܡܫܘܚܬܐ emph. st. of ܡܫܘܚܐ; see above.

ܡܫܘܚܬܢܝܐ rt. ܡܫܚ. *metrical.*

ܡܫܘܛܐ pl. ܛܐ̈ m. *a palmer* or *canker-worm, a creeping locust.*

ܡܫܘܠܐ pl. ܠܐ̈ rt. ܫܠܐ. *a gleaner.*

ܡܫܘܢܝܐ rt. ܫܘܐ. *levelling, simplifying.*

ܡܫܘܢܝܘܬܐ rt. ܫܘܐ. f. *levelling, making even;* ܡܫܘܢܝܘܬܐ ܕܐܘܪܚܬܐ *the levelling of the roads.*

ܡܫܘܦܦܘܬܐ rt. ܫܦܦ. f. *shrivelling, withering.*

ܡܫܘܦܪܬܐ rt. ܢܦܪ. f. *nostrils; a tumour, blister.*

ܡܫܘܥܐ rt. ܫܘܥ. m. *a plasterer's trowel.*

ܡܫܘܪܐ rt. ܫܪܐ. m. *a swine, boar, grunter.*

ܡܫܘܫܛܘܬܐ rt. ܫܛܚ. f. *progress, course* e. g. with ܙܒܢܐ̈ *of time;* ܡܫܘܫܛܘܬ ܐܝܕܐ *liberality.*

ܡܫܚ fut. ܢܡܫܘܚ, act. part. ܡܫܚ, ܡܫܚܐ, pass. part. ܡܫܝܚ, ܚܐ, ܚܬܐ. I. *a) to besmear, rub over;* ܡܫܘܚ ܠܨܪ̈ܝܬܐ *smear the cracks* with liquid pitch. *b) to anoint* at baptism; to the office of king, prophet, priest; *to administer unction* or *chrism; to consecrate to office;* ܡܫܚܝܢ ܡܥܡܕܢܐ *those who rebaptize.* Pass. part. *anointed, the Anointed One, the Messiah, the Christ;* ܡܫܝܚܐ ܕܓܠܐ—ܡܫܝܚܐ ܕܟܕܒܐ—ܡܫܝܚܐ ܫܢܝܐ *the false Christ, pseudo-Christ, Anti-Christ.*

II. *to measure, extend, stretch out;* ܐܪܥܐ *the land;* ܗܕܡ̈ܐ *the limbs.*

Ethpe. ܐܬܡܫܚ I. *to be anointed, receive unction* or *chrism, be consecrated.* II. *to be measured; to stretch oneself out;* ܕܠܐ ܡܬܡܫܚ *immense.* Pael ܡܫܚ *to measure, moderate, proportion;* ܡܡܫܚܝܢ ܡܫܡܥܝ̈ܬܐ ܠܚܛܗ̈ܐ *punishments in proportion to the sins.* Pass. part. ܡܡܫܚ, ܡܡܫܚܐ, ܚܬܐ *temperate, moderate, modest;* ܚܡܝܡܘܬܐ ܡܡܫܚܬܐ *moderate heat;* ܡܟܣܢܘܬܐ ܡܡܫܚܬܐ *a temperate* or *just reproof;* ܡܐܡܪܐ ܡܡܫܚܐ *a metrical sermon.* Ethpa. ܐܬܡܫܚ *to be measured, stretched out;* ܐܬܡܫܚ ܗܘ ܕܡܫܚ ܠܫܡܝܐ *He who stretched out the heavens is stretched out* on the Cross. Derivatives, ܡܫܘܚܐ, ܡܫܘܚܐ, ܡܫܘܚܬܐ, ܡܫܘܚܬܢܝܐ, ܡܫܚܐ, ܡܫܝܚܐ, ܡܫܝܚܘܬܐ, ܡܫܝܚܐܝܬ, ܡܡܫܚܢܘܬܐ, ܡܫܝܚܐ, ܡܫܝܚܐ.

ܡܫܚܐ pl. ܡܫܚ̈ܐ rt. ܡܫܚ. m. *a) ointment, oil, salve, unguent;* ܡܐܢܐ ܕܡܫܚܐ *a vase of ointment;* ܩܪܢܐ ܕܡܫܚܐ *a horn of oil;* ܡܫܚܐ ܕܒܣܡܐ *aromatic ointment;* ܡܫܚܐ ܕܙܝܬܐ *olive oil.* *b) unction;* ܡܫܚܐ ܕܛܝܒܘܬܐ *oil of grace* i. e. oil with which the sick were anointed; ܡܫܚܐ ܕܡܫܝܚܘܬܐ *anointing oil;* ܡܫܚܐ ܕܩܘܕܫܐ *chrism, unction.*

ܡܫܚܛܐܝܬ rt. ܫܚܛ. adv. *foully.*

ܡܫܚܛܘܬܐ rt. ܫܚܛ. f. with ܠܐ *innocence.*

ܡܫܚܛܢܐ, ܢܝܬܐ rt. ܫܚܛ. m. *a corruptor; corrupting, vicious.*

ܡܫܚܠܦܐܝܬ rt. ܫܚܠܦ. adv. *differently, in various ways.*

ܡܫܚܠܦܘܬܐ rt. ܫܚܠܦ. f. *variety;* ܡܫܚܠܦܘܬ ܡܘܗܒܬܐ *diversity of gifts.*

ܡܫܚܢܐ rt. ܡܫܚ. m. *a salve;* ܡܫܚܢܐ ܕܐܣܐ *myrtle salve.* Usually ܡܫܚܢܐ, ܡܫܚܢܝܢ, pl. of ܡܫܚܐ.

ܡܫܚܢܢܐ, ܢܝܬܐ rt. ܫܚܢ. *promoting warmth; inflaming, ulcerous.*

ܡܫܚܢܢܘܬܐ rt. ܫܚܢ. f. *heating, carrying heat.*

ܡܫܚܛ infin. of verb ܫܚܛ. *to flay.*

ܡܫܛ infin. of verb ܫܛ. *to despise.*

ܡܫܚܛܐ rt. ܫܚܛ. m. *skinning, peeling;* ܡܫܚܛܐ ܕܚܪ̈ܘܒܐ *stripping off the leaves of the locust-tree.*

ܡܫܛܘܚܐ pl. ܐ̈ rt. ܫܛܚ. m. *anything spread out to dry, a drying.*

ܡܫܛܝܢܐ, ܡܫܛܝܢܝܬܐ rt. ܫܛܐ. *infatuating.*

ܡܫܝܐ pl. ܡ̈ܫܝܐ rt. ܡܫܐ. m. pl. *sweepings, rubbish, refuse.*

ܡܫܝܓܢܐ rt. ܫܓ. *one who washes, used in washing.*

ܡܫܝܚܐ; see ܡܫܚ.

ܡܫܝܚܘܬܐ rt. ܡܫܚ. f. *anointing, unction, chrism;* ܩܒܠ ܡܫܝܚܘܬܐ *being anointed with chrism, receiving chrism.*

ܡܫܝܚܝܐ, ܡܫܝܚܝܬܐ rt. ܡܫܚ. *anointed, Christian, belonging to Christ; a Christian;* ܥܢܐ ܡܫܝܚܝܬܐ *the Christian fold;* ܟܘܡܪܘܬܐ ܡܫܝܚܝܬܐ *the Christian priesthood;* ܥܝ̈ܢܐ ܡܫܝܚܝ̈ܬܐ *Christian eyes* sc. *spiritual insight;* ܒܫܢܬܐ—ܡܫܝܚܝܬܐ *in the year—of the Christian era;* ܫܪ̈ܒܬܐ ܡܫܝܚܝ̈ܬܐ *the genealogies of Christ.*

ܡܫܝܛܢܐ, ܡܫܝܛܢܝܬܐ rt. ܫܛܐ. *ferocious, wanton, shameless.*

ܡܫܝܛܢܐܝܬ rt. ܫܘܛ. adv. *with contempt.*

ܡܫܝܛܢܘܬܐ rt. ܫܘܛ. f. *contempt.*

ܡܫܩܦܢܐ, ܡܫܩܦܢܝܬܐ rt. ܫܩܦ. *painful, hurtful, harmful;* ܐܘܠܨܢܐ ܡܫܩܦܢܐ *heavy sorrow;* ܡܚ̈ܘܬܐ ܡܫܩ̈ܦܢܝܬܐ *lacerating blows;* ܗܠܝܢ ܡܫܩ̈ܦܢܝܬܐ ܘܫܢ̈ܝܩܬܐ *these dreadful and distressing occurrences.*

ܡܫܩܦܢܘܬܐ rt. ܫܩܦ. f. *annoyance, harshness;* ܡܫܩܦܢܘܬܗ ܕܩܘܪܫܐ *the biting cold.*

ܡܫܝܢܐܝܬ from ܫܝܢ. adv. *peacefully, tranquilly.*

ܡܫܝܢܘܬܐ from ܫܝܢ. f. *peacefulness, tranquillity, gentleness, serenity; the taming* of wild animals; *civilization;* ܡܫܝܢܘܬ ܚܡܬܐ *the calming of wrath;* as a title ܡܫܝܢܘܬܟ *your Serenity.*

ܡܫܝܢܢܐ, ܡܫܝܢܢܝܬܐ from ܫܝܢ. *calm, peaceful, making for peace, exhorting to peace, a peacemaker;* ܠܡܐܢܐ ܡܫܝܢܢܐ *a calm haven;* ܡ̈ܠܐ ܡܫܝܢܢ̈ܝܬܐ *conciliatory words.*

ܡܫܝܢܢܘܬܐ from ܫܝܢ. f. *calming, reconciliation.*

ܡܫܝܦܐܝܬ rt. ܫܦܐ. adv. *clearly, right well.*

ܡܫܟܟܢܐ rt. ܫܟܟ. *sedative.*

ܡܫܟ fut. ܢܡܫܘܟ, act. part. ܡܫܟ, ܡܫܟܐ; pass. part. ܡܫܝܟ, ܡܫܝܟܐ. *to shrivel* as fruit or leaves, *to become shrivelled, flabby, flat;* ܢܡܫܟܘܢ ܐܝܟ ܩܫ̈ܝܫܐ *let them become shrivelled like raisins.* Derivatives, ܡܫܟܘܬܐ, ܡܫܟܐ, ܡܫܟܝܐ, ܡܫܟܐܝܬ, ܡܫܟܢܐ, ܡܫܟܢܘܬܐ.

ܡܫܟܐ pl. ܐ̈ rt. ܡܫܟ. m. *the skin, hide, fell; leather; skin, rind* of fruit; ܡܫܟܐ ܕܠܒܪ *the outer cuticle, epidermis;* ܡܫ̈ܟܐ ܕܥܙ̈ܐ *goat-skins;* ܡܫ̈ܟܐ ܣܡܘ̈ܩܐ *skins dyed red;* ܐܣܪܐ ܕܡܫܟܐ *a leathern girdle;* ܕܒܓ ܡܫ̈ܟܐ *a skinner, fellmonger;* ܥܠ ܡܫ̈ܟܐ ܕܚܝ̈ܘܬܐ *on animals' skins* i. e. *on parchment.*

ܡܫܟܘܬܐ pl. ܐ̈ m. rt. ܡܫܟ. a) *negligence, carelessness,* ܒܡܫܟܘܬܐ *negligently, carelessly.* b) pl. *trifles, follies, absurdities, nonsense;* ܡܫ̈ܟܘܬܐ ܥܠܡ̈ܢܝܬܐ *worldly follies.*

ܡܫܟܘܬܐܝܬ rt. ܡܫܟ. adv. *negligently, carelessly, perfunctorily.*

ܡܫܟܒܐ, ܡܫܟܒܬܐ pl. ܐ̈ rt. ܫܟܒ. f. *a couch, bedroom;* ܒܝܬ ܡܫܟܒܐ *sleeping apartment, bedroom; a garden bed, plot.*

ܡܫܟܚܢܐ, ܡܫܟܚܢܝܬܐ rt. ܫܟܚ. a) *a finder, inventor, author;* ܡܫܟܚܢܐ ܕܐ̈ܒܝܕܬܐ *Finder of the lost;* ܣܛܢܐ ܗܘ ܡܫܟܚܢܐ ܕܚܛܝܬܐ *Satan the author of sin.* b) *possible, productive, efficient;* ܥܠܬܐ ܡܫܟܚܢܝܬܐ *an efficient cause;* with ܠܐ *impossible;* ܠܐ ܡܫܟܚܢ̈ܝܬܐ *impossibilities.*

ܡܫܟܚܢܘܬܐ rt. ܫܟܚ. f. *invention, discovery; possibility;* with ܠܐ *impossibility.*

ܡܫܟܝܐ, ܡܫܟܝܬܐ rt. ܡܫܟ. *foolish, inept, out of order;* ܫܘ̈ܐܠܐ ܡܫ̈ܟܝܐ *preposterous inquiries;* ܫܐܠܬܐ ܡܫܟܝܬܐ *a foolish request.*

ܡܫܟܢ fut. ܢܡܫܟܢ, act. part. ܡܡܫܟܢ, pass. part. ܡܡܫܟܢ denom. verb from ܡܫܟܢܐ. *to pledge, pawn, to give* or *take in pledge* or *as a hostage;* ܡܡܫܟܢ ܗܘܐ ܠܘܬ ܗܘ̈ܢܝܐ *he was sent as a hostage to the Huns.* Ethp. ܐܬܡܫܟܢ *to be given in pledge, left in deposit;* metaph. *to be pledged, devoted to.*

ܡܫܟܢܐ pl. ܐ̈ rt. ܫܟܢ. m. *a tent, tabernacle, habitation; stage* of a theatre; ܡܫܟܢܐ ܕܣܥܪܐ *a tent of camel's hair;* ܥܡܘܪ̈ܝ ܡܫܟܢܐ *dwellers in tents, nomads;* ܩܡ ܡܫܟܢܐ *the tabernacle was set up;* ܡܫܟܢ ܙܒܢܐ *the tabernacle;* also

ܟܡ ܡܫܪܝܐ ܙܥܘܪܐ a temporary stay, sojourn; ܟܕ ܫܠܝܐ ܒܡܫܟܢܐ ܠܡܫܟܢܗ when he was safe at home again.

ܡܫܟܢܐ pl. ܢ̈ܐ rt. ܡܫܟܢ. m. a pledge.

ܡܫܟܢܘܬܐ rt. ܡܫܟܢ. f. pawning, a pawn or pledge, the condition of a hostage; ܐܝܬܘܗܝ ܗܘܐ ܠܘܬ ܡܠܟܐ ܕܗܘ̈ܢܝܐ ܒܡܫܟܢܘܬܐ he was with the king of the Huns as a hostage.

ܡܫܟܢܘܬܐ rt. ܫܟܢ. f. giving, bounty.

ܡܫܟܢܝܐ, ܢܝܬܐ rt. ܡܫܟ. leathery, membranaceous; ܓܦ̈ܐ ܡܫܟܢ̈ܝܐ membranaceous or webbed wings.

ܡܫܟܢܢܐ rt. ܫܟܢ. m. a giver; ܡܫܟܢܢܐ ܕܟܠ ܛܒ̈ܬܐ the Giver of all good gifts.

ܡܫܟܪܢܘܬܐ rt. ܫܟܪ. f. obscenity.

ܡܫ̈ܟܠܐ pl. of ܡܫܟܠܬܐ.

ܡܫܠܗܒܘܬܐ rt. ܠܗܒ. f. inflammation, glow.

ܡܫܠܗܒܢܐ rt. ܠܗܒ. feverish, febrile.

ܡܫܠܗܒܢܐ, ܢܝܬܐ rt. ܠܗܒ. flaming, burning; making to glow.

ܡܫܠܗܒܐ; see ܠܗܒ.

ܡܫܠܘ̈ܬܐ pl. of ܡܫܠܬܐ.

ܡܫܠܚܐܝܬ rt. ܫܠܚ. adv. a) stripped, despoiled; ܥܪܩ ܗܘܐ ܡܫܠܚܐܝܬ he fled bare. b) simply, downright.

ܡܫܠܚܬܐ Pael part. fem. emph. of ܫܠܚ. peeled off rind, cassia.

ܡܫܠܛܢܐܝܬ rt. ܫܠܛ. adv. freely, of his own will; authoritatively; despotically, violently.

ܡܫܠܛܢܘܬܐ rt. ܫܠܛ. f. power, rule, domination, free will, licence, full permission; a prefectship, principality; ܡܫܠܛܢܘܬ ܢܦܫܐ free agency, self-mastery.

ܡܫܠܛܢܝܘܬܐ rt. ܫܠܛ. f. judgement, power.

ܡܫܠܐ pl. ܡܫ̈ܠܘܬܐ rt. ܫܠܐ. f. a flesh hook or fork; ܡܫܠܐ ܕܬܠܬ ܩܪ̈ܢܝܢ a three-pronged hook or fork.

ܡܫܠܡܢ, ܡܫܠܡܢܐ, ܢܝܬܐ rt. ܫܠܡ. a) maker, perfecter, fashioner. b) perfect, complete, entire; full, whole, full grown; ܫܒ̈ܠܐ ܡܫܠܡܢ̈ܝܬܐ full ears of corn; ܓܒܪܐ ܡܫܠܡܢܐ an adult, man of full age i.e. of twenty-five years; ܐܘܢܓܠܝܘܢ ܡܫܠܡܢܐ an entire or complete copy of a Gospel. Fem. emph. a robe covering the whole body, a long garment.

ܡܫܠܡܢܐ rt. ܫܠܡ. m. a) a traitor, betrayer; a deserter. b) a Moslem, Mohammedan.

ܡܫܠܡܢܐܝܬ rt. ܫܠܡ. adv. entirely, fully, perfectly.

ܡܫܠܡܢܘܬܐ or with a helping vowel ܡܫܠܡܢܘܬܐ pl. ܘ̈, ܘ̈ܬܐ rt. ܫܠܡ. f. a) handing down, handing over, delivering, ceding, cession, capitulation, surrender, betrayal, treachery; ܩܢܕܝܢܘܣ ܕܡܫܠܡܢܘܬܐ danger of incurring the charge of treason. b) succession to the kingdom. c) tradition, translation, version; ܐܝܟ ܡܫܠܡܢܘܬܐ ܫܠܝܚܝܬܐ according to apostolic tradition; ܡܫܠܡܢܘܬܐ ܕܡܢ ܦܘܡܐ ܠܦܘܡܐ oral tradition; ܡܫܠܡܢܘܬܐ ܕܣܘܪ̈ܝܝܐ ܐܘ ܡܦܩܬܐ ܦܫܝܛܬܐ the Syriac or Peshita Version; ܡܫܠܡܢܘܬܐ ܕܫܒܥܝܢ the Septuagint. d) exposition, commentary; ܡܫܠܡܢܘܬܐ ܕܚܕܬܐ a commentary on the New Testament; ܡܫܠܡܢܘܬ ܫܝܪ ܫܝܪ̈ܝܢ commentary on the Song of Songs. e) dialect, traditional pronunciation. f) a summary, synopsis. g) Islam, Moslemism.

ܡܫܠܡܢܘܬܐ rt. ܫܠܡ. f. fullness, completion, full growth.

ܡܫܠܝܬܐ pl. ܡܫ̈ܠܝܐ a packing-needle, awl, punch.

ܡܫܡܪܘܬܐ pl. ܘ̈ܬܐ rt. ܫܡܪ. f. sloth, idleness, frivolity.

ܡܫܡܗܐܝܬ rt. ܫܡ. adv. by name, expressly, verbally.

ܡܫܡܗܢܘܬܐ rt. ܫܡ. f. reputation, celebrity.

ܡܫܡܗܘܬܐ Pael infin. emph. state of ܫܡܗ. to name.

ܡܫܡܠܝܐܝܬ rt. ܫܡܠ. adv. fully, completely.

ܡܫܡܠܝܢܐܝܬ rt. ܫܡܠ. adv. wholly, entirely, completely, altogether.

ܡܫܡܠܝܘܬܐ pl. ܘ̈ܬܐ rt. ܫܡܠ. f. completeness, entirety, perfection; fullness, abundance; wholeness, soundness, full growth, full number; ܡܫܡܠܝܘܬ ܙܝܢܐ ܪܘܚܢܝܬܐ spiritual panoply; ܡܫܡܠܝܘܬ ܦܘܩܕܢܐ fulfilment of a command; ܒܡܫܡܠܝܘܬܐ wholly, entirely.

ܡܫܡܠܝܢܐ rt. ܫܡܠ. one who perfects, effects, fulfils; perfecting, efficient, consecrating; ܡܫܡܠܝܢܐ ܕܥܒ̈ܕܐ a doer or fulfiller of the works of the law; ܡܫܡܠܝܢܐ ܕܨܒܝܢܗ a doer of his will; ܡܫܡܠܝ̈ܢܐ ܕܚ̈ܝܠܐ workers of miracles; ܩܪ̈ܝܢܐ ܡܫܡܠܝ̈ܢܐ lessons read at an ordination service.

ܡܫܡܢܢܐ, ܡܫܡܢܢܝܬܐ rt. ܫܡܢ. adj. *fattening.*

ܡܫܡܥ, ܡܫܡܥܐ rt. ܫܡܥ. m. often ܡܫܡܥ ܐܕܢܐ *hearing, obedience;* ܡܫܡܥܐ ܕܗܝܡܢܘܬܐ *obedience to the faith.*

ܡܫܡܥܬܐ, ܡܫܡܥܬܐ rt. ܫܡܥ. f. *the sense of hearing; hearing, obedience.*

ܡܫܡܥܢܐ rt. ܫܡܥ. *a teacher, exhorter.*

ܡܫܡܥܢܘܬܐ rt. ܫܡܥ. f. *instruction.*

ܡܫܡܪܝܢܝܬܐ rt. ܫܡܪ. f. *the starting-place* in a chariot-race.

ܡܫܡܫܢܐ, ܡܫܡܫܢܝܬܐ rt. ܫܡܫ. *a) a servant, minister, attendant;* ܡܫܡܫܢܗ ܕܡܘܫܐ Joshua *the servant of Moses;* the three lower orders of angels are ܡܫܡܫܢܐ ܕܒܪܝܬܐ ܡܫܡܫܝܢ *ministers ministering to creation.* O. T. *a minister* of the Temple Service; N. T. and eccles. *a minister;* ܡܫܡܫܢܝ ܡܕܒܚܐ *those who serve at the altar;* ܡܚܝܠܐ ܐܠܝܐ ܡܫܡܫܢܐ ܕܬܪܘܢܘܣ ܕܡܕܢܚܝܐ *weak Elias who administers the throne of the Easterns* i. e. *is Patriarch;* esp. *a deacon, deaconess;* ܪܫ ܡܫܡܫܢܐ *an archdeacon;* ܗܦܘܡܫܡܫܢܐ *a subdeacon;* ܡܫܡܫܢܝܬܐ ܡܝܬܪܬܐ *a venerable* or *influential deaconess. b) efficient, causing;* ܠܟܠܗ ܡܫܡܫܢܐ ܕܒܝܫܬܐ ܘܡܝܬܝ ܠܗ ܠܣܘܦܐ *he who caused all the evil and brought it to pass.*

ܡܫܡܫܢܘܬܐ rt. ܫܡܫ. f. *administration; diaconate, office of a deacon* or *deaconess;* ܐܣܡܟܗ ܠܡܫܡܫܢܘܬܐ ܥܡ ܐܚܪܢܐ *he ordained him deacon.*

ܡܫܡܫܢܝܐ, ܡܫܡܫܢܝܬܐ rt. ܫܡܫ. *a) of* or *belonging to a deacon. b)* gram. *servile;* ܡܫܡܫܢܝܬܐ *servile letters.*

ܡܫܢܐ also ܡܫܢܐ and other spellings, rt. ܫܢ. f. *a whetstone, hone.*

ܡܫܢܐ Ar. *fresh dates, dainties.*

ܡܫܢܝܢܐ, ܡܫܢܝܢܝܬܐ rt. ܫܢܐ. *changing, wandering, wavering, diffuse; furniture, movable property* opp. ܠܐ ܡܫܬܢܝܢܐ *fixtures;* gram. *transitive.*

ܡܫܢܝܢܐܝܬ rt. ܫܢܐ. adv. *subject to change, mutably;* with ܠܐ *immovably, immutably.*

ܡܫܢܩܢܘܬܐ rt. ܫܢܩ. f. *torment, emaciation, phthisis.*

ܡܫܢܩܢܐ, ܡܫܢܩܢܝܬܐ rt. ܫܢܩ. *torturing, excruciating; a torturer;* ܐܘܪܓܢܐ ܡܫܢܩܢܐ *instruments of torture.*

ܡܫܥܐ rt. ܫܥ. m. *a bricklayer's trowel.*

ܡܫܥܒܕܐܝܬ rt. ܫܥܒܕ. adv. *as a servant* or *subject, submissively.*

ܡܫܥܒܕܘܬܐ and ܡܫܥܒܕܢܘܬܐ rt. ܫܥܒܕ. f. *subjection.*

ܡܫܥܒܕܢܐ rt. ܫܥܒܕ. *one who reduces to servitude, an oppressor, taskmaster.*

ܡܫܥܝܢܐ pl. ܡܫܥܝܢܐ rt. ܫܥܐ. m. *a story-teller, jester.*

ܡܫܥܠܝܢ, ܡܫܥܠܝܢܐ, ܡܫܥܠܝܢܝܬܐ rt. ܥܠܐ. *conceited, overbearing, arrogant.*

ܡܫܥܠܝܢܘܬܐ and ܡܫܥܠܝܢܘܬܐ rt. ܥܠܐ. f. *self-conceit, arrogance.*

ܡܫܥܢܐ rt. ܫܥ. *an emollient, laxative, aperient.*

ܡܫܦܩܬܐ f. *a) a measure of land. b)* perh. *a bed.*

ܡܫܦܘܪܬܐ rt. ܫܦܪ. f. *a squirt, syringe.*

ܡܫܦܠܐܝܬ rt. ܫܦܠ. adv. *feebly.*

ܡܫܦܠܢܘܬܐ rt. ܫܦܠ. f. *feebleness, humiliation.*

ܡܫܦܠܢܐ, ܡܫܦܠܢܝܬܐ rt. ܫܦܠ. *wearisome, enfeebling.*

ܡܫܦܢܐ, ܡܫܦܢܝܬܐ rt. ܫܦ. *a harrow.*

ܡܫܦܢܘܬܐ rt. ܫܦ. f. *a) permission, leave, licence, assent, connivance;* ܡܫܦܢܘܬܐ ܐܝܬܝܗ *it is by favour. b) agreeableness, affability;* with ܠܐ *moroseness, disagreeableness.*

ܡܫܦܪܐ rt. ܫܦܪ. m. *an instrument for injecting oil into the nose.*

ܡܫܦܪܬܐ rt. ܫܦܪ. f. *a syringe.*

ܡܫܩܝܢܐ, ܡܫܩܝܢܝܬܐ rt. ܫܩܐ. *a canal for irrigation; a watered pasture; moist, plashy;* ܐܪܥܐ ܡܫܩܝܢܝܬܐ *watered* or *moist land.*

ܡܫܩܠܐ pl. ܡܫܩܠܐ rt. ܫܩܠ. *a) exaltation, honour. b) a load, burden* esp. of prophecy. *c) taking* of *a* city, *capture. d) journey, departure, march;* ܡܫܩܠܐ ܕܡܫܪܝܬܐ *the removal of the camp;* pl. with ܥܒܕ *to march, journey; to lay a burden on, to load.* For adj. ܡܫܩܠܐ *proud* see Pael part. of ܫܩܠ.

ܡܫܩܠܝܳܐܝܬ rt. ܫܩܠ. adv. *proudly.*

ܡܫܩܠܘܬܐ rt. ܫܩܠ. f. *journey, expedition.*

ܡܫܩܠܢܘܬܐ rt. ܫܩܠ. f. *pride, haughtiness.*

ܡܫܩܠܢܐ, ܢܝܬܐ rt. ܫܩܠ. a) *journeying, removing.* b) *a march, journey;* ܡܫܩܠܢܘܗܝ ܠܬܝܡܢܐ *his journey* was *southward.* Cf. pl. of ܡܫܩܠܐ.

ܡܫܩܠܢܐ, ܢܝܬܐ rt. ܫܩܠ. *proud, haughty.*

ܡܫܩܠܢܘܬܐ rt. ܫܩܠ. f. *removal.*

ܡܫܩܡܩܡ, ܡܫܩܡܩܡܬܐ *sick, ill* (doubtful).

ܡܫܩܦܩܐ rt. ܫܩܦ. *frenzy-stricken.*

ܡܫܩܪܐ pl. ܐ̈ rt. ܫܩܪ. *mere, genuine.*

ܡܫܪܐ pl. ܐ̈ rt. ܫܪܐ. *erysipelas.*

ܡܫܪܓܠܢܘܬܐ from ܫܪܓܠ. f. *a slip, error.*

ܡܫܪܘܪܝܬܐ f. *the disk of a spindle.*

ܡܫܪܘܓܝܬܐ pl. ܝܬܐ rt. ܫܪܓ. f. *slipperiness, a slippery place; a fall, offence.*

ܡܫܪܘܩܐ pl. ܐ̈ rt. ܫܪܩ. m. *a pipe, sound of the pipe.*

ܡܫܪܘܩܝܬܐ rt. ܫܪܩ. f. *hissing; piping, sound of the pipe.*

ܡܫܪܘܩܝܬܢܐ rt. ܫܪܩ. adj. *of* or *belonging to the pipe; hollow-sounding.*

ܡܫܪܝܐ pl. ܡܫܪܝ̈ܐ rt. ܫܪܐ. m. *a dwelling, habitation;* ܡܫܪܝܝ *my dwelling;* ܒܝܬ ܡܫܪܝܐ *a dwelling-place; a guest-chamber, lodging, inn.*

ܡܫܪܝ, ܡܫܪܝܐ *paralytic;* see Pael part. of ܫܪܐ.

ܡܫܪܝܘܬܐ rt. ܫܪܐ. f. *weakness, paralysis; laxity of conduct.*

ܡܫܪܝܢܐ, ܢܝܬܐ rt. ܫܪܐ. *an inn-keeper, tavern-keeper.*

ܡܫܪܝܢܐ, ܢܝܬܐ a) adj. *originating, having a beginning* opp. ܕܠܐ ܫܘܪܝܐ. b) subst. *an author, originator, inventor.*

ܡܫܪܝܢܳܐܝܬ rt. ܫܪܐ. adv. *having a beginning;* with ܠܐ *without a beginning, indissolubly.*

ܡܫܪܝܢܘܬܐ rt. ܫܪܐ. f. *beginning.*

ܡܫܪܝܢܝܬܐ rt. ܫܪܐ. f. *the whorl* of a spindle.

ܡܫܪܝܬܐ pl. ܡܫܪܝܢ, ܡܫܪܝ̈ܬܐ rt. ܫܪܐ. f. a) *a camp, encampment; a retinue; a troop, cohort; an army, host;* with ܢܩܠ or ܐܫܩܠ *to move the camp, strike encampment;* ܡܫܪܝܬܐ ܕܩܡܨܐ *a host of locusts;* ܡܫܪܝܬܐ ܫܡܝܢܝܬܐ *the heavenly host.* b) = ܡܫܪܝܐ *dwelling, habitation;* ܗܦܟ ܠܡܫܪܝܬܗ *he returned home;* astron. ܡܫܪܝ̈ܬܐ ܕܣܗܪܐ *the mansions of the moon.*

ܡܫܪܥܬܐ f. *a bedstead* raised to avoid reptiles.

ܡܫܪܪܐ rt. ܫܪ. *constant, trustworthy.*

ܡܫܪܩܘܬܐ rt. ܫܪܩ. f. *piping, whistling.*

ܡܫܪܩܢܐ, ܢܝܬܐ rt. ܫܪܩ. a) *a piper, whistler.* b) gram. *sibilant.*

ܡܫܪܪܳܐܝܬ rt. ܫܪ. adv. *firmly, strongly, entirely, truly.*

ܡܫܪܪܘܬܐ pl. ܘ̈ܬܐ rt. ܫܪ. f. *strength* of body or mind, *stability, steadfastness, constancy;* with ܠܐ *weakness, infirmity, inconstancy.*

ܡܫܪܪܢܐ, ܢܝܬܐ rt. ܫܪ. *confirmatory, affirmative.*

ܡܫܪܪܢܘܬܐ rt. ܫܪ. f. *confirmation, establishment.*

ܡܫܫܐ rt. ܡܫ. m. *touching, groping.*

ܡܫܬܐܠܢܐ, ܢܝܬܐ rt. ܫܐܠ. *interrogated, capable of being asked, an interlocutor;* with ܠܐ *inexorable, without intermission.*

ܡܫܬܐܠܢܳܐܝܬ rt. ܫܐܠ. adv. with ܠܐ *unavoidably.*

ܡܫܬܐܠܢܘܬܐ rt. ܫܐܠ. f. *reluctance, refusal, excuse, resignation of office; appeal;* ܡܫܬܐܠܢܘܬܐ ܕܡܢ ܒܝ̈ܫܬܐ *the eschewal of evil.*

ܡܫܬܒܗܪܢܘܬܐ rt. ܒܗܪ. f. *arrogance.*

ܡܫܬܒܠܢܐ from ܫܒܠ. *a pupil.*

ܡܫܬܒܩܢܐ rt. ܫܒܩ. with ܠܐ *lasting, enduring, indelible.*

ܡܫܬܒܩܢܘܬܐ rt. ܫܒܩ. f. *abandonment, desertion, dereliction; permission, leave;* ܗܘܬ ܠܗܘܢ ܡܫܬܒܩܢܘܬܐ *they had permission, were allowed.*

ܡܫܬܓܪܓܢܐ rt. ܓܪܓ. with ܠܐ *one who cannot be beguiled.*

ܡܫܬܓܪܓܢܘܬܐ rt. ܓܪܓ. f. *engrossing occupation.*

ܡܫܬܚܠܦܢܐ pass. part. Ethpaal of ܫܚܠܦ *disguised, mutable.*

ܡܫܬܚܠܦܢܘܬܐ and ܡܫܬܚܠܦܢܝܘܬܐ from ܚܠܦ. f. *permutation, mutability;* with ܠܐ *immutability.*

ܡܫܬܚܠܦܢܐ, ܢܝܬܐ from ܚܠܦ. *mutable;* with ܠܐ *immutable.*

ܡܫܬܚܠܦܢܝܐܝܬ from ܚܠܦ. adv. with ܠܐ *immutably.*

ܡܫܬܓܫܢܐ rt. ܓܫ. with ܠܐ *untroubled, calm.*

ܡܫܬܕܝܢܐ rt. ܫܕܐ. *cast out, cast off, exposed.*

ܡܫܬܕܝܢܘܬܐ rt. ܫܕܐ. f. *putting off;* with ܐܘܚܪܐ *delay.*

ܡܫܬܕܪܢܐ, ܢܝܬܐ rt. ܫܕܪ. *sent away, delegated, averting evil* as the scapegoat; *a delegate, ambassador; a missive.*

ܡܫܬܕܪܢܘܬܐ rt. ܫܕܪ. f. *a missive, letter.*

ܡܫܬܘܦܓܢܐ, ܢܝܬܐ rt. ܦܘܓ. with ܠܐ *inextinguishable, unquenchable.*

ܡܫܬܘܦܓܢܘܬܐ rt. ܦܘܓ. f. *cooling, refrigeration.*

ܡܫܬܘܚܠܦܐ, ܡܫܬܘܚܠܦܬܐ from ܚܠܦ. *variable, changeable.*

ܡܫܬܘܕܝܢܐ rt. ܝܕܐ. *self-convicted.*

ܡܫܬܘܕܝܢܘܬܐ rt. ܝܕܐ. f. *promising, a promise.*

ܡܫܬܘܕܥܢܐ, ܢܝܬܐ rt. ܝܕܥ. *significant, understanding, apprehending.*

ܡܫܬܘܕܥܢܘܬܐ rt. ܝܕܥ. f. *acquaintance, knowledge, recognition; a notification.*

ܡܫܬܘܙܒܢܐ, ܢܝܬܐ rt. ܫܘܙܒ. *freed, delivered, redeemed; escaping.*

ܡܫܬܘܙܒܢܘܬܐ rt. ܫܘܙܒ. f. *deliverance, redemption.*

ܡܫܬܘܬܐ Ar. *a carcass.*

ܡܫܬܘܚܪܢܘܬܐ rt. ܐܚܪ. f. *delay, tardiness.*

ܡܫܬܘܝܢܘܬܐ rt. ܫܘܐ. f. *equality;* with ܠܐ *unworthiness.*

ܡܫܬܘܕܪܢܘܬܐ rt. ܫܘܪ. f. *a conjunction* of the stars.

ܡܫܬܘܪܢܐ rt. ܫܘܪ. *that can be leaped, passable.*

ܡܫܬܘܪܢܘܬܐ rt. ܫܘܪ. f. *dancing, leaping.*

ܡܫܬܘܫܛܢܘܬܐ rt. ܫܛ. f. *advance, advancement, promotion.*

ܡܫܬܘܬܐ pl. ܬ̈ܐ rt. ܫܬܐ. f. *a feast, banquet* esp. *a wedding feast, marriage;* ܡܫܬܘܬܐ ܕܐܡܪܐ *the marriage of the Lamb;* ܒܝܬ ܡܫܬܘܬܐ *a house of feasting, banqueting-hall.*

ܡܫܬܘܬܦܢܐ, ܢܝܬܐ from ܫܘܬܦ *one who has been admitted to share, a partaker.*

ܡܫܬܚܠܦܢܐ, ܢܝܬܐ rt. ܚܠܦ. *mutable, variable, subject to change* or *alteration;* with ܠܐ *unchangeable, invariable, immutable, unmoved.*

ܡܫܬܚܠܦܢܐܝܬ rt. ܚܠܦ. adv. *variously;* with ܠܐ *immutably, constantly.*

ܡܫܬܚܠܦܢܘܬܐ rt. ܚܠܦ. f. *change, difference;* with ܠܐ *immutability, unchangeableness, steadfastness.*

ܡܫܬܚܡܢܘܬܐ rt. ܚܡܡ. f. *a becoming heated; hot fomentation.*

ܡܫܬܚܝܢܐ rt. ܫܚܐ *distracted.*

ܡܫܬܝ, ܡܫܬܝܐ pl. ܡܫܬ̈ܝܐ rt. ܫܬܐ. *drink, drinking, a draught, potion; feasting, a feast, banquet;* ܡܐܟܘܠܐ ܘܡܫܬܝܐ *food and drink, eating and drinking;* ܟܣ̈ܐ ܕܡܫܬܝܐ *drinking-cups, beakers;* ܡܫܬܝܐ ܪܘܚܢܝܐ ܐܫܬܝܘ *they drank a spiritual drink;* ܡܫܬܝܐ ܕܚܡܪܐ *a banquet of wine.*

ܡܫܬܝܢܐ pl. ܢ̈ rt. ܫܬܐ. m. *two beams to which the warp is fastened, a weaver's loom.*

ܡܫܬܚܢܐ rt. ܫܚܢ. *rabid.*

ܡܫܬܠܝܢܐ rt. ܫܠܐ. with ܠܐ *implacable, internecine.*

ܡܫܬܝܬܐ rt. ܫܬܐ. *a weaver's shuttle* or *beam, the thread, warp* or *web;* ܐܬܦܣܩܬ ܠܗ ܡܫܬܝܬܐ *the thread* of life *is cut short.*

ܡܫܬܡܚܢܐ rt. ܫܡܚ. *given, bequeathed.*

ܡܫܬܡܚܢܘܬܐ rt. ܫܡܚ. f. *munificence.*

ܡܫܬܠܗܒܢܐ rt. ܫܠܗܒ. *igneous, fiery.*

ܡܫܬܠܚܢܘܬܐ rt. ܫܠܚ. f. *a*) *removing, stripping off. b*) *a missive, embassy.*

ܡܫܬܠܡܢܐ, ܢܝܬܐ rt. ܫܠܡ. *a*) *finished, completed, delivered;* with ܠܐ *unending. b*) = ܡܫܬܠܡܢܐ ܐܢܐ *I am given* or *delivered up.*

ܡܫܬܠܡܢܐܝܬ rt. ܫܠܡ. adv. *infinitely, endlessly, absolutely.*

ܡܫܬܠܡܢܘܬܐ rt. ܫܠܡ. f. *abandonment, betrayal, completion.*

ܡܫܬܡܗܢܐ, ܢܝܬܐ rt. ܫܡ. *named, denominated;* gram. *the subject, object, a substantive qualified by an adjective.*

ܡܫܬܚܪܫܘܬܐ *shamming deafness.*

ܡܫܬܠܦܢܘܬܐ rt. ܫܠܦ. f. *the unsheathing* of a sword.

ܡܫܬܡܠܝܢܐܝܬ rt. ܫܡܠ. adv. *in perfection, in entirety.*

ܡܫܬܡܠܝܢܐ pl. ܐ̈ـ rt. ܫܡܠ. *those waiting for admission to full privileges* as catechumens and penitents; also a bishop *about to receive confirmation in office, a candidate* for the priesthood.

ܡܫܬܡܠܝܢܘܬܐ rt. ܫܡܠ. f. *ordination to the priesthood.*

ܡܫܬܡܥܢܐ, ܡܫܬܡܥܢܝܬܐ rt. ܫܡܥ. *a*) *to be attended to, obeyed. b*) *listening, willing to hearken, obedient. c*) *audible;* ܡܫܬܡ̈ܥܢܝܬܐ *things heard.*

ܡܫܬܡܪܝܢܘܬܐ rt. ܫܡܪ. f. *dismissal, letting go free.*

ܡܫܬܡܫܢܐ, ܡܫܬܡܫܢܝܬܐ rt. ܫܡܫ. *he who is served, the master, lord.*

ܡܫܬܢܩܢܐ rt. ܫܢܩ. *a torturer.*

ܡܫܬܢܝܢܐ pl. ܐ̈ـ rt. ܫܢܐ. pl. *movables, chattels.*

ܡܫܬܢܝܢܘܬܐ rt. ܫܢܐ. f. *removal, translation;* with ܠܐ *immobility, immutability.*

ܡܫܬܐܣܘܬܐ from ܫܬܐܣ. f. *a foundation.*

ܡܫܬܥܒܕܢܐ rt. ܥܒܕ. *reduced to subjection, obedient, broken in* as a horse; ܠܐ ܡܫܬܥܒ̈ܕܢܐ *rebels.*

ܡܫܬܥܒܕܢܘܬܐ rt. ܥܒܕ. f. *subjection.*

ܡܫܬܥܝܢܐ, ܡܫܬܥܝܢܝܬܐ rt. ܫܥܐ. *rehearsing, narrating; a merry maker.*

ܡܫܬܥܠܝܢܐ rt. ܥܠܐ. *overbearing.*

ܡܫܬܥܠܝܢܘܬܐ rt. ܥܠܐ. f. *arrogance, boasting.*

ܡܫܬܥܒܕܢܘܬܐ rt. ܫܥܒܕ. f. *complaisance, flattery.*

ܡܫܬܩܝܢܐ rt. ܫܩܐ. *watered, irrigated.*

ܡܫܬܩܦܢܘܬܐ rt. ܫܩܦ. f. *a being struck, hurt, damaged.*

ܡܫܬܪܓܠܢܘܬܐ from ܫܪܓܠ. *slip, error.*

ܡܫܬܪܕܠܢܐ from ܫܪܕܠ. *one who trembles.*

ܡܫܬܪܕܠܢܐܝܬ from ܫܪܕܠ. adv. *quiveringly.*

ܡܫܬܪܝܢܐ, ܡܫܬܪܝܢܝܬܐ rt. ܫܪܐ. *a*) *having a beginning. b*) *subject to dissolution, perishable;* with ܠܐ *insoluble; indissoluble, imperishable, that cannot be set aside* or *annulled.*

ܡܫܬܪܝܢܐܝܬ rt. ܫܪܐ. adv. with ܠܐ *indissolubly.*

ܡܫܬܪܝܢܘܬܐ rt. ܫܪܐ. f. *dissolution, destruction, abrogation.*

ܡܫܬܪܓܠܢܐ rt. ܫܪܓܠ. *prone to fall.*

ܡܫܬܪܓܠܢܘܬܐ rt. ܫܪܓܠ. *a fall, tendency; slipperiness;* ܦܩܚܘܬܐ ܡܫܬܪܓܠܢܘܬܐ ܠܘܬ ܚܛܝܬܐ *tendency* or *proneness to sin.*

ܡܫܬܝܢܐ, ܡܫܬܝܢܝܬܐ rt. ܫܬܐ. *drinkable, fit to drink;* ܡܝܐ ܡܫܬܝܢܐ *fresh water, drinking-water.*

ܡܫܬܐ pl. ܡܫ̈ܬܐ *fetters.*

ܡܬܐ or ܡܬܐ pl. ܡ̈ܬܘܬܐ and ܡܬ̈ܘܬܐ f. *native land, country, birthplace, domicile, home;* ܠܐ ܗܘܝܬ ܒܪ ܡܬܗܘܢ *I was not their fellow-countryman.* Pl. *little towns, townships.*

ܡܬܐܘܗ pl. of ܡܬܐܘܗܝ.

ܡܬܐܟܠܢܐ, ܡܬܐܟܠܢܝܬܐ, ܡܬܐܟܠܢܐ rt. ܐܟܠ. *fit for food, edible, esculent.*

ܡܬܐܠܗܢܘܬܐ from ܐܠܗܐ. f. *deification, divinity; the being made a partaker of the Divine Nature.*

ܡܬܐܡܐ, ܡܬܐܡܐ, ܡܬܐܡܝܐ *twin, double;* see Aphel pass. part. of ܬܐܡ.

ܡܬܐܡܢܘܬܐ rt. ܬܐܡ. f. *duplication;* gram. *conjunction.*

ܡܬܐܡܪܢܐܝܬ rt. ܐܡܪ. adv. with ܠܐ *ineffably.*

ܡܬܐܡܪܢܘܬܐ pl. ܬ̈ܐ rt. ܐܡܪ. f. *an utterance.*

ܡܬܐܢܝܢܘܬܐ rt. ܐܢܝ. f. *sloth.*

ܡܬܐܤܝܢܐ, ܡܬܐܤܝܢܝܬܐ rt. ܐܤܐ. *in need of healing, sick, ill;* with ܠܐ *incurable, without remedy.*

ܡܬܐܤܝܢܐܝܬ rt. ܐܤܐ. adv. with ܠܐ *incurably.*

ܡܬܐܤܝܢܘܬܐ rt. ܐܤܐ. f. with ܠܐ *an incurable disease.*

ܡܬܐܪܙܢܐ from ܐܪܙ. *one initiated into mysteries, instructed, a disciple; connected with the mysteries.*

ܡܬܐܪܙܢܘܬܐ, ܡܬܐܪܙܢܘܬܗ from ܐܪܙ. f. *initiation, instruction in holy things, secret intercourse, mystical consecration.*

ܡܬܐܫܕܢܐ rt. ܐܫܕ. adj. *liquid, fluid.*

ܡܬܐܫܕܢܘܬܐ rt. ܐܫܕ. f. *fluidity, pouring out.*

ܡܬܐܒܕܢܘܬܐ rt. ܐܒܕ. f. *annihilation.*

ܡܶܬܒܰܣܡܳܢܽܘܬܳܐ from ܒܣܡ. f. *shakiness* from drink.

ܡܶܬܒܰܝܢܳܢܳܐ rt. ܒܝܢ. *considering, discerning, understanding.*

ܡܶܬܒܰܝܢܳܢܽܘܬܳܐ rt. ܒܝܢ. f. *reflection;* with ܠܳܐ *stupidity.*

ܡܶܬܒܰܝܬܳܐ rt. ܒܝܬܐ. gram. *assimilated.*

ܡܶܬܒܰܝܬܳܝܳܐ rt. ܒܝܬܐ. gram. *an adjective derived from a substantive* as ܐܺܝܣܪܳܝܶܠܳܝܳܐ *Israelitish.*

ܡܶܬܒܰܝܬܳܢܽܘܬܳܐ rt. ܒܝܬܐ. f. *familiarity, fellowship.*

ܡܶܬܒܰܠܒܠܳܢܳܐ, ܢܺܝܬܳܐ rt. ܒܠ. with ܠܳܐ *imperturbable.*

ܡܶܬܒܰܣܪܳܢܳܐ, ܢܺܝܬܳܐ rt. ܒܣܪܐ. *contemptible.*

ܡܶܬܒܰܣܡܳܢܳܐ rt. ܒܣܡ. *pleasant, jocund.*

ܡܶܬܒܰܣܪܳܢܽܘܬܳܐ from ܒܣܪܐ. f. *becoming incarnate, incarnation.*

ܡܶܬܒܰܥܝܳܢܳܐ, ܢܺܝܬܳܐ rt. ܒܥܐ. *requisite, necessary, desirable.*

ܡܶܬܒܰܨܝܳܢܳܐ rt. ܒܨܐ. *that which can be examined into;* with ܠܳܐ *inscrutable, impenetrable.*

ܡܶܬܒܰܨܪܳܢܳܐ rt. ܒܨܪ. with ܠܳܐ *that which cannot be diminished.*

ܡܶܬܒܰܩܝܳܢܽܘܬܳܐ rt. ܒܩܐ. f. *observation, consideration, attention.*

ܡܶܬܒܰܪܝܳܢܽܘܬܳܐ rt. ܒܪܐ. f. *the being created, creation.*

ܡܶܬܒܰܪܟܳܢܳܐ, ܢܺܝܬܳܐ rt. ܒܪܟ. *blessed, one who receives a blessing* opp. ܡܒܰܪܟܳܢܳܐ.

ܡܶܬܬܒܰܪܳܢܳܐ rt. ܬܒܪ. *tangible, brittle.*

ܡܶܬܒܰܪܢܫܳܢܳܐ from ܒܪܢܫܐ; ܐܰܠܳܗܳܐ ܡܶܬܒܰܪܢܫܳܢܳܐ *God made man.*

ܡܶܬܒܰܪܢܫܳܢܽܘܬܳܐ from ܒܪܢܫܐ. f. *the assumption of human nature, becoming man.*

ܡܶܬܒܰܪܩܳܢܽܘܬܳܐ rt. ܒܪܩ. f. *flashing, coruscation, splendour.*

ܡܶܬܒܰܫܠܳܢܽܘܬܳܐ rt. ܒܫܠ. f. *ripeness* or *maturity* of fruit.

ܡܶܬܓܰܒܠܳܢܳܐ rt. ܓܒܠ. *pliable;* medic. *universal.*

ܡܶܬܓܰܒܢܳܢܳܐ rt. ܓܒܢ. *rugged, ridged.*

ܡܶܬܓܰܒܪܳܢܳܐ from ܓܰܒܪܳܐ. *virile, manly.*

ܡܶܬܓܰܘܙܠܳܢܳܐ, ܢܺܝܬܳܐ from ܓܘܙܠ. *burning, ardent.*

ܡܶܬܓܰܘܙܠܳܢܽܘܬܳܐ from ܓܘܙܠ. *kindling, inflaming, conflagration.*

ܡܶܬܓܰܘܢܳܢܽܘܬܳܐ rt. ܓܘ. f. *penetration.*

ܡܶܬܓܰܘܣܳܢܽܘܬܳܐ from ܓܘܣ. f. *a refuge.*

ܡܶܬܓܰܙܙܳܢܳܐ rt. ܓܙ. *shorn, ready for shearing.*

ܡܶܬܓܰܚܟܳܢܳܐ, ܢܺܝܬܳܐ rt. ܓܚܟ. *ridiculous, incongruous.*

ܡܶܬܓܰܠܓܠܳܢܽܘܬܳܐ rt. ܓܠ. f. *becoming round; globularity.*

ܡܶܬܓܰܠܙܳܢܽܘܬܳܐ rt. ܓܠܙ. f. *deprivation, lack.*

ܡܶܬܓܰܠܝܳܢܽܘܬܳܐ rt. ܓܠܐ. f. *a revelation, manifestation, transfiguration; pronunciation, explanation.*

ܡܶܬܓܰܢܒܳܢܳܐ = ܓܢܺܝܒܳܐ *elided;* ܐܳܬܘ̈ܳܬܳܐ ܡܶܬܓܰܢ̈ܒܳܢܝܳܬܳܐ *letters omitted in pronunciation.*

ܡܶܬܓܰܢܝܳܢܳܐ, ܢܺܝܬܳܐ rt. ܓܢܐ. *blameworthy.*

ܡܶܬܓܰܪܝܳܢܳܐ rt. ܓܪܐ. said to mean *an instigator.*

ܡܶܬܓܰܪܝܳܢܽܘܬܳܐ rt. ܓܪܐ. f. *provocation.*

ܡܶܬܓܰܪܣܳܢܽܘܬܳܐ rt. ܓܪܣ. f. *pulverization, destruction, annihilation.*

ܡܶܬܓܰܫܡܳܢܳܐ from ܓܘܫܡܐ. *endued with a body, corporeal;* ܐܰܠܳܗܳܐ ܡܶܬܓܰܫܡܳܢܳܐ *God incarnate.*

ܡܶܬܓܰܫܡܳܢܽܘܬܳܐ from ܓܘܫܡܐ. f. *the taking of a body* or *outward form, the incarnation.*

ܡܶܬܓܰܫܫܳܢܳܐ, ܢܺܝܬܳܐ rt. ܓܫ. *perceptible, palpable, tangible; comprehensible;* with ܠܳܐ *impalpable, intangible, incomprehensible, unfathomable.*

ܡܶܬܕܰܒܪܳܢܳܐ rt. ܕܒܪ. *a monk, an ascetic.*

ܡܶܬܕܰܓܠܳܢܳܐ, ܢܺܝܬܳܐ rt. ܕܓܠ. *lying, false;* with ܠܳܐ *true, trustworthy, firm, sure.*

ܡܶܬܳܕܳܘܣ pl. ܡܶܬܳܕܘ̈ܣ f. *μέθοδος, a method, system, dissertation, treatise.*

ܡܶܬܕܚܝܳܢܽܘܬܳܐ rt. ܕܚܐ. f. *being pushed* or *impelled, susceptibility to pressure.*

ܡܶܬܕܰܚܩܳܢܳܐ rt. ܕܚܩ. *he* or *that which is to be driven out, cast forth.*

ܡܶܬܕܰܝܘܳܢܳܐ from ܕܰܝܘܳܐ *a demoniac.*

ܡܶܬܕܰܝܢܳܢܳܐ rt. ܕܢ. *under censure, convicted, condemned.*

ܡܬܕܪܫܢܐ rt. ܕܪܫ. *one who is under discipline to restore him from sin.*

ܡܬܕܟܪܢܐ rt. ܕܟܪ. *one who commemorates, keeps in remembrance.*

ܡܬܕܟܪܢܘܬܐ pl. ܬ̈ܐ rt. ܕܟܪ. f. *a commemoration.*

ܡܬܕܠܚܢܐ, ܢܝܬܐ rt. ܕܠܚ. with ܠܐ *imperturbable, untroubled, unruffled, tranquil.*

ܡܬܕܠܝܢܘܬܐ rt. ܕܠܐ. f. *drawing out.*

ܡܬܕܠܠܢܘܬܐ rt. ܕܠܠ. f. *appropriation;* gram. *definition.*

ܡܬܕܠܩܒܠܢܘܬܐ from ܕܠܩܒܠ. f. *opposition, hostility.*

ܡܬܕܡܝܢܐ, ܢܝܬܐ rt. ܕܡܐ. *imitable;* with ܠܐ *inimitable, incomparable.*

ܡܬܕܡܝܢܘܬܐ rt. ܕܡܐ. f. *being imitated, imitation.*

ܡܬܕܡܪܢܐ and ܡܬܕܡܪܢܝܐ rt. ܕܡܪ. gram. *a mark, note of admiration;* ܡ̈ܠܐ ܡܬܕܡܪܢܝ̈ܬܐ *interjections* or *particles expressing amazement* or *admiration.*

ܡܬܕܡܪܢܐܝܬ rt. ܕܡܪ. adv. *wonderingly.*

ܡܬܕܡܪܢܘܬܐ rt. ܕܡܪ. *marvellousness.*

ܡܬܕܢܝܢܘܬܐ rt. ܕܢܐ. f. *compliance, obsequiousness, dissimulation.*

ܡܬܕܥܟܢܐ, ܢܝܬܐ rt. ܕܥܟ. *extinguishable;* with ܠܐ *inextinguishable, unquenchable.*

ܡܬܕܪܝܢܐ rt. ܕܪܐ. *a winnower.*

ܡܬܕܪܟܢܐ, ܢܝܬܐ rt. ܕܪܟ. *perceptible; conceivable* opp. ܡܬܪܓܫܢܐ *sensible.* With ܠܐ *incomprehensible, impregnable.*

ܡܬܕܪܟܢܐܝܬ rt. ܕܪܟ. with ܠܐ *incomprehensibly, in a way that cannot be comprehended.*

ܡܬܕܪܟܢܘܬܐ pl. ܬ̈ܐ rt. ܕܪܟ. f. *a*) with ܠܐ *incomprehensibility. b*) pl. *astronomical observations.*

ܡܬܕܪܥܢܘܬܐ from ܕܪܥܐ. f. *having the arms stretched out.*

ܡܬܕܪܫܢܘܬܐ rt. ܕܪܫ. f. *practice, training, discipline, abstinence.*

ܡܬܗܓܝܢܐ rt. ܗܓܐ. adj. *imaginative, imaginary, cogitative;* subst. *contemplation, cogitation.*

ܡܬܗܓܝܢܘܬܐ rt. ܗܓܐ. *meditation, cogitation.*

ܡܬܗܦܟܢܐ rt. ܗܦܟ. *reflective;* with ܠܐ *irreflective, lacking in the power of reflection* or *consideration.*

ܡܬܗܕܝܢܐ rt. ܗܕܐ. *one to be guided* or *led, a pupil.*

ܡܬܗܘܢܢܐ, ܡܬܗܘܢܢܐ, ܢܝܬܐ from ܗܘܢܐ. *a*) act. sense: *intellectual, understanding, wise;* with ܠܐ *stupid, unintelligent. b*) pass. sense: *intelligible, conceivable* opp. ܡܬܪܓܫܢܐ *perceptible by the senses;* ܟܝ̈ܢܐ ܡܬܗܘܢܢܝ̈ܐ *created intelligences = spiritual beings* often used of angels and of the unseen world opp. ܟܝ̈ܢܐ ܡܬܪܓܫܢ̈ܐ *creatures apparent to the senses = visible beings.*

ܡܬܗܘܢܢܐܝܬ from ܗܘܢܐ. adv. *intelligibly, by the intellect;* with ܠܐ *incomprehensibly.*

ܡܬܗܘܢܢܘܬܐ from ܗܘܢܐ. f. *the intellect; an understanding, comprehension.*

ܡܬܗܝܡܢܐ and ܡܬܗܝܡܢܢܐ, ܢܝܬܐ from ܗܝܡܢ. *credible;* with ܠܐ *incredible.*

ܡܬܗܝܡܢܢܘܬܐ from ܗܝܡܢ. f. *credibility, trustworthiness.*

ܡܬܗܠܟܢܐ, ܢܝܬܐ rt. ܗܠܟ. *permeable, possible of egress;* with ܠܐ *impassable.*

ܡܬܗܠܟܢܘܬܐ rt. ܗܠܟ. f. with ܠܐ *inaccessibility.*

ܡܬܗܦܟܢܐ, ܢܝܬܐ rt. ܗܦܟ. *pliant, convertible, transmutable.*

ܡܬܗܦܟܢܐܝܬ rt. ܗܦܟ. adv. with ܠܐ *straightforward, without turning back, without retrogression.*

ܡܬܗܦܟܢܘܬܐ pl. ܬ̈ܐ rt. ܗܦܟ. f. *turning from, changing, wavering, retrogression, perversion.*

ܡܬܗܬܠܢܐ, ܢܝܬܐ rt. ܬܗܠ. *witty, facetious.*

ܡܬܘܕܘܣ or ܡܬܘܕܘܣ = ܡܬܘܕܘܣ *a method.*

ܡܬܘܐ, ܡܬܘܝܐ, ܡܬܘܝܬܐ *sad;* see Aphel of ܬܘܐ.

ܡܬܘܝܢܐ rt. ܬܘܐ. *causing repentance.*

ܡܬܘܡ adv. of time. *without beginning, everlasting;* ܕܠܐ ܡܬܘܡ *lest ever, never, nor . . . ever;* ܡܢ ܡܬܘܡ usually contracted ܡܢܡܬܘܡ *from aforetime; from everlasting, formerly;* ܠܐ ܡܬܘܡ, ܠܐ ܡܢܡܬܘܡ or more emphatically ܠܐ ܡܢܡܬܘܡ

never, at no time; ܡܢ ܡܬܘܡ ܕܥܠܡܐ *from the beginning of the world;* ܩܒܝܪܐ ܕܡܢ ܩܕܝܡ ܩܡܝܢ *the buried of former times arise;* ܡܕܡ ܕܡܢ ܡܬܘܡ ܠܐ ܡܘܬܪ *a thing which has ever been profitless.* Derivatives, ܡܬܘܡܐܝܬ, ܡܬܘܡܝܐ, ܡܬܘܡܝܘܬܐ.

ܡܬܘܡܐܝܬ from ܬܘܡ. adv. *everlastingly, sempiternally, perpetually.*

ܡܬܘܡܝܐ, ܝܬܐ from ܬܘܡ. *without beginning, from everlasting, eternal;* ܡܬܘܡܝܐ ܕܠܐ ܫܪܝ ܘܠܐ ܡܫܠܡ *the everlasting which neither has begun nor ends;* ܡܠܬܐ ܡܬܘܡܝܬܐ *the everlasting Word;* ܬܠܝܬܝܘܬܐ ܝܬܝܪܐ ܘܡܬܘܡܝܬܐ *the self-existent* and *everlasting Trinity.*

ܡܬܘܡܝܘܬܐ from ܬܘܡ. f. *everlastingness, eternity;* ܒܪ ܡܬܘܡܝܘܬܗ *co-eternal.*

ܡܬܘܥܕܘܬܐ from ܘܥܕ. f. *keeping an appointment;* astron. *conjunction.*

ܡܬܘܡܨܐ, ܨܬܐ rt. ܡܨ. *a suckling, one who sucks;* ܢܦܫܐ ܕܡܪܪܬܐ ܡܬܘܡܨܢܝܬܐ *a soul which feeds on bitterness.*

ܡܬܘܪܐ; see ܡܬܪܐ.

ܡܬܙܘܓܘܬܐ from ܙܘܓ. f. *matrimony.*

ܡܬܚ fut. ܢܡܬܘܚ, act. part. ܡܬܚ, ܡܬܚܐ, pass. part. ܡܬܝܚ, ܚܐ, ܚܬܐ. *to stretch out, extend, prolong, lengthen, elongate; to reach out, hold out, present, offer.* With ܓܦܐ *to spread the wings;* ܐܘܠܝܬܐ *to make long lamentation;* ܐܘܪܚܬܐ *to lay out roads;* ܐܘܪܟܗ *to stretch to its full length;* ܚܝܪܐ, ܚܙܘܐ, ܡܚܫܒܬܐ, ܗܘܢܐ, &c. *to direct the gaze, thoughts, mind,* &c., *to consider attentively;* ܙܠܝܩܐ the sun *sends abroad its rays;* ܚܨܐ *to offer the back,* ܡܬܚ ܚܨܗ ܠܐܣܛܘܢܐ *he gives his back to the pillar* for scourging; ܝܬܪܐ *to stretch the bowstring;* ܣܕܪܐ *to open out the ranks, draw up in line of battle,* hence *to offer battle, stand up to fight,* with ܥܡ or ܠܘܩܒܠ; ܥܘܢܝܬܐ *to chant a long anthem;* ܨܘܡܐ *to prolong a fast;* ܩܫܬܐ *to draw the bow;* ܫܡܝܐ or ܫܡܝܐ *to stretch out the heavens;* ܡܬܚ ܪܩܝܥܐ ܐܝܟ ܫܥܠܐ ܕܐܝܕܗ *He stretcheth out the firmament as the hollow of His hand;* ܫܢܝܐ *to last* so many *years;* ܟܕ ܡܬܚܐ ܠܐ ܫܝܢܐ ܕܚܫܒܐ *when the discord of opinions increased.* Part. adj. *stretched out, extended, long drawn out, protracted, strained, tense, intense, attentive;* with ܒ *diffused through;* with ܥܠ *extended over.* With ܙܒܢܐ or ܥܕܢܐ *a very long time;* ܡܕܥܐ ܡܬܝܚܐ *an attentive mind;* ܡܬܝܚܬܐ ܡܬܝܚܬܐ *tense strings;* ܡܢܝܢܐ *a great number, long tale;* ܨܠܘܬܐ *earnest prayer;* ܫܘܠܛܢܐ *far reaching rule;* ܬܝܒܘܬܐ *protracted penance.* Ethpe. ܐܬܡܬܚ *to be spread out, reach far abroad; to reach, be directed towards, to extend* as a number, goodness; *to be stretched* in the stocks, ܥܠ ܩܝܣܐ *on a cross; to be prolonged, last, endure;* ܥܩܪܐ ܕܡܬܡܬܚ ܠܥܘܡܩܐ *a root that reaches deep into the earth;* ܐܬܡܬܚܬ ܡܚܘܬܐ ܐܚܪܬܐ *another blow befell him;* ܢܬܡܬܚ ܒܨܠܘܬܐ *let us pray intensely.* Derivatives, ܡܬܚܐ, ܡܬܚܬܐ, ܡܬܝܚܐ, ܡܬܝܚܐܝܬ, ܡܬܝܚܘܬܐ, ܡܬܡܬܚܢܐ.

ܡܬܚ, ܡܬܚܐ pl. ܚܐ rt. ܡܬܚ. m. *a*) *a length* of time or place, *length, duration, extent, reach, distance, height;* ܡܬܚܐ ܕܙܒܢܐ *a length of time;* ܡܬܚܐ ܕܬܡܢܐܝܢ ܫܢܝܢ *the space of eighty years, for eighty years;* ܡܬܚܐ ܕܚܝܐ *all one's life;* ܡܬܚܐ ܕܫܝܢܐ *the duration of the peace;* ܟܠܗ ܗܢܐ ܡܬܚܐ *all this time;* ܒܡܬܚܐ ܙܥܘܪܐ *with a short interval;* ܡܬܚܐ ܕܐܘܪܚܐ *the length of the journey;* ܡܬܚܐ ܕܫܬܝܢ ܦܪܣܢܓܝܢ *a space* or *distance of sixty leagues;* ܡܬܚܐ ܕܩܛܪܗܘܢ *the stretch of the axis* of a flight of locusts, *the space they covered;* ܒܘܨܝܐ ܕܡܬܚܐ *a long* or *far-reaching search.* *b*) *a nerve* or *tendon.*

ܡܬܚܐ pl. ܚܐ rt. ܡܬܚ. m. *stretching out, lengthening; being distended, distension.*

ܡܬܚܒܠܢܐ, ܢܝܬܐ rt. ܚܒܠ. *corruptible, destructible, subject to corruption* or *decay;* with ܠܐ *incorruptible, immortal.*

ܡܬܚܒܠܢܘܬܐ rt. ܚܒܠ. f. *ruin, destruction, debauching;* with ܠܐ *incorruptibility.*

ܡܬܚܡܢܐ, ܢܝܬܐ rt. ܚܡ. *limited, comprehended, restrained, subdued.*

ܡܬܚܘܝܢܐ, ܢܝܬܐ rt. ܚܘܐ. *demonstrable.*

ܡܬܚܘܝܢܐܝܬ rt. ܚܘܐ. adv. *demonstrably.*

ܡܬܚܘܝܢܘܬܐ rt. ܚܘܐ. f. *a manifestation, demonstration, expression, appearance.*

ܡܬܚܘܝܢܐ rt. ܚܘܐ. *ostentatious.*

ܡܬܚܘܝܢܘܬܐ rt. ܚܘܐ. f. *ostentation, boasting.*

ܡܬܚܙܝܢ, ܡܬܚܙܝܢܐ, ـܢܝܬܐ rt. ܚܙܐ. *visible;* with ܠܐ *unseen, invisible.*

ܡܬܚܙܝܢܐܝܬ rt. ܚܙܐ. adv. *visibly;* with ܠܐ *invisibly.*

ܡܬܚܙܝܢܘܬܐ rt. ܚܙܐ. f. *view, appearance;* with ܠܐ *being withdrawn from view, concealed; invisibility.*

ܡܬܚܝܕܢܐ rt. ܚܕ. with ܠܐ *irremediable, irreparable.*

ܡܬܚܝܕܢܘܬܐ rt. ܚܕ. f. *capability of union, reunion.*

ܡܬܚܟܡܢܐ, ـܢܝܬܐ rt. ܚܟܡ. *one with whom sexual intercourse is held.*

ܡܬܚܟܡܢܘܬܐ rt. ܚܟܡ. f. *experience, wisdom.*

ܡܬܚܛܦܢܐ, ـܢܝܬܐ rt. ܚܛܦ. with ܠܐ *inviolable, secure.*

ܡܬܚܛܦܢܘܬܐ rt. ܚܛܦ. f. *plundering, pillage, rapine.*

ܡܬܬܚܡܢܐܝܬ rt. ܬܚܡ. adv. *definitely.*

ܡܬܬܚܡܢܘܬܐ rt. ܬܚܡ. f. *limit, terminating, termination.*

ܡܬܬܚܡܢܐ, ـܢܝܬܐ rt. ܬܚܡ. *defining, definite.*

ܡܬܬܚܡܢܘܬܐ rt. ܬܚܡ. f. *definition, designation.*

ܡܬܚܦܪܢܘܬܐ rt. ܚܦܪ. f. *shamefacedness.*

ܡܬܡܬܚܢܐ, ـܢܝܬܐ rt. ܡܬܚ. *far-reaching, extensive, spacious;* ܪ̈ܘܡܐ ܡܬܡܬܚܢ̈ܐ *spacious heights.*

ܡܬܡܟܟ, ܡܬܡܟܟܢܐ, ـܢܝܬܐ rt. ܡܟ. *miserable, pitiable, pitiful.*

ܡܬܡܟܟܢܐܝܬ rt. ܡܟ. adv. *humbly.*

ܡܬܡܟܟܢܘܬܐ rt. ܡܟ. f. *humiliation.*

ܡܬܚܣܝܢܐ, ـܢܝܬܐ from ܚܘܣܝܐ. with ܠܐ *inexpiable, that cannot be atoned for.*

ܡܬܚܣܢܢܐ, ـܢܝܬܐ rt. ܚܣܢ. with ܠܐ *unconquerable, invincible.*

ܡܬܚܣܢܢܘܬܐ rt. ܚܣܢ. f. *defeat, shattering.*

ܡܬܚܦܛܢܐ rt. ܚܦܛ. *needing encouragement;* with ܠܐ *slack.*

ܡܬܚܦܝܢܘܬܐ rt. ܚܦܐ. f. *a covering, obscuration.*

ܡܬܚܦܪܢܐ rt. ܚܦܪ. m. *a mineral, metal;* with ܠܐ *too hard to dig.*

ܡܬܚܪܝܢܢܐ rt. ܚܪܐ. *spoken against, debatable; given to controversy;* gram. *expressing controversy.*

ܡܬܚܪܫܢܐ, ـܢܝܬܐ rt. ܚܪܫ. with ܠܐ *that cannot be charmed away; deaf to enchantments, implacable.*

ܡܬܚܫܒܢܐ rt. ܚܫܒ. *considered, estimated; mental;* pl. *objects of thought.*

ܡܬܚܫܒܢܘܬܐ rt. ܚܫܒ. f. *thought, the faculty of thought.*

ܡܬܬܚܝܬܘܬܐ rt. ܬܚܬ. f. *inferiority, abasement, humiliation.*

ܡܬܛܒܥܢܘܬܐ rt. ܛܒܥ. f. *impression, image.*

ܡܬܛܝܒܢܘܬܐ from ܛܝܒܘ. f. *supplication.*

ܡܬܛܚܢܢܐ rt. ܛܚܢ. *grain, cereal.*

ܡܬܛܟܣܢܐ from ܛܟܣܐ. *a candidate* for ordination.

ܡܬܛܠܝܢܘܬܐ rt. ܛܠܐ. f. *rejuvenescence.*

ܡܬܛܠܩܢܐ, ـܢܝܬܐ rt. ܛܠܩ. with ܠܐ *imperishable.*

ܡܬܛܠܩܢܘܬܐ rt. ܛܠܩ. f. *destruction.*

ܡܬܛܡܐܢܐ rt. ܛܡܐ. *polluted;* with ܠܐ *undefiled.*

ܡܬܛܢܦܢܐ rt. ܛܢܦ. with ܠܐ *uncontaminated.*

ܡܬܛܣܝܢܐ from ܛܣܐ *laminar.*

ܡܬܛܥܡܢܐ, ـܢܝܬܐ rt. ܛܥܡ. *sensible to the taste;* pl. f. *victuals.*

ܡܬܛܥܡܢܘܬܐ rt. ܛܥܡ. f. *ingrafting.*

ܡܬܛܥܢܢܐ, ـܢܝܬܐ rt. ܛܥܢ. *portable; tolerable;* ܡܘܒ̈ܠܐ ܝܩܝܪ̈ܐ ܡܬܛܥܢܢ̈ܝܢ ܠܚܝܠܬܢ̈ܐ *very heavy burdens can be borne* by the strong.

ܡܬܛܦܣܢܐ, ـܢܝܬܐ from ܦܝܣܐ. *obedient;* with ܠܐ *disobedient.*

ܡܬܛܦܣܢܘܬܐ from ܦܝܣܐ. f. *obedience, willing obedience, docility;* with ܠܐ *disobedience, unwillingness.*

ܡܬܛܘܦܣܢܘܬܐ from ܛܘܦܣܐ. f. *adumbration, that whereby something is shadowed forth.*

ܡܬܛܪܝܢܘܬܐ rt. ܛܪܐ. f. *beating back, driving away; an insult.*

ܡܬܛܪܢܢܘܬܐ from ܛܪܢܐ. f. *induration, petrifaction.*

ܡܬܛܪܦܢܐ rt. ܛܪܦ. *harassed, persecuted.*

ܡܬܠܐ m. *a packing-needle.*

ܡܬܐܬܐ; see ܡܬܐܠܐ.

ܡܬܐܒܒܢܘܬܐ and ܡܬܐܒܒܢܝܬܐ rt. ܐܒ. f. *longing, earnest desire.*

ܡܬܐܒܒܢܐ rt. ܐܒ. adj. *incentive, stimulative.*

ܡܬܐܒܒܢܐܝܬ rt. ܐܒ. adv. *eagerly.*

ܡܬܐܠܦܢܐ rt. ܐܠܦ. gram. *derived.*

ܡܬܦܢܝܢܘܬܐ rt. ܦܢܐ. f. *a*) *a reply. b*) *vomiting.*

ܡܬܣܒܪܢܐ, -ܢܝܬܐ rt. ܣܒܪ. *conceivable by the mind* opp. ܡܬܪܓܫܢܐ *perceptible to the senses; intellectual, spiritual, incorporeal, immaterial, mystical;* ܐܝܣܪܝܠ ܡܬܣܒܪܢܐ *the spiritual Israel;* ܒܒܠ ܡܬܣܒܪܢܝܬܐ *mystical Babylon;* ܡܬܣܒܪܢܐ ܐܝܬܝܗܘܢ ܡܠܐܟܐ *intelligences, spiritual beings, which are angels.*

ܡܬܣܒܪܢܐܝܬ rt. ܣܒܪ. adv. *intelligently, spiritually, in a figurative* or *mystical sense.*

ܡܬܣܒܪܢܘܬܐ rt. ܣܒܪ. f. *conventional usage of words.*

ܡܬܦܢܝܢܐܝܬ rt. ܦܢܐ. *in the dative case.*

ܡܬܦܢܝܢܘܬܐ rt. ܦܢܐ. f. *the apodosis* of a sentence.

ܡܬܝܚܢܐܝܬ rt. ܡܬܚ. adv. *earnestly, intensely.*

ܡܬܝܚܘܬܐ rt. ܡܬܚ. f. *extension, prolongation, extent, length, duration;* ܒܡܬܝܚܘܬ *at length.*

ܡܫܬܝܢܘܬܐ rt. ܫܝܢ. f. *quietness;* perh. *eye-ache.*

ܡܬܝܠܕܢܘܬܐ rt. ܝܠܕ. f. *nativity.*

ܡܐܬܝܢ dual of ܡܐܐ. *two hundred.*

ܡܬܝܢ, -ܢܐ, -ܢܬܐ; see ܡܬܢ.

ܡܬܝܢܐܝܬ rt. ܡܬܢ. adv. *slowly, tardily, slothfully, sluggishly.*

ܡܬܝܢܘܬܐ rt. ܡܬܢ. f. *slowness, sloth, laziness, leisure; patience, gentleness, placidity.*

ܡܬܦܪܣܢܐ, -ܢܝܬܐ rt. ܦܪܣ. *studied, laboured;* with ܠܐ *unaffected.*

ܡܬܨܝܪܢܐ from ܨܘܪܬܐ. *imaginable, that can be represented* or *delineated.*

ܡܬܨܝܪܢܘܬܐ from ܨܘܪܬܐ. f. *delineation, representation;* logic. *differentiation.*

ܡܬܚܡܬܢܐܝܬ rt. ܚܡܬ. adv. *furiously.*

ܡܬܝܬܐ; see ܡܬܐܬܐ.

ܡܬܝܬܪܢܘܬܐ rt. ܝܬܪ. f. *bounty, superfluity.*

ܡܬܟܒܫܢܐ, -ܢܝܬܐ rt. ܟܒܫ. with ܠܐ *impregnable* as ܫܘܪܐ *a wall,* ܚܣܢܐ *a fortress;* ܪܘܡܐ ܠܐ ܡܬܟܒܫܢܝܬܐ *untrodden, unsubdued* or *inaccessible peaks;* ܫܠܝܐ ܘܡܬܟܒܫܢܐ ܝܡܡܐ *tranquil and calmed seas.*

ܡܬܟܕܒܢܐ, -ܢܝܬܐ rt. ܟܕܒ. with ܠܐ *unimpeachable, undeniable;* ܣܗܕܘܬܐ ܠܐ ܡܬܟܕܒܢܝܬܐ *an undeniable testimony* or *evidence.*

ܡܬܟܕܢܢܐ, -ܢܝܬܐ rt. ܟܕܢ. *capable of being yoked;* ܚܝܘܬܐ ܡܬܟܕܢܢܝܬܐ *draught animals.*

ܡܬܟܗܢܢܐ rt. ܟܗܢ. *one consecrated, an ordained priest.*

ܡܬܟܗܢܢܘܬܐ rt. ܟܗܢ. f. *ordination to the priesthood; consecration* e. g. of chrism.

ܡܬܟܚܕܢܐ, -ܢܝܬܐ rt. ܟܚܕ. *shamefaced, modest, reverent;* ܡܬܟܚܕܢܝܬܐ *things to be ashamed of, disgraceful things.*

ܡܬܟܚܕܢܘܬܐ rt. ܟܚܕ. f. *a sense of shame, reverence, modesty;* with ܠܐ *impudence.*

ܡܬܟܝܢܘܬܐ rt. ܟܘܢ. f. *natural condition.*

ܡܬܟܠܝܢܐ, -ܢܝܬܐ rt. ܟܠܐ. adj. *hindered, forbidden.*

ܡܬܟܠܝܢܐܝܬ rt. ܟܠܐ. adv. *hardly, scarcely;* with ܠܐ *unhindered, unimpeded, without let.*

ܡܬܟܠܝܢܘܬܐ rt. ܟܠܐ. f. *prohibition, restraint, impediment, natural impossibility;* ܡܬܟܠܝܢܘܬܗ ܕܢܘܗܪܐ ܡܢ ܓܘܫܡܐ *occultation of light by* some intervening *body.*

ܡܬܟܠܠܢܐ rt. ܟܠܠ. *wearer of a crown.*

ܡܬܟܠܢܐ rt. ܬܟܠ. *one who makes to trust, wins confidence.*

ܡܬܟܠܢܘܬܐ rt. ܬܟܠ. f. *promising, threatening.*

ܡܬܟܢܝܢܐ rt. ܟܢܐ. *a person called by a* ܟܘܢܝܐ *kunyah* i. e. *son* or *father of* some one; gram. ܫܡܐ ܡܬܟܢܝܢܐ *a collective designation* as man.

ܡܬܟܢܫܢܐ, -ܢܝܬܐ rt. ܟܢܫ. *contracted, narrowed;* gram. with ܠܐ *incapable of forming a plural.*

ܡܬܟܢܫܢܘܬܐ rt. ܟܢܫ. f. *a coming together, meeting, conjunction* of the stars, elements, &c.

ܡܬܟܣܣܢܐ rt. ܟܣܣ. *a censor, censurer, restrainer.*

ܡܬܟܣܣܢܐ rt. ܟܣܣ. *reprehensible.*

ܡܬܟܦܦܢܐ, -ܢܝܬܐ rt. ܟܦ. with ܠܐ *inflexible.*

ܡܬܟܪܝܢܘܬܐ rt. ܟܪܐ. f. *shortening, abridging.*

ܡܬܟܪܟܢܐ, -ܢܝܬܐ rt. ܟܪܟ. *a*) *wandering,*

a vagabond, mendicant, wandering dervish. b) with ܐܓܪܬܐ *a circular letter. c) revolving, rotatory, according to the course of the year;* ܓܝܓܠܐ ܡܬܟܪܟܢܝܬܐ *a revolving wheel;* ܩܪܝܢܐ ܕܚܕܒܫܒܐ ܡܬܟܪܟܢܐ *the Sunday Lections in rotation.*

ܡܬܟܪܟܢܐܝܬ rt. ܟܪܟ. adv. *circularly, in rotation.*

ܡܬܟܪܟܢܘܬܐ pl. ܘܵܬܐ rt. ܟܪܟ. f. *revolving, revolution* of a sphere, *rotation, a period* of time; *winding up, folding, convolution;* eccles. *a procession;* ܡܬܟܪܟܢܘܬܐ ܕܒܝܬ ܣܦܪܐ *going regularly to school.*

ܡܬܟܫܦܢܐ, ܢܝܬܐ rt. ܟܫܦ. *a suppliant, intercessor; supplicatory, intercessory, deprecatory;* ܟܬܒܐ ܡܬܟܫܦܢܐ *a service-book.*

ܡܬܟܫܦܢܐܝܬ rt. ܟܫܦ. adv. *supplicatingly, as suppliants, earnestly beseeching.*

ܡܬܟܫܦܢܘܬܐ rt. ܟܫܦ. f. *supplication.*

ܡܬܟܬܒܢܐ, ܢܝܬܐ rt. ܟܬܒ. *written, literary; learned;* ܐܬܘܬܐ ܡܬܟܬܒܢܝܬܐ *written characters;* ܠܐ ܡܬܟܬܒܢܐ *unlettered, illiterate.*

ܡܬܟܬܒܢܘܬܐ rt. ܟܬܒ. f. *writing, enregistering, enrolling.*

ܡܬܟܬܫܢܐ, ܡܬܟܬܫܢܝܬܐ rt. ܟܬܫ. *one who strives, contends* ܚܠܦ *for; a combatant, wrestler, fighter, warrior, opponent;* ܦܘܩܕܢܐ ܡܬܟܬܫܢܐ *conflicting commands;* ܠܐ ܡܬܟܬܫܢܐ *unassailable.*

ܡܬܠ fut. ܢܡܬܘܠ, inf. ܡܡܬܠ, pass. part. ܡܬܝܠ, ܠܐ, ܠܬܐ. *to speak in parables, figuratively, compare,* with ܒ or ܠ; ܠܓܢܬܐ ܐܡܬܠܟ *he compared thee to a garden;* ܡܬܠ ܡܬܠܗ ܬܘܒ ܫܩܠ *he took up his parable again.* Part. *compared, represented, figured, likened;* ܡܫܚܐ ܩܕܝܫܐ ܡܬܝܠ ܠܪܘܚܐ ܩܕܝܫܐ *the consecrated oil represents the Holy Spirit;* ܥܡܡܐ ܡܬܝܠܝܢ ܠܚܝܘܬܐ ܕܕܒܪܐ *the Gentiles are compared to the beasts of the field;* ܡܠܐ ܡܬܝܠܬܐ *words used in a parable* or *figuratively;* ܡܠܦܢܘܬܐ ܡܬܝܠܬܐ *teaching by figures, in parables, symbolical doctrine.* Ethpe. ܐܬܡܬܠ *to be likened unto, compared to, described in a parable;* ܐܬܡܬܠܬܘܢ ܠܟܐܦܐ *you are compared to stones;* ܐܬܡܬܠ ܒܢܒܝܐ ܐܠܗܐ ܡܠܬܐ ܛܘܦܣܢܐܝܬ *God the Word was spoken of by the prophets under types.* Pa. ܡܬܠ *to liken, compare, express under symbols* or *parables;* ܡܬܡܬܠܝܢܢ ܠܐܠܓܐ *we are likened to vapour;* ܡܬܠ ܐܢܘܢ ܠܢܗܝܪܐ *he compared them to lights.* Ethpa. ܐܬܡܬܠ *to be made like, represented as, compared to;* ܫܪܪܐ ܘܛܘܥܝܝܐ ܡܬܡܬܠܝܢ ܒܬܪܬܝܢ ܡܟܝܠܬܐ *truth and error are represented under the figure of* two *measures;* ܫܡܘܥ ܡܬܡܬܠ ܒܐܪܣܝܘܛܐ ܕܡܩܪܒܝܢ ܥܡ ܥܡܢܘܐܝܠ *Shamuʿ is taken as the type of those heretics who war with Emmanuel.* Aphel ܐܡܬܠ *to utter parables, use a proverb* or *simile, speak fables* with ܒ, ܠ or ܥܠ; *to fable, speak foolishly;* ܐܡܬܠܬ ܡܬܠܐ ܗܢܐ *I told this fable, used this simile.* Derivatives, ܡܬܠܐ, ܡܬܠܢܐ, ܡܬܠܢܐܝܬ, ܡܬܠܝܐ, ܡܬܠܐ, ܡܡܬܠܢܐ.

ܡܬܠܐ pl. ܡܬܠܐ̈ rt. ܡܬܠ. m. *a proverb, parable, fable, myth;* ܡܬܠܐ̈ *the Proverbs of Solomon;* ܡܬܠܐ ܕܬܐܢܬܐ ܕܠܐ ܦܐܪܐ *the parable of the barren fig-tree.*

ܡܬܠܐ rt. ܬܠܐ. m. *giving;* cf. ܡܬܬܐ.

ܡܬܠܒܟܢܐ, ܢܝܬܐ rt. ܠܒܟ. *capable of being grasped, held, controlled;* with ܠܐ *uncontrollable, unrestrainable.*

ܡܬܠܒܟܢܐܝܬ rt. ܠܒܟ. adv. with ܠܐ *uncontrollably, immoderately, irresistibly.*

ܡܬܠܒܟܢܘܬܐ rt. ܠܒܟ. f. with ܠܐ *want of comprehension.*

ܡܬܠܓܓ from ܬܠܓ. *covered with snow;* ܬܠܓܐ ܡܬܠܓܓܐ *melted snow.*

ܡܬܠܓܓܘܬܐ from ܬܠܓ. f. *snowy whiteness.*

ܡܬܠܗܒܢܐ rt. ܠܗܒ. *burning, glowing.*

ܡܬܠܘܝܢܘܬܐ rt. ܠܘܐ. f. *companionship.*

ܡܬܠܚܝܢܐ, ܢܝܬܐ rt. ܠܚܐ. with ܠܐ *indelible.*

ܡܬܠܚܝܢܘܬܐ rt. ܠܚܐ. f. *blotting out, doing away with.*

ܡܬܠܛܫܢܐ, ܢܝܬܐ rt. ܠܛܫ. *adapted, smoothed, harmonious.*

ܡܬܠܝܐ, ܡܬܠܝܬܐ rt. ܡܬܠ. *parabolical, enigmatic.*

ܡܬܠܠܝܢܘܬܐ from ܬܠܠ. f. *evanescence, waning* of a star; *annihilation.*

ܡܬܠܡܕܢܐ rt. ܠܡܕ. *a teacher, instructor, missionary.*

ܡܬܠܢܐܝܬ rt. ܡܬܠ. adv. *in a parable, allegorically.*

ܡܶܬܡܰܬܠܳܢܳܐ, ܢܺܝܬܳܐ rt. ܡܬܠ. adj. *parabolical, expressed in a parable, figurative.*

ܡܬܠܥܒܢܐ rt. ܠܥܒ. *a jester.*

ܡܶܬܠܰܫܢܳܢܳܐ, ܢܺܝܬܳܐ from ܠܫܢܐ. *uttered with the tongue, pronounced.*

ܡܶܬܠܰܫܢܳܢܽܘܬܳܐ from ܠܫܢܐ. f. *pronunciation.*

ܡܬܠܬܝܐ from ܬܠܬܐ. *triple, triangular.*

ܡܶܬܢܰܟܠܳܢܳܐ rt. ܢܟܠ. *guileful, malicious, villainous.*

ܡܶܬܢܰܟܠܳܢܽܘܬܳܐ rt. ܢܟܠ. f. *craft, artifice, guile, malice.*

ܡܬܠܬܝܐ from ܬܠܬܐ. *trilateral.*

ܡܶܬܡܰܪܥܝܳܢܳܐ rt. ܪܥܐ. *rational, endowed with intelligence.*

ܡܶܬܡܗܳܢܽܘܬܳܐ and ܡܶܬܡܰܗܡܗܳܢܽܘܬܳܐ rt. ܬܡܗ. f. *astonishment.*

ܡܶܬܡܰܗܡܗܳܢܳܐ, ܢܺܝܬܳܐ rt. ܬܡܗ. *astounding, wonderful.*

ܡܶܬܡܰܙܓܳܢܳܐ, ܢܺܝܬܳܐ rt. ܡܙܓ. *mingled, diluted, tempered;* with ܠܐ *that will not mingle.*

ܡܶܬܡܰܚܝܳܢܳܐ rt. ܡܚܐ. *wounded, vulnerable.*

ܡܶܬܡܰܚܠܳܢܳܐ from ܡܚܠ. *feeble, dismayed;* with ܠܐ *invincible, indomitable.*

ܡܶܬܡܰܥܠܥܠܳܢܳܐ from ܡܥܠܥܠ. *stormy, tempestuous.*

ܡܶܬܡܰܥܠܥܠܳܢܽܘܬܳܐ pl. ܢ̈ܘܬܐ from ܡܥܠܥܠ. *tempestuousness; disquietude, distraction.*

ܡܬܡܐܬܝܩܐ or ܡܬܡܐܛܝܩܐ m. pl. μαθήματα, *learning, science* esp. *geometry.*

ܡܶܬܡܰܨܝܳܢܳܐ pl. ܢ̈ܐ rt. ܡܨܐ. m. *a lozenge.*

ܡܶܬܡܰܛܝܳܢܳܐ pl. ܢ̈ܐ rt. ܡܛܐ. *one who* or *that which may arrive;* with ܠܐ *unattainable, inaccessible, that cannot be arrived at.*

ܡܶܬܡܰܛܝܳܢܽܘܬܳܐ rt. ܡܛܐ. f. *approach, access;* ܥܰܣܩܳܐ ܠܡܶܬܡܰܛܝܳܢܽܘܬܳܐ *inaccessible, hard to attain.*

ܡܬܡܐܬܝܩܘܢ m. μαθηματικῶν, gen. pl. for τὰ μαθηματικά, *science* esp. *geometry.*

ܡܬܡܐܬܝܩܝܐ, ܩܝܬܐ pl. m. ܡܬܡܐܬܝܩܝ̈ܐ or ܡܬܡܐܬܝܩܝܬܐ f. ܩܝܬܐ μαθηματικός, *mathematical, learned in geometry.*

ܡܶܬܡܰܟܪܳܢܳܐ, ܢܺܝܬܳܐ rt. ܡܟܪ. *marriageable, sought in marriage.*

ܡܶܬܡܰܠܚܳܢܳܐ, ܢܺܝܬܳܐ rt. ܡܠܚ. *a) salt, seasoned with salt;* metaph. ܡܶܬܡܰܠܚܳܢܳܐ ܐܢܫܐ *a witty person, one of seasoned wits;* with ܠܐ *mere, utter;* ܗܰܘ ܕܗܰܝܡܳܢܽܘܬܳܐ ܗܽܘ ܠܐ ܡܶܬܡܰܠܚܳܢܳܐ *which is utter want of faithfulness. b) navigable.*

ܡܶܬܡܰܠܚܳܢܽܘܬܳܐ rt. ܡܠܚ. f. *piloting, being piloted* or *steered; the helm.*

ܡܶܬܡܰܠܟܳܢܳܐ rt. ܡܠܟ. *a) pertaining to council, senatorial; one who consults* or *asks advice. b) princely, in the line of succession to the throne.*

ܡܶܬܡܰܠܟܳܢܽܘܬܳܐ rt. ܡܠܟ. f. *deliberation, consultation.*

ܡܶܬܡܰܠܠܳܢܳܐ, ܢܺܝܬܳܐ rt. ܡܠܠ. with ܠܐ *unspeakable, ineffable, inexpressible, secret.*

ܡܶܬܡܰܠܠܳܢܳܐܺܝܬ rt. ܡܠܠ. adv. with ܠܐ *unutterably, ineffably, secretly.*

ܡܶܬܡܰܠܠܳܢܽܘܬܳܐ rt. ܡܠܠ. f. with ܠܐ *a secret, mystery, something which cannot be uttered* or *expressed in words.*

ܡܶܬܡܰܢܝܳܢܳܐ, ܢܺܝܬܳܐ rt. ܡܢܐ. *numerable, that may be counted* or *reckoned;* with ܠܐ *innumerable.*

ܡܶܬܡܰܣܝܳܢܳܐ rt. ܡܣܐ. *subject to decomposition.*

ܡܶܬܡܰܣܟܢܳܢܳܐ rt. ܡܣܟܢ. with ܠܐ *impoverishable, inexhaustible.*

ܡܶܬܡܰܣܪܳܢܽܘܬܳܐ rt. ܡܣܪ. f. *delation.*

ܡܶܬܡܰܨܝܳܢܳܐ, ܢܺܝܬܳܐ and ܡܶܬܡܰܨܝܳܢܳܐ rt. ܡܨܐ II. *possible, in one's power, potential;* with ܠܐ *impossible, powerless;* ܠܐ ܡܶܬܡܰܨܝܳܢܝܳܬܳܐ *impossibilities.*

ܡܶܬܡܰܨܝܳܢܳܐܺܝܬ rt. ܡܨܐ II. adv. *possibly, potentially.*

ܡܶܬܡܰܨܝܳܢܽܘܬܳܐ rt. ܡܨܐ II. f. *a) power, authority;* ܡܶܬܡܰܨܝܳܢܽܘܬܳܐ ܚܰܝܠܬܳܢܺܝܬܳܐ ܕܰܐܠܳܗܳܐ *the strong power of God;* ܐܰܝܟ ܡܶܬܡܰܨܝܳܢܽܘܬܝ *according to my ability, as I am able. b) possibility, potentiality.*

ܡܶܬܡܰܨܥܳܢܽܘܬܳܐ rt. ܡܨܥ. f. *intervening, intervention.*

ܡܶܬܡܰܪܝܳܢܳܐ rt. ܡܪܐ. m. *an imitator.*

ܡܶܬܡܰܪܝܳܢܽܘܬܳܐ rt. ܡܪܐ. f. *imitation, emulation.*

ܡܶܬܡܰܪܩܳܢܳܐ, ܢܺܝܬܳܐ rt. ܡܪܩ. with ܠܐ *indelible, that cannot be washed away* or *cleansed;* ܟܽܘܬܡܳܐ ܠܐ ܡܶܬܡܰܪܩܳܢܳܐ *an indelible stain.*

ܡܬܡܫܚܢܐ, ܢܝܬܐ rt. ܡܫܚ. *measured; with* ܠܐ *immense, immeasurable, infinite;* ܠܐ ܡܬܡܫܚܢܐ ܡܬܡܬܚ *the Infinite One is stretched* on the Cross.

ܡܬܡܬܚܢܐ rt. ܡܬܚ. with ܠܐ *relaxed, slack.*

ܡܬܡܟܡܟܢܐ from ܐܬܡܟܡܟ. *one who speaks through his nose* or *indistinctly; a mutterer.*

ܡܬܢ root-meaning *to wait.* PE. only part. adj. ܡܬܝܢ, ܡܬܝܢܐ *slow, sluggish, dull, inert; patient, placid, mild; still* (of wine); *cowardly;* ܕܒܐ ܡܬܝܢܐ ܡܢ ܐܪܝܐ *the bear is slower than the lion;* ܐܝܢܐ ܕܡܬܝܢ ܗܘܢܗ *one of sluggish mind, slow of understanding.* ETHPA. ܐܬܡܬܢ *to delay, linger, be late, slow;* ܬܘ ܘܠܐ ܬܬܡܬܢ *come without delay;* ܠܐ ܬܬܡܬܢ ܒܥܘܬܐ *let not supplication be tardy.* DERIVATIVES, ܡܬܝܢܐܝܬ, ܡܬܝܢܘܬܐ, ܡܬܢܬܐ.

ܡܬܢܒܝܢܐ rt. ܢܒܐ. *prophetic, endowed with the gift of prophecy.*

ܡܬܢܒܝܢܐܝܬ rt. ܢܒܐ. adv. *prophetically.*

ܡܬܢܒܥܢܘܬܐ rt. ܢܒܥ. f. *overflowing.*

ܡܬܢܒܪܫܢܘܬܐ rt. ܢܒܪܫ. f. *burning, conflagration.*

ܡܬܢܓܕܢ, ܡܬܢܓܕܢܐ rt. ܢܓܕ. *one who is to suffer torture.*

ܡܬܢܗܪܢܐ rt. ܢܗܪ. *enlightened, instructed; a pupil.*

ܡܬܢܗܪܢܘܬܐ rt. ܢܗܪ. f. *enlightenment, illumination.*

ܡܬܬܢܝܢܐ, ܢܝܬܐ rt. ܬܢܐ. gram. *indicative.*

ܡܬܬܢܝܢܐܝܬ rt. ܬܢܐ. adv. *repeatedly;* gram. *in the indicative mood.*

ܡܬܢܟܝܢܐ, ܢܝܬܐ rt. ܢܟܐ. *subject to hurt, exposed to danger;* with ܠܐ *inviolable, imperishable; invulnerable; unharmed, unhurt; safe, secure.*

ܡܬܢܟܝܢܐܝܬ rt. ܢܟܐ. adv. with ܠܐ *without harm, safely.*

ܡܬܢܟܝܢܘܬܐ rt. ܢܟܐ. f. *liability to hurt* or *injury.*

ܡܬܢܟܠܢܘܬܐ rt. ܢܟܠ. f. *being deceived, beguilement.*

ܡܬܢܟܣܢܐ rt. ܢܟܣ. *fit for sacrifice, due to be slain.*

ܡܬܢܟܪܝܢܘܬܐ from ܢܟܪܝ. f. *alienation, estrangement, separation, denial.*

ܡܬܢܣܒܢܐܝܬ rt. ܢܣܒ. adv. *metaphorically.*

ܡܬܢܣܝܢܐ rt. ܢܣܐ. *tempted, liable to temptation.*

ܡܬܢܣܟܢܘܬܐ rt. ܢܣܟ. f. *fusibility.*

ܡܬܢܩܠܢܐ rt. ܢܩܠ. f. with ܠܐ *stable, durable.*

ܡܬܢܩܠܢܐܝܬ rt. ܢܩܠ. adv. with ܠܐ *immutably.*

ܡܬܢܨܒܢܐ rt. ܢܨܒ. *fit for planting.*

ܡܬܢܗܝܢܐ, ܢܝܬܐ rt. ܢܗܐ. *lamentable.*

ܡܬܢܩܡܢܐ rt. ܢܩܡ. m. *an avenger.*

ܡܬܢܩܦܢܐ, ܢܝܬܐ rt. ܢܩܦ. *relating to, consequent upon;* gram. *a noun in the construct state; following, related.*

ܡܬܢܩܦܢܘܬܐ rt. ܢܩܦ. f. *intimacy.*

ܡܬܢܫܝܢܐ, ܢܝܬܐ rt. ܢܫܐ. *forgotten, unheeded.*

ܡܬܢܫܝܢܐܝܬ rt. ܢܫܐ. adv. *lethargically.*

ܡܬܢܫܝܢܘܬܐ rt. ܢܫܐ. f. *forgetfulness.*

ܡܬܢܬܐ pl. ܡܬܢܵܬܐ rt. ܡܬܢ. f. *the loins, side, ribs;* metaph. *the back, side* or *ridge of a hill, a shelf* of gravel.

ܡܬܩܐ pl. ܐ̈ m. *the thread which is first tied to the beam of a loom;* ܡܬܩܐ ܕܡܥܙܠܝ *the first thread of my web.*

ܡܬܥܒܕܢܐ rt. ܥܒܕ. *capable of being effected* or *carried out;* gram. *acted on, objective* opp. ܥܒܘܕܐ *active, nominative;* with ܩܠܐ *onomatopoetic.*

ܡܬܥܒܕܢܘܬܐ rt. ܥܒܕ. f. *action, effect;* gram. *objectivity, predicability; transitiveness.*

ܡܬܥܒܪܢܐ, ܢܝܬܐ rt. ܥܒܪ. *a*) *passable;* with ܠܐ *impassable* as ܢܚܠܐ *a torrent,* ܬܚܘܡܐ *a limit* metaph. *inviolable, inviolate, not to be transgressed* as ܢܡܘܣܐ *a law.* *b*) *a transgressor.*

ܡܬܥܒܪܢܘܬܐ pl. ܘ̈ܬܐ rt. ܥܒܪ. f. *transgression, violation.*

ܡܬܥܕܠܢܐ, ܢܝܬܐ rt. ܥܕܠ. *a*) adj. *culpable, reprehensible;* with ܠܐ *blameless.* *b*) subst. *a censor, faultfinder, disparager.*

ܡܬܥܕܪܢܐ, ܢܝܬܐ rt. ܥܕܪ. *needing help, receiving help;* ܡܥܕܪܢܐ ܐܘ ܡܬܥܕܪܢܐ *he that helpeth and he that is holpen;* ܗܘܢܐ ܠܐ ܡܬܥܕܪܢܐ *an obstinate mind, a mind that will not be helped.*

ܡܬܥܗܕܢܐ rt. ܥܗܕ. m. *memorable, pertaining to the memory, mindful;* with ܠܐ *unmindful, ungrateful.*

ܡܬܥܗܕܢܘܬܐ pl. ܘ̈ܬܐ rt. ܥܗܕ. f. *commemoration, rehearsal, memory, remembrance;*

a commentary; rit. *commemoration* of the Passion in the Holy Eucharist; ܩܘܕܫ ܡܥܗܕܢܘܬܐ *the consecration of the Commemoration* = celebration of Holy Communion.

ܡܬܟܠܝܢܐ, ܬܐ rt. ܟܠܐ. with ܠܐ *irresistible, resistless;* ܡܬܟܠܝܢܐ ܠܐ ܬܘܩܦܗ *its resistless impetus.*

ܡܬܟܠܝܢܐܝܬ rt. ܟܠܐ. adv. with ܠܐ *unimpeded.*

ܡܬܥܠܒܢܐ rt. ܥܠܒ. *susceptible of harm* or *violence;* with ܠܐ *unhurt, unconquerable, insuperable.*

ܡܬܥܠܝܢܐܝܬ rt. ܥܠܐ. adv. *in a higher sense, metaphorically.*

ܡܬܥܠܝܢܘܬܐ rt. ܥܠܐ. f. *ascent, elevation; the higher* or *metaphorical sense* of words.

ܡܬܥܠܠܢܐ rt. ܥܠܠ. gram. *causative.*

ܡܬܥܡܪܢܐ, ܬܐ rt. ܥܡܪ. *habitable, fit for habitation;* with ܠܐ *uninhabitable;* with ܐܪܥܐ or ellipt. *the habitable earth.*

ܡܬܥܢܘܝܢܘܬܐ rt. ܥܢܐ. f. *a*) *meekness. b*) *the ascetic life.*

ܡܬܥܣܩܢܘܬܐ rt. ܥܣܩ. f. *being multiplied, multiplication.*

ܡܬܥܨܝܢܐ rt. ܥܨܐ. with ܠܐ *irresistible.*

ܡܬܥܨܝܢܘܬܐ rt. ܥܨܐ. f. *stubbornness.*

ܡܬܥܩܒܢܐ, ܬܐ rt. ܥܩܒ. with ܠܐ *inscrutable.*

ܡܬܥܩܒܢܐܝܬ rt. ܥܩܒ. adv. with ܠܐ *inscrutably.*

ܡܬܥܩܒܢܘܬܐ rt. ܥܩܒ. f. with ܠܐ *inscrutability.*

ܡܬܥܩܪܢܐ, ܬܐ rt. ܥܩܪ. with ܠܐ *ineradicable, indestructible.*

ܡܬܥܩܪܢܘܬܐ rt. ܥܩܪ. f. *rooting out, extirpation, utter destruction;* with ܠܐ *impossibility of entire destruction.*

ܡܬܥܪܒܠܢܘܬܐ from ܥܪܒܠ. f. *a maze, confused heap.*

ܡܬܥܪܝܢܐ rt. ܥܪܐ. with ܠܐ *incomprehensible.*

ܡܬܥܪܡܢܐ rt. ܥܪܡ. *swelling, rising.*

ܡܬܥܪܩܠܢܐ from ܥܪܩܠ. with ܠܐ *safe from entanglement, that cannot be embarrassed.*

ܡܬܥܪܩܠܢܘܬܐ from ܥܪܩܠ. f. *perplexity.*

ܡܬܥܪܩܢܐ, ܬܐ rt. ܥܪܩ. *to be shunned, avoided;* with ܠܐ *inevitable, unavoidable.*

ܡܬܥܪܩܢܐܝܬ rt. ܥܪܩ. adv. with ܠܐ *without escape, inevitably.*

ܡܬܥܪܩܢܘܬܐ rt. ܥܪܩ. f. with ܠܐ *inevitableness.*

ܡܬܥܫܢܢܘܬܐ rt. ܥܫܢ. f. *oppression; might, power.*

ܡܬܥܫܩܢܐ rt. ܥܫܩ. *falsely accused.*

ܡܬܦܐܣܢܐ rt. ܦܐܣ. with ܠܐ *incomparable;* gram. *of comparison.*

ܡܬܦܐܣܢܐܝܬ rt. ܦܐܣ. adv. with ܠܐ *without comparison, incomparably.*

ܡܬܦܐܣܢܘܬܐ rt. ܦܐܣ. f. *confidence, exhilaration.*

ܡܬܦܪܟܢܐ, ܬܐ rt. ܦܪܟ. *friable, crumbled to dust.*

ܡܬܦܠܓܢܐ rt. ܦܠܓ. with ܠܐ *indivisible.*

ܡܬܦܠܓܢܐܝܬ rt. ܦܠܓ. adv. with ܠܐ *indivisibly.*

ܡܬܦܠܓܢܘܬܐ rt. ܦܠܓ. f. *doubt, hesitation.*

ܡܬܦܠܚܪܢܐ, ܬܐ rt. ܦܠܚܪ. *confused, scattered;* with ܠܐ *that cannot be disarranged, unchangeable, immutable.*

ܡܬܦܠܛܢܐ rt. ܦܠܛ. with ܠܐ *that which cannot be escaped, inevitable.*

ܡܬܦܠܣܦܢܐ from ܦܝܠܘܣܘܦܐ. *one who professes philosophy, calls himself a philosopher.*

ܡܬܦܢܛܣܢܐ from ܦܢܛܣܝܐ. *imaginable.*

ܡܬܦܢܝܢܐ, ܬܐ rt. ܦܢܐ. *brought back, made to return; persuading to return* or *be converted; that to which answer is given, answered.*

ܡܬܦܢܝܢܐܝܬ rt. ܦܢܐ. adv. with ܠܐ *without turning, inflexibly.*

ܡܬܦܢܝܢܘܬܐ rt. ܦܢܐ. f. *turning about, away* or *back, return, returning, conversion, renunciation, retractation.*

ܡܬܦܢܩܢܐ rt. ܦܢܩ. *luxurious, given to pleasures.*

ܡܬܦܣܠܢܐ rt. ܦܣܠ. *hewn;* with ܠܐ *unhewn, unquarried.*

ܡܬܦܣܩܢܐ, ܬܐ rt. ܦܣܩ. with ܠܐ *indivisible; an atom.*

ܡܬܦܣܩܢܐܝܬ rt. ܦܣܩ. adv. with ܠܐ *indivisibly.*

ܡܬܦܣܩܢܘܬܐ rt. ܦܣܩ. f. *section, intersecting.*

ܡܬܦܪܩܢܐ rt. ܦܪܩ. m. *a fugitive; one who has escaped.*

ܡܬܦܩܕܢܐ, ܬܐ rt. ܦܩܕ. *commanded, one who receives commands* opp. ܦܩܘܕܐ *one who issues orders.*

ܡܬܦܩܕܢܐܝܬ rt. ܦܩܕ. adv. gram. *in the passive voice* opp. ܦܩܘܕܐܝܬ.

ܡܬܦܪܓܢܐ rt. ܦܪܓ. *enjoying.*

ܡܬܦܪܢܣܢܘܬܐ from ܦܪܢܣ. f. *direction, administration.*

ܡܬܦܪܣܢܐ, ܬܐ rt. ܦܪܣ. *disclosed, openly shown.*

ܡܬܦܪܣܢܘܬܐ rt. ܦܪܣ. f. *conviction, detection.*

ܡܬܦܪܣܢܐ from ܦܪܘܣ. m. *a contriver, inventor.*

ܡܬܦܪܥܢܐ, ܬܐ rt. ܦܪܥ. with ܠܐ *that cannot be requited* or *repaid.*

ܡܬܦܪܩܢܐ rt. ܦܪܩ. *needing salvation.*

ܡܬܦܪܫܢܐ, ܬܐ *a*) *separate, distinguishable, distinct, separable;* with ܠܐ *inseparable. b*) *distinguished, illustrious. c*) *separate from the body, incorporeal;* ܗܘܢܐ ܡܬܦܪܫܢܐ ܡܢ ܦܓܪܐ ܡܠܐܟܐ *an incorporeal intelligence* i.e. *an angel.*

ܡܬܦܪܫܢܐܝܬ rt. ܦܪܫ. adv. with ܠܐ *inseparably, indivisibly.*

ܡܬܦܪܫܢܘܬܐ rt. ܦܪܫ. f. with ܠܐ *inseparability, indivisibility.*

ܡܬܦܪܬܢܘܬܐ rt. ܦܪܬ. f. *fissibility.*

ܡܬܦܫܟܢܐ, ܬܐ rt. ܦܫܟ. *equivocal, dubious, doubtful;* with ܠܐ *indubitable.*

ܡܬܦܫܟܢܐܝܬ rt. ܦܫܟ. adv. with ܠܐ *indubitably, unquestionably, incontestably.*

ܡܬܦܫܩܢܐ, ܬܐ rt. ܦܫܩ. with ܠܐ *incomprehensible, ineffable.*

ܡܬܦܫܩܢܐܝܬ rt. ܦܫܩ. adv. with ܠܐ *ineffably, unutterably.*

ܡܬܦܫܪܢܐ, ܬܐ rt. ܦܫܪ. *wasting away, soluble.*

ܡܬܦܫܪܢܘܬܐ rt. ܦܫܪ. f. *liquefaction, fusibility.*

ܡܬܦܬܚܢܐ rt. ܦܬܚ. *that which can be opened.*

ܡܨ fut. ܢܡܘܨ, act. part. ܡܐܨ, ܡܐܨܐ, pass. part. ܡܝܨ. *to suck, suck up, draw out* milk, water, rain; sweet or bitter; ܡܐܨܐ ܬܕܝܐ *sucking the breast;* ܡܨܘ ܚܠܝܘܬܐ ܕܡܢ ܝܘܠܦܢܐ *suck out the sweetness of the doctrine;* ܕܡܢܗ ܡܨܝܢ ܚܝܐ ܘܢܘܗܪܐ ܬܪܝܗܘܢ ܥܠܡܐ *from Whom both worlds derive life and light.* PAEL ܡܨܨ *to suck dry, exhaust.* APH. ܐܡܝܨ *to make to suck, let suck.* DERIVATIVES, ܡܨܬܐ, ܡܨܘܨܐ, ܡܨܘܬܐ.

ܡܨܝܐ rt. ܡܨ. m. *sucking, suckling.*

ܡܬܩܒܠܢܐ, ܬܐ rt. ܩܒܠ. *acceptable.*

ܡܬܩܒܠܢܘܬܐ rt. ܩܒܠ. f. *receiving, reception.*

ܡܬܩܝܡܢܐ rt. ܩܘܡ. *permanent;* with ܠܐ *transitory, evanescent.*

ܡܬܩܢܝܢܘܬܐ rt. ܩܢܐ. f. *possession.*

ܡܬܩܕܡܢܐ, ܬܐ rt. ܩܕܡ. with ܠܐ *unsurpassed, unprecedented.*

ܡܬܩܕܡܢܘܬܐ rt. ܩܕܡ. f. *prejudice.*

ܡܬܩܕܫܢܐ, ܬܐ rt. ܩܕܫ. *that which,* or *he who, is to be sanctified.*

ܡܬܩܕܫܢܘܬܐ rt. ܩܕܫ. f. *consecration.*

ܡܬܩܘܠܬܐ pl. ܬܐ rt. ܬܩܠ. f. *a*) *a plummet. b*) *a pouch.*

ܡܬܩܪܪܢܘܬܐ rt. ܩܪ. f. *coldness, frigidity.*

ܡܬܩܛܠܢܐ rt. ܩܛܠ. *one to be slain, one under sentence of death; the slain.*

ܡܬܩܦܣܢܘܬܐ rt. ܩܦܣ. f. *contraction, restriction.*

ܡܬܩܛܦܢܐ rt. ܩܛܦ. *downcast, rejected.*

ܡܬܩܛܦܢܘܬܐ rt. ܩܛܦ. f. *vintage, fruit-gathering;* metaph. *being cut off by an early death.*

ܡܬܩܛܓܪܢܐ, ܬܐ from ܩܛܓܪ. *a*) *the accused, the defendant. b*) *predicated, predicative, predicable.*

ܡܬܩܛܓܪܢܐܝܬ from ܩܛܓܪ. adv. *categorically.*

ܡܬܩܛܓܪܢܘܬܐ from ܩܛܓܪ. f. *a predicament.*

ܡܬܩܝܡܢܐ, ܬܐ rt. ܩܘܡ. *a*) *one who is raised from the dead. b*) with ܠܐ *irreparable.*

ܡܬܩܝܡܢܘܬܐ rt. ܩܘܡ. f. *being restored, raised up again.*

ܡܬܩܠܐ pl. ܝܢ, ܬܐ rt. ܬܩܠ. m. *a*) *a weight, scale, balance;* ܡܬܩܠܐ ܕܙܘܙܐ *the weight of a drachma;* ܡܬܩܠܐ ܕܢܟܠܐ *false weights;* ܢܬܩܘܠ ܒܡܬܩܠܐ *he will weigh in the balance. b*) a measure of weight or value, *a shekel* said to equal a drachma, but more exactly 7 ܡܬܩܠܝܢ = 10 zuze or drachmas and = 1 oz., also ܡܬܩܠܐ

ܡܰܠܟܳܝܳܐ ܕܡܰܬܩܳܠܳܐ *the royal shekel*=20 dirhems; ܡܰܬܩܳܠܳܐ ܕܩܽܘܕܫܳܐ *a shekel of the sanctuary*=60 zuze.

ܡܶܬܬܰܩܠܳܢܽܘܬܳܐ rt. ܬܩܠ. f. *a balance; weighing.*

ܡܶܬܬܰܩܠܳܢܳܐ rt. ܬܩܠ. *ponderable.*

ܡܶܬܬܰܩܠܣܳܢܳܐ from ܩܠܣ. *laudable, praiseworthy.*

ܡܰܬܩܢܳܐ, ܡܰܬܩܰܢ pl. ܐ̈ rt. ܬܩܢ. m. *a base, pedestal, support, a position, foundation.* Cf. Pael and Aphel parts. of ܬܩܢ.

ܡܰܬܩܢܽܘܬܳܐ rt. ܬܩܢ. f. *the coupling* or *opening of an ephod.*

ܡܶܬܩܰܢܝܳܢܳܐ, ܝܳܢܳܝܬܳܐ rt. ܩܢܐ. *a) procurable, purchasable, attainable. b) that can be tamed, domestic.*

ܡܶܬܩܰܢܝܳܢܽܘܬܳܐ rt. ܩܢܐ. f. *possession, acquisition, attainment.*

ܡܰܬܩܢܳܢܳܐ, ܢܳܝܬܳܐ rt. ܬܩܢ. *a) a founder, fashioner, artificer;* ܡܰܬܩܢܳܢܶܗ ܕܦܰܓܪܳܐ God *Who formed the body. b) a repairer, supporter; a reformer.*

ܡܰܬܩܢܳܢܽܘܬܳܐ rt. ܬܩܢ. f. *stability, orderly arrangement, disposition.*

ܡܶܬܩܰܦܣܳܢܳܐ, ܣܳܢܳܝܬܳܐ rt. ܩܦܣ. with ܠܳܐ *irrepressible, stubborn.*

ܡܶܬܩܰܦܠܳܢܽܘܬܳܐ rt. ܩܦܠ. f. *taking away, laying aside.*

ܡܰܬܩܦܳܢܳܐ rt. ܬܩܦ. *a strengthener.*

ܡܶܬܩܰܪܒܳܢܳܐ, ܒܳܢܳܝܬܳܐ rt. ܩܪܒ. with ܠܳܐ *unapproachable; not to be sought.*

ܡܶܬܩܰܪܒܳܢܽܘܬܳܐ rt. ܩܪܒ. f. *a) approach, access; nearness, propinquity, proximity. b) bringing near, presentation, offering.*

ܡܶܬܩܰܪܒܳܢܳܝܬܳܐ rt. ܩܪܒ. f. a term of prosody, perh. *tripping Bacchic measure.*

ܡܶܬܩܰܪܝܳܢܳܐ rt. ܩܪܐ. *a) legible. b) vocative;* gram. *a noun in the vocative case.*

ܡܶܬܩܰܬܽܘܠܝܩܳܢܳܐ from ܩܬܘܠܝܩܐ. *one eligible* or *elected to the dignity of Catholicos.*

ܡܰܬܪܳܐ, ܡܰܬܪܽܘܐܳܐ or ܡܰܬܪܺܝܳܐ m. *a long iron stake* or *rake, a long fork for turning sacrifices on the altar.*

ܡܰܬܪܳܝܳܐ, ܝܳܢܺܝܬܳܐ rt. ܬܪܐ. *an instructor, preceptor, pedagogue.*

ܡܶܬܪܰܒܝܳܢܳܐ, ܝܳܢܳܝܬܳܐ rt. ܪܒܐ. *that which grows* or *is nurtured.*

ܡܶܬܬܰܪܓܡܳܢܳܐ from ܬܪܓܡ. *an interpreter, translator, commentator.*

ܡܶܬܬܰܪܓܡܳܢܽܘܬܳܐ from ܬܪܓܡ. f. perh. *evidence given through an interpreter, the deposition* of a witness.

ܡܶܬܪܰܓܫܳܢܳܐ, ܫܳܢܳܝܬܳܐ rt. ܪܓܫ. *that which can be apprehended by the senses, perceptible, sensible* opp. ܡܶܬܝܰܕܥܳܢܳܐ *apprehended by the reason, intelligible;* ܡܰܝܳܐ ܡܶܬܪܰܓܫܳܢܶܐ *natural water;* ܠܰܚܡܳܐ ܡܶܬܪܰܓܫܳܢܳܐ *ordinary bread* opp. spiritual food; ܥܺܕܬܳܐ ܡܶܬܪܰܓܫܳܢܺܝܬܳܐ *the visible Church.*

ܡܶܬܪܰܓܫܳܢܳܐܝܬ rt. ܪܓܫ. adv. *sensibly, outwardly, as perceived by the senses.*

ܡܶܬܪܰܓܫܳܢܽܘܬܳܐ rt. ܪܓܫ. f. *sensibility, possibility of being perceived by the senses.*

ܡܶܬܪܰܕܝܳܢܳܐ rt. ܪܕܐ. *one under instruction, a pupil.*

ܡܶܬܪܰܕܦܳܢܳܐ rt. ܪܕܦ. *persecuted.*

ܡܶܬܪܰܗܒܳܢܳܐ rt. ܪܗܒ. *affrighted, frightened.*

ܡܶܬܪܰܗܛܳܢܳܐ rt. ܪܗܛ. *swift, careless.*

ܡܶܬܪܰܚܡܳܢܳܐ rt. ܪܚܡ. *merciful, pitied;* with ܠܳܐ *pitiless.*

ܡܶܬܪܰܚܩܳܢܳܐ, ܩܳܢܳܝܬܳܐ rt. ܪܚܩ. *one who secedes, revolts, is separate.*

ܡܶܬܪܰܚܩܳܢܳܐܝܬ rt. ܪܚܩ. adv. with ܠܳܐ *inseparably.*

ܡܶܬܪܰܚܩܳܢܽܘܬܳܐ rt. ܪܚܩ. f. *a) separation, distance, keeping aloof, putting away;* ܟܬܳܒܳܐ ܕܡܶܬܪܰܚܩܳܢܽܘܬܳܐ *a bill of divorce. b) secession, desertion, defection, revolt.*

ܡܶܬܪܰܘܙܓܳܢܳܐ rt. ܪܘܙܓ. *shaken* by the wind.

ܡܶܬܪܰܘܙܓܳܢܽܘܬܳܐ rt. ܪܘܙܓ. f. *being shaken to and fro; quivering.*

ܡܶܬܪܰܘܪܒܳܢܳܐ rt. ܪܒ. *boastful.*

ܡܶܬܪܺܝܛܳܐ or ܡܶܬܪܺܝܛܳܐ pl. ܡܶܬܪܺܝܛܶܐ, ܡܶܬܪܺܝܛܳܬܳܐ f. μετρητής, *a liquid measure, a bath;* ܡܳܐܐ ܡܶܬܪܺܝܛܺܝܢ ܡܶܫܚܳܐ *a hundred measures of oil.*

ܡܶܬܪܰܘܝܳܢܳܐ, ܝܳܢܳܝܬܳܐ rt. ܪܘܐ. with ܠܳܐ *implacable, unquenchable.*

ܡܶܬܪܰܟܒܳܢܳܐ, ܒܳܢܳܝܬܳܐ rt. ܪܟܒ. *a) fit for riding;* ܪܰܟܫܳܐ ܡܶܬܪܰܟܒܳܢܶܐ *riding horses. b) combinable, that which can be united. c) the material* or *substance* of a compound.

ܡܶܬܪܰܟܒܳܢܽܘܬܳܐ rt. ܪܟܒ. f. *cohesion.*

ܡܬܬܪܟܟܢܐ, ܢܝܬܐ rt. ܪܟ. with ܠܐ *hardened, implacable, relentless.*

ܡܬܬܪܟܢܢܐ rt. ܪܟܢ. *flexible;* with ܠܐ *inflexible.*

ܡܬܬܪܟܢܢܐܝܬ rt. ܪܟܢ. adv. *kindly, condescendingly.*

ܡܬܬܪܟܢܢܘܬܐ rt. ܪܟܢ. f. *compliance, submission, condescension;* gram. *inflexion.*

ܡܬܬܪܡܪܡܢܐ rt. ܪܡ. *lifted up, exalted.*

ܡܬܪܐܝܢܐ; see ܡܬܪܥܝܢܐ.

ܡܬܬܪܥܝܢܐ rt. ܪܥܐ. with ܠܐ *inconceivable.*

ܡܬܬܪܥܝܢܘܬܐ pl. ܬܐ rt. ܪܥܐ. f. *thought, reflection.*

ܡܬܪܣܝܢܘܬܐ and ܡܬܪܣܝܢܘܬܐ from ܬܪܣܝ. f. *nourishment.*

ܡܬܪܣܝܢܐ, ܢܝܬܐ from ܬܪܣܝ. *nourishing, nutritious; a nourisher, sustainer.*

ܡܬܬܪܦܝܢܐ, ܢܝܬܐ rt. ܪܦܐ. with ܠܐ *unrelaxed, unwearied.*

ܡܬܪܨܢܐ, ܢܝܬܐ rt. ܬܪܨ. *a director, corrector, reviser, regulator; one who puts to rights, restores to order.*

ܡܬܬܪܫܝܢܐ, ܢܝܬܐ rt. ܪܫܐ. *indictable;* with ܠܐ *irreproachable.*

ܡܬܬܪܫܠܢܘܬܐ rt. ܪܫܠ. f. *paralysis.*

ܡܬܬܪܫܡܢܐ rt. ܪܫܡ. *that which is to be signed.*

ܡܬܬܪܫܡܢܘܬܐ rt. ܪܫܡ. f. *drawing, delineation.*

ܡܬܬܐ pl. of ܡܬܐ.

ܡܬܬܒܥܢܐ, ܢܝܬܐ rt. ܬܒܥ. *a debtor; a culprit, one from whom punishment is exacted.*

ܡܬܬܒܪܩܢܘܬܐ rt. ܒܪܩ. f. *flashing, brightness.*

ܡܬܬܓܫܫܢܐ rt. ܓܫ. with ܠܐ *unfathomable, incomprehensible;* pl. ܡܬܬܓܫܫܢܬܐ *things perceptible to the senses.*

ܡܬܬܓܕܫܢܘܬܐ rt. ܓܕܫ. f. *meeting together, clashing.*

ܡܬܬܓܪܢܐ, ܢܝܬܐ rt. ܬܓܪ. *a*) *an earner, winner. b*) *that which is to be won* or *acquired.*

ܡܬܬܕܝܢܢܐ rt. ܕܝܢ. *arraigned, impleaded, under trial; convicted, condemned.*

ܡܬܬܕܝܢܢܘܬܐ pl. ܬܐ rt. ܕܝܢ. f. *the being indicted* or *arraigned.*

ܡܬܬܕܪܫܢܐ, ܢܝܬܐ rt. ܕܪܫ. with ܠܐ *untrodden, pathless, impassable.*

ܡܬܬܕܪܫܢܘܬܐ rt. ܕܪܫ. f. with ܠܐ *an untrodden* or *pathless place, a lonely waste.*

ܡܬܬܗܘܝܢܐ rt. ܗܘܐ. *capable of being created.*

ܡܬܬܗܘܝܢܘܬܐ rt. ܗܘܐ. f. *capability of creation.*

ܡܬܬܘܚܝܢܘܬܐ rt. ܘܚܐ. f. *delay.*

ܡܬܬܘܗܠܢܐ rt. ܗܠ. *an object of derision.*

ܡܬܬܘܒܠܢܘܬܐ rt. ܝܒܠ. f. *being led away, captivity; being brought.*

ܡܬܬܘܕܝܢܐ, ܢܝܬܐ from ܐܘܕܝ. rt. ܝܕܐ. *acknowledged, declared, manifest, certain.*

ܡܬܬܘܕܝܢܐܝܬ rt. ܝܕܐ. adv. *confessedly, avowedly, undeniably.*

ܡܬܬܘܕܝܢܘܬܐ rt. ܝܕܐ. f. *an acknowledged fact.*

ܡܬܬܘܗܝܘܬܐ rt. ܬܘܗ. f. *stupor.*

ܡܬܬܘܝܢܘܬܐ rt. ܬܘܝ. f. *grief.*

ܡܬܬܘܒܢܐ, ܢܝܬܐ rt. ܬܘܒ. *penitent,* with ܠܐ *impenitent.*

ܡܬܬܘܒܢܘܬܐ rt. ܬܘܒ. f. *penitence, compunction.*

ܡܬܬܘܬܒܢܘܬܐ rt. ܝܬܒ. f. *dwelling, habitation.*

ܡܬܬܙܝܥܢܐ, ܢܝܬܐ rt. ܙܘܥ. *movable;* ܩܢܝܢܐ ܡܬܬܙܝܥܢܐ *movables, movable property;* ܟܘܟܒܐ ܡܬܬܙܝܥܢܐ *a planet;* with ܠܐ *immovable, steadfast;* gram. *having a vowel.*

ܡܬܬܙܝܥܢܘܬܐ pl. ܬܐ rt. ܙܘܥ. f. *movement, motion, movableness, swift* or *continual motion* such as *surging, swelling* of the sea, *motion* of the heavenly bodies; *commotion;* gram. *vocalization;* pl. *points, vowels.*

ܡܬܬܐܚܝܕܢܐ, ܢܝܬܐ rt. ܐܚܕ. *tangible, that may be touched; liable, exposed to;* with ܠܐ *ungoverned, uncontrolled; not subject to, not exposed.*

ܡܬܬܐܚܝܕܢܐܝܬ rt. ܐܚܕ. adv. with ܠܐ *without control, uncontrollably.*

ܡܬܬܐܚܝܕܢܘܬܐ rt. ܐܚܕ. f. *arrest, seizing; apprehension.*

ܡܬܬܚܝܒܢܐ rt. ܚܘܒ. *due, incumbent* with ܠ *to* or ܥܠ *upon.*

ܡܬܬܚܝܒܢܐ, ܢܝܬܐ rt. ܚܘܒ. *obligatory, owing, due;* pl. *dues.*

ܡܬܬܚܝܒܢܐܝܬ rt. ܚܘܒ. adv. *duly.*

ܡܬܬܚܡܢܐ rt. ܬܚܡ. *definite, circumscribed, limited.*

ܡܬܬܚܡܢܐܝܬ rt. ܬܚܡ. adv. with ܠܐ *indefinitely.*

ܡܬܬܚܝܬܢܐܝܬ from ܐܬܚܬ. adv. *humbly.*

ܡܬܬܚܝܬܢܘܬܐ from ܐܬܚܬ. f. *condescension.*

ܡܬܛܥܝܢܐ rt. ܛܥܐ. m. *fallible;* with ܠܐ *infallible.*

ܡܬܝܬܝܢܐ rt. ܐܬܐ. gram. *derivative, superinduced, causal* of verbs opp. *primitive;* astron. *intercalar.*

ܡܬܝܬܝܢܘܬܐ rt. ܐܬܐ. f. *leading away; inclination, propensity.*

ܡܬܟܝܠܢܐ, ܢܝܬܐ rt. ܟܝܠ. *measurable;* with ܠܐ *immeasurable, immense;* pl. m. ܡܬܟܝ̈ܠܢܐ *things sold by measure.*

ܡܬܟܣܢܝܘܬܐ from ܐܟܣܢܝܐ. f. *travelling, sojourning.*

ܡܬܟܒܪܢܘܬܐ rt. ܟܒܪ. f. *an illness,* perh. *a thickening of the tissues.*

ܡܬܠܘܬܢܐ from ܠܘܬ. gram. *an enclitic, affix* pronoun as ܝ in ܥܒܕܝ *my work.*

ܡܬܠܘܬܢܘܬܐ pl. ܘ̈ܬܐ from ܠܘܬ. f. *a connexion of ideas.*

ܡܬܢܓܕܢܐ rt. ܢܓܕ *attractive.*

ܡܬܛܠܠܢܐ rt. ܛܠܠ. *moist.*

ܡܬܠܡܕܢܐ rt. ܠܡܕ. *a pupil, catechumen, novice.*

ܡܬܦܨܝܢܘܬܐ rt. ܦܨܐ. *possibility of escape;* with ܠܐ *that which is inevitable.*

ܡܬܓܚܟܢܐ rt. ܓܚܟ. m. *a laughing-stock.*

ܡܬܓܫܫܢܐ rt. ܓܫܫ. with ܠܐ *inscrutable, past finding out.*

ܡܬܬܢܝܚܢܐ rt. ܢܘܚ. *at rest, resting.*

ܡܬܬܢܝܚܢܘܬܐ rt. ܢܘܚ. f. *restfulness.*

ܡܬܡܠܠܢܐ, ܢܝܬܐ rt. ܡܠܠ with ܠܐ *indescribable.*

ܡܬܬܢܢܐ rt. ܬܢܢ. *smoky.*

ܡܬܬܚܡܢܘܬܐ rt. ܬܚܡ. f. with ܠܐ *indefiniteness.*

ܡܬܬܣܝܡܢܐ rt. ܣܝܡ. *a candidate for ordination* to the subdiaconate or to another of the lower orders, also a bishop *designate.*

ܡܬܬܣܝܡܢܘܬܐ rt. ܣܝܡ. f. *a) the laying on* of a burden, of a temptation. *b) an hypothesis.*

ܡܬܬܢܫܡܢܐ, ܢܝܬܐ rt. ܢܫܡ. *fit to breathe; perceptible to the sense of smell.*

ܡܬܣܪܚܢܢܐ rt. ܣܪܚ. *a candidate for ordination* to the diaconate or to the priesthood, *one about to be consecrated bishop.*

ܡܬܣܪܚܢܢܘܬܐ rt. ܣܪܚ. f. *ordination, consecration, designation, election* of a king, of a deacon, priest, bishop or patriarch.

ܡܬܥܒܕܢܐ rt. ܥܒܕ. *a) acted on, influenced, operated in* or *upon; that whereby anything is effected. b) energumenous, beset* or *possessed* by an evil spirit.

ܡܬܥܒܕܢܘܬܐ rt. ܥܒܕ. f. *formation, the being affected* or *influenced.*

ܡܬܬܥܝܪܢܘܬܐ rt. ܥܘܪ. f. *awakening.*

ܡܬܥܠܢܘܬܐ rt. ܥܠܠ. f. *bringing, presentation.*

ܡܬܥܦܦܢܘܬܐ rt. ܥܘܦ. f. *duplication.*

ܡܬܬܦܝܣܢܐ from ܦܝܣܐ. *easily entreated, docile, obedient.*

ܡܬܬܦܝܣܢܘܬܐ from ܦܝܣܐ. f. *obedience.*

ܡܬܬܦܝܪܢܐ rt. ܦܘܪ. *irascible, indignant.*

ܡܬܬܦܝܪܢܘܬܐ rt. ܦܘܪ. f. *irascibility.*

ܡܬܬܨܝܕܢܐ rt. ܨܘܕ. *intelligible.*

ܡܬܬܨܝܕܢܘܬܐ rt. ܨܘܕ. f. *capture, seizing.*

ܡܬܬܨܝܪܢܘܬܐ pl. ܘ̈ܬܐ rt. ܨܘܪ. f. *formation, imagination.*

ܡܬܨܠܚܢܐ rt. ܨܠܚ. *successful, prosperous.*

ܡܬܨܡܚܢܐ rt. ܨܡܚ. with ܠܐ *rayless, murky.*

ܡܬܨܡܚܢܘܬܐ rt. ܨܡܚ. f. *illumination.*

ܡܬܬܩܠܢܐ rt. ܬܩܠ. with ܠܐ *void of offence.*

ܡܬܩܪܩܪܢܘܬܐ rt. ܩܪܪ. f. *chipping* or *bursting open* as a bird from the egg, a bud from its sheath.

ܡܬܬܪܝܚܢܐ rt. ܪܘܚ. *that can be smelt.*

ܡܬܬܪܝܡܢܐ, ܢܝܬܐ rt. ܪܘܡ. with ܠܐ *that which cannot be taken away.*

ܡܬܬܪܝܡܢܘܬܐ rt. ܪܘܡ. f. *elevation, height, swelling, rising.*

ܡܬܪܘܝܢܐ, ܢܝܬܐ rt. ܪܘܐ. *soluble; permeated;* with ܠܐ *impermeable.*

ܡܬܪܘܝܢܘܬܐ rt. ܪܘܐ. f. *soakage, maceration.*

ܡܬܬܪܣܝܢܐ from ܬܪܣܝ. *one to be reared, nourished.*

ܡܬܬܪܦܢܐ rt. ܬܪܦ. with ܠܐ *uninterrupted, continuous.*

ܡܬܬܪܝܢܐ, ܢܝܬܐ rt. ܬܪܐ. subst. *a catechumen;* adj. with ܠܐ *incorrigible, incurable.*

ܡܬܫܠܡܢܘܬܐ rt. ܫܠܡ. f. *delivery* of goods to the purchaser, of payment to the creditor, of a deposit to its owner.

÷ ܫܠܡܬ ܐܬܘܬܐ ܕܡܝܡ. [illegible] ÷

ܬܘܒ ܥܡ ܐܠܗܐ ܡܫܪܝܢܢ ܐܬܘܬܐ ܕܢܘܢ. ܡܢ
ܐܘܨܪ ܠܫܢܐ ܣܘܪܝܝܐ

ܢ

ܢ, ܢܘܢ *Nun, n,* the fourteenth letter of the alphabet; the number 50, with ܂ *the fiftieth.* Nun is often elided at the end of a closed syllable, e.g. in ܐܢܬ *thou,* ܡܕܝܢܬܐ *a city,* ܣܦܝܢܬܐ *a ship;* it is omitted in a few words such as ܓܒܬܐ *cheese* for ܓܒܢܬܐ and ܐܢܬܬܐ the fem. form. of ܐܢܫܐ and constantly in ܦܣ verbs and their derivatives. Derivative, ܢܘܢܐ.

ܢܐ or ܢܝ particle of entreaty, *I beg, I pray thee, do, now;* ܩܪܘܒ ܢܐ *come near, I pray thee;* ܐܣܘܪ ܢܐ ܐܝܟ ܓܒܪܐ ܚܨܝܟ *gird up now thy loins like a man.*

ܢܐܒܐ 3 m. s. fut. *a)* of ܐܒܐ *to weep. b)* of ܐܒܐ *to be weary.*

ܢܐܒܐ and ܢܐܒܐ m. *nightmare.*

ܢܐܒܐ 3 m. s. fut. of ܢܒܐ *to sprout.*

ܢܐܩܪ 3 m. s. fut. of ܝܩܪ *to be heavy;* ܢܐܩܪ for ܢܩܪ 3 m. s. fut. of ܩܪ *to be cold.*

ܢܐܪܒ, ܢܐܪܒܐ pl. ܐ̈ m. *a peak, precipice; an abrupt valley, deep pool;* ܢܐܪܒܐ ܕܚܝܠܐ *a terrible precipice;* ܕܐܥܒܪ ܢܐܪܒܐ ܕܓܘܡܨܐ *that I may pass through the abysses of the pit.*

ܢܐܪܒ 3 m. s. fut. of ܪܒ *to become great,* &c.

ܢܐܪܕܘܣ usually f. νάρδος, *spikenard,* cf. ܢܪܕܝܢ and the following.

ܢܐܪܕܝܢܘܢ m. νάρδινον, *nard,* cf. ܢܪܕܝܢ.

ܢܒܐ Pa. ܢܒܝ *to prophesy;* ܡܢܒܝܐ ܗܘܐ ܗܘܐ *it had been prophesied.* Ethpa. ܐܬܢܒܝ *to prophesy, fulfil the office of a prophet, behave as a prophet, rave, predict;* ܐܬܢܒܝܘ ܒܒܥܠ *they prophesied by Baal, in the name of Baal;*

ܢܒܥ

ܐܬܢܒܝܬ ܕܓܠܘܬܐ—ܒܫܘܩܪܐ *thou hast prophesied deceit, falsely;* ܥܠܝܗܘܢ ܐܬܢܒܝ ܚܙܩܝܐܝܠ ܢܒܝܐ *concerning them did Ezekiel the prophet prophesy;* ܐܬܢܒܝ ܫܐܘܠ ܒܓܘ ܒܝܬܐ Saul *raved in the midst of the house.* Derivatives, ܢܒܝܐ, ܢܒܝܘܬܐ, ܢܒܝܬܐ, ܢܒܝܘܬܐ, ܢܒܝܬܐ, ܡܬܢܒܝܢܐ, ܡܬܢܒܝܢܘܬܐ.

ܢܒܐ pl. ܢܒܐ̈ m. *a nit, louse's egg.*

ܢܒܓ fut. ܢܢܒܘܓ, act. part. ܢܒܓ, ܢܒܓܐ. *to rise, arise* esp. out of the water, *to spring up* as a plant; *to break forth;* opp. ܛܒܥ and ܛܡܥ *to sink;* ܛܒܥܘ ܒܥܘܡܩܐ ܘܠܐ ܢܒܓܘ *they sank in the depth and arise no more;* ܐܝܠܢ ܚܝܐ ܢܒܓ ܗܘܐ *the tree of life had sprung up.* Ethpa. ܐܬܢܒܓ *to be divided* as a stream. Aph. ܐܢܒܓ *to diffuse, spread forth.* Derivatives, ܢܒܓܐ, ܢܒܘܓܐ, ܢܒܓܢܐ.

ܢܒܓܐ pl. ܐ̈ rt. ܢܒܓ. m. *a)* *a shoot, sprout, slip, sucker, growth;* ܢܒܓܘܗܝ ܕܒܝܫܬܐ *growths of evil. b)* *a fount.*

ܢܒܓܢܝܐ, ܢܒܓܢܝܬܐ rt. ܢܒܓ. gram. *derivative, secondary* opp. ܫܪܫܢܝܐ *radical.*

ܢܒܗ fut. ܢܢܒܗ, act. part. ܢܒܗ, ܢܒܗܐ root-meaning *to awake* from sleep. *To stir, begin to move, move, start; to arise, emanate, have their origin;* ܢܒܗ ܒܚܕܘܬܐ *he is stirred, agitated, with joy;* ܢܒܗܘ ܒܗ ܡܚܫܒܬܐ *thoughts arose in him;* ܚܝܐ ܠܥܠܡܝܢ ܢܒܗܝܢ ܡܢ ܐܠܗܐ *eternal life emanating from God;* ܡܢ ܥܒܪܝܐ ܢܒܗ *the word is of Hebrew origin;* geom. ܢܩܕܬܐ ܡܨܥܝܬܐ ܕܡܢܗ ܣܪܛܐ ܫܘܝܐ ܢܒܗܝܢ the centre *whence equal lines start to the circumference.* Aph. ܐܢܒܗ *to arouse, excite.* Derivatives, ܢܒܗܐ, ܢܒܗܢܐ, ܢܒܗܐ.

ܢܒܘܥܐ pl. ܐ̈ rt. ܢܒܥ. m. *emotion, impulse;* ܢܒܘ̈ܥܐ ܗܘܢܢܝ̈ܐ *mental impulses.*

ܢܒܘܥܐ rt. ܢܒܥ. m. *a stirring, arousing* of the thoughts or senses.

ܢܒܘܥܝܐ gram. *originative,* ܫܡܐ ܢܒܘܥܝܐ *a noun from which other words are derived* according to Syriac grammatical theory, as the verb ܫܡܫ from ܫܡܫܐ.

ܢܒܘܓܝܬܐ or ܢܒܘܓܝܬܐ rt. ܢܒܓ. f. *emerging* from water.

ܢܒܘܙܐ or ܢܒܘܙܐ pl. ܐ̈ m. *a centipede;* the plant *polypody.*

ܢܒܘܚܐ pl. ܐ̈ rt. ܢܒܚ. m. *one who barks;* ܢܒܘܚ̈ܘܗܝ *those who bark at him.*

ܢܒܘܪܐ rt. ܢܒܪ. m. *a beak.*

ܢܒܚ fut. ܢܢܒܘܚ and ܢܢܒܚ, inf. ܡܢܒܚ, act. part. ܢܒܚ, ܢܒܚܐ. *to bark;* ܠܐ ܢܒܚ ܟܠܒܐ *no dog barks;* ܢܢܒܘܚ ܥܠ ܟܠ ܢܘܟܪܝܐ *he will bark at every stranger;* metaph. *to speak roughly.* Aph. ܐܢܒܚ *to cause to bark.* Derivatives, ܢܒܘܚܐ, ܢܒܚܐ, ܡܢܒܚܐ.

ܢܒܚ, ܢܒܚܐ rt. ܢܒܚ. m. *barking;* ܢܒܚ ܟܠܒܢ *the barking of our dog.*

ܢܒܝܐ pl. ܢܒܝ̈ܐ, ܢܒܝܝܢ rt. ܢܒܐ. m. for fem. see ܢܒܝܬܐ. *a prophet;* ܒܢܝ̈ ܢܒܝ̈ܐ *sons of the prophets;* ܢܒܝ̈ܐ ܕܓܠܐ *false prophets.*

ܢܒܝܐܝܬ rt. ܢܒܐ. adv. *prophetically.*

ܢܒܝܙܐ Ar. m. *a drink made of dates* or *raisins.*

ܢܒܝܘ, ܢܒܝܘܬܐ pl. ܢܒܝܘ̈ܬܐ rt. ܢܒܐ. f. *prophecy, a prophecy, the gift* or *office of a prophet, prophetical writings,* ܒܢܒܝܘܬܐ ܕܐܫܥܝܐ *in the prophecy of Isaiah;* ܡܠܬܐ ܕܢܒܝܘܬܐ *the word of prophecy;* ܒܢܒܝܘܬܐ *prophetically, with prophetic inspiration.*

ܢܒܝܝܐ, ܢܒܝܝܬܐ pl. m. ܐ̈ f. ܬ̈ܐ rt. ܢܒܐ. *prophetic, prophetical;* ܟܬܒ̈ܐ ܢܒܝܝ̈ܐ *the prophetical Books;* ܬܫܡܫܬܐ ܢܒܝܝܬܐ *the religion of the Prophet* i.e. *Mohammedanism.*

ܢܒܝܬܐ pl. ܢܒܝ̈ܬܐ rt. ܢܒܐ. fem. of ܢܒܝܐ, *a prophetess.*

ܢܒܥ fut. ܢܢܒܥ, act. part. ܢܒܥ, ܢܒܥܐ. *to spring up, flow* as water, *to shoot up* as a plant, metaph. *to spring up, come to light, burst forth;* ܢܚܠܐ ܕܢܒܥ *a flowing brook;* ܢܒܥܝܢ ܗܪ̈ܣܝܣ *heresies sprang up;* ܡܢ ܫܠܝ ܢܒܥ ܠܝ ܒܥܠܕܒܒܝ *my enemy suddenly appeared to me.* Aph. ܐܒܥ *to pour forth, bring forth, eject, utter;* ܐܒܥ ܢܗܪܐ ܐܩܪ̈ܩܥܐ *the river brought forth frogs;* ܐܒܥ ܠܒܝ ܡܠ̈ܐ ܛܒ̈ܬܐ *my heart overflowed with good words;* ܡܥܨܪ̈ܬܟ ܢܒܥܢ ܚܡܪܐ *thy presses shall pour forth wine.* Derivatives, ܢܒܥܐ, ܡܒܘܥܐ, ܡܒܥܢܐ, ܡܒܥܢܘܬܐ.

ܢܒܥ, ܢܒܥܐ pl. ܐ̈ rt. ܢܒܥ. m. *a spring, source, fount;* ܪܕܝܐ ܕܢܒ̈ܥܝܗܘܢ *the flowing of their springs;* ܢܒܥܐ ܕܢܘܪܐ *a fount of fire;* ܢܒܥܐ ܕܢܝܠܘܣ *the source of the Nile;* ܢܒܥܐ ܕܒܘܪ̈ܟܬܐ *a fount of blessings.*

ܢܒܪ act. part. ܢܒܪ. *to scratch* the ground. Derivatives, ܢܒܘܪܐ, ܢܒܪܐ, ܢܒܪܐ.

ܢܒܪܐ pl. ܐ̈ rt. ܢܒܪ. m. *the spur* of a cock, *a hooked claw.*

ܢܒܪܐ pl. ܐ̈ rt. ܢܒܪ. *a*) *clawing* or *scratching* the ground. *b*) perhaps *tape,* something between ܚܘܛܐ *thread* and ܚܒܠܐ *cord.*

ܢܒܪܫ fut. ܢܢܒܪܫ. *to kindle, inflame;* ܢܒܪܫܬ ܐܢܘܢ ܚܘܒܐ ܕܐܠܗܐ *love of God inflamed them;* ܚܝ̈ܘܬܐ ܡܢܒܪܫܬܐ ܒܢܘܪܐ ܠܐ ܗܘܠܢܝܬܐ *living creatures burning with immaterial fire* i. e. in Ezekiel's vision. Ethpaal ܐܬܢܒܪܫ *to be set on fire, burning, flaming, to break forth into flames;* ܩܝܣܐ ܕܐܪ̈ܙܐ ܡܬܢܒܪܫ ܒܥܓܠ cedar-wood *easily takes fire, burns up;* ܪܬܚܐ ܕܐܬܢܒܪܫ ܗܘܐ ܒܝ *the fervour which had blazed up within me.* Derivatives, ܢܒܪܫܬܐ, ܢܒܪܫܬܢܐ, ܡܬܢܒܪܫܢܘܬܐ.

ܢܒܪܫܬܐ pl. ܢܒܪ̈ܫܬܐ f. *flame, blazing, bright fire;* ܢܒܪ̈ܫܬܐ ܕܢܘܪܐ ܡܠܐܟ̈ܐ angels are *flames of fiery ardour.*

ܢܒܪܫܬܢܐ, ܢܒܪܫܬܢܝܬܐ rt. ܢܒܪܫ. *flaming;* ܢܝ̈ܙܟܐ ܢܒܪܫܬܢܝ̈ܐ *fiery lances.*

ܢܓܒ fut. ܢܢܓܘܒ and ܢܢܓܒ, pass. part. ܢܓܝܒ, ܢܓܝܒܐ, ܢܓܝܒܬܐ. *to dry up, become dry;* ܥܕ ܠܐ ܢܓܒ ܛܝܢܐ ܕܦܚܪ̈ܐ *before the* potters' *clay has dried;* p. p. *dry, dried.* Pa. ܢܓܒ tr. *to dry up;* ܘܠܐ ܕܢܢܓܒ ܒܫܡܫܐ *we must dry* it *in the sun.* Ethpa. ܐܬܢܓܒ *to be dried up.* Derivatives, ܢܓܒܐ, ܡܢܓܒܐ, ܡܢܓܒܢܐ, ܡܢܓܒܢܘܬܐ.

ܢܓܒܐ rt. ܢܓܒ. m. *being dried up.*

ܢܓܕ fut. ܢܢܓܘܕ, inf. ܡܢܓܕ, imper. ܢܓܘܕ, act. part. ܢܓܕ, ܢܓܕܐ, pass. part. ܢܓܝܕ, ܐ, ܬܐ. *a*) *to draw* ܒܢܝܪܐ *with the yoke,* ܒܩܫܬܐ *to draw the bow,* ܡܨܝܕܬܐ *a net,* ܡܢ ܓܘܒܐ *out of a pit; to withdraw, to lead;* ܢܓܕܗ ܠܒܪ ܓܢܒܐ *he drew him aside;* ܓܕܘ ܢܦܫܟܘܢ ܠܒܪ ܡܢ ܡܕܝܢܬܐ *withdraw yourselves from the city.* b) *to attract, induce, persuade;* ܢܓܕܢܝ ܚܘܒܐ ܠܡܡܠܠܘ *love persuaded me to speak;* ܐܢܓܕ ܟܠܢܫ ܠܘܬܝ *I will draw all men unto Me;* ܟܘܟܒܐ ܢܓܕ ܠܡܓܘܫܐ ܕܢܐܬܘܢ *a star led the Magi to come.* c) *to stretch out, extend, prolong;* ܢܓܕ ܫܘܪܐ *he lengthened the walls* i. e. built further; pass. part. *drawn, long drawn out, long; enchased,* ܣܐܡܐ ܢܓܝܕܐ *chased silver;* ܢܓܝܕܝܢ ܦܪܣܐ *the curtains were drawn.* Ethpe. ܐܬܢܓܕ a) *to be drawn out, extracted,* ܒܡܨܝܕܬܐ *in a net;* ܡܪܪܬܐ ܡܬܢܓܕܐ *the poison is extracted.* b) *to be drawn aside, away, seduced;* ܠܛܘܥܝܝܢ *to error;* ܡܢ ܪܓܬܐ *by lust.* d) *to be long drawn out, lengthy.* e) *to be led, attracted, induced, impelled, compelled;* ܠܡܡܠܟܘ ܡܬܢܓܕ ܗܘܐ ܠܡܡܠܟܘ ܒܬܪ ܐܚܘܗܝ *he could hardly be induced to reign after his brother;* ܡܬܢܓܕ ܡܢ ܢܡܘܣܐ *he was compelled by law;* ܡܬܢܓܕܢܐ *docile;* ܠܐ ܡܬܢܓܕܢܘܬܐ *indocile.* Pa. ܢܓܕ a) *to draw.* b) *to beat, scourge;* ܢܓܕܘܗܝ ܒܥܪܩܬܐ *they scourged him with thongs;* metaph. *to scourge, plague;* ܠܡܨܪܝܐ ܢܓܕ ܒܡܚܘܬܐ *he scourged the Egyptians with plagues.* Ethpa. ܐܬܢܓܕ a) *to be drawn* or *torn away; to be compelled.* b) *to be beaten, scourged;* ܬܠܬ ܙܒܢܝܢ ܐܬܢܓܕܬ ܒܫܒܛܐ *thrice was I beaten with rods;* metaph. ܡܬܢܓܕ ܒܢܣܝܘܢܐ *plagued with temptations.* Aph. ܐܓܕ *to draw strongly, attract.* Derivatives, ܢܓܘܕܐ, ܢܓܕܐ, ܢܓܝܕܐ, ܢܓܕܐ, ܢܓܘܕܐ, ܡܢܓܕܢܐ, ܢܓܝܕܘܬܐ, ܡܬܢܓܕܢܐ, ܢܓܕܘܬܐ.

ܢܓܘܕܐ pl. ܐ̈ rt. ܢܓܕ. m. *one who draws, one who scourges; a thong, strap.*

ܢܓܕܐ pl. ܝܢ̈, ܐ̈ rt. ܢܓܕ. m. a) *the drawing up* ܕܡܨܝܕܬܐ *of a net.* b) *scourging, castigation, punishment, torment, pain;* ܐܣܝ ܠܗܘܢ ܡܢ ܢܓܕܝܗܘܢ *he washed their stripes;* ܢܓܕܐ ܕܫܘܝܐ ܠܣܟܠܘܬܗ *punishment befitting his fault;* metaph. ܢܓܕܐ ܕܡܣܟܢܘܬܐ *the scourge of poverty.* c) *a scourge, thong.*

ܢܓܕܐ rt. ܢܓܕ. m. *attraction, allurement; dragging, lengthening.*

ܢܓܗ fut. ܢܢܓܗ, act. part. ܢܓܗ, ܢܓܗܐ. *to dawn,* usually impers. ܟܕ ܢܓܗ ܨܦܪܐ *at dawn, very early in the morning;* ܩܕܡ ܕܢܓܗ *before dawn;* ܡܛܠ ܕܫܒܬܐ ܢܓܗܐ *because the Sabbath was dawning;* ܒܫܒܬܐ ܕܢܓܗ ܚܕ ܒܫܒܐ *on the Sabbath when Sunday was dawning, beginning to dawn.* Aph. ܐܢܓܗ a) *to be morning, to shine;* ܥܠ ܐܘܪܚܬܟ ܢܓܗ ܢܘܗܪܐ *light shall shine upon thy ways.* b) *to wait till dawn, remain all night;* ܐܢܓܗ ܗܘܐ ܒܨܠܘܬܐ ܕܐܠܗܐ *he continued till dawn in prayer to God.* Derivatives, ܢܓܗܐ, ܢܘܓܗܐ, ܡܢܓܗܐ.

ܢܓܗ, ܢܓܗܐ part. used as subst. a) *the dawn;* ܒܢܓܗ ܥܐܕܐ ܕܙܩܝܦܐ *at dawn on the feast of the Cross.* b) *twilight, vespers* which followed sunset and were before ܪܡܫܐ; ܕܢܓܗ *at vespers;* ܢܓܗ ܫܒܬܐ *Sabbath vespers.*

ܢܓܘܕܐ pl. ܐ̈ rt. ܢܓܕ. m. a) *a guide* esp. of the blind. b) *a piece of wood attaching a yoke* to the cart.

ܢܓܘܕܐ rt. ܢܓܕ. m. *a crooked stick to drive a ball with.*

ܢܓܘܕܘܬܐ rt. ܢܓܕ. f. *guiding, leading* esp. of the blind.

ܢܓܝܒܘܬܐ rt. ܢܓܒ. f. *being dried up, drought.*

ܢܓܝܕܐ rt. ܢܓܕ. m. *a guide.*

ܢܓܝܕܘܬܐ rt. ܢܓܕ. f. *length.*

ܢܓܝܠܐ, ܢܓܝܠܬܐ *foul, filthy.*

ܢܓܝܪ, ܐ, ܬܐ *long;* with ܪܘܚܐ *longsuffering;* see ܢܓܪ.

ܢܓܝܪܐܝܬ rt. ܢܓܪ. adv. *for a long time, patiently.*

ܢܓܝܪܘܬܐ rt. ܢܓܪ. f. a) *length of time, duration;* ܨܠܝܘ ܥܠ ܢܓܝܪܘܬ ܚܝܘܗܝ *they prayed for long life for him.* b) ܢܓܝܪܘܬ ܪܘܚܐ *longsuffering, patience.*

ܢܓܠ fut. ܢܢܓܘܠ. *to flee, take to flight;* ܢܓܠܘ ܡܢ ܩܕܡ ܒܪܒܪܝܐ *they fled before the barbarians.* Pael ܢܓܠ the same. ܢܓܠ is also Aphel fut. of verb ܓܠ *to unroll.*

ܢܓܪ fut. ܢܢܓܪ, act. part. ܢܓܪ, ܢܓܪܐ, pass. part. ܢܓܝܪ and ܢܓܝܪ, ܐ, ܬܐ. I) *to be long, lengthy* of time, *to continue, last;* ܢܓܪ ܬܡܢ ܝܘܡܬܐ ܣܓܝܐܐ *he had been there many days;* ܟܕ ܢܓܪܝܢ ܒܢ ܡܚܫܒܬܐ ܛܢܦܬܐ *when impure thoughts persist in us;* part. adj. ܢܓܝܪ *long, lengthy;* with ܚܝܐ, ܫܢܝܐ or ܝܘܡܬܐ *long-lived;*

ܡܘܬܐ ܐܘܪܚܐ ܢܓܝܪܬܐ *a long journey;* ܣܒܠ ܢܓܝܪܬܐ *he endured death by slow fire;* metaph. ܢܓܝܪ ܪܘܚܐ *longsuffering, patient.* 2) *to saw, hew, do carpenters' work;* with ܒܡܢܓܪܘܬܐ *to turn;* pass. part. ܢܓܝܪ, ܐ̈, ܬܐ *turned, hewn.* PA. ܢܓܪ 1) *to repress, restrain.* 2) *to saw, hew, carpenter.* APH. ܐܘܪܟ a) with ܝܘܡܬܐ expressed or understood, *to prolong his days, live long; to be a long time, remain, continue, last;* ܐܓܪ ܒܡܡܠܠܐ *he spoke for a long time;* ܐܓܪܘ ܠܢ ܥܕܡܐ *stay, we beg, until . . .;* ܐܓܪ ܒܟܘܪܗܢܐ ܫܒܥܐ ܝܘܡܝܢ *he continued ill for seven days;* ܠܐ ܡܓܪܝܢ ܓܘܡܪܝܗܘܢ *their coals do not last hot.* b) metaph. with ܪܘܚܐ or ellipt. and with ܥܠ or ܥܡ, *to be longsuffering, patient; to defer, delay;* ܚܘܒܐ ܡܓܪ ܪܘܚܐ *love is longsuffering;* ܐܓܪ ܪܘܚܗ ܒܨܠܘܬܐ *he continued patiently in prayer;* ܐܓܪ ܥܠܝ ܪܘܚܐ ܬܪܝܢ ܝܘܡܝܢ *be patient with me two days* or *grant me two days' delay.* ܐܓܪ is also the Pael conj. of ܐܓܪ *to hire.* DERIVATIVES, ܡܢܓܪܐ, ܢܓܪܘܬܐ, ܢܓܪܐ, ܢܓܘܪܬܐ, ܢܓܝܪܘܬ ܪܘܚܐ, ܡܢܓܪܢܘܬܐ, ܢܓܪܢܐ.

ܢܓܪܐ, ܢܓܪܐ pl. ܐ̈ rt. ܢܓܪ. m. *a workman* esp. *a carpenter;* ܢܓܪ̈ܐ ܘܢܣܪ̈ܐ *carpenters, sawyers;* ܒܪ ܢܓܪܐ *the carpenter's son* i.e. our Lord.

ܢܓܪܘܬܐ rt. ܢܓܪ. f. *the carpenter's art, wood-carving, carpentry;* ܦܠܚ ܢܓܪܘܬܐ *working as a carpenter.*

ܢܕ fut. ܢܢܕ, act. part. ܢܐܕ, ܢܐܕܐ, pass. part. ܢܕܝܕ, ܐ̈, ܬܐ *to loathe, abhor, turn from, reject* with ܡܢ; ܐܝܠܝܢ ܕܚܙܝܢ ܗܘܘ ܠܝ ܒܫܘܩܐ ܢܕܝܢ ܗܘܘ ܡܢܝ *they who saw me in the market-place turned from me;* ܢܕܘ ܗܘܘ ܡܢ ܐܝܣܪܝܠܝ̈ܐ the Egyptians *loathed the Israelites;* ܢܕܬ ܢܦܫܝ ܡܢ ܗܘܠܢܝ̈ܬܐ ܕܥܠܡܐ *my soul abhorred the material things of this world.* Usually impers. with ܠ and pron. suff. ܢܕܬ ܠܗ ܡܢ ܚܙܬܗ *she loathed the sight of him;* ܠܐ ܬܐܢܕ ܠܟ ܡܢܝ *do not abhor me.* Part. adj. *abominable, unclean, execrable, foul; an abominable thing, abomination;* ܢܕܝܕ ܣܪܝܐ *stinking;* ܡܐܟܘܠܬܐ ܢܕܝܕܬܐ *unclean food;* ܢܕܝܕܐ ܠܡܬܡܠܠܘ *unmentionable.* ETHPE. ܐܬܢܕܕ or ܐܬܢܕ *to be* or *become abominable;* ܗܠܝܢ ܠܘܐ ܕܢܬܢܕܕ ܒܥܝܢܝܢ ܗܘܐ *this ought to be abominable in our eyes.* PA. ܢܕܕ *to abhor, make to be abhorred.* ETHPA. ܐܬܢܕܕ *to become an abomination, be abhorred.* APH. ܐܢܕ a) *to be disgusted, abhor.* b) *to agitate, to chase away;* ܨܦܬܐ ܡܢܕܐ ܫܢܬܐ *care drives away sleep.* DERIVATIVES, ܢܕܝܕܘܬܐ, ܢܕܬܐ.

ܢܕܐ fut. ܢܢܕܐ, act. part. ܢܐܕܐ, ܢܕܝܐ, pass. part. ܢܕܝܐ, ܢܕܝܐ. a) *to break away, burst forth, drop down, splash;* ܢܕܐ ܕܡܗܘܢ ܥܠ ܡܐܢܝ *their blood splashed upon my garments.* b) *to project, be prominent,* ܟܐܦܐ ܕܢܕܝܢ ܠܒܪ ܡܢ ܒܢܝܢܐ *stones which project outwards from a building;* ܫܢ̈ܐ ܕܢܕܝܢ ܘܢܦܩܝܢ ܠܒܪ ܡܢ ܦܘܡܐ *tusks projecting and coming outside of the mouth;* ܐܬܪ̈ܘܬܐ ܕܢܕܝܢ ܘܪܡܝܢ *tracts of rising and lofty ground.* PA. ܢܕܝ only in part. ܡܢܕܝܐ, ܡܢܕܝܬܐ, ܡܢܕܝܢܘܬܐ. 1) *to jog, shake, bound along;* ܡܪܟܒܬܐ ܡܢܕܝܬܐ *a bounding chariot.* 2) adj. *vagabond, poor.* DERIVATIVES, ܢܕܝܐ, ܡܢܕܝܢܘܬܐ.

ܢܕܝܐ or ܢܕܝܐ pl. ܐ̈ rt. ܢܕܐ. m. *a prominence, eminence, high ground; a protuberance, roughness* of surface; *a bump, pustule;* ܫܢܢ̈ܐ ܘܢܕܝ̈ܐ *peaks and eminences;* ܡܢ ܚܣܝܪܘܬ ܢܕܝܐ ܕܒܣܬܪ ܪܝܫܐ ܚܘܣܪܢ ܥܘܗܕܢܐ *from the absence of bumps at the back* of the head come *defects of memory.*

ܢܕܝܕ, ܐ̈, ܬܐ *abominable; an abomination;* see ܢܕ.

ܢܕܝܕܘܬܐ pl. ܬܐ̈ rt. ܢܕ. f. *filth, abomination;* ܢܕܝܕܘܬ̈ܐ *foul crimes;* ܢܕܝܕܘܬ ܥܒܕ̈ܐ *foul actions, wickedness;* ܢܕܝܕܘܬܐ ܕܣܡ̈ܡܢܐ *nastiness, evil taste, of drugs.*

ܢܕܝܪܘܬܐ rt. ܢܕܪ. f. *a rapid flow, burst, torrent* of water, of tears.

ܢܕܠܐ m. a) *a field-mouse.* b) ܢܕܠܐ or ܢܕܠܐ *a centipede.*

ܢܕܪ 1) fut. ܢܢܕܘܪ, imper. ܢܕܘܪ, act. part. ܢܐܕܪ, ܢܕܪܐ. *to pour down* as water or tears; metaph. ܢܕܪ ܥܘܠܐ *pouring forth iniquity.* 2) fut. ܢܢܕܘܪ, pass. part. ܢܕܝܪ, ܐ̈, ܬܐ. *to vow, devote;* ܢܕܪ ܢܕܪܐ *to make a vow, take a vow;* ܐܝܠܢ̈ܐ ܢܕܝܪ̈ܝ ܠܫܐܕ̈ܐ *trees devoted to devils* i.e. planted near temples of idols. ETHPE. ܐܬܢܕܪ *to be vowed, devoted.* DERIVATIVES, ܢܕܪܐ, ܢܕܝܪܘܬܐ.

ܢܕܪܐ, ܢܕܪܐ pl. ܢܕܪ̈ܐ, rt. ܢܕܪ. m. *a vow;* ܢܕܪܐ ܕܢܕܪܬ ܠܐܠܗܐ *the vow which I have vowed unto God;* ܩܘܪܒܢ̈ܐ ܘܢܕܪ̈ܐ *oblations and alms* i.e. offerings which had been vowed.

ܢܕܝܘܬܐ rt. ܢܕܐ. f. *abomination, abhorrence.*

ܢܗܐ apoc. fut. of ܗܘܐ, for ܢܗܘܐ.

ܢܗܐ fut. ܢܢܗܐ *to cry* for food as a child.

ܢܗܩ fut. ܢܢܗܘܩ, act. part. ܢܗܩ. *to groan, roar.* Derivative, ܢܗܩܐ.

ܢܗܩܐ rt. ܢܗܩ. m. *groaning* of camels.

ܢܘܗܡܡܘܬܐ rt. ܢܗܡ. f. *murmuring, moaning.*

ܢܘܗܪ, ܢܘܗܪܐ rt. ܢܗܪ. m. *light.*

ܢܗܛ fut. ܢܢܗܛ and ܢܗܘܛ, act. part. ܢܗܛ, ܢܗܛܐ. *to disturb, annoy;* ܗܕܐ ܡܠܬܐ ܢܗܛܬ ܠܗܘܢ ܛܒ *this saying troubled them much.* Pa. ܢܗܛ *to grate, creak;* ܡܪܟܒܬܐ ܡܢܗܛܢܝܬܐ *creaking chariots.* Ethpa. ܐܬܢܗܛ *to be moved, shaken.* Derivatives, ܢܗܛܐ, ܢܗܘܛܐ.

ܢܗܛܐ rt. ܢܗܛ. m. *creaking* or *clatter* of chariots, *neighing* of horses.

ܢܗܝܪ, ܐ, ܬܐ adj. see under ܢܗܪ. subst. m. *light, a light, luminary* said of the sun, moon, stars; ܢܗܝܪ̈ܐ ܕܫܡܝܐ *the lights of heaven;* ܛܥܝܢܝ ܢܗܝܪ̈ܐ *bearers of lights, torch-bearers;* ܒܢܗܝܪܐ or ܒܢܗܝܪ̈ܐ *in the light* opp. ܒܚܫܘܟܐ *in the dark;* ܢܗܝܪܐ ܘܡܫܡܠܝܐ *light and perfection* i.e. *Urim and Thummim.*

ܢܗܝܪܐܝܬ rt. ܢܗܪ. adv. *clearly, luminously, lucidly, plainly;* ܚܙܐ ܗܘܐ ܟܠ ܡܕܡ ܢܗܝܪܐܝܬ *he saw all things clearly;* ܡܦܢܝܢ ܠܗ ܢܗܝܪܐܝܬ *they answer him plainly.*

ܢܗܝܪܘܬܐ rt. ܢܗܪ. f. *clearness, brightness, intelligence, lucidity, splendour;* ܢܗܝܪܘܬ ܓܘܢܐ *clear* or *bright colour;* ܫܪܓܐ ܕܠܐ ܚܣܝܪ ܡܫܚܐ ܕܢܗܝܪܘܬܗ *a lamp with unfailing oil to sustain its brightness;* ܥܒܕܐ ܕܝܕܥܬܢܘܬܐ ܘܢܗܝܪܘܬܐ *a work of knowledge and intelligence.*

ܢܗܡ or ܢܗܡ fut. ܢܢܗܘܡ, act. part. ܢܗܡ, ܢܗܡܐ. *a*) *to roar* as a lion or in anger, metaph. ܢܗܡܐ ܢܘܪܐ *the fire roars;* ܢܗܡܝܢ ܝܡ̈ܡܐ *the seas roar;* ܪܥܡܐ ܢܗܡ ܩܠܗ *the thunder roars.* *b*) *to moan* as a dove, *to murmur* as wizards. Pa. ܢܗܡ *to roar, bleat, moan.* Ethpa. ܐܬܢܗܡ *to roar.* Derivatives, ܢܗܡܐ, ܢܘܗܡܐ, ܢܗܡܬܐ, ܢܘܗܡܡܘܬܐ, ܡܢܗܡܢܐ.

ܢܗܡܐ rt. ܢܗܡ. m. *roaring, howling* of fire, of grief, *murmuring* of wizards.

ܢܗܡܐ, ܢܗܡܬܐ pl. ܬܐ̈ rt. ܢܗܡ. f. *roaring* of a lion, or in sorrow; ܢܗܡܬܗ ܕܠܒܝ *the disquietness of my heart; moaning, murmuring* of a dove.

ܢܗܪ fut. ܢܢܗܪ, act. part. ܢܗܪ, ܢܗܪܐ, pass. part. ܢܗܝܪ, ܐ, ܬܐ. *a*) *to be light, give light, shine;* ܥܕܡܐ ܕܢܗܪ ܨܦܪܐ *till the dawn shone, till daybreak;* ܗܝܕܝܢ ܙܕܝܩ̈ܐ ܢܢܗܪܘܢ ܐܝܟ ܫܡܫܐ *then shall the righteous shine forth as the sun;* ܒܐܪܒܥܐ ܒܫܒܐ ܕܢܗܪ ܚܡܫܐ *on Wednesday towards the dawn of Thursday;* ܢܗܪܝܢ ܠܡܦܐܕ̈ܝܗܘܢ *their lamps shine.* *b*) *to be lighted, alight, to burn,* ܫܪ̈ܓܐ ܦܫܘ ܟܕ ܢܗܪܝܢ *the candles remained alight;* metaph. *to be enlightened.* Part. adj. *a*) *light, bright, shining, clear, transparent, splendid, cheerful;* ܡܝ̈ܐ ܢܗܝܪ̈ܐ *clear waters;* ܢܗܝܪ ܚܙܘܗ *of splendid appearance.* *b*) *enlightened, wise, far-seeing, clear-sighted; illustrious;* ܡܕܥܐ ܢܗܝܪܐ *an enlightened mind;* ܛܠܝܐ ܢܗܝܪܐ *an intelligent boy.* *c*) *lucid, clear, plain, manifest.* *d*) subst. see ܢܗܝܪ above. Pa. ܢܗܪ *to bring to light, enlighten, make clear, show clearly, elucidate, explain* esp. *to annotate, write commentaries;* ܐܢܗܪ ܠܟܠܢܫ ܐܝܢܐ ܗܝ ܡܕܒܪܢܘܬܗ ܕܐܪܙܐ *I will make all men see what is the dispensation of the mystery;* ܡܢܗܪܐ ܗܘܬ ܠܣܓܝܐܐ ܒܡܠܬܗ ܕܐܠܗܐ *she enlightened many persons by the word of God;* ܡܢܗܪܐ ܒܡܪܢܝܬܐ *possessing marginal notes.* Ethpa. ܐܬܢܗܪ *to receive light, to be enlightened* esp. with teaching, *to receive the light* of the gospel; *to be sounded clearly* as a trumpet, *to be explained, elucidated,* ܡܬܢܗܪܝܢ ܡܢ ܙܠܝܩܘܗܝ ܕܡܠܬܐ ܐܠܗܝܬܐ *enlightened by the brightness of the Divine Word.* Aph. ܐܢܗܪ *a*) *to give forth light, to shine brightly;* ܢܗܘܘܢ ܡܢܗܪܝܢ ܒܪܩܝܥܐ ܕܫܡܝܐ ܠܡܢܗܪܘ ܥܠ ܐܪܥܐ *let them shine in the firmament of heaven to give light upon the earth;* ܢܗܘܘܢ ܡܢܗܪܝܢ ܫܪ̈ܓܝܟܘܢ *let your lamps be burning;* ܡܫܚܐ ܠܡܢܗܪܘܬܗ *oil for lighting;* ܩܠܐ ܘܡܢܗܪܐ ܒܠܠܝܐ *a firefly;* ܐܢܗܪ ܦܪܨܘܦܗ *his face shone.* *b*) *to light* a lamp. *c*) *to give light, lighten, enlighten, show clearly;* with ܚܫܘܟܐ *to give light in darkness, lighten darkness;* ܐܢܗܪ ܐܦܝܟ ܥ ... *let thy face shine upon . . .;* ܐܢܗܪܘ ܒܪ̈ܩܘܗܝ *his lightnings shone forth;* ܐܢܬ ܗܘ ܢܘܗܪܐ ܫܪܝܪܐ ܕܡܢܗܪ ܒܪ̈ܝܬܐ *thou art the true light which enlightenest thy creatures.*

ETHTAPH. ܐܬܬܢܗܪ *to receive light, be enlightened.* DERIVATIVES, ܢܘܗܪܐ, ܢܗܝܪܐ, ܢܗܝܪܐܝܬ, ܢܗܝܪܘܬܐ, ܢܘܗܪܐ, ܢܘܗܪܢܐ, ܢܗܪܢܐ, ܢܗܪܐ, ܢܗܪܐܝܬ, ܢܗܪܘܬܐ, ܢܘܗܪܐ, ܢܗܘܪܐ, ܢܗܘܪܢܐ, ܢܗܪܐ, ܡܢܗܪܢܐ, ܡܢܗܪܢܐ, ܡܢܗܪܢܘܬܐ, ܡܢܗܪܢܘܬܐ, ܡܢܗܪܢܐ, ܡܢܗܪܢܐܝܬ, ܡܢܗܪܢܘܬܐ.

ܢܗܪ, ܢܗܪܐ pl. ܢܗܪ̈ܘܢ, ܢܗܪ̈ܘܬܐ rt. ܢܗܪ. m. *a river, stream; a canal, branch* of a river; ܢܗܪ̈ܘܬܐ ܥܡܝܩܬܐ *deep rivers;* ܡܢ ܢܗܪܐ ܕܡܨܪܝܢ ܘܥܕܡܐ ܠܢܗܪܐ ܪܒܐ *from the Nile to the great river* i.e. the Euphrates; ܒܝܬ ܢܗܪ̈ܝܢ or ܒܝܬ ܢܗܪ̈ܘܬܐ *Mesopotamia.*

ܢܗܪܘܢܐ dim. of ܢܗܪܐ. m. *a rivulet, little stream.*

ܢܗܪܝܐ, ܢܗܪܝܬܐ rt. ܢܗܪ. *of* or *like a river, fluviatile, alluvial;* ܫܩܝ̈ܐ ܢܗܪ̈ܝܐ *river floods;* ܐܪܥܐ ܢܗܪܝܬܐ *alluvial soil; Mesopotamian,* i.e. with ܠܫܢܐ *the language of Mesopotamia,* ܐܠܦ ܒܝܬ ܢܗܪܝܬܐ *the Mesopotamian alphabet.*

ܢܗܪܢܐ rt. ܢܗܪ. m. *a faggot, a torch.*

ܢܗܪܐܝܬ rt. ܢܗܪ. adv. *as a river.*

ܢܗܪܢܘܬܐ rt. ܢܗܪ. f. *explanation, elucidation.*

ܢܗܫ m. a sort of *arum* or *sempervivum.*

ܢܘܓ pass. part. ܡܢܘܓ, ܡܢܘܓܐ ναυαγέω, *to shipwreck.* ETHPA. ܐܬܢܘܓ *to be wrecked, suffer shipwreck, be tempest-tost;* ܐܬܢܘܓܬ ܒܓܠ̈ܠܐ *I was driven about by the billows;* metaph. ܡܢܘܓ ܒܟܘܪ̈ܗܢܐ ܘܡܬܢܘܓ ܒܣܡ̈ܡܢܐ *tormented by diseases and broken down by drugs;* ܐܢܫ̈ܐ ܥܠ ܗܝܡܢܘܬܐ ܐܬܢܘܓܘ some *concerning the faith have made shipwreck.*

ܢܘܓܐ or ܢܘܘܓܐ ναυαγός, *shipwrecked;* ܗܢܘܢ ܕܢܘܓܝܢ *those who have suffered shipwreck.*

ܢܘܓܝܣܐ or ܢܘܓܝܣܐ pl. ܢ̈ܐ ναυαγῆσαι, *shipwrecked.*

ܢܘܓܝܐ rt. ܢܓܝ. m. a kind of hymn, the first troparion of an ode.

ܢܘܓܗܐ rt. ܢܓܗ. m. *early dawn, twilight before dawn;* ܟܘܟܒ ܢܘܓܗܐ *the daystar, morning star.*

ܢܘܓܪܐ rt. ܢܓܪ. m. *length, duration, a long time, long;* ܡܢ ܢܘܓܪܐ—ܡܢ ܢܘܓܪܐ ܪܒܐ—ܡܢ ܢܘܓܪܐ ܣܓܝܐܐ *for a long time, a very long time;* ܡܢ ܢܘܓܪܐ ܕܙܒܢܐ—ܕܫܢ̈ܝܐ *a long time ago, many years since;* ܠܐ ܗܘܐ ܒܢܘܓܪܐ *not long, without delay;* ܒܢܘܓܪܐ ܓܕܫܗ ܗܢܐ *this rarely, only once in a long time, happened to him;* ܢܘܓܪܐ ܕܬܠܬܐ ܝܘܡܝܢ *during three days;* ܢܘܓܪܐ ܕܝܘܡܐ *for the space of one day.*

ܢܘܓܪܝܐ m. *a house-sparrow, common sparrow.*

ܢܕ, ܢܘܕ fut. ܢܢܘܕ, infin. ܡܢܕ, imper. ܢܘܕ, act. part. ܢܐܕ, ܢܝܕܐ. *a*) *to wave to and fro* as a reed, a branch, *to toss* in sleep, *to roll* as a ship, *to stagger* as a drunken man, *to shake, tremble, quiver;* with ܒܐܪܥܐ *to wander to and fro on the earth;* with ܡܢ *to turn away from;* ܢܐܕ ܐܢܐ ܥܕܡܐ ܠܨܦܪܐ *I lie tossing till the morn;* ܟܠܗ ܦܓܪܗ ܢܐܕ ܗܘܐ *his whole body shook;* ܐܪܥܐ ܙܝܥܐ ܘܢܝܕܐ *the earth quakes and quivers. b*) *to be startled* in sleep, *start* out of sleep, *wake suddenly.* ETHPALPAL ܐܬܢܕܢܕ *to be shaken* to and fro, *be tossed.* APH. ܐܢܝܕ *to shake, toss, wag,* esp. the head; *to dandle; to cause to wander to and fro;* ܪܫܗ ܡܢܝܕ ܥܠܝܟ *he shakes his head at thee;* ܡܢܝܕ ܘܡܙܝܥ ܠܐܪܥܐ *he shakes the earth and makes it tremble.* DERIVATIVES, ܢܘܕܐ, ܢܕܢܕܐ, ܢܝܕܐ, ܡܢܝܕܐܝܬ.

ܢܘܕܐ pl. ܐ̈ rt. ܢܕ. m. *trembling, unrest, earthquake;* ܢܘܕܐ ܕܟܠܗ ܦܓܪܐ *the trembling of the whole body;* ܢܘܕܐ ܘܙܘܥܐ ܕܩܐܝܢ *unrest and fear like that of Cain.*

ܢܘܕܢܕܐ pl. ܐ̈ rt. ܢܕ. m. *shaking, quaking* of the earth.

ܢܘܗܐ rt. ܢܗ. m. *creaking, clattering, noise* of chariots.

ܢܘܗܡܐ pl. ܐ̈ rt. ܢܗܡ. m. *murmuring, humming, moaning, mourning.*

ܢܘܗܪ, ܢܘܗܪܐ pl. ܐ̈ rt. ܢܗܪ. m. *light, brightness, the light* ܕܪܩܝܥܐ *of the firmament,* ܕܢܘܪܐ *of the fire,* ܕܫܪܓܐ *of a candle,* ܕܐܘܢܓܠܝܘܢ *of the gospel;* ܠܒܝܫ ܢܘܗܪ *clothed in light;* ܢܘܗܪ̈ܐ ܬܢܝܢ̈ܐ *lights of the second rank = angels;* ܢܘܗܪܐ or ܕܢܘܗܪ̈ܐ ܥܐܕܐ *Epiphany.* Metaph. *sight, insight, enlightenment, brilliance, honour;* ܐܘܒܕ ܗܘܐ ܢܘܗܪܐ ܕܥܝܢ̈ܘܗܝ *he had lost his sight;* ܠܐ ܩܘ̈ܟܝܐ ܢܘܗܪܐ ܐܝܬ ܠܗܘܢ shellfish *have no eyesight;* ܥܠܝܡܐ ܦܝܐ ܢܘܗܪܐ *a brilliant youth;* ܠܒܫ ܢܘܗܪܐ *put on bright* or *festal attire.*

ܢܘܗܪ, ܢܘܗܪܐ pl. ܐ̈ rt. ܢܗܪ. m. *enlightenment, instruction, note, comment, commentary;* ܡܫܘܕܥܢܘܬܐ ܐܘ ܢܘܗܪܐ *a scholion* or *note;* ܢܘܗܪ ܡܙܡܘܪ̈ܐ *commentary on the Psalms.*

ܢܘܗܪܢܝܐ, ܢܝܬܐ rt. ܢܗܪ. *shining, splendid, luminous, illuminating.*

ܢܘܓܝܐ see ܢܓܝܐ.

ܢܘܓܝܐ pl. ܓ̈ܝܐ cf. ܢܘܓܐ. m. ναυαγία, *shipwreck, wreck, peril, misfortune, torment.*

ܢܘܕܠܐ rt. ܢܕܠ. m. *disease, misery.*

ܢܘܙ fut. ܢܢܘܙ, act. part. ܢܐܙ *to be restive, plunge, kick.*

ܢܘܙܐ or ܢܘܙܢܐ rt. ܢܘܙ. m. *plunging, kicking, restiveness; frenzy, epilepsy.*

ܢܘܕܠܐ rt. ܢܕܠ. m. *swaying up and down.*

ܢܚ, ܢܘܚ fut. ܢܢܘܚ, infin. ܡܢܚ, imper. ܢܘܚ, act. part. ܢܝܚ, ܢܝܚܐ, part. adj. ܢܝܚ, ܢܝܚܐ, ܢܝܚܬܐ. *to rest, be at rest, stay quiet; to cease, be stayed, assuaged;* ܢܚܘ ܓܠ̈ܠܐ—ܡܥܠܥܠܐ *the billows, the storm, ceased;* ܢܚ ܨܗܘܬܗ—ܪܘܓܙܗ *his thirst, his anger, was assuaged;* ܢܝܚ ܡܢ ܥܡܠܗ *resting from his labour;* ܙܠ ܐܚܘܢ ܘܢܘܚ ܩܠܝܠ *go, our brother, take a little rest.* Part. adj. *quiet, tranquil; gentle, meek; at rest = dead;* ܢܝܚ ܡܢ *preferable, more tolerable, less severe, better;* ܠܨܘܪ ܘܠܨܝܕܢ ܢܗܘܐ ܢܝܚ ܒܝܘܡܐ ܕܕܝܢܐ ܐܘ ܠܟܘܢ *it shall be more tolerable for Tyre and Sidon in the day of judgement than for you;* ܡܝܐ ܢܝܚܐ *still waters;* ܝܡܐ ܢܝܚܐ *a tranquil sea;* ܢܝܚ ܐܢܐ ܘܡܟܝܟ ܐܢܐ ܒܠܒܝ *I am meek and lowly of heart;* ܢܝܚ ܦܓܪܐ *courteous, affable;* ܢܝܚ ܢܦܫܐ *whose soul is at rest, the deceased.* Ethpe. ܐܬܬܢܝܚ rarely ܐܬܢܝܚ *to rest, be at rest, take rest* esp. of sleep and of death; *to refresh oneself; to be quiet, assuaged, satisfied, contented, pleased; to stay* or *stand still, settle down, remain, press heavily* with ܒ or ܥܠ *upon;* with ܡܢ ܟܘܪܗܢܐ *to recover from illness;* ܡܢ ܚܡܬܐ—ܪܘܓܙܐ &c. *to cease from anger;* ܡܢ ܩܪܒܐ *to have rest from war;* ܐܬܬܢܝܚܘ ܡܝܐ *the waters assuaged, subsided;* ܐܬܬܢܝܚܬ ܐܝܕܟ ܥܠܝ *Thy hand presseth me sore;* ܐܬܬܢܝܚ ܫܠܡܐ ܥܠܘܗܝ *he is dead, peace be on him!* ܐܝܠܝܢ ܕܒܛܘܒܐ ܐܬܬܢܝܚܘ *those who are at rest, the blessed dead;* ܥܬܝܩܬܐ ܐܬܬܢܝܚ *old things are at a standstill, have ceased;* ܚܕܐ ܘܡܬܬܢܝܚ *he is glad and content;* ܐܝܟ ܕܢܬܬܢܝܚܘܢ ܡܣ̈ܟܢܐ *that the poor may be relieved;* ܢܬܬܢܝܚ ܡܪܝܐ ܐܠܗܐ ܕܟܠ ܒܬܫܡܫܬܟܘܢ *may God the Lord of all be content with your ministrations.* Pa. ܢܝܚ *to assuage, relieve, give rest* or *pleasure.* Aph. ܐܢܝܚ *a) to give rest, to refresh; to satisfy* or *calm wrath, quiet the spirit; to assuage, relieve, satisfy, content, serve, please, gratify,* with ܨܒܝܢܐ *to content* or *do the will,* cf. ܡܢܝܚ below; ܐܢ ܨܒܐ ܐܢܬ ܕܬܢܝܚ ܨܒܝܢܝ *if thou desire to do my will;* ܡܫܝܚܐ ܢܢܝܚ ܡܫܟܒܟ Christ *give rest to thy death-bed;* ܡܪܝܐ ܢܢܝܚ ܢܦܫܗ *the Lord grant rest to his soul;* ܐܢܝܚ ܐܟܣ̈ܢܝܐ *relieve strangers;* ܡܢܝܚ ܗܘܐ ܠܗܘܢ ܒܠܚܡܐ ܘܒܡܝܐ *he satisfied, refreshed them with bread and water.* *b) to leave, leave off, lay aside, put down;* with ܙܝܢܐ *to lay down arms;* with ܛܥܢܐ *to unlade;* ܐܢܝܚܘ ܡܢܟܘܢ ܕܓܠܘܬܐ *put away falsehood;* ܐܢܝܚ ܠܩܘܠܬܐ ܡܢ ܟܬܦܗ *he put down the waterpot from his shoulders;* ܡܢܝܚܝܢ ܟܐܢ̈ܐ ܠܠܐܘܬܐ ܕܚܫ̈ܐ *the just lay aside the weariness of sufferings.* Act. part. ܡܢܝܚ, ܢܐ, ܢܝܬܐ *pleasing, agreeable; resting, contented, pleased;* ܡܢܝܚ ܠܨܒܝܢܗ ܕܐܠܗܐ *pleasing to God;* ܠܐ ܡܢܝܚܐ ܠܨܒܝܢܗ *unpleasant, disagreeable to him;* ܥܒܕܐ ܛܒܐ ܕܡܢܝܚ ܠܡܪ̈ܘܗܝ *a good servant giving satisfaction to his masters;* ܠܐ ܡܢܝܚܝܢ ܗܘܘ ܒܕܥܒܕ *they were dissatisfied, displeased, with what he had done;* pass. part. ܡܢܚ, ܢܐ, ܢܬܐ *at rest, at ease, contented, gratified, pleased, pleasing, agreeable;* ܨܒܘ̈ܬܐ ܡܢܝܚܬܐ *the pleasant circumstances of those who dwell at ease;* ܡܢܚ ܥܡ ܟܐܢ̈ܐ *living there quietly;* ܡܢܚ ܢܦܫܗ *at rest among the just;* ܡܢܚ ܢܦܫܗ *whose soul is at rest, dead;* ܕܡܢܝܚ ܒܗ ܐܠܗܐ or ܕܡܢܚ *with whom God is content, well-pleased;* ܐܢ ܡܢܚܐ ܠܟ or ܐܢ ܡܢܚܐ ܠܟܘܢ *if it please you;* ܠܐ ܡܢܚ ܗܘܐ *he did not consent, would not;* ܡܘܬܐ ܡܢܚ ܡܢ ܗܠܝܢ ܐܘܠܨܢܐ *death is far preferable to these miseries;* ܗܢܐ ܨܒܘܬܐ ܛܒ ܡܢܚ ܠܟܘܢ *you take great pleasure in, are delighted at, this matter.* Derivatives, ܢܘܚܐ, ܢܝܚܐ, ܢܝܚܘܬܐ, ܢܝܚܐܝܬ, ܡܢܝܚܐ, ܡܢܝܚܘܬܐ, ܡܢܚܐ, ܡܬܬܢܝܚܢܐ, ܡܬܬܢܝܚܢܘܬܐ.

ܢܘܚ *Noah.*

ܢܘܚܐ rt. ܢܘܚ. m. *rest, repose, a resting-place; serenity, calm weather.*

ܢܘܚܝܐ adj. from ܢܘܚ. *of Noah,* ܩܒܘܬܐ ܢܘܚܝܬܐ *Noah's ark.*

ܢܘܚܡܐ, ܢܘܚܡܐ rt. ܢܚܡ. m. *resurrection, raising to life; recovery, revival;* ܢܘܚܡܐ ܓܘܢܝܐ *the general resurrection;* ܢܘܚܡܗ ܕܠܥܙܪ

the raising of Lazarus; metaph. ܐܝܟ ܢܘܚܡܐ ܠܟܢܫܪܘܬܐ as a revival of idolatry.

ܢܘܚܡܬܐ rt. ܢܚܡ. f. resurrection.

ܢܘܚܡܬܐ rt. ܢܚܡ. f. resurrection.

ܢܘܚܪܐ rt. ܢܚܪ. m. snoring.

ܢܘܚܪܬܐ pl. ܬܐ̈ rt. ܢܚܪ. f. the nostrils.

ܢܘܚܫܐ pl. ܐ̈ rt. ܢܚܫ. m. augury, omen.

ܢܘܛܐ pl. ܐ̈ m. ναύτης, a sailor, seaman, mariner.

ܢܘܛܝܐ νοτία, moisture, damp.

ܢܘܛܠܐ pl. ܐ̈ rt. ܢܛܠ. m. doubt, hesitation.

ܢܘܛܦܬܐ pl. ܬܐ̈ rt. ܢܛܦ. f. a drop; dropping; ܢܘܛܦ̈ܐ ܕܡܛܪܐ drops of rain; ܢܘܛܦܬܐ ܕܩܝܩܢܝܬܐ fine drops; ܢܘܛܦܐ ܕܕܡ̈ܥܐ shedding of tears; ܢܘܛܦܐ ܕܒܪܢܫܐ seed of man. Metaph. a drop, a very little; instilling, infusion.

ܢܘܛܪܐ pl. ܐ̈ m. νοτάριος, a notary, public scribe.

ܢܘܛܪ, ܢܘܛܪܐ pl. ܐ̈ rt. ܢܛܪ. m. keeping, custody, saving, preservation; ܢܘܛܪܗ ܕܒܝܬ ܓܙܐ the keeping of the treasury; ܥܠ ܢܘܛܪܐ ܕܣܥܪ̈ܐ about the preservation of barley; ܨܠܘ ܥܠ ܢܘܛܪ ܚܝ̈ܘܗܝ pray that his life may be spared.

ܢܘܝܚܐ rt. ܢܘܚ. m. gentleness, calmness, modesty.

ܢܘܟܦܐ rt. ܢܟܦ. m. decency, decorum, chastity; shame.

ܢܘܟܪܝ, ܢܘܟܪܝܐ, ܢܘܟܪܝܬܐ from ܢܘܟܪ. a) subst. a stranger, foreigner, alien; ܢܘܟܪ̈ܝܐ ܐܢܘܢ ܒܐܪܥܐ they are strangers in the land. b) adj. foreign, strange, unusual, alien, alienated, ܐܪܥܐ ܢܘܟܪܝܬܐ a foreign land; ܠܐ ܢܗܘܐ ܠܟ ܐܠܗܐ ܢܘܟܪܝܐ thou shalt have no strange god; ܟܬܒ̈ܐ ܢܘܟܪ̈ܝܐ profane, ordinary books opp. ecclesiastical; ܠܐ ܐܝܬܝܗ ܢܘܟܪܝܬܐ it is not strange.

ܢܘܟܪܐܝܬ from ܢܘܟܪ. adv. like a stranger; gram. irregularly, abnormally.

ܢܘܟܪܝܘܬܐ from ܢܘܟܪ. f. strangeness, alienation, separation; ܚܕܬܘܬܗ ܘܢܘܟܪܝܘܬܗ its newness and strangeness; ܢܘܟܪܝܘܬ ܬܘܕܝܬܐ heterodoxy; ܢܘܟܪܝܘܬܐ ܕܡܢ ܐܝܩܪܐ deposition from honour.

ܢܘܟܪܝܛܐ pl. ܐ̈ m. ἀναχωρητής, an anchorite.

ܢܘܟܪܝܛܘܬܐ f. the life of an anchorite.

ܢܘܟܪܝܐ from ܢܟܪ. foreign.

ܢܘܟܬܐ, ܢܘܟܬܐ pl. ܬܐ̈ rt. ܢܟܬ. f. a bite, sting of a serpent; ܡܝܬܢܝܬܐ ܗܝ ܢܘܟܬܗ its sting is deadly.

ܢܘܠ root-meaning to suffer pain. Pa. ܢܘܠ to pain, torment, vex esp. with ܟܐܒܐ sickness, disease; pass. part. ܡܢܘܠ, ܡܢܘܠܐ suffering severe pain or long illness, ܩܘ ܡܢܘܠܐ ܝܘܡ̈ܬܐ he remained in pain for some days; ܦܓܪ̈ܐ ܡܢܘܠ̈ܐ ܘܡܟܪ̈ܗܐ sick and suffering bodies; ܠܝ ܕܡܢܘܠ ܒܚܛܗ̈ܐ to me tormented with sins. Ethpa. ܐܬܢܘܠ to suffer disease, hunger, be troubled, buffeted ܒܡܫܘܗ̈ܐ by the waves, ܒܡܣܟܢܘܬܐ in poverty. Derivatives, ܢܘܠܐ, ܢܘܠܢܐ, ܡܢܘܠܢܐ, ܡܢܘܠܢܘܬܐ, ܢܘܠܢܘܬܐ, ܡܢܘܠܘܬܐ.

ܢܘܠ, ܢܘܠܐ m. a) ܢܘܠܐ ܕܡܙܩܪܐ a weaver's beam. b) the web; ܢܘܠܐ ܕܡܛܝ ܠܡܬܦܣܩܘ a web nearly ready to be cut off, nearly finished; ܢܘܠܐ ܕܓܘܣܬܐ a spider's web, cobweb; ܢܘܠ ܚܝ̈ܐ the web of life.

ܢܘܠܢܘܬܐ rt. ܢܘܠ. f. a long illness.

ܢܘܠܢܝܐ from ܢܘܠܐ. adj. woven.

ܢܘܡ, ܢܡ fut. ܢܢܘܡ, act. part. ܢܐܡ, ܢܝܡܐ. to sleep heavily, slumber; ܢܡܘ ܟܠܗܘܢ ܘܕܡܟܘ they all slumbered and slept; ܢܛܘܪ̈ܐ ܢܝܡ̈ܐ slumbering guards. Pa. ܢܘܡ to put to sleep, make slumber. Aph. ܐܢܝܡ same as Pa. Derivatives, ܢܘܡܐ or ܢܘܡܬܐ, ܢܘܡܐ, ܢܘܡܐ, ܢܘܡܬܐ.

ܢܘܡܐ, ܢܘܡܬܐ pl. ܬܐ̈ rt. ܢܘܡ. f. slumber, deep sleep.

ܢܘܡܐ, ܢܘܡܣ or ܢܘܡܐ pl. ܢܘܡ̈ܐ and ܢܘܡܣ f. νομή, a) the spreading of a sore; usually with ܐܟܠ to consume, spread as a sore; metaph. to spread, lay hold, obtain; ܟܡܐܐ ܐܟܠ ܠܒܗܘܢ ܢܘܡܐ grief consumed their heart. b) pasture, territory. c) legal, usufruct; ܢܘܡܣ ܕܡܝ̈ܐ the use of the water; easements, the space to be left between buildings. d) pl. ܢܘܡܣ nummus, a small silver coin.

ܢܘܡܝܩܐ and ܢܘܡܝܩܐ pl. ܐ̈ m. νομικός, a lawyer, a scribe.

ܢܘܡܝܩܝܐ, ܢܘܡܝܩܝܬܐ from the above. relating to the law, about the law.

ܢܳܡܝܼܩܽܘܬܳܐ from ܢܳܡܝܼܩܳܐ f. *the legal profession.*

ܢܽܘܡܺܐܢܺܝܐ or ܢܽܘܡܺܢܝܳܐ *νεομηνία, new moon, the beginning of a lunar month.*

ܢܽܘܡܦܰܐܝܳܐ and ܢܽܘܡܦܳܝܳܐ m. *νυμφαία, nymphaea lotus, the water-lily lotus.*

ܢܽܘܡܶܪܽܘܢ m. *a cohort, column* of an army.

ܢܽܘܢ the letter *Nun.* See ܢܘܢ.

ܢܽܘܢܳܐ pl. ܢܽܘܢܶܐ, ܢܽܘܢܺܝܢ m. *fish;* ܢܽܘܢܰܝ ܝܰܡܳܐ *the fishes of the sea;* ܢܽܘܢܳܐ ܕܡܰܠܺܝܚ *dried fish;* ܢܽܘܢܳܐ ܕܡܶܠܚܳܐ *salt fish;* astron. ܢܽܘܢܶܐ *Pisces;* ܡܰܠܘܳܫܳܐ ܕܢܽܘܢܶܐ *the sign Pisces.*

ܢܽܘܢܽܘܢܳܐ or ܢܽܘܢܺܝܬܳܐ pl. ܶܐ dim. of the above. m. *a little fish.*

ܢܽܘܢܶܣ or ܢܽܘܢܳܐܣ *the nones.*

ܢܽܘܢܳܝܳܐ, ܢܽܘܢܳܝܬܳܐ from ܢܽܘܢ. adj. *belonging to the letter Nun, having the letter Nun;* ܡܶܠܬܳܐ ܢܽܘܢܳܝܬܳܐ *a plural ending in Nun* as ܐܢܳܫܺܝܢ; ܫܡܳܗܶܐ ܢܽܘܢܳܝܶܐ ܥܶܩܳܪܳܝܶܐ *nouns having a radical Nun.*

ܢܳܘܶܣ, ܢܽܘܣ act. part. ܢܳܐܶܣ. *to tremble, fear.*

ܢܰܘܣܳܐ pl. ܶܐ m. *ναός, a temple, shrine* of idol worship; *the sanctuary* of a church, *a chapel, shrine;* ܢܰܘܣܶܐ ܕܣܺܐܡܳܐ *silver shrines;* ܐܰܥܠܽܘܗ̈ܝ ܠܢܰܘܣܳܐ *they brought it into the temple;* ܐܶܬܢܓܶܕ ܦܰܪܣܶܐ ܕܢܰܘܣܳܐ *the curtains of the sanctuary are drawn;* ܢܰܘܣܳܐ ܕܰܟܢܺܝܫܬܳܐ *a mortuary chapel;* metaph. ܩܰܒܪܳܐ ܢܰܘܣܳܐ ܕܦܰܓܪܳܐ *the tomb is the shrine of the body;* ܢܰܘܣܳܐ ܕܟܝܳܐ ܕܪܽܘܚܳܐ a martyr is called *a pure shrine of the Spirit.*

ܢܽܘܣܝܳܐ, ܢܽܘܣܳܝܳܐ rt. ܢܣܐ. m. *trial;* ܢܽܘܣܳܝܳܐ ܕܕܶܝܽܘܬܳܐ *trial of the ink.*

ܢܽܘܣܟ݂ܳܐ pl. ܶܐ Ar. m. *a copy, manuscript, codex.*

ܢܽܘܣܟ݂ܽܘܬܳܐ Ar. f. *transcription.*

ܢܽܘܣܪܳܕܺܝܠ and ܢܽܘܣܪܕܺܝܠ the name of the first Sunday of summer, the seventh Sunday after Pentecost.

ܢܳܦ, ܢܽܘܦ fut. ܢܢܽܘܦ, act. part. ܢܳܐܶܦ. *to bend* or *move towards;* ܠܳܐ ܢܽܘܦ ܢܳܐܶܦ ܠܗܳܟܳܐ ܘܰܠܗܳܟܳܐ *let it not bend, waver, to and fro;* ܒܬܽܘܠܳܬܳܐ ܕܢܳܐܦܳܢ ܠܽܘܬ ܐܽܘܪܚܳܬܳܐ ܕܡܰܝܬܪܽܘܬܳܐ maidens *who incline to ways of virtue.* Ethpe. ܐܶܬܢܺܝܦ *to be shaken down, hurled down, brandished.* Ethpa. ܐܶܬܢܰܝܰܦ *to bend oneself, incline towards.* Aph. ܐܰܢܺܝܦ *to lift up, lay to, move, beckon,* esp. with ܐܺܝܕܳܐ; ܐܰܢܺܝܦ ܐܺܝܕܶܗ ܥܰܠ *he laid his hand to…;* ܡܢܺܝܦ ܗܘܳܐ ܠܗܽܘܢ ܒܐܺܝܕܶܗ *he beckoned to them with the hand;* ܐܰܢܺܝܦ ܐܺܝܕܶܗ ܥܰܠ *to wave the hand against, to menace;* ܐܰܢܺܝܦ ܠܰܟܢܶܫܳܐ *he beckoned to the crowd;* ܡܰܓܠܳܐ ܠܳܐ ܬܰܢܺܝܦ ܥܰܠ ܩܳܡܬܳܐ ܕܚܰܒܪܳܟ *thou shalt not lay a sickle to thy neighbour's standing corn;* ܡܢܺܝܦ ܪܽܘܡܚܳܐ *poising the lance.* Derivatives, ܢܰܘܦܳܐ, ܢܺܝܦܳܐ, ܡܢܺܝܦܽܘܬܳܐ.

ܢܰܘܦܳܐ pl. ܶܐ rt. ܢܘܦ. m. *a) beckoning, signing* esp. with the hand, hence *a sign, intimation;* ܪܽܘܚܳܐ ܪܡܰܙ ܠܶܗ ܢܰܘܦܳܐ ܕܢܺܐܙܰܠ *the spirit signed to him to go;* with ܪܶܥܝܳܢܳܐ or ܬܰܪܥܺܝܬܳܐ *bent* or *inclination of the mind, disposition. b) end;* ܕܡܳܛܶܐ ܢܰܘܦܳܐ *which arrives at an end.*

ܢܽܘܦܚܳܐ pl. ܶܐ rt. ܢܦܚ. m. *a blister, the rising* of a boil; *flatulency; rising, inflation;* ܬܡܳܪܶܐ ܥܳܒܕܺܝܢ ܢܽܘܦܚܳܐ ܘܪܽܘܚܳܐ *dates cause flatulency and wind.*

ܢܰܘܦܩܳܐ m. *pagan sacrifices, the use of anything which has been offered in pagan worship.*

ܢܽܘܦܳܨܳܐ pl. ܶܐ rt. ܢܦܨ. m. *a violent shaking;* med. *a clyster* or *drench; a discharge, evacuation.*

ܢܽܘܦܣܳܐ pl. ܶܐ rt. ܢܦܣ. m. *athletic* or *military exercises;* ܒܶܝܬ ܢܽܘܦܣܳܐ *the gymnasium;* ܕܘܟܬܳܐ ܕܒܶܝܬ ܢܽܘܦܣܳܐ ܕܦܰܪܳܫܶܐ *parade-ground;* usually metaph. *discipline, asceticism.*

ܢܳܨ, ܢܽܘܨ *to shoot, sprout, bud* as plants, leaves or flowers.

ܢܽܘܨܳܐ rt. ܢܨ. m. *shooting, budding, sprouting.*

ܢܽܘܛܳܦܳܐ rt. ܢܛܦ. m. *trickling down, oozing forth.*

ܢܽܘܓܗܳܐ rt. ܢܓܗ. m. *afterglow* opp. ܢܓܗܳܐ *the glimmer of light before dawn.*

ܢܽܘܙܳܕܳܐ rt. ܢܙܕ. m. *soft words, blandishments.*

ܢܽܘܙܳܕܬܳܐ pl. ܳܬܳܐ rt. ܢܙܕ. f. *a) lullaby, soft murmuring, fond words;* ܢܽܘܙܳܕܳܬܳܐ *joyful hymns* opp. ܐܽܘܠܳܝܳܬܳܐ *dirges. b) the chirping, twittering* or *singing of birds.*

ܢܽܘܩܙܳܐ, ܢܽܘܩܳܙܳܐ, ܢܽܘܩܙܬܳܐ pl. ܢܽܘܩܙܶܐ, ܳܬܳܐ rt. ܢܩܙ. f. *a point, puncture, mark* e.g. tattooed on the flesh; ܢܽܘܩܙܬܳܐ ܕܙܰܒܢܳܐ *a point of time;* ܣܪܳܛܳܐ ܬܪܺܝܨܳܐ ܐܰܩܦܳܣ ܡܶܢ ܢܽܘܩܙܶܐ a straight line is the shortest *between two points; a drop;* gram. *points.*

ܢܘܩܙܐ pl. ܐ̈ rt. ܢܩܙ. m. *a*) *a grammatical point;* the plural is denoted by ܢܘܩܙ̈ܐ *points* i.e. ܣܝܡܐ *Siami* or Ribbui; ܢܘܩܙܐ ܦܣܘܩܐ *a dividing point* i.e. dividing one phrase or paragraph from another; ܢܘܩܙܐ ܣܘܣܩܡܐ *a point in red ink* or *minium; vowel-points. b*) = ܢܩܙܐ *a beak, bill.*

ܢܘܩܙܬܐ, ܢܘܩܙ̈ܬܐ rt. ܢܩܙ. f. *a point;* ܡܨܥܝܘܬܐ ܢܘܩܙ̈ܬܐ ܕܟܠ ܟܪܟܐ *the centre i.e. the point in the middle;* ܢܘܩܙܬܐ ܕܙܒܢܐ *a moment of time, an instant.*

ܢܘܩܙܢܝܐ, ܢܝܬܐ rt. ܢܩܙ. gram. *expressed by points.*

ܢܘܩܣܐ pl. ܐ̈ rt. ܢܩܣ. m. *a libation, drink-offering;* ܕܒ̈ܚܐ ܘܢܘܩܣ̈ܐ *sacrifices and drink-offerings;* ܢܘܩܣ̈ܐ ܕܨܠܡ̈ܐ ܚܪ̈ܫܐ *libations to dumb images;* esp. *eucharistic wine and water,* ܠܚܡܐ ܘܢܘܩܣܐ *the bread and wine.*

ܢܘܩܠܪܐ ναύκληρος, *a ship-owner, ship-master.*

ܢܘܩܦܐ pl. ܐ̈ rt. ܢܩܦ. m. pl. *carnal ties;* gram. *a suffix.*

ܢܘܩܪܐ rt. ܢܩܪ. m. *a hole, cavity.*

ܢܘܩܫܐ pl. ܐ̈ rt. ܢܩܫ. m. *a*) *investigation, trying. b*) *throbbing,* ܢܘܩܫ̈ܐ ܕܡܟܝܫܘܬܐ *the throbs of disease.*

ܢܘܪ fut. ܢܢܘܪ, act. part. ܢܐܪ, ܢܐܪܐ, pass. part. ܢܝܪ, ܢܝܪܐ. *to shy at, be shy of, plunge, bolt;* ܓܡܠܝܗܘܢ ܡܢܗܘܢ ܢܘܪܝܢ ܡܢ ܟܠ ܚܙܘܐ ܢܘܟܪܝܐ *their camels shy at every strange sight;* metaph. ܢܐܪ ܡܢ ܡܫܘܚܠܦܘܬܐ ܕܒܢܝ̈ܢܫܐ *he is shy of, flees from, human intercourse.* Pa. ܢܘܪ same as Peal. Derivative, ܢܘܪܐ.

ܢܘܪ Pa. ܢܘܪ *to set light, kindle.* Ethpa. *a*) ܐܬܢܘܪ *to be set light to, kindled. b*) ܐܬܢܘܪ *to be ignited, inflamed, illuminated;* ܡܬܢܘܪܝܢ ܘܡܫܠܗܒܝܢ *flaming and blazing.* Derivatives, ܢܘܪܐ, ܢܘܪܐ, ܢܘܪܢܐ, ܢܘܪܢܝܘܬܐ, ܢܘܪܢܝܐ, ܢܘܪܝܘܬܐ, ܢܘܪܐ, ܡܢܪܬܐ.

ܢܘܪ, ܢܘܪܐ pl. ܢܘܪ̈ܘܬܐ rt. ܢܘܪ. f. *fire;* ܢܘܪ ܝܩܕܐ *burning fire;* ܒܝܬ ܢܘܪܐ *a fire-place, a beacon;* ܟܐܦܐ ܕܢܘܪܐ *pyrites;* ܢܘܪܐ ܕܐܣܛܘܡܟܐ *the heat of the stomach;* pl. *volcanoes.* Metaph. ܢܘܪ ܛܢܢܐ *the fire of zeal;* ܢܘܪܐ ܕܚܣܡܐ *the fire of envy;* ܦܠܓܘܢ ܢܘܪܐ *the fiery companies = Seraphim;* ܡܕ̈ܥܐ ܕܢܘܪܐ *fiery intelligences = Seraphim.*

ܢܘܪܐ or ܢܘܪܐ rt. ܢܘܪ. m. *a mirror.*

ܢܘܪܐ rt. ܢܘܪ m. *shying, starting* as a horse, *fright.*

ܢܘܪܒܐ pl. ܐ̈ m. *a sucker, shoot, offset, scion.*

ܢܘܪܢܐ, ܢܝܬܐ pl. ܐ̈ rt. ܢܘܪ. *fiery;* ܠܗܓ̈ܐ ܢܘܪܢ̈ܐ *fiery vapours;* ܣܦܣܪܐ ܢܘܪܢܝܬܐ *a fiery sword;* esp. of the angels ܢܘܪ̈ܢܐ ܘܪܘܚ̈ܢܐ *seraphs and cherubs;* ܛܟܣ̈ܐ ܕܢܘܪ̈ܢܐ *the seraphic ranks.*

ܢܘܪ̈ܢܐ pl. m. rt. ܢܘܪ. *white pepper.*

ܢܘܪܢܝܘܬܐ rt. ܢܘܪ. f. *igneous nature, inflammability.*

ܢܘܪܢܝܐ, ܢܝܬܐ rt. ܢܘܪ. *a*) *igneous, fiery;* ܥܡܘ̈ܕܐ ܢܘܪ̈ܢܝܐ *fiery pillars;* ܐܣܪܐ ܢܘܪܢܝܬܐ *the zone of fire. b*) geomet. *a pyramid.*

ܢܘܪܢܝܘܬܐ rt. ܢܘܪ. f. *igneousness, igneous nature.*

ܢܘܪܐ and ܢܘܪܐ pl. ܐ̈ rt. ܢܘܪ. f. *hay; a flower* perh. *a ranunculus; arsenic.*

ܢܘܫܓܐ rt. ܢܫܓ. m. *flaying, skinning.*

ܢܘܫܦܐ rt. ܢܫܦ. m. *a*) *the cleansing* of corn. *b*) *a sort of snake.*

ܢܘܫܩܬܐ pl. ܐ̈ rt. ܢܫܩ. f. *a kiss.*

ܢܘܬܐ impers. with ܠ and pron. suff. ܢܘܬܐ ܠܝ *it displeases, disgusts me.*

ܢܘܬܠܐ rt. ܢܬܠ. m. *the turning of the scale, weighing down of the scale.*

ܢܘܬܦܐ pl. ܐ̈ rt. ܢܬܦ. m. *attraction, distraction* of the mind; ܢܘܬܦ̈ܐ ܡܣܟܢ̈ܐ ܕܥܠܡܐ ܗܢܐ *the perilous attractions of this world;* ܢܘܬܦ ܡܘܫܚܠܦ ܪܥܝ̈ܢܐ *the distraction of varying opinions.*

ܢܘܬܦ, ܢܘܬܦܐ pl. ܐ̈ rt. ܢܬܦ. m. *tearing to pieces;* metaph. ܢܘܬܦ ܒܣܪܗܘܢ *the tearing of their flesh = calumnious detraction;* ܟܬܒܐ ܕܢܘܬܦ̈ܐ *a book of excerpts.*

ܢܙܘܪܐ rt. ܢܙܪ. m. *continence.*

ܢܙܝܪ, ܢܙܝܪܐ rt. ܢܙܪ. *a Nazirite,* a man separated from wine, &c., see Num. vi; hence, *abstinent, celibate, ascetic, a monk.*

ܢܙܝܪܐܝܬ rt. ܢܙܪ. adv. *like a Nazirite, ascetically.*

ܢܙܝܪܘܬܐ rt. ܢܙܪ. f. *Naziriteship;* ܣܥܪܐ ܕܢܙܝܪܘܬܗ *the hair of his separation* under the vow of a Nazirite; ܢܙܝܪܘܬܗ ܕܫܡܫܘܢ *the Naziritehood of Samson;* hence *abstinence, continence, chastity, the ascetic life;* ܢܙܝܪܘܬܗܘܢ ܕܡܢ ܒܣܪܐ *their abstinence from flesh;* ܨܘܡܐ ܘܢܙܝܪܘܬܐ ܘܫܗܪܐ *fasting and abstinence and vigils;* ܢܙܝܪܘܬܐ ܕܚܙܬܗ̇ *the modesty of her look.*

ܢܓܠ fut. ܢܢܓܘܠ, act. part. ܢܓܠ, ܢܓܠܐ, pass. part. ܢܓܝܠ, ܠܐ, ܠܬܐ. *to bend, turn, turn* the balance, *preponderate.* Pa. ܢܓܠ *to sway, hang down, swing; to lead down, make go* or *hang down;* ܢܓܠܬ ܘܫܕܬ ܦܬܟܪܐ *she shook off and cast away idols;* ܗܘܘ ܡܢܓܠܝܢ ܦܘܪܥܝܗܘܢ *they let their locks hang down.* Derivatives, ܡܢܓܠܢܐ, ܡܢܓܠܐ, ܢܓܠܐ, ܢܘܓܠܐ.

ܢܓܠܐ rt. ܢܓܠ. m. *swaying, dipping* of the balance, *turning* of the scale; ܐܬܩܠܬ ܐܢܘܢ ܒܢܓܠܐ ܕܡܐܙܢܝܟ *she weighed them in the poising of thy balance;* ܢܓܠܐ ܕܪܥܝܢܐ *vacillation;* ܫܘܝܐ ܢܓܠܐ *equal poise, equality;* ܫܘܐ ܒܢܓܠܐ *equal in the scales, of equal weight* usually metaph. *exactly equal.*

ܢܙܪ fut. ܢܢܙܘܪ, parts. ܢܙܪ, ܢܙܝܪ. *to separate, to be continent, to abstain* often with ܢܦܫܗ; ܢܙܪ ܢܦܫܗ ܡܢ ܠܚܡܐ *he abstained from bread;* ܢܙܪ ܕܩܢܗ ܐܝܟ ܢܙܝܪܐ *he let his beard grow* as a Nazirite. Ethpe. ܐܬܢܙܪ and Ethpa. ܐܬܢܙܪ *to separate oneself, to lead a life of abstinence, of continence, to abstain;* ܐܬܢܙܪܘ ܠܒܗܬܬܐ *they separated themselves unto the shameful thing;* ܡܬܢܙܪܢܐ *abstinent.* Pa. ܢܙܪ *to cause to abstain, to consecrate to be a Nazirite.* Derivatives, ܢܙܘܪܐ, ܢܙܝܪܐ, ܢܙܝܪܬܐ, ܢܙܝܪܘܬܐ.

ܢܚܠ fut. ܢܢܚܘܠ, act. part. ܢܚܠ, ܢܚܠܐ, pass. part. ܢܚܝܠ, ܠܐ, ܠܬܐ. *to grow lean, waste;* ܢܚܠܘ ܣܘܣܘܬܐ *the horses grew lean;* ܦܓܪܐ ܢܚܝܠ *a wasting body.* Pa. ܢܚܠ *to emaciate, make lean.* Derivatives, ܢܚܝܠܐ, ܢܚܠܐ, ܢܚܝܠܘܬܐ, ܢܚܘܠܘܬܐ, ܢܚܘܠܐ.

ܢܚܝܠ, ܢܚܝܠܐ rt. ܢܚܠ. *lean, meagre, dried up, squalid;* ܢܦܫܢ ܢܚܝܠܐ *our soul is dried up;* ܦܬܘܪܐ ܢܚܝܠܐ *a meagre table.*

ܢܚܠܐ rt. ܢܚܠ. m. *the scab, scurvy; weakness.*

ܢܚܝܠܘܬܐ rt. ܢܚܠ. f. *thinness, wasting, emaciation; squalor.*

ܢܚܘܠ, ܢܚܘܠܐ, ܢܚܘܠܬܐ rt. ܢܚܠ. adj. *dried up, thin, emaciated, meagre;* ܢܚܘܠܐ ܡܢ ܨܘܡܐ ܐܡܝܢܐ *emaciated from constant fasting;* ܡܐܟܘܠܬܐ ܢܚܘܠܬܐ *meagre food.*

ܢܚܘܠܘܬܐ rt. ܢܚܠ. f. *thinness, emaciation; drying up* and *roughness* of the skin.

ܢܚܪ fut. ܢܢܚܘܪ, act. part. ܢܚܪ, ܢܚܪܐ. *to snore.* Pa. ܢܚܪ the same. Derivatives, ܢܚܪܐ, ܡܢܚܪܢܐ.

ܢܚܪܐ pl. ܢܚܪ̈ܐ rt. ܢܚܪ. m. *a snore.*

ܢܚܝܪܐ pl. ܐ̈ rt. ܢܚܪ. m. *the nose, nostrils; nozzle* of a lamp; *the flange* of folding-doors.

ܢܚܠ fut. ܢܢܚܘܠ, imper. ܢܚܘܠ, act. part. ܢܚܠ, ܢܚܠܐ, pass. part. ܢܚܝܠ, ܠܐ, ܠܬܐ. *to sift, pass through a sieve;* metaph. *to rain, snow;* ܢܗܘܐ ܒܢܚܝܠܘ ܩܠܝܠܐܝܬ *it should be sifted fine;* ܩܡܚܐ ܠܐ ܢܚܝܠܐ ܕܣܥܪܐ *unsifted barley meal.* Ethpe. ܐܬܢܚܠ *to be sifted;* metaph. ܡܬܢܚܠܝܢ ܒܐܘܠܨܢܐ *sifted by tribulation.* Pa. ܢܚܠ *to sift; to make descend.* Derivative, ܡܢܚܠܬܐ.

ܢܚܠ, ܢܚܠܐ pl. ܠ̈ܐ m. *a torrent, the dry bed* of a torrent, *a gorge, valley;* ܢܚܠܐ ܠܐ ܡܬܥܒܪܢܐ *an impassable torrent;* ܢܚܠܐ ܕܕܡܐ *a torrent of blood;* ܢܚܠܐ ܕܒܪ ܗܢܘܡ *the valley of the son of Hinnom;* ܢܚܠܐ ܕܩܝܫܘܢ *the valley of Kishon.*

ܢܚܡ Pa. ܢܚܡ *to raise* the dead, *raise* to life, *resuscitate;* ܢܚܡ ܡܝ̈ܬܐ *he raised the dead.* Ethpa. ܐܬܢܚܡ *to be raised, to be revived, to be awaked;* ܗܢܘܢ ܕܐܬܢܚܡܘ ܒܚܝܠܗ ܕܡܫܝܚܐ *those who are raised to life by the power of Christ;* ܐܬܢܚܡܢ ܡܢ ܫܢܬܐ ܕܡܨܝܪܐ ܡܘܬܐ *we are roused from sleep which typifies death.* Aph. ܐܢܚܡ same as Pael. Derivatives, ܢܘܚܡܐ, ܢܘܚܡܬܐ, ܡܢܚܡܢܐ, ܢܚܡܬܐ, ܢܘܚܡܬܐ, ܡܢܚܡܢܘܬܐ.

ܢܚܡܬܢܐ m. *a dreamer.*

ܢܚܡܬܐ rt. ܢܚܡ. f. *resurrection.*

ܢܚܡܝܬܐ pl. ܬ̈ܐ f. *the tonsils.*

ܢܚܦ cf. ܚܦܝ. Aph. ܐܢܚܦ *to be unshod, barefoot; to be weary;* ܐܢܚܦ ܠܐ ܪ̈ܓܠܝܟ *thy feet did not go bare.*

ܢܚܪ fut. ܢܢܚܪ, act. part. ܢܚܪ, ܢܚܪܐ. *to breathe heavily* as from illness, *to snore.* Derivatives, ܢܚܪܐ, ܢܘܚܪܐ, ܢܚܝܪܐ.

ܢܚܪܐ rt. ܢܚܪ. m. *heavy* or *stertorous breathing* as in illness.

ܢܚܫ fut. ܢܢܚܘܫ, act. part. ܢܚܫ. *to whisper, mutter, divine.* Pa. ܢܚܫ *to practise augury* or *divination, to divine;* ܕܢܢܚܫ ܒܦܪ̈ܚܬܐ *to augur by birds.* Ethpa. ܐܬܢܚܫ *to be affected* or *influenced by divination.* Derivatives, ܢܘܚܫܐ, ܢܚܫܐ, ܢܚܫܐ, ܢܚܫܐ, ܡܢܚܫܢܐ.

ܢܚܫܐ pl. ܐ̈ m. *a*) rt. ܢܚܫ. *an augur. b*) *a worker in brass.*

ܢܚܫܐ pl. ܐ̈ rt. ܢܚܫ. m. *augury, divination* esp. by birds.

ܢܚܫܐ pl. ܐ̈ rt. ܢܚܫ. m. *an augur, diviner.*

ܢܚܫܐ m. *brass;* ܢܚܫܐ ܩܘܪܢܬܝܐ *Corinthian brass.*

ܢܚܫܝܐ, ܢܚܫܝܬܐ *brazen;* ܢܚܫܝܐ ܚܘܕܪܐ *brazen circles.*

ܢܚܫܝܪܐ pl. ܐ̈ Pers. m. *a*) *hunting, the chase; a battue, slaughter;* with ܥܒܕ *to hunt. b*) *a hunter, a strong man.*

ܢܚܫܝܪܘܬܐ and ܢܚܫܝܪܘܬܐ from ܢܚܫܝܪܐ. f. *hunting;* metaph. *endurance, fortitude.*

ܢܚܫܝܪܬܢܐ and ܢܚܫܝܪܬܢܐ pl. ܐ̈ from ܢܚܫܝܪܐ. m. *a hunter, warrior; strong, enduring, warlike;* ܢܚܫܝܪܬܢܐ ܓܢܒܪܐ *a mighty hunter;* ܢܚܫܝܪܬܢܐ ܒܣܗܕܐ *brave among the martyrs.*

ܢܚܫܝܪܬܢܐܝܬ from ܢܚܫܝܪܐ. adv. *bravely, with endurance.*

ܢܚܫܝܪܬܢܘܬܐ from ܢܚܫܝܪܐ. f. *hunting, the chase; courage, fortitude.*

ܢܚܬ fut. ܢܚܘܬ, imper. ܚܘܬ, act. part. ܢܚܬ, ܢܚܬܐ, part. adj. ܢܚܝܬ, ܢܚܝܬܐ, ܢܚܝܬܬܐ, opp. ܣܠܩ, *to go down, descend; to dismount, alight, get off, get down* from a horse, carriage, &c.; *to sink, fall* as a river, rain, &c.; *to descend from* by birth; ܢܚܬܝ ܝܡܐ *they who go down to the sea, sailors;* ܢܚܬܝ ܥܦܪܐ, ܢܚܬܝ ܓܘܒܐ *they that go down to the dust, to the pit;* ܢܚܬ ܠܦܩܥܬܐ *he went down to the open country;* ܢܚܬ ܥܠ ܐܢܛܝܘܟܝ *he marched against Antioch, went down to besiege Antioch;* ܡܢ ܢܚܬܝ ܕܡܥܘܗܝ *with falling tears;* ܡܪܝܡ—ܡܢ ܕܘܝܕ ܢܚܬܐ *Mary—descended from David;* ܢܚܬܝܢ ܗܘܘ *they went down;* ܢܚܝܬ ܓܢܣܐ *of plebeian descent.* Ethpe. ܐܬܢܚܬ *to be brought down, taken down.* Pael ܢܚܬ *to bring down; to lower, abase.* Ethpa. ܐܬܢܚܬ *to go down; to lower oneself, stoop, descend, humiliate oneself;* ܡܫܝܚܐ ܕܐܬܢܚܬ ܠܘܬ ܡܚܝܠܘܬܗܘܢ Christ *stooping to their weakness.* Aph. ܐܚܬ *to cause to come down, to send down, bring down, take down, cast down;* ܐܚܬ ܡܛܪܐ *He sent down rain;* with ܕܡܥܐ *to let tears fall;* ܐܚܬܘܗܝ ܠܡܫܟܢܐ *they took the tabernacle down;* ܡܚܬ ܢܦܫܗ ܡܢ *he claims descent from.* Derivatives, ܢܚܬܐ, ܢܚܬܘܬܐ, ܢܚܬܐ, ܡܢܚܬܐ, ܡܢܚܬܘܬܐ, ܡܬܢܚܬܢܐ, ܡܬܢܚܬܢܘܬܐ, ܡܬܢܚܬܢܐܝܬ, ܡܬܢܚܬܢܘܬܐ.

ܢܚܬܐ pl. ܐ̈ rt. ܢܚܬ. m. *a long outer garment* reaching to the feet; ܢܚܬܐ ܒܠܝܐ *a worn-out coat;* ܢܚܬܐ ܕܡܫܬܘܬܐ *wedding garments.*

ܢܚܬܘܡܐ pl. ܐ̈ m. *a baker.*

ܢܚܬܘܡܘܬܐ f. *baking.*

ܢܚܬܘܪܐ m. *a wooden mallet.*

ܢܚܬܘܬܐ rt. ܢܚܬ. f. *lowness, baseness; descent.*

ܢܛܐ act. part. ܢܐܛܐ, ܢܛܝܐ *to be damp.* Derivatives, ܢܛܝܐ, ܢܛܘܬܐ, ܢܛܝܬܐ.

ܢܛܘܦܐ or ܢܛܘܦܐ pl. ܐ̈ *unclean, foul; weak, lazy.*

ܢܛܘܠܐ, ܢܛܘܠܬܐ rt. ܢܛܠ. *a drawer* of water; *dewy, moist.*

ܢܛܘܠܘܬܐ and ܢܛܘܠܘܬܐ rt. ܢܛܠ. f. *moisture; pouring, sprinkling, wetting.*

ܢܛܘܦܬܐ usually ܢܛܘܦܬܐ rt. ܢܛܦ. f. *a drop.*

ܢܛܘܪܐ pl. ܐ̈ rt. ܢܛܪ. m. *a*) *a keeper, guard, watch, watchman, warder;* pl. *a guard, garrison;* ܢܛܘܪܐ ܕܦܘܩܕܢܐ *they who keep* God's *commandments;* ܢܛܘܪܐ ܕܩܢܘܢܐ *they who observe the canons;* ܡܪܝܐ ܗܘ ܢܛܘܪܟ *the Lord Himself is thy keeper;* ܡܓܕܠ ܢܛܘܪܐ *the tower of the watchmen. b*) *a vine shoot with two buds.*

ܢܛܘܪܘܬܐ pl. ܬܐ̈ rt. ܢܛܪ. f. *keeping, observance; a custom, rite, rule; a watch, vigil; guard, ward; protection;* astron. *observation;* ܢܛܘܪܘܬܐ ܕܠܫܢܐ *the keeping, bridling, of the tongue;* ܢܛܘܪܘܬܐ ܕܚܕܒܫܒܐ *the keeping* or *observance of Sunday;* ܢܛܘܪܘܬܐ ܕܚܕܒܫܒܐ ܘܕܥܪܘܒܬܐ *the observances* or *rites of Sundays and Fridays;* ܒܝܬ ܢܛܘܪܘܬܐ *a guard-house, prison;* ܒܝܬ ܢܛܘܪܘܬܐ ܕܟܬܒܐ *archives.*

ܢܛܘܪܢܐ rt. ܢܛܪ. m. *observance.*

ܢܛܪܬܐ pl. ܬܐ̈ rt. ܢܛܪ. f. *keeping, observance, precept, charge; ward, custody, a prison;* ܒܝܬ ܢܛܪܬܐ *guard-house, prison;* ܒܢܛܪܬܐ ܘܒܐܣܘܪܐ ܐܬܚܒܫ he was *confined under ward and in bonds;* ܢܛܪܬܐ ܟܝܢܝܬܐ *observance of natural law.*

ܢܛܫ act. part. ܢܐܛܫ, ܢܛܫܐ. *to glitter, shine;*

to spread, strike upon, be diffused, shed upon; to fall upon as rays of light; ܐܝܟ ܕܡܢ ܡܫܡܫܐ ܟܕ ܢܛܫܝܢ ܥܠ ܡܢܘܬܐ ܐܐܪܢܝܬܐ *the sun's rays striking upon aerial particles;* ܢܘܗܪܐ ܕܣܗܪܐ ܥܠ ܥܢܢܐ ܕܚܕܪܝܗ ܢܛܫ *the light of the moon is diffused over the clouds around its orb;* metaph. ܓܠܝܢܐ ܕܥܠܝܗܘܢ ܢܛܫܝܢ *the revelations which shine upon them.* PA. ܢܛܫ *to glitter.* ETHPA. ܐܬܢܛܫ *to shine brightly.* DERIVATIVE, ܢܛܝܫܐ.

ܢܛܝܫܐ, ܢܛܫܐ or ܢܛܫܐ pl. ܐ̈ rt. ܢܛܫ. m. *glittering, coruscation, brilliancy;* ܙܠܝܩܐ ܕܡܚܒܠܝܢ ܢܛܝܫܘܬܗܘܢ rays *which mutually destroy each other's brilliancy.*

ܢܛܘܒܐ rt. ܢܛܒ. m. *moisture.*

ܢܛܘܒܘܬܐ rt. ܢܛܒ. f. *moisture; lasciviousness.*

ܢܛܝܠܐܝܬ rt. ܢܛܠ. adv. *heavily; doubtfully, hardly.*

ܢܛܝܠܘܬܐ or ܢܛܝܠܘܬܐ rt. ܢܛܠ. f. *heaviness, weight; weighing, pondering; the drawing* of water.

ܢܛܝܒܐ rt. ܢܛܒ. m. *dampness.*

ܢܛܝܪܐܝܬ rt. ܢܛܪ. adv. *cautiously.*

ܢܛܝܪܘܬܐ rt. ܢܛܪ. f. *a) preservation, safe-keeping, safety, length of life. b) observance* ܕܢܡܘܣܐ *of the law; care, circumspection,* ܠܡܢܐ ܗܘܬ ܟܠܗ ܗܕܐ ܢܛܝܪܘܬܐ *to what end was all this care? c)* astron. *an observation. d) abstinence, continence.*

ܢܛܠ fut. ܢܛܘܠ, act. part. ܢܛܠ, ܢܛܠܐ. *a) to turn the scale, weigh heavy, be weighty;* ܢܛܠܘ ܡܥܘܢܝܗ ܕܐܪܡܠܬܐ *the widow's mites weighed heavy in the scales. b) to draw* water. Part. adj. ܢܛܝܠ and ܢܛܝܠ, ܠܐ, ܠܬܐ *weighty, ponderous; heavy, hesitating, divided; diuretic.* ETHPE. ܐܬܢܛܠ *to be weighty.* PA. ܢܛܠ *to make heavy, lay a burden upon.* The APHEL future of the verb ܢܛܠ has the same form. ETHPA. ܐܬܢܛܠ *to be weighed* in the mind, *be pondered over, doubtful.* DERIVATIVES, ܢܛܠܐ, ܢܛܘܠܐ, ܢܛܝܠܘܬܐ, ܢܛܝܠܐܝܬ, ܢܛܝܠܘܬܐ, ܢܛܠܐ, ܢܛܠܐ, ܡܢܛܠܐ, ܡܢܛܠܢܐ.

ܢܛܠܐ or ܢܛܠܐ rt. ܢܛܠ. m. *a measure* of weight $= 1\frac{1}{2}$ oz. or *one spoonful; a spoon, ladle.*

ܢܛܠܐ rt. ܢܛܠ. m. *drawing* of water, *pouring* of water over the head, body, and feet = *a shower-bath.*

ܢܛܦ fut. ܢܛܘܦ and ܢܛܦ, act. part. ܢܛܦ, ܢܛܦܐ. *to drop, flow in drops;* ܨܒܥܬܝ ܡܘܪܐ ܢܛܦ *my fingers dropped myrrh;* metaph. *to flow in, be instilled, insinuated;* ܠܐ ܢܛܦ ܒܝ ܨܢܐ ܣܪܝܩܐ *vain care did not creep into me.* PA. ܢܛܦ *to drop down abundantly.* ETHPA. ܐܬܢܛܦ *to fall in drops.* APH. ܐܛܦ *to drop, cause to drop, let fall in drops; to drop* or *lay salve* on a wound; *to distil, instil.* DERIVATIVES, ܢܛܘܦܬܐ, ܢܛܦܐ, ܢܛܘܦܬܐ, ܢܛܘܦܐ, ܡܛܘܦܬܐ, ܡܛܘܦܬܐ, ܡܛܦܬܐ, ܡܛܦܢܘܬܐ.

ܢܛܦܐ rt. ܢܛܦ. m. *a drop.*

ܢܛܘܦܬܐ and ܢܛܘܦܬܐ rt. ܢܛܦ. f. *a) stacte, oil of myrrh. b) resin, gum. c) mallow, malva officinalis* or *althea ficifolia.*

ܢܛܪ fut. ܢܛܪ rarely ܢܛܘܪ, imper. ܛܪ and ܛܘܪ, act. part. ܢܛܪ, ܢܛܪܐ, pass. part. ܢܛܝܪ, ܐ, ܬܐ. *a) to guard, watch, keep;* with ܡܛܪܬܐ or ܢܛܘܪܘܬܐ *to keep watch* or *ward;* ܐܛܪ ܦܘܡܝ ܡܢ ܒܝܫܬܐ *I will keep my mouth from evil;* ܛܪ ܠܫܢܟ *keep thy tongue. b) to keep, observe* a covenant, command, law; ܐܢܬ ܩܝܡܝ ܛܪ *do thou keep my covenant;* ܕܐܛܪ ܢܡܘܣܟ *that I may keep thy law;* ܢܛܪ ܫܬܩܐ *he kept silence;* with ܕܘܟܬܗ *to fill the place, assume the duty* or *office* of another. *c) to keep, retain, preserve, keep* in memory; ܠܐ ܬܛܪ ܒܥܠܕܒܒܘܬܐ *thou shalt not bear a grudge, keep enmity;* ܓܙܐ ܕܢܛܪܘ ܐܒܗܝܟ *the treasure which thy fathers laid up. d) to observe, take heed, watch, spy;* ܐܛܪ ܐܘܪܚܝ *I will take heed to my way;* ܢܛܪܘ ܘܐܫܟܚܘܗܝ ܠܕܢܝܐܝܠ ܟܕ ܒܥܐ *they watched and found Daniel making petition.* Act. part. *a keeper, guard, warder, custodian;* ܢܛܪ ܒܝܬ ܐܣܝܪܐ *a prison warder;* ܢܛܪ ܓܙܐ or ܒܝܬ ܓܙܐ *a treasurer, custodian of the treasury;* ܢܛܪ ܕܘܟܬܗ *a deputy, proxy, substitute; a successor;* ܢܛܪ ܓܪܒܝܐ the constellation *Arcturus* or *the Great Bear;* also *the polar regions;* ܢܛܪ ܡܐܢܐ *keeper of the wardrobe; a squire;* ܢܛܪ ܥܢܐ *keeper of sheep* = name of a star; ܢܛܪ ܟܡܐܢܐ *a spy;* ܢܛܪܝ ܦܓܪܐ *the body-guard;* ܢܛܪ ܦܪܘܣܘܦܐ same as ܢܛܪ ܕܘܟܬܗ; ܢܛܪ ܬܪܥܐ *the door-keeper, porter.* Pass. part. *a) guarded, kept, preserved, safe;* ܢܛܝܪ ܚܝܐ *whose life may God preserve. b) kept in memory, observed. c) laid by, stored, reserved.*

d) *watchful; abstinent, fasting.* Ethpe. ܐܬܢܛܪ *to be guarded, kept, observed, preserved, retained; to keep oneself* or *abstain* from food, *to be kept* or *remain.* Pa. ܢܛܪ *to keep* or *take as one's own; to keep safe, take care of, guard; to observe, keep* a commandment; *to leave unhurt, spare;* ܪ̈ܓܠܐ ܕܚܣܝܕܘܗܝ ܢܛܪ *He will keep the feet of His saints;* ܢܛܪܝܢܝ ܐܝܟ ܒܒܬܐ ܕܥܝܢܐ *keep me as the apple of the eye;* ܢܘܪܐ ܠܟܪ̈ܡܐ ܢܛܪܬ ܗܘܬ *the fire spared the vineyards.* Aph. ܐܛܪ *to put in a safe place, lay by, preserve;* ܡܛܪ ܢܦܫܐ ܠܡܣܘܒܪܘܬܐ *enough to preserve life;* ܐܟܠܘ ܒܟܝܠܐ ܡܛܪ ܢܦܫܐ *they ate by measure enough to preserve life.* Derivatives, ܢܛܘܪܐ, ܢܛܘܪ, ܢܛܘܪܘܬܐ, ܢܛܘܪܬܐ, ܢܛܘܪܬܐ, ܢܛܝܪܘܬܐ, ܢܛܪܐ, ܢܛܪܘܬܐ, ܡܢܛܪܢܘܬܐ, ܡܛܪܬܐ, ܡܛܪܢܘܬܐ, ܡܢܛܪܢܐ.

ܢܛܪܐ *a guard;* see ܢܛܪ act. part.

ܢܛܪܐ rt. ܢܛܪ. m. *keeping* of the law; *care, custody; a portion reserved.*

ܢܝ same as ܢܐ.

ܢܝܒܐ pl. ܐ̈ m. *a molar* or *a canine tooth, a tusk; crabs' claws.*

ܢܝܒܝ *the baggy part of drawers* or *breeches.*

ܢܝܒܢܐ *having tusks.*

ܢܝܕܐ rt. ܢܘܕ. m. *shaking, trembling;* ܢܝܕܐ ܕܪܝܫܐ *a shake of the head;* ܢܝܕܐ ܕܐܪܥܐ *an earthquake.*

ܢܝܡܐ, ܢܝܡܬܐ rt. ܢܘܡ. *slumbering.*

ܢܝܙܟܐ pl. ܐ̈ m. *a lance, spear, javelin;* ܩܢܝܐ ܕܢܝܙܟܐ *the staff of a spear;* ܚܢܝܐ ܕܢܝܙܟܐ *a spear-head;* ܐܚܝܕܝ ܢܝܙ̈ܟܐ *spearmen;* astron. *shooting stars, meteors.*

ܢܝܙܟܘܢܐ dim. of ܢܝܙܟܐ. m. *a short lance, a dart.*

ܢܝܙܪܐ m. *a sabre, scimitar.*

ܢܝܚ, ܢܝܚܐ pl. ܐ̈ rt. ܢܘܚ. m. a) *rest, calm, quiet;* ܝܘܡܐ ܕܢܝܚܐ *Sabbath, a day of rest;* ܘܬܫܟܚܘܢ ܢܝܚܐ ܠܢܦܫܬܟܘܢ *and ye shall find rest to your souls;* ܓܒܪܐ ܕܢܝܚܐ *a man of peace.* b) *appeasing, satisfaction;* ܢܝܚܐ ܕܪ̈ܓܫܐ *satisfaction of the senses;* ܠܡܢܝܚܘ ܪܘܓܙܗ *to appease his anger.* c) *will, pleasure;* ܠܡܥܒܕ ܢܝܚܗ *to do his will;* ܐܝܟ ܢܝܚܗܘܢ *according to their pleasure.* d) *ease, refreshment, pleasure, enjoyment;* ܢܝܚ̈ܐ ܦܓܪ̈ܢܝܐ *sensual pleasures;* ܢܚܐ ܒܢܝܚܐ *he may live at ease;* ܪܝܚܐ ܕܢܝܚܐ *a sweet savour;* ܫܢܬܐ ܕܢܝܚܐ *sweet sleep.*

ܢܝܚܐܝܬ rt. ܢܘܚ. adv. *gently, placidly, kindly; easily; softly, in a low voice.*

ܢܝܚܘ, ܢܝܚܘܬܐ rt. ܢܘܚ. f. *quietness, serenity, suavity, gentleness;* ܐܝܟ ܢܝܚܘܬܐ ܕܡܪܟ *according to thy clemency;* ܒܢܝܚܘܬܐ *gently* opp. ܒܩܫܝܘܬܐ *harshly;* ܢܝܚܘܬܐ ܕܦܘܪ̈ܫܐ *benignity, gracious manners.*

ܢܝܚܬܐ pl. ܐ̈ rt. ܢܘܚ. f. a) *repose, leisure, rest, a resting-place;* ܢܝܚܬܐ ܗܘ ܒܥܝܢ ܐܢܬܘܢ *ye seek repose;* ܢܬܚܦܛ ܕܢܥܘܠ ܠܗܝ ܢܝܚܬܐ *let us strive to enter into that rest;* ܠܠܝܐ ܕܢܝܚܬܐ *the night for rest.* b) *sleep, falling asleep, rest, death;* ܡܛܐ ܙܒܢܐ ܕܢܝܚܬܗ *the time of his rest drew near.* c) esp. *the rest* of Christ after the resurrection; ܒܥܐܕ̈ܐ ܕܢܝܚܬܗ ܕܡܫܝܚܐ ܡܨܝܪܝܢܢ *by feast-days we typify the rest of Christ;* hence Easter week is called ܢܝܚܬܐ: ܚܡܫܐ ܕܢܝܚܬܐ ܒܫܒܐ *Thursday in Easter week;* ܥܪܘܒܬܐ ܕܢܝܚܬܐ *Friday in Easter week;* &c. d) *the agape, love-feast;* ܐܝܠܝܢ ܕܒܢܝܚ̈ܬܟܘܢ *those who are at your love-feasts;* ܕܘܟܪܢ̈ܐ ܘܢܝܚ̈ܬܐ ܕܥܢܝ̈ܕܐ *memorials and agapes for the departed.*

ܢܝܛܪܘܢ and ܢܝܛܪܘ m. *νίτρον, nitre.*

ܢܝܠܐ m. *indigo.*

ܢܝܠܘܣ the river *Nile.*

ܢܝܠܘܣܝܐ adj. from ܢܝܠܘܣ. *of the Nile;* ܬܢܝܢܐ ܢܝܠܘܣܝܐ *the Nile crocodile.*

ܢܝܠܘܦܪ m. *the nymphaea, lotus* plant.

ܢܝܠܐ; see ܢܐܠ.

ܢܝܠܝ m. *indigo.*

ܢܝܢܘܐ *Nineveh* the capital of Assyria.

ܢܝܢܘܝܐ from ܢܝܢܘܐ. *a Ninevite;* ܒܥܘܬܐ ܕܢܝܢܘܝ̈ܐ *Rogation of the Ninevites,* a fast of three days in the tenth week before Easter.

ܢܝܢܝܐ and ܢܝܢܐ, in the lexx. ܢܝܢܐ 1) *hempen twine, cord, string;* fishing *tackle.* 2) a vegetable, *ammi copticum.*

ܢܝܢܪܐ, ܢܝܢܪܐ and ܢܢܪܐ m. *a sabre, scimitar; a swordstick.* Cf. ܢܝܙܪܐ.

ܢܝܣܢ *Nisan* the seventh month = April; ܒܙܒܢ ܢܝܣܢ *in spring.*

ܢܝܣܢܝܐ, ܢܝܣܢܝܬܐ adj. from ܢܝܣܢ. *of the spring;* ܥܣܒܐ ܢܝܣܢܝܐ *spring verdure.*

ܢܝܦܐ rt. ܢܘܦ. m. *loosely-hanging chains.*

ܢܝܪ, ܢܝܪܐ pl. ܢܝܪ̈ܐ, m. *a) a yoke* for oxen; metaph. *service, servitude, bondage;* ܫܩܘܠܘ ܢܝܪܝ ܥܠܝܟܘܢ *take my yoke upon you;* ܢܝܪܐ ܕܥܒܕܘܬܐ *the yoke of slavery;* ܒܪ ܢܝܪܗ *a yoke-fellow, husband, wife, colleague. b) the beam* of a weaver's loom, *the weft. c) the tie* of a vine to its prop.

ܢܝܪܬܐ same as ܢܐܪܬܐ.

ܢܝܪܘܦܠ and ܢܝܪܘܦܘܠ = ܢܝܠܘܦܪ m. *the nymphaea, lotus.*

ܢܝܪܬܐ pl. ܢܝܪ̈ܬܐ rt. ܢܘܪ. f. *white hairs.*

ܢܝܫ, ܢܝܫܐ pl. ܢܝܫ̈ܐ m. *a) an ensign, standard, banner;* ܢܝܫ ܡܠܟܘܬܐ *the royal banner. b) a monument, sign, portent, sign* of the Zodiac; ܢܝܫܐ ܕܨܠܝܒܐ *the sign of the Cross;* ܒܗܢܐ ܢܝܫܐ ܙܟܐ ܐܢܬ *in this sign thou conquerest. c) aim, end, goal, object, intention, purpose, disposition;* ܐܠܘܗܝ ܢܝܫܗ ܬܪܝܨܐ *his intention is right;* ܡܢܘ ܢܝܫܗ ܕܡܠܟܐ ܒܗܕܐ *what is the aim,* or *object, of the king in this?* ܣܡ ܒܢܝܫܗ *he proposed, intended;* ܗܘܐ ܢܝܫܗ ܠ *his mind inclined towards .... d) signification, sense, point; the subject, proposition, section* of a book, speech, poem, &c., ܢܝܫ̈ܐ ܕܒܥܘܬܐ *matters or points* in dispute; ܢܝܫ̈ܐ ܕܟܬܒܐ *the contents of the book;* ܢܝܫܐ ܩܕܡܝܐ ܡܚܘܐ *the first section demonstrates .... e) metre, mode, manner, appearance; example;* ܒܢܝܫܐ ܕܡܪܝ ܐܦܪܝܡ *in the metre of St. Ephrem;* ܒܢܝܫ ܪܚܡܬܐ *with an appearance of friendship;* ܢܝܫ̈ܝ ܓܪܡܛܝܩܝ *examples of grammar* i.e. of its rules. *f)* astron. *an observation. g)* gram. *sign, point, stop; the form* of a noun; ܫܡܐ ܕܒܚܕ ܢܝܫܐ a noun *of the same form.*

ܢܟܐ fut. ܢܢܟܐ, imper. ܟܝ, but when with a ܒܘܠܝܚ prefix ܟܐ, act. part. ܢܟܐ, ܢܟܝܐ. *to harm, hurt, injure; to be opposed to;* ܕܢܟܐ ܠܦܓܪܐ ܠܪܘܚܐ — *hurtful to the body, to the spirit.* Ethpe. ܐܬܢܟܝ and Ethpa. ܐܬܢܟܝ *to be harmed, injured, polluted;* ܐܬܢܟܝܘ ܗܠܝܢ ܡܣܟܢ̈ܐ ܡܢ ܛܘܪ̈ܝܐ *those poor people suffered harm from the mountain tribes.* Aph. ܐܟܝ *to harm, hurt, injure;* ܠܐ ܢܟܐ ܐܢܘܢ ܫܪܒܐ ܘܫܡܫܐ *the hot wind and sun shall not touch them;* ܗܘ ܕܒܗ ܡܟܐ ܗܘܐ ܠܚܒܪ̈ܘܗܝ the tongue *wherewith he had damaged his fellows;* ܠܐ ܡܟܐ ܠܗ ܚܘܝܐ *the serpent does not hurt him.* Ethtaph. ܐܬܬܟܝ *to be hurt, injured, suffer harm.* Derivatives, ܢܟܝܐ, ܢܟܝܢ, ܡܢܟܝܢܐ, ܢܟܝܢܐ, ܡܢܟܝܢܘܬܐ, ܡܬܢܟܝܢܘܬܐ, ܡܬܢܟܝܢܐܝܬ.

ܢܟܐ rare for ܢܟܐ *tin.*

ܢܟܘܝܐ, ܢܟܘܝܬܐ rt. ܢܟܐ. *injurious, harmful, destructive;* ܚܝܘܬܐ ܢܟܘܝܬܐ *ravenous animals.*

ܢܟܘܠܐ pl. ܢܟܘܠ̈ܐ rt. ܢܟܠ. *crafty, wily, deceitful;* ܝܘܢܝ̈ܐ ܢܟܝܠ̈ܐ ܘܢܟܘܠ̈ܐ *the crafty and wily Greeks.*

ܢܟܘܠܬܢܐ, ܢܟܘܠܬܢܝܬܐ, ܢܟܘܠܬܢ̈ܐ rt. ܢܟܠ. *deceitful, wily; a deceitful man;* ܣܦܘ̈ܬܐ ܢܟܘܠܬܢܝ̈ܬܐ *deceitful lips.*

ܢܟܘܠܬܢܘܬܐ rt. ܢܟܠ. f. *fraud, deceitfulness.*

ܢܟܘܣܐ rt. ܢܟܣ. m. *a slaughterer, butcher.*

ܢܟܘܦ, ܢܟܘܦܐ rt. ܢܟܦ. *modest, chaste, pious.*

ܢܟܘܦܬܢܐ, ܢܟܘܦܬܢ rt. ܢܟܦ. *modest, shamefaced.*

ܢܟܘܬܐ rt. ܢܟܬ. *pungent.*

ܢܟܘܬܬܐ rt. ܢܟܬ. *pungent, stinging.*

ܢܟܝܚ perh. *to treat courteously;* part. adj. ܢܟܝܚ and ܢܟܝܚ, ܢܟܝܚܐ, ܢܟܝܚܬܐ *meek, gentle, peaceable.* Derivatives, ܢܟܝܚܐܝܬ, ܢܘܟܚܐ, ܢܟܝܚܘܬܐ.

ܢܟܝܚܐܝܬ rt. ܢܟܚ. *calmly, gently.*

ܢܟܝܚܘܬܐ rt. ܢܟܚ. f. *gentleness, calmness, serenity.*

ܢܟܝܠܐܝܬ rt. ܢܟܠ. adv. *deceitfully, craftily.*

ܢܟܝܠܘܬܐ pl. ܢܟܝܠܘ̈ܬܐ rt. ܢܟܠ. f. *cunning, wiliness, perfidy; deception, deceit;* ܢܟܝܠܘܬܟܝ ܠܟܐܢ̈ܐ ܐܘܒܕܬ *thy guiles have brought true men to destruction.*

ܢܟܝܢ, ܢܟܝܢܐ rt. ܢܟܐ. m. *harm, hurt, damage, injury, pain, destruction;* ܕܠܐ ܢܟܝܢܐ *uninjured, inviolable.*

ܢܟܝܣܘܬܐ rt. ܢܟܣ. f. *being slain, being sacrificed.*

ܢܟܠ and ܢܟܠ fut. ܢܢܟܘܠ and ܢܢܟܠ, infin. ܡܢܟܠ and ܡܢܟܠ, act. part. ܢܟܠ, ܢܟܠܐ, pass. part. ܢܟܝܠ, ܢܟܝܠܐ, ܢܟܝܠܬܐ. *to deceive, defraud, act deceitfully, beguile, betray,* with ܒ or ܠ; ܬܠܡܝܕܐ ܕܢܟܠ ܠܗ ܠܪܒܗ *the disciple who betrayed his master;* ܢܟܠܘ ܠܚܒܪ̈ܝܗܘܢ ܒܥܘܠܐ *they defrauded their neighbours by oppression;* ܓܒܪ̈ܐ ܢܟܠ̈ܐ *deceitful men.* Pass. part. *deceitful, dishonest, crooked, treacherous, perfidious;* ܩܫܬܐ ܢܟܝܠܬܐ *a deceitful bow;*

ܦܥܠܐ ܢܟܝܠܐ *dishonest labourers.* Ethpe. ܐܬܢܟܠ usually with ܥܠ *to act deceitfully, treacherously, to dissemble; to be deceived.* Pa. ܢܰܟܶܠ *to beguile, defraud.* Aph. ܐܰܟܶܠ with ܥܠ *to deceive, to hold* or *state falsely; to suppose.* Derivatives, ܢܟܠܐ, ܢܟܘܠܬܢܐ, ܢܟܘܠܬܢܘܬܐ, ܢܟܘܠܬܢܐܝܬ, ܢܟܝܠܐ, ܢܟܝܠܘܬܐ, ܡܟܠܢܐ, ܢܟܠܬܐ, ܡܟܠܢܘܬܐ, ܡܬܢܟܠܢܘܬܐ.

ܢܶܟܠܐ pl. ܢܶܟܠܺܝܢ, ܢܶܟܠܶܐ rt. ܢܟܠ. *guile, deceit, perfidy, dissimulation, treachery; a plot;* ܐܡܰܪܘ ܒܢܶܟܠܐ *they spake with guile;* ܕܠܐ ܢܶܟܠܐ *not treacherously, unfeigned;* ܡܠܐ ܢܶܟܠܐ *deceitful, wily.*

ܢܟܰܣ ܢܟܰܣ fut. ܢܶܢܟܘܣ, infin. ܡܶܢܟܰܣ and rarely ܡܶܢܟܳܣܘ, imper. ܢܟܘܣ, act. part. ܢܳܟܶܣ, ܢܳܟܣܐ, pass. part. ܢܟܝܣ, ܢܟܝܣܐ, ܢܟܝܣܬܐ. *to slay, kill* for sacrifice or for food; ܢܟܘܣ ܢܟܣܬܐ ܘܐܛܝܒ *slay an animal and make ready;* ܢܟܘܣ ܦܶܨܚܐ *kill the passover;* ܢܟܰܣ ܢܰܦܫܗ *he slew himself;* ܐܶܡܪܐ ܗܘ ܢܟܝܣܐ *the lamb that hath been slain.* Ethpe. ܐܬܢܟܶܣ *to be slain, slaughtered, killed, sacrificed.* Pa. ܢܰܟܶܣ *to slay, put to death.* Ethpa. ܐܬܢܰܟܰܣ *to be slain, killed.* Ettaph. ܐܬܬܰܢܟܰܣ *to be dislocated.* Derivatives, ܢܟܘܣܐ, ܢܟܣܐ, ܢܟܘܣܐ, ܢܟܣܬܐ, ܢܟܝܣܘܬܐ, ܡܬܢܟܣܢܐ.

ܢܶܟܣܐ usually pl. ܢܶܟܣܺܝܢ, ܢܶܟܣܶܐ m. *a) a piece of flesh, portion of a victim. b) wealth, riches, goods; personal estate* opp. ܩܶܢܝܳܢܐ *real estate;* ܡܳܪܰܝ ܢܶܟܣܐ *wealthy men.*

ܢܟܳܣܐ rt. ܢܟܣ. m. *slaying, slaughter.*

ܢܶܟܣܘܣ or ܢܶܟܣܘܣ m. *birdlime.*

ܢܶܟܣܬܐ pl. ܢܶܟܣܳܬܐ rt. ܢܟܣ. f. *a) a victim, an animal killed* for sacrifice or for food, *flesh. b) slaying, slaughter, sacrifice.*

ܢܟܶܦ and ܢܟܰܦ fut. ܢܶܢܟܰܦ and ܢܶܢܟܘܦ, act. part. ܢܳܟܶܦ, ܢܳܟܦܐ. *a) to blush, be ashamed, modest; to fear, feel awe* or *respect;* ܢܟܶܦ ܐܢܐ ܡܶܢܟܘܢ *I blush for you;* ܢܟܶܦ ܗܘܐ ܕܠܡܐ *he feared lest.... b) to be sober, chaste, abstinent.* Pa. ܢܰܟܶܦ *to control, correct, chasten, teach to be chaste, enjoin chastity and modesty;* ܢܰܟܶܦܘ ܦܘܡܰܝܗܘܢ *they taught their mouths to be chaste, controlled their speech;* ܚܙܘܟܘܢ ܡܢܰܟܦܳܐ *your modest appearance.* Ethpa. ܐܬܢܰܟܰܦ *to be* or *become chaste, modest, sober; to be ashamed, refrain for shame* or *modesty; to be covered* or *sheltered;* ܐܰܝܟ ܡܳܠܐ ܡܛܰܠܢܟܦܐ *the wanton shall grow chaste;* ܢܳܟܦܐ ܐܢܐ ܕܐܦܘܩ *I am ashamed to go out.* Derivatives, ܢܟܦܐ, ܢܟܝܦܐ, ܢܟܝܦܐܝܬ, ܢܟܝܦܘܬܐ, ܢܟܦܬܐ, ܡܢܟܦܢܐ.

ܢܰܟܦܐ, ܢܰܟܦܐ, ܢܰܟܦܬܐ rt. ܢܟܦ. *modest, chaste, sober, religious,* often applied to monks and nuns; ܕܘܒܳܪܐ ܢܰܟܦܐ *honourable* or *pure life;* ܓܡܰܪܘ ܚܰܝܰܝܗܘܢ ܒܕܘܒܳܪ̈ܐ ܢܰܟܦܐ ܕܝܚܝܕܳܝܘܬܐ *they ended their lives in the pious practices of monasticism.*

ܢܰܟܦܳܐܝܬ rt. ܢܟܦ. adv. *modestly, discreetly, soberly.*

ܢܰܟܦܘܬܐ rt. ܢܟܦ. f. *chastity, modesty, discretion, prudence, honour, temperance, sobriety.*

ܢܶܟܦܬܐ rt. ܢܟܦ. f. *modesty, reverence, shame.*

ܢܰܟܰܪ fut. ܢܢܰܟܰܪ, act. part. ܡܢܰܟܰܪ, pass. part. ܡܢܰܟܰܪ. *to alienate, estrange, separate, remove; to make* or *be strange* or *foreign;* ܘܐܘܢ ܢܰܟܪܳܝܐ ܐܢܫ ܢܰܟܶܪ ܢܰܦܫܗ ܡܶܢ ܚܶܒܪܘܬܐ ܕܙܠܝܠܐ *a man should withdraw far from intercourse with the dissolute;* ܕܰܐܡܰܪ ܕܡܢܰܟܰܪ ܠܶܗ ܡܶܢ ܝܳܪܬܘܬܐ *saying that he deprived him of his right of inheritance;* ܡܢܰܟܪܺܝܢ ܡܶܢ ܗܰܝܡܳܢܘܬܐ *strangers to the faith;* ܐܰܬܪܐ ܡܢܰܟܪܳܝܐ ܡܶܢ ܪܶܓܠܐ ܕܒܰܪܢܳܫܐ *a place strange to the foot of man;* ܡܢܰܟܪܳܝܐ ܗܝ ܡܶܢ ܨܒܘܬܐ *it is foreign to the subject.* Ethpali ܐܶܬܢܰܟܰܪ *to be, become* or *be declared alien, strange, foreign; to be alienated, removed, dispossessed; to renounce, disown, reject, abstain.* Derivatives, ܢܘܟܪܐ, ܢܘܟܪܝܐ, ܢܘܟܪܝܘܬܐ, ܢܘܟܪܝܐܝܬ, ܡܢܟܪܢܘܬܐ, ܡܬܢܟܪܢܘܬܐ.

ܢܟܣ Aphel ܐܰܟܶܣ *to harm, do injury, chastise.*

ܢܟܰܬ fut. ܢܶܢܟܘܬ, act. part. ܢܳܟܶܬ, ܢܳܟܬܐ, pass. part. ܢܟܝܬ, ܢܟܝܬܐ, ܢܟܝܬܬܐ. *to bite, sting* esp. as a serpent or dog; ܢܶܟܬܶܗ ܒܪܶܓܠܶܗ *it bit him in the foot;* ܢܟܝܬ ܡܶܢ ܐܰܟܕܢܐ *stung by a viper;* ܟܟܐ ܢܟܝܬܐ *a decayed tooth.* Ethpe. ܐܶܬܢܟܶܬ *to be bitten, stung.* Pa. ܢܰܟܶܬ *to sting sharply, bite repeatedly, gnaw;* ܡܢܰܟܶܬ ܨܶܒ̈ܥܳܬܶܗ *biting his fingers.* Ethpa. ܐܶܬܢܰܟܰܬ *to be bitten* or *stung repeatedly.* Derivatives, ܢܟܬܐ, ܢܟܬܬܐ, ܢܟܘܬܐ, ܢܟܘܬܬܐ, ܡܢܟܘܬܐ and ܡܢܟܘܬܬܐ, ܡܢܟܘܬܬܐ, ܡܢܟܘܬܐ, ܡܢܟܬܢܐ.

ܢܠܐ m. *nightmare, incubus.*

ܢܳܡܘܣ, ܢܳܡܘܣܐ pl. ܢܳܡܘܣܐ, ܢܳܡܘܣܶܐ m. *a)* *νομός, a nome, prefecture* of Egypt. *b) νόμος, law, ordinance, custom, usage;* ܢܳܡܘܣܐ ܕܟܠܟܘܢ

a statute for ever; ܢܳܡܽܘܣܶܐ ܥܳܠܡܳܢܳܝܶܐ secular laws; ܢܳܡܽܘܣܳܐ ܕܚܺܐܪܽܘܬܳܐ privilege, exemption; ܕܠܳܐ ܢܳܡܽܘܣ lawless. DERIVATIVES, verb ܢܡܣܡܣ, ܢܡܘܣܐܝܬ, ܢܡܘܣܝܐ, ܢܡܘܣܘܬܐ, ܢܡܘܣܝܘܬܐ.

ܢܡܣܡܣ ETHPALPAL ܐܶܬܢܰܡܣܡܰܣ to become law, be proposed as a law.

ܢܳܡܽܘܣܳܐܝܺܬ from ܢܳܡܽܘܣܳܐ. adv. in accordance with law, lawfully, legally, legitimately.

ܢܳܡܽܘܣܳܝܳܐ, ـܝܬܳܐ from ܢܳܡܽܘܣܳܐ. lawful, legal, legitimate, rightful, of the law; ܐܰܢܬܬܳܐ ܢܳܡܽܘܣܳܝܬܳܐ a lawful wife; ܒܪܳܐ ܠܳܐ ܢܳܡܽܘܣܳܝܳܐ an illegitimate son; ܡܰܠܟܳܐ ܢܳܡܽܘܣܳܝܳܐ a rightful king; ܦܽܘܠܚܳܢܳܐ ܢܳܡܽܘܣܳܝܳܐ legal service i.e. observance of the law of Moses.

ܢܳܡܽܘܣܽܘܬܳܐ from ܢܳܡܽܘܣܳܐ. f. lawfulness; ܠܳܐ ܢܳܡܽܘܣܘܳܬܳܐ unlawful acts.

ܢܳܡܽܘܣܳܝܽܘܬܳܐ from ܢܳܡܽܘܣܳܐ. f. lawfulness, conformity to law, rectitude, rightfulness; with ܠܳܐ unlawfulness; iniquity; pl. ܠܳܐ ܢܳܡܽܘܣܳܝܘܳܬܳܐ unrighteous acts, transgressions.

ܢܰܛܪܺܝܩܳܐ ; see ܢܽܘܛܰܪܺܝܩܳܐ m. a notary.

ܢܡܠܐ, ܢܶܡܠܳܐ or ܢܡܶܠܳܐ pl. ܢ̈ـ a) m. an ant-heap. b) f. an ant; a rash.

ܢܶܡܝܳܐ m. ichneumon.

ܢܰܡܰܪ denom. verb Paal conj. from ܢܶܡܪܳܐ to growl. ETHPA. ܐܶܬܢܰܡܰܪ to growl, rage.

ܢܶܡܪܳܐ pl. ـܝܢ̈, ـܐ̈ m. a leopard; ܢܶܡܪܬܳܐ pl. ܢܶܡܪ̈ܳܬܳܐ f. a leopardess, she-leopard.

ܢܶܡܪܳܝܳܐ, ـܝܬܳܐ from ܢܡܪܐ. like a leopard.

ܢܰܡܪܬܳܐ f. a cage for wild beasts.

ܬܰܢܝܳܐ m. a rope; cf. ܬܰܢܝܳܢܳܐ.

ܢܰܢܥܳܐ m. mint.

ܢܣܣ PE. only found in verbal adj. ܢܰܣܺܝܣ, ܢܰܣܺܝܣܳܐ, ܢܰܣܺܝܣܬܳܐ weak, infirm, sickly; ܢܰܣܺܝܣܳܢ ܥܰܝ̈ܢܰܘܗܝ his eyes are weak; ܢܰܣܺܝܣ ܒܓܽܘܫܡܶܗ infirm in body; ܡܚܳܘܬܳܐ ܕܰܚܒܺܝܫܳܐ ܢܰܣܺܝܣ an unhealed sore. ETHPE. ܐܶܬܢܣܺܝܣ to become weak from illness. ETHPA. ܐܶܬܢܰܣܰܣ to be weak, broken by disease. DERIVATIVES, ܢܣܝܣܐܝܬ, ܢܣܝܣܘܬܐ.

ܢܣܐ root-meaning to weigh, try by weighing. PAEL ܢܰܣܺܝ to try, prove, tempt, make trial of, estimate, know by experience usually with ܠ; ܢܰܣܳܝܢܝ prove thou me; ܢܰܣܰܘܢܝ prove ye me; ܟܰܕ ܨܳܒܶܐ ܕܢܢܰܣܶܐ ܠܨܶܒܘܳܬܳܐ wishing to test the matter; ܣܳܛܳܢܳܐ ܗܰܘ ܡܢܰܣܝܳܢܳܐ the tempter Satan. Part. adj. a) tried, tempted, assailed, vexed by a devil, leprous; ܡܣܟܺܢ̈ܶܐ ܡܢܰܣܝܳܢ̈ܶܐ the poor leprous; ܥܺܝܠܳܐ ܠܳܐ ܡܢܰܣܝܳܐ an untried or unbroken-in colt. b) acquainted, accustomed, experienced; ܡܢܰܣܶܐ ܒܕܽܘܟܝ̈ܳܬܳܐ acquainted with the places; ܡܢܰܣܶܐ ܒܩܪܳܒܳܐ experienced in war, a veteran. ETHPA. ܐܶܬܢܰܣܺܝ to be tried, proved, tempted; to be afflicted, to be possessed by a devil. DERIVATIVES, ܢܣܝܐ, ܢܣܝܢܐ, ܢܣܝܘܢܐ, ܢܣܝܘܢ, ܡܢܣܝܢܐ, ܡܢܣܝܐ or ܡܢܣܝܢܘܬܐ, ܡܢܣܝܢܐܝܬ, ܡܢܣܝܘܬܐ.

ܢܶܣܳܐ or ܢܶܣܳܐ only pl. ܢܶܣ̈ܶܐ m. signs, portents.

ܢܣܒ fut. ܢܶܣܰܒ, imper. ܣܰܒ, infin. ܡܶܣܰܒ, act. part. ܢܳܣܶܒ, ܢܳܣܒܳܐ, pass. part. ܢܣܺܝܒ, ـܳܐ, ـܬܳܐ. a) to take, receive, assume; ܫܽܘܚܕܳܐ ܠܳܐ ܢܳܣܶܒ he takes no bribe; ܐܰܝܟ ܕܳܐܦ ܢܣܰܒܢܰܢ as we also have received; ܢܣܰܒܘ ܡܶܢ ܪܽܘܚܳܐ ܕܩܽܘܕܫܳܐ they were partakers of the Holy Spirit; ܐܶܢ ܠܢܽܘܚ ܬܶܣܰܒ for if you take Noah for an example. With nouns: ܐܰܢܬܬܳܐ or ܒܶܢܬܳܐ to take a wife, marry; ܢܣܰܒ ܠܶܗ ܒܪܳܐ—ܒܪܬܳܐ he adopted a son, a daughter; ܠܕܽܘܟܪܳܢܳܐ to take for a memorial, for a remembrance; ܙܳܟܽܘܬܳܐ to gain the victory; ܫܰܪܒܳܐ to make an onset; ܠܕܽܘܡܝܳܐ to take for an example; ܚܽܘܫܒܳܢܳܐ to take account; ܒܝܰܠܳܐ to take care of, protect; ܡܶܠܟܳܐ to take counsel; ܡܶܠܟܳܢܳܐ or ellipt. and ܒܢܰܦܫܶܗ to make a treaty that his life should be spared; ܣܰܝܦܳܐ to draw a sword; ܫܽܘܠܳܡܳܐ, ܣܽܘܦܳܐ, ܫܽܘܠܳܡܳܐ or ܚܽܘܪܳܐ to come to an end; ܩܪܳܒܳܐ to wage war; ܫܽܘܪܳܝܳܐ to begin. Pass. part. taken, derived, adopted, selected, assumed. b) to take away; ܗܳܢܳܐ ܢܳܣܶܒ ܚܛܳܗܰܝܟ this taketh away thy sins; with ܛܶܦܪ̈ܶܐ to pare the nails; ܡܰܕܥܳܐ to take away the understanding; ܪܺܫܳܐ to behead; ܢܣܺܝܒ ܗܰܘܢܳܐ bereft of his wits, insane. c) to take by force, take in war; ܢܣܰܒ ܚܶܣܢܳܐ he took the fortress. With preps.: ܠܘܳܬ to summon; ܡܶܢ to receive from, accept; also to take away from. Idioms: with ܒܐܺܝܕܶܗ to bring, carry; ܒܡܰܚܫܰܒܬܶܗ ܢܣܰܒ he thought, considered, had in his mind; ܒܰܐܦ̈ܶܐ or ܒܦܰܪܨܽܘܦܳܐ to accept the face or person of any one, be favourable to him; ܢܣܰܒ ܗܘܳܐ ܒܰܐܦ̈ܰܘܗܝ ܕܦܳܦܳܐ he took the part of the Pope; usually in a bad sense to regard outward appearance, be a *respecter of persons;* ܠܳܐ ܬܶܣܒܽܘܢ ܒܰܐܦ̈ܶܐ ܒܕܺܝܢܳܐ *ye shall not respect persons in judgement;* ܢܳܣܶܒ ܒܰܐܦ̈ܶܐ *one who puts on a false appearance, a hypocrite;* ܡܰܣܒܰܒ ܒܰܐܦ̈ܶܐ *dissimulation, hypocrisy.* Ethpeel ܐܶܬܢܣܶܒ *to be taken, received, accepted; to be partaker of, to be taken away; to be understood, to assume, take to oneself;* ܟܰܕ ܡܶܬܢܰܣܒܺܝܢ ܐ̈ܪܳܙܶܐ *while the mysteries are being received;* ܡܶܬܢܣܶܒ ܗܳܘܳܐ ܕܶܐ ܥܰܠ *this is to be taken, understood, as relating to . . .;* ܡܶܬܢܣܶܒ ܒܪ̈ܰܥܘܳܬܶܗ *he is received with favour;* gram. *to be derived.* Derivatives, ܢܣܘܒܐ, ܢܣܘܒܘܬܐ, ܡܣܒܐ, ܡܣܒܢܘܬܐ, ܢܣܒܬܐ, ܡܶܬܢܰܣܒܳܢܳܐܝܺܬ.

ܢܳܣܽܘܒܳܐ, ܢܳܣܽܘܒܬܳܐ rt. ܢܣܒ. *a recipient, partaker, communicant.*

ܢܣܽܘܒܽܘܬܳܐ rt. ܢܣܒ. f. *acceptance;* ܢܣܽܘܒܽܘܬ ܦܰܪ̈ܨܽܘܦܶܐ *hypocrisy.*

ܢܳܣܽܘܟܳܐ pl. ܐ̈ rt. ܢܣܟ. m. *a) a founder, metal-caster. b) a vessel for pouring oil into a lamp.*

ܢܶܣܺܝܐܳ m. Ar. *credit;* ܙܒܰܢ ܘܙܳܒܶܢ ܒܢܶܣܺܝܐܳ *selling on credit.*

ܢܣܺܝܳܐ rt. ܢܣܐ. m. *fear, alarm.*

ܢܣܺܝܒܳܐܺܝܬ rt. ܢܣܒ. adv. *in a derived* or *secondary sense.*

ܢܣܺܝܒܽܘܬܳܐ pl. ܬ̈ܳܐ rt. ܢܣܒ. f. *taking, taking possession, obtaining; receipts, income; acceptance, participation, communion* esp. *receiving* Holy Communion; ܢܣܺܝܒܽܘܬ ܙܰܝܢܳܐ *taking up arms;* ܢܣܺܝܒܽܘܬ ܐܰܦ̈ܶܐ *hypocrisy;* ܢܣܺܝܒܽܘܬ ܦܰܪ̈ܨܽܘܦܶܐ *respect of persons.*

ܢܶܣܝܳܢܳܐ rt. ܢܣܐ. *weak, morbid.*

ܢܶܣܝܽܘܢܳܐ pl. ܐ̈ rt. ܢܣܐ. m. *trial, temptation;* ܠܳܐ ܬܰܥܠܰܢ ܠܢܶܣܝܽܘܢܳܐ *lead us not into temptation.*

ܢܶܣܝܳܢܳܐ pl. ܐ̈ rt. ܢܣܐ. m. *proof, test, trial; experience, experiment, examination;* ܒܢܶܣܝܳܢܳܐ ܕܚܰܝ̈ܶܐ ܕܗܳܪܟܳܐ *by experience of life here below;* ܒܢܶܣܝܳܢܳܐ ܚܬܺܝܬܳܐ ܐܶܫܬܰܘܕܰܥ *it has been ascertained from close examination.*

ܢܶܣܝܳܝܳܐ from ܢܶܣܺܝܐܳ. adj. *on credit.*

ܢܶܣܝܳܢܳܝܳܐ rt. ܢܣܐ. adj. *learnt by experience.*

ܢܰܣܝܳܢܳܐܺܝܬ rt. ܢܣܐ. adv. *weakly, feebly* of eyesight.

ܢܰܣܝܳܢܽܘܬܳܐ rt. ܢܣܐ. f. *feebleness* esp. of sight.

ܢܣܺܝܪܳܐ rt. ܢܣܪ. *a prism.*

ܢܣܰܟ fut. ܢܶܢܣܽܘܟ, imper. ܣܽܘܟ, infin. ܡܶܢܣܰܟ, act. part. ܢܳܣܶܟ, ܢܳܣܟܳܐ, pass. part. ܢܣܺܝܟ, ܟ݂ܳܐ, ܟ݂ܬܳܐ. *a) to pour, pour out* water, oil, &c., ܢܳܣܶܟ ܚܰܡܪܳܐ *a butler, cupbearer.* Metaph. *to pour forth, pour into, instil, infuse* doctrine, love, &c.; ܛܰܝܒܽܘܬܳܐ ܕܪܽܘܚܳܐ ܕܶܐܬܢܣܶܟܰܬ ܥܠܰܘܗܝ *the grace of the Spirit which was poured forth upon him;* ܢܣܰܟ ܓܥܳܪ̈ܝܳܬܳܐ ܒܶܐܕ̈ܢܰܝܗܽܘܢ *he hurled threats at their ears. b) to flow into* the sea. *c) to smelt, cast, found* metal; ܢܳܣܶܟ ܕܰܗܒܳܐ *a goldsmith;* ܦܰܪܙܠܳܐ ܢܣܺܝܟܳܐ *cast iron;* ܨܰܠܡܳܐ ܢܣܺܝܟܳܐ *a molten image,* ellipt. ܥܒܰܕܘ ܠܗܽܘܢ ܢܣܺܝܟܳܐ *they have made them a molten image.* Metaph. ܢܶܢܣܽܘܟ ܐܶܢܽܘܢ *He will recast, remould them;* pass. part. *inherent.* Ethpe. ܐܶܬܢܣܶܟ *a) to be poured, poured out, shed abroad; to be instilled, infused, insinuated;* ...ܟܰܕ ܐܶܕܢܳܐ ܒܶܐܕܢܳܐ ܥܰܠ ܘܶܐܬܢܣܶܟ ܚܰܝ̈ܶܐ *by the ear . . . life entered and was instilled. b) to be melted, molten, tried in the fire;* ܡܶܬܢܰܣܟܺܝܢ ܐܰܠܳܗܰܝܗܽܘܢ *their gods are molten images. c)* from ܢܶܣܟܳܐ *to be copied out.* Derivatives, ܢܣܟܐ, ܢܣܘܟܐ, ܡܣܟܐ, ܡܣܟܬܐ, ܡܣܘܟܐ, ܢܣܟܬܐ, ܢܣܟܐ.

ܢܶܣܟܳܐ pl. ܢܶܣܟ̈ܶܐ rt. ܢܣܟ. m. *a) a fount, wellhead, flood-gate. b) a medicine injected* or *sprayed into the nose. c)* Ar. *a copy, codex.*

ܢܶܣܟܳܐ pl. ܐ̈ rt. ܢܣܟ. m. *pouring out* esp. *the casting of metals, foundery.*

ܢܶܣܟܬܳܐ rt. ܢܣܟ. f. *smelting, casting, founding;* ܕܢܶܣܟܬܳܐ *cast, molten.*

ܢܶܣܰܩ irreg. fut. of verb ܣܠܶܩ *to ascend.*

ܢܣܰܪ fut. ܢܶܢܣܽܘܪ, act. part. ܢܳܣܰܪ, ܢܳܣܪܳܐ, pass. part. ܢܣܺܝܪ, ܪܳܐ, ܪܬܳܐ. *to saw, cut asunder; to tear out* the hair; ܢܣܺܝܪ ܣܰܥܪܳܐ *with torn hair.* Ethpe. ܐܶܬܢܣܰܪ *to be sawn asunder; to be torn in two.* Derivatives, ܢܣܪܐ, ܢܣܘܪܐ, ܢܣܪܬܐ, ܡܣܪܐ or ܡܣܘܪܐ, ܡܣܪܬܐ.

ܢܶܣܪܳܐ pl. ܐ̈ rt. ܢܣܪ. *sawing; the part sawn, the cleft* of the wood; pl. *planks, sawn slabs.*

ܢܶܣܪܬܳܐ rt. ܢܣܪ. f. *sawdust.*

ܢܶܥܒܳܐ pl. ܢܶܥܒ̈ܶܐ m. *the breast* of animals.

ܢܥܳܒܳܐ pl. ܐ̈ m. *a crow, raven.*

ܢܥܰܓ fut. ܢܶܢܥܽܘܓ, act. part. ܢܳܥܶܓ, pass. part. ܢܥܺܝܓ, ܓܳܐ, ܓܬܳܐ. *to drag, hale* or *tear away;* ܟܰܠܒ̈ܶܐ ܢܥܰܓܘ ܠܥܶܢܳܐ *dogs worried the sheep.* Ethpe. ܐܶܬܢܥܶܓ *to be dragged* or *torn away, to be worried; to be ruined, come to ruin; to wallow;* ܢܥܓܠ ܠܐܒܕܢܐ ܥܘܠܐ *the evil-doer is dragged away to perdition.* Pael ܢܰܥܶܓ *to drag away, shake, worry, roll on the ground;* pass. part. ܡܢܰܥܓܳܐ *rolled in the mire, defiled.* Ethpa. ܐܶܬܢܰܥܰܓ same as Ethpe.; ܒܪ̈ܓܝܓܬܗ ܡܶܬܢܰܥܰܓ *he wallows in his lusts.* Derivative, ܢܥܓܐ.

ܢܶܥܓܳܐ rt. ܢܥܓ. m. *coming to naught, irreparable ruin.*

ܢܰܥܘܠܳܐ *slothful, negligent.*

ܢܰܥܘܠܽܘܬܳܐ f. *sloth, idleness.*

ܢܳܥܽܘܪܳܐ or ܢܥܘܪܐ m. and ܢܳܥܽܘܪܬܳܐ f. rt. ܢܥܪ. *a water-wheel.*

ܢܳܥܽܘܪܽܘܬܳܐ rt. ܢܥܪ. f. *roaring; braying.*

ܢܥܛ *to awaken.*

ܢܥܛ uncertain. *to strike, kick.*

ܢܰܥܶܠ denom. verb Pael conj. from ܢܰܥܠܳܐ *to shoe* horses.

ܢܰܥܠܳܐ pl. ܐ̈ *a horse-shoe.*

ܢܥܡ and Pael ܢܰܥܶܡ *to sound, utter.* Aph. ܐܰܢܥܶܡ *to rebuke, chide.* Derivatives, ܢܥܡܬܐ, ܢܥܡܬܢܐ.

ܢܰܥܡܳܐ pl. ܐ̈ f. *an ostrich;* ܒܢܬ ܢܰܥܡܳܐ *ostriches.*

ܢܶܥܡܬܳܐ pl. ܢܶܥܡ̈ܝܢ, ܬ̈ܐ rt. ܢܥܡ. f. *a musical note, modulation, gentle sound* or *voice, soft whisper, sound of the voice, tone of the voice;* ܟܢܳܪ̈ܐ ܚܠܝ̈ܢ ܢܶܥܡ̈ܬܐ *harps of sweet notes, melodious harps;* ܢܶܥܡ̈ܬܐ ܕܣܝܪ̈ܢܝܣ *sirens' melodies;* ܢܥܡܬܗ ܘܩܠܐ ܗܘܐ ܪܟܝܟ ܛܒ *his tone and voice were very soft;* ܢܘ̈ܢܐ ܕܠܐ ܢܶܥܡ̈ܬܐ *mute fishes.*

ܢܶܥܡܬܳܢܳܐ rt. ܢܥܡ. *melodious, harmonious.*

ܢܥܩ uncertain. *to grunt.*

ܢܥܪ fut. ܢܶܢܥܽܘܪ, act. part. ܢܳܥܰܪ. *to roar, growl, bray; to creak.* Ethpa. ܐܶܬܢܰܥܰܪ *to bray.* Derivatives, ܢܥܘܪܐ, ܢܥܘܪܘܬܐ, ܢܥܪܐ.

ܢܰܥܪܳܐ rt. ܢܥܪ. m. *braying.*

ܢܦܳܐܫܳܐ or ܢܦܫܐ E-Syr. ܢܝܐܫܐ rt. ܢܦܫ. m. *breathing; a breathing-space, pause, intermission, rest, refreshment;* ܐܝܬ ܒܗ ܢܦܐܫܐ ܕܚܝܐ *the breath of life is in him, he still breathes;* ܕܠܐ ܢܦܐܫܐ *breathless;* ܠܐ ܢܬܠܘܢ ܠܗܘܢ ܢܦܐܫܐ *they shall give them no rest;* ܢܦܐܫܐ ܠܐܚܝ̈ܕܐ *rest to the afflicted.*

ܢܦܐܫܢܳܐ rt. ܢܦܫ. *refreshing, of refreshment.*

ܢܦܽܘܚܳܐ rt. ܢܦܚ. m. *a blow-pipe, bellows.*

ܢܳܦܽܘܩܳܐ, ܢܦܘܩܬܐ rt. ܢܦܩ. *going forth, proceeding;* ܡܶܠܬܳܐ ܢܳܦܽܘܩܬܳܐ *a word proceeding* out of the mouth, *an uttered word.* Esp. *He Who proceedeth* = the Holy Spirit; ܪܘܚܐ ܢܦܘܩܐ *the Spirit Who proceedeth.*

ܢܳܦܽܘܩܽܘܬܳܐ rt. ܢܦܩ. f. *a) utterance;* ܒܢܦܘܩܘܬܐ ܐܘ ܒܠܘܬܟܝܢܐ ܡܠܦܝܢ *they teach expressly or implicitly;* ܢܦܘܩܘܬ ܡܶܠܬܳܐ *eloquence. b) the procession* of the Holy Spirit.

ܢܦܰܚ fut. ܢܶܦܘܽܚ, imper. ܦܘܽܚ, infin. ܡܶܦܰܚ, act. part. ܢܳܦܰܚ, ܢܳܦܚܳܐ, pass. part. ܢܦܺܝܚ, ܚܳܐ, ܚܳܐ, *to breathe, inbreathe, inspire; to blow, fan* a flame, *blow out; to puff up, swell;* ܢܦܰܚ ܒܢܚܝܪ̈ܘܗܝ ܢܫܡܬܐ ܕܚܝ̈ܐ *He breathed into his nostrils the breath of life;* ܢܳܦܰܚ ܐܢܐ ܒܟ ܪܘܚܐ ܕܩܘܕܫܐ *I breathe into thee the Holy Spirit;* ܢܦܚܐ ܕܢܦܚ ܢܘܪܐ ܒܡܦܘܚܐ the smith *who blows the fire with bellows;* ܦܘܚܘ ܫܪ̈ܓܐ *blow out the lamps;* ܢܦܚܬܗ ܫܘܒܗܪܐ *pride puffed him up.* Parts. ܢܳܦܰܚ ܬܘܪܐ *buprestis,* a beetle whose sting caused swellings in cattle; ܐܝܟ ܢܦܝܚܬܐ *an inflated bladder;* ܢܦܝܚ ܡܢ ܐܠܗܐ *inspired by God;* ܢܦܝܚܝܢ ܐܢܬܘܢ *ye are puffed up.* Ethpe. *to be blown upon, up* or *away, to be winnowed; to be wafted* as sweet odours; metaph. *to be inspired; to be puffed up, elated;* ܐܶܬܢܦܶܚ ܡܬܢܦܚܐ ܢܘܪܐ *the fire is fanned;* ܐܢ ܢܶܬܢܦܶܚ ܣܡܐ ܒܗ ܒܚܘܩܢܐ *if a drug be injected;* ܢܶܬܢܦܚ ܚܝܠܗܘܢ *their strength shall be blasted;* ܡܶܬܢܰܦܚܝܢ ܡܢ ܛܝܒܘܬܗ *being inspired by the grace* of God; ܐܶܬܢܦܶܚ ܒܪܘܚܗ *he was puffed up in spirit.* Pael ܢܰܦܶܚ *to winnow;* ܥܒܘܪܐ ܡܢܰܦܚܳܐ *winnowed corn.* Ethpa. ܐܶܬܢܰܦܰܚ *to swell, bubble up* as a cauldron, *to swell* with disease. Derivatives, ܢܦܚܐ, ܢܦܘܚܐ, ܢܦܚܐ, ܢܦܝܚܘܬܐ, ܢܦܝܚܐ, ܢܦܚܢܐ, ܢܦܝܚܘܬܐ, ܡܦܘܚܐ, ܡܦܘܚܬܐ, ܡܦܘܚܐ, ܡܦܚܢܘܬܐ, ܡܦܚܢܐ, ܡܦܘܚܬܐ, ܡܦܘܚܢܐ, ܡܦܘܚܬܐ, ܡܦܚܐ.

ܢܶܦܚܳܐ pl. ܐ̈ rt. ܢܦܚ. m. *the blowing* of the wind, *blowing* the fire; *inflation, elation; a snort, hiss.*

ܢܦܝܚܽܘܬܳܐ pl. ܬ̈ܐ rt. ܢܦܚ. f. *swelling, protuberance* of the iris.

ܢܰܦܛܳܐ E-Syr. ܢܶܦܛܳܐ m. νάφθα, *naphtha.*

ܢܰܦܛܽܘܪܳܐ pl. ܐ̈ـ Ar. m. *a pustule, pimple, blister.*

ܢܰܦܛܽܘܪܳܐ or ܢܰܦܛܺܝܪܳܐ pl. ܐ̈ m. *a torch, lantern.*

ܢܦܺܝܚܳܐܺܝܬ rt. ܢܦܚ. adv. *puffed up with vain fancies.*

ܢܦܺܝܚܽܘܬܳܐ rt. ܢܦܚ. f. *a swelling;* metaph. *being puffed up, vain elation.*

ܢܦܺܝܨܽܘܬܳܐ rt. ܢܦܨ. f. *shaking.*

ܢܦܺܝܩܽܘܬܳܐ rt. ܢܦܩ. f. *a*) *a translation, version. b*) *a swelling, prominence* of the paunch.

ܢܦܺܝܫܳܐ ; see ܢܦܳܫܳܐ.

ܢܦܺܝܫܽܘܬܳܐ rt. ܢܦܫ. f. *the animal life.*

ܢܦܰܠ fut. ܢܶܦܶܠ, imper. ܦܶܠ, infin. ܡܶܦܰܠ, act. part. ܢܳܦܶܠ, ܢܳܦܠܳܐ, part. adj. ܢܦܺܝܠ, ܠـ, ܠܳܐ. *a*) *to fall, fall down; to fall* in ruins, *collapse, fail, come to naught; to fall* in battle, *fall* sick, *lie down;* metaph. *to lapse, fall* into sin; ܐܶܢ ܬܶܦܶܠ ܬܶܣܓܽܘܕ ܠܺܝ *if thou wilt fall down and worship me;* ܢܦܰܠ ܡܢܳܗ ܣܰܓܺܝܐܳܐ ܕܐܰܢܛܺܝܽܘܟܺܝܐ *a great part of Antioch fell in that* earthquake; ܢܦܰܠ ܠܶܒܳܐ *the heart fails, fears;* ܢܦܰܠ ܒܦܶܣܩܰܬ ܣܰܒܪܳܐ *he fell into despair;* ܠܳܐ ܢܦܰܠ ܡܶܠܬܳܐ ܕܐܰܠܳܗܳܐ *the word of God has in no wise come to naught;* ܙܳܟܽܘܬܳܗ ܠܰܐܪܥܳܐ ܬܶܦܶܠ *her victory shall fall to the ground, come to naught;* ܓܰܢܒܳܪܰܝܟܝ ܒܚܰܪܒܳܐ ܢܶܦܠܽܘܢ *thy mighty men shall fall by the sword;* ܐܶܢ ܢܦܰܠ ܒܡܰܪܥܳܐ *if he fall sick;* also with ܒܟܽܘܪܗܳܢܳܐ *to fall sick;* ܗܳܢܽܘܢ ܕܢܳܦܠܺܝܢ ܠܐܰܪܥܳܐ *the epileptic;* ܥܽܘܠ ܘܦܶܠ ܘܕܡܽܘܟ ܒܢܝܳܚܳܐ *go in, lie down and sleep at thine ease;* ܐܳܘ ܢܰܦܫܳܐ ܕܢܶܦܠܰܬ ܒܕܰܒܪܳܬܳܐ *O soul fallen into evil ways. b*) *to be thrown, cast, laid;* ܡܨܺܝܕܬܳܐ ܢܦܰܠܬ ܒܝܰܡܳܐ *a net cast into the sea;* ܢܳܦܠܳܐ ܒܢܽܘܪܳܐ *it is cast into the fire;* ܢܦܰܠܘ ܒܫܽܘܫܠܳܬܳܐ *they were cast into chains;* ܒܒܶܝܬ ܐܰܣܺܝܪܶܐ *into prison;* ܢܦܰܠܘ ܫܶܬܶܐܣܶܐ *the foundations were laid;* ܬܶܦܶܠ ܢܽܘܪܳܐ ܒܩܰܝܣܳܐ *fire shall be set to the tree. c*) *to fall out, happen, occur, arise;* ܠܳܐ ܢܶܦܠܰܬ ܠܶܗ ܐܰܝܟ ܕܨܒܳܐ *it did not fall out as he wished;* ܦܽܘܠܓܳܝܽܘܬܳܐ ܢܶܦܠܰܬ ܒܝܰܬ *dissensions arose between ...,* ܢܦܰܠ ܚܶܪܝܳܐ ܒܥܰܡܳܐ *strife arose among the people.* Cf. *d. d*) with preps., with ܒ *to fall upon* or *into, befall, assail; to begin, arise; to be put upon* or *in;* ܢܦܰܠܘ ܚܰܕ ܒܚܰܕ *they fell upon each other;* ܢܶܦܠܰܬ ܢܽܘܪܳܐ ܒܒܰܓܕܰܕ *fire attacked Baghdad, arose in Baghdad;* ܐܳܘ ܟܡܳܐ ܫܓܽܘܫܝܳܐ ܢܦܰܠ ܒܰܢ *O what confusion has befallen us!* ܢܶܦܠܰܬ ܒܳܗ ܬܝܳܒܽܘܬܳܐ ܪܰܒܬܳܐ *great penitence laid hold of her;* ܒܺܐܝܕܰܝܳܐ *to fall into the hands of . . . ;* ܒܪܶܢܝܳܐ *to fall into deep thought.* N.B. construction ܒܩܶܛܠܳܐ ܬܶܦܠܽܘܢ *you shall be put to death;* ܫܽܘܫܠܳܬܳܐ ܕܢܦܰܠ ܒܗ *the chains which were put on him.* Cf. *b.* With ܒܳܬܰܪ *to follow;* with ܥܰܠ *to agree with;* ܐܳܣܝܽܘܬܳܐ ܕܢܳܦܠܳܐ ܠܶܗ *the medicine suitable for him;* cf. *c;* with ܠܘܳܬ *to fall off, fall away to, desert to;* with ܡܶܢ *to fall away from, desert, lapse;* ܡܶܢ ܗܰܝܡܳܢܽܘܬܳܐ *from the faith;* ܡܶܢ ܩܝܳܡܳܐ *to desert monastic vows;* ܡܶܢ ܛܰܟܣܶܗ *to be expelled from his order;* ܡܶܢ ܣܰܒܪܶܗ *to lose hope;* with ܥܰܠ *to fall upon, be imposed upon, fall sick, attack;* gram. *to refer to;* ܢܦܰܠ ܥܰܠ ܐܶܣܟܺܝܡܳܐ, ܢܦܰܠ ܥܰܠ ܥܰܪܣܳܐ *he took to his bed = fell ill;* ܢܦܰܠܘ ܥܠܰܝܗܽܘܢ ܓܰܝܳܣܶܐ *robbers fell upon them;* with ܥܰܡ *to lie with, have sexual intercourse with;* with ܩܕܳܡ ; ܬܶܦܶܠ ܒܳܥܽܘܬܝ ܩܕܳܡܰܝܟ *let my supplication be accepted before Thee;* with ܬܚܶܝܬ *to submit, subject oneself to.* Part. adj. *fallen, ruined, lying down, prostrate, slain; a deserter;* ܢܦܺܝܠܶܐ ܒܚܰܪܒܳܐ *slain with the sword;* ܢܦܺܝܠ ܥܰܠ ܐܰܦܰܘܗܝ, ܢܦܺܝܠ ܥܰܠ ܦܰܪܨܽܘܦܶܗ *fallen on his face, fallen prostrate;* ܡܩܺܝܡ ܠܗܳܢܽܘܢ ܕܢܦܺܝܠܺܝܢ *He will raise the fallen;* ܢܦܺܝܠ ܒ *placed in;* gram. *fallen away, lost.* Pael ܢܰܦܶܠ *to make fall, throw down;* part. ܡܢܰܦܠܳܐ *failing, enfeebled.* Ethpa. ܐܶܬܢܰܦܰܠ *to fall away, leave off, cease;* ܥܕܰܡܳܐ ܕܢܶܬܢܰܦܰܠ ܒܶܣܪܗܽܘܢ *till their flesh waste away;* ܫܰܪܺܝܘ ܟܽܐܒܰܝܗܽܘܢ ܠܡܶܬܢܰܦܳܠܽܘ *their pains began to abate.* Aphel ܐܰܦܶܠ *to cast down, overthrow; to omit* in writing or relating; *to seduce;* ܡܰܦܠܳܐ ܠܡܰܓܕܠܶܐ ܥܰܫܺܝܢܶܐ *it causes mighty towers to fall;* ܗܳܢܽܘܢ ܐܰܦܠܽܘܢܝ ܒܓܽܘܡܳܬܳܐ *these have made me fall into the ditch;* ܕܢܰܦܠܺܝܘܗܝ ܡܶܢ ܩܝܳܡܶܗ *that he might seduce him from his vows.* Derivatives, ܢܦܳܠܳܐ, ܢܦܺܝܠܳܐ, ܡܰܦܠܳܐ, ܡܰܦܰܠܬܳܐ, ܡܰܦܠܳܢܽܘܬܳܐ, ܡܰܦܠܳܢܳܐ, ܡܰܦܠܳܢܳܐܺܝܬ, ܡܰܦܠܳܢܝܳܐ, ܡܰܦܠܳܢܳܐܺܝܬ.

ܢܦܳܠܳܐ pl. ܐ̈ـ rt. ܢܦܠ. *a*) *fragment, scrap;* ܢܦܳܠܶܐ ܕܡܶܢ ܬܰܢܽܘܪܳܐ *scraps from the oven. b*) a plant *malabathrum indicum.*

ܢܦܳܠܳܐ pl. ܐ̈ـ rt. ܢܦܠ. m. *one who falls; a deserter.*

ܢܦܣ fut. ܢܢܦܘܣ, infin. ܡܢܦܣ, act. part. ܢܦܣ, ܢܦܣܐ, pass. part. ܢܦܝܣ. *to cast lots;* ܢܦܣܘ ... ܥܠ ... ܒܓܓܘܠܬܐ *they cast lots at Golgotha;* pass. part. *allotted; heckled, carded* of wool, cotton, &c. Pael ܢܦܣ *to hackle, comb, card.* Derivative, ܢܦܘܣܐ.

ܢܦܘܣܐ rt. ܢܦܣ. m. *the hackling, combing, carding* of wool, cotton, &c.

ܢܦܨ Aph. ܐܦܨ *to hatch* eggs. Ethtaph. ܐܬܬܦܨ *to be hatched.* Derivative, ܢܦܘܨܐ.

ܢܦܘܨܐ m. a bitter drug, *aristolochia rotunda, rhabarbarum* or *rheum palmatum.*

ܢܦܘܨܐ rt. ܢܦܨ. m. *the hatching* of eggs.

ܢܦܨ fut. ܢܢܦܘܨ, imper. ܦܘܨ, act. part. ܢܦܨ, ܢܦܨܐ. *to shake, toss; to shake out* or *off, empty* water; *to throw away* or *down; to impel;* ܢܦܨܬ ܩܘܠܬܗ *she emptied her pitcher;* ܦܘܨ ܥܦܪܐ *shake off the dust;* ܢܦܨܐ ܡܢܗ ܝܘܩܪܐ ܕܫܢܬܐ *she shakes off the heaviness of sleep;* ܢܦܨ ܐܝܕܗ ܡܢ ܫܘܚܕܐ *he shaketh his hand free of bribes;* ܡܢ ܐܬܪ ܠܐܬܪ ܢܦܨܬܢܝ *it drove me from place to place.* Ethpe. ܐܬܢܦܨ *to be tossed, shaken, shaken off; to be emptied; to rouse oneself from sleep.* Pael ܢܦܨ *to shake violently, break to pieces;* ܐܝܟ ܡܐܢܝ ܦܚܪܐ ܬܢܦܨ ܐܢܘܢ *as potter's vessels thou shalt dash them in pieces; to shake out* or *off, to empty;* ܢܦܨܘ ܠܡܨܪܝܐ *they cleared out the Egyptians;* with ܚܡܪܐ *to shake off* the effects of wine, *become sober; to rouse* the dead; med. *to purge, expel.* Ethpa. ܐܬܢܦܨ *a*) pass. *to be stirred up, emptied out, raised* out of the dust; *to be shaken* or *driven* as clouds by the wind; *to be withdrawn, drawn aside; to be cleansed, purged;* ܡܬܢܦܨܝܢ ܥܘܡܩܐ ܕܓܘܒܐ *the depths of the pit are emptied;* ܐܕܐ ܕܡܬܢܦܨ ܡܢ ܥܢܢܐ *vapour shaken out of the cloud;* ܐܬܢܦܨܘ ܡܢ ܡܕܝܢܬܐ *they were drawn away from the city.* *b*) refl. *to shake oneself; to void, discharge;* ܐܬܢܦܨ ܡܢ ܥܦܪܐ *shake thyself free of dust.* Derivatives, ܢܦܘܨܐ, ܢܦܘܨܘܬܐ.

ܢܦܩ fut. ܢܦܘܩ, imper. ܦܘܩ, infin. ܡܦܩ, act. part. ܢܦܩ, ܢܦܩܐ, pass. part. ܢܦܝܩ, ـܐ, ـܬܐ. *to go out, issue* or *proceed forth;* ܠܡܦܩ ܘܠܡܥܠ *to go out and come in;* ܢܦܩ ܡܢ ܩܕܡ ܦܪܥܘܢ *he went out of the presence of Pharaoh;* ܗܘ ܕܡܢ ܐܒܐ ܢܦܩ *who proceedeth from the Father.* Especially *a*) of the sun and stars *to shine forth, arise;* ܟܘܟܒܐ ܢܦܩ *the star appeared.* *b*) of plants and flowers *to come up, come out, bloom.* *c*) of time *to pass;* ܢܦܩ ܣܬܘܐ *the winter passed by;* ܢܬܘܐ ܥܠ ܝܘܡܘܗܝ ܕܢܦܩܘ ܒܒܛܠܢܐ let him regret *his days spent in idleness.* *d*) of events *to turn out, come to pass;* fully with ܠܡܫܘܠܡܐ, ܠܡܥܒܕ *it came to pass, was fulfilled;* ܢܦܩ ܗܘ ܚܠܡܐ *that dream came to pass;* ܠܐ ܐܝܟ ܪܓܝܓܘܬܗ ܢܦܩ ܣܘܥܪܢܐ *the affair did not turn out as he wished.* *e*) of a command, edict, sentence *to go forth, be issued, passed* with ܥܠ of the person. *f*) of books *to be put forth, published, translated, explained.* *g*) milit. *to make a sortie, to invade.* *h*) legal *to be emancipated, go out free* from slavery; of a wife *to leave her husband.* *i*) eccles. *to go right through, proceed, recite* or *read through;* ܟܕ ܕܢܦܩ ܩܪܝܢܐ ܩܕܡܝܐ *while the first lesson is being read.* *k*) arith. *to subtract;* with ܒ *to divide.* *l*) gram. *to be pronounced;* ܠܐ ܢܦܩܐ ܢܘܢ ܒܡܕܝܬܐ ܘܫܛܐ *nun is not sounded in m'dita and shata.* With preps.: ܠܐܘܪܚܐ *to set out, go on his way;* ܠܩܪܒܐ *to go to war;* ܠܫܒܝܐ *to be sent into captivity;* also *to consume,* ܐܢ ܒܝܬܐ ܢܦܩ ܒܗ ܐܡܪܐ *if* the house *be too small for a lamb* (Ex. xii. 4); ܢܦܩ ܠܚܝܠܐ *fit for military service;* with ܒܬܪ *to pursue, follow;* with ܠ *to proceed to, go towards; to fling himself, launch out into* ܠܒܝܫܬܐ *evil courses,* ܠܫܢܝܘܬܐ *madness;* also *to suit, be in accordance with;* with ܡܢ *to go out, go away from, to come from; to leave, desert; to go aside, be thrust out;* ܡܢ ܐܘܪܚܐ *to go aside from the way;* metaph. *to desert the ways* or *customs;* ܡܢ ܗܘܢܐ, ܡܢ ܪܥܝܢܐ *to go out of one's mind;* ܡܢ ܐܠܦܐ *to disembark;* ܡܢ ܟܘܪܣܝܗ *to leave* or *give up his see;* ܡܢ ܥܠܡܐ *to die;* ܡܢ ܥܡܠܐ *to lose his labour;* ܠܐ ܢܦܩ ܐܢܐ ܡܢ ܡܠܟܟ *I will not go aside from thy counsel;* ܢܦܩ ܡܢ ܥܕܬܐ ܩܬܘܠܝܩܝ Marcion *seceded from the Catholic Church;* with ܥܠ *to be in authority over; to cost, be spent, expended.* With substantives: ܛܒܐ *the rumour went abroad;* ܢܦܫܐ *to expire;* ܦܣܐ, ܦܣܬܐ *the lot* came out, fell; ܦܘܢܝܐ or ܒܦܘܢܝܐ to excuse, apologize, defend, with ܥܠ or ܡܛܠ ; ܠܐ ܢܦܩ ܐܢܐ ܦܘܢܝܐ ܡܛܠܬܗ I make no excuse for him; ܢܦܩ ܐܢܐ ܦܘܢܝܐ ܥܠ ܢܦܫܝ I make my defence; ܢܦܩ ܫܡܗ his name went abroad, he became famous. Part. a) verbal use ܢܦܩܝܢ ܢܦܩܝܢ ܗܘܘ they had gone out; ܢܦܝܩ ܗܘܐ ܫܐܕܐ ܡܢܗ̇ the devil was gone out of her; impers. ܢܦܝܩ ܠܗܘܢ have they come forth? b) adj. translated; of lines produced; ܢܦܩܬܐ ܡܢ ܡܨܥܬܐ eccentric. Pael ܢܦܩ a) to spend, go through, pass time; ܢܦܩܘܗܝ ܠܨܘܡܐ ܕܠܐ ܬܘܪܣܝܐ they passed Lent without nourishment. b) to train, instruct; pass. part. ܡܢܦܩ; ܡܢܦܩܐ ܒܝܘܠܦܢܐ instructed, learned; ܡܢܦܩ ܒܡܠܐ eloquent; ܡܢܦܩ ܒܩܪܒܐ experienced in war. Ethpa. ܐܬܢܦܩ to be sent out, driven out; to be instructed, learned, practised, exercised. Aphel ܐܦܩ a) to bring forth, put forth, produce; ܬܦܩ ܐܪܥܐ ܬܕܐܐ let the earth put forth grass; ܠܡܦܩܘ ܠܚܡܐ ܡܢ ܐܪܥܐ to bring forth food from the earth; ܡܦܩܐ ܗܘܬ ܦܪܥܐ it puts forth blossom; ܡܦܩܐ ܩܢܛܐ ܣܝܒܘܬܐ care causes white hairs. b) to lead out, take, bring or carry out; ܡܐ ܕܐܦܩܬ ܠܥܡܐ ܡܢ ܡܨܪܝܢ when Thou hast brought the people out of Egypt; ܗܘ ܡܦܩ ܡܢ ܡܨܝܕܬܐ ܪ̈ܓܠܝ He plucketh my feet out of the net; ܠܐ ܬܦܩܘܢ ܡܘܒܠܐ ܡܢ ܒ̈ܬܝܟܘܢ ye shall not carry forth a burden out of your houses. c) to cast out, remove, reject, repudiate; to put away a wife; to depose a bishop; ܡܦܩ ܢܦܩܘܢܟܘܢ ܡܢ ܫ̈ܐܕܐ casting out devils; ܢܦܩܘܢܟܘܢ ܡܢ ܟܢܘܫܬܗܘܢ they shall cast you out of their synagogues; ܚܪܝܡ ܘܡܦܩ ܡܢ ܕܝܦܛܘܟܐ anathematized and having his name removed from the diptychs. d) to make proceed, send forth; ܐܦܩ ܠܪܘܚܐ God the Father sent the Holy Spirit; to bring or let out of prison; to lead into captivity, lead captive; to bring to pass; to spread a rumour; to set forth, promulgate an edict, a law; to bring out, publish or translate a book; to spend money or time; ܒܣܪܝܩܘܬܐ ܡܦܩܝܢܢ ܝܘܡܬܢ we spend our days in vanity; also to extort money; to hatch; arith. to subtract; to compute. With ܥܠ to set over. With ܦܘܢܝܐ to excuse oneself. Ettapal ܐܬܬܦܩ to be taken away, to be cast out, to be extracted as an arrow from a wound; to be taken up, dragged out as bodies of the slain; to be spent, expended; to be translated; to be produced as lines; gram. to be pronounced. Derivatives, ܢܦܩܐ, ܢܦܩܐ, ܢܦܩܐ, ܢܦܩܐ, ܢܦܩܘܬܐ, ܢܦܩܬܐ, ܢܦܩܐ, ܡܦܩܘܬܐ, ܡܦܩܢܐ, ܡܦܩܐ, ܢܦܩܬܐ, ܢܦܩܐ, ܡܦܩܢܐ, ܡܦܩܢܐ.

ܢܦܩܐ or ܢܦܩܐ pl. ܐ̈ rt. ܢܦܩ. m. a) monks as those who leave the world. b) a rising, swelling in the groin.

ܢܦܩܐ pl. ܐ̈ rt. ܢܦܩ. m. a) a mine. b) ܢܦܩܐ ܕܚܨܪܡܐ the thickened juice of unripe grapes.

ܢܦܩܐ rt. ܢܦܩ. m. a spendthrift, prodigal.

ܢܦܩܐ rt. ܢܦܩ. m. fine parchment.

ܢܦܩܬܐ and ܢܦܩܬܐ pl. ܢ̈ܦܩܬܐ rt. ܢܦܩ. f. outgoings, expense, charge, cost; supplies, necessaries; ܐܦܩ ܢܦܩܬܐ I will pay expenses; ܚܫܒ ܢܦܩܬܗ he reckons the cost; ܝܗܒ ܠܗ ܢܦܩܬܐ ܠܐܘܪܚܐ he gave him supplies for his journey.

ܢܦܪ fut. ܢܢܦܘܪ, act. part. ܢܦܪ, ܢܦܪܐ. to snort, to shy as a horse; to shun, turn away from; to rage; ܢܦܪ ܡܢ ܡܐܟܘܠܬܐ ܡܐ ܕܣܒܥ he turns away from food when he is full; ܐܝܟ ܕܢܦܪ ܡܢ ܚܡܬܐ a man snorting with anger. Aph. ܐܦܪ to put to flight; pass. part. ܡܦܪ standing on end, towzled as hair. Derivative, ܢܦܪܐ.

ܢܦܪܐ pl. ܐ̈ rt. ܢܦܪ. m. snorting, neighing.

ܢܦܫ fut. ܢܢܦܘܫ, act. part. ܢܦܫ, pass. part. ܢܦܝܫ, ܢܦܝܫܐ. to breathe, be alive, have life. Ethpe. ܐܬܢܦܫ to breathe, respire; to take breath, to revive, be refreshed; ܙܒܢܐ ܚܕܐ ܐܬܢܦܫ he took breath for a moment. Pael ܢܦܫ to refresh; to give life. Ethpa. ܐܬܢܦܫ to be refreshed, revived, inspirited; ܡܢ ܥܩ̈ܬܗ after his troubles; ܡܢ ܟܘܪܗܢܐ after illness. Derivatives, ܢܦܫܢܝܐ, ܢܦܫܢܝܐ, ܢܦܫܘܬܐ, ܢܦܫܐ, ܢܦܫܐ, ܢܦܫܢܝܬ, ܢܦܫܢܘܬܐ, ܢܦܫܢܝܐ, ܢܦܫܢܘܬܐ, ܡܢܦܫܐ, ܡܢܦܫܢܘܬܐ.

ܢܦܫ, ܢܦܫܐ pl. ܢܦ̈ܫܢ, ܢܦ̈ܫܬܐ rt. ܢܦܫ. f. a) the breath of life, the animal soul, physical life, vital principle, opp. ܦܓܪܐ the body and ܗܘܢܐ the mind; ܢܦܫܐ ܡܠܝܠܬܐ the rational soul; ܢܦܫ ܚܝܐ, ܢܦܫܐ ܚܝܬܐ a living soul, living creature; ܥܕܟܝܠ ܢܦܫܐ ܒܗ breath is still in him, he still lives; ܕܡܐ ܢܦܫܐ ܗܘ the blood is the life;

ܡܦܨܐ ܢܦܫܬܗܘܢ ܡܢ ܡܘܬܐ He saves their soul from death; ܕܚܠܝܢ ܗܘܘ ܥܠ ܢܦܫܬܗܘܢ they feared for their lives; ܒܢܦܫܗ, ܒܢܦܫܢ at the peril of his, of our life, but ܒܢܦܫܗܘܢ for their lives, to save their lives; ܫܘܚܠܦ ܢܦܫܬܐ metempsychosis. b) a soul, living person, any one; ܟܠ ܕܢܦܫܬܐ ܕܐܢܫܐ persons; ܡܢ ܕܩܛܠ ܐܝܟ ܢܦܫܐ whoso killeth any person; ܫܒܘ ܐܝܟ ܚܡܫܝܢ ܐܠܦܝܢ ܢܦܫܬܐ they took captive about fifty thousand souls; ܢܦܫܐ ܕܡܝܬܬܐ a dead person. c) self, oneself; ܢܦܫܝ I myself; ܢܦܫܢ we ourselves; ܐܡܪܘ ܒܢܦܫܗܘܢ they said within themselves; ܡܢ ܢܦܫܗ, ܡܢ ܢܦܫܗ of himself, of his own accord; ܕܡܐ ܕܢܦܫܗܘܢ their own blood; ܐܬܪܘܪܒ ܒܥܝܢܝ ܢܦܫܗ he was exalted in his own eyes; ܐܝܬܝܐ ܕܢܦܫܗ self-existent; ܝܠܘܦܐ ܡܢ ܢܦܫܗ self-taught; ܩܛܘܠ ܢܦܫܗ suicide; ܨܠܘܬܐ ܕܢܦܫܗ silent prayer; ܚܘܝ ܢܦܫܗ he gave himself out to be; ܝܗܒ ܢܦܫܗ he professed; ܣܡ ܢܦܫܗ he set himself, determined; ܥܒܕ ܢܦܫܗ he feigned, pretended; ܫܪܐ ܢܦܫܗ he abdicated. d) a monument.

ܢܦܫܢܐ rt. ܢܦܫ. animate; endowed with a soul.

ܢܦܫܢܐܝܬ rt. ܢܦܫ. adv. according to nature, naturally opp. ܪܘܚܢܐܝܬ spiritually.

ܢܦܫܢܘܬܐ rt. ܢܦܫ. f. animate life.

ܢܦܫܢܝܐ, ܝܬܐ rt. ܢܦܫ. living, animal, natural; mental; ܡܙܕܪܥ ܦܓܪܐ ܢܦܫܢܝܐ . ܩܐܡ ܦܓܪܐ ܪܘܚܢܝܐ it is sown a natural body, it is raised a spiritual body; ܠܐ ܢܦܫܢܝܬܐ things without life; ܢܦܫܐ ܢܦܫܢܝܬܐ the natural soul; ܚܝܠܐ ܢܦܫܢܝܐ mental faculties; ܚܫܐ ܢܦܫܢܝܐ natural or animal passions; ܟܘܪܗܢܐ ܢܦܫܢܝܐ diseases of the soul or mind.

ܢܦܫܢܝܘܬܐ rt. ܢܦܫ. f. sensuality.

ܢܦܬܐ pl. ܢܦܬܐ f. refuse, rubbish, offscourings; ܐܝܟ ܢܦܬܐ ܕܡܫܬܕܝܐ ܡܢ ܒܝܬܐ as refuse cast out of the house; ܐܢܐ ܢܦܬܐ ܕܟܠܗܘܢ ܕܝܪܝܐ one who is the scum of all monks.

ܢܨܐ fut. ܢܢܨܐ, infin. ܡܢܨܐ, act. part. ܢܨܐ, ܢܨܝܐ. usually with ܥܡ to strive, contend, quarrel, be contrary; ܢܨܝܢ ܗܘܘ ܚܕ ܥܡ ܚܕ they strove one with another. Derivatives, ܢܨܝܐ, ܢܨܝܐ, ܢܨܝܢܐ, ܢܨܝܘܬܐ, ܡܢܨܝܢܐܝܬ, ܡܢܨܝܢܐ.

ܢܨܐ pl. ܢܨܐ m. a hawk; ܢܨܐ ܙܥܘܪ ܡܢ ܒܙܐ. ܘܨܐܕ ܨܦܪܐ ܘܦܪܘܓܐ a hawk is smaller than a falcon and catches sparrows and fledgelings.

ܢܨܒ fut. ܢܨܘܒ and ܢܢܨܘܒ, infin. ܡܢܨܒ and ܡܢܨܘܒ, imper. ܢܨܘܒ, act. part. ܢܨܒ, ܢܨܒܐ, pass. part. ܢܨܝܒ, ܐ, ܬܐ. to plant, implant, fix, found; of locusts to deposit eggs in the ground; ܢܨܒ ܡܪܝܐ ܐܠܗܐ ܦܪܕܝܣܐ the Lord God planted a garden; ܢܨܒ ܨܝܕܐ ܠܡܨܝܕܬܐ the fowler fixed the net; ܕܢܨܘܒ ܥܘܡܪܐ to found a monastery; metaph. of sowing seeds of sin, of virtue, implanting hope, love, envy, &c. Pass. part. ܐܝܠܢܐ ܕܢܨܝܒ ܥܠ ܦܨܝܕܐ ܕܡܝܐ a tree planted by a watercourse; ܩܡܨܐ ܢܨܝܒܐ ܒܚܩܠܬܢ the locust deposited in our fields, i.e. of which our fields are full; metaph. implanted, ingrafted, innate; ܡܠܬܐ ܕܢܨܝܒܐ ܒܟܘܢ the implanted word; ܪܚܡܬܐ ܕܗܢܝܘܬܐ ܢܨܝܒܬܐ ܒܢ the love of pleasure implanted in us. Ethpe. ܐܬܢܨܒ to be planted, implanted, firmly fixed. Pael ܢܨܒ to implant, plant firmly. Derivatives, ܢܨܒܬܐ, ܢܨܒܢܐ, ܢܨܘܒܐ, ܢܨܒܢܝܐ, ܢܨܒܘܬܐ, ܡܢܨܒܢܐ.

ܢܨܒܬܐ, ܢܨܒܐ pl. ܢܨܒܬܐ, ܢܨܒܐ rt. ܢܨܒ. f. planting, power of reproduction, the laying of locusts' eggs in the earth; a plant, sucker, slip; ܢܨܒ ܢܨܒܬܐ he planted, did planting; ܡܫܚܠܦܝ ܓܢܣܝܐ ܕܢܨܒܬܐ of different kinds of planting; ܐܫܩܝ ܢܨܒܬܗ: ܕܬܬܠ ܦܐܪܐ ܕܝܘܠܦܢܐ the springs of doctrine whence he watered her young plants that she might yield the fruits of doctrine; ܚܝܘܬܐ ܢܨܒܬܐ a zoophyte.

ܢܨܒܢܝܐ, ܢܝܬܐ rt. ܢܨܒ. vegetative, having the power to produce growth, implanted by nature, instinctive; ܢܦܫܐ ܢܨܒܢܝܬܐ the vivifying principle, principle of growth opp. ܢܦܫܐ ܡܠܝܠܬܐ the intellectual principle, rational soul; ܡܥܒܕܢܘܬܐ ܢܨܒܢܝܬܐ instinctive operations.

ܢܨܘܒܐ pl. ܐ̈ rt. ܢܨܒ. m. a gardener, vinedresser, planter; a founder; ܢܨܘܒܗ ܕܦܪܕܝܣܐ He who planted Paradise.

ܢܨܘܚܐ rt. ܢܨܚ. clear, liquid, sonorous of the voice.

ܢܨܘܦ, ܢܨܘܦܐ, ܢܨܘܦܝܬܐ E-Syr. ܢܨܘܦ &c. rt. ܢܨܦ. *red, reddish.*

ܢܨܘܦܘܬܐ or ܢܨ rt. ܢܨܦ. f. *clearness, brilliancy.*

ܢܨܘܪܐ pl. ܐ̈ rt. ܢܨܪ. m. *a*) *a running sore* in the corners of the eyes or on the gums, *a gumboil; piles. b*) *a sucker.*

ܢܨܘܪܘܬܐ same as ܢܨܘܪܐ *a*).

ܢܨܚ fut. ܢܶܢܨܰܚ, act. part. ܢܳܨܰܚ, ܢܳܨܚܳܐ, part. adj. ܢܨܝܚ, ܚܳܐ, ܚܬܳܐ. *a*) *to shine out, flame upwards, be brilliant. b*) *to be well known, distinguished, to become famous, celebrated; to conquer, triumph;* ܢܨܚ ܗܘܳܐ ܕܳܢܝܐܝܠ ܒܒܳܒܶܠ *Daniel was famous in Babylon;* ܢܨܚ ܗܘܳܐ ܒܩܪ̈ܳܒܐ *he was famous in war;* ܘܢܨܚܳܐ ܕܕܒܚܬܶܗ ܕܐܒܪܳܗܳܡ ܒܝܬ ܟܢ̈ܥܢܝܐ the fame of Abraham's sacrifice *which was well known among the Canaanites;* ܣܳܗ̈ܕܐ ܕܢܨܚܘ ܒܐܘܠܨ̈ܢܝܗܘܢ *martyrs who were glorious through their afflictions.* Part. adj. *a*) *bright, shining, brilliant, splendid, glorious;* ܐܣܦܝܪܐ ܢܨܝܚܬܐ *the shining sphere* of the sun; ܢܨܝܚܐ ܐܝܟ ܩܪܘܣܛܠܠܘܣ *bright as crystal;* ܟܬܳܢܳܐ ܕܟܝܐ ܢܨܝܚܐ *linen pure and bright;* ܛܘ̈ܒܐ ܢܨܝܚ̈ܐ ܐܝܠܝܢ *such glorious blessings. b*) *clear, sonorous* of the voice. *c*) *illustrious, victorious, triumphant;* ܢܨܝܚ ܙܟܘܬܐ *gloriously victorious;* ܢܨܝܚ ܩܕܝܫܐ *a very glorious saint. d*) subst. of God ܢܨܝܚܐ ܕܐܝܣܪܝܠ *the Victory of Israel;* frequently of martyrs; ܫܐܠܗ ܕܝܢܐ ܠܢܨܝܚܐ *the judge questioned the heroic martyr;* ܐܬܘܩܕ ܢܨܝܚܐ ܣܗܕܐ *the victorious martyr was burnt with fire.* Pael ܢܰܨܰܚ *to render celebrated, to distinguish, to make to triumph; to adorn, glorify; to celebrate, keep;* ܗܘ ܕܡܢܨܚ ܠܡܣܟܢܐ ܘܡܚܝܠܐ *He who makes the poor and feeble to triumph;* ܕܢܢܨܚܘܢܢܝ ܒܫܘ̈ܩܝܗ *that they may glorify me in her streets;* ܢܨܚܬ ܨܠܘ̈ܬܐ ܕܚܠܝܦܐ *I have celebrated public prayers for the Khalif;* ܢܨܚܘ ܢܕܪ̈ܝܟܘܢ *solemnize your vows.* Ethpa. ܐܬܢܨܚ *to be celebrated, renowned, glorious, triumphant; to excel, be victorious;* ܐܬܢܨܚ ܒܐܪ̈ܒܥ ܦܢ̈ܝܢ *he was celebrated in all four corners* of the earth; ܐܬܢܨܚ ܡܢ ܟܠܗܘܢ ܕܒܗܢܐ ܕܪܐ *he was renowned above all in this era;* ܐܬܢܨܚ ܒܡܝܬܪܘܬܐ *he excelled in virtue;* ܡܬܢܨܚ ܗܘܐ ܒܝܘܠܦܢܐ ܥܕܬܢܝܐ *he was celebrated for his ecclesiastical learning;* ܐܬܢܨܚ ܒܙܟܘ̈ܬܐ ܪܘܪ̈ܒܬܐ ܘܩܪ̈ܒܐ ܣܓܝ̈ܐܐ *he was glorious in great victories and many wars;* ܕܢܬܢܨܚ ܒܡܣܝܒܪܢܘܬܐ *that we may be victorious through patience;* ܕܢܬܢܨܚ ܩܝܛܐ ܒܦܐܪ̈ܘܗܝ *that summer may be glorious with fruits.* Aphel ܐܢܨܚ *to glorify, to be glorious, celebrated.* Derivatives, ܢܨܘܚܐ, ܢܨܝܚܐ, ܢܨܝܚܐܝܬ, ܢܨܝܚܘܬܐ, ܡܢܨܚܢܐ.

ܢܨܚܢ, ܢܨܚܢܐ pl. ܢ̈ܐ rt. ܢܨܚ. m. *a victory, triumph, trophy; an exploit, heroic deed; success, praise, pomp, splendour;* ܢܨܚܢܐ ܕܙܟܘܬܐ *trophy of victory;* ܚܕܝܘ ܒܢܨܚܢ ܗܝܡܢܘܬܗܘܢ they rejoiced *at the triumph of their faith;* ܟܬܒ ܢܨܚܢܝܗܘܢ ܕܣܗ̈ܕܐ *he wrote the heroic acts of the martyrs;* ܟܕ ܡܫܬܡܠܐ ܒܢܨܚܢ̈ܐ ܕܫܘܡܠܝܐ *he being fulfilled with the victories of the perfect life;* ܫܡܐ ܪܒܐ ܘܢܨܚܢܐ ܒܝܬ ܡܠܟ̈ܐ ܚܒܪ̈ܝܟ that thou shouldest gain *a great name and praise amongst the kings thy fellows.*

ܢܨܝ, ܢܨܝܐ, ܢܨܝܬܐ rt. ܢܨܐ. *contentious;* ܐܢܬܬܐ ܢܨܝܬܐ *a contentious woman;* ܠܐ ܢܨܝ *no brawler.*

ܢܨܝܐ rt. ܢܨܐ. m. *contention, strife.*

ܢܨܝܒܐܝܬ rt. ܢܨܒ. adv. *implanted by nature.*

ܢܨܝܒܘܬܐ rt. ܢܨܒ. f. *planting, plantation.*

ܢܨܝܒܝܢܝܐ from ܢܨܝܒܝܢ *Nisibene, a native of Nisibis.*

ܢܨܝܒܝܢ *Nisibis,* an ancient city of Northern Mesopotamia.

ܢܨܝܒܢܝܐ from ܢܨܝܒܝܢ *Nisibene, a native of Nisibis.*

ܢܨܝܚܐܝܬ rt. ܢܨܚ. adv. *excellently, gloriously, splendidly.*

ܢܨܝܚܘܬܐ rt. ܢܨܚ. f. *splendour, brilliancy, glory, pomp, excellence;* ܟܘܟܒܐ ܕܠܦܪܘܕܝܛܝ ܕܡܐ ܒܢܨܝܚܘܬܐ a star *resembling the planet Venus in brilliancy;* ܢܨܝܚܘܬܐ ܕܐܠܗܘܬܐ *the glory of the Godhead;* ܐܬܚܕܪ ܡܢ ܛܘܒܢܘܬܗ ܘܢܨܝܚܘܬܗ ܩܕܡܝܬܐ the devil *was cast down from his pristine state of blessedness and glory.*

ܢܛܘܦܬܐ rt. ܢܛܦ. f. *percolation.*

ܢܛܝܪܐ rt. ܢܛܐ. m. *dissension.*

ܢܛܝܦܐ m. *the linen cloth* worn on the head by Roman women.

ܢܛܦ fut. ܢܶܛܽܘܦ, act. part. ܢܳܛܶܦ, ܢܳܛܦܳܐ, pass. part. ܢܛܝܦ, ܢܛܝܦܳܐ, ܢܛܝܦܬܳܐ. *to let drop, to pour* oil or medicine; *to ooze.* Ethpe. ܐܶܬܢܛܶܦ *to be dropped, applied* as medicine to a sore. Derivatives, ܢܛܳܦܳܐ, ܢܛܘܦܬܳܐ, ܢܛܦܳܐ, ܢܶܛܦܳܐ.

ܢܛܦܳܐ or ܢܶܛܦܳܐ rt. ܢܛܦ. m. *a drinking-vessel.*

ܢܛܳܦܳܐ rt. ܢܛܦ. m. *pouring, dripping, distillation.*

ܢܨܒ fut. ܢܶܢܨܽܒ, act. part. ܢܳܨܶܒ, ܢܳܨܒܳܐ. *to hiss* as a serpent; *to shriek at* with ܒ, *scold, rage; to dilate, swell* as a sore or with anger. Also, in the Lexx. *to be strong, powerful; to be tasty, savoury, strong-flavoured; to be shrill, sharp* in sound. Ethpe. ܐܶܬܢܨܶܒ *to exude, perspire; to become strong.* Pael ܢܰܨܶܒ *to reject.* Derivatives, ܢܨܳܒܳܐ, ܢܨܝܒܳܐ, ܢܨܝܒܘܬܳܐ, ܢܨܒܳܐ.

ܢܨܒܳܐ or ܢܶܨܒܳܐ rt. ܢܨܒ. m. *a*) *hissing, sibilation.* *b*) *shrill, clear; clearness.* *c*) *a vine-branch, a caper twig, the caper* plant.

ܢܨܪ fut. ܢܶܢܨܽܪ, act. part. ܢܳܨܰܪ, ܢܳܨܪܳܐ, pass. part. ܢܨܝܪ, ܐ̈, ܬܳܐ. *to chirp, twitter* as birds; *to squeak, squeal* as a hog; *to shriek, utter shrill* or *broken sounds* as magicians; *to hum, croon* over a child; *to chant, praise, sing praises;* pass. part. *well known.* Pael ܢܰܨܰܪ same as Peal but in more frequent use: ܐܰܝܟ ܣܢܘܢܺܝܬܳܐ ܕܡܢܰܨܪܳܐ ܢܰܨܪܶܬ *as a swallow twittering so did I twitter;* ܡܶܢ ܥܰܦܪܳܐ ܡܢܰܨܪܳܢ ܡܶܠܰܝܟ *thy words quaver out of the dust;* ܐܶܡܶܗ ܕܣܺܝܣܪܳܐ ܡܢܰܨܪܳܐ the mother of Sisera *uttered shrill sounds of exultation.* With accusative, ܣܰܝܦܳܐ ܚܰܪܺܝܦܳܐ ܢܢܰܨܰܪ ܐܶܢܽܘܢ *the sharp sword shall whistle by them;* ܫܶܡܥܽܘܢ ܣܳܒܳܐ ܡܢܰܨܰܪ ܗܘܳܐ ܠܳܟ *aged Simeon crooned over Thee;* ܡܫܽܘܚܬܳܢܺܝܬܳܐ ܡܢܰܨܪܳܐ ܠܘܰܪܕܳܐ *the poetess sings the praises of the rose.* Ethpa. ܐܶܬܢܰܨܰܪ *to be chanted, praised, lauded; to be foretold, prefigured; to be caressed, lulled;* ܡܶܬܢܰܨܰܪ ܘܡܶܫܬܰܒܰܚ ܐܰܠܳܗܳܐ God *is lauded and praised;* ܒܚܶܘܝܳܐ ܕܡܽܘܫܶܐ ܦܰܓܪܳܐ ܕܡܳܪܰܢ ܡܶܬܢܰܨܰܪ ܗܘܳܐ *in the serpent of Moses the body of our Lord was prefigured;* ܡܶܢ ܣܶܦܘܳܬܳܐ ܕܒܬܽܘܠܬܳܐ ܡܶܬܢܰܨܰܪ ܐܰܢ̱ܬ *Thou art lulled by the Virgin's lips.* Derivatives, ܢܨܳܪܳܐ, ܢܨܺܝܪܳܐ, ܢܨܺܝܪܘܬܳܐ and ܢܨܺܝܪܽܘܬܳܐ, ܢܽܘܨܪܳܐ, ܢܽܘܨܳܪܬܳܐ, ܡܢܰܨܪܳܢܽܘܬܳܐ, ܡܢܰܨܪܳܢܺܝܬ, ܡܢܰܨܪܳܢܳܐ, ܡܢܰܨܪܳܢܺܝܬܳܐ, ܡܢܰܨܪܳܢܽܘܬܳܐ, ܡܶܬܢܰܨܪܳܢܺܝܬ, ܡܶܬܢܰܨܪܳܢܳܐ.

ܢܶܨܪܳܐ and ܢܽܘܨܪܳܐ rt. ܢܨܪ. m. *the chirping, twittering* of birds; *humming* or *shrill cries* of magicians; *squealing.*

ܢܳܨܪܳܝܳܐ pl. ܝ̈ܶܐ from ܢܳܨܪܰܬ. *a Nazarene, a Christian;* ܗܳܢܳܐ ܝܶܫܽܘܥ ܢܳܨܪܳܝܳܐ *this is Jesus of Nazareth;* ܦܳܪܽܘܩܗܽܘܢ ܕܢܳܨܪܳܝܶܐ *Saviour of the Nazarenes.*

ܢܽܘܨܪܳܝܽܘܬܳܐ rt. ܢܨܪ. f. *novelty, innovation.*

ܢܳܨܪܰܬ *Nazareth;* ܫܳܛܝܽܘܬܳܗ ܕܢܳܨܪܰܬ *the folly of Nazareth* = the Christian Faith.

ܢܩܐ act. part. ܢܳܩܶܐ. *a*) *to be oppressed in mind.* *b*) *to be adapted, ready, intent, inclined.* Pass. part. ܢܩܶܐ, ܢܩܺܝܳܐ. *a*) *apt, ready, eager; prone, disposed, bent on;* ܢܩܶܐ ܠܰܢ ܣܳܛܳܢܳܐ ܥܰܡ ܡܥܰܕܪܳܢܰܘܗܝ ܒܰܐܟܙܪܺܝܘܬܳܐ *for* Satan *with his helpers is cruelly intent on us;* ܢܩܺܝܳܐ ܗܺܝ ܠܰܢ ܐܰܠܳܗܽܘܬܳܐ ܐܰܝܟ ܡܪܰܒܝܳܢܺܝܬܳܐ ܠܡܶܚܙܳܐ ܠܰܛܠܳܝܳܐ *the Godhead is as ready to aid us as a nurse to see after a child;* ܒܪܺܝܬܳܐ ܢܩܺܝܳܐ ܠܫܽܘܚܠܳܦܶܐ *the creature is prone to variations;* ܠܶܫܳܢܶܗ ܢܩܶܐ ܠܒܽܘܙܳܚܳܐ *his tongue is apt to mock.* *b*) *sprinkled, prepared by sprinkling* as a sacrifice. Ethpe. ܐܶܬܢܩܶܐ *to be inclined.* Pael ܢܰܩܺܝ *to pour out* a libation, *make a drink-offering,* often with ܢܶܩܝܳܐ; *to consecrate, offer;* ܠܳܐ ܐܶܢܰܩܶܐ ܢܶܩܝܰܝܗܽܘܢ ܡܶܢ ܕܡܳܐ *their drink-offering of blood will I not offer;* ܡܢܰܩܶܝܢ ܢܶܩܝܶܐ ܥܰܠ ܡܰܕܒܚܳܐ *offering drink-offerings upon* this altar *to devils;* ܕܢܶܕܒܚܽܘܢ ܘܢܢܰܩܽܘܢ *that they may offer sacrifice and libations.* Ethpa. ܐܶܬܢܰܩܺܝ *to be poured out as a drink-offering; to consecrate oneself; to be inclined;* ܚܰܡܪܳܐ ܕܡܶܬܢܰܩܶܐ *wine that is offered.* Derivatives, ܢܶܩܝܳܐ, ܢܩܳܝܳܐ, ܡܢܰܩܝܳܢܳܐ.

ܢܩܒ fut. ܢܶܢܩܽܘܒ, imper. ܢܩܽܘܒ, pass. part. ܢܩܺܝܒ, ܐ̈, ܬܳܐ. *to bore, pierce, perforate, dig through;* ܢܶܢܩܽܘܒ ܡܳܪܶܗ ܐܶܕܢܶܗ ܒܡܰܩܒܳܐ *his master shall bore his ear through with an awl.* Pass. part. *bored* or *pierced through; hollowed out;* ܟܺܝܣܳܐ ܢܩܺܝܒܳܐ *a purse with holes in it;* ܟܺܐܦܳܐ ܕܢܩܺܝܒܳܐ *a stone with a hole in it* hung on for a punishment, hence *a weight, hindrance, fetter;* ܐܬܩܒܘ ܒܗ ܢܩܒܬܐ ܪܒܬܐ *they hung on him a great weight;* ܢܫܕܐ ܢܩܒܬܐ ܕܪܓܝܓܬܐ ܡܢ ܪܓܠܘܗܝ *let him cast off from his feet the weights of desire.* Ethpe. ܐܬܢܩܒ *to be bored through;* ܐܬܢܩܒܘ ܠܐܕܢܐ ܢܩܒܐ ܒܪܫܐ *holes have been prepared for the ears in the head.* Pael ܢܩܒ a) *to make a hole, an opening; to tattoo;* ܢܩܒ ܡܩܒܢܝܬܐ ܘܐܛܒܥ ܐܢܝܢ *he scuttled the ships;* ܡܢܩܒܝܢ ܗܘܘ ܕܪܥܝܗܘܢ ܐܝܟ ܚܢܦܐ *they tattooed their arms as the heathen do;* ܐܣܦܘܓܐ ܡܢܩܒܬܐ *a sponge full of holes.* b) gram. *to be* or *be placed in the feminine gender;* ܡܢܩܒܬܐ *of the feminine gender.* Ethpa. ܐܬܢܩܒ *to be pierced through.* Ethpalan ܐܬܢܩܒܢ denom. verb from ܢܩܒܬܢܐ *to be of the feminine gender.* Derivatives, ܢܩܒܐ, ܢܩܒܬܐ, ܢܩܒܐܝܬ, ܢܩܒܘܬܐ, ܢܩܒܝܐ, ܢܩܒܬܘܬܐ, ܢܩܒܬܢܐ, ܢܩܒܬܐܝܬ, ܢܩܒܬܢܘܬܐ, ܢܩܘܒܐ, ܢܩܒܬܢܝܐ, ܢܩܒܬܢܝܐܝܬ, ܢܩܒܬܢܝܘܬܐ, ܡܢܩܒܐ, ܡܢܩܒܬܢܐ, ܡܢܩܒܘܬܐ.

ܢܩܒܐ pl. ܢܩܒܐ, ܢܩܒܝܢ (ܒ hard) rt. ܢܩܒ. m. *a hole, opening, hollow, burrow, tunnel;* ܢܩܒܐ ܕܫܘܪܐ *a hole in the wall;* ܘܢܩܝܦܢ ܪܓܠܝܗܘܢ ܒܐܪܒܥܐ ܢܩܒܝܢ ܕܩܘܠܐ *their feet were stretched in four holes in the stocks.*

ܢܩܒܐ, ܢܩܒܬܐ pl. ܢܩܒܢ, ܢܩܒܬܐ (ܒ soft) rt. ܢܩܒ. f. *female, feminine* opp. ܕܟܪܐ, ܕܟܪ *male, masculine;* ܕܟܪ ܘܢܩܒܐ ܒܪܐ ܐܢܘܢ *male and female created He them;* ܢܩܒܬܐ ܕܩܡܨܐ *the female locust;* ܢܩܒܬܐ ܕܚܡܪܐ *a she-ass;* ܢܩܒܬܐ ܕܣܘܣܝܐ *mares.*

ܢܩܒܐܝܬ rt. ܢܩܒ. adv. a) *by means of a hole.* b) *in the feminine gender.*

ܢܩܒܘܬܐ rt. ܢܩܒ. f. *the female sex, the feminine gender.*

ܢܩܒܝܐ rt. ܢܩܒ. gram. *feminine.*

ܢܩܒܬܘܬܐ rt. ܢܩܒ. f. *the feminine gender.*

ܢܩܒܬܢܐ rt. ܢܩܒ. gram. *feminine.*

ܢܩܒܬܢܐܝܬ rt. ܢܩܒ. adv. gram. *in the feminine gender.*

ܢܩܒܬܢܘܬܐ rt. ܢܩܒ. f. *womanhood, effeminacy;* gram. *the feminine gender.*

ܢܩܒܬܢܝܐ rt. ܢܩܒ. *female, feminine.*

ܢܩܒܬܢܝܐܝܬ rt. ܢܩܒ. adv. *in the feminine gender.*

ܢܩܒܬܢܝܘܬܐ rt. ܢܩܒ. f. *the feminine gender.*

ܢܩܐ root-meaning a) *to prick, puncture, punctuate.* b) *to be pure.* Ethpe. ܐܬܢܩܝ *to be thin.* Pael ܢܩܝ *to clear away, cleanse;* pass. part. ܡܢܩܝܐ *cleansed.* Ethpa. ܐܬܢܩܝ *to be cleansed, purified;* ܐܢܐ ܡܛܠܫܬܐ ܐܬܢܩܝܬ *I spotted* with sin *was purified.* Derivatives, ܢܩܝܐ, ܢܩܝܐܝܬ, ܢܩܝܘܬܐ, ܢܩܝܐ, ܢܩܝܐ, ܢܩܝܢܐ, ܢܩܝܘܬܐ, ܡܢܩܝܢܐ, ܡܢܩܝܘܬܐ, ܢܩܝܘܬܐ.

ܢܩܐ, ܢܩܝܐ, ܢܩܝܬܐ rt. ܢܩܐ. a) *clean, pure, shining; unalloyed, sincere, free from taint* or *sin; fresh, wholesome, healthful;* ܟܬܢܐ ܢܩܝܐ ܘܕܟܝܐ *a clean strip of linen;* ܡܝܐ ܢܩܝܐ *pure water;* ܐܣܛܘܟܣܐ ܢܩܝܐ ܘܡܥܠܝܐ *the pure and ethereal element* i. e. *air;* ܐܬܒܚܪ ܙܘܙܗ ܘܐܫܬܟܚ ܢܩܝܐ *his coin was tried and found unalloyed;* ܡܐܟܘܠܬܐ ܢܩܝܬܐ ܘܒܣܝܡܬܐ *wholesome pleasant food;* ܐܕܢܐ ܢܩܝܬܐ ܫܡܥܬ *with ingenuous ears hast thou hearkened;* ܢܦܫܐ ܢܩܝܬܐ ܡܢ ܚܘܫܒܐ ܒܝܫܐ *a soul free from evil thoughts;* ܐܣܝܐ—ܟܘܡܪܐ ܢܩܝܐ *a revered physician, priest;* ܦܘܠܚܢܐ ܢܩܝܐ ܘܠܐ ܓܘܫܡܢܝܐ *pure and immaterial worship.* b) subst. *an embroidered shirt.*

ܢܩܝܐ pl. ܢܩܝܐ rt. ܢܩܐ. *a herdsman, sheepmaster.*

ܢܩܝܐܝܬ rt. ܢܩܐ. adv. *faultlessly, clearly, elegantly.*

ܢܩܝܘܢܐ rt. ܢܩܐ. *dainty, delicate.*

ܢܩܝܘܬܐ rt. ܢܩܐ. f. *cleanliness, purity, healthfulness.*

ܢܩܝܘܬܐ rt. ܢܩܐ. f. *herdsmanship.*

ܢܩܘܒܐ rt. ܢܩܒ. m. *a green locust* or *grasshopper.*

ܢܩܘܪܐ pl. ܢܩܘܪܐ rt. ܢܩܪ. a bird's *beak, bill.*

ܢܩܘܦܐ pl. ܢܩܘܦܐ rt. ܢܩܦ. m. *a follower, partisan;* gram. *agreeing with; affix.*

ܢܩܘܫܐ pl. ܢܩܘܫܐ rt. ܢܩܫ. m. *one knocking at the door; pulsating, throbbing* as a nerve; *a musical instrument; a player; a bell* or *sounding-board* used instead of a bell and struck with a mallet, same as Greek *semantron;* ܡܬܢܩܫ ܢܩܘܫܐ ܒܫܘܪܝ ܨܠܘܬܐ ܘܬܫܡܫܬܐ *the sounding-board is struck at the beginning of prayer and service;* ܩܝܣܐ ܕܢܩܘܫܐ *the mallet of the sounding-board.*

ܢܩܪ fut. ܢܢܩܘܪ. a) *to peck, wound.* b) *to point, add vowel-points.* Pael ܢܩܪ *to peck, prick, tattoo.* Derivatives, ܢܩܘܪܐ, ܢܩܘܪܬܐ, ܢܩܘܪܝܐ, ܢܩܪܐ.

ܢܩܚ part. ܢܳܩܶܚ, ܢܳܩܚܳܐ. *a*) *to peck, crack.* *b*) *to croak.* Aph. ܐܰܩܶܚ *to be audacious, obstinate.* Derivatives, ܢܩܚܐ, ܡܰܩܚܳܢܽܘܬܳܐ.

ܢܩܳܚܳܐ rt. ܢܩܚ. m. *a*) *cracking, fracture.* *b*) *croaking.*

ܢܩܝܐ pl. ܢܩܘܶ̈ܐ, ܢܩܘܳܬܳܐ f. *a*) *a sheep, ewe;* ܪܥܝ ܠܝ ܢܩܘܳܬܝ *feed my sheep;* the Blessed Virgin is called ܢܩܝܐ ܕܝܠܕܬ ܐܡܪܐ ܕܚܝܐ *the ewe which bare the Lamb of Life.* *b*) *the pole* of a mill to which an ass or mule is tied to turn it.

ܢܩܳܝܳܐ rt. ܢܩܐ. m. *aptitude, readiness, disposition, propensity.*

ܢܩܝܠܐ m. ܢܩܝܠܬܐ f. rt. ܢܩܠ. *a patch* on a shoe.

ܢܩܝܠܘܬܐ rt. ܢܩܠ. f. *clearing, levelling* or *smoothing* the road.

ܢܩܝܦܐܝܬ rt. ܢܩܦ. adv. *consequently, in accordance with.*

ܢܩܝܦܘܬܐ rt. ܢܩܦ. f. *a*) *connexion, relationship, affinity; copulation;* ܒܢܩܝܦܘܬܐ ܘܐܚܝܢܘܬܐ inheritance *according to affinity and relationship;* ܢܩܝܦܘܬܐ ܗܘܠܢܝܬܐ *material union.* *b*) used by the Nestorians to express the *conjunction* or *connexion* of the two natures in Christ without intermingling; ܢܩܝܦܘܬܐ ܠܐ ܡܬܦܪܫܢܝܬܐ *inseparable conjunction.* *c*) *adherence to* or *following of* opinion. *d*) *order, sequence;* ܟܬܒܐ ܚܕܬܐ ܥܡ ܥܬܝܩܐ ܒܢܩܝܦܘܬܐ *the books of the Old and New Testament in order;* ܢܩܝܦܘܬܐ ܕܡܠܘܫ̈ܐ *the order of succession of the signs of the zodiac;* ܗܦܟܐ ܕܢܩܝܦܘܬܐ *inverse order;* ܒܢܩܝܦܘܬܐ *in order, regularly.* *e*) gram. *being affixed, suffixed; an affix, suffix; the construct state;* ܢܩܝ̈ܦܘܬܐ ܕܡܠܬܐ *verbal affixes* i.e. denoting gender, number, tense, and person; ܢܩܝܦܘܬܐ ܕܐܬ̈ܘܬܐ *affixing of the* ܒܕܘܠ *letters.*

ܢܩܝܦܝܐ rt. ܢܩܦ. *of* or *by an affix, denoted by an affix.*

ܢܩܠ fut. ܢܶܩܘܽܠ, imper. ܩܘܽܠ, act. part. ܢܳܩܶܠ, ܢܳܩܠܳܐ, pass. part. ܢܩܺܝܠ, ܢܩܝܠܐ, ܢܩܝܠܬܐ. *to clear away, throw aside, reject; to make* a road *plain* or *smooth;* ܩܘܠܘ ܟܐܦ̈ܐ *clear away the stones;* ܢܩܠܬ ܢܗܝܪܘܬܟ ܫܒܝܠܐ ܡܢ ܟܐܦܐ *Thy splendour has cleared the path from stones;* ܟܠܗܘܢ ܡܕܢܚܝܐ ܢܩܠܘܗܝ *the Easterns rejected him* i.e. Manes; ܢܳܩܠܰܝ ܐܘܪܚܳܐ *they who clear away* stumbling-blocks from *the road.* Pass. part. *clear, even, smooth;* ܐܘܪܚܐ ܢܩܝܠܬܐ ܕܠܝܬ ܒܗ̇ ܟܐܦܐ ܘܬܘܩܠܬܐ *a smooth road without stones and stumbling-blocks;* ܡܪ̈ܓܢܝܬܐ ܘܟ̈ܐܦܐ ܢܩܝܠܝܢ ܠܩܛܝܢ ܡܢ ܬܡܢ *pearls and gems are picked up and cast away thence.* Ethpe. ܐܬܢܩܶܠ *to be cleared out of the way, cast aside;* ܠܚܫܘܟܐ ܡܬܢܩܠ *he is cast out into the dark.* Derivatives, ܢܩܝܠܐ, ܢܩܝܠܘܬܐ, ܢܩܠܐ.

ܢܩܳܠܳܐ rt. ܢܩܠ. m. *clearing, levelling* or *smoothing* the road.

ܢܩܡ Ethpe. ܐܬܢܩܶܡ usually with ܡܢ *to take vengeance;* ܡܶܬܢܩܶܡ ܐܢܳܐ ܡܶܢܟܘܿܢ *I take vengeance on you.* Ethpa. ܐܬܢܰܩܰܡ imper. West-Syr. ܐܬܢܰܩܶܡ *to take vengeance, be avenged* with ܒ or ܡܢ; *to be punished;* ܐܬܢܰܩܰܡ ܕܡܳܐ ܕܥܰܒ̈ܕܰܝ *the blood of my servants is avenged;* ܕܢܶܬܢܰܩܰܡ ܟܕ ܒܥܰܡܶܗ *that he might be avenged on his nation.* Derivative, ܢܩܡܬܐ.

ܢܶܩܡܬܳܐ, ܢܩܳܡܬܳܐ or ܢܶܩܡܬܳܐ rt. ܢܩܡ. f. *vengeance;* with ܥܒܰܕ or ܦܪܰܥ *to take vengeance, avenge, punish;* with ܬܒܰܥ *to demand* or *exact vengeance;* ܡܘܰܚܰܪ ܒܢܶܩܡܬܳܐ *he defers taking vengeance.*

ܢܩܰܣ *to cut up, cut in pieces.* Derivative, ܢܩܣܐ.

ܢܶܩܣܳܐ pl. ܢܶܩ̈ܣܶܐ rt. ܢܩܣ. m. *a piece, portion* of flesh; ܢܶܩܣܳܐ ܡܛܰܘܝܳܐ *a piece of roast meat.*

ܢܶܩܥܳܐ pl. ܢܶܩ̈ܥܶܐ m. *a cave, den, hole;* ܢܶܩ̈ܥܶܐ ܕܫܘܿܥ̈ܐ *holes of the rocks;* ܬܥܠ̈ܐ ܒܢܶܩ̈ܥܰܝܗܘܿܢ *foxes in their dens;* ܒܓܘ ܢܶܩܥܳܐ ܕܡܰܘܬܳܐ *in the innermost recess of death.*

ܢܶܩܥܬܳܐ f. *a dark-coloured* or *honey-coloured gem.*

ܢܩܦ fut. ܢܶܩܰܦ, imper. ܩܰܦ, infin. ܡܶܩܰܦ, act. part. ܢܳܩܶܦ, ܢܳܩܦܳܐ, pass. part. ܢܩܺܝܦ, ܢܩܝܦܐ, ܢܩܝܦܬܐ. *to cleave, stick to, be joined* in marriage; *to adhere, accompany, follow, agree with, be in accord with;* ܢܶܩܰܦ ܠܐܰܢܬܬܶܗ a man *shall cleave unto his wife;* ܒܡܰܠܦܳܢܘܬܶܗ *to adhere to* or *follow the teaching of* any one; ܢܶܩܦܘܗܝ ܟܢܫ̈ܐ ܣܓܝ̈ܐܐ *great multitudes followed him;* ܠܐ ܢܩܦ ܥܡܢ *he followed not us;* ܩܘܦ ܒܢܦܫܟ *keep yourself to yourself;* ܢܶܩܦܰܬ ܢܰܦܫܝ ܒܳܬܪܳܟ *my soul cleaveth unto the dust;* ܢܩܦܘ ܠܚܒܪܘܗܝ *they joined forces, made common cause;* ܡ̈ܠܐ ܕܢܩܦܢ *the words which follow;* gram. *to be joined, belong, consent;* fem. act. part. impers. ܢܩܦܐ *it is suitable, agrees, corresponds;* pass. part. *following, cleaving, joined, united, adjoining, contiguous, agreeing with;* ܢܩܝܦܝܢ ܗܘܘ ܠܗ *they followed him;* ܓܦܝܗܘܢ ܢܩܝܦܝܢ ܚܕ ܠܚܕ *their wings touched one another* (1 Kings vi. 27); ܢܩܝܦܝܢ ܠܗ ܠܦܓܪܐ ܕܘ̈ܢܐ ܒܝ̈ܫܐ *evil habits cleave to* the body; ܢܩܝܦ ܗܘܐ ܕܝܪܐ ܠܒܝܬ ܐܣܝܪ̈ܐ *a monastery was hard by the prison;* ܐܢܫܐ ܕܢܩܝܦܝܢ ܗܘܘ ܠܪܥܝܢܗ *some who adhered to his opinion;* ܠܡܦܣܩܘܬ ܡܠܬܐ. ܚܟܡܬܐ ܢܩܝܦܐ ܠܗ *to brevity of speech wisdom is united;* ܢܩܝܦܝܢ ܗܘܘ ܟܝ̈ܢܐ *the natures* of our Lord were *conjoined;* gram. *affix.* ETHPA. ܐܬܢܩܦ *to cleave to; to dote upon; to have sexual intercourse; to be conjoined, be united;* ܠܗ ܦܠܘܚ ܘܒܗ ܐܬܢܩܦ *serve Him and cleave unto Him;* ܘܠܗ ܐܠܗܐ ܕܡܬܓܫܡ ܡܘܕܝܢ ܠܗ: ܐܠܐ ܠܒܪ ܐܢܫܐ ܕܠܐܠܗܐ ܐܬܢܩܦ *they* (Nestorians) *do not confess Him to be God made flesh but man conjoined with God.* Gram. *to take an affix.* APHEL ܐܩܦ *a) to cause to cleave, to join, bring near;* ܚܘܒܐ ܡܩܦ ܠܢ ܠܐܠܗܐ *love brings us near to God;* ܐܩܦ ܠܗ ܐܠܗܐ ܡܠܬܐ ܠܒܪܢܫܐ ܕܡܢܢ *God the Word joined to Himself man of our nature;* ܕܟܪܐ ܐܩܦ ܠܢܩܒܬܐ *He made the male cleave to the female;* ܐܩܦܘ ܐܢܘܢ ܠܟܘܢ *associate them with yourselves. b) to be near, draw nigh;* ܐܩܦܢ ܠܡܐܒܕ *we are nigh to perishing;* ܟܕ ܐܩܦܘ ܝܘܡܝ ܡܫܬܘܬܐ *when the days of feasting came round. c) to apply himself, begin* esp. with verbs of speaking; ܐܩܦܘ ܠܡܡܠܠܘ *they began to speak;* ܐܩܦ ܠܡܐܟܠ *he began to eat. d) to add, continue;* ܚܛܝܬܐ ܠܚܛܝܬܗ ܐܩܦ ܫܐܘܠ Saul *added sin to sin;* ܐܩܦ ܘܐܡܪ *he went on to say;* part. ܡܩܦ or ܡܘܩܦ *he adds, continues, proceeds;* ܐܩܦ as adverb *then, next;* ܐܩܦ ܒܬܪ *next after, afterwards.* ETHTAPH. ܐܬܬܩܦ *to be joined.* DERIVATIVES, ܢܩܘܦܐ, ܢܩܦܐ, ܢܩܘܦܐ, ܢܩܘܦܐܝܬ, ܢܩܘܦܬܐ, ܢܩܦܬܐ, ܢܩܘܦܝܐ, ܢܩܦܐ, ܡܩܦܢܘܬܐ, ܡܩܦܢܘܬܐ, ܡܬܢܩܦܢܘܬܐ, ܡܬܢܩܦܢܐ.

ܢܩܦܐ rt. ܢܩܦ. m. *contact, intercourse* esp. *sexual; doting; society, company; sequence, cohesion;* ܢܩܦܐ ܒܣܪܢܝܐ *fleshly intercourse;* ܒܪܬ ܢܩܦܝ *my companion, my wife;* ܐܫܬܡܠܬ ܒܢܩܦܐ ܕܦܬܟܪ̈ܐ Samaria *was defiled by intercourse with idols;* ܒܢܝ ܢܩܦܐ *companions;* ܢܩܦܐ ܕܥܒ̈ܕܐ *a company of servants.*

ܢܩܦܐܝܬ rt. ܢܩܦ. adv. *in consequence, consequently, accordingly;* astron. *in onward order.*

ܢܩܦܝܐ, ܝܬܐ rt. ܢܩܦ. *a)* adj. *copulatory; congruous, consequent;* astron. *onward, forward;* gram. *suffix; an adverb. b)* fem. emph. = subst. *adjacent country;* ܢܩܦܝܬܗ ܕܨܘܪ *the confines of Tyre.*

ܢܩܦܘܬܐ rt. ܢܩܦ. f. astron. *a conjunction; a succession, series.*

ܢܩܦܬܐ pl. ܬܐ rt. ܢܩܦ. f. *cohesion.*

ܢܩܪ fut. ܢܢܩܘܪ, act. part. ܢܩܪ, pass. part. ܢܩܝܪ, ܐ. *to hew out, hollow out;* ܢܩܪܬ ܠܟ ܩܒܪܐ *thou hast hewed thee out a sepulchre;* ܩܒܪܐ ܕܢܩܝܪ ܗܘܐ ܒܫܘܥܐ *a tomb hewn in the rock;* ܢܩܪ ܩܝ̈ܣܐ *a woodpecker;* ܢܩܝܪܐ ܕܡܝ̈ܐ *a trough, tub.* ETHPE. ܐܬܢܩܪ and ETHPA. ܐܬܢܩܪ *to be hewn out, hollowed out;* ܡܥܪܬܐ ܒܫܘܥܐ ܐܬܢܩܪܬ ܗܘܬ *a cave had been hollowed out in the rock.* DERIVATIVES, ܢܩܪܐ, ܢܩܝܪܐ, ܢܩܘܪܐ, ܡܢܩܪܐ, ܡܢܩܪܐ, ܡܢܩܪܬܐ, ܡܢܩܪܢܐ.

ܢܩܪܐ rt. ܢܩܪ. m. *a cut, incision* in a tree to receive a graft.

ܢܩܫ fut. ܢܢܩܘܫ, imper. ܢܩܘܫ, act. part. ܢܩܫ, ܢܩܫܐ, pass. part. ܢܩܝܫ, ܐ. *a) to knock in* a nail or tent-peg, *to fix* a nail or stake, *to set up, pitch* a tent, *to encamp;* ܢܩܫ ܣܡܘ̈ܟܘܗܝ *he fixed the sockets of* the tabernacle; ܢܩܫ ܡܫܟܢܗ *he pitched his tent;* ܢܩܫ ܥܠ ܢܗܪܐ *he encamped by the river;* also with ܥܠ *to encamp against = besiege. b) to knock together* as the knees, *to chatter* as the teeth, *to clap* the hands; ܢܩܫܬ ܐܝ̈ܕܝܟ *thou didst clap thy hands;* ܢܢܩܫܘܢ ܟܦܐ *they shall clap their hands. c) to knock* at the door; ܢܩܘܫܘ ܘܢܬܦܬܚ ܠܟܘܢ *knock and it shall be opened unto you;* ܠܬܪ̈ܥܝ ܡܘܬܐ ܢܩܝܫܝܢ ܗܘܘ *they were at the doors of death. d) to strike, smite, batter;* ܟܐܦ̈ܐ ܕܢܩܫܝ *the stones which struck him;* ܢܩܫܘ ܠܫܘܪܐ ܒܚܝܠܬܢܐܝܬ *they battered the wall violently;* ܚܙܘܪ̈ܐ ܕܠܐ ܢܩܝܫܝܢ *apples without a bruise;* ܢܩܫ ܥܠ ܚܕܝܗ *he smote his breast;* ܢܩܫܘ ܒܐܦܐ

sorrow smote him. e) *to strike, clash, sound, play* a musical instrument; ܒܛܒܠܐ or ܒܦܠܓܐ *to beat the drum, sound the timbrels;* ܒܟܢܪܐ or ܢܩܫ ܒܟܢܪܐ ܢܩܫܐ ܕܢܩܫ ܚܟܝܡܐܝܬ *a cunning player on the harp;* ܢܩܫ ܢܩܘܫܐ *he struck the semantron;* ܢܩܫ ܠܐܚܐ ܠܟܢܘܫܝܐ *he rang the brethren to meeting.* f) of slight sounds *to touch, move, stir, vibrate;* ܩܠܐ ܕܛܪܦܐ ܕܢܩܫ *the sound of a leaf stirring;* ܐܢ ܪܘܚܐ ܬܢܩܫ ܒܚܩܠܐ *if the wind moves among the corn;* ܢܩܫܘ ܐܝܟ ܩܢܪܐ ܥܫܢܝܗܘܢ *his nerves quivered like harp-strings.* ETHPE. ܐܬܢܩܫ *to be pitched* as a tent, *driven in* as a nail; *to be battered, tossed about* by waves; *to be struck, played, harped* as a bell, semantron, musical instrument. PAEL ܢܩܫ a) intensive of Peal. b) *to search out.* ETHPA. ܐܬܢܩܫ same as Ethpeel but of repeated action. DERIVATIVES, ܢܩܘܫܐ, ܢܩܫܐ, ܢܩܫܬܐ, ܢܩܝܫܐ, ܢܩܫܬܐ, ܢܩܘܫܘܬܐ, ܡܢܩܫܢܘܬܐ.

ܢܩܫܐ pl. ܐ̈ rt. ܢܩܫ. m. *knocking; clash, clang, din; throbbing, palpitation;* ܢܩܫܐ ܕܙܝܢܝܗܘܢ *the clanging of their armour;* ܢܩܫܐ ܕܟܐܦܐ *stoning;* ܢܩܫ ܟܦܐ *clapping the hands;* ܢܩܫ ܪܫܐ *dispute, altercation; headache.*

ܢܩܝܫܐ rt. ܢܩܫ. gram. *of a vowel, sounded by a vowel.*

ܢܩܫܬܐ pl. ܬ̈ܐ rt. ܢܩܫ. f. gram. ܢܩܫܬ ܫܡܗܐ *the vocalization of nouns.*

ܢܩܫܬܐ pl. ܢ̈ܩܫܢ, ܬ̈ܐ rt. ܢܩܫ. f. *a beat, a vowel, a syllable;* ܚܡܫ ܢܩܫ̈ܬܐ *five vowels* in Syriac; ܡܫܘܚܬܐ ܬܡܢܐ ܢܩܫܢ *octosyllabic metre.*

ܢܪܓܐ pl. ܐ̈ m. *an axe;* ܩܢܝܐ ܕܢܪܓܐ *sugar-candy;* ܡܠܚܐ ܕܢܪܓܐ *rock-salt.*

ܢܪܓܘܢܐ dimin. of ܢܪܓܐ m. *a light hoe; a weeding-hook.*

ܢܪܓܝܠ m. *the cocoanut.*

ܢܪܕܘܣ, ܢܪܕܘܣ, ܢܪܕܝܢ, ܢܪܕܘܢ, ܢܪܕܐ, ܢܪܕ m. but f. in the Lexx. to agree with the gender of the Greek, νάρδος, *Indian spikenard, nard;* ܢܪܕܝܢ ܕܛܘܪܐ *mountain nard;* ܡܫܚܐ ܕܢܪܕܝܢ *ointment of spikenard;* ܫܒܒܬܐ ܕܢܪܕܝܢ *a stalk of nard.*

ܢܪܕܝܢܐ pl. ܐ̈ from ܢܪܕ m. *spikenard plants.*

ܢܪܕܘܦܢܣ m. *nerium oleander, the oleander.*

ܢܪܕܝܢ ܕܛܘܪܐ *polygonum, knot-grass.*

ܢܪܩܝܣܘܣ, ܢܪܩܝܣ, and ܢܐܪܩܝܣܘܣ f. *the narcissus.*

ܢܪܬܩܣ νάρθηξ, *narthex,* a part of a church to the west of the nave.

ܢܫ fut. ܢܢܫ and ܢܢܘܫ, act. part. ܢܐܫ, part. adj. ܢܫܝܫ, ܐ, ܬܐ. *to become feeble, slack, torpid, inert;* ܠܡܐܬܟܬܫܘ ܢܫܘ *they were too feeble to strive;* ܠܫܢܗ ܢܫ ܠܗ *his tongue failed;* ܢܫ ܐܝܕܝܗܘܢ *their hands became slack = they gave up in despair;* ܠܐ ܐܢܘܫ ܥܠܝܟܘܢ *I will not be burdensome unto you.* Part. adj. *feeble, listless, ineffective;* ܪܦܐ ܘܢܫܝܫ ܒܥܒܕܝܟ *slack and remiss in thy deeds;* ܡܟܣܢܘܬܐ ܢܫܝܫܬܐ *a feeble rebuke.* ETHPA. ܐܬܢܫܫ *to become inert, stiff, slack.* APH. ܐܢܫ *to make torpid, stupefy.* DERIVATIVES, ܢܫܝܫܐܝܬ, ܢܫܝܫܘܬܐ, ܡܬܢܫܫ.

ܢܫܐ fut. ܢܢܫܐ, act. part. ܢܫܐ, pass. part. ܢܫܐ. *to forget.* ETHPE. ܐܬܢܫܝ and ETHPA. ܐܬܢܫܝ *to forget; to be forgotten.* PAEL ܢܫܝ, part. ܡܢܫܐ. *to make forget.* APHEL ܐܢܫܝ, part. ܡܢܫܐ. *to make forget, make to be forgotten, consign to oblivion;* ܐܢܫܝܢܝ ܐܠܗܐ ܟܠܗ ܥܡܠܝ *God hath made me forget all my toil;* ܡܢܫܐ ܠܟܠܗܝܢ ܐܘܠܨܢܝܗܘܢ *He makes all their afflictions to be forgotten.* DERIVATIVES, ܢܫܝܐ, ܢܫܝܢܐ, ܡܢܫܝܢܐ, ܡܢܫܝܢܘܬܐ, ܡܬܢܫܝܢܐ, ܡܬܢܫܝܢܐܝܬ, ܡܬܢܫܝܢܘܬܐ.

ܢܫܐ, ܢܫܝܢ (abs. state rare) pl. of ܐܢܬܬܐ *women.*

ܢܫܒ fut. ܢܢܫܘܒ and ܢܢܫܒ, act. part. ܢܫܒ, ܢܫܒܐ. *to blow, breathe;* ܡܐ ܕܢܫܒܬ ܒܗ ܪܘܚܐ ܝܒܫ *when the wind has blown upon it, it withers;* ܡܢ ܟܠ ܕܢܫܒܐ ܪܘܚܐ *whencesoever the wind blows;* ܢܫܒ ܪܕܘܦܝܐ *persecution raged.* ETHPE. ܐܬܢܫܒ a) *to be tossed* or *driven by the wind.* b) *to be ensnared.* APH. ܐܢܫܒ *to cause to blow;* ܕܡܦܩ ܘܡܢܫܒ ܪܘ̈ܚܐ *He who brings forth the winds and lets them blow;* ܐܢܫܒ ܪܘܚܐ ܕܥܠܥܠܐ ܒܚܡܬܝ *I will send a stormy wind in my fury.* DERIVATIVE, ܢܫܒܐ, ܡܫܒܐ.

ܢܫܒܐ pl. ܐ̈ m. *a noose, snare, net;* ܦܪܣ ܢܫܒܘܗܝ *he stretches his snares;* ܢܫܒܐ ܕܨܝܕܐ *the meshes of the net.*

ܢܫܒܐ pl. ܐ̈ rt. ܢܫܒ. m. *the blowing* of the wind, *a storm, whirlwind.*

ܢܫܓܐ m. *a summer cloud.*

ܢܫܘܦܐ pl. ܐ̈ rt. ܢܫܦ. m. *a* bird's *beak; the jaws* or *nose* of a dog; *a snout.*

ܢܫܘܢܝܬܐ pl. ܢܫܘܢܝ̈ܬܐ fem. dimin. of ܢܫܐ. *a little woman.*

ܢܫܘܬܐ f. for ܐܢܫܘܬܐ. *manhood.*

ܢܫܝܘܬܐ from ܢܫܐ. f. *effeminacy.*

ܢܫܛ fut. ܢܢܫܘܛ, act. part. ܢܫܛ, ܢܫܛܐ, pass. part. ܢܫܝܛ, ܢܫܝܛܐ, ܢܫܝܛܬܐ. *to flay, skin, strip.* Ethpe. ܐܬܢܫܛ *to be flayed, skinned.* Derivatives, ܡܢܫܛܐ, ܢܫܛܐ, ܢܫܘܛܐ.

ܢܫܛܐ rt. ܢܫܛ. m. *flaying.*

ܢܫܝ, ܢܫܝܐ, ܢܫܝܬܐ from ܢܫܐ. *female; effeminate.* Pl. f. *the menses; a flow of blood* after childbirth.

ܢܫܝܫܐ pl. ܢܫܝܫ̈ܐ *feeble, inactive, listless, spiritless;* ܒܢܝ̈ ܕܪܢ ܢܫܝܫ̈ܐ ܘܡܥܝܩ̈ܐ *the men of our generation* are *poor-spirited and harassed;* ܗܘܢܐ ܢܫܝܫܐ *a feeble mind.*

ܢܫܝܢ, ܢܫܝܢܐ rt. ܢܫܐ. m. *forgetfulness, carelessness.*

ܢܫܝܢܢܐ rt. ܢܫܐ. *forgetful, careless;* gram. ܫܘܚܠܦܐ ܢܫܝܢܢܐ *misplacing* words *from carelessness.*

ܢܫܝܦܐ; see ܢܫܦ.

ܢܫܝܫܐܝܬ rt. ܢܫ. adv. *listlessly, feebly, slackly.*

ܢܫܝܫܘܬܐ rt. ܢܫ. f. *feebleness, slackness, inertness, effeminacy.*

ܢܫܡ fut. ܢܢܫܘܡ and ܢܢܫܡ, act. part. ܢܫܡ, ܢܫܡܐ. *to blow, breathe, respire, exhale; to blow* the nose; ܐܪ̈ ܢܫܡܢ animals which *breathe air;* ܚܡܬܐ ܢܫܡ ܠܘܩܒܠܗ *he breathed out anger against him;* ܢܫܡ ܡܘܬܐ *breathing out death = exhaling poison.* Ethpe. ܐܬܢܫܡ *to be breathed.* Derivatives, ܢܫܡܐ, ܢܫܡܬܐ, ܡܢܫܡܢܘܬܐ.

ܢܫܡܐ, ܢܫܡܬܐ pl. ܢܫܡ̈ܬܐ rt. ܢܫܡ. f. *breath, breathing; a living being, soul;* ܚܝܐ ܘܢܫܡܐ ܕܟܠ God is *the life and breath of all;* ܠܐ ܫܒܩ ܡܢܗܘܢ ܢܫܡܬܐ *he left no living soul of them;* ܥܠ ܢܫܡܬܐ ܐܚܪܝܬܐ ܐܝܬܝܗ *she is at her last gasp, breathes her last breath;* ܕܠܐ ܢܫܡܬܐ *lifeless.*

ܢܫܦ *to pound, smooth, pulverize;* pass. part. ܢܫܝܦܐ *fine;* ܣܡܝܕܐ ܢܫܝܦܐ *fine flour;* ܢܫܝܦܐ ܕܚܛܐ *fine wheat meal;* ܢܫܝܦܐ ܐܘܟܡܐ *black meal.* Pael ܢܫܦ *to smoothe, rub fine, pick clean.* Ethpa. ܐܬܢܫܦ *to be picked clean, cleansed* as corn. Derivatives, ܢܫܦܐ, ܡܢܫܦܐ.

ܢܫܦܐ rt. ܢܫܦ. m. *rubbing clean, purifying.*

ܢܫܩ fut. ܢܢܫܘܩ and ܢܢܫܩ, imper. ܫܘܩ, act. part. ܢܫܩ, ܢܫܩܐ. *to kiss;* ܢܫܩܬ ܥܪܦܐ ܠܚܡܬܗ *Orpah kissed her mother-in-law;* ܢܫܩ ܠܪ̈ܓܠܘܗܝ the deluge *kissed the feet of* Paradise. Ethpe. ܐܬܢܫܩ *to be kissed, receive a kiss.* Pa. ܢܫܩ *to kiss much* or *often;* ܠܐ ܫܠܝܐ ܡܢ ܕܬܢܫܩ ܠܪ̈ܓܠܝ *she hath not ceased to kiss my feet.* Derivative, ܢܘܫܩܬܐ.

ܢܫܪܐ pl. ܢܫܪ̈ܐ m. *a) the eagle;* ܒܪ ܢܫܪܐ *a young eagle;* astron. the name of various constellations: *the Eagle;* ܢܫܪܐ ܕܦܪܝܣ *the Spread Eagle;* ܢܫܪܐ ܕܝܬܒ *the Sitting Eagle* = Lyra. *b) a roof gabled in the centre with lower roofs slanting down to side walls.* Derivative, the following—

ܢܫܪܝܐ from ܢܫܪܐ. *of an eagle;* ܦܪܚܐ ܢܫܪܝܐ *an eagle's flight.*

ܢܬܘܦܐ, ܢܬܘܦܬܐ rt. ܢܬܦ. *attractive, inducing;* ܠܐܘܬܐ ܢܬܘܦܬܐ ܗܝ ܕܫܢܬܐ *labour induces sleep;* med. *calculated to draw out* humours; chem. *distillatory.*

ܢܬܘܦܘܬܐ rt. ܢܬܦ. f. *attraction;* ܢܬܘܦܘܬܐ ܕܡܓܢܝܛܝܣ ܠܦܪܙܠܐ *the attraction of the magnet for iron.*

ܢܬܘܪܐ, ܢܬܘܪܬܐ rt. ܢܬܪ. *deciduous.*

ܢܬܝܟܘܬܐ rt. ܢܬܟ. f. *dipping* of the balance; *inclining to one side.*

ܢܬܝܦܘܬܐ rt. ܢܬܦ. f. *attraction; evaporation* by the action of the sun.

ܢܬܟ fut. ܢܬܘܟ Heb. *to pour out.* Pael ܢܬܟ *to hurt, do harm.*

ܢܬܠ defective verb used to supplement ܝܗܒ: only fut. ܢܬܠ, 2 pers. ܬܬܠ, 1 pers. ܐܬܠ, and infin. ܡܬܠ *to give, impart, yield, make to be, put, lay;* ܕܬܬܠ ܐܪܥܐ ܦܐܪ̈ܐ *that the earth may yield fruit;* ܐܬܠܟ ܠܥܡܡ̈ܐ *I will make nations of thee;* ܢܬܠ ܟܗܢܐ ܡܢ ܕܡܐ ܥܠ ܩܪ̈ܢܬܗ ܕܡܕܒܚܐ *the priest shall put of the blood upon the horns of the altar;* ܐܬܠ ܢܡܘܣܝ ܒܓܘ ܟܘ̈ܠܝܬܗܘܢ *I will put my law in their inward parts;* ܘܠܢ ܟܝ ܕܢܬܠ ܢܦܫ̈ܬܢ *we ought to lay down our lives* for the brethren. With ܕܝܢܐ *to give* or *pronounce judgement;* with ܩܠܐ *to pronounce;* for constructions with other nouns see p. 188. DERIVATIVE, ܡܬܠܐ.

ܢܬܰܠ fut. ܢܶܬܽܠ, parts. ܢܳܬܶܠ, ܢܳܬܠܳܐ, and ܢܬܺܝܠ, ܢܬܺܝܠܳܐ. *to outweigh, incline* the balance, *turn* the scale, *exceed in weight, preponderate;* ܚܢܳܢܳܟ ܢܳܬܶܠ *Thy mercy weighs down* the balance; ܢܳܬܠܺܝܢ ܠܬܰܚܬ *they are weighed down, incline downwards;* ܢܶܬܠܰܬ ܣܰܢܓܳܐ ܘܰܬܠܳܬ ܥܰܡ ܚܰܒܪܬܳܗ ܫܰܘܝܳܐܺܝܬ *the scale inclined and hung equal with the other;* ܢܳܬܠܳܐ ܢܰܦܫܳܐ ܡܶܢ ܒܶܪܝܳܬܳܐ *the soul outweighs all created things.* PAEL ܢܰܬܶܠ *to give a turn to the scale, give the preponderance;* ܠܡܢܰܬܠܽܘ ܐܳܘ ܠܡܳܢ ܕܩܰܪܺܝܒ ܠܟܺܐܢܽܘܬܳܐ *the preponderance should be given to that which is most nearly just.* ETHPA. ܐܶܬܢܰܬܰܠ *to be made to depend, to be made to sink down.* APH. ܐܰܬܶܠ or ܐܰܬܺܝܠ *to make to incline downwards;* ܕܠܳܐ ܢܗܘܽܘܢ ܡܰܬܠܺܝܢ ܠܗܽܘܢ ܡܰܠܦܳܢܶܐ ܗܶܪܶܛܝܩܳܝܶܐ *that heretical teachers may not deflect their balance.* DERIVATIVES, ܢܬܳܠܳܐ, ܢܬܺܝܠܽܘܬܳܐ, ܢܬܳܠܳܐ, ܡܢܰܬܠܳܢܳܐ, ܡܢܰܬܠܳܢܽܘܬܳܐ.

ܢܬܳܠܳܐ or ܢܬܳܠܳܐ rt. ܢܬܠ. m. *the turning* of the balance, *inclination* of one scale.

ܢܬܰܓ fut. ܢܶܬܽܘܓ, imper. ܬܽܘܓ, act. part. ܢܳܬܶܓ, ܢܳܬܓܳܐ, pass. part. ܢܬܺܝܓ, ܓܳܐ, ܓܳܬܳܐ. *to draw on, out, in* or *up, to attract, entice; to drag* or *pull;* ܫܽܘܚܳܢܳܐ ܡܰܚܝܳܠܳܐܺܝܬ ܢܳܬܶܓ ܠܪܰܛܺܝܒܽܘܬܳܐ *heat powerfully draws out moisture, causes evaporation;* ܢܳܬܓܺܝܢ ܗܘܰܘ ܠܗܽܘܢ ܒܚܰܒܠܶܐ *they haul* the carts *with ropes;* ܕܠܳܐ ܢܶܬܽܘܓ ܡܰܠܝܽܘܬܶܗ ܡܶܢ ܗܰܘ ܢܚܳܬܳܐ *lest the patch tear away from the garment;* ܡܫܺܝܚܳܐ ܢܬܰܓ ܠܰܥܳܙܰܪ ܡܶܢ ܩܰܒܪܳܐ Christ *drew* Lazarus *from the tombs.* Pass. part. ܢܬܺܝܓ ܠܘܳܬ ܚܛܺܝܬܳܐ *enticed towards sin;* ܢܰܦܫܶܗ ܥܰܡ ܦܰܓܪܶܗ ܠܥܶܠ ܢܬܺܝܓܳܐ ܗܘܳܬ *his soul together with his body was drawn upward;* ܣܰܥܪܳܐ ܕܢܬܺܝܓ *plucked out hair;* ܪܽܘܚܶܐ ܢܬܺܝܓܳܬܳܐ *boisterous winds.* ETHPE. ܐܶܬܢܬܶܓ *to be attracted, drawn aside, dragged away;* ܕܢܶܬܢܬܶܓ ܪܶܥܝܳܢܟܽܘܢ ܠܘܳܬ ܕܽܘܒܳܪܳܐ ܓܡܺܝܪܳܐ *that your mind may be attracted towards a life of perfection;* ܐܰܝܠܶܝܢ ܕܠܳܐ ܡܶܬܢܰܬܓܺܝܢ ܒܟܽܠ ܪܽܘܚ ܡܰܠܦܳܢܽܘܬܳܐ *those who are not drawn away by every wind of doctrine.* PAEL *to drag, tear violently, seize;* ܡܰܟܺܝܪܳܐ ܒܥܶܠܕܒܳܒܳܐ ܡܢܰܬܶܓ ܠܝ *the crafty adversary tears at me;* ܨܒܰܘ ܕܢܢܰܬܓܽܘܢ ܠܗܽܘܢ ܡܰܠܟܽܘܬܳܐ *they wanted to seize the kingdom for themselves;* ܡܢܰܬܶܓ ܒܣܽܘܓܳܐܐ ܕܨܒܘܳܬܳܐ *dis-*

tracted by many things. ETHPA. ܐܶܬܢܰܬܰܓ *to be dragged about violently* or *often, to be driven in various directions, to be much harassed;* ܡܶܬܢܰܬܓܺܝܢ ܠܗܳܪܟܳܐ ܘܠܬܰܡܳܢ *dragged hither and thither;* ܟܰܕ ܡܶܬܢܰܬܓܺܝܢ ܘܡܶܬܛܰܠܡܺܝܢ *knocked about and roughly handled;* ܙܳܕܶܩ ܠܳܟ ܠܡܶܬܥܰܡܳܠܽܘ ܘܠܡܶܬܢܰܬܳܓܽܘ *thou must labour and suffer much tribulation.* DERIVATIVES, ܢܬܳܓܳܐ, ܡܢܰܬܓܳܢܳܐ, ܢܬܺܝܓܽܘܬܳܐ, ܢܳܬܽܘܓܳܐ, ܢܬܳܓܳܐ, ܡܢܰܬܓܳܢܽܘܬܳܐ.

ܢܬܳܓܳܐ rt. ܢܬܓ. m. *attraction.*

ܢܬܰܪ fut. ܢܶܬܰܪ, act. part. ܢܳܬܶܪ, ܢܳܬܪܳܐ, pass. part. ܢܬܺܝܪ, ܢܬܺܝܪܳܐ. *to fall off* as hair, fruit, withered flowers or leaves; *to fall* as a star, as flakes of fire; *to fall down* as crumbs, *to drop; to wither* or *waste away, to decay;* ܓܒܶܐ ܕܢܳܬܪܳܐ ܡܶܢܗܽܘܢ ܣܰܥܪܳܐ *eyelids from which the hair falls off;* ܐܰܝܟ ܩܰܫܳܐ ܕܢܳܬܪܳܐ ܥܒܰܕ ܩܶܫܬܶܗ He makes *his bow to be as stubble falling flat;* ܣܰܘܟܳܐ ܕܢܳܬܪܳܐ *a fallen branch;* ܕܠܳܐ ܢܶܬܪܽܘܢ ܥܶܢܒܶܐ ܡܶܢ ܣܶܓܘܳܠܰܝܗܽܘܢ *lest the grapes fall from their clusters;* ܬܺܐܢܶܐ ܕܢܬܰܪ ܡܶܢ ܬܺܐܢܬܳܐ *figs which fell off;* ܟܰܘܟܒܶܐ ܢܳܬܪܺܝܢ ܡܶܢ ܪܩܺܝܥܳܐ *stars fall from the firmament of heaven;* ܢܬܰܪ ܒܶܣܪܶܗ *his flesh fell away;* ܢܳܬܪܳܐ ܚܰܝܠܗܽܘܢ *all their strength fails.* Pass. part. *bald; fallen;* ܢܗܘܽܘܢ ܢܬܺܝܪܶܐ ܡܶܢ ܫܽܘܒܚܳܐ ܕܡܰܠܟܽܘܬܝ *they will be outcast from the glory of my kingdom;* ܢܬܺܝܪܺܝܢ ܡܶܢ ܣܽܘܓܳܐܐ ܕܙܰܒܢܳܐ *worn out by the lapse of time.* ETHPA. ܐܶܬܢܰܬܰܪ *to be fallen away, to be bald.* APH. ܐܰܬܰܪ *to shed, to shake off* or *down* as leaves; *to let drop;* ܦܶܐܪܶܐ ܡܰܬܪܺܝܢ ܦܶܐܪܰܝܗܽܘܢ *birds let* fruits *drop;* ܥܰܝܢܶܐ ܕܡܰܬܪܳܢ ܕܶܡܥܶܐ *eyes which let teardrops fall;* ܐܰܬܰܪܰܢ ܡܶܢ ܐܰܪܥܰܢ *He has cast us out of our land.* DERIVATIVES, ܢܬܳܪܳܐ, ܢܬܳܪܳܐ, ܢܬܳܪܳܐ, ܢܬܪܽܘܬܳܐ.

ܢܬܳܪܳܐ rt. ܢܬܪ. *a*) m. *fallen fruit, crumbs fallen* from the table, *crusts, leavings; a particle of* Eucharistic *bread;* ܢܬܳܪܳܐ ܕܦܳܬܽܘܪܶܗ ܠܳܐ ܝܰܗܒ ܠܡܶܣܟܺܝܢܳܐ *he gave no crumb from his table to the poor;* ܢܬܳܪܳܐ ܕܓܰܙܳܝܟ *a crumb from thy treasures;* ܢܬܳܪܳܐ ܕܚܰܨܦܳܐ *a potsherd.* *b*) *the* plant *teasel, dipsacus.* *c*) *a sort of poppy.*

ܢܶܬܪܳܐ Greek νίτρον, *nitre.*

ܢܬܳܪܳܐ rt. ܢܬܪ. m. *a*) *a falling off* of the hair; ܢܬܳܪܳܐ ܕܓܒܶܐ *falling off of the eyelashes.* *b*) *decay* of wood, *rot.* *c*) *anything fallen, a fragment.*

ܢܬܘܪܬܳܐ pl. ܬܶܐ dimin. of ܢܬܳܪܳܐ. m. *a fallen fragment.*

ܬܪܦ fut. ܢܬܪܘܦ, act. part. ܬܪܦ, ܬܪܦܐ, pass. part. ܬܪܝܦ, ܬܪܝܦܐ, ܬܪܝܦܬܐ. *to tear, lacerate, pluck;* ܝܘܢܐ ܕܬܪܦܘܗ ܢܨܐ *a dove which hawks have torn;* ܬܪܦܝܢ ܘܐܟܠܝܢ ܒܣܪܐ *they tear flesh and eat it;* ܦܬܘܬܐ ܕܬܪܝܦ ܡܢܗ ܒܬܢܘܪܐ *a loaf of which part has been torn off in the oven.* Metaph. *to excerpt;* ܟܬܒܐ ܕܬܘܪܦܐ ܐܝܟ ܨܒܝܢܗ ܬܪܦ ܘܣܡ *he put together books of excerpts as he thought fit.* ETHPE. ܐܬܬܪܦ *to be torn, convulsed; to be torn apart, separated;* ܡܬܬܪܦ ܗܘܐ ܡܢ ܪܘܚܐ ܒܝܫܬܐ *he was torn by the evil spirit.* PAEL *to tear in pieces, to tear* the hair, the flesh; *to mangle; to convulse;* ܠܐ ܢܬܪܦܘܢܗ ܕܐܒܐ ܚܛܘܦܐ *ravening wolves shall not tear her in pieces;* ܡܩܛܥܐ ܡܬܪܦܢܐ ܕܒܣܪܐ *flesh-tearing pincers;* ܡܬܪܦ ܣܥܪܗ ܘܪܫܗ *tearing his hair;* ܡܬܪܦܝܢ ܠܟ ܠܟܐ ܘܠܟܐ *they tear thee in different directions.* ETHPA. ܐܬܬܪܦ *to be torn in pieces, mangled;* ܐܬܐܟܠܘ ܠܚܝܘܬܐ ܘܐܬܬܪܦܘ ܠܦܪܚܬܐ *they were eaten by wild beasts and torn in pieces by birds of prey.* DERIVATIVES, ܬܘܪܦܐ, ܬܪܦܐ.

ܬܪܦܐ rt. ܬܪܦ. m. *the plucking out* of hair or feathers, *tearing* with pincers; *extirpation.*

∴ ܫܠܡ ܣܦܪܐ ܕܬܘ: ܒܡܥܕܪܢܘܬܐ ܕܐܠܗܐ ∴

∴ ܫܪܐ ܣܦܪ: ܣܡܟܬ ܕܐܣܟܝܡ ܐܬܘܬܐ ܗܕܐ ܕܣܡܟܬ. ∴

∴ ܣ ∴

ܣ, ܣܡܟܬ *semkath*, the fifteenth letter of the alphabet; the numeral 60; with a point, ܣ̇, 600. ܣ̄ is an abbreviation for the version of Symmachus.

ܣܐܐ emph. ܣܐܬܐ, dual ܣܐܬܝܢ, pl. ܣܐܝܢ, E-Syr. ܣܐܝܢ f. *a seah*, a dry measure containing about 1½ pecks; ܬܠܬ ܣܐܝܢ ܕܣܡܝܕܐ ܢܫܝܦܐ *three seahs of fine meal;* ܬܚܝܬ ܣܐܬܐ *under a bushel.*

ܣܐܒ fut. ܢܣܐܒ, part. ܣܐܒ, ܣܐܒܐ. *to grow old, to age, be aged, old;* ܣܐܒ ܘܣܒܥ ܝܘܡܬܐ *he was aged and full of days;* ܗܐ ܐܢܐ ܣܐܒܬ *lo! I have grown old;* ܣܒܐ ܕܣܐܒܘ ܬܡܢ *old men who had grown old there.* APH. ܐܣܐܒ *to bring to old age, come to old age.* DERIVATIVES, ܣܒܐ, ܣܝܒܐ, ܣܝܒܘܬܐ, ܣܝܒܘܬܐ, ܣܒܬܐ, ܣܒܘܬܐ.

ܫܒܬܐ pl. ܫܒܬܐ σάββατον -a, *the Sabbath, Saturday; a week.*

ܣܐܝܦ act. part. of verb ܣܘܦ.

ܣܐܢܐ rarely ܣܝܢܐ pl. ܣܐܢܐ rt. ܣܐܢ. m. *a sandal, shoe.*

ܣܐܘܪܐ, ܣܐܘܪܐ, ܣܐܘܪܘܣ or ܣܐܘܝܪܘܣ, also spelt ܣܘܝܪܐ, ܣܘܝܪܘܣ, &c., pr. n. *Severus;* esp. *Severus* patriarch of Antioch A.D. 512 to 519, a Monophysite. Hence—

ܣܐܘܪܝܢܐ pl. ܢ̈ܐ and ܣܐܘܪܝܢܘ *a follower of Severus, a Monophysite.*

ܣܐܝܓ act. part. of verb ܣܘܓ.

ܣܐܝܓ, ܣܐܝܓܐ rt. ܣܘܓ. *burnt up.*

ܣܐܠܐ; see ܣܠܐ *a basket.*

ܣܐܡ act. part. of verb ܣܘܡ.

ܣܐܡܐ no plural. m. *silver;* ܣܐܡܐ ܐܘܟܡܐ *lead;* ܣܐܡܐ ܚܘܪܐ *tin.* DERIVATIVE, ܣܐܡܢܐ.

ܣܐܡܢܐ pl. of ܣܡܐ.

ܣܐܡܢܐ, ܣܐܡܢܝܬܐ from ܣܐܡܐ. *silvern, silvery, of silver;* ܚܘܪܐ ܣܐܡܢܐ *silvery white.*

ܣܐܢ fut. ܢܣܐܢ, imper. ܣܐܢ, act. part. ܣܐܢ,

pass. part. ܣܐܝܢ. *to put on sandals* or *shoes;* ܗܢܘܢ ܕܣܐܝܢܝܢ ܣܐܘܢ̈ܐ *those who wear sandals;* ܣܐܝܢ ܡܣܐܢܐ *slippered;* ܣܐܝܢܝܢ ܒܪ̈ܓܠܝܗܘܢ *having* old sandals *bound on their feet.* Aph. ܐܣܐܢ *to give shoes, furnish with shoes* or *sandals.* Ethtaph. ܐܬܬܣܐܢ *to be shod.* Derivatives, ܣܐܘܢܐ or ܣܐܢܐ, ܡܣܐܢܐ and ܡܣܢܐ.

ܣܐܦܐ m. *the stomach of a ruminant.*

ܣܐܢܐ = ܣܢܐܐ *an enemy;* with suff. ܣܐܢܝ *they that hate me;* ܣܐܢܝܢ *our enemies.*

ܣܐܪܕܘܢܝܣ; see ܣܪܕ.

ܣܐܣܦܠܐ or ܣܘܣܦܠܐ *the medlar.*

ܣܐܦ act. part. of verb ܣܘܦ.

ܣܐܩܦܐ; see ܣܩܦܐ.

ܣܐܡ act. part. of verb ܣܘܡ.

ܣܐܪܐ; see ܣܪܐ.

ܣܐܪܕܘܢ m. *the sard;* oftener ܣܪܕܘܢ.

ܣܐܬܐ f. *a*) emph. state of ܣܐܐ. *b*) *a vine,* see ܣܝܬܐ; *a trailing plant;* ܣܐܬܐ ܐܘܟܡܬܐ *black bryony;* ܣܐܬܐ ܚܘܪܬܐ *white bryony. c*) *a mortar;* see ܣܝܬܐ.

ܣܒ imper. of verb ܢܣܒ. *to take.*

ܣܒ, ܣܒܐ, ܣܒܬܐ rarely ܣܐܒܐ, pl. ܣܒܝܢ, ܣܒ̈ܐ, ܣܒ̈ܬܐ, rt. ܣܐܒ. *a*) *an old man* or *woman, a grandfather* or *grandmother;* ܓܒܪܐ ܣܒܐ *an old man;* ܫܘܥܝ̈ܬܐ ܕܣܒ̈ܬܐ *old wives' fables. b*) *an elder, presbyter, a senior;* ܣܒ̈ܐ ܕܐܝܣܪܝܠ *elders of Israel;* ܣܒܐ ܕܥܘܡܪܐ *the prior of the monastery. c*) used as a proper name *Saba* or *Sabbas.*

ܣܒܗ fut. ܢܣܒܗ, act. part. ܣܒܗ. *to be* or *become like.* Pael ܣܒܗ *to make like, to liken.* Ethpa. ܐܬܣܒܗ *to be made like.* Aphel ܐܣܒܗ *to liken, compare, find a resemblance;* pass. part. ܡܣܒܗ, ܡܣܒܗܐ, ܡܣܒܗܬܐ *like, similar;* ܡܣܒܗ ܙܚܘܪܝܬܐ ܠܢܘܪܐ scarlet *resembles fire;* ܦܘܩܕ̈ܐ ܡܣܒܗ̈ܬܐ ܠܣܦܣܪܐ *arguments sharp as a sword.* Ethtaph. ܐܬܬܣܒܗ *to be likened.* Derivatives, ܣܘܒܗܐ, ܣܘܒܗܘܬܐ, ܣܒܗܝܐ, ܡܣܒܗܢܐܝܬ, ܡܣܒܗܢܘܬܐ.

ܣܒܗܐ rt. ܣܒܗ. m. *likeness, resemblance.*

ܣܒܗܘܬܐ rt. ܣܒܗ. f. *resemblance, appearance.*

ܣܒܗܝܐ, ܝܬܐ rt. ܣܒܗ. *like, resembling.*

ܣܒܘܟܝܬܐ; see ܣܒܟܝܐ f. *salt meat.*

ܣܒܘܟܐ rt. ܣܒܟ. *sticky, viscous.*

ܣܒܘܟܘܬܐ rt. ܣܒܟ. f. *tenacity, assiduity.*

ܣܒܘܠܐ, ܣܒܘܠܬܐ pl. ܝ̈ܢ, ܬ̈ܐ rt. ܣܒܠ. *one who carries,* esp. pl. *they who carry corn from the field to the threshing-floor.*

ܣܒܘܠܘܬܐ rt. ܣܒܠ. f. *the carrying of corn.*

ܣܒܘܠܐ rt. ܣܒܠ. m. *a*) *carrying. b*) *bearing, toleration.*

ܣܒܛܐ m. Pers. *a basket.* Cf. ܣܦܛܐ.

ܣܒܟܝܐ m. *salt meat.*

ܣܒܐ, ܣܒܬܐ rt. ܣܐܒ. *old, aged.*

ܣܒܝܟܝܐ *dried, preserved;* see ܣܒܟܝܐ.

ܣܒܝܟܘܬܐ rt. ܣܒܟ. f. *ascending, adhesion.*

ܣܒܠܝܘܣ and ܣܒܝܠܝܘܣ *Sabellius* the heresiarch.

ܣܒܝܠܘܬܐ rt. ܣܒܠ. f. *patience, toleration.*

ܣܒܝܠܝ̈ܢܐ pl. *Sabellians, followers of Sabellius.*

ܣܒܝܠܝܢܘܬܐ f. *Sabellianism, the heresy of Sabellius.*

ܣܒܝܢܐ σαβίνα, the shrub *savin,* a kind of juniper.

ܣܒܝܣܐܝܬ rt. ܣܒܣ. adv. *frequently, often, continuously;* gram. *joined together, in one,* of two words written in one, as ܐܝܟܢܐ for ܐܝܟ ܗܢܐ.

ܣܒܝܣܘܬܐ rt. ܣܒܣ. f. *density, closeness, thickness, multitude;* ܥܢ̈ܢܐ ܣܒܝܣܐ *dense clouds;* ܣܒܝܣܘܬܐ ܕܣܘ̈ܟܐ *denseness of branches, many branches;* ܣܒܝܣܘܬ ܡܥܒܕ̈ܢܘܗܝ *his many excellences;* ܣܒܝܣܘܬ ܩܠܐ *hoarseness;* ܣܒܝܣܘܬ ܢܦܫܐ *asthma;* ܒܣܒܝܣܘܬܐ *assiduously.* Gram. *being joined together, being written continuously, following immediately.*

ܣܒܣܒܐ Pers. the plant *atropa mandagora.*

ܣܒܪܘܬܐ pl. ܬ̈ܐ rt. ܣܒܪ. f. *imagination, illusion.*

ܣܒܪܝܢܝܐ *an inhabitant of Beth-Severina.*

ܣܒܟ fut. ܢܣܒܘܟ and ܢܣܒܟ, act. part. ܣܒܟ, ܣܒܟܐ, pass. part. ܣܒܝܟ or ܣܒܝܟ, ܟܐ, ܟܬܐ. *a*) *to fasten upon, set on, assail, attack* with ܒ or ܠ; ܣܒܟܘ ܒܗ ܐܝܟ ܚܝ̈ܘܬܐ ܩܛܘܠ̈ܬܐ *they set on him like wild beasts;* ܣܒܟܘ ܒܫܪܪܐ ܕܘܘܕܐܝܬ *they turbulently assailed the truth;* ܢܣܝܘܢܐ ... ܟܕ ܢܣܒܟ ܒܢ *when tempta-*

tion assails a solitary. *b*) *to set about, begin, rise to, attempt;* ܣܒܟ ܐܢܐ ܠܡܡܠܠܘ *I begin to speak;* ܣܒܟ ܘܣܠܩ *he rose and went up.* *c*) *to crawl up, touch, cling, settle* as an insect; ܐܝܟ ܩܡܨܐ ܕܣܒܟ ܒܣܝܓܐ *as a locust clinging on a hedge;* ܣܒܟܬ ܛܢܦܘܬܐ *dirt has settled.* Ethpe. ܐܣܬܒܟ *to fasten on, cling* with ܒ. Pael ܣܒܟ *a*) *to cling, seize, lay hold, catch in;* as insects or reptiles hang on a wall, as thorns catch in a dress, as dogs seize a person, as evil words fasten on any one. *b*) *to rise* in the air, *take flight.* *c*) caus. *to set on, incite;* ܕܢܣܒܟ ܐܚܐ ܠܚܪܝܢܐ the devil seeks *to set brethren at strife.* Derivatives, ܣܒܘܟܐ, ܣܒܘܟܘܬܐ, ܡܣܒܟܢܘܬܐ, ܣܒܟܐ, ܣܒܟܬܐ, ܣܒܟܘܬܐ.

ܣܒܟܐ rt. ܣܒܟ. m. *a*) *adhesion.* *b*) *a tire, headband, net.*

ܣܒܟܬܐ pl. ܣܒܟܬܐ rt. ܣܒܟ. f. *a tentacle.*

ܣܒܠ fut. ܢܣܒܘܠ, act. part. ܣܒܠ, ܣܒܠܐ, pass. part. ܣܒܝܠ, ܠܐ, ܠܬܐ. *a*) *to bear, carry* esp. to carry corn; ܣܒܠܝ ܡܘܒܠܐ *porters, carriers.* *b*) *to bear, suffer, endure;* ܚܫܐ ܕܣܒܠ ܡܫܝܚܐ *the sufferings which Christ bare;* ܕܢܣܒܘܠ ܠܚܫܚܬܐ *that he should suffer hardships;* ܣܓܝܐܬܐ ܢܣܝܘܢܐ ܣܒܝܠܝܢ ܗܘܘ ܠܗ *many trials were laid upon him.* Ethpe. ܐܣܬܒܠ *to be carried, conveyed.* Pael ܣܒܠ. *a*) *to fetch, cause to bring;* ܕܢܣܒܠܘܢ ܩܝܣܐ ܡܢ ܛܘܪܐ *to fetch wood from the mountain.* *b*) *to inflict;* ܡܣܒܠܝܢܢ ܠܗܘܢ ܒܝܫܬܐ *we make them endure evils.* Aph. *to make endure, lay upon, inflict;* ܐܘܒܠܘܢܝ ܢܓܕܐ ܗܠܝܢ *they made me endure those torments.* Derivatives, ܣܒܠܐ, ܣܒܠܬܐ, ܣܒܠܘܬܐ, ܣܒܘܠܐ, ܣܒܘܠܬܐ, ܣܒܠܢܐ, ܣܒܠܢܘܬܐ, ܣܒܘܠܐ, ܣܒܠܐ, ܣܒܠܐ, ܡܣܒܠܢܘܬܐ.

ܣܒܠܐ rt. ܣܒܠ. m. perh. *a straw mat.*

ܣܒܠܐ pl. ܠܐ Ephraimite pronunciation of ܫܒܠܐ *ears of corn* (see Jud. xii. 6).

ܣܒܠܐ rt. ܣܒܠ. m. *a*) *the carrying of corn.* *b*) *endurance.*

ܣܒܠܢܘܬܐ rt. ܣܒܠ. m. pl. *betrothal gifts.*

ܣܒܠܠܝܘܣ *Sabellius* the heresiarch; hence is derived—

ܣܒܠܝܢܐ m. pl. *Sabellians, followers of Sabellius.*

ܣܒܠܬܐ and with Mehagyono ܣܒܠܬܐ pl. ܣܒܠܬܐ rt. ܣܒܠ. f. *a*) *a staircase, ladder;* a sign of the zodiac; ܕܪܓܐ ܕܣܒܠܬܐ *the steps of the staircase.* *b*) *a kind of song.*

ܣܒܣ ܣܒܣ *to crowd, come frequently* or *thickly;* ܣܒܣܝܢ ܠܗܘܢ ܛܘܦܣܐ *types crowded on each other.* Part. adj. ܣܒܝܣ, ܣܒܝܣܐ, ܣܒܝܣܬܐ, ܣܒܝܣܬܐ, *oft, often, frequent, continuous, close, compact, crowded;* ܛܘܪܐ ܣܒܝܣܝ ܐܝܠܢܐ *thickly wooded mountains;* ܣܒܝܣ ܛܪܦܐ *leafy;* ܚܕ ܝܘܡܐ ܣܒܝܣܐ *one uninterrupted day* i.e. in northern regions; ܚܘܝܕܐ ܣܒܝܣܐ *close* or *intimate union;* ܒܒܝܫܬܐ ܣܒܝܣܝܢ ܗܘܘ *they abounded in wickedness, were given over to vice;* ܐܬܪܐ ܣܒܝܣ ܚܢܦܘܬܐ *a district full of paganism, given over to paganism;* ܣܕܪܐ ܣܒܝܣܐ ܕܣܪܦܐ *the serried ranks of seraphim;* ܣܒܝܣ ܩܘܪܝܐ *the scabious, scabiosa succisa.* Gram. *affix;* ܣܡܐ ܣܒܝܣܐ ܚܘܝܐ *nominal indicative affix* i.e. a letter added to a verb to indicate gender, person, and number, as the ܘ and ܝ of the imperative. Ethpe. ܐܣܬܒܣ *to be thick, tightly packed.* Pael ܣܒܣ *to greatly increase,* pass. part. ܡܣܒܣܐ *enriched* esp. in wisdom or knowledge. Derivatives, ܣܒܝܣܐܝܬ, ܣܒܝܣܘܬܐ.

ܣܒܣܛܐ and ܣܒܣܛܝ, also ܣܒܐܣܛܘܣ σεβαστός -ή, *belonging to Augustus* = Caesar, *Augustan.*

ܣܒܣܛܘܣ and ܣܒܣܛܘ σεβαστός -οῦ, *Augustus.*

ܣܒܣܠܝܐ *subsellium, a footstool.*

ܣܒܥ fut. ܢܣܒܥ, act. part. ܣܒܥ, ܣܒܥܐ, pass. part. ܣܒܝܥ and ܣܒܝܥ, ܥܐ, ܥܬܐ. *to be full, filled, satiated, satisfied;* esp. ܣܒܥ ܝܘܡܬܐ *he was full of days;* ܣܒܥ ܝܘܡܘܗܝ the same; ܕܢܣܒܥܘܢ ܙܕܝܩܐ ܚܝܝܗܘܢ *that the just might live out their full life;* ܠܚܡܐ ܠܡܣܒܥ *bread enough, bread to the full.* Pass. part. *full, satisfied, satisfying, sufficient;* ܣܒܝܥ ܐܢܐ *I am full;* ܡܫܬܝܗ ܡܝܐ ܘܣܒܝܥ *his drink is water and he is satisfied.* Ethpe. ܐܣܬܒܥ *a*) *to be fed, filled;* ܐܣܬܒܥ ܒܗܬܬܐ *he was filled, covered, with shame.* *b*) *to be satiating, annoying, wearisome;* ܠܐ ܡܣܬܒܥܐ ܗܘܬ *it did not satiate, weary, one could not have too much of it.* Pael ܣܒܥ *to fill, satisfy,* sate; ܝܫܘܥ ܣܒܥ ܐܪܒܥܐ ܐܠܦܝܢ ܒܚܡܫ ܠܚܡܝܢ Jesus satisfied 4000 with five loaves. Ethpa. ܐܣܬܒܥ to be filled, sated. Aph. ܐܣܒܥ to fill, satisfy. Derivatives, ܣܒܥܐ, ܣܒܥܬܐ, ܣܒܥܐܝܬ, ܣܒܥܘܬܐ, ܡܣܬܒܥܢܐ, ܡܣܬܒܥܢܘܬܐ, ܡܣܒܥܢܐ, ܣܘܒܥܐ.

ܣܒܥ, ܣܒܥܐ rt. ܣܒܥ. full.

ܣܒܥ, ܣܒܥܐ rt. ܣܒܥ. m. fullness, plenty opp. ܟܦܢܐ famine; ܐܫܬܝܘ ܡܝܐ ܠܣܒܥܗܘܢ they drank their fill of water; ܟܕ ܩܠܝܠ ܗܘܐ ܣܒܥܐ as there was little food.

ܣܒܥܐܝܬ rt. ܣܒܥ. adv. plentifully, to repletion.

ܣܒܥܘ, ܣܒܥܘܬܐ rt. ܣܒܥ. f. plenty, abundance opp. ܚܣܝܪܘܬܐ scarcity; ܦܐܪܐ ܕܣܒܥܘܬܐ fruit in plenty, abundant fruit; ܠܐ ܣܒܥܘ insatiable desire.

ܣܒܪ fut. ܢܣܒܪ, act. part. ܣܒܪ, pass. part. ܣܒܝܪ, ܣܒܝܪܐ, ܣܒܝܪܬܐ. to think, hold as true, be convinced, believe, suppose; ܣܒܪ ܐܢܐ I suppose; ܠܐ ܬܣܒܪܘܢ ܕ think not that . . .; ܣܒܪܝܢ ܒܢܦܫܗܘܢ ܕܚܟܝܡܝܢ ܐܢܘܢ thinking themselves to be wise; ܕܠܘܬܢ ܣܒܝܪܝܢ ܕܐܝܬܝܗܘܢ who are supposed by us to be . . . Ethpe. ܐܣܬܒܪ to be supposed, considered; impers. it seemed; ܐܣܬܒܪ ܠܟܠܢܫ every one supposed, it seemed to every one; ܕܠܐ ܐܣܬܒܪ that I may not seem; ܬܕܡܘܪܬܐ ܕܠܐ ܡܣܬܒܪܐ an unthought-of miracle. Pael ܣܒܪ a) to hope, trust, put trust with ܒ; ܫܪܝܪܐܝܬ ܣܒܪܬ ܒܡܪܝܐ truly I have hoped in the Lord. b) to announce, declare, tell, bring tidings, publish abroad; ܡܣܒܪ ܐܢܐ ܠܟܘܢ ܚܕܘܬܐ ܪܒܬܐ I bring you good tidings of great joy; ܐܙܠ ܣܒܪ ܡܠܟܘܬܗ ܕܐܠܗܐ go thou, preach the Kingdom of God; ܬܘܕܝܬܐ ܕܡܣܒܪܬ ܐܢܬ the profession of faith which you make. c) to consider, think; ܡܣܒܪܝܢܢ ܕܚܪܫܐ ܗܘ we think he is a sorcerer. Ethpa. ܐܣܬܒܪ a) to have good tidings brought; ܐܣܬܒܪܬ ܡܪܝܡ ܡܢ ܡܠܐܟܐ Mary received the message from the angel. b) to be preached, proclaimed, announced; ܐܣܬܒܪ ܝܘܚܢܢ ܘܐܬܝܠܕ the birth of John was announced and came to pass; ܡܣܬܒܪ ܡܘܬܗ his death was made known. c) to be considered, seem; ܠܝ ܡܣܬܒܪܐ ܝܬܝܪܬܐ it seems to me superfluous. Paiel ܣܝܒܪ to bear, endure; to wait; ܗܐ ܫܡܝܐ ܘܫܡܝ ܫܡܝܐ ܠܐ ܡܣܝܒܪܝܢ ܠܟ lo, heaven and the heaven of heavens cannot contain thee; ܒܦܓܪܐ ܣܝܒܪ ܟܠܗܝܢ ܗܠܝܢ ܟܕ ܐܠܗܐ ܗܘܐ in the body He endured all those things, yet being God; ܡܢ ܕܢܣܝܒܪ ܥܕܡܐ ܠܚܪܬܐ ܗܘ ܢܚܐ whoso shall endure unto the end, he shall be saved; ܣܝܒܪܘ ܝܘܡܐ they waited a day. With ܡܢ to refrain from; with ܠܘܩܒܠ to resist. Ethpaial ܐܣܬܝܒܪ a) to be borne, endured; ܠܐ ܡܣܬܝܒܪ ܗܘܐ ܠܗ ܕ he could not endure to . . .; ܕܠܐ ܡܣܬܝܒܪܢܐ unendurable, intolerable. b) denom. from ܣܝܒܪܬܐ to feed; ܡܣܬܝܒܪܝܢ ܡܢ ܦܐܪܐ ܕܐܝܠܢܐ they were sustained by the fruits of trees; ܠܐ ܡܣܬܝܒܪ ܗܘܐ ܐܠܐ ܠܚܡܐ he ate only bread. Aphel ܐܣܒܪ a) to think, suppose, expect; ܡܣܒܪ ܐܢܐ I think, it is my opinion; ܐܣܒܪܘ ܗܕܝܘܛܐ ܕ the ignorant supposed that . . .; ܠܐ ܐܣܒܪܘ ܠܗܘܢ ܐܦܠܐ ܩܠܝܠ they had not the least idea it was he. b) to make any one suppose, to seem; to declare oneself, profess to be; ܗܘ ܡܣܒܪ ܗܘܐ ܠܗܘܢ he made them think, made as if . . . Derivatives, ܣܒܪܐ, ܣܒܪܐ, ܣܒܪܬܐ, ܣܒܪܢܐ, ܣܒܪܐ, ܣܒܪܐ, ܣܒܪܬܐ, ܡܣܒܪܢܘܬܐ, ܡܣܒܪܢܐ, ܡܣܒܪܢܐܝܬ, ܡܣܒܪܢܘܬܐ, ܡܣܝܒܪܢܐ, ܡܣܝܒܪܢܘܬܐ, ܡܣܬܝܒܪܢܐ, ܡܣܬܝܒܪܢܐ.

ܣܒܪ, ܣܒܪܐ rt. ܣܒܪ. m. hope, trust, confidence, expectation; ܢܥܡܪܘܢ ܒܣܒܪܐ they shall dwell securely; ܥܠ ܣܒܪܐ in the hope, trusting; ܕܠܐ ܣܒܪ hopeless; also unhoped for, unexpected; ܦܣܩ ܣܒܪܐ he despaired; ܦܣܩܝܢ ܠܢ ܣܒܪܐ they throw us into despair.

ܣܒܪܐ rt. ܣܒܪ. m. opinion, conjecture, supposition.

ܣܒܪܐ pl. ܐ rt. ܣܒܪ. m. imagination, illusion; thought, opinion; ܣܒܪܐ ܬܪܝܨܐ ܕܥܠ ܐܠܗܐ right thought concerning God, orthodoxy.

ܣܒܪܢܝܐ, ܢܝܬܐ rt. ܣܒܪ. conjectural.

ܣܒܪܬܐ, ܬܐ rt. ܣܒܪ. f. a) tidings, good tidings, the Gospel; ܣܒܪܬܐ ܒܝܫܬܐ ܛܒ very sad tidings; ܣܒܪܬܐ ܡܠܐܟܝܬܐ the angelic message; ܣܒܪܬܐ ܕܡܠܟܘܬܗ ܕܐܠܗܐ the Gospel of the Kingdom of God. b) a copy of the Gospels, a lesson from one of the four Gospels; ܪܫ ܣܒܪܬܐ the chief Gospels, viz. ܐܝܠܝܢ ܕܩܝܡܬܐ the eleven lessons of the Gospel of the resurrection; ܫܒܬܐ ܕܣܒܪܬܐ or ܫܒܬܐ the Sabbath of the Gospel, i.e. Easter Eve, when these eleven lessons were read.

ܣܒܬܐ f. *froth, scum* of broth.

ܣܒܬܢܝܐ and ܣܒܬܢܝܬܐ rt. ܣܒܐ. *pertaining to an old woman, anile;* ܡܠܐ ܣܒܬܢܝܬܐ *old wives' tales.*

ܣܒܬܐܝܬ cf. ܫܒܬܐ. adv. *sabbatical* i. e. in a narrow or literal sense.

ܣܓܐ and ܣܓܝ fut. ܢܣܓܐ, act. part. ܣܓܐ, ܣܓܝܐ. *to increase, multiply, grow in number, spread;* ܣܓܐ ܗܘܐ ܡܢܝܢܐ ܕܬܠܡܝܕܐ *the number of the disciples increased;* ܣܓܝ ܠܗ ܬܡܢ ܝܘܡܬܐ *he passed many days there;* ܣܓܝ ܘܐܬܝܬܪ the widow's oil *increased and abounded;* ܣܓܐ ܬܪܬܝܢ ܥܦܝܦܢ ܡܢܝܢܐ *it is twice as many.* Pael ܣܓܝ *to make much of, extol, sing the praises of;* ܣܓܝܘ ܠܗ ܒܐܘܫܥܢܝܟܘܢ *magnify Him with your hosannas.* Ethpa. ܐܬܣܓܝ *to be extolled, to have one's praises sung.* Aph. ܐܣܓܝ *to make more, give more, increase, add, multiply:* ܡܣܓܐ ܦܪܘܩܐ. ܠܗܘ ܕܒܨܝܪ *the Saviour multiplies that which is too little.* Used adverbially with another verb: *very much, greatly, abundantly; the more, intensely, earnestly;* ܕܡܣܓܐ ܠܡܫܒܩ *Who will abundantly pardon;* ܐܣܓܝ ܐܪܝܡܗ God *hath highly exalted him.* Gram. *to form a plural, use in the plural.* Ethtaph. ܐܬܬܣܓܝ *to be multiplied;* gram. *to form the plural.* Derivatives, ܣܓܐ, ܣܓܝ and ܣܓܝܐ, ܣܓܝܐܘܬܐ, ܣܓܝܐܐܝܬ, ܣܓܝܐܢܐ, ܣܓܝܐܢܘܬܐ, ܣܓܝܐܢܐܝܬ, ܣܓܝܐܢܝܐ, ܣܘܓܐܐ, ܣܘܓܐܐ, ܣܘܓܝܢܐ, ܣܘܓܝܐܢܘܬܐ, ܡܣܓܝܢܐ, ܡܣܓܝܢܘܬܐ, ܡܣܓܝܐܢܐ, ܡܣܓܝܢܘܬܐ.

ܣܓܐ pl. ܣܓܝܢ rt. ܣܓܐ. m. *wool stuffing; clothes.*

ܣܓܕ fut. ܢܣܓܘܕ, act. part. ܣܓܕ, ܣܓܕܐ, pass. part. ܣܓܝܕ, ܐ, ܬܐ. *to bow oneself, do reverence* or *obeisance; to adore, worship;* ܣܓܕ ܥܠ ܐܦܘܗܝ ܥܠ ܐܪܥܐ *he bowed himself with his face to the earth;* ܟܗܢܐ ܟܕ ܣܓܕ ܠܡܕܒܚܐ ܐܬܠܬ ܙܒܢܝܢ *the priest when he bows thrice before the altar;* ܣܓܘܕܘ ܠܡܪܝܐ *worship the Lord.* Pass. part. *worshipped, adorable, august, an object of worship, divine;* ܐܪܙܐ ܪܒܐ ܘܣܓܝܕܐ ܕܡܬܒܪܢܫܢܘܬܐ *the great and adorable mystery of the Incarnation.* Ethpe. ܐܣܬܓܕ *to be worshipped, adored.* Aph. ܐܣܓܕ *to cause to worship, teach to adore.* Derivatives, ܡܣܓܕܐ, ܣܓܕܐ, ܣܓܕܘܬܐ, ܣܓܕܐ, ܡܣܓܕܢܐ, ܣܓܕܬܐ, ܣܓܕܢܝܬܐ.

ܣܓܕ ܠܫܡܫܐ m. *sun-worshipper* i. e. *the sunflower.*

ܣܓܕܡܘܢ *cardamomum, the spice cardamom.*

ܣܓܕܪܘܣ Pers. *as a dog.*

ܣܓܕܢܐܝܬ rt. ܣܓܕ. adv. *adoringly, in adoration.*

ܣܓܕܬܐ pl. ܬܐ rt. ܣܓܕ. f. *worship, adoration;* ܣܓܕܬܗ ܕܨܠܝܒܐ *the adoration of the Cross;* ܣܓܕܬܐ ܕܦܬܟܪܐ or ܣܓܕܬܐ ܕܦܬܟܪܘܬܐ *idolatry;* ܒܝܬ ܣܓܕܬܐ *place of worship.* Eccles. the name of a lection, John xiv. 15–31, read on Whitsun Eve and on the Eve of Good Friday.

ܣܓܘܕܐ, ܣܓܘܕܬܐ rt. ܣܓܕ. *a worshipper.*

ܣܓܘܣܓܘ m. *the teazle.*

ܣܓܘܠܐ, ܣܓܘܠܐ pl. ܣܓܘܠܝܢ, ܠܐ. m. *a bunch, cluster* of grapes, dates, &c.; ܣܓܘܠܝܢ ܣܓܘܠܝܢ *in clusters, clustering.* Metaph. ܣܓܘܠܐ ܕܚܝܐ *the life-giving cluster,* said of our Lord and of the holy martyrs; also of hair growing in clusters.

ܣܓܘܣܛܛܐ m. ζυγοστάτης, *a money-changer, banker;* cf. ܙܘܓܣܛܐ.

ܣܓܝ, ܣܓܝܐ, ܣܓܝܐܐ, ܣܓܝܐܬܐ pl. m. ܣܓܝܐܐܝܢ, ܣܓܝܐܐ, f. ܣܓܝܐܬܐ, ܣܓܝܐܬܐ rt. ܣܓܐ. *a*) adj. *much, many, great;* ܣܓܝܐܐ ܡܢ ܦܪܝܫܐ *many of the Pharisees;* ܚܝܠܐ ܣܓܝܐܐ *a great army;* ܡܕܝܢܬܐ ܣܓܝܐܬ ܥܡܐ *a populous city;* ܡܡܠܠܘܬܐ ܣܓܝܐܬܐ *much talking, talkativeness;* ܙܒܢܝܢ ܣܓܝܐܐܢ *oftentimes;* ܒܣܓܝܐܬܐ *in many things, with many words, very much.* In construction with nouns: ܣܓܝܐܝ ܐܠܗܐ *polytheists;* ܣܓܝ ܒܘܪܟܐ or ܣܓܝ ܪܘܟܐ the plant *polygonatum, Solomon's seal;* ܣܓܝ ܕܡܝܐ *costly, sumptuous;* ܣܓܝ ܫܢܝܐ *ancient;* ܣܓܝ ܢܫܐ *polygamous;* ܣܓܝ ܝܘܠܦܢܐ *learned;* ܣܓܝ ܝܘܡܬܐ *very aged, advanced in years;* ܣܓܝ ܙܢܝܢ *manifold;* ܣܓܝ ܩܢܝܢܐ *very wealthy;* ܣܓܝ ܪܓܠܐ *a polypod,* also the disease *polypus.* Gram. *plural, in the plural number;* ܫܡܗܐ ܣܓܝܐܐ ܢܩܘܙܐ ܢܩܝܢ nouns *in the plural take points.* *b*) adv. *very much, abundantly, extremely;* ܣܓܝ ܢܬܦܪܥ *he shall be greatly rewarded;* ܣܓܝ ܝܬܝܪ *much more;* ܣܓܝ ܪܚܝܩ *very far away;* ܡܢ ܣܓܝ *this long time;* ܡܢ ܟܕ ܣܓܝ ܛܠܐ ܗܘܝܬ *from my tenderest youth;* ܣܓܝ ܠܟܘܢ *it is enough, it is too much for you.* Imitating Greek construction, ܗܢܐ ܣܓܝ ܚܘܒܬܐ *this great debt.*

ܣܰܓܺܝܐܽܘܬܳܐ rt. ܣܓܐ. f. *a great number, multitude, increase;* ܣܰܓܺܝܐܽܘܬ ܐܰܠܳܗܶܐ *polytheism;* ܣܰܓܺܝܐܽܘܬ ܢܶܫ̈ܶܐ *polygamy;* ܒܣܰܓܺܝܐܽܘܬ ܐܽܘܪ̈ܚܳܬܳܐ *variously, in many ways;* ܣܰܓܺܝܐܽܘܬ ܒܺܝܫܳܬܳܐ *abounding evil;* gram. *plural.*

ܣܰܓܺܝܐܳܐܺܝܬ rt. ܣܓܐ. adv. *greatly, exceedingly.*

ܣܰܓܺܝܐܳܐܳܝܺܬ rt. ܣܓܐ. adv. *copiously;* gram. *plurally, in the plural.*

ܣܰܓܺܝܐܳܢܳܝܽܘܬܳܐ rt. ܣܓܐ. f. gram. *the plural number.*

ܣܰܓܺܝܐܳܢܳܝܳܐ rt. ܣܓܐ. gram. *plural;* ܫܡܳܗ̈ܶܐ ܣܰܓܺܝܐܳܢܳܝ̈ܶܐ *plural nouns.*

ܣܰܓܺܝܐܳܢܳܝܽܘܬܳܐ rt. ܣܓܐ. f. gram. *plurality, the plural number.*

ܣܰܓܦܽܘܬܳܐ rt. ܣܓܦ. f. *mutilation.*

ܣܶܓܳܐ, ܣܶܓܠܬܳܐ pl. ܣܶܓ̈ܠܳܬܳܐ f. *cyperus rotundus, a kind of rush.*

ܣܓܰܦ fut. ܢܶܣܓܽܘܦ. *to injure, maim, unnerve.* Pass. part. *impotent, maimed, injured, disabled;* ܣܓܺܝܦ ܒܪ̈ܶܓܠܰܘܗ̄ܝ *impotent in his feet.* Ethpe. ܐܶܣܬܓܶܦ and Ethpa. ܐܶܣܬܰܓܰܦ *to be injured, damaged, diminished, imperfect.* Pael ܣܰܓܶܦ *to injure, harm, damage; to diminish, detract from;* ܐܰܝܟܰܢܳܐ ܡܣܰܓܶܦ ܠܰܢ *how should he do us any harm?* ܪ̈ܓܺܝܓܳܬܳܐ ܕܣܰܟܠܳܢ ܘܡܣܰܓܦܳܢ *foolish and hurtful lusts;* ܠܳܐ ܡܶܕܶܡ ܡܣܰܓܦܳܐ *it in no way diminishes, detracts from* a truth, a parable, &c. Derivatives, ܣܓܺܝܦܽܘܬܳܐ, ܣܓܺܝܦܳܐ, ܡܣܰܓܦܳܐ, ܡܣܰܓܦܽܘܬܳܐ.

ܣܓܰܪ fut. ܢܶܣܓܽܘܪ, act. part. ܣܳܓܶܪ, pass. part. ܣܓܺܝܪ. *to shut up, keep in, confine, seclude,* esp. of keeping any one suspected of leprosy apart, see Lev. xiii passim; ܢܶܣܓܽܘܪ ܟܳܗܢܳܐ ܠܡܰܚܘܳܬܳܐ *the priest shall shut up the plague;* ܣܓܰܪ ܐܰܚܕ ܬܰܪ̈ܥܶܝ ܝܰܡܳܐ *He shut close the gates of the sea;* ܝܰܡ̈ܡܶܐ ܣܓܺܝܪܺܝܢ ܒܚܶܠܳܐ *seas enclosed by sand.* Ethpe. ܐܶܣܬܓܶܪ and Ethpa. ܐܶܣܬܰܓܰܪ *to be restrained, held back.* Derivatives, ܣܶܓܪܳܐ, ܣܶܓܪܳܐ, ܣܽܘܓܳܪܳܐ.

ܣܶܓܪܳܐ, ܣܓܶܪ rt. ܣܓܪ. m. *heavy rain.*

ܣܶܓܪܳܐ rt. ܣܓܪ. m. *confinement, seclusion.*

ܣܰܕܳܐ E-Syr. ܣܶܕܳܐ pl. ܣ̈ܕܺܝܢ m. *a) the stocks. b) grass.*

ܣܶܕܳܐ or ܣܶܕܳܐ pl. ܣ̈ܕܶܐ m. *the length of a furrow; a measure of* 100 *paces* equalling 400 cubits, three *seda* make one stadium, seven and a half *seda* go to a mile.

ܣܶܕܽܘܟܬܳܐ f. *a leathern bag, a nose-bag.*

ܣܕܘܡ Heb. pr. n. *Sodom.* Derivatives, the three following words.—

ܣܶܕܽܘܡܳܐܺܝܬ from ܣܕܘܡ. adv. *Sodomitically.*

ܣܶܕܽܘܡܳܝܳܐ, ܝܬܳܐ from ܣܕܘܡ. *Sodomite.* Fem. ellipt. for ܚܛܺܝܬܳܐ ܣܶܕܽܘܡܳܝܬܳܐ *the sin of Sodom.*

ܣܶܕܽܘܡܳܝܽܘܬܳܐ from ܣܕܘܡ. f. *Sodomy.*

ܣܽܘܕܳܪܳܐ rarely ܣܽܘܕܳܪܳܐ pl. ܝܢ, ܐ̈ ܣ m. *a cloth, loin-cloth, piece of cloth, towel;* ܣܽܘܕܳܪ̈ܶܐ ܪ̈ܰܒܪ̈ܒܶܐ ܕܟܶܬܳܢܳܐ *large cotton cloths;* ܚܰܝܶܨ ܗ̱ܘܳܐ ܣܽܘܕܳܪܳܐ *having a cloth round him.*

ܣܳܕܽܘܩܳܐ pl. ܐ̈ rt. ܣܕܩ. m. *a schismatic, author of schism* or *discord;* ܐܰܪܺܝܘܣ ܣܳܕܽܘܩܳܐ ܕܰܐܠܳܗܽܘܬܳܐ *Arius who divided the Godhead.*

ܣܶܕܽܘܪܳܐ m. *a corbel, projecting slab to hold a lamp.*

ܣܶܕܝܳܢܳܐ cf. ܣܰܕܝܳܢܳܐ, *the holm oak.*

ܣܶܕܝܩܽܘܬܳܐ rt. ܣܕܩ. f. *division, dissension;* ܣܶܕܝܩܽܘܬܶܗ ܕܥܳܠܡܳܐ ܗܳܢܳܐ *the divided state of this world.*

ܣܕܺܝܪܳܐܺܝܬ rt. ܣܕܪ. adv. *orderly, in good order.*

ܣܕܺܝܪܽܘܬܳܐ rt. ܣܕܪ. f. *arrangement, disposing, setting in order, array;* ܣܕܺܝܪܽܘܬ ܩܪܳܒܳܐ *drawing up a line of battle;* ܣܕܺܝܪܽܘܬ ܬܰܫܥܺܝܬܳܐ *the composition of a narrative.*

ܣܶܕܠܳܐ pl. ܐ̈ contracted from ܣܰܢܕܠܳܐ. m. *a sandal.*

ܣܰܕܢܳܐ, ܣܰܕܳܢ m. *the potter's wheel; an anvil;* ܕܰܗܒܳܐ ܡܬܡܚܶܐ ܥܰܠ ܣܰܕܢܳܐ gold *is struck on the anvil;* ܣܰܕܢܳܐ ܐܰܪܥܳܐ *horehound,* a fibrous plant used to make candle-wicks.

ܣܕܰܩ and ܣܕܶܩ fut. ܢܶܣܕܽܘܩ, act. part. ܣܳܕܶܩ, ܣܳܕܩܳܐ, pass. part. ܣܕܺܝܩ, ܩܳܐ, ܩܬܳܐ. *to tear asunder, divide, rive; to separate, cause a schism;* ܠܟܶܬܽܘܢܳܐ ܣܳܕܩܺܝܢ *they tear the vesture;* ܣܕܰܩܬܝܗ̇ ܠܩܰܒܪܳܐ *thou hast broken open a tomb;* ܦܳܪ̈ܚܬܳܐ ܣܕܺܝܩܳܢ ܓܶܦ̈ܝܗܶܝܢ birds *whose wings part into feathers;* ܣܕܺܝܩܺܝܢ ܡܶܢ ܚܰܒܪ̈ܰܝܗܽܘܢ *separated from their companions;* ܡܰܠܦܳܢܽܘܬܳܐ ܦܠܺܝܓܬܳܐ ܘܡܣܰܕܩܳܢܺܝܬܳܐ *doubtful and schismatical doctrine.* Ethpe. ܐܶܣܬܕܶܩ *to be rent, riven, parted, separated, divided; to separate, cause a schism;* ܚܰܕ ܐܺܝܬܽܘܬܳܐ ܕܠܳܐ ܡܶܣܬܰܕܩܳܢܺܝܬܳܐ *one un-*

divided concord; ܐܶܣܬܕܩܘ ܫܡܰܝܳܐ *the heavens were rent;* ܡܶܛܽܠ ܡܶܠܬܳܐ ܕܥܰܠܳܗ ܐܶܣܬܕܩܢ *the expression on account of which we separated* from the Church. Pael ܣܰܕܶܩ *to rend* the garments; *to rend, tear, lacerate; to cleave a way, divide;* ܠܒ̈ܽܘܫܶܐ ܡܣܰܕܩ̈ܶܐ *rent garments;* ܣܰܕܶܩ ܘܥܒܰܪ ܒܡܶܨܥܰܬ ܟܶܢ̈ܫܶܐ *he made a way and passed through the crowd;* ܫܡܰܝܳܐ ܣܰܕܶܩ ܘܣܰܕܩܶܗ ܚܶܪ̈ܝܳܢܶܐ *He rent the heavens and parted asunder the strife.* Ethpa. ܐܶܣܬܰܕܰܩ *to be torn, rent, separated;* used of clothes, of the heart, of schism. Derivatives, ܣܕܩܐ, ܣܶܕܩܳܐ, ܣܘܕܳܩܳܐ, ܡܣܰܕܩܳܢܳܐ, ܡܣܰܕܩܳܢܳܐܝܬ, ܣܕܘܩܝܐ, ܣܕܝܩܘܬܐ.

ܣܶܕܩܳܐ pl. ܣܶܕ̈ܩܶܐ rt. ܣܕܩ. m. *a rent, tear, division, schism, sect.*

ܣܘܕܳܩܳܐ rt. ܣܕܩ. m. *rending, laceration.*

ܣܕܰܪ fut. ܢܶܣܕܽܘܪ, act. part. ܣܳܕܰܪ, ܣܳܕܪܳܐ, pass. part. ܣܕܺܝܪ, ܪܳܐ, ܪ̈ܳܬܳܐ. *to arrange, lay* or *set in order; to marshal, set in array;* with ܠܘܳܬ or ܠܩܘܒܠܐ *to resist;* also *to follow in order, happen successively; to set forth, digest, revise;* eccles. *to repeat, recite;* ܣܕܰܪ ܩܕܳܡܰܘܗܝ ܢܳܡܽܘܣܳܐ ܕܚܰܝ̈ܶܐ *He set before him the law of life;* ܣܕܺܝܪ ܒܟܺܐܦ̈ܶܐ ܝܰܩܺܝܪ̈ܳܬܳܐ *set with rows of precious stones;* ܕܣܕܰܪ ܠܗܽܘܢ *those things which happened to them;* ܣܕܰܪܢ ܡܶܠ̈ܶܐ ܕܐܰܒ̈ܳܗܳܬܳܐ ܝܰܘ̈ܢܳܝܶܐ *we have revised the discourses of the Greek Fathers.* With ܩܪܳܒܳܐ *to prepare for combat;* ܡ̈ܶܠܶܐ *to marshal one's words, dispose arguments;* ܣܶܕܪܳܐ *to recite a sedra;* ܩܪܳܒܳܐ *to draw up in line of battle;* ܡܡܰܠܠܳܐ *to begin a conversation.* Ethpe. ܐܶܣܬܕܰܪ refl. *to draw up in line of battle, set the battle in array;* pass. *to be drawn up, set in array* esp. with ܩܪܳܒܳܐ; *to be laid, set;* ܐܶܣܬܕܰܪܘ ܥܰܠ ܒܳܒܶܠ *set yourselves in array against Babylon;* ܦܳܬܽܘܪ̈ܶܐ ܐܶܣܬܕܰܪܘ ܩܕܳܡܰܝܗܽܘܢ *tables were set before them.* Pa. ܣܰܕܰܪ *to set in array.* Ethpa. *to be drawn up, set in array.* Derivatives, ܣܶܕܪܳܐ, ܣܕܺܝܪܽܘܬܳܐ, ܣܕܺܝܪܳܐܝܬ.

ܣܶܕܪܳܐ pl. ܣܶܕ̈ܪܶܐ, ܪ̈ܝܢ rt. ܣܕܪ. m. *a*) *a hanging, curtain.* *b*) *a row, line, rank, array, order, series;* ܒܣܶܕܪܳܐ ܚܰܕ ܒܳܬܰܪ ܚܰܕ *in order, one after the other;* ܣܶܕܪܳܐ ܕܠܰܚܡܳܐ *rows of* shew-*bread;* ܣܶܕܪܳܐ ܠܩܘܒܠ ܣܶܕܪܳܐ *rank opposed to rank;* ܣܶܕܪܳܐ ܕܢܒ̈ܺܝܶܐ *the succession of prophets.* *c*) *a chant, prayer* or *anthem* having verses in alphabetical order.

ܣܶܕܪܳܐ ...

ܩܶܢܛܪܘܢ Pers. m. *a centurion.*

ܣܗܶܕ fut. ܢܶܣܗܰܕ, act. part. ܣܳܗܶܕ, ܣܳܗܕܳܐ, pass. part. ܣܗܺܝܕ, ܕܳܐ, ܕ̈ܳܬܳܐ. *to witness, testify* with ܥܰܠ or ܒ; *to suffer martyrdom;* ܠܳܐ ܬܶܣܗܰܕ ܣܳܗܕܽܘܬܳܐ ܕܰܓܳܠܬܳܐ *thou shalt not bear false witness.* Pass. part. *attested, of established reputation, acknowledged.* Ethpe. ܐܶܣܬܗܶܕ *to be witnessed to, approved by testimony;* ܒܚܰܫܳܐ ܘܰܒܩܝܳܡܬܶܗ ܕܡܳܪܰܢ ܐܶܣܬܗܶܕ ܕܰܐܠܳܗܳܐ ܫܰܪܺܝܪܳܐ by our Lord's passion and resurrection *witness is borne that He is very God.* Pael ܣܰܗܶܕ *to call to witness, charge, testify;* ܠܣܳܗܕ̈ܶܐ ܬܣܰܗܶܕ *thou shalt summon witnesses.* ܡܣܰܗܶܕ ܐ̱ܢܳܐ ܒܟܽܘܢ ܫܡܰܝܳܐ ܘܰܐܪܥܳܐ *I call heaven and earth to witness against you.* Ethpa. ܐܶܣܬܰܗܰܕ *to be confirmed by witnesses; to suffer martyrdom.* Aph. ܐܰܣܗܶܕ *to bear witness* with ܒ or ܥܰܠ; *to bring witness; to attest, protest; to be a martyr;* ܠܳܐ ܬܰܣܗܶܕ ܥܰܠ ܚܰܒܪܳܟ ܣܳܗܕܽܘܬܳܐ ܕܰܓܳܠܬܳܐ *thou shalt not bear false witness against thy neighbour;* ܡܰܣܗܕܺܝܢ ܥܰܠ ܚܬܳܡܳܐ *they attest by sealing.* Ethtaph. ܐܶܬܬܰܣܗܰܕ *to be summoned as a witness.* Derivatives, ܣܳܗܕܳܐ, ܣܳܗܕܽܘܬܳܐ, ܣܳܗܕܳܝܳܐ, ܣܳܗܕܳܝܬ, ܡܣܰܗܕܳܢܳܐ, ܡܣܰܗܕܳܢܽܘܬܳܐ, ܡܰܣܗܕܳܢܳܐܝܬ, ܡܰܣܗܕܳܢܽܘܬܳܐ.

ܣܳܗܕܳܐ, ܣܳܗܕ̈ܶܐ Peal act. part. in the emphatic state *a witness, martyr;* ܣܳܗܕ̈ܶܐ ܕܰܓܳܠܶܐ *false witnesses;* ܩܕܡܳܝܬ ܣܳܗܕܳܬܳܐ ܬܶܩܠܰܐ *the protomartyr Thekla;* ܒܶܝܬ ܣܳܗܕ̈ܶܐ *a martyrion, shrine* or *church where the remains of martyrs were laid;* ܡܕܺܝܢܰܬ ܣܳܗܕ̈ܶܐ *Martyropolis* = the city Maipheroat.

ܣܳܗܕܽܘ, ܣܳܗܕܽܘܬܳܐ pl. ܝ̈ܳܬܳܐ rt. ܣܗܕ. f. *a*) *witness, testimony, adjuration;* ܣܳܗܕܽܘܬܳܐ ܕܰܓܳܠܬܳܐ and ܣܳܗܕܽܘܬܳܐ ܕܰܓܳܠܬܳܐ *false witness;* ܬܰܪܬܶܝܢ ܠܽܘܚ̈ܶܐ ܕܣܳܗܕܽܘܬܳܐ *the two tables of testimony.* *b*) *attestation, evidence, cited* or *quoted witness;* ܒܣܳܗܕܽܘ̈ܳܬܳܐ ܢܗܺܝܪ̈ܳܬܳܐ ܚܰܘܺܝ ܐܶܢܽܘܢ *he showed them by clear evidence;* the Gospel of St. Matthew contains ܠܚ ܣܳܗܕܽܘ̈ܳܬܳܐ *thirty-eight quotations.* *c*) *confession, martyrdom;* ܟܬܳܒܳܐ ܕܣܳܗܕܽܘ̈ܳܬܳܐ *a martyrology.*

ܣܳܗܕܳܝܳܐ, ܣܳܗܕܳܝܬܳܐ rt. ܣܗܕ. *of* or *concerning a martyr;* ܐܰܓܽܘܢܳܐ ܣܳܗܕܳܝܳܐ *a martyr's conflict;* ܥܶܕܳܢܳܐ ܕܪܰܡܫܳܐ ܣܳܗܕܳܝܳܐ *the evening office for a martyr.*

ܣܰܗܪܳܐ com. gen. *the moon;* ܣܰܗܪܳܐ ܚܰܕܬܳܐ *new moon;* ܡܰܠܝܽܘܬܳܐ ܕܣܰܗܪܳܐ *full moon;* ܫܶܬܶܐܣܬܳܐ ܕܣܰܗܪܳܐ *the foundation of the* Paschal *moon* =

Angl. *the golden number* or *prime;* ܣܗܪܐ ܕܡܠܐ ܘܚܣܪ *the moon which waxes and wanes.* In chemistry ܣܗܪܐ is a name for *silver.* Derivatives, ܣܗܪܐ, ܣܗܪܢܐ, ܣܗܪܢܝܐ, ܡܣܗܪܢܐ.

ܣܗܪܢܝܐ, ܣܬܳܐ from ܣܗܪܐ. *lunar;* ܝܪܚܐ ܣܗܪܢܝܐ *a lunar month.*

ܣܗܪ̈ܘܢܐ from ܣܗܪܐ. m. pl. *crescents, crescent-shaped ornaments* hung on camels' necks.

ܣܗܪܢܝܐ, ܣܬܳܐ from ܣܗܪܐ. *lunar, of the moon, moonlike; moon-struck, lunatic;* ܫܢ̈ܝܐ ܣܗܪ̈ܢܝܬܐ *lunar years;* ܫܘ̈ܩܠܐ ܣܗܪ̈ܢܝܐ *lunar eclipses;* ܥܠܝ̈ܡܬܐ ܣܗܪ̈ܢܝܬܐ maidens *beautiful as the moon;* ܟܐܦܐ ܣܗܪܢܝܬܐ *selenite, crystalline gypsum.*

ܣ̄ܘ abbreviation of ܣܘܓܐܐ, of ܣܘܪܝܝܐ, &c.

ܣܘܐ fut. ܢܣܘܐ, part. ܣܘܐ, ܣܘܝܐ, ܣܘܝܐ. *to long, desire;* ܣܘܐ ܐܢܐ ܠܡܚܙܝܟܘܢ *I long to see you;* ܐܡܪ̈ܐ ܕܣܘܝܢ ܠܩܠܟ *the lambs who long for thy voice.* Ethpe. ܐܫܬܘܝ *to long, desire;* ܡܫܬܘܝܐ ܠܗܘܢ ܣܓܝ *it is sought by them, is greatly desired by them.* Aph. ܐܣܘܝ *to fill with longing;* ܠܝ ܡܚܝܠܬܐ ܫܘܦܪܗ ܐܣܘܝ *his loveliness filled me, the weak one, with longing.* Derivatives, ܣܘܝܐ, ܣܘܝܘܬܐ.

ܣܘܒ, ܣܒ root-meaning *to be impure.* Pael ܣܰܘܶܒ *to defile, profane;* ܗܠܝܢ ܐܢܝܢ ܕܡܣܘܒܢ ܠܒܪܢܫܐ *these are the things which defile a man.* Pass. part. ܡܣܘܒ, ܡܣܘܒܐ, ܡܣܘܒܬܐ. *defiled, unclean, common; filthy, abominable;* ܡܐܟܘܠܬܐ ܡܣܘܒܬܐ *common* or *unclean food;* ܠܒܐ ܩܕܝܫܐ ܘܠܐ ܡܣܘܒܐ *a holy and undefiled heart.* Ethpa. ܐܣܬܘܒ *to defile oneself, to be defiled;* ܐܣܬܘܒܘ ܒܗܢܐ ܣܘܪܚܢܐ *they have defiled themselves by this crime.* Derivatives, ܣܘܒܐ, ܡܣܘܒܘܬܐ.

ܣܘܒܪܐ rt. ܣܒܪ. m. *likeness.*

ܣܘܒܝܢܐ pl. ܣܘܒ̈ܝܢܝܬܐ f. Pers. *a spear.*

ܣܘܒܠܐ pl. ̈ܐ rt. ܣܒܠ. m. *a) a share, contribution, portion;* ܣܒ ܡܢ ܦܠܢ ܣܘܒܠܗ *take his contribution from so-and-so;* ܒܝܬ ܣܘܒܠܐ *a club;* ܝܬܒܝܢ ܒܣܘ̈ܒܠܐ *lounging at club-rooms. b) a fire-shovel, oven-rake.*

ܣܘܒܥܐ rt. ܣܒܥ. m. *compline;* ܒܝܬ ܣܘܒܥܐ *a supper-room, refectory.*

ܣܘܒܪܐ rt. ܣܒܪ. m. *preaching, annunciation;* the Syrians celebrate two feasts of Annunciation, ܕܡܪܢ or ܕܡܪܝܡ that of *our Lord* or *of Mary* answering to the season of Advent with us, ܚܕ ܒܫܒܐ ܩܕܡܝܐ ܕܣܘܒܪܐ *First Sunday of Advent;* and ܣܘܒܪܗ ܕܙܟܪܝܐ or ܕܝܘܚܢܢ *the Annunciation of Zacharias* or *of John.*

ܣܓ, ܣܓܐ fut. ܢܣܘܓ, act. part. ܣܐܓ, ܣܝܓܐ, pass. part. ܣܝܓ, ܣܝܓܐ, ܣܝܓܬܐ. *to hedge* or *fence in, enclose; to shut up, stop, repair;* ܣܓ ܠܗ ܐܘܪܚܐ *to stop the way;* ܣܐܓ ܬܪ̈ܥܬܐ *a repairer of breaches, he who repairs ruined places;* ܗܘ ܕܣܝܓܐ *the hindrance, impediment;* ܣܝܓܐ ܒܫܘܫܢ̈ܐ *set about with lilies;* ܣܓ ܝܡܐ ܐܘܪܚܐ ܩܕܡ ܥܒܪ̈ܝܐ *the sea barred the way of the Hebrews.* Ethpe. ܐܣܬܝܓ *to be stopped, blocked up, built up.* Pa. ܣܰܝܶܓ *to fence round; to repair, restore.* Aph. ܐܣܝܓ *to fence round; to stop, repair;* ܠܡܣܝܓܘ ܬܪܥܬܐ ܒܟܐ̈ܦܐ ܘܒܛܝܢܐ *to stop the breach with stones and mortar.* Derivatives, ܣܝܓܐ, ܣܝܓܬܐ, ܣܘܓܐ, ܣܝܓܘܬܐ.

ܣܘܓܐ m. *the black poplar.*

ܣܘܓܐܐ sometimes written ܣܘܓܐ pl. ܣܘ̈ܓܐܐ; with an affix loses one or both Aleps, ܣܘܓܗ *the greater part of it,* ܣܘܓܝܗܘܢ *the multitude of them;* construct state ܣܘܓܐ rt. ܣܓܐ. com. gen. *a multitude, a great part, the greater part, most part, very many;* ܣܘܓܐܐ ܕܛܝܒܘܬܟ *the multitude of Thy goodness;* ܣܘܓܐܐ ܕܟܢܫܐ *a great crowd;* ܣܘܓܐܐ ܕܩܛܝܢܐ *the most part of the throng;* ܐܢܫܐ ܣܘܓܐܐ *very many men;* ܓܢ̈ܐ ܣܘܓܐܐ *very many gardens;* ܣܘܓܐܐ ܕܟܪܝܘܬܗ *his very great sorrow;* ܐܝܟ ܕܒܣܘܓܐܐ *for the most part, usually.*

ܣܘܓܢܝܬܐ f. *a robe of honour.*

ܣܘܓܝܬܐ pl. ܣܘܓ̈ܝܬܐ rt. ܣܓܐ. f. *a song, canticle.*

ܣܘܓܦܢܐ pl. ̈ܐ rt. ܣܓܦ. m. *hurt, damage, injury, harm;* ܬܠܬܐ ܣܘܓ̈ܦܢܐ ܐܝܬ ܠܡܗܘܐ *three kinds of damage* may befall; ܕܠܐ ܣܘܓܦܢ *with impunity.*

ܣܘܓܪܐ rt. ܣܓܪ. m. *a clog* tied to a dog's neck.

ܣܘܕ, ܣܘܕܐ or ܣܘܕܪܐ pl. ̈ܐ Heb. and Ar. *a rug, divan-cushion.* m. *conversation* especially *quiet and intimate conversation* as of those sitting together; *speech;* ܚܙܘܗ ܘܣܘܕܗ ܗܘܐ *his appearance and mode of speech were pleasing;* ܣܘܕܐ ܡܥܪܒܝܐ *western manner of speaking;* ܣܘܕܐ ܛܘܪܝܐ *mountain dialect.* DERIVATIVES, verb ܣܘܕ, ܣܘܕܝܐ, ܣܘܕܢܝܐ, ܡܣܬܘܕܪܢܐ.

ܣܰܘܶܕ denom. verb Pael conj. from ܣܘܕܐ. *to talk, converse.* ETHPA. ܐܶܣܬܰܘܰܕ *to speak, talk, converse* with ܠ or ܥܡ of the pers., with ܥܠ or ܡܛܠ of the subject; ܥܡ ܐܢܫܝܢ ܐܣܬܘܕܢܢ *we talked with certain men;* ܐܝܟ ܗܢܘܢ ܕܒܠܫܢܐ ܢܘܟܪܝܐ ܡܣܬܘܕܝܢ *as those who converse in strange languages.* ETHTAPH. ܐܶܬܬܣܘܰܕ *to be said.*

ܣܘܕܐ or ܣܘܕܐ pl. ܐ̈ m. a measure of corn containing rather less than a pound.

ܣܘܕܝܐ, ܝܬܐ from ܣܘܕܐ. *vocative, allocutory.*

ܣܘܕܢܝܐ from ܣܘܕܐ. *colloquial, conversational.*

ܣܘܕܣܐ Arabic m. *a sixth, sixth part.*

ܣܘܕܩ, ܣܘܕܩܐ pl. ܐ̈ rt. ܣܕܩ. *a tear, rent, wound.*

ܣܘܕܪܐ pl. ܐ̈ m. sudarium, *a cloth, binder, linen girdle, loin-cloth; handkerchief; turban;* ܐܦܘܗܝ ܐܣܝܪܢ ܒܣܘܕܪܐ *his face was bound with a grave-cloth;* ܣܘܕܪܐ ܐܣܛܠܐ ܗܘ ܕܪܫܐ *a turban is the head-covering.*

ܣܘܕܪܬܐ fem. of ܣܘܕܪܐ. *a head-band, covering* worn by women.

ܣܘܗܕܢܐ rt. ܣܗܕ. m. *adjuration, calling to witness.*

ܣܘܘ; for words with two Wavs after the first radical, see the form spelt with one Wav.

ܣܘܙܘܓܐ or ܣܘܙܘܓܐ pl. ܣܘܙܘܓܝܣ συζυγία, *union; equal;* ܬܪ̈ܥܐ ܣܘܙܘܓܐ *two-fold doors.*

ܣܘܚ fut. ܢܣܘܚ, act. part. ܣܐܚ, ܣܝܚܐ, pass. part. ܣܝܚ. *to long for, earnestly desire; to eagerly meet* or *await* with ܠܘܬ or ܠܩܘܒܠܐ; ܕܣܘܚܬ ܒܗ ܢܦܫܝ *for whom my soul longed;* ܣܘܚܘ ܠܗܦܟܬܗ *they eagerly watched for the return of* the dove to the ark; ܣܐܚܐ ܣܓܝ ܐܢܐ *I greatly desire.* PAEL ܣܰܘܰܚ *to long for, eagerly desire.* ETHPA. ܐܶܣܬܰܘܰܚ the same. DERIVATIVES, ܣܘܚܐ, ܣܘܚܐܝܬ, ܣܘܚܝܐ, ܣܘܚܝܬܐ, ܡܣܬܘܚܢܐ, ܡܣܬܘܚܢܘܬܐ, ܡܣܘܚܢܐ, ܡܣܘܚܢܘܬܐ.

ܣܘܚܐ rt. ܣܚܐ. m. *dispersion.*

ܣܘܚܐ and ܣܘܘܚܐ rt. ܣܘܚ. m. *longing, earnest desire, eagerness;* ܠܒ̈ܘܬܐ ܕܣܘܘܚܐ *longing hearts.*

ܣܘܚܐܝܬ rt. ܣܘܚ. adv. *desirously, eagerly.*

ܣܘܚܝܐ pl. ܐ̈ rt. ܣܚܐ. m. *washing, ablution* esp. *magical ablutions.*

ܣܘܚܦܐ rt. ܣܚܦ. m. *destruction, demolition, overthrow.*

ܣܘܚܪܐ rt. ܣܚܪ. m. *vagrancy.*

ܣܛ, ܣܛ fut. ܢܣܘܛ, parts. ܣܐܛ, ܣܝܛܐ and ܣܝܛ, ܣܝܛܐ. *to burn, consume away;* ܣܐܛ ܫܪܓܐ *the candle burns away;* ܣܛܘ ܒܢܘܪܐ *they perished in the fire.* PA. ܣܰܘܶܛ *to burn up, destroy by fire, scorch, pinch with cold;* ܣܘܛܗ ܚܘܡܐ *the heat consumed it;* ܐܐܪ ܡܣܘܛ ܡܢ ܥܙܝܙܘܬ ܩܘܪܫܐ *the air is dried up from the fierce cold;* ܥܕܬܐ ܡܣܘܛܬܐ *a church destroyed by fire.* ETHPA. ܐܶܣܬܰܘܰܛ *to be burnt up, scorched, withered* by fire, sun, or cold wind. Metaph. *to be darkened, dazzled;* ܐܣܬܘܛ ܥܝ̈ܢܝ ܡܕܥܗ ܡܢ ܢܘܗܪܐ ܪܘܚܢܝܐ *the eyes of his mind were dim from spiritual light.* DERIVATIVES, ܣܘܛܐ, ܣܘܛܝܐ, ܣܘܛܬܐ, ܡܣܘܛܬܐ, ܡܣܬܘܛܘܬܐ.

ܣܘܛܡܐ pl. ܐ̈ rt. ܣܛܡ. m. *a shackle, fetter;* ܣܘܛܡ̈ܐ ܕܐܝ̈ܕܐ *manacles.* ܣܘܛܡ̈ܐ are lighter than ܩܘܠܐ and ܐܣܘܪܐ.

ܣܘܛܦܐ pl. ܐ̈ rt. ܣܛܦ. m. *a scratch, puncture; a small knife.*

ܣܘܝܐ rt. ܣܘܐ. m. *desire, longing.*

ܣܘܝܒܐ pl. ܐ̈ rt. ܣܘܒ. m. *uncleanness, defilement, abomination;* ܣܘܝܒܐ ܕܕܡܐ *blood-stain.*

ܣܘܝܬܐ rt. ܣܘܐ. f. *desire, craving.*

ܣܘܝܚܐ rt. ܣܘܚ. m. *strong desire, longing.*

ܣܘܚܝܬܐ rt. ܣܘܚ. f. *desire.*

ܣܘܝܛܐ rt. ܣܛ. m. *a burning, conflagration.*

ܣܘܟܡܐ pl. ܐ̈ rt. ܣܟܡ. m. *limitation, ending; a conclusion, the concluding clauses* of a prayer; arith. *the amount, sum total;* ܣܘܟܡܐ ܐܬܪܢܝܐ *limitation in space;* ܕܠܐ ܣܘܟܡܐ *limitless;* ܐܝܟ ܕܒܣܘܟܡܐ *finally, to sum up;* with ܢܣܒ *to be finished, concluded.*

ܣܘܟܪܡܐ rt. ܣܟܪ. m. *binding up* a wound; *a bandage, plaster.*

ܣܘܡܟܐ rt. ܣܡܟ. m. *support, succour.*

ܣܘܦ imper. of verb ܢܣܦ. *to pour.*

ܣܦ, ܣܦ fut. ܢܣܘܦ, pass. part. ܣܝܦ, ܣܝܦܐ. *to end;* ܣܦܘ ܡܐܡܪ̈ܐ *the sermons are ended, here end the sermons.* Pael ܣܰܝܶܟ *a) to bring to an end, conclude;* ܗܳܕܶܐ ܡܣܰܝܶܟ ܡܰܟܬܒܳܢܽܘܬܶܗ *herewith he brings his chronicle to an end. b) to limit; to contain, comprise, comprehend;* ܠܳܐ ܡܣܰܝܶܟ ܒܕܽܘܟܬܳܐ ܘܒܐܰܬܪܳܐ *not contained in a place and space, unlimited;* ܢܗܺܝܪܳܐ ܣܰܝܶܟ ܒܢܰܗܺܝܪ̈ܶܐ in the heavenly bodies God *collected together and set bounds to the light;* ܣܰܝܟܽܘܗ̇ ܒܟܠܺܝܠܳܐ *they set* or *confined* a pearl *in a crown;* ܦܰܪܙܠܳܐ ܘܢܚܳܫܳܐ ܡܣܰܝܶܟ ܒܶܗ *iron and brass are found therein;* ܠܳܐ ܡܣܰܝܟܳܐ—ܠܳܐ ܡܣܰܝܟܳܢܳܐ *limitless, infinite, incomprehensible. c) to define* in words, *to tell* or *rehearse completely;* ܠܳܐ ܐ̱ܢܳܫ ܐܶܫܟܰܚ ܠܡܣܰܝܳܟܽܘ ܡܶܢܝܳܢܗܽܘܢ *no one is able to tell the number of them;* ܠܰܝܬ ܠܝ ܚܰܝܠܳܐ ܕܐܣܰܝܶܟ *I have not the power to describe fully* his virtues in this book; ܒܡܰܟܬܒܳܢܽܘܬܳܐ ܡܣܰܝܟܳܐܝܬ *shortly, summarily.* Ethpa. ܐܶܣܬܰܝܰܟ *a) to be brought to an end, conclusion* or *consummation;* ܐܶܣܬܰܝܰܟܘ ܡܶܠܰܝܗܽܘܢ ܕܢܒܺܝ̈ܶܐ in the B.V.M. *were consummated the utterances of the prophets. b) to be bounded, limited; to terminate;* ܡܶܣܬܰܝܰܟ ܟܽܘܢܳܐ ܒܚܽܘܪܳܐ ܕܪܺܝܫܳܐ *a cone terminates at its apex;* ܒܪܢܳܫܳܐ ܗܽܘ ܐܶܣܬܰܝܰܟ our blessed Lord *as a man is limited* or *finite. c) to be contained, comprehended, included;* ܡܳܐܢܳܐ ܕܐܶܫܟܰܚ ܡܶܣܬܰܝܰܟ ܒܶܗ *a vessel in which the Maker can be contained;* ܒܶܗ ܐܶܣܬܰܝܰܟ ܟܽܠܗܶܝܢ ܡܰܝܬܪ̈ܳܘܳܬܳܐ *in him all virtues are comprised;* ܕܠܳܐ ܡܶܣܬܰܝܰܟ *countless, boundless, infinite.* Derivatives, ܣܘܟܐ, ܣܘܟܣܟܐ, ܣܘܟܝܐ, ܣܟܐ ܣܟܝ, ܣܟܝܐ, ܣܟܝܠܐ, ܣܟܝܬܐ, ܣܟܝܘܬܐ, ܣܘܟܝܐ, ܣܟܝܟܐ, ܡܣܝܟܢܐ, ܡܣܝܟܢܘܬܐ, ܡܣܝܟܐ, ܡܣܝܟܐܝܬ, ܡܣܬܝܟܢܐ, ܡܣܬܝܟܢܘܬܐ, ܡܣܬܝܟܢܘܬܐ.

ܣܘܟܐ, ܣܘܟܬܐ pl. ܣܘ̈ܟܐ, ܣܘ̈ܟܝܬܐ f. *a bough, branch, twig;* ܐܶܚܺܝܕ ܒܣܽܘܟܬܳܐ ܒܩܰܪ̈ܢܳܬܶܗ *a ram caught in the branches by his horns;* ܣܘ̈ܟܐ ܕܙܰܝܬܳܐ *olive-branches;* ܬܶܫܡܶܫܬܳܐ ܕܣܘ̈ܟܐ the office of *the Blessing of the Palms* ܕܚܕܒܫܒܐ ܕܣܘ̈ܟܐ *on Palm Sunday;* palms are also called ܣܘ̈ܟܐ ܕܐܘܫܥܢܐ *Hosanna branches;* ܣܘ̈ܟܐ ܕܫܢ̈ܐ *tooth-brushes* or *dentifrice.*

ܣܘܟܣܟܐ dimin. of ܣܘܟܐ m. *a small branch.*

ܣܘܟܝܐ rt. ܣܟܐ. m. *expectation;* ܒܣܘܟܝܐ ܗܘܘ ܩܝܡܝܢ *they were in expectation;* ܕܠܐ ܣܘܟܝܐ *unexpectedly.*

ܣܘܟܟܐ rt. ܣܟ. m. *nailing, fixing.*

ܣܘܟܠܐ pl. ܣܘ̈ܟܠܐ, ܐ̈ rt. ܣܟܠ. m. *the intelligence, understanding, intellect; a thought, consideration, opinion, note; the sense, meaning.*

ܣܘܟܠܢܝܐ, ܣܘܟܠܢܝܬܐ rt. ܣܟܠ. gram. *belonging to the sense.*

ܣܘܟܡܐ, ܣܘܟܡܢܐ from ܣܰܟܶܡ. m. *shaping, modifying, articulation* of letters.

ܣܘܟܢܐ pl. ܐ̈ m. *a helm, rudder;* ܐܶܠܦܶܗ ܛܳܥܝܳܐ ܒܝܰܡܳܐ ܕܠܳܐ ܣܘܟܢܐ *his ship errs rudderless among surging floods.*

ܣܘܟܢܝܐ a) from ܣܘܟܐ. *branching;* ܩܪ̈ܢܐ ܣܘܟܢܝ̈ܬܐ *branching horns.* b) from ܣܘܟܢܐ. *shaped like a rudder.*

ܣܘܟܪܐ pl. ܐ̈ rt. ܣܟܪ. m. *a bolt, bar, lock.*

ܣܘܠܒܐ, ܣܘܠܐܒܐ, ܣܘܠܐܒܝ, ܣܘܠܐܒܝ &c. pl. ܣܘܠܐܒܝܣ or ܣܘܠܠܒܘܣ f. συλλαβή, *a syllable.*

ܣܘܠܐ, ܣܘܠܝܐ also ܣܘܠܚܐ, ܣܘܠܚܢܐ pl. ܐ̈ rt. ܣܠܐ. m. *refuse, dross, offscouring, abomination; refusal, rejection.*

ܣܘܠܝܢܐ *small sheep.*

ܣܘܠܝܢܐ rt. ܣܠܐ. *adulterated, alloyed.*

ܣܘܠܛܝܡܐ from ܣܰܠܛܶܡ. m. *style, composition.*

ܣܘܠܘܓܝܣܐ pl. ܐ̈ συλλογίσαι, *syllogism.*

ܣܘܠܘܓܝܣܛܝܩܝܐ, ܐ̈ συλλογιστικός, *syllogistic.*

ܣܘܠܘܓܝܣܛܝܩܝܬܐ f. *a syllogism;* with ܚܟܡ *to infer by way of syllogism, to draw a conclusion.*

ܣܘܠܘܓܝܣܡܘܣ pl. ܣܘܠܘܓܝܣܡܘܣ and ܣܘܠܘܓܝܣܡܐ m. συλλογισμός, *a syllogism;* ܣܘܠܘܓܝܣܡܘܣ ܗܘ ܗܘܝܘ ܡܘܕܐ *a syllogism that is a mode of connected thought, an inference from premises.*

ܣܘܠܛܢ and ܣܘܠܛܢܐ Ar. m. *the sultan.*

ܣܘܠܛܢܝܐ pl. ܐ̈ adj. from ܣܘܠܛܢ. some coin; ܣܘ̈ܐܡܐ ܣܘܠܛܢܝ̈ܐ *silver sultan pieces.*

ܣܘܠܚܐ rt. ܣܠܐ. m. *rejection.*

ܣܘܠܩܐ pl. ܐ̈ rt. ܣܠܩ. m. *ascension* esp. *the ascension* into heaven of our blessed Lord; *ascent* of a mountain, metaph. ܣܘܠܩܐ ܕܡܢ ܡܝܬܪܘܬܐ ܠܡܝܬܪܘܬܐ *ascent from virtue to higher virtue.*

ܣܘܡ, ܣܳܡ fut. ܢܣܽܘܡ, imper. ܣܽܘܡ, infin. ܡܶܣܳܡ, act. part. ܣܳܐܶܡ, ܣܳܝܡܳܐ, pass. part. ܣܺܝܡ, ܣܺܝܡܳܐ. *to put, lay, set; to lay up, by* or *aside; to lay* in the grave; *to set up, constitute, determine, appoint, ordain; to affirm, declare, suppose* or *adduce* by way of argument, *understand* or *interpret; to price, reckon* at so much; *to compose* as an author, *edit, quote.* With nouns: ܐܺܝܕܳܐ *to lay the hands* on a scapegoat, a victim; *to lay hands on, seize; to ordain* by laying on of hands; ܐܰܦܶܐ *to turn towards, look for, desire; to journey towards; to turn towards;* ܒܠܶܐ or ܒܠܶܒܶܗ *to take heed, notice, lay to heart; to set one's mind,* with ܥܰܠ *on* or ܕ; ܒܽܘܪܟܶܐ *to kneel down;* ܒܶܣܡܶܐ *to burn incense;* ܓܙܺܝܪܬܳܐ *to ratify a decision;* ܕܝܳܬܺܝܩܺܐ *to make a covenant;* ܗܕܳܐ ܠܘܳܬ *to set out towards;* ܛܰܝܒܽܘܬܳܐ *to confer a favour;* ܛܺܝܡܶܐ *to put the price at, reckon the price;* ܟܪܡܳܐ *to plant a vineyard;* ܠܶܒܳܐ *to set the heart* i. e. *turn the mind, consider, care about;* cf. ܒܠܶܒܳܐ below; ܠܰܚܡܳܐ *to set on bread, bring food;* ܡܰܘܡܳܬܳܐ *to take an oath, affirm, accuse;* ܡܶܠܬܳܐ and ܥܰܠ *to lay a command upon;* ܢܽܘܪܳܐ *to lay a fire;* ܢܳܡܽܘܣܶܐ *to make laws,* ܣܳܐܶܡ ܢܳܡܽܘܣܳܐ *a lawgiver;* ܢܰܦܫܳܐ *to lay down one's life, devote oneself;* with ܒܐܺܝܕܳܐ also, *to take one's life in one's hands;* ܣܺܝܡܬܳܐ *to lay up treasure;* ܥܝܳܕܳܐ *to establish a custom;* ܥܶܠܬܳܐ *to allege a reason;* ܦܽܘܩܕܳܢܳܐ *to command;* ܩܝܳܡܳܐ = ܦܶܣܩܳܐ; ܩܽܘܝܳܡܳܐ *to make a covenant;* ܩܳܢܽܘܢܳܐ *to ordain* or *settle a canon;* ܩܪܳܒܳܐ *to make war;* ܫܡܳܐ or ܫܽܘܡܳܗܳܐ *to name, surname, give a name;* ܫܶܬܶܐܣܬܳܐ *to lay a foundation;* ܬܳܓܳܐ *to wear a crown;* ܬܰܚܘܺܝܬܳܐ *to make an example of;* ܬܚܽܘܡܳܐ *to set bounds, define a boundary;* ܬܫܡܫܬܳܐ *to appoint to service.*

With preps.: ܒ of place; ܒܠܶܒܳܐ, ܒܪܶܥܝܳܢܳܐ, ܒܪܶܥܝܳܢܳܐ, ܒܢܰܦܫܳܐ or ܒܬܰܪܥܺܝܬܳܐ *to make up one's mind, intend, resolve;* ܒܪܺܝܫܳܐ *to exact capital punishment, to punish;* also *to put at the head* i. e. *in authority;* also *to divide* a subject *into heads;* with ܒܳܬܰܪ *to set out after, pursue;* ܠ and pers. pron. *to resolve, propose;* ܠܒܪܳܐ *to adopt;* ܠܘܳܬܗܽܘܢ *to unite against* some one; ܠܘܳܬ or ܥܰܡ *to place with, put in the care of* some one; ܠܚܽܘܕ *to set aside, separate;* with ܥܰܠ *to place* or *lay upon; to set upon, attack;* ܣܳܡ ܩܕܳܡ *to set before* any one, but ܣܳܡ ܩܕܳܡ *to fore-ordain;* ܠܬܰܚܬ *to subject, consider inferior.*

Pass. part. *a) set, laid* esp. *laid* as a foundation, *laid up, laid by* as treasure, *laid* in the grave; ܣܺܝܡ ܒܐܽܘܪܝܳܐ *laid in a manger;* ܐܰܬܪܳܐ ܕܣܺܝܡ ܗܘܳܐ ܒܗ ܡܳܪܰܢ *the place where our Lord was laid;* ܒܶܝܢܰܝܢ ܠܒܶܝܢܰܝܟܽܘܢ ܣܺܝܡܳܐ ܗܘܳܬ *between us and you there is a gulf set;* ܦܶܠܳܐܬܳܐ—ܡܰܬܠܳܐ; ܣܺܝܡܳܐ ܕ *a lesson, a parable, set before* us; ܚܛܺܝܬܳܐ ܣܺܝܡܳܐ ܟܝܳܢܳܐܺܝܬ *sin is implanted by nature.* *b) laid down, determined, decreed* as a law, a rule; *set, intent* on doing or learning; with ܠ and pers. pron. *to intend, to have decided, determined. c) appointed, destined;* ܒܐܺܝܕܰܝܟܽܘܢ ܣܺܝܡܳܐ ܫܽܘܠܛܳܢܽܘܬܳܐ *in your hands is placed authority;* ܐܰܝܠܶܝܢ ܕܣܺܝܡܺܝܢ ܠܚܰܝܶܐ *those who were ordained to eternal life. d) written, composed, commented on, edited* with ܠ of the pers. ܣܺܝܡ ܒܟܬܳܒܳܐ *committed to writing. e)* idioms: ܣܺܝܡܳܐ ܒܒܺܝܫܳܬܳܐ *it is in evil plight;* ܣܺܝܡ ܒܽܘܪܟܶܐ *kneeling;* ܣܺܝܡܳܐ ܒܪܺܝܫܳܐ *punished. f)* gram. ܙܰܒܢܳܐ ܕܣܺܝܡ *present tense;* ܗܰܘ ܕܣܺܝܡ *the subject;* log. ܣܺܝܡܳܐ *affirmative* opp. ܡܣܰܬܪܳܐ *negative.* Ethpe. ܐܶܬܬܣܺܝܡ or ܐܶܬܣܺܝܡ *to be laid, set, placed; to be laid* in the grave, *buried; to be planted, set* as slips, cuttings; *to be composed, written; to be instituted, constituted, ordained* as a bishop, priest, exorcist, &c., *to be appointed, decreed, sanctioned; to be given, applied* of a name, *to be named* ܥܰܠ ܫܡܳܐ *after the name . . .;* log. *to be affirmed; to set on, attack.* With ܬܳܓܳܐ *to be crowned;* ܒܠܳܐ ܝܺܕܰܥܬܳܐ *to be in ignorance;* ܒܪܺܝܫܳܐ *to be punished;* ܒܳܬܰܪ *to pursue;* ܠܚܶܪܡܳܐ *to be anathematized.* Pael ܣܰܝܶܡ *to point* a book. Ethpa. ܐܶܬܣܰܝܰܡ *to be pointed.* Derivatives, ܣܺܝܡܳܐ, ܣܺܝܡܬܳܐ, ܣܺܝܡܽܘܬܳܐ, ܡܣܳܡܳܐ, ܣܳܐܶܡ, ܣܺܝܡ ܦܳܬܳܐ, ܣܺܝܡ ܢܳܡܽܘܣܳܐ, ܣܺܝܡ ܒܽܘܪܟܶܐ, ܡܣܺܝܡܳܐ, ܣܰܝܳܡܳܐ, ܣܰܝܳܡܽܘܬܳܐ, ܣܺܝܡܳܐܺܝܬ, ܣܰܝܡܬܳܐ, ܡܣܰܝܡܳܢܳܐ, ܠܳܐܡܣܰܝܡܳܢܽܘܬܳܐ, ܠܳܐܡܣܰܝܡܳܢܳܐ.

ܣܘܡܒܘܠܘܢ and ܣܘܡܒܘܠܝܢ σύμβολον, *a)* gifts sent by a king or emperor to other sovereigns at the beginning of a reign. *b) the symbol, creed.*

ܣܘܡܛܝܢ σωμάτιον, *parchment.*

ܣܘܡܛܘܣ pl. ܣܘܡܛܐ σώματος, σώματα,

bodies, corporeal beings opp. ܠܐ ܦܓܪܢܝܐ *incorporeal* = Syr. ܦܓܪܢܝܐ and ܠܐ ܦܓܪܢܝܐ.

ܣܘܡܛܝܩܘܢ σωματικός -όν, *corporeal.*

ܣܘܡܝܘܬܐ rt. ܣܡܐ. m. *blindness.*

ܣܘܡܟ, ܣܘܡܟܐ rt. ܣܡܟ. m. *reliance, dependence; sustenance, maintenance; a camel's howdah;* gram. *conjunction* of words.

ܣܘܡܣܡ, ܣܘܡܣܡܐ from ܣܡ, ܣܡܐ. m. *healing, medical attendance.*

ܣܘܡܣܪܘܬܐ *an agent's* or *broker's commission.*

ܣܘܡܣܟܢܘܬܐ from ܣܡܣܟܢ m. *voluntary poverty, asceticism, continence, denial; mean clothing.*

ܣܘܡܦܘܛܘܢ or ܣܘܡܦܘܛܘܢ m. the plant *comfrey, bone-set;* ܣܘܡܦܘܛܘܢ ܕܟܐܦܐ *symphytum saxosum.*

ܣܘܡܩ, ܣܘܡܩܐ, ܬܐ rt. ܣܡܩ. *a*) adj. *blood-red, dark red, reddish, ruddy;* ܬܘܪܬܐ ܣܘܡܩܬܐ *a red heifer;* ܣܘܡܩܝܢ ܠܒܘܫܘܗܝ *his garments are blood-red;* ܡܪܪܬܐ ܣܘܡܩܬܐ *bile.* *b*) subst. m. *red lentil, red pottage; red* or *purple dye, rouge,* metaph. *disguise; red ink, minium; the ruby* or *sard; rhus coriaria, the sumach.* f. *bile.*

ܣܘܡܩܡܩ, ܣܘܡܩܡܩܐ dimin. from ܣܘܡܩܐ. *little red man.*

ܣܘܡܩܡܩܘܬܐ rt. ܣܡܩ. f. *redness, ruddiness, red colour, a flush.*

ܣܘܡܩܪܐ pl. ܣܘܡܩܪܐ or ܣܘܡܩܪܝܐ a sort of small boat.

ܣܘܢ imper. of verb ܣܢ.

ܣܘܢ Pael ܣܘܢ *to fortify.*

ܣܘܢܐ *a sandal;* see ܣܐܢܐ.

ܣܘܢܕܝܣ or ܣܘܢܕܝܣ *cinnabar.*

ܣܘܢܕܝܐ *slothful repose.*

ܣܘܢܗܕܘܣ, ܣܘܢܗܕܘܣ; see ܣܘܢܘܕܘܣ *a synod.*

ܣܘܢܗܕܘܩܛܝܩܘܢ and ܣܘܢܗܕܘ συνδοκτικόν, *a pact, agreement.*

ܣܘܢܗܕܝܛܐ, ܣܘܢܗܕܝܛܐ, ܣܘܢܗܕܝܛܘ; see ܣܘܢܘܕܝܛܐ, &c.

ܣܘܢܗܕܝܣܐ συνοδῆσαι, astron. *conjunction;* with ܥܒܕ *to be in conjunction.*

ܣܘܢܗܕܝܩܘܢ *an eye-salve.*

ܣܘܢܗܘ; see ܣܘܢܣ.

ܣܘܢܘܕܘܣ, also ܣܘܢܗܕܘܣ, ܣܘܢܗܕܘܣ, ܣܘܢܘܕܘܣ, ܣܘܢܕܘܣ pl. ܣܘܢܘܕܘܣ, ܣܘܢܗܕܘܣ, also ܣܘܢܗܕܘ, ܣܘܢܘܕܘ, ܣܘܢܗܕܘ, &c. f. σύνοδος, *a*) *a synod, council,* esp. eccles. *a general council;* ܣܘܢܘܕܘܣ ܬܐܒܝܠܝܩܝܬܐ *an ecumenical council;* ܒܣܘܢܗܕܘܣ *in synodical writings.* *b*) astron. *conjunction;* ܟܢܘܫܝܐ ܕܟܘܟܒܐ ܥܡ ܫܡܫܐ ܘܥܡ ܚܕܕܐ ܣܘܢܘܕܘܣ ܡܬܩܪܐ *a conjunction of stars with the sun and with each other is called a synod.*

ܣܘܢܘܕܝܐ and ܣܘܢܘܕܝܐ f. συνοδία, *a party of travellers, a company,* astron. *conjunction.*

ܣܘܢܘܕܝܛܐ, ܣܘܢܗܕܝܛ, ܣܘܢܘܕܝܛ or ܣܘܢܗܕܝܛ pl. ܐ̈ συνοδίτης, *a follower of a council,* esp. of the Council of Chalcedon.

ܣܘܢܗܕܝܛܐ = ܣܘܢܗܕܝܛܐ.

ܣܘܢܘܕܝܩܐ, ܣܘܢܗܕܝܩ, ܣܘܢܘܕܝܩ, ܣܘܢܘܕܝܩܝ pl. ܐ̈ and ܣܘܢܘܕܝܩܝܬܐ συνοδικός, *synodical;* ܐܓܪ̈ܬܐ—ܩܢܘ̈ܢܐ ܣܘܢܘܕܝܩܝ̈ܐ *synodical epistles, canons.*

ܣܘܢܘܕܝܩܘܢ, ܣܘܢܗܕܝܩ or ܣܘܢܘܕܝܩ συνοδικόν, *synodical;* ܣܘܢܗܕܝܩܘܢ ܕܫܘܬܦܐ *acts of a council;* ܣܘܢܘܕܝܩܘܢ ܕܕܡܐܣܘܣ *the synodical of Damasus.*

ܣܘܢܘܕܝܩܝܐ, ܝܬܐ and ܣܘܢܗܕܝܩ *synodical, synodal, conciliar;* ܟܢܘܫܝܐ ܕܩܢܘ̈ܢܐ ܣܘܢܘܕܝܩܝ̈ܐ *a collection of conciliar canons.*

ܣܘܢܘܕܘܣ; see ܣܘܢܗܕܘܣ.

ܣܘܢܘܟܘܣ *a*) σύνοχος, *unintermittent* of a fever. *b*) σόγκος, *the sow-thistle.*

ܣܘܢܘܡܘܣܝܐ, ܣܘܢܘܡܘܣ ܕܝܢ, ܣܘܢܘܡܝܬܐ; see ܣܘܢܥܐ.

ܣܘܢܘܢܘܡܐܝܬ from συνώνυμος, *synonymously.*

ܣܘܢܘܢܘܡܝܐ συνωνυμία, *synonymy.*

ܣܘܢܛܐܟܣܝܣ, ܣܘܢܛܐܟܣܝܣ and ܣܘܢܛܟܣܐ f. σύνταξις, *a*) *ordering, arrangement;* esp. ܕܡܠܬܐ *arrangement of speech, syntax.* *b*) *section* of a book. *c*) *a treatise, compilation.* *d*) *valediction.* *e*) ܒܣܘܢܛܐܟܣܝܣ *compendiously.*

ܣܘܢܛܐܩܛܝܩܘܣ συντακτικός, *valedictory, a farewell.*

ܣܘܢܛܘܟܝܐ συντυχία, *interview, conversation.*

ܣܘܢܛܟܣܝܣ σύνταξις, *farewell addresses.*

ܣܘܢܛܩܛܝܩܝܐ, ܝܬܐ συντακτικός, *compendious.*

ܣܘܢܛܠܝܐ pl. ܣܘܢܛܠܝܣ and ܣܘܢܛܠܝܣ συντέλεια, *tribute, impost.*

ܣܘܢܛܩܛܐ same as the preceding.

ܣܘܢܛܩܛܝܪܝܘܢ συντακτήριον, *valedictory, a farewell address.*

ܣܘܢܘܦܛܪܘܢ σύνοπτρον, *a synopsis.*

ܣܘܢܘܦܛܪܝܩܝܐ, ܣܘܢܘܦܛܪܝܐ, ܣܘܢܩܝ, ܣܘܢܩܐ, &c., ܝܐ from σύνοπτρον. *collective, general, united, conjoint, compendious;* ܥܡܠܐ ܣܘܢܘܦܛܪܝܩܝܐ ܕܢܦܫܐ ܘܦܓܪܐ *the joint labours of the soul and body.*

ܣܘܢܘܦܛܪܝܩܘܬܐ f. from σύνοπτρον. *conjunction, comprehensiveness.*

ܣܘܢܘܦܛܪܝܩܐܝܬ συνοπτρικῶς, *briefly, comprehensively.*

ܣܘܢܩܛܪܝܢܐ *contagious.*

ܣܘܢܐܟܣܝܣ σύναξις, *synaxis, a meeting for worship,* esp. Eucharistic.

ܣܘܢܟܣܪܝܢ also ܣܘܢܐܟ and ܣܘܢܟܣܪܝܢ συναξάριον, *a lectionary, collection* of Gospels to be read at the Eucharist.

ܣܘܢܗܕܘܣ and other words in ܣܘܢܗ; see ܣܘܢܗܕ.

ܣܘܢܢܐ Ar. *the Sunnah* or traditions of Mohammed; ܛܝܝܐ ܕܣܘܢܢܐ *the Sunnite* or orthodox *Arabs.*

ܣܘܢܦܐ pl. ܐ̈ rt. ܣܢܦ. m. *alacrity, promptness; the girding up of the garments.*

ܣܘܢܦܪܐܣܡܐ, ܣܘܢܦܪ, ܣܘܢܦܪܣܡܐ and ܣܘܢܦܪܘܣܡܐ pl. ܣܘܢܦܪܐܣܡܛܐ συμπέρασμα, *the conclusion* of a syllogism.

ܣܘܢܦܘܢܘܣ perh. σύμφωνος, *agreeing.*

ܣܘܢܘܦܣܝܣ σύνοψις, *a synopsis, summary.*

ܣܘܢܩܠܐ and ܣܘܢܩܠܠܘܣ pl. ܐ̈ m. σύγκελλος, *syncellus, cell-mate* or *attendant* of a bishop or patriarch, later a high ecclesiastical dignitary.

ܣܘܢܩܠܝܛܐ, ܣܘܢܩܠܛܘܣ, ܣܘܢܩܠܝܛܘܣ, ܣܩܠܛܘܣ, &c. pl. ܣܘܢܩܠܝܛܘܣ — ܣܘܢܩܠܝܛܘܣ σύγκλητος -οι, *a*) m. *a senator, councillor; viceroy. b*) f. *the senate; the senatorial order.*

ܣܘܢܩܠܝܛܝܩܐ, ܣܘܢܩܠܝܛܝܩܘܣ pl. ܐ̈ and ܣܘܢܩܠܝܛܝܩܐ συγκλητικός, *senatorial, of the senate, a senator; of senatorial rank,* used of women as well as of men.

ܣܘܢܩܐ, ܣܘܢܩܢܐ pl. ܐ̈ rt. ܣܢܩ. m. *a*) *need, necessity; the thing needed, necessaries, a supply;* ܠܚܡܐ ܕܣܘܢܩܢܢ *bread for our needs, sufficient bread;* ܣܘܢܩܢܐ ܕܡܘܗܒܬܐ *the granting of supplies;* ܡܝܐ ܣܘܢܩܢܗ *water supply. b*) *frivolous conversation.*

ܣܘܢܩܢܝܐ rt. ܣܢܩ. *needful, necessary.*

ܣܘܢܩܪܝܛܐ, ܣܘܢܩܪܛܘܣ *joined, associated;* with ܥܒܕ *to associate with himself.*

ܣܘܢܩܪܝܛܐ pl. ܐ̈ συγκρίτης, *a judge's assessor.*

ܣܘܢܩܪܝܛܘܢ σύγκριτον, *a congregation.*

ܣܘܢܩܬܕܪܘܣ συγκάθεδρος, *an assessor.*

ܣܘܢܐܬܝܐ συνηθεία -ας, *wages, pay.*

ܣܘܢܬܪܘܢܝܐ with ܥܒܕ, *to enthrone.*

ܣܘܣܛܛܝܩܘܢ, ܣܘܣܛܛܝܩܐ, ܣܘܣܛܛܝܩܘܣ, ܣܘܣܛܛܝܩܐ pl. ܐ̈, ܝܢ συστατικός -όν, *a*) *commendatory,* letters of *commendation. b*) *systaticon, letters of election* of a patriarch subscribed by the electing bishops.

ܣܘܣܛܛܝܩܝܐ, ܣܘܣܛܝܩܝ, ܝܐ συστατικός, *commendatory.*

ܣܘܣܝ act. part. ܡܣܘܣܐ Saphel conj. from ܐܣܐ. *to heal, attend* as a physician, *to tend, cherish, foster; to fondle, caress, fawn on, coax;* ܕܣܘܣܝܬ ܠܟܪܝܗܝܟ ܣܘܣܐ ܟܘܪܗܢܝ *Thou who didst care for Thy sick, heal my sicknesses;* ܡܣܘܣܐ ܠܗܘܢ ܐܝܟ ܐܒܐ ܠܒܢܘܗܝ *he cherishes them as a father his children;* ܟܠܒܐ ܕܡܣܘܣܐ ܠܐܢܫ *a dog fawning on some one;* ܣܘܣܝܗܝ ܒܗܠܝܢ ܡܠܐ *wheedle him with these words.* Ethpa. ܐܣܬܘܣܝ *to be healed, tended, attended to, groomed;* ܢܣܬܘܣܐ ܒܡܣܝܒܪܢܘܬܐ *he shall be sustained with nourishment;* ܠܒܝ ܡܫܬܢܩ ܠܐ ܐܣܬܘܣܝ *my tormented heart is not soothed.* Derivatives, ܣܘܣܝܐ or ܣܘܣܝܐ, ܣܘܣܐ, ܣܘܣܝܐ, ܡܣܘܣܝܢܐ, ܡܣܘܣܝܢܘܬܐ.

ܣܘܣܝ, ܣܘܣܝܐ pl. ܣܘܣܘܬܐ, ܣܘܣܘܬ, ܣܘܣܝܬܐ m. ܣܘܣܝܬܐ pl. ܣܘܣܝܬܐ f. from ܣܘܣܝ *a horse, mare;* ܣܘܣܝ ܝܡܐ *sea-horse;* ܣܘܣܝܐ ܕܢܗܪܐ *hippopotamus;* ܦܪܘܛܘܣܘܣ name of some star; ܣܘܣܝܐ ܦܪܚܐ the constellation *Pegasus;* ܪܡܬܐ ܕܣܘܣܝܐ *the Quirinal Hill,* Ital. *Monte Cavallo.* Also, m. *a plank laid crosswise, a plank bridge.* f. pl. *worms* infesting vines.

ܣܘܣܝܐ from ܣܘܣܝ. m. *tending, care* of the sick; *regimen.*

ܣܘܣܦܪܢܘܣ, ܣܘܣܦܪܢܐ m. *a centaur.*

ܣܘܟ, ܣܟ not used in the Peal. PAEL ܣܲܘܸܟ *to uphold, support; to help, assist, succour, relieve;* ܝܲܡܝܼܢܵܟ ܣܲܘܟܲܬܢܝ *Thy right hand shall hold me up;* ܗܲܝܡܵܢܘܼܬܵܐ ܣܲܘܟܲܬ ܠܥܒ݂ܵܕܵܘܗ̈ܝ *faith upheld his works, wrought with his works;* ܡܸܠܹ̈ܐ ܕܡܣܲܘܟܝܼܢ ܠܟܠܢܵܫ ܠܘܵܬ ܣܘܼܥܪܵܢܵܐ ܕܟܹܐܢܵܬܵܐ *sayings helpful to every one towards the doing of upright deeds;* ܡܣܲܘܟ݂ܵܐ ܠܵܗ̇ ܢܵܡܘܿܣܵܐ *the law grants her redress.* ETHPA. ܐܸܣܛܲܘܲܟ *to be upheld, succoured, maintained;* ܒܥܘܼܕܪܵܢܵܐ ܕܡܵܪܗܘܿܢ ܐܸܣܛܲܘܲܟܘ *they were upheld by the aid of their Lord;* ܠܵܐ ܡܸܫܟܲܚ ܡܸܣܛܲܘܲܟ ܡܸܢ ܢܵܡܘܿܣܹ̈ܐ *he cannot be upheld by the laws;* ܐܸܢ ܡܸܢ ܡܲܡܠܠܝ ܬܸܣܛܲܘܲܟ *if thou wilt benefit by my conversation.* DERIVATIVES, ܣܘܼܟܵܠܐ, ܡܣܲܘܟܵܢ, ܡܣܲܘܟܵܢܘܼܬܵܐ, ܡܣܲܘܟܵܢܵܐ, ܡܣܲܘܟܵܢܝܼܬ.

ܣܘܼܥܪܵܢܵܐ rt. ܣܥܪ. m. *action, effect; visitation.*

ܣܘܼܥܪܵܢܵܐ, ܣܘܼܥܪܵܢ pl. ܝܼܢ, ܹ̈ܐ rt. ܣܥܪ. m. *a*) *an act, action, deed, thing; affair, business, administration;* ܣܘܼܥܪ̈ܵܢܲܝܗܘܿܢ ܕܫܠܝ̈ܚܵܐ *the Acts of the Apostles;* ܣܘܼܥܪ̈ܵܢܹܐ ܕܡܲܠܟܘܼܬܵܐ *affairs of the realm;* ܒܣܘܼܥܪܵܢܵܐ *in deed, actually;* ܒܗ ܒܣܘܼܥܪܵܢܵܐ *in the very act.* *b*) *a fact, reality* opp. ܕܡܸܬܚܲܫܒܵܐ *something imagined; the actual* or *literal sense.* *c*) *things = goods, possessions;* ܐܝܬ ܠܝ ܣܘܼܥܪ̈ܵܢܹܐ ܣܲܓܝܼܐܹ̈ܐ *I have many things.* *d*) *a category.* *e*) *working, effect;* ܕܠܵܐ ܣܘܼܥܪܵܢ *without effect.* *f*) *visiting* e.g. of the sick; *a visitation;* ܙܲܒܢܵܐ ܕܣܘܼܥܪܵܢܵܟ *the time of thy visitation.* *g*) gram. ܫܡ ܣܘܼܥܪܵܢܵܐ *a noun of action.*

ܣܘܼܥܪܵܢܵܐܝܼܬ rt. ܣܥܪ. adv. *actually, literally, in the literal sense.*

ܣܘܼܥܪܵܢܵܝܵܐ rt. ܣܥܪ. *literal; in actual existence;* gram. *active, of action.*

ܣܘܼܦ from the Egyptian word for *papyrus.* ܝܲܡܵܐ ܕܣܘܼܦ *the reedy sea* i.e. the Red Sea.

ܣܘܦ, ܣܦ fut. ܢܣܘܼܦ, act. part. ܣܵܐܹܦ, ܣܵܝܦܵܐ. *to come to an end, perish, be consumed; to cease, disappear, be no more* with ܠ; ܟܠ ܕܐܝܬ ܒܐܪܥܐ ܢܣܘܦ *everything that is in the earth shall perish;* ܥܕܡܵܐ ܕܣܵܦ ܟܠܗ ܥܲܡܵܐ *till all the nation were consumed;* ܥܢܵܢܵܐ ܣܵܝܦܵܐ *the cloud is consumed;* with ܡܸܢ ܟܲܦܢܵܐ, ܡܸܢ ܨܲܗܝܵܐ *to be consumed with hunger, with thirst, perish of hunger, of thirst.* ETHPE. ܐܸܣܬܸܝܦ *to be consumed.* APH. ܐܲܣܝܼܦ *to cause to disappear, consume away* or *cease to be; to consume, destroy;* ܢܲܣܝܼܦ ܟܲܦܢܵܐ ܠܐܪܥܐ *famine shall consume the land;* ܐܲܝܟ ܗܲܠܓܵܐ ܡܲܣܝܼܦ ܐܢܬ ܠܝ *as vapour dost Thou make me to consume away;* ܕܲܟܝܘܼܬܵܐ ܐܲܣܝܼܦܲܬ ܠܒܝܼܫܬܵܐ *purity has destroyed evil.* DERIVATIVES, ܣܘܼܦܵܐ, ܣܵܝܦܵܐ, ܣܘܼܦܵܠܵܐ, ܣܘܼܦܵܢܵܐ, ܣܵܝܦܘܼܬܵܐ, ܣܘܦܢܝܐ, ܡܣܝܦܢܘܬܐ, ܣܘܦܢܝܐ, ܡܣܝܦܢܐ.

ܣܘܼܦ, ܣܘܼܦܵܐ pl. ܝܼܢ, ܹ̈ܐ rt. ܣܘܦ. m. *the uttermost part, end, edge, border;* ܣܘܼܦܵܝܗ̇ ܕܐܪܥܐ or ܣܘܼܦܲܝܗ̇ ܕܐܪܥܐ *the borders of the land, ends of the world;* ܣܘܼܦܵܝܗ̇ ܕܡܲܕܒܪܵܐ *the edge, outskirts, of the wilderness;* ܠܡܲܠܟܘܼܬܹܗ ܣܘܼܦ ܠܵܐ ܢܸܗܘܹܐ *of his kingdom there shall be no end;* ܠܣܘܼܦ ܥܸܣܪܝܼܢ ܫܢܝܼܢ *at the end of twenty years;* ܠܣܘܼܦܵܐ *at the last;* ܒܟܠ ܣܘܼܦܝܼܢ *everywhere;* ܕܠܵܐ ܣܘܼܦ *boundless, infinite;* ܠܣܘܼܦܵܐ *utterly;* ܡܸܢ ܣܘܼܦܵܐ ܠܣܘܼܦܵܐ *from end to end.*

ܣܘܼܦܛܵܐ pl. ܹ̈ܐ rt. ܣܦܛ. m. *a filthy proverb* or *fable.*

ܣܘܼܦܝܼܐ and ܣܘܼܦܝܵܐ f. σοφία, *wisdom.* Eccles. an exclamation of the deacon in the Jacobite Liturgy.

ܣܘܼܦܵܝܵܐ, ܣܘܼܦܵܝܬܵܐ rt. ܣܘܦ. with ܠܵܐ *infinite.*

ܣܘܼܦܝܵܢܵܐ from ܣܘܼܦܝܵܐ. *wise, regarding wisdom.*

ܣܘܼܦܝܼܣܛܵܐ or ܣܘܼܦܝܣܛܐ pl. ܹ̈ܐ σοφιστής, *a sophist.*

ܣܘܼܦܝܼܣܛܝܼܩܵܐܝܼܬ σοφιστικῶς, *sophistically.*

ܣܘܼܦܝܼܣܛܘܼܬܵܐ from ܣܘܦܝܣܛܐ. f. *wisdom, sophistry, rhetoric.*

ܣܘܼܦܝܼܣܛܝܼܩܵܝܵܐ, ܣܘܼܦܝܼܣܛܝܼܩܵܝܬܵܐ σοφιστικός, *sophistical.*

ܣܘܼܦܝܼܣܛܝܼܩܘܿܣ and ܣܘܼܦܝܣܛܝܩܘܣ σοφιστικός, *of* or *like a sophist, sophistical.*

ܣܘܼܦܝܼܣܛܝܼܩܝܼ and ܣܘܼܦܝܼܣܛܝܼܩܹܐ σοφιστική, *a sophist's art, sophistry.*

ܣܘܼܦܝܼܣܛܝܼܩܵܝܵܐ, ܣܘܼܦܝܼܣܛܝܼܩܵܝܬܵܐ σοφιστικός, *sophistical, fallacious.*

ܣܘܼܦܵܢ, ܣܘܼܦܵܢܵܐ rt. ܣܘܦ. m. *a coming to naught, end, destruction;* ܐܸܥܒܸܕ ܣܘܼܦܵܢܵܐ ܒܟܠܗܘܿܢ ܥܲܡ̈ܡܹܐ *I will make a full end of all the nations;* ܣܘܼܦܵܢܵܐ ܡܲܟܪܸܙ ܢܒ݂ܝܼܵܐ *the prophet proclaims destruction.*

ܣܘܼܦܵܢܵܝܵܐ, ܣܘܼܦܵܢܵܝܬܵܐ rt. ܣܘܦ. with ܠܵܐ *infinite, endless.*

ܣܘܦܢܝܘܬܐ rt. ܣܘܦ. f. *end, ending.*

ܣܘܦܛܐ m. *a palm leaf, palm basket.*

ܣܘܩܒܪܐ rt. ܣܩܒܪ. m. *bidding, noisy bargaining, quarrelling over a bargain; talkativeness.*

ܣܘܩܒܪܘܬܐ rt. ܣܩܒܪ. f. *bidding; loquacity.*

ܣܘܦܐ rt. ܣܦ. m. *destruction* esp. *by fire.*

ܣܘܦܩܐ rt. ܣܦܩ. m. *evacuation, an emptying, discharge.*

ܣܘܦܩܢܐ rt. ܣܦܩ. m. *leisure.*

ܣܘܦܪܐ rt. ܣܦܪ. m. *shaving* the head, *tonsure, the rite of tonsure.*

ܣܘܦܪܬܐ rt. ܣܦܪ. f. *filings.*

ܣܘܦ, ܣܦ fut. ܢܣܘܦ, act. part. ܣܐܦ, ܣܐܦܐ. *a) to take breath, draw breath, breathe, inhale,* esp. with ܐܐܪ *air* or ܡܫܩܘܬܐ *breath;* ܣܦܬ ܪܘܚܐ ܐܝܟ ܬܥܠܐ *thou snuffedst up the wind as a jackal;* ܚܘܝܐ ܣܐܦܐ *a hissing serpent;* ܡܢ ܩܕܝܡ ܣܦܬ ܗܘܬ *she had already breathed her last;* ܥܕܟܝܠ ܣܐܦܝܢ *they still breathe = are still alive. b) to drink in, suck;* with ܡܪܬܐ *to suck poison. c) to smell, smell at, snuff up, scent* often with ܪܝܚܐ. Ethpe. ܐܬܣܝܦ *to be smelt, detected by its scent.* Pa. ܣܝܦ *to smell at, snuff at.* Derivatives, ܣܘܦܐ, ܣܘܦܢܐ, ܣܝܦܐ, ܣܘܦܝܢܐ, ܣܘܦܐ, ܣܘܦܢܘܬܐ, ܣܝܦܐ, ܡܬܣܝܦܢܐ.

ܣܘܦܐ pl. ܐ̈ rt. ܣܘܦ. m. *breathing, breath, the nostrils, sense of smell;* metaph. ܣܘܦܐ ܕܢܦܫܐ *the desire of the soul.*

ܣܘܦܚܠܐ rt. ܣܦܚܠ. m. *a chance;* ܒܣܘܦܚܠܐ *by chance.*

ܣܘܦܢܐ rt. ܣܘܦ. m. *a cupping-glass.*

ܣܘܦܢܐ rt. ܣܘܦ. m. *a cupper, surgeon.*

ܣܘܦܠܐ rt. ܣܦܠ. m. *adornment, decoration.*

ܣܘܦܣܦܐ from ܣܘܦܣܦܐ. m. *measurement, computation, a definite number, settled period; mean; direction.*

ܣܘܦܢܝܐ rt. ܣܘܦ. *that can be breathed.*

ܣܘܪܐ or ܣܘܪܐ f. σαύρα, *a lizard.*

ܣܘܪܐ *dross of copper.* Cf. ܣܘܦ.

ܣܘܪܝܓܐ pl. ܐ̈ σύριγξ, *fistula, a hollow sore, tubercles near the anus* or *in the nostrils.*

ܣܘܪܓܠܐ pl. ܐ̈ m. *a line, verse;* ܣܘܪܓܠܐ ܕܣܘܪܓܐ *a calendar.* Derivatives, verb ܣܪܓܠ, ܡܣܪܓܠܐ, ܡܣܪܓܠܐ.

ܣܘܪܓܠܝܐ from ܣܘܪܓܠܐ. *metrical.*

ܣܘܪܕܐ pl. ܐ̈ rt. ܣܪܕ. m. *terror, fright; an object of terror;* ܡܠܐ ܣܘܪܕܐ *terrific, horrible.*

ܣܘܪܕܝܢ usually ܣܪܕܝܢ *a sardine stone.*

ܣܘܪܕܢܐ rt. ܣܪܕ. *terrific, horrible.*

ܣܘܪܕܩܐ m. *a guile, wile.*

ܣܘܪܕܬܐ rt. ܣܪܕ. f. *quaking, agitation.*

ܣܘܪܗܒܐ rt. ܪܗܒ. m. *haste, hurry, trepidation, commotion, agitation;* ܒܣܘܪܗܒܐ *hastily;* ܠܐ ܚܣܝܪܝܢ ܗܘܘ ܒܢܣܝܢܐ ܕܣܘܪܗܒܐ ܕܓܠܠܐ *they were not wanting in experience of the turbulent billows;* ܣܘܪܗܒܐ ܕܫܒܝܐ *the imminence of the captivity.*

ܣܘܪܗܒܢܝܐ rt. ܪܗܒ. gram. *expressing haste.*

ܣܘܪܚܐ, ܣܘܪܚܢܐ rt. ܣܪܚ. m. *injury, laceration.*

ܣܘܪܚܢܐ pl. ܐ̈ rt. ܣܪܚ. m. *a) fault, defect, vice, crime. b) a defect, blemish, deformity* of the body. *c) a fault, corrupt place* in a text. *d) injury, harm, ravage. e) pernicious teaching.*

ܣܘܪܛܐ pl. ܐ̈, ܐ̈ rt. ܣܪܛ. m. *a line, letter, character;* ܣܘܪܛܐ ܬܪܝܨܐ *a straight line;* ܣܘܪܛܐ ܕܡܨܥܬ ܝܘܡܐ *the meridian line;* ܩܪܘܝܐ ܕܣܘܪܛܝ *the reader of my lines.* Gram. the four ܣܘܪܛܐ *lines* are ـ ܡܗܓܝܢܐ written under a vowel-less letter to show that it is not to be slurred over but to be pronounced with a half-vowel sound, ـ ܡܪܗܛܢܐ over a letter to mark a still slighter pronunciation, ܡܛܦܝܢܐ a slanting line below means that the voice is to be dropped, ܡܢܓܕܐ above, that the sound is to be sustained.

ܣܘܪܛܐ rt. ܣܪܛ. m. *delineation.*

ܣܘܪܛܘܢܐ dimin. of ܣܘܪܛܐ. m. *a small line.*

ܣܘܪܛܬܐ rt. ܣܪܛ. f. *an arrow-head, wound made by an arrow.*

ܣܘܪܝ Pers. m. *red vitriol, copperas water.*

ܣܘܪܝܐ f. *Syria;* ܣܘܪܝܐ ܓܘܝܬܐ *Farther Syria* i.e. Mesopotamia and Assyria, ܣܘܪܝܐ ܒܪܝܬܐ *Nearer Syria* viz. Palestine and the region north of the Euphrates. Hence are derived the three following words and verb ܣܪܝܐ:

ܣܘܪܝܝܐ and ܣܘܪܝܝܬܐ unusual spellings of ܣܘܪܝܝܐ.

ܣܘܪܝܐܝܬ from ܣܘܪܝܐ. adv. *Syriac, in Syriac;* ܒܣܘܪܝܐܝܬ the same; ܠܐ ܝܕܥ ܗܘܐ ܣܘܪܝܐܝܬ *he did not know Syriac.*

ܣܘܪܝܝܐ, ܣܘܪܝܝܬܐ from ܣܘܪܝܐ. a) *a Syrian, Palestinian;* ܟܠܕܝܐ ܐܘܟܝܬ ܣܘܪܝܝܐ ܥܬܝܩܐ *Chaldaeans* i.e. *ancient Syrians;* ܡܦܫܩܢܘܬܐ ܕܣܘܪܝܝܐ *the translation of the Syrians = the Syriac version.* b) *Syriac;* ܡܦܩܬܐ ܣܘܪܝܝܬܐ *the Syriac version;* two Syriac dialects ܠܫܢܐ ܣܘܪܝܝܐ ܐܘܟܝܬ ܢܗܪܝܐ *the Syriac* or *Mesopotamian language* and ܠܫܢܐ ܣܘܪܝܝܐ ܘܦܠܣܛܝܢܝܐ *Palestinian Syriac.* c) in the Lexx. f. *the storax of Damascus.*

ܣܘܪܝܝܘܬܐ from ܣܘܪܝܐ. f. *the Syriac language, Syriac letters, Syriac faith.*

ܣܘܪܢܓܢ Pers. *colchicum autumnale, meadow saffron.*

ܣܘܪܣܐ from ܣܪܝܣܐ. m. *castration, mutilation.*

ܣܘܪܓܦܐ pl. ܐ̈ rt. ܣܪܓܦ. m. *a branch, subdivision, ramification;* gram. *a conjugation, paradigm.*

ܣܘܪܓܦܝܐ rt. ܣܪܓܦ. gram. *of* or *belonging to a conjugation.*

ܣܘܪܦܐ, ܣܘܪܦܬܐ pl. ܣܘܪ̈ܦܬܐ rt. ܣܪܦ. f. *a sip, draught.*

ܣܘܪܩܐ rt. ܣܪܩ. m. *evacuation; privation, bereavement; voluntary poverty, renunciation* esp. used of our Lord with reference to Phil. ii. 7.

ܣܘܬܐ pl. ܣܘ̈ܬܐ f. *steam, smell, savour* esp. of the fat of a sacrifice, *a holocaust;* ܪܝܚ ܣܘܬܐ *a sweet savour;* ܡܢ ܢܘܪܐ ܣܠܩܐ ܣܘܬܗ ܐܝܟ ܒܣܡܐ *the smell from the fire rises up like spice;* ܣܘ̈ܬܐ ܕܐܠܗ̈ܐ ܕܚܢܦ̈ܐ ܡܩܪܒܝܢ *the holocausts which the heathen offered to idols.* Rarely *an evil smell.*

ܣܘܬܢܝܐ, ܣܘܬܢܝܬܐ from ܣܘܬܐ. *savoury.*

ܣܘܬܪܐ rt. ܣܬܪ. m. *covering, protection;* Jac. = Nest. ܣܘܬܪܐ *compline,* because at that service Ps. xc. 1, He that dwelleth ܒܣܬܪܗ ܕܡܪܝܡܐ *in the secret place of the Most High,* was recited.

ܣܘܬܬܐ, ܣܘܬܬܘܬܐ from ܫܬܬܐ. m. *a foundation, base; firmness, stability, constancy; taking root.*

ܣܚܣ PAEL ܣܚܣ *to make thin, rarefy.* DERIVATIVES, ܣܚܝܣܐ, ܡܣܚܣܐ, ܣܚܝܣܘܬܐ.

ܣܚܐ and ܣܚܝ fut. ܢܣܚܐ, act. part. ܣܚܐ, ܣܚܝܐ, pass. part. ܣܚܐ, ܣܚܝܐ. a) *to bathe, wash oneself;* metaph. *to be purified by baptism, baptized;* ܢܚܬܬ ܠܡܣܚܐ ܒܢܗܪܐ *she went down to bathe in the river;* ܣܚܐ ܗܘܐ ܠܒܗ *his heart was pure;* ܕܢܗܝܡܢ ܘܢܣܚܐ *that he may believe and be baptized.* b) *to swim, float;* ܥܕܡܐ ܕܐܢܫ ܒܚܝܠܐ ܣܚܐ ܒܗܢܐ ܝܡܐ *as long as a man swims vigorously in this sea;* ܣܚܝܐ m. and ܣܚܝܬܐ f. *creatures that swim;* ܣܚܝܐ ܦܪܚܬܐ ܒܐܐܪ *the bird floats in the air;* ܢܦܫܬܐ ܣܚܝܢ ܠܥܠ ܡܢ ܫܓܘܫܝܐ ܕܥܠܡܐ *human souls float above the tumult of earthly affairs;* ܣܚܝܢ ܒܕܡܐ *swimming in blood.* c) *to creep, spread* as leprosy, poison, plants; ܣܚܝܐ ܕܛܘܪܐ *thyme.* d) *to overspread, overrun, stray, roam;* ܣܚܘ ܠܐܪܥܐ ܘܐܬܒܘ ܒܗ *they overspread the country and settled in it.* ETHPE. ܐܣܬܚܝ *to be washed.* PA. ܣܚܝ trans. *to wash, purify;* ܡܣܚܝܢ ܒܪܘܚܐ ܕܩܘܕܫܐ *washed by the Holy Spirit.* ETHPA. ܐܣܬܚܝ *to be washed.* APH. ܐܣܚܝ trans. *to wash, bathe; to allow* or *admit to bathe;* ܐܣܚܝ ܐܢܘܢ ܒܡܝܐ *he washed them in water;* ܡܣܚܝܐ ܗܘܬ ܠܒܢܝܗ̇ *she bathed her children;* ܐܝܕܘܗܝ ܒܕܡܐ ܢܣܚܐ ܗܘܐ *he would have imbrued his hands in blood;* ܐܣܚܝܢܝ ܫܠܗܒܝܬܐ *he made me float through flame, dragged me through fire.* DERIVATIVES, ܣܚܝܐ, ܡܣܚܝܐ, ܣܚܘܐ, ܣܚܘܬܐ, ܣܚܝܐ, ܣܚܝܬܐ, ܣܚܝܐ, ܡܣܚܝܘܬܐ, ܡܣܚܝܐ.

ܣܚܘܐ rt. ܣܚܐ. m. *swimming;* ܒܝܬ ܣܚܘܐ *a swimming-bath;* ܥܒܪܘ ܢܗܪܐ ܒܣܚܘܐ *they swam over the river;* ܠܐ ܝܕܥܝܢ ܣܚܘܐ *those who cannot swim.*

ܣܚܘܦܐ pl. ܐ̈ rt. ܣܚܦ. m. *a destroyer;* ܣܚܘ̈ܦܝ *they who trouble me;* ܣܚܘܦܐ ܕܡܘܬܐ ܘܕܚܒܠܐ Christ is *the destroyer of death and corruption.* Gram. *negative.*

ܣܚܘܦܬܐ rt. ܣܚܦ. f. a) *a covering.* b) *overthrow.*

ܣܚܘܪܐ rt. ܣܚܪ. m. *a vagrant, vagabond.*

ܣܚܘܪܘܬܐ rt. ܣܚܪ. f. *mendicancy, vagrancy.*

ܣܚܘܬܐ pl. ܣܚܘ̈ܬܐ rt. ܣܚܐ. f. *washing, ablution.* Cf. ܣܚܝܐ.

ܣܚܝܐ m. *a*) = ܢܣܚܐ *a codex, copy of a book.* *b*) rt. ܣܚܐ. *fineness, transparency.*

ܣܚܐ Peal and ܣܚܐ Pael; see under ܣܚܐ.

ܣܚܝܐ, ܬܐ rt. ܣܚܐ. *a swimmer, diver;* ܡܝܬܐ ܣܚܝܬܐ and ܣܚܝܬܐ ܣܚܘܬܐ *swimming creatures, fish,* &c.; ܣܚܝܐ ܕܐܘܪܐ a sweet-smelling plant, perh. *wild thyme.*

ܣܚܝܐ rt. ܣܚܐ. m. *washing, swimming.*

ܣܚܝܢ, ܣܚܝܢܐ, ܬܐ rt. ܣܚܐ. *fine, subtle, transparent; liquid, fluid; loosely woven* as cloth; ܓܘܫܡܐ ܣܚܝܢܐ *fluid bodies;* ܓܦܐ ܣܚܝܢܬܐ *transparent wings.*

ܣܚܝܢܘܬܐ rt. ܣܚܐ. *tenuity, subtlety, transparency* of air; *phosphorescent putrefaction.*

ܣܚܝܦܘܬܐ rt. ܣܚܦ. f. *overthrow, destruction.*

ܣܚܝܦܬܐ rt. ܣܚܦ. f. *gangrene, cancer.*

ܣܚܡ fut. ܢܣܚܘܡ, act. part. ܣܚܡ, ܣܚܡܐ. *to press together, tie tightly.* Ethpe. ܐܣܬܚܡ *to be pressed hard.* Derivatives, ܣܚܡܐ, ܣܚܡܘܬܐ.

ܣܚܡܐ m. and ܣܚܡܘܬܐ f. rt. ܣܚܡ. *compression, tying tightly together.*

ܣܚܢܬܐ f. *a good complexion, beautiful natural colour.*

ܣܚܦ fut. ܢܣܚܘܦ, act. part. ܣܚܦ, ܣܚܦܐ, pass. part. ܣܚܝܦ, ܦܐ, ܦܬܐ. *to thrust, throw, cast* or *pull down; to overturn, overthrow, demolish; to defeat; to dethrone;* ܣܚܦܝܢ ܗܘܘ ܒܓܒܝܗܘܢ ܘܒܟܬܦܬܗܘܢ *they thrust with their sides and their shoulders;* ܠܡܕܒܚܐ ܣܚܦ *he pulled down the altar;* ܠܓܘܒܐ ܣܚܦܗ ܘܩܛܠܗ *he thrust him down a pit and killed him;* ܓܐܪܐ ܣܚܦܗ *an arrow laid him low;* ܣܚܦܬܢܝ ܠܚܕ *thou hast brought me very low;* ܐܠܗܐ ܣܚܦ ܠܦܪ̈ܣܝܐ ܢܟܝܠܐ *God overthrew the deceitful Persians.* Pass. part. *overthrown, ruined, prostrate; thrust down, degraded;* ܣܚܝܦ ܐܢܐ ܒܥܪܣܐ *I am lying in bed;* ܣܚܝܦ ܡܢ ܫܘܠܛܢܐ *thrust down from authority.* Ethpe. ܐܣܬܚܦ and Ethpa. ܐܣܬܚܦ *to be thrust* or *cast down, to be ruined, overthrown, defeated; to be outcast, rejected;* often with ܢܦܠ *to be cast down and fall;* ܒܒܝܫܘܬܗ ܢܣܬܚܦ ܥܘܠܐ *the wicked is thrust down in his evil-doing;* ܐܣܬܚܦ ܚܣܢܐ ܘܫܘܪܗ *the fortress and its wall were ruined;* ܟܘܪܣܝܗ ܐܣܬܚܦ *his throne is overthrown;* ܛܥܝܘܬܐ ܕܣܓܝܐܘܬ ܐܠܗ̈ܐ ܡܣܬܚܦܐ ܗܘܬ *the error of polytheism had been overthrown.* Pael ܣܚܦ *to utterly defeat, destroy, overthrow, ruin; to degrade, to thrust off* or *away; to urge, compel;* ܣܚܦ ܐܚܝܕ̈ܐ ܡܢ ܟܘܪ̈ܣܘܬܐ *He hath put down the mighty from their seats;* ܡܕ̈ܝܢܬܐ ܡܣܚܦܬܐ *ruined cities;* ܡܣܚܦܬܐ *ruins.* Derivatives, ܣܚܦܐ, ܣܚܝܦܐ, ܣܚܘܦܐ, ܣܚܘܦܬܐ, ܣܚܝܦܘܬܐ, ܣܚܝܦܬܐ, ܡܣܚܦܐ, ܡܣܚܦܢܘܬܐ, ܡܣܚܦܢܐ.

ܣܚܦ, ܣܚܦܐ pl. ܝܢ, ܐ rt. ܣܚܦ. m. *a*) *a course* of stones or wood. *b*) *reversion.*

ܣܚܦܘܦܐ pl. ܐ *a locust in the grub stage* or the *larval casing* of a locust-grub.

ܣܚܪ fut. ܢܣܚܘܪ, act. part. ܣܚܪ, ܣܚܪܐ. *to go round begging.* Pa. ܣܚܪ *to beg, be a beggar.* Derivatives, ܣܚܪܐ, ܣܚܘܪܐ, ܣܚܘܪܘܬܐ, ܣܚܪܐ, ܣܚܪܬܐ.

ܣܚܪܐ rt. ܣܚܪ. m. *a*) *vagrancy.* *b*) *peddling.*

ܣܚܪܬܐ or ܣܚܪܬܐ pl. ܣܚܪ̈ܬܐ rt. ܣܚܪ. f. *a walled enclosure, a palace.*

ܣܚܝܬܐ pl. ܣܚܝ̈ܬܐ rt. ܣܚܐ. f. *a cloth* or *rag for grooming horses.* *b*) *a bath, laver* often used of baptism, e.g. ܣܚܝܬܐ ܩܕܝܫܬܐ *the holy laver.*

ܣܛܐ fut. ܢܣܛܐ, act. part. ܣܛܐ. *to turn aside, turn in* with ܠ or ܡܢ; *to depart* from sin, from godliness; ܣܛܐ ܠܡܚܙܐ *he had turned aside to see;* ܣܛܐ ܗܘܐ ܠܬܡܢ ܠܡܐܟܠ *he turned in thither to eat;* ܠܡܣܛܐ: ܠܐ ܠܝܡܝܢܐ ܘܠܐ ܠܣܡܠܐ *to turn aside neither to the right hand nor to the left;* ܡܢ ܐܘܪܚܐ *from the way;* ܡܢ ܐܘܪܚܐ ܕܫܪܪܐ *from the way of truth;* ܣܛܝܬܘܢ ܡܢ ܦܘܩܕ̈ܢܝ *ye have turned aside from my commands.* Ethpe. ܐܣܬܛܝ *to be led aside;* ܣܟܠܐ ܒܥܓܠ ܡܣܬܛܐ ܒܡ̈ܠܐ a stupid man *is easily led aside by words.* Aph. ܐܣܛܝ *a*) trans. *to turn, turn aside, make to turn; to take* or *carry aside;* ܠܐܘܪܚܐ *into the way;* ܡܢ ܐܘܪܚܐ *from the way;* ܠܒܐ *the heart;* ܐܣܛܝ ܪܥܝܢܗ ܠܒܝܫܬܐ *he perverted his mind to evil;* ܡܢ ܚܕ ܐܠܗܐ ܡܣܛܐ ܠܢ *he turns us aside from monotheism.* *b*) intrans. *to turn aside, go astray, lapse, apostatize;* ܐܣܛܝ ܡܢܗܘܢ ܘܐܙܠ ܠܐܪܡܢܝܐ *he parted from them and went to Armenia;*

ܣܛܐ ܐܕܡ ܘܡܪܕ Adam *went wrong and rebelled;* with ܡܢ ܥܕܬܐ *to separate oneself from the Church.* Ettaph. ܐܬܣܛܝ *to be turned away.* Derivatives, ܣܛܝܐ, ܡܣܛܝܢܐ, ܡܣܛܝܢܘܬܐ.

ܣܛܕܝܘܢ usually ܐܣܛܕܝܘܢ pl. ܣܛܕܝܘܢܐ στάδιον, *a course, place of contest, arena.*

ܣܛܐܛܝܩܘܢ = ܐܣܛܐܛܝܩܘܢ.

ܣܛܐܟܘܣ, ܣܛܐܟܘܣ, and ܣܛܐܟܘܣ στάχυς, *Spica Virginis;* the sign of the zodiac *Virgo.*

ܣܛܐܠܐ; see ܣܛܝܠܐ.

ܣܛܐܣܝܣ; see ܣܛܣܝܣ.

ܣܛܒܠܪܐ and ܐܣܛܒܠܪ pl. ܐ̈ m. stabularius, *groom;* ܪܝܫ ܣܛܒܠܪܐ ܕܡܠܟܐ *superintendent of the imperial stables.*

ܣܛܪܘܢ for ܐܣܛܪܘܢ = ܣܛܪܘܣ.

ܣܛܕܝܘܢܐ pl. of ܣܛܕܝܘܢ.

ܣܛܘܐܝܩܐ pl. ܣܛܘܐܝܩܐ *a stoic.*

ܣܛܘܟܐ pl. ܐ̈ m. *a baby-boy, an infant.*

ܣܛܘܟܣܐ στοιχεῖα, *the elements.*

ܣܛܘܟܣܝܐ pl. ܝ̈ܐ *elementary, primary* as the particles ܠ, ܘ, ܕ, ܒ.

ܣܛܘܟܣܝܘܢܐ, ܢܝܬܐ *elementary, primary.*

ܣܛܘܡܢܩܠܘܣ and ܣܛܘܡܢܩܐܠܘܣ στῶμεν καλῶς, Jac. Malabar. *stand ye aright,* the deacon's cry to the congregation.

ܣܛܘܢܐ for ܐܣܛܘܢܐ *a pillar.*

ܣܛܘܪܐ Ar. *a butcher's knife.*

ܣܛܘܪܘܣ pl. the same with Ribui; σάτυρος, *a satyr.*

ܣܛܝܐ rt. ܣܛܐ. m. *declination, deflection.*

ܣܛܝܟܘܣ pl. ܣܛܝ̈ܟܘܣ στίχος, *a verse* esp. a verse of the Bible.

ܣܛܝܠܐ or ܣܛܝܠܐ also ܣܛܝܠܐ, ܣܛܐܠܐ, ܣܛܐܠܐ, ܣܛܠܐ, ܣܛܠܐ στήλη -ας, *a post, slab, column, statue.*

ܣܛܝܡܬܐ pl. ܡ̈ܬܐ rt. ܣܛܡ. f. *a narrow leathern pouch* or *bottle.* Cf. ܣܛܡܢܐ.

ܣܛܝܟܪܐ and ܐܣܛܝܟܪܐ pl. ܣܛܝܟܪ̈ܘܢ στιχηρόν -ά, *a verse of a hymn.*

ܣܛܠ denom. verb Pael conj. from ܐܣܛܠܐ. *to robe, clothe.*

ܣܛܠܐ, ܣܛܠܘܣ, and ܣܛܠܘܣ different spellings of ܣܛܝܠܐ.

ܣܛܡ fut. ܢܣܛܘܡ, act. part. ܣܛܐܡ, ܣܛܡܐ, pass. part. ܣܛܝܡ, ܣܛܝܡܐ; also Pael ܣܛܡ. *to close, bind, restrain, shackle;* ܣܛܘܡܘܗܝ ܠܦܘܡܗ ܫܘܩܪܐ *stop his lying mouth;* ܐܣܛܡܢܝ ܚܘܒܗ ܡܕܥܝ ܣܛܝܡܐ *my mind bound by love.* Gram. *to draw a line round* points to signify a mistake; ܢܘܩܙܐ ܕܣܛܝܡܝܢ ܘܕܚܠܦܝܗܘܢ ܐܬܬܣܝܡܘ *circumscribed points and those which are put instead of them;* ܢܘܩܙܐ ܕܠܐ ܣܛܡ ܫܦܝܪ *annotations which he had not well corrected.* Ethpa. ܐܣܛܡ *to be closed, stopped, restrained, shackled;* ܕܢܣܛܡ ܚܘܪܐ ܒܓܠܐ ܕܟܐܦܐ *that the hole be closed with a heap of stones.* Derivatives, ܣܛܡܐ, ܣܛܡܬܐ.

ܣܛܘܡܐ m. στόμωμα, *steel, a steel edge.*

ܣܛܡܢܐ pl. ܐ̈ m. ܣܛܡܢܝܬܐ pl. ܝ̈ܬܐ f. σταμνάριον, *a small wine-skin* or *bottle.*

ܣܛܢܐ m. *an adversary* often in the O. T.; ܘܩܡ ܡܠܐܟܐ ܕܡܪܝܐ ܒܐܘܪܚܐ ܕܢܗܘܐ ܠܗ ܣܛܢܐ *the angel of the Lord stood in the way to be an adversary to* Balaam; ܗܘܐ ܣܛܢܐ ܠܐܝܣܪܝܠ *he was an adversary to Israel. The Adversary, Satan* O. T. and N. T.

ܣܛܢܝܐ, ܢܝܬܐ from ܣܛܢܐ. *satanic, of Satan;* ܡܥܒܕܢܘܬܐ ܣܛܢܝܬܐ *satanic agency.*

ܣܛܣܝܣ, ܣܛܐܣܝܣ or ܐܣܛܣܝܣ στάσις, *sedition.*

ܣܛܣܝܢܐ *seditious.*

ܣܛܦ Pael ܣܛܦ *to cut, scarify, to puncture* sycamore fruit. Ethpa. ܐܣܛܛܦ *to be cut, scarified.* Derivatives, ܣܛܘܦܐ, ܣܛܦܐ.

ܣܛܦܐ rt. ܣܛܦ. m. *scratching open, scarification.*

ܣܛܩܛܐ and ܣܛܩܛܝ f. στακτή, *oil of myrrh.*

ܣܛܪ *to write, write down.*

ܣܛܪ denom. verb Pael conj. from ܣܛܪܐ. *to cut in two; to turn aside, avoid.* Ethpa. ܐܣܛܛܪ *to have divisions, to dispute.* Aph. ܐܣܛܪ *to lay on, ascribe* undeservedly.

ܣܛܪ, ܣܛܪܐ pl. ܐ̈ m. *the side* of animate and of inanimate objects; ܡܢ ܬܪܝܢ ܣܛܪ̈ܘܗܝ *on each side of him;* ܐܪܒܥܐ ܣܛܪ̈ܘܗܝ *the four sides of it;* ܐܬܦܠܚ ܣܛܪܗ ܒܠܘܟܝܬܐ Christ's *side was torn by the lance.*

Adverbial and prepositional uses: ܣܛܪ and

ܣܛܪ ܡܢ besides, beyond, except, without; ܣܛܪ ܡܢ ܗܠܝܢ besides those; ܣܛܪ ܡܢ ܗܕܐ other than this; ܣܛܪ ܡܢ ܢܡܘܣܐ outside the law, lawlessly; ܣܛܪ ܡܢ ܕܚܠܬܐ without fear, safely; ܣܛܪ ܡܢ ܪܘܓܙܐ without wrath; ܠܣܛܪ beside, near by; ܒܢܐ ܦܘܬܩܐ ܒܣܛܪܗ ܕܥܕܬܐ he built an inn by the side of the church; ܒܣܛܪܐ—ܒܣܛܪܐ on one side—on the other side; ܠܣܛܪ ܡܢ besides, beyond; ܕܠܣܛܪ other; ܠܣܛܪ on one side, apart; ܠܚܕ ܣܛܪ apart, aside, on one side; ܐܢܫ ܠܣܛܪܗ each to his own way; ܡܢ ܣܛܪܗ by its side; ܡܢ ܟܠܗܘܢ ܣܛܪܘܗܝ on every side. DERIVATIVES, verb ܣܛܪ, ܣܛܪܢܝܐ.

ܣܛܪܐ for words beginning thus, see ܐܣܛܪܐ.

ܣܛܪܐܛܘܣ stratum, a road; cf. ܐܣܛܪܛܐ.

ܣܛܪܛܝܓܘܣ pl. ܣܛܪܛܝܓܐ, ܣܛܪܛܝܓܘ m. στρατηγός, a commander, general oftener ܐܣܛܪܛܝܓܐ.

ܣܛܪܛܝܘܛܐ and ܐܣܛܪܛܝܘܛܐ pl. ܐ̈ m. στρατιώτης, a soldier.

ܣܛܪܛܝܠܛܐ, ܣܛܪܛܠܛܝܣ, ܣܛܪܛܝܠܛܝܣ, and ܐܣܛܪܛܠܛܐ m. στρατηλάτης, a commander, general.

ܣܛܪܛܝܐ στρατιά -ᾶς, an army.

ܣܛܪܢܝܐ, ܣܛܪܢܝܬܐ from ܣܛܪܐ. at or from the side, lateral; ܪܘܚܐ ܙܩܝܦܬܐ ܘܣܛܪܢܝܬܐ cross and side winds.

ܣܛܪܢܝܐ and ܐܣܛܪܢܝܐ στρηνία, luxury, lasciviousness.

ܣܛܪܦܐ and ܣܛܪܦܘܣ pl. ܐ̈ m. σατράπης, a satrap, governor.

ܣܛܪܦܘܬܐ and ܣܛܪܦܘܬ pl. ܬ̈ܐ f. a satrapy.

ܣܝܪ or ܣܝܪ̈ perh. abbrev. from σειρά. a section of a chapter.

ܣܝܒܐ m. pl. ܣܝܒܬܐ f. pl. rt. ܣܐܒ. white hairs.

ܣܝܒܘܠܐ f. Σίβυλλα, a sybil.

ܣܝܒܘܬܐ pl. ܣܝܒܘܬܐ rt. ܣܐܒ. f. old age.

ܣܝܒܪ Paiel conj. of ܣܒܪ.

ܣܝܒܪܬܐ pl. ܬ̈ܐ rt. ܣܒܪ. f. nourishment, food, provisions.

ܣܝܓ, ܣܝܓܐ pl. ܐ̈ rt. ܣܘܓ. m. a hedge, fence; a hindrance, obstacle, intervening space; a limit; repairing, stopping; ܣܝܓܗ ܕܬܪܥܘܬܢ the repairing of our ruin; ܚܛܗܝ ܗܘܘ ܣܝܓܐ ܒܝܢܝ ܠܛܝܒܘܬܟ my sins have separated me from Thy grace.

ܣܝܓܠܘܢ, ܣܝܓܝܠܘܢ, ܣܝܓܝܠܝܘܢ, and ܣܝܓܠܘܢ pl. ܣܝܓܝܠܠܐ m. σιγίλλιον, a seal, imperial diploma or letters patent, a state letter or document; ܣܝܓܝܠܠܐ ܕܚܐܪܘܬܐ ܡܢ ܡܕܐܬܐ royal letters of exemption from taxes.

ܣܝܓܪܐ pl. ܐ̈ m. a) some tree. b) a cave, cavern, mountain side or ridge.

ܣܝܓܬܐ pl. ܬ̈ܐ rt. ܣܘܓ. f. an enclosure, stronghold, fold, mandra, monastic precincts.

ܣܝܕܐ m. lime, plaster, any material except mud used for daubing buildings.

ܣܝܕܐ from ܣܝܕܐ. m. a plasterer; seller of lime or cement.

ܣܝܘܓܐ rt. ܣܘܓ. m. a repairer, builder up.

ܣܝܘܓܬܐ rt. ܣܓܐ. f. combustion.

ܣܝܘܡܐ, ܬܐ pl. ܐ̈ rt. ܣܘܡ. a) an author, writer. b) one who ordains, consecrates. c) a founder. d) a legislator; an umpire. e) a depositor, owner of goods deposited. f) gram. positive, affirmative, an affirmative proposition; hypothetical, an hypothesis; also ܡܠܬܐ ܣܝܘܡܬܐ ܕܣܝܘܡܐ the ablative case.

ܣܝܘܡܘܬܐ pl. ܬ̈ܐ rt. ܣܘܡ. f. a) authorship, composition, style; a treatise, book; ܟܬܒܐ ܕܣܝܘܡܘܬܗ the book he composed. b) ܣܝܘܡܘܬܐ ܢܡܘܣܐ legislation, lawgiving. c) ܣܝܘܡܘܬܐ ܒܢܝܐ adoption. d) gram. affirmation.

ܣܝܘܦܘܬܐ rt. ܣܘܦ. f. destruction, disappearance.

ܣܝܘܥܐ, ܬܐ rt. ܣܘܥ. breathing; smelling; ܪܓܫܐ ܣܝܘܥܐ the sense of smell.

ܣܝܘܥܘܬܐ rt. ܣܘܥ. f. smelling.

ܣܝܚܐ pl. ܐ̈ rt. ܣܚܐ. a swimmer, diver.

ܣܝܚܐ pl. ܐ̈ m. a shrub.

ܣܝܟ Pael conj. of ܣܘܟ.

ܣܝܟܐ a) Pers. m. a span. b) a kind of tumour.

ܣܝܟܘܬܐ = ܣܝܘܟܘܬܐ; see above.

ܣܝܛܠܐ situla, a bucket.

ܣܝܡ Pael conj. of ܣܘܡ.

ܣܝܡܘܠܐ dialect weak, feeble.

ܣܝܠܐ m. a water-pipe, runnel, ditch. Cf. ܣܝܠܘܢܐ.

ܣܠܢܛܝܪܝܘܣ or ܣܠܢܛܝܪܐ *silentiarius* an official of the Byzantine court, *a councillor*.

ܣܠܘܩܐ *poor, base.*

ܣܠܘܢ, ܣܠܘܢܐ pl. ܐ̈ m. σωλήν, *a channel, gutter, drain, pipe, tube; duct;* ܒܝܬܐ ܕܠܝܬ ܠܗ ܬܪܥܐ ܘܐܦܠܐ ܣܠܘܢܐ *a house with neither door nor gutters;* ܣܠܘܢܘܗܝ ܕܟܪܣܐ *the intestines.*

ܒܝܬ ܣܠܐ and pl. ܣܠܠܐ σέλλα -ας, *a latrine, privy.* Cf. ܣܠܠܐ.

ܣܠܝܓܢܐ f. σιλίγνιον -ια, *a loaf made from spring wheat.*

ܣܠܝܕܘܢ and ܣܠܝܕܝܢ pl. ܣܠܝܕܝܢ and ܣܠܝܕܣ σελίδιον, σελίδες, *a chronological list, table, schedule.*

ܣܠܝܕܝܐ, ܝܬܐ from the preceding. *in the form of a column* or *page.*

ܣܠܠܝܢ σελλίον, *seat, throne.*

ܣܝܡ imper. of verb ܣܘܡ.

ܣܝܡ, ܣܝܡܐ pl. ܐ̈ rt. ܣܘܡ. m. 1) *laying down, setting: a) planting, transplanting; a plantation. b) propounding;* ܣܝܡܐ ܕܡܬܠܐ *the setting forth of a parable. c) the composing, settling* e.g. of canons, *enactment; drawing up in writing.* 2) *that which is laid down: a) a proposition, statement, symbol, creed;* ܣܝܡܐ ܕܡܠܦܢܘܬܗܘܢ *the foundation of their teaching;* ܣܝܡܐ ܕܐܒܗܬܐ *writings of the Fathers;* ܣܝܡܐ ܕܗܝܡܢܘܬܐ ܕܗܘܐ ܒܢܝܩܝܐ *the statement of the faith made at Nicea, the creed drawn up at Nicea;* ܡܢ ܕܣܐܡ ܣܝܡܐ ܐܚܪܢܐ ܕܗܝܡܢܘܬܐ *whoso sets forth another creed. b) a portion, allowance* of food. *c) a faggot. d) position, situation, place; a reservoir, conduit. e)* gram. ܣܝܡܐ ܕܢܘܩܙܐ *the placing of points* but usually ellipt. *points, vowel points, plural points;* ܣܝܡܐ ܕܣܘܡܩܐ *points written in red ink.* Also ܒܝܬ ܣܝܡܐ, ܣܝܡܐ ܡܩܕܡܢܐ or ܡܩܕܡܢܝܐ *a preposition.* With other nouns: ܣܝܡ ܐܝܕܐ and ܣܝܡܝ ܐܝܕܐ pl. ܐ̈ or ܣܝܡ ܐܝܕܝܐ *the laying on of hands, ordination* ܕܡܫܡܫܢܘܬܐ *to the diaconate,* ܕܟܗܢܘܬܐ *to the priesthood; consecration* of a bishop, a patriarch; *a prayer said at the consecration* of a bishop; ܣܝܡ ܒܘܪܟܐ pl. ܐ̈ *kneeling, a genuflexion;* the name of one of the Whitsunday services; ܣܝܡ ܢܡܘܣܐ *legislation;* ܣܝܡ ܪ̈ܓܠܐ *stirrups.*

ܣܝܡܘܢܐ dimin. of ܣܝܡܐ. m. *a little book, a tract.*

ܣܝܡܘܬܐ pl. ܬ̈ܐ rt. ܣܘܡ. f. *a setting forth;* ܣܝܡܘܬ ܠܚܡܐ ܕܐܦܐ *the shew-bread;* ܣܝܡܘܬ ܒܢܝܐ *adoption of sons;* ܣܝܡܘܬ ܢܡܘܣܐ *the enacting of laws;* ܣܝܡܘܬ ܬܚܘܡܐ *a settling of boundaries.*

ܣܝܡܢܐ, ܢܝܬܐ rt. ܣܘܡ. *assumed, supposed, hypothetic;* ܟܝܢܝܐ ܐܢܘܢ ܘܠܐ ܣܝܡܢܝܐ the lunar months *are natural, not hypothetic.*

ܣܝܡܢܝܐ; see under ܣܝܡܐ.

ܣܝܡܝܘܢ or ܣܡܝܘܢ pl. ܣܝܡܝܐ or ܣܝܡܐ m. σημεῖον, *a sign, token, point, indication;* ܕܪܘܓܙܐ *a sign of wrath;* ܒܣܝܡܝܐ ܐܬܟܬܒܘ ܡܠܘܗܝ his words *were taken down in shorthand; a milestone; chiromancy.*

ܣܝܢ, ܣܝܢܐ m. *the moon; Sin,* the moon-god of the Chaldaeans; chem. *silver.*

ܣܝܢ, ܣܝܢܐ m. *mud, mire, filth;* ܣܝܢܐ ܕܫܘܩܐ *the mire of the streets;* ܡܒܘܥܐ ܕܣܝܢܐ *muddy springs;* ܣܝܢܐ ܕܚܛܝܬܐ *the filth of sin.*

ܣܝܢܢܐ, ܢܬܐ *miry.*

ܣܝܢܝ *Sinai;* ܛܘܪܐ ܕܣܝܢܝ *Mount Sinai;* ܡܕܒܪܐ ܕܣܝܢܝ *the wilderness of Sinai.* Derivative, ܣܝܢܝܐ.

ܣܝܢܝܐ, ܝܬܐ 1) *Sinaitic.* 2) *Sinite,* Gen. x. 17. 3) *Chinese.*

ܣܝܣܡܐ pl. ܐ̈ *a half-drachma.*

ܟܐܦܐ ܕܣܝܣܡܐ *whetstone.*

ܣܝܣܢܐ pl. ܐ̈ m. *a) a vine-shoot. b)* ܣܝܣܢܐ ܕܬܡܪܐ *clusters of dates.*

ܣܝܥܬܐ and ܣܝܥܬܐ pl. ܬ̈ܐ f. *a row, series, company;* ܣܝܥܬܐ ܕܙܕܝܩܐ *the company of the just.*

ܣܝܥܐ, ܣܝܥܬܐ pl. ܝܢ̈, ܬ̈ܐ rt. ܣܘܥ. f. *a) succour. b) a troop, band, company, choir;* ܒܢܝ ܣܝܥܬܗ *his retinue, his companions;* ܣܝܥܬܐ ܣܝܥܬܐ *in bands, by troops;* ܢܦܩܘ ܒܣܝܥܬܐ ܚܕܐ *they went forth in one band;* ܣܝܥܬܐ ܕܕܝܪܝܐ *a band of monks.*

ܣܝܥܬܐܝܬ rt. ܣܘܥ. adv. *in troops, in companies.*

ܣܝܦ, ܣܝܦܐ pl. ܝܢ̈, ܐ̈ m. *a sword, a blade;*

ܡܚܘܬܐ ܣܰܝܦܶܗ ܡܚܰܒܠܳܢܳܐ *his destroying sword;* ܡܰܘܬܳܐ ܕܣܰܝܦܳܐ *death by the sword.*

ܣܝܳܦܳܐ rt. ܣܘܦ. m. *slaughter, destruction.*

ܣܦܝܐ also ܣܦܝܐ, ܣܦܝܬܐ, ܣܦܝܐ, ܣܶܦܝܳܬܳܐ &c. σηπία, *cuttle-fish, squid;* also *a kind of crab;* also *sea-foam.*

ܣܺܝܦܽܘܢܳܐ m. *a*) dimin. of ܣܰܝܦܳܐ. *a small sword-blade.* *b*) σίφων, *a waterspout, a tempest; a trough between surging billows.*

ܣܝܦܐ *chaff.*

ܣܝܳܦܳܐ rt. ܣܘܦ. m. *breathing.*

ܣܺܝܩܳܪܺܝܣ pl. ܣܺܝܩܳܪܘܶܐ or ـܪ̈ܶܐ sicarius, *an assassin, bandit.*

ܣܺܝܩܽܘܡܳܐ pl. ـ̈ܶܐ m. σήκωμα, *amount, computation, era; metre;* ܒܣܺܝܩܽܘܡ ܝܰܘ̈ܢܳܝܶܐ *according to the Grecian era;* ܒܣܺܝܩܽܘܡ ܡܰܥܠܳܢܽܘܬܳܐ ܕܰܛܰܝܳܝܶܐ *dating from the Hejra.* Derivatives, verb ܣܩܡ, ܣܩܘܡܐ, ܣܩܘܡܐ, ܡܣܩܡܢܐܝܬ, ܡܣܩܡܢܘܬܐ.

ܣܺܝܩܠܳܘܣ, ܣܺܝܩܠܽܘܣ pl. ܣܺܝܩ̈ܠܶܐ m. σίκλος, the Hebrew *shekel;* ܣܺܝܩܠܳܘܣ ܡܰܬܩܰܠ ܠܬܪܶܝܢ ܙܽܘܙܺܝܢ *a shekel weighs two drachmas.* Cf. ܡܰܬܩܳܠܳܐ.

ܣܝܟܪܝܛܘܢ or ܣܝܟܪܝܬܘܢ secretum, the emperor's or patriarch's *privy chamber.*

ܣܺܝܪ, ܣܺܝܪܳܐ French sire, *sir.* For ܣܺܝ̈ܪܶܐ see ܣܺܝܪܳܐ.

ܣܺܝܪܳܐ or ܣܺܝܪܳܐ pl. ܣܺܝ̈ܪܶܐ, ܣܺܝ̈ܪܶܐ m. *a*) σειρά, *a cord, twist, plait, line; a small chain, chain armour; a thong, shoe-lace; the thread* of a loom; ܓܕܰܠ ܣܺܝܪܳܐ *weave a plait;* ܒܣܺܝ̈ܪܶܐ ܐܶܬܬܚܺܝܕܘ ܗܘܰܘ *they were caught in the toils;* ܣܺܝ̈ܪܶܐ ܕܚܰܛܺܝܬܳܐ *cords of sin.* *b*) *pickled fish.* *c*) *fine dust.* *d*) *a fine web.*

ܣܺܝܪܺܝܢ pl. ܣܺܝܪܺܝܢܰܘܣ, ܣܺܝܪܺܝܢܘܣ usually f. Σειρῆν, *a siren; a singing-bird; a screech-owl; a demon shaped like a woman* and preying on the dead.

ܣܺܝܪܺܝܩܽܘܢ, ܣܺܝܪܺܝܩܳܐ m. σιρικόν -ια, *minium, red lead, a red pigment.*

ܣܺܝ̈ܪܶܐ pl. of ܣܺܝܪܳܐ.

ܣܝܡ Pers. *arsenic.*

ܣܝܡ Pael ܣܰܝܶܡ *to nail, fix nails in;* ܠܽܘ̈ܚܶܐ ܡܣܰܝܡܺܝܢ ܒܫܽܘܪܳܐ *tablets nailed on the wall.* Ethpa. ܐܶܣܬܰܝܰܡ *to be nailed, held with nails;* ܐܶܣܬܰܝܰܡ ܐܺܝ̈ܕܰܝ ܘܪ̈ܶܓܠܰܝ *my hands and feet were nailed.* Derivatives, ܣܝܡܐ, ܣܝܡܬܐ, ܣܝܡܐ, ܡܣܝܡܢܘܬܐ, ܡܣܝܡܢܐܝܬ.

ܣܽܘܦ, ܣܳܦܳܐ pl. ܣܰܘ̈ܦܶܐ rt. ܣܘܦ. m. *a*) *end, bound, limit, extreme;* with ܢܶܣܰܒ or ܢܶܬܶܠ *to be at an end, be finished;* ܐܰܘܠܨܳܢܳܐ ܕܣܰܘ̈ܦܶܐ ܐܰܚܪ̈ܳܝܶܐ *extreme misery;* ܣܳܦܳܐ ܠܰܝܬ ܠܶܗ *it has no end, is innumerable;* ܡܶܕܶܡ ܕܣܳܦܳܐ ܠܰܝܬ ܠܶܗ *he has nothing at all.* *b*) *sum, summing-up, total;* ܣܳܦܳܐ ܕܫܢܰܘ̈ܗܝ *the sum of his years;* ܐܚܪܺܝܬܶܗ ܕܡܶܠܬܳܐ ܒܣܰܝܳܦܶܗ *the end of the matter in its summing up.* With preps. and ellipt. ܣܳܦܳܐ, ܒܣܳܦܳܐ and ܘܣܳܦܳܐ *in short, briefly, etcetera;* ܠܣܳܦܳܐ ܕ *to the point that . . ., to such an extreme;* ܡܶܢ ܣܽܘܦܶܗ *the whole, entire,* ܡܕܺܝܢܬܳܐ ܟܽܠܳܗ ܡܶܢ ܣܽܘܦܳܗ *the entire city;* ܡܶܢ ܣܽܘܦܗܽܘܢ *they gave themselves over entirely to evil;* ܠܒܺܝܫܬܳܐ ܡܶܢ ܣܽܘܦܗܽܘܢ *exceedingly, transcendently.* ܣܽܘܦ and ܠܳܐ ܣܽܘܦ *not at all, by no means, in no wise, ever, never;* ܠܳܐ ܣܽܘܦ ܐܶܬܕܟܰܪܢ ܠܗܳܢܳܐ ܫܡܳܐ *we made no mention at all of this name;* ܠܳܐ ܣܽܘܦ ܐܶܬܛܦܺܝܣ *he would in no wise obey;* ܕܠܳܐ ܫܽܘܚܠܳܦ ܓܰܘܢܳܐ ܣܽܘܦ *without changing colour at all;* ܡܶܢ ܣܽܘܦܗܽܘܢ—ܠܳܐ *not in any way, entirely not;* ܕܠܳܐ ܣܽܘܦ *unending, endless, innumerable, never-ceasing.*

ܣܟܐ Pael ܣܰܟܺܝ *to wait for, look for, expect; to lie in wait;* ܣܰܟܳܘ ܠܺܝ ܥܕܰܡܳܐ ܠܥܰܐܕܳܐ *wait for me till the feast;* ܟܽܠܗܽܘܢ ܡܣܰܟܝܶܐ ܠܣܰܒܪܶܗ *all they who wait in His hope;* ܡܣܰܟܶܐ ܒܺܝܫܳܐ ܠܙܰܕܺܝܩܳܐ *the evil man lies in wait for the righteous.* Ethpa. ܐܶܣܬܰܟܺܝ *to be awaited, expected;* ܟܡܰܪ ܕܠܳܐ ܐܶܣܬܰܟܺܝ ܡܢܳܗܘܢ *he was vexed that he had not been waited for;* ܡܶܣܬܰܟܝܳܢܳܬܳܐ *the things expected;* ܪܰܡܫܳܐ ܗܘܳܐ ܡܶܣܬܰܟܶܐ *evening was drawing near;* ܡܫܺܝܚܳܐ ܗܽܘ ܕܡܶܣܬܰܟܶܐ *Christ is He who is looked for.* Derivatives, ܣܟܝܐ, ܡܣܟܝܢܐ, ܡܣܬܟܝܢܐ, ܡܣܬܟܝܢܐܝܬ.

ܣܰܟܺܝܢ, ܣܰܟܺܝ̈ܢܶܐ pl. of ܣܟܺܝܢܳܐ.

ܣܳܟܳܐܝܬ rt. ܣܘܦ. adv. *generally, in entirety.*

ܣܽܘܟܳܪܳܐ pl. ـ̈ܶܐ m. *a money-changer.*

ܣܟܘܠܝ, ܣܟܘܠܝܢ pl. ܣܟܘܠܝܣ usually ܐܶܣܟܽܘܠܺܝ σχολή, *a school;* ܒܰܪ ܣܟܘܠܝ *a school-fellow.*

ܣܟܘܠܝܐ, ܣܟܘܠܝܐ, and ܐܶܣܟܘܠܝ *a scholar;* f. *a kind of hymn.*

ܣܟܘܠܝܢ, ܣܟܘܠ, and ܐܶܣܟܘܠ pl. ܣܟܘܠܝܐ,

ܣܟܘܠܝܢ m. σχόλιον, *a scholion, note, comment, gloss; enlightenment;* ܣܟܘܠܝܘܢ ܕܒܪܝܬܐ : ܕ ܕ *note on Genesis iv. 7.*

ܣܟܘܠܢܝܐ pl. m. *laborious.*

ܣܟܘܠܣܛܝܩܐ, ܣܟܘܠܣܛܝܩܘܣ, ܣܟܠܣܛܝܩܐ, ܣܟܘܠܣܛܝܩܐ, ܣܟܘܠܣܛܝܩܘܣ pl. ܐ̈ and ܣܟܘܠܣܛܝܩܘܣ m. σχολαστικός, *a scholar, a schoolmaster; a pleader, advocate.*

ܣܟܘܠܣܛܝܩܘܬܐ f. *advocateship.*

ܣܟܘܠܬܢܐ, ܣܟܘܠܬܢܐ, ܣܟܘܠܬܢ rt. ܣܟܠ. *understanding, intelligent, prudent, capable;* ܠܐ ܣܟܘܠܬܢܐ *without understanding.*

ܣܟܘܠܬܢܐܝܬ rt. ܣܟܠ. adv. *intelligently.*

ܣܟܘܠܬܢܘܬܐ rt. ܣܟܠ. f. *understanding, intelligence.*

ܣܟܘܣܝܪܐ = ܣܩܘܣܝܪܐ and ܣܟܘܪܐ.

ܣܟܝ Pael conj. of ܣܟܐ.

ܣܟܘܡܐ rt. ܣܟܡ. *last, final.*

ܣܟܝܕܪܝܐ m. pl. σχεδάρια, *memoranda tablets.*

ܣܟܝܢܐ pl. ܐ̈ rarely ܐ̈ f. *a knife, dagger.*

ܣܟܝܢܘܣ, ܣܟܝܢܘܣ, ܣܟܝܢܘܢ m. *a)* σχῖνος -ον, *mastich, the mastich-tree, pistacia lentiscus. b)* σχοῖνος, *an aromatic rush.*

ܣܟܝܪܘܬܐ rt. ܣܟܪ. f. *stopping* the ears, *shutting* the window.

ܣܟܠ act. part. ܣܟܠ. *to be stupid* or *foolish, to act foolishly, stupidly.* Ethpe. *to be known, understood;* ܡܪܝܐ ܡܢ ܒܪܝܬܗ ܡܬܣܟܠ *the Lord is known by His creation.* Pael ܣܟܠ *a) to make to understand, explain* with ܠ; *to advise; to signify;* ܣܟܠ ܠܗܢܐ ܚܙܘܐ ܗܢܐ *make this man to understand this vision;* ܡܢܐ ܡܣܟܠ ܫܡܐ *what is the meaning of the name?* ܟܕ ܡܣܟܠ *being admonished. b) to make foolish* or *stupid.* Ethpa. *to inspect, consider closely; to be capable, understanding; to understand, perceive, recognize;* ܡܣܬܟܠ ܥܒܕܝ *my servant deals wisely;* ܕܠܐ ܢܣܬܟܠܘܢ ܒܠܒܗܘܢ *lest they should perceive in their heart;* ܠܐ ܐܣܬܟܠܘ ܡܕܡ ܕܐܡܪ *they did not understand what he said;* ܕܠܐ ܡܣܬܟܠ *senseless.* Aph. ܐܣܟܠ intrans. *a) to act foolishly* or *perversely, to play the fool. b) to go astray, mistake;* ܠܐ ܐܢܫ ܢܣܟܠ ܟܕ ܩܪܐ *let any one not mistake if he read.* trans. *c) to offend, cause to fall; to be offensive, injure* with ܒ; ܐܢ ܐܣܟܠ ܒܟ ܐܚܘܟ *if thy brother have done thee wrong.* Ethtaph. *to be committed* as a sin, a transgression. Derivatives, ܣܘܟܠܐ, ܣܟܘܠܬܢܐ, ܣܟܘܠܬܢܐܝܬ, ܣܟܘܠܬܢܘܬܐ, ܣܟܠܐ, ܣܟܠܐܝܬ, ܣܟܠܘܬܐ, ܣܟܠܬܐ, ܡܣܟܠܢܐ, ܡܣܟܠܢܘܬܐ, ܡܣܬܟܠܢܐ, ܡܣܬܟܠܢܘܬܐ, ܡܣܬܟܠܢܐܝܬ.

ܣܟܠ or ܣܟܠ, ܣܟܠܐ, ܣܟܠܐ pl. m. ܐ̈, ܣܟܠܝܢ pl. f. ܐ̈, ܣܟܠܬܐ rt. ܣܟܠ. *stupid, foolish, void of understanding; a foolish person, fool;* ܣܟܠܐ ܓܒܪܐ *a foolish man;* ܣܟܠܬܐ ܗܝ ܠܡܣܒܪ ܗܕܐ *it is foolish to suppose this.*

ܣܟܠܐ rt. ܣܟܠ. m. *stupidity.*

ܣܟܠܐܝܬ rt. ܣܟܠ. adv. *stupidly, foolishly.*

ܣܟܠܘܬܐ, ܣܟܠܘܬܐ pl. ܐ̈ rt. ܣܟܠ. f. *folly, transgression, evil-doing, offence;* ܕܠܐ ܣܟܠܘ *innocent, innocently;* ܣܟܠܘܬܐ ܕܪܥܝܢܐ *want of reason, senselessness, folly.*

ܣܟܡ denom. verb Pael conj. from ܐܣܟܝܡܐ σχῆμα. *a) to form, shape, draw, delineate;* ܨܘܪܬܐ ܕܣܟܡܢܢ *the figure we have drawn out;* pass. part. *figured, formed, shaped;* ܗܘܢܐ ܠܐ ܡܣܟܡܐ *an unformed mind. b) to transform, put on, pretend, assume; to attribute;* ܕܐܒܐ ܡܣܟܡܝܢ ܠܒܘܫܐ ܕܐܡܪܐ *wolves assuming lambs' garments.* Ethpa. ܐܣܬܟܡ *a) to be formed, conformed, take shape* or *form;* ܡܣܬܟܡܝܢ ܒܡܠܐܟܐ ܕܙܕܝܩܘܬܐ *assuming the form of angels of righteousness;* ܦܪܙܠܐ ܕܢܣܬܟܡ *pig-iron. b) to feign, pretend, deceive;* ܡܣܬܟܡܝܢ ܠܟܬܒܐ *they feign to obey the scriptures.* Derivatives, ܐܣܟܝܡܐ, ܡܣܟܡܢܘܬܐ, ܡܣܬܟܡܢܘܬܐ, ܡܣܟܡܢܐ.

ܣܟܢ probable root of following. Maphel ܡܣܟܢ *to make poor, to weaken, reduce to poverty, pretend to be poor* often opp. ܐܥܬܪ *to enrich, give oneself out as rich;* ܡܪܝܐ ܗܘ ܡܡܣܟܢ ܘܡܥܬܪ *the Lord maketh poor and maketh rich;* ܐܣܬܪܩ ܘܡܣܟܢ ܗܘܐ ܠܗ *He emptied Himself and made Himself poor.* Ethmaphal ܐܬܡܣܟܢ *to grow poor* or *weak; to be impoverished, impaired, deprived of;* ܥܬܝܪܐ ܐܬܡܣܟܢܘ ܘܟܦܢܘ *the rich were im-*

poverished and hungered; ܠܐ ܡܬܡܣܟܢ ܡܥܬܪ ܟܠ *He who makes all rich suffers no diminution;* ܟܝܠܐ ܐܬܡܣܟܢ *the measure is lessened.* Derivatives, ܡܣܟܢܐ, ܡܣܟܢܐܝܬ, ܡܣܟܢܘܬܐ, ܡܣܬܡܣܟܢܢܐ.

ܣܟܢܐܝܬ rt. ܣܟܡ. adv. *finally.*

ܣܟܢܓܒܝܢ Pers. *oxymel, a mixture of vinegar and honey.*

ܣܟܢܝܐ, ܐ̈ ـܢܝܬܐ rt. ܣܟܡ. *final;* ܣܟܢܝܬܐ ܕܐܘܪܚܐ *the extremities.*

ܣܟܢܘܬܐ rt. ܣܟܡ. f. *conclusion;* ܣܟܢܘܬܐ ܕܣܟܘܡ *the final conclusion.*

ܣܟܪ fut. ܢܣܟܘܪ, act. part. ܣܟܪ, ܣܟܪܐ, pass. part. ܣܟܝܪ, ܐ', ܐ̈. *to shut, stop; to stop up, fill up, block* as ܐܘܪܚܐ *the way,* ܡܒܘܥܐ *a spring,* ܢܚܠܐ *a valley,* ܦܘܡܐ *the mouth,* ܬܘܪܥܬܐ *a breach,* ܬܪܥܐ *the door;* ܣܟܘܪ ܦܘܡܟܘܢ *shut your mouth;* ܐܕܢ̈ܐ ܕܣܟܝܪܢ ܒܫܥܘܬܐ *ears stopped with wax;* ܟܐܦ̈ܐ ܕܣܟܝܪܢ ܒܡܥܠܢ̈ܐ ܕܩܒܪ̈ܐ *stones set in the entrances of tombs.* Ethpe. ܐܣܬܟܪ *to be shut, stopped, repaired, silenced;* ܐܣܬܟܪ ܒܐܦܝܗܘܢ *it was shut in their faces;* ܐܣܬܟܪܬ ܨܗܝܘܢ *Zion was silent.* Pa. ܣܟܪ *to shut up closely, to shut up, block* or *stop* especially of the ears and mouth. Ellipt. ܣܟܪܘ ܒܐܦܘܗܝ *they shut* the door *upon him, bolted him in.* Also *to set close together; to fence off.* Ethpa. ܐܣܬܟܪ *to be stopped, shut fast, barred in.* Derivatives, ܣܟܪܐ, ܣܟܝܪܘܬܐ, ܣܟܪܐ, ܣܟܪܐ, ܡܣܟܪܢܐ, ܡܣܟܪܐ.

ܣܟܪܐ pl. ܝܢ̈, ܐ̈ rt. ܣܟܪ. f. *a round shield, a buckler, target.*

ܣܟܪܐ pl. ܐ̈ rt. ܣܟܪ. m. *a stopping, stoppage, obstacle, interposition;* esp. *an obstruction* in the liver; *a barrier, dam, mole.*

ܣܟܬܐ pl. ܣܟܝܢ, ܣܟܐ rt. ܣܟ f. *a pin, peg, pole, stake, nail, wedge, splinter;* ܣܟܐ ܕܦܪܙܠܐ *iron teeth, stakes* or *nails;* ܣܟܬ ܦܕܢܐ *a ploughshare* often ellipt.; ܣܟܬܐ ܕܛܒܥܐ some part of a die for coining.

ܣܠܐ pass. part. ܣܠܐ, ܣܠܝܐ but cf. ܣܠܝܐ below. *to despise, reject.* Ethpe. ܐܣܬܠܝ *to be rejected, thrown away;* ܢܣܬܠܘܢ ܐܝܟ ܡܝܐ ܕܡܬܐܫܕܝܢ *they shall be rejected as water that is poured away.* Pael ܣܠܝ *to reject* (rare).

Aph. ܐܣܠܝ *to reject, refuse, abhor, cast away, despise;* ܟܐܦܐ ܕܐܣܠܝܘ ܒܢܝ̈ܐ *the stone which the builders refused;* ܡܕܡ ܠܐ ܡܣܠܐ ܐܢܬ *Thou dost not despise aught.* Pass. part. ܡܣܠܐ, ܡܣܠܝܐ, ܡܣܠܝܬܐ *despised, rejected, reprobate, profane; an abomination;* ܡܣܠܝܐ ܒܝܢܝ ܥܡܡ̈ܐ *rejected amongst the nations;* ܐܝܟ ܫܘܒܛ̈ܐ ܡܣܠܝ̈ܐ ܡܬܦܣܩܝܢ *hewn down as worthless shoots;* ܙܘܘܓܐ ܡܣܠܝܐ *an abominable marriage* i. e. within prohibited degrees. Ethtaph. ܐܬܬܣܠܝ *to be rejected.* Derivatives, ܣܠܝܐ or ܣܘܠܝܐ, ܣܠܝܐ, ܣܘܠܝܐ, ܣܠܝܐ, ܡܣܠܝܐ, ܡܣܠܝܘܬܐ, ܡܣܠܝܢܐ, ܡܣܠܝܢܘܬܐ, ܡܣܬܠܝܢܐ, ܡܣܬܠܝܢܘܬܐ.

ܣܠܐ and ܣܠܠܐ, ܣܠܐ pl. ܣܠܝܢ, ܣܠܠܐ, ܣܠܝܐ com. gen. *a basket.*

ܣܠܐ, ܣܠܬܐ ܣܠܬ ܩܕܠܐ f. *the back hair.*

ܣܠܐ, ܣܠܬܐ f. *a) sea-weed, sedge. b) tree lichen.*

ܣܠܘܒ, ܣܠܘܒ &c.; see ܣܠܘܒ.

ܣܠܓܝܢܝܢ f. σιλίγνιον, *winter wheat, fine wheaten flour.*

ܣܠܓܣ denom. verb Palpel conj. from συλλογισμός. *to arrange words, compose, write.* Ethpalp. ܐܣܬܠܓܣ *to be arranged, composed.* Derivatives, ܣܠܓܣܐ, ܡܣܠܓܣܘܬܐ, ܡܣܠܓܣܢܐ.

ܣܠܕܐ or ܣܠܕܐ m. *a column* of writing.

ܣܠܘܐ m. *a thorn.*

ܣܠܘܝ f. *a quail.*

ܣܠܘܩ the city *Seleucia.*

ܣܠܘܩܝܐ *an inhabitant of Seleucia.*

ܣܠܘܚܝܬܐ f. mountain dialect. *the tortoise.*

ܣܠܘܩܐ pl. ܐ̈ rt. ܣܠܩ. m. *one who mounts up, ascends.*

ܣܠܘܩܘܣ, ܣܠܝܘܩܘܣ or ܣܠܘܩܘܣ *Seleucus* king of Syria 311 B. C., from whose reign the Greek chronology is dated.

ܣܠܘܩܝܐ or ܣܠܝܘܩܝܐ *Seleucia* the name of various cities.

ܣܠܘܩܝܐ *an inhabitant of Seleucia.*

ܣܠܘܩܝܣ σελευκίς -ιδα, *turdus seleucus,* a bird only found near Seleucia.

ܣܠܘܪܐ σίλουρος, *a river-fish.*

ܣܠܥܐ pl. ܐ̈ـ m. *a flint.*

ܣܠܚܬܐ (ܣܠܚܬ) rt. ܣܚܠ. m. *a draught-house, latrine.*

ܣܠܝܩ, ܣܠܝܩ or ܣܠܘܩ *Seleucia* on the Tigris, the capital of Parthia, almost always ܣܠܝܩ ܘܩܛܝܣܦܘܢ *Seleucia-Ctesiphon.*

ܣܠܝܩܬܐ *a drain, sewer.*

ܣܠܚܘܬܐ rt. ܣܚܠ. f. *refuse, filth.*

ܣܠܟܘ = ܣܠܘܩ and ܣܠܝܩ *Seleucia.*

ܣܠܡܢܕܪܐ and ܣܠܡܢܕܪܐ f. σαλαμάνδρα, *the salamander.*

ܣܠܢܛܝܢ and ܣܠܢܛܝܘܢ σιλέντιον, *an audience with the emperor.*

ܣܠܢܛܪܐ; see ܣܘܠܛܪ.

ܣܠܥܐ pl. ܣܠܥܝܢ a coin, *a shekel.*

ܣܠܦܐ Ar. *a husband's brother,* ܣܠܦܬܐ *a husband's sister;* cf. ܝܒܡ and ܝܒܡܬܐ.

ܣܠܩ fut. ܢܣܩ, imper. ܣܩ, infin. ܡܣܩ, act. part. ܣܠܩ, ܣܠܩܐ, part. adj. ܣܠܝܩ and ܣܠܝܩ. irreg. verb dropping the Lomad after a prefix, is conjugated like a ܦܢ verb. *a) to go up, ascend* opp. ܢܚܬ; ܣܠܩܝܢ ܠܗܝܟܠܐ *we go up to the temple;* ܣܠܩ ܠܘܬ ܡܨܪܝܢ *he went up towards Egypt;* ܣܠܩ ܠܫܡܝܐ *He ascended into heaven.* *b) to go to war* esp. with ܥܠ *against.* *c) to embark, disembark* e.g. with ܠܣܦܝܢܬܐ, with ܡܢ ܐܠܦܐ *from the ship.* *d) to arise, rise up, ascend* as the dawn, smoke, flame; as a spring, a flood, a storm. *e) to rise up, mount up* as a sacrifice = *to be offered.* *f) to rise* as a building, *to grow taller* as a tree. *g)* arith. *to result, amount to, to mount up, rise* as a number, a price. *h) to come out, result* from casting lots, *to fall to one's lot.* Idioms: ܨܒܥܐ *to turn out of the colour, be of the same colour;* ܠܪܫܐ *to come into effect, to succeed, prevail;* ܥܠ ܠܒܐ—ܥܠ ܪܥܝܢܐ *to come into the mind, to come to mind;* ܣܠܩ ܫܪܒܗ ܡܢ ܠܗ *his race arose from, had origin from;* ܣܠܩܬ ܢܦܫܗ *his soul ascended = he died.* ܣܠܝܩ act. *going up to war;* ܣܠܝܩ pass. *offered up; distilled.* Pa. ܣܠܩ *to lift up* with the winnowing-fan. Ethpa. ܐܣܬܠܩ *a) to be taken up, lifted up;* ܐܣܬܠܩ ܡܢ ܠܘܬܢ our Lord *was taken up from us.* *b) to go up, ascend;* ܐܣܬܠܩܘ ܒܫܘܪܐ *they climbed up by the walls.* Aph. ܐܣܩ *a) to make ascend, raise, bring up, take up, to bring up from the dead* cf. ܐܘܒܐ; ܫܒܝܠܐ ܫܦܝܐ ܕܡܣܩ ܠܪܘܡܐ *a smooth path leading up to the heights;* ܐܣܩܬ ܡܢ ܫܝܘܠ ܢܦܫܝ *Thou hast brought up my soul from Sheol;* ܕܢܣܩ ܟܝܢܐ ܐܢܫܝܐ ܠܥܘܬܪܗ *that He might raise human nature to His wealth.* *b) to lift up, pull out* of the water, out of a pit; ܐܣܩܘ ܡܝܐ ܠܩܒܘܬܐ *the waters lifted up the ark.* *c) to lift up, offer up* sacrifice, incense, praise, prayer. *d) to erect.* *e) to bring up = vomit.* *f) to pull up* ܡܢ ܥܩܪܐ *by the roots.* *g) to raise a levy, to pay tax, tribute;* ܡܣܩܝ ܡܕܐܬܐ *tributaries.* *h) to do raised work, carve in relief, emboss, overlay;* ܡܣܩܢ ܒܨܘܪܬܐ ܕܕܗܒܐ *embossed with gold ornament.* *i) to distil, sublimate;* ܡܝܐ ܡܣܩܐ *distilled water.* Idioms: ܠܪܫܐ *to bring* punishment *on the head* of any one; ܠܪܫܐ *to cause to succeed;* with ܥܠ *to attribute;* ܥܠ ܪܥܝܢܐ—ܥܠ ܠܒܐ *to bring to mind, call to mind;* ܡܚܫܒܬܐ *to suggest a thought.* Ethtaph. ܐܬܬܣܩ used as pass. of Peal *to be ascended.* Derivatives, ܐܣܩܐ, ܡܣܩܬܐ, ܡܣܩܘܬܐ, ܣܠܩܐ, ܣܘܠܩܐ, ܣܠܝܩܐ, ܡܣܩܢܘܬܐ, ܡܣܩܢܝܬܐ, ܣܘܠܩܢܐ, ܣܠܘܩܝܐ.

ܣܠܩܐ m. *beet, beetroot.*

ܣܠܩܐ rt. ܣܠܩ. m. *the lifting up in the air, winnowing* of corn.

ܣܠܩܐ m. *excuse, apology.*

ܣܠܬܐ, ܣܠܬܐ, ܣܠܬ ܣܠܬܐ; see ܣܠܐ and ܣܠܐ.

ܣܡ, ܣܡܐ pl. ܣܡܡܢܐ m. *a drug, medicine, remedy, poison, pigment;* ܣܡܡܢܐ ܡܪܟܒܐ *compound medicines;* ܡܪܟܒܝ ܣܡܡܢܐ *preparers of drugs, sorcerers;* ܣܡ ܚܝܐ *medicine of life* often said of our Lord; ܣܡ ܡܘܬܐ *a fatal drug, poison;* ܒܣܡܐ ܐܡܝܬܗ *he put him to death with poison;* ܐܫܩܝܗ ܣܡܐ ܕܡܘܬܐ *he gave him deadly poison to drink;* ܨܝܪܐ ܕܡܢ ܣܡܡܢܐ ܡܨܒܥܢܐ ܨܐܪ *a painter who paints with various pigments.* Derivatives, verbs ܣܡܡ, ܣܡܣܡ, and ܐܣܡ, ܣܡܡܐ, ܣܡܣܡܐ, ܣܡܣܡܢܐ, ܣܡܡܢܐ, ܣܡܡܢܝܐ, ܣܡܣܡܢܝܐ, ܡܣܡܡܢܐ, ܡܣܡܡܢܘܬܐ, ܣܡܣܡܢܘܬܐ.

Names of medicinal herbs:

ܣܡ ܫܘܪܐ *gentian.* ܣܡ ܟܠܒܐ *plantain.* ܣܡ ܣܡܐ also ܣܡ ܐܪܝܐ or ܣܡܐ ܕܪܩܘܢ *dragon's blood*, the thickened juice or resin of various plants, that of Calamus Draco has styptic qualities, another kind is from the tree Dracaena Draco. ܣܡܐ ܕܟܠܒܐ *dog's dung*.

ܣܡܐ, ܣܡܝ, ܣܡܐ fut. ܢܣܡܐ, pres. part. ܣܡܐ, cf. ܣܡܐ. *to be blind*; ܒܘܡܐ ܕܒܢܘܗܪܐ ܣܡܐ *the owl which is blind in the light*. PAEL ܣܡܝ *to blind, put out* the eyes, *deprive of sight*; ܣܡܝ ܠܥܝ̈ܢܘܗܝ *he put out his eyes*; ܣܡܝܗ ܢܘܗܪܐ ܠܚܙܬܗ *the light blinded his sight*. ETHPA. ܐܬܣܡܝ *to become blind, lose the sight, be maimed, disabled*; ܐܬܣܡܝ ܒܒܟܝܐ ܥܝ̈ܢܝ ܘܥܡܝ my eyes *were blinded with weeping, and became dim*; ܠܐ ܢܬܬܡܗ ܘܢܬܣܡܐ ܒܕܚܠ̈ܬܐ ܣܓܝ̈ܐܬܐ *let him not be stupefied and disabled by many terrors*. APH. ܐܣܡܝ *to deprive of one eye; to halt*; ܡܣܡܐ ܗܘܐ ܥܠ ܚܨܗ Jacob *halted upon his thigh*. DERIVATIVES, ܣܡܘܡܐ, ܣܡܐ, ܣܡܝܐ, ܣܡܝܘܬܐ, ܡܣܡܝܢܘܬܐ, ܡܣܡܝܢܘܬܐ.

ܣܡܝܐ, ܣܡܝܐ, ܣܡܝܬܐ, ܣܡܝܐ pl. m. ܣܡܝܢ, ܣܡܝܐ f. ܣܡܝܬܐ rt. ܣܡܐ. *blind; dark, concealed*; ܣܡܝܐ ܝܠܝܕ ܗܘܐ ܡܢ ܟܪܣܐ *he was born blind*; ܣܡܝܐ ܐܝܟ ܚܘܠܕܐ *blind as a mole*; ܣܡܝܐ ܚܕ ܝܬܒ ܗܘܐ ܘܡܚܕܪ *a blind man was sitting* by the wayside *begging*; ܣܡܝܢ ܪܘܚܢܐܝܬ *they are spiritually blind*; ܗܕܡ̈ܐ ܣܡܝ̈ܐ *the concealed members*.

ܣܡܒܘܩܐ σαμβύκη, *sambuca, a three-cornered stringed instrument*.

ܣܡܕܪ *to blossom, put forth blossoms*.

ܣܡܕܪܐ pl. ̈ܝܢ rt. ܣܡܕܪ. *the blossom* or *young shoots of the vine, tendrils, vine-buds*.

ܣܡܕܪܘܬܐ rt. ܣܡܕܪ. f. *the budding* or *blossoming* of the vine.

ܣܡܘܟܐ, ܣܡܘܟܬܐ rt. ܣܡܟ. *a stay, support, supporter*; ܐܘ ܣܡܘܟܐ ܕܡܚܝܠܘܬܝ *O Support of my weakness*.

ܣܡܘܪ, ܣܡܘܪܐ pl. ̈ܐ m. *mustela Scythica, the sable*.

ܣܡܘܪܝܐ from ܣܡܘܪ. adj. *sable*.

ܣܡܘܪܢܐ, ܣܡܘܪܢܝܬ or ܣܡܘܪܢܝܬ f. some amphibious animal.

ܣܡܘܪܢܐ m. σμύρνα, *myrrh*.

ܣܡܘܪܢܝܘܢ σμυρνίον, a kind of parsley resembling myrrh.

ܣܡܝܐ ܕܣܡܝ̈ܐ pl. ̈ܐ m. *a leader of the blind*.

ܣܡܝܕܐ pl. ̈ܐ m. *a fox*.

ܣܡܝܕܪܐ m. *beetroot*.

ܣܡܝܟܪܐ m. *a small bladder, inflated skin*.

ܣܡܝܢܐ rt. ܣܡܐ. m. *halting, limping*.

ܣܡܝܕܐ m. σεμίδαλις, *the finest wheaten flour, a meal offering* Lev. ii. 1, 3 and passim; ܣܡܝܕܐ ܘܢܣܟܐ *the meal offering and drink offering*; ܠܚܡܐ ܕܣܡܝܕܐ *fine white bread*.

ܣܡܝܕܝܐ, ܣܡܝܕܝܬܐ adj. *of fine flour*; ܓܪ̈ܝܨܬܐ ܣܡܝܕ̈ܝܬܐ *fine white loaves*.

ܣܡܝܘܬܐ rt. ܣܡܐ. f. *blindness*.

ܣܡܝܩܐ *the ichneumon*.

ܣܡܝܟܘܬܐ rt. ܣܡܟ. f. gram. *addition, an accessory proposition*.

ܣܡܝܡܐ from ܣܡ, ܣܡܐ. *poisoned, dipped in poison* as arrows.

ܣܡܟ fut. ܢܣܡܘܟ, act. part. ܣܡܟ, ܣܡܟܐ, pass. part. ܣܡܝܟ, ܣܡܝܟܐ, ܣܡܝܟܬܐ. *a*) *to stay, sustain*; ܒܠܚܡܐ *with bread*, ܒܚܡܪܐ *with wine*; ܣܡܘܟܘ ܠܒܟܘܢ *sustain your heart = refresh yourself with food*. *b*) *to uphold, support; to prop, shore up*; ܚܝܠܐ ܕܣܡܟ ܒܪ̈ܝܬܐ *the Power which upholds creation*. *c*) *to rest* the hand on the head of a victim; ܢܣܡܘܟ ܐܝܕܗ ܥܠ ܪܫ ܩܘܪܒܢܗ *he shall lay his hand upon the head of his oblation*. *d*) *to lean, support oneself, rest against* or *on*; *to press heavily* with ܒ, ܥܠ or ܠܘܬ; ܣܡܟ ܠܩܪܢܐ ܘܕܡܟ *he rested himself against* a corner of the wall *and slept*; ܟܦܢܐ ܩܫܝܐ ܣܡܟ ܗܘܐ ܥܠ ܡܕܝܢܬܐ *severe famine pressed upon the city*. *e*) *to recline at* table; ܟܕ ܣܡܝܟ *as he sat at table*; ܩܕܡ ܣܡܝ̈ܟܐ *before the guests*. *f*) *to lean over*; ܣܡܟܬ ܠܡܦܘܠܬܗ *it tottered to its fall*. *g*) *to lean away, leave*; ܥܘܬܪܐ ܣܡܟ ܡܢܗ ܘܠܘܬ ܥܠ *his riches passed away from him to ...* *h*) *to touch* as a ship the land, *to reach, arrive* at port, *arrive* at a conclusion; ܕܐܠܦܐ ܬܣܡܘܟ ܠܠܡܐܢܐ *that the ship may reach the haven*; ܣܡܟܘ ܠܡܢܕܪܐ *they arrived at the mandra*; ܥܕܡܐ ܕܣܡܟܝܢ ܠܐܪܥܐ ܕܚ̈ܝܐ *until they rest in the land of life*. *i*) *to dash* or *beat against*; ܣܡܟܝܢ ܓܠ̈ܠܐ ܥܠ ܬܚܘܡܐ ܕܐܪܥܐ *the surges beat against the limit of the land*; ܝܡܐ ܠܐ ܣܡܟ ܠܐܪܥܐ *the rain did not beat upon the earth.* Pass. part. *upheld, supported; firm, established, steadfast;* ܠܐ ܣܡܝܟ *unstable; depending from* a letter, *beginning with* one letter, as several verses; *lying at table,* see *e.* ETHPE. ܐܶܣܬܡܶܟ *a) to rest, recline* esp. at table; ܢܶܣܬܡܟܘܢ ܐܢܫܐ ܟܠܗܘܢ *make them all sit down. b) to support oneself, lean on* with ܥܠ, *to rely upon;* ܐܶܣܬܡܶܟ ܥܠ ܚܘܛܪܗ *he leant on his staff. c) to be supported, propped up;* ܐܶܣܬܡܶܟ ܚܕ ܪܝܫܐ ܕܩܝܣܐ ܥܠ ܐܣܬܐ *one end of the beam was supported by the wall;* gram. *to depend on, be connected with.* PA. ܣܰܡܶܟ *to uphold, support* step by step, continuously; ܣܰܡܶܟܬ ܡܰܟܬܒܰܝ *Thou hast upheld my steps;* ܐܰܢ̱ܬܬܐ ܡܪܚܡܢܝܬܐ ܡܣܡܟܐ ܐܝܩܪܐ ܕܒܥܠܗ̇ *a gracious woman upholds the honour of her husband.* ETHPA. ܐܶܣܬܰܡܰܟ *a) to lean on* with ܥܠ of the pers.; *to rely on. b) to be firmly knit, hold fast together. c) to be supported, sustained. d) to depend on* a letter, *begin with the same letter* as verses. APH. ܐܰܣܡܶܟ *to make recline* or *sit down; to prop up, support; to inspire confidence.* DERIVATIVES, ܣܡܟܐ, ܣܘܡܟܐ, ܣܡܝܟܘܬܐ, ܣܡܘܟܐ, ܣܡܟܬܐ, ܣܡܟܬ, ܡܣܡܟܢܐ, ܡܣܡܟܢܐ.

ܣܘܡܟܐ pl. ܐ̈, ܐ̈ rt. ܣܡܟ. m. *a prop, pillar, support, socket; a supporter, upholder;* ܬܪܝܢ ܣܘܡܟܝܢ ܠܚܕ ܕܦܐ *two supports* or *sockets under* each *board;* ܣܘܡܟܐ ܕܩܢܝܐ ܪܨܝܨܐ *the staff of the bruised reed;* metaph. ܣܘܡܟܐ ܕܥܕܬܐ *a pillar of the Church;* gram. *an accent* under the word marking that the voice is to be sustained.

ܣܡܟܐ pl. ܐ̈, ܐ̈ rt. ܣܡܟ. m. *a) stability. b) a couch, seat, cushion, place at table; a banquet, feast, company;* ܒܝܬ ܣܡܟܐ *a banqueting-room;* ܪܝܫ ܣܡܟܐ *the ruler of the feast,* also *the chief place;* ܪܝܫ ܣܡܟܐ ܒܡܫܬܘܬܐ *the chief place at feasts;* ܐܣܡܟܘ ܐܢܘܢ ܣܡܟܝܢ or ܣܡܟܝܢ ܣܡܟܝܢ *make them sit down in companies, in rows;* ܣܒ ܠܟ ܣܡܟܐ *take thy place at the feast;* ܚܝܪ ܒܗ ܟܠܗ ܣܡܟܐ *all the company looked at him.*

ܣܡܟܪܘܣ m. *shoemaker's paste, glue.*

ܣܶܡܟܰܬ rt. ܣܡܟ *Semkath,* name of the letter ܣ.

ܣܡܠܐ f. *the left, left hand* opp. ܝܡܝܢܐ *the right hand;* ܡܢ ܝܡܝܢܐ—ܡܢ ܣܡܠܐ *on the right, on the left;* ܒܪ ܣܡܠܐ the thief crucified *on the left* of our Lord. Constantly used with reference to Matt. xxv. 33 sqq. *of those on the wrong side, the enemies of the Lord, evil;* ܒܪܐ ܕܣܡܠܐ ܩܠܐ *the voice saying, depart ye to the left;* ܫܐܕܐ ܕܣܡܠܐ *devils belonging to the left hand;* ܥܡ ܣܡܠܐ ܗܘ ܐܬܟܬܫܗ *his conflict is with evil.* DERIVATIVES, ܣܡܠܐܝܬ, ܣܡܠܝܐ, ܣܡܠܝܘܬܐ, ܡܣܡܠܢܘܬܐ.

ܣܡܠܐܝܬ from ܣܡܠܐ. adv. *on the left.*

ܣܡܠܝܐ, ܐ̈ *a) left, on the left side,* ܓܢܒܐ ܣܡܠܝܐ *the left wing* of an army. *b) unlucky, unfavourable, inauspicious. c) wrong,* ܟܠ ܕܣܥܪ ܐܢ ܝܡܝܢܝܐ ܐܢ ܣܡܠܝܐ *all his actions whether right or wrong.*

ܣܡܠܝܘܬܐ from ܣܡܠܐ. f. *the being on the left side.*

ܣܰܡܶܡ denom. verb Pael conj. from ܣܡܐ, part. ܡܣܰܡܡܳܐ, ܡܣܰܡܡܬܐ. *to poison;* ܓܐܪܐ ܡܣܡܡܐ *poisoned darts.* ETHPA. ܐܶܣܬܰܡܰܡ *to be poisoned, die by poison.* PALPEL ܣܰܡܣܶܡ *to give medicine, heal, cure.* ETHPALP. ܐܶܣܬܰܡܣܰܡ *to take medicine.* APH. ܐܰܣܶܡ *to give poison.*

ܣܡܘܡܐ from ܣܡܐ, ܣܡܐ. m. *lamp-black,* used for ink.

ܣܡܘܡܝܬܐ from ܣܡܐ, ܣܡܐ. f. *a poisonous lizard.*

ܣܡܡܢܐ pl. of ܣܡܐ, ܣܡܐ.

ܣܡܡܢܝܐ from ܣܡܐ, ܣܡܐ. *medicinal.*

ܣܡܣܦܝܪ *sediment* of flour.

ܣܡܣܡܪܐ pl. ܐ̈ *pomegranate rind.*

ܣܡܣܡ; see under ܣܰܡܶܡ.

ܣܡܣܪܐ m. *a broker, agent.*

ܣܡܣܪܐ m. *wild thyme* or *mint.*

ܣܰܡܢܶܠ *to make pale* or *thin, to emaciate.* ETHPA. ܐܶܣܬܰܡܢܰܠ *to be emaciated, to lead an ascetic life.* DERIVATIVES, ܣܘܡܢܠܐ, ܡܣܡܢܠܢܘܬܐ, ܡܣܡܢܠܐܝܬ, ܡܣܡܢܠܐ.

ܣܡܩ W-Syr. ܣܡܶܩ, fut. ܢܶܣܡܰܩ, act. part. ܣܳܡܶܩ, ܣܳܡܩܳܐ. *to be red, turn red* intrans. as the sky or heavenly bodies; with disease or chemical change; of the face. PA. ܣܰܡܶܩ

to redden, turn red trans.; ܚܡܪܐ ܕܡܣܡܩ ܐܦܐ *wine which makes the countenance flushed.* ETHPA. ܐܣܬܡܩ *to become red.* APH. ܐܣܡܩ *to make red, dye red, make to blush;* ܡܣܡܩ ܐܝܟ ܦܪܙܠܐ ܒܢܘܪܐ *it glows red-hot as iron in the fire;* metaph. ܡܣܡܩ ܒܚܛܗܐ *dyed scarlet in sin.* DERIVATIVES, ܣܡܘܩܐ, ܣܘܡܩܐ, ܣܘܡܩܢܐ, ܣܡܩܬܐ.

ܣܡܩܪܝ, ܣܡܩܪܢܐ *red, ruddy, red-haired.*

ܣܡܩܪ denom. verb from ܣܡܩܪܝ. ESTHAPH. ܐܣܬܡܩܪ *to be red* of the face or hair.

ܣܡܩܪܢܘܬܐ from ܣܡܩܪܝ. f. *ruddiness.*

ܣܡܩܬܐ rt. ܣܡܩ. f. *a red sea-weed.*

ܣܡܪܓܕܐ and ܣܡܪܓܕܘܣ *an emerald,* oftener ܙܡܪܓܕܐ, ܐܙܡܪܓܕ or ܐܣܡܪܓܕ.

ܣܡܬܐܘܬ; see under ܣܡ, ܣܡܐ.

ܣܢܢ imper. ܣܢ *to strain, filter, clarify, purge;* ܣܢ ܡܝܐ ܡܢ ܡܪܟܒܐ *strain away the water from the preparation.* Part. adj. ܣܢܝܢ, ܣܢܝܢܐ *refined, purified, pure* esp. of gold.

ܣܢܐ fut. ܢܣܢܐ, imper. ܣܢܝ, act. part. ܣܢܐ, ܣܢܝܐ, pass. part. ܣܢܐ, ܣܢܝܐ, ܣܢܝܬܐ. *to hate* opp. ܪܚܡ; ܣܢܐܘܢܝ ܡܓܢ *they hated me without a cause;* ܣܢܝܢ ܠܒܝܫܬܐ *they hate evil;* ܣܢܝܢܢ *we hate.*

Part. adj. *hateful, detestable, odious, foul, bad, ugly;* ܣܢܐ ܡܕܡ ܕܣܢܐ *anything impious;* ܣܢܐ ܚܙܘܐ *ugly;* ܡܚܫܒܬܐ ܣܢܝܬܐ *a foul thought;* ܩܥܐ ܒܩܠܐ ܣܢܝܐ *he called out with a terrible cry.* Pl. f. emph. ܣܢܝܬܐ *foul deeds, vices, crimes.*

ETHPE. ܐܣܬܢܝ and ETHPA. ܐܣܬܢܝ *to be hated; to be disfigured; to be faulty* of metre. APH. ܐܣܢܝ *to render odious; to disfigure.* ETHPAU. ܐܣܬܢܘܝ *to be an object of hatred.* DERIVATIVES, ܣܢܝܐ, ܣܢܝܢܐ, ܣܢܝܐܘܬܐ, ܣܢܝܬܐ, ܣܢܝܢܘܬܐ, ܣܢܝܐ, ܣܢܝܐ, ܣܢܐܬܐ, ܣܢܐܝܢ, ܣܢܝܐܘܬܐ or ܣܢܝܘܬܐ.

ܣܢܐ, ܣܢܝܐ m. *a bush, thorn, bramble;* ܢܘܪܐ ܕܝܩܕܐ ܒܣܢܝܐ *a fire blazing in a bush;* ܡܢ ܣܢܝܐ ܗܘܐ ܘܪܕܐ *from the thorn sprang a rose;* ܣܢܝܐ ܕܒܪܐ *the wild-rose, dog-thorn.*

ܣܢܐܐ pl. ܣܢܐܐ rt. ܣܢܐ. *a hater, enemy, adversary,* drops one Alep before suffixes and the other quiesces, ܣܢܐܝ *my enemy,* pl. ܣܢܐܝ *my enemies;* ܣܢܐܝܢ *our enemies;* f. pl. ܣܢܐܬܟܝ *they that hate thee.*

ܣܢܐܓܪܐ, ܣܢܐܓܪܬܐ also spelt without the Alep or with Yodh, ܣܢܝܓܪܐ, pl. m. ܐ̈ f. ܬ̈ܐ συνήγορος, *an advocate, defender;* ܣܢܝܓܪܐ ܢܗܘܐ ܨܠܝܒܟ ܠܘܬܢ *let Thy cross be an advocate for us.*

ܣܢܐܓܪܘܬܐ συνηγορία, f. *advocacy, pleading; a defence;* with ܥܒܕ *to plead.*

ܣܢܐܬܐ, ܣܢܐܬܘܬܐ another spelling of ܣܢܬܐ.

ܣܢܐܬܐ; see ܣܢܘܬܐ and ܣܢܬܐ.

ܣܢܐܩܐ rt. ܣܢܩ. m. *introducing.*

ܣܢܐܬܐ pl. ܣܢܐܬܐ rt. ܣܢܐ. f. *hatred, enmity;* ܣܢܐܬܐ ܕܐܚ̈ܐ *hatred between brethren;* ܣܢܐܬܐ ܕܐܟܣܢܝܐ *ill-will towards strangers, inhospitality;* ܣܢܐܬܗ ܕܢܘܪܐ *opposition* or *contrary nature of fire* towards wax.

ܣܢܒܘܠ or ܨܢܒܘܠ Pers. *the resinous covering of the cedar fruit* or perhaps *the sheath of the betel-nut.*

ܣܢܓܪ denom. verb from ܣܢܐܓܪܐ. ETHPAL. ܐܣܬܢܓܪ *to have one's cause pleaded, to be interceded for.*

ܣܢܝܓܪܐ; see ܣܢܐܓܪܐ.

ܣܢܕܘܩܐ Pers. m. *a case, coffer, casket.*

ܣܢܕܝܩܐ m. σάνδιξ, *cinnabar, a bright red pigment.*

ܣܢܕܠܐ or ܣܢܕܠܐ pl. ܐ̈ m. σάνδαλον, *a sandal.*

ܣܢܕܠܪܐ m. *a sandal-maker.*

ܣܢܕܪ oftener ܨܢܕܪ. *santalum, sandal-wood.*

ܣܢܕܪܘܟܐ, ܣܢܕܪܟܐ, ܣܢܕܪܐܟܐ, ܣܢܕܪܐܟܝ &c. σανδαράχη, *sandarach, red sulphuret of arsenic.*

ܣܢܕܪܝ *seed of garden rue, peganum harmala,* possessing narcotic properties.

ܣܢܗܕܪܝܢ συνέδριον, *assemblage, council.*

ܣܢܗܕܘܣ, ܣܢܗܕܪܘܣ, and ܣܢܗܘܕܪܘܣ; see ܣܘܢܗܘܕܘܣ.

ܣܢܘܬܐ, ܣܢܘܬܐ also written ܣܢܐܬܐ, ܣܢܐܬܐ rt. ܣܢܐ. *odious, detestable; a hated person.*

ܣܢܘܩܐ or ܣܢܘܩܐ rt. ܣܢܩ. m. *beardless.*

ܣܢܘܩܐ m. *a large-meshed sieve.*

ܣܢܘܢܝܬܐ pl. ܝ̈ܬܐ f. *a*) *a swallow.* *b*) *a tortoise.* *c*) *an arch* or *hollow.* *d*) *a bat.* *e*) *the middle part of the breast.* *f*) ܕܐܠܥ̈ܐ *the lesser ribs, the abdomen.*

ܣܢܘܪܐ, ܣܢܘܪܬܐ f. *a cat, a wild cat.*

ܣܢܘܪܬܐ, ܣܢܘܪܬܐ or ܣܢܘܪܬܐ pl. ܬܐ̈ f. *a) the crown of the head. b) a head-covering, head-band, cap, helmet.* DERIVATIVE, verb ܐܣܬܢܘܪ; see ܣܢܪ.

ܣܢܝܘܬܐ and ܣܢܐܝܘܬܐ rt. ܣܢܐ. f. *hate, hatred.*

ܣܢܝܐ m. *pestilence.*

ܣܢܓ *to shake, quiver.* PAEL ܣܢܓ *to be beardless;* part. ܡܣܢܓܐ *beardless, having a scanty beard;* metaph. ܛܘܪܐ ܡܣܢܓܐ *a mountain bare of trees.* DERIVATIVES, ܣܢܘܓܐ, ܣܢܝܓܐ.

ܣܢܛܘܕܝܣ σιτώδης, τὰ σιτώδη, *a morning meal of wheaten food.*

ܣܢܛܘܪ m. *a senator.*

ܣܢܓܘܪܬܐ f. *the hump* of a camel, buffalo, &c.

ܣܢܝܐ emph. state of ܣܢܐ *a bush.*

ܣܢܝܐ, ܣܢܝܬܐ pl. m. ܣܢܝܐܝܢ, ܣܢܝܐܬܐ pl. f. ܣܢܝܐܬܐ rt. ܣܢܐ. *detested, hated, hateful, odious;* ܣܢܝܐܝܢ ܠܐܠܗܐ *hateful to God* or *haters of God;* ܡܫܬܥܠܝܢܘܬܐ ܣܢܝܬܐ ܠܐܠܗܐ *arrogance hateful to God.*

ܣܢܝܐܝܬ rt. ܣܢܐ. adv. *detestably, odiously.*

ܣܢܝܘܬܐ and ܣܢܐܝܘܬܐ rt. ܣܢܐ. f. *hatred, aversion; odiousness, detestability; bad condition* or *life, viciousness, rascality; odious aspect* or *sound, ugliness, hideousness.*

ܣܢܝܓܐ rt. ܣܢܓ. m. *propolis, bees' glue* with which they close the entrance to the hive.

ܣܢܩܪܘܢ m. *mixture, intermingling.*

ܣܢܓܘܪܬܐ same as ܣܢܓܘܪܬܐ.

ܣܢܝܩ, ܣܢܝܩܐ; see verb ܣܢܩ.

ܣܢܝܩܘܬܐ rt. ܣܢܩ. f. *need, necessity; poverty, want, indigence.*

ܣܢܦ fut. ܢܣܢܘܦ *to introduce, inject.* PAEL ܣܢܦ *to be prompt in action, diligent; to loop up, gird up* clothes. DERIVATIVES, ܣܢܦܐ, ܣܢܐܦܐ.

ܣܢܦܐ̈ m. pl. *billows, surges.*

ܣܢܩ PEAL only part. ܣܢܝܩ, ܩܐ, ܩܬܐ. with ܕ or ܠ and a following verb, with ܥܠ and a substantive, *to need, have need, be in need;* as adj. *in need, needy, indigent;* ܐܢܐ ܣܢܝܩ ܐܢܐ ܕܡܢܟ ܐܥܡܕ *I have need to be baptized of Thee;* ܠܐ ܣܢܝܩܝܢܢ *we have no need;* ܣܢܝܩ ܥܠ ܕܢܬܐܣܪ *he must needs be bound;* ܣܢܝܩܐ ܕܪܚܡܐ *in need of mercy;* ܡܣܟܢܐ ܘܣܢܝܩܐ *the poor and needy.* ETHPE. ܐܣܬܢܩ *to need, stand in need* with ܥܠ; *to find it necessary, be obliged; to become needy, suffer want.* ETHPA. ܐܣܬܢܩ *to be in great need; to find it indispensable, be compelled.* APHEL ܐܣܢܩ *to cause to be in need, make to need; to constrain, compel.* DERIVATIVES, ܣܘܢܩܢܐ, ܣܘܢܩܐ, ܣܢܝܩܘܬܐ, ܡܣܢܩܢܘܬܐ.

ܣܢܪ PAEL ܣܢܪ *to nod* or *shake* the head. ETHPA. ܐܣܬܢܪ denom. verb from ܣܢܘܪܬܐ. *to put on a helmet.*

ܣܢܪܝܐ or ܣܢܐܪܝܐ m. *a peak, summit of a mountain.*

ܣܢܪܦܐ m. *a fine white loaf.*

ܣܣ act. part. ܣܐܣ *to gnaw, fret.* PA. ܣܣܣ *to gnaw* as a worm. DERIVATIVES, ܣܘܣܝܐ, ܣܣܐ.

ܣܣܐ m. σώσσος, a period of time.

ܣܣܐ or ܣܣܐ m. *a vault; the stars of the Milky Way.*

ܣܣܐ rt. ܣܣ. com. gen. *a moth, maggot, worm; rottenness, decay.*

ܣܣܓܘܢܐ Pers. subst. *vermillion, sky-blue* or *blue-black.*

ܣܣܓܘܢܝܐ adj. *of the colour of* ܣܣܓܘܢܐ.

ܣܣܛܝܪܘܣ; see under ܐܣܛܝܪܘܣ.

ܣܣܛܪܐ pl. ܐ̈ m. σεῖστρον, *a rattle.*

ܣܣܢܓ Pers. *possession by evil spirits, illness resulting from the same.*

ܣܣܬܐ; see ܣܐܣܬܐ.

ܣܥܪ fut. ܢܣܥܪ, act. part. ܣܥܪ. *to assail, assault, fall suddenly on; to act with boldness* or *presumption, to attempt, to dare, presume against* with ܥܠ; ܚܝܘܬܐ ܣܥܪܝ ܥܠ ܚܝܐ wild beasts *dared to attack the living;* ܟܕ ܣܥܪܝܢ ܒܝܫܬܐ *when evils come suddenly;* ܣܥܪܘ ܘܢܣܒܘ *they dared to take;* ܐܡܪܚ ܘܣܥܪ ܥܠ *he presumptuously transgressed* the custom of the Church. PAEL ܣܥܪ *to embolden.* DERIVATIVE, ܣܥܪܐ.

ܣܥܕܐ or ܣܥܕܐ a thickly branching tree bearing round blossoms.

ܣܥܕܐ pl. ܐ̈ f. *cyperus, a kind of rush with*

fragrant roots; the root of the same, *the head* of a rush or of garlic.

ܣܥܘܬܐ perhaps *dung.*

ܣܳܥܽܘܪܳܐ, ܬܳܐ rt. ܣܥܪ. *a*) *efficient, effectual,* with ܠܳܐ *ineffectual; a maker, doer, worker, one who brings about;* ܣܳܥܽܘܪܳܐ ܐܳܦ ܡܶܠܬܳܐ the Word is *the efficient* power *of God;* ܣܳܥܽܘܪܳܐ ܕܪܽܚܡܬܳܐ ܕܡܶܣܟܺܢܶܐ *one who practises love of the poor. b*) *an overseer, director, curator,* esp. eccles. *a periodeuta, chorepiscopus, visitor.*

ܣܳܥܽܘܪܳܐܺܝܬ rt. ܣܥܪ. adv. *actually.*

ܣܳܥܽܘܪܽܘܬܳܐ pl. ܬܳܐ rt. ܣܥܪ. f. *a*) *doing, operation, action, transaction; business, practice;* ܣܳܥܽܘܪܽܘܬܳܐ ܒܺܝܫܬܳܐ *evil-doing;* ܣܳܥܽܘܪܽܘܬܳܐ ܛܳܒܬܳܐ or ܛܳܒܽܘܬܳܐ *well-doing;* ܣܳܥܽܘܪܽܘܬ ܬܶܕܡܪ̈ܳܬܳܐ *miracle working;* ܬܶܐܘܪܺܝܰܐ ܘܣܳܥܽܘܪܽܘܬܳܐ *theory and practice;* ܒܣܳܥܽܘܪܽܘܬܳܐ *indeed, actually. b*) *care, supervision, visitation;* ܣܳܥܽܘܪܽܘܬܳܐ ܕܟܪ̈ܺܝܗܶܐ *visiting the sick;* ܣܳܥܽܘܪ̈ܘܳܬܳܐ ܐܰܠܳܗܳܝ̈ܳܬܳܐ *divine visitations.* Eccles. *a visitation, the office of a visitor* or *chorepiscopus, the diocese of a chorepiscopus. c*) gram. *action;* ܡܶܠܬܳܐ ܕܣܳܥܽܘܪܽܘܬܳܐ *an active verb.*

ܣܥܽܘܪܳܐ rt. ܣܥܪ. m. *a visitation.*

ܣܳܥܽܘܪܳܝܳܐ, ܝܬܳܐ rt. ܣܥܪ. *practical;* with ܠܳܐ *ineffectual, idle.*

ܣܥܰܒ fut. ܢܶܣܥܽܘܒ, act. part. ܣܳܥܶܒ, ܣܳܥܒܳܐ, pass. part. ܣܥܺܝܒ, ܣܥܺܝܒܳܐ, ܣܥܺܝܒܬܳܐ. *to shudder; to loathe;* pp. *loathsome, disdained, ignoble;* ܣܥܰܒܘ ܠܛܽܘܥܝܳܝܗܽܘܢ *they loathed error;* ܡܶܢ ܓܶܢܣܳܐ ܣܥܺܝܒܳܐ *of ignoble race.* Pa. ܣܰܥܶܒ *to make loathsome.* Ethpa. 1) ܐܶܣܬܰܥܰܒ *to be disgusted; to be in doubt; to eject, reject.* 2) ܐܶܣܬܰܥܰܒ *to flap* the wings. Derivatives, ܣܥܒܳܐ, ܣܥܺܝܒܽܘܬܳܐ.

ܣܥܒܳܐ rt. ܣܥܒ. m. *loathing.*

ܣܥܳܝܳܐ pl. ܝ̈ܶܐ rt. ܣܥܐ. m. *an audacious attack, assault, attempt* upon some one; rhet. *an objection, argument.*

ܣܥܺܝܒܽܘܬܳܐ rt. ܣܥܒ. f. *loathing, aversion.*

ܣܥܣܥܳܬܳܐ m. *the back hair.*

ܣܥܰܪ fut. ܢܶܣܥܽܘܪ, act. part. ܣܳܥܰܪ, ܣܳܥܪܳܐ, pass. part. ܣܥܺܝܪ, ܪܳܐ, ܪܳܬܳܐ. *a*) *to visit, inspect, look after, care for, provide, heal;* ܣܥܰܪ ܡܳܪܝܳܐ ܠܥܰܡܶܗ *the Lord hath visited His people;* ܐܰܝܟ ܕܣܳܥܰܪ ܪܳܥܝܳܐ ܠܡܰܪܥܺܝܬܶܗ *as a shepherd careth for his flock;* ܣܥܰܪ ܒܶܝܬ ܐܰܣܺܝܪ̈ܶܐ *visiting the prison;* ܨܒܺܝܬ ܕܬܶܣܥܽܘܪ ܠܥܰܡܡ̈ܶܐ ܡܶܢ ܟܽܘܪ̈ܗܳܢܰܝܗܽܘܢ *Thou didst choose to heal the nations of their diseases.* Eccles. *to visit, hold a visitation. b*) *to do, deal, commit, act, effect, perform; to treat; to exact;* ܕܣܳܥܪܺܝܢ ܚܽܘܒܳܠܳܐ *who deal destruction;* ܢܶܣܥܽܘܪ ܐܳܦ ܥܰܠ ܡ̈ܶܠܶܐ ܕܠܳܐ ܢܳܡܽܘܣ *let us treat also of the irregular words;* with ܐܽܘܪܚܳܐ *to make a way;* ܣܳܥܰܪ ܚܽܘܒܳܐ *a creditor;* ܣܳܥܪ̈ܰܝ ܚܰܝ̈ܠܶܐ *workers of miracles;* ܣܳܥܰܪ ܛܳܒ̈ܳܬܳܐ *a well-doer, a benefactor;* ܥܒܳܕܳܐ ܕܐܶܣܬܥܰܪ ܒܝ *an action done by me.* Ethpe. ܐܶܣܬܥܰܪ *a*) *to be mustered* for war; *to be examined, inspected;* ܢܶܣܬܥܰܪ ܒܟܬܳܒ̈ܶܐ *let search be made in the records. b*) *to be done, worked, performed;* also act. *to work, effect;* ܚܰܝܠܶܗ ܕܡܶܣܬܥܰܪ ܒܰܢ *His power which worketh in us. c*) *to be, happen, come to pass;* ܗܳܕܶܐ ܠܳܐ ܡܶܫܟܚܳܐ ܕܬܶܣܬܥܰܪ *this cannot be;* ܗܳܢܶܝܢ ܕܐܶܣܬܥܰܪ ܐܰܝܟ ܢܒܺܝܽܘܬܶܗ *which came to pass according to the prophecy of* the saint. Pael ܣܰܥܰܪ 1) *to visit; to treat of* a subject, *to write.* 2) denom. verb from ܣܰܥܪܳܐ *to cut off the hair.* Ethpa. ܐܶܣܬܰܥܰܪ *to be visited; to be done, achieved.* Aph. ܐܰܣܥܰܪ *to visit* the sick. Derivatives, ܣܥܳܪܳܐ, ܣܳܥܽܘܪܳܐ, ܣܳܥܽܘܪܳܐܺܝܬ, ܣܳܥܽܘܪܽܘܬܳܐ, ܣܥܽܘܪܳܐ, ܣܳܥܽܘܪܳܝܳܐ, ܡܣܰܥܪܳܢܳܐ, ܡܣܰܥܪܳܢܽܘܬܳܐ, ܣܰܥܪܳܐ, ܣܰܥܪܳܢܳܐ.

ܣܥܰܪ, ܣܥܳܪܳܐ and ܣܰܥܰܪ, ܣܰܥܪܳܐ pl. ܪ̈ܶܐ m. *hair, the hair.* Fem. ܣܰܥܰܪܬܳܐ or ܣܰܥܪܬܳܐ pl. ܣܰܥܪ̈ܶܐ, ܪ̈ܳܬܳܐ *a hair, single hair.* Also ܣܰܥܪܳܐ ܚܕܳܐ ܕܣܰܥܪܳܐ *one single hair;* ܓܰܒܪܳܐ ܕܣܰܥܪܳܐ *a hairy man;* ܥܰܡܳܐ ܕܣܰܥܪܳܢܳܐ *a long-haired* or *unshorn nation;* ܣܰܥܪܳܐ ܕܢܶܙܺܝܪܽܘܬܶܗ *the hair of his Nazirite vow;* ܒܬܽܘܠܬܳܐ ܕܣܰܥܪܳܗ̇ *a maiden wearing her hair* i.e. not a nun. ܣܰܥܪܳܐ ܕܐܰܪܢܒܳܐ *hare's fur;* ܣܰܥܪܳܐ ܕܓܡܠܳܐ *camel's hair;* ܣܰܥܪܳܐ ܕܓܢܳܒܳܪ̈ܶܐ *giant hair, adiantum capillus veneris, maiden-hair fern;* ܣܰܥܪ ܫܶܦܘܬܳܐ *a moustache.* Metaph. *leaves, fibres;* also chem. ܣܰܥܪܳܐ ܕܟܽܘܟܒܳܐ *Saturn = lead.* Derivatives, ܣܰܥܪܳܢܳܐ, ܣܰܥܪܳܝܳܐ, ܣܰܥܪܳܢܺܝܬ.

ܣܥܳܪܳܐ rt. ܣܥܪ. m. *visitation.*

ܣܥܳܪܳܐ, ܣܥܳܪܬܳܐ pl. ܣܥܳܪ̈ܶܐ, ܣܥܳܪ̈ܺܝܢ f. *a*) *barley;* ܠܰܚܡܳܐ ܕܣܥܳܪ̈ܶܐ *barley bread;* ܚܕܳܐ ܣܥܳܪܬܳܐ *one grain of barley;* ܣܥܳܪ̈ܶܐ ܡܰܪܓܳܢܺܝܬܳܐ *pearl barley;* ܣܥܳܪ̈ܶܐ ܕܪܽܘܡܳܝܶܐ *spelt. b*) a disease of the eyes. *c*) *a barley-corn,* measure of weight.

ܣܥܪܢܝܬܐ pl. ܝܬܐ̈ f. *a litter.*

ܣܥܪܘܢܐ or ܣܥܪܢܘܢܐ from ܣܥܪܐ. *hairy, shaggy.*

ܣܥܪܢܐ, ܢܝܬܐ from ܣܥܪܐ. *a*) *hairy, made of hair* or *haircloth. b*) f. a plant, *clinopodium, wild basil.*

ܣܥܪܬܢܐ, ܬܢܝܬܐ from ܣܥܪܐ. *hairy.*

ܣܥܪܬܢܐ from ܣܥܪܐ. *hairy.*

ܣܦ fut. ܢܣܘܦ, act. part. fem. ܣܝܦܐ, pass. part. ܣܦܝܦ, ܐ, ܬܐ. prep. *to take fire slowly* or *gradually without flame; to burn up; to be kindled, heated; to smoulder;* metaph. of anger, love, &c.; ܣܦܬ ܚܛܝܬܐ ܐܝܟ ܢܘܪܐ *sin smouldered as a fire;* ܢܘܪܐ ܣܦܝܦܬܐ *a kindled fire, a smouldering fire.* Cf. ܣܦܝܦܐ. ETHPA. ܐܣܬܦܦ *to be hasty; to vaunt, boast.* APH. ܐܣܝܦ *to kindle, light, set fire to.* ETTAPH. ܐܬܬܣܝܦ *to be set on fire.* DERIVATIVES, ܣܦܘܦܐ, ܣܦܝܦܐ, ܣܦܝܦܐܝܬ, ܣܦܝܦܘܬܐ, ܣܦܦܐ, ܣܦܬܐ.

ܣܦܐ fut. ܢܣܦܐ, act. part. ܣܦܐ, ܣܦܝܐ. *to pick up, heap together, collect, accumulate; to carry* corn; ܣܦܘܗܝ ܘܛܥܢܘܗܝ *they picked him up and carried him;* ܣܦܐ ܥܘܬܪܐ *amass riches.* ETHPE. ܐܣܬܦܝ *to be collected.* ETHPA. ܐܣܬܦܝ *to be taken up, occupied.* DERIVATIVES, ܣܦܝܐ, ܣܦܝܐ.

ܣܦܬܐ, ܣܦܬܐ pl. ܣܦܘܬܐ̈, ܣܦܘܬܐ̈ f. *lip; brim, rim; the edge* of a valley, of a curtain, &c.; *the brink, shore* of the sea, of a river; *the rim* or *ledge* of a table; *the brim* or *rim* of a cup, &c.; ܡܡܠܠܐ ܕܣܦܘܬܐ *the utterance of the lips, speech;* ܒܣܦܘܬܗ ܬܢܐ ܗܘܐ *in a low voice he repeated;* ܣܦܬܐ ܕܦܝܠܐ *the proboscis of an elephant;* ܡܠܐ ܠܣܦܬܐ *full to the brim;* ܣܦܐ ܠܣܦܐ *from one side to the other, entirely.*

ܣܦܐ pl. ܣܦܐ̈ m. *a doorpost, sill, threshold, porch;* metaph. *approach* to a city or its *suburb.*

ܣܦܝܐ, ܣܦܝܘܢ or ܣܦܝܘܢܐ f. σηπία, *the cuttlefish* or *squid.*

ܣܦܩ *to tremble; to wring* the hands. PAEL ܣܦܩ *to make to tremble; to reject.*

ܣܦܝܕܐ Pers. m. *a*) *white pepper. b*) *white lead.*

ܣܦܝܕܘܢ σηπεδών, *a sore, gangrene.*

ܣܦܕ ETHP. ܐܣܬܦܕ denom. verb from ܣܦܕܐ. alchem. *to be reduced to the state of white lead.*

ܣܦܘܐ; see ܣܦܝܐ.

ܣܦܘܓܐ, ܣܦܘܓܝܐ, ܣܦܘܓܓܝܘܢ also ܐܣܦܘܓ m. *a sponge.*

ܡܝܐ ܕܣܦܘܓܐ *soap-suds, lye-water.*

ܣܘܦܣܦܐ m. *bran.*

ܣܦܘܩܠܛܪܐ pl. ܐ̈ m. σπεκουλάτωρ, *an executioner;* cf. ܐܣܦܩ.

ܣܦܪܐ m. pl. *coverings.*

ܣܦܩ ETHPE. ܐܣܬܦܩ *to be cut, slit.* DERIVATIVE, ܣܦܩܐ. ETHPA. ܐܣܬܦܩ *to use foul proverbs.* DERIVATIVE, ܣܦܩܐ.

ܣܦܩܐ m. *a cut, incision.*

ܣܦܩܐ pl. ܐ̈ m. Pers. *a small basket, small money-bag.*

ܣܦܝܐ rt. ܣܦܐ. m. *a harvester.*

ܣܦܝܐ *dry drugs.*

ܣܦܝܐ rt. ܣܦܐ. m. *carrying corn* i. e. from the shock to the threshing-floor.

ܣܦܝܕܐ and ܐܣܦܝܕܘܢ *white lead.*

ܣܦܝܠܐ also ܣܦܝܪ and ܣܦܝܠܐ, ܣܦܝܪܐ f. *the sapphire.*

ܣܦܝܠܢܐ and ܣܦܝܪ *sapphirine, sapphire blue.*

ܣܦܝܢܐ m. perhaps *a passenger in a ship.*

ܣܦܝܢܬܐ, ܣܦܝܢܬܐ pl. ܢܐ̈, ܢܬܐ̈. f. *a ship.* DERIVATIVES, ܣܦܢܐ, ܣܦܢܝܐ, ܣܦܢܘܬܐ, ܣܦܢܝܐ.

ܣܦܣܛܝܣ *a sophist,* usually ܣܘܦܣܛܐ.

ܣܦܝܩܐ rt. ܣܦ. *a*) *bold, headlong, headstrong. b*) = ܣܦܝܦܐ *kindled, alight, incensed.*

ܣܦܝܦܐܝܬ rt. ܣܦ. adv. *boldly, rashly, unadvisedly.*

ܣܦܝܦܘܬܐ rt. ܣܦ. f. *catching fire, being alight; passion, passionateness, mad folly, senselessness.*

ܣܦܝܩܐܝܬ rt. ܣܦܩ. adv. *a*) *empty handed; without cause. b*) = ܣܦܝܩܐܝܬ *sufficiently.*

ܣܦܝܩܘܬܐ rt. ܣܦܩ. f. *a void, an empty space; evacuation; nothingness, vanity; want; leisure, freedom* e. g. from cares or business.

ܣܦܝܪ, ܣܦܝܪܐ and ܐܣܦܝܪ f. *a*) σπεῖρα, *a cohort. b*) σφαῖρα, *a ball, a round mass.*

ܣܦܝܪܐ f. σφῦρα, *a large hammer.*

ܣܦܝܪܘܬܐ rt. ܣܦܪ. f. *skilfulness, learning.*

ܣܦܝܪܢܝܐ and ܐܣܦܝܪܐ from σφαῖρα, *spherical.*

ܣܦܝܠܐ f. *a jar with a twisted moulding round the brim.*

ܣܦܠܘܟܝܐ m. the plant *aristolochia.*

ܣܦܢܝܐ pl. ܝ̈ܐ from ܣܦܝܢܬܐ. m. *a mariner, sailor.*

ܣܦܢܝܘܬܐ from ܣܦܝܢܬܐ. f. *navigation, seamanship.*

ܣܦܢܝܐ from ܣܦܝܢܬܐ. *nautical.*

ܣܦܣܛ denom. verb Palpel conj. from ܣܘܦܣܛܐ. *to cavil, make use of sophisms.*

ܣܦܣܝܪܐ and ܣܦܣܝܪܐ pl. ܝܢ̈, ܐ̈ Pers. f. *a sword, a blade;* ܣܦܣܝܪܐ ܕܛܪܢܐ *a sharp flint, flint knife.*

ܣܦܣܠܐ pl. ܠ̈ܐ also written with other vowels. m. Lat. subsellium, eccles. *a footstool, stool, bench; the presbyters' seats; a stand* on which the bier rested while the office for the dead was sung.

ܣܦܣܠܝܐ, ܣܦܣܠܝܢܐ, &c. *a*) same as ܣܦܣܠܐ. *b*) *those occupying benches or seats in the church.*

ܣܦܣܪ *to make a bid, to bargain, to haggle* or *dispute* about the price; ܣܦܣܪ ܕܡܝ̈ܗܘܢ *he disputed over the price of it.* Derivatives, ܣܦܣܪܐ, ܣܦܣܪܘܬܐ, ܣܦܣܪܐ, ܣܦܣܪܘܬܐ, ܡܣܦܣܪܢܐ.

ܣܦܣܪܐ pl. ܐ̈ rt. ܣܦܣܪ. m. *a*) *a factor, broker, huckster.* *b*) *gabble, empty talk, fiction, fable.* For ܣܦܣܪܐ see ܣܦܣܝܪܐ.

ܣܦܣܪܘܬܐ rt. ܣܦܣܪ. f. *cunning, craftiness in bargaining; gabble.*

ܣܦܣܦܐ rt. ܣܦ. m. *burning, smouldering, taking fire.*

ܣܦܣܦܘܬܐ f. *cheese of kine.*

ܣܦܦܝܪܐ σάπφειρος, *a sapphire.*

ܣܦܩ fut. ܢܣܦܘܩ, act. part. ܣܦܩ, ܣܦܩܐ, part. adj. ܣܦܝܩ, ܩܐ, ܩܬܐ. *to suffice, be enough, sufficient; to be able, capable, competent; to be fit, adequate;* ܣܦܩ ܠܗ ܠܝܘܡܐ ܒܝܫܬܗ *sufficient unto the day is the evil thereof;* ܣܦܩ ܒܢܦܫܗ *he is capable, independent;* ܡܢ ܢܣܦܘܩ ܠܝ *how can I suffice? what can enable me to . . . ?* With ܩܢܝܢܘܗܝ *to have enough, possess sufficiency;* ܠܐ ܣܦܩܐ ܩܢܝܢܘܗܝ *he has not enough, does not possess enough;* ܐܝܟ ܕܣܦܩܐ ܩܢܝܢܘܗܝ *such as he has, according to his ability;* with ܠܡܫܩܠ *to be equal to the saying, able to comprehend* or *receive,* ellipt. ܡܢ ܕܡܨܐ ܕܢܣܦܘܩ ܢܣܦܘܩ *whoso is able to receive it let him receive it.* Act. part. *able, capable, competent* esp. with regard to learning; ܡܠܦܢܐ ܣܦܩܐ *an able teacher;* ܣܦܩܐ ܒܡܪܕܘܬܐ *learned;* ܣܦܩܐ ܐܘܪܗܝܐ *a learned Edessene;* ܣܦܩ ܠܟܠ ܕܒܥܐ *the Omnipotent.* Pass. part. *empty, vacant, vain, fruitless, devoid, lacking; unoccupied, at leisure;* ܣܦܝܩܝܢ ܐܘܨܪ̈ܝܢ *our treasuries are empty;* ܒܝܬܐ ܣܦܝܩܐ *an unoccupied house;* ܗܦܟܘ ܣܦܝܩܐܝܬ the ambassadors *returned having failed of effecting anything;* ܣܒܪܐ ܣܦܝܩܐ *vain hope;* ܠܐ ܣܦܝܩ ܐܢܐ *I am not at leisure.* Ethpe. ܐܣܬܦܩ *to be emptied, laid bare; to be at leisure, have time* for; *to cease* or *rest* with ܡܢ *from.* Pael ܣܦܩ *a*) *to empty, lay bare, clear out, evacuate; to withdraw from a* region; ܣܦܩܘ ܠܗܘܢ ܠܓܘܒ̈ܐ *they emptied the cisterns;* ܒܥܘ ܕܢܣܦܩܘܢ ܠܡܕܝܢܬܐ *they asked leave to withdraw from the city;* ܫܕܪ ܚܝܠܐ ܕܢܣܦܩܘܢ ܠܗ ܠܚܨܢܐ Saladin *sent* a force *to deprive the fortress of its stores.* *b*) *to empty out, pour out* e. g. ܡܢ ܡܐܢܐ ܠܡܐܢܐ *from one vessel into another; to lavish;* metaph. ܡܣܦܩ ܟܠܗ ܝܕܥܬܗ *he does all he knows;* ܟܠܗ ܚܝܠܗܘܢ ܒܟܘܢ ܡܣܦܩܝܢ *they concentrate their whole force upon you.* *c*) *to render empty, poor* or *futile;* ܣܓܝܐܬܐ ܠܡܫܩܠܘܬܢ ܕܠܗܕܐ ܢܣܦܩܢ *many things will render our endeavours towards this end futile.* Ethpa. ܐܣܬܦܩ *a*) *to be emptied, bare, devoid of, deprived of* with ܡܢ; ܐܣܬܦܩ ܕܘܟܬܗ ܕܬܐܢܬܐ ܕܠܐ ܦܐܪ̈ܐ *let the place of the unfruitful fig-tree be cleared;* ܐܣܬܦܩ ܪܥܝܢܟ ܡܢ ܪܚܡܬ ܟܣܦܐ *let thy mind be free from avarice.* *b*) *to deprive oneself, abstain.* *c*) *to be at leisure, find opportunity;* ܕܢܣܬܦܩܘܢ ܠܡܩܡ ܘܠܡܚܙܐ ܬܗܪܐ *so that they might be at leisure to stand and see the wonder.* *d*) *to be enabled, made fit.* *e*) *to be poured out, shed abroad, lavished;* ܐܣܬܦܩܬ ܥܠܘܗܝ ܡܘܗܒܬܐ ܕܟܗܢܘܬܐ *the gift of the priesthood was poured upon him;* ܐܣܬܦܩܘ ܟܠܗܘܢ ܚܕ̈ܘܬܝ *all my joys are scattered.* Aph. ܐܣܦܩ *a*) *to make fit* or *sufficient, to qualify;* ܐܣܦܩ ܠܢ ܕܢܗܘܐ ܡܫܡܫܢܐ ܕܕܝܬܩܐ ܚܕܬܐ

make us fit to be ministers of Thy covenant. b) *to empty out, throw out;* ܠܐ ܐܣܦܩܗ ܐܝܟ ܟܠܐ ܥܠ ܨܘܡܐ *it took up and scattered* the fishes *about in the market-place.* c) *to give, grant, yield.* Derivatives, ܣܦܘܩܐ, ܣܦܘܩܝܐ, ܣܦܩܘܬܐ, ܣܦܝܩܐܝܬ, ܣܦܝܩܘܬܐ, ܣܦܩܐܝܬ, ܡܣܦܩܢܐ.

ܣܦܝܩܐܝܬ rt. ܣܦܩ. adv. *sufficiently, capably, competently;* ܕܣܦܝܩܐܝܬ ܐܝܬ ܠܗܘܢ *which is sufficient for them.*

ܣܦܝܩܘܬܐ rt. ܣܦܩ. f. *sufficiency, fitness, ability.*

ܣܦܪ act. part. ܣܳܦܰܪ, ܣܳܦܪܳܐ, ܣܳܦܪܬܳܐ see below, pass. part. ܣܦܝܪ, ܐ, ܬܐ. root-meaning *to cut, shear.* a) *to study, practise;* ܣܳܦܪܳܐ ܣܦܝܪ ܢܳܡܽܘܣܳܐ *the scribe learned in the law.* b) *to cut* a pen. Pass. part. *skilful, learned;* with ܠܐ *uninstructed, unlearned;* ܐܝܕܝܐ ܣܦܝܪܬܐ *practised hands;* ܩܢܝܐ ܣܦܝܪܐ *a ready pen.* Pael ܣܰܦܰܪ and Aphel ܐܰܣܦܰܪ *to cut, crop, clip* the hair, *trim* the beard, *shear* the head, *take* or *give the tonsure;* ܣܰܦܰܪ ܣܰܥܪܶܗ ܘܠܒܶܫ ܐܶܣܟܺܝܡܳܐ ܕܝܺܚܺܝܕܳܝܽܘܬܳܐ *he cut off his hair and took the monastic habit.* Ethpa. ܐܶܬܣܰܦܰܪ *to be shorn; to take the tonsure;* ܗܰܘ ܕܡܣܰܦܰܪ *he who has the tonsure* = a monk. Derivatives, ܣܦܳܪܳܐ, ܣܦܰܪ, ܣܦܪܐ, ܣܘܦܪܐ, ܣܦܝܪܘܬܐ, ܣܦܪܬܐ, ܣܦܪܘܬܐ, ܡܣܦܪܐ, ܣܦܪܢܐ, ܣܦܪܢܝܐ, ܣܦܝܪܘܬܐ, ܣܦܪܐ, ܡܣܦܪܬܐ, ܡܣܦܪܢܐ, ܡܣܦܪܢܘܬܐ.

ܣܰܦܳܪܳܐ, ܬܐ rt. ܣܦܪ. *a barber.*

ܣܦܰܪ, ܣܶܦܪܳܐ pl. ܝܢ, ܐ rt. ܣܦܪ. m. a) *a writing, book;* ܣܦܰܪ ܙܰܒܢܶܐ *annals, chronicles;* ܣܦܰܪ ܥܒܳܕܰܘܗܝ *acts, records;* ܣܦܰܪ ܚܰܝܶܐ *the book of life,* i.e. the diptychs on which were enrolled the names of saints. Esp. *a book* of the Bible; ܣܶܦܪܳܐ ܕܒܪܺܝܬܳܐ *the Book of Genesis;* ܣܶܦܪܳܐ ܕܡܰܦܩܳܢܳܐ *the Book of Exodus,* &c. b) *letters, the art of writing; the letters* of the alphabet; ܠܐ ܝܳܕܰܥ ܐܢܳܐ ܣܶܦܪܳܐ *I cannot read;* ܠܡܰܠܳܦܽܘ ܐܶܢܽܘܢ ܣܶܦܪܳܐ *to teach them letters;* ܒܶܝܬ ܣܶܦܪܳܐ *a school;* ܣܶܦܪܳܐ ܕܰܟܬܺܝܒܽܘܬܳܐ *shorthand writing.* c) *speech, language;* ܣܶܦܪܳܐ ܣܽܘܪܝܳܝܳܐ *the Syriac language.*

ܣܳܦܪܳܐ, ܣܳܦܪܬܳܐ pl. m. ܐ pl. f. ܬܐ rt. ܣܦܪ. a) *a scribe, clerk, notary, lawyer.* b) *a learned* or *literary man, a writer, teacher, schoolmaster.*

ܣܦܳܪ, ܣܦܳܪܳܐ rt. ܣܦܪ. m. a) *the shore, coast, bank, border;* ܣܦܳܪ ܝܰܡܳܐ *the sea-coast, coast land, maritime district;* ܣܶܦܪܰܘܗܝ ܕܝܽܘܪܕܢܳܢ *the banks of Jordan;* ܣܶܦܪܰܝ ܬܺܐܒܶܠ *the borders of the inhabited world* = *remote regions.* b) *the edge, margin* of a book; ܟܳܬܒܺܝܢ ܥܰܠ ܣܶܦܪܳܐ ܕܦܰܬܳܐ *they write on the margin of a page.*

ܣܦܰܪܓܠܳܐ and ܐܣܦܪܓܠ *the quince.*

ܣܦܰܪܓܰܡܳܐ m. *an aromatic plant* esp. *ocymum basilicum.*

ܣܳܦܪܽܘܬܳܐ rt. ܣܦܪ. f. *the office of a scribe, grammar, learning.*

ܣܦܪܝܐ and ܣܦܪܢܝܐ, ܬܐ rt. ܣܦܪ. *learned, literary.*

ܣܦܪܡܟܐ and ܐܣܦܪܡܟ Pers. m. *sweet-smelling herbs* esp. *basilicum regium, sweet basil.*

ܣܶܦܪܬܳܐ emph. state of ܣܦܪܐ.

ܣܦܰܬܳܪܳܐ σπαθάριος, *a sword-bearer,* one of the body-guard of the Byzantine emperors.

ܣܦܛܪܘܡܝܢ *a royal enclosure* or *pleasure-ground.*

ܣܩ imper. of verb ܣܠܩ.

ܣܩ *vinegar.*

ܣܰܩ, ܣܰܩܳܐ pl. ܐ m. a) *sackcloth, hair-cloth;* ܐܰܣܰܩ ܣܰܩܳܐ ܒܚܰܨܰܘܗܝ *he put sackcloth on his loins;* ܥܳܡܰܪܰܝ ܣܰܩܶܐ *dwellers in sackcloth tents.* b) *a sack, bag, wallet;* ܣܰܩܶܐ ܒܠܰܝܳܐ *worn-out sacks.*

ܣܩܘܣܘܦ dialect of Harran. *a box, chest.*

ܣܩܪܘܣ and ܣܝܩܪܘܣ σικάριοι, *bandits.*

ܣܩܪܝܘܛܝܐ adj. from Iscariotes; *such as befel* Judas *Iscariot.*

ܣܰܩܒܳܐ pl. ܐ m. *a wound, an ulcer.*

ܣܰܩܒܶܠ Saphel conj. of verb ܩܒܠ and Estaphal ܐܶܣܬܰܩܒܰܠ *to be present, to happen;* see under ܩܒܠ.

ܣܩܒ Pael ܣܰܩܶܒ denom. verb from ܣܩܒܪܐ. *to make bitter; to harm, torment.*

ܣܩܘܣ σκεῦος, *a tool.*

ܐܣܩܘܒܝܛܘܪܐ and ܐܣܩܘܒܝܛܪܘܣ pl. ܣܩܘܒܝܛܘܪܐ and ܣܩܘܒܝܛܪܝܣ Lat. excubitor, *a guard, sentinel.*

ܣܰܩܽܘܒܠܳܐ pl. ܝܢ, ܬܐ, ܝ rt. ܩܒܠ. *opposite, contrary, adverse; an opponent;* ܣܰܩܽܘܒܠܳܐ *contradictory;* ܣܰܩܽܘܒܠܳܝܳܐ ܕܢܰܦܫܗܽܘܢ *self-contradictory, their own opponents;* ܪܽܘܚܶܐ ܣܰܩܽܘܒܠܳܝܳܢ ܗܘܰܝ *the winds were adverse.*

ܣܘܩܒܠܐܝܬ rt. ܩܒܠ. adv. *adversely, in opposition;* with ܐܬܐ *to contradict;* with ܩܡ and ܩܡ *to oppose, resist.*

ܣܘܩܒܠܢ, ܣܘܩܒܠܢܐ, ܢܝܬܐ rt. ܩܒܠ. *contrary, adverse, opposite; an opponent, adversary.*

ܣܘܩܒܠܢܘܬܐ rt. ܩܒܠ. f. *contrariety, opposition;* with ܡܠܬܐ or ܡܡܠܠܐ *gainsaying, contradiction;* with ܩܘܡܐ *resistance, strife;* with ܫܘܡܗܐ *antiphrasis.*

ܣܘܩܒܪܝܬܐ *a trumpet.*

ܣܘܩܪܐ *the bitter gourd; bitterness, annoyance.*

ܣܘܩܛܐ and ܣܘܩܛܐ *a) short, small, slender. b) a child, boy, youth. c) a curry-comb.*

ܣܘܩܠܐ rt. ܣܩܠ. m. *a polisher.*

ܣܘܩܪܝܐ *rheum ribes, rhubarb.*

ܣܘܩܠܩܐ pl. ܐ̈ m. σκούλκη, *a scout, reconnoitring party.*

ܣܘܩܢܐ m. *a surname, nickname.*

ܣܘܩܒܐ and ܣܘܩܒܐ rt. ܣܩܒ. m. *one who squats on his haunches, crouches.*

ܣܩܦܛܘܣ σκηπτοί, *thunderbolts.*

ܣܘܩܪܐ, ܪܬܐ rt. ܣܩܪ. *an ill-wisher, spiteful* or *malicious person, an enemy.*

ܣܘܩܘܪܕܝܘܢ σκόρδιον, *wild garlic* or *some plant smelling like garlic.*

ܣܘܩܪܝܐ *a)* rt. ܣܩܪ. f. *the evil eye, looking askance. b)* σκωρία, *dross, slag.*

ܣܘܩܪܬܢܐ rt. ܣܩܪ. *one looking with the evil eye.*

ܣܘܩܝܬܐ pr. n. *Scythia.*

ܣܘܩܘܬܝܐ pl. ܐ̈ and ܣܩܘܬܝܣ Σκύθης, *a Scythian.*

ܣܘܩܛܐ *avaricious, covetous.*

ܣܩܛܐ Pers. *a hedge round a vineyard.*

ܣܩܛܝܣ, ܣܩܛܝܢ, ܣܩܛܝܣ, ܣܩܛܐ and ܐܣܩܛܐ &c. *Scete*, a desert in Egypt.

ܣܩܛܝܐ ἀσκητής, *an ascetic.*

ܣܩܝܠܐ, ܣܩܝܠܠܐ and ܐܣܩܝܠ σκίλλα, *the squill*, a kind of onion.

ܣܩܝܠܘܬܐ rt. ܣܩܠ. f. *polish, brightness, lustre; a polished* or *elegant style;* ܣܩܝܠܬܐ ܡܠܘܗܝ *his polished words.*

ܣܩܝܬܝܐ pl. ܐ̈ *a Scythian;* cf. ܣܘܩܘܬܝܐ.

ܣܩܠ fut. ܢܣܩܘܠ, act. part. ܣܩܠ, ܣܩܠܐ, pass. part. ܣܩܝܠ, ܐ̈, ܬܐ. *to furbish, burnish, polish* esp. *to polish* or *adorn* speech, *speak in a polished* or *elegant style.* Pass. part. *polished, elegant, rouged;* ܡܚܙܝܬܐ ܣܩܝܠܬܐ *a burnished mirror;* ܣܩܝܠܐ ܡܣܢܐ *elegant sandals;* ܒܡܠܬܐ ܣܩܝܠܬܐ *polished diction.* Ethpe. ܐܣܬܩܠ *to be adorned, made elegant.* Pa. ܣܩܠ *to polish, adorn.* Derivatives, ܣܘܩܠܐ, ܣܩܠܐ, ܣܩܝܠܘܬܐ, ܣܩܠܐ, ܣܩܠܐ, ܣܩܠܐ, ܣܩܝܠܝܢ, ܡܣܩܠܢܘܬܐ.

ܣܩܠܐ rt. ܣܩܠ. m. *a furbisher, polisher* esp. *one whose business it was to polish and sharpen swords.*

ܣܩܠܐ rt. ܣܩܠ. m. *polishing; elegance* esp. of style.

ܣܩܠܐ *a)* σκάλα, *a landing-place, wharf. b)* ὀκλάξ, *squatting, sitting cross-legged and on the soles of the feet. c) a stirrup. d)* rt. ܣܩܠ. m. *adornment, embellishment;* ܓܕܠܐ ܘܣܩܠܐ ܕܣܥܪܐ *plaiting and hairdressing.*

ܣܩܠܪܐ; see ܣܩܠܪܐ.

ܣܩܠܛܘܢ Lat. scarlatum, *scarlet.*

ܣܩܠܝܘܢ σακκέλλιον, *a purse, treasury.*

ܣܩܠܝܢܐ pl. ܐ̈ rt. ܣܩܠ. gram. particles used to impart elegance to the style.

ܣܩܠܪܐ and ܣܩܠܠܪܐ σακελλάριος, *a bursar, keeper of the emperor's* or *empress's purse.*

ܣܩܡ denom. verb Pael conj. from ܣܘܩܡܐ. *to direct, adapt, apply, explain.* Pass. part. ܡܣܩܡ, ܡܣܩܡܐ *proportioned, tempered, measured, defined; a measure* of capacity. Ethpa. ܐܣܬܩܡ *to be measured out, defined, proportioned, computed.*

ܣܩܡܢܝܢ pl. ܣܩܡܢܝܐ Lat. scamnum, *a seat, bench.*

ܣܩܦ fut. ܢܣܩܘܦ, act. part. ܣܩܦ, pass. part. ܣܩܝܦ. *to crouch, to squat on the feet; to twist* or *pull awry a sandal.* Pa. ܣܩܦ *to crouch down, cower.* Derivatives, ܣܘܩܦܐ, ܣܩܦܐ, ܡܣܩܦܢܐ.

ܣܩܦܐ or ܣܩܦܐ rt. ܣܩܦ. m. *crouching, squatting on the soles of the feet.*

ܣܩܪ fut. ܢܣܩܘܪ, act. part. ܣܩܪ, ܣܩܪܐ, pass. part. ܣܩܝܪ, ܐ̈. *a*) *to look awry* or *askance, to look at with the evil eye, to envy, grudge, spite; give a perverted account* of any one; ܫܪܝ ܫܐܘܠ ܠܡܣܩܪܗ ܠܕܘܝܕ *Saul began to envy David;* ܥܝܢܐ ܣܩܪܬܐ *an evil eye, malignant look.* *b*) *to colour, smear with paint.* Ethpe. ܐܬܣܩܪ *to be envied, regarded with malignity.* Pa. ܣܩܪ and Aph. ܐܣܩܪ *to regard with malice* or *malignity.* Ethtaph. ܐܬܬܣܩܪ *to be hated, envied.* Derivatives, ܣܩܘܪܐ, ܣܩܘܪܐ, ܣܩܪܐ, ܣܩܪܬܐ, ܣܩܘܪܐ, ܣܩܘܪܬܐ, ܡܣܩܪܢܐ, ܡܣܩܪܢܘܬܐ.

ܣܩܪܐ or ܣܩܪܛܐ f. σάκρα, *a letter* esp. *an imperial rescript, edict, state letter of recommendation, passport; an official report.*

ܣܩܪܐ rt. ܣܩܪ. m. *envy;* ܥܝܢܐ ܕܣܩܪܐ *an envious eye.*

ܣܩܪܝܒܘܢܐ σκρίβωνες, *the imperial body-guard.*

ܣܩܪܘܣ *a*) m. σκάρος, a kind of sea-fish. *b*) perhaps σκωρία, *copper dross* or *scales.*

ܣܩܪܘܪܐ Pers. m. *a saucer, small dish* or *pan.*

ܣܩܪܘܪܐ rt. ܣܩܪ. *rabid, mad* as a dog.

ܣܩܪܝܡ; see ܣܩܪܡ.

ܣܩܪܐ pl. ܣܩܪܘܬܐ m. *the mast* of a ship.

ܣܩܪܝܦܘܣ m. σκάριφος, *an outline, delineation, ground-plan.*

ܣܩܪܬܐ and ܣܩܪܬܐ rt. ܣܩܪ. f. *red paint.*

ܣܪܐ oftener ܣܪܝ fut. ܢܣܪܐ, pass. part. ܣܪܐ, ܣܪܝܐ. root-meaning *to be stagnant* as water. *a*) *to be putrid, corrupt, to stink;* ܣܪܝܬ ܐܪܥܐ *the land stank* from the plague of frogs. *b*) *to be motionless* from terror. Part. *corrupt, putrid, ill-smelling, foul, fetid;* ܣܪܐ ܪܝܚܗ *its odour is foul;* ܪܝܚܐ ܣܪܝܐ *a bad smell, stink;* ܝܡܐ ܣܪܝܐ *the stagnant sea;* ܪܓܝܓܬܐ ܣܪܝܬܐ *foul lusts;* ܫܡܐ ܣܪܝܐ *a name of infamy.* An epithet of various plants: ܘܪܕܐ ܣܪܝܬܐ *anemone coronaria, rosa foetida;* ܣܟܬܐ ܣܪܝܬܐ *spina foetida;* or *ceratonia siliqua, the locust* or *carob-tree;* ܚܡܥܬܐ ܣܪܝܬܐ *rumex hydrolapathum, horse-sorrel.* Ethpe. ܐܣܬܪܝ *to become rotten.* Pa. ܣܪܝ *to cause to rot* or *stink; to make foul, defile.* Aph. ܐܣܪܝ *to leave to putrefy, make to stink.* Derivative, ܣܪܝܘܬܐ.

ܣܪܒ fut. ܢܣܪܘܒ, act. part. ܣܪܒ, ܣܪܒܐ. *to talk idly* or *foolishly, to prate, boast; to bring false accusations; not to confess, to deny, gainsay;* ܣܪܒܬ ܠܘܩܒܠܟ *I spoke impudently to thy face;* ܡܣܪܒܝܢ ܣܪܒܝܢ ܣܪܝܒܘܬܐ *they talk a lot of nonsense;* ܐܢ ܗܘ ܕܣܪܒܬ ܕܠܐ ܬܘܕܐ ܚܛܗܐ ܕܣܥܪܬ *if you refused to confess the sins you have committed;* ܥܡ ܡܣܪܒܢܐ ܠܐ ܬܣܪܘܒ *gainsay not with the froward.* Derivatives, ܣܪܒܐ, ܣܪܘܒܐ, ܣܪܘܒܘܬܐ, ܣܪܒܐ.

ܣܪܒܐ m. *syrup.*

ܣܪܒܐ pl. ܐ̈ *stakes, pales.*

ܣܪܓ fut. ܢܣܪܘܓ, act. part. ܣܪܓ, ܣܪܓܐ, pass. part. ܣܪܝܓ, ܐ̈, ܬܐ. *to set the warp in the loom, begin the web, to set firmly together, to fabricate; to interweave, entangle;* ܣܪܓܬܢܝ ܒܟܪܣܗ ܕܐܡܝ *Thou didst begin to frame me in my mother's womb;* ܢܣܪܘܓ ܢܚܬܐ *let him weave clothes;* ܐܘܪܚܐ ܕܡܟܫܘܠܐ ܣܪܝܓܐ ܗܘܬ *a road beset* or *entangled with stumblingblocks;* ܒܠܒܫ ܗܘܐ ܒܠܝܐ ܕܣܪܝܓܐ ܠܚܕܪܚܨܗ *he was clad in tatters tied together round his waist.* For ܣܪܝܓܬܐ see below. Ethpe. ܐܣܬܪܓ *to be knotted firmly, bound on, joined together.* Pa. ܣܪܓ denom. verb from ܣܪܓܐ. *to put on a saddle-cloth, to saddle, harness; to adjust armour, arrange* words. Ethpa. ܐܣܬܪܓ *to be harnessed.* Derivatives, ܣܪܘܓܐ, ܣܪܓܐ, ܣܪܝܓܬܐ, ܡܣܪܓܢܐ, ܡܣܪܓܢܘܬܐ.

ܣܪܓܐ pl. ܐ̈ Ar. m. *a saddle, saddle-cloth, housing, caparison.*

ܣܪܓܠ denom. verb Palpel conj. from ܣܪܓܠܐ. *to trace* or *write* lines.

ܣܪܕ fut. ܢܣܪܘܕ. *to remain alone; to quake, be terrified;* ܣܪܕܘ ܓܪܡܘܗܝ ܡܢ ܐܘܟܠܬܗ *his bones quaked with his emotion.* Pael ܣܪܕ *to make to quake, make afraid, terrify;* ܩܠܐ ܕܡܣܪܕ ܫܡܥܬܗ *a rumour the hearing of which terrifies greatly;* ܡܩܫ ܒܐܝܕܘܗܝ ܠܡܣܪܕܘ *he claps his hands to frighten away the mice;* ܡܘܬܐ ܡܣܪܕܢܐ *terrible deaths.* Ethpa. ܐܣܬܪܕ *to be made to quake, be struck with terror; to be terrified, alarmed;* ܐܣܬܪܕ ܡܢ ܚܝܠܐ ܕܪܘܪܒܢܝܟ *be alarmed at the power of thy nobles.* Derivatives, ܣܪܕܐ, ܣܪܘܕܐ, ܣܪܘܕܬܐ, ܣܪܕܐ, ܡܣܪܕܢܐ, ܡܣܪܕܢܘܬܐ.

ܣܪܕܐ m. *a sieve.*

ܣܪܕܐ rt. ܣܪܕ. m. *terror.*

ܣܪܕܐܒ Pers. m. *an ice-cellar, ice-house.*

ܣܪܕܘܢ or ܣܪܕܝܢ and other spellings. *a*) m. *a sard, sardius;* ܣܪܕܘܢ ܣܪܕܝܘܢ ܗ̇ ܟܐܦܐ ܣܘܡܩܬܐ ܘܡܨܡܚܢܝܬܐ *the sard or carnelian is a shining red stone.* *b*) the island *Sardinia.*

ܣܪܕܘܢܘܟܣ σαρδόνυξ, *the sardonyx.*

ܣܪܕܘܣ i. e *prow* of a ship.

ܣܪܕܝܢ *a*) σάρδιον, *the carnelian* or *sardine stone.* *b*) *the juice of the wild cucumber* or *a medicine prepared from it.*

ܣܪܗܒ and ܐܣܬܪܗܒ Saphel and Estaphal conjugations of verb ܪܗܒ *to hasten;* see under ܪܗܒ.

ܣܪܘܐ *the cypress.*

ܣܪܘܒܐ pl. ܝܢ̈, ܒܐ̈ rt. ܣܪܒ. m. *a caviller, gainsayer;* ܝܗܘܕܝܐ ܣܪܘܒܐ ܘܡܣܪܚܢܐ *the gainsaying and rebellious Jews.*

ܣܪܘܒܐܝܬ rt. ܣܪܒ. adv. *very rapidly, over-hastily* of a man talking so quickly that he cannot be understood.

ܣܪܘܒܘܬܐ rt. ܣܪܒ. f. *idle* or *foolish speech, trifling, impudence; calumny.*

ܣܪܘܒܐ rt. ܣܪܒ. m. *cavilling, disparagement.*

ܣܪܘܓ *a*) the patriarch *Serug.* *b*) *Sarug,* a district of Mesopotamia; its capital is ܒܛܢܢ or ܒܛܢܢ ܕܣܪܘܓ *Batna of Serug* also called *Sarug.*

ܣܪܘܓܝܐ, ܝܬܐ *of Sarug;* ܝܥܩܘܒ ܣܪܘܓܝܐ *James* Bishop *of Batna* or *Sarug;* ܒܡܫܘܚܬܐ ܣܪܘܓܝܬܐ *in the metre of Sarug* i. e. *in twelve-syllable metre* in which James of Sarug wrote.

ܣܪܘܓܐ rt. ܣܪܓ. m. *a porch* perhaps of lattice-work.

ܣܪܘܓܐ, ܣܪܘܓܝܬܐ pl. ܓܐ̈, ܝܬܐ̈ f. *a ladle; an iron pan.*

ܣܪܘܕ *rue-seed.*

ܣܪܘܚܐ, ܣܪܘܚܬܐ pl. m. ܝܢ̈, ܚܐ̈ pl. f. ܬܐ̈ or ܚܬܐ̈ rt. ܣܪܚ. *noxious, baneful, ravenous, devastating, vicious;* ܕܐܒܐ ܣܪܘܚܐ *ravening wolves;* ܫܐܕܐ ܣܪܘܚܐ *baneful demons;* ܥܒܕܐ ܣܪܘܚܐ *a wicked servant.*

ܣܪܘܚܐܝܬ rt. ܣܪܚ. adv. *fiercely, cruelly.*

ܣܪܘܚܘܬܐ rt. ܣܪܚ. f. *detriment, corruption, depravity.*

ܣܪܘܛܐ, ܣܪܘܛ rt. ܣܪܛ. m. *a writer.*

ܣܪܘܝܐ, ܣܪܘܝ rt. ܣܪܝ. *cohesive, obstructive;* ܟܝܡܘܣܐ ܕܣܪܘܝܢ *clogging humours.*

ܣܪܘܝܘܬܐ rt. ܣܪܝ. f. *adherence.*

ܣܪܝܢ denom. verb from ܣܘܪܝܝܐ, part. ܡܣܪܝܢ *to be well acquainted with the Syriac language.*

ܣܪܘܦܐ rt. ܣܪܦ. m. *one who sips.*

ܣܪܘܦܐ and ܣܪܘܦܘܬܐ rt. ܣܪܦ. f. *sipping, swallowing; a draught, gulp.*

ܣܪܘܦܐ, ܣܪܘܦܐ or ܣܪܘܦܐ rt. ܣܪܦ. m. *a particle* of mist, *a cloudy day.*

ܣܪܘܩܬܐ rt. ܣܪܩ. f. *a*) *a* weaver's *sley* or *reed.* *b*) *a rake, harrow.*

ܣܪܘܫ m. alchym. *refined and reddened brass.*

ܣܪܘܛܐ m. *malicious, malignant.*

ܣܪܚ fut. ܢܣܪܘܚ, act. part. ܣܪܚ, ܣܪܚܐ, pass. part. ܣܪܝܚ, ܚܐ, ܚܬܐ. *a*) *to hurt, injure, damage, devastate; to tear, wound, mangle* as wild beasts, as locusts, pestilence, a demon, &c. with acc. ܒ or ܥܠ; ܣܪܚ ܠܥܝܢܗ *he tore out* his *eye;* ܟܕ ܠܐ ܣܪܚ ܒܗ ܡܕܡ *having done him no harm;* ܩܠܐ ܕܣܪܚܝܢ *rending claps* of thunder. Esp. with ܒ, *to make an onslaught, onset* of a flood, the enemy, &c.; ܛܪܕ ܕܐܒܐ ܕܠܐ ܢܣܪܘܚ ܒܡܪܥܝܬܐ *he drove off the wolf that it might not attack the flock.* *b*) *to throttle, choke* as a noose, as weeds choke growth. *c*) *to defile, corrupt* esp. *to violate* a maiden; ܐܢܬܬܐ ܕܣܪܚܐ ܥܠ ܒܥܠܗ *a woman who trespasses against her husband;* ܣܪܚܗ ܠܣܝܦܗ ܒܕܡܐ *he made his sword foul with blood;* ܣܪܚ ܦܓܪܗ ܒܙܢܝܘܬܐ *he defiles his body* with fornication. *d*) absol. *to commit sin, do iniquity.* *e*) *to vitiate, corrupt* the text, the sense. *f*) *to indicate, signify.*

Pass. part. *a*) *corrupt, damaged, feeble, vicious, foul;* ܣܪܝܚ ܒܗܕܡܘܗܝ *enfeebled in his limbs;* ܡܚܫܒܬܐ ܣܪܝܚܬܐ ܘܠܐ ܡܛܟܣܬܐ *bad and disorderly thoughts;* ܦܘܚܡܐ ܣܪܝܚܐ *corrupt codices;* ܐܢܫܐ ܣܪܝܚܐ *wicked men;* ܡܣܟܢܐ ܘܣܪܝܚܐ *the poor and feeble.* Fem. pl. emph. ܣܪܝܚܬܐ *wicked actions, crimes, vices.* *b*) *consecrated* to office. Ethpe. ܐܣܬܪܚ *to be wounded, mangled, marred; to be damaged, laid waste, desolated.* Pa. ܣܰܪܰܚ *to grievously mar, maim, mutilate* esp. the limbs; *to destroy; to befoul.* Ethpa. ܐܶܣܬܰܪܰܚ *to be destroyed, mutilated, injured, maimed; to be corrupt.*

Aph. ܐܰܣܪܰܚ *a) to put forward, propound, express, utter* a riddle, a proposition, objection, question, answer, &c.; *to question, to object;* ܣܒܪܘܬܐ ܡܫܚܠܦܬܐ ܒܟܝܢܗ ܐܣܪܚܘ *they offered various suppositions about it;* ܡܰܣܪܚܺܝܢ ܒܡܫܡܥܬܐ ܩܠܐ *uttering fair words;* ܐܣܪܚ ܠܗܘܢ ܩܘܫܬܐ *he declared the truth unto them;* ܗܿܢܝܢ ܕܩܕܡܝܟܘܢ ܡܣܪܚ ܐܢܐ *that which I propound to you.* With ܚܣܕܬܐ *to reproach, recriminate. b) to brandish, cast* spears, &c.; *to dart, emit* vituperation. *c) to bring out, distribute, bestow;* ܡܣܪܚ ܡܢ ܓܙܟ ܘܡܦܠܓ ܠܡܣܟܢܐ *distributing out of Thy treasure and dividing to the needy;* ܐܣܪܚ ܫܡܗܐ ܐܕܡ Adam *bestowed names.* With ܫܘܒܩܢܐ *to pardon, to grant* or *pronounce pardon. d) to offer, proffer, tender* a request; ܟܠ ܕܩܪܐ ܢܣܪܚ ܨܠܘܬܐ ܥܠ ܕܘܝܘܬܝ *whoso reads let him proffer a prayer for my wretched self. e) to publish, edit, bring out* a book. *f) to spread out* snares. *g) to sprout out, grow luxuriantly* as a tree. *h) to designate, ordain, consecrate* a deacon, priest, bishop; *to appoint, make* a king, leader, a Caesar. *i) to inflict* pain or damage, *to corrupt* ܒܫܘܚܕܐ *with a bribe;* also same as Pael *to wound, injure.* Ethtaph. ܐܶܬܬܰܣܪܰܚ *a) to be elected, appointed;* esp. *to be ordained* deacon or priest, *to be consecrated* as a bishop or patriarch. *b)* gram. *to be expressed* as the plural. Derivatives, ܣܘܪܚܐ, ܣܘܪܚܢܐ, ܣܪܘܚܐ, ܣܪܘܚܐܝܬ, ܣܪܘܚܘܬܐ, ܣܪܚܐ, ܣܪܝܚܐܝܬ, ܣܪܝܚܘܬܐ, ܡܣܪܚܢܐ, ܡܣܪܚܢܐ, ܡܣܪܚܢܘܬܐ, ܡܣܪܘܚܐܝܬ, ܡܣܪܚܢܘܬܐ, ܡܣܪܚܢܘܬܐ, ܡܬܣܪܚܢܐ, ܡܬܣܪܚܢܐ, ܡܬܣܪܚܢܘܬܐ.

ܣܘܪܚܢܐ rt. ܣܪܚ. m. *corruption, depravity, violation of the marriage vow.*

ܣܪܰܛ and ܣܪܶܛ fut. ܢܶܣܪܘܿܛ, act. part. ܣܳܪܶܛ, ܣܳܪܛܳܐ, pass. part. ܣܪܺܝܛ, ܣܪܺܝܛܳܐ. *to scratch, make a line* or *stroke, indent; to draw* or *write a line, write down;* ܣܪܘܿܛ ܒܦܪܙܠܐ *scratch with steel;* ܠܡܶܣܪܰܛ ܒܟܬܝܒܬܐ ܨܒܘܬܐ *to note down matters in writing.* Ethpe. ܐܶܣܬܪܶܛ *to be abraded, torn off* as the skin; *to be inscribed.* Pa. ܣܰܪܶܛ *to tear off* skin; *to write down.* Ethpa. ܐܶܣܬܰܪܰܛ *to be lacerated, gashed; to be written.* Derivatives, ܣܘܪܛܐ, ܣܘܪܛܐ, ܣܘܪܛܢܘܬܐ, ܣܘܪܛܐܝܬ, ܣܪܘܛܐ, ܣܪܛܐ, ܣܪܛܐ, ܣܪܛܘܢܐ, ܣܪܛܘܢܘܢܐ, ܣܪܛܢܐ, ܣܪܛܢܐܝܬ, ܡܣܪܛܐ, ܡܣܪܛܢܘܬܐ.

ܣܶܪܛܳܐ pl. ܐ̈ rt. ܣܪܛ. m. *a scratch, gash; a line, character, tittle;* ܣܶܪܛܳܐ ܦܫܺܝܛܳܐ *the simple* or *ordinary character* i.e. Maronite script.

ܣܪܳܛܳܐ rt. ܣܪܛ. m. *an incision; writing.*

ܣܶܪܛܘܿܢܳܐ pl. ܐ̈ rt. ܣܪܛ. m. gram. *a short line* or *point* over a word, = the accent ܚܛܳܪܳܐ.

ܣܶܪܛܘܿܢܘܿܢܳܐ rt. ܣܪܛ. m. dimin. of ܣܶܪܛܘܿܢܳܐ. *a tiny line* or *mark.*

ܣܰܪܛܳܢܳܐ pl. ܐ̈ rt. ܣܪܛ. m. *the crab;* a sign of the Zodiac, *Cancer;* the disease *cancer.*

ܣܰܪܛܳܢܳܐܺܝܬ from ܣܪܛܢܐ. *crab-like, sideways.*

ܣܪܶܝ; see ܣܪܳܐ.

ܣܪܺܝܓܳܐ, ܣܪܺܝܓܬܳܐ pl. ܐ̈ܬܳ rt. ܣܪܓ. f. *net, net-work; wicker-work, a basket; a lattice before book-shelves; matting, a mat.*

ܣܪܺܝܓܳܐܺܝܬ rt. ܣܪܓ. adv. *intricately, interwoven* as a net.

ܣܪܺܝܓܘܼܬܳܐ rt. ܣܪܓ. f. *saddling, caparisoning; housings.*

ܣܪܺܝܕ, ܣܪܺܝܕܳܐ, ܣܪܺܝܕܬܳܐ rt. ܣܪܕ. *a fugitive, survivor; a remnant, remainder;* ܠܐ ܫܒܰܩ ܡܶܢܗܘܢ ܣܪܺܝܕܳܐ *he left none of them remaining;* ܣܪܺܝܕܳܐ ܕܥܰܡܡܳܐ *the remnant of the nation;* ܐܰܪ̈ܥܳܬܳܐ ܣܪ̈ܺܝܕܳܬܳܐ ܘܡܶܣܟ̈ܢܳܬܳܐ *neglected and poor lands.*

ܣܪܺܝܘܼܬܳܐ rt. ܣܪܐ. f. *stink, rankness, sewage; snivel, mucus; foulness, filthiness.*

ܣܪܙܠ Pers. *the medlar.*

ܣܪܺܝܚܳܐܺܝܬ rt. ܣܪܚ. adv. *savagely, cruelly.*

ܣܪܺܝܚܘܼܬܳܐ rt. ܣܪܚ. f. *harm, hurt; a vicious life, depravity.*

ܣܪܺܝܟܘܼܬܳܐ rt. ܣܪܟ. f. *attachment, addictedness; a burr.*

ܣܪܺܝܣܳܐ and ܣܰܪܝܣܳܐ pl. ܐ̈ m. *an eunuch; castrated.* Derivatives, verb ܣܪܣ, ܣܘܪܣܐ, ܡܣܪܣܐ.

ܣܪܺܝܒܘܼܬܳܐ rt. ܣܪܒ. f. *being deprived of the ears;* metaph. *hardness of heart.*

ܣܪܝܩܐܝܬ rt. ܣܪܩ. adv. *empty, empty-handed; vainly, in vain, without cause.*

ܣܪܝܩܘܢ = ܣܪܝܩܘܢ *minium.*

ܣܪܝܩܘܬܐ rt. ܣܪܩ. f. *vanity, nothingness, an idol;* ܦܬܟܪܐ ܕܣܪܝܩܘܬܐ *idols of naught;* ܒܣܪܝܩܘܬܐ *in vain, uselessly;* ܡܠܐ ܣܪܝܩܬܐ *idle talk;* ܚܘܫܒܐ ܣܪܝܩܐ *a vain thought, vanity;* ܥܡܠܐ ܣܪܝܩܐ *unprofitable labour.*

ܣܪܟ and ܣܪܟ fut. ܢܣܪܘܟ, parts. ܣܪܟ, ܣܪܟܐ, and ܣܪܝܟ, ܟܐ, ܟܬܐ. *to adhere, stick* as a plaster; *to cohere, combine* as quicksilver with other metals; metaph. *to be addicted;* ܬܢܢܐ ܣܪܟܝܢ ܠܐܐܪ *fumes unite with the air;* ܛܥܝܘܬܐ ܕܣܪܝܟ ܗܘܐ ܒܗ *the error to which he adhered;* ܗܝܡܢܘܬܐ ܕܣܪܝܟܐ ܒܪܚܡܬ ܐܢܫܘܬܐ *faith combined with philanthropy;* ܗܢܘܢ ܕܣܪܝܟܝܢ ܒܨܒܘܬܐ ܥܠܡܢܝܬܐ *those who are attached to worldly concerns.* Ethpe. ܐܣܬܪܟ *to be fastened, combined immediately.* Pa. *to stick, cling fast, cohere, adhere.* Ethpa. ܐܣܬܪܟ *to become gradually attached* or *addicted to.* Derivatives, ܣܪܘܟܐ, ܣܪܘܟܘܬܐ, ܣܪܝܟܘܬܐ, ܣܪܟܐ.

ܣܪܟܐ rt. ܣܪܟ. m. *glue; adhesion, attachment.*

ܣܪܟܘܣ or ܣܪܟܘܣ m. *a fern* probably *filix mas.*

ܣܪܡ fut. ܢܣܪܘܡ. *to cut off the tip of the nose.* Pass. part. ܣܪܝܡ, ܡܐ, ܡܬܐ. *flat-nosed, lop-nosed.* Derivatives, ܣܪܡܐ, ܣܪܡܘܬܐ, ܣܪܡܬܢܐ.

ܣܪܡ, ܣܪܡܐ rt. ܣܪܡ. m. *flat-nosed, having a part of the nose* or *of the lip cut off.*

ܣܪܡܝ Pers. the plant *orach, atriplex hortensis.*

ܣܪܡܘܬܐ rt. ܣܪܡ. f. *flatness of nose; mutilation of the nose* or *ear.*

ܣܪܡܬܢܐ rt. ܣܪܡ. m. same as ܣܪܝܡ and ܣܪܡܐ.

ܣܪܢܐ pl. ܢܐ m. *an axle, axis; the pole.*

ܣܪܢܝܐ = ܣܘܪܢܝܐ; see above.

ܣܪܣ denom. verb Pael conj. *a*) from ܣܪܣܐ. *to twist, twine;* part. ܡܣܪܣܐ *having a twisted ornament* round the brim. *b*) from ܣܪܝܣܐ. *to castrate, make an eunuch of.* Ethpa. ܐܣܬܪܣ *to be castrated.*

ܣܪܦܠܘܬܐ dialect of Tirhan. f. a bird's *crop.*

ܣܪܣܦ from ܣܪܦ. *to scrawl, spoil* paper.

ܣܪܣܩܐ and ܣܪܣܩܐ pl. ܩܐ m. French *saucisse, a sausage.*

ܣܪܣܠܐ pl. ܠܐ m. *a thread.*

ܣܪܦ perhaps *to choke, suffocate;* ܦܬܘܬܐ ܕܠܚܡܐ ܣܪܦܬܗ ܘܡܝܬ *a morsel of bread choked him and he died.* Pass. part. ܣܪܝܦ, ܣܪܝܦܐ *malformed* or *injured* in any way, *slit, bored through* esp. of the ear; ܐܡܪܐ ܕܣܪܝܦܐ ܐܕܢܗ *a lamb marked by a notch in its ear.* Derivatives, ܣܪܦܘܬܐ, ܣܪܦܐ, ܣܪܦܐ.

ܣܪܦܐ rt. ܣܪܦ. m. *the notch* of an arrow.

ܣܪܦܐ rt. ܣܪܦ. m. *obstruction of the gullet, choking.*

ܣܪܥܦ Parel conj. of root ܣܥܦ not used in Syr. *to branch out, increase* intrans., *propagate;* ܐܝܠܢܐ ܡܣܪܥܦܐ *spreading trees;* ܬܠܬܐ ܫܪܒܢ ܣܪܥܦܝ ܡܢ *three races branched out* from Noah. Gram. *to conjugate; to derive.* Ethparal ܐܣܬܪܥܦ *to put forth branches, branch out, subdivide;* ܗܕܐ ܕܪܝܫܐ ܐܣܬܪܥܦܬ ܠܬܪܬܝܢ ܗܪܣܝܣ this opinion *branches out into two heresies.* Gram. *to be conjugated; to be derived;* ܝܡܐ ܡܣܬܪܥܦܐ ܐܝܟ ܒܢܐ ܘܩܪܐ *imā (to swear) is conjugated like b'nā (to build) and q'rā (to read).* Derivatives, ܣܘܪܥܦܐ, ܣܘܪܥܦܘܬܐ, ܣܪܥܦܬܐ.

ܣܪܥܦܬܐ only pl. ܣܪܥܦܬܐ rt. ܣܥܦ. f. *branches, a branching out, fork; layers, suckers.*

ܣܪܛ fut. ܢܣܪܘܛ, act. part. ܣܪܛ, ܣܪܛܐ. *a*) *to sup up, swallow up, absorb;* ܡܘܬܐ ܣܪܛ ܠܢ *death swallows us up.* *b*) *to block up;* ܣܪܛ ܠܬܪܥܐ *he blocked the gates.* Ethpe. ܐܣܬܪܛ *to be blocked up;* ܢܣܬܪܛ ܦܘܡܗ ܕܡܥܪܬܐ ܒܟܐܦܐ *let the mouth* of the cave *be blocked with stones.* Pael ܣܪܛ *a*) *to gulp up, swallow greedily.* *b*) *to fill, obstruct.* Aph. ܐܣܪܛ *to make to swallow.* Derivatives, ܣܘܪܛܐ, ܣܪܘܛܐ, ܣܪܘܛܘܬܐ, ܣܪܛܬܐ, ܣܪܛܐ.

ܣܪܛܐ rt. ܣܪܛ. m. *gruel.*

ܣܪܦܐ pl. ܦܝܢ, ܦܐ m. *a seraph, seraphim,* the second order of angels.

ܣܪܦܘܫ Pers. *a tarboush, skull-cap.*

ܣܪܩ fut. ܢܣܪܘܩ, act. part. ܣܪܩ, ܣܪܩܐ, pass. part. ܣܪܝܩ, ܩܐ, ܩܬܐ. *a*) *to comb* the hair or cotton cloth; *to torture with an iron comb.* b) *to make to be in vain, to bring to naught.* Pass. part. a) *combed, carded, lacerated with combs.* b) *empty, vain, worthless;* ܓܘܒܐ ܣܪܝܩ ܗܘܐ *the pit was empty;* ܐ̈ܢܫܐ ܣܪ̈ܝܩܐ *worthless fellows;* ܦܬܓܡܐ ܣܪ̈ܝܩܐ *vain babbling;* ܫܘܒܚܐ ܣܪܝܩܐ *vain-glory;* ܣܪܝܩ ܫܘܒܚܐ *vain-glorious;* ܣܪ̈ܝܩܘܬܐ ܕܥܠܡܐ *worldly vanities.* ETHPE. ܐܣܬܪܩ a) *to be combed, to be torn with an iron comb.* b) refl. *to become empty, bare, lacking; to choose poverty* as monks; ܡܣܬܪܩ ܡܢ ܥܠܡܐ *he divests himself of the world,* i. e. *of worldly possessions;* ܐܣܬܪܩ ܡܢ ܙܝܢܐ *he lays aside his armour.* PAEL ܣܪܩ a) *to empty, toss out, lay bare, lay waste; to deprive, bereave;* ܠܐ ܣܪܩܘ ܡܢ ܡܐܢܐ ܠܡܐܢܐ *they have not emptied from one vessel to another;* ܣܪܩܬܟ ܡܢ ܥܘܬܪܐ *I have stripped thee of riches;* ܣܪܩ ܡܪܢ ܠܫܝܘܠ our Lord *spoiled Sheol.* b) esp. *to give up, renounce, make* oneself *poor;* ܣܪܩ ܢܦܫܗ ܡܪܢ our Lord *emptied Himself;* ܡܣܪܩ ܡܢ ܥܠܡܐ *one who has renounced the world.* c) *to evacuate, eject, clear out.* d) *to render null* and *void.* e) gram. *to deprive of, leave without* a point, a vowel. Pass. part. ܡܣܪܩ, ܡܣܪܩܐ. *empty, vain, devoid of; having given up worldly possessions;* ܡܣܪܩܐ ܡܢ ܢܘܩܙܐ *devoid of points.* ETHPA. ܐܣܬܪܩ a) *to be emptied out, left bare; to be deprived of* with ܡܢ, *to be impoverished;* ܐܣܬܪܩܘ ܟܠܗܘܢ ܡܢ ܡܕܝܢܬܐ *they poured out of the city;* ܐܣܬܪܩܘ ܡܢ ܪ̈ܟܫܐ *they were deprived of their horses, lost their horses.* b) *to renounce* worldly possessions; ܐܣܬܪܩܘ ܡܛܠ ܡܪܢ *renounce for our Lord's sake.* c) *to be made null* and *void.* ETHPAUAL ܐܣܬܪܘܩ denom. verb from ܣܪܘܩܐ. *to be overclouded.* DERIVATIVES, ܣܪܩܐ, ܣܪܘܩܐ, ܣܪܘܩܝܐ, ܣܪܩܘܬܐ, ܣܪܩܘܬܐ, ܣܪܝܩܐ, ܣܪܝܩܘܬܐ, ܣܪܝܩܐܝܬ, ܡܣܪܩܐ, ܡܣܪܩܢܐ, ܡܣܪܩܘܬܐ, ܡܣܪܩܢܘܬܐ, ܡܣܬܪܩܢܐ, ܡܣܬܪܩܢܘܬܐ, ܡܣܪܩܢܘܬܐ.

ܣܪܩܐ pl. ܐ̈ rt. ܣܪܩ. m. *a comb, a carding-comb, hackle; an instrument of torture with iron claws.*

ܣܪܩܐ pl. ܐ̈ rt. ܣܪܩ. m. a) *torturing with the iron comb, tearing the flesh, laceration.* b) *emptying out, evacuation.*

ܣܪܩܘܬܐ rt. ܣܪܩ. f. same as ܣܪܩܬܐ.

ܣܪܩܝ, ܣܪܩܝܐ, ܣܪܩܝܐ *oriental, Saracen, an Arab;* ܠܫܢܐ ܣܪܩܝܐ ܐܘ ܛܝܝܐ *the Saracenic or Arabic language.*

ܣܪܩܝܘܬܐ f. *the religion of the Saracens.*

ܣܪܩܝܢܐ m. *dung.*

ܣܪܩܬܐ rt. ܣܪܩ. f. *linen* or *cotton waste, tow, hards; refuse.*

ܣܪܒܪ = ܐܪܒܪܝܣ. *berberis, the common barberry.*

ܣܬܐ APHEL ܐܣܬܝ denom. verb from ܣܬܘܐ. *to winter, pass the winter;* ܐܣܬܝܢܢ ܥܡ ܚܕܕܐ *we have passed the winter together.*

ܣܬܐ or ܣܬܐܠܐ pl. ܣܬܝܢ, ܣܬ̈ܐ f. *a vine, a creeping plant, a vine-twig, sucker; a stem;* ܣܬܐ ܕܓܘܦܢܐ *a vine-sprout;* ܣܬ̈ܐ ܕܕܩܠܐ *palm-stems, palm-trees.*

ܣܬܐ, ܣܬܐ or ܣܬܠܐ f. *a mortar; a bell.*

ܣܬܘܐ pl. ܐ̈ m. *winter; stormy weather, a storm;* ܣܬܘ̈ܐ ܪܘܪ̈ܒܐ *great storms.* DERIVATIVES, verb ܐܣܬܝ see ܣܬܐ, ܣܬܘܝܐ, ܡܣܬܝܢܘܬܐ.

ܣܬܘܪܐ m. *a turban, cap, head-dress* worn by women.

ܣܬܘܝ, ܣܬܘܝܐ, ܣܬܘܝܬܐ from ܣܬܘܐ. *wintry, stormy, cold.*

ܣܬܘܪܐ, ܣܬܘܪܬܐ rt. ܣܬܪ. *destructive; a destroyer; a slanderer.*

ܣܬܘܪܘܬܐ pl. ܐ̈ rt. ܣܬܪ. m. *destruction, ruining; a slander, calumny; a refutation.*

ܣܬܝܠܐ m. *food prepared with vinegar, pickles.*

ܣܬܝܪܐܝܬ rt. ܣܬܪ. adv. *secretly.*

ܣܬܝܪܘܬܐ rt. ܣܬܪ. f. *secrecy.*

ܣܬܟܐ m. alchem. *iron, steel.* Cf. ܣܛܟܐ.

ܣܬܪ fut. ܢܣܬܘܪ, act. part. ܣܬܪ, ܣܬܪܐ, pass. part. ܣܬܝܪ, ܐ, ܬܐ. a) *to break down, pull down, destroy, ruin* opp. ܒܢܐ *to build up;* ܣܬܪܘܗܝ ܕܩܒܪܐ *riflers of the tomb;* ܢܣܬܘܪ ܛܘܪܢܘܬܗ ܕܐܟܠܩܪܨܐ *He will break down the tyranny of the Accuser.* b) *to refute, confute, reject* opp. ܒܢܐ *to establish;* ܣܬܪܝܢ ܡܚܫ̈ܒܬܐ *we refute reasonings;* ܢܣܬܘܪ ܐܢ ܚܝܠܐ ܕܩܢܘ̈ܢܐ if *he destroy the force of the canons.* c) *to ruin* a reputation, *speak against, traduce;* ܠܐ ܬܣܬܘܪ ܠܐܢܫ ܕܢܦܩ ܡܢ ܥܠܡܐ *thou shalt not speak against any one who has left this world;* ܐܝܠܝܢ ܕܣܬܪܝܢ ܠܝ *those who traduce me.* d) of a wound, *to break out again, break open.* e) *to cover; to shelter.*

Pass. part. a) *concealed, hidden, secret;* ܒܐܬܪܐ ܣܬܝܪܐ *in a secret place, in secret;* ܐܪ̈ܙܐ ܣܬܝܪ̈ܐ *hidden mysteries;* f. pl. *secrets.* b) f. pl. *ruined places, ruins.*

ETHPE. ܐܣܬܬܪ a) *to be thrown down, ruined, destroyed;* ܐܣܬܬܪ ܗܘܐ ܗܝܟܠܐ *the Temple was destroyed;* ܠܐ ܡܫܒܩܝܢܢ ܕܬܣܬܬܪ ܗܝܡܢܘܬܢ *we will not suffer our faith to be overthrown.* b) *to be traduced, calumniated.* c) *to break out* as sores. PA. ܣܬܪ a) *to conceal, cover, bury; to obscure, occult, eclipse;* ܡܣܬܪ ܐܦ̈ܘܗܝ ܒܚܫܘܟܐ *he conceals his face in the darkness;* ܥܪܦܠܐ ܣܬܪ ܠܢܘܗܪܗ *mist concealed the light of the moon and stars.* b) *to shelter, protect, defend;* ܠܡܟܣܝܘ ܘܠܡܣܬܪܘ ܡܢ ܐܪܥܫܐ *to cover over and shelter from storm;* ܬܚܝܬ ܟܢܦ̈ܝܟ ܣܬܪ ܠܢ *protect us under Thy wings.* Part. pass. *hidden, concealed, secret, sure, safe, protected;* ܕܘܟܬܐ ܡܣܬܪܬܐ *a safe place;* ܣܝܡܬܐ ܡܣܬܪܬܐ *hidden* or *safely guarded treasure;* ܡܕ̈ܝܢܬܐ ܡܣܬܪ̈ܬܐ ܡܢ ܡܚܒ̈ܠܐ fenced cities *safe from the spoilers.*

ETHPA. a) *to be concealed, sheltered, protected; to lie hid, seek shelter, take refuge;* ܬܚܝܬ ܟܢܦ̈ܘܗܝ ܬܣܬܬܪ *under His wings shalt thou take refuge;* ܐܣܬܬܪ ܡܢ ܛܝܒܘܬܐ ܐܠܗܝܬܐ *he was protected by divine grace.* b) *to be laid in the earth, buried.* c) astron. *to be obscured, in occultation.* DERIVATIVES, ܣܘܬܪܐ, ܣܬܘܪܐ, ܣܬܘܪܝܐ, ܣܬܝܪܐܝܬ, ܣܬܝܪܘܬܐ, ܣܬܪܐ, ܣܬܪܐ, ܣܬܪܐ, ܡܣܬܪܢܐܝܬ, ܡܣܬܪܢܘܬܐ, ܡܣܬܪܢܐ, ܡܣܬܪܐ, ܡܣܬܪܢܘܬܐ.

ܣܬܪܐ rt. ܣܬܪ. m. a) *a secret;* ܒܣܬܪܐ *in secret, secretly.* b) *ruin; calumny.* For ܒܣܬܪ subst. and prep. see under ܒ.

ܣܬܪܐ pl. ܐ̈ rt. ܣܬܪ. m. a) *a covert, shelter, hiding-place, refuge; protection.* b) *a cover, covering, wall-hanging.*

ܣܬܪܐ rt. ܣܬܪ. m. *destruction, ruin.*

ܫܬܬ denom. verb Pael conj. from ܐܫܬܐ, ܐܫܬܐܣܐ. *to set firmly, establish, stay, settle; to plant firmly, implant, to take root;* ܫܬܬܘ ܓܐܪ̈ܝܗܘܢ ܥܠ ܝܬܪܐ *they set their arrows to the bow-string;* ܫܬܬܘܢܢܝ ܒܒܣܡ̈ܐ *stay me with spices;* ܫܬܬ ܒܝܫܬܐ ܘܐܬܥܫܢܬ *evil has taken root and waxed sturdy.* Pass. part. *founded, stable, steady, sure;* ܒܝܬܐ ܡܫܬܬ ܫܦܝܪ *a house well founded;* ܠܐ ܥܕܟܝܠ ܗܝܡܢܘܬܐ ܡܫܬܬܐ ܗܘܬ ܒܗܘܢ *faith had not yet struck firm root in them.* ETHPA. ܐܫܬܬܬ *to be settled, established; to be rooted, implanted.* DERIVATIVES, ܫܬܬܐ, ܡܫܬܬܢܐܝܬ, ܡܫܬܬܢܘܬܐ, ܡܫܬܬܢܐ.

⁘ ܫܠܡ ܣܕܪܐ ܕܣܡܟܬ ܘܠܐܠܗܐ ܫܘܒܚܐ ⁘

⁘ ܒܪܝܟ ܡܪܝ، ܘܡܥܕܪܢ ܒܟܬܒܐ ܗܢܐ ܕܒܟ. ܕܥܠܟ ܐܬܟܠܬ
ܒܫܘܠܡܗ ܕܟܬܒܢ: ܘܡܥܕܪܢܝܟ ܘܛܝܒܘܬܟ
ܢܗܘܘܢ ܥܡܢ ܥܠ ܥܠܡ ܥܠܡܝܢ. ܐܡܝܢ ⁘

⁘ ܥ ⁘

ܥ

ܥ, ܥܐ *Ain*, the sixteenth letter of the alphabet; as a numeral 70; with ܕ prefixed *the seventieth;* with a line above, ܥ̄, 700.

ܥ̄

ܥ̄ contraction a) for ܥܒܪܝܐ *the Hebrew text.* b) for ܥܬܝܩܐ *ancient;* ܥ̄ ܒܨ̄ = ܒܨܚܚܐ ܥܬܝܩܐ *in an ancient codex.*

ܥܐܕܐ pl. ܥܐ̈ܕܐ rt. ܥܕ cf. Arab. m. *a day of assembly, a festival, feast, feast-day;* ܕܛܝ̈ܝܐ *the festival of the Arabs, the Bairam;* ܕܡܛܠ̈ܐ *the feast of tabernacles;* ܕܕܢܚܐ or ܕܕܢܚܐ *the festival of the Epiphany;* ܕܦܨܚܐ *Easter.*

ܥܐܕܢܝܐ, ܝܬܐ rt. ܥܕ. *festal;* ܐܓܪ̈ܬܐ ܥܐܕܢܝ̈ܬܐ *Festal Letters* e.g. letters about the special feast, Easter; ܫܝܦܘܪܐ ܥܐܕܢܝܐ *the festal trumpet.*

ܥܐܕܥܐܕ or ܥܐܕܥܐܕ = ܥܕܥܕ Palpel conj. of ܥܕ.

ܥܐܕܪܘܪܘܬܐ rt. ܥܕܪ, ܥܕ. f. *rooting up, stubbing.*

ܥܐܙ, ܥܐܙܐ *a*) act. part. of verb ܥܙ. *b*) ܥܐܙܐ = ܥܙܐ and ܥܙܐ pr. n. *Gaza*, the chief city of the Philistines.

ܥܐܛܘܦܘܬܐ rt. ܥܛܦ. f. *feebleness, languor.*

ܥܐܠ, ܥܐܠܐ *a*) act. part. of verb ܥܠ. *b*) ܥܐܠܐ = ܥܠܐ *a bramble.*

ܥܐܦܐ also spelt ܥܦܐ and ܐܥܦܐ pl. ܝܢ, ܐ̈ rt. ܥܦ. *double, multiplied;* ܡܐܐ ܥܐܦ̈ܐ *an hundredfold.*

ܥܒܐ and ܥܒܝ fut. ܢܥܒܐ. *to swell, thicken, harden.* Part. adj. ܥܒܐ, ܥܒܝܐ, ܥܒܝܬܐ. *swollen, thick, dense, gross, fat, heavy;* ܥܒ̈ܝܢ ܗܘܘ ܥܝ̈ܢܘܗܝ *his eyes were swollen;* ܥܒܝܬܐܝܬ ܡܩܦ *he is thick-set;* ܦܓܪ̈ܐ ܥܒ̈ܝܐ *heavy bodies;* ܥܪܦܠܐ ܥܒܝܬܐ *dense fog.* Metaph. *dense, dull, material, crass, uncultivated;* ܥܒ̈ܝܝ ܣܘܟܠܐ *dense of understanding;* ܬܚܘܡ̈ܐ ܥܒ̈ܝܐ *clumsy definitions;* ܐܬܪܐ ܥܒܝܐ *an unlearned country;* ܩ̈ܠܐ ܥܒ̈ܝܐ *flat* or *bass sounds* opp. ܡܩܛ̈ܢܐ *sharp, treble;* gram. ܐܬܘ̈ܬܐ ܥܒ̈ܝܬܐ *full* or *heavy letters.* Ethpe. ܐܬܥܒܝ *to swell.* Pa. ܥܒܝ *to make heavy, to harden; to be* or *become thick, to condense;* ܡܥܒܝܢ ܓܠܕܝܗܘܢ *their skin is thick;* ܡܛܠ ܕܠܒܗܘܢ ܡܥܒܝܐ ܗܘܐ *because their heart was hardened;* ܡܥܒܝܐ ܘܥܒܝܐ *it condenses.* Ethpa. ܐܬܥܒܝ *to become thick* as honey; *to be swollen* as the eyes, face, or body, as a wound; *to be hardened* as the heart; *to become dense, material;* ܡܠܬܐ ܕܠܐ ܥܒܝܐ ܐܬܥܒܝܬ ܒܒܣܪܐ *the immaterial Word became material in the flesh.* Aph. ܐܥܒܝ *to thicken* trans.; ܣܦܪ̈ܐ ܡܥܒܝܢ ܠܐܬܘ̈ܬܐ scribes *write the letters thickly.* Derivatives, ܥܒܐ, ܥܒܝܐ, ܥܒܝܐܝܬ, ܥܒܝܘܬܐ, ܥܒܝܢܐ, ܥܒܝܢܘܬܐ, ܥܒܘܝܐ, ܥܒܘܝܢܐ, ܥܒܘܝܐ.

ܥܒ, ܥܒܐ pl. ܥܒ̈ܐ rt. ܥܒܐ. m. *a thicket, thick wood, dense forest;* ܥܒܐ ܩܛܝܢܐ *a grove;* ܚܝܘ̈ܬ ܥܒܐ *forest animals.*

ܥܒܐ or ܥܒܐ m. *a lizard.*

ܥܒܕ fut. ܢܥܒܕ, act. part. ܥܒܕ, ܥܒܕܐ, pass. part. ܥܒܝܕ, ܐ, ܬܐ. contractions ܥܒܕ = ܥܒܕܢܐ, ܥܒܕܝܢ ܠܗ = ܥܒܕܝܢܠܗ, ܥܒܕ ܐܢܐ = ܥܒܕܢܐ, ܥܒܕܐ = ܥܒܝܕܐ ; ܥܒܕܝܢ ܐܢܘܢ = ܥܒܕܝܢܘܢ, ܐܢܬ. *a*) *to do, cause, effect, perform, bring to pass;* ܚܟܝܡܐܝܬ ܥܒܕܬ *thou hast acted wisely;* ܥܒܕ ܛܒܬܐ, ܥܒܕ ܛܒ̈ܬܐ *to do well, well-doing;* ܥܒ̈ܕܝ ܒܝܫ̈ܬܐ *evil-doers, malefactors;* ܟܘܟ̈ܒܐ ܒܝ̈ܫܐ *evil stars;* ܥܒܕ ܛܒ̈ܬܐ *a benefactor;* ܡܢ ܢܥܒܕ ܐܢ ܥܒܕ *O that . . . ! b*) *to do, make, work;* ܓܒܪܐ ܕܥܒܕܐ ܠܐ ܥܒܕ *a man who does nothing, a sluggard;* ܥܒ̈ܕܝ ܥܒܕܐ *the workmen;* ܥܒ̈ܕܝ ܥܒܕܐ ܕܡܠܟܐ *doing the king's business;* ܥܒ̈ܕܝ ܬܫܡ̈ܫܬܐ *filling offices, fulfilling ministries;* ܥܒ̈ܕܝ ܟܬܢܐ *linen-weavers;* ܥܒܕ ܣܐܡܐ *a silversmith;* ܥܒ̈ܕܝ ܩܫ̈ܬܐ *makers of bows. c*) *to build, construct, repair. d*) *to write, compose. e*) *to make to be, appoint* king, bishop, priest; spy, &c. *f*) *to make to be, hold* or *consider as;* ܥܒܕܝܢ ܠܢ ܫܒܗܪ̈ܐ *they make us out braggarts. g*) *to make ready, prepare* food, *slay, sacrifice;* ܓܕܥܘܢ ܥܒܕ ܓܕܝܐ ܕܥܙ̈ܐ *Gideon made ready a kid;* ܢܥܒܕܝܘܗܝ ܚܛܗܐ Aaron *shall offer* the goat *for a sin-offering. h*) *to bear* fruit, *yield* milk. *i*) *to be good* or *fit for* with ܠ; ܐܪܥܐ ܐܘܟܡܬܐ ܥܒܕ *black soil is good for, suits* certain plants; ܥܩܪܐ ܕܩܢܝܐ ܥܒܕ *cane-root is good for . . .;* ܐܘܟܡܬܐ ܕܥܒܕܐ ܠܕܝܪܐ ܐܬܪܐ *a site convenient for a monastery. j*) *to pass time, stay;* with ܫܢܬܐ *to pass a year;* ܥܒܕ ܩܠܝܠ ܙܒܢܐ *he stayed a little while.*

ܥܒܕ is used in conjunction with many nouns:

ܚܪܝܢܐ *to contend, strive.*

ܐܣܛܣܝܣ ܥܠ *to egg on the mob.*

ܐܣܛܣܝܣ *to stir up sedition.*

ܐܬܐ *to do* or *work a sign.*

ܒܛܝܠܘܬܐ ܥܠ *to take pains about, have care for.*

ܒܝܫܬܐ ; see under *a.*

ܩܪܒܐ *to combat, fight.*

ܕܘܟܪܢܐ *to commemorate, celebrate;* esp. *to keep a saint's day.*

ܕܝܢܐ to give judgement, hold judicial inquiry.

ܛܒܥܐ; see under a.

ܛܝܒܘܬܐ to act kindly; to gain favour.

ܚܦܝܛܘܬܐ to take trouble, do carefully.

ܟܢܘܫܝܐ or ܣܘܢܗܕܘܣ to convoke a synod.

ܡܡܠܠܐ to compose a speech; to execute a command; to have reason.

ܡܦܣܢܘܬܐ to grant permission.

ܢܚܫܝܪܐ to hunt.

ܢܦܫܐ to make oneself out, pretend to be.

ܥܐܕܐ—ܦܨܚܐ—ܥܐܕܐ ܕܩܝܡܬܐ to make, keep or celebrate a feast, the Passover, Easter, &c.

ܥܘܗܕܢܐ to make mention, record.

ܥܠܬܐ to find a pretext, an occasion.

ܥܢܝܢܐ to have to do with, hold intercourse with.

ܦܘܢܝܐ to reply.

ܦܘܠܚܐ to use wiles; ܥܒܕ ܦܘܠܚܐ wily, tricky, fraudulent.

ܦܝܠܣܘܦܘܬܐ to live ascetically, as a philosopher.

ܦܠܝܪܘܦܘܪܝܐ to make certain, confirm.

ܦܣܩܐ to pass sentence.

ܨܘܡܐ to fast.

ܨܠܘܬܐ to pray.

ܨܠܝܒܐ to make the sign of the Cross.

ܩܕܡ to set before.

ܩܘܪܒܐ to celebrate the holy Eucharist.

ܩܛܦܐ to gather in or tread the vintage.

ܩܝܢܕܘܢܘܣ to be in peril, run into danger.

ܩܪܒܐ to wage war.

ܩܬܐܪܣܝܣ to depose.

ܪܐܙܐ to take counsel; to celebrate the holy mysteries.

ܪܫܐ to make a beginning; to make a king, set a chief or head over them.

ܫܘܬܦܐ to make partaker.

ܫܠܡܐ to make peace, reconcile.

ܫܠܡܘܬܐ to make an agreement, agree with.

ܫܡܥܘܬܐ to vote for.

ܫܢܬܐ; see under j.

ܥܒܕ ܫܢܬܐ soporific.

ܬܒܥܬܐ to take vengeance.

ܥܒܕ ܬܕܡܪܬܐ a wonder-worker.

ܬܚܝܬܐ to subject.

ܥܒܕ ܬܘܒܐ an emetic.

ܬܪܥܐ to close the gate, shut the door; ܥܒܝܕ ܗܘܐ ܬܪܥܐ the door is shut.

Act. part. cf. above. Gram. ܥܒܕ active opp. ܚܫܐ passive. Pass. part. done, made, formed, become, committed, devised, composed, appointed, constituted; ܥܒܝܕ ܠ done, made, written &c. by . . .; ܥܒܝܕ ܠܝ—ܠܟ it was done by me, by thee = I have done, thou hast done &c.; ܟܠ ܥܒܝܕܐ everything created; ܥܒܝܕܢ ܐܝܕܝܐ made by hands i.e. idols; ܢܚܙܐ ܐܝܟ ܥܒܝܕܝܢ let us see how they fare; ܥܒܝܕܝܢ ܗܘܘ ܟܪܝܗܐ ill, sick, diseased; ܥܒܝܕܝܢ ܣܒܐ they have become old; ܥܒܝܕܬ ܐܝܟ ܫܢܝܬܐ thou becamest like a mad woman. Fem. emph. ܥܒܝܕܬܐ pl. ܬܐ subst. a) anything done or committed, a deed, action, thing. b) anything to be done, work, business, matter, occupation, office, service; ܥܒܝܕܬܐ ܙܥܘܪܬܐ a small matter, trifle; ܙܝܢܐ ܘܡܐܢܐ ܘܫܪܟܐ ܕܥܒܝܕܬܐ ܡܠܟܘܬܐ the armour and other imperial property.

Ethpe. ܐܬܥܒܕ a) to be done, carried out, effected; ܐܬܥܒܕܬ ܬܒܥܬܐ ܡܢ vengeance was taken upon . . . b) to be performed, celebrated as a feast, the passover, &c. c) to be ordained, consecrated bishop, priest, &c. Pa. ܥܒܕ denom. verb from ܥܒܕܐ to make serve (rare). Cf. Palpel. Aph. a) ܐܥܒܕ to make work, set to work. b) to impel, instigate, set on to do anything. c) to work, effect; ܗܘ ܕܡܥܒܕ ܟܠ ܒܟܠܢܫ He who worketh all things in each one; ܫܐܕܐ ܗܘ ܕܡܥܒܕ ܗܘܐ ܠܗ the demon who impelled him, possessed him; ܡܥܒܕ ܚܝܐ life-giving, vivifying; ܡܥܒܕܐ ܗܘܐ ܠܗ he must needs. Ethtaph. ܐܬܬܥܒܕ to be done, made, effected, formed; esp. to be impelled, possessed by an evil spirit. Palpel ܥܒܕܒܕ to make to serve, reduce to servitude; ܚܫܐ the passions; ܚܛܝܬܐ sin; ܥܒܕܒܕ ܠܦܪܢܓܝܐ ܒܡܘܗܒܬܐ he brought the Franks to his allegiance by gifts. Ethpalpal ܐܬܥܒܕܒܕ to be enslaved, reduced to slavery, to bondage; to be a servant or slave of. Shaphel ܫܥܒܕ to make serve, enslave, subdue, subject, bring into subjection; with ܥܒܕܘܬܐ to reduce to slavery; ܐܢܐ ܥܒܕܐ ܐܢܐ ܘܡܫܬܥܒܕܐ ܠܦܘܩܕܢܝܟ I am Thy servant and subject to Thy *command;* ܒܳܬܰܪ ܕܫܰܥܒܶܕ ܟܽܠܳܗ ܦܳܪܣ *after he had subdued all Persia;* ܠܡܶܫܥܒܳܕܽܘ ܐܶܢܽܘܢ ܠܦܽܘܠܚܳܢܳܐ ܕܙܰܕܺܝܩܽܘܬܳܐ *to bring them into the service of righteousness.* Pass. part. ܡܫܰܥܒܰܕ, ܡܫܰܥܒܕܳܐ *subject, subject to; a servant, dependent;* ܡܫܰܥܒܰܕ ܠܚܰܘܒܬܳܐ *a debtor;* ܠܡܰܘܬܳܐ *subject to death;* ܠܢܽܘܚܳܬܳܐ *a slave of pleasure;* ܛܰܝܳܝܶܐ ܡܫܰܥܒܕܶܐ *subject* or *tributary Arabs;* ܟܽܘܪܗܳܢܳܐ ܕܠܳܐ ܡܫܰܥܒܰܕ ܠܐܳܣܝܽܘܬܳܐ *an incurable disease.* ESHTAPH. ܐܶܫܬܰܥܒܰܕ *to be enslaved, in bondage, in subjection; to be subject, to submit; to be under control, restrained;* ܐܶܫܬܰܥܒܰܕ ܠܝܰܘܢܳܝܶܐ *he submitted to the Greeks;* ܠܳܐ ܡܶܫܬܰܥܒܕܳܐ ܥܽܘܫܢܳܐ ܕܛܰܘܦܳܢܳܐ *the onrush of the flood cannot be restrained;* ܒܪܺܝܬܳܐ ܓܶܝܪ ܐܶܫܬܰܥܒܕܰܬ ܠܣܰܪܺܝܩܽܘܬܳܐ *for the creation was subjected unto vanity.* DERIVATIVES, ܥܒܳܕܳܐ, ܥܒܳܕܳܐ, ܥܒܳܕܳܐܺܝܬ, ܥܒܺܝܕܽܘܬܳܐ, ܥܒܳܝܳܐ, ܥܒܳܕܳܝܳܐ, ܥܒܳܕܳܐܺܝܬ, ܥܒܳܕܳܢܳܐܺܝܬ, ܥܒܳܕܽܘܬܳܐ, ܥܳܒܽܘܕܳܐ, ܥܒܽܘܕܳܐܺܝܬ, ܥܒܽܘܕܳܝܳܐ, ܡܥܰܒܕܳܢܳܐܺܝܬ, ܡܥܰܒܕܳܢܳܐ, ܡܥܰܒܕܳܢܽܘܬܳܐ, ܡܫܰܥܒܕܳܐ, ܡܫܰܥܒܕܽܘܬܳܐ, ܡܫܰܥܒܕܳܢܳܐܺܝܬ, ܡܫܰܥܒܕܳܢܳܐ, ܡܫܰܥܒܕܳܢܽܘܬܳܐ, ܡܶܫܬܰܥܒܕܳܢܽܘܬܳܐ, ܡܶܫܬܰܥܒܕܳܢܳܐ, ܡܶܫܬܰܥܒܕܳܢܳܐ, ܡܶܫܬܰܥܒܕܳܢܽܘܬܳܐ, ܡܶܫܬܰܥܒܕܳܢܽܘܬܳܐ, ܡܥܰܒܕܳܐ.

ܥܒܶܕ, ܥܰܒܕܳܐ pl. ܝܢ‍, ܶܐ rt. ܥܒܕ. m. *a bondsman, serving-lad, servant;* ܥܒܶܕ ܥܰܒܕܺܝܢ *a servant of servants;* ܥܰܒܕܶܐ ܒܢܰܝ ܒܰܝܬܳܐ *slaves born in bondage;* ܠܚܰܫܶܐ ܕܢܰܦܫܶܗ ܗܘܳܐ ܥܰܒܕܳܐ *he was the slave of his own passions;* ܥܰܒܕܶܗ ܕܡܳܪܝܳܐ *the servant of the Lord;* ܥܰܒܕܝ ܡܽܘܫܶܐ *my servant Moses.* Often used to form proper names e.g. ܥܒܶܕ ܝܶܫܽܘܥ *Ebedjesus,* E-Syr. ܥܰܒܕܝܫܽܘܥ *Audishu, the servant of Jesus;* ܥܒܶܕ ܫܰܕܰܝ *the servant of the Almighty.*

ܥܒܳܕ, ܥܒܳܕܳܐ pl. ܶܐ rt. ܥܒܕ. m. *a*) *a deed, action, affair; work, occupation, business, employment; making, construction;* ܥܒܳܕܳܐ ܕܐܽܘܡܳܢܶܐ *skilled labour, the work of skilled hands;* ܥܒܳܕܳܐ ܕܐܺܝܕܰܝܳܐ *handiwork* esp. *idols;* ܐܰܠܳܗܶܐ ܥܒܳܕ ܐܺܝܕܰܝܳܐ *gods made by hand;* ܥܒ̈ܳܕ ܦܳܠܚܽܘܬܳܐ or ܕܚܰܩܠܳܐ *husbandry, agriculture, field labour;* ܥܒ̈ܳܕ ܒܪܺܝܬܳܐ *the work of creation;* ܥܒܳܕ ܠܰܚܡܳܐ *baking, bread-making;* ܥܒܳܕ ܕܢܽܘܚܳܫܳܐ *bakery, baked food;* ܥܒ̈ܳܕܶܐ ܕܢܶܣܟܳܐ *molten work, cast metal;* ܥܒܳܕܳܐ ܕܦܽܘܠܚܳܢܳܐ *servile work;* ܥܒܳܕܳܐ ܕܦܽܘܩܕܳܢܶܐ *the execution of commands;* ܥܒܳܕܳܐ ܕܨܶܒܥܳܐ *embroidery;* ܥܒܳܕܳܐ ܕܫܽܘܫܰܢܬܳܐ *lily work;* ܥܒ̈ܳܕܰܝ ܛܳܒ̈ܶܐ *my good deeds;* ܥܒܳܕܳܐ ܠܳܐ ܢܳܡܽܘܣܳܝܳܐ *an illegal action;* ܫܶܠܝܳܐ ܡܶܢ ܥܒܳܕܶܐ *leisure from business.* *b*) *substance, goods, possessions, wealth;* ܡܙܰܒܢܺܝܢ ܗܘܰܘ ܥܒ̈ܳܕܰܝܗܽܘܢ *they sold their possessions;* ܠܳܐ ܐܺܝܬ ܗܘܳܐ ܠܶܗ ܥܒܳܕܳܐ ܟܠܳܠ *he had no possessions at all, had nothing left;* ܥܒܳܕܳܐ ܕܡܶܣܟܺܢܶܐ *the property of the poor.* *c*) Arab. *a province;* ܡܶܢ ܥܒܳܕܳܐ ܕܕܰܪܡܣܽܘܩ *belonging to the province of Damascus.* *d*) gram. *action, active voice;* ܡܶܠܬܳܐ ܕܥܒܳܕܳܐ *the active voice.* *e*) adverbial use with ܒ, *indeed, really;* ܗܘܳܬ ܒܥܒܳܕܳܐ *it came to pass;* ܩܳܡ ܒܥܒܳܕܳܐ *it was realized, accomplished;* with ܠ after a verb; ܦܳܐܶܐ ܠܥܒܳܕܳܐ *it is useful for work;* ܐܶܬܳܐ ܠܥܒܳܕ or *it took effect;* ܐܰܝܬܺܝ ܠܥܒܳܕ ܢܰܦܫܶܗ *he carried through, accomplished, brought it about.*

ܥܒܳܕܳܐܺܝܬ = ܥܒܳܕܳܢܳܐܺܝܬ.

ܥܰܒܕܶܕ Palpel conj. of ܥܒܕ.

ܥܒܽܘܕ, ܥܒܽܘܕܽܘܬܳܐ rt. ܥܒܕ. f. *service, servitude, slavery, bondage;* ܦܳܠܰܚ ܐ̱ܢܳܐ ܥܒܽܘܕܽܘܬܳܐ *I serve, do service;* ܥܒܽܘܕܽܘܬܳܐ ܕܐܰܠܳܗܶܐ ܣܰܓܺܝܐܶܐ *polytheism.*

ܥܒܽܘܕܳܐܺܝܬ rt. ܥܒܕ. adv. *slavishly, like a servant* or *bondsman.*

ܥܒܳܕܳܢܳܐܺܝܬ rt. ܥܒܕ. adv. *really, in deed.*

ܥܒܽܘܕܳܝܳܐ, ܝܬܳܐ rt. ܥܒܕ. *servile, as becomes a servant* or *bondsman.*

ܥܒܳܕܽܘܬܳܐ rt. ܥܒܕ. f. *a household; substance, goods, wealth, property, baggage;* ܩܢܳܐ ܠܶܗ ܥܒܳܕܽܘܬܳܐ ܣܰܓܺܝܐܳܐ ܕܕܰܗܒܳܐ ܘܕܣܺܐܡܳܐ *he got himself much wealth in gold and silver.*

ܥܳܒܽܘܕܳܐ, ܬܳܐ rt. ܥܒܕ. *a*) *a doer, maker* esp. *the Maker* of all things; ܥܳܒܽܘܕܳܐ ܕܟܽܠܡܶܕܶܡ *the Maker of the ages;* ܡܶܠܬܳܐ ܥܳܒܽܘܕܬܳܐ *the creating Word;* ܥܳܒܽܘܕܳܐ ܕܢܳܡܽܘܣܳܐ *a doer of the Law;* ܥܳܒܽܘܕܳܐ ܕܩܰܪܛܺܝܣܶܐ *a paper-maker.* *b*) *efficient; an agent, factor;* ܚܰܝܠܳܐ ܥܳܒܽܘܕܳܐ *efficient force;* ܥܶܠܬܳܐ ܥܳܒܽܘܕܬܳܐ *the efficient cause.* Gram. *active* opp. ܚܰܫܽܘܫܳܐ *passive;* ܡ̈ܶܠܶܐ ܥܳܒ̈ܽܘܕܳܬܳܐ *active* or *transitive verbs; the subject* or *nominative.*

ܥܳܒܽܘܕܳܐܺܝܬ rt. ܥܒܕ. adv. *really, in effect;* gram. *in the active* or *transitive sense.*

ܥܳܒܽܘܕܽܘܬܳܐ rt. ܥܒܕ. f. *a*) *doing, working, operation, action, construction;* ܐܰܠܳܗܳܐ ܡܫܰܒܚܳܐ ܒܥܳܒܽܘܕܽܘܬܳܐ *God glorious in His working;* ܥܳܒܽܘܕܽܘܬ ܛܳܒ̈ܳܬܳܐ *beneficence.* *b*) *creative energy.*

c) gram. *active force* or *signification, action;* ܫܡܗ̈ܐ ܕܥܒܘܕܘܬܐ *nouns of action.*

ܥܒܘܕܢܝܐ, ܝܬܐ rt. ܥܒܕ. adj. gram. *active.*

ܥܒܘܬ, ܬܐ, ܬܬܐ rt. ܥܒܬ. *growing* or *standing thick, thick, dense, abounding, fertile;* with ܐܝܠܢܐ or ܩܝܣܐ *a shady* or *umbrageous tree;* ܥܢ̈ܢܐ ܥܒܘܬܐ *dense clouds;* ܡܪܥܝܬܐ ܥܒܘܬܬܐ *a crowded flock;* ܐܪܥܐ ܥܒܘܬܬܐ ܒܥܒܘܪܐ *land thick with corn.*

ܥܒܘܬܘܬܐ rt. ܥܒܬ. f. *density;* ܥ ܕܓܐܪ̈ܐ *a dense cloud of arrows.*

ܥܒܘܪܐ pl. ܐ̈ Heb. m. *a crop, produce, corn, food, victuals;* ܒܝܬ ܥܒܘܪܐ *a granary;* ܪ̈ܫܝܬܐ ܕܥܒܘܪܐ *the firstfruits of the crops.*

ܥܒܘܪܐ, ܪܬܐ pl. m. ܐ̈ f. ܥܒܘܪ̈ܝܬܐ rt. ܥܒܪ. a) *transgressing, a transgressor.* b) *a passer-by, wayfarer.* c) *transient, transitory, passing away;* ܐܘܢܐ ܥܒܘܪܐ *passing time;* ܥܠܡܐ ܥܒܘܪܐ this *transitory world;* pl. f. with ܨܒܘ̈ܬܐ or ellipt. *transitory things, affairs* opp. ܩܝ̈ܘܡܬܐ; ܡ̈ܠܐ ܥܒܘܪ̈ܝܬܐ *passing words* i.e. *quickly forgotten.*

ܥܒܘܪܘܬܐ rt. ܥܒܪ. f. *transgression; passing by* or *over.*

ܥܒܘܪܝܐ pl. ܝ̈ܐ rt. ܥܒܪ. m. a) *deviation, transgression* ܕܢܡܘܣܐ *of the law.* b) *transitoriness.* c) *migration, transmigration;* ܥܒܘܪܝܐ ܕܢܦܫܬܐ ܡܢ ܦܓܪ̈ܐ ܠܦܓܪ̈ܐ *metempsychosis.*

ܥܒܘܪܩܐ or ܥ, ܩܬܐ adj. *spotted black and white, piebald* as sheep or goats.

ܥܒܬ fut. ܢܥܒܘܬ *to grow thick.* Part. adj. ܥܒܝܬ, ܬܐ, ܬܬܐ. a) *thickly grown, thick, heavy;* ܐܝܠܢ ܕܥܒܝܬ *a leafy* or *shady tree;* ܥܒܝܬ ܛܠܠܗ *giving close shade;* ܥܒ̈ܐ ܥܒܝ̈ܬܬܐ *dense woods;* ܫܒ̈ܝܠܐ ܥܒܝ̈ܬܝܢ *overgrown paths.* b) *full, abundant, crowded;* ܫܒ̈ܠܐ ܥܒܝ̈ܬܬܐ *full ears;* metaph. ܡܕܝܢܬܐ ܥܒܝܬܬ ܥܒ̈ܕܐ ܕܙܕܝܩܘܬܐ a city *abounding in works of righteousness.* Pa. ܥܒܬ same as Pe. Derivatives, ܥܒܘܬ, ܥܒܘܬܘܬܐ, ܥܒܝܬܐ, ܥܒܝܬܘܬܐ, ܥܘܒܬܐ.

ܥܒܝܐ pl. ܝ̈ܐ rt. ܥܒܐ. m. *thickness; a swelling, tumour; the solid part.*

ܥܒܝܐܝܬ rt. ܥܒܐ. adv. *stupidly, in bungling fashion.*

ܥܒܝܕܘܬܐ rt. ܥܒܕ. f. *making, forming, creation;* ܐܬ̈ܘܬܐ *the working of signs;* ܦܐܪ̈ܘܦܐ *hypocrisy;* ܒܢ̈ܝܐ *the begetting of sons;* ܦܪܨܘܦܐ *prosopopeia, personification.*

ܥܒܝܘܬܐ rt. ܥܒܐ. f. *thickness, grossness, fatness; a swelling, thickening;* metaph. *denseness, dullness.*

ܥܒܝܬܐ or ܥܒܝܬܐ rt. ܥܒܬ. *a camel's saddle for women* tented over with a framework.

ܥܒܝܬܘܬܐ rt. ܥܒܬ. f. *thickness, denseness* of fumes, incense.

ܥܒܝܢܐ rt. ܥܒܐ. *a swelling.*

ܥܒܝܬܐ or ܥܒܝܬܐ rt. ܥܒܐ. f. a) *a woollen tunic.* b) a sort of thick bread.

ܥܒܢܢܐ rt. ܥܒܐ. *wooded, woody, leafy.*

ܥܒܪ fut. ܢܥܒܪ, act. part. ܥܒܪ, ܥܒܪܐ, pass. part. ܥܒܝܪ, ܐ̈, ܪܬܐ. a) *to pass on, by, over* or *beyond;* ܥܒܪ ܦܪܬ *he crossed the Euphrates;* ܥܒܪ ܥܠ ܝܕ ܢܗܪܐ *he walked by the river side;* ܥܒܪ ܒܡܨܥܬ ܡܕܝܢܬܐ *he passed through the city;* ܥܒܪ ܘܕ ܐܘܪܚܐ *a passer-by, wayfarer, traveller;* ܥܒܪ ܘܗܦܟ *one who passes by and returns, goes and comes* metaph. *one who transgresses and repents.* Gram. ܥܒܪܐ *transitive;* with ܠܐ *intransitive.* With preps.: ܥܒܪ ܠ *to go to* any place, *to invade;* with ܥܠ in relating or writing *to pass on* to; with ܡܢ *to pass away from, depart from, turn aside from;* ܡܢ ܗܕܐ ܬܪܥܝܬܐ *from this way of thinking;* ܡܢ ܕܘܟܪܢܐ *to escape the memory, be forgotten;* ܡܢ ܥܠܡܐ *to die.* With ܥܠ *to go close to, to flow near* or *by, to come upon, befall* as trouble, affliction; metaph. *to transgress, violate* ܥܠ ܦܘܩܕܢܐ *a command;* ܥܠ ܢܡܘܣܐ *the law;* ܥܒܪ ܥܠ ܚܡܪܐ *quarrelsome over wine, a brawler;* ܥܒܪ ܥܠ ܡܘܡܬܐ *a false swearer, perjurer.* b) *to pass away, vanish* esp. of time; ܥܒܪ ܙܒܢܐ *time passes away;* ܚ̈ܝܐ ܕܠܐ ܥܒܪܝܢ *life eternal;* ܕܩܝܡ ܐܘ ܕܥܒܪ ܐܘ ܕܥܬܝܕ *present, past* or *future;* ܙܒܢܐ ܕܥܒܪ *the past* or *preterite tense;* ܒܕܥܒܪ *in the preterite.* c) *to surpass, exceed, be beyond, overcome;* ܥܒܪܐ ܠܗܘܢ ܗܕܐ *this is beyond them, more than they can understand;* ܥܒܪ ܠܡܡܠܠܘ *surpassing speech, inexpressible;* ܠܡܢܝܢܐ *innumerable;* ܠܡܫܘܚܬܐ *beyond measure;* ܠܫܡܫܐ ܥܒܪܐ ܗܘܬ ܒܫܘܦܪܗ *she surpassed the sun in fairness.*

Ethpe. ܐܬܥܒܪ *to be passed over, crossed*

as a river; *to pass on, by* or *to, to turn aside to* with ܠܘܬ of the pers., *to be turned away* or *diverted* with ܡܢ *from; to neglect, fail* of accomplishment, *to transgress, sin*. Aph. ܐܥܒܰܪ *a) to cause to pass* ܢܘܪܐ ܒܢܘܪܐ *through the fire; to allow to pass* or *to depart; to transfer, remove, transport, transplant;* ܐܥܒܪܘ ܙܩܝܦܐ ܡܢ ܦܪܘܩܢ ܘܣܡܘܗܝ ܥܠ ܫܡܥܘܢ *they took the cross* from our Saviour *and laid it on* Simon; with ܠܒܝܬ ܩܒܘܪܐ *to bear to the sepulchre;* ܩܠܐ ܒ *to proclaim;* ܡܢ ܡܠܟܘܬܐ or ܡܢ ܫܘܠܛܢܐ *to depose;* ܡܢ ܫܘܠܛܢܐ *to remove from power, depose. b) to set aside* ܢܡܘܣܐ *the law. c) to pass over, remit* transgression, sin. *d) to transfer, translate* ܡܢ ܠܫܢܐ ܥܒܪܝܐ ܠܝܘܢܝܐ *from Hebrew into Greek;* from one bishopric to another; ܐܥܒܪܗ ܠܟܘܪܣܝܐ ܕܡܠܟܘܬܐ ܡܢ ܪܗܘܡܝ ܠܒܘܙܢܛܝܘܢ *he removed the seat of empire from Rome to Byzantium. e) to convert, turn from* paganism to the faith. *f)* logic. *to pass over* ܡܢ ܡܢܬܐ ܠܟܠ ܡܕܡ *from a part to the whole, from detail to generality;* ܚܫܐ ܠܘܬ ܐܒܐ ܐܥܒܪܘ *they attributed the Passion to the Father. g) to go beyond, exceed. h) to pass over, omit; to defer, put off* ܡܢ ܝܘܡܐ ܠܝܘܡܐ *from day to day; to pass* time. Ethtaph. ܐܬܬܥܒܰܪ *to be translated, removed, transferred; to be extended* (of a proposition). Derivatives, ܥܒܘܪܐ, ܥܒܪܐ, ܥܒܪܐ, ܥܒܘܪܐ, ܥܒܪܝܐ, ܥܒܘܪܘܬܐ, ܡܥܒܪܢܐ, ܡܥܒܪܢܘܬܐ, ܡܥܒܪܢܐ, ܥܒܪܢܐ, ܡܬܥܒܪܢܘܬܐ.

ܥܒܳܪ, ܥܒܳܪܳܐ rt. ܥܒܪ. m. *a) passing over;* ܥܒܳܪ ܢܗܪܐ *crossing the river. b) transgression* with ܢܡܘܣܐ *of the law* or ܦܘܩܕܢܐ *of the command*.

ܥܶܒܪܳܐ pl. ܐ̈ rt. ܥܒܪ. m. *a) passing over* esp. *crossing* a river, hence *a ford, strait; the further shore, the land beyond;* ܥܶܒܪܳܐ ܕܝܘܪܕܢܢ *beyond Jordan;* ܥܒܪܐ ܕܝܡܐ *the sea-shore, strand;* ܥܶܒܪ̈ܝܗ ܕܡܕܝܢܬܐ *the limits of the city;* ܥܒܪ̈ܝ ܐܪܥܐ *the ends of the earth. b)* m. *a stake, tent-peg*.

ܥܶܒܪܳܐܝܬ rt. ܥܒܪ. adv. *in Hebrew, in the Hebrew language*.

ܥܶܒܪܳܝܳܐ, ܥܶܒܪܳܝܬܳܐ rt. ܥܒܪ. *Hebrew, an Hebrew;* ܥܶܒܪ̈ܳܝܳܬܳܐ *Hebrew women;* ܒܪ ܥܶܒܪܳܝܳܐ *of Hebrew parentage;* ܥܰܡܳܐ ܥܶܒܪܳܝܳܐ *the Hebrew nation;* ܟܬܳܒ̈ܳܐ ܥܶܒܪ̈ܳܝܶܐ *Hebrew characters*.

ܥܒܳܪܬܳܐ or ܥܒܳܪܬܳܐ f. *dysentery*.

ܥܰܒܫܳܐ *parti-coloured, black and white* as sheep; *unbleached, unbleached* or *unfulled cloth*.

ܥܓܰܕ Pa. ܥܰܓܶܕ *to paralyze, afflict with paralysis;* ܡܥܰܓܕܳܐ *paralyzed, palsied; a paralytic, cripple*.

ܥܰܓܕܳܢ, ܥܰܓܕܳܢܳܐ or ܥܓܕ̈ *benumbed, torpid, stupefied*.

ܥܰܓܽܘܪܳܐ rt. ܥܓܪ. *rustic, rude, hard*.

ܥܰܓܽܘܪܽܘܬܳܐ rt. ܥܓܪ. f. *rusticity, rudeness*.

ܥܰܓܽܘܫܳܐ pl. ܐ̈ rt. ܥܓܫ. m. *wont to gore* or *butt* as a bull.

ܥܰܓܺܝܢܽܘܬܳܐ rt. ܥܓܢ. f. *lying prostrate, prostration, dejection*.

ܥܓܠ root-meaning *to be round*. Cf. ܥܓܠ and ܥܓܠ. Pa. ܥܰܓܶܠ *to roll round, roll away;* ܟܐܦܐ ܡܥܰܓܠܳܐ *a stone rolled away*. Parel ܥܰܓܪܶܠ *to roll about* or *roll violently;* ܕܡܥܰܓܪܶܠ ܟܐܦܐ ܥܠܘܗܝ ܬܗܦܘܟ *He who rolleth a stone it shall return upon him;* ܡܥܰܓܪܠ ܘܡܬܛܡܫ ܒܕܡܐ *rolled in and befouled with blood*. Ethparal ܐܶܬܥܰܓܪܰܠ *to be rolled, to roll down* as stones or water from a mountain, *to roll* or *turn oneself, to wallow* in the dust; ܡܬܥܰܓܪܠܝܢ ܒܣܝܢܐ ܕܚܛܝܬܐ *in the mire of sin;* ܐܝܟ ܢܗܪܐ ܡܬܥܰܓܪܰܠ ܕܝܢܐ *judgement shall roll down like a flood;* ܡܬܥܰܓܪܠܐ ܗܘܬ ܡܟܝܢܬܐ *the engine was turned round;* ܐܝܟ ܚܘܝܐ ܡܬܥܰܓܪܠܝܢ ܒܐܪܥܐ *they writhe on the earth like a serpent*. Derivatives, ܥܓܠܬܐ, ܥܓܠܐ, ܥܓܠܐ, ܥܓܘܠܐ, ܥܓܠܬܐ, ܥܓܘܠܐ, ܥܓܘܠܐ, ܥܓܠܐ, ܡܥܓܪܠܢܐ.

ܥܓܰܠ rt. ܥܓܠ. adv. usually with ܒ prefixed. *a) quickly, immediately, forthwith;* ܐܢܐ ܐܬܐ ܒܥܓܠ *I come quickly;* ܥܓܠ ܠܡܡܬ ܒܥܓܠ *he was on the point of death;* ܒܥܓܠ ܥܓܠ *very quickly. b) soon, easily;* with ܠܐ *hardly, with difficulty;* ܡܐܢܐ ܕܕܗܒܐ ܕܠܐ ܒܥܓܠ ܡܬܬܒܪ *a golden vessel which is not easily broken*.

ܥܶܓܠܳܐ pl. ܐ̈ rt. ܥܓܠ. m. *a calf; an antelope;* ܥܶܓܠܳܐ ܕܒܪܐ, see under ܒܪܐ. For fem. see ܥܶܓܠܬܳܐ.

ܥܶܓܠܽܘܢܳܐ m. dim. *a)* of ܥܶܓܠܳܐ *a little calf. b)* of ܥܓܠܬܐ *a small cart*.

ܥܶܓܰܠܬܳܐ pl. ܥܶܓܠܳܢ, ܥܶܓܠܳܬܳܐ rt. ܥܓܠ. f. *an*

heifer, a cow-calf sometimes ܬܘܪܬܐ ܕܥܓܠܬܐ; ܥܓܠܬܐ ܬܠܝܬܝܬܐ *an heifer of three years.*

ܥܓܠܬܐ or ܥܓܠܬܐ pl. ܥܓܠܢ, ܥܓܠܬܐ rt. ܥܓܠ. f. *a cart, wain, waggon;* the constellation *Charles' Wain, the Waggoner.*

ܥܓܡ or ܥܓܡ fut. ܢܥܓܘܡ, pass. part. ܥܓܝܡ, ܥܓܝܡܐ. *to cast down, to lie prostrate;* ܒܩܒܪܐ *in the grave.* Part. *lying down, prone, prostrate, the dead;* ܒܚܫܘܟܐ *lying in darkness;* ܒܓܘܡܨܐ *in the pit.* Metaph. *of low morals;* ܥܡܡܐ ܗܘܘ ܥܓܝܡܝܢ ܒܚܒܠܐ *the nations were lying in corruption;* ܥܘܒܕܐ ܥܓܝܡܐ ܕܣܡܝܘܬܐ *behaviour of blind baseness.* Ethpe. ܐܬܥܓܡ *to be cast down, fallen down, lying prostrate.* Pa. ܥܓܡ *to cast* or *throw down;* ܒܐܣܝܪܐ *into prison; to make fall into sin.* Derivatives, ܥܓܝܡܘܬܐ, ܥܓܡܐ.

ܥܓܡܐ pl. ܐ̈ rt. ܥܓܡ. m. *prostration, humiliation; the lower regions.*

ܥܓܪ root-meaning *to be dense, thick.* Derivatives, ܥܓܪܐ, ܥܓܝܪܐܝܬ, ܥܓܝܪܘܬܐ, ܥܓܪܘܢܐ, ܥܓܪܬܐ.

ܥܓܝܪ, ܥܓܝܪܐ rt. ܥܓܪ. adj. *stout, heavy, weighty, thick, dense, gross;* ܢܘܢܐ ܥܓܝܪܐ ܛܒ Leviathan is a *very ponderous fish;* ܚܛܗܐ ܥܓܝܪܐ *grievous sins;* ܚܫܐ ܥܓܝܪܐ ܘܚܝܘܬܢܝܐ *gross and bestial passions.*

ܥܓܝܪܐܝܬ rt. ܥܓܪ. adv. *strongly.*

ܥܓܝܪܘܬܐ rt. ܥܓܪ. f. *grossness, roughness.*

ܥܓܪܘܢܐ m. *inula helenium, fleabane.*

ܥܓܫ fut. ܢܥܓܘܫ. *to butt, gore* as a bull. Derivative, ܥܓܫܐ.

ܥܕ adv. of time *while, whilst, whilst yet, as long as; until, till; as far as, up to, unto;* ܥܕ ܕܐܬܐ *until he come;* ܥܕ ܗܘ ܡܡܠܠ *while he was speaking;* ܥܕ ܗܘ ܚܝ *during his lifetime;* ܥܕܐ or ܥܕ ܐܝܟ ܙܒܢܐ *for a time, a while;* ܥܕ ܙܒܢܐ ܩܠܝܠ *a little while;* ܥܕ ܝܘܡܬܐ *for a few days;* ܥܕ ܩܠܝܠ *nearly, almost, but a little.* Forms the compounds ܥܕܡܐ, ܥܕܟܝܠ, ܥܕܟܡܐ.

ܥܕ for ܘܥܕ ܥܕ *to fix a place* or *time of meeting, to assemble.* Palpel ܥܕܥܕ, ܥܐܕܥܕ or ܥܐܕܥܕ *to celebrate, keep* a feast; ܢܥܕܥܕ ܥܐܕܐ or ܥܐܕܐ *let us keep the feast.* Derivatives, ܥܐܕܐ, ܥܐܕܥܐܕܐ, ܥܕܥܐܕܐ, ܥܕܥܕܐ, ܥܕܥܕܘܬܐ, ܥܕܘܢܐ, ܥܕܐܝܬ, ܥܕܥܕܐܝܬ, verb ܥܕܝ, ܥܕܥܕܢܐ.

ܥܕܕ or ܥܕܕ root-meaning *to weed.* Pass. part. ܥܕܝܕ, ܐ, ܬܐ. *a) weeded, cleared of weeds, purged, pruned;* ܚܩܠܐ ܥܕܝܕܐ ܡܢ ܟܘܒܐ *a field cleared of thorns. b) bound together;* ܡܛܥܢܐ ܥܕܝܕܐ *loads packed up.* Ethpe. ܐܬܥܕܕ *to be weeded.* Derivatives, ܥܕܕܐ, ܥܕܘܕܐ.

ܥܕܐ, fut. ܢܥܕܐ, imper. ܥܕܝ, act. part. ܥܕܐ, ܥܕܝܐ with ܒ or ܠ. *to touch, pass near, come suddenly upon, affect, seize;* ܪܝܚܐ ܕܢܘܪܐ ܠܐ ܥܕܐ ܒܗܘܢ *the smell of fire had not passed upon them;* ܥܕܝܢ ܒܗܘܢ ܪܘܚܐ ܒܝܫܬܐ *evil spirits seize upon them;* ܠܐ ܥܕܐ ܒܗܘܢ ܡܘܬܐ *death does not touch* the angels. Pa. ܥܕܝ *to set free; to sustain.* Aph. ܐܥܕܝ *a) to lay hold, snatch, wrest;* ܡܢ ܦܘܡܐ ܕܬܢܝܢܐ *from the dragon's mouth;* with ܙܟܘܬܐ *to wrest a victory;* ܠܡܠܟܘܬܐ ܡܢ ܡܨܪܝܐ *to wrest empire from the Egyptians;* ܡܢܘ ܐܥܕܝ ܟܠܝܠܐ ܕܠܐ ܐܓܘܢܐ *who hath laid hold on the crown without strife? b) to wrest, extort. c) to snatch, pluck out, rescue, carry off* from wild beasts, captivity, peril, &c. Ethtaph. ܐܬܬܥܕܝ *to be snatched* or *torn away; to be taken away by force, rescued.* Derivatives, ܥܕܝܐ, ܥܕܝܢܐ, ܥܕܝܢܘܬܐ, ܥܕܝܬܐ, ܥܕܘܝܐ, ܥܕܘܝܢܐ, ܥܕܘܝܘܬܐ.

ܥܕܘܕܐ or ܥܕܕ pl. ܐ̈ m. *a wood-pigeon, stock-dove.*

ܥܕܘܕܐ rt. ܥܕܕ. m. *weeding, stubbing, removing the young shoots of fruit trees.*

ܥܕܘܠܐ pl. ܐ̈ rt. ܥܕܠ. m. *an accuser, fault-finder.*

ܥܕܘܪܐ pl. ܐ̈ rt. ܥܕܪ. m. *a helper, giver of aid, assistant.*

ܥܕܘܢܐ rt. ܥܕܐ. m. *a) distance;* ܒܥܕܘܢܐ *at a distance, far away. b) return, period,* ܕܩܘܪܫܐ *the cold fit of a fever* opp. ܕܡܫܚܢܘܬܐ *the hot fit.*

ܥܕܘܝܐ or ܥܕܝ, ܥܕܘܝܬܐ pl. m. ܥܕܘܝܐ̈ pl. f. ܥܕܘܝܬܐ̈ rt. ܥܕܐ. *a sojourner, wanderer, pilgrim.*

ܥܕܘܝܘܬܐ rt. ܥܕܐ. f. *wandering, staying a while, being a sojourner.*

ܥܕܘܠܐܝܬ rt. ܥܕܠ. adv. *culpably;* with ܠܐ *innocently, free of blame.*

ܥܕܘܠܘܬܐ rt. ܥܕܠ. *blameworthiness, culpableness.*

ܥܕܝܠܐ rt. ܥܕܠ. *culpable, blameworthy, reprehensible.*

ܥܕܝܢ = ܥܕܢ *Eden.*

ܥܕܝܢܝܐ = ܥܕܢܝܐ adj. *of Eden* or *Paradise.*

ܥܕܘܠܬܐ pl. ܠܬܐ rt. ܥܕܠ. f. *varicose veins; bloodshot state of the eyes; weak* or *blurred sight; vexation.*

ܥܕܠ or ܥܕܰܠ, fut. ܢܥܕܘܿܠ, act. part. ܥܳܕܶܠ, ܥܳܕܠܳܐ, pass. part. ܥܕܝܠ, ܠܐ, ܠܬܐ. *to find fault, blame, complain of;* ܡܥܕܠ ܥܳܕܶܠ ܗܘ ܠܢܦܫܗ *he blames himself thoroughly;* ܥܳܕܠܝܢ ܒܟܠ ܕܡܕܡ *finding fault with everything, inveterate grumblers.* Pass. part. *blamed, reproved; culpable, blameworthy, reprehensible;* with ܠܐ *harmless, innocent, unimpugned.* ETHPE. ܐܬܥܕܶܠ *to be blamed, accused, complained of;* ܠܐ ܐܝܬ ܠܗ ܡܕܡ ܕܢܬܥܕܠ *there is nothing to find fault with in him.* ETHPA. ܐܬܥܰܕܰܠ *to blame, find fault, complain,* with ܒܢܦܫܗ *to accuse himself; to find guilty, condemn* with ܒ or ܥܠ of the pers. APH. ܐܥܕܶܠ *to blame severely, find great fault.* PAREL ܥܰܪܕܶܠ *to blame* with ܒ. DERIVATIVES, ܥܕܘܠܐ, ܥܕܘܠܐ, ܥܕܠܐ, ܥܕܝܠܐ, ܥܕܝܠܘܬܐ, ܥܕܠܬܐ, ܥܕܝܠܬܐ, ܡܬܥܕܠܢܐ.

ܥܕܠܐ comp. of ܥܕ and ܠܐ. adv. of time, *before, until, while as yet, not yet, even now.*

ܥܕܠܐ pl. ܠܐ rt. ܥܕܠ. m. *blame, censure, accusation;* ܕܠܐ ܥܕܠܐ *blameless.*

ܥܕܡܐ comp. of ܥܕ and ܡܐ. *a*) adv. of time and place, usually followed by ܕ, *until, so far, so that.* *b*) prep. with ܠ *as far as, unto, until, to;* ܥܕܡܐ ܠܚܡܫܝܢ ܫܢܝܢ *till the end of fifty years, for fifty years;* ܥܕܡܐ ܠܥܠܡ *for ever, to eternity;* ܥܕܡܐ ܠܐܡܬܝ *how far? as far, as long as;* ܥܕܡܐ ܠܐܝܟܐ *how far? how long?* ܥܕܡܐ ܠܒܬܪ *until after . . ., until past . . .;* ܥܕܡܐ ܠܗܫܐ contr. ܥܕܡܫܐ, ܥܕܡܗܫܐ or ܥܕܡܫܐ *hitherto, till the present time.*

ܥܶܕܶܢ or ܥܕܝܢ Heb. *Eden;* ܦܪܕܝܣܐ ܕܥܕܶܢ *the Garden of Eden;* ܐܗܦܟܢ ܡܫܝܚܐ ܠܥܕܝܢ *Christ has brought us back to Eden.* DERIVATIVES, verb ܥܰܕܶܢ, ܥܕܢܐ, ܥܕܝܢܐ or ܥܕܢܝܐ, ܥܕܘܢܐ.

ܥܰܕܶܢ denom. verb Pael conj. *to make pleasant, delight, solace.* Pass. part. ܡܥܰܕܰܢ, ܡܥܕܢܐ, ܡܥܕܢܬܐ. *given to pleasures, delicate; abounding in delights.* ETHPA. ܐܬܥܰܕܰܢ *to enjoy delights;* ܒܦܘܢܩܗ ܕܥܕܢ ܓܢܬܐ *to enjoy the pleasures of the Garden of Eden.*

ܥܶܕܳܢ, ܥܶܕܳܢܳܐ pl. ܥܶܕܳܢܺܝܢ, ܥܶܕܳܢܶܐ m. *a moment, minute; a season* or *time,* esp. *a convenient season, fit* or *right time;* ܙܒܢܐ ܘܥܕܢܐ *times and seasons;* ܥܕܡܐ ܠܥܕܢ *until the time appointed;* ܒܥܕܢܗܘܢ *in their season, in due season;* ܕܠܐ ܒܥܕܢܗܘܢ *unseasonably;* ܥܕܢ ܨܦܪܐ or ܥܕܢ ܨܦܪܐ *daybreak, dawn;* ܒܥܕܢܐ ܕܪܡܫܐ *at supper-time;* ܥܕܢܐ ܕܡܛܪܐ *a rainy season;* ܥܕܢ ܒܥܕܢ *from season to season = an entire year;* ܒܥܕܢܐ ܙܥܘܪܐ *in a short time, a little while;* ܥܕܢܐ ܡܘܓܪܐ *a late season, long time;* ܥܕܢܐ ܥܒܪ ܠܗ *the hour is past;* ܒܟܠܗܘܢ ܥܕܢܝܢ *at all seasons, continually, ever;* ܐܝܟ ܥܕܢ *as formerly, heretofore;* ܕܥܕܢ *temporary;* ܕܥܕܢܢ *of our time, of our age;* ܫܒܥܐ ܥܕܢܝܢ *seven times;* ܥܕܡܐ ܥܕܢ ܥܕܢܝܢ ܘܦܠܓܗ ܥܕܢ *for a time, times and a half.* DERIVATIVE, ܥܕܢܝܐ.

ܥܕܢܝܐ or ܥܕܝܢܝܐ, ܥܕܝܢܝܬܐ adj. from ܥܕܢ. *of or belonging to Eden;* ܐܘܬܪ ܠܩܕܝܫܐ ܐܪܥܐ ܥܕܢܝܬܐ *He hath granted abundantly to the saints a land of Eden.*

ܥܶܕܳܢܳܝܳܐ, ܢܳܝܬܳܐ adj. from ܥܶܕܳܢ. *seasonable, fit, suitable.*

ܥܐܕܐ less commonly ܥܐܕܐ pl. ܐ rt. ܥܐܕ. m. *a feast, feast-day, holiday, festival.*

ܥܕܩܐ, ܥܕܩܬܐ pl. ܥܕܩܝܢ, ܥܕܩܐ f. *a curl, curled lock of hair, crisped bush of hair;* ܓܠܚܬ ܠܗ ܫܒܥ ܥܕܩܬܐ ܕܪܫܗ *she shaved off the seven locks of his head.*

ܥܕܰܪ fut. ܢܥܕܘܿܪ, act. part. ܥܳܕܰܪ, ܥܳܕܪܳܐ, pass. part. ܥܕܝܪ, ܐ, ܬܐ. *to help, assist, be of use* or *advantage;* ܐܝܟ ܕܥܕܪܐ ܠܗ *as is expedient;* ܠܐ ܥܳܕܪܳܐ *it is of no avail, of no use.* PA. ܥܰܕܰܪ *to help, bear aid, assist, favour; to be good* or *useful;* with ܥܠ *to take the part of;* ܡܫܚܐ ܡܥܕܪ ܠܟܪܝܗܐ *oil is good for the sick;* ܚܝܠܐ ܕܥܕܪ ܠܣܗܕܐ ܒܐܘܠܨܢܐ *O Might Who supported the martyrs in tribulation;* ܗܘ ܕܠܐ ܬܐܙܠ ܡܥܕܪܐ ܠܟ ܡܢ ܗܘ ܕܬܐܙܠ *it is better for you to stay than to go;* ܠܐ ܡܥܕܪܐ *it is useless, hurtful, prejudicial.* ETHPA. ܐܬܥܰܕܰܪ *to be helped, assisted, healed; to receive help, advantage; to be to the advantage* or *profit of . . .;* ܡܢܐ ܓܝܪ ܡܬܥܕܪ ܒܪܢܫܐ *what doth it profit a man?*

ܢܦܫܐ ܥܢܝܕܬܐ ܡܬܥܕܪܐ a departed soul *receives help from prayers.* Derivatives, ܥܘܕܪܐ, ܥܕܪܐ, ܡܥܕܪܢܘܬܐ, ܡܥܕܪܢܝܬܐ, ܡܥܕܪܢܐ, ܥܕܘܪܐ, ܥܕܪܢܐ, ܡܥܕܪܢܐ, ܡܬܥܕܪܢܐ, ܥܕܝܪܐ, ܐܬܥܕܪܘܬܐ.

ܥܘܕܪܐ pl. ܥܘܕܪ̈ܐ rt. ܥܕܪ. m. *help, aid, advantage;* ܥܘܕܪܐ ܠܐ ܙܥܘܪܐ *no small advantage;* pl. *auxiliary troops, reinforcements.*

ܥܕܪܐ pl. ̈ܐ Ezech. xxvii. 5 and in the Lexx. probably a mistake for ܐܣܪܐ *a mast* &c.

ܥܕܪܢܐ m. *saponaria officinalis, soapwort.*

ܥܕܬܐ W-Syr. ܥܕܬܐ constr. st. ܥܕܬ pl. ܥܕ̈ܬܐ or ܥܕܬ̈ܐ rt. ܥܕ. f. = ἐκκλησία. *a*) *an assembly, congregation, company, church;* ܬܠܬ ܥܕ̈ܬܐ ܫܡܝܢܝ̈ܬܐ *three heavenly companies;* ܟܕ ܐܫܬܪܝܬ ܥܕܬܐ *when the congregation broke up;* ܥܕܬܐ ܩܬܘܠܝܩܝ *the Catholic Church. b*) *a temple, church;* ܥܕܬܐ ܪܒܬܐ *a cathedral church.*

ܥܕܬܘܢܝܬܐ dim. of ܥܕܬܐ. f. *a little church.*

ܥܕܬܢܐܝܬ adv. from ܥܕܬܐ. *ecclesiastically, in the ecclesiastical sense.*

ܥܕܬܢܐ, ܢܝܬܐ adj. from ܥܕܬܐ. *of the church, ecclesiastical, clerical; an ecclesiastic, official, doctor of divinity;* ܡܟܬܒܢܘܬܐ ܥܕܬܢܝܬܐ *Church history.*

ܥܕܬܢܘܬܐ from ܥܕܬܐ. f. *ecclesiastical law, custom* or *learning.*

ܥܕܬ denom. verb from ܥܕܬܐ. *to congregate.*

ܥܗܕ fut. ܢܥܗܘܕ, imper. ܥܗܘܕ, act. part. ܥܗܕ, ܥܗܕܐ, pass. parts. ܥܗܝܕ and ܥܗܝܕ; E-Syr. ܥܗܕ &c. (In this and the following words beginning with ܥܗ West-Syrians pronounce the ܥ like Alep, East-Syrians keep the strong pronunciation.) *a*) *to remember, recall, come* or *call to mind;* with ܢܦܫܗ *to come to himself, come to a right mind. b*) *to mention, make mention of, recount, relate;* ܐܪܒܥ ܐܓܪ̈ܢ ܕܥܗܕ ܐܢܐ he wrote *the four epistles which I mention;* ܥܗܕܢܢ ܥܘܡܪ̈ܐ ܗܠܝܢ ܘܫܘܪܝܐ ܕܒܢܝܢܗܘܢ *we have recounted those monasteries and the founding of them.* Pass. part. *a*) act. sense ܥܗܝܕ *remembering, mindful of;* ܥܗܝܕ ܐܢܐ *I remember,* &c.; ܥܗܝܕܝܢܢ *we remember. b*) passive sense ܥܗܝܕ *mentioned, aforesaid.* Ethpe. ܐܬܥܗܕ *a*) *to remember, recollect;* ܗܪܟܐ ܐܝܬܘܗܝ ܟܠܗ ܩܘܪܒܢܐ ܕܢܬܥܗܕ ܘܢܐܡܪ ܡܕܡ ܕܥܒܕ ܠܢ ܡܫܝܚܐ *herein consists the whole oblation, that we should remember and say what things Christ did for us. b*) *to bring to remembrance, reflect upon, mention, make mention of;* ܬܫܒܘܚܬܐ ܕܐܬܥܗܕܬ *the above-mentioned hymn;* ܐܬܥܗܕܢ ܡܠܬܐ ܕܟܬܒܐ *we remember, reflect upon, the saying of scripture. c*) *to recall, remind;* ܐܬܥܗܕܬܢܝ ܥܠ ܠܟܣܝܩܘܢ *you have recalled to my remembrance the lexicon.* Pa. ܥܗܕ *to call to remembrance, mention;* ܟܬܒ̈ܐ ܕܡܥܗܕ ܐܢܐ the books *which I* here *mention.* Ethpa. ܐܬܥܗܕ *to be remembered, kept in remembrance.* Aph. ܐܥܗܕ *to call* or *bring to remembrance, to remind, mention, commemorate, record;* ܗܘ ܢܥܗܕܟܘܢ ܐܘܪܚܬܝ ܕܒܡܫܝܚܐ *he shall put you in remembrance of my ways which are in Christ;* ܡܥܗܕ ܐܢܐ ܒܟܬܒܐ ܗܢܐ *I record in this book;* ܡܥܗܕܝܢ ܗܘܘ ܡܘܗܒܬܐ ܕܢܡܘܣܐ *they commemorated the giving of the Law.* Derivatives, ܥܘܗܕܢܐ, ܥܗܕܢܐ, ܡܥܗܕܢܐ, ܡܥܗܕܢܘܬܐ, ܡܬܥܗܕܢܐ, ܡܬܥܗܕܢܘܬܐ.

ܥܗܘܕܢܐ, ܥܗܘܕܢܝܬܐ rt. ܥܗܕ. *endowed with a good memory.*

ܥܘܗܕܢܐ rt. ܥܗܢ. m. *opportunity.*

ܥܗܢ only used in the part. ܥܗܢ, ܥܗܢܐ. *convenient, suitable, opportune, fitting, agreeable;* ܥܕܢܐ ܥܗܢ *a convenient time, opportunity;* ܕܘܟܬܐ ܕܥܗܢܐ ܠܬܐܘܪܝܐ *a spot suitable for contemplation;* ܥܗܢ ܠܚܝ̈ܐ ܐܢܫܝ̈ܐ *fit to sustain human life.* Derivatives, the three following words and ܥܘܗܕܢܐ.

ܥܗܢܐܝܬ rt. ܥܗܢ. adv. *usefully, profitably.*

ܥܗܢܘܬܐ rt. ܥܗܢ. f. *suitability, aptitude, aptness;* ܥܗܢܘܬ ܥܕܢܐ *a fitting time* or *opportunity;* ܥܗܢܘܬ ܡܥܡܪܐ *suitableness for habitation;* ܥܗܢܘܬܐ ܕܟܪܘܙܘܬܐ ܥܕܬܢܝܬܐ *facility in preaching;* ܠܐ ܥܗܢܘܬܐ ܕܐܣܟܡܗܘܢ *the unsuitable character of their clothing.*

ܥܗܢܢܐ rt. ܥܗܢ. *fit, suitable, opportune, convenient, able;* ܒܙܢܐ ܥܗܢܢܐ *in a suitable manner;* ܕܪܫܐ ܥܗܢܢܐ *an able disputation.*

ܥܗܪ fut. ܢܥܗܘܪ, act. part. ܥܗܪ, ܥܗܪܐ, pass. part. ܥܗܝܪ, ܥܗܝܪܐ. *to be wanton, lustful* as horses or camels. Ethpa. ܐܬܥܗܪ the same. Derivative, ܥܗܪܘܬܐ.

ܥܗܪܘܬܐ rt. ܥܗܪ. f. *wantonness, lust.*

ܥܘܐ or ܥܘܐ, fut. ܢܥܘܐ, act. part. ܥܘܐ.

ܥܘܐ. *to howl* as wild beasts, *to wail* with ܠܘܬ; ܥܘܐ ܗܘܐ ܐܝܟ ܟܠܒܐ *he howled like a dog.* Pa. ܥܰܘܺܝ *to howl long* or *loudly.* Aph. ܐܰܥܘܺܝ *to cause to wail;* ܐܝܢܐ ܕܥܳܘܶܠ ܘܡܰܥܘܶܐ *whoso wrongs and causes wailing.* Derivatives, ܥܘܝܐ, ܥܘܝܬܐ, ܥܘܐܐ, ܥܘܝܬܐ, ܥܘܬܐ.

ܥܘܒ Pa. ܥܰܘܶܒ 1) *to smile, laugh at.* 2) *to grow gloomy;* pass. part. ܡܥܰܘܒܳܐ *overclouded.* Aph. ܐܰܥܺܝܒ *to overcloud, shroud in mist.* Derivatives, ܥܘܒܐ, ܥܘܒܝܐ, ܥܝܒܐ.

ܥܘܒ, ܥܘܒܳܐ pl. ܥܘܒܶܐ rt. ܥܘܒ. m. *a) the bosom, lap, womb, matrix;* ܝܺܚܺܝܕܳܝܳܐ ܐܰܠܳܗܳܐ ܗܰܘ ܕܐܺܝܬܰܘܗ̱ܝ ܒܥܘܒܳܐ ܕܐܰܒܽܘܗ̱ܝ *God Only-begotten Who is in the bosom of His Father;* ܥܘܒܳܐ ܕܥܺܕܬܳܐ *the bosom of the Church;* ܥܘܒܳܐ ܪܘܚܳܢܳܝܳܐ or ܕܡܰܥܡܽܘܕܺܝܬܳܐ *the spiritual* or *baptismal womb.* *b) a hollow, cavity, recess, inner part;* ܥܘܒܳܐ ܥܶܠܳܝܳܐ ܕܡܽܘܚܳܐ *the upper cavity of the brain;* ܫܰܪܳܐ ܕܒܥܘܒܳܐ ܕܐܺܝܠܳܢܶܐ *sap in the veins of trees;* ܡܶܬܦܰܬܚܺܝܢ ܥܘܒܶܐ ܕܣܰܘܟܶܐ *the branches swell and open;* ܥܘܒܳܐ ܕܟܰܝܠܳܐ *the hollow of a measure;* ܥܘܒܶܐ ܬܰܚܬܳܝܶܐ ܕܐܰܪܥܳܐ *the lowest recesses of the world;* ܥܘܒܳܐ ܕܫܝܘܠ *the gulf of Sheol.* *c) a gulf, bay, a land-locked lake* or *sea;* ܥܘܒܳܐ ܕܣܽܘܦ *the Red Sea;* ܥܘܒܰܝ ܝܰܡܡܶܐ *lagoons, inner seas.* *d) the bosom* of a robe, *a pocket, receptacle;* metaph. ܠܳܐ ܗܘܳܐ ܥܘܒܳܐ ܕܪܶܥܝܳܢܟ ܠܡܰܚܡܳܠܽܘ *your mind is not capacious enough* to hold . . . *e)* geometr. *a sine.* *f)* med. ܥܘܒܶܐ *piles, emerods;* ܥܘܒܳܐ ܕܫܘܚܢܳܐ *the opening* or *the bottom of a sore.*

ܥܘܒܝܳܐ rt. ܥܒܐ. m. *close growth, density, profusion; a crowd; condensing, an epitome;* ܥܘܒܝܳܐ ܕܐܺܝܠܳܢܶܐ ,ܥܘܒܝܳܘܗ̱ܝ ܕܐܺܝܠܳܢܶܐ *a thicket;* ܩܰܡܛܶܐ ܥܘܒܝܳܐ *trunks stuffed full of garments;* ܥܘܒܝܳܐ ܕܬܽܘܪܳܣܳܗ̇ ܕܦܰܓܪܳܐ *abundance of bodily nourishment;* ܥܘܒܝܳܐ ܕܐܰܪܥܳܐ *the fatness of the earth.*

ܥܘܒܝܳܐ rt. ܥܒܐ m. *thickness, consistency;* ܐܰܝܟ ܥܘܒܝܳܐ ܕܕܶܒܫܳܐ *about as thick as honey;* ܫܬ ܐܰܡܝܢ ܦܽܬܝܳܐ ܘܥܘܒܝܳܐ *six cubits in width and thickness.*

ܥܘܒܢܳܐ pl. ܢܶܐ rt. ܥܒܐ. m. *a swelling, tumour, gathering, fester;* ܥܘܒܢܶܐ ܩܫܶܐ *hard swellings.*

ܥܘܒܢܳܝܳܐ, ܝܬܳܐ adj. from the above. *festering, gathering.*

ܥܘܓܳܠܳܐ rt. ܥܓܠ. m. *rotation, rotatory motion.*

ܥܘܕ (1) ܥܰܘܶܕ = ܥܕܰܪ, fut. ܢܥܘܕ, act. part. ܥܳܐܶܕ. *to uproot* weeds, *tear up* thorns, *disbud* vines. Ethpa. ܐܶܬܥܰܘܰܕ *to be pruned off, disbudded.* Derivatives, ܥܘܕܪܳܐ, ܥܕܪܳܐ.

ܥܘܕ (2) not used in Pe. Pael ܥܰܘܶܕ *to accustom, habituate, use, exercise;* ܕܥܰܘܶܕ ܠܰܠܫܳܢܶܗ ܠܕܰܓܳܠܽܘܬܳܐ *one who has accustomed his tongue to falsehood.* Pass. part. ܡܥܰܘܰܕ, ܡܥܰܘܕܳܐ, ܡܥܰܘܕܳܐܺܝܬ with ܒ or ܕ *accustomed, used, wont, expert, usual;* ܨܶܒܘܳܐ ܗܘܳܐ ܕܡܥܰܘܕܺܝܢ ܗ̄ܘܰܘ ܒܶܗ *a matter to which they were well accustomed;* ܡܥܰܘܕܺܝܢ ܗ̄ܘܰܘ ܒܡܶܢܝܳܢܳܐ *they were practised in* observation of *the stars;* ܐܰܝܟ ܕܡܥܰܘܕܳܐ *as is usual, customary;* ܥܝܳܕܳܐ ܡܥܰܘܕܳܐ *custom.* Ethpa. ܐܶܬܥܰܘܰܕ *to be accustomed, to accustom oneself, grow used to* esp. of tamed animals; ܟܰܕ ܡܶܬܪܰܒܝܳܐ ܘܡܶܬܥܰܘܕܳܐ ܥܰܡ ܒܢܰܝܢܳܫܳܐ *when it has been brought up and used to be with men;* ܒܡܰܡܠܠܳܐ ܕܠܳܐ ܡܶܬܥܰܘܰܕ ܐ̱ܢܳܐ ܒܶܗ *you use a language to which I am not accustomed.* Aph. only part. ܡܥܺܝܕ, ܡܥܺܝܕܳܐ and oftener ܡܥܰܕ, ܡܥܰܕܳܐ, ܡܥܰܕܳܐܺܝܬ with ܒ *to be accustomed, used, wont;* ܐܰܝܟ ܕܡܥܰܕ ܐܢܬ = ܐܰܝܟ ܕܡܥܰܕܳܐ ܐܺܝܬ ܠܳܟ *as you are wont, as your habit is;* ܐܰܝܟ ܕܡܥܰܕܳܐ ܕܗܳܘܝܳܐ *as is usual, as usually happens;* with ܥܰܡ *to be familiar* or *intimate with* any one. Derivatives, ܥܝܳܕܳܐ, ܥܝܳܕܳܝܳܐ, ܡܥܰܕܳܢܽܘܬܳܐ, ܡܥܰܘܕܳܐ.

ܥܘܕ (3) Heb. not found in O. or N.T., often otiose, *viz., sc., forsooth, indeed, again, for.*

ܥܘܕ (4) Ar. *lign-aloes.*

ܥܘܕ (5) ܥܘܕܳܐ pl. ܥܘܕܶܐ com. usually masc. *an unclean bird, the owl, little owl, night-hawk;* ܐܰܝܟ ܥܘܕܳܐ ܕܚܽܘܪܒܬܳܐ *as an owl in the desert.*

ܥܘܕ (6) m. *a lock of wool, flock, nap.*

ܥܘܕܳܢܳܐ same as ܥܰܕܢܳܐ; see above.

ܥܘܕܪܳܐ pl. ܶܐ rt. ܥܘܕ (6). *a lock of wool, flock; woolliness, nap* of cloth; *flock, down* or *woolliness* of plants; *lint, a morsel of plucked wool.*

ܥܘܕܪܳܐ rt. ܥܕܪ. *the rooting up* of weeds, *weeding* fields.

ܥܘܕܪܽܘܬܳܐ rt. ܥܘܕ (6). f. *woolliness, fleeciness; the nap* of clothes; *a stopping, plug* of flock or wool.

ܥܘܕܪܳܢܳܐ pl. ܢܶܐ rt. ܥܕܪ. *liberation.*

ܥܘܕܪܳܢܳܝܳܐ, ܥܘܕܪܳܢܳܝܬܳܐ, ܥܘܕܪܳܢܳܝܶܐ rt. ܥܕܪ. adj.

without, outside, extraneous, foreign; gram. *irregular, anomalous, foreign;* ܡܠܬܐ ܥܘܒܪܝܬܐ *strange* or *foreign speech;* ܥܘܒܪܝ ܬܪܥܝܬܐ *heterodox, of strange opinions.*

ܥܘܒܪܝܘܬܐ rt. ܥܒܪ. f. with ܕܡܠܬܐ *strange speech, foreign* or *outlandish pronunciation.*

ܥܘܕܠܐ pl. ܐ̈ rt. ܥܕܠ. m. *complaint, blame, reproof.*

ܥܘܕܢܐ pl. ܐ̈ from ܥܕܢ. m. *softness, delicacy;* pl. *delicacies, cates.*

ܥܘܕܪܢܐ, ܥܘܕܪܢ pl. ܐ̈ rt. ܥܕܪ. m. *a) aid, succour, an auxiliary force. b) advantage, benefit;* ܠܥܘܕܪܢܢ *for our good, for our benefit;* ܐܝܕܐ ܕܥܘܕܪܢܐ *a helping hand;* ܥܘܕܪܢܐ ܪܘܚܢܝܐ *spiritual benefit. c) relief, remedy, healing;* ܥܘܕܪܢܐ ܕܐܣܝܘܬܐ ܕܣܥܪ ܡܪܗ ܒܐܝܕܗ *the acts of healing which his Lord worked through him;* ܥܘܕܪܢܐ ܕܡܢ ܣܚܝܬܐ *relief from taking baths;* ܦܪܕܝܣܐ ܕܟܠܗ ܥܘܕܪܢܐ *Paradise where all ills will be redressed. d)* rit. ܩܠܐ ܕܥܘܕܪܢܐ ܕܥܢܝܕܐ *suffrages in aid of the departed;* E-Syr. the concluding collects of the daily offices.

ܥܘܗܕܢܐ, ܥܘܗܕܢ pl. ܐ̈, ܝ̈ rt. ܥܗܕ. m. *a) the memory, remembrance,* with ܠܐ *forgetfulness, oblivion;* ܡܢ ܥܘܗܕܢܐ *from memory;* with ܐܥܠ or ܥܒܕ *to bring to remembrance, remind, mention. b) a memory, record;* ܟܬܒܐ or ܣܦܪ ܥܘܗܕܢܐ *a book of records;* ܥܒܕ ܥܘܗܕܢܐ *a recorder, chronicler;* ܥܘܗܕܢ ܟܬܒܐ *a list* or *catalogue of books. c) a memorial, commemoration, day of commemoration, monument.*

ܥܘܘܐ and ܥܘܘܝܐ rt. ܥܘܐ. m. *howling, wailing.*

ܥܘܘܩ, ܥܘܘܩܐ pl. ܝ̈, ܐ̈, rt. ܥܘܩ. m. *a hindrance, impediment, obstacle, difficulty;* with ܕܠܐ *unhindered, unimpeded, free.*

ܥܘܙܐ, ܥܘܙ rt. ܥܙ. m. *energy, strength, fervour* of heat, cold, fire; of anger, of disease; *vehemence, violence* ܕܡܚܘܬܐ *of the blows;* ܥܘܙܐ ܕܪܘܚܐ ܥܙܝܙܬܐ *of fierce winds;* ܥܘܙܐ ܕܛܠܝܘܬܐ *the flower of youth;* ܕܥܠܝܡܘܬܐ *the prime* or *vigour of age.*

ܥܘܙܙܐ rt. ܥܙ. m. *fervour, heat, vehemence.*

ܥܘܙܢܝ rt. ܥܙ. *harsh, hard.*

ܥܘܙܢܐ rt. ܥܙܐ. m. *fortitude.*

ܥܘܙܠܐ pl. ܐ̈ m. *a fawn, young roe.*

ܥܘܙܐ *a hog.*

ܥܘܙܪܢܐ pl. ܐ̈ m. *thorn, bramble, spina Christi;* ܟܠܝܠܐ ܕܥܘܙܪܢܐ *a crown of thorns.*

ܥܘܛ, ܥܛ root-meaning *to irritate.* Pael ܥܝܛ and ܥܘܛ *to provoke, irritate;* ܥܝܛܬܗ ܕܚܠܬܐ *fear made her angry;* pass. part. ܡܥܝܛܐ, ܡܥܝܛ *provoked, angry.* Ethpa. ܐܬܥܝܛ *to be annoyed, fretted, chafed, irritated.* Derivatives, ܥܝܛܐ, ܥܝܛܐ.

ܥܘܛܦܐ rt. ܥܛܦ. m. *a) the act of putting on;* ܕܦܓܪܐ *putting on clothes, dressing;* ܕܦܓܪܐ *incarnation. b) apparel, attire;* ܡܠܒܫ ܥܘܛܦܐ ܕܫܘܒܚܐ *in glorious apparel.*

ܥܘܛܫܐ, ܥܘܛܫܬܐ pl. ܬ̈ rt. ܥܛܫ. f. *sneezing, a sneeze; snuff.*

ܥܘܝܐ rt. ܥܘܐ. m. *howling, wailing.*

ܥܘܝܦܐ pl. ܐ̈ rt. ܥܘܦ. m. *swaying; fainting, languor.*

ܥܘܝܦܐ same as ܥܘܦܝܐ.

ܥܘܝܪ, ܥܘܝܪܐ, ܥܘܝܪܬܐ rt. ܥܘܪ. *blind, one-eyed;* ܫܘܩܐ ܥܘܝܪܐ *a blind alley;* ܥܘܝܪ ܗܘܢܐ ܥܘܝܪ ܠܒܐ—ܪܥܝܢܐ— *blind of understanding, heart, mind.*

ܥܘܝܪܐܝܬ rt. ܥܘܪ. adv. *blindly.*

ܥܘܝܪܘܬܐ rt. ܥܘܪ. f. *blindness,* esp. of the heart, mind, &c.

ܥܘܝܬܐ rt. ܥܘܐ. f. *a) wailing, grief. b) tattered* or *ragged cloth.*

ܥܘܩ, ܥܩ root-meaning *to hold back.* Pael ܥܘܩ, act. part. ܡܥܘܩ, pass. part. ܡܥܘܩ, ܡܥܘܩܐ, also ܡܥܝܩ, ܐ, ܬܐ. *to hinder, impede;* ܠܐ ܥܘܩ ܐܢܘܢ ܨܥܪܐ *contumely has not held them back;* ܡܥܘܩܝܢ ܗܘܘ ܣܘܥܪܢܘܗܝ *his affairs were entangled, did not prosper.* Ethpa. ܐܬܥܘܩ *to be stopped, hindered* with ܡܢ, *entangled* with ܒ; ܡܢ ܨܠܘܬܐ *from prayer;* ܡܢ ܩܒܠܬ ܒܘܪܟܬܐ *from receiving blessings;* ܠܐ ܡܬܥܘܩܐ ܥܘܩܬܐ *there is no impediment, it does not matter.* Aph. ܐܥܝܩ, act. part. ܡܥܝܩ. *to obstruct, stop.* Derivatives, ܥܘܘܩܐ, ܡܥܘܩܢܐ, ܡܥܘܩܢܘܬܐ, ܡܬܥܘܩܢܐ, ܡܬܥܘܩܢܘܬܐ.

ܥܘܩܐ, ܥܘܩܬܐ rt. ܥܩ. m. *a hindrance, let, impediment;* ܕܠܐ ܥܘܩܐ *without let* or *hindrance, unimpeded, without delay.*

ܥܘܠ root-meaning *to do iniquity.* Ethpa.

ܐܬܥܘܠ to suffer injury or wrong; ܗܘ ܕܙܟܐ ܠܐ ܢܬܥܘܠ ܡܢ ܡܘܬܐ ܗܘ ܬܢܝܢܐ he that overcometh shall not be hurt of the second death; ܦܪܘܩ ܠܗܘ ܕܡܬܥܘܠ deliver the wronged. Aph. ܐܥܘܠ to wrong, do or commit wrong or injustice with ܒ; to entice to sin; with ܕܝܢܐ or ܕܝܢܐ ܘܐܘܪܚܐ to pervert justice or judgement; ܐܥܘܠܝܢ ܕܡܥܘܠܝܢ ܒܪܐܙܐ those who trespass against the sacraments, i.e. receive them wrongfully. Derivatives, ܥܘܠܐ, ܥܘܠܐ, ܥܘܠܐܝܬ, ܥܘܠܘܬܐ, ܡܥܘܠܘܬܐ.

ܥܘܠ, ܥܘܠܝܢ imperative of verb ܥܠ to enter.

ܥܘܠ, ܥܘܠܐ, ܥܘܠܬܐ pl. ܝܢ, ܐ, ܬܐ rt. ܥܘܠ. unjust, unrighteous, lawless; an evil or wrong doer, wicked man; ܕܝܐܬܝܩܐ ܥܘܠܬܐ an unjust or unfair will; ܫܘܠܛܢܐ ܥܘܠܬܐ unrighteous rule; ܥܘܠܐ ܡܫܬܠܛ ܥܠ ܙܕܝܩܐ the wicked tyrannizes over the righteous.

ܥܘܠܐ pl. ܥܘܠܐ rt. ܥܘܠ. m. iniquity, injustice, injury, wrong against man opp. ܚܛܝܬܐ wickedness towards God; ܡܡܘܢܐ ܕܥܘܠܐ mammon of unrighteousness; ܦܥܠܝ ܥܘܠܐ or ܥܒܕܝ workers of iniquity; ܒܥܘܠܐ unjustly, wrongfully, iniquitously.

ܥܘܠܐ pl. ܥܘܠܐ m. the embryo, fetus; a newborn babe, swaddled baby; ܥܘܠܐ ܡܬܩܪܐ ܟܡܐ ܕܥܛܝܦ ܒܥܙܪܘܪܐ it is called ܥܘܠܐ so long as it is wrapped in swaddling clothes, cf. ܝܠܘܕܐ; ܥܘܠܐ ܥܠܐ an infant too young to speak; metaph. ܥܘܠܝܗܘܢ ܕܦܐܪܐ the immature fruits of the earth.

ܥܘܠܐܝܬ rt. ܥܘܠ. adv. unjustly, unfairly, wrongfully, iniquitously.

ܥܘܠܒܐ Ar. f. a basket, pail.

ܥܘܠܒܢܐ pl. ܐ rt. ܥܠܒ. m. a) committing fraud, wrong; ܥܘܠܒܢܐ ܕܡܣܟܢܐ the defrauding of the poor. b) extreme, excess, eminence, superiority.

ܥܘܠܘܬܐ rt. ܥܘܠ. f. wrong, injustice, unrighteousness, wickedness.

ܥܘܠܘܬܐ from ܥܘܠܐ. f. the embryonic or rudimentary stage, infancy; ܡܥܠܒܝܢ ܐܢܫܐ ܥܘܠܘܬܗ men impugn the abiding of our Lord in the womb.

ܥܘܠܝܐ pl. ܐ rt. ܥܠܐ. m. rising, elevation, ascent; sublimity.

ܥܘܠܠܐ rt. ܥܠ. m. entrance, access, arrival.

ܥܘܠܡܐ pl. ܐ from ܥܠܡܐ. m. renewed youth; youthful lusts or innovations.

ܥܘܠܥܠܐ from ܥܠܥܠܐ. m. raising a whirlwind, stirring up strife.

ܥܡ, ܥܡܡ root-meaning to be cloudy, overclouded. Ethpa. ܐܬܥܡܡ the same; ܟܕ ܡܬܥܡܡ ܐܐܪ when the air grew dark or misty. Ethpailal ܐܬܥܡܥܡ to be cloudy, overcast with clouds. Aph. ܐܥܡ to darken, render obscure; metaph. ܠܐ ܢܥܡ ܡܪܝ ܥܘܗܕܢܝ let not the memory of me, O my Lord, be clouded. Derivatives, ܥܡܡܐ, ܥܡܝܡܐ.

ܥܘܡܓܢܐ rt. ܥܡܓ. m. gloom.

ܥܘܡܙܐ rt. ܥܡܙ. m. a morsel ܕܠܚܡܐ of bread.

ܥܘܡܙܐ rt. ܥܡܙ. m. closing, shutting in.

ܥܘܡܩܐ pl. ܝܢ, ܐ rt. ܥܡܩ. m. a) the deep, depth, deepness; ܥܘܡܩܘܗܝ ܕܝܡܐ the depths of the sea; ܕܡܕܒܪܐ the innermost desert; ܕܣܝܒܘܬܐ extreme old age; ܕܦܠܐܬܐ the profundity of a parable. b) a vale, dale, low-lying country. c) a meteor.

ܥܘܡܩܩܐ rt. ܥܡܩ. m. deep research.

ܥܘܡܪܐ pl. ܐ rt. ܥܡܪ. m. a) living, life, course or manner of life; ܫܘܠܡܐ ܕܥܘܡܪܗ the end of his life. b) a habitation, dwelling-place, house = family. c) the monastic life, a monastery, cell.

ܥܘܡܪܢܐ rt. ܥܡܪ. m. a dweller in a monastery.

ܥܘܢܕܢܐ rt. ܥܢܕ. m. a) removal, transference ܕܡܠܟܘܬܗ ܕܐܠܗܐ of the kingdom of God from the Jews to the Gentiles. b) departing, departure ܡܢ ܥܡܐ ܕܝܠܗ from his own people. c) decease, death; ܕܦܓܪܝ the putting off of my body; ܟܘܪܗܢܐ ܩܕܡ ܥܘܢܕܢܐ illness before death; ܫܘܠܡܐ ܕܥܘܢܕܢܗ the end of his failing health.

ܥܘܢܝܐ pl. ܐ rt. ܥܢܐ. m. a refrain, response, alternate chant, antiphon.

ܥܘܢܝܬܐ pl. ܬܐ rt. ܥܢܐ. f. an anthem, chant, response, chorus, alternate verse or verses sung by the choir.

ܥܘܢܢܐ from ܥܢܢܐ. m. a clouding over.

ܥܘܣܩܐ pl. ܐ rt. ܥܣܩ. m. worrying, care.

ܥܘܣܟܬܐ pl. ܼܬܐ rt. ܥܣܟ. m. *a*) *the roughness* of wood after sawing. *b*) pl. *worldly cares, distractions.*

ܥܘܣܩܐ pl. ܼܐ and ܥܘܣܩܢܐ rt. ܥܣܩ. m. *difficulty, embarrassment, vexation, pain.*

ܥܘܣܪܐ rt. ܥܣܪ. m. *a tenth part.*

ܥܘܥܝ act. part. ܡܥܘܥܝܐ. *to cry* as an infant.

ܥܛܦ, ܥܛܦ cf. ܥܛܦ and ܥܛܦܐ, fut. ܢܥܛܘܦ, act. part. ܥܳܛܶܦ, ܥܳܛܦܳܐ, pass. part. ܥܛܝܦ, ܥܛܝܦܐ. *a*) intrans. *to be double, have double;* ܥܛܝܦܐ ܥܩܬܗܘܢ ܕܐܝܬܝܗܝܢ *their sorrow is double.* *b*) trans. *to double, render double;* ܥܛܘܦ ܠܗ̇ ܥܳܛܦܳܐ *render unto her double.* *c*) *to fold, enfold, wind round, twist, twine, connect;* with ܚܒܠܐ *to twist a rope;* with ܥܘܛܦܐ *to enfold in a veil;* ܥܛܦ ܥܙܩܬܐ ܕܐܝܬ ܗܘܝ ܒܐܝܕܘܗܝ ܘܝܗܒ ܠܗ̇ *he twisted off the rings on his hands and gave them to her;* ܥܛܝܦܝܢ ܐܝܟ ܗܕܡܐ ܒܪܫܐ *connected as the limbs with the head;* ܐܥܛܘܦ ܡܠܝ ܥܠ ܬܫܥܝܬܗ *I will twine my words into a tale of him.* *d*) *to fail in strength, faint, swoon;* ܥܛܝܦܝܢ ܒܐܘܪܚܐ ܡܢ ܟܦܢܐ *they faint on the way from hunger.* Ethpa. ܐܬܥܛܦ *to grow languid, faint, droop;* ܣܛܢܐ ܟܕ ܐܬܥܛܦ *Satan wearied and giving way.* Aph. ܐܥܛܦ *to enfeeble.* Derivatives, ܐܥܛܦܐ, ܥܛܝܦܘܬܐ, ܥܛܦܐ, ܥܘܛܦܐ, ܥܛܝܦ, ܥܛܝܦܘܬܐ, ܥܛܦܬܐ or ܐܥܛܦܬܐ.

ܥܘܦܐ m. *a*) collect. subst. *fowl, winged creatures,* esp. birds of prey; ܡܪܐ ܥܘܦܐ *possessing wings;* ܥܘܦܐ ܕܦܩܥܬܐ *wild fowl;* ܥܘܦܐ ܕܒܝܬܐ *domestic fowls.* *b*) pl. ܼܐ m. *a high branch, tree top, vine-shoots.*

ܥܘܦܝܐ rt. ܥܦܐ. m. *bloom, herb, flowers;* ܕܚܩܠܐ *the flowers of the field, wild flowers;* ܕܪܛܝܒܐ *tender herb.*

ܥܘܦܝܐ pl. ܼܐ rt. ܥܦܐ. m. *enshrouding, interment; a winding-sheet, shroud;* ܟܕ ܛܥܝܢ ܥܘܦܝܗ *carrying his shroud;* ܥܘܦܝܗܘܢ *their winding-sheets;* ܥܠ ܥܘܦܝܐ ܕܥܢܝܕܐ *burial of the departed.*

ܥܘܦܝܢܐ pl. ܼܐ rt. ܥܦܐ. m. *a*) *herb, growth;* ܥܘܦܝܢܐ ܕܐܪܥܐ *the green things of the earth.* *b*) *distraction.* *c*) in the Lexx. *a place of pitch and sulphur.*

ܥܘܦܦ, ܥܘܦܦܐ pl. ܼܐ rt. ܥܦ. m. *multiplication, reduplication, repetition;* rhet. *tautology;* ܥܘܦܦ ܠܐ *a double negative;* ܥܠ ܥܘܦܦܐ *genuflexions.*

ܥܘܦܩܐ pl. ܼܐ rt. ܥܦܩ. m. *an embrace.*

ܥܘܦܪܐ, ܥܘܦܪܬܐ rt. ܥܦܪ. f. *dust* or *refuse of the threshing-floor, gleanings.*

ܥܨܪ, ܥܨܪ act. part. ܥܳܨܰܪ, pass. part. ܥܨܝܪܐ. *to press* or *join together.* Pa. ܥܨܪ *to howl, cry.* Derivative, ܥܨܪܘܬܐ.

ܥܘܨܦܪ m. *the blossom of cnicus, blessed thistle,* or of *carthamus, saffron-thistle, safflower.*

ܥܘܨܪܐ pl. ܼܐ rt. ܥܨܪ. m. *a*) *pressing* or *squeezing out.* *b*) *stones, skins, kernels* or *husks* of olives or grapes.

ܥܩ, ܥܩ fut. ܢܥܘܩ, act. part. ܥܳܐܶܩ, ܥܳܩܳܐ. the adj. ܥܩܝܩ is used instead of the pass. part. *to loathe, be weary, be out of heart* with ܒ or ܥܠ; ܠܐ ܬܩܪܐ ܝܬܝܪܐܝܬ ܥܕܡܐ ܕܬܥܘܩ *do not read overmuch till you are weary;* ܢܦܫܢ ܥܩܬ ܒ *our soul loathes.* Impers. with ܠ of the pers. and ܒ of the thing; ܥܩܬ ܠܝ ܒܚܝܝ *I am weary of my life;* ܥܩܬ ܗܘܬ ܠܗܘܢ ܒܗܕܐ *they were distressed about it.* Ethpe. ܐܬܬܥܝܩ *a*) *to be out of heart, wearied, grieved, indignant;* ܐܬܬܥܝܩ ܩܐܝܢ ܛܒ *Cain was very indignant;* ܡܬܬܥܝܩܝܢ ܐܢܬܘܢ ܒܢܣܝܘܢܐ *ye are out of heart with temptations.* *b*) *to be straitened, pent in;* ܐܬܬܥܝܩ ܒܬܪܨܐ ܡܢ ܥܡܪܝ *Zimri was pent in in Tirzah by Omri.* Ethpa. ܐܬܥܝܩ *to become wearied* or *disgusted; to be deeply distressed.* Aph. ܐܥܝܩ *a*) *to annoy, be troublesome, weary, grieve, distress;* ܒܚܛܗܝܗܘܢ ܐܥܝܩܘ ܪܘܚܐ ܕܒܪܘܝܗܘܢ *by their sins they grieved the spirit of their Creator;* ܐܥܝܩܬܢܝ ܕܠܐ ܩܘܝ ܠܝ *I am distressed that he did not wait for me.* Pass. part. ܡܥܝܩ, ܼܐ, ܼܬܐ. *weary, distressed;* ܐܪܥܐ ܕܡܥܝܩܐ ܐܢܬ ܒܗ̇ *the land which thou loathest;* ܒܝܐܘ ܠܡܥܝܩܐ *comfort the distressed.* Derivatives, ܥܩܬܐ, ܥܩܬܢܐ, ܥܩ, ܥܩܘܬܐ, ܥܩܝܩ, ܥܩܝܩܘܬܐ, ܐܥܩܬܐ, ܡܥܝܩܢܐ, ܡܥܝܩܢܘܬܐ.

ܥܘܩܒܐ pl. ܼܐ, ܼܐ rt. ܥܩܒ. m. *searching, investigation, inquiry;* ܕܠܐ ܥܘܩܒܐ *untested, without investigation;* ܕܚܠܘ ܦܪܘܫܐ ܡܢ ܥܘܩܒܐ *fear, O ye prudent,* and shun *curious search* into Divine matters.

ܥܘܩܒܪܐ pl. ܥܘܩܒܪܝܢ, ܥܘܩܒܪ̈ܐ and ܥܘܩܒܪ̈ܐ com. gen. *a mouse, field-mouse, jerboa; a maggot;* ܥ̈ ܦܪܚܬܐ *a bat;* ܐܪ̈ܙܝ ܥܘܩܒܪ̈ܐ *marjoram;* ܡܠܐ ܥܘܩܒܪ̈ܐ *a small boil;* ܥ̈ ܕܩܢܝܐ *root of sedge* or *reed*, perh. *the node* or *joint* of a reed.

ܥܘܩܒܪܬܐ pl. ܬ̈ܐ f. *a) a muscle. b) a she-mouse.*

ܥܘܩܒ Pauel conj. of ܥܩܒ.

ܥܘܩܒܐ and ܥܘܩܒܐ rt. ܥܩܒ. m. *sinuous motion* of a worm or serpent, *wriggling, writhing.*

ܥܘܩܠܐ pl. ܠ̈ܐ rt. ܥܩܠ. m. *an intricacy* or *difficulty* in the way, *that which leads astray* or *trips up.*

ܥܘܩܡܐ pl. ܡ̈ܐ rt. ܥܩܡ. m. *crookedness, perversity, stratagem.*

ܥܘܩܣܐ pl. ܣ̈ܐ rt. ܥܩܣ. m. *a sting, goad, sharp stake.*

ܥܘܩܣܐ rt. ܥܩܣ. m. *stinging, goading; extracting a sting.*

ܥܘܩܪܬܐ rt. ܥܩܪ. *extraction* ܕܫܢ̈ܐ *of the teeth.*

ܥܘܪ Pa. ܥܘܪ *to put out* one or both eyes, *to blind;* ܥܘܪܬ ܐܢܘܢ ܒܝܫܘܬܗܘܢ *their own wickedness hath blinded them;* ܫܘܚܕܐ ܡܥܘܪ ܥܝ̈ܢܝܗܘܢ ܕܚܟܝ̈ܡܐ ܒܕܝܢܐ *a gift blindeth the eyes of the wise in judgement.* Pass. part. pl. ܡܥܘܪ̈ܐ, ܡܥܘܪ̈ܬܐ. *the blind.* Metaph. with ܥܘܦܝ̈ܐ *to disbud.* Ethpa. ܐܬܥܘܪ *to be blinded;* ܐܬܥܘܪ ܡܕܥܗܘܢ *their understanding was darkened.* Aph. ܐܥܘܪ *to put out* the eyes, *to blind.* Derivatives, ܥܘܝܪܐ, ܥܘܝܪܘܬܐ, ܥܘܝܪܐܝܬ, ܥܘܪܐ, ܥܘܪܐ, ܥܘܪܢܐ.

ܥܘܪ, ܥܪ, parts. ܥܐܪ, ܥܝܪܐ, ܥܝܪܐ; ܥܝܪ, ܥܝܪܐ, ܥܝܪ̈ܬܐ. *to wake, watch.* Part. adj. *a) waking, watchful, vigilant, attentive, diligent;* ܐܢܐ ܕܡܟܐ ܘܠܒܝ ܥܝܪ *I sleep but my heart waketh;* ܥܝܪ ܦܠܓ or ܦܠܓ ܥܝܪܐ *half-awake;* ܪ̈ܥܘܬܐ ܥܝܪ̈ܐ or ܥܝܪ̈ܝ ܪܥܝܢ *watchful shepherds;* ܥܝܪ ܪܥܝܢܐ or ܥܝܪ ܬܪܥܝܬܐ *sober, prudent. b)* subst. *a watcher, guardian angel, angel;* ܫܒܩ ܥܝܪܐ ܕܢܗܘܐ ܢܛܪ ܗܕ̈ܡܝܗܘܢ *He left an angel to guard their limbs.* Ethpe. ܐܬܬܥܝܪ rarely and wrongly ܐܬܥܝܪ *to awake; to be awaked, aroused, excited, stirred up* of the sword, of wind; *to be attentive, sober; to wake* from the dead; ܡܬܬܥܝܪܝܢ ܘܩܝܡܝܢ *they wake and watch;* ܐܬܬܥܝܪ ܥܠ ܥܡܠܐ ܐܠܗܝ̈ܐ *he bestirred himself to godly labours;* ܐܬܬܥܝܪ ܥܠܝ ܒܥܠܕܒܒܐ *an enemy rose up against me;* ܐܡܬܝ ܕܡܬܬܥܝܪ ܡܡܠܠܐ *when speech is aroused* or *begins.* Pa. ܥܝܪ *to wake, rouse;* ܕܠܐ ܬܥܝܪܘܢ ܘܠܐ ܬܥܝܪܘܢ ܚܘܒܐ *that ye stir not up nor awake love.* Aph. ܐܥܝܪ *to wake, awaken, arouse* out of sleep, from death; *to rouse up, stir up, excite* passion, the enemy, insurrection, war, persecution; to good works; ܡܥܝܪ ܩܒܝܪ̈ܐ *awakening the buried;* ܐܥܝܪܘ ܗܘܝܬܘܢ ܬܪܥܝܬܟܘܢ *become sober.* Derivatives, ܥܝܪܐ, ܥܝܪܐܝܬ, ܥܝܪܘܬܐ, ܥܝܪܢܐܝܬ, ܥܝܪܢܘܬܐ, ܥܝܪܬܐ, ܡܥܝܪܢܐ, ܡܥܝܪܢܘܬܐ, ܡܬܬܥܝܪܢܘܬܐ.

ܥܘܪ, ܥܪ, root-meaning *to descend into an enclosed valley* or *into the ground.* Derivative, ܡܥܪܐ.

ܥܘܪ, ܥܘܪܐ, pl. ܐ̈ rt. ܥܘܪ. f. any minute particle that hurts the eye as *chaff, fine dust, down, smoke;* ܥܘܪܐ ܕܦܩܠܐ *the husk of pulse;* ܥܘܪܐ ܕܪܕܐ ܪܘܚܐ *chaff which the wind scattereth;* ܡܬܛܢܦ ܒܥܘܪܐ ܕܦܓܪܐ *it is defiled with particles of the body.*

ܥܘܪܐ rt. ܥܘܪ. m. *blindness.*

ܥܘܪܒܐ pl. ܒ̈ܐ m. *a) a raven. b) willow.*

ܥܘܪܒܐ rt. ܥܪܒ. m. *mingling.*

ܥܘܪܒܠܐ from ܥܪܒܠ. m. *sifting, shaking in a sieve.*

ܥܘܪܒܝܐ rt. ܥܪܒ. m. *a) intermingling, admixture. b)* pl. ܐ̈ *willow.*

ܥܘܪܒܢܝܐ from ܥܘܪܒܐ. *corvine, of* or *belonging to ravens.*

ܥܘܪܓܠܐ pl. ܐ̈ rt. ܥܪܓܠ. m. *rolling, wallowing; fomentation.*

ܥܘܪܙܐ and ܥܘܪܙܙܐ rt. ܥܪܙ. *gnawing* or *craunching* of bones.

ܥܘܪܙܠܐ pl. ܠ̈ܐ rt. ܥܪܙܠ. m. *a tangle, entanglement, intricacy; connexion, a connected series;* ܥܘܪܙܠܐ ܣܓܝܐܝܢ ܥܘܪܙܠܝܢ *very intricate, tricky;* ܣܘܪܝܐ ܕܟܘܟܒ̈ܐ *the glad maze of the stars;* ܥܘܪܙܠܐ ܡܡܠܠܝ̈ܐ *verbal intricacies.*

ܥܘܪܛܐ m. ܥܘܪܛܬܐ f. pl. ܛ̈ܐ, ܛ̈ܬܐ. *wind ejected from the stomach, eructation.*

ܥܘܪܛܠܐ from ܥܪܛܠ. m. *stripping, denudation.*

ܥܘܪܬܐ rt. ܥܘܪ. pl. f. *button-holes.*

ܥܘܪܠܐ abs. and constr. st. ܥܪܠ pl. ܥܪܠܝܢ, ܠܐ̈ rt. ܥܪܠ. *uncircumcised; profane, a gentile;* ܥܪܠ ܒܠܒܗ. ܥܪܠ ܒܒܣܪܗ *uncircumcised in heart and in flesh.*

ܥܘܪܠܘܬܐ pl. ܬܐ̈ rt. ܥܪܠ. f. *the foreskin, uncircumcision.*

ܥܘܪܦܬܐ *the temples* of the head.

ܥܘܪܥܘܪܐ from ܥܪܥܪ. m. *a lotion for the teeth, a gargle; gargling.*

ܥܘܪܦܐ rt. ܥܪܦ. m. *money-changing.*

ܥܘܪܦܠܐ from ܥܪܦܠ. m. *rolling on the ground* as a horse or mule.

ܥܘܪܦܢܐ, ܥܘܪܦܢ pl. ܢܐ̈ rt. ܥܪܦ. m. *money, change, small money;* ܥܘܪܦܢܐ ܕܣܐܡܐ *silver money.*

ܥܘܪܙܐ pl. ܐ̈ rt. ܥܪܙ. m. *a kind of pottage.*

ܥܘܪܩܐ rt. ܥܪܩ. m. *gnawing, crunching* of bones.

ܥܘܪܩܠܐ pl. ܠܐ̈ from ܥܪܩܠ. m. *a twist, turn; perplexity.*

ܥܘܪܬܐ f. pl. *damaged goods, chipped and broken crockery.*

ܥܘܫ only used in the participle. *to talk nonsense;* ܡܢܐ ܥܘܫܝܢ ܐܢܬܘܢ *what nonsense you talk.*

ܥܘܫܐ or ܥܘܫܐ pl. ܫܐ̈ m. *a*) *a marsh, swamp, bog. b*) *rank growth. c*) *a buffoon. d*) *nonsense, buffoonery.*

ܥܘܫܢܐ rt. ܥܫܢ. m. *strength, force, power, multitude; strong current* or *swelling* of a river; *a stronghold.*

ܥܘܫܩܐ rt. ܥܫܩ. m. *calumny.*

ܥܘܫܪܐ pl. ܐ̈ cf. ܥܣܪܐ. m. *a tenth, tithe.*

ܥܘܬܐ rt. ܥܬܐ. f. *wailing, bitter weeping.*

ܥܘܬܕ, ܥܘܬܕܐ pl. ܐ̈ rt. ܥܬܕ. m. *preparation, plan, purpose; preface;* ܥܘܬܕܗ ܕܕܝܢܐ *supreme condemnation;* ܥܘܬܕ ܩܪܒܐ *equipment of war;* ܚܛܗ̈ܐ ܕܡܢ ܥܘܬܕܐ *deliberate sins.*

ܥܘܬܠܐ rt. ܥܬܠ. m. *fraud, fraudulence.*

ܥܘܬܩܐ rt. ܥܬܩ. m. *age, old age, antiquity;* ܒܥܘܬܩܐ *in old time;* ܥܘܬܩܐ ܕܙܒܢܐ or ܕܥܠܡܐ *ancient time.*

ܥܘܬܪܐ pl. ܐ̈ rt. ܥܬܪ. m. *riches, opulence.*

ܥܘܬܪܢܝܐ rt. ܥܬܪ. *pertaining to riches.*

ܥܙ fut. ܢܥܙ, act. part. ܥܐܙ, ܥܙܐ, ܥܙܝܢ, ܥܙܢ, pass. part. ܥܙܝܙ, ܥܙܝܙܐ, ܥܙܝܙܬܐ. *to be powerful, full of force, vehement; to wax powerful, gain force, surpass* or *exceed in power, overpower* with ܥܠ; ܪܝܚܐ ܕܫܘܫܢܐ ܥܙ ܗܘܐ *the scent of the lily was overpowering;* ܟܪܝܘܬܐ ܥܙܐ ܗܘܬ ܛܒ *the disease gained great force;* ܥܡ ܝܒܝܫܘܬܐ ܥܙܐ ܚܡܝܡܘܬܐ *with the drought the heat grows overpowering;* ܢܘܪܐ ܥܙܐ *the fire waxes vehement;* ܗܘܘ ܐܝܟ ܐܪܥܐ ܥܙܝܙܬܐ *be like fertile ground.* Pass. part. ܥܙܝܙ ܛܥܡܐ *strong flavoured* opp. ܦܟܝܗܐ *insipid;* ܥܙܝܙܐ ܪܝܚܗ ܠܣܛܢܐ ܚܠܐ ܠܐܠܗܐ *its fragrance is rank to Satan, sweet to God;* ܪܘܚܐ ܥܙܝܙܬܐ *a mighty wind;* ܒܫܡܗ̈ܐ ܥܙܝܙܐ ܡܟܪܟܝܢ ܠܗ ܠܫܐܕܐ *they exorcise the demon with potent names.* Pa. ܥܙܙ *to encounter with fortitude, resist* or *bear undauntedly* with ܠܘܩܒܠ or ܠ. Ethpa. ܐܬܥܙܙ *to be mighty, strongly moved, animated* ܒܓܘܗ *inwardly;* ܒܪܘܚܐ *in the spirit;* ܒܚܡܬܐ, ܒܪܘܓܙܐ *in anger, wrath, &c.;* ܟܕ ܒܚܢܦܘܬܐ ܡܬܥܙܙ ܗܘܐ *being strongly devoted to paganism.* Derivatives, ܥܙܘܙܐ, ܥܙܝܙܐ, ܥܙܝܙܘܬܐ, ܥܙܝܙܐܝܬ, ܥܙܐ, ܥܘܙܐ, ܥܘܙܐ.

ܥܙܐ pl. ܥܙܝܢ, ܐ̈ com. gen. *a goat; Capella,* a star in the left shoulder of the constellation Auriga.

ܥܙܐ or ܥܙܝ root-meaning *to endure.* Pael ܥܙܝ *to endure with constancy, withstand with fortitude,* with ܠܘܩܒܠ, ܩܕܡ of the enemy; *to sustain, persist, persevere;* ܟܦܢܐ *to endure hunger;* ܒܨܘܡܐ *to fast with constancy;* ܐܦܝܣܘܗܝ ܕܢܥܙܐ ܩܠܝܠ *they persuaded him to withstand a while;* ܠܡܥܙܝܘ ܒܕܪܫܐ ܥܙܝܙܐ *to hold strong disputations.* Ethpa. ܐܬܥܙܝ *to strive with fortitude.* Derivatives, ܥܙܘܝܐ, ܡܥܙܝܢܐ, ܡܥܙܝܢܐܝܬ, ܡܥܙܝܢܘܬܐ.

ܥܙܠܐ pl. ܠܐ̈ rt. ܥܙܠ. m. *thread.*

ܥܙܘܦ, ܥܙܘܦܐ *rough, harsh, bristly, unpleasant.*

ܥܙܘܦܘܬܐ f. *roughness, harshness.*

ܥܙܘܪܐ rt. ܥܙܪ. m. *a wooden bolt* or *pin* to hold pieces of wood together.

ܥܙܝܙܐܝܬ rt. ܥܙ. adv. *vigorously, vehemently, intensely;* ܡܪܕܝܢ ܥܙܝܙܐܝܬ *flowing with a strong current.*

ܥܙܝܙܘܬܐ rt. ܥܙ. f. *vehemence, intensity,*

severity of cold, heat, light; of misery, persecution, &c.; *strength, acridness* of taste or smell.

ܥܙܠ fut. ܢܥܙܘܠ, act. part. ܥܙܠ, ܥܙܠܐ, pass. part. ܥܙܝܠ, ܠܐ, ܠܬܐ. *to spin, twist, twine;* ܒܘܨܐ ܥܙܝܠܐ *fine twined linen;* ܥܙܝܠܢ ܢܦܫܬܗܘܢ ܚܕܕܐ *their souls were knit together;* ܐܪܙܐ ܥܙܝܠ ܒܗܢܐ ܕܒܚܐ *a mystery was interwoven with this sacrifice.* Pael ܥܙܠ *to entwine, interweave;* ܠܫܢܟ ܡܥܙܠ ܗܘܐ ܢܟܠܐ *thy tongue wove guile;* pass. part. *implicated, involved, entangled, complicated* opp. ܦܫܝܛܐ *simple* or *straightforward;* ܡܥܙܠ ܒܚܛܗ̈ܐ *entangled in sins.* Ethpaal ܐܬܥܙܠ *a) to be tangled, intertwined, knit together;* ܣܒܐ ܘܟܪܝܗܐ ܘܡܬܥܙܠ *old and infirm and contorted. b) to join together;* ܠܡܬܥܙܠܘ *to join in combat;* ܠܐ ܢܬܥܙܠ ܥܡ ܒܝܫܐ *let us hold no converse with the wicked. c) to be joined* in marriage. Derivatives, ܥܙܘܠܐ, ܥܙܠܐ, ܥܙܠܐ, ܥܙܝܠܐ, ܡܥܙܠܐ, ܥܙܝܠܘܬܐ, ܡܥܙܠܢܘܬܐ, ܡܬܥܙܠܢܘܬܐ.

ܥܙܠܐ or ܥܙܠܐ rt. ܥܙܠ. m. *spinning; a web, cloth.*

ܥܙܡ *to melt, refine* gold.

ܥܙܩܬܐ or ܥܙܩܬܐ pl. ܥܙܩܬܐ f. *a) a ring, signet-ring;* ܗܘ ܕܥܙܩܬܐ *keeper of the signet;* ܒܘܪܟ ܥܙܩܬܐ *Blessing of the rings,* the first part of the marriage service; ܥܙܩܬܐ ܕܣܥܪܐ *ringlets. b) the seat, anus.*

ܥܙܪ pass. part. ܥܙܝܪ. *to entangle;* ܣܥܪܗ ܥܙܝܪ ܐܝܟ ܢܘܡܪܐ *her hair was tangled like a wild dog's.* Palal ܥܙܪܙܪ *to involve, intertwine; to enswathe, swaddle;* ܠܐ ܡܥܙܪܙܪ ܥܡ ܡܬ̈ܠܐ ܘܦܠܐܬ̈ܐ discourse *not involved in proverbs and parables.* Ethpalal ܐܬܥܙܪܙܪ *to be environed, enwrapped* esp. in swaddling-bands; ܒܡ̈ܝܐ ܐܐܪ ܡܬܥܙܪܙܪ *the air is encompassed with water.* Derivatives, ܥܙܪܘܙܐ, ܥܙܪܙܐ.

ܥܙܪܙܐ pl. ܐ̈ m. and ܥܙܪܙܢܝܬܐ f. rt. ܥܙܪ. *a swathing-band,* pl. *swaddling-clothes;* ܡܢ ܚܕܘܗܝ ܕܥܙܪ̈ܙܐ *from the cradle.*

ܥܙܪܙܪܐ pl. ܐ̈ m. ܥܙܪܙܪܬܐ pl. ܬ̈ܐ f. *the service-tree* or *berry; the medlar.*

ܥܙܪܙܬܐ f. *marriageable, of marriageable age.*

ܥܛܐ fut. ܢܥܛܐ, imper. ܥܛܝ, act. part. ܥܛܐ, ܥܛܝܐ, pass. part. ܥܛܐ, ܥܛܝܐ, root-meaning *to cover. To blot out, efface, cancel;* opp. ܪܫܡ *to inscribe;* ܡܕܝܢܬܐ ܕܥܛܬ ܠܗ̇ ܠܡܠܬܐ *the city which expunged the phrase . . .;* ܥܛܐ ܥܘܗܕܢܗ *whose memory is blotted out;* ܥܛܝܢ ܚܘ̈ܒܝܟܘܢ *your debts, sins, are blotted out.* Ethpe. ܐܬܥܛܝ *to be blotted out, effaced* esp. ܚܛܗܐ or ܫܡܐ *sin,* ܫܡܐ *a name;* ܐܬܥܛܝܬ ܡܠܟܘܬܐ ܕܦܪ̈ܣܝܐ *the Persian empire,* i.e. the dynasty of the Sassanidae, *ceased, was blotted out;* ܡܘܕܝܢܘܬܐ ܕܚܛܗ̈ܐ ܒܝܢܬܟܘܢ ܐܬܥܛܝܬ *confession of sins has fallen into desuetude amongst you.* Pa. ܥܛܝ *to entirely efface, wholly obliterate.* Aph. ܐܥܛܝ *to cause to be blotted out.* Derivatives, ܥܛܘܝܐ, ܥܛܝܐ, ܥܛܝܢܐ, ܡܥܛܝܢܘܬܐ.

ܥܛܐ m. *a grass* of which baskets, huts, &c. are woven.

ܥܛܘܝܐ, ܥܛܘܝܬܐ rt. ܥܛܐ. *he* or *that which erases.*

ܥܛܘܦܝܐ rt. ܥܛܦ. gram. *copulative.*

ܥܛܘܦܝܐ pl. ܐ̈ rt. ܥܛܦ. m. *a) return; turn, winding* of a river. *b)* gram. *the connexion* of any word with that which precedes it; ܐܬܐ ܕܥܛܘܦܝܐ *a copulative conjunction.*

ܥܛܘܦܝܝܐ rt. ܥܛܦ. *a copulative* particle.

ܥܛܘܪ, ܥܛܘܪܐ, ܥܛܘܪܬܐ rt. ܥܛܪ. *smoking, steamy, vaporous.*

ܥܛܘܪܐ or ܥܛܘܪܐ m. *the ichneumon, mus indicus.*

ܥܛܝ, ܥܛܝܐ rt. ܥܛܐ. m. *a cancelling* ܕܚܘ̈ܒܐ *of debts* or *sins;* ܕܚܢܦܘܬܐ *the abolition of paganism.* Gram. *blotting* or *crossing out.*

ܥܛܝܢܐ rt. ܥܛܐ. m. *obliteration, negation.*

ܥܛܝܦܘܬܐ rt. ܥܛܦ. f. *a) return;* ܥܛܝܦܘܬܐ ܕܡܬܚܕܬܢܘܬܐ *renascence, second existence. b) a double cloak.*

ܥܛܝܦܬܐ rt. ܥܛܦ. f. *a double garment, lined cloak.*

ܥܛܠ fut. ܢܥܛܠ, act. part. ܥܛܠ, ܥܛܠܐ, pass. part. ܥܛܝܠ, ܠܐ, ܠܬܐ. *to be hard* of hearing, of heart, *slow* of tongue, *stupid; to be hard, difficult;* ܡܢܘ ܗܟܢ ܣܟܠ ܘܥܛܝܠ *who can be so silly and stupid?* ܠܐ ܥܛܝܠ ܠܐܠܗܐ ܡܕܡ *nothing is hard to God.* Ethpa. ܐܬܥܛܠ *to find anything hard* or *difficult;*

ܕܠܐ ܬܬܥܛܠ ܠܡܨܠܝܘ lest thou find it hard to *pray.* DERIVATIVES, ܥܛܠܐ, ܥܛܝܠܐܝܬ, ܥܛܝܠܘܬܐ.

ܥܛܠ, ܥܛܝܠܐ, ܥܛܝܠܬܐ rt. ܥܛܠ. *a) slow* in doing or understanding; *hard, difficult;* ܥܛܠ ܠܫܢܐ *indistinct* or *hesitating in speech;* ܥܛܠ ܡܡܠܠܐ speech *hard to understand. b) stiff, stubborn, obstinate;* ܟܘܪܗܢܐ ܥܛܝܠܐ *obstinate diseases;* ܥܛܠ ܠܒܐ *hard-hearted.*

ܥܛܝܠܐܝܬ rt. ܥܛܠ. adv. *hardly, with difficulty.*

ܥܛܝܠܘܬܐ rt. ܥܛܠ. f. *slowness* of apprehension, *hardness* of heart, *dullness, stubbornness.*

ܥܛܡܐ, ܥܛܡܐ pl. ܥܛܡܬܐ f. *the thigh;* ܓܝܕܐ ܕܥܛܡܐ *the femoral tendon;* metaph. *the side;* ܥܛܡܬܐ ܕܛܘܪܐ *the hill-sides.*

ܥܛܦ fut. ܢܥܛܘܦ, act. part. ܥܛܦ, ܥܛܦܐ, pass. part. ܥܛܝܦ, ܐ̈ܢ, ܬܐ. *a) to turn another way, turn back, return, to do anything again;* ܐܢ ܨܒܐ ܐܢܬ ܕܬܥܛܘܦ if *you choose to come back hither;* ܥܛܦ ܝܬܒ *he sat down again;* a genealogy ܕܥܛܦܐ *going backwards* i.e. *beginning at the end. b) to reflect, be reflected* as light. *c) to return* a purchase; ... *he may return* the slave *and recover the price. d) to clothe oneself, put on clothes.* Pass. part. *a)* impers. ܠܐ ܥܛܝܦ ܠܝ *I did not come back. b) clothed, arrayed; bearing, wearing;* ... *a white garment;* ... *victorious, arrayed in victory;* ... or ... *arrayed in light;* ... *crowned;* ... *having taken the name, bearing the name;* ... *souls who have put on* or *received Baptism.* Gram. ... *when it takes the plural form.*

ETHPE. ܐܬܥܛܦ *to be covered* as the lip of a leper; *to return.* PA. ܥܛܦ *a) to cover, deck, clothe, array;* ... *Who covereth the heavens with clouds. b) to add, insert* extra verses. *c) to assume* a name. Part. *having put on, clothed, wearing* ... *purple;* ... *golden ornaments;* ... *sackcloth;* ... *beauty.* ETHPA. ܐܬܥܛܦ *a) to wrap* or *shroud oneself, to put on, assume; to be covered, clothed* with ܒ or ܥܠ; ܠܐ ܬܬܥܛܦ ܥܠ ܣܦܘܬܟ *do not cover thy lips* i.e. in sign of grief. *b) to be covered* as a door with curtains. APH. ܐܥܛܦ *to cover as with a garment, wrap round, endue;* ... *Thou hast robed him in honour and glory;* ... *Thou hast covered me with shame. b) to interpolate* a verse. *c) to send back, return* a gift, a purchase; *to recall* words or actions; *to return, reciprocate* affection; ... *they sent him back to prison.* DERIVATIVES, ܥܛܘܦܐ, ܥܛܘܦܐ, ܥܛܘܦܐ, ܥܛܦܐ, ܥܛܦܬܐ, ܥܛܝܦܐ, ܥܛܝܦܘܬܐ, ܥܛܘܦܝܐ.

ܥܛܦܐ rt. ܥܛܦ. m. *a) clothing, a cloak. b) retrograde movement* of the stars.

ܥܛܦܬܐ rt. ܥܛܦ. f. *a) a mantle, cloak, shroud. b) putting on a cloak, enshrouding* the dead. *c) an interpolated verse. d) return.*

ܥܛܪ fut. ܢܥܛܪ, act. part. ܥܛܪ, ܥܛܪܐ, pass. part. ܥܛܝܪ. *to exhale, to rise up* as vapour, smoke or steam, *to steam, smoke;* ܕܥܛܪ ܒܬܢܢܐ *rising up in smoke;* ... *his lamentations rise up;* ... *lees of oil, muddy water* i.e. containing sediment after evaporation. ETHPA. ܐܬܥܛܪ *to be burned* as incense. APH. ܐܥܛܪ *to produce fumes, burn incense* or *perfume, make a fragrance;* ... *burn incense within the sanctuary;* ... *do Thou, O Lord, make fragrant within us the sweet odour of the pleasantness of Thy love.* DERIVATIVES, ܥܛܘܪܐ, ܥܛܪܐ, ܥܛܪܢܐ, ܥܛܪܢܝܐ, ܥܛܪܢܐ, ܥܛܪܐ, ܥܛܪܝܐ.

ܥܛܘܪܐ rt. ܥܛܪ. m. *a perfumer, preparer of perfumes.*

ܥܛܪܐ pl. ̈ܐ, ܐ̈ rt. ܥܛܪ. m. *vapour, fume, steam, incense* esp. of anything offered in sacrifice; ܥܛܪܐ ܕܒܣܡܐ *sweet incense;* ܥܛܪܐ ܕܟܒܪܝܬܐ *sulphur fumes;* ܥܛܪܐ ܕܢܘܪܐ *fiery vapour.*

ܥܛܪܢܐ pl. ܐ̈ rt. ܥܛܪ. *odorous, fragrant.*

ܥܛܪܢܐ or ܥܛܪܢܐ rt. ܥܛܪ. m. *cedar resin, oil of cedar, resin.*

ܥܛܪܢܝܐ, ܝܬܐ rt. ܥܛܪ. *vaporous, steamy;* ܡܢܘܬܐ ܥܛܪܢܝܬܐ *particles of vapour.*

ܥܛܫ root found in Chaldee and Arabic

to sneeze. DERIVATIVES, ܥܛܘܫܐ, ܥܛܫܐ, ܡܥܛܫܢܐ.

ܥܛܫܬܐ rt. ܥܛܫ. m. sneezing.

ܥܝܐ = ܘܝܐ mimet. woe; ܥܝܐ ܠܟ woe betide thee.

ܥܝܒ Pael conj. of ܥܘܒ.

ܥܝܒܐ pl. ܐ̈ rt. ܥܘܒ. m. a) a large leathern pouch or wallet; a trunk. b) thick clouds.

ܥܝܕ Pael conj. of ܥܘܕ.

ܥܝܕ, ܥܝܕܐ pl. ܐ̈ rt. ܥܘܕ. m. a) custom, habit, rite, use; ܐܝܟ ܥܝܕܐ as usual; ܐܝܟ ܥܝܕܐ ܕܚܢܦ̈ܐ according to the custom of the heathen; ܐܝܟ ܥܝܕܐ ܕܢܡܘܣܐ according to the law; ܥܝܕܐ usual, customary; ܐܪܝܟܝܢ ܗܘܘ ܩܫܬܗܘܢ ܡܢ ܥܝܕܐ their bows were longer than is usual; ܥܝܕܐ ܗܘ ܠܟܬܒܐ ܩܕܝܫܐ Holy Scripture is wont. b) pl. habits, customs, behaviour; ܥܝ̈ܕܐ ܚܢܦ̈ܝܐ heathen customs.

ܥܝܕܐ rt. ܥܘܕ, ܥܕ. m. extirpation of weeds.

ܥܝܕܢܝܐ, ܥܝܕܢܝܬܐ rt. ܥܘܕ. a) customary, usual, familiar; ܡܡܣܪܩܘܬܐ ܥܝܕܢܝܬܐ carelessness arising from familiarity; ܡܡܠܠܐ ܥܝܕܢܝܐ familiar conversation. b) ethical, moral. c) festal, cf. ܥܐܕܢܝܐ.

ܥܝܩܘܬܢܝܐ rt. ܥܘܩ. grievous, troublesome.

ܥܝܩܘܬܢܐܝܬ rt. ܥܘܩ. adv. hardly, painfully.

ܥܝܘܬܐ or ܥܝܘܬܐ m. the name of the star Aldebaran.

ܥܝܛ Pael of ܥܘܛ.

ܥܝܛܐ pl. ܐ̈ rt. ܥܘܛ. m. indignation, vexation, blustering; contumely, reproach.

ܥܝܛܪܐ rt. ܥܛܪ. m. cedar resin.

ܥܝܛܪܢܐ pl. ܐ̈ rt. ܥܛܪ. m. cedar resin or oil; a mixture of oil and pitch.

ܥܝܛܢܝ, ܥܝܛܢܝܐ rt. ܥܘܛ. irritating.

ܥܝܡܢ, ܥܝܡܢܐ rt. ܥܡܡ. dusky, gloomy.

ܥܝܦ, ܥܝܦܐ rt. ܥܘܦ. a) folded; ܐܘܪܪ̈ܐ ܟܕ ܥܝܦܦܝܢ stoles when doubled or folded. b) weary, fainting, failing.

ܥܝܦܘܬܐ rt. ܥܘܦ. f. weakness, faintness.

ܥܝܩ, ܥܝܩܐ, ܥܝܩܬܐ rt. ܥܘܩ. a) impers. verbal use ܥܝܩܐ ܠܢ it grieves us, we are straitened; ܟܕ ܥܝܩܐ ܠܗ grieving, distressed. b) usually in the construct state with ܠܒܐ, ܢܦܫܐ or ܪܘܚܐ grieved, distressed, sad.

ܥܝܩܐܝܬ rt. ܥܘܩ. adv. sadly.

ܥܝܩܘܬܐ rt. ܥܘܩ. f. sadness.

ܥܝܠܐ pl. ܥܝ̈ܠܝܢ or ܥܝ̈ܠܐ, ܥܝ̈ܠܐ m. a foal, colt.

ܥܝܡܐ pl. ܐ̈ rt. ܥܡܡ. m. mist, fog, cloud, mass of clouds; metaph. rit. a veil.

ܥܝܢ, ܥܝܢܐ pl. ܥܝ̈ܢܝܢ, ܥܝ̈ܢܐ, in the metaphorical senses ܥܝ̈ܢܝܢ, ܥܝ̈ܢܬܐ. f. the eye; ܥܝܢܐ ܒܝܫܬܐ an envious eye; ܒܝܬ ܥܝ̈ܢܐ the forehead. Metaph. a) of men: ܥܝܢܐ ܢܗܝܪܬܐ ܡܘܫܐ ܠܟܠܗ ܥܡܐ Moses was a clear eye to the whole nation; ܥܝ̈ܢܐ ܕܕܪܐ ܗܘ the lights of that generation. b) ܥܝܢܐ ܕܡܕܥܐ, ܕܪܥܝܢܐ &c. intelligence, the mental eye. c) a view, opinion. d) ܥܝܢܐ ܕܐܪܥܐ the surface of the earth. e) ܥܝܢܐ ܕܒܘܪܟܐ the socket of the knee. f) the opening or span of a bridge. g) the buds of a vine. h) the colour, sparkle of wine, of precious stones. i) ܥܝܢܐ ܕܡܝܐ usually ellipt. a spring, fount, fountain, source; ܥܝ̈ܢܬܐ ܕܡܝ̈ܐ springs of water; ܟܢܫ ܥܝ̈ܢܬܐ ܘܐܪܕܝ ܡܝ̈ܗܝܢ ܠܕܝܪܐ he collected the springs and conducted their waters into the monastery. ܥܝܢ often forms part of a proper name as in ܥܝܢ ܓܕܝ Engedi, ܥܝܢܘܪܕܐ 'Ain Warda, the Fount of Roses.

With preps.: ܒܥܝܢ, ܒܥܝ̈ܢܝ in the sight of, before; ܥܝܢ ܒܥܝܢ eye to eye; ܥܝܢ ܥܝܢܐ to the face, openly, publicly; ܥܝܢܐܝܬ ܚܙܘ ܠܬܕܡܪ̈ܬܐ they were eye-witnesses of these marvels; ܥܝܢ or ܠܥܝܢ in the sight of, before: with suffixes is often spelt ܠܥܝܢ: ܠܥܝܢܝ or ܠܥܝ̈ܢܝ in my sight, ܠܥܝܢܝܟ or ܠܥܝ̈ܢܝܟ in thy sight, &c.; ܠܥܝ̈ܢܝ ܥܡܐ in the sight of the people; ܥܝܢ ܠܟܠܢܫ ܠܐ ܬܚܘܐ ܠܗ show no one; ܠܥܝܢ ܥܠܡܐ ܟܠܗ before the whole world, publicly; ܠܥܝܢ ܫܡܫܐ in the open day. DERIVATIVES, verb ܥܝܢ, ܡܥܝܢܐ, ܡܥܝܢܐ, ܥܝܢܐ, ܥܝܢܘܬܐ.

ܥܝܢ ܥܓܠܐ calf's eye, some precious stone, perhaps sardonyx or amethyst.

ܥܝܢ ܬܘܪܐ buphthalmum, ox-eye, a composite flower.

ܥܝܢ denom. verb Pael conj. from ܥܝܢܐ. a) to eye, look at, perceive. b) to point out, show; ܥܝܢܗ ܠܚܒܪܗ ܥܠ ܩܢܝ̈ܢܘܗܝ he showed his companion his properties. ETHPA. ܐܬܥܝܢ to be pointed out, designated. ETHPALP. ܐܬܥܝܢܢ to be ingrafted.

ܥܝܢܬܐ; see under ܥܝܢ, ܥܝܢܐ.

ܥܝܢܘܢܬܐ dim. of ܥܝܢܐ. f. *a little eye, little spring.*

ܥܝܢܢܐ from ܥܝܢܐ. m. adj. *having large eyes.* subst. *budding.*

ܥܝܦܐ rt. ܥܘܦ. m. *folding up; a swoon;* a horse's *mane,* cock's *comb.*

ܥܝܦܐܝܬ oftener ܥܝܦܐܝܬ *doubly.*

ܥܝܦܘܬܐ rt. ܥܘܦ. f. *a mane.*

ܥܝܩܘܬܐ rt. ܥܘܩ. f. *a) urgency. b) nearness, propinquity.*

ܥܝܪ, ܥܝܪܐ, ܥܝܪܬܐ *vigilant; a watcher:* see under ܥܘܪ.

ܥܝܪܐ, ܥܝܪܬܐ pl. ܥܝܪ̈ܐ rt. ܥܘܪ. f. *vengeance* esp. ܥܝܪܐ ܕܕܡܐ *blood-vengeance, demand* or *penalty for bloodshed;* with ܣܡ *to be liable to a blood-feud,* with ܬܒܥ *to exact satisfaction* for the slain.

ܥܝܪܐ, ܥܝܪܬܐ for ܥܪܬܐ f. *a rival, second wife.*

ܥܝܪܐܝܬ rt. ܥܘܪ. adv. *watchfully, vigilantly.*

ܥܝܪܘܢ m. pl. *asphodel.*

ܥܝܪܘܬܐ rt. ܥܘܪ. f. *a) wakefulness, vigilance, diligence, attention;* ܕܡܠܐܟ̈ܐ *the angels' watch;* ܕܢܦܫܐ or ܕܗܘܢܐ *heed, vigilance;* ܕܬܫܡܫܬܐ *diligent service. b) rousing.*

ܥܝܪܘܬܢܝܐ, ܢܝܬܐ rt. ܥܘܪ. *pertaining to vigils.*

ܥܝܫܘܫܐ pl. ܫ̈ܐ m. *a pock-mark; a wart, callosity.*

ܥܟܘܪܐ rt. ܥܟܪ. m. *a troubler;* ܥܟܪ ܥܟܘܪܗ ܕܐܝܣܪܐܝܠ *Achar the troubler of Israel.*

ܥܟܒ Pael ܥܟܒ *to hinder, detain, prevent, obstruct;* ܥܟܒ ܠܐܝܓܕ̈ܐ *he detained the ambassadors;* ܠܐ ܡܕܡ ܥܟܒܝܢ ܠܚܕ̈ܕܐ day and night *in no wise hinder each other;* ܬܢܢܐ ܕܡܥܟܒ ܠܐܐܪ ܫܦܝܐ *smoke which clouds the pure air.* Ethpa. ܐܬܥܟܒ *to be hindered, prohibited* ܡܢ ܡܫܘܬܦܘܬܐ *from conjugal intercourse;* ܠܐ ܬܬܥܟܒ ܡܢ ܝܘܡ ܠܝܘܡ *put not off from day to day.* Derivatives, ܥܟܒܐ, ܥܟܒܘܬܐ, ܡܥܟܒܢܐ.

ܥܟܒܪܐ Num. xxiii. 10 and quoted thence in the Lexx. is a mistake for ܥܦܪܐ.

ܥܟܢܒܐ for ܥܝܢܒܐ. name of a plant.

ܥܠ fut. ܢܥܘܠ, imper. ܥܘܠ, infin. ܡܥܠ or ܡܥܠܠ, act. part. ܥܐܠ, ܥܐܠܐ, part. adj. ܥܠܝܠ, ܠܐ, ܠܬܐ. *a) intrans. to enter, come in;* ܠܐ ܥܐܠ ܘܢܦܩ ܠܡܥܠ ܘܠܡܦܩ *to go in and out;* ܠܐ ܥܐܠ ܘܠܐ ܢܦܩ ܠܘܬܗ = *to no one. b)* trans. with ܒ, ܠ, ܠܘܬ, ܩܕܡ, ܥܠ, ܠܘܬ &c.; ܥܐܠܐ ܥܠ ܚܝ̈ܐ ܠܗ *life returns to him;* ܥܠ ܥܠ ܥܡܠܗ *he entered into the labour* of another. With ܥܠ or ܠܘܬ *to come in* to a woman. *c) to attack, invade* with ܒ; with ܢܦܫܐ *to attempt to kill;* ܠܩܪܒܐ *to go to war;* ܥܠ ܚܙܝܪܐ ܥܠ ܓܒܪܐ *the pig came at the man. d) to begin;* ܡܢ ܡܥܠܬܐ ܕܫܢܬܐ *at the coming in of the year;* ܥܐܠ ܨܘܡܐ ܩܪܝܒ *the fast is coming, draws near. e) to come in, be carried in;* ܥܠܠܬܐ ܒܡܥܠܬܐ ܕܥܠܠܬܐ *at the bringing in of harvest. f) to go towards* as a road. With ܐܝܪܬܘܬܐ *to take possession;* ܠܓܙܘܪܬܐ *to undergo circumcision;* ܠܕܝܢܐ *to go to law;* ܒܢܦܫܐ see c; ܠܐ ܥܐܠܝܢ ܠܡܢܝܢܐ *they cannot be numbered;* ܚܠܦ *to be instead of, be substituted;* ܒܡܘܡܬܐ *to enter into a covenant by oath;* ܠܣܗܕܘܬܐ *to come to witness, to testify;* ܒܣܟܠܘܬܗܘܢ *to perceive* or *recognize their folly;* ܒܪܐܙܐ ܥܡ *to agree* or *conspire with;* ܒܫܢܝܐ *to advance in years, age;* ܥܠ ܒܫܢܬܐ ܕܬܠܬܥܣܪ *he had entered his thirteenth year;* ܠܡܫܘܡܬܗ *to have come to full age;* ܠܗܝܡܢܘܬܐ ܕܛܝܝ̈ܐ *to enter the religion of the Arabs, embrace Islam.*

Pass. part. *entered, brought in; advanced* ܒܕܘܒܪܐ *in the monastic life;* ܒܫܢܝܐ *in years;* ܥܠܝܠ ܒܗ ܫܐܕܐ *a devil entered into him;* ܟܕ ܗܝ ܡܢ ܥܠܝܠܐ ܗܘܬ ܠܥܕܬܐ *when* that opinion *had been introduced into the Church;* ܨܘܪܬܐ ܥܠܝܠܬܐ ܒܐܫܝܬܐ *a picture let into the wall.* Ethpe. ܐܬܥܠܠ *to be brought in, introduced; to enter; find entrance.* Pael ܥܠܠ pass. part. ܡܥܠܠ ܒܫܢܝܐ—ܡܥܠܠܬܐ *advanced in years;* in the Lexx. ܡܥܠܠܝܢܢ *we allege, bring an excuse.* Ethpa. ܐܬܥܠܠ *a) to enter;* ܐܬܥܠܠ ܒܗ ܣܛܢܐ *Satan entered into him. b) to allege, make a pretext, excuse;* ܐܬܥܠܠ ܒܣܬܘܐ *he excused himself on account of the winter;* ܐܬܥܠܠܘ ܒܥܠܠܬܐ *they made false excuses.* Aph. ܐܥܠ *a) to bring, put* or *carry in;* ܠܐ ܬܥܠܢ ܠܢܣܝܘܢܐ *bring us not into temptation;* ܡܥܠ ܐܝܕܗ ܒܡܝ̈ܐ *he puts his hand in the water;* ܐܥܠ ܢܦܫܗ ܒܥܢܝ̈ܢܐ ܥܠܡܝ̈ܐ *he got mixed up with worldly affairs;* ܠܐ ܬܥܠ ܬܫܡܫܬܐ ܒܬܫܡܫܬܐ *thou shalt not put one office on another* i.e. say prayers for two of the hours at one time. *b*) *to bring in, introduce* a custom, rite, opinion, doctrine, heresy. *c*) *to insert* notes from the margin into the text. With ܚܠܦ *to substitute, put instead;* ܥܠ *to bring* an accusation *against;* ܥܠܠܬܐ *to bring in the harvest.* Ethtaph. ܐܬܬܥܠ *to be brought* or *conducted in;* ܐܬܬܥܠ ܠܐܡܝܕ ܒܙܘܚܐ *he made his entrance into Amid with pomp.* Derivatives, ܡܥܠܐ, ܥܠܠܐ, ܥܠܠ, ܡܥܠܢܐ, ܥܠܠܬܐ, ܡܥܠܢܘܬܐ, ܥܠܬܐ, ܡܥܠܬܐ or ܥܠܢܐ, ܥܠܠܢܐ, ܥܠܠܢܘܬܐ, ܥܠܠܝܐ, ܥܠܠܐܝܬ, ܡܥܠܢܐ, ܡܥܠܐ, ܥܠܝܘܬܐ, ܥܠܝܢܐ, ܥܠܠܢܐ, ܡܥܠܢܘܬܐ, ܡܥܠܠܢܐ, ܡܥܠܠܢܘܬܐ.

ܥܠ rt. ܥܠܐ. prep. takes the suffixes of a noun in the m. pl. *a*) of place: *above, upon, on, near, by; opposite, against;* ܥܠ ܝܕ *close by, near;* ܐܬܪܥܐ *at* or *by the gate;* with ܣܡ *to lay upon.* *b*) of motion: *to, unto;* ܗܘܐ ܦܬܓܡܐ ܕܡܪܝܐ ܥܠ *the word of the Lord came unto;* with ܫܕܪ or ܫܠܚ *to send to.* *c*) of cause or subject: *for, as, because of, on account of, concerning, about, of;* ܥܠ ܐܦܝ *for the sake of;* ܥܠ ܗܕܐ *about* or *concerning this, on that account, therefore;* ܥܠ ܕ *because, on account of; in order to; whilst;* ܥܠ ܗܘ ܕ *because;* ܥܠ ܡܢܐ and ܥܠܡܢܐ *wherefore, on what account?* ܥܠܘܗܝ ܕܗܘ ܥܠܘܗܝ *of the same matter;* ܥܠ ܥܠܬܐ *on account of;* ܒܟܝܐ ܥܠ ܒܢܝܗ *weeping for her children;* with ܐܬܐܡܪ *to be said of* or *concerning;* with ܒܥܐ or ܫܐܠ *to inquire, ask about* or *concerning;* ܦܩܕ *to command* or *charge concerning;* ܨܠܝ *to pray for.* *d*) of war or enmity: *to, with, against;* ܥܒܕ ܩܪܒܐ ܥܠ *to make war;* ܟܢܫ ܥܠ *to collect* forces *against;* with ܣܠܩ *to go up to* or *against;* ܫܪܐ *to lay siege to;* ܪܓܙ *to be angry with;* ܡܪܝܪ ܥܠ *bitter against.* *e*) expressing number or distance: *to, over, more, beyond;* ܠܐ ܢܬܘܣܦ ܐܢܫ ܥܠ ܡܢܝܢܐ ܗܢܐ *let no one be added to that number;* ܡܦܠܓ ܥܠ ܐܪܒܥܐ *he divides by four;* ܡܬܦܠܓ ܥܠ ܬܪܝܢ ܡܢܘܢ *it is divided into two parts;* ܫܒܥܝܢ ܙܒܢܝܢ ܥܠ ܫܒܥ *seventy times seven;* ܥܠ ܫܬ ܡܝܠܝܢ ܡܢ *over six miles from …;* ܬܠܬܐ ܦܬܓܡܐ ܢܫܪܘܢ ܥܠ ܐܬܘܬܐ *three verses shall begin with each letter.* Idioms: *f*) expressing affliction: ܡܝܬܬ ܥܠܘܗܝ ܪܚܝܠ *Rachel died.* *g*) obligation: ܐܝܬ ܥܠܝ—ܥܠܝܟ *I ought, thou oughtest,* &c.; ܠܝܬ ܐܢܫ ܥܠܝ ܡܕܡ *no one has aught against me;* ܨܘܡܐ ܣܝܡ ܥܠܝܗܘܢ *abstinence is enjoined on them.* *h*) position or dignity: ܥܠ ܒܝܬܐ *over the household;* with ܐܡܠܟ *to reign over.* *i*) possession: ܐܝܬ ܥܠܝ—ܥܠܝܟ *I have, thou hast,* &c. *j*) close relation: *by, with, according to;* ܚܒܝܒ ܥܠܘܗܝ *beloved by him;* ܕܚܝܠ ܥܠ ܒܥܠܕܒܒܘܗܝ *feared by his enemies;* ܥܠ ܡܢ ܝܠܦܬ ܐܣܝܘܬܐ *under whom hast thou studied medicine;* ܥܠ ܫܡ *by the name,* with ܒܢܐ *to build a city and name it after some one;* ܥܠ ܫܘܘܕܝܐ *according to agreement, on condition.* *k*) in composition: ܥܠ ܡܡܠܠܐ *ineffable;* ܥܠ ܡܠܬܐ *an adverb.*

ܠܥܠ comp. of ܠ and ܥܠ. adv. *upward, above* opp. ܠܬܚܬ; ܕܠܥܠ *upper, higher, superior;* ܡܠܘ ܐܢܘܢ ܥܕܡܐ ܠܥܠ *they filled* them *up to the brim;* ܡܢ ܗܫܐ ܘܠܥܠ *henceforward;* ܬܓܡܐ ܕܠܥܠ *the companies above;* ܠܫܢܐ ܕܠܥܠ *mountain dialect;* ܡܢ ܠܥܠ *above, from above;* ܠܥܠ ܡܢ *above, upon, beyond;* ܠܥܠ ܡܢ ܡܠܬܐ *ineffable.*

ܥܠܐ or ܥܠܝܐ; see ܥܠܠܬܐ.

ܥܠܐ or ܥܠܝܐ, ܥܠܠܬܐ. f. *thorn, bramble.*

ܥܠܐ, ܥܠܝ not found in Peal. Pael ܥܠܝ *to raise, elevate, exalt; to offer a higher price;* with ܫܘܪܐ *to raise the wall, make it higher;* ܠܕܪܓܐ ܪܡܐ *to a high position.* Pass. part. ܡܥܠܝ, ܡܥܠܝܐ, ܡܥܠܝܬܐ. *lofty, exalted, sublime* opp. ܡܬܡܟܟܐ *low.* With ܡܢ *excelling, superior;* ܛܒ ܡܥܠܝܐ *most excellent;* ܐܠܗܐ ܟܠܗ ܡܥܠܝܐ *God wholly exalted;* ܟܝܢܐ ܡܥܠܝܐ *the Supreme Nature;* ܡܠܟܝܬܐ ܘܡܥܠܝܬܐ *royal and exalted matters;* ܬܕܡܘܪܬܐ ܡܥܠܝܐ ܡܢ ܚܝܠܐ ܐܢܫܝܐ *a miracle exceeding human power.* Ethpa. ܐܬܥܠܝ *a*) *to be raised, elevated, exalted* ܠܕܪܓܐ ܪܡܐ *to high degree; to be eminent, exalted, to excel* with ܒ, ܒܚܟܡܬܐ *in wisdom;* ܒܕܘܒܪܐ *in conduct;* ellipt. ܐܬܥܠܝ ܘܗܘܐ ܝܚܝܕܝܐ ܡܝܬܪܐ *he excelled and became a virtuous monk;* ܡܢ ܕܚܠܬܐ *to be raised above fear;* ܢܦܫܐ ܡܬܥܠܝܐ ܠܐܠܗܐ *the soul is lifted up to God.* *b*) *to go up higher, mount on high, ascend; to exalt oneself, boast.* *c*) *to be taken away, removed.* *d*) *to be referred to a higher court.* Aph. ܐܥܠܝ *a*) *to lift up.* *b*) perhaps denom. from ܥܘܠܐ *to act perversely, wickedly, do ini-*

quity; ܥܘܠܗܘܢ ܕܥܒܕܘ ܒܝ *their iniquity which they have committed against me.* SHAPHEL ܫܥܠܒ *to exalt;* ܫܥܠܒܬ ܥܠܝ *thou hast exalted over me, preferred to me.* ESHTAPH. ܐܫܬܥܠܒ *to exalt oneself, behave haughtily, be arrogant, haughty;* ܐܫܬܥܠܒ ܥܠ ܢܡܘܣܐ *to arrogantly violate the law;* ܐܫܬܥܠܒ ܡܘܬܐ ܥܠ ܒܢܝܢܫܐ *death bare haughty dominion over mankind.* DERIVATIVES, ܥܠܒܐ, ܥܠܒ, ܡܥܠܒܐ, ܥܠܘܒ, ܥܠܘܒܐ, ܥܠܝܒܐ, ܥܠܒܬܐ, ܥܠܘܒܬܐ, ܡܥܠܒܢܘܬܐ, ܡܥܠܒܐ, ܡܥܠܒܢܐ, ܡܥܠܒܢܐܝܬ, ܡܫܬܥܠܒܢܐ, ܡܫܬܥܠܒܢܘܬܐ, ܡܥܠܒܢܘܬܐ, ܡܫܬܥܠܒܢܐܝܬ, ܡܫܬܥܠܒܢܘܬܐ, ܡܥܠܒܢܐ, ܡܫܬܥܠܒܢܘܬܐ, ܡܥܠܒܐ.

ܥܠܒ fut. ܢܥܠܘܒ, act. part. ܥܠܒ, ܥܠܒܐ, pass. part. ܥܠܝܒ, ܒܐ, ܒܬܐ. *a) to have the upper hand, to overreach, take advantage; to defraud, wrong;* ܠܐ ܬܥܠܒܘܢ ܚܕ ܠܚܒܪܗ *ye shall not overreach* or *wrong one another. b) to surpass, exceed;* ܘܠܐ ܥܠܒ ܦܬܝܗ ܠܐܘܪܟܐ *the breadth of* a cube *does not exceed the length;* ܢܘܗܪܟ ܕܥܠܒ ܠܫܡܫܐ ܒܚܝܠܗ *Thy light which surpasses the sun in its strength.* Pass. part. *wronged, oppressed, snatched away* esp. *by premature death; iniquitous, unfair;* ܕܡܐ ܥܠܝܒܐ ܕܐܫܕܘ *the blood they wrongfully shed;* ܥܠܝܒ ܡܢ ܫܢܬܐ *overpowered by sleep;* ܥܘܠܠܐ ܘܥܠܝܒܐ *infants and prematurely slain.* ETHPE. ܐܬܥܠܒ and ETHPA. ܐܬܥܠܒ *to be defrauded, wronged; to suffer wrong, be overpowered* ܡܢ ܪܓܬܐ *by lust;* ܡܢ ܫܢܬܐ *by sleep;* ܐܢܫ ܕܡܟܝܟ ܘܡܬܥܠܒ *one who is meek and suffers wrong.* PAEL ܥܠܒ *to exceed;* ܕܪܬܐ ܠܐܟܕܢܐ ܡܥܠܒܐ *discussion is worse than a viper.* DERIVATIVES, ܡܥܠܒܢܐ, ܥܠܘܒܐ, ܥܠܘܒܬܐ, ܥܠܘܒܐܝܬ, ܥܠܒܢܐܝܬ, ܥܠܒܢܘܬܐ, ܡܥܠܒܢܐ.

ܥܠܒܐ or ܥܠܒܐ m. *a goat-skin, a small leathern bottle; a bellows.*

ܥܠܒܐ pl. ܥܠܒܐ or ܥܠܒܐ m. *a waking vision, something seen when half-awake, awakening* opp. ܚܠܡܐ *a dream.*

ܥܠܘܒ, ܥܠܘܒܐ rt. ܥܠܒ. *a grasping* or *overreaching person.*

ܥܠܘܒܐܝܬ rt. ܥܠܒ. adv. *oppressively, unjustly.*

ܥܠܘܒܘܬܐ pl. ܘܬܐ rt. ܥܠܒ. f. *a) fraudulence, greed, avarice; oppression, coercion. b) pre-eminence.*

ܥܠܘܒܝܐ pl. ܐ rt. ܥܠܒ. m. *fraud, wrong.*

ܥܠܘܝ m. *the aloe;* metaph. *bitterness.*

ܥܠܘܝ E-Syr. ܥܠܘܝ. *a) the upper part;* ܕܐܓܪܬܐ *the address on a letter, superscription. b) above, over;* ܥܠܘܝ ܡܫܟܢܝ *above my tent.*

ܥܠܘܠ, ܐ, ܬܐ rt. ܥܠ. *a) one who enters. b) brought in, introduced, foreign, adventitious, accidental.* Gram. *added, adopted* opp. *radical.*

ܥܠܘܠܘܬܐ rt. ܥܠ. f. gram. *adoption, insertion* of a non-radical letter.

ܥܠܘܩܐ and ܥܠܘܩܐ pl. ܐ rt. ܥܠܩ. m. *a) a leech. b) tough, tenacious, viscous, glutinous, sticky, greasy* as clay or dough.

ܥܠܘܩܘܬܐ and ܥܠܘܩ rt. ܥܠܩ. f. *lubricity, oiliness, slipperiness.*

ܥܠܝܟ, *a)* ܥܠܝܟ Pael conj. of ܥܠܐ. *b)* ܥܠܝܟ prep. ܥܠ with suffix pron. I pers. sing.

ܥܠܝ, ܥܠܝܐ, ܥܠܝܬܐ rt. ܥܠܐ. *a) exalted, supreme, heavenly;* ܐܠܗܐ ܕܥܠܝ ܡܢ ܟܠ *God exalted over all;* pl. m. *heavenly beings* opp. ܬܚܬܝܐ *mortals;* pl. f. ܥܠܝܬܐ *heavenly things* opp. *earthly. b) upper, superior;* ܫܡܝܐ ܥܠܝܐ *the highest heavens;* ܥܠܝܬܐ—ܬܚܬܝܬܐ *the upper and lower wells;* ܣܘܪܐ ܥܠܝܐ *the top line;* ܕܟܬܒܢ ܠܥܠܝܬܐ *we have written above;* ܒܝܬܐ ܥܠܝܐ *an upper story. c)* ellipt. *a lofty chamber;* ܥܠܝܬܐ ܪܘܪܒܬܐ *large and lofty rooms. d)* gram. ellipt. for ܢܘܩܙܐ ܥܠܝܐ *the points :* at the end of a phrase; ܐܬܘܬܐ ܥܠܝܬܐ *palatal letters.*

ܥܠܝܠܐ rt. ܥܠܐ. m. *malice, wanton wrong;* ܥܠܝܠܐ ܗܘ ܢܟܠܐ ܕܡܣܬܥܪ ܒܫܘܥܠܐ ܘܒܡܪܝܪܘܬܐ ܥܠ ܚܒܪܐ *treachery is deceit practised haughtily and spitefully on familiar friends.*

ܥܠܝܒܐܝܬ rt. ܥܠܒ. adv. *iniquitously.*

ܥܠܝܒܘܬܐ rt. ܥܠܒ. f. *fraudulence, oppression.*

ܥܠܝܘܬܐ rt. ܥܠܐ. f. *the higher* or *upper place.*

ܥܠܝܡܘܬܐ rt. ܥܠܡ. f. ܫܢܝܐ ܥܠܝܡܘܬܐ *full age.*

ܥܠܝܡܐ, ܥܠܝܡܬܐ pl. ܝܢ, ܬܐ. *a)* subst. *a youth, maiden;* pl. *the young* opp. ܣܒܐ *the aged* or ܩܫܝܫܐ *the elders; a serving-lad, handmaiden. b)* Greek *the New Academy. c)* adj. *young, youthful, juvenile;* ܥܠܝܡܝܢ ܗܘܦܟܐ *boyish behaviour.*

ܥܠܝܡܐܝܬ from ܥܠܝܡܐ. adv. *ardently, vigorously, valiantly.*

ܥܠܝܡܘܢܐ dimin. of ܥܠܝܡܐ. m. *a bachelor.*

ܥܠܝܡܘܬܐ from ܥܠܝܡܐ. f. *youth, youthfulness, youthful vigour;* collective. *youth, the young.*

ܥܠܝܡܝܐ from ܥܠܝܡܐ. *young, lusty, vigorous.*

ܥܠܝܬܐ pl. ܥܠܝ̈ܢ, ܥܠܝ̈ܬܐ. rt. ܥܠܐ. f. *a) an upper room, upper story;* ܥܠܝܬܐ ܕܐܪ̈ܙܐ *the upper chamber of the Mysteries* i.e. of the Last Supper. *b) a pinnacle.*

ܥܠܠܬܐ rt. ܥܠܐ. f. *the thigh.* Cf. ܥܠܠܐ, ܥܠܠܬܐ.

ܥܠܠ Pael conj. of ܥܠ.

ܥܠܠܐ, ܥܠܠܐ and ܥܠܠܐ rt. ܥܠ. m. *entrance, commencement;* ܕܨܘܡܐ *of Lent;* ܕܫܢܬܐ *of the year* = Oct. 1.

ܥܠܠܐ for ܥܠܐ; see ܥܠܠܬܐ.

ܥܠܠܡ, ܥܠܠܡܢܐ and ܥܠܡܢܐ pl. ـ̈ܝܢ, ـ̈ܐ rt. ܥܠ. m. *a) a pastor* esp. *a chief pastor of the Church, bishop, pontiff, prelate. b) a disciple;* ܥܠܡܢܐ ܗܘܐ ܠܗ Elisha *was disciple to* Elijah.

ܥܠܠܡ, ܥܠܠܡܬܐ pl. of ܥܠܐ, ܥܠܠܬܐ.

ܥܠܠܬܐ pl. ܥܠܠ̈ܬܐ and ܥܠ̈ܠܬܐ rt. ܥܠ. f. *ingathering, increase, harvest, crop, fruit, yield, produce.*

ܥܠܡ denom. verb Pael conj. from ܥܠܝܡܐ. *a) to grow young, be youthful, possess youthful vigour; to restore to youth, invigorate, renew;* ܥܠܡ ܥܠܡܝܗ ܒܥܕܝܢ ܕܒܘܣܡܐ *grant him fresh youth in the Eden of delight. b)* from ܥܠܡ. eccles. *to recite* the words *'for ever and ever';* ܡܫܒܚܝܢ ܘܡܥܠܡܝܢ *they repeat the Gloria Patri and In Secula.* Ethpa. ܐܬܥܠܡ *to grow up, come to maturity; to be renewed, grow young again.*

ܥܠܡܐ pl. ـ̈ܝܢ, ـ̈ܐ m. 1) constr. st. ܥܠܡ. *an age, generation, life-time, era; eternity, ever;* ܒܝܬ ܥܠܡܐ *a tomb;* ܡܪܝܡ ܒܬܘܠܬ ܥܠܡܝܢ Mary *ever-virgin;* ܥܠܡܐ ܚܕܬܐ *the new age;* ܙܒ̈ܢܐ ܥܠܡܝܐ *times eternal;* ܚܝ̈ܐ ܕܥܠܡܐ *eternal life;* ܡܠܟܘܬܐ ܥܠܡ *the kingdom of eternity;* ܩܝܡܐ ܕܥܠܡܐ *an everlasting covenant.* With preps.: ܠܥܠܡ *for ever;* ܠܥܠܡ ܥܠܡܝܢ *for ever and ever, in secula seculorum;* ܠܐ ܠܥܠܡ *never;* ܕܠܥܠܡ *eternal;* ܕܠܥܠܡ ܚܣܕܗ *for His mercy endureth for ever;* ܕܠܥܠܡܝܢ ܠܐ ܥܒܪܐ *which shall never pass away;* ܡܢ ܥܠܡ *of old time, of yore, ever;* ܡܢ ܝܘ̈ܡܬ ܥܠܡܐ *from the days of old, of old time;* ܠܐ ܡܢ ܥܠܡ *never before.*

2) const. st. ܥܠܡ *a) the world; temporal life; worldly* or *lay life* opp. monasticism; ܐܢܬܘܢ ܐܢܬܘܢ ܢܘܗܪܗ ܕܥܠܡܐ *ye are the light of the world;* ܟܠܗ ܥܠܡܐ *every one;* ܟܬܒܐ ܕܥܠܡܐ *a book of cosmography;* ܚܝ̈ܐ ܕܥܠܡܐ ܗܢܐ *life in the flesh, life in this world;* ܢܦܩ ܡܢ ܥܠܡܐ *he died;* ܕܠܐ ܕܚܠܐ ܬܕܒܪܝܘܗܝ ܠܥܠܡܟ *thou shalt lead thy temporal life, do thy worldly duties, fearlessly;* ܒܪ ܥܠܡܐ *a layman;* ܙܡܝܪ̈ܬܐ ܕܥܠܡܐ *secular* or *worldly songs;* ܩܫܝܫܐ ܕܥܠܡܐ *a secular priest.* Derivatives, verb ܥܠܡ *b,* ܥܠܡܐܝܬ, ܥܠܡܝܐ, ܥܠܡܝܘܬܐ, ܥܠܡܝܢܐܝܬ, ܥܠܡܝܢܐ, ܥܠܡܝܢܘܬܐ, ܥܠܡܢܐܝܬ, ܥܠܡܢܝܐ, ܥܠܡܢܝܘܬܐ. In the composition of Arabic names ܥܠܡ is frequent.

ܥܠܡܐܝܬ from ܥܠܡܐ. adv. *in lay* or *worldly fashion.*

ܥܠܡܝܐ, ܥܠܡܝܬܐ from ܥܠܡܐ. *temporal; secular, lay, worldly, common; a layman.*

ܥܠܡܝܘܬܐ from ܥܠܡܐ. f. *the course of this world; lay* or *secular life;* ܣܥܪܐ ܕܥܠܡܝܘܬܝ *the hair of my secular life* i.e. the long hair worn by laymen.

ܥܠܡܝܢܐܝܬ from ܥܠܡܐ. adv. *eternally.*

ܥܠܡܝܢܐ, ܥܠܡܝܢܝܬܐ from ܥܠܡܐ. *eternal, everlasting* opp. ܥܠܡܝܢܐ; ܥܠܡܝܢܐ ܘܡܠܘܫܐ *having neither beginning nor end.*

ܥܠܡܝܢܘܬܐ from ܥܠܡܐ. f. *eternity.*

ܥܠܡܢܐܝܬ from ܥܠܡܐ. adv. *in a worldly way, by a worldly standard.*

ܥܠܡܢܝܐ, ܥܠܡܢܝܬܐ from ܥܠܡܐ. *of this world, mundane; secular, lay; popular, common.*

ܥܠܡܢܝܘܬܐ from ܥܠܡܐ. f. *worldly nature* or *constitution.*

ܥܠܥܠ denom. verb Palpel conj. from ܥܠܥܠܐ. *to blow away.*

ܥܠܥܠܐ pl. ـ̈ܐ f. *a whirlwind, sudden gust, hurricane.*

ܥܠܥܠܢܐ, ܥܠܥܠܢܝܬܐ from ܥܠܥܠܐ. *tempestuous, whirling.*

ܥܠܥܠܐ; see ܥܠܥܠܢܐ.

ܥܠܩ Peal only found once in the imperative ܥܠܘܩ perh. a mistake for ܡܠܘܩ *boil.* Pael ܥܠܶܩ *to stick, adhere; be attached;* ܗܿܢܘܢ ܕܡܥܠܩܝܢ *adherents* of the Church. Ethpa. ܐܬܥܠܩ *a) to resist, strive with. b) to become sticky, glutinous.* Derivatives, ܥܠܘܩܐ, ܥܠܩܐ.

ܥܠܩܐ, ܥܠܘܩܬܐ or ܥܠܩܬܐ pl. ܬܐ̈ rt. ܥܠܩ. f. *a) a leech. b) colic,* a disease of cattle and horses. *c) anything clammy* or *sticky. d)* a metal *catch, a ward* of a lock.

ܥܶܠܬܳܐ rt. ܥܠܠ. emph. state and usual form of ܥܶܠܐ, constr. ܥܶܠܰܬ pl. ܥܶܠܠܶܝܢ, ܥܶܠܠܳܬܳܐ and ܥܶܠܝܢ, ܥܶܠܝܳܬܳܐ rt. ܥܠܐ. f. *cause, pretext; occasion, necessity; affair, thing, article; a fault, accusation; the argument, subject* of a book, *introduction, heading;* gram. *a primitive noun;* ܒܥܠܬ and ܡܢ ܥܠܬ *on account of, because.*

ܥܠܬܐ pl. ܥܠܘܬܐ, ܥܠܘ̈ܬܐ rt. ܥܠܐ. f. *a) an offering, oblation, holocaust, sacrifice. b) high place, altar.*

ܥܠܠܘܬܐ rt. ܥܠܠ. f. *causation.*

ܥܠܠܢܝܐ, ܢܝܬܐ rt. ܥܠܠ. *a) caused, effected; the effect, result. b) serving for a pretext.* c) gram. *causal, of causation.*

ܥܠܠܢܐܝܬ rt. ܥܠܠ. adv. *causally.*

ܥܠܠܢܘܬܐ rt. ܥܠܠ. f. *causation, cause.*

ܥܠܠܢܝܐ gram. *a) causal* as particles of causation. *b)* adjectives not formed immediately from a noun but from another adjective, as ܡܫܝܢܝܐ from ܡܫܝܢܐ.

ܥܠܠܢܝܘܬܐ rt. ܥܠܠ. f. *causality.*

ܥܡ prep. *a) with, together with, on, upon, at, at the moment;* ܥܡܝ *with me,* ܥܡܗ *in his presence, before him;* ܕܥܡܗ *those with him, his companions;* ܥܡ ܚܕܕܐ *together;* ܥܡ ܨܦܪܐ—ܪܡܫܐ *at dawn, at eventide;* ܥܡ ܡܥܠܢܗ *at his entrance;* ܥܡ ܗܘ ܕܐܬܬ *on her arrival, at the moment of her arrival;* ܥܡ ܨܒܝܢܐ ܕܐܦܣܩܘܦܐ ܘܪܘܪܒܢܐ *with the consent of the bishops and nobles;* ܕܥܡ ܫܡܐ *synonymous. b) besides, although, in spite of. c) along;* ܥܡ ܫܘܪܐ *along the wall;* ܥܡܗ ܕܢܗܪܐ *along the river. d)* after verbs of fighting, quarrelling, &c. *with. e)* with ܗܘܐ and a proper name *to belong to;* ܥܡ ܛܝܝܐ—ܪܗܘܡܝܐ ܗܘܬ the city *belonged to the Arabs, to the Romans.*

ܥܡ, ܥܡܐ pl. ܥܡܡܝܢ, ܥܡܡܐ m. *a) a people, nation;* ܥܡܝ *my people;* ܐܬܟܢܫ ܠܘܬ ܥܡܗ *he was gathered to his people;* ܥܡܡܐ ܛܝܝܐ *the Arab tribes. b)* pl. emph. *the Gentiles;* ܒܪ ܥܡܡܐ *a Gentile;* ܐܘ ܥܡܐ ܘܥܡܡܐ *a type of the Jews and Gentiles. c) the people, populace, a crowd;* ܥܡܐ ܕܡܕܝܢܬܐ *the people of the city.* Derivatives, ܥܡܡܐܝܬ, ܥܡܡܝܐ, ܥܡܡܝܘܬܐ.

ܥܡܐ Pael ܥܡܝ *to blind.* Aph. ܐܥܡܝ *to extinguish, extirpate.*

ܥܢܒܪ Arab. m. *ambergris.*

ܥܡܕ fut. ܢܥܡܕ, act. part. ܥܡܕ, ܥܡܕܐ, pass. part. ܥܡܝܕ, ܥܡܝܕܐ. *a) to dive, plunge, sink, set;* ܟܕ ܫܪܝ ܝܘܡܐ ܠܡܥܡܕ *when the day begins to set;* ܒܥܘܡܩܐ ܕܝܡܐ ܥܡܕ *he plunged into the depth of the sea;* ܥܡܕܝܢ ܘܣܠܩܝܢ *they dive and come up, sink and rise;* metaph. ܥܡܕ ܗܘܐ ܡܢ ܐܪܥܐ ܗܕܐ *he had sunk from this earth* = his day of life set. *b) to penetrate;* ܥܡܕ ܒܡܘܚܗ the point of the arrow *entered his brain. c) to dip* in or under water, *to bathe, wash;* ܥܡܕܐ ܗܘܬ ܒܡܥܝܢܐ *she bathed in the spring. d) to be baptized;* ܐܬܐ ܕܢܥܡܕ ܡܢܗ *He came to be baptized by him.* Pass. part. *plunged, immersed; set* beneath the horizon; *a candidate for baptism.* Ethpe. ܐܬܥܡܕ *to be baptized.* Aph. ܐܥܡܕ trans. *to dip, immerse* ܒܡܝܐ *in water; to baptize.* Pass. part. pl. ܡܥܡܕܝܢ ܒܕܡܐ *baptized in blood.* Derivatives, ܥܡܕܐ, ܥܡܘܕܐ, ܡܥܡܕܢܝܬܐ, ܡܥܡܕܢܐ, ܡܥܡܘܕܝܬܐ.

ܥܡܕܐ rt. ܥܡܕ. m. *the setting* of the sun or stars; *a plunge, somersault; dipping; baptism, the act* or *rite of baptism;* ܒܝܬ ܥܡܕܐ *a baptistery;* ܥܐܕܐ ܕܥܡܕܐ *the Feast of Baptism* = Epiphany.

ܥܡܘܕܐ, ܐ pl. ܐ̈ m. *a column, pillar; a platform; a meteor.*

ܥܡܘܕܐ pl. ܐ̈ rt. ܥܡܕ. m. *a) a diver. b) one to be baptized.*

ܥܡܘܕܘܬܐ rt. ܥܡܕ. m. *baptism.*

ܥܡܘܛ and ܥܡܘܛܐ, ܛܐ, ܛܬܐ rt. ܥܡܛ. *clouded over, misty, gloomy, dark; obscure.*

ܥܡܘܛܐܝܬ or ܥܡܛܐܝܬ rt. ܥܡܛ. adv. *obscurely, enigmatically.*

ܥܡܛܢܘܬܐ and ܥܡܛܢܐ rt. ܥܡܛ. f. *darkness, gloominess;* ܥܡܛܢܘܬ ܥܝܢܐ *dull* or *dim sight.*

ܥܡܘܠܐ, ܥܡܘܠܬܐ rt. ܥܡܠ. *laborious.*

ܥܡܘܠܬܢܐ rt. ܥܡܠ. *laborious, hard-working.*

ܥܡܘܢ pr. n. *Ammon* son of Lot; ܒܢܝ ܥܡܘܢ *the Ammonites.* DERIVATIVE, the following:—

ܥܡܘܢܝܐ, ܝܬܐ *an Ammonite, Ammonitess.*

ܥܡܘܨܘܬܐ rt. ܥܡܨ. f. *shutting, closing* esp. ܕܥܝܢܐ *of the eyes.*

ܥܡܘܩܘܬܐ rt. ܥܡܩ. f. *depth; the hollow* of the hand, *the sole* of the foot.

ܥܡܘܪ, ܥܡܘܪܐ, ܥܡܘܪܬܐ rt. ܥܡܪ. *a*) *a dweller, sojourner, settler; an inhabitant;* ܥܡܘܪܘܗ̈ܝ ܕܡܕܝܢܬܐ *the citizens.* *b*) f. emph. *a priest's housekeeper, priest's* or *bishop's concubine.*

ܥܡܘܪܐ pr. n. *Gomorrha.*

ܥܡܘܪܘܬܐ rt. ܥܡܪ. f. *a*) *a site.* *b*) *indwelling.*

ܥܡܘܪܢܐ rt. ܥܡܪ. m. *a dwelling-place; inhabiting; restoration, making habitable.*

ܥܡܛ fut. ܢܥܡܘܛ, act. part. ܥܡܛ, ܥܡܛܐ. *to become dark, cloud over;* ܕܢܥܡܘܛ ܚܫܘܟܐ *that darkness may gather;* ܥܡܛܐ ܘܠܐ ܡܬܚܙܝܐ the moon *becomes obscure and invisible.* Metaph. *to be clouded, thick with dregs.* PA. ܥܡܛ *to conceal, obscure.* ETHPA. ܐܬܥܡܛ *to be cast into shade, become dim, be darkened.* APH. ܐܥܡܛ *to darken, make dark, obscure, dim;* ܐܥܡܛ ܟܘܟܒܝܗܘܢ *I will darken the stars* of heaven; ܡܥܡܛ ܥܝܢܐ *it dims the eyes;* ܥܝܕܐ ܡܥܡܛ *custom dulls* the senses. ETHTAPH. ܐܬܬܥܡܛ *to be obscured, darkened.* DERIVATIVES, ܥܡܛܢܐ, ܥܡܘܛܐ, ܥܡܛܐܝܬ, ܥܡܛܢܘܬܐ, ܥܡܛܐ, ܥܡܛܢܐ, ܡܥܡܛܢܐ.

ܥܡܛܢܐ rt. ܥܡܛ. m. *thick darkness, gloom; a dark night;* ܥܡܛܢܐ ܕܚܫܘܟܐ *blackness of darkness.*

ܥܡܛܢܝܐ, ܝܬܐ rt. ܥܡܛ. *shrouded in darkness, gloomy.*

ܥܡܝܠܐܝܬ rt. ܥܡܠ. adv. *laboriously, with great pains.*

ܥܡܝܠܘܬܐ rt. ܥܡܠ. f. *laboriousness, painful exertion.*

ܥܡܝܡܐ *bastard, spurious.*

ܥܡܝܨܐ or ܥܡܝܨܐ *a*) pass. part. of ܥܡܨ. *b*) mistake for ܥܡܝܨܐ name of a plant.

ܥܡܝܨܘܬܐ rt. ܥܡܨ. f. *being closed* as the eyes; *suppression* or *restraint* of the senses.

ܥܡܝܩܐܝܬ rt. ܥܡܩ. adv. *deeply, profoundly.*

ܥܡܝܩܘܬܐ rt. ܥܡܩ. f. *deepness, profundity, intensity.*

ܥܡܝܪ, ܥܡܝܪܐ m. ܥܡܝܪܬܐ rare f. *grass, hay, fodder.*

ܥܡܠ fut. ܢܥܡܘܠ, act. part. ܥܡܠ, ܥܡܠܐ, pass. part. ܥܡܝܠ, ܠܐ, ܠܬܐ. *to labour, toil; take trouble, weary;* ܡܪܝ ܠܐ ܬܥܡܘܠ *Lord, trouble not Thyself;* ܥܡܠܬܗ ܚܒܢܢܘܬܐ *sloth made him feel weary;* with ܢܦܫܐ *to lead the hard life of an ascetic.* Act. part. *a toiler;* ܥܡܠ ܦܪܙܠܐ *a hammerer, smith.* Pass. part. *laborious, inured to toil; suffering hardship; toilsome, painful, diseased;* ܗܢܐ ܥܡܝܠ ܦܠܣܡܐ ܡܥܒܕܘ *they devised this foolish fiction;* ܚܝܐ ܥܡܝܠܐ *lives of hardship;* ܥܡܝܠܐ *ascetics* = *those who labour* in prayer. ETHPE. ܐܬܥܡܠ *to labour under, be exercised by* temptation or sin; ܡܐ ܕܡܬܥܡܠܝܢ ܒܡܚܣܪܢܘܬܐ ܕܒܟܪܝܗܘܬܐ ܕܟܝܢܐ ܐܢܫܝܐ *when they labour under shortcomings through the weakness of human nature.* APH. ܐܥܡܠ *to weary, worry, trouble;* ܐܥܡܠܬܗ ܒܡܠܝܗ̇ *she wearied him with her talk;* ܗܘ ܕܡܥܡܠ ܢܦܫܗ *one who worries himself.* DERIVATIVES, ܥܡܠܐ, ܥܡܘܠܬܢܐ, ܥܡܝܠܐܝܬ, ܥܡܝܠܘܬܐ, ܥܡܠܐ.

ܥܡܠ, ܥܡܠܐ pl. ܐ̈ rt. ܥܡܠ. m. *a*) *labour, travail, toil, pain, trouble, weariness;* ܕܠܐ ܥܡܠܐ *unruffled, easily, willingly;* ܪܚܡ ܥ̈ *laborious, industrious;* ܚܘܦܛܐ ܕܥ̈ *diligence, industry.* Often used of ascetic and religious exercises; ܥܡܠܐ ܕܒܬܪ ܙܕܝܩܘܬܐ *labouring after righteousness;* ܥ̈ ܕܬܝܒܘܬܐ *the work of repentance.* *b*) *a district, prefecture.*

ܥܡܠܐ Arab. m. *a prefect, official.*

ܥܡܡܐܝܬ from ܥܡܐ. adv. *after the manner of the Gentiles.*

ܥܡܡܝܐ from ܥܡܐ. *a*) *gentile, pagan.* *b*) *one of the people, a plebeian; a layman.* Pl. *the common people, the populace.* *c*) *plebeian,* common, popular; ܡܡܠܠܐ ܥܡܡܝܐ *the vulgar tongue, the vernacular.*

ܥܡܡܝܢ, ܥܡܡܝܬܐ pl. of ܥܡܐ, ܥܡ.

ܥܡܡܝܬܢܐ from ܥܡܐ. *endemic.*

ܥܡܡܬܐ f. Arab. *a mitre.*

ܥܡܡܬܐ pl. of ܥܡܬܐ.

ܥܡܨ fut. ܢܥܡܘܨ, imper. ܥܡܘܨ, act. part. ܥܡܨ, ܥܡܨܐ, pass. part. ܥܡܝܨ, ܥܡܝܨܐ. *to shut* esp. the eyes; *to shut up* as flowers. Pass. part. ܥܡܝܨܬܐ *closed eyes;* ܚܫܘܟܐ ܥܡܝܨܐ *dense darkness.* Ethpe. ܐܬܥܡܨ *to be closed.* Pa. ܥܡܨ *to close, shut* trans. esp. the eyes, *to close* the eyes of the dead; *to close* the ears; *to restrain* the senses. Ethpa. ܐܬܥܡܨ *to be closed, shut* as the eyes, *to have the eyes shut;* ܒܪܡܫܐ ܕܡܟ ܥܠܡܐ ܥܡܝܨܐܝܬ *at even the world sleeps with closed eyes;* ܗܘܝܢ ܒܐܘܪܚܬܐ ܐܬܥܡܨܢ *we were on the roads with our eyes shut,* i.e. *we could not see our way.* Aph. ܐܥܡܨ *a) to close the eyes* of the dying; ܡܢܘ ܢܟܢܫ ܘܢܥܡܨ *who will lay out* the dead *and close their eyes?* *b) to restrain, suppress* the senses. Derivatives, ܥܡܘܨܐ, ܥܡܘܨܐ, ܥܡܨܘܬܐ, ܥܡܝܨܘܬܐ, ܥܡܨܐ.

ܥܡܨܐ rt. ܥܡܨ. m. *closing* the eyes, ܥ ܕܥܝܢܐ *letting the eyelids fall.*

ܥܡܩ Peal only part. adj. ܥܡܝܩ, ܥܡܝܩܐ, ܥܡܝܩܬܐ. *a) deep, profound, hidden, difficult; hollow; very great, extreme;* ܬܗܘܡܐ ܥܡܝܩܬܐ *a profound abyss;* ܟܐܒܐ ܥܡܝܩܐ *deep-seated disease;* ܥ ܠܠܝܐ—ܒܪܕܝܐ ܥ *at dead of night, in the very early morning;* ܥ ܣܝܒܘܬܐ *extreme old age;* ܥ ܥܘܬܪܐ *very great riches.* *b)* m. *the cardiac artery.* Pa. ܥܡܩ *to go deep, excavate deeply; to deepen.* Used adverbially, *deeply, intensely;* ܚܦܪ ܘܥܡܩ *he digged deep down;* ܗܘ ܕܒܥܐ ܕܢܥܡܩ ܢܟܠܐ *he who seeks to lay deep wiles;* ܥܡܩܘ ܐܚܒܠܘ *they have deeply corrupted themselves.* Ethpa. ܐܬܥܡܩ *to be deeply sunken* of the eyes; of sleep; of planting deeply. Aph. ܐܥܡܩ *to go* or *hide far in, penetrate deeply.* Ettaph. ܐܬܬܥܡܩ *to search the depth, to fathom;* ܝܡܐ ܕܠܐ ܡܬܬܥܡܩ *a sea difficult to fathom.* Derivatives, ܥܘܡܩܐ, ܥܡܩܐ, ܥܡܝܩܘܬܐ, ܥܡܘܩܘܬܐ, ܥܘܡܩܐ, ܥܡܩܬܐ, ܡܥܡܩܬܐ, ܥܡܝܩܐܝܬ.

ܥܡܩܐ rt. ܥܡܩ. m. a name of the vowel ܘ $\bar{u}$ as being a deeper sound than ܘ $\bar{o}$.

ܥܘܡܩܬܐ pl. ܥܘܡܩܬܐ rt. ܥܡܩ. f. *a) a hollow, depression* in the surface of the ground. *b)* a kind of meteor.

ܥܘܡܩܬܐ rt. ܥܡܩ. f. *a valley.*

ܥܡܪ fut. ܢܥܡܪ, act. part. ܥܡܪ, ܥܡܪܐ, pass. part. ܥܡܝܪ, ܥܡܝܪܐ. *to dwell; to sojourn, stay;* with ܒ *to indwell, inhabit;* with ܥܡ and ܠܘܬ *to live with* esp. of married life; metaph. *to be immersed* in an occupation; ܕܫܠܝܐ ܘܫܝܢܐ ܚܝܐ ܢܥܡܪ *that we may lead a tranquil life;* ܫܐܕܐ ܕܥܡܪ ܒܗ *the demon which possessed him.* Act. part. *dwelling, a dweller, inhabitant, colonist;* ܥܡܘܪܝ ܐܘܪܫܠܡ *inhabitants of Jerusalem;* ܕܠܐ ܥܡܪ *uninhabited, houseless;* ܥܡܘܪܝ ܐܪܥܐ *dwellers on the earth;* ܥܡܘܪܝ ܡܫܟܢܐ *tent-dwellers, nomads.* Fem. emph. see below. Pass. part. impers. ܥܡܝܪ ܗܘܐ ܠܗ *he dwelt.* For ܥܡܝܪܐ *grass* see above. Ethpe. ܐܬܥܡܪ *to be inhabited.* Pa. ܥܡܪ *to cause to dwell, to settle.* Aph. *a) to cause to inhabit, cause to dwell; to colonise, settle;* ܒܢܐ ܩܪܝܬܐ ܘܐܥܡܪ *he built the city and peopled it;* ܐܥܡܪ ܒܠܒܘܬܢ ܚܕܘܬܐ *do Thou make joy to dwell in our hearts.* *b)* with ܥܡ *to give* or *take in marriage, to espouse;* ܐܥܡܪܬܘܢ ܥܡܟܘܢ ܢܫܐ ܢܘܟܪܝܬܐ *ye have taken strange women to dwell with you.* Ettaph. ܐܬܬܥܡܪ *to be made to dwell, be settled.* Derivatives, ܥܡܘܪܐ, ܥܡܘܪܬܐ, ܥܡܪܐ, ܥܡܪܬܐ, ܥܡܪܐ, ܥܡܝܪܐ, ܡܥܡܪܐ, ܡܥܡܪܢܘܬܐ, ܡܬܥܡܪܢܘܬܐ.

ܥܡܪ, ܥܡܪܐ m. *a) wool;* ܕܟܪܐ ܕܥܡܪܐ *unshorn rams;* ܠܒܘܫܝ ܥܡܪܐ *wearers of woollen* i.e. monks; ܠܒܫܬ ܥܡܪܐ *she put on wool* i.e. the habit of a nun. *b) pith;* ܥܡܪܗ ܓܘܝܐ *its inner pith.*

ܥܡܪ ܡܝܐ *green scum, pond-weed.*

ܥܡܪܐ ܕܓܡܐ *papyrus-pith.*

ܥܡܪ ܩܘܛܢܐ *cotton.*

ܥܡܪܐ ܕܝܡܐ *sea-weed.*

ܥܡܪܐ ܕܡܝܐ *water-weed.*

ܥܡܪ ܥܙܐ *goats' hair.*

ܥܡܪܐ ܕܩܘܒܐ *a fleece;* wool of the plant Spina Judaica.

Derivatives, ܥܡܪܢܐ, ܥܡܪܢܝܐ.

ܥܡܘܪܐ rt. ܥܡܪ. m. *inhabiting.*

ܥܡܪܢܐ, ܢܝܬܐ and ܥܡܪܢܝܬܐ, ܢܝܬܐ from ܥܡܪܐ. *woollen, woolly, fleecy; a blanket.*

ܥܡܘܪܬܐ pl. ܬܐ rt. ܥܡܪ. f. *habitable, an inhabited* region, usually ellipt. for ܐܪܥܐ ܥܡܘܪܬܐ *the habitable earth.*

ܥܡܣ *to dive.*

ܥܡܘܣܐ rt. ܥܡܣ. m. *diving.*

ܥܡܬܐ or ܥܡܬܐ pl. ܥܡ̈ܬܐ rarely ܥܡܘܡܬܐ f. *a father's sister, paternal aunt.*

ܥܢܐ fut. ܢܥܢܐ, act. part. ܥܢܐ, ܥܢܝܐ, pass. part. ܥܢܐ, ܥܢܝܐ, pl. ܥܢܝܢ, ܥܢܝ̈ܢܐ. *a) to answer, respond;* ܥܢܐ ܘܐܡܪ *he answered and said. b) to hearken, hear;* ܥܢܝܢܝ ܡܪܝܐ *hear me, O Lord;* ܥܢܝܢ *hear us;* ܠܐ ܐܝܬ ܕܥܢܐ *no one hearkens. c) to raise* a song or shout. *d) to converse, be occupied* with ܒ or ܥܡ; ܬܕܝܪܐܝܬ ܥܡܗ ܥܢܐ ܗܘܐ *he frequently conversed with him;* act. and pass. parts. *conversant, occupied, engrossed, engaged in;* ܥܢܐ ܗܘܐ ܒܨܒܘ̈ܬܐ ܕܩܪܒܐ *he was occupied with concerns of war;* ܒܬܐܘܪܝܐ ܥܢܝܢ ܗܘܘ *they were engrossed in contemplation;* ܥܢܐ ܚܛܝܬܐ *intimate with sin.* Ethpe. ܐܬܥܢܝ *a) to humble himself. b) to be heard, listened to* esp. of prayer. *c) to be occupied, busy, engaged in, engrossed, to attend;* ܥܢܝܢܐ ܕܢܬܥܢܘܢ ܒܗ *the business in which they will engage;* ܪ̈ܘܚܐ ܩܫܝ̈ܬܐ ܕܡܬܥܢܝܢ ships which *must encounter violent winds;* ܕܡܬܥܢܐ ܠܬܪܥܐ *he who attends to the door, the porter;* with ܠܥܕܬܐ *to attend church. d)* with ܥܡ *to have intercourse with, converse with,* esp. of marriage. Pa. ܥܢܝ *to raise* a shout or song, *to sing in alternate parts.* Ethpa. ܐܬܥܢܝ *to be sung, chanted.* Aph. ܐܥܢܝ *a) to lead* the singing, *teach singing; to raise a shout, make to rejoice;* ܗܢܘܢ ܕܡܥܢܝܢ ܙܟܘܬܐ *those who raise a shout of victory. b) to busy, cause to be occupied;* ܐܥܢܐ ܐܝܕܝܟ ܠܥܒܕܐ *apply thy hands to work.* Derivatives, ܥܢܝܢ, ܥܢܝܢܐ, verb ܥܢܘܝ, ܥܢܘܝܐ, ܥܢܘܝܘܬܐ, ܥܢܘܢܝܬܐ, ܥܢܝܐ, ܥܢܝܐ, ܥܢܝܢܐ, ܥܢܝܐ, ܥܢܝܘܬܐ, ܥܢܝܐ, ܡܥܢܝܢܘܬܐ, ܡܥܢܝܢܐ, ܡܥܢܝܢܘܬܐ, ܡܥܢܝܢܐ.

ܥܢܐ a collective noun, may be written with or without Ribui and with the verb in the sing. or in the pl. f. *a flock, small cattle* esp. *sheep;* ܥܢܝ *my sheep, my flock;* ܥܢܟ, ܥܢܢ *thy, our sheep,* &c.; ܥܢܐ ܕܥܙ̈ܐ *a herd of goats;* ܓܙܪܐ ܥܡܪܢܝܬܐ *a flock of sheep;* ܟܠܒ̈ܝ ܥܢܐ *sheep-dogs;* ܓܙܪܐ ܕܥܢܐ ܘܥܙ̈ܐ *a flock of sheep and goats.*

ܥܢܒܬܐ, ܥܢܒܐ pl. ܥܢܒܝܢ, ܐ̈ com. gen. in the pl. *berries, grapes, a cluster, bunch of grapes;* ܥܢܒ̈ܝ ܝܒܪܘܚܐ *mandrakes;* ܥ̈ ܬܥܠܐ *solanum nigrum, deadly nightshade;* ܥ̈ ܣܢܝܐ *black-berries;* ܥ̈ ܛܠܝܐ *atropa belladonna.* Fem. emph. *a single berry* or *grape;* also *a tubercle* in the eye, *a hemorrhoid* resembling a grape or mulberry; *the oval* of the eye.

ܥܢܒܬܢܝܬܐ from ܥܢܒܬܐ. *staphyloma, tubercles on the eye.*

ܥܢܕ fut. ܢܥܢܕ, act. part. ܥܢܕ, ܥܢܕܐ, part. adj. ܥܢܝܕ see below. *to depart, fail, be wanting, be taken away;* ܠܐ ܢܥܢܕ ܫܒܛܐ ܡܢ ܝܗܘܕܐ *the sceptre shall not depart from Judah;* ܠܐ ܬܥܢܕ ܛܝܒܘܬܟ ܡܢ ܥܕܬܟ *let not Thy grace depart from Thy Church;* ܥܢܕܘ ܡ̈ܝܐ *the waters fail;* ܬܠܓܐ ܡܢ ܪܝܫܗ ܕܛܘܪܐ ܠܐ ܥܢܕ ܠܗ *snow does not disappear from the summit of the mountain.* Esp. *to depart* ܡܢ ܚܝ̈ܐ *from life;* ܡܢ ܥܠܡܐ ܗܢܐ *from this world,* or ellipt. Ethpe. ܐܬܥܢܕ *to be lacking, missing.* Ethpa. ܐܬܥܢܕ *to be prepared for burial.* Aph. ܐܥܢܕ and perhaps Pael ܥܢܕ *to deprive of, cause to fail;* ܥܠܝ ܣܝܡܬܐ ܪܘܚܢܝܬܐ. ܡܢ ܐܥܢܕܟ ܡܢܢ *O our spiritual treasure, who has taken thee from us?* Derivatives, ܥܢܕܐ, ܥܢܝܕܐ, ܥܢܕܢܐ, ܥܢܝܕܐ, ܥܢܝܕܘܬܐ, ܥܢܕܘܪܐ.

ܥܢܝܕܐ rt. ܥܢܕ. m. some bird.

ܥܢܕܐ rt. ܥܢܕ. m. *departure* from this life, *decease.*

ܥܢܕܘܪܐ pl. ܐ̈ rt. ܥܢܕ. *a foreigner, absent from home.*

ܥܢܘܝ denom. verb Pali conj. from ܥܢܘܝܐ. *to make ascetic.* Ethpali ܐܬܥܢܘܝ *to practise, study* or *pursue with diligence; to lead the ascetic life;* ܐܬܥܢܘܝ ܒܦܝܠܘܣܘܦܘܬܐ *he diligently studied philosophy;* ܕܢܬܥܢܘܢ ܚܝ̈ܐ ܓܒܝ̈ܐ *that they might practise the elect life;* ܝܘܚܢܢ ܐܬܥܢܘܝ ܒܬܠܬ ܐܘܪ̈ܚܬܐ ܥܣܩ̈ܬܐ *John was an ascetic in the three difficult ways.*

ܥܢܘܝܐ, ܥܢܘܝܬܐ West-Syr. ܥܢܐ rt. ܥܢܐ. *a*) *poor, afflicted;* ܩܥܬܐ ܕܥܢܘܝܐ *the cry of the afflicted.* *b*) *self-contained, continent;* ܢܦܫܐ ܥܢܘܝܬܐ *a continent soul.* *c*) *ascetic, an ascetic, hermit.*

ܥܢܘܝܘܬܐ rt. ܥܢܐ. f. *self-denial, voluntary poverty, abstinence, continence, asceticism, the ascetic life;* ܥܢܘܝܘܬܐ ܕܦܘܠܚܢܐ *the practice of virtue;* ܥܢܘܝܘܬܐ consists in four things ܨܠܘܬܐ. ܥܘܗܕܢܐ. ܗܓܝܐ. ܗܪܓܐ *prayer, recollection, study, meditation.*

ܥܢܘܩܬܐ or ܥܢܘܩܬܐ rt. ܥܢܐ. f. *the maw* of a ruminant, *the craw* or *crop* of a bird.

ܥܢܐ denom. verb from ܥܢܢܐ. Ethpa. ܐܬܥܢܝ *to become a goat-herd.*

ܥܢܙܐ constr. st. ܥܢܙ and ܥܢܙ m. *a goat,* ܥܢܙ ܒܪܐ the same; ܥܢܙ ܛܘܪܐ *a mountain goat;* ܥܢܙ ܐܝܠܐ a fabulous animal *the goat-stag.*

ܥܢܙܝܐ from ܥܢܙܐ m. *a goat-herd.*

ܥܢܙܪܘܬ m. *sarcocolla,* a Persian gum.

ܥܢܚ *to smell* as the body from heat and sweat.

ܥܢܝܐ rt. ܥܢܐ. m. *a*) *a singer.* *b*) *the doxology.*

ܥܢܝܢܐ rt. ܥܢܐ. m. *a*) *anxiety, effort, study.* *b*) *a response.*

ܥܢܝܕ, ܐ̈, ܬܐ rt. ܥܢܕ. *a*) *absent, away from home.* *b*) *departed, deceased, defunct;* ܦܘܩܕܢܐ ܕܥܢܝܕܐ *dying commands;* ܥܘܗܕܢܐ ܕܥܢ̈ܝܕܐ *memorial of the departed;* ܚܕ ܒܫܒܐ ܕܥܢ̈ E-Syr. *Sunday of the Departed* = the Sunday before Lent.

ܥܢܝܕܝܐ, ܥܢܝܕܝܬܐ rt. ܥܢܕ. adj. *funeral, burial.*

ܥܢܝܘܬܐ rt. ܥܢܐ. f. *chanting.*

ܥܢܝܢ, ܥܢܝܢܐ pl. ܐ̈ rt. ܥܢܐ. m. *a*) *toil, business, travail;* ܥܢܝܢܐ ܒܝܫܐ *sore travail;* ܥܢܝܢܐ ܕܬܐܓܘܪܘܬܐ *trade, commerce.* *b*) *study;* ܒܥܢܝܢܐ ܐܡܝܢܐ ܕܟܬܒ̈ܐ ܩܕܝܫ̈ܐ *versed in constant study of the Scriptures.* *c*) *acquaintance, intimacy,* rarely of sexual intercourse, *converse, society;* with ܥܒܕ ܥܢܝܢܐ *to converse, hold intercourse;* ܒܪ ܥܢܝܢܐ *a companion;* ܪܚܡ ܥ̈ *social, fond of society;* ܚܝ̈ܐ ܕܠܐ ܥ̈ *a lonely life;* ܒܥܢܝܢܗ ܗܘܝܢ *we were intimate with him;* ܡܠܬܐ ܕܥ̈ *conversation;* ܥܢܝ̈ܢܐ ܫܪ̈ܝܐ *dissolute habits.* *d*) *an answer, report;* ܒܐܓܪܬܐ *by letter;* ܢܝܬܘܢ ܠܢ ܥܢܝܢܐ *let them bring us back word;* ܡܥܪܒܐ ܥܢܝܢܗ ܗܘ the Hebrew word for sea also *answers to west.* *e*) *an antiphon, anthem.*

ܥܢܝܢܝܐ rt. ܥܢܐ. *intimate, familiar.*

ܥܢܝܬܐ pl. ܥܢܝ̈ܬܐ rt. ܥܢܐ. f. *a*) *a shout* or *song.* *b*) pl. *liturgical responses.*

ܥܢܢ denom. verb Pael conj. from ܥܢܢܐ. *to collect* as clouds, *be clouded over.* Palp. ܥܢܥܢ *to cloud over.*

ܥܢܢܐ pl. ܐ̈ f. *a cloud;* ܥܢܢ̈ܐ ܕܡܛܪܐ *rain-clouds.* Alchym. *quicksilver.* Derivatives, ܥܢܘܢܐ, verb ܥܢܢ, ܥܢܢܝܐ.

ܥܢܢܐ m. *impotent, lacking the power of propagation.*

ܥܢܢܝܐ, ܥܢܢܝܬܐ from ܥܢܢܐ. *nebulous, cloudy.*

ܥܢܣ pass. part. ܥܢܝܣ. *tormented by a devil.* Ethpa. ܐܬܥܢܣ *to have a mane.*

ܥܢܦܐ or ܥܢܦܐ pl. ܐ̈, ܬܐ. f. *a*) a horse's *mane.* *b*) *the crest of a tree, top of a branch* esp. of a vine-branch.

ܥܢܦܐ pl. ܐ̈ f. *a*) *a sucker, offset, offshoot.* *b*) *a fibre, tie.*

ܥܢܦܐ ܕܪܘܡܐ f. *an ostrich.*

ܥܢܦܝܐ from ܥܢܦܐ. gram. *radical.*

ܥܢܫ, ܥܢܫܐ, ܥܢܫܬܐ pl. m. ܥܢ̈ܫܝܢ, ܐ̈ f. ܬܐ. Cf. ܥܫ and ܥܫܬܐ. *wicked, heinous, vicious, worthless; a knave, evil-speaker;* ܐܪܥܝܬܐ ܥܢܫܬܐ *a villainous frame of mind.* Derivatives, the two following words:—

ܥܢܫܐܝܬ from ܥܢܫܐ. adv. *evilly, viciously.*

ܥܢܫܘܬܐ from ܥܢܫܐ. f. *wickedness, criminality, immorality.*

ܥܣ fut. ܢܥܘܣ, act. part. ܥܐܣ. *to feel emotion; to be involved, be distracted with business.* Ethpe. ܐܬܥܣܣ *to be distracted with sorrow.* Pa. ܥܣܣ *to engage, occupy.* Ethpa. ܐܬܥܣܣ *to be occupied, engrossed, harassed with business.* Palp. ܥܣܥܣ *to distract, harass with business.* Ethpalp. ܐܬܥܣܥܣ *to be split, splintered.* Derivatives, ܥܣܘܣܐ, ܥܣܘܣܥܐ, ܥܣܘܣܐ, ܥܣܣܐ.

ܥܣܒ, ܥܣܒܐ but with aspirated *b* in the pl. ܥܣ̈ܒܐ m. *green herb, grass;* ܥܣܒܐ ܕܐܪܝܐ *orobanche.*

ܥܣܘܣܐ rt. ܥܣ. *evil.*

ܥܣܝܪܘܬܐ pl. ܘ̈ܬܐ rt. ܥܣܪ. f. *a decad.*

ܥܣܝܪܝܐ, ܥܣܝܪܝܬܐ rt. ܥܣܪ. *the tenth;* ܥܣܝܪܝܐ ܩܝܬܪܐ *a ten-stringed* harp; ܫܘܐܠܐ ܚܕ ܥܣܝܪܝܐ *question the eleventh.*

ܥܣܪܝܘܬܐ pl. ܘ̈ܬܐ rt. ܥܣܪ. f. *a decad, the number ten;* ܥܣܪܝܘܬܐ ܕܡ̈ܠܐ *the decalogue;* ܥܣܪ ܥܣܪܝܘܬܐ *ten times ten.*

ܥܣܟܪ, ܥܣܟܪܐ pl. ܐ̈ܬܐ Arab. f. *an army, a troop.*

ܥܣܩ, ܥܣܩܐ pl. ̈ܐ rt. ܥܣܩ. m. *a) harassment, trouble, pains, assiduity. b) idle talk, nonsense.*

ܥܣܩ fut. ܢܥܣܩ, pass. part. ܥܣܝܩ or ܥܣܩ, ̈ܐ, ̈ܬܐ. *to be difficult, to be vexed* with ܥܠ; ܠܡܥܣܩܘ ܒܡܠܐ ܕܚܪܝܢܐ *to be obstinate in a verbal strife.* Pass. part. *difficult, grievous;* ܥܣܩ ܠܡܬܕܪܟܘ *difficult to be understood;* ܗܟܢܐ ܥܣܝܩ ܗܢܐ ܥܩܬܐ *so grievous is this terrible trouble.* ETHPA. ܐܬܥܣܩ *a) to contend; to resist, withstand, dispute* with ܠ, ܥܠ or ܥܡ; ܛܒ ܡܬܥܣܩ ܥܠ ܡܠܬܐ *he strongly withstands this saying;* ܗܘ ܥܡܕܐ ܕܐܬܥܣܩ ܢܝܩܕܡܘܣ that baptism *with regard to which Nicodemus was difficult to convince;* ܐܢ ܥܠ ܟܣܝܐ ܬܬܥܣܩ *if thou obstinately dispute on a secret subject. b) to be unhappy, vexed, indignant* with ܒ or ܥܠ; ܐܬܥܣܩܬ ܪܘܚܝ ܒܓܘ *my spirit was vexed;* ܡܐ ܕܡܬܥܣܩ ܐܢܫ ܕܐܚܪܝܢ ܥܠܘܗܝ ܢܬܬܪܝܡ *when any one is indignant, takes it hard, that another is set above him. c) to be difficult, grievous;* ܡܬܥܣܩ ܠܡܥܩܪܘܢ *it is difficult to root them up. d) to be ill.* DERIVATIVES, ܥܣܩܐ, ܥܣܩܘܬܐ, ܥܣܝܩܐ, ܥܣܝܩܐܝܬ, ܥܣܝܩܘܬܐ.

ܥܣܩ, ܥܣܝܩܐ, ܥܣܝܩܬܐ rt. ܥܣܩ. *difficult, hard, rough; obstinate, perverse; grievous;* ܐܬܪܐ ܥ̈ *a rugged place;* ܟܘܪܗܢܐ ܥܣܝܩܐ *obstinate diseases;* ܟܦܢܐ ܥ̈ *a grievous famine;* ܥܣܩ ܠܡܣܝܒܪܘ *grievous to be borne;* ܥܣܩ ܠܡܦܫܩܘ *hard to interpret;* ܥܣܩ ܠܡܕܒܪܘ *ungovernable;* f. emph. pl. *hardships, difficulties; baggage.*

ܥܣܩܐ rt. ܥܣܩ. m. *troublesomeness.*

ܥܣܝܩܐܝܬ rt. ܥܣܩ. adv. *with difficulty.*

ܥܣܝܩܘܬܐ rt. ܥܣܩ. f. *difficulty, severity; heaviness;* ܥܣܝܩܘܬ ܐܘܪ̈ܚܬܐ *roughness of the roads;* ܥ̈ ܪܥܝܐ *perversity, morosity;* ܢܫܡܬܐ *asthma;* ܫܡܥܐ *deafness.*

ܥܣܪ f. ܥܣܪܐ m. *ten,* ܥܣܪܬܐ f. emph. collective *a ten* or *the ten, the tenth* esp. *the tenth day* of the month; pl. ܥܣܪܝܢ *twenty.* ܥܣܪ ܒ̈ܬܘܠܢ *ten virgins;* ܚܕ ܡܢ ܥܣܪܐ *one-tenth, a tenth part;* ܕܥܣܪܐ, ܕܥܣܪ, *the tenth;* ܕܥܣܪ ܩܝ̈ܛܪܝܢ *a ten-stringed* harp; ܥܣܪܬܝܗܘܢ *the ten of them;* ܥܣܪ ܡܕܝ̈ܢܬܐ *Decapolis.* DERIVATIVES, ܥܣܪ, ܐܥܣܪ &c., ܡܥܣܪ, ܥܣܘܪܐ, ܥܣܪܝܘܬܐ, verb ܥܣܪ, ܥܣܪܘܢܐ, ܥܣܪܢܝܐ, ܡܥܣܪܐ, ܡܥܣܪܢܘܬܐ.

ܥܣܪ denom. verb PAEL conj. from ܥܣܪ. *to tithe, offer* or *receive a tithe;* ܡܥܣܪܘ ܐܥܣܪ ܠܟ *I will surely give the tithe unto thee.* ETHPA. ܐܬܥܣܪ *to be tithed, made to pay tithes.*

ܥܣܘܪܐ pl. ܝ̈ܢ, ̈ܐ rt. ܥܣܪ. m. *a tenth part.*

ܥܣܪܝܢ; see ܥܣܪ. *twenty.*

ܥܣܪܝܢܝܐ, ܢܝܬܐ from ܥܣܪܝܢ. *the twentieth.*

ܥܟܢܬܐ pl. ܥܟܢܝܢ, ܥܟܢܝܬܐ f. *a battlement, pinnacle.* Cf. ܥܟܢܬܐ.

ܥܦ same as ܥܦܦ. fut. ܢܥܘܦ, infin. ܡܥܦ, imper. ܥܘܦ, act. part. ܥܐܦ, ܥܐܦܐ, pass. part. ܥܦܝܦ, ̈ܐ, ̈ܬܐ. *to double, fold over; to multiply, increase;* ܐܝܟ ܡܥܛܦܐ ܬܥܘܦ ܐܢܘܢ *as a vesture shalt Thou fold them;* ܐܬܥܦܦܬ ܙܟܘܬܗܘܢ *their victory was redoubled;* ܥܐܦܝܢ ܟܟܪܐ ܥܣܪ ܙܒܢܝܢ ܐܘ ܚܡܫܐ *they increase the talent ten times or five times;* ܡܐ ܕܣܓܝ ܥܦܬ *when thou art greatly increased.* Pass. part. *double, doubled, repeated;* ܥܦܝܦܐ ܠܬܠܬܐ *triple;* ܥܦܝܦܐ ܠܚܡܫܐ *quintuple;* ܥܦܝܦܐ ܠܬܡܢܝܐ *in the Octopla* of Origen; ܩܠܐ ܥܦܝܦܐ a chant ending in a *repeated word,* e.g. in two alleluias; ܒܘܪ̈ܟܐ ܥܦܝ̈ܦܬܐ *repeated kneelings* = prayers. Fem. emph. *a) a double* or *lined garment. b) double* or *outline writing.* ETHPE. ܐܬܥܦܦ or ܐܬܥܦ *to be doubled, repeated.* PA. ܥܦܦ *to double, repeat, do again and again;* ܣܓܝ ܡܥܦܦ ܗܘܐ ܠܫܡܐ ܗܢܐ *he often repeated this name;* ܥܦܦ ܡܕܐܬܐ *he imposed double tribute.* ETHPA. ܐܬܥܦܦ *to be doubled, repeated, multiplied,* with ܠܬܠܬܐ *to be tripled;* ܛܝܒܘܬܐ ܕܐܬܥܦܦܬ ܠܗ *the favour granted to him, being doubled;* ܠܡܬܥܦܦܘ ܘܠܡܬܦܫܛܘ *to draw together and to stretch out, to contract and expand.* APH. ܐܥܦ *to double, fold.* ETHTAPH. ܐܬܬܥܦ *to be multiplied.* DERIVATIVES, ܥܦܐ, ܥܘܦܦܐ, ܥܘܦܦܘܬܐ, ܥܦܝܦܐܝܬ, ܥܦܝܦܘܬܐ, ܡܥܦܦܢܘܬܐ.

ܥܦܐ = ܥܐܦܐ and ܥܦܐ *double.*

ܥܦܐ fut. ܢܥܦܐ, act. part. ܥܐܦܐ, ܥܦܝܐ, pass.

part. ܟܦܝܠ, ܟܦܝܠܐ. *a*) *to bloom, flourish.* *b*) *to double.* *c*) *to increase, gain, collect, amass* esp. with ܐܓܪܐ *wages* or *reward* and ܝܘܬܪܢܐ *gain, profit*; ܟܦܠܬ ܠܟ ܚܟܡܬܐ *thou dost gain wisdom.* Pass. part. *doubled, wrapped up, occupied*; ܟܦܝܠ ܫܘܢܩܗܘܢ *their torment is doubled*; ܗܘ ܕܝܢ ܟܦܝܠ ܗܘܐ ܒܕܐܡܝܢ *he was occupied and engrossed in similar matters.* Ethpe. ܐܬܟܦܠ *to be implicated, engaged.* Pa. ܟܦܠ *to cover over, envelop, enfold* esp. *to enshroud, prepare for burial*; ܡܟܦܠܝܢ ܗܘܘ ܦܓܪܗ ܘܥܒܕܝܢ ܠܘܝܐ *they enshrouded his body and formed a funeral procession*; ܐܢܫܐ ܟܦܠܬ ܒܚܕܘܬܟ *Thou hast enfolded, included, all men in Thy gladness.* Ethpa. ܐܬܟܦܠ *a*) *to be doubled, augmented.* *b*) *to be covered over, involved.* *c*) *to be enshrouded, laid in the grave.* Aph. ܐܟܦܠ *to put forth flowers, to blossom.* Derivatives, ܟܦܠܐ, ܟܦܝܠܐ, ܟܦܠܘܬܐ, ܟܦܠܐ, ܟܦܠܐ, ܡܟܦܠܐ.

ܟܦܝܦܘܬܐ rt. ܟܦ. f. *repetition, reduplication.*

ܟܦܘܦܐ rt. ܟܦܦ. m. *a*) *an embrace.* *b*) *the chin.*

ܟܦܘܦܐ rt. ܟܦܦ. m. *embracing, clinging.*

ܟܦܘܪܐ rt. ܟܦܪ. m. *a levinge, mosquito curtain; a wrapper.*

ܟܦܬܐ rt. ܟܦܬ. m. *putrefaction, stench.*

ܟܦܬܘܬܐ rt. ܟܦܬ. f. *stench.*

ܟܦܝܠܐܝܬ rt. ܟܦܠ. adv. *twice, doubly, in double measure.*

ܟܦܝܠܘܬܐ rt. ܟܦܠ. f. *a doubling, duplication; duplicity*; ܕܡܠܬܐ ܟܦܝܠܘܬܐ *repetition*; ܒܟܦܝܠܘܬܐ *a second time*; ܗܘܐ ܒܟܦܝܠܘܬܐ ܟܪܝܗܐ *he had a relapse.*

ܟܦܪܢ, ܟܦܪܢܐ from ܟܦܪܐ. *dusty.*

ܟܦܪܐ = ܐܦܪܐ m. *a gall, oak-apple.*

ܟܦܫ fut. ܢܟܦܘܫ, act. part. ܟܦܫ, ܟܦܫܐ, pass. part. but with act. sense ܟܦܝܫ, ܟܦܝܫܐ. *to embrace, cling, enclose*; ܟܦܝܫܝܢ ܗܘܘ ܚܕ ܒܚܕ *they embraced each other*; ܟܦܝܫܐ ܢܝܚܘܬܐ *I clung to my ease*; ܟܕ ܟܦܝܫ ܠܙܟܘܬܐ *having attained to victory.* Pa. ܟܦܫ *to embrace, clasp, grasp, handle*; ܡܟܦܫܐ ܗܘܬ ܠܗ ܠܘܬ ܥܘܒܗ *she clasped him to her breast*; ܚܢܦܘܬܐ ܟܦܫ *he embraced heathen worship.* Ethpa. ܐܬܟܦܫ *to embrace, be embraced*; ܟܪܝܘܬܐ ܐܬܟܦܫܝ *sorrows have laid hold on me.* Derivatives, ܟܦܘܫܐ, ܟܦܘܫܘܬܐ, ܟܦܫܘܬܐ.

ܟܦܪ root-meaning extant in Arabic *to veil.* Pael ܟܦܪ *a*) *to veil, cover the face.* *b*) denom. from ܟܦܪܐ. *to dust, sweep, pick out of the dust.* Ethpa. *a*) *to be veiled, covered, to wear a hood.* *b*) *to become dust* or *earth*; *to be dusted, swept.* Derivatives, ܟܦܘܪܐ, ܟܦܪܐ, ܡܟܦܪܐ.

ܟܦܪ, ܟܦܪܐ pl. ܐ m. *dust, earth, soil*; ܕܩܝܩܐ ܟܦܪܐ *fine dust*; ܕܠܒܘܢܬܐ ܟܦܪܐ *powdered incense, frankincense*; ܐܪܝܘܬܐ ܕܟܦܪܐ *chameleons.* Derivatives, ܟܦܪܢܐ, ܟܦܪܢ, verb ܟܦܪ, ܟܦܪܝܐ, ܟܦܪܢܝܐ, ܟܦܪܢܘܬܐ, ܡܟܦܪܐ.

ܟܦܪܐ pl. ܐ rt. ܟܦܪ. m. *a hood.*

ܟܦܪܝܐ pl. ܝܐ from ܟܦܪܐ. *earthy, earthly*; pl. *creatures of earth, mortals.*

ܟܦܪܢܘܬܐ from ܟܦܪܐ. f. *earthiness, nature of earth.*

ܟܦܪܢܝܐ from ܟܦܪܐ. *earthly, terrestrial.*

ܟܦܬܐ, ܟܦܬܐ or ܟܦܬܐ from roots ܟܦܦ, ܟܦ and ܟܦܠ. f. *a*) *a swoon, languor.* *b*) *a fold.*

ܟܦܬ act. part. ܟܐܦܬ root-meanings *to contract; to insert*; pass. part. ܟܦܝܬܐ. W-Syr. gram. *having the vowels* ˉ or ˊ *above* ‿ and ܘ respectively, ܝܘܕ ܟܦܝܬܬܐ *yud written with* ˉ, ܝ̈. Pael ܟܦܬ *to compel.* Derivatives, ܟܦܝܬܐ, ܟܦܝܬܘܬܐ, ܟܦܬܐ.

ܟܦܪ fut. ܢܟܦܪ, act. part. ܟܦܪ, ܟܦܪܐ, pass. part. ܟܦܝܪ, ܟܦܝܪܐ. *a*) *to compel, constrain, force*; ܟܦܪܬ ܢܦܫܗ *she forced herself*; ܟܦܪܗ ܚܘܒܗ ܕܢܬܓܠܐ ܒܒܣܪܐ *His love constrained Him to be revealed in the flesh*; ܠܐ ܟܦܪ ܠܚܐܪܘܬܢ *He will not do force to our free-will*; ܟܦܝܪ ܐܢܐ ܕܐܡܠܠ *I am constrained to speak.* *b*) *to resist, make resistance, fight against*; ܚܫܐ ܣܢܝܐܐ ܟܦܪ *he resists hateful passions*; ܠܐ ܟܦܪܘ ܗܘܘ ܦܘܩܕܢܗ *they made no resistance to his command.* Ethpe. ܐܬܟܦܪ *a*) *to be compelled, constrained, urged.* *b*) *to refuse, resist, oppose.* *c*) *to be tormented, molested, annoyed* with ܡܢ of the pers. or cause; ܡܢ ܚܒܠܐ *by pangs of childbirth*; ܡܢ ܩܘܪܫܐ *by severe cold*; ܡܢ ܪܚܫܐ *by vermin.* Pa. ܟܦܪ *a*) *to resist, refuse, be contumacious, wilfully disobedient*; ܐܢ ܡܟܦܪ ܢܟܦܪ *if he utterly refuse*; ܚܢܦܐ ܕܡܢ

ܠܡܠܝ ܡܟܒܝܢ ܐܢܬܘܢ ye resist my sayings; ܡܟܒܝܢ ܠܡܪܝܐ they set themselves against the Lord. b) to scrape up, claw up roots. ETHPA. ܐܬܟܒܝ a) to suffer violence, suffer pangs. b) to resist, refuse. DERIVATIVES, ܟܒܝܐ, ܟܒܝܢܐ, ܟܒܝܢܘܬܐ, ܟܒܝܢܐܝܬ, ܟܒܝܢܐ, ܟܒܝܘܬܐ, ܟܒܝܐ, ܡܟܒܝܢܐ, ܡܬܟܒܝܢܐ, ܡܬܟܒܝܢܘܬܐ.

ܟܒܣ fut. ܢܟܒܘܣ, act. part. ܟܒܣ, ܟܒܣܐ. to bind up, bandage ܡܚܘܬܐ a wound, ܬܒܪܐ a breach, fracture; to repair ܐܠܦܐ a ship. Metaph. to restore, strengthen, heal; ܡܢܘ ܟܒܣ ܠܟܘܪܗܢܝ who will bind up my weakness? ETHPE. ܐܬܟܒܣ to be bound up, strengthened. PAEL ܟܒܣ to bind up, heal; ܘܐܦܠܐ ܡܚܘܬܗܘܢ ܡܬܟܒܣܐ neither can their hurt be bound up. DERIVATIVES, ܟܒܣܐ, ܟܒܣܬܐ, ܟܒܘܣܐ.

ܟܒܣܐ pl. ܐ̈ rt. ܟܒܣ. m. a bandage; binding up; a remedy, prescription; ܚܕ ܡܢ ܐܢܫܝܢ ܟܒܣܐ ܐܘܣܝܐ one kind of remedy or drug.

ܟܒܣܬܐ rt. ܟܒܣ. f. a fillet, head-band.

ܟܒܘܣܐ pl. ܐ̈ rt. ܟܒܣ. m. one who binds up wounds, a dresser, surgeon, doctor.

ܟܒܘܝܐ rt. ܟܒܐ. m. one who uses force, an oppressor.

ܟܒܘܪܐ pl. ܐ̈ rt. ܟܒܪ. m. a pea.

ܟܒܘܫܐ rt. ܟܒܫ. m. a) one who treads the wine-press; metaph. one who wrings or racks.

ܟܒܘܫܐ, ܟܒܘܫܬܐ rt. ܟܒܫ. a large basin, cup, vial.

ܟܒܘܫܬܐ rt. ܟܒܫ. f. fresh cheese.

ܟܒܝܢܐ pl. ܐ̈ rt. ܟܒܐ. contumacious.

ܟܒܝܢܘܬܐ rt. ܟܒܐ. f. contumacy, stubborn resistance.

ܟܒܝܢܐ rt. ܟܒܐ. m. a) contumacy, contentiousness. b) compulsion, coercion; ܒܟܒܝܢܐ by compulsion. c) gram. a point over the middle of a sentence to indicate a slight pause; also written double —.

ܟܒܝܢܐܝܬ rt. ܟܒܐ. adv. against his will.

ܟܒܝܢܘܬܐ rt. ܟܒܐ. f. contumacy, stubborn disobedience or resistance.

ܟܒܝܢܢܐ rt. ܟܒܐ. contentious.

ܟܒܝܪܐ, ܬܐ; see ܟܒܪ.

ܟܒܝܪܘܬܐ W-Syr. gram. being written with the vowel ܥܨܨܐ etsotso; ܘܐܘ ܕܟܒܝܪܘܬܐ vav with ܼ above it, ܘܼ.

ܟܒܪܐ, ܟܒܪܐ rt. ܟܒܪ. m. W-Syr. the vowel ܼ.

ܟܒܫ fut. ܢܟܒܘܫ, act. part. ܟܒܫ, ܟܒܫܐ, pass. part. ܟܒܝܫ, ܟܒܝܫܐ. to trample, tread the wine- or oil-press; to squeeze, wring or press out; metaph. to crush, repress; ܟܒܫ ܡܪܪܬܐ ܒܥܝܢܘܗܝ press out gall in his eyes; ܫܩܝܐ ܕܚܝܐ ܟܒܫ he presses out a living draught; ܟܒܫܬ ܐܢܘܢ ܒܪܘܓܙܝ I have trodden them in my wrath. Pass. part. ܟܒܝܫܐ ܡܫܚܐ ܕܙܝܬܐ ܟܒܝܫܐ pure oil from trodden olives; ܡܫܚܐ ܟܒܝܫܐ beaten oil; also ܟܒܝܫܐ is used elliptically for the juice of olives or grapes, must. ETHPE. ܐܬܟܒܫ a) to be pressed out, expressed as oil, wine, &c. b) to be trampled upon, crushed; ܡܬܟܒܫܢ ܒܕܘܫܐ ܕܦܝܠܐ women crushed by the trampling of elephants. PA. ܟܒܫ to tread, press, squeeze, wring, keep under; ܐܢ ܬܟܒܫ ܢܚܝܪܐ if thou wring the nose; ܡܟܒܫ ܗܘܐ ܦܓܪܗ ܒܨܘܡܐ he subdued his body with fasts. ETHPA. ܐܬܟܒܫ to be coerced, subdued, oppressed; ܟܕ ܡܬܟܒܫ ܡܢ ܚܫܐ ܘܒܟܐ suffering force and weeping; ܡܬܟܒܫ oppressed by great heat. DERIVATIVES, ܟܒܫܐ, ܟܒܘܫܐ, ܟܒܘܫܐ, ܟܒܘܫܬܐ, ܟܒܫܬܐ, ܡܟܒܫܢܐ.

ܟܒܫܐ rt. ܟܒܫ. m. a) treading, pressing out ܕܥܢܒܐ of grapes. b) juice, extract; an infusion, decoction; with ܕܣܥܪܐ barley-water; ܕܓܘܙܐ walnut oil; ܕܙܝܬܐ olive oil; ܕܚܛܐ starch; ܕܥܢܒܐ grape juice, must; ܕܒܣܪܐ juice of unripe olives or grapes; ܕܩܘܡܐ gum arabic; ܕܬܘܬܐ mulberry juice.

ܟܒܫܬܐ pl. ܬܐ̈ f. Heb. a religious assembly.

ܟܒܫܬܐܘܦܘܪܝܘܢ agrimonia eupatorium, hemp agrimony.

ܟܒܝܬܐ rt. ܟܒܐ. f. force, compulsion.

ܟܒܦ fut. ܢܟܒܘܦ, act. part. ܟܒܦ, ܟܒܦܐ. to throw on the back, twist backwards; ܟܒܦܝܢ ܠܗ ܥܠ ܚܨܗ they throw him on to his back. ETHPE. ܐܬܟܒܦ and ETHPA. ܐܬܟܒܦ to lean *backwards* opp. ܐܬܦܩܣ *to lean forwards; to lie down on the back, to twist* or *bend backwards* as the fingers, the hand or foot. DERIVATIVE, ܥܩܡܐ.

ܥܩܐ pl. ܳܐ m. *a necklace, neck-chain, string of beads;* ܥܩܐ ܕܕܗܒܐ *a gold chain.*

ܥܩܐ, ܥܩܬܐ pl. ܥܩܝܢ, ܥܩܬܐ rt. ܥܘܩ. f. *sadness, grief, distress, adversity; harm, detriment;* ܕܠܐ ܥܩܐ *cheerful; unharmed.*

ܥܩܒ fut. ܢܥܩܘܒ, act. part. ܥܩܒ, ܥܩܒܐ. *a*) *to take by the heel, to hold back, to follow closely, to succeed* in office, esp. with ܕܘܟܬܐ *to supply the place of;* ܥܩܒܬ ܠܗ ܗܘ ܕܥܩܒܬܝܗܝ ܠܐܚܘܟ ܥܝܣܘ thy name shall be *Jacob because thou didst lay hold of thy brother Esau's heel.* *b*) *to trace* or *seek out* a way, ܟܕ ܥܩܒܘ ܘܐܬܘ *when they found out the way and came.* PA. ܥܩܒ *to trace, track, seek out, investigate* with ܒܬܪ; *to hold a judicial inquiry; to discuss, dispute* with ܥܡ, in a bad sense *to dispute* or *inquire too closely into holy matters;* ܒܟܠܗ ܠܒܝ ܥܩܒܬܟ *with my whole heart have I sought Thee;* ܕܝܢܐ ܘܡܥܩܒ ܕܝܢܐ *a judge and seeking judgement;* ܡܥܩܒܐ ܡܠܬܐ *the matter is discussed, inquired into;* ܢܫܒܚܘܢ ܒܢܝ ܥܕܬܐ ܘܠܐ ܢܥܩܒܘܢ let the children of the church *offer up praise and not be curious.* ETHPA. ܐܬܥܩܒ *to be investigated, sought out, inquired into; to make trial of, experience;* ܕܢܬܥܩܒܘܢ ܘܢܬܒܚܪܘܢ *that* the agitators *should be seized and tried;* ܗܘ ܡܫܒܚ ܘܠܐ ܡܬܥܩܒ the Holy Name *is glorious and unsearchable;* ܙܕܝܩܘܬܐ ... ܒܝܘܡܬܗ ܐܬܥܩܒܬ *justice was experienced, followed, was the rule, in the days of* King Josiah. DERIVATIVES, ܥܩܒܐ, ܥܩܒܐ, ܥܩܒܐ, ܥܩܒܢܘܬܐ, ܥܩܒܬܢܐ, ܥܩܘܒܬܢܘܬܐ, ܥܩܘܒܬܐ, ܥܩܘܒܬܢܘܬܐ, ܡܥܩܒܢܘܬܐ, ܡܥܩܒܢܐ, ܡܥܩܒܢܐܝܬ, ܡܥܩܒܢܐ, ܡܬܥܩܒܢܐ, ܡܬܥܩܒܢܐܝܬ, ܡܬܥܩܒܢܘܬܐ.

ܥܩܒ, ܥܩܒܐ pl. ܥܩܒܝܢ, ܥܩܒܐ m., ܥܩܒܬܐ pl. ܳܝܢ, ܳܬܐ f., rt. ܥܩܒ. up to 10 the m. pl. is used, above that number the f. pl. *a*) *a foot, heel, hoof;* ܐܝܕܗ ܐܚܝܕܐ ܒܥܩܒܗ ܕܥܝܣܘ *his hand took hold of Esau's heel;* ܥܩܒܗ ܕܣܘܣܝܐ *a horse-hoof.* *b*) *a footstep, footprint, trace, track, vestige* ܕܪܓܠܐ *of the feet,* ܕܡܪܟܒܬܐ *of chariots;* ܥܩܒܬܗ ܕܠܒܐ ܛܒܐ ܐܦܐ ܢܗܝܪܬܐ *the mark of a good heart is a shining countenance.* With ܐܚܕ ܒ *to follow closely;* ܗܦܟ ܠ *to retrace one's steps;* often with ܢܩܦ ܠ, ܗܠܟ ܒ or ܪܕܐ ܒ *to follow in the footsteps, follow the example;* ܩܪܝܒܐ ܒܥܩܒܗ ܒܥܩܒ *after, close after;* ܒܥܩܒ ܟܠ ܨܠܘܬܐ *directly after;* *after* or *at the end of each prayer.* *c*) *the lower part, extremity, end;* ܒܥܩܒܗ ܕܛܘܪܐ *at the extreme limit of the mountain;* ܥܩܒܗ ܕܚܘܛܪܐ *the end of the staff;* ܥܩܒܬܗ ܕܡܟܝܟܘܬܐ *the end of humility* is the fear of the Lord. In Jacobite Offices an ܥܩܒܐ was a variable *termination* of a prayer, also a short form of prayer at the conclusion of an Office. Gram. *the end* or *termination* of a word.

ܥܩܒܐ m. *succession; investigation.*

ܥܩܒܢܢܘܬܐ rt. ܥܩܒ. f. *supplanting.*

ܥܩܒܬܢܐ or ܥܩܒ rt. ܥܩܒ. *following a trace, tracking;* ܟܠܒܐ ܥܩܒܬܢܐ *a sleuth-hound, blood-hound.*

ܥܩܒܬܢܘܬܐ rt. ܥܩܒ. f. *a*) *tracking, investigation.* *b*) *succession.*

ܥܩܡ act. part. ܥܩܡ. *to fix, settle, solidify.* PAUEL ܥܘܩܡ *a*) *to coil* as a serpent, *to bend in sitting down;* part. ܡܥܘܩܡ *curved;* ܡܪܕܝܬܐ ܡܥܘܩܡܬܐ *the orbicular course* of the stars, opp. ܬܪܝܨܬܐ *straight.* ETHPAUAL ܐܬܥܘܩܡ *to coil, writhe, twist round;* metaph. *to be perplexed;* ܟܕ ܡܬܥܘܩܡ ܕܢܕܥ *being perplexed to know* whether. DERIVATIVES, ܥܘܩܡܐ or ܥܩܡܐ, ܥܩܡܐ, ܥܘܩܡܐ.

ܥܩܡܐ rt. ܥܩܡ. m. *solidification* of a liquid.

ܥܩܘܒܬܢܐ rt. ܥܩܒ. *a tracker, pursuer.*

ܥܩܘܒܬܢܘܬܐ rt. ܥܩܒ. f. *walking in the steps, following, searching out.*

ܥܩܘܡܐ pl. ܳܐ rt. ܥܩܡ. m. *a winding, twist, turn;* ܐܘܪܚܐ ܕܣܓܝܐܐ ܥܩܘܡܐ *a road with many turns.*

ܥܩܘܣܐ rt. ܥܩܣ. m. *a door-fastening.*

ܥܩܘܪܐ, ܳܬܐ rt. ܥܩܪ. *an uprooter, destroyer.*

ܥܩܘܪܝܐ pl. ܳܐ rt. ܥܩܪ. m. *eradication, razing to the ground, destruction, ruins.*

ܥܩܘܪܢܝܐ *restive, kicking.* Cf. ܥܩܪܢܐ.

ܟܦܳܦܳܐ rt. ܟܦܦ. m. *bending backwards* esp. the hand or finger; ܕܪܺܫܳܐ *turning the head round.*

 ܟܦܺܩܳܐ rt. ܟܦܩ. *solidified.*

ܟܦܺܝܫܽܘܬܳܐ rt. ܟܦܫ. f. *crookedness, craft.*

ܟܦܺܝܫܳܐ or ܟܶܦܫܳܐ rt. ܟܦܫ. m. *a crab, small lobster* or *prawn.*

ܟܦܺܝܫܽܘܬܳܐ rt. ܟܦܫ. f. *being twisted.*

ܟܦܠ Pael pass. part. ܡܟܰܦܠܳܐ, ܡܟܰܦܠܳܐ *awry, distorted, perverse;* ܕܶܚܠܬܳܐ ܡܟܰܦܠܬܳܐ *perverted religion.* Ethpalpal ܐܶܬ݂ܟܰܦܠܰܦ *to be twisted round.* Parel ܟܰܪܦܶܠ *to twist awry, tie up, trip up; to entangle, confuse; to embrace, bring together;* ܟܰܪܦܠܽܘܢܝ ܪ̈ܶܓ݂ܠܰܝ *they have tripped me up;* ܢܟܰܪܦܶܠ ܐܶܢܽܘܢ ܒܡܨܺܝܕܬܳܐ *he will entangle them in a net;* ܐܳܦܠܳܐ ܐܰܠܳܗܳܐ ܡܟܰܪܦܶܠ ܠܳܗ ܠܐܽܘܪܚܳܐ *neither does God render the way intricate.* Ethparal ܐܶܬ݂ܟܰܪܦܰܠ *to be entangled, involved, tripped up, perplexed, confused; to be enveloped* ܒܬܶܢܳܢܳܐ *in smoke;* ܢܶܬ݂ܟܰܪܦܠܽܘܢ ܫܒ̈ܺܝܠܶܐ ܕܐܽܘܪ̈ܚܳܬ݂ܗܽܘܢ *let the paths of their ways be perplexed;* ܐܶܬ݂ܟܰܪܦܰܠ ܓܶܐܪܶܗ ܒܺܐܝܕܶܗ *his arrow twists round in his hand,* i.e. *returns* and wounds him; ܐܶܬ݂ܟܰܪܦܰܠ ܪܶܕܝܳܐ ܕܡܶܠܬܳܐ *the flow of speech is confused.* Derivatives, ܟܦܳܠܳܐ, ܟܦܺܝܠܳܐ, ܟܶܦܠܳܐ, ܟܰܦܠܳܐ, ܟܰܦܠܳܐ, ܟܰܦܠܬܳܐ, ܟܰܦܠܬܳܐܺܝܬ݂, ܟܦܰܠܦܠܽܘܬ݂ܳܐ, ܡܟܰܪܦܠܳܐ, ܡܬ݂ܟܰܪܦܠܳܢܽܘܬ݂ܳܐ.

ܟܰܦܠܳܐ rt. ܟܦܠ. m. *the shank, leg.*

ܟܶܦܠܳܐ rt. ܟܦܠ. m. *a griping pain in the bowels; lassitude.*

ܟܰܦܠܬܳܐ rt. ܟܦܠ. *winding, crooked* as a serpent, a line; *forked* lightning. Metaph. *perverse, tortuous.*

ܟܰܦܠܬܳܐܺܝܬ݂ rt. ܟܦܠ. adv. *crookedly, windingly.*

ܟܦܰܠܦܠܽܘܬ݂ܳܐ rt. ܟܦܠ. f. *crookedness.*

ܟܦܰܢ Peal only part. adj. ܟܦܺܢܳܐ, ܟܦܺܢ *crooked, crafty, perverse;* ܥܰܡ ܟܦܺܢܳܐ ܬܶܬ݂ܟܰܦܰܢ *with the perverse thou wilt show thyself froward.* Pael ܟܰܦܶܢ *to turn aside, pervert,* esp. with ܐܽܘܪܚܳܐ *the way;* ܡܟܰܦܢܺܝܢ ܬܪܺܝܨܽܘܬ݂ܳܐ *they pervert equity.* Pass. part. ܡܟܰܦܰܢ, ܡܟܰܦܢܳܐ, ܡܟܰܦܢܬܳܐ *crooked, perverse;* ܐܽܘܪ̈ܚܳܬ݂ܳܐ ܡܟܰܦ̈ܢܳܬ݂ܳܐ *by-ways, devious* or *crooked ways;* ܫܰܪܒܬܳܐ ܕܠܳܐ ܡܗܰܝܡܢܳܐ ܘܡܟܰܦܢܬܳܐ *O faithless and perverse generation;* ܡܡܰܠܠܺܝܢ ܡܟܰܦ̈ܢܳܬ݂ܳܐ *speaking perverse things.* Ethpa. ܐܶܬ݂ܟܰܦܰܢ *to turn aside, be perverse;* ܘܳܝ ܠܗܽܘܢ ܠܰܕܡܶܬ݂ܟܰܦܢܺܝܢ ܡܶܢ ܡܳܪܝܳܐ *woe to them who turn perversely from the Lord.* Gram. *to twist round* in the throat; ܐܳܬ݂ܘ̈ܳܬ݂ܳܐ ܕܡܶܬ݂ܟܰܦ̈ܢܳܢ ܒܓܰܪ̈ܓܪܳܬ݂ܳܐ *guttural letters.* Derivatives, ܟܦܳܢܳܐ, ܟܦܺܝܢܽܘܬ݂ܳܐ, ܟܰܦܢܽܘܬ݂ܳܐ, ܡܟܰܦܢܳܐ, ܡܟܰܦܢܽܘܬ݂ܳܐ, ܡܟܰܦܢܳܐܺܝܬ݂.

ܟܦܺܝܢܽܘܬ݂ܳܐ rt. ܟܦܢ. f. *perversity, guile.*

ܟܦܰܫ Peal only pass. part. ܟܦܺܫ, ܟܦܺܫܳܐ. *twisted, bent, crooked;* ܚܽܘܛܪܳܐ ܕܟܦܺܫ *a crooked staff.* Ethpe. ܐܶܬ݂ܟܦܶܫ *to be stung* by a scorpion, serpent, &c.; *to be pricked* by thorns. Pa. ܟܰܦܶܫ *to wave* in the air; ܒܰܣ̈ܢܶܐ ܕܕܶܩܠܳܐ ܡܟܰܦܫܺܝܢ *waving palm-branches.* Pass. part. f. emph. ܡܟܰܦܰܫܬܳܐ *crooked.* Derivatives, ܟܦܳܫܳܐ, ܟܦܳܫܳܐ, ܟܶܦܫܳܐ, ܟܦܺܝܫܳܐ, ܟܦܺܝܫܽܘܬ݂ܳܐ, ܟܰܦܫܳܐ, ܟܰܦܫܰܦܫܳܐ, ܟܰܦܫܰܦܫܽܘܬ݂ܳܐ.

ܟܦܳܫܳܐ rt. ܟܦܫ. m. *lobster sauce.*

ܟܰܦܫܰܦܫܳܐ rt. ܟܦܫ. *crisp, curly.*

ܟܰܦܫܰܦܫܽܘܬ݂ܳܐ rt. ܟܦܫ. f. *crispness.*

ܟܰܦܶܩ Pael conj., Arab. *a) to adorn with cornelians. b) to hinder, impede.*

ܟܦܳܩܳܐ *oblique.*

ܟܦܰܪ fut. ܢܶܟܦܽܘܪ, inf. ܡܶܟܦܰܪ, act. part. ܟܳܦܰܪ, ܟܳܦܪܳܐ, pass. part. ܟܦܺܝܪ, ܐ, ܬܳܐ. *a) to uproot,* opp. ܢܨܰܒ *to plant; to pull out* teeth, *tear out* an eye; *to break down, pull down* foundations, buildings; metaph. *to extirpate* nations, opinions, &c.; *to utterly do away with;* ܟܦܰܪܘ ܩܶܝܡܬܳܐ ܕܒܰܥܠܳܐ *they brake down the pillar of Baal;* ܥܰܡ̈ܡܶܐ ܪ̈ܰܘܪܒܶܐ ܟܦܰܪ *it has extirpated great nations;* ܥܰܡܳܐ ܟܦܺܝܪ *a people uprooted, torn from their homes;* ܕܢܶܟܦܽܘܪ ܣܽܘܚܦܰܝ̈ܢ *that He may completely heal our scars. b) to be barren.* Ethpe. ܐܶܬ݂ܟܦܶܪ *to be plucked up, torn out, uprooted.* Pael ܟܰܦܰܪ same senses as Peal but more forcible. Ethpa. ܐܶܬ݂ܟܰܦܰܪ *to be utterly rooted up* or *destroyed;* ܐܶܬ݂ܟܰܦܪܰܬ݂ ܐܶܣܟܽܘܠܳܐ *the school* of Edessa *was totally ruined.* Aph. ܐܰܟܦܰܪ *to make barren.* Derivatives, ܟܦܽܘܪܳܐ, ܟܦܽܘܪܳܐ, ܟܦܽܘܪܬܳܐ, ܟܳܦܪܳܐ, ܟܦܺܝܪܳܐ, ܟܶܦܪܳܐ, ܟܦܳܪܳܐ, ܡܟܰܦܪܳܢܳܐ, ܟܦܺܝܪܽܘܬ݂ܳܐ, ܡܬ݂ܟܰܦܪܳܢܽܘܬ݂ܳܐ, ܟܦܰܪ.

ܟܦܰܪ, ܟܰܦܪܳܐ, ܟܰܦܰܪܬܳܐ rt. ܟܦܪ. *barren, sterile.*

ܥܩܪ ܚܩܠܐ = ܥܩܪܐ ܕܐܦܝܩ agrimony.

ܥܩܘܪܐ rt. ܥܩܪ. m. *an extractor;* ܥܩܘܪ ܟܟܐ *a dentist, a rogue.*

ܥܩܪܬܐ rt. ܥܩܪ. *a) germination. b) a medicine taken from a corpse.*

ܥܩܪ, ܥܩܪܐ pl. ܝܢ, ܐ̈ rt. ܥܩܪ. m. *a) a root, plant, sucker, shoot;* ܥܩܪ ܫܪ̈ܫܘܗܝ *the stump of his roots;* ܥܩܪ̈ܘܗܝ ܕܣܥܪ̈ܐ *the roots of the hairs;* ܡܢ ܥܩܪܐ *radically. b) stock, origin. c) the lower part* ܕܐܣܬܐ *of a wall;* ܕܣܒܠܬܐ *of a staircase. d)* ܥܩܪܐ ܕܡܠܚܐ *a salt-pit;* ܕܢܚܠܐ *the edge of a torrent. e) a herb, medicinal herb;* ܐܫܬܝ ܥܩܪܐ ܕܐܣܝܘܬܐ *he drank the physic.*

ܥܩܪܐ ܕܐܦܝܩ or ܕܫܒܬ ܐܦܝܩ *agrimonia eupatorium, hemp agrimony.*

ܥ̅ ܕܪܘܡܢܐ *root of the wild pomegranate.*

ܥ̅ ܕܐܪܝܐ *orobanche,* a parasitic plant.

ܥ̅ ܥܩܪܩܪܢܐ or ܥܩܪܩܪܢܐ *androsaces, a sea-plant.*

ܥ̅ ܕܦܘܬܐ the dye *madder.*

ܥ̅ ܕܝܘܢܐ a kind of verbena.

ܥ̅ ܦܘܢܝܐ *paeonia, peony.*

ܥ̅ ܟܠܝܕܘܢܝܘܢ *a) chelidonium, celandine. b) the corm of the autumn crocus.*

ܥ̅ ܕܐܣܪܘܢܐ *daphne oleoides, dwarf olive.*

ܥ̅ ܦܘܪܬܐ *anthemis pyrethrum, featherfew* or *camomile.*

ܥ̅ ܕܦܘܕܢܐ ܫܟܠܐ *paeonia, peony.*

ܥ̅ ܚܠܝܐ *glycyrrhiza, liquorice.*

ܥܩܪܐ rt. ܥܩܪ. m. *extirpation, eradication; extraction* of teeth.

ܥܩܪܒܐ pl. ܐ̈ m. *a scorpion; Scorpio,* a sign of the Zodiac; ܥܩܪܒܐ ܕܝܡܐ *a tortoise;* ܕܘܒܐ ܥܩܪܒܐ *heliotrope.*

ܥܩܪܒܢܐ *scorpiurus,* a kind of heliotrope with scorpion-like pods.

ܥܩܪܒܐ ܕܚܡܪܐ f. *asses' scorpion,* a plant.

ܥܩܪܩܥܐ pl. ܐ̈ m. *a frog.*

ܥܩܪܘܬܐ rt. ܥܩܪ. f. *barrenness..*

ܥܩܪܬܐ m. *kicking, restiveness.*

ܥܩܪܢܐ *restive, untamed, apt to throw.*

ܥܩܫܐ m. *erection* or *movement of the penis.*

ܥܩܫܘܬܐ = ܥܩܫܐ.

ܥܩܬܐ emph. state of ܥܩܐ, see above.

ܥܪ fut. ܢܥܘܪ, act. part. ܥܐܪ. *to be anxious;* ܥܐܪ ܠܒܗ *his heart is anxious.* Palpel ܥܪܥܪ see below. Derivatives, ܥܪܘܪܐ, ܥܪܘܪ, ܥܪܐ.

ܥܪܐ, ܥܪܝ fut. ܢܥܪܐ, act. part. ܥܪܐ, ܥܪܝܐ. *a) to contain, hold,* esp. of measures; *to have room for;* ܡܟܝܠܬܐ ܐܝܟܢ ܥܪܝܐ *a measure holds so much;* ܙܩܐ ܒܠܝܐ ܠܐ ܥܪܐ a worn-out wineskin *cannot contain new wine;* ܗܝ ܕܥܬܝܕܐ ܗܘܬ ܠܡܥܪܐ ܠܗܘ ܕܠܐ ܡܬܥܪܐ *she who was to contain Him who cannot be contained. b) to receive, grasp, comprehend;* ܠܐ ܟܠ ܗܘܢܐ ܥܪܐ ܚܝܠܐ ܕܡܠܬܐ *not every mind can fully comprehend the force of the saying. c) to hold, take hold;* ܥܪܝ ܟܣܐ ܡܠܝܐ ܠܗ *hold a full cup to him;* ܒܥܪܝܐ ܠܐ ܥܪܝܐ ܥܪܝܐ *in frosty weather a grasp cannot be maintained;* ܥܪܝ ܘܐܫܠܡܢܝ ܠܡܘܬܐ *take me and deliver me to a violent death;* ܦܐܪ̈ܐ ܕܦܪܕܝܣܐ ܥܪܝܢ ܚܕ ܒܚܕ *the fruits of* Paradise *follow each other in close succession;* with ܥܠܬܐ *to seize a pretext. d) to be seized with illness, to swoon;* ܢܦܠܬ ܥܪܝܐ ܠܗ *she fell down in a swoon.* Ethpe. ܐܬܥܪܝ *a) to be held, seized, arrested;* ܐܬܥܪܝ ܪܫܗ ܕܐܒܫܠܘܡ ܒܣܘܟܬܐ ܪܒܬܐ Absalom's *head was caught in a great branch. b) to become numb, rigid;* ܠܫܢܗ ܐܬܥܪܝ ܕܠܐ ܬܡܠܠ ܟܠܠ *her tongue became rigid so that she could not speak at all. c) to be contained, comprehended* used of God. Pa. ܥܪܝ *to grow numb with cold.* Aph. ܐܥܪܝ *a) to breakfast. b) to seize hold.* Derivatives, ܥܪܝܐ, ܥܪܐ, ܥܪܘܝܬܐ, ܥܪܝܢܐ, ܥܪܘܝܐ, ܥܪܝܬܐ, ܥܪܝܐ, ܥܪܘܝܬܐ, ܠܥܪܝܬܐ, ܡܥܪܝܢܐ, ܡܥܪܐ, ܥܪܝܬܐ.

ܥܪܐ rt. ܥܪ. m. *a) tamarix, the tamarisk* shrub. *b)* perh. *myrica, myrtle;* ܥܪܐ ܫܘܦܐ and ܥܪܐ ܕܝܡܐ *vitex agnus castus.*

ܥܪܐ rt. ܥܪ. m. *violence, intensity;* ܥܪܗ ܕܢܩܦܐ *violence of the throbbing* of a wound.

ܥܪܒ *a)* fut. ܢܥܪܘܒ, act. part. ܥܪܒ, ܥܪܒܐ, pass. part. ܥܪܝܒ, ܥܪܝܒܐ. *to set, go down;* ܗܘܐ ܫܡܫܐ ܠܡܥܪܒ *the sun was setting;* ܫܡܫܐ ܕܥܪܒ *the setting sun;* ܢܘܗܪܐ ܕܠܐ ܥܪܒ *light which does not go down. b)* fut. ܢܥܪܘܒ *to promise solemnly, to be surety, give security, pledge oneself,* with ܒ, ܠ or ܥܠ. Esp. *to stand sponsor* at baptism. ܐܢ ܥܪܒܬ ܠܚܒܪܟ *if thou art become surety for thy neighbour;*

ܥܪܒܘ ܦܘܠܚܢܐ ܗܘ ܠܐܠܟܣܢܕܪܘܣ *the three made themselves responsible for the money;* ܐܢܐ ܥܪܒܐ ܐܢܐ ܕܐܢ ܬܗܦܘܟ ܡܩܒܠ ܠܟ *I pledge myself that if thou return he will receive thee.* c) *to sift;* ܣܛܢܐ ܫܐܠ: ܕܢܥܪܒܟܘܢ ܐܝܟ ܕܠܚܛܐ *Satan hath desired to sift you as wheat.* d) *to mingle;* ܡܬܥܪܒܝܢ ܩܛܡܐ the ashes of those of differing degree are *mingled together in the earth.* Ethpe. ܐܬܥܪܒ *to stand surety* or *sponsor; to be sifted; to be mingled.* Pa. ܥܪܒ a) *to cause to set* as the sun; or metaph. of souls caused to go down into sleep or death. b) *to mingle;* ܢܦܫܐ ܘܦܓܪܐ ܡܥܪܒܝܢ ܐܝܟ ܚܕ ܥܡ ܚܕ *the soul and body are intermingled.* Aph. ܐܥܪܒ *to cause to set;* ܐܥܪܒ ܫܡܫܐ ܒܛܗܪܐ *I will make the sun to set at noon.* Derivatives, ܥܪܒܐ, ܥܪܘܒܬܐ, ܥܪܘܒ, ܥܪܒ, ܥܪܒܐ, ܥܪܒܐ, ܥܪܒܐ, ܥܪܒܐ, ܥܪܒܘܢܐ, ܥܪܒܘܬܐ, ܥܪܒܝܐ, ܥܪܒܝܐ, ܥܪܒܝܐ, ܥܪܒܐ, ܥܪܒܘܬܐ, ܡܥܪܒܐ, ܡܥܪܒܢܘܬܐ, ܡܥܪܒܐܝܬ, ܡܥܪܒܐ.

ܥܪܒ or ܥܪܒ rt. ܥܪܒ. f. *Araba,* part of Northern Mesopotamia between the Tigris and Nisibis and round Edessa.

ܥܪܒܐ pl. ܐ̈ rt. ܥܪܒ. f. a) *a large wooden bowl* or *vessel, a washtub, kneading-trough;* also *a cup, a measure; an olive-press.* b) *the west* (rare). c) *a vetch, chick-pea.* d) *a water-wheel* or *mill.*

ܥܪܒܐ, ܥܪܒܬܐ pl. ܥܪܒܝܢ, ܥܪܒܐ, ܥܪܒܬܐ, f. a) *a willow;* ܥܪܒܐ ܕܗܢܕܘ *piper cubeba.* b) *asparagus.*

ܥܪܒܐ, ܥܪܒܬܐ rt. ܥܪܒ. a) *a surety, sponsor, a god-parent;* also *one who gives in betrothal; a sponsor* at marriage, *groomsman.* b) *security, bail.*

ܥܪܒܐ pl. ܐ̈ m. but used generally, *a sheep;* ܥܪܒܐ ܝܡܝܢܝܐ *the sheep set at the* Lord's *right hand.*

ܥܪܒ, ܥܪܒܐ pl. ܐ̈ rt. ܥܪܒ. m. *sunset,* opp. ܕܢܚܐ *sunrise;* ܒܡܥܪܒ ܫܡܫܐ *at sunset.*

ܥܪܒܐ rt. ܥܪܒ. *the Arabah* i.e. the low desert tract of the Jordan and the Dead Sea; ܝܡܐ ܕܥܪܒܐ ܝܡܐ ܕܡܠܚܐ *the sea of the Arabah, the salt sea.*

ܥܪܒܝܐ pl. ܐ̈ m. *a ringdove.*

ܥܪܒܘܢܐ rt. ܥܪܒ. m. pl. *grinders, bolters* of corn.

ܥܪܒܘܢܝܬܐ pl. ܐ̈ perh. dimin. of ܥܪܒܐ. f. *a little cup* or *bowl.*

ܥܪܒܘܬܐ rt. ܥܪܒ. f. *suretyship; a pledge, surety.*

ܥܪܒܝܐ *centaurium, centaury.*

ܥܪܒܝܐ rt. ܥܪܒ. f. *Arabia;* ܥܪܒܝܐ ܛܘܒܢܝܬܐ *Arabia Felix.*

ܥܪܒܝܐ pl. ܐ̈ rt. ܥܪܒ. a) *an Arab, Arabian.* b) ܒܝܬ ܥܪܒܝܐ or ܐܬܪܐ ܕܥܪܒܝܐ *Araba* between the Tigris and Nisibis; cf. ܥܪܒ.

ܥܪܒܝܐ, ܥܪܒܝܬܐ from ܥܪܒܐ *of sheep;* with ܬܪܥܐ understood, *the sheep-gate.*

ܥܪܒܝܬܐ = ܥܪܒܝܬܐ f. *shivering* or *trembling with fever.*

ܥܪܒܠ *to sift, riddle.* Derivatives, ܥܪܒܠܐ, ܡܥܪܒܠܢܘܬܐ, ܥܪܒܠܐ.

ܥܪܒܠܐ from ܥܪܒܠ. m. *a sieve.*

ܥܪܓܠ Parel conj. of verb ܥܓܠ.

ܥܪܓܠܘܢܐ pl. ܐ̈ rt. ܥܓܠ. m. *a little ball.*

ܥܪܕ Ethpa. ܐܬܥܪܕ a) *to make patterns in the skin, to tattoo.* b) *to be unrestrained, unruly, savage* as a wild ass. Palel ܥܪܕܕ *to gnaw.* Ethpalal ܐܬܥܪܕܕ and ܐܬܥܪܕܕ a) *to gnaw, crunch.* b) *to be devoured* by dogs or wild beasts. Derivatives, ܥܪܘܕܐ, ܥܪܘܕܕܐ, ܥܪܕܐ, ܥܪܕܘܬܐ, ܡܥܪܕܕܘܬܐ, ܡܥܪܕܢܘܬܐ, ܡܥܪܕܐ.

ܥܪܕܐ Ar. m. *a mushroom, truffle.*

ܥܪܕܐ and ܥܪܕܐ pl. ܐ̈ Ar. *a mast; a column; a balk, timber; an engine of war* smaller than a battering-ram; *a wooden frame, peg; pasture left as uneatable.*

ܥܪܕܐ pl. ܐ̈, m. ܥܪܕܬܐ pl. ܬܐ̈, f. rt. ܥܪܕ. *a wild ass.*

ܥܪܕܘܬܐ rt. ܥܪܕ. f. *licentiousness.*

ܥܪܕܠ Parel conj. of verb ܥܕܠ.

ܥܪܘܒܐ rt. ܥܪܒ. m. a) *a swarm of vermin and insects.* b) *a mixed multitude, riff-raff, rabble.* c) ܥܪܘܒܐ ܕܡܠܐ *a confusion of words.*

ܥܪܘܒܬܐ pl. ܐ̈ and ܥܪܘܒܬܐ rt. ܥܪܒ. f. *the eve, day of preparation,* esp. *the eve of the Sabbath, Friday;* ܥܪܘܒܬܐ ܕܕܗܒܐ *the first Friday after Whitsunday* when S. Peter and S. John were commemorated [East-Syr.], S. Paul also

[West-Syr.], the name is an allusion to the lesson for the day, Acts iii. 6; ܥ̈ ܕܕܗܒܐ or ܥ̈ ܕܣܡܐ or ܕܐܣܩܦܘܠܘܬܐ *Good Friday;* ܥ̈ ܕܢܘܗܪܐ or ܕܦܨܚܐ *the Friday in Easter week.*

ܥܪܘܝܬܐ or ܥܪܘܝܬܐ rt. ܥܪܐ. f. *the shivering fit of an ague.*

ܥܪܘܝܬܐ pl. ܬ̈ܐ rt. ܥܪܐ. f. *the pin* of a loom which holds the woven cloth.

ܥܪܘܠܐ rt. ܥܪܠ. *uncircumcised.* Cf. ܥܘܪܠܐ.

ܥܪܘܦܬܐ = ܥܪܘܒܬܐ.

ܥܪܘܩܐ pl. ܐ̈ rt. ܥܪܩ. m. *a fugitive;* ܥܒܕܐ ܥܪܘܩܐ *a runaway slave;* chem. *volatile, quicksilver.*

ܥܪܘܩܘܬܐ rt. ܥܪܩ. f. *dirt of the teeth* or *ears, ear-wax.*

ܥܪܘܩܝܐ pl. ܐ̈ rt. ܥܪܩ. m. *flight;* ܒܝܬ ܥ̈ *a place of refuge, asylum;* ܥ̈ ܕܒܝܫܬܐ *avoidance of evil;* pl. *evasions, subterfuges.*

ܥܪܘܪܐ rt. ܥܪ. m. *a) fog, dark clouds, a whirlwind. b) manna.*

ܥܪܙܠ Parel conj. of ܥܙܠ.

ܥܪܙܠܐ pl. ܐ̈ rt. ܥܙܠ. m. *a booth* or *hut of interwoven branches; a lodge* in a cucumber-garden or vineyard.

ܥܪܙܠܠܐ rt. ܥܙܠ. *twisted, woven.*

ܥܪܓ Pael ܥܪܓ perh. *to neigh.*

ܥܪܛܠ *to strip, lay bare.* Ethparal ܐܬܥܪܛܠ *to be stripped, spoiled; to be bare of, despoiled of.* Derivatives, ܥܪܛܘܠܐ and the four following words:—

ܥܪܛܠ indeclinable, *bare, nude, naked, stripped;* ܥܪܛܠ ܥܐܠܝܢ *they come in naked.*

ܥܪܛܠܐܝܬ from ܥܪܛܠ adv. *smoothly; stripped, exposed; openly, simply, without disguise.*

ܥܪܛܠܝ, ܥܪܛܠܝܐ, ܥܪܛܠܝܬܐ from ܥܪܛܠ *bare, naked, exposed, unarmed, unadorned, simple;* ܥ̈ ܕܣܘܟܠܐ *deprived of meaning;* ܡܠܬܐ ܥܪܛܠܝܬܐ *spelt.*

ܥܪܛܠܝܘܬܐ from ܥܪܛܠ f. *nakedness, extreme poverty.*

ܥܪܛܢܝܬܐ *a cyclamen.*

ܥܪܛܢܝܬܐ or ܥܪܛܢܝ f. *leontice leontopetalon, lion's leaf* or *cyclamen europaeum.*

ܥܪܝ, ܥܪܝܐ rt. ܥܪܐ. m. *a) a grasp. b) a seizure, epileptic fit.*

ܥܪܝܐ pl. ܐ̈ rt. ܥܪܐ. m. *a)* adj. *cold. b) frost, severe weather;* ܥܪ̈ܝܐ ܕܣܬܘܐ *winter frosts;* ܥܪܝܐ ܕܒܗܬܬܐ *the chill of shame. c) severity, calamity.*

ܥܪܝܘܬܐ rt. ܥܪܐ. f. *nakedness.*

ܥܪܝܢܐ, ܥܪܝܢܬܐ rt. ܥܪܐ. *cold, stiff.*

ܥܪܝܣܘܬܐ rt. ܥܪܣ. f. *mixing flour, kneading.*

ܥܪܝܡܐܝܬ rt. ܥܪܡ. adv. *craftily, cunningly.*

ܥܪܝܡܘܬܐ, ܥܪܝܡܘܬ rt. ܥܪܡ. f. *craft, cunning, acuteness, subtilty, sagacity.*

ܥܪܝܙܐܝܬ rt. ܥܪܙ. adv. *a) accidentally. b) necessarily, of necessity, reluctantly.*

ܥܪܝܙܘܬܐ, ܥܪܝܙܘ rt. ܥܪܙ. f. *necessity, compulsion;* often with ܒ or ܡܢ *of necessity, by compulsion.*

ܥܪܝܐܝܬ rt. ܥܪܐ. adv. *cold.*

ܥܪܝܬܐ rt. ܥܪܐ. f. *a) breakfast. b) catching fire, burning up. c) power of endurance.*

ܥܪܣ act. part. ܥܪܣ, ܥܪܣܐ *to knead, stir up.* Derivatives, ܥܪܝܣܘܬܐ, ܥܪܣܐ.

ܥܪܣܐ rt. ܥܪܣ. m. *stirring, kneading.*

ܥܪܠ root-meaning *to circumcise.* Derivatives, ܥܘܪܠܐ, ܥܘܪܠܘܬܐ, ܥܪܘܠܐ.

ܥܪܡ *to stand up in a heap.* Pass. part. ܥܪܝܡ, ܐ, ܬܐ. *a) subtle, wily, adroit, astute, sagacious,* ܥܪܝܡ ܐܝܟ ܚܘܝܐ *wily as the serpent;* ܠܡܡܠܠܐ ܐܬܚܡܘ ܓܪܡܛܝܩܘ̈ ܚܟܝܡܐ ܘܥܪܝܡܐ *wise and astute grammarians have defined speech;* ܐܬܡܠܟܘ ܒܥܪܝܡܐ ܡܠܟܘܗܝ *it was discussed by his astute councillors. b) lofty.* Ethpe. ܐܬܥܪܡ *a)* perh. *to stand up on a heap;* cf. Ethpa. *b) to become astute; to ascertain.* Pa. ܥܪܡ *a) to steal subtilly; to make subtle* or *wise;* ܢܥܪܡ ܦܫܝܛܘܬܟ *he will make wise thy simplicity;* pass. part. *subtle. b) to cause to swell with excitement;* pass. part. *swollen, piled up, steep;* ܛܘܪܐ ܡܥܪܡܝܢ ܗܘܘ ܒܬܠܓܐ *the mountains were heaped with snow.* Ethpa. ܐܬܥܪܡ *a) to be piled up, rise high, swell* as the sea, the tempest; metaph. *to be swollen, inflated, exasperated;* ܐܬܥܪܡܘ ܡܢ ܪܘܚܐ ܕܗܦܘܟܝܘܬܐ *they were puffed up with the spirit of opposition. b) to become astute, sagacious.* Derivatives, ܥܪܝܡܐܝܬ, ܥܪܝܡܘܬܐ, ܥܪܡܐ,

ܡܥܪܡܘܬܐ, ܡܥܪܡܢܐ, ܥܪܡܬܐ, ܥܪܡܢܐ, ܡܬܥܪܡܢܐ.

ܥܪܡܐ pl. ܐ̈ rt. ܥܪܡ. *a*) adj. *steep, rugged. b*) subst. *a steep* or *rugged place, a heap; asperity;* ܥܪ̈ܡܐ ܐܫܘܐ *I will make the rugged places smooth. c*) *a dark cloud. d*) ܥܪܡܐ ܕܡܫܚܐ *an oil-flask, oil-press.*

ܥܪܡܢܐ rt. ܥܪܡ. *rugged, steep.*

ܥܪܡܣ pass. part. ܡܥܪܡܣ, ܡܥܪܡܣܐ *polluted.*

ܥܪܡܬܐ pl. ܬ̈ܐ rt. ܥܪܡ. f. *a heap, pile* of wheat, of stones.

ܥܪܢ Ethpe. ܐܬܥܪܢ *to become hard.* Derivatives, ܥܪܢܐ and ܥܪܢܝܐ, ܥܪܢܘܬܐ.

ܥܪܢܐ and ܥܪܢܝܐ rt. ܥܪܢ. *hard, obdurate.*

ܥܪܢܘܬܐ rt. ܥܪܢ. f. *hardness, obduracy.*

ܥܪܣܐ pl. ܥܪ̈ܣܝܢ, ܥܪ̈ܣܬܐ. f. *a couch, bed, litter, bier.* Astron. ܥܪܣܐ the four stars forming the body of Ursa Minor and ܒ̈ܢܬ ܥܪܣܐ the three of its tail; also ܒ̈ܢܬ ܥܪܣܐ the constellation *Cassiopea.*

ܥܪܣܘܢܝܬܐ pl. ܬ̈ܐ dim. of ܥܪܣܐ *a small couch.*

ܥܪܥܘܪܐ from ܥܪܥܪ m. *a*) *tempest, hurricane. b*) *manna.*

ܥܪܥܪ mimetic. Palpel conj. *to clean the teeth, wash out the mouth, gargle.* Derivative, ܥܪܥܘܪܐ.

ܥܪܥܪܢܐ *hypericum, St. John's wort.*

ܥܪܦ Pael ܥܪܦ *to change,* esp. *to change money.* Derivatives, ܥܪܘܦܐ, ܥܪܘܦܝܐ, ܡܥܪܦܢܐ, ܡܥܪܦܐ.

ܥܪܦܐ, ܥܪܦܐ, ܥܪܦܬܐ pl. ܬ̈ܐ f. *the willow;* ܒܝܬ ܥܪ̈ܦܬܐ *a willow-plantation, osier-bed.* Perhaps also *the elm, the pine.*

ܥܪܦܠ Ethparal ܐܬܥܪܦܠ *a*) *to roll on the ground* as a horse. *b*) denom. from ܥܪܦܠܐ *to cloud over, grow dark.* Derivative, ܥܪܦܠܐ.

ܥܪܦܠ, ܥܪܦܠܐ, ܥܪܦܠܐ pl. ܐ̈ f. *a*) *dark fog* or *mist, thick darkness. b*) ܥܪܦܠܐ ܚܘܪܐ *a white film* on the eyes. Derivatives, ܐܬܥܪܦܠ *b*, ܥܪܦܠܝܐ.

ܥܪܦܠܝܐ from ܥܪܦܠܐ. *dark, thick.*

ܥܪܩ fut. ܢܥܪܘܩ, act. part. ܥܪܩ, ܥܪܩܐ, cf. ܥܪܩܐ and ܥܪܩܬܐ below; pass. part. ܥܪܝܩ. *to occur, arise* as an occasion, *to come to pass; to happen, befall, come unexpectedly* with ܥܠ or ܠ; ܐܘܪܚܝܐ ܥܪܩ ܠܝ *a wayfarer came to me unexpectedly;* ܥܪܩ ܗܘܐ ܓܝܣܐ ܥܠ ܐܬܪܐ *the robber fell suddenly on the country;* ܐܢ ܐܬܥܪܩ *if there is occasion;* ܐܢ ܥܪܩܐ ܐܢܢܩܐ *if necessity arise.* Pass. part. *a*) *accidental, fortuitous,* f. emph. ܥܪ̈ܝܩܬܐ *unforeseen events, mischances. b*) *necessary.* Ethpe. ܐܬܥܪܩ *to receive a visitor at nightfall.* Derivatives, ܥܪܘܩܐ, ܥܪܝܩܐܝܬ, ܥܪܩܐ, ܥܪܩܐ, ܥܪܩܘܬܐ, ܥܪܩܬܐ, ܥܪܩܘܬܐ.

ܥܪܩܐ act. part. = subst. m. *a*) *a chance arrival, passer-by, stranger, alien. b*) adj. *necessary.*

ܥܪܩܐ rt. ܥܪܩ. m. *necessity, exigency.*

ܥܪܩܐܝܬ rt. ܥܪܩ. adv. *unexpectedly, by chance.*

ܥܪܩܘܬܐ rt. ܥܪܩ. f. *arrival of strangers, of guests; accident; exigency.*

ܥܪܩܬܐ pl. ܬ̈ܐ, act. part. f. emph. *a casual event; accident, non-essential property.*

ܥܪܩ fut. ܢܥܪܘܩ, act. parts. ܥܪܩ, ܥܪܩܐ, and ܥܪܝܩ. *to flee, escape, shun, avoid;* usually with ܡܢ and pers. pron. ܥܪܩ ܠܗ *he fled;* with ܡܢ, ܠܘܬ or ܩܕܡ of pers. and place; ܥܪܩ ܠܗ ܚܫܘܟܐ ܘܐܬܒܛܠ *darkness fled away and vanished;* ܫܡܥܘܢ ܪܝܫܐ ܘܪܫܐ ܕܫܠܝ̈ܚܐ ܥܪܩ ܗܘܐ Simon *head and chief of the Apostles had fled;* ܥܪܩܝܢ ܡܢ ܐܣܝܘܬܐ *they refuse medicine;* ܠܝܬ ܠܡܥܪܩ ܡܢܗ *it is inevitable;* chem. ܥܪܩ ܡܢ ܢܘܪܐ *it is volatilized by fire.* Pass. part. ܥܪܝܩ *gnawed.* Ethpe. ܐܬܥܪܩ *to shun.* Pa. *a*) *to take to flight; to scatter; to allow to escape;* ܕܢܥܪܩܘܢ ܥܢ̈ܢܐ *that they might disperse the clouds. b*) *to gnaw, crunch.* Aph. ܐܥܪܩ *a*) *to put to flight, drive away; to banish;* ܬܪܝܢ ܡܥܪܩܝܢ ܗܘܘ ܪܒܘܬܐ *two put ten thousand to flight;* ܡܥܪܩ ܛܠ̈ܠܐ ܫܦܪܐ dawn *makes the shadows flee away. b*) *to rescue, to put in a safe place;* ܕܢܥܪܩܘܢ ܡܢ ܛܘܦܢܐ ܐܝܠܝܢ ܕܐܫܟܚܘ ܠܡܥܪܩܘ *the things they were able to save from the flood.* Derivatives, ܥܪܘܩܐ, ܥܪܘܩܐ, ܥܪܘܩܘܬܐ, ܥܪܘܩܝܐ, ܡܥܪܩܢܐ, ܡܥܪܩܐ, ܥܪܩܐ, ܥܪܩܐ, ܡܥܪܩܐ, ܡܬܥܪܩܢܐ, ܡܬܥܪܩܢܘܬܐ.

ܥܪܩܐ pl. ܐ̈ rt. ܥܪܩ. m. *juniper, acacia* or *box-wood;* ܦܐܪ̈ܐ ܕܥܪܩܐ *juniper-berries.*

ܥܪܩܐ, ܥܪܩܬܐ pl. ܥܪ̈ܩܐ, ܥܪ̈ܩܝܢ, ܥܪ̈ܩܬܐ rt. ܥܪܩ. f. *a*) *a leathern strap, rein; a bell, band, fillet;* ܥܪ̈ܩܐ ܕܡܣܐܢܘ̈ܗܝ *his shoe-straps;* ܥܪܩܬܐ ܕܡܫܟܐ *a leathern belt;* ܐܣܪ ܥܪ̈ܩܐ *he tightens the reins;* ܢܦܠܬ ܠܗ ܥܪܩܬܐ ܒܦܘܡܗ *he was gagged.* *b*) *a transverse beam, thwart, joist, framework;* ܥܪ̈ܩܐ ܡܪܒܥܐ *squared timbers;* ܫܘܪ̈ܝ ܒܝܬܐ ܐܣܝܪܝܢ ܒܥܪ̈ܩܐ *the walls of the house are bound together with thwarts.* *c*) perh. *a lock* or *tuft of hair.*

ܥܪܩܘܒܐ pl. ܐ̈ m. *the tendon Achilles; the hollow of the knee.*

ܥܪܩܝܐ, ܥܪܩܝܬܐ *a*) rt. ܥܪܩ. *of juniper.* *b*) *Arkite, of Arce* in Lebanon.

ܥܪܩܠ Pael conj. of ܥܩܠ.

ܥܪܩܠܐ m. *grease and sweat from the tails of fat sheep.*

ܥܪܪܐ rt. ܥܪ. m. *a*) *the mast* of a ship, *an ensign, beacon.* *b*) *the female locust.* *c*) *the sound of sheep and camels at the pasture, bleating, lowing.*

ܥܪܫ Ethpe. ܐܬܥܪܫ *a*) dial. *to be fattened.* *b*) *to bite hard with the molar teeth, to grind with the teeth.* Ethpa. ܐܬܥܪܫ *a*) *to be fattened.* *b*) *to be hard and strong like a molar.* Derivatives, ܥܪܫܐ, ܥܪܫܘܬܐ, ܥܪܫܝܐ.

ܥܪܫܐ pl. ܐ̈ rt. ܥܪܫ. f. *a molar tooth, grinder.*

ܥܪܫܘܬܐ rt. ܥܪܫ. f. *fatness.*

ܥܪܫܝܐ rt. ܥܪܫ. *molar.*

ܥܪܬܐ pl. ܥܪ̈ܬܐ and ܥܪ̈ܘܬܐ rt. ܥܪ. f. *a second* or *rival wife* in polygamy.

ܥܫܘܡܐ rt. ܥܫܡ. m. *oppression, compulsion; the obligation* of dividing a heritage.

ܥܫܘܫܐ pl. ܐ̈ rt. ܥܫܫ. m. *an informer, false accuser, tale-bearer.*

ܥܫܘܫܘܬܐ rt. ܥܫܫ. f. *false witness, calumny.*

ܥܫܘܫܝܐ pl. ܐ̈ rt. ܥܫܫ. m. *misrepresentation, calumny, slander, false witness.*

ܥܫܦ, ܥܫܦܐ m. *a whetstone.*

ܥܫܝܢܐܝܬ rt. ܥܫܢ. adv. *mightily, violently.*

ܥܫܝܢܘܬܐ rt. ܥܫܢ. f. *strength, power.*

ܥܫܝܫܘܬܐ rt. ܥܫܫ. f. *frowardness, depreciation.*

ܥܫܡ fut. ܢܥܫܘܡ, act. part. ܥܫܡ, ܥܫܡܐ, pass. part. ܥܫܝܡ, ܥܫܝܡܐ. *a*) *to treat unjustly, wrong, oppress;* ܠܓܝܘܪܐ ܘܠܝܬܡܐ ܘܠܐܪܡܠܬܐ ܠܐ ܬܥܫܡܘܢ *the stranger, the orphan and the widow shall ye not oppress.* *b*) *to compel, repress, overcome;* ܠܚܐܪܘܬܗ *his freewill;* ܠܡܚܫܒܬܗ *his thoughts.* Ethpe. ܐܬܥܫܡ *to be compelled, coerced;* ܐܬܓܒܝ ܘܐܬܥܫܡ ܠܦܛܪܝܪܟܘܬܐ *he was elected and compelled* to be Patriarch *and consecrated.* Derivative, ܥܫܘܡܐ.

ܥܫܢ fut. ܢܥܫܢ, act. part. ܥܫܢ, ܥܫܢܐ, part. adj. ܥܫܝܢ, ܢܐ, ܢܬܐ. *to gain strength, prevail; to increase in number, be many, be more; to be sure, grievous,* with ܥܠ or ܒ; as ܟܦܢܐ *famine,* ܡܘܬܢܐ *pestilence,* ܟܘܪܗܢܐ *disease,* ܥܘܠܐ *iniquity.* ܐܙܠ ܘܥܫܢ *waxing stronger and stronger;* ܥܫܢܬ ܐܝܕܗ ܕܡܪܝܐ ܥܠ *the hand of the Lord was heavy upon . . .;* ܣܓܝ ܥܫܢܘ ܚܛܗܝܗܘܢ *their sins are very many* or *very grievous;* ܥܫܢ ܗܘܐ ܡܥܝܢܐ ܕܡܝܐ *the spring had increased in volume;* ܕܢܥܫܢ ܒܗܬܬܗ *that his shame might be the more grievous.* Part. adj. *a*) *strong, fortified* as ܚܨܢ̈ܐ *fortresses,* ܡܕܝܢ̈ܬܐ *cities.* *b*) *powerful, heroic; a mighty man, a warrior;* ܢܚܒܠ ܥܫܝܢ̈ܐ *he shall destroy the mighty ones;* ܥܫܝܢܝܢ ܐܢܘܢ ܡܢܗ *they are stronger than he;* ܥܫܝܢ ܚܝܠܐ *of mighty strength.* *c*) *sore, grievous, heavy, hard, severe;* as ܟܘܪܗܢܐ *sickness,* ܥܘܠܐ *iniquity,* ܐܘܠܝܬܐ *lamentation;* ܡܠܟܐ ܥܫܝܢܐ *a hard king;* ܥܫܝܢܝ ܠܒܐ *hard-hearted;* ܨܒܘܬܐ ܥܫܝܢ̈ܬܐ *weighty matters.* *d*) *large, loud, fierce, violent* as ܡܛܪܐ *rain,* ܪܘܚ̈ܐ *winds,* ܚܡܬܐ *anger;* rit. ܒܩܠܐ ܥܫܝܢܐ *with a loud voice.* Pa. ܥܫܢ *to strengthen; to repair* a wall, a ruin; *to magnify;* pass. part. ܡܥܫܢܐ *very great* or *strong;* ܥܫܢ ܩܪܒܐ ܛܒ *he continued the battle very sore;* ܠܐܠܗܐ ܕܐܝܣܪܝܠ ܢܥܫܢܘܢ *they shall magnify the God of Israel.* Ethpa. ܐܬܥܫܢ *a*) pass. *to be hardened* as the heart; *to be strengthened;* ܡܚܝ̈ܠܐ ܐܬܥܫܢܘ ܚܝܠܐ *the feeble are girded with strength.* *b*) *to strengthen oneself, wax strong, act strongly, bravely, do with all one's might;* ܐܬܚܝܠ ܘܐܬܥܫܢ ܛܒ *be strong and of good courage;* ܐܬܥܫܢܬ ܗܪܣܝܣ *heresy grew strong.* Aph. *to set firmly, harden* ܐܦ̈ܐ *the face,* ܠܒܐ *the heart; to make firm* or *strong, to strengthen* ܐܝܕܝܐ *the hands; to repair a wall;* ܡܥܫܢܝܢ ܩܠܗܘܢ *shouting loudly.* DERIVATIVES, ܥܫܝܢܐ, ܥܫܝܢܐܝܬ, ܥܫܝܢܘܬܐ, ܡܥܫܢܢܐ, ܡܬܥܫܢܢܘܬܐ, ܡܥܫܢܢܘܬܐ.

ܥܫܘܦܐ m. *an axe, hatchet.* DERIVATIVE, ܡܥܫܦܐܝܬ.

ܥܫܘܦܐ m. *cleaning grain.*

ܥܫܩ fut. ܢܥܫܘܩ, act. part. ܥܳܫܶܩ, ܥܳܫܩܳܐ, pass. part. ܥܫܝܩ, ܥܫܝܩܳܐ, ܥܫܝܩܬܐ. *to bring an accusation, charge, reproach* esp. *falsely; to misrepresent, slander, oppress;* esp. *to impugn, detract from* miracles or doctrines; *to falsify* a text; ܥܫܩ ܥܠ ܐܚܪܢ *he brought a false charge;* ܥܳܫܶܩ ܘܡܕܓܠ *he slanders and lies;* ܠܐ ܟܦܪ ܐܢܐ ܒܦܓܪܗ ܕܡܫܝܚܐ. ܐܝܟ ܕܥܫܩܝܢ ܠܝ ܕܓܠܐ *I do not deny the body of Christ, as liars accuse me;* ܥܫܩܘ ܠܫܘܒܚܗ ܟܕ ܐܡܪܝܢ *they impugned his glory, saying . . .* Pass. part. ܥܫܝܩ *one falsely accused;* ܥܫܝܩ ܒܙܘܥܐ—ܥܫܝܩܐ *shifty, perverse.* ETHPE. ܐܬܥܫܩ *to be falsely accused, oppressed.* PA. ܥܰܫܶܩ *a) to accuse falsely, impugn;* ܩܫܝܫܐ ܗܢܘܢ ܕܥܫܩܘܗ ܠܫܘܫܢ *those elders who accused Susanna. b) to be arrogant, haughty.* ETHPA. ܐܬܥܰܫܰܩ *to be accused, slandered, oppressed.* APH. ܐܥܫܩ *a) to slander, wrong. b) to boast, vaunt.* DERIVATIVES, ܥܫܘܩܐ, ܥܫܘܩܝܐ, ܥܫܘܩܘܬܐ, ܥܫܝܩܐ, ܥܫܝܩܘܬܐ, ܡܥܫܩܢܘܬܐ, ܡܥܫܩܢܐ, ܡܥܫܩܢܘܬܐ, ܡܬܥܫܩܢܐ.

ܥܫܘܪܐ Ar. m. *one who collects tithes, a publican.*

ܥܫܘܪܘܬܐ from the preceding. f. *the office of a publican.*

ܥܬ contracted from ܥܘܠ: cf. ܥܬܝܬܐ. fut. ܢܥܘܬ, act. part. ܥܐܬ, pass. part. ܥܝܬܐ, ܥܝܬܬܐ. *to defraud, be fraudulent, dishonest.* ETHPE. ܐܬܥܬܬ *to deal fraudulently.* DERIVATIVES, ܥܬܐ, ܥܬܝܐ, ܥܬܬܐ.

ܥܬܐ rt. ܥܬ. m. *deceit, knavery, villany, depravity;* ܢܟܡܘܢ ܠܙܟܝܐ ܒܥܬܐ *let us lie in wait wrongfully for the innocent;* ܣܝܡܬܐ ܕܥܬܐ *treasures gotten by knavery.*

ܥܬܐ same as ܥܬ. *to commit fraud, act deceitfully.* ETHPE. ܐܬܥܬܝ the same. PA. ܥܰܬܝ *to charge, accuse.* DERIVATIVE, ܥܬܘܝܐ.

ܥܬܕ *to be prepared.* PEAL only pass. part. ܥܬܝܕ, ܐ, ܬܐ *ready, prepared; to come, future;* ܥܬܝܕ ܕ expresses the future tense; ܥܬܝܕ ܕܢܐܬܐ *he shall come;* ܕܥܬܝܕ ܠܡܗܘܐ *that shall be;* ܕܝܢܐ ܕܥܬܝܕ *judgement to come;* ܥܬܝܕ ܙܒܢܐ *the future* tense; ܥܬܝܕܬܐ *things to come.* PAEL ܥܰܬܶܕ *to make ready, prepare, to bring to pass;* esp. *to equip* soldiers, also *to urge to prepare* for war; ܡܢܘ ܥܬܕ ܘܥܒܕ *who hath made ready and done it?* ܕܢܥܬܕ ܢܟܠܐ ܡܕܡ *in order to prepare some deceit.* ETHPA. ܐܬܥܬܕ *a) to be arranged, concerted, devised, brought to pass. b) to get ready, make ready* esp. for war. DERIVATIVES, ܥܬܝܕܐܝܬ, ܥܬܝܕܘܬܐ, ܥܬܝܕܐ, ܥܬܝܕܐ, ܡܥܬܕܢܐܝܬ, ܡܥܬܕܢܘܬܐ, ܡܥܬܕܢܐ, ܡܥܬܕܢܘܬܐ.

ܥܬܝܕܐܝܬ rt. ܥܬܕ. adv. *willingly, ready.*

ܥܬܝܕܘܬܐ rt. ܥܬܕ. f. *the future; readiness, preparation;* gram. *the future tense.*

ܥܬܝܕܝܐ rt. ܥܬܕ. *future.*

ܥܬܝܩܐܝܬ rt. ܥܬܩ. adv. *anciently.*

ܥܬܝܩܘܬܐ rt. ܥܬܩ. f. *old age, antiquity, old order, old habit.*

ܥܬܝܪܐܝܬ rt. ܥܬܪ. adv. *richly, abundantly.*

ܥܬܝܪܘܬܐ rt. ܥܬܪ. f. *wealth, richness, opulence.*

ܥܬܝܬܐ, ܬܐ rt. ܥܬ. *villainous, knavish.*

ܥܬܩ fut. ܢܥܬܩ, act. part. ܥܳܬܶܩ, ܥܳܬܩܳܐ, part. adj. ܥܬܝܩ, ܐ, ܬܐ. *to grow old; to become antiquated, out of date;* ܥܬܩܬ ܒܝܢ ܒܝܫܬܐ ܣܓܝܐܬܐ *I have grown old among many evils;* ܥܬܝܩܢ ܘܒܠܝܢ ܫܪܒܝܐ *obsolete and worn-out* chronicles. Part. adj. *old, ancient* ܥܬܝܩ ܝܘܡܬܐ *aged;* ܒܨܚܚܐ ܥܬܝܩܐ *in an ancient copy* or *codex.* Often ellipt. for *old provisions, old wine, old time, the Old Testament.* APH. ܐܥܬܩ *a) to make old, make stale. b) to become old, antiquated, ancient.* DERIVATIVES, ܥܬܝܩܐܝܬ, ܥܬܝܩܘܬܐ, ܥܬܩܐ, ܥܬܩܐ.

ܥܬܩܐ pl. ܐ rt. ܥܬܩ. m. *an edge, fringe.*

ܥܬܪ fut. ܢܥܬܪ, act. part. ܥܳܬܶܪ, ܥܳܬܪܳܐ, pass. part. ܥܬܝܪ, ܐ, ܬܐ. *to be* or *grow rich, to be enriched, increase, gain;* ܢܥܬܪ ܥܘܬܪܐ ܪܒܐ *he shall gain great riches, grow very rich;* ܘܩܡ

ܥܬܪܝܢ ܥܘܠܐ who make gain out of wickedness. Part. adj. *rich;* ܥܬܝܪ ܒܦܐܪܐ *very fertile;* ܥܬܝܪܐܝܬ ܒܐܝܕܐ *bountifully, munificently.* Aph. ܐܥܬܪ *to enrich; to make to abound;* with ܢܦܫܗ *to pretend to be rich.* Derivatives, ܥܘܬܪܐ, ܥܬܝܪܘܬܐ, ܥܬܝܪܐܝܬ, ܥܘܬܪܢܐ, ܥܬܪܐ, ܡܥܬܪܢܐ.

ܥܘܬܪܐ rt. ܥܬܪ. m. *riches, abundance.*

ܥܬܪܘܬܐ = ܥܘܬܪܐ.

∴ ܫܘܠܡܐ ܕܐܬܘܬܐ ܥܠܡ ܣܘܪܝܐ ܕܥܐ ∴

∴ ܫܘܪܝܐ. ܦܝܫ ܡܢ ܦܬܓܡܐ ܕܦܐ ∴

∴ ܦ ∴

ܦ ܦܐܛܪܝܩ

ܦ, ܦܐ f. *Pe*, the seventeenth letter of the alphabet; as a numeral *eighty;* with ܕ prefixed *the eightieth;* with a point above, ܦ̇, 800. ܦ̅ gram. abbreviation for ܦܘܩܕܢܐ *imperative.*

ܦܐܐ m. *a) the hyena.* *b)* pass. part. of verb ܦܐܐ.

ܦܐܘܦܝ Φαωφί, *Phaophi*, name of the second Egyptian month.

ܦܐܝܫ act. part. of verb ܦܘܫ.

ܦܐܝܓܢܘܢ; see ܦܝܓܢܐ *rue.*

ܦܐܪ, ܦܐܪܐ act. part. of verb ܦܪ.

ܦܐܘܛܐ, ܦܐܘܛܝܣ and ܦܐܘܛܝܐ, see ܦܘܐܝܛܐ *a poet.*

ܦܐܘܝܛܘܬܐ see ܦܘܐܝܛܘܬܐ *poetry.*

ܦܐܘܝܛܝܩܘܣ *a poet.*

ܦܐܘܝܛܝܩܝܐ, ܦܐܘܝܛܝܩܝܬܐ *poetical, of a poet.*

ܦܐܘܠܐ and ܦܐܘܠܘܣ; see ܦܘܠܘܣ.

ܦܐܘܢܝܐ *paeonia, the peony.*

ܦܐܘܩܐ pl. ܦܐܘܩܐ̈ πεύκη, *the fir.*

ܦܐܫ act. part. of verb ܦܘܫ.

ܦܐܛܪܣܝܛܝܣ πεταοίτης, a sort of coltsfoot.

ܦܐܛܪܝܩܐ, ܦܐܛܪܝܩܝܣ *patrician;* see ܦܛܪܝܩܘܣ.

ܦܐܛܪܝܩܝܐ *patrician.*

ܦܐܛܪܝܪܟܐ, ܦܐܛܪܝܪܟܝܣ pl. ܦܐܛܪܝܪܟܘ̈ ... *patriarch:* see ܦܛܪܝܪܟܝܣ.

ܦܐܐ fut. ܢܦܐܐ, act. part. ܦܐܐ. *to be becoming, comely.* Pass. part. ܦܐܐ, ܦܐܝܐ, ܦܐܝܐ pl. ܦܐܝܢ, ܦܐܝܢ, ܦܐܝܢ; a ܒܘܟܕ letter prefixed takes ◌̄, ܕܦܐܐ, ܕܦܐܐ. *proper, becoming, comely, seemly, convenient, fair;* ܦܐܐ ܠܢ ܕܢܐܡܪ *it becomes us to say;* ܠܐ ܦܐܝܐ ܗܕܐ *this is not proper;* ܦܐܐ ܙܟܘܬܐ *victorious, triumphant;* ܦܐܐ ܙܠܝܩܐ *radiant;* ܦܐܐ ܚܙܘܐ *of goodly appearance;* ܦܐܐ ܪܒܘܬܐ *of excellent majesty, magnificent;* ܦܐܐ ܒܨܘܪܬܐ *goodly, comely.* Pl. f. emph. *beautiful things, beauties, glories.* Pa. ܦܐܐ *to adorn.* Ethpa. ܐܬܦܐܐ *to be adorned, beautified.* Aph. ܐܦܐܐ *to beautify.* Ethtaph. ܐܬܬܦܐܐ *to be beautified.* Derivatives, ܦܐܝܐܝܬ, ܦܐܝܘܬܐ.

ܦܐܝܐܝܬ rt. ܦܐܐ. adv. *well, beautifully.*

ܦܐܝܘܬ, ܦܐܝܘܬܐ rt. ܦܐܐ. f. *beauty, comeliness, elegance;* comp. with adverbs; ܦܐܝܘܬ ܩܕܝܫܐܝܬ *befitting the holy;* ܦܐܝܘܬ ܡܛܟܣܐܝܬ *well arranged, orderly;* ܦܐܝܘܬ ܥܒܕܐܝܬ *as befits a slave, servilely.*

ܦܐܝܫ rt. ܦܫ. *erring, mistaken.*

ܦܰܐܚܘܢ Παχών, *Pachon*, the ninth Egyptian month.

ܦܰܐܠܰܛܺܝܢ and ܦܰܐܠܰܛܺܝܢ *a palace;* see ܦܰܠܳܛܺܝܢ.

ܦܰܐܠܰܩܬܳܐ for ܦܰܠܰܩܬܳܐ *a concubine.*

ܦܰܐܡܶܢܘܬ and ܦܰܐܡܶܢܘܬܳܐ *Phamenoth,* the seventh Egyptian month from about Feb. 25 to March 27.

ܦܰܐܢܶܐ and ܦܰܐܢܺܝܣ, Lat. pinnae, *bulwarks, ramparts.*

ܦܐܪܩܠܝܛܐ and ܦܰܐܪܰܩܠܺܝܛܳܐ; see ܦܰܪܰܩܠܺܝܛܳܐ.

ܦܰܐܪܰܣܬܳܐ and ܦܰܐܪܰܣܬܳܐ pl. ܦܰܐܪܰܣܬܳܣ; see ܦܰܪܰܣܬܳܐ.

ܦܰܐܪܰܣܘܣ *doubtless, positively;* see ܦܰܪܰܣܘܣ.

ܦܰܐܢܛܶܩܘܣܛܺܝ usually without the Alep, *Pentecost.*

ܦܐܢܬܝܪ = ܦܰܢܬܺܝܪ *a panther.*

ܦܰܐܣܳܐ pl. ܐ̈ܶ m. Lat. fossa, *a fosse, trench.*

ܦܐܣܝ πᾶσι, *to all;* ܐܺܝܪܺܝܢܺܝ ܦܐܣܝܢ εἰρήνη πᾶσιν, *pax omnibus.*

ܦܰܐܣܺܝܢܳܐ = ܦܰܣܺܝܢܳܐ *a pheasant.*

ܦܰܐܣܶܩ, Ar. *scoundrel.*

ܦܰܐܦܳܐ and ܦܰܐܦܰܐܣ; see ܦܰܦܳܐ *pope.*

ܦܶܐܦܪܘܡܶܢܺܝ πεπρωμένη, *fated, destined.*

ܦܰܐܦܘܪܘܣ, ܣ̈ܶܐ and ܦܰܐܦܺܝܪܘܣ m. *papyrus;* cf. ܦܦܘܪܘܣ.

ܦܶܐܦܶܪܰܛܰܣܬܰܐܝ πεπερατῶσθαι, *to have been fated.*

ܦܐܩܐ, ܦܰܐܩܳܐ and ܦܰܩܳܐ *tongue-tied, dumb, speaking indistinctly.*

ܦܰܐܩܳܐ, ܦܰܐܩܘܣ pl. ܦܰܐܩܶܐ, ܦܰܐܩܶܐ m. φακός, *the lentil; the lesser duckweed.*

ܦܰܐܩܘܬܳܐ from ܦܰܐܩܳܐ. f. *dumbness, stammering.*

ܦܰܐܪܳܐ, ܦܰܐܪܬܳܐ; see ܦܰܪܳܐ *a lamb.*

ܦܺܐܪܳܐ pl. ̈ܺܝܢ, ̈ܶܐ rt. ܦܪܐ. m. *fruit;* ܐܺܝܠܰܢ ܦܺܐܪܳܐ *a fruit-tree;* ܦܺܐܪ̈ܶܐ ܩܰܕܡܳܝ̈ܶܐ *first-fruits;* ܦܺܐܪܳܐ ܕܰܐܪܙܳܐ *a cedar-cone, fir-cone.* Metaph. *offspring; a knot in the flesh.*

ܦܰܐܪܺܝܘܕܶܘܛܳܐ and ܦܰܐܪܺܝܘܕܶܘܛܳܐ; see ܦܶܪܺܝܘܕܶܘܛܳܐ *periodeutes.*

ܦܐܪܐܛܝܣ περατής, *a foreigner.*

ܦܐܪܐܬܝܩܝ; see ܦܰܪܰܬܺܝܩܺܝ *a deposit.*

ܦܺܐܪܳܢܳܐ and ܦܺܐܪܳܢܳܝܳܐ, ܝܬܳܐ rt. ܦܪܐ. *fruit-bearing, fruitful, profitable.*

ܦܪܘܣܛܢ; see ܦܪܘܣܛܢ.

ܦܺܐܪܳܢܳܐܺܝܬ rt. ܦܪܐ. adv. *after the manner of fruit.*

ܦܰܐܪܗܶܣܝܳܐ, ܦܰܐܪܗܶܣܝܳܐ and ܦܰܐܪܗܶܣܝܳܐ *confidence;* see ܦܰܪܗܶܣܝܳܐ.

ܦܰܐܪܗܶܣܝܳܐܺܝܬ adv. *freely.*

ܦܰܐܫܪܺܝܣܛܘܢ a climbing plant, *bryony.*

ܦܰܐܬܳܐ and ܦܰܐܬܳܐ pl. ܦܰܐܬܘ̈ܳܬܳܐ f. *a) an edge, side, corner;* ܦܰܐܬ ܕܶܩܢܳܐ *the corner of the beard, hair on the lower lip, a mustache. b) the face* esp. *the forehead, the cheek.*

ܦܐܬܐ = ܦܐܬܐ.

ܦܰܓܳܐ and ܦܰܓܳܐ pl. ̈ܶܐ *a) an unripe fig, a sycamore fruit. b) cross-roads.*

ܦܓܐ Pael ܦܰܓܺܝ *to cajole, disturb, deceive.* Ethpa. ܐܶܬܦܰܓܺܝ *to take pleasure, enjoy oneself.* Derivative, ܦܘܓܝܐ.

ܦܓܐܬ; see ܦܰܓܬܳܐ.

ܦܓܕ *to harness, bridle.* Pa. ܦܰܓܶܕ *to make ready* a chariot, *to harness, bridle;* metaph. *to curb, restrain;* ܠܶܫܳܢܶܗ ܒܰܫܬܺܝܩܘܬܳܐ ܦܰܓܶܕ *he curbed his tongue with silence;* ܠܳܐ ܡܦܰܓܕܳܐ *unbridled.* Ethpa. ܐܶܬܦܰܓܰܕ *to be curbed, checked.* Derivatives, ܦܓܘܕܐ, ܦܓܕܐ, ܡܦܓܕܐ.

ܦܓܘܕܳܐ, ܦܓܘܕܬܳܐ pl. ̈ܶܐ f. *a bridle.*

ܦܓܘܡܳܐ rt. ܦܓܡ. *toothless.*

ܦܓܘܡܝܳܐ rt. ܦܓܡ. m. *waning* of the moon.

ܦܓܘܥܳܐ pl. ̈ܶܐ rt. ܦܓܥ. m. *a chance reader, one who meets with a book.*

ܦܓܘܪܳܐ *stale, mouldy, musty* as bread or other food.

ܦܓܘܪܘܬܳܐ f. *staleness, mouldiness.*

ܦܓܚ Ethpaal ܐܶܬܦܰܓܰܚ *to be hindered.* Derivatives, ܦܓܚܐ, ܦܘܓܚܐ, ܡܦܓܚܢܐ, ܡܦܓܚܢܘܬܐ.

ܦܓܚܳܐ rt. ܦܓܚ. m. *a hindrance.*

ܦܓܠܳܐ oftener ܦܘܓܠܳܐ. *radish.*

ܦܓܡ act. part. ܦܳܓܶܡ, ܦܳܓܡܳܐ. *to diminish, decay.* Derivatives, ܦܓܘܡܐ, ܦܓܘܡܝܐ, ܦܓܡܐ, ܦܘܓܡܐ.

ܦܓܳܡܳܐ rt. ܦܓܡ. m. *fracture* of a bone.

ܦܓܢܐ and ܦܓܢܐ pl. ܐ̈, Lat. paganus, *a villager, countryman, civilian.*

ܦܓܢܐ *rue;* see ܦܝܓܢܐ.

ܦܓܢܝܕܝܢ παιγνίδιον -α, *a game, sport.*

ܦܓܥ fut. ܢܦܓܥ, act. part. ܦܓܥ, ܦܓܥܐ, pass. part. ܦܓܝܥ, ܦܓܝܥܐ with ܒ in all its senses, *to meet with* a person, *arrive at* a place; *to fall in with, light upon, find, happen upon;* ܦܓܥܘ ܒܢܗܪܐ ܚܕ *they chanced on a river;* ܡܢ ܡܘܬܐ ܚܝܐ ܦܓܥܘ ܒܟ *out of death life has come to thee;* ܠܐ ܦܓܥ ܗܘܐ ܒܚܟܡܬܐ *he had not found wisdom.* Esp. used *a)* of disease or difficulty, ܐܘܠܨܢܐ ܕܦܓܥܘ ܒܗܘܢ *the afflictions which befel them;* ܦܓܥ ܒܟܘܪܗܢܐ *he fell sick.* *b) to meet with* a book, *chance to read; come across* a codex. *c) to meet = attack, oppose;* ܡܠܟ ܐܢܘܢ ܕܠܐ ܢܦܓܥܘܢ *he advised them not to attack;* ܦܓܥܘ ܗܘܘ ܚܕ ܒܚܕ *they fought, disputed.* Aph. ܐܦܓܥ *to cause to attack* or *fall upon; to lay upon* with ܒ; ܐܦܓܥ ܒܗ ܡܪܝܐ ܠܚܛܗܝܢ ܕܟܠܢ the Lord *hath laid upon him the iniquity of us all.* Derivatives, ܦܓܥܐ, ܦܘܓܥܐ.

ܦܓܥ, ܦܓܥܐ pl. ܐ̈ rt. ܦܓܥ. *a) a meeting, falling in with; a concourse; an interview, friendly meeting;* ܦܓܥܗ ܕܡܪܢ = Greek ὑπαπούτη, *the Meeting* of Christ by Simeon in the Temple, a W-Syr. Feast = the Purification of the B.V.M. in the Western Church. *b) presence, appearance.* *c) a hostile encounter, attack.* *d) occurrence, chance, accident;* ܒܝܫ ܦܓܥܐ *mischance, misfortune;* ܡܢ ܦܓܥܐ *by chance, accidentally.*

ܦܓܪ denom. verb Paal conj. from ܦܓܪܐ. pass. part. ܦܓܝܪ *embodied, incarnate.* Ethpa. ܐܬܦܓܪ *to become incarnate.*

ܦܓܪ, ܦܓܪܐ m. *the body, the flesh; a carcase;* ܟܕ ܐܝܬܝ ܒܦܓܪܐ *whilst I am in the flesh;* ܦܓܪܐ ܡܪܝܢܝܐ *the Lord's Body* = Eucharistic bread. Derivatives, ܦܘܓܪܐ, ܦܘܓܪܢܘܬܐ, verb ܦܓܪ, ܦܓܪܢܐ, ܦܓܪܢܐܝܬ, ܦܓܪܢܘܬܐ, ܦܓܪܢܝܐ.

ܦܓܪܢ, ܦܓܪܢܐ, ܦܓܪܢܝܬܐ from ܦܓܪܐ. *bodily, fleshly, carnal* opp. ܪܘܚܢܐ and ܪܘܚܢܝܐ *spiritual,* and ܢܦܫܢܐ *of the soul, natural.*

ܦܓܪܢܐܝܬ from ܦܓܪܐ. adv. *bodily, in the flesh; according to the flesh, carnally.*

ܦܓܪܢܘܬܐ from ܦܓܪܐ. f. *being in the flesh, bodily nature; the Incarnation, the human nature* of our Lord.

ܦܓܪܢܝܐ, ܦܓܪܢܝܬܐ from ܦܓܪܐ. *bodily, corporeal, carnal; according to the flesh; relating to the Incarnation;* ܚܬܐ ܦܓܪܢܝܬܐ *a sister-german.*

ܦܓܪܦ ἀπογράφειν, *to write down, transcribe.* Ethpalpal ܐܬܦܓܪܦ *to be copied, transcribed.* Derivative, ܦܘܓܪܦܐ.

ܦܕ, ܦܕ and ܦܕܐ cognate roots with the same meaning; fut. ܢܦܕ, act. parts. ܦܐܕ, ܦܕܐ also ܦܐܕܐ and ܦܝܕܐ, pass. part. ܦܕܝܕ, ܐ. *to stray; to miss, fall short of, fail, slip, shrink, swerve;* ܡܢ ܢܝܫܐ *from the aim;* ܡܢ ܣܒܪܗ *of his hope;* ܡܢ ܨܝܕܐ *of the prey;* ܡܢ ܫܪܪܐ *from the truth;* ܡܐ ܕܦܐܕܐ ܢܩܝܐ *when a sheep strays;* ܩܫܬܐ ܦܕܬ ܢܦܠܬ ܡܢ ܐܝܕܝܗܘܢ *the bow swerved and fell from their hands;* ܠܐ ܦܕ ܗܘܝ ܐܝܕܝܟܘܢ *your hands did not fail, were not unable.* ܦܕܝܕ ܐܢܐ ܡܢܗ *I am baulked, baffled, by him.* Ethpe. ܐܬܦܕܕ also ܐܬܦܕܕ and ܐܬܦܕܕ *to write incorrectly.* Palpel ܦܕܦܕ *to cause to err.* Ethpalpal ܐܬܦܕܦܕ *to be made to err.* Aph. ܐܦܕ *to cause to swerve* or *start aside, to lead astray, to deprive of* with ܡܢ; ܐܦܕܗ ܠܐܝܕܗ ܕܚܛܘܦܐ *he turned aside the hand of the grasper.* Derivatives, ܦܐܕܝܐ, ܦܕܘܕܐ, ܦܕܐ, ܦܕܝܕܘܬܐ, ܡܦܕܝܕܘܬܐ, ܦܕܕܐ, ܦܕܘܕܐܝܬ, ܦܕܝܕܐ, ܦܕܝܕܘܬܐ.

ܦܕܓܘܓܘܣ, ܦܕܓܘܓܐ, ܦܐܕܓܘܓܐ pl. ܐ̈ m. παιδαγωγός, *a pedagogue, tutor, schoolmaster.*

ܦܐܕܓܘܓܘܬܐ and ܦܕܓܘܓܘܬܐ f. παιδαγωγία, *education.*

ܦܕܓܪܐ m. ποδάγρα, *gout;* cf. ܦܘܕܓܪܐ.

ܦܕܓܪܐܝܐ *gouty.*

ܦܕܝܕܘܬܐ rt. ܦܕ. f. *error, deviation.*

ܦܕܘܣ a disease of the eye.

ܦܕܘܥܐ pl. ܐ̈ rt. ܦܕܥ. m. *an iron bar, club, mace, axe.*

ܦܕܘܪܬܐ f. *a lute, flute.*

ܦܕܝܐ rt. ܦܕ. m. *swerving, going astray, error.*

ܦܕܝܕܘܬܐ rt. ܦܕ. f. *distraction, frantic state.*

ܦܕܝܬܐ rt. ܦܕ. f. *error, aberration.*

ܦܕܝܢܬܐ pl. ܦܕܝܢܬܐ f. *a long sleeve.*

ܦܕܢ, ܦܕܢܐ pl. ܝܢ, ܐ̈ f. *a yoke, a plough;* ܦܕܢܐ ܕܬܘܪܐ *a yoke of oxen;* with ܕܒܪ *to yoke, to plough.*

ܦܕܚ fut. ܢܦܕܚ. *to break* the head, *to smash.* DERIVATIVES, ܦܕܚܐ, ܦܘܕܚܐ, ܦܕܚܐ.

ܦܕܚܐ rt. ܦܕܚ. m. *a broken skull, contusion.*

ܦܕܡܐ and ܦܕܡܐ m. *fastening a bit* or *bridle, tying up, pulling up an animal's head by the reins; hanging up.*

ܦܕܪ *to drive away* sleep. DERIVATIVE, ܦܕܪܐ.

ܦܕܪܐ m. Ital. padre, *father.*

ܦܕܪܐ pl. ܐ̈ m. *a cake.*

ܦܕܪܐ rt. ܦܕܪ. m. *dispersion.*

ܦܕܬܐ pl. ܦܕ̈ܬܐ. f. *an ephod.*

ܦܗܐ fut. ܢܦܗܐ, act. part. ܦܗܐ, ܦܗܝܐ, ܦܗ̈ܝܬܐ. *a) to roam, rove, wander about* esp. of the eyes and mind; act. part. *roving, vagabond, inconstant, unstable, distracted;* ܒܡܕܒܪ̈ܐ ܘܒܚܘܪ̈ܒܐ ܦܗܝܢ *wandering in wildernesses and deserts;* ܡܢ ܪ̈ܘܚܐ ܦܗܝܢ *driven about by the winds;* ܠܐ ܬܦܗܐ ܒܪܥܝܢܟ ܒܡܠܟܐ *be not of inconstant mind. b) to be absorbed; to permeate, pervade* as drugs the body, as atoms the air. *c) to be distracted with admiration,* ܦܗܘ ܚܙ̈ܝܐ ܒܟ *the beholders were distraught at* thy beauty. APH. ܐܦܗܝ *to cause to wander, lead astray; to wander; to drive crazy, bewilder, dazzle;* ܚܠܡ̈ܐ ܡܦܗܝܢ ܠܗ̇ *dreams set* the soul *wandering;* ܐܦܗܝ ܡܕܝܢܬܐ *roam about the city;* ܡܦܗܐ ܠܗܘܢ ܡܢ ܡܕܥܗܘܢ *he drives them out of their wits;* ܠܒܣܝܡܘܬܐ ܐܦܗܝܗ worldly pleasure *dazzled him.* DERIVATIVES, ܦܗܝܐ, ܦܗܝܐ, ܦܗܝܐ, ܦܗܝܐܝܬ, ܦܗܝܘܬܐ.

ܦܗܘܢܝܐ = ܦܐܘܢܝܐ *paeonia, the peony.*

ܦܗܕܐ m. Ar. *a panther, ounce.*

ܦܗܪܓܘܡܘܢ; see ܦܪܓܘܡܘܢ.

ܦܗܝܐ, ܦܗ̈ܝܐ rt. ܦܗܐ. *roving, wandering;* ܥܡ̈ܡܐ ܦܗ̈ܝܐ ܕܡܕܒܪܐ *desert nomads;* ܡ̈ܠܐ ܦܗ̈ܝܬܐ *raving* or *delirious words.* ܟܘ̈ܟܒܐ ܦܗ̈ܝܐ *planets, meteors.*

ܦܗܝܐ rt. ܦܗܐ. m. *wandering, aberration, error,* esp. *wandering* of the mind, *distraction, dissipation.*

ܦܗܝܐ rt. ܦܗܐ. *a)* = ܦܗܝܐ. *b) a cloudy substance in the urine.*

ܦܗܝܐܝܬ rt. ܦܗܐ. adv. *vaguely, unsteadily.*

ܦܗܝܘܬܐ rt. ܦܗܐ. f. *going astray, aberration, error.*

ܦܗܠܘܢܝܢ φελόνη, *a thick cloak.*

ܦܘܢܛܐ πέντε, *five;* ܦܢܛܩܝܕܩܛܐ πεντεκαιδεκάτη, *fifteenth.*

ܦܢܛܩܘܣܛܝ or ܦܢܛ Pentecost.

ܦܘܦܪܝ and ܦܦܪܝ πέπερι, *pepper.*

ܦܘܪ PAEL ܦܘܪ *to yawn.* ETHPA. ܐܬܦܘܪ *to yawn.* DERIVATIVE, ܦܘܪܐ.

ܦܘܫ abbrev. for ܦܘܫܩܐ *commentary.*

ܦܘ φοῦ, the plant *valerian.*

ܦܘܐܝܛܐ, ܦܘܐܛܐ, ܦܘܝܛܐ and ܦܘܐܝܛܐ, also ܦܘܐܛܝܣ and ܦܘܝܛܐ, pl. ܐ̈ and ܦܘܝ̈ܛܐ m. ποιητής, *a poet.*

ܦܘܐܝܛܐܝܬ and ܦܘܐܛ adv. *poetically.*

ܦܘܐܝܛܘܬܐ, ܦܘܐܛ and ܦܘܐܛ f. *poetry.*

ܦܘܐܝܛܝܩܝ f. *poetry, the art of poetry.*

ܦܓܝ, ܦܓܝ fut. ܢܦܓܐ, act. part. ܦܓܐ, ܦܓܝܐ. *a) to cool, grow cold, abate* as love, anger; *to be quenched* as thirst, fire; ܕ ܢܦܓܐ ܝܘܡܐ *until the day be cool;* ܥܕ ܠܐ ܦܓܝܐ ܛܠܝܘܬܟ *ere thy youth hath cooled down. b) to lose flavour, grow insipid; to grow slack, feeble;* ܡܘܪܐ ܕܠܐ ܦܓܐ *myrrh which does not lose its pungency;* ܦܓܝ ܢܡܘܣܐ ܕܪ̈ܘܫܡܐ *the law of foreshadowings waxed powerless.* ETHPE. ܐܬܦܓܝ *to be quenched.* PA. ܦܓܝ *to cool, refresh; to mitigate, assuage* cold, heat, anger, grief, torment; *to quench* thirst; med. *to check inflammation.* ETHPA. ܐܬܦܓܝ imper. W-Syr. ܐܬܦܓܝ *to be cooled, refreshed, quenched, mitigated; to be soothed, calm.* APH. ܐܦܓܝ *to quench* thirst, *to put away* or *shake off* drunkenness. DERIVATIVES, ܦܓܝܐ, ܦܓܝܐ, ܦܓܝܘܬܐ, ܡܦܓܝܢܐ, ܡܦܓܝܢܘܬܐ.

ܦܘܓܕܐ pl. ܐ̈ rt. ܦܓܕ. m. *a bridle, curb;* metaph. *curbing, restraining.* Gram. the vowel ܴ.

ܦܘܓܥܐ rt. ܦܓܥ. m. *an obstacle, hindrance.*

ܦܘܓܠܐ rt. ܦܓܠ. m. *enjoyment.*

ܦܘܓܠܐ pl. ܐ̈ Ar. m. *wild radish, horse-radish.*

ܦܘܓܡܐ pl. ܐ̈ rt. ܦܓܡ. m. *a sore.*

ܦܘܓܪܣܐ from ܦܓܪܣ. m. *a writing, description.*

ܦܘܕ, ܦܘ; see ܦܕ.

ܦܘܕܐ pl. ܐ̈ rt. ܦܕ. m. *a slip* of the pen, *fault, error.*

ܦܘܕܪܓܐ *a bird's crop.*

ܦܘܕܪܓܐ *a)* pl. ܐ̈ *a small leaden box. b)* = ܦܕܪܓܐ.

ܦܘܕܪܐ; see ܦܘܕܪܐ.

ܦܘܕܝܢܐ pl. ܐ̈ m. *the bandage folded round the chin of a corpse.*

ܦܘܕܓܪܐ also ܦܘܕܓܪܐ, ܦܘܕܓܪܐ and ܦܘܕܓܪܐ often with ܕ ܪ̈ܓܠܐ m. ποδάγρα, *gout in the feet.*

ܦܘܕܓܪܝܐ pl. ̈ܐ *gouty.*

ܦܘܕܐ probably a mistake for ܦܘܕܝܐ. m. *a bedstead, couch.* Cf. ܦܘܕܝܐ.

ܦܘܕܪܢܐ dialect m. *the loam* or *clay stopping of a wine-jar.*

ܦܘܕܪܝܩܘܢ, ܦܘܕܝܩܘܢܐ cf. ܐܦܘܕ and ܗܘܦܘ. m. *a subdeacon.*

ܦܘܕܪܢܐ, ܦܘܕܪܢܘܣ, ܦܘܕܪܢܐ; see ܦܘܕܪܐ.

ܦܘܕܝܬܐ pl. ܦܘܕܝܢ, ܦܘܕܝܬܐ and ܦܘܕܝܣ f. πούς, measure of length *a foot;* measure of time *two minutes;* member of the body *a foot* (rare in this sense).

ܦܘܕܐܝܬ rt. ܦܕ. adv. *erroneously.*

ܦܘܕܪܐ pl. ̈ܐ m. *a*) *a vulture.* *b*) *a lizard.* *c*) *a balcony.*

ܦܘܕܪܐ also ܦܘܕܪܐ and ܦܘܕܪܐ pl. ̈ܐ m. ποδήρης, *a priestly vestment reaching to the feet.*

ܦܘܗܐ or ܦܘܗܐ pl. ̈ܐ m. *an eruption in the mouth* of the nature of erysipelas.

ܦܘܗܝܐ *suffering from* ܦܘܗܐ; see the preceding.

ܦܘܗܪܐ rt. ܦܗܪ. m. *yawning.*

ܦܘܚܐ rt. ܦܘܚ. m. *an odour, waft of odour.*

ܦܘܩܐ rt. ܦܘܩ. m. *a hiccough, yawn, gasp.*

ܦܘܙܪܐ *a small wooden box.* Cf. ܦܘܙܪܐ.

ܦܘܚ, ܦܘܚܝ imper. of verb ܢܦܚ *to blow.*

ܦܚ, ܦܚ fut. ܢܦܘܚ, act. part. ܦܐܚ, ܦܝܚܐ. *a*) *to breathe, blow* usually with ܒ *upon* or *into,* rarely with ܥܠ; ܢܦܘܚ ܒܗܘܢ ܘܢܬܝܒܫܘܢ *he will blow upon them and they shall wither.* *b*) *to blow away, scatter* intrans. ܦܚܘ ܐܝܟ ܕܥܘܪܐ *they scattered like chaff.* *c*) *to exhale, give out odour;* ܦܩܚܐ ܕܦܐܚ ܪܝܚܗ *the blossom which sends forth its fragrance.* PA. ܦܝܚ *to breathe forth, exhale.* ETHPA. ܐܬܦܝܚ *to be exhaled.* APH. ܐܦܝܚ *to cause to exhale, shed abroad; to cause to pant, hasten after; to puff up;* ܡܦܝܚ ܢܦܫܗ *he puffs himself up.* DERIVATIVES, ܦܘܚܐ, ܦܚܐ, ܦܝܚܐ, ܦܘܚܐ, ܦܝܚ, ܡܦܘܚܐ, ܡܦܚܢܘܬܐ, ܡܦܝܚܢܘܬܐ.

ܦܘܚܐ rt. ܦܘܚ. m. *a breath of air, the air; inspiration, influence.*

ܦܘܚܐ m. *a*) rt. ܦܘܚ. *coolness, cold.* *b*) =ܦܘܚܐ, ܦܘܚܐ ܚܘܪܐ *a white pustule, sore in the mouth.*

ܦܘܚܙܐ pl. ̈ܐ m. *the jugular veins; the thighs, sinews of the thighs.*

ܦܘܚܡ, ܦܘܚܡܐ pl. ̈ܐ rt. ܦܚܡ. m. *comparison; collation; a similitude;* with ܠܘܬ *respect, ratio;* ܕܠܐ ܦܘܚܡ *incomparably.* Gram. *relation* of words to each other and of points; adverbs *of comparison; distinction;* ܢܘܩܙܐ ܕܦܘܚܡܐ *diacritic points,* hence *punctuation, vowel-points.*

ܦܘܚܡܝܐ rt. ܦܚܡ. gram. *diacritical.*

ܦܘܚܪܐ rt. ܦܚܪ. m. *breaking, smashing.*

ܦܘܚܪܐ pl. ̈ܐ rt. ܦܚܪ. m. *a banquet; a mess, company.*

ܦܘܚܪܝܐ rt. ܦܚܪ. *convivial.*

ܦܘܚܬܐ f. *a young gazelle.*

ܦܘܛ, ܦܛ only in the Lexx. *to scorn, deride.* ETHPE. ܐܬܦܛܛ *to be scorned.* PA. ܦܛܛ *to utterly scorn.* ETHPA. ܐܬܦܛܛ *to be utterly scorned.* APH. ܐܦܝܛ *to say pooh, to pooh-pooh, to treat lightly* with ܥܠ or ܒ; ܐܦܝܛܬ *I said pooh;* ܐܦܝܛܘ ܥܠ ܥܘܬܪܐ ܕܥܠܡܐ *they held* worldly *riches in light esteem.* DERIVATIVES, ܦܛܐ, ܦܛܝܐ, ܡܦܛܢܘܬܐ, ܡܦܛܝܛܘܬܐ.

ܦܘܛܐ *contemptible;* ܠܐ ܦܘܛܐ *not the very least.*

ܦܘܛܝܬܐ; see ܦܘܐܛܝܩܐ *poetry.*

ܦܘܛܠܐ *pitch.*

ܦܘܛܝܩܐ and ܦܛܝܩܐ pl. ̈ܐ m. *a jar.*

ܦܘܛܡܐ rt. ܦܛܡ. m. *fattening, increase.*

ܦܘܛܩܐ for ܦܘܬܩܐ *an inn.*

ܦܘܝ or ܦܘܝ interj. of contempt, *pooh, fie,* used with ܥܡ or ܥܠ; ܦܘܝ ܥܡ ܡܚܝܠܘܬܝ *out on my weakness.*

ܦܘܝܓܐ pl. ̈ܐ rt. ܦܝܓ. m. *cooling, ablution, alleviation, refreshment;* pl. *refreshing breezes.*

ܦܘܝܛܐ; see ܦܘܐܛܝܐ *a poet.*

ܦܘܟܟܐ rt. ܦܟܟ. m. with ܦܘܡܐ *washing out the mouth.*

ܦܘܟܪܐ rt. ܦܟܪ. m. *yawning.*

ܦܘܚܐ rt. ܦܘܚ. m. *anger, heat.*

ܦܘܚܚܐ rt. ܦܚ. m. *smashing, battering.*

ܦܘܚܢܐ m. *mixing, a confused heap.*

ܦܘܚܪܢܐ rt. ܦܚܪ. m. *a chafing-dish, receptacle for hot embers.*

ܦܠܠ, ܦܠ fut. ܢܦܘܠ, pass. part. ܦܠܝܠ, ܦܠܝܠܐ. *a) to sprinkle, strew, cover, bespatter, mingle* ܒܕܡܐ *with blood;* ܒܕܡܥܐ *with tears;* ܒܩܛܡܐ *with ashes;* ܒܛܢܦܘܬܟ ܦܠܠܬ ܐܢܘܢ *thou hast bespattered them with thy filth;* ܓܪܝܨܐ ܕܦܠܝܠܢ ܒܡܫܚܐ *cakes mingled with oil. b) to clean* the head from lice. ETHPE. ܐܬܦܠܠ *to be mingled; to sprinkle* the head with ashes. DERIVATIVE, ܦܠܐ.

ܦܘܠ imperative of verbs ܦܠܠ and ܦܠ.

ܦܘܠܐ; see ܦܘܠܘܣ.

ܦܘܠܩܛܝܪܝܘܢ pl. ܦܘܠܩܛܝܪܝܐ φυλακτήριον, *an amulet; a phylactery.*

ܦܘܠܩܐ pl. ܦܘܠܩܐ φυλακή, *a prison.*

ܦܘܠܓܐ, ܦܘܠܓܐ pl. ܐ̈ rt. ܦܠܓ. m. *dividing, division, distribution; distinction; hesitation, doubt, ambiguity; a segment, section, portion; a faction;* ܦܘܠܓ ܠܫܢܐ *the division of languages;* ܦܘܠܓ ܦܣܐ *distribution by lot, inheritance;* ܦܘܠܓܐ ܘܦܘܠܓܐ ܕܦܘܠܓܐ *divisions and subdivisions;* ܕܠܐ ܦܘܠܓܐ *without hesitation; undoubtedly, undeniably.*

ܦܘܠܕ, ܦܘܠܕܐ m. Pers. *steel;* cf. ܦܠܕܐ.

ܦܘܠܚܘܪܐ rt. ܦܠܚܪ. m. *dispersion, dissipation.*

ܦܘܠܐ pl. of ܦܘܠܘܣ.

ܦܘܠܝܛܝܐ, ܦܘܠܝܛܝܐ pl. ܦܘܠܝܛܝܘܬܐ πολιτεία, *the state, government, administration;* ܒܢܝ ܦ *citizens.* Metaph. *polity, conduct.*

ܦܘܠܛܝܢ, ܦܘܠܛܝܢ; see ܦܠܛܝܢ *a palace, the court;* ܒܢܝ ܦܘܠܛܝܢ *courtiers.*

ܦܘܠܘܣ and ܦܘܠܘܣ pl. ܦܘܠܐ m. πόλος, *the pole;* ܦ ܓܪܒܝܝܐ *the north pole;* ܦ ܬܝܡܢܝܐ *the south pole.*

ܦܘܠܘܣ, ܦܘܠܐ, ܦܘܠܘܣ and ܦܘܠܐ, ܦܘܠܐ pr. n. m. *Paul.*

ܦܘܠܘܣܝܐ, ܝܬܐ from ܦܘܠܘܣ. *of Paul, Pauline.*

ܦܘܠܚܢ, ܦܘܠܚܢܐ pl. ܐ̈ rt. ܦܠܚ. m. *a) service, labour, work, occupation;* with ܥܒܕܘܬܐ *servitude;* ܟܐܦܐ *stone-cutting;* ܗܘ ܦܘܠܚܢܐ *take pains;* ܐܢܫ ܦܘܠܚܢܐ *diligent. b)* ܦܘܠܚܢ ܐܪܥܐ or ellipt. *tillage, husbandry, cultivation;* ܬܘܪܐ ܕܦܘܠܚܢܐ *an ox fit for the plough. c)* religious *service, worship;* ܕܡܫܟܢ ܙܒܢܐ *service of the Tabernacle;* ܕܐܪ̈ܙܐ *administration of the sacraments;* ܕܦܬܟܪ̈ܐ *idolatry. d) exercise, practice* ܕܡܝܬܪܘܬܐ *of virtue;* ܕܫܠܝܐ *of the contemplative life.*

ܦܘܠܛ, ܦܘܠܛܐ rt. ܦܠܛ. m. *escape;* ܦܘܠܛ ܗܕܡ̈ܐ *paralysis* or *slipping out of the joints.*

ܦܘܠܝܛܝܐ; see ܦܠܛܝܢ.

ܦܘܠܠܘܢ and ܦܘܠܘܢ φύλλον, *malobathrum,* the aromatic leaf of an Indian plant, perhaps the *betel* or *areca.* Cf. ܦܠܐ.

ܦܘܠܠܘܣ; see ܦܘܠܘܣ and ܦܘܠܘܣ.

ܦܘܠܡܘܣ and ܦܘܠܡܘܣ; see ܦܠܘܡܘܣ *mullein.*

ܦܘܠܣܐ pl. ܐ̈ m. from ὀβολός through Arabic; *a small coin.*

ܦܘܠܦܠܐ rt. ܦܠ. m. *filth, pollution.*

ܦܘܠܩܐ; see ܦܘܠܩܐ.

ܦܘܠܩܛܪ̈ܝܐ *phylacteries;* see ܦܘܠܩܛܝܪܝܘܢ.

ܦܘܠܩܣ = ܦܠܩܣ.

ܦܘܠܫܐ m. *refuse from the wine-press, grape-skins* &c.

ܦܘܠܫܐ rt. ܦܠܫ. m. *the digging through* of a wall.

ܦܘܠܫܬܐ pl. ܦܘܠܫܢ, ܦܘܠܫ̈ܬܐ rt. ܦܠܫ. f. *breaking through* the wall of a house, *a breach, hole* in the wall, *aperture.*

ܦܘܡ, ܦܘܡܐ pl. ܝ̈ܢ, ܐ̈ m. *the mouth; a mouthful; mouth, orifice, hole, opening* of a well, cave, garment; *entering in, entrance* of a path, valley, desert; *edge* of a sword; ܕܐܪܥܐ *surface of the ground;* ܕܟܪܣܐ *the vent. A saying, command, mode of speech;* ܡܢ ܦܘܡܐ ܠܦܘܡܐ *oral tradition;* ܐܝܟ ܡܠܬ ܦܘܡ *according to the word, the command;* ܡܢ ܚܕ ܦܘܡ *with one accord;* ܦܘܡ ܠܘܬ ܦܘܡ *mouth to mouth, openly.* DERIVATIVES, the two following words:—

ܦܘܡ ETHPA. ܐܬܦܘܡ denom. verb from ܦܘܡܐ. *to be spoken in a full* or *round voice.* PALEL ܦܘܡܡ *to mouth, speak with a full or round voice.*

ܦܘܡܐܠܦܘܡ from ܦܘܡܐ. adv. *face to face, by word of mouth.*

ܦܘܢܐܣ and ܦܘܢܣ pl. f. φωνάς, *an outcry, shout, acclamation.*

ܦܘܢܝ, ܦܘܢܝܐ rt. ܦܢܐ. m. *return, restitution; conversion;* ܦܘܢܝ ܛܒܬܐ *recompense;* ܦܘܢܝ ܦܬܓܡܐ or ܦܬܓܡܐ or ellipt. *answer, reply;* ܕܦܘܢܝܐ *revocation of a command; the latter half of a verse of a psalm* in alternate recitation.

ܦܘܢܝܘܣ φόνιος, *murderous.*

ܦܘܢܝܩܣ, ܦܘܢܝܩܐ or ܦܘܢܝܩܘܣ φοίνιξ. *a*) *the phoenix.* *b*) *a palm-tree.* *c*) a kind of grass.

ܦܘܢܝܩܐ, ܦܘܢܝܩܝ and ܦܘܢܝܩܝܐ *Phoenicia.*

ܦܘܢܝܩܝ φοῖνιξ, *blister ointment.*

ܦܘܢܝܩܝܐ, ـــܝܬܐ *Phoenician.*

ܦܘܢܝܛܐ or ܦܘܢܛܐ m. *the lower* or *foundation threads* of a web.

ܦܘܢܣ; see ܦܘܢܐܣ.

ܦܘܢܛܐ; see ܦܢܛܐ *a torch.*

ܦܘܢܩܐ pl. ـــܐ, ـــܐ rt. ܦܢܩ. m. *delicacy, daintiness, pleasure.*

ܦܘܢܛܐ; see ܦܘܢܝܛܐ.

ܦܘܣܝܘܠܘܓܝܐ = Syr. ܡܠܬܐ ܟܝܢܝܬܐ *physiology, natural science.*

ܦܘܣܝܘܓܢܘܡܘܢܝܩܝܐ and ܦܘܣܝܘܓ̈, ـــܝܬܐ *physiognomical.*

ܦܘܣܝܘܓܢܘܡܘܢܝܩܘ pl. m. *physiognomists.*

ܦܘܣܝܘܠܘܓܘ̈ܣܐ *physiologists.*

ܦܘܣܝܣ and ܦܘܣܝܘܣ. f. φύσις, *nature.*

ܦܘܣܝܩܘܣ φυσικός, *a physicist, student of natural science.*

ܦܘܣܘܣ πόσος, *how much?*

ܦܘܣܟܐ rt. ܦܣܟ. m. *a coal-pan, censer.*

ܦܘܣܣܐ m. *biting, a bite.*

ܦܘܣܩܐ pl. ـــܐ rt. ܦܣܩ. m. *a*) *cutting down, slaughter; cutting off* a limb, *amputation.* *b*) *a division, section; intersection.* *c*) *oxymel, a drink made with vinegar.* *d*) *an eggshell.*

ܦܘܣܩܢܐ; see ܦܣܩܢ *a ditch, channel.*

ܦܘܣܩܢܐ rt. ܦܣܩ. m. *a portion; a decision, decree, ordinance, fate;* ܕܦܘܣܩܢܐ *precise.*

ܦܘܣܬܩܐ = ܦܣܬܩܐ.

ܦܘܣܬܩܝܐ, ـــܝܬܐ from ܦܣܬܩܐ. adj. *pistachio green.*

ܦܘܥ Pael ܦܘܥ *to wash out* the mouth. Derivatives, ܦܘܥܝܐ, ܦܘܥܐ.

ܦܘܥܝܐ rt. ܦܘܥ. m. *dropsical.*

ܦܘܥܪܐ rt. ܦܥܪ. m. *a*) *gaping.* *b*) *a cleft, chasm.*

ܦܘܩܝܐ m. *an eclipse.*

ܦܘܦܘܪܘܢ *papyrus;* see ܦܦܝܪܘܣ.

ܦܘܦܪܐ some aquatic creature.

ܦܘܨܝ, ܦܘܨܝܐ rt. ܦܨܐ. m. *deliverance.*

ܦܘܩ imper. of verb ܢܦܩ *to go out.*

ܦܘܩ *the owl.*

ܦܘܩ Ethpa. ܐܬܦܘܩ *to yawn, to hiccough.* Derivatives, ܦܘܩܐ, ܦܘܩܝܐ, ܦܘܩܬܐ.

ܦܘܩܐ f. φώκη, *a seal.*

ܦܘܩܐ m. *the partition between the nostrils, cartilage of the nose.*

ܦܘܩܕܢܐ pl. ـܐ rt. ܦܩܕ. m. *a*) *a command, commandment, precept, order, ordinance.* *b*) *a will, testament; a legacy.*

ܦܘܩܕܢܐ pl. ـܐ rt. ܦܩܕ. m. *a*) *visitation.* *b*) *command, commandment, decree;* ܕܡܘܬܐ *sentence of death.* *c*) *authority, rule, dominion, domination.*

ܦܘܩܘܣ *a*) = ܛܠܘܦܚܐ *lentil, duckweed.* *b*) φῦκος, *red seaweed.* *c*) with pl. points πεῦκαι, *fir-trees;* cf. ܦܩܘܬܐ.

ܦܘܩܚܐ pl. ـــܐ rt. ܦܩܚ. *counsel.*

ܦܘܩܛܝܩܝ πυκτική, *boxing.*

ܦܘܩܝܠܐ = ܦܩܝܠܐ. m. *a cap, wrap, kerchief* worn on the head, *kefiyeh.*

ܦܘܩܝܢܐ πεύκινος, *of fir-wood.*

ܦܘܩܪܐ pl. ـܐ perh. corrupt for ܦܩܝܠܐ. *a cap, kerchief.*

ܦܘܩܥܐ rt. ܦܩܥ. m. *cracking, crackling;* ܦܘܩܥ ܨܒܥܬܐ *snapping the fingers.*

ܦܘܩܩܐ pl. ـــܐ rt. ܦܩ. m. *chattering, nonsense.*

ܦܘܩܪܢܐ = ܦܩܪܢܐ *a warming-pan.*

ܦܘܩܬܐ rt. ܦܘܩ. f. *hiccough, hiccoughing.*

ܦܘܪ root-meaning *to boil*. Ethpe. ܐܬܦܪܝ or ܐܬܦܪ *to wax hot* as anger, *to be angry, enraged* with ܒ of the pers. Derivatives, ܦܘܪܐ, ܦܘܪܬܐ, ܦܘܪܝܐ, ܦܘܪܢܐ, ܡܬܦܪܢܐ, ܡܬܦܪܢܘܬܐ.

ܦܘܪܓܐ, ܦܘܪܓܘܣ and ܦܘܪܓܣܐ = ܦܘܪܓܣܐ *a tower*.

ܦܘܪܓܝܐ rt. ܦܪܓ. m. *pleasure*.

ܦܘܪܓܠܐ and ܦܘܪܓܠܢܐ pl. ܐ̈ from ܦܪܓܠ. m. *a command, order, charge; a warning, prohibition*.

ܦܘܪܕܪܐ rt. ܦܪܕ. m. *separation, forming into grains* or *seeds*.

ܦܘܪܕܝܣܐ; see ܦܪܕܝܣܐ.

ܦܘܪܕܫܐ from ܦܪܕܫ. m. *demonstration*.

ܦܘܪܗܕܐ m. *a warning, caution*.

ܦܘܪܘܣ pl. ܦܘܪ̈ܘܣ and ܦܘܪܘ f. *a*) πόρος, *a pore*. *b*) πόρος, *a bridge, ferry, ford*. *c*) πυρός, *wheat*.

ܦܘܪܘܬܐ pl. ܬ̈ܐ rt. ܦܘܪ. f. *wrath, raging*.

ܦܘܪܛܐ pl. ܦܘܪ̈ܛܣ m. Lat. porta, *a gate*.

ܦܘܪܝܐ and ܦܘܪܝܘܢ. m. *a*) φορεῖον, *a couch, litter, sedan-chair*. *b*) *palm-pith*.

ܦܘܪܐ pl. Heb. *Purim, lots*.

ܦܘܪܟܟܐ rt. ܦܪܟ. m. *crumbling*.

ܦܘܪܟܠܐ pl. ܐ̈ from ܦܪܟܠ. m. *a bond, strap, shackle*.

ܦܘܪܣܣܐ pl. ܦܪܣ. m. *dispersion*.

ܦܘܪܣܩܐ and ܦܘܪܣܩܐ also ܦܘܪܓܘܣ, ܦܘܪܓܣܐ, ܦܘܪܓܐ pl. ܐ̈ m. πύργος, *a tower*.

ܦܘܪܢܐ, ܦܘܪܢܘܣ, ܦܘܪܢܘܢ, and ܦܘܪܢܝ m. Lat. furnus, *an oven*.

ܦܘܪܢܐ pl. ܦܘܪ̈ܢܣ, f. πόρνη, *a prostitute*.

ܦܘܪܢܘܒܘܣܩܘܣ m. πορνοβοσκός, *a brothel-keeper*.

ܦܘܪܢܝܬܐ pl. ܬ̈ܐ from ܦܘܪܢܐ. f. *bread baked in the oven, a loaf*.

ܦܘܪܢܣܐ, ܦܘܪܢܣܐ pl. ܐ̈ from ܦܪܢܣ. m. *a*) *sustenance, support, supply;* pl. *supplies, revenues*. *b*) *control, management, administration; safeguard; guardianship*. *c*) *affair, action*. *d*) Divine *dispensation, providence*. *e*) *a province, diocese*.

ܦܘܪܣܐ emph. state of ܦܪܘܣ.

ܦܘܪܣܛܩܣܬܐ for ܦܘܪܣܛܩܣܘܬܐ pl. of ܦܪܣܛܩܣ.

ܦܘܪܣܝܐ rt. ܦܪܣ. m. *nakedness, shame, the privy parts*.

ܦܘܪܣܝܐ = ܦܪܣܝܐ *Persian*.

ܦܘܪܣܡܐ = ܐܦܘܪܣܡܐ m. *balsam, balm*.

ܦܘܪܣܢܐܝܬ from ܦܪܣ. adv. *craftily, prudently*.

ܦܘܪܣܢܐ from ܦܪܢܣ. m. *one who provides*.

ܦܘܪܣܩܐ from ܦܪܣܩ. m. *attenuation, rarefaction; the thing rarefied*.

ܦܘܪܣܬܢ, ܦܘܪܣܬܢܐ from ܦܪܘܣ. m. *astute, crafty*.

ܦܘܪܥܢ, ܦܘܪܥܢܐ pl. ܢ̈ܐ, ܐ̈ rt. ܦܪܥ. *a*) *retribution, vengeance, punishment*. *b*) *payment of* a debt. *c*) *recompense, reward*. *d*) *germination*. *e*) gram. *apodosis*.

ܦܘܪܥܢܘܬܐ rt. ܦܪܥ. f. *requital, remuneration, retribution, vengeance;* with ܥܒܕ, ܐܬܦܪܥ or ܐܫܬܠܡ *to requite*. Gram. *apodosis*.

ܦܘܪܦܘܪܐ and ܦܘܪܦܘܪܘܣ, ܦܘܪܦܘܪܐ πορφύρα, *purple; the murex* from which the purple dye is obtained. Cf. ܦܪܦܘܪܐ.

ܦܘܪܦܟܐ pl. ܐ̈ from ܦܪܦܟ. m. *a*) *plashing* of water, *floundering* of a fish. *b*) *luxury, pleasure*.

ܦܘܪܦܪܐ *a*) from ܦܪܦܪ. m. *death-struggle, agony, convulsion*. *b*) rt. ܦܘܪ. *an outbreak, a burst of passion*.

ܦܘܪܩ, ܦܘܪܩܐ rt. ܦܪܩ. m. *a*) *looseness, sunderings* of the limbs; ܦܘܪܩ ܒܘܪܟܐ *knocking together of the knees*. *b*) *a division* of a MS.

ܦܘܪܩܢܐ pl. ܐ̈ rt. ܦܪܩ. m. *redemption, ransom, salvation*.

ܦܘܪܩܢܝܐ rt. ܦܪܩ. *relating to salvation*.

ܦܘܪܩܣܐ = ܦܘܪܣܩܐ.

ܦܘܪܫ, ܦܘܪܫܐ pl. ܐ̈ rt. ܦܪܫ. m. *a*) *distinction, difference;* ܦܘܪܫ ܡܐܟܘܠܬܐ *distinction between foods* allowed and forbidden by the Mosaic Law; ܕܠܐ ܦܘܪܫ *without distinction*. *b*) *separation, divorce*. *c*) *interpretation* of a dream, *setting forth, explanation*. *d*) ܦ̈ ܩܪܝܢܐ *selected lessons, a lectionary;* ܦ̈ ܡܠܐ *an index*.

ܦܘܪܫܠܐ m. *a goat's hoof*.

ܦܘܪܫܢܐ pl. ܢ̈ܐ, ܐ̈ rt. ܦܪܫ. m. *a*) *division*,

separation, sundering, absence, departure; ܦܘܪܫܢܗ̇ ܕܢܦܫܐ ܡܢ ܦܓܪܐ the sundering of the soul from the body. b) separation, divorce. c) O.T. setting apart as an offering to God; an oblation; ܠܚܡܐ ܕܦ̈ shewbread. Hence: d) an offering, a gift. e) bread for the Eucharist; also an ordinary loaf. f) a portion set apart, a sum agreed upon. g) decision, discrimination, difference; ܕܠܐ ܦ̈ with no difference, indiscriminately; ܒܦ̈ separately, apart. h) manner, way, form; ܕܦ̈ manifold, ܣܓܝܐܐ ܦܘܪܫܢܐ multiform, various. i) distinction, excellence; ܐܝܟ ܕܒܦܘܪܫܢܐ as a mark of distinction, of honour; ܡܠܐ ܦ̈ distinctive, characteristic, extraordinary.

ܦܘܪܫܢܝܐ rt. ܦܪܫ. select, arranged.

ܦܘܪܬܐ rt. ܦܘܪ. f. wrath, fury.

ܦܘܪܬܐ rt. ܦܪܬ. m. crumbling, sundering.

ܦܘܪܬܬܐ pl. ܐ̈ rt. ܦܪܬ. m. a) fragment, particle, scale. b) uncertainty, anxiety.

ܦܘܪܬܥܢܐ pl. ܐ̈ m. a) a flea. b) ܙܪܥܐ ܦ̈ fleabane, plantago psyllium.

ܦܫ, ܦܫܫ fut. ܢܦܘܫ, act. part. ܦܐܫ, ܦܝܫܐ, part. adj. ܦܫܝܫ, ܦܫܝܫܐ. a) to remain, wait, stay behind, stay, persist; ܦܫ ܫܒܥܐ ܝܘܡܝܢ he waited seven days; ܦܘܫ ܠܟܘܢ ܗܪܟܐ stay here; ܦܫܐ ܒܠܚܘܕܘܗܝ it remains alone; ܦܫ ܚܝܐ to remain alive; ܥܒܕܐ to remain a slave; ܐܡܪ ܦܘܫ ܦܘܫ he said, cease, let be; ܦܘܫ ܒܫܠܡܐ farewell. b) with ܒ of a place, ܥܡ or ܠܘܬ of a person to stay, remain. c) = to be in a state; ܦܫܘ ܒܐܘܠܨܢܐ they were in distress; ܡܬܡܗ ܢܦܫܗ ܦܫ he was stupefied; ܦܫܝܫ ܡܫܟܢܐ ܕܢܦܫܝ without Thee the tabernacle of my soul is desolate. d) to remain over, be left; ܐܢ ܦܫܝܢ ܬܪܬܝܢ—ܬܠܬ if two—three be over. e) astron. to recede. f) with ܡܢ, to cease, leave off, desist from, fall short of, abstain; ܦܫ ܠܐ ܦܫ ܡܢ ܩܪܒܐ he did not desist from war; ܦܫ ܡܢ ܠܡܐܙܠ he did not go; ܦܐܫ ܡܢ ܒܬܪܟ he ceases to follow thee, forsakes thee; ܥܘܬܪܐ ܦܐܫ ܡܢܢ riches forsake us. Aph. ܐܦܝܫ to miss, lose; to forbear to do often with ܐܦܘܫܝ. Derivatives, ܦܘܫܐ, ܦܫܐ.

ܦܘܫܐ rt. ܦܫ. m. lingering, postponement, intermission, pause, delay; astron. recession.

ܦܘܫܪܐ pl. ܐ̈ m. a) oats; the round Egyptian bean. b) a canal.

ܦܘܫܟܐ pl. ܐ̈ rt. ܦܫܟ. m. breaking or tearing down, dislocation, tumbling of waves.

ܦܘܫܩ, ܦܘܫܩܐ rt. ܦܫܩ. m. a) embarrassment; uncertainty; ܕܠܐ ܦܘܫܩܐ undoubtedly, indisputably. b) ܦܘܫܩ ܐܝܕܝܐ clapping the hands.

ܦܘܫܩܝܐ rt. ܦܫܩ. gram. expressing doubt, as the particles ܕܟܒܪ, ܡܟܐ, &c.

ܦܘܫܟܠܐ from ܦܫܟܠ. m. having the legs twisted inwards.

ܦܘܫܠܐ rt. ܦܫܠ. m. crookedness, limping.

ܦܘܫܦܫܐ m. pl. tick, small vermin infesting birds.

ܦܘܫܩܐ, ܦܘܫܩܐ rt. ܦܫܩ. m. interpretation, translation, explanation, commentary; ܕܚܠܡܐ ܦ̈ interpretation of dreams; ܦ̈ ܕܡܠܐ a dictionary; ܕܠܐ ܦܘܫܩܐ inexplicable, incomprehensible.

ܦܘܫܩܝܐ rt. ܦܫܩ. explanatory.

ܦܘܫܩܠܐ same as ܦܘܫܟܠܐ.

ܦܘܫܪܐ rt. ܦܫܪ. m. fusion, liquefaction.

ܦܘܫܫ Pauel conj. of ܦܫ.

ܦܘܫܫܐ pl. ܐ̈ rt. ܦܫ. m. evaporation; daily loss, wearing away of the body.

ܦܘܬ always with ܠ prefixed; see under ܠ.

ܦܘܬܐ f. the plant madder, rubia tinctorum.

ܦܘܬܓܘܪܘܣ and ܦܝܬܓܘܪܣ Pythagoras.

ܦܘܬܓܘܪܝܐ from the above. Pythagorean.

ܦܘܬܚ, ܦܘܬܚܐ rt. ܦܬܚ. m. opening, esp. of the eyes of the blind, enlightenment.

ܦܘܬܚܐ rt. ܦܬܚ. m. pl. two wooden supports from which the beam of a loom hangs.

ܦܘܬܝܐ rt. ܦܬܐ. m. extension.

ܦܘܬܟܐ rt. ܦܬܟ. m. diversity; changing colours, iridescence.

ܦܘܬܠܐ pl. ܐ̈ rt. ܦܬܠ. m. crookedness, perversity, anxiety.

ܦܘܬܟܬܐ rt. ܦܬܟ. f. calumny.

ܦܘܬܩܐ pl. ܐ̈ a) from πανδοκεῖον, m. an inn, a tavern, hostelry; ܦܘܬܩܐ ܕܡܫܚܐ an oil-store. b) = ܦܬܩܐ a label, notice.

ܦܘܬܩܝܐ m. from ܦܘܬܩܐ. an innkeeper, a landlord, hostler; ܦܘܬܩܝܬܐ f. pl. landladies.

ܦܙ fut. ܢܦܘܙ. to leap, frisk as lambs and kids. Part. adj. ܦܙܝܙܐ, ܦܙܝܙܬܐ agile, nimble.

ETHPE. ܐܶܬ݂ܦܙܰܙ to be agile, quick. PAEL ܦܰܙܶܙ part. ܡܦܰܙܙܳܐ = ܦܰܙܺܝܙܳܐ. DERIVATIVE, ܦܙܝܙܘܬܐ.

ܦܰܙܳܐ pl. ܦܰܙܶܐ m. *barley-water.*

ܦܰܙܕܳܐ = ܦܰܐܙܕܳܐ m. *an uneven number*, but in the Lexx. also *even.*

ܦܰܙܕܶܕ denom. verb from ܦܰܙܕܳܐ. *to make uneven.*

ܦܰܙܳܐ or ܦܰܙܳܝܳܐ pl. ܶܐ adj. *a*) *light. b*) in the Lexx. *greedy, gluttonous.*

ܦܰܙܳܝܽܘܬܳܐ or ܦܰܙܽܘܬܳܐ f. *greediness, gluttony.*

ܦܰܙܺܝܙܽܘܬܳܐ rt. ܦܙ. f. *agility, nimbleness, friskiness.*

ܦܚ ETHPA. ܐܶܬ݂ܦܰܚܰܚ *to be shattered, dried up* or *porous* as a burnt bone. DERIVATIVES, ܦܚܚܐ, ܦܚܝܚܐ, ܦܚܝܚܘܬܐ.

ܦܚܐ denom. verb from ܦܰܚܳܐ. ETHPA. ܐܶܬ݂ܦܰܚܺܝ *to be ensnared.*

ܦܰܚܳܐ pl. ܶܐ f. *a snare, gin.* DERIVATIVES, verbs ܦܚܐ and ܦܚܡ.

ܦܰܚܚܳܐ or ܦܰܚ rt. ܦܚ. *weak, soft.*

ܦܰܚܬܳܐ pl. ܳܬ݂ܳܐ rt. ܦܚܬ. f. *an earthquake which makes chasms.*

ܦܚܙ PAEL ܦܰܚܶܙ *to act lewdly.* ETHPA. ܐܶܬ݂ܦܰܚܰܙ *to be voluptuous, licentious.* APH. ܐܰܦܚܶܙ *to cause to wanton, make to be impudent;* part. fem. ܡܰܦܚܙܳܢܺܝܬܳܐ *a wanton.* DERIVATIVES, ܦܰܚܙܳܐ, ܦܚܙܐ, ܦܚܙܐܝܬ, ܦܚܙܘܬܐ.

ܦܰܚܙܳܐ, ܦܰܚܺܝܙܳܐ, ܦܰܚܺܝܙܬܳܐ rt. ܦܚܙ. *voluptuous, wanton, licentious.*

ܦܽܘܚܙܳܐ rt. ܦܚܙ. m. *wantonness, lasciviousness.*

ܦܰܚܺܝܙܳܐܺܝܬ݂ rt. ܦܚܙ. adv. *licentiously.*

ܦܰܚܺܝܙܽܘܬܳܐ pl. ܘܳܬ݂ܳܐ rt. ܦܚܙ. f. *wantonness, lasciviousness.*

ܦܰܚܝܳܚܳܐ, ܝܳܬܳܐ rt. ܦܚ. *porous, hollow, empty, futile, untrustworthy;* ܗܰܘܳܐ ܦܰܚܝܳܚܳܐ ܐܰܝܟ ܥܰܠ ܗܰܘ ܪܶܥܝܳܢܶܗ ܐܰܝܟ ܩܰܢܝܳܐ *his mind is as hollow as a reed.*

ܦܰܚܝܳܚܽܘܬܳܐ rt. ܦܚ. f. *emptiness* of mind, *vacillation.*

ܦܚܰܠܬܳܐ = ܦܶܚܠܬܳܐ; see ܦܚܠܐ.

ܦܰܚܠܳܐ pl. ܶܐ m. *a stallion.*

ܦܚܠܐ, ܦܶܚܠܬܳܐ pl. ܳܬ݂ܳܐ f. (vowels uncertain) *testicle.*

ܦܚܡ Peal only act. part. ܦܳܚܶܡ, ܦܳܚܡܳܐ *to be like, comparable, to equal;* ܡܶܕܶܡ ܠܳܐ ܦܳܚܶܡ ܠܳܗ̇ *nothing is comparable to* wisdom. PA. ܦܰܚܶܡ *to compare, treat as equal, estimate; make comparison, collate;* ܠܳܐ ܦܰܚܡܶܬ ܠܥܽܘܬܪܳܐ ܠܘܳܬܳܗ̇ *I esteemed riches nothing in comparison of her;* ܡܦܰܚܡܳܐ ܠܗ ܟܬܳܒܳܐ ܩܰܕܺܝܫܳܐ *Holy Scripture compares the* chosen nation to . . .; ܡܦܰܚܡܳܐ ܠܘܳܬ ܨܚܳܚܶܐ ܝܰܘܢܳܝܶܐ *collated with Greek codices.* Gram. *to punctuate, add points.* ETHPA. ܐܶܬ݂ܦܰܚܰܡ *to be compared, estimated; to be collated; to become like, imitate;* ܠܳܐ ܡܶܬ݂ܦܰܚܡܳܢܳܐ *incomparable.* DERIVATIVES, ܦܘܚܡܐ, ܦܘܚܡܢܐ, ܡܦܚܡܢܘܬܐ, ܦܚܡܐ, ܦܚܡܐܝܬ, ܦܚܡܢܐ, ܦܚܡܢܝܐ, ܡܬܦܚܡܢܘܬܐ, ܡܬܦܚܡܢܐ, ܡܬܦܚܡܢܐܝܬ.

ܦܶܚܡܳܐ, ܦܚܡ pl. ܶܐ m. *a coal.*

ܦܽܘܚܳܡܳܐ rt. ܦܚܡ. m. *a*) *equal, like, similar* often with ܒ, ܒܰܪ ܦܽܘܚܳܡܶܗ *his equal. b*) *a copy of* or *answer to* a letter; *a written narrative. c*) *equality, proportion;* ܐܰܝܟ ܕܰܒܚܰܕ ܦܽܘܚܳܡܳܐ *as with one accord. d*) *comparison, analogy.* With ܒ, *in respect to, with regard to, like;* with ܠ, *in comparison with, in contrast to;* with ܕܠܳܐ, *incomparable, unlike.*

ܦܽܘܚܳܡܳܐܺܝܬ݂ rt. ܦܚܡ. adv. *comparatively.*

ܦܽܘܚܳܡܳܝܳܐ rt. ܦܚܡ. *comparative.*

ܦܽܘܚܳܡܳܢܳܝܳܐ rt. ܦܚܡ. *comparative, relative.*

ܦܰܚܶܡ denom. verb Pael conj. from ܦܰܚܳܐ. *to ensnare.*

ܦܰܚܰܪ denom. verb Pael conj. from ܦܰܚܳܪܳܐ. *a*) *to harden;* ܡܳܐܢܳܐ ܕܛܺܝܢܳܐ ܕܰܒܫܶܡܫܳܐ ܡܦܰܚܰܪ *a vessel of clay hardened in the sun. b*) *to crack.* ETHPA. ܐܶܬ݂ܦܰܚܰܪ *a*) *to be formed* as by a potter. *b*) *to be cracked, crumbling.*

ܦܰܚܳܪܳܐ m. *a potter;* ܡܳܐܢܳܐ ܕܦܰܚܳܪܳܐ *a potter's vessel.* DERIVATIVES, verb ܦܚܪ, ܦܘܚܪܐ, ܦܘܚܪܐ, ܦܚܪܝܐ, ܦܘܚܪܢܐ.

ܦܰܚܳܪܳܝܳܐ, ܝܬܳܐ from ܦܰܚܳܪܳܐ. *a*) m. *a potter. b*) adj. *earthen, of earthenware.*

ܦܫܦܫ, ܦܫܦܫܐ *friable, loose.*

ܦܚܰܬ fut. ܢܶܦܚܽܘܬ, act. part. ܦܳܚܶܬ. *to dig, burrow.* PA. ܦܰܚܶܬ *to dig through* a house, *to cleave, shatter* the head, the ground. ETHPA. ܐܶܬ݂ܦܰܚܰܬ *to be undermined, collapse; to be riven, to cleave* intr., *to part asunder* as by earthquake; ܐܰܪܥܳܐ ܕܡܶܬ݂ܦܰܚܬܳܐ *the riven land;* ܓܠܺܝܕܳܐ ܐܶܬ݂ܦܰܚܰܬ ܬܚܶܝܬܶܝܗ̇ *the ice opened under her.* DERIVATIVES, ܦܚܬܘܬܐ, ܦܚܬܐ, ܦܘܚܬܢܐ, ܦܚܬܬܐ.

ܦܰܚܬܳܐ E-Syr. ܦܶܚܬܳܐ, pl. ܶܐ rt. ܦܚܬ. m. *a chasm, gulf.*

ܦܫܠܘܢܐ dimin. of ܦܫܠܬܐ. m. *a fissure, pit, pool.*

ܦܫܠܬܐ pl. ܦܫܠܬܐ rt. ܦܫܠ. *fiery meteors.*

ܦܛܐܪܝܣ; see ܦܛܪܝܣ.

ܐܬܦܛܦܛ denom. verb Ethpalal conj. from ܦܛܦܛܐ *to feast on dainties.*

ܦܛܦܛܐ pl. ܐ̈ m. *a dainty, delicacy; confectionery.*

ܦܛܦܛܐ m. *a cook, confectioner.*

ܦܛܓܪܐ oftener ܦܘܕܓܪܐ. m. *gout.*

ܦܛܪܝܣ, ܦܛܝܪܝܣ and ܦܛܐܪܝܣ m. πτέρις, *filix mas, the male fern;* ܦ ܢܩܒܬܐ *filix femina, lady-fern.*

ܦܛܘܓ a disease of the eye.

ܦܛܘܚܐ *dry, rotten* as a tree.

ܦܛܘܚܐ m. *bread fallen into the oven.*

ܦܛܘܡܐ m. pl. *fattenings.*

ܦܛܘܢܐ rt. ܦܛܢ. *prudent, discreet, wise.*

ܦܛܘܢܘܬܐ rt. ܦܛܢ. f. *discretion, prudence.*

ܦܛܘܣܝܣ f. πτῶσις, gram. *a case;* logic. *the five predicaments,* sc. genus, species, difference, property, accident.

ܦܛܘܦܛܐ = ܦܛܦܛܐ *dainties.*

ܦܛܘܪܐ pl. ܐ̈ rt. ܦܛܪ. *passing away, dying.*

ܦܛܘܪܘܬܐ rt. ܦܛܪ. f. *passing away, decease, non-existence.*

ܦܛܘܪܝܐ, ܐܝܬܐ rt. ܦܛܪ. *transient.*

ܦܛܘܪܬܐ or ܦܛܪ pl. ܐܬܐ rt. ܦܛܪ. *a fungus.*

ܦܛܘܫܐ rt. ܦܛܫ. *oblong.*

ܦܛܝܫܐ = ܦܛܘܫܐ.

ܦܛܝܚܐ pl. ܐ̈ m. *a melon, pumpkin.*

ܦܛܝܪ, ܦܛܝܪܐ, ܦܛܝܪܬܐ rt. ܦܛܪ. *a*) *fresh, untanned, raw,* as hides. *b*) *unleavened, unleavened bread;* ܥܐܕܐ ܕܦܛܝܪܐ and often ellipt. *the feast of unleavened bread, the Passover, Easter;* metaph. *the Lord's Supper;* also *unleavened = sincere.*

ܦܛܝܫܐ rt. ܦܛܫ. *flat, snub-nosed.*

ܦܛܩܛܐ or ܦܛܝܫܐ m. *a praefect.*

ܦܛܩܛܘܬܐ f. *office, authority of a* ܦܛܩܛܐ.

ܦܛܠܐ *a briar, thorny shrub.*

ܦܛܠܐ, ܦܛܠܝܐ and ܦܛܠܝܬܐ pl. ܐ̈ πέταλον -α, *a sheet of writing; a sheet, plate* of metal.

ܦܘܛܠܝܐ = ܦܛܠܝܐ.

ܦܛܡ Pael ܦܛܡ. *to fatten, feed up, enrich;* ܦܛܡ ܐܢܘܢ ܒܒܘܪܟܬܐ ܕܡܠܟܘܬܟ *enrich them with the blessings of Thy kingdom.* Pass. part. ܡܦܛܡ, ܐ, ܬܐ *fattened; a fatling, fat beast.* Ethpa. ܐܬܦܛܡ *to be fattened, fed; to fare sumptuously;* ܟܕ ܡܬܦܛܡ ܒܥܐܕܐ ܕܐܠܗܘܗܝ *gorging at the feasts of his gods;* ܒܥܠܕܒܒܐ ܡܬܦܛܡܝܢ ܡܢ ܚܠܠܬܗ *enemies growing fat on the harvests* of the land. Derivatives, ܦܘܛܡܐ, ܦܛܡܐ, ܡܦܛܡܢܘܬܐ, ܡܦܛܡܢܘܬܐ.

ܦܛܡܐ rt. ܦܛܡ. m. *fattening; a fatling;* ܦܛܡܐ ܕܬܘܪܐ *fat oxen.*

ܦܛܢ fut. ܢܦܛܢ, parts. ܦܛܢ, ܦܛܝܢܐ and ܦܛܝܢ *to perceive, understand;* ܕܠܐ ܦܛܢ *senseless;* ܐܣܝܐ ܦܛܝܢ ܕܢܥܕܪ *a physician wise to help.* Derivatives, ܦܛܘܢܐ, ܦܛܘܢܘܬܐ, ܦܛܢܐ.

ܦܛܢܐ rt. ܦܛܢ. m. *good sense, understanding.*

ܦܛܫ denom. verb from ܦܛܫܐ. Ethpa. ܐܬܦܛܫ *to be stupid.*

ܦܛܫܐ, ܦܛܫܬܐ *stupid, senseless, silly, worthless.* Derivatives, verb ܐܬܦܛܫ, ܦܛܫܐܝܬ, ܦܛܫܘܬܐ.

ܦܛܫܐܝܬ from ܦܛܫܐ. adv. *stupidly.*

ܦܛܫܘܬܐ pl. ܘܬܐ from ܦܛܫܐ. f. *ignorance, stupidity, folly.*

ܦܛܫܐ m. *rank, degree.*

ܦܛܩܐ pl. ܝܢ m. *a*) πιττάκιον, *a slip of parchment, list, writing-tablet, label, inscription, written bond.* *b*) *a bowl.*

ܦܛܪ fut. ܢܦܛܪ, act. part. ܦܛܪ, ܦܛܪܐ. *a*) *to leave, quit, go away, return home* ܡܢ ܒܝܬ ܡܫܬܘܬܐ *from a banquet;* ܦܛܪ ܠܒܝܬܟ *return to thy house;* ܟܕ ܗܘܐ ܥܕܢܐ ܠܡܫܬܒܩܘ *when it was time to take leave.* *b*) *to leave,* ܦܛܪ ܚܝܠܗ ܡܢܗ *his strength left him.* *c*) *to pass away* ܡܢ ܚܝܐ *from life;* ܡܢ ܥܠܡܐ *from the world;* ܐܝܟܢ ܕܦܛܪ *the passing, the dying.* *d*) *to cease, desist* ܡܢ ܥܡܠܗ *from his labour; to be at an end, pass away;* ܦܛܪ ܥܐܕܐ *the feast is ended;* ܦܛܪ ܪܕܘܦܝܐ ܡܢ ܥܕܬܐ *persecution ceased from the Church;* ܚܝܐ ܕܠܐ ܦܛܪܝܢ *life which does not pass away;*

ܚܕܘܬܐ ܕܠܐ ܦܛܝܪܐ *unending gladness.* e) *to be* or *remain unleavened.* Aph. ܐܦܛܪ a) *to shoot out, thrust out* ܣܦܘܬܗ *the lips* in mockery, also sing. without ܒ, ܣܦܬܗ ܐܦܛܪ ܠܘܬܗ *he put out his lip to him.* b) *to bring to an end, bring to nought, do away with;* ܥܕܡܐ ܕܐܦܛܪ ܚܫܡܝܬܐ *until he had finished supper;* ܡܫܝܚܐ ܐܦܛܪ ܕܒܚܐ ܢܡܘܣܝܐ Christ *put an end to the sacrifices of the Law.* c) *to dismiss, separate, dissolve;* ܟܘܪܗܢܐ ܡܦܛܪ ܠܗܕܡܐ *sickness relaxes the joints;* ܡܘܬܐ ܡܦܛܪ ܠܟܠܗܘܢ *death dismisses them all.* Derivatives, ܦܛܘܪܐ, ܦܛܘܪܘܬܐ, ܦܛܘܪܐ, ܦܛܘܪܬܐ, ܦܛܝܪܐ, ܦܛܪܐ.

ܦܛܪܐ m. pl. *shank-bands, puttees.*

ܦܛܪܐ *Peter;* see ܦܛܪܘܣ.

ܦܛܪܐ rt. ܦܛܪ. m. *passing away.*

ܦܛܪܘܢ, ܦܛܪܘܢܐ, ܦܛܪܘܢܘܣ pl. ܦܛܪܘܢܐ m. Lat. patronus, *a patron, protector, defender, advocate.* Derivatives, the two following:—

ܦܛܪܘܢܘܬܐ from ܦܛܪܘܢ. f. *patronage, defence, advocacy.*

ܦܛܪܘܢܝܐ from ܦܛܪܘܢ. f. *patronage;* collect. *furtherers, promoters.*

ܦܛܪܘܣ, ܦܛܪܐ also spelt ܦܛܪܣ and ܦܛܪ. E-Syr. ܦܛܪ pr. n. *Peter.*

ܦܛܪܘܣܝܐ, ܦܛܪܘܣܝܬܐ from ܦܛܪܘܣ. *Petrine,* of or *derived from Peter;* ܪܫܢܘܬܐ ܦܛܪܘܣܝܬܐ *primacy derived from Peter.*

ܦܛܪܝܩܝܘܣ, ܦܛܪܝ and ܦܛܪܝܩܐ pl. ܦܛܪܝܩܝܘܣ m. ܦܛܪܝܩܝܐ, ܦܛܪܝܩܐ f. Lat. patricius, *patrician,* a Byzantine and Persian rank.

ܦܛܪܝܪܟܐ, ܦܛܪܝܪܟܝܣ, ܦܛܪܝܪܟܐ, ܦܛܪܟ &c. E-Syr. ܦܛܪܝܪܟܐ pl. ܐ̈ and oftener ܦܛܪܝܪܟܘ, m. πατριάρχης, *Patriarch* the highest ecclesiastical dignity. Derivatives, verb ܦܛܪܟ, and the four following words:—

ܦܛܪܝܪܟܘܬܐ f. *the patriarchate.*

ܦܛܪܝܪܟܝܐ, ܦܛܪܝܪܟܝܬܐ *patriarchal.*

ܦܛܪܟ denom. verb Palen conj. from ܦܛܪܝܪܟܐ. *to raise to the patriarchate, to elect Patriarch.* Ethpalan ܐܬܦܛܪܟ *to be elected* or *consecrated Patriarch.*

ܦܛܪܟܝܐ, ܦܛܪܟܝܬܐ *patriarchal.*

ܦܛܫ, ܦܛܫܐ *snub-nosed, flat-nosed;* ܦܛܫ ܢܚܝܪܘܗܝ *his nostrils were flat.* Derivatives, ܦܛܫܐ, ܦܛܘܫܐ, ܦܛܫܘܬܐ.

ܦܛܫܐ pl. ܐ̈ Chald. m. *leggings.*

ܦܛܫܘܬܐ from ܦܛܫ. f. *being snub-nosed.*

ܦܝ Ar. *in.*

ܦܝܒܘܪܐ m. *a balustrade.*

ܦܝܒܠܐ m. a) Lat. fibula, *a clasp, buckle.* b) *a thick thread.*

ܦܝܟ, ܦܝܟܐ pl. ܐ̈ Pers. m. *a runner; a foot-soldier.*

ܦܝܓܐ rt. ܦܘܓ. m. *cooling, refreshment, repose.*

ܦܝܓܢܐ pl. ܐ̈ m. Lat. paganus, *rustic, plebeian.*

ܦܝܓܢܐ, ܦܝܓܢܐ, ܦܠܓܢܘܢ, ܦܝܓܢܘܢ m. πήγανον, *peganum harmala, rue.*

ܦܝܓܐ = ܦܝܓܐ.

ܦܝܕܐ rt. ܦܕ. m. *error.*

ܦܝܪܝܘܢ πυρεῖον, *a stove.*

ܦܝܓܘܬܐ rt. ܦܘܓ. f. *cooling.*

ܦܝܚܐ rt. ܦܘܚ. m. *a cool, spacious* or *draughty place.*

ܦܝܘܪܐ m. ἐπίουρος, *a stake.*

ܦܝܙܐ Chinese, *a tablet,* Mongolian symbol of authority.

ܦܝܙܪܐ m. *a travelling merchant, a peddler.*

ܦܝܛܐ m. *an obolus.*

ܦܝܓܐ rt. ܦܓܓ. m. *contemptibility.*

ܦܝܚܐ rt. ܦܘܚ. *fragrant.*

ܦܝܚ; see verb ܦܘܚ.

ܦܝܩܪܝܐ m. Lat. vicarius, *the Vicar* apostolic.

ܦܝܠ, ܦܝܠܐ pl. ܝ̈ܢ, ܐ̈ m. ܦܝܠܬܐ pl. ܦܝܠܬܐ f. *an elephant;* ܫܢܐ ܕܦܝܠܐ, ܫܢܐ, ܫܢܐ ܕܦܝܠܐ *ivory.* Derivative, ܦܝܠܢܐ.

ܦܝܠܐ or ܦܝܠܐ, pl. ܝ̈ܢ, ܐ̈, ܬ̈ܐ, ܦܝܠܝܣ f. φιάλη, *a broad shallow dish; a paten, a cup, bowl,* esp. *a sacrificial bowl.* Cf. ܦܝܠܣܐ, ܦܠܐ and ܦܝܠܐ.

ܦܝܠܐ pl. ܐ̈ rt. ܦܠܠ. *anything sprinkled* or *mixed* e. g. with oil as a cake or dough.

ܦܝܠܘܛܐ and ܦܝܠܘܛܐ πιλωτός, *felt, a horse-cloth, girth;* a falcon's *hood.*

ܦܝܠܣܘܦܐ, ܦܝܠܣܘܦܐ, ܦܝܠܣܘܦܐ, ܦܝܠܣܦ, ܦܝܠܣܦܐ pl. ܝ̈ܢ, ܐ̈ m. ܦܝܠܣܘܦܝܬܐ f. φιλόσοφος, *a philosopher.*

ܦܝܠܘܣܘܦܘܬܐ and ܦܝܠܣܘܦܘܬ̈ f. φιλοσοφία, *philosophy;* ܦܝܠܘܣܘܦܘܬܐ ܐܠܗܝܬܐ or ܪܘܚܢܝܬܐ *divine* or *spiritual philosophy* = monastic counsels, the ascetic life.

ܦܝܠܘܣܘܦܝܐ and ܦܝܠܣܘܦܝ̈ f. *philosophy.*

ܦܝܠܘܣܘܦܝܐ *philosophical.*

ܦܝܠܘܣܘܦܝܣܐ f. φιλοσοφῆσαι, with ܥܒܕ *to study* or *treat systematically;* also *to live ascetically, plainly.*

ܦܝܠܢܝܐ, ܦܝܠܢܝܬܐ from ܦܝܠܐ. *elephantine, of elephants, ivory.*

ܦܝܠܝܢ; see ܦܝܠܐ *a vial.*

ܦܝܠܣܘܦܘܬܐ, ܦܝܠܣܘ— &c.; see above spelt with one ܠ only.

ܦܝܠܟܐ pl. ܦܝܠܟܐ = ܦܝܠܐ f. *a dish* esp. one for use at the altar, *a paten.*

ܦܝܠܟܐ m. *the whorl* of a spindle, *a spindle.*

ܦܝܠܪܓܐ and ܦܝܠܪܓ̈ pl. ܦܝܠܪܓܐ m. *the stork.*

ܦܝܠܪܓܘܬܐ from the above. f. *piety* such as that of the stork.

ܦܝܢܐ pl. ܦܝܢܐ φαινώλης, φελόνιον &c. m. *a priest's vestment, long and sleeveless.*

ܦܝܢܟܐ pl. ܦܝܢܟܐ m. πίναξ, *a*) *a trencher, dish, paten.* *b*) *a board, panel* for painting on, *a writing-tablet.* DERIVATIVES, ܦܢܟܝܬܐ, verb ܦܢܟ.

ܦܝܢܟܝܬܐ pl. ܦܝܢܟܝܬܐ dimin. of ܦܝܢܟܐ. m. *a small dish, platter.*

ܦܝܣ APHEL ܐܦܝܣ denom. verb from ܦܝܣܐ πεῖσαι, retains the hard pronunciation of the π. Act. part. ܡܦܝܣ, pass. part. ܡܦܝܣ. with ܒ, ܥܠ, ܕ, acc. *to persuade, convince, instruct; to desire, make petition, ask;* ܠܣܘܓܐܐ ܕܟܠܗ ܐܣܝܐ. ܐܦܝܣ ܗܢܐ ܦܘܠܘܣ *the greater part of all Asia hath this Paul persuaded;* ܐܦܝܣܢܝ ܥܠ ܐܠܝܐ *teach me about Elijah;* ܐܦܝܣ ܕܢܬܝܗܒ ܠܗ ܙܒܢܐ *he desired that time should be granted him;* ܒܟܠܙܒܢ ܡܦܝܣ ܐܢܬ ܠܐܠܗܐ ܡܛܠܝ *thou dost ever make petition to God for me.* Pass. part. *persuaded, acquainted with, conversant, expert;* the act. part. in ܡܦܝܣܝܢܢ = *we persuade* or *convince ourselves,* is sometimes found for ܡܦܝܣܝܢܢ *we are persuaded;* ܡܦܝܣܝܢܢ ܥܠܝܟܘܢ ܐܚܝ ܕ *we are persuaded concerning you, brethren, that . . .;* ܗܠܝܢ ܕܡܦܝܣܝܢܢ ܒܗܝܢ *of which we are fully persuaded;* ܡܦܝܣ ܛܒ *knowing well;* ܐܢܫ ܕܡܦܝܣ ܠܐܘܪܚܐ *one who knows the road;* ܡܦܝܣ ܗܘܐ ܠܬܠܬ ܠܫܢ̈ܐ *fairly well acquainted with three languages.*

ETHPE. ܐܬܦܝܣ oftener ܐܬܦܝܣ *to be persuaded, instructed; to consent, obey;* ܠܡܬܦܝܣܘ ܡܢܗ ܥܠ ܢܡܘܣܐ *to be instructed by him about the law;* ܕܠܐ ܡܬܦܝܣܝܢ ܠܐܒܗ̈ܝܗܘܢ *disobedient to parents.*

ܦܝܣ, ܦܝܣܐ and ܦܝܣܐ oftener ܦܐܣ, ܦܐܣܐ πεῖσις or πεῖσαι. m. *a*) verbal use: with ܥܒܕ *to persuade, to make petition;* with ܐܡܠܐ *to convince.* *b*) *persuasion, conviction, assurance, confidence;* ܦܐܣܐ ܕܡܠܐ *a bringing of persuasive arguments;* ܕܠܐ ܦܐܣ *disobedient,* but cf. *e.* *c*) *supplication, intercession.* *d*) *an explanation, answer, argument, reasoning, view.* *e*) *moderation;* ܕܠܐ ܦܐܣܐ *immoderate.* DERIVATIVES, verb ܐܦܝܣ, ܦܝܣܝܐ, ܦܝܣܝܬܐ, ܡܦܝܣܢܐ, ܡܦܝܣܢܘܬܐ, ܡܦܝܣܘܬܐ, ܡܬܦܝܣܢܐ, ܡܬܦܝܣܢܘܬܐ, ܠܐܡܬܦܝܣܢܐ, ܠܐܡܬܦܝܣܢܘܬܐ.

ܦܝܣܘܣ πίσος, *pulse, peas.*

ܦܝܣܛܘܩܐ pl. ܐ̈ m. *the crop* of a bird, *stomach* of a ruminant.

ܦܝܣܛܩܝܘܢ πιστάκιον: cf. ܦܣܬܩܐ.

ܦܝܣܛܝܣ πίστις, *faith.*

ܦܝܣܛܝܩܘܣ pl. ܦܝܣܛܝܩܐ for ܦܝܣܛܝܩܐ m. πιστικός, *a skipper.*

ܦܝܣܝܐ, ܦܝܣܝܬܐ from ܦܝܣܐ. *deprecatory, intercessory.*

ܦܝܣܘܕ from ψευδο-, with ܐܦܝܣܩܘܦܐ *a pseudo-bishop.*

ܦܝܣܩܐ, ܦܝܣܩܝܐ, ܦܝܣܩܝܬܐ Pers. *spotted, piebald, parti-coloured.*

ܦܝܣܩܐ = ܦܝܣܩܣܩܐ.

ܦܝܣܪܝܢ πισάριον, dimin. of ܦܝܣܘܣ. *a small sort of pulse.*

ܦܝܣܬܐ pl. ܦܝܣܬܐ from ܦܝܣܐ. f. *persuasion, conviction; a supplication, intercession.*

ܦܝܥܬܐ m. *bleating:* cf. ܦܥܝܐ.

ܦܦܝܪܘܣ, —ܪܐ; see ܦܦܘܪܘܣ. *papyrus.*

ܦܝܦ, ܦܝܦܐ = ܦܐܦܐ *stammering, a stammerer.*

ܦܝܩ, ܦܝܩܐ pl. ܦܝܩ̈ܬܐ rt. ܦܘܩ. f. *rage, threat, anger.*

ܦܝܫܩܐ and ܦܝܫܩܐ dialect of Tirhan, *a split, rupture.*

ܦܝܫܡܐ pl. ܝܢ, ܐ̈ m. *a censer, incense.*

ܦܝܫܢܐ *lazy.*

ܦܟܗܐ rt. ܦܟܗ. m. *pause, delay.*

ܦܝܫܟܠܘܬܐ rt. ܦܫܟܠ. f. *frying, cooking.*

ܦܝܫܦܝܫܝ pl. ܝܢ Pers. *a fore-runner:* cf. ܦܝܫܝܐ.

ܦܟܪ fut. ܢܦܟܘܪ *to break, bruise* the head. Ethpe. ܐܬܦܟܪ *to be crushed, shattered.* Pa. ܦܰܟܰܪ *to break to pieces, shatter.* Ethpa. ܐܬܦܰܟܰܪ *to be reduced to powder* or *ashes, to smoke.* Derivatives, ܦܟܘܪܐ, ܦܟܐ, ܦܟܝܪܘܬܐ, ܦܟܝܪܐ, ܦܟܪܐ, ܡܦܟܪܢܐ.

ܦܟ, ܦܟܐ pl. ܐ̈ rt. ܦܟܪ. m. *a) a blow, buffet, slap, box on the ear. b) a tusk; the jaw, cheek;* metaph. ܦܟܐ ܕܡܕܒܚܐ *the side of the altar.*

ܦܟܗ fut. ܢܦܟܗ, act. part. ܦܟܗ, ܦܟܗܐ, part. adj. ܦܟܝܗ, ܗܐ, ܗܬܐ. *a) to lose flavour, scent* or *colour* as fruit and flowers, *to fade* from the mind; ܐܢ ܡܠܚܐ ܢܦܟܗ *if salt lose its savour. b) to cool* as an oven; as love, anger &c.; *to abate* as suffering, persecution. *c) to grow pale* or *dim; to languish, grow weak* as prayer, faith &c.; *to lose interest, sense* or *meaning;* ܦܟܗ ܗܘܐ ܠܗ ܢܘܗܪܗܘܢ ܕܠܡܦܐܕܐ ܩܕܡ ܢܘܗܪܗ *the light of the torches waxed dim before his light;* ܦܟܗ ܝܘܡܐ ܘܐܘܪܟܘ ܛܠܠܐ *day faded and shadows lengthened.* Part. adj. *faded, dim; tasteless, insipid; senseless, foolish;* ܦܟܝܗ ܡܕܥܐ *senseless, foolish;* ܦܟܝܗܘܬ ܪܘܚܐ *spiritless, weak-spirited;* ܡܠܐ ܦܟܝܗܬܐ *silly fables;* ܫܡܐ ܦܟܝܗ *a meaningless name;* ܬܘܬܐ ܦܟܝܗܬܐ *a sycamore.* Pa. ܦܰܟܶܗ *to abate, temper, moderate* pungency, bitterness, intensity; *to relax, remit* ardour, desire; *to deprive* of meaning, *render meaningless.* Ethpa. ܐܬܦܰܟܰܗ *to be tempered, mitigated, counteracted.* Aph. ܐܦܟܗ *to moderate, soothe.* Derivatives, ܦܟܝܗܐܝܬ, ܦܟܝܗܘܬܐ, ܡܦܟܗܢܘܬܐ.

ܦܟܘܪܐ rt. ܦܟܪ. m. *one who binds.*

ܦܟܝܗܐܝܬ rt. ܦܟܗ. adv. *foolishly.*

ܦܟܝܗܘܬܐ rt. ܦܟܗ. f. *insipidity, folly, slackness, lukewarmness.*

ܦܟܝܟܘܬܐ rt. ܦܟ. f. *contusion, bruising* or *wounding of the head.*

ܦܟܝܪܘܬܐ rt. ܦܟܪ. f. *binding; a bond.*

ܦܟܟܐ rt. ܦܟ. m. *contusion.*

ܦܟܟ perhaps denom. verb from ܦܟܐ. *to jaw, gabble.* Ethpa. ܐܬܦܰܟܰܟ *to abuse, be insolent, gabble.*

ܦܟܡܢܐ, ܦܟܡܢܝܬܐ from ܦܟܡ. *loud-tongued, vociferous, clamouring.*

ܦܟܡܢܘܬܐ from ܦܟܡ. f. *vociferousness, impudence, clamour.*

ܦܟܪ fut. ܢܦܟܘܪ, act. part. ܦܟܪ, ܦܟܪܐ, pass. part. ܦܟܝܪ, ܐ, ܬܐ. *to bind;* with ܐܝܕܝܗܘܢ *to join* or *fold the hands* in prayer; ܦܟܝܪ ܘܐܣܝܪ *bound and tied;* ܡܘܡܬܐ ܕܦܟܝܪ ܗܘܐ ܒܗܝܢ ܐܒܘܗܝ *the oaths with which his father had bound him.* Ethpe. ܐܬܦܟܪ *to be bound,* ܒܫܫܠܬܐ *in chains;* ܒܚܒܠܐ ܕܚܛܝܬܐ *in the bonds of sin.* Pa. ܦܰܟܰܪ *to bind closely, to ensnare.* Ethpa. ܐܬܦܰܟܰܪ *to be bound* with many bonds or gradually, chiefly metaph. *to be entangled* with cares or lusts; ܡܬܦܟܪ ܒܨܒܘܬܐ ܕܥܠܡܐ *entangled in worldly matters.* Derivatives, ܦܟܝܪܘܬܐ, ܦܟܘܪܐ, ܦܟܪܬܐ, ܦܟܪܐ, ܦܟܪܐ.

ܦܟܪܐ, ܦܟܪܐ pl. ܐ̈ rt. ܦܟܪ. m. *a band, bond, obstacle; a hard question, subtle view.*

ܦܟܪܐ rt. ܦܟܪ. m. *a door-fastening, bolt, bar.*

ܦܟܬܐ rt. ܦܟ. f. *the handle of an auger* or *drill.*

ܦܐܟܗܬܐ pl. ܐ̈ f. Ar. *fruit.*

ܦܠ or ܦܝܠ Pers. *nymphaea lotus, the blue water-lily* or *its root.*

ܦܠ fut. ܢܦܘܠ, infin. ܡܦܠ, act. part. ܦܐܠ, pass. part. ܦܠܝܠ, ܐ. *a) to sprinkle,* ܒܩܛܡܐ *with ashes;* ܒܛܝܢܐ ܕܒܝܫܬܐ ܦܠܝܠ ܐܢܐ *I am bespattered with the mire of evil. b) to knead, press into a mass.* Palpel ܦܰܠܦܶܠ *to wallow* in blood, *imbrue* the hands in blood; *to bespatter, defile, cast aspersions;* ܡܦܠܦܠ ܒܕܡܐ *weltering in blood;* ܦܠܦܠܗ ܒܪܓܬܗ ܛܢܦܬܐ *he defiled her with his filthy lust;* ܦܠܦܠܬ ܠܡܚܒܢܝܟܝ ܒܨܥܪܐ ܛܢܦܐ *thou hast covered thy lovers with abominable scorn.* Ethpalp. ܐܬܦܰܠܦܰܠ *to be sprinkled* with ashes, *rolled* in the dust, *defiled* with blood, mire, sin. Derivative, ܡܦܠܚܠܐ.

ܦܠ imperative of verb ܢܦܠ *to fall.*

ܦܝܠܐ and ܦܝܠܐ m. *a large flask, cup, tumbler* of glass, leather or wood. Cf. ܦܢܝܠܐ and ܦܠܟܐ.

ܦܠܐ, ܦܠܐ or ܦܘܠܐ m. *laurus malobathrum*, an Indian plant from which a costly ointment was prepared.

ܦܠܐ fut. ܢܦܠܐ, act. part. ܦܐܠ, ܦܠܝܐ. *to pick out lice, search for vermin* in the head or clothes; *look over* an olive-tree for the remaining olives; metaph. *to search minutely;* ܦܠܝ ... ܐܝܟ ܒܠܡܦܕܐ *search out* the meanings *as with a lantern.* Pa. ܦܠܝ *to search closely;* ܦܠܝܗ ܘܐܫܟܚܗ ܠܐܓܪܬܐ *he searched him and found the letter.* Aph. ܐܦܠܝ *to shake* or *search thoroughly.* Derivative, ܦܠܝܐ.

ܦܠܐܛܘܢ; see ܦܠܛܘܢ *Plato.*

ܦܠܐܛܝܢ; see ܦܠܛܝܢ *a palace.*

ܦܠܐܩܣ and ܦܠܐܩܣ pl. f. πλάκες, *tables* of stone; see ܦܠܩܣ.

ܦܠܐܬ and ܦܠܬ denom. verb Pael conj. from ܦܠܐܬܐ *to speak parables, describe by a parable.* Ethpa. ܐܬܦܠܐܬ and ܐܬܦܠܬ *to be pronounced* as a parable, *to be compared.*

ܦܠܐܬܐ, ܦܠܐܬܐ pl. ܬܐ f. *a parable, allegory, proverb, illustration;* ܒܦܠܐܬܐ *in parables, allegorically.*

ܦܠܐܬܐܝܬ from ܦܠܐܬܐ. adv. *allegorically, mystically.*

ܦܠܐܬܢܝܐ, ܢܝܬܐ from ܦܠܐܬܐ. *allegorical, of the nature of a parable.*

ܦܒܘܠܪܝܐ corrupted from Lat. fabularius, *a fabler, teller of fables.*

ܦܠܓ and ܦܠܓ fut. ܢܦܠܘܓ and ܢܦܠܓ, act. part. ܦܠܓ, ܦܠܓܐ, pass. part. ܦܠܝܓ, ܓܐ, ܓܬܐ. a) *to divide, part in two;* ܦܠܓ ܝܡܐ *he divided the sea; to assign* ܐܝܩܪܐ *honour.* b) *to have a portion, go shares* with ܥܡ *with;* ܐܡܪ ܠܐܚܝ ܕܢܦܠܓ ܥܡܝ ܝܪܬܘܬܐ *bid my brother divide the inheritance with me.* c) *to be half through, to come to the middle;* ܟܕ ܦܠܓܘ ܝܘܡܬܐ ܕܥܐܕܐ *when half the days of the feast were passed.* Pass. part. a) *divided;* ܦܠܝܓ ܪܓܠܐ *cloven-footed.* b) ܦܠܝܓ ܫܢܝܐ *middle-aged.* c) *doubting, dubious, undecided, wavering* with ܒܠܒܐ *in heart;* ܒܪܥܝܢܐ *in mind;* ܒܡܚܫܒܬܐ *in thought.* d) *differing, at variance; schismatic;* ܡܠܦܢܘܬܐ—ܟܢܘܫܝܐ ܦܠܝܓܬܐ *schismatic doctrine, a schismatic synod.* Ethpe. ܐܬܦܠܓ a) *to be divided, parted in two, shared.* b) *to be divided, at strife, to separate from* with ܡܢ or ܥܠ of the pers.; ܢܬܦܠܓ ܐܒܐ ܥܠ ܒܪܐ ܘܒܪܐ ܥܠ ܐܒܘܗܝ *father shall be divided against son and son against father.* c) *to be doubtful, to doubt.*

Pael ܦܠܓ *to divide into many parts, to distribute* a portion, an inheritance, the spoil; ܠܐܪܒܥܐ ܦܠܓ *into four parts;* ܦܣܐ *to divide by lot, allot; to share, to assign;* ܦܠܓܘ ܢܚܬܝ ܒܝܢܬܗܘܢ *they parted my garments amongst them;* ܦܠܓ ܠܗܘܢ ܩܢܝܢܗ *he divided unto them his substance;* ܐܪ̈ܙܐ ܕܦܓܪܐ ܘܕܕܡܐ ܕܡܦܠܓ ܟܗܢܐ *the mysteries of the body and of the blood which the priest distributes;* ܡܣܟܢܐ ܡܦܠܓܝܢ ܠܗܘܢ ܥܘܬܪܐ *the poor to whom wealth is distributed.* Metaph. *to divide, make heretical distinctions;* ܡܦܠܓ ܠܐܠܗܘܬܐ ܡܢ ܦܓܪܐ *dividing the Godhead from the body.* With ܐܝܩܪܐ *to honour, show honour.* ܚܝܐ ܡܦܠܓܐ *the distracted life* of worldliness; ܣܦܘܬܐ ܡܦܠܓܢܝܬܐ *lying lips;* ܡܦܠܓ ܪܥܝܢܐ—ܪܥܝܢܬܐ *of wavering* or *doubtful mind.* Ethpa. ܐܬܦܠܓ a) *to be divided, distributed* as alms, as the holy mysteries; ܥܠܝܬܐ ܕܒܗ ܐܬܦܠܓܘ ܠܫܢܐ *the upper chamber wherein tongues were divided;* ܐܬܦܠܓ ܫܘܠܛܢܐ ܠܚܪܒܐ ܠܐܘܒܕܢܐ *power was granted to the sword to destroy;* ܠܐ ܡܬܦܠܓܢܐ *undivided.* b) *to divide oneself, separate;* ܡܬܦܠܓܝܢ ܢܗܪܘܬܐ *streams divide.* c) *to doubt, hesitate.* Derivatives, ܦܠܓܐ, ܦܠܓܐ, ܦܠܓܐ, ܦܠܓܘܬܐ, ܦܠܓܘܬܐ, ܦܘܠܓܐ, ܦܠܝܓܐܝܬ, ܦܠܝܓܘܬܐ, ܡܦܠܓܢܐܝܬ, ܡܦܠܓܢܘܬܐ, ܡܦܠܓܢܐ, ܦܠܓܢܐܝܬ, ܡܬܦܠܓܢܐ, ܡܬܦܠܓܢܐܝܬ, ܡܬܦܠܓܢܘܬܐ.

ܦܠܓ, ܦܠܓܐ pl. ܓܐ rt. ܦܠܓ. m. a) *a half, a part;* ܦܠܓܐ ܠܟܐ ܘܦܠܓܐ ܠܟܐ *half on one side half on the other, hither and thither;* ܦܠܓܐ ܒܦܠܓܐ *half and half, in equal quantities;* ܦܠܓܗ ܓܠܝܕ *half-congealed;* ܦܠܓܐ ܕܦܬܝܟܐ

half the dowry; ܦܠܓܗ ܕܫܒܛܐ *a half-tribe.* b) *the midst;* ܕܦܠܓ ܝܘܡܐ or ellipt. *midday;* ܕܠܠܝܐ *midnight;* ܦܠܓ ܫܢܝܐ *middle-aged.* c) *the middle* of the body = *the loins; half* the body; ܡܚܝܗܝ ܒܪܩܐ ܘܝܒܫܗ ܠܦܠܓܗ lightning *struck him and withered half his body* = *he had a paralytic stroke;* ܦܠܓ ܓܘܫܡܐ *partial paralysis, a stroke on one side, hemiplegia.* d) *a sect, school of thought.* e) Ar. *a two-humped camel.*

ܦܠܓܐ pl. ܐ̈ m. *a tambourine.*

ܦܠܓܐ, ܦܠܓܬܐ m. and f. rt. ܦܠܓ. *a phalanx, battalion, battle-array.*

ܦܠܓܐ pl. ܐ̈ rt. ܦܠܓ. m. *division, a division.*

ܦܠܓܘ, ܦܠܓܘܬܐ pl. ܦܠܓܘ̈ܬܐ, ܬܐ rt. ܦܠܓ f. a) *half* generally in composition; ܦܠܓܘܬ ܐܡܬܐ *half a cubit;* ܦܠܓܘܬ ܟܘܪܐ *hemisphere;* ܦܠܓܘܬ ܐܪܝܢܐ *semi-Arian;* ܦܠܓܘܬ ܒܪܢܫܐ *a puny creature, a pigmy;* ܦܠܓܘܬ ܚܘܕܪܐ *semi-circle;* ܦܠܓܘܬ ܚܡܪܐ *a mule;* ܦܠܓܘܬ ܠܠܝܐ *midnight;* ܦܠܓܘܬ ܡܝܬܐ *half dead;* ܦܠܓܘܬ ܡܫܡܫܢܐ *sub-deacon;* ܦܠܓܘܬ ܣܗܪܐ *full moon;* ܦܠܓܘܬ ܪܫܐ *pain on one side of the head, migraine;* ܦܠܓܘܬ ܥܠܝܡܘܬܐ *middle age;* ܦܠܓܘܬ ܫܥܬܐ *half an hour;* ܒܪ ܦܠܓܘܬܐ *co-heir.* b) *part, section* or *volume* of a book. c) ܫܪܝܐ ܕܦܠܓܘܬܐ *paralysis of one side, a stroke.*

ܦܠܓܘ, ܦܠܓܘܬܐ pl. ܦܠܓܘ̈ܬܐ, ܬܐ rt. ܦܠܓ. f. a) *a portion, part.* b) *a division* esp. of an army, *a rank, order;* ܕܠܐ ܦܠܓܘ *indivisible.* c) *a division, difference of opinion, dissension, faction.* d) *duplicity, deception.*

ܦܠܓܢܐ, ܦܠܓܢܝܬܐ pl. ܐ̈ f. ܬܐ̈ a) *a player on the tabor* or *tambourine.* b) rt. ܦܠܓ. m. *a sub-prefect, second in command.* c) *a soldier.*

ܦܠܓܝܡ, ܦܠܓܝܡ, ܦܠܓܝܡ and ܦܠܓܝܡ *artemisia maritima, mugwort, wormwood.*

ܦܠܓܡܐ pl. ܐ̈ and ܦܠܓܡܛܐ m. φλέγμα -τα, *phlegm, a cold, inflammation.*

ܦܠܓܡܢܝܐ, ܦܠܓܡܢܝܬܐ from ܦܠܓܡܐ *of the nature of phlegm, arising from phlegm.*

ܦܠܓܝܢܐ *inula helenium, elecampane.*

ܦܠܓܢܐܝܬ rt. ܦܠܓ. adv. *to half extent, at half-moon.*

ܦܠܓܬܐ rt. ܦܠܓ. f. *mid-lent, the middle of* the fast.

ܦܠܕܐ m. Pers. *steel.*

ܦܠܕܪ fut. ܢܦܠܕܪ. *to scatter, drive away, rout, separate; to lavish, scatter, squander* money; ܗܘ ܕܡܦܠܕܪ ܢܟܣܘܗܝ *he who squanders his riches;* ܡܫܝܚܐ ܕܦܠܕܪ ܚܫܘܟܐ *Christ who dispelled darkness;* ܦܠܕܪܘ ܡܢ ܪܥܝܢܝܟܘܢ ܚܘܫܒܐ ܐܢܫܝܐ *drive away from your minds human considerations.* Ethpa. ܐܬܦܠܕܪ *to disperse, be scattered* as an army, people, clouds; *to be squandered, dissipated,* as possessions; *to be distracted, disturbed;* ܐܬܦܠܕܪܘ ܒܐܬܪ̈ܘܬܐ ܣܓܝܐܐ *they were dispersed in* many *places;* ܐܬܦܠܕܪܘ ܗܘܘ ܠܗܘܢ ܠܡܫܠܚܘ ܩܛܝܠܐ *they had scattered to strip the slain;* ܨܘܐܐ ܡܬܦܠܕܪ ܒܡܫܝܓܬܐ *dirt is dispelled by the washtub;* ܐܬܦܠܕܪܘ ܡܚܫܒܬܗ *his thoughts are in confusion.* Derivatives, ܦܠܕܪܐ, ܡܦܠܕܪܢܐ, ܡܦܠܕܪܢܘܬܐ, ܡܬܦܠܕܪܢܘܬܐ.

ܦܠܚܐ, ܦܠܚܬܐ rt. ܦܠܚ. *one who serves God, pious; labouring;* ܥܒܕܐ ܦܠܚܬܐ *manual labour.*

ܦܠܚܐ Pers. *a door-ring, knocker.*

ܦܠܚܐ; see ܦܠܚܐ *felt; a felt rug.*

ܦܠܛܝܢ = ܦܠܛܝܢ *palace.*

ܦܠܘܡܐ m. Lat. pluma, *a feather.*

ܦܠܘܡܒܛܐ m. Lat. plumbatae, *scourges loaded with lead.*

ܦܠܘܡܘܣ, ܦܠܘܡܘܣ, ܦܠܘܡܘܣ and ܦܠܘܡܘܣ m. φλόμος, *verbascum, mullein,* the leaves of which were used for candle-wicks.

ܦܠܘܡܝܢ πλουμί, πλουμίον, *embroidery.*

ܦܠܡܘܢܝ or ܦܠܡܘܢܝ Heb. *such an one,* Dan. viii. 13.

ܦܠܠܘܢ; see ܦܠܠܘܢ.

ܦܠܚ fut. ܢܦܠܘܚ and ܢܦܠܚ, act. part. ܦܠܚ, ܦܠܚܐ, pass. part. ܦܠܝܚ, ܐ, ܬܐ. *to labour, work, cultivate, plough; to make, do, exercise* an art or occupation; *to do business; to teach; to serve* esp. *to serve God, to worship;* ܦܠܚܐ ܕܒܘܪܬܐ ܚܠܝܬܐ the bee *makes the sweet honeycomb;* ܦܠܘܚ ܣܡܡ̈ܢܐ *work* ingredients *in a mortar;* ܐܙܠܘ ܦܠܘܚܘ ܠܡܪܝܐ ܐܠܗܟܘܢ *go serve the Lord your God.* With ܐܪܥܐ *to till the ground;* ܦܠܚܘܬܐ *to do military service, serve as a soldier;* ܙܓܘܓܝܬܐ *to make glass;* ܙܪܥܐ *to sow;* ܡܚܫܒܬܐ *to reflect, meditate;* ܟܐܢܘܬܐ or ܙܕܝܩܘܬܐ *to work righteousness;* ܒܩܘܫܛܐ *to* trade; ܠܒܢ̈ܐ to make bricks; ܪ̈ܚܡܘܬܐ to show mercy; ܥܒܕܘܬܐ to be a slave, to serve; ܦܘܠܚܢܐ to do work, do service; ܦܘܠܚܢܘܬܐ to wage warfare, carry on war; ܦܬܟܪ̈ܐ to serve idols; ܡܘܗܒܬܐ to use a gift, an office; ܬܐܓܘܪܘܬܐ to trade. Also act. part. in comp. ܦܠܚ ܣܡ̈ܐ ܟܝܡܝܐ̈ alchemists; ܢܘܢ̈ܐ ܦܠܚ fishermen; ܦܠܚ ܡܫܟ̈ܐ a tanner. Pass. part. *cultivated, tilled; worked, wrought* as stone, wood, brass; *done with great pains, arduous* as writing, war; *committed* as sin; with ܠܐ *unhewn, unwrought; unprepared* as food. Gram. *in use.* ETHPE. ܐܬܦܠܚ *to be tilled, ploughed; to be practised, wrought, made, done; to be committed* as sins; *to be elaborated, reduced to method.* PA. ܦܠܚ *to labour; to serve* as a soldier; *to work, temper* clay. ETHPA. ܐܬܦܠܚ *to be worshipped; to be made, wrought; to be enlisted.* APH. ܐܦܠܚ *to cause to labour, enforce labour; to enlist; to serve as a soldier, do military service; to grant military decorations.* DERIVATIVES, ܦܘܠܚܢܐ, ܦܠܚܐ, ܦܠܚܐ, ܦܘܠܚܢܐ, ܦܘܠܚܢܘܬܐ, ܦܠܚܘܬܐ, ܦܠܚܐ, ܦܠܚܢܘܬܐ, ܦܠܚܢܐ, ܦܘܠܚܢܘܬܐ, ܡܬܦܠܚܢܐ.

ܦܠܚܐ, ܦܠܚܬܐ pl. up to ten ܦܠܚ̈ܐ, over ten ܦܠܚ̈ܘܬܐ rt. ܦܠܚ. a) *a servant, attendant, worshipper; a worker, artisan;* cf. act. part. of ܦܠܚ. b) *a soldier.*

ܦܠܚܐ, ܦܠܚܬܐ rt. ܦܠܚ. *a labourer, husbandman, vine-dresser.*

ܦܘܠܚܢܐ pl. ܦܘܠܚܢ̈ܐ rt. ܦܠܚ. f. a) *tillage, husbandry, agriculture.* b) *service;* with ܥܒܕܘܬܐ the same; ܦܘܠܚܢ ܦܬܟܪ̈ܐ *idolatry;* ܒܢ̈ܝ ܦܘܠܚܢܐ *attendants.* c) *occupation, office, ministry.* d) *an army, host; the military profession;* ܒܢ̈ܝ ܦܘܠܚܢܐ *fellow soldiers.*

ܦܠܚܘܬܐ rt. ܦܠܚ. f. *agriculture.*

ܦܘܠܚܢܝܐ rt. ܦܠܚ. *military.*

ܦܘܠܚܢܘܬܐ rt. ܦܠܚ. f. *agriculture.*

ܦܘܠܚܢܝܐ rt. ܦܠܚ. *military.*

ܦܠܛ fut. ܢܦܠܘܛ, act. part. ܦܠܛ, ܦܠܛܐ, part. adj. ܦܠܝܛ, ܦܠܝܛܐ, ܦܠܝܛܬܐ. a) *to escape, slip out* or *away;* ܦܠܛ ܡܢ ܗܘ ܕܚܫܐ *he has escaped suffering;* ܦܠܛܝ̈ ܐܝ̈ܕܝܗܘܢ ܡܢ ܟܠ *their hands have lost hold of all = all has slipped away from them;* ܠܐ ܦܠܛ ܠܗܘܢ ܡܕܡ *nothing escapes them* i.e. their notice; ܦܠܝ̈ܛܝ ܣܝܦܐ *escaped from the sword.* Cf. ܦܠܛܐ below. b) *to bring forth* young. ETHPE. ܐܬܦܠܛ *to be allowed to escape.* PA. ܦܠܛ a) *to save, deliver* with ܡܢ *from;* ܦܠܛ ܢܦܫܟ *save thyself.* b) *to let escape, throw up, eject;* ܢܘܢܐ ܕܦܠܛܗ ܢܒܝܐ *the prophet whom the fish disgorged.* ETHPA. ܐܬܦܠܛ a) *to make one's escape, save oneself, flee;* ܐܬܦܠܛ ܠܛܘܪܐ *flee to the mountain;* ܩܠܡܐ ܫܘܪ ܘܐܬܦܠܛ ܗܘܐ *the flea jumped out and made his escape.* b) *to be taken away.* APH. ܐܦܠܛ *to set free, let loose, let escape.* DERIVATIVES, ܦܠܛܐ, ܦܘܠܛܐ, ܡܦܠܛܢܐ, ܡܬܦܠܛܢܐ.

ܦܠܛܐ rt. ܦܠܛ. m. a) *escape.* b) *slipping out of place, dislocation* of a joint.

ܦܠܛܘܢ and ܦܠܐܛܘܢ. pr. n. *Plato.*

ܦܠܛܘܢܐܝܬ from ܦܠܛܘܢ. adv. *platonically, according to wise precept.*

ܦܠܛܘܢܝܐ, ܦܠܛܘܢܝܬܐ and ܦܠܐܛ pl. ܢ̈ܐ and ܦܠܐܛܘܢܝܘܬ from ܦܠܛܘܢ. *platonic, of Plato.*

ܦܠܛܝܐ pl. ܦܠܛܝ̈ܬܐ f. πλατεῖα, *a broad way, broad place.*

ܦܠܛܝܢ, ܦܠܐܛ, ܦܠܛ, ܦܠܛܘܢ, ܦܠܛܘܢ &c. f. Lat. palatium, *a palace, the court;* ܒܢ̈ܝ ܦ *courtiers.*

ܦܠܛܝܢܐ and ܦܠܛܝܢܘܣ m. palatinus, *an officer of the palace.*

ܦܠܛܝܩܐ pl. ܩ̈ܐ πολιτικός, *publicly distributed.*

ܦܠܛܝܘܡܢܘ and ܦܠܛ m. pl. πολιτευόμενοι, *public magistrates.*

ܦܠܝܐ rt. ܦܠܐ. m. *picking out* lice, *searching out* vermin; metaph. *scrutiny.*

ܦܠܝܓܐܝܬ rt. ܦܠܓ. adv. *in parts, separately; doubtfully.*

ܦܠܝܓܘܬܐ, ܦܠܝܓܘܬ rt. ܦܠܓ. f. *discord, division, schism; doubt, doubtfulness; double-mindedness, duplicity.* With ܪܥܝܢܐ *wavering* or *hesitation;* ܦܠܝܓܘܬ ܫܢ̈ܝܐ *middle age.*

ܦܠܓܝܘܣ and ܦܠܓܝܘܣ πλάγιος, *plagal,* belonging to the second set of tones in church music.

ܦܠܘܢܐ and ܦܠܘܢ m. φελόνιον, *a cloak, long garment; a eucharistic vestment worn by priests.*

ܦܠܚܘܬܐ rt. ܦܠܚ. f. with ܟܐܦ̈ܐ *stone-hewing, masonry.*

ܦܠܢܝܛܐ m. pl. πλάνητες, *the planets.* Cf. ܦܠܢܛ.

ܦܠܢܝܛܝܐ m. πλανητεία, *wandering.*

ܦܠܢܓܠܐ f. *trigonella, fenugreek.*

ܦܠܢܩܘܬܐ rt. ܦܠܩ. f. *crookedness* esp. of the beard.

ܦܠܢܦܘܢ or ܦܠܢܝܦܘܢ *mustard seed.*

ܦܠܢܪܘܦܘܪܝܐ pl. ܘܬ, f. πληροφορία, *full assurance, full conviction.*

ܦܠܢܪܘܦܘܪܝܣܐ with ܥܒܕ. πληροφορῆσαι, *to assure, to be fully assured.*

ܦܠܢܪܘܦܘܪܝܛܝܢܐ πληροφορηθῆναι, *to be assured, fully persuaded.*

ܦܠܢܪܝܣ πλήρης, *full;* with ܒ *in full.*

ܦܠܣܘܣ and ܦܠܣܘܣܐ *having the canine teeth projecting.*

ܦܠܩ Peal only part. ܦܠܝܩ, ܦܠܝܩܐ. *curved* as a vessel; *crooked* as a beard. Ethpe. ܐܬܦܠܩ *to be curved, crooked.* Derivative, ܦܠܢܩܘܬܐ.

ܦܠܡܘܣ; see ܦܠܣܘܣ.

ܦܠܡܘܠܝܢ m. pl. Lat. flammula, *a little banner.*

ܦܠܡܘܢܝ; see ܦܠܡܘܢܝ.

ܦܠܡܝܪܝܐ pl. ܦܠܡܝܪ̈ܝܐ or ܦܠܡ̈ Palmyrene, from ܦܠܡܝܪܐ *Palmyra.*

ܦܠܢ m. ܦܠܢܝܐ, ܦܠܢܝܬܐ f. *so and so, a certain one, such an one; such and such, some or other;* ܐܢܐ ܦܠܢ ܒܪ ܦܠܢ ܡܢ ܩܘܪܝܐ ܦܠܢ *I N. son of N. of N.,* ܓܘܗܪܐ ܦܠܢ ܕܒܥܩܕܐ ܕܦܠܢܝܬܐ ܐܢܬܬܐ *a certain gem in the necklace of a certain woman.*

ܦܠܣ = ܦܘܠܣܐ *a small copper coin.*

ܦܠܣܘܣ Lat. falsus, *forged.*

ܦܠܣܘܪܐ pl. ܐ̈ m. Lat. pressura, *a press, a mangle.*

ܦܠܣܘܪܘܬܐ f. *a strict fast, severe fasting.*

ܦܠܣܛܘܝ πλαστοί, m. pl. *forged.* Cf. ܦܠܣܛܘܣ.

ܦܠܣܛܝܢܐ, ܦܠܣܛܝܢ, ܦܠܣܛܝܢܐ, ܦܠܣܛ also ܦܠܣ f. *Palestine.*

ܦܠܣܛܝܢܝܐ pl. ܐ̈ from the above: *Palestinian, an inhabitant of Palestine.*

ܦܠܣܛܘܣ pl. the same, πλαστός, *forged, fictitious.*

ܦܠܣܦ denom. verb Palpel conj. from ܦܝܠܣܘܦܐ. *to live as a philosopher* = ascetically. Ethpalp. ܐܬܦܠܣܦ *to have studied philosophy, profess to be a philosopher.*

ܦܠܣܪܐ Lat. falsarius, *babbling, raving; false.*

ܦܠܣܪܘܬܐ f. *falsifying, falsification.*

ܦܠܛ fut. ܢܦܠܛ. *to shake off* the yoke; with ܐܘܪܚܐ *to turn out of the way.* Ethpe. ܐܬܦܠܛ *to be shaken off.* Pa. ܦܠܛ same as Peal. Aph. ܐܦܠܛ *to shake off, shake free;* ܐܦܠܛ ܩܕܠܗ ܡܢ ܢܝܪܐ *he shook free his shoulder from the yoke.* Derivatives, ܦܠܛܐ, ܦܠܛܐ, ܡܦܠܛܢܘܬܐ.

ܦܠܛ, ܦܠܛܐ rt. ܦܠܛ. m. *a) occasion, opportunity.* *b)* alchem. a name for tin.

ܦܠܛܐ rt. ܦܠܛ. m. *shaking off* the yoke.

ܦܠܦܠ Palpel conj. of ܦܠ.

ܦܠܦܠ, ܦܠܦܠܐ pl. ܐ̈ Sanskrit f. *pepper.*

ܦܠܦܠܡܘܪ Sanskrit *pepper-root,* an Indian drug.

ܦܠܨܘܪܐ m. *a bookbinder's press.* Cf. ܦܠܣܘܪܐ.

ܦܠܩܐ πάλλαξ -ίς -ή, f. *a concubine.*

ܦܠܩܐ pl. ܐ̈ πέλεκυς, m. *an axe.*

ܦܠܩܝܢܐ πελέκιον, m. *a hatchet.*

ܦܠܩܣ, ܦܠܩܘܣ- or ܦܠܩܝܢ, ܦܠܩܣ and ܦܠܐܩܣ f. pl. πλάξ, πλάκες, *tables of stone.*

ܦܠܫ fut. ܢܦܠܘܫ, act. part. ܦܠܫ, ܦܠܫܐ, pass. part. ܦܠܝܫ, ܐ, ܬܐ. *a) to break through, undermine, dig through a wall;* ܦܠܫܝ ܫܘܪܐ *housebreakers, burglars;* ܦܠܫ ܣܝܡܬܐ *he dug through to a treasure, found a treasure by digging.* Pass. part. *broken into, nicked, notched.* Metaph. *to see into, to fathom;* of dreams *to issue, result.* Ethpe. ܐܬܦܠܫ *to be dug through, broken into* as a house. Pa. ܦܠܫ *to force a way into, to pierce;* pass. part. ܡܦܠܫ *rent, worn, riddled.* Derivatives, ܦܠܫܐ, ܦܠܫܬܐ, ܦܘܠܫܐ, ܦܘܠܫܬܐ.

ܦܠܫܐ rt. ܦܠܫ. m. *violation.*

ܦܠܫܐ, ܦܠܫܬܐ rt. ܦܠܫ. f. ܦܠܫܬܐ ܕܐܘܪ̈ܚܬܐ *the parting of the ways.*

ܦܠܫܘܢܐ m. *a doorhandle.*

ܦܠܬܐ cf. ܦܠܐ. f. *a vial, vessel* of holy oil.

ܦܠܬܐܝܬ = ܦܠܐܝܬ *allegorically.*

ܦܠܬܪܐ pl. ܝܢ, ܐ̈ *a)* πλέθρον, a measure of land = 100 poles. *b) a sown field.* *c) a dish, basin.*

ܦܶܢܛܶܐ πέντε, *five.*

ܦܰܡܶܠܝܳܐ pl. ܐ̈ـ Lat. famulus, *a servant.*

ܦܶܢܳܐ φήνη, *the ossifrage.*

ܦܢܳܐ and ܦܢܳܝ, fut. ܢܶܦܢܶܐ, act. part. ܦܳܢܶܐ, ܦܳܢܝܳܐ. *to turn* with ܠ or ܠܘܳܬ *towards* or *upon; to decline* as the sun, the day; *to return; to repent;* with another verb *again, back;* ܕܦܳܢܶܐ ܠܬܰܝܡܢܳܐ *which turns towards the south;* ܦܢܳܐ ܠܶܗ ܝܰܘܡܳܐ *the day declined;* ܦܢܳܐ ܗܘܳܐ ܫܰܕܪܶܗ *he sent him back.* ETHPE. ܐܶܬܦܢܺܝ *a) to turn, turn towards, betake oneself* with ܠ, ܠܘܳܬ, ܠܘܳܬ of place or pers. esp. with the notion of heeding, regarding; ܐܶܬܦܢܰܝ ܡܳܪܝ ܦܰܪܩܳܗ ܠܢܰܦܫܝ *return, O Lord, deliver my soul.* Esp. in O. T. ܕܡܶܬܦܢܶܐ ܠܘܳܬܝ *he who has turned unto Me* i. e. to God, *a convert, proselyte.* *b) to turn back, return; to be converted;* ܡܶܢ ܡܰܘܬܳܐ ܠܚܰܝܶܐ ܐܶܬܦܢܰܝܰܬ *she returned from death to life;* ܐܶܬܦܢܰܘ ܡܶܢ ܐܽܘܪܚܳܬܟܽܘܢ ܒܺܝܫܳܬܳܐ *turn ye from your evil ways. c) to be returned, rendered* (rare, cf. Ethpaal); ܐܰܓܪܳܐ ܗܳܢܳܐ ܐܶܬܦܢܺܝ ܠܝ ܡܶܢܗܽܘܢ *this reward was rendered me by them.* PA. ܦܰܢܺܝ *to return, restore* a deposit, possession; *to give back, grant;* with ܦܶܬܓܳܡܳܐ, ܡܶܠܬܳܐ or ellipt. *to answer; to make responses* in the liturgy. ETHPA. ܐܶܬܦܰܢܺܝ *a) to be restored, given back, returned* to the owner; *to be rewarded. b)* with ܫܶܐܠܬܳܐ *a request, to be granted. c) to be answered, returned answer. d) to turn.* APH. ܐܰܦܢܺܝ *to cause to turn, turn* trans. *a) to make to return, bring back;* ܟܰܕ ܡܰܦܢܶܐ ܡܳܪܝܳܐ ܫܶܒܝܳܬܳܐ ܕܨܶܗܝܽܘܢ *when the Lord turns again the captivity of Zion. b) to give back, restore;* ܠܳܐ ܨܒܰܘ ܠܡܰܦܢܳܝܽܘ ܡܕܺܝܢܬܳܐ *they were unwilling to give back the city. c) to convert, turn* ܡܶܢ ܛܽܘܥܝܳܝܬܳܐ *from error;* ܠܘܳܬ ܡܳܪܝܳܐ *to the Lord.* With nouns: ܐܰܦܢܺܝ ܐ̈ܦܶܐ *to turn the face* away, also *to turn* towards; ܐ̈ܦܶܐ *to turn towards, set out; to expect;* ܚܨܳܐ, ܡܰܦܢܳܐ *to turn the back, to flee;* ܢܰܦܫܳܐ *to restore the soul.* DERIVATIVES, ܦܢܳܝܳܐ, ܦܳܢܝܳܐ, ܦܢܺܝܳܐ, ܦܢܺܝܬܳܐ, ܦܢܳܝܬܳܐ, ܦܢܳܝܘܬܳܐ, ܡܰܦܢܝܳܢܳܐ, ܡܰܦܢܝܳܢܘܬܳܐ, ܡܶܬܦܰܢܝܳܢܳܐ, ܡܶܬܦܰܢܝܳܢܳܐܝܬ, ܡܶܬܦܰܢܝܳܢܘܬܳܐ.

ܦܶܢܕܳܩܳܐ or ܩܺܐ pl. ܐ̈ـ m. *the filbert.*

ܦܰܢܕܶܩܛܶܣ and ܦܰܢܕܶܩܛܺܝܣ, ܦܰܢܕ̈ܩ πανδέκτης, *a) a complete copy of the Holy Scriptures. b) a place of burial for strangers.*

ܦܢܶܛܳܐ = ܦܶܢܛܶܐ, in the Lexx.

ܦܶܢܛܰܕܝܳܐ, ܦܶܢܛܰܕܺܝܰܐ πενταδία, *consisting of five.*

ܦܽܘܢܛܽܘܢܳܐ pl. ܐ̈ـ Lat. pontonium, *a heavy river boat;* also *a pontoon.*

ܦܰܢܛܽܘܣ πάντως, *altogether, by all means.*

ܦܶܢܛܺܝܩܽܘܣܛܺܐ, ܦܶܢܛ̈ܝ — ܦܢ̈ܛ — ܦܢ̈ܛ Πεντηκοστή, *Pentecost.*

ܦܰܢܛܶܣ denom. verb PALPEL conj. from ܦܰܢܛܰܣܝܰܐ. *to cause illusions, play juggling tricks, represent to the imagination.* ETHPALP. ܐܶܬܦܰܢܛܰܣ *to imagine, to represent to oneself.*

ܦܰܢܛܰܣܝܰܐ and ܦܰܢܛܰܣܝܰܐ pl. ܦܰܢܛܰܣܝܰܣ φαντασία, f. *a) display, ostentation. b)* one of the five mental senses, cf. ܪܶܓܫܳܐ; *imagination, power of forming mental images. c) a fancy, imagination, phantasm, apparition; an effigy; vain show;* ܒܰܦܢܛܰܣܝܰܐ *in appearance* opp. ܒܫܳܪܺܝܪܳܐܝܬ *in truth.* DERIVATIVES, verb ܦܰܢܛܶܣ, ܦܰܢܛܰܣܝܳܐ, ܦܰܢܛܰܣܛܳܐ, ܡܦܰܢܛܣܳܢܳܐ, ܡܶܬܦܰܢܛܣܳܢܳܐ.

ܦܰܢܛܰܣܝܳܢܳܐ and ܦܰܢܛܰܣܛܺܝܩܳܐ, ܐ̈ـ from ܦܰܢܛܰܣܝܰܐ. *of the imagination, imaginary, illusory.*

ܦܰܢܛܰܣܡܳܐ pl. ܦܰܢܛܰܣܡܰܛܳܐ φάντασμα -τα, *a phantom, illusion.*

ܦܢܳܐ, ܦܢܺܝܬܳܐ pl. ܦ̈ܢܝܳܢ, ܦ̈ܢܝܳܬܳܐ rt. ܦܢܐ. f. *region, district, quarter;* ܐܰܪܒܰܥ ܦ̈ܢܝܳܢ *the four quarters* of the globe; ܦܢܺܝܬܳܐ ܓܰܪܒܝܳܝܬܳܐ *the northern regions;* ܒܟܽܠ ܦ̈ܢܝܳܢ *everywhere;* ܠܦܢܺܝܬ *towards;* ܡܶܢ ܦܢܺܝܬܳܐ French *de la part de . . .; from, to represent . . . .*

ܦܢܳܝܳܐ rt. ܦܢܐ. m. with ܕܰܝܘܡܳܐ. *the turn of the day, declining day, early evening;* metaph. ܦܢܳܝܶܗ ܕܣܳܒܽܘܬܳܐ *declining age;* ܕܚܰܪܬܳܐ *the last age of the world.*

ܦܢܳܝܳܐ rt. ܦܢܐ. m. *turning, return, inclination; sound, cry.*

ܦܢܳܝܳܝܳܐ rt. ܦܢܐ. adj. *of the evening.*

ܦܢܳܝܬܳܐ rt. ܦܢܐ. f. *a) turning, return. b) early evening meal.*

ܦܢܺܝܬܳܐ; see ܦܢܳܐ above.

ܦܰܢܶܩ denom. verb Pael conj. from ܐܶܦܢܩܳܐ. *to depict.* ETHPA. ܐܶܬܦܰܢܰܩ or ܐܶܬܦܰܢܰܩ *to be made like, to be depicted; to be hindered, slackened.*

ܦܢܳܩܳܐ pl. ܐ̈ـ = ܦܝܢܳܟܳܐ *a paten, dish.*

ܦܢܺܝܩܳܐ *base; a bastard.*

ܦܢܳܩܳܐ or ܦܢܺܝܩܳܐ, ܦܶܢܩܶܣ, ܦܺܝܢܩܽܘܣ, ܦܺܝܢܩܳܐ pl. ܐ̈ـ

m. φανός, *a torch, lantern, lamp, candlestick, socket for a candle.*

ܦܢܛܦܝܩܘܣ = ܦܣܛܦܩܘܣ. *a parrot.*

ܦܢܣܠܝܢܘܣ, ܦܢܣܠܢܘܣ, ܦܢܣܠܢ &c. f. πανσέληνος, *full moon.*

ܦܢܩ Pael ܦܰܢܶܩ *to treat with affection, indulge, give pleasure, feed luxuriously.* Part. ܡܦܰܢܩܳܐ, ܡܦܰܢܩܳܐ, ܡܦܰܢܩܳܢܺܝܬܳܐ *delighting, delightful; luxurious, tender, delicate;* ܦܰܓ̈ܪܶܐ ܡܦܰܢܩ̈ܶܐ *pampered bodies;* ܡܦܰܢܩ̈ܶܐ *those who live in luxury* opp. ܟ̈ܢܳܫܳܐ *hermits.* Ethpa. ܐܶܬܦܰܢܰܩ *to delight oneself, enjoy to the full, live luxuriously, to revel; to be pampered;* ܬܶܬܦܰܢܰܩ ܢܰܦܫܟܽܘܢ ܒܕܽܘܗܢܳܐ *let your soul delight itself in fatness;* ܡܶܬܦܰܢܩܳܢ ܒܐܰܓܽܘ̈ܢܶܐ ܕܡܰܝܬܪܽܘܬܳܐ *revelling in struggles after virtue.* Derivatives, ܦܢܩܐ, ܡܦܢܩܢܐ, ܡܦܢܩܢܘܬܐ, ܡܬܦܢܩܢܘܬܐ, ܐܦܢܩܐ.

ܦܢܩܝܕܝܢ πινακίδιον, f. an old and rare form for ܦܢܩܝܬܐ *a volume.*

ܦܢܩܝܢܐ m. *writer of a codex.*

ܦܢܩܝܬܐ pl. ܦܢ̈ܩܶܐ, ܦܢܩܝ̈ܬܐ f. πίναξ, πινακίς, πινακίδιον, *a writing-tablet,* ܕܢܚܳܫܳܐ *a tablet of brass; a letter, volume, book.*

ܦܣܬܐ m. *a) the upper leather* of a shoe, *a leathern patch. b) the back* of the hand, *instep* of the foot.

ܦܢܬܝܪ or ܦܢܬܪ m. πανθήρ, *a panther, leopard.*

ܦܣܝܣ pass. part. ܦܣܝܣܐ, ܦܣܝܣܬܐ. *allowed, permitted;* with ܠܐ *forbidden* usually eccles. ܡܫܰܡܫܳܢܳܐ ܠܐ ܦܣܝܣ ܠܡܩܰܕܳܫܽܘ ܐ̄ܪ̈ܳܙܶܐ *a deacon is not allowed to consecrate the mysteries.* Ethpe. ܐܶܬܦܣܶܣ *to be allowed, permitted;* ܐܶܬܦܣܶܣ ܠܶܗ ܕܢܶܥܽܘܠ ܠܘܳܬ ܡܰܠܟܳܐ *he was allowed to enter the royal presence.* Pa. ܦܰܣܶܣ *to grant.* Aph. ܐܰܦܣܶܣ *a) to grant permission, give leave, allow, permit;* ܐܶܢ ܡܰܦܣܶܣ ܐܢ̄ܬ ܠܝ *if you allow me;* ܐܰܦܣܶܣ ܠܰܢ ܕܢܫܰܒܚܳܟ *grant that we may glorify Thee;* part. ܡܰܦܣܰܣ *it is permitted, allowed;* ܠܐ ܡܰܦܣܰܣ *it is forbidden, unlawful. b)* denom. from ܦܣܐ, ܦܣܬܐ. *to cast lots.* Ethtap. ܐܶܬܬܰܦܣܰܣ *to obtain by lot; to be allowed.* Derivatives, ܦܣܝܣܐ, ܦܣܝܣܘܬܐ, ܡܦܣܢܘܬܐ.

ܦܘܣܐ pl. ܦܘ̈ܣܐ = ܦܘܣܐ m. Lat. fossa, *a fosse, trench.*

ܦܣܐ, ܦܣܬܐ pl. ܦܣ̈ܐ, ܦܣ̈ܬܐ f. *a) the palm* of the hand, *sole* of the foot; a measure of length, ܚܕܳܐ ܦܶܣܬܳܐ ܕܪܶܓܠܳܐ *one foot. b) a towel, clout.*

ܦܣܐ, ܦܣܬܐ pl. ܦܣ̈ܐ a softened form of ܦܨܐ. generally f. *a) a lot, an allotted portion; casting lots, divining by lot; a ballot, suffrage;* with ܪܡܳܐ, ܐܰܪܡܺܝ or ܢܦܰܠ *to cast lots;* ܢܦܰܠ *the lot fell;* ܡܛܳܐ *the lot came,* &c. *b) wing* of an army, *line* of battle. *c) page* of a book.

ܦܣܐ m. pl. *freckles.*

ܦܣܘܠܐ pl. ܠܶܐ rt. ܦܣܠ. m. *a) a stone-cutter, stone-mason. b) an axe, a chisel.*

ܦܣܠܝܘܢ m. ψύλλιον, *plantago psyllium, flea-wort.*

ܦܣܘܩܐ, ܦܣܘܩܬܐ rt. ܦܣܩ. *cutting; one who cuts; a section* of a book, *an aphorism.* Gram. *a word* or *point breaking off* a phrase; *a full stop.*

ܦܣܝܩܐܝܬ rt. ܦܣܩ. adv. *absolutely.*

ܦܣܘܩܝܘܬܐ rt. ܦܣܩ. f. *excision.*

ܦܣܘܩܢܐ, ܦܣܘܩܢܝܬܐ rt. ܦܣܩ. *cutting;* ܫ̈ܢܶܐ ܦܣܘܩܢܝ̈ܬܐ *the incisors.*

ܦܣܛܓܐ βαστραγή, *baggage.*

ܦܣܛܝܠ *jujube syrup.*

ܦܣܛܘܠܐ or ܦܣܛܝܠܐ pl. ܠܶܐ ἐπιστύλιον, *a peristyle, colonnade.*

ܦܣܛܠ denom. verb from ܦܣܛܘܠܐ. *to surround with pillars.*

ܦܣܛܪܐ ξύστρα, m. *a plane.*

ܦܣܝܐ m. *a file; a whetstone.*

ܦܣܝܘܢܐ m. *a)* same as ܦܣܝܐ. *b) a river-bottom, deep hole in a river.*

ܦܣܛܩܘܣ, ܦܣܝܛܩܘܣ, ܦܣܛܩ &c. pl. ܦܣܛ̈ܩܐ f. ψίττακος, *a parrot.*

ܦܣܠܘܬܐ rt. ܦܣܠ. f. *stone-cutting, quarrying.*

ܦܣܠܝܡ rt. ܦܣܠ. Heb. m. *a stone-quarry* or *sculptures.*

ܦܣܠܬܐ rt. ܦܣܠ. f. *a stone-quarry; a hewn stone.*

ܦܣܡܝܬܝܢ ψιμύθιον, *white-lead.*

ܦܣܝܢܐ and ܦܐܣܢ pl. ܠܶܐ m. φασιανός, *a pheasant.*

ܦܣܢܐ m. *a ploughshare.*

ܦܣܝܣ and ܦܐܣܝܣ φάσις, f. *a) a declaration, decision. b) appearance.*

ܦܣܝܣ, ܦܣܝܣܬܐ; see under ܦܣ.

ܦܣܝܦܣܡܐ and ܦܣܦܣ ψήφισμα, *a decree, act, vote.*

ܦܣܝܩܐܝܬ rt. ܦܣܩ. adv. *shortly, concisely.*

ܦܣܝܩܘܬܐ rt. ܦܣܩ. f. *separation, refraining;* ܒܦܣܝܩܘ *briefly.*

ܦܣܝܩܐ pl. ܐ̈ rt. ܦܣܩ. *short, abridged, compendious.*

ܦܣܝܩܬܐ pl. ܬ̈ܐ rt. ܦܣܩ. f. usually pl. *a decision, thing determined, judgement;* ܝܘܡܐ ܕܦܣܝ̈ܩܬܐ *the day of judgement.* With preps. ܒܦܣܝ̈ܩܬܐ *briefly, shortly, in few words;* with ܥܒܕ *to abridge;* ܕܦܣܝ̈ܩܬܐ *in brief, abridged;* ܡ̈ܠܐ ܕܦܣܝ̈ܩܬܐ *apophthegms.*

ܦܨܚ, ܦܨܚܐ πάσχα = ܦܨܚܐ *the passover; Easter;* also *the fast before Easter,* ܨܘܡ ܬܠܬܝܢ ܕܦܨܚܐ *Lent.*

ܦܣܥ act. part. ܦܣܥ, ܦܣܥܬܐ. *to make a step,* perh. *to crawl.*

ܦܣܠ fut. ܢܦܣܘܠ, act. part. ܦܣܠ, ܦܣܠܐ, pass. part. ܦܣܝܠ, ܠܐ, ܠܬܐ. *to quarry, hew* stone; ܦܣ̈ܠܝ ܟܐ̈ܦܐ *hewers of stone;* ܟܐ̈ܦܐ ܦܣܝ̈ܠܬܐ and ellipt. *hewn stones, squared stones.* Ethpe. ܐܬܦܣܠ *to be hewn, quarried.* Derivatives, ܦܣܠܐ, ܦܣܝܠܘܬܐ, ܦܣܝܠܝܢ, ܦܣܝܠܬܐ, ܡܦܣܠܬܐ.

ܦܣܠܛܘܬܐ f. *psalmody.*

ܦܣܠܛܐ, ܦܣܠܛܝ, ܦܣܠܛܐ, ܦܣܠܛܝܣ pl. ܦܣܠܛܘ, ܦܣܠܛܐ m. ψάλτης, *a chanter, church singer.*

ܦܣܠܛܪܝܢ and ܦܣܠܛܪܝܘܢ m. ψαλτήρ, ψαλτήριον, *a psalter, book of psalms.*

ܦܣܡܐ m. *a moustache.*

ܦܣܢܣܢ m. *the male flower of the palm.*

ܦܣܣܐ rt. ܦܣ. m. *permission, favour;* ܐܝܟ ܦܣܣܐ *by favour.*

ܦܣܣܘܬܐ rt. ܦܣ. f. *permission.*

ܦܣܥ fut. ܢܦܣܘܥ, act. part. ܦܣܥ, ܦܣܥܐ. *a*) *to step* or *go forward, advance, proceed;* ܦܣܥ ܘܥܠ ܠܬܚܘܡܗܘܢ *he advanced and entered their border.* Metaph. with ܥܠ *to overstep, go beyond bounds, transgress;* ܥܠ ܡܫܘܚܬܐ *to go beyond measure;* ܦܣܥܝܢ ܥܠ ܗܘ ܢܡܘܣܐ ܕܡܢ ܩܕܝܡ *they transgress that ancient law of Moses. b*) *to take steps, make foolish attempts, presume;* ܡܠܟܐ ܕܦܣܥ ܥܠ ܡܘܬܪ̈ܬܐ ܘܠܐ ܪܘܪ̈ܒܬܐ *a king who attempts great things foolishly and unadvisedly. c*) *to step upon, tread under with scorn, trample upon;* ܟܕ ܦܣܥ ܥܠ ܡܘܬܐ *despising death;* ܦܣܥ ܥܠ ܫܝܛܘܬܐ *he trampled upon contempt.* Ethpe. ܐܬܦܣܥ *to advance.* Pa. ܦܣܥ *to tread out, tread apart.* Derivatives, ܦܣܘܥܐ, ܦܣܥܬܐ.

ܦܣܥܐ, ܦܣܥܬܐ or ܦܣܥܬܐ pl. ܦܣܥܝܢ, ܦܣܥ̈ܬܐ rt. ܦܣܥ. f. *a*) *a step, pace;* a measure of length, two ܐܡ̈ܝܢ *cubits* make one ܦܣܥܬܐ *pace,* 1000 paces make one ܡܝܠܐ *mile. b*) *a hole* or *opening* in the lappet of an under-garment.

ܦܣܦܣܐ pl. ܐ̈ m. ψῆφος -ίς, *dice; a pebble, a piece* in a game.

ܦܣܩ fut. ܢܦܣܘܩ, infin. ܡܦܣܩ, act. part. ܦܣܩ, ܦܣܩܐ, pass. part. ܦܣܝܩ, ܩܐ, ܩܬܐ. *to hew* wood, stones, *to cut down; to cut off, mutilate, castrate; to break off, come to an end; to interrupt, to decide, determine, decree, pass sentence; to excommunicate; to agree, make an agreement;* with ܠܬܪܝܢ *to cut in two, divide;* ܦܣܩܘ ܚܘܝܐ ܕܢܚܫܐ *they brake in pieces the brazen serpent;* ܦܣܩ ܫܘܠܡܐ ܕܢܒ̈ܝܐ *the line of prophets broke off, came to an end;* ܦܣܩ ܡܢ ܡܐܟܘܠܬܐ ܦܣܩܘ ܠܢܦܫܗܘܢ *he determined;* *they refrained from food.* With ܐܘܪܚܐ *to cross the road; to interrupt his journey; to close the way;* also *to open a way;* ܣܘܦܩܢܘܬܐ *to cut off supplies;* ܕܝܢܐ *to give judgement;* ܕܡܝܐ *to settle the price, value;* ܕܫ̈ܢܐ *to withhold gifts;* ܗܕܡ ܗܕܡ *to hew limb from limb;* ܕܘܟܪܢܐ *to stop the recitation of a Bishop's name in the liturgy;* ܡܕܐܬܐ *to refuse tribute* but with ܥܠ *to impose tribute upon;* ܡܘܬܐ *to be certain of death, resigned to death;* ܡܡܠܠܐ *to interrupt, break off* communications; ܣܒܪܐ *to despair;* ܣܥܪܐ *to cut the hair, give tonsure;* ܥܝܕܐ *to interrupt, break a custom;* ܪܫܐ *to behead;* ܦܣܩܝ ܚܕ̈ܬܬܐ *innovators.* Pass. part. *mutilated, castrated;* ܦܣܝܩ ܐܝܕܐ *maimed of one hand; excommunicate; settled, determined;* gram. *abbreviated.*

Ethpe. *to be cut, hewn down* as wood; *to be cut off, slain; to be cut out* or *off, mutilated; to be in rags* as clothes; *to be broken, interrupted* as a genealogy, line of succession; *to be shut up; to be excommunicate, under interdict;*

to be determined, decreed with ܥܠ *concerning;* with ܣܒܪܐ *hope was cut off, was lost;* ܦܣܝܩܬܐ ܕܠܐ ܡܬܦܣܩܢ *atoms.* PAEL ܦܰܣܶܩ *to cut to bits, hew up, cut off* the lesser members of the body, *break into fragments, cut* or *break many small things* as bonds, meshes of a net; pass. part. pl. ܡܦܰܣܩܳܐ *small change, clipped coin.* ETHPA. ܐܶܬܦܰܣܰܩ *to be cut to pieces; to be castrated.* DERIVATIVES, ܦܣܘܩܐ, ܦܣܘܩܝܐ, ܦܣܘܩܐ, ܦܣܘܩܝܬ, ܦܣܘܩܘܬܐ, ܦܣܘܩܐ, ܦܣܝܩܝܬ, ܦܣܝܩܘܬܐ, ܦܣܝܩܐ, ܦܣܩܬܐ, ܦܣܩܐ, ܦܣܩܐ, ܦܣܩܬܐ, ܡܦܣܩܢܐ, ܡܬܦܣܩܢܐ, ܡܬܦܣܩܢܝܬ, ܡܬܦܣܩܢܘܬܐ.

ܦܣܩ, ܦܣܩܐ pl. ܐ̈ rt. ܦܣܩ. m. *a) cutting, hewing; amputation, mutilation; excommunication, interdict; a decree, precept, sentence; interruption;* ܒܦܣܩܐ *in short, finally;* ܒܦܣܩܐ ܕܚܪܡܐ or ܬܚܝܬ ܦܣܩܐ *under anathema. b) a cut, part; a division. c)* in imitation of Arabic usage *a flock, herd.* With ܒܣܪܐ *concision, cutting of the flesh;* ܦܣܩܐ ܕܕܝܢܐ *a judicial decision;* ܦܣܩܐ ܕܕܡܐ *stopping a flow of blood;* ܦܣܩ ܣܒܪܐ *despair;* ܦܣܩ ܣܥܪܐ *hair-cutting;* ܦܣܩ ܪܫܐ *beheading;* ܦܣܩܐ gram. *an abbreviation.*

ܦܣܩܐ pl. ܐ̈ rt. ܦܣܩ. m. *a cloth, rag.*

ܦܣܩܝܢ, ܦܣܩܝܢܐ pl. ܦܣܩܝܢܣ or ܦܣܩܝܢܘܣ com. gen., Lat. piscina, *a fishpond, tank, cistern.*

ܦܣܩܝܬܐ pl. ܐ̈ܬܐ rt. ܦܣܩ. f. *a bed-quilt; a bandage, swathing-band, grave-clothes.*

ܦܣܩܦܣ ETHPALPAL ܐܶܬܦܰܣܩܦܰܣ denom. verb from ܐܦܣܩܘܦܐ. *to be made a bishop, be raised to the episcopate.*

ܦܰܣܰܪ PAAL conj. *to annul, render void* esp. *to reject* witness.

ܦܣܬܐ see ܦܣܬܐ; ܦܣܬܐ see ܦܣܬܐ.

ܦܣܬܘܩܐ pl. ܐ̈ Pers. m. *a narrow-necked wide-mouthed jug;* cf. ܒܣܬܘܩܐ.

ܦܣܬܠܐ pl. ܦܣܬܠܐ, ܦܣܬܠܐ *matting.*

ܦܣܬܩܐ pl. ܐ̈ m. πιστάκη, *the pistachio-tree, pistachio-nut;* ܦܣܬܩܐ ܕܗܢܕܘ *nutmeg.*

ܦܥܐ fut. ܢܦܥܐ, act. part. ܦܳܥܶܐ, ܦܳܥܝܐ, pass. part. ܦܥܝܐ, ܐ̈, ܝܐ̈. *a) to beat with a stick, to batter, strike down;* ܦܥܝܗ ܒܟܐܦܐ ܠܪܫܗ *he battered in his head with stones;* pass. part. *battered, beaten, bruised, worn. b) to hatch eggs;* cf. ܢܦܥ. ETHPE. ܐܶܬܦܥܝ *to be beaten with a stick* as a dog; *to be crushed.* PA. ܦܰܥܝ *to bruise, crush.* ETHPA. ܐܶܬܦܰܥܝ *to be badly bruised* or *crushed.* DERIVATIVES, ܦܥܝܘܬܐ, ܦܥܝܐ, ܡܦܥܝܢܘܬܐ.

ܦܥܐ and ܦܥܐ fut. ܢܦܥܐ, act. part. ܦܳܥܶܐ, ܦܳܥܝܐ. *to bleat, baa;* metaph. of children calling for their mother and of senseless speech. DERIVATIVES, ܦܥܝܐ, ܦܥܝܐ.

ܦܥܘܠܐ pl. ܐ̈ rt. ܦܥܠ. m. *a labourer.*

ܦܥܝܐ pl. ܐ̈ rt. ܦܥܐ. m. *one who bleats.*

ܦܥܝܐ rt. ܦܥܐ. m. *bleating.*

ܦܥܝܥܘܬܐ and ܦܥܝܥܘܬܐ rt. ܦܥ. f. *a broken head, bruise.*

ܦܥܝܪܘܬܐ rt. ܦܥܪ. f. ܦܥܝܪܘܬܐ ܕܦܘܡܐ *opening the mouth wide, gaping.*

ܦܥܠ fut. ܢܦܥܘܠ, act. part. ܦܳܥܶܠ, ܦܳܥܠܐ. *to labour.* DERIVATIVES, ܦܥܘܠܐ, ܦܥܠܐ, ܦܥܠܐ, ܦܥܠܘܬܐ.

ܦܥܠܐ rt. ܦܥܠ. m. *hired labour, day labour.*

ܦܥܠܐ pl. ܐ̈ rt. ܦܥܠ. m. *an hired labourer, day labourer.*

ܦܥܠܘܬܐ and ܦܥܠ rt. ܦܥܠ. f. *daily labour, service; course of action.*

ܦܥܥܐ rt. ܦܥ. m. *a broken head, a bruise.*

ܦܥܪ fut. ܢܦܥܘܪ, parts. ܦܳܥܶܪ, ܦܳܥܪܐ and ܦܥܝܪ, ܐ̈, ܬܐ̈. *to open wide, to gape* as the mouth, the earth, sores; ܦܥܝܪܝܢ ܥܝܢܘܗܝ *his eyes were distended;* ܚܟܐ ܦܥܝܪܐ *a craving palate.* ETHPA. ܐܶܬܦܰܥܰܪ *to be made to gape.* DERIVATIVES, ܦܥܪܐ, ܦܥܝܪܘܬܐ, ܦܥܪܐ, ܦܥܪܐ.

ܦܥܪܐ E-Syr. ܦܥܪܐ, pl. ܐ̈ rt. ܦܥܪ. m. *a cleft, chasm, gap;* ܦܥܪܐ ܕܡܥܪܬܐ *the opening of the cave.*

ܦܥܪܐ rt. ܦܥܪ. m. *opening wide* of the mouth.

ܦܥܪܬܐ f. *piper cubeba, cubeb.*

ܦܦܐ or ܦܐܦܐ pl. ܦܦܐ̈ πάππας, Papa, m. *pope, father,* a title of bishops and esp. of the patriarchs of Alexandria and Rome, also of Greek priests. ܦܦܐ ܕܪܗܘܡܝ *the pope of Rome;* ܦܦܐ ܕܡܥܪܒܐ *pope of the West* i. e. the patriarch of Antioch. Also a Christian name.

ܦܦܘ, ܦܐܦܘ, ܦܦܝܪܘܣ, ܦܦܘܪܘܣ, ܦܦܝܪ m. πάπυρος, *the papyrus.*

ܦܦܝܐ παπία, vocative, *O Father.*

ܦܪܘܿ imperative of verb ܢܦܰܪ to shake off.

ܦܶܪܳܐ, ܦܶܪܬܳܐ pl. ܦܶܪܺܝܢ, ܦܶܪܶܐ, cf. ܦܰܣܬܳܐ, f. a) a piece, part. b) a column, page of a book; ܒܦܶܪܬܳܐ ܫܒܺܝܥܳܝܬܳܐ on the seventh column; ܦܶܪܶܐ ܫܬܬܳܢܳܝܶܐ the Hexapla version; ܦܶܪܶܐ ܬܡܳܢܝܳܝܶܐ the Octapla. c) a lot, allotted portion, share, claim, title; ܦܶܪܬܳܐ ܕܡܰܠܟܽܘܬܳܐ ܠܟܠ ܡܶܢܝ ܚܛܰܦ he has robbed me of my title to the kingdom; ܗܳܕܶܐ ܦܶܪܬܳܐ ܕܝܰܩܺܝܕܽܘܬܳܐ ܡܫܰܘܬܦܳܐ ܠܳܟ this lot, sentence, of being burnt is assigned thee.

ܦܰܪܳܐ PAEL ܦܰܪܺܝ to deliver, set free; ܦܰܪܶܝܢ ܡܶܢ ܒܺܝܫܳܐ deliver us from evil; ܦܰܪܳܐ ܢܰܦܫܳܟ save thyself. Pass. part. ܡܦܰܪܝܳܐ, ܡܦܰܪܰܝ, guiltless, innocent; ܡܦܰܪܰܝ ܡܶܢ ܚܰܝܳܒܽܘܬܳܐ not liable to the blood-penalty. ETHPA. ܐܶܬܦܰܪܺܝ to be delivered; to escape. DERIVATIVES, ܦܽܘܪܳܝܳܐ, ܡܦܰܪܝܳܢܳܐ, ܡܬܦܰܪܝܳܢܳܐ.

ܦܪܰܕܶܫܬܳܐ Pers. a viceroy.

ܦܪܽܘܣܬܳܐ f. a mark on the forehead of a beast of burden.

ܦܪܰܚ fut. ܢܶܦܪܰܚ. to rejoice, cause rejoicing. Part. adj. ܦܰܪܺܝܚ, ܐ, ܬܳܐ glad, gay, merry; clear, bright, radiant; ܦܰܪܺܝܚ ܒܠܶܒܶܗ glad at heart; ܦܰܪܺܝܚܺܝܢ ܦܰܪܨܽܘܦܰܝܗܽܘܢ their countenances were radiant; ܨܰܦܪܳܐ ܦܰܪܺܝܚܳܐ bright dawn. ETHPE. ܐܶܬܦܪܶܚ to be glad, bright, cheerful; ܗܳܒܶܝܠ ܐܰܝܟ ܟܰܘܟܒܳܐ ܢܰܗܺܝܪܳܐ ܐܶܬܦܪܶܚ Abel was as bright as a shining star. ETHPA. ܐܶܬܦܰܪܰܚ a) to exult, burst forth into song; ܐܶܬܦܰܪܰܚܘ ܛܽܘܪܶܐ ܒܬܶܫܒܽܘܚܬܳܐ break forth into singing, ye mountains. b) to cease raging, become serene. c) to be inaugurated. APH. ܐܰܦܪܰܚ a) to gladden; to make bright, serene, cheerful; with ܐܰܦܶܐ or ܦܰܪܨܽܘܦܳܐ to make to be of a cheerful countenance; ܗܽܘܝܽܘ ܕܡܰܦܪܰܚ ܠܟܰܪܝܶܐ it is He who makes the mournful glad; ܫܽܘܦܪܳܐ ܕܐܰܦܪܰܚ ܠܟܠ the beauty which brought gladness to all. b) to make merry, to joke; ܐܶܡܰܪ ܠܝ ܟܕ ܡܰܦܪܰܚ he said to me in joke. c) from Heb. to keep the passover; ܢܰܦܪܰܚ ܡܳܪܝܳܐ ܥܰܠ ܬܰܪܥܶܐ the Lord will pass over the doors; God gave Moses a lamb ܕܢܰܦܪܰܚ ܥܰܠ ܥܰܡܳܐ to offer the passover for the nation. DERIVATIVES, ܦܽܘܪܚܳܐ, ܦܰܪܺܝܚܳܐܺܝܬ, ܦܰܪܺܝܚܽܘܬܳܐ, ܡܰܦܪܚܳܢܳܐ, ܡܰܦܪܚܳܢܳܐܺܝܬ.

ܦܶܪܚܳܐ pl. ܢ̈ܶܐ Heb. m. a) the passover, feast of the passover, the paschal lamb; ܢܶܟܣܘܽܢ ܦܶܪܚܳܐ slay the passover. b) the Paschal feast, Easter; E-Syr. Maundy Thursday. Cf. ܦܶܨܚܳܐ.

ܦܽܘܪܚܳܐ rt. ܦܪܚ. m. cheerfulness, merriment.

ܦܰܪܰܚ Pael conj.; see ܦܪܰܚ.

ܦܰܪܚܺܝܢ, ܦܰܪܚܳܢܳܐ m. a brook, watercourse, channel; a pond, tank, lake; ܦ̈ ܕܡܰܝܳܐ a pond &c. of water.

ܦܰܪܺܝܚܳܐܺܝܬ rt. ܦܪܚ. adv. gladly, readily, cheerfully, with alacrity.

ܦܰܪܺܝܚܽܘܬܳܐ rt. ܦܪܚ. f. cheerfulness.

ܦܪܰܛ fut. ܢܶܦܪܽܘܛ. to cleave, cut through, make a way through, to open a book; ܦܪܰܛܰܬ ܠܣܶܕܪܶܗ she made a way through the line; ܠܳܐ ܦܪܰܛܘ ܠܓܶܦܰܝܗܽܘܢ Seraphim did not make an opening among their wings, did not fold them asunder, so as to look through and behold the Deity. Pass. part. ܩܰܝܣܳܐ ܕܦܪܺܝܛ ܠܬܪܶܝܢ wood cleft in twain; ܦܪܺܝܛܰܝ ܦܰܪܣܳܬܳܐ cloven-footed. ETHPE. ܐܶܬܦܪܶܛ to be cleft, separated. PA. ܦܰܪܶܛ to cut asunder, divide. ETHPA. ܐܶܬܦܰܪܰܛ to be cut asunder. DERIVATIVE, ܦܶܪܛܳܐ.

ܦܶܪܛܳܐ rt. ܦܪܛ. m. cutting or sawing of wood into planks.

ܦܶܪܬܳܐ; see ܦܶܪܳܐ.

ܦܣܦܣ PAEL ܦܰܣܦܶܣ to babble, prate, talk idly, talk nonsense; ܡܦܰܣܦܣܺܝܢ ܒܡܶܠܶܐ ܣܰܓܺܝܐܳܬܳܐ they talk diffusely and noisily; ܠܳܐ ܬܦܰܣܦܶܣ ܡܶܠܶܐ ܣܪܺܝܩܳܬܳܐ ܘܪܘܓܙܳܢܝܳܬܳܐ do not utter vain and angry words. DERIVATIVES, ܦܣܦܣܳܐ, ܦܣܦܳܣܳܐ, ܦܣܦܳܣܳܐܺܝܬ, ܦܣܦܳܣܽܘܬܳܐ, ܡܦܰܣܦܣܳܢܳܐ.

ܦܩܰܕ fut. ܢܶܦܩܽܘܕ, act. part. ܦܳܩܶܕ, ܦܳܩܕܳܐ, pass. part. ܦܩܺܝܕ, ܐ, ܬܳܐ. a) to visit, inquire, review, see to; ܐܶܦܩܽܘܕ ܚܰܛܗܰܝܗܽܘܢ ܥܠܰܝܗܽܘܢ I will visit their sins upon them; ܦܩܽܘܕܘ ܘܚܙܰܘ ܡܰܢܽܘ ܐܶܙܰܠ ܡܶܢܰܢ number and see who is gone from us. b) to command, order, give command, give charge with ܠ or ܥܰܠ over; also with ܥܰܠ to have the command of, bear rule over; ܦܩܰܕ ܠܥܰܒܕܰܘܗܝ ܕܢܶܫܡܛܽܘܢ ܣܰܦܣܺܝܪܰܝܗܽܘܢ he ordered his servants to draw their swords; ܦܩܰܕ ܠܶܗ ... ܙܽܘܙܶܐ he ordered so many pieces of silver to be given to him; ܦܩܰܕܘ ܥܰܠ ܒܰܝܬܳܝܗܽܘܢ they gave orders concerning their households. Legal, to leave by *will; to adjudge;* with ܕܝܢܐ *to give judgement;* liturg. *to enjoin, to give a rubrical direction;* gram. *to use the imperative tense.* c) *to entreat;* ܦܩܕܝܢ ܬܠܡܝܕܝܟ Thy disciples *entreat Thee to hear them.* d) *to depart, die;* ܥܢܝܕܐ ܕܦܩܕܘ ܡܢܢ *the departed who have left us.* Pass. part. *commanded, ordained, appointed; under orders;* with ܒ or ܥܠ *appointed over, in authority over;* ܦܩܝܕܐ ܕܥܠ ܡܟܣܐ *a publican.* Ethpe. ܐܬܦܩܕ a) *to be sought for, to be missing; to be vacant, empty* as ܕܘܟܬܐ *a place,* ܡܘܬܒܐ *a seat.* b) *to be visited with punishment.* c) *to be commanded.* Pa. ܦܩܕ a) *to give a commission, a charge, a commandment;* ܠܡܠܐܟܘܗܝ ܢܦܩܕ ܥܠܝܟ *He will give His angels charge concerning thee;* with ܥܠ or abs. *to set over.* b) *to give last commands; bequeath;* ܐܢ ܢܦܩܕ ܠܦܛܪܘܣ ܓܢܬܐ *if he leave a garden to Peter.* Ethpa. ܐܬܦܩܕ a) *to be commanded, committed; to receive command;* with ܥܠ *to be set over, put in charge of;* with ܡܢ *to be commanded to abstain from;* ܐܝܠܢܐ ܕܐܬܦܩܕܘ ܡܢܗ *the tree* of knowledge of good and evil *which was forbidden them.* b) *to be bequeathed, devised by will;* ܠܗ ܐܬܦܩܕܬ ܡܠܟܘܬܐ *to him was the kingdom bequeathed.* Derivatives, ܦܘܩܕܢܘܬܐ, ܦܘܩܕܢܐܝܬ, ܦܘܩܕܢܐ, ܦܩܕܐ, ܦܩܝܕܐ, ܦܘܩܕܐ, ܦܩܝܕܘܬܐ, ܦܩܕܘܢܐ, ܦܘܩܕܢܐ, ܦܩܝܕܐܝܬ, ܦܘܩܕܢܘܬܐ, ܡܦܩܕܢܐ, ܡܦܩܕܢܘܬܐ, ܡܦܩܕܢܐܝܬ.

ܦܘܩܕܐ m. a) rt. ܦܩܕ. *a decree, mandate.* b) *a visitation, inquiry, demand.* c) Ar. *a kind of mead flavoured with the leaves and fruit of the Vitex agnus castus.*

ܦܘܩܕܢܐ, ܦܘܩܕܢܝܬܐ rt. ܦܩܕ. a) *a superintendent, director, officer,* esp. *a procurator;* eccles. *the ordinary.* b) gram. *the imperative mood.*

ܦܘܩܕܢܐܝܬ rt. ܦܩܕ. adv. *with command, imperatively;* gram. *in the imperative mood.*

ܦܘܩܕܢܘܬܐ rt. ܦܩܕ. f. *giving command, governing, directing, superintendence; an injunction;* gram. *the imperative mood.*

ܦܩܘܕܐ rt. ܦܩܕ. m. *visitation; seeking, missing.*

ܦܩܘܠܝܢ Lat. peculium, *private property of a slave.*

ܦܩܘܥܐ pl. ܐ̈ rt. ܦܩܥ. m. a) *wild cucumber or gourd;* also ܦܩܘܥ̈ܝܬܐ ܕܬܐܢܐ *unripe figs.* b) *cheese-maggot, cheese-mite.* c) *a bow-legged* or *bandy-legged man.*

ܦܩܘܬܐ = ܦܩܘܬܐ f. *stammering.*

ܦܩܚ *to be flourishing.* Part. fem. ܦܩܚܐ impers. *to be of advantage, be advantageous, suitable, expedient,* ܦܩܚܐ ܗܘ ܠܝ *it is better for me;* ܠܐ ܦܩܚܐ *it is not expedient;* ܐܝܬܝܗܝܢ ܦܩܚܢ ܕܪ̈ܘܫܐ ܕܡܪܕܘܬܐ *suitable modes of training.* Pa. ܦܩܚ a) *to flourish, produce blossoms.* b) *to cure, be good for.* Aph. ܐܦܩܚ *to bud, put forth blossoms.* Derivatives, ܦܩܚܐ, ܦܘܩܚܐ, ܦܩܚܐ, ܦܘܩܚܢܐ, ܦܘܩܚܢܐܝܬ, ܦܘܩܚܘܬܐ, ܦܘܩܚܢܘܬܐ, ܦܩܚܢܐ.

ܦܩܚ, ܦܩܚܐ usually in the abs. state, *useful, expedient;* ܦܩܚ ܗܘܐ ܠܢ *it were better for us;* ܦܩܚ ܠܝ ܒܒܝܬܟ *it is well with me in thy house;* ܠܐ ܒܥܐ ܐܢܐ ܕܝܠܝ ܕܝܠܝ ܦܩܚ *I seek not mine own advantage.*

ܦܩܚܐ E-Syr. ܦܩܚܐ pl. ܝܢ, ܐ̈ rt. ܦܩܚ. m. *a blossom;* ܦܩܚ̈ܐ ܕܐܝܒ̈ܐ *fruit-blossoms;* ܦܩܚ̈ܐ ܕܘܪ̈ܕܐ *flower-buds;* ܦܩܚ̈ܐ ܕܢܝܣܢ *spring blossoms;* metaph. ܦܩܚܘܗܝ ܕܡܠܬܐ ܡܠܝܠܬܐ *the choice flowers of rational speech.*

ܦܩܚܐܝܬ rt. ܦܩܚ. adv. *suitably, rightly, duly.*

ܦܩܚܘܢܐ pl. ܐ̈ dimin. of ܦܩܚܐ m. *a bud, floweret.*

ܦܘܩܚܘܬܐ rt. ܦܩܚ. f. *benefit, advantage.*

ܦܘܩܚܢܐ rt. ܦܩܚ. *suitable.*

ܦܩܚܢܝܐ rt. ܦܩܚ. *freely flowering, covered with blossoms.*

ܦܩܠܐ m. *leaping, bounding.*

ܦܩܝܗܐ Ar. m. *a Mohammedan lawyer* or *theologian.*

ܐܬܦܩܠ denom. verb from ܦܩܝܠܐ. *to put on a turban.*

ܦܩܝܠܐ, ܦܩܝܠܐ or ܦܩܝܠܐ pl. ܐ̈ φακιόλιον, m. a) *a cope* worn by E-Syrian bishops, same as the ܡܥܦܪܐ. b) *a cloth worn over the head, a turban.*

ܦܩܦܩܐ and ܦܩܦܩ pl. ܐ̈ Heb. m. *a capital* of a pillar; a brazen *boss* or *support.*

ܦܩܦܩܘܬܐ rt. ܦܩܦܩ. f. *being fissured, a cleft, chaps on the skin.*

ܦܩܝܪ, ܐ̈ *a*) Arab. *fakir, a religious mendicant.* *b*) = ܦܩܝܠܐ *a turban.* *c*) part. adj. see under ܦܩܪ.

ܦܩܠܐ Lat. faecula, *salt of tartar, the crust* of wine.

ܦܩܥ fut. ܢܦܩܘܥ, act. part. ܦܩܥ, ܦܩܥܐ. *a*) *to burst open, break asunder, shiver, shatter* intrans. as rocks, the heart; ܒܥܠܐ ܐܬܥܓܠܬ ܘܦܩܥܬ *the egg rolled round and broke;* ܦܩܥ ܡܢ ܪܫܗ ܘܠܬܚܬ a serpent *burst open from its head downwards;* ܦܩܥ ܡܢ ܚܡܬܐ *he exploded with anger.* *b*) *to be wide apart* as the legs. ETHPE. ܐܬܦܩܥ *to burst asunder, to be rent in shreds; to be wide apart, crooked* as the feet or legs. PA. ܦܩܥ *to beat; to cleave, part asunder; to crack* a whip, *to crack* as fire cracks the skin; ܡܠܚܐ ܕܡܦܩܥܐ *salt crackling* over a fire. ETHPA. ܐܬܦܩܥ *to be rent, torn* as flesh, *to be made to creak, rattle* as bones; *to be rent, fissured* as rock. APH. ܐܦܩܥ *to make a noise, to crack* the fingers; with ܢܚܝܪܐ *to snort;* with ܪܓܠܐ *to stamp; to cause fissures, to rend* rocks. DERIVATIVES, ܦܩܘܥܐ, ܦܩܥܐ, ܦܩܥܐ, ܦܩܥܬܐ, ܦܩܘܥܘܬܐ, ܦܩܥܐ, ܦܩܥܬܐ, ܡܦܩܥܬܐ, ܡܦܩܥܢܐ, ܦܩܥܝܐ, ܦܩܥܬܐ.

ܦܩܥܐ or **ܦܩܥܐ** pl. ܐ̈ rt. ܦܩܥ. m. *a*) *noise, crash, a thunderbolt.* *b*) *a crack, rift, fissure, cleft; chaps* of the hands or feet. *c*) *sea-weed, wrack.*

ܦܩܥܐ or **ܦܩܥܬܐ** rt. ܦܩܥ. f. *the cracking* of whips.

ܦܩܥܝܐ rt. ܦܩܥ. m. *a lowlander.*

ܦܩܥܬܐ pl. ܐ̈ rt. ܦܩܥ. f. *a plain, broad valley, level tract, expanse.*

ܦܩܥܝܬܐ, ܐ̈ rt. ܦܩܥ. *lowland; a lowlander.*

ܦܩܦܩ Pael conj. of ܦܩ.

ܦܩܦܩܐ, ܦܩܦܩܬܐ rt. ܦܩ. *talkative, garrulous; a babbler, gossip;* ܦܩܦܩܬܐ *babble, gossip.*

ܦܩܦܩܐܝܬ rt. ܦܩ. adv. *foolishly.*

ܦܩܦܩܘܬܐ rt. ܦܩ. f. *chattering, gossiping.*

ܦܩܪ fut. ܢܦܩܘܪ, act. part. ܦܩܪ, ܦܩܪܐ. *to be mad* as a dog; *to be furious, rabid, to rave, rage;* ܥܠ ܙܟܝܐ ܣܦܘܬܗ ܦܩܪܐ *against the innocent doth his lip rage.* Part. adj. ܦܩܝܪ, ܐ̈ *mad, rabid, infuriated;* ܥܠ ܚܕܕܐ ܦܩܝܪܝܢ ܗܘܘ *they were furious with each other;* ܕܒܐ ܕܦܩܝܪܐ ܡܢ ܟܦܢܐ *a bear wild with hunger.* ETHPE. ܐܬܦܩܪ and ETHPA. ܐܬܦܩܪ *to behave like a mad dog, to run riot;* ܡܬܦܩܪܝܢ ܒܪܘܝܘܬܐ ܘܒܚܡܬܐ ܘܒܪܓܝܓܘܬܐ *they were raging with drunkenness, anger and lust.* APH. ܐܦܩܪ *to drive wild, make rabid.* DERIVATIVES, ܦܩܪܐ, ܦܩܪܐܝܬ, ܦܩܪܘܬܐ, ܦܩܪܬܐ.

ܦܩܪܐ, ܦܩܪܬܐ rt. ܦܩܪ. *mad, rabid, furious, savage.*

ܦܩܪܐ pl. ܐ̈ Ar. m. *a vertebra, joint.*

ܦܩܪܐܝܬ rt. ܦܩܪ. adv. *rabidly.*

ܦܩܪܘܬܐ rt. ܦܩܪ. f. *rabies, frensy, fury, mad passion.*

ܦܩܪܢܐ or **ܦܩܪܢܐ** pl. ܐ̈ m. *a coal-pan, warming-pan.*

ܦܩܪܩܝܢ m. *a winter cloak or hood,* properly *a square of cloth worn on the shoulders or hanging from the head.*

ܦܩܪܬܐ rt. ܦܩܪ. *mad, rabid.*

ܦܪ fut. ܢܦܘܪ, act. part. ܦܐܪ. *a*) *to flee, fly away.* *b*) = ܦܪܐ *to abound.*

ܦܪܐ fut. ܢܦܪܐ, act. part. ܦܪܐ. *to be fruitful, beget, bear;* ܦܪܘ ܘܣܓܘ *be fruitful and multiply;* ܦܪܝܐ ܝܠܕܐ ܪܘܚܢܝܐ *she shall bear spiritual children.* ETHPE. ܐܬܦܪܝ *to redound, proceed* from a source. ETHPA. *to be promoted, advanced.* APH. ܐܦܪܝ *a*) *to make fruitful; to increase, make manifold, multiply;* ܐܦܪܝܟ ܘܐܣܓܝܟ ܛܒ *I will make thee exceeding fruitful;* ܚܝܠܘܬܐ ܫܡܝܢܝܬܐ ܡܦܪܝܢ ܬܫܒܚܬܗܝܢ ܕܠܐ ܫܠܝܐ *the* heavenly *hosts multiply* their *ascriptions of praise unceasingly;* ܡܦܪܝܐ ܡܠܬܐ ܪܘܚܢܝܬܐ ܘܡܬܪܣܝܐ ܠܟܦܢܝܗ the spiritual word *fructifies and feeds those who hunger for it.* *b*) *to bring forth, bear fruit;* ܐܪܥܐ ܕܡܦܪܝܐ ܝܬܝܪܐܝܬ *land abundantly fertile;* ܐܦܪܝܬ ܗܒܒܐ ܫܦܝܪܐ ܕܬܝܒܘܬܐ *she brought forth the fair flowers of repentance.* *c*) *to beget, generate, to regenerate.* *d*) *to produce, put forth* songs, homilies, writings. ETHTAP. ܐܬܬܦܪܝ *to be produced, put forth, published* as a book. DERIVATIVES, ܦܐܪܐ, ܦܐܪܢܐ, ܦܐܪܢܐܝܬ, ܦܐܪܘܬܐ, ܦܪܝܐ, ܦܪܝܬܐ, ܡܦܪܝܢܐ, ܡܦܪܝܢܘܬܐ, ܡܦܪܝܐ, ܡܦܪܝܢܐ, verb ܐܬܦܪܝ.

ܦܪܐ pl. ܐ̈ m. ܦܪܬܐ pl. ܐ̈ or fully written ܦܐܪܬܐ f. *a lamb;* usually in the f. *an ewe lamb;* ܦܪܬܐ ܒܪܬ ܫܢܬܐ *a yearling lamb.*

ܦܪܐ foreign, *an uneven number.*

ܦܶܪܳܐ, ܦܶܪܬܳܐ pl. ܦܶܪ̈ܶܐ f. *a) bran;* ܦܶܪܬܳܐ ܩܠܳܦܶܐ ܕܚܶܛܶܐ ܘܣܥܳܪܶܐ *bran is the husks of wheat and barley. b) scurf, dandriff.*

ܦܪܐ_ for words beginning thus, see under ܦܪ_.

ܦܪܐ_ for words beginning thus, see under ܦܪ_.

ܦܪܐܣ; see under ܦܪܣ.

ܦܪܒܘܠܪܐ pl. ܐ̈ Lat. parabolarius, *a hired fighter with wild beasts.*

ܦܰܪܰܒܰܛܶܣ or ܦܪܐܛܣ *παραβάτης, a transgressor.*

ܦܪܓ root-meaning *to be free from care.* Ethpe. ܐܶܬܦܪܶܓ *to be bright.* Aph. ܐܰܦܪܶܓ *a)* intrans. *to shine, gleam, glitter;* act. part. *gay, radiant, splendid, resplendent;* ܦܶܩܳܚܳܐ ܕܡܰܦܪܶܓ *a flower in bloom;* ܡܰܪ̈ܓܳܢܝܳܬܳܐ ܡܰܦܪ̈ܓܳܢܝܳܬܳܐ *gleaming pearls;* ܡܰܦܪܓܳܐ ܒܡܰܘܗ̈ܒܳܬܳܐ a banquet *resplendent with gifts;* ܐܶܣܛܠܳܐ ܡܰܦܪܓܳܐ ܕܨܶܒ̈ܥܶܐ *a robe gay with colours.* Metaph. *to be radiant, to rejoice;* ܢܥܰܕܶܐ ܘܢܰܦܪܶܓ ܒܝܰܘܡܳܐ ܕܕܘܟܪܳܢܗܘܢ *let us keep festival and rejoice in the day of their commemoration. b)* trans. *to make bright* or *joyful; to adorn; to give pleasure;* ܐܰܦܪܶܓܘ ܠܡܳܐܢܰܝܟܘܢ *make your garments gay;* ܩܳܠܶ̈ܐ ܩܰܕܺܝ̈ܫܶܐ ܡܩܰܪ̈ܝܳܢܶܐ ܕܡܰܦܪܓܺܝܢ *holy canticles calling us to gladness.* Pali ܦܰܪܓܺܝ *to delight, to recreate, reanimate;* ܡܦܰܪܓܝܳܐ ܗܘܳܬ ܠܗܘܢ ܘܡܒܰܣܡܳܐ shade *refreshed and solaced them.* Ethpali ܐܶܬܦܰܪܓܺܝ *to take pleasure, find recreation, delight oneself, divert oneself;* ܐܺܙܰܠ ܐܶܬܦܰܪܓܶܐ ܒܰܩܪܺܝܬܳܐ ܦܠܳܢܺܝܬܳܐ *I will go and divert myself in such and such a village;* ܒܰܪܓܳܝܳܬܳܐ ܣܰܪܝܳܬܳܐ ܡܶܬܦܰܪܓܺܝܢ *they delight in barren pleasure.* Derivatives, ܦܪܓܐ, ܦܘܪܓܐ, ܦܘܪܓܝܐ, ܦܪܓܘܢܐ, ܡܦܪܓܢܐ, ܡܦܪܓܢܘܬܐ, ܡܦܪܓܢܝܬܐ, ܡܦܪܓܢܘܬܐ.

ܦܰܪܓܳܐ m. a kind of millet.

ܦܘܪܓܐ rt. ܦܪܓ. m. *splendour.*

ܦܪܓܘܕܝܢ Arab. *a striped garment.*

ܦܰܪܓܡܳܛܘܬܳܐ from ܦܪܓܡ. f. *administration.*

ܦܰܪܓܡܳܢܝܬܳܐ *dumbfoundered.*

ܦܰܪܓܘܢܳܐ pl. ܐ̈ rt. ܦܪܓ. m. *a strigil, currycomb.*

ܦܰܪܓܺܝ and ܐܶܬܦܰܪܓܺܝ; see under ܦܪܓ.

ܦܪܓܝܢ, ܦܰܪܓܺܝܢܳܐ m. *sweet cane.*

ܦܪܓܣܘܢ *a tongue of sea; a channel, moat.* ܦܰܪܓܳܣܳܐ = ܦܰܪܓܳܣܳܐ *a ditch.*

ܦܰܪܓܶܠ *παρήγγειλε, to summon* an army; *to prescribe* a fast; *to command, charge;* ܡܦܰܪܓܠܳܐ ܒܟܽܠ ܕܽܘܒܳܪ̈ܝܢ *instructed in all good ways;* with ܕܠܳܐ or ܡܶܢ *to forbid, prohibit;* legal. *to challenge* a right. Ethpa. ܐܶܬܦܰܪܓܰܠ *to be commanded, admonished,* ܡܶܢ ܡܰܠܦܳܢܶ̈ܐ *by teachers;* with ܕܠܳܐ *to be forbidden.* Derivatives, ܦܘܪܓܠܐ, ܦܪܓܠܘܬܐ.

ܦܪܓܠܐ pl. ܐ̈ m. *φραγέλλιον, a whip, lash.*

ܦܪܓܡܛܘܛܐ m. *πραγματευτής, a) a merchant, trader. b) a skilled scribe. c) a beggar.*

ܦܪܓܡܛܝܐ or ܦܪܓܡܛܝܐ pl. ܦܪܓܡܛܝܣ ܐ̈ f. *πραγματεία, an undertaking, business, trade; a treatise.*

ܦܪܓܡܛܝܩܘܢ, ܦܪܓܡܛܝܩܘܢ *πραγματικόν, of state affairs, imperial;* with ܛܘܦܣܐ *an imperial decree.*

ܦܪܕ fut. ܢܶܦܪܽܘܕ, act. part. ܦܳܪܶܕ, ܦܳܪܕܳܐ, pass. part. ܦܪܺܝܕ, ܦܪܺܝܕܳܐ and ܦܪܶܕ, ܐ̈. *a) to flee* as sleep, *flee away, be scared away* as birds or sheep, *pass away* as a dream; ܦܪܺܝܕܳܐ ܫܶܢܬܳܐ ܕܟܽܠܗܽܘܢ ܪ̈ܚܡܰܝ ܟܣܦܳܐ *the sleep of all the avaricious is scared away;* ܦܳܪ̈ܕܳܢ ܥܶܢ̈ܳܐ ܡܶܢ ܩܳܠܶܗ *the sheep flee at his voice;* ܢܶܦܪܽܘܕ ܐܰܝܟ ܚܶܙܘܳܐ ܕܠܺܠܝܳܐ *he shall pass away as a vision of the night. b) to place apart, lay separately* as grapes. Pass. part. *sleepless, heavy with sleep, scared; crumbling, friable* as soil, sand. Ethpe. ܐܶܬܦܪܶܕ *to be crushed, reduced to grains.* Pa. ܦܰܪܶܕ *a) to scare away, drive away* as sheep. *b) to break up, crumble.* Ethpa. ܐܶܬܦܰܪܰܕ *a) to flee away, be driven away. b) to be friable, crumbled.* Palel ܦܰܪܕܶܕ *a) to break in pieces, disperse. b) to pick out pomegranate seeds.* Ethpalal ܐܶܬܦܰܪܕܰܕ *a) to be crumbled to pieces, become friable, loose. b) to be scared away* as sleep. Aph. ܐܰܦܪܶܕ *to make to flutter* of the heart; *to disturb, break* slumber. Derivatives, ܦܘܪܕܕܐ, ܦܪܕܐ, ܦܪܕܐ, ܦܪܕܕܐ, ܦܪܕܘܣܐ, ܦܪܕܝܐ, ܦܪܝܕܘܬܐ, ܦܪܝܕܘܬܐ, ܡܦܪܕܢܘܬܐ, ܡܦܪܕܕܐ.

ܦܰܪܕܳܐ or ܦܶܪܕܳܐ m. *a)* rt. ܦܪܕ. *a cake. b)* Arab. *uneven, odd.*

ܦܽܘܪܕܳܐ rt. ܦܪܕ. m. *an interval, separation; sleeplessness, fright.*

ܦܪܕܐ, ܦܪܕܬܐ pl. ܝܢ̈, ܐ̈ rt. ܦܪܕ. f. *a grain* of corn, sand, metal; *an atom; a berry, grape-stone, seed, pip;* ܦܪܕܐ ܕܚܪܕܠܐ *mustard-seed;* ܦܪ̈ܕܐ ܕܪܘܡܢܐ *pomegranate seeds;* ܦܪ̈ܕܐ ܕܒܪܕܐ *hail-stones;* ܦ̈ ܡܪ̈ܓܢܝܬܐ *seed-pearls.*

ܦܪܕܕ Palel conj. of ܦܪܕ.

ܦܪܕܘܪܐ pl. ܐ̈ rt. ܦܪܕ. m. *a granule.*

ܦܪܕܝܐ perh. περιδέεια, *terror.*

ܦܪܕܢܝܬ rt. ܦܪܕ. adv. *in separate grains.*

ܦܪܕܝܓܡܐ and ܦܪܕܝܓܡܐ m. παράδειγμα, *a model, pattern; exordium.*

ܦܪܕܝܣ, ܦܪܕܝܣ m. *a leopard.*

ܦܪܕܝܣ, ܦܪܕܝܣܐ pl. ܐ̈ Pers. m. *a paradise, park, garden.*

ܦܪܕܝܣܢܐ Pers. m. *a gardener, park-keeper.*

ܦܪܕܝܣܢܘܬܐ from the preceding. f. *gardening.*

ܦܪܕܝܣܐ pl. ܐ̈ m. *a cupboard, chest, shrine.*

ܦܪܕܢܐ, ܦܪܕܢܝܬܐ rt. ܦܪܕ. *producing grains, granulated.*

ܦܪܕܘܬܐ Pers. *a hunter's tent.*

ܦܪܕܫ *to demonstrate, explain.* Ethpa. ܐܬܦܪܕܫ *to be explained.* Derivative, ܦܘܪܕܫܐ.

ܦܪܗܘܣܝܐ; see ܦܪܗܣܝܐ.

ܦܪܗܣܝܐ, ܦܪܗܣܝܐ, ܦܪܗܣܝܐ, ܦܪܗܣܝܐ, ܦܪܗܣܝܐ, ܦܪܗܣܝܐ &c. f. παρρησία, *freedom of speech, confidence, boldness; liberty, familiarity.* With ܒ, *freely, openly, publicly, orally, by word of mouth.* Derivatives, ܦܪܗܣܝܐܝܬ and ܡܦܪܗܣ, ܡܬܦܪܗܣܢܘܬܐ.

ܦܪܘܒܠܝܡܐ pl. ܦܪܘܒܠܝܡܛܐ πρόβλημα -τα, *a proposition, premiss.*

ܦܪܘܓܐ and ܦܪܘܓܐ pl. ܐ̈ m. ܦܪܘܓܬܐ and ܦܪܘܓܬܐ pl. ܬܐ̈, ܝܬܐ̈ f. *a young bird, nestling, fledgeling, chick.*

ܦܪܘܕܘܪܐ m. *a royal patent, diploma.* Also = ܦܪܘܬܪܐ.

ܦܪܘܕܪܐ; see ܦܪܘܬܪܐ.

ܦܪܘܙܐ m. *sipping.*

ܦܪܘܚܐ, ܬܐ rt. ܦܪܚ. *a) flying;* ܦܪ̈ܘܚܐ *birds. b) quicksilver.*

ܦܪܘܚܘܬܐ rt. ܦܪܚ. f. *flying, flight.*

ܦܪܘܛܐ for ܦܪܛܐ. Lat. porta, *a gate, door.*

ܦܪܘܛܐ πρώτη, *the first* Indict.

ܦܪܘܛܐܣܝܣ, ܦܪܘܛܐܣܝܣ pl. the same. f. πρότασις, logic. *a proposition, the major premiss.*

ܦܪܘܛܪܘܢ; see ܦܪܛܪܘܢ.

ܦܪܘܝܐ = ܦܪܘܝܐ.

ܦܪܘܝܚܬܐ pl. ܬܐ̈ f. *a starling.*

ܦܪܘܟܣܝܡܘܣ, ܦܪܘܟܣܝܡܘܣ Lat. proximus, *a deputy, viceroy.*

ܦܪܘܟܬܐ Heb. f. *a veil, curtain.*

ܦܪܘܠܘܓܘܣ, ܦܪܘܠܘܓܘܣ, ܦܪܘܠܘܓܘܣ πρόλογος, *a preface, introduction.*

ܦܪܘܐܡܝܢ, ܦܪܘܐܡܝܢ, ܦܪܘܐܡܝܢ, ܦܪܘܐܡܝܢ, ܦܪܘܐܡܝܢ, ܦܪܘܐܡܝܢ pl. ܦܪܘܐܡܝܘܢ, ܦܪܘܐܡܝܢܘܬܐ &c. m. προοίμιον, *a preface, introduction.*

ܦܪܘܡܐ pl. ܐ̈ m. *a thong;* perh. *a lasso* or *a club.*

ܦܪܘܡܐ pl. ܐ̈ m. *a runner, king's messenger.*

ܦܘܪܣ emph. ܦܘܪܣܐ pl. ܦܘܪ̈ܣܐ, ܦܘܪܣܝܢ m. πόρος, *means, way, resource; a contrivance, stratagem, device, trick;* ܦܘܪܣܐ ܕܣܘܢܩܢܐ ܕܡܬܒܥܝܢ *resources for* obtaining *necessaries;* ܠܦܘܪܣܐ ܕܛܘܥܝܝܐ *as a means of* propagating *error;* ܒܦܘܪܣܐ ܨܕ ܨܦܪܐ *he caught birds by stratagem;* ܠܐ ܐܫܟܚ ܦܘܪܣܐ ܠܡܥܪܩܘܬܐ *he found no way of escape;* ܒܥܐ ܦܘܪܣܐ *seek means.* With verbs: ܐܢ ܐܝܬ ܦ̈ *if there be a way, if it be possible;* ܠܝܬ ܦܘܪܣ ܡܢ *there is no way of avoiding;* with ܥܒܕ, ܒܥܐ or similar verbs: *to contrive, plot, scheme.* Phrases: ܡܢ ܟܠ ܦܘܪ̈ܣܝܢ *in any way,* with ܠܐ *by no means;* ܒܟܠ ܦܘܪܣ *in every way;* ܡܢ ܟܠ ܦܘܪܣ, ܦܘܪ̈ܣܝܢ *by all means;* ܠܐ ܡܢ ܦܘܪܣ *by no means.* Derivatives, ܐܦܪܣ, verb ܦܪܣ, ܦܘܪܣܢܝܬ, ܡܦܪܣܢܝܬܐ, ܡܦܪܣܢܘܬܐ, ܡܦܪܣܢܐ.

ܦܪܘܣܛܓܡܐ, ܦܪܘܣܛܓܡܐ and ܦܪܘܣܛܓܡܐ pl. ܦܪܘܣܛܓܡܛܐ πρόσταγμα, *a mandate, edict, command.*

ܦܪܘܣܛܪܐ another spelling of ܦܪܘܣܛܪܐ; see below.

ܦܪܘܣܛܪܘܢ; see ܦܪܣܛܪ.

ܦܪܘܣܛܝܡܘܢ πρόστιμον, *a fine.*

ܦܪܘܣܦܘܢܝܛܝܩܘܢ προσφωνητικόν, *addressing, an address.*

ܦܪܘܣܦܘܢܝܣܝܣ and ܦܪܘܣܦܘܢܝܣܐ προσφώνησις, *an address, allocution.*

ܦܪܘܣܦܘܪܝܩܐ, ܣܩܐ, ܣܩܝ̈ προσφορικοί, *hymns chanted by the choir before the reception of the holy Eucharist.*

ܦܪܘܣܛܐܣ rarely ܦܪܘܣܛܐ pl. ܐ̈ m. *a*) προστάς, *a porch.* *b*) παραστάς, *door-post, lintel;* ܦܪܘܣܛܐܕ̈ ܬܪ̈ܥܐ *the door-posts.*

ܦܪܘܣܛܝܩܝ, ܦܪܘܣܛܝܩܐ from ܦܪܘܣ. *ingenious, crafty.*

ܦܪܘܥܐ rt. ܦܪܥ. m. *he who recompenses, requites; a rewarder, an avenger.*

ܦܪܘܥܘܬܐ rt. ܦܪܥ. f. *a*) *refutation; reparation.* *b*) *uncovering* the head.

ܦܪܘܦܫܝܣ ܦܪܘܦܫܝ̈ܣ; see under ܦܪܦ.

ܦܪܘܩ, ܦܪܘܩܐ rt. ܦܪܩ. m. *a saviour, deliverer, preserver, defender, guardian;* esp. *the Saviour* of mankind.

ܦܪܘܩܘܬܐ rt. ܦܪܩ. f. *salvation.*

ܦܪܘܩܝܐ, ܦܪܘܩܝܬܐ rt. ܦܪܩ. *of our Saviour, saving, bringing salvation;* ܚܫܐ ܦ *the Passion of our Saviour;* ܒܫܢܬ ܐܠܦ ܦܪܘܩܝܬܐ *in the year* 1579 *of our Saviour;* ܕܡܐ ܦܪܘܩܝܐ *the saving Blood.*

ܦܪܘܪܐ or ܦܪܘܪܐ. *a*) *broth.* *b*) *roof, upper storey.*

ܦܪܘܫ, ܦܪܘܫܐ, ܦܪܘܫܬܐ rt. ܦܪܫ. *a*) *separating, distinguishing* as gram. vowels, accents. *b*) *discerning, sagacious, prudent, capable of discernment, a person of discernment.* *c*) *distinguished, one of superior rank.* *d*) Heb. ܫܡ ܦܪܘܫ *the Separate Name* i.e. the Holy Name of the Most High.

ܦܪܘܫܐܝܬ rt. ܦܪܫ. adv. *a*) *discriminately, distinctly, particularly.* *b*) *discreetly, prudently, wisely.*

ܦܪܘܫܘܬܐ rt. ܦܪܫ. f. *a*) *power of discerning, discernment, discrimination, judgement;* with ܠܐ *want of judgement, folly.* *b*) *difference.* *c*) *the use* of arms. *d*) used as a title, ܦܪܘܫܘܬܟ *your discretion.*

ܦܪܘܫܝܐ pl. ܐ̈ rt. ܦܪܫ. m. *difference; separation, renunciation; excommunication.*

ܦܪܘܫܐ m. *a smelter.*

ܦܪܘܬܐ or ܦܪ̈ pl. ܬܐ̈ from ܦܪܐ. f. *a fur-coat* esp. *a lamb-skin coat, a sheep-skin, reindeer-skin.*

ܦܪܘܬܐ also ܦܪܘܬܐ and ܦܪܘܬܐ m. *a latrine.*

ܦܪܝܬܐ rt. ܦܪܐ. m. *rupture, hernia.*

ܦܪܘܬܐܣܝܣ πρόθεσις, *a proposition, statement; a preposition.*

ܦܪܘܬܐܣܡܝܐ, ܦܪ̈, ܦܪܬܣܡܝܐ f. προθεσμία, *a term, limit of time* for the bringing of an action, for payment &c., ܙܒܢܐ ܒܦܪ̈ *sale on credit.*

ܦܪܘܬܐܣܡܝܐ, ܝܬܐ from the above. *deferred; on credit.*

ܦܪܘܪܐ m. *pottage* or *pudding flavoured with almonds, honey* &c.

ܦܪܘܙܘܡܐ and ܦܪ̈ pl. ܐ̈ m. περίζωμα, *a girdle, loincloth, drawers.*

ܦܪܙܠܐ pl. ܐ̈ m. *iron; an iron* bar, tool, fetter &c.; ܦܪܙܠܐ ܩܘܡܘܢܐ *steel.*

ܦܪܙܠܝܐ, ܦܪܙܠܢܐ and ܦܪܙܠܝܢܐ, ܝܬܐ from ܦܪܙܠ. adj. *of iron, iron.*

ܦܪܙܠܐ m. *a piece of bread, crust of bread.*

ܦܪܚ fut. ܢܦܪܘܚ, act. part. ܦܪܚ, ܦܪܚܐ, pass. part. ܦܪܝܚ, ܐ. *a*) *to fly, flee* as birds, arrows &c.; ܦܪܚܬ ܢܦܫܗ *his spirit fled* = he expired; ܦܪܚܐ ܠܘܬܟ ܡܫܬܘܚܐ the soul *flies towards Thee;* ܪܘܚܐ ܕܦܪܚܐ *a whirlwind.* *b*) *to float, crawl;* ܦܪܚܬ ܥܠ ܛܘܦܢܐ ܐܠܦܐ ܕܡܪܐ ܟܠ *on the deluge floated the ship of the Lord of all;* ܦܪܚܝܢ ܥܠ ܐܪܥܐ ܘܐܪܥܢܝܐ *earthly and earth-bound.* *c*) *to spread* as a sore, leprosy, poison, as a rumour; *to pervade, become prevalent;* ܦܪܚ ܗܘܐ ܫܘܚܢܐ ܠܠܒܗ ܕܐܢܫܐ *the ulcer has crept into the heart of mankind;* ܒܟܠܗ ܐܪܥܐ ܣܒܪܬܐ ܦܪܚܬ *over the whole world the Gospel has spread.* Pa. ܦܪܚ *a*) *to flutter, fly about;* ܨܦܪܐ ܡܦܪܚܐ ܥܠ ܐܓܪܐ *a sparrow flying about on the roof.* *b*) *to squander, dissipate* ܢܟܣܐ *riches,* ܩܢܝܢܐ *possessions;* ܒܪܐ ܕܦܪܚ ܢܟܣܘܗܝ *the prodigal son;* ܦܪܚܬ ܝܘܡܝ *I have wasted my days.* Ethpa. ܐܬܦܪܚ *to be squandered, dissipated.* Aph. ܐܦܪܚ *a*) *to cause to fly, let* a bird *go free, scare away; to give wings, enable to soar, raise on high;* ܨܪܐ ܦܓܪ̈ܐ ܘܐܦܪܚ ܠܢܦܫܬܐ *He rent bodies and let souls soar free;* ܐܦܪܚ ܗܘܢܟ *let thy mind rise upward.* *b*) *to cause to spread, to diffuse, disseminate;* ܐܦܪܚܬܗ ܠܫܠܗܒܝܬܐ a violent wind *caused the flame to spread.*

Ethtaph. ܐܬܦܪܰܚ to be allowed to fly, to be let go. Derivatives, ܦܪܘܚܐ, ܦܪܚܘܬܐ, ܦܪܳܚܐ, ܦܪܚܐ, ܦܪܚܐܝܬ, ܦܪܚܕܪܐ, ܦܪܚܕܪܢܐ, ܦܪܚܬܐ, ܦܪܚܬܢܘܬܐ, ܦܪܚܬܐ, ܦܪܚܬܢܐ, ܡܦܪܚܢܝܬ, ܡܦܪܚܢܐ.

ܦܪܳܚܐ rt. ܦܪܚ. m. a) spendthrift, dissolute. b) a travelling merchant. c) capparis spinosa, the caper-tree.

ܦܪܚܐ pl. ܐ̈ rt. ܦܪܚ. m. a) flight of birds. b) a bud, sprout.

ܦܪܳܚܐܝܬ rt. ܦܪܚ. adv. prodigally, dissolutely.

ܦܪܚܕܪܐ pl. ܐ̈ rt. ܦܪܚ. m. a bat.

ܦܪܚܕܪܢܝܐ, ܝܬܐ from the above. batlike, of the nature of bats.

ܦܪܳܚܘܬܐ rt. ܦܪܚ. f. prodigality, dissipation.

ܦܪܚܬܐ, ܦܪܚܬܘܢܝܬܐ, ܚ̈ܬܐ rt. ܦܪܚ. f. a spark.

ܦܪܳܚܬܐ pl. ܚ̈ܬܐ rt. ܦܪܚ. f. a flying creature, insect, bird, fowl.

ܦܪܳܚܬܢܝܐ from the above. winged, of birds.

ܦܪܰܛ fut. ܢܶܦܪܘܿܛ, act. part. ܦܳܪܶܛ, ܦܳܪܛܐ, pass. part. ܦܪܝܛ, ܐ. to rend, tear away, burst open as a seam; to drop off as fruit; to speak while yawning; to be abrupt in speaking; ܦܳܪܛܝܢ ܡܡܠܠܐ ܠܕܘܟ ܐܚܪܝܢ they divert the conversation in another direction; ܦܪܰܛ ܩܛܝܢܐ ܣܓܝܐ the seam was partially rent; ܦܪܝܛܐ ܡܢ ܫܢܰܘܗܝ torn by the teeth of .... Ethpe. ܐܬܦܪܶܛ to be rent, gaping open. Pa. ܦܰܪܶܛ to give up entirely, make over. Derivative, ܦܪܛܐ.

ܦܪܛܐ rt. ܦܪܛ. m. rending, tearing.

ܦܪܛܐ πειρατής, a pirate.

ܦܪܛܘܪܝܘܢ, ܦܪܛܘܪܝܢ, ܦܪܐܛܪܝܢ, ܦܪܬܘܪ, ܦܪܘܛܘܪ and ܦܪܛܘܪܝܢܐ pl. ܦܪܛܘܪ̈ܝܢܐ f. Lat. praetorium, the prefecture, governor's residence, palace.

ܦܪܛܘܪܝܢܐ and ܦܪܘܛܘܪ pl. ܐ̈ from the above. a praetorian, soldier of the bodyguard.

ܦܪܛܘܡܐ m. snout, nose.

ܦܪܝܐ pl. ܐ̈ rt. ܦܪܐ. m. offshoot, offspring; fertility.

ܦܪܝܐ rt. ܦܪܐ. m. propagation, fertility.

ܦܪܝܒܛܘܡ Lat. privatum, the emperor's private property.

ܦܪܝܘܕܘܛܐ, ܦܪܝܘܕܘܛܐ, ܦܪܝܕܘܛ, ܦܪܐܕܘܛ, ܦܪܕܘܛ, ܦܪܝܘܛ &c. pl. ܐ̈ m. περιοδευτής, a visiting priest acting as the bishop's representative in visiting villages and monasteries.

ܦܪܝܘܕܘܛܘܬܐ from the above. f. the office of a periodeuta.

ܦܪܝܕܘܬܐ rt. ܦܪܕ. f. a) comminution. b) absent-mindedness.

ܦܪܝܕܘܣܘܣ f. περιόδευσις, περιοδεία, medical treatment.

ܦܪܝܘܬܐ pl. ܘ̈ܬܐ f. φορεῖον, a cradle, a litter for a child.

ܦܪܝܙܘܡܐ pl. ܦܪܝܙܘܡ̈ܛܐ = ܦܪܙܘܡܐ. m. girdle, short drawers.

ܦܪܝܟܐ olive juice, olive dregs.

ܦܪܝܣܐ rt. ܦܪܣ. m. the breastplate of the High Priest; the veil of the Temple; a mantle, cloak, wide wrapper; a Jacobite vestment, cloak or pall.

ܦܪܝܣܐ, ܦܪܝܣܬܐ pl. ܣ̈ܬܐ rt. ܦܪܣ. f. a) a flat cake of bread, a wafer esp. that used for the holy Eucharist, the host. b) a coverlet, wrapper, rug. c) a cloak.

ܦܪܝܣܛܝܪ m. πρηστήρ, a violent wind, hurricane, storm; a kind of meteor.

ܦܪܝܥܘܬܐ rt. ܦܪܥ. f. uncovering, baring the head.

ܦܪܝܦܛܛܝܩܐ, ܦܪܝܦܛܛܝܩܐ, ܦܪܦܛܛܝܩ, ܦܪܝܦܛܛ &c. ܛ̈ܝܩܐ pl. ܐ̈ or ܩܐ περιπατητικός -ή, a peripatetic philosopher, Aristotelian.

ܦܪܝܩܘܬܐ rt. ܦܪܩ. f. distance, separation.

ܦܪܝܟܐ or ܦܪܝ m. feeble-minded, half-witted.

ܦܪܝܟܘܬܐ f. shallowness of mind, imbecility.

ܦܪܝܫܐ pl. ܐ̈ rt. ܦܪܫ. m. a) a Pharisee. b) a noble; ܐܒܐ ܕܝܠܝ ܗܘܐ ܡܢ ܦܪܝܫܐ my father was a noble.

ܦܪܝܫܐܝܬ rt. ܦܪܫ. adv. separately, singularly; especially; distinctly, articulately; of weaving palm-leaves, loosely.

ܦܪܝܫܘܬܐ rt. ܦܪܫ. f. difference, diversity.

ܦܪܝܫܝܐ rt. ܦܪܫ. m. a Pharisee; pharisaic.

ܦܪܰܟ fut. ܢܶܦܪܘܿܟ, act. part. ܦܳܪܶܟ, ܦܳܪܟܐ. to rub, bruise; ܦܳܪܟܝܢ ܗܘܘ ܒܐܝܕܝܗܘܢ they rubbed ears of corn between their hands. Pass. part. ܦܪܝܟ, ܟܐ, ܟܬܐ. a) hard, dry, musty. b) f. pl. ܦܪܝܟܬܐ new corn rubbed from the ears. Ethpe. ܐܬܦܪܶܟ

to be rubbed, bruised; to be shaken out. PA. ܦܰܪܶܟ to shake out; to bruise, to soften. ETHPA. ܐܶܬ݂ܦܰܪܰܟ to be bruised, broken; to be brittle, crumbled, to become friable, loose as earth; ܐܰܝܟ ܡܶܢ ܝܽܘܩܕܳܢܳܐ ܐܶܬ݂ܦܰܪܰܟܘ they are crumbled as from burning. PALPEL ܦܰܪܟܶܟ to break in pieces; to crumble, loosen clods; to promote perspiration. ETHPALPAL. ܐܶܬ݂ܦܰܪܟܰܟ to be broken up, loosened, scattered as earth, to become brittle. DERIVATIVES, ܦܘܪܟܐ, ܦܪܟܐ, ܦܪܳܟܳܐ, ܦܰܪܟܳܐ, ܦܘܪܟܳܢܳܐ, ܦܘܪܟܳܢܘܬ݂ܳܐ, ܡܦܰܪܟܳܢܘܬ݂ܳܐ, ܡܶܬ݂ܦܰܪܟܳܢܳܐ.

ܦܰܪܟܳܐ, ܦܰܪܟܬ݂ܳܐ rt. ܦܪܟ. hard, savage.

ܦܶܪܟܳܐ, ܦܶܪܟܬ݂ܳܐ pl. ܦܶܪܟܳܬ݂ܳܐ f. an idol's shrine, small temple for idol-worship on the outskirts of a village; conventicle of heretics.

ܦܪܽܘܟܳܐ pl. ܦܪܽܘܟܶܐ rt. ܦܪܟ. easily broken open or picked out of the shell as almonds.

ܦܪܳܟܳܐ rt. ܦܪܟ. m. fragility, breakage.

ܦܳܪܽܘܟܳܐ pl. ܦܳܪܽܘܟܶܐ rt. ܦܪܟ. m. a bit of bread, slice of bread, morsel, crust; a clot of blood.

ܦܰܪܰܟܽܘܪܺܝܣܺܝܣ παραχορῆσαι, concession; with ܥܒܰܕ to cede possession.

ܦܳܪܽܘܟܽܘܬ݂ܳܐ rt. ܦܪܟ. f. dryness; inhumanity, unmercifulness.

ܦܰܪܟܶܟ Palel conj. of ܦܪܟ.

ܦܰܪܟܶܠ to shackle, hobble a horse; to impede; ܦܰܪܟܠܶܗ ܕܠܳܐ ܢܶܥܒܰܪ ܬܚܽܘܡܰܘܗ̱ܝ he shackled him so as not to let him go beyond bounds; ܠܶܒܶܗ ܦܰܪܟܶܠ he kept his heart in bonds. ETHPARAL ܐܶܬ݂ܦܰܪܟܰܠ to be ensnared, entangled ܒܡܨܺܝܕܬ݂ܳܐ in a net; ܠܳܐ ܐܶܬ݂ܦܰܪܟܰܠܬ݁ ܐܰܝܟ ܚܰܘܳܐ ܡܶܢ ܗܰܘ ܡܰܘܬܳܢܳܐ thou hast not been ensnared as was Eve by that agent of death. DERIVATIVE, ܦܘܪܟܠܐ.

ܦܰܪܟܶܣ to separate, annihilate, destroy; ܠܳܐ ܬܦܰܪܟܶܣ ܒܶܝܢ ܢܰܦܫܝ ܘܦܰܓ݂ܪܝ do not part asunder my soul and body. ETHPALPAL ܐܶܬ݂ܦܰܪܟܰܣ to be parted, destroyed. DERIVATIVE, ܦܘܪܟܳܣܳܐ.

ܦܰܪܡܰܫܬ݂ܳܐ m. a secret place, hiding-place, thicket.

ܦܪܰܟܣܺܝܣ pl. ܦܪܰܟܣܺܝܣ̈ܘܬ݂ܳܐ f. πρᾶξις, a deed, action, act; acts of a synod; an action at law, with ܗܘܳܐ to be brought; the Acts of the Apostles.

ܦܰܪܰܠܺܝܛܘܣ; see ܦܰܪܰܩܠܺܝܛܘܣ.

ܦܰܪܰܠܺܝܠܘܣ and ܦܰܪܰܠܺܝܠܳܐ, ܦܰܪܰܠܺܝܠܶܐ m. pl.

ܦܰܪܰܠܺܝܠܘ and ܦܰܪܰܠܺܝܠܳܐ f. pl. ܦܰܪܰܠܺܝܠܳܬ݂ܳܐ παράλληλος, parallel.

ܦܪܰܠܘܣ πάραλος, the coast district, maritime region.

ܦܪܰܡ fut. ܢܶܦܪܽܘܡ, act. part. ܦܳܪܶܡ, ܦܳܪܡܳܐ. a) to hack, hash, cut in little pieces; ܦܰܪܡܽܘܗܝ ܗܰܕܳܡ ܗܰܕܳܡ they hacked him limb from limb. b) with ܫܶܢ̈ܐ to lose the milk teeth, have a gap between the teeth. Pass. part. ܦܪܺܝܡ, ܦܪܺܝܡܳܐ hashed, chopped, splintered, having the partition of the nose pierced. ETHPE. ܐܶܬ݂ܦܪܶܡ a) to be chopped up; to be separate, stand apart. b) perhaps to be poured in, filled up as a jar with wine. PA. ܦܰܪܶܡ a) to slice up, cut up. Pass. part. ܡܦܰܪܡܳܐ, ܡܦܰܪܡܬ݂ܳܐ rent, tattered as clothes in sign of grief; also fringed, slashed for elegance; ܟܘܬܺܝܢܳܬ݂ܳܐ ܡܦܰܪܡܳܬ݂ܳܐ ܡܥܰܠ̈ܝܳܐ tunics with fringed borders. b) to fill up, fill full a jar with new wine. DERIVATIVES, ܦܪܳܡܳܐ, ܦܽܘܪܡܳܢܳܐ, ܦܪܳܡܬ݂ܳܐ.

ܦܪܳܡܳܐ m. and ܦܪܳܡܽܘܬ݂ܳܐ f. rt. ܦܪܡ. a) slashing, cutting, rending of garments. b) slicing, shredding vegetables. c) a gap among the teeth. d) filling a jar with must.

ܦܪܡܢ Pers. a firman.

ܦܪܡܫܟܬ݂ܳܐ a compound of musk and other perfumes.

ܦܰܪܰܡܽܘܢܳܪܺܝܣ and ܦܰܪܰܡܽܘܢܳܪܺܝܽܘܣ pl. ܐ̈ ܦܰܪܰܡܽܘܢܳܪܶܐ παραμονάριος, a verger, sacristan.

ܦܪܳܡܽܘܬ݂ܳܐ; see ܦܪܳܡܳܐ.

ܦܪܡܘܬܝ and ܦܪܡܘܬ Pharmuthi, the seventh Egyptian month, nearly answering to April.

ܦܰܪܰܡܽܘܬ݂ܺܝܰܐ f. παραμυθία, comfort, assistance.

ܦܽܘܪܡܰܣܬ݂ܳܐ pl. ܦܽܘܪܡܰܣ̈ܬ݂ܳܐ f. a button, buckle.

ܦܪܺܝܡܬ݂ܳܐ rt. ܦܪܡ. f. perh. a divided hoof, cloven hoof.

ܦܪܢ denom. verb from ܦܽܘܪܢܳܬ݂ܳܐ. APHEL ܐܰܦܪܶܢ to endow, portion.

ܦܰܪܢܳܐ m. big-bellied, a glutton.

ܦܪܰܢܓ݁ or ܦܪܰܢܓ݁ܳܝܳܐ from Frank; the country of the Franks, Western Europe.

ܦܪܰܢܓ݁ܳܐܺܝܬ݂ and ܦܪܰܢܓ݁ܺܝܬ݂ in Latin, in the Latin language.

ܦܪܰܢܓ݁ܳܝܳܐ, ܦܪܰܢܓ݁ܳܝܬ݂ܳܐ a Frank, Roman, one of Latin race; one belonging to the Western or Latin Church.

ܦܰܪܰܢܓ݁ܶܠܺܝܰܐ pl. ܦܰܪܰܢܓ݁ܶܠܺܝܣ a) παραγγελία, legal

an intimation, notice of a suit, charge. b) φαλάγγιον, *a venomous spider.*

ܦܪܢܘܝܐ and ܦܪܢܘܝܬܐ πρόνοια, *divine providence.*

ܦܰܪܢܺܝܫܳܐ m. *worn out with age, a decrepit old man.*

ܦܰܪܢܺܝܫܽܘܬܳܐ f. *decrepitude, extreme old age.*

ܦܰܪܢܺܝܫܳܝܳܐ, ـܝܬܳܐ *senile.*

ܦܰܪܢܽܘܬܳܐ from ܦܰܪܢܳܐ. f. *intemperance, gluttony.*

ܦܶܪܢܺܝܬܳܐ pl. ـܝܳܬܳܐ f. φερνή, *price paid to the father of the bride, dower, dowry, marriage settlements,* sometimes used of the portion brought by the bride from her father's house but usually of the dower settled by the bridegroom, hence a marriage ܕܠܳܐ ܦܶܪܢܺܝܬܳܐ *without settlements* and children of the same ranked lower than a marriage with dower and ܒ̈ܢܰܝܳܐ ܕܡܶܢ ܦܶܪܢܺܝܬܳܐ *legitimate children.* ܟܬܳܒܳܐ ܕܦܶܪܢܺܝܬܳܐ *marriage contract.*

ܦܪܘܢܘܡܝܐ προνομία, *privilege, exemption, remission of taxes.*

ܦܰܪܢܶܣ a) *to take the oversight, manage, rule;* to administer ܩܶܢܝܳܢܳܐ *property;* ܐܘܚܕܳܢܳܐ *the realm = to be regent; to be a guardian* of orphans, *bring up* children; ܦܰܪܢܶܣ ܦܽܘܪܫܳܢܰܢ ܕܡܶܢ ܚܕܳܕܶܐ God *has ruled our separation from each other;* ܡܦܰܪܢܶܣ ܗ̄ܘܳܐ ܣܽܘܥܪ̈ܳܢܶܐ ܕܡܰܠܟܽܘܬܶܗ *he managed the affairs of his kingdom;* ܩܰܫܺܝܫܶܐ ܕܡܦܰܪܢܣܺܝܢ ܡܕܺܝܢܬܳܐ *the elders who govern the town.* b) *to care for, provide for* the poor or sick; *to distribute;* ܟܽܠ ܕܐܺܝܬ ܗ̄ܘܳܐ ܦܰܪܢܶܣ ܠܡܣܟܺܢ̈ܶܐ *he distributed all* the gold and silver *he possessed to the poor;* ܦܰܪܢܣܰܬ ܫܡܰܝܳܐ ܥܰܠ ܬܰܚܬܳܝ̈ܶܐ *heaven dispensed to those below* dew and rain. c) *to appoint, ordain, arrange in order.* ETHPALAL ܐܶܬܦܰܪܢܰܣ *to be administered, managed* as affairs, revenues; *to be distributed* as alms; *to be provided, cared for, fully supplied* esp. with food; ܗܳܕܶܐ ܒܡܕܰܒܪܳܢܽܘܬܳܐ ܐܰܠܳܗܳܝܬܳܐ ܗܳܟܰܢ ܡܶܬܦܰܪܢܣܳܐ *this is so appointed by divine dispensation;* ܢܽܘܪܳܐ ܐܰܠܳܗܳܐ ܠܥܳܠܡܳܐ ܝܰܗ̄ܒ ܕܢܶܬܦܰܪܢܰܣ ܒܶܗ *God gave fire to the world that it might be sustained thereby.* DERIVATIVES, ܦܽܘܪܢܳܣܳܐ, ܦܰܪܢܳܣܳܐ, ܡܦܰܪܢܣܳܢܽܘܬܳܐ, ܡܦܰܪܢܣܳܢܳܐ, ܡܦܰܪܢܣܳܢܳܝܬ, ܠܳܐ ܡܦܰܪܢܣܳܢܽܘܬܳܐ.

ܦܰܪܢܳܣܳܐ pl. ـܣܶܐ from ܦܰܪܢܶܣ. m. *a steward, administrator.*

ܦܪܰܣ fut. ܢܶܦܪܽܘܣ, parts. ܦܳܪܶܣ, ܦܳܪܣܳܐ, ܦܪܺܝܣ: ܦܪܺܝܣ, ܦܪܺܝܣܳܐ cf. subst. ܦܪܺܝܣܳܐ, ܬܳܐ above. a) intrans. *to spread out, extend;* ܕܠܳܐ ܢܶܦܪܽܘܣ ܦܽܘܠܚܳܢ ܣܓܺܝܕܽܘܬܶܗ ܒܶܝܬ ܥܰܡ̈ܡܶܐ *lest the idolatry* of Israel *should spread amongst the nations.* b) trans. *to spread out, stretch out, unfold* the wings, the hands; a net; a veil, covering; *to unroll* a scroll, roll; *to shed abroad* light, darkness; *to diffuse;* ܦܪܰܣ ܦܪܳܣܳܐ ܥܰܠ *he spread a veil over . . .,* ܦܪܰܣ ܫܶܡܫܳܐ ܥܰܠ ܙܰܠܺܝܩܰܘ̈ܗܝ *the sun sheds its rays abroad;* ܦܪܰܣܘ ܠܗܽܘܢ ܐܺܝܕܰܝ̈ܗܽܘܢ *they stretched out their hands;* ܦܪܺܝܣܺܝܢ ܪ̈ܰܚܡܰܘܗ̄ܝ ܥܰܠ ܟܽܠܗܽܘܢ *His mercies are extended to all.* c) *to divide, distribute.* ETHPE. ܐܶܬܦܪܶܣ a) refl. *to spread, shed itself abroad.* b) pass. *to be spread out, diffused; to be made known abroad, promulgated.* c) *to be divided, classed.* PA. ܦܰܪܶܣ *to spread out* the hands *widely.* ETHPA. ܐܶܬܦܰܪܰܣ *to overspread, overrun* for plunder. DERIVATIVES, ܦܪܳܣܳܐ, ܦܪܳܣܬܳܐ, ܦܰܪܣܳܐ, ܦܳܪܣܳܐ, ܦܶܪܣܳܐ, ܡܰܦܪܣܳܐ.

ܦܰܪܶܣ denom. verb from ܦܽܘܪܣܳܐ, ܦܽܘܪܣܳܐ. ETHPAAL ܐܶܬܦܰܪܰܣ *to devise, plan, scheme;* with ܦܽܘܪܣܳܐ *to contrive a means* or *device; to attempt, invent, achieve; to use guile, do cunningly;* ܠܰܫܠܳܡܳܐ ܢܶܬܦܰܪܰܣ *let us compass peace;* ܡܶܬܦܰܪܰܣ ܕܢܶܕܪܶܟ ܐܺܝܩܳܪܳܐ ܪܰܒܳܐ *he schemes to attain great honour;* ܡܶܬܦܰܪܰܣ ܘܡܡܰܠܶܐ ܠܶܗ *he flatters him cunningly.*

ܦܳܪܣ pr. n. f. *Persia.* DERIVATIVES, ܦܳܪܣܳܝܳܐ and ܦܳܪܣܳܝܳܐ, ܦܳܪܣܳܝܬ.

ܦܰܪܣܳܐ, ܦܰܪܣܬܳܐ pl. ـܣܶܐ, ـܣܳܬܳܐ and ܦܰܪܣܳܬܳܐ rt. ܦܪܣ. f. a) *the sole of the foot, hoof* of men and beasts; *a footstep, trace;* ܡܦܰܫܚܳܐ ܦܰܪܣܬܳܐ *having the hoof undivided;* ܦܳܪܣܳܐ ܦܰܪܣܬܳܐ *cloven-hoofed;* ܦܰܪܣܳܬܳܐ ܡܣܰܪܓܳܢܳܝܳܬܳܐ *web-feet.* b) *the lupine.*

ܦܳܪܣܳܐ a) = ܦܪܳܣܳܐ c. b) fem. act. part. of verb ܦܪܰܣ. ܠܓܰܘ ܡܶܢ ܦܰܪܣܳܐ ܗܳܐ ܦܳܪܣܳܐ ܕܬܶܬܶܠ ܠܰܢ ܡܢܳܬܳܐ *within the tent lo she spreads the cloth to give us* our *portion.*

ܦܪܳܣܳܐ pl. ـܣܶܐ rt. ܦܪܣ. m. a) *a cloth, strip of cloth; a covering, carpet, tent-covering.* b) *a peach-tree.* c) = ܦܪܣܬܐ.

ܦܪܳܣܳܐ pl. ـܣܶܐ rt. ܦܪܣ. m. a) *a cover, curtain, veil, screen;* rit. *the veil placed over the conse-*

crated bread. b) a mat, rug, carpet. c) a measured allowance, portion, rations. d) a cedar-cone.

ܦܪܣܝܐ m. περσέα, *persea*, an Egyptian tree with the fruit growing from the stem.

ܦܪܣܐܝܬ adv. *a*) from ܦܪܣ. *naked. b*) from ܦܪܣ. *in the Persian language.*

ܦܪܣܬܐ pl. ܬܐ from ܦܪܣ. m. *a hoof, claw.*

ܦܪܣܐ pl. ܐ Pers. m. *a parasang, farsang* or *farsakh* = three or four miles according to the nature of the ground, an hour's journey.

ܦܪܣܓܢܐ; see ܦܪܘܣܓܢܐ.

ܦܪܣܛܝܢ, ܦܪܣܛܐ and ܦܪܘܣܛܐ pl. ܛܝܢ̈ m. προάστειον, *a suburban farm* or *estate.*

ܦܪܣܘܢܝܬܐ f. *a waiting-woman.*

ܦܪܣܝ Parel conj. *to strip naked, lay bare, expose, unmask, put to shame.* Pass. part. ܡܦܪܣܝ, ܡܦܪܣܝܐ *stripped* as corpses; *unseemly, shameful.* Ethpali ܐܬܦܪܣܝ *to be made known openly; to be exposed, disclosed* as treachery, hypocrisy; *to be detected* in, *convicted* of; *to come into bad repute.* Derivatives, ܦܘܪܣܝܐ, ܦܪܣܝܐܝܬ, ܡܦܪܣܝܢܝܬ, ܡܦܪܣܝܢܘܬܐ, ܡܦܪܣܝܐ, ܡܬܦܪܣܝܢܐ, ܡܦܪܣܝܢܘܬܐ, ܡܬܦܪܣܝܢܘܬܐ.

ܦܪܣܝܐ, ܦܪܣܝܬܐ from ܦܪܣ. *Persian, a Persian; a peach.*

ܦܪܣܬܢܐ pl. ܢܐ rt. ܦܪܣ. *a*) m. *having hoofs, hoofed. b*) f. pl. of ܦܪܣܬܐ, ܦܪܣܬܐ.

ܦܪܣܦܣ *to distend, rarefy, make loose; to place at some distance apart* as in planting out. Pass. part. ܡܦܪܣܦܣܐ, ܡܦܪܣܦܣܬܐ *thin, scanty; of loose cohesion; dissolute.* Ethpalpal ܐܬܦܪܣܦܣ *to be of loose texture; to be dispersed; to be rarefied.* Derivatives, ܦܘܪܣܦܣܐ, ܦܪܣܦܣܐ, ܡܦܪܣܦܣܘܬܐ, ܡܦܪܣܦܣܢܘܬܐ.

ܦܪܣܦܣܢܝܘܬܐ; see ܦܪܘܣܦܣܢܝܘܬܐ.

ܦܪܥ ܦܪܥ fut. ܢܦܪܘܥ, act. part. ܦܪܥ, ܦܪܥܐ, pass. part. ܦܪܝܥ, ܥܐ. *a*) *to spring up, bud, put* or *bring forth* leaves, flowers, fruit; *to show forth. b*) *to shave* the head. *c*) *to requite, repay, recompense, reward, bestow; to make restitution, pay compensation; to answer, be answerable for;* ܟܠ ܕܦܪܥܢܝ ܡܪܝܐ ܒܚܢܢܗ *all that* the Lord *hath bestowed on me in His mercy.* Esp. with ܐܝܩܪܐ *to render honour;* ܚܘܒܐ *to pay what is due;* ܛܝܒܘܬܐ *to return, requite,* ܦܪܥܘܗ ܛܝܒܘܬܐ ܛܒܬܐ *they requited* him *well;* ܚܘܒܬܐ *to pay a debt;* ܫܘܥܝܬܐ *to relate duly, bring a narration to its due end, come to an end;* ܢܕܪܐ *to pay a vow;* ܣܓܕܬܐ *to do due reverence, to salute, return greetings.* Ethpe. ܐܬܦܪܥ *a*) *to be avenged, to take vengeance* often with ܦܘܪܥܢܐ, ܚܛܝܬܐ &c. *b*) *to be recompensed, rewarded, repaid, to receive* ܐܓܪܐ *a reward;* ܕܗܒܐ *gold;* ܕܝܢܐ *judgement, punishment;* ܕܡܝܐ *the price;* ܚܕ ܒܡܐܐ *an hundredfold. c*) *to be performed* as a vow, a prayer.

Aph. ܐܦܪܥ *to germinate, bud, shoot forth, to put forth* buds &c., metaph. *to break forth* as water, *put forth, flourish.* Derivatives, ܦܪܥܘܬܐ, ܦܪܥܘܢܘܬܐ, ܦܘܪܥܢܐ, ܦܪܘܥܐ, ܦܘܪܥܢܘܬܐ, ܡܦܪܥܢܐ, ܡܦܪܥܢܐ, ܦܪܥܢܐ, ܦܪܥܐ, ܦܪܥܐ.

ܦܪܥܐ pl. ܥܐ rt. ܦܪܥ. m. *a*) *vengeance. b*) *a bud, shoot, sucker, blossom;* metaph. *a ramification, offshoot* of doctrine; gram. *a derived form. c*) *hypericum, St. John's wort; cucumis melo, melon.*

ܦܪܥܐ rt. ܦܪܥ. m. *a*) *produce, fruit. b*) *shaving* the head. *c*) *retribution.*

ܦܪܥܘܢ *Pharaoh.* Derivative, the following adjective:—

ܦܪܥܘܢܝܐ, ܢܝܬܐ *Pharaonic, Egyptian.*

ܦܪܥܢܝܐ, ܢܝܬܐ rt. ܦܪܥ. gram. *derived, derivative.*

ܦܪܥܢܝܬܐ f. *a starling.*

ܦܪܦܐ, ܦܪܦܐ pl. ܦܐ m. πόρπη, *a wooden clasp* or *curtain-hook;* also *a clamp, sill* of a tent.

ܦܪܦܐ pl. ܦܪܦܝܬܐ f. *utensils, pots.*

ܦܪܦܘܪ and ܦܘܪܦܘܪܘܢ = ܦܪܦܘܪܘܢ *purple.*

ܦܪܦܘܪܐ m. *the partridge,* also a kind of water-fowl.

ܦܪܦܚܝܢܐ pl. ܢܐ m. *portulaca, purslain.*

ܦܪܦܟܬܐ or ܟܐ pl. ܬܐ m. *a*) *wings, plumes. b*) *rubbing* or *crumbling* bread between the hands.

ܦܪܦܠܝ *calamus aromaticus.*

ܦܪܦܘܣܝܛܐ, ܦܪܦܘܣܛܐ, ܦܪܦܘܣ and ܦܪܦܘܣ m. Lat. praepositus, *prefect, chamberlain* at the Byzantine court.

ܦܰܪܦܶܣ a) *to rinse, rinse out* clothes &c., *to gargle.* b) *to lead a soft luxurious life.* Ethpalpal ܐܶܬ݂ܦܰܪܦܰܣ *to sport, frisk, run riot, luxuriate, feast to excess, revel;* ܦܳܪܚܳܬ݂ܳܐ ܕܰܫܡܰܝܳܐ ܕܡܶܬ݂ܦܰܪܦܣܳܢ ܒܰܐܐܰܪ *winged creatures of heaven disporting themselves in the air;* ܐܶܬ݂ܦܰܪܦܣܰܬ݂ ܢܰܦܫܰܢ ܒܛܳܒ݂ܳܬ݂ܳܐ ܘܰܒ݂ܡܶܛܰܠܠܳܬ݂ܳܐ *our soul hath revelled in good things and in shady retreats.* Derivative, ܦܘܪܦܣܐ.

ܦܰܪܦܰܪ *to flutter, quiver.* Ethpalpal ܐܶܬ݂ܦܰܪܦܰܪ *to writhe, to be in the agony of death.* Derivative, ܦܘܪܦܪܐ.

ܦܰܪܦܪܳܐ pl. ܐ̈ *a sheet* or *plate* of metal.

ܦܰܪܨܳܐ *intemperate, lascivious.*

ܦܰܪܨܘܦ̣, ܦܰܪܨܘܦܳܐ pl. ܐ̈ πρόσωπον, a) *face, countenance, presence;* ܢܗܰܪ ܦܰܪܨܘܦܶܗ ܐܰܝܟ ܫܶܡܫܳܐ *His face shone as the sun;* ܦ̄ ܠܘܳܬ݂ ܦ̄ *face to face;* ܡܶܢ ܦ̄ ܕ *in the presence of, before . . .,* cf. *f.* b) of inanimate objects *the face, surface* ܕܰܐܪܥܳܐ *of the earth,* ܕܰܫܡܰܝܳܐ *of the heavens,* ܕܫܶܡܫܳܐ *of the sun.* c) *his person, himself;* ܡܳܪܰܢ ܣܳܡ ܦܰܪܨܘܦܶܗ ܠܡܶܨܠܳܝܘܬ݂ܶܗ *our Lord set Himself to pray, betook Himself to prayer.* d) theolog. *a Person* of the Holy Trinity, πρόσωπον while ܩܢܘܡܳܐ is more often used for ὑπόστασις; the Nestorians acknowledge two ܩܢܘܡܶܐ one ܦܰܪܨܘܦܳܐ in Christ; ܥܕܰܡܳܐ ܕܬܰܘܕܶܐ ܬܪܶܝܢ ܟܝܳܢܺܝܢ ܕܗܘܰܘ ܚܰܕ ܦܰܪܨܘܦܳܐ *until thou confess two Natures which became one Person.* e) *a person, any one;* ܐܶܓܪ̈ܳܬ݂ܳܐ ܠܘܳܬ݂ ܦܰܪܨܘ̈ܦܶܐ ܡܫܰܚܠ̈ܦܶܐ letters *to various persons;* ܦܰܪܨܘ̈ܦܶܐ ܡܥܰܠܝ̈ܶܐ *illustrious men;* ܬܪܶܝܢ ܦ̄ ܕܰܐܚ̈ܘܳܬ݂ܳܐ *two sisters.* f) *person, personification; appearance, likeness;* with ܢܣܰܒ݂ *to represent, act in the person of . . .,* also *to personify, dramatize;* ܡܶܠܶܐ ܕܡܰܟܝܟ݂ܘܬ݂ܳܐ ܦ̄ ܛܥܺܝܢܺܝܢ ܗܘܰܘ words *bearing an appearance* or *pretence of meekness;* ܒܦܰܪܨܘܦ̣ ܐܰܟ݂ܣ̈ܢܳܝܶܐ angels appeared to Abraham *in the likeness of strangers;* ܐܶܡܰܪ ܠܶܗ ܒܦ̄ ܡܳܪܶܗ Moses spoke to Pharaoh *as representing his Lord;* ܡܶܢ ܦ̄ ܕ *in the person of, under the name of . . .,* ܦ̄ ܢܣܰܒ݂ see ܢܣܰܒ݂. g) *the sense, meaning* of a word. h) astron. = ܕܘܩܢܳܐ *a third part of each sign of the Zodiac.* i) gram. *person* of a verb. Derivatives, the three following words:—

ܦܰܪܨܘܦܳܐܺܝܬ݂ adv. *personally.*

ܦܰܪܨܘܦܳܝܳܐ, ܝܬܳܐ *of person, personal, personifying;* gram. *personal;* a letter *forming a person* of a verb.

ܦܰܪܨܘܦܳܢܳܐܺܝܬ݂ adv. *personally, in person.*

ܦܰܪܨܘܦܢܺܝܳܬ݂ܳܐ pl. f. *motes* in a sunbeam.

ܦܰܪܨܳܢܳܐ, ܦܰܪܨܳܢܬܳܐ or ܦ̄ܪܶܨ pl. ܦܰܪܨܳܢܘܳܬ݂ܳܐ f. *a grapestone, pomegranate seed; a raisin.*

ܦܰܪܨܳܢܘܢܺܝܬ݂ܳܐ pl. ܝܳܬ݂ܳܐ dimin. of ܦܰܪܨܳܢܳܐ. *an atom, particle, mote.*

ܦܪܰܩ fut. ܢܶܦܪܘܿܩ, act. part. ܦܳܪܶܩ, ܦܳܪܩܳܐ, cf. ܦܳܪܘܿܩܳܐ below; part. adj. a) ܦܪܺܝܩ, ܩܳܐ, ܩܬܳܐ. b) ܦܰܪܺܝܩ, ܩܳܐ, ܩܬܳܐ. a) intrans. *to separate from, break loose; to depart, go away, remove, withdraw, abandon* with ܡܶܢ; ܠܳܐ ܦܪܰܩ ܥܰܡܽܘܕܳܐ ܕܢܽܘܪܳܐ ܡܶܢ ܩܕܳܡ ܥܰܡܳܐ the pillar of fire *departed not from before the people;* ܦܪܰܩ ܠܶܗ ܚܰܝܠܶܗ ܡܶܢܶܗ *his strength forsook him;* ܠܳܐ ܦܪܰܩܘ ܡܶܢ ܥܒ݂ܳܕ݂ܰܝܗܘܿܢ ܒܺܝܫܶܐ *they did not abandon their evil deeds;* ܦܪܰܩ ܡܶܢ ܨܠܘܬ݂ܶܗ *he ceased praying.* Part. adj. ܦܰܪܺܝܩ *separate, lonely, distant, absent, remote, far off;* ܦܪܺܝܩܳܐ ܐܶܣܛܰܕܺܝܘܬ݂ܳܐ ܫܬܺܝܢ *sixty stadia distant;* ܡܶܢ ܝܰܡܳܐ *inland;* ܡܶܢ ܕܰܓܳܠܘܬ݂ܳܐ *free from falsehood;* ܡܶܢ ܚܛܺܝܬ݂ܳܐ *separate from sin;* ܡܶܢ ܟܽܠܳܗ ܝܺܕܰܥܬܳܐ *far from any knowledge, utterly ignorant.* b) trans. *to redeem, ransom, save;* ܡܙܰܒ݂ܢܶܗ ܢܶܦܪܘܿܩ ܐܰܚܘܗܝ *his kinsman shall redeem that which he hath sold;* ܦܳܪܩܺܝܢ ܫܒ݂ܝܳܐ *they ransom captives;* ܦܪܘܿܩ ܡܳܪܝܳܐ *save Lord;* ܦܪ̈ܺܝܩܰܘܗ݈ܝ ܕܡܳܪܝܳܐ *the ransomed of the Lord;* ܥܳܢܳܐ ܦܪܺܝܩܬܳܐ ܒܙܩܺܝܦܳܐ *the flock redeemed by the cross.* Ethpe. ܐܶܬ݂ܦܪܶܩ a) *to depart, abandon; to be torn away, dislocated, broken off.* b) *to be ransomed, redeemed, saved.* Pa. ܦܰܪܶܩ *to break off, rend, dislocate; to take away;* ܡܦܰܪܰܩ ܒܣܪܺܝܩܘܳܬ݂ܳܐ *distracted with vanities.* Ethpa. ܐܶܬ݂ܦܰܪܰܩ a) *to be rent, dislocated.* b) *to move to and fro, to be moved.* c) *to separate oneself, abandon, to be quit of.* Aph. ܐܰܦܪܶܩ a) *to rend;* ܪܘܚܳܐ ܐܰܠܺܝܨܬܳܐ ܡܰܦܪܩܳܐ ܠܛܘܪ̈ܶܐ *a strong wind rending the mountains.* b) *to cause to depart, drive away, take away, remove, to withdraw* an army; *to put away* ܚܶܪܡܳܐ *a devoted thing,* ܐܰܠܳܗ̈ܶܐ ܢܘܟ݂ܪ̈ܳܝܶܐ *strange gods;* ܠܡܰܦܪܳܩܘ ܝܺܗܘܕ̈ܳܝܶܐ ܡܶܢ ܦܘܠܚܳܢܳܐ ܕܰܐܠܳܗܗܘܿܢ *to turn aside the Jews from the worship of their God.* c) *to separate, cause to abandon, cause to abstain from* with ܡܶܢ.

DERIVATIVES, ܦܘܪܫܐ, ܦܘܪܫܢܐ, ܦܘܪܫܢܝܐ, ܦܪܝܫܐ, ܦܪܝܫܐܝܬ, ܦܪܝܫܘܬܐ, ܦܪܫܘܢܐ, ܦܪܫܢܐ, ܦܪܫܘܬܐ, ܡܦܪܫܢܘܬܐ, ܡܦܪܫܢܐܝܬ, ܦܪܫܬܐ, ܦܪܫܢܐ, ܦܪܫܐ, ܡܬܦܪܫܢܐ, ܡܬܦܪܫܢܘܬܐ.

ܦܪܘܫܐ pl. ܐ̈ rt. ܦܪܣ. m. *a strip, bandage; a piece of cloth, silk,* &c.

ܦܪܘܩܐ rt. ܦܪܩ. m. *the Saviour.*

ܦܪܘܩܐ rt. ܦܪܩ. m. *a division, juncture, joint.*

ܦܪܓܡ *to bend forward, fall down.*

ܦܪܘܣܬܐ dimin. of ܦܪܘܫܐ. m. *a small cloth, small strip of cloth.*

ܦܪܘܩܘܪܐ with ܥܒܕ, Greek infin. formed from Lat. procurare: *to give over the management.*

ܦܪܐܩܛܐ, ܦܪܐܩܛܣ m. pl. φράκτης -αι, *a screen.*

ܦܪܐܩܛܝܩܐ πρακτική, with ܐܓܪܬܐ *a Synodical Letter.*

ܦܪܐܩܛܝܩܘܣ, ܩܘܣ, ܩܘܢ πρακτικός -όν, *practical; active, energetic.*

ܦܪܐܩܛܝܩܝܐ, ܩܝܬܐ *practical.*

ܦܪܐܩܛܝܪ πρακτήρ = πράκτωρ, *tax-gatherer.*

ܦܪܘܢܐ pl. ܐ̈ f. *a moat, ditch, sewer.*

ܦܪܩܝܢܝܛܝܣ παρακινητής, *a disturber of the peace.*

ܦܪܘܩܣܣ, ܣܘܣ and ܦܪܘܣ m. Lat. processus, *an imperial progress,* also the emperor's *temporary stay* elsewhere than at Constantinople.

ܦܪܩܠܝܛܐ and ܦܪܩܠܝܛ pl. ܐ̈ m. παράκλητος, *an advocate, intercessor* esp. *the Comforter.*

ܦܪܩܠܝܛܝܐ from the preceding: *of the Paraclete.*

ܦܪܦܪ *to chatter, chirp* as birds. ETHPALP. ܐܬܦܪܦܪ *to be split.*

ܦܪܩܬܐ rt. ܦܪܩ. f. *the back of the neck, the vertebra of the neck.*

ܦܪܝܪܐ pl. ܐ̈ French frère, *a brother.*

ܦܪܗܣܝܐ; see ܦܪܗܣܝܐ.

ܦܪܗܣܝܐܝܬ, ܦܪܗܣ and ܦܪܗܣܝܐܝܬ from ܦܪܗܣܝܐ. adv. *freely, boldly.*

ܦܪܫ fut. ܢܦܪܘܫ, act. part. ܦܪܫ, ܦܪܫܐ, pass. part. ܦܪܝܫ, ܐ, ܬܐ *a*) trans. *to separate, sever, set apart, part, divide;* ܦܪܫ ܐܠܗܐ ܒܝܢ ܢܘܗܪܐ ܠܚܫܘܟܐ *God divided the light from the darkness;* ܠܡܦܪܫ ܠܦܘܩܕܢܐ ܕܡܠܐܟܐ *to set aside the angelic command. b*) *to set apart* for a special use or office, *to appoint;* ܠܡܦܪܫ ܢܕܪܐ ܐܘ ܡܫܡܠܝܐ ܠܡܪܝܐ *to set apart for a vow or whole offering unto the Lord;* ܗܘ ܕܩܕܡ ܦܪܫܗ ܕܒܐܝܕܘܗܝ *He Who fore-appointed him that by him . . .;* ܦܪܘܫܘ ܐܦܣܩܘܦܐ ܐܝܢܐ ܕܨܒܝܬܘܢ *appoint bishop whomsoever ye elect. c*) *to make a distinction, a difference, to distinguish;* ܠܦܘܪܫܢܐ ܕܦܪܫ ܡܬܩܢܢ ܟܠ *the distinctions which He who ordains all has made;* with ܐܝܩܪܐ *to distinguish, to honour.* Gram. ܦܪܫܐ ܠܓܠܠܐ ܗܢ ܠܡܕ ܡܢ ܫܡ ܓܠܐ *the Lomadh distinguishes galle,* waves, *from the noun gelo,* a straw. Adverbial use with another verb, *distinctly, clearly;* ܦܪܫ ܡܬܠܠ ܐܢܘܢ ܒ *he clearly compared them to . . . . d*) *to separate* from intercourse, *to excommunicate. e*) *to separate* from a wife, a husband. *f*) with ܢܦܫܗ or ellipt. *to separate oneself, go apart, away, secede, depart, die* with ܡܢ; ܦܪܘܫ ܡܢ ܥܡܐ *stand aloof from the people;* ܦܪܫ ܡܢܗܘܢ ܘܐܙܠ ܠܗ ܠ *he parted from them and took his way to . . .,* ܢܦܫܐ ܕܦܪܫܐ ܡܢ ܦܓܪܐ *the soul which departs from the body;* ܦܪܫܬܘܢ ܕܒܛܘܪܐ ܬܥܡܪܘܢ *ye have gone apart that ye might settle in mountains* i.e. become solitaries. Part. adj. *a*) *separated, separate, apart, different, diverse;* ܦܪܝܫ ܡܢ ܟܢܘܫܬܐ or ellipt. *excommunicate;* gram. *separate* letters i.e. *written separately. b*) *set apart, dedicated;* ܝܘܡܐ ܦܪܝܫ ܠܥܒܕܐ ܚܡܝܠܐ *the day is for work. c*) *special, singular, wonderful;* ܕܘܟܬܐ ܦܪܝܫܬܐ *a special place;* ܦܪܝܫܝܢ ܐܢܘܢ ܐܪ̈ܙܘܗܝ ܕܐܠܗܐ *wonderful are the mysteries of God;* ܫܡܐ ܦܪܝܫܐ *the Special Name* i.e. of God. Fem. pl. emph. *wonders, portents.* Cf. subst. ܦܪܝܫܬܐ. ETHPE. ܐܬܦܪܫ *a*) *to be divided, become separated;* ܕܠܐ ܡܬܦܪܫܝܢ the Persons of the Holy Trinity *who are inseparable. b*) *to be set apart, assigned. c*) *to be designated, elected, appointed* to office, also *to be constituted,* as a bishopric. *d*) *to be marked out, distinguished. e*) *to be divorced. f*) *to be excommunicated. g*) refl. *to separate oneself, stand aloof, depart.* PA. ܦܪܫ *a*) *to part asunder, separate; to make a difference, distinguish. b*) *to set apart, dedicate. c*) *to write distinctly, describe clearly, to explain.* Pass. part. ܡܦܪܫ, ܡܦܪܫܐ,

ܡܦܪܫܳܐ. *separate, distinct, defined, explained; various; special;* ܡܶܠܬܳܐ ܡܦܰܪܫܬܳܐ *a clear* or *articulate speech;* eccles. *selected, arranged in order;* ܡܰܙܡܽܘܪ̈ܶܐ ܕܕܳܘܺܝܕ ܡܦܰܪ̈ܫܶܐ *the Psalms of David in order;* ܩܶܪ̈ܝܳܢܶܐ ܡܦܰܪ̈ܫܶܐ ܚܰܕ ܒܳܬܰܪ ܚܰܕ *the lessons in following order* through the year; ܐܶܘܰܢܓܶܠܝܽܘܢ ܕܡܦܰܪ̈ܫܶܐ *the Gospels following separately*, opp. a diatessaron or harmony of the Gospels. ETHPA. ܐܶܬܦܰܪܰܫ *to be parted asunder, separated; to be assigned.* APH. ܐܰܦܪܶܫ *to set apart* as an offering to the Lord; *to separate oneself;* with ܠܶܒܳܐ *to prick the heart, cause compunction.* DERIVATIVES, ܦܪܫܐ, ܦܪܫܘܢܐ, ܦܪܫܘܬܐ, ܦܪܫܐܝܬ, ܦܪܝܫܐ, ܦܪܝܫܘܬܐ, ܦܪܝܫܐܝܬ, ܦܪܫܬܐ, ܦܪܫܐ, ܦܰܪܫܳܐ, ܦܪܫܘܬܐ, ܦܪܫܝܢܐ, ܦܪܫܐܝܬ, ܡܦܪܫܐܝܬ, ܡܦܪܫܘܬܐ, ܡܦܪܫܢܐ, ܡܦܪܫܢܘܬܐ, ܡܬܦܪܫܢܐ, ܡܬܦܪܫܢܐܝܬ, ܡܬܦܪܫܢܘܬܐ.

ܦܰܪܳܫܳܐ pl. ܐ̈ܶ, ܐ̈ rt. ܦܪܫ. m. *a horseman, mounted soldier;* ܦܰܪ̈ܳܫܶܐ ܘܰܦܰܓ̈ܪܶܐ *cavalry and infantry, horse and foot.*

ܦܽܘܪܫܳܐ rt. ܦܪܫ. m. *a) separation, selection;* ܟܬܳܒܳܐ ܕܦܽܘܪܫ ܩܶܪ̈ܝܳܢܶܐ *a lectionary. b) an ox-goad.*

ܦܰܪܳܫܟܳܐ pl. ܐ̈ Pers. m. *a copy* of a book, &c., an astronomical *table.*

ܦܰܪܳܫܽܘܬܳܐ rt. ܦܪܫ. f. *horsemen, cavalry; horsemanship.*

ܦܽܘܪܫܳܢܬܳܐ pl. ܐ̈ rt. ܦܪܫ. f. *a) an offering, thing dedicated. b) determination.*

ܦܰܪܫܶܓ or ܦܰܪܫܶܚ *to straddle.*

ܦܰܪܫܰܓܬܳܐ f. *having the feet wide apart, straddling.*

ܦܪܳܐ act. part. ܦܳܪܶܐ, ܦܳܪܝܳܐ. *to rip up.* ETHPE. ܐܶܬܦܪܺܝ *to burst* as a fruit with ripeness; *to burst asunder; to be ripped up;* metaph. *to burst* with anger. PA. ܦܰܪܺܝ *to tear open, rip up;* ܚܰܝܘܬܳܐ ܕܒܳܪܳܐ ܬܦܰܪܶܐ ܐܶܢܽܘܢ *a wild beast shall tear them;* ܦܰܓ̈ܪܶܐ ܡܦܰܪ̈ܝܶܐ *lacerated corpses.* ETHPA. ܐܶܬܦܰܪܺܝ *to burst;* ܐܶܬܦܰܪܺܝܬ ܟܰܪܣܶܗ *his belly burst open.* APH. ܐܰܦܪܺܝ *to tear to pieces.* PALI ܦܰܪܝܺܝ *to tear away* or *asunder.* ETHPALI ܐܶܬܦܰܪܝܺܝ same as ETHPEEL and sometimes confused with it. DERIVATIVES, ܦܘܪܝܐ, ܦܪܝܬܐ, ܦܪܬ, ܦܪܬܐ, ܦܪܬܐ, ܦܪܬܘܬܐ, ܡܬܦܪܬܘܬܐ.

ܦܪܳܬ rarely ܦܪܰܬ, rt. ܦܪܬ. pr. n. *the Euphrates.*

ܦܰܪܬܳܐ; see ܦܰܪܬܳܐ. ܦܶܪܬܳܐ; see ܦܶܪܬܳܐ.

ܦܰܪܬܳܐ rt. ܦܪܬ. m. *bread broken* or *crumbled to put into soup.*

ܦܶܪܬܳܐ (short e) rt. ܦܪܬ. m. *undigested food in the stomach, dung.*

ܦܶܪܬܳܐ (long e) rt. ܦܪܐ. f. = ܦܺܐܪܳܐ *fertility.*

ܦܰܪܬܰܘ or ܦܰܪܬܰܘܢ pr. n. *Parthia.*

ܦܰܪܬܳܘܳܐܝܬ from ܦܪܬܘ. adv. *in the Parthian language.*

ܦܪܬܘܡܐ; see ܦܪܬܘܡܩܐ.

ܦܰܪܬܘܳܝܳܐ pl. ܐ̈ from ܦܪܬܘ; *a Parthian.*

ܦܰܪܬܘܬܳܐ pl. ܐ̈ = ܦܰܪ̈ܬܽܘܬܳܐ *particles.*

ܦܰܪܬܽܘܬܳܐ pl. ܐ̈ rt. ܦܪܬ. m. *broken bits of bread, crumbs, fragments.*

ܦܪܬܡܐ; see ܦܪܬܘܡܩܐ.

ܦܰܪܬܶܟ *to crush.* ETHPAL. ܐܶܬܦܰܪܬܰܟ *to be crushed.*

ܦܰܪܬܺܝ PALI conj. of ܦܪܬ.

ܦܪܳܬܳܝܳܐ from ܦܪܳܬ. *from* or *of the banks of the Euphrates.*

ܦܰܪܰܬܺܝܩܺܝ, ܦܰܪܰܬܺܝܩܺܐ, ܦܰܪܰܕܺܝܩܺܝ, &c. pl. ܦܰܪܰܬܺܝܩܶܣ, ܦܰܪܰܬܺܝܩܺܣ, &c. f. παραθήκη, *a deposit, charge.*

ܦܰܪܬܶܟ ETHPALAL ܐܶܬܦܰܪܬܰܟ *a) to be split, cleft;* part. ܡܶܬܦܰܪܬܟܳܢܳܐ *fissile. b) to be doubtful, anxious;* ܡܶܬܦܰܪܬܟܳܐ ܗܘܳܬ ܪܶܥܝܳܢܶܗ ܒܰܩܢܳܝܳܐ ܕܡܰܥܒܕܳܢܘܳܬܳܐ *his mind was anxiously set on acquiring virtues.* DERIVATIVES, ܦܘܪܬܟܐ, ܦܪܬܟܐ.

ܦܶܪܬܳܟܳܐ pl. ܐ̈ rt. ܦܪܬܟ. m. *an atom, minute particle, crumb.*

ܦܶܪܬܳܢܳܝܳܐ from ܦܶܪܬܳܐ, ܦܶܪܬܳܐ *made of bran.*

ܦܰܪܰܬܺܝܩܺܐ pl. ܦܰܪܰܬܺܝܩܶܣ; see ܦܰܪܰܬܺܝܩܺܝ.

ܦܫ ETHPA. ܐܶܬܦܰܫܫ *to be relaxed, dissolved.* APH. ܐܰܦܶܫ pass. part. ܡܦܰܫ. *worn* or *wasted away.* PAUEL ܦܰܘܫܶܫ *a) to throw off by perspiration;* ܡܦܰܘܫܫܳܢܳܐ *diaphoretic, promoting perspiration. b) to disperse vapour;* metaph. *to dissipate;* ܢܦܰܘܫܶܫ ܟܪܝܘܬܗܘܢ *he will dispel their sadness.* ETHPAU. ܐܶܬܦܰܘܫܰܫ *a) refl. to waste away, consume;* ܐܰܝܟ ܕܡܶܬܦܰܘܫܫܳܐ ܦܰܓܪܳܐ ܒܥܰܡܠܳܐ ܘܰܒܨܰܘܡܳܐ *as the body wears away in labour and fasting. b) to be dissipated, dispersed, evaporated;* ܠܳܐ ܡܶܬܦܰܘܫܫܺܝܢ ܥܢ̈ܳܢܶܐ ܕܛܘܪ̈ܶܐ *mountain mists are not dispersed;* ܡܶܬܦܰܘܫܰܫ ܫܽܘܚܢܳܐ *the tumour can be dispersed.* DERIVATIVES, ܦܘܫܫܐ, ܡܦܘܫܫܢܐ.

ܦܫܚ part. adj. ܦܫܝܚܐ ,ܦܫܝܚ maimed, crippled in hand or foot. Derivatives, ܦܫܝܚܘܬܐ ,ܦܫܝܚܐܝܬ.

ܦܫܘܫܐ rt. ܦܫܫ. m. tasteless, insipid.

ܦܫܘܪܐ, ܪܬܐ rt. ܦܫܪ. a) explaining, discerning; an interpreter of dreams. b) digestive; suppurating, generating matter. c) lukewarm, pl. ellipt. warm water; metaph. insipid, senseless, silly.

ܦܫܘܪܘܬܐ rt. ܦܫܪ. f. a) liquefaction. b) senselessness, folly.

ܦܫܚ fut. ܢܦܫܘܚ and ܢܦܫܚ, act. part. ܦܫܚ, ܦܫܚܐ, part. adj. ܦܫܝܚ, ܚܐ. a) to tear, rend asunder, cut off; ܫܡܫܘܢ ܦܫܚ ܠܐܪܝܐ Samson rent the lion; ܦܫܚ ܫܒܘܒܐ ܡܢ ܐܝܠܢܐ he cut off a sucker from the tree. b) to throw down; ܦܫܚܘܗ ܘܦܫܚܘܗ throw her down, and they threw her down. c) to detach, seduce; ܒܥܐ ܕܢܦܫܚܟܘܢ ܡܢ ܢܟܦܘܬܐ he seeks to draw you away from a chaste life. d) to diminish, become remiss. Part. a) maimed, broken; less, more tolerable; ܕܬܗܘܐ ܦܫܝܚܐ ܠܗܘܢ ܡܠܟܐ ܒܝܘܡܐ ܕܕܝܢܐ that it may be more tolerable for them in the day of judgement; ܗܘܐ ܦܫܝܚ ܢܣܝܘܢܐ the temptation was less, the force of the temptation was broken. Ethpe. ܐܬܦܫܚ to be torn or broken off as branches; to be crippled, disjointed; metaph. to be enfeebled, knocked up. Pa. ܦܫܚ to cut in pieces as sacrificial animals, to cut off as branches; to tear asunder, tear to pieces; ܣܘܟܐ ܡܦܫܚܬܐ lopped off branches; ܠܡܠܒܫܗ ܘܠܡܦܫܚܘܬܗ ܡܬܚܡܬܝܢ ܠܗ they will threaten to seize him and tear him to pieces. Metaph. to perplex, distract. Ethpa. to be torn asunder; to be shattered; to be broken off, torn away; to be distracted, perplexed; ܟܠ ܝܘܡ ܕܠܐ ܝܘܬܪܢ ܡܬܦܫܚ every day is torn away from us, comes to an abrupt end without profit; ܕܠܐ ܬܬܦܫܚ ܪܥܝܢܟܘܢ lest your mind be distracted. Derivatives, ܦܫܝܚܘܬܐ ,ܦܫܝܚܐ ,ܦܫܚܐ ,ܦܘܫܚܐ.

ܦܘܫܚܐ pl. ܚܐ rt. ܦܫܚ. m. a) a section, part of a book. b) the fork of branches. c) a company of soldiers. d) a sect. e) either transverse line of a cross.

ܦܫܪ Ethpal. ܐܬܦܫܪ to be torn or broken away.

ܦܫܛ fut. ܢܦܫܘܛ, act. part. ܦܫܛ, ܦܫܛܐ, pass. part. ܦܫܝܛ, ܛܐ, ܛܬܐ. a) trans. to stretch out, extend, reach out, often with ܐܝܕܐ to spread out the hands in supplication, to reach out the hand to give; ܦܫܘܛ ܐܝܕܐ ܠܗܘܢ ܠܡܣܟܢܐ extend help to the needy; ܦܫܛ ܗܘܐ ܡܫܘܛ be large-minded; with ܩܘܡܬܐ or ܩܘܡܬܗ to stand erect but with ܢܦܫܗ also to offer oneself; ܦܫܛ ܢܦܫܗ ܠܡܘܬܐ ܕܪܫܝܥܐ He gave Himself up to the wicked; with ܨܘܪܐ to stretch forward, offer the neck. b) to make straight; ܦܫܛ ܥܩܡܬܐ He made the crooked to stand erect; ܦܫܛ ܠܫܢܐ ܕܚܪܫܐ He made the tongue of the dumb to speak. c) intrans. to reach, go forward, spread out; ܓܐܪܐ ܦܫܛ ܘܥܒܪ ܒ the arrow went on and passed through his body; ܦܫܛ ܚܝܠܐ ܐܪܥܗܘܢ the army overspread their land. Pass. part. a) erect, upright, esp. rit. opp. ܓܗܝܢ prostrate; ܨܠܘܬܐ ܕܒ ܦܫܝܛ a prayer said by the priest standing up. b) with ܐܝܕܐ a stretched-out hand; metaph. open, liberal; with ܠܫܢܐ ready of tongue. c) straight, plain, flat; ܦܫܝܛ ܩܕܡܝܢ straight before us. d) med. simple drugs, substances, illnesses, opp. ܡܪܟܒܐ compound. e) geomet. with ܛܠܠܐ explained as a simple or straight shadow, i.e. one which only widens or decreases, opp. ܗܦܝܟܐ a shadow which moves round the object which casts it. f) legal. with ܙܒܢܐ sale without warranty. g) simple; common, with ܡܡܠܠܐ prose; ܡܠܐ ܦܫܝܛܐ common, i.e. heptasyllabic measure; also the categories are called ܗܠܝܢ ܦܫܝܛܬܐ ܥܣܪ the ten simple matters; ܡܦܩܬܐ ܦܫܝܛܬܐ or ellipt. the Peshitto or Simple Version. h) simple, unlearned, pl. the common people; ܐܦܝܣܩܘܦܐ ܦ̈ an ordinary bishop, i.e. not a Metropolitan nor Patriarch. i) simple-minded, innocent, sincere, straightforward; ܠܒܐ ܦ̈ a simple heart; ܫܒܩ ܠܢܟܝܠܐ: ܓܒܐ ܠܦܫܝܛܐ He left alone the crafty and chose the simple. k) gram. a primary noun, intransitive verb, separate pronoun, cardinal number. E-Syr. the simple verb = Peal and Ethpeal conjj.

Ethpe. ܐܬܦܫܛ a) to be made straight, made able to move as the tongue, hand, body; ܡܫܪܝܐ ܐܬܦܫܛ the paralysed stood erect.

b) *to stretch out, spread out, extend; to expand* as flowers; ܩܕܡ ܕܢܬܦܫܛܘܢ ܛܛܪ̈ܝܐ ܒܗܠܝܢ ܐܬܪ̈ܘܬܐ *before* the Tartars *overspread those countries;* ܐܬܦܫܛܬ ܒܟܠܗ ܐܘܚܕܢܢ the Faith of Christ *has spread throughout our realm.* Pa. ܦܰܫܶܛ *to spread out; to set straight;* ܦܫܛܘܢܝ *compose* my limbs for burial. Ethpa. ܐܶܬܦܰܫܰܛ a) *to stretch out* the limbs, *to stand up, stand erect.* b) *to be extended, be made straight as a road.* Derivatives, ܦܫܛܐ, ܦܫܝܛܐ, ܦܫܝܛܐܝܬ, ܦܫܝܛܘܬܐ, ܡܦܫܛܢܘܬܐ, ܡܦܫܛܢܐ.

ܦܘܫܛܐ rt. ܦܫܛ. m. *extension, dilatation;* ܦ ܕܐܝ̈ܕܝܐ *the stretching out of the hands.*

ܦܘܫܛܐ, ܦܘܫܛܬܐ pl. ܬܐ̈ rt. ܦܫܛ. f. *a prayer* said by the priest *with outstretched hands* and *in a loud voice.*

ܦܫܛܝ̈ܐ m. pl. *swaddling clothes.*

ܦܫܝܓܐܝܬ rt. ܦܫܓ. adv. walking *with a limp, lamely.*

ܦܫܝܓܘܬܐ rt. ܦܫܓ. f. *paralysis of the hands.*

ܦܫܝܙܐ, ܦܫܝܙܐ or ܦܫܝܛܐ the middle form is probably correct, Pers. m. *a small coin.*

ܦܫܝܙܐ ܕܥܙܐ m. *the cloven hoof of a goat.*

ܦܫܝܚܘܬܐ rt. ܦܫܚ. f. *perplexity, a distracted mind.*

ܦܫܝܛܐܝܬ rt. ܦܫܛ. adv. *simply, directly, liberally; foolishly; generally* opp. specially; rit. ܩܐܡ ܦܫܝܛܐܝܬ *he rises and stands erect;* legal. with ܙܒܢ *to buy without warranty.*

ܦܫܝܛܘܬܐ rt. ܦܫܛ. f. *simplicity, innocence, ignorance;* with ܐܝܕܐ or ellipt. *openhandedness; unity of substance;* gram. *prose.*

ܦܫܝܛܬܐ a) *the Peshitto Version;* see under ܦܫܛ. b) *a branch.*

ܦܫܝܟ, ܦܫܝܟܐ, ܬܐ *held close together, pressed close.*

ܦܫܝܪܘܬܐ rt. ܦܫܪ. f. *tastelessness, insipidity.*

ܦܫܝܩܐܝܬ rt. ܦܫܩ. adv. *easily, with ease, freely, readily; plainly, distinctly.*

ܦܫܝܩܘܬܐ rt. ܦܫܩ. f. *ease, facility; readiness;* ܦܫܝܩܘܬܐ ܡܬܟܫܠܢܘܬܐ *proneness to offend.*

ܦܫܟ impers. ܦܫܟܬ ܠܗ usually with ܥܠ *to be all over with ...;* pass. part. ܦܫܝܟܐ *pressed closely together.* Pael ܦܰܫܶܟ *to make to doubt;* pass. part. ܡܦܫܟ, ܡܦܫܟܐ *nonplussed, at a loss, pressed by difficulties.* Ethpa. ܐܶܬܦܰܫܰܟ *to be doubtful, to hesitate, be in doubt* with ܒ or ܥܠ; ܠܐ ܢܬܦܫܟ ܐܢܫ ܒܚܕܐ ܡܢ ܗܠܝܢ ܬܪ̈ܬܝܢ *let him not be in doubt concerning either matter.* Derivatives, ܦܫܝܟܐ, ܦܫܝܟܘܬܐ, ܡܦܫܟܢܘܬܐ.

ܦܫܟ, ܦܫܟܐ m. *a handsbreadth* = half a cubit.

ܦܫܠ part. ܡܦܫܠ, ܡܦܫܠܐ *twisted, crooked, crookshanked.*

ܦܫܠ fut. ܢܦܫܘܠ, act. part. ܦܳܫܶܠ, ܦܳܫܠܳܐ, pass. part. ܦܫܝܠ, ܠܐ. *to twist, twine, spin;* metaph. ܢܦܫܘܠ ܠܟܠ ܓܒ̈ܝܢ *it will twist in every direction.* Ethpe. ܐܶܬܦܫܶܠ a) *to be twisted, spun.* b) = ܐܶܬܒܫܶܠ *to be cooked.* Pa. ܦܰܫܶܠ *to spin;* pass. part. a) *twined* or *spun linen.* b) *crooked, bending over to fall.* Ethpaal ܐܶܬܦܰܫܰܠ and Ethpaial ܐܶܬܦܰܝܫܰܠ a) *to be twisted, twined.* b) *to be cooked, fried.* Aph. ܐܰܦܫܶܠ a) *to twist, twine* ܚܒܠܐ *a rope.* b) *to twist, wring* the limbs. c) *to make great haste.* Ettaph. ܐܶܬܬܰܦܫܰܠ *to be spun.* Derivatives, ܦܫܠܐ, ܦܘܫܠܐ, ܦܫܝܠܘܬܐ, ܦܫܠܐ.

ܦܫܠܐ or ܦܘܫܠܐ a) *spinning.* b) *a thread.* c) *parching.*

ܦܫܡ, ܦܫܡܐ Ar. *tasteless.*

ܦܫܡܛܐ or ܦܫܡܘܛܐ pl. ܝ̈ܢ, ܐ̈. Pers. m. *a horse-cloth, pack-saddle.*

ܦܫܪ pass. part. ܦܫܝܪ, ܦܫܝܪܐ, ܬܐ. *lukewarm, tepid, tasteless.* Ethpa. ܐܶܬܦܰܫܰܪ *to become insipid, be spiritless.* Derivatives, ܦܫܝܪܘܬܐ, ܦܫܝܪܐ.

ܦܫܦܫܐ pl. ܐ̈ m. *a small reddish bug.*

ܦܫܦܫܐ m. *a wicket door.*

ܦܫܦܫ m. a great fish the skin of which is used for planing or polishing wood.

ܦܫܩ fut. ܢܦܫܘܩ only in the lexx. *to make plain* or *easy.* Part. adj. ܦܫܝܩ, ܩܐ, ܩܬܐ. *easy,* ܐܝܢܐ ܦܫܝܩܐ ܠܡܐܡܪ ... ܐܘ *whether is it easier to say,* &c.—*or* ...; ܦܫܝܩ ܠܐܘܪܓܙܐ *easy-tempered.* Pa. ܦܰܫܶܩ *to explain, expound; to write commentaries; to translate;* ܦܰܫܶܩ ܠܢ ܡܬܠܐ ܗܢܐ *explain this parable to us;* ܥܣܩܐ ܠܡܦܫܩܘܬܗ *hard of interpretation;* ܡܦܫܩ ܠܥܕܬܐ ܐܫܬܐ ܝܘܡܝ̈ ܒܪܝܬܐ *he expounds the Six Days of Creation to the congregation;* ܗܢܐ ܦܫܩ ܥܬܝܩܬܐ ܘܚܕܬܐ James of Sarug *wrote commentaries on the Old and New Testaments.* Ethpa. ܐܶܬܦܰܫܰܩ a) *to be declared, explained;* ܠܐ ܐܬܦܫܩ ܠܗ ܡܢܐ ܢܬܥܒܕ *it had not yet been declared what should be done.* *b) to be translated;* ܕܐܬܦܫܩ ܡܢ ܡܡܠܠܘܬܐ ܝܘܢܝܐ *which was translated from the Septuagint.* Derivatives, ܦܘܫܩܐ, ܦܫܝܩܐ, ܦܫܝܩܘܬܐ, ܦܫܩܐ, ܦܫܝܩܐܝܬ, ܡܦܫܩܢܐ, ܡܦܫܩܢܘܬܐ, ܡܬܦܫܩܢܐ, ܡܬܦܫܩܢܐܝܬ.

ܦܫܩܐ rt. ܦܫܩ. m. *an interpreter.*

ܦܫܩܠ pass. part. ܡܦܫܩܠܐ. *bandy-legged.* Cf. ܦܫܠ.

ܦܫܪ fut. ܢܦܫܘܪ, act. part. ܦܫܪ, ܦܫܪܐ, pass. part. ܦܫܝܪ, ܦܫܝܪܐ. *a) to interpret* a dream, *solve* a riddle. *b)* intrans. *to dissolve, melt, to liquefy, fuse* as metals; *to be macerated;* ܦܫܪ ܡܠܚܐ *the salt dissolved;* ܦܫܪ ܓܠܝܕܐ ܕܚܢܦܘܬܐ *the frost of heathendom disappeared;* metaph. ܚܡܬܐ ܕܠܒܟ ܠܐ ܦܫܪܐ *the anger of thine heart is not melted.* *c) to digest, to ruminate; to mature* as an ulcer; ܡܕܡ ܕܦܫܪ *a digestive;* ܫܘܚܢܐ ܠܐ ܦܫܝܪܝܢ *immature pustules.* Ethpe. ܐܬܦܫܪ *to melt, be melted;* of a dream *to vanish away, be of no effect.* Pa. ܦܫܪ *a) to interpret* a dream, *a parable.* *b)* trans. *to melt, smelt, liquefy* wax, glass, metals, *to run down* honey. *c) to digest.* Ethpa. ܐܬܦܫܪ *a) to melt, flow down, to be melted, liquefied; to be cracked;* ܫܘܪܐ ܘܒܬܐ ܐܬܦܫܪܘ ܡܢ ܝܩܕܢܐ the walls and *houses were cracked by the conflagration.* *b) to be explained* as a dream. *c) to be digested.* Aph. ܐܦܫܪ *a) to declare, explain;* ܗܠܝܢ ܐܦܫܪ ܐܫܥܝܐ ܒܡܬܠܐ ܕܟܪܡܐ *these things Isaiah declared in his parable of the vine.* *b) to relax, loosen* the limbs. Derivatives, ܦܘܫܪܐ, ܦܫܝܪܐ, ܦܫܝܪܘܬܐ, ܦܫܪܐ, ܦܫܪܬܐ, ܡܦܫܪܢܐ, ܡܬܦܫܪܢܐ, ܡܬܦܫܪܢܘܬܐ, ܐܦܫܪܬܐ.

ܦܫܪ, ܦܫܪܐ rt. ܦܫܪ. m. *interpretation* of dreams, *solution* of riddles; *rumination, digestion; melting;* ܦܫܪ ܠܒܐ *melting of the heart* = great sorrow; *mitigation, relaxation; foolishness.*

ܦܫܪܐ, ܦܫܪܬܐ rt. ܦܫܪ. f. *urine;* ܡܪܕܐ ܕ̈ܦ *diuretic.*

ܦܫܪܛܐܘܡ = ܦܪܛܐܘܡ *bryony.*

ܦܬ = ܦܬܓܡܐ.

ܦܬ or ܦܬܬ, ܦܬ, fut. ܢܦܬܘܬ, act. part. ܦܐܬ, pass. part. ܦܬܝܬ, ܦܬܝܬܐ. *to break bread in pieces;* ܦܬܘܬܘܗܝ *break* the cake *in pieces;* ܟܣܢܐ ܦܬܝܬܐ ܕܠܚܡܐ *broken bread.* Ethpa. ܐܬܦܬܬ *to be pounded, crushed.* Palpel ܦܬܦܬ *to tear* a reputation *to pieces, to disparage, calumniate.* Ethpalp. ܐܬܦܬܦܬ *to be broken, crushed, destroyed.* Derivatives, ܦܬܝܬܐ, ܦܬܬܐ and ܦܬܬܐ, ܦܬܦܬܘܬܐ.

ܦܬܐ and ܦܬܐ *to be enlarged, increased.* Pass. part. ܦܬܐ, ܦܬܝܐ, ܦܬܝܐ *wide, broad, ample;* ܦܬܝܐ ܬܪܥܐ *wide is the gate;* ܫܘܩܐ ܦܬܝܐ *a broad street;* ܡܐܢܐ ܕܦܬܝܐ ܦܘܡܗ *a wide-mouthed vessel;* ܦܬܐ ܪ̈ܓܠܐ *splay-footed;* with ܡܠܬܐ or ellipt. *long, lengthy;* ܒܦܬܝܘܬܐ ܟܬܒ ܠܘܩܐ ܐܘܢܓܠܝܘܢ *Luke wrote his Gospel at full length.* Pa. ܦܬܝ *to enlarge, enrich; widen* dresses, houses, territories; ܦܬܝ ܐܬܪܐ ܕܡܫܟܢܟ *enlarge the place of thy tent;* ܠܐ ܦܬܝܢ ܡܠܬܗ *we have not narrated it at length.* Ethpa. ܐܬܦܬܝ *to be enlarged, extended; to wax great, extend widely, spread abroad;* ܐܟܠ ܘܐܫܬܝ ܘܐܬܦܬܝ ܘܐܬܥܒܝ *he ate and drank and grew large and stout;* ܐܝܢܐ ܕܡܬܦܬܐ ܒܢܝܚܐ. ܐܘܠܨܐ ܕܬܪܥܐ ܡܕܚܐ ܠܗ *whoso relaxes in ease, the straitness of the gate repels him;* ܠܐ ܬܬܦܬܐ ܒܡܠܐ ܕܥܠܝܟ *do not talk big about thyself;* ܡܬܦܬܝܐ ܣܒܪܬܐ *the gospel spreads widely.* Aph. ܐܦܬܝ *to enlarge, make broad, spread out widely; to be verbose, lengthy;* ܕܪܚܡ ܠܡܦܬܝܘ ܡܠܟܘܬܗ *desirous of enlarging his dominions;* ܡܦܬܝܢ ܬܦܠܝܢܝܗܘܢ *they make broad their phylacteries;* ܐܦܬܝܬ ܫܝܘܠ ܦܘܡܗ *Sheol has opened widely.* Derivatives, ܐܦܬܐ, ܦܬܝܐ, ܦܬܝܬ, ܦܬܝܘܬܐ, ܦܬܝܢܐ, ܦܬܝܢܐ, ܡܦܬܝܢܘܬܐ, ܡܦܬܝܢܐ.

ܦܬܐ = ܦܬܬܐ.

ܦܬܐ, ܦܬܝܢ pl. of ܦܬܬܐ.

ܦܬܓܡ denom. verb from ܦܬܓܡܐ. *to say, speak.*

ܦܬܓܡ, ܦܬܓܡܐ pl. ܝܢ, ̈ܐ Pers. *a word, saying, phrase; a text* of Scripture; in poetry *a line, verse, half-verse, versicle, a foot; a matter, thing, affair;* with ܗܦܟ, ܦܢܝ, &c. *to return* or *give an answer, to answer for, be answerable.*

ܦܬܘܬܐ rt. ܦܬܐ. m. *largeness;* ܦܬܘܬܐ ܕܣܘܓܐܗܘܢ *their exceedingly large number.*

ܦܬܘܪܐ, ܦܬܪܐ rt. ܦܬܪ. m. *a) an originator;*

ܦܬܘܚܐ ܕܡܥܡܘܕܝܬܐ *he who first baptized.* b) *cow-dung.* c) a letter *taking P'thacha.*

ܦܬܘܪ, ܦܬܘܪܐ pl. ـܝܢ, ـܐ m. *a table, tray; a gift;* ܒܝܬ ܦܬܘܪܐ *a refectory.* Esp. *a Communion table, altar.*

ܦܬܟܘܢܐ or ܦܘܬܟܘܢܐ pl. ـܐ rt. ܦܬܟ. m. *ornaments, girdles or raiments dyed or wrought in various colours or of coloured gems, variegated marble or wood, agate, striped silk, brocade.*

ܦܬܚ fut. ܢܦܬܚ, imper. ܦܬܘܚ and ܦܬܚ, act. part. ܦܬܚ, ܦܬܚܐ, pass. part. ܦܬܝܚ, ـܐ, ـܬܐ. a) *to open, unlock, unbar, admit,* of a door *to be open;* ܡܪܢ ܡܪܢ ܦܬܚ ܠܢ *Lord, Lord, open to us;* ܡܢ ܐܦܩܐ ܕܬܘܪܥܝܬܝ ܦܬܚܬ ܗ̈ܠܝܢ ܠܡܫܬܝܟ *from my stream of thoughts I brought out these for thy drink.* Esp. with ܐܘܪܚܐ *to open a way, remove obstruction;* ܐܝܕܐ *to be liberal;* ܛܒܥܐ *to break a seal, unseal;* ܥܝ̈ܢܐ or ܣܡ̈ܝܐ *to open* the eyes of *the blind;* ܪܚܡܐ or ܡܪܒܥܐ *to open the womb, be first-born;* ܬܪܥܐ ܦܬܝܚ *the door opened, was open.* b) *to institute, originate.* c) Arab. *to take* a town *by storm.* d) gram. *to give* or *require the vowel P'thacha;* ܦܬܚ ܠܗܘ ܕܒܪܫܗ *write* or *pronounce its first letter with P'thacha.* Pass. part. *open, seeing;* ܐܓܪܬܐ ܦܬܝܚܬܐ *an open letter,* opp. secret instructions; also ܦܬܝܚܐ ellipt. *letters-patent.* Gram. a letter or syllable with the vowel *P'thacha.* Ethpe. ܐܬܦܬܚ a) *to be opened,* according to the lexx. used of gates and of being opened at once: ܐܬܦܬܚ ܠܗ ܫܡܝܐ *the heaven opened;* ܐܬܦܬܚ ܠܗ ܐܘܪܚܐ ܕܢܡܠܠ *a way was opened for him to speak.* b) *to be taken by storm.* Pa. *to open* windows; *to open the eyes* of the blind; with ܡܠܬܐ *to show* or *declare openly.* Ethpa. *to be opened,* used according to the lexx. of the eyes, ears, and other plural objects, and of opening gradually; ܣܡܝܐ ܕܐܬܦܬܚ *the blind man whose eyes were opened.* Aph. ܐܦܬܚ *to cause to open, to give vent.* Derivatives, ܦܬܘܚܐ, ܦܬܚܬܐ, ܦܬܚܐ, ܦܬܚܐ, ܦܬܝܚܐ, ܦܬܝܚܘܢܐ, ܦܬܝܚܘܬܐ, ܡܦܬܚ, ܡܦܬܚܢܐ, ܡܦܬܚܢܘܬܐ, ܡܦܬܚܢܘܬܐ.

ܦܬܚ, ܦܬܚܐ pl. ـܐ rt. ܦܬܚ. m. a) *a door, an opening.* b) *a commencement, institution.* c) *the place where a book opens,* i.e. *the two pages lying open.* d) *the taking of a city by storm.* e) pl. = ܣ̈ܡܟܬܐ *the supports* of a weaver's beam. f) gram. *the vowel P'thacha.*

ܦܬܚܐ pl. ـܐ rt. ܦܬܚ. m. a) *an opening.* b) *explanation.* c) *the royal sceptre.*

ܦܬܝ verb; see ܦܬܐ.

ܦܬܝ, ܦܬܝܐ pl. ـܐ rt. ܦܬܐ. m. *breadth; latitude;* ܒܦܬܝܐ *across, transversely.*

ܦܬܝܐܝܬ rt. ܦܬܐ. adv. of speaking or writing *at length, fully.*

ܦܬܝܘܬܐ rt. ܦܬܐ. f. a) *extent, abundance; enlargement, state of being at large, at ease,* opp. straits and distress; ܒܦܬܝܘܬܐ *amply, abundantly.* b) with ܡܠܬܐ *diffusiveness.*

ܦܬܝܚܘܢܐ dimin. of ܦܬܝܚܐ see under ܦܬܚ. m. *a short letter.*

ܦܬܝܚܘܬܐ rt. ܦܬܚ. f. *a doorway, gateway.*

ܦܬܝܢܐ, ܦܬܝܢܬܐ rt. ܦܬܐ. *broad, large.*

ܦܬܝܟܘܬܐ pl. ـܘܬܐ rt. ܦܬܟ. f. *variety, diversity; embroidery;* pl. a leopard's *spots.*

ܦܬܝܠܐܝܬ rt. ܦܬܠ. adv. *obliquely, sidewise.*

ܦܬܝܠܘܬܐ rt. ܦܬܠ. f. *crookedness;* ܕܠܐ ܦܬܝܠܘ *in a straight course.*

ܦܬܝܠܬܐ rt. ܦܬܠ. f. *a wick.*

ܦܬܝܢܝܐ rt. ܦܬܐ. *latitudinal, of latitude.*

ܦܬܝܣܝܣ, ܦܬܝܣ and ܦܬܝܣ φθίσις, *consumption,* also a disease of the eye, the pupil becomes small and dull.

ܦܬܝܣܝܩܐ pl. ـܐ φθισικός, *consumptive.*

ܦܬܝܬܐ fem. pass. part. a) of verb ܦܬ stat. abs. b) of verb ܦܬܐ stat. emph.

ܦܬܟ fut. ܢܦܬܘܟ. *to mix, mingle.* Pass. part. ܦܬܝܟ, ܦܬܝܟܐ, ܦܬܝܟܬܐ *intermingled, various, woven of different materials* or *colours, embroidered;* ܥܡ ܚܘܚܐ ܙܪܥܐ ܛܒܐ ܦܬܝܟ *the good seed is intermingled with briars;* ܐܠܒܫܬܝܗܝ ܦܬܝ̈ܟܬܐ *thou hast arrayed thyself in many-coloured raiment.* Pa. ܦܬܟ *to vary;* ܦܬܟܝܗܝ ܦܘܠܚܢܐ ܦܓܪܢܝܐ ܒܥܡ̈ܠܐ ܪܘܚܢܝ̈ܐ *vary thy physical service with spiritual labours.* Pass. part. ܡܦܬܟ, ܡܦܬܟܐ, ܡܦܬܟܬܐ *varied, mixed, confused; various, adorned, manifold,* esp. *many coloured, wrought in various colours;* ܡܪ̈ܓܐ ܡܦܬܟܝܢ ܒܓܘ̈ܢܐ ܕܦܩܚܐ ܘܕܘܒܪܐ *meadows with many-coloured blossoms and flowers;* ܟܠܝܠܐ ܕܡܦܬܟܪ ܒܟܐܦܐ ܝܩܝܪܬܐ *a crown adorned with precious beryls.* Ethpa. ܐܬܦܬܟܪ *to be curiously wrought, intermingled.* Derivatives, ܦܬܟܪܐ, ܦܬܟܪܬܐ, ܦܬܟܪܘܬܐ, ܦܬܟܪܐ, ܡܦܬܟܪܢܐ, ܡܦܬܟܪܢܘܬܐ, ܡܦܬܟܪܢܝܬ.

ܦܬܟܪܐ pl. ܐ̈ rt. ܦܬܟܪ. m. *interwoven, interwrought* or *embroidered cloth* or *silk; embroidery.*

ܦܬܟܪܐ, ܦܬܟܪܬܐ pl. m. ܝ̈ܢ, ܐ̈, f. ܬܐ̈. Sanskrit *an idol;* ܒܝܬ ܦܬܟܪܐ *a temple of idols;* ܦܠܚܝ ܦ̈ *idolators.*

ܦܬܟܪܘܢܐ dimin. of ܦܬܟܪܐ. m. *a small idol.*

ܦܬܟܪܘܬܐ pl. ܘ̈ܬܐ from ܦܬܟܪܐ. f. *idolatry.*

ܦܬܟܪܝܐ, ܝܬܐ from ܦܬܟܪܐ. *of* or *pertaining to idols.*

ܦܬܠ fut. ܢܦܬܘܠ, act. part. ܦܐܬܠ, ܦܬܠܐ. *to twist awry, pervert.* Pass. part. ܦܬܝܠ, ܠܐ, ܠܬܐ. *distorted, perverse, froward;* ܩܫܬܐ ܦܬܝܠܬܐ *a distorted bow;* ܣܟܠܐ ܦܬܝܠ ܣܦܘܬܐ *a fool of froward lips.* Ethpe. ܐܬܦܬܠ *to be crooked, distorted, awry* of the limbs, of furrows, &c. Pa. ܦܬܠ *to twist awry, distort, pervert, make crooked* usually metaph. often with ܐܘܪܚܐ *to make a way crooked, act frowardly.* Pass. part. *crooked, perverse, shifty, deceitful,* opp. ܬܪܝܨܐ *upright, straightforward;* ܕܪܐ ܡܥܩܡܐ ܘܡܦܬܠܐ *a crooked and perverse generation;* ܗܝܡܢܘܬܐ ܠܐ ܡܦܬܠܬܐ *unperverted faith.* Ethpa. ܐܬܦܬܠ *to be contorted, distorted, perverted;* ܐܬܦܬܠ ܦܘܡܗ *his mouth was awry;* ܐܬܦܬܠ ܫܒܝܠܐ ܕܝܠܕܐ ܬܡܝܡܐ ܒܝܕ ܡܗܝܪܐ *the path for innocent children was made crooked by the learned.* Derivatives, ܦܬܠܐ, ܦܬܠܬܐ, ܦܬܠܬܢܐ, ܦܬܠܬܢܘܬܐ, ܡܦܬܠܢܐ, ܡܦܬܠܢܘܬܐ, ܡܦܬܠܢܝܬ, ܦܬܠܬܢܝܬ.

ܦܬܠܐ rt. ܦܬܠ. m. *twisting; complication.*

ܦܬܠܘܢܐ dimin. of ܦܬܠܐ. m. pl. *fringes.*

ܦܬܢܐ m. *an asp, a deaf adder.*

ܦܬܢܐ Arab. *tumult, discord.*

ܦܬܦܬ Palpel conj. of ܦܬ.

ܦܬܩ fut. ܢܦܬܘܩ, act. part. ܦܐܬܩ, ܦܬܩܐ. *a) to burst, break open* as an ulcer. *b)* trans. *to penetrate, pierce* with an arrow. Ethpe. ܐܬܦܬܩ *to come to a head, burst* as sores. Derivative, ܦܬܩܐ.

ܦܬܩܐ = ܦܬܩܐ f. πιττάκιον, *a slip of writing, a memorandum, a letter.*

ܦܬܩܐ rt. ܦܬܩ. m. *the bursting of an ulcer, discharge.*

ܦܬܬܐ pl. ܦܬܝܢ, ܦܬܐ̈ rt. ܦܬ. m. *a morsel, slice, bit* of bread or meat, *scraps.*

∴ ܫܠܡ ܐܬܘܬܐ ܦܐ ܒܥܘܕܪܢܗ ܕܡܪܝܐ ∴

∴ ܥܡ ܐܬܘܬܐ ܨܕܐ ܕܐܝܬܝܗ ܕܐܬܘܬܐ ܬܡܢܥܣܪܐ ܒܡܢܝܢܐ ܘܒܣܕܪܐ ∴

∴ ܨ ∴

ܨ ܨܕܐ

ܨ, ܨܕܐ *Sodhe,* the eighteenth letter of the Syriac alphabet; the number 90, with a point above, ܨ̇, 900.

ܨ̄ abbrev. for ܨܚܚܐ *a codex;* ܨܠܘܬܐ *a prayer.*

ܨܐ for ܨܐܐ pass. part. of verb ܨܐܐ.

ܨܐܐ Pael conj. of ܨܐܐ.

ܨܐܐ pl. ܨܐܝܢ and ܨܐܐܝܢ, ܨܐܐ̈, m. ܨܐܐ, f. emph. ܨܐܝܬܐ and ܨܐܐܝܬܐ, pl. ܨܐܝܢ̈, ܨܐܝܬܐ̈ rt. ܨܐܐ. *filthy, foul, dirty, soiled, impure;* ܢܚܬܐ ܨܐܐ̈ *filthy garments;* ܡܚܫܒܬܐ ܨ̈ *foul thoughts.*

ܨܐܐܘܬܐ, ܨܐܘܬܐ or ܨܐܝܘܬܐ, pl. ܨܐܘ̈ܬܐ and ܨܐܝܘ̈ܬܐ rt. ܨܐܐ. f. *filth, dirt, defilement, uncleanness, impurity; dross, mire.*

ܨܐܒ act. part. of verb ܨܘܒ.

ܨܐܕ = ܨܝܕ.

ܨܐܚ act. part. of verb ܨܘܚ.

ܨܐܐ fut. ܢܨܐܐ, act. part. ܨܐܐ, ܨܐܝܐ, pass. part. ܨܐܝ, ܨܐܝܐ pl. W-Syr. ܨܐܝܢ, E-Syr. ܨܐܝܢ. *to be filthy, defiled;* ܨܐܘ ܓܒܪ̈ܐ ܘܟܠܗ ܫܪܒܬܐ ܐܢܫܝܬܐ ܨܐܝܐ *men were vile and the whole race of man was foul;* ܢܚܬ̈ܐ ܕܠܐ ܨܐܝܢ *garments undefiled.* Pa. ܨܐܐ, ܨܐܝ and ܨܝܐ *to defile, pollute, tarnish, sully;* ܨܐܝܬܝܗ ܠܡܪܓܢܝܬܟ *thou hast tarnished thy pearl.* Ethpa. ܐܬܨܐܝ, ܐܬܨܐܐ, ܐܬܨܐܝܐ *to be made filthy, to be defiled, sullied, tarnished;* ܫܡܫܐ ܠܐ ܡܨܬܐܐ ܟܕ ܥܒܪ ܥܠ ܩܩܠܬܐ *the sun is not sullied when it passes over dirt-heaps.* Derivatives, ܨܐܐ, ܨܐܝܘܬܐ, ܨܐܝ, ܨܐܝܐ, ܨܐܘܐ.

ܨܐܝܦ part. of verb ܨܘܦ. *eager,* &c.

ܨܐܪ, ܨܐܪܐ *a*) = ܨܐܪ act. part. of ܨܘܪ. *b*) *dazzled, dizzy.*

ܨܐܦܐ = ܨܦܬܐ *a mat.*

ܨܐܨܐ; see ܨܨܐ *tamarind fruit.*

ܨܐܪ, ܨܐܪܐ, act. part. of verb ܨܘܪ. ܨܐܪ, ܨܐܪܐ act. part. of verb ܨܪ.

ܨܐܝ denom. verb Pael conj. from ܨܐܝܬܐ; pass. part. ܡܨܐܝ *dirty, vile.*

ܨܐܝܬܐ rarely ܨܐܝܝܬܐ pl. ܨܐܝ̈ܬܐ rt. ܨܐܐ. f. *dirt, foulness, impurity.*

ܨܒܐ fut. ܢܨܒܐ, act. part. ܨܒܐ, ܨܒܝܐ. *a*) *to be willing, to will, wish, prefer, seek to;* with ܕ *to agree, consent;* ܨܒܝܢ ܗܘܝܢ ܕܢܡܘܬ *would that we had died;* ܨܒܝܢܢ ܕܢܚܙܐ ܡܢܟ ܐܬܐ *we would see a sign from Thee;* ܨܒܐ ܐܢܐ ܕܐܬܩܪܒ ܘܕܚܠ ܐܢܐ *I desire to draw nigh but I fear;* ܟܕ ܠܐ ܨܒܐ *unintentionally, unwillingly. b*) with ܒ *to have pleasure in, be pleased with, delight in;* ܨܒܐ ܒܒܝܫܬܐ *delighting in evil;* ܨܒܝ ܡܪܝܐ ܐܠܗܐ ܠܒܥܘܬܢ *Lord God, accept our prayers.* Ethpe. ܐܬܨܒܝ *to be willing, to consent;* with ܒ *to be well pleased, to choose;* ܐܦܣܩܘܦ̈ܐ ܘܥܠܡܝ̈ܐ ܐܬܨܒܝܘ ܒܡܪܝ ܒܗܢܡ *the Bishops and laity elected Bishop Behnam Patriarch;* with ܠܘܬ *to desire, be inclined;* with ܥܡ *to be of one will;* ܕܢܦܫܗ ܐܬܨܒܝܬ *what his soul desireth;* pass. part. ܡܨܛܒܝܢܐ *acceptable.* Derivatives, ܨܒܘܬܐ, ܨܒܝܢܐ, ܨܒܝܢܐܝܬ, ܨܒܝܢܝܐ, ܨܒܝܢܘܬܐ, ܡܨܛܒܝܢܐ, ܡܨܛܒܝܢܘܬܐ.

ܨܒܐ part. ܨܒܐ. *to dry up, wither.* Cf. ܨܘܐ.

ܨܒܐ m. *medicine.* Cf. ܨܒܝ.

ܨܒܘ, ܨܒܘܬܐ pl. ܨܒܘ̈ܢ, ܨܒܘ̈ܬܐ rt. ܨܒܐ. f. *a matter, affair, thing; a possession, property, goods;* ܕܐܬܬ ܨܒܘܬܐ *that she was come;* ܨܒܘܬܐ ܕܟܒܪܝܬܐ *sulphur;* ܨܒܘ̈ܬܐ ܕܒܝܬܐ *furniture;* ܡܢ ܨܒܘ ܠܨܒܘ *in some measure;* ܡܢ ܨܒܘ ܢܦܫܝ ܢܦܫܗ, *of my, of his, own accord;* ܡܛܠ ܨܒܘܬܐ *because.*

ܨܒܘܪܐ or ܨܒܘܪܐ, ܬܐ rt. ܨܒܪ. *witless, foolish.*

ܨܒܘܪܘܬܐ rt. ܨܒܪ. f. *vain talking, mad folly, depravity, witlessness.*

ܨܒܝܢ, ܨܒܝܢܐ pl. ܨܒܝ̈ܢܝܢ, ܢ̈ܐ rt. ܨܒܐ. m. *will, desire, device, delight;* ܚܐܪܘܬ ܨ *freedom of the will, free-will;* ܒܚܐܪܘܬ ܨܒܝܢܗ *of his free choice* or *will;* ܒܢܝ̈ ܨܒܝܢܗ *those who are on his side, partisans;* ܕܢܓܒܐ ܗܘ ܨܒܝܢܐ *he may choose, it may be as he will;* ܗܘܐ ܨܒܝܢܐ ܠ *he chose, willed; it was the will, mind* or *decision of...; it seemed good to ...;* ܠܝܬ ܠܝ ܒܗܘܢ ܨܒܝܢܐ *I have no pleasure in them.* With preps. ܒܨ or ܒܨܒܝܢ ܢܦܫܗ *willingly, of his own accord;* ܕܨ *voluntary; acceptable;* ܠܨ *with acceptance, acceptable.*

ܨܒܝܢܐܝܬ rt. ܨܒܐ. adv. *willingly, wilfully, voluntarily.*

ܨܒܝܢܝܐ, ܢܝܬܐ rt. ܨܒܐ. *voluntary, willing, of free will.*

ܨܒܝܢܘܬܐ rt. ܨܒܐ. f. *will.*

ܨܒܥ fut. ܢܨܒܘܥ, act. part. ܨܒܥ, ܨܒܥܐ, pass. part. ܨܒܝܥ, ܥܐ. *to dip, moisten, dye;* ܟܕ ܨܒܥܗ ܒܠܓܝܢܐ *when He had dipped* the sop *in the dish;* ܨܒܝܥ ܐܪܓܘܢܐ *dyed purple;* ܨܒܝܥܢ ܒܕܡܐ swords *wet with blood.* Ethpe. ܐܬܨܒܥ *to be dipped, dyed; to be baptized; to be moistened, wet;* ܐܪܥܐ ܐܬܨܒܥܬ ܡܢ ܕܡܥܘܗܝ *the ground was wet with his tears.* Pa. ܨܒܥ *to make wet, to water;* ܒܕܡܥܝܗ ܡܫܪܝܐ ܠܡܨܒܥܘ ܪ̈ܓܠܘܗܝ she began *to wet his feet with her tears.* Ethpa. ܐܬܨܒܥ *to be dipped, wetted, sprinkled* ܡܢ ܛܠܐ *with dew;* ܒܕܡܐ *with blood;* ܒܡܶܫܚܳܐ *with oil.* Derivatives, ܨܒܳܥܳܐ, ܨܶܒܥܳܐ, ܨܒܺܝܥܳܐ, ܨܒܺܝܥܽܘܬܳܐ, ܨܒܳܥܺܝܬܳܐ, ܨܒܽܘܥܳܐ, ܨܰܒܥܳܐ, ܨܽܘܒܥܳܐ, ܡܨܰܒܥܳܢܺܝܬܳܐ.

ܨܰܒܳܥܳܐ pl. ܐ̈ـ rt. ܨܒܥ. m. *a dyer.*

ܨܶܒܥܳܐ pl. ܐ̈ـ rt. ܨܒܥ. m. *a dye, pigment;* med. *an external application.*

ܨܶܒܥܳܐ, ܨܶܒܰܥܬܳܐ constr. st. ܨܒܰܥ, pl. up to ten ܨܶܒܥܳܬܳܐ, above ten ܨܶܒܥܳܬܳܐ, ܨܶܒܥܳܬܗܽܘܢ rt. ܨܒܥ. f. *a) a finger, toe, digit;* ܨܶܒܥܳܐ ܕܰܠܘܳܬ ܐܰܒܗܳܡܳܐ *the finger next the thumb, the forefinger* also called ܡܫܰܒܚܳܢܺܝܬܳܐ, ܡܶܨܥܳܝܬܳܐ is *the middle finger,* ܩܪܳܐ *the fourth,* and ܫܰܪܳܐ *the fifth finger.* *b)* a measure of length equalling six barley-grains placed side by side. *c)* ܨܶܒܥܳܐ ܕܒܰܪܙܠܳܐ *a thimble;* ܬܪܶܥܣܰܪ ܨܶܒܥܳܬܳܐ *the duodenum,* an intestine twelve fingers in length; ܨܶܒܥܳܬܳܐ ܕܗܶܪܡܺܝܣ *Hermes' fingers = meadow saffron;* ܨܶܒܥܳܬܳܐ ܕܒܬܽܘܠܳܬܳܐ *virgins' fingers, a long-shaped berry used in dyeing red.*

ܨܒܳܥܽܘܬܳܐ rt. ܨܒܥ. m. *dyeing.*

ܨܶܒܥܳܢܳܝܳܐ rt. ܨܒܥ. *of* or *done with the finger.*

ܨܒܰܪ fut. ܢܶܨܒܽܘܪ, act. part. ܨܳܒܰܪ, ܨܳܒܪܳܐ. *to talk foolishly, brawl, rave, twaddle;* ܨܒܰܪ ܘܡܰܠܶܠ *he uttered raving* blasphemies; ܐ̱ܢܳܫܳܐ ܨܳܒܪܶܐ *men of disordered minds.* Pa. ܨܰܒܰܪ *to rave.* Derivatives, ܨܒܽܘܪܳܐ, ܨܒܽܘܪܽܘܬܳܐ, ܨܰܒܳܪܳܐ, ܨܶܒܪܳܐ.

ܨܰܒܪܳܐ Ar. m. *the aloe.*

ܨܰܒܳܪܳܐ pl. ܐ̈ rt. ܨܒܪ. *a chatterer, witless.*

ܨܶܒܪܳܐ pl. ܐ̈ rt. ܨܒܪ. m. *a) prating, vain talk, gossip.* *b) bloodshot state of the eyes.*

ܨܰܒܬ denom. verb Pael conj. from ܨܶܒܬܳܐ. *to set in order, improve, decorate, embellish* buildings; *to adorn, dress, trim;* ܡܨܰܒܬ ܡܶܛܪܳܐ ܠܰܐܪܥܳܐ ܒܟܽܠ ܦܺܐܪܺܝܢ *rain adorning the earth with all sorts of fruit;* ܐܶܢ ܐܶܫܟܰܚ ܛܽܘܥܝܳܝܢܳܐ ܠܡܨܰܒܳܬܽܘܬܶܗ ܕܢܶܟܠܳܐ *if error be able to dress up deceit;* ܟܰܠܬܳܐ ܡܨܰܒܬܳܐ ܠܓܰܒܪܳܗ̇ *a bride adorned for her husband.* Ethpa. ܐܶܨܛܰܒܰܬ *to adorn* or *deck oneself; to be adorned.*

ܨܶܒܬ, ܨܶܒܬܳܐ pl. ܨܶܒܳܬܳܐ sometimes ܨܶܒܬܳܐ (soft p, ܨܶܦܬܳܐ *care* has hard p) m. *an ornament, decoration, embellishment; carved work; the gem of a ring.* Derivatives, verb ܨܰܒܬ,

ܨܽܘܒܬܳܐ, ܨܰܒܳܬܽܘܬܳܐ, ܡܨܰܒܬܳܢܳܐ, ܡܨܰܒܬܳܢܺܝܬܳܐ, ܡܨܰܒܬܳܢܽܘܬܳܐ, ܐܶܨܛܰܒܬܳܐ.

ܨܕܳܐ fut. ܢܶܨܕܶܐ and ܢܶܨܕܶܐ, parts. ܨܳܕܶܐ; ܨܳܕܶܐ ܥܰܝܢܳܐ *to fix* the eye, *cast the evil eye; to gaze intently, contemplate;* with ܒ, ܐܶܙܰܠ ܠܡܶܨܕܳܐ ܒܣܰܢܝܳܐ Moses *went to gaze at the bush;* ܫܳܬܶܩ ܘܨܳܕܶܐ *silent and contemplative.* Aph. ܐܰܨܕܺܝ *to fix* ܥܰܝܢܶܐ *the eyes,* ܗܰܘܢܳܐ *the mind,* ܬܰܪܥܺܝܬܳܐ *the thoughts,* &c.; also absolutely *to regard intently, consider* with ܒ; ܐܰܨܕܺܝ ܒܥܽܘܡܩܶܗ ܘܰܚܙܳܐ ܫܽܘܦܪܳܟ *he gazed intently into its depth and saw thy beauty;* ܐܰܨܕܺܝ ܒܟܬܳܒܳܐ ܗܳܢܳܐ *consider this book.* Derivatives, ܨܳܕܝܳܐ, ܨܕܳܝܽܘܬܳܐ, ܡܨܰܕܝܽܘܬܳܐ.

ܨܳܕܶܐ *Sodhe,* name of the letter ܨ.

ܨܕܳܐ, ܨܕܺܝ fut. ܢܶܨܕܶܐ, act. part. ܨܳܕܶܐ, ܨܳܕܝܳܐ, ܨܳܕܝܳܬܳܐ; pass. part. ܨܕܶܐ, ܨܕܺܝܳܐ, ܨܕܺܝܳܬܳܐ. *a) to grow rusty, worn out; to become deserted, desolate, lonely, void;* ܨܕܺܝܳܐ ܠܶܗ ܣܶܟܬܳܐ ܡܶܢ ܙܰܒܢܳܐ *the ploughshare has long been rusted;* ܨܕܺܝܳܐ ܡܶܢ ܐ̱ܢܳܫܳܐ the city *was left desolate;* ܨܕܺܝ ܚܰܩܠܳܬܳܐ *the fields were untilled;* ܨܕܺܝܳܐ ܡܶܢ ܡܰܝܬܪܳܬܳܐ *void of virtues;* ܨܕܺܝܬܳܐ *a lone woman, a desolate place.* *b) to snatch at, mock* with ܥܰܠ; ܕܠܳܐ ܢܶܨܕܶܐ ܥܠܰܝܟ ܚܶܫܽܘܟܳܐ *lest darkness snatch thee* or *taunt thee* in the pit. Pa. ܨܰܕܺܝ *a) to lay waste, depeople.* *b) to play the wanton.* Ethpa. ܐܶܨܛܰܕܺܝ *a) to be uninhabited, depopulated, deserted;* ܕܠܳܐ ܢܶܨܛܰܕܽܘܢ ܗܠܶܝܢ ܕܰܝܪܳܬܳܐ ܡܶܢ ܕܰܝܪܳܝܶܐ *may* these monasteries *never be uninhabited by monks.* *b) to make sport, make game of, mock; to trick, delude, beguile* with ܒ; ܐܶܨܛܰܕܺܝ ܒܶܗ ܥܳܠܡܳܐ ܒܫܽܘܥܒܳܕܰܘܗܝ *the world mocked him with its enticements;* ܡܶܨܛܰܕܶܐ ܒܢܰܦܫܶܗ *he deludes himself.* Aph. ܐܰܨܕܺܝ *to make desolate, deprive of inhabitants;* ܐܰܨܕܺܝ ܠܺܠܝܳܐ ܫܽܘܩܶܐ ܕܡܕܺܝܢܳܬܳܐ *night made the streets of the cities lonely.* Derivatives, ܨܕܳܝܳܐ, ܨܶܕܝܳܐ, ܨܰܕܝܳܐ, ܨܶܕܝܽܘܬܳܐ, ܨܳܕܝܳܐ, ܨܽܘܕܳܝܳܐ, ܡܨܰܕܝܳܐ, ܡܨܰܕܝܳܢܽܘܬܳܐ, ܡܶܨܛܰܕܝܳܢܳܐ, ܡܶܨܛܰܕܝܳܢܽܘܬܳܐ.

ܨܽܘܕܳܝܳܐ pl. ܐ̈ rt. ܨܕܐ. m. *sport, mockery; a laughing-stock; irony; a trick, beguilement.*

ܨܶܕܝܳܐ pl. ܐ̈ـ rt. ܨܕܐ. m. *rust; waste, uncultivation; a desert, solitude.*

ܨܕܳܝܳܐ *a)* rt. ܨܕܐ. m. *desolation.* *b)* Heb. *intent regard, attention.*

ܨܕܝܐܝܬ rt. ܨܕܐ. adv. *in ridicule, ironically.*

ܨܕܝܚܐ; see ܨܕܚ.

ܨܕܝܚܐ E-Syr. ܨܕܝܚܐ rt. ܨܕܚ. m. *a) the carbuncle. b) antimony, black lead, paint for the eyes.*

ܨܕܝܘܬܐ rt. ܨܕܐ. f. *lying waste, remaining uncultivated* or *uninhabited, desolation.*

ܨܕܝܢܝܐ rt. ܨܕܐ. *growing in waste places.*

ܨܕܥܐ pl. ܐ̈ m. *a rootlet, fibre.*

ܨܕܥܐ pl. ܐ̈ m. *the temples* of the head.

ܨܕܦ Ar. *mother-of-pearl.*

ܨܕܪ pass. part. ܨܕܝܪ. *to be drunken, be in a drunken sleep.* ETHPE. ܐܨܛܕܪ *to be seized with fear, flee from fright.* PA. ܨܕܪ, pass. part. ܡܨܕܪ. *intoxicated, giddy from drink.* ETHPA. ܐܨܛܕܪ *to be drowsy* or *giddy from drunkenness; ܐܨܛܕܪܬ ܐܝܟ ܗܘ ܕܡܨܕܪ ܒܚܡܪܐ I was as one stupified with drink.* APH. ܐܨܕܪ *to make drunken, make giddy.* DERIVATIVES, ܨܕܪܐ, ܨܕܪܘܬܐ, ܨܘܕܪܐ, ܡܨܕܪܐܝܬ, ܡܨܕܪܘܬܐ.

ܨܕܪܐ rt. ܨܕܪ. m. *sick headache, dizziness.*

ܨܕܪܘܬܐ rt. ܨܕܪ. f. *headache, pain in the temples.*

ܨܗܐ and ܨܗܝ, fut. ܢܨܗܐ, act. part. ܨܗܐ, ܨܗܝܐ, ܨܗܝܬܐ. *to thirst, to be dry, parched with thirst;* part. adj. ܨܗܐ, ܨܗܝܐ, ܨܗܝܬܐ *dry, thirsty;* ܐܪܥܐ ܨܗܝܬܐ *a thirsty land;* ܨܗܝ ܠܦܘܪܩܢܐ *thirsting for salvation;* ܨܗܐ ܐܢܐ ܠܚܙܘܗܘܢ *I thirst for the sight of them.* PA. ܨܗܝ intens. *to thirst;* ܠܕܡܐ *for blood.* ETHPA. ܐܨܛܗܝ *to thirst.* APH. ܐܨܗܝ *to make to thirst, cause to thirst.* DERIVATIVES, ܨܗܘܐ, ܨܗܘܝܐ, ܨܗܝܐ, ܨܗܝܐܝܬ, ܨܗܝܘܬܐ.

ܨܗܘܐ rt. ܨܗܐ. m. *thirst.*

ܨܗܘܠܐ, ܨܗܘܠܬܢܐ rt. ܨܗܠ. *neighing; lustful.*

ܨܗܘܠܬܢܘܬܐ rt. ܨܗܠ. f. *neighing, whinnying, braying.*

ܨܗܘܝܐ pl. ܐ̈ rt. ܨܗܐ. *thirst, drought; thirsty;* ܐܬܪ̈ܘܬܐ ܨܗܘܝܐ *dry places.*

ܨܗܝܐ, ܨܗܝܐ or ܨܗܝܐ rt. ܨܗܐ. m. *thirst.*

ܨܗܝܐܝܬ rt. ܨܗܐ. adv. *eagerly.*

ܨܗܝܘܢ pr. n. *Sion.*

ܨܗܝܘܢܝܐ ܐܝܬ from ܨܗܝܘܢ: *of* or *from Sion, Sionite.*

ܨܗܝܘܬܐ rt. ܨܗܐ. f. *thirst, thirstiness.*

ܨܗܠ fut. ܢܨܗܘܠ, act. part. ܨܗܠ, ܨܗܠܐ. *to neigh, whinny;* metaph. *to lust.* DERIVATIVES, ܨܗܘܠܐ, ܨܗܘܠܬܢܘܬܐ, ܨܗܠܐ.

ܨܗܠܐ or ܨܗܠܐ rt. ܨܗܠ. m. *a neigh, neighing.*

ܨܗܪܘܢܐ or ܨܗܪܘܢܐ m. *cicuta virosa, hemlock.*

ܨܗܪܝܓܐ m. *a cistern.*

ܨܘܐ fut. ܢܨܘܐ, act. part. ܨܘܐ, pass. part. ܨܘܐ. *a) to pile up* stones, *set up* a cairn, *block. b) to be silent* as an empty house. *c) to languish, begin to wither.* ETHPE. ܐܨܛܘܝ *to clash.* PA. ܨܘܝ trans. *to dry.* APH. ܐܨܘܐ same as Peal. DERIVATIVES, ܨܘܘܐ or ܨܘܝܐ, ܨܘܝܐ.

ܨܘܒ imper. of ܢܨܒ *to plant* and of the following verb.

ܨܘܒ, ܨܒ fut. ܢܨܘܒ, act. part. ܨܐܒ, ܨܐܒܐ. *to resort, frequent, visit, come* with ܠ, ܠܘܬ, ܥܡ or ܥܠ of place or pers. ܨܐܒܝܢ ܠܒܝܬ ܣܦܪܐ *they go to school;* ܟܠ ܚܕ ܨܐܒ ܗܘܐ ܠܬܪܥܗ *every one resorted to his door.* PA. ܨܝܒ *a) to summon, call* or *bring together; to recall, call to memory;* ܨܝܒ ܐܠܗܐ ܠܩܒܘܬܐ ܚܝܘܬܐ ܕܠܐ ܚܙܝܢ ܗܘܘ *God brought together to the ark animals which they had never seen. b) to fetch, obtain, procure, prepare;* ܡܨܝܒܘܬܐ *victuals;* ܡܨܝܒܢܘܬܐ *advantage.* ETHPA. ܐܨܛܝܒ *to resort, to be present, ready; to be found, obtained;* ܕܢܬܟܢܫܘܢ ܘܢܫܬܟܚܘܢ ܡܨܛܝܒܝܢ ܒܐܦܣܘܣ *that they should assemble and be present at Ephesus;* ܡܢ ܡܠܟܐ ܡܨܛܝܒܐ ܣܝܒܪܬܢ *our sustenance is derived from the king.* DERIVATIVES, ܨܘܒܐ, ܨܘܒܢܐ, ܨܝܒܐ, ܡܨܝܒܢܐ, ܡܨܝܒܢܐ, ܡܨܝܒܢܘܬܐ.

ܨܘܒܐ rt. ܨܘܒ. m. *a resort, rendezvous; meeting-place, approach, nearness;* ܒܝܬ ܨܘܒܐ *place of meeting;* ܠܨܘܒܟ *to meet thee;* ܩܪܝܒ ܨܘܒܐ ܠ *is in propinquity, approaches nearest to . . . ;* ܟܢܫ ܠܡܛܥܝܐ ܨܘܒܐ ܠܘܬܗ *He gathers wanderers near to Himself.*

ܨܘܒܥܐ rt. ܨܒܥ. m. *dye;* ܨ ܕܙܚܘܪܝܬܐ or ܕܙܚܘܪܝܬܐ *scarlet dye.*

ܨܘܒܥܐ pl. ܐ̈ rt. ܨܒܥ. m. *dyeing.*

ܨܘܒܥܢܐ pl. ܐ̈ rt. ܨܒܥ. m. *dye, colour; dyed wool, dyed raiment.*

ܨܘܒܬܐ rt. ܨܒܬ. m. *elegance.*

ܨܘܕ, ܨܕ fut. ܢܨܘܕ, act. part. ܨܐܕ, ܨܐܕܐ, pass. part. ܨܝܕ, ܐ, ܬܐ. *to hunt, chase, fish; to capture,* catch, take; ܢܘܢܐ ܕܨܕܘ *the fishes they had caught;* ܐܬܝܬ ܠܡܨܕ ܥܢܐ ܡܠܝܠܬܐ *Thou camest to take captive human sheep;* ܒܦܚܐ ܕܡܘܬܐ ܨܝܕܐ ܗܘܬ *she was fast held in the snares of death.* ETHPE. ܐܬܨܝܕ *to be caught, ensnared, netted, captured;* ܐܢ ܐܬܨܝܕ ܣܘܟܠܐ ܠܟܘܢ *was the sense caught by you? did you see the meaning?* ܢܬܨܝܕ ܒܪܓܝܓܬܐ *he will be captured by desire.* PA. ܨܝܕ *to hunt;* ܡܨܝܕ ܐܢܬ ܠܢܦܫܝ *thou huntest my soul;* ܦܪܚܬܐ ܡܨܝܕܢܝܬܐ *birds of prey.* APH. ܐܨܝܕ *to hunt, seize.* DERIVATIVES, ܨܝܕܐ, ܨܝܕܐ, ܨܝܕܐ, ܨܝܕܘܬܐ, ܨܝܕܢܐ, ܡܨܝܕܢܐ, ܡܨܝܕܢܝܬܐ, ܡܨܝܕܬܐ, ܡܨܛܝܕܢܐ, ܡܨܛܝܕܢܘܬܐ.

ܨܘܪܐ *a)* = ܡܐܡܪܐ *conversation.* *b)* = ܙܘܕܐ *victuals.*

ܨܘܪܝܐ pl. ܐ̈ rt. ܨܪܐ. m. *a trick, delusion.*

ܨܘܪܪܐ rt. ܨܪܪ. m. *drowsiness, heaviness, headache, drunken stupidity.*

ܨܘܪܬܐ rt. ܨܪ. *intention, effort.*

ܨܘܘܚܐ rt. ܨܘܚ. m. *smart, sharp pain.*

ܨܘܘܝܐ or ܨܘܝܐ rt. ܨܘܐ. *dried up, flabby, mouldy* as bread.

ܨܘܚ fut. ܢܨܘܚ. *a) to scream* as an eagle. *b) to feel a sharp pain* as when nitre or salt touches a sore; *to suffer* from a tubercle on the eye. PA. ܨܘܚ pass. part. ܡܨܘܚ. *to utter a shrill sound.* APH. ܐܨܘܚ *to pronounce clearly; to feel a sharp pain* or *smart; to clear* the thoughts, *purify* the mind. DERIVATIVES, ܨܘܚܐ, ܨܘܚܐ, ܨܘܚܢܐ, ܨܘܚܬܐ, ܨܘܚܢܐ, ܨܘܚܢܝܐ.

ܨܘܚܐ rt. ܨܘܚ. m. *a) pain, ache, giddiness. b) wailing sorrow. c) an alloy of brass and copper too soft to bear hammering.*

ܨܘܚܡܬܐ rt. ܨܘܚ. f. *pain from the probing* or *cauterization of an ulcer.*

ܨܘܚܢܐ rt. ܨܚܐ. m. *anxiety, profligacy.*

ܨܘܚܝܐ, ܨܘܚܝܬܐ pl. ܝܢ, ܝܬܐ rt. ܨܚܐ. f. *railing, abuse.*

ܨܘܚܢ, ܨܘܚܢܐ *red with shame.*

ܨܘܚܬܐ rt. ܨܘܚ. f. *an outcry, shrill cry.*

ܨܘܝܐ pl. ܐ̈ rt. ܨܘܐ. m. *a) a heap of stones, a cairn. b) a dry tree. c) desolation* of a forsaken house.

ܨܘܝܬܐ rt. ܨܝ. m. *filth.*

ܨܘܒܚܐ rt. ܨܒܚ. m. *preparation; the advent* of our Lord.

ܨܘܝܕܐ rt. ܨܕ. m. *the chase, hunting, fishing.*

ܨܘܢܚܐ rt. ܨܢܚ. m. *grief.*

ܨܘܝܪܐ rt. ܨܪ. m. *ornament.*

ܨܘܠܒܐ m. *liquorice root.*

ܨܘܠܚܐ rt. ܨܠܚ. m. *cleaving, splitting.*

ܨܘܠܝܐ rt. ܨܠܐ. m. *perversion* of justice.

ܨܘܠܠܐ, ܨܘܠܠܐ rt. ܨܠ. m. *a) clarifying, fining from dregs* or *lees,* metaph. of the soul. *b) clearness, lucidity.*

ܨܘܠܡܐ from ܨܠܡܐ. m. *an image, imagination.*

ܨܘܠܦܐ rt. ܨܠܦ. m. *fracture, fracturing.*

ܨܘܠܦܢܐ rt. ܨܠܦ. m. *the pounding* of drugs.

ܨܘܠܦܬܐ pl. ܦ̈ܬܐ rt. ܨܠܦ. f. *a wound, hurt; a bruise, contusion* esp. of the head.

ܨܘܡ, ܨܡ fut. ܢܨܘܡ, act. part. ܨܐܡ, ܨܝܡܐ. *to fast, abstain;* with ܨܘܡܐ *to keep, observe a fast;* ܨܘܡ ܡܢ ܒܝܫܬܐ *fast from evil.* ETHPE. ܐܬܨܝܡ *to be kept* of a fast; ܝܘܡܐ ܢܬܨܝܡ *the day shall be kept as a fast.* APH. ܐܨܝܡ *to enjoin a fast.* DERIVATIVES, ܨܘܡܐ, ܨܘܡܝܐ, ܨܝܡܐ, ܨܝܡܘܬܐ, ܨܘܡܝܢܐ.

ܨܘܡܐ pl. ܐ̈ rt. ܨܘܡ. m. *a fast.* 1 and 2. ܨ̈ ܕܐܪܒܥܒܫܒܐ and ܕܥܪܘܒܬܐ *the Wednesday and Friday fast* throughout the year; 3. ܨ̈ ܕܒܬܘܠܬܐ *the Virgins' fast,* on the three days following Epiphany; 4. ܨ̈ ܕܣܘܒܪܐ or ܕܒܪܝܐ *the fast of the Nativity* or *Annunciation* lasting through the four weeks before Christmas; 5. ܨ̈ ܕܫܘܢܝܐ ܕܝܠܕܬ ܐܠܗܐ *fast of the Assumption of the Deipara,* from Aug. 1–15; 6. ܨ̈ ܕܨܠܝܒܐ or ܕܡܪܝ ܐܠܝܐ *fast of the Cross* or *of Mar Elia,* from the First Sunday of Elijah = eighth Sunday after Pentecost, to the Seventh; 7. ܕܫܠܝܚܐ *fast of the Apostles,* from the third day after Pentecost till June 29; 8. ܨܘܡܐ ܪܒܐ also called ܨ̈ ܕܐܪܒܥܝܢ *Lent;* 9. = ܨ̈ ܕܢܝܢܘܝܐ ܒܥܘܬܐ ܕܢ̈, see above, under ܒܥܘܬܐ.

ܨܘܡܕܐ rt. ܨܡܕ. m. in the Lexx. *a tie, band, bond, obligation;* ܒܨܘܡܕܐ *firmly, constantly.*

ܨܘܡܝܐ and ܨܘܡܝܢܐ rt. ܨܘܡ. *of* or *belonging to a fast.*

ܨܘܡܚܬܐ from ܨܘܡܚܐ m. *shame, confusion.*

ܨܘܡܚܐ and ܨܘܡܚܬܐ plurals of ܨܘܡܚܬܐ.

ܨܘܢܒܐ perh. *anethum foeniculum, anise, dill, fennell.*

ܨܘܢܕܪ Pers. *red beet.*

ܨܘܢܥܐ m. *hard stone,* such as *flint, quartz, marble.*

ܨܘܐܬܐ rt. ܨܐܐ. m. *a) filth. b)* perh. *metaphysics.*

ܨܘܥܪܬܐ pl. ܬܐ rt. ܨܥܪ. m. *a) filth, defilement. b) reproach, calumny.*

ܨܘܥܪܢܐ rt. ܨܥܪ. m. *abuse, invective.*

ܨܘܦܝܢܐ rt. ܨܦܝ. m. *a sudden onslaught, encounter.*

ܨܘܦܝܢܬܐ (ܨܘܦܝܢܬܐ) *soap-stone.*

ܨܘܨܝ Pali conj. *to chirp, squeak, chink.* Derivatives, ܨܘܨܝܐ, ܡܨܘܨܝܐ.

ܨܘܨܝܐ from ܨܘܨܝ. m. *chirping, twittering.*

ܨܘܨܝܢܐ E-Syr. ܨܘܨܢܐ pl. ܐ m. with ܟܘܟܒܐ or ellipt. *a comet.*

ܨܘܨܝܬܐ usually pl. ܝܢ, ܬܐ f. *a) a lock of hair, fore-lock;* metaph. *tendrils, flames. b) the downy plume* of a reed. *c) fibrous roots. d) fringes, threads.*

ܨܘܨܠܐ pl. ܐ m. *a wood-pigeon, ringdove.*

ܨܘܨܦܬܐ f. pl. *forceps, tongs.*

ܨܘܨܪܐ m. *artemisia vulgaris, southern-wood, old man;* or *sium lancifolium,* an umbellifer producing edible roots.

ܨܘܪ m. *dust.*

ܨܘܪ imper. of verb ܨܪ *to bind* and of verb ܨܘܪ, ܨܪ.

ܨܘܪ pr. n. *Tyre.*

ܨܘܪ, ܨܪ fut. ܢܨܘܪ, act. part. ܨܐܪ, ܨܝܪܐ, pass. part. ܨܝܪ, ܨܝܪܐ, ܨܝܪܬܐ. *a) to form, fashion, paint, draw* often with ܨܠܡܐ, ܨܘܪܬܐ, ܕܡܘܬܐ, ܨܠܡܐ *figures, images; to describe, depict, delineate;* ܨܝܪܝܢ ܨܝܪܐ ܒܣܡܡܢܐ *painters paint with pigments;* ܥܓܠܐ ܕܨܪܘ *the calf they fashioned;* ܠܡܨܪ ܥܕܬܐ *to decorate the church with pictures;* ܨܝܪܐ ܝܘܢܐ ܡܢܐ *a ringdove. b)* with ܨܠܝܒܐ or ܨܠܝܒܐ *to make the sign of the cross. c) to represent, show forth, signify, typify;* with ܩܕܡ *to prefigure;* ܩܪܒܐ ܕܨܝܪܝܢ ܠܗ *the war they represented to him* as imminent; ܣܒܠܬܐ ܕܝܥܩܘܒ ܨܪܬ ܨܠܝܒܐ Jacob's *ladder typified Our Saviour's cross. d) to see confused images, be dim-sighted, dizzy.* Ethpe. ܐܬܨܝܪ and ܐܬܨܪ *to be formed, fashioned, depicted, represented, figured* ܒܡܬܠܐ *in a parable;* ܥܕܠܐ ܐܬܨܝܪ ܒܟܪܣܐ *before he was formed in the womb.* Pa. ܨܝܪ and ܨܘܪ *to paint, represent, imagine;* pass. part. ܡܨܝܪܐ, ܡܨܝܪܬܐ *speckled, variegated.* Derivatives, ܡܨܝܪ, ܨܝܪܐ, ܨܘܪܐ, ܨܘܪܬܐ, ܨܘܪܬܐ, ܨܘܪܬܐ, ܨܝܪܐ, ܨܝܪܐ, ܨܝܪܐ, ܨܝܪܐ, ܨܝܪܘܬܐ, ܡܨܝܪܢܐ, ܡܨܝܪܢܐ, ܡܨܝܪܢܘܬܐ.

ܨܘܪܐ pl. ܨܘܪܐ m. *the neck, throat;* ܒܝܬ ܨ *collar;* ܨ ܕܓܡܠܐ *a camel's hump;* ܨ ܕܪܘܡܢܐ *the top* or *the stalk of pomegranates;* ܪܡܘܬ ܨ *haughtiness.*

ܨܘܪܐ rt. ܨܘܪ. m. *dizziness.*

ܨܘܪܟܐ m. *tordylium officinale, the seed of the hartwort* or *meadow saxifrage.* Also *laserpitium, assafoetida.*

ܨܘܪܚܢܝܬܐ and ܨܘܪܚܢܬܐ rt. ܨܪܚ. f. *cry, scream* of an eagle, *peacock,* &c.

ܨܘܪܝܐ, ܬܐ from ܨܘܪ. *Tyrian.*

ܨܘܪܦܐ pl. ܐ rt. ܨܪܦ. m. *poverty, want.*

ܨܘܪܡܐ rt. ܨܪܡ. m. *a) cutting, harvesting* of the date crop. *b) resolution.*

ܨܘܪܢܐ pl. ܝܢ, ܐ rt. ܨܘܪ. m. *a swimming in the head, dizziness, consternation, terror;* usually pl. and often with ܐܚܕ *to be seized with giddiness.*

ܨܘܪܥ, ܨܘܪܥܐ Ar. m. *epilepsy.*

ܨܘܪܦܐ rt. ܨܪܦ. m. *constipation, astringent acidity.*

ܨܘܪܩܐ rt. ܨܪܩ. m. *hard frost.*

ܨܘܪܬܐ pl. ܨܘܪܝܢ, ܬܐ rt. ܨܘܪ. f. *a) a form, image; a statue* but also *a picture,* opp. ܨܠܡܐ *a statue;* ܐܘܢܓܠܝܘܢ ܕܨܘܪܬܐ *an illuminated gospel. b) figured work, embroidery. c) lineaments, features. d) form,* opp. substance and reality. *e)* moral *character. f)* ܨ ܕܟܬܒܐ or ܕܡܠܬܐ *writing, text,* esp. *the text* of Holy Scripture. *g)* ܨ ܕܟܠܒܐ *the dog-star, Sirius.*

ܨܘܬ, ܨܬ fut. ܢܨܘܬ, infin. ܡܨܬ, act. part. ܨܐܬ, ܨܝܬܐ, pass. part. ܨܝܬ, ܨܝܬܐ, ܨܝܬܬܐ. *to give ear, give heed, obey;* ܨܘܬ ܠܡܠܝ *hearken unto me;* ܨܠܝܬ ܐܕܢܟ *Thou hast inclined Thine ear.* Ethpe. ܐܨܛܘܬ part. ܡܨܛܘܬ or ܡܨܛܬ. *to be listened to.* Aph. ܐܨܝܬ *to hearken.* Derivatives, ܨܘܬܐ, ܨܘܬܐ.

ܨܘܬܐ (hard ܬ) rt. ܨܘܬ. m. *a) hearkening, attention, heed; sound* esp. the sound of a voice. *b)* ܨܘܬܐ (soft ܬ) *conversation, society, companionship.*

ܨܚ fut. ܢܨܘܚ, act. part. ܨܐܚ. *to glow, to strike, beat* as the rays of the sun; ܨܚܬ ܫܡܫܐ ܥܠ ܪܫܗ ܕܝܘܢܢ *the sun beat on Jonah's head.* Aph. ܐܨܚ *to express, pronounce, make known abroad* as ܣܒܪܬܐ *tidings; to publish* as ܦܘܩܕܢܐ *an edict.* Esp. *to write down, write out;* ܐܢ ܐܢܫ ܢܨܚ ܕܝܬܝܩܐ *if a man write a will;* ܦܩܕ ... ܕܢܨܚܘܢ ܬܪܝܢ ܨܚܚܐ *he commanded two copies to be made of it.* Ethtaph. ܐܬܬܨܚ *to be expressed, described; to be written down.* Derivatives, ܐܨܚܬܐ, ܨܚܐ, ܨܚܘܐ, ܨܚܚܐ, ܨܚܚܬܐ, ܨܚܚܐ, ܨܚܚܘܬܐ, ܡܨܚܚܘܬܐ.

ܨܚܐ or ܨܘܚܐ rt. ܨܚ. m. *burning heat.*

ܨܚܐ Pael ܨܚܝ. *to revile;* ܗܘ ܕܡܨܛܚܐ ܗܘܐ ܘܠܐ ܡܨܚܐ *Who was reviled and reviled not;* ܠܐ ܬܨܚܝܘܗܝ *do not revile him.* Ethpa. ܐܨܛܚܝ *to be reviled, to be accused of disgraceful sin.* Derivatives, ܨܘܚܝܐ, ܨܘܚܝܬܐ, ܡܨܚܝܢܐ, ܡܨܚܝܢܘܬܐ, ܨܚܝܐ.

ܨܚܘܐ rt. ܨܚ. m. *a clear sky, fair weather.*

ܨܚܚܐ pl. ܐ̈ rt. ܨܚ. usually m. *a) a copy, codex, manuscript,* ܒ and ܒܨܚܚܐ *in another copy;* ܨܚܚܐ ܕܦܬܓܡܐ *copies of articles, heads* of accusation. *b) a section, lesson, portion of scripture.* These are rather longer than our chapters.

ܨܚܚܬܐ rt. ܨܚ. f. *a document, note* ܕܙܒܢܘܬܐ *of sale.*

ܨܚܝܚܐ pl. ܨܚܝܚܝܢ, ܐ̈ rt. ܨܚ. *clear, bright, powerful* of sunlight.

ܨܚܝܚܘܬܐ rt. ܨܚ. f. *splendour.*

ܨܚܢ denom. verb from ܨܚܢܐ Pael conj. *a) to play the harlot. b) to use foul language.* Ethpa. ܐܨܛܚܢ *to defile oneself.*

ܨܚܢ, ܨܚܢܐ, ܨܚܢܬܐ *filthy, impure.* Derivatives, verb ܨܚܢ, ܨܚܢܘܬܐ.

ܨܚܢܘܬܐ from ܨܚܢܐ f. *harlotry, licentiousness, immodesty.*

ܨܚܢܬܐ f. *a fish snack, relish.*

ܨܚܪܐ *shamefaced.* Cf. ܨܘܚܪ.

ܨܛܐ pl. ܐ̈ m. *a) chips of wood, splinters, firewood, fuel. b) slices of dried meat, layers of salted meat.*

ܨܛܘܛܐ m. *the mouthpiece of a reed pipe.*

ܨܛܝܛܐ adj. *hard, dried* meat.

ܨܛܛܢܝܐ, ܢܝܬܐ from ܨܛܐ. *laminar.*

ܨܝܕ rarely ܨܕ, also ܨܐܕ and ܨܝܐܕ but only with pron. affixes, ܨܐܕܝ or ܨܝܕܝ, &c. prep. *to, with, at;* ܠܨܝܕ *to, up to;* ܠܨܝܕ ܩܠܝܠ *within a little;* ܠܝܬ ܨܝܕܝ ܡܕܡ *there is nothing against me;* ܐܢܚܢ ܡܢ ܨܝܕܢ, ܨܐܕܝܗܘܢ *for our part, their part; of our, of their own accord.*

ܨܝܕ, ܐ, ܬܐ pass. part. of verb ܨܘܕ.

ܨܝܕܐ (ܨܝܕܐ) rt. ܨܘܕ. m. *hunting, fishing; a snare; the prey; game, venison, food;* ܨܝܕܐ ܕܢܘܢܐ *a catch, haul of fish;* ܕ ܟܠܒܐ *hunting dogs;* ܕ ܦܪܚܬܐ *a bird of prey.* Metaph. *a chase, eager pursuit;* also ܚܣܪ ܡܢ ܨܝܕܐ *he failed to catch* the meaning.

ܨܝܕܐ (ܨܝܕܐ) pl. ܐ̈ rt. ܨܘܕ. m. *a hunter, fisher, fowler.*

ܨܝܕܘܬܐ rt. ܨܘܕ. f. *fishing.*

ܨܝܕܢ pr. n. *Sidon.*

ܨܝܕܢܝܐ, ܢܝܬܐ *a)* from ܨܝܕܢ. *Sidonian. b) an apothecary. c)* rt. ܨܘܕ. *of the chase.*

ܨܝܘܦܐ pl. ܐ̈ rt. ܨܘܦ. m. *a comer, a goer, one who habitually attends.*

ܨܝܘܡܐ rt. ܨܘܡ. m. *one who fasts.*

ܨܝܘܪܐ rt. ܨܘܪ. m. *one who forms, a maker.*

ܨܝܘܬܐ pl. ܐ̈ rt. ܨܘܬ. m. *a listener.*

ܨܝܚܐ rt. ܨܘܚ. m. *the sharp cry* or *shriek of* a hawk.

ܨܝܛܘܪܝܘܢ or ܨܝܛܘܪܘܢ *lepidium latifolium, broad-leaved cress.*

ܨܝܠܐ m. *reason, intellect.*

ܨܝܡܐ, ܨܝܡܬܐ pl. ܨܝܡܝܢ, ܨܝܡܢ rt. ܨܘܡ. *fasting, one who fasts, an abstainer.*

ܨܝܢ and ܨܝܢܣܬܐܢ pr. n. *China.*

ܨܝܢܕܘܦܝ m. *cinnamon.*

ܨܝܢܝܐ pl. ܨܝܢܝܐ from ܨܝܢ. *a Chinee, Chinaman.*

ܨܝܦܐ = ܨܘܦܐ, and ܨܝܦܢܝܬܐ = ܨܘܦܢܝܬܐ.

ܨܝܦܪܐ; see ܨܦܪܐ.

ܨܝܦܬܐ = ܨܦܬܐ *a mat, matting.*

ܨܝܨܠܐ pl. ܨܝܨܠܐ; see ܨܨܠܐ *a cymbal.*

ܨܝܨܪܐ; see ܨܨܪܐ *a cricket.*

ܨܝܪ, ܨܝܪܐ, ܨܝܪܬܐ pass. part. of verb ܨܘܪ.

ܨܝܪ, ܨܝܪܐ rt. ܨܘܪ. m. *a former, fashioner; a carver, painter, embroiderer.*

ܨܝܪܐ pl. ܨܝܪܐ rt. ܨܘܪ. m. *a painted idol, picture of an idol.*

ܨܝܪܐ pl. ܨܝܪܐ rt. ܨܘܪ. m. *a pen, pencil, brush, graving tool.*

ܨܝܪܐ rt. ܨܘܪ. m. *a suffusion of blood in the eyes from a blow; mental infirmity, weak brain* from a blow on the head.

ܨܝܪܘܬܐ rt. ܨܘܪ. f. *the art of painting.*

ܨܝܪܬܐ pl. ܨܝܪ, ܨܝܪܬܐ rt. ܨܘܪ. f. *the upper and lower sockets on which a door turned, the threshold or lower stone of a door.*

ܨܠ fut. ܢܨܘܠ, act. part. ܨܐܠ. *a) to tingle* as the ears. *b) to pour over*, med. *to foment;* metaph. *to be diffused* as fog. *c) to clear away;* ܢܨܘܠ ܟܐܒܐ ܕܥܘܩܒܝܟ *may he take away the pain of thy sorrows.* Part. adj. ܨܠܝܠ, ܨܠܝܠܐ, ܨܠܝܠܬܐ *strained, clarified* as wine, honey, ointment; *transparent, limpid, clear* as air, water, and metaph. ܨܠܝܠ ܡܘܚܐ *of clear brain;* ܡܫܟܚܬܐ ܨܠܝܠܬܐ ܡܢ ܪܢܝܐ *a mind free from anxiety.* Pa. ܨܠܠ *to draw from the lees, to strain* as wine; *to fine, free from dross,* ܡܨܠܠܝܢ ܒܩܐ *straining out the gnats;* ܦܝܠܣܘܦܐ ܟܣܝܝܬܗ ܢܛܪ ܡܨܠܠ *the philosopher keeps his outer self unsullied.* Pass. part. ܡܨܠܠ, ܡܨܠܠܐ, ܡܨܠܠܬܐ *strained, clear, limpid; fine, refined, exquisite; unsullied, uncontaminate;* ܦܪܕܝܣܐ ܡܨܠܠܐ ܘܩܕܝܫܐ *Paradise spotless and holy;* ܡܨܠܠܐ ܘܢܩܕܐ *free from earthly dross and pure.* Ethpa. ܐܬܨܠܠ *to be made* or *kept pure; to be filtered;* ܢܬܨܠܠܘܢ ܓܦܐ *let the pinions* of the soul *be kept from defilement.* Aph. ܐܨܠ *a)* prob. = Heb. Hiṣṣil *to deliver. b) to draw out* an arrow. Derivatives, ܨܠܘܠܐ, ܨܠܠܐ, ܨܠܠܘܬܐ, ܨܠܝܠܘܬܐ, ܡܨܠܠܢܘܬܐ, ܡܨܠܠܢܘܬܐ, ܡܨܠܠܐܝܬ, ܡܨܠܠܢܘܬܐ, ܨܠܠܬܐ, ܨܠܠܐ, ܡܨܠܠܐ, ܡܨܠܠܢܐ.

ܨܠܐ m. *a game, pastime.*

ܨܠܐ *a hide, leather.*

ܨܠܐ and ܨܠܝ fut. ܢܨܠܐ, act. part. ܨܠܐ, ܨܠܝܐ, pass. part. ܨܠܐ, ܨܠܝܐ, ܨܠܝܬܐ. *to incline, turn* aside or towards with ܠ or ܠܘܬ; *to slope; to lean towards, be prone to, to intend, mean;* ܨܠܐ ܝܘܡܐ *the day declines;* ܐܪܥܐ ܕܨܠܝܐ ܠܚܕܐ ܡܢ ܪܓܠܐ *ground sloping steeply beneath the feet;* ܨܠܝܢ ܠܡܫܬܝܐ *given to wine-bibbing;* ܨܠܘ ܥܠܝܟ ܒܝܫܬܐ *they intended mischief against thee.* With ܐܕܢܐ *to incline the ear, give heed, attend;* ܒܬܪ *to turn after, be a follower* of . . .; ܪܥܝܢܐ, ܗܘܢܐ &c. *to turn the mind to, to apply the thoughts;* ܕܝܢܐ *to pervert justice;* ܡܨܝܕܬܐ *to spread a net;* ܦܚܐ *to lay snares;* ܫܥܬܐ *the hour passes.* Of colours, *inclined to, verging towards;* ܨܠܐ ܠܚܘܪܘܬܐ *whitish, pale;* ܠܣܘܡܩܘܬܐ *inclined to red, reddish.* Ethpe. ܐܨܛܠܝ *a) to lean, bend one way or other;* ܠܐ ܐܨܛܠܝ ܘܠܐ ܐܣܬܡܟ *he did not lean about nor recline. b) to turn aside, incline towards, be prone to* with ܒ, ܒܬܪ, ܠ, ܠܘܬ; ܐܨܛܠܝܘ ܒܬܪ ܥܘܠܐ *they turned aside to dishonesty;* ܨܠܐ ܠܡܢܬܐ ܕܟܪܝܣܛܝܢܐ *he inclines to the Christian party. c) to decline* as shadows; from the right faith; also astron. *to decline.* Pa. ܨܠܝ *a) to pray* with ܠ, ܠܘܬ; with ܥܠ *to pray for, bless. b) to lay* a snare. Ethpa. ܐܬܨܠܝ *to be offered* of prayer; *to be prayed for, mentioned in prayer.* Aph. ܐܨܠܝ *to reach out, offer.* Derivatives, ܨܠܘܬܐ, ܨܠܘܬܢܐ, ܨܠܘܬܢܐ, ܨܠܝܐ, ܨܠܝܘܬܐ, ܨܠܝܬܐ, ܡܨܛܠܝܢܐ, ܡܨܛܠܝܢܘܬܐ, ܡܨܛܠܝܢܐܝܬ, ܡܨܠܝܢܐ.

ܨܠܒ fut. ܢܨܠܘܒ, act. part. ܨܠܒ, pass. part. ܨܠܝܒ, ܨܠܝܒܐ, ܨܠܝܒܬܐ *to crucify.* Ethpe. ܐܨܛܠܒ *to be crucified.* Aph. ܐܨܠܒ *to make the sign of the cross, cross oneself.* Derivatives, ܨܠܘܒܐ, ܨܠܒܐ, ܨܠܝܒܐܝܬ, ܨܠܝܒܘܬܐ, ܨܠܝܒܐ, ܨܠܝܒܘܬܐ.

ܨܠܒܐ m. *a rope of bark.*

ܨܠܒܘܒܐ m. *a reed flute* or *whistle.*

ܨܠܒܘܒܢܐ or ܨܠܒܘܒܝܬܐ m. *a cloth soaked in naphtha and oil and wound round a piece of iron or wood and lighted; brimstone.*

ܨܠܒ act. part. ܨܳܠܶܒ. *to prop up.* DERIVATIVE, the following word:—

ܨܶܠܒܳܐ pl. ܐ̈ rt. ܨܠܒ. m. *a prop, support.*

ܨܠܘܒ; see ܨܠܘܒܝܬܐ.

ܨܠܘܒܐ pl. ܐ̈ m. ܨܠܘܒܬܐ f. rt. ܨܠܒ. *a crucifier;* fem. ellipt. for ܟܢܘܫܬܐ ܨܠܘܒܬܐ *the synagogue of those who crucified.*

ܨܠܘܚܝܬܐ rt. ܨܠܚ. f. Heb. *a water-pot, horse-trough.*

ܨܠܘܠ, ܨܠܘܠܐ rt. ܨܠ. *transparent; innocent, guiltless.*

ܨܠܘܠܒܐ and ܨܠܘܠܝܒܐ pl. ܐ̈ *Palma Christi, ricinus communis, castor-oil plant.*

ܨܠܘܠܘܬܐ rt. ܨܠ. f. *clearness, limpidity.*

ܨܠܘܠܒܐ or ܨܠܘܒܠܐ m. *a scarecrow.*

ܨܠܘ, ܨܠܘܬܐ pl. ܨܠܘ̈ܬܐ, ܨܠܘ̈ܬܐ rt. ܨܠܐ. f. *prayer, a prayer;* ܒܝܬ ܨ̈ *an oratory.* Also *reconciliation, readmission to communion.*

ܨܠܘܬܢܐܝܬ rt. ܨܠܐ. adv. *by way of prayer, with a petition.*

ܨܠܘܬܢܝܐ, ܢܝܬܐ rt. ܨܠܐ. *of prayer, liturgical.*

ܨܠܚ fut. ܢܶܨܠܘܽܚ, act. part. ܨܳܠܰܚ, ܨܳܠܚܳܐ, pass. part. ܨܠܺܝܚ, ܚܳܐ. *to cleave* wood, *to crack* the head; met. ܫܪܒܗ ܕܗܒܝܠ ܨܠܚ ܠܝ ܟܐܒܐ *the story of Abel rent me with pain.* PA. ܨܰܠܰܚ *to cleave* wood; *to hew down* an altar; *to rip up, rive, rend* of animals fighting; ܨܰܠܰܚ ܦܝܠܐ ܠܓܘܫܡܗ ܕܐܪܝܐ ܒܫܢܘ̈ܗܝ the elephant *ripped up the lion's body with his tusks.* ETHPA. ܐܶܨܛܰܠܰܚ *to be rent, ripped open.* DERIVATIVES, ܨܠܘܚܝܬܐ, ܨܠܚܐ, ܨܠܚܘܬܐ, ܨܠܚܬܐ, ܨܠܝܚܐ, ܡܨܠܚܐ, ܡܨܠܚܘܬܐ.

ܨܠܚ fut. ܢܶܨܠܰܚ. *to prosper, succeed.* ETHPA. ܐܶܨܛܰܠܰܚ *to be successful.* APH. ܐܰܨܠܰܚ *a) to make prosperous, grant success;* ܐܬܚܦܛ ܕܢܨܠܚ ܡܕܒܪܢܘܬܐ ܥܕܬܢܝܬܐ *he attempted to conduct ecclesiastical matters successfully. b) to be prosperous, to succeed, flourish, do well; to be of good report, honoured;* part. *prosperous, lucky, well-to-do, wealthy;* ܐܪܐ ܥܡܗܘܢ ܕܡܨܠܚܝܢ *do they envy the successful?* ܐܨܠܚܘ ܒܗܝܡܢܘܬܐ *they were renowned in the faith.* ETHTAPH. ܐܬܬܨܠܚ *to be prosperous, go well* as an undertaking, a journey. DERIVATIVES, ܡܨܠܚܢܐܝܬ, ܡܨܠܚܢܘܬܐ, ܡܨܠܚܢܘܬܐ, ܡܨܠܚܢܐ.

ܨܠܚܐ rt. ܨܠܚ. m. *a) splitting, shivering* wood. *b) the frog* of a horse's foot.

ܨܠܚܢܘܬܐ rt. ܨܠܚ. f. *a splitting pain.*

ܨܠܚܬܐ pl. ܨܠܚ̈ܬܐ rt. ܨܠܚ. f. *cleaving, splitting; a cleft* of the head, *wound; headache on one side of the head.*

ܨܠܝ = ܨܠܐ; ܨܰܠܺܝ PAEL conj. of ܨܠܐ.

ܨܠܝܐ pl. ܐ̈ rt. ܨܠܐ. m. *inclination; a slope, depression, hollow* where water collects; astron. *declination.*

ܨܠܝܒܐ pl. ܝܢ, ܐ̈ rt. ܨܠܒ. m. *a cross, sign of the cross; the crucifixion;* ellipt. for ܥܐܕܐ ܕܨܠܝܒܐ *Holy Cross day.* Astron. ܐܪܒܥܐ ܕ̈ four stars in the constellation Aquila.

ܨܠܝܒܐܝܬ rt. ܨܠܒ. adv. *crosswise.*

ܨܠܝܒܘܢܐ dimin. of ܨܠܝܒܐ. m. *a small cross.*

ܨܠܝܒܘܬܐ rt. ܨܠܒ. f. *crucifixion.*

ܨܠܝܒܝܐ pl. ܐ̈ rt. ܨܠܒ. *of the form of a cross.*

ܨܠܝܘܬܐ rt. ܨܠܐ. f. astron. *declination.*

ܨܠܝܚܐ pl. ܐ̈ rt. ܨܠܚ. *split wood, fire-wood, a lath, chip.*

ܨܠܝܚܐ Ar. *stone on which perfumes are ground.*

ܨܠܝܠܘܬܐ rt. ܨܠ. f. *clearness, transparency, purity.*

ܨܠܝܬܐ rt. ܨܠܐ. f. *a line, snare.*

ܨܰܠܶܠ PAEL conj. of verb ܨܠ.

ܨܠܠܐ rt. ܨܠܠ. m. *a) a ringing* in the ears, *tingling. b) purity, pure condition.*

ܨܠܨܠܬܐ rt. ܨܠ. f. *a noise, rattling, clattering.*

ܨܰܠܶܡ denom. verb PAEL conj. from ܨܠܡܐ. *to impress an image* ܒܛܝܢܐ *on clay; to form, mould;* ܗܦܟ ܨܰܠܶܡ *to reform, form anew;* ܠܐ ܡܨܰܠܡܳܐ *shapeless.* ETHPA. ܐܶܨܛܰܠܰܡ *to be formed* in the womb; *to be impressed with an image* as coin; *to be prepared* for baptism. Ethpalp. ܐܬܨܛܠܡ to be expressed, represented.

ܨܠܡ, ܨܠܡܐ pl. ܐ̈ m. a) image, figure, form; a picture; ܨ̈ ܕܐܢܫܘܬܐ the human form; ܨ̈ ܕܟܐܦܐ a statue. b) an image on a coin; ܨܠܡܐ ܕܣܐܡܐ silver coins. c) an image, idol; ܦܘܠܚܢ ܨܠܡܐ image-worship, idolatry. d) astron. ܨ̈ ܩܫܬܐ Sagittarius, ܬܐܡܐ ܨܠܡܐ Gemini, signs of the Zodiac. Derivatives, verb ܨܠܡ, ܨܘܠܡܐ, ܨܠܡܘܢܐ, ܨܠܡܬܐ, ܨܠܡܝܘܬܐ, ܡܨܠܡܢܐ.

ܨܠܡܐ Ar. m. stone.

ܨܠܡܘܢ coriander.

ܨܠܡܘܢܐ dimin. of ܨܠܡܐ. m. a small idol; a doll.

ܨܠܡܘܢܝܐ m. a venomous insect, a tarantula.

ܨܠܡܘܢܝ̈ܬܐ f. pl. wasps.

ܨܠܡܢܘܬܐ from ܨܠܡܐ. f. fashioning, formation, conformation; figured work woven or embroidered.

ܨܠܡܬܐ fem. of ܨܠܡܐ. an idol, image.

ܨܠܦ fut. ܢܨܠܘܦ. to bruise, wound. Pass. part. ܨܠܝܦ, ܨܠܝܦܐ wounded; metaph. divided, dissentient ܨܒܝ̈ܢܐ wills, ܪܥܝܢܐ mind. Ethpe. ܐܬܨܠܦ to be wounded. Pa. ܨܠܦ a) to beat, wound, bruise, hurt esp. the head; ܡܨܠܦ ܢܦܫܗ ܒܟܐܦܐ cutting himself with stones; ܨܠܦܘ ܐܢܘܢ ܐܝܟ ܟܠܒܐ they beat them like dogs. b) to open a little way or gradually, set a door ajar; ܡܨܠܦ ܐܠܗܐ ܘܡܚܘܐ ܠܗ ܫܘܒܚܗ God opens a little chink and shows His glory to every one according to his strength; part. ܡܨܠܦ apparent, partly open, ajar. Ethpa. ܐܬܨܠܦ a) to be beaten, wounded esp. on the head. b) to be fissured, have chinks as a door. Aph. ܐܨܠܦ to open partly as a door; to open out, show partially, give a glimpse. Ethtaph. ܐܬܬܨܠܦ to be shown a little, to appear; ܐܬܬܨܠܦ ܠܗ ܨܡܚ ܗܘ ܢܘܗܪܐ ܗܢܐ a glimmer of that light appeared to him. Derivatives, ܨܘܠܦܐ, ܨܠܦܐ, ܨܠܦܬܐ, ܨܘܠܦܬܐ, ܡܨܠܦܢܐ.

ܨܠܦܐ or ܨܘܠܦܐ pl. ܐ̈ m. a) a chink, cranny of a door or window; a rift in armour; dissension. b) ܨܠܦܐ ܕܪܘܡܢܐ the first flowers of the pomegranate, first-ripe fruits of the same, pomegranate rind.

ܨܠܦܐ, ܨܠܦܬܐ pl. ܨ̈ rt. ܨܠܦ. f. a cleft, division.

ܨܠܪܘܢܐ pl. ܐ̈ m. a bird which preys on fish.

ܨܡܐ fut. ܢܨܡܐ to observe attentively, watch, guard. Pa. ܨܡܝ and Aph. ܐܨܡܝ the same.

ܨܡܐ pl. ܐ̈ Ar. dumb.

ܡܫܚܐ ܕܨܡܐܩܝ or ܕܙܐܒܩܝ Ar. jessamine oil.

ܨܡܚ̈ܐ pl. m. crescent-shaped ornaments, silver crescents.

ܨܡܓ, ܨܡܓܐ Ar. with ܥܪܒܝܐ. gum arabic.

ܨܡܕ fut. ܢܨܡܘܕ, act. part. ܨܡܕ to bind up a wound, bind together; ܨܡܕ ܪܫܗ he bound up his head. Pass. part. ܨܡܝܕ, ܐ, ܬܐ bound, closely joined, constricted, narrow; ܦܘܡܐ ܨܡܝܕܐ a narrow mouth; ܟܘܟܒܐ ܨܡܝܕܐ stars closely arranged in a constellation; ܐܝ̈ܕܝܐ ܕܨܡܝܕܢ the hands held closely together to receive; ܐܚܘܬܐ ܨܡܝܕܬܐ a brotherhood closely linked in love. Pa. ܨܡܕ to bind, fasten; to tie, strap or buckle on; pass. part. bound, fastened; compact; ܣܦܣܝܪܗ ܕܡܨܡܕ ܗܘܐ ܥܠ ܥܛܡܗ his dagger fastened on his thigh; ܓܘܫܡܐ ܡܨܡܕܐ the round and compact body of a bird. Ethpa. ܐܬܨܡܕ to be joined or fastened together, be made compact, connected; ܟܕ ܐܬܟܢܫܘ ܡܝ̈ܐ ܘܐܬܨܡܕܘ at the creation when the waters were gathered together and held united. Gram. to be connected. Aph. ܐܨܡܕ same as Pael. Derivatives, ܨܡܕܐ, ܨܡܕܐ, ܨܡܕܐ, ܨܘܡܕܐ, ܨܡܘܕܐ, ܨܡܝܕܐ, ܨܡܝܕܘܬܐ, ܨܡܝܕܬܐ, ܡܨܡܕܢܘܬܐ, ܡܨܡܕܢܐ, ܡܨܡܕܢܘܬܐ, ܡܨܡܕܢܝܬ.

ܨܡܕܐ rt. ܨܡܕ. m. in Isaiah iii. 23, is explained in the Lexx. as a casket to contain bridal array or a wrapper or cloak worn over full dress.

ܨܡܕܐ rt. ܨܡܕ. m. a bandage; the binding of a book.

ܨܡܕܐ pl. ܐ̈ rt. ܨܡܕ. m. a wardrobe-peg; peg in a weaver's beam.

ܨܡܘܕܐ rt. ܨܡܕ. m. a bone-setter.

ܨܡܘܕܝܐ rt. ܨܡܕ. m. binding up; closing the eyes of the dead.

ܨܡܘܚܝܐ pl. ܝܐ̈ rt. ܨܡܚ. *shining bright* as a star.

ܨܡܘܚܐ rt. ܨܡܚ. m. *a polisher.*

ܨܡܘܚܘܬܐ rt. ܨܡܚ. f. *shining brightness.*

ܨܡܘܚܢܐ, ܨܡܘܚܢܝܬܐ, ܢܝܬܐ̈ rt. ܨܡܚ. *shining, brilliant, resplendent.*

ܨܡܘܚܢܘܬܐ rt. ܨܡܚ. f. *brilliance.*

ܨܡܘܪܬܐ pl. ܬܐ̈ also ܨܡܪܐ and ܨܡܪܬܐ f. *a serpent's tooth, the large tooth in which a serpent's venom is contained.*

ܨܡܚ fut. ܢܨܡܚ, parts. ܨܡܚ, ܨܡܝܚܐ, and ܨܡܝܚܐ. *to spring forth, appear, shine;* ܐܝܠܝܢ ܕܨܡܚ ܥܠܝܗܘܢ ܢܘܗܪܐ ܕܡܫܝܚܐ *those on whom the light of Christ shines.* Ethpe. ܐܬܨܡܚ *to be illuminated.* Pa. ܨܡܚ *to make apparent, show, reflect.* Ethpa. ܐܬܨܡܚ *to shine; to obtain light.* Aph. ܐܨܡܚ *to cause to spring forth; to cause to shine; to shine, gleam, glitter;* ܐܨܡܚ ܠܒܘܫܐ ܗܘ ܫܦܝܪܐ ܐܝܟ ܫܡܫܐ *that beauteous raiment glittered like the sun;* ܡܢ ܕܠܐ ܡܨܡܚ ܒܕܟܝܘܬܐ ܪܥܝܢܐ *whoso has not a mind shining with purity.* Ethtaph. ܐܬܬܨܡܚ *to be illuminated, enlightened.* Derivatives, ܨܡܘܚܐ, ܨܡܘܚܝܐ, ܨܡܘܚܘܬܐ, ܨܡܘܚܢܝܐ, ܨܡܘܚܢܘܬܐ, ܨܡܚܐ, ܨܡܝܚܘܬܐ, ܡܨܡܚܢܐ, ܡܨܡܚܢܘܬܐ, ܠܐ ܡܨܡܚܢܐ, ܠܐ ܡܨܡܚܢܘܬܐ.

ܨܡܚܐ pl. ܚܐ̈ rt. ܨܡܚ. m. a) *a sprout, shoot.* b) *brilliancy, radiance, effulgence, splendour, reflection.* c) gram. *an elucidation, comment.*

ܨܡܚ Pael conj. of verb ܨܡܚ.

ܨܡܝܕܐܝܬ rt. ܨܡܕ. adv. *together, jointly.*

ܨܡܝܕܘܬܐ rt. ܨܡܕ. f. *close connexion* or *alliance, familiarity, coherence.*

ܨܡܨܡܐ Ar. m. *a sharp unyielding sword.*

ܨܡܟܐ m. *dirt, uncleanliness.*

ܨܡܟܘܬܐ f. = ܨܡܟܐ.

ܨܡܟܪ a strengthened form of root ܨܟܪ. Ethpamal ܐܨܛܡܟܪ *to be ashamed.* Derivative, ܨܘܡܟܪܐ.

ܨܡܪ denom. verb Pael conj. from ܨܡܪܐ. *to run, be watery, bleared* as the eyes. Ethpa. ܐܨܛܡܪ *to have bleared eyes.*

ܨܡܪܐ m. pl. *running of the eyes, bleared eyes.*

ܨܡܪܟܐ pl. ܟܐ̈ m. a) *dirt.* b) *calumny, detraction.*

ܨܡܪ root-meaning *to burst.* Ethpe. ܐܨܛܡܪ *to suffer from strangury.* Derivatives, the following five words:—

ܨܡܪ ܫܡܫܐ rt. ܨܡܪ. m. *the heliotrope.*

ܨܡܪܐ pl. ܪܐ̈ rt. ܨܡܪ. m. *strangury; stone in the bladder.*

ܨܡܪܘܬܐ rt. ܨܡܪ. f. *strangury.*

ܨܡܪܨܡܪܐ pl. ܪܐ̈ rt. ܨܡܪ = ܨܡܪܬܐ.

ܨܡܪܬܐ and ܨܡܪܬܐ rt. ܨܡܪ. f. a) *strangury, retention of urine.* b) *a whirlpool, gulf.*

ܨܢܐ *crooked, perverse.*

ܨܢܓܐ pl. ܨܢܓܝܢ and ܨܢܓܐ m. Ar. *castanets, cymbals.*

ܨܢܕܘܩܐ pl. ܩܐ̈ = ܣܢܕܘܩܐ Ar. *a box, chest.*

ܨܢܕܠ usually ܨܢܕܠ Ar. m. *sandal-wood.*

ܨܢܕܠܝܐ Turk. m. *a chair of state.*

ܨܢܕܠ Ar. m. *sandal-wood.*

ܨܢܓܐ; see ܨܢܓܐ.

ܨܢܝܥܐ pl. ܥܐ̈ rt. ܨܢܥ. *crafty.*

ܨܢܝܥܐܝܬ rt. ܨܢܥ. adv. *craftily.*

ܨܢܝܥܘܬܐ rt. ܨܢܥ. f. *craftiness.*

ܨܢܘܪܬܐ; see ܨܢܪܬܐ.

ܨܢܝܥ, ܨܢܝܥܐ rt. ܨܢܥ. *skilful, shrewd, astute, ready, crafty, cunning.*

ܨܢܝܥܐܝܬ rt. ܨܢܥ. adv. *artfully, cunningly.*

ܨܢܝܥܘܬܐ pl. ܘܬܐ̈ rt. ܨܢܥ. f. *prudence, cunning, slyness, artifice, artfulness.*

ܨܢܢܐ pl. ܢܐ̈ m. *savour, smell* esp. of roast meat; *smell* of the armpits.

ܨܢܪܬܐ and ܨܢܪܬܐ f. a) *a single hair* or *lock of wool.* b) *stench, stink.*

ܨܢܥ Paal ܨܢܥ *to act craftily, plot, scheme;* ܐܝܢܐ ܕܠܐ ܨܢܥ ܒܝܫܬܐ *whoso doth not plot evil.* Ethpa. ܐܨܛܢܥ *to contrive, plot; to act cunningly, skilfully, artfully; to be caught by guile;* with another verb *craftily, with guile;* ܐܨܛܢܥ ܘܫܚܠܦ ܐܬܘܬܐ *he craftily changed the letter.* Aph. ܐܨܢܥ *to devise artifices.* Derivatives, ܨܢܝܥܐ, ܨܢܝܥܐܝܬ, ܨܢܝܥܘܬܐ,

ܨܢܝܥܐ, ܨܢܝܥܘܬܐ, ܨܢܥܐ, ܨܢܥܬܐ, ܨܢܥܬܢܐ, ܡܨܛܢܥܢܘܬܐ, ܡܨܢܥܢܘܬܐ.

ܨܢܥܬܐ, ܨܢܥܬܐ pl. ܬܐ, ܢܐ rt. ܨܢܥ. f. *skill, craft; a doing, contrivance; a device, artifice, stratagem;* ܨܢܥܬܐ ܕܡܠܐ *sophisms.*

ܨܢܦ Heb. *to wind round.* Pael ܨܢܦ the same: ܐܬܩܪܝܬ ܡܨܢܦܬܐ ܡܢ ܗܘ ܕܡܨܢܦܐ ܘܡܬܟܪܟܐ ܥܠ ܪܫܐ *it is called a head-band from being bound and rolled round the head.* Derivative, ܡܨܢܦܬܐ.

ܨܢܪܐ pl. ܪܐ m. a wasp's *sting.*

ܨܢܪܬܐ, ܨܢܪܐ and ܨܢܪܐ pl. ܨܢܪܬܐ f. *a fish-hook, fishing-line.*

ܨܢܬܐ contraction of *a)* ܨܢܝܥܬܐ. *b)* ܨܢܥܬܐ.

ܨܐ parts. ܨܐܐ and ܨܐܝܐ *fetid, foul* as ulcers. Palpal ܨܐܨܐ pass. part. ܡܨܐܨܐ, ܝܐ, ܝܬܐ *fetid, foul, polluted;* ܫܘܚܢܐ ܡܨܐܨܝܐ *running sores.* Ethpalp. ܐܨܛܐܨܐ *to be bespattered* with mire or with calumny. Derivative, ܨܘܐܨܐ.

ܨܥܐ E-Syr. ܨܥܐ, Ar. *a) a dish. b) a measure* of fruit.

ܨܥܝܪܐܝܬ rt. ܨܥܪ. adv. *pitiably.*

ܨܥܝܪܘܬܐ rt. ܨܥܪ. f. *contemptibleness.*

ܨܐܠ perhaps denom. verb from ܨܐܐ. Pass. part. ܡܨܐܠ *defiled.*

ܨܐܐ, ܨܐܝܬܐ *soiled, dirty, impure, filthy.* Derivatives, ܨܘܐܬܐ, verb ܨܐܠ, ܨܐܝܐܝܬ, ܨܐܝܘܬܐ.

ܨܐܝܐܝܬ from ܨܐܐ. adv. *impurely, basely.*

ܨܐܝܘܬܐ pl. ܘܬܐ from ܨܐܐ. f. *dirt, filth, nastiness, ordure; foulness* of a sore, *foulness* of speech.

ܨܐܨܐ Palpal of ܨܐ.

ܨܥܪ *to be despised, bear disgrace.* Part. adj. ܨܥܝܪ, ܐ, ܬܐ *despised, despicable, vile, ignominious, disreputable.* Legal. *disreputable, debarred* from holding office or exercising certain honourable professions; also of a woman marrying again within ten months of her husband's death, thereby forfeiting money left by her first husband. Pa. ܨܥܪ *to be overbearing; to treat shamefully, abuse, contemn, dishonour; to outrage* a woman; ܨܥܪܬܗ ܣܪܐ *Sarah dealt hardly with* Hagar; ܡܚܐܘܗܝ ܘܨܥܪܘܗܝ ܘܫܕܪܘܗܝ *they beat him and handled him shamefully and sent him away;* ܚܝܐ ܡܨܥܪܐ ܚܝܐ ܗܘܐ *he lived an abject life.* Ethpa. ܐܨܛܥܪ *to be brought into contempt, be shamefully entreated, suffer dishonour; to be dishonoured, outraged.* Derivatives, ܨܘܥܪܐ, ܨܥܝܪܐܝܬ, ܨܥܝܪܘܬܐ, ܨܥܪܐ, ܨܥܪܢܘܬܐ, ܡܨܥܪܢܐ, ܡܨܥܪܢܐܝܬ, ܡܨܥܪܢܘܬܐ.

ܨܥܪܐ rt. ܨܥܪ. m. *shame, dishonour, insult, wrong.*

ܨܥܪܢܘܬܐ rt. ܨܥܪ. f. *insolence.*

ܨܦ fut. ܢܨܘܦ, parts. ܨܐܦ, ܨܝܦܐ and ܐܨܛܦܐ, ܨܛܦ *to be eager, rampant* as a lion; *to be inflamed* with thirst, with desire; ܨܛܦ ܡܢ ܨܗܝܐ *inflamed with thirst.* Pa. ܨܦܦ *to leap.* Derivative, ܨܘܦܐ.

ܨܦܐ Pael ܨܦܝ *to filter, strain.*

ܨܦܐ pl. of ܨܦܬܐ *a mat.*

ܨܦܪܐ m. pl. *fastening threads* of quires; *threads* used by women weavers.

ܨܦܪܐ or ܨܦܪܐ m. dial. of Tagrit, *a pewter wine-pot.*

ܨܦܪܐ m. *the staple* of a bolt.

ܨܦܝܢܐ rt. ܨܦܢ. *epidemic.*

ܨܦܘܢܐ m. *soap.*

ܨܦܘܪܐ *a flute.*

ܨܦܘܢܝܐ, ܨܦܘܢܝܬܐ pl. ܝܬܐ and ܝܬܐ f. perh. *συμφωνία, bagpipes;* also *a seven-stringed harp.*

ܨܦܨܦ *confused, distracted.*

ܨܦܨܦ, ܨܦܨܦܐ or ܨܦ. pl. ܦܐ m. *a pillory, iron collar.*

ܨܦܩ fut. ܢܨܦܘܩ, act. part. ܨܐܦܩ, ܨܐܦܩܐ. *a) to close suddenly, spring to* as a trap; ܠܐ ܨܐܦܩ ܦܚܐ ܥܠ ܐܪܥܐ ܟܕ ܠܐ ܐܚܕ ܡܕܡ *does a springe close to the ground without catching anything? b) to fall upon* as lightning; ܨܦܩܐ ܕܪܥܡܐ ܘܕܒܪܩܐ ܨܐܦܩ ܥܠ ܟܝܢܢ ܡܚܝܠܐ *the sudden vehemence of* thunder and *lightning strikes upon and stuns our feeble nature.* Metaph. [illegible] *muttering thunders, thundering* at him. *c) to come* suddenly upon, fall upon, overtake or attack suddenly with ܥܠ; as death, destruction, wrath, sorrow, evil; an invasion; an army; to arise suddenly as a rumour; ܨܦܥ ܒܗ ܡܘܬܐ ܒܠܠܝܐ death came upon him in the night; ܒܨܦܪܐ ܨܦܥܘ ܒܗܘܢ ܘܫܒܘ ܫܝܪܬܐ early in the morning they fell on them and captured a convoy; ܨܦܥܐ ܩܝܡܬܐ ܥܠ ܕܡܝܟܝ ܒܥܦܪܐ resurrection suddenly comes to those who sleep deep in the dust; ܣܗܕܘܬܐ ܕܡܠܘܗܝ ܡܚܝܒܐ ܠܕܓܠܐ the testimony of his own words shall quickly convict the liar. PA. ܨܦܥ intensive of Peal c, to come suddenly on, fall upon. ETHTAPH. ܐܬܬܨܦܥ to be afflicted with sudden misfortune. DERIVATIVES, ܨܘܦܥܐ, ܨܦܘܥܝܐ, ܨܦܥܐ, ܨܦܥܬܐ.

ܨܦܥܐ m. a) rt. ܨܦܥ. anything happening suddenly or unexpectedly; ܒܨܦܥ ܨܦܪܟ at thy sudden dawning. b) a plate, dish.

ܨܦܥܬܐ pl. ܨܦܥܬܐ rt. ܨܦܥ. f. a springe, gin, noose; a clap, crash; a sudden onslaught, surprise; an epidemic; ܨܦܥܬܐ ܕܪܘܓܙܐ sudden wrath.

ܨܦܝܚܐ Ar. a sheet, plate of metal.

ܨܦܝܐ, ܐ, ܬܐ rt. ܨܦܐ. a) burning ܒܓܗܢܐ in hell. b) ܥܢܐ ܕܨܦܝܢ ܒܨܗܝܐ flocks heated with thirst.

ܨܦܝ PAEL conj. of ܨܦܐ.

ܨܦܝܨܬܐ pl. instruments of torture.

ܨܦܪ, ܨܦܪܐ pl. ܨܦܪܘܬܐ m. early morning, daybreak, dawn; the third of the twelve divisions of the day; the second of the seven canonical hours; ܒܨܦܪܐ ܒܨܦܪ, ܒܟܠ ܨܦܪ ܨܦܪ and ܨܦܪ ܨܦܪ every morning; also ܒܨܦܪܘܬܐ ܐܙܠ ܗܘܐ in the mornings he used to go; ܕܨܦܪ ܝܘܡܐ early next day. DERIVATIVES, ܨܦܪܝܐ, ܨܦܪܢܐ.

ܨܦܪ, ܨܦܪܐ pl. ܝܢ, ܐ f. any small bird, sparrow, finch; ܟܠ ܨܦܪ ܘܟܠ ܦܪܚܬܐ every bird and winged creature; ܨܦܪ ܓܡܠܐ an ostrich; ܨ ܕܦܠܐ the bulbul, nightingale; ܨ ܟܘܫܝܐ the Ethiopian bird = parrot; ܡܠܟܘܬܒܪܐ = ܨ ܩܡܨܐ a bird which feeds on locusts, also a tomtit; ܨ ܩܘܩܝܬܐ a starling; ܨ ܓܡܠܐ the ostrich. DERIVATIVES, ܨܦܪܐ, ܨܦܪܘܢܐ.

ܨܦܪ, ܨܦܪܐ m. a bird-fancier.

ܨܦܪܕ Ar. m. a lark.

ܨܦܪܘܢܐ dimin. of ܨܦܪܐ m. a little bird.

ܨܦܪܝܐ, ܝܬܐ from ܨܦܪܐ. in the morning, early, morning (adj.); ܒܨܦܪܝܬܐ in the early morning.

ܨܦܝܪܐ, ܨܦܝܪ and ܨܦܝܪ, ܝܬܐ com. gen. a kid, yearling goat usually ܕܓܕܝܐ ܨ.

ܨܦܪܢܐ from ܨܦܪܐ. the part of the sky where the sun rises, the east.

ܨܦܪܬܐ f. the peg of an ox-yoke.

ܨܦܬܐ and ܨܦܝܬܐ pl. ܨܦܬܐ, ܨܦܝܬܐ f. a mat, matting.

ܨܦܬܐ pl. ܨܦܬܐ rt. ܨܦܐ. f. care, anxiety, solicitude.

ܨܦܬܐ f. a) the stone or setting of a ring. b) = ܨܒܬܐ ornament. c) ܨ ܕܟܬܒܘܬܐ a writing-case, desk.

ܨܨܐ or ܨܨܐ m. the tamarind.

ܨܨܐ pl. ܐ m. a) a nail. b) a wart, whitlow.

ܨܨܠܐ, ܨܠܨܠܐ or ܨܨܠܐ pl. ܐ m. cymbals, castanets; song of birds, cooing of doves.

ܨܨܨ denom. verb PAEL conj. from ܨܨܐ. to nail.

ܨܨܪܐ or ܨܪܨܪܐ and perhaps ܨܘܨܪܐ pl. ܐ m. a cricket.

ܨܪ fut. ܢܨܘܪ, act. part. ܨܐܪ, ܨܪܐ, pass. part. ܨܪܝܪ, ܨܪܝܪܐ. to tie up a purse, to bind fast e.g. in a cloth or in a corner of a garment; ܨܘܪ ܟܣܦܐ ܒܐܝܕܟ bind up the money in thine hand; ܨܪ ܠܗ ܡܕܥܝ ܘܐܬܕܘܕ my mind was constrained and confused; ܨܪܝܪܐ ܒܨܪܪܐ bound up in a bundle. ETHPE. ܐܬܨܪܝܪ and ETHPA. ܐܬܨܪܪ to be bound fast. PA. ܨܪܪ to bind up, sew up; ܙܩܐ ܡܨܛܪܝܢ ܘܡܨܪܪܝܢ wineskins rent and bound up. DERIVATIVES, ܨܪܘܪܐ, ܨܪܪܐ.

ܨܪܐ fut. ܢܨܪܐ, act. part. ܨܪܐ, ܨܪܝܐ, pass. part. ܨܪܐ, ܨܪܝܐ. to rip up, mangle with claws or knives; to rend asunder, rend clothes; to make a way through, pass through; to break through the enemy's ranks; to cleave the air as a bird, the ground as a plough, a river; to burst forth as tears; to break out of the womb, from the egg, from the calix as flowers. ETHPE. ܐܬܨܪܝ a) to be rent in twain, rent by earthquake; ܐܬܦܪܨ ܐܦ ܐܦܪܚܐ ܕܗܝܟܠܐ ܐܬܦܪܨ *the veil of the temple was rent in twain;* ܐܬܦܪܨ ܐܘܪܚܐ *a way was forced through the snow.* b) *to burst* with anger, *be torn* with vexation. c) *to take pleasure.* PA. ܦܪܨ *to rend* garments, *rend* rocks, walls, *to tear, lacerate* the flesh; *to burst open, tear, perforate.* ETHPA. ܐܬܦܪܨ a) *to be violently rent* as the earth; *to be rent, burst, torn* as wineskins, nets; as clouds, the sky. Also ܐܬܦܪܨܘ ܓܦܘܗܝ the bird's *wings grew to separate form* in the egg. b) denom. verb from στρηνία (cf. ܣܛܪܢܝܐ) *to be luxurious, lascivious; to wax wanton.* DERIVATIVES, ܦܪܘܨܐ, ܦܪܨܐ, ܦܪܨܘܬܐ, ܡܦܪܨܢܐ, ܡܦܪܨܢܘܬܐ.

ܦܪܨܘܡܐ or ܦܪܨܘܡܐ m. *the kermes worm* from which a crimson dye is obtained.

ܦܪܪ ETHPE. ܐܬܦܪܪ *to flutter about, tear about* as a frightened bird or beast.

ܦܪܘܐ m. a) *balsam, opobalsam.* b) *mace.* c) *gum* or *root of a resinous tree.* d) *pine kernels.*

ܦܪܘܝܐ rt. ܦܪܐ. m. *one who cleaves a way, the leader of a flock of birds.*

ܦܪ̈ܘܝܢ, ܦܪ̈ܘܝܬܐ rt. ܦܪܐ. f. pl. *torn pieces, tatters, rags.* Cf. ܦܪܝܐ.

ܦܪܘܦܐ pl. ܐ̈ rt. ܦܪܦ. m. a) *a metal-worker, refiner.* b) *astringent.*

ܦܪܘܦܘܬܐ and ܦܪܘܦܬܢܘܬܐ rt. ܦܪܦ. f. *astringency, contraction, congelation.*

ܦܪܘܦܬܢܐ rt. ܦܪܦ. *astringent, styptic.*

ܦܪܘܫܬܐ pl. ܬ̈ܐ f. *an eft, newt; a poisonous yellow lizard.*

ܦܪܚ fut. ܢܦܪܘܚ, act. part. ܦܪܚ, ܦܪܚܐ, part. adj. ܦܪܝܚܐ. a) *to catch* or *take fire; to set on fire; to crackle, crash, coruscate* all used of meteors and lightnings; ܐܬܝܪ ܢܘܪܐ ܗܘܐ ܐܚܕ ܠܗܠܝܢ ܠܗ̈ܓܐ ܡܫܚ̈ܢܐ ܘܦܪܚ *fiery ether seizes* those oily vapours *and sets them on fire;* ܚܝܠܐ ܢܘܪܢܝܐ ܕܦܪܚ ܒܥܢܢ̈ܐ *the fiery force which crackles in the clouds;* ܦܪܚ ܡܘܬܐ ܥܠ ܟܠܗܘܢ ܝܠܕ̈ܝ ܚܘܐ *death comes with a crash on all the offspring of Eve.* b) *to groan, to cry out.* APH. ܐܦܪܚ *to burst out* singing or sobbing, *to cry aloud; to scream* as an eagle; ܠܫܢܐ ܕܡܦܪܚ ܩܝ̈ܢܬܐ *the tongue which cries out lamentations;* ܐܦܪܚ ܘܩܥܝ *break forth and cry aloud.* DERIVATIVES, ܦܘܪܚܢܐ, ܦܪܚܐ, ܦܪܚܢܐ.

ܦܪܚܐ rt. ܦܪܚ. m. *coruscation, play of lightning.*

ܦܪܚܢܝܬܐ rt. ܦܪܚ. f. name of a bird.

ܦܪܝ, ܦܪܝܐ also ܦܪܝܐ pl. ܐ̈ m. and pl. f. ܦܪ̈ܝܢ, ܦܪ̈ܝܬܐ rt. ܦܪܐ. a) *rending asunder; dissection, anatomy.* b) *a crack, rift, cleft;* ܦܪܝܐ ܕܫܘܥܐ *a cleft in the rock;* ܦܪܝܐ ܕܬܪܥܐ *a crack in the door;* ܦܪ̈ܝܐ ܕܐܝ̈ܕܝܐ ܘܕܪ̈ܓܠܐ *chaps in the hands and feet.* c) *a fragment, chip, bit of broken glass.* d) f. pl. *a piece rent from a garment.*

ܦܪܝܓܐ *twisted, bent.*

ܦܪܝܘܬܐ rt. ܦܪܐ. f. *rending; a rent, cut.*

ܦܪܝܟܘܬܐ rt. ܦܪܟ. f. *poverty, need, distress.*

ܦܪܝܡܘܬܐ rt. ܦܪܡ. f. *insolence, violence.*

ܦܪܝܦܘܬܐ rt. ܦܪܦ. f. *flux, fusion* of metals.

ܦܪܟ *to lack, be in want.* Part. ܦܪܝܟ, ܦܪܝܟܐ, ܦܪܝܟܬܐ *lacking, needy, poor;* ܦܪܝܟ ܒܠܚܡܐ *lacking bread;* ܠܫܢܐ ܥܒܪܝܐ ܦܪܝܟ the Hebrew language *is very poor.* ETHPE. ܐܬܦܪܟ and ETHPA. ܐܬܦܪܟ *to suffer want, be in need.* APH. ܐܦܪܟ *to impoverish, reduce to poverty.* DERIVATIVES, ܦܘܪܟܢܐ, ܦܪܝܟܘܬܐ.

ܦܪܡ fut. ܢܦܪܘܡ, act. part. ܦܪܡ, ܦܪܡܐ. a) *to crop, cut off* the ears; *to crop* grass as cattle; *to cut grass* for cattle; *to pluck, tear up* plants; *to crop* or *cut back* branches, *prune.* b) *to venture, be determined.* PA. ܦܪܡ *to be persistent, carry through with perseverance.* APH. ܐܦܪܡ a) *to resort to.* b) *to dare to attempt, be firmly resolved.* DERIVATIVES, ܦܘܪܡܐ, ܦܪܝܡܘܬܐ, ܦܪܡܐ.

ܦܪܡܐ rt. ܦܪܡ. m. a) *resolution, determination.* b) *a cut, cut-off branch, place of a cut.* c) *half a skin of wine.*

ܦܪܡܝܢܩܐ Pers. m. *a leathern, glass,* or *stone bottle, a tumbler, glass.*

ܦܪܡܝܢܐ and ܦܪܡܢܐ same as ܦܪܨܘܡܐ.

ܦܪܢܟܐ E-Syr. ܦܪܢܟܐ m. *breasts* or *udders full of milk.*

ܦܪܦ or ܦܪܦ fut. ܢܦܪܘܦ and ܢܦܪܦ, act. part. ܦܪܦ, ܦܪܦܐ, pass. part. ܦܪܝܦ, ܦܪܝܦܐ. a) *to clear,* refine, purge; ܐܶܨܪܽܘܦ ܐܶܢܽܘܢ ܐܰܝܟ ܕܨܳܪܦܺܝܢ ܟܣܦܳܐ I will refine them as they refine silver; ܟܣܦܳܐ ܨܪܺܝܦܳܐ refined silver; ܫܶܢܩܳܐ ܨܪܰܦܬܶܗ suffering refined him. b) to straiten, chasten, pain, afflict; ܠܶܒܶܗ ܠܳܐ ܨܳܪܶܦ ܠܶܗ his heart does not misgive him. c) to astringe, be astringent. d) Arab. to change money; ܕܨܳܪܦܺܝܢ ܙܽܘܙܶܐ money-changers. Ethpe. ܐܶܨܛܪܶܦ a) to be purged, refined as silver; to be purged from sin. b) to contract, become of close texture. Pa. ܨܰܪܶܦ a) to clarify. b) to chastise, afflict. c) to render astringent. Ethpa. ܐܶܨܛܰܪܰܦ a) to be contracted, to have the lips drawn up or awry from a bitter taste. b) denom. from ܨܶܪܦܳܐ to be treated with alum. Aph. ܐܰܨܪܶܦ a) to chasten, chastise, punish; ܨܰܘܡܳܐ ܡܰܨܪܶܦ ܠܶܗ ܠܦܰܓܪܳܐ fasting chastens the body; ܟܳܐ ܒܶܗ ܘܰܐܨܪܶܦ ܠܶܗ he rebuked and chastised him. b) to bind fast, astringe, contract; ܚܰܝܠܳܐ ܕܡܰܨܪܶܦ styptic or astringent virtue; ܒܚܰܠܗܽܘܢ ܐܰܨܪܦܽܘ ܣܶܦܘ̈ܳܬܶܗ with their vinegar they made His lips contract. c) to gripe, pinch, pain; ܩܽܘܪܳܐ ܘܪܰܛܺܝܒܽܘܬܳܐ ܡܰܨܪܦܳܢ ܠܦܰܓܪ̈ܰܝܢ cold and wet pinch our bodies. Derivatives, ܨܪܳܦܳܐ, ܨܶܪܦܳܐ, ܨܪܺܝܦܽܘܬܳܐ, ܨܪܺܝܦܳܐܺܝܬ, ܨܪܺܝܦܳܝܽܘܬܳܐ, ܨܶܪܦܽܘܬܳܐ, ܨܳܪܽܘܦܳܐ, ܨܪܳܦܳܐ, ܨܪܳܦܽܘܬܳܐ, ܡܰܨܪܦܳܢܽܘܬܳܐ, ܡܰܨܪܦܳܢܳܐ, ܡܰܨܪܦܳܐ.

ܨܳܪܽܘܦܳܐ pl. ܐ̈ rt. ܨܪܦ. m. a) a refiner of silver. b) Arab. a money-changer, banker.

ܨܶܪܦܳܐ rt. ܨܪܦ. m. a) a fining-pot. b) an astringent salt, alum. c) constipation. d) ܨܶܪܦ ܠܶܒܳܐ oppression of the heart, palpitations.

ܨܰܪܦܳܩܬܳܐ from ܨܰܪܦܶܩ m. a buffet, blow.

ܨܶܪܦܬܳܐ = ܩܪܽܘܦܬܳܐ kermes.

ܨܰܪܦܶܩ to slap, buffet.

ܨܰܪܳܦܳܐ pl. ܐ̈ rt. ܨܪܦ. m. a goldsmith.

ܨܪܳܨܽܘܪܳܐ m. canker-worm, grub, locust.

ܨܪܳܨܪܳܐ and ܨܪܳܨܳܪܳܐ, ܨܪܨܽܘܪܬܳܐ m. a register.

ܨܪܳܪܳܐ rt. ܨܪ. m. a bundle, packet, money-bag, purse; a knot, tie.

ܨܪܳܬܡܳܐ and ܨܪܳܬܡܶܐ and perh. ܨܪܡ. m. tamarind fruit.

ܨܳܪܬܳܐ pl. ܐ̈ m. satureia thymbra, wild thyme.

⁘ ܫܠܡ ܣܕܪܐ ܕܨܕܐ ܘܠܐܠܗܐ ܫܘܒܚܐ ⁘

⁘ ܩܪܐ ܥܕܪܐ ܠܫܘܠܡܗ. ܡܪܝ ܥܕܪ ܠܝ ⁘

⁘ ܩ ⁘

ܩ, ܩܳܘܦ Qoph, the nineteenth letter of the Syriac alphabet; the numeral 100, ܕܩ̄ the one hundredth.

ܩ̄ abbrev. a) for ܩܰܠܺܝܠ somewhat, slightly. b) for ܩܶܪܝܳܢܳܐ a lection. c) ܩܳܠܳܐ a tone.

ܩܰܐܐܢ, ܩܰܐܢ or ܩܳܐܢ Tatar. m. Khan, lord, chief.

ܩܳܐܶܒ, ܩܳܐܒܳܐ act. part. of verb ܩܒ.

ܩܰܐܒܽܘܬܳܐ, ܩܺܐܒܽܘܬܳܐ or ܩܶܒܽܘܬܳܐ pl. ܬ̈ܳܐ f. κιβωτός, the ark; ܩ̄ ܕܕܺܝܰܬܺܩܺܐ or ܕܩܝܳܡܳܐ the ark of the covenant; a chest, coffer, coffin; a wooden cage for wild beasts.

ܩܳܐܨܽܘܕܳܐ rt. ܩܨܕ. m. a harvester, reaper.

ܩܳܐܶܪ act. part. of verb ܩܪ.

ܩܳܐܪܶܐ f. pl. swollen glands, glandular swellings.

ܩܳܐܕܺܝ pl. ܩܘܳܐܕܺܝ Ar. m. the Cadi, judge.

ܩܐܬܪܘܐ pl. ܐ̈ m. *a watercourse, channel.*

ܩܐܘܣܘܣ καῦσος, *a bilious remittent* fever.

ܩܐܐ act. part. of verb ܩܘܐ.

ܩܐܛܐ Greek κατά: for words beginning thus see under ܩܛ.

ܩܐܛܐ, ܩܐܛܘܣ pl. ܩܐ̈ܛܐ and ܩܝܛܘܣ pl. ܩܝ̈ܛܐ, ܩܝܛܐܣ m. κῆτος, *a huge fish, sea-monster, whale, leviathan.*

ܩܐܛܝܐ, ܩܐܛܝ or ܩܝܛܝ adj. from ܩܐܛܐ. *of* or *belonging to a whale.*

ܩܐܛܝܓܘܪܝܣ pl.; see ܩܛܝܓܘܪܝܐ.

ܩܐܝܡ m. ܩܝܡܬܐ and ܩܐܝܡܬܐ f. verbal adj. of ܩܘܡ. *standing.*

ܩܐܠܒ Ar. m. *the framework* of a roof.

ܩܐܠܢܕܝܢ, ܩܐܠܢܕܘܣ, ܩܐܠܢܕܝܢ; see ܩܠܢܕܝܢ *calends.*

ܩܐܠܬܐ pl. ܩܐ̈ܠܐ; see ܩܠܬܐ *a basket.*

ܩܐܡ, ܩܝܡܐ act. part. of verb ܩܘܡ.

ܩܐܡܘܣ rarely ܩܡܘܣ f. κημός, *a muzzle, snaffle, bit.* Derivative, verb ܩܡܣ.

ܩܐܡܘܢܐ a name for *sorcerers* in a Turkish tribe.

ܩܐܢ *Khan;* see ܩܐܢ.

ܩܐܢܐ = ܩܢܐ *a nest.*

ܩܐܢܐܘܣ, ܩܪܐܢܘܣ κρήνη -ας, *fountains.*

ܩܐܣܐ = ܩܣܐ.

ܩܐܣܝܣ Lat. cassis, *a helmet.*

ܩܐܣܛܪ = ܩܣܛܪ *a secretary.*

ܩܐܣܛܪܐ pl. ܩܐܣܛܪܘܢ; see ܩܣܛܪܐ *a camp.*

ܩܐܣܝܐ usually ܩܣܝܐ *cassia.*

ܩܐܦܐ the Greek letter κάππα.

ܩܐܦܐܠܐܘܢ pl. ܩܐܦܐܠܐ; see ܩܦܠܐܘܢ *a chapter.*

ܩܐܦܝܛܐ Lat. capita, with ܥܒܕ. *to take a census.*

ܩܐܦܛܘܠܝܢ; see ܩܦܛܘܠܝܢ.

ܩܐܦܠܘܛܐ; see ܩܦܠܛ.

ܩܐܦܘܪ and ܩܦܘܪ m. *camphor.*

ܩܐܪ, ܩܪܐ act. part. of verb ܩܪ.

ܩܐܪܐ = ܩܪܐ *end.*

ܩܐܕܝ = ܩܐܕܝ *a Cadi, judge.*

ܩܐܪ, ܩܪܐ act. part. of verb ܩܪ.

ܩܐܪܐ pl. ܐ̈ for ܩܪܐ *a gourd.*

ܩܐܪܒܘܣ pl. ܩܐܪܒܐ m. κάραβος, *a prickly crab.*

ܩܐܪܘܬܐ, ܩܐܪܘܣ oftener ܩܪܘܬܐ. κηρός, *a)* f. *wax; a wax candle;* ܩ̈ ܕܟܝܐ *clarified wax.* *b)* ܩܐܪܘܬܐ f. καρυῶτις, *a palm bearing fruit like walnuts.*

ܩܐܪܘܣ pl. ܐ̈ also spelt ܩܪܘܣ and ܩܝܪܘܣ καιρός, m. *a) the right time, occasion, opportunity. b) misfortune, calamity. c) fighting, battle, war.*

ܩܐܫ, ܩܫܐ act. part. of verb ܩܫ.

ܩܐܬ, ܩܬܐ act. part. of verb ܩܬ.

ܩܐܬܐܪܐ *Cathari,* heretics; see ܩܬܪܐ.

ܩܐܬܘܠܝܩܐ, ܩܐܬܘܠܝܩܐ pl. ܩܐܬܘܠܝܩܘܣ; see ܩܬܘܠܝܩܐ *catholic.*

ܩܐܬܝܛܐ, ܩܐܬܝܛܘܣ m. ἡ κάθετος, *a perpendicular line; plumb-line.*

ܩܐܬܐܪܣܝܣ and ܩܐܬܐܪ; see ܩܬܐܪܣܝܣ *deposition.*

ܩܒ fut. ܢܩܘܒ, parts. ܩܐܒ and ܩܒܝܒ. *a) to stand on end, bristle* as the hair from terror; ܩܐܡ ܩܘܒܬܗܘܢ *their hair stands on end.* *b) to over-arch, form a dome;* ܡܩܒܩܒܐ ܩܒܝܒܐ ܠܗ *flames of light form a dome over Him.* Part. adj. ܡܩܒܒ, ܐ *vaulted, convex;* ܪܩܝܥܐ ܕܩܒܝܒܐ ܘܡܩܒܒܐ *the arched and vaulted firmament.* Pa. ܩܒܒ *a) to be horrified. b) to vault;* ܒܝܬܐ ܡܩܒܒܐ *a vaulted house.* Ethpa. ܐܬܩܒܒ *a) to bristle, be rigid* with fear. *b) to shiver feverishly.* Derivatives, ܩܒܒܐ, ܩܘܒܒܐ, ܩܘܒܐ, ܡܩܒܒܢܐ, ܩܘܒܬܐ.

ܩܒ rt. ܩܒܐ. m. *a pool.*

ܩܒܐ fut. ܢܩܒܐ, act. part. ܩܐܒܐ, ܩܒܝܐ, pass. part. ܩܒܐ, ܩܒܝܐ. *a)* intrans. *to collect, run together* as liquids, secretions; ܡܝܐ ܩܒܝܢ ܒܓܘܡܨܐ ܘܒܩܒܝ̈ܐ *water collected in hollows and pools;* ܕܡܐ ܕܩܒܐ ܗܘܐ ܠܓܘ ܡܪܟܒܬܐ *the blood which had trickled down into* the chariot; ܡܘܓܠܐ ܕܩܒܐ ܒܚܕܝܐ *matter gathered in the chest.* *b)* trans. *to collect, gather, contain, hold;* ܓܘܒ̈ܐ ܬܒܝܪ̈ܐ ܕܠܐ ܡܫܟܚܝܢ ܠܡܩܒܝܘ ܡܝ̈ܐ *broken cisterns which can hold no water;* ܡܝ̈ܐ ܩܒܝ̈ܐ *standing water;* metaph. ܐܓܪ̈ܬܟ ܕܒܫܐ ܩܒܝ̈ܢ *thy letters drip honey;* ܩܒܝܐ ܠܒܝܫܬܐ *it gathers evil, is a receptacle for evil.* Ethpe. ܐܬܩܒܝ

a) to be collected, gathered together; ܩܕܡ ܕܢܬܩܒܐ ܝܡܡܐ *before the sea was gathered together.* *b) to be retained, held* ܒܦܘܡܐ *in the mouth.* Ethpa. ܐܬܩܒܝ *to betake oneself, secrete oneself.* Derivatives, ܩܒܐ, ܩܘܒܐ, ܩܒܐ, ܩܒܝܐ, ܩܒܝܬܐ, ܩܘܒܬܐ, ܩܒܘܝܐ, ܩܒܘܝܬܐ.

ܩܒܐ m. *a) an enclosure;* ܩ̈ ܕܦܪܙܠܐ *an iron cage.* *b)* Arab. *the womb;* ܩܒܐ ܩܒܐ *the last offspring* of a woman as closing the womb.

ܩܒܐ pl. ܩܒܝܢ Heb. *cab,* a dry measure equalling nearly two quarts; a liquid measure of nearly half a pint.

ܩܒܝܐ rt. ܩܒܐ = ܩܒܐ.

ܩܘܒܝܐ rt. ܩܒܒ. m. *a vault, dome; an arched cavity* e.g. in the body.

ܩܘܒܩܒܝܬܐ rt. ܩܒܒ. f. *a shivering fit, feverish rigour, shudder.*

ܩܒܘܠ; see ܩܒܘܠܐ.

ܩܒܘܠܐ rt. ܩܒܠ. m. *an accuser.*

ܩܒܘܠܝܐ rt. ܩܒܠ. m. *an accusation, impeachment.*

ܩܒܘܪܐ pl. ܐ̈ rt. ܩܒܪ. m. *a grave-digger, sexton.*

ܩܒܘܪܐ pl. ܐ̈ rt. ܩܒܪ. m. *burial, sepulture;* ܩ̈ ܒܝܬ and ellipt. *a burial-place, sepulchre.*

ܩܒܘܪܬܐ pl. ܬ̈ܐ rt. ܩܒܪ. f. *burying, a burial, funeral, funeral rites; a shroud.*

ܩܒܘܬܐ; see ܩܒܘܬܐ.

ܩܒܘܬܘܢܝܬܐ dimin. of ܩܒܘܬܐ. f. *a small chest.*

ܩܒܝܐ or ܩܒܝܐ rt. ܩܒܐ. m. *a) a pool, water-hole, cistern.* Metaph. ܩܒܝܐ ܕܦܬܟܪܘܬܐ *the swamp of idolatry.* *b) holding water in the mouth to rinse it out.*

ܩܒܝܘܬܐ rt. ܩܒܐ. f. *a gathering together, mass* of waters, of pus.

ܩܒܝܠܬܐ rt. ܩܒܠ. f. *a charge, accusation.*

ܩܒܝܢܐ pl. ܩ̈ rt. ܩܒܐ. m. *a bruise.*

ܩܒܝܥܐܝܬ rt. ܩܒܥ. adv. *fixedly, firmly.*

ܩܒܝܥܘܬܐ rt. ܩܒܥ. f. *a) putting up, setting up* ܕܡܛܠܐ *of booths* = feast of tabernacles. *b) fixedness, stability, coherence;* ܐܪܙܐ ܕܩܒܝܥܘܬܐ *the mystery of the standing* of our Lord at God's right hand; ܩܒܝܥܘܬܐ ܕܐܦ̈ܐ *cast of features, physiognomy.* *c) compactness, elegance* of style. *d) fixing* the mind, *attention, application.*

ܩܒܝܪܘܬܐ rt. ܩܒܪ. f. *burial.*

ܩܒܟܬܐ also ܩܘ̈ܒ and ܩܒ̈ pl. ܩܒ̈ܟܬܐ rt. ܩܒܐ. f. *a pool, standing water; a tank, reservoir, cistern;* ܩ̈ ܕܝܡܡܐ *the gathering together of the seas.*

ܩܒܟܬܐ pl. ܬ̈ܐ f. *a man's upper garment, overcoat.*

ܩܒܠ fut. ܢܩܒܘܠ, act. part. ܩܒܠ, ܩܒܠܐ, pass. part. ܩܒܝܠ, ܠܐ. *to accuse, impeach, complain of* with ܥܠ or ܡܢ of the pers. accused or of the cause and ܠ or ܠܘܬ of the pers. before whom the complaint is laid, also abs., ܕܢܩܒܘܠ ܠܗ ܥܠ ܗܠܝܢ *to lodge complaints with him about these matters;* ܠܗ ܠܡܩܒܠܢܐ ܕܥܠ ܕܝܢܐ ܢܩܒܘܠ ܩܕܡ ܕܝܢܐ *the plaintiff must carry his appeal before the judge;* ܟܕ ܒܟܐ ܘܡܩܒܠ ܕ *weeping and complaining that.* Pass. part. *a) accused;* ܚܒܪܟ ܩܒܝܠ ܡܢܟ *thy neighbour is accused by thee.* *b) opposite.* Ethpe. ܐܬܩܒܠ *to be accused.* Pa. ܩܒܠ *a) to receive, accept* as ܡܘܗܒܬܐ *a gift, an office;* ܒܒܝܬܐ *in the house;* ܐܟܣܢܝܐ *a guest;* ܓܢܝܒܬܐ ܕܓܘܢܒܐ *stolen goods;* ܐܘ ܪܘܫܡܐ ܕܡܥܡܘܕܝܬܐ *the signing of baptism, to be baptized;* ܐܝܕܐ ܣܝܡ *ordination;* ܐܣܟܝܡܐ ܕܝܚܝܕܝܘܬܐ *the monastic habit.* Special meanings: with ܒܛܢܐ *to conceive;* ܒܗܬܬܐ *to be put to shame;* ܚܘܒܐ — *to receive punishment for sin;* ܛܝܒܘܬܐ *to be grateful, render thanks;* ܘܝ *to be declared miserable;* ܫܘܕܝܐ *to accept a promise, make terms;* ܡܠܬܗ *to accept a* man's *word, believe him;* ܕܝܢܐ ܡܢ *to receive punishment;* ܬܘܪܣܝܐ *to take nourishment;* ܦܘܩܕܢܐ *to be commanded;* ܒܥܘܬܐ *to grant a petition;* ܩܒܘܠܝܐ legal. *to admit an accusation, receive a suit.* *b) to accept, admit, approve, assent;* with ܠ; ܚܘܐ ܩܒܠܬ ܠܚܘܝܐ *Eve consented to the serpent;* ܠܣܘܢܗܕܘܣ *to assent to a synod, to synodical decisions;* with ܡܢ of the pers. *to accept doctrine, opinion, information;* ܡܩܒܠܝܢ ܗܘܘ ܡܢܝ ܕ *they had learnt from me that;* with ܥܠ *to consent, agree upon;* with ܥܠ and pers. pron. *to determine, take upon oneself, agree to;* absol.

ܠܐ ܩܒܠ he would not agree. c) to oppose, attack; ܩܒܠ ܐܢܘܢ ܡܢ ܩܕܡܝܗܘܢ attack them in front. Pass. part. ܡܩܒܠ, ܡܩܒܠܐ, ܡܩܒܠܬܐ acceptable, gracious; ܠܐ ܡܩܒܠ ܛܝܒܘܬܐ ungrateful, ungracious. ETHPA. ܐܬܩܒܠ to be received, accepted, acceptable; to be admitted to communion; of commands, to be obeyed; legal. to be acquitted, opp. ܐܬܚܝܒ to be found guilty. APH. ܐܩܒܠ a) to be opposite, to face; ܬܪܥܐ ܡܩܒܠܝܢ ܚܕ ܠܘܩܒܠ ܚܕ doors facing each other. b) to go towards, meet, esp. with ܐܦܐ or ܦܪܨܘܦܐ; to be present; ܢܩܒܠ ܐܦܐ ܚܕ ܕܚܕ let us meet, i.e. in battle; ܐܘܪܐ ܕܡܪܥܝܬܗ ܐܡܩܒܠܗ it is a figure of the flock of Christ which goes to meet Him. c) to cause to meet, bring together. d) = PA. to receive; to agree; ܐܬܐ ܠܘܬܢ ܘܐܡܩܒܠܢܝܗܝ he came to us and we received him. e) to pronounce acceptable, commend. SAPHEL ܫܩܒܠ to go towards, to be present. ESTAPHAL ܐܫܬܩܒܠ a) to happen, to meet casually, to be present; ܗܘܐ ܐܫܬܩܒܠ ܠܡܕܝܢܬܐ ܚܕܐ he had happened to be in a certain city; ܐܝܠܝܢ ܕܥܡ ܣܘܥܪܢܐ ܗܠܝܢ ܐܫܬܩܒܠܘ those who had been present at these doings; ܐܢ ܢܫܬܩܒܠ ܡܐܬ if he chance to die. b) to stand contrary, set oneself in opposition; ܐܫܬܩܒܠ ܘܐܬܥܠܝ ܥܠ ܐܠܗܐ the devil set himself in opposition and exalted himself against God. DERIVATIVES, verb ܩܒܠ, ܩܒܘܠܐ, ܩܒܘܠܝܐ, ܩܒܠܬܐ, ܩܒܘܠܬܐ, ܩܒܠܐ, ܩܒܠܢܐ, ܩܒܠܢܘܬܐ, ܡܩܒܠܢܐ, ܡܩܒܠܢܘܬܐ, ܡܩܒܠܢܘܬܐ, ܡܩܒܠܢܐ, ܡܩܒܠܢܘܬܐ, ܡܬܩܒܠܢܘܬܐ, ܡܬܩܒܠܢܐ, ܡܬܩܒܠܢܘܬܐ, ܩܘܒܠܐ, ܩܘܒܠܐ, ܩܘܒܠܝܐ, ܩܘܒܠܐ, ܩܘܒܠܢܐ, ܩܘܒܠܢܘܬܐ, ܩܘܒܠ, ܩܘܒܠܐ, ܩܘܒܠܢܐ, ܩܘܒܠܢܘܬܐ, ܩܘܒܠܝܐ, ܩܘܒܠܢܐ, ܩܘܒܠܐ, ܩܘܒܠܐ.

ܩܒܠܡܐ and ܩܒܠܡܝܢ m. white lump sugar, sugar-candy.

ܩܒܠܒܠܐ or ܩܘܒܠܒܠܐ leontice leontopetalum, lion's leaf or lion's turnip.

ܩܒܠܬܐ rt. ܩܒܠ. f. a midwife.

ܩܒܥ fut. ܢܩܒܘܥ and ܢܩܒܥ, act. part. ܩܒܥ, ܩܒܥܐ, pass. part. ܩܒܝܥ, ـܐ, ـܬܐ. a) to fasten, fix, thrust in; ܣܟܐ to fasten with nails; ܩܒܥ ܩܒܥ ܡܘܩܠܘܗܝ he fixed its bolts; ܩܒܥܗ ܒܨܠܝܒܗ He nailed it to His cross; ܩܒܥܝ ܐܠܦܐ shipwrights. b) to set up as ܨܠܝܒܐ a cross; ܩܒܥ ܡܝܠܐ milestones; ܬܚܘܡܐ a boundary; to build ܩܢܐ a nest; to establish ܡܕܝܢܬܐ cities; ܩܒܥ ܗܘܐ ܠܘܩܐ ܥܕܬܐ Luke founded the church in that country. c) to make firm, consolidate; to make certain, settle; ܠܒܣܪܐ ܩܒܥܬ ܐܢܘܢ I made water and blood to become firm flesh. d) to impress; ܒܢܦܫܬܗܘܢ ܢܩܒܘܥ ܚܝܠܬܢܘܬܐ He will impress fortitude on their souls; ܩܒܘܥ ܒܠܒܟ fix within thy heart. Pass. part. fixed, fastened, stationary, established; invariable; joined together, well set, well wrought, compact, concrete; impressed; ܐܝܟ ܨܒܥܐ ܩܒܝܥܐ ܒܐܝܕܐ as a finger firmly jointed in the hand; ܕܡܐ ܩܒܝܥ coagulated blood; ܩܒܝܥ ܒܟܝܢܐ inherent, instinctive.

ETHPE. ܐܬܩܒܥ a) to be thrust in, driven in; to be firmly impressed on the heart, the mind. b) to be fastened, nailed; to be set up, erected; to be established as a custom. c) to be knit together, compacted in the womb; to be constructed as a ship. PAEL ܩܒܥ to thrust in, drive in nails, sharp points; to fix metal, set, stud with jewels; ܩܒܥܘ ܒܐܝܕܝ ܣܟܐ they thrust nails into my hands; ܡܩܒܥ ܒܟܐܦܐ ܝܩܝܪܬܐ set with precious stones. ETHPA. ܐܬܩܒܥ to stick fast, be firmly fixed, nailed; to be stabbed, transfixed; ܐܣܛܘܢܐ ܐܬܩܒܥ ܒܐܪܥܐ a column was firmly set in the ground; ܐܬܩܒܥ ܪܫܗ ܒܪܘܡܚܐ he was stabbed in the head with a spear. DERIVATIVES, ܩܒܥܐ, ܩܒܝܥܐ, ܩܒܝܥܘܬܐ, ܩܒܝܥܐܝܬ, ܩܘܒܥܐ, ܩܘܒܥܢܐ, ܩܘܒܥܢܝܐ, ܩܘܒܥܝܬܐ, ܩܘܒܥܐ.

ܩܒܥܐ rt. ܩܒܥ. m. fastening, nailing; setting up, erection; fixing in the memory; the growing together, becoming firm of the foetus.

ܩܒܥܐ rt. ܩܒܥ. m. pl. trimmings, ornaments, fringes of the collar, sleeves and skirts of a dress.

ܩܒܪ fut. ܢܩܒܘܪ, act. part. ܩܒܪ, ܩܒܪܐ, pass. part. ܩܒܝܪ, ـܐ, ـܬܐ. to bury, inter; ܩܒܪܘܢܝ or ܐܩܒܪ ܠܟܠܗܘܢ ܩܒܝܪܐ ܩܒܪܘܢܝ bury me; I will proclaim to all the buried. ETHPE. ܐܬܩܒܪ to be buried, interred; ܐܬܩܒܪܬܘܢ ܥܡܗ ܒܡܥܡܘܕܝܬܐ ye are buried with Him in baptism. PA. ܩܒܪ a) to bury many. b) to heap up; ܓܘܡܪܐ ܕܢܘܪܐ ܬܩܒܪ ܥܠ ܪܫܗ thou shalt heap coals of fire on his head.

Ethpa. ܐܬܩܒܪ to be heaped up. Derivatives, ܩܒܘܪܐ, ܩܒܘܪܬܐ, ܩܒܘܪܢܐ, ܩܒܘܪ, ܩܘܒܪܐ, ܩܒܪܐ, ܩܒܪܘܬܐ, ܩܒܪܢܐ, ܩܒܪܢܝܐ, ܩܒܝܪܐ, ܩܒܪܬܐ, ܩܒܪܝܬܐ, ܡܩܒܪܢܐ.

ܩܒܪܐ pl. ܐ̈ rt. ܩܒܪ. m. *a grave, tomb, sepulchre.*

ܩܒܪܐ rt. ܩܒܪ. m. *a ball of thread; a shock of corn.*

ܩܒܪܬܐ rt. ܩܒܪ. f. *a garden.*

ܩܒܪܢܝ Ethp. ܐܬܩܒܪܢܝ from ܩܘܒܪܢܝܛܐ. *to navigate.*

ܩܒܪܢܐ rt. ܩܒܪ. m. *an epitaph.*

ܩܒܬܐ or ܩܘܒܬܐ = ܩܘܒܬܐ f. *the scum* or *fat* of broth.

ܩܕ fut. ܢܩܕܘܪ, act. part. ܩܐܕ. *to tear* or *cut away;* ܩܐܕ ܟܘܣܬܐ ܡܢ ܡܐܢܐ *he rends a piece out of a garment.* Pa. ܩܕܕ *to cut off, tear up* ܐܓܪܬ ܚܘܒܐ *a bill of debts.* Ethpa. ܐܬܩܕܕ *to be torn up* of bonds. Derivative, ܩܕܕܐ.

ܩܕ, ܩܕܬܐ, ܩܕ ܩܕܐ and ܩܕܐ abbreviations for ܩܕܝܫ, ܩܕܝܫܬܐ and the pl.

ܩܕܐ verb: see ܩܕܚ.

ܩܕܐ *a*) Ar. m. *a leathern vessel, skin of milk, oil, wine. b*) imper. of verb ܩܕܐ.

ܩܕܕܐ rt. ܩܕ. m. *a strip of untanned leather; cutting* or *tearing to pieces.*

ܩܘܕܡܘܬܐ rt. ܩܕܡ. f. *priority, precedence.*

ܩܘܕܡܩܠܬܐ f. *a cap coming down low on the neck, a burnoose.*

ܩܕܘܪܐ, ܩܕܘܪܬܐ f. *a small pot, vase.*

ܩܕܘܫ absol. and construct state of ܩܕܘܫܐ.

ܩܕܚ fut. ܢܩܕܘܚ, act. part. ܩܐܕܚ, ܩܕܚܐ, pass. part. ܩܕܝܚ, ܐ. *a*) *to tear* the hair, *shave* the head as a sign of grief; ܠܐ ܢܩܕܚܘܢ ܩܕܝܚܬܐ ܒܪܫܝܗܘܢ *they shall not make bald patches on their heads. b*) fut. ܢܩܕܘܚ *to catch fire, blaze up;* ܩܕܚܬ ܫܠܗܒܝܬܐ ܕܢܘܪܐ *a flame of fire blazed up.* Metaph. *to rekindle, revive,* of error, of fever. *c*) *to set light, kindle* usually with ܢܘܪܐ; ܩܕܚܐ ܕܩܕܚܐ ܢܘܪܐ *the flint which lights a fire;* ܢܘܪܐ ܕܩܕܝܚܐ *a lighted fire. d*) *to bore, pierce; to make a cut* in grafting; ܩܕܚܘ ܐܝܕܘܗܝ ܒܣܟܪ̈ܐ *they pierced His hands with nails.* Ethpe. ܐܬܩܕܚ *a*) *to be kindled. b*) *to be cut, pierced.* Pa. ܩܕܚ *to light* ܢܘܪܐ *a fire.* Aph. ܐܩܕܚ *a*) *to light* a fire, *heat* a pot. *b*) *to pluck out* hair. Derivatives, ܩܕܚܐ, ܩܕܚܬܐ, ܡܩܕܚܢܐ, ܩܕܝܚ, ܩܕܘܚ, ܡܩܕܚܐ &c., ܩܕܚܢܐ, ܩܕܚܢܬܐ.

ܩܕܚܐ (vocalisation uncertain, perhaps ܩܕܚܐ or ܩܕܚܐ) pl. ܐ̈ rt. ܩܕܚ. m. *a*) *striking fire* from a flint. *b*) *a perforation, incision, cut. c*) *removal of cataract* from the eye. *d*) *a suture of the skull. e*) *crying, wailing. f*) *germination. g*) *black pocks* under the skin. *h*) chem. *a receiver, matrass.*

ܩܕܚ Pael ܩܕܚ *to keep possession of, not let go, hold fast, retain;* ܩܕܚ ܕܝܠܟ *keep thine own;* often of martyrs, ܩܕܚܘ ܟܠܝܠܐ ܕܙܟܘܬܗܘܢ *they did not let go the crown of their victory.* Of trees *to keep* fruit *hanging on* opp. ܫܪܐ *to let fall;* metaph. *to give abiding* or *enduring possessions;* ܐܘ ܥܠܡܐ ܡܠܝܐ ܥܡܠܐ ܕܠܐ ܡܩܕܚ ܠܡܢ ܕܪܚܡ ܠܟ *O world full of misery which givest nothing enduring to him who loves thee.* Ethpa. ܐܬܩܕܚ *to be held fast, possessed in perpetuity; to last, endure;* ܠܐ ܡܬܩܕܚ ܫܘܠܛܢܐ ܥܠܡܝܐ worldly *power is not long possessed;* ܘܠܐ ܡܬܩܕܚܐ *not lasting, not enduring.* Aph. ܐܩܕܚ *to make to endure, make permanent.* Derivatives, ܩܕܚܐ, ܡܩܕܚܢܘܬܐ, ܡܬܩܕܚܢܐ, ܡܬܩܕܚܢܘܬܐ.

ܩܕܚ subst.: see ܩܕܚ.

ܩܕܚܬܐ rt. ܩܕܚ. f. *a fire.*

ܩܕܚܬܐ pl. ܬ̈ܐ rt. ܩܕܚ. *red-hot coals.*

ܩܕܝܡ or ܩܕܡ also ܩܕܡ ܩܕܡ rt. ܩܕܡ. *first, former* qualifying the names of two months; see ܟܢܘܢ and ܬܫܪܝ.

ܩܕܡܘܬܐ rt. ܩܕܡ. f. *priority, precedence, pre-eminence, primacy;* in comp. usually *fore-, pre-;* ܩ ܝܕܥܬܐ *fore-knowledge;* ܡܩܕܡܘܬܐ *a prediction, fore-telling;* ܡܘܬܒܐ or ܡܘܬܒܐ *precedence, the first place at table;* ܛܘܝܒܐ *preparation;* also ܡܘܙܦܘܬܐ ܩ *advancing a loan;* ܣܝܡܐ or ܣܝܡܬܐ ܩ *a proposition, a design, purpose;* ܫܗܪܐ ܩ *a vigil.* Gram. ܣܝܡܐ ܩ *a preposition.*

ܩܕܡܝܐ or ܩܕܡܝ rt. ܩܕܡ. *former, pristine;* logic. *antecedent.*

ܩܕܫ, ܐ̈, ܬܐ rarely written without the Yudh, ܩܕܝܫ &c. rt. ܩܕܫ. *pure, holy; a holy one, saint;* ܩܕܝܫܐ ܕܐܝܣܪܝܠ *he Holy One of Israel;*

ܪܘܚܐ ܩܕܝܫܐ *the Holy Spirit;* ܐܪ̈ܙܐ ܩܕܝ̈ܫܐ *the holy mysteries* = the Eucharist; ܥܠܝܡܘܬܐ ܕܩܕܝ̈ܫܐ *relics of the saints.* Rit. ܩܕܝܫܐ ܐܢܬ ܐܠܗܐ *Holy art Thou, O God,* and ܩܕܝܫܬܐ *the Trisagion,* the hymn *Holy, Holy, Holy.* Botan. ܐܠܚܝܠܐ ܩܕܝܫܐ *Vitex Agnus-castus.*

ܩܕܝܫܐܝܬ rt. ܩܕܫ. adv. *with holy awe, solemnly.*

ܩܕܝܫܘܬܐ rt. ܩܕܫ. f. *holiness, sanctity, sanctification, consecration; chastity, virginity, celibacy.* As a title ܩܕܝܫܘܬܟ *your Holiness.*

ܩܕܠܐ, ܩܕܠ m. *a) the neck, nape of the neck, back;* with ܐܗܦܟ or ܐܦܢܝ *to turn the back;* ܩܫܐ ܩ̄ *stiff-necked, stubborn. b) the neck* or *opening* of a vessel, a river; *orifice, vent* of the bladder, stomach &c., *the top* or *end* of an egg. Derivative, the following word:—

ܩܕܠܢܝܐ from ܩܕܠܐ. *cervical.*

ܩܕܡ fut. ܢܩܕܘܡ, parts. ܩܕܡ, ܩܕܝܡܐ, and ܩܕܝܡ, oftener ܩܕܝܡ, ܐ̄ܐ, ܬ̄ܐ. *to go before, precede; to be beforehand, to do first;* ܩܕܡ ܐܢܐ ܠܟܘܢ ܠܓܠܝܠܐ *I go before you into Galilee;* ܩܕܡ ܝܕܥܝܢ *knowing beforehand;* martyrs ܩܕܝܡܝܢ ܠܣܝܦܐ *ready beforehand for the sword.* Pass. part. *a)* verbal use with ܠ *preceding, before;* sometimes with the substantive verb, *to go before, precede; to take precedence;* ܩܕܝܡ ܠܡܐܬܝܬܗ ܕܡܫܝܚܐ *preceding the coming of Christ;* ܩܕܝܡ ܗܘܐ ܠܗܘܢ *He went before them. b)* adj. *prior, preceding, anterior, pre-existing. c)* in comp. *pre-, fore-,* ܩ̄ ܦܣܝܩ *predestined;* ܩ̄ ܠܒܝܫ *pre-occupied. d)* 1st form with ܡܢ often written as one word, *at the first, of old, beforetime, formerly;* ܐܝܟ ܕܡܢܩܕܝܡ *as aforetime. e)* with names of months, see ܩܕܡ. Pa. ܩܕܡ *to rise early, to come, do* or *be early* or *beforehand, to precede, prevent, anticipate;* ܩܕܡ ܒܨܦܪܐ *he rose early in the morning;* ܩܪܒ ܡܩܕܡ ܘܡܚܫܟ *he drew near early and late;* ܢܩܕܡ ܐܦܝܟ ܒܬܘܕܝܬܐ *that we may come before Thee with thanksgivings.* With other verbs *before, afore, fore, first, pre;* ܐܚܘܝ *to foreshow;* ܐܡܪ *to tell beforehand, foretell, predict;* ܚܙܐ *to foresee;* ܦܣܩ, ܚܪܡ or ܣܡ *to predestine;* ܓܒܐ *to prefer in honour.* Also ܡܠܐ ܡܩܕܡܢܝܬܐ *predictions.* Ethpa. ܐܬܩܕܡ *to be beforehand with, to forestall, anticipate; to be prejudiced, prepossessed; to be outstripped, overtaken, caught* ܒܡܣܟܠܘܬܐ *in a fault;* ܕܝ̈ܢܐ ܕܠܐ ܢܬܩܕܡܘܢ ܠܫܡܥܐ *judges who do not anticipate the hearing* of a case. Derivatives, ܩܕܡܘܬܐ, ܩܕܡ, ܩܕܝܡ, ܩܕܡܐ, ܩܕܡܝܐ, ܩܕܡܝܐܝܬ, ܩܕܡܝܬܐ, ܩܕܡܝܘܬܐ, ܩܕܡܘܢ.

ܩܕܡ absol. and constr. st. of subst. ܩܕܡܐ = prep. of place and time, *before, in the presence of;* ܩܕܡ ܟܠ ܡܕܡ *before all things;* ܩ̄ ܙܒܢܐ *aforetime, of old;* ܩ̄ ܬܡܠܝ *yesterday;* ܩ̄ ܩܠܝܠ *lately;* ܩ̄ ܩܠܝܠ *a little while ago;* also ܩ̄ ܐܝܕܐ *at hand, near;* ܩ̄ ܬܪܥܐ *a porch, vestibule;* with ܩܡ *to stand firm before . . ., resist.* With ܕ *before that, before;* ܩܕܡ ܕܢܩܪܐ ܬܪܢܓܠܐ *before cock-crow;* ܡܢ ܩܕܡ ܕ *the same;* ܠܩܕܡ with verbs of movement, with ܐܬܐ *to come before; to forward, be of advantage; to surpass, exceed;* ܡܢ ܩܕܡ *from the presence; before;* pleonastic ܕܚܠ ܡܢ ܩܕܡܘܗܝ *he feared him;* ܐܪܓܙ ܩܕܡ ܡܪܝܐ *he provoked the Lord to anger.*

ܩܕܡܐ pl. ܐ̄ rt. ܩܕܡ. *first, early, primeval, ancient;* ܒܩܕܡܐ *at first;* ܠܩܕܡܐ ܩܕܡܐ *the first comer.*

ܩܕܡܐ rt. ܩܕܡ. m. *front, presence;* ܗܠܝܢ ܕܒܩܕܡܐ *those things which are in front, before;* ܡܢ ܩܕܡܐ *in front;* ܠܚܡܐ ܕܐܦܝ̈ܐ *shewbread.*

ܩܕܡܐܝܬ and ܩܕܡܝܐܝܬ rt. ܩܕܡ. adv. *foremost, first; at the first, in early times.*

ܩܕܡܘܢܝ̈ܐ m. pl. rt. ܩܕܡ. *the ancients.*

ܩܕܡܝ, ܩܕܡܝܐ, ܩܕܡܝܬܐ, pl. m. ܐ̄, pl. f. ܬ̄ܐ rt. ܩܕܡ. *first, fore; early, primitive, ancient;* ܩ̄ ܓܒܐ *the fore-part, fore-side;* ܪ̈ܓܠܐ ܩܕܡܝ̈ܬܐ *the fore-feet;* ܡܢ ܫܢܝ̈ܐ ܩܕܡܝ̈ܬܐ *of ancient times;* ܩ̄ ܝܠܝܕܐ *first-born.* Masc. pl. *those of former times, the ancients; the first* or *chief men.* Fem. emph. *the first state, beginning;* ܒܩܕܡܝܬܐ *first, at the first, at the beginning, formerly;* pl. *things of old, former things.*

ܩܕܡܝܘܬܐ rt. ܩܕܡ. m. *priority, precedence, first rank, former state.*

ܩܕܣܐ pl. ܐ̈ـ m. κάδος, *a metal pot, caldron.*

ܩܕܦ Pael ܩܰܕܶܦ and Ethpa. ܐܶܬܩܰܕܰܦ *to be anxious.*

ܩܕܪܕܪܢܐ pl. ܢ̈ܐ *spotted, mottled, particoloured.*

ܩܕܪ Pael ܩܰܕܰܪ *to cut, rend.* Ethpa. ܐܶܬܩܰܕܰܪ *to be torn up.*

ܩܕܪܐ m. *a runner, attendant.*

ܩܕܪܝܐ from ܩܕܪܐ m. *a potter.*

ܩܕܪܐ, ܩܕܪܬܐ pl. ܐ̈, ܬ̈ܐ f. *a pot.* Derivatives, ܩܕܪܝܐ, ܩܕܘܪܬܐ.

ܩܪܐ pl. ܐ̈ *ricinus, castor oil.*

ܩܕܪܐ; see ܩܕܪܝܐ cedar resin.

ܩܕܪܘܣ also ܩܕܪܐ, ܩܕܘܪ and ܩܕܪ pl. ܩܕܪ̈ܘܣ. m. κέδρος, *pinus cedrus, the cedar; juniper.*

ܩܕܫ* *to be pure, holy.* For ܩܰܕܺܝܫ see above. Pael ܩܰܕܶܫ *to keep* or *render holy, to hallow, sanctify, consecrate, to set apart for holy use; to celebrate holy rites, to give in marriage; to chant the Tersanctus, cry 'Holy, Holy, Holy'*; ܐܶܬܕܟܰܪ ܝܰܘܡܳܐ ܕܫܰܒܬܳܐ ܠܡܩܰܕܫܽܘܬܶܗ *remember the Sabbath day to keep it holy;* ܩܰܕܶܫ ܩܽܘܪܒܳܢܳܐ *he celebrated the holy Eucharist* often ellipt.; ܢܩܰܕܶܫ ܠܡܰܥܡܪܳܐ ܕܝܚܺܝܕܳܝܘܬܳܐ *he will consecrate* a building *to monastic purposes.* Ethpa. ܐܶܬܩܰܕܰܫ *to be sanctified, consecrated; to be joined in marriage.* Derivatives, ܩܕܝܫ, ܩܘܕܫܐ, ܩܕܫܐ, ܩܕܝܫܘܬܐ, ܩܕܝܫܐܝܬ, ܡܩܕܫܢܐ, ܡܩܕܫܐ, ܡܩܕܫܢܐ, ܡܩܕܫܢܘܬܐ, ܡܩܕܫܐ, ܡܬܩܕܫܢܘܬܐ, ܡܬܩܕܫܢܐ.

ܩܕܫܐ pl. ܐ̈ m. *an ear-ring, nose-ring.*

ܩܕܬܐ or ܩܕܝܬܐ m. *a*) *a thin sandal-strap* or *shoe-strap.* *b*) name of a plant.

ܩܗܐ and ܩܗܝ fut. ܢܶܩܗܶܐ, act. part. ܩܳܗܶܐ, ܩܳܗܝܳܐ, pass. part. ܩܗܶܐ, ܩܗܝܳܐ, ܩܗܝܳܬܳܐ. *to be blunt, dull* as iron, a sword, &c.; *to be set on edge* as the teeth; metaph. of the eye, mind; of death. Aph. ܐܰܩܗܝ *to blunt, turn the edge, set on edge;* ܡܰܩܗܶܐ ܥܽܘܩܣܳܗ ܕܡܰܘܬܳܐ *he blunts the sting of death;* ܕܢܰܩܗܶܐ ܒܨܶܡܚܶܐ ܢܗܺܝܪܶܐ ܕܝܺܕܰܥܬܳܐ ... *that he might turn the edge of error by bright rays of knowledge.* Derivatives, ܩܗܝܐ, ܩܗܝܘܬܐ.

ܩܕܪܝܐ κεδρέα, *cedar resin* or *oil.*

ܩܕܪܘܣ; see ܩܕܪܘܣ cedar.

ܩܗܝ, ܩܗܝܐ rt. ܩܗܐ. m. *numbness;* ܩܗܝ ܫܶܢܶܐ *bluntness* or *being set on edge* of the teeth.

ܩܗܝܘܬܐ rt. ܩܗܐ f. ܩܗܝܘܬܐ ܕܫܶܢܶܐ *bluntness of the teeth.*

ܩܗܠ fut. ܢܶܩܗܽܘܠ, act. part. ܩܳܗܶܠ, ܩܳܗܠܳܐ. *a*) *to come together, assemble* with ܠܘܬ. *b*) *to consider;* ܩܶܗܠܶܬ ܘܰܚܙܺܝܬ *I considered and saw.* Pa. ܩܰܗܶܠ *to bring* or *call together, summon, assemble; to compile* a book; *to consider attentively;* ܠܰܡܫܰܡܳܥܽܘ ܚܰܒܪܳܐ ܩܰܗܶܠ *he calls another to listen;* ܩܰܗܠܶܬ ܐܶܢܽܘܢ ܠܰܡܦܰܓܥܳܢܽܘܬܳܐ *I have brought them to meet together.* Ethpa. ܐܶܬܩܰܗܰܠ *to assemble from all sides, to collect, gather together;* ܐܶܬܩܰܗܰܠܘ ܟܽܠܗܽܘܢ ܓܽܘܕܶܐ ܕܛܰܝܳܝܶܐ *troops of Arabs collected from all sides;* ܟܽܠܗ ܥܰܡܳܐ ܐܶܬܩܰܗܰܠ *all the people came together.* Aph. ܐܰܩܗܶܠ *to levy troops; to gather.* Derivatives, ܩܗܠܐ, ܩܗܠܢܐ, ܩܗܠܢܘܬܐ, ܩܗܠܝܐ.

ܩܗܠ, ܩܗܠܐ rt. ܩܗܠ. m. *a gathering, assembly.*

ܩܗܠܢܐ, ܩܗܠܢܝܬܐ rt. ܩܗܠ. *one who gathers a crowd by shrieking, a brawler, scold, noisy person.*

ܩܗܠܢܘܬܐ rt. ܩܗܠ. f. *altercation, wrangling.*

ܩܗܠܢܝܐ rt. ܩܗܠ. *summoning* or *calling people together.*

ܩܗܣܪܝܘܢ *the Caesareum, temple of Caesar.*

ܩܗܪܘܢܘܣ κεραυνός, *a thunderbolt.*

ܩܘܐ Pael ܩܰܘܺܝ *to abide, continue, remain, await;* ܩܰܘܺܝ ܚܰܝܶܐ or ellipt. *to remain alive;* ܩܰܘܰܘ ܒܝ ܘܶܐܢܳܐ ܒܟܽܘܢ *abide in me and I in you;* ܡܩܰܘܶܝܢܰܢ ܠܟܽܘܢ *we await you;* ܡܕܺܝܢܬܳܐ ܕܡܩܰܘܝܳܐ *a continuing city;* ܐܶܠܦܳܐ ܡܩܰܘܝܳܐ ܠܪܽܘܚܳܐ *a ship waiting for* a fair wind. Derivatives, ܩܘܝܐ, ܡܩܘܝܢܐ, ܡܩܘܝܢܘܬܐ.

ܩܘܒ imper. of verb ܢܩܒ *to bore.*

ܩܘܒܐ pl. ܐ̈ rt. ܩܒ. m. *a reservoir, cistern.*

ܩܘܒܬܐ, ܩܘܒܬܐ pl. ܩܘܒ̈ܐ rt. ܩܒ. f. *a*) *a canopy, umbrella, tabernacle, pavilion.* *b*) *a dome, vault, arch;* metaph. ܩܘܒܬܐ ܕܫܡܝܐ *the dome of the heavens.* *c*) *apex, top, crown, centre.*

ܩܘܒܒܐ pl. ܐ̈ rt. ܩܒ. m. *ague, shivering fit.*

ܩܘܒܪܐ = ܩܘܒܪܐ.

ܩܘܒܘܣ pl. ܩܘܒܘܣ m. κύβος, *a cube.* Cf. ܩܘܒܣܐ.

ܩܘܒܩܠܪܐ, ܩܘܒܩܠܪܐ and other spellings,

ܬܐ pl. m. ܐ̈, pl. f. ܬ̈ܐ. Lat. cubicularius, *a chamberlain; chamber-servant, chambermaid.*

ܩܘܒܝܢ m. pl. *two obols* = ⅓ dram, *a grain* (measure).

ܩܘܒܠܢܐ pl. ܐ̈ rt. ܩܒܠ. m. *a gathering, swelling, tumour; white spots on the nails.*

ܩܘܒܠܐ, ܩܘܒܠ constr. st. = ܩܘܒܠܐ rt. ܩܒܠ. m. *face, visage, aspect; front;* ܦܐܝܐ ܩܘܒܠܐ *fair of face.* Adv. *a)* with ܡܢ: ܡܢ ܩܘܒܠ *opposite, against, over against; afar, far off. b)* with ܠ: ܠܩܘܒܠܐ usually with pron. suffix of 2 and 3 pers. sing. and of 1 pers. pl., with other pron. suffs. the form ܠܘܩܒܠ is used. *Opposite to, over against, in front of;* ܫܪܐ ܠܩܘܒܠܗ ܕܡܕܝܢܬܐ *he encamped over against the city;* ܢܦܘܩ ܠܩܘܒܠܗ *he shall go out opposite,* i.e. by a door opposite the entrance. *c) opposing, contrary to;* ܠܩܘܒܠܐ ܕܢܟܠܐ ܕܢܟܘܠܐ *in opposition to the tricks of deceivers;* ܪܘܚܐ ܠܩܘܒܠܗ ܗܘܬ *the wind was contrary to, right against* the ship. Cf. ܠܘܩܒܠ under ܠ.

ܩܘܒܠܐ pl. ܐ̈ m. *matricaria chamomilla; anthemis; the chamomile* or *earth-apple.*

ܩܘܒܠܐ pl. ܐ̈ rt. ܩܒܠ. m. *a flower-cup, calyx, bud; a cluster* of flowers.

ܩܘܒܠܐ pl. ܐ̈ rt. ܩܒܠ. m. *acceptance, approval, admission; fee for admission into a monastery; reception, entertainment, hospitality, a feast;* ܒܝܬ ܩܘܒܠܐ *an inn, guest-house;* ܩܘܒܠܐ ܕܥܐܕܐ *the day preceding a festival;* ܩܘܒܠ ܛܝܒܘܬܐ *gracious acceptance, thanksgiving;* ܡܣܝܒܪܢܐ ܩܘܒܠܛܝܒܘܬܐ *most gracious.*

ܩܘܒܠܢܐ, ܢܝܬܐ rt. ܩܒܠ. *opposite.*

ܩܘܒܠܐ rt. ܩܒܠ. m. *the face, countenance, aspect, appearance;* ܫܦܝܪ ܩܘܒܠܗ *of comely appearance.*

ܩܘܒܥܐ pl. ܐ̈ rt. ܩܒܥ. m. *a) the capital* of a column. *b) a felt cap; a hood;* metaph. *the covering, sheath* of a flower or fruit.

ܩܘܒܥܐ rt. ܩܒܥ. m. *nailing, driving in* nails.

ܩܘܒܥܘܢܐ dimin. of ܩܘܒܥܐ. m. *a black hood* worn by a bishop.

ܩܘܒܥܬܐ pl. ܥܬܐ̈ rt. ܩܒܥ. f. *a cap, hood.*

ܩܘܒܪܐ or ܩܘܒܪܐ or ܩܘܒܪܐ. m. *a) thick string* finer than ܚܒܠܐ *rope* and thicker than ܚܘܛܐ *a line* or *thread. b) a heap of wheat.*

ܩܘܒܪܢܛܐ, ܩܘܒܪܢܝܛܐ E-Syr. ܩܘܒܪܢܝܛܐ pl. ܐ̈, m. κυβερνήτης, *a shipmaster, helmsman, pilot.*

ܩܘܒܪܢܝܛܘܬܐ from the preceding. f. *steering, pilotage, direction.*

ܩܘܓܐ pl. ܐ̈ some part of the hand.

ܩܘܕܐ pl. ܐ̈ m. *a) a fetter, bond, chain.* In the Lexx. *b) the Milky Way. c) hoarfrost, rime; fine rain, drizzle.*

ܩܘܕܝܩܠܘܣ pl. ܩܘܕܝܩܠܐ and ܩܘܕܝܩܠܐ m. Lat. codicillus, *a writing, treatise.*

ܩܘܕܚܬܐ pl. ܚܬܐ̈ rt. ܩܕܚ. f. *tearing out the hair* as a sign of mourning esp. for the dead; *bald patches* on the head.

ܩܘܕܝܐ, ܩܘܕܝ rt. ܩܕܝ. m. *abiding possession, continuance.*

ܩܘܕܝܩܣ, ܩܘܕܝܣ, ܩܘܕܩܣ &c. m. Lat. codex, *index, table of contents.*

ܩܘܕܡܐ pl. ܡܝܢ rt. ܩܕܡ. m. *the fore part, front, first;* ܩܘܕܡܘܗܝ ܠܡܕܢܚܐ *facing east;* ܟܠܗ ܗܢܐ ܩܘܕܡܐ *all this chief part;* ... ܠܐ ܩܘܕܡܐ ܥܕܡܐ *not until.* With pron. suff. *before, in the presence of;* ܢܦܠ ܩܘܕܡܘܗܝ ܥܠ ܐܪܥܐ *he prostrated himself before him on the ground;* ܥܪܩ ܡܢ ܩܘܕܡܘܗܝ *he fled before him;* ܙܠ ܡܢ ܩܘܕܡܝ *depart from my presence;* ܡܢ ܩܘܕܡ ܘܡܢ ܒܣܬܪܐ *before and behind;* with ܠ, *facing front, in front, before, first,* usually written ܠܩܘܕܡ. Pl. ܕܪܐ ܩܕܡܝܐ *former generations;* ܡܢ ܠܩܘܕܡܝܢ *of old time, at the first.*

ܩܘܕܡܐ pl. ܐ̈ rt. ܩܕܡ. m. *a presumption, preconception, conviction;* astron. *precession.*

ܩܘܕܡܐܝܬ rt. ܩܕܡ. adv. *forward, previously.*

ܩܘܕܡܢܐ, ܢܝܬܐ rt. ܩܕܡ. *anterior, front, fore;* ܩܘܕܡܢܝ ܥܘܩܣܐ insects *having stings in front.*

ܩܘܕܡܬ rt. ܩܕܡ. prep. *before, in front of, in the presence of; against.*

ܩܘܕܪܐ m. *silk.*

ܩܘܕܪܐ pl. ܐ̈ m. κόδρα, *a mattress, thick mat.*

ܩܘܕܫܐ abs. and constr. st. ܩܘܕܫ, pl. ܫܝܢ, ܐ̈, rt. ܩܕܫ. m. *a) holiness, sanctity;* often used adjectivally ܟܬܒܐ ܕܩܘܕܫܐ *the Holy Scriptures;* ܡܕܝܢܬܐ ܕܩܘܕܫܐ *the holy city;* ܪܘܚܐ ܕܩܘܕܫܐ *the Holy Spirit. b) proclaiming holy;* ܬܠܬܐ ܩ *thrice holy, the hymn 'Holy, Holy, Holy.'* c) *holy things, dedicated offerings, a sacrifice;* hence *the shewbread;* ܩܽܘܕ̈ܫܶܐ ܕܡܶܬܦܪܫܝܢ ܠܡܳܪܝܳܐ *hallowed things separated unto the Lord,* Lev. xxiii. 15. d) *the holy place, sanctuary,* ܒܶܝܬ ܩ̄ the same; ܩܽܘܕܶܫ ܩܽܘܕ̈ܫܶܐ *the Holy of holies,* also ܩܽܘܕܶܫ ܩܽܘܕ̈ܫܝܢ *the most holy things* = the priest's part of the sacrifice. e) eccles. *consecration* to any office in the Church.

ܩܽܘܕܳܫܳܐ pl. ܐ̈ܶ rt. ܩܕܫ. m. a) *hallowing, sanctifying, the crying 'Holy'* of the angels. b) *dedication, consecration,* e.g. of an altar, of chrism; ܩܽܘܕܳܫ ܥܺܕܬܳܐ *consecration of the Church,* a feast kept on the 8th Sunday before Christmas; E-Syr. the season from this Sunday until Advent. c) *the liturgy, communion service.* d) *the oblation, Eucharist, the consecrated elements;* ܥܒܰܕ ܩܽܘܕ̈ܳܫܶܐ *to consecrate.*

ܩܽܘܕܫܳܢܳܐ rt. ܩܕܫ. *holy.*

ܩܽܘܕܫܳܢܳܝܳܐ rt. ܩܕܫ. *holy, sacred.*

ܩܽܘܗܳܝܳܐ rt. ܩܗܐ. m. *clamour* at a wedding or a funeral; *deep affliction.*

ܩܽܘܘܳܝܳܐ rt. ܩܘܐ. m. *continuance, abiding.*

ܩܽܘܙ fut. ܢܩܽܘܙ, act. part. ܩܳܐܶܙ. *to leap, bound; to palpitate,* ܒܩܽܘܠܳܐ *for fear.* Pael ܩܰܘܶܙ a) *to leap, skip;* ܗܳܝܕܶܝܢ ܢܫܰܘܰܪ ܚܺܓܺܝܪܳܐ ܐܰܝܟ ܐܰܝܠܳܐ *then shall the lame man leap as an hart.* b) *to cause to leap.* Derivatives, ܩܰܘܙܳܐ, ܩܰܘܳܙܽܘܬܳܐ.

ܩܽܘܙܳܐ and ܩܽܘܙܳܙܳܐ pl. ܐ̈ m. *a weasel.*

ܩܽܘܚ act. part. ܩܳܐܶܚ. *to mourn, sorrow.* Ethpa. ܐܶܬܩܰܘܰܚ a) *to cry out, raise an outcry, cry for help.* b) denom. from ܩܽܘܚܳܐ. *to put forth shoots, to bloom, blossom.* Derivatives, ܩܽܘܚܳܝܳܐ, ܩܽܘܚܳܬܳܐ.

ܩܽܘܚܳܐ E-Syr. ܩܽܘܚܳܐ pl. ܐ̈ܶ m. *a stem, stalk; a young shoot, top of a branch, leaf; expanding blossoms;* ܩ̄ ܕܚܰܣ̈ܶܐ *lettuce shoots;* ܩ̄ ܕܟܪܽܘܒܳܐ *the heart of a cabbage, a cauliflower;* ܩ̄ ܕܓܰܦܬܳܐ *tender vine-shoots, tendrils.*

ܩܽܘܚܩܳܚܳܐ from ܩܚܩܚ. m. *ripple* or *gurgle of water flowing over pebbles; gurgling laughter.*

ܩܽܘܚܳܬܳܐ rt. ܩܘܚ. f. *a cry for help; calamity.*

ܩܽܘܛ, ܩܳܛ fut. ܢܩܽܘܛ, act. part. ܩܳܐܶܛ, denom. verb Peal conj. from ܩܰܝܛܳܐ. *to evaporate, be dried up, dissipated* as water in summer. Pa. ܩܰܘܶܛ *to pass the summer.*

ܩܽܘܛܳܪܳܐ and ܩܽܘܛܳܪܳܐ rt. ܩܛܪ. m. *provocation, picking a quarrel.*

ܩܽܘܛܺܝ; see under verb ܩܛܐ.

ܩܽܘܛܳܝܳܐ pl. ܐ̈ܶ rt. ܩܛܐ. m. *a heap.*

ܩܽܘܛܝܢ a) *pawns, men* in chess. b) *costus albus,* an aromatic plant, perh. *tansy, costmary.*

ܩܽܘܛܠܳܒܳܐ from ܩܰܛܠܶܒ. m. *painstaking; being engaged in, engrossed in.*

ܩܽܘܛܠܳܒܳܐ from ܩܛܠܒ. *pre-occupied, anxious.*

ܩܽܘܛܳܡܳܐ pl. ܐ̈ܶ rt. ܩܛܡ. m. *the part of a fruit where it is broken or cut from the stem, footstalk, end of the stalk nearest the fruit.*

ܩܽܘܛܳܢܳܐ pl. ܐ̈ܶ rt. ܩܛܢ. m. a) *the mass* or *bulk* of the people, *the people, populace; the congregation, the laity.* b) ܩܽܘܛܳܢܳܐ ܕܟܺܐܦ̈ܶܐ *a mass of stones.*

ܩܽܘܛܳܥܳܐ rt. ܩܛܥ. m. a) *mutilation.* b) ܩܽܘܛܳܥ ܐܺܝܕܰܝܳܐ or absol. *listlessness, depression; shrinking, flinching, irksomeness, disgust.* c) E-Syr. an extra *hulala* or section of the Psalms said at matins in Lent.

ܩܽܘܛܳܦܳܐ pl. ܐ̈ܶ rt. ܩܛܦ. m. *depression, heaviness, fit of low spirits, losing heart,* ܒܩܽܘܛ̈ܳܦܶܐ ܕܚܶܫܳܐ *in the depths of despair, in extreme dejection.*

ܩܽܘܛܳܪ, ܩܽܘܛܳܪܳܐ rt. ܩܛܪ. m. *a tie, joint, connexion;* ܩܽܘܛܳܪ ܡܶܠܬܳܐ *connected argument;* ܩ̄ ܕܩܰܝ̈ܣܶܐ *jointed timbers.*

ܩܽܘܛܳܪܓܳܐ pl. ܐ̈ܶ from ܩܛܪܓ. m. a) *a charge, indictment, complaint.* b) logic. *denotation; predicate.*

ܩܽܘܝܳܐ pl. ܐ̈ܶ m. a) *a loom;* ܒܶܝܬ ܩܽܘ̈ܝܶܐ *a weaving shed; a ball of thread; a web.* b) = ܟܰܘܬܳܐ, ܟܰܘ̈ܶܐ *a window.*

ܩܽܘܝܳܙܳܐ pl. ܐ̈ rt. ܩܘܙ. m. *dancing, a dance.*

ܩܽܘܝܟܠܳܘܣ pl. ܩܽܘܝܟܠܳܘܣ *an amulet, charm.*

ܩܽܘܝܳܡ, ܩܽܘܝܳܡܳܐ rt. ܩܘܡ. m. *sustenance, subsistence, support, consistence, system, substance; structure, constitution, state; settlement, establishment; confirmation.*

ܩܽܘܟܡ said to mean *a spider.* Cf. ܓܽܘܟܳܐ.

ܩܽܘܫܝܳܐ from ܩܫܝ. *stiffness, a stiff neck.*

ܩܘܟܠܝܘܕܝܣ κοχλιώδης, *spiral, curved* as the ear.

ܩܘܟܠܝܐ pl. ܐ̈ـ m. κοχλίας, *a screw* or *vice; an instrument of torture; a fuller's press.*

ܩܘܟܠܝܐ = ܩܘܟܠܝܘܢ *a clothes-press; a press* or *vice* of torture.

ܩܘܟܠܝܘܢ κοχλίον, *a small snail, spiral shell.*

ܩܘܟܠܝܢܝܐ *snail-shaped, spiral.*

ܩܘܠ imper. of verb ܩܠ *to clear away.*

ܩܘܠ *a*) *dregs, sediment of* liquor. *b*) *a mule, an ass;* pl. ܩܘ̈ܠܐ *foals of asses.*

ܩܘܠܐ accus. ܩܘܠܢ κόλλα -ν, f. *glue.*

ܩܘܠܐ or ܩܘܠܐ pl. ܩܘ̈ܠܐ and ܩܘܠܝܬܐ or ܩܘܠ. m. κῶλον, *a limb, member* of the body, used chiefly of the larger limbs, the arms, legs, thighs, also of the hands and feet; *a corpse.* Metaph. *a member, portion* or *clause* of a sentence.

ܩܘܠܐ, ܩܘܠܬܐ pl. ـ̈ܢ, ـ̈ܐ. f. *a pitcher, ewer, cruse.*

ܩܘܠܒܐ pl. ـ̈ܐ m. *a*) *a bracelet.* *b*) = ܩܘܠܒܝܢ *a sleeveless coat.*

ܩܘܠܒܐ m. name of some bird.

ܩܘܠܓܪܐ = ܩܠܓܪܐ *a labourer.*

ܩܘܠܕܐ m. *a joining, a fastening, door-bolt; the lower part of a door-knocker.*

ܩܘܠܘܢ m. κόλον, *the colon,* part of the great intestines; ܟܐܒ ܩܘܠܘܢ *colic.*

ܩܘܠܘܢܝܐ Lat. colonia, *a colony.*

ܩܘܠܝܐ rt. ܩܠܐ. m. *contempt, disparagement.*

ܩܘܠܠܐ rt. ܩܠ. m. *swiftness; relief.*

ܩܘܠܣ, ܩܘܠܣܐ pl. ـ̈ܐ from ܩܠܣ. m. *good report, praise; an eulogy, panegyric;* ܫܡܗܐ ܕܩܘܠܣܐ *honourable titles.* Rit. E-Syr. the deacon's exclamation in the Liturgy.

ܩܘܠܣܣ pr. n. *Colossae* in Phrygia.

ܩܘܠܣܘܣ κολοσσός, *a gigantic statue,* esp. *the Colossus* of Rhodes.

ܩܘܠܣܝܐ pl. ـ̈ܐ from ܩܘܠܣܣ. *a Colossian.*

ܩܘܠܥܐ pl. ـ̈ܐ from ܩܠܥܐ. m. *a*) *a sling-stone, sling, projectile.* *b*) *a clod, lump of earth, earth, fallow land.*

ܩܘܠܣܐ pl. ـ̈ܐ rt. ܩܠܣ. m. *censure, a reproach.*

ܩܘܠܩܫܐ rt. ܩܠܩܫ. m. *sounding a bell.*

ܩܘܠܪܐ pl. ـ̈ܐ m. Lat. collare, *an iron band* or *chain for the neck.*

ܩܘܠܬ a drug, perh. *lithospermum, gromwell.*

ܩܘܠܬܐ emph. st. of ܩܘܠܐ.

ܩܘܡ, ܩܡ fut. ܢܩܘܡ, act. part. ܩܐܡ, ܩܝܡܐ, verbal adj. ܩܐܡ, ܩܝܡܬܐ see above. *a*) *to rise, arise,* esp. ܡܢ ܫܢܬܐ *from sleep; from death;* ܡܝ̈ܬܐ ܩܝܡܝܢ *the dead are raised up.* *b*) *to stand up, stand, be present;* ܩܐܡ ܗܘܐ ܒܫܠܝܐ *he stood silent.* *c*) *to stay, stop;* ܙܠ ܠܐ ܬܩܘܡ *go, stay not; to cease* with ܡܢ *from.* *d*) *to go on, last, remain;* ܟܕ ܩܝܡܐ ܚܫܡܝܬܐ *while supper is going on;* ܟܕ ܩܐܡ ܫܘܩܐ *while the market is open;* ܟܡܐ ܝܘܡ̈ܝܢ ܩܝܡܝܢ *how many days remain?* ܩܐܡ ܟܘܪܗܢܐ *the illness persists.* *e*) *to be, exist;* ܟܠ ܕܩܐܡ *everything that is;* ܡܐܡܪ̈ܘܗܝ ܩܝܡܝܢ *his homilies are extant;* ܩܐܡ ܡܚܘ̈ܬܐ ܦܓܪܗ his body *was scarred all over.* *f*) *to stand firm, be unchangeable* as a promise; also *to stand by, keep to* one's word, the law, with ܒ or ܥܠ. *g*) *to consist of* with ܒ or ܡܢ; ܫܘ̈ܪܐ ܓܘܝ̈ܐ ܩܝܡܝܢ ܗܘܘ ܒܩܝܣ̈ܐ *the inner walls were of wood.* *h*) *to become known, to flourish.* *i*) *to be made* king, bishop, patriarch, &c.; *to rule,* cf. below; ܫܪܝܘ ܡܠܟ̈ܐ ܠܡܩܡ ܒܐܘܪܗܝ *kings began to reign in Edessa.*

With preps. ܒ *to be over; to profess, stick to, be occupied in;* esp. ܩܐܡ ܒܐܦ̈ܐ *a protector, champion;* ܒܕܘܟܬܐ *to succeed;* ܒܚܝ̈ܐ *to remain alive;* ܒܡܘܡܬܐ *to stand by, keep oaths;* ܒܡܠܟܘܬܐ *to reign;* ܒܫܢܝ̈ܐ . . . ܕܫܢ̈ܝܐ *to be of the age of* so many *years;* ܒܨܠܘܬܐ *to persevere in prayer;* ܒܪܫܢܘܬܐ *to be chief, to rule.* With ܒܬܪ *to succeed.* With ܠ *to stand for, aid,* opp. ܩܡ ܥܠ; otiose ܩܡ ܠܗ *rise up;* of stars *to rule over.* With ܠܘܩܒܠ *to withstand, confront; to weigh as much.* With ܡܢ *to recover from; to be composed of.* With ܥܠ *to stand opposite = arrive at; to understand; to rise* or *break against* as a storm, a persecution; *to resist, oppose; to seize* for debt; *to be over, superintendent.* Cf. *f.* With ܥܡ *to help, co-operate, be coadjutor.* With ܩܕܡ *to stand in the presence of = to serve; to oppose.* Act. part. ܩܐܹܡ ܕܩܐܹܡ *present;* ܝܘܡܢܐ *to-day;* gram. ܙܒܢܐ ܕܩܐܹܡ *the present tense.*

Ethpe. ܐܶܬ݂ܩܺܝܡ *to be constituted, made* governor, king &c., *to be set* on the throne. Pa. ܩܰܝܶܡ *to establish, confirm, ratify; to erect; to constitute* a bishop, a patriarch &c.; *to be, to subsist;* with ܒܛܺܝܡܽܘܬ݂ܐ *to price, value;* ܡܩܰܝܶܡ ܥܺܕ̈ܳܬ݂ܐ *confirming the churches;* ܗܰܝܟܠܐ ܘܡܰܩܕܫܐ ܩܰܝܶܡ *he erected the temple and sanctuary;* ܬܚܘܝܬ݂ܐ ܕܡܩܰܝܡܳܢ ܠܡܶܠܬ݂ܐ *demonstrations which establish the point.* Pass. part. ܡܩܰܝܰܡ, ܡܩܰܝܡܳܐ, ܡܩܰܝܡܳܢܳܐ *subsisting, existing, consisting; abiding;* ܡܶܠܬ݂ܐ ܡܩܰܝܡܬ݂ܐ *the Word subsistent;* ܐܶܣܛܘܟܣܐ ܕܡܢܗܘܢ ܡܩܰܝܰܡ ܒܪܢܳܫܐ *the elements of which a man consists;* ܡܩܰܕܡ ܡܩܰܝܰܡ *pre-existent.* Ethpa. ܐܶܬ݂ܩܰܝܰܡ *to be established, strengthened, confirmed, ratified, to come to pass; to be erected; to be appointed; to consist, subsist* with ܒ; ܢܶܬ݂ܩܰܝܰܡ ܠܥܳܠܰܡ *he shall abide for ever;* ܘܶܐܬ݂ܩܰܝܰܡ ܡܶܠܰܝܗܘܢ ܕ *and the words of . . . were established, came to pass;* ܡܶܬ݂ܩܰܝܡܺܝܢ ܒܗܰܝܡܳܢܽܘܬ݂ܐ *stablished in the faith;* ܐܶܬ݂ܩܰܝܰܡܘ ܘܶܐܚܘܕܘ *stand fast and hold fast;* ܒܳܐܝܠܶܝܢ ܡܶܬ݂ܩܰܝܡܳܐ *wherein consists . . . .*

Aph. ܐܰܩܺܝܡ *a) to raise up, make to stand, set, place; to raise* ܡܶܢ ܒܶܝܬ݂ ܡܺܝ̈ܬ݂ܐ *from the dead;* ܐܰܚܕܳܗ ܒܺܐܝܕܳܗ ܘܰܐܩܺܝܡܳܗ *He took her by the hand and raised her up.* *b) to rouse up, stir up;* ܡܰܩܺܝܡܝܢ ܗܘܰܘ ܩܫܝܐ ܠܢܳܛܽܘܪ̈ܐ *they violently roused the guards.* *c) to erect, repair.* *d) to establish, appoint;* ܐܰܩܺܝܡܘ ܒܬܰܪܥܳܐ ܕܺܝܢܳܐ *establish judgement in the gate.* *e) to set up, set over, constitute* priest, king, prophet &c. *f) to promise, agree.* *g) to present* with ܠ or ܩܕܡ. Esp. with ܨܶܒܽܘܬ݂ܐ *to rebel;* ܬܶܓ݂ܪܳܐ *to provoke a conflict;* ܡܘܰܬ݂ܩܐ ܕܡܘܡܳܬ݂ܐ *to ratify oaths,* ܒܡܘܡܳܬ݂ܐ *to confirm with oaths;* ܟܶܣܦܳܐ *to raise an amount of money;* ܣܳܗ̈ܕܐ *to bring witnesses,* ܠܘܳܬ݂ ܣܳܗ̈ܕܐ *to appeal to witnesses;* ܫܺܘܬܳܘܬ݂ܐ *to make ready a banquet;* ܩܝܳܡܳܐ *to make a covenant, vow, devote;* ܡܢܳܬ݂ܐ *to appoint a portion;* ܩܪܳܒ݂ܐ *to make war;* ܪܕܘܦܝܐ *to arouse a persecution;* ܕܝܢܳܐ = *e;* ܫܠܳܡܳܐ *to intone the Pax vobiscum.* With preps. ܒܡܬ݂ܩܠܳܐ ܠܘܳܬ݂ *to weigh against;* ܥܰܠ *to set over; to bring to, place; to confirm, assure concerning; to stand to, regard, abide by* a command, law, determination. Derivatives, ܩܘܡܬ݂ܐ, ܩܝܳܡܳܐ, ܩܝܳܡܬ݂ܐ, ܩܝܡܐ, ܩܝܰܡܐ, ܩܝܳܡܘܬ݂ܐ, ܩܝܳܡܝܐ, ܩܝܡܘܬ݂ܐ, ܩܝܳܡܳܝܐ, ܩܝܳܡܬ݂ܐ, ܩܝܡܐ, ܡܩܝܡܢܐ, ܡܩܝܡܢܘܬ݂ܐ, ܩܘܝܳܡܐ, ܩܘܝܳܡܐ, ܡܩܝܡܢܐ, ܡܬ݂ܩܝܡܢܐ, ܡܬ݂ܩܝܡܢܘܬ݂ܐ.

ܩܽܘܡܳܐ pl. ܩܽܘܡܺܝܢ, ܩܽܘܡܶܐ rt. ܩܘܡ. m. *rising, standing, standing still; staying, remaining,* ܕܠܳܐ ܩܽܘܡܳܐ *unresting; state, position, station;* ܒܶܝܬ݂ ܩܽܘܡܳܐ *place, place of standing* or *meeting together; stability, abiding,* ܕܠܳܐ ܩ *unstable; a rising, insurrection; opposition.* Special meanings: *a) administration, tenure of office.* *b)* ܩ ܕܰܫܕܳܝܶ̈ܐ ܓܶܐܪ̈ܐ *a station of archers, battery.* *c) the standing-place, column* of a pillar saint. *d)* astron. *station, position* of the moon or stars. *e)* eccles. W-Syr. *a station* = a watch *of the night, hymns for these stations.* *f)* a measure, *the width of the outstretched arms* = about a fathom. *g) a category.* *h)* gram. *a point after a division of the sentence.*

ܩܽܘܡܬ݂ܳܐ, ܩܽܘܡܰܬ݂ܳܐ pl. ܩܽܘܡܶ̈ܝܢ, ܩܽܘܡܳܬ݂ܳܐ rt. ܩܘܡ. f. *a) height* of a tree, of corn. *b) height, stature, time of life; the body;* the three ܩܽܘܡܳܬ݂ܳܐ are ܛܠܳܝܽܘܬ݂ܳܐ *boyhood,* ܥܠܰܝܡܽܘܬ݂ܳܐ *youth,* ܕܣܰܝܒܽܘܬ݂ܳܐ *old age;* ܒܢܰܝ ܩܽܘܡܬ݂ܗܘܢ *those of the same age;* ܒܩ ܙܩܺܝܦܬ݂ܳܐ *erectly.* *c)* a measure of height or depth, perh. *a fathom;* ܩܽܘܡܰܬ݂ ܓܶܐܪܳܐ *an arrow's flight, bowshot.* Cf. ܩܽܘܡܳܐ above.

ܩܽܘܡܽܘܕܳܐ, ܩܽܘܡܳܘܕܳܐ and ܩܽܘܡܕܳܐ pl. ܐ̈ m. κωμῳδός, *a player, tragedian.*

ܩܽܘܡܳܘܕܺܝܐ and ܩܽܘܡܽܘܕܺܝܐ from the preceding. f. *comedy, satire, rhetorical use of ridicule.*

ܩܽܘܡܽܘܕܺܝܳܐ and ܩܽܘܡܽܘܕܺܝܐ f. κωμῳδία = the preceding.

ܩܘܡܘܣ; see ܩܽܘܡܣ.

ܩܘܡܣܝܢ dialect. *mist, darkness.*

ܩܘܡܣܢܐ rt. ܩܡܣ. *close, miserly.*

ܩܽܘܡܶܛܺܝܪܺܝܢ pl. ܩܘܡܝܛܪܝܐ, ܩܘܡܝܛܝܪܝܢ, ܩܽܘܡܺܝܛܺܝܪܺܝܘܢ m. κοιμητήριον, *a cemetery* esp. *a burial-place for strangers.*

ܩܘܡܡܝ *gum;* see ܩܽܘܡܺܝ.

ܩܘܡܝܛܐ and ܩܘܡܝܛܝܣ, ܩܽܘܡܺܝܛܺܝܣ, ܩܘܡܝܛܝܣ, ܩܽܘܡܺܝܛܳܐ pl. ܐ̈ m. κομήτης, *a comet* = Syr. ܕܘܢܒܳܢܳܐ.

ܩܘܡܝܛܐܛܘܣ m. Lat. comitatus, the emperor's *court, his retinue.*

ܩܘܡܝܛܝܣܐ Lat. comitissa, fem. of ܩܘܡܝܣ.

ܩܘܡܝܣ, ܩܘܡܝܣ, ܩܘܡܝܣ, ܩܘܡܣ and ܩܘܡܣ, ܩܘܡܝܣ, acc. ܩܘܡܝܛܐ pl. ܩܘܡܝܛܐ m. Lat. comes, *an official of the Byzantine court, chief officer, prefect, commander;* French *a count.*

ܩܘܡܝܩܘܣ, ܩܘܡܝܩܐ pl. ܐ̈ κωμικός, *a comedian, comic poet, satirist.*

ܩܘܡܠܐ = ܩܘܡܠܐ *a* and ܩܡܠܐ.

ܩܘܡܠܐ and ܩܘܡܠܐ rt. ܩܡܠ. m. *a) blue mould on bread. b) barley cakes baked in the embers and allowed to grow sour.*

ܩܘܡܩܡܐ Ar. m. *the nodes* of stalks, *seedpods, husks, refuse of vegetables.*

ܩܘܡܪܐ pl. ܐ̈ rt. ܩܡܪ. m. *a bond, belt.*

ܩܘܢܐ (rare), ܩܘܢܝܐ, ܩܘܢܝܐ pl. m. ܩܘܢܝܐ, pl. f. ܩܘܢܝܬܐ, ܩܘܢܝܬܐ = ܩܘܢܟܐ but is somewhat paler. adj. κυάνεος, *deep blue, purple, livid, dark, black and blue;* ܩܘܢܝܐ ܥܝܢܐ *black* = discoloured *eyes;* ܫܘܫܢܐ ܩܘܢܝܐ *blue lilies, irises.*

ܩܘܢܝܘܬܐ f. *a)* from ܩܘܢܐ. *deep blue, sad colour; the gloom, shadow* of an eclipse. *b)* in the Lexx. *a scabby eruption* on the skin, *ringworm.*

ܩܘܢܒܐ and ܩܘܢܒܠܐ *a sail.*

ܩܘܢܒܪܐ or ܩܘܢܒܪܐ pl. ܐ̈ *asclepias, swallow-wort,* a hot drug resembling mustard.

ܩܘܢܓܐ pl. ܐ̈ m. *a night watchman, city watchman.*

ܩܘܢܓܝܢ ܩܘܢܓܝܓܝܢ pl. the same and ܩܘܢܓܐ. m. κυνήγιον, *the hunt, chase; combats with wild beasts.*

ܩܘܢܕܐ = ܩܘܢܕܐ.

ܩܘܢܕܘܢܘܣ pl. ܩܘܢܕܘܢܘܣ = ܩܘܢܕܘܢܘܣ *peril.*

ܩܘܢܕܩܐ pl. ܐ̈ m. κόνταξ, *a pole.*

ܩܘܢܕܩܐ pl. ܝ̈ܢ m. *a)* κοντάκιον, *the stick* of a scroll, *a scroll, roll; an official writing; a short hymn* for a holy day. *b)* κῶνος, *a cone.*

ܩܘܢܝܐ, ܐ̈ from ܩܘܢܘܣ. *cone-shaped, conical.*

ܩܘܢܡܘܢܐ, ܩܘܢܡܘܡܘܢ, ܩܘܢܡܘܢ, ܩܢܡܘܡܘܢ, also ܩܢܡܘܢܐ, ܩܘܢܡܘܡܘܢ, ܩܢܡܘܡ, &c. m. κιννάμωμον, *cinnamon.*

ܩܘܢܘܣ pl. ܩܘܢܐ m. κῶνος, *a cone, cedar-cone, fir-cone;* geomet. *a cone.* Derivative, ܩܘܢܝܐ.

ܩܘܢܙܐ and ܩܘܢܘܙܐ and wrongly ܩܙܐ. f. κόνυζα, *a) inula, fleabane. b) the carob-tree. c) a kind of thorn.*

ܩܘܢܛܐ rt. ܩܢܛ. m. *fear.*

ܩܘܢܛܣܛܒܠ French connétable, *the high constable.*

ܩܘܢܛܪܐ pl. ܐ̈ m. κοντάριον, *a pole, javelin, short spear; an iron mace, iron-tipped staff;* metaph. *a spear-shaped meteor.*

ܩܘܢܝܐ m. κονία, *a) ashes. b) lye made of ashes and quicklime.*

ܩܘܢܝܓܐ pl. of ܩܘܢܓܝܢ.

ܩܘܢܝܢ f. κώνειον, *cicuta virosa, hemlock.*

ܩܘܢܝܢ pl. the same, and ܩܘܢܝܢܐ f. perh. κοινόν, *a concourse, party, factious meeting,* with ܥܒܕ and ܩܡ.

ܩܘܢܝܩܘܣ pl. ܩܘܢܝܩܘܣ κυνικός, *a)* the name of a tribe of Arabs. *b)* philosoph. *a Cynic.*

ܩܘܢܝܩܐ *canine; a Cynic.*

ܩܘܢܟܐ and ܩܘܢܟܠܐ = ܩܢܟܐ *a sacristan.*

ܩܘܢܡܘܢ, ܩܘܢܡܐ; see ܩܢܡܘܢܐ *cinnamon.*

ܩܘܢܣ, ܩܘܢܟܐ = ܩܘܢܝܐ. κυάνεος, *dark blue, ash-coloured, livid, black and blue;* f. pl. ܩܘܢܟܝܬܐ *blue tints; bruises.*

ܩܘܢܟܐ a woollen *veil.*

ܩܘܢܦܐ, ܩܘܢܦܐ m. *harmony.*

ܩܘܢܦܐ pl. ܐ̈ m. *harmony.* Derivative, verb ܩܢܦ; cf. ܩܘܢܦܐ.

ܩܘܦܐ m. *a) a little bit. b) a pot.*

ܩܘܣܘܡܒܘܛܘܢ κοσυμβωτός -όν, *fringed, bordered.*

ܩܘܣܘܡܒܘ κόσυμβοι, *fringes, borders.*

ܩܘܣܛܘܕܝܐ Lat. custodia, *the guard;* ܩܛܠܐ ܕܩܘ *death by execution.*

ܩܘܣܛܐ m. *a money-changer, banker.*

ܩܘܣܠܐ pl. ܐ̈ m. κασοῦλα, *a kind of hood worn by priests.*

ܩܘܣܡܘܣ m. κόσμος, *a) the ordered universe. b) decoration, an ornament.* Derivatives, ܩܘܣܡܐ, verb ܩܣܡܣ, ܡܩܣܡܣܢܘܬܐ.

ܩܘܣܡܣܐ from ܩܘܣܡܘܣ. m. *adornment.*

ܩܘܡܣܪܐ in the Lexx. *a worn-out ass.*

ܩܘܡܩܡܬܐ Ar. f. *a small pot.*

ܩܘܢܟܐ pl. ܐ̈ m. *a*) *bridge* of the nose, *partition between the nostrils.* *b*) *capital* of a column. *c*) *a bud.*

ܩܘܢܟܪܐ Ar. *a*) *an outer shell;* perh. *the bottom, extremity.* *b*) *a platter hollowed out of wood.*

ܩܘܦ *Qoph;* see ܩ.

ܩܘܦܐ pl. ܐ̈ m. *carrying staves* or *poles* esp. the poles by which the ark was carried; *the bars* of a bier.

ܩܘܦܐ pl. ܐ̈ m. *an ape.*

ܩܘܦܐ, ܩܘܦܬܐ pl. ܩܘܦܬ̈ܐ f. *a*) *the hoop* or *bezel* of a ring. *b*) = ܩܒܬܐ *an arch, arched recess.*

ܩܘܦܕܐ pl. ܐ̈ rt. ܩܦܕ. f. *hedgehog, porcupine;* ܩ̈ ܕܝܡܐ *sea-urchin.*

ܩܘܦܕܐ m. *a*) κοπάδιον, *a piece of meat.* *b*) *a long staff.*

ܩܘܦܕܐ, ܩܘܦܕܝܢ, ܩܘܦܩܝܢ *an owl.*

ܩܘܦܚܐ pl. ܐ̈ rt. ܩܦܚ. m. *buffeting, insult, humiliation, mortification, coercion, reprimand.*

ܩܘܦܛܐ m. *a white sweetmeat prepared from new wine boiled down and flavoured with young shoots of vine or other trees.*

ܩܘܦܝ *a*) *incense prepared in the temples and used as a medicine to strengthen the chest and vocal organs.* *b*) Chald. *a basket.*

ܩܘܦܝܐ rt. ܩܦܐ. m. *spume, foam, floatage, floating rubbish on rivers; scum* of broth.

ܩܘܦܝܐ pl. ܐ̈ from ܩܘܦܐ. m. *a carrier, porter.*

ܩܘܦܝܢܐ pl. ܝ̈ܢ, ܐ̈ m. κόφινος, *a large basket.*

ܩܘܦܠ *the Indian betel-tree and its nut.*

ܩܘܦܠܐ pl. ܐ̈, ܩܘܦܠܝܢ f. *a lock, bolt.*

ܩܘܦܣܐ pl. ܐ̈ m. κύβος, *a*) *a cube, a square tablet; a pebble; a tesselated pavement, checker-work.* *b*) *a die, piece* of a game, *chessman, chess.* Derivatives, verb ܩܒܣ, ܩܘܒܣ, ܐܩܒܣ. *c*) part of a verse consisting of four syllables, each line of the twelve-syllable metre of James of Sarug contained three ܩܘܦܣܐ. *d*) = ܩܘܦܣܐ *a cage.* *e*) = ܩܘܦܣܐ *the inner bend of the knee.*

ܩܘܦܣܝܐ *of chess.*

ܩܘܦܣܬܐ pl. ܩܘܦܣ̈ܬܐ f. *a woollen tunic.*

ܩܘܦܣܐ rt. ܩܦܣ. m. *brooding, sitting* on eggs.

ܩܘܦܪܐ = ܩܘܦܪܐ m. *pitch, bitumen.* Derivative verb ܩܦܪ.

ܩܘܦܪܘܣ pl. ܩܘܦܪܘ cypress-flowers, *henna.* Cf. ܩܘܦܪܐ.

ܩܦܪܘܣ, ܩܘܦܪܘܣ and ܩܘܦܪܘܣ *Cyprus.* Derivatives, ܩܘܦܪܝܐ, ܩܘܦܪܝܬܐ.

ܩܘܦܪܘܣ κόπρος, m. *dung.*

ܩܘܦܪܝܐ, ܩܘܦܪܝܬܐ from ܩܘܦܪܘܣ. *a Cypriot; of Cyprus.*

ܩܘܦܪܝܘܬܐ = the preceding.

ܩܘܦܬܐ m. *a fly-catcher* (bird).

ܩܘܦܬܢܐ pl. ܐ̈ m. *a fig-pecker, becafico;* perh. *a lark.*

ܩܘܦܬܐ; see ܩܘܦܐ.

ܩܘܨܐ m. *the washing of a soiled part of a garment.*

ܩܘܨܨܐ rt. ܩܨܨ. m. *shattering.*

ܩܘܨܪܐ rt. ܩܨܪ. m. *meanness, grudging.*

ܩܘܨܬܐ or ܩܘܨܬܐ pl. ܩܘܨ̈ܬܐ f. *a curl, ringlet.*

ܩܘܩܐ, ܩܘܩܬܐ pl. ܐ̈, ܩܘܩ̈ܬܐ f. *a*) *a water-pot, pitcher, urn.* *b*) *cells* of a honeycomb.

ܩܘܩܐ m. κόκκος, *a berry.*

ܩܘܩܝ mimetic verb *to caw, croak.*

ܩܘܩܝܐ, ܩܘܩܝܬܐ pl. ܐ̈, ܩܘܩܝ̈ܬܐ *a*) from ܩܘܩܐ. *a potter;* also used as a surname. *b*) *a kind of chant* probably first composed by ܫܡܥܘܢ ܩܘܩܝܐ *Simeon* surnamed the *potter.* *c*) from ܩܘܩ the name of their founder, *a Cuchite* = Aquarius, a sect of Gnostics. *d*) *a flat loaf* given to harvesters in the early morning. *e*) ܒܪ ܩܘܩܝܐ from Lat. praecox, *the apricot.*

ܩܘܩܝܘܬܐ f. *the potter's art.*

ܩܘܩܠܘܣ m. κύκλος, *a circle, cycle;* the Pharos of Alexandria, probably as being *a circular tower.*

ܩܘܩܠܝܘܢ and ܐܢܩܘܩܠܝܘܢ pl. ܩܘܩܠ̈ܝܢ, ܩܘܩܠܝܐ, ܩܘܩܠܝܐ m. κύκλιον = ἐγκύκλιον, *a cycle of hymns, a cycle of verses from the Psalms* recited after the Gospel.

ܩܘܩܠܘܢ Lat. cucullus, *a cowl.*

ܩܘܩܠܝܘܬܐ m. pl. *hymns sung in procession* round the altar.

ܩܘܩܢܘܣ pl. ܩܘܩܢܘ m. κύκνος, *a swan.*

ܩܘܪ *bdellium.*

ܩܘܪ̈ rit. abbreviation for ܩܘܪܝܐ ܐܠܝܣܘܢ.

ܩܘܪܐ pl. ܐ̈ rt. ܩܪ. m. *cold, frost.*

ܩܘܪܐ *a*) = ܟܘܪܐ *land* &c.; *a furnace.* *b*) *a handful, bundle* of corn. *c*) *the hollow* of a box.

ܩܘܪܐ for ܩܘܪܝܐ *lady.*

ܩܘܪܐ, ܩܘܪܬܐ rt. ܩܪ. f. in the phrase ܩܘܪܐ ܕܢܦܫܐ *cooling, refreshing, relief.*

ܩܘܪܐܢ and ܐܠܩܘܪܐܢ Ar. *the Koran.*

ܩܘܪܒܐ rt. ܩܪܒ. m. *nearness, intimacy, neighbourhood, vicinity* opp. ܪܘܚܩܐ *distance.* Usually with a prep. ܒܩܘܪܒܐ and ܡܢ ܩ̈ *shortly; near;* ܩܘܪܒܐ ܕ and ܠܩ̈ *near, nearly, about.*

ܩܘܪܒܐ rt. ܩܪܒ. m. *a*) act. *offering, oblation;* ܩܘܪܒ ܦܐܪ̈ܐ *an offering of fruit* upon the altar; ܩܘܪܒ ܩܘܪܒܢܐ *the offering of the oblation; the liturgy, Eucharistic office, anaphora;* ܩܘܪܒܐ ܕܥܢܝ̈ܕܐ *mass for the dead.* *b*) pass. *being brought near, access.*

ܩܘܪܒܝܣ m. pl. κύρβεις, *triangular tablets* inscribed with laws.

ܩܘܪܒܢܐ pl. ܝܢ, ܐ̈ rt. ܩܪܒ. m. *a*) *an offering, oblation* to God, *a sacrificial offering.* *b*) *the eucharistic oblation, eucharist, anaphora; oblate, consecrated bread;* ܩܘܪܒܢܐ ܒܬܘܠܐ *virgin oblate* = when given to a layman before the priest has communicated. *c*) *an offering, present;* ܒܝܬ ܩ̈ *the sacred treasury.*

ܩܘܪܒܢܝܐ, ܩܘܪܒܢܝܬܐ from ܩܘܪܒܢܐ. *eucharistic.*

ܩܘܪܕܝܐ from ܩܪܕܝ. m. *house-work, sweeping, making beds, putting to rights.*

ܩܘܪܕܝܢܐ or ܩܘܪܕܝܢܐ m. *a*) *a hypocrite, secret evil-doer.* *b*) *a puppy, whelp.*

ܩܘܪܕܝܐ pl. ܐ̈ m. a later form of ܩܪܕܘܝܐ *a Kurd.*

ܩܘܪܕܝܠܘܣ m. *a crocodile.* In the Lexx. *a puppy, whelp.*

ܩܘܪܕܡܢܐ pl. ܐ̈ m. *a wart, whitlow.*

ܩܘܪܕܝܬܐ m. *a cudgel, club.*

ܩܘܪܚܐ = ܩܪܚܐ *bald.*

ܩܘܪܚܬܐ rt. ܩܪܚ. f. *baldness, a bald head; the forehead.*

ܩܘܪܛܩܐ dialect. m. *a woollen jacket with wide sleeves; a long wrapper.*

ܩܘܪܛܒܐ usually pl. ܐ̈ m. *a thistle, thorn-bush, prickly shrub.*

ܩܘܪܛܘܪ or ܩܘܪܐܛܘܪ, ܩܘܪ̈ܐܛ, ܩܘܪ̈ܛ pl. ܩܘܪܛܘܪܐ, ܩܘܪܛܘܪܝܢ, ܩܘܪܛܘܪܣ and ܩܘܪܐܛܘܪܘܣ m. *curator, a legal guardian* = Syr. ܡܪܒܝܢܐ.

ܩܘܪܛܘܪܘܬܐ f. *curatorship, guardianship.*

ܩܘܪܛܡܐ or ܩܘܪܛܡܐ pl. ܐ̈ m. *carthamus tinctorius, the saffron thistle, safflower and its seed.*

ܩܘܪܛܝܬܐ Ar. f. *a snippet, small piece of meat.*

ܩܘܪܝܐ κυρία, *lady.*

ܩܘܪܝܐ pl. of ܩܪܝܐ, ܩܪܝܬܐ.

ܩܘܪܝܐ ܐܠܝܣܘܢ usually written as one word, ܩܘܪܝܠܝܣܘܢ, ܩܘܪܝܐܠܝܣܘܢ and ܩܘܪܝܐܠܝܣܘܢ κύριε ἐλέησον, *Lord have mercy.*

ܩܘܪ̈ܝܢ and ܩܘܪ̈ܝܢ pl. of ܩܪܝܐ, ܩܪܝܬܐ.

ܩܘܪܝܝ, ܩܘܪܝܝܐ, ܝܬܐ from ܩܪܝܐ, ܩܪܝܬܐ. *rustic, boorish; a villager, rustic, peasant;* ܐܢܫ ܩܘܪܝܝܐ ܦܠܚܐ *a field-labourer.*

ܩܘܪܝܝܘܬܐ from ܩܪܝܐ, ܩܪܝܬܐ f. *a country life; rusticity, boorishness.*

ܩܘܪܝܢܐ and ܩܘܪܝܢܝ *Cyrene.* Derivative, the following:—

ܩܘܪܝܢܝܐ pl. ܐ̈ from ܩܘܪܝܢܐ. *a Cyrenean.*

ܩܘܪܝܢܬܘܣ, ܩܘܪܝܢ, ܩܘܪܢ *Corinth.* Derivative, the following:—

ܩܘܪܝܢܬܝܐ and ܩܘܪܝܢ pl. ܐ̈ from ܩܘܪܝܢܬܘܣ. *Corinthian; a Corinthian.*

ܩܘܪܝܫ Ar. pr. n. *Koreish.*

ܩܘܪܝܫܝܐ and ܩܘܪܫܝܐ from ܩܘܪܝܫ. *a Koreishite, one of the tribe of Koreish.*

ܩܘܪܟܝܐ pl. ܐ̈ m. *a crane* (bird).

ܩܘܪܡܐ pl. ܝܢ, ܐ̈ m. κορμός, *trunk* of a tree, of the body; *a log.*

ܩܘܪܡܝܐ from ܩܪܡܝ. m. *frowning; a frown.*

ܩܘܪܢܝܬܐ f. *origanum, marjoram* or *mint;* ܩ̈ ܕܚܩܠܐ *field marjoram;* ܩ̈ ܕܛܘܪܐ *mountain mint;* ܩ̈ ܕܢܗܪܐ *mentha pulegium, pennyroyal.*

ܡܘܪܙܦܐ pl. ܐ̈ـ m. *a small hammer, mallet.* DERIVATIVE, verb ܡܪܙܦ.

ܡܘܪܙܢܬܐ m. *perfidy, calumny, villany.*

ܡܘܪܙܢܟܬܐ f. *a short hooded cloak* or *woman's large veil reaching to the shoulders.*

ܡܘܪܙܒܐ pl. ܐ̈ـ m. *a*) *a trough.* *b*) *a wallet, forage-bag, nose-bag.*

ܡܘܪܕܩܐ pl. ܐ̈ـ m. *the son of a slave.*

ܡܘܪܕܦܐ m. *a pointed cap worn by priests, a mitre.*

ܡܘܪܙܠܐ pl. ܐ̈ـ m. *the ankle, ankle-bone; the wrist.*

ܡܘܪܙܠܬܐ pl. ܠܬ̈ܐ f. = ܡܪܙܠܬܐ. *a lock of hair.*

ܡܘܪܙܦܐ m. *a*) *a halter; ring through a camel's nose.* *b*) *a gimlet, awl, borer.* *c*) rt. ܡܪܙܦ. *cackling* of a hen, *cackling laughter.*

ܡܘܪܙܡܠܐ m. *the gullet; crop* of a bird.

ܡܘܪܙܡܢܐ m. *a halter, muzzle.*

ܡܘܪܙܡܦܐ pl. ܢ̈ܝܢ, ܐ̈ـ m. *a ring, clasp, buckle, the tongue of a buckle;* astron. *a ring* of light. DERIVATIVES, ܡܪܙܡܦܐ, ܡܪܙܡܦܢܐ.

ܡܘܪܙܡܙܐ pl. ܐ̈ from ܡܪܙܡܙ. m. *a*) *the opening of the ear, a buzzing, humming* in the ears. *b*) *clucking* of a hen. *c*) *noise of wind* in the intestines, *rumbling.*

ܡܘܪܙܦܦܐ from ܡܪܙܦܦ. m. *clash, rattling.*

ܡܘܪܙܪ Pauel conj. of ܡܪ.

ܡܘܪܙܪܐ rt. ܡܪ. m. *cooling, cold; a cold, catarrh.*

ܡܘܪܙܪܐ pl. ܐ̈ـ rt. ܡܪܙ. m. *intense cold, frost, iciness; a chill, bad cold.*

ܡܘܪܙܪܢܐ rt. ܡܪܙ. *icy.*

ܡܘܪܙܡܠܐ pl. ܐ̈ـ m. *a lump;* ܘܐܠ ܡܘܪܙܡܠܐ *smoothly.*

ܡܘܫ imper. of verb ܡܫ *to knock.*

ܡܘܫܫ, ܡܘܫܫܐ rt. ܡܫ. m. *hardening;* gram. pronunciation of a letter without aspiration.

ܡܘܫܛܐ also ܡܘܫܛܘܣ and ܡܘܫܛܘܣ &c. m. κόστος, an aromatic plant, *costmary, tansy; ladanum.*

ܡܘܫܛܐ m. no pl. *truth, right, justice, rectitude;* with preps. ܒܡܘܫܛܐ *truly, verily, indeed;* ܕܡܘܫܛܐ *true, just, fair.* DERIVATIVES, the four following words and ܠܡܘܫܛܐܝܬ.

ܡܘܫܛܐܝܬ with ܒ or ܠ prefixed, from ܡܘܫܛܐ. adj. and adv. *true, very; truly, really, verily;* ܡܗܝܡܢܐ ܒܡܘܫܛ *a true believer* or *verily a believer.*

ܡܘܫܛܢܝܐ from the preceding. *true, very, real;* also with prefixed ܠ the same.

ܡܘܫܛܐܝܬ from ܡܘܫܛܐ. adv. *rightly, fairly.*

ܡܘܫܛܢܐ pl. ܐ̈ـ from ܡܘܫܛܐ. *true, upright.*

ܡܘܠܬܐ from ܡܠܠ. m. *immoderate laughter.*

ܡܘܠܐܬܐ from ܡܠܐܬܣ. m. *deposition* from office.

ܡܠ fut. ܢܡܘܠ, act. part. ܡܐܠ. *to loathe.* ETHPA. ܐܬܡܠܠ the same.

ܡܙ Ar. m. *raw silk, floss silk.* DERIVATIVE, ܡܙܙܐ.

ܡܙܘ a small song-bird with bright-coloured plumage.

ܡܙܘܢܬܐ f. *a skin of oil.*

ܡܙܙܐ from ܡܙ. m. *a silk manufacturer, mercer.*

ܡܙܡܐ, ܡܙܡܬܐ f. *a bottle, phial, jar, goblet, tumbler.*

ܡܙܡܘܠܐ f. *a pitcher with a narrow neck and wide mouth.*

ܡܙܙܐ m. *a skipper, ship-master; a driver.*

ܡܫܡܫ mimet. *to laugh.* ETHPALPAL ܐܬܡܫܡܫ *to gurgle, make a sound* as running water. DERIVATIVE, ܡܫܡܫܐ.

ܡܦ fut. ܢܡܘܦ, act. part. ܡܐܦ, ܡܐܦܐ. *a*) *to turn round, revolve;* ܩܛܪܐ ܕܡܐܦ *a turning axle;* ܫܡܫܐ ܕܡܐܦܐ *the revolving sun.* *b*) *to go about, go hither and thither, be occupied;* ܡܐܦܝܢ ܐܝܟ ܚܣܝܪ̈ܐ *they go about like beggars;* ܗܢܘܢ ܕܡܐܦܝܢ ܒܐܪ̈ܥܬܐ *those who wander abroad;* with ܒܬܪ *to run hither and thither in pursuit.* *c*) *to sprinkle,* ܡܠܚܐ ܡܐܦ ܥܠ ܪܫܗ *salt is sprinkled on his head.* APH. ܐܡܝܦ *to turn round, make to revolve, turn upside down;* ܡܡܝܦ ܦܚܪܐ ܓܝܓܠܐ the potter *turns the wheel;* ܒܝܫܐ ܡܡܝܦ ܟܠ *the Evil one upsets everything.* PAUEL ܡܘܦ *a*) *to make to go round; to go round* begging. *b*) *to pile up, heap up;* ܓܘܡܪ̈ܐ ܡܡܘܦܢܝܬܐ *heaped up live coals.* DERIVATIVES, ܡܘܦܐ, ܡܝܦܐ.

ܩܛܐ m. *a plummet, plumb-line.*

ܩܛܐ, ܩܛܘ usually m. *a cat*, pl. ܩܛܐ, ܩܛܘܬܐ.

ܩܛܐ, ܩܛܘ some bird, perh. *ardea stellaris, the heron.*

ܩܛܐ for ܩܛܝܐ pl. of ܩܛܝܬܐ.

ܩܛܐܪܟ *governor.*

ܩܛܐܪܘܢ = ܩܛܪܘܢ.

ܩܛܒ Pael ܩܛܒ *to pick a quarrel.* Derivatives, ܩܘܛܒܐ, ܩܛܒܐ.

ܩܛܓܪܝܐ, ܩܛܓܪܐ, ܩܛܓ &c.; see ܩܛܝܓ.

ܩܛܓܪܦܐ m. legal καταγραφή, *a conveyance, deed of transfer.*

ܩܛܕܝܩܐ pl. ܩܛܕܝܩܣ, legal καταδίκη, *a sentence, condemnation;* with ܝܗܒ *to punish, pronounce sentence.*

ܩܛܕܪܘܡܘܣ and ܩܛ… m. κατάδρομος -ον, *a race-course, lists; an onset, course.*

ܩܛܘ; see ܩܛܐ.

ܩܘܛܢ m. *flax.*

ܩܛܘܠܐ, ܩܛܘܠܬܐ rt. ܩܛܠ. subst. *a slayer, manslayer, homicide, murderer, executioner,* adj. *deadly, mortal, fatal,* as ܙܝܢܐ *a weapon;* ܚܘܝܐ *a snake.*

ܩܛܘܠܐ ܕܙܐܒܐ name of the plant from which ladanum is made.

ܩܛܘܠܘܬܐ rt. ܩܛܠ. f. *slaying, murder;* ܩܛܘܠܘܬ ܐܚܐ *fratricide.*

ܩܛܘܡܘܬܐ from ܩܛܡܐ f. *ashes.*

ܩܛܘܢܐ m. ܩܛܘܢܬܐ f. dimin. of ܩܛܐ. *a kitten.*

ܩܛܘܢܐ and ܩ ܪܝܙܐ Ar. *psyllium plantago, flea-bane.*

ܩܛܘܥܐ m. ܬܐ f. rt. ܩܛܥ. *a path, road, way.*

ܩܛܘܦܐ pl. ܐ rt. ܩܛܦ. m. *a grape-gatherer, vintager;* metaph. *a carper, caviller.*

ܩܛܘܪܐ pl. ܐ rt. ܩܛܪ. m. *a*) ܕܡܠܐ perh. *intricacy of language. b*) *a blow with the fist, a push.*

ܩܛܘܪܝܬܐ pl. ܬܐ f. *the groin, hair of the groin.*

ܩܛܘܬܐ and ܩܛ, ܩܛ pl. ܩܛܝܐ (rare), ܩܛܝܢ, ܩܛܝܬܐ constr. st. ܩܛܝܬ. f. *a cucumber, gourd;* ܩ ܕܒܪܐ *the wild gourd,* also called ܩܛܘܬ ܚܘܝܐ *the snake gourd* and ܩ ܚܡܪܐ *asses' gourd,* is the bitter *colocynthis citrullus, colocynth;* ܩ ܕܓܢܬܐ *the garden cucumber.* Derivative, ܩܛܝܝܐ.

ܩܛܘܬܐ pl. of ܩܛܐ *a cat.*

ܩܛܝܐ rt. ܩܛܐ. m. *a*) *rotation. b*) *joking, jesting.*

ܩܛܝܓܘܪܝܐ pl. ܐ, ܩܛܝܓܘܪܝܣ, also ܩܛܝܓ and ܩܛܓ κατηγορία, f. *a*) *a charge, accusation. b*) *a predicate, category.*

ܩܛܝܓܘܪܝܩܘܣ pl. ܩܛܝܓܘܪܝܩܘ κατηγορικός, *affirmative, categorical.*

ܩܛܝܓܘܪܐ and ܩܛ pl. ܐ from ܩܛܓܪ. m. *an assertion, argument.*

ܩܛܝܓܪܐ also ܩܛܝܓ, ܩܛܝܓ pl. ܐ from ܩܛܓܪ. m. *an informer, accuser, plaintiff.*

ܩܛܝܓܪܘܬܐ and ܩܛ, ܩܛ pl. ܬܐ from ܩܛܓܪ. f. *an accusation, complaint, charge, suit* with ܐܝܬܝ or ܩܪܒ *to bring.*

ܩܛܝܠܘܬܐ rt. ܩܛܠ. f. *being slain;* ܩܛܝܠܘܬܝ *my slain body.*

ܩܛܝܡܘܬܐ rt. ܩܛܡ. f. = ܩܛܡܐ.

ܩܛܝܢܐܝܬ rt. ܩܛܢ. adv. *sharply, minutely, exactly; in minute characters; sparingly.*

ܩܛܝܢܘܬܐ rt. ܩܛܢ. f. *fineness* of texture; *thinness, leanness; narrowness* of a path; ܩ ܕܗܘܢܐ *mental subtlety, fineness of wit.*

ܩܛܝܦܘܬܐ rt. ܩܛܦ. f. ܩܛܝܦܘܬ ܢܦܫܐ *anguish.*

ܩܛܝܦܬܐ pl. ܬܐ Ar. f. *a shaggy cloak* or *rug.*

ܩܛܝܪܐ pl. ܐ rt. ܩܛܪ. m. *a*) *compulsion, coercion, necessity, force, violence;* ܩ ܕܟܝܢܐ *natural need, necessity of nature;* ܩ ܓܒܪܐ *the violent man;* ܩܛܝܪܐ ܩܐܡ ܥܠܝ *I must needs;* with ܒ or ܡܢ *by force, by compulsion;* ܡܢ ܩ ܕܒܥܘܬܐ *constrained by entreaties. b*) = ܩܛܘܪܐ *b.*

ܩܛܝܪܐܝܬ rt. ܩܛܪ. adv. *of necessity, perforce, necessarily; by force, with violence.*

ܩܛܝܪܘܬܐ rt. ܩܛܪ. f. *condensation, coagulation; congelation.*

ܩܛܝܪܢܐ, ܢܝܬܐ rt. ܩܛܪ. *violent, forcible; by constraint, compulsory, necessary;* ܒܐܝܕܐ ܩܛܝܪܢܝܬܐ *by a strong hand, by force;* ܡܠܟܘܬܐ ܩܛܝܪܢܝܬܐ *the kingdom* of heaven *is to be taken by force.*

ܩܛܝܪܢܐ pl. ܐ rt. ܩܛܪ. *violent.*

ܩܛܝܪܬܐ a later writing of ܩܛܪܬܐ.

ܩܛܝܪܬܘܬܐ rt. ܩܛܪ. f. *compulsion, obligation.*

ܩܛܠ fut. ܢܩܛܘܠ, inf. ܡܩܛܠ, act. part.

ܩܛܠ, ܩܛܠܐ, pass. part. ܩܛܝܠ, ـܐ, ـܬܐ. *to kill, slay* usually of killing one; ܠܐ ܬܩܛܘܠ *thou shalt do no murder;* ܩܛܝܠܝ ܚܪܒܐ *slain with the sword;* ܩܛܠ ܐܢܫܐ *a homicide, murderer;* ܩܛܠ ܢܦܫܗ *a suicide.* ETHPE. ܐܬܩܛܠ *to be killed, slain, put to death.* PA. ܩܛܠ *to kill, slay* many; ܩܛܠ ܫܐܘܠ ܒܐܠܦܐ *Saul hath slain by thousands.* ETHPA. ܐܬܩܛܠ *to be slain* in numbers. DERIVATIVES, ܩܛܘܠܐ, ܩܛܘܠܘܬܐ, ܩܛܠܢܘܬܐ, plant names in ܩܛܠ, ܩܛܠܐ, ܡܩܛܠܢܐ, ܡܬܩܛܠܢܐ.

ܩܛܠ ܐܪܒܘܣ m. *arbutus unedo, wild strawberry-tree.*

ܩܛܠ ܕܐܒܐ m. *aconitum lycoctonum, wolf's bane.*

ܩܛܠ ܟܠܒܐ m. *cynanchus erectus.*

ܩܛܠܐ pl. ـܐ rt. ܩܛܠ. m. *slaughter, murder.*

ܩܛܠܒ from καταλαμβάνειν, *to take pains with; to engross;* ܡܐܡܪܐ ܕܩܛܠܒ ܓܒܪܐ ܗܢܐ *the discourses elaborated by this man.* ETHPA. ܐܬܩܛܠܒ *to be taken up with, engrossed in.* DERIVATIVES, ܩܛܠܒܐ, ܡܩܛܠܒܐ.

ܩܛܡ fut. ܢܩܛܘܡ, pass. part. ܩܛܝܡ. *to cut off, crop, lop* trees; ܩܛܝܡܝܢ ܒܣܘܟܝܗܘܢ trees *with lopped offshoots.* ETHPE. ܐܬܩܛܡ *to be cropped, lopped off.* PA. ܩܛܡ denom. from ܩܛܡܐ *to make pale.* DERIVATIVES, ܩܛܡܐ, ܩܛܡܐ, ܡܩܛܡܐ.

ܩܛܡ, ܩܛܡܐ m. *ash, ashes;* ܡܝ̈ ܩܛܡܐ *lye.* DERIVATIVES, ܩܛܡܢܐ, ܩܛܡܢܝܐ.

ܩܛܡܐ rt. ܩܛܡ. m. *a slice.*

ܩܛܡܐ rt. ܩܛܡ. m. *slicing, lopping off.*

ܩܛܡܢܐ from ܩܛܡܐ. *ashy.*

ܩܛܡܢܝܐ, ـܢܝܬܐ from ܩܛܡܐ. *ashy, ash-coloured; mixed with ashes* as soil.

ܩܛܢ fut. ܢܩܛܢ, act. part. ܩܛܢ, verbal adj. ܩܛܝܢ, ـܐ, ـܬܐ. *to be narrowed, grow thin, frail;* ܩܛܢ ܨܘܪܢ ܡܢ ܣܝܦܟ *our neck is too frail* to be worthy *of thy sword.* Verbal adj. *a*) *thin, lean, meagre* as ears of corn, food, cattle; also ܩܛܝܢܬܐ *small cattle.* *b*) *strait, narrow* as windows, paths, doors, &c.; ܩܛܝܢ ܨܘܪܐ *narrow-necked;* ܡܥܝ̈ܐ ܩܛܝܢ̈ܐ *the lesser intestines.* *c*) *fine, sharp, delicate;* ܣܘܥܪ̈ܢܐ ܩܛܝܢ̈ܐ *delicate* matters. *d*) *subtle, ethereal.* *e*) *high, shrill* as sounds. *f*) *keen, subtle, acute.*

ETHPE. ܐܬܩܛܢ *to be narrowed, contracted* as an arm of the sea. PA. ܩܛܢ *a*) *to reduce to powder, to particles; to attenuate, rarefy, subtilize.* *b*) *to emaciate.* *c*) *to restrict, straiten;* ܩܛܢ ܢܦܫܟ ܕܬܥܘܠ ܒܬܪܥܐ ܐܠܝܨܐ *straiten yourself that you may enter in by the strait gate.* Pass. part. ܡܩܛܢ, ܡܩܛܢܐ *rarefied, subtle; narrow, slender;* ܡܩܛܢܝܢ ܚܨܝܗܘܢ ܕܒܒ̈ܐ *wasps have slender waists.* Metaph. of the mind, *to refine, render keen* or *acute.* ETHPA. ܐܬܩܛܢ *to be drawn out fine* ܐܝܟ ܚܘܛܐ *as a thread; to contract, become narrow* as a strait; *to grow lean, emaciated; to become thin, subtle, ethereal.* DERIVATIVES, ܩܛܢܐ, ܩܛܢܐ, ܩܛܝܢܐܝܬ, ܩܛܝܢܘܬܐ, ܡܩܛܢܢܐ, ܡܩܛܢܢܘܬܐ, ܡܬܩܛܢܢܘܬܐ.

ܩܛܢܐ Arab. m. *a cotton-spinner* or *seller.*

ܩܛܣܛ from κατέστησε, PAEL conj. *to set in order.*

ܩܛܣܛܣܝܣ, ܩܛܐܣܛܐܣܝܣ, ܩܛܣܛ, &c. f. κατάστασις, *a settled state, condition* as health, sickness, widowhood, orphanhood, riches; *a settled state* of the weather, *serenity, peace, order; conduct; the constitution* of a state; *institution, appointment* of deacons, bishops, &c. Perh. *usury.*

ܩܛܥ fut. ܢܩܛܘܥ, infin. ܡܩܛܥ, act. part. ܩܛܥ, ܩܛܥܐ, pass. part. ܩܛܝܥ, ـܐ, ـܬܐ. *a*) *to tear* or *cut out* a leaf of a book; *to hew down* a tree, *hew* stones; with ܨܘܪܐ *to behead, wring the neck; to cut short, bring to an abrupt end* as a reign, dynasty. Pass. part. *cut, cut out, torn.* *b*) intrans. *to pause, cease, stop short, be intermitted;* ܩܛܥ ܡܫܚܐ ܘܠܐ ܗܘܐ ܪܕܐ *the oil ceases and flows no more;* ܒܟܝܟ ܕܠܐ ܩܛܥܐ *thy incessant weeping;* ܩܛܥܘ ܚܙܘܐ ܘܢܒܝ̈ܐ *visions and prophets have ceased.* *c*) impers. *to be weary, give up, be low-spirited;* ܩܛܥܐ ܠܗ *it is all over;* ܠܐ ܩܛܥܐ ܠܢ ܒܟܘܪܗܢܝܢ *we need not despond in our illnesses.* PA. ܩܛܥ *to mutilate, cut off, tear out* the hands, the tongue; pres. part. ܡܩܛܥ, ܡܩܛܥܐ *mutilated, severed; slack, poor-spirited.* Impers. *to sadden, make to despond.*

ETHPE. ܐܬܩܛܥ and ETHPA. ܐܬܩܛܥ *to be cut* or *torn out* as the tongue; *to be torn up* as tent cords; *to be disallowed* as legal rights.

With ܠܒܐ or ܬܐܘܪܝܬܐ *to be shaken in resolution, crushed in spirit, disheartened.* Impers. *to be disheartened, to lose hope, grow weary, shrink back;* ܚܙܘ ܕܠܐ ܬܬܩܛܦܘܢ ܒܢܣܝܘܢܐ *take heed that ye wax not weary in temptation.* Derivatives, ܩܛܦܐ, ܩܛܦܬܐ, ܩܛܘܦܐ, ܩܛܝܦܐ, ܡܩܛܦܢܐ, ܡܩܛܦܢܘܬܐ.

ܩܛܦܐ pl. ܐ̈ rt. ܩܛܦ. m. *a fragment, scrap, particle; a segment, piece.*

ܩܛܘܦܝܐ rt. ܩܛܦ. m. *intermission.*

ܩܛܘܦܝܐ rt. ܩܛܦ. m. *mutilated.*

ܩܛܦ fut. ܢܩܛܘܦ, infin. ܡܩܛܦ, act. part. ܩܳܛܶܦ, pass. part. ܩܛܝܦ. *to pluck, gather, pick* fruit, esp. grapes; ܩܛܘܦܘ ܠܣܓܘܠܐ ܕܟܪܡܐ *gather the clusters of the vineyard.* Metaph. *to gain, acquire, wrest* ܙܟܘܬܐ *victory,* ܝܘܬܪܢܐ *profit;* ܩܳܛܦܝܢ ܐܢܬܘܢ ܡܢ ܡܫܘܠܬܗܘܢ *you will profit by their opinion.* Pass. part. *troublesome, annoying;* ܩܛܝܦܐ ܗܘܐ ܠ *to annoy.* Ethpe. ܐܬܩܛܦ *a) to be plucked, gathered in* as the vintage. *b) to be gained, acquired. c) to be low-spirited, faint-hearted, depressed,* esp. with ܪܘܚܐ. *d)* impers. with ܠ *to be annoyed, vexed, disturbed.* Pa. ܩܰܛܶܦ *a) to pick, pluck* flowers, herbs. *b) to gather, tie up. c) to obtain, get. d) to annoy, vex, distress.* Ethpa. ܐܬܩܰܛܰܦ *a) to be gathered in, obtained, received* as ܬܘܟܝܬܐ *vexation,* ܫܐܠܬܐ *requests. b) to be weary, depressed, in low spirits. c)* impers. with ܠ, *to be restless, disquieted, depressed.* Derivatives, ܩܛܦܐ, ܩܛܘܦܐ, ܩܛܦܢܐ, ܩܛܦܢܘܬܐ, ܡܩܛܦܐ, ܡܬܩܛܦܢܐ, ܡܬܩܛܦܢܘܬܐ.

ܩܛܳܦܐ rt. ܩܛܦ. m. *a) ingathering, vintage. b)* ܩܛܦ ܠܒܐ *weakness* or *palpitation of the heart. c) atriplex hortensis, orach, a pot-herb.*

ܩܛܦܛܝܩܐܝܬ and ܩܛܦܛܝܩܘܣ καταφατικῶς, *affirmatively.*

ܩܛܦܛܝܩܘܬܐ = ܩܛܦܣܝܣ.

ܩܛܦܛܝܩܝܐ, ܝܬܐ καταφατικός, *affirmative.*

ܩܛܦܣܝܣ with ܥܒܕ καταφῆσαι, *to affirm.*

ܩܛܦܣܝܣ, ܩܐܛܐܦܣܝܣ f. κατάφασις, *an affirmation, affirmative proposition.*

ܩܛܘܦܬܢܐ *weak, distressed, poverty-stricken.*

ܩܛܩܛ *to gnaw.*

ܩܛܪ fut. ܢܩܛܘܪ, act. part. ܩܳܛܰܪ, ܩܳܛܪܐ, pass. part. ܩܛܝܪ, ܐ, ܬܐ. *a) to tie, bind, knot, interlace; to adjust, frame, form;* ܩܛܪܬ ܚܘܛܐ ܕܙܚܘܪܝܬܐ ܒܟܘܬܐ *she bound a thread of scarlet in the window;* ܠܐ ܬܬܩܛܪܘܢ ܒܟܬܢܐ *do not wind in silken shrouds.* With ܐܒܠܐ *to mourn;* with ܒ or ܥܠ *mourning befel . . .;* ܐܟܬܐ (uncertain) *to harbour wrath;* ܒܗܬܬܐ *to bring shame upon;* ܓܘܕܐ *troops formed, drew up;* ܓܢܘܢܐ *to interweave a bridal chamber,* i.e. *to enclose it with wickerwork;* ܐܠܝܬܐ *to raise cries of grief;* ܟܠܝܠܐ *to weave a crown; to gain* or *give the victory;* ܚܪܝܢܐ *to pick a quarrel;* ܢܟܠܐ *to weave wiles, to plot;* ܩܛܪܐ *to tie a knot;* ܩܛܪܐ *to knot, form nodes in the stem;* ܪܐܙܐ *to consult; to take secret council, conspire;* ܬܐܓܐ *to put on a crown;* ܩܛܝܪܝ ܬܐܓܐ *crowned heads. b)* intrans. *to harden, stiffen; congeal, curdle; grow thick,* ܩܛܰܪ ܗܘܐ ܓܠܝܕܐ ܒܡܥܝܢܐ *ice had formed on the pool;* ܩܳܛܰܪ ܐܝܟ ܚܠܒܐ *it curdles like milk;* ܩܛܰܪ ܥܠܝܗܘܢ ܚܫܘܟܐ *darkness closed in on them;* ܩܛܰܪ ܥܠܥܠܐ *a tempest gathered.* Part. adj. *a) bound, fastened, tied; knotted, intertwined,* &c.; ܥܨܒܐ ܩܛܝܪܝܢ ܒܪܫܝܗܘܢ *fillets bound on their heads;* ܨܪܪܐ ܩܛܝܪܐ *a tied-up money-bag;* ܟܘܟܐ ܩܛܝܪܐ *huts of wattle. b) condensed, congealed, curdled, coagulated, clotted;* as drops of water, milk, blood. *c) dense, gathering* as darkness.

Ethpe. ܐܬܩܛܪ *a) to be joined* or *linked together. b)* with ܬܐܓܐ and ܠ *to be crowned. c) to be condensed.* Pa. ܩܰܛܰܪ *to tie up, pack up; to condense;* pass. part. ܡܩܰܛܪܐ, ܡܩܛܪܬܐ *knotty, complicated, connected.* Ethpa. ܐܬܩܰܛܰܪ *a) to be tied up, tied* as a cord; ܐܬܩܛܪ ܓܫܪܐ ܥܠ *to make a bridge,* prob. *by linking boats together. b) to be rallied, brought together. c)* chem. *to be condensed, fixed;* ܙܝܘܓܐ ܕܐܬܩܛܪ *condensed mercury.* Aph. ܐܩܛܪ *a)* with ܟܠܝܠܐ *to put on a crown. b) to bring upon oneself, make oneself liable to* ܫܒܝܐ *captivity. c) to condense, curdle, coagulate.* Derivatives, ܩܛܪܐ, ܩܛܘܪܐ, ܩܛܝܪܐ, ܩܛܝܪܐܝܬ, ܩܛܝܪܘܬܐ, ܩܛܪܐ, ܩܛܪܢܐ, ܩܛܪܢܝܐ, ܩܛܪܢܘܬܐ, ܩܘܛܪܐ, ܩܛܪܬܐ, ܩܛܝܪܬܐ, ܡܩܛܪܐ, ܡܩܛܪܢܘܬܐ, ܡܩܛܪܢܐ, ܡܩܛܪܬܐ.

ܩܶܛܪܐ pl. ܐ̈ rt. ܩܛܪ. m. *a tie, bandage; knot, node* of a stem; *magic knots* used in divining; *interlaced patterns; joint, articulation; an enigma, perplexity;* ܩ̈ ܕܚܛܝܬܐ *bonds of sin;*

ܩ̈ ܕܩܛܪ̈ܐ knotty or perplexing queries; eccles. censure.

ܩܘܛܪܐ rt. ܩܛܪ. m. a) knotting, tying; ܩ ܕܓܒܝ̈ܢܘܗܝ the knitting of his eyebrows; eccles. ܛܟܣܐ ܕܩܘܛܪ ܓܢܘܢܐ Order of the Interweaving or Erection of the Bridal-chamber. b) a band, tie; ܩܘܛܪ ܪܫܐ head-band, fillet. c) chem. condensation.

ܩܛܓܪ from Greek κατηγορεῖν, a) to denounce, accuse, speak against with acc. of the pers. and ܥ of the cause; ܡܩܛܓܪ ܠܗܘܢ ܕܫܒܩܘ ܠܐܠܗܐ he accuses them of forsaking God; ܡ̈ܚܝܠܐ ܡܩܛܓܪܝܢ ܠܚܝܠܬܢ̈ܐ the weak speak against the powerful. b) to affirm, assert; ܐܝܟ ܕܐܡܪ ܠܗ ܒܪ ܙܢܝܘܬܐ ܩܛܓܪܗ he called him a bastard. Logic to affirm, predicate. Ethpal. ܐܬܩܛܓܪ a) to be accused, have a charge brought; ܡܬܩܛܓܪ ܥܡܐ ܕܠܐ ܢܛܪ ܦܘܩܕܢܗ ܕܐܠܗܐ the nation is charged with neglecting God's command; ܟܕ ܡܬܩܛܓܪ ܡܢ ܚܣܡܐ when an accusation is made by the envious. b) logic to be affirmed, predicated; ܗܘ ܕܣܝܡ ܘܗܘ ܕܡܬܩܛܓܪ the subject and the predicate. Derivatives, ܩܛܓܪܝܐ, ܩܛܓܘܪܐ, ܩܛܓܪܝܢܐ, ܩܛܓܘܪܝܢܐ, ܩܛܓܘܪܝܐܣ, ܩܛܓܪܝܢܘܬܐ all also spelt ܩܬܓܪ, ܩܛܝܓܪ, ܩܬܝܓܪ; ܡܩܛܓܪܢܐ, ܡܩܛܓܪܢܘܬܐ, ܡܬܩܛܓܪܢܐ, ܡܬܩܛܓܪܢܘܬܐ, ܡܬܩܛܓܪܢܐܝܬ.

ܩܛܪܘܢܐ dimin. of ܩܛܪܐ m. a knot or enigmatic figure.

ܩܛܪܘܢܐ pl. ܐ̈ـ I m. a) a brazier for incense, an incense burner with a cover and handles. b) = ܩܛܪܘܢܐ b.

ܩܛܪܢܐ rt. ܩܛܪ. m. a woody excrescence.

ܩܛܪܐ, ܩܛܪܐ and ܩܛܪܢܐ pl. ܐ̈ـ a) Pers. f. a quiver, case for arrows. b) m. the cypress or pine. c) = ܩܛܪܩܛܐ.

ܩܛܪܢܐ m. the almond-tree.

ܩܛܪܩܛܐ and other vocalizations pl. ܐ̈ـ m. καταράκτης, a sluice; a cataract, rush of water; a staircase.

ܩܛܪܬܐ pl. ܬ̈ܐ rt. ܩܛܪ. f. a) a knot, node; a joint, articulation; ܩܛܪ̈ܬܐ ܕܨܒ̈ܥܬܐ the knuckles. b) a bridge, pontoon. c) metaph. ܩܛܪܬܐ ܕܩܪܒܐ an aggression, onset, beginning of a fray. d) astron. a node, point of intersection of orbits; ܩ ܕܣܬܘܐ the winter solstice.

ܩܛܫܬܐ lichen.

ܩܛܬܝܣܝܣ, ܩܛܬܐ and ܩܬܬܐ f. κατάθεσις, a deposition, testimony, affidavit, used with ܥܒܕ.

ܩܛܬܐ with ܥܒܕ to depose, attest, attaint.

ܩܝܒܘܠܐ a rope.

ܩܝܒܘܪܝܢ, and ܩܝܒܘܪܐ pl. ܐ̈ـ f. κιβώριον, canopy, baldachin of the altar; shrine containing the host.

ܩܝܒܘܬܐ; see ܩܒܘܬܐ.

ܩܝܕܪܘܣ pl. ܩܕܪܘܣ and ܩܝܕܪܘܣ; see ܩܕܪܘܣ cedar.

ܩܝܕܪܝܣ, ܩ̈ـ and ܩܝܕܐܪܝܣ f. κίδαρις, a mitre.

ܩܝܕܪܝܢܐ κέδρινος, of cedar.

ܩܝܕܬܐ; see ܩܕܬܐ.

ܩܝܘܡܐ, ܬܐ rt. ܩܘܡ. a manager, superintendent; a governor, prefect; a patron, protector, succourer, upholder, stay, firm support; m. pl. a garrison.

ܩܝܘܡܘܬܐ rt. ܩܘܡ. f. protecting care; superintendence, government, presidency.

ܩܝܘܡܢܐ, ܢܝܬܐ rt. ܩܘܡ. supporting, upholding.

ܩܝܘܬܢܘܣ, &c.; see ܩܘܢܛܘܢܘܣ.

ܩܝܘܩܠܐܝܬ from ܩܘܩܠܘܣ. in or into a circle.

ܩܝܛ denom. verb Pael conj. from ܩܝܛܐ. to pass the summer.

ܩܝܛܐ pl. ܐ̈ـ m. summer, reckoned to begin with May. Derivatives, verb ܩܝܛ, ܩܝܛܐܝܬ, ܩܝܛܝܐ.

ܩܝܛܐ a wild boar; see ܩܛܝܐ.

ܩܝܛܐ m. a cinder.

ܩܝ̈ܛܐ; see ܩܐܛܐ.

ܩܝܛܐܝܬ from ܩܝܛܐ adv. during the summer.

ܩܝܛܘܢ, ܩܝܛܘܢܐ pl. ܐ̈ـ m. κοιτών, a sleeping-room, bed-chamber; an inner or private room; the women's apartments.

ܩܝܛܘܢܝܐ pl. ܐ̈ـ from ܩܝܛܘܢ m. a chamberlain.

ܩܝܛܘܣ pl. ܩܝ̈ܛܘܣ a whale; see ܩܐܛܐ.

ܩܝܛܐ = ܩܛܐ a cat.

ܩܝܣܐ κίσσα, a craving for strange food, green-sickness, the longing of pregnant women.

ܩܝܛܝܐ, ܩܝܛܝܬܐ from ܩܝܛܐ adj. of summer; ܟܬ̈ܒܐ ܩܝ̈ܛܝܐ service-books containing the offices used in summer.

ܩܝܕܘܢܐ, ܩܝܕܘܢܬܐ *a wild boar.*

ܩܝܠܐ = ܩܠܝܐ *a cell.*

ܩܝܠܘܢ *a drain.*

ܩܝܠܘܢܐ pl. ܐ̈ perh. κήλων, m. *a stallion.*

ܩܝܠܝܡ *a path.*

ܩܝܠܬܐ f. *intestinal* or *scrotal hernia.*

ܩܝܡ, ܩܝܡܐ rt. ܩܘܡ. *in being, existing, still alive; continuing, lasting;* ܩܝܡ ܝܘܡܐ ܥܕ *it is yet high day;* ܐܢ ܩܝܡܝܢ ܥܕܟܝܠ ܫܢܝܐ ܣܓܝܐܬܐ *if there be yet many years;* ܐܢ ܩܝܡ ܐܒܘܗܝ *if his father be yet alive;* ܩܝܡܐ ܠܥܠܡ *abiding for ever;* ܦܠܓܗ ܩܝܡܐ ܘܦܠܓܗ ܡܝܬܐ *half-alive;* ܟܘܪܗܢܐ ܕܩܝܡ *continuing sickness, chronic disease;* ܕܠܐ ܩܝܡ *uncertain;* legal *standing, valid;* ܩܝܡ ܙܒܢܐ *the sale is valid.*

ܩܝܡ, ܩܝܡܐ rt. ܩܘܡ. m. *a*) *standing, upright bearing; constitution; stability;* ܒܝܬ ܩ̈ *a standing place. b*) *a military post, station, garrison. c*) *a statute, covenant;* ܐܢܬܬܐ ܕܩ̈ *lawful wife;* ܩ̈ ܕܠܥܠܡ *an everlasting covenant. d*) *profession of the ascetic* or *monastic life, vow of chastity, celibacy. e*) *the minor orders, monkish orders, members of the minor orders. f*) ܒܪ ܩ̈ *one in minor orders, one vowed to a religious life;* ܒܢܬ ܩ̈ *church virgins, nuns,* rarely used of a *deaconess.*

ܩܝܡܐ = ܩܘܡܐ *a bit.*

ܩܝܡܐ pl. ܐ̈ rt. ܩܘܡ. m. *a door-post.*

ܩܝܡܐ, ܩܝܡܬܐ rt. ܩܘܡ. f. *a*) *standing firm, stability. b*) *rising up, resurrection;* ܝܘܡ ܩ̈ *the day of* our Lord's *resurrection* = *Sunday,* but usually = *Easter,* ܫܒܬܐ ܕܩ̈ *Easter week. c*) *a portion, ration, fixed allowance. d*) *a garrison, post.*

ܩܝܡܘܬܐ rt. ܩܘܡ. f. *a*) ܒܩܝܡܘܬܐ ܕܢܦܫܗ (rare) *of his own will. b*) ܩܝܡܘܬܐ ܕܩܠܐ or ellipt. *chanting, intoning music.*

ܩܝܡܝܢܘܢ and ܩܝܡܝܢ; see ܩܘܡܝܢܘܢ.

ܩܝܡܝܠܝܘܢ and ܩܝܡܠܐ pl. ܩܝܡܠܝܐ and ܩܝܡܠܐ m. κειμήλιον, *treasure, valuables, chattels.*

ܩܝܡܬܐ pl. ܩܝܡܬܐ, ܩܝܡܝܢ, ܩܝܡܬܐ rt. ܩܘܡ. f. *a*) *a post,* ܩ̈ ܕܬܪܥܐ *door-post; a pillar, obelisk, monument; a statue, image. b*) *stalk, stem, tree-trunk; standing corn.*

ܩܝܡܬܢܝܐ rt. ܩܘܡ. *relating to the resurrection.*

ܩܝܢܐ, ܩܝܢܬܐ pl. ܩܝܢܝܢ, ܩܝܢܬܐ f. *singing, wailing, melody; a song, chant, hymn; tone,* ܒܩ̈ ܩܕܡܝܐ *in the first tone; metre; a point.* DERIVATIVE, verb ܩܝܢ.

ܩܝܢܡܘܡܘܢ, ܩܝܢܐܡܘܡܘܢ, ܩܝܢܐܡܘܡܘܢ, ܩܝܢܐܡܘܡܘܢ, &c.; see ܩܘܢܡܘܢ *cinnamon.*

ܩܝܢܢܒܪܝܣ; see ܩܝܢܢܒܪܝܣ m. *cinnabar, minium.*

ܩܝܢܕܪܐ *the elm.*

ܩܝܢܕܘܢܘܣ, ܩܝܢܕܘܢܘܣ, ܩܝܢܕܘܢ, ܩܝܢܕܘܢ, ܩܝܢܕܘܢ, ܩܝܢܕܘܢܐ, ܩܝܢܕܘܢ, ܩܝܢܕܘܢ, and ܩܝܢܕܘܢܐ pl. ܩܝܢܕܘܢܐ, ܩܝܢܕܘܢܐ, &c. f. κίνδυνος, *peril; danger.*

ܩܝܢܕܘܢܝܐ, ܢܝܬܐ from ܩܝܢܕܘܢܘܣ *perilous, dangerous.*

ܩܝܢܕܘܢܝܘܬܐ, ܢܝܬܐ, ܢܘܣܐ, &c. pl. ܐ̈ m. κινδυνεῦσαι, *peril,* with ܥܒܕ *to be in peril, run a risk.*

ܩܝܢܘܢ = ܩܢܘܢ.

ܩܝܢܘܢ τὸ κοινόν, *the community, communion.*

ܩܝܢܝܐ pl. ܐ̈ m. *a smith, blacksmith, silversmith, goldsmith.* DERIVATIVES, verb ܩܝܢ, ܩܝܢܘܬܐ.

ܩܝܢܘܬܐ from ܩܝܢܝܐ. f. *the smith's art, metal-working.*

ܩܝܢܝܐ, ܩܝܢܝܐ pl. ܐ̈ from ܩܝܢ. *a Kenite.*

ܩܝܢ denom. verb from ܩܝܢܝܐ. *to work as a smith, to forge;* ܫܫܠܬܐ ܡܩܝܢܢܬܐ *forged chains, wrought fetters.*

ܩܝܢܣܘܣ m. Lat. census, *registration for taxation, poll-tax.*

ܩܝܢܪܐ and ܩܝܢܪܐ *cynara, the cardoon, globe artichoke.*

ܩܝܢܬܐ; see ܩܝܢܐ.

ܩܝܣ denom. verb PAEL conj. from ܩܝܣܐ. *to plank, cover with boards.* ETHPA. ܐܬܩܝܣ *to stiffen* refl., *become rigid.*

ܩܝܣܐ, ܩܝܣܐ pl. ܩܝܣܝܢ, ܐ̈ m. *a*) *wood, a piece of wood, a wooden vessel;* ܩ̈ ܕܐܪܙܐ *cedar-wood;* ܕܐܛܕܐ *white-thorn;* ܕܚܘܢܝܐ *asparagus;* ܕܙܝܬܐ *olive-wood;* in the Lexx. also *an ounce of oil, two drachms;* ܩ̈ ܕܐܣܦܠܬܘܣ *aspalathus,* a prickly shrub yielding a fragrant oil. *b*) *a tree; a cross, gibbet; a stick, stake. c*) rarer uses: *stocks; handle* of a bell, an axe, &c.; *rudder.* DERIVATIVES, verb ܩܝܣ, ܩܝܣܢܐ, ܩܝܣܢܝܐ, ܩܝܣܢܝܬܐ, ܩܝܣܘܢܐ, ܩܝܣܐ, ܡܩܝܣܢܘܬܐ, ܡܩܝܣܢܘܬܐ.

ܩܝܣܘܢܐ pl. ܐ̈ dimin. of ܩܝܣܐ. m. *a stick, piece of wood; a stem, twig, brushwood.*

ܩܝܣܘܣ, ܩܣܘܣ and ܩܝܣܘܣ, &c., f. κισσός, *ivy; a kind of vine.*

ܩܝܣܛܘܪܐ m. *a) arsenic. b)* cf. ܩܝܣܪܐ *pumice stone.*

ܩܝܣܘܡܐܬܐ, ܩܝܣ ܡܝܐ and ܩܝܣܘܡܐܬܐ, ܩܝܣ ܡܝܐ from ܩܝܣܐ. f. *sandal-wood* usually ܩܝܣ ܕܨ.

ܩܝܣܝܐ from ܩܝܣܐ. *wooden.*

ܩܝܣܢܐ from ܩܝܣܐ. *woody, hard.*

ܩܝܣܢܘܬܐ from ܩܝܣܐ. f. *woodiness, woodenness.*

ܩܝܣܢܝܐ, ܢܝܬܐ from ܩܝܣܐ. *wooden, woody.*

ܩܝܦܐ pr. n. *Caiaphas.*

ܩܝܪܛܐ m. *soot.*

ܩܝܪܘܐ ; see ܩܪܘܐ.

ܩܝܩܐ a bird, *the bee-eater.*

ܩܝܩܠܘܣܝܐ from κύκλος, *circular, rotatory.*

ܩܝܩܠܘܣܝܘܬܐ f. κύκλωσις, *circumvolution.*

ܩܝܩܠܬܐ E-Syr. ܩܩܠܬܐ or ܩܝܩܠܬܐ pl. ܩܝܩܠܝܬܐ f. *a dung-hill, dust-heap.*

ܩܝܢܐ and ܩܢܐ pl. ܩܝܢܐ m. *a plough-share, share-beam.*

ܩܝܪ m. κῦρ = κύριος, *lord, sir.*

ܩܝܪܐ and ܩܝܪܐ f. κυρά = κυρία, *lady, mistress.*

ܩܝܪܐ m. *pitch, tar, bitumen.*

ܩܝܪܛܐ ; see ܩܪܛܐ.

ܩܝܪܝܣܝܐ, ܩܝܪܝܣܝܬܐ *oblique.*

ܩܝܪܩܝܣ ; see ܩܝܪܩܝܣ.

ܩܝܪܬܐ f. *a whip of plaited hair smeared with pitch.*

ܩܝܢܬܐ rt. ܩܢ. m. *clinging, fixing the nails in.*

ܩܝܬܪ denom. verb Paiel conj. from ܩܝܬܪܐ. *to harp, play the harp, sing to the harp* or *guitar.* Ethp. ܐܬܩܝܬܪ *to be harped, played on the harp.*

ܩܝܬܪ, ܩܝܬܪܐ m. κιθάρα, *a stringed instrument, harp, cithern, lyre.* Derivatives, verb ܩܝܬܪ and the six following words :—

ܩܝܬܪܘܕܐ, ܩܝܬܪܘܕܘܣ κιθαρῳδός, *a player on the harp* or *cithern.*

ܩܝܬܪܘܕܘܬܐ from ܩܝܬܪܐ. f. *harp-playing.*

ܩܝܬܪܘܕܝܐ = ܩܝܬܪܘܕܐ.

ܩܝܬܪܘܢܐ dimin. of ܩܝܬܪܐ. *a small cithern.*

ܩܝܬܪܢܝܐ, ܢܝܬܐ from ܩܝܬܪܐ. *of* or *on the cithern.*

ܩܝܬܪܣܛܐ m. κιθαριστής, *a harp-player.*

ܩܠ fut. ܢܩܠ, act. part. ܩܐܠ, ܩܐܠܐ construed with ܡܢ. Verbal adj. ܩܠܝܠ see below. *a) to abate, diminish, lessen* as a flood, as pain. *b) to be swift, pass swiftly;* ܢܩܠܘܢ ܠܗܘܢ ܝܘܡܬܐ ܕܥܠܡܐ *oh may the days pass swiftly. c) to be lightened, relieved,* as ܡܘܥܢܐ *a weight;* ܩܐܠ ܠܗ ܦܓܪܗ *his body gains alertness.* Pa. ܩܠܠ *to lighten* a weight; *to make easier, expedite.* Pass. part. ܡܩܠܠ, ܡܩܠܠܐ *swift; bare, vile.* Ethpa. ܐܬܩܠܠ with ܡܢ *a) to be lightened, become light, swift. b) to be lightly esteemed.* Aph. ܐܩܠ *a) to lighten, relieve, assuage* ܚܫܐ *suffering,* &c.; ܐܩܠ ܡܢ ܥܝܢܝ ܥܦܪܐ ܕܐܪܥܐ *relieve mine eyes of* earthly *dust;* ܐܩܠܘ ܡܢ ܐܠܦܐ *they lightened the ship;* ܐܩܠ ܠܟ *it is a relief to thee. b) to hasten* ܪܗܛܐ *a course;* ܐܩܠ ܠܡܫܬܒܩܘ *haste to be forgiven. c) to rise above* as sounds; *to get the upper hand. d)* with ܥܠ *to make light of, disparage;* ܡܩܠܝܢ ܥܠ ܡܘܬܐ *they make light of death.*

Palpel ܩܠܩܠ *a) to distort, distract, throw into confusion. b) to bring shame upon;* ܛܘܒܘܗܝ ܠܡܢ ܕܠܫܢܗ ܠܐ ܩܠܩܠܗ *blessed is he whose tongue has brought no reproach upon him.* Ethpalp. ܐܬܩܠܩܠ *to be thrown into disorder; to be held in light esteem.* Derivatives, ܩܠܝܠܐ, ܡܩܠܠܐ, ܩܠܝܠܘܬܐ, ܩܠܩܠܐ, ܡܩܠܩܠܐ, ܩܠܝܠ, ܩܠܩܠܘܬܐ, ܩܠܘܠܐ, ܩܠܝܠܝܬ, ܩܘܠܩܠܐ, ܩܠܩܘܠܬܐ, ܡܩܠܩܠܘܬܐ.

ܩܠ, ܩܠܐ pl. ܩܠܝܢ, ܩܠܐ m. *a) voice, sound, noise, clamour;* ܩܠܐ ܪܒܐ or ܪܡܐ *a loud voice* or *cry;* ܩܠܐ ܕܩܘܩܢܣ *the swans' song;* ܩܠ ܫܝܦܘܪܐ *the sound of a trumpet;* ܩܠ ܪܓܠܐ *a footfall, trampling of feet;* with ܝܗܒ *to cry out, to sound;* ܐܪܝܡ *to lift up the voice, cry aloud;* ܕܠܐ ܩܠܐ *dumb, speechless;* gram. ܐܬܘܬܐ ܕܠܐ ܩܠܐ *a consonant. b) a saying, expression. c) a chant* properly one strophe with a versicle prefixed, *a hymn; a tone, tune;* ܩܠܐ ܡܫܚܠܦܐ *a hymn farced with alternate verses of another hymn or psalm,* ܩ ܕܩܦܠܐ *a hymn with double antistrophe to each verse;* ܒܩܠܐ or ܥܠ ܩܠ *to the tone, to the tune;* ܗܘ ܩܠܐ *the same tone;* ܩܠܐ ܚܕ *a word, term, expression,* cf. under ܒܪ, p. 54 *b.* Derivatives, ܩܠܢܐ, ܩܠܢܘܬܐ.

ܩܠܠ̈ܐ pl. of ܩܰܠܬܐ.

ܩܶܠܠܐ pl. ܩܶܠ̈ܠܐ Lat. cella, *a cell*. Cf. ܩܶܠܝܬܐ.

ܩܠܐ fut. ܢܶܩܠܶܐ, act. part. ܩܳܠܶܐ, ܩܳܠܝܳܐ, pass. part. ܩܠܶܐ, ܩܠܶܝܐ, ܩܠܶܝܬܐ, for pl. ܩܠܝ̈ܬܐ see below. *a*) *to roast, parch, fry;* ܫܶܒ̈ܠܐ ܕܩܠܶܝܢ ܒܢܘܪܐ *ears of corn parched by fire.* *b*) *to inflict severe pain, pain acutely, destroy;* ܒܥܰܛܗ ܘܩܰܠܝܶܗ ܘܡܝܬ *he kicked him and hurt him severely and he died.* Ethpe. ܐܶܬܩܠܝ *a*) *to be fried.* *b*) *to suffer agony, be in great pain.* Pa. ܩܰܠܝ *a*) *to fry, parch, dry up;* ܩܰܠܐ ܢܘ̈ܢܐ *fry fish.* *b*) *to quarrel.* *c*) *to make eager, make hot in pursuit.* Ethpa. ܐܶܬܩܰܠܝ *a*) *to be fried, scorched, burnt up;* ܓܰܪ̈ܡܐ ܢܶܬܩܰܠܘܢ *the bones shall be burnt.* *b*) *to be nipped, pinched* with cold. *c*) *to be consumed by desire.* *d*) perh. denom. from ܩܘܠܢܣ *to have the colic, suffer in the bowels;* ܐܶܬܩܰܠܝܘ ܡܢ ܣܰܓܝܐܘܬ ܡܶܐܟܠܬܐ *they were in agony from eating too much.* Aph. ܐܰܩܠܝ *a*) *to fry.* *b*) from ܐܰܩܶܠ *to lighten* a load. *c*) *to make light of, hold in light esteem* with ܒ; ܐܰܩܠܝܘ ܒܡܰܘܬܐ *they made light of death.* Derivatives, ܩܠܝܐ, ܩܠܝܬܐ, ܡܩܠܝܐ, ܩܠܝܐ, ܩܠܝ̈ܬܐ, ܩܠܝ̈ܬܐ.

ܩܰܠܝܳܢܳܐ, ܩܰܠܝܳܢ and ܩܰܠܝܰܢ pl. ܐ̈ perh. Pers. *a bricklayer's labourer, a navvy.*

ܩܠܝܡܛܝܪܝܢ = ܩܠܝܡܛܪܝܘܢ, ܩܠܝܡܛܝܪܝܣ.

ܩܰܠܒܳܐ = ܩܳܠܒ m. *a mould, form.*

ܩܠܝܐ dialect of Baghdad, m. *quick-lime.*

ܩܠܝܢܐ = ܩܰܠܝܳܢܳܐ.

ܩܠܒܐ pl. ܐ̈ m. *ring in a camel's nostrils.*

ܩܠܘܒܐ pl. ܩܠܘܒ̈ܐ m. *a birdcage, wicker cage; basket.*

ܩܘܠܒܝܢܐ, ܩܘܠܒܝܢ or ܩܘܠܒܝܢ pl. ܩܘܠܒܝ̈ܢܐ m. κολόβιον, *an outer garment without sleeves.*

ܩܠܘܒܝܐ from ܩܠܘܒܐ m. *a cage-maker, basket-weaver.*

ܩܘܠܒܐ m. *a door-fastening, bolt, ring.*

ܩܰܠܘܳܛ, ܩܰܠܘܳܛܳܐ, ܩܰܠܘܳܛܬܐ rt. ܩܠܛ. *avaricious, grasping.*

ܩܰܠܘܳܛܘܬܐ rt. ܩܠܛ. f. *avarice, niggardliness.*

ܩܰܠܘܳܛܳܐ rt. ܩܠܛ. *stingy, niggardly.*

ܩܰܠܘܳܠܳܐ rt. ܩܠ. *a*) *light in weight, swift.* *b*) *squint-eyed.*

ܩܰܠܘܳܠܘܬܐ rt. ܩܠ. f. *nimbleness, agility.*

ܩܠܘܦܐ m. *a long sharp blade.*

ܩܰܠܘܳܦܳܐ pl. ܝ̈ܢ rt. ܩܠܦ. *squint-eyed.*

ܩܰܠܘܳܦܘܬܐ rt. ܩܠܦ. f. *squinting.*

ܩܘܠܘܪܐ pl. ܝ̈ܢ, ܐ̈ m. κολλύρα, *a flat round loaf, small cake of bread.* Derivative, verb ܩܠܪ.

ܩܘܠܘܪܝܬܐ pl. ܝ̈ܬܐ, ܝ̈ܬܐ f. *a small cake.*

ܩܰܠܘܣܬܳܐ m. *giant fennel; a slender rod* or *stem swayed by the wind.*

ܩܠܛ Pael ܩܰܠܶܛ, part. ܡܩܰܠܛ. *close-fisted, mean.* Ethpa. ܐܶܬܩܰܠܰܛ *to be niggardly, grasping.* Derivatives, ܩܰܠܘܳܛܳܐ, ܩܰܠܘܳܛܘܬܐ, ܩܰܠܘܳܛ.

ܩܠܝܐ rt. ܩܠܐ. m. *alkali.*

ܩܠܝܐ rt. ܩܠܐ. m. *a*) *frying, parching* corn over the fire. *b*) *whipping with raw rods.* *c*) *the colic, pains in the bowels,* cf. Ethpa. of ܩܠܐ *d.*

ܩܠܝܕܐ and ܐܩܠܝܕܐ pl. ܝ̈ܢ, ܐ̈ m. κλείς, κλεῖδα, *a key;* ܩܠܝܕ ܩܕܡ ܨܘܪܐ *the collar-bone.*

ܩܠܝܕܢܐ m. *keeper of the keys, doorkeeper.*

ܩܰܠܝܠ, ܩܰܠܝܠܳܐ, ܩܰܠܝܠܬܐ rt. ܩܠ. *a*) *swift, light, rapid; hasty, headlong;* ܥܢ̈ܢܐ ܩܰܠܝܠܳܬܐ *fleeting clouds;* ܡ̈ܝܐ ܩܰܠܝܠܝܢ *rushing waters;* ܡܰܘܬܐ ܩܰܠܝܠܳܐ ܕܣܰܝܦܐ *swift death by the sword.* *b*) *little, small, brief;* ܩܰ ܗܘܳܐ ܒܥܰܝ̈ܢܰܘܗܝ *it was a little thing in his eyes;* ܒܩܰ ܟܣܦܐ ܙܳܒܶܢ *he buys for a small sum of money;* ܩܰ ܙܰܒܢܐ *a short time.* *c*) *a little, a few, somewhat;* ܩܰ ܒܩܰܠܝܠ ܗܰܝܡܶܢܬ *thou hast been faithful in a little;* ܩܰ ܪܓܶܙܶܬ *I was but a little angry;* ܩܰ ܡܰܪܗܝܒܳܐܝܬ *somewhat boldly;* ܦܘܕܐ ܩܰܠܝܠܳܐ *a slight error.* Phrases: ܩܰܠܝܠ ܒܪܰܡ *almost; partly;* ܩܰ ܝܰܬܝܪ ܘܩܰ ܒܨܝܪ *more or less, sooner or later;* ܩܰ ܒܳܬܰܪ *soon after;* — ܒܳܬܰܪ ܝܰܪ̈ܚܐ ܫ̈ܢܝܐ ܩܰܠܝܠ *after a few months, years;* ܩܰ ܒܩܰܠܝܠ *every little while;* ܒܩܰܠܝܠ ܩܰܠܝܠ *wellnigh;* ܩܰ ܒܩܰܠܝܠܘ *briefly, shortly; scarcely;* ܩܰ ܡܢ *shortly before;* ܩܰ ܠܘܬ *within a little, wellnigh, almost;* ܩܰ ܡܢ ܩܕܡ *a little before;* ܩܰ ܝܰܘ̈ܡܬܐ ܡܢ ܩܕܡ *a few days before;* ܩܰܠܝܠ ܩܰܠܝܠ and ܩܰ ܩܰ *a very little, little by little, gradually.*

ܩܰܠܝܠܳܐܝܬ rt. ܩܠ. adv. *swiftly, suddenly, hastily; easily.*

ܩܰܠܝܠܘܬܐ rt. ܩܠ. f. *a*) *swiftness, rapidity, facility;* ܩܰܠܝܠܘܬ ܙܰܒܢܐ *shortness of the time.* *b*) *lightness, subtilty;* ܩܰܠܝܠܘܬ ܪܶܥܝܳܢܳܐ *levity.*

ܩܠܝܡܐ pl. ܝܢ̈ـ, ܬܐ̈ـ and ܩܠܝܡܛܐ m. κλίμα, *a clime, zone, region, district;* the ancients divided the world into seven ܩܠܝܡܐ̈ *climes* or *zones*.

ܩܠܝܡܐ pl. ܐ̈ـ from ܩܘܠܡܐ. *of good report, honoured, praised.*

ܩܠܝܣܘܪܐ pl. ܐ̈ m. Lat. clausura, *a pass* or *narrow path* in the mountains.

ܩܠܝܣܝܣܛܝܩܐ, ܩܠܝܣܛܝܩܝܣ also ܩܠܐܣ and ܩܠܣ; see ܐܩܠܝܣܛܝܩܐ *church history.*

ܩܠܩܘܡ ܩܪܢܐ *a jug with one handle.*

ܩܠܝܪܘܣ and ܩܠܪܘܣ m. κλῆρος, *the clergy.*

ܩܠܠܪܝܛܝܣ m. κελλαρίτης, *cellarer, store-keeper.*

ܩܠܝܪܝܩܐ, ܩܘܣـ pl. ܐ̈ـ, ܩܠܝܪܝܩܘ m. κληρικός, *a clerk in holy orders, clergyman;* pl. *the secular clergy* opp. ܕܝܪ̈ܝܐ *the monastic orders.*

ܩܠܝܬܐ pass. part. emph. f. pl. of verb ܩܠܐ. *parched corn.*

ܩܠܝܬܐ pl. ܬܐ̈ـ f. κέλλα, *a cell, an alcove,* usually a *monk's cell;* used of the Patriarch's residence; ܒܢܝ̈ ܩܠܝܬܗ a bishop's or abbot's *cell-mates, attendants.*

ܩܠܝܬܐ pl. ܬܐ̈ـ rt. ܩܠܐ. f. *a) a challenge, combat, contention. b) a slight, insult.*

ܩܠܝܬܘܢܝܬܐ dimin. of ܩܠܝܬܐ f. *a little cell.*

ܩܠܩܕܘܢܐ pr. n. *a)* = ܩܠܩܕܘܢ *Chalcedon. b) Carthage.*

ܩܠܩܕܘܢܝܐ from the preceding. *a)* properly *an adherent of the Council of Chalcedon.* *b) a Carthaginian.*

ܩܠܩܠܐ rt. ܩܠ. m. *belittling, slighting, contempt, ignominy, shame;* ܫܩܠ ܩܠܩ or ܫܩܠ ܩ ܠ *to put to shame.*

ܩܠܡܐ pl. ܐ̈ـ com. gen. *a) a louse, parasite, weevil. b) morbus pedicularis.*

ܩܠܡܘܢܐ m. palma Christi, *castor-oil bean.*

ܩܠܡܣܡܐ f. *a well with steps down to it.*

ܩܠܡܪܐ m. Lat. calamarius, *a writing-case.*

ܩܠܢܐ = ܐܩܠܢܐ m. κλάνιον, *a bracelet.*

ܩܠܢܕܘܣ, ܩܠܢܕ, ܩܠܢܕܐ, &c. pl. ܩܠܢܕܘܣ com. gen. Lat. calendae, *the Calends, first day of the month* or *year.*

ܩܠܢܝܐ, ܬܐ̈ـ from ܩܠܐ. *sounding, resounding; vocal, vowel;* ܩܠܢܝܬܐ ܐܬܘ̈ܬܐ *the vowel-letters* ܐ ܘ ܝ.

ܩܠܢܝܐ *a) muddy, turbid. b)* from ܩܠܢܐ. *similar to a bracelet.*

ܩܠܢܝܘܬܐ from ܩܠܐ f. gram. *the quality of a vowel, vocalization.*

ܩܠܣ from Greek καλῶς. Pael conj. *to laud, extol, give praise, applaud;* ܐܝܟܢܐ ܩܘܠܣܐ ܪܘܪܒܐ ܩܠܣܬܗ ܩܕܡ ܟܠ *how greatly thou hast extolled him before all.* Pass. part. ܡܩܠܣ, ܐـ, ܬܐـ *laudable, commendable, excellent;* with ܠܐ *unworthy, improper;* ܠܐ ܡܩܠܣܬܐ ܗܝ *it is not thought suitable.* Ethpa. ܐܬܩܠܣ *to be praised, commended; to become illustrious.* Derivatives, ܩܘܠܣܐ, ܩܠܣܐ, ܡܩܠܣܢܐ, ܡܩܠܣܢܐ, ܡܩܠܣܢܐ, ܡܩܠܣܢܘܬܐ.

ܩܠܣܛܝܩܐ, ܩܠܣ, ܩܠܣܐ; see ܩܠܝܣܛܝܩܐ.

ܩܠܥ denom. verb Pael conj. from ܩܠܥܐ. *to sling, hurl.*

ܩܠܥ, ܩܠܥܐ m. *a) a sling;* ܫܕܝ ܒܩ̈ܠܥܐ *slingers;* ܩܠܥ ܩܫܬܐ *a catapult, ballista. b) a sail.* Derivatives, verb ܩܠܥ, ܩܘܠܥܐ, ܩܠܥܐ, ܡܩܠܥܢܐ.

ܩܠܥܐ pl. ܐ̈ـ from ܩܠܥܐ. m. *a slinger.*

ܩܠܥܐ or ܩܠܥܐ, ܩܠܥܬܐ pl. ܬܐ̈ـ Ar. *a fortress, fortification; castle.*

ܩܠܦ fut. ܢܩܠܘܦ, act. part. ܩܠܦ, ܩܠܦܐ, pass. part. ܩܠܝܦ, ܐ, ܬܐ. *to peel, pare, shell; to scrape off, strip off; to scale off* as the crust of a sore; ܗܘ ܩܠܦ ܚܙܘܪܐ ܒܣܟܝܢܐ *he peeled the apple with a knife;* ܩܠܦ ܦܬܟܪ̈ܐ *he stripped the idols,* i.e. of their gold casings; ܦܘܠܐ ܩܠܝܦܐ *shelled beans;* ܚܡܪܐ ܕܠܐ ܩܠܝܦ *must.* Ethpe. ܐܬܩܠܦ *to be pared, husked, lose the husk; to be scraped off, rubbed off.* Pa. ܩܠܦ *to scrape off, rub away, fret; lay bare.* Ethpa. ܐܬܩܠܦ *to be scraped* or *skinned off.* Derivatives, ܩܠܦܐ, ܩܠܦܬܐ, ܩܠܦܐ, ܩܠܦܢܐ, ܩܠܦܐ, ܩܠܦܬܐ, ܩܠܦܢܐ.

ܩܠܦܐ pl. ܐ̈ـ rt. ܩܠܦ. m. *a sheet of parchment, leaf.*

ܩܠܦܐ, ܩܠܦܬܐ, and ܩܠܦܬܐ pl. ܐ̈ـ, ܬܐ̈ـ rt. ܩܠܦ. f. *bark, rind; husk, peel, chaff, shells; scales* of fish, *scales* formed by disease such as cataract or leprosy; *talc, flakes of talc;* ܩܠܦܐ ܕܒܝܥ̈ܐ—ܕܚܠܙܘܢܐ *egg-shells, snail-shells;*

ܩܘܠܦܐ ܕܩܘܩܘܐ ܩܠܦܬܐ cinnamon; ܕܩܪܘܚܐ skin formed over a sore; ܕܢܚܫܐ brass filings, particles, dross; ܕܦܪܙܠܐ iron slag; ܕܪܘܡܢܐ pomegranate peel.

ܩܘܠܘܦܘܢܝܐ and ܩܠܦܘܢܐ from κολοφωνία, resin.

ܩܠܦܝܢ m. καλπίον, a tankard.

ܩܠܦܝܬܐ rt. ܩܠܦ. f. scab, scurf.

ܩܠܦܘܦܝܬܐ pl. ܬܐ rt. ܩܠܦ. bark, a leaf.

ܩܠܦܢܐ rt. ܩܠܦ. a) adj. flaky, laminar. b) a cutaneous disease.

ܩܠܦܢܕܪ = σκολόπενδρα, m. milliped.

ܩܠܦܢܝܐ, ܢܝܬܐ rt. ܩܠܦ. scaly.

ܩܠܐܩܣܝܣ and ܩܠܐܩ f. ἔκλειψις, an eclipse, = Syr. ܟܘܣܦܐ.

ܩܠܩ act. part. ܩܠܩ to show the white of the eye, look askance. Derivatives, ܩܠܩܘܬܐ, ܩܠܩܘܬܐ.

ܩܠܟܐ pl. ܐ m. κάχληξ, a pebble, gravel.

ܩܠܩܘܡܐ pl. ܐ corrupted from χαράκωμα, a mound, rampart, bulwark thrown up by a besieging force.

ܩܠܩܠܢܐ m. some small low-growing herb.

ܩܠܩܠ Palpel conj. of ܩܠ; see above.

ܩܠܩܠ = ܩܠܩ the acacia.

ܩܠܩܠܢܝܬܐ f. pl. forms, appearances.

ܩܠܩܫ to strike or sound a bell. Derivative, ܩܘܠܩܫܐ.

ܩܠܪ denom. verb Pael conj. from ܩܠܘܪܐ. to make cakes.

ܩܠܪܘܣ; see ܩܠܝܪܘܣ.

ܩܠܪܝܛܝܣ m. κελλαρίτης, a cellarer, storekeeper.

ܩܠܫ Peal, and ܐܩܠܫ Aph. to swell, surge said of the deep sea.

ܩܠܬܐ and ܩܐܠܬܐ pl. ܩܠܬܐ, ܩܠܐ and ܩܐܠܐ a) f. κάλαθος, a large basket. b) κήλη, hernia.

ܩܘܠܬܐ fem. form of ܩܘܠܐ. an anthem sung at Nocturns when the Eucharist is to follow.

ܩܡܐܐ maimed of one testicle.

ܩܡܐܠܘܢ m. a snail.

ܩܘܡܐܕܪܐ = ܩܘܡܘܕܪܐ an actor.

ܩܘܡܐ, ܩܘܡܝ and ܩܘܡܝܘܢ, ܩܘܡܐ, ܩܘܡܝ, ܩܘܡܝ f. gum, gum arabic.

ܩܡܘܛܐ rt. ܩܡܛ. wrinkled, rugged.

ܩܘܡܘܠܐ or ܩܘܡ = ܩܘܡܘܠܐ.

ܩܡܘܠܒܩܘܢ pl. ܐ καμελαύκιον, a kind of cap.

ܩܘܡܘܠܬܐ rt. ܩܡܠ. f. mould, mouldiness esp. on bread.

ܩܡܘܫܬܐ pl. ܬܐ rt. ܩܡܫ. f. a cake of bread, biscuit.

ܩܘܡܘܢ = ܩܘܡܪܐ b, and perhaps also = ܩܘܡܪܘ.

ܩܡܚܐ m. flour, meal.

ܩܘܡܚܢܝܬܐ from ܩܡܚܐ. f. blue mould.

ܩܡܛ fut. ܢܩܡܘܛ, act. part. ܩܐܡܛ, ܩܐܡܛܐ, pass. part. ܩܡܝܛܐ and ܩܡܝܛܐ. a) to lay fast hold of, to take; a dog ܩܡܛܗ ܠܟܘܟܘܡܝܬܐ ܘܚܢܩܗ laid hold of the weasel and strangled it. b) to contract, shrink; ܩܡܝܛܝܢ ܐܦܝܗ her face was contracted with pain. Ethpe. ܐܬܩܡܛ a) to be laid hold of. b) with ܐܦܐ to be contracted, drawn as the features with pain or disgust. Pa. ܩܡܛ to shrivel up tr. Ethpa. ܐܬܩܡܛ to fall in as the cheeks with old age, to become wrinkled, contracted. Derivatives, ܩܡܛܘܛܐ, ܩܡܘܛܐ, ܩܡܛܐ.

ܩܡܛܐ pl. ܐ rt. ܩܡܛ. a wrinkle, crease.

ܩܡܛܐ m. pl. Ar. swaddling-clothes.

ܩܡܛܘܣ = ܩܘܡܛܘܣ.

ܩܡܛܪܝܢ; see ܩܘܡܝܛܐ a comet.

ܩܡܛܪܝܐ κάμπτρια, a box, case.

ܩܡܛܐ or ܩܡܛ m. a) a baby's cradle. b) = ܩܘܡܝܛܘܣ a count. c) cf. verb ܩܡܛ.

ܩܘܡܝܛܘܣ = ܩܘܡܝܛܐ a comet.

ܩܡܝܢܐ E-Syr. ܩܡܝ m. κάμινος, a stove, fireplace, metal hearth.

ܩܘܡܝܣ = ܩܘܡܝܣ.

ܩܘܡܝܨܬܐ pl. ܬܐ f. Ar. a chemise, shirt, camisole, tunic.

ܩܡܝܥܐ pl. ܐ rt. ܩܡܥ. m. an amulet, charm, phylactery.

ܩܡܠ to moulder, become mouldy. Pa. ܩܡܠ to grow as the fungus of mould. Aph. ܐܩܡܠ to grow mouldy as bread. Derivatives, ܩܘܡܠܐ, ܩܡܠܐ, ܩܡܘܠܬܐ, ܩܡܠܢܝܬܐ, ܩܡܠܐ, ܩܘܡܠܐ.

ܩܘܡܠܐ pl. ܐ rt. ܩܡܠ. m. mould, dust.

ܩܡܠܐ = ܩܡܠܝܘܢ chattels.

ܩܡܣܡ denom. verb Pael conj. from ܩܐܡܣܐ. to bit, put a bit or bridle in the mouth.

ܩܘܡܣܐ and ܩܘܡܣ = ܩܘܡܣܝܣ *a commander*, &c.

ܩܡܥ *to tie* or *bind*; ܩܡܥܝ ܩܡܝܥܐ *those who bind on* or *who sew together amulets.*

ܩܡܦܓܝܢ καμπάγιον -ια, a kind of boot.

ܩܡܦܘܣ m. campus, *a plain.*

ܩܡܦܛܘܣ and ܩܡܦܛܪܘܣ m. καμπτός, καμπτήρ, *a turning-point, turning-post, goal.*

ܩܡܨܐ pl. ܐ̈ m. *a) the locust;* ܒ̈ܢܝ ܩܡܨܐ *young locusts* before the wings are developed. *b) pastinaca agrestis, parsnip.*

ܩܡܪ Peal and ܩܡܪ Pael *to strap, tie.* Derivatives, ܩܡܪܐ, ܩܘܡܪܐ.

ܩܡܪܐ pl. ܐ̈ and ܩܡܪ̈ܐ rt. ܩܡܪ. m. *a strap, shoe-strap, belt;* astron. *the belt* of Orion; or ܩ̈ ܕܙܘܕܝܐ ܕܡܠܘܫܐ *the zodiac; four points of intersection* of the epicycle.

ܩܢ denom. verb from ܩܢܐ, ܩܢ. Aphel ܐܩܢ *to nest, build a nest* used of ants and bees besides birds; *to breed* as worms.

ܩܢ, ܩܢܐ and ܩܢܢܐ pl. ܐ̈ m. *a) a nest, brood; a rookery; an ant's nest, ant-hill, a bee-hive. b)* ܩܢܐ ܕܡܠܘܫܐ; see ܩܢܡܠܘܫܐ. Derivative, verb ܐܩܢ.

ܩܢܐ I. fut. ܢܩܢܐ, parts. ܩܢܐ, ܩܢܝܐ and ܩܢܐ, ܩܢܝܢܐ. *to get, gain, purchase, possess, have; to obtain, attain;* ܐܢ ܢܩܢܐ ܥܠܡܐ ܟܠܗ *if he gain the whole world;* ܩܢܐ ܬܝܒܘܬܐ *attain to repentance.* With ܐܒܕܢܐ *to go to ruin, perish;* ܚܠܝܡܘܬܐ *to be healed, restored;* ܓܘܢܐ *to become of a colour;* ܙܗܝܪܘܬܐ *to exercise caution;* ܩܢܝܢܐ *to possess cattle;* ܪܚܡܐ *to have for a friend;* ܡܫܡܠܝܐܝܬ *to attain completely;* ܫܠܡܘܬܐ *to consent.* Both participles have active significance; *having, endowed with,* &c., *a possessor, owner;* ܡܟܝܟܘܬܐ ܕܩܢܐ ܗܘܐ *the humility to which he had attained;* ܩܢܐ ܫܡܝܐ ܘܐܪܥܐ *possessor of heaven and earth;* ܝܕܥ ܬܘܪܐ ܩܢܝܗ *the ox knoweth his owner;* ܥܬܝܪܐ ܘܡܣܟܢܐ ܩܢܝܐ *rich and poor;* ܩܢܝ ܡܠܬܐ—ܗܘܢܐ *intelligent, reasonable;* ܩܢܝ ܩܢܝܢܐ *cattle-owners.* Ethpe. ܐܬܩܢܝ *to be acquired, gained, purchased, possessed;* ܫܘܐ ܠܡܬܩܢܝܘ *worthy of attainment, desirable.* Pa. ܩܢܝ *to retain.* Aph. ܐܩܢܝ *to put in possession, enable to win; to confer, bestow, impart* ܚܝܐ *life,* ܚܝܠܐ *power,* &c.; *to impose* ܢܡܘܣܐ *rules,* ܫܠܝܘܬܐ *silence.* With ܦܘܣܐ *to persuade, convince.* Derivatives, ܩܢܝܐ, ܩܢܝܢܐ, ܩܢܝܢܘܬܐ, ܩܢܝܐ, ܩܢܝܢܐ, ܩܢܝܢܝܐ, ܡܩܢܝܢܘܬܐ, ܡܩܢܝܢܐ, ܡܩܢܝܢܘܬܐ, ܡܬܩܢܝܢܐ, ܡܩܢܝܢܐ.

ܩܢܐ II. perh. from ܩܘܢܝܐ. 3 m. pl. ܩܢܘ *they became pale as ashes.* Pa. ܩܢܝ pass. part. ܡܩܢܝܐ pl. ܡܩܢܝܢ *livid, dim.* Derivatives, ܩܢܝܐ, ܩܢܘܬܐ, ܡܩܢܝܢܘܬܐ.

ܩܢܐ, ܩܢܝܐ pl. ܩܢܝܢ, ܩܢܝܐ; see ܩܢܝܐ subst. ܩܢܐ, ܩܢܝܐ pl. ܩܢܝܢ, ܩܢܝܐ part. of verb ܩܢܐ I.

ܩܢܐ pl. of *a)* ܩܢ. *b)* ܩܢܝܐ.

ܩܢܘܬܐ rt. ܩܢܐ II. f. *lead colour.*

ܩܢܘܪܘܣ m. *a) the giraffe. b) cynara cardunculus, cardoon, globe artichoke.*

ܩܢܪܘܣ; see ܩܢܘܪܘܣ.

ܩܢܬܐ and ܩܢܝܬܐ pl. ܐ̈ rt. ܩܢܐ. f. *a) anger, indignation. b) enmity, rancour, virulence.*

ܩܢܒ Pael ܩܢܒ *to lie in ambush.* Aph. ܐܩܢܒ *a) to maraud. b) to lie in ambush.* Derivatives, ܩܢܒܐ, ܡܩܢܒܐ.

ܩܢܒܐ rt. ܩܢܒ. m. *an ambush.*

ܩܢܒܪܐ m. *a rope-maker.*

ܩܢܒܪܝܣ and ܩܢܐ, ܩܢܒܪܝܣ, ܩܢܢܒܪܝܣ κιννάβαρις, *cinnabar, red sulphuret of mercury, minium.*

ܩܢܒܘܠܐ *a tribute, fine.*

ܩܢܕܘܢܘܣ, ܩܢܕܘܢ— and ܩܢܕܝܢܘܣ pl. ܩܢܕܝܢܘ = ܩܝܢܕܘܢܘܣ *peril.*

ܩܢܕܘܣ and ܩܘܢܕܘܣ *saponaria officinalis, soap-wort;* or *veratrum album, white hellebore.*

ܩܢܕܝܠܐ pl. ܐ̈, ܩܢܕܠܐ and ܩܢܕܝܠܝܣ, ܩܢܕܝܠܐܣ m. and f. Lat. candela, *a candle, candlestick, lamp-stand, hanging lamp.*

ܩܢܘܒܝܐ pl. ܐ̈ m. *a cenobite, cloister-brother.*

ܩܢܘܒܝܢ, ܩܢܘܒܝܘܢ, ܩܢܐ and ܩܢܘܒ m. κοινόβιον, *a cloister, monastery.*

ܩܢܘܕܐ *the large middle pearl of a necklace.*

ܩܢܘܝܐ rt. ܩܢܐ. m. *possessor, owner.*

ܩܢܘܡ, ܩܢܘܡܐ pl. ܩܢܘܡܝܢ, ܐ̈ m. *a) hypostasis, substance, actual existence;* ܒܪܐ ܐܠܗܐ ܩܢܘܡܗ ܕܫܡܝܐ ܘܩܢܘܡܗ ܕܐܪܥܐ God created *the substance,* or *the true existence, of heaven and earth;* ܩܢܘܡ ܚܕܐ ܫܥܐ *one actual hour, one very hour. b) a person, individual, the individual self;* ܩ̈ ܕܡܠܟܐ *the king's person;* ܢܩܪܘܒ

ܩܢܘܡܝܢ ܬܪܝܢ ܩܫܐ ܘܡܫܡܫܢܐ he is to send two persons, a priest and a deacon; ܒܩܢܘܡܐ in person, personally; ܩܢܘܡ ܢܦܫܗ his very substance, himself = ܦܠܢ a certain person, any one; ܠܦܠܢܐ ܗ̄ ܕܐܒܗ̈ܬܐ office for such an one of the Fathers; ܠܦܠܢ ܗ̄ ܕܝܪܝܐ for a certain monk. With pron. suff. ܐܢܐ ܩܢܘܡܝ I myself; ܩܢܘܡܟ thyself; ܩܢܘܡܗ ܕܣܛܢܐ Satan himself; ܕܡܐ ܕܩܢܘܡܗ his own blood; ܠܐ ܩܢܘܡܐܝܬ not at all. c) theol. ܩܢܘܡܐ ܕܐܠܗܘܬܐ the persons of the Godhead; Nestorians distinguish between ܩܢܘܡܐ hypostasis and ܦܪܨܘܦܐ πρόσωπον; ܬܪܬܝܢ ܟܝ̈ܢܝܢ ܘܬܪܝܢ ܩܢܘܡܝܢ ܡܫܝܚܐ ܚܕ ܦܪܨܘܦܐ ܕܒܪܘܬܐ ܐܬܚܝܕܘ Christ is two natures and two qnumi united in the person of the Son (Ebedjesus Lib. Margaritae Par. 3. cap. 1). Derivatives, the five following words and verb ܐܬܩܢܡ:—

ܩܢܘܡܐܝܬ adv. in substance; in person, personally.

ܩܢܘܡܝܐ, ܩܢܘܡܝܬܐ a) actually existent; hypostatic. b) personal, proper, own. c) real, substantive.

ܩܢܘܡܝܘܬܐ f. and ܩܢܘܡܬܢܝܘܬܐ f. personality.

ܩܢܘܡܬܢܐ subsisting, existent, personal.

ܩܢܢ denom. verb from ܩܢܘܢܐ. Ethpaual ܐܬܩܢܘܢ to be prescribed in a canon, canonically pronounced or ordered.

ܩܢܘܢ, ܩܢܘܢܐ pl. ܐ̈ m. κανών. a) O. T. Hex. a measuring-rod. b) a section, paragraph of Scripture. c) a rule of life, of medicine, of grammar. d) a canon, rule of the Church; a canonical fine, penalty. e) the regular clergy. f) rit. a canon, a list of those to be prayed for or commemorated; an appointed chant, hymn esp. a short metrical farcing of a psalm; an expansion of the endings of certain prayers. Derivatives, verb ܐܬܩܢܘܢ and the four following words:—

ܩܢܘܢܐܝܬ adv. rightly, canonically; with ܠܐ uncanonically, irregularly.

ܩܢܘܢܝܐ, ܩܢܘܢܝܬܐ regular, canonical.

ܩܢܘܢܝܘܬܐ f. observation of the canons.

ܩܢܘܢܬܐ f. a mould.

ܩܢܙܬܐ f. a whip, scourge.

ܩܢܛ fut. ܢܩܢܛ, parts. ܩܢܛ, ܩܢܛܐ and ܩܢܝܛ, ܩܢܝܛܐ, ܩܢܝܛܬܐ. to fear, shrink from with ܡܢ, ܒ, ܕ; ܡܢ ܚܒܬܐ ܩܢܛ ܚܘܒܐ ܕܠܡܐ love feared lest . . ., ܩܢܛ ܐܢܐ ܡܢ ܒܢܝ̈ ܫܪܒܬܟ I fear thy fellow tribesmen. Pass. part. a) verbal use; ܩܢܝܛ ܐܢܐ ܡܢ ܕܝܢܐ ܪܒܐ I fear the great Judgement. b) afraid, timid. c) fearful, terrible; ܡ̈ܠܐ ܩܫܝ̈ܬܐ ܘܩܢܝ̈ܛܬܐ harsh and terrible words. Ethpa. ܐܬܩܢܛ to be afraid, alarmed with ܡܢ, ܒ, ܥܠ. Aph. ܐܩܢܛ to make afraid, make anxious; ܠܒܝ ܐܩܢܛܢܝ ܡܢܗ my heart made me afraid of him. Derivatives, ܩܘܢܛܐ, ܩܢܛܐ, ܩܢܛܐܝܬ, ܩܢܛܘܬܐ.

ܩܢܛܐ pl. ܐ̈ rt. ܩܢܛ. m. fear, suspicion; ܕܠܐ ܩܢܛܐ safe; safely, securely.

ܩܢܛܐ pl. ܐ̈ probably κελέοντες the beams in the upright loom of the ancients.

ܩܢܛܝܡܐ or ܩܢܛ pl. ܐ̈ m. κέντημα, a point, instant.

ܩܢܛܢܪܐ and ܩܢܛܢܪܝܢ &c. pl. ܐ̈ m. κεντηνάριον, a quintal, hundredweight.

ܩܢܛܪܘܢ and ܩܢܛ pl. ܩܢܛܪܐ m. κέντρον, the centre, middle point of a circle.

ܩܢܛܪܘܢܐ pl. ܩܢܛܪܘܢܝܢ, ܐ̈ m. Lat. centurio, a centurion, captain of a hundred.

ܩܢܛܪܘܢܘܬܐ from ܩܢܛܪܘܢܐ. f. centurionship.

ܩܢܝܐ abs. st. ܩܢܐ pl. ܩܢܝܢ, ܩܢܝ̈ܐ m. pl. f. ܩܢܘܬܐ (rare) a) a cane, reed; rope of twisted rushes; ܗ̄ ܕܒܣܡܐ or ellipt. aromatic cane, sweet calamus. b) a reed pen, pen; ܕܦܪܙܠܐ a style. c) stalk, straw, halm of corn. d) shaft, branch, pipe of a candlestick. e) a measuring rod; a rod (measure of land). f) beam of a balance, balance; Libra, sign of the zodiac. g) the shoulder. h) ܩܢܝܐ ܕܪܐܬܐ the wind-pipe. i) virga virilis.

ܩܢܝܐ pl. ܐ̈ rt. ܩܢܐ. m. a possessor, owner, purchaser, rich man.

ܩܢܝܢܬܐ pl. ܬ̈ܐ rt. ܩܢܐ. f. a) purchase, property, possessions; ܟܬܒܐ ܕܗ̄ deed of purchase. b) habit, constitution, condition, state ܕܦܓܪܐ of the body, ܕܢܦܫܐ of the soul; ܩܢܝܢܬܐ ܒܝܫܬܐ ܕܚܘܠܡܢܐ bad state of health. c) gram. a noun signifying a quality or state as ܟܘܪܗܢܐ sickness, ܫܘܦܪܐ comeliness, ܟܐܢܘܬܐ righteousness.

ܩܢܝܛ, ܐ; see ܩܢܛ.

ܩܢܝܛܐܝܬ rt. ܩܢܛ. adv. *timidly*.

ܩܢܝܛܘܬܐ rt. ܩܢܛ. f. *timidity*.

ܩܢܝܢ, ܩܢܝܢܐ pl. ܐ̈ rt. ܩܢܐ. m. *possessions, landed property* opp. ܩܢܘܡܐ *money; substance, goods, chattels* esp. *cattle, beasts of burden*.

ܩܢܝܢܐܝܬ rt. ܩܢܐ. adv. *habitually*.

ܩܢܝܬܐ pl. ܩܢ̈ܝܬܐ rt. ܩܢܐ. f. *a*) *an image, puppet, female idol*. *b*) *a shoot, sucker*. *c*) *a band* of robbers.

ܩܢܟܐ or ܩܘܢܟܐ usually pl. ܐ̈ also ܩܢ̈ܟܐ m. κόγχη, *the apse, chancel* of a church, approached by steps and containing the bema with the altar. DERIVATIVES, ܩܢܟܝܐ, ܩܢܟܝܬܐ, and ܩܢܟܐ.

ܩܢܟܝܐ or ܝܐ pl. ܐ̈ m. *a sacristan*.

ܩܢܢܩܘܢ, ܩܘܢܢܩܘܢ and ܩܢ̈ m. a gem, *reddish amber, jacinth*.

ܩܢܡ denom. verb from ܩܢܘܡܐ. ETHPA. ܐܬܩܢܡ *to subsist, to be personified*.

ܩܢܣܐ *poll-tax, tribute*.

ܩܢܝܐ pl. *a*) of ܩܢܬܐ. *b*) *chick-peas*.

ܩܢܝܢܝܐ pl. ܐ̈ from ܩܢܝܐ. *reed-like, reed-shaped*.

ܩܢܝܣܩܐ, ܩܢܣ̈, ܩܢܝ̈ pl. ܐ̈ m. κανίσκιον, *a basket woven of reeds* esp. *a bread basket* for use in the temple.

ܩܢܐ fut. ܢܩܢܐ, part. ܩܢܐ *to turn blue, livid, pale*. Cf. ܩܢܐ II. and ܩܘܢܐ. ETHTAPH. ܐܬܬܩܢܐ *to become blue*. APH. ܐܩܢܐ *to turn blue, become blue*. DERIVATIVES, ܩܢܝܐ, ܩܢܝܢܝܐ, ܡܩܢܝܢܐ.

ܩܢܐ APH. ܐܩܢܐ *to invest with the veil* called ܡܩܢܝܬܐ. DERIVATIVES, ܩܢܝܐ, ܡܩܢܝܬܐ.

ܩܢܝܐ or ܩܘܢܝܐ pl. ܐ̈ rt. ܩܢܐ I. m. *a*) *isatis tinctoria, woad*. *b*) = ܩܢܒܐ.

ܩܢܝܢܝܐ rt. ܩܢܐ. m. *flower of the woad plant; indigo blue*.

ܩܢܒܐ, ܩܘܢܒܐ, ܩܢ̈, ܩܢ̈ m. *hemp*; ܙܪܥܐ ܕ *hemp-seed*.

ܩܘܢܨܠ Lat. and French consul, *consul*.

ܩܢܩܠ denom. verb PAEL conj. from ܩܢܩܠܐ. *to enclose*.

ܩܢܩܠܐ or ܩܢ̈ pl. ܐ̈ m. Lat. cancelli, *a lattice, grating, trellis-work;* a brass *railing* or *screen* outside the chancel door; *a barred prison; the barrier* of a racecourse.

ܩܢܩܠܪܐ m. Lat. cancellarius, *doorkeeper*.

ܩܢܩܢ denom. verb PALPEL conj. from ܩܢܬܐ. *to chant, sing*. ETHPALP. ܐܬܩܢܩܢ *to be chanted, sung*. DERIVATIVES, ܩܢܩܢܐ, ܩܢܩܘܢܐ.

ܩܢܪܘܣ, ܩܢܪ̈, ܩܐܪܝܢܐ, ܩܐܪܘܣ m. κρήνη -ας, *a well, tank, fountain*.

ܩܢܝܐ ܡܟܝܠܐ rarely ܩܢܡܟܝܠܐ = ܩܢܐ ܡܟܝܠܐ *an even rod* or *beam of a balance*, m. *Libra*, a sign of the zodiac.

ܩܢܬܐ f. pl. ܩܢ̈ܐ, ܩܢܝܐ m. *the split* or *cleft of a nut, a kernel*.

ܩܣܝܐ, ܩܣ̈ ܩܐܣ f. Lat. cassis, *a helmet*. ܩܣܝܐ ܘܩܡܚܐ in Job xxxviii. 29 for *hoar-frost*, in the Lexx. *snowy* or *severe weather, a gloomy hard sky*.

ܩܣܝܢ, ܩܣܝܢܐ *hairless, scabby, having hard dry and stiff skin, having scanty hair or wool from old sores not come to a head or from sickness*.

ܩܣܝܢܘܬܐ f. *dry scab, hard skin*.

ܩܣܘܣܐ m. *a wart, horny skin, withered skin*.

ܩܣܘܣܘܬܐ f. *induration, callosity, thickness of skin*.

ܩܣܘܣ; see ܩܣܘܣ.

ܩܣܘܬܐ (ܩܣܐ ؛) *sandal-wood*.

ܩܣܛܐ pl. ܐ̈ ξέστης, f. *a*) *a pint*. *b*) *a pot*.

ܩܣܛܘܢܪܐ, ܩܣ̈ pl. ܐ̈ m. Lat. quaestionarius, *a guard, a gaoler; a torturer, executioner*.

ܩܣܛܘܢܪܘܬܐ from the preceding word. f. *execution, office of an executioner*.

ܩܣܛܘܪ and ܩܐܣ̈ m. *a*) Lat. quaestor, Byzant. *a secretary*. *b*) κάστωρ, *the beaver*.

ܩܣܛܢܐ pl. ܐ̈ κάστανα, *a chestnut*.

ܩܣܛܪܐ, ܩܐܣ̈, ܩܣܛܪܘܢ, ܩܐܣܛܪܘܢ pl. ܩܣܛܪ̈ܘܢ m. Lat. castrum, *a castle, fort, fortress, fortified place*.

ܩܣܛܪܘܡܐ perh. κατάστρωμα, m. *a porch; the base* or *raised floor* of the altar; *the chancel steps*.

ܩܣܛܪܝܣ and ܩܣܛܪܝܣܝܘܣ καστρήσιος, an

official of the Byzantine court, *a quarter-master, lord chamberlain.*

ܩܰܣܺܝܳܐ, ܩܣܝܐ m. Lat. casia, *an aromatic bark.*

ܩܣܩܣܐ *a pitcher with handles.*

ܩܰܣܩܶܣ denom. verb Palpel conj. from ܩܣܩܣܐ. *to adorn, be an honour.* Pass. part. ܡܩܰܣܩܣ, ܡܩܰܣܩܣܳܐ, ـܬܳܐ; ܡܩܰܣܩܣ ܒܝܰܕܥܬܳܐ *adorned with knowledge.* Ethpa. ܐܶܬ݂ܩܰܣܩܰܣ *to be adorned.*

ܩܰܣܦܳܝܳܐ and ܩܣܦܝܐ pl. ـܝܶܐ *Caspian, a dweller by the Caspian Sea.*

ܩܣܦܝܘܢ *the Caspian Sea.*

ܩܶܣܰܪ, ܩܺܣܰܪ, ܩܶܐܣܰܪ, ܩܶܐܣܳܪ; ܩܶܣܰܪܐ pl. ܩܶܣܰܪܶܐ, ܩܶܣܰܪܶܣ, pr. n. and title, *Caesar, a Caesar* = next to the throne.

ܩܣܛܪܝܣ κίσσηρις, *pumice stone.*

ܩܶܣܰܪܝܰܐ *a*) pr. n. of a woman, *Caesaria.* *b*) also spelt ܩܶܣܰܪܝܳܐ, ܩܐܣܪܝܐ, ܩܐܣܪܝܐ, ܩܐܣܪܝܐ, ܩܣܪܝܐ, ܩܣܪܝܐ, ܩܣܪܝܢ, name of various cities, *Caesarea.*

ܩܶܣܰܪܝܳܝܳܐ, ܩܐܣܪܝܝܐ, ܩܐܣܪܝܐ from ܩܶܣܰܪܝܰܐ. adj. *of Caesarea.*

ܩܶܣܰܪܝܳܘܣ *a*) *a Caesar.* *b*) pr. n. *Caesarius.*

ܩܥܳܐ = ܩܥܳܐ, fut. ܢܶܩܥܶܐ, act. part. ܩܳܥܶܐ, ܩܳܥܝܳܐ. *a*) *to call, cry out, shout;* ܩܥܳܐ ܒܩܳܠܳܐ ܪܳܒܳܐ *he cried with a loud voice;* ܫܪܺܝܗ̇ ܕܩܳܥܝܳܐ ܒܳܬܰܪܰܢ *send her away for she crieth after us.* *b*) *to cry, scream,* as an eagle, *to crow, to bleat.* *c*) *to sound* ܒܫܺܝܦܘܪܶܐ *trumpets;* also ܩܳܥܝܳܐ ܩܰܪܢܳܐ *the trumpet sounds.* Ethpe. ܐܶܬ݂ܩܥܺܝ *to be applauded.* Pa. ܩܰܥܺܝ *to cry out* curses. Aph. ܐܰܩܥܺܝ *a*) *to make to cry out;* ܐܰܩܥܺܝ ܠܟܺܐܦܶܐ *it made the stones cry out.* *b*) *to proclaim,* or *aloud.* Derivatives, ܩܥܳܝܳܐ, ܩܥܳܬ݂ܳܐ.

ܩܦܰܕ fut. ܢܶܩܦܰܕ W-Syr. and ܩܦܰܕ fut. ܢܶܩܦܘܿܕ E-Syr. pass. part. ܩܦܺܝܕ, ܐ̈. *to bend* ܒܘܪ̈ܟܶܐ the knees, *to kneel;* ܟܰܕ ܩܳܦܶܕ ܐ̱ܢܳܫ ܕܢܨܰܠܶܐ *when a man kneels to pray;* ܥܰܠ ܚܕܳܐ ܒܘܪܟܶܗ ܩܦܺܝܕ *kneeling upon one knee.* Ethpa. ܐܶܬ݂ܩܰܦܰܕ *to kneel down.* Aph. ܐܰܩܦܶܕ *to make to kneel;* ܐܰܩܦܶܕ ܥܰܠ ܐܰܪܥܳܐ ܒܘܪ̈ܟܰܘܗ̱ܝ *he bent his knees on the earth.* Derivatives, ܩܦܳܕܳܐ, ܩܦܳܕܬܳܐ.

ܩܦܳܕܳܐ rt. ܩܦܕ. m. *genuflexion, kneeling.*

ܩܦܳܕܬܳܐ rt. ܩܦܕ. f. *genuflexion.*

ܩܳܥܘܿܝܳܐ rt. ܩܥܐ. m. *the crier, herald,* name of the constellation Bootes.

ܩܦܘܿܠܳܝܳܐ, ܩܦܘܿܠܳܝܬܳܐ *expansile, expanding* as the lungs.

ܩܦܺܝܠܬܳܐ pl. ـܠܳܬ݂ܳܐ f. *a plait, braid* of hair; *rope* or *wreath pattern; stones linked together* to form the top course of a wall.

ܩܦܺܝܠܳܐ m. *an iron stove, fire-basket.*

ܩܦܰܪ fut. ܢܶܩܦܘܿܪ, act. part. ܩܳܦܶܪ, pass. part. ܩܦܺܝܪܳܐ. *to shell.*

ܩܶܠܦܳܐ, ܩܠܳܦܬܳܐ pl. ܩܠܳܦܶܐ rt. ܩܠܦ. f. *a*) *an acorn-cup; an egg-shell.* *b*) *a weal, wale* from beating, *bump* or *roughness* of the skin from exposure to bad weather.

ܩܥܳܬ݂ܳܐ pl. ܩܥܳܬ݂ܳܐ, ܩܥܳܝܳܬ݂ܳܐ rt. ܩܥܐ. f. *crying, shouting, an outcry, clamour, applause; blast* of a trumpet.

ܩܘܿܦ imper. of verb ܢܩܦ. *to follow.*

ܩܦܳܐ fut. ܢܶܩܦܶܐ, act. part. ܩܳܦܶܐ, part. adj. ܩܦܺܐ, ـܝܳܐ, ـܝܳܬ݂ܳܐ. *to settle down, subside, condense; to keep quiet, to sit* on eggs, *brood;* ܩܦܰܘ ܬܗܘܡ̈ܶܐ *the deeps were congealed;* ܩܦܺܝ ܒܒܰܝܬ݂ܳܟ *keep quiet at home;* ܐܰܝܟ ܦܳܪܚܬܳܐ ܕܥܰܠ ܦܰܪ̈ܘܓܶܝܗ̇ *a mother-bird brooding over her young.* Pael ܩܰܦܺܝ *to brood over.* Palp. ܩܰܦܩܶܦ *to brood, sit* as a hen. Derivatives, ܩܘܦܳܐ, ܩܘܦܳܝܬܳܐ, ܩܦܳܐ.

ܩܦܳܐ fut. ܢܶܩܦܶܐ, act. part. ܩܳܦܶܐ, ܩܳܦܝܳܐ, pass. part. ܩܦܶܐ. *a*) *to collect, gather in heaps; to skim off;* ܥܘܠ̈ܠܶܐ ܡܺܝܬ݂ܶܐ ܩܦܶܝܢ ܐܰܝܟ ܩܰܡܨܶܐ ܥܰܠ ܣܶܦܬ݂ܶܗ ܕܢܰܗܪܳܐ dead *infants lay in heaps like locusts on the river bank;* ܪܽܘܩܳܐ ܕܩܳܦܶܐ ܥܰܠ ܣܶܦܘ̈ܳܬ݂ܶܗ froth *which had collected on his lips.* *b*) *to float* as scum on the water, as dead bodies. *c*) *to reach, attain, touch* ܠܡܺܐܢܳܐ *the haven;* ܥܰܠ ܫܘܢܺܝܬ݂ܳܐ ܩܦܺܝܬ݂ *I clung to the steep rock.* Ethpe. ܐܶܬ݂ܩܦܺܝ *a*) *to be dispersed* as a cloud. *b*) *to reach* port. Pa. ܩܰܦܺܝ *a*) *to skim off.* *b*) *to catch* insects as a bird. Derivatives, ܩܘܦܳܐ, ܩܦܳܐ.

ܩܳܦܳܐ = ܩܳܦܳܐ κάππα.

ܩܦܰܣ and ܩܦܰܣ an old form of preterite, fut. ܢܶܩܦܘܿܣ, act. part. ܩܳܦܶܣ. *a*) intr. *to bristle, to contract, shrink, creep* from fear; ܩܦܰܣ ܡܶܫܟܳܐ *my very skin crept;* ܩܦܰܣ ܦܰܓܪܰܝܗܘܢ ܒܕܶܚܠܬܳܐ *their bodies bristled with fear.* *b*) tr. *to contract, make to shrink, confine;* ܫܶܡܫܳܐ ܡܝܰܒܶܫ ܘܩܳܦܶܣ ܠܰܐܦܰܝ̈ ܐܰܪܥܳܐ *the sun dries up the surface of the earth and draws it into folds;* ܩܦܰܣܬ݂ ܐܶܢܳܐ ܠܗܰܘ̈ܢܳܐ *I have drawn to one* centre *this light* of the moon. Ethpe. ܐܬܩܦܕ *to be shortened, cut off* as ropes; *to be shrunk, shrivelled;* ܐܬܩܦܕ ܡܫܟܝܗܘܢ ܥܠ ܓܪܡܝܗܘܢ *their skin over their bones was shrivelled.*

ܩܘܦܕܐ from ܩܦܕ. m. *contraction into wrinkles, shrunkenness; bristling, stiffening* from terror.

ܩܦܕܩܝܐ, ܩܦܕܘܩܝܐ, ܩܦܘܕܩܝܐ, ܩܦܕܩܝܐ &c. f. pr. n. *Cappadocia.*

ܩܦܕܩܝܐ, ܩܦܕܘܩܝܐ, ܩܦܕܩܝܐ, ܩܦܕܩܝܐ &c. pl. ܐ̈ *a Cappadocian.*

ܩܦܘܠܐ rt. ܩܦܠ. m. *a locksmith.*

ܩܦܘܦܐ pl. ܐ̈ m. an unclean night-bird, perh. *a crow* or *an owl.*

ܩܦܘܪ and ܩܐܦܘܪ m. *camphor.*

ܩܦܘܪܐ = ܩܦܘܪܐ m. *hellebore.*

ܩܦܚ ܩܦܚ fut. ܢܩܦܘܚ, act. part. ܩܐܦܚ, ܩܦܚܐ, pass. part. ܩܦܝܚ, ܚܐ, ܚܬܐ. *to beat on the head, slap, buffet, subdue;* ܪܥܒܬܢܘܬܐ ܩܦܚܬܢܝ *greediness has subdued me;* ܩܦܝܚܐ ܦܐܝ *may my face be slapped!* Pa. ܩܦܚ. a) *to slap, cuff, buffet, beat, treat with insolence;* ܒܩܢܝܐ ܩܦܚܘܗܝ *they smote* Christ *with a reed;* ܩܦܚ ܦܓܪܗ ܒܢܛܘܪܘܬܐ ܕܡܐܟܘܠܬܐ *he buffeted his body with abstention from food;* ܟܕ ܡܩܦܚܝܢ ܐܐܪ ܒܪܫܐ ܕܓܦܝܗܘܢ birds *beating the air with the tips of their wings.* b) *to trample upon, insult, bring low, humiliate;* ܩܦܚܬܘܢ ܠܡܣܟܢܐ *ye have trampled down the poor;* ܩܦܚ ܟܠܗܘܢ ܡܥܕܝܢܐ ܕܛܘܥܝܝܢ *he trampled down all growths of error;* ܕܢܩܦܚ ܠܪܡܘܬܐ ܕܝܗܘܕܝܐ *that he might humiliate the pride of the Jews.* c) *to check, reprimand* with ܥܠ of the fault. d) *to press, repress, oppress; pain;* ܣܡܘ ܟܠܝܠܐ ܕܟܘܒܐ ܥܠ ܪܫܗ ܘܡܩܦܚܝܢ ܠܗ *the crown of thorns was set on His head and pressed down on Him;* ܣܒܐ ܡܩܦܚ ܒܫܢܝܐ *an old man oppressed with age;* ܚܫܐ ܠܐ ܡܩܦܚܢܐ *unrepressed passions.* Ethpa. ܐܬܩܦܚ *to be slapped, cuffed, insulted, to suffer indignities; to be oppressed, brought low; to be repressed, coerced.* Derivatives, ܩܦܚܐ, ܡܩܦܚܢܐ, ܡܩܦܚܢܘܬܐ.

ܩܦܙܐ m. *leaping, jumping.*

ܩܦܙܐ m. *a leaper.*

ܩܦܚ Pael conj. of verb ܩܦܠ.

ܩܦܬܐ m. *the hinder part* of the neck, *vertebrae* of the neck.

ܩܦܝܐ or ܩܦܝܐ rt. ܩܦܐ. m. *a heap of rubbish, flotsam,* esp. *loose substances gathered from the surface of the water.*

ܩܦܝܙܐ m. a measure equalling about 48 bushels, *an ass-load.*

ܩܦܝܚܘܬܐ f. *a long strip of black* or *dark red silk two spans wide and seven ells long worn twisted round the head by women.*

ܩܦܝܛܘܠ, ܩܦܝܛܘܠܝܘܢ, ܩܦܛܘܠܝܘܢ, ܩܦܝܛܘܠܝܘܢ pl. ܩܦܝܛܘܠܝܢ m. *the Capitol, temple of Jupiter.*

ܩܦܝܠܐ pl. ܐ̈ m. a) κάπηλος, *a tavern-keeper, petty tradesman, huckster;* ܒܝܬ ܩ̈ *a tavern.* b) = ܩܦܝܠܐ and ܡܥܦܪܐ *a pall* or *cloak* worn by the Patriarch (E-Syr.). c) pass. part. of verb ܩܦܠ.

ܩܦܠܘܢ, ܩܦܠܝ, ܩܦܠܘܬܐ from καπηλεῦσαι, with ܥܒܕ *to adulterate, debase, corrupt.*

ܩܦܝܠܘܬܐ from ܩܦܝܠܐ. f. *huckstering, adulterating.*

ܩܦܝܠܘܬܐ rt. ܩܦܠ. f. *destruction.*

ܩܦܝܠܐ, ܠܬܐ from ܩܦܝܠܐ. *adulterated;* with ܠܐ *uncorrupt, genuine.*

ܩܦܠܢܘܬܐ *doing, business, stir.*

ܩܦܝܣܐܝܬ rt. ܩܦܣ. adv. *succinctly, briefly, compendiously.*

ܩܦܝܣܘܬܐ rt. ܩܦܣ. f. *relaxation, contraction; conciseness,* ܒܩܦܝܣܘܬ *concisely, in a shortened form.*

ܩܦܠ ܩܦܠ fut. ܢܩܦܘܠ, act. part. ܩܐܦܠ, ܩܦܠܐ, pass. part. ܩܦܝܠ, ܠܐ. *to strip, lay bare* walls; *to roll away* a veil, curtain; *to take off* or *away* ܡܘܒܠܐ *a burden,* ܐܬܟܣܝܬܐ *a covering; to remove, dispel* ܥܡܛܢܐ *darkness,* ܥܩܬܐ *distress.* Ethpe. ܐܬܩܦܠ a) *to be rubbed, peeled, torn off;* ܐܬܩܦܠ ܗܘܐ ܨܘܪܐ ܡܢ ܫܘܪܐ the painting *peeled off the wall;* ܩܝܣܐ ܡܬܩܦܠܝܢ *woods are torn up.* b) *to be drawn back, rolled aside;* ܡܬܩܦܠ ܪܩܝܥܐ ܐܝܟ ܬܢܝܬܐ *the firmament is rolled up like a curtain;* ܠܐ ܐܬܩܦܠܘ ܓܢܘܗܝܗܘܢ *their bridal chambers were not unveiled.* c) *to be dispelled, dissipated* as darkness, sadness. d) gram. *to be elided.*

Ethpa. ܐܬܩܦܠ a) *to be exterminated, done away with* as a dynasty. b) *to be rolled away, dispelled* as darkness. Aph. ܐܩܦܠ *to roll* or *fold up; to uncover.* Derivatives, ܩܦܠܐ, ܡܩܦܠܢܘܬܐ, ܩܦܠܐ, ܩܦܠܐ, ܩܦܠܐ, ܡܬܩܦܠܢܘܬܐ.

ܩܦܠܐ pl. ܐ̈ rt. ܩܦܠ. m. a) *an inmost recess, inner chamber, retreat, nook, secret corner, secret.* b) *anything laid up, stored away, a layer, treasure.*

ܩܦܠܐ or ܩܦܠܐ pl. ܐ̈ m. *a fillet, turban.*

ܩܘܦܠܐ pl. ܐ̈ m. a) *an armful, sheaf.* b) Ar. *a caravan.*

ܩܦܠܐ rt. ܩܦܠ. m. *stripping, tearing off.*

ܩܦܠܐ pl. ܐ̈, ܩܦܠܐ and ܩܦܠܐܣ m. κεφαλή, *a chapter.*

ܩܦܠܐܘܢ, ܩܦܠܐܘܢ, ܩܦܠܐ, ܩܦܠܐ, ܩܦܠܐܘܢ &c. pl. ܩܦ̈ܠܐܐ, ܩܦܠܐܐ &c. m. κεφάλαιον. a) *a chapter,* = Syr. ܪܝܫܐ. b) *a sum* of money.

ܩܦܠܘܛܐ pl. ܐ̈ κεφαλωτός. a) *a large-headed nail.* b) *a leek with a large head.*

ܩܦܠܡܣܐ pl. m. *bee-food made of raisins and thyme kneaded together.*

ܩܦܠܝܣ pl. ܐ̈ κεφαλίς -ίδα, *the capital* or *chapiter* of a pillar.

ܩܦܠܩܠܐ pl. ܐ̈ perhaps from κεφαλή. m. *a many-headed thing;* ܛ ܦܬܟܪܘܬܐ *many-headed idolatry.*

ܩܦܣ fut. ܢܩܦܘܣ, act. part. ܩܐܦܣ, ܩܐܦܣܐ, pass. part. ܩܦܝܣ, ܐ, ܬܐ. a) *to contract* the muscles; with ܝܕܐ *to close the hand, to desist; to draw back, hold in check, restrain;* ܩܦܘܣ ܐܝܕܟ *stay thine hand;* ܩܦܣ ܕܐܝܕܗ ܐܝܢܐ ܕܩܦܣ ܐܝܕܗ ܡܢ ܡܚܘܬܐ ܘܠܫܢܗ ܡܢ ܡܐܟܠ ܩܪܨܐ *one who restrains his hand from striking and his tongue from backbiting;* ܩܦܣ ܠܓܠܠܐ *He checked the waves.* b) *to bring close together, to lay by, store;* ܩܦܣ ܐܢܘܢ ܒܓܙܐ *he laid them in the treasury;* ܩܦܣ ܐܢܐ ܠܟ ܠܘܬ ܐܒܗܝܟ *I will gather thee to thy fathers.* c) *to take up, compose* the body for burial. d) *to shorten; to put shortly, say briefly;* ܩܦܣ ܐܘܪܟܗ *he made it short;* ܩܦܣ ܘܡܨܥܪ ܐܘܪܟܐ ܕܙܒܢܐ *He shortens and reduces the length of the time;* ܩܦܣ ܠܗ ܫܢܝܟ the angel of death *cuts short your life;* ܐܘܪܟܐ ܕܡܠܬܐ ܢܩܦܘܣ *let him avoid prolixity.* e) (rare) *to withdraw, remove.* f) intrans. *to restrain oneself, be self-contained, recollected; to contract;* of flowers, *to droop;* ܩܦܣ ܡܢ ܕܚܠܬܐ *it shrank from fear;* ܪܘܚܐ ܩܦܣܝܢ ܒܥܘܒܝܗܘܢ *winds stay quiet in their bosoms.* Pass. part. *contracted, brief, abbreviated; recollected;* ܛ ܠܡܬܠ *chary of giving, close;* ܬܪܥܝܬܐ ܩܦܝܣܬܐ *a restrained mind.* Ethpe. ܐܬܩܦܣ *to be drawn together, to be gathered* to the grave; *to be withdrawn, to stay* as troops from pursuing; *to draw in, be withdrawn* as light in the evening; *to recede* as the sea; ܐܬܩܦܣܬ ܐܝܕܗ *his hand was stayed* = *his power was checked.* Ethpa. ܐܬܩܦܣ *to be withdrawn, withheld; to be restrained; to draw* or *shrink back.* Aph. ܐܩܦܣ *to gather up, store; to withdraw, do away with.* Derivatives, ܩܦܣܐ c, ܡܩܦܣܢܐ, ܡܩܦܣܢܘܬܐ, ܩܦܣܐ, ܩܦܣܐ, ܡܩܦܣܢܐ, ܡܩܦܣܐ.

ܩܦܣ Aph. ܐܩܦܣ denom. verb from ܦܣܦܣܐ *to lay tesserae, make a tessellated pavement.*

ܩܦܣܐ m. *a birdcage; a basket.*

ܩܘܦܣܐ or ܩܦܣܐ pl. ܐ̈ rt. ܩܦܣ. m. *the inner bend of the knee-joint, the ham, haunch.*

ܩܦܣܐ and ܩܦܣܐ pl. ܐ̈ rt. ܩܦܣ. m. a) *contraction; a spasm, convulsion;* ܛ ܟܠܒܝܐ *canine convulsions = distortion of one side of the face.* b) *a store;* ܒܝܬ ܩܦܣܐ *a storehouse, barn, magazine.*

ܩܦܣܢܝܐ rt. ܩܦܣ. *convulsive.*

ܩܦܣܩܝܣ transliteration of καψάκης, *a cruse.*

ܩܦܩܦ Pael conj. of ܩܦ.

ܩܦܩܦܐ rt. ܩܦ. m. *incubation, brooding.*

ܩܦܩܦ Palpel conj. of ܩܦ.

ܩܦܪ denom. verb Pael conj. from ܩܘܦܪܐ. *to pitch, cover with pitch.*

ܩܦܪ m. *capparis spinosa, the caper.*

ܩܦܪܐ pl. ܐ̈ m. κάπρος, *the wild boar.*

ܩܦܪܐ m. *lawsonia inermis, the henna plant; pitch, bitumen.*

ܩܨ fut. ܢܩܘܨ and ܢܩܨ, act. part. ܩܐܨ, pass. part. ܩܝܨ, ܐ, ܬܐ. a) *to agree, make an agreement* with ܥܡ, ܠ or ܠܘܬ of the pers.

with ܒ, ܡܢ or acc. of the payment; with ܕܡܝܐ or ܦܘܪܩܢܐ *to settle a price, a ransom, value at so much;* ܡܕܐܬܐ ܩܨ *to impose a tribute;* ܦܪܢܝܬܐ *to make marriage settlements;* ܩܨ ܥܡܗܘܢ ܒܕܝܢܪܐ *he agreed with them for a penny;* ܠܐ ܬܩܘܨ ܠܢ ܚܛܗܝܢ ܩܕܡܝܐ *reckon not against us our former sins.* Also *to reckon, take into account* pain or penitence, hence *to acquit, excuse, pardon.* *b*) *to cut short, clip* the wings, the beard; ܩܨܝܨܝ ܕܩܢܐ *clipped-beards.* Ethpe. ܐܬܩܨ *a*) *to be reckoned, imputed* as sin. *b*) *to be stipulated, made a condition.* *c*) *to be clipped, docked.* Pa. ܩܨܨ *to cut off, hack, to pare* the nails, *clip* wings, *clip, trim* a beard. Ethpa. ܐܬܩܨܨ *to be reckoned, credited, creditable.* Aph. ܐܩܨ *to reckon against a debt, take into consideration; to repay, requite;* ܐܩܨ ܠܝ ܡܪܝ ܫܘܢܩܐ ܕܐܬܝܗܒܘ ܠܝ ܥܠ ܟܠ ܕܣܟܠܬ *reckon, O Lord, the torments inflicted on me against all that I have done wrong;* ܡܬܩܨ ܠܗ ܠܟܠܢܫ ܕܫܘܠܡܗ *his deserts are requited to every man;* ܚܛܝܢ ܠܟ ܠܐ ܬܐܩܨ ܠܢ *we have sinned against thee, reckon it not against us.* Derivatives, ܩܨܐ, ܩܨܬܐ, ܩܨܝܨܘܬܐ, ܩܨܨܐ, ܩܨܝܢܐ, ܩܨܝܨܘܬܐ, ܩܨܘܨܐ, ܡܩܨܢܘܬܐ.

ܩܨ, ܩܨܐ and ܩܨܬܐ rt. ܩܨ. m. *cutting off, end,* ܩܨܐ ܕܕܢܐ—ܕܚܨܒܬܐ *the* pointed *end of a wine-jar, bottom of a cask.* Esp. *the end* of life; ܩܨܐ ܕܫܘܠܡܐ *the final dissolution.* Adv. ܠܩܨ *to the end, for the sake of;* ܡܛܠ ܩܨ *because.*

ܩܨܐ fut. ܢܩܨܐ, act. part. ܩܨܐ, ܩܨܝܐ, pass. part. ܩܨܐ, ܩܨܝܐ, ܩܨܝܬܐ. *to break* bread, esp. at the Holy Communion, hence also *to celebrate;* ܬܩܨܐ ܠܟܦܢܐ ܠܚܡܟ *thou shalt break thy bread for the hungry;* ܩܨܐ ܘܪܫܡ ܐܪܙܐ *he breaks and signs the mysteries.* Ethpe. ܐܬܩܨܝ *a*) *to be broken;* ܗܢܘ ܦܓܪܝ ܕܥܠܝܟܘܢ ܡܬܩܨܐ *this is My body which is broken for you.* *b*) rarely = ܐܬܩܨܨ probably by mistake. Pa. ܩܨܝ *to break* bread. Ethpa. ܐܬܩܨܝ pass. of Pael. Derivatives, ܩܨܝܐ, ܩܨܬܐ, ܩܨܘܬܐ, ܩܨܝܬܐ, ܩܨܘܢ.

ܩܨܒܐ Ar. m. *a butcher.*

ܩܨܘܡܐ pl. ܐ̈ rt. ܩܨܡ. m. *a diviner, soothsayer; a bard.*

ܩܨܘܡܘܬܐ rt. ܩܨܡ. f. *augury, divination, soothsaying.*

ܩܨܘܡܬܐ pl. ܬܐ̈ fem. of ܩܨܘܡܐ. usually *a woman delivering oracles by ventriloquism.*

ܩܨܝܐ pl. ܐ̈ rt. ܩܨ. m. *a*) *a contract, a norm, settled standard.* *b*) *a maggot.*

ܩܨܝ, ܩܨܝܐ pl. ܐ̈ rt. ܩܨܐ. m. *a*) *breaking* esp. *the breaking of bread* at the Holy Eucharist. *b*) *a morsel* of bread, *a broken piece; a particle* of consecrated bread.

ܩܨܬܐ E-Syr. ܩܨܬܐ rt. ܩܨܐ. m. *a morsel, piece, crust* of bread.

ܩܨܝܬܐ, ܩܨܝܬܐ rt. ܩܨܐ. f. *the action of breaking* of bread.

ܩܨܘܬܐ rt. ܩܨܐ. f. *a morsel, scrap.*

ܩܨܝܥܐ pl. ܐ̈ rt. ܩܨܥ. m. *a*) *an empty eggshell, eggshell after hatching out.* *b*) *fine,* as linen.

ܩܨܝܥܘܬܐ rt. ܩܨܥ. f. *an eggshell; thinness, fine cloth.*

ܩܨܝܨ, ܬܐ, ܬܐ; see ܩܨ.

ܩܨܝܨܘܬܐ rt. ܩܨ. f. *clipping, paring.*

ܩܨܡ fut. ܢܩܨܘܡ, act. part. ܩܨܡ, ܩܨܡܐ. *to divine, use divinations, consult an oracle;* ܩܨܘܡ ܠܝ *divine for me;* ܠܡܩܨܡ ܠܡܠܟܬܐ *to divine for the queen;* ܩܨܡ ܒܓܕܐ *an observer of omens;* ܩܨܡ ܒܡܝܬܐ *a necromancer;* ܕܩܨܡܢ ܡܢ ܟܪܣܐ *women ventriloquists.* Ethpe. ܐܬܩܨܡ *to divine, presage.* Pa. ܩܨܡ *to give signs or omens.* Derivatives, ܩܨܘܡܐ, ܩܨܘܡܘܬܐ, ܩܨܘܡܬܐ, ܩܨܡܐ, ܩܨܡܐ.

ܩܨܡܐ pl. ܐ̈ rt. ܩܨܡ. m. *an augur, diviner.*

ܩܨܡܐ pl. ܐ̈ rt. ܩܨܡ. m. *a*) *divination; an omen, oracle.* *b*) *a piece of barley bread used for divination.* *c*) *barley meal, millet* or *vetch flour.* *d*) = ܩܛܡܐ *soot.*

ܩܨܡܢܐ m. *smoke from a stove.*

ܩܨܝܢܐ, ܩܨܝܢܬܐ rt. ܩܨ. *last, final.*

ܩܨܦ *to rout.* Ethpe. ܐܬܩܨܦ *to be shattered, routed.* Derivative, ܩܨܦܐ.

ܩܨܦܐ rt. ܩܨܦ. m. *wrinkling into folds; breaking into many pieces.*

ܩܪܦ and ܩܪܦ, fut. ܢܩܪܘܦ, act. part. ܩܳܪܶܦ, ܩܳܪܦܳܐ, part. adj. ܩܪܝܦ, ܐ̈, ܬܐ. *to grudge, to be jealous; to be sad, irritated; to dread, be anxious, worried, to take amiss, take it ill;* ܩܪܦܘ ܘܠܐ ܣܢܝܘ ܠܫܠܡܐ *they were jealous and hostile to peace;* ܠܐ ܩܪܦ ܒܡܠܘܗܝ *he did not take his words amiss;* ܠܐ ܩܪܦܬ ܠܗ ܒܗܕܐ *he was not annoyed, disheartened, by this.* Part. adj. *a) sad, worried, anxious;* ܟܘܡܪܐ ܩܪܝܦܐ *an irritable* or *angry sore. b) shelled, skinned;* cf. ܩܪܝܦܐ above. Ethpe. ܐܬܩܪܦ *to be sadly, poorly.* Pa. ܩܪܦ pass. part. ܡܩܪܦܐ *sad, anxious.* Ethpa. ܐܬܩܪܦ *a) to be vexed, take it ill. b) to be mean, grudging.* Aph. ܐܩܪܦ *to grieve, to grudge.* Derivatives, ܩܘܪܦܐ, ܩܪܝܦܐ, ܩܪܝܦܘܬܐ, ܩܪܦܐ.

ܩܘܪܦܐ rt. ܩܪܦ. m. *jealousy, grudging, meanness; sadness, anxiety.*

ܩܘܪܦܐ pl. ܐ̈ m. = ܩܘܦܦܐ.

ܩܪܦܐ rt. ܩܪܦ. m. *an agreement, contract, bargain; prepayment, discount.*

ܩܪܦܝܬܐ rt. ܩܪܦ. f. pl. *clippings, parings, shreds.*

ܩܨܪ fut. ܢܩܨܘܪ, act. part. ܩܳܨܰܪ, ܩܳܨܪܳܐ, pass. part. ܩܨܝܪܐ. *to scour, full* cloth. P. p. *a) scoured. b) sick.* Pa. ܩܨܪ *to full;* ܦܶܠܓܬܐ ܠܐ ܡܩܨܪܬܐ *a piece of unfulled cloth.* Ethpa. ܐܬܩܨܪ *to be purged* ܡܢ ܬܢܢܐ ܣܘܟܡܐ *from smokiness; to be thickened, condensed.* Derivatives, ܩܨܪܐ, ܩܨܪܐ, ܩܨܘܪܘܬܐ.

ܩܨܪܐ Ar. m. *a fortress.*

ܩܨܪܐ pl. ܐ̈ rt. ܩܨܪ. m. *a fuller.*

ܩܨܪܐ and ܩܨܪܐ pl. ܐ̈ m. *husk of a grain of wheat, knot, joint* in a straw, *piece of straw.*

ܩܨܪܐ rt. ܩܨܪ. m. *fulling, bleaching, scouring.*

ܩܨܘܪܘܬܐ rt. ܩܨܪ. f. *fulling.*

ܩܨܬ construct state of ܩܨܬܐ, ܡܛܠ ܩܨܬ. adv. *on account of.*

ܩܨܬܐ rt. ܩܨ. f. *extremity, outskirt.*

ܩܨܬܐ rt. ܩܨܐ. f. *the breaking of bread, a broken portion;* esp. *the bread to be consecrated for Holy Communion, the Holy Eucharist.*

ܩܩܐ m. *the pelican.*

ܩܩܐ κάκη, *bad.*

ܩܩܒܐ pl. ܐ̈ m. κακκάβη, *a three-legged pot, caldron.*

ܩܩܒܢܐ, ܐ and ܐ pl. ܐ̈ m. κακκάβη, *a partridge.*

ܩܩܘܢ m. *the jerboa, jumping mouse.*

ܩܩܘܡܐ, ܩܩܘܡܐ or ܩܩܘܡܐ m. *a glass flask.*

ܩܩܘܠ, ܩܩܘܠ and ܩܩܒܘܠ m. *mimosa nilotica, the acacia-tree.*

ܩܩܘܠܐ m. *salsola fruticosa.*

ܩܩܘܠܐ m. *cardamom.*

ܩܩܒܢܐ = ܩܩܘܢܐ.

ܩܩܘܬܐ f. *a cup, goblet.*

ܩܩܒܬܐ; see ܩܩܒܬܐ.

ܩܩܢܐ; see ܩܩܢܐ.

ܩܪ abbreviation for ܩܪܝܪܐ *cooling,* as a drug.

ܩܪ fut. ܢܩܪ and ܢܐܩܪ, act. part. ܩܐܪ, ܩܪܐ, part. adj. ܩܪܝܪ, ܐ, ܬܐ. *to grow cold, to cool;* ܩܪ ܪܚܡܘܬܗ *his friendship cooled;* ܟܕ ܩܪ ܝܘܡܐ *when the day grew cool.* Part. adj. *cool, cold;* ellipt. m. *dough before fermentation has made it warm,* m. pl. *cold water;* ܠܐ ܨܗܐ ܠܩܪܝܪܐ *he does not thirst for cold water;* f. emph. *cold fit* of ague, *a chill.* Aph. ܐܩܪ part. ܡܩܪ or ܡܩܐܪ, ܡܩܪܐ. *to cool; to put out* fire; *to dry* as the wind. Pauel ܩܘܪܪ *to cool; to become cool.* Ethpau. ܐܬܩܘܪܪ *to cool, grow cold.* Derivatives, ܩܪܐ, ܩܘܪܐ, ܩܘܪܪܐ, ܩܪܝܪܐ, ܩܪܝܪܘܬܐ, ܩܪܝܪܐ, ܩܪܝܪܘܬܐ, ܩܪܘܪܐ and ܡܩܪܪܢܐ, ܡܩܪܢܐ, ܡܩܪܢܘܬܐ, ܡܩܘܪܪܢܘܬܐ.

ܩܪܐ and ܩܪܝ fut. ܢܩܪܐ, act. part. ܩܪܐ, ܩܪܝܐ, pass. part. ܩܪܐ, ܩܪܝܐ, ܩܪܝܬܐ, pl. ܩܪܝܢ, ܩܪܝܐ, ܩܪܝܬܐ, *a) to call, invoke, to summon, invite; to proclaim, pronounce; to call to be bishop, to designate;* ܠܫܡܐ ܩܪܐ ܕܡܪܝܐ *to call on the name of the Lord;* ܩܪܐ ܠܬܠܡܝܕܘܗܝ *He called His disciples* unto Him; ܐܝܟܐ ܕܩܪܝܬܐ ܚܦܝܛܬܐ *where there is an urgent call. b) to crow, to croak. c) to read, recite; to study.* With ܩܕܡ *to appeal;* ܠܣܗܕܘܬܐ *to call to witness;* ܩܪܝܢܐ *to read the lesson;* ܒܩܪܢܐ—ܒܫܝܦܘܪܐ *to sound a horn, a trumpet;* ܫܠܡܐ *to proclaim peace;* ܫܠܡܐ *to salute;* ܡܠܟ *to proclaim, acknowledge* a ruler. Act. part. ܩܪܝܐ *a reader;* ܩܪܝ ܒܫܝܦܘܪܐ *trumpeters.* Pass. part. ܩܪܝܐ ܝܘܡܐ ܩܪܝܐ *a festal day;* ܝܘܡܐ ܩܪܐ

ܩܪܝܬܐ ܩܕܝܫܬܐ *a holy convocation;* ܩܪܝܐ ܘܩܕܝܫܐ *called and holy;* ܩܪܝܐ ܘܡܦܪܝܢܐ Maphrian *designate of the East.* Ethpe. ܐܬܩܪܝ *a) to be called, named;* ܡܬܩܪܐ ܫܡܐ ܥܠ *= it is called by the name of . . ., to be invoked; to be cited, summoned; to be called, elected* to the episcopate. *b) to be sounded,* of a trumpet. *c) to be read, recited, explained. d) to contend, fight doggedly.* Aph. ܐܩܪܝ *a) to have* any one *called, to summon; to make to read. b) to provoke, dispute.* Taphel ܬܩܪܝ *to read.* Ethtaph. ܐܬܬܩܪܝ *to oppose.* Derivatives, ܩܪܘܝܐ, ܩܪܝܘܬܐ, ܩܪܝܢܐ, ܩܪܝܬܐ, ܩܪܝܢܘܬܐ, ܩܪܝܒܐ, ܩܪܝܬܐ, ܩܪܐ, ܩܪܝܐ, ܩܪܝܐ, ܩܪܝܢܐ, ܡܩܪܝܢܐ, ܡܩܪܝ, ܡܩܪܝܢܐ, ܬܩܪܝܢܐ.

ܩܪܝܐ, ܩܪܝܬܐ constr. st. ܩܪܝܬ and ܩܘܪܝܬ, pl. ܩܘܪܝܢ, ܩܘܪܝܬܐ, and an ancient form of broken plural, ܩܘܪܝܐ also ܩܘܪܝܬܗܘܢ, ܩܘܪܝܗ f. *a town; a village, hamlet, district, a field, farm;* ܡܪܝ ܩܘܪܝܐ *landed proprietors, village masters;* ܩܘܪܝܬܐ ܕܩܘܕܫܐ *the holy city,* Jerusalem. Derivatives, ܩܘܪܝܢܐ, ܩܘܪܝܝܘܬܐ, ܩܪܝܬܢܝܘܬܐ.

ܩܪܐ pl. ܐ̈ m. *a gourd;* with pron. suff. ܩܪܐܗ or ܩܪܐܗ ܕܝܘܢܢ *Jonah's gourd.*

ܩܪܒ fut. ܢܩܪܘܒ, act. part. ܩܪܒ, ܩܪܒܐ, part. adj. ܩܪܝܒ see below. *to come near, draw nigh,* with ܒ, ܠܘܬ, ܥܠ, ܩܕܡ; *to touch; to come near, touch* a woman; ܩܪܘܒ ܠܗܪܟܐ *come hither.* Adv. use: *nigh, at hand, nearly;* ܩܪܒ ܠܡܫܬܠܡܘ ܗܘܐ *it was nearly completed.* Pa. ܩܪܒ *a) to bring, take, carry, lay near, apply,* ܢܩܪܒܝܘܗܝ ܡܪܗ ܠܘܬ ܕܝܢܐ *his master shall bring him before the judge;* ܩܪܒܘ ܐܠܦܝܗܘܢ ܠܝܒܫܐ *they brought their ships to land;* ܩܪܒ ܣܡܡܢܐ *he applied remedies. b) to offer* ܕܒܚܐ *sacrifice, to present* ܩܘܪܒܢܐ *an offering, gift, oblation;* metaph. *to offer* ܒܥܘܬܐ *supplication,* ܡܠܐ *remarks,* ܡܠܟܐ *advice;* with ܡܪܢܝܬܐ *to reprove;* ܬܝܒܘܬܐ *to show penitence. c)* esp. *to offer* the oblation, mass, *to celebrate* the liturgy with ܩܘܪܒܢܐ or absol. ܗܘ ܗܘ ܕܡܩܪܒ *the celebrant.* Ethpa. ܐܬܩܪܒ *a) to be brought near, come near, approach, touch;* ܠܐ ܬܬܩܪܒܘܢ ܒܗ *neither shall ye touch it;* ܚܝܠܐ ܕܐܬܩܪܒ ܠܒܗܘܢ ܐܠܗܐ *the host whose heart God had touched;* ܐܬܩܪܒܬ ܡܢ ܒܣܬܪܗ *she came behind him;* ܐܬܩܪܒ ܙܒܢܐ *the time had come. b) to go in* to a woman. *c) to attain to, apply oneself, betake oneself;* ܐܬܩܪܒ ܠܥܒܕܐ ܕܬܝܒܘܬܐ *he applied himself to works of repentance. d) to be offered up* as a sacrifice; *to be celebrated* as the Liturgy; *to be communicated, receive* Holy Communion; ܟܠ ܡܢ ܕܠܐ ܡܬܩܪܒ ܥܡܝ *whoso will not communicate with me. e) to seize, come at* a fort. Aph. ܐܩܪܒ *to join battle, to make war, fight,* with ܥܡ ,ܠܘܩܒܠ; with ܥܠ *to attack, besiege;* ܠܡܩܪܒܘ ܩܪܒܐ *to draw nigh to battle;* ܡܩܪܒ ܠܘܩܒܠ ܢܡܘܣܐ ܕܪܥܝܢܝ *warring against the law of my mind.* Ethtaph. ܐܬܬܩܪܒ *to be attacked;* ܩܪܒܐ ܢܬܬܩܪܒ *war shall be made;* ܢܬܬܩܪܒ ܒܫܝܢܐ *he will be assailed by annoyances.* Derivatives, ܩܘܪܒܐ, ܩܪܒܐ, ܩܪܒܬܢܐ, ܩܪܝܒܐ, ܩܪܒܐ, ܩܘܪܒܢܐ, ܩܘܪܒܢܐ, ܩܪܝܒܐ, ܩܪܝܒܘܬܐ, ܩܪܒܬܢܘܬܐ, ܩܪܒܬܢܝܬ, ܩܪܝܒܘܬܐ, ܩܪܝܒܐ, ܩܪܝܒ, ܩܘܪܒܐ, ܡܩܪܒܢܐ, ܡܩܪܒܢܘܬܐ, ܡܩܪܒܢܝܬ, ܡܩܪܒܢܐ, ܬܩܪܘܒܬܐ, ܬܩܪܘܒܐ, ܡܬܩܪܒܢܘܬܐ, ܡܬܩܪܒܢܐ, ܬܬܩܪܒܢܘܬܐ.

ܩܪܒܐ pl. ܐ̈ rt. ܩܪܒ. m. *a) nearness. b) war, battle;* ܙܝܢܝ ܩܪܒܐ *weapons of war;* construed with ܥܠ *an attack, siege. c)* ܩܪܒܐ pl. of ܩܪܒܢ.

ܩܪܒܘܢܐ m. Lat. carbo, *coal.*

ܩܪܒܝܐ pl. ܐ̈ rt. ܩܪܒ. *of war, military.*

ܩܪܒܝܢ pl. ܩܪܒܝܢܐ and ܩܪܒܐ m. *a ship's boat, skiff, dingey.*

ܩܪܒܬܢܐ, ܩܪܒܬܢܝ pl. ܐ̈ rt. ܩܪܒ. *a) warlike, brave; pugnacious, contentious. b) a man of war, warrior.*

ܩܪܒܬܢܐܝܬ rt. ܩܪܒ. adv. *warlike.*

ܩܪܒܬܢܘܬܐ rt. ܩܪܒ. f. *bravery, warlike strength.*

ܩܪܒܬܢܝܐ rt. ܩܪܒ. *military, valiant.*

ܩܪܕܐ or ܩܪܕܐ pl. ܐ̈ m. *ricinus communis, the castor oil* plant.

ܩܪܕܐ pl. ܐ̈ m. *a tick, louse* (parasite of sheep and cattle).

ܩܪܕܘ *the Kurds.*

ܩܪܕܘܝܐ and ܩܘܪܕܝܐ pl. ܐ̈ m. ܩܪܕܘܝܬܐ f. *a Kurd.*

ܩܪܕܘܢܐ dimin. of ܩܪܕܐ. m. *a louse, nit.*

ܩܪܕܚ Parel conj. from ܩܕܚ. *to cuff, cudgel, knock on the head.* Ethparel ܐܬܩܪܕܚ *to be made*, as glass. DERIVATIVES, ܩܪܘܙܐ, ܩܪܘܙܘܬܐ, ܩܪܘܙܘܬܐ.

ܩܪܙܝܐ pl. ܐ̈ *an artisan, smith*, esp. *one who makes small articles* opp. ܢܦܚܐ *a blacksmith.*

ܩܪܙܝܘܬܐ rt. ܩܪܙ. f. *working in iron; handicraft.*

ܩܪܕܠܝ κερδαλέη, m. *a fox.*

ܩܪܕܠܝܐ κερδαλέος, *craftily, cunningly.*

ܩܪܕܠܐ pl. ܐ̈ perh. corrupted from Lat. calidarium. usually m. *a large hanging pot, a pot* used to cook meat offered in sacrifice.

ܩܪܕܘܡܐ *hashed meat roasted with onions and eggs.*

ܩܪܘܒܐ pl. ܐ̈ rt. ܩܪܒ. m. *a communicant.*

ܩܪܘܒܐ rt. ܩܪܒ. m. *presentation, preferring* of a petition, charge, accusation.

ܩܪܘܛܝ κηρωτή, med. *a cerate* or *salve.*

ܩܪܘܛܐ m. in the Lexx. *ink.*

ܩܪܘܛܐ rt. ܩܪܛ. m. *a chisel, graving-tool, pencil.*

ܩܪܘܝܐ pl. ܐ̈ rt. ܩܪܐ. m. *a reader, reciter*, esp. *a reader* in church, one of the lower ecclesiastical orders.

ܩܪܘܝܐ, ܝܬܐ rt. ܩܪܐ. gram. *vocative.*

ܩܪܘܝܘܬܐ rt. ܩܪܐ. f. *a*) *calling by name, naming.* *b*) *readership, office of a reader.*

ܩܪܘܝܬܐ rt. ܩܪܐ. f. eccles. *a*) *a letter.* *b*) *a reading-desk, lectern.*

ܩܪܘܟܐ pl. ܐ̈ m. Lat. carruca, *a two-horse chariot.*

ܩܪܘܡܚܐ *having the eyebrows meeting.*

ܩܪܘܢܐ pl. ܐ̈ κορώνη, m. *a*) *a crow, jackdaw, magpie.* *b*) *a door-handle, bolt.*

ܩܪܘܢܝܬܐ pl. ܝܬܐ f. *a cruse with a handle and a curved spout*, used for oil or wine.

ܩܪܘܣܛܠܠܘܣ, ܩܪܘܣܛܠܘܣ κρύσταλλος, m. *rock crystal.*

ܩܪܘܣܘܣܐ perhaps κροσσοί, *tassels, a fringe.*

ܩܪܘܨܐ and ܩܪܨ rt. ܩܪܨ. m. *a spike, very large nail.*

ܩܪܘܩܣܬܐ f. *a felt cap* or *hat* worn by a deacon or priest.

ܩܪܘܪܐ pl. ܩܪܘܪܝܬܐ rt. ܩܪ. f. *a glass bottle, phial.*

ܩܪܘܫ, ܩܪܘܫܐ, ܫܬܐ rt. ܩܪܫ. *cold, icy.*

ܩܪܘܦܝܓ m. *the ibex, mountain goat.*

ܩܪܘܬܐ, ܩܪܐ, ܩܪܐ f. κηρός, *wax*; ܐܝ̈ܕܝܐ ܕܩܪܘܬܐ *hands like wax.*

ܩܪܙܐ m. *a ball of thread, a skein.*

ܩܪܚ fut. ܢܩܪܘܚ and ܢܩܪܚ *to become bald.* Metaph. *to describe baldly, expose, divulge*; ܠܐ ܨܒܐ ܐܢܐ ܕܐܩܪܘܚ ܐܢܝܢ ܠܚܛܗ̈ܐ *I do not choose to specify these sins distinctly.* Part. adj. ܩܪܝܚ, ܚܐ, ܚܬܐ *evident, specified, clearly known, prominent*; ܩܪܝܚܐ ܗܘ ܘܡܦܪܣܐ *it is publicly known*; ܕܘܟܬܐ—ܡܠܬܐ ܩܪܝܚܬܐ *a specified place, object*; ܫܡܗ ܕܢܘܚ ܩܪܝܚܐ the name Noah *is obviously Syriac*; ܩܪܝ̈ܚܐ ܕܦܪ̈ܣܝܐ *well-known, prominent Persians.* Gram. *expressed, pronounced* opp. ܡܬܚܒܠܐ *elided* and ܡܫܬܠܝܐ *quiescent.* APH. ܐܩܪܚ *a*) *to make bald.* *b*) *to declare expressly, disclose, specify, mention, exhibit.* Pass. part. ܡܩܪܚܐ *eloquent; quarrelsome.* ETTAPH. ܐܬܬܩܪܚ *to be clearly evident, commonly known, manifest*; ܠܐ ܡܕܢܚܐ ܘܠܐ ܡܥܪܒܐ ܐܬܬܩܪܚ ܒܐܣܛܘܟܣܐ *neither east nor west could it be discerned on the horizon*; ܕܢܬܬܩܪܚ ܝܘܬܪܢܐ *that the profit may be clear.* DERIVATIVES, ܩܪܚܐ, ܩܪܚܬܐ, ܩܪܚܘܬܐ, ܩܪܚܐ, ܩܪܝܚܐ, ܩܪܝܚܘܬܐ, ܡܩܪܚܢܐ, ܡܩܪܚܢܘܬܐ.

ܩܪܚ, ܩܪܚܐ, ܚܬܐ rt. ܩܪܚ. *a*) *bald.* *b*) *having a white spot on the forehead, hornless* as sheep. *c*) *bare* as a mountain.

ܩܪܚ, ܩܪܚܐ m. *broken skull, cleft in the head.*

ܩܪܚܐ pl. ܐ̈ rt. ܩܪܚ. m. *tempest, whirlwind.*

ܩܪܚܐ pl. ܐ̈ m. *a vetch; a pea-nut*; ܩ ܥܩܪܐ *pyrethrum, featherfew.*

ܩܪܚܘܬܐ rt. ܩܪܚ. f. *a*) *baldness.* *b*) *hornlessness* (sheep).

ܩܪܛ PAEL ܩܪܛ *to nibble, gnaw.* ETHPE. ܐܬܩܪܛ *to be nibbled, gnawed.* DERIVATIVE, ܩܪܘܛܐ.

ܩܪܛܐ pl. ܝ̈ܢ, ܐ̈, ܩܪܛܝܢܐ, ܩܪܛܝܢܘܢ &c. κερατέα, m. *a*) *the fruit of the locust* or *carob-tree.* *b*) *a carat* = the third part of an obol, also = 4 barleycorns.

ܩܪܛܐ pl. ܐ̈ m. *a leek.*

ܩܪܛܐ, ܩܪܛܝܣ &c. pr. n. *Crete.*

ܩܪܛܘܢܐ *a woollen tunic.*

ܩܪܛܝܐ, ܩܪܛܝܬ, ܩܪܛܝ from ܩܪܛܐ. *Cretan.*

ܩܪܛܡܐ *a line.*

ܩܪܛܡ m. *early breakfast given to reapers.*

ܩܪܛܢܣ *a very small coin;* cf. ܩܪܛܐ *b.*

ܩܪܛܝܣ, ܩܪܛܝܣܐ pl. ܐ̈ χάρτης, m. *paper, a sheet of paper, a book written in pages, a pamphlet.*

ܩܪܛܠܐ pl. ܐ̈ m. *a basket, a fruit-basket* used at the vintage. Cf. ܩܪܛܠܘܬܐ.

ܩܪܛܡ *to cut off.* Derivative, ܩܪܛܡܐ.

ܩܪܛܡܝܬܐ or ܩܪܛܡܝܬܐ f. *thin mist, vapour.*

ܩܪܝ = ܩܪܐ verb.

ܩܪܝ; see ܩܪܝܬܐ *a beam.*

ܩܪܝܐ rt. ܩܪܐ. m. *a) strife. b) an effusion during sleep,* usually ܕܒܠܠܝܐ or ܕܒܚܠܡܐ ܩ *nocturnal pollution.*

ܩܪܝܐ rt. ܩܪܐ. m. *a) crying;* ܠܐܝܬ ܒܩܪܝܐ *I am weary of crying. b) crowing* of a cock, *chatter* of a magpie. *c) election, designation* of a bishop.

ܩܪܝܢܐܝܬ and ܩܪܝܢܝܐܝܬ rt. ܩܪܐ. adv. *contentiously, contrarily, adversely.*

ܩܪܝܒ, ܒܐ, ܒܬܐ rt. ܩܪܒ. *a) near, nigh, neighbouring, present, contemporary; approaching, imminent;* ܩܪܝܒ ܠܡܡܬ *at the point of death;* ܩܪܝܒܐ ܗܘ ܕܬܫܡܥܘܢ *you are about to hear;* ܕܩܪܝܒܐ ܗܘ ܠܡܐܡܪ ܥܠܝܗܘܢ *of whom it may almost be said . . .,* ܩܪܝܒܐ *those of the present age* opp. ܐܚܪܝܐ *later generations. b) one who draws near, an attendant; a kinsman, neighbour;* ܩ ܕܡܠܟܐ *the courtiers;* ܩ ܒܚܝܢܐ *a near relation. c) a god-father, god-mother.*

ܩܪܝܒܐܝܬ rt. ܩܪܒ. adv. *near by, nearly, shortly.*

ܩܪܝܒܘ, ܩܪܝܒܘܬܐ rt. ܩܪܒ. f. *nearness, neighbourhood, proximity; affinity, kinsmanship* = right of redemption; *access; presence; juxtaposition, comparison;* ܕ ܩ *nearly, about;* ܒܩ ܕ *in the neighbourhood of, near.*

ܩܪܝܒܬܐ; see ܩܪܝܒܬܐ.

ܩܪܝܘܢ, ܩܪܝܘܢܐ pl. ܐ̈ m. rarely f. κηρίον, κηρίων, *a wax-light, wax candle.*

ܩܪܝܚܐܝܬ rt. ܩܪܚ. adv. *plainly, openly, obviously, expressly.*

ܩܪܝܚܘܬܐ rt. ܩܪܚ. f. *distinctness, perspicuity.*

ܩܪܝܛܐ, ܩܪܝܛܝܣ and ܩܪܛܐ, also ܩܪܝܛܣ. pr. n. *Crete.*

ܩܪܝܛܝܐ, ܩܪܝܛܝ, ܩܪܛܝ &c. pl. ܐ̈ *Cretan.*

ܩܪܝܛܝܣ m. κριτής, *a judge.*

ܩܪܝܢ, ܩܪܝܢܐ rt. ܩܪܐ. *quarrelsome, contentious, wrangling.*

ܩܪܝܢܘܬܐ rt. ܩܪܐ. f. *contentiousness, contrariety.*

ܩܪܝܡ, ܡܐ, ܡܬܐ; see verb ܩܪܡ.

ܩܪܝܡܬܐ, ܩܪܝܡܬܐ f. *a cake of raisins.*

ܩܪܝܡ *polished brass.*

ܩܪܝܢ, ܩܪܝܢܐ pl. ܐ̈ rt. ܩܪܐ. m. *a) calling, vocation; calling on, invocation. b) reading, study, erudition;* eccles. *a lection, lesson;* ܟܬܒܐ ܕܦܘܫܩ ܩܪܝܢܐ *a lectionary. c) disputation.*

ܩܪܝܦܬܐ, ܩܪܝܦܬܐ and ܩܪܦܬܐ κηριάπτης, *a lamp.*

ܩܪܝܪ, ܪܐ, ܪܬܐ; see under verb ܩܪ.

ܩܪܝܪܘܬܐ rt. ܩܪ. f. *severe cold, frost, coldness, chilliness.*

ܩܪܝܫܐ, ܩܪܝܫܬܐ rt. ܩܪܫ. f. *a) milk after parturition, beestings. b) brass.*

ܩܪܝܬܐ abs. st. ܩܪܝ pl. ܩܪܝܬܐ, f. *a beam, plank.*

ܩܪܝܬܐ f. a kind of locust.

ܩܪܝܬܐ pl. ܝܬܐ rt. ܩܪܐ. f. *a) a calling, vocation; invocation* esp. *the invocation* of the Holy Trinity at baptism. *b) an invitation;* legal *an appeal; recalling. c) cockcrow; braying* of trumpets. *d) designation* of a bishop. *e) a reading, rendering. f)* gram. *a mood; a sentence in the vocative.*

ܩܪܝܬܐ emph. state of ܩܪܝܐ.

ܩܪܝܬܐ or ܩܪܝܬ f. κριθή, *barley; a stye* in the eye.

ܩܪܝܬܘܢܬܐ dimin. of ܩܪܝܐ, ܩܪܝܬܐ. *a little village, hamlet.*

ܩܪܝܬܢܝܐ from ܩܪܝܬܐ. *beam-like.*

ܩܪܟܕܘܢܐ pl. ܐ̈ m. χαλκηδών, *chalcedony, carnelian.*

ܩܪܘܒܐ pl. ܐ̈ prob. = ܩܪܘܩܐ *a crow.*

ܩܪܡ fut. ܢܶܩܪܘܿܡ, act. part. ܩܳܪܶܡ, ܩܳܪܡܳܐ, pass. part. ܩܪܝܡ, ܡܳܐ, ܡܳܬܳܐ. *to overlay, plate, encrust,* ܕܗܒܐ or ܒܕܗܒܐ *with gold; to veneer, cover* with wood, stone, skin; *to spread, overspread;* ܢܚܫܐ ܩܪܘܡܝܗܝ *overlay it with brass;* ܬܪܒܐ ܕܩܳܪܶܡ ܠܓܘܐ *the fat that covereth the inwards;* ܩܳܪܶܡ ܚܶܫܘܿܟܳܐ ܥܰܠ ܥܰܝܢܰܝܟܘܿܢ *darkness lies upon your eyes;* ܚܕܘܬܐ ܩܪܘܡܘ ܠܠܒܟܘܢ *ye draw joy on to your heart.* Ethpe. ܐܬܩܪܶܡ *to be spread over, be overlayed* with ܥܰܠ. Pa. ܩܰܪܶܡ *to overlay, overspread.* Derivatives, ܩܪܡܐ, ܡܩܪܡܐ.

ܩܪܡ, ܩܪܡܐ also ܩܶܪܡܳܐ and ܩܰܪܡܳܐ pl. ܐ̈ m. *a layer, plate, covering* of metal, wood, skin; *a bed-spread; a membrane;* ܕܟܪܣܐ ܩ̄ *the peritonaeum;* ܩܪܡ ܕܩܝܣܐ *panelling;* ܩܪܡ ܚܡܪܐ *a saddle-cloth.*

ܩܪܡܫ Arab. *to contract, be drawn* as the face with grief.

ܩܪܡܝܕܐ, ܩܪܡܝܕܝܬܐ, ܩܪܡܝܕܐ or ܩܪܐܡܝܕܐ pl. ܐ̈ κεραμίδιον, *a tile, brick.*

ܩܪܡܠܐ = ܩܠܡܕܪܐ *a pen-case:* in the Lexx. *a brass inkstand.*

ܩܪܐܡܝܣܐ, ܩܪܡܝܣܐ, ܩܪܡܝܣܬܐ and ܩܪܐܡܘܣܐ pl. ܐ̈ m. κέραμος, *a pitcher.*

ܩܪܢ alchem. a compound of tin and lead.

ܩܪܢ, ܩܪܢܐ pl. ܩܪ̈ܢܝܢ, ܐ̈ when used of natural horns, ܢ̈ܝܢ, ܢ̈ܬܐ when used figuratively, f. *a*) *a horn* of an animal, *a horn* (trumpet), *horn* (vessel); ܩ̄ ܕܡܥܡܘܕܝܬܐ *the horn of baptismal oil.* With ܐܪܝܡ *to exalt the horn;* ܩ̄ ܪܡܬܐ *haughtiness. b*) *cornea* of the eye; *a corn, horny excrescence; claw* of a crab. *c*) *a corner, angle;* ܒܩܪܢܢܐ *obliquely. d*) *tip; arm* of a seat; *tittle* of a letter; *border* of a garment; *peak* of a mountain; *wing* of an army. *e*) *a capital sum;* ܩ̄ ܘܪܒܝܬܐ *principal and interest. f*) a measure = *twelve pints. g*) bot. *dictamnus, dittany.* Derivatives, ܩܪܢܝܐ, ܩܪܢ, ܩܪܢܢܐ, ܩܪܢܝܐ, ܡܩܪܢܢܐ.

ܩܒܐ ܩܪܢܐ = καρύϊνα κεράμια, *wine-bins.*

ܩܪܢܒܐ m. *a gardener.*

ܩܪܢ ܚܕܐ *the rhinoceros.*

ܩܪܢܢܐ pl. ܐ̈ from ܩܪܢܐ. *horned, horned cattle.*

ܩܪܢܢܝܐ, ܢܝܬܐ from ܩܪܢܐ. *horny, horn-coloured.*

ܩܪܢܣ denom. verb Palpel conj. from ܩܘܪܢܣܐ. *to hammer.*

ܩܪܣ fut. ܢܶܩܪܘܿܣ, act. part. ܩܳܪܶܣ. *to become dried up, rugged, harsh;* ܟܕ ܩܳܪܣܐ ܠܫܢܗ ܕܪܓܝܙܐ *when the tongue of the angry is exasperated.* Ethpe. ܐܬܩܪܶܣ *to be dried up, wrinkled, hard.* Pa. ܩܰܪܶܣ *to be rough, harsh.* Ethpa. ܐܬܩܰܪܰܣ perhaps denom. from ܩܪܒܐ. *to wage war.* Aph. ܐܩܪܶܣ *to dry, harden.* Derivatives, ܩܪܣܐ, ܩܪܝܣܘܬܐ, ܩܪܝܣܐ, ܩܘܪܣܐ.

ܩܪܣ, ܩܪܣܐ, ܩܪܣܬܐ rt. ܩܪܣ. *dry, hard; frigid, severe; harsh, rugged, rough-tempered.*

ܩܪܣܐ pl. ܣ̈ܝܢ, ܐ̈ m. κρᾶσις, *mixture, temper, combination.*

ܩܪܣܐ m. Lat. currus, *a chariot.*

ܩܪܣܐ; see ܩܠܐܘܣܐ.

ܩܪܣܒܢܐ pl. ܐ̈ m. *a robe.*

ܩܪܝܣܘܬܐ rt. ܩܪܣ. f. *harshness, asperity; frigidity;* ܩܪܝܣܘܬ ܡܡܠܠܐ *harsh language, disparagement.*

ܩܪܣܝܐ, ܩܪܣ and ܩܪܣ pl. ܐ̈ κερασέα, *a cherry, cherry-tree.*

ܩܪܣܦܬܐ pl. ܬ̈ܐ f. *cut branches.*

ܩܪܝܣ, ܩܪܝܣܐ rt. ܩܪܣ. *hardened, severe.*

ܩܪܣܬܐ rt. ܩܪܣ. f. *a piece of wood used as a lever to lift stones.*

ܩܪܥ, ܩܪܥܐ Ar. = ܩܪܐ. m. *a*) *the pumpkin gourd;* ܡܝܐ ܕܩܪܥ *pumpkin juice. b*) chem. *a cucurbit. c*) also Arab. *a blow, stripe.*

ܩܪܥܬܐ pl. ܬ̈ܐ f. *cucurbita sylvestris, wild gourd, colocynth.*

ܩܪܦ Ethpa. ܐܬܩܰܪܰܦ *to be roofed over.*

ܩܪܦܐ m. *a woman's veil.*

ܩܪܦܛܐ m. pl. *pustules.*

ܩܪܦܣ *to narrow, contract,* trans.

ܩܪܦܣܬܐ f. *an aromatic wood;* in the Lexx. *cubeb pepper.*

ܩܪܩܦܬܐ pl. ܐ̈ m. *a*) *paltry household stuff, trash. b*) *a gnat.*

ܩܪܩܘܛܢܐ from the preceding. m. *a broker, dealer in old goods.*

ܩܪܦܬܐ dial. f. *a torch, lamp.* Cf. ܩܪܝܦܬܐ and ܩܪܝܦܬܐ.

ܩܪܙ act. part. ܩܳܪܶܙ, ܩܳܪܙܳܐ. *to glance scornfully.* Pa. ܩܰܪܶܙ *to ridicule.*

ܩܪܳܙܳܐ *a gnawed* or *broken morsel;* metaph. *slander;* with ܐܶܟܰܠ *to backbite, slander.*

ܩܪܙܒܢܐ pl. ܐ̈ m. *a nettle.*

ܩܪܙܒܬܐ and ܩܪܙܒܢܝܬܐ pl. ܝ̈ܬܐ f. *a nettle.*

ܩܪܙܘܦܬܐ f. = ܩܪܙܘܬܐ.

ܩܪܙܘܬܐ f. *shivering fit* or *languor preceding an attack of fever; a sign.*

ܩܪܙܢܐ = ܩܪܙܐ m.

ܩܪܙܢܐ m. *ague.*

ܩܪܙܝܬܐ f. *a) chilblain. b) hoarfrost.*

ܩܪܙܠ denom. verb from ܩܘܪܙܐ. Ethpalp. ܐܶܬܩܰܪܙܰܠ *to follow on the heels of* . . . .

ܩܪܙܐ pl. ܐ̈ m. *hoarfrost, rime; sleet; severe cold.*

ܩܪܩܪ = ܩܪܩܪ *to cluck.* Derivative, ܩܘܪܩܪܐ.

ܩܪܛܐ pl. ܐ̈ m. *thin sandals.*

ܩܪܛܒܐ m. *a ford, shallow.*

ܩܪܛܒܢܐ = ܩܘܪܛܒܢܐ m. a bird's *crop.*

ܩܪܛܦܬܐ = ܩܪܛܦܬܐ f. *head; head* or *summit* of a mountain; *head, chief;* metaph. ܩܪܛܦܬܐ ܕܝܠܟ *thyself.*

ܩܪܛܘܡܢܐ m. *expense, cost.*

ܩܪܛܘܠܐ from σαρκοκόλλα. m. *glue.*

ܩܪܛܘܡܢܐ from ܩܘܪܛܘܡܐ. m. *a maker of nose-rings.*

ܩܪܩܘܦܐܢܛܘܣ and ܩܪܩܘܦܐܢܛܘܢ κροκυφάντωτος -ον, *a hair-net, network.*

ܩܪܛܘܪܐ pl. ܐ̈ f. *a light boat, ship's boat.*

ܩܪܛܘܪܝܬܐ dimin. of ܩܪܛܘܪܐ. f. *a little boat, skiff.*

ܩܪܛܦ *to smear* the face *with ashes, to make black* or *red streaks* on the face.

ܩܪܛܦܐ from ܩܪܛܦ. m. *blacking, dirt.*

ܩܪܝܣܛܘܢ some material.

ܩܪܩܣ, ܩܪܩܘܣ and ܩܪܩܝܣ pl. ܝ̈ܣ m. Lat. *circus.*

ܩܪܩܝܣܐ m. pl. κιρκήσια: *contests in the circus.*

ܩܪܩܠ f. *a grating.*

ܩܪܩܠܐ and ܩܪܩܠܢܐ m. *a)* vulg. *hook to which a sheep's carcase is slung for skinning. b)* Ar. *a chemise, child's shirt.*

ܩܪܩܡܝܢ m. *necklace* or *neck chain with pendent gems.*

ܩܪܩܣ; see ܩܪܩܣ.

ܩܪܩܦܐ and ܩܪܩܦܐ pl. ܐ̈ m. *a)* κόραξ, *a crow, raven. b)* dialect of Tirhan: pl. *tree-roots cast up by a flood. c)* pl. *chess-men, draughts.*

ܩܪܩܦܬܐ f. *a magpie.*

ܩܪܩܦ denom. verb Palpel conj. from ܩܪܩܦܬܐ. *to behead.*

ܩܪܩܦܬܐ pl. ܝ̈ܢ, ܝ̈ܬܐ and ܢ̈ܬܐ f. *a) a head, skull;* with ܦܣܩ or ܩܛܥ *to behead. b) top, crown, summit. c) a chief, prince.*

ܩܪܩܪ *to cluck, cackle* as a hen. Derivative, ܩܘܪܩܪܐ.

ܩܪܩܫ *to clash, rattle, rustle; to overthrow with a crash.* Ethpalp. ܐܶܬܩܰܪܩܰܫ *to be shaken, rattled, made to clash* or *rustle;* ܪܩܝܥܐ ܡܬܩܪܩܫ ܐܝܟ ܐܝܠܢܐ *the firmament is made to rustle as trees.* Derivative, ܩܘܪܩܫܐ.

ܩܪܘܪܐ m. *a driver.*

ܩܪܫ act. part. ܩܳܪܶܫ, ܩܳܪܫܳܐ. *to become chilled, frozen;* ܡ̈ܝܐ ܩܪܫܘ ܘܩܦܘ the waters become *frozen and hard bound.* Part. adj. *a)* ܩܪܝܫ *chilled, cold. b)* ܩܪܝܫ *coagulated,* ܚܠܒܐ ܩܪܝܫܐ *clotted milk.* Cf. ܩܪܝܫܐ. Pa. ܩܰܪܶܫ *to cool, ice* food or water; *to chill.* Ethpa. ܐܶܬܩܰܪܰܫ *to shade, put in the shade.* Derivatives, ܩܘܪܫܐ, ܩܘܪܫܢܐ, ܩܪܘܫ, ܩܪܝܫܬܐ, ܩܪܫܐ, ܩܪܫܐ, ܩܪܫܘܬܐ, ܩܪܝܫܬܐ.

ܩܪܫܐ rt. ܩܪܫ. m. *a) a chill, cold. b) a midden, muck-heap. c) refuse* of vegetables &c., *sweepings.*

ܩܪܫܐ rt. ܩܪܫ. m. *coagulation.*

ܩܪܫܘܬܐ rt. ܩܪܫ. f. *scum, incrustation* formed on the surface of wine, vinegar or pickle.

ܩܪܫܬܐ rt. ܩܪܫ. f. *biestings, first milk after calving.*

ܩܪܬܢܐ = ܩܪܕܢܐ.

ܩܫܬܐ pl. ܩܛܠܬܐ = ܩܘܫܬܐ *a wicker basket.*

ܩܫ fut. ܢܩܘܫ and ܢܩܫ, act. part. ܩܐܫ, ܩܫܐ and ܩܫܐ. *a) to grow old;* ܩܫܢ ܘܥܠܠܢ ܒܫܢܝܐ *we grew old and advanced in years. b) to collect, pick up* sticks, straw. Cf. ܩܫܐ. Ethpe. ܐܬܩܫܫ *to be the eldest.* Pa. ܩܫܫ *to place as eldest or first, give precedence;* pass. part. ܡܩܫܫܐ, ܡܩܫܫܬܐ *prior, preferred, first.* Ethpa. ܐܬܩܫܫ *to be declared elder, be given precedence, take precedence.* Derivatives, ܩܫܐ, ܩܫܐ, ܩܫܝܫ, ܩܫܝܫܘܬܐ, ܩܫܝܫܐ, ܩܫܝܫܘܬܐ.

ܩܫܐ Peal only part. adj. ܩܫܐ, ܩܫܝܐ, ܩܫܝܬܐ pl. m. ܩܫܝܢ, ܩܫܝܐ, pl. f. ܩܫܝܢ, ܩܫܝܬܐ. *a) hard, difficult, grievous;* with ܡܢ *too hard, too difficult; stronger than, more severe* &c.; ܡܠܬܐ ܩܫܝܬܐ *a hard saying. b) rough* as a road; *severe* as labour, winter, persecution; *violent* as wind, storm, earthquake. *c) strong* as a smell; *harsh* in taste; *tough* as meat; *drastic* as medicine; med. *hard, indurated* as a tumour. *d)* of men and beasts, *austere, stern, crabbed, stubborn, intractable;* ܩܫܐ ܠܒܐ *hardhearted;* ܩܫܐ ܐܦܐ *impudent;* ܩܫܐ ܨܘܪܐ *stiffnecked. e)* gram. *non-aspirated* letters (rare). *f)* cf. ܩܫܝܬܐ. Pael ܩܫܝ *a) to harden, stiffen;* ܐܢܐ ܩܫܝܬ ܠܒܗ ܕܦܪܥܘܢ *I have hardened Pharaoh's heart;* with ܐܦܐ *to be severe, inflexible;* with ܠܒܐ or ܨܘܪܐ *to be stubborn.* Pass. part. ܡܩܫܝ, ܡܩܫܝܐ, ܡܩܫܝܬܐ *callous, indurated;* gram. *not aspirated, hard in pronunciation. b)* with ܥܠ *to make grievous, press heavily upon;* ܩܫܝ ܩܫܝܐ ܥܠ ܐܘܪܗܝ *he laid grievous interdicts upon Edessa;* with ܢܝܪܐ *to make the yoke heavy.* Ethpa. ܐܬܩܫܝ *a) to be hardened* as the heart, as the hands with labour. *b) to become harder, more difficult, grievous, serious; to increase in severity, press heavily upon* with ܥܠ, as flood, famine, pain; ܥܕܠܐ ܬܬܩܫܐ ܨܒܘܬܐ *before the matter grows serious. c) to be harsh* with ܠܘܬ of the pers. *d) to become solid, congeal;* ܩܡܘ ܡܝܐ ܐܬܩܫܝܘ ܐܝܟ ܫܘܪܐ *the waters rose in a solid mass. e)* gram. *to be hard, unaspirated.* Aph. ܐܩܫܝ *to make grievous* as ܢܝܪܐ *a yoke; to be harsh, severe;* ܐܩܫܝ ܥܠܘܗܝ ܡܪܕܘܬܐ *give him severe discipline;* with ܐܦܐ and ܠܒܐ as Pael. Gram. *to pronounce a letter hard, without aspiration.*

Derivatives, ܩܫܝ, ܩܫܝܐܝܬ, ܩܫܝܘܬܐ, ܩܫܝܬܐ, ܡܩܫܝܢܘܬܐ, ܡܩܫܝܢܐ.

ܩܫܐ contracted from ܩܫܝܫܐ. m. *an elder, presbyter, priest.*

ܩܫܐ, ܩܫܬܐ rt. ܩܫ. f. *a) stubble, dry stalks, grass* or *leaves. b) picking up sticks, gathering dry leaves* &c.

ܩܫܒܐ pl. ܐ̈ m. *a) a sign, beckoning. b) a dried date.*

ܩܫܒܐ ܕܩܘܡܐ name of a medicine.

ܩܫܛ Pael ܩܫܛ *to shoot* an arrow. Act. part. ܡܩܫܛ *an archer.* Cf. ܩܫܛ and ܩܫܬܐ. Ethpa. ܐܬܩܫܛ *to be shot at with an arrow, to have an arrow aimed at one.*

ܩܫܛܐ = ܩܫܛܐ m. *an archer, bowman;* astron. *Sagittarius.*

ܩܫܛܐ m. *archery.*

ܩܫܝ Pael conj. of ܩܫܐ.

ܩܫܝܐܝܬ rt. ܩܫܐ. adv. *roughly, severely, harshly, grievously, violently, overpoweringly.*

ܩܫܝܘܬܐ rt. ܩܫܐ. *hardness, callosity; difficulty, severity, harshness, acerbity; grievousness, violence; stubbornness,* with ܠܒܐ *hardness of heart,* ܨܘܪܐ *stiffneckedness; fortitude.*

ܩܫܝܫ, ܐ, ܬܐ rt. ܩܫ. *a) eldest, older* with ܡܢ; *the elder, eldest* son, brother, sister; ܒܪܬܝ ܩܫܝܫܬܐ *my eldest daughter. b) full-grown, fully formed* as men, trees, the moon, at creation. *c) a grandfather, ancestor;* ܩܫܝܫܐ ܕܐܡܐ *a maternal grandfather. d) an elder, ancient;* ܕ ܩܫܝܫܘܬܐ *of great age;* ܕ ܡܢ ܟܠ ܩܫܝܫܘܬܐ = ܕܟܠ *the Ancient of all;* ܩܫܝܫܐ ܕܡܕܝܢܬܐ *the elders of the city;* ܡܫܠܡܢܘܬܐ ܕܩܫܝܫܐ *the tradition of the ancients. e) ancient, of old time;* ܩܫܝܫ ܗܘ ܡܠܦܢܘܬܐ ܡܢ ܡܠܦܢܐ *doctrine is more ancient than the doctors. f) a presbyter, priest;* ܩ ܕܥܠܡܐ *a secular priest;* ܩܫܝܫܐ ܕܩܘܪܝܐ *village priests.* Fem. *a presbyteress.*

ܩܫܝܫܘܬܐ pl. ܘ̈ܬܐ rt. ܩܫ. f. *seniority, primogeniture, precedence; priority, antiquity; the office of presbyter, priesthood.*

ܩܫܝܫܢܐ pl. ܐ̈ rt. ܩܫ. m. *a presbyter, priest.*

ܩܫܝܫܢܘܬܐ rt. ܩܫ. f. *the presbyterate, priesthood.*

ܩܫܥܬܐ or ܩܶܫܥܬܐ pl. ܝ̈ܳܬܐ rt. ܩܫܥ. f. *a fruit-stone, cotton-husk.*

ܩܫܩܫܐ *having deeply set eyes, sunken-eyed, squinting.*

ܩܫܩܫܐ Arab. m. *rubbish picked up, leaves and sticks lying about.*

ܩܫܩܫܬܐ f. a parasitic plant, *bindweed;* or perh. = ܩܘܫܬܐ or ܩܣܘܬܐ transliteration of *cuscuta.*

ܩܰܫܶܬ denom. verb Pael conj. from ܩܶܫܬܐ. *to shoot* an arrow *from the bow.*

ܩܶܫܬ, ܩܶܫܬܐ pl. m. ܩܶܫ̈ܬܐ (rare), pl. f. ܩܶܫ̈ܬܳܢ, ܩܶܫ̈ܬܳܬܐ *a*) *a bow;* with ܡܬܚ and ܢܓܕ *to draw the bow;* metaph. ܩ ܕܪܚܡܘܬܐ = *Cupid's bow.* *b*) ܩܶܫܬܐ ܕܥܢܢܐ and in the Lexx. ܩܫܬ ܡܛܪܐ *the rainbow.* *c*) *arch* of a building. *d*) *row, semi-circle.*

ܩܶܫܬܐ emph. state of ܩܶܫܬ.

ܩܫܬܐ f. dial. of Tirhan *a door-knocker;* cf. ܩܫܬܢܐ.

ܩܰܫܳܬܐ pl. ܐ̈ from ܩܶܫܬܐ. m. *an archer, bowman.*

ܩܶܫܬܳܢܳܝܐ, ܝܬܐ *a*) from ܩܶܫܬܐ. *arched, curved like a bow.* *b*) *a door-knocker;* cf. verb ܢܩܫ and ܢܩܘܫܐ.

ܩܰܬ fut. ܢܶܩܽܘܬ, act. part. ܩܳܐܶܬ, ܩܳܝܬܐ. *to remain fixed, stuck* ܒܰܐܪܥܐ *in the ground;* ܐܰܘܩܝܢܐ ܕܩܳܐܶܬ ܒܰܚܡܳܬܐ *the anchor which stays fast in the mud; to remain motionless* as eyes glazed in death. Part. adj. ܩܝܬ, ܩܝܬܐ *thrust in, stuck in* as claws; *intent, fixed* as the eyes; ܒܰܐܪܥܐ ܩܝܬ ܚܝܳܪܗ *his gaze was fixed on the ground.* Pa. ܩܰܝܶܬ *a*) *to fix* the claws in. *b*) in the Lexx. *to cause to wither.* Aph. ܐܰܩܝܶܬ act. part. ܡܰܩܝܶܬ and ܡܰܩܶܬ *a*) *to fix in, stick in* teeth, claws; iron tools; ܐܰܩܝܶܬ ܢܰܪܓܶܗ ܒܫܘܪܐ *he struck his axe into the wall.* *b*) *to fix* the eyes, the gaze, *to gaze steadfastly* with ܒ, often with ܚܙܘܐ, ܚܝܳܪܐ, ܣܘܟܳܝܐ; with ܗܰܘܢܐ *to contemplate, fix the mind.* Derivatives, ܩܝܬܐ, ܩܬܐ, ܩܬܢܐ, ܩܰܘܬܳܢܘܬܐ, ܡܩܝܬܳܢܘܬܐ, ܡܩܝܬܢܐ.

ܩܳܬܐ pl. ܩܳ̈ܬܐ m. *a handle.*

ܩܬܐ rt. ܩܬ. m. *the sticking in* of claws, *clawing.*

ܩܳܬܶܕܪܐ m. *καθέδρα, a seat, throne.*

ܩܬܘܠ abbrev. for ܩܳܬܽܘܠܝܩܐ.

ܩܳܬܽܘܠܝܩܐ, ܝܩܝ̈, ܩܝܩܐ, ܩܝܩ, ܩܘܣ and ܩܬܠܝܩܐ pl. ܩܳܬܽܘܠܝܩܳܘܣ *καθολικός -κή.* *a*) *catholic, general, universal;* ܥܕܬܐ ܩܰܕܝܫܬܐ ܩܳܬܽܘܠܝܩܝ *the holy catholic* Church; ܐܶܓܪ̈ܳܬܐ ܩܳܬܽܘܠܝܩܳܝܳܬܐ *the general epistles.* *b*) *the Catholicos, primate* ܕܡܰܕܢܚܐ *of the East;* ܕܐܰܪ̈ܡܢܳܝܐ *of the Armenians;* ܡܕܝܢ̈ܬܐ ܩܳܬܽܘܠܝܩܳܝܬܐ Seleucia Ctesiphon, *the see of the Catholicos.* *c*) *the principal* or *cathedral* church of a city. *d*) name of a *general prayer* in the Liturgy wherein the names of dead and living were briefly mentioned. *e*) *the median vein* of the hand. Derivatives, the two following words, verb ܐܶܬܩܰܬܠܰܩ, ܡܬܩܬܠܩܢܐ.

ܩܳܬܽܘܠܝܩܽܘܬܐ and ܩܬܠܩܘܬ f. *the office of a Catholicos, the primacy.*

ܩܳܬܽܘܠܝܩܳܝܐ, ܝܬܐ and ܩܬܠܩ *a*) *catholic; of the Catholicos.* *b*) ܟܬܒܐ ܩܳܬܽܘܠܝܩܳܝܐ *a book* containing both parts of the Bible.

ܩܰܬܩܳܬܐ or ܩܶܬܩܳܬܐ rt. ܩܬ. m. *a*) *loud laughter.* *b*) vulg. *pausing in weeping, gulping down sobs.* *c*) *blinking, an intent gaze* (of young children). *d*) = ܩܬܝܬܐ.

ܩܳܬܝܣܡܐ, ܡܐ̈ pl. ܩܳܬܝܣܡܛܐ, ܩܬܝܣܡܛܐ, ܩܳܬܝܣܡܛܳܐ &c., *κάθισμα -τα, a session,* W-Syr. one of the twenty *sections of the Psalms, hymns chanted while sitting.* Cf. E-Syr. ܡܰܘܬܒܐ.

ܩܰܬܝܬܐ; see under verb ܩܰܬ.

ܩܰܬܝܬܘܬܐ rt. ܩܬ. f. *attention, application.*

ܩܰܬܠܶܩ denom. verb from ܩܳܬܽܘܠܝܩܐ. Ethpa. ܐܶܬܩܰܬܠܰܩ *to be raised to the dignity of Catholicos.*

ܩܰܬܩܶܬ Palpel *to burst out laughing, laugh loudly.* Derivative, ܩܰܬܩܳܬܐ.

ܩܰܬܰܪ denom. verb from ܩܰܬܪܐ. *to be rocky.*

ܩܰܬܪܐ pl. ܐ̈ m. *a*) *a rock.* *b*) *a great candlestick.*

ܩܰܬܰܪܐ, ܪܐ pl. ܐ̈, ܩܰܬܰܪܘܣ and ܩܛܰܪܐ *καθαρός.* *a*) *clean, pure;* ܐܶܬܥܒܶܕ ܨܚܚܐ ܩܰܬܰܪܐ *a clean copy was made.* *b*) pl. *Cathari,* heretics.

ܩܰܬܪܶܢ Ethpalel ܐܶܬܩܰܬܪܰܢ *to be married:* perh. a mistake for ܐܶܬܡܰܟܪܰܢ.

ܩܰܬܪܰܢܕܝ m. *a giraffe.*

ܩܰܬܪܺܝܢܳܐ perh. κάνθαρος, m. *a water-pipe, duct.*

ܩܰܬܰܪܶܣ denom. verb PALPEL conj. from ܩܰܬܰܐܪܶܣܺܝܣ *to degrade, depose* esp. from the episcopate. ETHPALP. ܐܶܬܩܰܬܰܪܶܣ *to be deposed, degraded.*

ܩܰܬܰܐܪܶܣܺܝܣ, ܩܐܬܪܣܝܣ, ܩܬܐܪܣܝܣ, ܩܬܪܣܝܣ καθαίρεσις, f. *deposition, degradation from office,* esp. of a bishop. DERIVATIVES, verb ܩܰܬܪܶܣ, ܩܘܬܪܳܣܳܐ.

ܩܰܬܶܠ PAEL conj. of verb ܩܬܠ.

ܩܶܬܠܳܐ pl. ܩܶܬܠܶܐ m. *a covered watercourse, conduit, moat.*

ܩܶܬܠܶܐ pl. of ܩܶܬܠܳܐ.

ܩܬܠܘܓܝܣ *a firefly.*

:. ܐܬܦܪܒ ܡܫܡܠܝܐ ܣܕܪܐ ܗܢܐ ܕܩܘܦ :.

:. ܪܒܐ ܘܡܪܢܝܬܐ ܕܫܡܗ ܡܬܩܪܝܢ ܡܢ ܟܠ. ܐܬܪܫܡ ܟܠ
ܪܡܙܘܬܐ܂ ܘܡܕܒܪܢ ܒܐܬܘܬܐ ܗܕܐ ܕܪܫ :.

:. ܪ :.

ܪ ܪܐܘܒܐ

ܪ, ܪܺܝܫ E-Syr. ܪܺܫ *Resh,* the twentieth letter of the alphabet; the numeral 200, ܪ̈ *the two hundredth;* with a line beneath, ܪ̱, 2,000,000.

ܪܳܐܶܒ scriptio plena of verb ܪܰܒ; ܪܳܐܶܒ act. part. of the same; ܪܳܐܶܒ, ܪܳܐܒܳܐ act. part. of verb ܪܘܒ.

ܪܳܐܶܓ, ܪܳܐܓܳܐ act. part. of verb ܪܓ.

ܪܳܐܘܒܳܐ rt. ܪܒܝ. m. *a nursling, foster-son.*

ܪܳܐܘܢ Pers. = ܪܳܐܘܢ through Greek ῥῆον and ܪܰܒܳܐ m. *rheum rhaponticum, the root of a kind of rhubarb.*

ܪܳܐܶܙ act. part. of verb ܪܙ.

ܪܳܐܙ, ܪܳܐܙܳܐ also ܪܳܙ, ܪܳܙܳܐ and ܐܪܳܙ, ܐܪܳܙܳܐ (see under ܐ) pl. ܪ̈ܳܙܺܝܢ, ܐ̈ Pers. m. *a) a secret, mystery, mystical signification; a symbol, sign. b) a sacrament, the Eucharist, the mystical elements;* ܚܰܡܫܳܐ ܕܪܳܙܶܐ *Maundy Thursday;* ܫܰܒܬܳܐ ܕܪܳܙܶܐ *Passion week. c) conspiracy;* with ܥܒܰܕ and ܓܒܰܠ, with ܢܣܰܒ, ܥܒܰܕ or ܢܟܰܠ *to conspire;* ܒܪܳܙܳܐ or ܒܪܳܙ *secretly; mystically; in the likeness of, as.* DERIVATIVES, ܪܳܙܳܢܳܐܝܬ, ܪܳܙܳܢܳܐ, ܪܳܙܳܢܽܘܬܳܐ, ܡܪܳܙܳܢܳܐ, ܡܪܳܙܳܢܽܘܬܳܐ, ܡܶܬܪܳܙܳܢܳܐ, ܡܶܬܪܳܙܳܢܽܘܬܳܐ, verb ܪܳܙ, ܐܶܬܪܳܙ &c.

ܪܳܐܙܳܢܳܐܝܬ, ܪܳܙܳܢܳܐܝܬ, ܪܳܐܙ, ܐܪܳܙ &c. from ܪܳܐܙܳܐ. adv. *secretly; mystically, symbolically.*

ܪܳܐܙܳܢܳܝ, ܪܳܐܙܳܢܳܝܳܐ, ܪܳܐܙܳܢܳܝܬܳܐ from ܪܳܐܙܳܐ. *a) secret, mystical, symbolical, typical. b) liturgical, sacramental, eucharistic.* Fem. emph. pl. *sacramental mysteries.*

ܪܳܐܙܳܢܽܘܬܳܐ from ܪܳܐܙܳܐ. f. *mystical meaning, sense, virtue* or *efficacy.*

ܪܳܐܶܚ act. part. of verb ܪܘܚ, ܪܳܚ.

ܪܳܐܚܳܐ rt. ܪܘܚ. m. *odour.*

ܪܳܐܛܺܝܢܳܐ pl. ܪܳܐܛܺܝܢܶܐ = ܪܶܛܺܝܢܳܐ *resin.*

ܪܳܐܶܡ act. part. of verb ܪܳܡ.

ܪܳܐܶܣ, ܪܳܐܣܳܐ act. part. of verb ܪܳܣ.

ܪܳܐܘܣܶܢ and ܪܳܘܣܶܢ Arab. *inula helenium, fleabane.*

ܪܳܐܶܥ act. part. of verb ܪܘܥ, ܪܳܥ.

ܪܳܐܶܦ, ܪܳܐܦܳܐ act. part. of verb ܪܳܦ.

ܪܳܐܘܦܳܐ rt. ܪܦ. m. *blinking; fluttering.*

ܪܳܐܶܨ act. part. of verb ܪܳܨ.

ܪܳܐܶܩ, ܪܳܐܩܳܐ act. part. of verb ܪܳܩ.

ܪܳܐܩܳܐ usually ܪܰܩܳܐ *Raca.*

ܪܐܶܓ act. part. of verb ܪܓ.

ܪܳܐܶܐ, ܪܳܐܝܳܐ act. part. of verb ܪܐܐ.

ܪܐܬܳܐ and ܪܐܬܐ pl. (in the Lexx.) ܪܐܬܘܳܬܳܐ rt. ܪܐܐ. f. *the lungs.*

ܪܐܬܳܢܳܝܳܐ from ܪܐܬܳܐ. *lunged, furnished with lungs.*

ܪܒ fut. ܢܪܽܘܒ, act. part. ܪܳܐܶܒ. Cf. ܪܒܝ and ܪܒܳܐ. *to grow great, mighty;* ܪܳܐܶܒ ܘܰܫܡܰܗܬܳܢ *he increased in might and renown.* Palpel ܪܰܘܪܶܒ for ܪܰܒܪܶܒ *to give great occasion* ܥܰܠ *against; to talk big, magnify oneself* with ܥܰܠ of the pers. and often with ܡܶܠܶܐ. Ethpaual ܐܶܬܪܰܘܪܰܒ *a) to be magnified, increased in might* or *honour. b) to magnify oneself, to behave insolently, arrogantly;* with ܒ or ܒܰܬܫܡܶܫܬܐ and with ܥܰܠ *against, over.* Derivatives, ܪܒ, ܪܰܒܐ, ܪܰܒܳܐ, ܪܰܒܽܘܬܳܐ, ܪܰܒܳܢܳܐ, ܪܰܒܽܘܬܳܐ, ܪܰܒܪܒܳܢܳܐ, ܪܰܒܪܒܳܢܳܝܬ, ܪܰܘܪܒܳܐ, ܪܰܘܪܒܳܢܳܐ, ܪܰܘܪܒܳܢܽܘܬܳܐ, ܪܰܘܪܒܳܢܳܝܬ, ܪܰܒܪܒܳܢܳܐ, ܡܶܬܪܰܘܪܒܳܢܳܐ, ܡܪܰܒܪܒܳܢܳܐ.

ܪܰܒ, ܪܰܒܳܐ, ܪܰܒܬܳܐ no pl. when used as an adjective, cf. ܪܰܘܪܒܳܐ which is usual in the pl. form. With suff. 3 m. s. ܪܰܒ ܗܽܘ = ܪܰܒܽܘ; 3 f. s. ܪܰܒܳܐ ܗܺܝ *great is.* As subst. pl. m. ܪܰܒܶܐ (rare), ܪܰܒܳܢܶܐ, ܪܰܒܳܢܺܝܢ const. st. ܪܰܒܰܝ; pl. f. ܪܰܒܳܬܳܐ. Subst. with suff. 1 pers. ܪܰܒܝ, ܪܰܒܝ see under separate headings. rt. ܪܒ. *a)* adj. *great, loud, large, long, strong; important, grand; noble, of high rank;* ܡܰܥܡܰܕ ܡܰܥܡܽܘܕܺܝܬܳܐ ܪܰܒܳܐ *they recited Ps. cxix;* ܥܶܠܬܳܐ ܪܰܒܬܳܐ *the first cause; the major premiss;* ܠܡܶܬܠ ܒܺܐܝܕܳܐ ܪܰܒܬܳܐ *to give largely;* ܠܳܐ ܗܘܳܐ ܪܰܒܳܐ ܨܒܽܘܬܳܐ *it was no great matter. b) older, elder* son, daughter &c. *c)* subst. *king, duke, prince, chief, magistrate, prefect; master, teacher;* ܪܺܫܳܐ ܘܪܰܒܳܐ *head and chief;* ܪܰܒ ܐܰܟܬܺܝܢܶܐ *the prince of conquerors.* Used absolutely ܪܰܒܳܐ ܕܰܐܪܟܰܢ *the great one who became feeble.* Frequent in construction with other substantives:

ܪܰܒ ܐܰܠܦܳܐ *captain of a thousand, chiliarch.*

ܪܰܒ ܒܰܝܬܳܐ pl. ܪܰܒܰܝ ܒܳܬܶܐ *steward, manager, governor.*

ܪܰܒܽܘܬ ܒܰܝܬܽܘܬܳܐ *stewardship.*

ܪܰܒܳܐ ܕܕܰܝܳܢܶܐ *the chief justice.*

ܪܰܒ ܕܰܚܫܳܐ *captain of the guard.*

ܪܰܒ ܚܰܝܠܳܐ *captain of the host, commander, military governor, Amir.*

ܪܰܒܳܐ ܕܟܽܘܡܪܶܐ also ܪܰܒ ܟܽܘܡܪܶܐ and ܪܰܒܳܐ ܕܟܽܘܡܪܽܘܬܳܐ *high priest, chief priest.*

ܪܰܒ ܟܢܽܘܫܬܳܐ *ruler of the synagogue.*

ܪܰܒܳܐ ܕܡܳܐܬܳܐ pl. ܪܰܒܰܝ ܡܳܐܬܳܐ *centurion.*

ܪܰܒ ܡܗܰܝܡܢܳܐ *a)* = *Rab saris, head eunuch. b) leader of the faithful* i. e. *of the laity.*

ܪܰܒ ܡܶܠܶܐ *boastful, arrogant.*

ܪܰܒ ܡܰܠܐܰܟܳܐ *archangel.*

ܪܰܒܡܫܰܡܫܳܢܳܐ *archdeacon.*

ܪܰܒ ܡܰܫܪܝܳܬܳܐ *quarter-master.*

ܪܰܒ ܢܰܓܳܪܶܐ *master-builder, architect.*

ܪܰܒ ܢܰܚܬܽܘܡܶܐ *chief baker.*

ܪܰܒ ܢܰܦܫܳܐ *magnanimous.*

ܪܰܒ ܥܣܳܪܳܐ *decurion.*

ܪܰܒ ܥܒܳܕܽܘܬܳܐ *magnificent.*

ܪܰܒ ܩܰܫܺܝܫܳܐ *chief presbyter* or *priest.*

ܪܰܒ ܪܳܥܰܘܳܬܳܐ *chief pastor.*

ܪܰܒ ܫܳܩܶܐ *chief butler, chief cupbearer.*

ܪܒܳܐ and ܪܒܳܐ fut. ܢܶܪܒܶܐ, act. part. ܪܳܒܶܐ, ܪܳܒܝܳܐ. *to grow, grow up; to wax* opp. ܒܨܰܪ of the moon; *to increase, multiply; to be increased by usury, bear interest;* ܟܰܕ ܪܒܳܐ ܒܩܽܘܡܬܳܐ *when it has grown tall;* ܟܰܕ ܪܳܒܝܳܢ ܚܶܫܰܝܗܽܘܢ *as their passions grow strong;* ܟܶܣܦܳܟ ܪܳܒܶܐ ܘܡܰܥܬܰܪ *thy money bears interest and yields riches.* Pa. ܪܰܒܺܝ *to bring up, rear, breed, educate; to let grow; to make more, increase, enrich; to practise usury, lend on interest;* ܢܨܒܶܬ ܪܰܒܺܝܬ ܘܰܟܢܰܫܬ *I planted, watched the growth and gathered in;* ܡܰܪܒܶܐ ܗܘܳܐ ܣܰܥܪܶܗ *he let his hair grow;* ܠܟ ܐܰܫܠܶܡ ܐܶܢܽܘܢ ܕܬܪܰܒܶܐ *he entrusted them to thee to be brought up;* ܡܪܰܒܶܝ ܒܥܺܝܪܳܐ *cattle-breeders;* ܢܪܰܒܽܘܢܳܝܗܝ ܠܡܶܫܚܳܐ *they shall augment* the chrism *with oil;* ܡܪܰܒܝܳܐ ܗܘܳܐ ܙܰܒܢܶܐ *He gave fruitful seasons;* ܠܳܐ ܬܪܰܒܶܐ ܥܰܠ ܐܰܚܽܘܟ *thou shalt not lend upon usury to thy brother.* Ethpa. ܐܶܬܪܰܒܺܝ *to be brought up, to grow up, grow strong;* ܐܰܝܟ ܐܰܪܙܳܐ ܐܶܬܪܰܒܺܝܬ ܕܰܒܠܶܒܢܳܢ *I grew up like a cedar of Lebanon;* ܡܶܬܪܰܒܶܐ ܒܶܗ ܒܺܝܫܬܳܐ *evil waxes strong in it.* Aph. ܐܰܪܒܺܝ *to bring up; to let* the hair *grow; to lend on interest;* ܬܰܪܒܽܘܢ ܠܰܒܢܰܝܟܽܘܢ ܘܰܠܟܶܣܦܰܝܟܽܘܢ *you shall bring up your children and invest your money.* DERIVATIVES, ܪܒܝܐ, ܪܒܝܬܐ, ܪܒܝܢܝܐ, ܪܒܬܐ, ܪܘܒܐ, ܡܪܒܝܢܐ, ܡܪܒܝܬܐ, ܡܬܪܒܝܢܐ, ܪܒܝܬܐ.

ܪܒܝܬܐ = ܪܒ ܒܝܬܐ.

ܪܒܒܬܐ f. *a*) rt. ܪܒܒ. *confused cries, clamour, sound of many voices. b*) *thickened fruit-juice.*

ܪܒܕܝܢ ῥάβδιον, *an iron pin* or *style.*

ܪܒܘ, ܪܒܘܬܐ, ܪܒܘܬܐ pl. ܪܒܘܢ, ܪܒܘܬܐ rt. ܪܒ. f. *a myriad, ten thousand;* ܚܕ ܒܪܒܘ *ten thousand times more;* ܒܪܒܘ ܥܘܦܦܝܢ *ten thousandfold.*

ܪܒܘܒܝܬܐ pl. ܝܬܐ rt. ܪܒ. f. *a swelling in the groin.*

ܪܒܘܠܝ = ܪܒܘܢܝ. *my master:* both these are dimin. forms.

ܪܒܘܢܐ usually with pron. suff. ܪܒܘܢܝ. *master, lord.*

ܪܒܘܥܐ pl. ܥܐ rt. ܪܒܥ. m. *a square salver* or *dish, four-cornered flask.*

ܪܒܘܥܝܬܐ f. prob. dimin. of ܪܒܘܥܐ.

ܪܒܘ, ܪܒܘܬܐ pl. ܪܒܘܢ, ܪܒܘܬܐ rt. ܪܒ. f. *greatness, grandeur; size, magnitude; importance; majesty, magnificence, generosity; dignity, majesty;* ܗܒ ܪܒܘܬܐ ܠ *give glory to . . .;* as a title, ܦܘܩܕܢܐ ܕܪܒܘܬܟ *the commands of thy Excellence.* In construction: ܪܒܘܬ ܡܠܟܘܬܐ *magnificence;* ܪ ܟܘܡܪܘܬܐ or ܪ ܟܗܢܘܬܐ *the high-priesthood;* ܪ ܟܪܣܐ *gluttony;* ܪ ܠܒܐ *large-heartedness, courage;* ܪ ܢܦܫܐ *magnanimity;* ܪ ܥܒܕܘܬܐ *great deeds;* ܪ ܦܐܝܘܬܐ *magnificence;* ܪ ܬܪܥܝܬܐ *sagacity.*

ܪܒܘܬܢܝܐ rt. ܪܒ. *relating to myriads.*

ܪܒܚ fut. ܢܪܒܘܚ, act. part. ܪܒܚ, ܪܒܚܐ, part. adj. ܪܒܝܚ, ܚܐ. *to crumble away, moulder, rot;* ܪܒܚܘ ܘܐܬܒܕܪܘ ܐܝܟ ܪܘܚܐ ܚܘܪ̈ܒܐ ruins *mouldered away and were scattered like wind.* Metaph. *to diminish.* ETHPE. ܐܬܪܒܚ *to be decayed, rotten.* DERIVATIVE, ܪܘܒܚܐ.

ܪܒܚܐ Arab. m. *usury.*

ܪܒܚܐ rt. ܪܒܚ. m. *mould, putrefaction.*

ܪܒܝ rt. ܪܒ. *Rabbi, master.*

ܪܒܝ, ܪܒܝܐ rt. ܪܒܐ. m. *a usurer.*

ܪܒܝܬ, ܪܒܝܬܐ pl. ܝܬܐ rt. ܪܒܐ. f. *usury.*

ܪܒܝܐ rt. ܪܒܐ. m. *interest.*

ܪܒܝܢܝܐ rt. ܪܒܐ. *bearing interest, subject to interest.*

ܪܒܝܥ, ܪܒܝܥܐ, pl. ܥܐ rt. ܪܒܥ. *a*) *a square* or *oblong tabor hung from the neck and played on both sides, a timbrel. b*) *early rain, spring rain, spring time. c*) ܪܒܝܥ ܩܕܡܝܐ Arab. *fourth lunar month of the Arabs.*

ܪܒܝܥܐܝܬ rt. ܪܒܥ. adv. *fourfold, quadruply.*

ܪܒܝܥܝ, ܪܒܝܥܝܐ, ܪܒܝܥܝܬܐ also written ܐܪܒܝܥܝܐ rt. ܪܒܥ. *a*) *early, spring rain. b*) *fourth;* ܒܢܝ̈ܐ ܪܒܝܥܝ̈ܐ *sons of the fourth generation.* In comp. ܪܒܝܥܝ ܐܣܛܝܟܐ *quadrilateral;* ܪ ܓܦ̈ܐ *four-winged;* ܪ ܦܣܩ̈ܐ *tetrasyllabic;* ܪ ܝܘܡ̈ܐ *four days dead;* ܪ ܦܬܓܡ̈ܐ *tetraplar;* ܪ ܦܪ̈ܨܘܦܐ *having four faces;* ܪܒܝܥܝ ܪ̈ܓܠܐ *quadrupeds.*

ܪܒܝܥܝܘܬܐ and ܐܪܒܥ̈ rt. ܪܒܥ. f. *fourfold nature* or *quality; a body of four, quaternion; quaternity; quadrature.*

ܪܒܝܥܝܢܝܐ and ܐܪܒܥ̈, ܝܬܐ rt. ܪܒܥ. *quadragesimal.*

ܪܒܝܥܬܐ rt. ܪܒܥ. f. *a squared block of stone.*

ܪܒܝܪܘܬܐ rt. ܪܒܪ. f. *prominence* of the eyes.

ܪܒܝܬܐ or ܪܒܝܬܝܐ pl. ܪܒ ܒܝ̈ܬܐ contraction of ܪܒ ܒܝܬܐ *a steward.*

ܪܒܝܬܐ; see ܪܒܝ.

ܪܒܠ fut. ܢܪܒܘܠ, act. part. ܪܒܠ, ܪܒܠܐ. *to swell.* ETHPE. ܐܬܪܒܠ *to be swollen* with weeping, with disease. PA. ܪܒܠ *to swell up, gather;* ܡܪܒܠܝܢ ܗܘܘ ܐܦ̈ܝܗܘܢ their *faces were covered with abscesses.* SHAPHEL ܫܪܒܠ pass. part. ܡܫܪܒܠ, ܠܐ *draggled, shabby.* ESHTAPH. ܐܫܬܪܒܠ *to be draggled.* DERIVATIVES, ܪܒܠܐ, ܪܘܒܠܐ, ܡܪܒܠܐ, ܡܪܒܠܐ, ܡܪܒܠܘܬܐ.

ܪܒܠܐ rt. ܪܒܠ. *lax, dissolute.*

ܪܒܠܐ m. *palm-fibre.*

ܪܒܢ from ܪܒ with pron. suff. *our master.* Used as a title for priests, monks and abbats.

ܪܒܢܐ pl. of ܪܒ.

ܪܒܢܝܐ rt. ܪܒ. *of* or *belonging to a master* or *teacher.*

ܪܒܥ fut. ܢܪܒܥ, act. part. ܪܒܥ, ܪܒܥܐ, pass. part. ܪܒܝܥ, ܥܐ, ܥܬܐ. *a*) *to lie down, couch; to recline* at table; ܒܪܟ ܘܪܒܥ ܐܝܟ ܐܪܝܐ *he stooped down, he couched as a lion;* ܒܪܒܝܥܐ ܟܕ ܪܒܝܥܐ: ܐܝܠܢܐ ܐܦ ܗܘ ܒܪܒܝܥܐ *in the spring* time a woman reclining and singing to a timbrel. b) to drum, tabour, beat a tabor. Pa. only pass. part. ܡܪܰܒܰܥ, ـܐ, ـܬܐ square, four-cornered, four-sided, quadrangular, quadrilateral; geom. a square; arith. square of a number. Ethpa. ܐܶܬܪܰܒܰܥ to be squared, made square. Aph. ܐܰܪܒܰܥ a) to cause to lie down, to settle; ܪ̈ܳܥܘܳܬܳܐ ܡܰܪܒܥܺܝܢ ܠܡܰܪ̈ܥܝܳܬܗܽܘܢ shepherds causing their flocks to lie down. Derivatives, ܪܒܝܥܐ, ܐܪܒܥ, ܪܒܥܐ, ܪܒܝܥܝܐ, ܪܒܝܥܝܬܐ, ܪܒܥܐ, ܪܒܝܥܬܐ, ܪܒܝܥܝܢ, ܪܒܝܥܘܬܐ, ܪܒܥܝܐ, ܡܪܒܥܐ, ܡܪܒܥܘܬܐ, ܡܪܒܥܐ, ܪܒܥܐ, ܪܒܥܝܐ, ܡܪܒܥܝܬܐ, ܡܪܒܥܢܐ, ܡܪܒܥܐ.

ܪܒܥܳܐ pl. ـܐ, ـܝܢ rt. ܪܒܥ. m. a quadrantal, liquid measure of about nine gallons.

ܪܒܳܥܳܐ rt. ܪܒܥ. a sheep-fold, camel-stable.

ܪܒܰܥܬ rt. ܪܒܥ. four years hence.

ܪܒܰܨ fut. ܢܶܪܒܽܘܨ, act. part. ܪܳܒܶܨ, ܪܳܒܨܳܐ, pass. part. ܪܒܺܝܨ, ـܐ, ـܬܐ. a) to hold tight, grip, to confine within bounds; to stiffen; to oppress, depress; ܐܳܐܰܪ ܚܰܪܺܝܦܳܐ ܘܪܳܒܶܨ sharp air chills and grips; ܫܽܘܚܳܢܳܐ ܪܒܰܨܳܟ the heat oppressed thee; ܪܒܺܝܨܺܝܢ ܟܶܝܡܽܘܣܰܘܗܝ his humours have become clogged; ܬܰܪܥܺܝܬܳܐ ܪܒܺܝܨܬܳܐ ܒܚܰܫ̈ܐ a mind held in the grip of passions; ܪܒܰܨܰܢ ܒܥܰܘ̈ܠܳܬܳܐ it held us fast in transgressions. b) to pronounce with the vowel R'waṣa, ̈ e, ܐܳܠܰܦ ܕܪܒܺܝܨܳܐ Alep with e. Ethpe. ܐܶܬܪܒܶܨ a) to be squeezed tightly, gripped, wedged in; ܡܳܐ ܕܐܶܬܪܒܶܨ ܒܬܪ̈ܰܝܗܶܝܢ ܚܶܠ̈ܐ when it is wedged tight in both holes; ܐܶܡܰܬܝ ܕܡܶܬܪܒܨܳܐ ܚܺܐܪܽܘܬܰܢ ܒܝܰܬ ܢܛܳܪܬܳܐ ܠܰܥܒܳܪܬܳܐ ܕܦܽܘܩܕܳܢܳܐ when our free choice is in a strait between keeping and breaking the commandment; ܟܰܕ ܡܶܬܪܰܒܨܺܝܢ when they are forced, obliged. b) gram. to have the vowel ̈, R'waṣa. Pa. ܪܰܒܶܨ to check, repress. Ethpa. to be checked, repressed. Derivatives, ܪܒܝܨܘܬܐ, ܪܒܨܐ, ܪܒܘܨܐ, ܪܒܨܐ, ܪܒܨܐ.

ܪܒܳܨܳܐ rt. ܪܒܨ. m. pressure, strain.

ܪܒܳܨܳܐ rt. ܪܒܨ. m. R'waṣa, the vowel ̈ e, ܪܒܺܝܨ with Yudh having e, ܝ̈.

ܪܰܒܩܳܬܳܐ Arab. f. treading out grain by oxen without instruments.

ܪܰܒܪ̈ܒܳܢܶܐ an older spelling of ܪܰܘܪ̈ܒܳܢܶܐ pl. of ܪܰܘܪܒܳܢܳܐ.

ܪܰܒܳܬ rt. ܪܒ. adv. very much, very greatly.

ܪܰܒܬܳܐ fem. of ܪܰܒ. great, noble; a mistress, superior; a great lady.

ܪܓܳܐ fut. ܢܶܪܓܶܐ, parts. ܪܳܓܶܐ, ܪܳܓܝܳܐ or ܪܳܓܳܐ and ܪܓܶܐ, ـܐ, ـܬܐ frequently written with Alep as if the root were ܐܪܓ, fut. ܢܶܐܪܰܓ, part. adj. ܐܪܺܝܓ &c. to desire, covet, lust often with ܪܶܓܬܳܐ or the infin., ܪܓܳܐ ܡܶܪܓܳܐ also ܪܓܳܐ ܪܶܓܬܳܐ he desired earnestly, while ܪܓܳܐ ܪܶܓܬܳܐ is usually in a bad sense to lust; ܪܳܓܶܐ ܪܶܓܬܳܐ the lustful, but ܡܳܐܢܶܐ ܪ̈ܓܺܝܓܶܐ desirable or goodly vessels; ܠܳܐ ܬܶܪܓܶܐ ܐܰܢ̄ܬܬܶܗ ܕܚܰܒܪܳܟ thou shalt not covet thy neighbour's wife. Parts. a) first form fem. impers. with ܠ to be desirable, pleasant; to desire, to please; ܠܡܰܢ ܕܪܳܓܝܳܐ ܠܶܗ whom you please; ܐܰܝܟ ܡܳܐ ܕܪܳܓܝܳܐ ܠܳܟ as you please; ܡܳܢܳܐ ܪܳܓܝܳܐ ܠܳܟ what do you wish? ܪܳܓܝܳܐ ܠܗܽܘܢ ܕ they desire that.... b) second form, verbal use ܐܶܢܳܐ ܪܓܺܝܓ I desire; ܪܓܺܝܓܺܝܢ ܕܢܶܫܬܰܘܘܽܘܢ they desire to be worthy of.... c) adj. desirable, fair, pleasant; ܪܓܺܝܓ ܠܡܶܚܙܳܐ or ܠܚܶܙܘܳܐ pleasant to see, of agreeable appearance; ܚܰܝܶܐ ܪܓܺܝܓܺܝܢ ܠܶܗ life was pleasant to him. d) pl. subst. desires, lusts; desirable things, pleasures; ܥܰܡ ܪ̈ܓܺܝܓܳܬܳܐ ܐܶܬܟܰܬܰܫܘ they strove against lusts; ܒܟܽܠܗܶܝܢ ܪ̈ܓܺܝܓܳܬܳܐ ܕܢܰܦܫܳܟ with all the desires of thy soul. Palp. ܪܰܓܪܶܓ to make to long, rouse desires, yearnings; ܡܪܰܓܪܶܓ ܗܘܳܐ ܠܗܽܘܢ ܠܡܶܪܕܰܦ ܒܬܰܪ ܡܰܝܬܪܽܘܬܳܐ he made them long to pursue virtue. Ethpalp. ܐܶܬܪܰܓܪܰܓ to long sore, yearn, earnestly desire; ܪܳܓܝܳܐ ܢܰܦܫܝ ܘܐܶܬܪܰܓܪܓܰܬ ܠܡܶܥܰܠ ܠܕ̈ܳܪܰܘܗܝ ܕܡܳܪܝܳܐ my soul hath a desire and longing to enter into the courts of the Lord. Aph. ܐܰܪܓܝ to long, covet. Derivatives, ܪܶܓܬܳܐ, ܪܓܺܝܓܳܐ, ܪܓܳܓܳܐ, ܪܓܺܝܓܽܘܬܳܐ, ܪܰܓܳܓܽܘܬܳܐ, ܪܓܳܓܬܳܐ, ܪܓܝܓܝܬܐ, ܪܓܪܓܢܐ, ܪܓܪܓܢܘܬܐ, ܡܪܓܝܢܐ, ܡܪܓܪܓܢܐ, ܬܪܓܝܓܐ.

ܪܓܳܐ fut. ܢܶܪܓܶܐ. to moisten. Part. adj. ܪܰܓܺܝ, ܪܰܓܝܳܐ, ܪܰܓܝܳܬܳܐ moist, soft; tender, fresh, green; ܣܰܘ̈ܟܶܐ ܪ̈ܰܓܝܶܐ fresh branches; ܙܰܒܢܳܐ ܪܰܓܝܳܐ spring time; ܫܡܰܝܳܐ ܪ̈ܰܓܝܶܐ moist skies. Pa. ܪܰܓܺܝ to moisten, soften, freshen; ܗܰܘ ܕܐܰܫܟܰܚ ܕܢܪܰܓܶܐ ܬܕܰܝܳܐ ܥܩܺܝܪ̈ܳܬܳܐ He Who could make moist the barren breasts. Ethpa. ܐܶܬܪܰܓܺܝ to be moistened, softened; to grow fresh; ܩܰܢܝܳܐ ܕܢܶܬܪܰܓܶܐ ܐܰܝܟܰܢܳܐ ܫܳܟܰܚ ܕܠܳܐ ܡܰܝܳܐ can the reed shoot up fresh without water? ܐܶܬܪܰܓܺܝ ܒܛܰܠܳܟ ܪܶܥܝܳܢܝ my mind is freshened by Thy dew. Aph. ܐܰܪܓܺܝ a) to make to grow up fresh, make to flourish. b) act.

part. ܐܢܐ ܡܪܓܐ *I wish, I hope*, as if from verb ܪܓܐ. Derivatives, ܪܓܬܐ, ܪܓܝܓܐ, ܡܪܓܝܓܐ.

ܪܓܬܐ (abs. st. rare) ܪܓܬܐ rt. ܪܓܐ. f. *a*) *desire, longing, appetite, lust;* ܪܓܬܐ ܕܒܣܪܐ *fleshly desire;* ܐܝܟ ܪܓܬܟ *as you please.* *b*) *an object of desire;* ܥܝܢܐ ܪܓܝܐ ܟܠ ܪܓܬܐ *the eye desires every object of desire;* ܪܓܬܐ ܠܥܝܢܐ *a delight to the eyes.*

ܪܓܘܫܐ = ܪܓܘܫܐ *largess.*

ܪܓܒ Arab. *Rajab*, the third lunar month of the Arabs, accounted holy.

ܪܓܒܐ m. vernac. *mire* or *slime out of a well.*

ܪܓܝܓܐ, ܪܓܝܓܬܐ rt. ܪܓܐ. adj. *of desire, of appetite.*

ܪܘܓܙܐ rt. ܪܓܙ. f. *wrath.*

ܪܘܓܙܐ rt. ܪܓܙ. m. *anger, irritation.*

ܪܓܝܙܘܬܐ = ܪܓܝܙܢܘܬܐ.

ܪܓܝܙܢܐ rt. ܪܓܙ. *angry, wrathful, irascible.*

ܪܓܝܙܢܘܬܐ rt. ܪܓܙ. f. *proneness to anger, irascibility.*

ܪܓܠܐ pl. ܐ̈ m. *the narrow valley of a rivulet; a rivulet.*

ܪܓܘܡܐ pl. ܐ̈ rt. ܪܓܡ. m. *one who stones.*

ܪܓܘܡܝܐ rt. ܪܓܡ. m. *a*) *stoning,* ܡܘܬܐ ܕܪܓܡܐ *death by stoning.* *b*) *the disease of the stone.*

ܪܓܘܡܝܐ, ܪܓܘܡܝܬܐ rt. ܪܓܡ. with ܟܐܦܐ *stones for stoning, heavy stones.*

ܪܓܘܫ = ܪܓܘܫܐ *bounty.*

ܪܓܘܫܐ pl. ܐ̈ rt. ܪܓܫ. m. *endowed with senses, sentient, moved by the senses, sensitive.*

ܪܓܘܫܘܬܐ rt. ܪܓܫ. f. *sense, perception,* with ܠܐ *insensibility; sentient beings.*

ܪܓܘܫܐ rt. ܪܓܫ. m. *rushing sound* of water, *tumult.*

ܪܓܘܫܢܝܬܐ and ܪ rt. ܪܓܫ. f. pl. *nurses who rock and lull babies to sleep.*

ܪܓܘܫܬܢܐ, ܬܢܝܬܐ rt. ܪܓܫ. *sentient, sensitive.*

ܪܓܘܫܬܢܐܝܬ rt. ܪܓܫ. adv. *sensibly, perceptibly.*

ܪܓܘܫܬܢܘܬܐ rt. ܪܓܫ. f. *understanding, intelligence.*

ܪܓܙ fut. ܢܪܓܙ, act. part. ܪܳܓܶܙ, ܪܳܓܙܐ, pass. part. ܪܓܝܙ, ܐ, ܬܐ. *to be wroth, angry* with ܥܠ of the pers. or cause; with ܡܢ *to part in anger.* P.p. *prone to anger; at enmity.* Aph. ܐܪܓܙ *to provoke to anger, excite imagination* with ܒ or ܠ; ܐܬܪܥܐ ܥܡܢ ܕܐܪܓܙܢܟ *be reconciled to us for we have provoked Thee to anger.* Derivatives, ܪܘܓܙܐ, ܪܘܓܙܐ, ܪܓܝܙܘܬܐ, ܡܪܓܙܢܘܬܐ, ܡܪܓܙܢܐ, ܪܓܝܙܢܐ, ܪܓܝܙܢܘܬܐ, ܡܪܓܙܢܘܬܐ, ܪܓܙܢܐ.

ܪܓܙܐ, ܪܓܙܬܐ, ܪܓܙܬܐ or ܪܓܫܬܐ f. *a wallet of hair cloth* or *wool, a fodder-bag, nosebag; a plaited basket.*

ܪܰܓܺܝ Pael conj. of verb ܪܓܐ.

ܪܓܝܒ, ܪܓܝܒܐ *broad, spacious;* ܕܘܟܬܐ ܪܓܝܒܬܐ *a broad place for the erection of idols.*

ܪܓܝܓ, ܪܓܝܓܐ, ܪܓܝܓܬܐ; see under verb ܪܓܐ.

ܪܓܝܓܘܬܐ and ܪܰܓܝܳܓܘܬܐ pl. ܘ̈ܬܐ rt. ܪܓܐ. f. *appetite, desire, savouriness.*

ܪܓܝܓܘܬܐ rt. ܪܓܐ. f. *delightfulness.*

ܪܓܝܓܘܬܐ rt. ܪܓܐ. f. *moisture, greenness, freshness, softness.*

ܪܓܝܙܘܬܐ rt. ܪܓܙ. f. *indignation, enmity.*

ܪܓܝܫܘܬܐ rt. ܪܓܫ. f. *sensibility.*

ܪܓܝܬܐ rt. ܪܓܐ. f. perh. *young crops, spring corn.*

ܪܓܠ denom. verb from ܪܓܠܐ. Ethpa. ܐܬܪܓܠ *to come* or *go on foot, to dismount, to step forward;* ܢܦܩ ܠܐܘܪܥܗ ܘܐܬܪܓܠ ܘܢܫܩ ܠܐܪܥܐ *he went out to meet him and dismounted and kissed the ground.* Aph. ܐܪܓܠ *to go on foot.* Shaph. ܫܪܓܠ *to impede, ensnare, to drag* or *sweep off the feet;* ܫܪܓܠ ܒܚܪܫܐ *to ensnare in witchcraft;* ܠܚܘܡܪܐ ܫܪܓܠܘܢ *they dragged them down.* Eshtaph. ܐܫܬܪܓܠ *to slip, slide down, lose one's footing; to be made to swerve aside; to be impeded, ensnared;* ܡܢ ܓܘܡܨܐ ܠܓܘܡܨܐ ܐܫܬܪܓܠܘ *they slipped from one pitfall into another;* ܐܫܬܪܓܠ ܡܠܬܐ ܠܡܠܬܐ ܐܚܪܬܐ *the narration slid off into another subject;* ܒܐܘܪܚܬܐ ܒܝܫܬܐ ܡܫܬܪܓܠܝܢ ܗܘܘ *they had slid into evil ways.*

ܪܓܠ, ܪܓܠܐ pl. ܝܢ, ܐ̈ and in metaph. senses ܪܓܠܬܐ f. *a foot, hoof;* ܥܩܝܡ ܪܓܠܐ *crook-shanked;* ܪ ܕܐܪܒܥ and ܐܪܒܥ ܪܓܠܝܢ *four-footed, quadruped;* ܪ ܬܪܬܝܢ *biped.* Metaph. *foot, base, pier.* With preps. ܒܪܓܠ and ܡܢ ܪܓܠ *on foot;* ܠܪܓܠܘܗܝ *after him.* Derivatives, verb ܪܓܠ, and the six following words:—

ܪܓܠܐ f. pl. *astragalus, milk-vetch.*

ܪܓܠܐ, ܪܓܠܝܐ pl. ܐ̈, ܬܐ from ܪܓܠܐ. *a foot-soldier;* f. ܚܝܘܬܐ ܪܓܠܝܬܐ *a land animal.*

ܪܶܓܠܳܐ pl. ܳܬܳܐ from ܪܶܓܠܳܐ. m. *a footstool.*

ܪܶܓܠܳܐܺܝܬ from ܪܶܓܠܳܐ. adv. *on foot.*

ܪܰܓܠܽܘܬܳܐ from ܪܶܓܠܳܐ. f. *fighting on foot.*

ܪܰܓܠܳܝܳܐ pl. ܳܝܶܐ, ܳܝܳܐ from ܪܶܓܠܳܐ. m. *a foot-soldier, infantry.*

ܪܰܓܠܳܝܬܳܐ pl. ܳܝܳܬܳܐ, also ܐܶܪܓܠܳܝܳܬܳܐ (rare). f. *a torrent.*

ܪܓܰܡ fut. ܢܶܪܓܽܘܡ, act. part. ܪܳܓܶܡ, ܪܳܓܡܳܐ. *to stone, kill by stoning, hurl stones, heap stones;* ܪܓܰܡܽܘܗܝ ܒܟܺܐܦܶܐ ܘܡܺܝܬ *they stoned him with stones and he died;* ܪܓܰܡܘ ܩܰܒܪܶܗ *they defaced his tomb with stones.* Pass. part. ܪܓܺܝܡܳܐ *condemned to be stoned, deserving of death by stoning.* Ethpe. ܐܶܬܪܓܶܡ *to be stoned, to be subjected to stone-throwing.* Ethpa. ܐܶܬܪܰܓܰܡ *to be stoned.* Derivatives, ܪܓܳܡܳܐ, ܪܓܽܘܡܳܐ, ܪܓܽܘܡܝܳܐ.

ܪܓܳܡܳܐ rt. ܪܓܡ. m. *stoning.*

ܪܓܽܘܡܬܳܐ pl. ܳܡܳܬܳܐ = ܪܓܳܡܳܐ.

ܪܓܰܫ fut. ܢܶܪܓܽܘܫ, parts. ܪܳܓܶܫ, ܪܳܓܫܳܐ and ܪܓܺܝܫ, ܳܫܳܐ, ܳܫܬܳܐ. *a) to rage, be in an uproar;* ܕܬܶܪܓܽܘܫ ܪܶܓܬܳܐ ܒܦܰܓܪܶܗ *that desire might rage in his body. b) to feel, perceive, be conscious, aware of* with ܒ; ܠܳܐ ܪܳܓܶܫ ܐ̱ܢܳܐ ܒܢܰܦܫܝ ܕܥܒܶܕܬ ܡܶܕܶܡ ܒܰܗܬܬܳܐ *I am not conscious of having done anything disgraceful;* ܠܳܐ ܪܳܓܫܺܝܢ *they do not perceive;* ܟܕ ܠܳܐ ܪܳܓܫܺܝܢ *unawares;* ܪܳܓܫܳܢܶܐ *sentient beings. c) to curry, rub down.* Ethpe. ܐܶܬܪܓܶܫ *a) to be in commotion, toss;* ܡܶܬܪܰܓܫܺܝܢ ܡܰܝܰܘܗ̱ܝ *his waters toss. b) to be perceived, perceptible.* Aph. ܐܰܪܓܶܫ *a) to feel, perceive, to be sensible of, conscious of, aware of;* ܟܕ ܐܰܪܓܶܫ ܒܗܽܘܢ ܥܪܰܩ *when he was aware of them he fled;* ܟܕ ܐܰܪܓܫܘ ܐܰܠܶܟܣܰܢܕܪܳܝܶܐ *when the Alexandrians were apprised of this.* With ܟܽܐܪܳܐ, ܒܟܽܐܪܳܐ *to feel ill, feverish, be seized with illness, with fever. b) to make known, acquaint;* ܟܕ ܠܳܐ ܐܰܪܓܶܫ ܠܐ̱ܢܳܫ ܡܶܢ ܚܰܒܪܰܘܗ̱ܝ *making it known to none of his companions.* Derivatives, ܪܶܓܫܳܐ, ܪܶܓܫܬܳܐ, ܪܶܓܫܳܢܳܐ, ܪܶܓܫܳܢܽܘܬܳܐ, ܪܰܓܫܳܢܳܐܺܝܬ, ܪܰܓܫܳܢܳܝܳܐ, ܪܰܓܫܳܢܳܝܽܘܬܳܐ, ܪܓܺܝܫܽܘܬܳܐ, ܪܓܺܝܫܳܐ, ܡܪܰܓܫܳܢܳܐ, ܡܪܰܓܫܳܢܳܐܺܝܬ, ܡܪܰܓܫܳܢܽܘܬܳܐ, ܡܰܪܓܫܳܢܳܐ, ܡܰܪܓܫܳܢܳܐܺܝܬ, ܡܰܪܓܫܳܢܽܘܬܳܐ.

ܪܶܓܫܳܐ pl. ܳܫܺܝܢ, ܳܫܶܐ rt. ܪܓܫ. m. *a) uproar. b) a sense, the senses, organs of sense;* ܕܠܳܐ ܪܶܓܫܳܐ *senseless;* ܪܶܓܫܰܝ̈ ܦܰܓܪܳܐ *the bodily senses* are ܚܙܳܬܳܐ *sight,* ܡܶܫܡܰܥܬܳܐ *hearing,* ܡܽܘܪܳܚܳܐ *smell,* ܛܳܥܡܳܐ *taste,* ܡܓܰܫܫܽܘܬܳܐ *feeling;* ܪܶܓܫܶܐ ܓܰܘܳܝܶܐ or ܪܶܓܫܶܐ ܕܢܰܦܫܳܐ *the inner senses* or *the senses of the soul* are variously reckoned by Bar Bahlul as ܗܰܘܢܳܐ *mind,* ܡܰܚܫܰܒܬܳܐ *thought,* ܒܽܘܝܳܢܳܐ *discernment,* ܡܰܕܥܳܐ *understanding,* ܡܡܰܠܠܽܘܬܳܐ *speech,* by Ebedjesu as ܦܰܢܛܰܣܝܰܐ *imagination,* ܡܰܚܫܰܒܬܳܐ *thought,* ܥܽܘܗܕܳܢܳܐ *memory,* ܣܽܘܟܳܠܳܐ *intelligence,* ܡܰܕܥܳܐ *understanding.*

ܪܶܓܫܳܢܳܐ rt. ܪܓܫ. *perceptible to the senses.*

ܪܶܓܫܳܢܳܝܳܐ, ܳܝܬܳܐ rt. ܪܓܫ. *of the senses, sensible.*

ܪܶܓܫܬܳܐ rt. ܪܓܫ. f. *a) rustling noise. b) sense, sensation, perception, cognizance, movement.*

ܪܶܓܬܳܐ emph. state of ܪܶܓܳܐ.

ܪܰܓܬܳܢܳܐ rt. ܪܓ. *eager, covetous.*

ܪܰܓܬܳܢܳܐܺܝܬ rt. ܪܓ. adv. *greedily, eagerly.*

ܪܰܓܬܳܢܳܝܳܐ, ܳܝܬܳܐ rt. ܪܓ. *of desire, desirous, eager.*

ܪܕܳܐ fut. ܢܶܪܕܶܐ, act. part. ܪܳܕܶܐ, ܪܳܕܝܳܐ, pass. part. ܪܕܶܐ, ܪܕܶܝܳܐ, ܪܕܶܝܳܬܳܐ. *a) to journey, travel, go forward, proceed on the way, move along;* often with ܒܐܽܘܪܚܳܐ *to go on the road, travel;* ܪܳܕܶܝ ܒܐܽܘܪܚܳܐ *travellers;* but ܐܽܘܪܚܳܐ ܪܳܕܝܳܐ ܠ *the path leads to . . .;* with ܒܝܰܡܳܐ, ܒܝܰܡܡܳܐ *to journey by sea, sail, make a voyage;* ܢܶܪܕܶܐ ܠܦܰܩܥܬܳܐ *let us go into the open country;* ܪܕܺܝ ܩܕܳܡܰܝ *proceed before me;* ܪܳܕܝܳܐ ܢܽܘܪܳܐ ܠܦܺܝܬܺܝܠܬܳܐ *the fire runs along to the wick;* ܕܠܳܐ ܪܕܳܐ *motionless.* With ܒܳܬܰܪ *to seek, to follow after, pursue;* ܪܳܕܶܝ ܒܳܬܰܪ ܪܰܒܽܘܬܳܐ *ambitious men;* with ܒܥܶܩܒܳܬܶܗ *to follow, imitate;* with ܥܰܡ *to accompany. b) to go on, proceed, continue,* with ܥܝܳܕܳܐ or ellipt. *to obtain as a custom;* ܐܰܝܟ ܕܥܝܳܕܳܐ ܪܳܕܶܐ *as the custom is;* ܐܰܝܟ ܕܫܰܪܺܝ ܗܳܟܰܢ ܪܕܳܐ ܘܫܰܠܶܡ *as he began so he continued and ended;* ܡܶܠܬܳܐ ܗܳܕܶܐ ܪܕܳܬ ܥܕܰܡܳܐ ܠܗܳܪܟܳܐ *so far has the argument proceeded. c) to continue, live* ܒܚܛܺܝܬܳܐ *in sin,* ܒܫܪܳܪܳܐ *in truth;* ܟܽܠ ܐ̱ܢܳܫ ܐܰܝܟ ܕܨܳܒܶܐ ܗܘܳܐ ܫܰܪܺܝ ܪܳܕܶܐ *every one began to behave as he pleased. d) to flow, issue, emanate, derive, descend as a stream;* ܢܰܗܪ̈ܘܳܬܳܐ ܪܳܕܝܳܬܳܐ *flowing streams;* ܡܰܝܳܐ ܕܠܳܐ ܪܳܕܶܝܢ *stagnant waters;* ܐܰܝܟ ܢܽܘܪܳܐ ܪܕܳܐ ܡܶܢ ܪܰܘܡܳܐ *like fire did He issue forth from on high;* ܠܳܐ ܪܳܕܝܳܐ ܚܰܝܠܳܐ ܟܳܗܢܳܝܳܐ ܡܶܢ ܫܽܘܡܳܠܳܝܳܐ *the priestly power does not derive* from an uncanonical ordination. For act. part. m. pl. = subst. see under ܪܳܕܝܳܐ.

e) to instruct, chastise; ܐܪܕܘܢܟܘܢ ܚܕ ܫܒܥܐ ܥܠ ܚܛܗܝܟܘܢ I will chastise your sins sevenfold. Pass. part. well informed, experienced, cultivated, versed; ܩܘܦܐ ܪܕܝܢ trained apes; with ܠܐ ignorant, unlearned, undisciplined; ܛܠܝܐ ܕܠܐ ܪܕܐ a badly brought-up boy; ܡܠܬܐ ܠܐ ܪܕܝܬܐ an uncouth saying, rude speech. Often misprinted or confused with ܕܪܐ to scatter. Ethpe. ܐܬܪܕܝ a) to be chastened, corrected, instructed, learned; ܐܢ ܠܐ ܬܬܪܕܘܢ if ye will not accept discipline; ܡܢ ܗܘ ܫܐܕܐ ܐܬܪܕܝ he was punished by that demon; ܐܬܪܕܝܘ ܟܠܗ ܚܕܬܐ ܘܥܬܝܩܬܐ they had been taught the whole of the New Testament and of the Old. b) to be made fluid, to be liquefied. c) with ܒܐܘܪܚܐ to pursue a journey, a course. Pa. ܪܕܝ a) to pound. b) = Aph. to lead. Aph. ܐܪܕܝ a) to shed forth, let flow; to discharge; metaph. to supply abundantly; ܐܪܥܐ ܕܡܪܕܝܐ ܚܠܒܐ ܘܕܒܫܐ a land flowing with milk and honey; ܡܪܕܐ ܡܒܘܥܐ ܕܚܝܐ ܪܘܚܢܝܐ he sheds forth an abundant spring of spiritual life. b) to instruct, chastise, punish; ܕܝܢܐ ܩܫܝܐ ܘܪܘܓܙܢܐ ܐܪܕܝ ܠܬܪܝܗܘܢ he adjudged severe and wrathful punishment to both of them. c) = Peal to proceed, go with. d) to lead; ܐܘܪܚܐ ܕܡܪܕܝܐ ܠܫܡܝܐ the heavenward path. Derivatives, ܪܕܘܝܐ, ܪܕܝܐ, ܪܕܝܐ, ܪܕܝܐܝܬ, ܪܕܝܘܬܐ, ܡܪܕܐ, ܡܪܕܝܘܬܐ, ܡܪܕܝܐ, ܡܪܕܝܢܐ, ܡܪܕܝܬܐ, ܡܬܪܕܝܢܐ.

ܪܕܐܦܐ rt. ܪܕܦ. m. (rare) for ܪܕܘܦܝܐ persecution.

ܪܕܝܕܬܐ = ܪܕܝܕܐ.

ܪܕܘܝܐ, ܪܕܘܝܬܐ pl. ܐ̈ rt. ܪܕܐ. a) adj. fluid, liquid; med. running. Metaph. frail, perishable. b) subst. m. a traveller. c) an instructor, chastiser; apt to teach or guide.

ܪܕܘܢܐ pl. ܐ̈ Lat. raeda, a four-wheeled travelling carriage.

ܪܕܘܦ, ܪܕܘܦܐ, ܬܐ rt. ܪܕܦ. a persecutor.

ܪܕܘܦܘܬܐ rt. ܪܕܦ. f. persecuting, persecution.

ܪܕܘܦܝܐ and ܐܪܕܘܦܝܐ pl. ܐ̈ rt. ܪܕܦ. m. persecution, banishment.

ܪܕܝܐ pl. ܪ̈ܕܝܐ also ܪ̈ܕܝܐ rt. ܪܕܐ. m. a) a flow, current; running water, a stream. b) flux, fusion of metal; med. a flux, discharge, issue. c) a march, journey; ܪܕܝܐ ܩܫܝܐ a forced march; metaph. course, succession.

ܪܕܝܐܝܬ rt. ܪܕܐ. adv. skilfully; with ܠܐ ignorantly.

ܪܕܝܕ, ܪܕܝܕܐ and ܐܪܕܝܕܐ pl. ܐ̈ m. a bridal veil, a square veil of transparent stuff gathered at the top.

ܪܕܝܕܘܬܐ f. a cloak.

ܪܕܝܕܐ and ܪܕܝܕܬܐ f. a deacon's sleeveless surplice.

ܪܕܝܘܬܐ rt. ܪܕܐ. f. a) good breeding, culture; with ܠܐ ignorance, lack of education. b) course, continuance.

ܪܕܝܦܘܬܐ rt. ܪܕܦ. f. suffering persecution, being persecuted.

ܪܕܢ Ethpe. ܐܬܪܕܢ perh. to be spun into thread. Derivative, ܡܪܕܢܐ.

ܪܕܦ fut. ܢܪܕܘܦ, act. part. ܪܕܦ, ܪܕܦܐ, pass. part. ܪܕܝܦ, ܐ, ܬܐ. a) to urge on, drive on, to overdrive cattle; ܪܕܘܦܝ ܥܒܕܐ slavedrivers, taskmasters; ܐܠܦܐ ܕܪܕܦܐ a galley propelled by oars. b) to chase away, banish with ܡܢ from; ܥܘܬܪܐ ܪܕܦ ܫܢܬܐ riches have banished sleep; ܪܕܦܬ ܠܫܐܕܐ thou hast chased the demons away. c) to persecute with ܠ. d) to pursue an enemy, to pursue a desire, to seek after, long after with ܒܬܪ; ܚܢܢ ܪܕܦܝܢ ܚܘܪ̈ܒܬܐ we seek waste places. e) with ܥܠ or ܠܘܩܒܠ to rush upon, make an attack. Pass. part. driven, banished, persecuted; ܐܠܦܐ ܪܕܝܦܬܐ ܡܢ ܥܠܥܠܐ a storm-driven ship; ܐܠܗܐ ܢܒܥܐ ܠܪܕܝܦܐ ܘܠܡܛܪܕܐ God will seek him who is persecuted and outcast. Ethpe. ܐܬܪܕܦ to be driven away, banished, persecuted. Ethpa. ܐܬܪܕܦ a) to be put to flight. b) to be hurried on a journey. Derivatives, ܪܕܐܦܐ, ܪܕܘܦܐ, ܪܕܘܦܘܬܐ, ܪܕܘܦܝܐ, ܪܕܝܦܘܬܐ, ܡܪܕܘܦܝܐ.

ܪܕܩ fut. ܢܪܕܘܩ, act. part. ܪܕܩ, ܪܕܩܐ. to watch closely esp. from a lurking-place, to spy out, be on the look out for; ܬܘ ܢܬܒ ܒܝܢܬ ܐܝܠܢܐ ܗܠܝܢ ܘܢܪܕܩܝܘܗܝ ܠܣܒܐ let us settle ourselves among these trees and watch for the old man; ܦܪ̈ܚܬܐ ܪܕܩܢ ܠܚܘܘܬܐ birds are on the look out for snakes. Derivative, ܪܕܩܐ.

ܪܗܒ Peal only part. adj. ܪܗܝܒ, ܐ, ܬܐ.

a) verbal use: *to hasten;* ܐܘ ܚܝܐ ܠܐܝܟܐ ܪܗܒܝܢ ܐܢܬܝ *O life whither hastest thou?* b) *hasty, hurried; rapid, swift;* ܡܘܬܐ ܪܗܝܒܐ *a premature death;* ܢܗܪܐ ܪܗܝܒܐ *a swift stream.* c) *disquieted, agitated, perturbed, alarmed;* ܟܕ ܠܐ ܪܗܝܒ ܘܠܐ ܙܐܥ *composed and firm;* ܪܗܝܒܐ ܒܟܠܗ ܠܠܝܐ *uneasy all night;* ܪܗܝܒ ܐܢܬ ܥܠ ܣܓܝܐܬܐ *thou art careful and troubled about many things.* Ethpe. ܐܬܪܗܒ *to be disquieted, agitated with fear, to be afraid.* Ethpa. ܐܬܪܗܒ *to be greatly alarmed, terrified.* Aph. ܐܪܗܒ a) *to trouble, disquiet;* ܚܠܡܐ ܕܐܪܗܒܘ ܐܢܘܢ *the dreams that troubled them.* b) *to inspire awe, terror, to alarm, cause to tremble;* ܡܪܐ ܟܠ ܡܪܗܒ ܠܟܪܘܒܐ *the Lord of all inspires the cherubim with awe.* c) *to hasten, make to hasten;* ܐܢ ܗܘ ܕܡܕܒܪ ܠܟ ܡܪܗܒ ܠܟ *if he who is in charge of thee hurries thee on;* ܢܨܐ ܡܪܗܒ ܩܠܗ *the hawk utters hasty cries;* ܐܪܗܒܬ ܠܡܐܬܐ *she made haste to come.* Ettaph. ܐܬܬܪܗܒ *to be made to tremble.* Saphel ܫܪܗܒ *to hasten, impel, urge on;* ܪܗܒܘܬܐ ܕܡܘܬܐ ܡܫܪܗܒܝܢ ܗܘܘ ܠܬܠܡܝܕܐ *the terrors of death forced sudden action on the disciples;* ܩܪܢܬܐ ܡܫܪܗܒܝܢ *the trumpets haste to sound;* ܡܠܬܐ ܕܡܠܟܐ ܡܫܪܗܒܐ *the king's command brooked no delay;* ܫܪܗܒܬ ܛܒ ܠܡܘܒܕܘ ܠܥܒܕܟ *Thou hast been very hasty to destroy Thy servant.* Often with adverbial force; ܫܪܗܒ ܐܝܬܝ ܠܝ *hasten to bring me;* ܫܪܗܒ ܬܐ *come quickly;* ܫܪܗܒܘ ܥܪܘܩܘ *flee in haste.* P.p. *pressing, hurried, hasty, precipitate, unrestrained; quick, speedy;* ܡܫܪܗܒ ܠܡܫܡܥ *quick to hear;* ܚܕ ܡܢ ܡܫܪܗܒܝ ܡܠܬܐ *one of hasty speech;* ܓܘܚܟܐ ܡܫܪܗܒܐ *immoderate laughter.* Estaph. ܐܫܬܪܗܒ *to make haste, hasten; to be terrified;* ܐܫܬܪܗܒ ܡܠܟܐ ܘܩܡ *the king rose up hastily;* ܡܫܬܪܗܒ ܐܢܐ ܠܥܒܕܐ ܗܢܐ ܕܦܩܝܕ *I hasten to this appointed work.* Derivatives, ܪܗܒܐ, ܪܗܒܘܬܐ, ܪܗܒܬܐ, ܪܗܝܒܐܝܬ, ܪܗܝܒܘܬܐ, ܡܫܪܗܒܐܝܬ, ܡܪܗܒܢܐ, ܡܪܗܒܐ, ܡܫܪܗܒܘܬܐ, ܡܫܬܪܗܒܢܐ, ܫܪܗܒܢܐ.

ܪܗܒܐ rt. ܪܗܒ. m. *commotion; alarm.*

ܪܗܒܘܢܐ m. ἀρραβών, *arles, earnest-money, a pledge, earnest.*

ܪܗܒܘܢܐܝܬ from the preceding word. adv. *as an earnest.*

ܪܗܒܘܬܐ rt. ܪܗܒ. f. *trepidation.*

ܪܗܒܬܐ E-Syr. ܪܗܒܬܐ rt. ܪܗܒ. f. a) *haste, speed;* ܒܪܗܒܐ *speedily.* b) *commotion, consternation.*

ܪܗܘܛܐ pl. ܝ̈ܐ rt. ܪܗܛ. m. *a runner; a vivid flash of lightning.*

ܪܗܘܡܐ, ܪܗܘܡܝ rarely ܪܗܘܡ, also ܪܘܡܐ, ܪܘܡܝ *Rome, the Roman Empire.*

ܪܗܘܡܐ pl. ܪ̈ܗܘܡܐ and ܪ̈ܗܘܡܛܐ, also ܪܘܡܐ, m. ῥεῦμα, *a flux,* esp. *diarrhoea.*

ܪܗܘܡܐܝܬ from ܪܗܘܡܝ. adv. *in the Latin language.*

ܪܗܘܡܝܐ, ܝܬܐ pl. ܝ̈ܐ, ܝ̈ܬܐ from ܪܗܘܡܝ. a) *Roman, Latin.* b) *a Roman, Latin,* rarely *a Frank; a Greek* i. e. *a citizen of the Eastern Roman Empire.* c) *a soldier.*

ܪܗܘܡܝܘܬܐ and ܪܘܡܝ̈ from ܪܗܘܡܝ. f. a) *the right of Roman citizenship, being Roman.* b) *military service.*

ܪܗܘܡܝܢܝܐ and ܪܗܘܡܢܝܐ f. *the Roman Empire,* sometimes *the Eastern Empire.*

ܪܗܘܡܢܝܐ and ܪܘܡܝ̈ pl. ܝ̈ܐ *a Roman, a Greek.*

ܪܗܛ fut. ܢܪܗܛ, imper. ܪܗܘܛ and ܪܗܛ, parts. ܪܗܛ, ܪܗܛܐ and ܪܗܝܛ, ܪܗܝܛܐ, ܪܗܝܛܬܐ. *to run, to make haste, be swift; to have free course, make rapid progress; to occur, concur; to be active, eager, energetic, to endeavour, strive* esp. with ܪܗܛܐ ܡܪܗܒ or ܒܥܒܕܐ. With ܒܬܪ *to run after, follow, pursue;* with ܠ or ܠܘܬ *to run to, hasten towards;* with ܡܢ *to flow from;* with ܒ or ܥܠ *to assail, run at.* Adverbial use *quickly, speedily;* ܪܗܘܛ ܬܐ *come quickly;* ܪܗܛܬ ܥܠܬ *she rushed in;* ܗܦܟ ܪܗܛ *he returned quickly;* ܩܕܡ ܪܗܝܛ *immediately preceding;* ܪܗܛ ܠܐܘܪܥܗ ... *he ran to meet ...;* ܟܬܒܐ ܠܚܫܝܚܬܐ ܪܗܛܝܢ *the Scriptures pass on quickly to things of greater moment;* ܪܗܛܐ ܐܝܬܘܗܝ ܠܚܪܝܢܐ *a brawler;* ܪܗܘܛ ܒܛܠܝܘܬܟ *be eager in thy youth;* ܟܕ ܪܗܛܝܢ ܐܟܚܕܐ ܟܢܫܐ ܣܓܝܐܐ *a great crowd having run together;* ܚܦܝܛ ܘܪܗܝܛ *painstaking and energetic.* Aph. ܐܪܗܛ *to drive or urge forward, to move quickly, to do, go or bring with haste;* ܐܪܗܛܘܗܝ ܡܢ ܒܝܬ ܐܣܝܪܐ *they brought him hastily out of the dungeon;* ܓܢܒܪܐ ܡܪܗܛܝܢ ܠܗ ܒܚܝܠܐ *strong men drive it* (a battering-ram) *forcibly;* ܡܪܗܛܝܢ ܒܡܛܝܒܘܬܐ *they are actively engaged in preparations.* Esp. *to ride quickly, to gallop.* With ܥܠ ܪܫ and ܥܠ ܚܒܪܐ or ܥܘܠܐ *to throw the blame upon;* with ܥܠ or ܠܩܘܒܠܐ *to make a sudden attack.* Gram. *to let the voice pass on quickly* i.e. *to pronounce without a vowel.* Derivatives, ܪܗܛܐ, ܪܗܛܐ, ܪܗܛܐ, ܪܗܛܐ, ܪܗܛܢܐ, ܡܪܗܛܐ, ܡܪܗܛܐܝܬ, ܡܪܗܛܢܐ, ܡܪܗܛܢܐܝܬ, ܡܪܗܛܢܘܬܐ, ܡܬܪܗܛܢܐ.

ܪܗܛܐ pl. ܐ̈ rt. ܪܗܛ. a) m. *a runner, courier, letter-carrier, foot-guard; a fore-runner* esp. John the Baptist. b) *swift;* ܣܘܣܝܐ ܪ *a swift horse;* ܓܡܠܐ ܪ *a dromedary;* ܪܗܛܬܐ *a she-dromedary.*

ܪܗܛܐ E-Syr. ܪܗܛܐ rt. ܪܗܛ. m. a) *running, racing; rapidity, strenuousness;* ܪ ܕܪܟܫܐ *horse-racing;* ܒܝܬ ܪ *a racecourse;* ܒܪܗܛܐ *at a run, rapidly.* b) *a course, row, series;* ܚܝܛܝܢ ܒܪܗܛܐ *bound with rows of stitching.* c) *a rafter.* d) *course* of action, of nature, of years; esp. *the course* or *manner* of life, life, condition; ܕܢܕܥ ܪܗܛܗܘܢ *that he might know how they did;* ܛܝܒܬܐ ܕܪܗܛܝܗܘܢ *the good actions of their lives;* ܪܗܛܐ ܠܐܝܐ *wearisome runnings to and fro;* ܫܘܐ ܒܪܗܛܐ *equal, conjoint.*

ܪܗܛܐ pl. ܐ̈ rt. ܪܗܛ. m. *running waters, watercourse, stream.* Gram. the name of three points, ·.·, ‥, and .·. which accelerate the rhythm.

ܪܗܛܢܐ or ܪܗ rt. ܪܗܛ. m. *manual labour, gain from hard labour; a labourer;* perh. also *course of life.*

ܪܗܛܝܢܐ and ܪܗܛܝܢܘܢ also ܪܝܛܝܢܘܢ and ܪܐܛܝܢܐ &c. pl. ܐ̈ f. ῥητίνη, *resin, gum, balm.*

ܪܗܛܘܪܐ, ܪܐܛܘܪ, ܪܘܛܘܪ &c. pl. ܐ̈ m. ῥήτωρ, *a public speaker, pleader, orator.*

ܪܗܛܘܪܐܝܬ and ܪܗܛܘܪܝܩܝ from ܪܗܛܪܐ. adv. *eloquently.*

ܪܗܛܘܪܘܬܐ and ܪܗܛܘܪܝܩܝ from ܪܗܛܪܐ. f. *rhetoric, oratory, eloquence.*

ܪܘܝܐ rt. ܪܘܐ. m. *squalling* of a cat.

ܪܘܒܐܝܬ rt. ܪܘܒ. adv. a) *hastily, speedily, precipitately.* b) *timorously, weakly.*

ܪܘܒܒܐ, ܪܘܒܒܘܬܐ and ܪܘܒܐ rt. ܪܘܒ. *perturbation, trepidation; velocity.*

ܪܗܛܘܪܝܩܝܐ, ܝܩܝܬܐ from ܪܗܛܪܐ. *rhetorical, eloquent.*

ܪܗܠ Peal only act. part. ܪܗܠ. *to putrefy.* Ethpe. ܐܬܪܗܠ *to be putrid.* Pa. pass. part. ܡܪܗܠ, ܡܪܗܠܐ *putrid, foul.* Ethpa. ܐܬܪܗܠ *to discharge bloody matter.* Aph. ܐܪܗܠ *to putrefy, ooze blood.* Derivatives, ܪܗܠܐ, ܪܗܠܢܐ.

ܪܗܠܐ rt. ܪܗܠ. m. *festering, putrefaction; matter.*

ܪܗܠܢܝܐ pl. ܐ̈ rt. ܪܗܠ. *bilious; watery.*

ܪܗܙܐ m. *strength.*

ܪܘܐ, ܪܘܝ fut. ܢܪܘܐ, act. part. ܪܘܐ, ܪܘܝܐ. *to become drunken, intoxicated;* ܪܘܝܬ ܣܝܦܗ ܡܢ ܕܡܐ *his sword was drunken with blood.* Pass. part. ܪܘܐ, ܪܘܝܐ, ܪܘܝܬܐ pl. ܪܘܝܢ, ܪܘܝܐ, ܪܘܝܬܐ *irrigated, watered; drunken;* ܦܪܕܝܣܐ ܪܘܝܐ *a watered garden;* ܢܘܕܘ ܐܝܟ ܪܘܝܐ *they staggered like drunken men.* Ethpe. ܐܬܪܘܝ *to drink to excess, to be drunken.* Aph. ܐܪܘܝ *to give to drink, to water, satiate, intoxicate;* ܐܪܘܝܢܝ ܓܕܕܐ *He hath sated me with wormwood;* ܐܝܟ ܡܛܪܐ ܕܡܪܘܐ ܠܐܪܥܐ *as rain which watereth the earth;* ܡܫܩܠܢܗ ܕܚܩܠܐ ܡܝ̈ܐ ܣܓܝܐܐ ܡܪܘܐ the Nile *supplies its fields with abundant waters.* Derivatives, ܪܘܝܐ, ܪܘܝܐܝܬ, ܪܘܝܘܬܐ, ܡܪܘܝܐ.

ܪܘܐ a) *yellow amber.* b) ܪܘܐ and ܪܘܐ ῥόα, *pomegranate.*

ܪܘܒ, ܪܒ fut. ܢܪܘܒ, act. part. ܪܐܒ, ܪܐܒܐ. *to clamour, be in an uproar, resound;* ܪܒܘ ܥܠ ܡܘܬܗ *they clamoured for his death;* ܪܐܒܝܢ ܟܢܫܐ *the populace clamours.* Aph. ܐܪܝܒ *to make to resound; to clamour, cry aloud;* ܙܡܙܘܡܐ ܕܡܪܝܒܝܢ ܠܐܐܪ *buzzing sounds which make the air resound;* ܐܪܝܒ ܒܩܠܐ ܪܒܐ *he called out with a loud voice.* With ܥܠ *to clamour against, contend.* Ettaph. ܐܬܬܪܝܒ *to sound, resound.* Derivatives, ܪܘܒܒܐ, ܪܘܒܐ, ܡܪܝܒܢܐ.

ܪܘܒܐ pl. ܐ̈ rt. ܪܘܒ. m. *a row, clamour, confused noise* of a crowd; *sound, resounding.*

ܪܘܒܐ Arab. m. *juice thickened by boiling, thickened milk* or *honey.*

ܪܘܒܐ, ܪܘܒܝܐ rt. ܪܒܐ. m. *growth; augmentation; bringing up, education.*

ܪܘܒܠܐ rt. ܪܒܠ. m. *a swelling, tumour.*

ܪܘܒܥܐ pl. ܐ̈ rt. ܪܒܥ. m. *a quarter;* a measure *the fourth part of a cab.*

ܪܘܒܩܐ rt. ܪܒܩ. m. *repression;* ܒܪܘܒܩܐ ܕܡ̈ܠܐ *with repressive words.*

ܪܘܓܐ, ܪܘܓܝܣ, ܪܘܓܝܣܛܐ and ܪܘܓܝܣ m. ῥόγα, ῥογεῦσαι, *largess, a donative.*

ܪܘܓܪܓܐ rt. ܪܓ. m. *eagerness, enjoyment.*

ܪܘܕܐ m. ῥόδον, ῥόδα, *the rose.*

ܪܘܕܝܐ m. *a maker of rose conserve.*

ܪܘܕܕܦܢܐ, ܪܘܕܕܦ, ܪܘܕܕ and ܪܘܕܘܕܐܦܢ m. ῥοδαδάφνη, prob. *nerium oleander.*

ܪܘܕܝܐ pl. ܐ̈ *a Rhodian,* from ܪܘܕܘܣ *Rhodes.*

ܪܘܘܚܐ rt. ܪܘܚ. m. *ease, solace.*

ܪܘܙܓܐ rt. ܪܙܓ. m. *vibration.*

ܪܘܙܢܐ m. *solicitude, anxiety.*

ܪܘܙ fut. ܢܪܘܙ, act. part. ܪܐܙ, ܪܐܙܐ. *to exult, rejoice greatly; to flourish, thrive;* ܢܪܘܙ ܘܢܕܘܨ *let us rejoice and be exceeding glad;* ܢܘܗܪܐ ܕܙܕܝ̈ܩܐ ܢܪܘܙ *the light of the righteous shall rejoice;* ܦܪܕܝܣܐ ܕܪܐܙ ܒܟܠ ܦܐܪ̈ܝܢ *a garden rejoicing in all kinds of fruit;* ܬܘܪ̈ܡܣܐ ܟܡܐ ܕܡܬܒܣܪܝܢ ܝܬܝܪ ܪܐܙܝܢ lupines *the more they are neglected the better they thrive.* Aph. ܐܪܝܙ *to gladden, make joyful; to make to flourish;* ܡܪܝܙ ܐܒܐ ܠܩܕܝ̈ܫܘܗܝ *the Father makes his saints to rejoice;* ܗܢܐ ܢܗܪܐ ܡܪܝܙ ܠܐܝܠܢ̈ܐ *this* river of Eden *makes trees to flourish joyfully.* Derivatives, ܪܘܙܐ, ܪܘܙܢܐܝܬ, ܪܘܙܢܐ.

ܪܘܙܐ and ܐܪܘܙܐ rt. ܪܙ. m. *exultation, great rejoicing, merrymaking.*

ܪܘܙܐ and ܐܘܪܘܙܐ m. *rice.*

ܪܘܙܒܢܐ Pers. m. *an executioner.*

ܪܘܙܩܐ Arab. m. *rations, military stores.*

ܪܘܙܢܐܝܬ rt. ܪܙ. adv. *exultantly.*

ܪܘܙܢܐ rt. ܪܙ. *exultant.*

ܪܘܚ fut. ܢܪܘܚ, act. part. ܪܐܚ. *to be enlarged, relieved, to expand;* ܕܢܪܘܚ ܒܝܬܐ ܡܢ ܠܥܠ *that the house might be enlarged upward;* ܐܡܠܠ ܘܢܪܘܚ ܠܝ *I will speak to find relief.* Part. adj. ܪܘܝܚ, ܐ, ܬܐ also ܐܪܘܝܚܐ, ܬܐ *large, broad, spacious, vast;* ܪܘܝܚܐ ܐܘܪܚܐ ܕܡܘܒܠܐ ܠܐܒܕܢܐ *broad is the way which leadeth to destruction;* ܙܕܝ̈ܩܐ ܪܘܝܚ ܠܒܗܘܢ *the just are large-hearted,* but ܪܘܝܚ ܠܒܗ *his heart is swollen with pride.* Gram. *prolonged, long.* Pa. ܪܘܚ *to enlarge, widen, give free scope;* ܢܪܘܚ ܡܪܝܐ ܬܚܘܡܟ *the Lord shall enlarge thy border;* ܬܘܢ̈ܐ ܡܪܘܚܬܐ *spacious chambers.* Ethpa. ܐܬܪܘܚ *to be enlarged* as a building, *opened wide* as a door; *to spread widely* as a plant. Metaph. *to be relieved, set free* from pain, anxiety, distress; *to recover* from illness, *be delivered* of child; ܢܫܟܚܘܢ ܡܬܪܘܚܘ ܐܘ ܡܬܚܠܡܢܘ *may they find relief and be restored to health;* ܠܐ ܐܬܪܘܚܘ ܒܐܘܠܨܢܗܘܢ *they remained without relief in their misery.* Aph. ܐܪܘܚ *to enlarge, give space; to relieve, give relief, solace;* ܐܪܘܚ ܠܢ ܡܪܝܐ *the Lord hath made room for us;* ܠܐ ܡܪܘܚ ܘܠܐ ܡܬܪܘܚ *he neither gives nor receives benefits.* Derivatives, ܪܘܘܚܐ, ܐܪܘܚܐ and ܪܘܚܬܐ, ܪܘܚܐ, ܪܘܚܢܐܝܬ, ܪܘܚܢܘܬܐ, ܡܪܘܚܢܝܬ, ܡܪܘܚܐ.

ܪܘܚ, ܪܚ fut. ܢܪܘܚ, act. part. ܪܐܚ. *to take breath* metaph. *to revive;* ܢܪܘܚ ܠܒܟܘܢ *thy heart shall breathe freely.* Ethpe. ܐܬܪܝܚ *to smell, perceive odours.* Pa. ܪܝܚ *to soften, soothe, mollify, mitigate, appease;* ܡܠܬܐ ܕܡܬܡܟܟܐ ܡܪܝܚܐ *it calms the angry sea;* ܡܘܗܒܬܐ ܕܡܪܝܚܐ ܪܘܓܙܐ *a gift which appeases the wrathful man.* Ethpa. ܐܬܪܝܚ *to be quieted, relieved, appeased;* ܐܬܪܝܚ ܣܘܣܝܐ *the horse was quieted;* ܠܐ ܐܬܪܝܚܬ ܒܥܠܕܒܒܘܬܗ *his illwill was not appeased.* Aph. *to scent, smell, perceive a smell;* ܐܪܝܚܘ ܒܗ ܥܢܐ *the sheep smelt* the wolf; metaph. ܐܪܝܚ ܐܟܠܩܪܨܐ ܘܚܝܠܘܗܝ the devil and his hosts *scented out the coming of* our Lord. Pass. part. ܡܪܝܚ, f. pl. ܡܪܝܚܢ perh. denom. from ܪܘܚܐ *possessed by evil spirits.* Derivatives, ܪܘܚܐ, ܪܘܚܐ, ܪܘܚܢܐ, ܪܘܚܢܝܐ, ܪܘܚܢܐܝܬ, ܪܘܚܢܝܘܬܐ, ܪܘܚܢܝܐ, ܪܘܚܢܝܘܬܐ, ܪܝܚܐ, ܪܝܚܬܐ, ܪܝܚܢܐ, ܪܝܚܢܘܬܐ, ܪܝܚܢܬܐ, ܡܪܘܚܐ, ܡܪܘܚܬܐ, ܡܪܝܚܢܐ, ܡܪܝܚܐ, ܡܪܝܚܢܘܬܐ, ܡܬܪܘܚܢܐ, ܡܬܪܝܚܢܐ, ܡܪܝܚܢܘܬܐ.

ܪܘܚ, ܪܘܚܐ pl. ܪܘܚܐ, ܪܘܚܝܢ and ܪܘܚܢ, ܪܘܚܬܐ, also ܪܘܚܬܐ usually fem. except when used of the Holy Spirit. *a) breath, animal life;* ܪܘܚܐ ܕܚܝ̈ܐ *the breath of life. b) wind, vapour;* ܪܘܚܐ ܕܫܘܒܐ *sultry wind, simoom;* ܪ̈ܘܚܐ ܕܟܪܣܐ or ellipt. *wind in the belly, flatulence. c) spirit, a spirit, spiritual being; spectre, ghost;* esp. ܪܘܚ ܩܘܕܫܐ or ܪܘܚܐ ܩܕܝܫܬܐ *the Holy Spirit;* ܒܪܘܚ

spiritually; ܪܘܚܢܝ *spiritual;* ܪ̈ܘܚܐ ܕܬܫܡܫܬܐ *ministering spirits = angels;* ܪ̈ܘܚܐ ܒܝ̈ܫܬܐ *evil spirits.*

ܪܘܚܐ rt. ܪܘܚ. the E-Syr. vowel *Rwakha*, ܘ݁.

ܪܘܚܐ rt. ܪܘܚ. m. *a space, interstice.*

ܪܘܚܢܐ, ܪܘܚܢܝܬܐ rt. ܪܘܚ. *windy, of wind.*

ܪܘܚܡܬܐ for ܪܘܚܡܬܐ m. *a screech, shrill cry.*

ܪܘܚܢܐ, ܪܘܚܢܝܬܐ pl. m. ܪܘܚܢܝܢ, ܪ̈ܘܚܢܐ, pl. f. ܪ̈ܘܚܢܝܬܐ rt. ܪܘܚ. *spiritual.* ܪ̈ܘܚܢܐ is also the old form of pl. for ܪܘܚܐ in senses *b* and *c*.

ܪܘܚܢܐܝܬ. rt. ܪܘܚ. adv. *in a spiritual sense, spiritually, mystically.*

ܪܘܚܢܘܬ, ܪܘܚܢܘܬܐ rt. ܪܘܚ. f. *spiritual existence, spirituality.*

ܪܘܚܢܝܐ, ܪܘܚܢܝܬܐ rt. ܪܘܚ. *spiritual, mystical.* Gram. ܐܬܘ̈ܬܐ ܪ̈ܘܚܢܝܬܐ *sibilant letters* scil. ܙ. ܣ. ܨ. ܫ.

ܪܘܚܢܝܘܬܐ rt. ܪܘܚ. f. *spirituality.*

ܪܘܚܦܐ pl. ܐ̈ rt. ܪܚܦ. m. *brooding, incubation; pity, grace; the descent* of the Holy Spirit on the Eucharistic and Baptismal elements; rit. *a gentle waving of the hands.*

ܪܘܚܦܘܬܐ = ܪܚܦܘܬܐ f. *brooding.*

ܪܘܚܩܐ abs. and constr. ܪܘܚܩ. rt. ܪܚܩ. m. usually with a prep. ܠܪܘܚܩܐ or ܒ, ܕ *afar;* ܡܢ ܪ̈ *from afar, from the East; long ago, long beforehand.*

ܪܘܚܫܐ from ܪܚܫ. m. *a ring in water* made by a stone thrown in.

ܪܘܚܬܐ and ܪܘܚܬܐ rt. ܪܘܚ. f. *an open space, spaciousness; deliverance, relief.*

ܪܘܛ, ܪܛ. Ethpa. ܐܬܪܘܛ *to be tremulous, to vibrate, vacillate;* ܓܘܫܡܐ ܕܡܬܪܘܛ ܗܘܐ ܡܢ ܕܚܠܬܐ *the body tremulous with fear;* ܣܦܣܪܐ ܬܬܪܘܛ ܘܬܚܘܬ ܥܠܝܗܘܢ *the sword shall vibrate and descend upon them;* ܠܐ ܡܬܪܘܛܐ ܗܝܡܢܘܬܗܘܢ *their faith does not vacillate.* Ethpalp. ܐܬܪܛܪܛ *to deviate.* Derivatives, ܪܘܛܐ, ܪܛܐ, ܪܛܪܛܐ, ܡܬܪܘܛܘܬܐ.

ܪܘܛܐ pl. ܐ̈ rt. ܪܘܛ. m. *a flexible thin branch, a lath.*

ܪܘܛܒܐ rt. ܪܛܒ. m. *medicago sativa*, a kind of clover.

ܪܘܛܢܐ rt. ܪܛܢ. m. *complaint, dissatisfaction; murmuring* of magicians.

ܪܘܝ = ܪܘܐ verb.

ܪܘܝܐ, ܪܘܝܐ, ܪܘܝܬܐ and ܪ̈ rt. ܪܘܐ. *a drunkard; thirsty; enthusiastic.*

ܪܘܝܐܝܬ rt. ܪܘܐ. adv. *in drunken fashion.*

ܪܘܝܘܬܐ rt. ܪܘܐ. f. *drunkenness, intoxication, strong drink;* pl. ܪ̈ܘܝܘܬܐ *drinking-bouts.*

ܪܘܝܚ, ܚܐ, ܚܬܐ; see ܪܘܚ Peal conj.

ܪܘܝܚܐܝܬ rt. ܪܘܚ. adv. *amply; at great length.*

ܪܘܝܚܘܬܐ rt. ܪܘܚ. f. *open country, breadth, ampleness, vastness;* ܪܘܝܚܘܬ ܢܦܫܐ *magnanimity.*

ܪܘܟܒ, ܪܘܟܒܐ rt. ܪܟܒ. m. *construction, composition, arrangement, fabrication;* esp. *the compounding* of medicines, *a recipe; structure* of the body; literary *composition;* ܪܘܟܒ ܡ̈ܠܐ *composition, style;* ܪ̈ ܡܨܝܕ *elaborate.*

ܪܘܟܒܐ rt. ܪܟܒ. m. *a besom, broom.*

ܪܘܟܒܝܐ rt. ܪܟܒ. *structural.*

ܪܘܟܟܐ rt. ܪܟ. m. *a*) *an emollient, poultice, fomentation.* *b*) *hoeing, harrowing.* *c*) gram. *aspiration* of the ܒܓܕܟܦܬ letters.

ܪܘܡ, ܪܡ root-meaning *to be* or *become high.* Ethpe. ܐܬܬܪܝܡ *a*) *to go up;* ܐܬܬܪܝܡ ܐܠܗܐ ܡܢ ܐܒܪܗܡ *God went up from Abraham.* *b*) *to be lifted on high, exalted; to be lifted up, haughty;* ܫܩܐ ܕܦܪܫܘܬܐ ܕܐܬܬܪܝܡ *the thigh of the heave-offering which is heaved up;* ܗܟܢܐ ܥܬܝܕ ܠܡܬܬܪܝܡܘ ܒܪܗ ܕܐܢܫܐ *so shall the Son of man be lifted up;* ܟܠ ܕܡܟܟ ܢܦܫܗ ܢܬܬܪܝܡ *he that humbleth himself shall be exalted;* ܐܬܬܪܝܡ *the proud;* with ܩܪܢܗ *his horn was lifted up = he was exalted to honour.* *c*) *to be taken away;* with ܡܕܥܗ *he was bereft of his wits.* Gram. *to be suppressed* as a letter. Palp. ܪܘܡܪܡ *to lift up, exalt;* pass. part. *high, exalted, lofty;* ܕܢܪܘܡܪܡ ܠܐܕܡ ܕܐܬܡܟܟ *to exalt fallen man;* ܐܪܘܡܪܡܟ *I will exalt Thee.* Ethpalp. ܐܬܪܘܡܪܡ *a*) *to become great;* ܐܬܪܘܡܪܡ ܐܝܠܢܐ ܗܘ ܘܡܛܝ ܠܫܡܝܐ *that tree grew great and reached to the sky.* *b*) *to be exalted, extolled, magnified;* ܡܬܪܘܡܪܡ ܗܘܐ ܫܡܗ ܕܡܪܢ *the name of our Lord was magnified.* *c*) *to exalt oneself, be haughty.* Pael ܪܝܡ pass. part. ܡܪܝܡ, ܡܪܝܡܐ, ܡܪܝܡܬܐ *set on high, high, lofty;* ܐܠܗܐ ܡܪܝܡܐ or ellipt. *the Most High God;* ܡܪܝܡܐ ܡܕܥܢ ܕܐܝܬܘܗܝ ܡܪܝܡܐ *our mind which is the highest* part of us. Aph. ܐܪܝܡ to raise, set up, lift up, take up, exalt; to remove, take away; ܐܪܝܡ ܡܘܫܐ ܚܘܝܐ ܒܡܕܒܪܐ Moses lifted up the serpent in the wilderness; ܠܐ ܗܘܐ ܕܡܪܝܡ ܟܢܦܐ there was none that moved the wing; ܐܪܝܡ ܠܡܟܝܟܐ He hath exalted them of low degree; ܡܠܟܘܬܐ ܡܪܡܐ ܡܢܟ the kingdom is taken from thee. Chem. to evaporate, distil. Gram. to suppress a letter. With ܐܝܕ to lift up the hand = to swear; with ܐܝܕܐ and ܟܦܐ to raise the hand in wrath, in blessing; ܐܬܐ to set up a standard; ܢܦܫܗ to exalt oneself; ܣܝܦܐ and ܩܛܠ to cease slaughtering; ܡܠܬܐ to speak; ܥܝܢܐ to look towards; ܟܦܐ ܥܠ to injure; ܩܠܐ to cry aloud; ܩܪܢܐ to promote to honour; ܪܝܫܐ to exalt to honour; ܥܩܒܐ ܥܠ to rebel against. Derivatives, ܐܪܡܘܬܐ, ܪܘܡܐ, ܪܘܡܝܬ, ܪܡܐ, ܪܡܬܐ, ܪܡܫܐ, ܪܘܡܪܡܐ, ܪܘܡܢܐ, ܡܪܘܡܪܡܐ, ܡܪܘܡܢܐ, ܡܪܘܡܐ, ܪܡܝܐ, ܪܡܝܘܬܐ, ܡܪܝܡܢܐ, ܡܪܝܡܢܘܬܐ, ܡܪܝܡܢܐ, ܡܪܝܡܘܬܐ, ܡܬܪܘܡܪܡܢܐ, ܡܪܡܪܡܢܐ, ܡܪܡܪܡܐܝܬ, ܡܪܡܘܬܐ, ܡܬܪܡܪܡܢܘܬܐ, ܡܬܪܡܪܡܢܐ.

ܪܘܡܐ pl. ܐ̈ rt. ܪܘܡ. m. height, breadth, size; ܪ̈ ܕܐܝܕܐ raising the hand; exalted position, haughtiness, pride; a high place, summit; heaven.

ܪܘܡܐ also ܪܘܘܡܐ ῥεῦμα, catarrh, phlegm, a running; ܪ̈ ܕܥܝܢ̈ܐ ophthalmia; ܪ̈ ܕܐܪܙܐ bdellium.

ܪܘܡܐ m. a falsehood.

ܪܘܡܝܐ, ܪܘܡܝܬ, ܪܘܡܝܐ, ܪܘܡܝܬܐ, ܪܘܡܝܘܬܐ, ܪܘܡܐܝܬ, and ܪܘܡܢܝܐ; see ܪܗܘܡܐ Rome, ܪܗܘܡܝܐ &c.

ܪܘܡܐܝܬ rt. ܪܘܡ. adv. magnificently.

ܪܘܡܚܐ pl. ܐ̈ m. a spear, lance; ܐܚܝܕ̈ܝ ܪ̈ spearmen.

ܪܘܡܢܝܐ pl. ܐ̈ rt. ܪܘܡ. a) lofty, sublime. b) a gift, offering esp. marriage gifts.

ܪܘܡܢܐ pl. ܐ̈ m. the pomegranate; ܒܝܬ ܪ̈ a plantation of pomegranate trees; ܦܩܪܐ ܕܪ̈ the flower of the wild pomegranate; ܕܪ̈ ܡܨܪܝܐ the juice of the Egyptian poppy. Metaph. a round head at the end of a stalk, resembling a pomegranate.

ܪܘܡܢܢܝܐ like a pomegranate.

ܪܘܡܨܐ a smouldering fire, hot embers, perh. a chafing-dish, pan of hot coals.

ܪܘܡܪܡܐ rt. ܪܘܡ. m. high estate, exaltation, great dignity.

ܪܘܣ imper. of verb ܪܣ to sprinkle.

ܪܘܣܛܢܐ and ܪܘܣܛܩܐ m. a brass grating or lattice outside a door of wood; a chancel.

ܪܘܣܛܩܐ pl. ܐ̈ Pers. m. a village, hamlet, district.

ܪܘܥ, ܪܥ act. part. ܪܐܥ to talk idly. Derivative, ܪܘܥܐ.

ܪܘܥܐ m. a) rt. ܪܘܥ. idle talk, garrulity, nonsense. b) rt. ܪܥ. fracture, breaking into large pieces.

ܪܘܥܐ, ܪܘܥܬܐ pl. ܪܘܥܬ̈ܐ f. froth, foam; nonsense, gibberish; ܪ̈ ܕܣܗܪܐ or ellipt. selenite, talc; ܪ̈ ܕܬܢܟܪ borax; ܪ̈ ܕܣܐܡܐ a plaster made of silver and quicksilver. Derivatives, verb ܪܥܬ, ܪܘܥܬܢܐ, ܪܘܥܬܢܘܬܐ, ܪܥܬܐ, ܡܪܥܬܢܘܬܐ.

ܪܘܥܬܐ rt. ܪܥܐ. f. opinion.

ܪܘܥܠܐ, ܪܘܥܠ rt. ܪܥܠ. m. ܪ̈ ܕܗܕܡ̈ܐ trembling of the limbs.

ܪܘܥܡܐ pl. ܐ̈ rt. ܪܥܡ. m. indignation, resentment, murmuring; outcry, clamour; disagreement, discord with ܥܡ; ܕܠܐ ܪܘܥܡܐ without murmuring.

ܪܘܥܢܐ m. pl. wild herbs, pot-herbs esp. mallow.

ܪܘܥܥܐ rt. ܪܥ = ܪܘܥܐ b.

ܪܘܥܪܥܐ pl. ܐ̈ rt. ܪܥ. breaking open; a contusion.

ܪܘܥܬܢܐ from ܪܘܥܐ, ܪܘܥܬܐ. frothy, foamy.

ܪܘܥܬܢܘܬܐ from ܪܘܥܐ, ܪܘܥܬܐ. f. frothiness.

ܪܘܦܐ or ܪܘܦܝ f. ῥοπή, a moment.

ܪܘܦܝܐ rt. ܪܦܐ. m. softening of metal, rendering ductile.

ܪܘܦܣܬܐ in the Lexx. a broom.

ܪܘܦܣܐ pl. ܐ̈ rt. ܪܦܣ. m. a measure of time, twenty minutes.

ܪܘܦܪܦܐ rt. ܪܦ. m. twitching.

ܪܘܙ imper. of verb ܪܙ.

ܪܘܨܝܢܐ rt. ܪܨ. m. a rivulet, brooklet.

ܪܘܩ imper. of verb ܪܩ.

ܪܘܩ, ܪܩ root-meaning to be light. Ethpe.

ܐܬܪܩܩ *to be despised.* DERIVATIVES, ܪܩܩܘܬܐ, ܪܩܝܩܐ, ܪܩܝܩܘܬܐ.

ܪܘܩܐ pl. ܐ̈ rt. ܪܩ. m. *saliva, spittle; spitting, ignominy.*

ܪܘܩܥܐ pl. of ܐܪܘܩܥܬܐ (rare) and ܪܘܩܥܬܐ rt. ܪܩܥ. f. *a piece of worn cloth, a rag, tatter; a slip of paper;* ܪܘܩܥܐ ܕܡܫܝܘܬܐ *clouts, towels.*

ܪܘܪܐ m. dialect of Tirhan, *marrow, fat.*

ܪܘܪܒ PALPEL conj. of verb ܪܒ.

ܪܘܪܒܐ pl. m. *a)* ܪܘܪܒܝܢ, ܪܘܪܒܐ, *b)* ܪܘܪܒܢܐ; ܪܘܪܒܬܐ pl. f. *a)* ܪܘܪܒܢ, ܪܘܪܒܬܐ, *b)* ܪܘܪܒܢܝܬܐ. Sing. is rare; the shorter forms of pl. are chiefly used as adj., the longer (older) forms only as subst. rt. ܪܒ. *a) great, grown up;* ܪܘܪܒܐ ܘܙܥܘܪܐ *great and small;* ܕܡܢ ܪܘܪܒܐ ܥܕܡܐ ܠܙܥܘܪܐ *young and old.* Fem. emph. pl. *mighty works, great deeds* or *words;* ܡܠܠ ܪܘܪܒܬܐ *he spake haughtily.* *b)* pl. m. *princes, nobles, chiefs,* often constr., ܪܘܪܒܢܝ ܚܝܠܐ *captains of the host.* Pl. f. *princesses, great ladies.*

ܪܘܪܒܐܝܬ rt. ܪܒ. adv. *greatly, excessively, magnificently.*

ܪܘܪܒܘܬܐ rt. ܪܒ. f. *greatness;* ܪܘܪܒܘܬ ܬܪܥܝܬܐ *magnanimity.*

ܪܘܪܒܢܐ; see ܪܘܪܒܐ.

ܪܘܫܐ and ܪܘܫܢܐ m. *barley groats, barley water.*

ܪܘܫܟܢܐ and ܪܘܫܟܢܐ pl. ܐ̈ m. *a pad-saddle, pad under the saddle; panniers, saddle-bags.*

ܪܘܫܠܐ rt. ܪܫܠ. m. *convulsion, paralysis* of one side of the face.

ܪܘܫܡܐ const. st. ܪܘܫܡ rarely ܪܫܘܡ, pl. ܐ̈ rt. ܪܫܡ. m. *a sign, mark, token, indication, index; ascription, inscription; title* of a book, *copy* of a book, *annotation; setting down, committing to writing; description, design, plan* of a house; *signing with the sign of the cross;* ܚܡܝܪܐ ܕܪܘܫܡܐ *leavened bread marked with a cross* = Eucharistic bread; ܪ̈ ܕܚܝܐ *the sign of salvation* i.e. Baptism; ܪ̈ ܕܪ̈ܫܐ *index of chapters.*

ܪܘܫܡܢܝܐ rt. ܪܫܡ. *written, committed to writing.*

ܪܘܫܢ Pers. m. *a skylight, dormer window.*

ܪܘܫܥܐ rt. ܪܫܥ. m. *ungodliness, impiety, wickedness; an impious opinion, wicked deed.*

ܪܘܫܦܐ pl. ܐ̈ rt. ܪܫܦ. m. *a crawler, worm, insect.*

ܪܘܬܐ m. *a triplex halimus, orach,* a wild potherb.

ܪܘܬܠܐ rt. ܪܬܠ. m. *ravage, destruction.*

ܪܙ act. part. ܪܐܙ, denom. verb from ܪܐܙܐ. *to conspire.* ETHPE. ܐܬܪܙ and ܐܬܪܐܙ *to be initiated into mysteries; to receive secret information; to be mystically shown forth;* ܪܐܙܐ ܪܒܐ ܐܬܪܙ ܒܥܠܝܬܐ *the great mystery was mystically shown forth in the upper chamber.* In the LEXX. *to take secret counsel, plot.* PA. ܪܙܙ *to signify mystically, to teach by types or mysteries;* ܡܢܐ ܡܪܙܙ *what is the mystical meaning of . . .?* ܚܫܗ ܘܡܘܬܗ ܘܩܝܡܬܗ ܡܪܙܙܝܢܢ *we show forth in a mystery His passion and death and resurrection.* ETHPA. ܐܬܪܙܙ and ܐܬܪܐܙ *to be instructed in or made familiar with mysteries; to be signified in mysteries or sacraments;* ܐܬܪܙܙܘ ܠܢܒܝܐ ܐܪ̈ܙܐ ܐܠܗܝ̈ܐ *divine mysteries were mystically imparted to the prophets.* ETHPALEN ܐܬܪܙܢ or ܐܬܪܐܙܢ *to take secret counsel.* APH. ܐܪܙ and ܐܪܐܙ *to initiate into mysteries; to instruct, declare* esp. *by mysteries and symbols; to signify, imply, give secret instruction;* ܐܫܥܝܐ ܐܪܙܗ ܒܦܠܐܬܐ *Isaiah declared it in mystic parables;* ܡܪܙܝܢ ܡܢ ܪܘܚܐ ܕܩܘܕܫܐ *those who are instructed inwardly by the Holy Spirit.* Gram. ܥܠ ܡܪܙܐ ܕܠܘܩܒܠܘܬܐ *'al signifies opposition.*

ܪܙܙ ETHPE. ܐܬܪܙܙ *to be reduced, wasted away.*

ܪܙܘܦ *a vine root.*

ܪܐܙܐܝܬ, ܪܐܙܢܐ, ܪܐܙܢܝܘܬܐ; see ܪܐܙܢܐܝܬ &c.

ܪܙܦ fut. ܢܪܙܘܦ, act. part. ܪܐܙܦ. *to sprinkle, to rain gently;* ܪܙܦ ܡܘܫܐ ܕܡܐ ܥܠ ܥܡܐ *Moses sprinkled blood upon the people;* ܥܢܢ̈ܐ ܪܙܦ ܡ̈ܝܐ *the clouds dropped water.* ETHPE. ܐܬܪܙܦ *to be gently watered, sprinkled with water.* APH. ܐܪܙܦ *to sprinkle, cause to drop;* ܢܪܙܦܘܢ ܟܗܢ̈ܐ ܕܡܐ ܕܕܒܚܬܐ ܥܠ ܡܕܒܚܐ *the priests shall sprinkle the blood of the sacrifice upon the altar.* ETTAPH. ܐܬܬܪܙܦ *to be sprinkled.* DERIVATIVES, ܪܙܦܐ, ܪܙܘܦܐ.

ܪܙܦܐ rt. ܪܙܦ. m. *a) black and white poppy.* *b)* = ܪܙܘܦܐ *b.*

ܪܙܦܐ pl. ܐ̈ rt. ܪܙܦ. m. *a) sprinkling, ceremonial aspersion.* Metaph. ܫܘܐ ܠܪܙܦܐ ܕܚܝܐ ܕܡܥܡܘܕܝܘܬܐ *he was counted worthy that* on him should descend a sprinkling of the pangs of the Crucifixion. b) spattering, dirt. c) freckles, pox, white spots. d) the lower part of sandals.

ܪܚܝܡܐ, ܬܐ rt. ܪܚܡ. pass. *beloved, sweetheart, a friend.*

ܪܚܘܡܐ, ܬܐ rt. ܪܚܡ. act. *a lover, friend.*

ܪܚܘܡܐܝܬ rt. ܪܚܡ. adv. *lovingly, with goodwill.*

ܪܚܘܡܘܬܐ rt. ܪܚܡ. f. *love, affection.*

ܪܚܘܡܬܢܐ rt. ܪܚܡ. *loving, benign.*

ܪܚܘܡܬܢܐܝܬ rt. ܪܚܡ. adv. *kindly.*

ܪܚܘܦܐ rt. ܪܚܦ. *hovering* as a hawk before pouncing.

ܪܚܘܦܘܬܐ rt. ܪܚܦ. f. *incubation, brooding.*

ܪܚܘܩ; see ܪܚܘܩܐ.

ܪܚܘܩܘܬܐ rt. ܪܚܩ. f. *repelling.*

ܪܚܘܩܝܐ rt. ܪܚܩ. m. *renunciation.*

ܪܚܘܫܐ pl. ܐ̈ rt. ܪܚܫ. m. a) adj. *creeping, spreading* as an eruption. b) subst. *a reptile.*

ܪܚܘܫܘܬܐ rt. ܪܚܫ. f. *the act of creeping; spawning.*

ܪܚܘܫܬܢܐ rt. ܪܚܫ. *reptilian.*

ܪܚܘܫܬܢܐܝܬ rt. ܪܚܫ. adv. *after the manner of a reptile.*

ܪܚܝܐ pl. ܪ̈ܚܘܬܐ f. *a mill, millstone* esp. *the nether millstone;* ܪ̈ܚܝܐ ܕܐܝ̈ܕܐ *hand-mills.* Med. *a hard formation in the womb.*

ܪܚܝܝܐ m. *a miller.*

ܪܚܝܡܐܝܬ rt. ܪܚܡ. adv. *benignly, with loving-kindness.*

ܪܚܝܡܘܬܐ rt. ܪܚܡ. f. *affection.*

ܪܚܝܦܐ rt. ܪܚܦ. *benign.*

ܪܚܝܩ, ܐ, ܬܐ rt. ܪܚܩ. *far, afar, far off, remote, distant;* ܐܪܥܐ ܪܚܝܩܬܐ *a far country;* ܫܘܥܝܬܐ ܕܪ̈ܚܝܩܬܐ *a history of remote concern.* With ܡܢ *far removed, alien, without, apart;* ܣܓܝ ܪܚܝܩܝܢ ܐܢܬܘܢ ܡܢ ܟܪ̈ܝܣܛܝܢܐ *ye are very unlike Christians;* ܪܚܝܩ ܡܢ ܥܠܘܒܘܬܐ *devoid of greediness.* With ܠܐ it is *not unlikely, not a remote contingency.* Subst. m. abs. *a space, interval.*

ܪܚܝܩܘܬܐ rt. ܪܚܩ. f. *distance, remoteness, length; separation, immunity.*

ܪܚܡ fut. ܢܪܚܡ, act. part. ܪܳܚܡ, ܪܳܚܡܐ, ܪܳܚܡܬܐ, pass. part. ܪܚܝܡ and ܪܚܝܡ, ܐ, ܬܐ. *to love, delight in, desire;* ܪܚܡ ܠܩܪܝܒܟ ܐܝܟ ܢܦܫܟ *love thy neighbour as thyself;* ܠܒܐ ܕܒܪܢܫܐ ܪܳܚܡ ܡܪܝܐ the Lord *desires the heart of man.* Act. part. *loving, a lover, friend;* ܪ. ܫܪܝܪܐ *a trusty friend.* Frequent in construction: ܪܳܚܡ ܐܟܣ̈ܢܝܐ *hospitable;* ܪ. ܐ̈ܢܫܐ *philanthropic;* ܪ. ܡܠܦܢܘܬܐ *studious;* ܪ. ܥܡܠܐ or ܫܘܥܒܕܐ *laborious;* ܪ. ܬܘܟܚܬܐ *censorious;* ܪ. ܪ̈ܓܝܓܬܐ *pleasure-seeking;* ܪ. ܫܘܒܚܐ *ambitious.* P.p. *dear, beloved, lovely, lovable;* also ܐܝܟ ܡܐ ܕܪܚܝܡ ܠܐܠܗܐ *as pleases God;* ܗܘ ܕܪܚܝܡ ܠܗ *as seems good to him.* ETHPE. ܐܬܪܚܡ *to be beloved, be a friend.* PA. ܪܰܚܶܡ with ܥܠ, *to have mercy upon, be pitiful to;* ܪܰܚܶܡ ܥܠܝ *have mercy upon me,* often used as the title of Psalm li. ETHPA. ܐܬܪܰܚܰܡ *to have mercy, show pity, be moved with compassion,* with ܥܠ; ܐܬܪܰܚܰܡ ܥܠܝܢ ܡܪܝܐ *have mercy upon us, O Lord.* APH. ܐܪܚܶܡ *to show love; to obtain love or favour, render lovable; to crave for mercy;* ܐܪܚܡ ܢܦܫܟ ܠܟܢܘܫܬܐ *gain for thyself the love of the congregation;* ܗܕܐ ܣܓܝ ܐܪܚܡܬ ܠܗܘܢ ܠܟܪ̈ܣܛܝܢܐ *this conduct gained great favour for the Christians.* DERIVATIVES, ܪܚܡܐ, ܪܚܘܡܐ, ܪܚܘܡܐ, ܪܚܘܡܐܝܬ, ܪܚܘܡܘܬܐ, ܪܚܘܡܬܢܐ, ܪܚܘܡܬܢܐܝܬ, ܪܚܝܡܐܝܬ, ܪܚܝܡܘܬܐ, ܪܚܡܐ, ܪܚܡܢܐ, ܪܚܡܢܘܬܐ, ܪܚܡܢܐܝܬ, ܪܚܡܬܐ, ܪܚܡܬܢܐ, ܪܚܡܬܢܐܝܬ, ܡܪܚܡܢܐܝܬ, ܡܪܚܡܢܐ, ܡܪܚܡܢܘܬܐ, ܪܚܡܬܢܐܝܬ, ܡܬܪܚܡܢܐ, ܡܪܚܡܢܘܬܐ.

ܪܚܡ, ܪܚܡܐ pl. ܪ̈ܚܡܝܢ, ܐ̈ rt. ܪܚܡ. m. *the womb, a woman's privy parts; the bladder; testicles.* Usually pl. *bowels,* metaph. *tenderness, mercy, compassion, affection, favour;* ܕܠܐ ܪ̈ܚܡܐ *merciless;* ܕ. ܚܣܝܪܘܬ *cruelty;* ܡܠܐ ܕ *merciful;* ܕ. ܢܩܝܦ or ܣܓܝ *compassionate, tender-hearted;* ܟܐܦܐ ܕܪ̈ܚܡܐ *a precious stone.*

ܪܚܡܐܝܬ rt. ܪܚܡ. adv. *benevolently.*

ܪܚܡܘܬܐ or ܪܚܡܬܐ rt. ܪܚܡ. f. *kindness, friendship, amity;* ܥܒܕ ܕ ܥܡ *to make alliance.*

ܪܚܡܝܐ, ܝܬܐ rt. ܪܚܡ. *friendly, kindly.*

ܪܚܡܢܐ, ܢܝܬܐ rt. ܪܚܡ. *tender-hearted, merciful.*

ܪܚܡܢܐܝܬ rt. ܪܚܡ. adv. *mercifully.*

ܪܚܡܢܘܬܐ rt. ܪܚܡ. f. *mercifulness.*

ܪܚܡܬܐ pl. ܪ̈ܚܡܬܐ rt. ܪܚܡ. f. *love, friendship, kindness, desire;* ܪ̈ܚܡܬܐ ܗܘܠܢܝ̈ܬܐ *material desires;* metaph. *the attraction* of the magnet. Often in construction: ܪܚܡܬ ܐܢܫܘܬܐ *love towards man, philanthropy;* ܪ̄ ܡܥ̈ܝܐ *tender love, affectionateness;* ܪ̄ ܢܦܫܗ *self-regard;* ܪ̄ ܟܪܣܐ *gluttony;* ܪ̄ ܡܫܘܚܬܐ *contentment, moderation.*

ܪܚܡܬܢܐ E-Syr. ܪܚܡܬܢܐ or ܪܚܡܬܢܐ, ܬܢܐ rt. ܪܚܡ. *pitiful, compassionate, merciful, by love.*

ܪܚܡܬܢܐܝܬ rt. ܪܚܡ. adv. *with compassion, benevolently.*

ܪܚܡܬܢܘܬܐ rt. ܪܚܡ. f. *commiseration.*

ܪܚܦ PAEL ܪܲܚܸܦ *to brood, hover over; to cherish, pity, take care of* with ܥܠ; ܐܝܟ ܬܪܢܓܘܠܬܐ ܕܡܪܚܦܐ ܥܠ ܦܪ̈ܘܓܝܗ̇ *a hen brooding over her young;* ܡܪܚܦܐ ܥܠ ܐܦ̈ܝ ܡ̈ܝܐ the Spirit of God *brooded upon the face of the waters;* ܠܐ ܐܚܘܣ ܘܠܐ ܐܪܚܦ *I will not pity nor have compassion.* Eccles. Jac. *to wave, to move gently to and fro; to move the hand* in ordaining or consecrating; ܡܪܚܦ ܐܝܕܗ ܥܠ ܐܪ̈ܙܐ the priest *waves his hand gently above the elements;* ܪܚܦ ܥܠܘܗܝ ܦܛܪܝܪܟܐ *the Patriarch moved his hand above the head* of one to be ordained priest; ܡܪܚܦܢ̈ܝܬܐ ܡܪ̈ܘܚܐ *waving fans.* DERIVATIVES, ܪܘܚܦܐ, ܪܚܦܐ, ܪܚܘܦܐ, ܪܚܘܦܘܬܐ, ܪܘܚܦܘܬܐ, ܡܪܚܦܢܘܬܐ, ܡܪܚܦܢܐܝܬ, ܡܪܚܦܢܐ.

ܪ̈ܚܦܐ rt. ܪܚܦ. m. pl. *heated pebbles* or *small stones thrown into milk to heat it.*

ܪܚܩ for part. adj. ܪܚܝܩ &c. see above. PAEL ܪܲܚܸܩ *to put far away.* ETHPA. ܐܬܪܚܩ *to journey* or *abide afar; to avoid, abstain, renounce;* ܐܬܪܚܩ ܥܘܠܐ ܕܠܐ ܢܐܠܦ ܙܕܝܩܘܬܐ *the evildoer fled afar to avoid learning righteousness;* ܦܘܪܩܢܐ ܐܬܪܚܩ ܡܢܢ *salvation was far from us;* ܙܒܢܐ ܠܡܬܪܚܩܘ ܡܢ ܚܒܘܩܝܐ *a time to refrain from embracing;* ܠܟܢܫܐ ܕܒܝ̈ܫܐ ܡܬܪܚܩ ܐܢܬ *thou dost eschew the company of the wicked.* APH. ܐܪܚܩ *to depart afar, go to a distance; to abandon, forsake; to remove, put away, separate;* ܡܪܚܩܘ ܠܐ ܬܪܚܩܘܢ ܒܗܠܟܬܐ *ye shall not go very far away;* ܐܪܚܩ ܡܢ ܐܠܗܐ *he forsook God;* ܗܟܢ ܐܪܚܩ ܡܢܢ ܚܛܗܝܢ *so far hath He set our sins from us;* ܕܠܐ ܡܪܚܩ *inseparable.* ETTAPH. ܐܬܬܪܚܩ *to be removed* or *sent far away.* DERIVATIVES, ܪܘܚܩܐ, ܪܚܘܩܘܬܐ, ܪܚܝܩܐ, ܪܚܝܩܘܬܐ, ܪܚܩܐ, ܡܪܚܩܢܐ, ܡܬܪܚܩܢܐ, ܡܬܪܚܩܢܐܝܬ, ܡܪܚܩܢܘܬܐ, ܡܬܪܚܩܢܘܬܐ.

ܪܚܪܚ PALPEL conj. *to make rings in the water* as a stone. DERIVATIVE, ܪܘܚܪܚܐ.

ܪܚܫ and ܪܚܫ fut. ܢܪܚܫ, act. part. ܪܚܫ, ܪܚܫܐ. *a*) *to creep; to swarm, bring forth swarms;* ܟܠܗ ܪܚܫܐ ܕܪܚܫ ܥܠ ܐܪܥܐ *every creeping thing that creepeth upon the earth;* ܪܚܫܘ ܡ̈ܝܐ ܪ̈ܚܫܐ *the waters swarmed with reptiles. b*) *to move slowly, creep, throb, flutter;* ܨܒ̈ܥܬܐ ܕܐܝ̈ܕܝܗܘܢ ܠܐ ܪܚܫܢ *the fingers of their hands have no feeling;* ܘܠܐ ܪܚܫ ܒܗ ܕܡܐ ܚܝܐ *without living blood moving in it;* ܢܦܫܗ ܪܚܫܐ ܗܘܬ ܕܬܦܘܩ *his soul was fluttering to depart. c*) *to start growth, germinate, bourgeon;* ܥܕܡܐ ܕܪܚܫܐ ܥܝܢܗ ܕܓܦܬܐ *until the eye of the vine bourgeon.* APH. ܐܪܚܫ *a*) *to breed reptiles, swarm; to make to creep;* ܩܘܝܐ ܕܡ̈ܝܐ ܡܪܚܫ ܪ̈ܚܫܐ ܡܢ ܫܡܫܐ *a stagnant pool breeds creeping things from the influence of the sun;* ܢܪܚܫ ܢܗܪܐ ܥܘܪ̈ܕܥܢܐ *the river shall swarm with frogs. b*) metaph. *to insinuate, suggest;* ܐܪܚܫ ܒܠܒܘܬܗܘܢ *he put it into their hearts to . . . . c*) *to move;* ܠܐ ܡܕܡ ܗܘܐ ܕܢܪܚܫ ܚܕܐ ܡܢ ܐܝ̈ܕܘܗܝ ܐܘ ܪ̈ܓܠܘܗܝ *he could neither move hand nor foot. d*) *to cause germination;* ܡܪܚܫ ܠܓܦ̈ܢܐ ܙܒܠܐ ܕܝܘܢ̈ܐ doves' dung *encourages germination in vines.* DERIVATIVES, ܪܚܘܫܐ, ܪܚܘܫܘܬܐ, ܪܚܫܢܐܝܬ, ܪܚܫܐ, ܪܚܫܐ, ܪܚܫܢܐ, ܪܚܫܬܐ, ܪܚܫܢܘܬܐ, ܪܚܫܬܐ, ܡܪܚܫܢܐ.

ܪܚܫܐ rt. ܪܚܫ. collective noun, m. *a*) *reptiles, vermin, insects, creeping things;* the term includes fish and mice. *b*) *hoarseness, sore throat. c*) *gangrene, a spreading eruption, creeping pustules which develop into ulcers.*

ܪܚܫܐ rt. ܪܚܫ. m. *a*) *a creeping tumour. b*) *decay.*

ܪܚܫܘܢܐ dimin. of ܪܚܫܐ. m. *small vermin.*

ܪܚܫܬܐ pl. ܬܐ rt. ܪܚܫ. m. *a louse, vermin.*

ܪܚܫܬܐ pl. ܢܝܬܐ rt. ܪܚܫ. f. *myrobalsam.*

ܪܚܫܢܐ, ܢܝܬܐ rt. ܪܚܫ. *creeping, a creeping thing.*

ܪܛܒ fut. ܢܪܛܒ, act. part. ܪܛܒ. *to be* or *become*

moist. Part. adj. ܪܳܛܶܒ, ܒܳܐ, ܒܬܳܐ *moist, fresh, green;* ܩܢܒܳܐ ܪܰܛܺܝܒܳܐ ܟܰܕ ܪܰܟܺܝܟ ܗܽܘ *fresh hemp while still tender;* ܝܰܬܪܶܐ ܪܰܛܺܝܒܶܐ *new bowstrings;* ܪܰܛܺܝܒܶܐ ܡܶܬܩܪܶܝܢ such *are called rainy* winds. Ethpe. ܐܶܬܪܛܶܒ *to become wet, moist;* ܡܶܢ ܙܪܳܡܳܐ ܕܛܽܘܪܶܐ ܢܶܬܪܰܛܒܽܘܢ *they shall be wet with the showers of the mountains.* Pa. ܪܰܛܶܒ *to wet, moisten;* ܒܕܶܡܥܶܗ ܪܰܛܶܒ ܠܰܐܪܥܳܐ *he watered the ground with his tear;* ܡܪܰܛܰܒ ܒܡܶܫܚܽܘܬܳܐ *moistened with salve.* Ethpa. ܐܶܬܪܰܛܰܒ *to be made wet* or *moist.* Aph. ܐܰܪܛܶܒ *to wet, moisten;* ܕܢܰܪܛܶܒ ܠܶܗ ܠܠܶܫܳܢܝ *that he may moisten my tongue.* Derivatives, ܪܛܳܒܳܐ, ܪܛܒܳܐ, ܪܛܺܝܒܽܘܬܳܐ, ܪܛܒܬܳܐ, ܡܪܰܛܒܳܢܳܐ.

ܪܶܛܒܳܐ E-Syr. ܪܰܛܒܳܐ rt. ܪܛܒ. m. *moisture, wet ground; verdure.*

ܪܳܛܽܘܢܳܐ rt. ܪܛܢ. m. *prone to complain, a gainsayer;* ܒܶܣܪܳܐ ܪܳܛܽܘܢܳܐ *meat consecrated by the Magi.*

ܪܛܽܘܢܝܳܐ and ܐ̈ܶ pl. ܢܶܐ rt. ܪܛܢ. *murmuring, gainsaying, contradiction, disparagement.*

ܪܳܛܽܘܢܳܝܳܐ, ܢܳܝܬܳܐ rt. ܪܛܢ. *gainsaying, contradictious grumbling.*

ܪܰܛܺܝܒܽܘܬܳܐ pl. ܒܘ̈ܳܬܳܐ, ܬܳܐ rt. ܪܛܒ. f. *moisture, wetness; humour, saliva; sap, juice.*

ܪܛܝܢܣ m. *red nitre.*

ܪܺܛܠܳܐ and ܪܺܝܛܠܳܐ m. a weight, *one pound;* a measure, $2\frac{1}{2} = 1$ pint.

ܪܛܰܢ fut. ܢܶܪܛܽܢ, act. part. ܪܳܛܶܢ, ܪܳܛܢܳܐ. *to murmur,* with ܥܰܠ, rarely with ܒ or ܥܠܰܘܗܝ; ܪܳܛܢܺܝܢ ܗܘܰܘ ܦܪ̈ܺܝܫܶܐ ܘܳܐܡܪܺܝܢ the Pharisees *murmured, saying* .... Ethpe. ܐܶܬܪܛܶܢ *to be murmured against;* ܡܶܛܽܠ ܗܳܢܳܐ ܐܶܬܡܰܠܠܽܘ ܥܠܰܘܗܝ ܘܶܐܬܪܛܶܢ ܡܶܢ ܣܰܓܺܝܐܶܐ *on this account many spoke* against him *and murmured.* Pa. ܪܰܛܶܢ *to murmur very much, complain greatly;* ܪܰܛܶܢܘ ܥܰܠ ܡܰܢܢܳܐ ܠܰܚܡܳܐ ܕܡܰܠܰܐܟ̈ܶܐ *they complained of manna, the bread of angels;* ܝܗܰܒ ܚܣܺܝܣܳܐܺܝܬ ܘܟܰܕ ܡܪܰܛܶܢ *he gave sparingly and grumbling.* Aph. ܐܰܪܛܶܢ *to make to murmur, arouse complaints;* ܐܰܪܛܶܢܘ ܓܳܫܽܘܫ̈ܶܐ ܠܟܽܠܳܗ ܟܢܽܘܫܬܳܐ ܥܰܠ ܡܽܘܫܶܐ the spies *made all the congregation murmur against* Moses. Derivatives, ܪܛܳܢܳܐ, ܪܛܽܘܢܳܐ, ܪܛܽܘܢܝܳܐ, ܪܳܛܽܘܢܳܐ, ܪܳܛܽܘܢܳܝܳܐ, ܪܶܛܢܳܐ, ܡܪܰܛܢܳܢܳܐ.

ܪܶܛܢܳܐ pl. ܢܶܐ rt. ܪܛܢ. m. *murmuring, speaking against, a scruple;* ܪܳܛܽܘܢܳܐ = ܒܶܣܪܳܐ ܕܪ̈ܶܛܢܶܐ ܣ.

ܪܶܛܦܳܐ m. *filth.*

ܪܶܝܓܬܳܐ pl. ܓܳܬܳܐ rt. ܪܓ. m. *longing, yearning.*

ܪܶܝܓܬܳܢܳܐ rt. ܪܓ. m. *eager, sensual, greedy.*

ܪܶܝܓܬܳܢܽܘܬܳܐ rt. ܪܓ. f. *avidity.*

ܪܺܝܚ, ܪܺܝܚܳܐ pl. ܪ̈ܺܝܚܶܐ, ܪ̈ܺܝܚܰܝܳܐ rt. ܪܘܚ. m. *a smell, savour, odour, fragrance;* pl. *perfumes, spices, unguents;* ܪܺܝܚܳܐ ܕܓܰܪܒܳܐ *leprosy.*

ܪܺܝܚܽܘܬܳܐ rt. ܪܘܚ. f. *fragrance.*

ܪܺܝܚܳܢܳܐ, ܪܺܝܚܳܢܳܝܳܐ rt. ܪܘܚ. *spiced, fragrant, aromatic.*

ܪܺܝܚܳܢܽܘܬܳܐ rt. ܪܘܚ. *fragrance.*

ܪܺܝܚܳܢܳܝܳܐ rt. ܪܘܚ. *aromatic.*

ܪܺܝܛܘܪ; see ܪܽܘܛܪܳܐ.

ܪܺܝܛܽܘܪܺܝܩܽܘܣ *rhetorical.*

ܪܺܝܛܽܘܪܽܘܬܳܐ and ܪܺܝܛܽܘܪܺܝܩܺܝ f. *rhetoric.*

ܪܺܝܛܺܝܢܺܝ and ܪܺܝܛܺܝܢܳܐ; see ܪܽܘܛܺܝܢܳܐ *resin.*

ܪܰܝܶܡ Pael conj. of verb ܪܘܡ.

ܪܺܝܡܳܐ pl. ܡܶܐ m. *a wild bull, buffalo, unicorn.*

ܪܺܝܡܳܐ rt. ܪܘܡ. m. *raising, support;* ܪܺܝܡ ܐ̈ܺܝܕܰܝܳܐ ܪܺܝܫܳܐ— *lifting up the hands, the head.*

ܪܝܡܣܐ m. *ivory chips.*

ܪܺܝܡܬܳܐ pl. ܡܳܬܳܐ rt. ܪܘܡ. f. *a very large stone, an obstacle.*

ܪܺܝܦܽܘܕܺܝܢ pl. ܪܺܝܦܽܘܕܺܝܢܶܐ f. Lat. repudium, *a bill of divorce.*

ܪܺܝܦܽܘܬܳܐ rt. ܪܘܦ. f. *small gains, a 'tip.'*

ܪܺܝܩܳܢ, ܢܳܐ, ܢܬܳܐ rt. ܪܘܩ. *empty, vain, valueless.*

ܪܺܝܩܳܢܽܘܬܳܐ or ܪܺܝܩܽܘܬܳܐ rt. ܪܘܩ. f. *vanity, emptiness.*

ܪܺܝܪܳܐ m. *saliva, spittle, mucus, watery phlegm; mucilage.*

ܪܺܫ, ܪܺܫܳܐ pl. ܪܺܫܺܝܢ, ܫܶܐ constr. ܪܺܫܰܝ, also written without yudh, ܪܫ, ܪܫܳܐ &c. m. *a*) *head, poll, single person;* ܪܺܫܳܐ ܪܺܫܳܐ *one by one;* ܒܪ̈ܺܫܰܝܗܽܘܢ *by their polls;* ܡܳܐܐ ܪܺܫܺܝܢ ܒܥܺܝܪܳܐ *a hundred head of cattle;* ܟܣܶܦ ܪܺܫܳܐ *poll-tax.* *b*) *summit, point, tip, top, end;* ܪ ܛܽܘܪܳܐ *a mountain top;* ܪ ܨܶܒܥܳܐ *tip of the finger;* ܒܪ̈ܺܫ ܨܶܒ̈ܥܳܬܗ ܕܪ̈ܶܓܠܰܘܗܝ *on tiptoe.* *c*) *a division* of a discourse, *head, heading, chapter, treatise.* *d*) *the beginning, chief part;* ܪ ܐܶܘܰܢܓܶܠܝܳܘܢ *the beginning of the Gospel;* ܪܺܫ̈ܰܝ ܐܶܓܰܪ̈ܳܬܳܐ various ways of *beginning letters;* ܪܺܫ ܐܺܝܠܽܘܠ *beginning* or *first of September;* ܪ ܝܰܪܚܳܐ *first of the month* = new moon, calends; ܪ ܫܰܢܬܳܐ *New Year.* *e*) *a division, company* of soldiers. *f*) *first, best, chief, a capital* city, *initial* letter; *prince, chief, prefect, superior;* ܪ̈ܫܐ ܕܡܕ̈ܝܢܬܐ *the magistrates;* ܡ̈ܠܐ ܕܦܬܚܢ ܪܫܐ *words having Pthaka on the first letter.* In composition: ܪ̈ܫ ܐܒ̈ܗܬܐ O. T. *head of a family; patriarch; a bishop, pope, patriarch;* ܪܫ ܫܪܒܬܐ *founder of a race;* ܪܫ ܐܠܦܐ *a chiliarch, captain of a thousand;* ܪܫ ܐܣܛܘܡܟܐ *orifice of the stomach;* ܪܫ ܐܦܣܩܘܦܐ *archbishop;* ܪܫ ܒܣ̈ܡܐ *choice spices;* ܪܫ ܓܒܠܐ *cheiranthus incanus, gilliflower;* ܪܫ ܕܝܪܐ *abbat, archimandrite;* ܪܫ ܕܟܪܐ *battering-ram;* ܪܫ ܗܪܣܝܣ *heresiarch;* ܪܫ ܙܘܝܬܐ *chief corner-stone;* ܪܫ ܚܝܠܐ *commander-in-chief;* ܪܫ ܛܘܦܣܐ *archetype;* ܪܫ ܝܠܕܐ *first-born;* ܪܫܐ ܕܠܫܢܐ *the uvula;* ܪܫ ܟܠܟ̈ܠܐ *warts;* ܪܫ ܟܘܡܪ̈ܐ *high-priest;* ܪܫ ܡܐܐ *a centurion;* ܪܫ ܡܘܬܒܐ *president;* also *a chief seat;* ܪܫ ܡܠܐܟ̈ܐ *archangel;* ܪܫ ܡܫܡܫܢܐ *archdeacon;* ܪܫ ܢܒܥܐ—ܢܗܪܐ *source, head of a spring, a stream;* ܪܫ ܢܓܪ̈ܐ *master-builder, architect;* ܪܫ ܢܓܪܘܬܐ *architecture;* ܪܫ ܢܡܘܣܐ *Head of the Law,* a Moghul title; ܪܫ ܣܗ̈ܕܐ *protomartyr;* ܪܫ ܣܡܟܐ *ruler of the feast;* ܪܫ ܣܡܟ̈ܐ *chief seats;* ܪܫ ܥܠ̈ܠܬܐ = ܪܫ ܒܟܘܪ̈ܐ; ܪܫ ܥܠ̈ܠܬܐ *first-fruits;* ܪܫ ܦܘܠܚܢܐ = ܪܫ ܫܒܝܠܐ; ܪܫܐ ܕܐܪܒܥܐ *tetrarch;* ܪܫܐ ܕܘܙܝܪ̈ܐ *chief Vizir;* ܪܫ ܬܕܝܐ *nipple;* ܪܫ ܬܘܪܬܐ *initial letter of a stanza.* Idiom: ܠܝܬ ܠܗ ܪܫܐ ܕܢܚܐ *he has no business to live.* See ܩܡ, ܣܠܩ, ܝܗܒ &c. With preps. ܒܪܫܐ *before, representing; especially, briefly;* ܥܠ ܪܝܫܗ ܕܟܠ *headlong, head downwards;* ܡܢ ܪܝܫ *again;* ܡܢ ܕܪܝܫ *again;* ܡܘܠܕܐ ܕܡܢ ܕܪܝܫ *regeneration;* ܡܢ ܪܫܗ *upside down;* ܡܢ ܪܝܫ ܠܪܝܫ *from end to end, utterly.* Derivatives, the following sixteen words:—

ܪܫܐܝܬ from ܪܝܫ. adv. *especially.*

ܪܫܕܝܪܝܘܬܐ pl. ܪܫܕܝܪ̈ܝܘܬܐ cf. ܪܝܫ ܕܝܪܐ. f. *abbacy, office of archimandrite, rule over a mandra.*

ܪܫܘܢܐ dimin. of ܪܝܫ. m. *head, top* of a plant.

ܪܫܝܘܬܐ from ܪܝܫ. f. in construction *most high, supreme, chief;* ܪܫܝܘܬ ܐܠܗܘܬܐ *the Most High Godhead;* ܪܫܝܘܬ ܛܒܘܬܐ *the supreme good;* ܪܫܝܘܬ ܟܘܡܪܘܬܐ *the high-priesthood; the episcopate;* ܪܫܝܘܬ ܛܟܣܘܬܐ ܡܠܐܟܝܬܐ *the angelic hierarchy.*

ܪܫܝܐ, ܪܫܝܐ, ܪܫܝܬܐ from ܪܝܫ. *chief, best, fine, finest, choice, admirable.* Pl. f. *noble ladies; initial* letters.

ܪܫܝܘܬܐ from ܪܝܫ. f. *first rank, chief place* or *part, beginning.*

ܪܫܝ ܟܘܡܪ̈ܐ *high-priests, chief presbyters, bishops.*

ܪܫܝܬܐ pl. ܪ̈ܫܝܬܐ from ܪܝܫ. f. *a*) *beginning, first beginning, origin; chief part, principal part.* Gen. i. 1, *In the beginning,* is written ܒܪܫܝܬ by the West-Syrians, ܒܪܫܝܬ by the East-Syrians. *b*) usually pl. *first-fruits.*

ܪܫܟܘܡܪܝܐ *pontifical, episcopal.*

ܪܫܡܠܐ from ܪܝܫ. *principal sum, capital.*

ܪܫܢ E-Syr. ܪܫܢ denom. verb from ܪܫܢܐ. *to raise to power, constitute* king, patriarch &c.; ܪܫܢܘ ܗܘܘ ܒܗ *they seized the supreme power.* Ethpalan ܐܬܪܫܢ and ܐܬܪܫܢ *to be raised to power, set in authority over, made head; to hold rule.*

ܪܫܢܐ, ܪܫܢܝܬܐ from ܪܝܫ. *a ruler, magistrate, noble, prince; prefect, president, captain, general.*

ܪܫܢܐܝܬ from ܪܝܫ. adv. *originally, commandingly, authoritatively.*

ܪܫܢܘܬܐ pl. ܪܫܢ̈ܘܬܐ from ܪܝܫ. f. *principality, governorship, magistracy; dignity; principle; primacy, episcopacy, abbacy.*

ܪܫܢܝܐ, ܪܫܢܝܬܐ from ܪܝܫ. *chief, principal.*

ܪܫܬܐ constr. st. ܪܫܬ fem. form of ܪܫܐ. *head, chief;* ܪܫܬ ܕܝܪܐ *an abbess.*

ܪܟܟ fut. ܢܪܘܟ, act. part. ܪܐܟ. *a*) *to be soft, tender;* ܡܐ ܕܪܟܟ ܣܘܟܘܗܝ ܘܦܪܥܘ ܛܪ̈ܦܐ *when the branches* of the fig *grow tender and put forth leaves.* *b*) *to soften, moderate;* ܪܟܟ ܗܘܐ ܚܝܠܗ ܕܫܠܗܒܝܬܐ *he moderated the force of the flame.* Part. adj. ܪܟܝܟ, ܪܟܝܟܐ, ܪܟܝܟܬܐ *soft, fresh, gentle, mild;* ܥܪ̈ܣܬܐ ܪܟܝܟ̈ܬܐ *soft couches;* ܚܠܒܐ ܪܟܝܟܐ *fresh milk;* ܢܘܪܐ ܪܟܝܟܬܐ *slow fire;* ܡܛܪܐ ܪܟܝܟܐ *gentle rain;* ܟܐܦܐ ܪܟܝܟܬܐ *soft stone* opp. ܫܝܫܐ *marble;* ܬܗܘܐ ܡܠܬܗ ܪܟܝܟܐ *let his speech be mild.* Pl. f. *molluscs.* Pa. ܪܟܟ *to soften, mollify; to make tender, gentle;* ܢܪܟܟ ܒܣܪܗ ܐܝܟ ܕܛܠܝܐ *He will make his flesh tender as a child's;* ܪܟܟܘ ܠܒܘܬܗܘܢ ܒܬܝܒܘܬܐ *they made their hearts tender by penitence.* Gram. *to write* or *pronounce* the ܪܘܟܟܐ letters with Rukokh; ܡܪܰܟܟܳܐ pronounced softly i.e. aspirated. Ethpe. ܐܶܬ݂ܪܟܶܟ݂ and Ethpa. ܐܶܬ݂ܪܰܟܰܟ݂ a) to be soft, be softened, become tender; ܐܶܬ݂ܪܰܟܰܟ݂ ܡܶܠܰܝܗܽܘܢ ܝܰܬܺܝܪ ܡܶܢ ܡܶܫܚܳܐ their words are softer than oil. b) to be stirred, hoed as clods, earth. Aph. ܐܰܪܶܟ݂ a) to soften, soothe; ܐܰܪܶܟ݂ ܐܳܣܝܳܐ ܒܡܶܫܚܳܐ the physician soothed the sore with oil. b) to mitigate, moderate. Ethpalp. ܐܶܬ݂ܪܰܟ݂ܪܰܟ݂ to be softened, moderated. Derivatives, ܪܟܟܐ, ܪܟܝܟܐ, ܪܟܝܟܘܬܐ, ܪܟܝܟܐܝܬ, ܡܪܟܟܐ, ܡܪܟܟܘܬܐ, ܡܪܟܟܢܐܝܬ, ܡܬܪܟܟܢܐ.

ܪܟܶܒ݂ fut. ܢܶܪܟܰܒ݂, act. part. ܪܳܟ݂ܶܒ݂, ܪܳܟ݂ܒ݂ܳܐ, pass. part. ܪܟ݂ܺܝܒ݂, ܒ݂ܳܐ, ܒ݂ܳܬ݂ܳܐ. a) to mount, bestride, ride a horse, mule, camel &c. with ܥܰܠ; to mount a chariot, a throne; ܡܰܠܟܳܐ ܪܟܶܒ݂ ܠܨܰܝܕܳܐ the king went a-hunting; ܪܳܟ݂ܒ݂ܰܝ ܪܰܟ݂ܫܳܐ horse-riders; ܣܽܘܣܝܳܐ ܘܪܳܟ݂ܒ݂ܶܗ a horse with its rider; ܪܟ݂ܺܝܒ݂ ܗܘܳܐ ܥܰܠ ܚܰܨܶܗ ܕܦܺܝܠܳܐ riding on the back of an elephant; ܪܟ݂ܺܝܒ݂ ܠܶܗ ܫܺܐܕܳܐ demon-ridden. b) with ܐܶܠܦܳܐ, ܣܦܺܝܢ݈ܬ݂ܳܐ &c. to embark. c) to cover in breeding. Ethpe. ܐܶܬ݂ܪܟܶܒ݂ to be covered in breeding. Pa. ܪܰܟܶܒ݂ a) to compound, make up ܣܰܡܡܳܢܶܐ medicines. b) to put together, construct, make ܐܽܘܪܚܳܐ a road; ܡܪܰܟܒܺܝܢ ܗܘܰܘ ܡܰܓ݂ܕܠܶܐ ܕܩܰܝܣܳܐ they were constructing wooden towers; ܐܰܠܳܗܳܐ ܪܰܟܒܶܗ ܡܶܢ ܢܰܦܫܳܐ ܘܡܶܢ ܦܰܓ݂ܪܳܐ God made man of soul and body. c) to compose, write books, songs, odes, lamentations, parables; ܟܬ݂ܳܒ݂ܳܐ ܕܫܰܗܡܰܪܘܪܺܝܕ ܕܰܐܢܳܐ ܒܛܰܝܳܐܺܝܬ ܪܰܟܒܶܬ݂ܶܗ the Book of Shah Marurid which I wrote in Arabic. d) to fabricate, devise ܢܶܟ݂ܠܶܐ stratagems; ܪܰܟܶܒ݂ ܝܽܘܠܦܳܢܳܐ ܚܰܕܬ݂ܳܐ he devised a new doctrine; ܪܰܟܶܒ݂ܘ ܥܠܰܘܗ݈ܝ ܥܶܠܠܳܬ݂ܳܐ they trumped up charges against him. Pass. part. ܡܪܰܟܒܳܐ, ܡܪܰܟܒܳܐ, ܡܪܰܟܒܳܬ݂ܳܐ compound, composite opp. ܦܫܺܝܛܳܐ simple; ܡܪܰܟܒܳܐ ܡܶܢ ܐܰܪܒܥܳܐ ܐܶܣܛܽܘܟܣܶܐ composed of the four elements. Gram. compound noun, ordinal number, affix pronoun, transitive verb. E-Syr. any conjugation other than Peal. Ethpa. ܐܶܬ݂ܪܰܟܰܒ݂ a) to be constructed, composed, framed as a building, a ship, the body. b) to be devised, invented as a story, a wile. c) to be composed, arranged; ܐܶܬ݂ܪܰܟܰܒ݂ ܒܣܶܦܪܳܐ ܦܶܬ݂ܓܳܡܶܐ scattered sayings were arranged in a book. d) gram. to be formed, derived; to take affixes. Aph. ܐܰܪܟܶܒ݂ a) to make to ride, to mount, set with ܥܰܠ upon a beast, with ܒ in a chariot; to cause to embark. b) to set, to fasten; ܐܰܪܟܶܒ݂ ܐܺܝܕܳܟ ܥܰܠ ܩܶܫܬܳܐ set thy hand upon the bow. c) to admit, copulate animals. Derivatives, ܪܳܟ݂ܒ݂ܳܐ, ܪܟ݂ܺܝܒ݂ܳܐ, ܪܟ݂ܺܝܒ݂ܬܳܐ, ܪܰܟ݂ܳܒ݂ܳܐ, ܪܶܟ݂ܒ݂ܳܐ, ܪܶܟ݂ܒ݂ܬܳܐ, ܪܶܟ݂ܽܘܒ݂ܳܐ, ܪܶܟ݂ܽܘܒ݂ܽܘܬ݂ܳܐ, ܡܰܪܟܒ݂ܳܐ, ܡܰܪܟܒ݂ܳܢܳܐ, ܡܪܰܟܒ݂ܳܢܳܐܺܝܬ, ܡܪܰܟܒ݂ܽܘܬ݂ܳܐ, ܡܰܪܟܰܒ݂ܬܳܐ, ܡܶܬ݂ܪܰܟܒ݂ܳܢܳܐ, ܡܶܬ݂ܪܰܟܒ݂ܳܢܽܘܬ݂ܳܐ, ܡܶܬ݂ܪܰܟܒ݂ܳܬ݂ܳܐ.

ܪܳܟ݂ܒ݂ܳܐ, ܪܳܟ݂ܶܒ݂ pl. ܒ݂ܶܐ Peal act. part. = subst. m. a rider, horseman.

ܪܳܟ݂ܒ݂ܳܐ pl. ܒ݂ܶܐ rt. ܪܟܒ. m. the upper millstone; the iron axle of a millstone.

ܪܰܟ݂ܳܒ݂ܳܐ pl. ܒ݂ܶܐ rt. ܪܟܒ. m. a horseman, mounted soldier, the fighting-man in a chariot.

ܪܟ݂ܳܒ݂ܳܐ pl. ܪܟ݂ܳܒ݂ܶܐ ܕܣܽܘܟܳܢܶܐ rudder-bands, Acts xxvii. 40.

ܪܶܟ݂ܒ݂ܬܳܐ rt. ܪܟܒ. f. covering, impregnating of animals; ܣܽܘܣܝܳܐ ܕܪܶܟ݂ܒ݂ܬܳܐ a stallion.

ܪܶܟ݂ܽܘܒ݂ܳܐ pl. ܒ݂ܶܐ m. ܪܶܟ݂ܽܘܒ݂ܬܳܐ pl. ܒ݂ܳܬ݂ܳܐ f. rt. ܪܟܒ. a) conveyance, means of transport, vessel; ܐܐܰܪ ܗܽܘ ܕܐܺܝܬ݂ܰܘܗ݈ܝ ܪܶܟ݂ܽܘܒ݂ܳܐ ܕܦܳܪܰܚܬܳܐ air which is the transport of birds. b) a mount, any animal for riding, horse; ܪܶܟ݂ܽܘܒ݂ܳܬ݂ܳܐ ܛܰܝܳܝܳܬ݂ܳܐ Arab steeds or perh. dromedaries. c) riding, horsemanship; ܪ ܕܝܰܡܳܐ travelling by sea.

ܪܶܟ݂ܽܘܒ݂ܽܘܬ݂ܳܐ rt. ܪܟܒ. f. riding, horsemanship.

ܪܰܟ݂ܽܘܒ݂ܳܐ pl. ܒ݂ܶܐ rt. ܪܟܒ. m. a) = ܪܶܟ݂ܒ݂ܬܳܐ. b) perh. a horse-cloth.

ܪܟ݂ܺܝܟ݂, ܟ݂ܳܐ, ܟ݂ܳܬ݂ܳܐ; see ܪܰܟ݂ Peal conj.

ܪܟ݂ܺܝܟ݂ܳܐܺܝܬ rt. ܪܟ. adv. softly, gently, in a low voice, noiselessly.

ܪܟ݂ܺܝܟ݂ܽܘܬ݂ܳܐ rt. ܪܟ. f. tender growth; softness.

ܪܟ݂ܺܝܢܽܘܬ݂ܳܐ or ܪܟ̈ pl. ܢ̈ܘܳܬ݂ܳܐ rt. ܪܟܢ. f. an inclination, bending; ܪܟ݂ܺܝܢܽܘܬ݂ ܒܽܘܪܟܳܐ genuflexion; lowliness.

ܪܶܟ݂ܟ݂ܳܐ m. pl. rt. ܪܟ. mildness.

ܪܰܟ݂ܠܳܐ or ܪܳܟ݂ܠܳܐ pl. ܠܶܐ m. a herb-gatherer, dealer in drugs, huckster.

ܪܳܟ݂ܠܽܘܬ݂ܳܐ f. pharmacy.

ܪܳܟ݂ܠܳܢܳܐ pl. ܢܶܐ m. a druggist.

ܪܟܶܢ fut. ܢܶܪܟܰܢ, parts. ܪܳܟܶܢ and ܪܟ݂ܺܝܢ, ܢܳܐ, ܢܳܬ݂ܳܐ. to turn, bend downwards, sink, decline, incline; ܪܟܶܢ ܝܰܘܡܳܐ the day declined, the day was far spent; ܪܟܶܢܘ ܛܶܠܳܠܰܝ ܪܰܡܫܳܐ the evening shadows lengthened; ܐܰܠܳܗܳܐ ܒܪܰܚܡܰܘܗ݈ܝ ܪܟܶܢ ܘܢܚܶܬ God in His mercy leaned towards us and descended.

Part. 1st form: verbal use *inclining, bending* in prayer; ܠܐܪܥܐ ܪܳܟܢܺܝܢ ܚܙܘܗܘܢ *casting their looks downwards.* 2nd form: *prone, inclined to; lowly; downcast;* ܪܟܝܢ ܠܨܶܒܬܐ *inclined to adornment;* ܣܓܕܬܐ ܪܟܝܢܬܐ *prostrate adoration.* Ethpe. ܐܶܬܪܟܶܢ *a) to incline oneself, bend, be bent;* ܐܶܬܪܟܶܢ ܘܣܓܶܕ *he bent and did obeisance. b) to dismount, light down;* ܐܶܬܪܰܟܢܰܬ ܡܶܢ ܚܡܳܪܐ *she lighted down from the ass. c) to descend, condescend;* ܐܶܬܪܟܶܢ ܡܫܝܚܐ ܒܚܘܒܗ ܘܐܬܳܐ ܠܘܳܬܰܢ *Christ in His love descended and came to us;* ܟܕ ܒܳܥܶܐ ܕܢܶܬܪܟܶܢ ܠܡܶܥܰܠ ܠܒܰܝܬܶܗ *begging that he would condescend to enter his house. d) to yield, agree;* ܠܐ ܐܶܬܪܰܟܢܰܬ ܠܒܳܥܘܬܗܘܢ *she did not yield to their entreaty. e)* gram. *to be subject to, agree with* a rule. *f)* denom. from ܪܶܟܢܳܐ *to modulate, chant.* Aph. ܐܰܪܟܶܢ *a) to lower, let down;* ܐܰܪܟܶܢ ܠܝ ܩܘܠܬܟ ܘܐܶܫܬܶܐ *let down thy pitcher that I may drink; to take down* a tent opp. ܐܰܩܺܝܡ *to erect. b) to incline, bend* esp. ܐܶܕܢܳܐ *to incline the ear, hearken;* ܐܺܝܕܳܐ *to stretch out the hand, set the hand* to work; ܚܰܨܳܐ, ܟܬܦܬܐ *to turn the eyes;* ܪܺܫܳܐ and ܨܰܘܪܳܐ *to bend the neck, the head, to submit, obey;* with ܡܶܢ *to turn away, avert.* Pass. part. *bent, abased, humbled;* ܡܰܪܟܰܢ ܨܰܘܪܳܐ ܕܦܬܟܪܘܬܐ *vain idolatry.* Derivatives, ܪܟܝܢܘܬܐ, ܪܶܟܢܳܐ, ܪܟܳܢܳܐ, ܪܟܝܢܳܐ, ܪܟܝܢܳܐܝܬ, ܡܬܪܟܢܳܢܳܐ, ܡܰܪܟܢܘܬܐ, ܡܬܪܟܢܳܢܘܬܐ.

ܪܶܟܢܳܐ pl. ܐ̈ rt. ܪܟܢ. m. *inflection, modulation; metre; a tone* in music, ܬܡܳܢܝܳܐ ܪ̈ܟܢܐ *octoechus, hymnbook of the eight tones.*

ܪܶܟܢܳܐ rt. ܪܟܢ. m. *side, slope;* ܪ ܕܡܰܝܳܐ *a waterfall, the sound of falling water.*

ܪܟܳܢܘܬܳܐ rt. ܪܟܢ. f. *subsiding.*

ܪܟܳܢܳܝܳܐ pl. ܐ̈ rt. ܪܟܢ. *inflexional.*

ܪܰܡܟܳܐ pl. ܪ̈ܡܟܐ m. *a horse;* ܪ̈ܡܟܐ ܐܰܪ̈ܚܫܬܐ or ܐܰܚܫܬܪ̈ܢܐ *stallions;* ܒܝܬ ܪ *a stable.*

ܪܰܡܟܬܳܐ fem. of ܪܰܡܟܳܐ, only pl. *mares.*

ܪܳܡ, ܪܳܡܳܐ, ܪܳܡܬܳܐ rt. ܪܘܡ. *tall, high; exalted, sublime; proud;* ܪܳܡ ܓܒܝܢܘܗܝ *supercilious;* ܪܳܡ ܥܰܝܢܶܐ *having prominent eyes,* also *haughty.*

ܪܡܳܐ Peal only parts. Act. ܪܳܡܶܐ, ܪܳܡܝܳܐ pl. m. ܪܳܡܶܝܢ pl. f. ܪܳܡܝܳܢ *a) to put, place, pour, to cast* ܡܨܝܕܬܐ *a net,* ܚܰܟܬܳܐ *a hook;* ܢܰܗܪ̈ܘܬܐ ܪܳܡܝܳܢ ܠܝܰܡܳܐ *rivers run into the sea;* ܥܦܪܐ ܪܳܡܶܐ ܥܠ ܡܺܝ̈ܬܐ the priest *casts dust on the dead. b) to lay, set, lay low, lay or leave on the ground;* ܟܕ ܪܳܡܶܐ ܩܰܪܳܝܬܐ *as he was felling a beam;* ܟܘܣܝܬܐ ܪܳܡܶܐ ܠܐܦܣܩܘܦܐ *he sets the mitre on the* bishop's *head. c)* with ܚܪܝܢܐ *to sow discord, set at variance;* ܪܳܡܶܐ ܚܪܝܢܐ *a sower of discord. d)* with ܥܠ *to add, multiply; to impose* a fine, tribute &c. *e)* with ܐܺܝܕܳܐ ܒ *to set the hand to; to subscribe;* ܐܺܝܕܳܐ ܥܠ *he lays his hand upon . . .;* ܙܰܝܢܳܐ *to lay down arms;* ܛܰܝܒܘܬܐ *to requite, oblige, lay under an obligation;* ܪܳܡܶܐ ܚܶܡܬܳܐ *venomous;* ܪܳܡܶܝܢ ܢܰܦܫܳܬܗܘܢ *they lay down their lives;* ܪܳܡܶܝܢ ܡܶܫܬܘܬܐ *feasters, riotous livers;* ܦܓܘܕܐ *to bridle;* ܪܳܡܶܝܢ ܩܺܝܢܳܬܳܐ *they utter laments;* ܒܳܥܘܬܳܐ *to lay or offer a petition.* Pass. part. ܪܡܶܐ, ܪܡܶܝܳܐ *fallen, lying, prostrate, cast out, set;* ܬܫܢܝܩܐ ܕܪܡܶܝܢ ܒܶܗ *the torment in which they lie;* ܪܡܶܐ ܗܘܳܐ ܠܗ ܠܣܛܢܐ ܒܠܒܶܗ *the devil having put it in his heart;* ܪܡܶܝܢ ܥܠ ܐܘܪܚܐ *fallen by the way;* ܥܠ ܥܰܪܣܳܐ *lying in a cradle;* ܒܐܫܬܐ *ill with fever;* ܒܟܘܪܗܢܐ *lying sick;* ܒܥܪܣܐ or ܥܠ ܥܪܣܐ *lying on a couch.* Idiom: ܡܢܐ ܪܡܐ ܠܟܘܢ *what does it concern you? what do you care?* Ethpe. ܐܶܬܪܡܺܝ *a) to be lying down, lying ill. b) to be poured, thrown, cast out;* ܐܶܬܪܡܺܝ ܒܝܰܡܳܐ *it was cast into the sea. c) to submit, yield; to give heed, give way, to be given up to, occupied with;* ܡܶܬܪܡܶܐ ܠܡܶܫܬܰܡܥܘ *yielding to persuasion;* ܐܶܬܪܡܺܝ ܒܣܘܥܪܢܐ ܐܝܢܐ ܕܗܘ *he was engaged in some business or other;* ܠܐ ܡܶܬܪܡܶܐ ܗܘܳܐ ܠܓܘܚܟܐ *he seldom gave way to laughter. d) to be allowed to stand, left* to ferment. Pael ܪܰܡܺܝ *to tell tales, traduce, calumniate,* with ܥܠ of the pers. Ethpa. ܐܶܬܪܰܡܺܝ *a) to be tricked, deceived. b) to agree, acknowledge.* Aph. ܐܰܪܡܺܝ *to throw, cast, pour, impart; to cast down, lay low, make to fall; to lay, set, place, put, add,* with ܥܠ *on, to set upon, attack; to impose* a tax, tribute; with ܩܕܡ *to lay before, offer;* with ܒܳܬܰܪ *to pursue.* With ܐܘܪܚܐ *to set out, undertake a journey;* ܐܺܝܕܳܐ *to set the hand to, undertake, subscribe;* ܐܺܝ̈ܕܝܐ ܥܠ *to lay hands on;* ܠܓܠܘܬܐ *to send into exile;* ܒܐܠܦܐ *to take ship;* ܒܝܬ ܐܣܝܪ̈ܐ *to cast into prison;* ܒܘܪܟܐ *to kneel;* ܒܥܘܬܐ *to offer a petition;* ܒܝܥܬܐ *to lay an egg;* ܙܝܢܐ *to take up arms;*

ܫܘܠܡܐ to requite, oblige; with ܥܠ to exact, extort; ܚܡܪܐ ܥܠ ܣܓܕܐ to saddle an ass; ܒܣܝܦܐ, ܚܪܒܐ to put to the sword; ܠܒܢܐ to make bricks; ܡܨܝܕܬܐ to cast a net; ܒ ܢܘܪܐ to set fire to; ܢܦܫܗ to cast oneself down, lay oneself open to, take upon oneself; ܣܗܕܘܬܐ to take to witness, adjure; ܣܝܦܐ to gird on a sword, cf. ܚܪܒܐ; ܥܝܢܐ, ܚܙܘܐ to cast the eyes on, cast a look; ܦܓܘܕܐ to bridle; ܚܪܝܢܐ ܒܝܬ to sow discord; ܦܣܐ or ܦܘܪܐ to cast lots; ܩܠܐ to raise the voice; ܥܩܡܬܐ ܒܗ or ܒܫܫܠܬܐ to urge forwards; ܒܫܫܠܬܐ to throw into chains; ܫܢܐ to knock out a tooth; ܡܠܬܐ to undertake a matter, set forth a tale; ܫܬܐܤܬܐ to lay a foundation. Ettaph. ܐܬܪܡܝ a) to be cast, cast out, outcast, exposed as infants; ܐܬܪܡܝܘ ܠܟܠܒܐ they were thrown to the dogs. b) to be laid, laid aside, stored up. With ܪܓܠܐ to be tripped up. Derivatives, ܪܡܝܐ, ܪܡܝܐ, ܪܡܝܐ, ܪܡܝܘܬܐ, ܪܡܝܘܬܐ, ܡܪܡܝܘܬܐ, ܡܪܡܝܢܐ, ܡܪܡܝܬܐ, ܡܪܡܝܬܐ, ܬܪܡܝܬܐ.

ܪܡܐ pl. of ܪܡܬܐ.

ܪܡܐܝܬ rt. ܪܘܡ. adv. greatly, sublimely, proudly.

ܪܡܛܢ, ܪܡܛܐܢ and ܪܡܛܘܢ Ramadan, the Arab month of fasting.

ܪܡܘܟܐ m. ܪܡܘܟܬܐ f. rt. ܪܡܟ. a syringe for injecting oil into the nostrils.

ܪܡܘܡܐ = ܪܡܘܡܬܐ hot embers.

ܪܡܘܬܐ rt. ܪܘܡ. f. elevation, height, altitude; elation, pride. Gram. suppression of a letter.

ܪܡܙ fut. ܢܪܡܘܙ, act. part. ܪܡܙ, ܪܡܙܐ, pass. part. ܪܡܝܙ, ܪܡܝܙܐ. to make signs, beckon, wink ܒܥܝܢܐ with the eyes; ܒܨܒܥܬܐ with the fingers; to mean, point out, indicate, with ܥܠ; ܪܡܙ ܠܗ ܕܢܡܠܠ he beckoned to him to speak; ܪܡܙ ܐܒܘ ܓܥܦܪ ܘܐܬܩܛܠ Abu Jafar gave a sign and he was put to death; ܡܢܐ ܪܡܙ what is the meaning of . . . ? ܐܝܟ ܕܪܡܙܐ ܟܬܒܐ as Scripture indicates; ܓܠܝܐ ܗܝ ܕܫܒܛܐ ܪܡܙ ܠܫܘܠܛܢܐ it is clear that the sceptre indicates power; ܪܡܝܙܝܢ ܒܡܬܠܐ signified in parables. Ethpe. ܐܬܪܡܙ to be indicated, signified; ܦܠܐܬܐ ܕܐܬܪܡܙܝ ܒܥܒܕܐ ܕܡܘܫܐ ܥܡ ܚܘܛܪܐ allegories indicated by Moses' actions with the rod. Pa. ܪܡܙ to beckon, make signs ܒܥܝܢܐ with the eyes; to intimate, signify.

Aph. ܐܪܡܙ to beckon with the eyes, to glance. Derivatives, ܪܡܙܐ, ܪܡܙܐܝܬ, ܪܡܙܢܐ, ܪܡܙܢܐ.

ܪܡܙܐ pl. ܐ̈ rt. ܪܡܙ. m. a sign, hint, gesture, a dark saying; suggestion, symbol; ܪ ܕܓܒܝܢܐ a motion of the eyebrow; ܪ ܕܥܝܢܐ a glance, wink; ܟܬܒܐ ܕܪܡܙܐ Book of Symptoms of disease; ܪ ܕܥܝܢܐ a moment. Metaph. the Divine will, command.

ܪܡܙܢܐܝܬ rt. ܪܡܙ. adv. by way of a sign or hint, suggestively; mystically, symbolically.

ܪܡܙܢܐ, ܢܝܬܐ rt. ܪܡܙ. allusive, symbolical. Gram. demonstrative; indicating.

ܪܡܝ Pael conj. of ܪܡܐ.

ܪܡܝܐ pl. ܝܢܐ rt. ܪܡܐ. m. a) ܪ ܕܙܠܝܩܐ shedder of rays i.e. the sun. b) a whisperer, slanderer: cf. ܪܡܐ c. c) fraudulent, a sharper.

ܪܡܝܐ constr. st. ܪܡܝ and ܐܪܡܝ, rt. ܪܡܐ. m. a throw, cast of a missile, a bolt; ܪ ܕܐܪܩܥܬܐ a laid-on piece of stuff = a patch; ܪ ܕܠܒܢܐ bricklaying; ܪܡܝ ܦܓܘܕܐ, ܪܣܢܐ putting on of a bit, a bridle; ܪܡܝ ܐܝܕܐ undertaking, subscribing.

ܪܡܝܘܬܐ rt. ܪܡܐ. m. a place to receive things in.

ܪܡܝܘܬܐ rt. ܪܡܐ. f. a) fraud. b) casting out, exposing.

ܪܡܝܣܐܝܬ rt. ܪܡܣ. adv. sagaciously, soberly, placidly, with composure.

ܪܡܝܣܘܬܐ rt. ܪܡܣ. f. soberness, moderation, composure, cool reasoning.

ܪܡܟܐ collective noun. f. a herd of swine, camels &c.; a troop of demons; a crowd, multitude.

ܪܡܟܐ from ܪܡܟܐ. m. a herdsman.

ܪܡܟܐ m. Arab. the musk of commerce i.e. adulterated.

ܪܡܟܢܐ from ܪܡܟܐ. of the common herd, vulgar.

ܪܡܠ; see ܐܬܪܡܠ to be a widow.

ܪܡܣ Peal only part. adj. ܪܡܝܣ, ܣܐ, ܣܬܐ rt. ܪܡܣ. sedate, sober, moderate, temperate; gentle of speech, placid opp. ܥܩܝܣ morose; ܒܪܥܝܢܐ ܪܡܝܣܐ with composed mind; composedly, ܒܡܚܫܒܬܐ ܪܡܝܣܬܐ with cautious thought, cautiously; ܠܐ ܒܪܥܝܢܐ ܪܡܝܣܐ ܠܐ

ܒܪܘܚܘܬܗܘܢ *childish and of ill-regulated behaviour.* Ethpe. ܐܬܪܡܫ *to be placid, composed.*

ܪܡܫܐ pl. ܐ̈ m. *a white secretion in the corners of the eyes; a mote in the eyes.*

ܪܡܪܡ Palpel conj. of ܪܘܡ, ܪܡ.

ܪܡܫ fut. ܢܪܡܫ denom. verb from ܪܡܫܐ. *to grow towards evening, to become evening.* Pa. ܪܡܫ *to stay till the evening.* Aph. ܐܪܡܫ *to grow late, grow dark;* ܡܪܡܫ ܘܡܩܕܡ *early and late.*

ܪܡܫ, ܪܡܫܐ pl. ܪܡܫܐ̈ and in the Lexx. ܪܡܫܘܬܐ m. *evening, eventide;* ܒܪܡܫܐ ܠܪܡܫܐ *late in the evening;* ܕ ܪܡܫܐ ܕܫܒܬܐ *the eve of the Sabbath.* Rit. ellipt. for ܨܠܘܬܐ ܕܪܡܫܐ *vespers;* ܕ ܪܡܫܐ ܕܦܨܚܐ *Easter Eve;* ܕ ܚܡܫܐ or ܕܐܪܙܐ *the evening of Maundy Thursday.* Derivatives, verb ܪܡܫ, ܪܡܫܐ.

ܪܡܫܝܐ, ܪܡܫܝܬܐ from ܪܡܫܐ. adj. *a) evening;* ܨܘܡܐ ܪܡܫܝܐ *a fast kept till evening;* ܪܡܫܐܝܬ *towards evening* i. e. *before sunset. b) Western.*

ܪܡܬܐ or ܪܡܬܐ pl. ܪܡܐ f. *a pool, pond;* ܕ ܪܡܬܐ ܕܡܛܪܐ *a rainpool.*

ܪܡܬܐ constr. st. ܪܡܬ pl. ܪ̈ܡܬܐ rt. ܪܘܡ. f. *a) a high place, hill, height.* Pr. n. of many places such as *Rama, Arithmathea. b)* see ܪܡ.

ܪܡܬܐ f. *a) a worm,* collect. *worms. b) dust.*

ܪܢܐ fut. ܢܪܢܐ, act. part. ܪܢܐ, ܪܢܝܐ. *to think, reflect, meditate; to heed, attend to, intend; to devise* with ܒ; with ܣܪܝܩܘܬܐ *to regard vanity;* ܪܢܘ ܒܡܪܝܐ *think on the Lord;* ܪܢܘ ܒܢܦܫܟܘܢ *take heed to yourselves;* ܐܢܬܬܐ ܪܢܝܐ ܕܥܠܡܐ a married woman *is careful for the things of the world;* ܦܘܪܥܢܐ ܕܠܐ ܪܢܝܢ *unexpected retribution;* ܠܡܪܢܐ ܒܝܫܬܐ *to plan evil.* Ethpe. ܐܬܪܢܝ *to be thought, considered, deemed;* ܢܒܝܘܬܐ ܡܬܪܢܝܐ this prophecy *is considered to refer to the captivity.* Ethpa. ܐܬܪܢܝ *to consider, reflect, contemplate, conceive;* ܗܘ ܡܐ ܕܐܬܪܢܝ ܠܡܥܒܕ *that which he contemplated doing;* ܡܬܪܢܝܢ ܥܠܝ ܟܠ ܒܝܫܢ *they imagine all kinds of evil against me.* Aph. ܐܪܢܝ *to insinuate a thought, direct the thoughts;* ܠܥܡܠܐ ܡܪܢܝܐ ܡܪܢܝܬܐ. ܘܚܕܘܬܐ ܠܚܛܗܐ *industry directs the thoughts towards action, gaiety leads them into sin.* Derivatives, ܪܢܝܐ, ܡܪܢܝܢܐ, ܡܬܪܢܝܢܐ, ܡܬܪܢܝܢܘܬܐ.

ܪܢܝܐ pl. ܪ̈ܢܝܐ rt. ܪܢܐ. m. with suff. 1 pers. W-Syr. ܪܢܝ E-Syr. ܪܢܝ. *reflection, meditation, subject of thought; mocking; thought, anxiety, care;* ܪܢܝܗ ܕܥܠܡܐ *worldly care.*

ܪܣ fut. ܢܪܘܣ, act. part. ܪܐܣ, ܪܣܐ, pass. part. ܪܣܝܣ, ܐ. *to besprinkle, drop, to purify by sprinkling,* with ܥܠ; ܐܪܘܣ ܕܡܐ ܥܠ ܡܕܒܚܐ ܚܕܪܢܝܬ *sprinkle the blood upon the altar round about;* ܛܠܐ ܪܣܝܣ ܥܠ ܦܩܥܬܐ *dew falls gently on the blossoms.* Ethpe. ܐܬܪܣܝܣ *to be sprinkled;* ܡܐܢܐ ܕܡܬܪܣܝܣ ܒܕܡܐ *a garment which has been sprinkled* with blood. Pa. ܪܣܣ *to sprinkle, moisten, bedew;* ܪܣܣܘ ܡܢ ܕܡܐ ܥܠ ܐܣܩܘܦܬܐ *they sprinkled some of the blood on the thresholds;* ܚܢܢܟ ܪܣܣ ܐܝܟ ܛܠܐ *Thy mercy dropped like dew.* Derivatives, ܪܣܝܣܐ and ܐܪܣܝܣܐ, ܪܣܣܐ.

ܪܣܘ Pers. m. *a weasel.*

ܪܣܢܐ m. *a neck* or *head chain.*

ܪܣܦܐ ܕܪܝܫܐ vulgar. *a tap* or *slap on the back of the head.*

ܪܣܣܐ usually pl. ܪ̈ܣܣܐ and ܐܪܣܣܐ rt. ܪܣ. m. *small drops, fine rain, gentle showers; a sprinkling.*

ܪܣܡ fut. ܢܪܣܡ, act. part. ܪܐܣܡ, ܪܣܡܐ, pass. part. ܪܣܝܡܐ. *a)* intrans. *to drop* or *flow gently, fall in drops;* ܢܪܣܡ ܐܝܟ ܡܛܪܐ ܡܠܦܢܘܬܝ *my doctrine shall drop as the rain. b)* trans. *to let drop, shed, pour forth;* ܪܣܡܬ ܠܥܠܡܐ ܒܣܡ̈ܐ *Thou didst drop spices on the world;* ܒܢܝ ܫܠܗܒܝܬܐ ܕܪܣܡܝܢ ܓܘܡܪ̈ܐ ܝܩܝܕ̈ܐ *sons of flame dropping hot burning coals;* ܡܣܘܟܠܢܘܬܗ ܪܣܡ ܗܘܬ ܬܘܕܝܬܐ *her comprehension murmured gentle thanksgiving.* Ethpe. ܐܬܪܣܡ *to be sprinkled, bedewed.* Derivative, ܪܣܡܐ.

ܪܣܡܐ E-Syr. ܪܣܡܐ pl. ܐ̈ rt. ܪܣܡ. m. *dew, dewdrops, moisture.*

ܪܣܡ; see ܐܪܣܡ.

ܪܣܣ Pael conj. of verb ܪܣ.

ܪܣܣܐ pl. ܐ̈ rt. ܪܣ. m. *ceremonial sprinkling, lustration.*

ܪܥ fut. ܢܪܘܥ, act. part. ܪܐܥ, ܪܥܐ. *to beat, break to pieces;* ܢܪܥܘܢ ܣܝܦܝܗܘܢ ܠܣܟܐ ܕܦܕܢܐ *they shall beat their swords into ploughshares.* Metaph. *to defeat, confute.* Pass. part. ܪܥܝܥܐ, ܐ̈ and ܪܥܝܥܬܐ *broken, ruined, leaky;*

bruised; ܓܘܒ̈ܐ ܪ̈ܥܝܥܐ *broken cisterns;* ܡܠܚܐ ܪܥܝܥܐ *pounded salt.* Metaph. *disordered, defective;* ܬܪ̈ܥܝܬܐ ܪ̈ܥܝܥܬܐ *irregular opinions.* Ethpe. ܐܬܪܥܥ *to be bruised, broken to pieces, brought to naught;* ܡܢ ܕܢܦܠ ܥܠ ܟܐܦܐ ܗܕܐ ܢܬܪܥܥ *he that falleth on this stone shall be broken to pieces.* Pael act. and pass. parts. ܡܪܥܥ *shattering; shattered, bruised.* Ethpa. ܐܬܪܥܥ *to be fractured, shattered;* ܗ̈ܕܡܝܗ ܐܬܪܥܥܘ *her limbs were shattered* by the fall. Palp. ܪܥܪܥ *to dash together, to shatter.* Ethpalp. ܐܬܪܥܪܥ *to be dashed together, broken to bits;* ܐܬܪܥܪܥܝܢ ܐܠܦ̈ܐ ܘ... ships *collided and were broken to pieces.* Derivatives, ܪܥܘܥܐ, ܪܘܥܪܥܐ, ܪܘܥܥܐ, ܪܥܝܥܐ, ܪܥܪܥܐ, ܡܪܥܪܥܐ.

ܪܥܐ fut. ܢܪܥܐ, act. part. ܪܥܐ, ܪܥܝܐ, ܪܥܝܬܐ cf. ܪܥܝܐ subst., pass. part. ܪܥܐ, and ܐܬܪܥܐ, ܪܥܝܬܐ, ܪܥܝܐ. Two different roots. i. *a) to feed, tend, herd, keep;* metaph. *to rule, lead, govern* of bishops, pastors, rulers; ܪܥܝ ܘܕܒܪ ܠܡܪܥܝܬܟ *feed and lead thy flock;* ܪ̈ܥܘܬܐ ܪ̈ܥܝܐ *shepherds;* ܡܕ̈ܒܪܢܐ ܘܚܝ̈ܠܘܬܐ *leaders and forces. b) to feed, feed on, graze, browse, eat up;* ܪܥܝܘܗ̇ ܚܝܘܬܐ ܕܒܪܐ *the beasts of the field devoured it;* ܪܥܐ ܥܣܒܐ *graminivorous;* ܗܘܐ ܪܥܐ ܥܣܒܐ *he fed on grass;* ܪܥܝܢܢ ܕܡܣܒܪܐ ܪܥܝܢܢ *our mind which we sustain on hope;* ܕܪܥܐ ܠܙܢܝܬܐ *he who flocks,* or *companies, with harlots.* ii. *to be contented, pleased, willing;* ܠܐ ܪܥܝܢ ܗܘܘ ܒܗ *they were unwilling to accept him;* ܐܝܠܝܢ ܕܗܘܝܢ ܠܢ ܟܕ ܠܐ ܪܥܝܢܢ *the things which happen to us against our will.* Pass. part. ܠܐ ܪܥܐ *he is unwilling;* ܛܒ ܪܥܐ ܐܢܐ ܕܐܫܡܥ (for ܐܪܥܐ) *I am very willing to hear.* Ethpe. ܐܬܪܥܝ *a) to feed, to be fed; to be governed* by a bishop. *b) to think, suppose;* ܐܝܟ ܕܡܬܪܥܐ ܐܢܬ *as you suppose.* Pa. ܪܥܝ *a) to please, to be pleasing;* ܙܕ̈ܝܩܐ ܡܪ̈ܥܝܢܐ ܠܡܪܝܐ *the just who are well-pleasing to the Lord. b) to appease, reconcile; to heal;* ܐܬܐ ܡܪܢ ܠܡܪܥܝܘ ܠܒܪܝܬܐ ܠܘܬܗ *our Lord came to reconcile the creation unto Himself.* Ethpa. ܐܬܪܥܝ *a) to be accepted; to be reconciled, to agree with, make agreement;* with ܒ, ܥܠ, ܥܡ or ܠ; ܩܘܪܒܢܗ ܢܬܪܥܐ ܠܗ *his offering shall be accepted for him;* ܡܬܪܥܝܢ ܠܡܫܦܝܪܘ ܥܡ ܚܕ̈ܕܐ *agreeing well together;* ܐܬܪܥܝ ܠܢ ܐܠܗܐ ܒܡܘܬܗ ܕܒܪܗ *God was reconciled with us by the death of His Son. b) to think, be minded, be of opinion; to reason; to purpose;* with ܬܪܥܝܬܐ *to take counsel, have a purpose, determine;* ܟܕ ܗܠܝܢ ܐܬܪܥܝ *while he thought on these things;* ܕܡܬܪܥܝܢ ܥܡܝ *who think with me, who are of my opinion.* Aph. ܐܪܥܝ (cf. Peal *c*) *to appease, pacify; to be pleasing, acceptable;* ܠܡܪܥܝܘ ܠܒܥܠܕܒܒܐ *to appease the adversary.* Ettaph. ܐܬܬܪܥܝ *to be fed upon, eaten off* of pasture. Derivatives, ܪܥܝܐ, ܪܥܝܐ, ܪܥܝܘܬܐ, ܪܥܝܐ, ܪܥܝܐ, ܪܥܘܬܐ, ܪܥܝܢܐ, ܡܪܥܝܬܐ, ܪܥܝܐ, ܪܥܝܬܐ, ܪܥܝܢܐ, ܪܥܝܬܐ, ܡܪܥܝܐ, ܡܪܥܝܬܐ, ܬܪܥܝܬܐ, ܬܪܥܝܬܐ, ܬܪܥܝܢܝܬܐ, ܡܪܥܝܢܘܬܐ.

ܪܥܐ *rhubarb:* see ܪܐܘܣ.

ܪܥܒ Pe. only part. ܪܥܝܒܐ *tender, flexible.* Ethpe. ܐܬܪܥܒ *to become flexible, pliable;* ܦܪܙܠܐ ܡܬܪܥܒ ܒܢܘܪܐ *iron becomes pliant in the fire.* Derivatives, ܪܥܒܐ, ܪܥܒܘܬܐ, ܪܥܒܢܐ, ܡܪܥܒܐ, ܪܥܒܘܬܐ, ܪܥܒܢܐ.

ܪܥܒܐ, ܪܥܒܬܐ rt. ܪܥܒ. *tender.*

ܪܥܒܘܬܐ rt. ܪܥܒ. f. *suppleness, softness, freshness.*

ܪܥܒܐ m. *a sheep which lags behind the others, the last to follow of the flock.*

ܪܥܒܢܐ or ܪܥܒܢܐ rt. ܪܥܒ. m. *a) the pith of a palm-tree. b) cowardly.*

ܪܥܒܢܐ rt. ܪܥܒ. *a) tender, supple, flexible* as a reed. *b) weak, shaky.*

ܪܥܒܢܘܬܐ rt. ܪܥܒ. f. same as ܪܥܒܘܬܐ.

ܪܥܒܢܐ *weak, unsteady.*

ܪܥܘܝܐ rt. ܪܥܐ. m. *a wether.*

ܪܥܘܠܠܐܝܬ rt. ܪܥܠ. adv. *quiveringly.*

ܪܥܘܡ, ܪܥܘܡܐ, ܪܥܘܡܬܐ and ܪܥܡ rt. ܪܥܡ. *quivering with emotion, piteous;* ܪܥܘܡܐ ܗܘܬ *she was lamenting, uttering laments;* ܩܝ̈ܢܬܐ ܪܥܘܡܬܐ *laments, dirges.*

ܪܥܘܡܐܝܬ rt. ܪܥܡ. adv. *stormily, passionately; mournfully.*

ܪܥܘܦܬܐ f. Ar. *a wide-mouthed jar.*

ܪܥܝ Pael conj. of verb ܪܥܐ.

ܪܥܝܐ rt. ܪܥܐ. m. *pasture, fodder, food;* ܒܝܬ ܪܥܝܐ *pasturage, feeding-place;* ܪܥܝܐ ܕܓܡܠܐ *pastinaca sativa, carrot* or *parsnip;* ܪ̈ܝܘܬܐ ܕ probably *verbena officinalis, common vervain.*

ܪܥܝܐ pl. ܪ̈ܥܘܬܐ, ܪ̈ܥܝܐ = act. part. emph. st. m. *a shepherd; a pastor, chief pastor, bishop.*

ܪܥܝܘܬܐ rt. ܪܥܐ. f. *tending, shepherding, pastoral care, charge, supervision, office of a pastor.*

ܪܥܝܢܝܐ, ܝܬܐ rt. ܪܥܐ. *pastoral.*

ܪܥܝܠܘܬܐ rt. ܪܥܠ. f. *agitation, trepidation.*

ܪܥܝܢܐ, ܪܥܝܢ rt. ܪܥܐ. m. *a) mind, intellect, conscience;* ܪ ܫܪܝܪܘܬܐ *folly;* ܪ ܡܟܝܟܘܬܐ *lowliness of mind. b) a way of thinking, opinion, doctrine; a sentence, maxim; a vote;* ܐܝܟ ܪܥܝܢܝ *in my judgement, in my opinion. c) sense, meaning.*

ܪܥܝܢܐܝܬ rt. ܪܥܐ. adv. *from the mind, from the soul.*

ܪܥܝܢܝܐ, ܝܬܐ rt. ܪܥܐ. *mental.*

ܪܥܝܥܐ, ܥܬܐ; see verb ܪܥ.

ܪܥܝܥܘܬܐ rt. ܪܥ. f. *collision, shattering.*

ܪܥܝܦܬܐ = ܪܥܦܐ *a cake baked in the embers.*

ܪܥܝܬܐ or ܪܥܬܐ rt. ܪܥܐ. f. *the elephant's trunk, proboscis.*

ܪܥܝܬܐ pl. ܪ̈ܥܝܬܐ rt. ܪܥܐ. f. *a) a pasture. b) sheep, cattle, stock.*

ܪܥܠ fut. ܢܪܥܠ, act. part. ܪܥܠ, ܪܥܠܐ, pass. part. ܪܥܝܠܐ and ܪܥܝܠ, ܠܐ, ܠܬܐ. *to oscillate, reel, quiver; to be swayed, shaken;* ܪܥܠܬ ܐܪܥܐ *the earth quaked;* ܨܘܪܬܐ ܕܣܗܪܐ ܪܥܠܐ *the reflection of the moon quivering* in the water; ܒܘܪ̈ܟܐ ܪ̈ܥܝܠܬܐ *palsied knees;* ܐܦ ܐܪܬܥܠܘ ܒܕܚܠܬܐ *they trembled and quaked for fear.* Pass. part. *a)* ܪܥܝܠܐ *shaken, shattered. b)* ܪܥܝܠ *quivering, trembling, shuddering.* Aph. ܐܪܥܠ *to make to quake, to terrify;* ܢܚܒܛ ܠܒܝܬܐ ܪܡܐ ܘܢܪܥܠܝܘܗܝ *He will smite the lofty house and cause it to quake;* ܢܪܥܠ ܐܢܘܢ ܒܩܠܐ ܥܫܝܢܐ *he will terrify them with a violent noise.* Derivatives, the four following words, also ܪܘܥܠ, ܪܥܠܬܢܐܝܬ and ܪܥܠܬܢܘܬܐ.

ܪܥܠܐ and ܪܥܝܠܐ rt. ܪܥܠ. m. *a) oscillation, quaking, earthquake. b) trembling, terror.*

ܪܥܠܬܐ rt. ܪܥܠ. f. *quaking, shuddering, tremor.*

ܪܥܠܬܐ pl. ܠܬܐ rt. ܪܥܠ. f. *an egg half-cooked, not set.*

ܪܥܠܬܢܐܝܬ rt. ܪܥܠ. adv. *with oscillation; quiveringly.*

ܪܥܡ fut. ܢܪܥܡ, act. part. ܪܥܡ, ܪܥܡܐ, pass. part. ܪܥܝܡ, ܪܥܝܡܐ. *a) to thunder, sound, resound, ring, to rise* as a sound, clamour; ܪܥܡ ܒܫܡܝܐ ܡܪܝܐ *the Lord thundered in the heavens;* ܕܢܗܘܘܢ ܬܚܘܡܝܗ ܪܥܡܝܢ ܒܥܡܘܪ̈ܐ *that her borders may resound with inhabitants;* ܪܥܡܘ ܩܠܐ ܕܬܫܒܘܚܬܐ ܒܟܠܦܢܝܢ *sounds of praise arose on every side. b) to feel pity, have compassion;* ܪܥܡܬ ܢܦܫܗ ܥܠ ܚܒܝܒܘܗܝ *his soul moved with compassion for his darlings.* Ethpe. ܐܬܪܥܡ *to be angry, enraged, indignant.* Pael ܪܥܡ *to rage; to make to resound.* Ethpa. ܐܬܪܥܡ *a) to proclaim. b) to clamour, to be enraged, indignant; to complain;* with ܥܠ, ܒ, ܠܘܩܒܠ; ܒܗܕܐ ܫܐܠܬܐ ܐܬܪܥܡ *at this demand he was indignant;* ܐܬܪܥܡ ܥܠ ܐܠܗܐ Cain *complained angrily against God.* Aph. ܐܪܥܡ *to make to resound;* ܐܪܥܡ ܗܝܟܠܝܗܘܢ ܒܬܫܒܘܚܬܐ *he made their temples resound with praise.* Ettaph. ܐܬܬܪܥܡ *to be made angry, indignant,* with ܒ. Derivatives, ܪܘܥܡܐ, ܡܪܥܡܢܘܬܐ, ܪܥܡܐ, ܪܥܡܬܢܐܝܬ, ܪܥܡܬܢܐ, ܡܪܥܡܢܐ.

ܪܥܡܐ, ܪܥܡ pl. ܝܢ, ܐ rt. ܪܥܡ. m. *thunder, thundering; resonance, sonorousness;* ܒܢܝ ܪܥܡܐ *Boanerges, sons of thunder;* ܒܢܬ ܪܥܡܐ *truffles.*

ܪܥܡܣ Ethpe. ܐܬܪܥܡܣ perh. *to be overwhelmed.*

ܪܥܡܣܐ m. *dispersion.*

ܪܥܥ Pael conj. of verb ܪܥ.

ܪܥܥܐ pl. ܐ rt. ܪܥ. m. *a violent blow, a crash.*

ܪܥܦܐ pl. ܐ m. *a flat cake, bread baked on a girdle or in the ashes of a fire on the ground* opp. ܬܢܘܪܝܐ *bread baked in an oven.*

ܪܥܦܐ m. *gargling, rinsing out the mouth.*

ܪܥܦܘܢܬܐ dimin. of ܪܥܦܐ. f. *a cake baked in the embers.*

ܪܥܪܥ Palpel conj. of verb ܪܥ.

ܪܥܪܥܐ rt. ܪܥ. m. *dashing two things together, a collision.*

ܪܦܣ fut. ܢܪܦܘܣ. *to rend, trample* as a wild beast, *to convulse* as a demon. Pass. part. ܪܦܝܣܐ *bruised, shattered.*

ܪܦܬ denom. verb from ܪܘܦܬܐ, ܪܘܦܬܐ. Aphel ܐܪܦܬ *a) to foam* at the mouth; ܡܚܪܩ ܫܢܘܗܝ ܘܡܪܦܬ *he gnashes his teeth and foams. b) to make to palpitate.* Ettaph. ܐܬܬܪܦܬ *to be made to foam.*

ܪܦܬܐ rt. ܪܦܬ. m. *foaming.*

ܪܦ fut. ܢܪܘܦ, act. part. ܪܐܦ, ܪܝܦܐ. *a) to move the eyelids, wink, blink. b) to flap the wings, move gently;* ܦܪܚܬܐ ܕܦܪܚܐ ܟܕ ܠܐ ܪܐܦ *a bird flying without flapping the wings;* ܣܦܘܬܗ ܪܦܝܢ ܗܘܝ *his lips moved gently.* Pa. ܪܦܦ *to flutter.* Ethpa. ܐܬܪܦܦ *to be fluttered, twitched.* Aph. ܐܪܝܦ *to move slightly, to twitch, touch lightly;* ܡܪܝܦ ܠܗܕܡܐ dreaming *makes the limbs twitch.* Palp. ܪܦܪܦ *to move to and fro;* ܪܦܪܦ ܢܦܝܠܐ ܘܢܦܠ a wounded elephant *staggered and fell.* Ethpalp. ܐܬܪܦܪܦ *to oscillate.* Derivatives, ܪܦܦܐ, ܪܦܦܐ, ܪܦܦܘܬܐ, ܪܦܐ, ܪܦܐ, ܪܘܦܪܦܐ, ܪܦܪܦܐ, ܪܦܦܬܐ.

ܪܦ m. *a lizard.*

ܪܦܐ and ܐܪܦܐ pl. ܝܢ, ܐ rt. ܪܦ. m. *a nest, brood, flight* of birds, *a shoal* of fishes, *swarm* of lice; ܪܦܝܢ ܪܦܝܢ *in flocks, in flights.*

ܪܦܐ rt. ܪܦ. m. *a slight motion, twitch, fluttering.*

ܪܦܐ Peal only part. adj. ܪܦܐ, ܪܦܝܐ, ܪܦܝܬܐ. *a) loose, porous, friable, soft* as air, earth, *unstable* as water; *flabby* as flesh. *b) loose, slack, effeminate, dissolute;* ܡܝܬܪܐ ܪܦܝܬܐ *slack harpstrings;* ܐܠܦܐ ܪܦܝܬܐ *badly built ships;* ܠܐ ܗܘܝܢ ܒܛܝܠܐ ܐܦܠܐ ܡܪܦܝܢܐ ܘܪܦܝܐ ܘܕܠܐ ܥܒܕܐ ܐܝܬܝܢ *we are not to be idle nor slack and ineffectual.* Pael ܪܦܝ *a) to loosen, slacken, relax; to weaken, enfeeble;* ܡܪܦܐ ܗܘܐ ܦܓܪܗ *his body was enfeebled;* ܐܝܢܐ ܕܡܪܦܐ ܐܝܕܘܗܝ ܡܢ ܥܒܕܗ *he that is slack in his work;* ܡܪܦܝܢ ܐܝܕܘܗܝ ܘܠܐܐ *weary and exhausted;* ܡܪܦܝܢܘܬܐ *softnesses, relaxations, luxuries. b) to leave, desert;* ܠܐ ܡܪܦܐ ܐܢܐ ܠܬܫܡܫܬܐ ܕܡܫܝܚܐ *I will not leave the ministry of Christ. c) to concede, allow, induce;* ܪܦܝܬܘܢ ܠܗܘܢ ܕܢܡܠܠܘܢ ܒܓܠܝܐ *you allowed them to speak publicly.* Ethpa. ܐܬܪܦܝ *a) to become loose, weak;* ܒܢܝܢܐ ܐܬܪܦܝ ܗܘ ܚܕܬܐ ܘܢܦܠ *the part newly built became loosened and fell;* ܡܬܪܦܝܢ ܡܢ ܟܦܢܐ *weakened with hunger. b) to be slack, remiss, to succumb;* with ܡܢ *to fall away from, be overcome by;* ܘܠܐ ܬܬܪܦܐ ܪܥܝܢܟ ܡܢ ܐܓܘܢܟ *nor let thy purpose relax from thy conflict;* ܐܬܪܦܝ ܣܘܥܪܢܐ *the matter was conducted slackly. c) to be left* as a legacy. Aph. ܐܪܦܝ *a) to leave, let alone;* ܐܪܦܐ ܠܢ ܫܒܥܐ ܝܘܡܝܢ *give us seven days' respite;* ܐܪܦܝܢܝ ܒܒܝܫܬܝ *leave me to my misery;* ܐܪܦܐ ܢܩܘܡ *let it settle;* ܡܕܡ ܒܬܪܗܘܢ ܠܐ ܢܪܦܘܢ *they will leave nothing behind.* Often with ܐܝܕܐ *to loose hold, let go, allow; to weaken;* with ܐܝܕܐ and ܡܢ *to lose hold of, to become weak. b) to leave, desert, renounce;* ܐܢ ܬܪܦܘܢ ܐܬܪܐ ܡܬܪܦܝܢ *if you leave the country;* ܠܐ ܐܪܦܝܟ ܘܠܐ ܐܫܒܩܟ *I will not leave thee nor forsake thee. c) to leave out, neglect;* ܐܪܦܝ ܠܗܘܢ ܕܠܐ ܟܬܒ *the matters which he omitted to write about;* ܐܪܦܝ ܕܢܡܠܟ ܡܠܟܬܗܘܢ *he neglected their advice. d) to give leave, allow;* ܘܠܐ ܐܪܦܝ ܠܐ ܠܐܢܫ ܠܡܥܠ ܬܡܢ *he allowed no one to enter there.* Imper. ܐܪܦܐ *allow, grant; let alone, much less;* ܠܡܣܒܠ ܩܫܝܐ ܡܣܝܒܐ ܐܪܦܐ ܕܥܠܝܡܐ ܘܛܠܝܐ *hardly can the aged endure, let alone youths and boys. e) to let loose;* ܒܥܝܢ ܕܢܪܦܐ ܐܪܝܐ ܥܠ *begging him to let loose the lion on* the martyr. *f) to leave* an inheritance, a legacy; *to leave* children, disciples, after him. *g)* rare uses: *to set* fire to; *to let* blood; *to utter* words. Derivatives, ܪܦܝܐ, ܪܦܝܐ, ܪܦܝܘܬܐ, ܪܦܝܘܬܐ, ܡܪܦܝܢܐ, ܡܪܦܝܢܐ, ܡܪܦܝܢܘܬܐ.

ܪܦܩ part. ܪܐܦܩ. *to lurk, crawl* as a serpent. Derivative, ܪܦܩܐ.

ܪܦܩܐ m. *gentle motion, palpitation.*

ܪܦܝܣܐ rt. ܪܦܣ. *supple, flabby.*

ܪܦܝܣܘܬܐ rt. ܪܦܣ. f. *distension.*

ܪܦܝܬܘܬܐ rt. ܪܦܬ. f. *a) impulse, incentive. b)* ܪܦܝܬܘܬܐ ܕܨܦܪܐ *the beginning of dawn.*

ܪܦܣ fut. ܢܪܦܘܣ. *to bubble, heave, burst open;* ܪܦܣܬ ܚܘܠܕܐ ܘܢܦܠܬ *the mole* undermined by fire, *heaved open and fell in.* Ethpe. ܐܬܪܦܣ *to be distended, swelled.* Derivatives, ܪܦܝܣܐ, ܪܦܣܐ, ܪܦܝܣܘܬܐ.

ܪܦܣܐ pl. ܐ rt. ܪܦܣ. m. *rising up, swelling, surging.*

ܪܦܝ PAEL conj. of ܪܦܐ.

ܪܦܝܐܝܬ rt. ܪܦܐ. adv. *carelessly, slackly, negligently.*

ܪܦܝܘܬܐ rt. ܪܦܐ. f. *softness, weakness, want of cohesion, laxity, levity, dissoluteness.*

ܪܦܝܢܘܬܐ rt. ܪܦܐ. f. *condescension.*

ܪܦܝܣܬܐ; same as ܪܦܝܦܬܐ.

ܪܦܪܢܕܪܐ Lat. Referendarius, an official of the Byzantine Court, *a lord in waiting.*

ܪܦܣ fut. ܢܪܦܘܣ, act. part. ܪܦܣ, ܪܦܣܐ, pass. part. ܪܦܝܣ. *a) to beat the ground in dancing, to dance in a ring, to prance, stamp, paw;* ܢܦܩܝܢ ܠܡܪܦܣ ܪܩܕܐ *they go out to tread dances;* ܪܦܣ ܒܪܓܠܘܗܝ ܥܠ *he stamped upon . . .;* ܐܪܝܐ ܒܪܓܠܘܗܝ ܪܦܣ ܒܐܪܥܐ *the lion pawed the ground. b) to fasten, make fast;* ܢܓܪܐ ܢܪܦܣܘܢ ܟܘܐ *carpenters are to make the windows secure with bars.* DERIVATIVES, ܡܪܦܣܐ, ܪܦܣܐ, ܪܦܘܣܐ.

ܪܦܣܐ or ܪܦܣܐ pl. ܐ̈ rt. ܪܦܣ. m. *a) a beat of the foot, a stamp. b) a choral dance;* ܡܙܕܘܓܝܢ ܪܦܣܐ ܘܡܪܝܡܝܢ ܩܠܗܘܢ *they weave a dance and raise shouts. c)* a measure of time, *twenty minutes.*

ܪܦܦ PAEL conj. of ܪܦ.

ܪܦܦܐ pl. ܐ̈ rt. ܪܦ. *a) vibration, balancing* of the scales. *b) a twitch, jerk, quivering, slight motion, involuntary movement* (observing these was a mode of divination); ܪܦܦ ܒܟܢܦܘܗܝ *fluttering the wings;* ܪܦܦܐ ܕܡܚܫܒܬܐ *agitation of the thoughts, impulses. c)* ܪܦܦ ܥܝܢܐ *a blink, twinkling of the eye, a second. d)* = ܪܦܦܐ *a throng, shoal.*

ܪܦܦܝܐ rt. ܪܦ. *momentary.*

ܪܦܝܦܘܬܐ and ܪܦܦܘܬܐ rt. ܪܦ. *an itch, twitch.*

ܪܦܪܦ PALPEL conj. of verb ܪܦ.

ܪܦܫܐ pl. ܐ̈ m. *a) a winnowing-fan. b) the shoulder-blade.*

ܪܦܫ fut. ܢܪܦܘܫ and ܢܪܦܫ, act. part. ܪܦܫ, ܪܦܫܐ, pass. part. ܪܦܝܫ. *a) to glide, wriggle, wind along; to throb, pulsate, palpitate; vibrate; to move, show signs of life;* ܚܘܝܐ ܕܪܦܫܐ ܒܕܘܢܒܗ *the snake with sinuous tail;* ܦܓܪܐ ܢܪܦܫ ܒܪܦܫܐ ܚܝܐ *the body will throb with living pulses;* ܥܘܠܐ ܒܟܪܣܐ ܪܦܫ *the embryo stirred in the womb;* ܘܠܐ ܠܒܪ ܡܢܟ ܪܦܫܝܢ ܬܢܘܥܬܐ *neither apart from Thee do impulses stir in the soul. b) to swarm, breed;* ܪܦܫܬ ܐܪܥܐ ܪܚܫܐ *the earth swarmed with reptiles;* ܪܦܫ ܬܘܠܥܐ *it bred worms;* ܪܦܝܫ ܗܘܐ ܩܠܡܐ *he was covered with lice.* DERIVATIVES, ܪܦܫܘܬܐ, ܪܦܫܐ, ܡܪܦܫܢܐ.

ܪܦܫܐ and ܪܦܫܬܐ pl. ܐ̈ rt. ܪܦܫ. m. *a) a throb, palpitation, vibration, slight stirring, an impulse;* ܪܦܫܐ ܕ *agitation. b) a moment. c) a creeping thing.*

ܪܨ fut. ܢܪܘܨ, act. part. ܪܐܨ, pass. part. ܪܝܨ, ܐ, ܬܐ. *to bruise, crush;* ܪܨ ܚܘܝܐ ܒܙܩܝܦܘܬܗ *He crushed the serpent by His crucifixion;* ܪܨܬܗ ܠܩܪܩܦܬܗ *she brake his skull.* ETHPE. ܐܬܪܨ *to be bruised, crushed.* PA. ܪܨܨ *a) to bruise, crush;* ܪܨܨ ܦܬܢܐ *he crushed the asp. b) to strain, sprain;* ܪܨܨ ܚܘܠܝ ܚܨܐ *he dislocated the vertebrae of the back.* ETHPA. ܐܬܪܨܨ *to be entirely crushed, bruised;* ܢܬܪܨܨ ܪܫܗ ܕܬܢܝܢܐ *may the dragon's head be utterly crushed.* APH. ܐܪܨ pass. part. ܡܪܨ *torn.* DERIVATIVES, ܪܨܘܨܘܬܐ, ܪܨܨܐ, ܡܪܨܐ.

ܪܨܨ Arab. *lead.*

ܪܨܥ only pass. part. ܪܨܝܥ, ܐ, ܬܐ *pieced together, patched, patchwork, a patched garment;* ܠܒܝܫ ܒܓܠܐ ܪܨܝܥܬܐ ܡܢ ܣܩܐ *clothed in a horsecloth patched together of pieces of sacking.* DERIVATIVES, ܪܨܥܐ, ܡܪܨܥܐ.

ܪܨܥܐ rt. ܪܨܥ. m. *a patch, piece sewn on.*

ܪܨܘܦܐ rt. ܪܨܦ. m. *making costive, astringent.*

ܪܨܘܢܐ dimin. of ܪܨܝܐ m. *a tiny rill.*

ܪܨܝܐ and ܪܨܐ pl. ܐ̈ rt. ܪܨܝ. m. *a slender trickling stream, a brooklet, rill.*

ܪܨܝܢܘܬܐ, ܪܨ or ܪܨ rt. ܪܨܝ. f. *a)* dimin. of ܪܨܝܐ. *b) scurf, dandriff.*

ܪܨܝܢܝܐ, ܐܝܬܐ rt. ܪܨܝ. *oozing, marshy.*

ܪܨܝܦܘܬܐ rt. ܪܨܦ. f. *closeness, density* of air, of foliage.

ܪܨܝܦܬܐ pl. ܐ̈ܬܐ rt. ܪܨܦ. f. *a pavement.*

ܪܨܝܨܘܬܐ rt. ܪܨ. f. *being bruised, sprained.*

ܪܨܝ fut. ܢܪܨܐ, act. part. ܪܨܐ, ܪܨܝܐ. *to ooze, trickle; to let trickle, let drop;* ܡܝܐ ܕܪܨܝܢ ܡܢ ܡܥܪܐ *water which trickles forth from caves;* ܐܣܦܘܓܐ ܕܪܨܝܐ ܚܠܐ *a sponge moist with vinegar;* ܓܦܢܐ ܕܙܪܦܢ *vines which shed their grapes.* ETHPE. ܐܬܪܙܦ *to trickle, ooze.* DERIVATIVES, ܡܪܙܦܢܐ, ܪܙܦܘܬܐ, ܪܙܦܢܐ, ܪܙܦܢܘܬܐ, ܪܙܦܬܐ, ܪܙܦܐ, ܪܙܦܐ.

ܪܙܦܐ rt. ܪܙܦ. m. *a slender rill, oozing drops.*

ܪܙܦܐ rt. ܪܙܦ. m. *scurf, scab, dirt.*

ܪܨܦ fut. ܢܪܨܘܦ, act. part. ܪܨܦ, ܪܨܦܐ. *to set closely, to ram in, to crowd; to make solid;* ܠܐ ܐܪܘܩ ܠܡܨܪܦܘ ܢܨܒܬܐ *young plants should not be crowded together;* ܪܨܦ ܐܘܪܚܬܐ *he made the roads firm.* Part. adj. ܪܨܝܦ, ܦܐ, ܦܬܐ. *set close together, dense, compact, solid, paved, shaded by thick foliage;* ܓܦܢܐ ܪܨܝܦܢ ܒܬܘܟܠܐ *vines closely covered with clusters;* ܦܬܘܚܐ ܗܘܐ ܒܝܬܗ ܘܪܨܝܦ ܘܡܠܐ ܢܘܗܪܐ *his room was spacious and leafy and full of light;* ܚܒܠܐ ܪܨܝܦܐ *thick ropes;* ܟܐܦܐ ܦܣܝܠܬܐ ܪܨܝܦܢ *hewn stones set closely together;* ܥܪܣܬܐ ܪܨܝܦܢ ܒܟܐܦܐ ܝܩܝܪܬܐ *couches set with precious stones;* f. emph. *a pavement.* ETHPE. ܐܬܪܨܦ *to be condensed* as air, vapour; *to be set close together,* of planks or stones, *to be paved.* APH. ܐܪܨܦ *to condense, contract.* DERIVATIVES, ܪܨܘܦܐ, ܪܨܝܦܘܬܐ, ܪܨܝܦܬܐ, ܪܨܦܐ.

ܪܨܦܐ pl. ܐ̈ = ܪܫܦܐ m. *the sole of a sandal.*

ܪܨܦܐ pl. ܐ̈ rt. ܪܨܦ. m. *a) a pavement. b) density.*

ܪܨܨܐ rt. ܪܨ. m. *a) a bruise, contusion; a sprain, strain. b) a fragment. c) contrition.*

ܪܨܨܬܐ rt. ܪܨ. m. *tinware, a leaden vessel.*

ܪܩ pl. ܪܩܐ f. *thin parchment.*

ܪܩ fut. ܢܪܘܩ, act. part. ܪܐܩ, ܪܩܐ, pass. part. ܪܩܝܩ, part. adj. ܪܩܝܩ, ܐ, ܬܐ. *to spit* with ܒ or ܥܠ, *to spit up* or *out, expectorate;* ܪܩ ܒܐܦܝܗ̇ *he spit in her face;* ܪܐܩ ܡܪܬܐ *spitting out phlegm;* ܪܩܝܩ ܒܗ ܒܐܦܘܗܝ *his face spat upon.* Part. adj. *fine, thin, thin-drawn, shallow; rejected, scorned;* ܡܝܐ ܪܩܝܩܐ *shallow water;* ܡܐܢܐ ܪܩܝܩܐ ܕܩܝܛܐ *a thin summer dress.* ETHPE. ܐܬܪܩܝܩ *to be spat upon* with ܒ or ܒܐܦܐ; *to be vomited; to be rejected with contumely* with ܡܢ. PA. ܪܩܩ *to make thin, draw fine.* ETHPA. *to be thinned, set far apart.* PALP. ܪܩܪܩ *to drivel, talk in a contemptible manner.* APH. ܐܪܩ *to make thin; to attenuate;* ܐܪܩܘ ܛܣܐ ܕܕܗܒܐ *they beat out thin plates of gold.* DERIVATIVES, ܪܩܘܩܐ, ܪܩ, ܪܩܐ, ܪܩܘܬܐ, ܪܩܝܩܘܬܐ, ܡܪܩܩܐ, ܪܩܪܩ, ܪܩܪܩܐ.

ܪܩܐ rt. ܪܩ. Aramaic through Greek ῥακά, *Raca, contemptible, an object of contempt, fool, empty fellow.*

ܪܩܐ or ܪܩܐ pl. ܐ̈ m. *a tortoise;* ܪܩܐ ܕܐܪܥܐ *land tortoises.*

ܪܩܐ pl. ܐ̈ m. *a leathern bottle;* ܪܩܐ ܕܡܝܐ *a skin of water.*

ܪܩܐܬܐ m. pl. *stone brackets, corbels.*

ܪܩܕ fut. ܢܪܩܘܕ, act. part. ܪܩܕ, ܪܩܕܐ (rare in Peal). *to dance.* PA. ܪܩܕ *to dance, prance, skip; to make to skip;* ܐܥܕܢܐ ܠܡܪܩܕܘ: ܘܐܥܕܢܐ ܠܡܪܩܕܘ *a time to mourn and a time to dance.* APH. ܐܪܩܕ *to mourn, make lamentation* with ܥܠ; ܐܬܐ ܐܒܪܗܡ ܠܡܪܩܕܘ ܥܠ ܣܪܐ ܘܠܡܒܟܝܗ̇ *Abraham came to mourn for Sarah and to weep over her.* ETTAPH. ܐܬܬܪܩܕ *to be mourned, lamented;* ܠܐ ܢܬܬܪܩܕܘܢ ܘܠܐ ܢܬܩܒܪܘܢ *there shall be no mourning for them nor shall they receive burial.* DERIVATIVES, ܪܩܕܐ, ܪܩܕܐ, ܪܩܕܐ, ܪܩܘܕܐ, ܪܩܘܕܘܬܐ, ܡܪܩܕܢܘܬܐ, ܡܪܩܕܢܐ, ܡܪܩܕܢܘܬܐ, ܡܪܩܕܢܝܬܐ.

ܪܩܕܐ pl. ܐ̈ rt. ܪܩܕ. m. *a dancer, mime.*

ܪܩܕܐ E-Syr. ܪܩܕܐ m. *the dance, pantomimic dancing; a revel, revelling; jerking, convulsive movements* of fish out of water.

ܪܩܕܐ rt. ܪܩܕ. m. *mourning.*

ܪܩܘܕܐ rt. ܪܩܕ. m. *a dancer, skipper.*

ܪܩܘܕܘܬܐ rt. ܪܩܕ. f. *the dance.*

ܪܩܘܩܣܝܢ in the Lexx. *a milking-pail.*

ܪܩܘܬܐ rt. ܪܩ. f. *a) vileness, contemptibility. b)* vernac. of Mosul, *mentha siccata, mint.*

ܪܩܝܥܐ and ܐܪܩܝܥܐ rt. ܪܩܥ. m. *the expanse of heaven, the firmament; a zone, sphere* of the heavens.

ܪܩܝܥܘܬܐ rt. ܪܩܥ. f. *a) squeezing out, wringing out. b) spreading out. c)* ܪܩܝܥܘܬܐ ܕܕܡܐ *hardening, coagulation of blood.*

ܪܩܝܥܝܐ rt. ܪܩܥ. *of the firmament, heavenly.*

ܪܩܝܩ, ܩܐ, ܩܬܐ; see verb ܪܩ.

ܪܩܝܩܘܬܐ rt. ܪܩ. f. *thinness, shallowness* ܕܐܪܥܐ *of soil;* ܕܡܝܐ *of water.*

ܪܩܘܡܐ Arab. *an embroidered robe.*

ܪܩܢܐ ῥυκάνη, m. *a carpenter's plane.*

ܪܩܥ fut. ܢܪܩܘܥ, act. part. ܪܩܥ, ܪܳܩܥܐ, pass. part. ܪܩܝܥ, ـܐ, ـܬܐ. *to spread out; to press down, make firm; to plug;* ܪܩܥ ܐܪܥܐ ܥܠ ܡܝܐ *Who spread forth the earth above the waters;* ܪܩܥܗ̇ ܠܫܬܐܣܬܐ ܗܘܬ *he set it firmly for a foundation;* ܪܩܘܥ ܠܦܘܡܗ ܕܟܕܐ ܒܐܣܦܘܓܐ *plug the mouth* of the jar *with a sponge.* Pass. part. *a)* ܪܩܝܥ ܪ̈ܓܠܐ *web-footed. b) firm, impervious, compact;* ܡܟܝܠܬܐ ܛܒܬܐ ܘܪܩܝܥܬܐ *good measure pressed down;* ܐܪܥܐ ܪܩܝܥܬܐ *stiff soil,* also *the solid earth;* ܐܘܪܚܐ ܪܩܝܥܬܐ ܘܕܝܫܬܐ *a hard and trodden road. c)* subst. see above. Ethpe. ܐܬܪܩܥ *to be pressed together, solidified;* ܡܢ ܡܝܐ ܐܬܪܩܥ ܗܘܐ the firmament *was compacted out of the waters;* ܐܬܪܩܥܘ ܫܬܐܣ̈ܝܗ̇ ܕܐܪܥܐ *the foundations of the earth grew solid.* Pa. ܪܰܩܰܥ *to make solid, lay firmly.* Ethpa. ܐܬܪܰܩܰܥ *to be pressed together, coagulated;* ܡܝܐ ܕܐܬܪܰܩܰܥܘ ܐܝܟ ܓܒܬܐ ܡܢ ܚܠܒܐ *the waters which were coagulated as cheese from milk.* Aph. ܐܪܩܥ *a) to patch, sew cloth to . . . . b) to press together, make solid;* ܪܩܝܥܐ ܡܢ ܡܝܐ ܡܪܩܥ *the firmament compacted out of water.* Derivatives, ܐܪܩܘܥܬܐ, ܪܘܩܥܐ, ܪܩܥܐ, ܪܩܝܥܐ, ܪܩܝܥܘܬܐ, ܪܩܥܐ.

ܪܘܩܥܐ rt. ܪܩܥ. m. *a) a piece of cloth. b) expansion, extension.*

ܪܩܦ pass. part. ܪܩܝܦ. *to floor, lay a floor;* ܢܗܘܐ ܪܩܝܦ ܒܩܝ̈ܣܐ ܓܘܠ̈ܠܐ *let it be floored with round timbers.* Derivative, ܪܩܦܐ.

ܪܩܦܐ or ܪܘܩܦܐ rt. ܪܩܦ. m. *planking, roof-covering of rounded timbers set closely above the joists.*

ܪܰܩܶܩ Pael conj. of verb ܪܩ.

ܪܘܩܩܐ rt. ܪܩ. m. *a) a shallow. b) expectoration, vomit;* ܪܩܩ ܕܡܐ *spitting blood.*

ܪܰܩܪܶܩ Palpel conj. of verb ܪܩ.

ܪܰܩܪܺܩ rt. ܪܩ. *thin, meagre.*

ܪܫܢ fut. ܢܪܘܫܢ, act. part. ܪܳܫܶܢ, pass. part. ܪܫܝܢ, ـܐ, ـܬܐ. *to bray, pound, decorticate;* ܚܛܐ ܩܠܝܬܐ ܪܫܝܢܬܐ *husked parched corn.* Ethpe. ܐܬܪܫܢ *to be pounded, beaten, hammered.* Pa. ܪܰܫܶܢ *to crush, chew, masticate.* Ethpa. ܐܬܪܰܫܰܢ *to be husked.* Ettaph. ܐܬܬܪܫܢ *to be broken small.* Derivatives, ܪܫܢܐ, ܡܪܫܢܬܐ.

ܪܰܫ, ܪܰܫܐ pl. ܪܰܫܝܢ, ܪܰܫܶܐ E-Syr. spellings of ܪܫܐ &c.; see above.

ܪܫܐ fut. ܢܪܫܐ, act. part. ܪܳܫܐ, ܪܳܫܝܐ, pass. part. ܪܫܝܐ. *to find fault, blame; to accuse, lodge a complaint;* ܡܢܐ ܥܕܟܝܠ ܪܫܐ *why doth he yet find fault?* ܪܫܝܘ ܠܗ̇ ܘܕܘܢܘ ܠܥܒܪ ܢܡܘܣܐ *accuse and judge the transgressor.* Ethpe. ܐܬܪܫܝ *to be censured, accused, prosecuted,* with ܡܢ of the pers.; ܗܝ ܕܡܬܪܫܐ ܥܠܝܗ̇ *that of which he is accused;* ܡܬܪܫܝܢܐ ܡܢ ܢܡܘܣܐ "*infamis*" *disfranchised.* Pa. ܪܰܫܺܝ *to present;* ܪܰܫܺܝܘ ܠܠܘܝ̈ܐ ܠܦܨܚܐ ܐܠܦܐ ܥܪ̈ܒܐ *they gave to the Levites for the Passover a thousand sheep.* Aph. ܐܪܫܝ *a)* with ܛܝܒܘܬܐ and ܒ of the pers. *to confer a favour;* ܐܪܫܝ ܒܝ ܛܝܒܘܬܐ *he did me the kindness. b) to accuse* with ܒ or ܥܠ; ܪܫܝܢܐ ܕܡܪܫܝܢ ܗܘܘ ܥܠܝܢ *the accusations they brought against us.* Derivatives, ܪܫܝܐ, ܪܫܝܐ, ܪܫܝܢܐ, ܪܫܝܢܘܬܐ, ܡܪܫܝܢܘܬܐ, ܡܪܫܝܢܘܬܐ, ܡܬܪܫܝܢܐ.

ܪܳܫܽܘܝܐ rt. ܪܫܐ. m. *a censor, faultfinder, accuser.*

ܪܫܘܡ *a)* imper. of verb ܪܫܡ. *b)* abs. and constr. st. of ܪܘܫܡܐ; see above.

ܪܳܫܽܘܦܐ rt. ܪܫܦ. m. *a crawler, reptile.*

ܪܳܫܽܘܦܘܬܐ rt. ܪܫܦ. f. *crawling.*

ܪܫܝܐ rt. ܪܫܐ. m. *a) a grievance, ground of complaint. b) the conferring of a favour.*

ܪܰܫܝܐ; see ܪܰܫܺܝ.

ܪܫܝܠܘܬܐ rt. ܪܫܠ. f. *relaxation; ambiguity.*

ܪܶܫܝܢ, ܪܶܫܝܢܐ pl. ܐ̈ rt. ܪܫܐ. m. *censure, rêprehension; accusation, indictment;* ܕܠܐ ܪܶܫܝܢ *found blameless.*

ܪܫܝܢܘܬܐ rt. ܪܫܐ. f. *culpability.*

ܪܰܫܝܥܐ, ܬܐ rt. ܪܫܥ. often pl. *the lawless, wicked, impious, criminal;* f. emph. *crimes.*

ܪܰܫܝܥܐܝܬ rt. ܪܫܥ. adv. *wickedly, impiously.*

ܪܰܫܝܥܘܬܐ rt. ܪܫܥ. f. *wickedness, impiety, superstition.*

ܪܰܫܝܥܬܐ; see ܪܰܫܝܥܐ.

ܪܫܠ fut. ܢܪܫܘܠ. *to be feeble, palsied; to be tremulous* with age. Ethpe. ܐܬܪܫܠ *a)* with

ܐܶܬܪܰܫܰܠ ܗ̈ܰܕܳܡܶܐ to be paralysed; but ܐܶܬܪܰܫܰܠ ܗܰܕ̈ܳܡܶܝܗ her limbs relaxed opp. ܐܶܬܩܰܫܰܚ to become rigid. b) to be slack, relaxed from moisture; to be disabled, to flag; to give way; ܐܶܬܪܰܫܰܠ ܬܰܪܥܺܝܬܗܽܘܢ their resolution faltered; ܐܰܝܠܶܝܢ ܕܡܶܬܪܰܫܠܺܝܢ ܠܘܳܬ ܪ̈ܰܦܝܽܘܬܳܐ those who give way to dissolute habits. PA. ܪܰܫܶܠ pass. part. ܡܪܰܫܰܠ, ܡܪܰܫܠܳܐ slack, relaxed as the stomach; weak as stale medicine; palsied. ETHPA. ܐܶܬܪܰܫܰܠ with ܐܺܝ̈ܕܰܝܳܐ to wax feeble; to falter, yield; ܐܶܬܪܰܫܰܠ ܗܘܳܘ ܡܶܢ ܩܕܳܡܰܝܗܽܘܢ they gave way before them. APH. ܐܰܪܫܶܠ a) to give up; to let go; ܐܰܪܫܠܶܗ ܗܘܳܐ ܡܳܪܳܐ ܚܰܘܒܳܐ the creditor had let him go free; ܐܰܪܫܶܠ ܘܰܫܒܰܩ ܟܽܠܗ ܩܶܢܝܳܢܶܗ ܗܘܳܐ he gave up and left all that he possessed. With ܐܺܝ̈ܕܰܝܳܐ to falter, flag, be slack. b) to permit with ܠ. SHAPHEL ܫܰܪܫܶܠ part. ܡܫܰܪܫܠܳܐ perh. loose, dragging of dress. DERIVATIVES, ܪܰܫܠܳܐ, ܪܳܫܠܳܐ, ܪܶܫܠܽܘܬܳܐ, ܡܰܪܫܠܳܐ, ܡܪܰܫܠܳܐ, ܡܪܰܫܠܽܘܬܳܐ, ܡܶܬܪܰܫܠܳܢܽܘܬܳܐ.

ܪܰܫܠܳܐ rt. ܪܫܠ. m. a) flabby, disabled, feeble; flap-eared. b) subst. flabbiness, languor.

ܪܫܰܡ fut. ܢܶܪܫܽܘܡ, act. part. ܪܳܫܶܡ, ܪܳܫܡܳܐ, pass. part. ܪܫܺܝܡ, ܪܫܺܝܡܳܐ, ܪܫܺܝܡܬܳܐ. a) to grave, engrave, inscribe on the rock; to note, set down; ܪܫܺܝܡܳܐ ܥܰܠ ܠܽܘܚܳܐ ܕܠܶܒܗܽܘܢ graven upon the table of their heart; ܪܫܽܘܡ ܐܶܢܽܘܢ ܒܰܟܬܳܒܳܐ ܕܚܰܝܶܐ inscribe them in the book of life; ܗܳܢܽܘܢ ܕܪܫܰܡܢ ܠܥܶܠ whom we mentioned above; ܪܽܘܫܡܶܐ ܕܰܥܠ ܣܶܦ̈ܬܳܐ annotations, marginal notes. b) to draw, delineate, trace the plan of a building; to represent, denote, indicate; ܪܫܰܡܶܗ ܒܕܽܘܡܝܳܐ ܕܨܰܠܡܳܐ ܕܒܰܪܢܳܫܳܐ he fashioned it like the image of a man; ܪܫܽܘܡ ܩܕܳܡ ܥܰܝ̈ܢܰܝܟܽܘܢ ܫܽܘܒܚܳܐ ܕܰܢܛܺܝܪ set before your eyes the glory which is reserved; ܐܶܠܳܐ ܕܣܰܘܟܳܐ ܕܙܰܝܬܳܐ ܢܪܫܽܘܡ ܠܰܢ ܠܫܠܳܡܳܐ the olive branch should represent to us the sign of peace; ܦܛܺܝܪܳܐ ܬܡܺܝܡܽܘܬܳܐ ܪܫܺܝܡܳܐ by unleavened bread a guileless life is indicated. c) to assign, appoint, ordain; ܪܫܰܡ ܐܶܢܽܘܢ ܒܫܽܘܠܳܡܳܐ ܕܰܟܬܳܒܳܐ ܝܰܘܡ̈ܳܬܳܐ ܕܩܰܕܺܝ̈ܫܶܐ the Saints' days which he arranged at the end of the Service Book; ܪܫܺܝܡ ܐܰܢ̄ܬ ܒܛܰܝܒܽܘܬܳܐ ܕܬܶܬܟܰܬܰܫ ܘܬܶܙܟܶܐ thou art ordained by grace to strive and to conquer. With ܩܕܳܡ to prefigure, fore-ordain. d) to entitle, call; Psalms i and ii are ܠܳܐ ܪܫܺܝܡܺܝܢ without title, without the name of the writer. e) to sign, make the sign of the cross; ܪܫܰܡ ܪܽܘܫܡܳܐ set a mark; ܪܳܫܶܡ ܐܳܬܳܐ he makes the sign of the cross over the elements; ܫܳܡܽܘܥܶܐ ܘܪܫܺܝܡܶܐ the hearers and the signed i.e. catechumens and those who have received chrism and are about to be baptized. ETHPE. ܐܶܬܪܫܶܡ a) to be engraved, inscribed, written down; ܢܶܬܪܫܡܽܘܢ ܒܪܶܥܝܳܢܳܟ let them be inscribed on thy mind; gram. ܐܳܬ̈ܘܳܬܳܐ ܕܠܳܐ ܡܶܬܪܰܫܡܳܢ letters pronounced but not written, as an Aleph supplied before initial Yudh. b) to be imprinted, marked; ܐܶܬܪܫܶܡ ܙܽܘܙܳܐ ܒܫܡ̈ܳܗܶܐ ܕܰܬܠܳܬܳܐ ܡܰܠܟܶ̈ܐ coin was stamped with the names of three rulers; ܗܳܢܽܘܢ ܕܶܐܬܪܫܶܡܘ ܡܫܺܝܚܳܐ those who had the imprint of Christ i.e. were marked as His. c) to be signed, receive the sign of the cross, receive chrism; to be ordained; fore-ordained; ܢܶܬܪܫܡܽܘܢ ܒܡܰܝ̈ܳܐ ܕܡܰܥܡܽܘܕܺܝܬܳܐ let them be signed with the waters of baptism; ܐܶܬܪܫܶܡ ܦܠܳܢ ܕܢܶܗܘܶܐ ܩܳܪܽܘܝܳܐ N. is ordained Reader. d) to be indicated, figured, shown by types; ܐܳܪ̈ܳܙܶܐ ܕܒܪܳܐ ܐܶܬܪܫܶܡܘ ܒܒܶܪܝܳܬܳܐ the mysteries of the Son shadowed forth in creation. PAEL ܪܰܫܶܡ pass. part. ܡܪܰܫܰܡ, ܡܪܰܫܡܳܐ, ܡܪܰܫܰܡܬܳܐ drawn, marked out by lines; ܠܽܘ̈ܚܶܐ ܡܪܰܫܡܶܐ ruled boards, chess- or draught-boards. ETHPA. ܐܶܬܪܰܫܰܡ to be delineated, imprinted; to be signed with chrism; ܢܶܬܪܰܫܰܡ ܒܗܽܘܢ ܢܽܘܗܪܳܐ ܕܦܰܪܨܽܘܦܳܟ may the light of Thy countenance be imprinted on them. DERIVATIVES, ܪܽܘܫܡܳܐ, ܪܽܘܫܡܳܝܳܐ, ܪܫܺܝܡܳܐ, ܡܪܰܫܡܳܢܳܐ, ܡܪܰܫܡܳܢܽܘܬܳܐ, ܡܶܬܪܰܫܡܳܢܳܐ, ܡܶܬܪܰܫܡܳܢܽܘܬܳܐ.

ܪܳܫܡܳܐ, ܪܫܳܡ rt. ܪܫܡ. m. signing with the sign of the cross; indicating, foreshadowing.

ܪܫܰܡ and ܐܶܬܪܫܶܡ; see verb ܪܫܰܡ.

ܪܫܥ APHEL ܐܰܪܫܰܥ to speak or act impiously, to do wickedness; ܐܰܪܫܰܥ ܟܽܦܪܳܢܳܐ ܕܡܫܺܝܚܳܐ he committed the wickedness of denial of Christ; ܟܰܕ ܡܰܪܫܥܺܝܢ ܗܘܰܘ ܘܳܐܡܪܺܝܢ saying impiously .... SHAPHEL ܫܰܪܫܰܥ to conceal wickedness. DERIVATIVES, ܪܽܘܫܥܳܐ, ܪܰܫܝܳܐ, ܪܰܫܺܝܥܳܐ, ܪܶܫܥܽܘܬܳܐ, ܪܶܫܥܳܐ.

ܪܶܫܥܳܐ rt. ܪܫܥ. m. impiety.

ܪܚܰܫ fut. ܢܶܪܚܽܘܫ, act. part. ܪܳܚܶܫ, ܪܳܚܫܳܐ, pass. part. ܪܚܺܝܫܳܐ, ܬܳܐ (uncertain). to crawl, creep as a snake, worm, insect, to grovel often with ܥܰܠ ܐܰܪܥܳܐ on the ground; ܕܶܚܠܬܳܐ ܠܳܐ ܪܳܚܫܳܐ ܒܠܶܒܶܗ fear does not steal into his heart; ܦܰܓܪ̈ܳܢܶܐ ܘܪܳܚܫܺܝܢ ܥܰܠ ܐܰܪܥܳܐ carnal and earthbound.

ETHPE. ܐܬܪܚܫ *to drag oneself along.* APH. ܐܪܚܫ *to allow to crawl, to humble.* DERIVATIVES, ܪܚܫܐ, ܪܚܫܐ, ܪܚܫܘܬܐ, ܪܚܘܫܐ, ܪܚܫܐ.

ܪܚܫܐ pl. ܐ̈ rt. ܪܚܫ. m. *a reptile.*

ܪܚܫܐ rt. ܪܚܫ. m. *crawling, slow movements, insinuation.*

ܪܚܫ ETHPE. ܐܬܪܚܫ *to be hurled to a distance.* DERIVATIVE, the following word:—

ܪܚܫܐ m. *a*) *a cast, bow-shot.* *b*) ܕ ܘܪܕܐ *rose seed.*

ܪܚܫܐ rt. ܪܚܫ. m. *pounding, braying.*

ܪܬ fut. ܢܪܬܘܬ, act. part. ܪܐܬ, ܪܐܬܐ and ܪܬܐ, part. adj. ܪܬܝܬ, ܪܬܝܬܐ. Two Grammars and a Lex. add the form ܪܬ, saying that ܪܬ is used of the natural world and ܪܬ of sentient beings, e.g. ܪܬܘ ܫܡܝܐ ܘܒܪܝܬܐ ܪܬܘ *heaven and created beings trembled; to tremble, shudder, quake, shake;* ܗܘܬ ܐܪܥܐ ܪܬܐ ܘܙܝܥܐ ܠܗܠ ܘܠܗܠ *the earth was quaking and shaking to and fro;* ܪܬܝܢ ܗܘܘ ܦܓܪܝܗܘܢ *their bodies shook* with ague. Part. adj. ܪܬܝܬ ܠܒܗ *fainthearted;* ܪܬܝܬܐ ܘܙܝܥܬܐ *trembling with fear.* PA. ܪܬܬ *to cause to tremble;* ܫܐܕܐ ܡܪܬܬܝܢ ܡܢ ܩܕܡ ܫܡܗ ܕܡܫܝܚܐ *evil spirits made to quake before the name of Christ.* APH. ܐܪܬ *to terrify, to cause to shake;* ܫܢܘܗܝ (for ܐܪܬ) ܐܪܬܬ *his teeth chattered.* DERIVATIVES, ܪܬܬܐ or ܪܬܐ, ܪܬܝܬ, ܪܬܘܬܐ, ܪܬܝܬܐ, ܪܬܝܬܘܬܐ, ܪܬܝܬܐܝܬ.

ܪܬܐ APH. ܐܪܬܝ *to admonish, advise, instruct;* ܐܪܬܝܗ ܒܚܘܒܐ *he admonished him lovingly;* ܡܢܗܘܢ ܐܪܬܝ ܘܐܥܠ ܠܕܝܪܬܐ *some of them he instructed and admitted to monasteries;* ܐܪܬܝ ܘܐܟܪܙ ܠܥܡܐ *he expounded and preached to the people.* ETTAPH. ܐܬܬܪܬܝ *to be admonished; to be under instruction* before baptism; ܗܘ ܕܡܬܪܬܐ *a catechumen.* DERIVATIVES, ܪܬܝܐ, ܡܪܬܝܢܐ, ܡܪܬܝܢܝܬ, ܡܪܬܝܢܘܬܐ, ܡܬܪܬܝܢܐ.

ܪܬܐ = ܪܐܬܐ *the lungs.*

ܪܬܐ m. *a filbert.*

ܪܬܝܘܬܐ rt. ܪܬ. f. *lung disease, consumption.*

ܪܬܚ fut. ܢܪܬܘܚ, act. part. ܪܐܬܚ, ܪܬܚܐ, part. adj. ܪܬܝܚܐ. *to seethe, bubble up, grow hot, heave; to ferment, to heat* as manure; *to break out* as a boil; ܪܬܚ ܙܝܢܗ ܒܚܘܡܗ ܕܝܘܡܐ in the heat of the day *his armour grew hot;* ܡܝܐ ܪܬܚܝܢ *boiling water;* ܚܡܪܐ ܚܕܬܐ ܪܬܚܐ *new wine working in fermentation;* ܟܐܦܐ ܪܬܝܚܬܐ *fire-coloured stones.* Metaph. *to be greatly moved, be fervent, heated;* ܪܬܚ ܕܡܗ *his blood boiled* with anger, also *his blood bubbled up;* ܪܬܚܘ ܪܚܡܐ ܕܪܘܡܐ *mercy on high was fervently moved;* ܪܬܝܚ ܒܪܘܚ *fervent in spirit;* ܪܬܝܚܐ *fervent, enthusiastic.* APH. ܐܪܬܚ *to set to boil, heat; to make fervent, inflame* with zeal, lust &c., ܐܪܬܚ ܘܐܪܬܚ ܠܡܝܐ ܘܐܦܩ ܚܝܐ *to heat the waters and cause them to ferment and bring forth life;* ܠܠܫܢܝ ܐܪܬܚ *endow my tongue with fervency.* ETTAPH. ܐܬܬܪܬܚ *to be heated, brought to boiling point.* SHAPHEL ܫܪܬܚ *to make to abound, supply abundantly;* parts. *abundant, ample, copious, numerous;* ܠܪܥܝܢܝ ܫܪܬܚ *grant exuberance to my mind;* ܡܫܪܬܚ ܗܘܐ ܠܚܡܐ ܒܒܝܬܗ no one *had a superfluity of bread in his house;* ܐܢܫܐ ܡܫܪܬܚܐ *opulent persons;* ܚܝܐ ܢܝܚܐ ܘܡܫܪܬܚܝܢ ܒܫܠܡܐ ܫܪܬܚ ܠܢ *grant us lives of leisure abounding in peace.* ESHTAPH. ܐܫܬܪܬܚ *to be made to abound; to acquire opulence, power; to flourish exceedingly, be very numerous;* ܐܫܬܪܬܚ ܡܢܝܢܐ ܕܟܗܢܐ ܡܢ *the number* of priests *surpassed that* of the laity. DERIVATIVES, ܪܬܚܐ, ܪܬܝܚܐ, ܪܬܝܚܘܬܐ, ܡܫܪܬܚܢܝܬ, ܡܫܪܬܚܢܘܬܐ, ܡܫܪܬܚܢܐ, ܡܫܪܬܚܢܘܬܐ, ܡܫܬܪܬܚܢܐ, ܡܫܬܪܬܚܢܐ.

ܪܬܚܐ E-Syr. ܪܬܚܐ m. *a*) *bubbling up, working, fermentation; fervent heat.* *b*) *breakings out, discharging boils, gangrene.* *c*) *fervour, enthusiasm, excitement.*

ܪܬܚܢܐ rt. ܪܬܚ. *fervid, enthusiastic.*

ܪܬܝܐ or ܪܬܝܐ rt. ܪܬܐ. m. *warning, admonition.*

ܪܬܝܚܘܬܐ rt. ܪܬܚ. f. *fervour* of the sun; *boiling heat.*

ܪܬܝܬܐ and ܐܪܬܝܬܐ pl. ܪܬܝܬ̈ܐ rt. ܪܬ. com. gen. *trembling, fear;* pl. *violent shocks* of earthquake. Cf. ܪܬܝܬ part. adj. of verb ܪܬ.

ܪܬܝܬܘܬܐ rt. ܪܬ. f. *trembling, shuddering.*

ܪܬܝܬܐܝܬ rt. ܪܬ. adv. *tremulously.*

ܪܬܡ fut. ܢܪܬܘܡ, act. part. ܪܐܬܡ, ܪܬܡܐ, pass. part. ܪܬܝܡܐ. *to speak very softly* or *indistinctly, to whisper, stammer,* ܪܬܘܡ ܒܢܝܚܘܬܐ *whisper gently;* ܠܐ ܡܨܝܐ ܠܫܢܐ ܠܡܪܬܡ *no tongue can tell;* ܢܪܬܡܢ ܣܦܘܬܟ ܡܘܕܝܢܘܬܐ *let thy lips stammer praise.* Pass. part. *mumbling, toothless.* ETHPE. ܐܬܪܛܢ *to be uttered, mentioned.* PA. ܪܛܢ *to utter gently;* rit. ܡܪܛܢ *he says gently.* DERIVATIVE, ܪܛܢܐ.

ܪܛܢܐ, ܪܛܘܢܐ or ܪܛܢܬܐ rt. ܪܛܢ. m. *movement of the lips, a gentle murmur, whisper, utterance.*

ܪܦܐ *to droop;* only part. ܪܦܐ, ܪܦܝܐ, ܪܦܝܢ, ܪܦܝܢ ܣܘܟܝܟ *thy branches droop.* APH. ܐܪܦܝ *to wrench loose* as ܟܬܦܐ *the shoulder; to make to hang loose;* ܐܘܕܢܝܗܘܢ ܡܪܦܝܢ the bulls' *ears droop.* DERIVATIVES, ܪܦܝܘܬܐ, ܪܦܝܐ.

ܪܦܝܐ rt. ܪܦܐ. m. *violence* of the wind, *a violent shaking, shock.*

ܪܦܣ APHEL ܐܪܦܣ *to prick, make a puncture.*

⁘ ܫܠܡ ܡܫܠܡܢܘܬܐ ܕܐܬܘܬܐ ܕܪܝܫ ⁘
⁘ ܬܘܒܐ ܕܡܫܝܚܐ ܟܠܗ ܟܠܗ ⁘

⁘ ܒܫܡ ܡܪܢ ܡܫܪܝܢܢ ܐܬܐ ܕܫܝܢ ⁘

⁘ ܫ ⁘

ܫ ܫܐܠ

ܫ, ܫܝܢ *Shin,* the twenty-first letter of the alphabet. The number *three hundred,* with ܕ, ܕܫ, *the three hundredth.*

ܫ̄ abbrev. for ܫܠܡ *finis, here endeth* a book or lesson.

ܫܐܒ act. part. *a)* of verb ܫܒ *to let down. b)* of verb ܫܘܒ *to burn.*

ܫܐܕ, ܫܐܕܐ act. part. of verb ܫܘܕ.

ܫܐܕܐ pl. ܝܢ, ܐ m. *a demon, devil, evil spirit,* often ܫܐܕܐ ܒܝܫܐ. DERIVATIVES, the following three words:—

ܫܐܕܢܐ pl. ܢܐ from ܫܐܕܐ. *demoniac, possessed by a demon; a demon.*

ܫܐܕܘܬܐ from ܫܐܕܐ. f. *diabolical cunning.*

ܫܐܕܢܝܐ, ܢܝܬܐ from ܫܐܕܐ. *of* or *caused by an evil spirit* or *by demoniacal possession; diabolical, devilish;* also ܐܬܟܬܫܘܬܐ ܫܐܕܢܝܬܐ *conflicts with evil spirits.*

ܫܐܗ Pers. *Shah, King;* ܫܐܗܢܫܐܗ *King of Kings, Emperor.*

ܫܐܘ Mongol paper money, worth from one to twenty dinars.

ܫܐܒܘܬܐ rt. ܫܒ. f. *letting down* a bucket.

ܫܐܘܠ, ܫܐܘܠ and ܫܐܘܘܠ Heb. pr. n. *Saul.*

ܫܐܘܠܐ pl. ܠܐ rt. ܫܐܠ. m. *an asker, beggar, petitioner.*

ܫܐܘܠܐ pl. ܠܐ rt. ܫܐܠ. m. *an inquiry, interrogation; a riddle.*

ܫܐܙܐ m. pl. = ܫܐܙܘܬܐ *jujubes.*

ܫܐܛ act. part. of verb ܫܘܛ.

ܫܐܛܝܢܐ (ܘܩܝܬܐ) *lenticula stagnina, marsh lentil.*

ܫܐܓ, ܫܐܓܐ act. part. of verb ܫܘܓ.

ܫܐܘܦ = ܫܐܘܦܐ.

ܫܐܠܐ, ܫܐܠܬܐ; see verb ܫܐܠ.

ܫܐܝܠܐܝܬ, ܐܫܐܝܠܐܝܬ and ܫܐܝܠܐܝܬ rt. ܫܐܠ. adv. *supposed, reputed, putatively* opp. ܟܝܢܐܝܬ *by nature; feignedly; in a borrowed or secondary sense, tropically* opp. ܡܢ ܟܝܢܐܝܬ *properly,* ܐܟܝܢܐܝܬ *exactly* and ܫܪܝܪܐܝܬ *truly.*

ܫܐܠܬܐ, ܫܐܠܬܘܬܐ rt. ܫܐܠ. f. *a)* with ܒ: *tropically, by personification. b)* ܫܐܠܬܘܬܐ ܦܪܨܘܦܐ *pretence.*

ܫܐܠ fut. ܢܫܐܠ, imper. ܫܐܠ, act. part.

ܫܳܐܶܠ, ܫܳܐܠܳܐ, pass. part. ܫܺܐܝܠ, ܫܺܐܝܠܬܳܐ and with prosthetic Aleph ܐܶܫܺܐܝܠ &c. *a) to ask, entreat; to beg, borrow;* ܫܰܐܶܠ ܡܶܢܝ ܘܶܐܬܶܠ ܠܳܟ *ask of me and I will give thee;* ܫܶܐܠܺܝܢܝ ܡܶܢ ܡܰܠܟܳܐ *ask the king's permission for me;* with ܫܶܐܠܬܳܐ *to make a request;* with ܒܰܩܛܺܝܪܳܐ *to extort.* *b) to inquire, interrogate;* with ܫܠܳܡܳܐ or ܒܰܫܠܳܡܳܐ *to inquire after the health, salute;* ܫܳܐܶܠ ܫܠܳܡܶܗ *my friend.* With ܬܶܫܢܺܝܩܳܐ *to examine by torture.* *c) to ask counsel, consult* with ܒ or ܠ; ܫܶܐܠܘ ܒܰܐܠܳܗܳܐ—ܒܡܳܪܝܳܐ *they asked of God, of the Lord;* ܫܳܐܶܠ ܠܒܰܥܠܶܝ ܙܰܟܽܘܪܳܐ *one who divines by familiar spirits, a necromancer.* Pass. part. *borrowed, pretended, assumed, putative, reputed; in a secondary sense, tropical;* ܫܽܘܒܚܳܐ ܫܺܐܝܠܳܐ *borrowed splendour;* ܫܽܘܒܚܳܐ ܫܺܐܝܠܳܐ ܕܰܥܠ ܦܰܪܨܽܘܦܶܗ *the reflected glory on the countenance of* Moses; ܐܰܒܳܐ ܫܺܐܝܠܳܐ *the reputed* or *supposed father;* ܫܡܳܐ ܫܺܐܝܠܳܐ *an assumed name;* ܐܶܣܟܺܝܡܳܐ ܫܺܐܝܠܳܐ *fancy dress;* ܚܰܝܶܐ ܫܺܐܝܠܶܐ ܘܡܶܬܥܰܒܪܳܢܶܐ *unreal and fleeting life;* ܫܺܐܝܠܳܐܝܬ or ܒܰܫܺܐܝܠܽܘܬܳܐ *in pretence, feignedly;* gram. ܡܶܬܚܫܚܳܢܽܘܬܳܐ ܫܺܐܝܠܬܳܐ *secondary* or *tropical use.* ETHPE. ܐܶܫܬܐܶܠ imper. W-Syr. ܐܶܫܬܐܰܠ *to excuse oneself, to decline; to eschew, abstain from; to resign;* with ܡܶܢ, ܐܶܫܬܐܶܠ ܕܢܶܥܽܘܠ *he excused himself from going in;* ܡܶܢ ܥܪܳܒܽܘܬܳܐ *refuse suretyship;* ܐܶܫܬܐܶܠ ܡܶܢ ܟܽܠܗ *he absolutely declined;* ܡܶܫܬܐܠܳܢܳܐ ܡܶܢ ܫܽܘܒܚܳܐ ܣܪܺܝܩܳܐ *eschewing vainglory;* ܕܠܳܐ ܡܶܫܬܐܠܳܢ *inevitable, necessary.* With ܡܶܢ ܡܶܐܟܽܘܠܬܳܐ—ܡܶܢ ܙܽܘܘܳܓܳܐ *to abstain from food, from marriage;* ܡܶܢ ܦܰܛܪܺܝܰܪܟܽܘܬܳܐ *to resign the office of Patriarch.* Legal *to refuse to receive* a purchase, *to disallow, cancel.* PA. ܫܰܐܶܠ sometimes with Yudh inserted before ܠ. *a) to ask questions, to inquire, question* with ܠ or acc. of the pers., with ܥܰܠ *for, about* or *concerning;* ܫܰܐܶܠ ܡܰܢ ܗܽܘ *he asked who it was;* ܫܰܐܶܠܘ ܥܰܠ ܒܰܝܬܳܐ *they inquired for the house;* ܡܳܪܳܐ ܕܦܽܘܩܕܳܢܳܐ ܫܰܐܶܠ ܥܰܠ ܓܰܒܪܳܐ *the owner of the deposit asked concerning the man* with whom he had left it. With ܦܶܠܐܬܳܐ *to propose a question, propound an enigma.* *b) to call in question, debate.* ETHPA. ܐܶܬܫܰܐܰܠ *a) to be questioned, interrogated, examined, tried* at law; with ܒܫܽܘܐܳܠܶܐ *to be put to the question.* *b)* = ETHPEEL *to excuse himself, refuse; to abstain;* with ܡܶܢ, ܡܶܢ ܐܶܣܛܪܰܛܺܝܐܳܐ ܘܡܶܢ ܬܶܫܡܶܫܬܳܐ *we beg to be excused from military duty and service.* APH. ܐܰܫܐܶܠ act. part. ܡܰܫܐܶܠ or ܡܰܫܐܠܳܐ. *to lend, bestow; to lend, grant a loan;* ܐܰܫܐܶܠܶܝܢܝ ܬܠܳܬ ܓܪܺܝܨܳܢ *lend me three loaves;* ܡܰܢ ܡܰܫܐܶܠ ܠܝ ܙܶܕܩܬܳܐ *who will grant me an alms.* DERIVATIVES, ܫܽܘܐܳܠܳܐ, ܫܰܐܳܠܳܐ, ܫܺܐܝܠܳܐܝܬ, ܫܐܶܠܬܳܐ, ܫܺܐܝܠܽܘܬܳܐ, ...

ܫܶܐܠܬܳܐ and ܫܶܐܶܠܬܳܐ, ܫܶܐܠܳܐ, ܫܺܐܠܳܐ, ܫܶܐܠܬܳܐ pl. ܫܶܐܠܳܬܳܐ, ܫܶܐܠܳܢ &c. rt. ܫܐܠ. f. *a request, petition, object of desire, requisite; consultation; a loan; the appropriation* of a name, *a trope;* ܫܶܐܠܳܬܳܐ ܕܒܰܝܬܳܐ *household requisites;* ܫܶܐܠܬܳܐ ܕܫܠܳܡܳܐ *a salutation;* ܫܡܳܐ ܗܳܢܳܐ ܒܫܶܐܠܬܳܐ *he borrowed* or *assumed that name;* ܫܶܐܠܬܳܐ ܕܡܰܪܺܝܳܐ *the fruit of cordia myxa,* a kind of plum.

ܫܳܐܡ, ܫܰܐܡ rarely ܫܳܡ Arab. *Damascus; Syria.*

ܫܳܐܡܳܝܳܐ and ܫܰܐܡܳܝܳܐ from ܫܳܐܡ. *a Damascene, a Syrian.*

ܫܳܐܶܦ, ܫܳܐܦܳܐ act. part. of verb ܫܘܦ.

ܫܳܐܦܳܐ Arab. m. *a mill-stone.*

ܫܳܐܶܦ, ܫܳܐܦܳܐ act. part. of verb ܫܘܦ *to rub.* ܫܳܐܶܦ, ܫܳܐܦܳܐ or ܫܳܐܦܳܐ act. part. of verb ܫܦ *to crawl.*

ܫܳܐܦܳܐ rt. ܫܦ. m. *a crawling locust, unfledged locust.*

ܫܳܐܶܪ *a)* for ܫܳܘܶܪ act. part. of ܫܘܪ *to leap.* *b)* act. part. of ܫܪ *to be strong, firm.*

ܫܶܐܪܳܐ or ܫܺܐܪܳܐ pl. ܐ̈ Heb. m. *a chain, ankle-chain, bangle, bracelet.*

ܫܶܐܪܳܐ, ܫܶܐܪܳܝܳܐ, ܫܶܐܪܳܝܳܐ rarely ܫܶܪܳܝܳܐ pl. ܐ̈ subst. and adj. *silk, silken, silken attire, a silken hanging, a piece of silk;* ܡܰܚܶܐ ܫܶܐܪܳܝܶܐ *a silk-weaver, mercer.*

ܫܺܐܪ ܗܰܫܺܐܪܺܝܡ Heb. *the Song of Songs;* cf. ܫܺܝܪܳܐ.

ܫܳܐܬܳܐ; see ܫܬ.

ܫܶܐܬܶܐܣ = ܫܬܶܐܣ verb.

ܫܶܐܬܶܐܣܬܳܐ; see ܫܬܶܐܣܬܳܐ.

ܫܒ imper. of verb ܢܫܒ *to blow.*

ܫܰܒ fut. ܢܶܫܒܽܘܒ, act. part. ܫܳܐܶܒ. a) *to let down* ܠܓܽܘܒܳܐ *into a pit;* ܡܶܢ ܟܰܘܬܳܐ *from a window;* ܫܰܒܘ ܠܡܰܝܳܐ ܒܚܶܣܢܳܐ *they let the water rush out with violence.* b) *to descend, condescend;* ܡܰܢ ܢܶܫܒܽܘܒ ܘܢܶܬܡܰܠܰܠ ܥܰܡܝ *who will come down and converse with me?* Pa. ܫܰܒܶܒ *to let down.* Derivative, ܫܽܘܒܳܒܳܐ.

ܫܰܒܳܐ, ܫܰܒܬܳܐ pl. ܫܰܒܶܐ, ܫܰܒ̈ܐ; see ܫܰܒܬܳܐ.

ܫܒܳܐ fut. ܢܶܫܒܶܐ, imper. ܫܒܺܝ, act. part. ܫܳܒܶܐ, ܫܳܒܝܳܐ pl. ܫܳܒܶܝܢ, ܫܳܒ̈ܝܳܐ, pass. part. ܫܒܶܐ, ܫܒܺܝܳܐ, ܫܒܺܝܬܳܐ pl. ܫܒܶܝܢ, ܫܒ̈ܝܳܐ, ܫܒ̈ܝܳܬܳܐ cf. ܫܒܺܝܬܳܐ. *to take* or *lead away captive, to bring into captivity; to depopulate, lay waste; to capture, take possession of,* with ܠ; ܫܒܳܐ ܫܒܺܝܬܳܐ *he led away captives;* ܫܒܰܘ ܟܶܣܦܰܢ *they seized our silver.* Metaph. ܫܒܳܬܶܗ ܒܫܽܘܦܪܳܗ̇ *she captivated him by her beauty;* ܫܳܒܶܝܢܰܢ ܟܽܠ ܡܰܚܫܰܒܬܳܐ *we bring every thought into captivity.* Act. part. *a captor, spoiler, robber;* ܫܳܒܶܝ ܒܥܺܝܪܳܐ *cattle-lifters.* Pass. part. *captured, a captive;* ܫܒ̈ܝܳܬܳܐ ܫܦܺܝܪ̈ܳܬܳܐ ܢܶܗܘܝܳܢ ܫܳܒ̈ܝܳܬܳܐ ܕܫܳܒ̈ܝܰܝܗܶܝܢ ܪ̈ܚܽܘܡܰܝܗܶܝܢ *beautiful captives may become the capturers of their enamoured captors;* ܫܒܶܐ ܠܪ̈ܰܓܝܳܬܶܗ *enslaved by his lusts;* ܫܒܶܐ ܗܽܘ ܪܶܥܝܳܢܝ ܠܘܳܬ ܐܰܠܳܗܳܐ *my mind is ravished unto God;* ܫܒܶܐ ܠܒܳܐ *bereft of wit.* Ethpe. ܐܶܫܬܒܺܝ *to be carried into captivity, captured; to be taken by the enemy; to be laid waste, plundered;* ܐܶܫܬܒܺܝ ܠܒܳܒܶܠ *he was led away captive to Babylon;* ܐܽܘܪܗܳܝ ܐܶܫܬܒܝܰܬ ܡܶܢ ܡܰܝܳܐ *Edessa was devastated by floods;* ܐܶܫܬܒܺܝ ܟܽܠܶܗ ܩܽܘܢܝܳܢܗܽܘܢ *all their baggage was carried off.* Metaph. *to be captivated, enslaved, subject* with ܒ, ܡܶܢ, ܠ; ܐܶܫܬܒܝܰܬ ܒܚܽܘܒܶܗ ܕܓܰܒܪܳܐ; ܠܓܰܒܪܳܐ *she was captivated by love of him;* ܟܽܠ ܙܳܟܽܘܬܳܐ ܢܶܫܬܒܝܳܢ ܠܳܟ *every victory shall be in thy power, be possible to thee.* Aph. ܐܰܫܒܺܝ act. part. ܡܰܫܒܶܐ. a) *to deliver into captivity, to send* or *lead away captive.* b) *to take a catch* of fish. Derivatives, ܫܒܺܝܳܐ, ܫܶܒܝܳܐ, ܫܒܺܝܬܳܐ, ܫܒܺܝܬܳܐܝܬ, ܡܶܫܬܒܝܳܢܽܘܬܳܐ.

ܫܒܳܐ pr. n. *Sheba, Sabaea,* kingdoms of Arabia.

ܫܒܳܒ, ܫܒܳܒܳܐ, ܫܒܳܒܬܳܐ *neighbouring, a neighbour.* Derivatives, ܫܒܳܒܽܘܬܳܐ, ܫܒܳܒܳܐܺܝܬ, &c.

ܫܒܳܒ ܢܰܗܪܳܐ *potamogeton natans, pondweed.*

ܫܒܳܒܽܘܙܳܐ or ܫܰܒܳܒܽܘܢܳܐ m. *nigella sativa,* a kind of fennel the black seeds of which were used to spice bread and for a medicine.

ܫܒܳܒܽܘܬܳܐ f. a) *neighbourhood, nearness, vicinity;* ܫܒܳܒܽܘܬܳܐ ܥܰܠܡܳܢܳܝܬܳܐ *social intercourse.* b) *a district, quarter of a town;* ܕܝܺܗܽܘܕ̈ܳܝܶܐ ܫ *the Jews' quarter.*

ܫܰܒܗܰܪ and ܐܶܫܬܰܒܗܰܪ Shaphel and Eshtaphal conjugations; see under ܒܗܰܪ.

ܫܰܒܗܪܳܢܳܐܺܝܬ from ܫܰܒܗܰܪ. adv. *arrogantly.*

ܫܰܒܗܪܳܢ, ܢܳܐ, ܢܺܝܬܳܐ from ܫܰܒܗܰܪ. *boastful, vainglorious.*

ܫܰܒܗܪܳܢܳܐܺܝܬ from ܫܰܒܗܰܪ. adv. *vaingloriously.*

ܫܰܒܗܪܳܢܽܘܬܳܐ from ܫܰܒܗܰܪ. f. *boastfulness, vainglory.*

ܫܰܒܳܒܽܘܢܳܐ; see ܫܒܳܒܽܘܙܳܐ.

ܫܰܒܽܘܛܳܐ pl. ܛ̈ܶܐ rt. ܫܒܛ. m. a) *a thin plate of metal.* b) *a large fish found in the Nile.*

ܫܰܒܽܘܥ, ܫܰܒܽܘܥܳܐ, ܫܰܒܽܘܥܬܳܐ pl. ܥ̈ܶܐ, ܥܺܝܢ, ܥ̈ܳܬܳܐ m. f. (rare) rt. ܫܒܥ. *the number seven; a week.* E-Syr. ܫܳܒܽܘܥܳܐ (soft b) a division of the ecclesiastical year, properly seven weeks.

ܫܰܒܽܘܩܳܐ pl. ܩ̈ܶܐ rt. ܫܒܩ. m. *a shoot, sprig, slip, sucker, rod;* —ܫܰܒܽܘܩ̈ܶܐ ܕܳܐܣܳܐ—ܕܓܦܶܬܳܐ—ܕܘܰܪ̈ܕܳܐ—ܕܪ̈ܘܡܳܢܶܐ *myrtle sprigs, vine-shoots, rose-stems, rods of pomegranate;* ܡܶܢ ܫܰܒܽܘܩ̈ܶܐ ܓܕܺܝܠ *woven of osiers, wicker.*

ܫܰܒܽܘܩܳܐ pl. ܩ̈ܶܐ rt. ܫܒܩ. m. *pardoning, forgiving, ready to forgive;* ܫ ܕܚܰܛܳܗ̈ܶܐ *He who forgives sins.*

ܫܒܽܘܩܝܳܐ rt. ܫܒܩ. m. *liberation.*

ܫܰܒܽܘܩܳܢܳܐ from ܫܰܒܽܘܩܳܐ. *like a rod, striped.*

ܫܰܒܽܘܩܬܳܐ pl. ܩ̈ܳܬܳܐ rt. ܫܒܩ. f. *a staff,* and esp. *a pastoral staff.*

ܫܰܒܽܘܪܳܐ, ܫܰܒܽܘܪܬܳܐ from ܫܒܰܪ. *simple, childish; a simpleton, innocent.*

ܫܒܽܘܪܓܳܢ Pers. *steel.*

ܫܒܰܚ Peal only part. adj. ܫܒܺܝܚ, ܚܳܐ, ܚܬܳܐ. *glorious, illustrious, celebrated; splendid, goodly, stately; praiseworthy, excellent;* ܟܝܳܢܳܐ ܫܒܺܝܚܳܐ ܕܰܐܠܳܗܽܘܬܶܗ *the glorious nature of His Godhead;* ܒܶܢܝܳܢ̈ܶܐ ܫܒܺܝܚ̈ܶܐ *stately edifices;* ܫܒܺܝܚ ܒܩܽܘܡܬܶܗ *of goodly stature.* Fem. emph. pl. ܫܒܺܝܚܳܬܳܐ *glories, glorious deeds.* Pa. ܫܰܒܰܚ a) *to praise, glorify, sing praises* often with ܬܶܫܒܽܘܚܬܳܐ; *to hold in honour;* eccles. *to say the Gloria.* b) *to keep in good repute, sustain the credit of;* ܫܰܒܰܚ ܠܥܺܕܬܳܐ ܘܢܰܛܪܳܗ ܡܶܢ ܫܺܝܛܽܘܬܳܐ *he served the Church and guarded it from discredit.* c) like Gk. δοξάζειν, cf. derivs. *to think, hold opinions;* ܐܰܝܠܶܝܢ ܕܠܰܘܳܬܶܗ ܡܫܰܒܚܺܝܢ *those of his opinion.* Pass. part. a) *glorious, illustrious, in high position* opp. ܡܶܫܬܰܥܒܕܳܐ *a commoner;* ܦܰܛܪܺܝܰܪܟܳܐ ܡܫܰܒܚܳܐ *the illustrious Patriarch.* b) *splendid, precious;* ܠܒܽܘܫܶܐ ܡܫܰܒܚܶܐ *magnificent array;* ܡܫܰܒܚܳܬܳܐ ܕܗܰܝܟܠܳܐ *the glories, precious ornaments, of the temple.* Ethpa. ܐܶܫܬܰܒܰܚ a) pass. *to be praised, glorified, glorious.* b) refl. *to adorn oneself; to glory.* c) *to resound.* Derivatives, ܫܘܒܚܐ, ܫܒܝܚܘܬܐ, ܡܫܒܚܐ, ܡܫܒܚܢܘܬܐ, ܡܫܒܚܢܐܝܬ, ܡܫܒܚܘܬܐ, ܡܫܬܒܚܢܘܬܐ, ܡܫܬܒܚܢܐ, ܡܫܬܒܚܢܐ, ܡܫܬܒܚܢܘܬܐ, ܬܫܒܘܚܬܐ, ܬܫܒܘܚܬܐ.

ܫܰܒܚܶܫܳܐ (ܩܰܩܢܶܐ) *the ostrich.*

ܫܒܰܛ fut. ܢܶܫܒܽܘܛ, act. part. ܫܳܒܶܛ, ܫܳܒܛܳܐ. *to float, to fly loose, stream.* Derivative, ܫܶܒܛܳܐ.

ܫܰܒܶܛ Pael conj. *to beat out, hammer;* ܣܺܐܡܳܐ ܡܫܰܒܛܳܐ *beaten silver.* Ethpa. ܐܶܫܬܰܒܰܛ *to be beaten out;* ܠܳܐ ܡܶܫܬܰܒܛܳܢܳܐ *unyielding, stubborn.* Derivatives, ܫܒܘܛܐ, ܫܰܒܛܳܐ, ܫܘܒܛܐ.

ܫܒܳܛ E-Syr. ܫܒܰܛ m. the Syrian month *Shebat* or *Shwat* from February new moon to that of March.

ܫܰܒܛܳܐ pl. ܫܰܒܛܺܝܢ, ܶܐ rt. ܫܒܛ. m. a) *a rod, staff, branch, sceptre;* ܫ̈ ܕܪܽܘܡܳܢܶܐ *a pomegranate rod;* ܓܠܺܝܡܳܐ ܕܫܰܒܛܶܐ *a cloak of wickerwork;* ܡܢܰܪܬܳܐ ܕܫܰܒܥܳܐ ܫܰܒܛܺܝܢ *a seven-branched candlestick.* Pl. *the fasces* of Roman lictors. b) *a stripe, scourging;* metaph. *a scourge, plague;* ܫ̈ ܕܡܰܝܳܐ *the plague of waters, the deluge;* ܫ̈ ܕܠܶܫܳܢܳܐ *the scourge of the tongue;* ܐܰܕܪܟܶܗ ܫܰܒܛܳܐ ܕܟܺܐܢܽܘܬܳܐ *a just judgement overtook him.* c) *a tribe;* ܦܰܠܓܶܗ ܕܫܰܒܛܳܐ ܕܡܢܰܫܶܐ *the half-tribe of Manasseh.* d) = ܫܳܦܛܳܐ *a Judge* of Israel. e) *a measuring-rod; a rod* (measure). f) *a stripe, streak* of light, of colour; *a meteor;* ܡܫܰܟܶܗ ܕܢܶܡܪܳܐ ܫܰܒܛܺܝܢ ܫܰܒܛܺܝܢ *the skin of the panther is striped.* g) *the arum.* h) *salt pork.*

ܫܶܒܛܳܐ rt. ܫܒܛ. m. *flowing hair, straight locks* opp. ܩܘܨܘܬܐ *curls.*

ܫܰܒܛܰܒܛܳܐ m. *polygonum seminale, knot-grass.*

ܫܒܺܛܳܐ com. gen. *level;* ܐܰܪܥܳܐ ܫ̈ *a table-land.*

ܫܳܒܝܳܐ pl. ܶܐ m. ܫܳܒܺܝܬܳܐ pl. ܝܳܬܳܐ f. rt. ܫܒܐ. a) *a captor, capturer, kidnapper, marauder, robber.* b) E-Syr. ܫܒܳܝܳܐ *a Sabaean.*

ܫܶܒܝܳܐ rt. ܫܒܐ. m. a) collect. *captives, captivity.* b) *devastation, depopulation, harrying.*

ܫܰܒܺܝܒܳܐ pl. ܶܐ m. a) *a ray, spark;* ܫܰܒܺܝܒܶܐ ܕܨܰܦܪܳܐ *the rays of dawn.* b) in the Lexx. *a mountain path.*

ܫܰܒܺܝܒܽܘܬܳܐ f. *sparkling, glittering.*

ܫܒܺܝܚܳܐܝܬ rt. ܫܒܚ. adv. *gloriously, nobly, excellently.*

ܫܒܺܝܚܽܘܬܳܐ rt. ܫܒܚ. f. *splendour, magnificence, goodliness.*

ܫܒܺܝܠ, ܫܒܺܝܠܳܐ pl. ܶܐ m. *a path, pathway, way, road, trace;* ܫܒܺܝܠܶܐ ܥܰܬܺܝܩܶܐ *the old ways, ancient paths;* ܫ̈ ܕܬܶܒܢܳܐ *the Milky Way,* lit. *the way of chaff.*

ܫܒܺܝܥܳܐܝܬ from ܫܒܰܥ. *seven times, sevenfold.*

ܫܒܺܝܥܳܝ, ܫܒܺܝܥܳܝܳܐ, ܝܬܳܐ from ܫܒܥ. *seventh, consisting of seven, sevenfold;* ܫܒܺܝܥܳܝܶܐ *the seven planets.*

ܫܒܺܝܥܳܝܽܘܬܳܐ from ܫܒܥ. f. *the number seven, a number of seven.*

ܫܒܺܝܩܽܘܬܳܐ rt. ܫܒܩ. f. *desertion, abandonment, being abandoned.*

ܫܒܺܝܪܬܳܐ; see ܫܒܪܬܳܐ.

ܫܒܺܝܬܳܐ rt. ܫܒܐ. f. a) collect. *captives, captivity;* ܣܠܶܩܘ ܫܒܺܝܬܳܐ ܡܶܢ ܒܳܒܶܠ *those of the captivity came up from Babylon.* b) *the prey, booty; a theft; a take of fishes.*

ܫܰܒܶܠ I. denom. verb Pael conj. from ܫܒܺܝܠܳܐ. a) *to show the way, direct;* ܡܫܰܒܠܺܝܢ ܡܰܝܳܐ ܡܶܢ ܕܘܟܝܳܬܳܐ ܪ̈ܚܺܝܩܳܬܳܐ *conveying water from considerable distances;* ܢܰܚܠܶܐ ܠܳܐ ܡܫܰܒܠܺܝܢ *pathless ravines.* b) *to instruct, train* in the spiritual life. II. denom. verb from ܫܶܒܠܬܳܐ *to form spikes.* Ethpa. ܐܶܫܬܰܒܰܠ *to be directed, instructed;* ܗܘܳܐ ܡܶܫܬܰܒܰܠ ܡܶܢ ܡܳܪܰܢ *he was under the direction of our Master.*

ܫܰܒܠܳܐ, ܫܰܒܠܳܢܳܐ from ܫܰܒܶܠ. *a director, spiritual guide.*

ܫܶܒܠܳܐ, ܫܶܒܶܠܬܳܐ or ܫܶܒܠܬܳܐ pl. ܫܶܒܠܺܝܢ, ܫܶܒܠܶܐ constr. states ܫܶܒܶܠ and ܫܶܒܠܰܬ f. *a spike, blade, an ear* of wheat; ܫܒ̈ܠܐ ܕܚܛܐ *blades of corn, young green corn;* ܫܒܠܬܐ ܕܢܪܕܐ or ܢܪܕܐ *spikenard;* ܫܒܠܬܐ ܛܘܪܝܬܐ *mountain nard.* Astron. a sign of the Zodiac, *Virgo spicifera.* Derivatives, verb ܫܒܠ, ܫܒܠܐ, ܫܘܒܠܐ, ܫܒܠܢܐ, ܫܒܠܢܘܬܐ, ܫܒܠܬܢܐ.

ܫܒܥ f. ܫܒܥܐ m. *seven;* ܕܫܒܥ or ܕܫܒܥܐ *the seventh;* ܫܒܥ ܙܒܢܝܢ *seven times;* ܫܒܥ ܐܘ ܬܡܢܐ *seven or eight;* ܫܒܥܐ ܥܠܡ̈ܐ or ellipt. *the seven aeons* of Bardesanes' heresy; *the seven planets;* ܫܒܝܥܝܐ pl. ܫܒܝܥ̈ܝܐ *the seventh* day of the month; the collective *number seven;* ܫܒܥܬܝܗܘܢ *the seven of them.* Derivatives, the four following words, and ܫܒܘܥܐ, ܫܒܥܬܐ, ܫܒܝܥܐ, ܫܒܝܥܝܘܬܐ.

ܫܒܥܝܢ *seventy;* ܫܒܥܝܢ ܕܫܒܥܝܢ ܐ̈ܢܫܐ *the Septuagint version.*

ܫܒܥܝܢܝܐ, ܫܒܥܝܢܝܬܐ with ܫܒܥܝܢ̈ܐ or oftener ellipt. *of the Septuagint;* ܐܫܥܝܐ ܫܒܥܝܢܝܐ *Isaiah in the LXX version.*

ܫܒܥܡܐܐ *seven hundred.*

ܫܒܥܣܪ or ܫܒܥܬܥܣܪ m. ܫܒܥܣܪܐ f. *seventeen.*

ܫܒܪܐ m. *mixing, confusing.*

ܫܒܩ fut. ܢܫܒܘܩ, act. part. ܫܒܩ, ܫܒܩܐ, pass. part. ܫܒܝܩ, ܫܒܝܩܐ, ܫܒܝܩܬܐ. *a) to leave, go away;* ܫܒܩܬܗ ܐܫܬܐ *the fever left her.* With ܕܡܐ *to let blood;* with ܪܘܚܐ *to expire;* also ܫܒܩܬܗ ܢܦܫܗ *his soul departed.* Otiose with verbs of motion: ܫܒܩܘ ܘܐܙܠܘ *they went away, took leave;* ܫܒܩ ܘܢܦܩ *he went out;* ܫܒܩ ܘܥܪܩ *he took to flight. b) to leave over, leave behind, leave* by will; ܠܐ ܫܒܩ ܫܪܟܐ *he left none remaining;* ܐܫܒܘܩ ܛܘܦܣܐ ܛܒܐ *I shall leave a good example;* ܥܘܬܪܐ ܕܫܒܩܘ ܠܗ ܐܒܗ̈ܘܗܝ *the riches his parents had left him. c) to give leave, allow, let alone;* ܫܒܘܩܝܢܝ ܐܫܕܪ *permit me to send;* ܫܒܘܩܝܢܝ *leave me alone. d) to send away, let go, dismiss* from school, *set free* from prison, *manumit* a slave, *put away, repudiate* a wife; ܟܪ̈ܘܙܐ ܫܒܝܩܝܢ ܠܡܠܟܐ *heralds have been sent out by the king;* ܫܒܝܩܬܐ ܕܒܢܡܘܣܐ *a legally divorced woman. e) to let go, let loose;* ܦܩܕ ܕܚܝ̈ܘܬܐ ܢܫܒܩܘܢ ܠܘܬܗ *he ordered the wild beasts to be let loose at him;* with ܢܘܪܐ *to set fire to. f) to remit, forgive* ܚܘ̈ܒܐ, ܚܘܒ̈ܠܬܐ *debts,* ܚܛܗ̈ܐ *sins;* ܡܟ̈ܣܐ *taxes. g) to leave, forsake, desert, abandon;* ܫܒܩ ܐܢܘܢ *he forsook them;* ܫܒܩܬ ܚܘܒܟ ܩܕܡܝܐ *thou hast left thy first love;* ܒܝ̈ܥܐ ܫܒܝܩ̈ܬܐ *forsaken eggs. h) to leave out, omit;* ܫܒܩ ܕ *to say nothing about, except.* Ethpe. ܐܫܬܒܩ imper. W-Syr. ܐܫܬܒܩ passive of Peal in all its senses: *to be left, deserted, repudiated; to be permitted, allowed; to be remitted, forgiven; to be left out, passed over, omitted;* also *to be deferred; to be reserved* as the Eucharist. Derivatives, ܫܒܩܐ, ܫܒܘܩܐ, ܫܒܘܩܝܐ, ܫܒܩܢܐ, ܫܒܘܩܬܐ, ܫܒܝܩܘܬܐ, ܫܒܩܐ, ܫܘܒܩܢܐ, ܫܘܒܩܢܘܬܐ, ܡܫܬܒܩܢܐ, ܡܫܬܒܩܢܘܬܐ.

ܫܒܩܐ or ܫܒܩܐ pl. ܐ̈ ܀ rt. ܫܒܩ. m. *a) a source, channel* or *pool* of water. *b) a rush, onslaught, charge. c)* ܫܒܩ ܕܡܐ *blood-letting. d) desertion, abandonment.*

ܫܒܪ act. part. ܫܒܪ, ܫܒܪܐ *to be childish, infantile, simple, foolish, to behave childishly;* ܥܕܟܝܠ ܗܘܘ ܒܪܥܝܢܗܘܢ ܫܒܪܝܢ *they are even yet childish in mind.* Ethpa. ܐܫܬܒܪ *to behave as a child, pretend to be a simpleton.* Aph. ܐܫܒܪ *to feign childishness.* Derivatives, ܫܒܪܐ, ܫܒܪܐ, ܫܒܪܐܝܬ, ܫܒܪܘܬܐ, ܫܒܪܘܢܐ, ܫܒܪܝܐ, ܫܒܪܢܝܐ, ܫܒܪܘܢܐ.

ܫܒܪ, ܫܒܪܐ, ܫܒܪܬܐ from ܫܒܪ. *a)* subst. *an infant, young child, little boy* or *girl* under five years old. *b)* ܫܒܪܘܬܗ *her infancy. c)* adj. *infantile, childish, innocent, simple, silly, stupid.*

ܫܒܪܐ and ܫܒܪܘܪܐ, ܫܒܪܐ and ܫܒܪܐ. m. *peganum harmala, Syrian rue* used for wicks, *a wick.*

ܫܒܪܐܝܬ from ܫܒܪ. adv. *childishly, foolishly.*

ܫܒܪܘܢܐ, ܫܒܪܘܢܐ and ܫܒܪܘܢܝܐ dimin. of ܫܒܪܐ. m. *a little boy, tiny child.*

ܫܒܪܘܬܐ from ܫܒܪ. f. *infancy, childhood, youth; innocence, simplicity, childishness, silliness, folly.*

ܫܒܪܝܐ, ܫܒܪܝܬܐ from ܫܒܪ. *infantile, childish, puerile;* ܥܘܕܪܢܐ ܫܒܪܝܐ *tender age;* ܡܠܦܢܘܬܐ ܫܒܪܝܬܐ *teaching suited to children.*

ܫܒܪܢܝܐ, ܫܒܪܢܝܬܐ from ܫܒܪ. *infantile, childish.*

ܫܒܫ Pael ܫܒܫ *to wheedle.* Ethpa. ܐܫܬܒܫ *to be coaxed, wheedled.*

ܫܒܫܬܐ, ܫܒܫ̈ܐ and ܫܒܫ̈ܬܐ pl. ܫܒܫ̈ܝܢ, ܐ̈ܬ usually f. *a vine-shoot, sucker, slip, layer, branch, twig.*

ܫܒܫܬܐ f. *sorbus domestica, the service-tree.*

ܫܒܫܬܢܐ, ܐ̈ܬܐ from ܫܒܫܬܐ. *having long creeping branches.*

ܫܒܬ denom. verb Pael conj. from ܫܒܬܐ. *to keep the Sabbath.* Aph. ܐܫܒܬ *to keep Sabbath, take Sabbath rest;* ܐܫܒܬܬ ܐܪܥܐ *the land kept Sabbath.*

ܫܒܬܐ and ܫܒܐ pl. ܫܒ̈ܝܢ, ܫܒ̈ܐ f. *a*) *the Sabbath, Saturday;* ܝܘܡ ܫܒܬܐ or ܝܘܡܐ ܕܫܒܐ *the Sabbath day;* ܫܢܬܐ ܕܫܒܬܐ *the Sabbatical year;* ܒܝܬ ܫܒܬܐ *a synagogue,* also *a refectory. b*) *a week;* ܫܒܬܐ ܩܕܝܫܬܐ *Holy week;* ܫܒܬ ܫܒ̈ܐ *the week of weeks* i.e. *Easter week;* ܫܒܬܐ ܕܫܒܬܐ ܕܚܕܬܐ *Saturday in Easter week;* ܒܚܕ ܝܘܡ ܕܫܒܐ *on the first day of the week;* ܚܕ ܒܫܒܐ *Sunday;* ܚܕ ܒܫܒܐ ܚܕܬܐ *the First Sunday after Easter.* Derivatives, verb ܫܒܬ, ܡܫܒܬܢܐ, ܫܒܬܝܐ, ܫܒܬܐܝܬ, ܫܒܬܢܐ.

ܫܒܬܐ f. *anethum graveolens, dill.*

ܫܒܬܝܐ pl. ܐ̈ from ܫܒܬܐ. m. *a*) *the officer of the week, hebdomadary* of a monastery. *b*) *a Sabbatarian,* a heretic who observed the Jewish Sabbath.

ܫܒܬܐܝܬ from ܫܒܬܐ. adv. *on each Sabbath.*

ܫܒܬܢܝܐ pl. ܐ̈ from ܫܒܬܐ. *Sabbatical, on the Sabbath.*

ܫܒܬܒܫܒ̈ܐ; see ܫܒܒܫܒ̈ܐ.

ܫܓܐ fut. ܢܫܓܐ, act. part. ܫܓܐ, ܫܓܝܐ. *to stray, wander, err, swerve;* ܡܢ ܐܘܪܚܐ *from the way;* ܡܢ ܫܪܪܐ *from the truth;* ܐܣܒܪܘ ܕܫܓܐ ܗܘܐ *they thought he was wandering, delirious.* Aph. ܐܫܓܝ *to lead astray, mislead, delude;* ܪܘ̈ܚܐ ܒܝ̈ܫܬܐ ܡܫܓܝܢ ܠܥܠܡܐ *evil spirits leading the world astray;* ܪܘܚܐ ܕܡܫܓܝܐ ܠܚܙܘܐ *a wind blowing athwart the vision.* Derivatives, ܫܓܝܐ, ܫܓܝܐ, ܡܫܓܝܢܐ.

ܫܓܐ m. *teak-wood.*

ܫܓܕܐ, ܫܓܕܬܐ pl. ܫܓ̈ܕܐ f. *the almond* tree and fruit, esp. *the bitter almond* opp. ܚܠܝܐ *sweet almonds* but ܫܓ̈ܕܐ ܡܪ̈ܝܪܬܐ *bitter almonds;* ܩܠܦܐ ܫܓ̈ܕܐ ܬܪ̈ܝܐ *fresh almonds.*

ܫܓܘܠܐ m. *absorption, pre-occupation.*

ܫܓܘܡܐ rt. ܫܓܡ. m. *craft, subtlety.*

ܫܓܘܪܐ pl. ܐ̈ rt. ܫܓܪ. m. *a stoker.*

ܫܓܘܫܐ pl. ܐ̈ rt. ܫܓܫ. m. *a*) *troublesome, disturbing;* with ܠܐ *mild. b*) *factious, seditious, a partisan, revolutionary. c*) *soothing.*

ܫܓܘܫܘܬܐ rt. ܫܓܫ. f. *turbulence, disorderliness, unsteadiness.*

ܫܓܘܫܝܐ rt. ܫܓܫ. m. *a*) *commotion, tumult, sedition. b*) ܫ̈ ܕܐܐܪ̈ܐ, ܕܝܡܐ ܫ̈ *a tempest.*

ܫܓܘܫܬܢܐ rt. ܫܓܫ. *turbulent, seditious.*

ܫܓܘܫܬܢܘܬܐ rt. ܫܓܫ. f. *a*) *turbulence. b*) *soothing words, flattery.*

ܫܓܝܐ or ܫܓܝܐ rt. ܫܓܐ. m. *error, misleading.*

ܫܓܝܐ rt. ܫܓܐ. m. *a seducer, deceiver.*

ܫܓܝܡܘܬܐ rt. ܫܓܡ. f. *a venture, surmise.*

ܫܓܝܪܘܬܐ rt. ܫܓܪ. f. *glowing heat, ardour.*

ܫܓܝܫܐܝܬ rt. ܫܓܫ. adv. *violently, hastily.*

ܫܓܝܫܘܬܐ rt. ܫܓܫ. f. *commotion, disturbance, tumult;* ܝܡܐ ܕܫܓܝܫܘܬܐ *the boisterous sea;* ܦܪ̈ܨܘܦܐ ܕܫ̈ *frightful masks.*

ܫܓܠ m. Pers. *a jackal.*

ܫܓܠܐ perh. *a pier, jetty.*

ܫܓܡ fut. ܢܫܓܘܡ, act. part. ܫܓܡ, ܫܓܡܐ, pass. part. ܫܓܝܡ, ܐ̈. *a*) *to engage in, be occupied with, take to;* ܫܓܡܝܢ ܒܗܠܝܢ ܐܘܡܢܘ̈ܬܐ *they are engaged in these arts. b*) *to cajole, pervert, distract;* ܟܕ ܣܒܪ ܕܫܓܡ ܠܗ ܒܡ̈ܠܐ ܪ̈ܟܝܟܬܐ *thinking to cajole him with soft words.* Pass. part. *a*) *occupied, given up to, intent, engrossed;* ܫܓܝܡ ܗܘܐ ܒܩܪܝܢܐ *he was engrossed in study. b*) *cajoled, distracted;* ܐܝܟ ܐܢܫ ܐܢܐ ܕܫܓܝܡ ܒܠܒܗ *I am as one distraught.* Ethpe. ܐܫܬܓܡ *a*) *to occupy oneself, to be engaged in, intent upon, given up to;* ܒܨܒܘ̈ܬܐ ܡܕܝܢܝ̈ܬܐ ܡܫܬܓܡ ܐܢܐ *I am occupied in affairs of state;* ܠܐ ܡܢ ܐܟܘܠܘܬܐ ܘܡܢ ܙܢܝܘܬܐ ܐܫܬܓܡ *he attended to nothing but gluttony and vice. b*) *to be cajoled, deluded;* ܒܪܢܫܐ ܕܡܫܟܚ ܕܢܫܬܓܡ *a human being capable of being deluded.* Aph. ܐܫܓܡ *to occupy the attention, keep engaged;* ܐܫܓܡܘ ܠܗܘܢ ܕܥܠ ܫܘܪܐ *the assailants kept those on the ramparts fully engaged.* Derivatives, ܫܓܘܡܐ, ܫܓܝܡܘܬܐ, ܫܓܝܡܐ, ܡܫܬܓܡ, ܡܫܬܓܡܢܐ, ܡܫܬܓܡܢܘܬܐ.

ܫܓܘܫܝܐ pl. ܐ̈ rt. ܫܓܫ. m. a) *occupation, employment;* ܢܘܚܐ ܡܢ ܫܓܘܫܝܐ ܕܐܝܡܡܐ *rest from the labours of the day.* b) *cajolery, artifice.* c) *chance, haphazard, fortune;* ܒܫܓܘܫܝܐ *by chance, possibly, casually, indiscriminately, rashly;* ܕܫܓܘܫܝܐ *casual, chance, uncertain, fortuitous.*

ܫܓܘܫܝܐܝܬ rt. ܫܓܫ. adv. *regardlessly, without reflection.*

ܫܓܠܐ m. *a stone-cutter's saw.*

ܫܓܢܝ Pahli conj. from ܫܢܐ see verb ܫܢܐ. *to remove from its place; to alter, transform, translate;* ܟܠ ܕܡܫܓܢܐ ܟܬܒܐ ܡܢ ܕܝܪܐ ܗܢܐ *whoso removes a book from this monastery;* ܪܘܓܙܐ ܫܓܢܝ ܬܪܥܝܬܟ *wrath hath altered thine intent;* ܠܐ ܐܢܫ ܢܡܪܚ ܘܢܫܓܢܐ ܠܠܒܘܫܗܘܢ *let no one dare to alter their clothing.* Pass. part. ܡܫܓܢܝ, ܡܫܓܢܝܐ, ܡܫܓܢܝܬܐ *different, dissimilar; diverse, various;* ܦܩܥܐ ܡܫܓܢܝ̈ܢ ܪ̈ܝܚܐ *blossoms of varied odours;* ܕܡܫܓܢܝܢ ܒܡܫܡܥܘܬܐ *those of various hearing* i.e. *of different languages.* With ܠܐ *immutable.* Ethpahli ܐܫܬܓܢܝ a) *to be removed, displaced;* ܐܫܬܓܢܝܬ ܫܘܩܗ *his thigh was dislocated,* cf. ܫܢܬ ܫܘܩܗ. b) *to become different; to be altered in appearance, to change colour* or *expression; to disguise oneself;* ܐܫܬܓܢܝܬ ܡܕܝܢܬܐ ܒܥܝܢܘܗܝ *the city appeared changed to him.* c) *to change sides, desert one's party.* d) *to be distracted, confused;* ܐܫܬܓܢܝ ܗܘܢܝ *my mind was distracted.* e) *to be alienated* with ܡܢ of the pers. f) *to be subject to change, mutable.* Derivatives, ܫܘܓܢܝܐ, ܡܫܓܢܝܢܘ, ܡܫܓܢܝܢܘܬܐ, ܡܫܬܓܢܝܢܘܬܐ, ܡܫܬܓܢܝܢܐܝܬ, ܡܫܬܓܢܝܢܐ, ܡܫܬܓܢܝܢܘ.

ܫܓܓܐ pl. ܐ̈ m. *the murmur of running water.*

ܫܓܪ fut. ܢܫܓܘܪ, infin. ܡܫܓܪ, act. part. ܫܓܪ, ܫܓܪܐ, pass. part. ܫܓܝܪ, ܐ. a) *to kindle, heat* a bath, furnace, &c.; *to burn* incense; *to be hot, heated, warm, glowing;* ܬܢܘܪܐ ܕܫܓܪ *a glowing oven;* ܬܡܘܙ ܫܓܪ ܗܘܐ *July glowed.* Metaph. *to heat, inflame; to glow* of anger, desire, &c.; ܛܢܢܐ ܫܓܪܟ *zeal inflamed thee.* Pass. part. *burnt, fired; inflamed, ardent;* ܡܐܢܐ ܕܦܚܪܐ ܕܠܐ ܫܓܝܪ *an unburnt* i.e. *sun-dried potter's vessel;* ܟܠܣܐ ܫܓܝܪܐ *quick-lime;* ܣܕ̈ܪܐ ܫܓܝܪ̈ܐ ܕܪܒ ܚܝܠܐ ܡܝܟܐܝܠ *the ardent ranks of Michael.* b) *to pour forth, let run;* ܫܓܪ ܥܝ̈ܢܐ ܕܡ̈ܥܐ ܕܟܘܪܗܢܐ *eyes poured forth tears of misery.* Ethpe. ܐܫܬܓܪ a) *to be kindled, heated, to seethe; to be burnt, baked* as pottery; ܩܕܪܐ ܕܡܫܬܓܪܐ *a seething pot.* b) *to burn, glow* with fever, zeal, &c. c) *to come, present oneself, be at;* ܟܠܢܫ ܠܬܪܥܢ ܢܫܬܓܪ *every one should come to our gate.* Pa. ܫܓܪ a) *to let down* ܚܒܠܐ ܠܝܡܐ *a line into the sea.* b) perh. *to leave, quit.* Aph. ܐܫܓܪ *to remove, quit.* Derivatives, ܫܓܘܪܐ, ܫܓܝܪܘܬܐ, ܫܓܪܐ, ܫܓܪܐ, ܫܓܝܪܐ, ܫܓܝܪܘܬܐ, ܡܫܓܪܐ, ܡܫܓܪܢܐ.

ܫܓܝܪܐ rt. ܫܓܪ. m. *awakening, rousing.*

ܫܓܪܐ or ܫܓܝܪܐ rt. ܫܓܪ. usually ܫܓܪ ܡܝܐ *a drain, ditch, gutter.* Cf. ܫܩܝܐ.

ܫܓܕܐ better ܫܩܕܐ *an almond, a pistachio-nut.*

ܫܓܪܐ rt. ܫܓܪ. m. *kindling, heat, flame.*

ܫܓܝܪܘܬܐ rt. ܫܓܪ. f. a) *throwing away, throwing down.* b) *kindling.*

ܫܓܫ fut. ܢܫܓܘܫ, act. part. ܫܓܫ, ܫܓܫܐ, part. adj. ܫܓܝܫ, ܐ, ܬܐ. a) *to trouble, ruffle; to stir up* tumult, strife, sedition; *to provoke* war; ܫܓܫܘ ܠܥܡܐ ܘܠܩܫܝ̈ܫܐ *they stirred up the people and the elders;* ܠܐ ܕܚܠܬܐ ܫܓܫܐ ܠܢ *nor can fear disturb us.* b) *to be rough, boisterous, to rage* as the sea, with ܥܠ; ܫܓܫܘ ܥܠܘܗܝ ܥܠܥܠܐ ܩܫ̈ܝܐ *violent tempests broke over him.* c) *to stir, move, rustle;* ܐܝܟ ܚܝܘܬܐ ܕܫܓܫܐ ܒܓܘ ܚܘܫܒܐ *like a wild creature stirring in the wood.* d) *to dandle, coax, fawn on;* ܫܓܫܬܢܝ ܐܝܟ ܠܛܠܝܐ *she coaxed me as a child.* Part. adj. a) *troubled, perturbed, disorderly, boisterous;* ܝܡܐ ܫܓܝܫܐ *the troubled sea;* ܐܘܪ̈ܚܬܐ ܫܓܝܫܢ ܗܘܝ *the roads were disorderly, dangerous;* ܛܘܪ̈ܐ ܫܓܝܫܐ *mountains infested with robbers;* ܪ̈ܘܚܐ ܫܓܝܫܬܐ *boisterous winds.* b) act. sense *troubling, ruffling, stirring up strife.* c) *flattering, fawning.* Ethpe. ܐܫܬܓܫ *to be troubled, perturbed, uneasy, in uproar, noisy; to be tossed, ruffled;* chiefly of storm, tumult, war; ܐܫܬܓܫܘ ܡܫܪ̈ܝܬܐ ܒܚܘܠܛܢܐ *the hosts were mingled in confusion;* ܡܠܟܘܬܐ ܐܫܬܓܫܬ *the empire was in uproar.* Also

ܐܫܬܓܫ ܫܘܝܘܬܗ his health was upset; ܐܫܬܓܫ ܗܘܐ he was perturbed; ܘܠܐ ܡܫܬܓܫܢ ܡܢ ܡܕܡ untroubled, imperturbable. Pa. ܫܓܫ a) to stir up strife, rebellion; to throw into confusion. b) to wheedle, coax, soothe, assuage; ܡܫܓܫ ܫܓܫ ܚܝܘܬܐ he coaxed and soothed the wild beasts; ܫܓܫܗ ܠܟܘܡܪܐ ܟܕ ܐܣܪܗ ܠܗ he eased the sore by dressing it. Ethpa. ܐܫܬܓܫ a) to be troubled; to be clouded, turbid as wine. b) to be fawned on, cringed to, flattered; ܣܟܠܐ ܟܕ ܡܫܬܓܫ ܡܬܝܬܪ ܒܣܟܠܘܬܐ a fool flattered becomes yet more a fool. Derivatives, ܫܓܘܫܐ, ܫܓܘܫܘܬܐ, ܫܓܘܫܝܐ, ܫܓܘܫܝܬܐ, ܫܓܘܫܝܐܝܬ, ܫܓܫܝܬ, ܫܓܫܐ, ܫܓܝܫܐ, ܫܓܫܬܐ, ܡܫܓܫܢܐ, ܡܫܓܫܢܘܬܐ.

ܫܓܫܐ, ܫܓܫܬܐ rt. ܫܓܫ. cringing, fawning.

ܫܓܫܐ rt. ܫܓܫ. m. a) tumult, trouble. b) adulation.

ܫܓܝܫܐ, ܬܓܝܫܐ blear-eyed.

ܫܓܝܫܘܬܐ f. soreness of the eyes.

ܫܕܐ fut. ܢܫܕܐ, act. part. ܫܕܐ, ܫܕܝܐ, pass. part. ܫܕܐ, ܫܕܝܐ. a) to hurl, throw esp. to shoot an arrow, cast a stone, sling; ܫܕܝ ܓܐܪܐ or ܒܩܫܬܐ archers, bowmen; ܫܕܝ ܒܩܠܥܐ slingers; ܬܫܕܐ ܥܠܘܗܝ ܘܠܐ ܬܚܘܣ thou shalt hurl at him and not spare; ܫܕܐ ܗܘܐ ܨܘܚܝܬܐ ܥܠ ܛܛܪܝܐ he hurled abuse at the Tatars. With ܡܢ to throw away or cast off; with ܥܠ to add, impute. b) to cast out, expose infants, corpses; ܫܠܕܐ ܟܕ ܫܕܝܢ bodies cast abroad. c) of a horse to throw its rider; of a bull to toss. d) to pour, flow, empty itself; ܢܗܪܐ ܫܕܐ ܒܗܕܐ ܝܡܬܐ the stream empties itself into this lake. e) to drop unripe fruit; to cast, miscarry. f) to drop, upset; to throw down, ruin. g) to reject, eject, expel, depose with ܡܢ; ܫܕܝܘܗܝ ܡܢ ܡܕܝܢܬܐ—ܡܢ ܪܫܢܘܬܐ he expelled him from the city, from the magistracy; ܠܓܠܘܬܐ or ܠ to exile; ܫܕܐ ܡܢ ܥܕܬܐ ܘܡܢ ܫܘܬܦܘܬܐ he excommunicated. With ܐܝܕܐ to lay hands on, seize; ܐܠܦܐ to launch a ship; ܙܝܢܐ to lay down arms; ܬܪܣܐ to throw away a shield; ܟܣܦܐ to invest money; ܡܪܪܬܐ to be venomous; ܢܦܫܗ to cast himself down, throw himself on the earth; to expose himself, cast himself; ܡܨܝܕܬܐ to cast a net; ܫܪܫܐ or ܥܩܪܐ to take root; ܦܣܐ to cast lots, choose; ܦܝܢܟܐ to drop a tray; ܪܥܝܢܐ to apply the mind. Pass. part. cast, laid, lying; ܫܕܐ ܥܠ ܩܩܠܬܐ cast on the dungheap; ܚܙܐ ܚܘܝܐ ܪܒܐ ܫܕܐ ܒܐܘܪܚܐ he saw a great snake lying in the road. Ethpe. ܐܫܬܕܝ a) to be shot, discharged as an arrow; to be shot by an arrow. b) to be cast down to the ground; ܠܐܪܥܐ ܡܢ ܡܝܐ to be cast up by water; to be thrown away, cast out to perish; to be exposed ܠܥܩܬܐ to great trouble; ܠܫܝܛܘܬܐ to contempt. c) to be rejected, expelled, banished, exiled; to be deposed ܡܢ ܡܠܟܘܬܐ from the throne; ܡܢ ܬܫܡܫܬܐ from office. d) with ܒܬܪ to go after, yearn after. Pa. ܫܕܝ a) to hurl words, reproaches. b) to cast off clothes. Ethpa. ܐܫܬܕܝ to be cast out, exposed. Aph. ܐܫܕܝ to cast out, banish. Derivatives, ܫܕܘܝܐ, ܫܕܝܐ, ܫܕܝܐ, ܫܕܝܬܐ, ܫܕܝܬܐ, ܡܫܕܐ, ܡܫܕܝܢܐ, ܡܫܕܝܢܘܬܐ.

ܫܕܓܘܢܐ m. mace.

ܫܕܘܪܐ m. the thread on the shuttle; ܫ ܕܥܪܒܐ the thread of the woof.

ܫܕܘܝܐ rt. ܫܕܐ. m. a hurler, shooter of an arrow; a chucker out.

ܫܕܝܐ pl. ܐ̈ rt. ܫܕܐ. m. a) cloak, habit of a monk or nun. b) a thrower of stones, an archer, a sower.

ܫܕܝܐ rt. ܫܕܐ. m. a) hurling, throwing away; deposing. b) a throw, cast; a bowshot. c) ܫ ܕܡܝܐ a spout, conduit.

ܫܕܝܬܐ pl. ܬ̈ܐ rt. ܫܕܐ. f. a missile, dart, slingstone.

ܫܕܟ Pael ܫܕܟ to make proposals of marriage, offer marriage gifts. Pass. part. f. ܡܫܕܟܬܐ engaged to be married, promised in marriage. Ethpa. ܐܫܬܕܟ to be founded. Derivative, ܫܕܟܐ.

ܫܕܟܐ pl. ܐ̈ rt. ܫܕܟ. m. a) proposals of marriage, gifts before marriage. b) also written ܫܬܟܐ the laying of a foundation, preparation of a foundation or of an undertaking.

ܫܕܡܘܢܐ the edge of a sword-blade.

ܫܕܠ fut. ܢܫܕܘܠ, act. part. ܫܕܠ, pass. part. ܫܕܝܠ, ܐ. to soothe; to cajole, allure; ܫܕܠ ܘܡܐܣܐ it soothes and heals; ܨܒܬܐ ܫܕܝܠܬܐ ܕܛܠܝܘܬܗ the alluring ornaments of her youthfulness. Pa. ܫܕܠ to cajole, beguile, entice; to seduce; ܫܰܕܶܠ ܢܰܦܫܳܟ ܘܰܦܢܺܝ ܠܶܒܳܟ *indulge thyself and refresh thine heart;* ܡܫܰܕܶܠ ܠܰܐܪܥܳܐ ܘܡܪܰܟܶܟ man *coaxes the earth and softens it.* ETHPA. ܐܶܫܬܰܕܰܠ *to be cajoled, enticed;* ܐܶܫܬܰܕܰܠ ܒܶܗ ܐܳܕܳܡ ܡܶܢ ܚܶܘܝܳܐ Adam *was enticed by the serpent;* ܐܰܝܟ ܥܽܘܠܳܠܳܐ ܡܶܫܬܰܕܰܠ ܗܘܳܐ *he was cajoled like an infant.* DERIVATIVES, ܫܕܳܠܳܐ, ܫܽܘܕܳܠܳܐ, ܫܽܘܕܳܠܬܳܐ, ܫܰܕܳܠܳܐ, ܡܫܰܕܠܳܢܳܐ.

ܫܰܕܳܠܳܐ pl. ܶܐ rt. ܫܕܠ. *enticing, beguiling; a beguiler.*

ܫܽܘܕܳܠܳܐ and ܫܽܘܕܳܠܳܐ pl. ܶܐ rt. ܫܕܠ. m. *enticing, solicitation; a lure, bait.*

ܫܽܘܕܳܠܬܳܐ pl. ܳܬܳܐ rt. ܫܕܠ. f. *allurement.*

ܫܳܕܢܳܐ Pers. m. *bloodstone, haematite.*

ܫܕܪ PAEL ܫܰܕܰܪ *to send, send away, dismiss; to refer; to send forth* roots; *to send* word, a messenger, soldiers; with ܒ, ܠ, ܠܘܳܬ, ܡܶܢ; with ܒܳܬܰܪ *to send for, summon;* ܫܰܕܪܽܘܗܝ ܒܰܫܠܳܡܳܐ *they let him depart in peace;* ܫܒܺܝܝ ܢܫܰܕܰܪ *he shall let my captives go;* ܫܰܕܰܪ ܡܰܓܠܳܟ *send forth thy sickle;* ܫܰܕܰܪ ܕܰܠܝܳܐ *he let* a bucket *down into the well.* Often with other verbs: ܫܰܕܰܪ ܐܶܡܰܪ *he sent to say;* ܫܰܕܰܪ ܐܶܚܰܕܗ *he sent and seized him;* ܫܰܕܰܪ ܦܣܰܩܗ ܠܪܺܫܶܗ *he sent and cut off his head.* Pass. part. ܡܫܰܕܰܪ, ܡܫܰܕܪܳܐ *a messenger, legate, commissioner.* ETHPA. ܐܶܫܬܰܕܰܪ *a) to be sent out, commissioned;* ܗܘܳܐ ܓܰܒܪܳܐ ܕܶܐܫܬܰܕܰܪ ܡܶܢ ܐܰܠܳܗܳܐ *there was a man sent from God. b) to be thrown away.* DERIVATIVES, ܫܽܘܕܳܪܳܐ, ܡܫܰܕܪܳܢܳܐ, ܡܫܰܕܪܳܢܽܘܬܳܐ, ܡܫܰܕܪܳܢܺܝܬ, ܫܘܕܪܬܐ, ܫܰܕܪܽܘܬܳܐ.

ܫܶܕܝܳܐ rt. ܫܕܐ. m. *a) position, place, office. b)* dial. of Tacrit. *an earthen pot with two handles.*

ܫܗܳܐ, ܫܗܳܝ fut. ܢܶܫܗܶܐ, parts. ܫܳܗܶܐ, ܫܳܗܝܳܐ, ܫܳܗܝܳܬܳܐ and ܫܗܶܐ, ܫܗܶܝܳܐ, ܫܗܶܝܬܳܐ. *to grow cool, burn low, abate, relax;* ܫܗܳܬ ܢܽܘܪܳܐ *the fire burnt low;* ܡܶܢ ܢܰܦܫܶܗ ܫܗܳܬ the storm *fell of itself.* Both parts. = adj. *burning slowly; untilled, void, waste, lonely;* ܢܽܘܪܳܐ ܕܫܳܗܝܳܐ *a slow fire;* ܐܶܫܳܬܳܐ ܕܫܳܗܝܳܐ *a wasting fever;* ܙܳܘܺܝܬܳܐ ܫܗܶܝܬܳܐ *an obtuse angle;* ܡܰܕܒܪ̈ܳܐ ܫܗ̈ܶܝܳܐ *desolate wildernesses;* ܐܰܬܪܳܐ ܕܫܳܗܶܐ ܡܶܢ ܟܰܘܟܒ̈ܶܐ *a starless space;* ܫܳܗܶܐ ܡܶܢ ܙܰܘܥܳܐ *motionless.* PA. ܫܰܗܺܝ *a) to cool, abate, moderate;* ܫܰܗܰܘ ܢܽܘܪܳܐ ܕܚܶܡܬܟܽܘܢ *moderate the fire of your anger;* ܫܰܗܺܝ ܠܥܰܡܠܳܐ ܕܰܐܓܽܘܢܳܟ *he mitigated the labours of thy conflict. b) to make slack, weary;* ܐܶܢܳܐ ܡܫܰܗܝܳܐ ܐ̱ܢܳܐ *I am worn out;* ܡܚܺܝܠܳܐ ܘܡܫܰܗܝܳܐ *weak and languid.* ETHPA. ܐܶܫܬܰܗܺܝ *to be cooled, abated, allayed; to be overcome with weariness, wearied out;* ܐܶܫܬܰܗܝܰܬ ܡܶܙܓܳܗ ܛܳܒ *his temperature fell very low;* ܐܶܫܬܰܗܺܝ ܚܰܝܠܰܢ *our strength is worn out.* APH. ܐܰܫܗܺܝ *to allay* anger. DERIVATIVES, ܫܰܗܝܳܢܳܐ, ܫܗܳܝܳܐ, ܫܗܺܝܘܬܳܐ, ܫܳܗܝܳܐ, ܫܳܗܝܽܘܬܳܐ, ܡܫܰܗܝܳܢܳܐ, ܫܰܗܝܳܢܽܘܬܳܐ, ܡܫܰܗܝܳܢܳܐ, ܡܶܫܬܰܗܝܳܢܽܘܬܳܐ.

ܫܳܗܺܝܢܳܐ pl. ܶܐ m. *a falcon; parti-coloured, red and white.*

ܫܗܳܝܳܐ pl. ܶܐ rt. ܫܗܐ. m. *loss of heat.*

ܫܳܗܬܰܪܓ Pers. king's herb, perhaps *fumaria officinalis, fumitory,* used to soothe inflamed sores.

ܫܗܶܝܳܐ, ܫܗܶܝܬܳܐ Peal pass. part. emph. state of verb ܫܗܐ.

ܫܗܳܝܳܐ rarely ܫܗܺܝܳܐ rt. ܫܗܐ. m. *vacancy, loneliness;* ܫܗܳܝܳܐ ܕܢܰܦܫܳܐ *depression, sadness.*

ܫܳܗܝܽܘܬܳܐ pl. ܳܬܳܐ rt. ܫܗܐ. f. *emptiness, vacuity, a vacant space.*

ܫܗܰܪ fut. ܢܶܫܗܰܪ, act. part. ܫܳܗܰܪ, ܫܳܗܪܳܐ, ܫܳܗܪܳܬܳܐ, pass. part. ܫܗܺܝܪ. *to watch, keep vigil;* ܫܳܗܪܳܐ ܗܘܳܬ *she was awake;* ܫܳܗܪܺܝܢ ܫܰܗܪܳܐ *they say nocturns.* PA. ܫܰܗܰܪ *to keep diligent watch* with ܥܰܠ. APH. ܐܰܫܗܰܪ *to cause to watch; to be wakeful;* ܕܰܗܒܳܐ ܡܰܫܗܰܪ ܠܡܳܪ̈ܰܘܗܝ *gold makes its owners wakeful.* DERIVATIVES, the following words:—

ܫܗܰܪ, ܫܰܗܪܳܐ rt. ܫܗܪ. m. *a) a vigil, watch, watching;* ܫܰܗܪܳܐ ܘܨܰܘܡܳܐ *vigil and fast. b) the office of the night, nocturns. c) watching by the dead, a funeral feast, wake.*

ܫܰܗܳܪܳܐ, ܶܐ rt. ܫܗܪ. m. *vigilant; observing vigil.* Eccles. E-Syr. *a priest whose office it was to intone nocturns.*

ܫܳܗܪܳܐ part. Peal of verb ܫܗܪ = ܫܰܗܳܪܳܐ.

ܫܰܗܪܳܝܳܐ and ܫܰܗܪܳܢܳܝܳܐ, ܝܬܳܐ rt. ܫܗܪ. *nocturnal; of vigils* or *nocturns; keeping vigil.*

ܫܰܗܪܽܘܬܳܐ rt. ܫܗܪ. f. *vigils.*

ܫܘ abbreviation of ܫܽܘܒܚܳܐ.

ܫܘܳܐ fut. ܢܶܫܘܶܐ, act. part. ܫܳܘܶܐ, ܫܳܘܝܳܐ, ܫܳܘܝܳܬܳܐ, pl. m. ܫܳܘܶܝܢ, ܫܳܘܝܳܢܶܐ, pl. f. ܫܳܘܝܳܢ, ܫܳܘܝܳܬܳܐ, pass. part. ܫܘܶܐ, ܫܘܶܝܳܐ, ܫܘܶܝܬܳܐ, pl. ܫܘܶܝܢ, ܫܘܶܝܳܐ,

ܫܘܳܐ to be even; usually metaph. with ܕ or ܠ to be equal, sufficient; to be worth; to deserve, to be esteemed worthy; to agree with; ܗܳܢܳܐ ܟܽܠܶܗ ܠܳܐ ܫܳܘܶܐ ܠܺܝ all this does not suffice me; ܐ̱ܢܳܐ ܠܳܐ ܫܘܺܝܬ ܕܬܶܐܬܶܐ ܠܘܳܬܳܟ I was not worthy to come unto Thee; ܫܘܳܬ ܐܽܘܪܗܳܝ ܠܡܶܩܒܰܠ ܒܽܘܪܟܬܳܐ ܡܶܢ ܡܳܪܰܢ Edessa was deemed worthy to receive a blessing from our Lord; ܫܳܘܶܐ ܬܠܳܬܡܳܐܐ ܕܺܝܢܳܪܺܝܢ ܡܶܫܚܳܐ the oil is thought worth three hundred pence; ܫܳܘܶܐ ܘܙܳܕܶܩ it is meet and right; ܫܳܘܶܐ ܠܬܶܗܪܳܐ—ܠܬܶܕܡܽܘܪܬܳܐ remarkable, admirable; ܫܳܘܶܐ ܠܫܽܘܒܚܳܐ praiseworthy. Pass. part. a) level, even opp. ܡܥܰܡܩܳܐ depressed; ܐܰܦ̈ܶܐ ܫܘܰܝܳܬܳܐ ܕܠܶܒ̈ܢܶܐ level surfaces of bricks; ܡܶܢܝܳܢܳܐ ܫܘܶܐ an even number; ܫܢܬܳܐ ܫܘܺܝܬܳܐ an even year opp. ܟܒܺܝܫܬܳܐ bissextile. Gram. ܫܘܶܐ ellipt. for ܢܽܘܩܙ̈ܶܐ ܫ̈ the even points : serving to divide members of a sentence, ܫܘܰܝ ܦܣܽܘܩܳܐ these same points when at the end of a sentence. b) equal, in compos. fellow-, co-, con-, like-, ܫܘܶܐ ܠܐܰܒܳܐ equal to the Father; ܫܘܶܐ ܒܐܽܘܣܺܝܰܐ or ܫܘܶܐ ܒܐܽܘܣܝܳܐ co-essential, consubstantial = ὁμοούσιος; ܫܘܶܐ ܦܽܘܠܚܳܢܳܐ a fellow workman; ܫܘܰܝ̈ ܝܳܪ̈ܬܶܐ—ܦܠܚ̈ܶܐ fellow heirs, fellow soldiers; ܫ̈ ܪܶܥܝܳܢܳܐ like-minded; ܫ̈ ܡܶܨܥܳܝܳܐ concentric; ܫ̈ ܪܗܳܛܳܐ concurrent, accompanying; ܫ̈ ܫܡܳܐ homonymous; ܫ̈ ܫܰܪܒܬܳܐ of the same race; contemporary; ܫ̈ ܬܚܽܘܡܳܐ adjoining, contiguous.

Ethpe. ܐܶܫܬܘܺܝ a) to be equal, like, placed on an equality. b) to deserve, to be made or esteemed worthy esp of office, spiritual gifts &c.; ܐܶܫܬܘܺܝܬ ܕܐܶܚܙܶܐ I was counted worthy to see; ܐܶܫܬܘܺܝ ܠܐܶܦܺܝܣܩܽܘܦܽܘܬܳܐ he was preferred to the episcopate. c) to be of the same opinion, to agree, make an agreement, conspire with ܥܰܡ of the pers. and ܥܰܠ of the object; ܐܶܫܬܘܺܝܘ ܥܰܠ ܕܢܰܘܒܕܽܘܢܳܝܗ̱ܝ they conspired to ruin him; ܐܶܢ ܐܶܫܬܘܺܝ ܥܰܡ ܡܙܰܒܢܳܢܳܐ if he has come to terms with the seller. Pa ܫܰܘܺܝ pass. part. ܡܫܰܘܶܐ, ܡܫܰܘܝܳܐ. a) to lay even, spread over esp. to lay the table, make a bed, spread out a rug; ܫܰܘܺܝ ܥܰܠ ܚܡܳܪܳܐ he saddled the ass; ܫܰܘܺܝܬ ܥܰܪܣܝ I have made my bed; ܫܰܘܺܝܘ ܠܶܗ ܘܰܝܬܶܒ they made his place ready and he sat down; ܥܶܠܺܝܬܳܐ ܡܫܰܘܝܳܐ ܘܰܡܛܰܝܒܳܐ an upper room laid and set in order; ܡܫܰܘܝܳܐ ܒܟܺܐܦ̈ܶܐ paved; ܠܡܫܰܘܳܝܽܘ ܡܫܺܝܚܳܐܝܬ to smooth, soften. b) to wipe: ܠܡܫܰܘܳܝܽܘ ܪ̈ܶܓܠܰܘܗ̱ܝ ܒܣܰܥܪܳܗ̇ to wipe His feet with her hair. c) to treat as equal, treat alike; to proportionate; ܡܫܰܘܝܳܬܳܐ ܡܫܰܘܝܳܬܳܐ couplets. d) to agree, be like-minded with ܥܰܡ. Ethpa. ܐܶܫܬܰܘܺܝ to be laid low; to lie down at table; to be smoothed as a vine-cutting; to agree with ܥܰܡ; ܐܶܫܬܰܘܺܝܘ ܒܰܚܕܳܕ̈ܶܐ they held familiar intercourse. Aph. ܐܰܫܘܺܝ a) to level, make even, make equal, treat alike, make agree; ܐܰܫܘܰܘ ܠܫܒܺܝ̈ܠܰܘܗ̱ܝ make His paths level; ܐܰܫܘܰܘ ܐܺܝܕ̈ܰܝܟܽܘܢ spread out your hands; with ܒܶܝܢܳܬ ܐܰܚ̈ܶܐ ܠܡܰܫܘܳܝܽܘ to put things straight between brothers, make them agree; ܐܰܫܘܺܝܬ ܠܐ̱ܚܪ̈ܳܝܶܐ ܥܰܡ ܩܰܕ̈ܡܳܝܶܐ thou hast made the last equal to the first. b) to take part with, with ܥܰܡ. c) to make or deem worthy, to deign; ܠܳܐ ܐܰܫܘܺܝܘ ܠܡܶܥܒܰܕ ܦܶܨܚܳܐ they might not keep the Passover on account of pollution; ܐܰܫܘܳܢ ܕ or ܐܰܫܘܳܐ ܠܰܢ ܕ make us worthy to . . .; ܐܰܫܘܳܢܝ ܠܢܝܳܚܳܟ make me worthy to enjoy Thy rest; ܠܳܐ ܫܳܘܶܐ ܐܰܢ̱ܬ ܠܡܫܰܒܳܚܽܘ ܡܶܕܶܡ thou dost not deign to praise anything; ܠܚܰܕܒܫܰܒܳܐ ܐܰܫܘܺܝܘ they dedicated the first day of the week to the sun. Derivatives, ܫܘܳܝܳܐ, ܫܘܳܝܽܘܬܳܐ, ܫܘܰܝ, ܫܘܳܝܳܐܝܬ, ܫܘܝܽܘܬܳܐ, ܫܘܳܝܽܘܬܳܐ, ܫܘܺܝܬܳܐ, ܫܘܶܐ, ܫܘܳܝܬܳܐ, ܫܘܳܐ, ܫܘܝܳܐ, ܡܫܰܘܝܳܐ, ܡܫܰܘܝܽܘܬܳܐ, ܡܫܰܘܝܳܢܽܘܬܳܐ, ܫܘܳܝܘܬܳܐ.

ܫܽܘܐܳܠ, ܫܘܳܐܠܳܐ, ܫܽܘܐܠܳܐ, ܫܽܘܐܳܠܳܐ, ܫܽܘܐܳܠܳܐ pl. ܫܽܘܐ̈ܠܶܐ, ܫ̈ rt. ܫܐܠ. m. a) a petition, prayer. b) question, inquiry, query, case, debate; ܫܽܘܐ̈ܠܶܐ ܘܦܽܘܢܳܝ̈ܶܐ questions and answers, cases for discussion with their solutions; ܕܠܳܐ ܫܽܘܐܳܠ unquestionable, certain. c) cross-examination, questioning by torture. d) gram. interrogation.

ܫܰܘܳܠ the tenth Arabian month.

ܫܰܘܳܠ; see ܫܐܘܠ.

ܫܽܘܐܳܠܳܝܳܐ or ܫܽܘܐܳܠܳܝܳܐ rt. ܫܐܠ. gram. interrogative.

ܫܘܰܒ, ܫܳܒ ܫܘܒ part. ܫܳܐܶܒ, ܫܝܺܒܳܐ. a) to wither, be scorched esp. by hot wind; ܕܠܳܐ ܢܫܽܘܒܽܘܢ ܐܰܕܪ̈ܶܐ lest the young crops wither from heat. b) to hatch by heat as fishes. Pa. ܫܰܝܶܒ to blight with heat. Ethpa. ܐܶܫܬܰܝܰܒ to be blighted, scorched by strong sun. Derivatives, ܫܰܘܒܳܐ, ܫܽܘܒܳܐ, ܫܘܳܒܳܐ, ܫܽܘܒܳܐ, ܫܽܘܒܳܐ, ܫܽܘܒܳܬܳܐ.

ܫܰܘܒܳܐ rt. ܫܘܒ. m. parching or sultry heat,

sultriness, blight; ܪܘܚܐ ܕܫܘܒܐ or ellipt. *a sultry wind, the Simoom.*

ܫܘܒܗܪܐ from ܫܒܗܪ. m. *pride, pomp; boast, ostentation;* ܫܘܒܗܪܐ ܕܟܠܗ ܐܪܥܐ *the glory of the whole earth;* ܐܓܪܬܐ ܕܫܘܒܗܪܐ *a most pompous letter.*

ܫܘܒܚܐ pl. ܐ̈ rt. ܫܒܚ. m. *a) praise, honour, glory, splendour;* ܟܐܦܐ ܕܫܘܒܚܐ *precious stones;* ܟܠܝܠܐ ܕܫܘܒܚܐ *a crown of glory. b) a hymn of praise, ascription of glory, the Gloria Patri, doxology;* ܫܘܒܚܐ ܠܐܠܗܐ *Glory to God. c) a division of the Psalms* according to the Jacobites who divided the Psalter into XV ܡܪ̈ܡܝܬܐ each ܡܪܡܝܬܐ comprising four ܫܘܒ̈ܚܐ. *d)* = δόξα, *tenet, opinion;* ܬܪܝܨܘܬ ܫܘܒܚܐ *orthodoxy.*

ܫܘܒܚܘܢܐ pl. ܐ̈ dimin. of ܫܘܒܚܐ. m. *a boast.*

ܫܘܒܛܐ rt. ܫܒܛ. m. *a thin plate of metal;* ܫ ܕܕܗܒܐ *gold-leaf.*

ܫܘܒܠܐ from ܫܒܠ. m. *direction* in the monastic life; ܪܫ ܫܘܒܠܐ *the chief director, archimandrite.*

ܫܘܒܐ pl. ܐ̈ rt. ܫܘܒ. m. *sultriness, sultry wind.*

ܫܘܒܩܢܐ rt. ܫܒܩ. m. *a) release* from debt, sin, prison, *forgiveness;* ܫܢܬܐ ܕܫ *the year of release. b) being forsaken, left; repudiation;* ܟܬܒܐ ܕܫ *a bill of divorce;* ܫܘܐ ܠܫܘܒܩܢܐ *deserving to be abandoned,* also *venial, pardonable.*

ܫܘܒܪܐ = ܫܒܪܐ.

ܫܘܒܒܐ rt. ܫܒܒ. m. *coaxing, wheedling.*

ܫܘܒܬܐ rt. ܫܘܒ. f. *heat spots, eruption.*

ܫܘܒܬܐ from ܫܒܬܐ. m. *the keeping of the Sabbath.*

ܫܓ, ܫܐܓ root-meaning *to rub.* Pael ܫܝܓ *to wash.* Aph. ܐܫܝܓ act. part. ܡܫܝܓ, pass. part. ܡܫܝܓ, ܡܫܝܓܐ. *to wash, wash away, scour; to purify, expiate;* ܟܕ ܠܐ ܡܫܝܓܢ ܐܝܕܘܗܝ *with unwashen hands;* ܐܫܝܓ ܐܝܕܝܟ ܡܢܝ *wash thy hands of me;* ܛܘܦܢܐ ܐܫܝܓ ܠܟܠܗ ܕܪܐ *the flood swept away that whole generation.* Ettaph. ܐܬܬܫܝܓ *to be washed, scoured; to be purified, expiated.* Derivatives, ܫܝܓܬܐ, ܡܫܝܓܬܐ, ܡܫܝܓܬܐ, ܡܫܝܓܢܐ, ܡܬܫܝܓܢܘܬܐ.

ܫܘܓܢܝܐ pl. ܐ̈ from ܫܓܢ. m. *change, alteration, variation, transformation;* ܫ ܕܗܘܢܐ *mental confusion, aberration;* ܕܠܐ ܫ *invariable.* Logic. *a conversion.*

ܫܘܓܪ; see under ܫܓܪ.

ܫܘܓܪܐ rt. ܫܓܪ. m. *a hollow where water collects, a reservoir.*

ܫܘܓܪܐ rt. ܫܓܪ. m. *vileness.*

ܫܘܓܫܐ pl. ܐ̈ rt. ܫܓܫ. m. *a) uproar, tumult. b) blandishment, allurement.*

ܫܘܓܫܐ rt. ܫܓܫ. m. *pleasure, enjoyment.*

ܫܕܐ, ܫܕ act. part. ܫܕܐ, ܫܕܝܐ probably *to devastate;* ܫܕܝܐ ܕܛܗܪܐ Ps. xci. 6. But cf. ܫܐܕܐ.

ܫܕܪ Eshtaphal ܐܫܬܕܪ; see under ܫܕܪ.

ܫܘܕܠܐ or ܫܘܕܠ pl. ܐ̈ rt. ܫܕܠ. m. *wheedling, flattery; a compliment, bait.*

ܫܕܠ Shaphel conj. of verb ܫܕܠ.

ܫܘܕܪܐ pl. ܐ̈ rt. ܫܕܪ. m. *an embassy; expulsion; a portion.*

ܫܘܕܫܐ m. *a sixth part.*

ܫܘܕܝܐ rt. ܫܕܐ. m. *calming, a free space.*

ܫܘܕܠܐ and ܫܘܕܠܐ; see ܫܘܕܠܐ.

ܫܘܕܝܐ or ܫܘܕܝܐ pl. ܐ̈ rt. ܫܕܐ. m. *a promise; a declaration.* Gram. *protasis.*

ܫܘܕܥܬܐ and ܫܘܕܥܬܐ pl. ܐ̈ rt. ܫܕܥ. m. *a sign, mark, indication, signification; a narration; a catalogue, list.* Gram. *a predicate.*

ܫܘܙܒܐ and ܫܘܙܒܐ from ܫܘܙܒ. m. *deliverance, preservation, safety, refuge;* ܒܝܬ ܫ *an asylum, refuge;* ܫ ܕܡܫܝܚܐ *the salvation of Christ.*

ܫܘܚܐ rt. ܫܘܚ. m. *germination, origin.*

ܫܘܚܕܝܐ or ܫܘܚܕܝܐ rt. ܫܚܕ. m. *solitude.*

ܫܘܚܠܦܐ and ܫܘܚܠܦܐ pl. ܐ̈ rt. ܐܚܠ. m. *a) delay, tardiness. b) a gap, omission.*

ܫܘܛܚܐ m. *the spreading out* of the hands.

ܫܘܛܬܐ dial. of Tirhan. f. *a weaver's comb* or *shuttle.*

ܫܘܝܐ rt. ܫܘܐ. m. *a pavement.*

ܫܘܝܬܐ rt. ܫܘܐ. f. *a reel for winding yarn.*

ܫܘܝܘܢܐ; see ܫܘܝܢܐ.

ܫܘܝܪܐ; see ܫܝܪܐ.

ܫܘܘܙܐ rt. ܫܘܙ. m. *dancing; singing in chorus.*

ܫܘܙܦܬܐ oftener ܫܘܦܬܐ.

ܫܘܙܒ *to deliver, preserve, redeem, ransom;* ܡܫܘܙܒܐ *a refugee.* Eshtaph. ܐܫܬܘܙܒ *a) to be preserved, delivered; to escape. b) to be hatched* as fishes.

ܫܘܚ fut. ܢܫܘܚ, act. part. ܫܐܚ, ܫܝܚܐ. *to sprout, spring up, have origin, flourish;* ܙܪ̈ܥܐ ܕܫܝܚܝܢ *sprouting crops;* ܡܢ ܐܒܐ ܫܚ ܐܝܟ ܚܝ̈ܐ ܡܢ ܚܝ̈ܐ Christ *sprang from the Father as life from life;* ܡ̈ܠܐ ܕܡܢ ܦܘܡܗ ܫܝܚܝܢ ܗܘܝ *the words which sprang from her mouth;* ܢܫܘܚ ܒܝܘܡܘܗܝ ܙܕܝܩܐ *in His days shall the right flourish.* Aph. ܐܫܝܚ *a) to make to spring up; to foster;* ܡܛܪܐ ܕܡܫܝܚ ܠܙܝܙ̈ܢܐ *rain which makes the tares spring up. b) to bring forth;* ܐܫܝܚܬ ܠܡܫܝܚܐ Mary as a blessed field *brought forth* Christ. Derivatives, ܫܘܚܐ, ܫܘܚ, ܫܘܚܬܐ, ܡܫܘܚܐ, ܡܫܘܚܘܬܐ.

ܫܘܚ, ܫܚ act. part. ܫܐܚ, ܫܝܚܐ. *to melt* intrans., *to waste away, be consumed;* ܐܝܟ ܫܥܘܬܐ ܫܐܚ ܗܘܐ ܫܐܚ *it melts like wax;* ܫܚ ܠܒܝ ܒܓܘܝ *my heart melted within me;* ܫܚ ܟܠܗ ܒܣܪܗ ܡܢ ܢܘܪܐ *all his flesh was consumed by the fire.* Pa. ܫܚܚ *a) to waste away. b)* in the Lexx. *to dare, to attempt.* Aph. ܐܫܝܚ *a) to melt* trans., *to cause to waste;* ܦܪ̈ܢܣܘܬܐ ܡܫܝܚܢ ܠܦܓܪܐ *cares which waste the body. b) to presume, attempt; to defy, treat contemptuously* with ܥܠ; ܥܒܕܘ ܕܐܫܝܚܘ ܡܚܫܒܘ *they effected that which they boldly designed;* ܐܫܝܚܘ ܥܠ ܫܘܠܛܢܗ *they defied his power.* Derivatives, ܫܘܚܐ, ܫܚܚܐ, ܫܝܚܐ.

ܫܘܚܐ rt. ܫܘܚ. m. *a slip, shoot.*

ܫܘܚܠܦ Shaphel conj.; see ܚܠܦ.

ܫܘܚܕܐ pl. ܐ̈ rt. ܫܚܕ. m. *a bribe; blood-money; a forced contribution.* ܫܘܚܕܐ; see ܫܘܚܕܐ.

ܫܘܚܛܐ pl. ܬܐ̈ rt. ܫܚܛ. m. *perversity, perverse folly; a corrupt passage; deflowering.*

ܫܘܚܠܦ, ܫܘܚܠܦܐ pl. ܫܘܚܠܦ̈ܝܢ, ܬܐ̈ rt. ܚܠܦ. m. *a) change, alteration, variation, transformation;* ܥܐܕܐ ܕܫܘܚܠܦܐ *the Feast of Transfiguration. b) difference, variety, kind, species;* ܫܘܚܠܦ ܐܘܪ̈ܚܬܐ *various ways, different methods;* ܟܠ ܫܘܚܠܦܝܢ *all sorts of things, every manner of form. c) variation* in temperature, *season, solstice, tropic;* ܐܪܒܥܐ ܫܘܚܠܦܐ ܕܫܢܬܐ *four seasons of the year. d)* astron. *parallax;* music *modulation;* ܫܘܚܠܦ ܩܠܐ *hymns with variable tones;* gram. part of the names of various points.

ܫܘܚܠܦܐ rt. ܫܚܠ. m. *a) disorder. b) the strawberry-tree, arbutus.*

ܫܘܚܢܐ pl. ܐ̈ rt. ܫܚܢ. m. *an ulcer, abscess;* ܫܘܚܢܐ ܒܝܫܐ *cancer* or *elephantiasis.*

ܫܘܚܢܐ rt. ܫܚܢ. m. *fomentation, application of hot cloths.*

ܫܘܚܢܢܐ, ܢܝܬܐ rt. ܫܚܢ. *ulcerous.*

ܫܘܚܪ Shaphel conj. of ܐܚܪ.

ܫܘܚܪܐ pl. ܫܘܚܪ̈ܝܢ, ܐ̈ rt. ܫܚܪ. m. *a) blackness, foulness;* usually pl. *lampblack, soot, coals. b) forced labour. c)* for ܫܘܚܪܐ, see above.

ܫܘܚܪܐܝܬ rt. ܐܚܪ. with ܒ *slowly, deliberately.*

ܫܘܚܬܐ pl. ܬܐ̈ rt. ܫܚܬ. m. *rust, verdigris; tartar* on the teeth; *venom;* metaph. *foulness.*

ܫܘܚܬܢܐ rt. ܫܚܬ. *rusty, foul.*

ܫܘܛ, ܫܛ fut. ܢܫܘܛ, inf. ܡܫܛ, act. part. ܫܐܛ, ܫܝܛܐ, part. adj. ܫܝܛ, ܫܝܛܐ, ܫܝܛܬܐ. *to treat with contempt, to neglect;* ܡܫܛ ܫܛܗ *he treated him as beneath contempt;* ܐܢܬܘܢ ܫܛܬܘܢ ܠܡܣܟܢܐ *ye have dishonoured the poor;* ܫܛ ܠܡܫܪܝܬܐ ܘܠܐ ܝܗܒ ܠܗܘܢ ܐܦܣܢܝܐ *he neglected the army and gave them no pay.* Part. adj. *despised, contemptible, mean, worthless;* ܫܝܛ ܗܘ ܕܡܟ ܒܥܝܢܘܗܝ *Thy blood is as nothing in his sight;* ܒܩܐ ܫܝܛܐ *a wretched gnat;* ܪܟܫܐ ܫܝܛܐ *a sorry nag.* Ethpe. ܐܫܬܝܛ *to be despised, held in contempt, insulted.* Pa. ܫܘܛ *to treat with contempt.* Aph. ܐܫܝܛ *to treat with contempt, to render contemptible.* Derivatives, ܫܝܛܐ, ܫܝܛܘܬܐ, ܫܝܛܐܝܬ, ܫܘܛܐ, ܡܫܝܛܐ, ܡܫܝܛܘܬܐ, ܡܫܬܝܛܢܐ, ܡܫܬܝܛܢܘܬܐ.

ܫܘܛܐ pl. ܫܘܛ̈ܝܢ, ܐ̈ m. *a whip, lash, scourge, stroke.*

ܫܘܝܐ rt. ܫܘܐ. m. *a hilt, handle;* ܫ ܕܢܝܙܟܐ *the shaft of a spear.*

ܫܘܝܐܝܬ rt. ܫܘܐ. adv. *equally, alike, in like manner* or *proportion; at the same time, together.*

ܫܘܝܘ, ܫܘܝܘܬܐ rt. ܫܘܐ. f. *a plane, level surface; equality, agreement; equity;* with ܠܐ *disagreement, inequality;* ܒܫܘܝܘ *equally, together, alike;* ܫܘܝܘ ܚܕܐ *with one consent.* In construction *like-, co-, con-, equi-;* ܐܘܣܝܘܬܐ ܫ *consubstantiality;* ܐܝܬܘܬܐ ܫ *co-essentiality;* ܫ ܕܐܝܡܡܐ ܘܕܠܠܝܐ *the equinox;* ܫ̈ ܕ ܡܕܝܢܬܐ *the equator;* ܫ ܕܬܫܪܝܢ *the autumnal equinox;* ܫ ܡܥܡܪܐ *co-habitation;* ܫ ܬܩܠܐ *equipoise;* ܫ ܢܦܫܬܐ *unanimity;* ܫ ܩܠܐ *harmony, a concert;* ܫ ܪܗܛܐ *a concourse;* ܒܫܘܝܘܬ ܫܡܐ *having the same name.*

ܫܘܝܘ, ܫܘܝܘܬܐ rt. ܫܘܐ. f. *dignity, worth;* ܠܐ ܒܕܠܐ ܫܘܝܘ *unmerited;* ܠܐ ܫܘܝܘܬܝ *my unworthy self.*

ܫܘܝܘܬܢܝܐ adj. from ܫܘܝܘܬܐ. *equinoctial.*

ܫܘܚܢ, ܫܘܚܢܐ rt. ܫܚܢ. m. *melting, softening.*

ܫܘܚܢܘܬܐ rt. ܫܚܢ. f. *vital force, growth.*

ܫܘܚܠܐ *artemisia arborescens,* a healing herb.

ܫܘܝܢܐ from ܫܝܢ. m. *pacification.*

ܫܘܝܦܐ pl. ܐ̈ rt. ܫܘܦ. m. *a) rubbing, friction.* Metaph. *stroking, coaxing. b) a rein.*

ܫܘܝܬ = ܫܘܝܐܝܬ and ܫܘܝܐ: rt. ܫܘܐ. adv. *simultaneously, together.*

ܫܘܝܟܘܬܐ rt. ܫܘܐ. f. *reduction, low price.*

ܫܘܝܬܐ pl. ܫܘܝ̈ܬܐ rt. ܫܘܐ. f. *a thick cord* esp. *a measuring-line;* ܫ ܕܦܪܙܠܐ *a wire rope.*

ܫܘܫܦܐ or ܫܘܫܦܢܐ m. pl. dial. = ܫܘܫܡܦܐ *a rash.*

ܫܘܟܠܠܐ rt. ܟܠܠ. m. *completion, finishing;* ܫ ܕܟܠܗܘܢ *the best of all.*

ܫܘܟܢܐ less commonly ܫܘܟܘܢܐ pl. ܐ̈ rt. ܫܟܢ. m. *a) a gift, grace* esp. *a spiritual gift, office, holy orders;* ܗܢܘܢ ܕܠܐ ܦܠܚܘ ܫܘܟܢܝܗܘܢ *those who have not cultivated their gifts. b) a charitable bequest, legacy.*

ܫܘܟܢܝܐ rt. ܫܟܢ. *relating to legacies.*

ܫܘܟܦܐ m. *covering over.*

ܫܘܟܪ, ܫܘܟܪܐ rt. ܫܟܪ. m. *abuse, insult, dishonour; a disgrace, shameful deed.*

ܫܘܟܬܐ rt. ܫܟܬ. m. *sediment, lees* of wine or oil; *secretions, faeces.* In the Lexx. *skin disease, eruption, erysipelas.*

ܫܘܟܬܢܐ, ܫܘܟܬܢܝܬܐ rt. ܫܟܬ. *sedimentary, feculent.*

ܫܘܠܐ; see ܫܘܠܐ.

ܫܘܠܒܒܐ pl. ܐ̈ *a) bird's fat;* ܫ ܕܘܙܐ *goose-grease. b) the glutinous matter secreted in the corner of the eye and on the eyelashes.* Cf. ܫܘܠܒܦܐ.

ܫܘܠܒܝܐ pl. ܐ̈ m. = ܫܘܠܒܦܐ.

ܫܘܠܗܒܐ pl. ܐ̈ rt. ܠܗܒ. *a)* m. *heat, inflammation; a conflagration;* ܫܘܠܗܒ ܕܡܥܐ *burning tears. b) the hearth of an altar.*

ܫܘܠܗܘܒܐ from ܫܠܗܒ. m. *blowing* upon any object, as a magician does.

ܫܘܠܚܢܐ rt. ܫܠܚ. m. *degradation from office.*

ܫܘܠܛܦܬܐ, ܫܠܛܦܬܐ f. *lathyrus sativa, everlasting pea.*

ܫܘܠܛܢ, ܫܘܠܛܢܐ pl. ܐ̈ rt. ܫܠܛ. m. *a) power, authority, right;* ܫܘܠܛܢ ܐܪܥܐ *the temporal power;* ܫ ܢܦܫܐ *free-will;* ܠܝܬ ܫ ܕ *it is not allowed, he has not the right to . . . . b) rule, government, sway; charge, office; a province, diocese;* ܫ ܕܦܠܚܘܬܐ *military rule;* ܫ ܙܥܘܪܐ *oligarchy;* ܫ ܕܐܘܪܗܝ *the diocese of Edessa. c) a ruler, commander, prince, sultan. d)* pl. *dominions* the sixth order of angels.

ܫܘܠܛܢܘܬܐ rt. ܫܠܛ. f. *power, empire, the sultanate.*

ܫܘܠܛܢܝܐ rt. ܫܠܛ. adj. *conferring authority; imperial.*

ܫܘܠܡ, ܫܘܠܡܐ rt. ܫܠܡ. m. *the end of a fixed period* as ܫܒܬܐ, ܫܢܬܐ, ܨܘܡܐ ܫ *of a week, the year, Lent;* often = ܫܪܝܐ and opp. ܫܘܪܝܐ or ܪܫܐ *the beginning. End, completion, consummation;* with ܚܝܐ or ܫܢ̈ܝܗ̇ *end of life;* ܥܠܡܐ or ܙܒܢܐ ܫ *the consummation of this age* or *world;* ܟܕ ܫܘܠܡ ܙܒܢܐ *when the time was fully come;* ܐܝܟ ܫܘܠܡܐ ܕܣܘܥܪܢܐ ܗܘܐ *as the event showed;* ܒܫܘܠܡܐ *at the end, after, finally;* ܕܠܐ ܫ *endless.* With ܡܛܐ *to come to an end, cease;* with ܢܣܒ or ܩܒܠ *to be fulfilled, completed.*

ܫܘܠܦܐ rt. ܫܠܦ. m. *a) the blade* of a knife. *b)* = ܫܠܦܐ.

ܫܘܠܦܦܐ and ܫܘܠܒܦܐ m. *rump-fat* of partridges, pheasants, or pigeons.

ܫܘܠܩܦܐ pl. ܐ̈ from ܫܠܩ = ܢܦܚ *to blow,*

swell. m. *a) a floating bubble. b) a blister, boil, swelling; inflammation of the eye; smallpox.*

ܬܘܡܒܥܬܐ pl. ܬܵܐ f. = ܬܘܡܒܥܳܐ *b.*

ܬܘܡܟܠܐ rt. ܡܟܠ. m. *a decoction.*

ܬܘܡܟܠܐ from ܡܟܠ. m. *progressive desire.*

ܬܘܡ pass. part. ܬܡܝܥܐ. *stricken, pain-stricken.* Aph. ܐܬܡܥ *to inflict pain, to cut, wound;* ܚܛܗܐ ܕܡܬܡܥ ܘܡܬܡܥܐ ܠܢ *sin which strikes and wounds us.* Derivatives, ܬܘܡܥܬܐ, ܡܬܡܥܢܐ, ܬܡܥܢܘܬܐ.

ܬܘܡܗܐ, ܬܘܡܗܬܐ rt. ܬܡܗ. m. *a name, surname, appellation, title; fame, renown;* ܒܬܘܡܗܐ ܕܫܡܐ *nominally;* ܪܡ ܬ̈ *of high fame;* ܩܢܐ ܬ̈ *he gained a name, renown;* ܬ̈ ܕܣܘܩܒܠܐ *antiphrasis.* Gram. *an epithet, attributive adjective* opp. ܫܡܐ *a substantive.*

ܬܘܡܗܐܝܬ rt. ܬܡܗ. adv. *nominally* opp. ܒܫܪܪܐܝܬ *really.*

ܬܘܡܗܝܐ, ܬܵܐ rt. ܬܡܗ. *nominal, appellative.*

ܬܘܡܬܐ f. perh. *the upper part of the body.*

ܬܘܡܠܝܐ pl. ܬܵܐ rt. ܬܡܠ. m. *a)* in the O. T. *consecration, perfection;* ܕܟܪܐ ܕܬ̈ *the ram of consecration;* ܥܐܕܐ ܕܬ̈ *the feast of ingathering;* ܬܘܡܝܡ ܘܐܘܪܝܡ *Thummim and Urim. b) completion, complement, fulfilment, accomplishment, conclusion, finality;* ܬܘܡܠܝܐ ܕܒܢܝܢܐ *completion of a building;* ܬ̈ ܕܫܢܬܐ *end of the year. c)* eccles. *perfection* in the religious life; *performance, conclusion, consummation* of a rite; *confirmation* of a bishop by the Patriarch; ܬ̈ ܕܟܗܢܘܬܐ ܪܒܬܐ *ordination, confirmation. d) full age, ending* of life; *maturity, ripeness* of fruit. *e)* gram. *termination.*

ܬܘܡܠܝܢܐ and ܬܘܡܠܝܢܝܐ, ܬܵܐ rt. ܬܡܠ. *efficient, complementary.*

ܬܘܡܫܢܐ rt. ܬܡܫ. m. *fat, fatness, plumpness; the best part;* ܬܘܡܫܢܗ ܕܚܠܒܐ *cream;* ܬ̈ ܕܐܪܥܐ *the fat of the land;* ܬ̈ ܕܚܛܐ *the best wheat;* ܚܛܐ ܕܐܦܝܩ ܫܒܠܐ ܘܐܬܡܫܢ *wheat which has formed ears and filled out;* ܬ̈ ܕܡܘܪܐ *stacte, oil of myrrh.*

ܬܘܡܫܢܐ rt. ܬܡܫ. m. *obesity.*

ܬܘܡܬܐ or ܬܡܬܐ m. *anethum foeniculum, anise.*

ܬܘܦܪܐ pl. ܬܵܐ rt. ܬܦܪ. m. *a)* eccles. *reservation, inhibition. b)* in the Lexx. *discharge* of arrows; *being emptied out, poured out.*

ܬܘܦܪܢܝܐ rt. ܬܦܪ. *spilt, overflowing.*

ܬܘܨܦܬܐ pl. ܬܘܨܦܐ, ܬܵܐ rt. ܬܨܦ. f. *a) a sore, swelling, spot, scurvy spot, plague spot; a scab, scar;* ܬ̈ ܚܘܪܬܐ *a white rising* in the skin; ܬ̈ ܕܟܘܝܐ *scar over a burn;* ܬܘܨܦܬܗ ܕܡܫܝܚܐ *marks of Christ, scars of sufferings borne for His sake;* ܬ̈ ܕܒܐܦܝ ܣܗܪܐ *spots on the face of the moon. b)* pl. *whiskers;* ܬ̈ ܕܕܩܢܐ *the beard;* ܛܠܝܐ ܕܠܐ ܬܘܨܦܬܐ *a beardless boy;* ܢܦܩܘ ܬܘܨܦܬܗ *his beard sprouted. c)* pl. *crumbs* of the Eucharistic bread.

ܬܘܪܐ = ܬܘܪܐ *torment.*

ܬܘܢܝ, ܬܘܢܝܐ rt. ܬܢܐ. m. *a) change, changing, transition, vicissitudes. b) removal, migration, departure* esp. from this life; ܥܐܕܐ ܕܬ̈ *the Festival of the Assumption* of the B. V. M.; ܬܘܢܝ ܢܦܫܬܐ *transmigration. c) translation* from one see to another; of relics. *d) defection.*

ܬܘܢܐ or ܬܘܢܝܐ m. *vitex agnus castus, tree of chastity.*

ܬܘܢܝܐ pl. ܬܵܐ rt. ܬܢܐ. m. *suffering, punishment, torment, torture, bad usage.*

ܬܘܢܝܢܐ rt. ܬܢܐ. m. = ܬܘܢܝܐ.

ܬܘܪܐ m. *a cat.*

ܬܘܫ, ܬܫ fut. ܢܬܘܫ, act. part. ܬܐܫ, ܬܐܫܐ, part. adj. ܬܝܫ, ܬܝܫܐ, ܬܝܫܬܐ. *to daub, besmear, pitch; to stop up, obstruct* with clay, wax, pitch; *to rub with ointment;* metaph. *to stop* the eyes, ears, nostrils, heart; ܬܐܫ ܠܬܪܥܐ ܕܐܬܘܢܐ *he stops up the doors* of the furnace *with clay;* ܬܐܫܐ ܥܝܢܐ *the eye is dulled.* Part. adj. *a) daubed over, covered; closed, stopped;* ܠܘܚܐ ܕܬܝܫܝܢ ܒܩܪܘܬܐ *tablets covered with wax;* ܬܝܫ ܒܡܕܥܐ *dull of understanding;* ܩܒܪܐ ܬܝܫܐ *a sealed sepulchre. b) headlong, ill-considered.* Ethpe. ܐܬܬܝܫ *to be smeared over; to be dull* as the eyes. Aph. ܐܬܝܫ *to smear with clay.* Derivatives, ܬܝܫܐ, ܬܝܫܐܝܬ, ܬܝܫܘܬܐ.

ܬܘܫ Ettaphal ܐܬܬܘܫ denom. from ܬܘܫܐ. *to be petrified.*

ܫܘܥܳܐ pl. ܳܐ m. *rock, a rock;* ܬܶܠܳܐ ܕܫܽܘܥܳܐ *a rocky hill.*

ܫܽܘܥܒܳܕ, ܫܽܘܥܒܳܕܳܐ rt. ܥܒܕ. m. *a) subjection, oppression, servitude. b) submission, obedience;* ܕܠܳܐ ܫ *unruly;* ܡܫܰܥܒܕܺܝܢ ܠܗ ܫܽܘܥܒܳܕܶܗ *subject to him. c) domination, tyranny. d) the district subject to a city, its dependencies.*

ܫܽܘܥܳܢܳܝܳܐ, ܝܬܳܐ from ܫܽܘܥܳܐ. adj. *rocky, stony, growing on rocks;* ܢܽܘܢܶܐ ܫܽܘܥܳܢܳܝܶܐ *fishes living on a gravelly bottom.* Metaph. *firm, solid.*

ܫܽܘܥܠܳܝܳܐ rt. ܫܥܠ. m. *scurrility.*

ܫܽܘܥܺܝܬܳܐ pl. ܝܳܬܳܐ rt. ܫܥܐ. f. *a) talk, talking, discourse; chatter. b) a tale, story, fable. c) the plot* of a tragedy.

ܫܽܘܥܠܳܐ m. *the hollow of the hand, a handful.*

ܫܽܘܥܠܳܝ, ܫܽܘܥܠܳܝܳܐ rt. ܫܥܠ. m. *magnificence, pride, arrogance.*

ܫܽܘܥܳܢܳܝܳܐ, ܝܬܳܐ from ܫܽܘܥܳܐ. *made of stone.*

ܫܽܘܥܳܢܳܝܽܘܬܳܐ from ܫܽܘܥܳܐ. f. *rocky hardness.*

ܫܽܘܥܠܳܝܳܐ rt. ܫܥܠ. m. *making glossy* or *smooth.*

ܫܘܦ, ܫܳܦ fut. ܢܫܽܘܦ, act. part. ܫܳܐܶܦ, ܫܳܝܦܳܐ, pass. part. ܫܺܝܦ, ܫܺܝܦܳܐ. *a) to file, scrape; to rub;* ܒܺܐܝܕܳܐ *with the hand;* ܒܫܽܘܦܺܝܢܳܐ *with a file;* ܟܠܰܚ ܫܳܝܦܳܐ ܒܶܐܠܶܐ ܒܺܐܝܥܶܐ ܘܝܳܬܒܳܐ ܥܠܰܝܗܶܝܢ the halcyon *scrapes her eggs about in the sand and sits upon them. b) to rub, apply salve* or *massage;* ܫܳܐܶܦ ܢܰܦܫܶܗ ܒܺܐܝܠܳܢܶܐ *he rubs against trees;* ܫܳܦ ܠܶܗ ܠܟܪܺܝܗܳܐ ܡܫܺܝܚܳܐ *he rubbed the patient* with embrocation; ܕܢܶܫܽܘܦܽܘܢ ܣܺܐܩܳܐ ܥܰܠ ܚܰܨܰܝܗܽܘܢ *that they should rub red ochre on their loins.* Ethpe. ܐܶܫܬܺܝܦ *a) to be rubbed;* ܩܰܝܣܳܐ ܟܰܕ ܡܶܫܬܺܝܦ ܫܳܚܶܢ *wood grows hot with friction b) to be rubbed on, applied* as oil or salve. Pa. ܫܰܘܶܦ *to rub, chafe, polish; to lick* wounds as a dog; *to stroke, fondle;* ܢܶܟܠܶܐ ܡܫܰܘܦܶܐ *polished wiles.* Ethpa. ܐܶܫܬܰܘܰܦ and wrongly ܐܶܫܬܰܘܰܦ *to be rubbed in; to be rubbed with oil &c.;* metaph. ܚܽܘܣܳܕܳܐ ܕܐܶܫܬܰܘܰܦ ܒܶܗ *the opprobrium that has been fastened on him.* Aph. ܐܰܫܺܝܦ *to rub, make plain, to accommodate* ܠܘܳܬ ܢܰܦܫܶܗ *to himself.* Derivatives, ܫܽܘܦܳܐ, ܫܽܘܦܳܝܳܐ, ܫܽܘܦܳܢܳܐ, ܫܺܝܦܳܐ, ܫܽܘܦܳܝܳܐ, ܫܽܘܦܳܦܳܐ, ܫܽܘܦܳܦܽܘܬܳܐ, ܫܳܝܽܘܦܳܐ, ܫܺܝܦܬܳܐ, ܡܫܰܘܦܳܢܺܝܬ.

ܫܽܘܦܳܐ or ܫܽܘܦܳܐ pl. ܳܐ rt. ܫܘܦ. m. *a) friction, attrition. b) polish. c) chafing, inflammation of the skin caused by riding* or *walking;* ܫ ܕܡܣܳܢܶܐ *the galling* or *wringing of shoes. d) filings;* ܫ ܕܦܰܪܙܠܳܐ *steel* or *iron filings;* ܫ ܕܩܺܝܣܶܐ *embers, wood-ash. e) brooding;* ܫ ܐܰܠܳܗܳܝܳܐ *the fostering care of God. f)* ܫ ܕܡܰܥܰܝܳܐ *moving* or *slipperiness of the intestines, dysentery.*

ܫܽܘܦܳܐ = ܐܶܫܽܘܦܳܐ.

ܫܽܘܦܳܝܳܐ rt. ܫܘܦ. m. *lubricating grease;* ܫ ܕܚܙܺܝܪܳܐ *hog's grease, lard.*

ܫܽܘܦܳܦܳܐ rt. ܫܘܦ. m. *scrubbing, rubbing, shampooing, massage.*

ܫܽܘܦܺܝܢܳܐ pl. ܳܐ rt. ܫܘܦ. m. *a file.*

ܫܽܘܦܠܳܐ rt. ܫܦܠ. m. *exhaustion, utter weariness, collapse.*

ܫܽܘܦܠܳܐ rt. ܫܦܠ. m. *a footstool.*

ܫܽܘܦܳܢܳܐ rt. ܫܘܦ. m. *oil, polish.*

ܫܽܘܦܝܢܳܝܬܳܐ, ܫܽܘܦܝܢܳܝܳܐ, ܫܽܘܦܝܢܺܝܢ pl. ܺܝܢ, ܳܐ m. and f. *a turtle-dove, pigeon.*

ܫܽܘܦܳܟ, ܫܽܘܦܳܟܳܐ pl. ܳܐ rt. ܫܦܟ. m. *a) pouring* e.g. of oil upon the head; ܫܽܘܦܳܟ ܕܡܳܐ *bloodshed;* ܫ ܕܪܽܘܚܳܐ *outpouring of the Holy Spirit. b)* in the Lexx. *injection* by the nostrils.

ܫܽܘܦܳܦܳܐ rt. ܫܘܦ. m. *a covering, veil.*

ܫܽܘܦܳܪܳܐ pl. ܺܝܢ, ܳܐ rt. ܫܦܪ. m. *a) grace, fairness, beauty;* ܡܠܶܐ ܫܽܘܦܪܳܐ *full of grace, most fair;* ܫ ܕܐܰܪܥܳܐ—ܕܥܳܢܳܐ *the best of the land, of the flock. b) a fair deed, virtue; a grace, favour;* ܫ ܐܰܠܳܗܳܝܶܐ *divine virtues.*

ܫܽܘܦܳܪܕܶܩܢܳܐ pl. ܳܐ rt. ܫܦܪ. *a flatterer, fawner.*

ܫܽܘܦܳܪܕܶܩܢܽܘܬܳܐ rt. ܫܦܪ. f. *flattery, adulation.*

ܫܽܘܦܳܪܳܐ rt. ܫܦܪ. m. *complacence; obsequiousness.*

ܫܽܘܦܪܳܝܳܐ rt. ܫܦܪ. adj. *of beauty* or *virtue;* ܫ ܡܫܰܒܗܪܳܐ *glorying in beauty or in virtue.*

ܫܽܘܦܪܳܢܳܐ rt. ܫܦܪ. *a) the act of pleasing, cringing. b) obsequious, vain.*

ܫܽܘܦܪܳܢܳܐܺܝܬ rt. ܫܦܪ. adv. *obsequiously.*

ܫܽܘܦܪܳܢܽܘܬܳܐ rt. ܫܦܪ. f. *flattery, adulation, currying favour.*

ܫܽܘܦܪܳܢܳܝܳܐ rt. ܫܦܪ. *obsequious.*

ܫܽܘܦܳܪܬܳܢܳܐ rt. ܫܦܪ. m. *a flatterer.*

ܫܽܘܦܬܳܐ rt. ܫܦ. f. ܫ ܕܢܚܺܝܪܶܐ *the partition, cartilage of the nostrils.*

ܫܘܩܪܐ and ܫܘܩܪ m. *mugwort, artemisia*.

ܫܘܩ imper. of verb ܢܫܩ *to kiss*.

ܫܘܩ, ܫܘܩܐ pl. ܶܐ m. *a*) *an open space;* with ܒ or ܠ *abroad, out-of-doors, out.* *b*) *a street, square, market-place, market, bazaar;* ܫܘܩܐ ܕܢܚܬܘܡܐ *the bakers' quarter, bread-market;* ܫܘܩܐ ܠܓܝܪܐ *alleys;* ܫ̈ ܕܠܐ ܡܦܩܢܐ ܣܡܝܐ *blind alleys;* metaph. ܫ̈ ܕܝܡܐ ܕܡܝܐ *the watery ways of the sea.* *c*) *forum, place of assembly, court.* *d*) *a laura*, row of monastic cells. *e*) *a quarter* of a city; ܫ̈ ܬܠܝܬܝܐ ܕܒܓܕܕ *the third quarter of Baghdad.*

ܫܘܩܝܐ, ܫܘܩܝܬܐ from ܫܘܩܐ. *a*) *a huckster, petty trader; a sutler, camp-follower.* *b*) *a court-day, a public pleader.*

ܫܘܩܠܐ rt. ܫܩܠ. m. *arrogance.*

ܫܘܩܦܐ pl. ܶܐ rt. ܫܩܦ. m. *a*) *buffeting, beating, dashing to the ground, slaughter; castigation, tribulation.* *b*) *a blow, bruise;* ܫܘܩܦ ܦܟܐ *a slap on the cheeks, box, cuff.* *c*) *being beaten to the ground* as crops, *meagreness* of a crop. *d*) *a contention.*

ܫܘܩܪܐ pl. ܶܐ rt. ܫܩܪ. m. *lying, falsehood;* ܫ̈ ܕܡܘܡܬܐ *perjury;* ܫ̈ ܕܣܗܕܘܬܐ *false witness.*

ܫܘܪ fut. ܢܫܘܪ, act. part. ܫܐܪ, ܫܐܪܐ. *a*) *to leap, bound, spring, jump; to spring to* as a trap; ܕܢܫܘܪ ܠܡܥܒܪ̈ܐ *to jump the ditches;* ܫܘܪ ܗܘܐ ܠܐܠܦܐ *he leapt into the ship;* ܓܐܪ̈ܐ ܕܫܝܪܝܢ ܡܢ ܩܫ̈ܬܐ *arrows darting from the bows;* ܫܘܪ ܥܝܢ̈ܘܗܝ ܠܒܪ *his eyes started out;* ܫܘܪ ܘܥܪܩ *he bounded away;* ܫܘܪ ܠܥܠ *he leapt up.* *b*) *to rise, swell, mount up;* ܐܦ ܙܦܬܐ ܫܘܪܬ ܘܣܠܩܬ *the pitch bubbled up;* ܠܡܐܐ ܕܡܛܐ ܫܐܪ *it mounts up to a hundred.* *c*) *to rise, aspire;* ܠܪܝܫܢܘܬܐ ܫܘܪ *he aspired to the supreme power;* ܫܘܪ ܥܠܥܠܐ ܕܢܫܘܪ ܥܠ ܐܠܦܐ *a tempest burst forth against the ship.* ETHPE. ܐܫܬܘܪ *to rise, spring up;* ܐܫܬܘܪܬ ܠܥܠ *she sprang upright;* with ܥܠ *to oppose.* PA. ܫܘܪ *to dance, to skip, gambol* as young animals; *to dart, leap up* as fish; *to start, palpitate* as the heart; *to startle.* DERIVATIVES, ܫܘܪܐ, ܫܘܪܐ, ܡܫܬܘܪܢܐ, ܡܫܬܘܪܢܘܬܐ.

ܫܘܪܐ = ܫܝܪܐ *a wick, a plant from which wicks are made.*

ܫܘܪܐ pl. ܶܐ m. *a city wall, fortification, bulwark, defence;* ܡܕܝܢ̈ܬܐ ܚܣܝܢ̈ܬܐ ܕܫܘܪܐ *walled cities;* ܫܘܪܐ ܒܪܝܐ *an outer wall, rampart.*

ܫܘܪܐ m. *the navel.*

ܫܘܪܐ rt. ܫܪܐ. m. *a pulley, axle-tree, leathern bucket of a water-wheel.*

ܫܘܪܐ, ܫܘܪܬܐ pl. ܶܐ rt. ܫܘܪ. f. *a spring, leap, bound.*

ܫܘܪܒܐ pl. ܶܐ from ܫܪܒ. m. *planting, propagation.*

ܫܘܪܒܝܢܐ, ܫܘܪܒܝܢܬܐ = ܫܪܒܝܢܐ f. *the cypress.*

ܫܘܪܓܐ from ܫܪܓ. m. *a slip, error.*

ܫܘܪܕܐ from ܫܪܕ. m. *alarm, trepidation, a shock.*

ܫܘܪܛܐ pl. ܶܐ Ar. m. *a city watchman, guard;* pl. *the Praetorian guard.*

ܫܘܪܝܐ pl. ܫܘܪܝܬܐ f. *peas, pulse; oats.*

ܫܘܪܝ ESHTAPHAL ܐܫܬܘܪܝ from a root ܫܪܐ not found in Syriac. *a*) *to be arrogant, insolent;* with ܥܠ *to attack.* *b*) *to happen to be, to be present;* ܐܝܠܝܢ ܕܐܫܬܘܪܝܘ ܬܡܢ *those who happened to be present.* *c*) astron. *to be in conjunction.* DERIVATIVE, ܡܫܬܘܪܝܢܘܬܐ.

ܫܘܪܝ, ܫܘܪܝܐ pl. ܶܐ rt. ܫܪܐ. m. *a*) *beginning, origin* opp. ܫܘܠܡܐ *end;* ܕܠܐ ܫܘܪܝܐ *without beginning, eternal;* ܡܢ ܫ̈ *from the beginning.* *b*) *a preface, exordium, introduction.* E-Syr. a few verses of the Psalms introducing an anthem or a clause from the Psalter prefixed to a verse of an anthem. *c*) gram. *the subject of a nominal sentence.*

ܫܘܪܝܦܐ pl. ܶܐ rt. ܫܪܦ. m. pl. *flashing beams* of sun or fire-light.

ܫܘܪܠܐ pl. ܶܐ m. in the Lexx. *a white film, white spots on the eye.*

ܫܘܪܡܐ Ar. m. *the rectum.*

ܫܘܪܢܐ m. *a weasel.*

ܫܘܪܢܩܐ pl. ܶܐ m. *a*) *the calyx* of a flower; *a seed-vessel, pod, cod; rind* of a pomegranate. *b*) *casing, sheath* of the brain. *c*) *the bag* or *case* of locusts' eggs. *d*) *scab, crust* of an ulcer. *e*) *a watery bladder* in the eye. *f*) a poison made of various bitter herbs.

ܫܘܪܥܬܐ, ܫܘܪܥܬܐ pl. ܶܬܐ rt. ܫܪܥ. f. *a slip, fall, offence, fault* lit. or metaph.; *a slippery slope;* ܫ̈ ܕܠܫܢܐ *slips of the tongue.*

ܫܘܪܒܒܐ from ܫܪܒܒ. m. *quivering, palpitation.*

ܫܘܪܙܐ *mespilus germanica, the medlar.*

ܫܘܪܕܐ *a) grape-gleaning. b) free access, permission.*

ܫܘܪܪܐ rt. ܫܪ. m. *a) strength, support. b) confirmation, ratification; proving* of a will; *satisfaction* of a debt. *c) an agreement. d)* gram. *emphasis, corroboration, the adding of force* by words such as ܗܟܝܠ, ܐܝܟܢܐ, ܕܝܠܗ &c.

ܫܘܪܪܝܐ pl. ܝܐ̈ rt. ܫܪ. adj. *affirmative, confirmatory* e.g. an adverb such as ܐܡܝܢ *Amen.*

ܫܘܪܪܬܐ rt. ܫܪ. f. *reflection, deliberation.*

ܫܘܪܝܐ rt. ܫܪܐ. m. *a) looseness* of the bowels, *a flux, issue. b) becoming easy, making smooth.*

ܫܘܪܬܐ f. *the navel, the umbilical cord.* Cf. ܫܘܪܐ and ܫܪܐ.

ܫܘܪܬܐ; see ܫܘܪܐ.

ܫܘܪܬܢܐ pl. ܢܐ̈ rt. ܝܬܪ. m. *superabundance, opulence, numerousness.*

ܫܘܫ Pael 1st form, ܫܘܫ *to confuse, put in disorder.* 2nd form, ܫܫܝ *to repress, refrain, curb* the heart, anger, &c. Ethpa. ܐܫܬܘܫ *to be quieted; to be put out* as a blaze. Aph. ܐܫܝܫ *to abate, to quiet.* Derivatives, ܫܘܫܐ, ܫܘܫܝܐ.

ܫܘܫܐ rt. ܫܘܫ. m. *a) disorder. b)* in the Lexx. *self-restraint, gentleness, patience.*

ܫܘܫܐ or ܫ̈ ܩܝܣ m. *liquorice.*

ܫܘܫܐ — ܫܫܐ m. *a worm.*

ܫܘܫܒܝܢܐ m. ܫܘܫܒܝܢܬܐ f. from a root ܫܒܢ, cf. ܫܒܒܐ. *the bridegroom's friend, groomsman; the bridesmaid; a godparent, sponsor.*

ܫܘܫܒܝܢܘܬܐ or ܫ̈ ܫܘܫ from the preceding. f. *sponsorship; relationship of a godparent; office of a groomsman* or *bridesmaid.*

ܫܘܫܒܝܢܝܐ, ܫܘܫܒܝܢܝܬܐ from ܫܘܫܒܝܢܐ. *pertaining to sponsorship, sponsorial.*

ܫܘܫܓ Shaphel conj.; see ܫܓ.

ܫܘܫܓܐ rt. ܫܓ. m. *advance, growth, progress, course;* ܫ̈ ܕܛܠܝܘܬܐ *youth.*

ܫܘܫܦ part. ܡܫܘܫܦܐ. *to grunt.*

ܫܘܫܢܐ and ܫܘܫܢܝܐ m. *a muleteer, caravan attendant.*

ܫܘܫܢܘܬܐ f. *caravan hiring, care of caravan horses* or *mules.*

ܫܘܫܠܬܐ pl. ܫܘܫܠܬܐ, ܫܘܫܠܢܝܬܐ f. *a tape-worm.*

ܫܘܫܡܐ pl. ܫܘܫܡ̈ f. *sesame;* pl. *sesame seed.*

ܫܘܫܡܢܐ *a)* = ܫܘܫܡܢܝܬܐ. *b) a crocodile; a lizard.*

ܫܘܫܡܢܐ and ܫ̈ ܫܘܫ pl. ܫ̈ *a) an ant;* ܫܘܫܡܢ ܐܪܝܐ *the lion ant. b) roughness of the skin from cold, tingling, irritation.*

ܫܘܫܡܢܝܬܐ f. *amomum granum paradisi,* an aromatic shrub whence a spice used in embalming was prepared.

ܫܘܫܢ (collective), ܫܘܫܢܬܐ (noun of unity) pl. ܫܘܫܢ̈ܐ f. *a lily;* ܫܘܫܢ ܕܚܘܠܐ *the lily of the valley;* ܓܠܦܐ ܕܫܘܫܢܬܐ *carved lily work.*

ܫܘܫܦܐ pl. ܫ̈ rt. ܫܦ. f. *a) a veil, covering; chalice veil. b) a napkin, towel, handkerchief; the towel* in which the baptised are held. *c) vestment, robe* of a judge, king, priest.

ܫܘܬܐ and ܫܘܬܐ perh. contr. from ܫܘܝܬܐ. adv. *equally, together;* ܫܘܬܐ ܥܡ *rashly, commonly.*

ܫܘܬܐܣܬܐ from ܫܬܐܣ. m. *foundation;* ܫܘܬܐܣ ܓܪܡܛܝܩܐ *an elementary grammar.*

ܫܘܬܦ *a) to make a partaker, to communicate; to associate* with ܥܡ; ܐܚܘܗܝ ܫܘܬܦ ܥܡܗ ܒܡܠܟܘܬܐ *he associated his brother with himself in the royal power;* ܫܘܬܦ ܐܢܘܢ ܡܪܝ ܒܚܝܐ *make them partakers, Lord, of life. b) to administer* the Holy Eucharist; ܫܘܬܦܗ ܒܐܪ̈ܙܐ ܩܕ̈ܝܫܐ *he administered the Holy Mysteries to him.* Pass. part. ܡܫܘܬܦ, ܡܫܘܬܦܐ, ܡܫܘܬܦܬܐ *a) a partaker, sharer, associate;* ܡܫܝܚܐ ܟܝ̈ܢܐ ܡܫܘܬܦ Christ *is a partaker of both natures. b) shared, in common;* ܪܥܝܢܐ ܡܫܘܬܦܐ *common sense. c) a married person. d)* gram. *a participle.* With ܠܐ *excommunicate; not shared, not in common; a bachelor.* Ethpaual ܐܫܬܘܬܦ *a) to be made a partaker; to share, have part in; to be an accomplice; to communicate;* ܕܚ̈ܝܐ ܕܠܥܠܡ ܪ̈ܚܡܝܢ ܕܢܫܬܘܬܦܘܢ *who desire to be made partakers of eternal life;* ܠܐ ܐܫܬܘܬܦ ܒܩܛܠܗ *he had no part in his murder;* ܥܡ ܓܢ̈ܒܐ ܘܚܪ̈ܫܐ ܠܐ ܢܫܬܘܬܦ *let us have no fellowship with thieves and sorcerers;* ܡܫܬܘܬܦܝܢ ܠܣܘܢܩܢܘܬܐ ܕܩܕ̈ܝܫܐ *communicating to the necessities of the saints;* with

ܒܐܪ̈ܙܐ or ellipt. *to receive the Holy Communion.* *b*) *to have conjugal intercourse.* Derivatives, ܫܘܬܦܐ, ܫܘܬܦܘܬܐ, ܡܫܬܘܬܦܐܝܬ, ܫܘܬܦܘܬܐ, ܡܫܬܘܬܦܢܐ, ܡܫܬܘܬܦܢܘܬܐ.

ܫܘܬܳܦܳܐ, ܫܘܬܦܬܐ pl. m. ܫܘܬܦܝܢ, ܫܘܬܦܢ. *a partaker, partner, associate, colleague; a companion, consort, husband, wife.*

ܫܘܬܳܦܘܬܳܐ from ܫܬܦ. f. *a*) *participation, partnership;* O.T. with ܙܒܢܐ *a bargain.* *b*) *fellowship, communion, communicating;* esp. *Holy Communion;* ܫ̈ ܕܪܘܚܐ ܕܩܘܕܫܐ *the fellowship of the Holy Spirit.* *c*) *a charitable contribution.* *d*) *intercourse, familiarity* esp. *conjugal intercourse, marriage;* ܫ̈ ܙܢܝܬܐ *impure carnal intercourse.*

ܫܘܬܳܩܳܐ rt. ܫܬܩ. m. *silence, taciturnity; cessation; apoplexy.*

ܫܘܬܬܘܬܐ from ܫܬ. f. *a sixth part.*

ܫܚ = ܫܘܚ, ܫܚ.

ܫܚܐ fut. ܢܫܚܐ, act. part. ܫܳܚܐ, ܫܚܝܐ = ܫܘܚ, ܫܚ. *to melt, waste away* used esp. of the eyes; ܫܳܚܐ ܦܓܪܗ *his body wastes away;* ܫܚܘ ܟܠܗܘܢ ܥܡܘܪܝܗ *all the inhabitants melted away.* Ethpe. ܐܬܫܚܝ perh. *to treat with contempt.* Aph. ܐܫܚܝ *a*) *to melt away, refine* silver. *b*) *presume against, defy* with ܠܘܬ. Derivative, ܫܚܝܐ.

ܫܚܕ fut. ܢܫܚܘܕ, inf. ܡܫܚܕ, act. part. ܫܳܚܶܕ, pass. part. ܫܚܝܕ, ܫܚܝܕܐ. *to give a gift, a bribe; to bribe, corrupt with a gift;* ܕܝܢܐ ܐܡܪ ܫܚܘܕ *the judge says, bring a gift;* ܫܚܝܕܝܢ ܒܪܚܡܬ ܟܣܦܐ *corrupted by avarice;* ܫܚܝܕܝܢ ܦܣܩܝ ܕܝܢܝܗܘܢ *the judges' sentences are corrupt.* Ethpe. ܐܬܫܚܕ *to be bribed.* Pa. ܫܰܚܶܕ *to bribe often* or *habitually, to be addicted to bribery.* Ethpa. ܐܬܫܚܕ *to receive many bribes;* ܡܢ ܟܠܗܘܢ ܠܡܫܬܚܕܘ ܡܣܟܐ ܗܘܐ *he hoped to receive bribes from all of them.* Derivative, ܫܘܚܕܐ.

ܫܚܘܩܐ, ܫܚܘܩܬܐ rt. ܫܚܩ. *wearisome; an annoying person.*

ܫܚܘܪܐ, ܫܚܘܪܬܐ rt. ܫܚܪ. *rough, stony.* Fem. *a steep place, bad bit of road.*

ܫܚܘܪܘܬܐ or ܫܚ̈ rt. ܫܚܪ. f. *roughness, difficulty* of a road.

ܫܚܘܬܐ = ܫܚܘܬܐ *rust.*

ܫܚܘܬܐ pl. of ܫܚܬܐ.

ܫܚܛ Pael ܫܰܚܶܛ *a*) *to harm, mar, abuse; to impair, vitiate;* ܟܬܒܐ ܡܫܚܛܐ *damaged codices;* ܬܘܡ̈ܐ ܠܐ ܡܫܚܛܝܢ ܠܚܘܕܪܢܘܬܗ ܕܐܪܥܐ *prominences do not detract from the sphericity of the earth.* *b*) *to infringe, violate* a law; *to abuse, violate* a virgin. Ethpa. ܐܫܬܚܛ *to suffer harm, detriment; to be damaged, impaired, depraved; to fall away from, fall into desuetude;* ܘܠܐ ܢܫܬܚܛ ܡܢ ܫܡܫܐ ܘܡܢ ܓܠܝܕܐ *that he should suffer no harm from sun or sleet;* ܐܫܬܚܛ ܒܗܕܐ ܗܪܣܝܣ *he was infected by this heresy;* ܘܠܐ ܢܫܬܚܛܢ ܕܝܠܝܬܐ *lest the special attributes suffer detraction;* ܒܬܪ ܙܒܢܐ ܐܫܬܚܛ ܗܢܐ ܢܘܡܘܣܐ *after a time this ordinance fell into desuetude.* Derivatives, ܫܘܚܛܐ, ܫܚܛܐ, ܫܚܛܘܬܐ, ܫܘܚܛܢܐ.

ܫܚܛܐ rt. ܫܚܛ. m. *a swelling, sore.*

ܫܘܚܛܢܘܬܐ rt. ܫܚܛ. f. *violation* of a woman; *depravity.*

ܫܘܚܛܢܘܬܐ rt. ܫܚܛ. f. *abomination.*

ܫܚܝܐ rt. ܫܚܐ. m. *wasting, consumption of the bowels.*

ܫܚܝܡܐ; see under verb ܫܚܡ.

ܫܚܝܡܐܝܬ rt. ܫܚܡ. adv. *simply, plainly, in a simple style, in an ordinary way; merely; extempore, without forethought, unadvisedly.*

ܫܚܝܡܘܬܐ rt. ܫܚܡ. f. *a*) *a dark mass, swarthiness.* *b*) *plainness, frugality; boorishness; absence of style;* ܫܚܝܡܘܬܐ ܐܣܟܡܐ *secular dress;* ܫ̈ ܕܝܘܠܦܢܐ *want of learning.*

ܫܚܝܢ, ܫܚܝܢܐ, ܫܚܝܢܬܐ; see verb ܫܚܢ.

ܫܚܝܢܘܬܐ rt. ܫܚܢ. f. *warmth, heat.*

ܫܚܝܪܐ, ܫܚܝܪܬܐ rt. ܫܚܪ. m. and f. *a*) *vitriol, verdigris, copperas;* ܡ̈ܝܐ ܕܫ̈ *copperas water* used in making blacking and ink. *b*) *black liquid, ink.*

ܫܚܝܬܐ rt. ܫܚܐ. f. vulg. *a sauce, condiment.*

ܫܚܠ fut. ܢܫܚܘܠ, and ܫܚܠ fut. ܢܫܚܠ, act. part. ܫܳܚܶܠ, ܫܚܠܐ, pass. part. ܫܚܝܠ, ܫܚܝܠܐ. *to drip, trickle, exude, emit moisture; to run down, fall, overflow* of tears, *to let tears fall; to strain, filter;* metaph. *to desist;* ܐܝܟ ܫܥܘܬܐ ܕܬܫܬܪܐ ܬܫܚܘܠ *it will drop like melted wax;* ܟܕ ܗܕܡܘܗܝ ܫܚܠܝܢ ܕܘܥܬܐ *his limbs dripping with sweat;* ܫܚܘܠ ܒܣܕܝܢܐ ܕܟܬܢܐ *strain through* a cotton rag; ܕܡ̈ܥܐ ܫܚܝܠܬܐ welling tears. Ethpe. ܐܫܬܚܠ and Ethpa. ܐܫܬܚܠ to be strained, poured off from the dregs, purified; ܡ̈ܝܐ ܡܢܗ ܡܫܬܚܠܝܢ the water is to be strained off. Pa. ܫܚܠ to liquefy, fine metal; to strain, pour off. Aph. ܐܫܚܠ to cause to shed tears; to pour, let trickle. Derivatives, ܫܚܠܐ, ܫܚܠܐ, ܫܚܠܐ, ܫܚܠܐ, ܫܘܚܠܐ, ܫܚܠܬܐ, ܫܚܠܬܐ, ܫܚܠܬܐ.

ܫܚܠܐ and ܫܚܠܐ pl. ܐ̈ rt. ܫܚܠ. m. a strainer, filter, colander; firepan, sprinkler for sacrificial use; the saucer of a lamp.

ܫܚܠܐ pl. ܐ̈ rt. ܫܚܠ. m. a dripping, leak, trickle, trickling, fine drops; dregs; ܫ̈ ܕܟܘܪ̈ܬܐ drippings from honeycomb; ܫ̈ ܕܐܪܥܐ marshy exudation, muddy overflow; ܪ̈ܕܝܐ ܘܫܚ̈ܠܐ ܕܡ̈ܝܐ rills and trickling waters.

ܫܚܠܐ m. a) act. part. emph. of verb ܫܚܠ. b) = ܫܚܠܐ, = ܫܚܠܐ, = ܫܚܠܐ. In most of these senses at least two ways of vocalization are found.

ܫܚܠܐ rt. ܫܚܠ. m. discharge, exudation; ܫ̈ ܕܡܛܪ̈ܐ ܣܓܝ̈ܐܐ heavy rainfall; ܫ̈ ܕܕܡ̈ܥܐ the trickling down, running down of tears; ܫ̈ ܕܒܣ̈ܡܐ the distillation of perfumes while ܫܚܠܐ ܕܒܣ̈ܡܐ is probably prepared perfumes; ܫ̈ ܕܕܗܒܐ deposit, veins of gold.

ܫܚܠܘܢܐ dimin. of ܫܚܠܐ. m. a tricklet.

ܫܚܠܬܐ rt. ܫܚܠ. m. a strainer, searce.

ܫܚܠܢܝܐ rt. ܫܚܠ. wasting, running.

ܫܚܠܦ Shaphel conj. of verb ܚܠܦ.

ܫܚܠܬܐ pl. ܬ̈ܐ rt. ܫܚܠ. liquefaction, distillation, ooze.

ܫܚܡ fut. ܢܫܚܡ, act. part. ܫܚܡ, ܫܚܡܐ to become dusky, swarthy; to be black with sin; ܢܫܚܡ ܓܘܢܗ ܕܡܪ̈ܓܢܝܬܐ the pearls will acquire a dusky tone; ܡܫܚܡܝܢ ܐܝܟ ܗ̈ܢܕܘܝܐ dusky as Hindoos. Part. adj. ܫܚܝܡ, ܡܐ, ܡܬܐ. a) dusky, swarthy; ܫܚܝܡܝ ܓܘܢܐ dusky-hued. b) awkward, rude; simple, sincere; ܬܘܪܣܝܬܐ ܫܚܝܡܬܐ ܘܒܨܝܪܬܐ rude and scanty fare; ܡܦܩܬܐ ܦܫܝܛܬܐ ܫܚܝܡܐ the Pshitta Version of the Syrians is unscholarly. c) common, ordinary, mere; ܐܬܚܙܝ ܡܪܝܐ ܐܠܗܐ ܐܝܟ ܒܪܢܫܐ ܫܚܝܡܐ ܠܐܒܪܗܡ the Lord God appeared as an ordinary person to Abraham; ܠܐ ܒܪܢܫܐ ܗܘܐ ܫܚܝܡܐ Christ did not become a mere man; ܠܐ ܒܡܠ̈ܐ ܫܚܝܡܬܐ not merely in words. d) common, ordinary, secular, lay opp. consecrated, of bread, oil, water, places &c.; a common soldier; a lay brother, a monk opp. a priest. e) ferial opp. festal, also ܥܐܕ̈ܐ ܫܚܝ̈ܡܐ ordinary festivals opp. those connected with Our Lord; ܝܘ̈ܡܬܐ ܫܚܝ̈ܡܐ week-days; ܫ̈ ܫܚܝܡܬܐ and fem. emph. ellipt. the daily office. f) gram. name of a point or accent. Pa. ܫܚܡ a) to darken, blacken. b) to sully, defame, disparage; ܐܪܥܐ ܛܒܬܐ ܫܚܡܘܗ the spies disparaged a good land; ܡܘ̈ܡܐ ܣܢ̈ܝܐ ܕܫܚܡܘܗܝ ܗܘܘ ܠܗ hateful vices which disfigured him. c) to make common, profane; ܫܚܡ ܠܐܪ̈ܐܙܐ ܐܠܗܝ̈ܐ he profaned the Divine Mysteries. Ethpa. ܐܫܬܚܡ a) to be darkened, fouled, sullied, defamed; ܐܫܬܚܡ ܫܘܦܪܗ its beauty was sullied; ܒܛܘܥܝܐ ܕܚܫܘܟܐ ܐܢ ܢܫܬܚܡܘܢ if they become dark from dark error. b) to be profaned. Derivatives, ܫܘܚܡܐ, ܫܚܝܡܐܝܬ, ܫܚܝܡܘܬܐ, ܫܚܡܐ, ܫܘܚܡܬܐ.

ܫܚܡܐ pl. ܐ̈ rt. ܫܚܡ. dusky, swarthy, olive-coloured.

ܫܚܡܘܬܐ rt. ܫܚܡ. f. swarthiness.

ܫܚܢ fut. ܢܫܚܢ, act. part. ܫܚܢ, ܫܚܢܐ. a) to grow warm, feel warm; ܟܕ ܫܠܡ ܝܘܡܐ ܫܚܢܐ ܐܪܥܐ as the day waxes hot the earth grows warm. b) to warm oneself, bask ܒܫܡܫܐ in the sun. Part. adj. ܫܚܝܢ, ܫܚܝܢܐ warm, hot pl. hot water. Pa. ܫܚܢ. a) to warm, keep warm trans.; ܕܢܫܚܢ ܦܓܪܗ he may take a hot bath to warm his body; ܡܫܚܢܐ ܬܪܢܓܘܠܬܐ ܠܒܝܥ̈ܐ the hen keeps her eggs warm; ܦܪܘܬܐ ܕܡܫܟܐ ܡܫܚܢܢܐ a warm fur cloak. b) to have ulcers. Ethpa. ܐܫܬܚܢ a) to be warmed, kept warm; ܡܢ ܓ̈ܙܐ ܕܥܢ̈ܢ ܐܫܬܚܢܘ they were warmed with the fleeces of my sheep. b) to be inflamed with love. Ethpalp. ܐܫܬܚܢܢ to suffer from ulcers. Paiel ܫܚܝܢ to enrage, excite with drink. Ethpaial ܐܫܬܚܝܢ often miswritten ܐܫܬܚܢ. to rage, rave; to burn with desire; ܐܫܬܚܝܢܘ ܚܪ̈ܫܐ ܕܦܪܥܘܢ Pharaoh's sorcerers raved like drunkards. Aph. ܐܫܚܢ a) to make warm; ܫܡܫܐ ܡܢܗܪ ܘܡܫܚܢ the sun gives light and warmth. b) to ulcerate, cause inflammation. Derivatives, ܫܘܚܢܐ, ܫܘܚܢܐ,

ܫܘܚܠܦܐ, ܫܘܚܠܦܘܬܐ, ܫܚܠܦܐ, ܫܚܠܦܘܬܐ, ܫܚܠܦܢܐ, ܫܚܠܦܘܬܐ, ܡܫܚܠܦܢܐ, ܡܫܚܠܦܢܘܬܐ, ܡܫܬܚܠܦܢܘܬܐ.

ܫܚܡܐ rt. ܫܚܡ. m. perh. *a hot potion.*

ܫܚܢܟܐ Pers. m. *governor of a town* or *province, satrap.*

ܫܚܢܘܬܐ rt. ܫܚܢ. f. *ulceration of the stomach.*

ܫܚܦܐ m. *first milk after parturition, beestings; a flow of milk; sucking.*

ܫܚܩ fut. ܢܫܚܘܩ and ܢܫܚܩ, act. part. ܫܚܩ, ܫܚܩܐ, pass. part. ܫܚܝܩ, ܐ̈ܢ, ܬܐ. *a) to break up small, shatter, triturate, pound;* ܫܚܩ ܠܗܘܢ ܐܝܟ ܡܘܪܓܐ ܠܟܥܒܪܐ *he tears them as a threshing-instrument tears chaff;* ܦܠܚܕܐ ܫܚܩ Christ *shattered idols;* ܫܚܩ ܐܣܝܐ ܣܡܡܢܘܗܝ *the physician pounds his drugs. b) to wear away, fret, harass, vex, importune;* ܫܚܩܝܢ ܫܘܐܠܐ *they thresh out questions;* ܫܚܘܩܝܗܝ ܠܬܪܥܐ ܕܕܝܢܐ *be importunate at the judge's doors. c) to wear oneself out, drudge, take trouble;* ܫܚܩ ܐܢܐ ܒܝܘܠܦܢܝ *I drudge at my learning;* ܠܐ ܫܚܩ ܗܘܐ ܠܡܫܪܝܬܐ *he did not trouble about an army.* Pass. part. *a) triturated, pounded, broken;* ܙܓܘܓܝܬܐ ܫܚܝܩܬܐ *pulverized glass;* ܠܒܐ ܫܚܝܩܐ *a contrite heart. b) wearied out, harassed, sad, anxious; wearisome;* ܒܣܝܒܘܬܗ ܗܘܐ ܫܚܝܩܐ *he was worn out with age;* ܚܝܐ ܫܚܝܩܐ *miserable life;* ܫܚܝܩܝܢ ܗܘܘ ܥܠ ܩܢܝܢܗܘܢ *anxious about their wealth.* ETHPE. ܐܫܬܚܩ and ETHPA. ܐܫܬܚܩ *a) to be broken to pieces, pounded. b) to be harassed, in trouble, molested, vexed* with ܥܠ or ܡܢ; ܐܠܦܐ ܕܡܫܬܚܩܐ *a ship which has suffered many shocks;* ܐܫܬܚܩܘ ܩܢܝܢܝܗܘܢ *their possessions were damaged;* ܡܫܬܚܩ ܒܦܓܪܗ ܘܒܢܦܫܗ *uneasy in body and soul;* ܓܒܪܐ ܕܡܫܬܚܩ ܥܡ ܚܒܪܗ *a man vexed with his friend. c) to be wearied, worn out; to trouble oneself, take trouble;* ܐܝܟ ܣܒܐ ܢܝܚ ܕܐܫܬܚܩ *as a wearied old man takes rest;* ܢܫܬܚܩܘܢ ܚܦܝܛܐ *the diligent will weary themselves out;* ܕܬܫܬܚܩ ܠܘܬܝ ܒܥܝܬ I besought you *to trouble yourself to come to me.* PA. ܫܚܩ *a) to shatter, shiver. b) to molest, disturb;* ܠܐ ܐܢܫ ܫܚܩܗ ܕܝܠܗ ܩܢܝܢܗ *no one has disturbed his possession, has questioned his title to the property.* APH. *to weary.* DERIVATIVES, ܫܚܩܘܬܐ, ܫܚܩܐ, ܫܚܝܩܐ.

ܫܚܩܐ rt. ܫܚܩ. m. *a pelican.*

ܫܚܩܐ pl. ܐ̈ rt. ܫܚܩ. m. *a)* ܛܒ ܕܩܠܝܦܝܢ *pounding in a mortar. b) wear and tear, detriment. c) fatigue, wearisomeness;* ܫܚܩ ܕܚܝܐ *being weary of life. d) vexation, misery, adversity;* ܫܚܩܐ ܕܢܦܫܐ ܛܒ *anguish of mind. e) bickering, strife. f)* ܕܠܐ ܫܚܩܐ *without disturbance, untroubled, calmly.*

ܫܚܪ fut. ܢܫܚܪ, act. part. ܫܚܪ. *a) to become black, sooty;* ܡܫܟܢ ܕܝܠܢ ܐܝܟ ܬܢܘܪܐ ܫܚܪ *our skin is blackened like a furnace;* ܫܚܘܪ *add soot. b) to be alarmed.* PA. ܫܚܪ. *a) to blacken, foul, char; to make gloomy;* ܩܕܪܐ ܕܡܫܚܪܢ ܒܩܛܪܐ *pots foul with soot;* ܦܟܐ ܡܫܚܪܬܐ *sooty cheeks;* ܥܕܡܐ ܠܐܡܬܝ ܡܫܚܪ ܐܢܬ ܐܦܝܟ how long *wilt thou blacken thy face with misery? b) to levy forced service, to compel, impress;* ܫܚܪ ܓܡܠܘܗܝ *he commandeered his camels;* ܡܢ ܕܡܫܚܪ ܠܟ ܡܝܠܐ ܚܕ *whosoever shall compel thee to go one mile.* ETHPA. ܐܫܬܚܪ *a) to be blackened, fouled;* ܐܦܝܗܘܢ ܡܫܬܚܪܢ ܒܒܗܬܬܐ *their faces were covered with shame. b) to be forced, compelled. c)* cf. Eshtaphal conj. of ܫܚܪ. APH. ܐܫܚܪ *to blacken, foul;* ܡܫܚܪ ܓܝܚܘܢ ܫܝܢܐ ܡܝܘܗܝ ܕܟܝܐ Nile *mud fouls its limpid waters.* DERIVATIVES, ܫܚܘܪܐ, ܫܚܪܐ, ܫܚܪܘܬܐ, ܫܚܪܐ, ܫܚܪܐ, ܫܚܪܐ, ܫܚܪܘܬܐ, ܫܚܪܬܐ, ܡܫܚܘܪ.

ܫܚܪܐ and ܫܚܪܐ pl. ܐ̈ f. Arab. *a pannier* or *hurdle* for carrying corn on beasts to the threshing-floor.

ܫܚܪܐ pl. ܝܢ̈, ܐ̈ rt. ܫܚܪ. com. gen. *a herd* of swine, *a troop* of demons; *a drove, crowd, sect.*

ܫܚܪܐ pl. ܐ̈ rt. ܫܚܪ. m. *burnt crusts* of bread.

ܫܚܪܐ, ܫܚܪܬܐ rt. ܫܚܪ. f. *vitriol.*

ܫܚܪܘܪܐ Arab. m. *a blackbird.*

ܫܚܪܘܬܐ rt. ܫܚܪ. f. *forced labour.*

ܫܚܪܩܐ vernac. m. *the last child born to a woman.*

ܫܚܬ fut. ܢܫܚܬ. *to rust* intr., *to contract rust, grow dull;* ܢܦܫܐ ܕܫܚܬܐ ܒܟܘܒܐ̈ ܥܬܝܩܐ̈ *the soul rusted with its old sores.* APH. ܐܫܚܬ trans. and neut. *to cover with rust, to tarnish, sully;* ܕܗܒܐ ܕܡܫܚܬ ܥܠܘܗܝ *tarnished gold;* ܐܫܚܬ ܬܢܢܐ ܠܫܢܝܗܘܢ *smoke has blackened their teeth;* ܚܛܝܬܐ ܠܢܦܫܐ ܡܫܚܬܐ *sin destroys the lustre of the soul.* DERIVATIVES, ܫܚܝܬܐ, ܫܚܝܬܢܐ, ܫܚܝܘܬܐ.

ܫܚܝܬܐ f. a marsh plant, *sium lancifolium.*

ܫܚܝܬܐ pl. ܫܚܝܬܳܐ f. *the armpit, armhole.*

ܫܚܝܬܐ m. pl. *rising ground, eminences.*

ܫܚܝܢ, ܫܚܝܢܬܐ f. *barley-meal, barley porridge, made of barley-meal, honey and fat.*

ܫܛܐ fut. ܢܫܛܐ, act. part. ܫܳܛܐ, ܫܳܛܝܐ, ܫܳܛܝܬܐ. *to go wrong, misbehave, be infatuated* esp. of conjugal infidelity; *to play the fool, be out of one's wits, beside oneself;* ܐܢ ܣܛܝܬܝ ܠܒܪ ܡܢ ܒܥܠܟܝ *if thou hast gone wrong with another not thy husband.* Act. part. *infatuated, crazy, a born fool, madman, low fellow;* ܥܒܕ ܢܦܫܗ ܫܳܛܝܐ *he feigned madness.* Pl. f. ܫܳܛܝܳܬܐ *prostitutes; vain folly;* ܫܳܛܝܐ ܫܳܛܝܳܬܐ ܡܡܠܠ *a fool utters folly.* ETHPE. ܐܫܬܛܝ *to act foolishly, take to bad ways.* ETHPA. ܐܫܬܛܝ *to take to wicked folly, take to vile* or *wrong ways, to misconduct oneself* esp. of fornication; *to become* or *be considered foolish* or *vile;* ܐܫܬܛܝ ܥܡܗ ܒܗ *he committed wicked folly with her;* ܟܕ ܐܫܬܛܝ ܝܪܬܐ *when the heir took to evil ways;* ܫܠܡ ܪܗܛܟ ܕܠܐ ܬܫܬܛܐ *finish thy course lest thou be accounted a fool.* APH. ܐܫܛܝ *to infatuate; to besot, to accuse of folly, to make to appear foolish;* ܐܫܛܝܬܗ ܒܠܒܗ ܒܠܒܗ *she despised him in her heart, thought him a fool;* ܐܫܛܝܗ ܐܠܗܐ ܠܚܟܡܬܗ ܕܥܠܡܐ *hath* not *God made foolish the wisdom of the world?* ܐܫܛܝ ܠܟܠܗܘܢ ܐܢܫܐ *it has driven every one crazy.* DERIVATIVES, ܫܛܝܐܝܬ, ܫܛܝܘܬܐ, ܡܫܛܝܢܐ, ܡܫܛܝܢܘܬܐ.

ܫܛܐ Arab. m. *brink, margin, shore.*

ܫܛܘܚܐ rt. ܫܛܚ. m. *ground fig, wolf's milk,* a sort of spurge.

ܫܛܘܚܐ rt. ܫܛܚ. m. pl. *cups, goblets.*

ܫܛܘܚܝܬܐ rt. ܫܛܚ. f. *wild fig;* cf. ܫܛܘܚܐ.

ܫܛܘܝܐ, ܫܛܘܝܬܐ or ܫܛ̈ rt. ܫܛܐ. *a) frivolous, vapid, stupid, inane* esp. of conversation; ܫܛܘܝܐ ܡܡܠܠܐ *vapid talk;* ܙܢܓܐ ܫܛܘܝܐ ܩܠܐ *a clattering cymbal;* ܣܒܬܐ ܫܛܘܝܬܐ *silly old women.* *b) one bereft of sense, witless, a driveller.*

ܫܛܘܝܐܝܬ or ܫܛ̈ rt. ܫܛܐ. adv. *frivolously, at random.*

ܫܛܘܝܘܬܐ pl. ܫܛܘܝܘܬܳܐ rt. ܫܛܐ. f. *mental confusion, raving, drivel, random talk, humbug.*

ܫܛܚ fut. ܢܫܛܘܚ, act. part. ܫܳܛܚ, ܫܳܛܚܐ, part. adj. ܫܛܝܚ, ܫܛܝܚܐ, ܫܛܝܚܬܐ. *to spread out, lay out* on the ground; *to strike down, lay dead* on the ground; ܢܫܛܚܘܢ ܐܢܘܢ ܒܫܡܫܐ *they shall lay* the fruit *out in the sun;* ܫܛܚ ܐܠܗܐ ܒܣܪܐ ܩܕܡܝܗܘܢ God *spread flesh before them;* ܠܒܢܝܗܘܢ ܫܛܚ ܡܝܬܐ ܥܠ ܐܪܥܐ *their children he stretched dead on the ground.* Part. adj. *trailing* as plants, *prone; broad, ample; diffuse;* ܫܛܝܚ ܥܡܪܗܘܢ sheep *with long fleeces* opp. curly; ܦܩܥܬܐ ܫܛܝܚܬܐ *a broad plain,* ellipt. ܫܛܝܚܐ *open country.* Geomet. *plane.* ETHPA. ܐܫܬܛܚ *to be spread out* on the ground, *laid flat.* DERIVATIVES, ܫܛܚܐ, ܫܛܘܚܐ, ܫܛܘܚܝܬܐ, ܫܛܝܚܐ, ܫܛܝܚܐܝܬ, ܫܛܝܚܘܬܐ, ܡܫܛܚܐ.

ܫܛܚܐ pl. ܫܛ̈ rt. ܫܛܚ. m. *a) an open space* esp. *the land beyond the walls of a city;* ܒܬܐ ܕܒܫܛܚܐ *houses without the walls;* ܩܘܪܝܐ ܕܫܛܚܐ *unwalled villages;* ܫܛܚܐ ܘܛܘܪܐ *open country and mountains.* *b) open space* round a house, *unwalled courtyard.* *c) open expanse* of smooth sea, *a pool; a reach* of a river.

ܫܛܛܐ m. *a shallow in which turtles are caught.*

ܫܛܝܐܝܬ rt. ܫܛܐ. adv. *stupidly, impertinently, tactlessly.*

ܫܛܝܘܬܐ rt. ܫܛܐ. f. *senselessness, folly, misconduct; madness; contempt.*

ܫܛܝܚܐܝܬ rt. ܫܛܚ. adv. *plane, flat.*

ܫܛܝܚܘܬܐ rt. ܫܛܚ. f. *breadth, extent, surface, superficies;* geomet. *a plane, plane figure;* ܫ̄ ܕܡܠܐ *prolixity.*

ܫܛܝܦܬܐ pl. ܫܛ̈ rt. ܫܛܦ. f. *a small tapering vase of glass* or *alabaster, an ointment-box, incense-boat.*

ܫܛܠܚܢܐ m. *a polo-mallet.*

ܫܛܦ fut. ܢܫܛܘܦ, act. part. ܫܳܛܦ. *to cleave asunder, cut obliquely;* ܫܛܦܝܢ ܩܢܝܐ *they cut reeds across.* Pass. part. ܫܛܝܦ, ܫܛܝܦܐ, ܫܛܝܦܬܐ *sloping, slanting, splayed;* ܟܘܐ ܫܛܝܦܬܐ ܠܓܘ ܘܥܨܝܪܬܐ *windows broad within and narrow without.* DERIVATIVES, ܫܛܝܦܬܐ, ܫܛܦܐ.

ܫܛܦܐ rt. ܫܛܦ. m. *plucking, skinning, flaying.*

ܫܛܐ fut. ܢܫܛܐ, act. part. ܫܳܛܶܐ, ܫܳܛܝܳܐ. *to lose one's senses; to talk at random, talk foolishly, madly;* ܟܠܒܐ ܕܐܝܟ ܫܛܝܐ ܠܟܠܗܘܢ ܡܪܘܬܐ ܦܐܫ ܘܠܐ ܡܗܝܡܢ ܠܚܕ *senseless is the word they use of a dog who will follow any master and not stay faithful to one;* ܐܚܪܢܐ ܕܒܠܐ ܝܕܥܬܐ ܕܫܪܪܐ ܫܳܛܶܝܢ *others who in ignorance of the truth talk at random.* DERIVATIVES, ܫܛܝܐ, ܫܛܝܐܝܬ, ܫܛܝܘܬܐ.

ܫܛܪ, ܫܛܪܐ and ܐܫܛܪܐ pl. ܐ m. *a handwriting, deed;* ܫ̈ ܕܙܒܢܬܐ *a deed of sale;* ܫܛܪ ܚܘܒܐ *promissory note, bond, bill;* metaph. ܫ̈ ܕܚܐܪܘܬܐ *ratification of liberty.*

ܫܛܪܐ pl. ܫܛܪܐ Pers. m. *a great honour.*

ܫܛܚܐ usually pl. ܫܛܚܐ ܕܪ̈ܚܝܐ or ܕܪ̈ܚܝܐ m. *a mill-stream, mill-race.*

ܫܝܒܘܛܐ; see ܫܒܘܛܐ *a kind of fish.*

ܫܝܚܐ rt. ܫܘܚ. m. *a thin garment.*

ܫܝ̈ܚܬܐ m. pl. in the Lexx. *hastiness, error.*

ܫܝܚܘܪܐ m. in the Lexx. *a weaver's beam to which the woof is attached with clay.*

ܫܝܚܐ *a*) usually m. pl. ܫܝ̈ܚܐ ܕܦ̈ܘܡܐ *the gums.* *b*) ܫ̈ ܕܡܝ̈ܐ *drains.* Cf. ܫܝܚܐ.

ܫܝܚܬܐ pl. ܫܝ̈ܚܬܐ rt. ܫܘܚ. f. *a*) *washing, ablution, rinsing;* ܐܘܢܓܠܝܘܢ ܕܫ̈ the Lection for Maundy-Thursday, John xiii. 1–19; ܫ̈ ܕܪ̈ܓܠܐ *the washing of feet* on the same day. *b*) *a wash, soap, lye; the water in which anything has been washed, suds.* *c*) ܫܝܚܬ ܡܥ̈ܝܐ *wasting away of the bowels from chronic dysentery.*

ܫܝܦܐ (ܕ ܫܝܦܐ); see verb ܫܘܦ.

ܫܝܦܐ pl. ܐ m. *the first corn threshed out.*

ܫܝܦܐ in the Lexx. m. *a great ship.*

ܫܝܦܘܪܐ m. *haematite, blood-stone.*

ܫܝܘܦܐ, ܫܝܘܦܬܐ rt. ܫܘܦ. *parched, blasted, dried up, mildewed; shrivelled.*

ܫܝܘܦܘܬܐ rt. ܫܘܦ. f. *sultriness; havoc wrought by sultry winds.*

ܫܝܘܚܐ pl. ܐ rt. ܫܘܚ. *liquid.* In the Lexx. *insipid.*

ܫܝܘܛܐ, ܫܝܘܛܬܐ rt. ܫܘܛ. *a despiser, scorner.*

ܫܝܘܛܘܬܐ rt. ܫܘܛ. f. *contempt.*

ܫܝܘܠ Heb. rt. ܫܐܠ. f. *Sheol, the pit* = Greek *Hades, limbus, the lower regions;* ܫ̈ ܬܚܬܝܬܐ *the lowest hell.*

ܫܐܘܠܐ rt. ܫܐܠ. m. *one who asks, a petitioner.*

ܫܝܘܠܝܐ from ܫܝܘܠ. *of or relating to Sheol, lower, infernal.*

ܫܝܘܦܘܬܐ rt. ܫܘܦ. f. *filing, polishing.*

ܫܝܘܬܐ f. *complexion, natural colour, state of health, appearance, beauty;* ܢܫ̈ܐ ܨܗܝܘܢ̈ܝܬܐ ܫܝܘܬܐ ܕܣܗܪܐ *women shining like the moon;* ܫ̈ ܕܡܝܬܪܘܬܐ *the beauty of virtue.*

ܫܝܘܬܢܝܐ from the above. adj. *relating to the complexion.*

ܫܝܙܦܐ pl. ܐ m. *a*) *zizyphus, the jujube-tree.* *b*) *cordia sebestana, a kind of plum.*

ܫܝܙܦܝ Pers. *bats' guano.*

ܫܝܚ PAEL conj. of verb ܫܘܚ.

ܫܝܚܐ m. *a*) *a ditch, a water-pit.* *b*) *abrotonon, artemisia, southern-wood.*

ܫܝܚܐ rt. ܫܘܚ. m. *liquefaction.*

ܫܝܚܘܪ Heb. rt. ܫܚܪ. *Sihor, Black River* = the Nile.

ܫܝܚܘܪܝܐ from the above. perh. *black.*

ܫܝܚܘܬܐ f. perh. = ܫܝܚܘܬܐ.

ܫܝܚܘܬܐ f. perh. *a district under a sheikh,* a district of Egypt.

ܫܝܚܡ PAIEL conj. of verb ܫܚܡ.

ܫܝܚܡܐ rt. ܫܚܡ. *ferocious.*

ܫܝܚܡܘܬܐ rt. ܫܚܡ. f. *savagery, wildness.*

ܫܝܛ, ܫܝܛܐ, ܫܝܛܬܐ; see verb ܫܘܛ, ܫܛ.

ܫܝܛܐ m. *a stye in the eye.*

ܫܝܛܐܝܬ rt. ܫܘܛ. adv. *contemptuously.*

ܫܝܛܘܬܐ pl. ܬ̈ܐ rt. ܫܘܛ. f. *contempt, scorn; desecration; contemptibility;* ܫܝܛܘܬ ܢܦܫܐ *self-contempt;* ܫܝܛܘܬܝ *my contemptible self.*

ܫܝܛܬܐ pl. ܫܝ̈ܛܬܐ f. *a branch, rod;* ܫ̈ ܕܐܣܐ *a myrtle-branch.*

ܫܝܟ Arab. *a sheikh.*

ܫܝܣܬܐ f. *a blossom.*

ܫܝܠ rare form for ܫܐܠ verb.

ܫܝܠܐ perh. *a seam.*

ܫܝܠܐ, ܫܝܠܬܐ; see verb ܫܐܠ.

ܫܝܠܝܬ = ܫܐܠܝܬ.

ܫܝܠܘܚܝ̈ܐ m. pl. *locusts' legs.*

ܫܝܠܘܚܐ, ܫܝܠܘܚܬܐ Lexx. *a bastard.*

ܫܘܠܡܘܣ, ܫܘܠܡܘܣܐ and ܫܘܠܡܐ Arab. m. *lolium, darnel.*

ܫܘܠܡܝܬܐ ,ܫܘܢܡܝܬܐ f. *a Shunammite* or *Shulammite,* woman of Shunem, now Sûlem.

ܫܝܡ pr. n. m. *Shem.*

ܫܝܢ *Shin,* name of the letter ܫ.

ܫܝܢ probably from a root ܫܠܡ. Pael *a) to make peace, conciliate, reconcile, appease* with ܥܡ, ܒ, ܠ; ܫܝܢ ܡܪܝܐ ܠܥܕܬܟ *grant peace, Lord, to Thy Church;* ܫܝܢ ܐܘܪ̈ܚܬܐ *he rendered the roads safe;* pass. part. ܫܠܝܐ ܘܡܫܝܢܐ *quiet and peaceable;* ܚܝܐ ܡܫܝ̈ܢܐ *a peaceful life;* ܡܘܬܐ ܠܐ ܡܫܝܢܐ *a violent death;* ܡܫܝ̈ܢܬܐ or ellipt. *a favourable answer, soft words. b) to calm* ܠܥܠܥܠܐ *the tempest;* ܫܝܢ ܢܦܫܟ *be calm;* ܕܢܫܝܢ ܠܪ̈ܥܝܢܝܗܘܢ *to quiet their minds, pacify them;* ܩܘ̈ܝܐ ܡܫܝ̈ܢܐ *tranquil pools;* ܠܡܥܢܐ ܕ̈ܫܝܢ *a calm haven. c) to cultivate, reclaim, tame;* with ܐܪ̈ܥܬܐ *to bring lands under cultivation,* also *to render peace to a country;* ܝܘܪ̈ܩܢܐ ܡܫܝ̈ܢܐ *garden vegetables;* ܠܐ ܡܫܝ̈ܢܬܐ *untamed* animals. Ethpa. ܐܫܬܝܢ *a) to be at peace, find peace; to be pacified, reconciled, to live peaceably* with ܠ, ܥܡ; ܐܫܬܝܢܬ ܒܪܝܬܐ *creation was at peace. b) to make peace, make a treaty of peace. c) to be calmed, tranquillized, tamed.* Derivatives, ܐܫܬܝܢܘܬܐ, ܫܝܢܐ, ܫܝܢܝܐ, ܫܝܢܝܬܐ, ܡܫܝܢܢܘܬܐ, ܡܫܝܢܝܐ, ܡܫܝܢܘܬܐ, ܡܫܝܢܢܐ.

ܫܝܢ, ܫܝܢܐ, rt. ܫܠܡ. m. *a) peace* (answers to Lat. pax; cf. ܫܠܡܐ salus), *tranquillity. b) a treaty of peace, a truce, capitulation;* to take a city ܒܫܝܢܐ *by surrender* opp. ܒܩܪܒܐ *by storm. c) cultivated* or *inhabited land* opp. ܚܘܪܒܐ and ܡܕܒܪܐ; ܕܫܝܢܐ *cultivated; tame, domestic.*

ܫܝܪܓܐ Arab. m. *anchusa tinctoria, alkanet,* a plant yielding a red dye.

ܫܝܢܝܐ rt. ܫܠܡ. *a) peaceful;* ܕܒܚ̈ܐ ܫܝܢ̈ܝܐ *peace-offerings. b) cultivated, garden;* ܐܦܘܪܫܢܐ ܫ *cinnamon.*

ܫܝܥ, ܫܝܥܐ, ܫܝܥܬܐ; see verb ܫܘܥ.

ܫܝܥܐ rt. ܫܘܥ. m. *daubing, plastering; a layer of mud over a graft.*

ܫܝܥܐ and ܫܝܥܗ Arab. *the Shi'ah,* followers of Ali.

ܫܝܥܐܝܬ rt. ܫܘܥ. adv. *headlong, indiscreetly, rashly.*

ܫܝܥܘܬܐ rt. ܫܘܥ. f. *headlong hurry, temerity, ungovernableness.*

ܫܝܦܐ pl. ܐ̈ rt. ܫܘܦ. m. *a) salve, eye-salve;* ܥܒܕܗ ܫܝܦܐ *reduce it to a paste. b) a little swelling under the tongue. c)* ܫ ܕܡܫܠܠܢܘܬܐ perh. *a purgative. d)* ܫ ܕܡܡܝܬܐ *glaucium, celandine. e)* in the Lexx. *filing.*

ܫܝܦܐ rt. ܫܘܦ. *a caulker, one who smears with pitch.*

ܫܝܦܘܪܐ pl. ܐ̈ m. *a trump, trumpet.*

ܫܝܦ denom. verb from ܫܘܦܢܐ. *to file, saw.*

ܫܝܦܬܐ rt. ܫܘܦ. f. *filings.*

ܫܝܪ denom. verb Pael conj. from ܫܝܪܐ. ܫܝܪܝ. *to sing.*

ܫܝܪܐ m. *fine dust; the first corn trodden out of the ear.*

ܫܝܪܘܣܐ in BB. *leavings, residuum.*

ܫܝܪܐ; see ܫܝܪܝܐ *silk.*

ܫܝܪܓ Arab. *sesame oil.*

ܫܝܪ ܫܝܪܝܡ Heb. *the Song of Songs* = Syr. ܬܫܒܘܚܬ ܬܫܒ̈ܚܬܐ.

ܫܝܪܬܐ pl. ܐ̈ f. *a caravan.*

ܫܝܫ Pael conj.; see ܫܘܫ.

ܫܝܫܐ pl. ܐ̈ m. *marble;* ܫ ܚܘܪܐ *white marble.* Cf. ܫܝܫܬܐ.

ܫܝܫܘܪܐ pl. ܐ̈ m. *a palm-spathe, a rope of palm-fibre.*

ܫܝܫܠܬܐ, ܫܝܫܠܬܐ or ܫܫ or ܫܫ pl. ܢ̈, ܬܐ̈. f. *a) a chain, bond, fetter;* ܐܪܡܝ ܥܠܝܗܘܢ ܫܝܫ̈ܠܬܐ *he put fetters upon them = cast them into bonds. b) a line, series.*

ܫܝܫܠܢܝܐ, ܢܝܬܐ from ܫܝܫܠܬܐ. adj. *of chain-work.*

ܫܝܫܡܐ = ܫܘܫܡܐ *grains of sesame.*

ܫܝܫܢܐ *butomus, the flowering rush.*

ܫܝܫܬܐ pl. ܫܝ̈ܫܐ f. *an alabaster vase, a flagon.*

ܫܝܬ = ܫܬ *six.*

ܫܝܬ pr. n. m. *Seth.*

ܫܝܬܐ m. *a mound of earth, a grave.*

ܫܝܬܝܐ, ܫܝܬܝܬܐ probably from ܫܬ. *primaeval, pristine.*

ܫܰܝܟܳܢܳܝܽܘܬܳܐ from the preceding. f. *antiquity*.

ܫܰܟܳܐ = ܐܶܫܟܳܐ.

ܫܟܶܒ fut. ܢܶܫܟܽܘܒ, parts. ܫܳܟܶܒ, ܫܳܟܒܳܐ; ܫܟܺܝܒ and ܫܟܺܝܒ, ܫܟܺܝܒܳܐ. *to lie down, fall asleep, take rest; a*) of natural sleep: ܐܶܢܳܐ ܫܶܟܒܶܬ ܘܕܶܡܟܶܬ ܘܐܶܬܬܥܺܝܪܶܬ *I laid me down and slept and rose up again;* ܠܳܐ ܫܳܟܶܒ ܠܶܒܶܗ *his heart taketh no rest;* part. ܫܟܺܝܒ *lying down. b*) of death: esp. with ܡܶܢ ܥܳܠܡܳܐ *to rest from this world;* with ܒܰܫܠܳܡܳܐ *in peace;* ܫܟܶܒ ܥܰܡ ܐܰܒܳܗܰܘܗ̱ܝ *he slept with his fathers.* Act. and pass. parts. *dead, buried;* ܫܳܟ̈ܒܶܐ or ܫܟܺܝ̈ܒܶܐ ܕܥܰܦܪܳܐ *those that lie in the dust;* ܫܟܺܝ̈ܒܶܐ ܥܰܬܺܝ̈ܩܶܐ *those who have long been at rest.* ETHPE. ܐܶܬܫܟܶܒ *to be laid out,* part. ܡܶܫܬܰܟܒܳܐ *divided into beds* or *plots* for irrigation. APH. ܐܰܫܟܶܒ *a*) *to make to lie down, to send to sleep;* ܡܰܫܟܶܒ ܥܰܠ ܥܰܪܣܳܐ *laid upon the bed. b*) *to situate;* ܐܰܪܥܳܐ ܕܡܰܫܟܒܳܐ ܥܰܠ ܡܰ̈ܝܳܐ ܣܰܓܺܝ̈ܐܶܐ *open land lying by abundant waters.* DERIVATIVES, ܡܫܟܒܘܬܐ, ܡܫܟܒܐ, ܡܫܟܒܬܐ.

ܫܶܟܒܳܐ or ܫܶܟܒܳܐ m. *a louse.*

ܫܶܟܒܽܘܬܳܐ rt. ܫܟܒ. f. *sediment; subsidence; repose.*

ܫܟܺܝܒܺܝܢ only pl. m. rt. ܫܟܒ. *sunk, subsided, calmed down;* ܫ̄ ܥܰܠ ܬܽܘܠܰܝܗܽܘܢ *settled on the lees.*

ܫܟܰܚ anomalous verb usually with prosthetic Aleph, ܐܶܫܟܰܚ, fut. ܢܶܫܟܰܚ, inf. ܡܶܫܟܳܚܽܘ, act. part. ܡܶܫܟܰܚ, ܡܶܫܟܚܳܐ, pass. part. ܫܟܺܝܚ, ܫܟܺܝܚܳܐ. *a*) *to find, meet with, happen; to attain, acquire; to find out, invent, discover;* ܠܳܐ ܐܶܫܟܚܰܬ ܠܳܗ̇ ܝܰܘܢܳܐ ܢܝܳܚܳܐ *the dove found no rest;* ܐܶܢ ܐܶܫܟܰܚ ܠܚܰܕ *if thou meet any one;* ܕܢܶܫܟܚܽܘܢ ܚܰܝܶܐ ܒܡܫܺܝܚܳܐ *that they may find life in Christ;* ܡܶܫܟܚܳܢܶܐ ܕܒܺܝܫܳܬܳܐ *inventors of evil.* With ܥܶܠܬܳܐ or ܥܰܠ *to find occasion against* any one; ܠܳܐ ܡܶܫܟܰܚ ܠܳܟ *he is no match for thee;* with ܪ̈ܰܚܡܶܐ *to find mercy, grace, pardon. b*) with ܐܰܬܪܳܐ *to find room* or *opportunity,* with ܚܰܝܠܳܐ *to find strength* (cf. above), hence auxil. verb *to be able, to find it possible, he can, he may;* construed with fut. or inf. or with the same tense immediately following; ܐܶܢ ܐܶܫܟܰܚ ܐܶܕܪܶܟ ܠܳܟ *if by any means I may attain;* ܡܰܢܽܘ ܡܶܫܟܰܚ ܡܣܰܝܒܰܪ *who may abide it?* ܠܳܐ ܡܶܫܟܚܳܐ ܐ̱ܢܳܐ *I cannot.* Impers. ܡܶܫܟܰܚ *it may be;* ܠܳܐ ܡܶܫܟܚܳܐ *it is impossible. c*) part. adj. *a*) *to be found, present, occurring, existing, extant; remaining over;* ܐܺܝܠܶܝܢ ܕܫܟܺܝܚܺܝܢ *the Found* = Christians opp. ܐܺܝܠܶܝܢ ܕܛܳܥܶܝܢ *the erring;* ܫܟܺܝܚܺܝܢ ܗܘܰܘ *there were present;* ܫܟܺܝܚܺܝܢ ܒܟܽܠ ܙܒܰܢ *ever-present;* ܕܫܟܺܝܚܺܝܢ ܠܐܺܝܬܽܘܬܶܗ *essential attributes;* ܫܟܺܝܚ ܠܶܗ *there is found in him, it is natural to him;* ܫܟܺܝܚܳܐ ܠܝ *I have something* to say; ܫܟܺܝܚܺܝܢ ܥܶܣܪܺܝܢ ܘܚܰܡܫܳܐ ܟܬ̈ܳܒܺܝܢ ܕܚܽܘܢܰܝܢ *twenty-five books by Honein are extant.* β) *possible;* ܠܳܐ ܫ̄ *impossible.* ETHPE. ܐܶܫܬܟܰܚ *a*) *to be found, be present, exist, be; to happen;* ܐܶܫܬܟܰܚ ܡܗܰܝܡܢܳܐ *he was found faithful;* ܐܰܒܺܝ̈ܕܶܐ ܕܐܶܫܬܟܚܽܘ *the lost who are found;* ܐܶܫܬܟܰܚ ܕܐܶܬܳܐ *there came by chance;* ܐܶܫܬܟܚܽܘ *there were;* ܐܶܫܬܟܰܚܢܰܢ ܒܐܶܣܩܺܝܛܺܝܣ *we were at Scete;* ܡܶܟܺܝܠ ܡܶܫܬܟܰܚ *hence it follows;* ܟܽܠ ܡܳܐ ܕܡܶܫܬܟܰܚ ܠܝ *whatsoever I possess. b*) *to be found out, discovered, detected;* ܐܶܢ ܡܶܫܬܟܚܳܐ *if the theft be found in his hand;* ܥܰܠ ܕܐܶܫܬܟܰܚ ܢܶܣܛܽܘܪܝܳܢܳܐ *because he was convicted of Nestorianism. c*) *to be able.* DERIVATIVES, ܫܟܚܬܐ, ܫܟܝܚܘܬܐ, ܫܟܝܚܘܬܐܝܬ, ܫܟܝܚܘܬܢܝܐ, ܡܫܟܚܢܐ, ܡܫܟܚܢܘܬܐ.

ܫܟܳܚܬܳܐ pl. ܫܟ̈ܳܚܳܬܳܐ rt. ܫܟܚ. f. *finding, discovery, recovery* = *salvation; an invention, idea, notion, occasion;* ܕܠܺܝܠܳܐ ܠܡܶܫܟܳܚܬܳܐ *easy to find;* ܫ̄ ܕܡܰܪ̈ܡܝܳܬܳܐ *on Foundlings;* ܫ̄ ܕܥܶܠܠܳܐ *inventing excuses;* ܫܟ̈ܳܚܳܬܗܽܘܢ *their inventions, imaginations;* ܫ̄ ܕܙܩܺܝܦܳܐ *the Invention of the Cross.*

ܫܟܺܝܒܽܘܬܳܐ rt. ܫܟܒ. f. *falling asleep* = *death;* ܬܠܳܬܺܝܢ ܝܰܘܡܺܝܢ ܒܳܬܰܪ ܫܟܺܝܒܽܘܬܶܗ *thirty days after he had entered into rest.*

ܫܟܺܝܒܬܳܐ pl. ܫܟܺܝ̈ܒܳܬܳܐ f. *a quail.*

ܫܟܺܝܚܽܘܬܳܐ rt. ܫܟܚ. f. *finding, discovery, attainment; existence.* With ܠܳܐ *absence, lack.*

ܫܟܺܝܚܽܘܬܳܐܺܝܬ rt. ܫܟܚ. adv. *actually.*

ܫܟܺܝܚܽܘܬܳܢܳܝܳܐ, ܢܳܝܬܳܐ rt. ܫܟܚ. adj. *of* or *belonging to existence, essential.*

ܫܟܺܝܢܽܘܬܳܐ rt. ܫܟܢ. f. *a halt, stay; residence.*

ܫܟܺܝܢܳܢܳܐ rt. ܫܟܢ. *perpetual, constantly abiding.*

ܫܟܺܝܢܬܳܐ pl. ܫܟܺܝ̈ܢܳܬܳܐ rt. ܫܟܢ. f. *a*) *a resting-place, habitation; a tabernacle, temple. b*) Neo-Heb. *the Shechinah,* the visible glory of the Divine Presence; ܩܰܕܺܝܫܳܐ ܕܐܰܫܪܺܝ ܫܟܺܝܢܬܶܗ ܥܰܠ ܛܽܘܪ ܨܶܗܝܽܘܢ *the Holy One who let His glory abide on Mount Zion.* c) *a sepulchre, shrine, reliquary, relics* of Saints; *a shrine* or *temple* of idols.

ܫܟܝܪ̈ܐ rt. ܫܟܪ. m. pl. *freckles, pimples.*

ܫܟܝܪܐܝܬ rt. ܫܟܪ. adv. *disgracefully.*

ܫܟܝܪܘܬܐ pl. ܘ̈ܬܐ rt. ܫܟܪ. f. *disgrace, disfigurement, unseemliness, foulness, obscenity; absurdity;* ܫܟܝܪܘܬ ܡܡܠܠܐ *foul language;* ܡܠܦܢܘܬܐ or ܝܘܠܦܢܐ ܫ̄ *corrupt doctrine, heresy.* Pl. *foul deeds, crimes.*

ܫܟܝܪܬܐ rt. ܫܟܪ. f. *the fat under the skin.*

ܫܟܝܠܘܬܐ rt. ܫܟܠ. f. *faeces.*

ܫܟܠܠ Shaphel conj.; see ܟܠܠ.

ܫܟܢ fut. ܢܫܟܘܢ, act. part. ܫܟܢ, ܫܟܢܐ, part. adj. ܫܟܝܢ, ܢܐ. *to alight, perch, settle* or *rest upon* with ܥܠ; ܕܒܘܪܬܐ ܥܠ ܟܠ ܗܦܪ̈ܚܝܢ ܫܟܢܐ *the bee alights on every flower;* ܫܟܢܬ ܥܠ ܡܫܟܢܐ ܥܢܢܐ *the cloud rested on the tabernacle;* ܟܕ ܪܘܚܐ ܕܩܘܕܫܐ ܐܝܟ ܝܘܢܐ ܦܪܚܬ ܘܥܠ ܪܫܗ ܫܟܢܬ the Holy Spirit *like a dove flew down and settled on His head;* ܥܕܡܐ ܕܫܟܢ ܥܠ *till it settles;* ܣܦܣܪ̈ܝܢ ܒܐܪܥܐ ܫܟܢܘ *our swords sank to the ground.* Pa. ܫܟܢ a) *to bestow, confer,* esp. *to impart a spiritual gift, to confer office* in the Church; *to bequeath;* ܫܟܢ ܠܗ ܡܪܝܐ *grant to him, Lord;* ܫܟܢܗ ܠܟܬܒܐ ܠܕܝܪܐ *he bequeathed a codex to the monastery.* b) *to gratify, humour;* ܕ ܠܡܫܟܢ ܠܗ *to gratify him,* also, ܕ ܡܫܟܢ *gratuitously, with no reason.* c) perh. *to pledge, pawn:* cf. Aphel. Ethpa. ܐܬܫܟܢ a) *to be bestowed, granted, imparted; to be bequeathed;* ܪܓܫܐ ܘܙܘܥܐ ܠܗܕ̈ܡܐ ܡܫܬܟܢܝܢ *feeling and movement are bestowed upon the limbs.* b) *to be condoned;* ܢܫܬܟܢ ܡܢܗܘܢ ܕܝܢܐ *punishment shall be remitted.* Aph. ܐܫܟܢ a) *to make to settle, cause to dwell, to place, set;* ܐܫܟܢ ܥܠܝܟ ܟܠܗ ܦܪܚܬܐ ܕܫܡܝܐ *I will cause all the fowls of heaven to settle upon thee.* b) *to pledge, pawn;* ܐܫܟܢ ܟܘܬܝܢܗ *he pawned his shirt.* See verb ܡܫܟܢ. Ethtaph. ܐܬܬܫܟܢ *to be pawned, to be given in pledge.* Derivatives, ܫܟܢܐ or ܫܘܟܢܐ, ܫܘܟܢܐ, ܫܘܟܢܬܐ, ܫܟܝܢܐ, ܫܟܝܢܬܐ, ܫܟܢܐ, ܫܟܢܐ, ܫܟܢܬܐ, ܫܟܝܢܬܐ, ܡܫܟܢܐ, ܡܫܟܢܢܐ, ܡܫܟܢܘܬܐ, ܡܫܟܢܢܘܬܐ, ܡܫܟܢܢܐ, ܡܫܬܟܢܢܐ, ܡܫܬܟܢܢܘܬܐ.

ܫܟܢܐ pl. ܢ̈ܐ rt. ܫܟܢ. m. pl. *demons inhabiting human beings.*

ܫܟܢܐ rt. ܫܟܢ. m. a) *the settling, alighting* of a bird &c. b) *dwelling, residence, staying;* ܡܘܪܟ ܫܟܢܗ *he prolongs his stay.* c) *deposit, settlings, faeces* esp. of urine.

ܫܟܢܬܐ rt. ܫܟܢ. f. *descent.*

ܫܟܢ̈ܬܐ rt. ܫܟܢ. f. pl. *birds' nests, roosts.*

ܫܟܦܐ m. *a saddler, maker of packsaddles.* Cf. ܐܫܟܦܐ.

ܫܟܪ fut. ܢܫܟܪ, act. part. ܫܟܪ. a) *to be dull, dizzy;* ܫܟܪܬ ܚܙܘܗܘܢ ܕܪ̈ܥܘܬܐ ܡܢ ܚܫܘܟܐ *the sight of the shepherds was dizzy from the darkness.* b) *to insult, dishonour, treat as vile;* ܠܡܠܟܗܘܢ ܫܟܪܘ *they dishonoured their king.* Part. adj. ܫܟܝܪ, ܐ, ܬܐ. a) *foul, vile, disfigured;* ܫܟܝܪ ܚܙܘܐ *hideous.* b) *disgraceful, dishonourable, shameful;* ܪ̈ܓܝܓܬܐ ܫܟܝܪ̈ܬܐ ܕܒܣܪܐ *the shameful lusts of the flesh;* ܕܘܒܪܐ—ܥܒܕܐ—ܐܪܚܐ ܫܟܝܪܐ *disgraceful conduct, behaviour;* ܡܡܠܠܐ ܫܟܝܪܐ *an abuse.* Fem. emph. *a foul deed, crime.* c) *absurd;* ܡܘܒܠܢܘܬܐ ܠܗܕܐ ܫܟܝܪܬܐ *reductio ad absurdum;* ܗܘ ܕܫܟܝܪ *which is absurd.* d) *unlucky, inauspicious.* Ethpe. ܐܫܬܟܪ and Ethpa. ܐܫܬܟܪ *to be disfigured, marred; to be dishonoured, treated as vile;* ܕܠܐ ܢܫܬܟܪ ܫܘܦܪܗܘܢ *lest their beauty be marred;* ܐܫܬܟܪܬ ܕܚܠܬ ܐܠܗܐ *religion was dishonoured.* Pa. ܫܟܪ *to mar, disfigure; to defame, dishonour;* ܛܥܫ ܘܫܟܪ ܠܟܬܒܐ ܗܢܐ *he blotted and spoiled this codex;* ܠܐ ܡܫܟܪ ܠܐܢܫܐ ܚܛܝܐ *not accounting sinners vile;* ܫܘܒܗܪܐ ܡܫܟܪܐ ܗܘ ܠܚܟܝܡܐ *vainglory is a disgrace to the wise.* Pass. part. ܡܫܟܪ, ܐ, ܬܐ *foul;* ܡܫܟܪ ܚܙܘܐ *ill-featured, of hideous appearance;* ܠܒܘܫܐ ܡܫܟܪܐ *filthy attire;* ܗܘܠܐ ܡܫܟܪܬܐ *vile matter;* ܚܘܫܒ̈ܐ ܡܫܟܪ̈ܐ *base thoughts.* Derivatives, ܫܟܝܪܐ, ܫܟܝܪ̈ܐ, ܫܟܝܪܐܝܬ, ܫܟܝܪܘܬܐ, ܫܟܝܪܬܐ, ܡܫܟܪܢܘܬܐ.

ܫܟܪ, ܫܟܪܐ m. *sugar;* ܩܢܝܐ ܕܫܟܪ *sugar-cane;* ܫܟܪ ܕܢܒܝܬ *crystallized sugar.*

ܫܟܪ, ܫܟܪܐ m. *strong drink other than wine,* esp. a liquor made from dates or from honey.

ܫܟܪܘܢܐ m. *henbane,* a soporific herb.

ܫܟܪܬܐ Arab. f. *a field* or *garden plot, a piece of ground ready for sowing.*

ܫܟܬ fut. ܢܫܟܘܬ, act. part. ܫܟܬ, ܫܟܬܐ, pass.

part. ܫܠܐ and ܫܠܝܐ. *a*) *to sink, settle* as dregs; ܫܠܝ ܫܠܘܬܐ ܕܚܡܪܐ *throw away the sediment;* ܚܡܪܐ ܓܒܝܐ ܘܫܠܝܐ ܒܡܐܢܗ *choice wine clear in its vessel.* *b*) *to settle down, rest, stay quiet, cease from war;* ܠܐ ܢܫܠܐ ܥܠ ܐܪܥܐ *let us not rest on the earth.* Ethpe. ܐܫܬܠܝ *to sink, subside;* ܐܫܬܠܝ ܒܥܘܡܩܐ ܕܣܝܢܐ ܕܙܢܝܘܬܐ *he sank deep into the filthy slough of lewdness.* Pa. ܫܠܝ *a*) *to let sink.* *b*) *to tranquillize, give rest.* Ethpa. ܐܫܬܠܝ *to find rest, be led to rest.* Aph. ܐܫܠܝ *to tranquillize, bring rest.* Derivatives, ܫܠܘܬܐ, ܫܠܝܐ, ܫܠܝܘܬܐ, ܫܠܝܐܝܬ, ܫܠܝܘܬܐ, ܫܠܝܐ.

ܫܠܘܬܐ rt. ܫܠܐ. *a*) *grounds, lees.* *b*) *repose.*

ܫܠܠ part. ܫܠܝܠ. *to ooze slowly;* ܫܠܝܠܢ ܕܡܥܝܟ *thy slow tears well up.* Derivatives, ܫܠܠܐ, ܫܠܝܠܐ.

ܫܠܠ with ܡܢ; see ܫܠܡ, ܫܠܠܐ.

ܫܠܐ fut. ܢܫܠܐ, act. part. ܫܠܐ cf. ܫܠܝ. *to draw out* ܡܢ ܒܐܪܐ ܘܓܘܒܐ ܘܝܡܐ ܘܢܗܪܐ ܘܬܗܘܡܐ *from a well and a pit and the sea and a river and an abyss;* ܚܛܘ ܘܫܠܐܘܟ ܡܢ ܥܘܡܩܐ *they dived and brought thee, O pearl,* out of the depth; ܟܕ ܫܠܐ ܘܡܫܠܐ ܚܫܘܟܐ ܫܡܫܐ the sun *as it draws up and dissipates darkness.* Ethpe. ܐܫܬܠܝ *to be taken out* of the water; ܐܫܬܠܝܢ ܡܢ ܝܡܐ *we were rescued from the sea.* Aph. ܐܫܠܝ *to draw out, pull out.* Derivatives, ܫܠܝܐ, ܫܠܝܐ, ܫܠܐ ܢܘܢܐ, ܫܠܐ, ܫܠܝܬܐ, ܫܠܝܐ, ܫܠܐ ܒܣܪܐ.

ܫܠܐ pl. ܫܠܐ m. Arab. *a*) *a sack.* *b*) *a shawl.* c) Pael imper. of verb ܫܠܝ.

ܫܠܐ ܒܣܪܐ pl. ܫܠܝ ܒܣܪܐ rt. ܫܠܐ. m. *a flesh-hook.*

ܫܠܐ ܢܘܢܐ pl. ܫܠܝ ܢܘܢܐ rt. ܫܠܐ. m. *a pelican, gannet; a heron.*

ܫܠܐܠܐ = ܫܠܐܠܬܐ.

ܫܠܘܒ and ܫܠܘܒܐ pl. ܐ̈ m. *a mountain pass, defile, gully.*

ܫܠܓܡ, ܫܠܓܡܐ Arab. m. *turnip.*

ܫܠܕܐ pl. ܝ̈ܢ, ܐ̈ f. *a corpse, body, carcass; the trunk;* ܫܠܕ̈ܐ ܡܝ̈ܬܐ *dead bodies.*

ܫܠܗܒ ܫܠܗܒ Shaphel conj.; see ܠܗܒ.

ܫܠܗܒܝܬܐ pl. ܝ̈ܢ, ܫܠܗܒܝ̈ܬܐ rt. ܠܗܒ. f. *a*) *a flame, blaze;* ܫ̈ ܕܢܘܪܐ *a flame of fire.* *b*) *the flash* of arms, *a bright blade.* *c*) *a burning fever.*

ܫܠܗܒܝܬܢܐ from ܫܠܗܒܝܬܐ. *flaming, blazing.*

ܫܠܗܒ ܫܠܗܒ Shaphel conj.; see ܠܗܒ.

ܫܠܘܐ rt. ܫܠܐ. m. *cessation, intermission;* ܕܠܐ ܫܠܘܐ *unceasing, incessant.*

ܫܠܘܐ or ܫܠܘܐ m. *a cave, chasm, hollow;* cf. ܫܠܘܒܐ.

ܫܠܘܐܝܬ rt. ܫܠܐ. adv. with ܕܠܐ *unintermittently.*

ܫܠܘܚܐ rt. ܫܠܚ. m. *one who sends, a sender;* ܣܠܩ ܠܘܬ ܫܠܘܚܗ Christ *ascended to Him who sent Him.*

ܫܠܘܚܝܬܐ = ܫܠܚܝܬܐ f. *skin, slough.*

ܫܠܘܝܐ *a*) pl. ܐ̈ rt. ܫܠܐ. *a bucket for drawing water.* *b*) ܫܠܘܝܐ, ܫܠܘܝܬܐ rt. ܫܠܐ. with ܠܐ *unceasing.* *c*) from ܫܠܘܐ m. *a cave-dweller.*

ܫܠܘܡܐ, ܫܠܘܡܝܬܐ rt. ܫܠܡ. with ܠܐ *infinite, endless.*

ܠܐ ܫܠܘܡܐܝܬ rt. ܫܠܡ. adv. *endlessly.*

ܫܠܘܡܝܬܐ = ܫܠܡܘܬܐ.

ܫܠܘܡܝܬܢܐ, ܫܠܝܡܐ rt. ܫܠܡ. logic. *granted, admitted* as a premiss.

ܫܠܘܦܚܐ pl. ܐ̈ = ܫܠܘܦܚܐ m. *a boil, swelling, blister.*

ܫܠܘܩܐ pl. ܐ̈ rt. ܫܠܩ. m. *a pot-herb.*

ܫܠܚ act. part. ܫܠܚ, ܫܠܚܐ, pass. part. ܫܠܝܚ, ܐ, ܬܐ. i. fut. ܢܫܠܘܚ *to send* a messenger, letter, answer; with ܠ or ܠܘܬ of the pers. ܫܠܚ ܠܩܘܐܕ ܕ *he sent word to Cavad that . . .;* ܫܠܚܬ ܠܢ ܠܡܐܡܪ *she sent to inform us of . . . .* ܫܠܝܚܐ subst., see below. ii. fut. ܢܫܠܚ opp. ܠܒܫ. *a*) *to doff, take off, strip off* clothes; ܫܠܚܘ ܥܪܛܠܝܢ *strip yourselves bare;* ܫܠܚܘ ܫܘܒܚܐ ܘܠܒܫܘ ܛܪ̈ܦܐ Adam and Eve *laid aside glory for a clothing of leaves.* With ܙܝܢܐ *to lay aside armour;* ܦܓܪܐ *to put off the body;* ܚܛܝܬܐ *to put off sin.* *b*) *to abjure the monastic life;* ܕܝܪܝܐ ܕܫܠܚ *a monk who lays aside his habit, an unfrocked monk.* *c*) *to slough, shed a slough, cast a skin* as an insect or reptile; ܫܠܚܝܢ ܘܦܪܚܝܢ *they shed their skins and fly.* Pass. part. *stripped, bare, naked;* ܫܠܝܚܝܢ ܓܪ̈ܡܘܗܝ *his bare bones;* ܣܘܣܘܬܐ ܫܠܝܚܬܐ *barebacked horses;* ܠܐܝܠܢܐ ܫܠܝܚܐ ܡܠܒܫ Nisan *clothes the bare trees;* ܫܠܝܚ ܡܢ ܫܘܒܚܗ *despoiled of his glory;* ܫܠܝܚܝ ܥܠܡܐ *those who have cast off the world.* Fem. emph. = subst., see below. Ethpe. ܐܶܫܬܠܶܚ to be sent with ܥܰܡ, ܠ, ܡܶܢ; ܡܰܒܘܥܳܐ ܕܶܐܫܬܠܶܚ ܠܚܘܣܳܝܶܢ the fountain sent for our pardoning. Pa. ܫܰܠܰܚ to strip, lay bare, spoil, loose from, divest of clothes, armour; with ܠ, ܡܶܢ. With ܡܶܫܟܳܐ to flay. Eccles. to unfrock, deprive of habit or orders. Pass. part. unarmed, naked, bare, destitute; ܕܰܐܝܕܰܝܳܐ ܡܫܰܠܚܳܢ empty-handed; ܡܫܰܠܚܺܝܢ ܡܶܢ ܕܶܚܠܬܶܗ ܕܰܐܠܳܗܳܐ having put aside the fear of God; ܡܶܠܬܳܐ ܡܫܰܠܰܚܬܳܐ ܗܽܘ ܡܶܢ ܦܰܓܪܳܐ the Word alone apart from the flesh. Ethpa. ܐܶܫܬܰܠܰܚ a) to be stripped, despoiled, laid bare; ܡܶܢ ܡܶܫܟܶܗ to be skinned; ܡܶܢ ܟܽܘܡܪܽܘܬܳܐ to be deprived of priests' orders. b) refl. to divest oneself, lay aside, put off; ܠܒܽܘܫܳܐ ... ܡܶܫܬܰܠܚܺܝܢܰܢ ܐܰܝܟ we strip for gymnastics; ܡܶܫܬܰܠܰܚܬ ܐܰܢ݈ܬ ܘܫܳܒܶܩ ܐܰܢ݈ܬ ܡܰܠܟܽܘܬܳܐ thou dost depose thyself and abdicate. Aph. ܐܰܫܠܰܚ to strip, lay bare, take off, despoil; ܐܰܫܠܚܰܢܝ ܐܺܝܩܳܪܝ He hath stripped me of my glory; ܠܶܒܳܐ ܡܫܰܠܚܳܐ ܡܶܢ ܦܺܐܪܶܐ ܛܳܒܶܐ a heart bare of good fruit. Ettaph. ܐܶܬܬܰܫܠܰܚ to be sent. Derivatives, ܫܠܺܝܚܳܐ, ܫܠܳܚܳܐ, ܫܠܺܝܚܽܘܬܳܐ, ܫܠܚܳܐ, ܫܠܰܚܬܳܐ, ܫܠܺܝܚܳܐ, ܫܠܺܝܚܳܐܺܝܬ, ܫܠܺܝܚܽܘܬܳܐ, ܫܽܘܠܳܚܳܐ, ܫܽܘܠܳܚܳܐ, ܡܫܰܠܚܳܢܺܝܬ, ܡܫܰܠܚܳܢܳܐ, ܡܫܰܠܚܳܢܽܘܬܳܐ.

ܫܠܰܚ, ܫܠܚܳܐ pl. ܶܐ rt. ܫܠܚ II. m. a) a swarm ܕܕܶܒܳܒܶܐ of flies, ܕܕܶܒܽܘܪܝܳܬܳܐ of bees. b) a hide, skin; ܫܠܚܶܐ ܕܶܐܡܪܶܐ lamb skins. c) in BB. bank of a river.

ܫܠܚ, ܫܠܳܚܳܐ rt. ܫܠܚ II. m. putting off, laying aside of clothes.

ܫܠܳܚܳܐ, ܫܠܳܚܬܳܐ pl. ܳܬܳܐ rt. ܫܠܚ II. f. a) undressing. b) a cast skin, exuviae esp. ܫ̈ ܕܚܶܘܝܳܐ a serpent's slough.

ܫܠܚܰܠܳܘܢܳܐ m. ligusticum, lovage or the flower of laserpitium, laserwort.

ܫܠܶܛ fut. ܢܶܫܠܰܛ. to bear rule, bear sway, have the mastery, prevail with ܒ or ܥܰܠ; ܠܫܶܡܫܳܐ ܠܡܶܫܠܰܛ ܒܐܺܝܡܳܡܳܐ ܘܒܠܺܠܝܳܐ God set the sun and moon to rule over the day and over the night; ܐܰܝܟ ܢܽܘܪܳܐ ܒܰܚܒܳܠܳܐ ܫܠܶܛܬ ܚܰܪܒܳܐ ܒܗܽܘܢ as fire among the stubble so had the sword sway amongst them. Part. adj. ܫܰܠܺܝܛ, ܫܰܠܺܝܛܳܐ, ܫܰܠܺܝܛܬܳܐ a) ܫܰܠܺܝܛ ܗܘܳܐ he bare rule; ܫܰܠܺܝܛ ܥܰܠ in authority, in charge of or over; ܫܰܠܺܝܛ ܗܽܘ ܠܡܶܫܒܰܩ ܚܛܳܗܶܐ he hath power to forgive sins; ܫܰܠܺܝܛ ܐ̱ܢܳܐ I have power; ܒܝܰܨܺܝܒܽܘܬܶܗ ܫ̈ or ܒܢܰܦܫܶܗ endowed with free-will, free. b) impers. it is lawful, he may; ܠܳܐ ܫܰܠܺܝܛ ܐ̱ܢܳܫ ܕ it is not lawful for any one, no one may. c) subst., see below. Pa. ܫܰܠܶܛ to set to rule, give power, put in authority with ܒ or ܥܰܠ; ܡܫܰܠܶܛ ܡܰܠܟܳܐ ܠܐ̱ܢܳܫܺܝܢ ܥܰܠ ܨܒܘ̈ܬܳܐ ܕܡܰܠܟܽܘܬܶܗ when a king sets men in authority over the affairs of his kingdom. Pass. part. ܡܫܰܠܰܛ, ܳܐ, ܬܳܐ. a) authoritative, in authority, set over with ܥܰܠ; ܐܰܝܟ ܡܫܰܠܛܳܐ as one having authority; ܡܫܰܠܛܳܐ ܗܘܳܬ ܡܶܠܬܶܗ his word was with authority; ܟܰܦܢܳܐ ܡܫܰܠܰܛ ܗܘܳܐ ܥܰܠ ܡܰܕܢܚܳܐ famine prevailed over the East; ܦܽܘܩܕܳܢܳܐ ܡܫܰܠܛܳܐ absolute power. With ܢܰܦܫܳܐ, ܨܶܒܝܳܢܳܐ, ܚܺܐܪܽܘܬܳܐ, ܝܰܨܺܝܒܽܘܬܳܐ or absol. master of himself, having free-will, free. b) perh. = Aph. pass. part. Ethpa. ܐܶܫܬܰܠܰܛ a) to bear sway, rule, have dominion, authority, power with ܥܰܠ. b) to have the right, be allowed, be able; to be lawful; ܠܳܐ ܫܰܠܺܝܛ ܐ̱ܢܳܫ ܐܳܘ ܡܶܫܬܰܠܰܛ no one has either the power or the right to .... c) to take possession, take, occupy; ܥܰܠ ܦܳܪܣܳܝܶܐ ܐܶܫܬܰܠܰܛܘ ܐ̱ܚܪܺܢܳܐ ܡܰܓܕܠܳܐ the Persians took yet another tower; ܐܶܫܬܰܠܰܛ ܥܠܰܘܗ̱ܝ ܟܶܡܪܳܐ ܐܳܘܟܳܡܬܳܐ melancholy took possession of him. Aph. ܐܰܫܠܶܛ to set in authority, set over work or business; to give power, permission. Pass. part. ܡܰܫܠܰܛ permitted, lawful. Ethtaph. ܐܶܬܬܰܫܠܰܛ to be under dominion. Derivatives, ܫܽܘܠܛܳܢܳܐ, ܫܽܘܠܛܳܢܽܘܬܳܐ, ܫܰܠܺܝܛܳܐ, ܫܰܠܺܝܛ, ܫܰܠܺܝܛܽܘܬܳܐ, ܫܠܺܝܛܳܐܺܝܬ, ܡܫܰܠܛܳܢܳܐ, ܡܫܰܠܛܳܢܽܘܬܳܐ, ܡܫܰܠܛܽܘܬܳܐ.

ܫܰܠܛܳܐ pl. ܶܐ m. a quiver.

ܫܠܳܐ fut. ܢܶܫܠܶܐ, act. part. ܫܳܠܶܐ, ܫܳܠܝܳܐ, pass. part. ܫܠܶܐ, ܫܠܶܝܳܐ, ܫܠܶܝܬܳܐ pl. m. ܫܠܶܝܢ, ܫܠܶܝܶܐ, pl. f. ܫܠܝܳܢ, ܫܠܝܳܬܳܐ. Cf. ܫܠܐ. to cease, desist; to be silent, still, to abate; to dwell in peace; ܫܠܰܘ ܪܘܚ̈ܐ ܘܓܰܠ̈ܠܶܐ—ܓܰܠܠܶܐ the winds, the waves were still; ܫܠܝ m. ܫܠܝ ܠܟܝ f. be still, keep silence; ܬܰܡܳܢ ܪ̈ܫܺܝܥܶܐ ܫܠܰܘ ܡܶܢ ܪܽܘܓܙܳܐ there the wicked cease from troubling; ܕܫܳܠܶܐ ܐ̱ܢܳܐ ܥܠܰܝܗ̇ respecting which I am silent; ܕܠܳܐ ܫܳܠܶܐ incessant sorrow or pain. Pass. part. quiet, silent, mute; immovable; inert, unemployed; ܫܠܶܐ ܗܘܳܐ ܒܥܽܘܡܪܶܗ a hermit dwelt at peace in his abode; ܒܟܳܝܳܐ ܫܠܶܝܳܐ ܘܕܠܳܐ ܕܶܡܥ̈ܶܐ quiet tearless weeping; ܐܰܝܟ ܕܫܠܶܝܢ ܡܰܝܳܐ ܘܡܰܫܩܶܝܢ

where the water was still and deep. Gram. *quiescent, vowelless;* ܫܡܐ ܕܪܫܗ ܫܠܐ *a noun with quiescent initial.* Pa. ܫܰܠܺܝ a) *to quiet, calm, still; to reduce to silence, make an end of;* ܝܶܫܽܘܥ ܕܰܫܠܺܝ ܓܰܠܠܶܐ ܫܰܠܺܝ ܚܶܡܬܳܐ *Jesus who didst calm the billows, calm angry passions;* ܫܰܠܝܽܘܗ̱ܝ ܒܠܶܒܗܽܘܢ *he made them keep it secret in their hearts;* ܫܰܠܺܝ ܡܡܰܠܠܽܘܬܶܗ *he made an end of speaking.* b) *to stay, stanch;* ܦܶܐܪܳܐ ܕܚܰܫܚܳܫܳܐ poppy juice *assuages pain;* ܫܰܠܝܶܗ ܠܕܡܳܐ *he stanched the blood.* c) gram. *to write* or *pronounce without a vowel, to make quiescent.* Ethpa. ܐܶܬܫܰܠܺܝ *to cease; to be stilled, quieted.* Gram. *to be quiescent, be without a vowel.* Aph. ܐܰܫܠܺܝ *to calm, to quiet; to allow to remain at rest;* ܡܰܫܠܶܝܢ ܗ̱ܘܰܘ ܓܶܦܰܝܗܽܘܢ *they let their wings hang motionless.* Derivatives, ܫܶܠܝܳܐ, ܫܰܠܝܳܐܺܝܬ, ܫܠܳܝܳܐ, ܫܠܺܝܳܐ, ܫܠܺܝܽܘܬܳܐ, ܫܠܳܝܳܐ, ܫܠܳܝܘܬܳܐ, ܫܠܝܳܐ.

ܫܶܠܝ, ܫܶܠܝܳܐ rt. ܫܠܐ. m. a) *stillness, quiet, calm; deep sleep, stupor, immobility;* ܗ̱ܘܳܐ ܫܶܠܝܳܐ *there was a calm;* ܫܶܠܝܳܐ ܠܰܝܬ *it ceases not, there is no pause;* ܐܰܪܡܺܝ ܫܶܠܝܳܐ ܥܰܠ ܐܳܕܳܡ the Lord God *caused a deep sleep to fall upon the man;* ܒܫܶܠܝܶܗ ܕܐܰܪܥܳܐ *when the earth is at rest;* ܫܶܠܝܳܐ ܕܣܽܘܥܪܳܢܳܐ *the end of the affair.* b) *silence, private life; the solitary life;* ܕܫܶܠܝܳܐ ܚܰܝܶܐ *the life of an anchorite;* ܒܫܶܠܝܳܐ ܕܳܝܪ̈ܶܐ *solitaries, eremites, recluses;* ܥܳܡܰܪ ܒܫܶܠܝܳܐ *living in retirement.* Adverbial use: c) ܒܫܶܠܝܳܐ *in silence, at peace, securely; tranquilly, silently, secretly;* ܒܫܶܠܝܳܐ ܕܢܶܟܠܶܗ *in his secret guile;* rit. ܗܘܰܘ ܒܫܶܠܝܳܐ *be still, keep silence.* d) ܡܶܢ ܫܶܠܝ, ܡܶܢ ܫܶܠܝܳܐ, ܒܫܶܠܝ, ܒܫܶܠܝܳܐ, ܡܶܢ ܫܶܠܝ, ܡܶܢ ܫܶܠܝܳܐ, ܡܶܢ ܟܽܠ ܫܶܠܝܳܐ or ܡܶܢ ܫܶܠܝ ܐܶܢܫ *sudden, unexpectedly, all at once;* ܡܰܘܬܳܐ ܕܡܶܢ ܫܶܠܝ *sudden death.*

ܫܠܳܝ, ܫܠܳܝܳܐ m. a) rt. ܫܠܐ. *taking out of the water;* ܫ ܕܡܰܝ̈ܳܐ *drawing water.* b) rt. ܫܠܐ. gram. *quiescence* of a letter, not pronounced as ܐ in ܐܰܪܙܳܐ or not vocalized as ܘ in ܢܰܦܫܳܐ.

ܫܠܳܝܳܐܺܝܬ rt. ܫܠܐ. adv. a) *silent, quiet; quietly, noiselessly, in a low voice.* b) *in retirement, in the solitary* or *eremite life.* c) gram. *without a vowel.*

ܫܠܳܝܽܘܬܳܐ rt. ܫܠܐ. f. *stillness, calmness, calm; the eremite life.* Gram. *the quiescence* of a letter.

ܫܠܺܝܚܳܐ pl. ܶܐ rt. ܫܠܚ I. m. a) *a messenger, emissary, missionary;* esp. *an apostle;* ܫܳܒܽܘܥܶܐ ܕܫܠܺܝܚܶܐ the seven weeks following Whitsunday; ܚܕܒܫܒܳܐ ܬܠܺܝܬܳܝܳܐ ܕܫܠܺܝܚܶܐ *the third Sunday of the Apostles* = first Sunday after Trinity. b) *the Epistles of St. Paul, a lection from the Epistles.* c) fem. ܫܠܺܝܚܬܳܐ *a go-between, bearer of messages.*

ܫܠܺܝܚܳܐ, ܫܠܺܝܚܬܳܐ rt. ܫܠܚ II. f. *a skin* = ܫܠܳܚܳܐ; a serpent's *slough.*

ܫܠܺܝܚܳܐܺܝܬ rt. ܫܠܚ. II. adv. *bare, despoiled; barely; in private station.*

ܫܠܺܝܚܽܘܬܳܐ f. a) rt. ܫܠܚ I. *shoots, suckers, palm-branches.* b) *an embassy, message;* ܐܬܺܝܬ ܒܫܠܺܝܚܽܘܬܳܐ ܡܶܢ *I am come on an embassy from ....* c) *the office of an apostle, apostleship, the Apostolate;* ܓܽܘܕܳܐ ܕܫܠܺܝܚܽܘܬܳܐ *the company of the Apostles.* d) rt. ܫܠܚ II. *nakedness, nudity, bareness.*

ܫܠܺܝܚܳܝܳܐ, ܫܠܺܝܚܳܝܬܳܐ rt. ܫܠܚ I. *apostolic;* ܟܽܘܪܣܝܳܐ ܫ W-Syr. *the Apostolic see* i.e. the Patriarchate of Antioch.

ܫܠܺܝܚܬܳܐ; see ܫܠܺܝܚܳܐ and ܫܠܚ II.

ܫܰܠܺܝܛ, ܫܰܠܺܝܛܳܐ pl. ܶܐ, ܺܝܢ and ܫܰܠܺܝܛܳܢܶܐ, ܳܢܺܝܢ rt. ܫܠܛ. m. *a taskmaster; a ruler, leader, governor, prefect, prince;* ܫܰܠܺܝܛܳܢܰܝ ܚܰܝܠܳܐ *captains;* ܫܰܠܺܝܛܳܢܶܐ ܕܐܰܪܥܳܐ *temporal rulers.* Pl. the sixth order of angels = ܫܽܘܠܛܳܢܶܐ.

ܫܰܠܺܝܛܽܘܬܳܐ rt. ܫܠܛ. f. *rule, governorship;* ܫܰܠܺܝܛܽܘܬ ܢܰܦܫܳܐ *self-mastery, free-will;* ܫܰܠܺܝܛܽܘܬ ܢܰܦܫܳܐܺܝܬ *freely, independently.*

ܫܰܠܺܝܛܳܢܳܐ; see ܫܰܠܺܝܛ.

ܫܰܠܝܳܐ rt. ܫܠܐ. m. *a dweller; a recluse, hermit.*

ܫܠܶܝܡܽܘܢ also spelt ܫܠܶܝܡܘܢ, ܫܠܡܘܢ, ܫܠܰܝܡܽܘܢ &c. pr. n. *Solomon.*

ܫܠܶܝܡܽܘܢܳܝܳܐ, ܢܳܝܬܳܐ adj. from the preceding. *Solomitic;* ܗܰܝܟܠܳܐ ܫ *the temple of Solomon.*

ܫܠܺܝܦܳܐ m. a) *a large fodder-bag, corn-sack.* b) pass. part. of verb ܫܠܦ b.

ܫܠܺܝܬܳܐ pl. ܫܠܳܝܳܬܳܐ rt. ܫܠܐ. f. a) *a caul, membrane enveloping the foetus, after-birth.* b) *the thin covering of an egg, egg-skin; membranaceous casing of roe.*

ܫܠܳܟܳܐ pl. ܶܐ rt. ܫܠܟ; see ܫܠܳܟܬܳܐ. a) Chald. and Arab. *a skein,* perhaps *intricacy, detail;* ܫܠܳܟܰܝ ܡܳܪܽܘܬܳܐ *the details* or *discipline of war;* also *the fray, contest.* b) *involution, knot;* ܩܛܪ̈ܐ ܕܐܣܝܪܝܢ ܗܘܘ *the knots with which they were held together;* ܟܪ̈ܟܐ ܥܒܝ̈ܐ ܕܠܠܝܐ *the dense folds of night.* c) Chald. *spoils.*

ܫܠܡ fut. ܢܫܠܡ, act. part. ܫܠܡ, ܫܠܡܐ, pass. part. ܫܠܝܡܐ. a) opp. ܫܪܐ *to come to an end, be finished, concluded;* ܫܠܡܘ ܫܡܝܐ ܘܐܪܥܐ *the heavens and the earth were finished;* ܫܠܡܘ ܛܠܝܐ ܟܠܗܘܢ *are these all thy sons?* ܒܫܘܠܡܗ ܕܫܢܬܐ *at the end of the year;* ܫܠܡܬ ܡܠܟܘܬܐ *the kingdom came to an end;* ܫܠܡ ܠܗ ܥܠܡܐ *the world has come to an end;* ܟܕ ܫܠܡ ܩܘܪܒܐ *when the Eucharist is concluded;* ܡܢ ܒܬܪ ܕܫܠܡ ܐܘܢܓܠܝܘܢ *after the reading of the Gospel;* ܫܠܡ ܒܥܘܕܪܢܗ ܕܡܪܢ ܟܬܒܐ ܗܢܐ *by the help of our Lord this book is completed;* absol. ܫܠܡ *Finis, the End.* b) *to come to the end of life, to die.* Cf. Pael. c) *to be complete, fulfilled* as a tale, number, measure, time, prophecy, with ܟܠ, ܒ, ܠ, ܥܠ; ܫܠܡܬ ܡܠܬܗ ܕܡܪܝܐ *the word of the Lord was fulfilled;* ܟܠ ܒܡܪܢ ܫܠܡܐ *it is fulfilled in our Lord.* d) *to agree with, consent, assent;* with ܠ or ܥܡ; ܠܦܘܩܕܢܗ *to obey his command;* ܫܠܡܘ ܠܫܝܢܐ *to consent to a truce;* ܫܠܡܘ ܕܢܪܡܘܢ ܦܣ̈ܐ *they agreed to cast lots;* ܬܪ̈ܥܝܬܐ ܕܠܐ ܫܠܡܢ *different dispositions.* e) *to agree to, approve, ratify* an election, appointment, canons &c., with ܠܐ *to refuse;* ܠܐ ܫܠܡܘ ܠܗ ܥܡܐ *the people would not receive him* as Patriarch; ܫܠܡ ܗܢܐ ܫܘܪܪܐ *this ratification was made.* f) *to follow, be a follower of, adhere to* esp. with regard to doctrine; ܠܗܝܡܢܘܬܐ *to follow the faith* or *confession;* ܟܠ ܕܠܐ ܫܠܡ ܠܣܘܢܗܕܘܣ *whoso does not adhere to the Council;* ܫܠܡ ܫܒܝܠܐ ܢܫܠܡ *let us follow the same path.* g) *to follow, succeed, be contiguous;* ܠܒܢ̈ܝ ܥܡܘܢ ܫܠܡܝܢ ܒܢ̈ܝ ܡܘܐܒ *the Moabites come next to the Ammonites;* ܟܬܒܐ ܕܫܠܡ *the following book.* h) *to correspond, resemble;* ܫܠܡ ܫܡܥܘܢ ܠܫܡܥܘܢ ܟܐܦܐ ܒܫܡܐ ܘܒܥܒܕܐ S. Simeon *resembled Simon Peter in name and in deed.* i) *to yield, surrender;* ܫܠܡ ܢܦܫܗ ܠܐܠܗܐ ܘܠܥܕܬܐ *he gave himself up for God and the Church.* j) impers. use ܫܠܝܡܐ ܫܠܡ *it was agreed, settled.* Act. part. *whole, entire; following, agreeable* &c.; ܠܐ ܫܠܡܐ *contrary, discordant.* Ethpe. ܐܫܬܠܡ a) *to be given up, delivered up;* ܐܫܬܠܡ ܗܘܐ ܡܫܝܚܐ ܚܠܦ ܦܘܪܩܢܗ ܕܥܠܡܐ Christ *was delivered up for the salvation of the world;* ܠܫܛܝܘܬܐ ܕܛܠܝܘܬܐ *he was given over to childish folly.* b) *to be put to death.* Pa. ܫܠܡ a) opp. ܫܪܝ *to make an end, end, finish, conclude;* ܕܠܐ ܫܘܪܝܐ ܘܠܐ ܫܘܠܡܐ *without beginning or end* = *eternal;* ܟܕ ܫܠܡ ܝܫܘܥ ܡܬ̈ܠܐ ܗܠܝܢ *when Jesus had ended these parables.* b) with ܚܝܘܗܝ, ܝܘܡ̈ܘܗܝ, ܪܗܛܗ, ܐܓܘܢܗ *to end his days, life, course, conflict, to die;* ܫܠܡ ܒܣܝܒܘܬܐ ܛܒܬܐ *he died in a good old age;* ܒܩܛܠܐ ܢܫܠܡ *he shall be put to death;* ܫܠܡ ܡܢ ܚܝ̈ܐ—ܡܢ ܥܠܡܐ *he departed this life, left this world.* c) *to fulfil, perform* a vow, promise, law, divine service, a prediction; ܫܠܡ ܠܡܪܝܐ ܢܕܪ̈ܝܟ *fulfil unto the Lord thy vows.* d) *to make restitution, restore, recompense;* ܚܕ ܒܬܪܝܢ ܢܫܠܡ *he shall restore double.* e) *to deliver up, hand over.* f) *to set* gems. g) *to salute, give peace* with ܠ or ܥܠ. Pass. part. ܡܫܠܡ a) *perfected, finished;* ܗܐ ܡܫܠܡ *it is finished.* β) *whole, entire;* ܟܐܦ̈ܐ ܡܫܠܡܬܐ *whole* or *unhewn stones.* Ethpa. ܐܫܬܠܡ a) *to be brought to an end, finished, completed, accomplished* as a book, vow, service, number, prophecy; ܟܕ ܐܫܬܠܡܬ ܬܫܡܫܬܐ *at the conclusion of the office;* ܐܫܬܠܡ ܨܒܝܢܐ ܕܡܪܝܐ *the will of the Lord was accomplished.* b) *to be given* or *delivered up, surrendered, to surrender* with ܠ. c) *to be brought into a state of peace;* ܐܫܬܠܡ ܥܠܡܐ ܒܡܘܬܗ ܕ *peace was restored to the world at the death of* Julian the Apostate. Aph. ܐܫܠܡ a) *to bring to completion, to achieve;* ܒܗܕܐ ܐܫܠܡ ܘܫܠܡ *herewith he completed and ended* his labours. b) *to give up, give in, surrender, make peace;* ܩܕܡ ܕܐܫܠܡ ܐܪܡܢܝܐ ܠܪܗܘܡܝ̈ܐ *before Armenia made peace with Rome.* c) *to deliver, hand over, commit, consign, to betray;* ܐܫܠܡ ܐܠܗܐ ܠܒܪܗ ܚܠܦܝܢ God *gave up His Son for us;* ܚܕ ܡܢܟܘܢ ܢܫܠܡܢܝ *one of you shall betray Me.* With ܒܐܝܕܐ *to entrust* but ܐܫܠܡ ܐܝܕܐ *to yield, surrender;* with ܚܨܐ *to turn the back, flee;* ܠܡܘܬܐ *to deliver up to death;* ܢܦܫܗ ܪܘܚܐ *to give oneself up, devote oneself;* ܪܘܚܐ *to expire.* d) *to commit* to writing, to memory; *to hand down;* ܣܦܪ̈ܐ ܕܡܫܠܡܝܢ ܝܘܠܦܢܐ ܠܕܪ̈ܐ *the learned who transmit knowledge to the young.* e) *to become a Moslem.* Ettaph. ܐܬܫܠܡ a) *to be given up, handed over, surrendered, delivered.* b) *to be surrendered to, to take possession* of a surrendered place or force; ܐܬܫܠܡ ܪܝܫܐ ܕܚܝܠܘܬܐ *he took command of the army.* c) *to receive, take possession of* a purchase. d) *to be handed down, prescribed; to receive* by tradition. Derivatives, ܫܠܡܐ, ܫܠܡܐ, ܫܘܠܡܐ, ܫܘܠܡܐܝܬ, ܫܘܠܡܢܐ, ܫܠܡܬܐ, ܫܠܡܘܬܐ, ܫܠܡܐܝܬ, ܫܠܡܐ, ܫܠܡܢܐ, ܫܠܡܢܘܬܐ, ܫܠܡܢܐܝܬ, ܫܠܡܢܘܬܐ, ܫܠܡܢܐ, ܡܫܠܡܢܐ, ܡܫܠܡܢܐ, ܡܫܠܡܢܐܝܬ, ܡܫܠܡܢܘܬܐ, ܡܫܠܡܢܘܬܐ, ܡܫܠܡܢܘܬܐ, ܡܫܬܠܡܢܘܬܐ, ܡܫܬܠܡܢܐܝܬ, ܡܫܬܠܡܢܐ, ܡܫܬܠܡܢܘܬܐ.

ܫܠܡ, ܫܠܡܐ, ܫܠܡܬܐ rt. ܫܠܡ. *whole, entire, perfect, full, complete;* ܛܝܡܐ ܫܠܡܐ *the full price;* ܫܢܬܐ ܫܠܡܬܐ *a full* or *entire year;* ܓܒܪܐ ܫܠܡܐ *a man of full age, adult;* ܢܟܣܐ ܫܠܡܐ often ellipt. *whole burnt-offerings, peace-offerings;* ܢܘܗܪܐ ܘܫܠܡܐ *Urim and Thummim.*

ܫܠܡ, ܫܠܡܐ pl. ܐ̈ rt. ܫܠܡ. m. a) *peace, safety, health, welfare;* ܫܠܡ ܗܘ *is he well?* ܫܠܡ ܠܟ or ܫܠܡܐ ܠܟ *peace be with thee, hail, greeting;* ܦܘܫ ܒܫܠܡܐ *farewell.* b) *a greeting, salutation;* with ܝܗܒ, ܫܐܠ, ܐܡܪ and ܠ *to greet, salute;* ܫܐܠ ܒܫܠܡܗ *to inquire of the health* or *welfare;* ܫܠܡܐ ܘܐܓܪܬܐ ܕܪܚܡܘܬܐ *greetings and friendly letters.* c) eccles. *the invocation of peace, Pax nobiscum; the pax* or *kiss of peace.* d) ܡܕܝܢܬ ܫܠܡܐ *the City of Peace,* the Arabic name of Baghdad given to it by its founder, Almansor, the second Abbasside Khalif.

ܫܠܡܐܝܬ rt. ܫܠܡ. adv. *entirely, fully; unanimously.*

ܫܠܡܘܬܐ or ܫܠܡ̈ rt. ܫܠܡ. f. a) *soundness of body, full age.* b) *consummation* of marriage. c) *the setting* of gems. d) *agreement, concord, common consent, unanimity;* ܒܚܕܐ ܫ̈ *unanimously;* ܒܪ ܫ̈ *agreeing, consenting.* e) *vote, suffrage, assent* to the election of a Patriarch, Maphrian &c. or to the succession of a Khalif; ܫ̈ ܣܘܢܗܕܝܩܝܬܐ *synodical ratification* of an election; ܫ̈ ܕܟܬܒܐ *written assent* or *vote* sent by bishops not present at an election. f) ܫܠܡܘܬܐ ܕܡ̈ܠܐ *harmony, agreement of expressions* in the four Gospels. g) *convention, technical* or *conventional meaning.*

ܫܠܡܘܬܢܝܐ, ܢܝܬܐ rt. ܫܠܡ. *conventional.*

ܫܠܡܠܡܐ, ܫܠܡܠܡܬܐ rt. ܫܠܡ. *whole, entire, perfect;* ܟܐܦ̈ܐ ܫܠܡܠܡ̈ܬܐ *whole stones* i.e. undressed stones, also *squared, ready-hewn stones.*

ܫܠܡܠܡܘܬܐ rt. ܫܠܡ. f. *entirety, completeness.*

ܫܠܡܠܡܢܝܐ rt. ܫܠܡ. *complete, containing all.*

ܫܠܡܢܐ and ܫܠܡܢܐ pl. ܐ̈ m. *jutting out, projecting stones.*

ܫܠܦ fut. ܢܫܠܘܦ, act. part. ܫܳܠܶܦ, ܫܳܠܦܳܐ. a) *to dry up, languish.* b) in BB. *to shoot up, form blades* or *ears.* c) *to draw* a sword, *to extract, pull out* splinters, nails, a lance-head. Ethpe. ܐܫܬܠܦ *to go out of doors.* Pa. ܫܰܠܶܦ *to dry up;* ܬܘܡ̈ܐ ܡܫܰܠܦܶܐ *dry garlic stalks.* Ethpa. ܐܫܬܠܦ *to be drawn* of a sword. Derivatives, ܫܘܠܦܐ, ܫܠܦ ܙ̈ܓܐ, ܫܠܦܐ, ܫܠܦܐ, ܫܠܦܬܐ.

ܫܠܦ ܙ̈ܓܐ rt. ܫܠܦ. *pincers.*

ܫܠܦܐ rt. ܫܠܦ. m. *a blade without hilt or handle.*

ܫܠܦܐ m. *a brother-in-law, sister's husband.*

ܫܠܦܐ rt. ܫܠܦ. m. a) *extraction* of an arrow &c. from a wound. b) *a bread-trencher.*

ܫܠܦܘܚܝܬܐ cf. ܫܠܦܘܚܝܬܐ. f. *a bladder, the renal bladder;* ܫ̈ ܕܢܦܝܚܐ *an inflated bladder.*

ܫܠܦܬܐ rt. ܫܠܦ. f. *a double-edged knife.*

ܫܠܩ fut. ܢܫܠܘܩ, act. part. ܫܳܠܶܩ, ܫܳܠܩܳܐ, pass. part. ܫܠܝܩ, ܩܐ, ܩܬܐ. *to cook, boil, broil, to soak, steep;* ܚܛ̈ܐ ܫܠܝ̈ܩܬܐ *sodden grain.* Ethpe. ܐܫܬܠܩ *to be boiled, soaked.* Ethpa. ܐܫܬܠܩ *to be sodden, stewed; scalded;* ܐܫܬܠܩ ܗܘܐ ܦܐܪܐ ܡܢ ܫܡܫܐ *the fruit was scalded* by the sun. Aph. ܐܫܠܩ *to scald* linen, *to steep in boiling water.* Derivatives, ܫܘܠܩܐ, ܫܠܩܐ, ܫܠܩܐ, ܫܠܩܬܐ.

ܫܠܩܐ pl. ܐ̈ rt. ܫܠܩ. m. *boiling, a decoction; fruit-juice thickened by boiling;* ܐܟܠܝܢ ܠܗ ܒܫܠܩܐ *they eat it boiled.*

ܫܠܩܩܬܐ or ܫ̈ rt. ܫܠܩ. f. *small-pox.*

ܫܠܫܠ ETHPALPAL ܐܫܬܠܫܠ *to follow in succession.*

ܫܠܫܠܐ *a*) pl. ܫܠܫܠܐ and ܫܠܫܠܐ rt. ܫܠ. m. *a clot* of blood. *b*) pl. ܫܠܫܠܬܐ; see ܫܠܫܠܬܐ.

ܫܠܡ; see ܫܠܡ.

ܫܡ, ܫܡܐ ܫܡܐ irreg. pl. ܫܡܗܐ, ܫܡܗܐ, ܫܡܗܝܢ, ܫܡܗܘܬܐ m. *a*) *a name, appellation, title;* ܒܫܡܗܘܗܝ ܫܡ ܫܡ ܡܕܟܪ ܐܢܐ *I mention each by name;* ܫܡܐ ܕܢܦܫܗ *a proper* or *personal name* = opp. ܫܡܐ ܕܫܪܒܬܗ *gentilic* or *family name.* *b*) *an empty name, pretext, pretence;* ܒܫܡ ܐܦܣܩܘܦܐ—ܕܝܪܝܐ *a bishop, a monk in name only, nominally.* *c*) *fame, reputation, renown;* ܫܡܐ ܕܫܡܗܘܬܐ *very famous, of great renown;* ܫܡܐ ܒܝܫܐ *infamy.* With preps. ܒܫܡܐ ܕ *in the name of, for the sake of;* ܐܬܩܛܠ ܒܫܡܐ ܛܒܐ ܡܛܠ ܝܫܘܥ *he was slain gloriously for Jesus;* ܐܬܒܢܝ ܥܠ ܫܡ ܕ *the building was named after, dedicated to ....* *d*) gram. *a word, part of speech, noun;* ܫܡܐ ܟܢܘܫܝܐ *a collective noun;* ܫܡܐ ܩܢܝܢܐ or ܫܡܐ ܩܢܝܢܐ *a noun substantive;* ܫܡܗܐ ܚܘܘܝܢܐ *demonstrative pronouns.* DERIVATIVES, verbs ܫܡܗ and ܫܡܝ, ܫܡܗܝܐ, ܫܡܗܝܐܝܬ, ܫܡܗܝܘܬܐ, ܫܡܗܐܝܬ, ܫܡܗܝܐ, ܫܡܗܘܬܐ, ܡܫܡܗܐܝܬ, ܡܫܡܗܘܬܐ, ܡܫܬܡܗܢܐ.

ܫܡܛ PAEL ܫܡܛ perh. *a*) *to mislead; to allow to be idle* or *inattentive;* ܡܠܦܢܐ ܕܬܠܡܝܕܗ ܘܒܚܢܢܐ ܠܐ ܡܫܡܛ ܠܗ ܡܥܠܡ ܠܗ *a teacher compels his pupil to learn and in kindness does not allow him to idle.* *b*) *to excommunicate, execrate;* ܢܐܣܘܪ ܘܢܫܡܛ ܟܗܢܐ *the priest shall bind and excommunicate them.* Pass. part. ܡܫܡܛ, ܡܫܡܛܐ *idle, dissipated; execrable, excommunicate.* ETHPA. ܐܫܬܡܛ *to be weakened, divided; to be repudiated.* DERIVATIVES, ܫܡܛܐ, ܡܫܡܛܘܬܐ.

ܫܡܛܐ rt. ܫܡܛ. m. *imprecation; exultation over the misfortunes of others.*

ܫܡܗ and ܫܡܝ denom. verb PAEL conj. from ܫܡ. *to name, call, denominate; to give a surname, nickname; to take* or *assume a name* with ܒܫܡܗ or ܥܠ ܫܡܗ; ܐܥܡܕܗ ܘܫܡܗܗ ܓܝܘܪܓܝܣ *he baptized him by the name of George;* ܫܡܗ ܠܡܕܝܢܬܐ ܥܠ ܫܡܗ *he called the city after his own name;* ܝܥܩܘܒ ܕܫܡܗ ܐܝܣܪܝܠ *Jacob to whom he gave the name of Israel.* Pass. part. ܡܫܡܗ, ܡܫܡܗܐ, ܡܫܡܗܬܐ *named, mentioned; famous, renowned, illustrious;* ܕܡܫܡܗ ܠܥܠ *the above-named;* ܐܦܣܩܘܦܘܬܐ ܕܠܐ ܡܫܡܗܐ *an unnamed bishopric* viz. when a bishop was consecrated without a cure; ܠܐ ܡܫܡܗܐ *nameless, anonymous.* ETHPA. ܐܫܬܡܗ and ܐܫܬܡܝ *to be called, named; to have* or *assume a name* or *title; to be designate; to be renowned, famous;* ܕܡܫܬܡܗ *called, surnamed;* ܩܕܡ ܕܐܫܬܡܗ *above-named, aforesaid.*

ܫܡܗܐܝܬ from ܫܡ. adv. *by name, expressly.*

ܫܡܗܝܐ, ܫܡܗܝܬܐ from ܫܡ. gram. *of* or *pertaining to a noun.*

ܫܡܗܝܘܬܐ from ܫܡ. gram. *the mentioning of a noun; nominality.*

ܫܡܘܛܐ rt. ܫܡܛ. m. *thread wound on the spindle, a ball of thread.*

ܫܡܘܛܘܬܐ rt. ܫܡܛ. f. *peeling, skinning.*

ܫܡܘܪܚܐ m. *a mill-house, mill-shed.*

ܫܡܘܢܐ pl. ܝܢ, ܐ m. *a very small coin, a farthing* or *the fourth part of an as* or *farthing, an obol;* ܕܢܫܐ ܫ is said to be equivalent to a half as which weighs 36 carats, also to a mina i.e. an obol or 31 carats. Troy weight one ܫܡܘܢܐ = $1\frac{1}{2}$ grains.

ܫܡܘܢܐ in the Lexx. m. *sadness, depression.*

ܫܡܘܥܐ pl. ܐ rt. ܫܡܥ. *a*) *a hearer, hearkener, listener; attentive.* *b*) *an official appointed to hear law-suits.* *c*) *a pupil;* eccles. *one under instruction;* ܙܠܘ ܫܡܘܥܐ *go ye hearers* = Ite missa est. *d*) Arab. *coating* or *incorporating with wax.*

ܫܡܘܥܬܐ pl. ܬܐ rt. ܫܡܥ. f. *news, tidings; a report, rumour; hearsay, tattling.*

ܫܡܛ fut. ܢܫܡܘܛ, act. part. ܫܡܛ, ܫܡܛܐ, pass. part. ܫܡܝܛ, ܐ, ܬܐ. *a*) *to draw, unsheathe;* ܫܡܘܛ ܣܦܣܪܟ *draw thy sword.* *b*) *to draw out, tear out, pluck out* hair, feathers, a weapon from a wound &c., ܫܡܛ ܣܟܐ ܡܢ ܪܓܠܗ *he pulled out a thorn from his foot;* ܒܪܩܐ ܫܡܛ ܕܦܐ ܡܢ ܐܠܦܐ lightning *tore a plank out of* the boat; ܐܠܥܐ ܕܫܡܛ ܥܒܘܕܐ *the rib which the Maker drew out.* *c*) *to pull off* shoes, bracelets &c. Pass. part. *unsheathed, drawn, bare, unshod, barefoot;* ܠܫܢܐ ܫܠܝܚܐ *a tongue like a drawn sword;* ܟܬܦܐ ܕܫܠܝܚ ܓܪܡܗ *a boned shoulder of meat;* ܫܠܝܚ ܠܒܐ *discouraged, senseless.* Ethpe. ܐܫܬܠܚ *to be unsheathed, drawn* as a sword; *to be pulled* or *drawn out;* ܢܫܬܠܚ ܦܪܙܠܐ ܡܢ ܩܝܣܐ *the iron may slip from the helve;* ܢܫܬܠܚ ܩܝܣܐ ܡܢ ܒܝܬܗ *let a beam be pulled out from his house.* Ethpa. ܐܫܬܠܚ *to get loose from harness, throw off the yoke.* Aph. ܐܫܠܚ *to draw off* sandals. Derivatives, ܫܠܚܬܐ, ܫܠܝܚܘܬܐ, ܫܠܚܐ, ܫܠܘܚܐ, ܫܠܘܚܘܬܐ, ܡܫܠܚܘܬܐ, ܫܠܚܠܚܘܬܐ.

ܫܠܚܬܐ rt. ܫܠܚ. m. *a great axe, woodman's axe.*

ܫܠܘܚܐ rt. ܫܠܚ. m. *the drawing* of a sword; *plucking out* of feathers; *extraction* of an arrow from a wound.

ܫܠܘܚܘܬܐ rt. ܫܠܚ. f. *drawing a sword; extraction.*

ܫܠܫܠ and ܐܫܬܠܫܠ Pael and Ethpaal; see ܫܫܠ.

ܫܠܡܝܐ from ܫܐܡ. *Damascene, a Syrian.*

ܫܡܝܐ pl. ܫܡܝܐ rarely ܫܡܝܢ. com. gen. usually m. and sing. *a*) *heaven;* ܫܡܝ ܫܡܝܐ *the heaven of heavens;* ܐ̈ ܣܡܝܩ *sky-blue, azure.* *b*) *the ceiling, roof, eaves; the height, highest part;* ܫܡܝ ܒܝܬܐ *the roof* or *ceiling;* ܫܡܝ ܡܫܟܐ *a shelter roofed with skins;* ܫܡܝ ܚܢܟܐ *the roof of the palate;* ܫܡܝ ܦܘܡܐ *the roof of the mouth;* ܫܡܝܐ ܕܡܘܚܐ *the upper part of the brain;* ܫܡܝ ܐܦܘ̈ܐ *the vaults, ceilings.* Derivatives, ܫܡܝܢܐ, ܫܡܝܝܐ, ܫܡܝܢܘܬܐ.

ܫܠܝܚܘܬܐ rt. ܫܠܚ. f. *being unsheathed; being plucked out; being unshod.*

ܫܡܝܢ, ܐ, ܬܐ *fat;* see ܫܡܢ.

ܫܡܝܢܐ, ܝܬܐ from ܫܡܝܐ. *heavenly, celestial.*

ܫܡܝܢܘܬܐ rt. ܫܡܢ. f. *fatness.*

ܫܡܝܢܝܐ, ܫܡܝܢܝܐ, ܝܬܐ from ܫܡܝܐ. *heavenly.*

ܫܡܝܢܝܘܬܐ from ܫܡܝܐ. f. *heavenliness.*

ܫܡܝܥܘܬܐ rt. ܫܡܥ. f. *the being heard, acceptableness* of prayer.

ܫܡܝܪܐ or ܟܐܦܐ ܕܫ̈ m. *a*) *adamant;* ܫ̈ ܕ ܛܦܪܐ *a diamond point, steel graver.* *b*) *emery.*

ܫܡܝܪܝܐ, ܝܬܐ from ܫܡܝܪܐ. *adamantine.*

ܫܡܝܫܛܝܐ pl. ܝܐ̈ from ܫܡܝܫܛ or ܫܡܫܛ *Samosata, Samosatene, of* or *from Samosata.*

ܫܡܟܐ and ܫ̈ܡܟ m. pl. *onions, garlic bulbs, bulbous roots.*

ܫܡܟܐ m. pl. *the smell of the armpits.*

ܫܡܟܘܬܐ f. *the stink of a cavern.*

ܫܡܠܝ Shaphel conj. of verb ܡܠܐ.

ܫܡܢ fut. ܢܫܡܢ, act. part. ܫܡܢ, ܫܡܢܐ. *to be* or *grow fat; to fill out, ripen* as fruit; *to be fertile; to swell up* as a tumour; ܫܡܢ ܘܒܥܛ *he waxed fat and kicked;* ܥܕܡܐ ܕܫܡܢ ܦܐܪܐ ܒܟܪܡܐ *until the fruit be ripe in the vineyard;* ܫܡܝܢܐ ܡܢܬܗ *his portion is fat* or *large.* Part. adj. ܫܡܝܢ, ܐ, ܬܐ *fat, full, rich, ripe, fertile;* ܥܢܐ ܫܡܝܢܬܐ *fat sheep;* ܫܒܠܐ ܫܡܝܢܬܐ *a full ear;* ܐܪܥܐ ܡܙܒܠܐ ܘܫܡܝܢܐ *manured and fertile soil;* ܓܒܪ̈ܐ ܫܡܝܢܝ ܟܝܣܐ *men with fat* or *well-filled purses.* Ethpe. ܐܫܬܡܢ *to grow fat; to grow luxuriantly.* Pa. ܫܡܢ *to fatten, ripen;* ܡܐܟܘܠܬܐ ܡܫܡܢܢܝܬܐ *fattening food.* Derivatives, ܫܡܝܢܐ, ܫܡܝܢܘܬܐ, ܡܫܡܢܐ.

ܫܡܥ fut. ܢܫܡܥ, act. part. ܫܡܥ, ܫܡܥܐ, pass. part. ܫܡܝܥ, ܐ, ܬܐ. *to hear, hearken, listen, attend, understand, obey;* with ܒ or ܥܠ *of, about;* with ܠ or ܡܢ of the pers. or ܒܩܠܗ *to attend to, consent, comply with.* Imper. with suff. I pers. ܫܡܥܝܢܝ (sing.) *attend to me;* ܫܡܥܘܢܝ (pl.) *hearken unto me;* ܡܢ ܕܐܝܬ ܠܗ ܐܕܢܐ ܕܢܫܡܥ ܢܫܡܥ *he that hath ears to hear let him hear;* ܠܒܪ ܡܢ ܣܘܪܝܝܐ ܡܕܡ ܠܐ ܫܡܥ *he understands nothing beyond Syriac.* Pass. part. *heard, accepted* as a prayer; *understood, intelligible; audible; obedient;* with ܠܐ *unheard of;* ܫܡܝܥ ܠܟ *thou hast heard;* ܒܩܠܐ ܫܡܝܥܐ *audibly;* ܫܡܝܥܐ ܒܥܠܡܐ ܟܠܗ *world-renowned.* Ethpe. ܐܫܬܡܥ *to be heard, hearkened unto; to be obedient, obey;* ܐܫܬܡܥܬ ܨܠܘܬܟ *thy prayer is heard;* ܟܐܢܘܬܐ ܕܠܐ ܐܫܬܡܥܬ *disregarded justice;* ܐܫܬܡܥܘ ܠܐܒܗܝܟܘܢ *obey your parents.* Aph. ܐܫܡܥ *to let* or *make hear, cause to hear, tell; to announce, proclaim;* ܐܫܡܥܝܢܝ ܩܠܟܝ *let me hear thy voice;* eccles. with ܩܠܐ *to speak audibly, proclaim aloud;* ܕܬܡܢ ܢܫܡܥ ܣܒܪܬܐ *that he might there proclaim the Gospel.* Derivatives,

ܫܡܥܐ, ܫܡܘܥܐ, ܫܡܘܥܬܐ, ܫܡܝܥܐ, ܡܫܡܥܢܐ, ܡܫܡܥ, ܡܫܡܥܬܐ, ܡܫܬܡܥܢܐ, ܡܫܬܡܥܢܐܝܬ, ܡܫܬܡܥܢܘܬܐ, ܡܫܬܡܥܢܘܬܐ.

ܫܡܥܬܐ pl. ܬܐ̈ rt. ܫܡܥ. m. *a*) *hearing, the sense of hearing.* *b*) *a sound, noise, report;* ܩܝܬܪ̈ܐ ܕܫܡܥܬܐ *loud cymbals.* *c*) *a report, narration;* ܡܢ ܫܡܥܬܐ *by hearsay.* *d*) Arab. *wax.*

ܫܡܥܘܢ Heb. pr. n. *Simeon, Simon;* ܫ̈ ܟܐܦܐ *Simon Peter.*

ܫܡܥܘܢܝܐ, ܢܝܬܐ from ܫܡܥܘܢ. *a*) *of the tribe of Simeon.* *b*) *a follower of St. Peter; Petrine;* ܗܝܡܢܘܬܐ ܫܡܥܘܢܝܬܐ *faith like Peter's.*

ܫܡܥܢܝܐ, ܢܝܬܐ rt. ܫܡܥ. *of the hearing; auditory, audible.*

ܫܡܪ fut. ܢܫܡܪ, act. part. ܫܡܪ. *to guard, keep.* Pa. ܫܡܪ *a*) *to send forth* or *out, to dispatch, dismiss, let go, let loose, let down;* ܫܡܪ ܠܐܘܪܥܗ ܕܝܠܗ *he sent to meet him;* ܫܡܪ ܩܘܪ̈ܒܢܐ ܘܫܡܪܗ *he gave him gifts and dismissed him;* ܡܐ ܕܢܫܡܪ ܒܥܝܪܗ *when* any one *lets his cattle loose;* ܫܡܪ ܫܒܝܗ ܫܒܝ̈ܐ *he let his captives go free;* ܫܡܪ ܘܡܫܡܪ ܫܒܝ̈ܠܐ *he despises and discards* evil ways; ܫܡܪ ܠܢ ܒܓܠ̈ܠܐ ܕܥܩܬܐ *he threw us into floods of grief.* With ܐܠܦܐ *to launch a ship;* ܓܐܪ̈ܐ *to discharge arrows;* ܡܨܝܕܬܐ *to let down a net.* *b*) *to send forth, emit* breath, smoke, vapour, light, water, sound; ܦܢܝܬܢ ܡܫܡܪܢܝܬܐ ܢܘܗܪܐ *our region which sheds light abroad.* *c*) *to break out into* weeping, curses &c., *to utter;* ܫܡܪܬ ܩܠܐ ܒܟܝܐ *I gave vent to loud sobbing;* ܠܐ ܢܫܡܪ ܠܘܛܬܐ *let him not hurl imprecations at me.* *d*) *to direct* the mind, the gaze, the attention; ܫܡܪܬ ܚܙܝܐ ܕܝܠܝ ܠܪܘܚܩܐ *I gazed afar.* Ethpa. ܐܫܬܡܪ *a*) *to be dismissed, sent away; to be discharged, released* from prison; ܡܢ ܕܢܬܢܟܣ ܐܫܬܡܪ the scapegoat *was sent away unslaughtered.* *b*) *to let loose, let go; to be diffused, to be given free vent;* ܡܫܬܡܪܢܐ ܡܪܟܒܬܐ *the chariot is started* in the race; ܟܠ ܠܫܢܐ ܐܫܬܡܪ ܥܠܝ *every tongue was let loose at me;* ܢܣܝܘܢ̈ܐ ܡܫܬܡܪܝܢ ܥܠ ܡܚܝܠܘܬܟ *temptations let loose against thy weakness;* ܠܕܝܢܐ ܕܝܢܐ ܡܫܬܡܪ *he shall be delivered over to judgement.* *c*) gram. *to be found, to be in use;* ܢܬܠ ܡܫܬܡܪ ܗܘ ܒܥܬܝܕ ܘܠܐ ܒܥܒܪ *Nethel is used in the future but not in the past tense.* Derivatives, ܫܡܪܐ, ܫܡܪܬܐ, ܫܘܡܪܐ, ܡܫܬܡܪܢܘܬܐ, ܡܫܡܪܢܝܬܐ, ܡܫܡܪܢܐ, ܫܡܪܐ.

ܫܘܡܪܐ = ܫܡܪܐ m. *fennel;* ܫ̈ ܕܣܘܣܝܐ *horse-fennel.*

ܫܡܪܐ rt. ܫܡܪ. m. *thick smoke, soot.*

ܫܡܪܐ rt. ܫܡܪ. m. *dispatching; setting at liberty, discharging.*

ܫܡܪܝܐ, ܝܬܐ from ܫܡܪܝܢ. *Samaritan, a Samaritan.*

ܫܡܪܝܘܬܐ from ܫܡܪܝܐ f. *Samaritanism,* a half-Judaic, half-heathen form of worship.

ܫܡܪܝܢ pr. n. f. *Samaria.*

ܫܡܪܡܪܐ pl. ܐ̈ m. *unable to see after sunset.* Pl. *nyctalopia, night-blindness.*

ܫܡܪܢܝܐ rt. ܫܡܪ. *sooty.*

ܫܡܫ Pael ܫܡܫ. *a*) *to serve, minister to, wait upon; to attend to, supply;* ܡܫܡܫܐ ܗܘܬ ܠܟܪ̈ܝܗܐ *she ministered to the sick;* ܐܬܘܢܐ ܕܡܫܡܫ ܠܐܦܝܐ *the oven which serves for baking.* With ܥܒܕܘܬܐ *to serve as a slave;* ܨܒܝܢܐ *to do the will.* *b*) *to perform the duties of an office, to administer,* with ܐܝܙܓܕܘܬܐ *to discharge an embassy;* ܡܠܟܘܬܐ *to fill the throne, reign.* Eccles. with ܐܦܝܣܩܘܦܘܬܐ, ܟܘܡܪܘܬܐ, ܩܫܝܫܘܬܐ, ܟܗܢܘܬܐ &c. or absol. *to perform the duties, fill the office of a priest, bishop* &c.; ܥܘܡܪܐ ܕܒܗ ܫܡܫܬ *the monastery which I administered;* ܡܐ ܕܫܡܫ ܫܢܝܢ ܥܣܪܝܢ ܘܬܠܬ *when he had been Patriarch for twenty-three years.* With ܐܪ̈ܙܐ *to administer the Holy Mysteries.* c) with ܡܙܡܘܪ̈ܐ, ܡܕܪ̈ܫܐ, ܬܫܒ̈ܚܬܐ or absol. *to chant* or *recite the Psalter;* ܟܠܗ ܕܘܝܕ ܡܫܡܫܝܢܢ *we recite the whole Psalter;* ܡܫܡܫ ܒܠܒܗ *he repeats the Psalms to himself.* *d*) idiom. ܫܒܗܪܘܬܐ ܕܡܫܡܫܐ ܩܕܝܫܘܬܟܘܢ *the pride your Holiness exhibited.* Ethpa. ܐܫܬܡܫ *a*) *to be served, ministered to.* *b*) *to be administered, performed, celebrated* of rites, divine service &c., ܥܪܘܒܬܐ ܕܕܗܒܐ ܐܝܟ ܥܐܕܐ ܡܫܬܡܫܐ *Golden Friday is kept as a feast.* *c*) *to be said, recited, chanted* as psalms, creeds. *d*) *to be done, performed, perpetrated, effected, to take place, come to pass;* ܟܠܗ ܐܝܟ ܐܫܬܡܫ

how was his death brought about? ܐܝܟܢܐ ܐܫܬܡܠܝ ܡܘܬܗ; ܣܘܪܚܢܐ ܕܐܫܬܡܠܝ ܒܡܕܝܢܬܢ the sin committed in our city; ܐܫܘܝܘܬܐ ܕܐܫܬܡܠܝ ܒܝܢܬܗܘܢ the treaty that was concluded between them; ܥܒ̈ܕܐ ܕܐܫܬܡܠܝ ܒܚܪܬܐ ܕܥܠܡܐ the stupendous events at the end of the world. e) to be cultivated, reverenced; ܐܝܟܐ ܕܢܟܦܘܬܐ ܡܫܬܡܫܐ where purity was reverenced. DERIVATIVES, ܫܡܫܐ, ܫܡܫܘܬܐ, ܡܫܡܫܢܐ, ܡܫܡܫܢܘܬܐ, ܡܫܡܫܢܝܬܐ, ܡܫܬܡܫܢܐ, ܡܫܬܡܫܢܘܬܐ, ܡܫܬܡܫܢܝܬ.

ܫܡܫ, ܫܡܫܐ pl. ܫܡܫܝܢ com. gen. usually masc. the sun; ܣܥܪܐ ܫܡܫܝܐ sunny or red hair. Chem. a name for gold. DERIVATIVES, ܫܡܫܝܐ, verb ܫܡܫܡ, ܫܡܫܝܐ, ܫܡܫܝܐܝܬ, ܫܡܫܢܝܐ.

ܫܡܫܐ, ܫܡܫܬܐ pl. ܫܡܫܐ̈, ܫܡܫܬ̈ܐ rt. ܫܡܫ. a) a servant, minister. b) = ܡܫܡܫܢܐ a deacon; rarely = a priest; ܫܡܫܐ ܕܩܘܕܫܐ a minister of holy things. c) f. a hand-maid, a deaconess.

ܫܡܫܘܬܐ rt. ܫܡܫ. f. the diaconate (rare).

ܫܡܫܡ denom. verb from ܫܡܫܐ. to expose to the sun, leave in the sun.

ܫܡܫܢܐ, ܫܡܫܢܝܬܐ from ܫܡܫܐ. solar.

ܫܡܫܢܐ from ܫܡܫܐ. ܫܡܫܢ ܓܘܢܐ sunny-coloured.

ܫܡܫܐܝܬ from ܫܡܫܐ. adv. like the sun, sunnily.

ܫܡܫܝܐ, ܫܡܫܝܬܐ from ܫܡܫܐ. a) of the sun, sunny, solar; ܡܢܝܢܐ ܫܡܫܝ̈ܐ those who count by solar months; metaph. ܫܡܫܝܐ ܒܫܘܦܪܐ radiant, sunlike in beauty. b) pl. sun-worshippers = Yezidees.

ܫܡܫܪ, ܫܡܫܪܐ m. the juniper.

ܫܢ, ܫܢܐ pl. ܫܢܝܢ, ܫܢ̈ܐ of animal teeth, ܫܢܐ, ܫܢܬܐ when used figuratively, const. st. ܫܢܬ pl. ܫܢܝ f. a) a tooth, tusk; ܣܕܪܐ ܕܫܢ̈ܐ ܠܥܠܝܬܐ the upper row of teeth; ܚܝܘܬܐ ܫܢܢܬܐ a wild beast. Gram. ܐܬܘܬܐ ܕܫܢ̈ܐ dental sibilants i.e. ܙ ܣ ܨ ܫ. As in Arabic ܒܪ ܫܢܐ, ܒܪܬ ܫܢܐ of the same age. b) ellipt. for ܫܢܐ ܕܦܝܠܐ ivory; ܓܠܦܐ ܕܫܢܐ ivory carving. c) a steep rock, jutting crag, mountain peak; ܫܢܐ ܕܫܘܥܐ the crag of the rock. d) a spike ܕܬܘܡܐ of garlic; a prong; ܬܠܬ ܫܢ̈ܝܢ three-pronged. e) compounds: ܫܢܬ ܐܪܝܐ or ܫܢܝ ܟܠܒܐ pointed eryngium; ܫܢܬ ܟܠܒܬܐ burning sores, furuncles, usually near the nails; ܫܢܝ ܬܢܝܢܐ dragon arum, snake-plant.

ܫܢܐ Arab. great honour, sublimity.

ܫܢܐ fut. ܢܫܢܐ, act. part. ܫܢܐ, ܫܢܝܐ, ܫܢܝܬܐ, pass. part. ܫܢܐ, ܫܢܝܐ. a) to be altered for the worse; ܫܢܐ ܓܘܢܐ ܕܚܙܘܗ̈ܝ ܫܦܝܪ̈ܐ its fine colour fades. b) to be displaced, dislocated; ܫܢܬ ܚܨܗ his hip was dislocated. c) to change from one place to another, to remove, depart; ܦܩܕ ܠܝ ܕܐܫܢܐ he ordered me to move. d) to be changed in mind, go mad, rave. Parts. insane, frantic, mad, foolish; ܫܢܝܐܝܬ ܡܫܬܢܐ ܐܢܬ thou ravest wildly; ܫܢܝܐ ܡܐܢܝ mad Manes. ETHPE. ܐܫܬܢܝ to rave, rage, act wildly, go on madly; ܐܝܟ ܫܐܕ̈ܐ ܡܫܬܢܝܢ ܗܘܘ they raved like frantic demons. PA. ܫܢܝ a) to change, alter, remove from one place to another; ܠܒܐ ܕܒܪܢܫܐ ܡܫܢܐ ܐܦ̈ܘܗܝ the heart of a man changeth his countenance; ܟܬܒܐ ܕܠܐ ܡܫܢܐ a written decree which altereth not. With ܛܥܡܐ to change his manner = feign madness; ܠܬܚܘܡܐ to remove a landmark. b) to be dislocated, to slip out of the socket. c) trans. to transfer, convey, remove, take away; ܫܢܝܗ ܐܠܗܐ God translated Enoch; ܕܢܫܢܐ ܡܢܗ ܡܘܬܐ in order to avert death. d) intrans. to remove, migrate, depart with ܠ and ܡܢ, often with ܠ and pron. suff., ܫܢܝ ܠܟ ܡܢܟ take thyself off; ܫܢܝ ܠܗ ܡܢ ܡܘܬܐ ܠܚܝ̈ܐ he hath passed from death unto life; ܐܡܪ ܠܛܘܪܐ ܗܢܐ ܫܢܝ thou shalt say to this mountain, Remove hence and it shall remove; ܦܪܚܬܐ ܕܡܫܢܝܐ ܡܢ ܕܘܟܬܐ a migratory bird; ܫܢܝ ܡܚ̈ܘܬܐ ܡܢ ܦܓܪܗ the stripes disappeared from his body. Metaph. to leave, fall off from, desert; ܡܢ ܬܠܡܝܕܘܬܐ discipleship; ܡܢ ܐܓܘܢܐ the conflict; with ܛܥܝܘܬܐ to be converted from error; ܠܗܕܝܘܛܘܬܐ to apostatize. Also ܫܢܝܬ ܡܢܗ ܛܝܒܘܬܐ grace departed from him. e) to depart ܡܢ ܚܝ̈ܐ ܗܠܝܢ from this life; ܠܘܬ ܡܪܗ to his Lord; ܡܢ ܦܓܪܐ from the body; ܢܦܫܗ ܫܢܝܬ ܡܢܗ he expired; ܝܥܩܘܒ ܟܕ ܚܙܐ ܟܘܬܝܢܗ ܕܝܘܣܦ ܫܢܝܬ ܢܦܫܗ when Jacob saw Joseph's coat he swooned. ETHPA. ܐܫܬܢܝ a) to be changed, troubled with ܚܙܘܐ, ܐܦ̈ܐ, ܓܘܢܐ &c. of the colour or expression of the countenance; ܡܫܬܢܝܢ ܥܡ ܟܠ ܪܘܚ changing with every wind. b) to depart, be taken away, translated as relics, as a Bishop. Esp. to depart hence ܠܐܪܥܐ ܕܚܝܐ to the land of life; ܐܫܬܢܝ ܚܢܘܟ Enoch was translated. Aph. ܐܫܢܝ a) to madden; ܚܡܪܐ ܡܪܘܐ ܘܡܫܢܐ ܘܡܒܙܚ wine intoxicates and maddens and exposes to scorn; ܗܘ ܡܫܢܝܐ ܢܦܫܗ he feigns to be demented. b) to cause to change, cause to be perverted, converted. Pahli ܫܢܚܝ and Ethpahli ܐܫܬܢܚܝ; see above under ܫܢܐ. Derivatives, ܫܘܢܝܐ, ܫܢܝܐ, ܫܢܝܐ, ܫܢܝܐܝܬ, ܫܢܝܘܬܐ, ܫܢܝܢܐ, ܡܫܢܝܢܐ, ܡܫܢܝܢܘܬ, ܡܫܬܢܝܢܐ, ܡܫܬܢܝܢܘܬܐ.

ܫܢܐ, ܫܢܬܐ pl. ܫܢܝܢ, ܫܢܝܐ f. a) a year; ܫܢܐ ܒܫܢܐ or ܡܢ ܫܢܐ ܠܫܢܐ year by year, yearly; ܒܪܝܫ ܫܢܬܐ at the beginning of the year; ܒܫܘܠܡܗ ܕܫ̈ towards the end of the year; ܫ̈ ܕܒܬܪܗ the following year. b) age; ܡܫܡܠܝܐ ܒܫܢܝܐ of advanced age. c) era; ܫܢܬ ܝܘܢܝܐ, ܕܛܝܝܐ, ܕܐܪܡܢܝܐ the year of the Greeks, Arabs, Armenians. Derivatives, ܫܢܬܢܝܬ, ܫܢܬܢܝܐ, ܫܢܬܢܝܘܬܐ.

ܫܢܐ a) a tooth; see ܫܢ. b) sleep; see ܫܢܬܐ.

ܫܢܓ fut. ܢܫܢܓ to wound with love, to enrapture. Part. adj. ܫܢܝܓܐ love-sick; ܫܢܝܓܐ ܫܘܦܪܗ ܠܒܒܢܝ her loveliness made me love-sick. Pa. ܫܢܓ to be in love; part. ܡܫܢܓܐ in love, a lover; ܡܫܢܓܐ ܛܠܝܐ a youthful lover, lovelorn youth. Ethpa. ܐܫܬܢܓ to be love-sick, be in love, be struck to the heart. Derivatives, ܫܢܓܐ, ܫܢܘܓܐ, ܫܢܓܘܬܐ.

ܫܢܓܐ, ܫܢܓܬܐ pl. ܫܢܓܝܢ variously vocalized. rt. ܫܢܓ. f. love, desire, passion; ܫܢܓܬ ܦܓܪܐ voluptuousness.

ܫܢܕ Pael ܫܢܕ to torment, execute. Ethpa. ܐܫܬܢܕ a) act. sense with ܒ of the pers. to torment, punish, ill-use, abuse; to inflict torture, put to the question; ܫܢܕܐ ܕܐܫܬܢܕܬܘܢ ܒܝ the torments you inflicted upon me. b) pass. to be tortured, tormented. Derivatives, ܫܢܘܕܐ, ܫܢܕܐ, ܡܫܬܢܕܢܐ, ܫܢܕܘܬܐ.

ܫܢܕܐ pl. ܐ̈ rt. ܫܢܕ. m. torment, torture.

ܫܢܕܠܐ, ܫܢ̈ &c. Pers. m. a small seafaring vessel, a boat supplying larger ships.

ܫܢܘܓܐ rt. ܫܢܓ. m. a lover.

ܫܢܘܕܐ pl. ܐ̈ rt. ܫܢܕ. m. a charioteer; a helmsman, steersman; a leader.

ܫܢܘܝܐ rt. ܫܢܐ. m. a) the redemption of a pledge. b) gram. anomaly, exception.

ܫܢܘܪܐ insipid.

ܫܢܐ fut. ܢܫܢܐ and ܢܫܢܐ, act. part. ܫܢܐ. a) to swerve, deflect, turn aside; ܡܢ ܟܝܢܗ from its nature; ܡܢ ܢܝܫܐ from the aim. Gram. ܫܢܐ ܡܢ ܥܢܝܢܐ irregular. b) to wander as the thoughts, as the mind. c) to be redeemed as a pledge by the payment of a debt. Aph. ܐܫܢܝ to redeem. Derivatives, ܫܢܘܝܐ, ܫܢܘܝܐ, ܫܢܝܐ.

ܫܢܝܐ rt. ܫܢܐ. m. swerving, failure.

ܫܢܝ Pael conj. of verb ܫܢܐ.

ܫܢܝ, ܫܢܝܐ rt. ܫܢܐ. raving, frantic.

ܫܢܝܐ rt. ܫܢܐ. m. frenzy, infatuation.

ܫܢܝܐܝܬ rt. ܫܢܐ. adv. foolishly, frantically.

ܫܢܝܓܘܬܐ rt. ܫܢܓ. f. love, passion.

ܫܢܝܘܬܐ rt. ܫܢܐ. f. madness, insanity, frantic folly, senseless rage; ܫ̈ ܕܬܪܥܝܬܐ mental aberration.

ܫܢܝܢܐ rt. ܫܢܐ. frantic.

ܫܢܝܢܐ pl. ܝ̈ܢ, ܢܐ̈ from ܫܢ. sharp, sharp-pointed; ܓܐܪ̈ܐ ܫ̈ sharp arrows.

ܫܢܢܐ, ܫܢܢܬܐ pl. ܢ̈ܐ, ܬ̈ܐ from ܫܢ. a) a sharp point, ܫ̈ ܕܣܝܦܐ a sword's point; ܫ̈ ܕܪܘܡܚܐ a spear-head, point of a lance; a lance, javelin. b) a mountain peak, crag, sharp rock, rocky point. c) a spike, ear of corn; the beard of grain; a spike, spire of grass.

ܫܢܩ cf. ܐܢܩ, ܚܢܩ, ܫܢܕ. Pael ܫܢܩ to punish, abuse, to inflict severe pain, punishment, torture; ܫܢܩܘ ܠܪ̈ܫܢܐ ܕܢܓܠܘܢ ܣܝܡܬܗܘܢ they tortured the chief men to make them disclose their hoards; ܡܪܚܘܬܟ ܫܢܩܬܟ thy impudence has brought punishment on thee; ܡܫܢܩܐ ܒܟܦܢܐ famine-stricken; ܐܪܥܐ ܗܕܐ ܡܫܢܩܬܐ ܘܟܪܝܗܘܬܐ this earth subject to pain and sickness. Ethpa. ܐܫܬܢܩ a) to be paired, tormented, oppressed ܒܟܦܢܐ by hunger; ܒܕܚܠܬܐ by fear; ܒܡܦܩܢܐ ܥܫܝܢ̈ܐ by terrible exactions; to suffer chastisement, pain, torment; ܠܐ ܠܥܠܡ ܡܫܬܢܩܝܢ ܪ̈ܫܝܥܐ not for ever will the wicked be in torments. b) to labour painfully; ܡܫܬܢܩܐ ܒܚܒ̈ܠܐ in the pains of labour. Derivatives, ܫܢܘܩܐ, ܫܢܘܩܝܐ, ܫܢܩܐ, ܡܫܢܩܢܘܬܐ, ܡܫܢܩܢܐ, ܫܢܩܘܬܐ.

ܫܢܩܐ rt. ܫܢܩ. m. phthisis, consumption.

ܫܢܝܢܐ m. pl. perh. *blades* or *ears of corn when they first shoot up.*

ܫܢܝܪܬܐ Arab. f. *a cat.*

ܫܢܝܪ ܟܠܒܐ, ܫܢܝܪ ܒܘܡܒܐ, ܫܢܝܪ ܐܪܙܐ; see under ܫܢܝܪ, ܫܢܝܪܐ.

ܫܢܝܬܐ Arab. f. *tree-moss, lichen.*

ܫܢܬܐ *a year;* see ܫܢܐ.

ܫܢܬܐ abs. st. ܫܢܐ (rare) rt. ܝܫܢ. found in Heb. f. *sleep.*

ܫܢܬܐܝܬ from ܫܢܬܐ. adv. *yearly, annually.*

ܫܢܬܢܝܐ, ܫܢܝܐ and ܫܢܬܝܐ from ܫܢܐ, ܫܢܬܐ. *yearly, annual, of the year.*

ܫܢܬܢܝܘܬܐ from ܫܢܬܐ. f. *annual circuit, period.*

ܫܥܐ fut. ܢܫܥܐ *to smooth, plaster;* ܢܫܥܘܢ ܫܪܘܬܐ *let them smooth the roughness.* Part. adj. ܫܥܝܥ, ܫܥܝܥܐ, ܫܥܝܥܬܐ *a*) of stones, shells &c. *smooth, bare.* *b*) of plants *glabrous.* *c*) ܫܥܝܥܝ ܢܚܝܪܐ *flat-nosed.* Pa. ܫܥܥ *to smooth.* Ethpa. ܐܬܫܥܥ *to be smoothed.* Aph. ܐܫܥ *to make smooth* or *bare;* ܐܫܥܘ ܡܝܐ ܟܐܦܐ *water wore the stones smooth;* ܢܦܫܬܐ ܕܐܫܥܝ ܡܢ ܦܓܪܐ souls *which have shuffled off the body.* Palp. ܫܥܫܥ *to smooth, plane.* Derivatives, ܫܥܝܥܐ, ܫܥܝܥܘܬܐ, ܫܥܫܥܢܐ, ܫܥܫܥܐ, ܫܥܫܥܘܬܐ, ܫܥܝܢܐ, ܡܫܥܝܢܐ, ܡܫܥܐ, ܡܫܥܝܢܐ.

ܫܥܐ, ܫܥܬܐ, ܫܥܬܐ constr. st. ܫܥܬ pl. ܫܥܝܢ, ܫܥܐ (abs. state only in ܫܥܫܥ) f. *an hour, moment, time, season;* ܦܠܓܘܬ ܫܥܬܐ *half an hour;* ܒܬܠܬ ܫܥܝܢ *at three o'clock, at the third hour,* ܒܫܬ ܫܥܝܢ *at the sixth hour,* ܒܬܫܥ ܫܥܝܢ *at the ninth hour,* these were three of the seven hours of prayer; ܫܥܬܐ ܕܡܘܬܝ *the hour of my death;* ܒܝܬ ܫܥܐ *a clock* or *clock tower;* ܚܙܝܐ ܕܫܥܐ *a horoscope.* Astron. *a degree.* A weight = 5 ozs. With preps. ܒܗ ܒܫܥܬܐ, ܡܢ ܫܥܐ, ܠܫܥܐ and ܒܗ ܒܫܥܬܗ *that same hour, that very moment, directly;* ܕܫܥܬܐ *now, at the same time; for a moment, passing;* ܐܟܣܢܝܐ ܕܫܥܬܐ *the guest of an hour;* ܡܘܬܐ ܕܫܥܬܐ *instantaneous death;* ܐܘܪܚܐ ܕܫܥܬܐ *an hour's journey;* ܐܝܟ ܗܕܐ ܫܥܬܐ ܠܡܚܪ *to-morrow at this time;* ܫܥܫܥ *hourly, always, perpetually;* ܫܥܫܥ ܡܫܒܚܐ *for ever glorified;* ܡܢ ܗܝ ܫܥܬܐ *from that time.* Compounds, ܫܥܐ, ܒܪܫܥܐ; see under ܒܪܫܥܐ.

ܫܥܐ act. part. ܫܥܐ. *a*) *to smooth down, please.* *b*) *to stop up* holes. Cognates ܫܥܥ and ܫܥܐ. Ethpe. ܐܫܬܥܝ *to play* ܒܦܣܦܣܐ *at ball;* ܒܩܘܒܝܐ *at dice, to gamble; to sport, engage in sports, in warlike exercises; to divert himself* ܒܟܠܒܐ ܨܝܕܐ *with hounds; to mock, make a mock of.* Ethpa. ܐܫܬܥܝ *to relate, narrate, tell; to discuss, discourse, talk;* with ܒ or ܥܠ; ܐܫܬܥܝ ܚܠܡܗ *he told his dream;* ܡܫܬܥܝܢܐ ܕܫܘܥܝܬܐ ܡܬܠܐ *fable-writers, story-tellers.* Ethpeel and Ethpaal are often confused. Ettaph. ܐܬܬܫܥܝ *to mock* with ܒ. Derivatives, ܡܫܬܥܝܢܐ, ܡܫܬܥܝܢܐ, ܫܥܝܐ, ܫܥܝܐ, ܫܥܝܘܬܐ, ܫܥܝܐ, ܫܥܝܢܐ, ܫܥܝܬܐ, ܫܘܥܝܬܐ, ܡܫܥܝܢܐ, ܡܫܥܝܢܐ, ܡܫܥܝ, ܡܫܥܝܬܐ, ܡܫܥܝܢܘܬܐ, ܡܫܥܝܢܐ.

ܫܥܒܐܢ Arab. m. name of the eighth Arab month.

ܫܥܒܕ Shaphel conj. of verb ܥܒܕ.

ܫܥܘܪ Pehlevi *a jackal.*

ܫܥܘܦܐ pl. ܐ̈ rt. ܫܥܦ. m. *aquatic animals having fins, fish.*

ܫܥܘܠܐ rt. ܫܥܠ. m. *a cough, coughing.*

ܫܥܘܣܐ only in the Lexx. *having an unpleasant flavour, loathsome.*

ܫܥܘܣܘܬܐ only Lexx. f. *loathsomeness.*

ܫܥܘܬܐ or ܫܥܐ no pl. *wax, sealing-wax, a wax light;* ܢܢܗܪ ܥܕܬܐ ܒܫܥܘܬܐ *we will light* the church *with wax candles.* Derivatives, the two following words:—

ܫܥܘܬܢܝܐ from ܫܥܘܬܐ. *wax-coloured;* ܕܒܫܐ ܫ̈ *pale honey.*

ܫܥܘܬܢܝܬܐ from ܫܥܘܬܐ. f. *waxen, wax-coloured.*

ܫܥܦ fut. ܢܫܥܘܦ, act. part. ܫܥܦ, ܫܥܦܐ, pass. part. ܫܥܝܦ. *to float* ܒܐܐܪ *in the air,* ܒܡܝܐ *in the water; to swim, crawl.* Parel see ܫܪܥܦ. Derivatives, ܫܥܘܦܐ and the three following words:—

ܫܥܦܐ pl. ܐ̈ rt. ܫܥܦ. m. *a newly hatched bird* or *reptile, a young snake, viper, brood of vipers* generally metaph.

ܫܥܦܐ rt. ܫܥܦ. m. *floating.*

ܫܥܦܬܢܝܐ rt. ܫܥܦ. *webbed, finny,* ܫܥܦܬܢܝܐ ܓܦܐ *having webbed wings* or *fins.*

ܫܥܝܳܐ pl. ܫܥܝܶܐ rt. ܫܥܐ. m. *a*) *a game, a play, show, amusement;* ܫ̈ ܕܪܽܘܡܳܝܶܐ *a play;* ܫ̈ ܕܪܡܙܶܐ *a pantomime;* ܫ̈ ܕܦܨܳܐ *a game of hazard, gaming;* ܫ̈ ܥܳܒܶܕ *a juggler;* ܕܫܥܝܳܐ *ludicrous, amusing.* *b*) *trumpery, nonsense.* *c*) *jesting, mockery.* *d*) in the Lexx. *dimness of sight.*

ܫܥܝܳܐ dial. of Tirhan. m. *squinting.*

ܫܥܝܽܘܬܳܐ or ܫܥ̈ rt. ܫܥܐ. f. only Lexx. *a game, show.*

ܫܥܝܢܳܐ m. *mire, filth;* ܐܰܝܟ ܫܥܝܢܳܐ *to a paste.*

ܫܥܝܳܢܳܝܳܐ rt. ܫܥܐ. *playing, of play.*

ܫܥܝܢܽܘܬܳܐ f. *muddiness, defilement.*

ܫܥܝܥ, ܫܥܝܥܳܐ, ܫܥܝܥܬܳܐ; see verb ܫܥ.

ܫܥܝܥܳܐ rt. ܫܥ. m. ܫ̈ ܕܝܰܡܳܐ *sea-weed.*

ܫܥܝܥܽܘܬܳܐ rt. ܫܥ. f. *a*) *smoothness, glossiness.* *b*) ܫܥܝܥܽܘܬܳܐ ܕܡܥܰܝܳܐ *looseness of the bowels, dysentery.*

ܫܥܶܠ fut. ܢܶܫܥܽܘܠ, act. part. ܫܳܥܶܠ, ܫܳܥܠܳܐ. *to cough, have a cough.* Derivatives, ܫܥܳܠܳܐ, ܫܥܠܢܳܐ, ܫܥܠܳܐ.

ܫܥܳܠܳܐ pl. ܫ̈ rt. ܫܥܠ. m. *a cough, coughing.*

ܫܰܥܒܶܕ Shaphel conj.; see ܥܒܕ.

ܫܥܠܳܢܳܐ rt. ܫܥܠ. m. *tussilago, colt's foot.*

ܫܰܥܢܶܢ denom. verb from ܐܽܘܫܰܥܢܳܐ: ܡܫܰܥܢܢܝܢ *shouting Hosanna.*

ܫܰܥܶܥ Pael conj. of verb ܫܥ.

ܫܥܥ, ܫܥܥܳܐ pl. ܫ̈ ܝܢ, ܫ̈ rt. ܫܥ. m. *a*) adj. *beardless, without hair;* ܓܰܒܪܳܐ ܫܥܥ *a smooth man.* *b*) *a smooth stone, a pebble.*

ܫܥܥܽܘܬܳܐ rt. ܫܥ. f. *smoothness;* ܫܥܥܽܘܬܳܐ ܕܨܰܘܪܳܐ *the smooth part of the neck.*

ܫܥܥܳܢܳܐ, ܫܥܥܳܢܳܝܳܐ rt. ܫܥ. *smooth, waterworn, rounded.*

ܫܥܪܳܐ or ܫܥܪܳܐ *soft hair, down, wool.*

ܫܰܥܫܰܥ Palpal conj. of verb ܫܥ.

ܫܥܬܳܐ emph. state of ܫܳܥܳܐ. *an hour.*

ܫܥܝܬܳܐ rt. ܫܥܐ. f. = ܫܥܝܳܐ *a game.*

ܫܥܝܬܳܐ rt. ܫܥܐ. f. *a*) *a joke, a game, play, spectacle, sport; the public games.* *b*) *a laughing-stock, object of mockery.*

ܫܦܰܐ fut. ܢܶܫܦܶܐ, act. part. ܫܳܦܶܐ, ܫܳܦܝܳܐ or ܫܳܦܝܳܐ. *to move softly, to crawl;* ܟܽܠ ܕܫܳܦܶܐ ܥܰܠ ܟܰܪܣܶܗ *whatsoever goeth upon the belly;* ܐܰܝܟ ܕܫܳܦܶܐ ܘܠܳܐ ܦܳܪܰܚ ܠܗ ܓܽܘܒܳܐ *a wingless crawling locust;* ܫܦܺܝܬ ܒܰܢܝܳܚܳܐ ܥܕܰܡܳܐ ܕܡܶܛܺܝܬ *I crept softly till I reached . . .;* ܫܦܳܐ ܪܰܡܫܳܐ ܒܢܝܳܚܳܐ *the evening passed slowly;* ܫܦܰܘ ܐܶܓܰܦܰܝܗܽܘܢ *they gently moved their wings.* Pa. ܫܰܦܺܝ *to crawl on the ground;* ܐܰܝܟ ܥܽܘܠܳܠܳܐ ܡܫܰܦܝܳܢܳܐ *like a crawling infant.* Aph. ܐܰܫܦܺܝ or ܐܰܫܦܶܐ, act. part. ܡܰܫܦܶܐ and ܡܰܫܦܝܳܐ. *a*) *to turn gently aside, to bring down;* ܐܰܫܦܺܝ ܐܶܢܽܘܢ ܡܶܢ ܪܳܡܽܘܬܳܐ ܠܡܰܟܺܝܟܽܘܬܳܐ *he turned* their thoughts *from ambition to humility;* ܡܶܢ ܚܰܡܫܺܝܢ ܠܥܶܣܪܳܐ ܐܰܫܦܺܝܗ ܠܕܰܝܳܢܳܐ ܕܟܽܠ Abraham *induced the Judge of all to give way from fifty to ten;* ܐܶܢ ܬܰܫܦܶܐ ܡܶܢ ܫܪܳܪܳܐ *if thou diverge from the truth.* *b*) with ܢܰܦܫܶܗ *to adapt oneself; to deal gently, be indulgent, give way, yield* with ܠܘܳܬ; ܐܰܫܦܺܝ ܠܘܳܬ ܡܚܺܝܠܽܘܬܶܗ ܕܕܳܪܳܐ *make allowance for the weakness of the age;* ܠܙܰܒܢܶܐ ܐܰܝܟ ܠܡܶܫܬܰܘܚܳܦܽܘ ܢܰܫܦܶܐ *to accommodate himself to circumstances;* ܐܶܢ ܡܰܫܦܝܢ ܠܘܳܬܟܽܘܢ *if they are indulgent towards you;* ܐܰܫܦܶܐ ܠܘܳܬ ܒܥܶܠܕܒܳܒܳܟ ܩܰܠܺܝܠ *concede a little to thy adversary.* *c*) *to give assent, consent, grant;* ܒܰܥܘܳܬܳܐ ܙܥܽܘܪܬܳܐ ܐܰܫܦܶܐ *concede a small boon;* ܐܰܠܳܗܳܐ ܐܶܢ ܡܰܫܦܶܐ *God permitting;* ܐܳܦܠܳܐ ܚܕܳܐ ܩܰܠܺܝܠܳܐ ܡܰܫܦܶܐ ܗܘܳܐ *he would not yield one jot;* with ܠܳܐ *to refuse, decline.* Eccles. *to allow, give permission, grant dispensation; to consent* to the election of a Patriarch. Derivatives, ܫܦܳܐ, ܡܫܦܝܳܢܳܐ, ܫܦܝܳܐ, ܫܦܝܳܐ, ܫܦܝܽܘܬܳܐ, ܡܫܦܝܳܢܽܘܬܳܐ, ܫܦܝܽܘܬܳܐ.

ܫܦܳܐ fut. ܢܶܫܦܶܐ, act. part. ܫܳܦܶܐ, ܫܳܦܝܳܐ. *a*) *to plane* wood. *b*) *to become clear* from dregs, from sin; ܢܶܫܒܩܽܘܢܳܝܗܝ ܠܡܶܫܚܳܐ ܥܰܠ ܫܦܳܝܳܐ *let them leave the oil to settle.* Pass. part. ܫܦܶܐ, ܫܦܝܳܐ, ܫܦܝܳܐ pl. ܫܦܶܝܢ, ܫܦܝܳܢ. *a*) *plain, cleared, bare;* ܐܽܘܪܚܳܐ ܫܦܝܳܐ ܡܶܢ ܟܺܐܦܶܐ *a road clear of rocks;* ܦܶܩܥܬܳܐ ܫܦܺܝܬܳܐ *a bare plain;* ܢܶܗܘܶܐ ܥܰܪܰܡܬܳܐ ܠܫܦܝܳܐ *the rough place shall become a plain.* *b*) *clarified, clear, transparent, limpid, serene;* ܫܦܝܳܐ ܡܶܢ ܚܰܡܪܳܐ ܡܫܰܘܚܠܳܐ *clearer than strained wine;* ܠܳܐ ܛܥܶܡ ܡܶܕܶܡ ܐܶܠܳܐ ܐܶܢ ܗܘܳܐ ܫܦܝܳܐ ܒܡܰܪܘܰܕܳܐ *he took nothing but a spoonful of liquid;* ܡܰܒܽܘܥܶܐ ܕܡܰܝܳܐ ܫܦܝܳܐ *clear springs;* ܫܦܶܐ ܝܰܘܡܳܐ ܡܶܢ ܥܢܳܢܶܐ *a cloudless day.* *c*) metaph. *simple, pure, sincere, single-minded;* ܫܦܶܐ ܡܶܢ ܡܽܘܡܳܐ *clear from the rust of sin;* ܫܦܶܐ ܡܶܢ ܚܶܠܕܳܐ ܕܚܛܺܝܬܳܐ *guileless;* ܫܦܝܳܐ ܒܪܶܥܝܳܢܳܐ *single-minded;*

ܫܦܝܐ ܒܬܪܥܝܬܐ *simple-minded, sincere.* d) *serene, calm, equable;* ܐܘ ܫܦܝܐ ܫܦܝ ܠܡܚܫܒܬܝ *O Thou who art ever calm, calm my meditations;* ܡܨܠܝܢܐ ܫܦܝܐ ܐܢܐ *I am quietly praying.* e) *plain, innocent, ingenuous, simple, silly, worthless;* ܛܠܝܐ ܫܦܝܐ *innocent children;* ܫܦܝܐ ܒܡܠܘܗܝ *simple in his expressions;* ܝܘܢܐ ܫܦܝܬܐ *the innocent dove;* ܚܟܡܬܐ ܕܒܪܬ ܠܢܘܚ ܒܩܝܣܐ ܫܦܝܐ wisdom *directed the course of Noah in a piece of wood of small value.* Pael ܫܦܝ a) *to hew smooth, shave off;* ܩܝܣܐ ܕܡܫܦܝܢ ܗܘܐ ܡܢܗ *the shavings, refuse wood;* ܫܒܛܐ ܕܪܘܡܢܐ ܟܕ ܠܐ ܡܫܦܝܢ ܟܘܒܝܗܘܢ *pomegranate rods with the thorns not scraped off.* b) *to make plain, even, smooth* ܐܘܪܚܐ *a road,* ܥܪܩܐ *a rugged place.* c) *to clarify, strain; to separate from refuse, purge from dross;* used of oil, of iron; ܥܒܘܪܐ ܕܡܫܦܝ ܡܢ ܬܒܢܐ *corn freed from the chaff;* ܫܦܝ ܡܫܪܝܬܟ ܡܢ ܢܨܪܝܐ *purge thy army of Nazarenes.* d) *to calm, settle* ܫܦܝܘܗܝ ܠܪܥܝܢܝ ܒܡܙܡܘܪܝܟ *calm my mind with thy psalms.* Ethpa. ܐܫܬܦܝ a) *to be hewn smooth, planed; to be made plain, level.* b) *to be cleared of dregs, cleansed, purged, purified;* metaph. ܡܢ ܬܘܪܝܐ *from dregs* of false doctrine; ܡܢ ܚܫܐ *from passions.* c) *to be made calm, serene;* ܚܙܘܐ ܫܦܝܐ ܠܥܝܢܐ ܢܫܬܦܐ *may serene vision be restored to the eyes* after alarming apparitions. Derivatives, ܫܦܝܐ, ܫܦܝܘܬܐ, ܫܦܝܐܝܬ, ܫܘܦܝܐ, ܡܫܦܝܢܘܬܐ, ܫܦܝܢܐ.

ܫܦܬܐ m. *a coffin, case.*

ܫܦܬܐ, ܫܦܝܬܐ pl. ܫܦܬܐ rt. ܫܦ. f. a) *upper part of a slipper.* b) *the nostril.*

ܫܦܕ fut. ܢܫܦܘܕ, act. part. ܫܦܕ, ܫܦܕܐ, pass. part. ܫܦܝܕܐ. a) *to pierce, transfix* with an arrow or dart. Pa. ܫܦܕ same as Peal. Metaph. ܐܘܣܦ ܫܦܕܗ ܒܡܠܬܐ ܚܪܝܦܬܐ *he pierced him still more with sharp words.* Ethpe. ܐܫܬܦܕ and Ethpa. ܐܫܬܦܕ *to be transfixed, pierced;* ܓܐܪܐ ܕܐܫܬܦܕ ܒܦܓܪܐ *an arrow which had penetrated the body.* Derivatives, ܫܦܕܐ, ܫܦܕܐ, ܫܦܘܕܐ.

ܫܦܕܐ rt. ܫܦܕ. m. *a large sieve.*

ܫܦܕܐ rt. ܫܦܕ. m. *piercing.*

ܫܦܗ for ܝܫܦܗ *jasper.*

ܫܦܘܕܐ pl. ܐ̈ rt. ܫܦܕ. m. a) *a dart.* b) *a spit, broach; a poker;* ܕܙܓܘܓܝܬܐ ~ *a glass tube;* pl. *palings.*

ܫܦܘܟܐ rt. ܫܦܟ. m. *emptying out.*

ܫܦܘܟܝܬܐ rt. ܫܦܟ. f. *a syringe, funnel.*

ܫܦܘܠܐ pl. ܐ̈ rt. ܫܦܠ. m. usually pl. *skirts, outskirts, uttermost parts, borders, lower parts* ܕܛܘܪܐ *of a mountain;* ܕܡܕܒܚܐ *base of an altar;* ܕܫܘܥܐ *foot of a rock;* ܕܟܘܬܝܢܐ *skirt of a dress;* ܚܝܛܐ ܕܫܦܘܠܐ *seam of a robe;* ܫܦܘܠܐ sing. *lowland.*

ܫܦܘܦܐ or ܫܦܦܐ pl. ܐ̈ rt. ܫܦ. m. a) *crawling;* ܛܠܝܐ ܫܦܘܦܐ ܘܠܐ ܡܗܠܟܢܐ *infants crawling before they can walk;* ~ ܩܡܨܐ *a wingless locust.* b) *a reptile;* ~ ܕܝܒܫܬܐ *a land reptile.*

ܫܦܘܦܘܬܐ rt. ܫܦ. f. *crawling.*

ܫܦܘܪܐ rt. ܫܦܪ. m. *complaisance, obsequiousness, adulation.*

ܫܦܘܪܢܐ pl. ܐ̈ rt. ܫܦܪ. *desirous to curry favour, obsequious; a flatterer.*

ܫܦܘܪܢܘܬܐ rt. ܫܦܪ. f. *adulation, obsequiousness.*

ܫܦܛܐ m. pl. Heb. the Book of *Judges.*

ܫܦܝܐ or ܫܦܝܐ pl. ܐ̈ rt. ܫܦܐ. m. *a sharpened stake, splinter, thorn; an offence, hindrance;* ~ ܒܒܣܪܝ *a thorn in my flesh;* ~ ܕܬܘܩܠܬܐ *a cause of offence.*

ܫܦܝܐ rt. ܫܦܐ. m. a) *clearing, levelling, smoothing.* b) *sincerity.*

ܫܦܝܐܝܬ rt. ܫܦܐ. adv. *straight on, straightforward, simply, sincerely.*

ܫܦܝܘܬܐ rt. ܫܦܐ. f. *serenity, limpidity, transparency, sincerity;* ~ ܒ *simply, sincerely.*

ܫܦܝܥܐܝܬ rt. ܫܦܥ. adv. *abundantly, liberally, bountifully.*

ܫܦܝܥܘ, ܫܦܝܥܘܬܐ rt. ܫܦܥ. f. *abundance, profusion, plenitude; prodigality; exaggeration;* ܫܦܝܥܘܬ ܡܘܗܒܬܐ or ܐܝܕܐ *liberality, munificence;* ܒܫܦܝܥܘ *abundantly.*

ܫܘܦܢܬܐ rt. ܫܦ. f. *oil, unguent.*

ܫܦܝܪ, ܐ, ܬܐ rt. ܫܦܪ. a) *fair, good, lovely, pleasing;* ܫܦܝܪ ܚܙܘܐ *fair to look upon;* ܘܚܙܐ ܐܠܗܐ ܕܫܦܝܪ *and God saw that it was good.* b) *honourable, noble, excellent, virtuous, right;* ܐܓܘܢܐ ܫܦܝܪܐ *a well-fought contest;* ܡܕܒܪܢܘܬܐ

ܫܦܝܪܘܬܐ *a right faith;* ܡܗܝܡܢܐ ܫܦܝܪܐ *orthodox believers;* ܡܗܝܡܢܐ ܫܦܝܪܐ ܕܗܢܕܘ *the orthodox Syrians of India;* ܥܒ̈ܕܐ ܫܦܝܪ̈ܐ *good works.* F. emph. usually pl. *a virtue, merit, advantage, noble deed, fine saying;* ܥܒܕ ܫܦܝܪ̈ܬܐ *beneficent;* also *Euergetes.* c) in compos. ܫܦܝܪ is often equivalent to Greek εὖ, *well,* &c.; ܫ ܕܚܠܬܐ *pious, devout;* ܫ ܕܝܘܒܢ *virtuous;* ܫ ܓܢܣܐ or ܫ ܡܘܠܕܐ *well-born;* ܫ ܠܒܐ *glad of heart;* ܟܘܢܝܐ ܫܦܝܪܐ ܠܒܐ *a well-merited rebuke.* Adv. *well, rightly, piously, properly, correctly;* ܫܦܝܪ ܐܡܪܬ *thou hast well said;* ܩܒܠ ܐܢܘܢ ܫܦܝܪ *he received them kindly, made them welcome;* rit. the deacon says ܩܘܡܘ ܫܦܝܪ *stand aright, in due order, reverently.* Interj. *bravo, well done.*

ܫܦܝܪ ܝܪܘܩܐ *spinach.*

ܫܦܝܪܐܝܬ rt. ܫܦܪ. adv. *well, finely, beautifully.*

ܫܦܝܪܘܬܐ rt. ܫܦܪ. f. *pleasure, loveliness, goodliness.* Usually in constr. answering to Greek εὖ: ܫܦܝܪܘܬ ܐܘܡܢܘܬܐ *skill;* ܫ ܕܚܠܬܐ *piety, devoutness, orthodoxy;* ܫ ܓܒܪܘܬܐ *manliness, virility;* ܒܫܦܝܪܘܬ ܙܒܢܐ *at a convenient time, suitable opportunity;* ܫ ܐܣܟܡܐ or ܫ ܡܛܟܣܘܬܐ *orderliness, moderation;* ܫ ܚܙܬܐ *goodly appearance, comeliness;* ܫ ܨܒܝܢܐ *good pleasure, approval.*

ܫܦܝܪܬܐ rt. ܫܦܪ. f. *the fat under the skin* of human beings.

ܫܦܟ fut. ܢܫܦܘܟ *to pour from one vessel into another, empty out;* ܫܦܘܟ ܥܠ ܐܪܥܐ *pour it out on the ground.* Ethpa. ܐܫܬܦܟ *to be transfused, transmitted;* ܢܦ̈ܫܬܐ ܕܒܢܝ̈ܢܫܐ ܒܟܝ̈ܢܐ ܕܚܝ̈ܘܬܐ ܡܫܬܦܟܢ *human* souls *pass into the natures of animals* (by transmigration). Derivatives, ܫܦܘܟܐ, ܫܦܟܬܐ, ܫܦܟܐ, ܡܫܦܟܢܐ, ܫܦܘܟܝܬܐ, ܡܫܦܟܐ.

ܫܦܘܟܐ or ܫܦܟܐ pl. ܐ̈ rt. ܫܦܟ. m. a) *a funnel, the tube of a syringe; a water-pipe, spout.* b) *pouring out, transfusion.*

ܫܦܠ fut. ܢܫܦܠ. *to be weary, give way, faint;* ܕܠܐ ܢܫܦܠܘܢ ܡܢ ܩܕܡ ܒܥܠܕܒܒܐ *lest they give way before the enemy.* Pael ܫܦܠ *to humble, bring low, cast down, give trouble;* ܡܫܦܠ ܠܓܢܒܪܐ *he lays low the mighty warrior;* ܫܦܠ ܠܪ̈ܡܬܐ *he cast down the high places;* ܠܐ ܬܫܦܠ *do not lose heart;* ܫܦܠܬܟܘܢ ܠܡܐܬܐ *I have given you the trouble of coming hither.* Pass. part. ܡܫܦܠ, ܡܫܦܠܐ *weary, weak, humble, low, base;* ܩܠ̈ܐ ܡܫܦܠ̈ܐ ܘܡܫܦܠ̈ܐ *low weak voices;* ܐܘ ܟܡܐ ܡܫܦܠܐ ܚܝ̈ܐ *Oh how base a thing is life!* Ethpa. ܐܫܬܦܠ a) *to be wearied; to give oneself trouble, labour to weariness;* ܒܢܝܢܐ ܕܐܫܬܦܠܘ ܒܗ *the building at which they had laboured;* ܐܫܬܦܠܬ ܠܡܐܬܐ *I took the trouble of coming.* b) *to be worn out, weakened, overcome; to be abased, humbled;* ܐܫܬܦܠ ܒܝܫܐ *the Evil One is overcome;* ܥܠ ܕܐܫܬܥܠܝܢ ܐܫܬܦܠܢ *because we were arrogant we were brought low.* Aph. ܐܫܦܠ a) *to bring low, humble, overpower;* ܐܙܟܝܟ ܘܐܫܦܠܟ *I will vanquish and humble thee.* b) *to be wearied out, to succumb, give way; to take trouble;* ܠܐ ܐܫܦܠ ܠܘܬ ܚܕܐ ܡܢ ܥܣܩܘܬܐ *he succumbed to no difficulty;* ܐܫܦܠܘ ܛܘܪ̈ܟܝܐ ܡܢ ܩܛܠܐ *the Turks were weary of slaughter.* Derivatives, ܫܦܠܐ, ܫܦܘܠܐ, ܫܦܠܐ, ܫܦܠܐ, ܫܦܠܐ, ܫܦܠܐܝܬ, ܫܦܠܘܬܐ, ܡܫܦܠܘܬܐ, ܡܫܦܠܐܝܬ, ܡܫܦܠܢܐ.

ܫܦܠ or ܫܦܠ, ܫܦܠܐ, ܫܦܠܬܐ rt. ܫܦܠ. *feeble, mean, low, humble, wretched, cowardly;* ܫܦܠ ܐܢܫܝܢ *the meanest of men;* ܐܝܟ ܚܕ ܫܦܠܐ ܩܒܪܘܢܝ *bury me as one of low estate.*

ܫܦܠܐ pl. ܐ̈ rt. ܫܦܠ. m. a) = ܫܦܘܠܐ *skirts.* b) *a depression, low-lying land;* ܫܦܠܘܗܝ ܕܢܝܠܘܣ *the delta of the Nile.* c) *fatigue, weariness, exhaustion.* d) *low estate, humiliation, fall.* e) *ignominy, cowardice.*

ܫܦܠܐ rt. ܫܦܠ = Heb. *the Shephelah, lowland.*

ܫܦܠܐܝܬ rt. ܫܦܠ. adv. *basely, meanly.*

ܫܦܠܘܬܐ pl. ܐ̈ m. in the Lexx. a) *a wick.* b) *an acorn.* c) *eye-salve.* d) *a syringe.*

ܫܦܠܘܬܐ rt. ܫܦܠ. f. a) *feebleness* of the voice, the limbs, *debility, slackness.* b) *lowliness, poverty.* c) *cowardice.*

ܫܦܦ act. part. ܫܐܦ, ܫܐܦܐ. perh. denom. verb from ܫܘܦܦܐ. Cf. rts. ܫܘܦ and ܫܦܐ. *To harrow, to make even* or *smooth;* ܫܦ ܐܪܝܐ ܒܕܘܢܒܗ ܥܩܒ̈ܘܗܝ the lion to conceal his traces from the hunter *smoothes* the ground *with his tail.*

ܫܦܦܐ from ܫܦܦ. m. *harrowing.*

ܫܦܥ fut. ܢܫܦܥ, act. part. ܫܦܥ, ܫܦܥܐ. *to pour forth, overflow, run over, rise* as a river in flood; *to abound;* ܢܫܦܥܘܢ ܡܒܘܥ̈ܐ ܡ̈ܝܐ

ܘܡܥܨܪܬܐ *the presses shall overflow with wine and oil;* ܫܦܥܬ ܡܟܝܠܬܐ *the measure ran over;* ܫܦܥܝܢ ܕܡܥܘܗܝ *his tears flow freely;* ܐܪܥܐ ܕܫܦܥܐ ܒܦܘܢܩܐ *a land abounding in delights.* Act. part. *redundant, superfluous.* Part. adj. ܫܦܝܥ, ܐ̈ ܐ *abundant, copious, lavish;* ܫܦܝܥ ܒܡܘܗܒܬܐ *copious streams;* ܢܗܪ̈ܐ ܫܦܝ̈ܥܐ *munificent;* ܪ̈ܚܡܐ ܫܦܝ̈ܥܐ *abounding mercy.* PA. ܫܰܦܰܥ *to pour out, shed abroad, give abundantly;* ܛܠ̈ܐ ܡܫܦܥ̈ܐ *copious dews.* ETHPE. ܐܶܬ݂ܫܦܰܥ and ETHPA. ܐܶܬ݂ܫܰܦܰܥ *a) to overflow, rush forth;* ܟܕ ܐܬܫܦܥܘ ܡܝ̈ܐ ܠܥܠ ܡܢ ܫܘܪܐ *when the water rose higher than the wall;* ܡܫܬܦܥܐ ܗܘܬ ܫܠܗܒܝܬܐ ܠܥܠ ܡܢ ܐܬܘܢܐ *the flames leapt up above the furnace. b) to be poured forth, shed* or *given freely; to be abundantly supplied;* ܡܛܪܟ ܥܠ ܟܠ ܢܫܬܦܥ *let Thy rain descend abundantly upon all. c) to be as weak as water, to be unnerved.* APH. ܐܰܫܦܰܥ *a) to pour forth, shed, run over, give abundantly* with ܥܠ; ܐܫܦܥܬ ܡܘܪܘܢ ܥܠ ܪܫܗ *she poured the ointment upon his head;* ܐܫܦܥ ܘܝܗܒ *he gave liberally;* ܡܫܦܥܝܢ ܙܕܩ̈ܬܐ *they give abundant alms. b) to make to abound;* ܡܫܦܥ ܟܗ̈ܢܐ *he consecrates many priests.* DERIVATIVES, ܫܦܥܐ, ܫܦܝܥܐܝܬ, ܫܦܝܥܘܬܐ, ܫܦܥܐ, ܡܫܦܥܢܐ, ܡܫܦܥܢܘܬܐ.

ܫܶܦܥܳܐ pl. ܐ̈ ܐ, ܝܢ rt. ܫܦܥ. m. *abundance of water, a full spring, copious shower, rushing stream, strong current, flood;* ܡܛܟܣܘܬܐ ܕܫܦܥܗ *regularity of the* Nile *rising;* ܫܦܥܐ ܕܡܠܬܐ *fluency of speech;* ܫܦܥܐ ܕܠܫܢܐ *eloquent.*

ܫܰܦܶܦ Pael conj. of verb ܫܦ.

ܫܦܘܦܐ, ܫܦܘܦܬܐ rt. ܫܦ. *creeping, crawling;* ܓܦ̈ܢܐ ܫܦܘ̈ܦܐ *trailing vines.*

ܫܦܝܦܐ rt. ܫܦ. m. *a) crawling. b)* ܫ ܕܡܝ̈ܐ *oozing, trickling.*

ܫܦܰܪ ܫܦܰܪ fut. ܢܶܫܦܰܪ, act. part. ܫܳܦܰܪ, ܫܳܦܪܳܐ. For part. adj. ܫܰܦܝܪ see above. *a) to be fair, bright, beautiful;* ܫܡܢܘ ܘܫܦܪܘ *they grew fat and fair;* ܫܦܪ ܐܝܟ ܕܗܒܐ *as bright as gold;* ܫܦܪ ܥܣܒܐ *grass throve beautifully. b)* ܫܦܪ ܠܒܗ ܒܚܡܪܐ *to be exhilarated, merry with wine. c) to please, to be pleasing* with ܒܥܝܢ̈ܐ or ܩܕܡ *in the sight of* and with ܥܠ or ܠ of the pers., ܫܦܪܘ ܡܠܝܗܘܢ ܒܥܝܢܝ *their words pleased . . .,* ܟܠܗܘܢ ܕܫܦܪܘ ܩܕܡ ܐܠܗܐ *all who were well-pleasing to God;* hence abs. *to act well, do right* opp. ܣܪܚ. *d) to make oneself agreeable, please, court;* ܒܝܕܘ ܐܘܕܝ ܒܡܫܠܡܢܘܬܐ ܕܢܫܦܪ ܠܗܘܢ *Baidu professed Islam to court their favour. e)* impers. ܐܢ ܫܦܪܐ ܠܟܘܢ *if it seem good to you;* ܐܝܟ ܕܫܦܪ ܠܗ *as he pleases;* ܫܦܪܐ ܠܪܘܚܐ ܕܩܘܕܫܐ ܘܠܢ *it seemed good unto the Holy Spirit and unto us* (exordium of Canons). ETHPE. ܐܶܬ݂ܫܦܰܪ *to be pleased; to seek to please.* ETHPA. ܐܶܬ݂ܫܰܦܰܪ *to be pleasing, to find favour; to try to please, make oneself agreeable, curry favour.* APH. ܐܰܫܦܰܪ *a) to do well, act becomingly, improve;* ܐܢ ܬܫܦܪܘܢ ܐܘܪ̈ܚܬܟܘܢ *if you amend your ways. b) to make fair, pleasing, to adorn;* ܠܫܢܐ ܕܚܟܝܡ̈ܐ ܡܫܦܪ ܝܕܥܬܐ *the tongue of the wise makes knowledge pleasing;* ܐܫܦܪ ܨܒܝܢܟ *do as you please. c) to make himself agreeable.* DERIVATIVES, ܫܘܦܪܐ, ܫܘܦܪܢܐ, ܫܘܦܪܢܝܐ, ܫܘܦܪܢܝܬܐ, ܫܘܦܪܢܘܬܐ, ܫܦܝܪܐ, ܫܦܝܪܐܝܬ, ܫܦܝܪܘܬܐ, ܫܦܪܐ, ܫܦܪܢܐ, ܫܦܪܢܘܬܐ, ܡܫܦܪܢܐ, ܫܦܪܐ, ܫܦܪܐ, ܫܦܪܐ, ܫܦܪܘܬܐ, ܫܦܪܐܝܬ, ܡܫܬܦܪܢܘܬܐ.

ܫܰܦܪܳܐ, ܫܦܪܐ rt. ܫܦܪ. m. *early dawn, twilight before dawn, the first glimmer of light;* ܒܫܦܪܐ ܠܩܠܐ ܬܪܢܓܠܐ *at cockcrow, before the break of dawn.*

ܫܰܦܳܪܳܐ m. *a)* rt. ܫܦܪ. *a flatterer. b)* Neo-Heb. *a tailor.*

ܫܰܦܪܳܝܳܐ, ܫܦܪܝܬܐ rt. ܫܦܪ. *early, matutinal;* ܒܫܦܪܝܬܐ *in the morning twilight* opp. ܒܪܡܫܝܬܐ *at fall of night.*

ܫܩܐ Peal only parts. = subst., see below. Cf. ܫܩܝܐ. ETHPE. ܐܶܬ݂ܫܩܝ *to be watered.* PA. perh. *to water drop by drop.* APH. ܐܰܫܩܝ *to water, irrigate; to give to drink, serve as a cupbearer;* ܐܫܩܝܘܗܝ ܡܝ̈ܐ *they gave him water to drink;* ܠܓܡܠܝܟ ܐܫܩܐ *I will water thy camels;* ܚܩܠܐ ܡܫܬܩܝܐ ܡܝ̈ܐ *a watered field.* ETTAPH. ܐܶܬ݁ܬ݁ܰܫܩܝ *to be made to drink; to be watered.* DERIVATIVES, ܫܩܝܐ, ܫܩܝܘܬܐ, ܫܩܝܐ, ܫܩܝܐ, ܫܩܝܘܬܐ, ܫܩܝܬܐ, ܫܩܝܬܐ, ܡܫܩܝܢܐ, ܡܫܬܩܝܢܐ.

ܫܩܐ rarely ܫܩܐ pl. ܐ̈ ܐ f. *a) the shin-bone, shank, fore-leg, leg; the fore-arm;* ܫܩܐ ܘܟܬܦܬܐ *a haunch* or *a shoulder. b) a greave, legging. c) branch* or *stem,* metaph. *stem, stock, lineage;*

ܫܩܐ ܕܡܠܟܘܬܐ *royal lineage.* *d*) *a division, limb.* *e*) *side of* a triangle; ܫܘܝ ܫܩܐ *equilateral.* *f*) *a line, verse.*

ܫܩܐ pl. ܫܩܐ, f. *a mound of earth; a sarcophagus.*

ܫܩܐ *diarrhoea* in fowls.

ܫܩܝܐ, ܫܩܝܬܐ, ܫܩܝܐ pl. m. ܫܩܝܬܐ pl. f. ܫܩܝܬܐ rt. ܫܩܐ. *a*) *a cupbearer, butler; a water-seller.* *b*) f. emph. *a watercourse, canal.*

ܫܩܒܐ or ܫܩܦܐ pl. ܐ̈ only Lexx. m. *an entrance.*

ܫܩܩܝܬܐ m. pl. *rattles.*

ܫܩܕܬܐ Heb. f. *the bitter almond.*

ܫܩܘܩܘܪܐ *avaricious, envious.*

ܫܩܘܠܐ pl. ܐ̈ rt. ܫܩܠ. m. *a*) *a bearer.* *b*) *a partaker.*

ܫܩܘܠܐ rt. ܫܩܠ. m. *an impost.*

ܫܩܘܠܐܝܬ rt. ܫܩܠ. adv. *arrogantly.*

ܫܩܘܠܬܐ pl. ܬ̈ܐ rt. ܫܩܠ. f. *a*) *an elevation, rising-ground; exaltation.* *b*) *conveyance, transport; a burden, baggage;* ܓܡܠܐ ܠܫܩܘܠܬܐ *baggage* or *transport camels.*

ܫܩܘܝܬܐ pl. ܬ̈ܐ rt. ܫܩܐ. f. *a*) *watering, irrigation; a watercourse, channel.* *b*) *drink, drinking; a drink, potion, draught; savour.*

ܫܩܘܬܐ perhaps *stupor, amazement.*

ܫܩܝܐ, ܫܩܝܐ rt. ܫܩܐ. m. *a waterer, irrigator; a water-carrier; a butler.*

ܫܩܝܐ pl. ܐ̈ rt. ܫܩܐ. m. *a*) *watering, irrigation;* ܓܢܬܐ ܕܫܩܝܐ *a watered garden.* *b*) *a watercourse, channel, trough.* *c*) *drink, drinking, a drink.*

ܫܩܝܘܬܐ rt. ܫܩܐ. f. *irrigation.*

ܫܩܝܠܘܬܐ rt. ܫܩܠ. f. *derivation.*

ܫܩܝܦ, ܐ, ܬܐ rt. ܫܩܦ. *precipitous; bristling with difficulties; headlong, stubborn.*

ܫܩܝܦܐ pl. ܐ̈ rt. ܫܩܦ. m. *a steep rock, crag, precipice.*

ܫܩܝܦܘܬܐ rt. ܫܩܦ. f. *emaciation, pallor.*

ܫܩܝܦܐ pl. ܐ̈ rt. ܫܩܦ. m. *a*) *abstruse, arduous.* *b*) *one who dwells in rocky places.*

ܫܩܝܦܘܬܐ in the Lexx. f. *a*) *nausea, dizziness.* *b*) *a fell, hide.*

ܫܩܝܬܐ pl. ܬ̈ܐ rt. ܫܩܐ. f. *a draught, purge; remedy.*

ܫܩܝܬܐ pl. ܬ̈ܐ rt. ܫܩܐ. f. *a*) see ܫܩܐ. *b*) Lexx. *a thick measuring-rod.*

ܫܩܠ fut. ܢܫܩܘܠ, parts. ܫܩܠ, ܫܩܝܠ and ܫܩܝܠ, ܫܩܝܠܐ. *a*) *to lift up, carry, bear* ܥܠ ܟܬܦܐ *on the shoulder;* ܥܠ ܓܡܠܐ *on a camel;* hence *to pack up, to break up a camp* opp. ܫܪܐ, *to march, start* with ܡܢ or with verbs of motion, ܫܩܠ ܡܢ ܬܡܢ *he marched thence;* ܫܩܠ ܘܐܙܠ *he started and went.* Metaph. *to proceed from, arise out of, begin;* ܫܩܠܬ ܠܡܡܠܠܘ *I began to speak.* *b*) *to take, partake, receive; to take* in war, *capture, carry off; to take away* with ܡܢ; ܫܩܠ ܗܘܐ ܠܛܠܝܐ ܒܐܝܕܗ *he took the child by the hand.* *c*) rarer uses: *to bear* a crop; *to put on, wear; to borrow; to subtract, to omit; to take as the meaning, interpret;* with ܥܡ *to increase.* Examples: with ܐܓܪܐ *to receive a reward;* ܐܘܠܝܬܐ *to make lamentation;* ܐܬܐ *to raise a standard;* ܐܢܬܬܐ or ܢܫܐ *to marry;* ܕܘܟܬܐ *to fill* or *take the place;* ܙܝܢܐ *to take up arms;* ܙܟܘܬܐ or ܙܟܝܘܬܐ *to gain the victory;* ܚܛܝܬܐ *to bear* or *take away sin;* ܚܝܠܐ *to regain strength;* ܛܥܢܐ *to take up a burden = to take trouble, undertake;* ܡܕܐܬܐ *to exact tribute;* ܡܕܝܢܬܐ *to take a city by storm;* ܡܥܡܘܕܝܬܐ *to receive Baptism;* ܡܦܣܢܘܬܐ *to obtain permission;* ܡܫܩܠܐ *to take up a burden = utter a prophecy;* ܢܝܪܐ *to bear the yoke;* ܢܣܝܢܐ *to make trial or proof;* ܢܦܫܐ *to take away life; to hold in suspense;* ܣܐܡܐ *to wear silver* ornaments; ܣܦܣܪܐ *to draw the sword;* ܣܟܐ or ܣܘܟܠܐ *to come to an end, be finished;* ܥܝܢܐ *to lift up the eyes;* ܥܠܬܐ *to originate, take its rise;* ܦܓܪܐ *to receive Holy Communion;* ܪܝܫܐ *to behead;* ܥܘܗܕܢܐ *to call to mind;* ܫܘܚܕܐ *to take a bribe;* ܫܘܪܝܐ *to begin;* ܬܘܟܠܢܐ *to be encouraged.* Idioms: after ܣܘܥܪܐ *to be eager, carried away,* ܫܩܠܘ ܣܘܥܪܐ ܚܙܝܪܐ lit. *the swine took a furious rush = they rushed vehemently;* ܛܢܢܐ *to be carried away by zeal;* ܙܘܥܐ *to feel incited, urged, impelled;* ܪܘܚܐ *a wind arose.* Parts. *a*) active sense: both forms are used thus: ܫܩܠ ܡܐܢܐ or ܫܩܝܠ ܙܝܢܐ *an armour-bearer;* ܫܩܠܝ ܚܘܛܪܐ *lictors;* ܫܩܝܠ ܗܘܐ or ܫܩܠ ܒܚܘܛܪܐ *he had received authority;* ܡܶܢ ܡܫܰܩܠܺܝܢ ܡܶܢ *excepting;* ܫܳܩܶܠ ܐ̱ܢܳܐ *I take.* *b*) passive sense: *derived; captured, taken;* ܫܩܺܝܠ ܒܩܽܘܛܪܳܐ *taken by force;* ܫܩܺܝܠ ܗܰܘܢܳܐ *bereft of reason.* Ethpe. ܐܶܫܬܩܶܠ *a*) *to be lifted up* on the cross, *crucified;* also *to be taken down* from the cross. *b*) *to be borne* ܒܟܰܪܣܳܐ *in the womb; to be carried, brought.* *c*) *to be captured, taken by storm; to be exacted* as tribute. *d*) *to be taken away, be abolished, come to an end, cease;* ܐܶܫܬܩܶܠ ܡܰܢܢܳܐ *manna was no longer given;* ܩܽܘܪܛܳܐ *fear ceased.* *e*) *to be cut off* as the feet, *cut out* as the tongue; ܡܶܢ ܚܰܝܶܐ *from life.* *f*) *to be accepted* as the meaning, *understood;* ܡܳܐ ܕܡܶܫܬܩܠܳܐ ܪܽܘܚܳܢܳܐܝܬ *when it is taken in a spiritual sense.* Pael ܫܰܩܶܠ *to lift, raise* ܥܰܪܦܶܐ *the eyelids; to carry* in the arms. Part. adj. ܡܫܰܩܰܠ, ܡܫܰܩܠܳܐ, ܡܫܰܩܠܽܘܬܳܐ *uplifted, lofty, proud; high-spirited, prancing.* Ethpa. ܐܶܫܬܰܩܰܠ imper. W-Syr. ܐܶܫܬܰܩܰܠ *to lift himself up* ܐܰܝܟ ܐܰܪܝܳܐ as a lion; *to be exalted, to prevail over;* ܡܶܫܬܰܩܰܠ ܥܰܠ ܒܥܶܠܕܒܳܒܰܘܗ̱ܝ *he is exalted over his enemies; to set himself above, be uplifted with pride, be arrogant, haughty* with ܥܰܠ. Aph. ܐܰܫܩܶܠ *a*) caus. *to break up* a camp, *cause to set forward;* ܐܰܫܩܶܠ ܠܥܰܡܶܗ ܐܰܝܟ ܥܳܢܳܐ *He led forth* His *people like sheep; to force to receive.* *b*) = Peal *to carry, remove; to set forward, set off, remove, march, journey;* ܐܰܫܩܶܠ ܡܰܪܗܝܳܐܝܬ ܠܘܳܬ ܐܽܘܪܗܳܝ *he marched rapidly towards Edessa;* ܐܰܫܩܶܠ ܡܶܢ ܗܳܪܟܳܐ ܠܡܰܠܟܽܘܬܳܐ ܕܠܥܶܠ *depart hence to the kingdom above.* *c*) with ܓܶܦܶܐ *to spread the wings, fly away.* Derivatives, ܫܩܳܠܳܐ, ܫܩܳܠܳܐ, ܫܩܳܠܳܐ, ܫܩܳܠܽܘܬܳܐ, ܫܰܩܠܳܐ, ܫܰܩܳܠܳܐ, ܫܩܳܠܳܐ, ܫܩܺܝܠܽܘܬܳܐ, ܫܰܩܳܠܳܐ, ܡܰܫܩܠܳܐ, ܫܩܳܠܳܐ, ܫܰܩܳܠܽܘܬܳܐ, ܫܰܩܳܠܽܘܬܳܐ, ܡܫܰܩܠܳܢܳܐ, ܡܫܰܩܠܳܢܳܐ, ܡܫܰܩܠܳܢܽܘܬܳܐ, ܡܫܰܩܠܳܢܽܘܬܳܐ.

ܫܩܳܠ, ܫܩܳܠܳܐ pl. ܶ̈ܐ rt. ܫܩܠ. m. *a*) *taking;* ܫܩܳܠ ܢܰܦܫܳܐ *putting to death;* ܕܝܽܘܚܰܢܳܢ ܫ̱ *the translation of S. John;* ܕܥܶܩܳܪܳܐ ܫ̱ *uprooting.* *b*) *a burden; a portion, assigned provision.* *c*) *a syllable;* ܡܫܰܩܠܳܐ ܬܪ̈ܶܥܣܰܪ ܫܩܳܠܶܐ *dodecasyllabic metre.* *d*) usually with ܒܶܢܳܐ *care, pains, diligence;* with ܗܘܳܐ or ܥܒܰܕ *to bestow endeavour, take pains, be careful;* ܒܫܩܳܠܒܶܢܳܐ *carefully, diligently.* Chem. *a mortar.*

ܫܩܳܠܳܐ pl. ܶ̈ܐ, ܺܝܢ rt. ܫܩܠ. m. *a*) pl. *takings, receipts, gains;* ܫܩܳܠܳܐ ܘܰܝܗܳܒܳܐ *trade, commerce.* *b*) *a tax, impost; an assessed district.* *c*) *a robe with a train.*

ܫܰܩܠܳܐ pl. ܶ̈ܐ Heb. m. *a shekel* = Syr. ܡܰܬܩܳܠܳܐ.

ܫܩܳܠܽܘܬܳܐ rt. ܫܩܠ. f. *a baggage-animal.*

ܫܩܳܠܬܳܐ rt. ܫܩܠ. f. with ܕܟܰܬܦܳܐ *the lower part of the shoulder.*

ܫܰܩܺܝܡ, ܫܰܩܺܝܡܳܐ pl. ܫܰܩܺܝܡܺܝܢ *ill, sad.*

ܫܩܡܬܳܐ E-Syr. ܫܩܡܬܳܐ pl. ܺܝܢ, ܶ̈ܐ f. *the sycamore tree* and *fruit, a wild fig, unripe grape.*

ܫܩܰܩ fut. ܢܶܫܩܽܘܩ, act. part. ܫܳܩܶܩ, ܫܳܩܩܳܐ, pass. part. ܫܩܺܝܩ, ܫܩܺܝܩܳܐ, ܫܩܺܝܩܬܳܐ. *to beat, bruise, dash against the ground; to blight, make pale;* ܫܩܽܘܩ ܥܰܠ ܚܰܕܝܳܟ *beat thy breast;* ܫܶܒ̈ܠܶܐ ܕܫܩܺܝܩܺܝܢ ܒܪܽܘܚܳܐ *ears blasted by the wind;* ܫܩܺܝܩܺܝܢ ܒܕܶܚܠܬܳܐ *pale with fear.* Pa. ܫܰܩܶܩ *a*) *to dash against the ground, to batter;* ܢܶܫܩܽܘܠ ܘܢܫܰܩܶܩ ܠܥܽܘܠܳܠܰܝܟܝ ܒܟܺܐܦܳܐ *he will take and dash thy little ones against the rock.* *b*) *to buffet, slap, knock;* ܡܫܰܩܶܩ ܦܰܟܰܘ̈ܗܝ the teacher *slaps* the boy's *cheeks.* *c*) *to make pale, to afflict;* ܡܫܰܩܶܩ ܗܘܳܐ ܐܰܝܟ ܓܰܘܢܶܗ *pale i.e. in colour;* ܥܺܕܬܳܐ ܡܫܰܩܰܩܬܳܐ ܕܡܰܕܢܚܳܐ *the stricken Church of the East.* Ethpe. ܐܶܫܬܩܶܩ and Ethpa. ܐܶܫܬܰܩܰܩ *a*) *to be dashed in pieces, dashed against the ground; to be buffeted, knocked about;* ܐܰܠܦܳܐ ܕܡܶܫܬܰܩܩܳܐ ܡܶܢ ܓܰܠܠܶܐ *a ship buffeted by the billows.* *b*) *to be blighted, pale;* ܗܰܒܳܒܳܐ ܕܡܶܢ ܪܽܘܚܳܐ ܡܶܫܬܰܩܰܩ *a flower beaten down* or *blighted by the wind;* ܡܶܫܬܰܩܩܺܝܢ ܒܟܰܦܢܳܐ *prostrated by famine, pale with hunger.* *c*) *to be pushed, thrust out;* ܚܦܰܪܘ ܓܽܘܡܳܐ ܗܰܘ ܕܒܶܗ ܐܶܫܬܰܩܰܩܘ *they dug that pit into which they were thrust.* Derivatives, ܫܩܳܩܳܐ, ܫܰܩܺܝܩ, ܫܰܩܺܝܩܽܘܬܳܐ, ܫܩܳܩܳܐ, ܫܩܳܩܳܐ, ܡܫܰܩܩܳܐ, ܡܫܰܩܩܳܢܽܘܬܳܐ.

ܫܩܳܩܳܐ rt. ܫܩܩ. *a*) *state of health, habit of body.* *b*) *impact, encounter.*

ܫܩܰܩܰܝܬܳܐ f. *the hoopoo.*

ܫܩܳܩܳܐ pl. ܶ̈ܐ m. *a narrow passage, lane, alley;* ܫ̱ ܥܨܺܝܪܳܐ *a blind alley.*

ܫܩܘܩܝܬܐ dimin. of ܫܩܳܩܳܐ m. *a*) *a slype, narrow passage* esp. in a church. *b*) *dwarf walls* in a church.

ܫܩܪ Pael ܫܰܩܰܪ to lie, deceive, assert falsely, do wickedness secretly; ܫܰܩܰܪ ܥܰܠ ܒܰܣܪܳܐ ܕܝܼܠܶܗ. ܐܰܝܢܳܐ ܕܡܫܰܩܰܪ ܒܛܶܫܝܳܐ one who commits lewdness in secret. Ethpa. ܐܶܫܬܰܩܰܪ to tell lies. Derivatives, ܫܰܩܳܪܳܐ, ܫܘܼܩܪܳܐ, ܫܰܩܳܪܘܼܬܳܐ, ܡܫܰܩܪܳܢܳܐ.

ܫܰܩܳܪܳܐ, ܫܰܩܳܪܬܳܐ rt. ܫܩܪ. lying, perjured, perfidious; ܢܒܺܝܶܐ ܫܰܩܳܪܶܐ lying prophets; a liar, hypocrite, secret sinner. Fem. emph. a lie.

ܫܰܩܳܪܘܼܬܳܐ rt. ܫܩܪ. f. falseness, perjury.

ܫܰܩܪܳܩܳܐ pl. ܶܐ Ar. m. perh. a kind of thrush or a woodpecker.

ܫܪܰܪ fut. ܢܶܫܪܰܪ or ܢܫܪܰܪ, act. part. ܫܳܪܰܪ, ܫܳܪܪܳܐ. a) to be strong, get well; ܫܪܰܪ ܒܚܰܝܠܶܗ he recovered his strength. b) with ܫܪܳܪܳܐ, ܡܶܠܬܳܐ, ܫܪܺܝܪܘܼܬܳܐ &c. to be proved true, to stand firm, come to pass; with ܚܬܳܡܳܐ to be proved, ratified; ܒܬܰܪܥܺܝܬܳܐ to be fixed. Impers. ܫܪܰܪ it was certain, proved; it was established, settled; ܢܶܫܪܰܪ ܠܟ be assured. c) to tell the truth. Part. adj. ܫܰܪܺܝܪ, ܐ, ܬܳܐ a) whole, sound; firm, solid; strong, lasting; legal, valid; ܐܶܙܰܠ ܟܰܕ ܫܰܪܺܝܪ ܐܢܬ ܘܚܰܠܺܝܡ depart safe and sound; ܟܺܐܦܳܐ ܫܰܪܺܝܪܬܳܐ the solid rock; ܡܶܐܟܘܼܠܬܳܐ ܫܰܪܺܝܪܬܳܐ solid food; ܣܳܗܕܘܼܬܳܐ ܕܠܳܐ ܫܰܪܺܝܪܳܐ an invalid deposition. b) with ܠ and pers. pron. assured, certain; with ܠ legal, lawful; ܫܰܪܺܝܪܳܐ ܠܒܰܪܢܳܫܳܐ ܕܢܶܫܒܽܘܩ ܕܝܳܬܺܝܩܶܗ it is lawful for a man to set aside his will. c) true, genuine, trustworthy, steadfast, faithful; ܨܶܒܝܳܢܳܐ ܫܰܪܺܝܪܳܐ a steadfast will; ܥܰܒܕܳܐ ܫܰܪܺܝܪܳܐ a trusty servant; ܪܶܢܝܳܐ ܫܰܪܺܝܪܳܐ a true or right opinion; ܗܰܝܡܳܢܘܼܬܳܐ ܫܰܪܺܝܪܬܳܐ the true faith; ܐܰܠܳܗܳܐ ܫܰܪܺܝܪܳܐ ܡܶܢ ܐܰܠܳܗܳܐ ܫܰܪܺܝܪܳܐ very God of very God. Subst. m. a confidential servant, a commissioner, prefect; pl. the faithful, the orthodox. Fem. emph. truth; a confirmation, sanction. Pa. ܫܰܪܰܪ a) to fix or set firmly; ܫܰܪܰܪ ܣܶܟܬܰܝܟ strengthen thy stakes; ܡܫܰܪܰܪ ܫܶܢܰܘܗܝ ܒܓܰܪܡܳܐ he sets his teeth into the bone. b) to assure, assert, affirm; ܫܰܪܰܪ ܐܶܢܽܘܢ ܕ he assured them that . . .; ܫܰܪܰܪ ܦܰܘܠܳܘܣ ܟܰܕ ܐܳܡܰܪ Paul affirmed. c) to strengthen, confirm, ratify; ܒܡܰܘܡܳܬܳܐ with oaths; ܫܰܪܪܘܼܗ ܠܓܽܘܒܳܝܳܐ ܘܠܦܽܘܪܫܳܢܳܐ they confirmed the election and designation to the patriarchate; ܩܰܒܠܽܘܗ ܘܫܰܪܪܽܘܗ they approved and confirmed the Creed. d) denom. from ܫܪܳܪܳܐ to speak the truth. Part. adj. robust, strong, firm, solid, sure, steadfast; ܡܫܰܪܪܺܝܢ ܚܬܳܡܶܝܗ ܡܫܰܪܪܺܝܢ ܗ̱ܘܰܘ its seals were entire; ܫܶܬܶܐܣܬܳܐ ܡܫܰܪܰܪܬܳܐ a firm foundation; ܡܫܰܪܪܺܝܢ ܒܗܰܝܡܳܢܘܼܬܳܐ steadfast in the faith. Ethpa. ܐܶܫܬܰܪܰܪ a) to become strong, get well; to show himself strong, prevail. b) to become solid, firm as clay in the fire. c) to be firmly set, fixed or laid as a building; ܐܶܫܬܰܪܪܘܼ ܡܰܚܫܒܳܬܝ ܥܰܠ ܥܶܪܘܩܝܳܐ my thoughts were fixed on flight. d) to be established ܥܰܠ ܟܘܼܪܣܝܳܐ, ܒܡܰܠܟܘܼܬܳܐ on the throne, in possession of the kingdom; to be determined upon, settled as war, peace; to be confirmed, ratified as a testament, deed, canon. e) to be certain, assured, made known; ܗܰܝܡܶܢܘ ܐܰܝܟ ܕܬܶܫܬܰܪܪܽܘܢ believe and be certain; ܐܶܫܬܰܪܰܪܢ ܡܶܢܳܟ ܥܰܠ we received information of . . . . Aph. ܐܰܫܪܰܪ a) to set firmly; to make strong, restore to health; ܡܰܪܓܳܢܝܳܬܳܐ ܡܫܰܪܪܳܢ ܒܕܰܗܒܳܐ gems set in gold. b) to confirm, establish, make true, keep one's word, a promise, vow, command, dream; ܡܫܰܪܪܺܝܢ ܡܶܠܰܝܗܽܘܢ ܒܳܐܬܘܳܬܳܐ confirming their words with signs; ܡܨܶܐ ܐܢܬ ܠܡܫܰܪܳܪܽܘ ܚܶܠܡܶܐ Thou canst make dreams come true. c) to credit, give credence, believe firmly, be convinced; ܠܳܐ ܬܰܫܪܰܪ ܠܡܶܠܬܳܐ ܕܓܰܠܬܳܐ thou shalt give no credit to a false report; ܡܰܫܪܰܪ ܐܢܳܐ ܠܟ I believe you fully. d) to assert, affirm; ܟܰܕ ܡܰܫܪܰܪ ܕܗܳܟܰܢܳܐ ܐܺܝܬܰܘܗܝ affirming that it was even so. Gram. with ܥܰܠ to signify, refer to. e) to speak the truth, be true; ܗܶܪܣܺܝܣ ܡܶܢܗܶܝܢ ܡܫܰܪܪܳܢ ܘܡܶܢܗܶܝܢ ܡܕܰܓܠܳܢ these heresies are partly true and partly false. Ettaph. ܐܶܬܬܰܫܪܰܪ to make himself believed, assert strongly. Derivatives, ܫܪܳܪܳܐ, ܫܰܪܺܝܪܳܐ, ܫܰܪܺܝܪܘܼܬܳܐ, ܫܪܺܝܪܳܐܺܝܬ, ܡܫܰܪܪܳܢܳܐ, ܡܫܰܪܪܳܢܘܼܬܳܐ, ܡܫܰܪܪܳܢܺܝܬ, ܡܫܰܪܪܳܢܳܐܺܝܬ, ܡܫܰܪܪܳܢܘܼܬܳܐ, ܡܫܰܪܪܳܢܳܐ, ܡܫܰܪܪܽܘܬܳܐ, ܫܘܼܪܳܪܳܐ.

ܫܪ̈ abbrev. for ܫܰܪܟܳܐ: ܘܫܪ̈ etcetera.

ܫܪܳܐ fut. ܢܶܫܪܶܐ, parts. ܫܳܪܶܐ, ܫܳܪܝܳܐ and ܫܪܶܐ, ܫܪܶܝܢ, ܫܪܰܝܬܳܐ. i. trans. to loosen opp. ܐܶܣܰܪ in many senses. a) to loosen, untie, unfasten, unbind; ܫܪܶܐ ܣܰܥܪܳܐ with dishevelled hair; ܫܪܶܐ ܡܣܳܐܢܶܐ unshod. With ܚܰܨܳܐ to ungird the loins; ܠܶܫܳܢܳܐ to unloose, set free the tongue; to paralyse the limbs. With ܚܬܳܡܳܐ, ܐܶܓܰܪܬܳܐ &c. to unseal, break open, open a will, letter, book. Metaph. to lay open the sense, expound. With ܩܶܛܪܳܐ or ܐܽܘܚܕܳܬܳܐ to untie a knot, solve a difficulty, a riddle. b) to let loose from bonds, unburden, *unharness* with ܡܢ; *to let go, dismiss; to disband* an army, *dismiss* from office, *depose, allow to resign,* with ܢܦܫܗ *to abdicate. To repudiate, put away* a wife, *disown a son.* With ܚܝ̈ܐ *to depart from this life;* with ܡܢ ܚܝ̈ܐ *to deprive of life.* c) *to loose* from sin, *absolve* from ordinances, *give dispensation; to loose* from consecration, as oil of chrism, water of Baptism after the service is over. *To break* ܩܢܘܢܐ, ܦܘܩܕܢܐ, ܫܠܡܐ *a rule, commandment, treaty of peace.* With ܡܟܘܪܝܐ *to break* or *set free from betrothal;* ܨܘܡܐ *to break* or *finish a fast,* hence *to eat, feast. To violate* ܒܬܘܠܘܬܐ *virginity,* ܢܕܪܐ *a vow,* ܫܒܬܐ *the Sabbath.* ܐܢ ܫܪܐ ܐܢܫ ܠܗ ܫܘܬܦܘܬܗ *if a man dissolve partnership;* with ܕܝܢܐ *to break off a lawsuit;* ܚܪܝܢܐ *to adjust a quarrel; to transact* business. *To abrogate, rescind* ܦܘܩܕܢܐ *a decree,* ܡܢܘܝܘܬܐ *an ordination;* with ܟܠܗ *to render null and void. To refute, confute* an opinion, argument. *To destroy;* ܐܘ ܫܪܐ ܗܝܟܠܐ *O Thou that destroyest the temple.* d) *to dissolve* chemically, *resolve* into vapour, *thaw, soften, liquefy.* Pass. part. a) *loose, open, fluid, free;* ܦܨܝ̈ܠܬܐ ܫܪܝ̈ܬܐ ܕܐܐܪ *the open regions of the air.* Metaph. *relaxed, dissolute.* β) *common, profane, null and void.* II. intrans. e) *to dwell, lodge, stay* with ܒ, ܠܘܬ *at* or *with,* ܠܘܬ *near; to reside, be situated; to rest upon* with ܒ, ܥܠ; ܫܪ̈ܝܢ ܡܫܟ̈ܢܐ *nomads;* ܫܪܐ ܥܡ ܟܐܢ̈ܐ *having his habitation among the just, deceased.* f) *to pitch* a camp, *encamp, halt,* with ܒ, ܠܘܩܒܠ *by, opposite, against,* hence *to besiege.* g) *to be at a standstill, break up;* ܟܕ ܫܪܐ ܥܕܬܐ *when church is over.* Ethpe. ܐܫܬܪܝ a) *to be loosed* as ܐܣܘܪ̈ܐ *bonds; to be unsealed, opened.* With ܦܪ̈ܩܐ *to be paralysed, dislocated;* ܠܫܢܐ *to have the tongue loosed, speak freely;* ܡܥܝ̈ܐ *to have the bowels relaxed;* metaph. *to be loosened, relaxed* as ܫܪ̈ܝܢܐ *the joints;* ܚܝܠܐ *the strength* or ellipt. from fear, grief or weariness, *to faint. To be taken* or *broken to pieces.* b) *to be let loose, released; to be dismissed,* as catechumens, *to break up* as ܥܕܬܐ, ܟܢܘܫܬܐ, ܣܘܢܗܕܘܣ a congregation, a synod, *be over* as ܥܐܕܐ *a festival,* ܫܘܩܐ *a market; to be finished, concluded, settled* as ܕܝܢܐ *a lawsuit,* ܨܒܘܬܐ *an affair.* Gram. *to end.* Fem. impers. *it was settled, resolved upon, permitted.* Also refl. *to depart* usually with ܡܢ ܚܝ̈ܐ; ܠܐ ܡܫܬܪܝܢܐ *indissoluble, imperishable.* c) *to be rejected, deposed, divorced.* d) *to be absolved; to be loosed from consecration* ܐܫܬܪܝܬ ܡܥܡܘܕܝܬܐ *Baptism is over* i.e. the holy water has been declared free and poured away. e) *to be broken, violated, revoked* as a law, an oath, the Sabbath, peace. f) *to be dissolved, resolved, melted, softened;* metaph. ܐܫܬܪܝܬ ܐܦܘܪܝܐ *the difficulty was solved.* Pa. ܫܪܝ a) *to begin* with fut., infin., act. part., subst. with ܒ, or absol. ܫܪܝܘ ܡܫܐܠܝܢ *they began asking;* ܫܪܝ ܒܟܘܪܗܢܐ *he fell ill;* ܥܒܕ ܫܘܪܝܐ *make a beginning;* ܡܫܪܐ ܡܢ *it begins with. To be introduced, to take its rise.* Eccles. *to recite a* ܩܢܘܢܐ. b) *to relax, paralyse* usually pass. part. ܡܫܪܝ, ܡܫܪܝܐ, ܡܫܪܝܬܐ *loose, dissolute; paralysed, paralytic;* ܐܒܪܐ = ܩܣܛܝܪܐ ܡܫܪܝܐ *tin.* Ethpa. ܐܫܬܪܝ a) *to be begun.* b) *to be paralysed, to be destroyed.* c) *to dine, sup, feast.* Aph. ܐܫܪܝ a) *to call a halt, command to encamp, place, set, assign quarters, billet* soldiers; ܥܡܘܕܐ ܕܥܢܢܐ ܕܗܘܐ ܡܫܘܕܥ ܠܡܫܪܝܬܐ ܘܠܡܫܩܠܬܐ *the pillar of cloud which gave the signal for encamping and for setting forward;* ܐܫܪܝ ܐܢܝܢ ܠܘܩܒܠ ܠܩܪ̈ܒܐ ܕܨܘܪ *he drew up the ships of war opposite Tyre.* b) *to make to dwell, make to rest; to instil, infuse, affect, ascribe;* ܐܫܪܝ ܠܡܠܐܟ̈ܐ ܒܗܘ ܢܘܗܪܐ ܕܠܐ ܡܫܓܫܢܐ *He hath appointed the angels to dwell in untroubled light;* ܐܫܪܐ ܫܠܡܟ ܒܓܘ ܥܕܬܟ *may Thy peace dwell within Thy Church;* ܐܫܪܝ ܚܝ̈ܐ ܒܡܝ̈ܐ *He sent life into the waters;* ܐܫܪܝ ܬܗܪܐ ܥܠ ܒ ܫܪܝܬܐ *to amaze, alarm.* c) = Pael *to paralyse.* Derivatives, ܫܪܝܐ, ܫܪܝܘܬܐ, ܫܪܘܝܐ, ܫܪܝܐ, ܫܪܝܘܬܐ, ܫܪܝܬܐ, ܫܪܝܢ, ܫܪܝܢ, ܫܪܝܬܐ, ܫܪܝܘܬܐ, ܫܪܝܬܐ, ܡܫܪܐ, ܡܫܪܝܢܘܬܐ, ܡܫܪܝܢܐ, ܡܫܪܝܢܘܬܐ, ܡܫܪܝܐ, ܡܫܪܝܬܐ, ܡܫܪܝܢܝܬܐ, ܡܫܪܝܘܬܐ, ܡܫܪܝܢܐ, ܡܫܪܝܢܝܬܐ, ܡܫܪܝܢܘܬܐ, ܡܫܬܪܝܢܐ, ܡܫܬܪܝܢܝܬܐ, ܡܫܬܪܝܢܘܬܐ.

ܫܪܐ a) = ܫܪܪܐ m. *the navel.* b) = ܫܝܪܐ *a chain, ornament.*

ܫܪܒ pass. part. ܫܪܝܒܐ. *to become dry, sapless.* Ethpe. ܐܫܬܪܒ a) *to be dried up.* b) *to be approved.* c) = Ethpa. Pa. ܫܪܒ a) *to dry.*

b) denom. from ܫܪܒܬܐ *to propagate, generate; to found* a city, *fill* it *with families*. ETHPA. ܐܫܬܪܒ *a*) *to be reckoned by genealogy, counted according to families; to be propagated, continued; to divide* a subject *under heads;* ܠܐ ܬܫܬܪܒ ܗܝ ܡܠܦܢܘܬܐ ܒܐܬܪܢ *let not this doctrine be propagated in our country*. *b*) perh. *to set up*.

ܫܪܒ, ܫܪܒܐ pl. ܫܪܒܝܢ, ܫܪܒܐ m. *a*) *generation, genealogy, history, a story, deed, action;* ܓܠܐ ܘܟܣܐ ܫܪܒܟ *Thy generation is revealed and yet hidden;* ܫܪܒܗ ܕܗܒܝܠ *the history of Abel;* ܒܫܪܒܐ ܩܕܡܝܐ *in the foregoing account*. *b*) *a matter, affair; subject, argument, discourse, essay; supposition, hypothesis;* legal *a cause, action, suit;* ܒܫܪܒܐ ܕ *for, touching, with regard to;* ܥܠ ܫܪܒܐ ܕ *concerning*.

ܫܪܒܐ in the Lexx. m. rt. ܫܪܒ. *sultry wind, the simoom*.

ܫܪܒܐ rt. ܫܪܒ. m. *drought*.

ܫܪܒܬܐ, ܫܪܒܬܐ pl. ܫܪܒܢ, ܫܪܒܬܐ f. *a*) *generation, genealogy; a family, tribe, race, nation;* ܝܘܠܦܢܐ ܕܫܪܒܬܐ or ܡܠܬܐ ܕ *genealogical science*. *b*) *order, rank*. *c*) gram. *origin*.

ܫܪܒܘܢܐ dimin. of ܫܪܒܐ m. *a minor matter, small affair*.

ܫܪܒܘܛܬܐ pl. ܫܪܒܘܛܬܐ f. *a*) *a noose, snare*. *b*) *a loop, dress-fastening*.

ܫܪܒܘܬܐ rt. ܫܪܒ. f. *aridity*.

ܫܪܒܠ Shaphel conj. of verb ܪܒܠ.

ܫܪܒܠܐ pl. ܫܪܒܠܐ m. *wide trousers*.

ܫܪܒܘܒܐ dimin. of ܫܪܒܐ. m. *a trifle, small sum*.

ܫܪܓ act. part. ܫܪܓ, ܫܪܓܐ. *a*) *to be dim* as the eyes. *b*) *to light*. ETHPA. ܐܫܬܪܓ *to be illuminated*. ETHPALPAL ܐܫܬܪܓܪܓ *a*) *to have the sight dim* or *confused*. *b*) *to imagine, dream*. *c*) *to hasten*. APH. ܐܫܪܓ *to dazzle*. DERIVATIVES, ܫܪܓܐ, ܫܪܓܝܐ, ܫܪܓܪܓܐ, ܫܪܓܪܓܬܐ, ܫܪܓܪܓܝܐ, ܫܪܓܝܢܐ, ܫܪܘܓܝܐ.

ܫܪܓܐ pl. ܫܪܓܝܢ, ܫܪܓܐ m. *a lamp*.

ܫܪܓܠܣ m. *myristica moschata, the mace and nutmeg-tree*.

ܫܪܓܪܓ Shaphel conj.; see ܪܓܓ.

ܫܪܓܝܐ rt. ܫܪܓ. adj. *of a lamp*.

ܫܪܓܪܓ, ܫܪܓܪܓܐ rt. ܫܪܓ. m. *a phantasm, hallucination*.

ܫܪܓܪܓܬܐ pl. ܫܪܓܪܓܬܐ rt. ܫܪܓ. f. *a*) *twinkling, sparkling*. *b*) usually pl. *hallucination, illusion, phantom;* with ܕܚܝܠܐ *mirage;* ܫܪܓܪܓܬܐ ܕܚܪܫܐ *conjuror's tricks*.

ܫܪܓܪܓܝܐ rt. ܫܪܓ. *fantastic, hallucinatory*.

ܫܪܓܝܢܐ rt. ܫܪܓ. *having charge of the lamps*.

ܫܪܕܐ m. *the bitter almond*.

ܫܪܕܘܪܐ pl. ܐ m. *a skeleton, corpse*.

ܫܪܘܝܐܝܬ rt. ܫܪܐ. adv. *for the first time, newly, recently; as a candidate, probationer*.

ܫܪܘܒܘܬܐ rt. ܫܪܒ. f. *being dried up, mustiness*.

ܫܪܘܝܐ, ܫܪܘܝܬܐ rt. ܫܪܐ. *a*) *early, fresh, young, first-ripe;* ܡܛܪܐ ܫܪܘܝܐ *early rain*. *b*) *new, recent, initial, newly made, built* or *appointed*. *c*) *a beginner, tyro, postulant, novice;* ܡܠܦܢܘܬܐ ܫܪܘܝܬܐ *rudimentary teaching, instruction for beginners*. Fem. *a mother bearing her first child*.

ܫܪܘܝܐ, ܫܪܘܝܬܐ rt. ܫܪܐ. *a*) *solvent*. *b*) *one who dissolves, loosens, unbinds, violates* &c. *c*) *a dweller, sojourner*. *d*) = ܫܪܘܝܬܐ ܕܡܬܢܝܬܐ *the whorl* of a spindle.

ܫܪܘܝܘܬܐ rt. ܫܪܐ. f. *commencement, rudiments; novitiate*.

ܫܪܘܝܢܐ rarely ܫܘܪܘܝܢܐ *the cypress;* also a species of cedar.

ܫܪܘܪܐ = ܫܘܪܪܐ and ܫܘܪܪܐ Ar. m. *a cat; a squirrel*.

ܫܪܘܦ, ܫܪܘܦܐ, ܫܪܘܦܬܐ rt. ܫܪܦ. *slippery; gliding*.

ܫܪܘܦܘܬܐ rt. ܫܪܦ. f. *viscidity, slipperiness*.

ܫܪܘܦܢܝܐ rt. ܫܪܦ. *gliding, rapid* as water.

ܫܪܘܦܬܢܘܬܐ rt. ܫܪܦ. f. *instability*.

ܫܪܘܦܬܐ f. *a*) rt. ܫܪܦ. *absorption*. *b*) *a woollen tunic*.

ܫܪܘܪܐ and ܫܪܐ pl. ܐ rt. ܫܪܐ. m. *a tender shoot, young plant;* ܫܪܐ ܕܩܪܐ *a young gourd-plant*.

ܫܪܘܓܝܐ rt. ܫܪܓ. m. *dimness of sight*.

ܫܪܘܬܐ pl. ܫܪܘܬܐ abs. state ܫܪܘ rt. ܫܪܐ. f. *a meal, repast, feast, banquet; the meal eaten by reapers at* 3 *p.m.*

ܫܪܝܘܬ and ܫܪܝܘܬܝ usually with ܕ prefixed. rt. ܫܪܐ. adv. *recently, lately; first.*

ܫܪܐܪܐ or ܫܪܪܐ m. some bird.

ܫܪܓ only Lexx. ETHPA. ܐܫܬܪܓ *to tremble, be alarmed.* DERIVATIVES, ܫܘܪܓܐ, ܡܫܬܪܓܢܐ, ܡܫܬܪܓܢܘܬܐ.

ܫܪܚ *to range;* ܫܪܚܬ ܠܐܘܪܚܬܐ ܕܢܘܟܪܝܐ *thou hast taken to roving ways.* Part. adj. ܫܪܝܚ, ܫܪܝܚܐ, ܫܪܝܚܬܐ *immoderate, unrestrained, lascivious;* ܦܘܢܩܐ ܫܪܝܚܐ *excessive luxury;* ܫܪܝܚܝܢ ܦܠܚܝ ܦܬܟܪܐ *fanatical idolaters;* ܢܟܦܐ ܘܠܐ ܫܪܝܚܐ *chaste and modest.* ETHPE. ܐܫܬܪܚ and ETHPA. ܐܫܬܪܚ *to be immoderate, run riot, commit excesses; to be overjoyed, ravished with joy;* ܐܫܬܪܚ ܠܫܢܝ ܒܗ *my tongue exceeds;* with ܙܢܝܘܬܐ, ܪܓܬܐ, ܒܣܝܡܘܬܐ *to indulge in debauches, in lust.* PA. ܫܪܚ *to provoke lust, excite excesses;* ܒܩܝܢܬܐ ܘܒܢܥܡܬܐ ܫܪܚ ܠܛܠܝܘܬܐ *with songs and melody* Bardesanes *excited the passions of the youthful.* APH. ܐܫܪܚ *to ravish, enrapture, fascinate, captivate;* ܐܫܪܚ ܠܝ ܝܬܝܪ ܒܫܝܢܗ ܡܢ ܕܒܫܘܦܪܗ Paradise *enraptured me yet more by its peace than by its loveliness.* DERIVATIVES, ܫܪܝܚܐܝܬ, ܫܪܝܚܘܬܐ.

ܫܪܛܐ pl. ܐ̈ Arab. = ܫܘܪܛܐ. m. *a watchman, guard; the Pretorian guard.*

ܫܪܝ, ܫܪܝܐ rt. ܫܪܐ. m. *a) release, liberation; acquittance, remission;* ܫ ܕܥܩܬܐ *relief.* Eccles. *abrogation, dispensation;* ܫܪܝܐ ܕܡܝܐ *loosing the* Baptismal *water from its consecration. b) dismissal; repudiation;* ܫ ܕܡܠܟܘܬܐ or ellipt. *abdication. c) dissolution, destruction;* ܫ ܕܡܘܬܐ *abolition of death;* ܫܪܝܐ ܕܟܪܣܐ *consumption, dysentery. d) end, termination; the concluding verses* of an antiphon. *e) solution, resolving of* ܫܘܐܠܐ *a query,* ܡܣܟܠܐ *an objection; explanation, exposition, interpretation* ܕܚܠܡܐ *of dreams;* ܕܩܘܪܐܢ *of the Quran; confutation, refutation,* with ܫܪܐ *to confute, refute. f)* the points :.

ܫܪܝܐ; see ܫܪܐ.

ܫܪܝܐܝܬ rt. ܫܪܐ. adv. *loosely, freely, dissolutely.*

ܫܪܝܘܬܐ rt. ܫܪܐ. f. *a) solubility, fluidity, liquidness. b) liberty, laxity, license. c)* ܫܪܝܘܬܐ ܕܦܓܪܐ *paralysis;* ܫܪܝܘܬܐ ܕܠܫܢܐ *loquacity.*

ܫܪܝܚܐܝܬ rt. ܫܪܚ. adv. *wantonly, lecherously.*

ܫܪܝܚܘܬܐ rt. ܫܪܚ. f. *intemperance, excess, wantonness, lasciviousness.*

ܫܪܝܟ, ܫܪܝܟܐ; see verb ܫܪܟ.

ܫܪܝܟܘܬܐ and ܫܪܟܐ rt. ܫܪܟ. f. *persistence, continuance.*

ܫܪܝܡܐ *having the nose split.*

ܫܪܝܢ, ܫܪܝܢܐ pl. ܐ̈ m. *a) a corselet, cuirass, breastplate;* ܫ ܕܦܪܙܠܐ *a coat of mail. b) a joint, articulation. c) a nerve, a membrane. d) an artery, vein, pulse; a vein in the rocks, a fissure.*

ܫܪܝܢܝܐ, ܫܪܝܢܝܬܐ from ܫܪܝܢܐ. *of a joint, articulation.*

ܫܪܝܩܘܬܐ rt. ܫܪܩ. f. *hollowness, emptiness.*

ܫܪܝܪ, ܫܪܝܪܐ, ܫܪܝܪܬܐ; see verb ܫܪ.

ܫܪܝܪܐܝܬ rt. ܫܪ. adv. *truly, verily, indeed, firmly, steadfastly.*

ܫܪܝܪܘܬܐ rt. ܫܪ. f. *a) firmness, soundness, health. b) reality, truth, fidelity, steadfastness.*

ܫܪܝܬܐ pl. ܫܪܝܬܐ̈ rt. ܫܪܐ. f. *a)* ܫ ܕܟܪܣܐ *laxness of the bowels, diarrhoea. b) laxity, lasciviousness. c) a joint, articulation;* gram. *a member* of a sentence.

ܫܪܟ fut. ܢܫܪܘܟ and ܢܫܪܘܟ, act. part. ܫܪܟ, ܫܪܟܐ, pass. part. ܫܪܝܟ and ܫܪܝܟ, ܐ. *a) to be left, to remain, be reduced to, come to; to turn out, result, end in;* ܢܘܗܪܐ ܠܟ ܠܚܫܘܟܐ ܫܪܟ *light is turned into darkness for thee;* ܣܪܝܩܘܬܐ ܢܫܪܘܟ ܠܗ *vanity shall be his recompense;* ܠܓܠܘܬܐ ܫܪܟ *he was doomed to banishment.* Esp. ܫܪܟ ܠܐܒܕܢܐ—ܠܕܘܘܢܐ—ܠܡܣܟܢܘܬܐ *to be reduced to destruction, to misery, to be ruined;* with ܠܛܥܝܘܬܐ *to be left to oblivion;* ܥܠ ܠܐ ܡܕܡ *to come to naught, be spoiled;* ܠܬܚܬܝܬܐ *to drift downwards;* ܠܨܒܝܢܐ *to be left to choice, be optional.* With ܨܒܘܬܐ or ܫܪܟܐ *to refer the matter;* ܫܪܟܬ ܥܠܬܗܘܢ ܠܘܬ ܣܘܠܛܢܐ *their cause was referred to the Sultan;* but ܠܐܝܟܐ ܫܪܟ ܫܪܟܐ *how the thing would end* or *turn out. b) to remain, be found, persist* with ܒ or ܠܘܬ of the pers. ܐܢ ܠܘܬܟ ܫܪܟܐ ܣܟܠܘܬܐ *if the fault is brought home to you, if you are found guilty;* with ܠܘܬ of the thing *to incline to, tend towards;* ܫܪܟ ܠܘܬ ܡܠܟܐ *he inclines to, abides by, my opinion.* c) *to be left over, left remaining, survive;* ܫܪܟܘ ܨܒܘ̈ܬܐ ܣܓܝ̈ܐܬܐ *many things remained unfinished;* ܗܢܘܢ ܕܫܪܟܘ *the survivors;* ܡܫܬܪܟܢܐ ܕ̈ *the residue, remainder;* ܡܫܬܪܟܢܐ ܕ (in an argument) *the remaining alternative is, it results that* . . . . APH. ܐܫܪܟ *to leave, commit, abandon* ܠܒܣܪܐ *to contempt;* ܠܐܠܗܐ ܡܫܪܟ ܐܢܬ ܕܝܢܟ *thou committest thy cause to God.* ETTAPH. ܐܬܬܫܪܟ *to be committed, entrusted.* DERIVATIVES, ܫܪܟܢܘܬܐ, ܫܪܟܐ, ܫܪܟܐ, ܫܪܟܢܐ.

ܫܪܟܐ no pl. rt. ܫܪܟ. m. *the remnant, remains, the rest;* ܫܪܟܐ ܕܥܡܐ *the rest of the people;* ܫܪܟܐ ܕ *the rest, the others;* ܘܫܪܟܐ, ܘܫ̄ *etcetera.*

ܫܪܟܐ only Lexx. m. a) *a young calf.* b) *foundation, root, base.*

ܫܪܟܐ rt. ܫܪܟ. m. *tendency, result.*

ܫܪܟܢܐ pl. ܐ̈ rt. ܫܪܟ. m. *a remainder, remnant, residue, the rest;* ܫ̄ ܕܚܝ̈ܝܢ *the rest of our lives.*

ܫܪܟܢܝܐ rt. ܫܪܟ. *remaining, of the remainder.*

ܫܪܝܓܐ, ܫܪܝܓܬܐ *empty, exhausted.*

ܫܪܡܠܝ Sanskrit: *the silk-cotton tree.*

ܫܪܛ fut. ܢܫܪܛ, act. part. ܫܪܛ, ܫܪܛܐ, pass. part. ܫܪܝܛ. a) *to slip, slip away, slide, glide;* ܐܬܠܝܛܐ ܡܫܚ ܢܦܫܗ ܕܢܫܟܚ ܢܫܪܘܛ ܡܢ ܐܝ̈ܕܘܗܝ ܕܒܥܠܕܒܒܗ a gymnast oils himself *that he may be able to slip from the grasp of his antagonist;* ܫܪܫܐ ܕܡܝ̈ܐ *aquatic creatures.* b) *to slip, stumble, lapse* ܫܪܛ ܡܢ ܫܪܪܐ *from the truth;* ܕܫܪܛ ܘܢܦܠ ܒܦܚ̈ܐ ܕܚܛܝܬܐ *one who has slipped and fallen into the pitfalls of sin,* ܫܪܛܬ ܐܢܬ *thou hast erred.* ETHPE. ܐܫܬܪܛ = Peal b; ܐܫܬܪܛ ܒܣܟܠܘܬܐ *he fell into a fault;* ܐܫܬܪܛܬܘܢ ܒܡ̈ܠܐ *ye have offended in words.* APH. ܐܫܪܛ *to make ready to fall, cause to waver, shake;* ܥܠܬܐ ܕܡܫܪܛܢܘܬܗܘܢ ܘܡܦܩܢܘܬܗܘܢ *the cause of their fall and expulsion* from Paradise. DERIVATIVES, ܫܪܛܢܝܐ, ܫܪܛܐ, ܫܪܛܢܘܬܐ, ܫܪܛܐ, ܫܪܝܛܘܬܐ, ܫܪܛܐ, ܡܫܪܛܢܘܬܐ, ܡܫܪܛܢܐ, ܡܫܬܪܛܢܘܬܐ.

ܫܪܛܐ, ܫܪܛܬܐ pl. ܢ̈ܐ, ܬܐ̈ rt. ܫܪܛ. f. a) *a slippery place, a slide.* b) *a slip, lapse, fault.* c) *slipping out* of the joints, *dislocation.*

ܫܪܛܘܡܐ pl. ܐ̈ m. *a plague-spot, the plague.*

ܫܪܟܒ PAREL conj. from ܫܟܒ. *to quiver, palpitate* as fishes.

ܫܪܩܐ pl. ܐ̈ m. a) *dung, droppings.* b) *cinders.*

ܫܪܨ fut. ܢܫܪܘܨ, act. part. ܫܪܨ. *to creep.* DERIVATIVES, ܫܪܨܐ, ܫܪܨܐ, ܫܪܨܢܐ.

ܫܪܨܐ rt. ܫܪܨ. collect. m. *creeping things, vermin,* opp. ܪܚܫܐ *large reptiles.*

ܫܪܨܝܐ, ܫܪܨܝܬܐ and ܫܪܨܢܝܐ, ܫܪܨܢܝܬܐ rt. ܫܪܨ. *creeping, reptilian.*

ܫܪܩ Peal only act. part. ܫܪܩ, ܫܪܩܐ, ܫܪܩܬܐ and part. adj. ܫܪܝܩ, ܫܪܝܩܐ *hollow, hollow-sounding, empty;* ܫܪܝܩ ܡܘܚܐ *brainless, empty-headed;* ܐܝܠܢܐ ܕܫܪܝܩ *a hollow tree.* APH. ܐܫܪܩ a) *to whistle, hiss;* ܪܘܚܐ ܕܡܫܪܩܢ *whistling winds;* ܟܕ ܡܫܪܩ ܠܗ ܚܘܝܐ the serpent *hissing deceit to* Eve; ܡܫܪܩܝܢ ܒܐܒܘܒܐ *piping.* DERIVATIVES, ܫܪܘܩܬܐ, ܫܪܩܘܬܐ, ܫܪܩܐ, ܫܪܩܬܐ, ܫܪܩܬܐ, ܫܪܩܘܩܐ, ܡܫܪܘܩܝܬܐ, ܡܫܪܘܩܝܬܐ, ܡܫܪܘܩܘܬܐ, ܡܫܪܩܢܘܬܐ.

ܫܪܩܐ rt. ܫܪܩ. m. a) *hissing, whistling.* b) *swallowing, gulping.*

ܫܪܩܘܦܐ *a resounding box on the ears.*

ܫܪܩܪܩܐ Ar. m. *a green magpie* or *bee-eater.*

ܫܪܩܪܩܬܐ = ܫܪܩܬܐ *a.*

ܫܪܩܬܐ pl. ܬܐ̈ rt. ܫܪܩ. f. a) *a shell, eggshell;* ܫܪܩܬܐ ܕܒܝ̈ܥܐ *empty eggshells.* b) *husk* of a pomegranate.

ܫܪܪܬܐ rt. ܫܪ. f. ܫܪܪܐ ܕܚܝܠܐ *vote, assent.*

ܫܪܫ denom. verb from ܫܪܫܐ. APHEL ܐܫܪܫ *to root, establish.* PALI ܫܪܫ *to take root; to root up, eradicate; to loosen, relax.* ETHPALI ܐܫܬܪܫ a) *to strike root.* b) *to settle, make smooth, facilitate.*

ܫܪܫܐ pl. ܐ̈ m. a) *a root;* ܓܕܡܐ ܕܫܪܫܘܗܝ *the stump of its roots;* ܫܪܫܐ ܕܒܪܩܐ *thunderbolts.* Often metaph. *root, base, foundation, ground;* ܡܢ ܫܪܫܐ *radically, from the foundations.* b) *a ball* of thread or cotton. DERIVATIVES, verb ܐܫܪܫ and ܫܪܫ, ܫܪܫܢܐ, ܫܪܫܝܐ.

ܫܪܫܠ Shaphel conj. of verb ܪܫܠ.

ܫܪܫܢܝܐ, ܫܪܫܢܝܬܐ from ܫܪܫܐ. gram. *radical, principal.*

ܫܪܬܚ Shaphel conj. of verb ܪܬܚ.

ܫܬܐ; see ܫܝܬܐ.

ܫܬܕܠ Shaphel conj. of verb ܕܠܠ.

ܫܛܚܐ or ܫܛܝܚܐ m. *a*) *a raft.* *b*) *a cotton jacket.*

ܫܬܬܐ or ܫܬܬܐ = ܫܘܫܬܐ m. *a worm, maggot, wood-worm.*

ܫܫܠܬܐ, ܫܫܠܬܐ pl. ܫܫܠܬܐ, ܫܫܠܬܐ; see ܫܫܠܬܐ *a chain.*

ܫܫܠܬܢܝܐ, ܫܫܠܬܢܝܬܐ; see ܫܫܠܬܢܝܐ.

ܫܫܠܘܦܐ, ܫܫܠܘܦܐ *a tortoise.*

ܫܬ f. ܫܬܐ or ܫܬܐ m. also ܐܫܬܐ and ܐܫܬ *six;* ܫܬ ܫܬ *by sixes, six in a row;* ܕܫܬ, ܕܫܬܐ *the sixth;* ܦܫܝܛܬܐ ܕܫܬܐ *the Hexapla.* Pl. ܫܬܝܢ and ܐܫܬܝܢ *sixty;* ܫܬܡܐܐ *six hundred.* Derivatives, ܫܬܝܬܐ, ܫܬܐܝܬ, ܫܬܝܬܝܐ, ܫܬܝܬܝܘܬܐ, ܫܬܢܝܐ, ܫܬܣܕܪܐ, ܫܬܝܬܐ, ܫܬܬܣܪ.

ܫܬ root together with ܐܫܬܐ of ܫܬܐ, ܫܬܐܣܬܐ, ܫܬܐܣܬܐ, ܫܬ, verb ܫܬܩ, ܫܬܩܘܬܐ.

ܫܬ W-Syr. ܫܬ E-Syr. rt. ܫܬ. perhaps construct st. of ܐܫܬܐ *the lowest part, bottom;* ܫܬ ܕܚܨܒܐ *the bottom of a cask;* ܫܬ ܐܕܪܐ *refuse of the barn floor;* ܫܬ ܫܩܕܐ pl. ܫܬܝ ܫܩܕܐ *almond.*

ܫܬܐ the pret. and imper. are always written with prosthetic Aleph, pret. ܐܫܬܝ, imper. ܐܫܬܝ, fut. ܢܫܬܐ, act. part. ܫܬܐ, ܫܬܝܐ. *a*) *to drink, imbibe, suck in;* ܫܬܐ ܗܘܐ ܚܡܪܐ ܥܬܝܩܐ *he was drinking old wine;* ܣܝܦܐ ܫܬܝܐ ܕܡܐ *the sword drenched with blood;* ܐܫܬܝܢ ܡܠܝ *ye shall receive my words.* *b*) *to give drink, water, be watered;* ܡܫܩܝܢ ܠܗܘܢ ܫܬܝܢ *they give it to them to drink;* ܐܪ̈ܥܬܐ ܫܬܝܢ ܡܢ ܓܘܒܐ *fields watered from tanks.* Ethpe. ܐܫܬܬܝ *to be drunk, swallowed, imbibed;* ܟܕ ܡܫܬܬܝܐ *when it is drunk;* ܡܐܢܐ ܕܡܫܬܬܝܢܘܬܐ ܒܗ *a drinking-vessel;* ܡܝܐ ܕܡܫܬܬܝܢ *drinking-water.* Aph. ܐܫܬܝ i. *to cause to drink.* ii. *to weave, intertwine, plait;* ܢܫܐ ܕܡܫܬܝܢ ܡܙܥܪ̈ܝܗܝܢ *women braiding their hair;* ܒܟܠܗ ܦܓܪܐ ܡܫܬܐ ܓܝܕܐ ܘܥܪ̈ܩܐ *through the whole body he weaves nerves and veins.* Ettaph. ܐܬܬܫܬܝ *to be woven.* Derivatives, ܫܬܘܝܐ, ܫܬܝܐ, ܫܬܝܐ, ܫܬܝܐ, ܡܫܬܘܬܐ, ܡܫܬܝܐ, ܡܫܬܝܢܐ, ܡܫܬܝܬܐ, ܡܫܬܬܝܐ.

ܫܬܐܣ verb; see ܫܬܣ.

ܫܬܐܣܬܐ pl. ܫܬܐܣܬܐ, E-Syr. ܫܬܐܣܬܐ, also ܫܬܐܣܬܐ and ܐܫܬܐܣܬܐ from ܫܬ and ܐܣܐ, ܐܣܬܐ. f. *the base of a wall; a foundation, groundwork, base;* with ܣܡ, ܐܩܝܡ and ܐܘܬܒ *to lay.* Metaph. ܫܬܐܣܬܐ ܕܡܠܬܐ ܒܡܠܬܐ ܫܬܐܣܬ *I have based my dissertation on —;* ܫܬܐܣܬܐ ܕܥܕܬܐ *foundations of the Church* = Anglice *foundation truths;* ܫ ܕܕܗܒܐ *the golden number;* ܫ ܕܫܢܬܐ *the last day of the year.*

ܫܬܘܝܐ pl. ܝ̈ rt. ܫܬܐ. m. *one who drinks, a drinker.*

ܫܬܘܩܐ from ܐܫܬܘܩ m. *desire; attachment.*

ܫܬܝܩܐܝܬ rt. ܫܬܩ. adv. *silently.*

ܫܬܝܐ pl. ܝ̈ rt. ܫܬܐ. m. *a drinker;* ܫ ܕܚܡܪܐ *a wine-bibber.*

ܫܬܝܐ pl. ܝ̈ rt. ܫܬܐ. m. *a*) *drink.* *b*) *thread, the warp* opp. ܥܪܒܐ *the woof;* ܫܬܝܐ ܩܛܝܢܐ *fine threads.*

ܫܬܝܐ rt. ܫܬܐ. m. *drinking; a drink, beverage.*

ܫܬܝܩܐܝܬ rt. ܫܬܩ. adv. *silently.*

ܫܬܝܩܘܬܐ rt. ܫܬܩ. f. *silence, inaction, taciturnity.*

ܫܬܝܬܐܝܬ from ܫܬ adv. with ܙܘܝܬܐ *hexagonally.*

ܫܬܝܬܝܐ, ܫܬܝܬܝܬܐ from ܫܬ *sixth; sextuple, of* or *consisting of six;* ܫܬܝܬܝ ܓܦܐ *six-winged;* ܫܬܝܬܝ ܦܫܝܛܐ *Hexaplar.*

ܫܬܝܬܝܘܬܐ from ܫܬ. f. *the number six; the consisting of six;* ܫܬܝܬܝܘܬ ܦܐܬܐ *six-sided;* ܫܬܝܬܝܘܬ ܡܫܘܚܬܐ *hexameter.*

ܫܬܠ fut. ܢܫܬܘܠ, act. part. ܫܬܠ, ܫܬܠܐ, pass. part. ܫܬܝܠ, ܫܬܝܠܐ, ܫܬܝܠܬܐ. *to plant, transplant, lay down, set, insert;* ܢܫܬܠܘܢ ܦܪܕܝܣܐ *they shall lay out gardens;* ܐܘܪܚܐ ܫܬܝܠܐ ܐܝܠܢܐ *a road planted with trees;* ܐܫܬܘܠ ܫܡܗܝܟܘܢ ܒܦܢܩܝܬܐ *I will insert your names on the schedule.* Ethpe. ܐܫܬܬܠ *to be planted, transplanted, grafted, inserted; to be rooted, grounded.* Derivatives, ܫܬܠܐ, ܫܬܠܬܐ.

ܫܬܠܐ rt. ܫܬܠ. m. *planting, laying out.*

ܫܬܠܬܐ pl. ܫܬ̈ܠܬܐ rt. ܫܬܠ. f. *a plantation, nursery garden; grove.*

ܫܬܐܣܝܘܬܐ rt. ܫܬ. f. *fundamentality.*

ܫܬܢܝܐ contraction of ܫܢܬܢܝܐ *yearly.*

ܫܬܝܬܝܐ from ܫܬ. *sixth.*

ܫܬܐܣ, ܫܬܐܣ, ܐܫܬܐܣ, or ܐܫܬܐܣ denom. verb Pael conj. from ܫܬܐܣܬܐ. *to found, ground, establish;* ܕܢܫܬܐܣ ܫܪ̈ܫܘܗܝ ܒܐܪܥܐ *that it may fix its roots firmly in the ground;* ܠܐ ܡܫܬܐܣܐ ܒܕܚܠܬܐ ܕܐܠܗܐ *not firmly established in the fear of God;* ܠܐ ܡܫܬܐܣܢܘܬܐ *unfounded, unrealities.* Ethpa. ܐܫܬܐܣ and ܐܫܬܐܣ *to be founded, firmly set;* refl. *to settle, establish oneself;* ܐܬܢܝܚ ܗܘܐ ܒܩܪܝܬܐ ܘܐܫܬܐܣ ܬܡܢ *he found rest in the village and settled there;* ܥܝܕ̈ܐ ܕܐܫܬܐܣܘ ܠܟܝܢܐ ܕܡܝܢ *established habits are like nature.*

ܫܬܒܝܢܐ = ܐܫܬܒܝܢܐ *a game, play.*

ܫܬܒܪܘܪ = ܫܬܐܒܪܘܪ.

ܫܬܩ fut. ܢܫܬܘܩ, act. part. ܫܬܩ, ܫܬܩܐ, part. adj. ܫܬܝܩ, ܩܐ, ܩܬܐ. *to cease, be still, to keep silence, hold his peace;* ܟܕ ܫܬܩ ܡܢ ܡܡܠܠܘ *when he had ceased speaking;* ܢܫܬܘܩ ܠܗ ܠܫܢܐ *let him hold his tongue;* ܫܬܩܬ ܠܗ ܡܥܝܢܐ *the spring ceased, ran dry.* Part. adj. *still, silent, mute, speechless;* ܫܬܝܩܝܢ ܐܝܟ ܟܐܦ̈ܐ *motionless as stones;* ܒܪܝܬܐ ܫܬܝܩܬܐ *the mute creation;* ܢܡܘܣܐ ܗܘܐ ܫܬܝܩ *the law kept silence on this point.* Pa. ܫܬܩ *to still, stop, suppress, make to cease; to silence, reduce to silence;* ܒܟܣܦܐ ܡܫܬܩ ܦܘܡܗܘܢ *he stops their mouth with silver;* ܨܠܝܒܐ ܡܫܬܩ ܥܘܠܐ *the Cross which makes wickedness cease;* ܫܬܩ ܐܢܘܢ ܠܙܕܘܩܝ̈ܐ *He put the Sadducees to silence.* Ethpa. ܐܫܬܬܩ *to be silenced, stilled, speechless, mute; to be stopped, to cease, come to an end;* ܐܫܬܬܩܘ ܓܠ̈ܠܐ *the billows are stilled;* ܐܫܬܬܩ ܢܦܫܐ ܡܢܗ *he became inanimate, lifeless;* ܐܫܬܬܩܬ ܪܫܢܘܬܐ ܡܢ ܡܬܒ ܒܣܠܝܩ ܩܛܝܣܦܘܢ *the primacy ceased to be seated at Seleucia Ctesiphon.* Derivatives, ܫܬܩܐ, ܫܬܝܩܘܬܐ, ܫܬܩܬܐ, ܫܬܝܩܐܝܬ, ܫܬܩܐ, ܫܬܩܐ.

ܫܬܩܐ rt. ܫܬܩ. m. *a) silence. b) privation of motion, apoplexy.*

ܫܬܘܩܐ, ܫܬܘܩܐ rt. ܫܬܩ. *mute, speechless.*

ܫܬܪ Pers. *a tent.*

ܫܬܐ and ܐܫܬܐ from ܫܬ. f. *the number six;* usually with suffixes, ܫܬܝܢ *the six of us, we six;* ܘܥܒܕܘ ܗܟܢܐ ܫܬܝܗܘܢ ܝܘ̈ܡܝܢ *they did thus for six days;* ܡܐܡܪܐ ܥܠ ܫܬܬ ܝܘ̈ܡܐ *a discourse on the six days of* Creation.

ܫܬܬܥܣܪ or ܫܬܥܣܪ and ܐܫ m. ܫܬܬܥܣܪܐ, ܫܬܬܥܣܪܐ or from ܫܬ. *sixteen.*

⁘ ܫܠܡ ܣܘܪܐ ܕܫܝܢ ⁘

⁘ ܘܐܬܐ ܕܬܪܝܢܐ ⁘

⁘ ܬܘܒ ܐܬܚܠܬ ܠܡ ܬܪܝܢܘܬܐ ܕܡܫܬܝܬܝܢ ܕܝܘܢܝܐ ܡܢܗ ܕܬܘ ⁘

⁘ ܬ ⁘

ܬ ܬܐܒܐ

ܬ, ܬܘ or ܬܐܘ pl. ܬܘ̈ܐ, ܬܘ̈ܝܢ *Tau,* the twenty-second and last letter of the alphabet, *t, th.* The numeral 400; with ܕ, ܬܕ *the four hundredth;* with a line beneath, ܬ̱, 4000.

.ܬ abbrev. for *the version of Theodotion,* in the Tetrapla and Hexapla versions of Holy Writ.

ܬܐ imper. m. s. of verb ܐܬܐ *to come.*

ܬܐܐ pl. ܬܐܐ, ܬܐܝܢ Hex. transliteration from Heb. through Greek, *a room, lodge, chamber.*

ܬܐܒܝܐ, ܬܒ and ܬܒ pl. ܝܐ from ܬܐܒܐܝܣ. *a) a dweller in the Thebais, a hermit of the Theban desert. b) a Theban.*

ܐܬܐܒܪ̈ܐ, ܬܐܒܐܪܐ, ܬܐܒܐܪܘܣ, ܬܐܒܪܘܣ &c.; see ܬܐܒܪ̈ܘܣ.

ܬܐܒܝܠ, ܬܐܒܠ, ܬܐܒܠ, ܬܐܒܝܠ f. *the habitable earth, the earth, the world.* Derivatives, ܬܐܒܠܝܐ and ܬܒ, ܬܒܠܝܬ.

ܬܐܒܝܠܝܐ, ܬܐܒܠܝܐ, ܬܒܝܠ, ܬܒܠ, ܬܒܠܝܘܬ, ܬܐ̈ܐ from ܬܐܒܝܠ. *of the whole earth, universal.* Eccles. *a*) *ecumenical*, esp. *belonging to the first Ecumenical Council, a Father present at the Council of Nicaea;* ܗܝܡܢܘܬܐ ܕܬܐܒܝܠܝ̈ܐ *the Creed of the Nicene Fathers.* *b*) ܡܝܛܪܦܘܠܝܛܐ ܬܐܒܝܠܝܐ a metropolitan bishop with no special see but authorized to exercise metropolitical functions wherever any of his flock were found. *c*) as a title: ܡܠܦܢܐ ܬܐ *Universal Doctor.*

ܬܐܒܠܬܐ; see ܬܒܠܬܐ.

ܬܐܓܐ; see ܬܓܐ.

ܬܐܓܘܪܬܐ const. st. ܬܐܓܪܬ pl. ܬܐܓܪ̈ܝܢ, ܬܐܓܖ̈ܬܐ from ܬܓܪ. f. *commerce, merchandise, trade, business, endeavour, pursuit;* ܒܝܬ ܬ *a mart, market, market-place.*

ܬܐܓܘܪܬܢܐ from ܬܐܓܘܪܬܐ. *commercial.*

ܬܐܓܡܐ &c.; see under ܬܓܡ.

ܬܐܓܪܐ oftener ܬܓܪܐ; see below.

ܬܐܓܪܘܣܩܘܬܐ, ܬܐܓܪ, or ܬܓܪ rt. ܓܪܡ. f. *a skeleton.*

ܬܐܓܪܝܬ or ܬܓܪܝܬ *Tagrit* or *Tekrit*, a city on the Tigris between Mosul and Baghdad.

ܬܐܓܪܝܬܢܝܐ or ܬܓܪ from ܬܐܓܪܝܬ. *an inhabitant of Tagrit.*

ܬܐܕܪܐ and ܬܐܕܪ; see ܬܕܪܐ *spring.*

ܬܐܕܪܝܐ or ܬܐܕܪܢܝܐ also ܬܐܕܪܢܝܐ, ܬܕܪ or ܬܕ, ܬܐ̈ from ܬܐܕܪܐ. *vernal, of the spring.*

ܬܐܘ; see ܬ.

ܬܐܘܡܐ or ܬܐܘܡܐ; see ܬܐܘܡܐ.

ܬܐܘܛܪܘܢ pl. ܬܐܘܛܪ̈ܐ; see ܬܐܛܪܘܢ.

ܬܐܘܠܘܓܘܣ rarely ܬܐܘܠܘܓܐ pl. ܬܐܘܠܘܓܘ̈ܣ, ܬܐܘܠܘܓܘ̈ܣܐ &c. θεολόγος, *a theologian, divine, apostle.* Esp. used of S. Gregory Nazianzen.

ܬܐܘܠܘܓܝܐ, ܬܐܘܠܘܓܝܐ θεολογία, *theology* = Syr. ܡܡܠܠܘܬ ܐܠܗܘܬܐ.

ܬܐܘܡܐ or ܬܐܘܡܐ, ܬܐܘܡܐܝܠ, ܬܐܘܡܐܝܘܣ and ܬܐܘܡܐ from ܬܐܡܐ through Greek, pr. n. *Thomas, Didymus.*

ܬܐܘܡܐ = ܬܘܡܐ *garlic; thyme.*

ܬܐܘܡܝܐ and ܬܐܘܡܢܝܐ, ܬܐ̈ from ܬܐܘܡܐ *of* or *belonging to Thomas.*

ܬܐܘܢܐ = ܬܘܢܐ.

ܬܐܘܦܘܪܘܣ pl. ܬܐܘܦܘܪ̈ܘܣ θεοφόρος -οι, *the God-bearer* = Syr. ܛܥܝܢ ܐܠܗܐ.

ܬܐܘܪܝܐ from θεωρία, f. *metaphysics.*

ܬܐܘܪܝܐ, ܬܐܪ and ܬܐܘܪ pl. ܬܐܘܪ̈ܝܣ, ܬܐܘܪܝܣ, ܬܐܘܪܝܐ θεωρία, *a*) *philosophic speculation, theory* opp. ܦܪܟܣܝܣ *action, practice; method of study* or *observation, research.* *b*) *spiritual contemplation, intuition, ecstasy.* *c*) *a concept, idea, view, estimate.* *d*) *a theory, inner meaning, hypothesis, argument.*

ܬܐܘܪܛܝܩܘܣ, ܬܝܩܐ, ܬܝܩܘܢ, pl. ܬܐܘܪܛܝܩܘܝ θεωρητικός -ή -όν -οί. *a*) *contemplative.* *b*) *a researcher, investigator.*

ܬܐܘܪܛܝܩܝܐ, ܬܐ̈ *theoretic, speculative.*

ܬܐܘܪܝܐ pl. ܬܐܘܪܝܡܛܐ m. θεώρημα -ατα, *a theorem.*

ܬܐܘܪܝܣܐ θεωρῆσαι, *theorizing, contemplating.* With ܥܒܕ *to investigate, research.*

ܬܐܪ, ܬܐܪܐ act. part. of verb ܬܪ.

ܬܐܛܪܐ, ܬܐܛܪܐ, ܬܐܛܪܘܬܐ &c.; see ܬܛܪܐ.

ܬܐܛܪܘܢ or ܬܐܛ, ܬܐܘܛ, ܬܐܛܪܐ, ܬܐܛܪ, ܬܛ pl. ܬܐܛܪܐ, ܬܐܛܪܐ θέατρον, f. *a*) *a theatre.* *b*) *the spectators.* *c*) *a show, play, game.*

ܬܐܛܪܘܬܐ from ܬܐܛܪܐ. f. *dregs, impurities.*

ܬܐܛܪܐ from ܬܐܛܪܐ. *turbid, thick.*

ܬܐܛܪܘܬܐ from ܬܐܛܪܐ. f. *foulness.*

ܬܐܛܪܢܝܐ, ܬܐ̈ from ܬܐܛܪܐ. *turbid, foul, faecal.*

ܬܐܠܝܢ pl. ܬܐܠܐ; see ܬܠܝܢ, ܬܠܐ.

ܬܐܠ, ܬܐܠܐ act. part. of verb ܬܘܠ *to cease;* ܬܐܠ act. part. of verb ܬܠ *to harm.*

ܬܐܡ, ܬܐܡܬܐ, ܬܐܡܝܐ; see ܬܐܡ.

ܬܐܡ denom. verb from ܬܐܡܐ. Ethpa. ܐܬܬܐܡ *to be coupled, paired.* Aph. ܡܬܐܡ act. part. ܡܬܐܡ *to double, to bear twins;* ܬܐ̈ ܡܬܐܡ̈ܬܐ ܕܓܙܝܙ̈ܢ *shorn ewes bearing twins.* Usually pass. part. ܡܬܐܡ, ܡܬܐܡܐ, ܡܬܐܡܬܐ *paired, double, twofold, fitted to each other;* ܣܩܐ ܥܠ ܣܩܐ ܡܬܐܡ ܗܘܐ (= ܡܬܐܡ) *sackcloth was added upon sackcloth.* Palel ܬܐܡܡ *to double.*

ܬܐܘܡܐ, ܬܐܘܡܬܐ pl. ܝ̈ܢ, ܡ̈ܐ, ܬ̈ܐ *twin, double;* ܒ̈ܝܥܐ ܕܬܐܘܡܐ *eggs with double yolks;* ܐ̈ܚܐ ܬܐܘ̈ܡܐ *twin brothers;* ܚܡܫܐ ܬܐܘ̈ܡܐ ܕܠܐܝܢ *the five twins who laboured* i. e. the hands of a scribe. Pl. m. astron. *Gemini*, a sign of the Zodiac. Pl. f. *valves* of a door, *double doors.* Derivatives, verb ܬܐܡ, ܬܐܘܡܐ, ܬܐܘܡܐܝܬ, ܬܐܘܡܘܬܐ, ܡܬܬܐܡܢܘܬܐ.

ܬܐܘܡܘܬܐ from ܬܐܘܡܐ. f. *twin-ship, being double or a pair;* ܒܪ ܬ *twin-born;* ܬܐܘܡܘܬܗܘܢ *both of them, the pair of them.*

ܬܐܡܢܘܣ pl. ܬܐܡ̈ܢܐ and ܬܐܡ̈ܢܘܣ θάμνος, *a bush, shrub.*

ܬܐܝ act. part. of verb ܬܘܝ and of verb ܬܝ.

ܬܐܢܐ; see ܬܐܢܬܐ.

ܬܐܢܚܬܐ = ܬܢܚܬܐ *a groan, sigh.*

ܬܐܢ̈ܐ m. pl. *blisters, dimples.*

ܬܐܢ̈ܐ rt. ܬܢ. m. pl. only in BB. *vapours, exhalations.*

ܬܐܢܬܐ, ܬܐܬܐ, ܬܬܐ pl. ܬܐ̈ܢܐ, ܬ̈ܐܢܐ f. *a) the fig-tree* and fruit; ܬ̈ܐܢܐ ܒ̈ܟܝܪܐ *untimely figs;* ܬ ܦܘܩܠܐ *the sycamore. b) a hard red swelling.*

ܬܐܢܬܐ = ܬܝܢܬܐ.

ܬܐܢܝܬܐ pl. ܬܐܢ̈ܝܢ, ܬܐܢ̈ܝܬܐ f. *a curtain-loop.*

ܬܐܦܐ = ܬܦܐ.

ܬܐܦܐ = ܬܦܐ.

ܬܐܩܢܐ = ܬܩܢܐ; see verb ܬܩܢ.

ܬܐܪ act. part. ܬܐܪ. *to contemplate, meditate.* Pa. ܬܐܪ *to suggest, intimate.* Ethpa. ܐܬܬܐܪ *to be directed* or *prompted by instinct.* Derivatives, ܬܐܪܐ, ܬܐܪܬܐ.

ܬܐܪ prep.; see ܬܐܪ.

ܬܐܪܐ and ܬܐܪܬܐ; see ܬܪܬܐ.

ܬܐܪܘܬܐ rt. ܬܐܪ. f. *discipline, system of education.*

ܬܐܪܘܢܐ = ܬܪܘܢܐ.

ܬܐܪܢܐ, ܬܐܪܢܝܬܐ from ܬܐܪܬܐ. *conscientious.*

ܬܐܪܘܦܐ with ܕܬܒܢܐ *a heap of straw.* Only in the Lexx.

ܬܐܪܬܐ rarely ܬܪܬܐ pl. ܬܐܪ̈ܬܐ rt. ܬܐܪ. f. *a) the conscience, consciousness, mind;* ܒܬܐܪܬܐ ܕܐܒܗܘܬܐ *as a brother, in paternal wise. b) the abdomen.*

ܬܐܪܝܢܘܬ = ܬܪܝܢܘܬ *the second time.*

ܬܐܬܐ; see ܬܐܢܬܐ.

ܬܒܝܣ, ܬܐܒܝܣ, ܬܐܒܘܣ, ܬܐܒܐܝܣ, ܬܒܐܝܣ, ܬܒܐܝܣ and other spellings *a) Thebes, the Thebais, Upper Egypt. b) Thebes* in Boeotia.

ܬܒܘܥܐ pl. ܝ̈ܐ rt. ܬܒܥ. m. *a) an avenger, one who vindicates a right,* hence *a near kinsman. b) a creditor, a tax-gatherer; a punisher. c) an inquirer, inquisitor, detective.*

ܬܒܝܐ; see ܬܒܘܐ.

ܬܒܝܪܐ pl. ܐ perh. Pers. *vile, abandoned.*

ܬܒܝܠ = ܬܐܒܝܠ *the habitable earth.*

ܬܒܝܠܝܐ, ܬܒܠ = ܬܐܒܝܠܝܐ.

ܬܒܝܪܘܬܐ rt. ܬܒܪ. f. *a wound;* ܬܒܝܪܘܬ ܠܒܐ *sadness, depression.*

ܬܒܝܪ̈ܬܐ rt. ܬܒܪ. f. pl. *an eruption, rash.*

ܬܒܠܐ pl. ܐ̈ usually ܬܒܠܐ ܩܦܠܐ *tordylium, hartwort, meadow saxifrage.*

ܬܒܝܠܐܝܬ from ܬܒܝܠ. adv. *universally.*

ܬܒܝܠܝܐ = ܬܐܒܝܠܝܐ *universal, ecumenical.*

ܬܒܢܐ *straw;* ܬ ܦܘܠܐ *bean haulm.* Astron. ܫܒܝܠ ܬܒܢܐ *the Milky Way.*

ܬܒܢܐ pl. ܐ̈ from ܬܒܢܐ. m. *one who carries straw.*

ܬܒܥ fut. ܢܬܒܥ and ܢܬܒܘܥ, imper. ܬܒܥ and ܬܒܘܥ, act. part. ܬܒܥ, ܬܒܥܐ, pass. part. ܬܒܝܥ, ܥܐ, ܥܬܐ. *a) to seek, demand, desire, beg* with acc. of the thing, ܡܢ or ܠ of the pers. ܬܒܥ ܚܘܠܦܐ ܕܫܒ̈ܝܐ *he sought an exchange of prisoners;* ܟܝܢܐ ܦܓܪܢܝܐ ܬܒܥ ܠܢ *bodily nature makes demands on us.* With ܡܥܡܘܕܝܬܐ *to desire baptism;* with ܩܛܝܪܐ *to compel, coerce. b) to require, claim, exact, avenge* with ܡܢ or ܡܢ ܐܝܕܝܗ *of* any one. With ܕܡ *to require or avenge blood;* ܡܕܐܬܐ *to levy tribute;* ܢܦܫܐ *to require the life,* also *to avenge oneself;* ܢܩܡܬܐ, ܕܝܢܐ or ܬܒܥܬܐ *to demand vengeance.* Pass. part. *he on whom judgement is done, the guilty party.* Act. part. ܬܒܥ ܝܪܬܘܬܐ *one whose right it is to redeem an inheritance, the next of kin;* ܬܒܥ̈ܝ ܕܝܢܐ *avengers, near kinsmen.* Hence *c) to perform the duty of a kinsman. d) to ask, inquire* with ܥܠ of the thing and ܡܢ of the pers. Ethpe. ܐܬܬܒܥ *a) to avenge oneself, be avenged* with ܡܢ *on;* with ܕܝܢܐ or ܬܒܥܬܐ *vengeance is taken. b) to be required* to give satisfaction; *to be required, compelled, exacted, claimed;* ܡܢ ܐܬܬܒܥ

ܘܡܬܒܥ ܗܘܐ ܡܢܗ ܠܡܦܪܥܘ when a claim was made on him and he had not wherewith to pay; ܬܬܬܒܥ ܟܣܦܐ the money may be claimed; ܠܐ ܡܬܬܒܥܐ ܐܢܬܬܐ a wife is not liable; ܡܬܬܒܥܝܢܢ ܕܢܗܘܐ ܠܢ ܙܘܗܪܐ we are required to be careful. c) to be inquired. DERIVATIVES, ܬܒܘܥܐ, ܬܒܥܐ, ܬܒܥܐ, ܬܒܥܬܐ, ܬܒܥܬܢܐ, ܡܬܬܒܥܢܐ, ܡܬܬܒܥܢܘܬܐ.

ܬܒܘܥܐ rt. ܬܒܥ. m. *demanding, requiring.*

ܬܒܥܬܐ, ܬܒܥܬܐ pl. ـܬܐ, ܬܒܥܝܬܐ or ܬܒܥܘܬܐ rt. ܬܒܥ. f. a) *vengeance, punishment;* ܕܠܐ ܬ̈ *unavenged.* b) O.T. *redemption, right* or *custom of redemption of inheritance.* c) *a legal inquiry, judgement.* d) *a requisition, demand, exaction;* with ܡܕܐܬܐ *the levying of a tribute.* e) *inquiry, a question.*

ܬܒܥܐ rt. ܬܒܥ. f. a female demon who strangled women and children.

ܬܒܥܬܢܐ rt. ܬܒܥ. *litigious.*

ܬܒܪ fut. ܢܬܒܪ and ܢܬܒܘܪ, act. part. ܬܐܒܪ, ܬܒܪܐ, pass. part. ܬܒܝܪ, ܐ, ܬܐ. a) *to break, bruise, fracture;* ܪܘܚܐ ܠܐܝܠܢܐ ܬܒܪܐ *the wind breaks the tree.* Metaph. *to break the power, break down, defeat;* ܬܒܪܘ ܠܚܝܠܐ *they defeated the army* but usually with ܚܝܠܐ *to weaken;* ܬܒܪܝܢ ܠܗ ܠܚܡܪܐ ܒܡܝܐ ܣܓܝܐܐ *they weaken* the wine *with plenty of water.* With ܠܒܐ *to discourage;* ܬܒܝܪ ܠܒܐ *broken-hearted, dispirited;* ܡܟܝܟܝܢ ܘܬܒܝܪܝܢ *sad and broken down.* b) *to rend, tear;* ܬܒܝܪ ܚܝܘܬܐ *torn of wild beasts.* c) with ܛܝܡܐ *to pay a price.* ETHPE. ܐܬܬܒܪ and ETHPA. ܐܬܬܒܪ a) *to be broken, rent, torn, fractured, wrecked;* ܩܫܬܐ ܕܓܢܒܪܐ ܢܬܬܒܪܢ *the bows of the mighty shall be broken.* b) *to be routed, discomfited, defeated;* ܐܬܬܒܪܘ ܛܝܝܐ ܬܒܪܐ ܪܒܐ *the Arabs were crushingly routed.* c) *to be broken-hearted.* BB. says Ethpeel is used of physical objects and Ethpaal metaphorically. PAEL ܬܒܪ *to break, shatter, shiver* stones, bones, weapons; ܬܒܪ ܡܘܟܠܝܗ ܕܫܝܘܠ *he brake the bars of Sheol;* ܓܒܪܐ ܡܬܒܪܐ *a wounded man.* APH. ܐܬܒܪ *to rout, defeat.* DERIVATIVES, ܬܒܘܪܐ, ܬܒܪܐ, ܬܒܪܐ, ܬܒܪܐ, ܬܒܪܬܐ, ܬܒܘܪܐ, ܡܬܒܪܢܐ.

ܬܒܪܐ pl. ܐ̈ rt. ܬܒܪ. m. *a fragment, broken piece;* ܬܒܪ̈ܐ ܕܦܬܟܪ̈ܐ ܕܚܨܦܐ *shards of earthenware idols.*

ܬܒܪܐ pl. ܐ̈ rt. ܬܒܪ. m. a) *breaking, crushing; shipwreck, discomfiture, ruin;* ܬܒܪ ܠܒܐ *heart-breaking.* b) *a fracture, bruise, wound; a part, piece; the prey.*

ܬܒܪܬܐ pl. ܬ̈ܐ rt. ܬܒܪ. f. *rout, defeat.* Pl. *broken hymns* i. e. short clauses.

ܬܒܠܬܐ, ܬܒܠܬܐ or ܬܒܠܬܐ = ܙܒܠܐ rt. ܙܒܠ. f. *dung, excrement, filth.*

ܬܓܐ, ܬܓܐ or ܬܐܓܐ pl. ـܝܢ, ـܐ m. a) *a diadem, the band* or *fillet* beneath the crown; *a Persian king's head-dress, tiara.* Metaph. *regal power; the summit, crown.* b) Jac. Syr. *fillet* or *mitre* of the Patriarch. DERIVATIVE, verb ܬܓܓ.

ܬܓܐ τάγος, *a ruler, king.*

ܬܓܓ denom. verb Pael conj. from ܬܓܐ. *to crown, set a diadem on the head;* ܡܬܓܓܐ *diademed.* ETHPA. ܐܬܬܓܓ *to be crowned, diademed.* APH. ܐܬܓ *to set on a diadem.*

ܬܓܡ denom. verb from ܬܓܡܐ. ETHPA. ܐܬܬܓܡ *to be drawn up in line.*

ܬܓܡܐ, ܬܓܡܐ or ܬܐܓܡܐ pl. ـܝܢ, ـܐ τάγμα, m. a) *a division, legion.* b) *a rank, class, order* of angels. c) *class, rank, sex, company;* ܒܪ ܬ̈ *an equal, companion.* d) *a precept.* e) *sort, fashion.*

ܬܓܪ denom. verb from ܬܐܓܪܐ. ETHPA. ܐܬܬܓܪ a) *to earn wages.* b) *to trade, carry on commerce, engage in business;* ܢܥܡܪܘܢ ܒܐܪܥܐ ܘܢܬܬܓܪܘܢ ܒܗ *let them dwell in the land and trade therein.* c) *to acquire, obtain, gain, make gains;* ܠܐ ܐܬܬܓܪ ܒܟܪܗ *his talent has gained nothing;* ܡܫܚܐ ܕܒܗ ܡܬܬܓܪܝܢ ܚܛܝܐ ܫܘܒܩܢܐ ܕܚܛܗ̈ܐ *chrism by means of which sinners obtain remission of sins.* With ܢܦܫܗ *to gain for himself,* also *to gain his soul.* Ironically *to get, make, acquire* harm; ܡܬܬܓܪ ܐܢܐ ܡܢ ܚܘܣܪܢܐ ܕܟܢܫܐ *I shall gain my advantage at the expense of the community;* ܫܢܩܐ ܘܢܣܝܘܢܐ ܡܬܬܓܪ ܠܢܦܫܗ *he lays up for himself suffering and temptation.*

ܬܓܪܐ rt. ܓܪܐ. m. *strife, contention.*

ܬܓܪܐ or ܬܐܓܪܐ, ܬܓܪܐ pl. ܐ̈ *a merchant.*

Alchem. a name of the planet Mercury. Derivatives, verb ܬܓܪ, ܬܓܪܐܝܬ, ܬܓܪܘܬܐ, ܬܓܪܐ, ܡܬܬܓܪܢܐ.

ܬܰܓܳܪܳܐܝܬ from ܬܓܪܐ. adv. *commercially.*

ܬܰܓܪܽܘܡܽܘܬܳܐ = ܬܓܪܡܘܬܐ.

ܬܰܓܳܪܽܘܬܳܐ from ܬܓܪܐ. f. *trade, commerce.*

ܬܰܓܳܪܳܝܳܐ, ܝܬܳܐ from ܬܓܪܐ. *commercial.*

ܬܰܓܪܺܝܬ and ܬܰܓܪܺܝܬܳܐ; see under ܬܓܪ.

ܬܕܐ rarely ܬܕܝܐ, usually pl. ܬܕܶܐ m. *a breast, the breasts, paps.*

ܬܕܐܐ, ܬܕܐܐ, ܬܕܐ, ܬܕܐ E-Syr. ܬܕܐܐ m. *a) sprouting grass* or *corn, tender grass. b) the spring.* Derivatives, ܬܕܐܝܐ, ܬܕܐܝܢܐ and ܬܕܐ, ܬܕܐܢܐ.

ܬܕܐܝܢܳܐ pl. ܝܢܶܐ dimin. of ܬܕܐ *pulse.*

ܬܰܕܟܺܝܬܳܐ rt. ܕܟܐ. f. *a) cleansing, purification, expiation;* ܬ̈ ܕܚܛܗܐ *a sin-* or *trespass-offering. b) evacuation of excrement, excrement.*

ܬܰܪܕܡܳܐ from Heb. m. *deep sleep.*

ܬܕܡܘܪܬܐ pl. ܬܕܡܪ̈ܬܐ rt. ܕܡܪ. f. *a marvel, wonder, portent;* ܕܬ ܓܒܪ̈ܐ *men set for a sign;* ܕܬ̈ ܫܒܘܥܐ *the week of miracles* = the fifth week of Lent; ܒܬ̈ *in a wonderful way.*

ܬܕܐܝܐ, ܝܬܐ = ܬܕܐܝܐ *vernal.*

ܬܗܐ Pael ܬܰܗܺܝ *to waste time, delay, defer, retard, arrest;* ܬܗܘܢܝܗܘܢ ܡܢ ܝܘܡܐ ܕܕܒܚܐ *they would make him too late for the day of sacrifice;* ܬܗܝ ܡܐܬܝܬܗ *he put off his arrival;* ܬܗܝ ܠܡܥܡܪ̈ܢܐ ܕܚܝܠܐ *he restrained the garrison.* Absol. ܡܬܗܝܢܢ ܡܢ ܝܘܡ ܠܝܘܡ *we delay from day to day.* Ethpa. ܐܬܬܗܝ *a)* refl. *to delay, be tardy, desist,* absol. or with ܡܢ; ܐܬܬܗܝܘ ܡܢ ܩܪܒܐ *they ceased making war. b)* pass. *to be hindered, retarded, deferred; to be at a loss;* ܐܬܬܗܝ ܨܒܐ ܡܢ ܣܚܝܗ *the tortoise swam slowly.*

ܬܶܗܶܐ apoc. fut. for ܬܶܗܘܶܐ 3 f. s. and 2 m. s. of verb ܗܘܐ.

ܬܗܠܗܠܐ = ܬܐܠܐܠܐ.

ܬܗܘܡܐ pl. ܡܶܐ, ܡܳܬܳܐ (rare) Heb. m. *a) chaos, deep abyss, the bottomless pit;* ܬ ܕܐܒܕܢܐ *the pit of perdition. b) the depth, bottom* of a well, river, the sea. Derivatives, the three following words and verb ܬܗܡ.

ܬܗܘܡܘܬܐ from ܬܗܘܡܐ. f. *depth, profundity.*

ܬܗܘܡܝܐ and ܬܗܘܡܢܝܐ from ܬܗܘܡܐ. *very deep, abysmal.*

ܬܗܝܪܐܝܬ rt. ܬܗܪ. adv. *marvellously, miraculously.*

ܬܗܝܪܘ, ܬܗܝܪܘܬܐ rt. ܬܗܪ. f. *marvellousness;* ܬܗܝܪܘ ܡܥܒܕܢܘܬܐ *wonderful.*

ܬܗܠܬܐ rt. ܗܠ. m. *derision.*

ܬܗܠܘܠܬܐ rt. ܗܠ. f. *derision, mockery; a jest, object of derision;* ܒܬ *in jest, in mockery.*

ܬܗܠܘܠܢܝܐ rt. ܗܠ. *expressing derision.*

ܬܰܗܶܡ denom. verb Pael conj. from ܬܗܘܡܐ. Pass. part. ܡܬܗܡܐ *profound.* Ethpa. ܐܬܬܗܡ *to be submerged, sunk in the depths.*

ܬܗܰܪ fut. ܢܶܬܗܰܪ, parts. ܬܳܗܰܪ, ܬܗܪܐ and ܬܗܝܪ, ܐ, ܬܐ, part. adj. ܬܗܝܪ, ܐ, ܬܐ. *to wonder, marvel, be astonished;* with ܒ *to regard with wonder, marvel at;* ܬܗܪ ܘܫܘܪ ܘܬܗܪ *he was confounded, astounded and stupefied;* ܬܗܪܝܢ ܗܘܘ ܘܐܡܪܝܢ *they marvelled saying . . . .* Part. adj. *marvelling, marvellous, miraculous, delightful;* ܬܗܝܪܐ ܩܕܝܫܐ *marvellously holy;* ܬܗܝܪܐ ܒܛܢܗ *the miraculous conception* of the B. V. M. Pl. f. *miracles.* Ethpa. ܐܬܬܗܪ *to marvel* with ܒ *at.* Aph. ܐܬܗܪ *to make to marvel, to entrance, fascinate, delight;* ܐܬܗܪ ܐܢܘܢ ܒܡܣܝܒܪܢܘܬܗ *he astounded them by his endurance;* ܐܬܗܪ ܫܘܦܪܗ ܠܥܝܢܝܢ *his beauty entranced our eyes;* ܘܛܥܡܗ ܘܪܝܚܗ ܐܬܗܪ ܐܢܘܢ ܠܫܡܝܢܝܐ *its taste and scent delighted heavenly beings.* Derivatives, ܡܬܗܪܢܐ, ܬܗܝܪܘܬܐ, ܬܗܪܐ, ܬܗܪܐ, ܬܗܝܪܐ.

ܬܶܗܪܳܐ, E-Syr. ܬܗܪ pl. ܝܢ, ܐ rt. ܬܗܪ. m. *a) astonishment. b) a wonder, miracle;* ܡܠܐ ܬ *wondrous, miraculous;* ܒܬ *miraculously;* ܬܗܪܐ ܠܡܫܥܝܘ *wonderful to relate.*

ܬܗܪܐ rt. ܬܗܪ. m. *dismay, terror.*

ܬܘ or ܬܐܘ letter *Tau;* see ܬ.

ܬܰܘ imper. m. pl. of verb ܐܬܐ *to come.*

ܬܘܐ fut. ܢܬܘܐ, act. part. ܬܘܐ, ܬܘܝܐ. *to be sorry, to regret, feel compunction, remorse,* with ܠܒܐ or ܢܦܫܐ in the nom. and with pers. pron. ܬܘܝܗ ܠܒܗ ܕܕܘܝܕ *David's heart smote him;* ܬܘܬ ܠܢܦܫܗ *he repented himself;* also with ܒܢܦܫܗ and absol. Ethpe. ܐܬܬܘܝ sometimes ܐܬܘܝ *to regret, rue, repent, be moved to regret,* with

ܠܐ ܢܬܘܒܘܢ ܡܢ ܥܒܕܝܗ̇ ;ܐܠܐ and ܡܢ ܥܒܕܝܗ̇ *except they repent of her works.* PA. ܬܘܝ *to soften, affect, move to regret;* ܠܐ ܡܬܘܝܐ ܠܗ ܩܠܐ ܕܒܟܝܐ *the sound of weeping does not move him;* ܟܪܝܗܘܬܐ ܡܬܘܝܐ ܚܝܠܐ *illness reduces the strength.* APH. ܐܬܘܝ *to suggest sorrowful reflections, to sadden, bring to penitence;* part. ܡܬܘܝ, ܡܬܘܝܐ, ܡܬܘܝܬܐ *downcast, sad, melancholy;* ܚܫܐ ܡܬܘܝܐ *in melancholy sorrow.* DERIVATIVES, ܬܘܝܐ, ܬܘܝܘܬܐ, ܬܘܝܬܐ, ܡܬܘܝܢܐ, ܡܬܘܝܢܐܝܬ, ܡܬܘܝܢܘܬܐ.

ܬܘܝܪܘܣ; see ܬܐܘܪܘܣ.

ܬܘܒ, ܬܒ fut. ܢܬܘܒ, act. part. ܬܐܒ, ܬܝܒܐ. *a) to return, come again;* ܥܒܪ ܘܬܐܒ *one who passes by and returns. b) to flow back, ebb. c) to turn to God, be converted, repent, do penance;* ܕܢܬܘܒܘܢ ܘܢܬܦܢܘܢ ܠܘܬ ܐܠܗܐ *that they should repent and turn to God;* ܬܐܒ ܐܢܐ ܒܝ *I repent me;* ܬܝܒܝܢ ܕܬܝܒܝܢ *penitents.* APH. ܐܬܝܒ *a) to turn, convert. b) to vomit, disgorge, throw up, eject;* ܡܬܝܒܐ ܪܘܛܒܘܬܐ ܐܘܟܡܬܐ the cuttle-fish *discharges an inky fluid. c)* with ܠܒܐ ܥܠ *to take to heart, bring to mind;* with ܦܬܓܡܐ *to bring word, answer.* ETTAPH. ܐܬܬܝܒ *a) to be vomited, disgorged. b) to be restored.* DERIVATIVES, ܬܘܒ, ܬܘܒܐ, ܬܝܒܐ, ܬܝܒܘܬܐ, ܬܝܒܬܐ, ܬܝܒܘܬܐ, ܬܘܒܝܢ, ܬܝܒܐܝܬ, ܬܘܒܬܐ, ܬܝܒܐ, ܬܘܒܐ, ܬܘܒܢܐ, ܬܘܒܢܘܬܐ, ܡܬܝܒܢܘܬܐ.

ܬܘܒ rt. ܬܘܒ. *a) again, back, on the other hand;* ܠܐ ܐܘܣܦ ܬܘܒ *I will not again;* ܗܦܟܬ ܬܘܒ ܠܡܕܝܢܬܐ *she returned back to the city;* ܬܘܒ ܘܬܘܒ *again and again;* ܬܘܒ ܠܐ *no more, never again, never;* ܠܐ ܗܘܐ ܕܬܘܒ ܚܙܐ *no one had ever seen.* Often stands at the beginning of a narrative, ܬܘܒ ܟܬܒܝܢ *again we write;* ܬܘܒ ܕܝܠܗ ܕܗܘ ܡܢ ܕܡܟܬܒ *by the same author. b) also, yet, even;* ܬܘܒ ܗܒ ܠܝ ܡܪܝ *grant also to me, O Lord;* ܬܘܒ ܝܬܝܪܐܝܬ *yet more;* ܘܬܘܒ ܝܬܝܪ *and even greater.*

ܬܘܒܐ rt. ܬܘܒ. m. *the ebb, ebb-tide, reflux.*

ܬܘܒܐ or ܬܐܒܐ pl. ܐ̈ m. *the wild fig.*

ܬܝܒܐ rt. ܬܘܒ. m. *vomit.*

ܬܘܒܐ Arab. m. *a robe.*

ܬܘܒܢ = ܬܘܒ *again, afresh.*

ܬܘܒܪܐ rt. ܬܒܪ. m. *breaking, a fracture;* ܬ̈ ܕܫܩܐ *breaking the legs,* a punishment of slaves; ܬܘܓܪܐ ܕܚܪܝܢܐ *disputatiousness;* ܬܘܓܪܐ ܕܫܢ̈ܐ *toothache.*

ܬܘܓܐ or ܬܘܓܬܐ pl. ܐ̈ m. *a raindrop, dewdrop, snowflake.*

ܬܘܓܝܐ from ܬܘܓ. m. *profound meditation, anxiety.*

ܬܘܕܝܬܐ, ܬܘܕܝܬܐ pl. ܬ̈, ܬܐ from ܝܕܐ rt. ܝܕ. f. *acknowledgement, profession, thanksgiving, praise, a confession* esp. of faith, hence *faith, religion, doctrine, a sect;* ܒܢ̈ܝ ܬܘܕܝܬܐ *sectaries;* ܬ ܬܪܝܨܬܐ *the orthodox;* ܬܘܕܝܬܐ ܬܪܝܨܬܐ ܡܘܫܚܬܐ *the orthodox faith.*

ܬܘܕܝܬܢܝܐ from ܝܕܐ. *religious; expressive of thanksgiving.*

ܬܘܕܪܐ Arab. m. *bugloss* = Syr. ܠܫܢ ܬܘܪܐ.

ܬܘܗ fut. ܢܬܘܗ, parts. ܬܐܗ and ܬܝܗ. *to be alarmed, startled, astounded;* ܬܘܗ ܐܝܟ ܕܡܢ *he was startled as it were from* ܫܢܬܐ ܥܡܝܩܬܐ *sound sleep;* ܬܘܗܐ ܗܘܘ ܒܗ *they were in great consternation.* PA. ܬܘܗ *to alarm, stun;* ܡܚܘܬܐ ܕܡܬܘܗܐ ܠܗܘܢ *the blow which stuns them.* ETHPA. ܐܬܬܘܗ *to be troubled, perturbed, dismayed; in consternation;* ܐܢ ܐܢܫ ܢܡܚܐ ܠܨܠܡܐ ܕܡܠܟܐ ܡܬܬܘܗܝܢ ܚܙܝܐ *if any one strike the* emperor's *statue the spectators are dismayed.* APH. ܐܬܘܗ *to dismay, discomfit, alarm;* ܡܘܬܐ ܡܬܘܗ ܠܣܓܝܐܐ *death dismays many an one.* Pass. part. ܡܬܘܗܐ, ܡܬܘܗܬܐ *stunned, stupefied, stupid;* ܐܝܟ ܡܬܘܗܐ ܕܠܐ ܪܓܫ ܒܟܐܒܐ *as stunned and unconscious of pain.* DERIVATIVES, ܬܘܗܬܐ, ܬܗܝܘܬܐ, ܡܬܘܗܢܘܬܐ.

ܬܘܗ interj. *begone;* with ܠ *away with it.*

ܬܘܗ ܘܒܘܗ Heb. Tohu-we-Bohu, *chaos.*

ܬܘܗܒܘܗܝܐ, ܬܐ from the preceding word. *chaotic.*

ܬܘܗܝ, ܬܘܗܝܐ rt. ܬܗܐ. m. *a) delay, tardiness;* ܕܠܐ ܬ *without delay, immediately. b) a prodigy, marvel;* ܡܢ ܬܘܗܝܐ ܕܡܠܘܗܝ *from His marvellous words. c)* perh. for ܬܘܝܐ or ܬܘܝܬܐ. *remorse.*

ܬܘܗܬܐ, ܬܘܗܬܐ or ܬܘܗܬܐ pl. ܬ̈ rt. ܬܘܗ. f. *a) a prodigy. b) confusing* or *stunning noise;* ܬ ܕܓܠ̈ܠܐ ܕܝܡܐ *roaring of the sea. c) alarm, consternation, perturbation, amazement.*

ܬܘܘܢܐ or ܬܘܢܐ and ܬܘܢ pl. ܐ̈ rt. ܬܘܢ. m. *an inner room; a garner.*

ܬܘܙ fut. ܢܬܘܙ, act. part. ܬܐܙ. *to leap, exult.* Ethpe. ܐܬܬܘܙ with ܥܠ *to assail.* Derivative, ܬܘܙܐ.

ܬܘܙܐ rt. ܬܘܙ. m. *leaping; assault, victory.*

ܬܘܚ Peal only part. adj. ܬܘܚܐ *moaning.* Ethpa. ܐܬܬܘܚ *to sigh, regret;* ܐܬܬܘܚ ܡܪܝܐ ܕܥܒܕ ܠܐܕܡ *it repented the Lord that He had made man.* Derivatives, ܬܘܚܬܐ, ܡܬܬܘܚܢܘܬܐ.

ܬܘܚܝܐ rt. ܐܚܝ. m. *dry rubbish.*

ܬܘܚܠܐ m. pl. *palm-leaf baskets for dates.*

ܬܘܚܫܠܬܐ rt. ܚܫܠ. f. *despondency.*

ܬܘܚܡܐ from ܬܚܘܡܐ. m. *a) a set limit of time. b) a resolution, determination, order. c)* log. *a definition;* ܕܠܐ ܬܘܚܡ *indeterminate, indefinite.*

ܬܘܚܡܝܘܬܐ from ܬܚܘܡܐ. f. *termination.*

ܬܘܚܪܬܐ pl. ܬܐ rt. ܐܚܪ. f. *delay, tardiness.*

ܬܘܚܬܐ rt. ܬܘܚ. f. *bemoaning, regret.*

ܬܘܚܬܝܐ from ܬܚܬ. m. *condescension, courtesy.*

ܬܘܝ Pael conj. of verb ܬܘܐ.

ܬܘܝܐ adj. from ܬܘ; ܡܠܐ ܬܘܝܬܐ *words to which* ܬ *is added.*

ܬܘܝܐ rt. ܬܘܐ. m. *compunction.*

ܬܘܝܗܘܬܐ rt. ܬܘܗ. f. *consternation.*

ܬܘܝܬܐ rt. ܬܘܐ. f. *compunction.*

ܬܘܝܪܘܬܐ rt. ܬܘܪ. f. *amazement, confusion, embarrassment.*

ܬܘܟ, ܬܟ fut. ܢܬܘܟ, act. part. ܬܐܟ, ܬܐܟܐ, pass. part. ܬܝܟ, denom. verb from ܬܟܐ. *a) to be contained, enclosed;* ܟܠ ܗܘ ܬܐܟ ܒܥܘܗܕܢܐ *all is contained in the* memory; ܬܐܟ ܗܘܐ ܒܫܠܝܘܬܐ *he was enclosed, protected, by serenity. b) to be kept within bounds, to restrain, give over;* ܠܐ ܬܐܟ ܡܢ ܐܣܛܠܝܘܬܗ *his impiousness was unbounded. c) to be abashed, disconcerted;* ܒܝܫܘܬܐ ܕܠܐ ܬܟܐ *unabashed wickedness;* ܠܐ ܡܢܢ ܐܢܫ ܒܗܬ ܘܬܟ *no one of us was ashamed, not one gave in.* Pa. ܬܝܟ *to rail* or *fence in; to coerce, hold in check;* ܐܪܥܐ ܡܬܝܟܬܐ *enclosed land;* ܬܝܟܗ ܡܢ ܕܢܪܕܘܦ ܠܕܝܪܝܐ *he forbade him to persecute the monks.* Ethpa. ܐܬܬܝܟ *to be restrained, kept within bounds;* ܠܫܢܐ ܕܠܐ ܡܬܬܝܟ *an unbridled tongue.* Aph. ܐܬܝܟ *a) to put a stop to. b)* ܡܬܝܟܐ ܠܫܢܐ Sir. xviii. 18 uncertain, in the Lexx. *to hurt, to abash.*

ܬܘܟܐ pl. ܬܘܟܝܢ, ܬܘܟܐ rt. ܬܟ. m. *harm, loss, injury; a trick, fraud; misery.*

ܬܘܟܣܐ pl. ܐ rt. ܬܟܣ. m. *heavy care.*

ܬܘܟܠܢܐ rt. ܬܟܠ. m. *trust, confidence;* ܒܬܘܟܠܢܐ ܕܠܐ ܡܫܬܪܪ *uncertain;* ܐܢܫ ܕܬ *a trusty friend;* ܬ ܥܠܬ *a source of confidence;* ܓܢܒܪܐ ܕܬ *steadfast heroes.*

ܬܘܟܡܘܣ Arab. m. *sourness in the stomach, indigestion.*

ܬܘܟܢܐ rt. ܬܟ. only in BB. m. *harm, loss.*

ܬܘܟܣܐ rt. ܬܟܣ. m. *reining in, coercion, reproof.*

ܬܘܠܒܫܐ rt. ܠܒܫ. m. *induing, putting on;* ܬ ܕܐܣܟܝܡܐ *the taking of the monastic habit.*

ܬܘܠܕܬܐ pl. ܬܘܠܕܬܐ rt. ܝܠܕ. f. *generation, descent, origin, race, stock, kindred.*

ܬܘܠܚܐ pl. ܐ rt. ܬܠܚ. m. *rending, tearing asunder;* ܬܘܠܚ ܩܝܪܐ *rupture.*

ܬܘܠܡܕܐ rt. ܠܡܕ. m. *a) training, discipline, instruction of catechumens, catechizing;* ܡܐܡܪܐ ܕܬܘܠܡܕܐ *a catechetical homily. b) making disciples, conversion. c) discipleship, novitiate; a monastic school;* ܒܪ ܬ ܕܥܘܡܪܐ *a novice, pupil of the monastery;* ܩܒܠ ܬ *he received instruction, was a pupil.*

ܬܘܠܥܒܐ rt. ܠܥܒ. m. *ridicule, scoffing.*

ܬܘܠܥ denom. verb from ܬܘܠܥܐ. Ethpaual ܐܬܬܘܠܥ *to swarm with worms.*

ܬܘܠܥܐ, ܬܘܠܥܬܐ pl. ܬܘܠܥܐ usually fem. *a) a worm, tape-worm. b) cochineal kermes, scarlet dye, murex. c) a firefly. d) a grub, larva, embryo;* ܬ ܕܬܘܬܐ *a silkworm.*

ܬܘܠܥܢܐܝܬ from ܬܘܠܥܐ. adv. *as if dyed scarlet.*

ܬܘܠܥܢܝܐ from ܬܘܠܥܐ. *vermicular;* ܡܫܚܐ ܬ *gum arabic.*

ܬܘܠܬܐ from ܬܠܬܐ. m. *a third time, doing anything a third time.*

ܬܘܠܬܐ pl. ܐ from ܬܠܬܐ. com. gen. *three years old, a three-year old.*

ܬܘܠܬܐ pl. ܬܐ from ܬܠܬܐ. m. *a third*

part; ܬܪܬܝܢ ܬܘܠܬܝܢ ܕܡܝܠܐ two-thirds of a mile.

ܬܘܡܘܬܐ pl. ܬܐ̈ perh. an unripe ulcer.

ܬܐܘܡܐ; see ܬܐܘܡܐ Thomas.

ܬܘܡܐ or ܬܐܘܡܐ pl. ܐ̈ m. garlic.

ܬܘܡܘܣ, ܬܐܘܡܘܣ (rare), ܬܘܡܘܡܘܣ, ܬܘܡܘܣ, ܬܘܡܘܣ θύμος, thyme = Syr. ܨܥܬܪܐ.

ܬܘܡܚܐ from ܬܡܚ. m. weighing, measuring.

ܬܘܡܚܬܐ from ܬܡܚ. m. hammering.

ܬܘܡܠܐ θυμέλη, an altar.

ܬܘܡܠܝܢ θυμέλην, an altar-shaped platform, the theatre.

ܬܘܡܢܝܐ from ܬܡܢ. m. an eighth part.

ܬܘܡܢܝܐ, ܬܐ̈ from ܬܘܡܐ. garlic-like.

ܬܘܢ, ܐܬ part. ܐܬܢ to make water. Ethpe. ܐܬܬܢܝ to be passed of urine. Derivatives, ܬܢܢܐ, ܬܘܢܐ, ܬܢܝܐ, ܬܢܝܬܐ.

ܬܘܢ, ܬܘܢܐ; see ܬܘܢܐ an inner chamber.

ܬܘܢܝܐ rt. ܬܘܢ. m. pl. urine.

ܬܘܢܒܐ rt. ܬܢܒ. in BA. pestilence, epidemic; dearth.

ܬܘܢܝܐ pl. ܐ̈ rt. ܬܢܐ. m. a tale, byword; a story, history, narration; ܬ ܕܦܘܡܐ oral tradition. Gram. the indicative mood.

ܬܘܢܢܐ = ܬܢܢܐ rt. ܬܢ. m. smoke.

ܬܘܣܦܬ, ܬܘܣܦܬܐ pl. ܬܐ̈ rt. ܝܣܦ. f. an addition, increase, growth; support, relief. Pl. a supplement, appendix. Gram. a predicate; ܐܬܘܬܐ ܕܬ servile letters.

ܬܘܣܦܢܐ rt. ܝܣܦ. m. augmentation, surplus.

ܬܘܦܪܐ pl. ܐ̈ light smooth-grained wood, used in Tirhan for making spindles.

ܬܘܩܠܐ, ܬܘܩܠܬܐ pl. ܝ̈, ܬܐ̈ rt. ܬܩܠ. f. a stumbling-block, offence, scandal; ܕܠܐ ܬ giving no offence.

ܬܘܩܝܐ (ܕܪܕܐ) rt. ܬܩܐ. m. only Judges ix. 27, variously explained in the Lexx. as a plain; centre; soft mire.

ܬܘܩܢܐ pl. ܐ̈ rt. ܬܩܢ. m. a) the work ܕܒܪܝܬܐ of creation; the making ܕܫܡܝܐ of the heavens, ܕܝܡܡܐ of the seas, ܕܒܪܢܫܐ of man. b) making, construction, structure; ܬ ܕܐܘܪܚܐ road-making; ܬ ܕܐܠܦܐ ship-building; ܬ ܕܐܪܥܐ husbandry. c) a thing made, formed or constructed, a structure, handiwork. d) preparation, making ready of a meal, a meal, banquet. e) preparation, making up of medicines or chemicals. f) establishment, institution, ordinance. g) repairing, restoration, putting to rights.

ܬܘܩܦܐ const. st. ܬܘܩܦ rt. ܬܩܦ. m. a) bottom, base. b) force, power, strength; ܬ ܕܚܩܠܐ goodness of the fields; ܕܛܘܪܐ immensity of the mountains; ܕܩܪܒܐ warlike strength; ܕܥܠܝܡܘܬܗ the flower of his age; ܩܘܪܝܐ ܕܬܘܩܦܟ thy fenced cities.

ܬܘܗ fut. ܢܬܘܗ, pass. part. ܬܝܗ, part. adj. ܬܘܝܗ. to be dazed, amazed, shocked, confounded; ܟܕ ܢܦܩܗ ܗܘܐ ܒܗ ܬܘܝܗ ܐܝܟ ܬܠܬܝܢ ܝܘܡܝܢ ܟܕ ܐܬܐ when he recovered consciousness he remained dazed for thirty days. Aph. ܐܬܝܗ pass. part. ܡܬܝܗ, ܡܬܝܗܐ. to confound, daze, bewilder. Derivatives, ܬܘܗܝܐ, ܬܘܗܐ.

ܬܘܪ, ܬܪ to stir. Aph. ܐܬܝܪ to plough.

ܬܘܪܐ pl. ܝ̈, ܐ̈ m. for fem.; see ܬܘܪܬܐ. a bull, ox; a sign of the Zodiac, Taurus, the Bull. Derivative, ܡܬܪܝܢܬ.

ܬܘܗܪܐ rt. ܬܗܪ. m. bewilderment, confusion.

ܬܘܪܐ, ܬܘܪܬܐ pl. ܬܐ̈ f. in the Lexx. a swelling, plague-spot.

ܬܘܪܕܐ rt. ܪܕܐ. m. erudition.

ܬܘܪܓܡܐ pl. ܐ̈ from ܬܪܓܡ. m. interpretation, an allegory, commentary, homily, funeral oration; a discourse, speech, harangue. E-Syr. an expository anthem preceding the Epistle and Gospel.

ܬܪܝܩܐ or ܬܪܝܩܐ θηριακή, a) antidote. b) poison opp. ܐܬܪܝܩܐ.

ܬܘܪܟܐܝܬ adv. Turkish.

ܬܘܪܟܝܐ, ܬܐ̈ or ܬܘܪܟܝܐ, also ܬܘܪܟ. a Turk.

ܬܘܪܡܘܣܐ, ܬܪܡ, ܬܪܡܣ pl. ܐ̈ θέρμος, m. a kind of lupine.

ܬܘܪܝܐ, ܬܐ̈ from ܬܘܪܐ. bovine, savage.

ܬܘܪܢܝܬܐ f. the cypress.

ܬܘܪܣܝܐ from ܬܪܣ. m. nourishment, victuals, provisions, means of subsistence, support.

ܬܘܪܥܐ (rare), ܬܘܪܥܬܐ W-Syr., ܬܪܥܬܐ E-Syr. pl. ܝ̈, ܬܐ̈ rt. ܬܪܥ. f. a breach, rift, gap, mountain pass; a strait, creek, channel; a hole; ruin, slaughter.

ܬܘܪܦܐ rt. ܬܪܦ. m. *dyed wool.*

ܬܘܪܨܐ pl. ܐ̈ rt. ܬܪܨ. m. *a) direction, arrangement; right action, uprightness. b) reformation, a remedy;* ܬ ܕܗܘܢܐ *sanity. c) correction, emendation;* ܬ ܚܕܬܐ or ܬ ܫܪܝܪܬܐ *revised version;* ܬ ܕܩܪܝܢܐ *the right reading, correct text;* ܬܘܪܨ ܡܡܠܠܐ *grammar.*

ܬܘܪܬܐ or ܬܘܪܬܐ pl. ܬ̈, ܬ̈ f. *a cow, heifer;* ܬ ܕܚܠܒܐ *a milch cow;* ܬ ܕܓܡܘܫܐ *a buffalo cow.*

ܬܫܐ fut. ܢܬܫܐ. *to wander, rave.* Pa. ܬܫܐ *to lead astray.* Part. ܡܬܫܝܐ *tainted.* Ethpa. ܐܬܬܫܝ *to hesitate, deviate, be led astray.* Derivatives, the three following words:—

ܬܫܝܐ pl. ܬ̈ rt. ܬܫܐ. m. *a trackless waste, pathless desert; wandering;* ܒܬܫܝܐ *astray.*

ܬܫܝܐܝܬ and ܬܫܝܘܬܐܝܬ rt. ܬܫܐ. adv. *astray, deviously.*

ܬܘܫܥܐ rt. ܬܫܥ. m. *a ninth part.*

ܬܘܬ *Thoth,* name of the first Egyptian month.

ܬܘܬܐ often ܬܘܬ ܢܦܫܐ rt. ܬܘܐ. f. *compunction, regret, remorse.*

ܬܘܬܐ pl. ܐ̈ m. *the sycamore; the mulberry; a swelling near the anus like a mulberry.*

ܬܘܬܒܐ, ܬܘܬܒܬܐ rt. ܝܬܒ. *a sojourner, stranger, foreigner; a settler, a lodger.*

ܬܘܬܒܘܬܐ rt. ܝܬܒ. f. *pilgrimage, sojourning, dwelling in a strange country.*

ܬܘܬܝܐ Arab. *antimony.*

ܬܘܬܪ, ܬܘܬܪܐ pl. ܐ̈ rt. ܝܬܪ. m. generally pl. *the remainder, rest, leavings; fullness, superfluity.*

ܬܙ fut. ܢܬܘܙ, act. part. ܬܐܙ, ܬܐܙܐ. *to swell up, to be boiling hot, to be indignant;* ܠܒܗ ܬܐܙ ܒܚܕܘܬܐ *his heart swells with joy.* Part. adj. ܬܙܝܙ, ܐ, ܬܐ *raging hot, fervid.* Ethpe. ܐܬܬܙܝܙ *to be greatly excited, act with extreme fervour.* Pa. ܬܙܙ *to make to swell* with ܠܒܐ *the heart.* Ethpa. ܐܬܬܙܙ *to be swollen with pride; to be enraged; to be greatly alarmed.* Derivatives, ܬܙܝܙܐܝܬ, ܬܙܝܙܘܬܐ.

ܬܙܝܙܐܝܬ rt. ܬܙ. adv. *angrily.*

ܬܙܝܙܘܬܐ rt. ܬܙ. f. *raging heat, fervour, vehemence, commotion.*

ܬܚܕܩ *water-peppermint.*

ܬܚܒ fut. ܢܬܚܒ, act. part. ܬܚܒ, ܬܚܒܐ. *to be brought low, be enfeebled; to succumb, give way;* ܠܐ ܬܚܒ ܡܠܟܘܬܐ ܕܪܗܘܡܝܐ ܕܬܫܕܪ ܡܕܐܬܐ ܠܦܪܣܝܐ *the Roman Empire has not sunk so low as to send tribute to the Persians.* Pa. ܬܚܒ same as Aphel. Ethpa. ܐܬܬܚܒ *to appear weak.* Aph. ܐܬܚܒ *to bring low, enfeeble, depress;* ܕܚܠܬܐ ܐܬܚܒܬ ܢܦܫܢ *fear made us irresolute.* Derivatives, ܬܚܒܐ, ܬܚܒܐ, ܬܚܒܘܬܐ, ܬܚܒܘܬܐ, ܡܬܚܒܢܐܝܬ.

ܬܚܒܐ rt. ܬܚܒ. m. *infirmity.*

ܬܚܘܒ, ܐ, ܬܐ rt. ܬܚܒ. *infirm, feeble, helpless, wretched, of low degree, mean;* ܬܚܘܒ ܚܙܬܐ *having impaired vision;* ܝܪܚܐ ܬܚܘܒܝܢ *unhealthy months.*

ܬܚܘܒܐܝܬ rt. ܬܚܒ. adv. *weakly.*

ܬܚܘܒܘܬܐ rt. ܬܚܒ. f. *impotence, incompetence, wretchedness, feebleness;* ܬܚܘܒܘܬܝ *my wretched self.*

ܬܚܘܝܐ, ܬܚܘܝܬܐ pl. ܬܚܘܝܬܐ rt. ܚܘܐ. f. *an appearance, showing forth, manifestation; a token, example, specimen; a demonstration, argument.*

ܬܚܘܡܐ pl. ܐ̈ m. *a) limit, boundary, border; a limit, set time. b) a precept, regulation, penalty. c) limitation, extreme; definition, term;* ܕܠܐ ܬ *indefinitely.* Derivatives, ܬܚܘܡܐ, ܬܚܘܡܘܬܐ, verb ܬܚܡ, ܡܬܚܡܢܐ, ܡܬܚܡܢܘܬܐ, ܡܬܚܡܢܐ, ܡܬܚܡܢܘܬܐ, ܡܬܬܚܡܢܐ, ܡܬܬܚܡܢܐܝܬ.

ܬܚܘܬ; see ܬܚܬ.

ܬܚܠܐ pl. ܐ̈ f. *lepidium sativum, garden cress.*

ܬܚܠܘܦ, ܬܚܠܘܦܐ rt. ܚܠܦ. m. *a) an exchange; the thing exchanged or given in return;* ܚܠܦ ܬ *in exchange, instead, for. b) a vicegerent, deputy, substitute.*

ܬܚܠܘܦܘܬܐ rt. ܚܠܦ. f. *change, substitution.*

ܬܚܠܘܨܐ pl. ܐ̈ rt. ܚܠܨ. m. *spoil, prey, plunder;* ܬ ܕܩܘܕܫܐ *sacrilege;* ܕܠܐ ܬ *unhurt, untouched, inviolate.*

ܬܚܡ denom. verb Pael conj. from ܬܚܘܡܐ. *a) to mark out a boundary, set a limit, to limit, border; to keep within bounds, confine; to forbid, restrict, inhibit;* ܬܚܡܢ ܠܗܘܢ

ܬܬܚܡܘܢ ܬܚܘܡܟܘܢ *ye shall mark out your border;* ܬܚܡܗ ܠܪܘܚܐ ܒܝܫܬܐ—ܢܘܪܐ—ܡܒܘܠܐ *he forbade the evil spirit; stayed the fire, the flood. b) to settle, fix, determine; to lay down, define;* ܬܚܡܬ ܠܗ ܙܒܢܐ *I fixed a time for him;* ܡܬܚܡܐ ܘܡܬܚܡܐ *destined and determined.* With ܩܕܡ *to fore-determine.* Eccles. of determining questions of faith or practice, ܬܚܡܢ ܘܐܫܪܢ ܠܗܢܐ ܩܢܘܢܐ *we have laid down and confirmed this canon;* ܬܚܡܝܢ ܡܢ ܫܘܠܛܢܐ ܘܡܠܬܐ ܚܝܬܐ ܕܐܠܗܐ *we determine by the authority and living word of God.* Log. and gram. *to define, determine.* Ethpa. ܐܬܬܚܡ *a) to be terminated, to have a set limit; to be kept within bounds. b) to be determined, fore-determined; to be laid down, settled, defined.*

ܬܬܚܡ 2 m. s. fut. of verb ܚܡܡ.

ܬܚܡܨܘܬܐ rt. ܚܡܨ. f. *bashfulness, modesty, reverence;* ܬ ܕܓܢܒܐ *honour among thieves;* ܕܠܐ ܬ *impudent.*

ܬܚܢܢܬܐ rt. ܚܢ. f. *fervent prayer, supplication, intercession.*

ܬܚܦܝܬܐ pl. ܬܚܦܝܬܐ rt. ܚܦܐ. f. *a veil, covering; an eggshell.* Metaph. *a disguise, mask, cloak;* ܕܠܐ ܬ *openly, frankly.*

ܬܚܝܬ, ܬܚܘܬ and ܬܚܝܬ, the 1st form is properly an adverb used with the preps. ܠ and ܡܢ, the 2nd a prep. with pron. suffixes, ܬܚܘܬܝ *under me,* &c. The 3rd form precedes a noun and is without suffixes, but these distinctions are not constant. *Under, beneath;* ܠܬܚܬ *down, downward, under, below, here below;* ܕܠܬܚܬ *the lower place, beneath* opp. ܕܠܥܠ; ܡܢ ܠܬܚܬ ܠܥܠ *from below upward.* Of place usually with ܡܢ, ܠܬܚܬ ܡܢ ܡܘܨܠ *below Mosul;* ܕܡܬܐܡܪܝܢ ܡܢ ܠܬܚܬ *which are mentioned below;* of age, ܡܢ ܒܪ ܬܪܬܝܢ ܫܢܝܢ ܘܠܬܚܬ *from two years old and under;* of rank, ܟܠ ܐܢܫ ܕܡܬܚܡ ܘܠܬܚܬ ܡܢܗ *any one inferior to him;* ܬܚܝܬ ܐܚܪܝܐ *late-born;* ܬ ܚܘܒܬܐ *in debt;* ܬ ܚܘܒܐ *guilty, culpable;* ܬ ܠܘܛܬܐ *under a curse;* ܬ ܫܘܥܒܕܐ *subject;* ܡܢ ܬܚܝܬ ܥܕܢܐ *suddenly.* Logic. ܬܚܝܬ ܦܪܘܫܐ *sub-alternate;* ܬܚܝܬ ܣܘܩܒܠܝܐ *sub-contrary.* Derivatives, ܬܚܬܝܐ, verb ܬܚܬ, ܬܚܬܝܐ, ܬܚܬܝܘܬܐ, ܡܬܬܚܬܢܘܬܐ, ܡܬܬܚܬܢܘܬܐ, ܡܬܬܚܬܢܐ.

ܬܚܬܪܘܬܐ rt. ܬܚܬܪ. m. *haughtiness, pompousness.*

ܬܚܬܝܢ and ܬܚܬܝܢ = *a)* ܠܬܚܬ *down,* and *b)* ܬܚܝܬ *under.*

ܬܚܬܝ denom. verb Pali conj. from ܬܚܬ. *to bring low, bring into subjection, to abase, humble, despise;* ܡܢܘ ܬܚܬܝܟ ܡܢ ܫܡܝܐ *who brought Thee down from heaven?* ܬܚܬܝܬܗ ܠܫܒܗܪܘܬܐ *it humbled pride;* ܡܨܥܪ ܘܡܬܬܚܬܝ *vile and despised.* Ethpali ܐܬܬܚܬܝ *a)* pass. *to be brought down, suppressed; to be made to hang down;* ܒܡܠܬܐ ܡܟܝܟܬܐ ܡܬܬܚܬܝܐ ܚܡܬܐ *by meek speech anger is subdued. b)* refl. *to humble himself, to submit;* ܐܬܬܚܬܝ ܘܛܥܡ ܡܘܬܐ *He humbled Himself and tasted death.*

ܬܚܬܝܐ, ܬܝܬܐ from ܬܚܬ. *a) lower, inferior, lowest, earthly;* ܬ ܥܠܡܐ *this lower world, here below;* ܬܚܬܝܐ opp. ܥܠܝܐ *those below, earthly beings;* also *the lower stories* of a house. Masc. *a lowlander;* ܬ ܕܪܓܠܐ *the sole of the foot.* Fem. *this world;* also *humiliation, indignity.* Fem. pl. *earthly things.* Gram. the points ܊ at the end of a sentence; these sometimes signify interrogation.

ܬܚܬܝܘܬܐ from ܬܚܬ f. *descent; lower position, low estate.*

ܬܛܘܫܬܐ rt. ܛܘܫ. f. *pollution, a polluted thing.*

ܬܛܝܪܐ or ܬܛܪ, ܬܐ from ܬܛܪܐ. *clouded, foul, turbid, perturbed.*

ܬܛܝܪܘܬܐ from ܬܛܪܐ. f. *turbidity.*

ܬܛܢܦܘܬܐ rt. ܛܢܦ. f. *contamination.*

ܬܛܠܝܠܐ pl. ܐ̈ rt. ܛܠܠ. m. *a roof, rafters; a panelled ceiling.*

ܬܛܪ denom. verb from ܬܛܪܐ. *to render gloomy, to foul.*

ܬܛܪܐ and ܬܛܪ pl. ܐ̈ constr. st. ܬܛܪܝ m. *dregs, lees, sediment; refuse, filth; earwax,* thought to be dregs of the brain. Derivatives, ܬܛܝܪܘܬܐ, ܬܛܝܪܐ, ܬܛܝܪܘܬܐ, ܬܛܝܪܐܝܬ, ܬܛܪܐ and ܬܛܪ, ܬܛܪܘܬܐ, verb ܬܛܪ.

ܬܝ pl. ܬܝܝܢ imper. 2 f. of verb ܐܬܐ *to come.*

ܬܝܐ pl. of ܬܘܝ.

ܬܝܒܐ, ܬܝܒܬܐ rt. ܬܘܒ. *a) a backslider, apostate. b) a penitent. c) one who can be moved by entreaty, relenting. d)* ܬܝܒܐ ܘܬܝܒܐ *those who frequented* the place *and returned to it, visitors.*

ܬܐܒܐ and ܬܐܒܝܐ pl. ܝ̈ܐ = ܬܐܒܝܐ *a Theban.*

ܬܝܒܐܝܬ rt. ܬܘܒ. adv. *penitently.*

ܬܝܒܘ, ܬܝܒܘܬܐ rt. ܬܘܒ. f. *backsliding; recantation; return, conversion, repentance, penitence.*

ܬܝܒܘܬܐ rt. ܬܘܒ. f. *vomit.*

ܬܝܒܘܬܢܐ rt. ܬܘܒ. *penitential.*

ܬܝܒܬܐ rt. ܬܘܒ. *a) vomiting, sickness, nausea. b) vomit, spittle. c) returning;* with ܦܬܓܡܐ *an answer.*

ܬܝܒܬܐ = ܬܐܒܬܐ, ܬܘܒܬܐ.

ܬܝܘܒܐ pl. ܐ̈ rt. ܬܘܒ. m. *vomiting.*

ܬܝܘܒܐ rt. ܬܘܒ. m. *vomit, saliva, spittle.*

ܬܝܘܒܢܐ, ܬܝܘܒܢܝܬܐ rt. ܬܘܒ. *nauseous, sickening.*

ܬܝܡܣܬܐ from ܬܐܡܐ. f. pl. *two-valved, double doors.*

ܬܝܘܢ and ܬܐܝܐ pl. ܬܝ̈ܐ and ܬܐ̈ܝܐ θεῖον, θεῖα, f. *brimstone, sulphur.*

ܬܝܪܐ pl. ܐ̈ m. *battlements, a parapet; paling, railing, fence* round a well. Derivative, verb ܬܘܪ.

ܬܝܪܬܐ f. *a water-skin, large leathern bottle.*

ܬܝܡܢ, ܬܝܡܢܐ or ܬܝܡܢܐ from ܝܡܝܢ. f. *the south;* ܡܢ ܬܝܡܢ ܡܕܢܚ *south-east.*

ܬܝܡܢܝܐ or ܬܝܡܢܝܐ, ܬܝܡܢܝܬܐ from ܝܡܝܢܐ. *southern;* ܪܘܚܐ ܬܝܡܢܝܬܐ *south wind.*

ܬܝܢܐ rt. ܬܘܢ. m. pl. *urine.* Chem. *oil of sulphur, sulphuretted water;* ܬܝܢܐ ܕܟܠܒܐ a name for mercury.

ܬܝܢܬܐ rt. ܬܘܢ. f. *urine.*

ܬܝܩܐ also ܬܐܝܩܐ and ܬܝܩܐ pl. ܬܝ̈ܩܐ f. θήκη, *a receptacle, case, scabbard; a shrine, a grave.*

ܬܝܪܐ pl. ܐ̈ Arab. m. *the surface of the sea.*

ܬܝܪܩܢ = ܬܪܝܩܢ.

ܬܝܪܬܐ pl. ܬܐ̈ f. in the Lexx. *a bubo, inguinal swelling;* cf. ܬܘܪܐ, ܬܘܪܬܐ.

ܬܝܫܐ pl. ܐ̈ m. *a) a he-goat. b)* in the Lexx. *the hoarse voice of a youth when it first grows deep.*

ܬܟ fut. ܢܬܘܟ, infin. ܡܬܟ, act. part. ܬܐܟ. *to harm, injure, oppress;* ܠܐ ܬܬܘܟ ܠܡܣܟܢܐ *thou shalt not oppress the poor.* Ethpe. ܐܬܬܟ *to be humiliated.* Aph. ܐܬܟ *a) to do harm, bring harm;* ܬܘܟܐ ܕܐܬܟܘ ܚܛܗܝ *the harm which my sins have caused. b) to suffer harm* or *loss;* ܬܓܪܝܗ ܡܬܟܝܢ ܟܠܝܘܡ *its merchants suffer daily loss.* Palpel ܬܟܬܟ *to injure;* part. ܡܬܟܬܟ *mischievous.* Derivatives, ܬܘܟܐ, ܬܟܘܟܐ.

ܬܟ̈ܐ pl. of ܬܟܬܐ.

ܬܟܦ fut. ܢܬܟܘܦ, act. part. ܬܟܦ, ܬܟܦܐ, pass. part. ܬܟܝܦ, ܦܐ, ܦܬܐ. *a) to press hard, come heavily, to grow frequent, throng, to grow worse, weigh upon;* ܪܕܘܦܝܐ ܥܠ ܟܪܣܛܝܢܐ ܬܟܦ ܗܘܐ *persecution pressed hard on the Christians;* ܬܟܦܐ ܡܚܘܬܐ *the wound becomes worse;* ܬܟܦܘ ܡܛܪܐ ܬܟܝܦܐ *heavy rains fell;* ܬܟܦ ܪܡܫܐ *evening sets in;* ܐܓܪ̈ܬܐ ܬܟܦܝܢ ܠܘܬܟܘܢ *letters pour in on you;* ܬܟܦܘ ܥܠܘܗܝ ܚܙܘ̈ܢܐ *visions thronged upon him. b) to be urgent, pressing, assiduous;* ܟܕ ܬܟܦ ܥܠܝܗ *when he greatly urged her;* ܬܟܦ ܘܚܦܪ ܚܘܠܕܐ ܒܐܪܥܐ the mole *labours assiduously in the earth.* Pass. part. *heavy, frequent, continuous, assiduous;* ܬܠܓܐ ܬܟܝܦܐ *heavy snow;* ܬܟܫܦܬܐ ܬܟܝܦܬܐ *continuous supplication.* Ethpe. ܐܬܬܟܦ and Ethpa. ܐܬܬܟܦ *to be oppressed, troubled, weighed down;* ܡܢ ܟܘܪ̈ܗܢܐ *by diseases.* Aph. ܐܬܟܦ *to frequent, visit frequently; to urge, oppress;* ܠܐ ܬܬܟܦ ܠܡܚܝܒܟ *do not press* thy debtor; ܡܬܟܦܢܐ *task-masters;* ܐܬܟܦܘ ܒܗ ܒܬܟܫܦܬܐ ܡܬܟܦܬܐ *they urged him with repeated supplication.* Derivatives, ܬܘܟܦܐ, ܬܟܦܐ, ܬܟܝܦܐܝܬ, ܬܟܝܦܘܬܐ.

ܬܟܦܐ rt. ܬܟܦ. m. *frequency, heaviness.*

ܬܟܦܢܐ rt. ܬܟܦ. m. *one who restrains, forbids.*

ܬܟܝܦܐܝܬ rt. ܬܟܦ. adv. *earnestly, urgently, hastily, voraciously, frequently.*

ܬܟܝܦܘܬܐ rt. ܬܟܦ. f. *vehemence, assiduity, persistence.*

ܬܟܝܠܐܝܬ rt. ܬܟܠ. adv. *trustfully, confidently, with assurance, assuredly; faithfully, steadfastly.*

ܬܟܝܠܘܬܐ rt. ܬܟܠ. f. *reliance, assurance, trustfulness, trustworthiness;* ܒܬܟ̈ *assiduously, confidently.*

ܬܟܝܫ prob. dial. for ܬܟܝܫ. *perturbed.*

ܬܟܝܫܘܬܐ from ܬܟܝܫ. f. *perturbation.*

ܬܟܠ Peal only part. ܬܟܝܠ, ܠܐ, ܠܬܐ. *a) to*

trust, place confidence in, rely on with ܒ or ܥܠ; ܡܢ ܕܬܟܝܠ ܥܠ ܠܒܗ *he that trusteth in his own heart;* ܬܟܝܠܝܢܢ ܥܠ *we put our trust in . . . .* b) *secure, safe;* ܓܫܪܐ ܬܟܝܠܐ *a safe bridge;* ܢܗܘܐ ܬܟܝܠܐ ܘܫܠܝܐ *may we be in safety and tranquillity.* Ethpe. ܐܬܬܟܠ *to trust, put trust in, rely upon; to state assuredly; to be assured, certain, confident;* ܐܬܬܟܠܘ ܥܠ ܙܟܘܬܐ *they were confident of victory;* ܐܬܬܟܠ ܠܡܥܒܕ ܟܢܘܫܝܐ ܕܠܐ ܫܘܠܛܢܐ *he had the assurance to hold a council without authorization.* Aph. ܐܬܟܠ *to lead* or *exhort to trust, to assure, promise;* ܟܕ ܡܬܟܠ ܠܗ ܕܠܐ ܢܕܚܠ *exhorting him not to fear;* ܐܬܟܠܬܟ ܥܠ ܣܝܡܬܐ ܟܣܝܬܐ *I promised thee secret treasures.* Derivatives, ܬܘܟܠܢܐ, ܬܟܝܠܐܝܬ, ܬܟܝܠܘܬܐ, ܬܟܠܐ, ܡܬܬܟܠܢܐ, ܡܬܬܟܠܢܘܬܐ.

ܬܟܠܐ rt. ܬܟܠ. m. *confidence;* ܥܠ ܬܟܠܐ ܕ *trusting that . . . .*

ܬܟܠܐ m. *bereavement, barrenness, loss of children.*

ܬܟܠܬܐ pl. ܬܟܠܬܐ f. *dark blue, violet, purple;* pl. *purple robes, fringes.*

ܬܟܣ fut. ܢܬܟܘܣ, act. part. ܬܟܣ, ܬܟܣܐ. a) *to strike* ܟܢܪܐ *the harp;* ܒܡܥܩܬܐ *to strike with goads.* b) *to hold* or *keep back, forbid, control, restrain, stop;* ܦܓܘܕܐ ܕܟܐܢܘܬܐ ܕܬܟܣܝܢ ܡܢ ܬܘܩܠܬܐ *the reins of justice which restrain from offence;* ܬܟܣܗ ܠܩܪܘܝܐ *he stopped the reader.* Often with ܐܝܕܐ *to withhold,* ܫܘܪܝܐ *to restrain the impetus.* c) perh. a mistake for ܦܩܕ *to exhort, ordain.* Ethpe. ܐܬܬܟܣ a) *to be coerced, deterred, prevented, restrained;* ܡܢ ܓܘܥܪܝܗܘܢ ܠܐ ܡܬܬܟܣܝܢ *they were undeterred by his threats;* ܕܠܐ ܡܬܬܟܣܢܐ *unbridled, uncontrollable.* b) *to be jerked back, dislocated;* ܐܬܬܟܣ ܨܘܪܗ ܡܢ ܡܦܪܩܬܗ *his neck was jerked out of joint.* Pa. ܬܟܣ *to suppress, keep back, drive back;* ܠܐ ܡܫܟܚܝܢ ܗܘܘ ܠܡܬܟܣܘ ܡܠܘܗܝ *they could not rebut his words;* ܬܟܣ ܬܢܚܬܟ *control* thy *sobs.* Aph. ܐܬܟܣ perh. for ܐܬܩܣ: ܐܬܟܣ ܪܥܝܢܗ *he repressed his opinion.* Derivatives, ܬܘܟܣܐ, ܬܟܘܣܐ, ܬܟܣܐ, ܬܟܣܐ, ܬܟܣܢ, ܡܬܟܣܢܐ.

ܬܟܣܐ rt. ܬܟܣ. m. W-Syr. gram. *the moderator,* name of the points ◌̤ which express reprehension or lamentation.

ܬܟܣܐ rt. ܬܟܣ. m. *opposition, coercion.*

ܬܟܣܝܬ, ܬܟܣܝܬܐ pl. ܬܟܣܝܬܐ rt. ܟܣܐ. f. *a covering, garment, vesture, cloak; a kerchief; an awning;* ܠܐ ܡܢ ܚܕܐ ܬܟܣܝܬ *without any covering at all.*

ܬܟܣܢ, ܬܟܣܢܐ rt. ܬܟܣ. adj. *of reproof.*

ܬܟܪ = ܕܟܪ *to remember.*

ܬܟܪܣܐ only in the Lexx. m. *satiety.*

ܬܟܪܬܐ rt. ܟܪܐ. f. *sorrow.*

ܬܟܫ; see ܬܟܝܫ.

ܬܟܫܦܢܐܝܬ rt. ܟܫܦ. adv. *as a suppliant.*

ܬܟܫܦܬܐ pl. ܬܟܫܦܬܐ rt. ܟܫܦ. f. *supplication, intercession, entreaty, request;* ܬ ܕܟܬܒܐ *a written petition.* Pl. lit. *solemn metrical litanies.*

ܬܟܫܦܬܢܝܐ rt. ܟܫܦ. *supplicatory.*

ܬܟܬܐ pl. ܬܟܐ f. *a belt.*

ܬܟܬܘܫ, ܬܟܬܘܫܐ pl. ܝܢ, ܫܐ rt. ܟܬܫ. m. *a contest, fight, conflict, strife;* ܬ ܕܐܘܠܘܡܦܝܩܐ *the Olympian contests;* ܕܐܠܦܐ or ܒ *a naval battle;* ܬ ܕܡܕܒܪܢܘܬܐ *to strive after the ascetic life;* ܬܟܬܘܫ ܡܠܐ *a strife of words.*

ܬܠܠ Peal only pass. part. ܬܠܝܠ, ܠܐ, ܠܬܐ. *damped, deadened* as sounds; *damp, moist, watery* as land; air. Metaph. *tainted.* Pa. ܬܠܠ part. ܡܬܠܠ *to taint.* Ethpa. ܐܬܬܠܠ *to be wetted, soaked.* Derivatives, ܬܠܝܠܘܬܐ, ܡܬܠܠܢܐ.

ܬܠܐ fut. ܢܬܠܐ, act. part. ܬܠܐ, ܬܠܝܐ, pass. part. ܬܠܐ, ܬܠܝܐ. a) trans. *to lift up, hang up, suspend, make depend from;* with ܥܠ ,ܒ ,ܠܘܬ ,ܠܥܠ; with ܡܢ *to draw back, take away;* ܣܢܬܐ ܕܬܠܐ ܒܗ ܡܐܢܐ *a peg whereon to hang vessels;* ܢܬܠܐ ܐܪܙܐ ܥܠ ܦܬܘܪܐ *he shall elevate the sacrament.* Often with ܐܝܕܐ *the hands* and ellipt. ܬܠܐ ܕܢܡܚܝܘܗܝ *he raised his hand to strike him;* ܥܝܢܐ or ܥܝܢܝܢ *to lift up the eyes;* ܢܦܫܗ *to get up, stand erect;* ܩܠܐ *to raise the voice;* ܪܫܐ *to lift the head;* with ܚܨܕܐ or ܥܠܠܬܐ *to carry the harvest;* with ܡܬܠܐ *to take up a parable.* Metaph. ܬܠܐ ܒܗ ܥܠܬܐ ܕܡܘܬܗ ܕܫܐܘܠ *he laid the blame of Saul's death upon him;* ܬܠܐ ܐܢܘܢ ܒܣܒܪܐ ܣܪܝܩܐ *he let them depend on an empty hope.* b) *to fix, prop up, fasten, wear;* ܬܠܐ ܦܩܘܕܐ ܒܫܘܩܐ *he fixed* the notice *up in the streets;* ܬܠܝܢ ܗܘܘ ܡܪܓܢܝܬܐ *they wore pearls.* c) *to hang, crucify;*

ܙܩܦܘܗܝ ܥܠ ܙܩܝܦܐ they hung him on the cross. *d*) in pass. part. *to hang, depend on, be dependent;* ܬܠܐ ܘܡܬܕܠܕܠ *hanging dangling;* ܟܒܪܝܬܐ ܬܠܝܬܐ *sulphur in suspension;* ܦܪܕܝܣܐ ܬܠܝܐ *hanging gardens;* ܪ̈ܓܫܐ ܬܠܝܢ ܚܕ ܒܚܕ *the senses are interdependent.* Ethpe. ܐܬܬܠܝ *a*) *to be hung up, suspended* ܒܐܐܪ *in the air;* ܒܣܢܬܪܐ *on a nail; to hang, cling;* ܡܬܬܠܝܐ ܥܘܠܢ ܒܨܘܪ̈ܝܢ *our iniquity clings round our necks.* Esp. *to be hung on the cross.* *b*) *to be lifted up, removed;* ܡܢ ܫܠܝ ܐܬܬܠܝ ܦܪܣܐ ܕܬܪܥܐ *the door-hanging was suddenly drawn back;* ܠܐ ܐܬܬܠܝ ܪܫܗ *his head was not lifted up,* Anglice *turned.* Ethpa. ܐܬܬܠܝ or ܐܬܠܝ *a*) *to seize, clutch, lay hold of* ܒܐܝܕܗ *by the hand;* ܒܐܕܢܐ *by the ear;* ܐܬܠܝ ܒܠܒܘܫܝܗܘܢ ܘܨܪܐ ܐܢܘܢ *he caught at their clothes and tore them.* Metaph. *to adhere, cling to;* ܥܡܐ ܫܢܝܐ ܕܝܗܘܕܝܐ ܐܬܬܠܝ *the mad* Jewish nation *adhered to Caesar.* *b*) *to drag, draw, pull;* med. *to draw, draw out.* Metaph. ܪ̈ܓܝܓܬܐ ܕܡܬܬܠܝܢ ܠܟܘܢ *lusts which drag you down.* Aph. ܐܬܠܝ *to unload.* Derivatives, ܬܠܝܐ, ܬܠܝܘܬܐ, ܬܠܝܢܐ, ܬܠܝܬܐ, ܡܬܠܝܢܐ.

ܬܠܐ, ܬܠܠܐ or ܬܠܐ, rarely ܬܠܠܐ pl. ܬܠܝܢ, ܬ̈ܠܐ m. *a*) *a hill, mound, pile, earthwork;* ܬܠܝܠܝܢ *heaped up.* *b*) pr. n. *Tela,* a city west of Nisibis. Derivatives, ܬܠܘܠܝܬܐ, ܬܠܝܠܝܬܐ, ܬܠܝܐ.

ܬܠܒܘܣܐ m. pl. in the Lexx. *pickles.*

ܬܠܒܘܬܐ pl. ܬ̈ܠܒܘܬܐ f. in the Lexx. *conversation.*

ܬܠܒܘܫܬܐ pl. ܬ̈ܠܒܘܫܬܐ rt. ܠܒܫ. f. *apparel, clothing, armour; a shroud.* Rit. *the Eucharistic veil, corporal.*

ܬܠܓ denom. verb Pael conj. from ܬܠܓܐ. pass. part. ܡܬܠܓܐ. *covered with snow, mixed with snow.* Ethpa. ܐܬܬܠܓ *to become white as snow.* Aph. ܐܬܠܓ *to make shining white; to be white as snow, to glitter; to grow hoary;* ܬܠܓܘ ܠܒܘܫܘܗܝ ܐܝܟ ܬܠܓܐ *his garments shone like snow.* Ettaph. ܐܬܬܬܠܓ *to be made snow-white.*

ܬܠܓܐ pl. ܬ̈ܠܓܐ m. *snow;* ܬ̈ܠܓܐ ܥܠܥ̈ܠܐ *violent snowstorms.* Derivatives, verb ܬܠܓ, ܬܠܓܢܘܬܐ, ܡܬܠܓܢ, ܡܬܠܓܢܐ, ܡܬܠܓܢܘܬܐ.

ܬܠܓܢܬܐ from ܬܠܓܐ. f. *a*) *a chilblain.* *b*) Lexx. *numbness of the bowels.*

ܬܠܗܘܢܐ and ܬܠܗܘܢܐ in the Lexx. *cancer.*

ܬܠܘܝܐ pl. ܬ̈ܠܘܝܐ rt. ܬܠܐ. m. *a hangman.*

ܬܠܘܠܝܬܐ pl. ܬ̈ܠܘܠܝܬܐ dimin. of ܬܠܐ f. *a little hill.*

ܬܠܘܠܝܬܐ dimin. of ܬܠܐ f. *a hillock.*

ܬܠܘ̈ܬܐ rt. ܬܠܐ. f. pl. *a*) *the heart-strings.* *b*) *a bruise, weal; a bald patch.*

ܬܠܚ fut. ܢܬܠܘܚ, act. part. ܬܠܚ, ܬܠܚܐ, pass. parts. ܬܠܝܚ and ܬܠܝܚ, ܬܠܝܚܐ, ܬܠܝܚܬܐ. *a*) *to be rent, to burst asunder;* ܬܠܚ ܟܠܗ ܦܓܪܗ *his bowels burst asunder.* *b*) *to rend, part asunder;* ܨܗܝܐ ܕܕܗܒܐ ܬܠܚ ܛܘܪ̈ܐ thirst for gold *rends open the mountains;* ܟܕ ܬܠܝܚܝܢ ܡܐܢܝܗܘܢ *with their clothes rent.* *c*) *to tear up, do away with;* ܬܠܚ ܫܛܪܐ ܕܚܘܒܝܗܘܢ *He tore up their bill of debts.* *d*) *to wear away.* Pass. parts. ܬܠܝܚ *rent, torn;* ܬܠܝܚ *fissured, ruined.* Pa. ܬܠܚ = Peal *b. to rend asunder, tear to pieces, lacerate, flay;* ܬܠܚ ܒܪܩܐ ܛܘܪ̈ܐ *lightning rent the mountains.* Ethpe. ܐܬܬܠܚ and Ethpa. ܐܬܬܠܚ pass. *a*) *to be rent, burst asunder;* ܐܬܬܠܚܬ ܐܪܥܐ *the earth was riven;* ܥܪ̈ܩܐ ܕܡܬܬܠܚܝܢ *ruptured veins.* *b*) *to be torn up, blotted out;* ܫܛܪ̈ܐ ܕܚܛܗ̈ܐ ܡܬܬܠܚܝܢ *records of sins are wiped out.* *c*) *to burst open* as ܫܘܚ̈ܢܐ *sores; to gush forth.* Derivatives, ܬܘܠܚܐ, ܬܠܚܐ, ܬܠܚܐ.

ܬܠܚܐ pl. ܬ̈ܠܚܐ rt. ܬܠܚ. m. *a*) *rupture, hernia;* ܬܠܚܐ ܕܫܪ̈ܝܪܐ ܘܥܫܝܢ̈ܐ *overstrained* or *lacerated muscles.* *b*) *a rag, tatter, torn strip.*

ܬܠܚܐ pl. ܬ̈ܠܚܐ rt. ܬܠܚ. m. *a rent, fissure, chasm; a laceration, rupture, a humpback.*

ܬܠܝܐ and ܬܠܝ from ܬܠܐ. *of the city of Tela.*

ܬܠܝܐ pl. ܬ̈ܠܝܐ rt. ܬܠܐ. m. *a*) *hanging.* *b*) *a hook, loop, noose;* ܬ݀ ܕܐܕܢܐ *an ear-ring, pendant;* ܬ݀ ܕܐܣܟܠܐ *a vine-branch with pendant clusters.*

ܬܠܝܠ, ܬܠܝܠܐ, ܬܠܝܠܬܐ; see verb ܬܠܠ.

ܬܠܝܠܘܬܐ pl. ܬ̈ܠܝܠܘܬܐ rt. ܬܠܠ. f. *moisture, wateriness, humour; a gush, rush;* ܬ݀ ܕܛܢܦܘܬܐ *taint of pollution.*

ܬܠܝܦܐ *a shell, shell-fish.*

ܬܠܝܦܐ Arab. m. *a bag.*

ܬܠܝܦܐ pl. ܬ̈ܠܝܦܐ m. *the eyelid.*

ܬܠܝܬܐ pl. ܬ̈ܠܝܬܐ rt. ܬܠܐ. f. *a*) *a handle by*

which a vessel is suspended. *b*) eccles. *a prayer said with uplifted voice* opp. ܡܫܠܝܢܐ *a secret prayer.*

ܬܠܝܬܐܝܬ from ܬܠܝܬܐ. adv. *thrice, triply, threefold; thirdly; triunely;* ܬ̄ ܩܕܝܫܐ *the Ter Sanctus.*

ܬܠܝܬܝܐ, ܬܠܝܬܬܐ constr. st. m. ܬܠܝܬܝ, f. ܬܠܝܬܝܬ from ܬܠܬ. *a*) *third, threefold, triple, treble, tertian.* *b*) *triune, trine;* ܬܠܝܬܝ̈ܐ *the Three Persons* of the Holy Trinity; ܐܠܗܐ ܬܠܝܬܝ *the triune God;* ܬܠܝܬܝܬ ܩܢܘܡܐ ܐܠܗܘܬܐ ... *the chant Holy, Holy, Holy.* *c*) *third, the third in command; the third day.* *d*) perh. *eating only once in three days.* *e*) *a go-between, mediator.* *f*) the sixtieth part of a second. *g*) in compos. ܬܠܝܬܝ ܐܠܗ̈ܐ *tritheists;* ܬܠܝܬܝ ܐܬ̈ܘܬܐ *triliteral;* ܬ̄ ܙܘܝܬܐ *triangular;* ... *trisyllabic;* ܬܠܝܬܝ̈ ܙܘܘܓܐ *those who marry three times;* ܬ̄ ܛܘܒܐ *thrice-blessed;* ܬ̄ ܡܫ̈ܟܢܐ *three-storied;* ܬ̄ ܦܠܓܐ *tripartite;* ܬ̄ ܡܫܘܚܬܐ *one in the third division of life* = ܥܠܝܡܐ *a youth.*

ܬܠܝܬܝܘܬܐ, ܬܠܝܬܝܘܬ pl. ̈ܬܐ from ܬܠܬ. f. *a triad; the Trinity.* In comp. ܬܠܝܬܝܘܬ ܐܠܗܘܬܐ *tritheism;* ܬ̄ ܙܘܝ̈ܬܐ *a triangle;* ܬ̄ ܙܘܘܓܐ *a third marriage;* ܬ̄ ܝܘ̈ܡܬܐ *a space of three days;* ܒܬܠܝܬܝܘܬ ܡܚ̈ܘܬܐ *with triple blows.*

ܬܠܝܬܝܘܬ from ܬܠܬ. adv. *for the third time.*

ܬܠܠܐ and ܬܠܐ *a hill;* see ܬܠ.

ܬܠܡܐ pl. ̈ܐ dial. m. *an earthen vessel, pitcher.*

ܬܠܡܕ Taphel conj. of ܠܡܕ. *to make disciples, teach the Faith, give instruction.*

ܬܠܡܝܕܐ, ܬܠܡܝܕܬܐ, ܬܠܡܝܕܬܐ rt. ܠܡܕ. *a disciple, follower, servant of a prophet.*

ܬܠܡܝܕܘܬܐ rt. ܠܡܕ. f. *a*) *teaching, education.* *b*) *discipleship, pupillage, novitiate.* *c*) *the company of the disciples.*

ܬܠܡܝܬܐ dimin. of ܬܠܡܐ. f. *a little pitcher, jug.*

ܬܠܥܒ Pael ܬܠܥܒ *to deride, scoff.* Derivatives, ܬܘܠܥܒܐ, ܡܬܠܥܒܢܐ.

ܬܠܥܘܠܬܐ f. *a*) *the scab, mange.* *b*) *birds' dung.*

ܬܠܫ fut. ܢܬܠܘܫ and ܢܬܠܫ, act. part. ܬܠܫ *to tear up, pluck up;* ܬܠܫܗ ܡܢ ܥܩܪ̈ܘܗܝ *he tore it up by the roots.* Ethpe. ܐܬܬܠܫ *to be plucked* or *torn up.*

ܬܠܬ denom. verb Pael conj. from ܬܠܬ. *a*) *to divide by three, to multiply by three, to triple;* ܥܒܕ ܥܘܬܪܗ ܘܬܠܬ *he doubled and tripled his riches.* *b*) *to do a third time, repeat thrice;* ܬܢܐ ܘܬܠܬ *he did it again and again.* Pass. part. ܡܬܠܬܐ *triangular, triliteral.* Ethpa. ܐܬܬܠܬ *a*) *to be thrice repeated.* *b*) *to become triune, be made a trinity.*

ܬܠܬ f., ܬܠܬܐ m. *three;* ellipt. for ܬܠܬ ܙܒ̈ܢܝܢ *thrice;* ܬܠܬ ܙܒ̈ܢܝܢ ܒܝܘܡܐ *thrice daily;* ܬܠܬܐ ܬܠܬܐ *three each;* ܚܕ ܬܠܬܐ ܥܠ *three times more;* ܚܕܐ ܠܬܠܬܐ ܝܘ̈ܡܝܢ *once in three days;* ܬܠܬܐ ܒܫܒܐ *Tuesday, market-day;* ܬܠܬ ܛܪ̈ܦܐ *artemisia arborescens, southern-wood;* ܒܬܠܬ ܫܥ̈ܝܢ *at three o'clock.* In gen. with ܕ, *the third;* ܝܘܡܐ ܕܬܠܬܐ *on the third day; threefold;* ܕܬܠܬ ܦܐܬ̈ܐ *triangular.* Pl. ܬܠܬܝܢ *thirty;* ܬ̄ ܕܟܣܦܐ *thirty pieces of silver;* ܒܬ̄ or ܕܬ̄ *thirtyfold.* Derivatives, ܬܘܠܬܐ, ܬܘܠܬܐ, ܬܠܝܬܝܐ, ܬܠܝܬܐ, ܬܠܝܬܝܘܬ, ܬܠܝܬܝܘܬܐ, verb ܬܠܬ, ܡܬܠܬܐ.

ܬܠܬܐ = ܬܠܝܬܝܘܬܐ.

ܬܠܬܡܐܐ and ܬܠܬ ܡܐܘ̈ܢ *three hundred.*

ܬܠܬܥܣܪ m. ܬܠܬܥܣܪܐ f. *thirteen.*

ܬܡ part. adj. ܬܡܝܡ, ܬܡܝܡܐ, ܬܐ *innocent, perfect, harmless, guileless* as ܐܡܪܐ *a lamb,* ܝܘܢܐ *a dove;* ܡܛܥܝܢ ܠܬܡܝ̈ܡܐ *deceiving the guileless.* Pael ܬܡܡ *to make entire, to perfect;* ܡܬܡܡ ܐܢܬ ܐܘܪ̈ܚܬܟ *Thou makest Thy ways perfect.* Ethpa. ܐܬܬܡܡ *to become innocent.* Derivatives, ܬܡܝܡܐܝܬ, ܬܡܝܡܘܬܐ.

ܬܡܐ rare form of ܬܐܡܐ.

ܬܡܗ fut. ܢܬܡܗ, parts. ܬܡܗ and ܬܡܝܗ; part. adj. ܬܡܝܗ, ܐ, ܬܐ. *a*) *to be numb, torpid, rigid; dumb, speechless;* ܬܡܗܘ ܒܒ̈ܬܐ *the pupils were rigid;* ܩܝܡܝܢ ܗܘܘ ܬܡܝܗܝܢ *they stood speechless.* *b*) *to stare, to be struck dumb, stupefied, amazed,* with ܒ, ܥܠ, ܩܕܡ, ܕ and absol. ܥܕܡܐ ܕܟܠܗܘܢ ܢܛܘܪ̈ܐ ܬܡܗܘ ܒܢܘܗܪܗ *till all the guards were stupefied at his light;* ܥܝܢܐ ܕܡܚܫܒܬܐ ܟܕ ܩܪܒܐ ܠܗ ܬܡܗܐ ܘܡܬܕܡܪܐ *the eye of thought, approaching it, is amazed and dazed.* *c*) *to regard with awe, to reverence;* ܘܵܠܹܐ ܕܢܬܡܗ ܒܚܟܡܬܗ *we ought to reverence his wisdom.* Part. adj. *stupendous, amazing;* ܢܒܝܐ ܕܬܡܝܗܐ ܚܙܘܢܐ *prophet of wondrous visions;* ܐܬܘܬܐ ܬܡܝܗܬܐ *stupendous signs.* Ethpe. ܐܬܬܡܗ *to be admired.* Ethpa. ܐܬܬܡܗ *to be stupefied, amazed* with ܒ or ܥܠ. Aph. ܐܬܡܗ *a) to stop the growth* of a plant. *b) to stupefy, make amazed;* ܡܬܡܗܝܢ ܠܫܡܘܥܐ *amazing those who hear. c) to do wondrously.* Derivatives, ܬܗܡܐ, ܬܡܗܐ, ܬܡܝܗܐܝܬ, ܬܡܝܗܘܬܐ, ܬܡܗܘܬܐ, ܡܬܡܗܢܘܬܐ, ܡܬܡܗܢܐ, ܡܬܡܗܢܐܝܬ.

ܬܗܡܐ pl. ܝ̈ܢ rt. ܬܡܗ. m. *torpor, insensibility, stupor; amazement, reverence; a prodigy.*

ܬܗܡܢܝܐ, ܢܝܬܐ rt. ܬܡܗ. gram. *expressing admiration* as ܐܘ *Oh!*

ܬܡܘܙ *Thammuz,* the tenth Syrian month, answering to July.

ܬܡܘܙܝܐ, ܝܬܐ from ܬܡܘܙ. *in* or *of the month of July.*

ܬܡܝܢ = ܬܡܢ.

ܬܡܚ only in BB. *rice.*

ܬܡܚܝ from ܡܚܐ. *to weigh, measure.* Derivatives, ܬܘܡܚܐ, ܬܡܚܝܐ.

ܬܡܚܝܬܐ rt. ܡܚܐ. f. *destruction.*

ܬܡܝܗ and ܬܡܝܗ, ܗܐ, ܗܬܐ; see Peal of ܬܡܗ.

ܬܡܝܗܐܝܬ rt. ܬܡܗ. adv. *admirably.*

ܬܡܝܗܘܬܐ rt. ܬܡܗ. f. *a hard swelling on the eyelids.*

ܬܡܝܗܘܬܐ rt. ܬܡܗ. f. *stupefaction, amazement, admiration;* ܬܡܝܗܘܬ ܬܘܩܢܐ ܕܫܡܝܐ *the awe-inspiring structure of the heavens.*

ܬܡܝܡ; see verb ܬܡ.

ܬܡܝܡܐܝܬ rt. ܬܡ. adv. *innocently, simply, unwittingly, not aiming at any special object, not addressing any one in particular.*

ܬܡܝܡܘܬܐ rt. ܬܡ. f. *guilelessness, harmlessness, simplicity, innocence, integrity, perfectness.*

ܬܡܝܢܐܝܬ from ܬܡܢܐ. adv. *eight times as much.*

ܬܡܝܢܝܐ, ܢܝܬܐ from ܬܡܢܐ. *eighth;* ܒܬܡܝܢܝܐ *on the eighth day;* ܬܡܝܢܝ ܙܘܝܬܐ *octangular.*

ܬܡܝܢܝܘܬܐ from ܬܡܢܐ. f. *the number eight, being* or *consisting of eight.*

ܬܡܪܝܐ *meat cooked with dates.*

ܬܡܠ adv. of time, oftener ܐܬܡܠܝ *yesterday;* ܐܝܟ ܕܐܬܡܠܝ ܘܩܕܡ *recently, formerly;* ܐܝܟ ܕܐܬܡܠܝ ܘܕܡܢ ܬܡܠܝ *as beforetime, as heretofore.*

ܬܡܡ Pael conj. of ܬܡ.

ܬܡܢ denom. verb Pael conj. from ܬܡܢܐ. *to divide into eight parts.*

ܬܡܢ, rarely ܬܡܢܝ adv. of place. *there, yonder;* ܡܢ ܬܡܢ *thence, whence;* ܠܬܡܢ *thither;* ܕܬܡܢ *of that place;* ܫܢܐ ܠܗ ܡܢ ܬܡܢ *he departed thence; Heaven, the life beyond* opp. ܗܪܟܐ *here below.*

ܬܡܢܐ f. ܬܡܢܝܐ m. rarely ܬܡܢܝܐ f., ܬܡܢܝܐ m. *eight;* ܒܬܡܢܝܐ *on the eighth day;* ܬܡܢܐ ܩܠܝܢ *Octoechus* i.e. a book in which hymns are arranged according to the eight tones. Pl. ܬܡܢܝܢ and ܬܡܢܐܝܢ *eighty.* Derivatives, ܬܘܡܢܐ, ܬܡܢܝܐ, ܬܡܝܢܝܐ, ܬܡܝܢܝܘܬܐ, verb ܬܡܢ.

ܬܡܢܘܣ; see ܐܬܡܢܘܣ.

ܬܡܢܝܐ from ܬܡܢ. *of that place, yonder;* ܚܝܐ ܬܡܢܝܐ *the life beyond.*

ܬܡܢܡܐܐ or ܬܡܢܐ ܡܐܐ *eight hundred.*

ܬܡܢܥܣܪ or ܬܡܢܬܥܣܪ m., ܬܡܢܥܣܪܐ f. *eighteen.*

ܬܡܣܝܘܬܐ rt. ܡܣܐ. f. *putrefaction, decay, rottenness, stink, pus, matter.* Metaph. *corruption.*

ܬܡܣܚ Arab. *the crocodile.*

ܬܡܪ denom. verb from ܬܡܪܐ. Aph. ܐܬܡܪ only Lexx. *to blink, wink.*

ܬܡܪ ܗܢܕܝ pl. ܬܡܪܐ ܗܢܕܝܐ f. *the tamarind.*

ܬܡܪܐ pl. ܐ̈ m. *eyelid, eyelash;* ܬ or ܬ ܡܚܝܕܐ *the twinkling of an eye, a moment.* Derivative, verb ܐܬܡܪ.

ܬܡܪܬܐ pl. ܬܡܪ̈ܐ f. *the date-palm, the date.*

ܬܡܬܡ *to mutter, murmur, to speak through the nose.* Derivatives, ܬܡܬܡܢܐ, ܡܬܡܬܡܢܐ.

ܬܡܬܡܢܐ pl. ܢܐ from ܬܡܬܡ. m. *a mutterer, magician; one who speaks through his nose.*

ܬܢ fut. ܢܬܢ, part. ܬܐܢ, ܬܢܐ. *a) to be numb, rigid, to stiffen;* ܬܐܢ ܟܠܗ ܦܓܪܗ *his whole body becomes rigid. b) to smoke;* ܐܬܘܢܐ ܕܬܐܢ *a smoking furnace.* Ethpe. ܐܬܬܢ *to smoulder, be reduced to smoke, to emit smoke;* ܬܢܢܐ

ܕܡܬܬܢܢܐ ܟܬܢܐ *smoking flax.* Pa. ܬܢܢ pass. part. ܡܬܢܢ, ܡܬܢܢܐ *smoked, driven out by smoke* as bees. Ethpa. ܐܬܬܢܢ *to be stupefied, to be smoked out* as bees, *to be mixed with smoke.* Aph. ܐܬܢ *to cause smoke, fumigate, burn for fumigation;* ܡܐ ܕܡܬܢܢ ܐܢܬ ܩܘܠܩܘܢܬܐ ܥܩܒܪܐ ܥܪܩܝܢ *when you burn* colocynth, mice *rush away.* Derivatives, ܬܢܢܐ, ܬܢܢܐ, ܬܢܢܐ, ܬܢܢܐ, ܬܢܢܐ, ܬܢܢܘܬܐ, ܡܬܢܢܐ, ܡܬܢܢ.

ܬܢܐ fut. ܢܬܢܐ, imper. ܬܢܝ, act. part. ܬܢܐ, ܬܢܝܐ, pass. part. ܬܢܐ, ܬܢܝܐ. i. *a) to repeat, do again;* ܬܢܐ ܘܬܠܬ *he struck again and yet again;* ܐܟܪܐ ܕܟܪܒ ܘܬܢܐ *a ploughman who ploughs twice;* ܠܐ ܐܝܬ ܕܬܢܐ ܠܗ *no one is like him. b) to repeat, recite, intone, learn, recapitulate;* ܬܢܐ ܡܢ ܠܒܗ *he repeats by heart;* ܬܢܝܢ ܡܢ ܣܦܪܐ *they learn from books;* ܬܢܐ ܣܝܡܝ ܐܝܕܐ *he intones the Ordination Service;* ܬܢܐ ܒܦܣܝܩܬܐ ܐܢܐ *I recapitulate briefly. c) to tell, narrate; to rehearse, to recriminate; to divide;* ܐܘܣܦ ܬܢܐ *he told them further;* ܠܐ ܬܬܢܐ ܥܡܝ *do not bandy words with me.* ii. denom. verb from ܬܢܘܝܐ *to make a compact, agree.* Ethpe. ܐܬܬܢܝ and Ethpa. ܐܬܬܢܝ *a) to be repeated, doubled; to recur. b) to be repeated, rehearsed, related, narrated, told;* ܡܡܠܐ ܗܢܐ ܕܐܬܬܢܝ *this conversation which has been repeated.* Pa. ܬܢܝ *a) to narrate, rehearse, report, recount, extol, tell, say;* ܬܢܝ ܠܘܬ ܐܚܐ ܥܠ ܐܘܪܚܗ *he told the brethren about his journey;* ܡܢܘ ܡܫܟܚ ܠܡܬܢܝܘ ܓܙܝܟ *who can worthily recount Thy treasures? b)* with ܥܡ, ܠܘܬ, ܥܡ *to talk, converse.* Derivatives, ܬܢܝܐ, ܬܢܝܐ, ܬܢܝܐ, ܬܢܝܢܐ, ܬܢܝܢܐ subst., ܬܢܝܢܐ adj., ܬܢܝܢܘܬܐ, ܬܢܝܢ &c., ܡܬܢܝܢܐ, ܡܬܢܝܢܝܬ, ܡܬܢܝܢܐ.

ܬܢܝܐ = ܬܢܢܐ pl. of ܬܢܢܬܐ.

ܬܢܒ fut. ܢܬܢܒ. *to become stiff, rigid.* Pa. ܬܢܒ and Aph. ܐܬܢܒ *to benumb, deaden.* Parts. ܡܬܢܒ and ܡܬܢܒ *narcotic.* Derivatives, ܬܢܘܒܐ, ܬܢܒܐ, ܬܢܘܒܘܬܐ, ܬܢܒܬܐ.

ܬܢܒܪܬܐ = ܬܢܘܒܪܬܐ.

ܬܢܒܝܠ *soot* on a spit or shovel.

ܬܢܝܒ, ܬܢܝܒܐ, ܬܢܝܒܬܐ E-Syr. ܬܢܒ rt. ܬܢܒ. *torpid, benumbed with cold.*

ܬܢܘܒܘܬܐ rt. ܬܢܒ. f. *numbness, torpidity;* ܬܢܘܒܘܬ ܥܝܢܐ *glassy eyes.*

ܬܢܘܒܬܐ rt. ܬܢܒ. f. *a)* = ܬܢܘܒܘܬܐ. *b)* see ܬܢܘܝ.

ܬܢܘܝ, E-Syr. ܬܢܘܝ f. no pl. *a) an agreement, contract, covenant, marriage settlement;* ܬ̈ ܕܡܙܒܢܢܘܬܐ *contract of sale with warranty;* ܬ̈ ܕܙܒܢܐ *sale without warranty.* With verbs: ܥܒܕ *to make,* ܣܡ *to settle,* ܥܒܪ *to infringe a contract. b) a condition;* ܒܬܢܘܝ ܕ or ܥܠ ܬܢܘܝ *on condition, on the pretext.* Gram. ܕܬ̈ *conditional. c) a term, stated time, truce. d) a watchword, signal.*

ܬܢܘܝ denom. verb Pali conj. from ܬܢܘܝ. *to make a contract, settle terms, agree, stipulate;* ܚܐܪܘܬܐ ܡܬܢܘܝܬܐ *stipulated manumission.* Ethpali ܐܬܬܢܘܝ *to be agreed upon, stipulated, covenanted.*

ܬܢܘܡ, ܬܢܘܡܐ *Cannabis sativa, hemp.*

ܬܢܘܪܐ *a) furnace, oven, baking-pit. b) a lamp, bowl* of a candlestick. *c) the pectoral cavity. d) breastplate, cuirass.*

ܬܢܘܪܝܬ from ܬܢܘܪܐ *d.* adv. *doubled.*

ܬܢܚܬܐ and ܬܢܚ usually pl. ܬܢܚܬܐ rt. ܐܢܚ. f. *a groan, sigh.*

ܬܢܝ Pael conj. of ܬܢܐ.

ܬܢܝ imper. of verb ܬܢܐ.

ܬܢܝܐ rt. ܬܢܐ. m. *a) repetition;* ܬ̈ ܕܩܪܝܢܐ *recital, reading;* ܕܬܢܝܢ or ܕ *a second time, again. b) narration, a narrative.*

ܬܢܝܐ rt. ܬܢܐ. m. *learning by heart, repetition.*

ܬܢܝܢܐ rt. ܬܢܐ. *a)* log. *double, consisting of two propositions. b)* gram. *expressing exception* as particles.

ܬܢܝܢ, ܬܢܝܢܐ pl. ܬ̈ rt. ܬܢܐ. m. *iteration, repetition, recitation; a tale, tale-bearing;* ܬ̈ ܕܫܡܗܐ *a list of names;* ܬܢܝܢ ܢܡܘܣܐ *Deuteronomy.*

ܬܢܝܢܐ pl. ܬ̈ m. *a dragon;* met. *the devil.* Astron. the constellation *Draco;* a sign of the Zodiac. Alchem. *a slender perforated bronze vessel to hold dried herbs, spice-box;* ܕܡ ܬ̈ *dragon's blood,* a drug; ܡܪܪܬܐ ܕܬ̈ *dragon's gall,* a name for quicksilver.

ܬܢܝܢܐ, ܬܢܝܢܬܐ rt. ܬܢܐ. *a) second, double; again, a second time;* ܬܢܝܢ ܡܠܐ *ambiguous. b) two years old, a two-year-old. c) a mate, cell-mate; second in authority, representative; sub-prior;* ܬ̈ ܕܡܠܟܐ *viceroy.*

ܬܢܝܢܐܝܬ, ܬܢܝܢܘܬܐ rt. ܬܢܐ. f. *second rank* or *course, second place, second year of age.* Constr. st. adv. *for the second time, again, anew; twice.* Gram. ܬܢܝܢܘܬ ܡܫܬܥܝܢܘܬܐ *exception.*

ܬܢܝ Pael conj. of verb ܬܢܐ.

ܬܢܢ adv. of place *here, in this place;* ܕܬܢܢ *of this place,* also *the things of this life* opp. ܕܠܗܠ and ܕܥܬܝܕܝܢ *the things to come;* ܚܝܐ ܕܬܢܢ *this present life.*

ܬܢܢܐ rt. ܬܢܢ. m. *a) smoke, steam, reek, fumes. b)* a stone used for polishing glass.

ܬܢܢܐܝܬ from ܬܢܢ. adv. *in this world.*

ܬܢܢܝܐ from ܬܢܢ. *of this life, present.*

ܬܢܢܢܐ, ܬ̈ rt. ܬܢܢ. *smoky, vaporous.*

ܬܢܢܢܘܬܐ rt. ܬܢܢ. f. *smokiness, reek, fumes.*

ܬܦܦܠܬܐ, ܬܦܦܠܐ or ܬܝܦܠ f. pl. a kind of plum.

ܬܢܩܪ or ܬܢܩܐܪ Pers. *gold soldering, borax.*

ܬܣܠܘܢܝܩܐ, ܬܣܠܘܢܝܩܐ, ܬܣܠܘܢܝܩ, ܬܣܠ pr. n. *Thessalonica.*

ܬܣܠܘܢܝܩܝܐ and ܬܣܠ pl. ̈ *Thessalonian.*

ܬܘܣܠܘܣܐ Lexx. *a sample, pattern.*

ܬܣܠܘܬܐ rt. ܣܠܐ. f. *refuse, abomination.*

ܬܣܡܐ pl. ܬܣܡܐ Pers. f. *a strap.*

ܬܣܦܘܬܐ BB. f. *filth.*

ܬܣܩܐ BA. f. *a commission, contract.*

ܬܥܕܝܠ Arab. *proportionate taxation* opp. poll-tax.

ܬܥܕܪܐ pl. ̈ rt. ܥܕܪ. m. *help, assistance, aid, service rendered;* milit. *an adjutant.*

ܬܥܒܘܢܐ pl. ̈ rt. ܬܥܒ. m. *a toiler.*

ܬܥܝܒܐܝܬ rt. ܬܥܒ. adv. *assiduously.*

ܬܥܝܒܘܬܐ rt. ܬܥܒ. f. *weariness, lassitude, distressfulness.*

ܬܥܠ denom. verb Pael conj. from ܬܥܠܐ. *to fawn, wag the tail.*

ܬܥܠ, ܬܥܠܐ pl. ܬܥܠܝܢ, ̈ m. ܬܥܠܬܐ pl. ܬ̈ f. *a fox;* ܬܥܠܐ ܕܠܠܝܐ *night foxes;* ܥܢܒܐ ܬ̈ *solanum nigrum.*

ܬܥܠܘܬܐ from ܬܥܠܐ. f. *a)* a disease like mange in foxes. *b) slyness.*

ܬܥܠܝܐ, ܬ̈ from ܬܥܠܐ. *vulpine, fox-like, sly.*

ܬܥܪܬܐ rt. ܥܪܪ. f. *a) cold, cold fit. b) sweepings.*

ܬܥܒ fut. ܢܬܥܒ, act. part. ܬܥܒ, ܬܥܒܐ, part. adj. ܬܥܝܒ, ܬ̈, ܬ̈. *a) to toil, labour, be wearied, distressed;* ܬܥܒܝܢ ܒܩܪܒܐ *they are sore put to it in the war. b) to be troublesome, to annoy;* ܬܥܒ ܠܢ ܩܠܗܘܢ ܕܡܙܡܘܪܝܬܐ ܕܝܠܘܕܐ *it annoys us to hear schoolboys' songs.* Part. adj. *wearisome, toilsome, wearied out, distressing;* ܦܘܠܚܢܐ ܬܥܝܒܐ ܕܠܒܢܐ *the hard labour of brick-making;* ܥܠܡܐ ܬܥܝܒܐ *the weary world.* Derivatives, ܬܥܘܒܐ, ܬܥܝܒܐܝܬ, ܬܥܝܒܘܬܐ, ܬܥܒܐ.

ܬܥܘܒܐ pl. ̈ rt. ܬܥܒ. m. *toil, labour, exertion, effort; troublesomeness, annoyance;* ܡܠܝ ܬ̈ *laborious.*

ܬܦܐ or ܬܐܦܐ pl. ̈ (hard p) com. gen. *a stream* smaller than a river, usually ܕܡܝܐ ܬ̈; ܬܦ̈ܐ ܕܕܡܥܐ *streams of tears.* Derivatives, verbs ܬܦܐ and ܬܦܦ.

ܬܦܐ denom. verb Peal conj. from ܬܦܝܐ. pass. part. ܬܦܐ, ܬܦܝܐ. *to set on, put on* the pot; ܬܦܝ ܩܕܪܐ *set on the caldron.* Ethpe. ܐܬܬܦܝ *to be set on.*

ܬܦܝ denom. verb Pael conj. from ܬܦܐ. *to cause to flow, to pour.*

ܬܦܝܐ and ܬܦܝܐ pl. ̈, ܬ̈ rt. ܐܦܐ. f. *a bake-house, oven; a kettle, a three-legged caldron.*

ܬܦܠܐ pl. ̈, ܬ̈ (soft p) m. *a phylactery, a scroll, tablet.*

ܬܦܢܝܬܐ and ܬܦܢܝܬܐ pl. ̈ Pers. m. *a prototype, exemplar, idea, original; figure.*

ܬܦܢܝܬܝܐ and ܬܦܢܝܬܐ from ܬܦܢܝܬܐ. *primary, typical.*

ܬܦܢܘܩܐ pl. ̈ rt. ܦܢܩ. m. *good cheer, luxury.*

ܬܦܢܝܬܘܬܐ from ܬܦܢܝܬܐ. f. *the thing itself, reality.*

ܬܦܝ denom. verb Pael conj. from ܬܦܐ. *to cause to flow.* Ethpa. ܐܬܬܦܝ *to be poured.*

ܬܦܦ Pael ܬܦܦ *to knock, thump, tap;* ܐܢ ܚܙܝܢܢ ܐܚ̈ܐ ܕܢܥܣܝܢ ܢܬܦܦ ܐܢܘܢ *if we see any brethren slumbering let us nudge them.*

ܬܦܫܘܪܬܐ rt. ܦܫܪ. f. *urine.*

ܬܨܒܝܬܐ pl. ̈ rt. ܨܒܬ. f. *decoration, carved* or *decorative work; adornment, ornament, toilet necessaries, elegant dress.*

ܬܩܐ *a)* Arab. *necklace. b)* some kind of dress. *c)* ܬܩܐ = ܬܝܩܐ θήκη, *a case.*

ܬܘܩܐ pl. ̈ m. *a) a staff, sceptre, pastoral*

staff; ܐܚܝܕ ܬ̈ he *who bears rule.* *b*) in the Lexx. *a standard.*

ܬܩܘܠܐ pl. ܐ̈ rt. ܬܩܠ. m. *a weigher, balancer, banker; a balance.*

ܬܩܘܠܐ pl. ܐ̈ rt. ܬܩܠ. m. *a tax, impost.*

ܬܩܘܡ constr. st. of ܬܩܘܡܐ.

ܬܩܝܠܐܝܬ rt. ܬܩܠ. adv. *exactly, evenly balanced.*

ܬܩܠܘܬܐ rt. ܬܩܠ. f. *weighing.*

ܬܩܝܡܘܬܐ rt. ܬܩܡ. f. *stability, position.*

ܬܩܝܦܐܝܬ rt. ܬܩܦ. adv. *violently.*

ܬܩܝܦܘܬܐ rt. ܬܩܦ. f. *force, weight, intensity;* ܒܬ̈ *heavily.*

ܬܩܠ I. fut. ܢܬܩܘܠ, act. part. ܬܩܠ, ܬܩܠܐ, pass. part. ܬܩܝܠ, ܠ̈, ܠܐ̈. *a*) trans. *to weigh* ܒܡܣܐܬܐ *in the balance; to fathom, sound; to balance, counterpoise, compare.* *b*) *to weigh out, pay,* ܟܣܦܐ *silver,* ܫܘܚܕܐ *a bribe.* *c*) intrans. *to weigh, be equal to;* ܬܩܠ ܐܠܦ ܠܝܛܪܝܢ *it weighed a thousand pounds;* ܬܩܝܠ ܐܒܠܗ ܠܚܘܒܗ *his sorrow equals his love;* ܡܫܘܚܬܐ ܬܩܝܠܬܐ *even measure, metre.* Ethpe. ܐܬܬܩܠ and Ethpa. ܐܬܬܩܠ *to be weighed* in the balance. Pa. ܬܩܠ *to balance, compare, equalize;* ܬܩܠ ܡܘ̈ܒܠܐ *he made the loads equal.* Derivatives, ܬܩܘܠܐ, ܬܩܘܠܐ, ܬܩܝܠܐܝܬ, ܬܩܠܘܬܐ, ܬܩܠ, ܬܩܠܐ, ܬܩܠܘܬܐ, ܡܬܩܠܢܘܬܐ, ܡܬܩܠܐ, ܡܬܩܠܢܘܬܐ, ܡܬܩܠܢܐ.

ܬܩܠ II. Ethpe. ܐܬܬܩܠ and Ethpa. ܐܬܬܩܠ *to stumble;* ܒܟܐܦܐ *against a stone;* ܚܕ ܒܚܕ *one upon another; to be scandalized, to take exception.* Aph. ܐܬܩܠ *to cause to stumble, to let fall* into sin. Derivatives, ܬܘܩܠܬܐ, ܡܬܩܠܢܐ.

ܬܩܠ, E-Syr. ܬܩܠ rt. ܬܩܠ. *Tekel,* Dan. v. 27.

ܬܩܠܐ pl. ܐ̈ rt. ܬܩܠ. m. *a weight, weighing; a ponderous mass, bulk.*

ܬܩܠܬ, ܬܩܠܬܐ rt. ܬܩܠ. f. *a weight, measure of weight, weighed amount.*

ܬܩܠܢ a name of mountain spikenard.

ܬܩܢ fut. ܢܬܩܢ, act. part. ܬܩܢ, ܬܩܢܐ, part. adj. ܬܩܝܢ, ܢ̈, ܢܐ̈. *a*) *to be in good order, established, settled* ܥܠ ܟܘܪܣܝܐ *on the throne;* ܒܡܠܟܘܬܐ ܥܠ *in the kingdom;* ܬܬܒܢܐ ܘܬܬܩܢ ܡܕܝܢܬܐ *the city shall be built and settled.* *b*) *to be stable, steady, erect;* ܬܩܢ ܘܝܬܒ *he sat up;* ܥܕܡܐ ܕܬܩܢ ܛܗܪܐ *till high noon* i.e. when the sun seems to stand still; but ܬܩܢ ܛܗܪܐ ܕܥܐܕܐ *the day of the feast was fixed.* *c*) *to be put right, to be restored, healed, to regain the use of* ܗܘܢܗ *his mind;* ܒܒ̈ܬܐ ܕܥܝ̈ܢܐ *the pupils of the eyes;* ܬܩܢ ܣܘܪܚܢܐ ܗܘ ܕܐܬܚܒܟ *that tangled business has been put to rights.* Part. adj. *set ready, prepared; firm, stout, sturdy, stanch; unsullied.* Pa. ܬܩܢ *a*) *to construct, frame, fashion, furnish.* Used esp. of the work of the Son, ܐܒܐ ܒܪܐ. ܒܪܐ ܬܩܢ. ܪܘܚܐ ܨܒܬ *the Father created, the Son formed, the Spirit adorned;* ܬܩܢܢ ܒܩܕܡܝܐ ܒܛܝܒܘܬܗ *He formed us first by His grace;* ܨܠܡܐ ܡܢ ܩܝܣܐ ܬܩܢ *he fashioned an image out of wood;* ܡܬܩܢܝܢ ܒܕܗܒܐ ܘܒܡܪ̈ܓܢܝܬܐ robes *wrought with gold and pearls;* ܢܦܫܐ ܡܬܩܢܬܐ *the soul prepared* for our Lord opp. His Eternal Godhead; ܠܐ ܡܬܩܢܐ *unwrought, in the rough, formless.* *b*) *to restore, repair, set to rights;* ܬܩܢ ܠܒܪܝܬܐ ܕܐܫܬܓܫܬ *He set disordered creation straight.* *c*) *to arrange, set right, get ready* as ܡܐܟܘܠܬܐ *food,* ܕܘܟܬܐ *a place;* ܕܢܬܩܢܘܢ ܙܘܕܐ ܕܡܪܕܝܬܗܘܢ *to get ready for their journey;* ܬܩܢ ܡܫܪܝܬܗ *he equipped his army.* Ethpa. ܐܬܬܩܢ *a*) *to be formed, framed, fashioned* as ܥܠܡ̈ܐ *the ages;* ܒܪܝܬܐ *the creation;* ܗܝܟܠܐ *the temple; to be constituted, instituted* as ܒܬ̈ܝ ܕܝܢܐ *law-courts.* *b*) *to be equipped, furnished.* *c*) *to be repaired, set to rights.* *d*) *to be made, prepared* ܡܢ ܩܡܚܐ *from flour; prepared* as drugs, *medicated.* Aph. ܐܬܩܢ *a*) *to set in order, construct, fix, adapt, fit;* ܠܡܬܩܢܘ ܘܠܡܩܡܘ ܡ̈ܝܠܐ *to make and set up milestones;* ܐܬܩܢ ܩܫܬܗ ܘܫܕܐ *he fitted his bow and shot;* ܡܬܩܢ ܟܠ *the Maker of all things;* ܡܪܝܐ ܢܬܩܢ ܣܘܥܪ̈ܢܝܟܘܢ *the Lord make your affairs prosperous.* *b*) *to furnish, fashion, fit up* often with ܒܢܐ, ܒܢܝ; ܒܢܐ ܥܕܬܐ ܘܐܬܩܢܗ ܒܟܠ ܕܝܐܝܢ ܠܗ *he built a church and provided it with suitable fittings;* ܓܢ̈ܐ ܐܬܩܢ *he laid out gardens;* ܡܬܩܢܝܢ ܒܐܘܡܢܘܬܐ ܕܚܟܡܬܐ *wrought with cunning workmanship.* *c*) *to make ready, prepare* a tent, a bedroom, supper; *to make up* medicines; ܥܢ̈ܐ ܡܬܩܢ̈ܢ *sheep ready dressed;* ܡܫܚܐ ܡܬܩܢܐ *prepared ointment.* *d*) *to correct, restore, make firm* or *whole;* ܒܪܝܟ ܕܐܬܩܢ ܚܙܘܐ *blessed be He who restored sight.* Derivatives, ܬܘܩܢܐ, ܬܩܝܢܐ, ܬܩܝܢܐܝܬ, ܬܩܝܢܘܬܐ, ܬܩܢܐ, ܡܬܩܢܐ, ܡܬܩܢܘܬܐ, ܡܬܩܢܢܐ, ܡܬܩܢܢܘܬܐ.

ܬܩܢ Aphel fut. 3 f. s. and 2 m. s. of verb ܩܢ *to nest.*

ܬܩܝܢ, ܬܩܝܢܐ, ܬܩܝܢܬܐ *a) firmly set, stable, steady, reliable, firm, steadfast, honest, trusty, good, thorough.* Fem. emph. pl. *excellent handiwork, right words* or *actions, honest* or *respectable women.* *b)* ܬܩܝܢܐ ܕܛܘܪܐ *a table-land.*

ܬܩܝܢܐܝܬ rt. ܬܩܢ. adv. *firmly, steadily, straightforwardly, thoroughly, honestly.*

ܬܩܝܦܐ pl. ܐ̈ *decrepit.*

ܬܩܝܦܘܬܐ f. *advanced age, decrepitude.*

ܬܩܢܘܬܐ rt. ܬܩܢ. f. *stability, steadfastness; integrity, honesty, probity; excellent fashioning.*

ܬܩܦ fut. ܢܬܩܘܦ, act. part. ܬܩܸܦ, ܬܩܦܐ, part. adj. ܬܩܝܦ, ܐ̈, ܬܐ. *to wax strong, prevail;* with ܪܘܓܙܐ *anger waxed strong;* ܥܡܐ ܣܓܝ ܘܬܩܦ ܒܡܨܪܝܢ *the nation increased and waxed strong in Egypt.* Part. adj. *a) strong, powerful, valiant;* ܬܩܝܦܗ ܕܝܥܩܘܒ *the Mighty One of Jacob.* *b) strong, fortified* as ܕܪܬܐ *a courtyard,* ܡܕܝܢܬܐ *a city.* *c) vast, ample, enormous;* ܬ ܕܗܒܐ *an enormous sum of money.* *d) heavy, grievous* as ܢܝܪܐ *a yoke;* ܡܚܘܬܐ *a plague; pungent* as ܚܠܐ *vinegar.* *e) severe, rigorous* as ܚܘܡܐ *heat,* ܩܘܪܐ *frost,* ܡܪܕܘܬܐ *discipline.* Pa. ܬܩܸܦ *to strengthen, repair, refresh,* ܬܩܦܗ ܠܕܝܪܗ *he repaired his monastery;* ܐܢܬ ܬܩܦܬܗ ܟܕ ܠܐܝܐ *Thou refreshedst it when it was weary.* Ethpa. ܐܬܬܩܦ *to wax lusty, increase in strength,* with ܥܠ *to prevail over.* Aph. ܐܬܩܦ *to increase, augment.* Derivatives, ܬܘܩܦܐ, ܬܩܝܦܐܝܬ, ܬܘܩܦܬܐ, ܡܬܩܦܢܐ.

ܬܩܘܦ 3 f. s. and 2 m. s. fut. of verb ܢܩܦ *to adhere.*

ܬܪ f. a bird inhabiting the river-bank, feeding on gnats and flies, and which, whether perching or flying, has the wings in constant movement, perhaps *a water-wagtail.*

ܬܪ prep. = ܠܘܬ *at, near, with; by, on account of.*

ܬܪܐ Pael ܬܪܝ and ܬܪܝ *to instruct, admonish, guide, discipline;* ܟܠ ܚܕ ܡܬܪܐ ܢܦܫܗ ܒܕܚܠܬܐ ܕܐܠܗܐ *each disciplines himself in the fear of God.* Ethpa. ܐܬܬܪܝ and ܐܬܬܪܝ *to be instructed, disciplined;* ܠܐ ܐܬܬܪܝ *he would not receive instruction.* Derivatives, ܬܪܝܐ or ܬܘܪܝܐ, ܬܘܪܝܬܐ, ܬܪܘܝܐ, ܡܬܪܝܢܐ, ܡܬܪܝܢܘܬܐ.

ܬܪܐ and ܬܪܝ fut. ܢܬܪܐ, pass. part. ܬܪܐ, ܬܪܝܐ. *a) to be damp, soaked; to grow in the water;* ܡܠܚܐ ܕܬܪܝܐ ܒܡܝ̈ܐ *lenticula stagnina, marsh-weed;* ܠܐ ܬܪܝܬ ܓܙܬܗ ܕܓܕܥܘܢ ܡܢ ܡܛܪܐ Gideon's fleece *did not become soaked by rain.* *b) to be dissolved, reduced to mud.* *c)* = ܬܪܥ *to burst, burst forth.* Ethpe. ܐܬܬܪܝ *to become soaked, steeped;* ܟܕ ܢܬܬܪܘܢ ܡܢ ܡܛܪܐ ܘܢܦܪܥܘܢ *when they become soaked with rain and sprout.* Aph. ܐܬܪܝ *to soak, steep, macerate* ܒܡܝ̈ܐ *in water,* ܒܚܠܐ *in vinegar,* ܒܡܫܚܐ *in oil;* ܝܪ̈ܩܐ ܡܬܪ̈ܝܐ *steeped pot-herbs.* Derivatives, ܬܪܝܐ, ܬܪܝܐ, ܬܪܘܝܐ, ܬܪܝܐ, ܡܬܪܝܢܐ, ܡܬܪܝܢܘܬܐ.

ܬܪܐ B A. *a flame.*

ܬܪܝܐ E-Syr., ܬܪܝܐ, ܬܪܝܐ W-Syr. pl. ܬܪ̈ܝܐ, ܬܪ̈ܐ and ܬܪܝܐ (rare) rt. ܬܪܐ. m. *a tutor, pedagogue, master, instructor, guide.*

ܬܪܒ, ܬܪܒܐ m. *fat, fat parts* of an animal offered in sacrifice, *the adipose membrane;* ܬ ܕܚܛܐ *the fat of wheat; the fleshy part of fruit, pulp.* Derivatives, verb ܬܪܒ, ܬܪܒܢܐ, ܬܪܒܢܐ.

ܬܪܒ denom. verb from ܬܪܒܐ. Ethpa. ܐܬܬܪܒ *a)* = Ethpalal ܐܬܬܪܒܒ *to be fattened, to grow fat.* *b)* in the Lexx. *to be drawn* or *dragged away.* Aph. ܐܬܪܒ *to become fat.*

ܬܪܒܝܬܐ rt. ܪܒܐ. f. *growth, increase, up-bringing, education;* ܬ ܒܪ *a foster-child, pupil.*

ܬܪܒܢܐ and ܬܪܒܢܢܐ from ܬܪܒܐ. *fat, fleshy; fatty, adipose.*

ܬܪܒܨܝܢܐ pl. ܐ̈ Pers. m. pl. *breeches.*

ܬܪܓܘܢܐ *sirens, sea-monsters.*

ܬܪܒܝܨܐ rt. ܪܒܨ. m. BB. *a fore-court, entry.*

ܬܪܓܡ perh. denom. verb from ܬܘܪܓܡܢ. *a) to act as interpreter, to interpret, translate.* *b) to hold forth, harangue, to preach, deliver a homily, a eulogy;* ܡܬܪܓܡ ܠܡܐܡܪܐ ܬܪܝܢܐ ܠܥܡܐ *he delivers the Second Homily to the congregation.* Ethpal. ܐܬܬܪܓܡ *to be interpreted, translated, expounded; to be the subject of a sermon;* ܡܠܬܐ ܕܡܠܝܠܘܬܢ ܠܐ ܡܬܬܪܓܡܐ *the Word not to be interpreted into our speech.*

ܬܪܓܡܢ, ܬܪܓܡܢܐ m. *an interpreter.* Derivatives, verb ܬܪܓܡ, ܬܘܪܓܡܐ, ܡܬܪܓܡܢܐ, ܡܬܪܓܡܢܘܬܐ.

ܬܘܪܒܘܣ θόρυβος, *a disturbance.*

ܬܪܘܦܪܝܢ τροπάριον, *troparion.*

ܬܪܘܕܐ pl. ܬܐ m. *a*) *a spoon, spoonful.* *b*) *a probe.* *c*) a measure, *one* ܬܪܘܕܐ (*small teaspoonful*) = *two* ܡܬܩܠܐ *mathqalas*, and *five* ܬ̈ = *one* ܡܩܒܣܬܐ *tablespoon.*

ܬܪܘܫܐ, ܬܪܘܫܬܐ *a mountain goat, capra Caucasiaca, the chamois* of Kurdistan.

ܬܪܘܢܘܣ, ܬܪܘܢܘܣ, ܬܪܢܘܣ, ܬܪܘܢܘܣ, ܬܪܘܢܘܣ pl. ܬܪܘܢܘܣ m. θρόνος, *a throne; the altar, the middle of the altar* where the chalice and paten stand; *the episcopal* or *patriarchal throne.*

ܬܪܘܢܝܣܡܐ θρονίσαι, *enthronization.*

ܬܪܘܥܐ, ܬܪܘܥܬܐ rt. ܬܪܥ. *a breaker, housebreaker.* Med. *clearing away obstructions, opening.*

ܬܪܘܨܐ rt. ܬܪܨ. m. *one who directs, corrects.*

ܬܪܘܨܐ rt. ܬܪܨ. *firm.*

ܬܪܙ Peal only parts. Act. ܬܐܪܙ *to fill over-full, to burst.* Pass. part. ܬܪܝܙ, ܬܪܝܙܐ *crammed, replete, distended, bursting.* Pa. ܬܪܙ *to rip* or *chip open;* ܐܕܘܢܝܣ ܕܬܪܙܗ ܚܙܝܪܐ ܒܪܐ *Adonis whom a wild boar ripped open;* ܦܪܘܓܐ ܬܪܙܗ ܠܒܝܥܬܐ the chick *grew and chipped open the egg.* Ethpe. ܐܬܬܪܙ *to be crammed, distended, riven open;* ܐܬܬܪܙܬ ܫܝܘܠ ܘܢܦܩܘ ܛܓܡܐ ܕܚܒܝܫܝܢ *Sheol was rent and the confined ranks issued forth.* Ettaphal ܐܬܬܬܪܙ *to be riven.* Pali ܬܪܙ *to transfix.* Derivatives, ܬܪܙܐ, ܬܪܝܙܘܬܐ, ܡܬܬܪܙܢܘܬܐ.

ܬܪܙܐ rt. ܬܪܙ. m. *repletion, surfeit;* ܐܬܡܠܝܬ ܬܪܙܗ *she gorged herself.*

ܬܪܫܐ = ܬܪܘܫܐ *a chamois.*

ܬܪܚܝܢܐ or ܬܪܚܝܢܐ Pers. *barley and wheaten meal prepared with sheep's milk.*

ܬܪܝ; see verb ܬܪܐ.

ܬܪܝܢ; see ܬܪܝܢ.

ܬܪܝܐ τρία, *three.*

ܬܪܝܐ rt. ܬܪܐ. (rare) = ܬܪܝܢܐ *juice.*

ܬܪܝܐ rt. ܬܪܐ. m. *steeping, maceration.*

ܬܪܝܬܐ rt. ܬܪܐ. m. pl. *loaves made from soaked wheat.*

ܬܪܝܙܘܬܐ rt. ܬܪܙ. f. *bursting asunder.*

ܬܪܝܢ emph. st. ܬܪܝܢܐ (rare), constr. st. ܬܪܝܢ, m. ܬܪܬܝܢ, f. rt. ܬܢܐ. *two; a couple, brace;* with suffixes ܬܪܝܢ, ܬܪܬܝܢ *we two;* ܬܪܝܗܘܢ, ܬܪܬܝܗܝܢ *they two, the two of them,* &c.; ܬܪܝܢ ܐܘ ܬܠܬܐ *two or three;* ܬܪܝܢ ܬܪܝܢ, ܬܪܬܝܢ ܬܪܬܝܢ *two each;* ܚܕ ܬܪܝܢ or ܚܕ ܒܬܪܝܢ *double;* ܬܪܬܝܢ ܙܒܢܝܢ or ellipt. *twice.* With ܕ, *second, another; secondly, for the second time;* ܬܪܝܢ ܒܫܒܐ or ellipt. *Monday.* In comp. ܬܪܝܢ ܐܝ̈ܕܝܐ *ambidexter;* ܬܪܝܢ ܐܝܬܘ̈ܬܐ *dualists, Manichaeans;* ܬ̈ ܟܝܢܐ *Diophysites.*

ܬܪܝܢܐ pl. ܬܐ rt. ܬܪܐ. m. *juice from steeped raisins, dates* or *figs.*

ܬܪܝܢܐ, ܬܪܝܢܬܐ from ܬܪܝܢ. *second; double, lined.* Masc. *second in command* or *rank, vicegerent, viceroy; sub-prior; the second Person* of the Holy Trinity. Fem. *the second letter* of a word; *a second,* the sixtieth part of a minute; *the after-birth.*

ܬܪܝܢܐܝܬ from ܬܪܝܢ. adv. *secondly, in the second place; twofold, doubly.*

ܬܪܝܢܘܬܐ from ܬܪܝܢ. f. *the second rank* or *order; the dual number, duality, double-dealing, duplicity;* ܬܪܝܢܘܬܐ ܕܐܝܬܘ̈ܬܐ *dualism, Manichaeanism;* ܬ̈ ܕܟܝܢܐ *Diophysitism;* ܬ̈ ܕܙܘܘܓܐ *remarriage.*

ܬܪܝܢܝܐ, ܬܪܝܢܝܬܐ from ܬܪܝܢ. *secondary, inferior; dual.* In compos. ܬܪܝܢܝ ܐܬܘ̈ܬܐ *biliteral;* ܬܪܝܢܝ ܦܣܘ̈ܩܐ *disyllabic;* ܬܪܝܢܝ ܙܘܘܓܐ *bigamists;* ܬ̈ ܕܝܢܪܐ *didrachma;* ܬܪܝܢܝ ܚܝ̈ܐ *amphibious;* met. *having divided aims in life;* ܬ̈ ܠܫܢܐ or ܬ̈ ܡܠܬܐ *double-tongued;* ܬ̈ ܦܘܡܐ *two-edged, having two openings;* ܬܪܝܢܝ or ܬ̈ ܢܦܫܐ *double-minded;* ܬ̈ ܩܠܦܐ *bivalves.*

ܬܪܝܥܘܬܐ rt. ܬܪܥ. f. *rupture;* ܬܪܝܥܘܬ ܕܡܐ *haemorrhage;* ܬ̈ ܕܕܡܥܐ *a burst of tears;* ܬ̈ ܡܠܬܐ *garrulousness.*

ܬܪܝܨܐܝܬ rt. ܬܪܨ. adv. *rightly, uprightly, straightforwardly; in a straight line, straight opposite; right way up.*

ܬܪܝܨܘ, ܬܪܝܨܘܬܐ rt. ܬܪܨ. f. *uprightness, rectitude, integrity, straightforwardness; the direct road; a carpenter's rule.* With ܕܒܪܐ *upright conduct;* ܬܪܝܨܘܬ ܡܪܕܝܬܐ *a direct course;* ܬ̈ ܢܫܡܬܐ *asthma;* ܬ̈ ܗܝܡܢܘܬܐ *orthodoxy.* With preps. ܒ *in a straight line; correctly; straightforwardly, sincerely;* ܕ *right, exact, true.*

ܬܪܝܩܐ, ܬܪܝܩܢ or ܛܪܝ θηριακή, *an antidote, medicine.*

ܬܪܙܐ or ܬܪܙ m. *a layer of straw under* or *over a stack of corn, thatch.*

ܬܪܡܘܣܢܐ BA. *indigent, poverty-stricken.*

ܬܪܡܘܣܝܐ from ܬܪܡܣ. *idle, incapable; an idler, good-for-nothing.*

ܬܪܡܘܣܘܬ, ܬܪܡܘܣܘܬܐ from ܬܪܡܣ. f. *idling, carelessness, incapacity.*

ܬܪܡܘܬܐ f. *a dimple.*

ܬܪܡܣ Ethpa. ܐܬܬܪܡܣ *to dawdle, idle.*

ܬܪܡܝܬܐ pl. ܬ̈ rt. ܪܡܐ. f. *a*) *a foundation. b*) ܬ̈ ܕܙܪܥܐ *the sowing of seed;* metaph. *conception.*

ܬܪܡܠܐ rt. ܪܡܠ. m. *a wallet, scrip; a bag, case.*

ܬܪܡܨܝܬܐ f. pl. *moles, beauty-spots, freckles.*

ܬܪܢܐ Lexx. *whey.*

ܬܪܢܓܘܠ, ܬܪܢܓܠܐ pl. ܐ̈ m. *a cock;* ܬܪܢܓܘܠܬܐ, ܬܪܢܓܠܬܐ pl. ܬ̈ f. *a hen, fowl;* ܬܪܢܓܘܠ ܛܘܪܐ *a hoopoe;* ܬ̈ ܗܢܕܘܝܬܐ *a turkey.*

ܬܪܢܝܢܐ = ܬܪܝܢܐ and ܬܪܢܐ.

ܬܪܣܝ probably Taphel conj. from rt. ܪܣܐ. *to nourish, support, rear; to supply* with ܒ; ܡܬܪܣܐ ܒܥܝܪܐ—ܩܢܝܢܐ *one who rears cattle, a herdsman;* ܬܘܪܐ ܡܬܪܣܝܐ *a fatted ox.* Ethpali ܐܬܬܪܣܝ *to be nourished, sustained, fed; to feed upon* with ܒ, ܡܢ; ܡܢ ܢܘܢܐ ܡܬܬܪܣܝܢ *they feed on fish.* Derivatives, ܬܘܪܣܝܐ, ܬܪܣܝܬܐ, ܬܪܣܝܘܬܐ, ܡܬܪܣܝܢܐ, ܡܬܬܪܣܝܢܐ.

ܬܪܣܝܬܐ pl. ܬ̈ from ܬܪܣܝ. f. *nourishment, sustenance, food, victuals, supplies.*

ܬܪܥ fut. ܢܬܪܘܥ, act. part. ܬܳܪܰܥ, ܬܳܪܥܳܐ, pass. part. ܬܪܝܥ, ܐ, ܬܐ. *a*) trans. *to force a passage, break through* with ܒ or ܠ; with ܣܝܓܐ *to break down a fence,* ܬܘܪܥܬܐ *to make a breach,* ܢܡܘܣܐ *to break a law, transgress. b*) *to rive* ܓܒܗ ܒܠܘܓܚܬܐ *his side with a lance;* with ܥܪܩܐ *to open a vein, bleed. c*) intrans. *to find a vent, burst forth* as ܕܡܥܐ *tears,* ܡܒܘܥܐ *springs;* ܬܪܥ ܥܠܥܠܐ *the tempest burst;* ܥܝܢܐ ܬܪܝܥܬܐ *streaming eyes;* ܡܛܪܐ ܬܪܝܥܐ *copious rain. d*) caus. *to let flow, cause to flow, give vent to;* ܕܡܥܐ *tears,* ܕܡܐ *blood;* ܬܪܘܥ ܡܝܐ ܘܐܫܩܐ ܓܢܬܐ *turn on water and water the garden.* Ethpa. ܐܬܬܪܥ *to be riven, rent, broken through, to have a breach made* in the walls, *be ruined; to be given vent to, to burst* or *break forth;* ܡܠܟܘܬܟ ܡܬܬܪܥܐ ܒܩܛܠܐ ܕܚܝܠܐ *thy kingdom is rent with terrible slaughter;* ܐܬܬܪܥܘ ܣܕܪܝܗܘܢ *their ranks were broken;* ܡܝܐ ܐܬܬܪܥܘ *waters burst forth.* Pael ܬܪܥ only parts., ܡܬܪܥ, ܡܬܪܥܐ, ܡܬܪܥܬܐ. Act. *to tear asunder, make a breach;* ܡܬܪܥܝܢ ܡܝܐ ܫܘܪܝܗ *the flood breaks down her walls.* Pass. *broken down, ruined.* Derivatives, ܬܘܪܥܐ, ܬܪܥܘܬܐ, ܬܪܥܐ, ܬܪܥܐ, ܬܪܥܐ, ܬܪܥܐ, ܬܪܥܘܢܐ, ܬܪܥܢܐ, ܡܬܬܪܥܢܐ.

ܬܪܥܐ constr. state ܬܪܥ pl. ܝ̈ܢ, ܐ̈ rt. ܬܪܥ. m. *a*) *a gate, door, entrance;* ܬܪܥܐ ܐ̈ܦܝ *double doors, folding-doors;* ܠܒܪ ܡܢ ܬܪܥܐ *out of doors;* ܡܢ ܠܓܘ ܬ̈ *indoors;* ܥܠ ܬ̈ *close to, very near. b*) ܬ̈ ܕܡܠܟܐ, ܬܪܥ ܡܠܟܘܬܐ and ellipt. *the court, palace. c*) *an opening, outlet, vent; a gateway, avenue, ingress; a mountain pass. d*) as in Arabic باب *a division* of a book, *chapter; a stanza* each verse of which begins or ends in a special letter.

ܬܪܥܐ m. ܬܪܥܬܐ f. rt. ܬܪܥ. *a porter, portress* (rare).

ܬܪܥܐ m. ܬܪܥܬܐ f. rt. ܬܪܥ. *a doorkeeper, porter, janitor.*

ܬܪܥܐ rt. ܬܪܥ. m. *a rent.*

ܬܪܥܘܙܐ pl. ܐ̈ m. *a small melon.*

ܬܪܥܘܢܐ dimin. from ܬܪܥܐ. m. *a little door, outlet.*

ܬܪܥܘܬܐ rt. ܪܥܐ. f. *reconciliation; a truce, peace; agreement, goodwill, benevolence;* legal *consent.*

ܬܪܥܝܐ pl. ܐ̈ rt. ܬܪܥ. m. *a janitor, doorkeeper.*

ܬܪܥܝܬܐ pl. ܬܪܥܝܢ, ܬ̈ rt. ܪܥܐ. f. *the mind, intelligence, sense; reflection; opinion, doctrine, belief; sense, meaning.*

ܬܪܥܝܬܢܝܐ from ܬܪܥܝܬܐ. *intellectual.*

ܬܪܥܣܪܘܬܐ f. *the number twelve.*

ܬܪܥܣܪ m. ܬܪܬܥܣܪܐ f. *twelve;* ܬܪܥܣܪܝܬܐ abstract noun, *the number twelve, a company of twelve,* usually = *the twelve Apostles.*

ܬܪܟܠܬܐ f. a plant used for washing, perh. *mallow*.

ܬܪܦ act. part. *to dip*. Derivative, ܬܪܘܦܐ.

ܬܪܨ fut. ܢܬܪܘܨ, act. part. ܬܳܪܶܨ, ܬܳܪܨܳܐ, part. adj. ܬܪܝܨ, ܐ̈, ܬܐ. *a) to direct, make straight* or *right; to steer a ship, aim* an arrow; ܬܪܘܨܘ ܫܒܝ̈ܠܐ *make the paths straight;* ܬܪܘܨ ܠܒܟ *set thy heart aright.* With ܚܙܘܐ *to direct the gaze.* Often with ܐܘܪܚܐ, ܡܪܕܝܬܐ or ellipt. with ܠ, ܠܘܬ, ܠܘܩܒܠ *to direct one's course, make straight for, go in the direction of;* ܬܪܨܘ ܠܐܦܝ ܕܝܪܐ *they went in the direction of the monastery.* *b) to erect, set up, sit up straight;* ܬܳܪܶܨ ܘܝܳܬܶܒ *he sits up.* *c) to set straight, correct.* Part. adj. *straight, direct;* ܣܘܪܛܐ ܬܪܝܨܐ *a straight line;* ܙܘܝܬܐ ܬܪܝܨܬܐ *a right angle.* Metaph. *upright, straightforward, right, honest;* ܬܪܝܨܝ ܠܒܐ *upright in heart;* ܒܥܠܟܝ ܬ *thy legitimate husband;* ܠܐ ܡܫܟܚܝܢ ܠܡܡܠܠܘ ܬܪܝܨܬܐ *they cannot speak the truth.* With ܫܘܒܚܐ or ellipt. *orthodox.* F. emph. pl. *honesty, uprightness.* Pa. ܬܰܪܶܨ *a) to do rightly, set right, direct;* with ܕܝܢܐ *to judge aright, give right judgement;* ܨܒܝܢ ܕܢܬܪܨܘܢ ܚܝ̈ܐ *desiring to lead right lives.* *b) to set upright, rebuild.* *c) to amend, reform* ܥܝܕ̈ܐ *manners,* ܠܥܠܡܐ *the age; to emend* ܨܚܚܐ *a codex,* ܛܥܘ̈ܬܐ *errors.* With ܡܠܐ or ܡܡܠܠܐ *to make* or *observe rules of grammar.* Ethpa. ܐܬܬܪܨ *a)* refl. *to stand erect, stand up.* *b)* pass. *to be directed, guided aright; to be straightforward;* ܢܨܒܬܐ ܪܟܝܟܬܐ ܒܦܫܝܩܘ ܡܬܬܪܨܐ *a young plant is easily trained right;* ܠܐ ܡܬܬܪܨ ܠܒܗܘܢ ܘܢܝܫܗܘܢ ܠܡܦܠܚ *their heart and aim will not be sincere.* *c) to be emended, corrected.* Aph. ܐܬܪܨ (rare), *to correct.* Derivatives, ܬܪܘܨܐ, ܬܪܘܨܘ, ܬܪܝܨܐ, ܬܪܝܨܘܬܐ, ܬܘܪܨܐ, ܡܬܪܨܢܐ.

ܬܪܨܐ = ܬܘܪܨܐ *direction.*

ܬܪܩܐ, ܬܪܩܐ or ܬܪܩܝܐ, also ܬܪܩ, ܬܪܟ, ܬܪܩ, ܬܪܩܝܣ (rare). pr. n. *Thrace.*

ܬܪܩܝܐ pl. ܐ̈ from ܬܪܩܐ. *a Thracian.*

ܬܪܪܐ BA. *tares.*

ܬܪܫܝܫ *a)* pr. n. *Tarshish.* *b) chrysolith.*

ܬܪܬܐ = ܬܪܬܝܐ.

ܬܪܬܝܢ *a)* and ܬܪܬܝ from ܬܪܝܢ. *second, for the second time.* *b)* = ܛܛܪܐ *Tatar.*

ܬܫܒܘܚܬܢܘܬܐ pl. ܬܐ̈ rt. ܫܒܚ. f. *pomp, splendour.*

ܬܫܒܘܚܬܐ pl. ܬܫܒܚܢ, ܬܫܒܚ̈ܬܐ rt. ܫܒܚ. f. *a) praise, honour, glory, magnificence; a hymn, chant, canticle;* ܬܫܒܚܬܐ ܬܫܒܚ̈ܬܐ *the Song of Songs;* ܡܐܢ̈ܝ ܬ̈ *musical instruments;* ܬ ܕܥܠܝܐ W-Syr. *the hymn* Gloria in Excelsis. *b)* = δόξα, *opinion;* ܬܪܝܨܘܬ ܬ *orthodoxy.*

ܬܫܒܝܐ and ܬܫܒܝܝܐ from ܬܫܒܐ *Thisbe.* *a Tishbite.*

ܬܫܕܪܬܐ rt. ܫܕܪ. f. *sending, a mission, embassy; a letter.*

ܬܫܘܝܬܐ and ܬܫܘܝ pl. ܬܫܘܝܢ, ܬܐ̈ rt. ܫܘܐ. f. *a) a rug, carpet, mattress, bedding, bed.* *b) the deck* of a ship.

ܬܫܝܥܝܐ, ܬܐ from ܬܫܥ. *ninth; the ninth day.*

ܬܫܪܝܢܘܬܐ from ܬܫܪܝܢ. f. *autumn.*

ܬܫܡܫܬܐ pl. ܬܫܡܫܢ, ܬܐ̈ rt. ܫܡܫ. f. *a) serving, service, attendance, ministration;* with verb of going *to go to do homage, to pay one's respects;* ܬ ܕܡܟܐ *a pilgrimage to Mecca.* *b) service, office, rite, worship;* ܬ ܕܐܪ̈ܙܐ or ܕܩܘܪܒܢܐ *administration of Holy Communion, the mass, liturgy;* ܬ ܕܠܠܝܐ *nocturns,* ܬ ܕܨܦܪܐ *matins,* ܬ ܕܪܡܫܐ *vespers;* ܬ ܕܥܠ ܥܢܝ̈ܕܐ *burial service.* *c) office, ministry, administration;* ܬ ܕܟܘܡܪܘܬܐ *the priestly ministry;* ܒܪ ܬ *a fellow servant, fellow worshipper, fellow minister, colleague;* ܬ ܕܦܛܪܝܪܟܘܬܐ *the Patriarchal office.*

ܬܫܡܫܬܢܝܐ rt. ܫܡܫ. *ministerial; an attendant.*

ܬܫܢܝܩܐ pl. ܐ̈ rt. ܫܢܩ. m. *torment, torture.*

ܬܫܢܩܐ pl. ܐ̈ rt. ܫܢܩ. m. *torment, torture, severe pain, anguish.*

ܬܫܥ f. ܬܫܥܐ m. *nine;* ܬܫܥܬܐ f. emph. *the ninth day* of the month; ܬܫܥܐ ܡܘܙܘܓܐ alchem. *lead.* Pl. ܬܫܥܝܢ *ninety.* Derivatives, verb ܬܫܥ, ܬܫܘܥܐ, ܬܫܝܥܝܐ, ܬܫܥܝܢܝܐ, ܬܫܥܣܪ, ܬܫܥܣܪܝܬܐ.

ܬܫܥ denom. verb Pael conj. from ܬܫܥ. *to multiply by nine.* Ethpa. ܐܬܬܫܥ *to be multiplied by nine.*

ܬܫܥܝ Taphel conj. of ܫܥܐ. *to tell, relate;* ܬܫܥܝ ܠܢ *tell us, rehearse to us.*

ܬܫܥܝܢܝܐ, ܬܐ from ܬܫܥ. *ninth.*

ܬܫܥܝܬܳܐ pl. ܬܫܥ̈ܝܳܬܐ or ܬܫܥܝܳܬܳܐ rt. ܫܥܐ. f. a) *relation, narration, account; story, history, biography;* ܬ ܟܡܝܪܬܐ *a sad story;* ܬ̈ ܕܩܕ̈ܝܫܐ *Lives of the Saints.* Gram. *the indicative mood.*

ܬܫܥܝܬܳܐܝܬ from ܬܫܥܝܬܐ. adv. *narratively;* gram. *in the indicative mood.*

ܬܫܥܝܬܳܢܳܝܳܐ from ܬܫܥܝܬܐ. adj. *narrative, historical.*

ܬܫܥܡܐܐ *nine hundred.*

ܬܫܥܣܪ and ܬܫܥܬܥܣܪ m. ܬܫܥܣܪܐ f. *nineteen.*

ܬܫܥܣܪܝܘܬܐ from ܬܫܥܣܪ. f. *a nineteenth part.*

ܬܫܥܝ denom. verb from ܬܫܥܝܬܐ. *to make up a story.*

ܬܫܦܘܟܐ rt. ܫܦܟ. m. *transfusion;* ܬ ܕܢܦ̈ܫܬܐ *transmigration of souls.*

ܬܫܦܘܟܝܐ from ܬܫܦܘܟܐ. m. one of a sect who believed in the transmigration of souls.

ܬܫܪܩ *the alphabet backward* i.e. from the last letter to the first.

ܬܫܘܪܝܬܐ in the Lexx. f. *wish, desire.*

ܬܫܪܝ or ܬܫܪܝܢ pl. ܬܫܪ̈ܝܬܐ f. the name of two months, ܩܕܡ or ܩܕܡܝ, ܬ ܩ *October;* ܬ ܒ ܐܚܪܝ or ܐܚܪܢ *latter Tishrin, November.* Pl. *the autumn months, autumn.* DERIVATIVES, ܬܫܪܝܘܬܐ, ܬܫܪܝܐ, ܬܫܪܝܢܐ.

ܬܫܪܝܐ, ܬ̈ܐ and ܬܫܪܢܝܐ, ܬ̈ܐ from ܬܫܪܝ. *autumnal.*

ܬܬܐ or ܬܐܬܐ f. *glue.*

ܬܬܐ = ܬܬܝܬܐ.

ܬܬܘܪܐ *a small awl, small tool.*

ܬܬܠ 3 f. and 2 m. fut. of verb ܝܗܒ *to give.*

ܬܬܪ 2 s. fut. Aphel of verb ܢܬܪ *to fall.*

ܬܬܪ̈ܝܐ m. pl. *Tatars.*

܀ ܒܥܘܕܪܢܐ ܕܝܫܘܥ ܡܪܢ ܫܠܡܬ ܟܬܒܬܐ ܗܕܐ ܕܡܦܫܩܢܘܬܐ ܕܡ̈ܠܐ
ܣܘܪ̈ܝܝܬܐ ܒܡܦܫܩܢܘܬܐ: ܡܕܝܢ ܢܬܒܥܘܢ ܠܗ ܦܘܪܥܢܐ ܘܛܘܒܐ
ܠܗܘܢ ܒܕܪܫܡܬܗ. ܠܗ ܫܘܒܚܐ ܘܥܠܝܢ ܪ̈ܚܡܘܗܝ،
ܐܡܝܢܐܝܬ ܘܠܥܠܡ ܥܠܡܝܢ ܐܡܝܢ ܀

ADDENDA

Page 4 ܐܪܙܦ add *to hammer*. Derivatives, ܐܪܙܦ, ܡܪܙܦܐ, ܡܪܙܦܘܬܐ.

5 ܐܘܒܠܐ rt. ܝܒܠ. f. *the pole* of a litter.

ܐܘܪܝ read Aph. conj. of rt. ܝܪܐ.

7 *b* ܐܘܩܦܬܐ or ܐܘܩܘܦܬܐ f. *a net, head-dress.*

12 *b* ܐܝܒܐ *a flood* of water.

13 *b* ܐܝܠܠܬܐ commoner than ܝܠܠܬܐ rt. ܝܠܠ. f. *wailing; a shout, cry.*

17 *b* ܐܠܘܐ m. *the aloe.*

ܐܠܘܐ or ܐܠܒܐ m. *first milk after calving.*

19 ܐܡܘܡܐ add *a bit.*

24 *b* ܐܣܦܬܐ f. *an oven-rake; a branch; the spathe* of a palm.

ܐܣܩܐ rt. ܣܠܩ. m. *distillation, sublimation.* Gram. the point above ܘ̇.

ܐܣܩܦܬܐ pl. ܬ̈ܐ f. σκάφος, *a mattock.*

25 ܐܣܪܐ add astron. *a node, intersection* of the ecliptic.

26 ܐܦܝܐ m. ܐܦܝܬܐ f. rt. ܐܦܐ. *a baker.*

26 *b* ܐܦܛܪܘܦܘܬܐ rt. ܦܛܪ. f. *government, authority.*

ܐܦܪܣܐ; see ܦܪܘܣ. m. *a plan, plot, artifice;* with ܥܒܕ or ܣܡ *to plot;* ܝܬܒ ܒܗ *to sit in council.*

27 ܐܩܠܐ m. *the handle* of a bucket.

ܐܩܦܬܐ pl. ܬ̈ܐ rt. ܢܩܦ. f. *a sequence.*

29 *b* ܐܪܝܒܘܩܘܢ for Lat. read Greek.

ܐܪܢܝܬܐ *vitex agnus castus.*

31 ܐܫܦܫ = ܫܦܫ.

31 *b* ܐܫܚܩܢܝܬܐ or ܐܫܚܩܢܝܬܐ rt. ܫܚܩ. m. *a game; public games, plays, shows.*

ܐܫܚܩܢܝܬܐ rt. ܫܚܩ. *pertaining to games, belonging to one faction of the circus.*

37 ܒܘܕܪܐ or ܦܘܕܪܐ pl. ܐ̈ m. *a vulture.*

Page 37 *b* ܒܘܬܐ Arab. m. *a crucible.*

55 ܒܪܐ for Ethpa. read Ethpe.

66 *b* ܓܠܘܬܐ f. *the inner rind of an acorn.*

68 ܓܢܚ Aph. for *cease* read *cause.*

70 ܓܒܘܬ or ܓܒܘܬ *sea-foam.*

79 *b* ܓܫܘܪܐ pl. ܐ̈ from ܓܫܪ. m. *the bridging joist* of a roof.

85 for ܕܘܟܠܐ correct ܕܘܟܠܐ.

88 ܕܘܪܟܬܐ add *treading out* wheat.

ܕܘܪܟܐ m. *a*) from ܕܪܟ. *stretching out the arms.* *b*) Arab. *a coarse upper garment.*

91 ܕܝܩܠܐ δίκελλα, *a mattock with two points.*

91 *b* ܕܠܝܬܐ add *a thick branch.*

93 *b* ܕܠܩܘܒܠܐܝܬ rt. ܩܒܠ. adv. *contradictorily, on the contrary.*

ܕܠܩܘܫܛܐܝܬ from ܩܘܫܬܐ. adv. *verily, indeed.*

98 *b* ܕܡܢܘܚܕܝܢ rt. ܚܕܐ. adv. *recently.*

106 *b* ܗܘܦܟܘܬܐ rt. ܗܦܟ. f. *activity.*

110 ܙܢܓܢܓܐ from ܙܢܓܐ m. *resounding, a ringing* in the ears.

113 ܙܘܛܐ BA. m. *a little boy.*

ܙܘܪܦܐ or ܙܘܦܪܐ m. a bird of prey, perh. *the ossifrage.*

116 ܙܠܓ fut. ܢܙܠܓ *to shine forth.*

116 *b* ܙܠܝܩܐ rt. ܙܠܩ. m. *a shower* ܕܢܘܪܐ *of sparks.*

118 ܙܥܘܪܐ pl. ܐ̈ m. *an ulcer.*

ܙܢܓ denom. verb Pael conj. from Nasar. ܙܢܓܐ *a bell, to jingle;* pass. part. ܡܙܢܓܐ *having bells on the harness.* Cf. ܙܢܓܐ.

118 *b* ܙܢܩܐ rt. ܙܢܩ. m. *archery, shooting* with arrows.

Page 118 *b* ܙܢܳܐ m. *the running of mucus from the nose, catarrh.*

119 ܙܥܶܦ fut. ܢܶܙܥܘܿܦ *to scold, blame.* Part. adj. ܙܳܥܶܦ, ܙܳܥܦܳܐ *wrathful, furious.* Pa. ܙܰܥܶܦ *to be furious, reprove sharply.*

ܙܰܩܘܿܩܺܝܬܳܐ pl. ܝܳܬܳܐ dimin. of ܙܰܩܳܐ f. *a small leathern bottle.*

119 *b* ܙܰܩܳܝܳܐ, ܝܬܳܐ from ܙܰܩܳܐ. *dropsical.*

123 ܣܚܺܝܦܘܼܬܳܐ rt. ܣܚܦ. f. *the violence* of a torrent.

124 *b* ܣܰܚܠܰܒܠܳܐ m. *a water-weed,* perh. *pellitory.*

125 ܫܚܳܡܳܐ m. *ink.*

128 ܚܰܕܥܶܣܪܳܝܳܐ, ܝܬܳܐ from ܚܕܥܣܪ. *eleventh.*

129 ܚܡܶܣ add Derivatives, ܚܡܘܿܣܳܐ, ܚܡܳܣܬܳܐ, ܚܡܳܣܳܐ, ܚܡܺܝܣܳܐ, ܡܚܰܡܣܳܢܘܼܬܳܐ, ܡܚܰܡܣܳܢܳܐ, ܡܚܰܡܣܳܢܳܐܝܬ, ܡܚܰܡܣܳܢܺܝܬ.

137 ܚܪܶܦ add Pael ܚܰܪܶܦ *to be austere, make rough.*

157 ܚܢܳܐ, ܚܢܺܝܬܳܐ; see ܐܶܚܢܳܐ.

166 *b* ܛܰܒܠܳܐ add properly *a tambourine hung with jingles.*

175 *b* ܛܰܒܠܘܼܠܳܐ pl. ܠܶܐ m. *a grub, insect* on herbs.

208 ܟܰܥܟܳܐ and ܟܥܟܳܐ m. *a cake;* ܟ̈ ܕܣܥܳܪܶܐ *a barley-cake.*

210 ܟܘܿܢܳܐ χώνη, m. *a funnel, hopper* of a mill, *a bucket tied to the mill to receive the flour.*

ܟܘܿܣܳܣܳܐ rt. ܟܣܣ. add *a crunching.*

211 *b* ܟܘܼܪܣܝܘܿܢܳܐ dimin. of ܟܘܼܪܣܝܳܐ m. *a chair of state.*

213 *b* ܟܝܳܪܳܐ pl. ܶܐ Turk. m. *a cucumber.*

225 ܟܳܪܘܳܝܳܐ m. κάρον, *caraway seed.*

227 *b* ܟܘܳܐ *to brand.*

228 ܟܘܼܡܬܳܐ pl. ܡܳܬܳܐ rt. ܟܘܡ. f. *a coping; capital, abacus.*

228 *b* ܟܘܼܦܳܬܳܐ pl. ܦܳܬܳܐ f. *furniture, utensils; old and broken goods* esp. *broken crockery.*

241 *b* ܟܰܪܟܘܼܫܳܐ pl. ܫܶܐ m. *a weasel; ichneumon.*

244 *b* ܠܘܼܩܒܠܳܐܝܬ rt. ܩܒܠ. adv. *on the contrary;* logic. *in the way of opposition.*

Page 244 *b* ܠܘܼܩܒܠܳܝܳܐ rt. ܩܒܠ. *opposed, opposite.*

ܠܘܼܩܒܠܳܝܘܼܬܳܐ rt. ܩܒܠ. f. *opposition, contradiction.*

251 *b* ܡܓܰܫ add pass. part. ܡܓܺܝܫ; ܒܶܣܪܳܐ ܕܡܓܺܝܫܳܐ *meat consecrated by Magi.*

260 *b*, line 7 for *ten* read *nine.*

266 ܡܰܚܬܳܐ rt. ܢܚܬ. m. *a*) *descent.* *b*) *dripping, a fall of rain.* *c*) *catarrh.*

ܡܰܚܬܘܼܬܳܐ rt. ܢܚܬ. f. *descent.*

ܡܰܚܬܳܢܳܐ rt. ܢܚܬ. *a*) *causing to descend.* *b*) subst. *a descent, way down.*

ܡܰܚܬܳܢܺܝܬܳܐ pl. ܝܳܬܳܐ rt. ܢܚܬ. f. *descending, descent, going down, journey.*

267 *b* ܡܰܬܩܠܳܐ pl. ܠܶܐ rt. ܬܩܠ. m. *a balance; a weight.*

271 ܡܛܰܟܣܳܐ usually ܡܬܰܟܣܳܐ.

272 *b* ܡܩܰܨܨܬܳܐ rt. ܩܨܨ. f. *a pruning-knife.*

273 ܡܟܰܘܝܳܢܳܐ from ܟܘܳܐ. m. *a brander.*

285 ܡܩܰܡܩܶܡ for Palpel conj. read *see* —. Next three words, dele rt. ܩܡܡ.

286 *b* ܡܣܰܪܗܒܳܐܝܬ rt. ܪܗܒ. adv. *hurriedly, inconsiderately.*

ܡܣܰܪܗܒܘܼܬܳܐ rt. ܪܗܒ. f. *haste.*

294 *b* ܡܪܰܘܚܳܐ rt. ܪܘܚ. m. *the gradual opening of a door.*

ܡܪܰܡܕܳܢܘܼܬܳܐ rt. ܪܡܕ. f. = ܪܶܡܕܳܐ *a peg* fastening the web to the beam.

ܡܪܰܡܕܳܢܳܐ, ܢܺܝܬܳܐ rt. ܪܡܕ. m. *repressive.*

ܡܪܰܡܕܳܢܘܼܬܳܐ rt. ܪܡܕ. f. *fastening.*

ܡܪܰܡܫܘܼܬܳܐ rt. ܪܡܫ. f. *radiance.*

ܡܪܰܡܫܳܢܘܼܬܳܐ rt. ܪܡܫ. f. *radiance; polishing.*

297 *b* ܡܫܰܪܓܳܢܳܐ *crafty, fraudulent.*

300 *b* ܡܺܝܙܳܒܳܐ Arab. m. *a conduit, canal.*

302 *b* ܡܰܪܓܳܐ rt. ܪܓ. m. *a marsh, water-meadow.*

304 ܡܙܰܦܬܳܐ m. *a seller of pitch.*

304 *b* ܡܫܰܒܗܪܳܢܘܼܬܳܐ rt. ܫܒܗܪ. f. *glory, boast.*

305 ܡܫܰܘܬܦܳܐܝܬ from ܫܘܬܦ. adv. *in common.*

ܡܫܰܘܬܦܘܼܬܳܐ from ܫܘܬܦ. f. *communion, fellowship, harmony;* with ܠܳܐ *excommunication.* Gram. *a participle; homonymity.*

Page 305 ܡܫܘܬܦܢܐ from ܫܘܬܦ. *sharing;* gram. *expressing participation.*

306 ܡܡܪܚܢܘܬܐ rt. ܡܪܚ. f. *presumption.*

307 *b* ܡܥܛܦܬܐ pl. ܬ̈ܐ rt. ܥܛܦ. f. *a linen robe covering the whole body.*

309 *b* ܡܝܬܪܢܐܝܬ rt. ܝܬܪ. adv. *copiously, abundantly.*

ܡܝܬܪܢܘܬܐ rt. ܝܬܪ. f. *plenteousness, opulence, superabundance, exuberance.*

ܡܝܬܪܢܢܐ rt. ܝܬܪ. *making copious* or *redundant.*

ܡܝܬܪܢܢܘܬܐ rt. ܝܬܪ. f. *superabundance.*

ܡܫܬܒܚܢܐ, ܚܢܬܐ rt. ܫܒܚ. *glorified, of good repute.*

ܡܫܬܒܚܢܘܬܐ rt. ܫܒܚ. f. *glory, gloriousness.*

ܡܫܬܥܒܕܢܘܬܐ rt. ܥܒܕ. f. *bondage.*

310 *b* ܡܫܬܘܬܦܢܘܬܐ from ܫܘܬܦ. f. *participation.*

311 ܡܫܬܡܥܢܐܝܬ rt. ܫܡܥ. adv. *obediently.*

Page 311 ܡܫܬܡܥܢܘܬܐ rt. ܫܡܥ. f. *obedience, heed;* ܡܫ̈ ܕܫܡܘܥ̈ܐ *the instruction of catechumens.*

313 *b* ܡܬܟܒܫܢܘܬܐ rt. ܟܒܫ. f. *repression.*

315 ܡܬܚܡܬܢܘܬܐ rt. ܚܡܬ. f. *irascibility.*

323 ܡܬܚܡܡܢܐ rt. ܚܡܡ. *that which can admit of great heat* as a metal.

ܡܬܚܝܒܢܘܬܐ rt. ܚܘܒ. f. *liability.*

324 *b* ܡܬܚܦܝܢܘܬܐ rt. ܚܦܐ. f. *ablution.*

ܡܬܒܣܪܢܐ rt. ܒܣܪ. *despicable.*

ܡܬܒܣܪܢܘܬܐ rt. ܒܣܪ. f. *indignity, insult.*

368 *b* read ܣܘܣܘܢ, ܣܘܣܢܐ.

375 *b* ܣܝܡܬܐ pl. ܬ̈ܐ rt. ܣܝܡ. f. *a*) *a treasure, treasury, hoard, store, case, casket. b*) ܣ̈ ܕܟܪܡܐ *planting a vineyard. c*) *adoption,* usually ܣܝܡܬ ܒܢܝܐ. *d*) *a precept, statute. e*) *a thesaurus, dictionary.*

383 *b* ܫܬܝܢܐ add *a period of sixty years.*

390 ܣܘܪܝܓܣ σῦριγξ, *a fistula, hollow sore.*

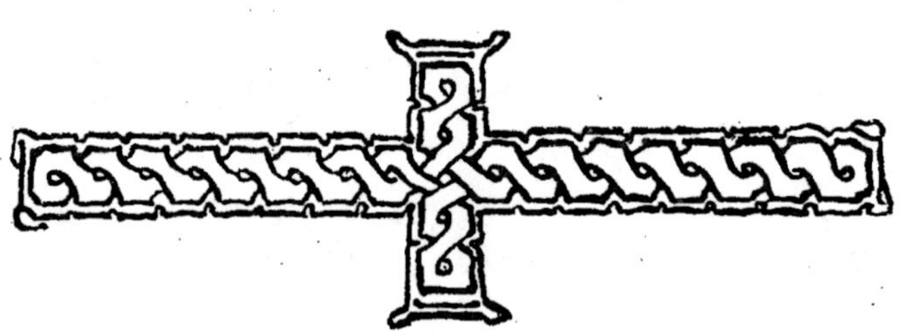